P9-DTS-029

Handbook of Clinical Psychology

EDITED BY
Benjamin B. Wolman

with
Consulting Editors:

Gordon F. Derner · *James G. Miller*
Molly Harrower · *O. Hobart Mowrer*
Robert R. Holt · *Henry A. Murray*
Silvan S. Tomkins

McGRAW-HILL BOOK COMPANY
New York St. Louis San Francisco Toronto London Sydney

HANDBOOK OF CLINICAL PSYCHOLOGY

Library of Congress Catalog Card Number 64–8976
ISBN 07–071539–4

78910 KPKP 79876543

"Savoir pour prévoir," dit Auguste Comte.
"Mais non!" je dis. "Savoir pour aider autrui."
B. B. W.

Preface

The field of clinical psychology is rapidly expanding. Clinical psychologists today engage in a great many activities, among them scientific research, teaching, hospital service, and private practice. Diagnostic work, individual and group therapy, teaching and training, and research in mental health centers are among these areas to which clinicians devote their time and energies. Even greater diversity can be found in regard to rationale and theoretical approach. Some clinical psychologists are Freudian, Sullivanian, or Adlerian psychoanalysts; others subscribe to the learning theories of Pavlov, Hull, or Skinner; some of them try to bridge the gap between learning theory and psychoanalysis. Clinical psychologists have also gained prominence in the study of organic, neurological, and biochemical aspects of mental disorders; and recently several clinical psychologists have made a substantial contribution to the study of sociopsychological factors in psychopathology.

It is almost paradoxical that, in spite of the growth and ascendency of clinical psychology, there is no authoritative and representative source of information about this large and diversified field. There are handbooks in several other areas of psychology, but the greatest group of psychologists do not have a source to turn to for reliable, comprehensive, and authoritative information. Psychologists taking the Ph.D. in clinical psychology or preparing themselves for the various professional examinations, academic psychologists, and clinical practitioners badly need an objective and comprehensive presentation of the great body of scientific research and practical experience in clinical psychology.

The time has come, therefore, when a handbook of clinical psychology has become a necessity. The *Handbook* has been planned and organized in such a way as to represent the various areas of specialization and the diversified points of view. The purpose of the *Handbook* is to acquaint clinical psychologists and other professionals with the tremendous scope of research, experience, theory, and practice in this rapidly growing field. The aim of the *Handbook* is to represent the profession of clinical psychology and to demonstrate its vitality, its vigorous pursuit of scientific truth, and its willingness and capacity for serving those who need it. It is hoped that the *Handbook* will stand as positive evidence of the moral and scientific unity of the profession, despite diversity in theoretical viewpoints, research methods, and areas of specialization.

The *Handbook* is composed of six parts. Part 1 deals with *Research Methods.* A critical analysis of basic concepts of scientific method is followed by a detailed examination of the four major scientific tools used in clinical research: the case-study method, experimentation, measurement, and statistics.

Part 2 of the *Handbook* deals with the *Theoretical Foundations* of clinical psychology. The opening chapter outlines the history of clinical psychology. The nine ensuing chapters analyze the contributions of various disciplines to understanding the nature of mental disorders. Three chapters on genetics, neurology, and biochemistry describe organic factors. Two following chapters analyze sociological and anthropological factors. Learning theory and various theories of personality, including Freudian and non-Freudian analytic theories, are presented in the last four chapters.

The nine chapters in Part 3 describe *Diagnostic Methods.* The introductory chapter deals with problems of differential diagnosis, and the chapters following it describe in detail interviewing techniques, personality inventories, intelligence tests, and the various projective techniques, especially the Rorschach and the TAT. The last two chapters analyze diagnostic methods in childhood disorders and the problems of psychiatric diagnosis, nomenclature, and classification.

Part 4 is the largest, comprising fifteen chapters devoted to *Clinical Patterns.* The first three chapters give a detailed analysis of various organic mental disorders, including brain lesions and convulsive disorders. Speech disorders, physical disability, clinical patterns of old age, mental deficiencies and psychosomatic problems are analyzed in five separate chapters. The various psychoneuroses, schizophrenia, and related disorders, and the various depressive states are discussed in three consecutive chapters. Two chapters are dedicated to psychopathic condition, addictions, perversions, and delinquency. A separate chapter describes mental disorders in childhood. The concluding chapter in this section provides an analysis of the concepts of mental health, mental disorders, and classification of mental disorders.

Methods of Treatment are analyzed in the twelve chapters in Part 5. An introductory chapter analyzes psychotherapy in general and describes certain psychotherapeutic methods. Two chapters describing the Freudian and non-Freudian psychoanalytic techniques are followed by a chapter each on client-centered therapy, behavior therapy, group psychotherapy, and hypnosis. Two separate chapters describe chemotherapy and the treatment of childhood disorders. Mental hospitals and psychological aspects of general hospital practice are described in two consecutive chapters. The concluding chapter in Part 5 discusses the problems of prevention of mental disorders.

Part 6 describes *Clinical Psychology as a Profession.* The first two chapters describe undergraduate, graduate, and postdoctoral training programs. The legal status and organization of clinical psychology and the duties and responsibilities of clinical psychologists are taken up in the next two chapters. Relations with other professions and international resources of clinical psychology are the subject matter of the two following chapters. The chapter on ethical standards for clinical psychologists concludes the *Handbook.*

From its inception, it has been clear that a work of this magnitude could not represent the efforts of any one person or any single point of view. The *Handbook* has been written to be used as a reference book for psychologists and related professionals such as psychiatrists, social workers, clergymen, and others. Although it is aimed primarily at the professional level, it has been prepared in such a way as to be appropriate for use as a text in doctoral and postdoctoral psychological training programs. Each chapter, except for those covering certain special topics, has been written so as to present a systematic and objective survey of a particular subject-matter area rather than the viewpoint or philosophy of a particular contributor.

Five years ago, when I conceived this project, I conducted a series of conversations with several of my colleagues about the feasibility of assembling between the covers of one book the bewildering variety of facts, philosophies, theories, techniques, and viewpoints which presently constitute the subject matter of contemporary clinical psychology. At that time it became clear to all of us that precisely this diversity and confusion mandated the massive undertaking of which this *Handbook* is the fruition.

The *Handbook* has been a truly cooperative enterprise. Seven leading authorities served as consulting editors, participating individually and jointly in the planning and the editing of the *Handbook.* Each contributor was selected by the committee of consulting editors, and each chapter was then read and criticized first by me and then by one consulting editor. It was then revised and submitted for final editorial approval by me. If there are any errors, and such are unavoidable in a manuscript of this size, the responsibility is surely mine, for the consulting editors and the contributors have done a splendid and conscientious job.

Sixty-one outstanding members of our profession and related fields spared neither time nor effort in preparing the fifty-eight chapters of the *Handbook.* My gratitude extends also to several other scholars who provided help and guidance. I am especially grateful to Paul H. Hoch, Bernard H. Kalinkowitz, George A. Kelly, Lawrence C. Kolb, N. Houston Merritt, Gardner Murphy, Carl R. Rogers, and Laurence F. Shaffer for their most friendly suggestions.

It is with deep regret that I report that the splendid chapter on psychosomatic disorders, which Franz Alexander coauthored with Glenn Flagg, was Dr. Alexander's last work. The passing of this great mind is a loss to all of us. Ruth L. Munroe had undertaken the writing of the chapter on non-Freudian psychoanalytic theories, but her untimely death prevented her from completing the work and grieved us all.

I should also like to acknowledge the diligent and faithful work of five young people who, in the latter stages of the work, served as editorial assistants. They are Alvin Dichter, Esther Feinman, Marrietta V. Lee, Jerome Liblit, and Sylvia Sandowsky.

To all my editors, contributors, consultants, assistants, and friends I would like to convey my warmest personal thanks.

Benjamin B. Wolman

Contents

Part 5 Methods of Treatment

Part 6 Clinical Psychology as a Profession

Contributors

Samuel Abrams, M.D., Clinical Instructor (Psychiatry), State University of New York, Downstate Medical Center, Brooklyn, N.Y.

Franz Gabriel Alexander, M.D. (deceased), formerly Director of Division of Psychiatry, Mount Sinai Hospital, Los Angeles, Calif.

Irving E. Alexander, Ph.D., Professor of Psychology, Director of Clinical Training, Acting Chairman, Duke University, Durham, N.C.

Arnold Bernstein, Ph.D., Associate Professor of Psychology, Queens College of the City University of New York, Flushing, N.Y.

Hedda Bolgar, Ph.D., Chief Psychologist and Director of the Clinical Psychology Training Program, Cedars-Sinai Hospitals, Mount Sinai Division, Los Angeles, Calif.; Associate Clinical Professor of Psychiatry (Psychology), University of Southern California, Los Angeles, Calif.

Henry Brill, M.D., Director Pilgrim State Hospital, West Brentwood, Long Island, N.Y.

Jacob Cohen, Ph.D., Professor of Psychology, New York University, New York, N.Y.

Henry P. David, Ph.D., Associate Director, World Federation for Mental Health, Geneva, Switzerland.

Gordon F. Derner, Ph.D., Professor of Psychology and Director of Clinical Psychology Program and Postdoctoral Program in Psychotherapy, Aldelphi University, Garden City, Long Island, N.Y.; Consultant V.A., New York City Civil Service Commission; Pontiac (Michigan) Childrens Court; Field Selection Officer, Peace Corps.

Jon Eisenson, Ph.D., Professor of Speech Pathology and Audiology, Stanford University, Palo Alto, Calif.; Director, Scottish Rite Institute for Childhood Aphasia.

Aaron H. Esman, M.D., Director of Psychiatric Training, Jewish Board of Guardians Lecturer in Psychiatry, Columbia University School of Social Work, New York, N.Y.; Associate Attending Psychiatrist, Montefiore Hospital, New York, N.Y.

Glenn Willard Flagg, M.D., Director of Psychiatric Research, Mt. Sinai Hospital, Los Angeles, Calif.

Sol Louis Garfield, Ph.D., Professor of Psychology and Director of the Clinical Psychology Training Program, Teachers College, Columbia University, New York, N.Y.

Haim G. Ginott, Ed.D., Adjunct Associate Professor, Graduate Department of Psychology, New York University, New York, N.Y.; Consultant in Child Psychotherapy, North Shore Child Guidance Center, Manhasset, N.Y.; Consultant in Group Psychotherapy, Hartley-Salmon Child Guidance Clinic, Hartford, Conn.; Consultant, Connecticut Valley Hospital, Middletown, Conn.

Eli S. Goldensohn, M.D., Professor of Neurology, School of Medicine, University of Pennsylvania, Philadelphia, Pa.

Milton Greenblatt, M.D., Superintendent, Boston State Hospital, Boston, Mass.; Professor of Psychiatry, Tufts University School of Medicine, Medford, Mass.

Florence Halpern, Ph.D., Associate Professor in Clinical Psychology, New York University, Graduate School of Arts and Sciences, New York, N.Y.; Consultant, Veterans Administration.

Ernest Harms, Ph.D., Consultant, Credmoore State Hospital, Long Island, N.Y.

Ross Harrison, Ph.D., Professor of Psychology, Hunter College of the City of New York, New York, N.Y.

Molly R. Harrower, Ph.D., Professor of Research in Clinical Psychology, Temple University Medical Center, Philadelphia, Pa.; Visiting Professor of Psychology, New School for Social Research, New York, N.Y.; Chairman, Advisory Council in Psychology, University of the State of New York; Editor, American Lecture Series in Psychology.

Starke R. Hathaway, Ph.D., Professor and Director, Division of Clinical Psychology, Department of Psychiatry and Neurology, University of Minnesota Medical School, Minneapolis, Minn.

Karl Florien Heiser, Ph.D., Consulting Psychologist in private practice.

Nicholas Hobbs, Ph.D., Chairman, Division of Human Development, George Peabody College for Teachers, Nashville, Tenn.

Erasmus L. Hoch, Ph.D., Professor and Administrative Officer, Department of Psychology, University of Michigan, Ann Arbor, Mich.

Audrey Rose Holliday, Ph.D., Assistant Professor and Director of Psychopharmacology Research Program, Department of Pharmacology, School of Medicine, University of Washington, Seattle, Wash.

Robert R. Holt, Ph.D., Professor of Psychology and Co-Director, Research Center of Mental Health, New York University, New York, N.Y.

William A. Hunt, Ph.D., Professor of Psychology, the Biological Sciences, and Education, and Chairman of the Department of Psychology, Northwestern University, Evanston, Ill.

Lewis Alfred Hurst, M.D., Ph.D., Head, Department of Psychiatry and Mental Hygiene, University of the Witwatersrand, Johannesburg, South Africa; Chief Psychiatrist, Johannesburg Hospital and associated Teaching Hospitals.

Irving L. Janis, Ph.D., Professor of Psychology and Director of Graduate Studies, Department of Psychology, Yale University, New Haven, Conn.

Harry I. Kalish, Ph.D., Professor and Chairman, Department of Psychology, State University of New York at Stony Brook, Long Island, New York.

Milton V. Kline, M.A., Ed.D., Director, The Institute for Research in Hypnosis; Chairman, Committee on Hypnosis, New York State Psychiatric Association; Editor Emeritus, *The International Journal of Clinical and Experimental Hypnosis.*

Walter George Klopfer, Ph.D., Professor of Psychology and Director of Clinical Training, University of Portland, Portland, Oreg.

Samuel Benjamin Kutash, Ph.D., Consultant in Psychotherapy, Veterans Administration Hospital, East Orange, N.J.; Mental Hygiene Clinic, Newark, N.J.; Faculty Institute for Analytic Psychotherapy, N.J.; Consultant, Selection Division, Peace Corps, Washington, D.C.

Howard Leventhal, Ph.D., Associate Professor, Department of Psychology, and Research Associate, School of Nursing, Yale University, New Haven, Conn.

Daniel J. Levinson, Ph.D., Director, Center for Sociopsychological Research, Massachusetts Mental Health Center, Boston, Mass.; Assistant Professor of Psychology, Department of Psychiatry, Harvard Medical School, Cambridge, Mass.

Alexander R. Luria, M.D., Ph.D., Professor of Psychology, University of Moscow, Moscow, USSR.

Robert M. MacIver, Ph.D., President, New School for Social Research, New York, N.Y.

Horace Winchell Magoun, Ph.D., Professor of Anatomy and Dean of the Graduate Division, University of California, Los Angeles, Calif.

Joseph D. Matarazzo, Ph.D., Professor of Medical Psychology and Chairman, Department of Medical Psychology, University of Oregon Medical School, Portland, Oreg.

Ivan Norman Mensh, Ph.D., Professor of Medical Psychology and Head, Division of Medical Psychology, Department of Psychiatry, UCLA Center for the Health Sciences, Los Angeles, Calif.; Consultant, Surgeon General, U.S. Navy; Veterans Administration; Los Angeles County Department of Mental Health and County Hospitals; USN Medical Neuropsychiatric Research Unit; California State Department of Mental Hygiene.

James Grier Miller, M.D., Ph.D., Professor of Psychology and Psychiatry and Director, Mental Health Research Institute, The University of Michigan, Ann Arbor, Mich.

O. Hobart Mowrer, Ph.D., Research Professor of Psychology, University of Illinois, Urbana, Ill.; Consultant, State Research Hospital, Galesburg, Ill.

Patrick Mullahy, M.A., Lecturer in Psychology, Manhattan College, New York, N.Y.

Henry Alexander Murray, M.D., Ph.D., Professor Emeritus, Department of Social Relations, Harvard University, Cambridge, Mass.

Walter S. Neff, Ph.D., Professor of Psychology, Graduate School of Arts and Science, New York University, New York, N.Y.

Marvin K. Opler, Ph.D., Professor of Social Psychiatry, School of Medicine, State University of New York at Buffalo, N.Y.; Professor, Departments of Sociology and of Anthropology, State University of New York at Buffalo, N.Y.; Editor, *The International Journal of Social Psychiatry;* Associate Editor, *The American Anthropologist.*

Zygmunt A. Piotrowski, Ph.D., Professor of Psychology in Psychiatry, The Jefferson Medical College, Philadelphia, Pa.

Albert I. Rabin, Ph.D., Professor of Psychology, Michigan State University, East Lansing, Mich.

Max Rosenbaum, Ph.D., Education Director, Association for Group Psychoanalysis and Process; Consultant, group psychotherapy, Protestant Episcopal Diocese of Newark and Jersey City.

Nathaniel Ross, M.D., Clinical Professor of Psychiatry, State University of New York College of Medicine, Downstate Medical Center, Brooklyn, N.Y.; Co-Editor, *Annual Survey of Psychoanalysis;* Associate Editor, *Journal of the American Psychoanalytic Association.*

Roger Walcott Russell, D.Sc., Professor and Chairman, Department of Psychology, Indiana University, Bloomington, Ind.

Nevitt Sanford, Ph.D., Director, Institute for the Study of Human Problems, Professor, Departments of Psychology and Education, Scientific Director, Cooperative Commission on the Study of Alcoholism, Stanford University, Palo Alto, Calif.

Emanuel K. Schwartz, Ph.D., D.S.Sc., Associate Dean, Postgraduate Center for Mental Health, New York, N.Y.; Adjunct Professor of Psychology, Graduate School, New York University, New York, N.Y.; Clinical Professor, Postdoctoral Program in Psychotherapy, Institute of the Behavorial and Social Sciences, Adelphi University, Garden City, Long Island, N.Y.

Julius Seeman, Ph.D., Professor of Psychology, George Peabody College, Nashville, Tenn.

Edwin S. Shneidman, Ph.D., Co-Director, Suicide Prevention Center, Los Angeles, Calif.; Professor of Psychiatry (Psychology), University Southern California School of Medicine, Los Angeles, Calif.

Ross Stagner, Ph.D., Professor and Chairman, Department of Psychology, Wayne State University, Detroit, Mich.

Edwin Stainbrook, M.D., Ph.D., Professor and Chairman, Department of Psychiatry, University of Southern California, Los Angeles, Calif.; Chief Psychiatrist, Los Angeles County General Hospital.

Silvan Samuel Tomkins, Ph.D., Director, Center for Research in Cognition and Affect, City University of New York, New York, N.Y.

John Goodrich Watkins, Ph.D., Professor of Psychology and Director of Clinical Training, Montana State University, Missoula, Mont.

Samuel Abraham Weiss, Ph.D., Associate Project Coordinator, Amputee Psychology Research, New York University, New York, N.Y.; Psychological Consultant (Associate Professor), Stern College for Women, Yeshiva University, New York, N.Y.; Psychological Consultant, New York State Division of Vocational Rehabilitation.

J. Richard Wittenborn, Ph.D., Professor of Psychology and Education and Director of the Rutgers Interdisciplinary Research Center, Rutgers—The State University, New Brunswick, N.J.

Benjamin B. Wolman, Ph.D., Clinical Professor of Psychology, Post Doctoral Program in Psychotherapy, Adelphi University, Garden City, Long Island, N.Y.; Dean of Faculty, Institute for Applied Psycoanalysis; Lecturer in Psychology, Hunter College, New York, N.Y.; Associate Editor, *American Imago*.

George Kassimer Yacorzynski, Ph.D., Professor and Head, Division of Psychology, Department of Neurology and Psychiatry, Northwestern University Medical School, Chicago, Ill.; Courtesy Staff, Evanston Hospital.

part 1

Research Methods

1

Clinical Psychology and the Philosophy of Science

BENJAMIN B. WOLMAN

EPISTEMOLOGICAL PROBLEMS

Three Types of Science

It is generally agreed that the business of scientific inquiry is to seek truth. However, one need not be a scientist to seek truth. For example, when a person looks up a telephone number in a telephone book, the result of his search will be a truthful statement, but neither the search nor its results are science.

Sciences do not deal with the known and the obvious. No one builds telescopes to check the contents of a show window in a department store. Science seeks to produce new knowledge and endeavors to discover precise and valid information hitherto unknown.

Scientists have no monopoly on truth. Average men know a lot without practicing science, but the main difference between science and common knowledge is that scientists *adduce proof* for their statements. Thus, whenever men seek to discover unknown facts and to prove their findings, they are scientists. In short, science is an action that aims at discovering truth and at bringing evidence that truth has been discovered.

Scientific search or research is an action producing truthful information about things and what happened to them (i.e., about events). The results of scientific inquiry can be presented or described in singular statements, such as "Rome was conquered by the Germans in 476"; in general statements, such as "All animals take in food"; in mathematical formulas, such as $E = mc^2$; or in other types of statements. All these statements or propositions contain information pertaining to things or objects and to happenings or events. Sciences, such as physics and chemistry, geology and geography, anatomy and physiology, psychology and sociology, history and archeology, are *empirical* (or descriptive) *sciences*. All empirical sciences contain information arrived at through research and supported by evidence pertaining to bodies and events. The degree to which they are scientific depends upon the amount of evidence; the more their propositions are proved to be true, the more they are scientific.

There are, however, sciences that report their findings in propositions that are neither true nor false. Consider education. Such propositions as "Children should prepare their homework" and "Teachers should encourage intellectual curiosity in students" are neither true nor false. They are suggestions, instructions, beliefs, or norms. They are not empirically true or false statements, and they do not describe objects or events. Medicine is another example of a science that operates not exclusively with empirically true statements. For example, "A physician should examine the patient before giving him a prescription" and "Nurses should wash their hands" are not empirical statements.

Thus, there are two categories of sciences.

To the first category belong all sciences that make true or false statements concerning objects and events. To the second category of *praxeological sciences* belong sciences such as medicine, political science, education, etc., that state what should be done and how. But there is also a third category of sciences that are neither empirical nor praxeological. These are the *formal* sciences.

The first two classes of sciences deal with objects and events. The empirical or descriptive class describes objects and events in true or false propositions. The propositions of the praxeological class of sciences suggest goals and means of actions related to objects and events. The third class of sciences are propositions not related to objects and events. They deal with signs, symbols, propositions, meanings, etc. Consider a proposition taken out of a textbook of logic: "If p then q." Using logical signs, it reads: "$p \supset q$." This proposition does not describe objects or events, nor does it prescribe them. Or consider the following equation:

$$(a + b)^2 = a^2 + 2ab + b^2$$

Although they contain no information pertaining to objects or any suggestion of action, both the logical and the mathematical statements are true statements. Moreover, their nonempirical truth is applicable to many real situations.

Formal sciences, such as mathematics and symbolic logic, can be of help in the analysis of procedures and results of empirical and praxeological sciences. But before one discusses this nonempirical meaning of truth, some explanatory remarks are necessary in regard to the use of formal sciences in empirical research.

Philosophy of Science

Contemporary philosophy is not a science in the sense that other sciences are. Philosophy has gradually given up all specific areas of study. At present there is no room for metaphysics as a study of nature or for mental philosophy as a study of man; physics, chemistry, astronomy, and geology have rendered metaphysics superfluous and obsolete. Even the traditional stronghold of philosophy, the study of man and his society, has rebelled against it. Herbart (1776–1841), the last metaphysical psychologist, believed psychology should be based on "metaphysics, empiricism, and mathematics" (Herbart, 1824, 1825; Wolman, 1942). Wundt, the founder of the first psychological laboratory, was no less a philosopher than a psychologist; his *Principles of Physiological Psychology*, originally published in 1873, was as indebted to Kant and Herbart as to Fechner and Helmholtz (Wundt, 1874). Barth (1922) believed that sociology is a "philosophy of history."

The radical changes in the methods and content of research make one feel that not decades, but centuries, have since past. Contemporary behavioral sciences have come far indeed since Wundt and Barth. Psychology and sociology are presently empirical sciences independent of any philosophical systems and not related to any traditional philosophical thought. One need not, however, get the impression that philosophy itself has not changed.

Contemporary philosophy, although it has given up all research areas to the highly specialized scientific disciplines, has never renounced its own aim and *raison d'être.* Philosophy is, as it has been in the past, the guardian of truth, and its main aim is, as it has ever been, the *search for truth.* While other sciences study rocks, molecules, locomotion, insects, and behavior, philosophy *studies these studies.* Philosophy became the science of sciences, a research on scientific research. Philosophy is today the science of the scientific tools, methods, and procedures; it is a science that criticizes the methods and results of scientific research.

Philosophers have to develop their own research methods, plans, and strategies. Contemporary philosophy is devoted to the processes of cognition (epistemology), reasoning (logic), communication (semantics), etc., and to analysis of the procedures of scientific research and theory formation (methodology of science). These main areas cover a great many specific problems and research tasks. It is the philosopher's task to analyze the tools used by the scientist in his search for empirical truth; it is the task of the philosopher to analyze the methods of communication, semantics, and semiotics. It is the philosopher, or scientist of science, who studies the sciences; his science is neither empirical nor praxeological: it is a *formal* science of propositions, procedures, and signs.

In this new road philosophers have met new partners, the theoretical scientists or philosophically minded research workers.

The newest developments in physics forced scientists to take a fresh look at the problems philosophers tried to solve. The new discoveries and new theoretical constructs forced physicists not only to abandon old physics but also to develop a new system of epistemological and methodological concepts. Theoretical physicists became philosophers of physics, and the rapidly growing systematic explanations of methods of observations, induction, inference, causation, probability, etc., became the core of the new philosophy of science. Einstein, Eddington, Jeans, Schrödinger, Bohr, and others are the philosophers and scientists of our times.

Simultaneously, several professional philosophers of science, logicians, and epistemologists have joined in the search for better methods and more precise tools of reasoning in order to arrive at a thorough analysis of the concepts sciences use. Russell, Nagel, Carnap, Feigl, Scriven, and others are today's philosophers of science.

The growth of philosophy of science and the growing awareness of philosophical problems involved in psychological research also brought a rapprochement between philosophically minded psychologists and philosophers of science. There seems to be more and more evidence that philosophy without science may easily turn into metaphysical speculation, while science without philosophy may become hopelessly naïve. The increased number of works devoted to philosophical problems in psychology well represents the *Zeitgeist* (cf. Feigl & Scriven, 1956–1962; Marx, 1951; Marx, 1963; Pratt, 1948; Wolman, 1960; Wolman & Nagel, 1964; and the multivoluminous works of Piaget).

It has been adequately proved that formal or philosophical disciplines are not superior to empirical sciences. There is no reason to assume that philosophers or mathematicians know more about stars than astronomers do, or about earthquakes than geologists do, or about brains than neurologists do. Yet empirical sciences look for guidance to the philosophers of science because they analyze the tools other sciences use.

Kant's Heritage

Science has been defined as the search for truth and the resulting system of true propositions. The definition of truth is therefore of paramount importance.

The epistemological controversy is well represented by Locke and Hume on one side and by Descartes and Spinoza on the other. To Locke and Hume, sensory perception was the only source of knowledge, while Descartes and Spinoza assumed that truth was not given by sensory apparatus but could be reasoned out or stated a priori. This controversy between empiricism and rationalism was of utmost importance for the development of psychology. The sensualistic approach gave rise to associationism, while the rationalistic philosophy fostered the traditional philosophy of mind.

A settlement to this controversy was proposed by Kant. Kant seemingly agreed with the empiricists that sensory perception is the prime source of knowledge but that this knowledge is not a knowledge of things as they really are. True knowledge is given a priori in a rationalistic fashion; mathematical propositions are true and yet are independent of any empirical validation.

Kant's system was an effort to restore the primacy of philosophy over empirical sciences. In 1787 he stated: "There can be no doubt that all knowledge begins with experience" (1881, p. 1), but he added that it "does not arise out of experience." Knowledge arises in the "thinking subject," for the corporeal world is "nothing but an appearance in the sensibility of the subject."

The mind sets the rules for the cognition of the world. Its rules need no proof, for they are the prerequisite for any proof. Time and space are not derived from experience; they are the ways the mind perceives the world. Also relationships, including causality, quantity (thus all mathematics), quality, and modality, are terms or categories of the perceiving mind, the a priori forms of perception and reasoning. Philosophy, as Kant saw it, was not an all-encompassing science, but the queen of sciences, the prolegomena to all science.

When Wundt embarked upon his daring program for the new discipline of scientific psychology, he had to make historic decisions in regard to the triple heritage of the soul, mental faculties, and introspection. Wundt discarded the first two, but he could not renounce the Kantian emphasis on introspection.

Kantianism, as such, never was and never could become one of the leading currents in psychology. First, there was the matter of timing. Kant's *Critique of Pure Reason* (*Kritik der reinen Vernunft*) appeared in 1781; the second edition of this book (1787) starts with the above-quoted statement: "There can be no doubt that all knowledge begins with experience," but, according to Kant, "it does not arise out of experience" (1881). For he came too late for a nonempirical psychology. His contemporaries in France and Britain paved the road for a new psychology of sensation and association. The nineteenth century, the century of Comte, Spencer, Darwin, and Michelson, was too late a time for a Kantian psychology of reason, emotion, and will.

Yet Kant's impact on psychology has been in terms of more than just his psychological ideas. Either psychology had to abandon all empirical research and dwell on the mysteries of the superb, cognizant mind, with its a priori given knowledge, or it had to become an empirical observation of "phenomena" that were remotely related to real things-in-themselves (Wolman, 1960, pp. 391ff.). Kant left a narrow passage open for such an "empirical" or "pragmatic" psychology conceived as a part of anthropology, or the science of man. His "empirical psychology" was meant to be based on observation of phenomena by the mind that observes what it can within the limits of its a priori terms of space, time, and other categories. One of the categories is quantity. Kant believed that mathematical propositions were synthetic and a priori, and most psychologists influenced by him seem to trust that mathematics will make their systems valid. Brett wrote about Kant as follows:

> Many would regard the legacy of Kant as a disaster for psychology. It perpetuated the rigid distinction between the outer and the inner with its accompanying assumptions both that there is a radical difference between what we know of our own minds and what others know of them, and that overt behavior alone can be scientifically described. It also led people to believe that they were not doing science unless they were using mathematics. We have therefore the tendency developing for psychologists to explore all methods of obtaining quantifiable "data" often without any fruitful assumptions to test (1953, p. 508).

Kant's revolution was not Copernican, as Kant claimed, but rather anti-Copernican, for he enthroned the perceiving subject and made him the center of the universe. His most consistent disciple was undoubtedly Schopenhauer, to whom the world became the "will and idea" of the cognizant and volitionary (1923). The error in Kant's distinction between thing-in-itself and phenomenon had been discovered already by Maimon, who explained that since the thing-in-itself is a cause (at least a partial one) of the phenomenon, causality cannot be an a priori category (1790; Wolman, 1938; Wolman, 1948).

Space does not permit us to analyze the impact on psychology of the Marburg neo-Kantians, such as Herrman Cohen, Paul Natorp, Ernst Cassirer, and others, or of the Baden group of neo-Kantians, such as Wilhelm Windelband, Heinrich Rikert, and others. The fact remains that whoever studied psychology in Germany in the nineteenth century became enmeshed in various brands and shades of neo-Kantianism. Wundt and Külpe, Mach and Brentano, Avenarius and Dilthey—all struggled with the problems posed by Kant and perhaps created by him. Throughout generations of disciples, some of them accepting and some rejecting Kant's ideas, the Kantian heritage has survived and still looms large in the writings of philosophers and psychologists who may or may not be aware of the fact that they struggle with problems posed by Kant.

Some of these problems make no sense today. Kant's mathematical ideas became meaningless after Russell and Whitehead published their *Principia Mathematica.* Mach's theory was closely related to introspection, today largely discredited as a scientific method. Dialectics was accepted by Hegel as a system of logic and applied toward an interpretation of history prior to the development of mathematical logic. But the history of superstitions and sciences proves that errors die hard.

Transcendent Truth

Modern logic, epistemology, and methodology of science have developed along other lines. Men like Russell (1935), Einstein (1934), Kotarbinski (1929), M. R. Cohen (1944), Nagel (1961), and others bypassed Kantian dichotomies and developed epistemological systems free of metaphysics and geared to empirical research. These systems are not necessarily identical, but all of them represent the principles of epistemological realism in a more or less radical version.

These principles can be briefly described as follows: Whatever exists, exists irrespective of whether it is or is not perceived by men. An assumption such as Berkeley's (1901) *esse est percipi* ("To be is to be perceived") contradicts whatever the perceivers know. For there is no doubt that distant planets in the solar system existed before men discovered them or that America was where it is now before Columbus's voyage.

An assumption that the universe is but a conglomeration of perceptions, as Mach believed it to be, leads to self-contradictions. Mach said: "Nature is composed of sensations as its elements. . . . Sensations are not signs of things. . . . The world is not composed of things as its elements, but of colors, tones, pressures, spaces, times, in short, what we ordinarily call sensations" (1960, p. 482).

But why then must perceptions be Mach's perceptions? Were his perceptions the sole source of knowledge, no one could be sure that the perceptions of other people were the same as Mach's. Mach's world consists of Mach's perceptions; there is no way to prove (using Mach's perceptions) that the perceptions of other people are the same as his.

One may follow Schopenhauer at this point and assume that the world is the way "I" see it. In such a case, any further pursuit of truth is futile.

Scientific inquiry can continue only on the assumption that there is something to inquire into and that this something exists irrespective of observing scientists and independently of them. There is no empirical evidence for such an assumption, but it is necessary to postulate it, for any other assumption leads inevitably to inner contradictions and renders impossible any further search for truth.

The position defended here is the position of *radical epistemological realism.* Were the world a cluster of sensations, all sciences would have shrunk to psychology. However, such a panpsychologism, as developed by Berkeley or Mach, would render scientific psychology impossible. A psychologist would have to observe the way in which he observes, and so on, *ad infinitum.* He and his own perceptions would have become the sole source of information. There is no other way but to assume that other individuals exist independently of their perceivers. This is merely an assumption, for there is no empirical evidence for empirical evidence. But radical realism is the only assumption free of inner contradictions.

On the basis of the epistemological realism, further scientific considerations become possible. A clinical psychologist observing the behavior of disturbed individuals assumes that he does not observe his own sensations, but the actions of other individuals. More psychologists may join in the process of observing, and all observers may observe the same phenomenon. Their observations can be checked against one another, and the knowledge thus acquired becomes objective, provided certain canons of scientific procedure are observed.

The rules of scientific procedure are described in detail in the following four chapters. The first common principle of all these rules is that of *transcendent truth.* A proposition conveys transcendent truth whenever, and only when, its content corresponds to reality. The principle of transcendent truth requires that all propositions of empirical science be checked against reality.

Radical realism is not naïve and does not assume an infallibility of human perceptions. Human perception can be improved by the use of scientific apparatus, by precision, by control, and by several other devices explored in detail in the following four chapters. The aim of all these devices is to prove the correspondence between scientific propositions made by clinical psychologists and the objects of their inquiry. The objective of all these inquiries is to establish transcendent truth.

Immanent Truth

Science, to paraphrase Poincaré's famous dictum, is not a collection of facts, just as a house is not a pile of bricks. Scientific propositions must form a coherent system, a system of connected and interrelated statements. Formal logic is needed at this point to answer the question: What are the principles of cohesive systems?

The logical principles—namely, identity, contradiction, and excluded middle (Cohen & Nagel, 1934, pp. 181ff.)—offer together the necessary over-all principle. This principle of *immanent truth* means that scientific propositions must be free of inner contradictions and, within a given system, must not contradict one another. Thus, a scientific system is *formally* true whenever it is free of inner contradictions; then and only then does it meet the requirements of immanent truth. A scientific system is *empirically* true when it does not contradict the body of well-established empirical data and meets the requirements of transcendent truth.

Formal sciences, such as logic and mathematics, must meet the criterion of immanent truth only. Empirical sciences must meet both criteria (cf. Wolman, 1960, chap. 14).

Remarks on Mathematics

It is an open question how strictly clinical psychology can abide by these two rules. One could say that the more a science adheres to the rules of transcendent and immanent truth, the more it is scientific. Hence the justified tendency to describe clinical data in empirically proved propositions and to present them in a quantified way.

Mathematics does not deal with objects and events. It is a system of signs and a set of agreed-upon rules. In geometry there are several systems; so are there in algebra. Mathematics, wrote Jeffreys, "can display connections between scientific statements; it does not prove the statements by itself" (1957, p. 11).

Mathematical systems operate strictly on the principle of immanent truth. Hence their scientific usefulness. A set of empirical propositions ordered to, and represented in, some sort of mathematical relationships can be readily tested in regard to its inner consistency.

The more quantification in empirical data, the more consistency and precision in the scientific system. The use of mathematics adds clarity and testability to scientific propositions. The ever-growing application of mathematics to research in behavioral sciences is described in detail in two chapters of the *Handbook* ("Measurement in Clinical Research" and "Some Statistical Issues in Psychological Research," Chapters 4 and 5), and some of its advantages are analyzed in detail by Meehl (1954, 1956) and Lazarsfeld (1954).

Yet one must express some reservation in regard to the application of mathematics to clinical research. Some of the problems have been pointed out by J. Cohen (1962), Meehl (1958), and Rozeboom (1960) and are analyzed by J. Cohen in "Some Statistical Issues in Psychological Research," Chapter 5 below. Additional questions have been raised by Wolman (1960, chap. 14).

The core of the problem lies in the Kantian overemphasis on the role of mathematics, giving the impression that whoever does not use mathematics is not practicing science. It is worthwhile to remember that the greatest scientific discoveries in psychology have been made by Pavlov, Freud, and Piaget, none of them a mathematician. Certainly mathematics adds precision to propositions describing empirical data, but it does not offer any consolation when the empirical findings are meager, lack precision, are not objective, or lack adequate proof.

As Goedel has shown, even mathematics is not perfect because in any arithmetical system that is not self-contradictory, there are true propositions that cannot be derived from it. Thus, the highly mathematical research reports in clinical psychology sometimes give the impression of overplaying mathematics with inadequate knowledge of fact.

It seems to be more in agreement with the highly complex nature of abnormal behavior to start research with a detailed and most thorough study of the individual case. The next step may be a cautious and tentative generalization. High-powered mathematics too eagerly and too early applied to the clinical field is not the best research procedure. Clinical psychology has to learn to walk before it may start running.

Idiophenomena

Any quantification is based on a system of classes, i.e., on an assumption that the entities included in a class belong there logically. Physics operates on such systems of classes, for it is generally agreed that the elements of physics belong to certain classes.

No such agreement seems to be feasible in contemporary psychological theory, not even on the level of empirical generalizations, often called "experimental laws" (Feigl, 1951). Questions have been raised in regard to the generality of psychological propositions. Could they be stated in such a way that if behavior n belongs to class N and all designates of the class N are a result of the event M, then whenever M occurs, behavior n will take place?

Obviously, this is not always the case. Let us

use punishment (any infliction of pain) as M and withdrawal as n. One may hypothesize that whenever M occurs, some withdrawal action (a member of class N) will take place. But in several cases, punishment (burning the skin in Pavlov's experiments or pain in severe schizophrenics) will cause no withdrawal. Apparently individual differences are here of great importance. Consider reactions to stress, to anxiety, to sexual frustration, etc. Certainly humans behave in a more individualized way than Skinner's pigeons (cf. Scriven, 1956b).

The stress on individual differences, put by Stern in terms of *unitas multiplex* (1938) and reemphasized by Allport (1942; 1961), certainly deserves careful consideration. Were psychological events true and unrepeatable idiophenomena, the case study method would be the sole justified method of research.

The problem of idiographic versus nomothetic sciences (cf. Allport, 1942; Allport, 1961; Holt, 1962; Wolman, 1960, chap. 14) requires additional elucidation. This problem was crucial in the medieval discussion between "realists" and "nominalists." Realists ascribed existence to "generalia" such as rocks, houses, trees, etc., in general. Nominalists rejected the notion that there is such a thing as a rock, a house, a tree, in general. There are peculiar rocks, houses, and trees; the name "rock" or "house" is merely a *name* (hence nominalism) of a class of objects put together on the basis of a certain similarity between them. The only things that exist are *certain* rocks, houses, trees, etc.

A similar discussion was started by both the Baden and the Marburg schools of neo-Kantians. Are all objects and events single and unrepeatable, or are they categories and classes of events, whether they are studied by physics or history, astronomy or psychology?

In 1894 Windelband introduced the distinction between the natural and the historical sciences. The units of the natural world, he said, are atoms. Atoms are "colorless and soundless, without any smack of the sensible qualities" (quoted after Hodges, 1952, p. 227). Atoms are homogeneous and lack individual character. Natural sciences seek universal laws (nomos); science "seeks not the changeful as such but the changeless form of change." Thus natural sciences are *nomothetic*. History, in contradistinction to natural science, seeks the unique, individual, and unrepeatable idiophenomenon (Windelband, 1904).

It seems that Windelband unwittingly repeated the error of medieval realists. It can be easily shown that each atom, each speck of dust, and each drop of water is an idiophenomenon. Whatever is, was, or will be is a unique and unrepeatable event. History, as well as astronomy and physics, deals with idiophenomena. Thus not only Napoleon's march on Moscow in 1812 was an idiophenomenon, but the winter of 1812, the snow that covered the roads, and each particular revolution of earth at that time were also unique events. Whoever exists is an idiophenomenon, but sciences abstract or overlook the individual differences and group together objects and events on the basis of at least one common trait. Thus, though each rock and each tree and each earthquake is an idiophenomenon, they are grouped into classes of rocks, trees, and earthquakes.

In two essays, one devoted to natural sciences (Wolman, 1938) and the other to behavioral sciences (Wolman, 1948), I have tried to prove that *all phenomena are idiophenomena but that all sciences are nomothetic.* This rule applies to clinical psychology also. The case of "Dora" was an idiophonomenon, but so was Freud's treatment of her. Yet there have been many similar cases, and several therapists have repeated Freud's method. Clinical psychology starts from the study of single cases, compares them, classifies them, and forms general statements.

These general statements have been called by Feigl (1951) "empirical laws" and by Nagel (1961) "experimental laws." I prefer to call them "empirical generalizations" because only some of the psychological data have been derived from experimental procedures, but all psychological data are empirical, or they are not data at all. Experiment is one of the empirical methods and not the only one. I prefer the term "generalization" to the term "law" because the latter is ambiguous, while "generalization" merely implies a logical prodedure.

Empirical generalizations must be validated by proper empirical procedures. The method of choice is controlled experiment, but the question of research procedure leads to the next section of this chapter, devoted to methodological problems.

METHODOLOGICAL PROBLEMS

Psychological Propositions

Several authors have pointed to differences between propositions of behavioral and physical sciences (Kotarbinski, 1964; Scriven, 1956a; Wolman, 1964a; and others). A detailed analysis of propositions of clinical psychology may be advisable.

All propositions of clinical psychology can be divided into five categories:

1. Propositions describing *observable behavior*, such as nervous tics, stuttering, excessive perspiration, bed-wetting, compulsive acts, impotence, violence, suicidal attempts, etc. This very large class of behavioral patterns is called "symptoms." Clinical studies start usually from symptomatology, i.e., from the observation of, and/or experimentation with, *observable patterns* of abnormal behavior. Symptomatology is certainly the oldest part of psychopathology.

2. Propositions describing *introspectively observable phenomena,* i.e., human behavior that is not easily observed from without, such as toothache, headache, worry, hunger, and fear. One may doubt the objectivity of introspective data, but their existence is undeniable. Whether the patient fears real or imaginary dangers and whether he complains about true or imaginary aches and pains, the content of his communication must not be overlooked. Clinical psychology cannot omit these valuable clues. A good empiricist studies not only the smoke but also the hidden fire. Not only an attempted suicide, but also suicidal thoughts—not only hostile acts, but also hostile feelings—belong in the realm of clinical study.

3. Propositions describing *unconscious processes,* i.e., those mental processes which are not accessible even to the experiencing individual himself. Kant, Mach, Husserl, and Wundt dealt with conscious phenomena. Whenever the subject was unaware of his feelings, the existence of such feelings was readily denied. Psychology was a science of the Bewusstsein (consciousness) and of nothing else.

The studies of Janet, Charcot, and Freud; the experimental research in hypnosis; and the experimental studies in unconscious, interoceptive conditioning (to be discussed later on) proved that unconscious processes are not a theory but an empirical fact. Thus the third category of psychological propositions emerged.

4. Propositions describing hypotheses, models, constructs, and other nonempirical elements. The first three categories of propositions deal with factual data; they are all *empirical generalizations.* However, the fourth category, *theoretical propositions* (to be discussed later on), differs substantially from empirical propositions. For example, "Schizophrenics avoid people" is an empirical proposition of the first type; it is or is not empirically true. The proposition "The schizophrenic's superego is overdemanding" is not an empirically true or false statement, for superego is not a behavioral pattern but a theoretical construct.

5. Clinicopsychological propositions dealing with what ought to be done to help the patients. For example, "A psychotherapist must side with his schizophrenic patient" is not an empirical or a theoretical proposition. It is a device, a norm, a rule to obey or disobey. It belongs in the fifth category, praxeological propositions (Wolman, 1964d).

The Observables

The study of overt symptoms raises a host of questions. Can symptoms be put together on the basis of similarities? Are symptoms symptomatic? Consider elation.

It took the genius of a Kraepelin to put together, in 1899, two seemingly opposite patterns of overt behavior and coin the term "manic-depressive psychosis" (cf. Kraepelin, 1921).

In manic-depressive psychosis, the patient who is depressed may seem or later become elated, and vice versa. This is not a violation of the logical law of identity, for in Kraepelin's description the patient was either elated or depressed at a certain time. The change of moods proved merely the changeability and fluidity of moods, but it did not mean that "a" is "not a."

However, later observations of depressive disorders (Rado, 1928; Wolman, 1959) indicate that the elated patient is actually depressed while he is elated. He may be, at a certain moment, profoundly depressed, but trying to overcome his depression by agitated elation.

This seemingly logical contradiction is not a contradiction at all. It is an arbitrary assumption that pain and pleasure, joy and sorrow, tears and smiles, and love and hate are pairs of mutually exclusive terms. Freud's observations of ambivalences point to the fact that, at least at some moments, organisms are capable of experiencing the allegedly contradictory experiences. Pavlov's (1928, p. 228) experiments with salivation as a reaction to electrical destruction of skin offered significant support to this observation and challenged the idea that pain and pleasure are mutually exclusive. Studies of masochism offer most conclusive evidence at this point (Reik, 1941).

Logicians are often impatient with this branch of psychology that deals with irrational behavior (cf. Nagel, 1959). Often they say that one can read in psychoanalysis many different and apparently contradictory statements. Freud's language was a language of case studies, full of historical data, and not free of what look like ambiguities. Consider symptom formation. Fixation can be caused by frustration or by abundant gratification. Anxiety can arise in inhibition of impulse and in overindulgence. The first child in the family can be overindulged or overprotected; so can any other child. Schizophrenics' performance on mental tests depends on their mood (Wolman, 1959) and on who examines them (Kaufman, 1962). (See also "Schizophrenia and Related Disorders," in Part 4.)

One can bring a great deal of empirical evidence in support of these apparently contradictory statements. The business of scientific inquiry is not to ascribe rationality to men but to study in a rational way the irrational ways of mankind. Psychological propositions representing empirical generalizations require a great many qualifications, such as "Men do this and this, provided. . . ." The list of "provisions" is far from complete. The fact that human behavior is often irrational and sometimes self-contradictory does not make clinical psychology irrational. It is the method of research and not the subject matter that makes science.

Comparative Data

Comparative psychology offers a great many useful comparisons and clues in regard to abnormal behavior in humans. It is wholly objective, and all its propositions belong in the first category that describes observable data. Observable animal behavior is the most reliable foundation for comparative research. Pavlov's description of what happened to a dog exposed to conflicting stimuli is a valuable contribution to the understanding of mental disorder. Wrote Pavlov: "The whole behavior of the animal underwent an abrupt change. The hitherto quiet dog began to squeal in its stand, kept wriggling about, tore off with its teeth the apparatus for mechanical stimulation of the skin. . . . In short, it presented all the symptoms of a condition of acute neurosis" (1927, p. 291). No less interesting are the studies of Maier (1949) on frustration in rats, Liddell's research (1956), and scores of other works. The experimental design and the results obtained in comparative psychology have earned well-deserved esteem.

Caution might be advisable in regard to the conclusions arrived at about animal behavior, but even greater caution is necessary when making comparisons to human behavior. One may or may not be convinced that what happened in experimental animals under stress was a neurosis. One may question whether the experimental neuroses were actually caused by conflicting stimuli acting upon the nerve centers. Pavlov's neurology is composed of (1) observable data on the level of independent and dependent variables and (2) theoretical constructs that come in as intervening variables in experimental structure. (Intervening variables are discussed further in the section on theory formation.) Observable data can be confirmed or refuted, and the works of the Soviet research workers (cf. Winn, 1961) offered substantial support to Pavlov's experimental data. However, Pavlov's *theory* of mental disorder is merely a theory and not a statement of fact. Experimental data obtained in a laboratory are, as a rule, more reliable than observational data gathered in a clinic. This laboratory superiority does not, however, extend to logical inferences. Whether one deduces from clinical, behavioral, experimental, or neurological data, it is always a speculation. The trustworthiness of speculative or theoretical propositions will be discussed later on.

Granted that Maier's rats went into seizures *because* of frustration (some workers doubt it) and that Pavlov's dogs suffered nervous breakdowns *because* of stress in discriminatory processes, the question of whether all that applies to human beings is still open. Would a man break down whenever he could not discriminate between a circle and an ellipse? Are happy-go-lucky, unambitious men who have no goal necessarily frustrated? Do they inevitably head toward a nervous breakdown?

The logic of these inferences requires close

scrutiny. The fact that $a + x = m$ does not prove that $b + x = m$ just because there is x in both cases. $a + x$ and $b + x$ have a common element x; humans and birds walk on two feet, but even their walking processes are different. Inferences drawn from one species may be entirely wrong when projected onto another.

The closer to Homo sapiens the species under investigation is, the better the chances for proper inferences are. Consider some of the recent experimental work with monkeys (Harlow, 1962; Harlow & Harlow, 1962; Harlow & Zimmerman, 1959). Analogy has been and still is a useful heuristic method; the closer the similarity, the more justification for the use of analogies. However, analogy is not a method of adducing evidence, and an indiscriminate use of analogies may lead to grave logical errors.

Harlow and Harlow's monkeys were raised without mothers and without a peer group. Several behavioral disorders were observed. "Of course, research on nonhuman animals, even monkeys, will never resolve the baffling complex roles of various kinds of early experiences in the development of human personality," stated the Harlows. However, they believe that "important theoretical and practical questions in the realm of interest can be resolved by the use of monkeys" (1962, p. 10).

Certainly the "close behavioral semblance" between monkeys and humans speaks in favor of comparative studies of that kind. One should perhaps stress the fact that Harlow had in mind a *human problem* such as maternal or peer deprivation and tested it on animals similar to humans. One may doubt whether comparative research could ever solve human problems, but if it is conducted properly, it may offer valuable clues and insights of a heuristic nature.

Yet even the best comparative studies cannot substitute for studies with humans. The effect of maternal deprivation in man has still not been determined. A great many variables have to be taken into consideration, among them the age when deprivation started, the nature and degree of deprivation, the type of compensation received, etc. Although a great deal of valuable research has been conducted in that area by Bender, Bowlby, A. Freud, Goldfarb, H. L. Rheingold, Spitz, and others, the issue is by no means simple or resolved. Especially crucial is the problem of irreversibility of damage caused by a prolonged deprivation. In a recent review of pertinent literature, Yarrow (1961) pointed to the fact that conclusive evidence is still not available.

Introspective Data

Psychology is a science that studies certain aspects of what happens with living organisms. Human psychology observes and explains what people do and how and why they do it; hence it is often called a science of behavior. If "behavior" is used broadly to include also covert and unobservable elements of what goes on with men, it is a satisfactory name.

Many things and events go into this broad term. When John perspires, runs, goes to school, feels persecuted, and refuses to go to work, or when he feels fine and sings, plans to become a physician or a lawyer, and applies to a graduate school—all that is behavior. Yet certain aspects of his behavior, such as running, vomiting, and writing, are as observable as a falling stone, a burning campfire, thunder, or a foul smell. On the other hand, John's feeling, planning, fearing, or suffering is not directly observable but can be *inferred* from (1) his verbal or nonverbal communication (e.g., when he says he is afraid, he probably is); (2) external observation of his observable performance (e.g., when he replies correctly on a mental test, he is probably capable of doing so, and his intelligence is probably high); and (3) the resulting action (e.g., when he took a train to Philadelphia, he probably decided to do so).

Moreover, there is no reason to doubt that John knew about his decision to go to Philadelphia before he actually went. This knowledge of one's own feelings, thoughts, decisions, and fears is called "introspection."

Introspection need not be confused with introexplanation. Introexplanation is a pseudoscientific subjective procedure without any possibility for validation. For example, if Jones says, "I hate people *because* they hate me" or "I fear cats *because* they scratch" or "I have a pain in my tooth *because* I have root infection," his explanation may not be based on, or related to, fact. But if Jones merely introspects to register his own experiences, there is no good reason to disqualify his witness. When he says, "I hate people" or "I have a toothache" or "I dislike cats," this presents an empirical statement.

When a patient says, "I spoke to God," one may doubt whether such a conversation ever took place, but it is quite possible that the patient experienced a hallucinatory conversation. In fact, research in the so-called "experimental psychoses" (Linton & Langs, 1962; Savage & Cholden, 1956) makes good use of subjective, introspectionistic data reported by subjects who said that they felt dizzy, hallucinated, etc. The subjective reports based on introspection are highly correlated with objective data obtained independently with the same subjects.

On the other hand, the use of the plethysmograph and the objective measure of constriction of vessels (Bykov, 1957) make it possible to check introspective data regarding pain and pleasure. Recent experimentation in interoceptive conditioning (Razran, 1961) opens new vistas in a dual research methodology that includes both introspective and objective experimentally tested data. Introspective data are a matter of fact; "personal" experiences are part of behavior and, as such, need not be excluded from scientific inquiry. Clinical psychology, and probably other areas of psychology as well, will not benefit by a blind imitation of physics. Behavioral problems are a part of biology, and biology is a part of natural science. There are problems in biology that physics does not know of, such as intake of food, metabolism, respiration, etc. There are problems in behavioral sciences that neurology and physiology do not know of, such as reasoning, comprehension, decision, fear, etc. Psychology is only remotely related to physics and is closely related to biology. Psychology may learn little from physical sciences and more from biology, but mostly it must learn from its own research area. The fact that there is no room or need for introspection in physiology does not prove that introspection must be abandoned in scientific psychology.

The aversion for introspection had its good points when it was taken at face value by such avowed introspectionists as Wundt and Titchener. When it is taken for what it is and checked against other, more objective research methods, it is valuable in assessing some aspects of covert behavior. In fact, interviewing techniques and, to some extent, also inventories and projective methods (described in detail in Part 3 of the *Handbook*) use the subject's statements about his thoughts and feelings.

A refusal to include "private" events in psychological research (Skinner, 1950) does not necessarily imply good empiricism. An empiricist studies *all* factual data, irrespective of their nature and of the way in which he must assess them. If there is such a thing as private events, science must study them. Hypnotic phenomena were expelled from science in 1784 by the French academies of science and medicine. Notwithstanding this verdict, hypnotism is a matter of fact. So are "private" experiences.

Unconscious Processes

A similar plea has to be made in regard to unconscious processes. Since they are unconscious, these processes do not fit too well into the usual research patterns established by natural sciences. Logic, mathematics, and philosophy did not develop in a vacuum; there has always been an interrelationship and interdependence between the various empirical disciplines and the formal sciences. Present-day logic and mathematics serve physics better than psychology. Psychological propositions may require their own philosophy of science (cf. Wolman, 1964a).

In a volume dedicated to psychoanalysis and philosophy, Pap (1959, p. 292) concluded that since psychoanalytic propositions do not fit into what he believed to be the proper system of psychological data, the unconscious does not exist. Pap distinguished between "intrinsic qualities" and "causal properties" of mental states. Whether his formal division of the content of psychological science is right or wrong is here immaterial. It is, however, worthwhile to say that Pap's reasoning follows Cartesian logic. Things that do not fit into one's rational scheme are pushed out of existence. Needless to say, the formal sciences are sciences of signs, symbols, etc. They may play an exceedingly useful role in analysis and criticism of the scientific procedures of empirical sciences, but they are not the supreme judge in empirical matters. What is and what is not must be resolved by empirical research itself.

The Psychosocial Field

Although experimental studies enjoy the reputation of being objective, the objectivity of clinical observations has always been a controversial issue. A great many data pertaining to the behavior of abnormal individuals have been assessed in clinics, hospitals, and private offices by observers who have observed their patients while trying to help them. Such a *participant observation* gave rise to legitimate doubts in regard to its objectivity. Not only do the difficulties stem from the possible theoretical bias of the observer, but they are directly related to the vantage point of observation. One may say, in a truly Einsteinian sense, that the social position of the therapist-observer compared with that of the patient-observed greatly influences the results of the observation.

Consider the differences in data reported by Freud and Sullivan. Both were keen observers; however, not only their interpretations but even their mere descriptions of the behavior of mental patients were not the same.

The reclining position of the neurotic patient and the sparse communication from the mostly silent psychoanalyst facilitated transference phenomena. Freud, the keen observer, noticed them and made them the cornerstone of his therapeutic method (cf. "The Psychoanalytic Technique," in Part 5). However, when a psychotic patient was asked to recline, with a psychoanalyst sitting behind his couch and watching him, a different reaction took place. Silence was probably perceived as a rejection, and the invisible analyst became a threatening figure. The patient withdrew even more into his shell, and if he did communicate, he would not dare to communicate his true feelings. Such a behavior gave the impression of narcissistic withdrawal and lack of transference feelings toward the psychoanalyst (S. Freud, 1946).

Sullivan worked in a hosptial where patients were moving back and forth and were acting out their feelings. He saw his patients in interpersonal relations, and being a keen observer, he did not fail to notice the socially induced changes in their behavior. The here-and-now interaction became the clue to the understanding of the psychotic patient (Sullivan, 1947; Sullivan, 1953). Most probably what has been observed in participant observations was not the patient as an isolated entity but the patient in interaction with the therapist, a *psychosocial* field situation.

Even a nonparticipant observation cannot escape the field situation. Caudill (1958), Stanton and Schwartz (1954), Wolman (1964c), and others conducted extensive nonparticipant observations in mental hospitals. The observers did not treat the patients they observed, nor did they directly participate in making decisions in regard to the observed patients. Yet their very presence influenced, to some extent, the patients' actions.

Needless to say, this influence grows when the interaction is direct and intense. Several research workers have noticed that mental patients, especially schizophrenics, are highly sensitive to who administers a test and how. Shakow (1946), Garmezy (1952, Winder (1960), Rabin and King (1958), Wolman (1959), and scores of others have noticed that the performance of schizophrenics largely depends on who tests them and how it is done and on who interviews or interacts with them. In other words, schizophrenic performance has its ups and downs, depending on rapport. This should not be surprising. Pavlov's dogs became conditioned not only to the metronome but also to the footsteps and to the presence of Pavlov's coworkers. It should be expected that human reactions depend on who the person interacts with and on the emotional tone of such an interaction.

Interaction includes the totality of social experiences of an individual in his lifetime. Whether one stresses or minimizes the importance of hereditary factors, the fact remains that humans do not live in a vacuum and that they interact with others all their lives.

The striking differences in performance between patients who have been recently admitted to a hospital and the long-time "chronic" patients illustrate this. Some students of this issue go as far as to hypothesize that the grave deterioration is a result of hospitalization. Noyes and Kolb (1958, p. 419) remark about the chronic, unemployable schizophrenic patients in the back wards of mental hospitals that their "deterioration is, to a considerable degree, often a hospital artifact."

In physics, under Einstein's influence, there has been a growing awareness of the fact that any observer-observed situation represents a field. Wrote Jeans: "Every observation involves a passage of a complete quantum from the observed object to the observing subject, and a complete quantum constitutes a not negligible coupling between the observer and the observed. We can no longer make a sharp division between the two. . . . Complete objectivity can only be regained by treating observer and observed as parts of a single system" (Jeans, 1958, p. 143).

Field studies in clinical psychology must include not only the here-and-now observer versus observed situation, but also the totality of the past social experiences of the patient. Humans are what they are as a result of (1) inherited factors and (2) interaction with their physical and social environment.

This field type of research has nothing to do with Lewin's field-at-a-given-time (Lewin, 1936; Wolman, 1960, chap. 13). The interactional fields are changeable, and a snapshot taken at a certain time may give only a fraction of truth. Psychological research must be painstaking, thorough, preferably longitudinal, and geared to the aim of discovering the total truth. There is no substitute for, or shortcut to, a detailed study that unravels all aspects and all facets of a problem.

CLINICAL THEORIES

Theory Formation

Empirical generalizations describe what things happen, how they happen, and how often they happen. Science, however, must reach beyond observables and make inferences regarding connections, relationships, etc. A collection of data is not a scientific system, just as a pile of bricks is not a house, said Poincaré. Science is composed of facts and theories that *explain* the facts.

Yet not all psychologists are in agreement on this issue. The dissidents are divided into two important groups. The first group, led by Skinner, sees no need for theory; the second group, starting with Lewin, disagrees with the explanatory notion of theory.

A radical opposition to theory formation was introduced by Skinner (1931; 1938; 1950). The business of science is, as Mach suggested, to describe observable phenomena. In Mach's system "explanation is reduced to description and the notion of function substituted for that of causation. The full description of an event is taken to include a description of its functional relationship with antecedent events" (Skinner, 1931).

Skinner's opposition to theories is rooted in a profound dislike for armchair speculation and, as such, deserves proper credit. In the struggle of empiricism against rationalism (briefly described in the first section of this chapter), it was Hume who wrote the emphatic words that follow: "All ideas, especially abstract ones, are naturally faint and obscure; the mind has but a slender hold of them . . . . All impressions, that is, all sensations, either outward or inward, are strong and vivid" (1894, par. 2). Ideas must be derived from sensations and checked against them.

Certainly armchair theories that do not rest on empirical data have been more a handicap than a help in the progress of sciences. Yet this aversion to theory, so pronounced in Skinner's works, does not necessarily guarantee a fruitful research. Skinner's system "confines itself to description rather than explanation. Its concepts are defined in terms of immediate observations. . . . A reflex is not an arch, a drive is not the state of a center. . . . Terms of this sort are used merely to bring together groups of observations, to state uniformities, and to express properties of behavior which transcend single instances . . ." (Skinner, 1938, p. 44).

The question of why things happen—why overt behavior is a function of external condition—has been left out by Skinner and his school. A Skinnerian can very well describe what happens in abnormal behavior and how it happens, but he refuses to look into causes and explain why what happened, happened.

Another opposition to explanatory theories in psychology was introduced by Lewin. According to Lewin, a theory is a system of concepts that represent empirical data. Conceptualization is the key to every theory. Scientific theories use two types of concepts. The first-order concepts are mathematical; they "represent the logical structure of empirical relationships." Lewin chose topology as the mathematics psychology has to be ordered to. The second set of concepts are dynamic concepts such as force, force field, valence, etc. Conceptual representation of empirical data, "of what is, is at the same time an explanation of what happens" (Lewin, 1936, p. 11).

Lewin shied away from generalization and classification. He tried to solve the problem of idiophenomena as posed by Dilthey and Windelband. Lewin believed that the determination of scientific laws "involves the task of representing concrete situations in such a way that the actual event can be derived from them according to the principles which are given in the general laws." Each given situation is unique, and the business of constructive psychology is to "predict individual cases." For "a complete representation of one situation would mean that the whole task of psychology is completed. . . . The representation of a situation implies no less theory than the laws which it presupposes" (Lewin, 1936, p. 82).

Lewin did not like a question such as "Do all children do that, or is it at least *common?*" Such a question seemed to him to be "Aristotelian," the class defining the essential nature of the object (Lewin, 1935, p. 82). To represent the totality of a situation at a given time was to Lewin tantamount to making a complete analysis of a problem.

At the present time the antitheoretical bias is perhaps in vogue among clinical psychologists. The multiude of explanatory theories introduced by psychiatrists such as Freud, Adler, Jung, and Sullivan is, to some extent, a contributing factor to this antitheoretical bias. Clinical psychologists (cf. chapters in the *Handbook* by M. Harrower, O. H. Mowrer, and others) are becoming wary of the inability to prove or disprove any of the abovementioned and other theories. Purely descriptive-behavioristic terms are presently more often used than before (cf. Bachrach, 1962; Eysenck, 1961). It reminds one of the early years of post-Newtonian physics, with the almost general aversion to theory.

Physical Theory

At this point, a comparison with the status of physical theory may be useful. "The physical theory of relativity has now shown that electric and magnetic forces are not real at all; they are mere mental constructs of our own, resulting from our rather misguided efforts to understand the motion of the particles" (Jeans, 1958, p. 200).

As Einstein remarked, theories are not a result of empirical generalizations. They are "free inventions of the human spirit, not logically derivable from what is empirically given" (1959, p. 684). Einstein did not accept Bridgman's idea that theories must be described in operational terms, i.e., in terms of acts performed by the research worker. "In order to be able to consider a logical system as physical theory it is not necessary to demand that all of its assertions can be independently interpreted and 'tested operationally'; *de facto* this has never yet been achieved by any theory and can not at all be achieved" (1959, p. 679).

Theoretical propositions are neither true nor false in the empirical sense. They do not state facts; they *explain* facts. A theory does not say, "It is so-and-so" or "All hysterics tend to exaggerate." A theory explains *why* it is so-and-so and *why* hysterics tend to exaggerate. The phenomena of light are *described* by empirical generalizations; the same phenomena are *explained* by the wave and molecular theories of light.

The fact that there is more than one theory of light is not earthshaking to physicists. Although human behavior is certainly more complex than physical phenomena could ever be, some psychologists seem to expect theories to fit in a simple and indisputable way into their empirical findings and are eager to reject a theory at the drop of an experimentalist's hat.

Actually a theory does not copy empirical data. Deductively formulated constructions deal with "empirically unobservable, purely imaginative or intellectually known, theoretically designated factors, related in very complicated ways to the purely empirically given" (Northrop, 1959, p. 389).

A theory is a system of hypotheses. Hypotheses explain, and their explanations should be open to factual verification. "Yet most often hypotheses cannot be directly proven. An indirect and by far incomplete proof is available through deduction from the hypothesis that could be experimentally tested" (cf. Cohen & Nagel, 1934, pp. 207ff.).

The complexity of psychological data is not too conducive to simple generalizations and easily proved hypotheses. Consider Pavlov. Although his theory has had a tremendous research backing in thousands of experiments conducted by Pavlov himself and by scores of workers, his neurological interpretations of conditioning that form the *core* of his theory have not been directly proved. The specific hypotheses deduced from Pavlov's laws of irradiation, concentration, and induction have been successfully tested, but the main body of theory of conduction and connection and of analyzers and neuroses is, and perhaps must remain, a useful hypothetical system (cf. "Behavior Therapy," in Part 5).

Tolman has coined the term "intervening variables." The observable causes of behavior, the objectively definable factors, are grouped together under the name "independent variables." The resulting observable behavior of the organism is the "dependent variable." Intervening variables "are to behavior as electrons, curves, or whatever it may be, are to the happenings in inorganic matter," wrote Tolman (1932, p. 414).

MacCorquodale and Meehl (1948) distinguished between intervening variables and "hypothetical constructs." They believed hypothetical constructs are far more elaborated than intervening variables.

Feigl (1951) called the hypothetical constructs "existential hypotheses." Existential hypotheses "fill out" the space assigned to intervening variables. They should be introduced on the basis "of some new and heterogeneous area of evidence."

Actually the differences in the concepts used are differences in language. Whenever one talks about observational or experimental procedures, the proper terms are the "observable independent variables," the "observable dependent variables," and the "inferable intervening variables." Whenever one discusses theoretical propositions, the term to be used is "theoretical constructs" or "hypothetical constructs." Freud's ego and libido are not empirical facts but theoretical (or hypothetical) constructs. Ego or libido could serve as a variable if one could design an experiment in which these constructs could be interpolated between the independent and dependent variables.

Operationism

Basically, theoretical propositions, like any other scientific propositions, should meet the criteria of immanent and transcendent truth (cf. Wolman, 1960, chap. 14). However, no science could apply these two criteria rigorously.

The criterion of immanent truth was believed to be applicable to mathematics until the studies of Russell (1948) undermined the rationalist belief in the infallibility of mathematics. Russell has shown that mathematical propositions are not, as Kant believed them to be, a priori and synthetic propositions, but mere symbolic definitions. Definitions can be set at will; the rules of operations can also be set at will. A consistent application of the system of symbols and rules may lead to absolutely certain conclusions, free of contradictions. However, Goedel (1931) has shown that this certainty is not as absolute as it seemed to be and that even mathematics is not the perfect haven for an absolute immanent truth.

It may seem that a theory coated in terms of its empirical data would have a better chance of meeting the criterion of transcendent truth. Hence the natural tendency of clinical psychologists to formulate their theories in the language of empirical observations and experimentation. It is therefore not surprising that many psychologists accepted Bridgman's operationism. According to Skinner's definition, operationism is "the practice of talking about (1) one's observations, (2) the manipulative and calculational procedures involved in making them, (3) the logical and mathematical steps which intervene between earlier and later statements, and (4) nothing else" (1945).

Carnap believed that operationism "has contributed to the clarification of many concepts and has helped to eliminate unclear or even unscientific concepts. On the other hand, we must realize today that the principle is too narrow. . . . The requirement of testability and of operationism excludes some empirically meaningful terms . . ." (1956, p. 65).

Operationism, by its insistence on the study of observations, imposes unnecessary limitations in research. Unconscious phenomena cannot be operationally defined, but there is no good reason to study the visible smoke and overlook the hidden fire.

There is, moreover, no evidence that the research worker's observation of his own behavior or operations is more objective and therefore scientifically more valid than his observation of the behavior of other humans. An operationally minded clinical research worker will trust his data more if they are in terms of his own activities. Such a preferential treatment of oneself can be traced to the Kantian tradition, which ascribed intelligibility to the "inner" observation and questioned the validity of observation of the outer world. It was Mach who "insisted on the direct discussion of observations and regarded scientific laws as the description of observations in the most economical way" (Jeffreys, 1957, pp. 15–16). Mach implied that the perception of outer phenomena is questionable and that the observation of the observer's own sensations is the only true science. Science deals with observables, and the only observables are our own sensations. Kant told scientists to look into their own perceiving minds; Mach requested them to look into their own sensations; Bridgman ordered them to look at their own hands.

None of them could have proved that looking at oneself is more valid than looking at others (cf. Plutchik, 1963; Wolman, 1964a).

Some psychologists insist that not only observational and experimental data and empirical generalizations of observable data but also theoretical systems be presented in operational terms. Such a demand, if rigorously applied, would wreck theory, for both physics and psychology operate with theoretical constructs not derived from, or expressed in terms of, experimental research. Consider neutrons. Bridgman was critical of quantum theory because "it is not obvious how one would construct an idealized laboratory apparatus for making any desired sort of measurement" (1936, p. 189). Thus Bridgman (1959) accepted relativity theory, but Einstein (1959, p. 679) never approved of operationism.

Furthermore, the language of empirical findings and even of empirical generalizations in psychology deals with observable phenomena of animal and human behavior, while psychological theory must account for inferable data and interpolate empirical findings with a great many constructs, models, etc.

Some rules must be established to enable one to distinguish between "good" and "bad" theories. Since formal logic may safeguard immanent truth, and mathematical symbols and operations are far more logical than any spoken language, quantification of theories substantially enhances their scientific value. Thus whenever measurement and statistics are applicable to clinical research, they should be applied (cf. "Measurement in Clinical Research" and "Some Statistical Issues in Psychological Research," Chapters 4 and 5 below).

Far more complicated is the problem of the "correspondence rules" (Nagel, 1961, pp. 97ff.) to be established between a theory and the empirical data it tries to explain. Despite thirty years of solid experimental work and a great deal of theorizing, no learning theory has been either generally accepted or discredited and abandoned (cf. Miller, 1959; Ritchie, 1964). Theories are competitive; apparently preference should be given to those which are more consistent, more in agreement with empirical data, more explanatory, and more heuristic.

In the history of physics some concepts, such as the phlogiston theory, have been discredited. Newton's theory yielded to the more general and more explanatory theory of relativity. One may expect a similar process in psychology, but at the present time there is no superior theory that has rendered all others obsolete (cf. Wolman, 1960, chap. 14).

Clinical Theories

Thus clinical psychology is not unique among other fields in psychology in regard to the wide range of disagreement among the various theories. There is, however, less disagreement among learning theorists in regard to the nature of reinforcement than among clinicians in regard to the nature of schizophrenia.

As was mentioned above, the inability to reach an agreement on a theory is probably a contributing factor to an antitheoretical bias. Since psychology has become experimental, psychologists have been conditioned to a streamlined way of proving and disproving their findings, often expecting the impossible. There is no clear-cut method of "proving" a clinical theory, and it is quite possible that there is more than one way of explanation. There is but one empirical truth, but a theory is not an empirical truth.

Theories are accepted or rejected on formal and methodological grounds (cf. Jeffreys, 1957; Nagel, 1961; etc.). When a theory contains gross inner contradictions, it is useless and must be rejected; also when its main propositions evade empirical test or are contradicted by empirical evidence, a theory is useless. When a theory is formulated so as to be untestable, it is not necessarily wrong; it is merely useless, for the task of science is to find truth and adduce evidence. When a theory is contradicted by empirical data, the data and the theory must be rechecked. Ultimately a theory must be explanatory of an established body of empirical findings; sometimes a modification of a theory, a rewording of its propositions, and an elaboration of correspondence rules between the theoretical propositions and empirical data may increase its testability.

The reader will soon notice that this *Handbook* incorporates several theoretical systems. In fact, neither it nor any other volume can at the present time offer a generally accepted theory. Luria, Yacorzynski, Mowrer, Hurst, Ross, Seeman, and others write from highly diversified viewpoints representative of the variety of opinions in this field.

Although it is natural to hope that truth will ultimately prevail, this is possible with empirical data only. One can prove or disprove whether a certain precisely defined category of "patients" or disturbed individuals had or did not have certain experiences; one can prove or disprove by a painstaking and controlled study whether certain physical or chemical noxious agents are or are not associated with a certain mental disorder. No one, however, can "prove," in the empirical sense of the word, that in schizophrenia the ego is hard pressed by the superego, that the ego boundaries are impaired, that the self-system is damaged, that the interindividual cathexes are disbalanced, or that protective inhibitions developed in the cerebral cortex. One cannot prove all that because Freud's superego, Federn's ego boundaries, Sullivan's self-system, Wolman's interindividual cathexis, and Pavlov's protective inhibitions are all theoretical constructs and not things or events (cf. "Schizophrenia and Related Disorders," in Part 4).

The theoretical controversy in the study of mental disorders takes, however, a new turn as soon as the theorists realize that they are battling not for the sake of empirical truth but for the sake of epistemological, logical, and methodological convenience. Certainly the search for empirical data must be pursued with utmost rigor and controls; e.g., one must make sure whether schizophrenia is or is not associated with tuberculosis or whether psychosomatic symptoms occur in all or some disorders. This empirical research leads to empirical generalizations.

Theoretical discussions are being conducted on a different level. One cannot answer such a question as "Do people have self-system (Sullivan), or do they have instead an id-ego-superego system (Freud)?" The question to be resolved is "Which hypothetical system is more consistent, is more in agreement with the established body of empirical data, explains more facts, and thus is heuristically more fruitful and methodologically more convenient?"

Some of the research aimed at proving Freud's theoretical propositions operated with poorly defined concepts and oversimplified the issue. "The triviality of determined differences in this field makes a most discouraging picture: and the coarseness of the experimental methods so far available does not augur well for the future," wrote Sears about repression (1943; cf. also Barker, Dembo, & Lewin, 1941; Farrell, 1954; A. Freud, 1951; Hilgard, Kubie, & Pumpian-Mindlin, 1952; Wolman, 1960, pp. 337ff.; Wolman, 1964b). Nagel's (1959) verdict in regard to psychoanalytic propositions, stating that they were not proved, is applicable to all theories of mental disorders and perhaps to all theories, for theories cannot be proved. They may, however, be backed up by a substantial body of empirical evidence.

PRAXEOLOGY

Some methodological problems of clinical psychology stem from its two distinct scientific traditions. Clinical psychology is an empirical science as a psychology and a praxeological science as a clinical discipline. It resembles, therefore, a combination of empirical science, physics, and engineering (praxeology).

A division of clinical psychologists into "physicists" and "engineers" may prove detrimental to both groups, as has been mentioned in the preface to the *Handbook*. Those clinical psychologists who try to follow the pattern of physics may overlook crucial issues, and they often spend their valuable time and effort studying trivialities. A substantial part of clinical research falls into this category, as a perusal of doctoral dissertations and published journal articles will prove. Some research workers seem to be satisfied with the mere exercise of scientific tools and procedures, even when their efforts do not produce knowledge beyond the scope of what is already known. Consider the following statement, summarizing four years of intensive hospital research: "Much of what we have learned from our carefully controlled experiments appears in retrospect to be composed of things that skilled, experienced clinicians 'knew' all the time. . . . But remember that we now have the advantage of measuring these things automatically in the laboratory" (Lindsley, 1960, p. 15). Yet even automatic measurement of the obvious does not produce knowledge (cf. the first paragraph of this chapter).

The academically oriented psychologists have been, in a vast majority of cases, trained in experimental procedure with animals. The experimental animals have usually been white rats, pigeons, or dogs. The experimenter has exercised full mastery over the independent variables and could easily isolate and variate all the experimental variables; hence precision, automation, and streamlined designs.

Experimentation with humans, for practical and ethical reasons, has been limited to simple and emotionally rather neutral issues. Whenever experimenters dealt with human feelings, they had to use volunteers. The experimental design had to be limited to unoffensive and unharmful procedures. Even the experiments with the so-called "model psychoses" did not produce a true psychosis; who would dare to create a life-long and possibly incurable schizophrenia in his volunteers? In all these experiments, experimenters and subjects have been reasonably sure that no real psychosis was experimentally produced (cf. Abood, 1960; Rinkel, Hyde, Solomon, & Hoagland, 1955; etc.).

Despite Skinner's optimism in 1955 about "the bright future to which research in psychiatry is now pointing" that could eventually lead to "prediction and control" of human behavior (1959), so far no significant results have been reported (cf. Lindsley, 1960; Lindsley, 1963; "Experimental Methods in Clinical Psychology," Chapter 3 below; "Learning Theory and Behavior Therapy," in Part 2; "Behavior Therapy," in Part 5).

In general, however, the impact of the objective, quantitative, and experimental scientific approach has been beneficial in clinical research as an antidote against the tradition of drawing far-reaching conclusions from an anecdotal description of a single case. Apparently the "physicists" have introduced good and bad points into clinical research, and each side may learn a lot from the other.

The fact that clinical psychology is a "science in service of those who need help" makes the praxeological type of research more relevant. Whoever *treats* patients must focus on their true problems. He must find the genuine causes to be able to remedy them.

However, the clinicopraxelogical tradition also has its strong and weak points. Since it is often urgently necessary to *do* something to remedy a painful situation, the clinician may become a sort of hurried handyman whose repair work is not based on a thorough knowledge but on the necessity to help immediately, even if the value of the help is dubious.

Clinical psychology, since it deals with human problems and tries to remedy them, has been greatly influenced by the scientific tradition of medicine. Medicine is a praxeological science *par excellence*. Its research has been predominantly case study research; medical books and journals have been full of descriptions of cases and treatment procedures and techniques. The history of medicine is notorious for its long list of trials and errors. It took the genius and perseverance of many great physicians to develop experimental medicine (cf. Bernard, 1949) and to establish the scientific, empirical foundations for the medical praxeology.

In clinical psychology the physics-like quantitative research may sometimes lead to statistically significant but otherwise irrelevant findings, while the engineering type of case study may lead to a collection of highly interesting anecdotal data that lack scientific evidence. And if the gulf increases, there is the danger that the "physicists" in clinical psychology will amass a great deal of precise and valid data about nothing and that the "engineers" will amass nothing of scientific value in regard to most relevant phenomena. The sad truth has to be stated that as long as these two approaches are kept apart, not much progress can be expected.

Obviously the problem lies in the necessity of combining the *truth-seeking* experimental and quantitative research methods borrowed from physics with the clinical methods geared to the *necessity of helping*. Research must be objective, yet geared toward helping each suffering human. It seems, therefore, that there is no substitute for a thorough, detailed, painstaking study of a single case (cf. "The Case Study Method," below). This is the necessary first step; the other steps must lead to experimental checking of data and to measurement, generalization, and quantification. The detailed case study will determine the relevant issues, point to significant problems, single out the research variables, and permit the formulation of tentative hypotheses. Thorough, well-controlled, objective, and rigorous observation, measurement, and experimentation will check the findings, lead to empirical generalization, and make possible the formulation of testable theories.

Clinical Norms

Praxeological propositions can be divided into two categories, namely, norms and techniques. Consider another praxeological discipline, e.g., education. The propositions stating educational aims and goals are normative.

They read: "Children must be educated for democracy" or "Education must be adjusted to the needs of each individual."

As was said before, such propositions are neither true nor false. They are norms. Some philosophers call them "value judgments," thus excluding any possibility of studying them objectively. Philosophers of education expose their philosophies in a more or less arbitrary fashion (cf. Brameld, 1955), for there is, seemingly, no way to prove or disprove their respective viewpoints.

A similar situation seems to exist in the area of mental health. Although to some workers the purpose of treatment is cure, to others it is merely a correction of behavior patterns. Whenever research workers undertake studies of results of treatment, lack of agreement in regard to what is actually studied is quite a handicap.

It seems, though, that the agreed-upon goal of treatment of mental patients is the restoration or creation of a state of "mental health" in them. "Mental health," however, is a most ambiguous term.

The concept of mental health will be discussed in detail in "Mental Health and Mental Disorders," in Part 4. Suffice it to say here that unless mental health is defined in an objective and generally agreed-upon way, any kind of assessment of success or failure of treatment becomes a matter of subjective judgment. The apparent difficulty lies in the praxeological and nonempirical nature of the problem. The question "Who is mentally healthy?" reminds one of the question "Who is well-educated?" or "What social system is the best?" And yet, if one assumes that mental health norms are value judgments established at will, one must predict great difficulties for scientific research in treatment. K. Horney wrote: "With us a person would be neurotic or psychotic who talked by the hour with his deceased grandfather, whereas such communication with ancestors is a recognized pattern in some Indian tribes" (1937, p. 15). Does this prove cultural relativism?

An analysis of praxeological propositions can offer some useful clues. Empirical sciences offer no direct guidance in the choice of human goals and ideals. Man decides, rationally or irrationally, what is good or bad—what should be good education, good mental health, good government, etc. Value judgments are arbitrarily set, often dogmatically upheld, and, as a rule, lacking in clarity. Consider social and educational philosophies and the perennial discussion of what is the best social system or what the goal of education should be.

The way out is not to try to establish scientific value judgments; such an effort is self-contradictory, for value judgments are not scientific. The way out is to study the *reasons* for, and *methods* of, human judgments and decisions. Value judgments, whether they apply to ethics, social philosophy, education, or mental health, are ultimately *generalized or objectified attitudes of a certain group.* How men develop value judgments is a legitimate subject matter of empirical study. The question of what men do and how they do it is an empirical one. Science cannot determine what is right or wrong, but it can study how and why people feel as they do. By doing this, it introduces empirical causation instead of praxeological teleology.

Obviously, each society or distinct part of it develops its own so-called "set of values." Human values can be ascribed to supernatural beings, to Platonian ideas, to Kant's thing-in-itself, to Hegel's "objective spirit," to ancestors, or to any other factor. Yet, empirically speaking, no matter where a society gets its values or to whom it ascribes them, it is the society, the *human group*, that establishes its rights or wrongs. Consider Sherif's studies of social norms (1936), Asch's research on group pressures (1951), or Lewin's studies of group decisions (1951).

As a rule, people make their choices in accordance with their *needs*. Men may go wrong in their choices, for they act in accordance with their needs as they perceive them, and they may err in their perceptions. Scientific research cannot establish human norms and goals, but it may look into what caused men to make one or another particular choice in regard to their ethical, political, educational, and mental health values (Wolman, 1964d).

Certainly various societies offer different answers to these questions. Thus there are several social and educational systems and philosophies. Yet there has been and there will always be a *common* element in these choices, for all societies want to survive, and *all* societies want their children to grow and mature. There are definite differences in the way various groups interpret public well-being and educational maturity, but no society wants to perish or wants its children to stay children. Continuity of a group and the growth of an individual are the common elements. Thus there is a culture-free element in educational values, namely, the desire to help children grow. (For a detailed discussion, see Wolman, 1949; Wolman, 1958.)

A similar reasoning is applicable in the mental health area, for no matter how diversified our views are, practically all students of human behavior agree that the most general and universal need is *survival,* all other needs being subordinated to, or derived from, this over-all need. Whether it is called Pavlov's "instinct for life," Freud's "Eros," Goldstein's "self-realization," Hull's "drive," or any other name, it always means that organisms fight to stay alive, and this criterion applies to mental health also. Mental health is not a luxury or a whim but a bare necessity and a prerequisite for survival.

This objective criterion could be compared with analogous criteria in other praxeological disciplines. What is the aim of "treatment" of physical ailments, social ills, or sensory handicaps? The term "cure" is applicable to certain cases only; when a physician prescribes glasses or a hearing aid, when a dentist puts in artificial teeth or bridges, when a social worker helps to find a job—all these are actions aimed at the *optimum adjustment.* The aim is always survival, and survival under the best possible conditions. This is also the aim of the psychotherapist, whether he is a clinical psychologist, a psychiatrist, a psychiatric social worker, or a psychiatric nurse.

Clinical Technique

Several treatment techniques are said to give satisfactory results, although there are workers who question whether treatment gives any results whatsoever.

According to Eysenck's (1952) analysis of 19 treatment reports, the more treatment—especially of the psychoanalytic type—the smaller the recovery rate. His estimate of spontaneous remission was 72 per cent, as compared to 44 per cent for improvement produced by psychoanalytic treatment.

The term "spontaneous recovery" is one of those loosely used concepts that may disappear once light is thrown upon them. Over fifty years ago, Bleuler noticed that some schizophrenic patients rapidly improved ("spontaneously") after a visit from a relative, a change of attendants, etc. (1950). A thorough examination of the alleged "spontaneity" will uncover profound environmental and interactional patterns, no less therapeutically significant than a treatment offered by a good therapist (cf. Rosen, 1953; Schwing, 1954; Stevenson, 1961; Wolman, 1964c).

As far as the results of treatment are concerned, the accounts of treatment are wholly subjective essays. In addition to the absence of generally accepted clinical norms, the clinician's evaluation of his own patients' progress largely depends upon his school of thought, his professional standards, and the level of expectation of achievement in his work. An ill-trained, euphoric, hyperoptimistic worker may praise his achievements, while a highly skilled and successful worker may be dissatisfied with the results of his treatment.

The controversy over treatment methods leaves no stone unturned. Mowrer rejects the basic tenets of psychoanalysis and believes that the very issue of transference is a misconception (1963), while Wolman (1964b) believes that the criticism of psychoanalytic technique lacks objective criteria. Dollard and Miller (1950), Rogers and Dymond (1954), Eysenck (1960), Frankl (1962), and Wolpe (1958), to mention only a few, claim good results whenever they have used their own therapeutic methods. A recently published book by Andreev (1962) claims that satisfactory results were obtained with sleep therapy.

In short, one may be a Freudian or a non-Freudian psychoanalyst; one may be a Pavlovian or a non-Pavlovian therapist; or one may apply gestalt, nondirective, existentialist, or Zen Buddhist methods and yet believe oneself to be always right and successful (see all chapters in Part 5 of the *Handbook*). Certainly something, somewhere, went wrong, either in the assessment of data or their interpretation or in the logic of inferences.

Elsewhere a hypothesis is forwarded (see "Mental Health and Mental Disorders," in Part 4) that underscores the common interactional elements in all types of treatment. More clarification of the terms "health," "cure," "treatment," etc., is necessary before a truly objective evaluation will be possible.

Apparently, objective evaluation of results of treatment is an exceedingly important and controversial issue, as is borne out by the increasing number of research works in this area. The reports of the psychotherapists themselves cannot be used as an objective basis. Sometimes the degree of success is adversely related to one's own estimate of what success should be. Freud himself was certainly less optimistic about the outcome of psychoanalytic treatment at the time he wrote (1937) the paper "Analysis Terminable and Interminable" than he was in earlier years. Actually, in the early years Freud's "cathartic" treatment resulted in removal of symptoms rather than in a thorough reshaping of personality. Certain placebos, suggestions, and reassurances may bring substantial alleviation of symptoms. Is this the aim of psychotherapy?

Freud's concept of "cure" underwent substantial changes with the passing years (cf. S. Freud, 1950; Thompson, 1951). Adler, Jung, Ferenczi, Rank, Sullivan, Horney, and others did not necessarily agree with Freud or with one another. Orthodox and deviant psychoanalytic literature includes hundreds of works discussing the objectives and techniques of treatment. The differences include both goals and means.

Despite these difficulties, a great deal of useful research is going on, testing the methods and results of psychotherapy. Although a detailed description of these methods is given in several chapters in Part 5 of the *Handbook*, the limitations of such research have to be mentioned here.

The discrepancy in results is perhaps the most puzzling element in this research. Some authors, as mentioned above, claim little, if any, results in psychotherapy, while others truly believe the results are highly satisfactory (for references, see all chapters in Part 5).

And yet the truth is probably somewhere in between, somehow related to removal of symptoms, to better functioning, and to a host of highly relevant and still controversial concepts of mental health and mental disorder. There are apparently no shortcuts in this research, nor could anyone at this time claim to have a monopoly on truth or be sure that his truth is *the* truth. Either whoever evaluated the results of treatment was wrong, or, if everyone was right, no treatment was specifically useful. In view of the lack of agreement on such matters as the concept of mental health, what can be accomplished, and how lasting the results must be to be counted as satisfactory, no one can be sure that this or another method is absolutely superior to all others (cf. Bachrach, 1962; Bandura, 1962; Eysenck, 1960; Rogers, 1963; Rogers & Dymond, 1954; Strupp & Luborsky, 1962; Winn, 1962; Wolman, 1964b; Wolpe, 1958). As inconclusive as the research is, it certainly deals with the most crucial issues: Is psychotherapy helping people, and how can it be made more efficient?

Summary

Summarizing the results obtained in praxeological research, one cannot help feeling that achievements have been modest. Wolpe wrote in 1963: "After sixty years of expanding influence, psychoanalytic theory still, in almost every particular, consists of nothing more than speculation" (p. 24). One can only say that if speculation means empirically unproved hypotheses, then certainly there is much speculation in psychoanalytic theory (Wolman, 1964b). But this is also true of the theories of Wolpe, Eysenck, and Pavlov and of any other theory. Wolpe's "reciprocal inhibition" is not an empirical fact but a speculative explanatory principle introduced as a part of his theoretical system.

Thus, since no one can claim a monopoly on truth, especially in the praxeological area, no one has too much to be proud of. All of us grope in darkness. The darkness has been pierced, here and there, by rays of light coming from a Freud, a Pavlov, a Sullivan, and others. What is the *true* great light, we do not yet know. We may have certain preferences, but we must watch our preferences lest they turn into biases and prevent us from making a continuous and objective search for truth.

Philosophy of science can be of great help in the much-needed improvement of research methods and sophistication of reasoning.

REFERENCES

Abood, L. G. A chemical approach to the problem of mental disease. In D. D. Jackson (Ed.), *The etiology of schizophrenia.* New York: Basic Books, 1960.

Allport, G. W. The use of personal documents in psychological science. *Soc. Sci. Res. Council Bull.,* 1942, No. 49.

Allport, G. W. *Pattern and growth in personality.* New York: Holt, 1961.

Andreev, B. V. *Sleep therapy in the neuroses.* New York: Consultants Bureau, 1962.

Asch, S. E. Effects of group pressure upon the modification and distortion of judgments. In H. Guetzkov (Ed.), *Groups, leadership, and men.* Pittsburgh, Pa.: Carnegie Hall, 1951.

Bachrach, A. J. (Ed.) *Experimental foundations of clinical psychology.* New York: Basic Books, 1962.

Bandura, A. Psychotherapy as a learning process. *Psychol. Bull.*, 1961, **58**, 143–159.

Barker, R. G., Dembo, T., & Lewin, K. Frustration and regression: an experiment with young children. *Univer. Iowa Stud. Child Welf.*, 1941, **18**, No. 1.

Barth, P. *Die Philosophie der Geschichte als Soziologie.* 1922.

Berkeley, G. In A. C. Fraser (Ed.), *Principles of human knowledge.* London: Oxford Univer. Press, 1901.

Bernard, C. *An introduction to the study of experimental medicine.* (Tr. by H. C. Greene.) New York: H. Schuman, 1949.

Bleuler, E. *Dementia praecox or the group of schizophrenias.* New York: International Universities Press, 1950.

Brameld, T. *Philosophies of education in cultural perspective.* New York: Dryden Press, 1955.

Brett, G. S. *History of psychology.* (R. S. Peters, Ed.) London: Allen & Unwin, 1953.

Bridgman, P. W. *The nature of physical theory.* Princeton, N.J.: Princeton Univer. Press, 1936.

Bridgman, P. W. Einstein's theories and the operational point of view. In P. A. Schilpp (Ed.), *Albert Einstein: philosopher—scientist.* Vol. I. New York: Harper & Row, 1959. Pp. 333–354.

Bykov, W. H. *The cerebral cortex and the internal organs.* New York: Chemical Publishing, 1957.

Carnap, R. The methodological character of theoretical concepts. In H. Feigl & M. Scriven (Eds.), *Minnesota studies in the philosophy of science.* Vol. I. Minneapolis, Minn.: Univer. of Minnesota Press, 1956.

Caudill, W. *The psychiatric hospital as a small society.* Cambridge, Mass.: Harvard Univer. Press, 1958.

Cohen, J. The statistical power of abnormal–social psychological research. *J. abnorm. soc. Psychol.*, 1962, **65**, 145–153.

Cohen, M. R. *A preface to logic.* New York: Holt, 1944.

Cohen, M. R., & Nagel, E. *An introduction to logic and scientific method.* New York: Harcourt, Brace & World, 1934.

Dollard, J., & Miller, N. E. *Personality and psychotherapy.* New York: McGraw-Hill, 1950.

Einstein, A. *The world as I see it.* New York: Friede, 1934.

Einstein, A. Remarks on the essays appearing in the collective volume. In P. A. Schilpp (Ed.), *Albert Einstein: philosopher—scientist.* New York: Harper & Row, 1959.

Eysenck, H. J. The effects of psychotherapy: an evaluation. *J. consult. Psychol.*, 1952, **16**, 319–324.

Eysenck, H. J. (Ed.) *Behavior therapy and the neuroses.* New York: Pergamon Press, 1960.

Eysenck, H. J. (Ed.) *Handbook of abnormal psychology.* New York: Basic Books, 1961.

Farrell, B. A. Scientific testing of psychoanalytic findings and theory. In H. Brand (Ed.), *The study of personality: a book of readings.* New York: Wiley, 1954.

Feigl, H. Principles and problems of theory construction in psychology. In W. Dennis (Ed.), *Current trends in psychological theory.* Pittsburgh, Pa.: Univer. of Pittsburgh Press, 1951. Pp. 179–213.

Feigl, H., & Scriven, M. (Eds.) *Minnesota studies in the philosophy of science.* Minneapolis, Minn.: Univer. of Minnesota Press, 1956–1962. 3 vols.

Frankl, V. E. *Man's search for meaning.* Boston: Beacon Press, 1962.

Freud, Anna. The contribution of psychoanalysis to genetic psychology. *Amer. J. Orthopsychiat.*, 1951, **21**, 476–497.

Freud, S. Analysis terminable and interminable. *Int. J. Psychoanal.*, 1937, **18**, 373.

Freud, S. On narcissism: an introduction (1914). In *Collected papers of. . . .* Vol. 4. London: Hogarth Press, 1946.

Freud, S. A case of successful treatment by hypnotism (1892–1893). In *ibid.* Vol. 5. 1950.

Garmezy, N. Stimulus differentiation by schizophrenic and normal subjects under conditions of reward and punishment. *J. Pers.*, 1952, **20**, 253–276.

Goedel, K. Ueber formal unentscheidbare Saetze der *Principia Mathematica* und verwandter Systeme. *Monatshefte Math. Physik*, 1931, **28**, 173–198.

Harlow, H. F. The heterosexual affectional system in monkeys. *Amer. Psychologist,* 1962, **17,** 1–9.

Harlow, H. F., & Harlow, Margaret K. Social deprivation in monkeys. *Scientif. Amer.,* 1962, **203,** 2–10.

Harlow, H. F., & Zimmerman, R. Z. Affectional responses in the infant monkey. *Science,* 1959, **130,** 421–432.

Herbart, J. F. Psychologie als Wissenschaft (1824–1825). In *Sämmtliche Werke.* Langesalza: Kehrbach, 1891.

Hilgard, E. R., Kubie, L. S., & Pumpian-Mindlin, E. *Psychoanalysis as science.* New York: Basic Books, 1952.

Hodges, H. A. *The philosophy of Wilhelm Dilthey.* London: Routledge, 1952.

Holt, R. R. Individuality and generalization in the psychology of personality. *J. Pers.,* 1962, **30,** 377–404.

Horney, Karen. *The neurotic personality of our time.* New York: Norton, 1937.

Hume, D. *An enquiry concerning the human understanding.* Oxford: Clarendon Press, 1894.

Jeans, J. *Physics and philosophy.* Ann Arbor, Mich.: Univer. of Michigan Press, 1958.

Jeffreys, H. *Scientific inference.* (2nd ed.) London: Cambridge Univer. Press, 1957.

Kant, I. *Critique of pure reason.* London: Macmillan, 1881.

Kaufman, I. Crimes of violence and delinquency in schizophrenic children. *J. Amer. Acad. child Psychiat.,* 1962, **1,** 269–283.

Kotarbinski, T. *Elementy logiki, theorii poznania, i metodologii nauk.* (Polish.) Warszawa: Atlas, 1929.

Kotarbinski, T. Psychological propositions. In B. B. Wolman & E. Nagel (Eds.), *Scientific psychology: principles and approaches.* New York: Basic Books, 1964.

Kraepelin, E. *Manic-depressive insanity and paranoia.* Edinburgh: Livingstone, 1921.

Lazarsfeld, P. F. (Ed.) *Mathematical thinking in the social sciences.* New York: Free Press, 1954.

Lewin, K. *A dynamic theory of personality.* New York: McGraw-Hill, 1935.

Lewin, K. *Principles of topological psychology.* New York: McGraw-Hill, 1936.

Lewin, K. *Field theory in social science.* New York: Harper & Row, 1951.

Liddell, H. S. *Emotional hazards in animals and man.* Springfield, Ill.: Charles C Thomas, 1956.

Lindsley, O. R. Characteristics of the behavior of chronic psychotics as revealed by free-operant conditioning methods. *Dis. nerv. System,* 1960, **21,** 66–78.

Lindsley, O. R. Free-operant conditioning and psychotherapy. *Current psychiatr. Ther.,* 1963, **3,** 47–56.

Linton, Harriet B., & Langs, R. J. Subjective reactions to lysergic acid diethylamide (LSD-25). *Arch. gen. Psychiat.,* 1962, **6,** 352–368.

MacCorquodale, K., & Meehl, P. E. On a distinction between hypothetical constructs and intervening variables. *Psychol. Rev.,* 1948, **55,** 95–107.

Mach, E. *The science of mechanics.* (6th ed.) La Salle, Ill.: Open Court, 1960.

Maier, N. R. F. *Frustration: the study of behavior without a goal.* New York: McGraw-Hill, 1949.

Maimon, S. *Versuch über die Transcedentalphilosophie.* Leipzig: 1790.

Marx, M. H. (Ed.) *Psychological theory.* New York: Macmillan, 1951.

Marx, M. H. (Ed.) *Theories in contemporary psychology.* New York: Macmillan, 1963.

Meehl, P. E. *Clinical vs. statistical prediction.* Minneapolis, Minn.: Univer. of Minnesota Press, 1954.

Meehl, P. E. Wanted—a good cookbook. *Amer. Psychologist,* 1956, **11,** 263–272.

Meehl, P. E. When shall we use our heads instead of the formula? In H. Feigl, M. Scriven, & G. Maxwell (Eds.), *Minnesota studies in the philosophy of science.* Vol. 2. Minneapolis, Minn.: Univer. of Minnesota Press, 1958.

Miller, N. E. Liberalization of basic S-R concepts: extensions to conflict behavior, motivation, and social learning. In S. Koch (Ed.), *Psychology: a study of a science.* Vol. 2. New York: McGraw-Hill, 1959. Pp. 196–292.

Mowrer, O. H. Transference and scrupulosity. *J. Relig. ment. Hlth.,* 1963, **2,** 313–343.

Nagel, E. Methodological issues in psychoanalytic theory. In S. Hook (Ed.), *Psychoanalysis, scientific method and philosophy.* New York: New York Univer. Press, 1959.

Nagel, E. *The structure of science.* New York: Harcourt, Brace & World, 1961.

Northrop, F. S. C. Einstein's conception of science. In P. A. Schilpp (Ed.), *Albert Einstein: philosopher—scientist.* New York: Harper & Row, 1959.

Noyes, A. P., & Kolb, L. C. *Modern clinical psychiatry.* (5th ed.) Philadelphia: Saunders, 1958.

Pap, A. On the empirical interpretation of psychoanalytic concepts. In S. Hook (Ed.), *Psychoanalysis, scientific method and philosophy.* New York: New York Univer. Press, 1959.

Pavlov, I. P. *Conditioned reflexes.* London: Oxford Univer. Press, 1927.

Pavlov, I. P. *Lectures on conditioned reflexes.* New York: Liveright, 1928.

Piaget, J. *Logic and psychology.* New York: Basic Books, 1957.

Piaget, J. *Introduction à l'épistemologic génetique: T. III. La pensée biologique, la pensée psychologique et la pensée sociologique.* Paris: Presses Universitaires de France.

Plutchik, R. A. Operationism as methodology. *Behav. Sci.,* 1963, **8,** 234–241.

Pratt, C. C. *The logic of modern psychology.* New York: Macmillan, 1939.

Rabin, A. I., & King, G. F. Psychological studies. In L. Bellak (Ed.), *Schizophrenia: a review of a syndrome.* New York: Logos, 1958.

Rado, S. The problem of melancholia. *Int. J. Psychoanal.,* 1928, **9.**

Razran, G. Observable unconscious and inferable conscious. *Psychol. Rev.,* 1961, **68,** 81–147.

Reik, T. *Masochism in modern man.* New York: Grove Press, 1941.

Rinkel, M., Hyde, R. W., Solomon, H. C., & Hoagland, H. Experimental psychiatry. II. Clinical and physio-chemical observations in experimental psychosis. *Amer. J. Psychiat.,* 1955, **111,** 881–895.

Ritchie, B. F. Concerning an incurable vagueness in psychological theories. In B. B. Wolman & E. Nagel (Eds.), *Scientific psychology: principles and approaches.* New York: Basic Books, 1964.

Rogers, C. R. Psychotherapy today. *Amer. J. Psychother.,* 1963, **17,** 5–16.

Rogers, C. R., & Dymond, Rosalind F. *Psychotherapy and personality change.* Chicago: Univer. of Chicago Press, 1954.

Rosen, J. N. *Direct analysis.* New York: Grune & Stratton, 1953.

Rozeboom, W. W. The fallacy of the null-hypothesis significance test. *Psychol. Bull.,* 1960, **57,** 416–428.

Russell, B. *Our knowledge of the external world.* La Salle, Ill.: Open Court, 1935.

Russell, B. *Human knowledge: its scope and limits.* New York: Simon and Schuster, 1948.

Savage, C., & Cholden, L. Schizophrenia and model psychoses. *J. clin. exp. Psychopathol.,* 1956, **17,** 504–418.

Schwing, Gertrud. *A way to the soul of the mentally ill.* New York: International Universities Press, 1954.

Scriven, M. A possible distinction between traditional scientific disciplines and the study of human behavior. In H. Feigl & M. Scriven (Eds.), *Minnesota studies in the philosophy of science.* Vol. I. Minneapolis, Minn.: Univer. of Minnesota Press, 1956. (a)

Scriven, M. A study of radical behaviorism. In H. Feigl & M. Scriven (Eds.), *Minnesota studies in the philosophy of science.* Vol. I. Minneapolis, Minn.: Univer. of Minnesota Press, 1956. (b)

Sears, R. R. Survey of objective studies of psychoanalytic concepts. *Soc. Sci. Res. Council Bull.,* 1943, No. 51.

Shakow, D. The nature of deterioration in schizophrenic condition. *Nev. ment Dis. Monogr.,* 1946, No. 70.

Sherif, M. *The psychology of social norms.* New York: Harper & Row, 1936.

Skinner, B. F. The concept of the reflex in the description of behavior. *J. gen. Psychol.,* 1931, **5,** 427–458.

Skinner, B. F. *The behavior of organisms: an experimental analysis.* New York: Appleton-Century-Crofts, 1938.

Skinner, B. F. The operational analysis of psychological terms. *Psychol. Rev.,* 1945, **52,** 270–277, 291–294.

Skinner, B. F. Are theories of learning necessary? *Psychol. Rev.,* 1950, **57,** 193–216.

Skinner, B. F. *Cumulative record.* New York: Appleton-Century-Crofts, 1959.

Stanton, A. H., & Schwartz, M. *The mental hospital.* New York: Basic Books, 1954.

Stern, W. *General psychology from the personalistic standpoint.* New York: Macmillan, 1938.

Stevenson, I. Processes of "spontaneous" recovery from the psychoneuroses. *Amer. J. Psychiat.,* 1961, **117,** 1057–1064.

Strupp, H. M., & Luborsky, L. (Eds.) *Research in psychotherapy.* Washington, D.C.: American Psychological Association, 1962.

Sullivan, H. S. *Conceptions of modern psychiatry.* Washington, D.C.: Allen White Foundation, 1947.

Sullivan, H. S. *The interpersonal theory of psychiatry.* New York: Norton, 1953.

Thompson, Clara. *Psychoanalysis: evolution and development.* New York: Hermitage, 1951.

Tolman, E. C. *Purposive behavior in animals and men.* New York: Appleton-Century-Crofts, 1932.

Windelband, W. *Geschichte und Naturwissenschaft.* (3rd ed.) Tubingen: 1904.

Winder, C. L. Some psychological studies of schizophrenics. In D. D. Jackson (Ed.), *The etiology of schizophrenia.* New York: Basic Books, 1960.

Winn, R. B. (Ed.) *Psychotherapy in the Soviet Union.* New York: Philosophical Library, 1961.

Wolman, B. B. The chance: a philosophical study. (Hebrew.) *Tarbitz Hebrew Univer. Quart.,* 1938, **10,** 56–80.

Wolman, B. B. Johann Friedrich Herbart. (Hebrew.) *Hachinuch Quart.,* 1942, **15,** 1–23.

Wolman, B. B. *Prolegomena to sociology.* (Hebrew.) Jerusalem: Kiryat Sefer, 1948.

Wolman, B. B. Scientific study of educational aims. *Teach. Coll. Rec.,* 1949, **50,** 471–481.

Wolman, B. B. Education and leadership. *Teach. Coll. Rec.,* 1958, **59,** 465–473.

Wolman, B. B. The continuum hypothesis in neurosis and psychosis and the classification of mental disorders. Paper read at East. Psychol. Ass., 1959.

Wolman, B. B. *Contemporary theories and systems in psychology.* New York: Harper & Row, 1960.

Wolman, B. B. Toward the science of psychological science. In B. B. Wolman & E. Nagel (Eds.), *Scientific psychology: principles and approaches.* New York: Basic Books, 1964. (a)

Wolman, B. B. The evidence in psychoanalytic research. *J. Amer. Psychoanal. Ass.,* 1964. (b)

Wolman, B. B. Non-participant observation on a closed ward. *Acta Psychother.,* 1964. (c)

Wolman, B. B. Psychoanalysis as an applied science. *Amer. Imago,* 1964, **21,** 153–164. (d)

Wolpe, J. *Psychotherapy by reciprocal inhibition.* Stanford, Calif.: Stanford Univer. Press, 1958.

Wolpe, J. Psychotherapy: the nonscientific heritage and the new science. *Behavior Res. Ther.,* 1963, **1,** 23–28.

Wundt, W. *Principles of physiological psychology.* London: Macmillan, 1874.

Yarrow, L. J. Maternal deprivation: toward an empirical and conceptual re-evaluation. *Psychol. Bull.,* 1961, **58,** 459–490.

2
The Case Study Method

HEDDA BOLGAR

The case study method is the traditional approach of all clinical research. It is essentially exploratory in nature; it focuses on the individual, and it aims primarily at discovering and generating hypotheses. It is the preferred method of the clinical psychologist, who is concerned with complex interrelationships between many variables and whose subject matter, i.e., the clinical situation involving human beings, makes experimental manipulation difficult and often impossible.

Much of the knowledge common to all clinicians today was discovered by the case study method. Starting with Kraepelin's minute descriptions of many cases of mentally disturbed patients, all psychiatric diagnostic classification is based on the case study in its simplest form, namely, carefully recorded observation. Psychoanalytic theory was developed through, and continues to be refined largely by, the case study method. Similarly, the development of psychotherapeutic techniques as we know them today originated with Breuer and Freud's (1957) conscientiously recorded observations of the therapeutic process in their famous *Studies in Hysteria.* Since then the case study method has been applied to areas of human life which are not primarily concerned with pathology. Although problems of etiology and the process of psychotherapy are still of greatest interest to the clinical psychologist, child development, the effect of social change on the individual, the formation of personality, and communication and interaction between people are also areas of investigation in which the case study method has led to useful hypotheses. Whenever the investigator approaches a new area in which relatively little is known, the case study is his first methodological choice. The term "case study" itself is ambiguous. It originates in medicine, and clinical psychology has inherited it from psychiatry. The use of the word "case" to designate a human being who is suffering from any kind of physical or emotional disorder has been offensive to many clinicians, but custom dies hard, and all too often a person becomes a case. Case history originally meant the history of a patient's current illness or of several illnesses which added up to his medical history. Social scientists usually speak of the "life history" of a person, and they refer to the data from which a life history is culled as "personal documents." With the advent of the psychologist in the clinic, the case history became the medical as well as the social history of a person, supplemented by personal documents and psychological test data. The clinic case was "studied" in staff meetings and training conferences. It was also studied by means of interviews and special techniques, and occasionally such studies were published. Thus the process of collecting the data and the body of data itself and their clinical and didactic use were all called "case study." For the purposes of this chapter "case history" will designate the raw data, and "case study method" will designate the scientific use that is made of the case history. Personal documents, test protocols, medical records, and transcripts of psychotherapy sessions make up a case history, but they do not represent the case study method of research.

AREAS OF INVESTIGATION

Although the case study method originates in the medical sciences and in psychiatry, not all case study research is concerned with psychopathology and its alleviation. In looking over the literature, one is struck by the fact that there seem to be two branches of case study research which, until recently, developed relatively independently of each other. One is the already mentioned medical, psychiatric, and psychoanalytic clinical research, with its particular genetic emphasis. The other is the study of human development represented by academic child psychology, sociology, and anthropology. Roughly at the same time that Freud was struggling with the seduction theory of the etiology of hysteria, Preyer (1898) was keeping a careful diary of the development of his own child. In general, child psychology represents one of the earliest nonmedical uses of case material. Bechterew (1925), Gesell (1925), and C. Buhler (1935) were among the investigators who applied the method of continuous recorded observation to the study of individual children. Stern (1929) and the Buhlers (K. Buhler, 1918) kept diaries on the development of their own children. Piaget's observations of his three children led to his monumental work on the intellectual development of the child (1952; 1954).

Bohne (1922), Stern (1925), and C. Buhler (1934) investigated diaries of adolescents. C. Buhler (1933) evolved her theories of intentionality and goal-directed tendencies in human life, based on a study of 200 life histories. Frenkel (1936) provided a presentation in English of the methods and findings of this as yet untranslated study.

Sociologists first became interested in the scientific use of life histories following the publication of Thomas and Znaniecki's *The Polish Peasant in Europe and America* (1927). In this five-volume study the authors explore the change and reorganization of the individual, the family, and the community under the influence of rapid transition from one form of social organization to the other. The authors based this investigation almost entirely on personal documents such as letters and autobiographies, and they stated that "personal life records as complete as possible constitute the *perfect* type of sociological material." This method was so new in sociology that Blumer (1939), in his appraisal of Thomas and Znaniecki's work, devoted almost as much space to a discussion of the methodology as he did to the authors' social theory. Since then, life-history material has been widely used in sociological research, particularly in criminology. Works by Healey and Bronner (1945), Shaw (1962), and Sutherland (1937) are good examples. Anthropologists have always used case histories in the form of either spoken autobiographies or interview records. (For the most complete bibliography on the use of personal documents in sociology and anthropology, see Gottschalk, Kluckhohn, & Angell, 1945.)

Social scientists and child psychologists did not use the term "case study" or "case history," but the questions they asked were in essence not too different from those of the clinicians. From the concern with childhood, adolescence, and the psychological experience of human life itself, the trend of investigative curiosity turns to problems of aging (Cummings & Henry, 1961; Neugarten, 1962; Neugarten & Kraines, 1962; Wood & Neugarten, 1962).

Recently the case study method has invaded two of the most taboo areas of human experience—death and suicide. Certainly the questions asked by Feifel (1959) and Shneidman and Farberow (1957) deal with relevant areas in which the interests of clinicians and humanistic psychologists merge.

Unusual individuals or individuals in unusual circumstances seem to challenge the clinical as well as the nonclinical investigator. The question that is asked about the unusual person is: How did he get to be this way? And this may apply to the etiology of psychopathology or organic pathology as well as to the etiology of creativity. Roe (1952), Eiduson (1962), and Gertzel and Gertzel (1962) explored the life histories of eminent scientists and other creative individuals in a first attempt to formulate some hypotheses about the development and functioning of these unusual people. In order to understand the modes in which people cope with unusual or stressful political situations, personality patterns were studied on the basis of life histories by Allport, Bruner, and Jandorf (1941) and Eitinger (1962).

While these are admittedly relevant areas

of psychological study, the clinical psychologist's major preoccupation has been the understanding of the individual with emotional problems. Problems of etiology still constitute one of the major areas of case study research. However, as we get to know more about the problem areas and can move on to ask somewhat more specific questions, case study methods are combined with more experimental approaches, as in the study of Biber et al. (1962) on the etiology of homosexuality or of Jackson (1960) on the etiology of schizophrenia. At the present time, case study research has moved into a new and, to all clinicians, extremely vital area, i.e., the study of the psychotherapeutic transaction. Here the "case" which is studied is not the patient but the interactional process between two people which is designed to produce change in at least one of them. Psychotherapy research, if it is to understand the essential aspects of the process and not just some minor variable, must be approached by the basic methodology of the case study. As in every initial reconnaissance in a new area of investigation, we do not know enough to ask specific questions, and as a result we must study the entire case.

UNIQUENESS VERSUS GENERALITY

The case history, by definition, is the story of one person, and much of the criticism leveled against the case study method of research is based on the accepted canon that it is impossible to generalize from one case. Most investigators agree that the power of this method lies in its ability to open the way for discoveries. Very few claim that it is the function of the case study method to provide experimental validation of a hypothesis. Most clinical researchers will be content with developing initial leads for further investigation. Some will want to pursue their hunches by experimentation; others will leave this type of scientific endeavor to those of their colleagues who are more concerned with experimental rigor. The scientific value of the single case study, beyond the development of hunches or hypotheses, has been upheld in this country primarily by Allport (1942; 1955; 1961). He emphasizes that the understanding of one single person in his uniqueness is a legitimate scientific enterprise and that the interest of the psychologist should be riveted on the individual more often than it is. Allport represents the idiographic point of view, which claims that each single life is lawful and that lawfulness does not depend on the frequency with which an event occurs in different individuals. This point of view stresses the fact that the human individual is more than a representative of any group or class and that he is more than a point of intersection of abstract variables. Accordingly, the whole person must be studied. Understanding, not dissecting, is the true goal of psychology. In recent years this position has received strong support through the development of statistical methods which make possible the quantitative manipulation of the complex interrelationships between a number of variables within one individual. Stephenson (1953); Mendelson, Kubzansky, Liederman, Wexler, and Solomon (1961); Chassan (1961); and Lustman (1962) have stated that the chief advantage of the intensive study of individuals is that it makes possible investigation without the often insurmountable difficulties involved in matching several subjects. The nomothetic point of view demands that generalizations be made to large numbers of individuals and usually by means of large-scale statistics. Allport points out that the difference between nomothetic and idiographic research lies in the coarseness and fineness of the generalizations which are looked for. For precision and refinement, he claims that "a specialized law in personal form is needed."

The current position of some psychologists is best exemplified by Beck's (1963) discussion of the Rorschach method, which "both penetrates human life in its intimate reality and as a scientific tool within the framework of the behavioral sciences." Beck claims that in the Rorschach method, nomothetic and idiographic approaches merge through the use of empirical, inductive method for the study of individual persons. Because of the importance of investigating "human nature at its core," dependable statistics are essential. They are the guarantee for differentiating the patient from the experimenter, or as Beck says, "they take the experimenter out of the experiment." It seems that the framework of diagnostic assessment lends itself well to a productive concern for both the unique and the general. Murray's (1938) classic study of 50 men of college age combined clinical and experimental approaches and at the same time presented psychology with a number of new investigative techniques. However, the argument between the idiographic and the nomothetic points of view is by no means resolved by pointing out that the tools that we employ in studying the unique individual were nomothetically derived and validated. The question still remains the same: Does one single individual represent an acceptable field of study? Holt (1962) argues vigorously and convincingly in favor of laying the ghost of the controversy, claiming that it results from an "anachronistic methodological confusion." However, he does not really address himself to the basic issue. The question is not whether the scientific method can be applied to the individual, but whether the results obtained with a single individual are a scientifically acceptable contribution to knowledge (cf. Hirsch, 1963). The crux of the problem is the idiographic emphasis on precisely that aspect of the individual which is unique to him and which therefore cannot be explored further by replication of the same study with other individuals. Perhaps this is the same kind of controversy as the one about whether psychotherapy is an art or a science.

Psychoanalytic investigators, and particularly Freud, are firm representatives of the nomothetic point of view. Unlike many contemporary humanistic theorists and therapists, Freud, as a scientist, was not interested in the unique experience of one individual nor in any unique pattern of growth or adaptation. He stated: "If we had to deal with only one case like that of my patient, we should turn away from it with a shrug of the shoulders. It would not occur to anyone to base a belief which has such far-reaching implications on an isolated observation, but I can assure you that this is not the only case in my experience" (Freud, 1933).

DISCOVERY VERSUS PROOF

It is pretty generally accepted that experimentation is mainly concerned with proof and rarely leads to discovery and that in the rigid attention to hypothesis testing, the researcher often overlooks unexpected outcomes which might be discoveries. On the other hand, there seems to be universal agreement about the fact that the case study method is the ideal way to generate hunches, hypotheses, and important discoveries. It seems pointless to try to decide which of the two forms of scientific activity is more important or more virtuous. Obviously there comes a time when every discovery, no matter how plausible and appealing, has to be tested against reality (see Holt's discussion of the place of experiment in clinical psychology in "Experimental Methods in Clinical Psychology," below). In fact, a discovery really is only a hunch until its existence in reality can be demonstrated by the methods which all scientists employ in their search for certainty. Clinicians traditionally are more inclined than experimentalists to trust their hunches and to accept them as discoveries even in the absence of experimental evidence. Their confidence is based on the conviction that the clinician's investigative methods of careful, unbiased observation of many instances or many cases are as good as, or superior to, the experimental method.

The methods available for validation of a hunch or a hypothesis determine the status of a discovery at any given time. Freud, in spite of what seems to us today a somewhat circular approach to the problems of assumption and evidence, actually proceeded in the best scientific tradition of his time. He observed and recorded events in the course of the therapeutic work with his patients. He arrived at an explanation that seemed to fit the events and from then on conscientiously perused his case material for events supporting or invalidating his original explanation. The fact that he lacked proper recording methods and that he did not employ any quantitative measures does not alter the basically scientific approach to his clinical work.

For the clinician, the prototype of all case study research is the development of the psychoanalytic theory of personality and psychopathology by Freud. Freud's case studies originated, like all other medical case studies, in the clinician's urgent need to help a suffering patient, but the data gathered in the psychoanalytic method grew far beyond the discovery of therapeutic technology and led to a theory of general human behavior. Or perhaps it would be more accurate to say that the body of psychoanalytic theory aims at the explanation of human behavior in general. It is far from complete, and Freud has always cautioned against prematurely freezing issues and discontinuing investigation.

Each of Freud's published case histories demonstrates the discovery of either a special technique or a new theoretical insight, e.g., the use of dreams, in the case of "Dora" (1925b), or the first analysis of a child, in the case of "Little Hans" (1925a). The case of the "Rat Man" (1925d) led to some of the discoveries concerning the obsessional neuroses, particularly the "omnipotence of thought." In the Schreber case (1925e), which was based on the patient's autobiographic account of his illness and not on his analysis, Freud developed the distinction among different forms of repression, the breaking down of the repression, and the resulting "return of the repressed." In the case of the "Wolf Man" (1925c) Freud demonstrates the impact of transference and countertransference problems on the course of psychoanalytic treatment and his experimentation with a time-limiting-technique type of analysis.

Most students of psychoanalytic literature are well acquainted with the story of Freud's original theory concerning the genesis of the neurosis. It will be repeated here briefly, mostly for its value in illustrating the fate of a famous clinical discovery. Freud (1896a) originally stated that the roots of subsequent neurosis lay in early sexual childhood experiences. He assumed then that his female patients had been seduced sexually by their fathers or some other older male relative. With his later observations and the experience of his self-analysis, he began to doubt his original assumption, and he was led to the now famous revision of the seduction hypothesis. Freud (1954) described in great detail both the thinking that led to "the error into which I fell for a while and which might well have had fatal consequences for the whole of my work" and the reasoning which led him out of it. In the sixty-ninth letter to Wilhelm Fliess, he stated that his reasons for rejecting his own theory were his continual failure to bring his analyses to a real conclusion, the loss of patients who for awhile seemed most promising, the lack of success which he had expected, and the fact that his partial successes could be explained in other ways. Furthermore, Freud reasoned that it was hardly credible that perversion or sexual acts against children should have been so frequent. Finally, Freud wrote, there was the definite realization that there is no indication of reality in the unconscious and that it is impossible to distinguish between truth and emotionally charged fiction. At that point Freud felt he had to abandon the complete solution of a neurosis and the tracing of its etiology into infancy. Freud himself comments with some surprise about his state of mind. Still in the same letter to Fliess, he states that although the occasion might require that he feel disgraced, he actually had a feeling "more of triumph than of defeat." In a footnote added in 1924 to his *Further Remarks on the Neuro-psychoses of Defense,* Freud wrote about this error: "This section was written while I was under the ascendancy of an error which I have since then repeatedly acknowledged and corrected. I had not yet found out how to distinguish between patients' fantasies about their own childhood and real memories. I consequently ascribed to the etiological factor of seduction an importance and general validity which it does not possess" (1896b). Today, of course, we know that the discovery of this error led Freud to the insight into the nature of infantile sexuality and to his most important "discovery," namely, the Oedipus complex. Freud himself, incidentally, usually used the term "insight into" or "understanding of" a psychological event, rather than "discovery."

Murphy's (1956) comments seem pertinent to the general discussion of the relative merits of the case study method. He suggests that "the capacity to observe with open eyes and to test empirically has been part of Freud's approach from the beginning and that despite many premature conclusions, the entire system can be pushed gently in the direction of science." And "while I think the experimental testing of psychoanalytic hypotheses will have *some* value, it has become evident by now that the experimental is only one of several and by no means necessarily the most suitable method to be used in the development of such a science." Murphy goes on to say that in biological phenomena and where large time spans are involved, as in the case of human life, the genetic and comparative methods often take precedence over the experimental.

THE DATA OF THE CASE STUDY

The data of the case study are characteristically communications or observations of events which were not planned or intentionally altered by the investigator for the purpose of research. Even where the communications are elicited rather than produced spontaneously, they usually have not been elicited in an investigative context for the purpose of a specific research project. Responses obtained in the normal course of clinical interviews, diagnostic psychological testing, and psychotherapeutic sessions are naturalistic data unless the diagnostic or therapeutic procedures are systematically varied for the purpose of experimental control. In addition to naturalistic clinical data, case studies also make use of "personal documents" (Allport, 1942) of all kinds. These are generally of greater interest to the historian, the biographer, and the personologist than to the clinical researcher. Nevertheless, as the lines between "illness" and "health" become less sharply drawn and as a rapprochement develops between those who are interested in pathology and those who are interested in human behavior in general, personal documents will again be of value to clinical research.

Personal documents are either first-person or third-person accounts. First-person documents include spontaneous communications, such as letters, diaries, and autobiographies; responses to interviews; free association; and communication of dreams and other matters made during the course of psychotherapy. Third-person accounts are biographies, including clinical case histories and systematic here-and-now observations of behavior.

Diaries, letters, and most autobiographies have in common that they were produced as part of the author's life rather than as data in a clinical or experimental investigation. Allport (1942), Blumer (1939), and Garraty (1957) have discussed the advantages and disadvantages of these documents for psychological, sociological, and historicobiographical research. The use to be made of the personal document very largely determines whether or not some of its characteristics are considered disadvantages. If letters are used to obtain factual information about real conditions in a given place at a given time, the correspondent's veracity and accuracy of observation are of paramount importance. The same is true if the experiences described in a diary or in a letter are to be accepted as having actually occurred or if the reminiscences of an old man at the end of his life are to be taken as evidence of how he felt as a young man. Usually in the case of such ready-made data there is no dependable way of establishing the author's trustworthiness. Indirect methods for checking, and if possible correcting, errors and distortions must be found.

It is important to understand what motivated the author to produce the document in the first place. A large number of possible motivations have been suggested. Those mentioned by Allport (1942; 1961), Garraty (1957), and Krueger (1925) include catharsis, drive for immortality, stocktaking and integration, justification, atonement, cover-up, exhibitionism, financial return, and scientific interest. Closely related to the motive is the question about the nature of the audience to whom the communication is directed. In the case of letters, the recipient is known at least as far as his realistic identity is concerned. The diary, while allegedly written for no one in particular, is often addressed to a more or less consciously fantasied reader. Autobiographies also may be directed at posterity in general, but at times they are written for a specific purpose with a definite audience in mind. Entrance requirements for many professional schools include a written autobiography, and many business organizations require written autobiographical accounts from applicants for executive positions. In that type of situation the writer would most certainly slant his statements with a view to the reader, even if he could not be sure of what is actually expected. A document produced in that way might be a better indication of the writer's expectation and assessment of a school's admissions committee or a company's personnel manager than a full account of his own life. Certainly the usefulness of personal documents is greatly increased if the researcher can make allowances for distortions due to the relationship between the writer of the document and the real or imaginary audience. E. Jones (1955) points out that in Freud's voluminous correspondence with many colleagues and friends, there was a great deal of difference in the contents of his letters and even in the scientific points he discussed in them, depending on the person to whom they were addressed.

In exploring Freud's correspondence in a longitudinal fashion, Jones also found that the early letters were written to relieve tension, while in later life Freud was concerned with helping his friends. Collections of letters written by one person over a long period of time and to a stable set of correspondents are an excellent source of data for studies in which changes in behavior are related to the variable of maturation or aging. In a study based on more than two thousand letters covering most of the adult life of three different individuals, Bolgar (1934) has traced transitions and changes in needs, goals, and values in significant areas of human existence. The use of letters made it possible to learn about the thoughts, feelings, and spontaneous concerns of the authors at the time they were experienced and to observe the changes with maturation and aging. No other type of personal document provides such immediate here-and-now, firsthand reporting continued over long periods of time.

Diaries share with letters the advantage of immediacy of recording, but unless one has other sources of information, it is difficult to decide what range of experiences a diary covers. Biographers have pointed out that some people resort to expressing themselves in diaries only under certain special circumstances of their lives and that very few adults make complete and consistent entries in their diaries over a sufficiently large part of their lives.

Autobiographies, particularly those written late in life, have the major disadvantage that they are retrospective and are usually more an indication of the aging author's state of mind at the time of writing than a reliable account of past events and experiences. Unfortunately for case study research, particularly of longitudinal developmental processes, both letters and diaries are rapidly disappearing. Garraty (1957), along with other biographers, bemoans the fact that the telephone and the secretary have replaced the more personal document.

Angell and Freeman (1953) and Gottschalk, Kluckhohn, and Angell (1945) state that the advantage of using personal documents is that they help in identifying significant variables and are not dominated by the conceptual scheme of the investigator. Also, they offer data for scientific analysis from remote times and places which may otherwise not be accessible to the investigator. The main advantage for the clinical researcher of the spontaneously produced first-person document is that it opens up relatively unknown areas of life experience for systematic exploration. Accounts of the intensely personal experience of adolescence (Anonymous, 1921; C. Buhler, 1934); mental illness (Beers, 1938); physical illness (Dda, 1939); mastery of unusual physical handicaps (Keller, 1903); social isolation (Burney, 1952); imminent death (Gollwitzer et al., 1956); and others have often been the first stimulus for clinical investigators.

Interivews and questionnaires are not specifically clinical methods and are not limited to the collection of case study data. They are major instruments in all social science research and usually serve to test hypotheses about attitudes, opinions, or perceptions of individuals in a given sample. At the same time, a single individual's answers to the questions in the interview, particularly if accompanied by observations of his behavior during the interview, may well become part of a case history. The clinical diagnostic interview is a classic technique for the collection of case study data. It usually covers the medical history of an individual; his life history; his interpersonal relations; his sexual patterns; his feelings, thoughts, fantasies, conscious attitudes, early memories, and dreams; his interests, goals, plans, and values; his intellectual, emotional, physical, and social resources; his conflicts and ways of solving them; and any other behavior which the interviewer considers relevant. If the interview is conducted primarily for clinical purposes, the information will be used to arrive at a diagnosis, to decide upon a method of treatment, and to predict the patient's response to treatment. If the interview is conducted as a method of collecting research data, there should be an explicit connection between the specific area of exploration and the information gathered.

All elicited data, whether collected in face-to-face situations, such as interviews or projective tests, or by indirect communication, such as requested autobiographies or biograms (Abel, 1947), have the advantage of greater completeness and of being clearly related to a definite area of exploration. The disadvantages center around the subject's defensiveness, transference feelings, or fantasies and the often unknown ideal image of himself which he tries to present.

The communications in psychotherapy and psychoanalysis are a combination of spontaneous and elicited first-person data. Although the free associations, fantasies, and dreams occur spontaneously, the patient is under contract, as it were, to communicate them. French (1952; 1953; 1958) demonstrated that data of this type can be used most successfully in case study research. He based his extensive study of the psychotherapeutic process exclusively on the dreams and free associations of one patient. Interpreting the patient's dreams in keeping with his theory of the problem-solving function of the dream, he traced the patterns and cycles of conflicts and their solutions throughout the patient's psychoanalysis. He applied a systematic and consistent method of analysis to naturalistic data which were obtained by another analyst in the usual psychoanalytic situation.

The potentially most complete form of case study data is probably the third-person account of the story of a person's life—the case history or the biography. It is not easy to write a good scientific case history. Allport, Dollard (1935), Polansky (1941), Kelly (1955), S. E. Jones (1944), Louttit (1947), Richard (1946), Shaffer and Lazarus (1952), Watson (1951), and Menninger, Mayman, and Pruyser (1962) have all offered suggestions for the presentation of case material. Allport's rules, as published by Garraty (1957) from an unpublished manuscript, include the following: The biography must be written from a clearly stated theoretical point of view, but the data must not be distorted to fit the writer's bias. It must be complete, but there must be no overemphasis on details. The genetic factors must be considered, but the importance of early experiences must be proved rather than assumed. Conflicts must be given more space than periods of "calm," but the conflict must not be overemphasized. In describing personality traits, each trait should be illustrated by concrete examples. Understandably, Allport decided to "write off" his rules as an unsuccessful experiment. He found that in following them, he turned out a lifeless, wooden description of a person. Dollard's set of criteria for the writing of a life history also seem to be unsatisfactory. He combines a culturalist approach and psychoanalytic theory, stressing the importance of viewing the subject as a specimen in a cultural series. He states that the role of the family in transmitting culture, the social relevance of the organic motors of action, the continuity of experience in the developmental sequence, and the importance of the social situation must be spelled out. Like Allport, he stresses the importance of conceptualizing the life-history data. He demonstrates the application of his criteria to six different case presentations and finds that only Freud's case of "Little Hans" meets an adequate number of them.

As the concern of therapists and investigators is directed toward interactional and transactional processes and toward problems of communication, the therapeutic dialogue is rapidly becoming one of the most important forms of case study data. Although the therapist of a decade ago was quite comfortable when he presented a case study exclusively in terms of the patient's life history, dynamics, pathology, transference, resistance, insight, and eventual working through, today he would feel obligated to include at least some statement about his own participation in the therapeutic process. He might even produce some tape recordings, if not sound films, in which the interaction and the communication pattern between him and the patient would become available for observation.

METHODOLOGY OF THE CASE STUDY

In spite of its venerable history and undeniable contribution to psychological theory, the case study method is a controversial issue and is often referred to as prescientific rather than scientific, particularly by researchers whose major commitment is to hypothesis validation rather than hypothesis generation. While this may be an artificial dichotomy and while many researchers cross lines or attempt to combine the two commitments, there are differences between the two attitudes. These differences appear with regard to the problems of data collection, rigorousness of design, and interpretation of the data. It is probably appropriate to consider the clinical researcher who is primarily committed to the case study approach a "naturalist," in perhaps somewhat artificial contrast to the experimentalist.

All researchers agree that the basic data of all scientific investigation are observations of events and the explanations or inferences derived from the observations. These inferences in turn lead to conceptualizations and hypotheses. The specific problems in the case study research stem from the complexity of the events which the clinician investigates and from his commitment to the totality of the event. He feels that by reducing the number of variables in a given clinical situation, he will "fragment" it and lose some essential information. He also tends to feel either that quantification and precision of measurement will do violence to the data or else that only the unimportant variables can be measured. Since the clinician approaches terra incognita more often than not, he feels that he cannot decide which variables are relevant and which are not. As a result, case studies usually represent "global data."

Observation is often referred to as naturalistic, the implication being that the observer observes events which occur freely in nature and not as a result of the researcher's manipulation. The assumption is that the phenomenon would have occurred in exactly the same manner without the observer's presence or intention to use the data for any investigatory purpose. In psychotherapy research this has led to much discussion concerning the possible factors which might disturb the naturalistic situation of the psychotherapeutic interaction. The question was raised whether a therapist, knowing that he is part of a research situation, could and would function as he does in the privacy of his own office—whether the fact that the therapeutic interaction was recorded or observed would in and by itself alter the phenomenon. Some researchers have objected to the use of the word "naturalistic," claiming that psychotherapy is a highly contrived situation and that there is nothing naturalistic about it (see Butler, Rice, & Wagstaff, 1962, editors' summary). Ever since Sullivan (1953) introduced the term "participant-observer," borrowed from cultural anthropology, clinical researchers have tried to differentiate between participant- and nonparticipant-observers, particularly Alexander (1957), who emphasizes the importance of the nonparticipant-observer in *A Study of the Psychotherapeutic Process.* The participant-observer in this case is the therapist, who is free to observe the patient but who is too involved to observe himself and his part in the interaction. In order to correct for this, the design of one project (Levy, 1961) called for two trained observers to observe, through one-way screens, the interaction between therapist and patient throughout the analysis. Whether or not they are truly nonparticipant remains to be seen. It is very probable that their observations, too, are distorted by their countertransference reactions. The so-called "nonparticipant-observer" is involved with the patient and with the therapist, as they are with each other. He formulates his own diagnostic evaluation of the patient and sees subsequent events in the light of such conceptualizations. He likes or dislikes the patient, and he likes or dislikes the therapist. His observations reflect his critical competitive or respectful feelings toward the therapist whom he is observing and his empathy or impatience with the patient. He is anxious about "how well he is doing" as compared with other observers; he feels compelled to make predictions and then cannot help but scrutinize subsequent therapeutic sessions to test his own powers of prediction. One is tempted to ask who observes the observer. However, in spite of the obvious difficulties in the observation of the interpersonal transactions in psychotherapy, there is likely to be considerably greater agreement between the nonparticipant-observers than between any nonparticipant-observer and the participant-observer (the therapist). Considering that most of the information concerning the psychotherapeutic process has so far come from participant-observers, this is a promising beginning.

While naturalistic observation is the major data-collecting method of the case study, relatively little attention is being paid to the very real difficulties of recording observations. Psychoanalytic literature abounds in references to the analyst's observations during the psychoanalytic process, but except for Freud, very little is said about how the analyst selects and records what he observes. Freud discussed at great length the difficulties of taking notes during the analytic session and the dangers of recording from memory at the end of the day, after having seen many patients. Note-taking during the hour interferes with the analyst's "hovering attention," and reporting from memory obviously reduces accuracy. Freud was also concerned with the discretionary problems of recording and particularly reporting observational data. On the other hand, Hartmann (1959) speaks repeatedly of the "great number of actual observations on which we base in every individual case the interpretations. . . of a person's character." He also claims that every single clinical case represents "hundreds of data of observed regularities in hundreds of respects." However, he does not elaborate on the method by which these observations are recorded, classified, or correlated.

While tape recorders and sound films are now being used increasingly to replace the human observer and while this certainly helps avoid the problems involving the observer's distortions, even accurately transcribing the recorded clinical event does not solve the problem of ordering the observed phenomena and classifying them according to a conceptual system. In fact, in view of the tremendous difficulties of data reduction, it is questionable whether the unselective quality of observation and recording of our electronic devices contributes to case study research or hinders it. The question of meaningful units has not been solved, although several units have been suggested, such as main themes, time, and syntactic units. Butler (1962) proposed a classification system which could serve as an ideal model for the theory and methodology of the case study method. Holt (1951) has exemplified a simple method of ordering a case study in terms of a single topic of interest.

Whether the case study deals with the psychotherapeutic process, with a diagnostic evaluation, or with the presentation of an unusual "case," once the observations are made and recorded, the researcher must take the final step, which is the interpretation of the data. Since the purpose of the case study research is to develop hypotheses, the researcher must rely on clinical inference. The major problem of the clinical inference is that of reliability, i.e., the question of whether two or more independent investigators would make the same judgment on the basis of the same data. Clinical judgments, unfortunately, are only as good as the judges, and the training of judges is a time-consuming and difficult task. Strupp and Luborsky (1962) point out that relatively little systematic research has been devoted to the process of clinical inference. One noteworthy exception is the recent paper by Engel and Blatt (1963) (see also Holt, 1961). The development of systems of content analysis is another approach to the interpretation of clinical data common to both case study and experimental research (see "Experimental Methods in Clinical Psychology," Chapter 3 below).

By and large, case study research seems to have entered a phase of increased concern with problems of method. The traditional controversy between experimentalists and naturalists appears to have lost much of its old fervor, and there seems to be general agreement among all clinical researchers that the entire field needs new methods which are more appropriate for psychological problems than those originally derived from the physical sciences. Clinicians most likely will continue to learn from case histories, not only from Freud's, but from their own. They will still try to bring a theoretical system to their observations and to bank on the power of clinical evidence and prediction. However, the most important advance in case study research occurs in the area of the ever-greater refinement of observational techniques.

REFERENCES

Abel, T. The nature and use of biograms. *Amer. J. Sociol.*, 1947, **53**, 111–118.

Alexander, F. A study of the psychotherapeutic process. Paper read at 1957 Western Division Meeting, Amer. Psychiatr. Ass., Los Angeles, Calif., November, 1957.

Allport, G. W. The use of personal documents in psychological science. *Soc. Sci. Res. Council Bull.*, 1942, No. 49.

Allport, G. W. *Becoming*. New Haven, Conn.: Yale Univer. Press, 1955.

Allport, G. W. *Pattern and growth in personality*. New York: Holt, 1961.

Allport, G. W., Bruner, J. S., & Jandorf, E. M. Personality under social catastrophe: an analysis of 90 German refugee life histories. *Charact. & Pers.*, 1941, **10**, 1–22.

Angell, R. C., & Freeman, R. The use of documents, records, census materials and indices. In L. Festinger & D. Katz (Eds.), *Research methods in the behavioral sciences*. New York: Dryden Press, 1953.

Anonymous. *A young girl's diary*. Prefaced with a letter by Sigmund Freud. New York: Thomas Seitzer, 1921.

Bechterew, W. *New studies in reflexology and physiology of the nervous system*. 1925.

Beck, S. J. Rorschach's Erlebnistypus: an empiric datum. Separata aus Beheft zur *Schweiz. Z. Psychol. Rorschachiana*, 1963, **7**, No. 45.

Beers, C. W. *A mind that found itself: an autobiography*. (5th ed.) New York: Doran, 1938.

Biber, I., et al. *Homosexuality*. New York: Basic Books, 1962.

Blumer, H. *An appraisal of Thomas and Znaniecki's* The Polish Peasant in Europe and America. New York: Social Science Research Council, 1939.

Bohne, G. *Die religiöse Entwicklung der Jugend in der Reifzeit. Auf Grund autobiographischer Zeugnisse.* Leipzig: Hinrich, 1922.

Bolgar, Hedda. The structure of emotional experience in the course of human life. Doctoral dissertation, Vienna, 1934.

Breuer, J., & Freud, S. *Studies in hysteria.* New York: Basic Books, 1957.

Bühler, Charlotte. *Der menschliche Lebenslauf als psychologisches Problem.* Leipzig: Hirzel, 1933.

Bühler, Charlotte. *Quellen und Studien zur Jugendkunde.* Vol. 11. *Drei Generationen im Jugendtagebuch.* Jena: Fischer, 1934.

Bühler, Charlotte. *From birth to maturity: an outline of the psychological development of the child.* London: Kegan Paul, Trench, Trubner & Co., 1935.

Bühler, K. *Die geistige Entwicklung des Kindes.* Jena: Fischer, 1918.

Burney, C. *Solitary confinement.* New York: Coward-McCann, 1952.

Butler, J. M., Rice, Laura N., & Wagstaff, Alice K. On the naturalistic definition of variables: an analogue of clinical analysis. In *Research in psychotherapy.* Vol. II. 1962. Pp. 178–705.

Chassan, J. B. Stochastic models of the single case as the basis of clinical research design. *Behav. Sci.,* 1961, **6** (1), 42–50.

Cummings, Elaine, & Henry, W. E. *Growing old.* New York: Basic Books, 1961.

Dda, C. F. Psychological states resulting from parathyroid deficiency. *J. abnorm. soc. Psychol.,* 1939, **34,** 481–496.

Dollard, J. *Criteria for the life history: with analyses of six notable documents.* New Haven, Conn.: Yale Univer. Press, 1935.

Eiduson, Bernice T. *Scientists: their psychological world.* New York: Basic Books, 1962.

Eitinger, L. Concentration camp survivors in the postwar world. *Amer. J. Orthopsychiat.,* 1962, **32** (3), 367–375.

Engel, Mary, & Blatt, S. J. Clinical inference in psychological assessment. Paper read at Amer. Psychol. Ass., Philadelphia, 1963.

Feifel, H. (Ed.) *The meaning of death.* New York: McGraw-Hill, 1959.

French, T. *The integration of behavior.* Vols. 1–3. Chicago: Univer. of Chicago Press, 1952–1958.

Frenkel, E. Studies in biographical psychology. *Charact. & Pers.,* 1936, **5,** 1–34.

Freud, S. *The etiology of hysteria* (1896a). In *The standard edition of the complete psychological works of Sigmund Freud.* Vol. 3. London: The Hogarth Press and the Institute of Psycho-Analysis., 1962.

Freud, S. *Further remarks on the neuropsychoses of defense* (1896b). In *ibid.*

Freud, S. Analysis of a phobia in a five year old boy. In *Collected papers of. . . .* Vol. 3. London: Hogarth Press, 1925. (a) Pp. 149–289.

Freud, S. Fragment of an analysis of a case of hysteria. In *ibid.* 1925. (b)

Freud, S. From the history of an infantile neurosis. In *ibid.* 1925. (c) Pp. 473–605.

Freud, S. Notes upon a case of obsessional neurosis. In *ibid.* 1925. (d) Pp. 296–383.

Freud, S. Psycho-analytic notes upon an autobiographical account of a case of paranoia (dementia paranoides). In *ibid.* 1925. (e) Pp. 390–470.

Freud, S. *New introductory lectures on psychoanalysis.* New York: Norton, 1944.

Freud, S. *The origins of psychoanalysis: letters to Wilhelm Fliess, Drafts and Notes: 1887–1902.* Edited by Marie Bonaparte, Anna Freud, and Ernst Kris. Authorized translation by Eric Mosbacher and James Strachey. New York: Basic Books, 1954.

Garraty, J. A. *The nature of biography.* New York: Knopf, 1957.

Gertzel, V., & Gertzel, Mildred G. *Cradles of eminence.* Boston: Little, Brown, 1962.

Gesell, A. *The mental growth of the pre-school child.* New York: 1925.

Gollwitzer, H., et al. (Eds.) *Dying we live.* New York: Pantheon, 1956.

Gottschalk, L., Kluckhohn, C., & Angell, R. *The use of personal documents in history, anthropology and sociology.* New York: Social Science Research Council, 1945.

Hartmann, H. Psychoanalysis as a scientific theory. In S. Hook (Ed.), *Psychoanalysis, scientific method, and philosophy.* New York: New York Univer. Press, 1959. P. 370.

Healey, W., & Bronner, Augusta. *Judge Baker Foundation case studies,* Series 1, Cases 1–20. Cited by C. R. Shaw, *The jack-roller.* Chicago: Univer. of Chicago Press, 1945.

Hirsch, J. Behavior genetics and individuality understood. *Science,* 1963, **142,** 1436–1442.

Holt, R. R. An inductive method of analyzing defense of self-esteem. *Bull. Menninger Clin.,* 1951, **15,** 6–15.

Holt, R. R. Clinical judgment as a disciplined inquiry. *J. nerv. ment. Dis.*, 1961, **133**, 369–382.

Holt, R. R. Individuality and generalization in the psychology of personality. *J. Pers.*, 1962, **30** (3).

Jackson, D. D. (Ed.) *The etiology of schizophrenia.* New York: Basic Books, 1960.

Jones, E. *The life and work of Sigmund Freud.* Vol. 2. New York: Basic Books, 1955.

Jones, S. E. In J. McV. Hunt (Ed.), *Personality and the behavior disorders.* New York: Ronald, 1944.

Keller, Helen. *The story of my life.* New York: Doubleday, 1903.

Kelly, G. A. *The psychology of personality constructs.* New York: Norton, 1955.

Krueger, E. T. *Autobiographical documents and personality.* Chicago: Chicago Univer. Library, 1925.

Levy, N. A. An investigation into the nature of the psychotherapeutic process: a preliminary report. In J. H. Masserman (Ed.), *Psychoanalysis and social process.* Vol. IV. New York: Grune & Stratton, 1961.

Louttit, C. M. *Clinical psychology.* New York: Harper & Row, 1947.

Lustman, S. L. Defense, symptom and character. In *Psychoanalytic study of the child.* Vol. 17. New York: International Universities Press, 1962.

Mendelson, J. H., Kubzansky, P., Liederman, H., Wexler, D., & Solomon, P. Physiological and psychological aspects of sensory deprivation: a case analysis. In *Sensory deprivation: a symposium at Harvard Medical School.* Cambridge, Mass.: Harvard Univer. Press, 1961. Pp. 91–113.

Menninger, K. A., Mayman, M., & Pruyser, P. *A manual for psychiatric case study.* (Rev. ed.) New York: Grune & Stratton, 1962.

Murphy, G. The current impact of Freud on American psychology. *Amer. Psychologist,* 1956, **2**, 663.

Murray, H. A., et al. *Explorations in personality: a clinical and experimental study of fifty men of college age.* New York: Oxford Univer. Press, 1938.

Neugarten, Bernice L. Personality changes during the adult years. *Conf. Adult Educ.* Sagamore Conference Center, Syracuse Univer., Oct. 2, 1962.

Neugarten, Bernice L., & Kraines, Ruth J. Factors related to the mental health of women in the climacteric years. Paper read at Amer. Psychol. Ass., St. Louis, 1962.

Piaget, J. *The origins of intelligence in children.* New York: International Universities Press, 1952.

Piaget, J. *The construction of reality in the child.* New York: Basic Books, 1954.

Polansky, N. A. How shall a life-history be written? *Charact. & Pers.*, 1941, **9**, 188–207.

Preyer, W. *Die Séele des Kindes.* 1898.

Richard, T. W. *Modern clinical psychology.* New York: McGraw-Hill, 1946.

Roe, Anne. A psychologist examines 64 eminent scientists. *Scientif. Amer.*, 1952, **1** (87).

Shaffer, G. W., & Lazarus, L. S. *Fundamental concepts in clinical psychology.* New York: McGraw-Hill, 1952.

Shaw, C. R. The case study technique: value of a delinquent boy's own story. In M. Wolstang, L. Savitz, & N. Johnston (Eds.), *The sociology of crime and delinquency.* New York: Wiley, 1962.

Shneidman, E. S., & Farberow, N. L. (Eds.) *Clues to suicide.* New York: Blakiston, 1957.

Stephenson, W. *The study of behavior.* Chicago: Univer. of Chicago Press, 1953.

Stern, W. *Anfänge der Reifezeit.* Leipzig: 1925.

Stern, W. *Intelligenz der Kinder und Jugendlichen.* Leipzig: 1929.

Strupp, H. H., & Luborsky, L. (Eds.) *Research in psychotherapy.* Washington, D.C.: American Psychological Association, 1962.

Sullivan, H. S. *Interpersonal theory of psychiatry.* New York: Norton, 1953.

Sutherland, E. H. *The professional thief.* Chicago: Univer. of Chicago Press, 1937.

Thomas, W. I., & Znaniecki, F. *The Polish peasant in Europe and America.* Boston: Gorham Press, 1918–1920. 5 vols. New York: Knopf, 1927, 2 vols.

Watson, R. *The clinical method in psychology.* New York: Harper & Row, 1951.

Wood, Vivian, & Neugarten, Bernice L. Social-role change and mental health in the climacteric years. Paper read at Amer. Sociol. Ass., Washington, D.C., 1962.

3

Experimental Methods in Clinical Psychology[1]

ROBERT R. HOLT

Large books have been written on experimental method, but surely the last word has not been said. In a single chapter, there is little point in trying to recapitulate the logic of the experimental method, outlining standard experimental designs, or otherwise trying to compete with the books in a highly condensed manner. A handbook can and should include a guide to available literature that does this kind of job, and the references at the end of the chapter contain a section intended to guide the reader to sources where he can learn about general methods of experimental research.

However, even someone who has read all the works listed in the references and who has a good general grasp of experimental research methods is likely to experience some difficulty when he tries to apply these methods within the broad territory known as clinical psychology. The principal aim of this chapter, therefore, is to focus on the role of experimentation in clinical psychology, to consider the kinds of special problems encountered in clinicoexperimental research, and to suggest a number of ways of coping with these problems.

THE PLACE OF EXPERIMENT IN CLINICAL PSYCHOLOGY[2]

For the purposes of this chapter, the term "experiment" will be used in its broadest sense, following Fisher, to mean "only experience carefully planned in advance." "This simple phrase," comments Kaplan (1964), "already makes reference to the two most general and fundamental traits of scientific inquiry—that [it] . . . is both empirical and rational. . . . Experiment is the consummation of the marriage of reason and experience, and though it is not in itself the [entire] life of the mind, it is the most passionate and fruitful expression of our intellectual life and loves."

This seductive phraseology ought to raise some doubts about the common assumption that experimentation is the pedantic and austere preoccupation of bloodless compulsives, an antithesis to the way of the clinician. There are more conflicts of outlook here than the above passage implies, even beyond the obvious personal and political ones, but the diversity that they express may as easily be complementary as competitive (cf. Holt, 1958). Let us begin, then, by examining the

[1] Preparation of this paper was supported by a Public Health Service research career program award (number K6–MH–12, 455) from the National Institute of Mental Health.

[2] This section is much indebted to secs. 17–19 of Kaplan, 1964. In particular, the various types of experiment listed follow Kaplan's classification and definitions.

differences in outlook connoted by the terms "clinical" and "experimental."

The clinical orientation grows out of the traditions of medicine, especially the medicine of the working physician at the bedside, who is directly involved in real problems about which he is obligated to do something and who must intervene as much as possible in the causal sequences he sees. The good clinician is a keen naturalistic observer, not afraid to rely on subjective—even intuitive—judgments and predictions; his approach is qualitative, holistic, molar, and personal. If he records his observations, it is a distinctly secondary activity of a participant-observer hoping to increase his future effectiveness by organizing his impressions and experience, usually as "recollected in tranquility."

By contrast, the experimental tradition grows out of the laboratory work of academic scientists, whose concern has always been with knowledge rather than action, with precise and objective measurement rather than sensitive and comprehensive looking, and thus with the precise handling of small, manageable segments of behavior rather than the struggle to do justice to the richness of a real-life encounter. The experimental researcher often relies on instruments and tests to help him record observations at once and with a minimum of bias. For the sake of objectivity, he strives to intervene as little as possible in what he sees. The experimentalist's ideal is to know what he knows as exactly as he can or with a known margin of error; the clinician's cognitive ideal is to know what it is *important* to know about a person. Moreover, the experimentalist worships truth monotheistically, while for the clinician truth is but one of a pantheon including service and social responsibility.

But clinical psychology is a science as well as a profession, and it needs to learn and use all it can that is of value from experimentation. The experimenter who hopes to learn something about personality and its disorders stands to gain a great deal from the clinical viewpoint, too. The trick is to keep the best of both worlds with a minimum of the faults of each. When he turns to the experimental method, the clinician should try to hold on to his sensitivity, his ability to see the relevance to important human issues, the breadth and richness of his outlook, his motivational orientation, and his flexibility. He should try to put aside his distaste for measurement and for objective methods of gathering data, his emotional reaction against the allegedly dry and dusty academic traditions of careful control, his resistance to analysis of such sacred confines as clinical judgment, and his nervousness about brass instruments.

The clinical psychologist will discover that his training and orientation provide him with a number of advantages when he tries his hand at controlled investigation. Even in a rigorously planned laboratory experiment, the clinician will notice that as long as the subjects are people, they have the capacity to understand communications on many levels simultaneously and to react in equally many-layered complexity. Since we are always being faced with the unexpected, it helps to be prepared for it. The "evenly hovering attention" of the therapist can be most useful in picking up incidental bits of laboratory behavior that may explain why a whole experiment went awry. His intuition, too, should not be left at the couch-side; the experimenter needs to have plenty of it and to be willing to *listen* to his intuition without being carried away by it. (Ironically, physicists tend to respect intuition more than traditional experimental psychologists do!)

Hunches may tell us where or how to look, but looking alone is not research. Whether the clinical psychologist is primarily interested in pursuing a theoretically important topic or in trying to learn the answer to a practical problem in his clinical work, he must eventually pass from the initial phase of merely keeping his eyes and ears open, to the discipline of systematic research. The experimental method is essentially reality testing refined and systematized, and therefore it is neither intrinsically arcane nor difficult. It is largely a matter of focusing on answerable questions and of introducing enough controls so that it is possible to trust and understand the answers.

Let us turn from such very general characterizations of experiment and examine some of the types of investigation that merit this proud name. To begin with, "some experiments are *methodological* (so-called): they serve to develop or to improve some particular technique of inquiry" (Kaplan, 1964). For example, after Aserinsky and Kleitman (1955) first verified the hunch that rapid eye movements during sleep indicate dreaming, it was necessary for Dement and Kleitman (1957a; 1957b) to conduct a series of experiments in order to develop efficient techniques of identifying the objective indicants of dreaming. When Shapiro, Goodenough, and Gryler (1963) studied the effects of different methods of awakening the S to obtain his dream report, their experiment was a methodological one. Tooling up of this kind can and should be experimental simply because there is no equally good way of getting empirical knowledge with a known margin of error.

When a methodological experiment focuses on establishing the limits of variables to be studied more systematically in a later series of projects, Kaplan calls it a "pilot study." Before he could explore the ramifications of dream deprivation, Dement (1960) had to discover through a pilot study whether it was possible to keep awakening a sleeper as soon as REMs began and thus prevent an appreciable amount of dreaming while still retaining his cooperation, how many times a night this would be necessary and for how many nights before any effect could be demonstrated, and so forth.

Initial investigative forays at times have the aim of opening up possible new fields of research, proceeding from the hunch or the theoretically engendered guess that a certain kind of controlled observation and intervention might yield fruitful results. Lilly (1956) was embarked on such a heuristic or exploratory experiment when he decided to immerse himself in a tank of tepid water and minimize all sources of external sensory stimulation. He was guided by some theoretical notions concerning sleep, but in large part he was simply curious to know what would happen in such an unusual situation; the effect was to provide many leads that have been followed up by other investigators. Notice that although not all exploratory research is experimental (see, for example, "The Case Study Method," above), a heuristic investigation may follow the general experimental model in that a phenomenon is studied under controlled conditions and with some attempt to manipulate one or more variables.

The fact-finding kind of research is often not considered experimental at all, since, for example, surveying the mental health of a community does not in any obvious way constitute an intervention. Contrast, however, the precise and reliable findings of such surveys as those of Hollingshead and Redlich (1958) and of Srole, Langer, Michael, Opler, and Rennie (1962) with the unsystematic impressions of a literary observer who visited American cities and their insane asylums almost a century ago (Dickens, 1842), and it begins to be apparent why the careful procedure of a modern sample survey can be called "experimental." Controlled interviewing and testing, as opposed to unsystematic conversation, intervene in the communicative processes of the respondents in a way precisely analogous to the sequences of controlled stimuli introduced in, say, psychophysical experiments. To want to know what would happen if you asked a probability sample of a city "What do you understand by mental illness?" is not intrinsically different from wanting to know what would happen if you gave a sample of people a new drug; both are properly called "experiments," and many of the same principles and techniques of research apply to both and to the most classical laboratory test of a rigorously derived hypothesis. But fact-finding experiments include a good deal more than surveys. Systematic studies of the natural course of a clinical syndrome like hysteria—a too-much neglected type of psychopathological research—or of the typical stages of ego development are fact-finding experiments, too. Much of Piaget's developmental research is experimental in this sense, in contrast to Erikson's (e.g., 1963), which is essentially retrospective reflection on unsystematically obtained clinical experience.

In the *boundary experiment*, an attempt is made to discover the range of application of certain known laws or functional relations. When does anxiety function as a generalized drive in learning experiments, as K. W. Spence and his coworkers have painstakingly shown (Taylor & Spence, 1952), and when does it start to become disruptive or paralyzing terror? At what degree of impoverishment of a supraliminal stimulus does the paradoxical limiting effect of awareness described by D. Spence and Holland (1962) give way, and what are the other parameters of what seems to be a phase change in the cognitive reverberations of a stimulus? A great many boundary experiments are called for to establish the precise limits of such relationships.

When we set up an explicit model of some

real-life situation and manipulate it, we are involved in a *simulation or analogue experiment*. This is the strategy of choice when we want to investigate conditions that are beyond our current reach in real life (e.g, perceptual isolation experiments as simulacra of space travel to enable us to study its cognitive effects) or matters that are closed to direct study for ethical reasons (compare the use of animals in the first clinical trials of potentially dangerous drugs—many experiments with animals as Ss may be considered simulations of the same thing with human beings). The well-known study by Keet (1948) compared miniature replicas of several psychotherapeutic techniques on their ability to uncover an experimentally induced repression, achieving thereby great economies and some advantages of control, as compared with an attempt to do the same experiment with real patients and real therapy. A different type of simulation with interesting possibilities for clinicians is the programming of high-speed computers to simulate personological processes such as free association (Tomkins & Messick, 1963; see especially chapter by Colby). Even though the behavior of no actual persons is observed, computer simulation makes possible the testing and clarification of theory in a way that should prove most salutary.

The ideal type of experiment, in the minds of many of us, is the specific one that Kaplan calls "nomological," to which most of the written methodological discussions are directed: the experiment that tests some hypothesis or, more specifically, attempts to decide between a null hypothesis and one or more alternatives. This is the kind of experiment that makes it possible "to transform an empirical generalization into a law . . . that is, to identify what is both necessary and sufficient for the empirically given connection, by varying the experimental conditions" (Kaplan, 1964). Usually, it will take a series of interrelated experiments to establish a law in this way; very exceptionally, a single *crucial experiment* can settle a theoretical issue—at least temporarily—by decisively altering "the balance of probabilities," such as between alternative explanations for a phenomenon. Thus, Fiss, Goldberg, and Klein (1963) set up an experimental situation in which the "partial cues" theory of Goldiamond, Eriksen, and others yielded diametrically opposite predictions from the conception that stimuli may affect behavior without the involvement of conscious awareness, and they verified the latter. By the time these words are in print, yet another theory may have been found more comprehensive and better able to predict than either of these, but that is the way science grows.

Finally, there are illustrative experiments—replications motivated by didactic purposes, as in the training of researchers, or by the wish to see with one's own eyes a reported phenomenon or relationship that seems important, puzzling, or otherwise interesting. Replication is so important and so neglected in clinical psychology, as well as in other branches of behavioral science generally, that it is good to see it included in such an authoritative classification as Kaplan's. It not infrequently happens that failures to replicate originally reported results lead to important discoveries or at least suggest that the initial publication neglected to point out significant parametric limitations on its findings. See, for example, the various attempts to replicate the 1948 experiment of Keet (Grummion & Butler, 1953; Heim, 1951; Merrill, 1952), which failed through an inability to reproduce his experimental analogue of repression. These may hopefully result in redoubled investigative attention to this side issue in Keet's work, which is important in its own right.

A dozen types of experiment may be described without even touching on the issue of pure versus applied research, for essentially the same methods are used whether the question addressed to nature grew out of theory, out of simple curiosity about concrete clinical phenomena, or out of practical necessity. A great deal of clinical research seeks to explore the reality of human lives and may help us formulate relatively precise questions. Whenever a clear-cut question can be posed, however one has arrived at it, experimentation is the method of choice to provide precise and reliable answers. Therefore, it can and must play a growing role in clinical psychology.

SPECIAL PROBLEMS OF CLINICAL RESEARCH

As we shall see, many of the problems that seem to be unique to clinical psychology turn out to exist, in disguised or attenuated form, in *any* kind of experimental research. Yet there are at least enough quantitative differences to make the following more outstandingly problematical for the clinical experimentalist than for his nonclinical brother.[3]

Problems arising from the nature of the subject matter and basic orientation. For the purposes of this chapter, clinical psychology will be understood to differ from the rest of psychology in that it has a major commitment to understand and deal with the major "real-life" issues and problems of living, striving, suffering human beings. Thus, general experimental psychology is concerned with perception; clinical psychology is interested in it too, but with an emphasis on the nature of the person who is perceiving and the role of his ways of contacting and testing reality in his pattern of adjustment or maladjustment. Both are concerned with learning, but the experimentalist wants to analyze learning processes in the laboratory, where he can control all the variables specified by theory, while the clinician wants to find out how the person learns his major motives, his styles of coping with challenge, and his mechanisms of defense and how he can unlearn maladaptive or self-destructive ways of behaving and replace them with ways that are more generally satisfactory to others and to himself. The social psychologist wants to learn how people in general respond to the manipulations of power in human relations, while the clinical psychologist more characteristically seeks to learn how and why individuals differ in their relations to authorities and what such styles are related to in other departments of personality.

As a practitioner, the clinician learns to look for the fox without getting too fascinated by each bit of fur; his practical experience forces him to develop the habit and techniques of keeping his eye on the main point, the fact that all the phenomena in front of him are part of a unique, valuable, and staggeringly complex human life. As a scientist, however, he is up against a basic paradox: most of the principles of scientific method seem predicated on gaining control over knowledge by limiting vision, whereas he is convinced that he will betray his first principles if he loses sight of the entire panorama. Here, then, is the first and most fundamental problem of experimental research in clinical psychology—how to discipline observation so that questions can be answered with some known degree of confidence without abandoning a commitment to ask humanly *important* questions (cf. Loevinger, 1963).

Problems of value judgments. Experimenters are understandably loath to rush into the area of good and bad, where only angels are at home. Yet clinical psychology is interested in personality and its pathology: the patterning of behavior viewed in the large and from the perspective of a life as a whole, with an emphasis on the difficulties and problems people encounter in living, the ways they function badly, and the types of intervention that can significantly affect major trends of behavior. This emphasis on pathology and dysfunction leads inevitably to a parallel concern with patterns of "normal," adaptive, and comfortable or creatively struggling life. One has to have some conception of normality to understand the abnormal, some grasp of health in order to know how to ameliorate disease. As Jahoda (1958) has argued—and I agree with her conclusion—the very concept of mental health is an unavoidably normative one, ultimately a statement of socially valued forms of behavior. The further one gets from the reduction screen of the laboratory, which narrows one's focus of observation down to a precise and isolated function, the more insistently questions of value raise themselves. Even the term "personality" itself, in common parlance, refers to a social ideal of attractiveness.

Problems of temporal scope. As Murray (1938) and White (1952) have defined it, personology is the study of lives, scientific biography. Freud's genetic emphasis has convinced the majority of psychopathologists that the disorders they are concerned with cannot be understood without the reconstruction of the person's past, preferably back to earliest childhood. Longitudinal studies of child development (see, for example, Kagan & Moss, 1962; MacFarlane, Allen, & Honzik, 1955) have been made in attempts to broaden observation to include a substantial segment of the life cycle. But it remains a heavy burden to be obliged to take into account the whole sweep of a subject's life, when the experimenter himself belongs to the same mortal species.

[3] This listing owes a good deal to the survey of clinical research made by Hilgard, Gill, and Shakow for the Ford Foundation (unpublished).

Some means must be found to take account of the genetic dimension in cross-sectional, brief experiments.

Problems of situational embeddedness. Once we admit to an interest in who our subjects are and how they are doing, we cannot ignore such homely but troublesome matters as where they live, where they came from, what they do for a living and how, whom they interact with, and what kinds of opportunities, dangers, or predicaments these others present. In short, we have to face the fact that psychology must be supplemented by sociology, anthropology, economics, political science, linguistics, and history—i.e., with *all* the social and behavioral sciences. The kinds of variables they deal with affect human behavior, and thus they cannot be ignored by clinical research.

Problems arising from the personality's relations with a body. The only behavior we need to concern ourselves with in clinical psychology is indulged in by human organisms prominently characterized by bodies: organized, mobile, sensitive, space-occupying aggregations of matter. The more we learn about any one person, the less we can ignore the far-reaching interdigitation of his behavior with the biochemical, physiological, anatomical, biophysical, and neurological nature of his soma. Moreover, we learn to recognize that there are many bodily nonverbal channels of communication and expression, which often convey the message or betray the reaction for which the clinician is listening. Thus, the body is of concern as a source of both independent and dependent variables.

Problems of objectivity about the subjective. It was perfectly possible for Watson to decide to ignore and deny the importance of anything about the behaving subject that could not be externally and objectively observed. It is equally possible today to put a schizophrenic into a room where he has nothing to do but pull a lever and then to concentrate one's attention entirely on the quantitative data generated by this apparatus. By my definition, however, this is not clinical psychology, though I would not deny that it is as legitimate an object of scientific curiosity as any other specifiable aspect of nature. The clinician's commitment forces him to be as much interested in the delusions and hallucinations that occupy the patient's consciousness while he is or is not pulling the lever as in any easily quantifiable aspect of his functioning. Clinicians have preoccupied themselves with these mentalistic phenomena, not because of any allegiance to Wundt or Titchener, but because they have found empirically that patients do talk a good deal about dreams, fantasies, moods, and other subjective states when allowed to discuss whatever is on their minds and because they have discovered that these kinds of data are indispensable in the therapeutic enterprise. Yet the requirements of intersubjectivity in science are valid and cannot be ignored.

Practical and ethical problems of privacy. It follows immediately from the above that the clinical researcher must have some means of gaining access to inner, subjective experiences of his subjects. This is not easy to do, for most people are reluctant to reveal their dreams, their daydreams, their longings and fears, and their private beliefs and values to a stranger. And serious ethical questions are raised: Does a human being have the right, even in the name and for the cause of science, to require other persons to reveal to him the aspects of their personalities of which they are most ashamed and about which they feel most guilty? Even if the experimenter can spare his subjects the embarrassment of directly revealing such secrets by the use of projective and other indirect techniques, is it ethical for him to peek through their defenses in this way? What, for example, is he to do if the subject reveals—wittingly or not—some antisocial acts, past or contemplated?

Problems of nonconscious determinants of behavior. The one great lesson that clinical psychologists of all persuasions have learned from Freud is that behavior is determined, on the *psychological* level (quite in addition to the levels of determination just alluded to), by motives, defenses, and controls of which the subject is not fully aware at the time and which he thus cannot report on even if he wishes to. The problems posed by this state of affairs have the same dual practical and ethical nature as those just discussed.

Problems of the interactional nature of clinical data—"countertransference." The subject is not the only fallible, driven, unconsciously motivated participant in an experiment; the experimenter is just as much a human being. This is true, incidentally, whether he is a clinician or not; his own hopes, anxieties, or prejudices may bias the data even when he is interested only in some isolated segment of objectively measurable behavior. But the clinician has learned that he has to look out for his own defenses and for the distorting influences of his current life problems and the residues of infantile experience alike, and so he is more likely to become aware that these sources of error exist in the laboratory too. There can be "acting out in the countertransference" in an experiment, just as there can be in a clinical encounter. The data may be affected by the tendency of *both* parties in an experiment to react in terms of unconscious repetition of old patterns of response to significant people in their personal pasts. The experimenter's blind spots and patterns of systematic distortion may be particularly troublesome when he has to analyze ambiguous and subjective data of the kind so often generated in clinical experiments.

Problems of the interpersonal setting: the lone investigator versus interdisciplinary team research. Most clinical research has always been done by single investigators, typically private practitioners of psychoanalysis or psychotherapy who used their clinical work as an opportunity to observe people and their problems and to form hypotheses about functional relationships. Although the research methods used in the typical clinical case study are not within the purview of this chapter (see "The Case Study Method," above), many of the same difficulties dog the steps of the lone investigator who is pursuing one of the kinds of experimentation listed above. He lacks the stimulation and correction of his ideas afforded by daily interchange with colleagues. Because of his involvement with his patients, he has the greatest difficulty in gathering data without biases and contamination; the problems of countertransference, blind spots, and the necessity to intervene for therapeutic reasons make systematic experimentation difficult indeed. So many of the phases of research require independent observation to establish the reliability (intersubjectivity) of judgments that the isolated experimenter's range of researchable problems is severely restricted.

Plainly, a consequence of many points already made is that much clinical research requires the cooperation of several experimenters with a variety of talents and training. Despite its advantages, such cooperative group research has several drawbacks: (1) It is expensive, not only in salaries, but also in the time and effort that investigators must put into administration. (2) As some wit pointed out, interdisciplinary research makes possible not only cross-fertilization of ideas but also cross-sterilization—a reduction of diverse contributions to their greatest common denominator, which may be disappointingly small. (3) Difficulties in communication are the primary source of trouble. People who have different contributions to make also use different jargons and approach things from subtly different points of view, which may require quite a lot of talking at cross-purposes to discover. Learning how members of other professions talk and think may be valuable educationally, but it does not directly contribute to getting research done. (4) It is difficult to plan an interdisciplinary experiment to the satisfaction of all concerned and to coordinate the work of many hands in carrying it out when different parts of a problem are divided among people with a variety of ways of working. (5) Finally, problems of interpersonal relations always obtrude themselves when people are dependent on one another in something as important as their work. It frequently happens in clinical research that the members of a team represent disciplines having different levels of prestige; thus, there are obvious barriers to maintaining equality in a group of psychologists and psychiatrists in a hospital setting, where the physician is the traditional authority. This kind of problem can be particularly severe when the person who is nominally in charge is actually less qualified to direct the total research enterprise than someone with less power.

Problems in the analysis of data. Clinical experiments often generate such data as verbal protocols, drawings or other graphic records of expressive movement, and qualitative notes from the observation of nonverbal behavior. Free associations and projective test responses are wonderfully rich and sensitive behavioral products; yet anyone who has ever struggled to reduce them to some manageable form so that they yield dependent variables that can be entered into a statistical formula knows that many of the headaches of clinical research are located precisely here. The main problem boils down to coping objectively with symbolic (meaningful) *content*.

The easy availability of tape recording has transformed the problem of analyzing qualitative data from a persistent nuisance to a crisis of glut in many clinics. Closets are filling to overflowing with reels of raw, untranscribed, primary data from psychotherapeutic interviews but also from projective testing, diagnostic interviews, and experimental sessions. Just to get such recordings transcribed is often a herculean task, to say nothing of subjecting them to a content analysis.

Some Suggested Solutions

It would be presumptuous to imply that there are many real solutions to the difficulties listed above. The following paragraphs are in a number of cases only orientations toward coping with the problems and tolerating the lack of clear guidelines.

Fortunately, with respect to the most *basic issues*, some reassurance can be given. There is no intrinsic reason why rigorous experimental research cannot be done on important human problems as well as on isolated, segmental functions. Psychoanalysts and academic personologists who have otherwise seemed poles apart have agreed on a pessimistic outlook in this respect, but the doubt that there can be scientific study of individuals grows out of an anachronistic methodological confusion (cf. Holt, 1962b). Many other disciplines (e.g., astronomy, meteorology) apply the scientific method to the study of individuals, and it is indisputable that the subject matter of all science is in principle as infinitely complex as personality. Other biological sciences have succeeded in dealing analytically with the intricate interrelatedness of living organisms (which are surely *Gestalten*), so that it is possible in fact as well as in principle to abstract for experimental study single aspects of the most complexly organized totalities. There remains some danger that the experimenter may lose sight of the fact that pieces have to be put back together again and that the lawful relationships he discovers probably apply within narrow parametric limits; but the clinician ought to be less prey to this shortsightedness than other psychologists. His problem is more likely to be that his professional commitment to considering "the whole patient" and respecting the interactive nature of human transactions will make him react emotionally against the thought of trying to "reduce this human richness to a set of numbers." An almost equally unfortunate, but widespread, reaction occurs when working clinicians concentrate their research efforts entirely on "safe," simple problems and neglect the experimental approach to the sorts of problems that concern them professionally.

There are some specific research strategies for applying the experimental method and simultaneously keeping the characteristically clinical breadth of outlook. Murray and his coworkers at the Harvard Psychological Clinic (1938) pioneered in one such strategy that has been successfully applied by many other experimenters: the simultaneous clinical and experimental study of the same group of Ss by a team of investigators. Various specific functions are studied and hypotheses tested in controlled laboratory experiments; but the Ss' personalities are clinically assessed by means of tests and ratings based on qualitative data. The experimental findings may then be illuminated and their limitations understood in relation to the extraexperimental data. To some extent, this kind of understanding may be attained by scrutinizing life histories or clinical syntheses of case data on Ss who are extreme on experimental measures; by statistically relating experimental results (taken as measures of individual difference) to measures of personality; or by relating the dependent variables from one experiment to those from another. The logic of this strategy is to try to achieve control of sources of variance that are not experimentally manipulated by learning their values for each S through independent measurement. For any given S, then, his assessed ego strength, authoritarianism, *n* Achievement, or paranoid tendency is a parameter for the degree of relation found between the experimental variables.

The other principal strategy is to attempt to control experimentally as many of the important sources of variance as possible, in a multivariate design (see Cohen, 1964). Theoretically, many independently measurable and manipulable variables may be studied simultaneously in a factorial design, from which measures of main effects and interactions can be obtained. Practically, however, this strategy is more difficult to apply than the preceding, since as more variables are added, the computation becomes very laborious (if one does not have a high-speed computer available), the number of cells to be filled and thus the number of subjects required grows rapidly, and it becomes more and more difficult to maintain true experimental independence of measurement.

The demand for degrees of freedom is actually just as great in the first approach, but it is less obvious; the more measures one adds without increasing the number of Ss, the less confidence can be put in the obtained patterns of statistical relationship because of the cumulation of alpha errors (see "Some Statistical Issues in Psychological Research," below)—if you are computing 500 correlation coefficients, you must expect to get five times as many apparently significant at the 5 per cent level by chance alone as from 100 *r*'s, and some of these randomly generated coefficients will be quite high. Likewise, as compared with multivariate factorial experimentation, it offers an only apparently easier approach to the problem of getting independent measures of independent variables, such as personality traits: Measure them by whatever tests or ratings are the best available, and then control the inevitable redundancy by intercorrelating the measures and factor analyzing them. This solution, too, calls for many cases if the answers are to be trusted. And of course the objection to large numbers is not due merely to human laziness; it is extremely difficult to apply a complex experimental design or a set of multiform assessments—especially when clinical judgment is involved—in a uniform way so that the hundredth S actually receives the same treatment as the first.

There is no easy way out. The ultimate solution, however, is *replication.* A complex clinical experiment usually cannot hope to provide definitive answers, but it can provide valuable leads, which can then be followed up by more focused experiments with larger groups of Ss, in which the experimenter manipulates only the independent variables that the exploratory study had suggested were probably crucial.

Value-laden areas are as subject to scientific study as any other, since the essence of science is its method rather than its subject matter. Another fallacy to guard against is the mistaken belief that science can *decide* questions of value (cf. Parsons, 1949). The scientific method can, for example, be applied to the study of persons socially adjudged delinquent or creative, but a scientific study cannot in itself decide whether an act is positively or negatively valuable. Thus, clinical psychology as a science cannot hope to discover the intrinsic nature of mental health or mental illness, since these are ultimately value judgments external to the behavior that the scientist studies (cf. Szasz, 1961). Even if he chooses to study evaluative behavior, his research cannot uncover the truth about the values in question. In all other respects, however, valuing is as subject to scientific study—including experiment—as anything else.

The need to consider the *genetic roots* of behavior does not have to pose insuperable problems. A great deal of behavior is situationally determined, or at least its determinants have a substantial autonomy from infantile events. Consider, for example, a fact that Fisher (1954) has pointed out: that the voyeuristic implications of a tachistoscopic exposure are important to consider in understanding some Ss' responses to this teasing partial glimpse. Yet one need not know any of the actual details of an S's possible exposure to primal scenes in his early childhood in order to take this kind of thing into account adequately; a contemporary, cross-sectional assessment of his motives will tell all that we need to know about the strength of the wish to look, the degree of its involvement in conflict, and the nature of the S's defenses against it.

For many problems, our need for a reconstruction of the S's personal history will be adequately met by having him write an autobiography, by interviewing him, or by administering a biographical inventory. These direct data, when supplemented by the judicious and cautious use of projective test responses, can often fill in the essential elements of the story to the necessary degree of approximation. When we pass from clinical studies of individuals (see "The Case Study Method," above), however, it is usually desirable to introduce some control over personal history by means of content analysis, which will enable us to abstract from many unique lives the aspects of general significance. Again, Murray et al. (1938) were the first to show how life histories could be analyzed in terms of such rated variables as amount of parental love (*p* Nur), degree of castration threat experienced by S, parental ego idealism, etc., and how these variables could be related to contemporary experimental findings.

To some extent, the same kind of approach can deal with the complexities of the S's *life situation* and its effect on his experimental behavior. The underlying principle remains: Be aware that any dependent variable in an experiment can be determined in part by uncontrolled factors, and find ways of assessing such a variable so as to investigate its degree of statistical association with the behavior in question. The further step is always desirable in case a notable degree of association is found (not just a significant one; cf. "Some Statistical Issues in Psychological Research," below): Replicate the experiment either holding the situational variable in question constant or systematically varying it. Even such a peripheral function as differential threshold for brightness may be affected by a contemporary crisis of discrimination against the S because of the shade of his complexion; this variable could be controlled by *selecting* Ss, either so that all have the same attitudes toward skin color or so that there are two contrasting groups otherwise treated identically. Clinicians are at times too ready to assume that because a variable such as the S's contemporary living arrangements *can* affect behavior in the laboratory, it probably does and needs to be controlled. Fortunately, Murphy's law ("Anything that can happen to foul things up will happen") is not that universally valid. The shrewdness or intuition of a good experimenter is in part his gift for informally and even unconsciously assessing the need to control or take account of the many kinds of possible contaminants of experimental measures.

It still remains true that you are not likely to consider the possibility that such a situational variable as barometric pressure can affect your GSR results unless you have at least a minimal grasp of the relevant but tangential sciences (in this case, meteorology and biophysics). The example is based on an actual finding (Watson, DiMascio, Kanter, Suter, & Greenblatt, 1957): The psychophysiological data from repeated measurements taken over the course of some months of psychotherapy did not make sense until the significant effect of barometric pressure, temperature, etc., on sweating was partialed out—despite the fact that the experiment was conducted in an air-conditioned room! Therefore, the more you can know about the possible relevance of other sciences—behavioral and physical—to your data, the better chance you have of holding down your error variance. It may be too hard to get all the necessary knowledge within one head, in which case the interdisciplinary team approach will be necessary.

Logically, the problem of the behaving organism's *somatic involvement* is the same as its being part of an ecosphere or a social system. We should reflect that there would not be a separate science of psychology if there were not considerable autonomy, if behavior were not to a large extent and most of the time essentially independent from the intrusive effects of nonpsychological determinants. The need to consider biochemistry is much greater for someone who is working on motivational problems than for his colleague who is interested in psycholinguistics, just as the contemporary closeness of a nation to nuclear disaster may have more impact on the data of someone studying adult anxiety than on those of the student of social conditioning in infancy. In a certain sense, everything is ultimately related to everything else, but most conceivable sources of error remain below the threshold of detectability. When measurement in any realm has proceeded to a certain stage of precision, it becomes possible to consider seemingly unrelated phenomena with some hope of finding that they actually do have an effect. But granted the crudeness with which it is possible today to measure latent homosexuality, for example, it would probably be a waste of time to test even as plausible a hypothesis as that this covert need is related to the balance of sex hormones in the blood. Yet the fact that many such physiological variables can be rather precisely and objectively measured encourages a good deal of psychosomatic research, in which the behavioral measures are so crude as to preclude the discovery of any but the grossest relationships. The greatest need of psychosomatic research is probably better measurement in the psychological realm.

It is indeed difficult to work with *subjective meanings* rather than objective movements or with implicit and hardly verbalizable private experiences like dreams or images rather than externally defined achievements. In principle, however, there are no fundamental methodological differences (Holt, 1961). Though psychologists avoided such subjective "mentalistic" concepts as imagery, states of consciousness, and attention during the early decades of the behavioristic "American revolution" (Hebb, 1960), there are many signs of a revival of interest in these peculiarly psychological matters, even among psychologists (Holt, 1964). What is needed to work with them is essentially a faith that they are real and worthy objects of study; the rest comes relatively easily. This is not to say that the experimenter sits back and introspects to get his prime data, in the style of the old structural psychology of consciousness. We still must be operational in our approach. In large part, this reduces simply to getting verbal, introspective reports from our Ss and applying to them the same kinds of judgmental analyses that we use on other qualitative data.

The *ethical problems* alluded to have been adequately dealt with by the American Psychological Association's code of ethics (1953); it should go without saying that any clinical experimenter must be thoroughly familiar with the ethics of research. The practical barrier set up by the issue of the research S's privacy is not easily taken care of. One must anticipate the S's feelings of not wanting to reveal everything he knows about himself—and *what he does not know*—and make it amply clear to him that his confidences will be respected. Here is the great advantage of research in a clinical context. When the S is also a patient, the data usually serve a diagnostic or therapeutic purpose as well as research purpose, so that he is motivated by self-interest to cooperate as fully as his defenses will let him. If the S has no such opportunity to get help with his own conflicts and anxieties from participating in a project, the usual motivations that can be induced—the desire to help a friend or to contribute to science and the wish for monetary gain—may be insufficient to counterbalance the psychic pain, shame, and other negative affects the S will have to suffer in the process of directly confessing the aspects of his life he is least happy about. At times it is possible to supplement the conventional motivators (which may also include satisfying a course requirement) by offering to let the S know what you find out about him. Such a feedback session is a delicate matter, not to be undertaken by experimenters without clinical experience and skills; Ss can be severely disturbed by being told too much too bluntly or by getting false impressions about themselves. It is almost equally undesirable and unethical to frustrate the S by leading him to expect an enlightening self-confrontation and then telling him only a few overgeneral or completely bland items (see Part 4, "Ethics in Clinical Psychology").

Because of these difficulties, it is usually helpful to the S, as well as necessary for the success of the experiment, not to demand too much direct self-revelation and to supplement direct with indirect approaches. When projective techniques are used for research purposes, Ss should not be deceived about the nature of the information desired, for example, by presenting such techniques as "tests of a kind of intelligence" or the like; it should be clearly understood that they are "personality tests." If the S has some guilty secrets that he fears he may give away, he can then refuse to proceed further with the experiment. Best of all, when the S is recruited for the research in the first place, he should have a general understanding of the nature of the investigation and the type of data needed, so that he comes in knowing that he is going to reveal himself and assenting to it.

The psychotherapist or psychoanalyst is truly a participant-observer, and he is often so much *involved emotionally* with the patient or with his clinical role that it is exceedingly difficult for him to achieve the disinterested and dispassionate distance that is necessary for carrying out research. It is generally advisable in any experiment, such as in research on psychotherapy, for the responsible experimenter to be a third party who has no relation to the patient other than an investigative one. This division of labor is often desirable for clinical reasons, too, to maintain an unambiguous role for the therapist without incurring any conflict of loyalties, real or fancied, to the goals of treatment and to the goals of research.

Even without any mixture of roles, the clinical experimenter is more likely than most other researchers to become intensely involved with his Ss. To the extent that the data he elicits touch on affectively important aspects of his own life, he runs the danger of distorting the facts or his interpretations of them. The sovereign remedy offered the therapist for such countertransference difficulties is equally applicable here: self-knowledge and mastery of tendencies to act out in rigid, inappropriate ways, through a personal therapeutic experience. The clinician who tends to see castration anxiety everywhere can, after successful treatment, often turn such a proclivity to good account. Once he calibrates himself, so to speak, and does not project unconsciously, he can make use of his own special sensitivity to minimal indicators of castration complexes, or whatever, in his Ss. Even without undergoing psychoanalysis, the well-trained clinician will often learn from supervision of his diagnostic and therapeutic work to know his characteristic patterns of relationship, something of his own stimulus value for others, and the kinds of blind spots he has. If he makes the effort to transfer this knowledge to the laboratory, he can be considerably ahead of the nonclinically trained investigator in his sensitivity to what is going on between the main parties in an experiment. For example, a physiologist without clinical training was conducting an experiment that involved keeping male Ss in the laboratory all night and awakening them when there were EEG indications of dreaming. He was using the technique of entering the bedroom and shaking one very sound sleeper by the shoulder, when to his astonishment and dismay, the S started to act as if a homosexual approach were being made to him. Fortunately, a clinician friend was able to show the physiologist the many elements of seductiveness there were in the situation and to point out to him some indicators in the S's behavior outside the dream laboratory of strong latent homosexual wishes, so that this situation did not arise again.

The preceding incident also exemplifies one of the advantages of *team research*. The various members can not only supplement one another's skills but also help counteract the effects of blind spots, acting out in relation to Ss, and other personal problems summed up under the heading "countertransference." The many levels of determination that enter into personality and its disorders have already led to the prescription of interdisciplinary cooperation.

In many ways, the ideal interdisciplinary team conference takes place within a single skull. Multidisciplinary training is one solution to the problems outlined earlier, albeit a heroic one. Even such a protean experimenter cannot provide several fresh perspectives on a problem, as separate persons can. And when the S has a variety of human beings with whom he must interact, a more complete sample of his behavioral repertory is elicited. For many kinds of research, the requirements of controls, sampling, respecting the complexity of data, getting reliability of judgments, and the like make it difficult to avoid the judgment that a group effort is necessary.

There are many virtues in solitude which should not be sacrificed on the altar of togetherness. Many investigators seem to be lone wolves by temperament. Working alone may foster originality and depth of penetration into a problem—the results of prolonged immersion and of thinking matters through—instead of large-scale but shallow coverage. Perhaps there is even a general relationship between being truly generative and being inner-directed. The task of the research administrator, then, is to create a kind of institutional structure within which people can get what they need from one another without constantly being in one another's hair. In such a setup, the person in authority will not necessarily have the most prestige, but he will be the one who has the requisite administrative and research skills. Truly democratic leadership is needed, not the authoritarian domination of a tyrant who will not let others develop their own ideas and thus contribute their best or the wishy-washy *laissez faire* of someone who is unwilling or unable to take responsibility and who refers everything back to the team for a group decision.

To a lesser degree, the headaches of interdisciplinary research come up in any collaborative intellectual enterprise. [Compare the statement by the authors of *Frustration and Aggression*—Dollard, Doob, Miller, Mowrer, and Sears (1938)—that collaborative writing is intrinsically frustrating.] Representatives of different schools of psychology may have as much trouble understanding one another as different kinds of scientists. There is always a need for a clearly understood structure of authority and responsibility in any working group, and it is desirable that there be clarity in advance about who gets what kind of credit in the published report. Collaboration demands a good deal of frankness between people, true respect for one another, and a willingness to compromise; it works best if there is a natural complementarity of skills and thus a congenial division of labor. In sum, the point is that tact, skill in human relations, and plain decency play a surprisingly large role in the desirable equipment of an experimenter, though this is rarely stressed in books on research method.

But what about the plight of the experimenter faced with the opposite problems, those of isolation? What can he do? Fortunately, he can protect himself against his most serious danger—ignorance and self-deception—by knowing what the limitations of his work are. Just as long as the clinician is not unaware of the restrictions on the conclusions he can reach that are imposed by the conditions under which he must work, he can go ahead and learn a good deal. His first guide should be Freud's remark in regard to the many difficulties attending dream interpretation: It is always possible to make *some* progress. Perfectionism is the enemy of enterprise, just as it is the ultimate guardian against error. If you must work alone, by all means do not give up in despair, just because you cannot perform complex, crucial experiments. Go ahead and learn what you can, realizing that all knowledge is relative and probabilistic and that larger probable errors attach to your findings than to those of many other investigators. The psychotherapist has one great advantage that can do much to compensate for his problems with objectivity—close contact with the great issues of human life and extended, repeated opportunities to observe, which give him the chance to make important discoveries. He should learn as much as possible about experimental method, asking always how the principles of control can be applied to the kinds of study he wants to undertake and instituting as much system, order, and objectivity as possible into his gathering and analysis of data. Even if you must work from notes taken after interviews, record them in a uniform manner, file them carefully, and try to systematize them as much as you can so as to make your collection of data maximally pertinent to the objectives of your study.

Some therapists who know about a number of techniques of testing and recording that are available are nevertheless reluctant to use them because they fear that they may contaminate the therapeutic relationship. No doubt there are times during the treatment of some patients when the greatest pains have to be taken to maintain trust, allay suspicion, and refrain from antagonizing the patient or giving him excuses to quit. Many clinicians have found that their anxieties about tape recording were wholly unfounded, and successful psychotherapy and psychoanalysis have been carried out while the entire process was being recorded on a sound movie or while both patient and therapist were hooked up to psychophysiological measuring equipment! Another clinical catchphrase is the keynote here: "It's all grist for the mill."

Cohen (1964) has a number of suggestions about ways that Q sorting (see below) and multivariate methods such as P technique (Cattell & Luborsky, 1950) can be used by the lone investigator. Snyder (1959) gives a useful example of the extent to which a therapist can use systematic ratings made by himself and by the patient.

Finally, there is a good deal to be said about ways of coping with the kinds of *qualitative data* that are typically generated by clinical research. Note that qualitative data may include any kind of verbal report by the S (ranging from free association or the description of a mystical experience, to the answer "Johnson" to the question "Who is President of the United States?" or "male" to a question about one's sex), a free drawing or copy of a presented design, a recording of the sounds made by the S or a movie of his expressive movements, or a verbal description of some aspect of his behavior, such as his nonverbal communications.

To consider a problem mentioned earlier, unanalyzed qualitative data may be less likely to pile up if the experimenter always makes sure that he has a clear idea of how he is going to analyze the responses he photographs or records before he begins doing so. A healthy respect for the frustrations and tediums of content analysis can do a lot to make a man think twice before he decides to "tape everything—we'll decide later what we are going to use out of it." That way lie enormous secretarial expenditures and usually interminable waits while typists struggle to reduce sounds on tape to words on paper (a process that takes at least three or four hours for every hour of recording). After he gets the typescript, the experimenter will frequently find that swallowed words and side remarks have been overlooked entirely, personal style and faults in speaking that point to such pathological indicators as anxiety and defensiveness have been automatically edited out, and "inside" references that are perfectly clear to him have been entirely misinterpreted by the brightest of typists because she was ignorant of petty details of the procedure. Then he must take more hours to listen to the tape and edit the typescript, kicking himself for not having made a decision earlier about just what it was he wanted to measure anyway. Often he ends up with ratings made less easily and validly than could have been done if he had had an observer on hand at the time the original data were produced. In many a routine structured interview, it is easy and quite adequate for the interviewer simply to jot down the substance of the S's replies, selecting at the moment the wheat from volumes of chaff, which would take a typist just as long to transcribe from a recording as the few kernels that are wanted. Where a verbatim text is required, there is usually no substitute for modern electronic gadgets, but the experimenter must always remember that scientific observation is always and intrinsically selective and at times may advantageously be severely selective.

There are two basic methods of translating discursive or presentational symbols, as S. K. Langer (1942) calls them, into quantitative form: content analysis (measurement by counting) and rating (measurement by scaling). The essential operation of content analysis is assignment of a symbol (meaning) to a category. It is objective in that different persons can learn to perform this operation with satisfactory reliability, and it is systematic, orderly, and comprehensive. Various forms of content analysis have been used for decades in a number of disciplines, so that there is a substantial literature on it containing many helpful procedures and techniques (see the references).

Briefly, content analysis consists of the following six steps:

1. Decide on the units into which to break the data (for example, the behavior observed in a given period of time, the sentence, the answer to a question, the word). This step may seem simple, but it is often extremely vexatious (cf. Guetzkow, 1950; Leary & Gill, 1959).

2. Decide on the aspects of these units to be categorized, which will usually be dictated by the objectives of the research. "Headings" (groups of categories) may be derived mainly from theory or mainly from observed regularities and recurrent themes in the data or from some combination of both.

3. Build a scoring guide [code, manual, or what Cartwright (1953) calls an "analysis outline"] on the basis of a sample of the materials to be analyzed. The guide lists each heading and its categories with operational definitions. It may be necessary to give examples of scored and not-scored material for each category and a general set of rules to guide decisions.

4. Train coders or judges to do the scoring until a satisfactory level of agreement has been attained, preferably with another sample of the *kind* of data that will finally be used.

5. Have the judges score the critical data, maintaining a constant spot checking of reliability. The proportion of cases needing to be coded twice will depend on the level of reliability attained and needed and on the extent to which the judges tend to develop different interpretations of the categories ("drift").

6. For ease of quantitative analysis, the specified types or categories under each heading are numbered arbitrarily from 1 to k, and the judges enter only the numbers on large cross-ruled coding sheets set up so that the lines represent Ss and the columns the various headings. For example, suppose the data being analyzed are initial psychotherapeutic interviews: the first two columns on the coding sheet are for the identifying case number, and the third column might be assigned to such a heading as "Nature of Complaints Verbalized." The scoring manual would indicate that in column 3, the number 1 indicates somatic complaints; 2 indicates sexual difficulties; 3 indicates overt anxiety; etc. It would then list the next heading for the next column and would give the new specific meanings assigned to these numbers for this context. From such sheets, the rows of coded numbers are easily punched on cards for machine analysis, usually a separate card for each S (or row).

Rating is a notoriously fallible approach to quantification (cf. "Measurement in Clinical Research," below), and yet it remains an indispensable tool for the clinical experimenter. The essential operation of rating is a psychophysical type of judgment: more, equal, or less. Thus, operations as seemingly different as Q sorting, ranking, quantitative scaling, and paired comparison are basically techniques of making ratings.

Ratings are subject to the same errors as other judgments, plus some of their own, all of which can be reduced to constant or systematic errors and random errors. Each kind calls for more or less specific countermeasures.

Contamination is the confounding of the judgment required of the rater by other cognitive contents. Note that there are two subtypes here: contamination by the intrusion of unwanted but true information (e.g., knowledge of the criterion when predictive ratings are being made and contamination by intrusion of inaccurate information or other biasing cognitive content relative to the S in question. Since raters are not able to set up artificial information-tight compartments in their minds, various kinds of steps have to be taken to ensure that each rating is based only on the intended data. It is ideal when raters have no other information beyond what you furnish them, thus running no risk of recognizing Ss; when they cannot discern any systematic differences among Ss that might indicate what your independent variables are; and when they do not concern themselves with hypotheses about what the experiment is trying to prove. But it may be that the only available raters who have the requisite skills already know more than you want them to about at least some of the Ss. The problem is still not serious if this information is irrelevant to the kind of rating being made; any influence on their ratings will simply constitute random error. Likewise, if raters have no way of discriminating subgroups of Ss who are homogeneous with respect to an independent variable, no harm will be done by their notions of what hypotheses are being tested. But if raters believe that they see common elements of some independent variable in the data from a subgroup of Ss, all of whom do happen to have the same experimental treatment, then whether or not the raters *correctly* guess the common element, their ratings are likely to be contaminated.

Let us consider some concrete examples. In an attempt to predict performance as psychiatric residents of young physicians on the basis of personality assessments at the time of application, external circumstances made it necessary for test data to be analyzed by psychologists who had a certain amount of social and professional contact with the Ss after they entered the school of psychiatry (Holt & Luborsky, 1958). These contacts occasionally provided information directly relevant to the criterion of psychiatric performance, though more frequently the contact merely affected the psychologists' feelings of liking or disliking, or supplied information irrelevant to the criterion (e.g., eye color, wife's maiden name). The first of these three types of information would have directly contaminated predictive judgments; the second might have indirectly contaminated them (since liking would probably bias ratings in a positive direction), though it could have led to spurious error or to spurious success of prediction; and the third kind of information would probably contribute only a small amount of random variation to the ratings. Obviously, contamination had to be prevented or kept to a minimum. The first, most obvious step was to code all the data to be analyzed, replacing all names by numbers and blotting out other possibly revealing data. This is not quite as simple as it sounds; it was a task which took a good deal of judgment and which could not safely be left to a secretary who might not realize that if there was only one resident from Alaska, all references to the Far North had to be expunged from the test data. Second, the raters made a prolonged effort to keep to a minimum all their contacts with the Ss until after the predictive ratings had been completed so that any possible recognition would not have serious consequences. Finally, the raters were instructed to make a note as soon as any hypotheses about the identity of any S occurred to them. Such notes included the name of the possibly recognized S, the data suggesting the hypothesis, and all criterion-relevant information the rater had about him. The design involved making a series of ratings of personality traits and predictive ratings at each of several levels of information as the raters worked their way through a thick dossier on each S. Consequently, the later stages of analysis inevitably contained more recognitions and pseudorecognitions—as well as repudiations of earlier guesses about Ss' identities—and the earlier stages were more unambiguously uncontaminated. Outright certain recognitions were rare; but when they occurred, raters made the usual notes and then stopped any further analysis of the case in question.

This procedure made it possible to study the effects of contamination of various degrees on the ratings, principally by correlating predictions and criteria with and without contaminated cases. As it happened, the "information" that raters had about Ss they thought they recognized was as often misleading as helpful, so that adding the partly contaminated cases in did not significantly affect the validity coefficients.

Halo—the biasing of ratings by an impression of liking-disliking or general positiveness-negativeness of reaction—is a second source of error in ratings. It is a sobering and instructive experience to intercorrelate a set of supposedly quite differentiated ratings of many separately defined aspects of personality or predictions about diverse sorts of behavior and then discover one enormous general factor that accounts for most of the variance. If the ratings have included any frankly evaluative traits or judgments (good-bad, attractive-unattractive, choose-reject as friend, etc.), they will usually be found at the center of this general halo factor. Since it seems to be a human necessity to express this type of basic emotional adience or abience with respect to another person, it is advisable to get such a rating as social desirability or "general goodness" along with the desired variables. If necessary, you can then partial it out afterward, or you can instruct raters to be quite aware of their feelings and to record them before going on to make additional and independent judgments about aspects of the person or his productions. But as Bingham (1939) pointed out, there is such a thing as "valid halo"; the aspects of the data that arouse the judges' admiration or antipathy may be the very ones that are most relevant to performance on some independent behavioral criterion. In the experiment on selecting psychiatric residents already referred to (Holt & Luborsky, 1958), *liking* was rated along with predictions about various types of psychiatric performance so as to make possible the elimination of its expected interference. To our surprise, however, the ratings of liking turned out to be consistently more highly correlated with the principal criteria of performance than any of the direct predictions (Holt, 1958)!

In many experimental contexts, however, halo is a nuisance that tends to swamp any other source of variation in the ratings. It can be controlled to some extent by the following measures:

1. Do not ask raters to make large numbers of independent judgments of the same material. Even well-trained psychologists find it difficult, for example, to judge many separate aspects of a drawing or to predict many discrete forms of behavior on the basis of an interview. Specific rules cannot be dogmatically legislated, for a single brief TAT story may be said to contain a great many independently discriminable bits of information capable of supporting separate ratings (e.g., the hero's needs, press, his adequacy in attaining his goals, optimism of the outcome, degree to which the teller complied with instructions, literary quality, etc.). The more that such ratings are pinned to specific, easily identifiable informational units, the more one can include; see, for example, the carefully specified scoring criteria for *n* Achievement, *n* Affiliation, and a few other needs described by McClelland, Atkinson, Clark, and Lowell (1953), Atkinson (1958), and their collaborators. On the other hand, raters find it onerous to have to make more than half a dozen over-all judgments that are based on an impression of the story as a whole.

2. Define all variables to be rated as concretely and clearly as possible. Provide examples of data that fit and do not fit *each rated point* on a continuum, with general rules or principles involved in the ratings, to the extent that you can without providing an excess of reading matter. Often it will help to clarify the theory underlying the choice of variables and of criteria for scoring. [See Holt & Havel (1960) for an example of an attempt to apply this principle to the scoring of the primary process in Rorschach responses. The Fels Scales of Parental Behavior (Baldwin, Kalhorn, & Breese, 1945) are excellent examples of highly reliable rating scales, each of them containing examples of concrete behavior illustrative of several orienting points along the continuum involved.] It is particularly important to anchor high and low points of scales with concrete examples.

3. Keep all scales as unidimensional as possible. When a single aspect of the data has to be considered, the judgment to be made is a great deal easier than when a number of more or less correlated criteria must be mentally weighted and balanced. This principle is closely related to the next.

4. Require as few stages of inference as possible between the data and the ratings. Sometimes the objectives of a research project

require the rating of constructs that are several inferential removes from the data (for example, mental health—see Luborsky, 1962a). As Schafer has pointed out (1949), clinical diagnosis typically involves essentially the same sort of chains of inference. We directly judge the degree of effort a patient seems to make in handling color and form simultaneously, infer from that the degree of emotional inappropriateness, and then put together a number of such primary inferences to enable us to make the secondary inferential step to schizophrenia. In research, we do well to follow his suggestion and require explicit rating at each such level. In using the Health-Sickness Rating Scale (Luborsky, 1962a), for example, raters first record their judgments on the specific criteria before casting a balance and inferring from these first-level ratings what the S's over-all degree of health may be.

5. Do not overload raters with data. Clinicians who are accustomed to working with as much information as can be obtained about a patient and who are dedicated to the study of the "whole man" are especially liable to strain raters' integrative capacities by giving them too many data to work with. It is all too possible to overload any data-processing system's channel capacity by an excessive informational input, in which case a variety of types of inefficiency result (Miller, 1960). It may seem harmless to furnish essentially irrelevant but orienting background information to set the stage for the sort of data that are most relevant to the judgments needed, but it has been found that even skilled clinicians become confused and perform less well when given information beyond a rather low optimal level (Bavelas, 1952; Kelly & Fiske, 1951). This kind of problem is particularly acute when raters have few specific guidelines, must make extensive inference, and do not have much experience in processing the particular types of data for the purpose in question. With too much to hold in mind at once and not enough knowledge to help one sift wheat from chaff, it is no wonder that many raters oversimplify, fall back on halo, or otherwise fail at their task.

6. Consider carefully the number of points to be rated on each scale. It is all too common a custom to make all rating scales of some standard length or degree of differentiation because of a local tradition or some other irrational basis of preference. A scale should not have more points than will ever conceivably be used, for that will tend to overload the judges, requiring them to make a wasteful number of discriminations, and it will greatly increase the size of the job of preparing the scale. (A research team can easily spend years of hard work producing a set of well-designed and "debugged" rating scales; cf. Baldwin et al., 1945.) Obviously, if a scale's degree of differentiation requires judges to make finer discriminations than they are in fact capable of, ratings will be unreliable and subject to influence by irrelevant sources of variance.

On the other hand, if judges are capable of making fine discriminations and are accustomed to doing so, they may find it frustrating to be given too coarse an instrument—a pair of pliers with which to sort pearls. The shortest and simplest rating scale contains two points: present and absent, yes and no. At this point, quantitative analysis and qualitative, or categorical, analysis meet. Such a binary scale contains but a single bit of information and therefore may throw away much usable and even needed information that may be easily obtainable from the data. In general, it is desirable to err on the side of providing more differentiation in the rating scales than you think you may need. It is always possible later on to collapse a fine scale into a coarse one, with a gain in reliability (and often more reliability in the final rating than could have been attained if the raters had made only the smaller number of discriminations to begin with). Holt and Luborsky (1958) used a 51-point scale for predictive ratings, subsequently testing the effect of collapsing it to varying degrees; in the end, they reduced it to nine points, primarily to get each variable into a single column on IBM cards, although there was a demonstrable loss of information and of predictive power in the reduction. [Since a 10-point scale can also be punched in one column, we might have saved a bit of this lost information by following Canfield (1951) in adopting "sten" scores, which are also easier to dichotomize.] On the grounds of a mathematical and information-theoretical analysis, Tukey (1950) argues that if more than 10 per cent of two judges' ratings agree exactly, the scale is *too coarse,* and usable discriminations are being sacrificed.

7. Get as good judges as possible to make the ratings. It is generally reported (Taft, 1955) that the good judge of personality is an

intelligent, sensitive, and highly differentiated person who is motivated by an intrinsic interest in the subject matter and whose efforts will therefore be maintained at an even high level. Other things being equal, raters should be objective, mature people; but to list such vague criteria amounts to little more than the redundant advice to "get good judges." In the end, there is no certain way of predicting who will be best able to perform any specific task of rating, and when it is possible to validate ratings against an external, face-valid criterion, by far the best technique of selection is a trial at the actual job. Samuels (1952) found that graduate students did as well (i.e., as badly) as famous and highly experienced clinicians in predicting performance in clinical psychology from projective test data; Holt and Luborsky found no evident pattern of relation between the validity of interviewers' predictive ratings and their years of experience, confidence in their ability to do the task, or general status as clinicians. Yet in all such research, large individual differences in the ability to rate predictively have been found.

8. Train raters intensively in the task with materials of the kind they are ultimately to use. The sort of procedure described above for the training of coders applies here too, *mutatis mutandis*. By dint of intensive training and practice with two talented undergraduate students, Murray once obtained reliabilities above .9 in the rating of needs on six-point scales from TAT stories (Tomkins, 1947). In reporting such results, one should not give the impression that any reasonably intelligent person could attain a similar level of reliability by briefly studying a scoring system and applying it without any apprenticeship. The reported reliability attributed to many a rating scale is more properly a function of extended practice by raters who have worked together enough to learn to think alike.

9. If ratings are stubbornly low in reliability despite the above measures, add more raters. As Ebel (1951) has demonstrated, the reliability of the *mean* rating produced by a group of judges goes up steeply as the number of individual ratings per S increases, even though none of the judges agrees with any other particularly well. Pine and Holt (1960) found, for example, that pairs of clinical raters could not easily be trained to agree with one another in ratings of the humorousness of titles supplied cartoons by Ss. We therefore used seven raters, and the reliability of their average judgment rose to the acceptable level of .865.

Response sets in raters are the third major source of systematic error in ratings. A rater's freedom to be sensitive to nuances of meanings and to extract the quantitative variations of genotypic constructs in the phenotypes of clinical data also permits him to express and record his own personal rating behavior. Such behavior may be a legitimate object of study, but when it obtrudes itself and becomes confounded with independent variations in the behavior of Ss, it is a major source of error.

Several types of response sets in rating behavior may be distinguished, some of them so widespread as to be considered typical (Allport, 1961). In a number of the early investigations of ratings, a cautious tendency to stay close to the mean and not spread ratings enough was noted; for example, when children's intelligence is rated, the IQs of the retarded are usually overestimated, and those of the gifted underestimated. The oft-given advice, after this discovery, that raters be bold and step up their sigmas leads to even more error, however. Cronbach (1955) and Meehl and Rosen (1955) have demonstrated that the rating process in predictive and diagnostic investigations works best when judges are conservative and stick to *base rates*—that is, assume that each case is like the known central tendency in the population from which he is drawn—unless the information supplied gives positive indication that this one is different. As long as prediction is not perfect, *any* error will result in the underestimation of cases at the high extreme and overestimation at the low, as a brief reflection on the relation of regression to correlation will verify. It is a false inference, therefore, that most people have a mean-hugging response set that must be resisted. Clinicians particularly may be prone to infer spring from a single robin and to glory in their inability to explain an intuitive hunch that a man who looks ordinary enough to the uninitiated is actually about to sprout a florid psychosis. One does not earn a reputation as a diagnostic wizard by hewing to the base rates. When the boast of one's colleagues is, "When I make a mistake, it's a beaut," it takes a perverse kind of courage to persist in playing it safe with one's ratings. There are plenty of opportunities during the course of scientific research to vent one's intuitive flair and place the rent money on long shots; in the humble process of transforming qualitative data into quantitative ratings, however, it pays to play the favorite to show.

A common response set is overrating, giving the Ss the benefit of the doubt on any evaluatively tinged scale. Since most people abide by the law, are decent, and conform to culturally shared standards of good behavior, it is hard to resist the feeling that they should be rated not at the mean but above it on any facet of being a "good guy." Raters should be well aware of this tendency and of the emotional need to demonstrate their own benevolence by saying nice things about others. Notice that this point is closely related to the halo problem, with the focus now interindividual rather than intraindividual. Many of the same kinds of recommendations hold, therefore. It is helpful to keep the variables to be rated as free from connotations of value judgment as possible. A good deal of attention in psychometric circles has been given to the biasing effects of social desirability on test items in recent years (cf. Edwards, 1962; Messick & Ross, 1962). Since the cognitive process involved in taking most personality tests is essentially the same judgmental one that is involved in quantitatively rating someone else, the experimenter who needs to use ratings can learn a good deal from the sophisticated strategems of the psychometricians (see "Measurement in Clinical Research," below).

These mischievous effects of response sets would not be troublesome if it were not for the fact that judges differ so with respect to them; otherwise, we could simply apply a correction factor. To some extent, judges can be calibrated and a constant subtracted, for example, from the ratings of someone who consistently and persistently overrates everyone. Even this procedure has a limited range of applicability, however; raters are disappointingly human in their proneness to such errors as the interaction of their response sets with individual differences in the Ss being rated. Since it has often been found that most of the variance in both the elevation and scatter in sets of ratings is contributed by the rating behavior (or response sets) of the judges, it is a logical enough step to the procrustean bed of the Q sorter.

Stephenson's (1953) Q-sort procedure, for all its pretentions to being a "methodology," something uniquely "idiographic" (Beck, 1953; cf. Eysenck, 1954; Holt, 1962b), or otherwise special, is a technique of getting ratings. It contains a few valuable contributions—well stated by Block (1961)—notably, the fact that the ratings of every judge are forced into the same distribution and thus have identical means and standard deviations. The Q sort is usually presented as a "package deal," however, in which you have to buy the so-called "ipsative scaling," the normal distribution, factor analysis, the physical sorting of cards into piles, and correlating persons, along with the device of eliminating raters' response sets. It is worth emphasizing, therefore, that each of these features may be detached and considered on its own merits for the piece of research in question. There is nothing sacred about normal distributions for ratings; a rectangular distribution gives even more spread and may be better suited to the nature of some kinds of problems. There is no intrinsic reason why one might not decide on an asymmetrical distribution, too.

Suppose, for example, that you want to assess the defenses of patients applying to a clinic for therapy as part of an attempt to predict who will remain in treatment and who will fail to return after a single interview. As part of its regular procedure, the clinic has a diagnostic work-up, so that there are decided advantages to introducing a systematic evaluation of these data at the time the diagnosticians have them freshly in mind. This means considering each case one at a time, the sort of situation to which ipsative rating is well adapted. Instead of considering each trait individually and distributing the cases with respect to one another, you take a set of traits as the population to be distributed within the single case, giving highest ratings to the ones that are outstanding for this person. With a mixed bag of several dozen miscellaneous items, such as the California Q set (Block, 1961), it works quite well to rate the population of traits on a normal curve for each S. Surprisingly, the resulting ratings on a given trait may be extracted from the total group of sorts and found to be reasonably well distributed across Ss and thus quite usable as an interindividual variate. In our particular example, however, the hypotheses under test deal with defenses and do not call for assessing all the other aspects of personality that are included in typical Q sets, so that it would be wasteful of diagnostic effort to embed the defenses in a larger group of items that had to be rated too. It is in the nature of defenses, however, that they are rarely conspicuous by their absence; it is easy to identify the ones that a patient relies on most heavily, but it is not possible to say which defensive strategies are *least* used. Why not, therefore, present a comprehensive list of defenses to be evaluated for each patient, requiring the raters to select the two most outstanding (most heavily relied on by the S) defenses and from three to six second-line but still characteristic defenses and let the rest simply be called "not noteworthy"?

Long before Q technique was proposed, Murray and his coworkers (1938) developed a similar technique of controlling response sets using normative rather than ipsative scales. The experimenters studied a group of a dozen or two Ss intensively, independently rating each on a large number of simple scales and attempting to use all points of each scale and to distribute them normally within the sample. Next, a series of diagnostic conferences were held on each S in which the independent ratings were pooled, differences were discussed, and an internally well-distributed set of consensual ratings was decided on. Finally, at another set of meetings, the resulting distributions of Ss were considered variable by variable, and the ratings on each trait were forced into a roughly normal distribution; in addition, when the samples were small enough, Ss were rank-ordered on each variable. Though this procedure consumed a great deal of time, it resulted in highly differentiated ratings, free from distortion by the response sets of any raters and ideally suited to being correlated with independent experimental results. Horn (1944) contributed one further step, which he called "syndrome analysis": rated variables of a given type (e.g., needs, defenses) were intercorrelated, and combined distributions were prepared for highly interrelated clusters of items. Such a simplified version of factor analysis can eliminate a good deal of the redundancy in a group of ratings and present the researcher with a reduced set of variables that cover the domain of personality, as the research group was able to perceive it, with a negligible sacrifice of information.

The method of paired comparison was developed in psychophysics as a way of systematizing judgment and has been used in social psychology (as in the construction of attitude scales) but as yet rather little in clinical research. Through the vigorous advocacy of Sargent (1956), it was adopted by the Menninger Foundation research project on psychotherapy (Wallerstein, Robbins, Sargent, & Luborsky, 1956) as a means of quantifying a number of aspects of clinical case folders. If a diagnostic tester has, for example, a battery of psychological tests given a patient before and after treatment, he can make a judgment "improved," "no change," or "worse," but it is difficult for him to quantify such a global concept on much more of a rating scale than that. But he can examine two such pairs of test batteries and make a simple comparative judgment—"this one shows more improvement, on the whole, than that"—or he can make the judgment in terms of such specific variables as anxiety level, severity of symptoms, insight, and ego strength. In the Menninger project, systematically extracted and condensed clinical assessment data from a whole team's evaluation were used and entered onto research forms as the basis of the clinical judgments.

> In Sargent's form of the paired comparisons procedure, the name of each patient was paired with every other in a batch of only 12 patients. The 42 cases [in the total project] had been broken down by random sorting into overlapping batches of 12 patients each. . . . The clinician had only to decide for each pair "Which of these two patients has more (of the variable)?" The clinician was not expected to make a new assessment of the patient but rather to refer constantly to the forms compiled by the research team. . . . Clinicians find themselves quite comfortable in making these choices, much more so than when they are asked for ratings of the variables (Luborsky, 1962b, p. 118).

Yet the pairings can rapidly be consolidated to produce "a scale that is more than ordinal but less than equal interval." (On the question of ordinal and equal-interval scales, see "Some Statistical Issues in Psychological Research," below.) Reliabilities of two judges doing this task independently were consistently over .85 (Luborsky, 1962b). This is a method of considerable power that deserves to be tried more widely.

When all is said and done, ratings remain at best a crude, laborious method of quantifying data, always prone to the intrusion of many sources of error and never any better than the clinical skill of the available raters. Wherever possible, they should be replaced by better methods of measurement. For the immediate future, however, it is difficult to see how clinical research can do without them. When the techniques outlined above are followed with care and understanding, rating makes possible the quantitative treatment of data thus far intractable to any other kind of measurement. Moreover, even in areas that have been industriously worked over by psychometricians, ratings often turn out to have more construct validity, better correlations with independent criteria, and more predictive efficiency than competing objective tests.

STAGES IN EXPERIMENTAL RESEARCH

In the remainder of this chapter, we shall briefly run through the main stages of research as they are usually or ideally described. In practice, seasoned experimenters rarely plan as meticulously as will be implied here, so that it is tempting to push aside all such prescriptions as smelling more of the lamp than the laboratory. But the situation is like that of most other highly skilled endeavors: the master is allowed to break rules that an apprentice does well to obey until he learns and understands them thoroughly. It is fatal for the novice to flout the laws of perspective or harmony until he can see from the inside how the logic of his work of art requires them. So it is in experimentation. When after the investigator is so experienced that he no longer needs to consult checklists such as the following, he can afford to settle into a personal style of investigation that may be quite different from the sequence recommended here.

To help concretize things a bit, the discussion will make frequent reference to a specific (though hypothetical) clinical experiment: the comparison of two forms of treatment. Just to make things difficult enough for ourselves, let us suppose that a form of psychotherapy and a psychoactive drug are to be evaluated.

By choosing a practical, applied problem, I do not wish to minimize in any way the importance or the problematical nature of experimental research that is concerned with theoretical issues. As Ackoff (1953) has argued, almost any research problem can be viewed as an attempt to decide which of two or more means is the most efficient way of attaining some specific end. Most of the problems of clinical experimentation will come up in this, one of the most difficult types of research.

Defining the Problem

Research begins with a problem; a problem well stated is a research partly completed. How can one learn to ask good questions?

A good way to start is to *clarify objectives*. Try to find out what the "real problem" is, why the issue as first posed came up, and why anyone is interested in it. Usually, in applied or operations research, whoever is paying for the research is the one whose ultimate interests need to be inquired into in the process of clarifying what the research is to be focused on. Suppose a psychologist in a hospital has been presented, by the hospital administrator, with the task of therapeutic evaluation alluded to above. On making discreet inquiries, he may learn that the main objective in the administrator's mind is to get some research going as a way of sprucing up the staff and making the various disciplines work together more closely. This information may in turn lead to the discovery that interprofessional rivalries have grown administratively bothersome, which actually may indicate that any experiment requiring the coordinated effort of the several staffs runs the danger of being greatly delayed or even sabotaged. Another possibility is that a drug company has offered a grant to support evaluative research. The administrator is attracted by the prospect of drug therapy that will be cheap and easy, but the professional staff is so committed to psychotherapy that he believes they will not cooperate properly unless the comparison is included. A third possibility is that there has been a series of troublesome minor episodes of acting out on the part of patients in psychotherapy, and an administrator who much prefers sedately sedated patients wants to show that a tranquilizer will produce better results.

In the first of these hypothetical instances, more direct action to improve morale and interprofessional relations will be a better means of attaining the true objective than carrying out any research at all. In the other two, the project as originally proposed may be carried out, but with different emphases

TABLE 1. CHECKLIST OF QUESTIONS TO BE ASKED ABOUT A RESEARCH PROPOSAL

1. What is the problem?
   a. Is it clearly stated?
   b. Is it focused enough to facilitate efficient work (i.e., are hypotheses directly testable)?
2. What are the underlying objectives?
   a. Is the problem clearly related to the objectives?
3. What is the significance of the proposed research?
   a. How does it tie in with theory?
   b. What are its implications for application?
4. Has the relevant literature been adequately surveyed?
   a. Is the research adequately related to other people's work on the same or similar topics?
5. Are the concepts and variables adequately defined (theoretically and operationally)?
6. Is the design adequate?
   a. Does it meet formal standards for consistency, power, and efficiency?
   b. Is it appropriate to the problem and the objectives?
   c. Will negative results be meaningful?
   d. Are possibly misleading and confounding variables controlled?
   e. How are the independent and dependent variables measured or specified?
7. What instruments or techniques will be used to gather data?
   a. Are the reliabilities and validities of these techniques well established?
8. Is the sampling of subjects adequately planned for?
   a. Is the population (to which generalizations are to be aimed) specified?
   b. Is there a specific and acceptable method of drawing a sample from this population?
9. Is the sampling of objects (or situations) adequately planned for?
   a. To what population of objects (situations) will generalizations be aimed?
   b. Is there a specific and acceptable method of drawing a sample from this population?
10. What is the setting in which data will be gathered?
    a. Is it feasible and practical to carry out the research plan in this setting?
    b. Is the cooperation of the necessary persons obtainable?
11. How are the data to be analyzed?
    a. What techniques of "data reduction" are contemplated?
    b. Are methods specified for analyzing data qualitatively?
    c. Are methods specified for analyzing data quantitatively?
12. In the light of available resources, how feasible is the design?
    a. What compromises must be made in translating an idealized research design into a practical research design?
    b. What limitations or generalizations will result?
    c. What will be needed in terms of time, money, personnel, and facilities?

and different problems of control. In the second situation, there will be special problems of equating the attitudes and enthusiasm of the staff for the different treatment modalities being compared; moreover, in light of the prevailing preference for psychotherapy, it will probably be necessary to show that the drug is significantly *better* than psychotherapy to convince the staff, even though the administrator would be content to switch to the drug if it could be shown to be not significantly worse (see "Some Statistical Issues in Psychological Research," below, for implications in terms of setting alpha and beta values). In the third hypothetical case, the designer of the research will have to keep in mind that the administrator's objective will call for a short-term criterion emphasizing ease of ward administration, whereas the ultimate good of the patients might better be served by a criterion based on a longer-run follow-up and emphasizing personal adjustment rather than administrative convenience.

These are only a few of the more obvious possibilities that can be uncovered by the attempt to clarify objectives. Often, the result will be that the original statement of the problem will be significantly altered, to the greater ultimate satisfaction of all concerned. Ackoff (1953) has described how to go about asking questions so as to find out what the real underlying need of the "research consumer" is.

Finding a problem. To digress a bit from the topic, suppose that the underlying need is to *find* a problem of theoretical importance to work on. Examples of psychologists who may feel this way are a graduate student looking for a dissertation topic and a clinical psychologist who has managed to clear some time from clinical responsibilities because he feels a general urge to "get back into research" but who does not have a specifically formulated target.

The first advice to be given such a person is to concentrate on areas of greatest interest to him, personally. It is all very well to consider the needs of psychology generally, but the fact is that any research involves work, and it is likely to turn into pure drudgery unless one finds it intrinsically interesting. To choose a problem because it seems to be convenient or expedient or possible to complete with a minimum of time and effort is to ask for trouble. Any problem has its knotty aspects; research usually takes longer than one most liberally estimates, and you have to *believe* in, and care about, a problem to get over the rough spots.

Yet as our hypothetical instances suggested, *too much* commitment to a hypothesis is a serious difficulty for the researcher. It not infrequently happens that after his clinical and academic education and some years of clinical experience, a man develops strong convictions and then wishes to undertake research in order to develop objective data to coerce others into sharing his beliefs. In our example, the persons who design and carry out the research may themselves be committed to a faith in the efficacy of the particular form of psychotherapy under study, and so deeply committed that it is extremely difficult to avoid motivated errors. Let us assume that they have planned as controlled a study as possible, in which patients are randomly assigned to the drug or to psychotherapy and then, after a period of treatment, are interviewed and tested by a team of clinicians who do not know which therapy has been used. In practice, it is exceedingly difficult to accomplish what can be so simply stated. Physicians in charge of the wards will argue that clinical responsibility to the patient has an overriding importance, and who can deny that ultimately they are right? The trouble is that a controlled experiment to find out how well therapies work *must* involve some predictable therapeutic failures (if existing clinical lore has any predictive validity at all). If the responsible physicians are allowed to intervene at all on the grounds that "this patient is special" and really must or must not have the randomly assigned treatment, a critically important feature of the experiment is lost. Note that unless assignment to treatments is truly random (determined by rigid adherence to some unbiased method decided on in advance, preferably the use of a table of random numbers), judgment will creep in, and unconscious bias will have a chance to foul up the works. Another type of error to which the described design is vulnerable is the accidental discovery of a patient's treatment at the time he is being evaluated. The interviewers may start out uncontaminated (though it is difficult for them to, if they work at the same hospital), and the patients may know that they are not supposed to reveal what kind of therapy they have received, but it is easy for the patient to let a hint drop which neither party to the discussion takes explicit note of; yet the harm will be done, and the criterion judgment of improvement will be contaminated.

It is so hard for ordinary mortals to overcome the biasing influence of their emotional convictions that it is better not to undertake a piece of research if you cannot honestly contemplate without disturbance the prospect of having the results come out either way. When you feel tempted to use a one-tailed test because an equally large effect in the opposite direction seems inconceivable, that is a warning signal to stop and ask yourself whether you are honestly able to *let* it happen that way. Suppose your study proved that psychoanalytic psychotherapy made a sample of patients *worse* off than they were before treatment—could you publish that and still face your colleagues? Would you examine your data with an equally fishy eye, looking for sources of error and reasons to doubt the findings no matter what the results? Of course not; and I do not want to argue that only completely isolated, compulsive-schizoid personalities without any sense of clinical identity should do research. Just remember that it is in the end self-defeating to invest the time and labor that research demands if you are in danger of biasing your results. The truth wins out, ultimately. We know today that administering limewater and pulling out all a patient's teeth are irrational and ineffective therapies for schizophrenia. Yet many earnest and hopeful investigators managed to produce and publish remarkable series of "cures" by these means. Advances in experimental method make such fiascoes somewhat less likely today, but only somewhat. Choosing a research topic can still be a steering between Scylla and Charybdis, between the stony aridity of uninteresting topics and the whirlpool of too great emotional involvement. For most of us, the passage is fortunately wide enough, and there is plenty to study with enthusiasm but not fanaticism.

The second requisite of any researchable problem is that it be within the powers of the investigator to carry out the research to completion. If it will take too much time, too much money, special skills you do not have, collaborators you cannot line up—and sew up!—ahead of time, or equipment that cannot be made available to you, then it is best eschewed.

Completed research in clinical psychology seldom resembles the original germinative idea very exactly. When closely examined, the initial formulation of the problem is frequently too sweepingly grandiose or too trivial to be worth carrying out. Neither state of affairs means that it should be abandoned forthwith. If the interest is there, mulling over a problem, reading about it, and discussing it with friends will usually result in a practicable and worthwhile approach if you keep at it long enough. For someone who has not had a great deal of experience in research, the first job is usually to narrow down the scope of an interest into something researchable. This can be done in several ways: in terms of the particular focus of your interest, in terms of what is feasible for your resources, and in terms of other intersecting theoretical problems.

Originality in research, as in any kind of thinking, is largely a matter of synthesis: putting together familiar elements in new combinations. Wide reading, plus acquaintance with a range of issues and problems in psychological theory and research, can interact with more specifically clinical studies and experience to yield a new approach.

The besetting antagonist of originality is rigidity, stubborn clinging to one way of organizing experience when many others are potentially possible. The trouble is that we so often are unaware of what our assumptions are and thus cannot see how they blind us to a host of possible fresh questions to ask of nature. For about two thousand years, the Empedoclean-Hippocratic doctrine of the four humors and four corresponding temperaments so completely shaped the educated man's conception of personality that there was a virtual inability to see any other form of diversity in people. Every now and then, however, someone suggests a way of asking questions that can be extended to open up many researchable topics. Thus, in the late 1930s and during the 1940s, several people hit on the idea of taking seriously the error term in most standard psychological experiments as representing valid variance due to individual differences. W. Langer (1938), for example, showed that the individual differences in all the usual measures generated in rote-learning experiments could be treated as indications of various types of personality organization and could be meaningfully related to independent assessments of personality. This kind of insight played an important role in the whole "new look" movement in perceptual research, and it still has a good deal of research applicability. The fruitful concept and research area of cognitive style (cf. Gardner, Holzman, Klein, Linton, & Spence, 1959) is essentially based on this idea, married to the concept of ego structure as developed by Rapaport (cf. Rapaport, Gill, & Schafer, 1945–1946).

Klein and his coworkers have shown how the ego-structural viewpoint can give rise to a great number of theoretically meaningful experiments. The central point Rapaport stressed clinically was that the same dynamic conflict could lead to very different behavioral outcomes (e.g., symptom-pictures) in patients with different types of favored defenses and adaptive, controlling structures. In research terms, this outlook can lead to asking what the structural differences are between people for whom a given dynamic proposition holds and those for whom it does not. Klein (1954) found such differences between persons whose perceptual judgment was "autistically" influenced by the aroused drive-state of thirst and those who were not so influenced. Alper (1946) similarly found ego-structural differences between subjects who remembered their failures and those who forgot them. Probably most testable psychoanalytic propositions will turn out to be valid under certain conditions and for persons of specifiable structural characteristics; at least a generation of researchers can be kept busy discovering the parametric limits of psychoanalytic theories (cf. also Sarnoff, 1962).

Another good set-breaking generative principle for research is to take any apparently established experimental or clinical fact and retranslate its theoretical statement into concrete terms with a different set of operational definitions from the usual ones. When a new technique of measuring an important construct is introduced, it tends to be taken up and widely adopted by a generation of researchers, most of whom assume that it solves the problem of operational definition for the construct in question and who generalize freely in terms of that construct. Consider, for example, the amount of research on anxiety that used the Taylor scale of so-called "manifest anxiety" before a few skeptical souls started asking what some of the results would look like if a different set of operations were used, perhaps closer to clinical reality. It is usually healthy in psychology to be cautious in assuming that any one set of operations provides a sufficient measure of a construct. A great deal of useful research can be generated by the attempt to replace a standard measure by looking at the concept in question as naïvely as possible, asking yourself what would be the most direct and ideally face-valid way of getting at it.

Ideally, research should grow out of an interest in the phenomena under observation themselves and should also be relevant to theory. In practice, researchers tend to be more interested in one side or the other of this dichotomy, either becoming fascinated by some empirical problem and pursuing it as long as they can find new questions to ask about it or trying to test only propositions that have direct bearing on theoretical issues. Though the latter style has more scientific prestige in many quarters, both can lead to excellent research. What matters is to find one's own style and make the most of it.

There are many published sources of specific research topics. Unsolved problems, often already formulated in experimentable form, abound in reviews of literature such as are found regularly in the *Psychological Bulletin*, the *Annual Reviews of Psychology*, *Progress in Neurology and Psychiatry*, *Progress in Clinical Psychology*, the *Annual Survey of Psychoanalysis*, the annual surveys in the *American Journal of Psychiatry* and the *Journal of Clinical Psychology*, or in works such as the present one or Eysenck's *Handbook of Abnormal Psychology*. Yet it rarely works well simply to comb through such a source and pick a nice, manageable-looking problem. The choice has to be guided by preexisting, genuine interest in a problem area.

Reviewing the Literature

Reading is an activity that should never cease for the researcher. Fairly early in his pursuit of a specific project, however, there should be a phase of redoubled activity in the library, for several reasons. Reading what has been done and thought by others in your area will help specify the hypotheses and questions that define your problem sharply. You may even find that what you are thinking of doing has already been carried to publication by others or has been tried and found impractical. Just because a piece of research has been carried out once is no reason not to do it again; on the contrary, one of the greatest needs in psychological research is more replication of experiments (see below). Why worry, then, and why bother to find out whether someone has anticipated you? It is always poor scientific manners to barge into an area and write as if you were the first one ever to think about it, but far more than politeness is involved; if psychology is to make progress as a science, we must build on one another's work. Science is one of the largest and most complicated human enterprises ever to go on for so many years and in so many places without some kind of central control, but it would be a complete anarchy without its main mechanism of social control, its literature. This mechanism does not work unless people use it, which means prompt reporting of all potentially useful parts of one's own work—including negative findings!—and a conscientious effort to keep up with the work of others, at least in areas of immediate interest. Without constant efforts at scientific communication, researchers duplicate one another's work unnecessarily, with unplanned and unintelligible variations in technique and instrumentation, so that an ultimate synthesis becomes impossible. Two apparently similar studies with different findings turn out to have many seemingly arbitrary differences in design and execution, so that the variables that are actually responsible for the difference are too confounded to be discerned.

If, however, you have a good grasp of where research stands in your field of interest, what its major unsolved problems are, what the standard techniques of experimentation have been, and what the usual methods of varying and measuring independent and dependent variables are, then you can design an experiment which will be rationally related to an existing body of work and which will make a useful contribution to it. One of the most valuable types of research is a complete replication of an outstanding study with one crucial variation; this is J. S. Mill's method of difference in pure form. No one is compelled to follow in the footsteps of predecessors, and there may be good reasons why your investigation uses different methods to get a new type of data on unusual types of subjects, but such a foray is a gamble. If it yields better results, it may set a new style of experimentation, but if not, it may open up only a private blind alley.

Our hypothetical example touches on one enormous literature, that of experimental pharmacotherapy, and a smaller but rapidly growing one in psychotherapeutic research. The clinical psychologist who is accustomed to leaning on the *Psychological Abstracts* will be surprised to find, if he looks conscientiously, that much of both types of research (but especially the work on drugs) is not covered at all in this source. Fortunately, there is an excellent guide to the important books in this field in the *Mental Health Book Review Index*. A couple of bibliographic journals in medicine, the *Index Medicus* and the *Current List of Medical Literature*, provide good entries into the literature of psychopharmacology and various forms of therapy. A good entry into the other literature is provided by the two APA volumes, *Research in Psychotherapy* (Rubinstein & Parloff, 1959; Strupp & Luborsky, 1962). The principal way to go at it is to look up the references cited in the papers or books you do know and note down relevant-sounding titles from their reference lists. In this way, you quickly find out which are the most frequently cited reports, which you can read first, extending the same process. Thereby you also learn the names of journals in which the kind of paper that interests you is published; to find the current literature, scan the most recent volumes (usually there is a lag of at least a year before papers are cited in bibliographic journals, and sometimes the *Psychological Abstracts* runs as many as five years behind). Other journals can be found by consulting a librarian in a good psychological, psychiatric, or medical library.

A lazier but occasionally effective technique is to write to a prominent center of the kind of research in question and ask if a ready-made bibliography is available. Drug manufacturers are usually happy to send you lists of publications dealing with their products, though you may have to write to quite a few in order to find all the work on any widely manufactured drug, such as many of the ataractics. Books and journals devoted to reviews and surveys are other obvious sources. Buros's *Mental Measurements Yearbooks* contain cumulative bibliographies on all psychological tests, and a number of (non-APA) journals, such as the *American Journal of Psychotherapy*, abstract or list current references likely to be of interest to their readers.

If you get interested in collecting a complete bibliography and in reading in an area that has not recently been reviewed, you can do the field a great service by preparing an article that collects, organizes, and critically evaluates a specifiable segment of literature. With the growing realization that science is in danger of being choked by its own output, we are all becoming increasingly dependent on such reviews, and they are becoming recognized as important contributions.

Problems of Designing Research

Experimental design has become a highly technical subdiscipline in itself, on which a number of books and articles are readily available; perhaps the best brief guide to it is the paper by Campbell (1957). This section will therefore deal with just a few miscellaneous points that bear stressing.

A useful procedure, recommended by Ackoff (1953), is to begin a research project by drawing up an idealized research design. From your initial formulation of the problem in terms of the underlying objectives there will follow indications for the types of data needed to attain each objective. The review of previous research (plus correspondence, visits, or other communication with others who are active in similar work) will suggest specific procedures and instruments as well as needed improvements, such as controls of previously ignored possible sources of error. Putting all this together with your knowledge of experimental design, plan a study which would be proof against all criticism and which would provide definitive results, regardless of expense or feasibility. Then make your compromises; scale it down to what your resources allow, and you will be aware of your project's actual limitations to a much greater extent than if you had never gone through the exercise of making an idealized design. The latter may show the need for a series of studies, each going at a piece of the total job to be done; it may even persuade you that you cannot get any unequivocal results at all. This last outcome is melancholy, but a far better one than to invest time, money, and effort in actually going through with something that will be unusable in the end.

An important minor part of designing research is to define your terms. All too often, this step is omitted until the writing up of the final report, when it may be too late. The process of definition should be twofold: All major terms should have both theoretical (conceptual) and operational definitions—the specification of data-gathering methods—which need to be carefully coordinated. It sometimes happens, for example, that an experimenter gives an excellent treatment of the concept of anxiety in theory and then adopts a conventional, available measure like GSR without making any linkage between the two types of definition, which leaves it an open question whether his work has any relevance to theory or not. For it is at this critical juncture that the bearing of empirical work on conceptual models and propositions derived from them is established. It is a serious but common error to think that the problems of definition are solved simply by the declaration that a specified measure is the operational definition of a term from some theory, which the experimenter then proceeds to bandy about, taking advantage of all its surplus meaning in the theory and in common usage, little of which may have any relation to the operation in question.

In designing research, the hardest thing to make oneself do and the most necessary is to be sufficiently specific and concrete. In a way, this is the central point of operationalism; but even the most objective and operationally minded experimenters at times settle for a too *general* description of operations to be used. Consider our hypothetical project. If two types of treatment are to be compared, it will be necessary to measure the effectiveness of each in modifying outcome; in other words, a criterion measure will be needed. It may sound operational to say that "expert ratings of outcome will be the criterion," but such a statement is a long way from being concrete enough to give any idea of how to proceed. Who will rate what, how, when, and on the basis of what information? A review of publications on experimental therapeutics in clinical psychology and psychiatry will show that the obvious and easy ways of getting such criterion measures have many serious drawbacks. Indeed, the lesson of much predictive research is that the heart of the matter is getting a good criterion and that a great deal of the initial research effort ought to go into developing adequate criterion measures (cf. Holt & Luborsky, 1958; Horst et al., 1941; Kelly & Fiske, 1951). Facing this issue squarely will frequently result in a considerable scaling down of the original scope of the project. In our example, it might result in a decision to concentrate on studying the comparative merits of the drug and the psychotherapy at issue in bringing about reduction of acting out in character disorders as assessed after six months and at discharge. It will not be easy to define acting out objectively enough so that nurses, psychiatric aides, psychiatrists, psychologists, and social workers can agree in rating the same behavior the same way, but the effort to sharpen the definition will be instructive and may yield a contribution in itself.

A final word of warning about research design. Investigators who know about research primarily from reading books like this one or from having taken courses in experimental design rather than from actual experience not infrequently lose sight of the fact that design is a means and not an end in itself, and they plan highly complex experiments using multivariate models or analysis of variance. When they try to carry them through, they find that such designs are extremely demanding of precision and meticulous adherence to plan, allowing for little serendipity and no spontaneity in execution. The more complex the design, the easier it is to get confused about just what treatment to apply to each S, and the more costly each such error is. Moreover, a design in which very few Ss get the same treatment will confound some of the independent variables that a clinical experimenter is likely to want to investigate; he will not be able to measure the personalities of his Ss and correlate the resulting variates with experimental findings in the way advocated above (cf. Holt & Goldberger, 1959, for an example of correlates of isolation, etc.). Unless there are compelling reasons, therefore, it is generally wise to err on the side of simplicity of design and not try to investigate many aspects of a problem at once.

Sampling

No part of research planning is more often slighted and more important than the drawing of samples. For *sampling is the key determinant of how findings can be generalized.* Since Brunswik's (1956) important expositions of representative design, it has become evident that the selection of subjects is only half of sampling, which must concern itself with the selection of the other determinants of the behavior under study—situations, objects, experimental stimuli, persons. If our criterion behavior were to be acting out, it would become necessary to define the situations in the patients' lives in which this kind of behavior typically takes place and the kinds of persons and provocations involved so that we could make sure to obtain meaningful measures. Suppose, for example, that we decided to use only ratings of observed behavior in the ward and in the OT shop (assuming a population of hospitalized subjects). We might arrange to have professional personnel observe a great deal of behavior directly, which would be in a number of ways a good basis for a criterion and which might yield interpretable results. Yet there are few hospitals in which patients never have *any* unobserved moments, and those are the very ones in which certain forms of acting out take place almost exclusively, such as drinking and sexual behavior. Thus, it would be necessary either to sample situations more representatively or to restrict generalization to ward behavior.

In the therapy, also, considerations of representative design (sampling of objects) are important. A single project is not likely to be able to compare more than one form of psychotherapy and one drug. It would be tempting, if the results were clear-cut and in line with our preexisting prejudices, to publish conclusions that "drugs are inferior [or superior] to psychotherapy in controlling acting out in psychiatric wards." It is a little more obvious that a single ataractic cannot stand for all drugs, but it is easily overlooked that the psychotherapy practiced in a given hospital by a certain group of staff members has just as little claim to represent the probable achievements of all other therapists elsewhere. The range of techniques covered by the one term "psychotherapy" is staggering; moreover, one cannot simply accept the word of the therapist that he used "classical x technique." Empirical studies of the behavior of psychotherapists who claim adherence to the same schools have shown great diversity (Strupp, 1960). Then, too, researchers in psychotherapy are increasingly recognizing that the personality of the specific practitioner who applies a technique is a major determinant of the effectiveness of therapy (see, for example, Holt & Luborsky, 1958; Betz & Whitehorn, 1956). To be able to make valid statements about client-centered therapy, for example, one would have to study a representative sample of all the therapists who are currently using this technique. To return to the pharmacological side of the problem for a moment, considerations of dosage are as important as the nature of the specific ataractic and again set limits on what claims can be made for the results.

The principle that the nature of his samples limits the generalizations an experimenter can make extends to the sample of personological items contained in a Q sort. Writers who cite Fiedler's (1950) well-known study showing more similarity among expert therapists of different schools than among experts and tyros within the same point of view usually neglect to mention the marked limitations imposed by the items in the Q sort used, which all referred to a few aspects of the psychotherapeutic relationship. Many of the critical points of technique that usually come to mind when one thinks about therapy of the kinds

Fiedler studied were not touched on at all in the Q set. Block (1961) has argued that if two Q sets both include a heterogeneity of items covering many aspects of personality, findings with both will be similar, and he performed a little study that supported his point. Nevertheless, it is logically inescapable that the concept of "similar personalities" is meaningless without reference to the specific points of identity or near-identity (Cronbach & Gleser, 1953). In Block's demonstration study, the Q set made up by the secretary by a commonsense selection of adjectives describing people contained no items dealing with specific mechanisms of defense; even though descriptions of people with this set acted statistically very much like descriptions in terms of the California Q set, which does contain defenses, the former might be seriously misleading if used in a problem for which just this aspect of personality happened to be crucial. Moreover, since there is no rational way of getting a complete inventory of all items describing personality, there can be no sure way of sampling them in a representative way.[4]

Until the advent of sample surveys, experimental psychologists were mostly blithely unconcerned with sampling subjects. The old tradition used the *E* himself, his wife, plus a few lab cronies and on this basis solemnly concluded general laws about all mankind. More recently, psychologists have begun to be aware that getting a large enough sample is a problem, but even today the size of the *n* is usually the only question that is considered (for that, see "Some Statistical Issues in Psychological Research," below). Experimenters who work with clinical groups of Ss must perforce be aware of more sampling variables than *n* and availability, but we still lack a firm tradition of responsibility in this connection.

The essential point about sampling is that we study a few persons and wish to find out about the many, so that the sample must *represent* the target population in relevant ways. Thus, in a sample survey to predict an election, the relevant sampling variables are those that are known to determine voting behavior: party affiliation, income, age, sex, ethnic-group membership, and education. These are not the only determinants, but they account for most of the variance, and information about them is obtainable for the target population and the sample. Therefore, one can draw a sample in such a way as to create a miniature replica of the population in these respects. The validity of generalization is a function of the adequacy with which the determinants of the behavior in question has been identified, the accuracy with which one knows their distribution in the target population (that is, the group whose behavior is to be predicted), and the fidelity or representativeness with which the sample duplicates the population in these respects. Note that *n*, the size of the sample, enters only as a determinant of the power of the statistical tests one can make and thus of the size of the random error of measurement; it has in itself nothing to do with how representative or "valid" a sample is.

The example may be misleading, since in most psychological research we are not trying to predict concretely what a specific population will do but are looking for general laws of behavior. It is vital to realize, however, that the logic of sampling still holds in the same way. A psychological law amounts to a prediction that, given conditions *c*, people will react with behavior *b*—but not just any people. The laws of verbal learning, for example, despite the virtually universal neglect of this issue in the experimental literature, are tacitly assumed to hold for persons with roughly normal sensory and motor capacities, normal intelligence, and normal familiarity with English and the ability to read and speak it. It may very well be that to a much larger extent than is generally recognized, they also hold only within certain limits of other parameters, such as capacity to get interested in abstract, intellectual problems; education; social class; and ego structure. These limitations (which are only suppositions, or hypotheses, at this point, because the issues are largely uninvestigated) result from the *de facto* restriction of the population sampled in most academic experiments and are not a result of an intention to sample in this way. The burden of proof is therefore on anyone who generalizes unrestrictedly to demonstrate that the actual limitations of his sample are irrelevant to the behavior he is studying.

In the days when psychology was the

[4] I am aware of Hilden's (1954) efforts to provide such representative Q sets by randomly sampling Allport and Odbert's (1936) listing of all personologically descriptive terms from an unabridged dictionary, but for a number of reasons, I do not consider the listing an adequate parent population of personality descriptions.

science of the average adult human mind, the target population was always normal, mature mankind, visualized (if considered at all) as well-educated, white, male, and American or Western European. There was thus a special psychology of women, one of children, one of members of off-brand ethnic groups ("ethnopsychology"), and one of hospitalized people ("abnormal psychology"). As psychology comes of age, it will become less ambitious, seeking to generalize about the behavior of more restricted groups, and also more ambitious, seeking to unify all these special psychologies into one science of behavior in which laws will have sampling parameters attached to them but will be otherwise general. For many of its laws, sex, ethnic-group membership, eye color, and many other characteristics of the subjects will be irrelevant, and the fact that they were first studied in United States college sophomores will turn out not to be restrictive. But just as comparative psychology has to broaden its purview beyond the cage of the white rat (Beach, 1950), human psychology must sooner or later find out the parameters that limit its generalizations, too.

There are essentially two ways of getting representative samples: probability sampling and stratified sampling. If you know the population values of the important variables to control, you can look for specifiable people who will create your miniature, that is, a form of quota or stratified sampling. In psychology, however, for the most part we do not know what are the appropriate constraints to put on our samples, and we have no way of finding out their distribution in the populations about which we wish to generalize. Logically, therefore, we should turn to the other technique, random or probability sampling. Such a sample can attain representativeness, not because efforts are made to include certain sorts of people, but because efforts are made *not* to *exclude* anyone in the population. When everyone in the parent population (the one from which a sample is drawn) has an equal chance of being included, a probability sample results. Randomness is an essential part of the technology involved, since considerable pains have to be taken not to proceed in an unconsciously biased and selective way. To pick people at random sounds extremely easy but is actually quite difficult. Buttonholing people in a park, for example, will get you a sample of mostly unemployed people who are not actively involved in community activities, who have few hobbies and other interests, who have smaller families than average, and who probably would turn out to have a restricted range of personality structures. Active, involved, busy people do not have an equal opportunity to be included, so the method is a biased one.

The simplest random way of selecting a sample is to give every member of the parent population a number and then enter a table of random numbers until you have as many as you need, using the people corresponding to the resulting set of numbers. This technique is practicable only with relatively small, captive populations that are already listed, such as students in a school or patients in a hospital. Even so, as far as institutions are concerned, you have a sample of only one, so that a randomly drawn sample of schizophrenics in a state hospital in Blackfoot, Idaho, may be a poor basis for generalizing about the people carrying a similar diagnosis at Chestnut Lodge or Manhattan Veterans Administration Hospital. And we typically want to be able to reach conclusions about relationships between variables x and y in schizophrenics, generally, or at least in adult Americans so diagnosed by a competent clinician and declared relatively free of other types of disorder. Nevertheless, it is usually helpful to introduce randomness whenever possible in drawing samples (Cochran, Mosteller, & Tukey, 1953).

What ways out of this dilemma are at hand? Ignoring it, while traditional, accomplishes nothing except to reduce anxiety, and it perpetuates one of the prime sources of the recurrent nuisance in psychology: that different experimenters get different results. More than a nuisance is involved, for this phenomenon means that we have not begun to locate some of the most important sources of variance in the behavior we study. First of all, we should describe our samples as completely as possible with respect to possibly relevant variables.[5] In a study of catechol amine secretion in relation to mood fluctuation, the texture of the Ss' hair and their clerical aptitudes can safely be neglected, but not their cultural

[5] Titles particularly tend to claim far more generality than is justified by the sample, a practice that should be discouraged. True, "the sexual behavior of contemporary Indiana white men" is less resounding and impressive than "the sexual behavior of the human male," but it would have been a bit more accurate.

backgrounds or diagnoses. Diagnosis, in turn, should be given in terms of a standard nosology and a specified set of criteria (such as those published by the American Psychiatric Association, 1952). One of the reasons for the widespread (and, in my view, unjustified) rejection of diagnostic classification of patients is the tendency to develop local idiosyncrasies of category and criteria, so that you have to know that 90 per cent of the patients at a certain hospital are diagnosed schizophrenic and only half that proportion at another one, which draws on an apparently similar population, before you can interpret disparate findings from the two institutions. In addition to the bald label "schizophrenia," one needs to know the type, whether acute or chronic, and the history of previous hospitalizations and remissions and of previous therapy, not to mention the current therapeutic regimen, its type and duration. Age; sex; number of years of education; religion; geographic, ethnic, and cultural origin; occupation; and marital status are other easily obtained facts that should routinely be included in the published descriptions of samples and of subsamples. Experimental and control groups need to be matched on every such sampling parameter that might affect the dependent variable.

This may seem a tedious amount of detail, though it can usually be rather compactly stated; but without it, we shall continue to flounder in ignorance of how far our results are a function of unknown sampling parameters. This is another way in which we can make sure that our results will add up with those of others and be of some ultimate scientific value.

As far as the actual selection of Ss is concerned, we should first of all become aware of the nature and implications of the sampling problem and know what we are doing. To a large extent, any experimenter is limited by the necessity to use available Ss, though often less so than he realizes. If you are not studying clinical groups and are working in an academic setting, do not settle for the easily obtainable students every time. The surrounding community contains sources that are hardly more difficult to exploit: clubwomen of many kinds, firemen, prisoners, recuperating patients in general hospitals, people in homes and day centers for the aged, and many others. Whatever the population you are drawing on, try to sample them in as unbiased a way as possible; if you have to use every volunteer you can get, make it clear in your paper that the sample *was* self-selected, and do not imply that it was random. A number of studies have shown that volunteers differ strikingly from nonvolunteers (cf. Lasagna & von Felsinger, 1954). Just this device of using a variety of samples, each carefully described, will help psychology expand its horizons.

The maximum benefit will be obtained, however, if you *replicate every experiment with a different sample of* Ss *before attempting to generalize* from its results. The more divergent the samples, the more safely can you assume that cross-validated results are generally true or are limited only by the few features both samples have in common. Any replication is better than none, and if you have any reason to doubt that a result was more than a fluke in the first place, you should cross-validate it as exactly as possible, including a sample drawn in the same way. Otherwise, however, replication with the same type of Ss does *not* make it more legitimate to generalize beyond the descriptive characteristics of those Ss' parent population. When Bach and Klein (1957) found essentially the same influence of a subliminally presented word on descriptions of a pictured face as Smith, Spence, and Klein (1959) had, they gambled by changing the experimental technique while simultaneously going from male VA schizophrenics to female summer students of education; if the results had been negative, it would not have been possible to tell what was responsible. As it was, however, they increased the generalizability of their results quite markedly. When Goldberger and I (1961) replicated an earlier study (Holt & Goldberger, 1959) of personological correlates of reactions to perceptual isolation, we changed from first-year undergraduates in the NYU School of Education to unemployed members of Actors' Equity. There had been a striking correlation of an adaptive pattern of reaction with measures of femininity in the earlier sample; among the actors, the relationship reversed completely, the adaptive pattern now correlating with masculinity. At the same time, measures of ego strength continued to show significant positive correlation with the adaptive pattern. This example illustrates both the futility of relying on results at the .01 level when going outside the bounds of the original sample and the way that the strategy of replication advocated here can fractionate the stable from the unstable findings, so that the later study illuminates the earlier one.

Planning Qualitative and Quantitative Analysis of the Data

The conventionally given advice in this area is so often and so unfortunately ignored as to make it worth repeating: Plan ahead *specifically,* in advance of collecting your final data, just how you are going to analyze them—all of them. This step will pay for itself in labor saved gathering unnecessary data alone. The time to get expert statistical consultation is before the results are in, not after. The same advice applies when performing a content analysis of qualitative data.

Except in the simplest experiments, it is virtually impossible to foresee all relevant and useful analyses of the data. Discoveries are made only by those who keep their eyes open. The experimenter who compulsively follows his original plan to the letter and stops there will rarely learn anything new, though he will turn out better work than the freewheeling impressionist who cannot be bothered to gather and analyze his data in a uniform manner. The best style is a mixture of discipline and freedom, responsibly sticking to what is essential in a design but flexibly taking advantage of the unexpected opportunity for exploration.

The Pilot Study

Whenever possible, it is usually helpful to have a dry run of an experiment with a few Ss as comparable as possible to the ones who will actually be used, going through as many parts of the total research process as you can before finally crystallizing the design and procedures. In this way, by trying out several versions you can work out exact instructions to Ss, collect sample data on which to develop a coding system for a content analysis, train your raters, check reliabilities, etc., without sacrificing any of your final data. In our exemplary project, a pilot study might help work out dosages of the drug and alert us to any side effects.

A pretest of this kind is particularly important in any large-scale study in which many Ss are to be used over quite some period of time or, in general, whenever a major investment will be made in an investigation. Once the gathering of the final data has begun, it may be too late to turn back and start again, so that all procedures need to be checked out before they are fixed. Under these circumstances, it is tempting to make a change in some instruction or what not after having analyzed the pretest data and then go ahead and use it, overlooking the fact that it is still untried and may have just as many unanticipated "bugs" as the original, discarded one. Pretesting then should ideally continue until every part has been tried out in its final version and the decision has been made that nothing more needs changing.

Last Steps

Collecting the crucial data, analyzing them, performing the statistical analyses, writing up the findings for publication—these are of course the critical steps of experiment; yet if planning has proceeded adequately, they usually may be run through relatively uneventfully. If not, there is little by way of general advice that can be given other than such homiletic stereotypes as to keep your head, note down everything untoward that happens, be accurate, try to understand the deviant cases as well as the ones that behave in predicted fashion, and have the courage to write up and publish negative findings. What, then, is the final step, the end point? An argument could be made that it should be a replication of the entire experiment or the publication of the written report. The fact is that there is no logical stopping place in experimentation; since science does not know any final truths, any study points inevitably to further problems that need to be investigated. That is one reason why research can be such an endlessly fascinating pursuit.

REFERENCES

The references are divided into two sections. The first is an alphabetical listing of all works referred to in the text; the second is a classified list of additional useful sources which have *not* been cited specifically. Therefore, to find a reference cited above, such as Kaplan (1964), look in the first section. To find a group of references on a given topic, such as the design of experiments, look in the second section under the appropriate heading, where you will find a cross-reference to each work of this kind in the first section, plus additional sources.

Works Referred to in Text

Ackoff, R. L. *The design of social research.* Chicago: Univer. of Chicago Press, 1953.

Allport, G. W. *Pattern and growth in personality.* New York: Holt, 1961.

Allport, G. W., & Odbert, H. S. Trait names: a psycho-lexical study. *Psychol. Monogr.,* 1936, No. 211.

Alper, Thelma G. Memory for completed and incompleted tasks as a function of personality: an analysis of group data. *J. abnorm. soc. Psychol.,* 1946, **41**, 403–420.

American Psychiatric Association. *Mental disorders: diagnostic and statistical manual.* Washington, D.C.: Author, 1952.

American Psychological Association. *Ethical standards of psyshologists.* Washington, D.C.: Author, 1953. (See also briefer, revised version in *Amer. Psychologist,* 1963, **18**, 56–60.)

Aserinsky, E., & Kleitman, N. Two types of ocular motility occurring in sleep. *J. appl. Physiol.,* 1955, **8**, 1–10.

Atkinson, J. W. (Ed.) *Motives, in fantasy, action and society.* Princeton, N.J.: Van Nostrand, 1958.

Bach, S., & Klein, G. S. The effects of prolonged subliminal exposures of words. *Amer. Psychologist,* 1957, **12**, 397–398.

Baldwin, A. L., Kalhorn, J., & Breese, F. H. Patterns of parent behavior. *Psychol. Monogr.,* 1945, **58**, No. 268.

Bavelas, A. Communication patterns in problem-solving groups. In H. van Foerster (Ed.), *Cybernetics: circular causal and feedback mechanisms in biological and social systems.* New York: Josiah Macy, 1952.

Beach, F. A. The snark was a Boojum. *Amer. Psychologist,* 1950, **5**, 115–124.

Beck, S. J. The science of personality: nomothetic or idiographic? *Psychol. Rev.,* 1953, **60**, 353–359.

Betz, Barbara, & Whitehorn, J. C. The relationship of the therapist to the outcome of therapy in schizophrenia. *Psychiat. Res. Rep.,* 1956, **5**, 89–105.

Bingham, W. Halo: invalid and valid. *J. appl. Psychol.,* 1939, **23**, 221–228.

Block, J. *The Q-sort method in personality assessment and psychiatric research.* Springfield, Ill.: Charles C Thomas, 1961.

Brunswik, E. *Perception and the representative design of psychological experiments.* Berkeley, Calif.: Univer. of California Press, 1956.

Campbell, D. T. Factors relevant to the validity of experiments in social settings. *Psychol. Bull.,* 1957, **54**, 297–312.

Canfield, A. A. The "sten" scale: a modified C-scale. *Educ. psychol. Measmt.,* 1951, **11**, 295–297.

Cartwright, D. P. Analysis of qualitative material. In L. Festinger & D. Katz (Eds.), *Research methods in the behavioral sciences.* New York: Dryden Press, 1953.

Cattell, R. B., & Luborsky, L. B. P-technique demonstrated as a new clinical method for determining personality and symptom structure. *J. gen. Psychol.,* 1950, **42**, 3–24.

Cochran, W. G., Mosteller, F., & Tukey, J. W. Statistical problems of the Kinsey Report. *J. Amer. statist. Ass.,* 1953, **48**, 673–716.

Cohen, J. Multivariate methods in clinical psychology. In R. B. Cattell (Ed.), *Handbook for multivariate experimental psychology.* New York: Rand McNally, 1964.

Cronbach, L. J. Processes affecting scores on "understanding of others" and "assumed similarity." *Psychol. Bull.,* 1955, **52**, 177–193.

Cronbach, L. J., & Gleser, Goldine C. Assessing similarity between profiles. *Psychol. Bull.,* 1953, **50**, 456–473.

Dement, W. The effect of dream deprivation. *Science,* 1960, **131**, 1705–1707.

Dement, W., & Kleitman, N. Cyclic variations in EEG during sleep and their relation to eye movements, body motility, and dreaming. *EEG clin. Neurophysiol.,* 1957, **9**, 673–690. (a)

Dement, W., & Kleitman, N. The relation of eye movements during sleep to dream activity: an objective method for the study of dreaming. *J. exp. Psychol.,* 1957, **53**, 339–346. (b)

Dickens, C. *American notes for general circulation.* New York: Harper, 1842.

Dollard, J., Doob, L. W., Miller, N. E., Mowrer, O. H., & Sears, R. R. *Frustration and aggression.* New Haven, Conn.: Yale Univer. Press, 1938.

Ebel, R. L. Estimation of the reliability of ratings. *Psychometrika,* 1951, **16**, 407–423.

Edwards, A. L. The social desirability hypothesis: theoretical implications for personality measurement. In S. Messick & J. Ross (Eds.), *Measurement in personality and cognition.* New York: Wiley, 1962.

Erikson, E. *Childhood and society.* (Rev. ed.) New York: Norton, 1963.

Eysenck, H. J. The science of personality: nomothetic! *Psychol. Rev,* 1954, **61**, 339–342.

Eysenck, H. J. (Ed.) *Handbook of abnormal psychology.* New York: Basic Books, 1961.

Fiedler, F. E. A comparison of therapeutic relationships in psychoanalytic, non-directive, and Adlerian therapy. *J. consult. Psychol.,* 1950, **14,** 436–445.

Fisher, C. Dreams and perception: the role of preconscious primary modes of perception in dream formation. *J. Amer. psychoanal. Ass.,* 1954, **2,** 389–445.

Fiss, H., Goldberg, F., & Klein, G. S. Effects of subliminal stimulation on imagery and discrimination. *Percept. mot. Skills,* 1963, **17,** 31–44.

Gardner, R., Holzman, P. S., Klein, G. S., Linton, Harriet B., & Spence, D. P. Cognitive control: a study of individual consistencies. *Psychol. Issues,* 1959, **1,** Monogr. No. 4.

Goldberger, L., & Holt, R. R. A comparison of isolation effects and their personality correlates in two divergent samples. *USAF ASD tech. Rep.,* 1961, 61–417. 54 pp.

Grummion, D. L., & Butler, J. M. Another failure to replicate Keet's study, "two verbal techniques in a minature counseling situation." *J. abnorm. soc. Psychol.,* 1953, **48,** 597.

Guetzkow, H. Unitizing and categorizing problems in coding qualitative data. *J. clin. Psychol.,* 1950, **6,** 47–58.

Hebb, D. O. The American revolution. *Amer. Psychologist,* 1960, **15,** 735–745.

Heim, R. B. An attempt to repeat the Keet counseling-comparison experiment. Paper read at Western Psychol. Ass., San Jose, April, 1951.

Hilden, A. H. *Manual for Q-sort and random sets of personal concepts.* Webster Groves, Mo. (628 Clark Ave.): Author, 1954.

Hollingshead, A. B., & Redlich, F. C. *Social class and mental illness: a community study.* New York: Wiley, 1958.

Holt, R. R. Clinical *and* statistical prediction: a reformulation and some new data. *J. abnorm. soc. Psychol.,* 1958, **56,** 1–12.

Holt, R. R. Clinical judgment as a disciplined inquiry. *J. nerv. ment. Dis.,* 1961, **133,** 369–382.

Holt, R. R. A clinical-experimental strategy for research in personality. In S. Messick & J. Ross (Eds.), *Measurement in personality and cognition.* New York: Wiley, 1962. (a)

Holt, R. R. Individuality and generalization in the psychology of personality. *J. Pers.,* 1962, **30,** 377–404. (b)

Holt, R. R. Imagery: the return of the ostracized. *Amer. Psychologist,* 1964, **19,** 254–264.

Holt, R. R., & Goldberger, L. Personological correlates of reactions to perceptual isolation. *USAF WADC* tech. Rep., 1959, No. 59-735. 46 pp.

Holt, R. R., & Havel, Joan. A method for assessing primary and secondary processes in the Rorschach. In Maria A. Rickers-Ovsiankina (Ed.), *Rorschach psychology.* New York: Wiley, 1960.

Holt, R. R., & Luborsky, L. *Personality patterns of psychiatrists.* New York: Basic Books, 1958. 2 vols.

Horn, D. A study of some syndromes of personality. *Charact. & Pers.,* 1944, **12,** 257–274.

Horst, P., et al. The prediction of personal adjustment. *Soc. Sci. Res. Council Bull.,* 1941, No. 48.

Jahoda, Marie. *Current concepts of positive mental health.* New York: Basic Books, 1958.

Kagan, J., & Moss, H. A. *Birth to maturity: a study of psychological development.* New York: Wiley, 1962.

Kaplan, A. *The conduct of inquiry: methodology for behavioral science.* San Francisco: Chandler, 1964.

Keet, C. D. Two verbal techniques in a minature counseling situation. *Psychol. Monogr.,* 1948, **62,** No. 7 (Whole No. 294).

Kelly, E. L., & Fiske, D. W. *The prediction of performance in clinical psychology.* Ann Arbor, Mich.: Univer. of Michigan Press, 1951.

Klein, G. S. Need and regulation. In M. R. Jones (Ed.), *Nebraska symposium on motivation.* Lincoln, Nebr.: Univer. of Nebraska Press, 1954.

Langer, Suzanne K. *Philosophy in a new key.* Cambridge, Mass.: Harvard Univer. Press, 1942.

Langer, W. Sensorimotor learning. In H. A. Murray et al., *Explorations in personality.* New York: Oxford Univer. Press, 1938.

Lasagna, L., & von Felsinger, J. M. The volunteer subject in research. *Science,* 1954, **120,** 359–361.

Leary, T., & Gill, M. The dimensions and a measure of the process of psychotherapy: a system for the analysis of the content of clinical evaluations and patient-therapist verbalization. In E. A. Rubinstein & M. B. Parloff (Eds.), *Research in psychotherapy.* Washington, D.C.: American Psychological Association, 1959.

Lilly, J. C. Mental effects of physical restraints and of reduction of ordinary levels of physical stimuli on intact healthy persons. *Psychiat. Res. Rep.,* 1956, **5,** 1–9.

Loevinger, Jane. Conflict of commitment in clinical research. *Amer. Psychologist*, 1963, **18**, 241–251.

Luborsky, L. Clinicians' judgments of mental health: a proposed scale. *Arch. gen. Psychiat.*, 1962, **17**, 407–417. (a)

Luborsky, L. The patient's personality and psychotherapeutic change. In H. H. Strupp & L. Luborsky (Eds.), *Research in psychotherapy.* Washington, D.C.: American Psychological Association, 1962. (b)

McClelland, D. C., Atkinson, J. W., Clark, R. A., & Lowell, E. L. *The achievement motive.* New York: Appleton-Century-Crofts, 1953.

MacFarlane, Jean W., Allen, Lucille, & Honzik, Marjorie. *A developmental study of the behavior problems of normal children between 21 months and 14 years.* Berkeley, Calif.: Univer. of California Press, 1955.

Meehl, P. E., & Rosen, A. Antecedent probability and the efficiency of psychometric signs, patterns, or cutting scores. *Psychol. Bull.*, 1955, **52**, 194–216.

Merrill, R. M. On Keet's study, "two verbal techniques in a miniature counseling situation." *J. abnorm. soc. Psychol.*, 1952, **47**, 722.

Messick, S., & Ross, J. (Eds.) *Measurement in personality and cognition.* New York: Wiley, 1962.

Miller, J. G. Information input overload and psychotherapy. *Amer. J. Psychiat.*, 1960, **116**, 695–704.

Murray, H. A., et al. *Explorations in personality.* New York: Oxford Univer. Press, 1938.

Parsons, T. *The structure of social action: a study in social theory with special reference to a group of recent European writers.* (2nd ed.) New York: Free Press, 1949.

Pine, F., & Holt, R. R. Creativity and primary process: a study of adaptive regression. *J. abnorm. soc. Psychol.*, 1960, **61**, 370–379.

Rapaport, D., Gill, M., & Schafer, R. *Diagnostic psychological testing.* Chicago: Year Book Medical Publishers, 1945–1946. 2 vols.

Rubinstein, E. A., & Parloff, M. B. (Eds.) *Research in psychotherapy.* Washington, D.C.: American Psychological Association, 1959.

Samuels, H. The validity of personality-trait ratings based on projective techniques. *Psychol. Monogr.*, 1962, **66**, No. 5 (Whole No. 337).

Sargent, Helen D. Insight test prognosis in successful and unsuccessful rehabilitation of the blind. *J. proj. Tech.*, 1956, **20**, 429–441.

Sarnoff, I. *Personality dynamics and development.* New York: Wiley, 1962. (Contains examples of, and suggestions for, research problems.)

Schafer, R. Psychological tests in clinical research. *J. consult. Psychol.*, 1949, **13**, 328–334. Reprinted in R. P. Knight & C. R. Friedman (Eds.), *Psychoanalytic psychiatry and psychology: clinical and theoretical papers.* Vol. 1. New York: International Universities Press, 1954.

Shapiro, A., Goodenough, D. R., & Gryler, R. Dream recall as a function of method of awakening. *Psychosom. Med.*, 1963, **25**, 174–180.

Smith, G. J. W., Spence, D. P., & Klein, G. S. Subliminal effects of verbal stimuli. *J. abnorm. soc. Psychol.*, 1959, **59**, 167–176.

Snyder, W. U. Some investigations of relationship in psychotherapy. In E. A. Rubinstein & M. B. Parloff (Eds.), *Research in psychotherapy.* Washington, D.C.: American Psychological Association, 1959.

Spence, D. P., & Holland, B. The restricting effects of awareness: a paradox and an explanation. *J. abnorm. soc. Psychol.*, 1962, **64**, 163–174.

Srole, L., Langner, T. S., Michael, S. T., Opler, M. K., & Rennie, T. A. *Mental health in the metropolis: the midtown Manhattan study.* Vol. 1. New York: McGraw-Hill, 1962.

Stephenson, W. *The study of behavior.* Chicago: Univer. of Chicago Press, 1953.

Strupp, H. H. *Psychotherapists in action.* New York: Grune & Stratton, 1960.

Strupp, H. H., & Luborsky, L. (Eds.) *Research in psychotherapy.* Washington, D.C.: American Psychological Association, 1962.

Szasz, T. S. *The myth of mental illness.* New York: Hoeber-Harper, 1961.

Taft, R. The ability to judge people. *Psychol. Bull.*, 1955, **52**, 1–23.

Taylor, Janet A., & Spence, K. W. The relationship of anxiety level to performance in serial learning. *J. exp. Psychol.*, 1952, **44**, 61–64.

Tomkins, S. S. *The Thematic Apperception Test.* New York: Grune & Stratton, 1947.

Tomkins, S. S., & Messick, S. (Eds.) *Computer simulation of personality: frontier of psychological theory.* New York: Wiley, 1963.

Tukey, J. W. Discussion. *J. clin. Psychol.*, 1950, **6**, 61–74.

Wallerstein, R. S., Robbins, L. L., Sargent, Helen D., & Luborsky, L. The psychotherapy research project of the Menninger Foundation. *Bull. Menninger Clin.*, 1956, **20**, 221–278.

Watson, P. D., DiMascio, A., Kanter, S. S., Suter, E., & Greenblatt, M. A note on the influence of climatic factors on psychophysiological investigations. *Psychosom. Med.*, 1957, **19**, 419–423.

White, R. W. *Lives in progress.* New York: Dryden Press, 1952.

Additional References

Research methods and techniques (See also Ackoff, 1953; Brunswick, 1956*)

Ackoff, R. L., Gupta, S. K., & Minas, J. S. *Scientific method: optimizing applied research decisions.* New York: Wiley, 1962.

Edwards, A. L. Experiments: their planning and execution. In G. Lindzey (Ed.), *Handbook of social psychology.* Vol. I. *Theory and method.* Cambridge, Mass.: Addison-Wesley, 1954.

Festinger, L., & Katz, D. *Research methods in the behavioral sciences.* New York: Dryden Press, 1953.

Fisher, R. A. *The design of experiments.* (6th ed.) New York: Hafner, 1951.

Good, C. V., & Scates, D. E. *Methods of research.* New York: Appleton-Century-Crofts, 1954.

Jahoda, Marie, Deutsch, M., & Cook, S. W. *Research methods in social relations.* New York: Dryden Press, 1951. 2 vols.

Lindzey, G. (Ed.) *Handbook of social psychology.* Vol. I. *Theory and method.* Cambridge, Mass.: Addison-Wesley, 1954.

Selltiz, Claire, Jahoda, Marie, Deutsch, M., & Cook, S. W. *Research methods in social relations.* (Rev. ed.) New York: Holt, 1961.

Wilson, E. B., Jr. *An introduction to scientific research.* New York: McGraw-Hill, 1952.

Methodology and the nature of scientific inquiry (See also Holt, 1962 b; Kaplan, 1964)

Bechtoldt, H. P. Construct validity: a critique. *Amer. Psychologist,* 1959, **14**, 619–629.

Boring, E. G. Psychological factors in the scientific process. *Amer. Scientist,* 1954, **42**, 639–645.

Brunswik, E. Organismic achievement and environmental probability. *Psychol. Rev.*, 1943, **50**, 255–272.

Brunswik, E. *The conceptual framework of psychology.* Chicago: Univer. of Chicago Press, 1952.

Conant, J. B. *On understanding science.* New Haven, Conn.: Yale Univer. Press, 1947.

Cronbach, L. J. The two disciplines of scientific psychology. *Amer. Psychologist,* 1957, **12**, 671–684.

* These references are to works cited above.

Feigl, H., & Sellars, W. *Readings in philosophical analysis.* New York: Appleton-Century-Crofts, 1949. (See especially Feigl, Operationalism and scientific method, p. 498; Feigl, Some remarks on the meaning of scientific explanation, p. 510; Schlick, Causality in everyday life and in recent sciences, p. 515; Ducasse, Explanation, mechanism, and teleology, p. 540)

MacCorquodale, K., & Meehl, P. E. On a distinction between hypothetical constructs and intervening variables. *Psychol. Rev.*, 1948, **55**, 95–107.

Merton, R. K. The bearing of empirical research upon the development of social theory. *Amer. sociol. Rev.*, 1948, **13**, 505–515.

Skinner, B. F. A case history in scientific method. *Amer. Psychologist,* 1956, **11**, 221–233.

Stevens, S. S. Mathematics, measurement and psychophysics. In S. S. Stevens (Ed.), *Handbook of experimental psychology.* New York: Wiley, 1951.

Tryon, R. C. Reliability and behavior domain validity: reformulation and historical critique. *Psychol. Bull.*, 1957, **54**, 229–249.

Wolfle, D., Likert, R., Marquis, D. G., & Sears, R. R. Standards for appraising psychological research. *Amer. Psychologist,* 1949, **4**, 320–328.

Wolman, B. B. *Contemporary theories and systems in psychology.* New York: Harper & Row, 1960. (See especially chap. 14, The scientific method.)

Wolman, B. B. Toward a science of psychological science. In B. B. Wolman & E. Nagel (Eds.), *Scientific psychology; principles and approach.* New York: Basic Books, 1964.

Special problems of clinical research (See also Cronbach, 1955; Holt, 1962a; Loevinger, 1963; Meehl & Rosen, 1955; Murray et al., 1938; Schafer, 1949)

Brenman, Margaret, et al. Problems in clinical research: round table, 1946. *Amer. J. Orthopsychiat.*, 1947, **17**, 196–236. (Contributors: Kris, Kubie, Murray, Brenman, Gill, and discussants.)

Bronner, Augusta F., et al. The objective evaluation of psychotherapy: round table, 1948. *Amer. J. Orthopsychiat.*, 1949, **19**, 463–492. (Contributors: Kubie, Hendrick, Kris, Shakow, Brosin, Bergman, E. Bibring, and discussants.)

Campbell, D. T., & Fiske, D. W. Convergent and discriminant validation by the multitrait-multimethod matrix. *Psychol. Bull.*, 1959, **56**, 81–106.

Chein, I. The logic of prediction: some observations on Dr. Sarbin's exposition. *Psychol. Rev.*, 1945, **53**, 175–179.

Cole, J. O., et al. Recommendations for reporting studies of psychiatric drugs. *Publ. Hlth. Rep.*, 1957, **72**, 638–645.

Flanagan, J. C. The critical incident technique. *Psychol. Bull.*, 1954, **51**, 327–358.

French, T. M. Clinical approach to the dynamics of behavior. In J. McV. Hunt (Ed.), *Personality and the behavior disorders.* New York: Ronald, 1944.

Gregg, A. A critique of medical research. *Proc. Amer. phil. Soc.*, 1944, **87**, 317.

Hammond, K. R. Representative vs. systematic design in clinical psychology. *Psychol. Bull.*, 1954, **51**, 150–158.

Heyns, R. W., & Lippitt, R. Systematic observational techniques. In G. Lindzey (Ed.), *Handbook of social psychology.* Vol. I. *Theory and method.* Cambridge, Mass.: Addison-Wesley, 1954.

Holt, R. R. Some statistical problems in clinical research. *Educ. psychol. Measmt.*, 1950, **10**, 609–627.

Horn, D. Intra-individual variability in the study of personality. *J. clin. Psychol.*, 1950, **6**, 43–47.

Howe, Louisa P. Problems in the evaluation of mental health programs. In Ruth Kotinsky & Helen L. Witmer (Eds.), *Community programs for mental health.* Cambridge, Mass.: Harvard Univer. Press, 1955.

Klein, G. S. A clinical perspective for personality research. *J. abnorm. soc. Psychol.*, 1949, **44**, 42–50.

Leuba, C. Hypnosis as a method of controlling variables in psychological experiments. *Amer. J. Psychol.*, 1946, **59**, 686–690.

Meehl, P. E. *Clinical vs. statistical prediction.* Mineapolis, Minn.: Univer. of Minnesota Press, 1954.

Money, J. Observations concerning the clinical method of research, ego theory and psychopathology. *Psychiatry*, 1951, **14**, 55–66.

Murray, H. A. Research planning: a few proposals. In S. S. Sargent & M. W. Smith. (Eds.), *Culture and personality.* New York: Viking Fund, 1949.

Orne, M. T. The nature of hypnosis: artifact and essence. *J. abnorm. soc. Psychol.*, 1959, **58**, 277–299.

Orne, M. T. On the social psychology of the psychological experiment. *Amer. Psychologist*, 1962, **17**, 776–783.

Rapaport, D. The structure of psychoanalytic theory: a systematizing attempt. In S. Koch (Ed.), *Psychology: a study of a science.* Study I. *Conceptual and systematic.* Vol. 3. *Formulations of the person and the social context.* New York: McGraw-Hill, 1959. Pp. 55–183. Also in *Psychol. Issues*, 1960, **2**, No. 2, Monogr. 6.

Schafer, R. *Psychoanalytic interpretation in Rorschach testing.* New York: Grune & Stratton, 1954. (See especially chap. 2)

Schmidt, H. O., & Fonda, C. P. The reliability of psychiatric diagnosis: a new look. *J. abnorm. soc. Psychol.*, 1956, **52**, 262–267.

Windle, C. Psychological tests in psychopathological prognosis. *Psychol. Bull.*, 1952, **49**, 541–574.

The design of experiments (See also Campbell, 1957; Cattell & Luborsky, 1950; Horst et al., 1941)

Boring, E. G. The nature and history of experimental control. *Amer. J. Psychol.*, 1954, **67**, 573–589.

Canter, R. R., Jr. The use of extended control-group designs in human relations studies. *Psychol. Bull.*, 1951, **48**, 38–45.

Cronbach, L. J. A validation design for qualitative studies of personality. *J. consult. Psychol.*, 1948, **12**, 365–374.

Solomon, R. L. An extension of control group design. *Psychol. Bull.*, 1949, **46**, 137–150.

Multivariate designs (See also Cohen, 1964)

Cattell, R. B. Personality measurement functionally related to source trait structure. In S. Messick & J. Ross (Eds.), *Measurement in personality and cognition.* New York: Wiley, 1962.

Cattell, R. B., & Scheier, I. H. *The meaning and measurement of neuroticism and anxiety.* New York: Ronald, 1961.

Cooley, W. W., & Lohnes, P. R. *Multivariate procedures for the behavioral sciences.* New York: Wiley, 1962.

Experimental study of the single case

Chassan, J. B. Statistical inference and the single case in clinical design. *Psychiatry*, 1960, **23**, 173–184.

Shapiro, M. B. The single case in fundamental clinical psychological research. *Brit. J. med. Psychol.*, 1961, **34**, 255–262.

Sidman, M. *Tactics of scientific research.* New York: Basic Books, 1960.

Administrative and financial problems of research

Campbell, A. A. Administering research organizations. *Amer. Psychologist*, 1953, **8**, 225–230.

Rapaport, D. The future of research in clinical psychology and psychiatry. *Amer. Psychologist*, 1947, **2**, 167–172.

Interpersonal and interdisciplinary aspects of research (See also Dollard, Doob, Miller, Mowrer, & Sears, 1938; Fisher, 1954)

Caudill, W., & Roberts, B. H. Pitfalls in the organization of interdisciplinary research. *Hum. Organization*, 1951, **10**, 12–15.

Easton, J. W. Social pressures of professional teamwork. *Amer. sociol. Rev.*, 1951, **16**, 707–713.

Polansky, N., et al. Problems of interpersonal relations in research on groups. *Hum. Relat.*, 1949, **2**, 281–291.

Redlich, F. C., & Brody, E. B. Emotional problems of interdisciplinary research in psychiatry. *Psychiatry*, 1955, **18**, 233–239.

Analysis of qualitative data (See Cartwright, 1953; Guetzkow, 1950; Holt, 1961; Holt & Luborsky, 1958; S. K. Langer, 1942; Leary & Gill, 1959)

Ratings (See also Allport, 1961; Allport & Odbert, 1936; Atkinson, 1958; Baldwin, Kalhorn, & Breese, 1945; Bavelas, 1952; Beck, 1953; Bingham, 1939; Block, 1961; Canfield, 1951; Ebel, 1951; Edwards, 1962; Eysenck, 1954; Hilden, 1954; Holt & Havel, 1960; Horn, 1944; Luborsky, 1962a; Luborsky, 1962b; McClelland, Atkinson, Clark, & Lowell, 1955; Messick & Ross, 1962; Sargent, 1956; Stephenson, 1953; Taft, 1955; Tomkins, 1947; Tukey, 1950; Wallerstein, Robbins, Sargent, & Luborsky, 1956)

Lorr, M. Rating scales and check lists for the evaluation of psychopathology. *Psychol. Bull.*, 1954, **51**, 119–126.

Finding a research problem; research strategies (See also Sarnoff, 1962)

Eysenck, H. J. (Ed.) *Experiments in personality.* New York: Humanities Press, 1960. 2 vols. (Contains examples and suggestions of various types.)

Marquis, D. G. Research planning at the frontiers of science. *Amer. Psychologist*, 1948, **3**, 430–438.

Maslow, A. H. Problem-centering vs. means-centering in science. *Phil. Sci.*, 1946, **13**, 326–331.

Rose, A. M. The selection of problems for research. *Amer. J. Sociol.*, 1948, **55**, 219–227.

The bibliographic phase of research

Bry, Ilse, Doe, Janet, & Kinney, Margaret M. Guidebooks to psychological literature. *Amer. Psychologist*, 1954, **9**, 584–585.

Daniel, R. S., & Louttit, C. M. *Professional problems in psychology.* Englewood Cliffs, N.J.: Prentice-Hall, 1953. (See especially chap. 4, Bibliographic problems in psychology. See also chap. 3 and appendix A.)

Sampling (See also Beach, 1950; Cochran, Mosteller, & Tukey, 1953; Lasagna & von Felsinger, 1954)

McNemar, Q. Sampling in psychological research. *Psychol. Bull.*, 1940, **37**, 331–365.

4
Measurement in Clinical Research

JANE LOEVINGER

Clinical psychology today has inherited two disparate traditions, that of Binet and that of Freud. The heirs of the Freudian tradition often proclaim that they would rather be right (or deep?) than quantitative. The heirs of Binet often seem to say that what they cannot measure with scientific objectivity they would as soon not measure. Yet it was Freud, not Binet, who began his career with a "project for a scientific psychology" (Freud, 1954), and he only gradually moved away from a reductionist view as his clinical insights and successes impelled him to emphasize qualitative, meaningful aspects of behavior. And it was Binet to whom Cattell and others flung the challenge: If we cannot be more scientific than that, let us not measure at all (Peterson, 1925).

The one great practical success of psychometrics has been the measurement of general ability, stemming from the contributions of Binet. Differential prediction of abilities, as distinct from measurement of general ability, has often been proclaimed to be within reach as a result of the development of factor analysis. It has, however, failed to materialize in many instances to a significant extent (Super, 1957). Nevertheless, measurement of ability is simple compared with measurement of personality traits. The practical value of current measures of ability and personality will be treated elsewhere in this volume. For the sake of evaluating these contributions in perspective and of encouraging more fundamental work in the future, basic theoretical issues underlying all such measures will be examined here.

In the natural sciences, measurement and evaluation are not separate sections or subdisciplines but are integrally related to theory and experiment. By contrast, the development of intricate psychometric theory as a special branch of psychology has been almost entirely sterile of yield for clinical psychology. In recent years there has been a trend, under the heading "construct validity," toward returning measurement to its integral place in theory and substantive research (Cronbach & Meehl, 1955). In this move there is a return to the spirit of Binet.

POLAR VARIABLES AND MILESTONE SEQUENCES

There are many differences between abilities and other traits which have bearing on the problems of measurement. The most fundamental is the problem of curvilinearity. Curvilinear regressions, although occurring occasionally in ability measurement, as will be illustrated presently, have not been a major problem there, either in the relation of one ability to another or in the relation of an ability to a criterion. By contrast, curvilinear and even multivalued regressions are as much the rule as the exception in relations of personality traits to one another and to external criteria. There are many ways to discuss this difference, e.g., in terms of the dialectical nature of

[1] Preparation of this chapter was supported by research grant number MH-05115 from the National Institute of Mental Health, Public Health Service.

personality growth as contrasted with the essentially nondialectical accretion of abilities. However one may see the cause of the curvilinearities, the result is the failure of a coherent science of personality and clinical psychology to emerge. General laws or relations are exceedingly difficult to find or to state; every combination of circumstances requires a new predictive statement. In this chapter, the writer will present as a working hypothesis the view that only the surface manifestations of personality have this intricate pattern of interactive relationships—that in principle there exist inferable traits in terms of which interrelationships of traits with one another and with at least some criteria will assume a simple, if not precisely rectilinear, form. Every science faces the propaedeutic task of discovering those constructs in terms of which its laws can be stated most simply; only when attention has been paid to this task will there be an access of vitality in clinical research.

An intuitive, if not explicit, appreciation of the foregoing point led one cohort of clinical researchers to assume that the basic constructs must be "deep" in the psychoanalytic sense, i.e., deeply unconscious. There are obvious difficulties in measuring unconscious traits. In addition, results of such research did not support the hope that unconscious motives are the variables in terms of which observable phenomena of personality are most simply ordered. For example, no simple relation appeared between psychosexual constitution and presence or absence of authoritarianism (Adorno, Frenkel-Brunswik, Levinson, & Sanford, 1950). Similarly, authoritarian family ideology does not hinge on problems of any particular psychosexual type or stage (Loevinger, 1962). Current attempts to formulate regnant constructs for personality and clinical theory stress ego and character aspects rather than psychosexual ones; in doing so, psychologists are not so much departing from the psychoanalytic tradition as they are catching up with contemporary psychoanalytic ego psychology.

Use of measurements in clinical research is intimately tied to the search for those constructs in terms of which the laws of personality are best formulated. In this chapter primary stress is on methodological aspects of the search. In particular, attention is called to the consequences of the distinction between *polar variables* and *milestone sequences,* a distinction by no means novel but much neglected in personality measurement. Manifestations of ability are almost always *polar functions* of age during the years of development; i.e., the probability that a given problem will be solved increases constantly with age. Conspicuous manifestations of many personality traits, on the contrary, comprise *milestone sequences;* i.e., they tend to increase with age up to some point, after which they tend to decrease. Once one has assembled a set of items all of which measure a given ability, then older children will, other things being equal, answer more of them correctly. By turning this reasoning around, the total number of correct items can be used as a measure of ability, regardless of age. This is the logic of cumulative tests (Loevinger, 1948; but compare Coombs, 1953; Thurstone & Chave, 1929). The psychometric properties of such tests have been explored extensively.

The distinction being made here is one to which many words in the psychometric vocabulary almost apply; yet something remains to be said by way of clarification. Psychometricians have terms for test scores and their interrelations; the terms "polar" and "milestones" are intended to describe kinds of traits rather than test scores, traits whose manifestations are the data from which scores are constructed. Prototypically, abilities are polar traits, while interests are milestones. Abilities tend to be positively correlated or, at worst, uncorrelated. No doubt situations could be discovered or contrived in which abilities are negatively related; nonetheless, an intrinsic positiveness characterizes the notion of ability. This fact was utilized by factor analysis in requiring a positive manifold as a criterion for rotation of axes. Interests, on the other hand, may be correlated positively or negatively. No one has an unlimited attention span; thus to some extent unrelated interests oppose each other.

Note that in making inferences or predictions from tests of ability, major emphasis is on total score. Inferences drawn from patterns of subtest scores are of limited or questionable validity; success on one subtest compensates for failure on another, so far as our best verified predictions are concerned. In many interest and personality tests, on the contrary, primary emphasis in making inferences or predictions rests on the pattern of subscales.

Indeed, some tests have been constructed so that the sum of all subscores is the same or nearly the same for all subjects. This occurs when a forced-choice format is used and the two or more alternatives for a single item are scored in separate scales. On any given item a person then adds to one of his subscores, but not more than one. A high score on one subscale does not compensate for a low score on another; precisely such differences in subtest scores are the basis for predictions from tests of this type. In such tests there is no significance to "general level"; only the pattern of subtests is significant. Examples are the Kuder Preference Record, a vocational interest test; the Allport-Vernon-Lindzey Study of Values, an attitude test; and the Edwards Personal Preference Schedule, a personality test. The dependence of these tests on pattern rather than general level demonstrates an implicit recognition of the inappropriateness of the polar (cumulative) model for the traits concerned.

During the years of development, abilities are ordinarily cumulative. Thus, if members of group A have an ability that members of group B do not and if we know that they are samples drawn from populations similar except for age, we guess that group A is older. But if group A has an interest (say, in cowboy hats) that group B does not share, we cannot infer which group is older. Group B may have outgrown interest in cowboy hats or may not yet have become interested in them. Thus ability to do problems in algebra tends to be a monotonically increasing function of age during the school years, at least. The tendency to wear a cowboy hat increases with age and then decreases; it is a nonmonotone function of age during years of rapid development. Thurstone used the terms "increasing probability" and "maximum probability" for tests constructed for these two models; Loevinger (1948) used the terms "cumulative" and "differential"; Coombs (1953) used the terms "monotone" and "nonmonotone" for a related distinction.

Suppose we correlate two such variables. The ability to spell *cat* rises sharply with age; the tendency to wear a cowboy hat is also dependent on age. At age 1, cat and hat are both low. At age 3, few can spell cat, but many children wear hats. At age 5, hat is going down, but cat is now coming up. At age 7, the latter trend continues. The relation between spelling cat and wearing a cowboy hat will thus depend on age range.

Now suppose we are concerned with two manifestations of a personality trait, *X*. Trait *X* now takes the place of age as the underlying causative variable; but unlike age it must be inferred from the intercorrelations of its manifestations. Use of a melange of monotone and nonmonotone functions will result in a hodgepodge of curvilinear and even multivalued relations, possibly in correlations not significantly different from zero, obscuring the underlying causal factor. The point of this digression is that it is descriptive of the current situation in personality measurement.

The logic of cumulative tests applies to polar variables; most of psychometric theory has been developed for, and properly applies only to, cumulative tests. Thurstone and Chave (1929) worked out a method of attitude testing appropriate to the maximum probability model, i.e., milestone sequences. Many other possibilities exist, including use of milestones as identifying points on a rating scale of maturity. This has been done in work at the Naval Retraining Command at Camp Elliott, based on a scale of ego development of Sullivan, Grant, and Grant (1957). However, there has not been extensive psychometric interest in noncumulative models, and such interest has rarely been integrated with work in personality measurement.

One may ask, why introduce the terms "polar" and "milestone"? The term "cumulative" refers primarily not to a trait but to a scoring model, to be sure, the model appropriate for polar traits. The terms "monotone" and "nonmonotone" refer to relations between variables and do not make sense as applied to traits in isolation. Again, a polar trait is ordinarily a monotone function of age during the years of development, at least, while the stages in a milestone sequence are, with the exception of the extreme stages, nonmonotone functions of age.

What is here called a "polar variable" has sometimes been called "bipolar." The term "bipolar" has been used to describe tests or variables in which both ends of the scale are meaningful and opposite in meaning, in contrast to scales which are meaningful at one extreme but not at the other. Thus a scale of conformity is often, and probably necessarily, unipolar. High conformity is meaningful, but low scores may be obtained by individuals whose nonconformity or failure to conform has arisen on varied and contradictory bases; thus while the implications of a high score may be clear, those of a low score are equivocal.

If one has a single vocabulary to describe tests and the traits underlying them, one is at a loss to consider the question whether the appropriate model is being used for the trait; yet this is one of the central questions that must be asked. Consider again the trait of conformity. Usually in psychological research this has been treated as a polar variable, i.e., each subject is characterized in terms of how much conformity he has. In careful studies of character development, however, such as those of Sullivan, Grant, and Grant (1957) and Peck and Havighurst (1960), conformity emerges as a middle stage, with amoral, impulse-ridden persons at a lower stage and with autonomous persons having internalized consciences at a higher stage. Thus conformity, in this view, is a milestone of character development rather than a polar variable.

There is no one evidently right way to decide what are polar variables and what are milestones. Any unipolar scale, a scale with only one meaningful pole, is a strong candidate for consideration as a milestone of development. No coefficient or test of significance can answer the question. There does not seem to be any more objective approach than to take a broad view of human personality in its many aspects and to ask: What concepts lead to the simplest, most parsimonious, and most inclusive view of observable relations? This method was used in establishing the basic concepts of physics and chemistry. Seen in broad perspective, polar aspects of development appear to coincide with the nondialectical, largely conflict-free functions. Milestones characterize those aspects of development that are dialectical in their course.

Psychologists have an understandable, indeed commendable, preference for approaches that are objective and quantifiable. The result has been that they have meticulously treated as polar variables many traits or putative traits that are better viewed as stages in milestone sequences. The cumulative test model, derived for ability tests, does not yield meaningful results when it is applied to milestone sequences. The statement that most objectively accessible personality traits are milestones rather than polar variables is, of course, only an opinion, not subject to rigorous proof or crucial test. Precisely for this reason the psychometric psychologists have turned their backs on the problem, along with related questions of meaningfulness and salience of traits. Although there is no single test for such importance properties, a simple and easily employed criterion has only seldom been used, i.e., the tendency of the trait to increase or decrease constantly with age during the developmental years.

Sanford, Webster, and Freedman (1957) found inferential evidence in a cross-sectional study that impulse expression rises from the freshman to the senior years in college and later falls among older alumnae of the same college. Similarly, seniors are more willing to admit symptoms than freshman (Sanford, 1956), although the tendency to describe oneself in socially desirable terms generally rises between ages 8 and 13 (Getzels & Walsh, 1958). If these are rare instances, the cause seems not to be the rarity of milestones of development, of trends that rise and then fall, but rather the neglect of that possibility in the pursuit of measurable, i.e., polar, variables. The frustration that besets personality measurement, plagued by negligible correlations and curvilinear relations even where clinical experience indicates causation, may well be traceable chiefly to this fundamental confusion.

There are indeed personality traits, such as emotional maturity, that can be construed as polar variables, but in general they are accessible only by inference from patterns of observations, a fact the clinician takes into account intuitively. The obvious and palpable manifestations are the milestones. Thus when one approaches the measurement of personality with predilections in favor at once of quantification and of observation of objectively verifiable behavior, one is immediately caught in an impasse. One ends by misconstruing a stage in a sequence as if it were a polar variable.

OBSERVATION

The place of observation and of inference in clinical measurement is a crucial issue. In order for the study of personality—in which every child and adult is perforce engaged—to qualify as scientific research, there must be basic observations on which minimally qualified persons will agree. To the extent that the qualifications for agreeing on observations include agreeing on theoretical issues, the force of the research, its claim to scientific objectivity, is lost. A related point is that as far as possible, no surplus meanings must be built into the observations.

Much that passes for observation in psychoanalytic research does not qualify according to the foregoing definition. Consider the following observation concerning a girl 7 years old, which is used to illustrate suffering due to self-punishment: "She was unable to use the treatment for her own benefit because she had bragged at home about being the only one in the family to have a nice Clinic lady. Her inability to talk in the session is related to her need for punishment" (Sandler, Kawenoka, Neurath, Rosenblatt, Schnurmann, & Sigal, 1962, p. 117). To make such "observations" one must be trained in psychoanalytic technique and theory, a requirement not altogether different from the medical training required to read x rays. But one must also believe in aspects of psychoanalytic theory that are controversial among equally well-trained psychiatrists of different persuasions; no similar requirements are acceptable elsewhere in science.

The issue is not whether the observations and the theory on which they are based are wrong or whether psychoanalysis can be subjected to research or whether its variables are measurable by ingenuity outside the framework of psychoanalysis proper. The point is that what psychoanalysts call "observations" are not simple observations. They contain much inference; they are not the simple data that are basic to scientific research and measurement.

The simplest observations are present-absent and more-less. These are the fundamental observations on which all measurement must be based, whether the judgment "present" or "more than" is made by the clinician or the subject. Dichotomous items are thus observations. Many clinicians, however, are uncomfortable with the present-absent character of such items. They feel that too much is lost in neglecting the quantitative differences. Two children having the same symptom do not necessarily have it to the same degree; two people agreeing to the same opinion may agree with different intensities. Clinicians intuitively want every item to incorporate such differences of degree; each item is a miniature measurement, and a test is in essence an average of many miniature tests. Where each item is considered an observation rather than a measurement, as in the present view, the quantitative trait that presumably underlies the observations is reconstructed from the number of observations present in a given direction or from the pattern of observations. Where each item is considered a miniature measurement, we are not told what the basic observations are or how they are combined to constitute a measure, i.e., a score. The underlying logic is closed to view.

Ability Test Items

Items used in paper-and-pencil tests of ability often have three to five alternative answers, from which the subject is to choose one. The scorer is the observer. He matches the response with the scoring key to decide whether the right answer is present or not. Some critics of such tests have objected that a youngster who is very sophisticated and has unusually deep insights into the problems might choose for correct reasons an answer keyed wrong. In such a case, the most able and the least able would be scored wrong, while those of intermediate ability would be scored right. Teacher-constructed tests cannot be guaranteed against such defects, but professionally constructed tests used on a national scale are constantly evaluated to protect against this and other defects, which may be assumed to affect few items. The point is raised to illustrate the problem of curvilinearity, rare in ability tests but pervasive in tests of personality.

Checklist and Paired Choice

Dichotomous items for personality tests are of two types. In one case the subject is asked to choose which of two statements is truer or applies better to him or to some situation; in the other, the subject chooses or does not choose a single statement. Psychometrically the properties are identical, since each can be construed as presence-absence of assent to the first statement. Psychologically they are quite different. The single statement has always been the preferred item form, and superficially it appears to be far simpler. Reflection suggests that psychologically the checklist of statements is more complex and inferential than picking the preferred of two statements. Consider the following pair of statements (Loevinger, 1962):

A. No child should be permitted to strike his mother.
B. A mother should not be harsh with a small child who strikes her.

When presented as alternatives, this item is highly correlated with authoritarianism in mothers ($r_{bis} = .56$). If the first alternative were presented alone, a subject would almost have to construct an alternative to decide whether he agrees. Naturally the implied alternative will be different for different subjects. Anyone who imagines that the alternative is "A child should be encouraged to hit his mother" will probably choose the original statement.

From the viewpoint of the tester, a checklist of statements is a series of present-absent observations. From the viewpoint of the subject, they are probably converted into more-than judgments before being answered. The advantage of the paired-choice-item form is that the nature of the subject's observation is made explicit, and the same pair of alternatives is offered every subject. Experience has demonstrated, too, that many subjects tend to agree, others to disagree, with statements in partial disregard of content. This response bias affects a checklist of statements, while paired-choice items, since they call for an equal number of agreements from each subject, are unaffected by a tendency to say "yes" or "no."

Many personality tests that use paired-choice items are constructed in blind imitation of the psychophysical method of paired comparisons. In order to do this, each statement must be paired with many or all others. Items such as the following, taken from the Edwards Personal Preference Schedule, result:

A. I like to judge people by why they do something—not by what they actually do.
B. I like my friends to show a great deal of affection toward me.

Edwards (1953) scores each such item twice. If the "A" alternative is chosen in the item above, one point is added to the intraception score; if the "B" alternative is chosen, a point is added to the succorance score. The subject, however, has made only one choice, and it is logically erroneous to try to extract two bits of information where only one exists. The relations between items built into scoring keys in this manner interfere with the next step, the inference leading from a set of observations to a scoring key. Psychologically, the arbitrary pairing and repetition of items is onerous and unreal, lacking in convincingness as a task.

Rating Scales

The most frequently used quantification in clinical research is the rating scale, despite the long accumulation of evidence that it is virtually worthless unless used with great care and sophistication. Many otherwise excellent studies have yielded little return because of use of ratings at a pivotal point. Ordinarily a trait is named, say, "introversion" or "social adjustment," and the subject or clinician is asked to rate himself or some other person on a scale ranging from little at one end to much at the other. The scale may be a continuous line segment, a set of numbers, or a set of quantitative adjectives ("very little," "little," "about average," "much," "very much"). The number of points discriminated may range from three to nine or more. (If there are only two points, the scale becomes a dichotomous item.) The rater is required to assess the trait in himself or another and then assign a number or a quantitative adjective. From a psychometric point of view, the judgment is not a simple observation but a miniature measurement, already incorporating a quantitative inference. Hence it is not a solid, appropriate basis for research. The difficulty with rating scales can also be stated in terms of empirical findings; e.g., some people are inclined to use extreme ratings, some rate near the middle, some have favorable or high biases, and some rate in the unfavorable or lower part of the distribution, in partial disregard of content. Such response biases vitiate the purpose of rating.

Many attitude tests—and many personality tests, such as the Berkeley F scale, that are more or less disguised as attitude tests—utilize a series of statements with which the subject is to express the degree of his agreement. Such items are in effect rating scales and have frequently been shown to suffer from the corresponding defects. The presence of a systematic error factor running through all the items tends to raise the test homogeneity as well as its correlation with other tests having the same error (Loevinger, 1954). These high correlations have seduced many psychologists into clinging to this weak item form long past the time when its weaknesses have been widely documented.

One way of improving rating scales is to designate the several points on the scale by comparison persons known to all raters. This has been called the "man-to-man" rating scale. The man-to-man scale may, however, encourage another failing which is especially conspicuous in rating scales, i.e., halo effect. Halo effect is the tendency for judgments on one characteristic to influence judgments on others. To put it crudely, one tends to ascribe all good traits to those one likes and all bad traits to those one dislikes. Subtler forms of halo effect also occur. (Further discussion of ratings can be found in "Experimental Methods in Clinical Psychology," above.)

An interesting way to deal with some of the problems ratings present without giving up their evident advantages is the Q-sort technique. In this method a list of attributes is rated according to how characteristic or salient each one is for each subject. Often the attributes must be fitted into a quasinormal distribution, with a small number of attributes rated highly characteristic or highly uncharacteristic, large numbers in the central portion of the distribution indicating slightly characteristic or uncharacteristic.

There are two logical difficulties in the method. One is that although instructions call for comparing each individual only with himself, entirely intraindividual comparison is not possible. How salient a trait is within a person's personality is bound to reflect an implicit comparison with a reference group. Whether fluent use of the English language is a remarkable characteristic depends on whether one is 2 or 20 years old, whether one is English or Russian. Failure to make the reference group explicit is a logical weakness. Nonetheless, under some circumstances the technique can be shown to yield reliable results in the hands of trained raters (Block, 1961). Hence it has practical utility.

A second weakness of the method lies in the arbitrary choice of attributes to be rated, which is left to the investigator to make. Results of any study using Q sort will naturally depend on the list of traits rated. Block (1961) has met this difficulty by resort to the experience of many psychiatrists and psychologists, each of whom can be presumed to draw on experience with many types of patients. The standard CQ set which has emerged from an essentially collaborative test-construction endeavor can be presumed to have wide application and indeed has been shown to be useful in a number of contexts.

The utility of Block's CQ set, despite the logical weaknesses of the method, brings up a point to which we shall return. Any method of measurement which has been used extensively and in a variety of circumstances and which has been subjected to repeated revision on the basis of such results will at least partially overcome its initial weaknesses. It will evolve into a useful instrument by successive approximations as a result of experience properly utilized. Thus the position of this chapter in outlining a puristic view of clinical measurement is subject to reservation: Existing, established instruments that incorporate much experience in successive revisions and in normative or quasinormative data are vastly preferable to *ad hoc* tests. The temptation a research worker using Block's CQ set might feel to delete a few uninteresting attributes and substitute those that sound relevant to his own problem is to be resisted. Changing a few items here and there, in the CQ set or other instruments on which appreciable work has been done, will render the new research noncomparable with the old to an unknown extent. Moreover, the aim of making data more relevant to a problem in hand is unlikely of success. Block's list was evolved in reference to many problems with many criteria in mind. The novice would most likely introduce nonfunctioning or poorly functioning items. Obviously, the same considerations hold for other tests and diagnostic instruments.

Projective Tests[2]

The basic observations in projective tests are variations of the former types. One may score the presence of signs, count the occurrence of a given sign, or rate the degree of some trait that is manifested. A neat and automatic quantification appears to be available in such indices as the number of movement (M) or color responses (C) on the Rorschach protocol. An unfortunate difficulty is that the total number of responses (R) varies widely. Should one partial out the effect of R on the various scores, for example, by dividing C and M by R? Some writers believe so. Others believe that the number of responses in the various scoring categories determine R, rather than vice versa (Harris, 1960).

[2] A detailed analysis of projective tests as diagnostic tools is given in Part 3 of the *Handbook*.

Evidently, in considering the significance of a given value of M, it is not quite satisfactory either to disregard R or to partial out R. The situation is, in fact, even more complicated than already suggested, since, as Cronbach (1949) and Fiske and Baughman (1953) have pointed out, some of the relations involved are curvilinear. Hence no linear correction could be adequate.

Projective tests, such as the Rorschach, which are pervaded with ambiguity about the number of times a sign may or may not appear elude rigorous psychometric analysis. This fact was one of the major considerations impelling Holtzman (Holtzman, Thorpe, Swartz, & Herron, 1961) to construct an inkblot test that would capture as much as possible of the clinical richness of the Rorschach in a psychometrically precise format. The Holtzman Inkblot Test has two parallel forms, each with 45 blots. The subject is instructed to give one response to each blot, an instruction that minimizes, though it does not entirely eliminate, differences in responsiveness. Scoring standards are given for each of 22 variables, and norms are given for each of the variables for groups as varied as 5-year-olds, college students, chronic schizophrenics, and mentally retarded subjects. Many clinicians will not be persuaded by the superior psychometric properties of the Holtzman test to give up the Rorschach, with which their own experience lies. For research purposes, however, the Holtzman is far preferable. Research already complete has demonstrated that it captures much of what is measured by similar scores on the Rorschach (Bock & Haggard, 1963; Holtzman et al., 1961). There remains a part of the variance of Rorschach scores not predictable from the Holtzman test, just as there is part of the variance of Holtzman scores not predictable from the Rorschach. The question is: Does it matter? Perhaps the overlapping variance is just what is valid. The question is not an easy one, since measurable criteria which will demonstrate the validity that many clinicians feel the Rorschach does indeed possess have been difficult to find.

Holtzman anticipates that some clinicians will argue that R itself is a source of information. The answer to this argument is that whatever information is encoded in number of responses is in principle encoded elsewhere and can be obtained reliably even when R is held constant. That the Rorschach R has a multiple correlation of only .63 with the Holtzman variables (Bock & Haggard, 1963) is not decisive, for the unpredicted variance may not be information in any important sense; i.e., it may not be information about anything other than response to the Rorschach. A similar problem occurs in the context of other tests. Response biases such as acquiescence and describing oneself in socially desirable terms are artifacts of some paper-and-pencil tests, as number of responses is a methodological artifact of the Rorschach. Response biases also encode valid information, but they are less useful indices than some nonartifactual scores. Generally, methodological artifacts should be minimized or eliminated, and efficient scores constructed for whatever useful information they may encode.

Despite the psychometric competence and the great advance which the Holtzman technique represents, the scoring manual goes only partway toward filling the gap which all projective test manuals have left between their rules and their reasons. Why, for example, does "microscopic life" receive a score of 0 on Animal Content, while "bugs or insects" receives a score of 1 (Holtzman et al., 1961, p. 67)? Neither evidence nor reasoning is adduced to bolster this somewhat arbitrary discrimination. Indeed, there is as yet no program for what kind of evidence would be relevant.

A group of psychologists working with the writer at Washington University are constructing a scoring manual for judging ego development from sentence completions; they are attempting to account for every scoring decision in terms of theory or evidence or, preferably, both. The few unusual responses for which it has been necessary to make an arbitrary scoring decision are listed as such. Evidence consists of ratings of the total protocols from which the response came. More rigorous would be ratings of total protocols excluding the response at issue. Still better would be ratings of case history or other data from outside the test situation as a validating criterion. Obvious practical considerations make the more rigorous validation usable only on a small scale, necessary though it is.

SCORES: THE PSYCHOMETRIC TASK

The psychometric task is to construct a meaningful score out of a set of minimally inferential observations. In principle every response in some way reflects every aspect of the respondent's personality; hence, behavior as it is observed is a confounding of many sources of variance. The psychometric task, to put it another way, is to sort out the variance from the several sources. The principle on which scores that are good measures of a trait are contrived from items that are poor measures of the trait has been known at least since the early work of Spearman: If the trait to be measured occurs in all items, its effect cumulates; if the irrelevant factors occur in only one or a few items, their effects tend to cancel out.

Cumulative Tests: Criterion Keying

Many test constructors seek to carry through the entire test-construction process on a minimal inferential level. In constructing the Minnesota Multiphasic Personality Inventory (MMPI), keys were arrived at by selecting items that differentiated at a statistically significant level between a standard control group and each of several pathological groups. The original aim was to substitute a test for the diagnostic interview, but the test was not able to reproduce diagnostic categories. A second version of the significant-difference method was used in constructing the California F scale for authoritarianism. The scoring key comprised those items significantly differentiating groups high and low on authoritarianism. However, groups extreme with respect to authoritarianism also differ in other ways, and the selected items may measure the wrong differences. In fairness, both the Minnesota and the California groups made use of other considerations; nonetheless, there was primary dependence on discrimination of extreme groups.

Another minimally inferential method is to take some criterion and then select items and sometimes also weight them so as to maximize the correlation with the criterion. It comes as a surprise to psychometricians who have built their science around external criteria that there happens not to be an infallible criterion in every particular instance; indeed, available criteria often have little more prima-facie validity than the test.

Still another method of constructing scoring keys with minimum inference is to set up a construct or criterion which can itself be defined statistically; e.g., one can use a statistical definition of normality and abnormality. Thus, an infrequent response is, by definition, "deviant," and a key for a putative trait of deviance can be set up at the minimal inferential level.

Cumulative Tests: Content Validity

At the opposite extreme from those test constructors who take no responsibility for the content of their test but shift it all to their operations are those test constructors who choose items entirely on the basis of content. An interesting example, and one which deserves more attention than it has received, is the Myers-Briggs Type Indicator, which is being used in research at the Educational Testing Service. The subtests are constructed to measure postulated entities in the Jungian system of psychology. The antithetical traits of Jung, introversion-extroversion, judgment-perception, sensing-intuition, and thinking-feeling, are well adapted to the dichotomous-item form.

Cumulative Tests: Construct Validity

To give a score on a trait implies that the trait is indeed an entity in some sense, a fact evaded by the minimal-inference testers and decided by fiat by those who use content alone. A step toward rationalizing key construction is to determine empirically whether an entity is there. Factorial methods are relevant to this purpose. Factor analysis proper, however, assumes multivalued rather than dichotomous items. A factorial method specifically evolved for dichotomous items is the homogeneous keying method of Loevinger, Gleser, and DuBois (1953). [A number of psychometricians, such as Guttman and Coombs, have constructed rigorous nonprobabilistic models presumably for psychological data. Their inappropriateness, particularly in the clinical field, is discussed elsewhere (Loevinger, 1957; Loevinger, in press).]

Homogeneous keying and other factorial methods of demonstrating an empirical basis for a score are but way stations on the road to what has currently come to be known as "construct validity" ("Technical Recommendations for Psychological Tests and Diagnostic Techniques," 1954). Although construct validity was proposed originally in terms of test evaluation (Cronbach & Meehl, 1955), it has also been developed in terms of test construction (Jessor & Hammond, 1957; Loevinger, 1957). One program for test construction based on the concept of construct validity is as follows: The original pool of items should sample broadly some area of content. Items are selected from the pool to constitute a scoring key or keys in accord with empirically determined structural relations. The structural model must be consistent with what is known of the structural characteristics of nontest manifestations of the trait to be measured. Some accounting must be made for the content of items included in each key, in contrast with items included in other keys and possibly also in contrast with unkeyed items. The latter, however, may simply be nondiscriminating items, in which case accounting for their content would be unprofitable. Finally, interpretations thus generated should be confirmed by relations with other variables. Criterionlike variables should show a significant correlation or significant differences in the expected direction. Artifactual variables such as response bias and in some cases demographic variables like age should be shown not to account for the results (Loevinger, 1957).

This program has been applied to the study of maternal attitudes in a heterogeneous sample of 202 women, yielding results of clinical interest which are in line with results from other studies but which add details not previously found (Loevinger, 1962; Loevinger & Sweet, 1961). Use of the structural relations of the items to clarify a construct is illustrated by the fate of the putative trait, "acceptance of woman's role." All items which had some a priori relation to the problem of acceptance of sex roles were placed in a single pool. Two distinct clusters emerged from the homogeneity analysis, one of which referred to acceptance of woman's social role and one to acceptance of woman's biological role; moreover, there was a slight negative correlation (−.23), confirmed on a subsequent sample (−.15). Thus, acceptance of woman's role is not a unitary trait.

Another substantive result of the homogeneous keying was demonstration of the salience and clarification of the content of the chief trait measured by the test, authoritarian family ideology. It incorporated the systematic variance which was attributed a priori to punitiveness-permissiveness, but there were a number of indications that the original prima-facie characterization was inappropriate. Items that clearly referred to punitiveness or permissiveness were in some cases not correlated with the cluster, while some items which proved to be good measures of the cluster had no such connotations. Theoretical considerations led to a further inference that authoritarian family ideology is a measure of ego development. The developmental interpretation was supported by a subsequent analysis of variance, in which the score was shown to vary significantly with age, with educational level, and with experience in child rearing, but not with religion.

Configural Scoring

Homogeneous keying, like the methods of maximizing correlation with a criterion and choice of items displaying significant differences, implies a cumulative or polar model. For nonpolar variables, an exact solution to the problem of maximizing correlation with an external criterion is found by pattern analysis, as has been known for some years. "Every individual in an answer pattern is assigned the same score, the mean criterion score for that answer pattern. This set of scores is called a *configural scale* . . . [and] is, in the least squares sense, the best prediction of his criterion score" (Lubin & Osburn, 1957, p. 64). Lubin and Osburn (1957) have summarized some relevant contributions and drawn out their implications. For a test composed of t dichotomous items, there are 2^t possible patterns of response; i.e., for eight items there are 256 patterns of response. Since information is obtained only for those patterns in which several individuals fall, large numbers of cases are needed even when the number of items is small. Thus pattern analysis is feasible only when there is a drastic reduction of admissible patterns, a reduction which must stem from theoretical, a priori considerations.

There have been a number of large-scale attempts using computer search of large numbers of items to find patterns of items which will be superior to linear (cumulative) scoring keys. Despite many programmatic articles proclaiming the merits of configural scoring, the accessions of predictive power have failed to materialize. The few studies that have been reported have shown no consistent superiority of configural keys over linear scoring models. The unreported studies presumably fared no better (Loevinger, 1959a).

While a blindly empirical, atheoretical search for patterns of items is theoretically impractical and empirically fruitless, the formulas of pattern analysis can be used to test whether the cumulative model is adequate (i.e., whether there are significant interactions between items) and to test for the significance of some few patterns which theory says should be present. With nonpolar variables, even more than with polar ones, an empirical, minimally inferential approach to scoring keys cannot work.

Implied in the Lubin-Osburn discussion is an additional answer to the vexing question of why the cumulative model continues to be widely used for personality measurement. It is the most specific structural model and hence gives reproducible results with fewer cases than other models. The more indeterminate the model, the more cases will be needed to get results that will hold true for a new sample.

PATTERN SEARCH: A DILEMMA OF CLINICAL RESEARCH

The foregoing remarks apply to pattern analysis in prediction of a criterion. The equivalent of homogeneous keying, the use of empirical data to find clusters of items that constitute a pattern of response, requires the use of some specific structural model. For every set of items yields *some* kind of response patterning. Discovery of the most frequent patterns is of little avail. They often represent no more than artifacts of measurement, and they may also mark common responses to the several items without indicating an intrinsic connection among the items. The clinician, moreover, is in many contexts only slightly interested in what most people do most of the time, which is what frequent response patterns show. The clinician is alert to rare and unique responses; precisely here the research worker is of little help, for research can handle only replicated responses. Meehl (1954) has discussed related problems.

Consider the following problem, which arose in making a scoring manual for judging ego development from sentence completions. The stem "A woman's body . . ." usually yields responses that can be classed with minimum inference in such categories as "is a thing of beauty," "is her chief asset," "should be kept covered," and so on. A response that occurred only once and to which no others in about one thousand cases approximated is "should be placed in a casket when dead." The former, replicated responses can be studied statistically, but they are of modest interest to a clinician. The last response, in which a clinician suspects many clues may be found, cannot be studied statistically. Too little attention has been paid to this methodological gulf. The way to bridge it is, again, by using inferential categories arrived at on a more or less theoretical basis. Thus the clinically significant response can be classed as hostile humor and also as concern with death and destruction. Both types of response can be shown to occur more frequently at low levels of ego development than at higher ones, though rarely in answer to this particular stem (and not often both in a single response).

EVALUATION AND VALIDITY

In many accepted texts on test theory (e.g., Gulliksen, 1950, p. 88), the validity of a test is described as its correlation with some criterion. There are then as many validities for a test as there are criteria it might be used to predict. Construct validity as a program for test evaluation arose in part because convincing criteria rarely materialized. In wake of a new wave of test theory, precipitated by publication of "Technical Recommendations for Psychological Tests and Diagnostic Techniques" (1954), classical theory of validation has been further weakened. It now appears that a single correlation between a test and a criterion or other variable can rarely, if ever, be evaluated by itself.

Convergent and Discriminant Validity

The most important contribution to this insight is the proposal by Campbell and Fiske (1959) that to evaluate a test, one must always have at least two quite different traits measured by at least two methods that are as different as possible. All the intercorrelations should be computed and displayed in a multitrait-multimethod matrix. Coefficients that refer to the same trait as measured by different methods are usually referred to as *validity coefficients;* in this matrix they constitute the validity diagonal. The values should certainly be larger than others in the same row and column of the heteromethod quadrant, since the latter values refer to different traits measured by different methods; this discrepancy is termed *convergent validity*. The monomethod triangles are identical with those used in homogeneous keying of multiple-scored tests. Diagonal values should be homogeneity coefficients (Kuder-Richardson formula 20) and should exceed appreciably the heterotrait coefficients in corresponding rows and columns (Loevinger et al., 1953). This is *discriminant validity* in Campbell-Fiske terms. Campbell and Fiske examined many published data on test validity. Many instances in which correlations were interpreted as supporting test validity were shown not to support the claim when the data were rearranged in the form of a multitrait-multimethod matrix. In many other instances the crucial comparative coefficients were not computed, although clearly data sufficient for their computation were available to the researcher. To the extent that monomethod-heterotrait values exceed heteromethod-heterotrait values, instrumental factors such as response bias can be assumed to be operating.

In factor-analytic studies utilizing several measures from each of several tests, such as Rorschach, TAT, MMPI, etc., it has regularly been found that the most salient factors statistically are specific to a single test; i.e., there are Rorschach factors, TAT factors, MMPI factors, and so on. If the tests really measure basic personality traits, why should not the same factors appear in different tests? Apparently in projective as well as in objective tests, artifacts obscure measurement to a large extent.

One suggestion made by Campbell and Fiske has been largely ignored in subsequent literature; this is their assertion that in many instances arranging the data in a multitrait-multimethod matrix will take the place of factor analysis and may even display the relevant information more clearly. (The writer has indeed seen papers in which laborious factor analyses have yielded only results that could have been discerned more clearly from the original matrix of correlations.) To clinicians this suggestion should be particularly appealing, since it enables one to stay close to one's original data rather than interposing complex statistical operations, whose appeal indeed is too often that of the magical and mysterious.

Incremental Validity

The relativity of validity coefficients is shown by Sechrest (1963) from another viewpoint which supplements that of the approaches already mentioned. Sechrest (following suggestions of Conrad, Cronbach, Gleser, and others) adds that a test must be evaluated in terms of *incremental validity*, i.e., how much it adds to prediction which can be made on the basis of more easily obtained information, such as age, sex, education, marital status, grade-point average, and so on. In an earlier paper aimed primarily at the problem of predicting dichotomous criteria, Meehl and Rosen (1955) concluded that the predictive efficiency of a test must always be measured against prediction on the basis of base rates. Does the test do better than simply to assign every case to the more numerous class (e.g., not brain-damaged, not schizophrenic, etc.)? Most tests, even those which provide significant differences between groups, do not. More germane, the evidence cited by many authors to show predictive efficiency actually showed no improvement over base rates, with which the predictions had not been carefully compared.

A THEORY OF TEST RESPONSE

No matter what the test constructor says he wishes to measure, one has the impression that a hidden hand guides the answers. Response bias in its various forms is a considerable part of the "hidden hand." Recently there has been a florid hypertrophy of studies of response bias, though the basic phenomena have been known since the work of Lorge (1937) and Rundquist and Sletto (1936). Study of response bias has been much encouraged by the repeated demonstration that there is some valid variance in it. But every voluntary action must have some valid variance. This does not mean that actions chosen at random are good measures of important traits. Surely it would be a most remarkable coincidence if the very artifacts of the testing situation should prove to be the best clues to vital human traits. What seems more likely is that, like other poorly or accidentally chosen measures, they will be curvilinear and even multivalued functions of humanly significant traits. Thus the position here is that attention should be directed to the salience, the importance of traits to be measured in clinical research; instead of forever studying response bias, we should devise methods to minimize it, such as the paired-choice item (Loevinger, 1962). Psychological and statistical considerations converge in this methodological area (Campbell, 1950; Loevinger, 1955).

Elsewhere the writer has argued that there is a natural order to the discovery and measurement of traits: that the most pervasive and effective ones must be taken into account before those which account for less variance can be effectively measured (Loevinger, 1959b). Intelligence is the most pervasive determinant of manifest behavior and was also the first trait to be measured. There are reasons to think that the second trait in the hierarchy is ego development. The artifacts of current measures are in considerable part functions of it; thus we are always measuring it, but never well. As in the case of intelligence, the only hope of measuring anything else well is first to concentrate on ego development and to learn to understand it and measure it.

To be more specific, acquiescence and tendency to describe oneself in socially desirable terms, two components of response bias, are instances of a more general tendency to response stereotypy, which is a more psychologically meaningful trait and can be expected to be manifest in situations other than that of testing. Stereotypy as such appears to be a polar, constantly decreasing function of ego development. The latter statement is by no means easy to prove, for the measurement of stereotypy presents difficulties. One can easily assess adherence to a particular stereotype, but adherence to an unusual one may appear exactly like original opinions. A stereotyped tendency to say "yes" or "no" can be detected if one is alert to the possibility and constructs a proper measure. A stereotyped tendency to describe oneself in socially approved terms often can be detected but may be missed if the subject is not socially sensitive enough to know what is socially approved in many circumstances. Another possible problem is that the subject's social stereotypes may refer to a different cultural group from that utilized by the test constructor, as is the case when foreign students are included in college research populations and more subtly in other instances. Nonconformist attitudes can also be stereotyped, as is frequently the case in adolescence; such attitudes would most likely be scored as nonstereotyped on any instrument constructed to detect stereotyped conformity. And of course the investigator's sterotypes are indistinguishable from well-reasoned opinions; it is to the credit of the California group (Adorno et al., 1950) that they noted the presence of "rigid lows" among their nonauthoritarian subjects. Apparently, then, stereotypy as a general tendency cannot be measured directly; it must be inferred from a variety of indicators. A recent attempt partially to meet these problems is the work of Rokeach on dogmatism (1960); a similar earlier attempt can be found in the work of Watson (1925).

Social sensitivity, which appears to be a constantly increasing function of ego development, also offers great difficulties in measurement. There is a midway point in development where stereotypy, though decreasing, is still appreciably present and where social sensitivity, though increasing, is still far from acute. The conjunction of stereotypy and social sensitivity has been referred to as "conformity" both in common speech and in the work of a number of psychologists. A large minority of the population, if not a majority, never develops beyond this stage. This is the stage in which the tendency to describe oneself in socially desirable terms is at a maximum.

This theory of test response is presented here (and it is not pure theory but is based on extensive evidence which cannot be reviewed in present compass), not only because it provides a parsimonious explanation of data in an overworked research area, but also because it illustrates treating a milestone of development as a polar variable. While being high on "social desirability"—or, indeed, on other measures of conformity—can be interpreted unequivocally, a low score is ambiguous. Is the subject too socially insensitive to know what is desirable, or is he too mature and differentiated to describe himself in those terms? Now ego development is an extremely important—and largely neglected—area of individual differences, while tendency to describe oneself in socially desirable terms is prima facie a minor trait. Here is a typical instance of the problems of personality measurement: What is important is difficult to measure and can only be inferred from diverse indicators. What is easily (and frequently) measured is unimportant and is a curvilinear function of the more important underlying trait. Being directly measurable by a paper-and-pencil test does not render a trait important or sensible for research. Neither does it prove that the trait is unimportant. Experience, however, uniformly suggests that traits directly and objectively measurable are highly equivocal in their clinical significance.

SOME PRACTICAL IMPLICATIONS

Psychologists have achieved a number of valuable tests of general ability. Beyond that, the number of well-validated tests is small indeed, as attested by such able reviews as those of Super (1957), covering differential prediction of abilities; Meehl and Rosen (1955), covering prediction of dichotomous criteria such as delinquency and pathology; and Campbell and Fiske (1959), covering convergent and discriminant (i.e., construct) validity, particularly as related to personality measurement. The psychologist or psychiatrist initiating a research project in the clinical field may be tempted to think that since no well-established test exists for exactly the trait he wants to measure, his best course is to make his own test. This view is particularly tempting to those who do not know a great deal about the effort that has been expended on many more or less unsuccessful tests. [For a virtually complete and critically annotated index of tests, the volumes edited by Buros (1941; 1949; 1953; 1959) should be consulted.]

Ad Hoc Tests

As this chapter has shown, the pitfall of professional test making repeatedly has been that superficial simplicity masks psychological complexity. Examples can be found in rating scales, checklists of items, degree-of-agreement items, and the many attempts to measure milestones of development as if they were simple polar variables, as in the case of conformity and "social desirability." If the professional psychometrician makes this mistake, how much more likely is the clinician who is an amateur in the field of measurement to make it also? The absence of good tests of many personality traits results not from lack of interest or of willingness to make a good test but from the intrinsic difficulties of personality measurement.

Persons without extensive training in the area of tests and measurements are prone to believe that a test, as every schoolboy knows, is a more or less clever set of items. Professional workers in the field, however, tend to borrow one another's items rather freely, on the grounds that the items alone do not constitute a test, but only the items together with a scoring key and appropriate norms. The number of cases needed even for a modest normative study is now recognized as being so great that for some types of test not only expertise but also commercial backing is necessary. To construct a scoring manual for a projective test, even larger numbers are required to get adequate empirical validation. We may conclude that for short-term (say, less than three years) or small-scale (less than about one thousand cases) research, tests that other investigators have studied empirically, however fallible they may be, are almost necessarily better than *ad hoc* tests. To say this, however, is not to condone taking the claims implied in the title or in the promotional literature at face value.

Random and Systematic Errors

Campbell and Fiske have emphasized what some early texts on statistics and tests obscured, i.e., that a test whose correlations with criterion measures are numerically low (say, .3) may still possess real and usable validity. Just at this point the clinician finds it difficult to adjust himself to the contradictory requirements of the objectives of research and the objectives of clinical practice (Loevinger, 1963). The clinician's commitment is to be as right as possible about each individual case; the research worker's commitment is to be as right as possible about the nature of things. Correlated errors in separate observations, small errors of bias, and errors that systematically prejudice the outcome of a study are fatal to the research enterprise. On the other hand, comparatively large errors that are random with respect to the variables under study will, to be sure, attenuate the relationships found, but they will not distort them, and the extent of the attenuation can often be estimated and hence approximately corrected.

Consider the problem of assessing in-patient psychiatric treatment in relation to diagnosis. The clinician is likely to favor diagnosis several weeks after admission, on discharge, or even one to five years after discharge on the grounds that the later the diagnosis, the more accurate it will be. The researcher must insist, however, that only intake diagnosis, no matter how fallible, be used for such a study. Errors in individual cases will be larger, but they will be random with respect to the dependent variable, treatment outcome, whereas the more accurate diagnosis on discharge will be contaminated to an unknown degree by knowledge of outcome. Established statistical methods do not enable one to estimate or to correct the effect of such contamination of judgment.

To carry the point even further, diagnosis on intake by a psychiatrist may incorporate social class and other biases that will also enter the treatment program. Thus for research purposes, use of such diagnostic information as can be gleaned from the MMPI or a similar instrument has distinct value in preference to diagnosis by a psychiatrist. There are biases in pencil-and-paper tests too, but they are unlikely to be the same kind of thing as the biases of the attendant psychiatrists. If indeed diagnosis by a psychiatrist is more likely to be accurate than diagnosis by MMPI, that is reason for use of the psychiatrist's opinion in individual cases; the more fallible but objective test may still be preferable for research purposes if it has any validity at all.

Summary

Measurement in clinical research is beset by paradoxes. First, if one wishes to measure only what is objectively observable and can be formulated on a strictly quantitative basis, one will surely end with nothing but trivialities. If one insists on being concerned only with important traits, one surrenders first strict quantification and then strict objectivity. Second, the clinician seizes on rare symptoms as the keystone of diagnosis; the research worker cannot deal with single or rare instances, but only with frequently replicated symptoms or responses. Third, the clinician always wants as much information as possible before expressing an opinion about a case; the researcher must insist that only limited sources of knowledge be available to clinicians taking part in a research program, or else the research is vitiated.

There are no easy or magical formulas for overcoming these dilemmas. In meeting the problems, the standard paraphernalia of the statistical consultant—his factor analysis, analysis of variance, and computer search for patterns—are of as little avail as the unbridled intuition of the clinician. To meet such problems requires evolving a mature science in which measurement, theory, and empirical verification are integral parts of a single enterprise. What the methodologist should bring into the clinical field is not a bag of statistical tricks, but the habit of rigorous and precise thought and a sense of where to look for errors that bias the result. The clinician must bring to the research area his problems and concerns as they impinge on him, his sense of the relative importance of different questions and of the genuineness or spuriousness of proposed approaches.

To be truly scientific requires more investment in constructs and theories than many psychologists find congenial; yet the great sciences of modern times are shaped in terms of theory. The basic observations on which measurement rests should be as little inferential as possible, but meaningful scores must correspond to and be arrived at by reference to constructs. In a similar way, the gap between the unique clinical sign and the empirically testable diagnostic hypothesis can be bridged by construct and theory.

REFERENCES

Adorno, T. W., Frenkel-Brunswik, Else, Levinson, D. F., & Sanford, R. N. *The authoritarian personality.* New York: Harper & Row, 1950.

Block, J. *The Q-sort method in personality assessment and psychiatric research.* Springfield, Ill.: Charles C Thomas, 1961.

Bock, R. D., & Haggard, E. A. *A comprehensive psychometric study of the Rorschach and Holtzman ink blot techniques.* Chapel Hill, N.C.: Psychometric Laboratory, Univer. of North Carolina, 1963. (Mimeographed)

Buros, O. K. (Ed.) *The nineteen forty mental measurements yearbook.* Highland Park, N.J.: Gryphon Press, 1941.

Buros, O. K. (Ed.) *The third mental measurements yearbook.* New Brunswick, N.J.: Rutgers Univer. Press, 1949.

Buros, O. K. (Ed.) *The fourth mental measurements yearbook.* Highland Park, N.J.: Gryphon Press, 1953.

Buros, O. K. (Ed.) *The fifth mental measurements yearbook.* Highland Park, N.J.: Gryphon Press, 1959.

Campbell, D. T. The indirect assessment of social attitudes. *Psychol. Bull.,* 1950, **47,** 15–38.

Campbell, D. T., & Fiske, D. W. Convergent and discriminant validation by the multitrait-multimethod matrix. *Psychol. Bull.,* 1959, **56,** 81–105.

Coombs, C. H. Theory and methods of social measurement. In L. Festinger & D. Katz (Eds.),

Research methods in the behavioral sciences. New York: Dryden Press, 1953. Pp. 471–535.

Cronbach, L. J. Statistical methods applied to Rorschach scores: a review. *Psychol. Bull.*, 1949, **46,** 393–429.

Cronbach, L. J., & Meehl, P. E. Construct validity in psychological tests. *Psychol. Bull.*, 1955, **52,** 281–302.

Edwards, A. L. *Manual for the Edwards Personal Preference Schedule.* New York: Psychological Corporation, 1953.

Fiske, D. W., & Baughman, E. E. Relationships between Rorschach scoring categories and the total number of responses. *J. abnorm. soc. Psychol.*, 1953, **48,** 25–32.

Freud, S. *The origins of psychoanalysis.* New York: Basic Books, 1954.

Getzels, J. W., & Walsh, J. J. The method of paired direct and projective questionnaires in the study of attitude structure and socialization. *Psychol. Monogr.*, 1958, **72,** No. 1 (Whole No. 454).

Gulliksen, H. *Theory of mental tests.* New York: Wiley, 1950.

Harris, J. G., Jr. Validity: the search for a constant in a universe of variables. In Maria A. Rickers-Ovsiankina (Ed.), *Rorschach psychology.* New York: Wiley, 1960. Pp. 380–439.

Holtzman, W. H., Thorpe, J. S., Swartz, J. D., & Herron, E. W. *Inkblot perception and personality.* Austin, Tex.: Univer. of Texas Press, 1961.

Jessor, R., & Hammond, K. R. Construct validity and the Taylor anxiety scale. *Psychol. Bull.*, 1957, **54,** 161–170.

Loevinger, Jane. The technic of homogeneous tests compared with some aspects of "scale analysis" and factor analysis. *Psychol. Bull.*, 1948, **45,** 507–529.

Loevinger, Jane. Effect of distortions of measurement on item selection. *Educ. psychol. Measmt.*, 1954, **3,** 441–448.

Loevinger, Jane. Some principles of personality measurement. *Educ. psychol. Measmt.*, 1955, **15,** 3–17.

Loevinger, Jane. Objective tests as instruments of psychological theory. *Psychol. Rep.*, 1957, **3,** 635–694.

Loevinger, Jane. Theory and techniques of assessment. *Annu. Rev. Psychol.*, 1959, **10,** 287–316. (a)

Loevinger, Jane. A theory of test response. *Proc. 1958 Invitational Conf. on Testing Problems.* Princeton, N.J.: Educational Testing Service, 1959. Pp. 36–47. (b)

Loevinger, Jane. Measuring personality patterns of women. *Genet. Psychol. Monogr.*, 1962, **65,** 53–136.

Loevinger, Jane. Conflict of commitment in clinical research. *Amer. Psychologist,* 1963, **18,** 241–251.

Loevinger, Jane. Psychological tests in the conceptual framework of psychology. In K. R. Hammond (Ed.), *Egon Brunswik memorial volume,* in press.

Loevinger, Jane, Gleser, Goldine C., & DuBois, P. H. Maximizing the discriminating power of a multiple-score test. *Psychometrika,* 1953, **18,** 309–317.

Loevinger, Jane, & Sweet, Blanche. Construction of a test of mothers' attitudes. In J. C. Glidewell (Ed.), *Parental attitudes and child behavior.* Springfield, Ill.: Charles C Thomas, 1961. Pp. 110–123.

Lorge, I. "Gen-like": halo or reality? *Psychol. Bull.*, 1937, **34,** 545–546.

Lubin, A., & Osburn, H. G. A theory of pattern analysis for the prediction of a quantitative criterion. *Psychometrika,* 1957, **22,** 63–73.

Meehl, P. E. *Clinical versus statistical prediction.* Minneapolis, Minn.: Univer. of Minnesota Press, 1954.

Meehl, P. E., & Rosen, A. Antecedent probability and the efficiency of psychometric signs, patterns, or cutting scores. *Psychol. Bull.*, 1955, 52, 194–216.

Peck, R. F., & Havighurst, R. J. *The psychology of character development.* New York: Wiley, 1960.

Peterson, J. *Early conceptions and tests of intelligence.* Tarrytown-on-Hudson: World, 1925.

Rokeach, M. *The open and closed mind.* New York: Basic Books, 1960.

Rundquist, E. A., & Sletto, R. F. *Personality in the depression.* Minneapolis, Minn.: Univer. of Minnesota Press, 1936.

Sandler, J., Kawenoka, Maria, Neurath, Lily, Rosenblatt, B., Schnurmann, Anneliese, & Sigal, J. The classification of superego material in the Hampstead index. In *The psychoanalytic study of the child.* Vol. 17. New York: International Universities Press, 1962. Pp. 107–127.

Sanford, N. (Ed.) Personality development during the college years. *J. soc. Issues,* 1956, **12,** No. 4.

Sanford, N., Webster, H., & Freedman, M. Impulse expression as a variable of personality. *Psychol. Monogr.*, 1957, **71,** No. 11 (Whole No. 440).

Sechrest, L. Incremental validity: a recommendation. *Educ. psychol. Measmt.*, 1963, 23, 153–158.

Sullivan, C., Grant, Marguerite Q., & Grant, J. D. The development of interpersonal maturity. *Psychiatry*, 1957, **20**, 373–385.

Super, D. E. The multifactor tests: summing up. *Personnel Guidance J.*, 1957, **36**, 154–161.

Technical recommendations for psychological tests and diagnostic techniques. *Psychol. Bull. Suppl.*, 1954, **51** (2), Part 2, 1–38.

Thurstone, L. L., & Chave, E. J. *The measurement of attitude.* Chicago: Univer. of Chicago Press, 1929.

Watson, G. B. The measurement of fairmindedness. *Teach. Coll. Contr. Educ.*, 1925, No. 176.

5

Some Statistical Issues in Psychological Research[1]

JACOB COHEN

This chapter is made up of four essays, each bearing on one aspect of contemporary statistical analysis as it is used by psychologists. The essays are opinionated, perhaps at points cranky, and undoubtedly controversial. I chose to meet the editor's request for a chapter on statistics by focusing on some matters that I believe are in need of attention, rather than by attempting a condensed rehash of the content of the popular statistical textbooks, in the knowledge that I would find the former far more rewarding and the hope that the reader would.

Statistical analysis is a tool, not a ritualistic religion. It is for use, not for reverence, and it should be approached in the spirit that it was made for psychologists rather than vice versa. As one of many tools in the psychologist's kit, it is frequently not relevant and is sometimes of considerable utility. It is certainly not as important as, nor can it even partly replace, good ideas or well-conceived experimental strategems, although it may be virtually indispensable in testing out an idea or rounding out a good experiment.

In what follows, I assume in the reader no more than a lowest-common-denominator budget of graduate "psychological" statistics. The treatment is informal and nonmathematical; I have gladly sacrificed statistical rigor and pedantic qualification in the exposition in an attempt at clarity, brevity, and a smooth reading flow.

[1] The preparation of this chapter was largely supported by grant MH 06137 from the National Institute of Mental Health, United States Public Health Service.

STATISTICAL POWER: THE OTHER KIND OF ERROR

First, a review of the logic and strategy of statistical inference. Consider the following typical situation: Dr. Doe believes on theoretical grounds that a certain experimental effect "exists," specifically, that two population means differ. He mounts an appropriate experiment and organizes the resulting data to yield a decision with regard to the validity of his belief. Following the rules of the game, he posits the *null* hypothesis—which we shall throughout understand to mean "the hypothesis that the phenomenon to be demonstrated is in fact absent" (Fisher, 1949, p. 13)—that is, that the population means are equal, and he sets an α risk, taking a prudently small value such as 5 per cent or 1 per cent. This is the risk that he will *mistakenly reject* the null hypothesis when it is true, that is, the risk of a *spuriously positive* conclusion. He performs the appropriate t test on his data. He may find that the difference between his sample means is significant, whereupon he rejects the null hypothesis and thus concludes that the population means do differ, subject to the α risk. Or, he may find that this difference is not significant, and thus the null hypothesis is accepted as tenable, whereupon he should conclude that the evidence does not support the proposition that the population means differ.

Note that Dr. Doe has been engaged in a procedure oriented around the null hypothesis: He either rejects it or fails to reject it, while controlling the probability or mistakenly rejecting it. Because of this control of the long-run error rate, all is well. All is well, that is, provided that the null hypothesis is true! As a responsible scientist, he has guarded himself and the scientific fraternity to whom he will communicate by controlling at a low level the risk of making a spurious positive claim. All right and proper.

But what if, in fact, the phenomenon *does* exist, the null hypothesis is *false,* and the population means *do* differ, say, by one-half σ. It is of course by no means certain that his obtained sample difference will be significant and that he will correctly conclude that the null hypothesis is false. Indeed, a recent survey suggests that under such circumstances, about half the time the present-day abnormal-social psychological researcher will, indeed, *not* find the sample difference to be significant and will thus accept the null hypothesis as tenable (Cohen, 1962). Assume that this is the case with our Dr. Doe, who then fails to reject (or accepts as tenable) a false null hypothesis. He has a spuriously negative result and has in fact committed the other kind of error, that is, a type II error, so called to distinguish it from the error of rejecting a true null hypothesis, the type I error. But if he is a typical psychological researcher, not only has he exerted no prior control over his risk of committing a type II error, but he will have no idea what the magnitude of this risk is. Thus, when the null hypothesis is false, all is not well in Dr. Doe's procedure.

My concern here is with this neglected other side of the coin of statistical inference as psychologists generally use it, some of the implications and consequences of this neglect, and some proposals to rectify this imbalance.

The central point is that β, the probability of committing a type II error, *can* be controlled in the planning of an experiment or can at least be determined after an experiment is planned. For some time now, the popular statistics texts used in psychology have discussed the logic of inference reviewed above and have illustrated it with regard to normal curve statistical tests. Unfortunately, this is done early in the book, and the issue is largely dropped thereafter. By the time the student has caught the swing of statistical manipulation, in the absence of reinforcement, type II errors are much like the weather—he can talk about them (on comprehensive examinations), but he cannot do anything about them. Nor does the conferring of the doctoral degree improve matters, if our published research is taken as evidence.

Any given statistical test of a null hypothesis can be viewed as a complex relationship between the following four parameters:

1. The *power* of the test, defined as $1 - \beta$, i.e., the probability of rejecting the null hypothesis.
2. The region of rejection of the null hypothesis as determined by the α level and whether the test is directional or nondirectional, e.g., one-tailed or two-tailed. This is merely the criterion value of the test statistic which leads to rejection. As α increases, power increases.
3. The sample size n. As n increases, power increases.
4. The magnitude of the effect in the population, or the degree of departure from the null hypothesis. The larger this is, the greater the power.

These four parameters are so related that when any three of them are fixed, the fourth is completely determined. Thus, when an investigator decides for a given experimental plan his significance criterion and the sample size he will use, the power of his test is determined, even though he does not in general know what it is. The difficulty lies in (4) above.

There are two ways of stating the hypothesis that is alternative to the null. The Fisherian alternative is simply that the null hypothesis is false; e.g., the difference between the population means is *any* nonzero value, the population r is *any* nonzero value, etc. This alternative dominates present practice in psychology and partly accounts for the neglect of power considerations. The Neyman-Pearson alternative to the null specifies an exact alternative; e.g., the difference between the population means is .5 σ (e.g., eight score units), the population r is .40, etc. This exact form of alternative hypothesis provides the fourth parameter above and makes power analysis possible.

How does Dr. Doe decide the size of the population effect he is trying to detect; how does he choose an exact alternative? When clinical psychology has evolved to the point of exact quantitative formulations and mathematical models, this problem will automatically be solved, since the model will specify an exact value alternative to the null; indeed, the usual problem will be to choose between two exact values specified by two competing theories, neither of them zero.

Still, our contemporary Dr. Doe is not so helpless here as he may at first think. Even in the absence of mathematical models, his knowledge of the research area in which he is working (the theory, the construct validity of his variables, past findings) may at least suggest to him whether his sought-for effect is "small," "medium," or "large." To operationalize these concepts, I have suggested elsewhere certain arbitrary but reasonable quantities to attach to these adjectives, a set for each of the main kinds of statistical tests used by psychologists (Cohen, 1962). For example, a small difference between population means is defined as .25 σ, a medium difference as .5 σ, and a large difference as 1 σ; population *r*s of .20, .40, and .60, respectively, define these levels; for differences between proportions and between *r*s, these levels are .10, .20, .30, and so on.

A medium difference between population means, .5 σ, is illustrated by an eight-point difference in mean IQ between two populations, such as is the case for clerical and semiskilled workers (Super, 1949, p. 98). This difference is large enough to be noticeable. A small difference in these terms would be illustrated by the four-point difference (.25 σ) between twins and nontwins, favoring the latter (Husén, 1959). This scientifically meaningful difference is relatively imperceptible; that is, a clinician cannot call upon his experience with twins to validate it. Finally, the large (16-point, 1 σ) difference between college graduates and marginal high school graduates (Cronbach, 1960, p. 174) is so apparent as to render a statistical test virtually superfluous.

Using this frame of reference, Dr. Doe can ask himself of which order of magnitude he believes his population mean difference to be. If this is not helpful, he can simply take the criterion for the medium effect size as a convention, or, better still, he can select a series of reasonable effect sizes and work with them as a conditional manifold. If the effect size is *A*, power is P_1; if *B*, power is P_2; etc.

Once an investigator has an exact alternative hypothesis or a set of such, he can proceed. Using various accessible references (Cohen, in press; Dixon & Massey, 1957; Mosteller & Bush, 1954), he can study the implications of the relationships between the four parameters noted above as they apply to his situation *before* the experiment is performed. Since any three determine the fourth, four formal possibilities suggest themselves.

1. He can set a specific alternative (size of effect to be detected), an α rejection criterion, and the sample size he plans to use and determine the power of the eventual significance test. This was the procedure used in a review of a volume of the *Journal of Abnormal and Social Psychology*, where the definitions of small, medium, and large effect sizes were applied to the research plans, using the 5 per cent nondirectional α criterion and the actual sample sizes employed (Cohen, 1962). This procedure is appropriate in appraising research plans, one's own or others, or in evaluating completed research in order to assess the a priori probability of positive results (null-hypothesis rejection) under various levels of hypothetical effect size. Or, if an investigator is limited by his resources to a given sample size and is the victim of a dogma which dictates that his α risk cannot exceed 5 per cent (an orthodoxy, incidentally, inherited from agronomy), he can proceed as above to determine the power he can expect under alternatives appropriate to his research. If his power is feeble, he can abandon the research as planned or forearm his ego against the negative results which will probably eventuate and at least warn the scientific community (if he succeeds in getting his results published) that these negative results must be at least partially discounted in the light of his high a priori β risk. I here intend no advocacy of a policy of doing low-power studies and then saying they do not count, but if the exigencies of reality put a psychologist in the position of reporting a statistical test of trivial power, he owes it to himself and to his audience to point the fact out. What I do advocate is that he *know* the power of the test.

2. A far happier way to proceed in experimental planning is to set the specific alterna-

tive, the α criterion, and the *desired power* which will then determine the sample size to be used. This is, of course, the only rational basis for deciding the sample size (n) to employ in an investigation. As far as I can tell, decisions about n in much psychological research are generally arrived at by such considerations as local tradition ("At Old Siwash U., 30 cases are enough for a dissertation"); subject-matter precedent ("I'll use samples of 20 cases, since that's how many Hook and Crook used when they studied conditioning under anxiety"); data availability ("I can't study more *idiots savants* than we have at the clinic, can I?"); intuition or one of its more presumptuous variants, "experience"; and negotiation ("If I give them the semantic differential, too, then it's only fair that I cut my sample to 40"). However understandable these bases for decision are, they have nothing to do with the vital center of most present-day research, the rejection of false null hypotheses. When these considerations are taken together with Zipf's principle of least effort, in the absence of knowledge of the power of planned statistical tests, one would expect that *n*s would come to be used which are too small to yield respectable power values for reasonable effect sizes. This expectation is fully borne out. The average total n used to test the major hypotheses in the 70 research reports in a recent volume of the *Journal of Abnormal and Social Psychology* was 68. This resulted in mean power values (5 per cent nondirectional tests) of .83 against large-effect alternatives, but only .18 against small effects and .48 against medium effects (Cohen, 1962). Taking medium effects as a conventional reference point, only one-fourth had as good as .60 power, and the lowest quarter had less than .32 power! (Were the 1 per cent α level to be used, the results would be far worse.) It seems very unlikely that these investigators were aware of this state of affairs.

Increasing n is no panacea for what ails psychological research. Problems should be well conceived, and variables of good construct validity and optimally efficient experimental designs should be employed for power to be maximal. But it is clear that much improvement in power values is available through increasing n. Indeed, once statistical power analysis in experimental planning becomes general, investigators will need no urging to increase their *n*s.

To return to a consideration of this second alternative, it requires setting in advance the power value desired, thereby controlling the value of β. Naturally, the greater the power, the better; but if the desired power is set very high, say, at .99, the required n will be very large for the size of effect which can usually be expected. If at all possible, the investigator should render a judgment of the amount of type II error he can tolerate and see what n this demands (for the fixed α risk and alternative hypothesis effect size). If the required n turns out to exceed his resources, he can try again with a more modest power value. If the required n turns out to be well within his resources, he might consider setting his power value higher. By studying the relationship between n and power *for his situation*, taking into account the increase in cost to achieve a given increase in power, he can arrive at a rational solution to the sample-size problem. Although the pure researcher cannot place a dollar utility value on the consequence of type II (and type I) errors, as can, for example, the industrial quality control engineer, he can, by a subjective weighing of the consequences of an error in inference and the effort involved in producing data, approximate this approach.

Statistical conventions, although frequently misused, are nevertheless useful, and I would suggest that if a conventional value for β is desired, .20 be taken, i.e., that power of .80 be sought when no other basis is available. Like all conventions, this value is arbitrary, but it is, I believe, reasonable. It is consonant with several considerations.

First, I believe that generally the consequences of false positive claims (rejections of null hypotheses) *are* more serious than those of false negative results (acceptances of null hypotheses). This is in accord with the conventional scientific view of these matters. Present practice, which concerns itself solely with the former, by ignoring the latter implicitly treats them as if they were of no, or at least little, consequence. My proposal maintains the usual emphasis but keeps the relation between the two risks within reasonable bounds. Since the convention of the 5 per cent level for α has come to be generally used, my proposal implies a setting of a "subjective general relative seriousness" of 20 per cent/5 per cent = 4. The second consideration, then, in setting the β risk convention of .20 is that it is consonant with a rough guess that type I errors are in general about four times as serious as type II errors. I would, of course, have no serious quarrel with anyone who claimed that the factor should be three or five (or even two or six), but such is the nature of conventions. I offer this convention so diffidently because I would prefer to see power values set *ad hoc* wherever possible. I deplore the slavish adherence to the quasiofficial convention of 5 per cent for type I errors, which has resulted in its implicit equation with scientific truth for the positive claim and with respectability, if not ethical purity, for the claimant. But however abused, conventions have their uses.

The third consideration leading to the recommended .80 power convention is a practical one. The aforementioned survey (Cohen, 1962) indicated that medium effects were detectable under nondirectional 5 per cent α conditions with an average power of .48; the mean total n was 68. As much as one would like the assurance of statistical tests of .95 power, this would demand an increase in ns over what is now being reported by a factor of three. This may simply not be feasible, and even when feasible, it will not be deemed worth the effort by most investigators. The proposed .80 power convention would demand doubling present ns. This strikes me as frequently feasible and worth the effort, since under the stated conditions it means moving from a 1:1 chance of rejecting the null hypothesis in the presence of a medium effect to a 4:1 chance. If the effect should be "slight," under the assumed nondirectional 5 per cent α conditions, doubling currently typical ns would mean improving from a 1:6 chance to about a 1:3 chance of rejecting the null. If the effect is "large," it means going from a 6:1 chance to perhaps a 50:1 chance, which may not be worth the trouble; but then, how frequently can one reasonably anticipate large effects?

To summarize this second *modus operandi* in experimental planning, the investigator sets an α value and a desired power value, formulates an effect size, and determines the necessary n for these conditions. It is deemed desirable that these values be set in accordance with the specific content of the experiment, but as a convention, I propose that α be 5 per cent nondirectional, power be .80, and the effect size be medium as previously operationally defined. For a t test between independent means, this leads to samples of 64 cases each (Cohen, in press). This would mean approximately doubling the ns currently employed.

3. If n is fixed in advance and the investigator also fixes the power desired, a given anticipated effect size then implies a level of α, which can be solved for. The α convention is so strong in psychology that this possibility may escape one's notice or, if noticed, may be rejected out of hand. Logically, however, there is no bar to this procedure, and some experimental circumstances may call for it. For example, Dr. Doe may have devised a new treatment method. He has available a total of 80 patients and plans to divide them randomly into two equal groups, E and C, and compare them on a criterion measure following treatment. (Better designs are certainly available, but they would unnecessarily complicate the point.) Now, he expects that a medium (.5 σ difference) effect exists in the population and is understandably eager to keep low the probability of failing to conclude that a difference exists (the type II error). Let us say that he accordingly sets his desired power as .80. All is now specified except his significance criterion, which is, of course, fully determined by these conditions. He finds this to be 17 per cent as a nondirectional (two-tailed) test. Note that no experiment has yet been performed: 17 per cent is *not* the significance level he obtained from his data, but the significance criterion he is setting in advance as part of the decision rules by which he is going to play his game with nature. Thus, he must plan to work with this unconventionally large α risk. Should he?

As stated, he has no choice. *If* he expects an effect of medium size and no larger, and *if* he wants power of .80 and no less, and *if* he is restricted to a total n of 80 cases, with this plan he must reject the null hypothesis with 17 per cent α risk. Formally, no problem exists; an eventual positive conclusion must carry a one-in-six risk of being spurious. However, his social risks may run rather larger. That is, he may find some reluctance to publish his results among journal editors, and colleagues may whisper behind his back about his sloppy standards. The real question is: Should he undertake the research as planned, change his specifications, or abandon the research and retreat into his consulting room to use the new treatment method without organizing any formal research around it?

The last alternative is beneath consideration

in an empirical science. As for the second, how can he change his specifications? He can trade off between types of risk. For the sake of respectability, he can hue to the 5 per cent α criterion, whereupon he discovers that power drops to .60; i.e., this means a doubling of his originally desired β risk from .20 to .40 and in absolute terms a not much better than 50–50 chance of rejecting the null hypothesis when there is the assumed medium difference. Despite his reluctance, he may choose to do this.

With some tentativeness, I would endorse his carrying out the original plan, despite the large α risk. As I have noted, I am for scientific caution and prudence in setting risks of false positive claims (and generally against sin), but if in his judgment as an investigator he wants to control his type II risk at .20 because of the harm which would result if he were to fail to find a real difference in methods and if he believes that this is worth a 17 per cent risk of a false claim of a difference, I believe he should so proceed. After all, his audience is forewarned of the order of magnitude of the α risk and can place their own assessment on the validity of a positive claim, should one result. Furthermore, no single psychological experiment, whatever its α criterion, constitutes a crucial experiment which will finally settle an issue. His results communicated, other researchers can pursue the issue and can replicate, revise, and extend this line of inquiry. A mistaken positive claim should be discovered fairly quickly.

Is this study publishable? It should be. Consider our current practice. If Dr. Doe is tyrannized by the 5 per cent α level, accepts it passively, does the experiment, and fails to reject the null hypothesis (of which there is a .40 chance), there is a strong possibility that his report will never be published anyway. The reluctance of investigators to offer for publication reports of negative results is exceeded only by that of editors in regard to publishing them. [An incidental consequence of not publishing negative results is that the actual rate of spuriously "significant" reports in published research is higher than conventional α levels (Cohen, 1962; Sterling, 1959).] The present practice in assessing research is to set α low and let β remain unknown, which too frequently means high. I am proposing that for fixed n, a reasonable choice for both β and α be made, which may necessitate a relaxation of the conventional stringency of the α criterion.

The tentativeness of this recommendation stems from some anxiety lest the above be taken as an endorsement of inadequately small samples and worthlessly high α risks. There is nothing in the above reasoning to justify the use of small samples; it is appropriately applied only when small samples are necessitated by other considerations *and* when the risks finally run are not so large as to make the results so ambiguous as to be scientifically worthless.

4. A final form of analysis results when n, α, and power are fixed. Dr. Doe, restricted to a total n of 80, plans to perform a nondirectional 5 per cent t test and wants .80 power. This now determines the fourth parameter, the size of the difference in population means he can expect to detect under these circumstances. The solution which results is .63 σ. Thus, the difference between E and C population means must be almost two-thirds of a standard deviation for Dr. Doe to have .80 probability of rejecting the null hypothesis at the two-tailed 5 per cent level. If this is rather larger than he has reason to expect, he will need to reconsider the specifications. This form of analysis is also useful in assessing completed experiments. In published work, n is fixed, and the 5 per cent α level can be assumed as a convention. With the addition of a conventional .80 power requirement, the magnitude of the "detectable" effect can be determined. This would be useful as a means of assessing the meaningfulness of negative results or in comparing researches with "contradictory" findings. Clearly, if in two researches bearing on the same issue, A has had positive results and B negative, this is hardly contradictory if A in the sense above had a detectable difference of .5 σ and B a detectable difference of 1.5 σ.

Although I have discussed four formal kinds of analysis involving power, in practice one can juggle these parameters into a series of conditional statements which surround the specific research circumstances, using conventional standards where necessary, to arrive at an efficient experimental plan. Generally, the first two of these (where power is solved for and where n is solved for) will prove the most useful, particularly the second. To facilitate such analyses, I have prepared a handbook which makes these determinations a simple matter of looking up a table (Cohen, in press).

Some thoughtful consideration of these

relationships involving power leads to an interesting discovery. The inhibition that surrounds the interpretation of nonsignificant results bears another look. We know that failure to reject a null hypothesis, or its "acceptance," does not justify its affirmation; i.e., we *cannot* say that the population difference or correlation or variance of means is exactly zero or even near zero (although the error is frequently made implicitly in discussions of results). Thus, there is an asymmetry in the inductive process. We can say the effect is *not* zero when we reject, but we cannot say it *is* zero when we accept. This problem arises as a necessary part of the Fisherian form of the alternative, which is not an exact value, as is the null hypothesis, but merely states that the effect is nonzero. If we adopt the Neyman-Pearson form of alternative, which states exactly the size of the nonzero effect, we can approach a more symmetrical situation. If we have set β to be relatively small, say, .05, and α at the same level and if we have defined the size of the effect we want to detect (the alternative hypothesis) at a value D, such that if the effect is smaller than this we deem it negligible in some appropriate sense, then failure to reject the null hypothesis takes on more substantive meaning. If the effect is as large as D, then we had at least an a priori .95 probability of rejecting the null hypothesis. Having failed to reject the null hypothesis, we can with a .05 risk (β) conclude that the size of the effect is less than D and therefore negligible (although still not necessarily zero). This comes fairly close to affirming the null hypothesis with a controlled error rate (β) and is what is really intended in present practice when null hypotheses are incorrectly affirmed. It has the singular advantage over present practice of being a rational, valid procedure. In this useful sense, then, proper attention to power makes possible the attribution of positive meaning to negative results.

The difficulty that will be encountered in this maneuver lies in the conception of a negligible effect. In much "pure" research, in principle, *any* nonzero effect, no matter how small, may be meaningful in relation to a theory; i.e., no negligible effects exist. This would limit the applicability of the idea of the previous paragraph to research, mostly "applied," where negligible effects can be meaningfully defined.

To summarize:

1. Present practice in statistical inference has neglected the error of falsely accepting null hypotheses, β, and its complement, the power of the statistical test.

2. This neglect has resulted in both wasted research effort because of low power and errors in the interpretation of research results.

3. An exposition of the relationships between power, α (type I) risk, sample size, and the magnitude of effects was presented; using this matrix of relationships, I have described various kinds of analysis involving power applicable to research planning and the evaluation of completed research.

4. Certain conventions and operational definitions to further these analyses were presented, among them the setting of .80 as the conventional power requirement and .5 σ difference between means as the operational definition of a medium effect size. These conventions and definitions notwithstanding, investigators are encouraged to specify conditions relevant to their specific research circumstances.

5. One thing above all else is urged, namely, that investigators *know* and if possible *control* the β risks they incur and that consumers of the research literature also become sophisticated with regard to these issues.

SIGNIFICANCE AND DEGREE: WHETHER AND HOW MUCH

An elementary distinction learned in even the most undistinguished undergraduate course in statistics is that which must be made between the size of an effect in a sample, on one hand, and its statistical significance, on the other. Because the naïve tendency to accept the observed effect at its face value needs to be counteracted, the status of its significance is greatly stressed. The usual result is some formulation by the student that the size of the effect does not matter and that what matters is its significance. A neat semantic trap has been set: "What matters is significance—what is significant is significance—that which is significant, matters." Finally, the trap is sprung: "If it is significant, it *matters;* it is important, large." The initial naïve confusion of believing that a large sample effect is necessarily real (statistically significant or nonchance) is replaced by a "sophisticated" (hence all the more dangerous) confusion that a demonstrably real effect is necessarily large!

Stated in such bald terms, this is so clearly erroneous that one would think that certainly by the time our undergraduate student reaches his final exams for the doctorate these issues will have been sorted out and the distinction between the magnitude of an effect (or its relative magnitude, or the proportion of the variance of the dependent variable attributable to the independent variable) and its significance (the rejectability of the hypothesis of no effect in the population) clearly understood.

If the contents of the research reports in our journals and monographs are accepted as evidence, we must conclude that when it is at issue, this distinction is most often not made. Again and again, the "results" section of an article describing an effect as significant or highly significant is followed by a "discussion" section which (usually implicitly) proceeds to treat the effect as if it had been found to be large or very large.

Many factors go to perpetuate this error, apart from simply poor training. Significant results are hard to come by in clinical research. The independent variables are almost never quite what we want them to be, and the dependent variables even less so. Thurstone once said that in psychology we measure men by their shadows. Indeed, in clinical psychology we often measure men by their shadows while they are dancing in a ballroom illuminated by the reflections of an old-fashioned revolving polyhedral mirror. Our independent variables include such semiphantoms as psychiatric diagnosis (a classification scheme arrived at by majority vote of a committee of the American Psychiatric Association) and "anxiety" as "induced" under sterile laboratory conditions. With such marked validity attenuation between our constructs and the means by which we operationally measure them, the 5 per cent level comes to be viewed as the top of a virtually sheer rock face which must somehow be climbed. It is understandable that when success is achieved under these most difficult circumstances, the correct interpretation of significance may be cognitively dissonant and never reach consciousness and, instead, may be interpreted as large magnitude.

There are circumstances where the reality principle so obtrudes as to inhibit this error. One readily identifiable class of these occurs when the relationship between independent and dependent variables (or simply two variables of equal status), i.e., the experimental effect, is indexed by the familiar product-moment correlation coefficient r. This is *first* found and *then* tested for significance. If it should prove significant, the actual value of r serves as a guide to the magnitude of the effect or degree of relationship, and if small, it will tend to preclude the usual misinterpretation of significance. Thus, with 42 cases an r of .30 is (barely) significant at the two-sided 5 per cent level, and even if the investigator fails to think of it as representing only .09 (i.e., $.30^2$) of the variance shared by the two variables, the .30 value itself is small enough to restrain him from overinterpreting the order of magnitude of the effect.

Thus, if the experimental design "naturally" yields a correlation coefficient, misinterpretation of significance is more likely to be avoided. But more often than not, research issues are carried by differences between or among means. The units in which we measure our dependent variables are not only arbitrary but also without absolute meaning, not at all like inches or pounds or degrees Fahrenheit, which we have all experienced in many contexts. They are also frequently *ad hoc,* with lives that do not extend over more than one or a few experiments. How much is a difference of 13.6 points on Professor A's Regression in the Service of the Ego (RISE) scale, or a difference of .07 on Professor B's Distress Ratio as scored from spontaneous speech? Or, to use nonfictitious variables, how large is a mean difference of 4.7 on the MMPI depression scale, or a mean difference of 1.4 in Rorschach originals? With by far most of our variables, we do not have any ready conception of how large a point or a unit is, which again invites recourse to the significance test as arbiter of the decision of the effect's magnitude.

Consider the following: Smith studies the relationship between scores on the RISE scale and ratings by supervisors of creativity for a sample of 60 research chemists by finding $r = .38$, which he tests by the t test, and finds $t = 3.13$, significant at the two-tailed .01 level. Jones, at another university, studies the same problem by selecting high and low halves of the RISE scores among *his* sample of 60 research chemists and finding their creativity rating means. Let us assume that he finds the high RISE group's mean to be 5.1 and the low RISE group's mean to be 4.4 and that the resulting t of 2.67 is significant at the two-tailed .01 level. Smith and Jones have studied the same problem using the same variables, but Smith, since he has an r to refer to, knows the size of the effect; i.e., he knows that the RISE score accounts (linearly) for about 14 per cent ($.38^2$) of the variance in creativity ratings in the sample, and he also knows that it is very unlikely that in the hypothetical population there is no relationship. He can also, by well-known methods (Edwards, 1960, pp. 78–82; McNemar, 1962, p. 139), set confidence limits on the population value of r. Jones knows, with Smith, that it is very unlikely that there is no relationship in the population, but he has only the difference between means of 4.4 and 5.1 on an *ad hoc* rating scale, very likely used for the first and last time in this investigation. How large *is* .7 of a point on this rating scale? The question may never even arise in his mind, or if it does, it is unlikely to be answered, at least not correctly. After all, the difference is "highly significant." In his discussion of the meaning of his findings, Jones is likely implicitly to overestimate the size of this effect; certainly he is more likely to do so than Smith is, with his $r = .38$, $r^2 = .14$ before him.

I am not advocating that all clinical research be so cast that it yields rs on continuous variables. Not all variables are conceptually continuous or measurable continuously, nor are the versatility and power of the analysis of variance and related methods to be so cavalierly abandoned. Nor need they be to achieve our aim.

Before a solution to this problem is suggested, further clarity might be achieved and the foundation prepared if the issues are generalized. Two kinds of pure numbers issue from our research. One kind is made up of numbers which reflect models used for statistical tests, which I shall call τ (tau, for test) values. These include t and F ratios, normal curve deviates, and χ^2. Since their information provides a basis for inference about the status of a null hypothesis in the population, they are functions not only of the magnitude of the effect in the sample but necessarily also of the size of the sample. Obviously, therefore, a small effect with large n and a large effect with small n may lead to identical levels of significance. Thus, τ values are ambiguous in regard to size of effect or degree of relationship, which, of course, they are not supposed to index.

The other kind of numbers reflect the relative size of the effect, the degree of relationship, or the proportion of variance or uncertainty for which we can account; these I shall call ρ (rho, for relationship) values. These include all varieties of correlation coefficients, correlation ratios, contingency coefficients, concordance coefficients, etc. These are sole and therefore unambiguous functions of the relative magnitude of the effect (or, equivalently, of the relationship) and do not depend upon the size of the sample on which they are determined.

In these terms, Jones has only a τ value ($t = 2.67$, $p < .01$), while Smith has both a ρ value ($r = .38$) and a τ value ($t = 3.13$, $p < .01$).

The principle being advocated here is that *routinely*, whenever a τ value is reported, the ρ value should also be reported. This restores symmetry in the demands of good practice in reporting psychological research, since this has always dictated that every ρ value be accompanied by the relevant τ value and its statistical significance. Present practice is invariably to report τ values, ρ values being reported only when the design happens to yield a correlation coefficient.

How to effectuate this principle? Any data which yield a τ value can also be made to yield a ρ value. Moreover, the ρ values are standard, well-known coefficients, although they may be the kind which the statistics instructor did not cover in his lectures or which were forgotten because they were presented in a way which suggested that they were somehow special or rarely used (true, unfortunately).

For example, *any* set of data which yields a t test of the difference between means can be made to yield a point biserial correlation coefficient (r_{pb}), i.e., a ρ value. Consider again the Smith-Jones situation. Jones can find the r_{pb} between membership in the high versus low RISE group and creativity rating and report it as the relevant ρ value, making his results as unambiguous and interpretable as Smith's. (If Jones prefers to consider the RISE construct to be continuously and more or less normally distributed, he can instead report the biserial correlation coefficient r_b between

RISE and creativity rating.) Then, with such a ρ value before him, he is less likely to misinterpret his t test, at least no more likely than Smith is.

This does not require a prodigious amount of additional calculation. It is demonstrable that for any such t ratio, the following simple formula applies:

$$r_{pb} = \sqrt{\frac{t^2}{t^2 + df}} \qquad (1)$$

where df is degrees of freedom for the t test, i.e., total sample $n - 2$.

r_{pb}, the point biserial correlation coefficient, is one of those "special" correlation coefficients. It is the familiar product-moment r applied to the case where one variable (group membership) is two-valued and the other variable is continuous. If one were to give membership in the high group one score (say, 1) and membership in the low group another score (say, 0) and if one were then to use any of the familiar computing formulas for r, one would get the value r_{pb} yields; thus, it is simply a shortcut formula for r for the case in which it is applied and not really special at all. If r_b is wanted, it is readily obtainable from r_{pb}, the *n*s of the two samples, and a table of the normal curve (Guilford, 1956, p. 304).

r_{pb} is from an experimentally important point of view more general than r or r_b in that the two-valued variable need not be segments of a continuous distribution, but literally a "point" distribution, such as schizophrenic-normal, male-female, or married-single. This is what makes its use appropriate whenever a t test between independent means is found. It is the correlation between the continuous variable and *group membership,* no matter how the groups are constituted. If the groups result from a cut in a continuous distribution, it still gives the relationship with group membership, which will then underestimate the relationship with the underlying score which formed the basis for grouping. This is the case where, if normality is not an unreasonable assumption for the dichotomized variable, the r_b can be used to estimate the correlation with the underlying score.

Given any t test between means, the r_{pb}, and hence a ρ value, is only a few minutes away. By way of example, returning to Jones, if he substitutes $t = 2.67$ with $df = 58$ in the formula, he finds

$$r_{pb} = \sqrt{\frac{2.67^2}{2.67^2 + 58}} = .33$$

and has a ρ value to work with. It is the correlation with group membership, which is a cruder measure of the latent continuum underlying RISE than the actual scores would be. If this latent continuum is taken as approximately normal, he can estimate the correlation of ratings with this continuum by finding r_b, which is here .41. (Incidentally, if the high and low groups on RISE were constituted by omitting average subjects, say, the middle third or half of the distribution, the r_{pb} and not the r_b would be the appropriate value, since r_b computed in this instance would overestimate the correlation with the latent continuum; such high-low distributions are more like point distributions than continuums.)

Finally, although the example involved independent means, Eq. (1) can also be used for dependent means with the appropriately computed t and df (McNemar, 1962, pp. 101–102). Under these conditions, the resulting coefficient represents the correlation between group membership and the continuous dependent variable with individual differences (variability from pair to pair) partialed out.

With the principle illustrated, other translations of τ values to ρ values can be quickly described. What happens when there are more than two means or, more generally, when the design results in an analysis of variance (or covariance) and the τ value is an F ratio? Another "special" kind of correlation coefficient, the η (eta) coefficient or *correlation ratio,* serves as the value and bears the same relationship to F that r_{pb} bears to t. η^2 is the proportion of the total sum of squares of the dependent variable (Y) that is associated with independent variable (X) group membership, hence the "between groups" sum of squares. η^2 can equally be interpreted as the proportion of total Y variance which is predictable from the Y means of the various X groups or as the proportionate amount by which prediction of Y scores is improved when one has knowledge of the Y means of the various X groups. η, itself, is an index of correlation whose limits are zero and one and is analogous to r, except that it describes any form of relationship involving a continuous dependent variable, while r indexes linear relationship between two continuous variables.

In the treatments of η which one encounters in our statistics textbooks, the case where X is a continuous variable is usually stressed, and η is presented in reference to curvilinear correlation between two continuous variables where X has been broken into class interval groups. As useful as this application is, it is a special case; more generally, the X groups need not be segments along a continuous variable but can constitute any kind of scale, including a purely nominal one. This brings it into alignment with the analysis of variance situation where means on Y are contrasted. η provides the ρ value to accompany the τ value provided by F. Again, the translation of an F ratio to η is simple:

$$\eta = \sqrt{\frac{df_b F}{df_b F + df_w}} \tag{2}$$

where df_b is the number of degrees of freedom associated with the numerator of the F ratio, and df_w is the number of degrees of freedom associated with the denominator of the F ratio.

It must again be stressed that *any* source of variation which yields an F ratio can equally yield η as an index of "how much" relationship there is between this source and the dependent variable, other nonerror sources of variation being partialed out, or η^2 as the proportion of the relevant sum of squares for which this source accounts.

As an example, in a recent investigation of attitudes toward the mentally ill of various occupational groups in two hospitals (Cohen & Struening, 1962), F ratios based on 9 and 500 to 600 df were found in the case of most of the attitude factor scales to be highly significant, generally far higher than required by the most stringent significance criterion available in published tables ($F = 3.16$ at the 0.1 per cent level). These F ratios varied up to as high as 41.1, which meant that the authors could conclude with confidence ranging from high to very, very, very, *very* high, depending upon hospital and scale, that the hypothetical population means of the occupational groups in fact differed! I submit that one is less interested in counting the "very's" in the authors' confidence than in knowing the degree of relationship between occupational-group membership and attitude; the η values ranged here from .21 and .23 for belief in interpersonal etiology of mental illness to .65 and .50 for authoritarian attitude toward the mentally ill.

Incidentally, the similarity of form of Eqs. (1) and (2) is no accident; Eq. (1) is actually a special form of Eq. (2), since F for one numerator df equals t^2. Thus Eq. (2) reduces to Eq. (1) in the case where there are two groups. It therefore also follows in this case that $r_{pb} \equiv \eta$.

It should also be pointed out that the expected value of η computed from a sample is larger than the population η value, in a way directly analogous to that of multiple R. A "shrunken" (or unbiased) value of η is provided by

$$\epsilon = \sqrt{\frac{df_b (F - 1)}{df_b F + df_w}} \tag{3}$$

Thus, when there is no relationship in the population, the expected F value equals unity, and ϵ (epsilon) equals zero, while η would have a nonzero value depending on the df. (When F is less than unity, the value under the radical is negative, but ϵ is taken as zero, since in the usual analysis of variance model, such a value of F would result only as a chance departure from a zero or small effect size.) For a more extended discussion of η, the reader is referred to Diamond (1959) and McNemar (1960); and for both η and ϵ, to Peters and Van Voorhis (1940).

One final τ statistic will be considered, χ^2 when used in contingency tests with frequencies. This is the case where X and Y are treated as categorical either because one or both of them are nominal scales or for reasons of convenience. In general, the appropriate ρ statistic is the coefficient of mean square contingency C. It, too, is a simple function of its τ statistic χ^2:

$$C = \sqrt{\frac{\chi^2}{\chi^2 + n}} \tag{4}$$

where n is the sample size.

C is not part of the product-moment r family (except under highly restricted circumstances) and has a maximum possible value which is a function of the numbers of rows and columns in the table and which does not quite reach 1.00. These deficiencies notwithstanding, it is a serviceable index of degree of relationship, where other than 2×2 frequency tables are being assessed. In the latter case, one would normally prefer for the ρ statistic the available product-moment coefficient ϕ, which can also be written as a function of χ^2:

$$\phi = \sqrt{\frac{\chi^2}{n}} \tag{5}$$

Again, ϕ is nothing but a shortcut formula for the product moment r which one would get with the usual formula applied to two variables each scored 0 and 1.

The principle discussed here can be extended to other statistical models, including the nonparametric. For example, where the τ statistic is the Friedman χ_r^2 (Siegel, 1956, pp. 166–172), the relevant ρ statistic is Kendall's coefficient of concordance W (Siegel, 1956, pp. 229–238).

When one becomes accustomed to working and thinking in terms of ρ values, a frequently occurring problem in data interpretation becomes clarified and soluble. Currently, when an investigator finds two τ statistics in two experiments, for example, two F ratios, and the substantive nature of the research demands that these two results be compared, he is likely to flounder. The comparison is likely to take the form of comparing the degrees of significance of the two F ratios and concluding that they are "about the same" or that one is "more statistically significant" than the other. He may be satisfied with this, or, with some statistical insight, he may ask himself whether it is "statistically more statistically significant" than the other. This question is as meaningless statistically as it is awkward verbally. If the two p values differ at all, it literally means that he can reject one null hypothesis with less risk than he can the other, and there is no meaning to be attached to the statistical significance of the difference in his respective risks.

However, what is actually intended is *not* a comparison of the p values at all, but rather of the magnitudes of the relationships, i.e., of the two relevant ρ values; in the present instance, what is required is a test of the null hypothesis that the two population η (or ϵ) values are equal. This is readily available, since the standard erros of η for large samples (σ_n) is approximated by $1 - \eta^2\sqrt{n}$, and the usual normal curve test for independent statistics can be performed:

$$z = \frac{\eta_1 - \eta_2}{\sqrt{\sigma_{\eta 1}{}^2 + \sigma_{\eta 2}{}^2}} \tag{6}$$

Similar procedures can be followed for other ρ statistics.

In summary, an investigator who finds and reports only τ values and/or their significance levels seriously risks misleading himself and his readers. We have seen that the relevant ρ values are easily conceived and even more easily computed and substantially reduce this risk. Further, ρ values can be meaningfully compared statistically, while the p values associated with τs cannot. It is strongly recommended that relevant ρ values be *routinely* reported when τ values or their significance levels are reported. When the ρ values are not given, enough information is usually reported so that, armed with the formulas presented above, the sophisticated consumer can readily determine them for himself.

HOW MANY TAILS HATH THE BEAST?

For simplicity and clarity of exposition, and perhaps to provide a pinch of dramatic tension, I shall initially review the issues of one-tailed versus two-tailed tests in terms of two protagonists, using an example involving a difference between means. Generalization will come later.

Drs. One and Two, unknown to each other, organize exactly the same experiment bearing on the same theoretical issue and involving the status of the difference between population means m_A and m_B based on samples of 100 cases. Both use the 5 per cent α criterion. Having taken the same theoretical route, both strongly expect that m_A is larger than m_B.

Dr. Two, in his preliminary thinking, reasons as follows: "If the null hypothesis is true, then I will be taking a long-run 5 per cent risk of mistakenly rejecting it if I follow the rule of rejecting it when t is *absolutely* equal to, or larger than, 1.97, since in this case, 2½ per cent of the time $\bar{A}$ (the mean of the A sample) will be that much larger than $\bar{B}$, and another 2½ per cent of the time $\bar{B}$ will be that much larger than $\bar{A}$." Thus, his null hypothesis is that $m_A - m_B = 0$, and the alternative hypothesis is that $m_A - m_B \neq 0$; he is guarding against mistaken null rejections by allowing for the 5 per cent possibility of sampling errors in either direction. His test is nondirectional, which, when t or a normal curve deviate (z) test is used, means that he is distributing his risk equally in the two tails of the sampling distribution which would obtain if the null hypothesis were true. Thus it is a two-tailed test.

Dr. One reasons differently: "If the null hypothesis is true, then I will be taking a long-run 5 per cent risk of mistakenly rejecting it if I follow the rule of rejecting it when t has been formed with $\bar{A} - \bar{B}$ in the numerator and turns out to be greater than +1.65, since if the null is true, 5 per cent of the time $\bar{A}$ will be that much larger than $\bar{B}$. It is of course possible, if the null hypothesis is true, to find that $\bar{B}$ is larger than $\bar{A}$, but if my data turn out that way, I will not reject the null hypothesis; hence I run no risk of that kind of error and can reserve my 5 per cent risk for the $\bar{A}$ greater than $\bar{B}$ case." Thus, his null hypothesis is actually that $m_A - m_B \leq 0$, and his alternative hypothesis is $m_A - m_B > 0$. Note that by guarding against risks of mistaken null rejection in only one direction, both his alternative hypothesis *and* his null hypothesis have changed. If when Dr. One runs his experiment he finds a t value algebraically smaller than +1.65, the null hypothesis which he sustains includes the possibility that m_B is larger than m_A as well as their equality. His test cannot result in the conclusion that m_B is larger than m_A, only the reverse, as stated in his alternative hypothesis. His statistical test is directional, which for test statistics that can take on negative values (t or z) involves putting his risk on only one end of the sampling distribution. Thus it is a one-tailed test.

Now, if the sample means differ in the anticipated direction, Dr. One needs a smaller discrepancy ($t = 1.65$) than Dr. Two ($t = 1.97$) to reject the null at the "same" 5 per cent level of significance.

They run their experiments. Both find $\bar{A}$ larger than $\bar{B}$, and, since we are more concerned about the statistics than the dramaturgy (or melodramaturgy), they obtain identical t value of +1.80. Dr. One writes up his significant results exultantly, Dr. Two writes up his negative results diffidently, and the two reports arrive in the same mail at the office of a journal editor. (Were this not a parable, Dr. Two would likely not have bothered.) The busy editor is struck by the coincidence, accepts Dr. One's manuscript for publication, and returns Dr. Two's with a kind letter mentioning Dr. One's paper and the funny coincidence. (My apologies to some journal editors who would have followed a more constructive course, such as offering joint publication, but that would spoil the story.) To infuse our cardboard characters with some life, let us assume that Dr. Two's depression is relieved by the fury he experiences upon the receipt of the editor's letter.

A few weeks later at the annual APA convention, Dr. Two, still smoldering, tracks Dr. One down and introduces himself, and the following dialogue ensues in a hotel lobby, heard by an artificial potted fern:

DR. TWO: It strikes me, quite impersonally and, mind you, solely from the point of view of research craftsmanship, that one-tailed tests imply a kind of shoddiness, a debasing of the research coin—at worst, a form of cheating in one's game with nature. As far as I'm concerned, you were really operating at the 10 per cent level and calling it 5 per cent. Your results couldn't be any more significant than mine—after all, they were identical!

DR. ONE: I refuse to be put on the defensive. You don't know the distinction between a research and an inquiry, between just "finding-out" and "finding-out-if-a-hypothesis-is-consistent-with-fact," such as Marks (1951) and Jones (1952) make. My experiment and yours were for the purpose of finding out whether m_A was larger than m_B, as theory suggested, not merely whether they differed. I wasn't using a more *lenient* test; you were using the *wrong* test for your purpose. My long-run α risk was 5 per cent, the same as yours, but you were wasting half of yours in a direction which is meaningless from theory. See Kimmel (1957)! Furthermore, with this same α risk, the power of my test was greater than yours. For example (*hastily referring to some notes*), if m_A is .25 σ larger than m_B, you had only a .42 chance of rejecting your null, while I had a .56 chance of rejecting mine; if m_A is .5 σ larger than m_B, my power was .97, yours only .93. You got what you deserved—nonsignificance—because you asked the wrong question, and you're acting out your pique by calling me a charlatan.

Dr. Two surely got the worst of *that*. He vaguely remembers reading somewhere that two-tailed tests are generally better (probably Burke, 1953b; Burke, 1954) or that one-tailed tests could create problems in interpretation (Goldfried, 1959), but he cannot remember the details. What bothers him most is a sense of injured virtue. He cannot get over the feeling that Dr. One is trading research integrity for statistical sophistry, and since they performed the same operations and got the same results, their results must mean the same thing, regardless of the statistical flimflam with which they are embroidered.

And he is right! (My inexperience as a playwright has resulted in my losing control of the drama, so I shall revert to a more familiar form and simply intervene in Dr. Two's behalf.) It must first be said that Dr. One is correct in every particular in his statistical argument; the risks and power are as he describes them. Yet, in my judgment, the research philosophy and experimental strategy implicit in his argument are of dubious validity for psychology in its current state of development, and even more so for clinical psychology. Two sets of considerations lead me to this position.

First, I would join Burke in his distinction between private judgments from experimental results and the public status of these results (1954). Their theory may lead Drs. One and Two to expect that m_A is greater than m_B, and *both* of them may privately consider that they risk no more than 5 per cent when they so conclude from a t of $+1.80$, since their shared theory (belief) rules out m_B greater than m_A as "impossible" or theoretically meaningless. Furthermore, this private conclusion may serve as a basis for further research from which other such private conclusions may follow. But, to quote Burke: "Experimental scientists must have for data a permanent respect that transcends their passing interest in the stories they make up about their data" (1954, p. 587), and, I would add, a respect that transcends the stories they can tell about how they came to do the experiment, which they call "theories." Once a research is to be communicated, its results go into the scientific public domain and have a standing that is quite independent of the reasons for their collection or the meanings which their collectors ascribe to them, no matter how enriching the latter may be to the "understanding" of the results. But this is precisely the distinction which Dr. One loses when he permits his theory to dictate that he is not interested in the left-tail risk. *He* is not interested, and that is *his* business. But his results should have the same status whether his reader next month or ten years hence shares his theory, entertains another which predicts that m_B is larger than m_A, or entertains still another which would predict their equality. Kimmel advocates the use of one-tailed tests when "results in the opposite direction are not deducible from coexisting psychological theory" (1957, p. 353). But facts in the sense of research results, no matter how trivial or irrelevant from the purview of some later theory, are nevertheless timeless, even when probabilistic. In this public sense, then, Dr. One (like Dr. Two) has found significance at the 10 per cent level, but (also, indeed, like Dr. Two) he can import prior or subjective probability considerations and privately conclude at the 5 per cent level. This strikes me as eminently reasonable, as it satisfies Dr. Two's (and my own) intuitive demand that having done the same thing and found the same thing, the two men should conclude the same thing!

Another, even more compelling consideration puts me on the two-tailed side of this controversy. Dr. One's argument presupposed that he would find $\bar{A}$ larger than $\bar{B}$ or, if smaller, only slightly so. Dr. Two, imprisoned in the same theory as Dr. One, shared this assumption. Had he conceived the possibility of the "impossible," namely, that $\bar{B}$ would turn out to be so much larger than $\bar{A}$ that a large *negative t* would result, and pursued the consequences thereof, he might not have been left floundering in the dialogue. Consider what happens if, say, $t = -5$. Dr. Two can simply conclude that m_B is larger than m_A. He will reconsider his theory in the light of this unexpected result and possibly offer another. But what happens to Dr. One in this eventuality?

The statistically proper conclusion, of which Dr. One presumably is fully aware since he talks so knowledgeably about research philosophy and power and all, is that his results do not warrant the conclusion that m_A is larger than m_B; indeed, he draws this same conclusion whether $t = -5$ or $-.5$ or $+.5$! This statistically impeccable conclusion which is demanded by the logic of one-tailed tests is experimentally irresponsible! How can he treat such a result as meaning nothing different from a t near zero? Indeed, it is from a broader statistical viewpoint equally irresponsible, since if the population means were in fact equal, the probability of such a result would be of the order of .0000001! But this broader statistical viewpoint is, in fact, the two-tailed strategy, and his one-tailed commitment bars its use.

The chances are pretty good that Dr. One will not let this t of -5 pass by without some comment that at least suggests that m_B is larger than m_A. After all, he is a psychologist, not a digital computer, and although I have carefully refrained from concretizing the nature of A and B and the psychological issue involved, Dr. One will certainly be strongly engaged by the evidence that m_B is larger than m_A and what it might mean to theory, and he will, in his "discussion" section, so conclude. I would not have it otherwise.

So he has broken the statistical rules of one-tailed tests. But this is not a case for the committee on ethics of the American Psychological Association or even of the American Statistical Association (if it has one). But a little thought will reveal that Dr. One *never was* operating on a one-tailed basis, after all.

To simplify the argument, let us agree on a degree of tolerance for unexpected results, or negative t values for one-tailers. I suggest, on the basis of experience, that a modal value would be the t value at the lower 2½ per cent point, i.e., the value of t which would have been dictated as a criterion by a two-tailed 5 percent α risk, here -1.97. Now, recall the nature of the α level. It is the long-run rate of mistakenly rejecting null hypotheses. But if Dr. One and his ilk not only will reject when t falls in the upper 5 per cent tail but also will (at least implicitly) conclude that m_B exceeds m_A when t falls in the lower 2½ per cent tail, then they are operating at a long-run α risk of 7½ per cent. Notice that this is true *whatever* the actual value of t might prove to be in the specific experiment being considered. Once the readiness is there to accept negative ts more extreme than -1.97 as a basis for positive conclusions, they were *never* operating at the 5 per cent level, after all, but at the 7½ per cent level. And so well greased are the skids to perdition, that the one-tailer may not be able to resist the temptation to draw positive conclusions from lower 5 per cent tail values (-1.65 or less in our example), and he is in fact then operating at the 10 per cent level!

I repeat that the one-tailed procedure is statistically valid. The researcher who really does not need to distinguish $m_B > m_A$ from $m_A = m_B$ so that they together comprise the null hypothesis can test $m_A > m_B$ as an alternative hypothesis and validly go his one-tailed way. He must renounce all interest in $\bar{B} > \bar{A}$ results of any magnitude. I acknowledge some very rare instances of this kind in psychology. It is frequently said that in applied psychology such instances occur; e.g., is the new treatment method A better than the old method B? One hears it argued that as long as B is not worse than A, no decision for change to A is warranted, and therefore the case of B's superiority to A need not be distinguished from that of equality. Perhaps. But if our applied psychologist remains true to his scientific heritage, whether it will affect the immediate decision he must make or not, he will want to be able to *know* the fact, if it is a fact, that B is superior to A; this should mean something quite different from their equality. In short, he too should be operating on a two-tailed basis.

Yet another kind of inferential logic is possible. Let us introduce into our aborted drama a new character, a sort of cousin to Dr. One, Dr. One-and-a-Quarter. He offers us a kind of middle position between our protagonists: "Look, fellows. Nobody wants to be in the position of having to ignore ts of -5, or working at the actual 7½ per cent level when you claim 5 per cent. I work at the 5 per cent level and am not embarrassed by large negative ts, and my power is almost as large as Dr. One's. I accomplish this simply by not putting my 5 per cent all in one tail, but also by not dividing it equally: I put 4 per cent in the predicted tail and 1 per cent in the other. So in the experiment you ran, I would reject with ts greater than $+1.76$ and less than -2.35. I would have called your t of $+1.80$ significant at my 5 per cent level, doing a 1¼-tailed test."

Again, one cannot quarrel with the statistics. I repeat the point about the distinction between the experimenter's belief and the status of findings in the public domain. Dr. One may find this reasoning acceptable, since his reasoning allows him to import into his statistical inference considerations of prior or subjective probability. The position advocated here would no more permit a 4:1 distribution of the α rate than a 5:0 distribution. Thus, this solution largely meets the second objection (large negative ts), but not the first. I might here raise a question I suppressed earlier: With all due deference to their originators, what is the scientific status of the theories in clinical psychology from which one-tailers draw their directional hypotheses? Merely to raise the question is virtually to answer it. Playing the hypothetico-deductive game with verbal counters is a necessary feature of our still primitive state of development. It provides us with ideas (which we call "hypotheses") which in turn lead us to make observations which lead to factual conclusions. (Indeed, it is by no means unheard of for a clinical investigator to plan a research first and *then* contrive a "theory" or "hypothesis" *post hoc* and *ad hoc!*) Only if these conclusions are interesting is the process which led up to them of value. It therefore strikes me as singularly wrongheaded to make our "theories," with their directional "predictions," dictate these factual conclusions, which is what one-tailed and 1¼-tailed tests amount to. The reader can make his own estimate of the frequency among (two-tailed) significant results of unanticipated ones; when I feel depressed, I figure it for about one in five. And I find researchers quite able to account for these unanticipated results when they occur, sometimes more convincingly than for their original anticipations.

There are some loose ends to be tied. First, our example was concerned with a difference between means. Obviously, our conclusions would hold for the difference between samples with regard to any other statistic. They would also hold for a test of the hypothesis that a population correlation coefficient is zero, since the departure from the null hypothesis can occur in either direction.

The terms "two-tailed" and "two-sided" can engender confusion, since they are tied to the symmetrical statistical functions of the normal curve and *t*, where the expected value is zero. When an investigator performs the usual χ^2 text of the equality of relative incidence of some characteristic between A and B groups and refers his χ^2 (with one *df*) value to the standard table, he is doing a *non*directional test, even though he refers to the upper tail of the χ^2 distribution. The lower tail here, i.e., near-zero χ^2 values, results from near-zero sample differences, which are, of course, rare but which do not lead to rejection of the null hypothesis. The upper tail of the χ^2 distribution represents departures from the null of both the A > B and the A < B variety; the test is thus literally one-tailed, but nondirectional. The incorrigible "one-tailer" in the previously used sense, to realize his purpose here, should halve the tabled p values he reads from the table: his 5 per cent test criterion is read off at the tabled $p = .10$ point as 2.706. Of course, again, he should do this *only* if the difference is as predicted; if the difference is in the direction opposite to prediction, the χ^2 value, no matter how high, is not significant. (The "1¼-tailer" at the 5 per cent level would call "significant" predicted differences yielding χ^2 values greater than 3.065 and nonpredicted differences yielding values greater than 5.412.) That these relationships hold can be readily seen if one recalls that the one *df* χ^2 function equals z^2 (the square of the normal curve deviate). Thus, the square of the normal curve *two*-tailed 5 per cent point (1.96^2) equals the upper-tailed 5 per cent point of the one *df* χ^2 distribution (3.841).

The same holds for the *F* distribution. It, too, is computed so that differences (for one numerator *df*) in both directions are reflected in the upper tail. Analogously, the one-tailer's intent would demand halving the tabled p values. Again this can be seen from the relationship $F = t^2$ for the same number of error *df*.

The problem becomes more complicated when k (more than two) samples are being compared, either by F or χ^2 tests. While two means can be ordered in only two ways, k means can be ordered in $k!$ ways, k (k-1) (k-2) . . . (2) (1). The man who predicts the order of four means is entitled on statistical grounds to divide a tabled p value by $4! = 24$, *if* the outcome is as predicted and "one-tailed" thinking prevails. However, with these ground rules, any departure from the predicted order renders his results nonsignificant no matter what the size of *F*. A much better procedure in general would be to devote one of his three *df* for "between groups" to a test of the linear component of the predicted trend (Edwards, 1960; McNemar, 1962). This is a less stringent hypothesis, since it permits departures from the exact anticipated order, but the statistical test is accordingly more powerful against the class of alternatives that would likely be meaningful in the context of the research hypothesis.

In 1954, Burke wrote: "Once they have the assurance of the mathematical statistician that the procedure is logically defensible, experimenters seem so eager to employ one-tailed tests that, sociologically speaking, I have lost the argument almost before it has been joined" (p. 590). Things are not as bad as he foretold, partially because of an unforeseeable development. We have seen that the F test as routinely applied is nondirectional, i.e., "two-tailed," in Burke's context. The rapidly increased popularity of the analysis of variance which results in automatically nondirectional F tests has served to preserve experimental virtue. It is ironic.

I conclude with Burke's advice: "We counsel anyone who contemplates a one-tailed test to ask of himself (before the data are gathered): 'If my results are in the wrong direction and significant at the one-billionth of 1 per cent level, can I publicly defend the proposition that this is evidence of no difference?' If the answer is affirmative, we shall not impugn his accuracy in choosing a one-tailed test. We may, however, question his scientific wisdom" (1953b, pp. 386–387).

NONPARAMETRIC, NONPANACEA

It is not immediately clear to whom one should turn for an explanation of the *succès fou* which nonparametric statistics have had in psychology over the last decade. Whether such a diagnosis is best made by a mathematical statistician on the one hand or by a social or clinical psychologist on the other, I shall leave to the reader to judge. Certainly, each can put forth a diagnostic claim.

The chief protagonists of these methods naturally offer primarily statistical reasons for them to be preferred in many (possibly most) situations which the psychologist encounters in the analysis of research data. The psychological nonparametricists would look upon the popularity of these methods as a simple consequence of their frequent superiority to parametric procedures. This section will be largely concerned with a review of these claims.

A sociopsychological diagnosis might depend on some such explanatory construct as "faddism." Thus, McNemar uses the phrases "keep up with the Joneses" and "an urge to be up-to-date" in his assessment (1960, pp. 297, 298). I am reminded that some years ago, a fellow graduate student planned (and executed) a doctoral research in psychosomatic personality based on samples of only 20 cases because of the added luster which would be lent to his research by the use of "small-sample" statistics, then coming into widespread use in psychology! It *did* add luster, not only for his fellow graduate students, but for his doctoral committee as well. (It may come as no surprise to the reader that his results were negative. If it does, please refer to the first section of this chapter.)

But the clinical psychologist might claim that the reason for the prevalence of nonparametric statistics lies within *his* ken. He might argue somewhat as follows: Psychologists labor under a sense of inferiority in their claims for psychology as science vis-à-vis their colleagues in physics or chemistry. An unconscious doubt about the relevance of numbers to their substantive concerns may poison the wellsprings of their research behavior. One form this may take is a pervasive sense of guilt when they measure aspects of behavior in samples and draw inferences to populations. This burden of guilt may take the overt form of a syndrome which includes such defensive operation as worry about statistical assumptions and a search for precision. Symptomatic relief is apparently afforded by following the nonparametric banner—no assumptions, precise alpha probabilities. Can you visualize a conscientious psychologist trying to convince himself that, in the population made up of all artists of the past, present, and future (Da Vinci to Kandinsky to those yet unborn), the scores on a 20-item regression-in-the-service-of-the-ego scale are distributed according to

$$y = \frac{N}{\sigma\sqrt{2\pi}} c^{-x^2/2\sigma^2}$$

i.e., normally? Consider his anxiety level when he encounters such statements as "The conditions which must be satisfied . . . before any confidence can be placed in any probability statement obtained by the use of the t test [include:] . . . the observations must be drawn from normally distributed populations" (Siegel, 1956, p. 19). And consider his relief when he is told: "Probability statements obtained from most nonparametric tests are *exact* probabilities . . . regardless of the shape of the population distribution from which the sample was drawn" (Siegel, 1956, p. 32)!

Since, whatever their dynamics, psychologists are fundamentally rational (an article of faith I require as an axiom), the place of nonparametric statistics in the psychologist's methods kit will be determined by a careful assessment of their properties as tools of research inference. What is the present status of their claimed advantages and disadvantages in comparison with the parametric techniques?

Part of their claim arises out of an analysis of levels or scales of measurement and permissible statistical operations at each level, particularly the nominal-ordinal-interval-ratio-scale formulation of Stevens (1951). This measurement system has been used as a basis of organization of psychological statistics textbooks (e.g., Senders, 1958; Siegel, 1956) and, moreover, has been used proscriptively, in that the scale of measurement of the data is taken to dictate the appropriate statistical procedures for summarization, correlation, and inference to populations. There is an undeniable intuitive appeal to the proposition that not much meaning can be attached to the mean of a set of telephone numbers (nominal) or to the mean of a set of numbers that reflect measurement on an ordinal scale. One has only to draw a line on a sheet of paper, divide it into grossly unequal segments, and number the division points successively. If the resultant "crazy yardstick" is used to measure two sets of objects, their means may be equal, while the groups of objects differ substantially in mean true length, or, conversely, the means may differ greatly, while the sets of objects may be the same in mean true length. As presented, the problem boils down to that of adding quantities based on unequal units or intervals. Now not only means but variances and correlation coefficients require adding. The upshot of this is, among other things, that these authors proscribe the use of these statistics and their parametric inferential procedures (F and t tests) unless the data came about by measurement with equal-interval scales. Since relatively few psychologists (and even fewer clinical psychologists) working with relatively few dependent variables can confidently claim that the units of their scales are equal (but see below), the implication is clear that parametric tests are only infrequently appropriate. Since we are relatively confident in our ability to classify data and to rank them, the appropriate nonparametric techniques can be used without a qualm.

Looked at in this way, the argument seems impregnable. But it has been pointed out repeatedly that among the numerous and troublesome assumptions in the mathematical derivations of parametric methods, one does *not* find any assumptions with regard to the nature of the scale, equal-interval or otherwise. The mathematics is concerned with the properties of certain classes of numbers, and "*the numbers don't remember where they came from.*"

The quotation is from a delightful parable by Lord, "On the Statistical Treatment of Football Numbers" (1953), which illustrates the point brilliantly (and which should be savored in the original). What could be more devoid of arithmetic properties than the numbers worn on the uniforms of football players, Stevens's own example of a nominal scale (1951)? Lord tells the story of a Professor X, who professed psychometrics, loved numbers, and would guiltily and behind locked doors for hours on end compute means and standard deviations on test scores, guiltily because he taught his students that such scores were merely ordinal and could not be added. The guilt led finally to a nervous breakdown and retirement, and in appreciation of his devoted service, he was given the university's "football numbers" concession, with a large (100 quadrillion) supply of two-digit cloth numbers and a vending machine. He resisted the temptation to add them up, since they were not even ordinal numbers and were peculiarly distributed (over two quadrillion 69s and only six 68s), but merely shuffled them randomly and put them in the machine. The sophomores got their numbers the first week and the freshmen the second, and soon a scandal broke that the numbers in the vending machine had been tampered with, the freshmen claiming that the 1,600 numbers they had bought were too low. Alarmed, Professor X, hoping that this was a chance result, hastily consulted a statistician, who proceeded to compute means and standard deviations of the population and the freshman sample, computed a critical ratio of 10, and concluded that it was implausible that the freshmen's numbers were a random sample and that they were, in fact, too low. The statistician met Professor X's bewildered objections that the numbers were not even ordinal, were merely nominal, and could not be added, multiplied, etc., by pointing out to him that since "the numbers don't know that . . . they always behave the same way, regardless." He further advised the professor that if he doubted his conclusions, he should perform sampling experiments with his population. Professor X did so and found that these numbers obey "the same laws of sampling as they would if they were real honest-to-God cardinal [interval scale] numbers." Lord concludes his parable happily with Professor X cured of his neurosis and resuming teaching. "He will no longer lock his door when he computes the means and standard deviations of test scores" (1953, p. 751).

A more sober treatment of this issue by Burke leads him to conclude: "The statistical technique begins and ends with the numbers and with statements about them. The psychological interpretation given to the experiment does take cognizance of the origin of the numbers but this is irrelevant for the statistical test as such" (1953a, p. 74).

"Ah!" the nonparametricist-on-measurement-grounds (cf. Senders, 1953) may retort, "the point lies in the second sentence, where the issue of psychological interpretation arises. Unless what is true of the numbers is also true of the objects, we can make no psychological interpretation, which is, after all, our original purpose."

A full reply to this argument would take us into issues of philosophy of science and measurement far beyond the scope of this chapter. Briefly, I would point out that, at least at the present time, the question of "truly" equal units of measurement for most psychological *constructs* such as personality traits is meaningless. If we could assume that such a construct as neuroticism, if measured "truly," is distributed normally (or rectangularly, or any other specified way) in some given population, we could monotonically transform our observed measures to this shape, whereupon the units would be "truly" equal. Or, conversely, if we had a measure whose units were "truly" equal, we could discover the "true" distribution shape of the construct. We are caught in the kind of meaningless bind which the operationalists warn us about. Taking a leaf from their book, we must for the present accept the units in which we measure, be they items or seconds or errors, as equal by dint of the operations we performed to obtain them, and we must treat them, at least provisionally, as equal on the construct as operationally defined. When the same theoretical construct leads to alternative measures, we must be prepared for the eventuality that, with measure A taken as standard, measure B does not have equal units, and conversely. These conflicting claims should eventually be resolved in the crucible of theoreticoexperimental advance, perhaps by following Cattell's recent (1962) suggestions, a simple form of which would dictate that that scale is most nearly equal-interval which gives rise to a maximum sum of linear relationships (rs) with other variables. The main point is that the demonstrations that crazy yardsticks yield crazy results relative to real yardsticks are beside the point in the absence of "true" measures, which is our present condition. Until true measures exist, our conclusions must relate to the numbers our available measures yield, the numbers which "don't remember where they came from."

And what if we *had* equal-interval scales? Anderson (1961) demonstrated how two scales with interval properties, time and speed, could lead to quite different conclusions for the same experimental data. Thus, interval or even ratio level measurement offers no guarantee of invariance of conclusions; two groups may differ in mean time of performance but not in mean speed of performance, or conversely. Further, he showed how even an ordinal scale (with its modest measurement assumptions) that is a complex of two or more dimensions might prove not to have the desirable invariant properties on the underlying dimensions. From these and other considerations, Anderson concluded that "the type of measuring scale used [has] little relevance to the question of whether to use parametric or nonparametric statistics" (1961, p. 316).

Probably the most important claimed advantage of nonparametric procedures is the modesty of the assumptions they make about the population being sampled, relative to those of parametric methods. The terms "nonparametric" and "distribution-free" are both used in connection with the methods we are considering, but they are not identical either connotatively or denotatively. Methods of statistical inference are nonparametric if they do not involve the comparison or estimation of population values (parameters) as, for example, the t test involves a comparison of population means. Methods are distribution-free if they make no assumptions with regard to the shape of the population(s) being sampled. It is clearly the freedom from distribution assumptions which is attractive to the psychologist. Indeed, as we shall see, the comparison of entire distributions rather than specific parameters thereof is likely to be disadvantageous.

Freedom from distribution assumptions, then, is the positive claim for the advantage of these methods over the parametric methods. The latter, in this context, assume that populations are distributed normally and with equal variances. The nonparametric advocates (e.g., Moses, 1952; Senders, 1958; Siegel, 1956) either say or imply that the failure of the populations to meet these assumptions renders the parametric tests invalid. If assumption failure renders the parametric tests invalid and if such assumptions are not made by "distribution-free" tests, then since one can hardly ever know that these assumptions are met, the choice is obvious.

The first proposition is, to say the least, questionable. Starting at least some thirty-five years ago (Pearson, 1929; Pearson, 1931), evidence has been accumulating which long ago suggested that under most of the conditions encountered by psychologists that they would judge as constituting rather severe departure from parametric assumptions, the validity of t and F tests is hardly impaired. These conclusions have been reached on the basis of both analytic and empirical investigations. [Scheffé (1959) provides a detailed summary for the mathematically sophisticated.] In the psychological literature, evidence along these lines came much later, but its first appearance was over a decade ago in Lindquist's text (1953, pp. 78–90), where he summarized in considerable detail Norton's empirical study on the F test in the analysis of variance. Boneau's (1960) empirical study of the t test under assumption failure completed the picture for psychologists, or should have.

Several issues must be put in perspective for the following summary to be useful. First, the statistical test which concerns us is that between two (t) or more (F) means and, by extension, other functions of means such as interactions, trends, and regression components. Second, one aspect of the question of validity under assumption failure relates to the α level: What is the *actual* rate of false rejection of the null hypothesis when one uses the *nominal* (tabled) criterion; e.g., what proportion of t ratios exceeds the tabled 5 per cent criterion when the null hypothesis is true? If 1 per cent, the test is overconservative; if 25 per cent, the test is grossly overliberal, and this is the usual concern. Another aspect of validity concerns power under assumption failure: if, in fact, the null hypothesis is false, is the probability of rejecting it much different from what would obtain if the assumptions were met?

A review of both analytic and empirical work with regard to alpha validity of t and F tests under assumption failure (Boneau, 1960; Box, 1954a; Box, 1954b; Lindquist, 1953; Pearson, 1929; Pearson, 1931; Scheffé, 1959; Welch, 1937) yields the following conclusions:

1. The effect of nonnormality of the population being sampled is generally trivial. For example, in the Norton study, drawing three samples of three cases each from populations ranging from J-shaped to rectangular to extremely leptokurtic, the nominal 5 per cent F point gave actual levels from 4.8 to 7.8 per cent (Lindquist, 1953). As another example, Boneau's (1960) small samples from J-shaped and rectangular distributions yielded ts at the nominal two-tailed 5 per cent level at a rate running between 3.1 and 7.1 per cent. As still another example, quite extreme degrees of skewness and kurtosis in populations sampled with five groups of five cases each yielded F ratios on the means at the nominal 5 per cent level between 4.8 and 5.3 per cent (Scheffé, 1959, p. 350).

2. Sampling from populations having *different* shapes from each other also seems to have a practically negligible effect. Comparing small samples from J-shaped with normal and rectangular populations, Boneau (1960) found actual ts at the tabled two-tailed 5 per cent level to occur 5.1 to 7.1 per cent of the time. Norton computed F ratios on samples of three and six cases from each of three populations, of which two were markedly skewed in opposite directions and the third was symmetrical, and found 5 per cent F ratio rates of 6.7 and 6.8 per cent (Lindquist, 1953).

3. Provided that sample sizes are about the same, even extreme degrees of inequality of variance in the population have tolerably small effects on alpha validity. Scheffé (1959, p. 353) gives analytic results for the two-tailed t test with samples of seven cases indicating that with one population having *ten* times the variance of the other, the actual type I error rate at the nominal 5 per cent level is 7.0 per cent. Boneau (1960) found empirically that t tests under conditions of 4.1 population variance heterogeneity with small samples gave actual percentages of 4.9 and 6.4. Box (1954a) found analytically with samples of five cases drawn from three and five populations with

variance heterogeneity of 1:2:3, 1:1:3, and 1:1:1:1:3 actual ranges of 5.6 per cent, 5.9 per cent, and 7.4 per cent at the nominal 5 per cent level. In a companion article on the F ratio in two-way analysis of variance, using designs ranging from 3×11 to 11×3 with row population variance heterogeneity of the same order, Box (1954b) found actual F ratio rates at the nominal 5 per cent level to run from 5.5 to 7.1 per cent for the row test and from 3.8 to 4.9 per cent for the column test.

4. When both extreme shape and variance heterogeneity obtain in the populations, for very small samples the effects may be a bit more serious. Thus, drawing samples of three cases from each of four populations varying in shape from J-shaped to normal and such that the variance heterogeneity for the extremes was 1:46, Norton found 10.0 per cent of the Fs exceeding the nominal 5 per cent level. But with samples of 10 cases under the same extreme circumstances, the value dropped to 8.1 per cent (Lindquist, 1953).

5. The above results are all the more impressive in that they were found with small samples, usually of three to five cases, and never exceeding 15. Small as the distortions on type I error estimates were, they decline rapidly toward zero as samples increase because of the operation of the central limit theorem. We have earlier in this chapter seen that psychologists generally need to use samples of several times 15 for reasonable power to reject their null hypotheses. At the order of sample size with which we should be operating, we can virtually ignore the effect of violations of parametric assumptions on our alpha levels.

6. Note that there are two circumstances which qualify the above conclusions. In the presence of variance heterogeneity which is at all marked, inequality of sample sizes may produce fairly gross departures of actual from nominal type I error rates. For example (Scheffé, 1959, p. 353), with samples of 15 and 5 cases drawn respectively from populations having variances in 5:1 ratio, the actual rate of ts at the nominal 5 per cent is 0.8 per cent; if the variances are reversed, 18.0 per cent. As the variance ratio increases, the respective limits are 0.2 per cent and 32.0 per cent. For another extreme case, one-way analysis of variance F ratios from three normal populations with 1:1:3 ratio of population variances, sampled respectively with nine, five, and one cases, yield a 17.0 per cent rate at the nominal 5 per cent level, and with one, five, and nine cases, a 1.3 per cent rate (Box, 1954a). Nor are such distortions mitigated with increase in sample size, since they are a function of the ratio of sizes and not their absolute magnitude.

7. The other qualification is that the relatively good fit of actual to nominal type I error rates when populations of *different* skew are subjected to t test holds for *two-tailed*, but not one-tailed, ts, since such circumstances produce skewed t distributions. Chalk up yet another point against one-tailed tests!

So much for the alpha validity of parametric tests under assumption failure. What about beta validity; i.e., what happens to the power of these tests to detect differences in population means under nonnormal and/or heterogeneous variance conditions?

Although not as voluminous as for alpha validity, the evidence here (Boneau, 1962; Scheffé, 1959; Srivastava, 1958; Wetherill, 1960) clearly points in the same direction: The power of parametric tests is *not* materially affected by assumption failure, and, furthermore, it retains its superiority, in general, over that of nonparametric tests.

1. For example, from an analytic study of the power function of the t test with samples of from five to twenty from nonnormal population distributions, Srivastava concludes: "For practical purposes, the power of the t test is not seriously invalidated even if the samples are from considerably nonnormal populations" (1958, p. 428). Furthermore, he states: "With increase in sample size, the effect of nonnormality on the power of the t test diminishes" (p. 429).

2. Scheffé (1959, pp. 356-358) presents results from Horsnell's analytic study of the effect of the power of the F test when four populations having variances of 1:1:1:3 are sampled with differing patterns of sample size totaling 40 and with all means but one being equal. The power-function charts reveal the fact that when the sample sizes are equal (i.e., 10 in each group), there is virtually no departure from the theoretical (i.e., equal variance) power values when the discrepant mean is that of the low variance population. When the discrepant mean is that of the high variance population, the values agree closely up to power of .50 and then gradually diverge, the theoretical value being the higher, with a maximum discrepancy at high power values of

about .07. When the sample sizes are unequal, the distortion may occur at any power value but nowhere exceeds .09, generally being far smaller. Such discrepancies as do occur can occur in *either* direction; e.g., assumption failure may result in greater power. The reader is referred to the detailed material in Scheffé for a discussion of how to capitalize on this possibility, but in any case, we can conclude that the amount of distortion that assumption failure can produce on power estimates of F tests is quite tolerable. Scheffé recommends that sample sizes generally be kept equal when population variances are substantially heterogeneous (p. 358), which we have seen is also a prudent measure to take for the sake of alpha validity. Here, too, the use of larger sample sizes yields not only greater power but also closer approximations to the nominal power values.

The above material can be summarized by saying that F and t tests are *robust,* a term invented by Box (1953) to denote a statistical test which is not sensitive to the failure of its nuisance assumptions (e.g., normality and variance equality for F and t tests) but which *is* sensitive to the falsity of the null hypothesis it is used to test (equality of means, in this case). An ironically good example of a *non*-robust test is Bartlett's test for variance homogeneity, which is as sensitive to nonnormality as it is to variance heterogeneity (Box, 1953). In the light of what we have seen about the robustness of F and t tests, consider the folly of the practice of using them only if the Bartlett test is nonsignificant!

More specifically, it can be concluded that barring only (1) an extremeness of assumption failure which mathematicians can posit but which psychologists rarely encounter in real data and (2) the case of *simultaneous* substantial variance heterogeneity with substantial sample size inequality, F and two-tailed t tests are *functionally* distribution-free with regard to both alpha risk and power. The research psychologist need lose no sleep over their use despite possible heterogeneity of variance, nonnormality, or heterogeneity in shape of the populations sampled. His actual type I and type II error rates will depart minimally from what he looks up in the usual tables. At worst, he may need to exercise some prudence in avoiding the use of very small or very unequal sample sizes. As we saw earlier, he need not be inhibited about their use because of doubts about the equality of his measurement units.

Once this argument is accepted, much of the attraction of the nonparametric methods is lost. The nonparametric buff may try to retain part of his argument by pointing out that although under assumption failure the parametric alpha values may not change *much,* they are still not precise. "Probability statements obtained from most nonparametric statistical tests are *exact* probabilities (except in the case of large samples, where excellent approximations are available), regardless of the shape of the population distribution from which the random sample was drawn" (Siegel, 1956, p. 32).

I cannot resist beginning my rebuttal with a quotation from I. J. Good: "Statistics is not primarily for making objective statements, but rather for introducing as much objectivity as possible into our subjective judgments. It is only in limited circumstances that fully objective statements can be made, although the literature of theoretical statistics is mainly concerned with such circumstances. The notion that it must all be precise is harmful enough to be worth naming. I shall call it the 'precision fallacy'" (1958, p. 799). I might add that Good is a mathematical statistician, not a clinical psychologist.

With regard to the "excellent approximations" to the exact probabilities available in nonparametric methods for "large" samples, Kogan wryly points out how commonly the nonparametricists invoke "the remarkably rapid potency of the central limit theorem . . . when the N goes over 10 or 15" (1960, p. 209). This is, of course, the same central limit theorem which assures the robustness of the parametric tests with similarly "large" samples.

In this connection, too, Sawrey (1958) points out that approximate nonparametric tests may be in greater error than parametric tests. A good example of this is the Wilson nonparametric χ^2 analogue of factorial design analysis of variance (1956). Apart from its very poor power efficiency demonstrated empirically (McNemar, 1957), Ylvisaker (1960) additionally points out that, in general, the function is not distributed as χ^2, does not lead to valid (alpha error) tests, and may lead to arbitrarily low power independent of sample size! One therefore need not be shocked by Cochran's recommendation that F tests be used as an approximation in preference to χ^2 even when the data are ones and zeros (1950, p. 262)!

Now, finally, let us look more closely at the claim for the validity of nonparametric tests "regardless of the shape of the population distribution from which the random sample was drawn" (Siegel, 1956, p. 32). The truth of this statement depends on some very narrow definitions of terms. In any case, as it has come to be widely misinterpreted, it is at least misleading.

First of all, let me assume that our interest lies in testing for differences between or among means of populations or, more generally, for differences in "location," which we can take to mean central tendency. Other differences between populations, their spread, symmetry, peakedness, etc., I shall refer to by the all-inclusive term "shape." Now, shape differences between populations (unless they are specifically of interest, which we are not assuming) are simply nuisances which may get in the way of a valid test of location. The researcher usually reads "distribution-free" to mean that he can safely ignore possible shape differences in populations in performing a test on location. This is *not* what distribution-free means. The rank tests make the assumption that the populations being sampled are of *identical* shape; they are free only of the assumption that this shape is *normal.* They are more properly called "normal-free" than distribution-free (Lubin, 1962). The nonparametricist who intends to test for difference in location two or more populations which are at the same time different in variance and/or skewness and/or kurtosis and/or any other shape function is violating the assumption of the nonparametric method! If, and only if, the shapes are nonnormal but identical, it is better (but not much better) in the two-sample case to use the Wilcoxon (or its equivalent, the Mann-Whitney *U*) nonparametric ranks test to test for a location difference. But Wetherill goes on to point out that this fact "give[s] the impression, wrongly, as it turns out, that the Wilcoxon test may be less sensitive to other types of departure from assumption, such as differences in shape between the two populations" (1960, p. 404). Indeed, following a comparative analysis of the Wilcoxon and *t* tests under nonnormal conditions, he concludes that "the size and . . . power of the Wilcoxon test are much *more* sensitive to differences of shape in skewness and kurtosis than is the *t* test" (p. 416)! (Not only the exclamation point, but the italics, are mine, since mathematical statisticians rarely so indulge themselves.) Finally, he sums up: "The [two-sample] Wilcoxon test is not a test of medians or of means. It is a [very] little more robust than the *t* test to differences in population variance, but is much more sensitive to skewness and kurtosis than the *t* test" (p. 418).

Reporting recently in the psychological literature the result of an empirical comparison of the *t* test and the nonparametric Mann-Whitney *U* test based on ranks, Boneau comes to similar conclusions: "Somewhat surprising . . . is [the fact] that the *U* test is not truly distribution free. It is always sensitive to differences in distributions, and sometimes seems more affected by differences (other than mean differences) than is the *t* test" (1960, p. 256).

Although the evidence offered above concerns the two-sample case, it is a reasonable inference that it would also apply generally to the *k*-sample case, e.g., that the Kruskal-Wallis *H* test, the nonparametric analogue (using ranks) to a one-way analysis of variance *F* test, is not sensitive solely to location differences but to shape differences as well and is thus not distribution-free in the sense understood by the consumer.

Thus, *both* barrels of the nonparametric shotgun—invalidity of parametric tests under assumption failure and freedom from nuisance assumptions of nonparametric methods—are seen to be loaded with blanks. This statement is probably a little stronger than is strictly warranted; nevertheless, as a working proposition it is quite close to the truth.

There are still other problems attendant upon the choice of nonparametric over classical statistical methods as practical aids to the research psychologist in drawing useful conclusions from data.

From my point of view, the most important of these is the serious limitation in the kinds of research questions they can help answer. Nonparametric methods can (within their already noted limitations) validly test only simple issues about data: the presence of simple correlation or of differences in location, and little more. Thus, in experimental design terms, nonparametric methods do not usefully go beyond the unreplicated two-way (subjects × treatments) design. The versatility of factorial design, with its possibilities for studying interactions and for using factors for control purposes (e.g., experimenters, subject populations, order of treatment, etc.) is lacking (Anderson, 1961). Nonparametric analogues of the highly efficient analysis of covariance and of nested, Latin square, and partially confounded designs do not exist. When one leaves simple correlation and looks for nonparametric alternatives to factor analysis, multiple and partial regression analysis, and trend analysis, one is faced with a methodological desert with, here and there, a stunted clump of mesquite (e.g., partial tau, of unknown sampling distribution and hence without any valid means of testing significance).

Even in more modest experimental structures, nonparametric methods are deficient. If one does a simple one-way comparison of k samples for location differences and wants then to make pairwise or other linear contrasts (multiple comparisons), no generally accepted procedures are offered by nonparametric methods (Anderson, 1961; Gaito, 1959).

Another problem with nonparametric methods is their power relative to functionally comparable classical methods. It is known that under the usual parametric assumptions, parametric methods are more powerful than nonparametric methods for any given sample size, or, equivalently, the parametric method requires fewer cases to have power equal to the nonparametric method. (The randomization test is an exception but is computationally infeasible beyond very small samples.) The percentage of cases needed by the parametric method to have power equal to the analogous nonparametric method is called the "power efficiency" of the latter (Siegel, 1956, pp. 20–21).

Now, it is true that the figures given for power efficiency are computed under the assumptions that normality and equal variance conditions prevail and that mathematical statisticians can contrive conditions in which a given nonparametric method is more powerful than its parametric analogue. However, the available evidence (Boneau, 1962; Scheffé, 1959; Srivastava, 1958; Wetherill, 1960) suggests that with the types and degrees of assumption failure the psychologist is apt to encounter with real data, the parametric procedures retain their superiority in power. Moreover, their power functions are regular and well behaved, following their actual alpha rates. The boogeyman assumptions seem no more potent with regard to beta than with regard to alpha.

Following are the power efficiencies of the major nonparametric methods in the detection of medium to large mean differences, the ranges being from very small to very large samples:

1. Rank-sum tests (Mann-Whitney, Wilcoxon, Kruskal-Wallis, Friedman): 90 to 95 per cent. Boneau (1962) concludes from his empirical results under nonnormal unequal variance that in the long run the t test would result in about 5 per cent more rejections than the Mann-Whitney U. From the point of view of power efficiency, the tests based on ranks are tolerably efficient.

2. Sign and median tests: 95 to 62 per cent. For the range of size of mean difference, sample size, and alpha level which characterize most psychological research, one can expect power efficiency of the order of 65 to 70 per cent.

3. Run and Kolmogorov-Smirnov tests: less than 50 per cent. This is not surprising, since these tests are designed to test for *any* difference between two populations and are therefore weak for the specific difference (between means) which is here at issue.

Thus, the psychologist who with the usual difficulty has collected 100 cases and who chooses a nonparametric test may be throwing away from five to over fifty of them. I have shown earlier in this chapter that even with parametric methods, the sample sizes psychologists use are generally inadequate for their purpose. The injudicious use of nonparametric methods greatly exacerbates an already bad situation.

Boneau (1962) encountered an interesting bit of nonparametric pathology in the U test comparison of normal with skewed populations. The test showed a *reduction* in power as the population mean difference increased between 0 and .25 σ; that is, the test for a difference in means is biased. Tests based on ranks are sensitive to median differences, but in an asymmetric population, the mean and median do not coincide. Thus, two populations of opposite skewness with equal means will have unequal medians, and conversely. I doubt the value of shifting our habitual frame of reference for central tendency from the mean to the median to accommodate this peculiarity.

In this last point I come full circle to the concern of the first section of this chapter, where various strategies that took power into account were described. Under different sets of conditions, we saw that methods were available to estimate power, sample size, and detectable effect size. It was neither accident nor bias that resulted in that discussion's being limited to parametric tests. With the exception of χ^2, such methods are generally not available for nonparametric statistics. This, too, is no accident. Power is a function of the size of an effect, which is most directly indexed through differences among means or ratios between variances, i.e., parameters, and the awkwardness of assessing the ability of nonparametric tests to detect parametric differences is self-evident. The problem may not be insoluble, but it has proved sufficiently difficult for the mathematical statisticians that there is as yet no discernible yield from their labors in the form of routine methods of power analysis in statistical textbooks. This lack would be sufficient reason to avoid their routine use.

In the fire of advocacy, I may have left the impression that I find no use for nonparametric methods in psychological research. Such is not the case:

1. For χ^2 with nominal data, there *is* no parametric alternative.

2. When data come originally in the form of ranks, rank tests should be performed if they are available for the research design, rather than routinely assuming "underlying" normality and normalizing the ranks. I would take the latter course (unless it was patently unreasonable) if the experimental structure could not be fully exploited by a rank test, e.g., a factorial design.

3. The computations generally demanded by nonparametric methods are generally quick and relatively foolproof. When one wants to learn quickly the major contours of a set of data, these methods are quite useful. (Wilcoxon's 1949 monograph, in which many psychologists first encountered nonparametric methods, was titled "Some Rapid Approximate Statistical Procedures.") If one is performing many statistical tests, these methods can be used to screen out the clearly nonsignificant comparisons (say, $p > .20$-$.30$) probably more efficiently than by inspection. At the other extreme, when an investigator notes that 48 out of 50 differences are positive, it would both smack of pedantry and waste his time not to accept the evidence of the implicit sign test but to go on to a laborious *t* test of the null hypothesis. But with few exceptions, this type of use is for the researcher's convenience; final reports in the literature should normally contain the results of follow-up parametric tests.

4. Finally, there are conceivable circumstances where the judged severity of the degree of assumption failure or its nature would make the use of nonparametric methods a prudent course. The most noteworthy example is simultaneous disparity in variance and size. This can also be cured sometimes by scale transformation and should be so handled for complex designs (e.g., factorial design, covariance analysis), but for simple designs, the suitable rank test is a reasonable procedure. The rank test is not wholly immune to these conditions, but it is more robust than its parametric analogue (Boneau, 1962).

The major points made in this section are, first, that parametric tests (1) are quite robust to assumption failure over a wide range of practical conditions and (2) are not crucially dependent on scaling assumptions; and second, that nonparametric tests (1) are not distribution-free in the sense desired, (2) lack relative power and adequate methods of power analysis, (3) lack the development necessary for any but the simplest of experimental designs and data-analytic forms, but (4) are useful as shortcut techniques and in certain special circumstances. I would conclude, therefore, that since the premises which underlie the current widespread use of nonparametric methods are generally false, they be relegated to those restricted and infrequent circumstances where they are uniquely appropriate.

FOR HIM WHO READS AND RUNS, SOME RECOMMENDATIONS

In this concluding section, I want to make a few terse recommendations to the typical research psychologist which emerge from the detailed exposition above:

1. Use larger samples. This not only will improve the power of your statistical tests but also assure their immunity from most failures of parametric assumptions.

2. Keep clearly in mind the distinction between statistical significance and degree of association, and do not neglect to make your data yield information on the latter score.

3. Shun one-tailed tests for many reasons, but mostly to avoid embarrassment and the temptation to second-guess.

4. Think twice before using a nonparametric test. The chances are good that your purposes (versatility, power, incisiveness) will be better served by the classical parametric method you would have turned to ten years ago.

REFERENCES

Anderson, N. H. Scales and statistics: parametric and nonparametric. *Psychol. Bull.,* 1961, **58,** 305–316.

Boneau, C. A. The effects of violations of assumptions underlying the *t* test. *Psychol. Bull.,* 1960, **57,** 49–64.

Boneau, C. A. A comparison of the power of the *U* and *t* tests. *Psychol. Rev.,* 1962, **69,** 246–256.

Box, G. E. P. Non-normality and tests on variances. *Biometrika,* 1953, **40,** 318–335.

Box, G. E. P. Some theorems on quadratic forms applied in the study of analysis of variance problems. I. Effect of inequality of variance in the one-way classification. *Ann. math. Statist.,* 1954, **25,** 290–302. (a)

Box, G. E. P. Some theorems on quadratic forms applied in the study of analysis of variance problems. II. Effects of inequality of variance and of correlation between errors in the two-way classification. *Ann. math. Statist.,* 1954, **25,** 484–498. (b)

Burke, C. J. Additive scales and statistics. *Psychol. Rev.,* 1953, **60,** 73–75. (a)

Burke, C. J. A brief note on one-tailed tests. *Psychol. Bull.,* 1953, **50,** 384–387. (b)

Burke, C. J. Further remarks on one-tailed tests. *Psychol. Bull.,* 1954, **51,** 587–590.

Cattell, R. B. The relational simplex theory of equal interval and absolute scaling. *Acta psychol.,* 1962, **20,** 139–158.

Cochran, W. G. The comparison of percentages in matched samples. *Biometrika,* 1950, **37,** 256–266.

Cohen, J. The statistical power of abnormal-social psychological research: a review. *J. abnorm. soc. Psychol.,* 1962, **65,** 145–153.

Cohen, J. *Statistical power analysis for behavioral sciences.* New York: Wiley, in press.

Cohen, J., & Struening, E. L. Opinions about mental illness in the personnel of two large mental hospitals. *J. abnorm. soc. Psychol.,* 1962, **64,** 349–360.

Cronbach, L. J. *Essentials of psychological testing.* (2nd ed.) New York: McGraw-Hill, 1960.

Diamond, S. *Information and error.* New York: Basic Books, 1959.

Dixon, W. J., & Massey, F. J., Jr. *Introduction to statistical analysis.* (2nd ed.) New York: McGraw-Hill, 1957.

Edwards, A. E. *Experimental design in psychological research.* (Rev. ed.) New York: Rinehart, 1960.

Fisher, R. A. *The design of experiments.* (5th ed.) New York: Hafner, 1949.

Gaito, J. Nonparametric methods in psychological research. *Psychol. Rep.,* 1959, **5,** 115–125.

Goldfried, M. R. One-tailed tests and "unexpected" results. *Psychol. Rev.,* 1959, **66,** 79–80.

Good, I. J. Significance tests in parallel and in series. *J. Amer. statist. Ass.,* 1958, **53,** 799–813.

Guilford, J. P. *Fundamental statistics in psychology and education.* (3rd ed.) New York: McGraw-Hill, 1956.

Husén, T. *Psychological twin research.* Stockholm: Almquist & Wiksell, 1959.

Jones, L. V. Tests of hypotheses: one-sided vs. two-sided alternatives. *Psychol. Bull.,* 1952, **49,** 43–46.

Kimmel, H. D. Three criteria for the use of one-tailed tests. *Psychol. Bull.,* 1957, **54,** 351–353.

Kogan, L. S. Statistics. *Annu. Rev. Psychol.,* 1960, **11,** 199–224.

Lindquist, E. F. *Design and analysis of experiments in psychology and education.* Boston: Houghton Mifflin, 1953.

Lord, F. M. On the statistical treatment of football numbers. *Amer. Psychologist,* 1953, **8,** 750–751.

Lubin, A. Statistics. *Annu. Rev. Psychol.,* 1962, **13,** 345–370.

McNemar, Q. On Wilson's distribution-free test of analysis of variance hypotheses. *Psychol. Bull.,* 1957, **54,** 361–362.

McNemar, Q. At random: sense and nonsense. *Amer. Psychologist,* 1960, **15,** 295–300.

McNemar, Q. *Psychological statistics.* (3rd ed.) New York: Wiley, 1962.

Marks, M. R. Two kinds of experiment distinguished in terms of statistical operations. *Psychol. Rev.,* 1951, **58,** 179–184.

Moses, L. E. Non-parametric statistics for psychological research. *Psychol. Bull.,* 1952, **49,** 122–143.

Mosteller, F., & Bush, R. R. Selected quantitative techniques. In G. Lindzey (Ed.), *Handbook of social psychology.* Vol. 1. Cambridge, Mass.: Addison-Wesley, 1954. Pp. 289–334.

Pearson, E. S. The distribution of frequency constants in small samples from non-normal symmetrical and skew populations. *Biometrika,* 1929, **21,** 259–286.

Pearson, E. S. The analysis of variance in cases of non-normal variation. *Biometrika,* 1931, **23,** 114–133.

Peters, C. C., & Van Voorhis, W. R. *Statistical procedures and their mathematical bases.* New York: McGraw-Hill, 1940.

Sawrey, W. L. A distinction between exact and approximate nonparametric methods. *Psychometrika,* 1958, **23,** 171–177.

Scheffé, H. *The analysis of variance.* New York: Wiley, 1959.

Senders, Virginia L. A comment on Burke's additive scales and statistics. *Psychol. Rev.,* 1953, **60,** 423–424.

Senders, Virginia L. *Measurement and statistics.* New York: Oxford Univer. Press, 1958.

Siegel, S. *Nonparametric statistics for the behavioral sciences.* New York: McGraw-Hill, 1956.

Srivastava, A. B. L. Effect of non-normality on the power function of *t* test. *Biometrika,* 1958, **45,** 421–429.

Sterling, T. D. Publication decisions and their possible effects on inferences drawn from tests of significance—or vice versa. *J. Amer. statist. Ass.,* 1959, **54,** 30–34.

Stevens, S. S. Mathematics, measurement, and psychophysics. In S. S. Stevens (Ed.), *Handbook of experimental psychology.* New York: Wiley, 1951. Pp. 1–49.

Super, D. E. *Appraising vocational fitness.* New York: Harper & Row, 1949.

Welch, B. L. The significance of the difference between two means where the population variances are unequal. *Biometrika,* 1937, **29,** 350–362.

Wetherill, G. B. The Wilcoxon test and non-null hypotheses. *J. roy. statist. Soc.,* Series B, 1960, **22,** 402–418.

Wilson, K. V. A distribution-free test of analysis of variance hypotheses. *Psychol. Bull.,* 1956, **53,** 96–101.

Ylvisaker, N. D. On the Wilson tests. *Psychometrika,* 1960, **25,** 297–302.

part 2

Theoretical Foundations

6
Historical Introduction

SOL L. GARFIELD

Clinical psychology is in many respects an unusual and unique field. Being a part of the broader field of psychology and deriving from it, it has, of necessity, been influenced by developments within psychology proper. At the same time, it has worked closely with, and been influenced by, other disciplines which are involved with the treatment and understanding of emotionally disturbed individuals. In a sense, one can say that clinical psychology has been part of two worlds—the academic and the clinical.

In the past, as well as at present, there has been some concern with the definition of clinical psychology. Some of the concern has centered around the use and meaning of the word "clinical." This word originally pertained to the bedside and has long been associated with the practice of medicine. It has, however, acquired other meanings. Currently, for example, the word "clinic" denotes an outpatient setting rather than an inpatient hospital regime. Nevertheless, psychologists, including Witmer (1907a) and those who followed him (Louttit, 1939; Wallin, 1919; Woodworth, 1937), have been somewhat less than pleased with the designation "clinical." A better term, however, has not been discovered, and at present the name "clinical psychology" appears here to stay.

Much of the concern about definition has been related also to what the psychologist does and how this differs from other related professional disciplines. In this connection, one can mention briefly some basic features which will be discussed in more detail later in this chapter as well as in other chapters. These deal with the functions of the clinical psychologist, his training, his values, and his relations to other professions.

Broadly speaking, clinical psychology can be defined as that branch of psychology which is concerned with problems of personality adjustment and modification. The clinical psychologist is first of all a psychologist and owes his basic loyalty to psychology. He receives most of his training in academic departments of psychology and shares many of the value systems derived from the basic field of psychology. His original and basic training in clinical psychology is provided in a department of psychology within a university graduate school and is augmented by a period of internship training in a clinical setting. The clinical psychologist thus is first oriented and educated with reference to the basic field of psychology and its emphasis on research methodology. Later, the clinical psychology student begins to specialize in the clinical aspects of his field. Clinical psychology, therefore, differs from other applied fields or professions in that it attempts to be both a science and a profession. The social worker and the psychiatrist, for example, are trained primarily as practitioners and not as researchers. The latter receives his basic training in medicine and then, like other specialists in medicine, receives additional training in the care of the mentally ill. Medicine itself makes a distinction between the basic sciences and the clinical areas of practice. While clinical psychology can in some ways be considered an applied field of psychology, it does not see itself solely as a practicing profession. Some of its members may be extensively engaged in practice, but others are concerned with research or with academic teaching. The emphasis on research, however, permeates the training of the clinical psychologist, and the completion of a research dissertation is a required part of this training.

The clinical psychologist today works in a variety of different settings and is mainly involved with four primary functions: diagnosis, psychotherapy, research, and training. Some of these functions are shared with other professions, while some are more unique to psychology. In the area of diagnosis, the psychologist's contribution has centered around the utilization of psychological tests. With regard to research, the psychologist generally receives more extensive training than other professionals in related areas. In terms of treatment, psychologists generally limit themselves to some form of individual or group psychotherapy. Somatic therapies and the use of drugs are the province of the physician, although the psychologist may play an important role in research with reference to these treatment activities.

We have described briefly, thus far, what clinical psychology is and the main functions in which clinical psychologists are engaged. With this as an orientation, let us now turn our attention to the sources from which clinical psychology derived and the influences which helped shape it in its present form.

ACADEMIC PSYCHOLOGY AND THE EXPERIMENTAL TRADITION

It is difficult to specify a precise date or place which marks the initial development of clinical psychology. It has many roots and has been influenced by developments occurring in a variety of fields. Foremost among these is the academic field of psychology. Beginning with the establishment of a psychological laboratory in 1879 by Wilhelm Wundt, psychology has emphasized an experimental tradition. The early psychologists were largely in academic settings and were attempting to model their science after the older and more developed fields of science. While some clinical psychologists have not always displayed positive feelings about this experimental and scientific tradition, it has, nevertheless, left a definite impact on psychology, including clinical psychology. The emphasis during this early period clearly was on laboratory procedures and on the development of a science of psychology. However, in spite of the fact that such an atmosphere may not have been particularly conducive to the development of clinical viewpoints, at a relatively early period there were attempts to apply psychological procedures to practical problems (Boring, 1950; Hunt, 1956), and we shall refer to them shortly.

Although the academic tradition, as such, did not contribute directly to the actual development of clinical psychology, the growth of academic departments of psychology did tend to foster other developments pertaining both to applied psychology and to the study of abnormal behavior. In addition, some of the theoretical points of view and emphases which grew from, and developed in, academic departments of psychology also had an impact on developments in clinical psychology. By providing a field and specific points of view, academic psychology provided a firm basis for other developments as well as a tradition and value system for such expanding developments.

In the next two sections, attention will be devoted to two developments within psychology which contributed directly to the growth of clinical psychology. However, some additional mention should be made of more general but contemporaneous movements within general psychology which had an indirect influence on clinical psychology. Boring (1950) has emphasized the practicality of the early functionalistic movement in American psychology. In a comparable manner, Hunt (1956) has stressed also the importance of behaviorism and gestalt psychology in providing a soil which allowed for the developments which occurred later. Space does not permit elaboration of these statements. However, it can be mentioned that J. B. Watson's work on the conditioning of fears was directly pertinent to clinical and abnormal psychology, and recent work on "behavior therapy" is historically related to this earlier work (Wolpe, 1958).

Mention should also be made of G. Stanley Hall, who founded the psychology laboratory at John Hopkins in 1883, the *American Journal of Psychology* in 1887, and the *Journal of Applied Psychology* in 1915 (Boring, 1950). Besides bringing Freud and Jung to lecture in America in 1909, Hall also contributed to the development of child and adolescent psychology and to the establishment of the psychological laboratory at McLean Hospital. Furthermore, such important figures in the early development of clinical psychology as Goddard and Terman were students of Hall's (Shakow, 1945). Another important academic figure was Cattell, about whom we shall have more to say later. However, it is of interest that he did try to establish a psychological clinic in the 1890s and was one of the first individuals to be concerned with the certification of psychologists (Cattell, 1937).

LIGHTNER WITMER AND THE FIRST PSYCHOLOGICAL CLINIC

If anyone has a claim to the title "founder of clinical psychology" it is undoubtedly Lightner Witmer. Witmer received his Ph.D. degree from the University of Leipzig in 1892, and upon returning to this country was made director of the laboratory of psychology at the University of Pennsylvania, succeeding Cattell, who moved to Columbia. Four years later, in 1896, he presented a new method of research and instruction at the annual meeting of the American Psychological Association. He referred to this method as "the clinical method in psychology and the diagnostic method of teaching." This was based on the case of a "bad speller" who was brought to Witmer at the psychological laboratory at the University of Pennsylvania. "With this case, in March 1896, the work of The Psychological Clinic was begun" (Witmer, 1907a, p. 4). This historic occasion thus instituted the founding of the first psychological clinic and what can be viewed as the formal beginning of clinical psychology.

In his address to the American Psychological Association in 1896, Witmer outlined "a scheme of practical work in psychology," and the following summer he was able to put most of this plan into operation at the University of Pennsylvania. Because of its historical interest, it may be worthwhile to reproduce the four main points outlined by Witmer:

> 1. The investigation of the phenomena of mental development in school children, as manifested more particularly in mental and moral retardation, by means of the statistical and clinical methods.
> 2. A psychological clinic, supplemented by a training school in the nature of a hospital school, for the treatment of all classes of children suffering from retardation or physical defects interfering with school progress.
> 3. The offering of practical work to those engaged in the professions of teaching and medicine, and to those interested in social work, in the observation and training of normal and retarded children.
> 4. The training of students for a new profession—that of the psychological expert, who should find his career in connection with the school system, through the examination and treatment of mentally and morally retarded children, or in connection with the practice of medicine (1907a, p. 5).

In line with the above, a four-week summer course was given. In addition to the usual courses in experimental and physiological psychology, "a course in child psychology was given to demonstrate the various methods of child psychology, but especially the clinical method" (Witmer, 1907a, p. 5). A psychological clinic was conducted daily in which children were seen, and a training school was also in operation.

In addition to establishing a psychological clinic and giving the name "clinical psychology" to the activity in which he was engaged, Witmer made several other noteworthy contributions. Besides providing courses dealing with child and abnormal psychology, his course "The Psychological Clinic" was probably the first course in clinical psychology. A description of it was published in 1907 and was as follows:

> PSYCHOLOGY 8. The Psychological Clinic.—Children will be examined in the presence of the students taking this course. The object of the course is to illustrate various mental and physical defects found in school children, to discuss the causes, to point out the nature of the consequent retardation and to propose the appropriate treatment. The course will also serve to make the student acquainted with the methods of examination. A daily clinic will be conducted by Professor WITMER and his assistants or by medical specialists for the eye, the ear, the nose and throat, the nervous system, orthopedics and internal medicine.
>
> A training school for backward and defective children will also be in daily session. One or more classes will be taught by com-

> petent instructors. Clinical study will also be carried on through visits to neighboring institutions for the training of special classes of children—the Pennsylvania Training School for Feeble-minded Children at Elwyn, the House of Refuge, and the Pennsylvania Institutions for the Instruction of the Blind and Deaf (Witmer, 1907c, p. 35).

Witmer also founded, edited, and contributed much of the material for the journal *The Psychological Clinic.* This journal, first published in 1907, continued until 1935. The material in it reflects Witmer's tremendous energy and commitment to clinical psychology, as well as providing a clear impression of the clinical psychology of those days.

Witmer (1907b) also set up and supervised a hospital. It was his belief that many children could not be properly understood without a period of observation during which attempts were also made to modify or improve their behavior. Particular emphasis was put on special types of remedial and educative efforts, although other procedures were utilized as well. Witmer was interested also in the physical condition of the child and apparently conducted some physical examinations on the basis of which he was able to request more specialized medical examinations. A physician, however, was utlized at the hospital and appeared to work in close collaboration with Witmer. The latter, apparently, was able to interest a number of educators and physicians in the work that he was doing. In examining all the articles and notes in the first two volumes of *The Psychological Clinic,* one finds no reference to problems of interdisciplinary rivalry or conflict. Witmer himself was highly successful in securing the support of many individuals in other fields. It is of interest that Meyer, the leading psychiatrist of his day, published a paper in one of the early issues of the *The Psychological Clinic* (1908).

In Witmer's clinical work the emphasis was clearly on children. From his accounts and the accounts of those who worked with him, it appears that the greatest emphasis was on cases of suspected intellectual subnormality, sensory difficulties, educational retardation, and speech problems (Brotemarkle, 1931). Related to this work were later developments which emphasized personal counseling with college students and the broad area of vocational counseling. Although reference is also made to "moral" and conduct disorders, severe personality disturbance is not as frequently mentioned as some of the other problems. Nevertheless, as has been pointed out by Sarason and Gladwin (1958), Witmer himself was aware of the diagnostic problems concerning mental deficiency and psychosis, and he worked therapeutically with what appeared to be psychotic children.

It is interesting to compare current emphases and practices with those of Witmer's day. There is now more professional time devoted to work with adult patients than with children (Kelly, 1961). The emphasis is on psychopathology and on psychotherapy, rather than on specific disabilities and what may be termed "remedial approaches." It is also of interest to note that some of the areas emphasized by Witmer and other early clinical psychologists have been somewhat neglected by clinical psychologists today, with the result that these activities are now engaged in by other specialists, e.g., school psychologists, remedial teachers, speech pathologists, and vocational counselors.

Although it is clear that Witmer was the founder of clinical psychology and pioneered in the development of this field, his influence on subsequent developments in clinical psychology has been surprisingly small. Joseph Collins, a collaborator and close personal friend of Witmer's, commented also on this lack of recognition of Witmer's contribution in his biographical sketch of him in the volume commemorating the thirty-fifth anniversary of the first psychological clinic. Collins stated: "No more do I understand why the genuine and substantial contribution that Witmer has made to psychology should not be mentioned when the status of that science in this country is reviewed" (1931, p. 5).

It is interesting to speculate on why Witmer's influence was somewhat limited. As both Watson (1953) and Shakow (1948) point out, Witmer was to a great extent concerned with intellectual functioning related to educational retardation and suspected mental deficiency. He also tended to be interested in the physical and neurological aspects of the cases referred to him. In contrast, the child guidance movement, to be referred to later, gave attention to a variety of behavioral difficulties, was more influenced by the thinking of Freud, and generally focused more on the noncognitive aspects of personality. Although Witmer had considerable influence on his students and the university community, his "influence did not spread beyond Philadelphia to any considerable degree" (Watson, 1953, p. 328). Certainly, it is remarkable that such an unusual pioneer and innovator as Witmer did not have a greater impact on subsequent developments in clinical psychology and is remembered primarily as a figure of historical importance.

OTHER EARLY CLINICAL PSYCHOLOGISTS

Besides Witmer, there were other individuals who functioned as clinical psychologists during this early period. Wallin (1961) has published a brief list of psychologists with the Ph.D. degree who functioned as clinical psychologists between 1896 and 1910. Some of them played important roles in the development of clinical psychology, while others are relatively unknown today. It is of interest that probably the first psychologist to work in a state hospital was William O. Krohn. He received his Ph.D. degree from Yale University in 1889 and was a psychologist at the Eastern Hospital for the Insane at Kankakee, Illinois, from 1897 to 1899. Daniel P. MacMillan, with a Ph.D. from Chicago, functioned as an assistant in the department of child study and pedagogic investigation of the Chicago public schools in 1900 and was director of that department from 1902 until 1935. He may have been the first school psychologist.

One of the most influential psychologists in this early group was Henry H. Goddard. Goddard contributed significantly both to the work with the mentally retarded and to the use of intelligence tests in clinical psychology. He introduced the Binet-Simon Scale in this country in 1908 and is known also for his restandardization of this scale in 1910 on 2,000 American children. "This revision of Goddard's remained for a long time the standard for American practice" (Pintner, 1931, p. 36). From 1906 to 1918 he was director of research at Vineland Training School in New Jersey, which "became the Mecca of all those interested in the new clinical psychology, and the storm center around which much of the heated discussion as to the validity of the Binet-Simon Scale raged" (Pintner, 1931, p. 36).

Frederick L. Wells, another pioneer in clinical psychology, functioned as an assistant in pathological psychology at McLean Hospital in 1907 and was preceded there by Shepard I. Franz. Grace Fernald, the first psychologist in a child guidance clinic, worked at the Juvenile Psychopathic Institute in Chicago in 1909 after receiving her Ph.D. degree from the University of Chicago. Frederick Kuhlmann, known for his revision of the Binet-Simon Scale and other tests, performed research and clinical duties as director of psychological research, Minnesota School for the Feeble-minded, in Faribault in 1910. Wallin himself had done some counseling work with "backward children" in 1907 and became director of the laboratory of clinical psychology at the New Jersey State Village for Epileptics in 1910. Altogether, 16 psychologists with the Ph.D. are identified by Wallin as functioning as clinical psychologists during this period.

Wallin (1961) also mentions that Jacob D. Heilman, who took his Ph.D. degree at the University of Pennsylvania in 1908, directed a psychological clinic at the State Teachers College, Greeley, Colorado, that same year. It is interesting in this connection that Seashore states that the psychological clinic at the University of Iowa, established about 1910, was patterned after Witmer's clinic in Pennsylvania and "became the second psychological clinic in an American university" (1942, p. 124). This clinic was conducted by Sylvester, who had been trained both at Iowa and with Witmer. There appears, however, to be some discrepancy between Seashore's account and that of Wallin (1914), who found approximately twenty psychological clinics in existence in 1914. As Watson (1953) points out, it does not appear likely that all these developed between 1910 and 1914, and it is possible that some of these clinics developed apart from the developments initiated by Witmer. However, the clinic directed by Heilman was undoubtedly influenced by the Pennsylvania clinic, since he took his graduate training at Pennsylvania.

It is of interest, too, that developments in related fields were also limited during this early period. Seashore mentions that there was no psychiatrist in Iowa at the beginning of this century. "The heads of the insane asylums were primarily business managers; their institutions were primarily for detention and safekeeping" (1942, p. 123). He also mentions that even as late as 1920, there did not appear to be adequate training available for clinical psychologists, and technically trained clinicians were few.

THE DEVELOPMENT OF PSYCHOLOGICAL TESTS

One of the most important developments within psychology, as far as clinical psychology is concerned, was the development of psychological tests. One of the earliest attempts in this area was made by Cattell prior to 1890 (Peterson, 1925). Apparently, he was the first to use the term "mental tests," publishing a paper in 1890 entitled "Mental Tests and Measurements" (Cattell, 1890). Cattell's tests were largely tests of sensory and perceptual response and of reaction time. Many of these tests were used with college students and were largely unsuccessful as predictors of academic achievement. Nevertheless, Cattell's work had a practical emphasis and was concerned with individual differences.

In connection with other early attempts to utilize tests prior to 1900, mention can be made of Kraepelin, who had studied with Wundt and who was professor of psychiatry at Heidelberg. Around 1895 he devised certain tests to measure what he regarded as basic traits in the individual. These included such things as memory, fatigue, and learning ability. The proposed tests dealt chiefly with arithmetical processes and were to be given over long periods of time (Peterson, 1925). They represent an early attempt to utilize psychological procedures in the study of psychopathology.

The person who had a more direct and important impact on the later development of clinical psychology was Alfred Binet, who, with Simon, developed the first usable test of intelligence. Since the mental age scale developed by Binet and Simon is so well known and is currently represented by the 1960 revision of the Stanford-Binet (Terman & Merrill, 1960), not too much need be said about the scale itself. In any event, a workable scale was published in 1905 and revised in 1908. As noted previously, Goddard published a translation of these scales which appeared in 1910. Other individuals also published translations of these scales at about the same time in this country. Kuhlmann in 1911 published a somewhat condensed and modified version of the 1908 scale, and Wallin published a similar version the same year (Peterson, 1925). However, it was Terman's revision of the Binet scale in 1916 which had the greatest impact on psychological testing and clinical work in this country. Before proceeding further, however, it is worth mentioning that Binet was very much interested in the study of the individual case, which, to many, personifies the clinical approach. As Peterson points out: "The environment in which Binet had grown up was favorable to a strong emphasis on the whole individual in psychological study. Itard, Seguin, and others had led out in the line of the subnormal, too, and in Binet this tendency is combined with that of studying the dissociated personality. So in this period the new tendency to emphasize individual psychology is most strongly expressed in Binet" (1925, p. 99).

With the advent of the various revisions of the Binet scale, particularly the 1916 Stanford revision, the testing movement developed rapidly. There is no need to discuss this here except to mention that a variety of psychological tests were developed. The use of tests in World War I acted as an additional stimulus, and in the 1920s and 1930s the use of psychological tests was widespread. The examination of children with reference to possible mental retardation and in relation to difficulties in school became an important activity of the clinical psychologist. Not only was the psychological evaluation of intellectual abilities and related appraisals seen as an important contribution to the clinical study of the individual, but as Louttit (1939) points out, the administration of the Binet scale was seen as synonymous with clinical psychology. The writer also can recall that during the 1930s a clinical psychologist was identified by his ability to give the Stanford-Binet.

During this period there was evident a growing emphasis on quantitative methodology and objectivity in psychology, and psychological testing was seen as the application of this orientation to the clinical situation. This objective and scientific emphasis was thus associated with psychological testing and the clinical psychologist. Positions became available in clinics and other institutions for psychometricians and psychological examiners. In this connection, it is interesting that whereas some leading clinical psychologists reacted strongly to the equating of clinical psychology with psychometric evaluation, "some physicians lamented the fact that non-medical men were allowed to usurp the field of mental testing" (Louttit, 1939, p. 379).

The development and growth of psychological testing activities thus provided an important impetus to the development of clinical psychology. The clinical psychologist tended to be identified with his use of psychological tests, and although changes in this function have occurred in the past twenty years, the use of the tests remains a unique activity of the psychologist in the clinical situation.

THE MENTAL HYGIENE MOVEMENT AND THE CHILD GUIDANCE CLINIC

Shortly after the beginning of Witmer's work and the development of the mental age scale by Binet, other movements were begun which have had some influence on the subsequent development of clinical psychology. Reference is made here to the mental hygiene movement initiated by Clifford Beers in 1908 and the development of the first child guidance clinic in the following year. Both of these were important events, but before saying more about them, it is worthwhile to take a quick glance at what was being done for the severely disturbed individual prior to these developments.

Without reviewing matters in any detail, mention can be made of the influence of Pinel on the care and treatment of the "insane" at the end of the eighteenth century. Pinel, appointed physician at the asylum at Bicêtre in 1793, reacted against the misery of the patients, many of whom were in chains. He did much, not only to improve the lot of the incarcerated patients for whom he was responsible, but also to influence the general attitude toward such individuals. Partially as a result of his influence, there developed in the nineteenth century a more humane attitude toward the care and treatment of the mentally ill. More detailed descriptions of these and related developments are available elsewhere (Bromberg, 1954; Deutsch, 1949; Zilboorg & Henry, 1941). Nevertheless, it can be said that, as contrasted with our more treatment-oriented hospitals today, the care and treatment of hospitalized patients left much to be desired. In fact, it was because of his reaction to his own hospitalization that Beers published his famous book, *A Mind That Found Itself* (1908). The book was a dramatic portrayal of his hospitalization and a criticism of his treatment.

Soon afterward, The National Committee for Mental Hygiene was formed to publicize the need for improving the care of mental patients and to foster the prevention of mental illness. William James was instrumental in this movement in its early stages through both personal support and financial contributions. Beers's book tended to act as a catalyst which stirred up "mental hygiene chain reactions which have increased to the present point of national and international concern" (Bromberg, 1954, p. 242).

Closely related to this development was the child guidance movement in this country. In 1909, the Juvenile Psychopathic Institute, later known as the Institute for Juvenile Research, was founded in Chicago to work with delinquent children. The first director was William Healy, a psychiatrist who had also been a student of James's. The professional staff of the clinic at first consisted of Healy and Dr. Grace Fernald, the psychologist. The psychologist thus preceded the psychiatric social worker in the child guidance clinic. Performance tests such as the Seguin were used, and in 1910 Healy introduced the Binet-Simon Scale into the clinic. Watson (1953) even credits Healy with introducing the Binet-Simon Scale into this country simultaneously with Goddard in 1910. However, as noted previously, Goddard had translated the 1905 edition in 1908. It is interesting, also, that Healy, in visiting around the country in 1908, found only two places where psychological testing of the child was done in addition to a physical examination. He mentions specifically Witmer's clinic and Goddard's laboratory at Vineland (Healy & Bronner, 1948).

The child guidance movement proceeded slowly for a few years but developed more rapidly after World War I. In 1912, a children's clinic was opened in connection with the recently established Boston Psychopathic Hospital, and in the next year the Henry Phipps Clinic opened in Baltimore with a unit for children (Deutsch, 1949). In 1917, Healy moved to Boston to organize and direct what is now known as the Judge Baker Guidance Center. Although the early clinics were greatly concerned with delinquency, they gradually broadened their scope of activities to include a wide variety of behavioral problems in children. In this development, the pattern of the clinic team emerged, which included the psychiatrist, the clinical psychologist, and the psychiatric social worker. While the psychologist's main function was that of psychological testing, other functions were also engaged in, depending upon the particular setting. As we have noted previously, Healy's clinic activity has had a greater influence on subsequent developments than is true of Witmer. In part, this seems related to the fact that Healy was more influenced than Witmer by certain developments to which we now turn our attention.

THE DYNAMIC MOVEMENT

In the latter half of the nineteenth century and during the early years of the present one, there occurred developments which represented a greater interest in man as a dynamic, striving organism and a greater awareness of psychological factors in psychopathology. These have sometimes been referrred to as the development of "dynamic psychology," although this term has been applied to diverse movements within psychology and psychiatry. Of these, psychoanalysis has been the most influential. The history of psychoanalysis has been set down by Freud (1938), and accounts of other related events are available in the writings of others (Boring, 1950; Bromberg, 1954; Zilboorg & Henry, 1941). Here we shall sketch only the historical importance of some of these developments as they pertain to clinical psychology.

Within psychology, reference is made to the influence of James, the functionalist school, G. Stanley Hall, and R. S. Woodworth, among others. Hall, as we have noted, was influential in making the views of Freud known to psychologists and others in this country by bringing him and Jung to this country and publishing their lectures in the *American Journal of Psychology* (1910). Within psychiatry and neurology, reference can be made to Charcot and Bernheim. Both were teachers of Freud and shared his interest in hypnosis and hysteria. Although basically a neurologist, Charcot helped focus greater attention on neurotic disturbances and admitted the importance of psychological factors in hysteria. Bernheim was able to demonstrate the importance of suggestion in hypnosis and to show that hypnotic phenomena were not necessarily related to hysteria. He also extended the therapeutic use of hypnosis.

Another significant figure in the development of dynamic psychology was Pierre Janet. A former student of Charcot's, he eventually became his successor. Janet, after completing his doctorate in 1889, became director of the psychological laboratory at the Salpêtrière and then received his M.D. degree in 1893. He contributed greatly to our understanding of hysteria and was a leading figure in both psychology and psychiatry (Boring, 1950). Nevertheless, his work has not had the impact that it perhaps might have had if Freud had not been a contemporary of his. However, it should be mentioned also that Janet, in spite of his psychological orientation, still saw hysteria as a hereditary or degenerative disease (Zilboorg & Henry, 1941).

The impact of psychoanalysis on contemporary thought and practice in psychology is probably too well known to need much elaboration in this brief account. Of basic importance was the emphasis which psychoanalysis placed on the psychological causation of a variety of personality disturbances. Above all else, Freud emphasized this, not only in neurosis, but also in everyday mistakes and errors. In addition, Freud dealt with a wide variety of adjustment difficulties which were of concern to people and for which there were no adequate explanatory accounts. He provided a comprehensive and dynamic theory for understanding human personality, a method for investigating psychological processes, and a method of psychotherapy. All these have been of primary importance for later developments in clinical psychology, including the development of projective techniques. In Boring's words: "It was Freud who put the dynamic conception of psychology where psychologists could see it and take it" (1950, p. 707).

These developments tended to highlight the importance of psychological factors in the development of personality disturbance. The psychoanalytic concepts of repression, unconscious motivation, defenses, and symptom formation added to our understanding of these psychological processes. This not only gave strong impetus to viewing disturbances from a psychological frame of reference but also emphasized a psychological approach to treatment. Psychoanalysis as an approach to the treatment of neuroses and related conditions was clearly a psychological treatment, and Freud himself, although a neurologist, considered this movement a psychological one.

Although some psychologists were responsive to Freud's ideas, most of those in academic circles were not favorably disposed toward this point of view. Nevertheless, this development was a major influence in the later development of clinical psychology. Certainly, psychoanalytic theory became one of the major theoretical orientations in clinical psychology, if not the dominant one. It is worth noting, also, that although Freud was not well received by his medical colleagues, psychoanalysis in this country has been largely a medical movement, an M.D. being a prerequisite for acceptance into a psychoanalytic institute. This occurred in spite of the fact that psychologists were among the first supporters of psychoanalysis in this country (Watson, 1953).

We can conclude our brief account of dynamic psychology with mention of two other contributors to this movement. Morton Prince, a contemporary of Janet's, is credited by Boring (1950) to continuing Janet's attempt to bring academic and clinical psychology closer together. He is probably best known for his work on multiple personality, his editorship for many years of the *Journal of Abnormal and Social Psychology,* and his founding of the Harvard Psychological Clinic in 1927. Henry Murray, still a contemporary and influential figure in clinical psychology, succeeded Prince as director of the Harvard clinic in 1928, made important contributions to the study of personality, and fathered the Thematic Apperception Test in 1935 (Morgan & Murray, 1935). He was also one of the charter members of the Boston Psychoanalytic Society (Hall & Lindzey, 1957).

EARLY PROFESSIONAL CONFLICTS

Even though the growth of clinical psychology was relatively modest during the first three decades or so of the present century, a certain amount of conflict with medical groups was apparent. Since professional relationships will be treated in another chapter, only a few references will be made to some of the early difficulties in this area.

It is of interest that even before 1920, there were published references to problems with the medical profession concerning the role and responsibility of clinical psychologists. In 1916, for example, the New York Psychiatrical Society appointed a committee "to inquire into the activities of psychologists and more particularly of those who have termed themselves 'clinical psychologists' in relation to the diagnosis and treatment of abnormal conditions" ("Activities of Clinical Psychologists," 1917, p. 224). This committee acknowledged the usefulness of psychological knowledge for education, vocational problems, advertising, and other industrial pursuits, but it expressed concern over "the growing tendency of some psychologists . . . to deal with the problem of diagnosis, social management and institutional disposal of persons suffering from abnormal conditions" ("Activities of Clinical Psychologists," 1917, p. 225). The committee was critical of the training of some psychologists and referred somewhat disparagingly to the "so-called 'psychological clinics.'" They were also critical of the fact that two states had enacted laws which permitted judges to commit mentally defective individuals to institutions "upon the so-called expert testimony of 'clinical psychologists'" ("Activities of Clinical Psychologists," 1917, p. 225). In general, they expressed their disapproval of psychologists' participating responsibly in clinical work with mentally disturbed or defective individuals, except under supervision of a qualified physician.

Franz (1917) replied to the previously mentioned statement with a thoughtfully considered presentation. He commented on the mutual distrust of the two professions and the need for cooperation between them. "The psychiatrist would have the psychologist barred from dealing with abnormal persons, and the psychologist insists that the psychiatrist is not competent to give and to interpret mental tests" (1917, p. 226). In addition to pointing out some of the limitations in psychiatric practice and the scarcity of competent psychiatrists at that time, Franz also emphasized the lack of psychological knowledge among physicians. It is of interest, also, that he called attention to the fact that only one psychologist was included among the 90 members of the National Committee for Mental Hygiene.

To supplement this brief account, we can refer to two other reports. Wallin (1919), presented the view that the best field of work for the clinical psychologist was "the field of mental deviation" rather than mental disorder. He was of the opinion that the latter area belonged more clearly to the "neuro-psychiatrist and the neuro-psychopathologist." On the other hand, he felt that the medical profession was trying to stop psychologists from playing a responsible role in the field of mental deficiency. On this point, he stated:

> But let us not lose sight of the fact that with the interest which the psychologists have recently awakened in the medical profession in the problem of mental deficiency, there has been inaugurated a vigorous campaign to convince the public that the psychologist has surreptitiously invaded the sacred precincts of the physician, that the diagnosis and treatment of the forms of mental deviation to which we have referred above are purely medical matters, that even the highly trained psychologists are entirely incompetent in this field, that their work at best is entirely secondary and subordinate to the work of the physician, and that they must be summarily ejected from the field (1919, p. 467).

Finally, we can note that Seashore (1942) mentions that around 1920, "organized psychology and psychiatry were at swords' point, and the time had come for a truce . . . " (p. 126). Clearly, ambiguity and conflict existed regarding professional roles and responsibilities. As a result there was a conference in 1920 at which delegates from nine professional associations, representing psychiatry, psychology, and related areas, were present to discuss these problems. At the conference it was clear that there was an overlapping area of theory and practice which was difficult to define. All groups expressed a determination to improve the qualifications of their practitioners. The view was also expressed that "to deal competently with the situation . . . persons should be trained both as psychologists and as psychiatrists, the ideal being a combination of the two" (Seashore, 1942, p. 132). Needless to say, the latter provision has never received wide adherence, and some of the same issues have tended to recur at various times since.

THE PRE–WORLD WAR II ERA

As we have seen, clinical psychology had shown some development, spurred on to a large extent by the development and acceptance of psychological tests. This helped contribute to the setting up of a number of psychological clinics in universities and to the employment of psychologists in child guidance clinics, institutions for the retarded, and state hospitals. Nevertheless, clinical psychology still played a relatively modest role in the study and treatment of individuals with personality difficulties. Many of the university clinics functioned only during the academic year and were combined with courses related to psychological tests and remedial work with children. In the institutions in which clinical psychologists were employed, they tended to spend much of their time in psychological testing (Kinder, 1937; Louttit, 1939), and even around 1930 there was a shortage of qualified clinical psychologists (Selling, 1952). Therapeutic activities on the part of psychologists were somewhat limited, and only in some institutions was research a major activity. Thus, while there was during the 1930s some recognition of clinical psychology, many of the psychologists who actually worked in clinical situations did not have the status or recognition accorded their colleagues in the academic setting. Nevertheless, there were indications of dissatisfaction with the state of affairs in clinical psychology. This was manifested in various attempts to create special organizations to represent the interests of clinical psychologists. It may be of interest, therefore, to sketch briefly some of these developments and their antecedents.

In 1917 a group of 45 psychologists with the doctorate degree held an organizational meeting in Pittsburgh to establish the American Association of Clinical Psychology. Prof. Leta S. Hollingworth played a major role in this project. Two years later, the American Psychological Association accepted a report which established this group as the section of clinical psychology within the national association. In 1921 the New York State Association of Consulting Psychologists was formed and this led eventually to the formation of the Association of Consulting Psychologists in 1932. This latter group included psychologists from 21 states and the District of Columbia and in 1937 founded the *Journal of Consulting Psychology* (Symonds, 1937). The aim of the journal was to provide an outlet for the interests of clinical psychologists and other applied psychologists. J. P. Symonds was the first managing editor, and among the corresponding editors were E. Lowell Kelly and George A. Kelly.

In 1937, a committee, entitled the National Committee for the Affiliation and Association of Applied and Professional Psychology, was formed to consider the formation of a national association for applied and professional psychologists. This committee was given the task of forming an organization which would build upon and incorporate the previously existing groups of clinical psychologists. The Association of Consulting Psychologists was asked to serve as the parent organization of the new national society and to contribute its journal and charter of incorporation. The committee also recommended: "That the proposed national society of applied psychology should incorporate its development as a professional association with the American Psychological Association, Inc., which is organized as a scientific society, so that their mutual interests may strengthen psychology as a whole" (Bernreuter, Maxfield, Patterson, Reymert, & Fryer, 1937). Thus was formed the American Association for Applied Psychology (AAAP). The new organization had four sections, one of which was the clinical section. Until 1945, when a new organizational framework within the American Psychological Association (APA) was provided, the AAAP was the main organization representing applied psychologists.

The clinical section of the AAAP held its first meeting in Minneapolis in 1937. In addition to forming a committee on the definition of clinical psychology, attempts were made to set up separate committees on psychological services in penal institutions, the courts, "hospitals for the insane," institutions for the mentally retarded, and state schools for girls and boys. These committees were clearly oriented to clinical settings (Brown, 1938).

Although clinical psychology appeared to be somewhat better organized in the late 1930s and to have a journal in which its interests were represented, it is difficult fully to characterize its status as a profession. Varying accounts had referred to the profession of clinical psychology for at least two decades previously, but apart from the organizations referred to, professional developments do not appear to have been very pronounced. The most influential people in the field, for the most part, still functioned in academic settings, although there were some well-trained and experienced psychologists in the field. Much of the work still centered around intellectual and related psychological examinations. Typical work patterns are reported in a survey by Louttit (1939) of 111 psychologists in child guidance clinics. Although the survey does not indicate the amount of time devoted to specific activities, it is obvious that "psychometrics" was the most frequent activity of the psychologist, with over 86 per cent of the group performing this kind of function. Educational guidance and vocational guidance were the next most frequent activities. Psychotherapy was the sixth most frequent activity, being listed by slightly under one-third of the psychologists, and it was exceeded in frequency by remedial teaching.

During this time the Stanford-Binet was undoubtedly the most widely used clinical instrument. Interest in projective techniques was developing very slowly. The Rorschach method was introduced into this country by David Levy around 1924 (Klopfer & Kelley, 1942). He also influenced Samuel Beck, who became the first American psychologist to use this method shortly before 1930. Hertz and Klopfer were other leaders in this development during the 1930s. Nevertheless, as far as psychology is concerned, the impact of projective techniques during this period was not very marked, and instruction in these techniques was not generally given in the universities. The Thematic Apperception Test appeared in 1935 and thus was still a fairly novel technique (Morgan & Murray, 1935).

A number of potential employers of clinical psychologists also did not appear to be utilizing them to any great extent. Ridenour (1938) surveyed the situation in New York State and presented some interesting findings. Among 21 state institutions for the mentally ill and mentally retarded, with over ninety thousand patients, there were apparently positions for four psychologists. "Occasionally the Superintendent of the Hospital is able to use a social worker's or an attendant' item for a psychologist" (Ridenour, 1938, p. 138). Other social agencies did not present a much different picture. A survey of 167 general and special hospitals revealed 16 psychologists working in these institutions. In fact, it was found that there were more psychologists doing nonpsychological work in social agencies than there were doing psychological work. Almost half of the 30 mental hygiene clinics had no psychologists at all.

Thus, clinical psychology during the late 1930s appeared to be far from a strongly established profession. Some psychiatrists, in fact, protested that psychology was not a "curative science" and labeled the psychologist's efforts at treatment as "charlatanism" (Zilboorg, 1943). Nevertheless, there were some aspects which are worth mentioning in comparison with clinical psychology today.

Clinical psychology then was concerned mainly with children and appeared to be heavily identified with psychological tests. According to Louttit (1939), there had been few significant changes in the field in the twenty years preceding his 1939 appraisal. Some of Louttit's other comments, however, are surprisingly current. For example, he pointed out the difficulties in trying to decide the boundaries between psychology and medicine. He was critical also of the training which the student received in the graduate school and which he saw as mainly academic. Others, previously, had also emphasized the need for more practical training and for an internship experience. (Poffenberger, 1938; Shakow, 1938; Wallin, 1919). However, as Dashiell (1939) noted, American academic psychology had been dominated by the laboratory and not the clinic. As a result of his evaluation, Louttit concluded: "For a real professional dealing with problems of behavior, the future must produce a new specialist. This behavior specialist will be the product of an entirely new curriculum which will include pertinent materials from psychology, medicine, education, sociology and social work. It may even be necessary to establish a new degree as a symbol of the curriculum" (1939, p. 384).

WORLD WAR II AND ITS IMMEDIATE AFTERMATH

As indicated, clinical psychology, despite a relatively early beginning, progressed somewhat slowly. At various times there was evident a desire on the part of clinical psychologists for professional identity, for specialized training, and for some definition of their field. Organizationally, these developments culminated in the formation of AAAP with a separate section for clinical psychology. At that time there appeared to be some awareness of clinical psychology as an emerging profession and of the need for developing more adequate training programs. Shortly after these happenings, however, psychology was faced with the advent of World War II, an event which greatly influenced the subsequent development of clinical psychology.

With the outbreak of World War II in 1941, there was a demand for a variety of psychological services pertaining to the national war effort. During World War I, psychologists had played an important role in the selection and assignment of military personnel and had first utilized group tests on a wide scale. Similar demands were made of psychologists in the 1940s. The developments of particular significance for clinical psychology centered around the high incidence of rejection of selectees for emotional disturbance and the high occurrence of psychiatric casualities as the war progressed. Psychologists were utilized at induction stations to help detect and screen candidates who were potentially unsuited for military service. They also participated in a variety of other settings requiring clinical psychological skills. Some commissions were available for clinical psychologists in the Navy, and in 1944 commissions were offered clinical psychologists in the Army. These events were of definite importance. Not only was clinical psychology recognized on an official basis, but opportunities were provided for training and participation in actual clinical work with patients.

During this period there were also other developments which deserve mention. One was the introduction by Rapaport and his colleagues of the use of a comprehensive psychological test battery in the diagnostic evaluation of patients (Rapaport, Gill, & Schafer, 1945). Rapaport's contribution was the development of a theoretical framework for interpreting test patterns as a means of understanding more fully the personality dynamics and psychopathology of the patient. Wechsler (1939) had previously produced the first adult intelligence scale and had called attention to the diagnostic possibilities of the scale. Rapaport extended this notion within a theoretical orientation and included a variety of psychological tests including projective techniques. The use of the psychological test battery was a much more complex and clinically oriented activity than the mere giving of tests in the traditional fashion and required a high level of clinical knowledge and skill. This type of diagnostic evaluation was also more in keeping with "dynamic psychology" and the diagnostic framework of psychiatry, and it appeared to be relatively well received by psychiatrists and other professional disciplines.

Another development of some consequence was the utilization of clinical psychologists as psychotherapists during World War II. Although some psychologists had been engaged in psychotherapeutic activities prior to the war and although Carl Rogers's influential *Counseling and Psychotherapy* appeared in 1942, a large number of clinical psychologists had had limited contact with this activity. As indicated earlier, diagnostic testing and remedial work were engaged in more frequently. However, with the great need for treatment and the shortage of trained therapists, psychologists were eventually given an opportunity to participate in various types of psychotherapeutic activities. Group psychotherapy, for example, received particular impetus during the war, and psychologists were active in this activity. Consequently, at least several hundred clinical psychologists gained some type of psychotherapeutic experience during the war. Furthermore, this type of activity was officially recognized, although in most instances the work was done within a medical framework and under some type of medical supervision or collaboration.

THE POSTWAR PERIOD

At the end of World War II there were other developments which served to spur a rapid expansion of clinical psychology. One of the most important came from the Veterans Administration. The VA was faced with a large number of emotionally disturbed veterans who were in need of both hospitalization and outpatient care. The prewar services of the VA were not adequate to cope with this new need. As a result, there was a reorganization within the VA, and positions were set up for clinical psychologists which were patterned somewhat after those provided by the military services. The first impact was thus the creation of many jobs for trained clinical psychologists. At first, positions were available for individuals without the Ph.D. degree as well as with the doctorate. Around the end of 1951, however, the VA, which had by then become the largest single employer of clinical psychologists, required the Ph.D. for all staff clinical psychologists. The positions set up for psychologists recognized the functions of diagnosis, psychotherapy, and research.

Another important innovation was the training program set up by the VA. Because of the scarcity of qualified clinical psychologists, the VA set up a training program in cooperation with approved universities which at its peak included 700 psychology graduate students. In this program, an opportunity was provided for graduate students to receive the equivalent of two years of clinical training in VA installations while they were concurrently enrolled as graduate students at the university. Fairly liberal stipends were paid to the students for the time spent at the clinical installations.

The U.S. Public Health Service also played an important role in providing financial support for graduate training at universities and stipends to internship centers outside of the VA. What developed very quickly, therefore, was a marked expansion of training in clinical psychology. At the same time, and with relatively great rapidity, changes were occurring in the university training programs.

Various groups and committees of clinical psychologists had been concerned with matters of training at various times in the past. However, little was done in any organized fashion about this until shortly after World War II. In 1947, a committee on training in clinical psychology of the American Psychological Association, with Shakow as chairman, recommended a program of graduate training in clinical psychology (American Psychological Association, Committee on Training in Clinical Psychology, 1947). This program emphasized six primary areas of study: (1) general psychology, (2) psychodynamics of behavior, (3) diagnostic methods, (4) research methods, (5) related disciplines, and (6) therapy. In addition, this program was to include a one-year internship in an appropriate clinical situation and thus require a minimum of four years of graduate work. The committee also emphasized that the clinical psychologist was first and foremost a psychologist and was to be acquainted with the basic body of psychological theory, research, and methods. The role of the clinical psychologist in research was emphasized. The report also stressed the importance of broad areas of competence as opposed to the learning of specific techniques or skills.

The particular objectives emphasized in 1947 were generally accepted in later discussions and conferences on training and are reflected in contemporary programs (Raimy, 1950; Strother, 1956). These recommendations thus have constituted both an official acceptance and a definition of training in clinical psychology. Furthermore, the APA later set up an educational and training board, which has had the responsibility for evaluating both university and internship programs. This was a novel departure in American psychology and clearly reflected the growth and importance of clinical psychology. Originally, about forty universities were approved for graduate training in clinical psychology, and in 1962 there were 60 such universities with approved programs leading to the Ph.D. degree in clinical psychology (Ross, 1962).

Another important development was a major reorganization within the APA. In 1945, it was decided to have the APA represent all the interests of psychologists, both scientific and professional, and to organize divisions to represent the more specialized interests within psychology (Wolfle, 1946). As a result, the AAAP was disbanded, and the *Journal of Consulting Psychology* was taken over as a clinical journal by the APA. The Division of Clinical and Abnormal Psychology was formed to represent the interests of clinical psychologists. Later, the name was changed to the Division of Clinical Psychology. At present, the Division of Clinical Psychology is the largest division within the APA, is responsible for planning four days of programs during the annual meeting of the APA, conducts an annual postdoctoral institute, and publishes a newsletter for its members. Representatives of the division also participate in the council of representatives of the APA, the main governing body of the association.

In addition to developments in training and professional organization, other developments also have taken place with some rapidity during this period. Since many of these will be covered in more detail in later chapters, only brief references to them will be made here.

The rapid growth of clinical psychology has been accompanied by a change in the pattern of professional roles and activities. Clinical psychologists have shifted from an emphasis on children to a greater concentration on work with disturbed adults. They have participated increasingly in therapeutic activities and have engaged more frequently in private practice. Although some psychologists have engaged in private practice previously, the postwar period revealed a marked increase in this activity. In a recent survey of the members of the Division of Clinical Psychology, Kelly (1961) reported that 17 per cent listed private practice as their primary professional working situation. Along with this, there has been a marked change in the relative importance of the activities of clinical psychologists. In the past, diagnostic testing was the primary activity of the clinical psychologist and, as we have seen, has been a major identifying activity of the clinical psychologist through the years. However, by 1961, psychotherapy was clearly the primary activity to which clinical psychologists were devoting their professional time (Kelly, 1961).

The increasing professionalization of psychology led to greater concern on the part of psychologists with their social and professional responsibilities. One manifestation of this was the publication of a code of ethics by the APA (1953). This was a rather lengthy booklet of 171 pages which attempted to indicate clearly the ethical responsibilities of the psychologist in a variety of situations. This code has since undergone revision, and a briefer version is now available ("Ethical Standards of Psychologists," 1963). In many ways it is a model of professional responsibility.

There has also been much activity in the area of legislation, certification, and legal definition of psychology. Without some type of legislation, anyone, regardless of training, can call himself a psychologist. As a result, psychologists, organized at the state level, have tried hard to enact various types of licensing or certification laws. At the present time there is some type of statutory certification or licensure in 16 states. Attempts to secure such legislation have frequently met with opposition from medical groups (Garfield, 1957). As a result, some type of nonstatutory certification has been tried in about twenty states. The latter designation refers to attempts by state associations of psychologists to set up their own procedures for certifying qualified psychologists to interested groups or individuals within the state.

Another aspect of this concern with professional standards was the creation of the American Board of Examiners in Professional Psychology in 1947 (Kelley, Sanford, & Clark, 1961). This board, patterned after the medical specialty boards, was set up to examine and certify psychologists in three areas of specialization, one of which is clinical. The present requirements for the diploma from the board include a Ph.D. degree, five years of experience, and written and oral examinations.

At the present time, clinical psychology appears to be relatively well established as one of the major professions in the so-called "mental health field." The functions of diagnosis and psychotherapy with emotionally disturbed individuals are reasonably well accepted and are even portrayed on a regular TV program. The competence of clinical psychologists to testify as experts in the field of mental disorder has received increasing recognition from the courts (Hoch & Darley, 1962). Conflicts with medicine appear less acute, and the demand for qualified clinical psychologists far exceeds the supply. The Division of Clinical Psychology of the American Psychological Association currently has approximately three thousand members, most of whom have the Ph.D. degree. There is probably an equally large number of members of the American Psychological Association who for one reason or another have not officially joined the Division of Clinical Psychology. There are 60 approved university doctoral training programs in clinical psychology. Psychologists function on important governmental committees and in research groups pertaining to personality adjustment and disturbance. Training programs for clinical psychologists are supported financially by several agencies of the Federal government as well as by many states. Most of this has occurred since 1945. It is a rather striking development, which few would have predicted twenty years ago. Nevertheless, there is still much concern about the training, future roles, and social utility of clinical psychologists and about the conflict between science and profession and similar matters. These problems perhaps reflect the diverse sources from which clinical psychology has developed. They may also be viewed as manifestations of the maturation of a unique profession.

REFERENCES

Activities of clinical psychologists. *Psychol. Bull.*, 1917, **14**, 224–225.

American Psychological Association. *Ethical standards of psychologists.* Washington, D.C.: 1953.

American Psychological Association, Committee on Training in Clinical Psychology. Recommended graduate training program in clinical psychology. *Amer. Psychologist*, 1947, **2**, 539–558.

Bernreuter, R. C., Maxfield, F. N., Patterson, D. G., Reymert, M. C., & Fryer, D. Progress report of the National Committee for Affiliation and Association of Applied and Professional Psychology. *J. consult. Psychol.*, 1937, **1**, 14–16.

Boring, E. G. *A history of experimental psychology.* (2nd ed.) New York: Appleton-Century-Crofts, 1950.

Bromberg, W. *Man above humanity: a history of psychotherapy.* Philadelphia: Lippincott, 1954.

Brotemarkle, R. A. (Ed.) *Clinical psychology: studies in honor of Lightner Witmer to commemorate the thirty-fifth anniversary of the founding of the first psychological clinic.* Philadelphia: Univer. of Pennsylvania Press, 1931.

Brown, A. W. Reports of the AAAP: organization of the clinical section. *J. consult. Psychol.*, 1938, **2**, 77–82.

Cattell, J. McK. Mental tests and measurements. *Mind*, 1890, **15**, 373–381.

Cattell, J. McK. Retrospect: psychology as a profession. *J. consult. Psychol.*, 1937, **1**, 1–3.

Collins, J. Lightner Witmer: a biographical sketch. In R. A. Brotemarkle (Ed.), *Clinical psychology: studies in honor of Lightner Witmer to commemorate the thirty-fifth anniversary of the founding of the first psychological clinic.* Philadelphia: Univer. of Pennsylvania Press, 1931, Pp. 3–9.

Dashiell, J. F. Some rapprochements in contemporary psychology. *Psychol. Bull.*, 1939, **36**, 1–24.

Deutsch, A. *The mentally ill in America.* New York: Columbia Univer. Press, 1949.

Ethical standards of psychologists. *Amer. Psychologist*, 1963, **18**, 56–60.

Franz, S. I. Psychology and psychiatry. *Psychol. Bull.*, 1917, **14**, 226–229.

Freud, S. The history of the psychoanalytic movement. In *The basic writings of Sigmund Freud.* New York: Modern Library, 1938.

Garfield, S. L. *Introductory clinical psychology.* New York: Macmillan, 1957.

Hall, G. S., & Lindzey, G. *Theories of personality.* New York: Wiley, 1957.

Healy, W., & Bronner, A. F. The child guidance clinic: birth and growth of an idea. In L. G. Lowrey (Ed.), *Orthopsychiatry 1923–1948. Retrospect and prospect.* New York: American Orthopsychiatric Association, 1948. Pp. 14–49.

Hoch, E. L., & Darley, J. G. A case at law. *Amer. Psychologist*, 1962, **17**, 623–654.

Hunt, W. A. *The clinical psychologist.* Springfield, Ill.: Charles C Thomas, 1956.

Kelley, N. H., Sanford, F. H., & Clark, K. E. The meaning of the ABEPP diploma. *Amer. Psychologist*, 1961, **16**, 132–141.

Kelly, E. L. Clinical psychology—1960: report of survey findings. *Newsltr., Div. clin. Psychol.*, Winter, 1961, 1–11.

Kinder, Elaine F. Psychological work at Letchworth Village, Thiells, New York. *J. consult. Psychol.*, 1937, **1**, 76–80.

Klopfer, B., & Kelley, D. M. *The Rorschach technique.* Tarrytown-on-Hudson, N.Y.: World, 1942.

Louttit, C. M. The nature of clinical psychology. *Psychol. Bull.*, 1939, **36**, 361–389.

Morgan, C. D., & Murray, H. A. A method for investigating fantasies: the Thematic Apperception Test. *Arch. Neurol. Psychiat.*, 1935, **34**, 289–306.

Meyer, A. What do histories of cases of insanity teach us concerning preventive mental hygiene during the years of school life? *Psychol. Clin.*, 1908, **2**, 89–101.

News notes. *J. consult. Psychol.*, 1938, **2**, 26–28.

Peterson, J. *Early conceptions and tests of intelligence.* Tarrytown-on-Hudson, N.Y.: World, 1925.

Pintner, R. *Intelligence testing: methods and results.* (New ed.) New York: Holt, 1931.

Poffenberger, A. T. The training of a clinical psychologist. *J. consult. Psychol.*, 1938, **2**, 1–6.

Raimy, V. C. (Ed.) *Training in clinical psychology.* Englewood Cliffs, N.J.: Prentice-Hall, 1950.

Rapaport, D., Gill, M., & Schafer, R. *Diagnostic psychological testing.* Vol. 1. Chicago: Year Book Medical Publishers, 1945.

Ridenour, Nina. Notes on the status of clinical psychology. *J. consult. Psychol.*, 1938, **2**, 137–142.

Rogers, C. R. *Counseling and psychotherapy.* Boston: Houghton Mifflin, 1942.

Ross, S. APA approved doctoral programs in clinical and in counseling psychology, 1962. *Amer. Psychologist*, 1962, **17**, 501–502.

Sarason, S. B., & Gladwin, T. Psychological and cultural problems in mental subnormality: a review of research. *Genet. Psychol. Monogr.*, 1958, **57**, 3–290.

Seashore, C. E. Pioneering in psychology. *Univer. Iowa Stud.*, 1942, No. 398.

Selling, L. S. Development of clinical tests in psychopathology. In P. H. Hoch & J. Zubin (Eds.), *Relation of psychological tests to psychiatry.* New York: Grune & Stratton, 1952, 15–25.

Shakow, D. An internship year for psychologists (with special reference to psychiatric hospitals). *J. consult. Psychol.*, 1938, **2**, 73–76.

Shakow, D. One hundred years of American psychiatry: a special review. *Psychol. Bull.*, 1945, **42**, 423–432.

Shakow, D. Clinical psychology: an evaluation. In L. G. Lowrey (Ed.), *Orthopsychiatry 1923–1948. Retrospect and prospect.* New York: American Orthopsychiatric Association, 1948. Pp. 231–247.

Strother, C. R. (Ed.) *Psychology and mental health.* Washington, D.C.: American Psychological Association, 1956.

Symonds, J. P. Toward unity. *J. consult. Psychol.*, 1937, **1**, 23–24.

Terman, L. M., & Merrill, Maud A. *Stanford-Binet intelligence test.* Boston: Houghton Mifflin, 1960.

Wallin, J. E. W. *The mental health of the school child.* New Haven, Conn.: Yale Univer. Press, 1914.

Wallin, J. E. W. The field of the clinical psychologist and the kind of training needed by the psychological examiner. *Sch. & Soc.*, 1919, **9**, 463–470.

Wallin, J. E. W. Ph.D's. in psychology who functioned as clinical psychologists between 1896 and 1910. *Psychol. Rec.*, 1961, **11**, 339–342.

Watson, R. I. A brief history of clinical psychology. *Psychol. Bull.*, 1953, **50**, 321–346.

Wechsler, D. *The measurement of adult intelligence.* Baltimore: Williams & Wilkins, 1939.

Witmer, L. Clinical psychology. *Psychol. Clin.*, 1907, **1**, 1–9. (a)

Witmer, L. The hospital school. *Psychol. Clin.*, 1907, **1**, 138–146. (b)

Witmer, L. University courses in psychology. *Psychol. Clin.*, 1907, **1**, 25–35. (c)

Wolfle, D. The reorganized American Psychological Association. *Amer. Psychologist*, 1946, **1**, 3–6.

Wolpe, J. *Psychotherapy by reciprocal inhibition.* Stanford, Calif.: Stanford Univer. Press, 1958.

Woodworth, R. S. The future of clinical psychology. *J. consult. Psychol.*, 1937, **1**, 4–5.

Zilboorg, G. *Mind, medicine, & man.* New York: Harcourt, Brace & World, 1943.

Zilboorg, G., & Henry, G. W. *A history of medical psychology.* New York: Norton, 1941.

7

Genetic Factors

LEWIS A. HURST

By way of historical introduction to our main theme, namely, genetics in relation to the psychological sciences, I should like to indicate that the notion of heredity in psychiatry has undergone many vicissitudes in the course of the last 100 years. During the closing decades of the nineteenth century, the predominant trend was to consider all forms of mental disorder and defect to be hereditary in an undiscriminating, nonspecific manner. With the development of scientific genetics, dating from the time of the rediscovery of Mendel's work at the beginning of the twentieth century (Mendel, 1959), there came a reaction against so crude a view from within the science itself, encouraged by the environmentalistic mental climate of the age and fostered in particular by the caricature of Freud's ideology evolved by many of his followers ("Psychoanalysis," 1962) and by an unverified personal dogma with which Watson saddled his behaviorism (1930).

Psychiatric genetics became established upon a firm scientific foundation only toward the end of the fourth decade of this century, through the extensive and systematic twin and family studies in the field of schizophrenia by Kallmann (1938; 1946; 1953) in the United States and Slater (1953) in England. This rendered possible the more discriminating insight that where psychiatric deviations are hereditary, they are so in a specific way, such that through inheritance schizophrenia can give rise only to schizophrenia, manic-depressive psychosis only to manic-depressive psychosis, and epilepsy only to epilepsy. The notion of a hereditary general "neuropathic taint" which could manifest indiscriminately in descendants in a variety of guises had perforce to be abandoned.

This achievement was possible only because of the steady development of basic and human genetics, whose history, concepts, and methods we now review as a basis for what is to follow.

Evolution of modern genetics[1]

To evaluate the general ideological orientation of modern genetics, one can do no better than to review, however briefly, the evolution of this science to its present, or third, stage, known as physiological and biochemical genetics.

[1] Condensed from Hurst, 1958.

FIRST STAGE

The first phase of scientific genetics was ushered in by the publication in 1866 by the Abbott Gregor Mendel in a rather obscure journal (from which it was only unearthed thirty-four years later independently by Correns, Tschermak, and De Vries) of his hybridization experiments with the garden pea. Mendel noted the proportion of characteristics—or, as they are technically known, "characters"—resulting from various crosses, of which he kept precise numerical records. His data gave him a firm basis for inferring the existence of hypothetical hereditary factors (later christened "genes" by De Vries) which preserve their identity from generation to generation, even if temporarily masked, and which appear in predictable proportions in crosses of a specified type.

In the course of his work, Mendel came across the phenomena of dominance, recessiveness, and the intermediate hybrid. In the case of dominant heredity, the trait is normally received from one parent and is transmitted in the direct line of descent, and 50 per cent of unaffected children cannot transmit the trait because there is no question of its remaining latent, as in the case of a recessive trait. In the case of recessive inheritance, most affected children are born of parents both overtly normal, each of whom, however, harbors a recessive gene which cannot manifest in the unpaired state. A further point of interest is that the expectancy figure for manifestation among children of parents with a single gene each for the trait in question, technically known as "heterozygotes," is 25 per cent. Moreover, transmission is often in the collateral rather than in the direct line of descent, so that siblings with latent genes are a large source of dissemination of the trait. In the case of the intermediate hybrid, the trait resulting from crossing is a compromise between the characters entering into the cross, for example, white and red yielding pink, instead of redness overriding the effect of whiteness completely as might occur classically in the case of redness dominant and whiteness recessive. In actual practice, one gets gradations in the dominance-recessiveness situation and in that of the intermediate hybrid.

As this question of dominance and recessiveness has special relevance to the discussion that follows, it would be well to quote a passage from Fraser Roberts in which he sets the question of dominant, recessive, and intermediate inheritance into historical and evolutionary perspective, at the same time relating the concepts to that of mutation, or the origin of new genes. Roberts states the position as follows:

> It has already been mentioned that when a new mutant gene appears, early in the history of a species, it does not usually display dominance or recessiveness. The presence of the mutant gene at one locus of the chromosome pair concerned produces a certain effect, while the presence of both loci produces a greater effect. And as we have just seen the simplex state will tend to be more variable in its expression than will the duplex.
>
> This variability of expression of the simplex state is in all probability an important factor in evolution. If the new mutation is disadvantageous, as will usually be the case, those heterozygous individuals who display lesser degrees of abnormality will be favoured in comparison with those more severely affected. The differences between heterozygotes are due to modifying genes and also perhaps to genes producing further independent effects; the differences will also be due to environmental influences in some cases. To the extent that the differences are genetic, this process of selection will increase in the species the proportion of genes exercising a diminishing influence upon the effect of the new mutant gene. Thus, as generations succeed each other and as the mutant gene keeps cropping up at its own characteristic mutation rate, its manifestation in the simplex state becomes less and less evident; the gene has started on its long course towards recessiveness (1959).

This quotation from Roberts, anticipating as it does some concepts yet to be defined, does give a picture of the relativeness of dominance and recessiveness and an explanation of how examples of both mutations may occur in one and the same mental condition, and it should do much to explain why acrimony need not arise when in certain diseases some workers tend to the dominant and others to the recessive explanation, for in different material of the same condition, a greater degree of dominance or recessiveness may objectively exist.

SECOND STAGE

From this digression let us return to the characteristics of the second and third stages of modern genetics. The cardinal feature of the second stage was the identification of the physical basis of inheritance, associated with the name of Thomas Hunt Morgan and his coworkers. It will be remembered that with Mendel, the hereditary units, now known as genes, were merely conceptual or hypothetical entities inferred from the ratios resulting from crossbreeding. It was left to Morgan to locate these entities in linear order—in the banana fly, *Drosophila melanogaster*—on the chromosomes, the advantages of this organism over man as an experimental animal residing in the facts that the number of chromosome sets is four instead of 23, that several generations are completed in a year, and that mating at the dictates of experimental design is possible in a way which would not be acceptable in human societies. Details about genetic linkage, chromosome maps, and the phenomenon of "crossing-over," upon which such maps are based, are beyond the scope of so general a chapter as this. Up to the present, only small beginnings have been made on the construction of maps of human chromosomes, owing to the large number of genes and chromosomes and certain difficulties of technique. There is no doubt about the value of such maps, for through their agency the potential carrying of a pathological gene of late manifestation, e.g., that of Huntington's chorea or manic-depressive psychosis, could be inferred early through associated common genes detectable early, such as those responsible for blood groups. There is also every assurance that this work, having begun in earnest, will now proceed rapidly. It is possible to investigate genetic linkage only if the genes whose relationship in transmission is to be explored are studied simultaneously in the same subjects. With rare traits the opportunity will hardly ever occur. As Roberts has pointed out, if brachydactyly and Osler's disease were to appear in an animal species, it would be a very simple matter to carry out breeding experiments to discover whether they were linked or not; but in the human species, the chance of intermarriage between sufferers from the two conditions is minute. The difficulty, however, can be met by utilizing common genes. For example, if sufficient cases were accumulated, it would not be difficult to discover whether the gene for Osler's disease was linked to the genes responsible for the blood groups A, B, and O. In this way the blood-group genes could be used as pointers or markers for one chromosome pair; any rare genes found to be linked to them would of necessity be linked to each other, and a beginning would have been made in the construction of a map of the chromosomes of that particular pair. Unfortunately, however, clearly recognizable differences between normal human beings due to the action of single genes are uncommon. Genetic differences between normal human beings are usually due to the combined action of many genes, the effects of which cannot be individually distinguished; examples that come to mind are height, weight, intelligence, and the graded tendency to epileptic seizures, and the designation of the underlying genetic mechanism is multifactorial or polygenic. A few useful markers do exist, however. To the A, B, and O blood groups and their genes were added the M and N blood groups and their genes, which do not exhibit linkage. The extensive work on blood groups by Race and Sanger and many others, which formed so substantial a contribution at the 1956 Congress at Copenhagen, where Sir Ronald A. Fisher gave them such pointed application to our theme, promises yet further developments in this direction. The ability or the inability to taste phenylthiocarbamide, 70 per cent of persons registering a bitter taste and 30 per cent no taste at all, has been shown to be dependent on a single gene pair, the ability to taste being dominant. With this gene pair and those responsible for the A, B, and O blood groups and for the M and N blood groups, we have three admirable indicators for three chromosome pairs.

In every species there is a nonhomologous pair of chromosomes, known as the "sex chromosomes," which are all-important in sex determination. The associated phenomenon of sex-linkage merits passing comment. Slater raises the question in a paper entitled "Sex-linked Recessives in Mental Illness," based on an analysis of 233 cases and their relatives, appearing in Frederick Mott's "heredity index" card-filing system for the L.C.C. mental hospitals, without arriving at any conclusions of a specific kind or of comprehensive applicability. This mechanism, however, has been reported in neurological conditions, as we shall see later. Two well-known pedigrees, presented by Bell and Haldane, show that genetic linkage in man is related to the sex chromosome, upon which the genes for both color blindness and hemophilia are situated. Detailed considerations based upon the cross-over value indicate that the loci of the two genes are situated close together upon the X chromosome. It is indeed the sex chromosome that can lay the highest claim to having been mapped. Haldane's tentative map of this chromosome reflects six conditions assigned their relative positions on the basis of cross-over values in the following order: total color blindness, xeroderma pigmentosum, Oguchi's disease, recessive epidermolysis bullosa, and dominant and recessive retinitis pigmentosa.

The term "partial sex-linkage" is also in need of explanation. It is shown by genes residing on the homologous or pairing portions of the X and Y chromosomes. The mode of transmission is superficially similar to that of ordinary dominant and recessive genes, and this type of mechanism was discovered only recently, and then as a result of deliberate search. The somewhat subtle difference from autosomal transmission is briefly this: A man who receives such a gene from his father hands it on to more than half his sons and less than half his daughters, and conversely if he receives it from his mother.

THIRD STAGE

We now turn our attention to the third stage in the history of modern genetics, in the unfolding of which we are still involved. This phase is best designated as that of physiological and biochemical genetics. It took its inception from Goldschmidt in his developmental studies on butterflies and moths. In principle, what his work showed is that the genes are not static units with inevitable mechanical results in the phenotype or developed organism; rather, they are the initiators of trains of biochemical events, each of which occurs in the context of innumerable trains of biochemical events initiated by other genes: These accordingly may further frustrate the manifestation of the trait or disease associated with the gene, gene pair, or gene complement in question. It is the vision of this vast dynamic biochemical system, with specific trends within it, which is the basis for the paradox of the reversibility of heredity, which we have already stressed, and the challenge to research and therapy to correct derailed trends such as are revealed, for example, in enzyme blocks.

The picture we have of the organism in terms of physiological and biochemical genetics provides the rationale and background; indeed, it leads very positively to the presumption of variability in the effects produced by genes. Significant from our point of view are the concepts of penetrance and expressivity. By penetrance is meant the percentage of cases in which, given the requisite gene, gene pair, or gene complement for the trait or disease in question, it in fact manifests itself in the fully developed organism at all. Before the third stage of modern genetics, a figure of 100 per cent was assumed *ex hypothesi,* whereas now the figure of 70 per cent claimed for schizophrenia is regarded as a very high rate of penetrance, and figures as low as 3 per cent for the gene for color blindness when in the simplex state in heterozygous females, or a fraction of 1 per cent in leukemia, have a substantial body of proof behind them. The term "expressivity," in contrast to "penetrance," indicates the degree to which the trait in question, having manifested at all in the phenotype (penetrance), does so; thus we have to do with degree of expression as opposed to frequency of expression (penetrance).

A nonpsychiatric example of penetrance is provided in a pedigree (Bulloch, after Gee in Roberts, 1940) of diabetes insipidus in which we see the occasional nonexpression of a dominant, autosomal gene. Expressivity is illustrated in a pedigree (Mohr & Wriedt, 1919) of brachydactyly in which cases of the full abnormality and others detectable only by careful measurement are found. Under the concept of expressivity, we may consider the cases where the gene concerned produces manifold effects, not all of which are manifested in a particular case. An example is Darier's disease (keratosis follicularis), in which the components of skin condition, small stature, and mental deficiency may be expressed in various constellations in individual cases. It is found with genes with manifold effects (the term used is "pleiotropy") that the less serious, such as the skin lesion in Darier's disease, tend to be more regularly expressed, since the constitutional effects in Darier's disease are sufficiently common to ensure that the mutation rate of the gene is considerable compared with the frequency of the disease.

The most important application of the concepts of penetrance and expressivity in psychiatry is doubtless in schizophrenia, where with the postulated double dose of recessive genes, there is a 70 per cent manifestation or 30 per cent defective expressivity of the requisite gene complement. The genes postulated as bringing about such frustration or limitation in expressivity are often called "modifiers."

Short of an exhaustive consideration of the variation in the effects produced by genes, one may comment on the situation, which in a sense is the obverse of pleiotropy, of the frustration of the manifestation of a gene by modifiers, namely, the case where an accessory gene is necessary to, or assists the manifestation of, the main gene, as has been demonstrated in a rare form of brachydactyly. One should perhaps also mention that there are additional influences of a nongenetic nature conditioning the expression of main genes. These are developmental in character. They are illustrated by sex-linked microphthalmia, in which the gene regularly produces blindness among the males who bear it but in which, apart from the blindness, there is marked variability in mentality, ranging from superior intelligence to idiocy. The variety of the cerebral effects within a single family makes it unlikely that these effects are genetic, but they must be due to influences operating during prenatal life. A reasonable hypothesis in this as in many other instances is that the gene makes the developing embryo especially susceptible at a particular stage (phenocritical period) to influences, variations in which would be without effect on the normal fetus. It may well be that the effect on the gene is to reduce the margin of safety, so that small and normally unimportant variations in environmental stimuli may make all the difference between normality and various types of abnormality. It is by no means unlikely that many cases of variability in the expression of genes will ultimately be found to fall into this group, although more will have to be learned about the pathology of early uterine life before there is much hope of identifying the nongenetic factors concerned.

A final example of factors influencing the expression of genes is to be seen in sex-limited as opposed to sex-linked inheritance. In sex-limitation the same genotype expresses itself differently in the male or female. This condition differs from sex-linkage inasmuch as in the latter the genotype is different, and we are dealing with an essentially genetic phenomenon. In sex-limitation, however, we have the state of affairs that the male or female organism affords a different medium or background for the manifestation of the trait concerned. Partial sex-limitation is much commoner than complete sex-limitation, which is a rare condition—e.g., pseudohermaphrodism, which occurs only in males. Perhaps the best example of incomplete sex-limitation in psychiatry is the higher incidence of depression, especially of the involutional type, in women.

The biochemistry of genetics

Haldane poses three questions concerning genes which raise certain fundamental issues:

1. What do genes do, or what are the differences in biochemical, physiological, and developmental behavior between organisms with different genes? We have moved from the purely conceptual or topological structural notions of the earlier phases of genetics, in which genes were regarded merely as factors for unit characters or strings of beads, to a functional one, in which each gene is conceived as controlling a unit process, biochemically describable and possibly playing its part in several genetic processes. It explains the phenomenon of pleiotropy already alluded to, in which a single gene acts on very different characters, a good example being the gene which is responsible in mice for microcytic anemia, flexed tail, and a white spot on the belly.

2. How do genes do what they do? The evidence is along the lines warranting the working hypothesis that the genes act by controlling enzymes (each of which determines a single biochemical step, as is well illustrated in sickle-cell anemia). Now all enzymes are proteins, which leads to the further conclusion that each gene makes one protein. If we put our generalization in aphoristic form, we may say "one gene—one enzyme." An illustration from human medicine is found in the condition of galactosuria, in which the infant is unable to metabolize lactose properly owing to the absence of the appropriate enzyme to change lactose into glucose, resulting in the production of galactose. These children, however, do quite well when they are provided with sucrose to make good their disability in coping with lactose. Another example is that of children who were

subject to recurrent infections to which they eventually succumbed and who were found, owing to deficiency of enzyme, to be unable to manufacture gamma globulin. These children overcame their disability when fed on gamma globulin.

3. What are genes biochemically? Genes are nucleoproteins like molecular viruses manufactured by the cell by some (unknown) process. It seems likely that genes (chromatin) may be characterized more specifically as deoxyribonucleoproteins.

There is much fascinating speculation leading out of the above, into which we cannot here go afield. There is, for instance, the hypothesis of the mating of a cell and an enzyme to render pneumococci and streptococci sensitive instead of resistant, so that we may veritably be able to practice genotherapy. There are, moreover, speculations arising from a consideration of protein structure which open a vista analogous to cybernetics, in which we may think of the communication of information and of protein words dependent on the order of component amino acids, nucleotides, etc. The study of DNA (deoxynucleic acid) and RNA (ribonucleic acid) makes a detailed contribution in this connection, including a picture of how RNA can carry genetic specificity. A final application of this new concept of protein language is that a mutation may be regarded as a misprint in a message which is perpetuated. Thus instead of a series of protein components 1221 . . . 2, we may get the misprint 1221 . . . 3. Translating this into biochemical terms, the appearance of "3" instead of "2" may mean that no enzyme is produced, with dislocation of the chemical economy of the organism and possibly death (lethal genes).

ENZYME BLOCKS

We have dealt with the question of absence of an enzyme; let us now consider the concept, so important for our purpose, of enzyme blocks. This takes us into the field of the inheritance of nutritional requirements, investigated by Beadle and Tatum, Horowitz, Pontecorvo, Catcheside, and Ephrussi, using the fungus *Neurospora* as the experimental organism. The nutritional mutants of these investigators have proved valuable in studying pathways of biological synthesis of nutritionally important metabolites, since different mutations appear to block different chemical steps in the many series of biochemical reactions which make up the pattern of metabolism. It should be recognized, however, that this method, like others, has its own characteristic limitations.

It had been advantageous to use organisms with simple growth requirements, since these have capacities for wider varieties of biosynthesis. *Neurospora,* for example, will grow on a medium containing inorganic salts, sugar (as a source of carbon and energy), and the one B vitamin biotin. During its growth it synthesizes all the great variety of amino acids, vitamins, nucleic acid constituents, polysaccharides, lipids, and other substances contained in its protoplasm. Since many of the pathways of biosynthesis by which essential metabolites are formed are very similar in different organisms, much information on the details of these processes can be obtained by studies of mutants of microorganisms.

We shall not be able to go into the experimental details here. However, the general principle of this work is, after having induced mutations by x ray, ultraviolet ray, or chemical means, to establish for the different mutants the compound required to maintain existence on the minimum medium noted above, as well as the compounds or compound specifically accumulated by each mutant. Examples of the findings bearing on the details of amino acid synthesis were that 12 mutants not growing on the minimal medium do so when cystine, methionine, and threonine are added. An elaborate process was disclosed whereby the S atom is transferred by the three-C chain of cysteine to the four-C chain of homoserine; Emerson has demonstrated in three different mutants that the step from homoserine to cystathionine is blocked with the accumulation of substances allowing growth without methionine or threonine.

The phenomenon of leakage was discovered, by which is meant that a mutant not viable on the minimal medium can survive by manufacturing the substance during the process of growth.

Genetic blocking of a reaction owing to accumulation of a product of intermediate metabolism is also seen in connection with the competitive utilization of a needed substance or intracellular enzyme by related substances (lysine with arginine or ornithine) in the course of purine and pyrimidine synthesis.

With regard to nonnitrogenous metabolites,

certain "acetateless" mutants have been discovered in which there is some product of the normal utilization of glucose for acetate formation—cases of suppression. *Neurospora* synthesizes over 90 per cent of its ergosterol and most of its fatty acids from labeled acetate. Here we have proof of partial metabolic blocks apart from leakage.

Examples occur also in which the deflection of metabolic processes through enzyme blocks leads to the accumulation of abnormal substances in the organism; the known positions of genetic interference in reaction series are as many as 23 in the biosynthesis of the aromatic amino acids.

Wagner and Mitchell make this analysis of one of the series of arginine-requiring mutants of *Neurospora,* which brings together a number of considerations in connection with genetically determined blocks:

> Of 3 genetically different mutants 3 will utilize ornithine, citrulline or arginine, 2 will utilize citrulline or arginine and 1 will use only arginine. These facts suggest that arginine can be produced from ornithine in vivo through a linear series of reactions. Thus it is considered that the genetically different mutants which will utilize the same metabolite frequently have effective blocks at different steps in biochemical reaction series. This is not necessarily always true, since each step is chemically complex and each can very likely be blocked in a number of different ways. Nevertheless the overall principle is sound, as has been established by investigations of many reaction series. By this principle nutritional mutants will utilize intermediate compounds that come after the block and not before it. This is an idealized situation, and very frequently the blocks are only partial in nature and subject to a variety of internal and external environmental changes of the completeness of expression.
>
> Some mutants pile up substances before the block that are related in biosynthesis to the nutrient required for growth, and, by isolation and identification of these, further circumstantial evidence concerning a pathway of biosynthesis can be obtained (1955).

Haldane splits up genetically determined blocks into the categories of (1) failure to produce a catalyst and (2) inhibition of metabolic products either by another B enzyme being unduly active and producing inhibition of the normal biochemical reaction or by a C enzyme being absent, with the result that the B enzyme is converted into something else.

Wagner and Mitchell provide the following general perspective, which is helpful in understanding the role of genetically determined blocks:

> The experimental results provide a variety of examples which demonstrate that one effect of gene mutation is to produce changes in cellular chemical composition in specific ways and in varying degrees. It is apparent that this comes about by causing changes in the rates of conversion of chemical substances into other chemical substances, and frequently it appears that a specific gene corresponds in its action to a specific reaction. Such a simple direct relation does not mean that the mechanism of control is also simple and direct. The chemical composition of the cell is in general the over-all result of the relative rates of reaction, and a genetic block merely shifts the intensity of reactions into different channels. Whenever relative reaction rates permit accumulation of some substance in noticeable quantities, then a characteristic chemical composition becomes manifest. These comments are made to emphasize that it is not just chemical differences that are inherited, but it is the processes which result in the chemical composition of the cells of the individual.

The question of genetically determined (enzyme) blocks has been dealt with at some length because of its crucial importance as regards research into the etiology of certain major psychoses through the avenue of the model psychoses, to be explored later in the course of this chapter.

At the First International Congress of Human Genetics, Copenhagen, 1956, R. J. Williams stressed the distinctive metabolic patterns (biochemical individuality) which must be related to specific enzymatic efficiency genetically determined, corresponding to distinctive patterns of nutritional needs among "normal" human beings. He emphasized the need of an appreciation of the tremendous social applications of this fact on the part of social scientists, who, to his mind, should develop a genecologic point of view. It was his belief that implications of human biochemical genetics in this connection are extremely broad and encompass such diverse topics as dental caries, obesity, alcoholism, mental disease, juvenile delinquency, divorce, race relations, and certainly politics and philosophy.

DNA, RNA, AND THE GENETIC CODE[2]

The latest phase of biochemical genetics concerns DNA (deoxyribonucleic acid), RNA (ribonucleic acid), and the genetic code, all intimately related to the chemistry of the nucleic acids and proteins.

In 1953 Watson and Crick proposed a model for the structure and replication of DNA and in so doing initiated the science of microbiology. As a result of the rapid advances of the intervening ten years, it can be seen that the general principles governing the controlled functioning and self-replication of living systems depend on three species of macromolecules: DNA, RNA, and protein. We shall here attempt a summary of what is known about the structure and replication of DNA, the transcription of DNA to messenger RNA, the coding of protein by messenger RNA, and, in conclusion, some of the ways in which these various processes are organized and controlled in living systems.

DNA

Structure and replication. That the DNA molecule is a repository of genetic information was established by the chemical identification of the bacterial transforming principle and the demonstration that some bacterial viruses inject their nucleic acid into the host bacterium to initiate infection. This rendered it apparent that there must be some precise mechanism for duplicating DNA so that the information within it can be handed down unchanged from generation to generation.

DNA is a polymer with a chain consisting of a five-carbon sugar, deoxyribose, and phosphate, a nitrogenous base being attached to the first carbon atom of each sugar. The four common bases are the two purines, adenine (A) and guanine (G), and the two pyrimidines, thymine (T) and cytosine (C). Vary as the relative proportions of these four bases in DNA do, the proportion of A is always the same as that of T, and the proportion of G is always the same as that of C. This phenomenon, coupled with x-ray diffraction data and evidence for hydrogen bonding between the bases, led Watson and Crick to devise their renowned model for the structure and replication of DNA.

Their proposal was to the effect that the DNA molecule consists of two polynucleotide chains wound spirally about a common axis and held together by hydrogen bonds between the bases; that there are two possible hydrogen-bonded base pairs, adenine-thymine and guanine-cytosine; and that the information contained in the molecule resides in the precise sequence of the base pairs. This absolute restriction in possible base pairs has the result that the sequence of bases in one chain specifies absolutely the sequence in the other—A in one chain implies T in the other, and vice versa, and similarly with G and C. This led to the further proposal by Watson and Crick that the replication of DNA involves separation of the two chains, with the creation of new complementary chains along the old ones, ensuring the preservation of the precise sequence of bases from one generation to the next.

Among important confirmatory data as to the correctness of this model are the isolation of the enzyme responsible for the polymerization of deoxyribonucleoside triphosphates and proof of its ability to replicate DNA *in vitro*, evidence from replication showing that each finished DNA molecule can be thought of as a hybrid of a parental strand and a new strand, and the demonstration that replicating DNA contains a fork whose two new daughter limbs each contain one strand of old material and one new strand.

Organization. The amount of genetic material required by different organisms varies greatly. The smallest DNA-containing viruses have only one molecule of 2 million molecular weight, while larger bacterial viruses contain approximately fifty times as much. It is not certain whether DNA molecules become larger and larger as the demand for genetic information increases or whether some factor sets an absolute upper limit to the size of DNA molecules. Duplication of DNA always begins at the end of the molecule and proceeds from there, the time required for the completion of the process thus depending on the length of the molecule. This may have forced higher organisms to have divided their genetic material among several chromosomes and to have developed a special mechanism, the mitotic apparatus, for ensuring that each daughter cell receives a copy of each chromosome. Accordingly a bacterium takes about twenty minutes to duplicate its chromosome; a human cell con-

[2] Condensed from Davern & Cairns, 1963.

tains about one thousand times as much DNA, and so at this rate it could duplicate its genetic material only once every two weeks. However, in view of the fact that the genetic material of a human cell is partitioned among 46 chromosomes, it can be duplicated in eight hours.

Little is known about the organization of DNA within the chromosomes of higher organisms. Sometimes the behavior of this DNA suggests that each chromosome may contain a single molecule or set of molecules which, in effect, are linked end to end. Be this as it may, it is clear that the DNA in certain chromosomes is packaged in a highly complete and yet ordered manner into regions of high and low concentrations, most neatly demonstrated in the giant chromosomes of the salivary glands of *Diptera*.

We have seen how DNA acts as a repository of genetic information. We now turn to the mechanism that translates this information into action, that is, translates the sequence of base pairs in DNA into the sequence of amino acids in a protein. This process is carried out by different species of RNA acting in concert.

With regard to the structure of RNA, like DNA it contains only four common bases: adenine, guanine, and cytosine, as in DNA, with uracil (U) replacing the thymine of DNA. As in DNA, these bases are linked by a sugar-phosphate chain, but the sugar is ribose instead of deoxyribose. The significance of these apparently minor chemical differences—loss of a methyl group of thymine to make uracil and addition of a hydroxyl group to make ribose—is unknown. Furthermore, RNA does not show the strict proportionalities of the different base pairs characteristic of DNA and the consequence of base pairing. Finally, all RNA is probably single-stranded, although each such molecule tends to fold back and pair with itself under appropriate ionic conditions.

We now turn to a consideration of the major species of RNA and the role that each may play in the execution of the message held in DNA.

Ribosomes. In the late 1940s it became apparent that protein synthesis occurs mainly in association with ribosomes, particles of ribonucleoprotein present in the cytoplasm. These particles can readily be extracted from bacteria and have been shown to consist of two unequal parts, each containing RNA and a protein and held together by divalent cations. It became increasingly obvious, however, that ribosomal RNA could not itself be the specific intermediary between DNA base sequence and protein amino acid sequence because (1) ribosomal RNA base composition does not reflect the great variability of over-all base composition of the DNA of different organisms; (2) ribosomal RNA lacks the versatility demanded in a hypothetical intermediary by the biochemical versatility of bacteria; and (3) ribosomal RNA has been shown in bacteria to be complementary to, and hence presumably coded by, a specific faint region of the bacterial chromosome.

Transfer RNA. In 1958, in the course of studies on the reaction sequence involved in protein synthesis, a low-molecular-weight RNA was found which had the unique property of binding enzymically with amino acids. This species of RNA has come to be known as "transfer RNA" or soluble or activating RNA. It is now known that there is at least one specific transfer RNA for each amino acid. Only the complexes of amino acids with their specific transfer RNAs constitute the immediate precursors for protein synthesis. Indeed, there is now proof of the fact that at the stage of polymerization, each amino acid is selected by virtue of its structure, namely, its base sequence of the attached transfer RNA, and not by virtue of its own structure. Thus one can convert cysteine, while attached to its transfer RNA, into alanine so that alanine will be incorporated into polypeptide in the positions normally occupied by cysteine.

Each transfer RNA contains about ninety bases, which have the sequence ACG . . . XYZ . . . G, where X, Y, and Z are unknown bases. It is probably folded back on itself in the form of a hairpin. The terminal bases (ACG at one end and G at the other) are common to all transfer RNA molecules, and the specificity at the time of activation of the amino acid is doubtless determined by the subterminal base sequence, which is known to be different for the different kinds of transfer RNA. The specificity, at the time of polymerization of the amino acid, is probably determined by the three bases (X, Y, and Z) that are located centrally at the bend of the molecule.

Messenger RNA. Although bacterial ribosomes and transfer RNA both survive unchanged during phage infection and serve for synthesis of foreign phage proteins, there is a small fraction of the bacterial RNA that does undergo rapid turnover after infection. This fraction has the same base composition as phage DNA, if we take the uracil of RNA as equivalent to the thymine of DNA. Going even further, it probably has the same base sequence as one of the two strands of the phage DNA, since artificial RNA-DNA hybrids can be formed between them *in vitro*. It may be detected, in infected bacteria, attached to the phage DNA (where it is presumably being synthesized), free (in transit), or attached to ribosomes (where it is assumed that it executes its information). For these and other reasons, it has been termed "messenger RNA."

Messenger RNA has since been found in every organism examined and, unlike ribosomal and transfer RNA, has a base composition which invariably reflects the base composition of the organism's DNA. The enzyme responsible for its synthesis has been isolated. Although *in vitro* this enzyme has been shown to copy both strands of DNA, there is some evidence that *in vivo* only one strand of DNA is copied into RNA.

Virus RNA. The genetic material of many viruses is RNA and not DNA. In one respect this RNA behaves like a messenger RNA, since it will code for virus protein *in vitro*. However, it differs from a simple messenger in coding for more than one distinct protein and, of course, in being replicated by the infected cell. For these reasons it should probably be placed in a class by itself.

The Genetic Code

The preceding argument may be crystallized into the formulation that inherited information resides in the precise sequence of bases in DNA and that this information is transferred to messenger RNA, which can then specify the sequence of amino acids in some particular protein. We now proceed to details of this genetic code which translates base sequence into amino acid sequence.

Although the variability in DNA base composition observed among different species suggests at first sight that each species has its own code, various experiments on protein synthesis *in vitro* show the code to be universal.

Clearly if the sequence of bases in messenger RNA is to be grouped in some way in words, the language not only must contain enough words to specify each of the twenty or so amino acids but also must allow for various forms of punctuation. With an alphabet of four letters, U, A, G, and C, there are only 16 possible two-letter words, so that the words must be longer than this. In fact, recent experiment has shown that the genetic code is a triplet one. There are several methods that could be used, if needs be in conjunction, to show which of the 64 possible three-letter words should be allocated to each amino acid.

The use of synthetic RNA molecules to code the synthesis of polypeptides *in vitro* has given rise to a kind of dictionary, which is unordered in the sense that the letters of each word are known but not their order in the word. This dictionary has in fact been extended to cover all amino acids.

To achieve order in this dictionary, we may turn to those instances in which mutation is known to change, in protein, one amino acid to another, a procedure which promises ultimately to give an unconditionally ordered dictionary and which does not depend on guessing the order, for one amino acid is best described symbolically with precise examples. Terminal addition of A or AA to poly-U gives an RNA which codes for a polyphenylalanine with one terminal tyrosine. Since random U-A copolymers code for polypeptides containing isoleucine, lysine, leucine, and asparagine, as well as tyrosine, it follows not only that the order for tyrosine is AUU . . . but that none of the others are coded by AAU. . . . A similar experiment with GUU . . . showed that the order for cysteine is GUU.

Although the language of the code is apparently universal, what may be called "word frequency" clearly differs for different species. Thus, the relative frequency of the two base pairs, A-T and G-C, is characteristic for the entire DNA of each species, and this is correlated with amino acid usage in accordance with the common dictionary. Since different species have much in common in their basic metabolisms, this variation in usage means that there must be many ways of building the same functional unit. This is illustrated by the composition and properties of the enzyme alkaline phosphatase, produced by *Escherichia coli* and *Serratia marcescans*. These two enzymes have identical function and similar geometry, and yet they are profoundly different in amino acid sequence.

Punctuation and transcription. The molecular weight of messenger RNA is rather variable but may reach about one million; that is, it may contain 3,000 bases and so be able to code a polypeptide chain of about one thousand amino acids. It is therefore now appropriate to consider the mechanism that punctuates the continuous body of information contained in DNA to give separate messenger RNA molecules, each of which can code single polypeptide chains. In thinking of the many possible ways in which the genetic message may be punctuated, it should be borne in mind that all require some special base sequence in DNA that codes for punctuation. Oddly enough, there is definite evidence that the punctuation mark separating regions that code for separate messengers is itself susceptible to deletion by mutation and that when such a deletion occurs, the two adjacent regions behave as if they were executed by a single messenger. Turning to the question of how the punctuated message is read, there is evidence, too detailed and complicated to enter into here, that RNA is loaded with activated amino acids from one end, in an orderly manner, the coding unit being a triplet.

Organization and control. It is believed that messenger RNA codes solely for proteins and that other polymers, no matter how complex, are not coded directly but are merely the specific products of enzyme action. Genetic information does not, however, merely dictate enzymatic or structural proteins; much of it is concerned with the problem of control. When a bacteriophage invades its host, different kinds of messenger RNA are made at different times. If this is a fair indication of how fast a single region of the genetic material can be expressed, it follows that the expression of most regions must, at any moment, be partly or totally restricted. What we know of such restricting control comes largely from the genetics of lactose utilization in *E. coli.* We cannot enter into details here, but genetic analysis of the system has revealed two kinds of genetic element—the structural genes, which code for permease and B-galactosidase, and two controlling elements, a regulator and an operator gene. The system which controls lactose utilization is one in which the structural genes are active only when the regulator substance is occupied by the inducing substance. Other systems are known in which the structural genes are active only when the regulator substance is free. Such is the arginine-synthesizing system of *E. coli,* in which a set of seven synthesizing enzymes is made only when arginine is not present. This system also differs from the other in that the seven structural genes, under common control, are not next to each other but are scattered throughout the genetic material, presumably being watched over in each case by a copy of the common operator gene. The nature of the regulator substance is not known, although there is some slight evidence that it may be yet another species of RNA.

The versatility of the arrangement whereby control of function may be exercised at the level of production of messenger RNA is ensured by the continual destruction of these molecules of messenger RNA in order to make way for new ones which may better reflect the needs of the occasion. The extent of this versatility is, however, itself under genetic control, for the stability of messenger RNA is different in different kinds of cells. A further regulator mechanism is found for certain enzymes, the catalytic activity of which is specifically repressed by substances which may or may not be related to their substrates. Thus apparently remote biochemical events may influence one another, not only through genetic control mechanisms, but also through a sensitivity built into the gene products themselves.

This diversity of regulator mechanisms and the multiplicity of their possibilities of interaction provide a basis for interpreting the complex sequence of events which characterize the process of differentiation, as well as all the responses to change in environment, and also provide a framework for the rapid development of cell cybernetics in the near future.

Cytogenetics, or chromosomal genetics

Of comparable importance to the discovery and exploration of the biochemical facet of genetics is the recent recognition of the significance of anomalies in the number and structure of chromosomes in the inheritance of pathological conditions, quite prominently in the psychiatric field. This new vista dawned as a result of improved and novel techniques in the field of cytogenetics, leading to the discovery in 1956 by Tjio and Levan that the normal chromosomal complement in man is 46 and not 48, as had been accepted for many decades. An extensive development of karyotyping occurred almost overnight. This has already yielded a rich harvest in psychiatry, for not only has Down's syndrome, or mongolism, yielded her secret to this technique, but other forms of mental defect, with and without congenital bodily deformity, have received fundamental clarification on the basis of chromosomal abnormality. The very tangibility of these findings has lent conviction to the role of genetics in psychiatry in the eyes of those whose psychogenic orientation or inability to grasp the remote intricacies of gene action rendered them inhospitable to genetic interpretations in this area.

Later in this chapter we shall take up the details of the role of chromosomal abnormality in mental defect, in the realm of achieved fact, and in schizophrenia, in the area of incipient research.

Statistical methods[3]

PEDIGREE, OR FAMILY-HISTORY, METHOD

This method is mainly of historical interest and of preliminary suggestive significance. Even before the Mendelian era, certain traits or disorders were observed to "run in families," paving the way for the more effective methods of assessing the fact of heredity and the type of hereditary mechanism involved. Sir Ronald Fisher gave interesting examples of such pedigrees that had pointed the way in his address at a plenary session of the 1956 Congress at Copenhagen. Pedigrees, from the pattern of distribution of affected or unaffected members of varying degrees of relationship within the family, may provide an indication as to whether the trait concerned is transmitted as a Mendelian dominant (transmission in the direct line of descent, a 50 per cent rate of children of one affected parent similarly affected, and descendants of nonaffected members not affected themselves), as a Mendelian recessive (transmission in the collateral line of descent, a 25 per cent rate of affected children of two overtly normal parents, raised consanguinity rate in parents, and skipping of generations in respect of affected members), or as one of the varieties of sex-linked traits (in the commoner of which, e.g., hemophilia, the condition is transmitted by the female and suffered by the male).

Such pedigrees, however, can at most be regarded as of preliminary value because the small size of human families does not statistically warrant the drawing of firm conclusions about the genetic mechanisms involved, and the pedigrees that draw attention to themselves often do so by virtue of their unduly heavy loading (not representative of the average family) with cases exhibiting the trait or disease in question.

From the cue given by pedigrees, we are driven on to the more precise and more statistically adequate methods, which have been called the "contingency method of statistical prediction" and the "twin study method," the two methods gaining in effectiveness in combination in the "twin family method" of Kallmann.

CONTINGENCY METHOD

Before proceeding to the more technical aspect of this method, it should be stressed what care is taken in modern genetic methods in collecting a representative, unselected sample. Perusal of Kallmann's 1938 monograph will give an idea of how painstaking such work can be. In the contingency method, large samples of consanguineous groups are used, distinguished by specified degrees of blood relationship to a statistically representative number of probands or index cases (carriers of the trait under investigation who form the starting point of inquiry for the particular family being studied) and considered suitable

[3] Condensed from Hurst, 1958.

TABLE 1

Age group	*All consanguineous persons observed*	*All cases of disease X observed (net figure)*	*Corrected rate of reference (expectancy figure)*
0–20	100		
20–40	100	10	50
Over 40	100	20	100
Total	300	30	150

Morbidity rate: 10 per cent (net, or uncorrected); 20 per cent (corrected, or expectancy figure).

for comparison with a normal, average population group. The technical procedures employed in such an assessment are Weinberg's proband and sibship methods.

In order to arrive at expectancy figures from the net figures of a particular investigation, which involves correcting for statistical inequalities in age distribution and in the process of collecting index cases for a survey to be analyzed according to the contingency method, the most elementary corrective methods used are those of Weinberg. The system of proband methods for correcting any bias in the selection of cases has been referred to but cannot be elaborated here. It may be instructive, however, to review his abridged method, which corrects for inequalities of age distribution. Let us consider a consanguineous group being investigated in respect of disease X, which has been found to have a manifestation period ranging from age 20 to age 40. Table 1 shows that although the divisor in calculating the net, or uncorrected, figure is 300, the divisor in calculating the corrected, or expectancy, figure is only 150, yielding a result which is twice the net figure.

The reasons for reducing the divisor are as follows: 100 of the 300 cases cannot be counted at all as they are under 20 years of age and can thus not have reached the minimal age at which the disease can develop. The 100 in column 2 of the table denoting the age group 40 and over all count because they have passed the manifestation period for the disease. The 100 denoting those distributed throughout the age period 20 to 40 may, on the assumption of even distribution throughout this period, be taken as having on the average reached the age of 30, thus having been exposed to only half the risk of developing the condition, so that instead of this figure's contributing a full 100 to the denominator, it contributes only 50. Adding our three figures together, we arrive at a figure of 150 instead of 300.

More refined methods have been devised by Bernstein, Ilse, Strömgren, and Lenz, which take cognizance of an uneven or irregular distribution through the risk period. Kallmann has moreover devised what is probably the most precise method in the form of morbidity statistics analogous to the mortality tables used in life insurance statistics.

TWIN STUDY METHOD

This method is based on the fact that monozygotic, monovular, one-egg, or identical twins originating from the same fertilized ovum have essentially the same genotypes—genetic constitution or hereditary equipment—whereas dizygotic, biovular, two-egg, or fraternal twins have no greater chance of having a similar combination of hereditary characters than any pair of ordinary siblings. If, therefore, in a study of a series of twins collected on the basis of the fact that at least one of every pair exhibits the trait or disease under consideration, the one-egg twins show a higher proportion of cases in which both members of the twin sets manifest the condition (concordance) than the two-egg twin sets, we have presumptive evidence of the operation of hereditary factors in the determination of the trait.

With regard to the establishment of the zygocity of twins, i.e., whether the twins are monozygous or dizygous, the similarity method (due to Siemens) is now generally used. According to this method, twins are classified as monozygotic if they are strikingly similar in general appearance and, in particular, if they are alike in the color of eyes, hair, and skin; hair texture; blood groups; facial features; dental irregularities; finger proportions; and the microscopic character of fingerprints (cross resemblance exceeding internal resemblance) and palm patterns. The presence of reversed asymmetry in handedness, dentition, and fingerprints, when present, is confirmatory evidence of monozygocity. The old fetal-membrane method is unreliable and is no longer used since monozygotic twins may have separate placentas.

A variety of minor criticisms of inferences from twin studies in special cases on the basis of anomalies of development have been raised by Zlotnikoff, Bronson Price, Newman, Dahlberg, N. F. Walker, Waardenburg, Meyer, Curtius, and von Verschuer, but the phenomena are so rare as not to raise any question about the validity of the main premise involved in twin studies. Of more general scope is the criticism based on the contention that in view of the fact that one-egg twins share a much more similar socioeconomic and psychological environment, it is unwarranted to attribute higher concordance figures which may be found in this type of twin, as compared with the two-egg variety, entirely to the greater similarity in genetic equipment. Slater's formulation is to this effect:

> It is sometimes assumed that any similarities shown by uni-ovular twins can be attributed to heredity, and differences to the environment, but only the latter half of this assumption can safely be held. From this, however, it does not follow that deductions about the importance of heredity in causing some characteristic cannot be based on the examination of a series of uni-ovular twins, provided that there is no biased selection and that controls, i.e. binovular twins, are available.

The co-twin control method was used by Gesell and Thompson for the study of variations such as those of intelligence produced in selected pairs of monozygotic twins by prearranged differences in training and other environmental influences. As applied to our special problem, this method leads to the investigation of whether the concordance rates for the trait or disease in question differ between the one-egg sets reared together and those reared apart under different psychological and socioeconomic circumstances. A significant difference in these figures would provide a measure of the contribution of environmental factors to the causation of the trait in question.

The twin family method of Kallmann includes the combination of the twin and family methods, which permits of the bringing together of certain significant figures, making this method an immeasurably more powerful analytic tool than either of the component methods separately. The main categories of relationship for which morbidity figures are obtained in this method are one-egg twins, two-egg twins, full siblings, half-siblings, step-siblings, and the general population. This method demonstrates whether or not the individual's chance of developing a given trait increases in direct proportion to the degree of blood relationship to an index case affected by the trait in question.

A specific example is the best way of conveying the force of this method. The figures for schizophrenia in Kallmann's American study are as follows: one-egg twins, 86.2 per cent; two-egg twins, 14.5 per cent; siblings, 14.2 per cent; half-siblings, 7.1 per cent; children, 16.4 per cent; general population, 0.85 per cent.

Inferences from these figures are:

1. The morbidity figures of all degrees of blood relationship are much higher than in the general population; even in half-siblings, the incidence is eight times greater.

2. With increasing degree of blood relationship, there is increasing degree of morbidity—from 7.1 per cent in half-siblings and 14.2 per cent in full siblings to 86.2 per cent in one-egg twins. Of additional special interest is the fact that the incidence for full siblings is exactly double that for half-siblings.

3. The concordance rate for one-egg twins is very high (86.2 per cent) and is approximately six times the figure for two-egg twins. Beside this, the finding in another study that the concordance of separated one-egg schizophrenic twins is slightly lower than that of nonseparated one-egg twins—65.0 per cent as compared with 71 per cent—fades into insignificance as regards the implication of environmental factors in causation of the condition.

4. The essential similarity of the figures for siblings and two-egg twins (14.2 per cent and 14.5 per cent) is of intrinsic interest because of postulated lack of significant differences in average genetic equipment. Further, there is an obvious analogy here to the greater similar-

ity of the environment shared by one-egg as compared with two-egg twins; in this case there is a presumption that two-egg twins are on the average likely to share a more common environment than any two siblings taken at random, and yet here this environmental factor has exerted no effect on the comparative morbidities.

Behavior genetics[4]

Before examining defined diseases and syndromes, let us consider the range of behavior related to such areas as intelligence, temperament, personality, neuroticism, and anxiety, with regard to the role of a possible genetic component.

This relatively new field of endeavor within human genetics, which has now been raised to the status of a department of its own and has been christened "behavior genetics," has been comprehensively surveyed in its ideological aspect as well as from the standpoint of its foundation in animal and human experiment by Fuller and Thompson (1960) in their excellent work entitled *Behavior Genetics,* upon which I shall draw heavily in my subsequent recital.

At the outset we should adduce salient methodological considerations in this field. With regard to experimental design, heredity as an independent variable can be incorporated in a psychological experiment, as is the case with physiological or experiential factors. The dependent variable can be any form of behavior which interests the investigator. The simplest experiment is to take two groups of different heredity, treat them alike in all other respects, and administer a behavior test. The results are compared against the prediction from the null hypothesis, i.e., that the groups differ no more than two independent samples drawn from the same population. If the null hypothesis is not supported, evidence for heritability of the behavior variation has been obtained.

PATHWAYS BETWEEN GENES AND BEHAVIOR

A fundamental ideological problem is that of the pathways between genes and behavior. The ordinary technique of physiological genetics research is to start with a specific, well-developed phenotypic difference and work backward toward genetic sources of variation. The reverse order is more suited to the presentation of general principles. Behavior is the response of an organism to stimulation of external or internal origin. Genes operate at the molecular level of organization, but they are peculiar kinds of molecules, highly individuated carriers of information, whose effects are describable in psychophysiological as well as chemical terms. Enzymes, hormones, and neurones may be regarded as successively complex intermediaries between genes and psychological characters. Instances of the path through enzymes are hyperphagia in the genetically obese mouse, strain differences in audiogenic seizures in mice, superior performance in the Krech hypothesis apparatus by rats with high brain cholinesterase levels, and, in man, phenylketonuria and Williams's genetotrophic theory of alcoholism. The approach to the gene-behavior-character relationship through enzyme studies has the advantage of being close to the gene end of the chain, but this advantage is counterbalanced by distance from behavioral events. One may employ genetic lesions to naturally dissect the nervous system at the metabolic level, but this dissection is not the same as separating natural units of behavior. More must be learned regarding the relationship between biochemical individuality and behavior before the findings of the biochemist can have psychological meaning. In the expanding area of psychochemistry, genetics will have a unique role, for genes are the only way in which permanent chemical characteristics can be built into an organism.

Beach (1948) has summarized the potential mechanisms through which hormones might control behavior as follows:

1. Through effects upon the organism's normal development and maintenance activities. Such effects, exemplified by the multiple deficiencies of the cretin, are relatively nonspecific.

2. Through stimulation of structures employed in specific response patterns; for example, the postnatal growth of genital organs is dependent upon hormones, and adult sexual

[4] Condensed from Hurst, 1962.

behavior cannot occur until these structures are fully developed.

3. Through effects upon peripheral receptors, sensitizing them to particular forms of stimulation—a comparatively little-explored area.

4. Through effects on the integrative functions of the central nervous system, investigated by direct injections of hormones into the brain (Fisher, 1956; Harris et al., 1958).

With these generalizations in mind, one should reinforce one's critical attitude by distinguishing between psychophysiological actions of hormones in normal concentrations and psychopharmacological effects of large doses applied in artificial ways, which latter type of effect has little significance for the genetics of normal variation. An additional complication in the analysis of the gene-hormone-behavior relationship is that genes might operate upon the source of the hormone, affecting the quality and quantity of the product, or upon the target organs, affecting their response. Furthermore, the endocrine system is physiologically complex, with much interaction between components. None of the four types of mechanism described by Beach, or the two means by which genes might act, are mutually exclusive. The availability of pathways is more than adequate.

Despite the importance of variation in the nervous system as a path along which genes might come to influence behavior, few studies have dealt directly with the problem. Genes which lead to major neurological defects have been found in many species and show a considerable uniformity in their manifestations. One group of these, the lipidoses, is characterized by abnormal lipid deposition in the brain, but these have not yet been related to specific enzymatic processes. A promising area of investigation in this field is the individual variation in the fine structure of the central nervous systems of higher vertebrates and its genetic components and behavioral significance.

GENES AND PSYCHOLOGICAL COMPONENTS

One final ideological consideration must engage our attention before we turn to details of the psychological behavior genetics field. It is the general logicostatistical question of the interrelationship of genes and psychological components. The search for anatomical and physiological channels through which genes contribute to variation in behavior has had the limited success just indicated. Physiological and anatomical techniques have the limitation that the measuring devices themselves impair the intactness of the subjects. This has provided a gap, which psychologists have been able to fill by using behavior tests themselves to define psychological components that could have genetic significance. The idea is that traits might be found by methods such as factor analysis which are biologically more real than test scores chosen empirically (Blewett, 1954; Cattell, 1953; Eysenck & Prell, 1951; Royce, 1957; Thompson, 1956; Thurstone, Thurstone, & Strandskov, 1953).

Although we cannot discuss the whole field of factor analysis here, we can perhaps bring home that part of it where we are concerned with the relationship between multifactor constellations at various levels, behavioral, physiological, and genetic. In their substantial work *The Meaning and Measurement of Neuroticism and Anxiety*, Cattell and Scheier (1961) stress the importance of multivariate analysis of a comprehensive array of test-response measurements in personality assessment. As an extension of this theme to various levels and their interrelationships, the reader is referred to Royce's congruent and noncongruent models reproduced in Fuller and Thompson (1960). In his congruent model, using general intelligence as an example, he illustrates his concept of the relationship between the multiple-factor theory of psychology and the multiple-factor theory of genetics. The model is called "congruent" because of the part-for-part correspondence between gene blocks and the three psychological components of general intelligence selected—space factor, memory factor, and other factors—manifested in the behavioral phenotypes. In contrast to this, the second model is noncongruent, inasmuch as there is no precise correspondence between genes and traits defined at the physiological and behavioral levels. The correlation between the traits ϕ and θ is a function of the contribution of the physiological character ι to each. This character is in turn controlled by gene D. Both ϕ and θ have genetic variances (from genes A, B, C, D, E, F) which are either specific or shared with other traits. The figure also has a portion illustrating chromosomal communality. The covariation between traits θ and Σ is dependent upon the linkage of genes F and G. The noncongruence in this model implies multiple-factor control of psychological traits and the existence of complex gene interactions in the development of phenotypes. In spite of this complexity, the evidence for lawful genetic effects upon behavior has been amply demonstrated. Further analysis of the gene-character relationship may be possible from experiments in which genotypes are manipulated and phenotypic effects measured.

Genetic factors in intelligence

We cannot here enter into a critical evaluation of the rival definitions of intelligence or of the dispute as to whether it is made up of a general factor as well as specific components.

FAMILY STUDIES

The first systematic examination of familial correlation with respect to mental ability was made by Karl Pearson around the turn of the century. Using teachers' rankings based on a seven-point scale of intellectual capacity, he found the correlations between brothers to be .52; between sisters, .51; and between brother and sister, .52. The correlations were in line with those obtained with physical characteristics such as height, hair color, and cephalic index. Cattell and Willson (1938), using a so-called "culture-free intelligence test," obtained the figures of .91 for parent-child and .77 for sibling correlations, concluding that parents and children have nine-tenths of their respective levels in common and that four-fifths of the variability in intelligence among families is due to heredity.

As representative of work on special abilities within intelligence, we may take the investigation of Carter (1932) into family resemblance in verbal and numerical abilities. He found that if both parents were superior, they tended to have a high proportion of superior children; if one or both were inferior, this proportion was correspondingly less.

Fuller and Thompson (1961) come to the following conclusions as a result of their survey of these family studies of intelligence.

> In the first place, resemblance in intelligence appears to depend in most populations more on hereditary than environmental or experiential factors. Second, degree of resemblance is not different in different kinds of populations, such as urban or rural, superior or average, except insofar as these may influence the homogeneity of the sample. If cultural influences on test score are eliminated (Cattell and Willson, 1938), degree of resemblance is increased. Third, there is some evidence to show that resemblances even in school abilities are affected by heredity at least as much as those in general intelligence.

TWIN STUDIES

In the sphere of twin studies, those based on intellectual resemblances of dizygotic and monozygotic twins reared together and apart are of the most definitive value. Those of Newman et al. (1937) and of Gardner and Newman (1940), in which intrapair correlations in respect of Binet, Otis, and Stanford achievement tests are recorded, are the best known, but there are four others (Burks, 1942; Saudek, 1934; Stephens & Thompson, 1943; Gates & Brach, 1941). In summary, the evidence on twins reared apart supports the hereditary hypothesis, though there is also little doubt that large differences in environment can affect similarity of monozygotic twins.

A host of studies on special abilities are in line with the broad conclusions in respect of general intelligence. Thus Holzinger (1929), who used among other indices five tests of school ability—namely, word meaning, arithmetic, nature study, history and literature, and spelling—found correlations that ranged from .73 to .87 in monozygotic pairs and from .56 to .73 in dizygotic pairs.

Genetic factors in temperament and personality

Genetic work in the wide field of temperament and personality stems from Galton's (1874) pedigree studies. More precise work has been made possible by family correlations and twin resemblances between the results (often including components) of such tests as the Bernreuter, several attitude scales, Maller Character Sketches, Allport Ascendance-Submission, tests of personal tempo (e.g., speed of tapping), the Rorschach (coarctative, introversive, and extroversive), and tests of perceptual and sensory capacities. These investigations may in general be said to support the view that a number of testable dimensions of personality depend on inheritance. However, conclusions such as the nature-nurture ratio are by no means as clear as they are in the case of intelligence. Obviously, much remains to be done, particularly in the matter of obtaining a rational and parsimonious description of personality. Experimentation on such points as activity and inactivity and emotionality and nonemotionality in rats offers promise in this direction and has already given rise to precise genetic hypotheses (Brody, 1942; Brody, 1950; Hall, 1951).

Genetic factors in neuroticism and anxiety

Our next theme is that of genetic factors in neuroticism and anxiety. Eysenck (1956) has by methods of factorial analysis given conclusive evidence that neuroticism and psychoticism are different dimensions of personality. Moreover, Eysenck and Prell (1951) have, on the basis of their study of 25 monozygotic and 25 dizygotic twin pairs, classified the "neurotic personality factor" as a biological and largely gene-specific entity, estimating the genetic contribution to this neurotic unit predisposition to be 80 per cent.

Anxiety, that frequent concomitant of neurosis, is brought together with it (i.e., neurosis) by Cattell and Scheier (1961) for critical statistical scrutiny, and both items are enriched by their treatment. Not only do they confirm Eysenck's finding that neuroticism and psychoticism are separate dimensions, but they establish the multifactor nature of neurosis on the basis of the method of multivariate analysis. In contrast to neurosis, both trait definition and type definition attach the clinical concept of anxiety to a single second-order factor. The main first-order components in this factor are ergic tension, ego weakness, guilt-proneness, low self-sentiment strength, and protension or suspiciousness, and on these components a valuable clinical test of anxiety has been devised. The general point their analysis has established is that anxiety is part, but not all, of neurosis, which is a broader and more complex concept.

Moving now from the general psychological dimension "neuroticism" to clinically overt neurosis, we meet Slater's earlier work, in which he brings together neurotic and psychopathic reactions, viewing them in terms of different grades of adjustment to stress. Genetically he considers that his figures suggest the hypothesis of nonspecific polygenic deficiencies in relation to stress. Moreover, in the neuroses he found that the form of the symptoms is not as closely related to the form of stress as to the basic personality . In his recent Maudsley Lecture (1961) on hysteria 311, Slater reviews twin data of his own and of Ljungberg (1957), illustrating the heterogeneity of this group and dethroning it from the status of a nosological entity.

Genetic findings in psychiatry and neurology[5]

This section consists of a condensed description of some of the main findings and recent research in the fields of psychiatry and neurology, including consideration of the condition phenylpyruvic amentia, where something substantial on the biochemical side is already known.

FINDINGS IN PSYCHIATRY

With the review of principles already given, Table 2 on pages 160–161 should be meaning-

[5] Condensed from Hurst, 1961; Hurst, 1962; Hurst, 1963.

ful. Something may profitably be said in elaboration of the following items.

Manic-depressive Psychosis

The genetic mechanism is irregularly dominant with a high degree of penetrance and with a pronounced tendency to a relatively mild symptomatology in the presence of stabilizing constitutional modifiers. The diagnostic classification should be restricted to cases with acute, self-limited mood swings before the fifth decade of life and without progressive or residual personality disintegration before or after psychotic episodes. So diagnosed, the disease is correlated with a tendency toward obesity, cardiovascular disorders, gout, and diabetes and with high resistance to tuberculosis, and it is apparently based on a strictly specific genotype. This condition is genetically unrelated to reactive or neurotic depression, to menopausal and presenile depressions, and to other nonperiodical forms of depressive behavior in the involutional period. The dysfunction may be looked upon as one of regulatory instability, but present information about the biochemical constituent of the underlying genotype, as well as about the range of its compensatory adaptiveness, is still far from complete (Kallmann, 1950; Kallmann, 1951; Kallmann, 1953a: Kallmann, 1954).

Schizophrenia

The implications of the figures appearing in Table 2 have been studied in connection with a review of the twin family method. One additional statistic in relation to the question of dominance or recessiveness of the schizophrenic genotype is that in his studies, Kallmann has found figures of 16.4 per cent in children with one schizophrenic parent and 68.1 per cent in children with both parents schizophrenic. The most cogent view, according to Kallmann, is that the condition is determined by an autosomal and single recessive unit factor, the penetrance (70 per cent) and phenotypical expressivity of which are limited by polygenic (nonspecific) constitutional modifiers, measurably correlated with the compensatory capacities of the athletic component of physique (Kallmann, 1946).

A close relationship between constitutional resistance to the schizophrenic genotype and graded resistance to pulmonary tuberculosis has been found. Only homozygous bearers of the specific (predisposing) genotype for schizophrenia are capable of reacting with a true schizophrenic psychosis. Other features emerging from an analysis of the detailed figures of Kallmann's work are reduced reproductivity rate, increased rate of consanguinity in the parents, and transmission in the collateral line of descent. Schizoid personality traits may be found in homozygotes with very high resistance or in heterozygotes with relatively low resistance (homozygotes having a double and heterozygotes a single dose of the gene).

Of the other serious workers and thinkers in this field, none dispute the fact of heredity in schizophrenia and its great importance, but there are those who favor some other type or additional type of genetic mechanism. In Germany during the 1930s, a simple dominant mode of inheritance was favored and became the basis for eugenic sterilization laws. Lenz, Koller, and Slater still support the dominance theory as covering some or all of the cases.

Koller's argument cannot be presented here in detail, but it culminates in the contention that if the gene were recessive, the incidence of schizophrenia would be lower in the children than in the sibs, whereas the reverse is the case. Slater (1953) likes this argument, inclines to the view that dominant as well as recessive forms exist, and adopts a view of genetic heterogeneity to explain the subgroups of schizophrenia, which Kallmann deals with more effectively, in my opinion, in terms of the modifying effect of the polygenic resistance mechanism. Penrose's theory of a multifactorial genetic determination of the disease does not conflict formally with Kallmann's hypothesis of a specific single recessive predisposing mechanism plus a multifactorial constitutional resistance mechanism, for after all, one plus many equals many, but Kallmann's theory is much richer in detailed content and in its fruitfulness as a research hypothesis.

In bringing together findings in respect to manic-depressive psychosis and schizophrenia, it is interesting to note the cumulative effect of the evidence of the specificity and distinctness of the two genotypes. In reviewing the work of Kallmann's department in 1952, Hurst (1952) was able to report that among a total of 1,232 twin index cases, no pair of one-egg twin partners was found whose clinical symptomatology warranted

TABLE 2. GENETIC FINDINGS IN PSYCHIATRIC CONDITIONS

Psychiatric condition	*Investigator*	*General population*	*Half-sibs*	*Sibs*	*Two-egg twins*	*One-egg twins*	*Parents*	*Children*	*Postulated genetic mechanism*
Neurosis and psychopathic personality	Slater			M 2.4 F 0.0	M 42.1% F 7.4%	M 80.0% F 0.0%			Polygenic
Manic-depressive psychosis	Kallmann	0.4%	16.7%	23%	26.3%	95.7%	23.4%	24.4%	Autosomal; irregular dominant
	Luxenburger			12.7%	1:16	31:33			
	Rosanoff				11:67	16:23			
	Stenstedt			c. 15%			c. 15%	c.15%	
Schizophrenia	Kallmann	0.85%	7.1%	14.2%	14.5%	86.2%	9.3%	16.4%	Autosomal recessive; 70% penetrance
	Slater				14.0%	76.0%			Recessive and dominant cases
Childhood schizophrenia	Kallmann & Roth			12.2%	17.1%	70.6%	12.5%		Similar to adult form
Involutional psychosis	Kallmann	1.0%	4.5%	6.0%	6.0%	60.0%	6.4%		Heterozygous carriers of schizophrenic genotype
Senile psychosis	Kallmann	Less than 1.0%		6.5%	8.0%	42.8%	3.4%		Gene-specific biochemical factors plus adaptive personality traits
Presenile psychosis									
Pick's disease	Sjögren	0.1%		6.8 ± 2.9%			19 ± 5%		Autosomal dominant; polygenic
Alzheimer's disease	Sjögren			3.8 ± 2.1%			10 ± 4%		
Suicide	Kallmann et al.				1:28	1:28			None demonstrated
Adult male homosexuality	Kallmann et al.				42.3%	100%			Genetically disarranged balance between male and female maturational tendencies

TABLE 2. (Continued)

Psychiatric condition	*Investigator*	*General population*	*Half-sibs*	*Sibs*	*Two-egg twins*	*One-egg twins*	*Parents*	*Children*	*Postulated genetic mechanism*
Huntington's chorea	Rosanoff & Handy				1:2	3:3			Autosomal dominant
	Haldane								
Epilepsy	Conrad			4.0%	4.3%	86%			Polygenic (Kallmann)
	Alstrom			1.5%			1.5%	3.5%	Not genetic, except rarely single dominant
	Gibbs et al. (EEG)				25%	100%			Single dominant
Mental defect (high-grade)	Brugger & Juda		23.4%	35.9%	54%	86%			Polygenic; special single recessive and single dominant forms
Mongolism	Lejeune, Gautier, & Turpin								Trisomic condition demonstrated cytologically

placing the two members of the pair into different diagnostic categories. Recently published observations of three different workers—Elsässer (1952), Slater (1953), and Stenstedt (1952)—point in the same direction.

The relative infrequency of manic-depressive psychosis in modern populations may be partly due to factors of selection which reduce the reproductive rate of the carriers without affecting the social level of their families (Kallmann, 1946; Stenstedt, 1952). At least there seems to be no tendency toward a social decline of the magnitude typical of schizophrenic family units.

Childhood schizophrenia. In their paper entitled "Genetic Aspects of Pre-adolescent Schizophrenia," Kallmann and Roth (1956) provide the following conclusions from their study of 52 twins and 50 singletons under age 15 (quoted in part):

> (a) These findings indicate an early effect in childhood schizophrenia of the same genotype (gene-specific deficiency state) assumed to be responsible for the basic symptoms of adult schizophrenia. The conclusion is supported by the observation that the psychoses in the co-twins of early schizophrenia cases occur sometimes before and sometimes after adolescence.
>
> (b) While the etiological mechanisn underlying the relatively infrequent activation of a schizophrenic psychosis before adolescence has not yet been adequately identified, it would seem to be connected with variable constellations of secondary factors lowering constitutional resistance. . . .
>
> (c) Because of a dearth of statistically comparable data, it is difficult to appraise the part played by a poor home with disturbed intra-family relationships in the etiology of childhood schizophrenia, as compared with that of adult schizophrenia. . . .

Recent trends in the genetics of schizophrenia. Two areas of recent study in Kallmann's department of medical genetics (Columbia University) worth reports are mating and fertility trends and the relationship between deafness and schizophrenia. These are discussed in chap. 6, "Mating and Fertility Trends," and chap. 7, "Deafness and Schizophrenia: Interrelation of Communication Stress, Maturation, Lag and Schizophrenic Risk," in *Expanding Goals of Genetics in Psychiatry* (Kallmann, 1962).

Under the design of the study of mating and fertility trends, a random sample of schizophrenic patients admitted to New York State mental hospitals during the three-year period from 1934 to 1936 is compared with a like sample admitted between 1954 and 1956. The most significant finding, reviewed in a preliminary communication on 1,552 cases, or one-third of the proposed final sample, is that of relatively greater increases in marriage and total reproduction among schizophrenics than in the general population, in this era of improved therapy and socialization of schizophrenic mental hospital patients. The implications of this for the health of future generations call for careful appraisal by geneticists and psychiatrists alike.

Of those workers reporting on deafness and schizophrenia, only D. Sank had worked extensively on the genetics of early total deafness as such. The others had devoted themselves more specifically to the theme indicated in the chapter title. On the basis of their statewide survey, the authors conclude that the severe and varied stresses associated with early total deafness apparently do little to increase the chance of developing the clinical symptoms of schizophrenia, whereas sibship consanguinity to a schizophrenic person results in a marked increase in schizophrenic morbidity risk.

A living monument to this seven-year intensive research program (recently embodied in a monograph) is a clinical facility, the deafness unit, which is now a going concern at Rockland State Hospital, New York.

Another significant recent work in the realm of population genetics is that of Garrone ("Statistical Genetic Study of Schizophrenia in the Geneva Population between 1901 and 1950"), confirming the conclusions of Kallmann's studies, including the genetic homogeneity of schizophrenia in respect of its clinical subgroups and a simple recessive mode of inheritance with a homozygous penetrance of 67 per cent. The crude incidence of schizophrenia in the Geneva population is estimated at 1 per cent, the morbidity risk at 2.4 per cent, and the prevalence of the schizophrenia gene at 19 per cent.

The paper of Essen-Möller, "On the Frequency of Schizophrenia in Mothers of Schizophrenics," demonstrates that the doubled frequency of affected mothers as compared with fathers in the ancestry of schizophrenics is not to be interpreted as supporting a psychogenetic view of schizophrenia but, in terms of statistical bias, as relating to the fraction of the risk period in the two sexes, between the time of entering systematic observation and the birth of the probands. This explanation fits in with the observation that among children, those descended from male probands become schizophrenic quite as often as those descended from female probands.

Chromosomal studies in schizophrenia. Raphael and Shaw (1963) point out that within the past three years, the causes of an increasing number of clinical disorders have been elucidated by the study of human chromosomes. It is understandable and desirable, therefore, that schizophrenics should be studied from this point of view, in spite of the strong evidence that we are here dealing with a single autosomal gene effect. We shall report briefly on three papers.

Money and Hirsch (1963), in a survey of 784 female and 916 male mentally defective patients, picked up three triple X and two triple X-Y patients. Two of these patients were schizophrenic, and their pedigrees were traced as far as possible. The authors, while concluding that schizophrenia when coexistent with mental deficiency in the triple X syndrome could not be ascribed to the tripling of the X chromosome, surmise that "perhaps there is a closer genetic linkage between schizophrenia and mental deficiency than can so far be demonstrated."

Tedeschi and Freeman (1963), in a study of sex chromosomes in male schizophrenics, while finding in two cases a count of sex-chromatin cells far above the expected frequency in the normal male (but lower than in the normal female), demonstrated that percentage-wise in the series as a whole, there was a frequency of positive sex chromatin "not too dissimilar from that found by others in normal and mentally defective males."

The paper by Raphael and Shaw (1963) describes chromosome studies of 10 adult schizophrenics (5 men and 5 women), followed by a more extensive series of 100 male and 100 female cases, and presents, in compendious form, 27 sex chromatin surveys (3 on newborn infants, 18 on mental defectives, and 6 on schizophrenics).

The authors conclude that one Klinefelter and one triple X syndrome in their series of 210 patients suggest that specific abnormalities of sex chromosomes are more frequent among schizophrenics than in the general population. With regard to the sex-chromatin studies, they comment that although the difference between the mental defectives and the newborn is statistically significant, in the case of the schizophrenics numbers are still insufficient to confirm a trend that appears suggestive.

Summarizing one's own impression of these studies, it may be said that to date chromosomal anomalies have been demonstrated in only a very small minority of schizophrenic cases.

Involutional Psychosis

According to Kallmann (1951), the implication of comparative data "would seem to be that the principal genetic derivation of involutional psychosis is from an indirect relationship to the entity of schizophrenia, and not from a specific type of predisposition producing a particular impairment of the adjustive plasticity of aging persons."

Senile and Presenile Psychoses

The severe maladjustment to aging resulting in the symptomatology of a senile psychosis would appear to depend on a combination of etiological components, including age-susceptible personality traits and decreasing adaptational plasticity and socioeconomic security. From their relation to those gene-specific biochemical phenomena which control growth and decline, these may be expected to coexist more frequently in genetically alike persons (one-egg twins). The genetic mechanism is in all probability polygenic in nature, despite Haldane's speculatively attractive attempt to assimilate it to the heterozygous state of phenylketonuria.

Of the presenile psychoses, we shall confine ourselves to the brain atrophies of Pick and Alzheimer. The evidence from the investigation of the Sjögrens and Lindgren (1952) that makes it probable that polygenic or multifactorial inheritance operates in Alzheimer's disease fits in with the graded nature of the clinical picture in terms of varying degrees of dementia and of degenerative neuropathological changes. In Pick's disease a dominant gene is almost certainly implicated. Grünthal's work (1930 to 1931) which had been suggestive of this, was clinched by the Sjögrens and Lindgren (1952). In attempting to account for the preponderance of women in Pick's as well as Alzheimer's disease, Sjögren rejected the hypothesis of sex-linked inheritance in favor of the thesis that either a reduced manifestation of the specific genetic factors in males is responsible, or there is an inhibiting gene on the X chromosome which prevents manifestation in men but which must be present in homozygous form before it can do so in women.

Suicide

In suicide, that final and irrevocable failure to adjust to life, there has been a widespread tendency to assume an inheritable type of unfitness in the general personality structure. This has not been borne out by the investigations of Kallmann and his coworkers (Kallmann & Anastasio, 1946; Kallmann et al., 1949). The first 27 sets of twin subjects were discordant as to suicide. In 1950 this run was broken by a pair of schizophrenic and overtly homosexual World War II veterans who became concordant as to suicide, albeit at different ages—25 and 29—and by different methods—drowning and gas. A single instance of this type in a sample of this size is clearly within the range of chance expectation. The general conclusion from this study of suicide in twins, as well as from another one by the same group in only children, is that there is no statistically valid support for the notion of hereditary or familial occurrence of suicide.

Adult Male Homosexuality

The twin family method provides a means of contributing to a scientifically validated elucidation of this condition, about which highly speculative psychodynamic theories have long held the field. Kallmann (1952) in his study used Kinsey's six-point scale in rating adult homosexuality.

One salient finding (reflected in Table 2) was that in 40 one-egg twin pairs showing a high degree of homosexuality (Kinsey ratings of 3 or more), there was 100 per cent concordance for the trait in question, while for the 45 two-egg pairs, the concordance was 11.5 or 42.3 per cent, according to whether the two highest homosexual ratings (5 and 6) or the whole range (1 to 6) was taken as the criterion. (These figures are only slightly higher than Kinsey's estimates of 10 per cent and 37 per cent of the total population.) A point of further interest is the fact that most of these twin pairs claimed to have developed their sexual deviation independently and far apart from each other and that all of them denied categorically any history of mutuality in overt sex relations.

An important conclusion also emerges from a consideration of sex ratios in the sibships of homosexuals (not reflected in Table 2). In the single-born and twin index samples alike, there is a fairly consistent tendency for this to deviate toward an excess of males. In the sibships studied by Kallmann, a ratio of 126 males to 100 females was obtained (as compared with 106 males to 100 females in the corresponding general population). This is in line with Lang's demonstration of a statistically significant deviation in the direction of a preponderance of males in the sibships of a large sample of some 1,015 German homosexuals, where the ratio for all ages was 121.1 males to 100 females and for subjects over the age of 25 was 128.3 males to 100 females. The inference from this is that adult male homosexuality is a biologically determined phenomenon on a genetic basis, i.e., is due to a genetically disarranged balance between male and female maturational tendencies.

Huntington's Chorea

This, the first psychiatric condition to be recognized as hereditary in nature, is found in all parts of the world and affects whites and nonwhites alike. It has been shown to be due to a single dominant gene of close to 100 per cent penetrancy, for it rarely skips a generation. Rosanoff and Handy (1935) have recorded five pairs of twins from affected families. The three monozygotic pairs were concordant for the condition, while in the case of the two dizygotic pairs, one was concordant and the other discordant. Haldane (1941) has advanced the thesis that there may be sex-linked modifiers which tend to raise the age of onset in males. Commenting on Bell's figures (1934) on the differential distribution of affected progeny of affected fathers and mothers, he finds that the difference is highly significant for the children of affected fathers. On the supposition that there are one or more sex-limited modifiers tending to lower the age of onset in males, it is clear that a man carrying such a modifier would be more likely than the average man carrying the main gene to develop the disease, and his sons would also, on the average, develop it before his daughters. Both allelomorphs of the modifier must be fairly common, or alternatively there must be a number of not very rare dominant modifiers. They cannot have any conspicuous effect on normal people, but they may have some. He goes on to speculate along the lines of Fisher's theory of dominance, i.e., that in conditions like Huntington's chorea, where modifiers are important, selection will cause them to spread. The present age of onset of this disease may mean merely that primitive men and women seldom lived much beyond 40, so that postponement of onset beyond this age had no selective advantage. If the unfavorable modifiers are not disadvantageous, they will spread until the disease becomes one of old age. Then the gene frequency will be increased by mutation until unions of persons carrying it become fairly common. The homozygous form will be a severe and perhaps lethal disease, and then perhaps other modifiers will be selected.

Epilepsy

In contrast to the unequivocal findings as to specific unit factor genetic mechanisms in the major psychoses, schizophrenia, and manic-depressive psychosis, extensive work in the sphere of epilepsy has not resulted in the same clear-cut conclusions. In fact, the findings of certain substantial studies are in such striking conflict that we are faced with the serious problem of how they are to be reconciled.

Work stressing the importance of the genetic factor comes from two sources: (1) Conrad's comprehensive pioneer study of epileptics diagnosed as idiopathic, where the expectancy rates were 4.0 per cent for siblings, 4.3 per cent for two-egg twins, and 86.0 per cent for one-egg twins, and (2) the studies of Lennox and the Gibbses, employing dysrhythmia in the EEG as the criterion of epilepsy, in which 100 per cent concordance was found for one-egg twins and 25 per cent concordance for the two-egg variety—the ideal figure for a fully penetrant single dominant gene.

In 1950, in striking contrast to this, came the publication of work by Alström, based on the study of epileptic patients and their families admitted from 1925 to 1940 to a university clinic for neurology in Sweden at the Serefimer Hospital. Salient findings of this study were as follows: In the first place, the expectancy figures for parents (1.3 ± 0.27 per cent), for siblings (1.5 ± 0.25 per cent), and for children (3.0 ± 0.93 per cent) were not significantly higher than those in the general population. Second, families with epilepsy in members, other than in the index case, were lacking in the majority (i.e., 0.92 per cent) of cases. Third, among the 16 pairs of twins in this study, two of which were monozygotic, there was not a single case of concordance as to epilepsy. All this notwithstanding, examination of individual pedigrees in Alström's series discloses, according to his own submission, a single-factor genetic mechanism in approximately 1 per cent of cases—11 index cases belonging to eight families in his sample of 897 index cases and their families. This is compatible with the type of genetic mechanism postulated by the Gibbses as being operative throughout their series instead of in only 1 per cent.

With a view to finding further evidence toward settling the dispute, Hurst, Reef, and Sachs undertook a study at the Meadowlands Clinic (1959 to 1961), where the clinical material held out the special advantage for genetic study of large sibship size (average, 5.8; range, 1 to 16).

The preliminary pilot study produced evidence along the following two lines: (1) the percentage of families showing one or more members exhibiting epilepsy in addition to the index case, for comparison with Alström's low figure cited above, and (2) the types of genetic mechanism exhibited in the pedigrees making up the material.

With regard to the first point, there is an incidence of 13 out of 46 families, i.e., a figure of 28.3 per cent in contrast to Alström's 0.8 per cent—a difference significant at the 0.1 per cent level. This comes down very heavily on Conrad's and on Lennox's and the Gibbses' side of the dispute.

Turning to the second point, analyses of the 13 positive pedigrees (of the 46) show that three are suggestive of a penetrant single dominant mechanism and one of irregular dominance, while the remaining nine are equally compatible with recessiveness—or irregular dominance. Therefore, at least a portion of these results is in line with the thesis of single dominance of Lennox and the Gibbses.

Metrakos (1961) offers a solution which resolves the problem in a most ingenious fashion. On the basis of the EEG of the parents and siblings of 211 probands and 112 controls, he claims that epilepsy of the centrencephalic type may be explained on the basis of a single dominant gene showing a variable penetrance with age, such that the penetrance is low at birth, rises rapidly to almost complete penetrance between the ages of 4 and 16, and declines gradually to almost zero penetrance after the age of 40.

Mental Defect

The sphere of mental defect provides particularly fine examples of the two new methodologies, chemical and chromosomal, to which we shall now refer.

Chemical aberrations. Garrod's concept of inborn errors of metabolism, enunciated in 1902, bore fruit in the domain of mental defect in 1934, when Fölling drew attention to the association of phenylketones in the urine with mental retardation. To date, 3.5 per cent of mental defectives have been shown to possess some presumably etiologically associated biochemical abnormality. They may be broadly divided into errors of carbohydrate, lipid, and protein metabolism. The amino acid urias are the common denominators of most diseases of protein metabolism, and classification is in terms of blood amino acid level and chromatographic abnormality.

Phenylketonuria, which may be classified as a single overflow amino acid uria, has become the paradigm of the chemical mode of action of single gene effects and enzyme blocks.

The complex of biochemical events disclosed in this condition is as follows: Phenylalanine hydroxylase, an enzyme concerned in the conversion of the essential amino acid phenylalanine to tyrosine, is at fault. Consequences of this are the following: (1) There is an accumulation of phenylalanine in the blood and CSF and overflow in the urine; (2) phenylpyruvic and phenylacetic acids and phenylacetylglutamine are therefore in excess and, as the renal threshold is low, are excreted in the urine; and (3) the administration of excess phenylalanine to normals produces a rise in blood tyrosine levels, but none follows in phenylketonurics.

The matter of how directly or completely the mental retardation in this condition is related to failure of conversion of phenylalanine to tyrosine has often been canvassed. Confirmation of the central etiological role of this mechanism comes from two sources (Hsia, Knox, Quinn, & Paine, 1956; Moncrieff & Wilkinson, 1961), where treatment commenced early (in which dietary phenylalanine was maintained at a bare minimum) gave indications of the prevention of mental retardation.

A test for the detection of carriers in this disease has been evolved, based on the plasma phenylalanine levels one, two, and four hours after a standard test dose of levo-phenylalanine.

Chromosomal aberrations. Our remarks will be confined very largely to Down's syndrome, or mongolism, the condition in which the new chromosome work won its spurs, with some slight allusion to other conditions.

DOWN'S SYNDROME, OR MONGOLISM. In Down's syndrome, in 1959, Lejeune et al. and Jacobs et al. showed independently that a trisomy of

Figure 1. Block in metabolism of phenylalanine to tyrosine.

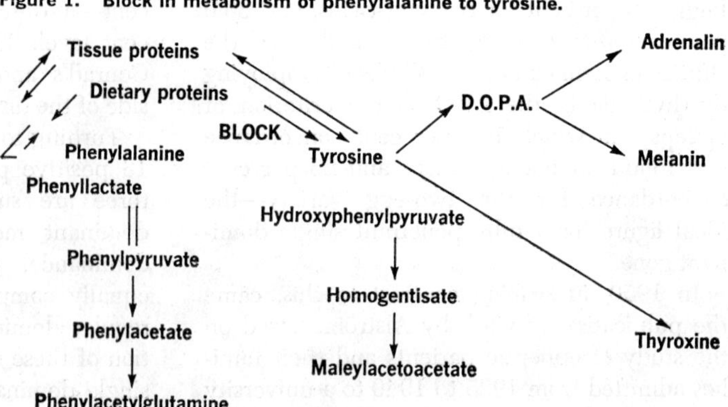

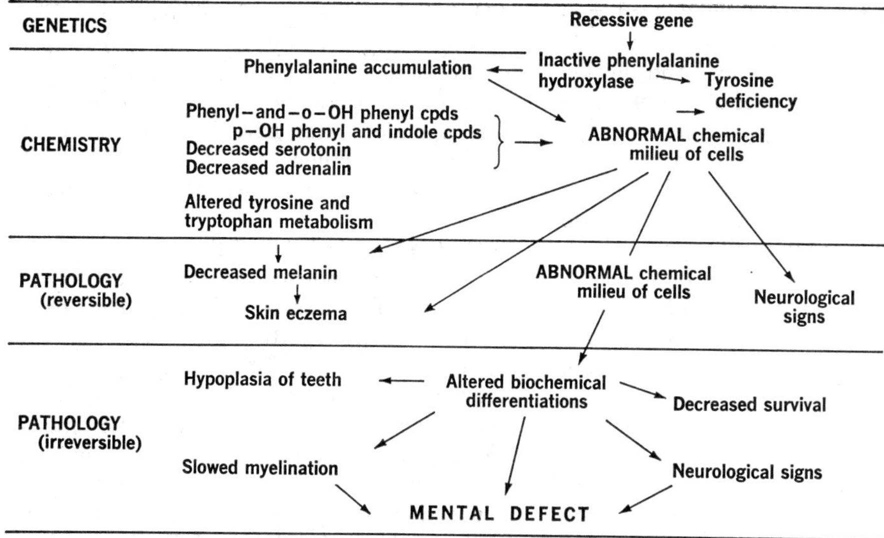

Figure 2. Possible mode of production of mental defect in phenylketonuria. *After Knox* (1960).

chromosome No. 21 exists; i.e., this chromosome is present in triplicate instead of in duplicate. The two mechanisms postulated as bringing this about are nondisjunction and translocation. The usual process is nondisjunction during meiosis, where two homologous No. 21 chromosomes, instead of separating and each migrating to its own pole, stick together and move to the same daughter cell. Much rarer is nondisjunction occurring during mitosis, resulting in normal trisomy 21 mosaicism, as described by Clarke et al. in 1961. Clinically, only certain mongoloid features appear in these cases.

Translocation involves breakage of nonhomologous chromosomes (one of which is No. 21) and an exchange of fragments between them—a reciprocal translocation, as described by Polani et al. in 1960 and more commonly seen in cases born to young mothers.

OTHER FORMS OF MENTAL DEFECT. A survey by Maclean et al. of 4,514 mental defectives discloses an excess of cases with an extra X chromosome in both males and females. Trisomy 22 has been reported in connection with the Sturge-Weber syndrome but has not been confirmed.

POLYGENIC MECHANISM. Despite the special interest attaching to chemical and chromosomal aberrations in mental defect, it is probable that the great majority of mental defectives, especially those of higher grade, represent the tail end of the normal curve of distribution of intelligence and are accounted for on the basis of polygenic mechanisms. There are, of course, the comparatively rare single recessive and single dominant mechanisms, typified by amaurotic family idiocy and epiloia, in which the underlying chemical basis has not as yet been defined.

To answer the question of what proportion of mental defect cannot be ascribed to genetic or chromosomal factors of any kind, one may cite Penrose's Colchester study, which gives a figure of 15 per cent of cases attributable to such nongenetic factors as cerebral birth injuries and anoxia, cerebral infections, and hemorrhage.

FINDINGS IN NEUROLOGY

I should like to commence this section by indicating general perspectives that have come from the application of genetic principles and insights to neurology. First, the fundamental etiology of a long list of neurological conditions has been established by demonstrating them as being due to single dominant, single recessive, or sex-linked genetic mechanisms. Secondly, examining the constellation and varying prominence of the signs and symptoms in stated neurological syndromes, in the light of the genetic concepts of penetrance and expressivity, makes these more understandable and also shows that cases with only a fraction of the total symptomatology are classifiable with the more fully fledged syndrome, the missing features being explicable in terms of deficient penetrance. And, finally, the now fully recognized fact of the chemical basis of all single-factor genetic mechanisms, such as underlie a long list of neurological disorders, has brought a reasoned hope of reversibility and cure in an area hitherto regarded as chronic and without hope.

We refer here to two reviews of this field. The first is the 1953 *Proceedings of the Association for Research in Nervous and Mental Disease*. The main contributions were those of Tyler, on muscular dystrophies and neural atrophies; of Schut, on the hereditary ataxias; of Herndon, on the lipidoses; and of Goodell, Lowentin, and Wolff, on migraine.

The more current review of Haberlandt and Glanville appearing in the work *Expanding Goals of Genetics in Psychiatry* (Kallmann, 1962), already referred to, will engage our attention in some detail. After surveying the question of hereditary myopathies in animals, the authors turn to the genetics of muscular dystrophies in man.

Among the pure muscular dystrophies of Morton and Chung, four genetic types were distinguished by them:

1. Duchenne: sex-linked, occurring exclusively in males
2. Facioscapulohumeral: autosomal dominant
3. Limb-girdle: autosomal recessive form including most "sporadic" cases, without known affected relatives
4. Limb-girdle: etiologically undetermined; may represent occasional pathological expression in the heterozygote or may be phenocopies without a simple genetic etiology

There is now little doubt that there is a form of dystrophy which is clinically indistinguishable from the Duchenne type but which can affect both boys and girls. The importance of distinguishing this type from the sex-linked form from a eugenic point of view is stressed by the authors of the review, and clinical criteria (including ECG pattern) are indicated by them.

The prevalence, mutation, and fertility rates for the four genetically determined forms of muscular dystrophy vary considerably. The prevalence of the types in the order mentioned is (1) 66 living cases per 1 million males, (2) 2 living cases per 1 million males, (3) 12 living cases per 1 million males, and (4) 8 living cases per 1 million males. The corresponding fertility rates are (1) 4 per cent of normal, (2) nearly normal, (3) 25 per cent of normal, and (4) 25 per cent of normal. The mutation rates have been estimated at (1) 89 per 1 million gametes, (2) 50 per 1 million gametes, and (3) 31 per 1 million loci.

On the chemical side of the serum enzymes, with a known tendency to increased activity in neuromuscular disease, aldolase has been found to be particularly increased in dystrophic patients. Other enzymes in this category are phosphohexose isomerase, lactic dehydrogenase, glutamic oxaloacetic transaminase, and glutamic pyruvic transaminase. Increased aldolase activity seems most pronounced in rapidly progressing forms, especially in the early phases of Duchenne dystrophy, and may precede the onset of clinical symptoms. It has been suggested that excess enzyme may leak into the serum from the muscles because of an abnormal permeability of cell walls. The potentially greater value of creatine phosphokinase—due to its more important role in muscular contraction—both in clinical diagnosis and in the identification of carriers has been preached by Okinara, Dreyfus, and others.

Other Myopathies

Apart from these classic inherited muscular dystrophies, several other related conditions can be distinguished both genetically and histologically. Since a striated muscle has many enzymatic functions, it presents multi-

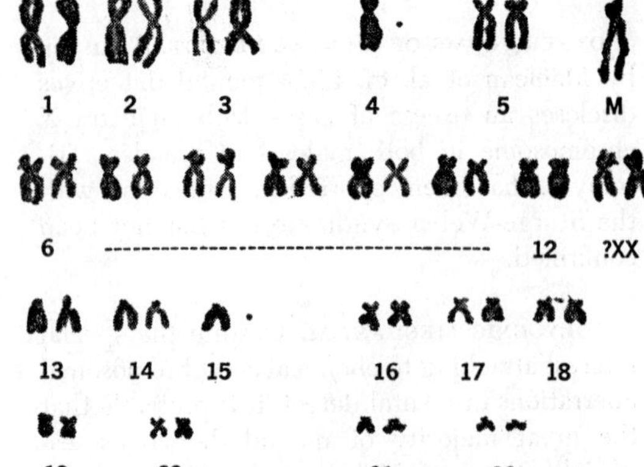

Figure 3. Human chromosome abnormality. Note the large translocation chromosome M, which consists of chromosomes Nos. 4 and 15 fused together. Note presumptive female X chromosomes. *I. F. Anderson and C. Wallace.*

ple possibilities for genetically determined dysfunctions. In this area, recent work has been done on McArdle's syndrome and muscle core disease, both of which, unlike dystrophy, are not related to primary defects in the muscle nucleus but to defects in the mitochondrial enzymes and the structure of the myofibrils, respectively. In McArdle's syndrome (myophosphorylase deficiency glycogenosis), which is inherited as an autosomal recessive, excessive amounts of glycogen are deposited in the muscles because of the deficiency in myophosphorylase. This syndrome presents clinically as weakness, pain, and stiffness after exercise. The enzyme appears to be completely inactive in the homozygote. In muscle core disease as described by Shy and Magee (1956), we have to do with a congenital nonprogressive myopathy, inherited as an autosomal dominant, in which, as yet, no biochemical basis has been determined. And, finally, in this category, there is the recent study on congenital myotonia by Becker (1961), which showed a fairly even distribution of the condition throughout Germany. Familial cases could be distinguished from sporadic ones, and they showed an earlier onset (before the age of 10) and were equally distributed between a dominant mode of inheritance with no difference between the sexes and a recessive one with excess of males.

There has been much recent work on the neuropathies and other neurological syndromes in the fields of dystonia musculorum deformans, multiple sclerosis, syringomyelia, tuberous sclerosis, and Charcot's disease, but from considerations of space, we limit ourselves to two conditions in which there has been an advance into the biochemical genetics—familial periodic paralysis and Wilson's disease (hepatolenticular degeneration).

In familial periodic paralysis, where an autosomal dominant mode of inheritance has been established, attacks may occur spontaneously or may follow administration of salt-retaining adrenocortical steroids. While an increase in serum aldosterone and 17-ketosteroids tends to precede the attack, the serum potassium level is found to be decreased during the paralysis. The condition may, therefore, be connected with defective permeability of the muscle membrane, resulting in an abnormal Na/K balance "triggering" hypersecretion of aldosterone; conversely, it may well be that an increase of aldosterone induces the observed electrolyte imbalance. A genetically distinct but clinically similar variant is adynamia episodica hereditaria, also inherited as an autosomal dominant. The main differences are an increased serum potassium level during attacks, ECG abnormalities, and provocation of the episodes by hunger or KCl administration.

Turning away from the review of Glanville and Haberlandt, we direct our attention to the especially effective studies, genetic and chemical, of Wilson's disease that have been undertaken by Bearn and his associates. Bearn postulates a single recessive gene mechanism, but differences in age of disease onset, consanguinity, and fertility and variance in serum copper and ceruloplasmin levels, as between cases of Eastern European and Mediterranean origin, lead him to suggest a modifying gene in the former group or, alternatively, the presence of more than one allele at the Wilson's locus.

Evidence is as yet insufficient as to whether ceruloplasmin is the primary gene product of Wilson's disease; the incorporation of copper into ceruloplasmin may be of more importance than the synthesis of ceruloplasmin itself.

On the hypothesis of two different alleles, the common allele is associated with a decreased serum ceruloplasmin, whereas the less common allelomorph is associated with a normal or near-normal level of ceruloplasmin synthesis. Heterozygotes similarly show marked depression of ceruloplasmin and serum copper levels but vary from marked depression to relatively normal values. Furthermore, a diminished serum ceruloplasmin level in a heterozygous parent is not apparently associated with earlier age of onset in affected offspring. Radioactive data provide the insight that although total ceruloplasmin levels are normal in both patients and heterozygotes, abnormalities in the rate of synthesis may be present (Sass-Kortsak, 1959).

The question of the normality of structure of the Wilson disease ceruloplasmin molecule came under investigation by means of the techniques of chromatography and immunophoresis in 1959. In 1961, Poulik and Bearn were in a position to comment on the heterogeneity of ceruloplasmin. They reported that in line with the increasing awareness of the heterogeneity of serum proteins, previously regarded as homogeneous (particularly the haptoglobins and transferrins), Morell and Scheinberg had demonstrated the existence of polymeric forms of ceruloplasmin possessing different electrophoretic mobilities in the starch gel system. They go on to canvass the possibility that these differences may be genetically based. According to reports of McAlister et al. and of Parker and Bearn, a family study extending over four generations showed that a quickly migrating band segregated as a dominant character. In one preparation, seven distinct ceruloplasmin bands were observed. Bearn has also shown that the lability of ceruloplasmin with regard to its oxidase activity is related to a particular part of the molecule.

Eugenics

Although we find mention of eugenics in Plato's *Republic* and although there were practical experiments in this direction in Sparta and in the Oneida Community in New York (the latter dating from 1841), the first exponent of systematic eugenics in modern times was that eclectic genius Francis Galton (1869; 1874; 1883; 1889; 1908). Inspired by the evolutionary vista provided by the publication in 1859 of the *Origin of Species* by his cousin Charles Darwin, and inspired also by the striking cases of apparently hereditary genius among Cambridge men who had been at the university at about his time, he first evolved the statistical theory and established the anthropological laboratories necessary to the study of man as a science. Then, feeling very strongly the importance of applying his findings to race improvement, he launched out into the dissemination of eugenic ideas.

It is clear from his writings that Galton's program included both negative eugenics—the elimination of stocks afflicted with serious hereditary disease—and positive eugenics—the favoring of propagation of stocks of superior abilities by providing suitable inducements to this end.

The subjoined formulation of his advocacy of negative eugenics shows his concern for doing so in a democratic setting:

> As in most other cases of novel views, the wrong-headedness of objectors to Eugenics has been curious. The most common misrepresentations now are that its methods must be altogether those of compulsory unions, as in breeding animals. It is not so. I think that stern compulsion ought to be exerted to prevent the free propagation of the stock of those who are seriously afflicted by lunacy, feeblemindedness, habitual criminality and pauperism, but that is quite different from compulsory marriage. A democracy cannot endure unless it be composed of able citizens; therefore it must in self-defence withstand the free introduction of degenerate stock (Galton, 1908).

Relative to positive eugenics, he says:

> I also hope that social recognition of an appropriate kind will be given to healthy, capable and large families, and that social influence will be exerted towards the encouragement of eugenic marriages (1908).

Galton repeatedly stresses the importance of eugenic theory and practice. Thus he says:

> I hence conclude that the improvement of the breed of mankind is no insuperable difficulty. If everybody were to agree on the improvement of the race of man being a matter of the very utmost importance and if the theory of hereditary transmission of qualities in men was as thoroughly understood as it is in the case of our domestic animals, I see no absurdity in supposing that in some way or other, the improvement would be carried into effect (1908).

and again:

> I take Eugenics very seriously, feeling that its principles ought to become one of the dominant motives in a civilised nation (1908).

Galton's advocacy of eugenics never degenerated into fanaticism or bigotry, as can be inferred from such statements as the following:

> What I desire is that the importance of eugenic marriages should be reckoned at its just value, neither too high nor too low, and that Eugenics should form one of the many considerations by which marriages are pro-

moted or hindered, as they are by social position, adequate fortune, and similarity of creed (1908).

In his *Enquiries into Human Faculty and Its Development* (1883), Galton emphasizes:

> The eugenic aim is the amelioration of average human qualities through the observation of heredity, rather than the production of a few exceptional record-breakers.

It is clear that when we are considering a program of negative eugenics for the elimination of serious hereditary disease (in our case, serious hereditary mental disorder or defect or incapacitating neurological disorder), the new vista provided by physiological and biochemical genetics immediately raises an approach which limits or negates negative eugenics; for if genetics points the way to curing a condition by locating the significant enzyme blocks and reversing them, are we justified in attempting—or, indeed, is it logical to attempt—elimination by eugenic means? The answer is unequivocally in the negative as I see the matter. We can therefore regard negative eugenics merely as a temporary measure, pending the fruition of our more fundamental hope.

With this limitation let us consider some features of a program of negative eugenics, with special reference to neuropsychiatry.

In the first place, action is clearly indicated only where the trait is very seriously disabling and incurable.

Second, negative eugenic action must be based in each individual case on the specific genetic mechanism reflected in the empirical risk figures. In a single dominant condition, such as manic-depressive psychosis, we are clearly confronted with a different situation from that in schizophrenia, where a single recessive mechanism is postulated. In the first case we have transmission of the disease in the direct line of descent and manifestation in approximately half of the offspring, the other half not carrying the gene and being incapable of transmitting the disease to their offspring in turn ("once free, forever free"). In the second case, however, most schizophrenics are the children of overtly normal parents, each of whom is a carrier of one schizophrenic gene. The manifestation rate in such children is 16 per cent (the 25 per cent expected for full penetrance being reduced by the 70 per cent penetrance of the schizophrenic genotype). Overtly unaffected children, as well as brothers and sisters of the first generation, are a rich source of carriers of "one gene," ready to manifest in the case of marriage with a similarly constituted person. This fact, coupled with the finding that, on the average, 70 per cent of the children due to be born to a schizophrenic are born to him before the disease manifests and he is hospitalized for it, accounts for the low estimate that only 2 to 4 per cent of schizophrenics would be eliminated by ensuring that the affected schizophrenic does not reproduce. This figure may well be increased when the mapping of the human chromosome now in progress becomes more complete, enabling us to identify the potential schizophrenic before the condition develops. If, however, we wish to follow the logic of the situation quite ruthlessly, we are compelled to concentrate on the brothers, sisters, and children of schizophrenics as the crux of the eugenic situation.

Cousin marriage, marriage into other schizophrenic families, or marriage with a markedly introverted individual is especially undesirable for members of schizophrenic families, as it is likely to bring two recessive genes together to produce a proportion of frank schizophrenics.

Where the type of hereditary mechanism is in dispute, the empirical risk figures form an objective basis for eugenic procedure.

Third, as regards the procedure of attaining the nonpropagation of the scientifically contraindicated types of persons, let us lay the ghost of sterilization at the very outset. Sterilization is so outmoded in the sphere of eugenics that at the 1956 Congress at Copenhagen there was not one reference to it! No, the modern approach in our democratic societies is to advise the afflicted person and/or his spouse (the latter particularly in the case of mental illness, where the patient himself may not be capable of understanding the position) what the risk is, in percentage terms, that any contemplated child or children will be affected by the hereditary trait concerned. Kallmann's experience with heritable mental disease is that in the metropolitan communities in which he has worked the application of birth control methods has been quite adequate to the objective envisaged, rendering the consideration of sterilization unnecessary.

In cases where religious objections render contraceptive methods unacceptable, abstention from marriage is often recognized as the best course to pursue.

HEREDITY COUNSELING

This brings us to the question of heredity counseling services and centers. H. G. Hammons (1956) lists 15 such centers for the United States and Canada, one in Denmark, five in England, one in France, one in Germany, two in Holland, one in India, two in Italy, one in Japan, one in Norway, three in Sweden, and one in Switzerland; two of these are primarily concerned with neuropsychiatric cases, and Reed (1963) extends the list.

Dice (1952), in a presidential address to the American Society of Human Genetics, gave many data about the functions and operations of such clinics, which I now proceed to summarize:

1. The problems presented to clinics are diverse, including questions from engaged couples with possibly hereditary disease in one or both families, from married couples with one or more children already affected by possibly hereditary disease, and from children's placement bureaus regarding chances of a child showing an adverse parental trait.

2. Drawing up of kindred pedigrees includes a system of record sheets with data by sibships, graphic pedigrees, and sources of information.

3. Mode of inheritance is then postulated on the basis of genetic principles.

4. Firsthand examination of near relatives, by a competent specialist, may be necessary. This involves financial considerations.

5. Records and documents should be detailed and precise in order to be understandable ten or 100 years hence. Abbreviations and scientific jargon are to be avoided. Professional persons referring the case should be encouraged to supply detailed written reports, including a formulation of the problem.

6. Professional secrecy and confidence are necessary. Special care should be taken in this regard concerning the disclosure, even to relatives, of illegitimate births, adoptions, age of elderly women, and results of clinical examinations not duly authorized by parent or guardian.

7. Information and advice to patients (clients) are limited to the restrained technique of stating the risk (in percentage terms) of the trait under consideration. Under no circumstances should the counselor tell a couple whether they should or should not have a child. In certain cases he will have to confess that he can make no sort of prediction on the basis of the information available. In many cases he will be in the happier position of being able to reassure the parents and advise them that there is no risk of the feared hereditary disease manifesting in the children.

8. Weight should be given to positive eugenics and desirable hereditary traits. Although the heredity clinic focuses its attention on the elimination of undesirable traits, the counselor does not lose sight of positive eugenics, e.g., in weighing up positive qualities of intelligence and temperament against an only moderately undesirable genetic trait.

9. Inasmuch as each heredity clinic acts as the archives of hereditary disease, there is a duty of publication so that human geneticists the world over may pool their information, especially as regards rare traits.

10. The clinic has a duty of education. Comparatively few medical schools instruct their students in genetics—especially human genetics—and yet, with the conquering of infectious and nutritional disease, heredito-constitutional disease is growing in volume and relative importance. Every heredity clinic should therefore provide lectures for undergraduates and facilities to direct the work of postgraduate students.

11. Concerning the organization of clinico-practical aspects, the minimal staffing is one geneticist, one physician, one laboratory assistant, and one secretary. There should be access to various clinical laboratories and a liaison with clinics of a well-equipped hospital. The minimum space is a general office, a waiting room, and one office for each member of the staff. It is, however, possible to share with other units a medical examination room, laboratories, a photographic studio and darkroom, a library, and seminar rooms. Fees should not be asked from patients or clients, except that fees for cooperating specialists should be paid when they can be afforded. The budgeting includes provision for traveling by distant relatives coming for examination and an item for staff transport for fieldwork as well as for staff salaries.

Reed's (1963) book on hereditary counseling and that edited by H. G. Hammons (1959) are commended to those students requiring a more detailed picture of heredity clinics.

POSITIVE EUGENICS

Little more need be said about positive eugenics. Eugenicists have been alarmed by the apparent trend of persons of lower ability to have, on the whole, larger families than those of higher ability. Positive eugenics advocates attempting to reverse this trend by devising ways of encouraging persons of above-average ability to marry earlier and to have larger families. It is recognized that such an objective cannot be tackled in an isolated fashion but takes us deep into problems affecting the structure of society as a whole. Kallmann summarizes positive eugenic measures as follows: (1) Larger families should be secured from eugenically desirable classes by using educational methods; by giving economic support to eugenically desirable families (proper housing at low rentals); by increasing the income of eugenically desirable families at the birth of each child; by instituting differential taxation in relation to family size; and by lowering the wages of single and childless workers. (2) Birth control measures should be practiced for sociological reasons.

Viewing the progress of eugenics historically, there have been signs in recent years of a sound and vigorous development of a separate science of human genetics, embodied in such concrete phenomena as the foundation in 1949 of the American Society of Human Genetics, with its own journal, following on the pioneer work of the journal *Eugenical News* (now *Eugenics Quarterly*), under the leadership of Frederick Osborn; the formation of the Population Council, Inc.; the institution of the heredity clinics mentioned above and of academic centers like the Galton Laboratory (University of London); and the holding of the First International Congress of Human Genetics in Copenhagen in 1956 and of the second in Rome in 1961.

Osborn (1956), in an article entitled "Galton and Midcentury Eugenics," gives point and perspective to the advance in eugenics that we are considering by attempting to appraise how the founder of modern eugenics would react to the situation if he were to return to the present-day scene:

> Galton, who died in 1911, would have been fascinated with the last half-century's progress in the science of genetics, which had become a subject of controversy during the last few years of his life. He would have given his powerful backing to the further advancement of human genetics. He would have been present at the . . . Congress to be held in Copenhagen. . . . He would have urged exhaustive studies on the identification of carriers of harmful recessive genes. He would have supported heredity clinics.

While Galton would have been disappointed at the little progress that has been made in the study of the genetic factors which affect the development of personality and intelligence, Osborn feels he would have been pleased with the methodologies of modern psychology, of which he is one of the pioneers, and with the applications of new measures in personnel selection. He would have been puzzled by the relatively small pure-research appropriations for the social as compared with the physical sciences. Osborn, in elaborating Galton's emphasis on directing "forces under social control," feels that he would not have been skeptical of the possibility of establishing the differential of larger families for the better-endowed. To achieve his aims, Osborn feels that eugenics will have to drop the idea of assigning genetic superiorities to social or racial groups and even of designating individuals as superior or inferior. "Let's stop telling anyone that they have a generally inferior genetic quality, for they will never agree. Let's base our proposals on the desirability of having children born in homes where they will get affectionate and responsible care, and perhaps our proposals will be accepted." This attitude clearly squares with Galton's emphasis on the idea that eugenic policies would fail unless geared to "existing conditions of law and sentiment."

Osborn concludes: "It seems to me that if it is to progress as it should, eugenics must follow new policies and state its case anew, and that from this rebirth we may, even in our own lifetime, see it moving at last towards the high goals Galton set for it."

CONCLUSION

In conclusion I should like to express my own views about the psychiatric dimension in genetic counseling. In the first place, there is a special climate attaching to counseling in the psychiatric sphere, originating from the ancient terrors clinging to matters psychiatric since medieval times, with their cruel practices, and from the abuses introduced in the name of eugenics in the thirties, still fresh in living memory. This underlines the need for scientific counseling which takes cognizance of the specific difference in the genetic mechanisms underlying schizophrenia and manic-depressive psychosis and which reflects this in the counsel given. Second, as Kallmann and Rainer have stressed, there is a psychological dimension in all genetic counseling, whether it concerns psychiatric conditions, or diseases and defects falling within any area of medicine. This renders psychiatric training additionally desirable for the genetic counselor. Obviously, in a sphere of such profound significance to the client, he comes to the counselor with a load of anxiety, often only partially recognized by himself, and this anxiety is a vital part of the situation to be handled by the counselor. In this context, it has been discussed whether giving the empirical risk figure to the client is the whole duty of the counselor or whether indeed it is his duty at all. It is questionable, in the first place, how meaningful such a statement is to any but a critical mind trained in statistical theory and how traumatic it might be in certain instances to any type of mind. A conclusion that would seem apposite is that genetic counseling is a synthetic art, to which the counselor should bring scientific genetic knowledge, psychological insight, and, if possible, medical and psychiatric orientation and training.

It might also lend perspective and reveal a vista for the future to raise the curtain a little on the basic work going on at the chemical level, which through pinpointing the enzyme block underlying individual psychiatric and neurological disorders promises hope of fundamental pharmacological cure, even though the question of when in the next few decades the breakthroughs will occur is a matter for conjecture. Studies involving psychotropic drugs and psychopharmacological agents, as well as direct neurochemical investigation, have suggested a number of clues, which require further elucidation and synthesis. Success has been achieved in phenylketonuria along lines already indicated, and this may serve as the model of what may be hoped for in psychiatric diseases of single gene etiology, notably schizophrenia and manic-depressive psychosis. We may call to mind the leads in this area that have appeared in recent years: derailed metabolism of adrenalin (Hoffer, Osmond, & Smythies, 1954; Osmond & Smythies, 1952); anomalies in serotonin production (Udenfriend, Woolley, & Shaw, 1954); abnormal serum protein or substance attached to it (Frohman, Tourney, Beckett, & Gottlieb, 1960; Heath, Leach, Cohen, & Feigley, 1958) denaturation of protein through disordered nucleotide sequences in the DNA code (Denber & Teller, 1964; Harrington, 1900); special amine appearing in the urine—3,4-demethoxyphenylethylamine (Friedhoff & van Winkle, 1962); shifting of carbohydrate into the shunt less effective for energy liberation (Gottlieb & Frohman, 1962); exploration of other areas of carbohydrate metabolism (Heyman & Merlis, 1962); electrolyte imbalance and possible role of glutathione (Easterday, Featherstone, Gottlieb, Nosser, & Hogg, 1952; Harrington, 1900); and electron donation and the metabolism of hem (Szent-Gyöngyi, 1960).

Hurst (1961c) has suggested another line of approach, namely, attempting a linkup with the underlying gene-determined enzyme block in manic-depressive psychosis and schizophrenia by tracing back the precursors of substances in the phenotype (e.g., noradrenaline and serotonin) influenced by effective neuropharmacological agents. We may instance the antidepressants (with the special advantage of two converging chemical paths in the case of MAO inhibitors and imipramine) and high-dosage insulin and high-dosage tranquilizer therapy in schizophrenia.

Finally, allow me to underline the reciprocal relationship obtaining between genetic counseling and fundamental cure directed at the genetically determined enzyme block underlying the psychiatric disorder in question. With the establishment of the latter, namely, specific gene-centered fundamental cure, the need for the former (genetic counseling) disappears. A word of caution is necessary, however, for when a specific breakthrough for one of the psychiatric disorders occurs, the therapeutic chemical may require a long period of refinement before it is effective *in vivo*, and even then the sufferer may be condemned to lifelong use of the medicament.

In our era, with its breathtaking possibilities stemming from the splendid paradox of modern biochemical genetics, this is the discrimination with which we must temper our enthusiasm over the fact that the hereditary nature of a condition actually opens the way to its fundamental pharmacological cure by pinpointing the genetically determined biochemical anomaly underlying it.

GLOSSARY OF CHEMICAL TERMS NOT EXPLAINED IN THE TEXT

(grouped under major chemical categories)

Aldosterone

a steroid principle isolated from the amorphous fraction of the adrenal cortex and from human urine; potent in causing sodium retention and potassium loss.

Amine

a substance derived from ammonia by the replacement of one or more of the hydrogen atoms by hydrocarbon radicals.

Amino Acids

relatively small molecules obtained when a protein is subjected to hydrolysis.

1. Sulfur-containing amino acids:
   - Cysteine
   - Cystine
   - Methionine
   - Cystathionine—an intermediate in the conversion of methionine to cysteine.
2. Arginine, ornithine, and citrulline:
   - Arginine—particularly abundant in basic proteins, the histones, and protamines.
   - Ornithine—formed when arginine is hydrolyzed under the catalytic influence of arginase.
   - Citrulline—formed from ornithine in the course of the urea cycle.
3. Phenylalanine, tryptophan, tyrosine, and phenylpyruvic acid:
   - Phenylalanine—an aromatic amino acid occurring in protein hydrolysis.
   - Tryptophan—a heterocyclic amino acid.
   - Tyrosine—an aromatic amino acid.
   - Phenylpyruvic acid and its precursors, phenyllactic acid and phenylacetylglutamine, which accumulate in phenylketonurics owing to a genetically determined enzyme block.
4. Glutamine and glutamic acid—monoaminodicarboxylic acids.
5. End products of amino metabolism—urea and uric acid.

Carbohydrates

organic compounds all containing carbon, hydrogen, oxygen, and some nitrogen and sulfur as well.

1. Monosaccharides: include the five-carbon compounds, or pentoses (e.g., D-ribose), and the six-carbon compounds, or hexoses (e.g., D-glucose and D-galactose).
2. Oligosaccharides: composed of two or more monosaccharide units linked together through glycosidic linkage (e.g., lactose, a disaccharide, and raffinose, a trisaccharide).
3. Polysaccharides: large aggregates of monosaccharide units joined by glycosidic bonds (e.g., starch).

Catalyst

a substance which in small, often minute amounts accelerates or retards a chemical reaction but which does not itself combine permanently with the reacting substances and appears to remain unchanged after the reaction has taken place.

Ceruloplasmin

a blue copper-containing alpha globulin of blood plasma, with a molecular weight of 150,000 and a complement of eight copper atoms per molecule. It catalyzes the oxidation of amines, phenols, and ascorbic acid.

Enzyme

a protein secreted by body cells that acts as a catalyst, inducing chemical changes in other substances, while remaining itself apparently unchanged in the process. There has been an attempt to introduce a nomenclature, calling each enzyme after the substance on which it acts or the reaction catalyzed, and adding the termination *-ase* (e.g., beta-galactosidase, which catalyzes the hydrolysis of galactosides).

Haptoglobins

two carbon-containing alpha-2-globulins isolated from human serum, so called because of their ability to combine with hemoglobin.

Hydrocarbons

organic compounds containing only hydrogen and carbon (e.g., ergosterol, an unsaturated hydrocarbon of the sterol group, derived from ergot, yeast, mushrooms, and other fungi, and similar in composition to cholesterol).

Lipids

a comprehensive term including those compounds characterized by insolubility in water and the capacity to be metabolized by the body—notably fats and oils. On hydrolysis they yield long chain fatty acids or nonpolar molecules of a dozen carbon atoms or more (e.g., cholesterol).

Proteins and Related Substances

1. Proteins: constitute the greater part of the nitrogen-containing compounds of animals and vegetables. They are highly complex and contain carbon, hydrogen, nitrogen, and oxygen; some contain iron, phosphorus, and sulfur as well. Chemically they are peptides or polypeptides or combinations of amino acids and their derivatives.
2. Peptide: a secondary protein derivative; a definitely characterized combination of two or more amino acids, the carboxyl group of one being united with the amino group of the other, with the elimination of a molecule of water.
3. Polypeptide: a peptide formed by the union of an indefinite (usually large) number of amino acids.
4. Nucleic acids: a family of substances of large molecular weight, found in chromosomes, mitochondria, and viruses. They are now thought to be the ultimate carriers of inheritance and to control the enzyme pattern of the cells of which they form a part. In combination with proteins they form nucleoproteins. On hydrolysis they yield purine bases, pyrimidine bases, phosphoric acid, and a pentose, which may be D-ribose or D-deoxyribose.
5. Nucleoproteins: one of the group of conjugated proteins consisting of a compound of simple protein with nucleic acid. Chromosomes, mitochondria, and viruses are largely nucleoprotein in nature.

6. Ribonucleoprotein: a conjugated protein containing ribonucleic acid as prosthetic group.
7. Purines: the parent substance of the uric acid group of bodies. It is not known to exist as such in the body.
   Classification:
      Oxypurines, e.g., xanthine and uric acid.
      Aminopurines, e.g., adenine and guanine.
      Methylpurines, e.g., caffeine, theophylline, and theobromine.
8. Pyrimidines: a heterocyclic substance; the parent substance of several bases present in nucleic acids—uracil, thymine, and cytosine—as well as of the barbiturates.
9. Globulin: a simple protein, insoluble in water but soluble in a 0.5 to 1 per cent solution of a neutral salt and coagulable by heat. By electrophoresis, three fractions, the alpha, beta, and gamma, may be separated. The last named is closely associated with immune bodies.
10. Transferrins: a beta-globulin of the plasma, capable of associating reversibly with up to 1.25 mg of iron per gram of protein and acting as iron-transferring protein.

Vitamins

a group of organic substances, some of which are of unknown composition, present in minute amounts in natural foodstuffs and essential to normal metabolism. The lack thereof results in deficiency diseases.

Biotin: formerly designated factor H of vitamin B_2 complex. The methyl ester has been crystallized from raw egg white. It is a growth factor for most yeast organisms.

REFERENCES

Alström, C. A. A study of epilepsy in its clinical, social and genetic aspects. *Acta psychiat. et neurol. scandinav.*, 1950, Suppl. 63.

Association for Research in Nervous and Mental Disease, Research Publications, No. XXXIII. *Genetics and the inheritance of integrated neurological and psychiatric patterns.* Baltimore: Williams & Wilkins, 1953.

Beach, F. A. *Hormones and behavior.* New York: Hoeber-Harper, 1948.

Becker, P. E. *Proc. 2nd int. Conf. human Genet.*, Rome, 1961. In *Die Heterogenie der Myotonien.* Vol. III. Amsterdam: Excerpta Medica, 1961. Pp. 1547–1552.

Bell, J. *Treas. human Inher.*, 1934, **4**, 1.

Blewett, D. B. An experimental study of the inheritance of intelligence. *J. ment. Sci.*, 1954, **100**, 922–933.

Brody, E. G. A note on the genetic basis of spontaneous activity in the albino rat. *J. Comp. physiol. Psychol.*, 1950, **43**, 281–288.

Brody, E. G. Genetic basis of spontaneous activity in the albino rat. *Comp. Psychol.*, 1942, Monogr. 17, No. 5, 1–24.

Burks, B. S. In Q. McNemar and M. A. Merrill (Eds.), *Studies in Personality.* New York: McGraw-Hill, 1942.

Carter, H. D. Family resemblances in verbal and numerical abilities. *Genet. Psychol.*, 1932, Monogr. 12, 1–104.

Cattell, R. B. Research designs in psychological genetics with special reference to the multiple variance method. *Amer. J. human Genet.*, 1953, **5**, 76–93.

Cattell, R. B., & Scherer, J. H. *The meaning and measurement of neuroticism and anxiety.* New York: Ronald, 1961.

Cattell, R. B., and Willson, J. L. *Brit. J. educ. Psychol.*, 1938, **8**, 129–149.

Clarke, C. M., Edwards, J. H., & Smallpiece, V. *Lancet*, 1961, **1**, 1028.

Davern, C. G., & Cairns, G. Nucleic acids and proteins. *Amer. J. Med.*, 1963, **34** (5), 600.

Denber, H. C. B., and Teller, D. N. *Dis. nerv. System*, 1965.

Dice, Lee R. Heredity clinics: their value for public service and for research. *Amer. J. human Genet.*, 1952, **4** (1), 1–13.

Easterday, D. D., Featherstone, R. M., Gottlieb, J. S., Nosser, M. L., & Hogg, R. V. *Arch. Neurol. & Psychiat.*, 1952, **68**, 48.

Elsässer, G. *Die Nachkommen geisteskranker Elternpaare.* Stuttgart: Thieme, 1952.

Essen-Möller, E. Schweiz. *Arch. Neurol, Neurochir. ü. Psychiat.*, 1963, **91** (1), 260–266.

Eysenck, H. J. The inheritance of extraversion-introversion. *Acta psychol.* 1956, **12**, 95–110.

Eysenck, H. J., & Prell, D. B. The inheritance of neuroticism: an experimental study. *J. ment. Sci.*, 1951, **97**, 441–465.

Fisher, A. E. Maternal and sexual behavior induced by intracranial chemical stimulation. *Science,* 1956, **124**, 228–229.

Friedhoff, A. J., & van Winkle, Elnora. *J. nerv. & ment. Dis.*, 1962, **135** (6), 550–555.

Frohman, C. E., Tourney, G., Beckett, P. Y. S., & Gottlieb, J. S. *Amer. J. Psychiat.*, 1960, **117**, 401.

Fuller, J. L., & Thompson, W. R. *Behavior genetics.* New York: Wiley, 1960.

Galton, F. *Hereditary genius.* London: Macmillan, 1869.

Galton, F. *English men of science: their nature and nurture.* London: Macmillan, 1874.

Galton, F. *Inquiries into human faculty and its development.* London: Macmillan, 1833.

Galton, F. *Natural inheritance.* London, Macmillan, 1889.

Galton, F. *Memories of my life.* London: Methuen, 1908.

Gardner, I. C., & Newman, H. H. *J. Hered.*, 1940, **31**, 119–126.

Garrone, G. Statistical genetic study of schizophrenia in the Geneva population between 1901 and 1950. *J. Génét. humaine,* 1962, **11**, 89–219.

Gates, N., & Brash, H. *Ann. Eugenics,* 1941, **11**, 89–101.

Gottlieb, J. S., & Frohman, C. E. In T. T. Tourlentes, S. L. Pollack, & H. E. Himmich, *Symposium on research approaches to psychiatric problems, 1960.* New York: Grune & Stratton, 1962. Pp. 129–139.

Grünthal, E. Clinical and genealogical study on the heredity of Pick's disease. *Z. ges. Neurol. Psychiat.*, 1930, **136**, 464.

Haberlandt, W. F., & Glanville, E. V. Progress in neurological genetics. In F. J. Kallmann, *Expanding goals of genetics in psychiatry.* New York: Grune & Stratton, 1962. Pp. 126–135.

Haldane, J. B. S. The relative importance of principal and modifying genes in determining some human diseases. *J. Genet.*, 1941, **41**, 149.

Hall, C. S. The genetics of behavior. In S. S. Stevens (Ed.), *Handbook of experimental psychology.* New York: Wiley, 1951. Pp. 304–329.

Hammons, Helen G. *Heredity counseling: its services and centers.* New York: American Eugenics Society, 1956. P. 16.

Hammons, Helen G. (Ed.) *Heredity counseling by 17 authors.* New York: Hoeber-Harper, 1959.

Harrington, C. S. Personal communication.

Harrington, J. S. Personal communication.

Harris, G. W., Michael, R. P., & Scott, P. P. In Ciba Foundation Symposium, *Neurological basis of behaviour.* Boston: Little, Brown, 1958. Pp. 236–251.

Heath, R. G., Leach, B. E. Cohen M., & Feigley, C. A. *Amer. J. Psychiat.*, 1958, **114**, 917.

Heyman, J. J., & Merlis, S. In *Recent advances in biological psychiatry.* Vol. 5, New York: Plenum Press, 1962.

Hoffer, A., Osmond, H., & Symthies, J. *J. ment. Sci.*, 1954, **100**, 29.

Holzinger, K. J. The relative effect of nature and nurture influences on twin differences. *J. educ. Psychol.*, 1929, **20**, 241–248.

Hsia, D. Y., Knox, W. E., Quinn, K. V., & Paine, R. S. *Pediatrics,* 1958, **21**, 178.

Hurst, L. A. Research in genetics and psychiatry: New York State Psychiatric Institute, Columbia University. *Eugenics News,* 1952, **37**, 86–91.

Hurst, L. A. Applications of genetics in psychiatry and neurology. *S. Afr. J. lab. clin. Med.*, 1958, **4** (3), 169.

Hurst, L. A. Applications of genetics in psychiatry and neurology. *Eugenics Quart.*, 1961, **8** (2), 61. (a)

Hurst, L. A. Classification of psychotic disorders from a genetic point of view. *Acta genet. med. gemellol.*, 1961, **11** (3), 321. (b)

Hurst, L. A. Research implications of converging advances in psychiatric genetics and the pharmacology of psychotropic drugs. *Proc. 3rd World Congr. Psychiat.*, Montreal, 1961, 538–542. (c)

Hurst, L. A. The current status of psychiatric genetics. *Leech,* 1962, **32** (5), 120.

Hurst, L. A. Genetics in relation to psychiatry and neurology. *Proc. 44th S. Afr. Med. Congr.*, Johannesburg, 1963, and *S. Afr. med. J.*, 1964, **38**, 339–346.

Hurst, L. A., Reef, H. E., & Sachs, S. B. Neuropsychiatric disorders in the Bantu. I. Convulsive disorders: a pilot study with special reference to genetic factors. *S. Afr. med. J.*, 1961, **35**, 750–754.

Jacobs, P. A., Baikie, A. G., Court Brown, W. M., & Strong, J. A. The somatic chromosomes in Mongolism. *Lancet*, 1959, **1**, 710.

Kallmann, F. J. *The genetics of schizophrenia.* Locust Valley, N.Y.: Augustin, 1938.

Kallmann, F. J. The genetic theory of schizophrenia—an analysis of 691 twin index families. *Amer. J. Psychiat.*, 1946, **103** (3), 309–322.

Kallmann, F. J. *Genetics of psychoses.* Paris: Hermann, 1950.

Kallmann, F. J. Biological aspects of mental health and disease. In Milbank Fund Symposium. New York: Hoeber-Harper, 1951. (a)

Kallmann, F. J. Lecture given to post-graduate trimester in psychiatry and neurology, College of Physicians and Surgeons, Columbia University, New York, 1951. (b)

Kallmann, F. J. Comparative twin study on the genetic aspects of male homosexuality. *J. nerv. & ment. Dis.*, 1952, **115** (4), 283–298.

Kallmann, F. J. *Heredity in health and mental disorder.* New York: Norton, 1953.

Kallmann, F. J. In P. Hoch & J. Zubin (Eds.), *Genetic principles in manic-depressive psychosis.* New York: Grune & Stratton, 1954. P. 1.

Kallmann, F. J. (Ed.) *Expanding goals of genetics in psychiatry.* New York: Grune & Stratton, 1962.

Kallmann, F. J., & Anastasio, M. Twin studies on the psychopathology of suicide. *J. Hered.*, 1946, **37** (6), 171.

Kallmann, F. J., Porte, J. de, Porte, Elizabeth de, & Feingold, Lissy. Suicide in twins and only children. *Amer. J. human Genet.*, 1949, **1** (2), 113.

Kallmann, F. J., & Roth, B. Genetic aspects of preadolescent schizophrenia. *Amer. J. Psychiat.*, 1956, **112** (8), 599–606.

Lejeune, J., Gautier, M., & Turpin, R. Étude des chromosomes somatiques de neuf enfants mongoliens. *C. R. Acad. Sci., Paris,* 1959, **248**, 1721.

Lejeune, J., Turpin, R., & Gautier, M. Le mongolisme, premier exemple d'aberration autosomique humaine. *Ann. Génét.*, 1959, **1**, 41.

Ljungberg, L. *Acta psychiat. scandinav.*, 1957, **32**, Suppl. 112.

Maclean, N., Mitchell, J. M., Harnden, D. G., Williams, J., Jacob, P., Buckton, K., Baikie, A. G., Strong, J. A., Close, H. G., & Jones, D. G. *Lancet*, 1962, **1**, 293.

Mendel, G. Experiments in plant-hybridization. In J. A. Peters (Ed.), *Classic papers in genetics.* Englewood Cliffs, N.J.: Prentice-Hall, 1959.

Metrakos, J. D. The centrencephalic EEG in epilepsy. *Proc. 2nd internat. Conf. human Genet.*, Rome, 1961, **3**, 1792–1795.

Mohr, O. L. & Wriedt, C. Carnegie Inst. of Washington Publ. 295, 1919.

Moncrieff, A., & Wilkinson, R. H. *Brit. Med. J.*, 1961, **1**, 763.

Money, J., & Hirsch, S. R. *Arch. gen. Psychiat.*, 1963, **8**, 242–251.

Newman, H. H., Freeman, F. N., & Holzinger, K. J. *Twins: a study of heredity and environment.* Chicago: Univer. of Chicago Press, 1937.

Osborn, F. Galton and midcentury eugenics. *Eugenics Rev.*, 1956, **48**, 15.

Osmond, H., & Smythies, J. *J. ment. Sci.*, 1952, **98**, 309.

Polani, P. E. Briggs, J. H., Ford, C. E., Clarke, C. M., & Berg, J. M. *Lancet*, 1960, **1**, 721.

Poulik, M. D., & Bearn, A. G. Heterogeneity of ceruloplasmin. *Clin. Chim. Acta,* 1962, 374–382.

Psychoanalysis. In *Encyclopaedia Britannica.* Chicago: Encyclopaedia Britannica, 1962. P. 673.

Rainer, J. D., Altshuler, K. Z., & Kallmann, F. J. (Eds.) & Deming, W. E. (Asst.) *Family and mental health problems in a deaf population.* New York: New York State Psychiatric Institute, 1963.

Raphael, T., & Shaw, Margery, W. *J.A.M.A.*, 1963, **183**, 1022–1028.

Reed, S. C. *Counseling in medical genetics.* Philadelphia: Saunders, 1963.

Roberts, J. A. Fraser. *An introduction to medical genetics.* New York: Oxford, 1940.

Roberts, J. A. Fraser. *An introduction to medical genetics.* (2nd ed.) New York: Oxford, 1959.

Rosanoff, A. J., & Handy, L. M. Huntington's chorea in twins. *Arch. neurol. Psychiat.*, 1935, **33**, 839.

Royce, J. R. Factor theory and genetics. *Educ. psychol. Measmt.*, 1957, **17**, 361–376.

Sass-Kortsak, A., Jackson, S. J., & Charles, A. F. *Vox Sanguinis,* 1960, **5**, 88.

Saudek, R. A British pair of identical twins reared apart. *Charact. & Pers.*, 1934, **3**, 17–19.

Shy, G. M., & Magee, K. R. *Brain*, 1956, **79**, 610.

Sjögren, T., Sjögren, H., & Lindgren, A. Morbus Alzheimer and Morbus Pick. *Acta psychiat. et neurol. scandinav.*, 1952, Suppl. 82.

Slater, E. *Psychotic and neurotic illness in twins.* M.R.C. Special Report Series No. 278. London: H. M. Stationery Office, 1953.

Slater, E. *J. ment. Sci.*, 1961, **107**, 359.

Stenstedt, A. The care of Milan and George, identical twins reared apart. *Acta psychiat. et neurol. scandinav.*, 1952, Suppl. 79, 1.

Stephens, F. E., & Thompson, R. B. *J. Hered.*, 1943, **34**, 109–114.

Szent-Györgyi, A. *Introduction to submolecular biology.* New York: Academic, 1960.

Tedeschi, L. G., & Freeman, H. *Arch. gen. Psychiat.*, 1963, **6**, 109–111.

Thompson, W. R. The inheritance of behavior: activity differences in five inbred mouse strains *J. Hered.*, 1956, **47**, 147–148.

Thurstone, T. G., Thurstone, L. L., & Strandskov, H. H. Chapel Hill: Univer. of North Carolina Psychometric Laboratory, 1953, No. 4.

Udenfriend, S. In R. D. Brady & D. B. Gower (Eds.), *The neurochemistry of nucleotides and amino-acids.* New York: Wiley, 1960.

Wagner, R. P., & Mitchell, H. K. *Genetics and metabolism.* New York: Wiley, 1955.

Watson, J. B. *Behaviorism.* (Rev. ed.) New York: Norton, 1930.

Woolley, D. W., & Shaw, E. *Brit. med. J.*, 1954, **2**, 122.

8

Brain Mechanisms for Innate and Emotional Behavior

HORACE W. MAGOUN

From early times, man has sought a somatotopic reference for his faculties as well as a conception of their mode of operation in mechanistic terms. In antiquity, the processes of the body were thought to be managed by spirits, and the major body cavities were logically proposed as their seat (Figure 1). In sequential order, vegetative activities servicing appetite and nutrition were placed lowest, in the pelvis and belly. Vital functions were located next above, in the chest. Fittingly, the crowning rational faculties were assigned the highest elevation in the body and were referred to the brain ventricles within the head. More recently, two ideological lines have contributed importantly to current views of the organization and function of brain mechanisms for innate and emotional behavior.

The broad biological background was provided by Darwin (1871), who proposed a view of evolution in which each living form adapted to its environment by staking out a territory, in which it obtained food and shelter and so preserved its individual life and where it sought a mate and reproduced and reared its young and so preserved its race. For survival of the fittest in this struggle for life, each form also found it necessary to combat enemies or predators and, when overpowered, to preserve itself by flight. It was in relation to these basic biological activities, Darwin proposed, that the brain came to contain mechanisms for the management of feeding, fighting, fleeing, and undertaking mating activity (MacLean, 1958b).

A second line of development was begun by Bernard (1859), when he called attention to the preservation of stability of the internal environment as a condition of all higher and freer life. The general principle of homeostasis was later proposed by Cannon (1939) in explanation of this internal stability, and with Wiener's (1948) formulation of automatic control theory, it became possible to seek analogies between the physiological processes serving homeostasis and the functioning of a mechanical homeostat. The latter's component parts include a sensor, a central mechanism possessing a gain-setting bias, and an effector (Figure 2). Alterations in the internal or external environment, detected by the sensor, set in motion effector processes which oppose the change. The arrangement forms a feedback loop in which the output of the system continually serves to influence its ongoing performance, by means of the sensor, by changing the bias on the central mechanism, or both. In their provision for adjustment to change as well as for stabilization of performance around an optimal norm, such feedback principles account for most of the features of innate behavior (Brobeck, 1963; Deutsch, 1960; Pribam, 1961).

As Kubie (1948) has pointed out, activity related both to feeding and to reproduction has a "biochemical core" and is primarily con-

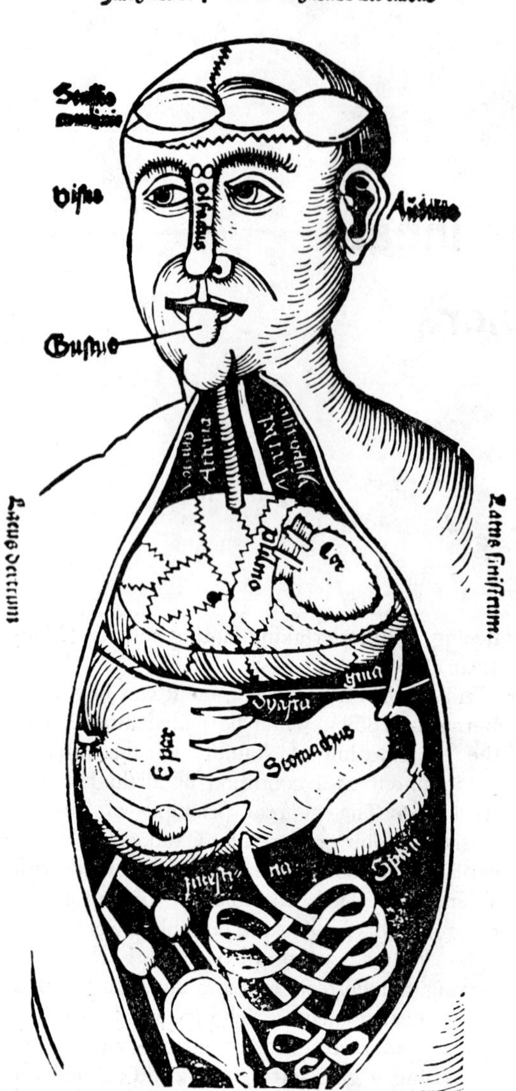

Figure 1. Renaissance anatomical figure showing the classical division of the body into the head, chest, belly, and pelvis. Note the ventricles of the brain with their faculties labeled above. *From Peyligk* (1518).

cerned with "the translation of bodily needs into behavior." As a feature of their feedback regulation, these needs are conspicuously cyclic, and their periodicity is a feature characteristic of innate behavior. When the activity of the rat is recorded (Richter, 1927), a three-hour cycle can be observed in relation to food intake, and a four-day cycle, with a doubling of running activity, in relation to recurring estrous periods (Figure 3).

Sequential steps have been differentiated within each such behavioral cycle (Tinbergen, 1951). An initial appetitive or exploratory stage is marked by plasticity, adaptiveness, and complex integration. In many species, exploration for food or a sexual partner often involves prolonged motor expenditures and, on the perceptual side, enhanced alertness and responsiveness to stimulation. By contrast, the consummatory act itself is usually brief and stereotyped. Following it, satiety develops, which typically involves "a state of rest, of disinterest in the outside world, and even of sleep which is in marked contrast to the heightened activity of the appetitive phase" (Dell, 1958). While the exploratory stages of innate behavior must implicate all major components of the brain, integrative mechanisms for the consummatory act and for satiety are more focal.

The obtrusive presence of these life- and race-preserving pursuits of innate behavior throughout the animal series implies their management by neural levels established early in phylogeny. The studies of Bard and Rioch (1937), Ranson (1940), and Hess (1954) established the significance of the hypothalamus for these functions, and the interconnections of the cephalic brainstem with the bordering limbic portions of the cerebral hemisphere were proposed by Papez (1937) as a circuit for emotion (Figure 4). A succeeding

Figure 2. Feedback organization by which the constancy of the internal environment is preserved in homeostasis. *From Deutsch* (1960).

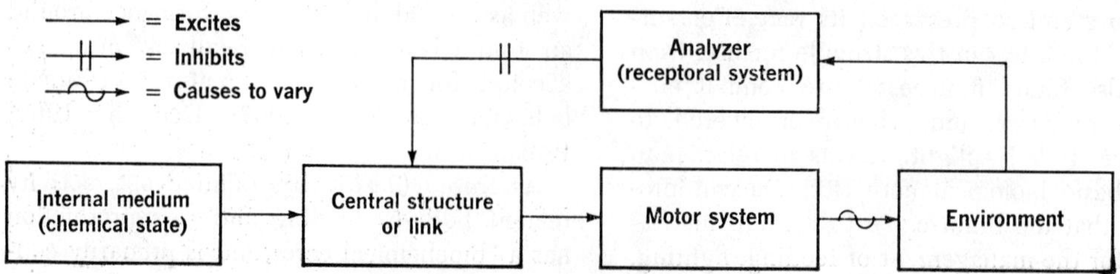

series of contributions by the Yale school (Fulton, 1953; Kaada, 1951; MacLean, 1949) has contributed significantly to current views.

REINFORCEMENT OF BEHAVIOR

Within this limbic forebrain and cephalic brainstem, Olds (1958) has recently discovered mechanisms for the positive and negative reinforcement of performance which do much to explain the impelling nature of innate behavior in terms of built-in drive or motivation. Much has been learned of factors which modify behavior through use of the Skinner box, in which an animal pushes a lever to obtain a reward, such as a pellet of food or a drop of milk. Closure with neurophysiology occurred when Olds and Milner (1954) arranged a Skinner box so that by pushing a lever, an animal with chronically implanted electrodes could deliver a stimulus directly to a part of its own brain (Figure 5). This inspired innovation revealed the existence of a previously unsuspected positively reinforcing mechanism in the basal forebrain, excitation of which appeared to have all the features of primary reward. With appropriate electrode placements, the animal repeatedly stimulated its own brain to the exclusion of all other activity for long periods of time (Olds, 1958). Stimulation rates reached the astronomical figure of 8,000 self-stimuli per hour when electrodes

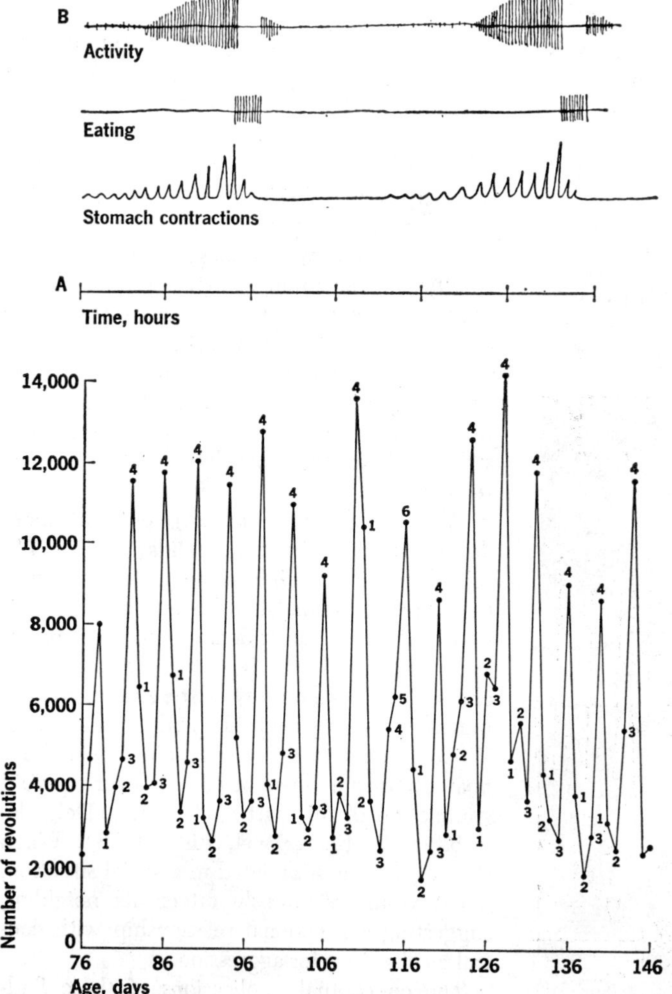

Figure 3. Records of running activity of the rat, showing the three-hour cycle related to food intake (above) and the four-day cycle related to recurring estrous periods (below). ***From Richter* (1927).**

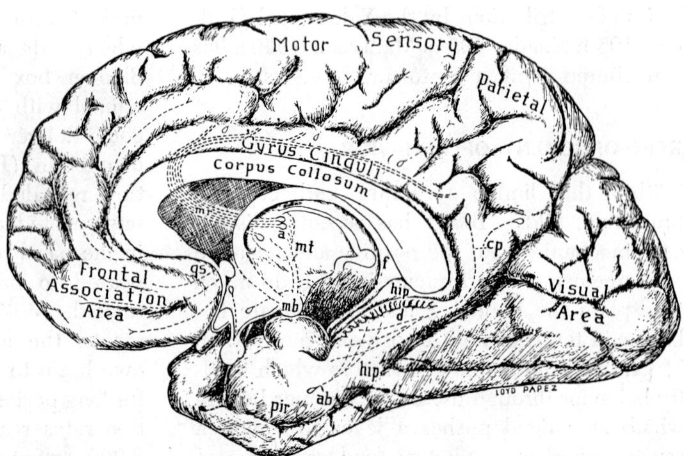

Figure 4. **Medical aspect of the cerebral hemisphere of man, showing Papez's emotional circuit and the limbic or visceral brain.** ***a*****, anterior thalamic nucleus;** ***ab*****, angular bundle;** ***cc*****, corpus callosum;** ***cp*****, posterior cingulate gyrus;** ***d*****, dentate gyrus;** ***f*****, fornix;** ***gc*****, cingulate gyrus;** ***gh*****, hippocampal gyrus;** ***gs*****, subcallosal gyrus;** ***hip*****, hippocampus;** ***mb*****, mammillary body;** ***mt*****, mammillothalamic tract;** ***pr*****, pyriform area.** ***From*** **Papez (1937).**

were in the posterior hypothalamus and midbrain; lower rates of self-stimulation were characteristic of more rostral sites (Figure 6). Pharmacological distinction was also possible, for tranquilizing agents, such as reserpine and chlorpromazine, reduced or abolished self-stimulation of the posterior hypothalamus but not of more cephalic structures.

Figure 5. **Rat with electrodes implanted in brain and with foot upon bar (above). Rat presses bar (below) and delivers stimulus to its own brain. Animal must release lever and press again to repeat stimulus. Some animals have stimulated themselves for twenty-four hours without rest and as often as 8,000 times an hour.** ***From*** **Olds (1958).**

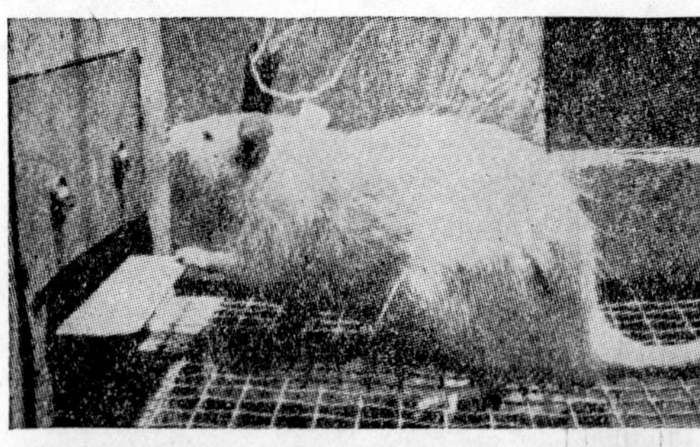

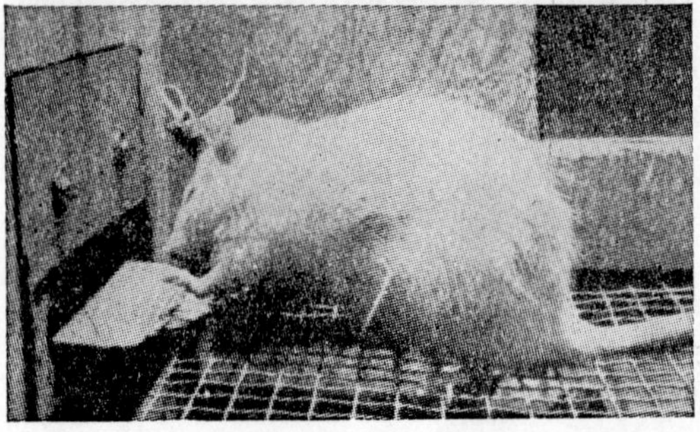

Olds's (1958) animals ran a maze as fast for self-stimulation as for food reward, and they ran a runway faster. When tested by being made to cross a painful grid, the drive for self-stimulation was at least twice that of a twenty-four-hour hunger drive. Some differentiation of hunger- and sex-reward systems was possible, for rates of self-stimulation of the medial hypothalamus were influenced by hunger or its satiety, while administration of sex hormones or castration modified the rates of self-stimulation of more lateral hypothalamic regions.

With electrodes in an adjacent but more dorsal diencephalic zone, Olds (1958) observed negative reinforcement, in the sense that after an animal had once stimulated this region, it would never do so again (Figure 6). When this area was repeatedly excited in a characteristic laboratory setting, anticipatory unrest was soon provoked by the setting alone. When trained to do so, an animal would repeatedly turn a wheel or press a lever to avoid stimulation of this part of its brain (Delgado, Roberts, & Miller, 1954; Lilly, 1958). When this region was stimulated in a social situation, a cat would vigorously attack its neighbor, suggesting a functional relationship with central mechanisms for aggression.

The conceptual implications of these findings are of the greatest interest. Do these dual, reciprocally antagonistic half-centers for positive and negative reinforcement serve subjective pleasure and pain and their elaborations as reward and punishment? Are slight feelings of pleasure or unpleasantness associated with liminal activity in these systems, while more exquisite or orgiastic enjoyments, on the one hand, and intensities of rage and terror, on the other, are related to their full-blown excitation? In these studies, have heaven and hell been located in the animal brain?

ALIMENTARY BEHAVIOR

Recently, a remarkably active program of experimentation has been exploring the limbic and hypothalamic management of alimentary behavior (Anand, 1963). Feeding can be induced by direct electrical stimulation of the lateral hypothalamus (Figure 7), even in the satiated animal (Andersson, Jewell, & Larsson, 1958; Larsson, 1954). Aphagia follows lesions here, and the lateral portions of the hypothalamus (Anand & Brobeck, 1951) or connections to this region from the globus pallidus (Morgane, 1961) are importantly involved in feeding. Reciprocally, the ventromedial hypothalamic nucleus or region is implicated in satiety. Its direct stimulation stops feeding behavior, even in the hungry animal, while lesions in it are followed by hyperphagia, leading to pronounced obesity (Figure 8; Hetherington & Ranson, 1940). A negative feedback appears operant in alimentary behavior, by which peripheral stores relay information concerning their inventory to hypothalamic regulatory mechanisms. After lesions were made in the hypothalamic ventromedial nucleus, with resultant hyperphagia and obesity, in one of a pair of parabiotic rats, the other responded to its mate's overfeeding by eating less and becoming thin (Hervey, 1959).

Food intake tends generally to be correlated with drinking, and although hypothalamic mechanisms for the two are adjacent, they appear to act separately and indeed to depend, respectively, upon contrasting adrenergic and cholingergic excitation (Grossman,

Figure 6. Parasagittal sections through the brain of the rat showing the distribution of areas for positive (crosslined) and negative (stippled) reinforcement. *C. Cort,* cingulum cortex; *CC,* corpus callosum; *S;* septum; *HPC,* hippocampus; *A,* anterior commissure; *FX,* fornix; *MT,* mammillothalamic fasciculus; *HTH,* hypothalamus; *CB,* cerebellar; *MB,* mammillary body; *AM,* amygdala; *Prepyr,* prepyriformis cortex. *From Olds* (1958).

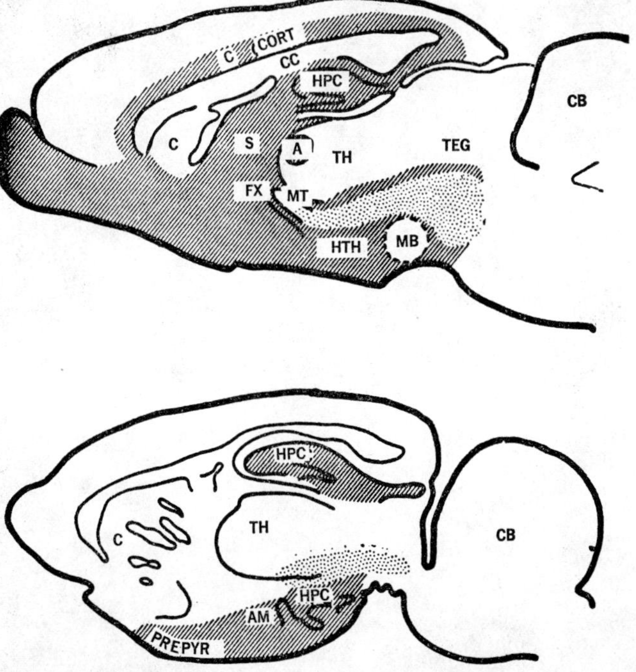

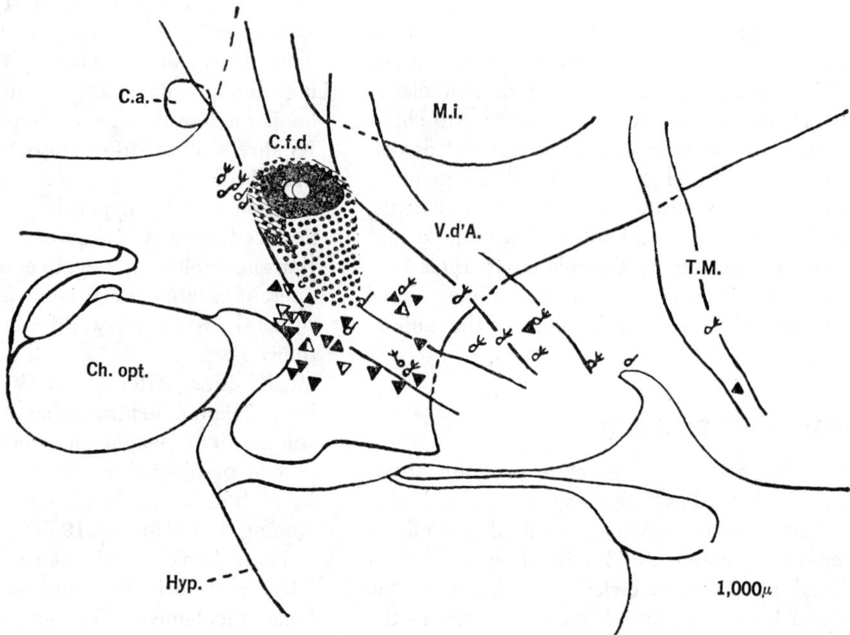

Figure 7. Midsagittal view of the hypothalamus of the goat. Black triangles mark the sites where electrical stimulation caused feeding and the solid black area marks the site where it caused drinking. Microinjection of hypertonic NaCl, in the dotted area, also caused polydipsia. *From Andersson, Jewell, & Larsson* (1958); *Andersson & McCann* (1955).

Figure 8. Obesity in the rat following lesions in the hypothalamic ventromedial nucleus (above) in comparison with the littermate control (below). *From Hetherington & Ranson* (1940).

1960). Andersson and McCann (1955) have identified a region near the paraventricular nucleus of the goat where electrical stimulation or the injection of hypertonic solutions evokes a gargantuan polydipsia in which as much as 16 liters of water may be drunk in a single experiment (Figure 7).

The increased firing of single supraoptic neurons has been observed on intracarotid injections of hypertonic sodium chloride or glucose (Cross & Green, 1959). In addition to these osmotic and glucostatic factors, however, such a variety of other means of influencing these mechanisms has been proposed—by shifts in serum lipids or amino acids, by changes in temperature, and by afferent stimuli from the oropharynx or digestive tract—that a multiple-factor theory of regulation of feeding and drinking seems presently most acceptable (Brobeck, 1963).

A number of contributions, which have been reviewed elsewhere (Magoun, 1963), point to the existence of a nonspecific thalamocortical system responsible for evoking large slow waves, recruiting responses, and spindle bursting in the EEG. These characteristically bear a close relation to internal inhibition, behavioral drowsiness, and sleep. This thalamocortical system can be driven from a number of parts of the brain, and its excitation from hypothalamic and limbic structures appears to provide a means of terminating innate behavior by satiety. In a study of feeding behavior, Anokhin (1961) has observed an EEG arousal pattern in the frontal cortex and hypothalamus of dogs deprived of food. When food is tubed directly into their stomachs and glucose injected into their bloodstreams, their EEG arousal patterns give way promptly to records of pronounced synchrony in both cortical and hypothalamic channels (Figure 9). Feeding is initiated by hunger and appetite and is terminated by satiety. In showing how its termination, in inactivity, lassitude, drowsiness, and often sleep, is associated with synchrony and spindle bursting in the electrical activity of the brain, these findings suggest that satiety may be the expression of a type of internal inhibition which, after consummation is achieved, plays an important role in bringing innate behavior to an end.

MATING BEHAVIOR

Turning now from food to sex, the recent work of Sawyer (1963) and others has differentiated a hypothalamic mechanism for mating behavior from one regulating pituitary-gonadotropic and target reproductive system functions. The latter involves tuberal structures located just above the median eminence of the stalk. In both the female rabbit and female cat, ovulation can be induced by direct electrical stimulation of this region, while experimental lesions here block ovulation following coitus and lead to atrophy of the ovaries and reproductive tract. Implantation of crystals of estrogen in this region gives similar results, although the animals continue to accept the male eagerly and display an unusual frequency of mating behavior. In the dog, analogous findings were obtained with the

Figure 9. Records of electrical activity of the frontal cortex of the cat under urethane anesthesia shows an aroused EEG during hunger (above) and contrasting EEG synchrony (below) after glucose and filling of the stomach with milk. *From Anokhin* (1961).

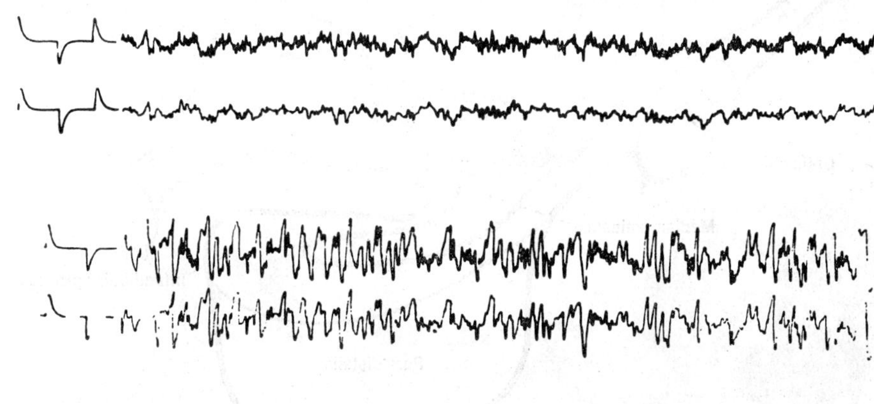

male, implantation of testosterone into this same region resulting in aspermia and testicular and prostatic atrophy.

In the manner of automatic control theory, this neuroendocrine system appears to employ inverse feedback to regulate performance, for circulating gonadal hormones normally act back upon the tuberal hypothalamus to check the further secretion of gonadotropins (McCann, 1963). These findings are relevant to the development of an effective oral contraceptive, for the new antifertility agents which prevent conception in women block the hypothalamic gonadotropin-releasing mechanism in the rabbit, while leaving unaffected the brain mechanisms serving libido and the appetitive and consummatory aspects of sexual behavior. Both the inclination for mating and its behavioral performance are unaffected, while consequent gonadotropin release and ovulation fail to occur. The action of these antifertility agents thus resembles that of the progestational steroids normally elaborated by the ovary during gestation, which prevent ovulation throughout pregnancy. Paradoxically, the human female is now able to stimulate an aspect of pregnancy in order to prevent conception.

In the male monkey, MacLean (1963) has identified preoptic and anterior hypothalamic areas in which electrical stimulation evokes penile erection, pelvic movements, and ejaculation.

In the female cat and rabbit, the hypothalamic mechanisms for mating behavior lie, respectively, in front of and behind those regulating pituitary gonadotropic functions (Figure 10; Sawyer, 1963). Lesions here are followed by permanent loss of estrous behavior, impossible to overcome by estrogens, although the hypothalamic-pituitary system remains viable, and ovarian atrophy fails to occur. The enhanced alertness and augmented motor performance during the appetitive or exploratory stage of sexual behavior are associated with an increased excitability of these systems. For several hours after administration of progesterone (Figure 11), the EEG arousal threshold was markedly lowered, with a succeeding elevation above the control (Sawyer, 1963). This increased responsiveness was associated with estrus and mating behavior, while the secondary

Figure 10. Midsagittal view of hypothalamus and pituitary showing the common tuberal area controlling release of pituitary ovulating hormone in both the cat and the rabbit (*CR*, tropic) and the areas concerned with sexual behavior in the anterior hypothalamus of the cat (*CB*) and the posterior hypothalamus of the rabbit (*RB*). *From Sawyer & Kawakami* (1961).

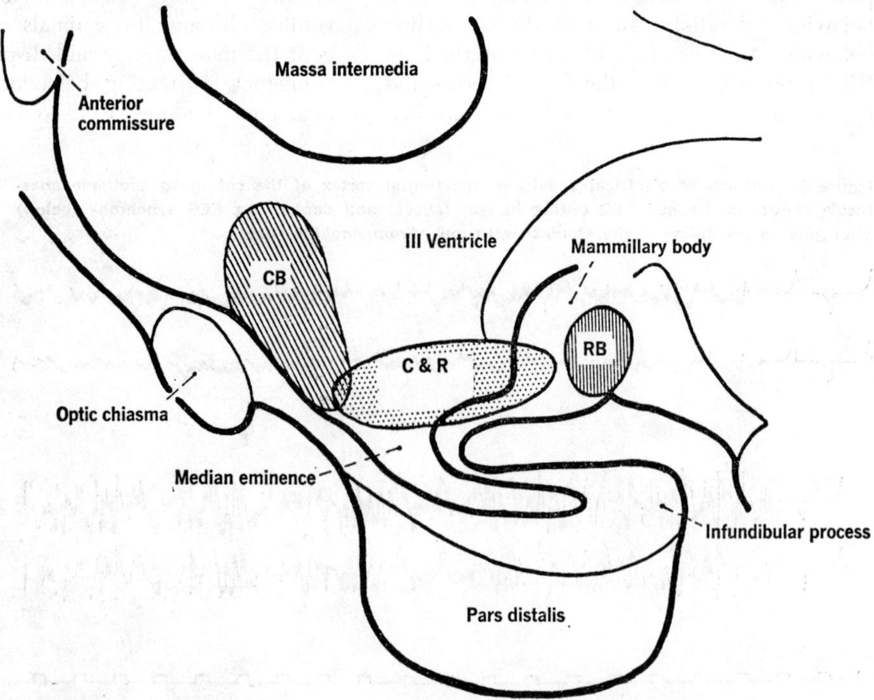

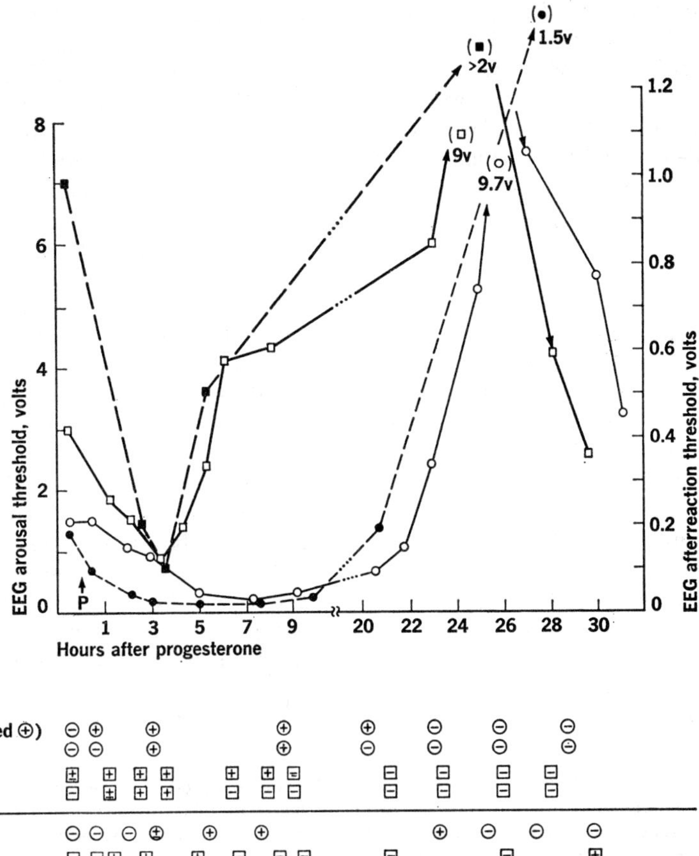

Figure 11. Marked initial increase in excitability and the subsequent pronounced elevation of threshold of the reticular formation and hypothalamus following injection of progesterone (P) in the rabbit. ***From Sawyer & Kawakami*** **(1961).**

elevation of threshold was correlated with anestrus and absence of sexual responsiveness. This striking modification of neural function, together with that which occurs after implanting sex hormones (Lisk, 1963; Michael, 1963), suggests that the induction of sexual behavior and the management of its remarkable periodicity in the estrous cycle may in large part be accounted for in terms of direct endocrine modification of excitability of the brain.

In the female rabbit, there is a period of several minutes following coitus during which the animal displays a languid relaxation, inactivity, and sleep, which terminate abruptly in a rebound burst of feeding (Figure 12). During this period, the EEG first shows spindle bursting, followed by the pattern of paradoxical sleep, associated with a prodigious hypersynchrony in limbic structures.

In the case of mating, therefore, as in feeding, satiety following consummation may be the consequence of activity in the EEG synchronizing thalamocortical system responsible for internal inhibition, which brings each cycle of innate behavior to an end.

AGGRESSIVE-DEFENSIVE BEHAVIOR

Much earlier evidence points to the hypothalamic integration of patterns of aggressive-defensive behavior. In the surviving decortical cat, vigorous patterns of sham or quasi rage may often be evoked by trivial afferent stimulation (Bard & Rioch, 1937); such activity is only fragmentary after lower decerebration (Bard & Macht, 1958). In a docile cat, focal lesions of the hypothalamic ventromedial nucleus are followed by an exaggeration of aggressive tendencies to the point of savagery (Wheatley, 1944). In aggression, as in feeding, the medial hypothalamus thus appears to be inhibitory of behavior, while the lateral area is excitatory. Stimulation of the latter yields coordinate "affective-defensive" responses (Figures 13 and 14), in which vocalization and autonomic discharge are associated with directed attack or flight, which in every way appears identical with the animal's natural emotional behavior (Hess, 1954; Hunsperger, 1956; Masserman, 1943).

AMYGDALA

At about the same time that Papez (1937) proposed a limbic circuit for emotion, Klüver and Bucy's (1939) observations of the consequence of bilateral temporal lobectomy initiated current study of this part of the brain. Among the striking alterations in their monkeys, tameness, docility, and emotional unresponsiveness were related to a reduction or loss of fear and anger, while hypersexuality and hyperphagia indicated an exaggeration of these latter categories of behavior. These changes now seem referable to ablation of the amygdala and/or the adjacent pyriform lobe. The work of Spiegel et al. (1940) and that of Bard and Mountcastle (1947) have indicated that injury to the limbic forebrain is the major factor leading to increased rage behavior after decortication. A similar exaggerated display of emotional behavior was observed during experimental limbic seizures (MacLean, 1958), in which mildly noxious stimuli evoked increased responsiveness leading to states of wild excitement, while enhancement of pleasure reactions might later appear.

In intact animals, stimulation of the amygdala induces fear and rage responses (Kaada, Andersen, & Jansen, 1954; Ursin & Kaada, 1960), components of which can be evoked along the course of its efferent stria terminalis to the hypothalamus and midbrain (Figure 14; Fernandez de Molina & Hunsperger, 1959; Fernandez de Molina & Hunsperger, 1962). When the two regions are excited concomitantly, the amygdala may suppress attack behavior elicited by hypothalamic stimulation (Egger & Flynn, 1962). Focal lesions of the amygdala or pyriform cortex are followed by docility and hypersexuality in a variety of animals (Schreiner & Kling, 1953). In the cat,

Figure 12. Behavior of female rabbit following coitus (*a*). (*b*), the eyes close, and at this time frontal spindle bursts appear. (c) to (e), the head sinks to the floor, the ears droop, and behavioral depression is complete; at this time the EEG is that of paradoxical sleep. (*f*), the animal suddenly recovers and feeds ravenously for a few moments. *From Sawyer & Kawakami* (1961).

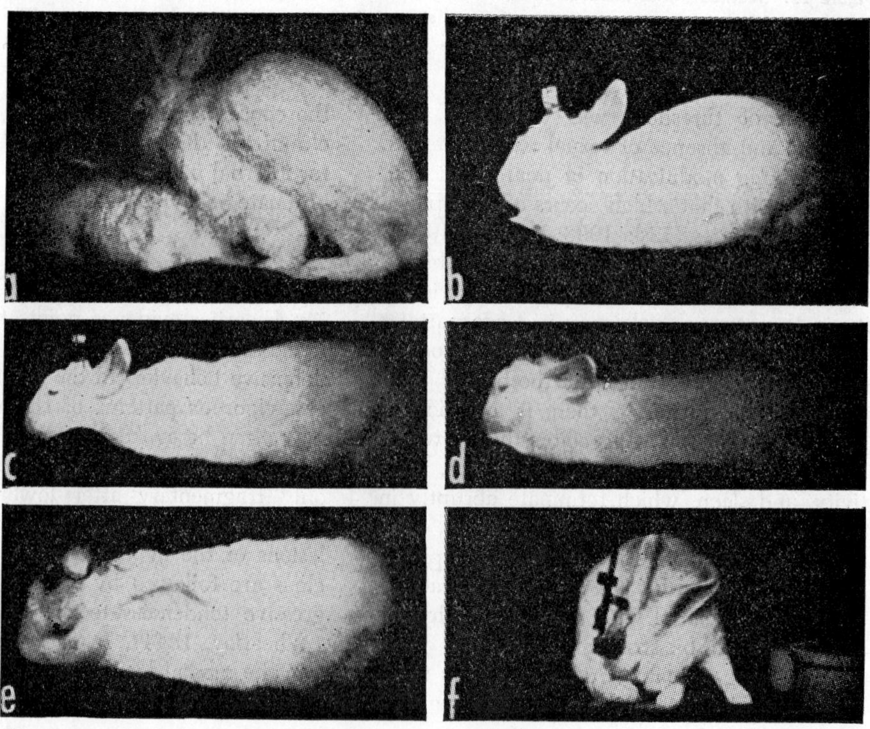

Figure 13. Affective-defensive reactions induced by stimulation of the diencephalon through implanted electrodes. ***From Hess*** **(1954).**

however, exaggeration of sexual behavior appeared to consist largely of the display of a normally wide-ranging repertoire outside of the usual territorial limits (Green, Clemente, & de Groot, 1957). From a social point of view, amygdala lesions in the monkey are followed by changes of position in the dominant to submissive spectrum of group hierarchy (Figure 17; Rosvold, Mirsky, & Pribram, 1954).

When the electrical activity of the amygdala is recorded (Figure 15), bursts of 40-per-second activity are characteristically observed during states of vigilance or excited behavior (Adey, Dunlop, & Hendrix, 1960; Freeman, 1960; Lesse, 1960). Although such burst discharge is induced in a variety of situations, its elicitation is by no means stereotyped but varies with the state of the animal. The presentation of food or water is evocative in deprived animals (Figure 16) but becomes ineffective after satiety. During the establishment of a conditioned avoidance response, this burst discharge appears earlier and, in subsequent extinction, persists longer than the motor performance itself.

Figure 14. Reconstruction of the relations of the amygdala and hippocampus to the cephalic brainstem of the cat. Black shading indicates the amygdala and the hypothalamic and periaqueductal regions from which affective-defensive responses can be evoked. ***From Fernandez de Molina & Hunsperger*** **(1959).**

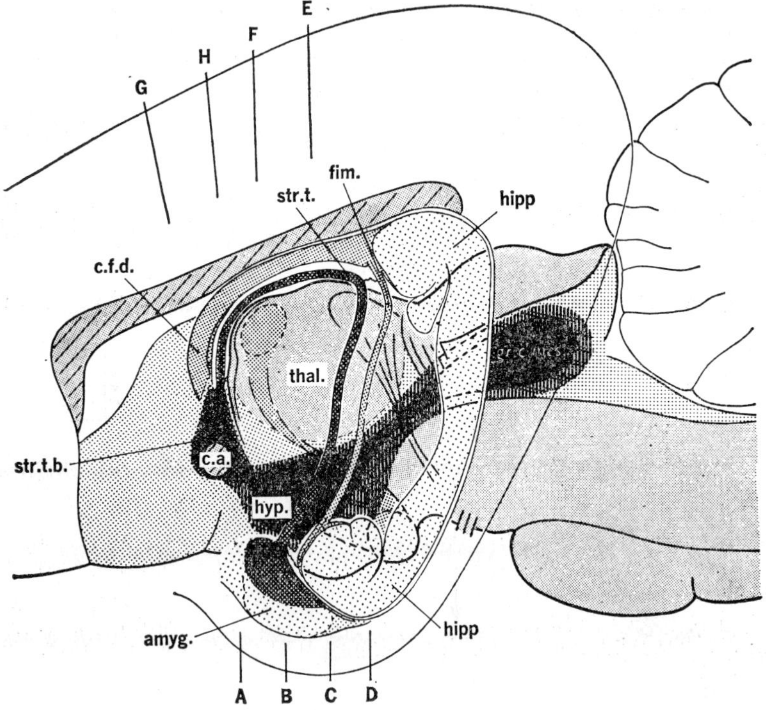

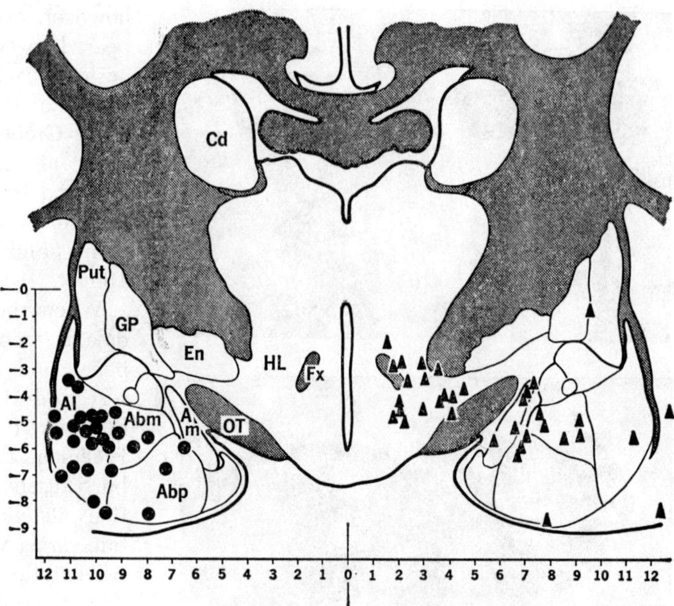

Figure 15. Transverse section through forebrain of the cat. Circles (left) mark sites in the amygdala from which forty per second bursts were recorded during excited behavior, and triangles (right) mark sites from which such activity was not recorded. *Abm*, basal amygdaloid nucleus (magnocellular); *Abp*, basal amygdaloid nucleus (parvocellular); *Al*, lateral amygdaloid nucleus; *Am*, medial amygdaloid nucleus; *Cd*, caudate nucleus; *En*, entopeduncular nucleus; *HL*, lateral hypothalamus; *Fx*, fornix; *GP*, globus pallidus; *OT*, optic tract; *Put*, putamen. *From Lesse* (1960).

Figure 16. Records of electrical activity from the region of the amygdala of the cat, showing the high-frequency bursts induced by fish odors in the hungry animal (*A*) and their virtual absence after feeding to satiety (*B*). *From Freeman* (1960).

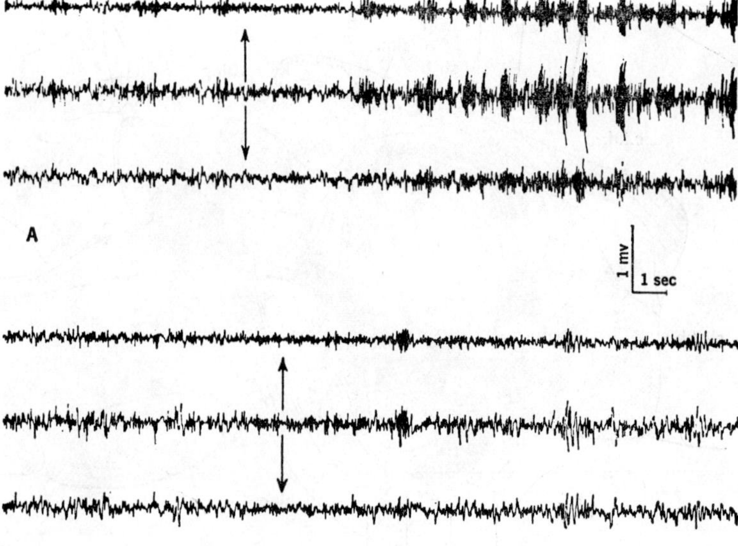

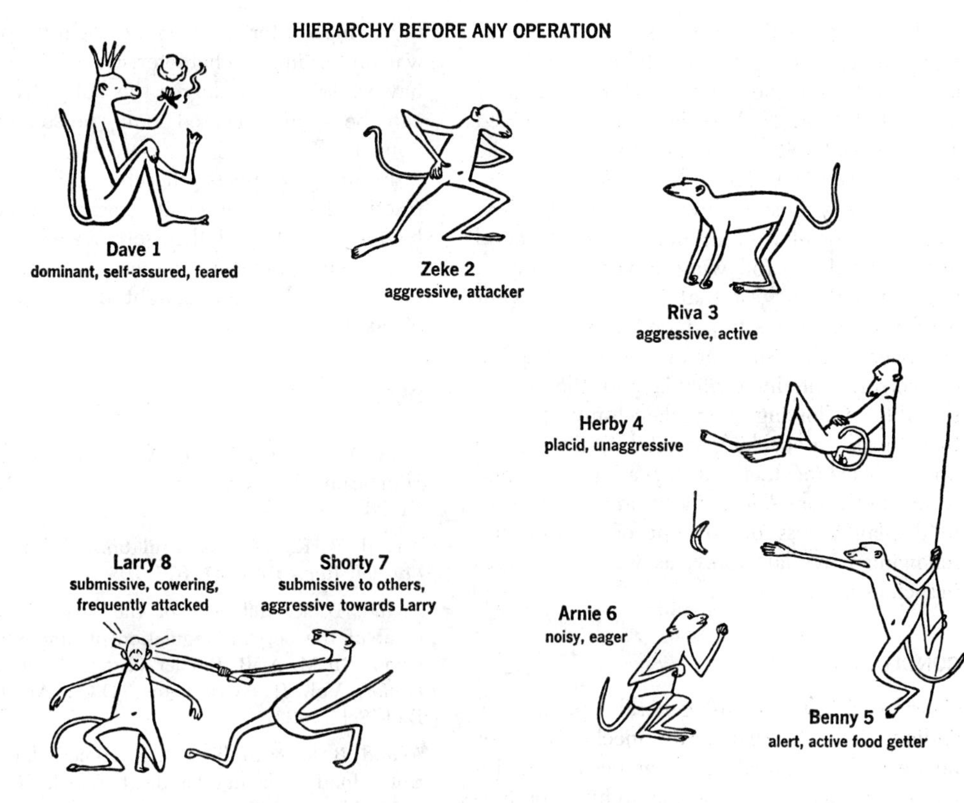

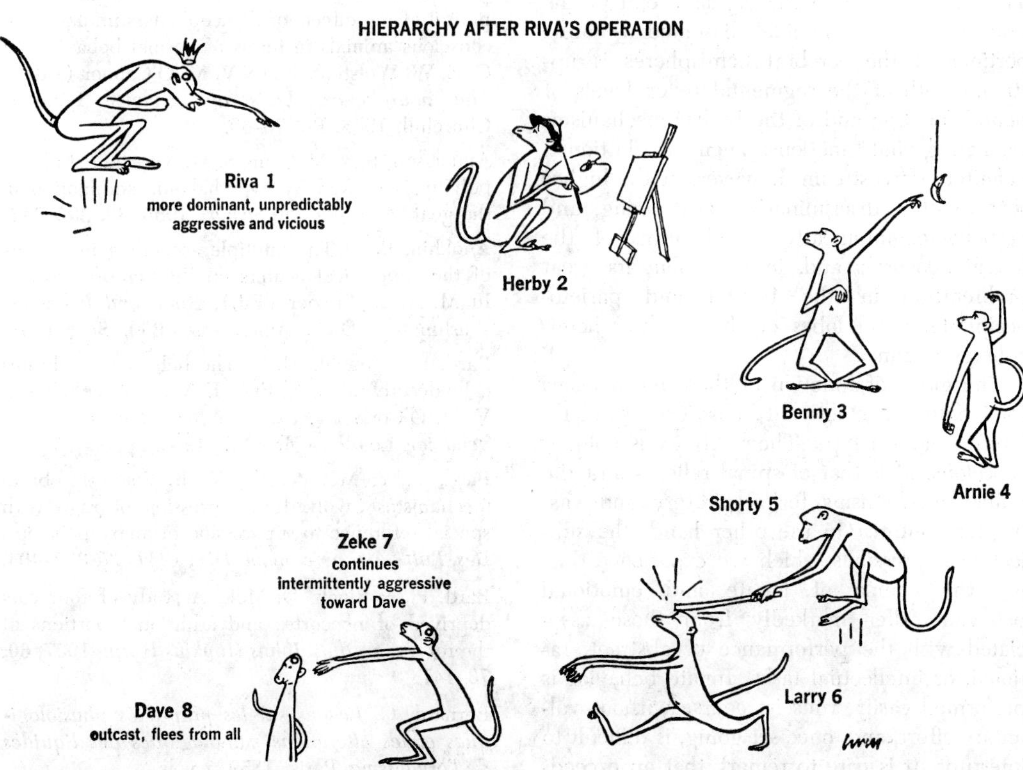

Figure 17. Change in group hierarchy in a colony following amygdala lesions in the monkey. *From Rosvold, Mirsky, & Pribram (1954).*

The amygdala thus appears to serve importantly in regulating the excitability of lower mechanisms for the consummatory phases of innate behavior. If these latter are conceived as homeostats, it can be proposed that the amygdala sets the bias on their central mechanisms so as to raise or lower their excitability. The tameness of wild animals and the general loss of aggression following amygdalectomy in some animals suggest that it or the adjacent pyriform cortex exerts a facilitatory influence on lower mechanisms for aggressive behavior. Conversely, the hyperphagia and the hypersexuality following amygdalectomy suggest that it exerts a checking or inhibiting influence upon lower mechanisms for alimentary and sexual behavior. Additionally, animals appear to display a loss of concept of territoriality following amygdalectomy, as well as changes in social status.

CONCLUSION

Considered in their most general aspect, these findings indicate that brain mechanisms for innate and emotional behavior occupy an intermediate position in the hierarchy of organization within the central nervous system. Their distribution in the cephalic end of the brainstem and in the older, basomedial, limbic portions of the cerebral hemispheres is upstream both of the segmental reflex levels of neural function and of the bulbar mechanisms regulating vital functions. Their distribution is definitely downstream, however, of the higher sensorimotor, discriminative, abstracting, and verbally communicative mechanisms of the lateral neocortex and, in particular, its great proliferation in the frontal and parieto-occipitotemporal lobes of the cerebral hemispheres of man.

The mode of function of these mechanisms for innate and emotional behavior is similarly intermediate in type. Their activity is not unconscious, as is that of spinal reflexes and the bulbar mechanisms for respiratory and vasomotor control. On the other hand, the subjective impressions which we experience during the course of innate and emotional behavior differ markedly from those associated with the performance of abstract, rational, or intellectual tasks. Innate behavior is performed easily, runs its course without voluntary effort, and, once set going, is difficult to interrupt. It is trite to remark that an exceedingly high titer of stirring feeling forms a warmly intimate characteristic of innate behavior. To a large degree this subjective affect can be communicated only personally and nonverbally.

In many respects, therefore, the most attractive features of innate and emotional behavior do not lend themselves well to handbook exposition but, rather, are among the most enjoyable and sought-after experiences of our lives.

REFERENCES

Adey, W. R., Dunlop, C. W., & Hendrix, C. E. Hippocampal slow waves. *Arch. Neurol.*, 1960, **3**, 74–90.

Anand, B. K. Nervous regulation of food intake. *Physiol. Rev.*, 1961, **41**, 677–708.

Anand, B. K. Influence of the internal environment of the nervous regulation of alimentary behavior. In M. A. B. Brazier (Ed.), *Brain and behavior.* Vol. II. Washington, D.C.: Amer. Inst. Biol. Sci., 1963.

Anand, B. K., & Brobeck, J. R. Hypothalamic control of food intake in rat and cat. *Yale J. Biol. Med.*, 1951, **24**, 123–140.

Andersson, B., Jewell, P. A., & Larsson, S. An appraisal of the effects of diencephalic stimulation of conscious animals in terms of normal behavior. In G. E. W. Wolstenholme & V. M. O'Connor (Eds.), *The neurological basis of behavior.* London: Churchill, 1958. Pp. 76–89.

Andersson, B., & McCann, S. M. A further study of polydipsia evoked by hypothalamic stimulation in the goat. *Acta physiol. Scand.*, 1955, **33**, 333–346.

Anokhin, P. K. The multiple ascending influences of the subcortical centers on the cerebral cortex. In M. A. B. Brazier (Ed.), *Brain and behavior.* Washington, D.C.: Amer. Inst. Biol. Sci., 1961.

Bard, P. & Macht, M. B. The behavior of chronically decerebrate cats. In G. E. W. Wolstenholme & V. M. O'Connor (Eds.), *The neurological basis of behavior.* London: Churchill, 1958. Pp. 55–75.

Bard, P., & Mountcastle, V. B. Some forebrain mechanisms involved in expression of rage with special reference to suppression of angry behavior. *Res. Publ. Ass. nerv. ment. Dis.*, 1947, **27**, 362–404.

Bard, P., & Rioch, D. McK. A study of four cats deprived of neocortex and additional portions of the forebrain. *Bull. Johns Hopkins Hosp.*, 1937, **60**, 73–147.

Bernard, C. *Leçons sur les propriétés physiologiques et les alterations pathologiques des liquides de l'organisme.* Paris: 1859. 2 vols.

Brobeck, J. R. Neural regulation of food intake. *Ann. N.Y. Acad. Sci.*, 1955, **63**, 44–55.

Brobeck, J. R. The internal environment and alimentary behavior: synthesis. In M. A. B. Brazier (Ed.), *Brain and behavior*. Vol. II. Washington, D.C.: Amer. Inst. Biol. Sci., 1963.

Cannon, W. B. *Wisdom of the body*. New York: Norton, 1939.

Cross, B. A., & Green, J. D. Activity of single neurons in the hypothalamus: effect of osmotic and other stimuli. *J. Physiol.*, 1959, **148**, 554–560.

Darwin, C. *The descent of man and selection in relation to sex*. London: J. Murray, 1871.

Delgado, J. M. R., Roberts, W. W., & Miller, N. E. Learning motivated by electrical stimulation of the brain. *Amer. J. Physiol.*, 1954, **179**, 587–593.

Dell, P. C.: Some basic mechanisms of the translation of bodily needs into behavior. In G. E. W. Wolstenholme & M. O'Connor (Eds.), *The neurological basis of behavior*. London: Churchill, 1958. Pp. 187–203.

Deutsch, J. A. *The structural basis of behavior*. Chicago: Univer. of Chicago Press, 1960.

Egger, M. D., & Flynn, J. P. Amygdaloid suppression of hypothalamically elicited attack behavior. *Science*, 1962, **136**, 43–44.

Fernandez de Molina. A., & Hunsperger, R. W. Central representation of affective reactions in forebrain and brain stem: electrical stimulation of amygdala, stria terminalis, and adjacent structures. *J. Physiol.*, 1959, **145**, 251–265.

Fernandez de Molina, A., & Hunsperger, R. W. Organization of subcortical system governing defense and flight reactions in the cat. *J. Physiol.*, 1962, **160**, 200–213.

Freeman, W. J. Correlation of electrical activity of prepyriform cortex and behavior in cat. *J. Neurophysiol.*, 1960, **23**, 111–131.

Fulton, J. F. The limbic system: a study of the visceral brain in primates and man. *Yale J. Biol. Med.*, 1953, **26**, 107–118.

Green, J. D., Clemente, C. D., & de Groot, J. Rhinencephalic lesions and behavior in cats. *J. comp. Neurol.*, 1957, **108**, 505–545.

Greep, R. O. Steroid control of pituitary-gonadal function. In M. A. B. Brazier (Ed.), *Brain and behavior*. Vol. III. Berkeley, Calif.: Univer. of California Press, 1963.

Grossman, S. P. Eating or drinking elicited by direct adrenergic or cholinergic stimulation of hypothalamus. *Science*, 1960, **132**, 301–302.

Harris, G. W., Michael, R. P., & Scott, P. P. Neurological site of action of stilbestrol in eliciting sexual behavior. In G. E. W. Wolstenholme & M. O'Connor (Eds.), *The neurological basis of behavior*. London: Churchill, 1958. Pp. 236–254.

Hervey, G. R. The effects of lesions in the hypothalamus in parabiotic rats. *J. Physiol.*, 1959, **145**, 336–352.

Hess, W. R. *Diencephalon, autonomic and extrapyramidal functions*. New York: Grune & Stratton, 1954.

Hetherington, A. W., & Ranson, S. W. Hypothalamic lesions and adiposity in the rat. *Anatom. Rec.*, 1940, **78**, 149–172.

Hunsperger, R. W. Affektreaktionen auf elektrische Reizung im Hirnstamm der Katze. *Helvet. physiol. Acta*, 1956, **14**, 70–92.

Kaada, B. R. Somato-motor, autonomic and electrocorticographic responses to electrical stimulation of "rhinencephalic" and other structures in primates, cat and dog. *Acta physiol. Scand. Suppl.* 83, 1951, **24**, 285.

Kaada, B. R., Andersen, P., & Jansen, J., Jr. Stimulation of the amygdaloid nuclear complex in unanesthetized cats. *Neurology*, 1954, **4**, 48–64.

Klüver, H., & Bucy, P. C. Preliminary analysis of functions of the temporal lobes in monkeys. *Arch. Neurol. Psychiat.*, 1939, **42**, 979–1000.

Kubie, L. S. Instincts and homeostasis. *Psychosom. Med.*, 1948, **10**, 15–30.

Larsson, S. On the hypothalamic organization of the nervous mechanism regulating food intake. I. *Acta physiol. Scand. Suppl.* 115, 1954, **32**.

Lesse, H. Rhinencephalic electrophysiological activity during "emotional behavior" in cats. *Psychiat. Res. Rep.*, 1960, **12**, 224–237.

Lilly, J. C. Learning motivated by subcortical stimulation the "start" and "stop" patterns of behavior. In H. H. Jasper (Ed.), *Reticular formation of the brain*. Boston: Little, Brown, 1958.

Lisk, R. D. Control of sexual behavior by gonadal steroids. In M. A. B. Brazier (Ed.), *Brain and behavior*. Vol. III. Berkeley, Calif.: Univer. of California Press, 1963.

McCann, S. M. Neural control of pituitary-gonadal functions. In *ibid*.

MacLean, P. D. Psychosomatic disease and the "visceral brain": recent developments bearing on the Papez theory of emotion. *Psychosom. Med.*, 1949, **11**, 338–353.

MacLean, P. D. Contrasting functions of limbic and neocortical systems of the brain and their relevance to psychophysiological aspects of medicine. *Am. J. Med.*, 1958, **25**, 611–626. (a)

MacLean, P. D. The limbic systems with respect to self-preservation and the preservation of the species. *J. nerv. ment. Dis.*, 1958, **127**, 1–11. (b)

MacLean, P. D. The limbic system with reference to two life principles. In M. A. B. Brazier (Ed.), *CNS and behavior.* New York: Josiah Macy, 1959.

MacLean, P. D. Cortical, limbic and hypothalamic regulation of sexual behavior. In M. A. B. Brazier (Ed.), *Brain and behavior.* Vol. III. Berkeley, Calif.: Univer. of California Press, 1963.

Magoun, H. W. *The waking brain.* Springfield, Ill.: Charles C Thomas, 1963.

Masserman, J. H. *Behavior and neurosis.* Chicago: Univer. of Chicago Press, 1943.

Michael, R. Control of sexual behavior by gonadal steroids. In M. A. B. Brazier (Ed.), *Brain and behavior.* Vol. III. Berkeley, Calif.: Univer. of California Press, 1963.

Morgane, P. J. Medial forebrain bundle and "feeding centers" of the hypothalamus. *J. comp. Neurol.*, 1961, **117**, 1–25.

Olds, J. Self-stimulation of the brain. *Science*, 1958, **127**, 315–324.

Olds, J., & Milner, P. Positive reinforcement produced by electrical stimulation of septal area and other regions of rat brain. *J. comp. physiol. Psychol.*, 1954, **47**, 419–427.

Papez, J. W. A proposed mechanism of emotion. *Arch. Neurol. Psychiat.*, 1937, **38**, 725–745.

Peyligk, J. Compendiosa capitis physici declaratio. In *Philosophiae naturalis compendium.* Lipsi: Imp. Wolfgangus Monacensis, 1518.

Pribram, K. H. Implications for systemic studies of behavior. In D. E. Sheer (Ed.), *Electrical stimulation of the brain.* Austin, Tex.: Univer. of Texas Press, 1961. Chap. 39.

Pribram, K. H. Control systems in behavior. In M. A. B. Brazier (Ed.), *Brain and behavior.* Vol. II. Washington, D.C.: Amer. Inst. Biol. Sci., 1963.

Ranson, S. W. *The hypothalamus and central levels of autonomic function.* Baltimore: William & Wilkins, 1940.

Richter, C. P. Animal behavior and internal drives. *Quart. Rev. Biol.*, 1927, **2**, 307–342.

Rosvold, H. E., Mirsky, A. F., & Pribram, K. H. Influence of amygdalectomy on social behavior in monkeys. *J. comp. physiol. Psychol.*, 1954, **47**, 173–178.

Sawyer, C. H. Neural mechanisms in the steroid feedback regulation of sexual behavior and pituitary-gonadal function. In M. A. B. Brazier (Ed.), *Brain and behavior.* Vol. III. Berkeley, Calif: Univer. of California Press, 1963.

Sawyer, C. H., & Kawakami, M. Interactions between the central nervous system and hormones influencing ovulation. In C. A. Villee (Ed.), *Control of ovulation.* New York: Pergamon Press, 1961. Pp. 77–97.

Schreiner, L., & Kling, A. Behavioral changes following rhinencephalic injury in the cat. *J. Neurophysiol.*, 1953, **16**, 643–659.

Spiegel, E. A., Miller, H. R., & Oppenheimer, M. J. Forebrain and rage reactions. *J. Neurophysiol.*, 1940, **3**, 538–548.

Tinbergen, N. *The study of instinct.* Oxford: Clarendon Press, 1951.

Ursin, H., & Kaada, B. R. Functional localization within the amygdaloid complex in the cat. *EEG Clin. Neurophysiol.*, 1960, **12**, 1–20.

Wheatley, M. D. The hypothalamus and affective behavior in cats. *Arch. Neurol. Psychiat.*, 1944, **52**, 296–316.

Wiener, N. *Cybernetics or control and communication in the animal and machine.* Paris: Herman & Cie, 1948.

9

Biochemical Factors in Mental Disorders[1]

ROGER W. RUSSELL

Those who are interested in the complexities of interactions between behavioral and somatic variables will find the search for biochemical factors in mental disorders both exciting and challenging. Those who are eager for clinical applications of knowledge in this area must be patient. The rate of development of knowledge in any field of science or technology is, in part, a function of man's ability to solve perplexing problems of research methods and techniques. As one of its stronger supporters (Osmond, 1958) has so baldly stated, for nearly fifty years the search for biochemical factors in mental disorders was confused by "the immense difficulties not merely of looking for a needle in a haystack, but of searching for a needle in a heap of needles—for this is what hunting in the body for minute quantities of an unknown chemical compound resembles." The search has also been seriously handicapped by a lack of theoretical models for interactions between biochemical events in the body and behavior, models from which specific, testable hypotheses could be derived. The fairly recent history of interest in this field has seen times when the search might have been abandoned had it not been for the conviction of a few that indeed there were interactions between biochemical events and behavior if man had the insight and could develop the skills needed to discover them. This was, of course, an article of faith and not in itself a testable hypothesis. The faith was reinforced by the prospect that discoveries of such interrelations could contribute most significantly to knowledge in the biological sciences and, in turn, to the application of that knowledge in the solution of important clinical problems.

Recent developments in the several disciplines upon which the search for biochemical factors in mental disorders depends have led to a clarification of the issues involved and, thus, to a significant increase in research effort. From these developments may come the definitive body of knowledge we seek. In the meantime, a survey of the field must be oriented primarily in the direction of problems and methods, illustrating them with examples from present empirical findings. The discussion which follows begins with a brief history of the search for biochemical factors in mental disorders. It then proceeds to a general consideration of biochemical events and their interactions with behavior. Against this background, theories and hypotheses of how such interactions may operate in the mental disorders can be more clearly understood. The discussion continues with an evaluation of research methods designed to test the hypotheses, and it ends with a survey of present empirical findings.

HISTORY

An essay by Thudichum (1884), the founder of modern neurochemistry, clearly stated the basic concept of the role of "toxic" substances

[1] The preparation of this chapter was supported by grant number MH 06997–01 from the National Institute of Health to Indiana University.

in interactions between biochemical systems and mental disorders:

> Many forms of insanity are unquestionably the external manifestations of the effects upon the brain substance of poisons fermented within the body, just as mental aberrations accompanying chronic alcoholic intoxication are the accumulated effects of a relatively simple poison fermented out of the body.

This was consistent with the then prevailing view in medicine that disease involves the breakdown of normal function due to structural damage or chemical change produced by mechanical injuries or by the invasion of poisonous substances, "toxins." With developments in the basic medical sciences, this view evolved into a broader biological approach to disease based upon the concept of an organism's maladjustment to its total environment. It is within this broader view of disease that the modern history of our present topic has developed.

The ups and downs in the search for biochemical factors in mental disorders during the present century have been described by several of those who have themselves witnessed the trends during some of their critical phases. Osmond (1958) perceives three such phases, the first and last being periods of progress, and the second, a period of research effort which contributed an "enormous and confusing literature." The first period, prior to World War I, was characterized by a scattering of essays and some research, particularly on what have more recently been termed the "model" or "experimental" psychoses. The results of such work and of clinical studies of psychotic patients led, at the time, to cautious support, by such leading figures as Kraepelin and P. E. Bleuler, of an endotoxic theory of mental disorder. The boldest supporting statement appears to have come from Jung (1909), based upon his observations of schizophrenia, which led him to speculate on the possible roles of a "neurotoxin." In 1957 Jung wrote, as honorary president of a symposium on chemical concepts of psychosis (Rinkel & Denber, 1958):

> To make myself clear, I consider the etiology of schizophrenia to be a dual one, namely, up to a certain extent psychology is indispensable to explain the nature and the causes of the initial emotions, which give rise to metabolic alterations. These emotions seem to be accompanied by chemical processes causing specific temporary or chronic disturbances or destructions.

We shall have occasion later to consider in greater detail this reciprocal nature of interactions between biochemical systems and behavior, but the main point for the moment is the emphasis upon the involvement of biochemical events in the processes underlying behavior disorders. Obviously any tests of theoretical models based upon such a view would require that the existence of some biochemical fault or abnormality be established in as specific terms as possible. The big questions were: Where should one look for such faults, and how should they be studied, even if one had a good hunch as to where they might be?

After World War I, developments in biochemistry began to provide techniques for studying such faults. The search was on, but still the lack of theoretical models left it without sound direction. The general approach was a purely empirical one in which comparisons were made between the states of particular chemical substances as they were found in the body fluids of psychotic and control subjects. A further refinement involved studies of the toxic effects of these fractions after administration to infrahuman animal subjects. Some significant differences came to light, but they were difficult to interpret. Reviews (Bellak, 1948; Hoskins, 1946; Lewis, 1936; Richter, 1957) show that much work was done. "But what resulted? Not very much, and what there was tended to be contradictory" (Osmond, 1958).

Contradiction can be interpreted as failure, and this was particularly easy in a *Zeitgeist* which was strongly influenced by the distinction between "organic" and "functional" disease and by psychoanalytic theory, which could offer a highly structured model for the dynamics of behavior disorders. The empirical search for biochemical factors continued, but with even less social reinforcement than it had previously received. In 1937 McFarland and Goldstein began a series of reviews on the biochemistry of the psychoneuroses (1937), of dementia praecox (1938), and of manic-depressive psychosis (1939). The reviews not only surveyed what was then known but also called attention to some of the major uncontrolled factors contributing to confusion among research results. The cautions they urged upon research workers are still being raised in criticisms of some of today's investigations. They recognized the "chaotic state" of the literature and attempted to put it into some order. Because of the empirical nature of the research, their order was structured in terms of the "biochemical constituents that have been most frequently investigated . . . blood sugar, acidity and alkaline reserve, blood oxygen and carbon dioxide, calcium and phosphorus, nitrogenous substances (proteins, total nitrogen, nonprotein nitrogen, ammonia, uric acid, etc.), cholesterol and chlorides" (McFarland & Goldstein, 1938). Although there were many contradictions, the research reports they reviewed appeared to indicate a greater variability in biochemical constituents in disturbed than in normal individuals. In cases of dementia praecox, there was evidence for disturbed carbohydrate and lipoid metabolism. But, as they clearly recognized, these and other differences could have resulted from the many uncontrolled factors which plagued the research.

McFarland and Goldstein cited some five hundred references in their reviews; there were others which could have been included, and many more were added to the literature during the next twenty-five years. Yet no central theses or patterns appeared to thrust themselves forward in an indisputable way. The future of progress in the search for biochemical factors in mental disorders looked so black that Bleuler (1955) could write: "It is possible that as a consequence of these negative results the search for a specific basis foı schizophrenia will be given up for a long time to come if not permanently."

This prediction did not come to pass. In fact, the search is on with more vigor than ever. Why? There are probably three good reasons: First, the "psychochemist's" continued adherence to his article of faith that man can develop the insight and skills needed to discover the nature of interactions between behavior and biochemical events, both of which are properties of the same biological systems. This faith has been reinforced by the broader biological concept of disease in terms of an organism's adjustment to its total environment. A second reason is the exciting new developments in biochemistry, which have already made it possible to understand how information is transmitted at a molecular level. New knowledge and new techniques make possible much more specific and precise analyses of biochemical events than have ever been possible in the past. A third reason comes from psychochemistry itself. At last some approximations to the development of theories and hypotheses have been achieved; they are still rough-and-ready, but they have suggested rational hypotheses for test as substitutes for the purely empirical approach of the past, which had a hazy beginning and apparently no end.

This brief history should not end smugly. Even the most recent reviews are still quite pessimistic about the present state of knowledge, although not about future prospects (Benjamin, 1958; Kety, 1959a; Kety, 1959b; Smythies, 1958). Indeed, so strongly worded has been the work of two of these critics, Benjamin and Kety, that they have been referred to as "biochemical nihilists" (Hoffer, 1960). In view of the many fruitless efforts in the past, it would seem particularly important that all new ideas and research results be examined as critically as possible. There certainly appears to be no problem for proponents in arranging "equal time," and evidence which needs protection against criticism is not likely to prove very convincing.

Science progresses by series of successive approximations. The search for biochemical factors in mental disorders is in the midst of a new such series. It is unlikely that it is yet prepared for an *experimentum crucis*, but neither are many areas of research in which psychologists and their colleagues from sister sciences have mutually vested interests. If problems are of sufficient importance, as they are in the present instance, attacks on them will begin somewhere. The history of psychochemistry clearly shows the need to attack with imagination and with attention to the details of research method which make the difference between results which are interpretable and those which are not.

BIOCHEMICAL EVENTS AND BEHAVIOR

Quite obviously, it is a basic assumption in the search for biochemical factors in mental disorders that interactions occur between biochemical events and behavior. If this assumption is not justified, there is no point in continuing the search; therefore, it is important to examine existing knowledge for evidence in its support. Since "disorder" refers to a disturbance of normal structure or function, such a survey can also be helpful in understanding the normal state of affairs in the body's biochemistry from which deviations, qualitative or quantitive, may occur. The purpose of this section is to examine some of the basic characteristics of biochemical systems and the nature of their reciprocal relations with behavior.

Without a living organism there is no "behavior" in the psychological sense. With the advent of modern scientific psychology, behavior became one of the measurable properties of living organisms, to be added to such others as the organism's anatomical structures, its biochemical systems, and its electrophysiological characteristics. Under normal circumstances all these properties are highly integrated, and all are involved in an organism's responses while adapting to its environment. The state of an organism at a particular time is a function of the interactions between all properties, a point to keep in mind even though, for the moment, our attention is turned to interactions between only two: biochemical events and behavior. Why focus attention on biochemical events?

Biochemical Systems

Research in comparative biochemistry has lent strong support to the notion that living organisms closely resemble one another at the molecular level—that there is a fundamental biochemical ground plan which characterizes them all and upon which more complex biochemical superstructures have been built in the process of surviving in a variety of different chemical environments (Baldwin, 1949; Blum, 1961). This notion implies the occurrence, very early in the history of the earth, of a chemical evolution, which must have preceded the more familiar biological evolution that resulted in the various forms of plants and animals as we know them today (Bernal, 1962). Recently several experiments, using a mixture of gases approximating in composition the primitive atmosphere believed to have existed during the early history of the earth (Miller & Urey, 1959), have been designed to study the possible formation of biologically important substances under the influence of electric discharges. Among the products of these experiments there have been isolated a variety of chemical substances of the kind which even today are the starting materials for the synthesis of many elaborate organic compounds. These views give an order of priority to the biochemical properties of living organisms. They suggest that other properties—including behavior—are, in a sense, "dependent upon" biochemical events. In the same sense, this priority evidences itself during the development of an individual organism, which is controlled by biochemical processes.

Biochemical events are involved in the production of energy upon which behavior depends. They take part in the sensory processes by which energy from the environment is transduced into afferent nerve impulses. They are basic to the transmission of nerve impulses within the central nervous system. They underlie the actions of muscles and glands. They are present wherever we look: within cells, within tissues and organs, within blood and body fluids. Taken together, these numerous and diverse chemical processes which underlie the activities of a living organism constitute its "metabolism." Taken as separate systems, they consist of series of chemical reactions, in some instances widely dispersed throughout the body, and in others localized in particular tissues or organs. To attain the rates characteristic of biological systems, chemical reactions are catalyzed by numerous enzymes, which are characterized by their high degree of specificity for the substrates upon which they act. The basic characteristics of such systems are illustrated in the principal features of the metabolism of acetylcholine, which has an important role in neuronal activity:

Acetyl coenzyme A + choline
↓ ← choline acetylase
Acetylcholine
↓ ← cholinesterase
Acetate + choline

Acetylcholine produced from acetylation of choline by the enzyme choline acetylase is present in brain almost entirely in a "bound" form. On nerve stimulation, acetylcholine is released and, in its "free" form, is rapidly inactivated by the enzyme cholinesterase through hydrolysis to acetate and choline. Here the interactions between enzymes and their substrates are seen as constituting the primary features in a series of chemical reactions. Such series may be long and complicated, and there are many of them.

In this complex of biochemical events, the question arises as to where to search for factors related to mental disorders. All answers to this question make assumptions about which tissues and organ systems of the body are "necessary" in behavior. Top priority has gone to those two great coordinating systems, the nervous and the endocrine systems. Biochemical events characterize cell-to-cell transmission of nerve impulses from sensory receptors to brain cells to effector organs and are involved in intracellular processes within a single neuron (Nachmansohn, 1959). Hormones, synthesized in the endocrine glands, may be carried to all the tissues of the body before becoming inactive metabolites, but they are transported to their sites of action through the circulatory system, and the liver and kidneys are involved in metabolism and excretion of metabolic by-products. On a priori grounds, the limits on where to search are not excessively restrictive! Indeed, as we shall see, the search has been extended in all these directions.

Interactions between Biochemical Events and Behavior

Biochemical events are an essential property of living organisms. But how are they related to behavior? Answers to this question came from experimental studies of two kinds: In one, biochemical events are varied, and concomitant changes in behavior are measured; in the other, variations in behavior constitute the independent variable, and changes in biochemical events constitute the dependent variable.

Effects of biochemical lesions on behavior. The general dependence of behavior on biochemical events within the body has been demonstrated in many ways, but the issue before us is one which involves the possibility of much more specific interactions between these two classes of variables. One step toward being more specific is to examine effects on behavior of conditions in which a particular biochemical event, rather than general metabolism, is altered. Both clinical and experimental studies show that changes in hormonal secretion due to abnormalities in the functioning of particular endocrine glands—e.g., extreme hypothyroidism, hypogonadism, deterioration of the adrenal cortex, and malfunction of the pituitary—are associated with alterations of behavior. One of the most dramatic present examples of the widespread effects of a very specific biochemical fault appears in phenylketonuria (Harris, 1955). For many years it has been known that inherited metabolic faults observable in man are understandable if we assume that in each case the body fails to carry out one particular step in a normal series of biochemical events. This failure could be accounted for in terms of a congenital absence of the enzyme required for the biochemical step affected. In phenylketonuria there occurs a defect in the breakdown of the amino acid phenylalanine, characterized by failure of its normal conversion to tyrosine. On the behavior side, this disorder is associated with intellectual impairment, typically to the level of imbecility; one noticeable behavioral feature is an accentuation of reflexes, and often seizures and spasticity appear. The effects of two closely related faults, alkaptonuria and tyrosinosis, in contrast do not appear to be associated with significant behavioral effects of any kind. In instances like these, specific biochemical events are seen to be associated with fairly general, or nonspecific, patterns of behavior.

To specify interactions between biochemical events and behavior more precisely requires the ability to vary selectively a particular feature, e.g., enzyme activity level or substrate concentration, of a biochemical system and to measure particular behavior patterns presumed to be related to it. The research literature contains a number of examples of this approach in which chemical agents have been used to create "biochemical lesions" (Peters, 1948). Because of its nature, much of the research has required the use of infrahuman animal subjects. For example, one series of studies (Russell, Watson, & Frankenhaeuser, 1961) has shown that reduction in activity of the enzyme cholinesterase, so essential to normal chemical transmission in the central nervous system, is related to differential effects upon behavior. Speed of conditioning was not altered significantly, whereas speed in the extinction of conditioned responses was so affected. The behavioral effects began to appear at a level of reduction in enzyme activity corresponding to a critical point where the enzyme starts to lose its control over its substrate, the transmitter substance, and the latter accumulates instead of being inactivated in the normal manner (Aprison, 1962). Other experiments (e.g., Essig, Hampson, McCauley, & Himwich, 1950; Feldberg & Sherwood, 1954) have shown that a variety of behavioral effects on the sensory or the motor side, or on both, can be elicited by injecting directly into particular sites in the brain chemical agents which presumably affect different biochemical systems. Recently Grossman (1962) has reported:

> The results of the present series of studies demonstrate clearly that the placement of adrenergic substances into a circumscribed region of the diencephalon elicits specific changes in one type of motivated behavior (food intake) while the placement of cholinergic agents into the same area of the hypothalamus evokes pronounced changes in a different type of motivated activity (water intake).

The multiple effects in the body of most chemical agents and our present lack of full knowledge about their biochemical modes of action call for caution in basing conclusions on any single experiment or series of experiments of this kind: "The likelihood of a point of view being correct can be assessed only in terms of the total weight of indirect evidence in its favor" (Carlton, 1963). The indirect evidence now available certainly suggests that particular biochemical events may interact with particular dimensions of behavior.

Effects of behavior on biochemical events. There is also evidence to suggest that this interaction is a reciprocal one, i.e., that behavior may influence the nature of biochemical events. Behavior may initiate changes which subsequently are measurable in biochemical systems. This view is a basic assumption underlying the diagnosis and treatment of the so-called "psychosomatic" illnesses in which behavioral stresses appear to precede signs of organic disorder. It is central in several lines of basic research which are seeking to understand how learning occurs and how experience is stored in memory. It has entered into the search for biochemical factors in mental disorders in ways we shall consider later. Our present purposes can be served by referring briefly to three studies which give some indication of the range of research now providing experimental evidence in support of this view.

One series of studies has shown how interactions between individuals in their social environments may produce lasting changes in biochemical events (Chitty, 1955; Clark, 1953). By ingenious techniques, the researchers were able to vary systematically in their laboratory the frequency of interactions between experimental animals and to demonstrate significant bodily changes, which were characterized by a pronounced increase in weight of the adrenal glands and the spleen and a decrease in weight of the thymus. Significant effects of behavior on biochemical events have been found in experiments where subjects have been exposed to different regimens of training and experience. One study in which the enzyme cholinesterase was the biochemical variable measured (Krech, Rosenzweig, & Bennett, 1960) provides a good example. The results showed a measurable and consistent change in the patterning of cholinesterase as a function of environmental stimulation, leading the investigators to state: "We have now shown that cerebral ChE activity, as well as helping to determine learning behavior, can in turn be modified by behavioral and environmental circumstances."

The third illustration comes from a very new and challenging area of research: behavioral modifications at the *molecular* level. Hydén (1961) has reported that, following several short periods of rotation, nerve cells from the division of the rabbit's acoustic nerve associated with the sense of equilibrium showed a significant production of RNA (ribonucleic acid). Since RNA mediates the synthesis of cell protein, it was not surprising that significant production of proteins and of certain cell enzymes was also found. In later experiments (Hydén & Egyhazi, 1962) it appeared that during the learning of an approach to food problems, there occurred a change in RNA bases. This area of research has been receiving increasing attention during the past three years, and further possibilities for interactions between behavior and biochemical events at a molecular level have been speculated upon (e.g., Gaito, 1961).

The purpose of this section of our discussion was to examine some of the basic characteristics of biochemical systems and the nature of their reciprocal relations with behavior. It is clear that biochemical events constitute an essential property of living organisms, that these events are complicated in nature, and that there are many of them. It is also clear that behavior is another basic property of biological systems and that it interacts reciprocally with biochemical events, sometimes changing as a consequent of variations in these events and sometimes preceding and producing changes in them. Against this general background we can now examine more specifically the theories, hypotheses, and empirical findings of those who have sought among the bewildering array of possibilities for biochemical factors which are in fact involved in behavior disorders.

THEORIES AND HYPOTHESES

One of the reasons given earlier for the present vigor in the search for biochemical factors in mental disorders was that the search is achieving some approximation to the development of theories and hypotheses which help to give it direction. Tests of hypotheses lead to the establishment of facts, but a systematic body of knowledge typically goes beyond facts. The lack of any theoretical framework means the piling up of facts which may lead nowhere. It is a moot point whether any of the so-called "theories" presently being proposed in the search for biochemical factors in mental disorders really meet fully the requirements for theory construction. Be this as it may, certain recent efforts have brought together a number of related observations in such ways as to enable predictions to be made which can be put to test.

The paragraphs which follow examine the major characteristics of current hypotheses and theories relating to biochemical factors in mental disorders.

Hypotheses

Etiology of mental disorders. Hypotheses are developed as alternative answers to questions. The basic questions within our present frame of reference are those which concern the *etiology* of mental disorders. Answers to these questions have typically fallen into two major classes of hypotheses: those in which the precipitating factors are considered to be psychological or behavioral in nature and those in which biochemical factors are considered to be the antecedents. In the usual terms in which hypotheses are stated, psychological processes constitute the independent variables in the former, and biochemical events, in the latter. For both classes of hypotheses, mental, or behavioral, disorders are the dependent variables.

Since, as we saw earlier, behavioral and biochemical events are closely integrated in living organisms, it might be anticipated that the task of establishing which is a "cause" or antecedent and which is an "effect" or consequent in the etiology of mental disorders might be a difficult one—and so it has proved to be, particularly in disorders such as schizophrenia. In other disorders, e.g., "toxic" psychoses, the chemical nature of the precipitating factor is known, even though its mode of action within the body is not fully understood. To conduct a critical test of hypotheses from either of the two classes would require controlling one of the two variables—biochemical events or psychological processes—while independently varying the other. Since the two are so intimately related, this has not been successfully accomplished. Those who favor the psychological hypothesis have pointed to the "functional" disorders as examples of disorders in which predominant psychological factors are present without discernible biochemical abnormalities. Their adversaries have replied that adequate steps have not been taken to search for possible biochemical factors. They, in turn, have made much of the fact that the psychotomimetic drugs, e.g., mescaline and LSD, produce temporary behavior disorders in normal human subjects and that psychotropic drugs, e.g., chlorpromazine and reserpine, make the disturbed psychotic more manageable. These kinds of facts, they claim, are consistent with a biochemical basis for mental disorders. But they have been accused of overlooking the difference between "analogy" and "homology" in cases of the "model" psychoses; i.e., the mescaline and LSD syndromes differ in many respects from the "natural" psychoses, and therefore the former may not be satisfactory working models for the latter. It is also still doubtful that the basic mental disorder is affected by psychotropic drugs (Margolis, 1957). There is considerable evidence that psychotics do differ from normal in certain biochemical dimensions, but because of the difficulties in unambiguously testing either psychological or biochemical hypotheses concerning precipitating factors, the question of whether the differences are primary or secondary is still in doubt. In either case, they are important features of mental disorders;

their identification need not await answers to the questions of etiology, although such answers would be of great assistance in suggesting where to look for significant biochemical factors and how they might be altered during the course of therapy.

Origin of biochemical factors. Much attention has been given to questions of the origin, exogenous or endogenous, of biochemical factors involved in mental disorders. Hypotheses have fallen into three general classes: those in which the critical biochemical factor is introduced into the body from sources external to the organism; those which attempt to identify toxic substances manufactured within the body as a function of some metabolic abnormality; and those which consider the critical factor to be an imbalance in homeostatic processes normally occurring within the body.

The classical alcoholic and drug psychoses are familiar examples of disorders arising from the actions of exogenous toxic agents introduced into the body. A more recent example is the schizophrenic- and depressive-type reactions reported to result from chronic exposure of agricultural workers to organophosphorus insecticides. The experimental production of behavioral abnormalities by administration of psychotomimetic drugs provides another example of the effects of biochemical factors exogenous in origin. Disorders may also arise from biochemical transformations induced by invading microorganisms. Here the psychoses associated with syphilitic infection are a classical example, although other sources of infection have received considerable attention, e.g., tuberculous bacilli, specific types of alpha streptococci, viral agents, etc. Hypotheses in which exogenous toxic substances constituted the precipitating factor in mental disorders were very popular at one time; recently, however, they have been much less prominent in the literature.

We may view all biochemical factors which are not introduced specifically from external sources as being *endogenous* in origin. This view is quite straightforward when we consider biochemical faults, such as phenylketonuria, which are determined genetically. Semantic confusions may arise when changes in biochemical events follow an organism's behavioral interactions with its external environment—when "A stress deriving from the external environment is reflected in alterations of the internal environment at the neuronal, endocrine and metabolic levels" (Sackler, Marti-Ibanez, Saeklen, & Sackler, 1958). In such instances, the biochemical factor itself has its origin and runs its course in the organism; i.e., it is not a function of infection or of chemical agents introduced into the organism. The possibility of endogenous origins of biochemical factors in mental disorders is particularly challenging and will occupy most of our attention when we consider in detail the empirical findings of current research within our present frame of reference.

Nature of biochemical factors. The search for the nature of biochemical factors in mental disorders begins with decisions as to where among the multitude of possibilities attention should be directed. Hunches as to where to look have come from several sources. Some have come from recognition of close chemical resemblances between substances which produce psychoticlike disorders, e.g., mescaline, and naturally occurring substances in the body, e.g., adrenaline. Others have resulted from observations that antimetabolites of a naturally occurring substance cause behavioral disturbances when administered to man. Other hypotheses have been suggested by discoveries of abnormal substances in the blood or urine of patients in whom behavioral disorders already existed. Phenylketonuria is a good illustration. The discovery of high levels of phenylalanine in the urine of affected patients led to the initial hypothesis that the characteristic behavioral abnormalities are associated with a severe disturbance of phenylalanine metabolism within the body.

Predisposing factors. It seems reasonable to hypothesize that in the highly integrated relations between the biochemical and behavioral properties of biological systems, predisposition to mental disorders may exist in the form of biochemical factors. Predisposing factors of a biochemical nature might be present as inborn metabolic variations which, under normal circumstances, are not sufficiently variant to produce significant disturbances of behavior but which might do so if environmental conditions induced more extreme variation. Information relevant to this general hypothesis has come from genetic studies of schizophrenia and from studies of biochemical changes accompanying exposure to "stress."

Evidence that genetic factors do operate has come from studies of human genetics in which the investigation of mental disorders in twins has played a dominant role. In reporting an early study, Kallmann (1946) concluded: "As far as the *specific predisposition* to schizophrenia is concerned, that is, the inherited capacity for responding to certain stimuli with a schizophrenic type of reaction, the findings of the present study are conclusively in favor of the genetic theory." Slater's (1953b) more recent research "confirms previous views on the importance of genetical factors in the psychoses." The question of pinpointing the biochemical factors involved does not follow easily from the data now available; Slater (1953a) has stated: "There is, for instance, a good deal to indicate the significance of endocrine factors, but none at all to show which aspect of endocrine metabolism is worth special investigation."

Evidence was presented earlier that lasting changes in biochemical systems may result from an organism's behavioral interactions with its environment. Both clinical and experimental studies show that behavior may become disorganized under conditions where the organism's capabilities or skills are being severely taxed in the course of adjusting to changes in its environment ("frustration") and where competition arises between incompatible response tendencies, resulting in a delay in making adaptive responses or in a failure to make them ("conflict"), conditions frequently referred to as exposure to "stress" (Russell, 1953). Considerable research has been done on biochemical changes accompanying exposure to stress (Selye, 1950). Included among the studies have been comparisons between normal and psychotic subjects, which implicated the pituitary-adrenal mechanism in differences between the two groups (Elmadjian, 1959; Pincus & Hoagland, 1950a; Pincus & Hoagland, 1950b). The results of such studies show that behavioral interactions between an organism and its environment may produce significant changes in biochemical events and that differences in these reactions may exist between normal subjects and patients with mental disorders. Although present data are not adequate to establish it as a fact, the possibility does exist that the differences in reactions are functions of inborn metabolic variations brought to light under certain environmental conditions.

Theories

As opposed to hunches which lead to specific testable hypotheses, theories are attempts to bring together isolated facts into frameworks which emphasize their interrelationships and enable further predictions to be made. The search for biochemical factors in mental disorders has led to some attempts at theory construction, all of which have come under strong criticism, primarily because of apparent contradictions with regard to the facts upon which they were based. A brief description of two such models will illustrate the lines along which thinking has gone in the past. In both cases the basic elements of the models are given without critical evaluation, of which each has received its share; both will be considered further when present empirical findings are discussed.

The serotonin model. In this model, first proposed by Woolley and Shaw in 1954, *quantitative variation of a normally occurring biochemical event* is the key to abnormal behavioral effects. Therefore, its description begins with the fact that serotonin, a biologically active amine, is normally present in the brain, with highest concentration in the brainstem, especially in the hypothalamus, and lowest in the cortex and cerebellum. The enzymes for its synthesis and inactivation are also present in these areas. Starting with the existence of the biochemical system, the model then states, in very general terms, relations between the system and behavior: first, ". . . serotonin has an important role to play in mental processes . . ." and second, ". . . suppression of its action results in mental disorder. In other words, it is the lack of serotonin which is the cause of the disorder" (Woolley & Shaw, 1954). It then proceeds to describe the mechanism for the deficiency as the result of a metabolic failure to form or maintain enough of the amine. Since its original statement in this form, many tests have been made of deductions from the model. Some have led to such questions about the model itself as "whether too much or too little serotonin causes the disturbance in schizophrenia" (Woolley, 1958).

The taraxein model. The central theme of the taraxein model is the *presence in the blood of a toxic substance* uniquely associated with schizophrenia. The extraction of the substance, taraxein, as a protein fraction from the plasma of schizophrenic patients was reported by Heath in 1957; it is a chemically unstable substance, a protein falling in the range of the alpha and/or beta globulins (Heath, 1961). The model states (Heath, 1959) that this blood protein does not exist in normal subjects; rather, it is considered to be the chemical manifestation of an inborn error of metabolism. The model goes on to postulate a mode of action in which taraxein inhibits an essential interaction between a brain enzyme and a chemical which is liberated in increasing quantities when the organism is under conditions of psychological stress; the specific chemical liberated is considered to be a diamine, and presumably taraxein performs the role of a diamine oxidase inhibitor (Heath, 1959). It is this inhibitory action that presumably underlies the appearance of the mental disorders. It is further postulated that, as far as behavior is concerned, the site of action is primarily in the septal region and possibly in other parts of the limbic system. The model also includes the suggestion of a quantitative relation between the amount of taraxein and the extent of behavior disorder: "The patients who display less schizophrenic symptomatology seemingly have less taraxein . . ." (Heath, 1959).

As models, both of those just described are chiefly concerned with the identification and with the possible mode of action of a biochemical factor which may be involved in mental disorders. Both fail to be comprehensive, particularly in the sense that neither attempts to answer the puzzling question of how the biochemical factor involved is transduced into changes of behavior. But both have encouraged a considerable amount of thought, research, and controversy, all of which will have contributed to developments in knowledge even if the models themselves are discarded.

RESEARCH METHODS

Hypotheses define supposed relations between independent and dependent variables—biochemical events and mental disorders in our present frame of reference. Support for such hypotheses requires evidence that variations of the independent variable are associated with concomitant variations of the dependent variable, when the effects of other factors can be ruled out of consideration. Several research approaches have been used in the search for biochemical factors in mental disorders, each attempting to meet these requirements in different ways.

Approach via Existing Individual Differences

By far the most popular approach has been one which depends upon demonstration, in the same subjects, that existing individual differences in behavior are related to individual differences in biochemical events. In this "correlational" approach no attempt is made to manipulate conditions experimentally; the major task is to measure individual differences in the two variables presumed to be related.

Because of difficulties in defining and quantifying degrees of mental disorder, the procedure most often used has been to divide subjects into two broad classes, e.g., those with schizophrenia and those without, and to determine the significance of the differences between the two classes in regard to the biochemical event(s) under study. The assumption seems apparent in many studies that the two behavioral classes are mutually exclusive, i.e., that a schizophrenic group is entirely distinct qualitatively from a control group in terms of the relevant behavioral variables. If this assumption is inaccurate and overlap occurs in the degree to which these variables are represented in the two classes, treating the groups as qualitatively distinct will tend to hide relations which may actually exist between specific behavioral variables and specific biochemical events. Similar problems of overlap may arise when there is dependence upon the conventional diagnostic categories for distinguishing among the various mental disorders because of the lack of precision in the definition of the categories themselves. In very few instances have attempts been made to apply quantitative methods for measuring the behavioral variables. Similar assumptions have also been made in regard to the qualitative or quantitative nature of the biochemical factors studied. The real power of the individual-differences, or correlational, approach could be more fully realized, and possible misinterpretations due to the combining of heterogeneous variables could be minimized, if more attention were given to quantitative measurements of the behavior and biochemical factors presumed to be related. When this approach is used, it would be very desirable to find more statements such as: "The patients who display less schizophrenic symptomatology seemingly have less taraxein . . ." (Heath, 1959), but put into more precise statistical language which would facilitate further tests of their validity.

Even if a significant relation is found, the correlational approach may not provide adequate information to support a clear interpretation. The biochemical factors may be the "cause" *or* the "effect" of the mental disorder, *or* both may be consequents of some other condition. Significant correlations between individual differences in biochemical events and individual differences in behavior give some information but may leave many questions about the nature of the relationship unanswered. There are, for example, instances in which biochemical differences among patient and nonpatient subjects were ultimately discovered to be due to dietary deficiencies, e.g., iodine (Kelsey, Gullock, & Kelsey, 1957), to differences in water intake (McDonald, 1958), and to other such uncontrolled factors. The need for adequate information about relevant variables is as essential to the correlational as to the experimental approach. The issue of controls is so basic and important to the search for biochemical factors in mental disorders that it will receive special attention later.

Inborn Biochemical Variations

Individual differences in biochemical processes may result from effects of environmental conditions during man's life-span or from inborn factors of a genetic nature. In the latter instance, there may occur a very specific biochemical lesion, such as the lesion underlying phenylketonuria, to which reference has already been made. Characteristically the lesions divide human beings into two sharply distinct groups; they appear to persist relatively unchanged throughout life (Harris, 1955). When such a lesion is discovered, comparisons may be made between individuals with and those without the lesion in order to study the effects of the particular biochemical event involved on behavioral variables, including mental disorders. Advantage can be taken of this naturally occurring condition in which an important independent variable, a specific biochemical event, has been altered in a manner frequently beyond the freedom of an experimenter to reproduce in human subjects.

The opportunities to conduct studies of this kind are restricted by our limited knowledge about inborn biochemical lesions. More is being learned, and the main reason for including this approach in the present discussion is its potentialities for the future. The notion of "molecular disease" as discussed by Zuckerkandl and Pauling (1962) has its implications for mental as well as somatic disorders: "Life is a relationship between molecules, not a property of any one molecule. So is therefore disease which endangers life. While there are molecular diseases, there are no diseased molecules." In this context "molecular disease" is defined in terms of altered relations among molecules due to altered genes or, in view of recent concepts of inheritance, to altered protein and nucleic acid molecules. Such alterations have abnormal enzymatic or other biochemical properties, which may, in turn, be reflected in abnormalities of behavior. The nature of the environment is also closely linked to the notion of molecular disease. For example:

> If phenylalanine happened to be present only in low amounts in our usual diet, the mutation leading to phenylketonuria, characterized by the inability to convert toxic amounts of phenylalanine into tyrosine, would also not be experienced as a molecular disease, whereas it actually is one under the prevailing circumstances (Zuckerkandl & Pauling, 1962).

New techniques as well as new concepts may soon make it possible to look at a molecular level for biochemical factors in mental disorders, for predisposing conditions of a genetic nature, and for the control that environmental conditions may have as precipitating factors.

Toxic Accidents

Accidental exposure of man to chemical agents can provide opportunities to observe behavioral correlates of the biochemical changes produced. Both chronic and acute toxic episodes are not infrequent, particularly when chemical agents employed in agriculture and industry are involved. As in the case of inherited metabolic variations, the independent variables—biochemical events—are not varied systematically by the investigator, nor is he able to control all the conditions under which his observations are made. The approach is analogous to action research in social sciences, where the investigator is prepared to observe but where he must await the occurrence of events beyond his control to vary the independent variable of his hypothesis before he can observe changes of dependent variables in which he is interested. This approach has seen good use in clinical studies of toxic psychoses but has not been employed to its full value in the search for interactions between biochemical events and specific behavior patterns quantitatively measured. Examples of situations in which this approach might be usefully applied are instances involving exposure to organophosphorus insecticides, studies of which, Gershon and Shaw (1961) suggest, might aid in determining "the role of cholinesterase and the levels of acetylcholine in mental disease."

Experimental Approaches

The use of an experimental approach in the search for biochemical factors in mental disorders is obviously limited by the kinds of treatments to which human subjects can be exposed; chronic behavior disorders cannot be produced experimentally in order to study concomitant changes in biochemical events. It is for this reason that research workers have been so enthusiastic about the possibilities provided by the psychotomimetic agents for producing "model" or "experimental" psychoses and by the psychotropic drugs for treating mental disorders, drugs which presumably act by reestablishing the organism to a normal physiological and chemical balance.

To employ the experimental approach to its full advantage would require that measures of the biochemical events under study be taken while "mental disorder" was being produced in experimental subjects; the results would be compared with measures of the same biochemical events in the same subjects prior to their experimental treatment and in comparable control subjects not undergoing the treatment. Comparison of measurements during and after a recovery period would add useful information, and preferably the mental disorder should be produced in varying degrees for different experimental groups in order to obtain information about quantitative relations between it and changes in biochemical events. The possibility of using psychotomimetic drugs as "tools" to produce the mental disorder required by such a design led several years ago to the development of what was termed "experimental psychiatry." Generalizations were made from results obtained during studies of experimental or "model" psychoses to what might be the state of affairs in the "natural" psychoses. The extent to which such generalizing is valid depends upon the comparability of the mental disorder in the two situations. Attention was called earlier to the very considerable controversy, which still rages, over the basic issue of whether the experimental models and the psychoses are truly homologous or only superficially alike in form. In terms of the usefulness of the models for experimental purposes, an answer to this question would seem to lie in empirical tests of the validity with which information derived from the models can, in fact, be applied to the psychoses. Evidence at present is controversial in this regard; for example, not all drugs which are useful in the treatment of schizophrenia have similar effects upon the model psychoses (Wikler, 1959).

Experimental studies in psychopharmacology approach the basic problem from the opposite direction. They begin with the existence of a mental disorder and attempt to reestabilsh normal biochemical conditions using drugs as tools (Russell, 1960). When successful, an understanding of a drug's mode of action will lead to knowledge about biochemical factors associated with the mental disorder.

Behavorial Variables

One of the persistent problems in clearly formulating testable hypotheses is that of defining "mental disorders." It is clear that the primary data available to the clinician and the research worker are not "mental" events in the lay sense of that term, but observations of behavior, verbal and nonverbal. As was pointed out earlier, one approach to defining mental disorders has been to classify a patient's over-all behavior pattern or syndrome in one of several diagnostic categories, which are assumed to be qualitatively distinct. In fact, there are few, if any, experts who would seriously contend that the classical psychiatric categories do not show significant overlap. As Kline (1958) has so clearly stated:

> There is a strong tendency . . . to accept such diagnostic categories as being more substantial and valid than they are in actuality. . . . The tremendous variability of diagnosis from one hospital to another, and the fact that a patient in the course of a

single hospitalization may exhaust all the available diagnostic categories as his condition changes, should be a warning as to the tentative nature of such labeling.

It is likely that much confusion and apparent contradiction in results can be laid to inadequacies in specifying the particular "mental disorders" studies.

Very little use has been made of available techniques for the quantitative measurement of behavior. A wide variety of psychological tests are capable of measuring behavior patterns which cut across the traditional diagnostic categories. Rinkel, Hyde, and Solomon (1954), in discussing a new chemical concept of psychosis, reported that the use of standardized tests helped to "uncover new phenomena such as the subject's reduction in organization and integration, loss of emotional control, decrease in orientation to past and future."

Eysenck (1947) called attention to the possibility that "dimensions of behavior derived from data provided by psychological measuring instruments may be related to biochemical factors such as cholinesterase activity." Unfortunately such examples are few, despite recognition that behaviorial variables must be defined more adequately if there is to be any real hope of refining present research approaches in the search for biochemical factors in mental disorders.

Controls

The problems of providing adequate controls have proved to be particularly troublesome in the search for biochemical factors in mental disorders, and recently they have been receiving special attention. Earlier the point was made that biochemical factors may be the "cause" or the "effect" of mental disorders, or both may be consequents of some other condition. In order to rule out the third possibility, all potentially relevant variables must be controlled or measured in order that their possible contributions to a particular set of research observations may be eliminated or, at least, estimated by appropriate statistical procedures. Since it may be that all such variables affecting a particular study are not known, fully adequate control precautions may not be built into the initial research design. However, relevant variables, which are clearly important, are often left uncontrolled in studies reported even in the contemporary research literature. General reference can be made here to some of these variables; more detailed consideration has been given to them in such critical surveys as those by Kline (1958) and Kety (1959a; 1959b).

Problems associated with the selection of subjects from what is in fact a heterogeneous population even within a single diagnostic category, e.g., "schizophrenia," have already been discussed in some detail. Other difficulties arise from the fact that cross-sectional studies may overlook "spontaneous" changes in both behavior and biochemical events, thus complicating attempts to replicate results. Reiss (1958b) has emphasized this point in his paper "Uses and Abuses of Statistics in Biochemical Investigations of Psychotic Patients": "Considering the enormous diurnal variations in the biochemistry of some schizophrenics, statisticians will agree that statistics based on a single biochemical finding, even if the investigation is carried out on a thousand patients, is useless." Other factors associated directly with the patient are recognized to be potentially relevant variables: the chronicity of the mental disorder, prolonged periods of hospitalization, lack of exercise and physical activity, amount of attention from hospital personnel, therapeutic procedures to which he is being or has been exposed, etc.

Of particular importance in any biochemical study are possible effects of dietary and infectious factors. "There is little question that some of the biochemical deviations reported in the literature are the result, not of mental disease, but of the food intake with its metabolic consequences" (Kline, 1958). For example, Kelsey et al. (1957) have demonstrated for their population that the reported increased uptake of iodine in psychotic patients was due to deficiencies in dietary iodine in institutionalized patients, who, when fed normal amounts of iodized salt, showed no greater uptake than noninstitutionalized control subjects. Many reports of this kind have alerted investigators to the importance of controlling dietary factors, perhaps the most elaborate procedure being that of the schizophrenia research program at the NIMH Laboratory of Clinical Science, for which a ward of clearly diagnosed schizophrenic patients and a ward of normal control subjects have been maintained under comparable conditions. Other reports have pointed to the existence in mental hospitals of undetected low-grade or even acute infectious processes, e.g., endemic amebiasis, which could have significant effects on biochemical factors under study.

Concern has been expressed over the selection of control subjects, since variations in "normal" individuals make them also a heterogeneous population in terms of the behavioral and biochemical variables relevant to a particular study. Difficulties arising from the requisitioning of students and institutional personnel and from the use of volunteers have been clearly recognized in other areas of research; similar limitations may affect research within our present frame of reference: "The nutritional, psychological, and biochemical status of such a special group . . . usually make them unfit to be used as comparable norms for the patient population . . ." (Kline, 1958).

Research results are functions of the operations by which they were obtained. Among those who are presently searching for biochemical factors in mental disorders, there is general agreement about the importance of planning and executing operations with care. Perhaps the best way to end this section on research methods is to quote from the comments of one of these people (McDonald, 1958):

> At present we need more emphasis on methodology and research design. . . . We need fewer claims based on inadequate data; we need more studies critically conceived, carried out, and communicated. . . . Some of the current confusion can be dispelled by the assertion of a critical, scientific attitude on the part of the investigator.

SOME RECENT EMPIRICAL FINDINGS

The historical introduction to this discussion had as a central theme the fact that a great many substances have been nominated as biochemical factors in schizophrenia and similar mental disorders, but none has been unequivocally elected. For our present purposes, it is inappropriate even to try to review the present status of all candidates: the status is often confused and contradictory, and reference has already been made to several of them. However, some further details about a few items which have attracted particular attention will serve to illustrate further the nature of recent findings.

Cerebral Metabolism

One obvious candidate to check would seem to be the biochemical processes involved in providing the sources of energy for the complex functions of the brain. Kety and Schmidt's (1948) nitrous oxide method provided a means for the quantitative determination of cerebral blood flow and oxygen consumption in conscious human subjects and thus for the study of cerebral metabolism under various experimental and naturally occurring conditions. Of particular interest in our present context is the failure of schizophrenic patients to show any deviation from normal subjects (Kety, Woodford, Harmel, Freyban, Appel, & Schmidt, 1948); nor were any changes found associated with model psychosis produced by LSD (Kety, 1961). In contrast, significant reductions in consumption were found in cases of organic psychoses, e.g., senile psychosis. Kety's (1961) conclusion "that it takes just as much oxygen to think an irrational thought as it does to think a rational one . . ." is supported by observations in which clinically significant changes in behavioral symptoms following administration of barbiturates and following electroshock therapy were not associated with measurable changes in cerebral metabolism: ". . . the most striking finding is the lack of correlation of the degree of clinical improvement, the presence of confusion, and the cerebral blood flow and metabolism" (Wilson, Schieve, & Scheinberg, 1952). Carbohydrate, glutamic acid, and phosphorus metabolism have all been implicated in mental disorders at one time or another. However, contradictory results and the rational difficulty in believing "that a generalized defect in energy metabolism—a process so fundamental to every cell in the body—could be responsible for the highly specialized features of schizophrenia" (Kety, 1959a) have given emphasis to the search for more specific biochemical factors.

Specific Biochemical Factors

At present the modal points of interest are centered on the biogenic amines, the blood proteins, and certain of the endocrine secretions.

Biogenic amines. During recent years much research effort has been concentrated on testing hypotheses which relate mental disorders to disturbances in the metabolism of this class of biologically active compounds, which are produced in the body. The majority of the research has investigated the possible roles of the adrenaline and serotonin systems. From evidence now available it is reasonable to conclude that two amines from these systems, noradrenaline and serotonin, have important functions in the brain. Do they have any direct association with mental disorders?

From the recognition by Hoffer, Osmond, and Smythies (1954) that the psychotomimetic agent mescaline has a chemical structure similar to that of adrenaline came the hypothesis that ". . . one of the aetiological agents in schizophrenia might be a substance or substances lying between these two; with the psychological properties of mescaline but effective in concentrations nearer to those of adrenaline." In other words, a major biochemical defect in schizophrenia was conceived as existing in the metabolism of adrenaline. As elaborated, the defect was viewed as resulting in the increased production of substances which interfere with cerebral functions. Two oxidized derivatives of adrenaline, adrenochrome and adrenolutin, were implicated as the substances involved. Evidence from studies on human and animal subjects was presented that both had psychotomimetic properties. According to the "adrenochrome model" (Hoffer & Osmond, 1959), the defect results in increased production of adrenochrome. Exposure to stress raises the level of activity of the sympathetic nervous system, which leads to discharge of adrenaline and to increased production of adrenochrome. In the schizophrenic this could be a vicious cycle of events: his behavioral abnormality would expose him to frequent stresses, which would in turn lead to increased production of the biochemical substance associated with the disorder. The model is an imaginative one, but it involves difficulties arising from controversies about certain basic facts. For example, the original evidence for the presence of adrenochrome in the plasma of normal subjects and, to an elevated degree, in schizophrenic patients has been brought into question by other results (Szara, Axelrod, & Perkins, 1958) which have failed to find adrenochrome in the plasma of either category of subjects.

The serotonin model was described earlier. The hypothesis upon which the model is based was suggested by the fact that many indoles, e.g., LSD, antagonize serotonin. It was also noted that these antimetabolites caused behavioral disturbances when administered to human and animal subjects. These observations suggested the possibility that abnormal levels of brain serotonin might underlie mental disorders. Evidence to support or refute this hypothesis was sought from many sources. Research designed to study the characteristics of serotonin as a possible chemical mediator in the central representation of the parasympathetic nervous system has established that the amine has some important function in the brain, although its specific role as a neurohumor is still not firmly based on direct evidence. Other studies have shown that certain psychotropic drugs, e.g., reserpine, displace serotonin from the brain and from other organs; the mechanism by which they produce their effects on aberrant behavior may therefore involve the serotonin system. Changes in the system produced experimentally in animals have been shown to be related quantitatively to behavioral effects (e.g., Aprison & Ferster, 1961). These latter kinds of evidence are only indirect supports of the basic hypothesis, and some of the results obtained are even then contradictory. For example, recent studies (Feldstein, Hoagland, & Freeman, 1961) have cast doubt upon the existence of significant differences between schizophrenic and normal control subjects in the metabolism of serotonin.

Blood proteins. Numerous protein fractions have been reported to be present in schizophrenic blood, and there is evidence that at least certain of these are altered under conditions of psychological stress. One of these, taraxein, has been the subject of considerable attention and controversy during the past few years.

In 1957, Heath (1959) reported in considerable detail on the extraction of a protein fraction from the plasma of schizophrenic patients which produced psychoticlike reactions when injected into nonpsychotic volunteers. From these original observations there developed the "taraxein model" described earlier. This model met at first with great skepticism, particularly when results could not be replicated even with fractions obtained from those who had conducted the initial studies. Recently, however, the pendulum appears to have swung somewhat in the other direction, as evidenced, for example, in a review by Hoagland, Pennell, Bergen, Sarvcus, Freeman, & Koella (1962) of the work of four independent groups: "In contrast to many investigations, these studies refreshingly tend to confirm each other." The research reviewed concentrated primarily upon extraction and purification of the blood fraction and upon various tests in animals. The evidence suggests that the instability of the original taraxein and the uncertain reliability of extraction procedures are factors which could account for early failures to confirm the Heath results. Refinement of procedures has now produced data

> . . . indicating the existence of a globulin in human blood probably associated with a tightly bound small molecule. This active complex displays, on the average, considerably greater activity by several test procedures if it is extracted from the plasma of schizophrenic patients in contrast to that from normal controls (Hoagland et al., 1962).

There is still much work to be done before this globulin fraction, or the small molecule bound to it, is likely to be fully accepted as a biochemical factor in mental disorders. Further studies must be conducted on human subjects; questions about generalization from one animal test or from a very limited number of them must be answered. But even some agreement in research results is encouraging.

Endocrine Factors

The importance of the endocrine system in coordination of bodily functions and the well-known abnormalities which malfunctions of its components may produce make the system a particularly attractive place to look for biochemical factors in mental disorders. Indeed, "psychoendocrinology" has become an established term. Although many investigators agree that endocrinological abnormalities occur in mental disorders, there are diversities of view as to their nature. It appears that, in many instances, the abnormalities are secondary rather than primary factors in the disorder. The picture is clouded by the several problems of research design and controls we considered earlier (Reiss, 1958a).

Receiving special attention have been the adrenal hormones, both cortical and medullary, with which some of the best-organized studies have been concerned. The distinguishing feature of one series of studies, which began twenty years ago and are still in progress, has been the ingenious use of various stress conditions to compare hormonal steroid metabolism in normal subjects and neuropsychiatric patients (e.g., Elmadjian, 1959; Pincus & Hoagland, 1950a; Pincus & Hoagland, 1950b). The psychological stresses to which subjects have been exposed include both life situations and experimental laboratory procedures; the physiological stresses have involved hypoxia and the administration of chemical agents known to stimulate the sympathetic nervous system, e.g., insulin, methacholine, and LSD. Changes in hormonal output have been measured by metabolic indices in the urine and blood.

It is not feasible here to try to summarize all the findings of such an extensive series of studies, but some of the central features can be given briefly. Age differences appeared in adrenocortical responses. Young men showed very little use of the adrenocortical mechanisms in meeting stresses which increased the responses in older men. The better the level of performance was under stress, the smaller was the percentage increase in 17-ketosteroid output. The sensitivity of adrenocortical activity to stress was shown in one study (Berkeley, 1952) in which significant changes in the activity occurred under conditions no more severe than failing to reach stated levels of aspiration in performance of a simple motor task. In contrast to normal subjects, schizophrenic patients as a group "showed a striking inability to respond to our tests with enhanced steroid output as measured by our blood and urinary indices despite the fact that their resting 17-ketosteroid excretion was not different from that of the general population" (Pincus & Hoagland, 1950a). Support was obtained for the hypothesis that the two medullary hormones are differentially related to different types of emotional reactions: excretion of noradrenaline increases with aggressive emotional displays, and increased excretion of adrenaline with normal excretion of noradrenaline is associated with passive emotional displays.

Molecular Changes

Opportunities for new developments often come with technological advances in research methods. Recent advances in cytochemistry which make it possible to analyze the contents of single cells measured in micromicrograms seem destined to move the search for biochemical factors in mental disorders in the direction of molecular events. Hydén (1961) has already begun to speak of interactions between behavior and effects at this level: "In every case analyzed we found that an increase of the brain activity introduced by emotion-producing stimuli—for example, sounds or tones, and even motor activities—was correlated with a production of RNA and protein. . . ." He has also reported that persons suffering from certain mental disorders appear to have smaller amounts of RNA and proteins in ganglion cells of the central nervous system than persons not so afflicted (Davidson, 1960). Whether or not such differences will withstand the rigorous test requirements we considered earlier remains to be seen, but the prospects that mental disorders and their treatments may be more clearly understood by research at the molecular level is so challenging as to be worth the major effort which will be required.

PROSPECTS

This discussion began with the realistic admission that, at present, the search for biochemical factors in mental disorders has more prospects than definitive knowledge. Firm information is available for certain disorders, i.e., the "organic" psychoses, but very little is yet known about biochemical bases of others, such as schizophrenia. So little is known, and the possibilities of where to look among the many biochemical events within the body are so great, that in the past only a relatively few hardy souls persisted in their attempts to find specific factors. Recently, however, the search has acquired new vigor; the volume of research—and of controversial points of view—has increased.

Encouragement has come from several sources. Developments of knowledge and techniques in biochemistry have provided new leads as to where biochemical factors in mental disorders may be found and have made possible much more precise analyses of biochemical events than have been possible in the past. Basic research on the reciprocal interactions between biochemical events and behavior is building a general background of information upon which to project the peculiar problems of behavioral disorders. The broader biological concept of disease in terms of an organism's adjustment to its total environment has helped to relax the strong parochial ideas of psychological *or* biological processes in favor of interactions of the two. The search for biochemical factors in mental disorders has itself become more systematic through the use of hypotheses and theoretical models, which, although often crude and eventually disproved, are steps toward lending order to empirical data and direction to the search.

Whether or not these recent developments will lead to some firm answers to questions of etiology, of predisposing and precipitating factors, and of mechanisms of action remains to be seen. So far efforts have helped more to clear the air in regard to the definition of problems and the requirements of adequate research approaches than to provide unequivocal information. But this in itself constitutes a significant advance and encourages further efforts. The prospects of contributing not only to the solution of important clinical problems but also to the development of basic knowledge in the biological and behavioral sciences are strong sources of motivation.

REFERENCES

Aprison, M. H. On a proposed theory of the mechanism of action of serotonin in brain. *Recent Advances biol. Psychiat.*, 1962, **4**, 133–146.

Aprison, M. H., & Ferster, C. B. Serotonin and behavior. *Recent Advances biol. Psychiat.*, 1961, **3**, 151–162.

Baldwin, E. *An introduction to comparative biochemistry*. London: Cambridge Univer. Press, 1949.

Bellak, L. *Dementia praecox: the past decade's work and present status: a review and evaluation.* New York: Grune & Stratton, 1948.

Benjamin, J. D. Some considerations in biological research in schizophrenia. *Psychosom. Med.*, 1958, **20**, 427–445.

Berkeley, A. W. Level of aspiration in relation to adrenal cortical activity and the concept of stress. *J. comp. physiol. Psychol.*, 1952, **45**, 443–449.

Bernal, J. D. Biochemical evolution. In M. Kasha & B. Pullman (Eds.), *Horizons in biochemistry.* New York: Academic, 1962. Pp. 11–22.

Bleuler, M. Research and changes in concepts in the study of schizophrenia: 1941–1950. *Bull. Isaac Ray med. Library*, 1955, **3**, 1–132.

Blum, H. F. On the origin and evolution of living machines. *Amer. Scientist,* 1961, **49,** 474–501.

Carlton, P. L. Cholinergic mechanisms in the control of behavior by the brain. *Psychol. Rev.,* 1963, **70,** 19–39.

Chitty, D. Adverse effects of population density upon the viability of later generations. In J. B. Cragg & N. W. Pirie (Eds.), *The numbers of man and animals.* London: Oliver & Boyd, 1955.

Clarke, J. R. The effect of fighting on the adrenals, thymus and spleen of the vole (*Microtus Agrestis*). *J. Endocrinol.,* 1953, **9,** 114–126.

Davidson, J. N. *The biochemistry of the nucleic acids.* New York: Wiley, 1960.

Elmadjian, F. Excretion and metabolism of epinephrine and norepinephrine in man. In F. A. Gibbs (Ed.), *Molecules and mental health.* Philadelphia: Lippincott, 1959.

Essig, C. F., Hampson, J. L., McCauley, A., & Himwich, H. E. An experimental analysis of biochemically induced forced circling behavior. *J. Neurophysiol.,* 1950, **13,** 269–275.

Eysenck, H. J. *Dimensions of personality.* London: Routledge, 1947.

Feldberg, W., & Sherwood, S. L. Injections of drugs into the lateral ventricle of the cat. *J. Physiol.,* 1954, **123,** 148–167.

Feldstein, A., Hoagland, H., & Freeman, H. Radioactive serotonin in relation to schizophrenia. *Arch. gen. Psychiat.,* 1961, **5,** 246–251.

Gaito, J. A biochemical approach to learning and memory. *Psychol. Rev.,* 1961, **68,** 288–292.

Gershon, S., & Shaw, F. H. Psychiatric sequelae of chronic exposure to organophosphorus insecticides. *Lancet,* 1961, **1,** June, 1371–1374.

Grossman, S. P. Direct adrenergic and cholinergic stimulation of hypothalamic mechanisms. *Amer. J. Physiol.,* 1962, **202,** 872–882.

Harris, H. *An introduction to human biochemical genetics.* London: Cambridge Univer. Press, 1955.

Heath, R. G. Physiological and biochemical studies in schizophrenia with particular emphasis on midbrain relationships. *Int. Rev. Neurobiol.,* 1959, **1,** 299–331.

Heath, R. G. Reappraisal of biological aspects of psychiatry. *J. Neuropsychiat.,* 1961, **3,** 1–11.

Hoagland, H., Pennell, R. B., Bergen, J. R., Sarvais, C. A., Freeman, H., & Koella, W. Studies of plasma protein factors that may be involved in psychoses. *Recent Advances biol. Psychiat.,* 1962, **4,** 329–346.

Hoagland, H., Pincus, G., Elmadjian, F., Romanoff, L., Freeman, H., Hope, J., Bollan, J., Berkeley, A., & Carlo, J. Study of adrenocortical physiology in normal and schizophrenic men. *Arch. Neurol. Psychiat.,* 1953, **69,** 470–485.

Hoffer, A. Abnormalities of behavior. *Annu. Rev. Psychol.,* 1960, **11,** 351–380.

Hoffer, A., & Osmond, H. The adrenochrome model and schizophrenia. *J. nerv. ment. Dis.,* 1959, **128,** 18–35.

Hoffer, A., Osmond, H., & Smythies, J. Schizophrenia: a new approach. II. Result of a year's research. *J. ment. Sci.,* 1954, **100,** 29–45.

Hoskins, R. G. *The biology of schizophrenia.* New York: Norton, 1946.

Hydén, H. Biochemical aspects of brain activity. In S. M. Farber & R. H. L. Wilson (Eds.), *Control of the mind.* New York: McGraw-Hill, 1961.

Hydén, H., & Egyhazi, E. Nuclear RNA changes of nerve cells during a learning experiment in rats. *Proc. nat. Acad. Sci.,* 1962, **48,** 1366–1373.

Jung, C. G. The psychology of dementia praecox. *Nerv. ment. Dis. Monogr. Ser.,* 1909, No. 3.

Kallmann, F. J. The genetic theory of schizophrenia. *Amer. J. Psychiat.,* 1946, **103,** 309–322.

Kelsey, F. O., Gullock, A. H., & Kelsey, F. E. Thyroid activity in hospitalized psychiatric patients. *Arch. Neurol. Psychiat.,* 1957, **77,** 543–548.

Kety, S. S. Biochemical theories of schizophrenia. I. *Science,* 1959, **129,** 1528–1532. (a)

Kety, S. S. Biochemical theories of schizophrenia. II. *Science,* 1959, **129,** 1590–1596. (b)

Kety, S. S. Chemical boundaries of psychopharmacology. In S. M. Farber & R. H. L. Wilson (Eds.), *Control of the mind.* New York: McGraw-Hill, 1961. Pp. 79–91.

Kety, S. S., & Schmidt, C. F. Nitrous oxide method for quantitative determination of cerebral blood flow in man: theory, procedure and normal values. *J. clin. Invest.,* 1948, **27,** 476–483.

Kety, S. S., Woodford, R. B., Harmel, M. H., Freyhan, F. A., Appel, K. E., & Schmidt, C. F. Cerebral blood flow and metabolism in schizophrenia. *Am. J. Psychiat.,* 1948, **104,** 765–770.

Kline, N. S. Nonchemical factors and chemical theories of mental disease. In M. Rinkel & H. C. B. Denber (Eds.), *Chemical concepts of psychosis.* New York: McDowell-Obolensky, 1958. Pp. 401–410.

Krech, D., Rosenzweig, M. R., & Bennett, E. L. Effects of environmental complexity and training on brain chemistry. *J. comp. physiol. Psychol.,* 1960, **53,** 509–519.

Lewis, N. D. C. *Research in dementia praecox.* New York: National Committee for Mental Hygiene, 1936.

McDonald, R. K. Problems in biological research in schizophrenia. *J. chron. Dis.*, 1958, 8, 366–371.

McFarland, R. A., & Goldstein, H. Biochemistry of the psychoneuroses: a review. *Amer. J. Psychiat.*, 1937, **93**, 1073–1095.

McFarland, R. A., & Goldstein, H. The biochemistry of dementia praecox: a review. *Amer. J. Psychiat.*, 1938, **95**, 509–552.

McFarland, R. A., & Goldstein, H. The biochemistry of manic-depressive psychosis: a review. *Amer. J. Psychiat.*, 1939, **96**, 21–58.

Margolis, L. H. Pharmacotherapy in psychiatry: a review. *Ann. N.Y. Acad. Sci.*, 1957, **66**, 698–718.

Miller, S. L., & Urey, H. C. Organic compound synthesis on the primitive earth. *Science*, 1959, **130**, 245–251.

Nachmansohn, D. *Chemical and molecular basis of nerve activity.* New York: Academic, 1959.

Osmond, H. Chemical concepts of psychosis: historical contributions. In M. Rinkel & H. C. B. Denber (Eds.), *Chemical concepts of psychosis.* New York: McDowell-Obolensky, 1958. Pp. 3–26.

Peters, R. A. Pharmacological and biochemical lesions. *Proc. roy. Soc. Med.*, 1948, **41**, 781–792.

Pincus, G., & Hoagland, H. Adrenal cortical responses to stress in normal men and in those with personality disorders. I. Some stress responses in normal and psychotic subjects. *Amer. J. Psychiat.*, 1950, **106**, 641–650. (a)

Pincus, G., & Hoagland, H. Adrenal cortical responses to stress in normal men and in those with personality disorders. II. Analysis of the pituitary-adrenal mechanism in man. *Amer. J. Psychiat.*, 1950, **106**, 651–659. (b)

Reiss, M. Psychoendocrinology. In M. Reiss (Ed.), *Psychoendocrinology.* New York: Grune & Stratton, 1958. Pp. 1–40. (a)

Reiss, M. Uses and abuses of statistics in biochemical investigations of psychotic patients. In M. Rinkel & H. C. B. Denber (Eds.), *Chemical concepts of psychosis.* New York: McDowell-Obolensky, 1958, Pp. 411–417. (b)

Richter, D. Biochemical aspects of schizophrenia. In *Schizophrenia: somatic aspects.* New York: Pergamon Press, 1957. Pp. 53–75.

Rinkel, M., & Denber, H. C. B. *Chemical concepts of psychosis.* New York: McDowell-Obolensky, 1958.

Rinkel, M., Hyde, R. W., & Solomon, H. C. Experimental psychiatry. III. A chemical concept of psychosis. *Dis. nerv. System*, 1954, **15**, 259–264.

Russell, R. W. Behaviour under stress. *Int. J. Psychoanal. Suppl.*, 1953, **34**, 1–12.

Russell, R. W. Drugs as tools in behavioral research. In L. Uhr & J. G. Miller (Eds.), *Drugs and behavior.* New York: Wiley, 1960. Pp. 19–40.

Russell, R. W., Watson, R. H. J., & Frankenhaueser, M. Effects of chronic reductions in brain cholinesterase activity on acquisition and extinction of a conditioned avoidance response. *Scand. J. Psychol.*, 1961, **2**, 21–29.

Sackler, M. D., Marti-Ibanez, F., Saeklen, R. R., & Sackler, A. M. A physiodynamic perspective on the etiology and therapy of the functional psychoses. In M. Rinkel & H. C. B. Denber (Eds.), *Chemical concepts of psychosis.* New York: McDowell-Obolensky, 1958. Pp. 389–400.

Selye, H. *Physiology and pathology of exposure to stress.* Montreal: Acta Press, 1950.

Slater, E. Genetic investigations in twins. *J. ment. Sci.*, 1953, **99**, 44–52. (a)

Slater, E. *Psychotic and neurotic illnesses in twins.* London: H. M. Stationery Office, 1953. (b)

Smythies, J. R. Biochemical concepts of schizophrenia. *Lancet*, 1958, **2**, 308–313.

Szara, S., Axelrod, J., & Perkins, S. Is adrenochrome present in the blood? *Amer. J. Psychiat.*, 1958, **115**, 162–163.

Thudichum, J. W. L. *A treatise on the chemical constitution of the brain.* London: Tindall & Cox, 1884.

Wikler, A. The loci and mechanisms of action of phrenotropic drugs considered in relation to screening procedures. In J. O. Cole & R. W. Gerard (Eds.), *Psychopharmacology.* Washington, D.C.: National Research Council, 1959. Pp. 213–223.

Wilson, W. P., Schieve, J. F., & Scheinberg, P. Effect of series of electric shock treatments on cerebral blood flow and metabolism. *Arch. Neurol. Phychiat.*, 1952, **68**, 651–654.

Woolley, D. W. Participation of serotonin in mental processes. In M. Rinkel & H. C. B. Denber (Eds.), *Chemical concepts of psychosis.* New York: McDowell-Obolensky, 1958. Pp. 176–189.

Woolley, D. W., & Shaw, E. A biochemical and pharmacological suggestion about certain mental disorders. *Proc. nat. Acad. Sci.*, 1954, **40**, 228–231.

Zuckerkandl, E., & Pauling, L. Molecular disease, evolution, and genic heterogeneity. In M. Kasha & B. Pullman (Eds.), *Horizons in biochemistry.* New York: Academic, 1962. Pp. 189–225.

10

Society and Individual Behavior

EDWARD STAINBROOK

The culture of our time is characterized by an intensifying and socially urgent commitment to the values and uses of scientific imagination and logical discipline in conceiving and understanding all humanly meaningful happenings. Such an ascendancy of science complicates intricately contemporary social and political action. The tasks created by the interaction of science and social processes are largely those of integrating and maintaining scientific knowledge and scientists in the stabilizing social systems of the institutions of society. As part of this innovative and maintenance action there is, of course, a specific sociology of clinical psychology, as there is, indeed, of every pure and applied scientific profession. The social implications of professional roles will be explored at a later point.

Our more fundamental initial purpose is to arrive at an adequate theoretical statement into which to fit the relevance of social factors in defining the specific conditions under which individual behavior happens. And as a prelude to this, we must recognize how the value systems of scientists themselves and the structures and functions of science-influenced institutions—such as educational, research, and health organizations—determine, implicitly and explicitly, the hierarchy of research emphasis, the preferences for theoretical models, and (especially in relation to human behavior) the desirable intervening action to control, alter, or facilitate individual thinking, feeling, and doing.

All this is to say that scientific theory is not above or beyond the society whose approach to itself and to the world it proposes to explain. Thus the creation of a comprehensive theory of the behavior of man is being slowly achieved in a disputatious atmosphere determined not only by the existing founded and experimentally validated knowledge or by the intellectual capacities of scientists, but also by general social needs and demands, by offered or available research and application resources, by specific organizational objectives, and by—not insignificantly—the psychodynamic functioning of individual scientists. Thus it comes about, among other consequences, that the internal sociology of a university conditions, wittingly and unwittingly, the theory of human behavior taught there.

Since clinical psychology has been so closely associated with both the theory and the practice of psychiatry, these reflections upon the social and cultural determinants of behavior theory itself should not be read too casually. For some time in the history of clinical psychology, the reproach could be made legitimately either that an applied technology was substituting for basic science theoretical and research activity or that at least it should also have been accompanied by it. Now, with clinical psychology risking increasingly its own professional separateness from psychiatry and medicine, there has come also a widening participation of basic science psychology into theory making and experimental action in engaging directly with all human behavior. The contemporary clinical psychologist, more certain of himself as a psychologist and more inaugurated, confirmed, and expanding in his social-professional role, is now more eager to rely on basic psychological theory and research, which, reciprocally, are developing for him more fundamental, experimentally validated knowledge of relevant clinical value, as, for example, from the research study of psychotherapy.

Nevertheless, the education and training of the clinical psychologist still occur in both a university and a medical or hospital setting, each with its unique pattern of emphasis concerning the nature of man. Insofar as the clinical training situations are psychiatric, there will be some influence regarding the significant variables to be considered in understanding human action coming from the present effort of much of current medical school psychiatry to introduce an adequate representation of the basic behavioral sciences into both undergraduate and postgraduate medical education.

However, the university-embedded doctorate program of basic knowledge for the clinical psychologist may be based on quite different theoretical assumptions about the nature of behavior from those guiding the diagnostic and therapeutic activities of the clinic and hospital. And, sadly, many times it is not only the medical school but the university, too, where it is darkest under the lamp and where, particularly, the biologists feel no need to map into their theoretical models of body the information and change added to biological processes by the individual's learning to be human. And the psychologists ignore or, perhaps even worse, are content with journalistic, not scientific, information about how culture and society organize and control individual psychodynamics. And the social scientists may show little or no interest in the ways in which values and the social conditions of being human modify and get modified, as Mr. Auden puts it, "in the guts of the living."

For most logical situations, Nagel has succinctly stated: "No statement containing a given term 'p' can be deduced from a class of statements unless the latter also contain that term." In order to assure that the total molarity of a behavioral event—all the information that is there—is associated with its specific molecular processes requires that theory capture totally the molar happening. Otherwise one will not know adequately either how the molarity is twisting the molecule or how the molecule is twisting the molarity.

The task, therefore, is not so much to deplore reductionism as it is to ensure that students of human behavior, wherever educated and trained, acquire the theoretical sensitivity and capacity to see and to conceptualize what is there. Then even the molecular biologist will be in no danger of excluding anything relevantly human. He will have to "save" it in his logic because it will be a fact in his natural system.

But such theoretical integrity about human behavior not only must be achieved in the mind of the occasional scholar but also must be organized into the educational process. This may not be achieved by reorganizations of separate behavioral science departments into divisions of human behavior or institutes of behavioral science. University politics, power, and scholarly objectives are not easily modified. But programs of integrated teaching and learning about human behavior for both undergraduate and graduate students, composed of a faculty of molar and molecular biologists, psychologists, and social scientists who, in fact, are comfortable and reciprocally supporting in a communality of behavioral theory, must be somehow acceleratingly innovated into the educational organization of both medical schools and the general university.

THE SOCIAL CONTEXT AND THE INDIVIDUAL

The older, simpler dichotomy of organism and environment is no longer, most all agree, an adequate perception of a person and his situation. Some stimulus-response theories, with the emphasis varying according to national and cultural affiliation, seem to state at least implicit assumptions about the character and interactions of organisms and their surround in the syntax of the billiard-ball physics of the nineteenth century. But most students of behavior are now aware of the complicated transactional cross-organization of body, self, and social environment. How to catch hold theoretically of these intricate, dynamic, and constantly changing action systems constituting behavior may be a more actively controversial task.

Fortunately, since our objectives here are to suggest the relevancy of social space and its organization to the preventive, diagnostic, treatment, and research activities of clinical psychology, we may present only a map of the theoretical territory rather than any complete theory in itself.

Considered both as a developmental beginning and as the basic structure-function process of behavior, biological action is the fundamental referent of individual behaving. Much of embryological and very early infantile biological action can be described as occurring as a result of genetic constitutional programming and the associated maturational and intrinsic feedback processes. For how long in developmental time we can talk about body as organization and action existing prior to any effects of learned change depends somewhat upon what one chooses to call "learning." Psychologists, particularly, can understand the extent to which students of human learning have allowed their theories to select the phenomena. It is evident, however, to those who look directly at the human newborn that self-transactional and self-interactional behavior begins to modify the given action of body within the first hours and days after the infant's birth.

The child is born most immediately into the dyadic social system of himself and mother, but also into the socially organized human group of his family. Hence, at least from birth onward, culture and society, as particularly specified for any individual family in its unique social space, are imposing a significant determination upon the process and the organization of individual learning. This individual experience-changing and experience-gaining result in the organization, control, and direction of biological action. In this way cultural patterns of value and meaning and the institutionalized conditions determining the transactions between persons as they activate and maintain social organizations also influence biological action.

For the subsequent consideration of some psychosomatic problems, it is necessary to remark here that this social and cultural influence may be differentiated into specific cultural meanings and specific social transactions in relation to specific organ systems, such as the gastrointestinal, or to specific physiological processes within the body.

It would seem, therefore, that from birth onward the conceptualization and the intellectual monitoring of biological action cannot be done exclusively by the language and methods of physiology or biochemistry without losing critical information about the specificity and individuation of biological process and structures. We speak by necessity, therefore, not only of an organism but also of personality, self, or—more sophisticatedly—an unreified psychological system.

As already indicated, not only do values and the general culture determine largely what is learned, but, by their determination of social transactions, they also condition significantly how learning occurs. Culture and society, therefore, "move into" personality.

Parsons (1959; Parsons & Shils, 1951) has most ably worked out the interpenetrating and integrating relationships of body and the psychological, social, and cultural systems. As he suggests:

> Social systems provide the most immediate set of conditions on which the functioning and development of cultural systems depend, psychological systems provide a set of conditions underlying the functioning of social systems, and the organism provides conditions underlying psychological systems.

He further states:

> When a plurality of interacting organisms tend to interact in systematically organized ways in relation to each other as the result of learning, we may speak of a social system.

Additionally, as he indicates:

> All concrete behavior belongs to some psychological system and a very large part of it at the same time belongs to some social system. Yet the same organism participates in a plurality of social systems; conversely, the same social system—over a period of time—may be "composed" of different behaving actors and yet remain "the same system."

Cultural orientations and socially structured action are, therefore, "internalized" and integrated into personality. No adequate understanding of the differentiated and organized functioning of individually experienced history into the presently acting self can be obtained without, at every behavioral moment, being both retrospectively and immediately aware of the transactional system-complex of body, self, social group, and institutionalized culture. History as a conscious conceptualization of prior experience, whether of an individual or of a political group, exists only in the uniquely personal behavior of the rethinking and the refeeling. That is to say that history, as awareness, does not appear in the present moment of experience unless it is invited. Moreover, even with the psychotherapeutic invitation to reconstruct his history symbolically, and, perhaps, also to conceptualize for the first time feelings and sensorimotor percepts never before associated with conceptual symbols, an individual reports himself from "behind his eyes" and sees the truth from where he stands. Hence it is easy for both the history-repossessing person and an interested other to consider the internalized experience as if it were determined by nothing but the genetic, psychodynamic, intrapsychic happenings of the person or as if, particularly, childhood experiences were determined wholly out of the behavior of two or more psychological persons, the determinants of whose action with each other were to be found exclusively in their reactions as individuals and not also in the social and cultural organization of their relationships.

What I am suggesting here is that the influence on individual behavior of the social context and culture is much more obvious to both pure and applied scientists of human behavior when their scrutiny is on the actual behavior of a present person in his here-and-now circumstances. The manner in which society and culture have determined the person's past original and prior learning and experience is too frequently left undifferentiated in the genetic explanation of how the past has influenced the present.

TRANSACTIONS BETWEEN PERSONS AND SOCIAL ORGANIZATIONS

General sociology is concerned mainly with the conceptualization and study of the functions and structure of social institutions as they integrate into patterned communities and into a national polity. Needless to say, there is also a comparative sociology of national societies and a sociology, however embryonic, of international relations.

With clinical concerns, we are interested usually in a specific person and his transactions with a particular family and a particular work, school, or other formal or informal social group. We are concerned also with this individual behavior as it may occur within a certain building in a particular geographical and social space in a specific community. From the clinical point of view, we are closer to the discipline of social psychology than of general sociology in the emphasis upon how social organizations structure and prescribe, explicitly and implicitly, much of the individual behavior that happens within them.

The idea of role is a basic concept for comprehending the behavior occurring in the interpenetrating cross-organization of a psychological and social system—of a person and a social group. The social role of an individual in a defined social situation is, for him, a pattern of already learned or to-be-learned behavior which is dependent upon, and related to, the status or position he occupies in the situation. Since most social behavior by definition involves two or more persons, either actually or referentially, role-determined activity involves a self-other system of reciprocal expectations. Either the actors are learning for the first time, or they have already learned from some earlier socialization, how to behave according to socially and organizationally defined goals and appropriate role action. Additionally, of course, adequate role learning and behavior not only imply knowing how oneself is expected to act but also entail an awareness of how others are going to behave in complemental action and reaction.

An individual, therefore, is named by his social position and his locus in the "anatomy" of the social structure, and he contributes his action to the total "physiology" of the organization through the associated role guidance and control.

Sarbin (1954) has been exceptionally cogent in discussing the relationships between the institutionalized structuring for behavior subsumed under the designation "social role" and the psychologically internalized, and hence also biologically integrated, symbolization and organization of experienced behavior conceived and constantly, but varyingly, restated as the self.

Sarbin's definition of personality as "the action systems arising out of the interplay of self and role" may or may not be wholly acceptable. Nevertheless, it is of crucial importance in the understanding of behavior to differentiate, as clearly as possible, self-action and role-determined action in the total behavior ascribed to the person. Otherwise, as is seen so frequently, particularly in psychiatric hospitals, attempts are made to explain totally the patient's action as being due entirely to his self-dynamics. The significant determination of his behavior arising out of the "organizational conditions of life" in the social system of the hospital is consequently overlooked. The patient, presumably an already vulnerable personality, is thus made additionally responsible for behavior which may be occurring actually as a consequence, perhaps quite unintentional, of the administration of the hospital system.

Another way of using helpfully the concepts of self and of role is to assume that the experiencing self constructs itself, cognitively and symbolically, within its role action. The perceived and symbolized action is then organized as memory, becoming at any subsequent moment a component in some later reconstruction of the remembered self. This is, perhaps, a more elaborate statement of the assumption that the self is an organization of internalized roles.

From this point of view, the enactment of specific role behavior over time might be presumed to exercise a generalizing effect on self-behavior in a wide range of other role situations. The extent to which current role action affects the ongoing organization of self depends importantly upon the motivational and capacity factors involved as well as upon the general psychodynamics and the developmental vicissitudes which the self-organization has undergone historically.

Merton cites what he calls the "depersonalization" and the "rigidity" developing in persons with long work experience in bureaucratic organizations. Similarly, one can point to the effects of long role participation in "total" institutions, such as prisons and psychiatric hospitals, on both characteristic self-action and subjective self-perception and self-experiencing.

Only very recently has it become clear how much of the nineteenth-century conception of the schizophrenic reactions as signifying progressive personality dilapidation and deterioration was based on a failure to recognize the contributions of the hospital socialization process to the behavior of the person.

In *Individualism Reconsidered,* David Riesman suggests another variation on the theme of self and role. There he writes: "Many of the motives which were in earlier decades built into the character structure of individuals are now built into the institutional structure of corporate life." Increasingly, and partly as a result of the expanding utilization of social science knowledge in administration, work organizations are structuring their various role actions in order to engender more motivational excitement about commitment to organizational tasks. This is, in effect, a countertrending against the generalization into character of the behavior learned in other social roles, notably in contemporary school organizations. In urban and suburban schools, particularly, the single classrooms have grown to the proportion of sociological crowds. There is an absence of any compensating enduring small-group context in which personal and emotional problems of self-delineation, role acceptance, and role learning can be mastered with minimal use of avoidance and social distancing and with minimal distortion of self and others.

Hence if adult work tasks demand self-behavior which has not been internalized previously out of earlier role socialization, then the work organization must not only institutionalize the demanded action but also provide for the dynamics of commitment to it.

A closely allied consideration is the understanding that not only does social role involve motivations and rewards and more or less definite prescriptions for action, but it also provides or fails to provide facilitation and support for a wide spectrum of ego functioning. From the subjective point of view, self and role are experienced ordinarily as a unity. And even from an objective position, the role characteristics have to be abstracted conceptually from the social setting. A role is, nevertheless, not only part of the structure but also part of the dynamic functioning of the social self.

A distinct sociopsychological system was introduced by Wolman (1960). Wolman has combined experimental studies in social psychology with the psychoanalytic frame of reference. Freud's logical construct, "cathexis," has been applied to interindividual relations. The new construct, "interindividual cathexis," permits one to distinguish three types of relationships: the receiving libido-cathexis, or "instrumental"; the receiving and giving, or "mutual"; and the giving, or "vectorial."

Within the usual family structure the relative social positions determine the social roles, i.e., the expected behavioral patterns of each individual. Parent-child relationships should be vectorial, parent-parent relationships mutual, and child-parent relationships instrumental.

Reversal and confusion in intrafamilial social roles have been singled out by Wolman as relevant pathogenic factors. For example, when intraparental interaction is instrumental, as when overdemanding (instrumental) parents force the child to assume an abnormal, hypervectorial, protective attitude toward them, a schizophrenic development is believed to start (Wolman, 1957; Wolman, 1961).

Within this frame of reference, Wolman has classified mental disorders into the hyperinstrumental or psychopathic type, the paramutual or cyclic type, and the hypervectorial or schizoid type. (See "Mental Health and Mental Disorders," in Part 4.)

All these considerations are especially significant in understanding and in dealing therapeutically with deviant and psychopathological behavior. The perceptual and cognitive construction of the environment and of environing people depends, among other conditions, upon the biological integrity of ego capacities and functions, upon prior learning and its ego organization, upon motivation, upon rewards, and upon the transactions of information-gaining from others and from the setting.

In other words, possible social-role action and the characteristics of socially organized behavior facilitate or impair the ego functions of perceiving, conceiving, organizing, and maintaining integrative and predictive stability and ego actions of effective and resourceful doing.

The Cummings (1962), in their extraordinarily valuable book *Ego and Milieu*, describe at least three basic facilitations of role structure for increasing the adaptation of the patient. Role structure, they suggest, provides the psychologically impaired patient with a lucid environment; second, it mirrors back to him widely varied aspects of his own nature; and third, through a delegation of a vast amount of task content, it provides him with numerous problems to solve."

If one reflects on the personality action involved in reality construction, it seems basic that conceptualization of self, others, and general reality always involves some varying balance of both the organized, internalized information provided by the self and the external information, much of which, too, is presented as already organized by culture and social context. The goal of "conceptual closure" and the associated feeling of certainty of knowing cannot be achieved if the external situation is unclear and ambiguous. The ambiguity of the external information may occur because of its paucity, because of its incongruity, because of its inadequate contextual organization, or because of its overabundance.

It is helpful to remember, incidentally, that under the influence of strong psychobiological drive-states, such as anxiety, the amount of potentially relevant information, internal as well as external, is both intensively and extensively increased. Hence, delusional thinking may be a derivative not only of a primary or secondary reactive disturbance of regional or integrative neurophysiology or of conflicting and regressive behavior but also of an attempt to master by conceptual organization the anxiety-created plethora of threatening information from both without and within.

Many psychiatric patients, particularly those who are hospitalized, suffer acute anxiety. For such persons, it is necessary for the psychiatric hospital as a social structure to minimize ambiguity and maximize confidence in the predictable certainty of both the behavior of self and the behavior of associated others. When, in the hospital, these goals can be achieved through the structural clarity and adequacy both of the patient's role and of the roles of the interrelating others, then the panic, the acute anxiety, of the psychotic experience is reduced. Then the troubled patient, although still impaired, can begin to use with increasing adaptability the resources provided in the hospital's response to his illness.

The brain-damaged patient, also, may be constantly threatened by his inability to differentiate and organize the informational input from the investing world and so require the supporting clarity, concreteness, and unambiguous organization of his own role action and, particularly, of the complementary role behavior of the relating others around him.

The ambiguity and informational inadequacy conditioned by role and general social structure have importance for individual behavior, especially for psychopathological behavior, with reference to paranoid and similar relatively enduring distortions of reality construction.

When there exists a relative paucity of communication from and with the environment, either because the social structure provides inadequate channels or because provided channels are not used, the social reality of the environment may be constructed largely with the internalized information—with the assumptions—brought to the situation by the person. The more the external reality is symbolically and conceptually constructed by information coming only from the "internal reality" of the person, the more likely this constructed external reality of other persons and of things and events will be idiosyncratically distorted by him. His responses to his organizations of the contemporary reality may be quite adaptive to his distorting assumptions, and yet such responses may be perceived as madness by others with a different balance of internal and external information in their own constructions. Moreover, for individuals already motivationally pushed or forced because of ego-capacity impairment, however engendered, to exclude relevant information or to include irrelevant cues, communicative inadequacy structured into role actions further impairs ego functioning and reinforces pathological behavior.

Within the large psychiatric hospital, the increase of the social structure and action of communication by organizational programs of "therapeutic milieu" and of group therapy has significantly augmented the informational transactions among patients and patients, staff and staff, and patients and staff. This restructuring of role action for the various role takers in the hospital organization is basically an administrative adaptation of the whole hospital system in order to create the most effective social processes for the achievement of the therapeutic goals of the hospital.

It is frequently difficult to make distinctions in the definitions of therapy between the most effective social structure of a psychiatric hospital, administratively achieved and maintained, and the more professionally usual structure and activity of individual and group psychotherapy. Yet it is sometimes helpful to keep in mind that the social behavior of the dyadic, or larger, psychotherapeutic group is also at the same time part of the behavior occurring in the more inclusive social system of the treatment organization, whether hospital, clinic, or other social agency. Group therapy, for example, happening on a ward of chronic, long-hospitalized schizophrenic persons often is given up by the professional staff or is continued in a desultory fashion after an initial enthusiasm because it is evaluated only with reference to an end point of "cure." Such therapeutic activity, however, must also be seen as part of the organizational reparation of social isolation and of the previous contact, informational, and communicative failure. It is almost always true that the individual and group psychotherapy of these iatrogenically desocialized chronic schizophrenic patients does not lead to a quickly demonstrable remission of psychotic behavior. Even so, such professional action may be justified as an organizational response to enhance impaired ego functioning and to stimulate and reward the transactional needs of patients.

There is another aspect worth mentioning of these relations between the small-group treatment processes and the administration, therapeutically sensitive or otherwise, of a whole hospital. This is the occasional tendency to try to repair the ambiguity and the general social inadequacy of the hospital by introducing group therapy alone into significantly deprived and poorly organized areas of the organization. There then exists little facilitation of any reinforcing generalization for the ego-aiding discrimination, integration, or predictive confidence that might, hopefully, be engendered in patients specifically in the small-group experience.

In fact, large public psychiatric hospitals, like prisons and other "total institutions," may use, unwittingly, the existence of psychotherapy, or even of pharmacologic treatment, as a rationalization. The limited employment of such specific ameliorative and therapeutic procedures allows them to remain administratively adamant about the rigidity of control and the sociological emptiness of what, for the psychiatric hospital at least, our culture has voted strongly to call a "therapeutic society."

The effect of role action on self-experience and on self-conceptualization is apparent also in the construction and stable maintenance of self-image and self-identity. The closely associated imagery, concepts, and feelings of self-value, of self-esteem, are determined largely by both present and past self-appraisal and by the psychodynamically processed, and hence possibly more or less distorted, appraisal of others. These appraisals, by both self and others, are emotionalized assessments not only of social-role performance but also of the socially conceived valuations of the position of the enacted role in specific organizations and in the general society.

These role relationships and self-relationships affecting self-identity and self-esteem are pertinent to both informal and formal role delineations. The informal roles arise out of the expression of deviant behavior, such as "delinquent," "drug addict," "alcoholic," "queer," or "crazy." The formal roles of patient or criminal are achieved in the action of the offered or imposed social control of deviance.

The self-image of the drug addict, the alcoholic, or the homosexual is composed of both the already internalized and the currently reflected social valuations of the self.

There exists frequently, too, a delinquent, criminal, addictive, or homosexual social group and subculture in which the deviant roles are being enacted. Hence, the psychodynamic resolutions of the deviance-conformity conflict, whatever its genetic causes, and the psychological state of the motivational commitment to change behavior are stabilized by at least two basically social factors.

One of these factors is the contribution of social role to the formation of the self-image. Out of this interrelation, frequently, motivations for the destructive use of the low-valued, low-esteemed self may be continually induced.

Second, the physical, social, and cultural resources of the deviant subsociety provide satisfactions for the needs associated with addicting biochemical short circuits to pleasure gain and psychophysiological satiety. Equally important, such informal social organizations assure the gratification of the urges for valued and meaningful identity and for socially sustained and evident reasons to feel good, or at least not to feel bad, about the self.

Not only in Paris is the "milieu" both the creature and the creator of its inhabitants. Studies of the ecology of deviant behavior and of the social action of prevention, control, and treatment must therefore be conceived in a theoretical matrix comprehensive enough to include all these self-transactions and society transactions.

SICK ROLE, PATIENT ROLE, AND THE SOCIAL HELPING RESPONSE

Illness is bred in the heart and in the head and in the body politic. Moreover, illness is not an entity; it is all the processes of ailing.

It is worth remarking parenthetically here on how the English language and our implicit cultural preferences in thinking conspire subtly to impair our experience of behavior as action and process. As a well-known nineteenth-century physicist complained, "English is a language for solids."

From an orthodox medical point of view, and considered etiologically, illness is a happening, sometimes unperceived by the self, in the biological action of the person. The initiating and sustaining causes of a biological dysfunction or structural alteration may reside only in the biological system itself and be genetic, maturational, or "intrinsic." Or some contribution to both the initiation and the maintenance of a physiologically detected illness may come from the patterning of biological action by the individually learned psychological organization, which, itself, was also partially determined by the cultural and social conditions imposed upon the individual's learning how to be human. Some influence on the creation of the incipient biological state defined as illness and on its continuation may come from the current social system or systems with which self and body are in transaction.

From the viewpoint of illness experienced in the total processes of ailing, sickness begins as a self-perceived uneasiness. This ill-at-easeness is the conscious or "preconscious" representation of biological action, however etiologically influenced. The highly variable individual response to this perception of "dis-ease" immediately becomes part of the illness and has its impact on both the biological action and the behavior of the person in relation to himself as well as to others.

The perception of unease may be denied or distorted, and the individual may refuse, at least for the time being and in his present circumstances, to conceptualize himself as ill. Or he may accept himself as sick and yet refrain from any informal or formal socialization of himself as ailing. Or he may validate his own sick role and accordingly alter his participation in various social groups—family, work, or school—in conformity with his self-validated compromise.

He may communicate his uneasiness to one or more of a large number of socially defined sources of potential response. Depending upon what he communicates and to whom he communicates it and upon the social structure and organization of their transactions, he may or may not, directly or by referral, be inducted into a legitimate sick role with some medical agency of the socially organized helping resources of the community.

In a jocular spirit, we may say that anyone, anywhere, may define himself as ill. It takes a doctor, however, to make him formally sick, that is, to validate him into the social sick role, with the help, the assurances, the privileges, the indulgences, and the responsibilities such a role implies.

It may be clarifying for some of our problem seeing and problem solving in contemporary community health and welfare and in some of the interprofessional collaboration and conflict between clinical psychologists and psychiatrists to reflect upon some aspects of the general sociology of the sick role.

The increasingly popular decision in Western European and American society is to impose social control and reparative attempts at the prevention and amelioration of all kinds of deviant behavior through the utilization of sick-role socialization in medical and paramedical social organizations. Thus, "organic" illness, psychological illness, crime, divorce, accident frequency, school and work failure, unhappiness, and less than optimal creativity may all be subsumed under the general rubric "illness."

Insofar as this trend is supported by the emergence in the general culture of some superordinating values about the nature of man and about the understanding of human behavior in terms of the contemporary sciences of social man, such social action is rationally and humanistically motivated. However, the dialectic of progress requires that every trend be challenged by an intelligent and anticipatory countertrend. Otherwise, unplanned and informal counteraction appears which, in itself, may create a considerable amount of social deviance.

Almost exclusively, psychiatry is that division of medicine which must respond to the expanding definition of social pathology as the expression of individual illness. In responding, psychiatry is presented with several problems. If the treatment response is shared with psychologists and social workers, for example, then shall the different role-associated therapeutic skills and knowledge be differentiated in treatment relations to patients according to the patient's diagnosis, according to the social setting in which therapist and patient come together, according to the relationship of superordination and subordination established between the professional roles, or according to the unique and exclusive skills which each role can employ?

Shall the creation and introduction into the psychiatric medical setting of "subprofessional" roles be accelerated, as has already happened for nursing, social work, and, to a certain extent, psychology? Or would it be more rational to seek, by intensified laboratory, clinical, and especially social-action research, the extent to which the dissemination of behavioral-science knowledge into all social organizations—into the home and into school, work, religious, recreational, penal, reformatory, medical, and legal groups—might prevent and ameliorate a good deal of behavioral deviation without the provision of any formal therapeutic role action?

Behavioral-science knowledge in our society is still too narrowly applied through psychiatric and social welfare agencies, is too exclusively used for the treatment or amelioration of severe human distress, and is too monotonously recommended as a preventive of mental illness and as a promoter of mental health. Perhaps a voluntary national association on human behavior should be instituted, complementary to the National Association on Mental Health.

More specifically, with reference to the conflicts and ambiguity arising out of decisions about illness, sick role, and treatment, many adaptations of the social helping response can occur. If a good deal of individual maladaptation is conditional upon the past but inadequate learning and socialization of a person, that is to say, upon how the psychological system has been organized, then, in the broadest sense, helping becomes a matter of additional learning and relearning and of additional socialization and resocialization. The person suffers from faulty learning and socialization, not from an "illness." He may not need to come to a medical source, petition for a sick role, or be diagnosed or treated.

Whether such a nonmedical model is feasible for the effective control and change of some deviant behavior must be evaluated carefully. Hopefully, it may provide a rationale for an effective countertrend against the present tendency to make all deviants sick. Not only does such a trend impose an almost impossible burden on psychiatry, but in contemporary society, changing so rapidly and expanding so greatly as to be constantly outrunning its own capacity for effectively integrated organization, such a trend may also make the individual responsible for much more than he can possibly control.

A somewhat related aspect is the preference of some social caricaturists for using the metaphor of illness in describing a "sick society." Here, as with the too inclusive range of sick individual behavior, it may be thought proper to perceive social problems as if they were exclusively medical problems. But societies are obviously not treatable by doctors or, indeed, by social engineers. The unduly stressing, conflict-engendering, depriving, or freedom-constraining society is not sick; it is wrongly or inadequately differentiated and organized to promote and facilitate the optimal actualization of the individual human potential. Society can be changed and guided, not by "treatment," but by democratically innovated decisions about the necessary social and political action.

A more specific structuring of the sick role is achieved when the person is inducted as a patient into a treatment or caretaking process. The role of being a patient may interfere hardly at all with the concomitant enactment of other social roles, or it may prohibit, temporarily or permanently, any other effective role behavior.

If the patient enters a hospital, he organizes himself and is organized into the social-role structure as it is defined, both formally and informally, in that specific hospital. He—his body and himself—has been integrated into the social system of the hospital. His illness, originally biologized and then psychologized, is now socialized. Hence it follows that what happens, perhaps quite remotely, in the social action of the hospital may affect, not always with pathological significance, the physiological action of perhaps already vulnerable somatic organs and processes. To be therapeutically relevant, such effects need not be positively pathogenic; they need only interfere, as either biological or psychological action, with the optimal conditions for healing and repair.

Striking, related evidence of the influence of patient role upon illness comes from the comparison of lengths of stay for similarly diagnosed diseases in different hospitals. In some community general hospitals, the average length of stay may be ten to twelve days. In some public hospitals, where, it is true, there may exist much greater diagnostic thoroughness, the average stay may be twenty-five to thirty-five days.

Hence, differences in structuring the social transactions between patients and the organized medical helping response may cut in half the time during which people may be sick with a similar illness.

Other important considerations about the social perception of illness and the social structuring of the sick role relate to the differentiation of sick-role action, particularly within a hospital, and to the discrimination of closely associated roles from the sick role.

The variety of role action associated with being a patient in a general hospital is not great. Most hospitals feel that they can best indicate their size by enumerating their "beds," thus explicitly relating most patient action, or inaction, to a bed. Hence too, there is permitted very little individuation of the patient role, either in terms of different ways of being in the hospital or in terms of paying attention to the way in which role action supports or impairs identity, self-respect, and self-esteem. Most patients, initially at least, in general hospitals as a rule and in psychiatric hospitals frequently, are stripped of much self-identifying and self-presenting informational cues and symbols.

Unlike the increasing provision in psychiatric hospitals for a wide range of ways of being a patient, role action for patients in general hospitals tends to occur completely within the hospital and as close as possible to the patient's bed.

Imaginative experimentation with day patients without beds, for example, might reduce the twenty-four-hour census of the general hospital by as much as one-third or more and significantly alter the pressure for costly expansion.

One additional problem related more particularly to disablement and to what is conceived as chronic illness is the possibility of creating clear role distinctions between active illness and residual or arrested disability. Since almost everyone over 50 is suffering from some latent disability, at least relative to an earlier state, it is also obvious that there exists a good deal of pre-illness as well as post-illness disability. Rehabilitation is usually conceived as part of the incapacitating illness; the individual with permanent residual impairment frequently never leaves the sick role, nor is he considered by others or by the medical system to have done so. Hence, the more socially restricting and more self-demeaning sick role is maintained, and disablement becomes indistinguishable from chronic illness.

There are many other consequences for individual behavior, pathological or normal, arising out of the conditions and characteristics of patient role action. In the psychiatric setting, the patient may accept himself as troubled or ill but protest the acceptance of what he perceives as a threatening, coercive, or hopeless patient experience. Most persons have very little previous experience in how to be a patient in even a general hospital. How much more unprepared they are to feel confident about being a patient in a psychiatric hospital. Yet psychiatrists often talk about the uncooperative patient without insight as if the patient is denying his illness. Frequently the person is not refusing to be troubled and in need of help; he is protesting about being a patient "our way." And his perception of the threat and the despair in "our way" is not all distortion.

So, too, once in the hospital, the patient learns both the intended and the unintended and incidental expectations of others concerning his behavior, and he learns what to expect from them. Since the "natural course" of any illness, but especially of behavioral illness, is determined partly by the social structure of its happening, the psychiatric hospital, we can say, will succeed in getting the kind of schizophrenia it deserves. The self-fulfilling expectation is of the very essence of structured role interaction.

To discuss adequately other facets of behavior in a hospital or, indeed, in any social organization, we now need to consider a simple conceptual model of an organization.

THE ORGANIZATION AND INDIVIDUAL BEHAVIOR

The familiar organizational chart can serve as a simple sketch of some of the structural aspects of an organization, whether medical, educational, governmental, or industrial. All the formal social and occupational roles and their positional loci can be placed in such a chart, but often they are not. Hospital organizational diagrams, for instance, seldom include patients, and educational organizations frequently omit students.

These maps of organizational structure display a good deal of the formal communication network of the system and so indicate potential areas of task deviance as a possible consequence of the way these positions are organized into the communication systems of the establishment.

The diagram of the organization may show also the positions in which, because of administrative structure, stress is likely to occur. The responses to organizationally induced conflict result in altered motivational states and in the evocation of characteristic coping strategies in people occupying such positions. These psychodynamic reactions almost always, in some measure, influence the overt task performance and role action within the organization.

As a paradigm, let us consider the position of a charge nurse, the executive nurse directing the patient care and managing the general organizational transactions on a ward in a hospital. Let us assume that her motivational state is optimal—that she is maximally committed to doing what it is best to do. Superordinating her in the structure of the hospital may be at least five different sources with the status and power to control her by directives and prescriptions for action. These may be the business manager of the hospital, the medical director, the director of nursing services, the director of nursing education, and the attending medical staff.

Let us further suppose that, directly or mediately, the nurse has received directions for the same task, some of which are conflicting, from all five of these superiors. The nurse's first reaction of anxiety or worry may be transformed immediately or more gradually into resentment, a fusion of anxiety and anger, or into some other emotive change in her assumed optimal motivational state. This change may be situationally specific and of short and episodic duration and frequency and therefore affect task doing a relatively small part of her time. If such occurrences are frequent, that is to say, structured into superior-subordinate relationships, then more permanent and more generalized coping preferences may lead to psychological and physical avoidance of the stress-inducing encounters and perhaps also to a de-emotionalized, "don't care" attitude as part of the enduring motivational engagement with the organizational tasks.

As bulwarked by this illustration, it must be considered that the social structure of an organization constantly conditions the motivational state of the people within it. When motivation is altered, action is apt to be. Hence not only are people affected psychodynamically by the conditions of institutional life, but the task performance within the organization, the organization's activities, are influenced too. If people do what it is best to do, but with resentment, then the desirable task action may also be the pathway for the expression of resentfulness.

Moreover, since task action frequently involves transactions with others, the changed motivational state, being also communication, elicits countermotivational needs in others. In this way, through emotional and cognitive messages, organizational stress on one position can be communicated to many others, with the consequent wide effect on behavior in the organization.

The recognition of the contribution which each person's way of being in the structure and functions of the organization makes to his behavior both with regard to himself and with regard to his task performances with others is highly relevant to the understanding of psychotherapeutic transactions. Too often, particularly within the psychiatric hospital, the therapist, his supervisor, and others tend to analyze the behavior constituting the psychotherapeutic process as if it were exclusively a two-or-more-person system of nothing but the involved individuals. Then it frequently happens that some of the behavior, interminably analyzed as the transference or countertransference attitudes and action of the participants, can be understood only as being motivated by the characteristics of the broader organizational context in which the psychotherapy is happening.

Somewhat similarly, personnel directors and executives generally tend to define individual deviant behavior in the organization as personal neurosis instead of raising questions about the possible influence the social structure and organization of the company may be having on the behavior of the people working in it.

Social organizations, by the way in which they are structured, by the processes of action which they provide, and by the products and goals they achieve, may be said to demand certain behavior from the individuals who participate in them or who relate to them. By shifting the perceptual stance, it may also be said that individuals create and structure social institutions and organize their action in order to get to products and goals they need.

Some theorists, therefore, in discussing individual personality and society, stress a modal psychodynamic character—arising out of child-rearing and early socialization actions, goals, values, and appraisals—being projected into and maintaining social institutions. Others place the emphasis on the individual character which the institutions of the society require. Obviously, some balance of this bifurcation of what is at basis a reciprocal relationship will be struck, depending on what argument is to be pursued.

All this is a prelude to the consideration of the "behavioral fit" between individual character and organizational role and position. Upward mobility in the organizational power-responsibility hierarchy may mean the initiation or the intensification of individual strain and consequent difficulties both for the person and for the organization. A dependency-yearning person, for example, with anxiety about independency sufficiently inhibiting to prevent mastery-achieving learning and with characteristic interpersonal strategies of being pleasing, placating, and pliant, may have no conflict with the demands of some roles and positions. If he is promoted, however, he may come progressively into conflict with the assertive, independent behavior demanded by the organization.

This is, I suggest, a paradigm for thinking about the conditions under which a characteristic pattern of behavior may be defined as "illness" at some time and for some circumstances in an individual's life and not others. The situation is somewhat similar for the relations between age, life-style, and social role in the episodic occupancy by an individual of the deviant, sometimes sick, role of being mentally retarded.

Some hypotheses about the correlation of psychosomatic illness, or at least about the correlated psychophysiology, and the personality or organizational adaptations to the stress of upward mobility can be made. The experimental validation is complicated and difficult and, thus far, is ambiguous.

SOCIAL CLASS AND THE INDIVIDUAL

The industrial development of contemporary American society has culminated both in highly differentiated and fluid social-class subsystems and in the urbanization of much of our physical and social space.

The social-class concept is difficult to use precisely in our society, and, admittedly, the behavior of any specific individual may not be described too comprehensively by the cluster of traits and values used to designate a whole class. Nevertheless, there seems little doubt that individual behavior is conditioned significantly by the way in which the class system, and its associated subcultures, structures the child-rearing transactions and subsequently dictates the individual's access to, perception of, and perception by the rest of his community and society.

As is the case with human behavior wherever we encounter it, we have the task of distinguishing between the action to be attributable to the self and that ascribed to the current social roles. Thus, the lower-class behavior of intolerance for frustration delay and for long-range economic and educational goal deferment is frequently explained on a psychodynamic character basis evolving out of early childhood socialization. However, the lower-class adolescent and adult may have to settle for "taking the cash and letting the credit go" mostly because there may be so few available alternatives to taking an unskilled job and quickly foreclosing an educational career already at a dead end. Contrastedly, the adolescent period can be prolonged defiantly as delinquency and crime into early adulthood. This may be done not only out of character but also out of an attempt to forestall and postpone the ultimate commitment to a despairingly narrow range of occupational and social roles.

So, too, as Reissman (1959) has suggested, the conformity behavior in an affluent, consumer-seeking society may not be so much character similarity as a response to an elite-managed range of consumer goals and services.

Social-class correlation with a broad spectrum of deviant behavior, ranging from premature pregnancy, infant mortality and morbidity, mental illness, mental retardation, crime and delinquency, accident readiness, addiction, and longevity, has been validated and supported by a mass of expanding research.

Historically, it is interesting to reflect that in relation to that most sensitive index of a secure and intelligent society—the infant mortality rate—the upper social classes of Europe already had achieved by the middle of the nineteenth century the rate only just now being attained generally in our society.

Hollingshead and Redlich (1958) and their associates, Myers and Roberts (1962), have made psychiatrists and others well aware of the relatively much greater incidence of schizophrenic reactions, chronic brain disease, addiction, and senile impairment among lower-social-class persons. Prison populations, too, are comprised largely of the lower class. A nineteenth-century French writer lumped together proletarians and criminals as the "dangerous classes." Contrastingly, neurotic persons, at least those who take a formal sick role, tend preponderantly to have middle-class backgrounds.

Psychologists and psychiatrists understandably are most interested in how social-class determinants enter into the formative psychodynamics of personality and so make their contribution to the predisposition to subsequent adaptive vulnerability. They may also be concerned about the social and cultural context in which stress, adaptive failure, and disorganization are occurring.

Redlich and Hollingshead chose to emphasize socialization and early child-rearing transactions in the integration of social-class knowledge into the understanding of schizophrenic reactions and neurotic behavior. Another important consideration, particularly with reference to the schizophrenic illness, is the relation of social class to medical resources and to attitudes toward past and contemplated experiences with the sick role.

Under ideal auspices, the sick role is a stress-reducing, helping offer made to a troubled person by the medical institutions of a society. But, as Hollingshead and Redlich documented, the therapeutic resources of the medical culture are differentially distributed according to social class.

It is possible to view many schizophrenic psychotic reactions as the decompensation of a schizophrenic character, which may be produced by one or a combination of several different causative factors. Many such "schizophrenic" personalities of the middle and upper classes when threatened by the symptoms of an impending psychosis may seek effective sick-role support and so recompensate and escape both the diagnosis and the experience of a frank psychotic disorganization. Similar lower-class persons may not seek, for various economic, social, and cultural reasons, the prodromal sick role and so not come to the formal medical helping resource until the psychosis is full-blown and undeniable.

Similarly, the lower-class person with neurotic symptoms may avoid a formal sick-role petition, not only because of the paucity or the threat of psychiatric resources, but also because the enactment of his social roles may not be too painfully incompatible with his symptoms. The lower-class individual may also be more apt to seek nonmedical control and explanation of his distress.

It is salutary to remember that in psychiatry, especially, diagnosis and methods of treatment depend tangibly upon the reasons why patient and psychiatrist have come together in a specific social context, upon what therapeutic process they contemplate with each other, and upon their recipocal social-class perception of each other.

Another interesting aspect of the influence of social class on illness and the adaptational use of the sick role can be seen in the differential mortality between social class I and social class V during the same length of formal sick-role experience with fatal disease. Some studies have shown that during a given period of time elapsing from a patient's formal induction into the sick role because of neoplastic malignancy, only 90 class I persons will die, while 135 class V patients will die. For Southern whites and nonwhites, the ratio is of the order of 115:170. Males and females have a differential favoring less mortality for females in all social classes except the lowest class of unskilled, economically marginal persons in which women may, apparently, tend to defer their entrance into the sick role longer than men.

The effects of social-role discontinuity and transition may also need a social-class referent in order to be understood adequately. For middle-class and, particularly, for upper-middle-class persons, the occupational role provides the major resources for impression management and for status and prestige. The job role, therefore, significantly supports self-esteem and identity. Retirement and the loss of such social support severely challenge the adaptational creativity of both the individual and our whole society.

The concepts of upward and downward social mobility are somewhat conceptually loose and ambiguous. One's social-class position at any one time is defined by a pattern of economic, residential, educational, and other social and cultural factors. Some may be independent variables, and others, dependent variables. Mobility usually means some change in the occupational, standard-of-living, and residential cluster of defining signs. From this point of view, retirement or prolonged or chronic illness may involve downward social mobility.

Upward class mobility, with its associated social-role conflicts between past socialization and present expectations and social situations, will lead to stressful experience to the extent to which neurotic or character problems interfere with learning adequate adaptational behavior. Stress on the upwardly mobile person may become particularly severe when, as in times of economic depression, he is threatened with downward mobility. There exists some suggestive evidence, for example, that the rate of suicide associated with economic reversal among middle-class males is greater for those who, in their lifetime, moved up into the middle class than for those who had always been in that social stratification.

SOCIAL ORGANIZATION OF THE CITY

The architecturally beautiful, well-landscaped, and serene city would not, for those characteristics alone, be the socially adequate and culturally resourceful city. We are quite aware now, after doing a sociological double take and seeing the obvious, that some slums may be organized quite resourcefully for the needs of the people who live there. This does not mean that urban renewal and urban planning are not crucially urgent. It does mean that we must keep aware constantly of the distinction between substance and dynamics. The social structure and functions of the city as a complicated interlocking social system must be abstracted from the physical and architectural definition. Otherwise, as is now too generally the practice, city planning and even the public administration of the "wholeness" of the city become the exclusive captive of the real estate developer, the financier, the engineer, the architect, and, of course, the politician.

Moreover, the human behavior in the city is probably influenced more significantly by the structure and functions of the urban social system than by buildings, parks, or freeways, important for human action though they may be.

An overview of the recent history of the city suggests that the incidence of social pathology in the urban setting may be associated with the rate of population influx. At a high quantity of input, the system is stressed to maintain its essential services. With more refinement, it may be proper to say that the incoming residents find themselves isolated both from the informational interaction with the neighborhood and wider social environment and from access to social resources.

The extent of this "integrative failure" may be related, among other things, to social class. The middle-class migrant may enter an already prepared nexus of potential relationships, especially organized around his occupational position. Utilization of already existing voluntary citizens' associations is already part of the social skill of the middle-class newcomer in contrast to the lower-class person.

The housewife may be more severely stressed by isolation, anonymity, informational deprivation, and resource failure than the occupied husband. Again, the working-class housewife may have fewer opportunities and resources for adapting effectively to her new neighborhood and community than the middle-class wife.

In general it can be said that to the extent to which the environing neighborhood is either intentionally or unintentionally not organized to respond with recognition and positive evaluation, the impersonal, isolating response of the environment may be met by avoidance and counterisolation on the part of the newcomer.

From the standpoint of general ecology, population density may add variables which make social pathology increase faster than in a one-to-one relation with increasing numbers of people. It is the experience generally in metropolitan and regional urban areas that some kinds of social pathology, such as crime, are increasing beyond expectation from population growth.

The highest rates of delinquency, suicide, tuberculosis, nonvehicular accidental deaths, alcoholic deaths, and infant mortality occur generally in the central core of New York City, according to Srole, Langrer, Michael, Opler, and Rennie (1962). This observation has had a long history of substantiation from general public health studies. The highest incidence of sick-role taking for schizophrenia, being highly correlated with low social class, is associated with the central city also.

The population composition which Srole and his colleagues outlined for central New York City is found, with some changes, in most central urban areas. The physical setting of the central residential core is close to the central business district. There is an excess of single people, particularly females, and a high percentage of women in the working force. In many central city areas, there are considerable numbers of working widows or separated mothers with children.

The characteristics of the central city have some relevance to the incidence of old persons being defined as senile and entering psychiatric hospitals or sanitariums. There may be many single dwellings and much personal isolation in the central city. The aged person, lacking supporting relationships and living in relative isolation, may suffer more impairment of ego capacities because of loss of social-role support for ego functions and so become unable to live outside a total sick-role institutionalization.

Comparative studies of the sociology of aging populations show that in Liverpool, England, for example, the incidence of psychiatric hospitalization is very much less than in our cities.

Comprehensive ecological knowledge of the city and intelligent public administration based upon this knowledge must be our adaptive response to what man has wittingly and unwittingly made of the city. A department of social behavior is an urgently needed innovation for urban administration.

REFERENCES

Ackerman, N. W. *The psychodynamics of family life.* New York: Basic Books, 1958.

Bell, N. W., & Vogel, E. F. *A modern introduction to the family.* New York: Free Press, 1960.

Caudill, W. *The psychiatric hospital as a small society.* Cambridge, Mass.: Harvard Univer. Press, 1958.

Clausen, J. A. *Sociology and the field of mental health.* New York: Russell Sage, 1956.

Cumming, J., & Cumming, Elaine. *Ego and milieu.* New York: Atherton Press, 1962.

Duhl, L. J. (Ed.) *The urban condition.* New York: Basic Books, 1963.

Freeman, H. E., Levine, S., & Reeder, L. G. *Handbook of medical sociology.* Englewood Cliffs, N.J.: Prentice-Hall, 1963.

Greenblatt, M., Levinson, D. J., & Williams, R. H. *The patient and the mental hospital.* New York: Free Press, 1957.

Grotjahn, M. *Psychoanalysis and the family neurosis.* New York: Norton, 1960.

Hollingshead, A. B., & Redlich, F. C. *Social class and mental illness: a community study.* New York: Wiley, 1958.

Jaco, E. G. (Ed.) *Patients, physicians, and illness.* New York: Free Press, 1958.

Kirkpatrick, C. *The family as process and institution.* (2nd ed.) New York: Ronald, 1963.

Leighton, A. H., Clausen, J. A., & Wilson, R. N. *Explorations in social psychiatry.* New York: Basic Books, 1957.

Merton, R. K. Bureaucratic structure and personality. *Soc. Forces,* 1940, **18**, 560–568.

Myers, J. K., & Roberts, B. H. *Social class, family dynamics and mental illness.* New York: Wiley, 1962.

Nagel, E. Principles of the theory of probability. In O. Neurath, R. Carnap, & C. Morris (Eds.), *International encyclopedia of unified science.* Vol. I. Chicago: Univer. of Chicago Press, 1955.

Parsons, T. *The social system.* New York: Free Press, 1951.

Parsons, T. An approach to psychological theory in terms of the theory of action. In S. Koch (Ed.), *Psychology: a study of a science.* Vol. 3. New York: McGraw-Hill, 1959.

Parsons, T. General theory in sociology. In R. K. Merton, L. Broom, & L. S. Cottrell, Jr. (Eds.), *Sociology today.* New York: Basic Books, 1959.

Parsons, T., & Shils, E. A. (Eds.) *Toward a general theory of action.* Cambridge, Mass.: Harvard Univer. Press, 1951.

Reissman, L. *Class in American society.* New York: Free Press, 1959.

Rose, A. M. (Ed.) *Mental health and mental disorder: a sociological approach.* New York: Norton, 1955.

Sarbin, T. R. Role theory. In G. Lindzey (Ed.), *Handbook of social psychology.* Reading, Mass.: Addison-Wesley, 1954.

Srole, L., Langner, T. S., Michael, S. T., Opler, M. K., & Rennie, T. A. *Mental health in the metropolis:* the midtown Manhattan study. New York: McGraw-Hill, 1962.

Stanton, A. H., & Schwartz, M. S. *The mental hospital.* New York: Basic Books, 1954.

Wolfgang, M. E., Savitz, L., & Johnston, N. *The sociology of crime and delinquency.* New York: Wiley, 1962.

Wolman, B. B. Explorations in latent schizophrenia. *Amer. J. Psychother.,* 1957, **11**, 560–588.

Wolman, B. B. *Contemporary theories and systems in psychology.* New York: Harper & Row, 1960.

Wolman, B. B. The fathers of schizophrenic patients. *Acta Psychother.,* 1961, **9**, 193–210.

11

Cultural Determinants of Mental Disorders

MARVIN K. OPLER

The clinician, be he psychiatrist, general practitioner, clinical psychologist, or researcher in behavioral sciences, is always caught in the web of his own conditions of existence. Today, in the decade of the sixties, in what has been called the "shrinking" world of new nations arising on all continents, of clashing ideologies and political philosophies, and of rapid technological novelty and dire social necessities, it seems vapid and curiously academic to hope that findings in behavioral sciences will lead the way in coping with enormous social problems. Yet the scientist attracted to human problems, like the artist and humanist in their roughly parallel efforts, holds firm to the belief that it is, after all, the uniquely human element that really matters. We lack a word for the human element in all its diversity. On the one hand, if we allude to man, or even man's fate, as our central concern, we miss the very diversity that art or humanism, in broad strokes, is able to depict and convey. On the other hand, when we describe the differences and variety in any detail, especially that of scientific quantification, we lose the impact of a vaster generality and a more summary statement.

There are those who find a bifurcation of science and art more convenient and comfortable in these circumstances. For them, we suggest that all serious fields of science first define the area to be investigated.

A plan of research in any field of science must depend, in the last analysis, upon the phenomena being investigated. By this we mean that if psychopathological states are the concern of social psychiatry—as they are the concern of any branch of psychiatry—we must begin with the character of such states at least insofar as present-day psychiatry understands them.

It has been argued that "what is normal," or some relativistic concept of normality, lies at the root of such questions since conduct and behavior vary noticeably from one community to another. A few decades ago, R. Benedict stated that the "normals" of one culture might seem to be the "abnormals" of another; that is, their behavior would seem strange in alien cultural contexts. This passing and plausible observation had added to it the astonishing corollary that out-and-out abnormals of one cultural context could "fit in" somewhere else, something which later authors had occasion to test and which they found to be incredibly naïve.

Illness, in short, represents impairments in functioning destructive of any individual's integration in his adaptation to *any* context or in his adjustment to *any* scene. The accurate point, from culture to culture, is not that such deviancy can find a haven elsewhere, but that it is etiologically traceable to *stresses implicit in a social and cultural background.*

In contrast with this last point, psychiatry has its time-honored classifications of mental disorders, which date back to the last century and which have undergone little modification. These categories are based not upon etiology or dynamics, but upon clusters of symptoms. The fact that many such symptoms, such as hallucinations, feelings of depersonalization, etc., are found cross-culturally argues, of course, for the existence of general illness classifications (the schizophrenias, neuroses, and the like). At the same time, the overlapping of many elements such as "asocial withdrawal," "restlessness," and "sexual identification problem" or their incorporation into illness states of varying degrees of seriousness links up very well with what we know of culturally varying types within such single or generic classifications as the schizophrenias. Both sets of facts denote or point to a necessity for new, etiological classifications within the more generalized rubrics.

If this is so, most studies of generic categories such as the schizophrenias, alcoholism, character disorder, etc., have been, statistically speaking, studies of apples and oranges which do not sort out the predominant, descriptive, and independent variables which cut most deeply. Social psychiatry has exactly these etiological interests, for it is concerned *ab initio* with the impact of culture, social environment, and family type upon the developing personality. It can reach this goal only if it maintains a focus upon both facets of the problem: the incidence and the variations of psychiatric disorders. Both of these focuses are important at the same time.

There is a growing faith among social psychiatry personnel that all is well if the study is one of incidence of psychiatric disorders *in general.* In the midtown study in New York (Srole, Langner, Michael, Opler, & Rennie, 1962), where we sought the prevalence, treated and untreated, of mental ills throughout a whole population, even criteria like "impairment in life functioning," together with symptoms, did not describe wholly the degrees of adjustment or adaptation or the measure of seriousness of an illness. A psychiatrist knows this insofar as he knows the history of a case in its total setting. The quality of knowing is preeminently important. There is no good substitute for studies in depth of the individual in settings of family and sociocultural environment; these are the methods used both by anthropology and social psychiatry. In measuring degrees of seriousness of an illness, one requires in psychiatry, as in other branches of medicine, some knowledge of the total case, of prognostic indicators, and of personality assets and liabilities in a known family and community environment—in short, a wide variety of information involving etiology and dynamics.

In health sciences, as in any field of knowledge, man's discovery of himself and of his meaningful social experiences comes late in human history. One need not recall that Galileo's discovery or that of Copernicus, of planetary motion, preceded Lyell's founding of earth sciences. The acceptance of Darwin's discoveries and the acceptance of Freud's follow in that order.

Concerning his conception of health and illness, also, first man had cosmic and astrological theories and later more earthy ones. Next he discovered illnesses internal to himself and, finally, illnesses stemming from his experiences in his own societies and cultures. The sequence was from those things which are most remote to our most immediate and commonplace concerns and interests. Plato's cosmic concept of disease involved disharmony and disproportion of the four universal elements, earth, water, fire, and air. He projected illness far out to an anonymous universe, with which the sick individual was out of step or out of tune. Stoics, like Buddhist thinkers, believed any happiness or suffering was just a matter of individual judgment and urged calm detachment in the face of pain. The Hippocratic version of disease made it more a part of human existence but limited it to its own sphere in the life processes in order to isolate it and study its manifestations. Not till Galen were the brave words spoken: "Man is a whole with his environment." Even later, at the time of the Black Death in the Middle Ages, the Paris medical faculty was speaking of atmospheric causation of these disasters, and the Italians contributed *mala aria* (literally, "bad air") to the miasmic theory of diseases (Ackerknecht, 1955; Riese, 1953).

From cosmic, universal theories to theories of gross, noxious agents in the earthly environment, one goes from fate and fatalism to the long theory advance which places man in his earthly environment. Yet these theories, propounded in a long age of agriculture, stressed man's dependence on nature and on wind and weather. Not till microorganic life was understood better, with Koch and Pasteur, did the pawn-of-nature theories lose ground to theories of internal assault. With Bernard, Cannon, and Freud, the unity or integration of the human being, physiologically and psychologically, was emphasized, and the door was opened to awareness that human values, attitudes, emotions, and habits play a part in the disease process. A sociologist like Parsons could locate the roots of various psychological patterns and influences in human societies and cultural conditions, or a psychiatrist like Kardiner could speak of different kinds of social emotions as being patterned in cultural experience (Galdston, 1954).

It was not, then, until man's protective and reactive functions were revealed by Cannon and Freud that the control and prevention of disease were extended beyond the germ theory or beyond those illnesses having a specific, isolated pathogenic agent. Halliday, in his book *Psychosocial Medicine* (1954), has therefore defined illness generally as reactions or responses of an individual to those forces encountered as he functions and develops in time.

However, with humans, we are all too prone to assume that these responses are the isolated reactions of individual organisms. As an anthropologist working in the interdisciplinary field of social psychiatry, we can report that individual reactions are mediated by a whole system of values, attitudes, and behaviors that are not exclusively possessed by any person in any culture. We may even go further, since cross-cultural studies indicate that even such ills as heart disease, hardening of the arteries, and the human organism's reactions to amoebic infection are anything but inevitable and invariable organ reactions. F. S. C. Northrop, of Yale, reports on a Latin-American country which has a pleasant lack of our efficient conceptions of time and where there is also a pleasant rarity of heart disease and sclerotic conditions. In Burma and Thailand, American health teams have to be eternally vigilant about water supply and about certain amoebic conditions, but the village populations, even down to the smallest children, seem immune to many of these conditions either through natural selection over time or through the immunity built up from the earliest years. On a broad, worldwide basis, the physical anthropologists Coon, Garn, and Birdsell (1950) have demonstrated how the Eskimo pyknik, or barrel-shaped, build—even down to small noses and fat cheeks—is ideal for circumpolar survival, whereas the tall, asthenic build of Sahara dwellers is better adapted to the heat they endure. Alfred Hess's studies of diet-deficiency diseases and of vitamins could be adduced for a modern urban example. Certainly the individual and his environment are not mutually exclusive systems.

While most organisms react directly to inborn potentials and outer stimuli, humans are both more sensitive reacting systems and more complex self-regulating systems. One of Cannon's most interesting papers, which appeared in the *American Anthropologist*, was called "Voodoo Death." It discusses schizophrenic fear reactions in different cultures resulting from the breaking of social-group taboos. The guilty individuals, impressed by the taboos and their magical death sanctions, literally wasted away and died. Any psychiatrist can think of similar modern occasions where unmet and extravagant emotional needs of one or more parents were fulfilled at the expense of a child. Lindner's *Rebel without a Cause* deals with such a case, though a less serious one, and it is significant that the author states in the first two pages that psychopathic behavior is relative to, or stems from, the culture in which it develops. The illness of Harold, his patient, is really measurable by the prevailing ethic and morality. Any prevailing psychopathology is relative to the culture in which it flourishes (Cannon, 1942; Lindner, 1944; Opler, 1956).

In a book published recently by the Russell Sage Foundation on community reactions to public health programs, John Cassel reports the difficulties of promoting milk and egg consumption and restriction of grazing lands among South African Zulus, to whom cattle are important in ancestor worship and are connected with ideas of proper conduct. The same difficulties were encountered among Navajos in the American Southwest because of emphases on the desirability of a mobile existence and the importance of sheep as tangible property. In the same book, the Cummings reveal social attitudes and beliefs about mental illness in a Canadian community which, no more rationally than Zulus or Navajos, "solved" the problem by putting the mentally ill in a class apart and keeping them, albeit most guiltily, in isolation. Lyle Saunders and Julian Samora discuss the failure of a cooperative health association plan in rural Colorado among 7,000 Spanish Americans who felt that it was a violation of established community leadership practices and individualized methods of dealing with sickness, which they preferred to the less personalized, less intimate system (Paul, 1955). In a more optimistic vein, we recall the tremendous success of the Japanese American community hospitals set up in relocation centers and ministering to health needs of barracks towns of 10,000 or more people, where hospital committees developed almost spontaneously to ensure a central focus of insecurity—their health—in a totally insecure population (Spicer, Opler, Luomala, & Hansen, 1946). Here ancient and folk methods of healing were revived, along with the most efficient hospital organization, in a general drive toward good health in a community where other forms of security—economic, social, and political—had virtually disappeared (Opler, 1950).

There can be no doubt, however, that all peoples value health, though their conceptions of what good health is and how it can be obtained vary with each ethnic group. Action programs aimed at health improvement or illness prevention must start with existing health practices and behavior and the functions these perform for those who practice them. A knowledge of a community and its people is as important to a successful public health program as a knowledge of epidemiology and medicine.

In 1945, Henry B. Richardson, in his book *Patients Have Families,* reported the results of two years of study of the concept of the family as a unit of practice. In this study, the value of approaching an entire family through the concerted efforts of a team representing medicine, psychiatry, nursing, and social work is assessed. The evidence is convincing that such an approach leads to a more accurate diagnosis, a better chance for successful treatment, less pressure for repeated clinical visits, and faster progress toward medically sound solutions. Unfortunately, such a team is complicated in structure and is most readily available in institutional settings such as hospitals. Even so, education of such teams requires knowledge of the cultures in a community. In 1940, Baumgartner suggested that an understanding of cultural backgrounds of various ethnic groups provided a shortcut to more effective public health service, and Saunders illustrates the importance of providing medical advice in a way that is culturally acceptable in the community for which it is intended.

In one Italian case[1] involving a urinary disturbance in a small girl, the public health nurse reported the mother's refusal to have the child referred to the hospital from a child health station. After months, the mother reluctantly took the child to a neighborhood physician, avoided the clinic, and was finally reluctant to admit even the nurse on routine call. Besides taking the child to the physician's office for a general, nonrevealing checkup, she prayed for strength "to give" the little girl. Many cultural beliefs are indicated here. Southern Italians, especially in the first generation, have an almost reverent attitude toward anything relating to the reproductive system. Girls are to be especially protected and shielded or, as P. Williams indicates, chaperoned by older male and female relatives during the nubile years and safeguarded by mothers and older sisters when younger. Moreover, in later matchmaking, such things as venereal infection or mental disorder and tuberculosis are literally blots on the family escutcheon. In this case, the mother's menstrual periods were scant and irregular, which in this same folk system means low fertility and impaired femininity. In some areas of southern Italy, feminine boasting will be of exactly such matters, and women with scant flow wash their napkins with those of better-favored women to increase fertility. Joffe reports the alacrity with which such information is imparted to the young and the early age at which it is included in the learning of sex role, or the insignia that are worn by women at such times. In this case, we can well imagine the shame and worry of the mother and the consequent discomfort and guilt of the child.

Earl L. Koos, working with the Committee on Food Habits investigating the place of nutrition in social patterns of various nationality groups, noted that the Irish, even over generations, tend to adhere to a pork-potato-cabbage or beefsteak diet; Czechs, to a heavy meat and potato-dumpling plate; Italians, to a pasta, red vegetables, and tomato or meat-sauce diet; and so on down the list. Italian Americans tell us that one of the worst aspects of going to a

[1] Much of this material has been drawn from fieldwork in New York and compares favorably with Williams, 1938.

hospital is having little Italian food. Again, the Italians from southern, rural sections of Italy or from Sicily lay great stress on producing and raising strong children. Red vegetables "make blood." Bread and pasta are "natural foods." Fresh vegetables rather than canned ones maintain the health and vigor essential for men and women. Among the Japanese, who prize vigor and potency, particularly for males, we recall the necessity of having pickled daikon (a phallic-shaped root vegetable) accompany practically every meal for about the same psychosexual reasons that rural Italians like red, "blood-producing" foods or rural Puerto Ricans see a reflection on a husband's potency if his wife fails to have children. The historical roots of these marginal farm economies favor the having of children to care for one in old age, and respect patterns toward parents are jealously guarded in each case. Each geographically separated culture—Japanese, Italian, and Spanish–Puerto Rican—tends also to favor male children and male virtues and values since the son, who once tilled or planted in his turn, carries on the family name and fortune.

Besides these similarities in diverse ethnic groups, there are also differences. One is struck by the restraint, sobriety, and dignity of most Japanese social occasions, and by the social life and emotional expression among southern Italians pitched at a high intensity. Social life in southern Italy centers in small towns that serve as the meeting ground of the surrounding locale. Robert Lowie, in his *Social Organization,* remarks on the *campanilismo,* or community feeling, which unites the persons who can hear the bells of a common church building. The central piazza is usually flanked by this church, by a school or monastery, and often by an opera house. According to Williams, no door is closed except at mealtimes. Children rise and retire with their elders, and much of the social life for the young and old alike is carried on out-of-doors, and promotes an air of intimacy and frank expression "from the heart" that few other people possess in the same degree. The scarcity of water makes the village fountain a pleasant place for general gatherings, and strong ties between the families of a village often persist long after the inhabitants have migrated to a foreign country. Indeed, marriages usually take place between inhabitants of the same village or locale, or among *paisani.* Because of dialect differences in larger districts, settlement and intermarriage patterns continue this sense of intimacy and local autonomy in this country. Here, people from one locale might settle in one street, and across the street or on another live those from a different district. While second-generation districts, such as we have been studying in New York, vary this pattern to one of relatives or of mothers and daughters living contiguously, the sense of intimacy, the willingness to express emotions directly, high rates of marriage, and a sharp sexual division of labor and of social functions will mark this community more than others. The family, including unmarried sons and daughters, collateral relatives, and sometimes even godparents, is more in evidence and wider in affective extent than the narrow, nuclear family of parents and children found among English or German descendants.

While in Irish families, a mother, grandmother, or aunt is usually central in affairs pertaining to children and to home, the Italian biological family recognizes the father as breadwinner and head, and the mother as the delegated authority, closer to the children and their problems and managing the home scene on a budget provided by the husband and older unmarried sons. While this devotion to male needs and the expectation of marrying early and producing large families have varied in this country, there is still more emphasis on sexual differentiation in family or social roles, more male dominance and aggressiveness, and more family-centered living than characterize Irish families and individuals. Studies of pain-threshold differentials have stressed the low tolerance standards of Italians, for whom bodily functions are so important and body image so clear that stoical equanimity is out of the question. Any visitor to a postoperative recovery room can note this, particularly where female patients are involved. Obstetricians have contrasted again and again the variance between the young Japanese American mother, who views birth almost as a battle where pain cannot be conceded to, and the young Italian American girl, who may be more relaxed about the whole process and more openly exultant about feminine functions but who does not believe that the least part of male fortitude is necessary for women where pain might be involved.

In southern Italy or Japan, marriages were arranged by parents, often with the good offices of a go-between who minimized interfamily friction and embarrassment. The prospective couple, in Italy, saw each other at family Sunday conclaves and dinners, or the boy, if impetuous, conversed through the doorway with the whole protective armament of the girl's family in solemn array. In the United States, where family honor is less a matter of local gossip, these customs wear away, but families maintain a lively interest especially in a daughter's or younger sister's marriage. While children of the second and third generation do not arrange births at home, with forty-day house confinements, as in Italy, and with midwives, the interest in prenatal care, hospital lying-in procedures, and large babies may appear too lively and irksome to some clinics. Attempts to inculcate the necessity of a protein diet instead of a high-calorie pasta diet for expectant mothers meet opposition from a grandparental generation, which in many instances becomes busy with the cooking at this time. Oils; "natural foods," like pasta, made from grain; and the blood-making vegetables can be bound up, in ideology, with reminiscences that heavy people are vigorous and that thin people are ill-tempered or, if female and elderly, are witches with the "evil eye." Happily in this case, higher-protein pastas are now manufactured, not exactly for the purpose of reducing intergeneration conflicts—though they do.

As we have suggested, the birth of a malformed or stillborn child is not only a family tragedy but also a sign of physical and sexual weakness and a personal disgrace for the parents concerned. Besides large babies, which Japanese or Irish would consider no great gain and perhaps a physical hazard, males are preferred to females, a matter which is left up to personal preference in Irish families. As with Puerto Ricans, the Italians traditionally allowed a double standard to prevail in sexual conduct, enjoining chastity and submissiveness upon the subordinate distaff side and at the same time stressing male escapades and impulsivity. While, therefore, southern Italian matrons wore red kerchiefs to announce the fact of menstruation, menstruating virgins were expected to hide the fact from men, except for first menses, which marked overnight maturation with assumption of women's dress and household occupations. With the Irish, the event frequently went unnoticed even among women of the family, and only sacramental events like marriage marked matronhood in a household group. Indeed, only the birth of a child marked the true assumption of the status of matron, or mother, which was a lifelong status position of enhanced authority and control in the Irish home. Thus, first-generation Italians have many folk beliefs and particular health practices surrounding menstruation, whereas the Irish have none. Since such women are vulnerable in colder seasons, as little children are, they are bundled, like infants, to prevent a chill. On the other hand, a godmother's help is needed at such times, since menstruation injures or is antithetical to babies. It can even cause mares to abort or "cure" skin growths and warts.

Although pain or hypochondriac ailments are ventilated, especially by Italian women, diseases which are conceived of as being incurable are family disgraces, hindering children's marriages, and are therefore hidden. Venereal disease carries the same social sanctions of shame rather than personalized guilt. The same fears of family "weakness" or vulnerability can be found among rural Japanese families, both peoples adding mental illness to the list of marriage deterrents. Among Irish, personalized guilt as well as publicized shame sanctions attach to the very areas, for men and for women, that Italian men or Puerto Rican men consider proper extramarital escapades. The exchanging of gifts, the donating of money to a family in need (*la pieta*), and the bestowing of help upon a family which has suffered a death (*il consolo*) further illustrate the solidarity of the extended family group and the close network of community relationships.

In viewing mental illnesses, both in extent and typology, psychiatrists trained in one tradition or working in a single unicultural group must have recourse to a terminology which developed largely in a Western European setting in the late nineteenth century. Our alternative is to describe laboriously the different psychodynamic profiles encountered in our studies. This we have done in two books (Opler, 1956; Opler, 1959); in various papers on schizophrenias among Italians, Irish, Puerto Ricans, and Japanese; and in papers on other disorders. Our friends in psychiatry have often themselves had cross-cultural experiences in their own life histories, or their practices have provided them with such perspectives if the literature and their training did not. Our friends among practitioners, impressed as we are by the range within an assumed entity, like the schizophrenias, or the constant encounter with admixtures, for example, schizophrenia with obsessive compulsive traits, tell us that really, for them, schizophrenia means mainly "very sick," "out of contact with reality," or, finally, "a flooding of impulse from primary processes." We know what we mean, each of us, and we *do* communicate after a fashion. But there is no scientific precision or consensus built initially into the science. Ripe clinical experience fills the gap. But pity the patient with the novice!

Obviously, questions of diagnosis, prognosis, and therapy are connected queries which apply to the tremendous numbers of people to whom we alluded at the outset. If half of all illnesses treated in United States hospitals are mental illnesses, if one out of two in midtown Manhattan shows some disability, and if rural and cross-cultural studies extend the problem even beyond our shores, then, to begin with, psychiatry is woefully short of trained personnel, "the ripe clinical experience" of which we spoke, and the institutional modalities or mechanisms for this enormous task. Rennie wrote years ago of this problem in an article entitled "Wanted: 10,000 Psychiatrists." That is one way to allude to the personnel shortage. But another way is to broaden the plea for a larger number of interdisciplinary social psychiatrists able to cope with cultural and class variations in what is today at last recognized as a much vaster problem in "transcultural psychiatry." Another method is to broaden the scope of such research in sociocultural backgrounds of mental illnesses. Since 1955, social psychiatry has had its journal, the *International Journal of Social Psychiatry*. Last but not least is the problem of new diagnostic categories.

Lest this seem iconoclastic or threatening to those inured to present terminology, it can be said that psychiatry requires *two,* not one, systematic attempts at diagnosis, and for one of these purposes the present system is good enough. This present system we shall call our "descriptive and classificatory system." It was largely inherited from the late nineteenth century, from such pioneers as Kraepelin and others. One often thinks of this system as heavily indebted to German, Swiss, and French sources with additional descriptions coming later, for instance, Bleuler's generalized descriptions of common aspects in various schizophrenias. Such systems of nomenclature and their accompanying descriptions are still useful in teaching, in designating clusters of symptoms, or, in short, in classifying. The revised nomenclatures of the Veterans Administration and of the American Psychiatric Association would serve as examples. One task of science, especially in early stages, is to describe and classify. This is, of course, an initial stage in teaching and training as well. Biology had its Linnaeus.

But most sciences go through a descriptive, classificatory stage to a second phase. Biology also had its Darwin. While no one decries the work of a Linnaeus, a Linnaeus is not a Darwin. *Descriptive-classificatory* procedures do indeed help in training a novice, and there is no doubt that they help to populate the world of psychopathology with some rather rigid models of what really goes on. But most important, a description is not a dynamic process of analysis, nor is it a dynamic analysis of process. One can learn terminology about symptom clusters, something which has gone on in European psychiatry for decades, and one will continue to describe rather than analyze. As a matter of fact, descriptive classifications, by their varied compartmentalizations, force one to describe further. This tends to resolve into further descriptions of subparts, the symptom clusters themselves, and down to the symptoms. An environmentalist, such as B. F. Skinner, of Harvard, in psychology, will castigate psychiatry generally for overconcern about "mere symptoms." Without adopting his somewhat mechanistic notions of learning and machine reorientation (called "reinforcement"), one knows what he means. In clinic conference, the novice schooled in such methods is more comfortable when discussing something as "concrete" as symptom or when labeling the specimens using something as "learned" and time-honored as Kraepelinian terminology, APA nomenclature, or the VA system. While we are not in the least opposed to careful description or designation of clusters of symptoms in rough-and-ready fashion, we feel that the novice mistakes this for an analysis of process in the case or for the exploration of dynamics. At least, he should know what he is doing, and he is only roughly describing and classifying.

Perhaps this is hard on the novice. There are other, well-seasoned examples. The most illustrious efforts at description, classification, and renaming are those of Adolf Meyer, in the twentieth century. It is not too early to sense that Meyer will be remembered for emphases on biosocial integration, total personality assessments, and the influence of environmental factors. These were challenging when they occurred, and even today they enjoy a certain influence. But already the elaborate renaming and classification in strange Greek terminology is almost forgotten, and his new manuals of classified descriptions strike one as being old before their time, as being wasted effort. This is all the more true because, we felt, even when they first appeared and before they became dust-covered tomes, new analytic demonstrations of general process were being successfully promulgated by the Freudians and neo-Freudians, and soon other interests in general processes were multiplying in the interpersonal theories of Sullivan, in the first cultural theories of Horney, and among the dissidents like Rado, Kardiner, and the European phenomenologists. These more analytic and dynamic views all showed more interest in process.

We ourselves propose a *second analytic-dynamic system when referring to diagnostic estimates that have primarily an etiological interest in process.* We imply that historically the earlier descriptive and classificatory system is typically the first product in the history of any science. A Linnaeus usually precedes a Darwin. A Kraepelinian (Meyerian) kind of classification usually brings some order out of chaos and paves the way for more analytically inclined attempts such as those of Freud, the neo-Freudians, or those interested in social psychiatry.

The first kind of system, the descriptive-classificatory system, is designed to answer the question of "what." It is naturally preoccupied with what the symptoms are, which systems of symptoms go together, and what the prognosis may be. Because it devolves attention ultimately upon parts of behavior, and hence parts of people, it is atomistic in tendency. It was not until recently that Hoch and Polatin saw a necessity to break through rigid boundaries and add pseudoneurotic schizophrenia to the nomenclature. Franz Alexander worked on character disorder similarly. Because classifications have compartments and a certain rigid neatness about them, there is a further tendency toward premature closure, codifications, and presumptions about a kind of prognosis always going with a kind of diagnosis. Rennie noted in a study at Henry Phipps Psychiatric Clinic that neuroses often mature into psychoses. And conversely, clinical experience often shows some psychoneuroses more recalcitrant in treatment than many psychoses. In *Culture, Psychiatry and Human Values* (Opler, 1956), after surveying the cross-cultural materials from nonliterate cultures, we turned away completely from the notion that schizophrenias occurred only in the familiar Western European forms. Some in so-called "primitive" cultures, with echolalia, echopraxia, disorientation, confusion, hallucinatory experiences, and so forth, were nuclear forms often surprisingly amenable to spontaneous remission. There were, for example, no paranoid defenses in depth. Affectivity levels might be high. Delusions might be only fleeting and never fixed or highly systematized. This disagrees fundamentally and completely with P. Benedict and I. Jacks, who have presented similar materials in the journal *Psychiatry* and who lose the sense of cross-cultural variance, of remarkable differences in schizophrenias, by referring to an overgeneralized classification system. Again, to repeat, our overgeneralized categories of the late nineteenth century do not analyze, do not explore dynamics, and only roughly describe. Consequently, they touch upon problems of integration and disintegration only lightly, never reaching the level of analysis of dynamic process.

Preoccupation with the question of "what" in psychiatry does in no way yield answers as to "how" and "why." The latter are etiological questions which belong in an analytic, dynamic system interested in process. One of the values of Sullivan's scheme, for instance, is that it showed interest in the interpersonal *process.* There is no question that a Freudian system dealing with unconscious, preconscious, and conscious interrelations likewise illuminates what is going on inside people. But we should like to emphasize that both these systems, no matter how helpful in illuminating *process,* tend to ignore the preexisting classifications in favor of the uniqueness of individual experience. Freud's altogether remarkable illumination of intrapsychic dynamics, truly a work of genius, was just that. Sullivan's interpersonal process had reference to affective response wholly within the individual, who indeed thought, felt, hoped, or despaired accordingly. True, he sometimes spoke of a psychiatry "of peoples," and yet no such method was produced. The existentialists, similarly, inveigh against overweighting unconscious dynamisms, and some exhort us to forget unconscious motivations entirely while entering into the system of current meanings for the patient. But the hallmark of all these methods, despite their differences, feuds, and special exhortations, is at base a very rugged individualism which agrees quite well with a disillusionment with bankrupt classifications of the nineteenth century, a growing interest in process in the twentieth century, and a curious desire to generalize about man through individual examples.

Of course, one cannot generalize about man through individual examples. The generalizing science within psychiatry is *social* psychiatry by its very definition. Social psychiatry is interested in meanings and significances of conduct for the individual, as we pointed out long ago. But like other behavioral sciences, and we are thinking of current anthropology, psychology, and sociology, social psychiatry has no confidence in building a generalizing science upon such slender reeds as individualized meanings. It is willing to commend and to imitate, if you will, the existentialist interest in *meanings* in assessments of individual cases. However, we find just as much usefulness in the Freudian or neo-Freudian drive to discover fundamental panhuman *processes*. The Freudian movement, the Sullivan interest in interpersonal process, and even Horney's stress on the "culture" of our time are each eminently correct in direction in that they stress process; yet they fail to examine specific cultures and groups systematically.

This, we think, has been the tragedy of psychiatric theory and method. Modern psychiatry for decades described and classified. It held jealously to fatalistic theories about genetics, and in some circles and for some illnesses it still does, although complete genetic studies throughout populations are conspicuous by their absence. It maintained a studied air of therapeutic nihilism. Each new movement interested in process, Freudian or neo-Freudian, has had to develop against odds, and some have in turn developed their own air of "cloak-and-dagger strategic service" cultism.

Especially tragic has been the fact that the very movements most concerned with process and faced with organicist and nihilistic emphases elsewhere in the profession have tended to develop final theories and formulations about man generically far too fast and with too many presumptions about generic man. Social psychiatry is interested, to be sure, in the behavioral study of man from biological, psychological, and sociocultural aspects; and it is these very factors which show historical and cultural variation. To study an illness in an individual or a group, one must investigate the group culture, the family and social life, and the larger networks of relationship which impinge upon the individual. Modern studies in social psychiatry deal with such complex variables as typology of illness, diagnosis, treatment, and outcome as elements in both a social and psychological process. It becomes necessary in this kind of research design to include an equal emphasis on the types of persons—both patients and therapists—who operate in a given social and cultural milieu. For this reason, social psychiatry lays claim to being a more complete research method.

In *Culture, Psychiatry and Human Values*, we dealt with these broad questions of illness and therapy, concluding that no fact about human conduct, normal or disturbed, "well" or "ill," could achieve a final significance without reference to an individual's culture, values, and social status. The study of Redlich and Hollingshead in New Haven has indicated how social status and cultural background influence the tendency of psychiatrists to administer certain kinds of treatment to various groupings in the class structure. Types of diagnoses are also significantly connected with class structure and ethnic-group membership. Finally, the prevalence of treated mental illness is also related to groupings in the social system. This study deals with backgrounds determinative of the diagnosis, kind of treatment, and outcome of cases that come into therapy. In an essay entitled "Epidemiological Studies of Mental Illness" (Opler, 1958) for the Walter Reed Army Institute of Research *Symposium on Preventive and Social Psychiatry*, it is indicated that our New York City studies were interested in an epidemiology of mental illness throughout a whole series of populations—not just those in treatment, but the vast numbers of those untreated as well, considered together. In *Culture and Mental Health* (Opler, 1959), we have been joined by almost two dozen authors in social psychiatry, each producing studies on mental health and illness from various continents and island areas of the world. Not only have cultural and social status played a part in the treatment process, but they strongly influence etiology, dynamics, and the epidemiology of disorders around the world.

In this light, social psychiatry formulates problems of this type which reach beyond the individual patient to social and cultural groups. While the older diagnostic classifications roughly describe, the newer formulations relate to the processes which are really important in psychiatric illnesses, namely, the etiology and dynamics of a more specific illness process in a given group. When social psychiatry goes in the latter direction of types of illnesses within the older groupings, such as the schizophrenias, it is obviously going beyond categories of symptoms in nomenclature derived from Kraepelin and others to social and cultural roots and is redefining dynamic profiles of illness structure and functioning. When this happens, one is pointing beyond static notions of therapy and prognostic estimates as fixed formulas to a more creative approach including social variables that structure the entire communicative process and milieu. Thus, social psychiatry has been thought of not only as a process of redefining illness entities but also as a new adventure in therapy with broader goals in the community than hitherto. Man is a social and cultural animal, and that first and foremost. Whether people function in hospitals or outside, they are functioning in social situations which are structured and predictable. Human responses cannot be adjusted to diagnostic formulations which have already changed both conceptually and in the light of increased clinical and cultural knowledge. Neither are human responses reducible to objectively defined stimuli. Even diagnoses historically have varied with social and cultural factors, as a cross-cultural survey of psychiatry would easily show. As to the symptoms themselves, their actual coloring, affective force, and use in the psychic economy have always arisen from experience in a social and cultural milieu or background. Social psychiatry must therefore continue its more precise definition of these social and cultural variables and their effects on diverse illness forms. This means not only clearer social and cultural classifications of patients, rather than atomistic listings of the symptoms, but also more attention to what these differentiations mean in the etiology and dynamics of that half of all illness known as "psychiatric disorder."

REFERENCES

Ackerknecht, E. H. *A short history of medicine.* New York: Ronald, 1955.

Cannon, W. B. Voodoo death. *Amer. Anthropologist,* 1942.

Coon, C. S., Garn, S. M., & Birdsell, J. B. *Races.* Springfield, Ill.: Charles C Thomas, 1950.

Galdston, I. (Ed.) *Beyond the germ theory.* New York: New York Academy of Medicine, 1954.

Gilbert, G. W. Toward a comprehensive bisocial theory of human behavior. *Int. J. soc. Psychiat.,* 1963, 9, 85–93.

Halliday, J. L. *Psychosocial medicine.* New York: Norton, 1948.

Hollingshead, A. B., & Redlich, F. C. *Social class and mental illness.* New York: Wiley, 1958.

Lindner, R. *Rebel without a cause.* New York: Grune & Stratton, 1944.

Opler, M. K. Japanese folk beliefs and practices. *J. Amer. Folklore,* 1950, 385–397.

Opler, M. K. *Culture, psychiatry and human values.* Springfield, Ill.: Charles C Thomas, 1956. (See especially chapters on epidemiology and etiology of disorders.)

Opler, M. K. Epidemiological studies of mental illness. In *Symposium on preventive and social psychiatry.* Washington, D.C.: Walter Reed Army Institute of Research, 1958.

Opler, M. K. (Ed.) *Culture and mental health.* New York: Macmillan, 1959.

Paul, B. D. (Ed.) *Health, culture and community.* New York: Russell Sage, 1955.

Riese, W. *The conception of disease.* New York: Philosophical Library, 1953.

Spicer, E. H., Opler, M. K., Luomala, K., & Hansen, A. T. *Impounded people.* Washington, D.C.: Government Printing Office, 1946.

Srole, L., Langner, T. S., Michael, S. T., Opler, M. K., & Rennie, T. A. *Mental health in the metropolis: the midtown Manhattan study.* New York: McGraw-Hill, 1962.

Williams, Phyllis H. *South Italian folkways in Europe and America.* New Haven, Conn.: Yale Univer. Press, 1938.

12

Learning Theory and Behavior Therapy

O. HOBART MOWRER

Although a review article or handbook chapter is not the place to advance an original idea or argument, it always lends interest and vitality to such a work if an organizing principle can be found with at least some semblance of theoretical novelty. Add to this the fact that in the area of our immediate concern excellent summaries and compendia are already available (see, for example, Bandura, 1961; Eysenck, 1960), and we have reason for searching with special diligence for such a device. Therefore, without further apology, a thesis will be set forth which will not only help to order the relevant empirical data but will also challenge the various interpretations which have previously been advanced to account for them.

I

The view most often espoused by those who have approached the domain of psychopathology from the standpoint of learning theory has been to the effect that here the basic trouble lies in some anomaly in the *emotional* (or "attitudinal") life of the afflicted individual and that any irregularities in overt behavior are merely symptomatic of the underlying affective problem. More specifically, the assumption has been that psychoneurotic individuals have suffered from "traumatic" emotional malconditioning of some sort, as a result of physical accidents or overly harsh, perverse training at the hands of others. Irrational or irresponsible behavior on the part of the victims of such unfortunate treatment is thus merely an expression of the irrationality and abnormality of their emotions. This, then, is supposed to be the essence of "neurosis" and "mental illness" in the most pervasive sense of these terms.

Despite the great insight and practical control which this (essentially Freudian) way of conceptualizing the problem is supposed to have provided, sober appraisal of our situation suggests that, in point of fact, it has contributed very little to the more effective management and prevention of psychopathology. A plausible case can, indeed, be made for the surmise that this theoretical position merely reinforces a perception which the neurotic is himself almost certain to have. He will be quick to tell you how bad he feels, and he will not be averse to the suggestion that others are somehow responsible for his present unfortunate state and thus ought to treat him in such a way as to make him "feel better." Also, he will readily fall in with the idea, which flows naturally from the foregoing assumptions, that he himself is *not responsible* for what he now does. This type of theory—to the effect that so-called "neurotic" individuals act strangely (compulsively, irrationally) because their emotions have been perverted and warped—is thus part and parcel of the "disease" itself and is by no means its cure. Increasingly we are getting reports of iatrogenic (treatment-exacerbated) personality disorder. And it also appears that great social institutions (viz., home, church, school, courts) which have assimilated this philosophy are afflicted by a mysterious, creeping paralysis and loss of confidence—to such a degree that our whole society is commonly said to be sick (LaPiere, 1959; Schoeck & Wiggins, 1962).

Where, then, can we find a sounder and more effective way of thinking about this type of problem? On the basis of various clinical reports and experimental studies (see, for example, Mowrer, 1964), the induction is emerging that so-called "emotional" disturbance, discomfort, or "dis-ease" is the lawful, well-earned, and eminently normal result of abnormal (in the sense of socially and morally deviant) behavior—and not the other way around, as has been so often assumed. Once an individual becomes fearful and guilt-ridden because of his misconduct, it is true that he may then develop "symptoms" which reflect his inner malaise and apprehension. But this is not to say that his emotional responses are the original source of his difficulty. It will instead be our thesis that in psychopathology the primary, basic cause is deliberate, choice-mediated behavior of a socially disapproved, reprehensible nature which *results* in emotional disturbance and insecurity (because the individual is now objectively guilty, socially vulnerable, and, if caught, subject to criticism or punishment). The symptoms which then ensue represent ways in which the individual is trying to defend himself against and *hide* his disturbing and suspicion-arousing emotions (of moral fear and guilt). Thus, a deliberate misdeed is the original, or primary, cause, and emotional disturbance follows, which may then produce symptoms of a more or less behavioral type. That is, we assume that emotional disturbance is the second in a three-link chain of consequences, rather than the original, or first, link in a two-link chain.

To be more precise, we should perhaps put the matter a little differently and say that *both* approaches imply three links in the "chain of circumstances" which eventuates in the more manifest aspects of what we call "psychopathology." If one wishes, one can easily think of emotional disturbance (or disturbing emotions) as the second link in both frames of reference; but in the one case the first link would be the foolish, unthinking, harmful behavior of others, whereas in the other case the first link is the foolish, unthinking, harmful behavior of the individual himself. This is the distinction which is behind the suggestion of certain contemporary writers to the effect that in neurosis and functional psychosis the element of *personal responsibility* is probably far greater than has been commonly supposed; and if this is true, there is also a corresponding opportunity—indeed, obligation—for the individual to help himself if he has fallen into a pathological state.

To epitomize the matter still further, one might take the position that it is not the emotions that are being experienced by patients in mental hospitals which constitute their "craziness." Given their personal history and life-style, the presumption is that (in the absence of gross neurological lesions, toxic states, and hormonal disorders) their emotions (however turbulent and painful) are, in an ultimate sense, reasonable and proper. What *is* crazy is the behavior which these persons have previously engaged in—and the ways in which they (and, very likely, their therapists) are now trying to deal with the resulting emotional "dis-ease."

This perception of the situation is in direct contrast to the still widespread view that the essence of mental illness is the inappropriate, disproportional, and irrational nature of the individual's emotional reactions. Our assumption is rather that it is the individual's behavior, both originally and now symptomatically, that has been "off" and that his emotions have been, and are now, in no way unsuited to the circumstances, when the latter are fully known and understood. And by this route we arrive at the view that the therapy of choice is necessarily *behavior therapy*, in the sense of (1) changing the behavior which originally got the individual into trouble and (2) changing what the individual has since been trying to do about his trouble or "dis-ease," i.e., his symptoms. This approach is manifestly different from the view that a neurotic's trouble is the fact that he is *having* trouble, emotional trouble (troubling emotions), a view which still dominates large segments of both psychiatric and psychological precept and practice. Our assumption is that the capacity to be troubled in this way is the hallmark of the individual's basic humanity and is potentially his salvation and deliverance (see Figure 1).

Our view, in short, is that the "sick" individual's problem lies not in how he is feeling

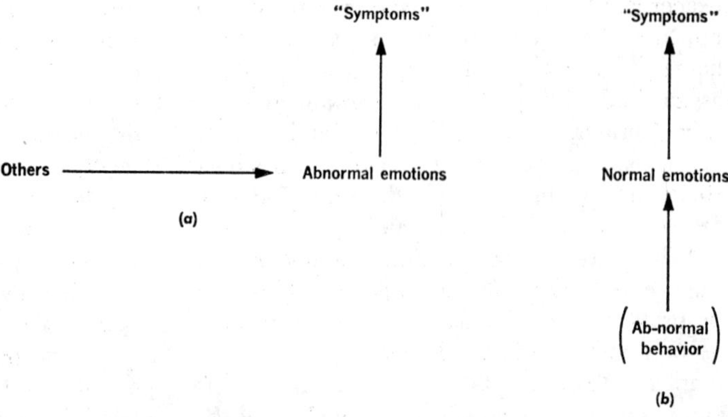

Figure. 1. Schematic representation of two conceptions of psychopathology. (*a*) According to the more conventional of these, the essence of neurosis or mental illness is an *emotional* disturbance or disorder which has been produced by inappropriate, irrational behavior on the part of others (parents, teachers, husbands, wives, employers, etc.). (*b*) The alternative position holds that the crux of the problem is not emotional but *behavioral.* Given the deviant, duplicitous life style of the individual himself, his emotional suffering (insecurity, anxiety, inferiority feelings, guilt) is seen as thoroughly natural, appropriate, normal. The abnormality in the situation consists of the individual's secret deviations from the norms, standards, rules, "values" of his reference group. In the first conceptual scheme, one's own behavior is never seen as "causal," only the behavior of others (which, if one is consistent, must in turn have been caused by others, and so on, to an infinite regress). And whatever the individual does, if it is in any way objectionable or "bad," is interpreted as "merely symptomatic of deep, underlying emotional problems." Thus, attention is focused almost exclusively upon emotions, with little or no responsibility accruing to the individual. In the other frame of reference, so-called "symptoms" (see Figure 2) arise from emotional discomfort which is appropriate and well "earned," considering what the individual has done in the past, is still doing, and is *hiding* (a fact denoted by the parentheses). Attention is thus shifted from emotions to conduct and from what others have done to one's own actions.

but in what he has been, and perhaps still is, doing. And we further assume that no therapy can be ultimately successful which involves a direct attack (by chemical or whatever other means) upon the patient's emotions, as such. They can be effectively modified, it seems, only through systematic changes in behavior. As Glasser (1963) succinctly says: "No one can help another person *feel* better." Neurotic persons do not act irresponsibly because they are sick; instead, they are sick (sick of themselves) and *feel* bad because they act badly, irresponsibly. So the strategy of choice for the therapist is to help the other person become more responsible (even though it temporarily "hurts"). This, of course, is in direct contradiction to the more traditional (but manifestly unsatisfactory) view that human beings become emotionally ill because they have been morally overtrained and are, in consequence, trying to be too good.[1]

If others are truly responsible for our emotional difficulties, then it would perhaps follow that we could recover only through treatment (that is, a so-called "corrective emotional experience") which would likewise have to come from without. This is, of course, tanta-

[1] Twenty-five years ago, in the heyday of Freudianism, most psychologists, if they were interested in the phenomenon of conscience at all, were concerned only to the extent of discovering how to get rid of it (on the assumption that it was likely to be the repository of all manner of unrealistic, "archaic" fears and scruples). As further indication of the collapse of this tendency to derogate conscience—and of the collapse of the whole Freudian philosophy—attention should be called to a small but rapidly growing literature on the question of how conscience and character and moral competence are acquired. This literature (mainly in the areas of child development and child training) is manifestly pertinent to our general thesis, but only tangentially, so it will not be specifically considered here. However, the interested reader will find a collection of readings in this area in *Conscience and Character* (Johnson & Mowrer, 1965).

mount to saying that psychopathology is due to false, unrealistic guilt, a mere "guilt complex." But a kind of revolution is now in progress which puts the responsibility—both for one's having gotten into a neurotic impasse in the first place and for one's getting out of it—much more squarely upon the individual himself. That is, we are here assuming that psychopathology involves *real* guilt, i.e., fear of being "found out," which is generated by actions which the individual's reference group (cf. Mowrer, 1965b) condemns and negatively sanctions.[2]

In other words, this newly emerging point of view attributes to human beings the capacity for choice: the capacity, in the first place, to choose either to behave or not to behave and, having chosen misbehavior, the further capacity to choose either to conceal or reveal this fact. Manifestly, we do not, cannot, choose or control our emotions, directly or voluntarily. Given the appropriate (conditioned) stimulus, they occur automatically, reflexly. So the question of control and choice exists only at the level of overt, voluntary behavior. And this is why behavior therapy opens up vistas and potentialities which are forever closed if one thinks of the problem of psychopathology as being essentially emotional. But there has been, in recent decades, some question as to whether the concept of choice or volition is justified even in respect to overt, instrumental behavior. We shall have to pause momentarily to consider this matter, for the validity of our whole analysis importantly hinges upon it.

Much of the skepticism concerning the possibility of human freedom of choice comes from stimulus-response psychology, or primitive behaviorism, which held that, given a specific stimulus S, the organism (be he man or mouse) must respond with whatever R happens to be most directly connected, or conditioned, to S. On the basis of evidence which has been reviewed in detail elsewhere (Mowrer, 1960a; Mowrer, 1960b; Mowrer, 1961), it can now, with good reason, be maintained that stimuli never produce or cause behavioral (as opposed to emotional) responses in the manner implied by S-R connectionism or reflexology. A stimulus S may suggest (i.e., provide an image or memory of) a particular response R. But the fact that S is present does not at all mean that the subject is obliged or "forced" (cf. Loeb, 1912) to make a particular R—or, indeed, any R at all. A given S may, as noted, suggest a particular R—that is, it may remind the subject of a certain possibility—but whether or not the individual responds to the suggestion ("yields to the temptation") is dependent upon prudential factors (hopes and fears) which are complexly determined by the individual's total life experience, knowledge (including that which is gained vicariously), and objectives—in a word, by character. Whatever else gestalt psychologists may have meant when they spoke of an organism's responding as a whole—totally, rather than segmentally—this is surely an important part of what they should have meant.

In the foregoing analysis, we are not repudiating determinism in the sense of denying that the universe (including the principles governing the human mind) is orderly and lawful; but we *are* saying that as far as the overt responses which human beings make are concerned, they are very intricately, very complexly determined. Their occurrence is dependent not merely upon the presence or absence of any given S, or even upon a particular pattern or concatination of stimuli comprising a situation, but also upon everything which, as Krechevsky (1932) has phrased it, the organism "brings to" the situation—and, we may add, upon the information (sensory feedback) which is provided while a response is in progress. In other words, the reflexological, connectionistic model of behavior which was postulated by Pavlov, Watson, Thorndike, and others is grossly inadequate—that is, it is not isomorphic with the reality it is supposed to represent—and we must have instead a model which, at the very least, recognizes the reality of mediating processes and higher-order "habits" (even the Russian reflexologists are now speaking of "the *second* signal system") which

[2] Our view does not for a moment overlook or deny the fact that others may be the source of great anguish and heartache for a given individual, but this is not neurosis and is not what "destroys" us. The assumption is rather that we are destroyed (in the sense of losing self-esteem and self-acceptance) only as a result of those things for which we, personally, are responsible. Society holds no one accountable and is in no sense inclined to punish one for what others have done to him. It is our *own conduct* which, if deviant, can be our downfall. If others are unreasonable, harsh, or unfair, the whole, healthy person may suffer acutely; but he will have durability and resiliency. Objective stress is usually episodic, and when it is over, the person whose self-regard is intact soon "bounces back." (The question of autism and childhood schizophrenia will be considered later in this chapter.)

make possible the deliberate weighing and balancing of alternative possibilities (Miller, Galanter, & Pribram, 1960; Mowrer, 1960b, especially chap. 6; Osgood, 1953). This way of thinking about the problem very largely resolves the conflict between determinism and teleology, or purpose. We may say, in effect, that we have now discovered (in contemporary learning theory) the mechanics of teleology. As long as we are able to respond to the circumstances of our existence with flexibility and intelligence, rather than in a fixed and essentially "stupid" manner, do we not have all the freedom we need or should, for that matter, desire?

Now we are in a position to ask what it is that human beings do, i.e., what choice or choices they make, which precipitates the state known, ambiguously, as "neurosis." Manifestly, this term is just a medical euphemism and does not at all mean what it would literally seem to mean, namely, an "osis" or disorder of the nerves or the nervous system. The term "psychosis" comes closer to carrying the implication which is obviously in point here. And it would not, perhaps, be too bad if it gradually replaced the term "neurosis." However, Erikson (1958) has suggested an expression which is more appropriate still, namely, "identity crisis," for it fits in nicely with the answer to the question: What is it that human beings do which leads to the personal condition with which we are here concerned? The answer to this question seems to be that (1) they choose to do socially forbidden things and then (2) they hide and deny what they have done. In other words, they refuse to say who they "really are"; i.e., they deny their true identity to others. Francis Thompson ends the first stanza of his "Hound of Heaven" with this memorable line: "All things betray Thee who betrayest Me." That is, if we for long deny who we are to others (that is, "betray" them), the time comes when we no longer know ourselves (cf. Jourard, 1963), and this is the state of psychic nonbeing or anxiety [cf. Frankl's (1962) concept of "existential vacuum," or "meaninglessness"] which we commonly call "neurosis" or "psychosis" and which we could, it seems, so much more pertinently and precisely call "identity crisis."

This way of thinking about the problem obviously represents a radical departure from the prevailing medical emphasis. In mental hospitals, both public and private, the doctor typically tries to reassure the patient (i.e., make him or her feel better) by saying something like this: "Now you should realize, first of all, that you do *have a disease*. And this is just like any other disease or sickness, of an organic nature, which you might have. It is not associated with anything you have done or not done. That is, you are in no way responsible for it—and you can't do anything about it, yourself. In other words, you should not worry or blame yourself for anything—instead, just relax and leave everything to us. We understand these things and will completely take over the 'treatment.' Simply do as you are told." If it is true that the individual does have a responsibility, and perhaps a very sizable one, for both the cause and the cure of the condition here under discussion, how tragically nonfunctional all this is! Such an approach has served to create what someone has aptly called the "healing industry," but it has not, it seems, accomplished much else.

Understandably, there is thus growing skepticism concerning the appropriateness of the medical model (of illness, sickness, and treatment) in the whole psychiatric area (cf. Glasser, 1965). And psychologists, while probably willing enough to accept this development, are, however, faced by the necessity of deciding whether they will go on trying to keep the "patient" (see how inveterate the medical language is!) in another deterministic frame of reference—not that of disease but of S-R bondage—or liberate him, in the sense of granting to him a significant role in both the production and the elimination of his difficulties. As already noted, the simple, unelaborated S-R learning model can only make of man a robot; but, for reasons cited, this model is inherently unsatisfactory and is today being replaced by a model in which freedom of choice is a definite (though qualified) possibility. The real element of determinism, compulsion, constraint, necessity comes, it seems, not so much from the biological, neurological, or even psychological nature of the individual as from the fact that man is a social being, operating within a social system, and that this system puts very definite and inevitable constraints and restraints upon him.

In such a system, the individual still has a number of choices open to him. He can, for example, choose (at least within limits) the particular social system in which he is going to function (cf. the concept of "social mobility"). And he can also choose whether he is going to function, within a given system, honestly or dishonestly. But if he chooses the latter course, there is, it seems, an inevitable consequence: he becomes prey to that special variety of fear and personal misery which we call "guilt," and if he does not deal with this in a realistic and constructive way—that is, by confession and restitution—he will soon be trying to deal with it in ways which we call "symptomatic." This is not the place to elaborate on the meaning of the latter term (cf. Mowrer, 1964, chap. 11), but it can be said that so-called "symptoms" represent (1) an effort on the part of the guilty (uneasy, "dis-easy," apprehensive, anxious) individual to deny and hide such feelings, lest they arouse suspicion—"*Why* are you so fearful?"—and (2) an effort to lessen the subjective intensity of such feelings because they are inherently unpleasant and painful. Hence, the appropriateness of referring to symptoms as "defenses," not against a fear of a return of repressed impulses of sex and hostility (as Freud supposed), but against the danger of having one's guilty secrets known to others and against the subjective experience of the emotion of guilt by the individual himself.

Thus one arrives at the view that there is no possibility of a successful private treatment of neurosis (in either a religious or a secular context—cf. Mowrer, 1963c), for the reason that privacy, concealment, secrecy, and "defensiveness" are the essense of the difficulty. Here both psychiatrists and psychologists have, it seems, made the error of engaging in treatment procedures which are more congruent with the premises of the disease than with those of health. It is not surprising that such procedures have been salable, for they promise the neurotic an opportunity to get well *on his own terms.* But neither should it surprise us that such procedures have not been truly effective, for they have not adequately recognized the true nature of an identity crisis (see Figure 2).

Thus, in the final analysis, a rational and effective therapy must be a behavior therapy, which involves (1) admission rather than denial, to the significant others in one's life, of who one genuinely is and (2) rectification of, and restitution for, past deviations and errors. Thus one must again traverse the same path which led him into neurosis in the first place, but now in the reverse direction. If it is by sinning and then trying to conceal the sinning that one progressively destroys his social relatedness (i.e., his identity), the only possibility of recovering it is to move back in the opposite direction, toward openness, cooperation, community, and fellowship.

But is this the shape of science in the domain of psychopathology or an awful retrogression? In the story of the temptation and fall of man, as set forth in the third chapter of Genesis, the essential facts of the case are, familiarly, that man (Adam, Everyman) sins and then hides his sin. If, after violating the *one* rule (remember, this was Paradise) that had been put upon him, man had gone to the Lord (his "significant others") and admitted his mistake, the outcome would presumably have been very different. But instead, after having chosen to eat of the forbidden fruit, man—and woman—further decided to deny and conceal what he had done. Banishment from Eden is the penality that is inflicted upon them, just as loss of peace of mind and a pervasive insecurity are the price that is still exacted of all of us if we violate our social obligations and then pretend that we have not done so. We, too, are "banished," no longer belong, because we have thus disqualified ourselves for the privilege of membership and group participation. But we alone know this, and our "neurosis" consists of this knowledge, of the fear of being found out which it engenders, and of the constant vigilance which is needed lest this should happen.

But why should man, if he is truly free, ever choose to violate rules? Rules always involve a restriction or sacrifice, which has the effect of ensuring a long-term advantage of some sort; and whenever an individual is not experienced or intelligent enough to see the logic of a rule, he is, understandably, tempted to violate it. In a land of wonderful abundance, it was certainly no great physical imposition upon Adam and Eve not to eat of the forbidden fruit, but it was perhaps something of an affront to their vanity and pride to be told there was something they should not do.[3] So, they ate. And then, instead of admitting what they had chosen to do, each, in his own way,

[3] Not long ago, a "sick" college girl said to me: "But if I confess this thing to my parents, I will lose my independence," meaning the complete autonomy and authority she had arrogated unto herself. Is this the age-old sin of pride?

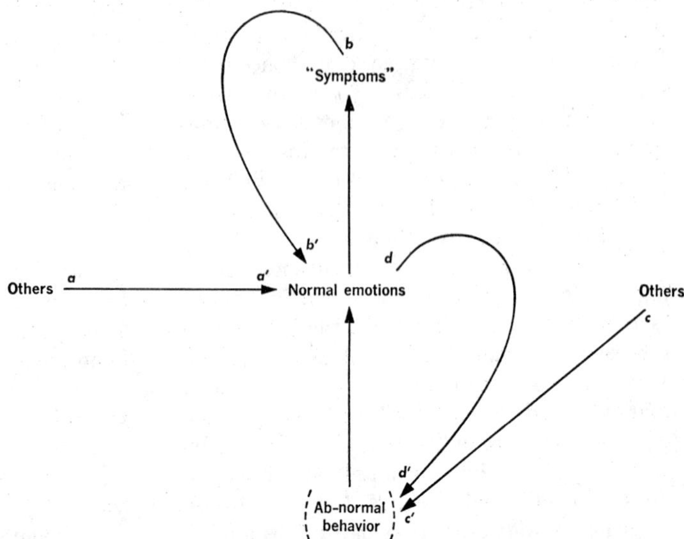

Figure 2. Combination and elaboration of the two diagrams shown in Figure 1. If, in the conventional frame of reference, the basic problem is an abnormality of emotions which has been produced by others, then "therapy" ($a \rightarrow a'$) would require some sort of treatment by others which would offset the mistreatment to which the individual has been previously exposed. Oddly, this is precisely what the individual's own symptomatic efforts ($b \rightarrow b'$) are designed to do: i.e., make him *feel* better, without necessarily *being* better. Thus, "symptoms" may be defined as an individual's own attempt at self-cure which, like most professional treatment, assumes that the basic problem is wrong emotions, bad "nerves." If, however, the other hypothesis is correct and if the neurotic individual's emotional reactions (considering his on-going life style) are essentially normal, we see how sadly misdirected such treatment is. Surely it is suggestive in this connection that, on the average, the apparent effectiveness of professional treatment does not exceed the incidence of "spontaneous remissions" in untreated persons. But if it is really the individual's behavior rather than his emotions which is abnormal, then therapy, i.e., the efforts of others to help him, ought to be directly toward behavior change ($c \rightarrow c'$), rather than emotional reeducation. And to the extent that this point of view begins to make sense to the suffering person himself, he will then start letting his emotional discomfort motivate him ($d \rightarrow d'$) to eliminate the questionable behavior and life strategies which have been producing the emotional upset, rather than seeking to eliminate the emotional discomfort directly ($b \rightarrow b'$). When an emotionally disturbed person is able to see his predicament in this light, he will actively, independently, effectively set about "curing" himself (through confession and restitution) and will not need protracted treatment from others. Instead of continuing to be weak and needing to "receive," he will become strong and able to *give*.

denied it: "And the man said, The Woman whom thou gavest to be with me, she gave me of the tree, and I did eat. . . . And the woman said, The serpent beguiled me, and I did eat." Because they both refused to confess their mistake and to accept the responsibility for it, they found no restoration, no redemption, no recovery, no reconciliation, no return to innocence: "Therefore the Lord God sent [man] forth from the Garden of Eden, to till the ground from whence he was taken . . . and he placed at the east of the garden of Eden Cherubims, and a flaming sword which turned every way, to keep the way to the tree of life."

The story of the fall of man is one of the great allegories of all time. It is like a finely cut diamond: no matter how one turns and looks at it, it reflects a bright and illuminating light. So, taking the particular facet of the story which we have chosen, does it not suggest that so many of our current efforts to help "fallen" (neurotic) individuals to "rise" (recover) are to no avail because we do not sufficiently recognize man's true nature and destiny?

On the assumption that man is today no less

(potentially, at least) than the author of Genesis understood him to be, we shall use this classical conception as the standard of comparison for latter-day theories and practices in this domain.[4]

Before proceeding further, the reader should perhaps be reassured that the conception of neurosis and recovery (or sin and salvation) which will be taken as a kind of benchmark in this chapter is not conventionally religious. In one sense, of course, this approach is deeply and inveterately religious. One of the roots of the word "religion" is the Latin term *ligare,* from which our words "ligament" and "ligature" come. Religion thus, literally, implies a binding to, a connectedness, a relationship, a belonging; and in this sense, we shall assume that the normal, "healthy" man is necessarily "religious" and that an abnormal, "sick" one is suffering from a tragic form of brokenness and alienation.

But religion, in the more institutional sense —particularly Protestant religion (which I am best qualified to appraise)—suffers, it seems, from some of the same presuppositions that have so seriously handicapped secular therapeutic approaches. Perhaps the most fatal of these is the assumption that in an identity crisis the individual's emotions are in some way out of kelter, inappropriate, disordered. As we have seen, an excellent case can be made for the alternative view that the neurotic is suffering, not from an emotional disorder, but from a disorderly, irresponsible way of life. And, as we have also seen, it is in itself neurotic to view the emotions as the source of the trouble. Thus, we are led to the inference that much contemporary religion is itself sick, just as psychiatry and clinical psychology—and the neurotic—are (Mowrer, 1961).

But is it true, is it fair, to say that contemporary Protestantism stresses wrong emotions as the source of suffering man's condition? Protestantism has long taken a dim view of "works" (your own efforts and actions) as a means of salvation ("lest any man should boast," as Paul put it), and now we find that many ministers have become so advanced in their thinking that they do not even talk about sin and guilt anymore. All is forgiveness and love: first love of God, then of one's fellow men, and then of oneself. And what is "love"? As ordinarily understood it is an emotion. And if you do not have it, cannot experience it, you are quite as helpless as you are if you have some negative emotion (such as anxiety) and want to get rid of it. Operationally, such a theology hamstrings the lost, alienated, suffering individual about as effectively as the doctrines of disease (in psychiatry) or reflexology (in psychology). The main difference is that now, in the religious context, one is supposed to see a theologian for help instead of a secular healer of some sort.

What we are talking about, and will be talking about recurrently in this chapter, is thus an approach which exemplifies the much discussed but seldom actualized Protestant doctrine of the "priesthood of all believers," i.e., the ability and the obligation, on the part of everyone, to be a priest ("therapist") to himself and to others.

Actually, there is excellent biblical support for this point of view. In classical Judaism, and in Orthodox Judaism of today, one appears before God (on the Day of Atonement) only after having spent a month making right one's transgressions against one's fellow men during the preceding year. And in the New Testament we read: "Therefore if thou bring thy gift to the altar, and there rememberest that thy brother hath ought against thee, leave there thy gift [to God] before the altar, and go thy way; *first be reconciled to thy brother, and then come and offer thy gift*" (*Matthew,* 5:23–24, italics added).

There is a familar couplet which goes:

> I sought my soul, I sought my God;
> but neither could I see;
> But then I sought my brother,
> and then I found all three.

This may not be very exalted poetry, but it is, it seems, excellent psychology and also "theology." And it is, in essence, the philosophy which we shall use as the touchstone for the ensuing discussion in this chapter. It puts behavior—interpersonal, social, *moral* behavior —first and says that everything else will follow from this.[5] Why have we professionals, in both psychology and religion, been so reluctant to acknowledge and emphasize this time-honored approach? Can it be that we have not

[4] It is interesting to observe how many psychologists (and psychiatrists) are today asking the existential question: "What, then, *is* man?" See, for example the book published by Meehl, 1958.

[5] Cf. "Seek ye first the Kingdom of God and his righteousness; and all these things shall be added onto you." (*Matthew,* 6:33)

liked it precisely *because* it gives the layman —Adam, Everyman—more freedom and responsibility and "power" than we wish him to have? Does it, in other words, make him too independent of us? If there is even a trace of professional chauvinism in this transcendently important human area, we should surely divest ourselves of it as promptly and completely as possible. Behavior therapy, as it has been outlined in this section, and as it will be further elaborated in the pages to follow, can, hopefully, be a useful instrument to this end.

II

When did interest in behavior therapy first appear? Nothing, it seems, in the realm of ideas is so old as not to have been, in one way or another, anticipated. But for our purposes, it can be said that William H. Burnham's book *The Normal Mind* was the first extended and relatively systematic attempt to base a theory of psychopathology—and of its prevention and treatment—on learning principles. Preliminary gestures in this direction had, of course, been made by various ancient and medieval writers and, more recently, by James (1899), Terman (1914), Watson (1919), Franz (1923), and others. However, the Burnham book, which appeared in 1924, marked the coalescence and fruition of many strands of thought and inquiry in such a way as to make it singularly important.

Not only did this book capture and coordinate much of the earlier and then emergent thinking in this field, but also its author saw, and to a significant degree helped set, the pattern of thought and action in the whole mental health area which was destined to become and to this hour remain the dominant point of view. But the bright hopes and promises which this approach initially held out have not, in the course of four decades, been fulfilled, with the result that there is today growing skepticism with respect to it. Consequently it becomes incumbent upon us to ask: Just what is it that we have thus believed and practiced for the past forty years? In what ways is it inadequate and mistaken? And what can we now appropriately put in its place?

Everyone, says Burnham in his preface, was (in 1924) "pathetically interested in the health of his own mind and in the healthful development of his children" (p. vii). But "the still small voice of simple, scientific teaching" had not as yet, he thought, been generally heard. He was not above citing an occasional aphorism by a man such as Lincoln or Grant or interspersing his own brand of common sense; but he saw it as his special mission to make available, particularly in the domain of child rearing and education, such new scientific findings and concepts as he deemed particularly pertinent and helpful.

A glance at the author index quickly reveals the cast of Burnham's general orientation. Here one finds 10 references to John Dewey, 18 (some of them quite extended) to Freud, 22 to Watson, 12 to Pavlov, and 9 to Krasnogorski. The only other writer cited with comparable frequency is William James. Hence we can anticipate a prevailing emphasis upon progressive education, permissive child rearing, and psychoanalytic theory and therapy, phrased and formulated in the language of behaviorism and reflexology.

In a supplementary bibliography, Burnham lists a book by E. R. Groves entitled *Personality and Social Adjustment,* which was published in 1922. But it is significant that in the text proper this book is not once alluded to. As we have already seen (in section I), one can take either of two very different orientations with respect to psychopathology: (1) that it represents a *biological* deprivation and disorder (caused by "cultural interference") of the kind posited by Freud. (2); that it represents a *sociological* dislocation of the afflicted individual (as a result of mismanagement of biological needs).[6] Thus, it would seem clear from the outset where Burnham himself is aligned and what his conception of mental illness and health is going to be.

Somewhat parenthetically, it is interesting to speculate on why the biological emphasis so decisively triumphed over the sociological emphasis during the first half of the twentieth century. It is hardly a question of the one being scientific and the other not. Both are, or at least can be, equally empirical, objective, and naturalistic. But the sociological approach, with its unavoidable stress on such concepts as obligation and integrity, has an unmistakable

[6] Another way to put this is to say that according to the second of these approaches, the "categorical imperative" in human existence—psychologically considered—is moral and social; according to the first, it is instinctual, biological. One can also say the question is that of where one's "supreme duty" lies: to his instincts or his human commitments? See Boisen, 1936.

aura of kinship with theology, so that, in a period of active rebellion against religion, this approach was almost certainly at a disadvantage.

But it should also be noted that there was already, at the turn of the century, a well-organized profession of practitioners, namely, physicians, and a system of special schools for training them in applied biological science, whereas the social sciences had not as yet established a powerful and distinctive applied discipline (social work was only just emerging and was soon to break away from its mother science, sociology), so there was no one to claim and contend for this area (as it became detached from its more traditional religious moorings). Moreover, no one had as yet articulated the sociological conception of personality disorder as Freud had done for the biological interpretation. So, the field "went" to the physicians. A considerable part of the revolution which now seems to be in progress involves a realization that this was a grave (though, at the time, probably inevitable) error. The present trend is to rethink the whole problem in interpersonal, moral, sociological terms (cf. London, 1964; Glasser, 1959).

A glance at the table of contents of Burnham's book shows that in one way or another there is reference to the concept of conditioning in the titles of five chapters (chaps. 3–7)—clear indication of the importance which was going to be attached thereto. And in the preface we encounter such statements as these:

> [The author] is not concerned with the conditioned reflex as the basis of any theory of psychology, but recognizes it as an objective method of such significance for the study of childhood and mentally disordered adults that, without a knowledge of it, the mental hygiene of today cannot be adequately understood (p. viii).
>
> The writer believes that the application of the simple knowledge we already have of the conditions of mental health would improve human health everywhere—that it would be helpful to schools, would prevent many neuroses, and favor the mental health and increase the efficiency of all normal children, and afford a social training vitally important for the health of the state (p. xi).

A similar sentiment is expressed in chap. 1 and elsewhere throughout this volume:

> The most important contribution of psychology to mental hygiene, providing a method of unique application, is probably the modern study of the conditioned reflex by the Russian school of Pavlov and his followers (p. 14).

However, it is not immediately evident how or why the concept of conditioning was to be so important in the area of mental hygiene. It took a special theory of neurosis to make Pavlovian theory and methodology uniquely relevant here; and this, oddly, was never supplied by the Pavlovians. It came instead from Freud. It is true that Pavlov did some research on what he called the "experimental neuroses," i.e., behavioral disturbances which were precipitated either by accident or by deliberate laboratory procedures, but the effects thus produced Pavlov explained in terms of the destructive neurological consequences of "the clashing of neural excitation and inhibition" in the central nervous system (1927). This, to be sure, implied the notion of conflict, but the injurious effects were seen as definitely structural, organic. The theory of neurosis which Freud evolved was, by contrast, strictly functional.

Obliquely, in chap. 1, Burnham adumbrates the conception of neurosis he is going to accept. Here he says:

> The studies of psychoanalysis made by Freud and his followers have contributed much to mental hygiene by showing the great importance of normal emotional and instinctive life in early childhood, the persisting evil results that may come from any unfortunate emotional shock, even in the days of infancy, and the danger from abnormal domestic relations—undue dependence on father, or mother, undue repression by the parents, or the like.
>
> These studies are significant, not merely because the psychoanalysts have shown the widely irradiated effects of disturbances of normal emotional life, but because this work furnishes illustration of the great principle that opportunity for normal reaction to emotional or instinctive stimuli should be furnished, and of the pathological effects that may occur when such opportunity is not given (pp. 15–16).

By implication, the author is saying, first of all, that he accepts the emotional basis of neurosis, rather than a behavioral one (as these terms have been defined in section I). He is voting for expressiveness as the basis for mental health, but *instinctive* expressiveness, rather than personal openness and, when need be, confession. Also, he is subscribing to the view that neurosis is caused by the untoward actions of others, rather than by one's own doings. Despite his emphasis on the psychological principle of conditioning, Burnham (and scores of other early mental hygienists) thus played into the hands of the medical profession. The instinctual and emotional forces in the life of an individual are associated with the involuntary physiological processes much more directly than with consciousness and voluntary behavior, so the physician might indeed seem best qualified to deal with disorders in this realm. And since the theory held that such disturbances were produced by the untoward actions of others, it follows that others should treat and correct them—and only physicians are authorized to engage in treatment.

Burnham seemed to accept all this without question. For example, he says: "Psychoanalysis is a special branch of psychiatry, a subject for the physician and the hospital, not for the teacher and the school" (p. 638)—or for the psychologist, presumably. But this was hardly surprising, for in 1924 clinical psychology as we know it today was hardly imagined. Unfortunately (as indicated in section I), clinical psychology is still not what it is potentially capable of being because of its continued preoccupation with the emotions rather than with behavior, in the sense of interpersonal conduct and integrity.

A few months before this chapter was written, I submitted to a technical journal a paper which advanced both empirical evidence and logical considerations which are incompatible with psychoanalytic premises; one of the consulting editors who read the paper advised the editor not to publish it because it was so "recriminatory." Today, in some quarters, psychoanalysis has become such an idol that to question or challenge it in any way is unspeakable treason. But let us note what a massive criticism and "recrimination" psychoanalysis itself originally directed and still directs (though less confidently) against conventional education and morality. Already, in 1924, Burnham had gotten the message and was transmitting it as follows:

> Formal education is largely made up of inhibitions. Necessarily this is so. The child's social education is chiefly a matter of acquiring inhibitions. To inhibit or delay reaction is a mark of the educated man.
>
> Thus it comes to pass that sometimes repression *goes too far,* and an *abnormal and exaggerated* habit of repression is developed. This may be distinctly injurious to a person's character; and probably in not a few cases the most serious handicap to one's efficiency is such *a habit of inhibition* (p. 360, italics added).

In the paper alluded to (Mowrer, 1964; see chap. 3) the results of recent studies were cited which indicate that neurotic individuals, in comparison with normal persons, are not "oversocialized." One of the editoral consultants in response said: "The author sets up a moldy straw-man and then attempts to knock him down but without success. I don't know where in even the earliest Freud one would find the contention that neurotics are 'above' normals on some scale of values." What a remarkable statement! There are literally hundreds of places in Freud's writings (see, for example, Peterson, 1965) where, either explicitly or by implication, he takes the position that the neurotic's trouble is, quite specifically, that his superego is too severe and needs to be made more lenient. And it is also abundantly clear how Burnham has read Freud:

> It may be humiliating to our professional pride [Burnham was an educational psychologist], but it is necessary to face the facts; if we do, it must be recognized that many unfortunate inhibiting conditioned reflexes and associations are likely to be formed in connection with teachers themselves. . . . This may happen because the teacher resembles some individual who has aroused aversion in the child or suggests one of the child's parents who has aroused unfortunate conditioned reflexes (pp. 379–380).
>
> School education consists largely in training into habits of doing and thinking the conventional. This is important both for education and for the mental health. Thus we soon become slaves of convention and can think even only in narrow limits and inhibit all other thinking. The repression of disagreeable thoughts and the like, illustrated so profusely by the Freudians, merely indicates in large letters what all of us do in a large part of our mental activity. Whatever is not agreeable, what does not harmonize

with our emotional and habitual mental set or attitude, we are likely to inhibit (pp. 382–383).

Still more pointedly, Burnham says:

> Since for thousands of years the custom of developing certain forms of inhibition has been the work of the home and the schools, and a large number of conventional inhibitions have resulted, it is not strange that there is a tendency in the schools to *overdo the matter* and *undue repression and inhibition* are often the result.
>
> This scholastic inhibition, repression, continued interference and exhortation, has become in many schools a serious handicap to education and the mental health of children. It appears in all the methods of discipline and the various forms of instruction and training. Mental hygienists and psychiatrists see the serious significance of it, because they have seen the disastrous results of repression and the unfortunate character of the overinhibited type (pp. 385–386, italics added).

Then the whole argument is summed up:

> As education and formal training are necessary to give an individual the benefit of the wisdom of the past [superego?] and to fit one for the practical situations of life [ego?], and since the power of inhibition [over the id?] is the mark of the educated man, almost inevitably this training is carried so far that injurious inhibitions and repression are developed; and so it comes to pass that in many cases the most important thing is for the teacher [and parent?] *to discover and remove the child's inhibitions, and for an adult to remove the accumulated inhibitions of a lifetime* (p. 286, italics added).

Thus, psychoanalysts set themselves up as arch critics of conventional educational practices (with respect not only to method but also to content) in home, school, and church. And in so doing they have created a vast market for their special services on the grounds that they alone know how to undo the destructive effects of past miseducation and malconditioning.

And how was all this to be accomplished? Burnham gives part of the answer in a chapter colorfully entitled "Inhibition of the Inhibitions." If too much inhibition is the root of all our neurotic difficulties, then obviously we need to "inhibit" or otherwise eliminate the inhibitions. But the argument does not take final form until the next chapter, which is entitled "Inhibition: Fear." Here we learn, for the first time, precisely what an inhibition is. It is a fear which has been associated with (conditioned to) the gratification of some normal, natural, instinctual need; that is, it is an abnormal emotion which has been inflicted upon an individual (usually as a child) by his overzealous, unwise educators and socializers. Some fear responses, says Burnham, are unavoidable and indeed useful. "Fear at the wrong time, however, is a serious and apparently universal inhibition. Usually it is the wrong time. Hence in mental hygiene it demands special study" (p. 417). More specifically the argument is:

> Even without quantitative data the evidence is convincing that the development of injurious inhibitions during the period of home and school training is one of the most serious handicaps to efficiency and health. These persist and are often aggravated by the development of new inhibitions in the difficult situations of adult life. The injury from such conditions is not confined to the weakly endowed and the mentally disordered, but many who are deemed practically normal suffer from such inhibition (p. 442).
>
> In extreme cases of worry we usually find an hypertrophied bump of prevision and of caution. All this is distinctly unhygienic. Many a man and woman under the stress of great duties and responsibilities would be able to work better and without injury to health if it were possible to cast caution to the wind and act spontaneously with attention fixed upon the present. Caution is a late development in the race; and with this development is correlated the tendency to nervous disorder and insanity (pp. 646–647).

The specific tie-up between the psychoanalytic conception of neurosis (as delineated in the foregoing excerpts) and the Pavlovian principles of conditioning is then made as follows:

> The methods of removing conditioned emotional responses, as summed up by Watson from the point of view of his laboratory studies, are distinctly in harmony with what has been stated. Among the methods suggested are the following: (1) constantly confronting the child with the stimuli that called out the fear responses, in order that dulling by habituation would occur; (2) by trying to recondition by showing objects

> which call out fear responses simultaneously with stimulation of tactual erogenous zones; (3) by trying to recondition by feeding candy or other food simultaneously with the fear-exciting stimulus; (4) by building up constructive activities around the object by imitation by putting the hand through the motions of manipulation (p. 419).

It is immediately apparent that Burnham's first method is what would today be termed "extinction," that his second and third methods are forms of counterconditioning, and that his fourth method is that of substitution or putting through. As we shall later see (section IV), there is today widespread and active interest in the use of extinction and counterconditioning as means of eliminating supposedly neurotic emotions, which is predicated on the assumption that these procedures are something new and different. The underlying conceptions, as Burnham's book clearly indicates, are not new; and we shall have occasion even sooner (section III) to see that extinction (reality testing) and counterconditioning (love, acceptance) are, in reality, the chief tools employed since its inception by psychoanalysis itself.

It should be pointed out that "the methods of removing conditioned emotional responses, as summed up by Watson," to which Burnham refers were largely hypothetical and programistic; for the little boy, Albert, with whom Watson and Raynor (1920) carried out their studies, became unavailable as a subject before they were able to get to the fourth stage of their investigation, which was to see "if after a reasonable period such emotional responses have not died out, what laboratory methods can be devised for their removal" (p. 3). To the related question, "What is the effect of time upon such conditioned emotional responses?" Watson and Raynor did succeed in getting an answer. As a result of tests made after the lapse of one month, these investigators say:

> These experiments would seem to show conclusively that directly conditioned emotional responses as well as those conditioned by transfer [i.e., generalized responses] persist, although with a certain loss in the intensity of the reaction, for a longer period than one month (p. 12).

One of the presuppositions of the conditioned-response theory of neurosis is that unrealistic ("neurotic") fears do *not* disappear or weaken with the mere passage of time and that, furthermore, they are not subject to extinction through repeated, unreinforced arousal. In order for a neurotic fear to be troublesome, it must be repeatedly experienced. And if it is truly unrealistic, then each time it is experienced without confirmation, it ought to undergo some extinction and eventually disappear. Although Watson and Raynor were unable to carry out actual extinction or counterconditioning procedures with Albert, there is not much question what their findings would have been if they had. Innumerable experiments (with animal subjects) have shown that laboratory-induced fears are regularly subject to elimination through extinction, and observations reported by Jones (1924), the same year that Burnham's book appeared, indicate that counterconditioning (by means of candy and ice cream) is an effective means of getting rid of simple fears in children.

Thus, by 1924, Freudian theory had been explicitly translated into the idiom of the conditioning laboratory; and, on the assumption that a neurotic inhibition is just an unrealistic fear, two presumably powerful therapeutic techniques had been suggested, namely, extinction and counterconditioning. The fact that this understanding of the problem has now been put into effect and extensively tried out, without the hoped-for results, suggests that the whole Freudian diagnosis of the condition called "neurosis" may be mistaken and in need of systematic reconsideration.[7]

In the foregoing pages, we have limited ourselves to what might be termed the "rudiments" of Burnham's argument; but he ramified and elaborated it in such a way as to cover psychosomatic and somatopsychic disturbances, pseudofeeblemindedness, discipline, delinquency, self-analysis, "negative practice" (Dunlap, 1917), and a wide array of other related topics. Thus it cannot be said that Burnham's approach was either superficial or unsophisticated. In fact, it would be hard to

[7] As indicated in section I, the basic error in the Freudian approach was the assumption that in neurosis guilt is illusory and false rather than fully justified and real. Once we grant that for the neurotic the "danger" (of social discovery and discipline) is always there, it is no mystery why the associated fears do not readily extinguish. They are constantly being reinforced, at least vicariously (by observation of others) and in at least minor ways directly (cf. footnote 13).

find in later works on behavior therapy any idea which is not given at least passing attention in this volume. However, after forty years, we cannot now say that our mental health is noticeably better than it was in 1924. Indeed, there are some observers who are prepared to argue that it is worse and that the very philosophy which Burnham (following Freud and Watson) expounded is directly (though not exclusively) responsible for this worsening.

Burnham himself seemed to have entertained some misgivings on this score, even though he had not had the opportunity to witness the course of events in this field over the last four decades. Just in the process of writing this book, his confidence that contemporary science held all the answers seems to have dimmed perceptibly. For example, in chap. 1 he says:

> Although in the minds of some, [mental hygiene] may still be associated with certain fads and vagaries, it now rests on a solid foundation of scientific fact, and has already made important contributions to the mental health of normal children and adults (p. 9).
>
> Recent studies in psychiatry . . . have shown the possibility of preventing many forms of mental disorder. . . . They have shown that in many cases the best means of cure is some form of re-education involving the development of wholesome interests (p. 13).

And a little later, in the same chapter, we read:

> Mental hygiene brings its quiet gospel based upon scientific fact and offers the aid of our vastly increased knowledge to those in need of sympathy and aid, a gospel as significant in peace as in war, as important for children as for adults, as helpful for normal children as for the defective. . . . Thus the various contributions mentioned above have placed mental hygiene and the hygiene of school instruction on a scientific foundation, and emphasized the far-reaching practical significance of these new subjects (p. 22).

However, in the concluding chapter of this volume, the mood is more restrained and cautious:

> We have not yet a sufficient nucleus of scientific knowledge in regard to mental health, and it is impossible to formulate principles where the essential data are not available . . . no general principles. . . . It takes considerable rashness, with our present meager knowledge, to attempt any formulation even of the conditions of mental health (p. 641).

What was it, then, that had this sobering effect upon the author of this volume as he thought through the many issues considered in its nearly seven hundred pages? In the first place, he seems never to have resolved what he terms the "dilemma" which arises from the assumption that education is both necessary and dangerous. That is to say, with too little of it we are inhuman (sociopathic), and with too much of it we are ill (neurotic, psychotic). The Freudian conception of neurosis, despite its often involved terminology and imagery, is extremely simple: it results from a little *too much* inhibition (education), which results in repression rather than mere control, which in turn can be removed only by treatment involving "inhibition of the inhibition," namely, extinction or counterconditioning.

But Burnham was never, it seems, quite able to persuade himself that this was all there was to it. Although paying lip service to the new psychology, he never fully emancipated himself from an older way of thinking and feeling. An argument that covers the better part of a chapter is to the effect that neurosis depends not upon disordered or distorted emotions but upon behavior, performance, and conduct. The following excerpts catch the essence of the fuller context:

> Thus Meyer says: "This growing conviction that personality is fundamentally determined by performance rather than by mere good will and good intention, rapidly becomes the backbone of our psychology and psychopathology."
>
> Thus the great thing in mental hygiene is to give opportunity for significant tasks, and the great problem for the psychiatrist is in devising means to obtain performance when it fails to come spontaneously. The role of the psychiatrist "consists of giving opportunities rather than prescriptions." It is the same with the teacher and hygienist (p. 615).

In fact, Burnham thought that even psychoanalysis, with a little ingenuity, was capable of being subsumed under this "doctrine of work." He says:

> In many cases what the patient needs is a task worthwhile—some interesting work to

> do. But often the patient is not interested in work. No task appeals to him. He is interested only in his own experience and his own symptoms. Go to, then, says psychoanalysis, your task shall deal with yourself. Thus psychoanalysis may be just the thing; for it concerns itself with the patient's own experience, and gives the task of studying precisely that (p. 614).

And finally, under this heading—"The Need for a Task"—we read:

> At a recent term of a court in a Massachusetts district it is said that one of the jurors drawn applied to Judge Webster Thayer to be excused on the ground of serious nervous breakdown. The judge thought the man looked better than his report would indicate, and refused to excuse him. As a result he was forced to serve for two weeks, and the result was so beneficial that when discharged he was a different man physically and mentally. He had gained eight pounds, and his nervous condition was so improved that the judge was said to be ready to recommend jury service for nervous breakdown (p. 636).

What is being said here? The hypothesis of "best fit" would seem to be this: that sometimes the best therapy for a neurosis is work—and so much the better if it involves a worthwhile task or social service of some sort.[8] On what conception of neurosis could such a therapy be predicated? Only, it seems, on one which takes *real guilt*, i.e., a kind of social debt or obligation, as the basis of personal disturbance—a view which is quite antithetical to that of psychoanalysis and its conditioned-reflex equivalent. But this sounds so much less "scientific" and is so reminiscent of religion that one is perhaps loath to give it serious consideration. Burnham tried to be fair and open-minded on this score. For example, he says:

> Although, as we have seen, a child is at the mercy of any incident or any accidental change in its environment, on the other hand, perhaps an equally slight incident or change in the environment may inhibit or take the place of the inhibition itself. The inhibiting associations or obsessions are apt to be repressed. At least, *the child keeps them secret and does not talk about them.* In such cases the mere description of the experience to another, the mere expression in words of the repressed experience, may be quite enough to bring about the inhibition and cure of the trouble. *Confession is only the best known example of this* (p. 410, italics added).

Analysts typically ask for free association in their patients, not as a means of eliciting a "confession"—since it is assumed that the patient has not done anything which is really wrong—but rather as a means of obtaining the information which is needed for the treatment. Can it be that the greatest benefit from analysis (when there is any) comes from the fact that here (despite the poor example set by the analyst) is the beginning of an openness that is then extended (often against the analyst's advice, on the grounds that it will "weaken the transference") to other, more significant persons? Burnham, like the analysts, seems to see the benefit of confession not in these interpersonal terms, but rather in terms of what it accomplishes, so to speak, intrapsychically; but he does note the factor of secrecy in an identity crisis and at least mentions confession as a means of correction.

More specifically, what does Burnham have to say about religion? One might wish that he had found in it support for the therapeutic philosophy of work, performance, service; but instead he sees it primarily as supporting the analytic emphasis upon wrong emotions. He says:

> Religion, though in primitive forms appealing largely to fear, in its most highly developed forms, like Christianity, has as its special aim to remove fear. The fundamental message of the Christian gospel is that love casteth out fear, and the aim of a million churches today is the elimination of fear. The aim of psychiatry is the same, and the work of thousands of sanitariums is to dispel the fears of their patients (p. 433).

Having thus established what he takes to be a basic congruence between psychiatry and religion (cf. such contemporary organizations as the Academy of Religion and Mental Health), Burnham then returns to his concerns with formal education. He says:

[8] It is perhaps pertinent to note that Burnham was writing at a time when the activity program in schools and occupational therapy in psychiatry were being developed. Here was a behavior therapy of sorts, but the emphasis tended to be upon activity for its own sake. Our emphasis—and the one which Burnham also at times seems to favor, at least obliquely—is different.

> Why, it may naturally be asked, should not the school join with religion, psychiatry, and hygiene for the protection of children against fear. Of course, it will do this, as soon as teachers and schoolmen have an adequate knowledge of mental hygiene. . . . The school has been historically, in large measure, an institution where fears developed (p. 444).

There are manifestly two ways of conceiving of neurotic fears and, depending upon which of these one accepts, two very different approaches to therapy. There is, in the Judeo-Christian tradition, abundant emphasis upon the view that fear arises through "sin" and that the way to eliminate this type of fear (known as "guilt") is to confess and rectify or make restitution for whatever it is that one has done wrong. But Protestant Christianity (as noted in section I), in its attempt to gain the multitude, has offered a softer doctrine, which holds that if you will only "believe" (have faith), you will be forgiven, without the inconvenience of confession and restitution. Thus, whereas it was possible for Burnham to say that psychiatry and "highly developed" Christianity are joining forces in fighting false and unrealistic fear, we can today say that the new understanding of behavior therapy is congruent with an older, sterner, but more truly redemptive religion which stresses works (behavior) rather than mere faith (emotions).

Burnham, interestingly enough, also cites the great Garden of Eden allegory, except that he views it in a way that is very different from the one suggested in section I:

> Adam and Eve in the Garden of Eden were not afraid. They reacted without restraint to their natural impulses. They adjusted normally to a natural environment. They were frankly and naively self-confident. Satan tempted them. . . . Thereafter, like all mankind subject to the imperative law of association, they could never rid themselves of worry. Thus fear, like death, came into the world with our first parents, and, unless removed by mental training shall last until the heavens be rolled away as a scroll (pp. 444–445).

Burnham speaks of the "imperative law of association" (conditioning) and of the irreversibility of its impact, "unless removed by mental training" (special treatment). The alternative interpretation which we have suggested attributes to each individual choice, responsibility, and "power." Which of these theories of man is likely to be the more functional, the more viable? Reformation theology, Freudian psychoanalysis, and Watsonian behaviorism have been in the undisputed ascendancy for the past fifty years. If one is satisfied and pleased with the contemporary scene, he manifestly has no reason for wishing for a change. But if he is disillusioned and alarmed, a different orientation and approach may be welcome to him.

Burnham, as we have seen, was in conflict on this score. He was dedicated to the empirical, pragmatic approach of science, but he also had some lingering loyalty to traditional social and ethical values. For example, in the very first chapter of his book, he says:

> If much of all this seems a form of social service in the field of morals, that is not strange, for sound morals and mental hygiene are in large part identical. Morality is by no means indifferent to hygiene, for it assumes that health is the basis of a sound morality, for it assumes that health will be used for worthy ends; and without health a sane morality is hardly possible (p. 20).

Burnham's error consisted in equating the scientific approach to personality disturbance with the medical model of illness and health. If it is true that man is preeminently a social creature, rather than a "mere" animal, our conception of psychological efficiency and stamina is bound to change. We will not see mental hygiene as dominating personal and social values, but the other way around: we will see moral existence (interpersonal relationships, obligation, and loyalty) as setting the conditions for mental health. And such a view is intrinsically no less scientific or naturalistic than the biomedical approach. In fact, considering the probable nature of the problem, the sociological frame of reference seems to be decidedly more scientific (in the sense of having real pertinence and power) than the biological approach.

III

Twenty-six years after the publication of Burnham's *The Normal Mind,* another volume appeared which is likewise a milestone in the history of that facet of applied science which we are here tracing: *Personality and Psycho-*

therapy: An Analysis in Terms of Learning, Thinking, and Culture, by John Dollard and Neal E. Miller. Like the Burnham volume, it too is essentially an attempt to translate psychoanalysis into the idiom of learning theory, and it is, significantly, dedicated to "Freud and Pavlov and their students." But the Burnham book is not once cited. Evidently it was not known to the authors, or else it was regarded as hopelessly outdated. However, the underlying conception of psychopathology and its treatment, being basically Freudian in both instances, is strikingly similar; so, in principle at least, the 1950 volume represents no major advance over the earlier one. Our reference to it here can be accordingly brief.

Since Freudian psychoanalysis, when restated in the simpler, more explicit language of learning theory, is rather starkly uncomplicated, one can catch the essense of the Dollard-Miller approach from any of several chapters in their book. But for our purposes a chapter entitled "Ways of Getting Rid of Symptoms" will be particularly useful. In fact, we find the authors' whole conception of neurosis, symptom formation, and therapy excellently summarized in the following few sentences:

> The patients that reach a therapist probably are a highly selected group that have especially strong inhibitions blocking their adaptive goal responses. Therefore merely interfering with their symptoms will not be likely to produce a favorable result. After the inhibitions blocking the more adaptive goal responses have been sufficiently reduced, however, we might expect different results. Then the increased drive produced by interfering with the symptoms might cause the goal response to become stronger than the weakened inhibition. In fact, this often seems to occur; after the fears motivating the inhibitions have been reduced, therapists often find it desirable to interfere with a symptom by an unfavorable interpretation. This is especially true if the immediate effects of the symptom, like an addiction or a perversion, are so drive-reducing that it is strongly reinforced and the motivation for new responses is kept low (p. 386).

Here we see, first of all, the standard Freudian assumption (cf. also Burnham) that the essense of neurosis is inhibition, which in practice turns out to be a socially (morally) instilled fear of gratifying either the impulse of sex or the impulse of aggression. A symptom, in this frame of reference, is basically a form of surreptitious gratification of the otherwise blocked impulse; but this gratification is disguised by an overlay of (superego-inflicted) suffering. Hence the so-called "biphasic" (Freud's term) nature of symptoms. The explicit aim of therapy is therefore (1) to get rid of the fear that is blocking the natural, normal gratification of the impulse in question and (2) then redirect the individual's behavior away from the unsatisfactory, substitutive, symptomatic form of gratification to a more "normal" form of satisfaction. The first task, in other words, is to inhibit the inhibition, i.e., to extinguish (or countercondition) the too strong and unrealistic social fear which is blocking the route to normal, healthy gratification and then gradually invoke the so-called "rule of abstinence" (also Freud's term), i.e., "interfere with the symptom by an unfavorable interpretation."[9]

By way of illustrating the foregoing principles in action, Dollard and Miller refer (as they often do throughout the course of their book) to the case of "Mrs. A":

> When Mrs. A came to the therapist, her main concern was about her symptoms, especially her great fear that her heart would stop beating if she did not constantly concentrate on counting its beats. She was not thinking about her basic difficulty, the conflict that produced the high drives motivating the symptoms. The therapist did not focus his attention on these symptoms but concentrated on getting at the conflict.
>
> By his permissive attitude he got her to talk more freely. When she told him how her foster brother had seduced her as a child, he maintained his calm, warm, accepting silence without giving her the punish-

[9] Burham's not very different description of "what the psychoanalyst does" reads as follows: "Briefly, what the psychoanalyst does is to find if possible the source of the mental experience of the disagreeable or disgusting memory and attitude, then to bring it clearly into consciousness, lower the threshold so that one will think of it without repression, then associate a rival stimulus with the disagreeable memory, a rival stimulus of agreeable, or humorous, or idealistic character, which will serve to inhibit the disagreeable idea or attitude itself" (p. 635). In other words, the analyst, by his passivity and permissiveness, i.e., by means of extinction, helps the patient to unlearn his inhibiting fears to the extent of at least being able to talk about them (and the impulses which they are presumably blocking); and then, by the more active process of counterconditioning, he makes an effort to dissolve the forces of inhibition still further.

> ment or disapproval that she seemed to expect. This produced a marked reduction in her fear. With this reduction in her fear, the symptoms abated. At the same time her sexual adjustment with her husband improved somewhat (pp. 391–392).

How well, actually, does this clinical account illustrate the underlying theory? One can see, readily enough, the element of inconvenience and suffering in the symptom, namely, the patient's "great fear that her heart would stop beating if she did not constantly concentrate on counting its beats." But wherein was the libidinal satisfaction? The authors do not, with respect to this particular symptom at any rate, presume to say. One might conjecture (in typical Freudian fashion) that the heart was a "displacement upward" of the patient's "throbbing, pulsating vagina"—and thus get the sexual element into the picture. And the compulsive counting of each heartbeat might be seen as a way of measuring, limiting, and controlling the forbidden, hidden sexual satisfaction thus obtained.

A much less contrived (and inherently more plausible) interpretation would run as follows: As a child, Mrs. A had been "seduced" by her brother. If her role in this incident had been as completely innocent as the case presentation would imply, why had she never before given herself the satisfaction of reporting it? And why, in later life, had she (though married) engaged in such flagrantly provocative behavior as hitchhiking rides with truck drivers at night and going on drinking parties with single girls? No, the more likely explanation was that Mrs. A was deeply and realistically guilty and was afraid that, as a punishment for her unconfessed misdeeds, she was going to die—and counting each heartbeat was a way of painfully reminding herself how little time she had left. The death penalty for serious sin and crime is by no means unknown in the history of mankind, and the symptom, thus interpreted, can be seen as a different type of "compromise formation," not between sexual impulse and unrealistic fear, but between deep guilt and the wish to confess and thus be restored socially (cf. her admission of the symptom) and the prideful resolution *not* to make such a confession. Hence the conversion of the problem into heart trouble, which indeed it was, metaphorically.

But what about the (at least qualified) success of the therapeutic strategy which Dollard and Miller describe? "This produced a marked reduction in her fear. . . . At the same time her sexual adjustment with her husband improved somewhat." When, after great hesitation, Mrs. A had originally admitted to a history of incest (p. 251), the therapist had "maintained his calm, warm, accepting silence without giving her the punishment or disapproval that she seemed to expect." Was not this a classical instance of extinction of an unrealistic fear? And was not the patient's improved sexual adjustment with her husband the direct and tangible consequence? The authors, in support of this supposition, say:

> Since Mrs. A's tendency to get into situations where she was likely to be seduced or raped was exposing her to real danger, the therapist labeled this behavior for her as soon as he thought her fear was reduced to a point where she could accept his interpretation. Pointing out that she was seeking situations in which she could get sexual gratification without being responsible also helped to focus her attention on the basic conflict (p. 392).

Mrs. A does not give one the impression of having been a particularly inhibited person in the sexual realm. But she did manifestly have trouble speaking the simple truth about herself. So may we not plausibly interpret her "confession" to the therapist (elsewhere, p. 246, Dollard and Miller themselves use this term) as a first tentative step in a good direction, which deserved the therapist's warm approval? But on the assumption that the basic difficulty was fear which was specifically associated with normal sexual gratification, he maintained a "calm, warm, accepting silence." Would it not have been far more helpful if, instead of thus trying to *extinguish* a supposedly unrealistic fear, he had actively *reinforced* this budding habit of honesty? And if he had then suggested to Mrs. A that she "generalize" her confession to her husband and a few significant others, the improvement in the patient's sexual adjustment with her husband might have been facilitated even more markedly. As her legitimate, socially approved sexual partner, he was undoubtedly a tangible reminder of her accumulated guilts; and if she could have been helped to improve her moral and spiritual relationship with *him*, her sexual responsiveness should have improved as a matter of course. Such minimal improvement in the patient's sexual adjustment with her husband as was actually observed came, it would seem, because she had made at least a beginning step in clearing her conscience by admitting her "identity" to at least one person (the therapist) instead of trying to continue to hide it completely.

How differently one proceeds, as a therapist, depending upon whether one assumes that the patient is suffering from an unrealistic fear of gratifying some natural, biological drive such as sex or aggression *or* from a fully realistic fear and apprehension lest his past improper gratification of such impulses come to light and result in at least some of the consequences which would have ensued had he been "caught in the act"! Both theories of neurosis make the afflicted individual out as something of a coward: a "stupid" (Dollard and Miller's term), needlessly self-limiting coward in the one case, and a simple moral coward in the other. So the role of the therapist is, in both instances, to help the other person develop courage. But the nature of this courage is very different, depending upon one's conception of "neurosis." In the Freudian framework, it is courage to be "independent" and *go against* certain conventional values, whereas in the other context it is the courage to "surrender" and *go with* such conventions as those which say that one should not live duplicitously.[10]

If at the point at which Mrs. A admitted to the perverse relationship with her brother and other sexual irregularities, she had been encouraged also to start honestly interacting with her husband and other members of her family (or perhaps the members of an artificial therapy group), it seems probable that her recovery would have moved forward swiftly and dramatically. But, as so often happens when classical (or even modified) analytic theory is followed, the actual course of Mrs. A's treatment was protracted and full of vicissitudes. On this score Dollard and Miller say:

> As Mrs. A began to think more fear-arousing thoughts and to do more fear-provoking things, to become a more sexually responsive woman and a more aggressive, less subdued person, some of her fears returned. For example, she became afraid of going out alone and acquired a fear of pregnancy. By labeling the clearly sexual elements in her wishes when clear-cut opportunities came up, and by failing to punish such sexual thoughts as she was able to express, the therapist helped her to become able to think about the real problem, namely, how to achieve good sexual relations with her husband. As she became able to put this into words, the generalized fears responsible for her irrational phobic symptoms, such as being afraid to go out on the street, were weakened. Securing more sexual satisfaction with her husband also tended to reduce the strength of the sex drive that motivated her to do foolish and frightening things on the street. The summation of both of these sources of fear reduction eliminated the phobia of going out alone on the street (p. 392).

In order not to protract comment on what seems to have been (typically, for psychoanalytically oriented therapies) an unduly circuitous course of treatment, whose end result is still open to question, suffice it to say that instead of working directly with the patient for improved sexual adjustment with her husband, one might have more expeditiously worked for an improved *moral* adjustment with him and other meaningful persons. When this had been achieved, along lines already suggested, it is likely that improved sexual adjustment would have been a not inconsiderable by-product. One wonders how basic or lasting a purely "sexual" recovery is ever likely to be, when the moral and interpersonal problems which were involved are dealt with only in the therapeutic context—and then in a rather inverted fashion. Analysts, when they wish to be particularly enigmatic, sometimes say: "Patients don't get well in analysis; they get well in life." But in the same breath, they are likely to admonish their patients, whatever they do, *not* to discuss the content of the analysis with other persons, lest it "weaken the transference." Elsewhere (Mowrer, 1963c; Mowrer, 1963d) an attempt has been made to show that the whole concept of transference is probably a misconception and that it can be

[10] Lest a hasty reading of the foregoing paragraph lead to the inference that the condition of emotional recovery is here being equated to a stodgy, unrelieved social conformity, it should be pointed out that all that this conception demands is that whatever role one chooses to play, he play it with *integrity*. If one *must* be socially deviant or defiant, then let him at least be honest rather than duplicitous in this role. This seems to be the simple but inexorable requirement of mental hygiene (cf. Mowrer, 1964).

mercifully circumvented by the cultivation of radical honesty, not just with a therapist, but with significant others as well.

Therefore, in no fundamental sense do we find Dollard and Miller differing from, or going substantially beyond, the position which was taken a quarter of a century earlier by Burnham. They had, of course, the benefit (if such it was) of Freud's later writings; and, by 1950, Hull (1943) had also refined and elaborated upon the work of Pavlov, Watson, and Thorndike, thus making available a somewhat more sophisticated form of learning theory than was extant in 1924. However, the basic concepts, in both psychoanalysis and the psychology of learning, which Dollard and Miller drew upon were already well known to, and "applied" by, Burnham.

Only in one respect may Dollard and Miller be said to have specifically surpassed Burnham, namely, in their more explicit and detailed concern with therapy. Burnham, it will be recalled, had explicitly assigned this enterprise to "the physician and the hospital," keeping only mental hygiene as a legitimate field for psychologist and educator. However, even Dollard and Miller report that Mrs. A was treated by a psychiatrist, rather than by either of them, thus tacitly accepting the restriction of treatment to the medical profession. This, actually, is not difficult to understand, for Dollard and Miller (like Burnham) start with the assumption that neurosis is essentially a *biological* problem; that is, they assume that the "misery" which is neurosis arises specifically from the "pain" of unsatisfied primary drives which are blocked by unrealistic, mislearned fears. Thus, the "illness" is one of emotion (with its physiological overtones), coupled with instinctual, bodily, biological privation. As long as this theory of personality disturbance is accepted, the physician can legitimately claim "ultimate authority and responsibility" in this field. But if the problem is, rather, one of unacknowledged misconduct and ensuing social apprehension and guilt, we may well ask, with Shakespeare, whether a person so afflicted "needs more the physician or the divine." Except that now we would think about the problem interpersonally—horizontally, rather than in a vertical, supernaturalistic manner.

But does not the psychoanalytic approach also have an ethical message and aim? Was not the objective of treatment in the case of Mrs. A to get her to abandon such irresponsible behavior as nocturnal hitchhiking and promiscuous drinking and to become capable of a conventional sexual relationship with her husband? The difference may thus appear to be one of means rather than ends; but the means are such, it seems, as to shape, or "misshape," the ends. As long as one assumes that sexual inhibition and deprivation are the source of neurotic anguish and ignores the alternative possibility that this anguish stems instead from the chronic *moral* vulnerability which we call "guilt," just so long will the means be wide of the mark, and the goal of genuine personality change achieved only by chance. If, on the other hand, one assumes that in so-called "neurosis" one is dealing not with instinctual pressures but with an *identity* crisis, i.e., a crisis at the very core of a person's being (or existence), steps can then be taken which are much more specifically relevant—and correspondingly more effective.

It so happens that while this chapter was being written, a married woman graduate student came into my office. She had recently completed a seminar and had had one personal interview with me. On the occasion of her second visit, she reported that (after the previous one) she had taken the initiative in "talking" with her physician, a close woman friend, and her husband. She had previously suffered from severe psychosomatic difficulties and diffuse anxiety. After an honest conversation with her physician, this woman reported him as saying: "Fine, now we have something to work on, some basis for understanding your physical problems." The relationship with her husband was so much improved that the woman added: "I can see it already redounding to the benefit of our children." And whereas this woman had initially done poor work in the seminar, she finished it with greatly improved confidence and efficiency. She herself summed the situation up by saying: "I didn't need specialized psychological or psychiatric treatment. All I needed was a little encouragement in doing what I could, *and should,* have done a long time ago: namely, start being honest, rather than hypocritical." This is a kind of responsibility—a "response-ability," i.e., the capacity to help oneself—which remains in total eclipse so long as the problem is seen as one of *wrong emotions*. When it is recast in terms of *wrong actions* and refusal to set them right, a much fuller measure of accountability and responsibility is restored to the individual, with results such as those just described.[11]

IV

As we have seen, the interest and excitement aroused by the publication of Burnham's book in 1924 had so far died down as to permit Dollard and Miller, in their 1950 volume, to make no reference to it. Their book enjoyed a lively vogue for a few years and then, also, was sufficiently "forgotten" to permit the publication, in 1958, of another book which was, in certain respects, also strangely oblivious of the past. That book was Joseph Wolpe's *Psychotherapy by Reciprocal Inhibition.* The following appraisal is taken from a recent paper entitled "Freudianism, Behavior Therapy, and 'Self-Disclosure'" (Mowrer, 1963a):

> Dr. Wolpe is at pains, in the volume which we shall take as the principal basis for our discussion, to give the reader, quickly and clearly, the essence of his argument. He has prepared a concise introductory statement for this purpose; and I shall largely confine myself, as far as Wolpe's views are concerned, to what is said therein.
>
> At the outset Dr. Wolpe contrasts his concepts and procedures with those of Freudian psychoanalysis. The latter is protracted and only minimally effective, whereas his methods work swiftly and surely. Psychoanalysis is predicated on the assumption that repression is the "primal pathogenic act," and its reversal is regarded as the essence of cure. Dr. Wolpe says he is presenting "a new theory of psychotherapy" (p. ix) which is based "on modern learning theory" and is, purportedly, very different. Its central thesis: "Since neurotic behavior demonstrably originates in learning, it is only to be expected that its elimination will be a matter of unlearning" (p. ix); "most neuroses are basically unadaptive conditioned anxiety reactions" (p. xi).[12]

Neurosis, according to Wolpe, originates when a human being (or laboratory animal) is arbitrarily punished for behavior which is motivated by hunger, sex, or some other bodily need or drive. The result is that the subject, when the pertinent need recurs, experiences "anxiety" and is unable to *act* in a manner appropriate to the need: i.e., is *inhibited.* Therapy, for Wolpe, therefore involves what he calls "reciprocal inhibition" which, in practice, turns out to be either "experimental extinction" or "counter-conditioning." In other words, it consists of enticing the subject (in fantasy or fact) to perform the previously punished act and then either showing that this act is not really dangerous or else arranging so that it will be followed by reward of some nature. The negative expectancies previously associated with the performance (or mere contemplation) of the act are thus progressively weakened and the attendant inhibitions eliminated.

Although the language is different, this conception of neurosis and its treatment is deeply—one can almost say "classically"—psychoanalytic. In what has come to be known as his *first* theory of neurotic anxiety, Freud held that sexual energy ("libido") which is arbitrarily denied expression and satisfaction becomes directly transformed into anxiety. But Freud soon moved on to the view (his *second* theory) that anxiety is, to use Pavlovian terms, simply a fear that has become conditioned to an impulse as a result of that impluse having previously eventuated in behavior which was punished. Thus, when

[11] If the reader is disposed to wonder how representative the Dollard-Miller book is of the total field at the time of its publication (1950), he may wish to consult the paper by Shoben (1949) entitled "Psychotherapy as a Problem in Learning Theory." Here the position, buttressed by some 66 references, is that "clinical cases share in common (a) anxiety touched off by (b) unverbalized, unsuccessfully repressed impulses to act in ways that have met with punishment, and (c) persistent non-integrative behavior of many kinds, which reduces the anxiety but does nothing about eliminating its objective causes" (p. 6). On the assumption that the individual has thus acquired inappropriate, unrealistic fears, the therapist tries to provide "a corrective emotional experience" in an interpersonal atmosphere characterized by "warmth, permissiveness, and complete freedom from moralistic and judgmental attitudes on the part of the counselor" (Dollard & Miller, 1950, p. 16). The Dollard-Miller conception of neurosis and its treatment may thus be said to represent faithfully, but not go substantially beyond, the prevailing (and predominantly Freudian) views of the period. (Shoben, incidentally, also makes no reference to the Burnham book.) The author, although himself long identified with psychoanalysis and the attempt to articulate it with learning theory (cf. Mowrer, 1939; Mowrer, 1940), had, by mid-century, largely abandoned this frame of reference (see Mowrer, 1948; Mowrer, 1950; Mowrer, 1953b). The conception of psychopathology which is set forth in this chapter has thus been in the process of development and elaboration for more than fifteen years.

[12] It is interesting to note that a similar but very much better justified claim to novelty was made, in 1924, by Burnham. He said: "The far-reaching result of the fact that any associated or conditioned stimulus may produce fear has been appreciated only by a few. No extended studies have been made. Psychiatrists, however, have plenty of illustrations of this indirect cause of fear" (p. 422).

this impluse subsequently starts to re-emerge into consciousness and to instigate consummatory behavior, the subject experiences the associated fear without recognizing the instigating impulse. Such a conditioned fear or "anxiety" was seen by Freud as the primary energy of the superego (or archaic, infantile conscience); and the goal of therapy, in the "transference relationship," was to extinguish or counter-condition this fear ("soften" the superego) so that inhibition would be replaced by freedom of choice and "spontaneous" action. Stripped of terminological peculiarities and converted into the same standard notation (such as that of symbolic logic), this conception of neurosis and its management differs, it seems, in no significant particular from the "new" interpretation put forward by Dr. Wolpe.

Dr. Wolpe says that psychoanalysis and related therapies are successful in only 50% of the cases (which is no better than can be expected on the basis of spontaneous remission), whereas his own methods, he claims, are 90% successful. It is to be hoped that this high level of effectiveness is substantiated and maintained, but there are reasons for skepticism. Since theory and technique seem basically so similar in both psychoanalysis and the Wolpian version of behavior therapy, it is not immediately clear why one procedure should work so poorly and the other so well. Both approaches involve a long-recognized enigma: In the laboratory and in ordinary life it has been found that fears which are not reinforced, at least occasionally, "spontaneously" extinguish.[13] Both psychoanalysis and behavior therapy are predicated on the contrary assumption of the essential permanence of some (why not *all*?) fears unless they are subjected to special "treatment" procedures.

[13] For a review of some of the empirical evidence on this score, see the original, unabridged version of the paper from which the above discussion is taken. The notion that responses which are learned through "aversive" conditioning are essentially permanent (unless subjected to special treatment procedures) is, of course, essential to the whole logic of Freudian psychoanalysis and all ancillary therapeutic strategies. In a recent paper by Lovibond (1963), reference is made to "the well-known resistance to extinction of conditioned avoidance response" (p. 17). Conditioned fears do indeed have a certain durability—otherwise they would not offer living organisms much of an advantage biologically. But they do eventually undergo *spontaneous* extinction, unless reinforced at least occasionally. The assumption of permanency leads to what has been called the "neurotic paradox" (Mowrer, 1948) and has never been satisfactorily resolved within the Freudian framework. Its resolution appears to lie along very different lines (cf. section II and footnote 7).

Even more remarkably, Dr. Wolpe regards his approach as "new"—"nobody else tries to treat patients on the reciprocal inhibition principle" (p. xi). At least ten years ago I recall having heard the Canadian psychiatrist, Dr. Ewen Cameron, in a lecture at the V. A. Hospital at North Little Rock, Arkansas, speak of using the method of "desensitization" (a term which Dr. Wolpe also applies to his approach). A nurse presented herself with complaints of acute anxiety. Inquiry revealed a masturbatory conflict. By means of reassurance and suggestion, the conflict was "desensitized," i.e., the fears associated with the masturbatory behavior were extinguished, and the patient was purportedly cured. When I was a graduate student, more than 30 years ago at Johns Hopkins University where Knight Dunlap was Departmental Head, I was exposed to his concept of "negative practice," which is essentially an extinctive technique (cf. Dunlap, 1932); and Burnham published a book on mental hygiene, in 1924, which reflects similar thinking—he even spoke of "inhibition of the inhibitions" (pp. 388ff). Manifestly, the Wolpian approach is neither "different" nor "new," and it goes contrary to some well-established principles in the very field from which it purports to draw its main scientific justification. Yet it is enjoying considerable popularity and exciting widespread interest.

The record of therapeutic effectiveness claimed by Wolpe and many of his associates (cf. Eysenck, 1960) is admittedly impressive, and in the light of the foregoing considerations, it is presently difficult to know quite how to evaluate such claims. Time alone will tell the whole story, but there are at least some hints as to what the situation may actually be. Let us consider the following case history, first reported by Wolpe in 1954:

"Mr. S., a 40-year-old accountant, was sent to me for the treatment of impotence by a psychoanalyst whom he had told that he could not wait the two years estimated to be necessary for psychoanalytic treatment. He said that his relationship with the woman he loved "could not be kept on ice for so long. . . ."

"About a year before coming for treatment Mr. S. had fallen progressively more deeply in love with a girl of 24 called May who worked in his office. She was responsive to him and one day, despite ejaculating prematurely, he managed to deflorate her. Finding that he had made a good impression in this act he used all sorts of excuses to avoid further intercourse. After 6 months, when May was about to go on holiday, he felt obliged to make another attempt but ejaculated before entry. During May's absence, Mr. S. tried to seduce two other women but was thwarted by failure of erection. He then saw a psychiatrist who gave him massive injections of testosterone [male hormone]. He was still receiving the hormone when May returned but his performance was worse than ever, for he could not even muster an erection. May began to show signs of coolness towards Mr. S. when later coital attempts were also unsuccessful. It was for this reason that Mr. S. was anxious to find a quick resolution of his sexual difficulties. . . .

"The simplicity of the treatment described will be surprising to many. . . . At the fourteenth interview Mr. S. stated that he had twice had successful intercourse—slightly premature on the first occasion but very prolonged on the second. He was much encouraged—to the extent that he had married May by special licence! Two days later he reported that they had had simultaneous orgasms on two successive nights" (pp. 110–111).

It is not inconceivable that a major reason for improvement in this situation was that Mr. S. *married* May, thus legitimizing their relationship and assuaging the *guilt* which might very well have been a factor in his prior sexual incapacity. But Mr. S., it could be pointed out, had been impotent in a previous marriage, which had ended in divorce, so this interpretation, without further information, is not entirely persuasive. Or it may be that here was a man with only a fragment of conscience in the sexual area—not enough to induce him to observe the conventions but enough to impair his sexual abilities—a man who, by means of psychotherapy, was divested of what little inner constraint he had previously had and thus "freed" in the way that a sociopath is free. Can it be that when Dr. Wolpe and his followers report therapeutic successes they are speaking of the disappearance of specific "symptoms" at the price of a general corrosion of character? Stekel (1938) reports the case of a traveling salesman who was impotent with all women except his wife. Would removal of *this* "symptom" have been counted a great therapeutic and moral victory? On the assumption that symptoms are the very legitimate protests by conscience against an odious life style, can we be certain that mere symptom removal is either a social or an individual service? *Moral* as well as "purely medical" (biological) considerations are manifestly involved in situations of this kind and need to be taken into account in judging therapeutic effectiveness.

The reader who wishes to familiarize himself more fully with Wolpian concepts and methods (and the very considerable influence they have had in psychiatry and clinical psychology in recent years) may consult a volume entitled *Behavior Therapy and the Neuroses,* which was published in 1960 under the editorship of H. J. Eysenck. Wolpe's writings and general approach have inspired a number of symposia (see, for example, Franks et al., 1962) and conferences, and a new journal called *Behavior Research and Therapy,* under the editorship of Eysenck, also heavily reflects the Wolpian emphasis. In the first issue of this journal, Wolpe himself has a paper entitled "Psychotherapy: The Nonscientific Heritage and the New Science." Here he says that "after 60 years of expanding influence, psychoanalytic theory still, in almost every particular, consists of nothing more than speculation" (p. 24). But what Wolpe fails to mention is that his own approach has had eloquent advocates since at least 1924 (a period of 40 years) without the utopian results which he feels it can produce.

Rachman (1963), writing in the same issue of *Behavior Research and Therapy,* begins an article with the ebullient statement that, in the Wolpian version of behavior therapy, treatment procedures "vary from aversion conditioning to desensitization" (p. 3). When one remembers that "desensitization" is merely another name for extinction and that "aversion conditioning" (as employed, for example, in the treatment of alcoholism) is simply an instance of counterconditioning, one is reminded of an evaluation which a critic once made of Katherine Hepburn's acting: He said it "ran the emotional gantlet from A to B." In 1924 Burnham, extrapolating from certain laboratory studies by Pavlov and Watson, suggested that the essence of the interpersonal operation called "psychotherapy" is "inhibition of the inhibitions," by means of either extinction or counterconditioning. This same theme was reiterated in 1950 by Dollard and Miller (see also Shoben, 1949). Now it is enjoying another revival, at the hands of Wolpe and his associates. It can be anticipated that this beguilingly simple hypothesis will, after a brief popularity, again drop into desuetude. The difficulty, it seems, is that both it *and* psychoanalysis involve a crucial misconception concerning the nature of so-called "neurosis"—and of human nature itself.

V

Writing in 1956, Wolpe explicitly claimed that, with the aid of conditioning concepts (notably those of extinction and counterconditioning), he had developed a *new* theory and method of treating personality disorders (cf. Masserman, 1943; Salter, 1949). Six years earlier, Dollard and Miller (see also Shoben, 1949) made a more modest claim, namely, that they were merely translating psychoanalytic concepts into the language of learning theory and then drawing the implications for therapy which seemed to follow therefrom. As we have now seen, Burnham, in 1924, had already made such a translation and, in elaboration of preliminary ideas advanced by Watson, had suggested that extinction and counterconditioning constitute the core procedures in all rational therapy.

In contrast to the recurrent intimations of novelty and innovation which have thus been made without adequate foundation, Skinner and his collaborators began, about the time of the publication of Wolpe's book, a program of "diagnosis and treatment" which, in at least two major ways, broke with the tradition which has here been traced. Skinner and his associates assumed that it is scientifically and practically idle to stress the *emotional* factor in pathological states, and they focused attention instead upon actual, objective *behavior*. They also assumed that neurosis is less a state of emotional overlearning than of behavioral underlearning or mislearning, and they embarked upon a series of attempts to reshape behavior. They thus shifted the emphasis from the extinction or counterconditioning of supposedly "abnormal" emotions to *positive behavioral learning* under conditions of controlled stimulation and reinforcement.

In a book entitled *Cumulative Record,* Skinner (1959) has a section entitled "The Analysis of Neurotic and Psychotic Behavior," wherein he reproduces three papers which were published, respectively, in 1953, 1954, and 1955. In the first of these papers (entitled "A Critique of Psychoanalytic Concepts and Theories"), he characterizes Freud's conception of neurosis as follows:

> [Freud represented] each of the causal relationships he had discovered as a series of three events. Some environmental condition, very often in the early life of the individual, leaves an effect upon the inner mental apparatus, and this in turn produces the behavioral manifestation or symptom. Environmental event, mental state or process, behavioral symptom—these are the three links in Freud's causal chain. He made no appeal to the middle link to explain spontaneity or caprice. Instead he used it to bridge the gap in space and time between the events he had proved to be causally related (pp. 187–188).[14]

Here is a description of Freudian theory which coincides well with the characterization given in section I (see especially Figure 1). By contrast, Skinner, as a latter-day proponent of "the American movement called Behaviorism," took the position that "the individual organism simply reacts to its environment, rather than to some inner experience of that environment" (p. 188). Thus, the student of psychopathology was to give no thought to hypothetical inner states and would instead undertake the *"explicit shaping of behavioral repertoires"* (p. 191).

In the 1954 article ("Psychology in the Understanding of Mental Disease"), Skinner held that the defining ("operational") criterion of mental disease is that the individual manifests behavior which someone finds "troublesome or dangerous" (p. 198). And then he adds:

> By manipulating the event called reinforcement, it is possible not only to shape up many novel forms of behavior but also to sustain almost any given level of activity for long periods of time. . . . It is reasonable to suppose that such an experimental science will eventually produce a technology capable of modifying and sustaining any given pattern of behavior almost at will (p. 198).

In the paper which appeared in 1955 ("What Is Psychotic Behavior?"), Skinner reports that he and Dr. Ogden R. Lindsley had started some research with patients at the Metropolitan State Hospital at Waltham, Massachusetts; and he concludes on the following ebullient note:

> In that bright future to which research in psychiatry is now pointing, we must be pre-

[14] Elsewhere Skinner says that "many of the causal relationships which he [Freud] so convincingly demonstrated" were more in the nature of "inventions" than "discoveries." "He carried the day with sheer persuasion . . ." (p. 185).

> pared for the possibility that increasing emphasis will be placed on immediately observable data and that theories of human behavior will have to adjust themselves accordingly. It is not inconceivable that the mental apparatus and all that it implies will be forgotten. It will then be more than a mere working hypothesis to say—to return at long last to my title—that psychotic behavior, like all behavior, is part of the world of observable events to which the powerful methods of natural science apply and to the understanding of which they will prove adequate (p. 219).

This, of course, is to denignate completely the premise that man is a *self*-directing (and *mis*directing) organism and to affirm instead that he is a mere automaton which is directed and determined entirely from without.[15] But if the direction *does* come from without, who then supplies it? Earlier in the same paper Skinner speaks of "the prediction and control" (p. 204) of human behavior. Control *by whom?* Presumably by behavioral scientists. And suppose the scientists differ among themselves on what is good for the masses? A recent issue of the *Atlantic Monthly* carried a feature story on Skinner in which the author quotes him as having written (in one of his innumerable "daybooks" or diaries): "It may all be up to me." It has been said that "one goes mad if one goes too far alone." Skinner and Carl Rogers have engaged in a series of debates on the issues thus raised. Here we shall not pursue them, but it *is* useful to see where Skinner stands, philosophically and politically.

Lindsley's first major report on the work at Metropolitan State Hospital appeared in 1956 and was entitled "Operant Conditioning Methods Applied to Research in Chronic Schizophrenia." Like many of his later papers, it was largely methodological in nature, but there were at least allusions to both presuppositions and empirical findings. Since there are today "many suggestions of how patients become psychotic, many suggestions about how to cure them, but surprisingly few quantified descriptions of exactly how and under what conditions they are psychotic" (p. 119), the first objective was to get precise behavioral comparisons of psychotic and nonpsychotic human subjects in a "free-operant" conditioning procedure (namely, that provided by an enlarged, room-size version of the device known as a "Skinner box," which was originally designed for use with laboratory rats).

> In two and a half years we have collected approximately 4,500 hours of data from 60 psychotic patients (p. 132).
>
> The primary purpose of our investigations has not been to produce therapy through automatic reinforcement of an isolated segment of a patient's behavior, although such a development would be more than welcome. Our purpose has been to develop a basic research tool for measurement of the simple and complex, individual and social behavior of psychotic patients, and then to proceed with an analysis of behavior anomalies found in psychosis (pp. 135–136).

Except for the fact that psychotic subjects were more erratic and harder to motivate than normal subjects, no very clear finding had emerged from Lindsley's studies as of this juncture.

Four years later, Lindsley (1960) published a paper entitled "Characteristics of the Behavior of Chronic Psychotics as Revealed by Free-operant Conditioning Methods." Despite an expansive introduction, this paper concludes, modestly enough, as follows:

> Much of what we have learned from our carefully controlled experiments appears in retrospect to be composed of things that skilled, experienced clinicians "knew" all the time. . . . But remember that we now have the advantage of measuring these things automatically in the laboratory (p. 15).

The most recent paper by Lindsley to which I have access was published in 1963 and is entitled "Free-operant Conditioning and Psychotherapy." This, too, begins optimistically:

> Free-operant conditioning principles can provide a fresh, exciting, and highly relevant theoretical background for the practice of office, group, and ward psychotherapy (p. 49).

But the author's concluding remarks indicate that this line of investigation is still largely programmatic:

[15] At a time when even the machines which we employ in factories and elsewhere are changing from the open-circuit (stimulus-response) to the closed-circuit (feedback) principle, Skinner and his followers are still arguing that human beings themselves are *less* self-directing and self-regulating than the mechanical contrivances they produce. For a systematic application of the servo (feedback) principle to learning theory, see Mowrer, 1960a; Mowrer, 1960b.

> Exploratory experiments have shown that free-operant principles and methods have wide application in social and clinical behavioral research. The method shows promise in the analysis of psychotherapy behavior and process [i.e., in quantifying the behavioral changes produced by *other* forms of psychotherapy] (p. 55).

In 1955 Leonard Krasner published a paper entitled "The Use of Generalized Reinforcers in Psychotherapy Research" in which he advanced the following argument:

> As both Shaw (1948) and Shoben (1949) point out in their applications of learning theory to psychotherapy, one means of extinguishing previously repressed behavior, and all the anxiety it evokes, is to have it verbalized (symbolically produced) and followed by no disapproval. But, before the patient can find out that his speech is not going to be disapproved or punished, he must actually verbalize and see for himself that no negative reinforcement follows.
>
> [Therefore], a secondary problem is for the therapist to use his techniques to guide the patient's verbalizations into certain areas which he feels will eventually be beneficial to the patient. He does this by a variety of reinforcing techniques such as suggestion, interpretation, questioning, or other ways of indicating that he is interested in or paying particular attention to certain aspects of the patient's verbalizations. Thus, since verbalization is of such importance in therapy, and since it is a segment of general behavior which is measurable, it would seem to be the logical dependent variable with which to start an experimental approach to the problem of psychotherapy (p. 22).

Here we see an attempt to combine the classical Freudian assumption of emotional malconditioning (and repression) with certain Skinnerian behavior-shaping methods. Krasner has published a number of intervening papers, both alone and with associates, but for our purposes we may limit discussion to a 1963 paper entitled "Reinforcement, Verbal Behavior, and Psychotherapy" (which, incidentally, has a good bibliography and review of related studies; cf. also Bandura, 1961; Bandura, 1963) and to one entitled "The Effects of Reinforcement on Pleasantness of Emotional Words Used by Normal and Psychiatric Subjects" (Ullmann, Krasner, & Gelfand, 1962). The first of these papers begins by saying that a "revolution" appears to be in progress in "ways of conceptualizing psychotherapy":

> The key concepts in this "new" approach to psychotherapy are social reinforcement and behavior control. . . . Psychotherapy is viewed as a lawful influence process within the broader context of studies of behavior control (p. 601).
>
> Behavior control studies represent a view of personality as being primarily a function of the outside-environmental stimuli, social interactions, social roles. It is at once a highly optimistic, as well as highly threatening view of man (p. 602).

Turning from the hortatory aspect of Krasner's writings, we find, again, that empirical accomplishments are modest. Here, in the paper by Ullmann, Krasner, and Gelfand, we read:

> In our work with the verbal conditioning of emotional words, we observed the phenomenon, repeated with a variety of examiners, subjects, and experimental conditions, that reinforcement not only increased the frequency of use of emotional words, but that it also led to the use of pleasanter words. There were not only changes in frequency but also changes in content. Further, we found that subjects' use of relatively pleasanter emotional words was significantly associated with test measures of anxiety. Finally, we obtained evidence that the relative pleasantness of emotional words used by subjects was influenced by experimental conditions.
>
> From theory, from similarities to Dollard and Mowrer's 1947 work, from the manner in which the emotional word variable has been derived, and from our own previous research on changing perceptual defence and adequacy of interpersonal behavior in group therapy, we believe that we are dealing with an important category of human behavior (p. 4).

The significance of certain aspects of this line of inquiry remains to be evaluated, but in other ways the findings are not surprising. Beginning in 1951, Greenspoon (in a series of studies which have recently been reviewed, Greenspoon, 1962) has convincingly shown that *verbal behavior,* like behavior in general, can indeed be "shaped" by the appropriate use of positive and negative reinforcers with normal subjects. To date, Krasner and his associates have apparently done little more than to show that similar effects can be produced with hospitalized patients. If behavior therapists would shift their attention from Freud's conception of neurosis to the view (suggested in section I; see also section VI) that neurosis begins with socially deviant action which is then protected by systematic deception with respect to that action, efforts to modify verbal output might take on real significance. Here actual practice has already advanced far beyond anything that Skinner and his followers seem to have contemplated (cf. Krasner, 1961). There is already ample evidence for believing (cf. Mowrer, 1964, and Mowrer, 1956b) that radical honesty on the part of the would-be helping person ("therapist") provides both the greatest incentive and the maximal reinforcement for a change in verbal habits (pertaining to honesty) *and* in the behavior which such dishonesty has previously shielded. In his 1955 paper, Krasner refers to a study in which "Peters (1952) used fudge candy as reinforcers with psychotics who had first been deprived of sugar" (p. 24). In psychosis and neurosis, "fudg(ing)" is the problem, not the cure. And there appears to be no more powerful incentive for a patient to modify his verbal habits in this regard than a "relationship" with a person whose own behavior provides a model of integrity and openness (Jourard, 1963; O'Connell, 1962).

There is already a large and rapidly proliferating literature (see, for example, Dinoff, Rickard, Salzberg, & Sipprelle, 1960; Isaacs, Thomas, & Goldiamond, 1960; King, Armitage, & Tilton, 1960; Rickard, Digman, & Horner, 1960; Robertson, 1958; Rogers, 1960; Sarason, 1958; Waskow, 1962) on Skinner-type investigations in the area of psychopathology and psychotherapy.[16] But much of it remains in the methodological and promotional stages, and despite the continuing air of excitement, one sees no substantial practical effect of accomplishment. In many respects the most impressive study known to me is one reported in a paper by Wolf, Mees, and Risley (1963) entitled "Application of Operant Conditioning Procedures to the Behavior Problems of an Autistic Child." Here, without going into detail, it can be said that the results obtained were truly dramatic. But, as Kanner (1935) has long since pointed out, there is a fundamental distinction between autism and childhood schizophrenia and other more highly evolved types of adult personality disorders. In autism we are dealing with the lowest possible degree of socialization (or, conversely, with the highest degree of socialization *failure*), i.e., the consequences of systematic and protracted neglect and mismanagement. Personality and character are minimally developed, and the individual is least removed from the "animal" level. It should therefore not surprise us, perhaps, if behavior-modification methods which have been developed in the animal laboratory should find effective application here.[17] But once *character* has developed to a substantial degree (as it normally has by the age of five or six years), it seems that neurosis has dimensions and complexities which many contemporary investigators completely overlook. Manifestly, we must have a conception of the problem which is more congruent with the facts than has thus far been given us either by Freudian psychoanalysis or by the study of laboratory animals. Neurosis, as indicated in section I, is preeminently a disturbance in a human being's *sociality* (interpersonal relatedness, personal identity, reputation, morality); and *any* treatment method, no matter how sound it may be in some other frame of reference, cannot prove highly effective until there is an accurate diagnosis in the sense of an accurate conceptualization of the nature of the problem itself.[18]

[16] I am greatly obliged to Prof. William F. Oakes for the courtesy of making his excellent reprint library in this area available to me at the University of Hawaii during the summer of 1963.

[17] In this connection it is also pertinent to note that the same general methodology employed by Wolf, Mees, and Risley has given good results in improving the "social competence" of feebleminded children (cf. Bijou, 1961; Birnbrauer, 1963).

[18] Since this chapter went to press, some other developments have come to my attention which should be cited. Ullman et al. (1965) have explored the possibility of modifying the conversation of schizophrenic patients away from "sick talk" toward more healthy, normal, responsible utterances. The authors' hypothesis is that in mental hospitals (and in the culture at large), sick talk (complaining, referring to oneself as sick, blaming others, etc.) commonly gets reinforced, and if one could *change* patients' way of talking, by selective reinforcement, it would have a constructive effect upon their behavior and the course of their careers as patients. This investigation, although hardly more than a pilot study as far as empirical findings are concerned, is noteworthy because it focuses on a problem that is a good deal more significant than those upon which other experiments on verbal conditioning have commonly centered. Further research along these lines is well worth

VI

In March of 1962, when the Polish psychiatrist Dr. C. Dabrowski was in the United States, he spoke with me about an interest in what he called "self-education," by which he meant concepts and practices which will permit an individual to initiate and direct his own change and growth as a person along constructive, "healthy" lines. And while the preceding section of this chapter was being written, I received a letter from a state hospital research psychologist who reports that he is "presently developing a treatment program for alcoholism based on a learning approach to self-control." These two events bracket the appearance of several papers which are laying the groundwork for a *new kind* of behavior therapy—or at least a kind which has been of very little interest to psychologists and psychiatrists in recent decades.

In the summer of 1962, Dr. Willard A. Mainord published a paper entitled, simply, "A Therapy." (The title originally submitted by the author, but editorially modified, was "A Therapy for Crazy—Not Sick—People.") In this paper appear the following paragraphs:

> Much time is spent [in the form of group therapy, which has been described] upon the concept of freedom of choice. While the author is philosophically a complete determinist, the concept of freedom of choice seems an essential one to obtain motivated patients who will behave in ways that can be reinforced. Thus, the group will never accept the idea that "I can't help myself when I want a drink," etc. It is at such times that the "You're not sick—you're crazy" technique seems dramatically useful. Our patients can comfortably be sick, but when they are making crazy choices merely because it is easier that way, they typically respond with vigorous efforts to prove their ability to be responsible.
>
> Historical material is not sought for, although typically much is spontaneously offered and discussed. However, when the patient offers some reason out of the distant past for current feelings of guilt, the group denies the validity of such an explanation and insists upon examining current reasons for guilt which are assumed to be deserved. No group member can get the group to accept the idea that guilt is the result of an over-punitive superego.
>
> It is always assumed that much of the patient's behavior is designed to manipulate others, and the group is constantly alert to such manipulations which are usually in evidence right on the ward and within the group. Bids for sympathy and collections of injustices are brusquely and directly counterattacked (pp. 88–89).
>
> This perhaps sounds grim and harsh, but in practice the group is more active, engages in more humor, and is more intimately involved in both the group and in therapy than any group seen by the author over an 8-year span. Patient reaction to the therapist is often initially hostile, but soon changes to an apparently relaxed yet respectful at-

pursuing. Also the work of Dr. Teodoro Ayllon and associates (Ayllon & Michael, 1959; Ayllon & Haughten, 1962; and Ayllon, 1963) will justify continued interest. Previously at a Saskatchewan provincial hospital and now at the State Hospital at Anna, Illinois, extensive ward management programs have been put into effect which use reinforcement principles in an effort to discourage regressive, irresponsible behavior and to reward the opposite kinds of responses. The weakness of the approach seems to be that its proponents do not sufficiently distinguish between "symptoms" and deviant behavior which originally generated the patient's guilt and the defenses against it (see section I, especially Figure 1). Although it is true that symptoms are often of such a nature as to create more guilt (and thus produce a kind of downward spiral, or vicious circle), it is nevertheless useful to differentiate between guilt-producing deviant behavior and the defenses a person subsequently employs to counteract and deny guilt. At this juncture it appears that the Ayllon approach may be helpful in combatting the institutionalizing effects which conventional mental hospitals often have upon patients, but it is not clear that it fathoms or effectively deals with the forms of behavior which bring people into mental hospitals. Nursing personnel (who are actively involved in Ayllon's procedures) seem to sense this shortcoming when they wonder if anything *fundamental* happens: "We've changed her behavior. So what? She's still psychotic, isn't she?" In other words, Ayllon's methods seem better designed to facilitate the institutional management of patients (in the sense of circumventing deterioration) than it is to deal with the character defects and faulty interpersonal strategies which cause people to come into mental hospitals in the first place. It is conceivable that a *total* rehabilitative program for mental hospital inmates would be one which combined the two types of behavior therapy described, respectively, in sections I and V of this chapter. Behavior therapy, of the kind discussed in sections II, III, and IV, by contrast, seems to involve important misconceptions and to lead only to misfortunes when put into practical effect. Behavior therapy in the manner of sections II, III, and IV, it should be noted, implies the medical model of sickness, *emotional* sickness; whereas the other two approaches assume *behavioral* incompetence and *social* irresponsibility. They do not imply the medical, or disease, model and are indigenously psychological—and sociological. Two books will be published shortly (Ullman & Krasner, 1965; and Krasner & Ullman, 1965) which should provide a very comprehensive and useful survey of fact and theory in this field. They have not, however, been available in the preparation of this chapter.

> titude. The group feels free to express itself with a bit of hostile humor; thus the therapist found in his chair a printed sign advertising his services for five cents (p. 90).
>
> It may be wondered what we do about the traditional problems of transference, repressed materials, symptom substitution, etc. The answer is, consciously, nothing. All the materials are there for a more traditional therapy, but we do not look for any particular course of therapy; we merely look for improved behavior which always seems accompanied by improved emotional states. *We believe that the consequences of behavior determine emotional tone; so if we can control the behavior, we believe we also control the feeling.* Then, with Eysenck, we are arguing that the so-called symptoms are the illness, and that if they are given up, therapy is complete.
>
> It should not be concluded that we believe that the apparent success of this therapeutic technique [empirical evidence of its effectiveness is presented] necessarily implies anything about the genesis of emotional disorder. There has never seemed any logical necessity for psychotherapy to be determined by theories of the development of psychopathology. However, the hint is there that Mowrer (1961) may have contributed a valid notion when he suggests that we have been in error in thinking of the mental patient as a victim of too rigid standards.
>
> It seems to us that perhaps the chief reason that this approach appeals to the patient is that *it gives him hope.* If he is sick, he is really quite bewildered as to what he might do about his plight. If, however, he is being irresponsible, evasive, dishonest, and deceitful and if this is causing his emotional pain, it seems obvious to him what he must do; luckily it is something he believes that he can do (p. 91, italics added).

This conception of psychopathology and its remediation is in fundamental agreement with the position taken in section I of this chapter. Only in one respect is there divergence, and this may be partially semantic. Mainord says: "With Eysenck, we are arguing that the so-called symptoms are the illness, and that if they are given up, therapy is complete." To me, clarity seems to demand that we distinguish among (1) "symptoms," (2) the underlying emotional disturbance or guilt, and (3) the misbehavior ("crazy decisions") which originally made the individual guilty. If we call the original behavior deviance "symptomatic," are we not using the same term to cover two different orders of event? One does not have to be "sick" in order to "sin" (some writers to the contrary notwithstanding—compare Szasz, 1961). It is only *after* the sin that one is sick, i.e., frightened and sick of himself; and it is presumably then and only then that symptoms of (defenses against) this fear and "sickness" appear. It is certainly true that the sin or sins may continue along with the sickness and the symptoms, and the symptoms may also be (and often are) of such a nature as to augment still further the patient's guilt (e.g., consider the individual who becomes alcoholic rather than confess and rectify what he has done which is guilt-producing). Thus, disruption of the symptomatic adjustment offers a double advantage: (1) It reduces at least *one* source of guilt, and (2) it helps the afflicted individual (and those who are attempting to help him) to "get back" to the guilt which precipitated the symptomatic behavior.

Therefore, Mainord's emphasis upon *present behavior* and the urgency of its modification can be defended for the reasons just suggested. But there is yet another justification. Even though a neurotic individual may not at the moment be practicing the particular form of behavior which originally precipitated his guilt, the chances are (if he is still disturbed and sick) that he is carefully hiding and denying the earlier misconduct and has done nothing by way of either confession or restitution (except insofar as they occur involuntarily in the form of sickness and symptoms—cf. Mowrer, 1964, chap. 11). Thus, the disturbed person is, here and now, at the very least a hypocrite and a moral coward; and if he can be persuaded to become *honest* (this is strongly emphasized in the Mainord approach), the needed "movement" is almost certain to occur.

Until October, 1962 (when I had the pleasure of introducing them), Willard Mainord and William Glasser did not know or know of each other. But these two men, working in complete independence (except for the reality of the present crisis in psychotherapy, which is impinging upon many of us), have arrived at strikingly similar positions. Since he is a psychologist, it is perhaps not surprising that Mainord has reached the conclusion that neurotic and functionally psychotic persons are not sick, in the Freudian (and general psychiatric) sense, but are *crazy,* i.e., have been and still are (in one way or another) making some very foolish, socially distressing, and self-defeating decisions. But it *is* remarkable that a psychiatrist with Glasser's training and background should today be saying to "mentally ill" persons: "You're not irresponsible because you're sick; you are sick *because you are irresponsible.*" For more than eight years, Glasser (in collaboration with another Los Angeles psychiatrist, Dr. G. L. Harrington) has been evolving and clinically validating his approach, which he has recently summarized in a paper entitled "Reality Therapy: A New Approach" (see also Glasser, 1961; Glasser, 1965). The following excerpts will give the flavor and direction of Glasser's thought and practice:

> Reality Therapy . . . is a method of psychiatric treatment in which the psychiatrist develops a strong, active relationship with the patient, the patient is held responsible for his present behavior, only conscious behavior is important and the unconscious completely disregarded. Excuses for irresponsible acts are never accepted because these acts appear to be the result of a bad environment, emotional disturbance, or unconscious conflicts coming to the surface (p. 2).
>
> We believe that all people, very early in life, begin to learn a basic sense of right and wrong from which their values are derived, and in most cultures these basic values are remarkably similar. Few indeed are societies where murder, lying, cheating, stealing, cowardice, incest, promiscuity, or illegitimacy are accepted as right. Tolerated to some degree in every society, they are never considered correct behavior.
>
> It seems logical to us, then, that right and wrong must be derived from essential human needs. Following this argument a step farther, we postulate that there are two needs basic to all humans. There is first the need for closeness with oneself, to feel that we are unique and worthwhile to ourselves. Second there is the need for closeness to others, to give and receive love and friendship with others, to feel others are worthwhile to you and you to them. When a person is responsible enough to live in a way which fulfills these two needs, he will do right much more than wrong (pp. 7–8).
>
> We are not concerned with isolated feelings. If the patient is sad, depressed, angry, empty, fearful, or anxious, he must relate these feelings to what he is now doing and determine whether his behavior is responsible. No one can help a patient *feel* better; he can only be helped to *do* better, which means live a more responsible life. Never claiming that therapy can make anyone happy, we do not concern ourselves with happiness, only with responsibility (p. 8).
>
> The technique of doing Reality Therapy [although teachable to "aids, counselors, technicians and nurses"] is more difficult to learn than the theory. It takes practice and discipline not to fall into the trap of looking for reasons for deviant behavior, reasons which in all cases are grasped by the patient to avoid responsibility. Patients treated by Reality Therapy never sing the familiar refrain "I'm this way because of my mother." We feel that regardless of what the patient's mother was like, the patient still is responsible for the way he is, and only he can change. Perhaps, if he changes his behavior, his mother may change hers, but whether she does or not, he must. . . . We think the classical question of "Why?" has led psychiatry down a blind alley because it helps the patient evade reality. Its use condones present irresponsibility and promotes further deviant behavior by making the unconscious a psychological scapegoat for irresponsible behavior (Glasser, 1963, p. 13).

The parallels between the positions of Glasser and Mainord are thus numerous and striking, and both writers are in essential agreement with the conceptions of psychopathology and behavior therapy set forth at the outset of this chapter. Both agree that behavior—the patient's *own* behavior and *not* his emotions—is the basic cause of his difficulties. They both reject injustice collecting and the nursing of grudges and grievances against others. They both reject many of the traditional "psychodynamic" concepts and stress instead "responsibility" and personal choice and accountability. And instead of looking for reasons and explanations in the remote past (or on the part of others), they emphasize defects in the individual's own character and conduct, here and now.

It would be possible, if space permitted, to cite various other writers in the field of clinical psychology, psychiatry, and social work (here see, for example, London, 1953) who are moving in much the same direction. However, as a means of rounding out this discussion, it will be pertinent to allude to an article which a Canadian acquaintance (Mr. Keither Staebler) recently sent to me. It appeared in the Canadian magazine *Maclean's* (June 15, 1963) and is entitled "The Triumphant Spirit of Man." Here, by way of the editor's introduction, we read: "June Callwood's four-year study of new learning in the sciences of man has led her to this conviction; by acts of will and wisdom, any adult can change himself for the better" (p. 13). Here are a few excerpts from the article itself:

> A prominent trend in modern psychology is the cynical manipulation of emotions, poking at the brain or plying the bloodstream with chemicals to produce an a-la-carte order of any emotion the scientist desires. . . . For lasting benefit, man must still rely on his inner resources. . . . The results are less spectacular, being tediously slow, but they are permanent (pp. 13–14).
>
> It's a process that most psychologists are only beginning to admit is possible, and none can fully explain. People who mature themselves "have so much to teach us that sometimes they seem almost like a different breed of human beings," commented the eminent Brandeis University professor of psychology, Dr. Abraham H. Maslow.
>
> European psychologists have come to believe that the adult personality can change, but most North American psychology is still strongly influenced by Sigmund Freud's concept that life-long character is decided before the age of three (p. 14).

Psychologists will be busy for some time to come revising their philosophical presuppositions and conceptual models in such a way as to harmonize with some recently neglected but seemingly immutable facts concerning the nature of man and of social reality. Mainord, though "philosophically a complete determinist," has found that he has to operate on the basis of other assumptions in order to motivate disturbed individuals and give them something to hope and work for. Glasser, though trained as a physician, has found that he has to think in terms of *ir*responsibility rather than "illness." And the Callwood article indicates that Glasser and Mainord are not alone in this regard but are instead part of what seems to be a definite trend, which has been necessitated by the inadequacy and failure of other approaches.

This is not the place to explore the ideological ramifications of this change in emphasis and approach, but the reader will find a sophisticated and literate discussion of these matters in a (badly neglected) book by Cherbonnier (1955). I have, on other occasions, also ventured some suggestions that may likewise be pertinent (Mowrer, 1953; Mowrer, 1956; Mowrer, 1960b).

SUMMARY

As a summary for the person who has just read this chapter and as a preview for the prospective reader, the following paragraphs (numbered to correspond with the chapter's six sections) epitomize the over-all argument:

I. For roughly half a century, the term "psychopathology" has been almost synonymous with "emotional disorder." Now there is growing recognition that there is nothing diseased or abnormal in the emotional reactions of so-called "neurotic" or "psychotic" individuals. Given the *life-style* (i.e., the character and the conduct) of such persons, their emotions are eminently appropriate. Thus, interest is now centering upon psychotherapy as *behavior change,* rather than upon the manipulation or modification of an individual's "emotional life," as such.

II. Despite recurrent excitement, during the past thirty years, over what can be accomplished by "translating" psychoanalytic concepts into the language of learning theory, the fact is that such a translation (and a rather *good* one) was made in 1924 by William H. Burnham in a book called *The Normal Mind.* The Burnham book had considerable impact on the mental hygiene and counseling movement in schools, but it has otherwise been strangely ignored and is today almost never cited in clinical psychology or psychiatry. The practical difficulty with this book is that it, like many later efforts of a similar nature, accepted the Freudian assumption that the way to change "abnormal" behavior is (for someone else, through "treatment") to change the "underlying emotions." Exactly the opposite assumption now appears to be more valid, namely, that the way to change disturbed (and disturbing) emotions is for the individual himself to change his *behavior.*

III. Although making no reference to the Burnham book, Dollard and Miller, in a widely read volume which was published in 1950, take a basically similar position: neurotic "symptoms" are produced by "anxiety," which, in turn, is caused by a conflict between an instinctual pressure (sex or aggression) which is inhibited by a fear established by inappropriate, unrealistic punishment. Therapy, they (like Burnham) hold, calls for extinction and counterconditioning. This section ends with the following conclusion: "As long as one assumes that sexual inhibition and deprivation are the source of neurotic anguish and ignores the alternative possibility that this anguish stems instead from the chronic *moral* vulnerability which we call 'guilt,' just so long will the means be wide of the mark, and the goal of genuine personality change achieved only by chance. If, on the other hand, one assumes that in so-called 'neurosis' one is dealing not with instinctual pressures but with an *identity* crisis, i.e., a crisis at the very core of a person's being (or existence), steps can then be taken which are much more specifically relevant—and correspondingly more effective."

IV. In 1958 Wolpe published a book entitled *Psychotherapy by Reciprocal Inhibition,* in which he laid claim to both a new theory of, and a new method for treating, personality disturbances. Actually the theory, despite the use of a different terminology (and protestations to the contrary), is basically Freudian, and the method of treatment has been extensively anticipated by Burnham, Dollard and Miller, and others. Wolpe, while conceding the poor therapeutic results obtained by other workers, claims excellent results for himself and those using "his" methods. It is not yet certain how we are to evaluate this optimism. One or two suggestions are offered on this score.

V. The first real break with the Burnham-Dollard-Miller-Wolpe tradition came about a decade ago, when Skinner and his coworkers started looking at psychopathology, not in terms of emotional mislearning or overlearning, but in terms of "behavior which is troublesome or dangerous" and which needs to be *reshaped* by means of positive reinforcement. Despite the genuine conceptual novelty here involved, the clinical and research reports thus far available are mainly methodological and programmatic. In Skinner's frame of reference, the aim of psychological science is the "prediction and control" of behavior; but the question of *who* is to do the controlling is a moot one. In contrast with both Skinner's approach and that of earlier writers, a movement is now afoot to help wayward, guilt-ridden persons improve their *self*-control.

VI. The type of behavior therapy which is today in the process of emerging involves a number of assumptions which have been delineated at the outset of this chapter (section I). Here (in section VI), the work of Mainord and Glasser is taken as representative and is reviewed in some detail. In both instances, responsibility—for both the cause and the correction of a "neurotic" state—is placed directly on the afflicted individual himself. Correspondingly little attention is given to the patients' emotions, only to his *conduct.* While using predominantly objective and naturalistic language, Mainord, Glasser, and others seem to be recapturing some of the great insights of traditional morality and religion, which religionists themselves have very largely lost. Perhaps a psychological *and religious* revolution is in process, but one which will emphasize naturalistic and humanistic considerations rather than the traditional metaphysics and mythology.

REFERENCES

Alexander F., & French, T. M. *Psychoanalytic therapy.* New York: Ronald, 1946.

Ayllon, T. Intensive treatment of psychotic behavior by stimulus satiation and food reinforcement. *Behav. Res. Therapy,* 1963, **1,** 53–61.

Ayllon, T., & Haughten, E. Control of the behavior of schizophrenic patients by food. *J. exper. Anal. Behav.,* 1962, **5,** 343–352.

Ayllon, T., & Michael, J. The psychiatric nurse as a behavior engineer. *J. exper. Anal. Behav.,* 1959, **2,** 323–334.

Bandura, A. Psychotherapy as a learning process. *Psychol. Bull.,* 1961, **58,** 143–159.

Bandura, A. *Behavioristic psychotherapy.* New York: Holt, 1963.

Bijou, S. W. Discriminative performance as a baseline for individual analysis of young children. *Child Developm.,* 1961, **32,** 163–170.

Birnbrauer, J. S. Applications of reinforcement theory to clinical problems. Paper read at Amer. Ass. Ment. Def., Portland, Oregon, 1963. (Mimeographed)

Boisen, A. T. *Exploration of the inner world.* New York: Harper & Row, 1936.

Burnham, W. H. *The normal mind.* New York: Appleton-Century, 1924.

Callwood, June. The triumphant spirit of man. *Maclean's* (Canada), 1963, **76,** 13ff.

Cherbonnier, E. LaB. *Hardness of heart.* Garden City, N.Y.: Doubleday, 1955.

Dinoff, M., Rickard, H. C., Salzberg, H., & Sipprelle, C. N. An experimental analogue of three psychotherapeutic approaches. *J. clin. Psychol.*, 1960, **16**, 70–73.

Dollard, J., & Miller, N. E. *Personality and psychotherapy: an analysis in terms of learning, thinking, and culture.* New York: McGraw-Hill, 1950.

Dollard, J., & Mowrer, O. H. A method of measuring tension in written documents. *J. abnorm. soc. Psychol.*, 1947, **42**, 3–32.

Dunlap, K. The stuttering boy. *J. abnorm. Psychol.*, 1917, **12**, 44–48.

Dunlap, K. *Habits: their making and unmaking.* New York: Liveright, 1932.

Eriksen, E. H. *Young man Luther.* New York: Norton, 1958.

Eysenck, H. *Behavior therapy and the neuroses.* New York: Pergamon Press, 1960.

Frankl, V. E. *Man's search for meaning.* Boston: Beacon Press, 1962.

Franks, C. M., et al. Symposium: the application of learning theory principles to the treatment and prevention of abnormal behavior. *Amer. Psychologist,* 1962, **17**, 343.

Franz, S. I. *Nervous and mental re-education.* New York: Macmillan, 1923.

Glasser, W. *Mental health or mental illness.* New York: Harper & Row, 1961.

Glasser, W. Reality therapy: a new approach. *Thirty-second Annu. Gov's Conf. Youth,* Chicago, 1963. (Mimeographed)

Glasser, W. *Reality therapy.* New York: Harper, 1965.

Greenspoon, J. Verbal conditioning and clinical psychology. In A. J. Bachrach (Ed.), *Experimental foundations of clinical psychology.* New York: Basic Books, 1962.

Groves, E. R. *Personality and social adjustment.* New York: Longmans, 1921.

Hull, C. L. *Principles of behavior.* New York: Appleton-Century-Crofts, 1943.

Isaacs, W., Thomas, J., & Goldiamond, I. Application of operant conditioning to reinstate verbal behavior in psychotics. *J. Speech Hearing Disorders,* 1960, **25**, 8–12.

James, W. *Talks to teachers.* New York: Henry Holt, 1899.

Johnson, R. C., & Mowrer, O. H. (Eds.) Conscience and character. 1965. (To be published.)

Jones, Mary C. The elimination of children's fears. *J. Exp. Psychol.*, 1924, **7**, 382–390.

Jourard, S. M. *The transparent self.* Princeton, N.J.: Van Nostrand, 1963.

Kanner, L. *Child psychiatry.* Springfield, Ill.: Charles C Thomas, 1935.

King, G. F., Armitage, S. G., & Tilton, J. R. A therapeutic approach to schizophrenics of extreme pathology: an operant-interpersonal method. *J. abnorm. soc. Psychol.*, 1960, **61**, 276–286.

Klaw, S. Harvard's Skinner: the last of the utopians. *Harper's,* 1963, **226**, 45–51.

Krasner, L. The use of generalized reinforcers in psychotherapy research. *Psychol. Rep.*, 1955, **1**, 19–25.

Krasner, L. The therapist as a social reinforcement machine. *Res. Psychother.*, 1961, **2**, 61–90.

Krasner, L. Reinforcement, verbal behavior, and psychotherapy. *Amer. J. Psychother.*, 1963, **33**, 601–613.

Krasner, L., & Ullman, L. P. *Research in behavior modification.* New York: Holt, Rinehart & Winston, 1965.

Krechevsky, I. "Hypotheses" in rats. *Psychol. Rev.*, 1932, **19**, 425–462.

LaPiere, R. *The Freudian ethic.* New York: Duell, Sloan & Pearce, 1959.

Lindsley, O. Operant conditioning methods applied to research in chronic schizophrenia. *Psychiat. Res. Rep.*, 1956, **5**, 118–139.

Lindsley, O. Characteristics of the behavior of chronic psychotics as revealed by free-operant conditioning methods. *Dis. nerv. System,* 1960, **21**, 66–78.

Lindsley, O. Free-operant conditioning and psychotherapy. *Current psychiat. Ther.*, 1963, **3**, 47–56.

Loeb, J. *Forced movements, tropisms, and animal conduct.* Philadelphia: Lippincott, 1918.

London, P. *The modes and morals of psychotherapy.* New York: Holt, Rinehart & Winston, 1964.

Lovibond, S. H. The mechanism of conditioning treatment of enuresis. *Behav. Res. Ther.*, 1963, **1**, 17–22.

Mainord, W. A. A therapy. *Res. Bull. ment. Hlth. Res. Inst. Ft. Stilacoom, Wash.*, 1962, **5**, 85–92.

Masserman, J. H. *Behavior and neurosis.* Chicago: Univer. of Chicago Press, 1943.

Meehl, P. E. (Ed.) *What, then, is man?* St. Louis: Concordia, 1958.

Miller, G. A., Galanter, E., & Pribram, K. H. *Plans and the structure of behavior.* New York: Holt, 1960.

Mowrer, O. H. A stimulus-response analysis of anxiety and its role as a reinforcing agent. *Psychol. Rev.*, 1939, **46,** 553–565.

Mowrer, O. H. An experimental analogue of "regression," with incidental observations on "reaction-formation." *J. abnorm. soc. Psychol.*, 1940, **35,** 56–87.

Mowrer, O. H. Learning theory and the neurotic paradox. *Amer. J. Orthopsychiat.*, 1948, **18,** 571–610.

Mowrer, O. H. *Learning theory and personality dynamics.* New York: Ronald, 1950.

Mowrer, O. H. Freedom and responsibility: a psychological analysis. *J. legal Educ.*, 1953, **6,** 60–78. (a)

Mowrer, O. H. *Psychotherapy: theory and research.* New York: Ronald, 1953. (b)

Mowrer, O. H. *Learning theory and behavior.* New York: Wiley, 1960. (a)

Mowrer, O. H. *Learning theory and the symbolic processes.* New York: Wiley, 1960. (b)

Mowrer, O. H. The rediscovery of moral responsibility. *Atlantic Mon.*, 1961, **208,** 88–91.

Mowrer, O. H. Freudianism, behavior therapy, and "self-disclosure." *Behav. Res. Ther.*, 1963, **1,** 321–337. (a)

Mowrer, O. H. *The new group therapy.* Princeton, N.J.: Van Nostrand, 1963. (b)

Mowrer, O. H. Payment or repayment? The problem of private practice. *Amer. Psychologist*, 1963, **18,** 577–580. (c)

J. Relig. Hlth., 1963, **2,** 313–343. (d)
Mowrer, O. H. Transference and scrupulosity.

Mowrer, O. H. (Ed.) *Morality and mental health.* Chicago: Rand McNally, 1964.

Mowrer, O. H. *Identity and community.* 1965. (To be published.)

O'Connell, W. E. Identification and curability of the mental hospital patient. *J. indiv. Psychol.*, 1962, **18,** 68–76.

Osgood, C. E. *Method and theory in experimental psychology.* New York: Oxford Univer. Press, 1953.

Pavlov, I. P. *Conditioned reflexes.* (Tr. by G. V. Anrep.) London: Oxford Univer. Press, 1927.

Peters, H. N. An experimental evaluation of learning vs. therapy in schizophrenia. *Amer. Psychologist,* 1952, **7,** 354. (Abstract)

Peterson, D. R. The insecure child: over-socialized or under-socialized? In O. H. Mowrer (Ed.), *Morality and mental health.* Chicago: Rand McNally, 1965.

Rachman, S. Introduction to behaviour therapy. *Behav. Res. Ther.*, 1963, **1,** 3–16.

Rickard, H. C., Digman, P. J., & Horner, R. F. Verbal manipulation in a psychotherapeutic relationship. *J. clin. Psychol.*, 1960, **16,** 364–367.

Robertson, J. P. S. The operant conditioning of speech and drawing behavior in chronic schizophrenics. *Swiss Rev. Psychol. Applications,* 1958, **17,** 309–315.

Rogers, J. M. Operant conditioning in a quasi-therapy setting. *J. abnorm. soc. Psychol.*, 1960, **60,** 247–252

Salter, A. *Conditioned reflex therapy.* New York: Creative Age Press, 1950.

Sarason, I. G. Interrelationships among individual difference variables, behavior in psychotherapy, and verbal conditioning. *J. abnorm. soc. Psychol.*, 1958, **56,** 339–344.

Schoeck, H., & Wiggins, J. W. *Psychiatry and responsibility.* Princeton, N.J.: Van Nostrand, 1962.

Shaw, F. S. Some postulates concerning psychotherapy. *J. consult. Psychol.*, 1948, **12,** 426–432.

Shoben, E. J., Jr. Psychotherapy as a problem in learning theory. *Psychol. Bull.*, 1949, **46,** 366–392.

Skinner, B. F. *Cumulative record.* New York: Appleton-Century-Crofts, 1959.

Stekel, W. *Technique of analytical psychotherapy.* New York: Liveright, 1938.

Szasz, T. S. *The myth of mental illness.* New York: Hoeber-Harper, 1961.

Terman, L. M. *The hygiene of the school child.* Boston: Houghton Mifflin, 1914.

Ullman, L. P., Krasner, L., & Gelfond, Donna M. The effects of reinforcement on pleasantness of emotional words used by normal and psychiatric subjects. Paper read at the Western Psychol. Ass., San Francisco, 1962.

Ullman, L. P., et al. Selective reinforcement of schizophrenics' interview responses. 1965. (To be published.)

Ullman, L. P., & Krasner, L. *Case studies in behavior modification.* New York: Holt, Rinehart & Winston, 1965.

Waskow, Irene E. Reinforcement in a therapy-like situation through selective responding to feelings or content. *J. consult. Psychol.,* 1962, **26** (1), 11–19.

Watson, J. B. *Psychology from the standpoint of a behaviorist.* Philadelphia: Lippincott, 1919.

Watson, J. B., & Raynor, Rosalee. Conditioned emotional reactions. *J. Exp. Psychol.*, 1920, **3**, 1–14.

Wolf, M., Mees, H., & Risley, T. Application of operant conditioning procedures to the behavior problems of an autistic child. Paper read at *West. Psychol. Ass.*, 1963. (Mimeographed)

Wolpe, J. Reciprocal inhibition as the main basis of psychotherapeutic effects. *Arch. Neurol. Psychiat.*, 1954, **72**, 205–226.

Wolpe, J. *Psychotherapy by reciprocal inhibition.* Stanford, Calif.: Stanford Univer. Press, 1958.

Wolpe, J. Psychotherapy: the nonscientific heritage and the new science. *Behav. Res. Ther.*, 1963, **1**, 23–28.

13
Theories of Personality

ROSS STAGNER

Clinicians would no doubt agree, as a broad generalization, that personality theory has some relevance for practice and research in clinical psychology. It is, on the other hand, relatively difficult to document this assertion with regard to most of the theoretical writing in this field. In this chapter I propose to indicate some links relating personality theories to diagnostics, to therapy, and to research on clinical problems.

Before doing this I find it necessary to delimit the field of discourse to some extent. There are many kinds of speculative doctrines which may be classified as "personality theory"; separate chapters will deal with S-R theory, orthodox psychoanalytic theory, and the neoanalytic approaches. There are others which seem to me inappropriate for inclusion here. Let me specify the criteria used in selecting theories for consideration.

WHAT IS A THEORY OF PERSONALITY?

A theory is a logical device for arranging empirical data in an orderly fashion. It may be defined as a network of hypothetical constructs and principles of interaction which serve to link stimulus input to, and response output from, the organism. In this broad sense we may have theories of learning, of perception, of thinking, of motivation, etc.

The very phrase "theory of personality" implies that personality is an event in nature, an observable phenomenon upon which competent observers can agree. This is not to say that all observers agree on the dimensions of variation of personality, any more than they agree on the intervening variables and constructs which should be incorporated into a theoretical formulation. They do show reasonable agreement on certain operational definitions of observations which can be classified under the rubric "personality."

From this it seems logically to follow that a theory of personality must offer some conceptualization of the total event in addition to its component parts or processes. Thus a theory of personality is not merely a theory of learning or of perception. (To the extent that such part-processes play an important role in the theory, the conceptualization of the whole should be compatible.) We may say, therefore, that the class "theories of personality" is composed of those theories which offer a logical formulation of the total personality; using the language of systems theory, we may say that there must be a concept of a bounded system which can be differentiated from other events observable at the same time.

By a bounded system I mean that each personality is unique in time and space; it has an operationally determinable zone of interaction with the environment and a relatively unchanging or slowly changing nucleus. Boundaries are revealed by resistance to change, by constancy of attitudes and sentiments, and by restrictions on communication. This is more than calling habit strength by a new name. The individual may reveal his unchanging inner core by doing something he has never done before in his life. We need theories which will conceptualize for us the nature of this inner organization and its resistance to modification. This kind of criterion discriminates S-R theories, which generally offer no speculations about the total personality, and Freudian views, which concentrate heavily on part-processes, from gestalt, phenomenological, and other views summarized in later pages.

A theory of personality which stops with a concept of the totality is of course unsatisfactory. The scientist, at least, does not wish simply to admire an event in nature; he wants to analyze it, work out functional interrelationships with the environment, and identify invariant part-processes. The whole should have emergent properties which are not identical with those of the parts, and the parts should have continuing identity even though they behave differently in one total personality from the way they do in another. To take an analogy from biochemistry, the DNA molecule is composed of nucleic acids, and these do not lose their chemical properties when organized into DNA. Nevertheless, the properties of the whole molecule are quite different in varying species; horse and man have the same nucleic acids, but the emergent wholes are not very similar in the two cases.

Theories of personality must also offer a formulation of the individual-environment interaction. As von Bertalanffy has argued so cogently, the human organism is an open system; homeostatic balance is preserved as a rule, but there is a constant interchange with the milieu. At the personality level we are concerned with the effects upon the individual of surrounding significant persons and with his responses which modify the environment. It is at this point that general psychological theories of learning and perception have greatest relevance.

A good personality theory deals with the internal differentiation of the whole and offers principles for understanding the interaction of these segmental aspects. It probably will involve some kind of hierarchical principle governing the relations of parts to whole. It is, then, a conception of a *differentiated* system, permitting studies to be made of parts across individuals or of the interrelations of parts within a single person. Obviously most American empirical research has been of the first type, but the work of the practicing clinician requires knowledge in the second category. Theoretical formulations in this area leave much to be desired, but I hope to show that considerable material of relevance can be found in the writings of personality theorists.

There are, of course, other usages of the term "personality" in scientific psychology which provide criteria we might apply in deciding what theories are relevant to this chapter. When Leeper (1963), for example, says that "people have great difficulties in changing any of their personality habits," it would seem that he is really pointing to language usage, that, when a habit is deeply rooted and hard to eradicate, we are likely to assign it to the rubric "personality." Allport (1937) proposes a distinction between "persona" or "mask" and the deeper personality, the one changing readily and the other only under extreme pressure. Lewin (1936) has made the same point with his "peripheral" and "central" regions. It is obvious, in terms of our purposes here, that clinicians have little interest in superficial, transitory habits or actions but are very much concerned with stubborn, persistent, and pervasive manifestations of individuality. It is almost correct to say that any change in a person which can be induced quickly is by definition not a "real" change in personality.

A second and fairly obvious point in this connection is that "personality" is employed as a label for phenomena which involve certain categories of individual differences. If, for example, we find in a learning experiment that two persons meet the criterion in the same number of trials but that one has consumed much time and made many errors, while the other has worked steadily and efficiently, we may speak of a personality trait affecting the learning process. Many studies of selective perception, selective memory, etc., fall into this phase of personality research. And once more it is appropriate to comment that the clinician is concerned with precisely such phenomena. The client comes because he is unable to function efficiently in certain areas of his life. His request is that persisting modes of perceiving, responding, learning, or remembering be modified so that his adjustment will improve. To be useful to the clinician, therefore, a theory must have some relevance to such problems.

Dimensions of Variation of Theories

It is helpful, in examining a number of different theories, to establish certain yardsticks by which they can be compared. One psychologist may emphasize the whole more than the parts, the organism more than the environment, or the general as opposed to the unique. It is then informative to group together those theorists who agree with respect to a given dimension, even though they may differ sharply on some other point.

In a book which merits more attention than it has received, Angyal (1941) developed the notion of personality as a polar relationship of organism and environment which became intrinsically meaningless when either term was ignored. Attempting to develop a logically consistent theory on this basis, he found it necessary to shift the focus of attention successively to the biological organism, to the social milieu, and to the interaction processes. Angyal is apparently unique in his industrious effort to emphasize at all times the bipolar nature of the total personality; most authors lean more heavily upon either the biology or the sociology of personality.

Among those emphasizing the biological end of this dimension we may cite Sheldon (1942) as relatively extreme, although his position has been exaggerated by his critics. In a less extreme spot we may place Lersch (1954) and the German "stratification" theorists; and near the center, but leaning to the biological side, Allport (1961). In this same general area we must locate writers like Goldstein (1939) and Maslow (1962). They stress biological determinants without minimizing social pressures as important factors to be considered.

At an extreme position of deemphasizing the biological side we may put Lewin (1935) and probably the existentialists, as exemplified in the volume by May, Angel, and Ellenberger (1958). Both Lewinians and existentialists pay lip service to the importance of man's biological nature, but they promptly drop the topic.[1] Somewhere toward the center of this dimension, but leaning to the environmental side, seems to be an appropriate locus for Murphy (1947), who develops more explicitly the place of biology in his framework.

Whole versus parts. A second logical dimension is that of molar versus molecular, or holistic versus segmental, theories. Some authors have laid greatest stress on the total personality, others on part-processes.

Lewin and his followers have perhaps been most insistent upon the necessity of conceptualizing the total personality and then establishing a basis for analyzing it into partial processes for detailed study. Conversely, the factor analysts (Cattell, Eysenck, etc.) have asserted the primacy of the parts, specific behavior sequences which can be observed and counted, and have treated the whole as a derivative of the summed parts. Again I would place Allport and Murphy in a middle-of-the-road position on this dimension. Goldstein is somewhat unique as a "biological holist."

Structure versus striving. Every psychologist must face up to the problem of structures versus dynamics in explaining behavior. To a question about the primacy of these, the safest answer is that we must take account of both. Theories, however, tend to emphasize one approach or the other.

Cattell, Eysenck, and others of a behavioristic trend necessarily place greater emphasis on structure. They are concerned with enduring habit patterns, with organized sequences. Drive, insofar as it must be mentioned, is likely to be treated in a rather generalized form (Hull's *D* function) or ignored. On the other hand, Allport and the existentialists have tended to ignore questions about organized habits and to emphasize striving toward some state other than that in which the person now finds himself. On a dimension formulated in this fashion, Lewin probably must be assigned to an intermediate position, since he deals extensively with both the dynamic forces inducing movement and the organized regions within the person which restrain and direct the expression of energy.[2]

Historical versus ahistorical. Another dimension in personality theory often is described as that ranging from great emphasis on historical determinants to stress on the ahistorical factors, the contemporary influences molding be-

[1] Since the existentialists speak of the importance of the individual as against his environment, this placement may seem inappropriate. However, the theoretical treatment emphasizes so much the dialectical process of individual versus environment that I prefer to locate it as indicated.

[2] Many of the theories to be discussed in this chapter have been tested by various kinds of empirical investigations. Insofar as the research has no clinical implications, it will be ignored; this leaves very few items for consideration. This chapter therefore deals with the content of theories, a comparison of assumptions made by different theorists, and some comments about potential applications to diagnostics, therapy, and research on clinical problems.

havior. Freudian theory is of course the classical form of historical exposition, with its great concern for infantile trauma, cathexis, and fixation and with many therapists holding that successful modification of the personality is impossible without real exploration of the infantile roots of present difficulties.

In sharp contrast to this view are, first, the Lewinians, with their explicit statement that behavior is always determined by contemporary forces, and secondly, the reference-group theorists, who deal primarily with the external group pressures operative at a specific point in time.

In my opinion this dimension of variation is of minimal importance. All the ahistorical theorists, Lewin included, admit that to understand the present situation one must have some knowledge of the past. Further, the writers who stress early determination of personality concede that it is not the past but the residues of past experience carried forward into the present which are decisive.

As regards the different writers whose views will be examined in this chapter, there is no real problem. All of them, with minor variations, belong to the ahistorical category. And, as noted above, the divergences among theories tend to break down when examined closely. This dimension will therefore not be treated formally in the present survey.

CLINICAL PSYCHOLOGY AND THE TOTAL PERSONALITY

The problem which I wish to pose in the following pages is that of relevance. Does a theoretical conception of the total personality have any value for the clinician? Not surprisingly, I shall argue that it does. The situation may be phrased as follows: individuals A and B may show quite similar processes in regard to trauma, fixation, defense, and so forth, and yet the particular functionings of the personality will be different. Two boys may be correctly characterized, for example, as showing an unresolved Oedipus complex, but in the one case the behavioral manifestations are those of overt rebellion and delinquency, whereas in the alternate case they take the form of intellectualized rebellion against social standards, against political institutions, or against orthodoxy in some scientific sphere. We need to know something about the personality structure in which the complex is embedded if we are to predict its behavioral consequences.

The problem is the familiar one in the logic of science, namely, that the same stimulus does not necessarily produce an invariant response. When responses to identical stimuli are found to vary, we assume the operation of *intervening variables* which differ in the cases under observation. The total personality may be considered to be an intervening variable which modifies responses to conflicts, to threats, and to positive goals. We may go further and speculate that the total personality has an inhibitory or exaggerating function, modifying the operation of such subsystems as fixations, defenses, and coping mechanisms.

In the following pages we shall examine various widely discussed theories of personality and consider to what extent they meet the requirements of this kind of formulation. In general, this means considering the relevance of the theory to psychodiagnosis, to therapy, and to clinical research.

HOLISTIC THEORIES

Kurt Lewin

Manifestly, if there are as many dimensions of variation among theoretical formulations as have been sketched, and if these are relatively independent, we cannot neatly order the theories to be examined here. Somewhat arbitrarily, therefore, I propose to begin with the extremes of holistic theory and then consider some variants of this approach, gradually moving into theories with a strong biological flavor and thence into the relatively molecular views of the factor analysts. It is not, however, possible to maintain a neat, logical progression of the presentation. With this apology, let me turn to an examination of the approach which is often considered the extreme of holistic theories, that of Lewin.

It is unfortunate for the field of personality research that Lewin did not live to write a formally connected exposition of his views about personality. There are several logical gaps in his formulations, and it would have been very satisfying to know what route he would have adopted in bridging them. On the other hand, it gives the commentator a free hand to offer his own interpretation at such points, and I shall proceed to do so.

Lewin's basic postulate, which is developed in all his writings (1935; 1936; 1938), is that we cannot define the person except in relation to his environment. As was noted of Angyal, reality includes both person and milieu, and we start logically by differentiating the one from the other. This leads to the primacy of the whole person over any part systems, a major contrast between this view and behavioristic approaches. It also requires the concept of a *boundary,* that which delimits person from environment. This boundary must be permeable because stimuli flow into the organism (for example, food, oxygen, etc.) and because actions are emitted by the person into the environment, modifying it. At times the boundary may be fluid and difficult to determine as when the individual is caught up in external events and loses his self-awareness; at other times he may be encapsulated and almost impervious to outer influences.

The person plus his psychological environment, the "totality of possible events" (Lewin, 1936, p. 14), make up the life space. The life space is an important portion of Lewinian theory, but since our concern is primarily with the person as distinguished from his context, I shall not explore this topic in detail. One problem, however, demands consideration because of its implications for the clinician. This is the relation between "perceived reality" and "objective reality" in the life space.

As critics have noted, Lewin did not distinguish systematically between these two classes of events. It would have been proper for him to have done so, but it is also easy to demonstrate that both are important. If I perceive tomatoes as poisonous, I am blocked from eating them just as if they were locked up in a warehouse, although one barrier is "inside" the person and the other is outside. While behaviorists would like to define stimuli in terms of energies (in the frame of reference of physics), it is pretty obvious that the perceiver may modify the incoming cues to fit into his own image of reality: to the young man in love, his sweetheart is beautiful, even if impartial observers agree that she is quite homely. Conversely, the extreme subjectivists ignore the fact that my failure to perceive an onrushing automobile does not prevent it from having a drastic effect on my behavior. In other words, the life space within which behavior occurs must allow for both perceived barriers and unperceived but "real" barriers.

This point is relevant to Lewin's personality theory. Although his approach to personality emphasizes the phenomenological side, the importance of the perceived self and the awareness of self-environment relations, he does not exclude biological determinants. The perceived self takes on attributes which reflect biological endowment to some extent. Likewise, Lewin's concern for an ahistorical analysis (the determinants of behavior are always contemporary) has been misinterpreted to suggest that he denies the importance of past experience. Actually both his research and his writings indicate that a present life space may be modified by rewarding or painful experience, thus being transformed into a new life space *the properties of which can best be understood in terms of the individual's history.* (For example, consider Barker, Dembo, & Lewin, 1941; Lewin, Lippitt, & White, 1939.) He also recognizes that the phenomenal attributes of present situations may be functions of unconscious influences.

The life space is differentiated also into valences, positive and negative pressures upon the person for locomotion toward or away from the valence. As was implied above, Lewin sometimes tends to treat these as if they can be defined objectively, i.e., by impartial observers, and at other times he emphasizes that they are determined by the person and must be defined phenomenally. By a process about which he is quite vague, the externally presented valences get incorporated into the inner structure of the person and become ambitions, aspirations, values, and ideals. At this point one is wiser to rely upon Allport or Murphy than upon Lewin for insights into the development of motivation.

Our main interest, however, is in Lewin's theory of the structure of the total personality. Obviously the scientist is not content simply to admire the gestalt of the individual person; he wants to develop a set of concepts which will enable him to differentiate various aspects or functions of this totality so that he can manipulate, experiment, and establish invariant relationships. Lewin accepts this necessity. The person is differentiated into regions, bounded from one another in somewhat the same fashion as the total is bounded from the psychological environment. Each region, it would seem, corresponds to a set of interrelated habits (perhaps a social role); perceptual and motor processes correspond to peripheral regions, in contact with the milieu. The self is a deeply central region. A phase of the person's life which "touches him deeply," which is close to his ego, would be represented as far from the periphery, near to the center. Thus a man whose professional work is intensely important to his self-evaluation would be represented with his professional habits and percepts as a region in contact with the central ego or self.

In a wide scattering of articles, Lewin proposed various hypotheses about this inner structuring of the person. At one time I drew together (Stagner, 1948, chap. 4) a set of concepts which seemed to represent adequately the Lewinian view of personality structure. Although the point was not made at that time, these concepts are helpful to the clinician who wishes to benefit from this theoretical approach.

Since the personality is a bounded whole, one of its major attributes must necessarily be the extent of internal differentiation. Individuals may be said to differ in *complexity*, or the trend toward homogeneity or heterogeneity of inner structure. A person of simple tastes, few activities, and a (perhaps) oversimplified view of life would be judged relatively homogeneous. The "man of many parts" is complex, highly differentiated internally. It seems plausible to suggest that a given symptom or defect in a simple structure must be interpreted rather differently from one phenomenally similar but embedded in a complex personality. An excessively simple statement of this would be that, in a person with five "regions" within his personality, an aberration in any one would be more salient and more readily observed and would affect a larger proportion of his behavior than if he showed 50 such regions.

The properties of the organism-environment boundary may also be expected to vary. This may be conceptualized as *accessibility*, or the receptivity of the individual to external influences. To use a traditional term, the highly accessible person would be extroverted, easily stimulated, and relatively responsive; or to use Riesman's term, the accessible personality is outer-directed. Since clinical literature offers extensive discussions of such differences, it is unnecessary to expand upon them here. Certainly both diagnostic and therapeutic conclusions will be affected by the over-all evaluation of such tendencies in the patient.

It would appear from Lewin's writings that personalities differ also with respect to the permeability of boundaries between subsystems or regions. This is true also of the same person at different times; e.g., repression is treated as strengthening the boundary around a painful memory or set of associated ideas, and the individual under stress is considered to undergo a weakening of internal boundaries with consequent loss of differentiation of percepts and skills (this probably corresponds to the extreme polarization of emotions and attitudes under stress, as in panic or as in the case of the paranoid who concludes that "all who are not for me are against me"). The construct of *fluidity* has been used by Lewin to identify this dimension of difference among persons. A person of low fluidity would seem to be predisposed to use dissociation as a device for dealing with conflicts, whereas the other end of the continuum would be characterized by a ready spread of emotion from one habit system or social relationship to logically independent areas of the personality.

Since both accessibility and fluidity relate to the more general construct of boundary permeability, research is desirable on the extent to which the distinction between the two is unnecessary. Some of Jung's assertions about extroversion, as well as the work of Eysenck, would lead to the interpretation that only a single construct is needed here. Systematic work is also needed on the extent to which such openness to the environment modifies the therapeutic approach which will be most successful.

Lewin has also been concerned (1936, p. 185) with the fact that personalities differ not only in the number of inner subsystems but also in their topological relationships to one another. A set of five tangent regions is not equivalent to four regions incorporated within a more inclusive region nor to a set of five concentric regions, four of which must be penetrated successively to affect the fifth, or most central, one. For such a dimension of personalities, the construct of *centrality* seems relevant; it is related to Allport's concept of cardinal disposition, discussed below, and perhaps to Maslow's concept of need hierarchies.

Lewin and the clinicians. Lewin's personal interests were directed toward social psychology and the interaction of persons rather than clinical problems and the structure of the individual. In much of his theorizing he liked to treat persons as interchangeable; i.e., he was seeking universal principles of behavior. The clinician must be aware of such laws, but he is likely to be more concerned with how these generalizations work out in a specific case. Lewin made notable contributions to the analysis of conflict situations (cf. Barker, Dembo, & Lewin, 1941), and some of his work on social pressures affecting individual decision has influenced group therapy.

It seems likely, however, that Lewin's main influence in the clinical area has been mediated through others. An important channel here would seem to be the team of Snygg and Combs (Combs & Snygg, 1959; Snygg & Combs, 1949), whose ideas bear a strong Lewinian imprint. They must be given credit for remolding the theory into more of a cognitive structure and for developing specific applications to the tasks of the clinician. With regard to therapeutic procedures and theory, they also incorporate much of the work of Rogers (1939; 1951), whose indebtedness to Lewin is less clear. However, the close compatibility of Lewin's ideas about personality and of Rogers's about therapy is obvious, and the fusion in Combs and Snygg has undoubtedly been influential in much clinical training, at least in the United States.

The Existentialists

It is difficult to be sure that existentialism represents a personality theory in the sense employed here. On the other hand, the writings of this school, as exemplified in May, Angel, and Ellenberger (1958), for example, make it clear that the personality is a unified whole. Like Lewin, they take primarily a phenomenological approach (the environment is that which is real for the perceiving, experiencing person) and so, like Lewin, get into some logical problems with unperceived but objective factors affecting the individual. Again like Lewin, they are relatively more concerned with individual-environment interactions than with the enduring structure of habit systems, which is the concern of other theorists.

Unlike Lewin, the existentialists postulate certain inner strivings, which are presumably biologically determined. May et al. quote approvingly Nietzsche's objection to theories of motivation as being pleasure-seeking; "this power, this expansion, growing, bringing one's inner potentialities into birth in action is the central dynamic and need of life" (1958, p. 31). We shall note that other personality theorists have utilized this same concept of inner striving for growth, but in quite different contexts.

The existentialists also differ from the Freudian analysts in placing much greater emphasis on the immediate situation facing the patient. They thus correspond more to the ahistorical approach mentioned earlier; they reject the notion that therapy requires detailed exposure and interpretation of infantile motives. The task of the therapist is presented as that of understanding, and helping the patient to understand, the world in which he lives, the world of perception and phenomena. This phenomenal reality is unquestionably affected by residues of earlier experience, but these may have been fantasied rather than objectively "real." (May cites Freud's discomfiture upon learning that vivid memories of childhood sexual trauma often proved to be products of fantasy.)

The attitude of the existentialists toward the temporal dimension in motivation is also distinctive. "They do not neglect the past, but they hold it can be understood only in the light of the future" (May et al., 1958, p. 69). Whereas the Freudians emphasize the past, and Lewinians the immediately given, the existentialist stresses the personality as a structure oriented toward future events.

There is much to appeal to the average observer in such a conception. Normal behavior includes a substantial concern with the future, with threats, aspirations, ambitions, goals. However, experienced clinicians will recall countless cases of individuals who are obsessed with the past to such an extent that even the immediate present is somewhat shadowy and who cannot develop a coherent point of view with respect to the future. And still another category of individual will be found to lack any evidence of affect with regard to past or future; he truly "lives in the present." These empirical observations do not, in and of themselves, confirm or reject the theories mentioned, if only for the reason that definitions may be so phrased as to comprehend more than one temporal segment (cf. my comment on Lewin, page 280). It is, however, of importance to the clinician to be aware of the significance of temporal orientations and to evaluate diagnostic or therapeutic material in the light of such distinctions.

A major consequence of this type of thinking has been the existentialist emphasis upon the patient as a unique person, in contrast to the Freudian view of the patient as an assembly of oral, anal, and oedipal conflicts. It is in this respect that they merit consideration in this chapter. Without offering us any formal theory of the unique individual, their overhauling of traditional analytic therapy points the way to the clinician's need for just such a theory.

Gordon Allport

The holists, as Hall and Lindzey (1957) have commented, can be subdivided according to how comprehensive a whole the theory comprehends. Lewin took into consideration the life space, the person in his psychological environment. By contrast, Allport (1937; 1955; 1961) has developed a theoretical conception which puts the focus more clearly on what happens inside the organism. His stress is not so much on the environment as represented phenomenally; rather, he emphasizes the fact that every act of an individual may be understood only against a background of his other acts (perhaps, in the extreme, of *all* his other acts). For this reason it seems proper to classify Allport as leaning more toward the biological end of the organism-environment continuum than Lewin and the phenomenologists.

Like the existentialists, Allport conceives of the human personality as oriented toward the future, as striving rather than as responding in terms of habits. Nevertheless, he devotes considerable attention to a theory of personality structure.

The key concept in his formulation is that of the proprium, which corresponds to Lewin's nuclear self or to Combs and Snygg's self-concept. Allport demonstrates that the significance of a habit, attitude, or value varies according to whether it is deeply, slightly, or not at all ego-involved, or, as he labels this, "propriate." Although the concept of the proprium has some of the connotations of Fisher's (Fisher & Cleveland, 1957) term "body image," for Allport the proprium may include one's name, one's family identification, and other closely associated items. Especially important is the fact that we can identify those attributes which are propriate *only by the study of this specific individual.* Religion may be a propriate value for one person, but quite peripheral for another. One boy's attachment to his mother may be propriate, deeply ego-involved, but another's not nearly so significant. Now obviously any good clinician will be aware of the difference in intensity in the two cases just cited, but he may very easily miss Allport's point, which is that the kind of proprium, or ego structure, characterizing a specific individual is far more significant for diagnosis and for therapy than his relationship to his mother. Readers who have experienced analytic-type therapy well know how the theoretical preconceptions of the therapist cause him to encourage certain kinds of associations; although the client is told to talk freely of whatever occurs to him, some topics encounter critical comments about resistance and intellectual defensiveness, whereas others elicit more enthusiasm. Thus, through verbal reinforcement, the therapist may impose his theoretical views on the client's associative flow.

Allport would argue that a person may be so organized that his concern with his business or his profession or with esthetic or religious values is so central to the proprium that a libido theory is inappropriate. As noted above, this seems to have been one of the major contributions of existential therapy. Although Allport himself has written little about problems of therapy, he seems to endorse the existentialist concept of a striving for growth and the notion that therapy should release growth potential. He says: "Some kind of continual growth and development into the stage of maturity is what fully fashioned human beings seek. . . . The goals of psychotherapy should be framed in these terms" (1961, p. 305).

A second major concept in Allport's thinking is that of *personal disposition.* This concept is closer to traditional clinical thinking insofar as it relates to strivings, emotional fixations, and fundamental motivations. The personal disposition is rather similar to Murray's concept of need, but it also spreads to include traits (as this term is used by Cattell and Eysenck) and values. A personal disposition is an observable unity, an invariance across situations, characteristic of this individual. It is identified by *intrapersonal reliability* rather than by reliability across individuals.

We are accustomed, of course, to dealing with the concept of reliability of observations in terms of the fact that the same phenomenon can be replicated in different individuals or different groups. In dealing with the concept of the personality as a unique bounded system, Allport argues that we must change our approach and seek the phenomena of uniformity and reliability in terms of uniform actions by the same individual when a particular stimulus context is repeated in a form perceived as identical. Despite the urgings of Allport and others interested in this problem, deplorably little research has been done on the occurrence of such uniformities within a single person. Every clinician, however, is aware of this phenomenon and must take account of it in his dealings with a specific client.

Allport suggests that personal dispositions form a hierarchy. A personality may be organized around a single, outstanding, pervasive disposition, in which case he proposes that we call it a "cardinal" disposition. When we speak of a man as a Don Juan or a Beau Brummel, we are implying that one particular striving has become, for this individual, such an outstanding feature that he can be indentified by it. In other cases there may be a few "central" dispositions, and of course the adjective here refers to those strivings which are propriate in character, i.e., ego-involved, to use a more familiar term. Finally, there are "secondary" dispositions, which appear frequently in a person's behavior but which can be overridden fairly easily when one of them conflicts with a central or cardinal disposition. The Hullian concept of a response hierarchy is obviously appropriate here, except that for Allport the personal disposition is much more than a response. It is a perceptual-motivational-behavioral unit, and its functional unity depends more on perceived similarity of person-environment relations than upon muscle movements.

Personal dispositions may also be categorized in terms of genotypical and phenotypical dispositions. Allport borrows these terms from Lewin and uses them to identify superficial versus underlying, intrinsic unities. (He is not, of course, using them in the sense of hereditary gene patterns and somatic expressions thereof, but the analogy helps us to get his meaning.) Allport is concerned here to emphasize that the underlying, highly predictable personal disposition may require continued and thoughtful observation. He notes, for example, that the Freudian concept of an anal-erotic character may aptly describe a pattern of striving in one person, but in another, miserliness may be a basic pattern all its own, without the obsessive concern for detail, the sadistic hostility, and other attributes of the anal individual. In this case, Allport argues, we misinterpret the genotype if we ascribe the behavior to anal eroticism. Miserliness may be a phenotype in one case, a genotype in another. To determine which is correct requires intensive study of the individual personality.

At this point one may ask: What is the connection with clinical psychology? My answer would be that clinical psychology is concerned with psychodiagnosis, psychotherapy, and clinical research and that Allport's conceptual framework can be useful for all three. Sound diagnostic practice calls for more than identifying T scores above 60 on MMPI, unusual *dd* scores on the Rorschach, or frequently appearing themata on the TAT. The significance of these attributes depends on how they are related to the proprium (or self), on where they stand in a hierarchy of dispositions, and on whether they show phenotypical or genotypical characteristics. The personality is not an additive total which can be gotten by counting the number of deviant scores or responses. Those clinicians who criticize the use of devices such as MMPI, Rorschach, and TAT for diagnostic purposes may well be correct in their conclusions, although they are often—in my view, at least—correct for the wrong reasons. It is not bad psychology to use standard stimuli in probing the personality, but it is bad psychology to ignore the total organization within which these specific symptoms are embedded.

Applications of Allport's thought to psychotherapy would follow somewhat the same pattern. Therapeutic work on superficial symptoms is wasted work, as Freud noted sixty years ago. The difficulty with many practitioners of analytic therapy is that they have too readily assumed that Freud classified and labeled for all time the deep, or significant, and the superficial, or trivial, manifestations of personality. Allport would certainly agree that, in many individuals, the Freudian framework labels for us the propriate strivings and the central dispositions. But he would equally assert that many therapeutic failures occur because the therapist keeps doggedly probing for infantile motivations in a personality where the propriate dispositions are organized around roles and conflicts of the adult situation. Essentially what I am saying is that excessive devotion to any theory opens the possibility of blinding oneself to better alternatives for specific cases. The danger of this happening is increased as the theory becomes more specific about crucial strivings, significant figures, critical stages in development, and so on. A highly generalized theory, such as that of Allport and even more that of Lewin, minimizes this danger because it merely provides a set of categories and postulates certain relationships but leaves the specific details to be filled in from an examination of the unique individual.

This brings me to the third point, the utility of such a theory in clinical research. Actually, I think that anyone who tries to study real, live individuals necessarily begins by using a theory of personality (in the rather comprehensive way I have defined that term). But when he tries to organize and systematize his observations, he is likely to fall back on theoretical categories, such as that he discovered so many oral erotics, so many cycloids, so many dysthymics, or whatever. Now it is of the very essence of the Allport approach that any such label does violence to the unique personality. Research, Allport would argue, should aim at identifying invariant response tendencies (more correctly, invariant strivings) within a specific person and at relating these to the pattern of events in his life, rather than taking a hypothetical developmental sequence and adapting all the observational material to fit this framework. Stephenson (1953) has offered a technique, the Q sort, which helps us to deal with the individual as a patterned organization, and Cattell (1957) has devised a statistic, the P technique, by which underlying factors can be found for individuals (as contrasted with R technique, which locates common factors in a population). These methods and others offer promise of major advances in clinical psychology; it is a matter of considerable regret, to me at least, that so little has been done with them.

Gardner Murphy

One of the most important figures in American personality research is Gardner Murphy. He has been particularly effective in sparking new and significant lines of investigation, such as the studies of autistic perception, which began with Levine, Chein, and Murphy (1942) and Schafer and Murphy (1943). Since these and subsequent studies did not involve clinical material, they will not be reviewed in any substantive way here; however, comments offered with respect to the implications of theory for clinical practice will in many cases reflect the findings of such research.

Murphy's magnum opus is his 1947 book, *Personality: A Biosocial Approach to Origins and Structure*. One must admit at the outset that it is not a tightly reasoned development from a few basic principles, comparable, for example, to Dollard and Miller's *Personality and Psychotherapy*. By the same token, it is incomparably better than Dollard and Miller's book at dealing with the more complex phases of personality organization. Murphy's viewpoint would have to be described as eclectic, since he utilizes, as his strategy dictates, principles of response elicitation and conditioning, cognitive principles, typological principles, and so on. The chaos, however, is more apparent than real. Much of what he does has already been spelled out in earlier pages of this chapter; i.e., he recognizes the existence of different levels of functioning and asserts the operation of different principles at these various levels. He states, for example:

> There are three developmental stages in the organization of tissue systems. . . . The stages comprise (1) a homogeneous, undifferentiated, global mass; (2) a differentiation, a cleavage between qualitatively distinct parts or ingredients; and (3) the establishment of functional relations between the differentiated parts so as to constitute a system (1947, p. 619).

He notes that the validity of these three stages can be demonstrated in response analysis, in the development of perception, and in the examination of the personality as a whole. In considering phenomena at the first stage, with regard to any class of events, gestalt principles are relevant and useful; at the second stage, molecular or atomistic principles may be more appropriate; and at the third stage, cognitive or hypothesis-learning principles may best fit the data. In effect this is no more of a logical problem than the fact that electrons and protons have their own distinctive laws of behaving but that it makes a good deal of difference whether they are organized into an atom of aluminum or an atom of plutonium. Laws relevant to one level of discourse may be virtually irrelevant to another.

Perhaps the major virtue of the Murphy

contribution is that it deals explicitly with just about every problem beyond the level of the trivial in the area generally identified as "personality." Further, he explores each of these problems in terms of principles and of empirical research; it is therefore a valuable guide to the clinical student who wishes to integrate theoretical and factual approaches to personality.

A listing of Murphy's contributions in specific problem areas would be too long for the space available here. Let me concentrate on a few which are particularly useful for the clinician. First is the process of "canalization." Needs are likely to possess undifferentiated, generalized properties in the infant; with experience, however, a need is likely to become canalized so that it focuses upon a particular stimulus or class of stimuli. The canalization of the sex drive upon a specific member of the opposite sex, in the form of marital love, is the classic instance. This has been preceded in time by many other and perhaps truly more important canalizations, upon culturally defined roles, upon family figures, upon classes of activity, and so on. This is obviously close to Freud's concept of cathexis, but the development is perceptibly more systematic and more closely tied to research on observable behavior. It is also related to Lewin's concept of differentiation of specific needs out of generalized tensions.

Murphy is alert to the implications of early learnings for later learnings and of the establishment of a hierarchy of conditioned responses. Referring to Razran's studies, which indicated that an attitude favorable or unfavorable to the experimenter might determine the outcome of a conditioning experiment, Murphy comments: "*Attitudes—which are themselves conditioned responses—determine what responses may later be conditioned*" (1947, p. 227). Certainly this points directly to the Freudian emphasis on infantile experience and the role of primacy in restricting what can be learned from a complex, variable environment. In relation to therapy it indicates a major problem which must be faced by learning theory as applied to therapy—for example, Eysenck's assertion that simply learning a new response for the stimulus which has initiated neurotic symptoms causes the whole neurosis to disappear. By Murphy's formulation, the neurosis is the learning which prevents new, adaptive learning—which constrains the individual to learning phobic, obsessive, or psychosomatic symptoms. Most clinicians, of course, spontaneously use some kind of hierarchical concept to subsume the fact that some responses are easier to modify than others, that modification of one may cause others to disappear, and so on. This formulation is also comparable to Lewin's notion of peripheral (easily changed) and central (resistant to modification) systems. Lewin, however, implied that central patterns were necessarily closely tied to the ego or self; Murphy's view would leave room for the idea that mere primacy in learning, plus perhaps an intensity factor, might account for the greater resistance of these traits to extinction or relearning.

For Murphy the *self* is primarily an object of perception, an image, a phenomenal reality. The individual is first of all an organism, and the organism has built into it the attributes of observing, remembering, and organizing percepts. Thus, from repeated experiences of body, of action, of naming, the gestalt of a perceived self is evolved. This is closely comparable to the conception of the ego in Koffka as a differentiated system within the behavioral environment or of the self for Lewin. The development of the self-percept obeys perceptual laws; specifically, it differentiates out from a mass of sensory inputs including proprioceptive and visceral as well as exteroceptive stimuli.

There is one important difference between the self as conceived by Murphy and as conceived by Lewin. For Lewin the self is a bounded subsystem within the total field, and the firmness of the boundary is an important variable which can be used logically for systematizing certain observations, such as the tendency to include possessions as part of the self, variations in ability to keep to a course of action in the face of attractive distractions, and so on. It is possible that Murphy can deal with these phenomena under some other rubric, but he does not explicitly incorporate the boundary concept into his system.

There are many other important concepts in Murphy's system, but I have space for only one more. This is the notion of uniqueness, his concept of individuality. He notes that in geometry we can have different kinds of figures, such as triangles, squares, pentagons, etc. All are composed of common elements (straight lines), but each has its own distinctive laws (e.g., within a triangle the sum of the angles must be180°, but this is not true for any other polygon). Likewise, individuals may be composed of common traits, but each person may have his own emergent principles which dominate the expression of these lower-level habits. Murphy also allows for the occurrence of "types," or categories of individuals who resemble one another in some important respects more than they resemble persons not included in the type. His best example is sex typing, which is of course reasonably discontinuous. However, when he comes to clinical types, such as those described by Freud or Abraham, he shows a natural skepticism because it is difficult to find a true discontinuity between the average personality and the hypothesized type. Such types may be only extremes of a normal distribution. There is, he concedes, also a defensible place in clinical psychology for ideal types, such as those of Kretschmer or Spranger. But in such cases we must demonstrate that there is a true functional coherence, a necessary interdependence, of the traits which define the type. This is the problem of functional unity, about which more will be said in connection with factor-analytic approaches.

Murphy's work has probably had considerable impact upon clincial psychology in the United States, if only because of his great prestige and the large number of graduate students who have been exposed to his ideas. It would be difficult to establish this by reference to the literature or even by interviews because much of his contribution has been in welding together into a congruent theoretical structure ideas and hypotheses which are also part of other systems. It is also noteworthy, however, that clinicians are constantly finding statements in Murphy's writings which summarize or epitomize their daily observations. Whether this process can be reversed, so that the theory helps in selecting observations which should be made for diagnostic purposes or manipulations which should be made in therapy, is a matter which has not yet been explored.

BIOLOGICALLY ORIENTED HOLISTIC THEORIES

I have sketched what I consider to be the essence of holistic approaches to personality and have illustrated these briefly. Let me now turn to some variants of this kind of theory, namely, theories in which the organism as a whole is the central concept.

Goldstein is no doubt the most respected member of the group of authors I shall categorize as biological holists. His long and distinguished research career and his incisive logic combine to give him this status. His major book, *The Organism,* incorporates many valuable contributions which can only be sketched here.

In an important respect Goldstein devotes himself to the destruction of a distorted image which has grown up around C. S. Sherrington. From Watson to Hull, the respected model of physiological research on reflex processes has been cited as support for molecular conceptions of the behavior process and hence of personality.

Not so, says Goldstein: "The results of reflex investigations do not offer the fundamentals for building up a concept of the organism" (1939, p. 213). "*With a change in any one locality in the organism, simultaneous changes occur in other localities*" (1939, p. 213). "Whenever a change is induced in one region," he writes, "we can actually *observe simultaneous changes in whatever part of the organism we may test*" (1939, p. 214). The organism is a unit, and the designation of responses or organs as separable units is arbitrary and heuristic, not logical.

The key question is: What happens when the carefully defined operational stimulus of the molecular psychologist is applied to an organism? "There are situations," he notes, "in which an individual endures pain, etc., for the sake of 'higher' interest" (1939, p. 218). And in another connection he refers to the biological similarities of man to lower animals:

> This similarity would not necessarily signify equality. It could, at the most, refer to a unitary, basic plan which manifests itself in similar details in man and animal. The details could then have different meanings in each instance, since all phenomena gained by the isolating method achieve significance only by virtue of their relationship to their respective whole (1939, pp. 477–478).

Goldstein, then, is an unmitigated holist, and a quite conscious one. He emphasizes the concept of a hierarchy, of dominance of higher over lower levels, and shows how this makes a simplistic S-R formulation absurd. Furthermore, he has some principles (which in my opinion have been grossly neglected) with regard to the hierarchical functioning of different aspects of the organism and the way in which this gives a certain uniqueness to each individual. The concept of hierarchy, particularly when it involves any substantial number of specific reaction patterns, implies so many alternative arrangements that the concept of uniqueness is easily assimilated to an ordinary doctrine of a nonreplicated ordering of magnitudes. I believe that Goldstein meant more than this, but this is what he says. Speaking physiologically, he comments: "The new principle of articulation tries to do greater justice to the idea of a functional organization of the whole organism" (1939, p. 481).

Another notable contribution is his demonstration that behavior varies along a dimension from abstract to concrete and that there is a shift toward the concrete that accompanies certain kinds of damage. This has been of considerable influence on clinical thinking. Not so much has been done with what seems to be implicit in his development of this idea, namely, that psychic damage can likewise bring about such shifts in the patterning of behavior.

Another holistic concept introduced by Goldstein (very similar to one of Lewin's concepts) is that of "*dedifferentiation.*" It is easier to explain this by beginning with differentiation. The organism progresses from a pattern of large-muscle, body-wide movements to a pattern of precise, segmented, relatively isolated responses. The child acquiring a skill uses far more muscles than are necessary and much excess energy. With skill, the response becomes segregated or differentiated from the total ongoing behavior. Dedifferentiation, then, refers to the fact that, under stress or damage, the organism reverts to diffuse, inefficient modes of functioning. While Lewin likewise utilizes this concept, Goldstein deserves credit for showing how it operates with regard to specific behavioral changes. An injury to the central nervous system simplifies, rather than complicates, the total behavioral pattern. Not only do we find a loss of reflexes which are "specific" to the area excised, but we often discover an accentuation of other reflexes which are not normally mediated by the injured area. This points to a normal "balance" of homeostatic process which has been disrupted by the injury and which is restored in a simpler form.

The total organism may, for example, decline to recognize the significance of an injury. This phenomenon is quite independent of the type of neurological defect under investigation. The individual simply erects defenses which protect against excessive concern with, or interference by, such injuries. It is clear that in such instances we are dealing with a function of the total organism.

This implies that we must, wherever possible, interpret the behavior of a person in terms of his own norms. As Goldstein puts it, we must always be alert to the "characteristics of the organism with which we are dealing, certain norms and constants of its nature" (1939, p. 364). This theme has been more explicitly elaborated by Allport and others; it is even recognized at the verbal level by the factor analysts, although (as we shall see) they later tend to lose sight of its importance.

Among the attributes of the total person which Goldstein considers important, "centering" deserves particular attention in the present context. Centering is a phenomenon descriptive of the kind of organization manifested by the entire personality. Goldstein suggests that it may be communicated by attributes such as "freedom, meaningfulness, action springing from the whole personality, productivity, capacity to meaningful actions, capacity to adequate shifting in attitude, and capacity to absorb milieu expansions or modifications" (1939, p. 491). If I may refer back to Lewin's conceptualization, I would suggest that a high degree of centering occurs in that person whose "nuclear self" is in easy communication with all the skills, attitudes, values, and social roles he has acquired. Statistically we might say that he would show a high degree of intrapersonal correlation (or congruence, as defined by Allport), whereas a person with less centering would have segmental responses relatively independent of one another.

This point enables us to identify a scarcely explicit assumption in Goldstein's thinking. Organisms vary in the amount or degree of centering; however, he implicitly assumes that the highest type of personality, that which is most truly human, is the one showing high centering. He would argue that the segmental, somewhat dissociated pattern of responses identifies a damaged organism or one which has matured and then regressed. (Children show high centering because differentiation has not yet occurred.) This suggests a value judgment rather than an operationally established fact, since it is clear from his writing that persons who are not, in the usual sense, damaged may nevertheless show less than maximum centering; and it is also clear that these are somehow "inferior" specimens.

The superior personality manifests *ordered* behavior, that in which pattern is clearly imposed upon the response sequences. "The individual himself experiences them with a feeling of smooth functioning, unconstraint, well-being, adjustment to the world, and satisfaction" (Goldstein, 1939, pp. 36–37). These subjective criteria, obviously, are not logically sufficient; the feebleminded and the psychotic individual may report such feelings along with obviously inefficient behavior. Goldstein's formulation, nonetheless, seems to have influenced Maslow, Rogers, and others with regard to the criteria of growth, adjustment, and the normal personality.

Maslow: Deficiency and Growth Motivation

Maslow (1954) has elaborated on some of the points mentioned above and has added one concept which seems particularly relevant. This is his distinction between deficiency motivation (needs for oxygen, food, water, etc.) and growth motivation. Because man is a biological organism, the deficiency needs will dominate behavior if they are activated. But when these animal motives are gratified, the person does not go to sleep; instead, he shows new dynamic processes—strivings toward self-actualization, knowledge, understanding, and esthetic gratification.

This implies that there is a dominance principle operating, a hierarchy of need-states. Maslow arranges this hierarchy as follows: physiological needs (homeostatic demands for essential substances); safety needs (freedom from pain); belongingness and love needs; esteem needs; and self-actualizing needs. He suggests that this is a rigid order and that gratification of needs at one level tends immediately to release needs at the next higher level. Offhand this looks much too simple; it is probable, in fact, that personalities differ with respect to the hierarchy described. Some persons are so dominated by fear that even basic physiological needs are frustrated; others seek esteem at the expense of love; and so on. In general, on a statistical average, the hierarchy as Maslow offers it would certainly hold.

In a later book, Maslow (1962) has concentrated on the implications of basic need gratification for the development of healthy personalities:

> So far as motivational status is concerned, healthy people have sufficiently gratified their basic needs for safety, belongingness, love, respect and self-esteem so that they are motivated primarily by trends to self-actualization (defined as ongoing actualization of potentials, capacities and talents, as fulfillment of mission . . . as a fuller knowledge of, and acceptance of, the person's own intrinsic nature (1962, p. 23).

It is important to recognize that the growth motives are weak, the deficiency needs strong; thus in a subsistence culture, motivation may appear to be purely deficit-based. As a few people achieve positions of economic and emotional security, they are freed to grow, in the sense of developing inner potentials to the fullest extent. I am not sure whether Maslow can find any substantial increase in self-actualizing, healthy personalities in nations where these basic needs are widely gratified; perhaps he would not concede that this is a relevant test of his theory. In any event, growth theory is an aspect of personality theory which will demand more attention in the future.

Growth Theory and the Clinician

Goldstein utilized numerous concepts from biology in developing his ideas about personality, and the notion of growth as an orderly developmental function is one of the more important. This, of course, is not new in clinical psychology; Freud made much of an unfolding of the individual through oral, anal, and genital stages, and at times he gave the impression that these were inevitable. Neo-analytic critics have undermined this kind of growth concept. Goldstein was more interested in the notion that the whole determines development of parts; e.g., whether an epithelial cell becomes skin, hair, fingernail, cornea, etc., depends on its locus and the organizing center dominating this area. This would suggest that such principles may operate in the development of personality, but Goldstein is not very specific in this respect.

Allport and Maslow have also utilized the growth concept but in a similarly vague manner. Allport often refers to the need for a morphogenetic approach to personality, but makes no use of biological models in spelling out what these might be. One assumes that he may have been thinking of gradients of development, organizing centers, critical periods, inhibitory influences, etc., but this is difficult to verify.

At an opposite extreme, Kent (1961) postulates a degree of identity of psychological and biological growth which is somewhat disturbing. He makes startling claims to the effect that his patients in psychotherapy undergo changes in bodily sensations, usually beginning at the head and gradually spreading downward, and that these phenomenal changes are correlated with genuine measurable bodily growth. On a purely verbal level this sounds plausible, especially in the light of our knowledge of somatic damage from psychic injury, but operationally we are likely to be a bit upset by the idea that removal of psychic inhibitions can induce new physical growth.

Kent takes his morphogenesis seriously and holds that a psychic trauma in childhood can truly block an innate growth potential. This potential has the same status (in his schema) as the potential of dermal tissue to become a fingernail or an eyelid under appropriate organizer stimulation. Further, he holds that this growth potential is not necessarily lost when inhibited; the fixation may be reversible. The cells still are capable of being organized, and full maturation may yet be possible. Thus he reports that in his patients prolonged psychotherapy has been associated with development of greater bodily symmetry, growth of new hair, flaking off of bunions, etc. He holds that such bodily changes are to be conceptualized as consequences of the unblocking of growth potentials.

Maslow, Rogers, and Combs and Snygg have also stressed the notion of therapy as releasing the individual from restraining forces so that he is free to grow, to become the person he might have been without these hindrances. Most of these men would probably be dubious about the extreme position taken by Kent, but they seem to believe that there is a true biological growth potential, manifestations of which, at least on the psychic level, can be released in therapy.

Do we really believe that mental and physical growth are processes obeying the same laws? If so, we ought to be studying morphogenic biology and applying relevant principles in our clinical practice. For example, is the restimulation of growth merely a negative matter of removing blockages, or can we discover positive procedures which will have a stimulating effect? Little has been done about trying to formulate analogies between personality and biological growth and to verify these empirically.

It must be conceded in advance that it will not be feasible to pursue the organismic analogy very far. Psychology deals with emergent properties beyond the scope of biological conceptualizing. The classic book by Thompson, *On Growth and Form,* for example, deals mainly with interrelations between size, shape, and function. The phenomena of personality do not lend themselves to analysis in terms of size and shape; hence we are going to be studying mainly the covariance of one function with another. While this has the appearance of putting psychologists on more shaky terrain, I do not believe we are irretrievably handicapped by this situation. Certainly the biological growth analogy ought to be pursued to see how far it can be helpful.

Sheldon's Biotypology

Whereas most of the theorists so far described have emphasized the uniqueness of each individual personality, it is also appropriate to consider in this chapter theories which propose typological classifications. To take a very crude analogy, within the class of quadruped mammals, dogs and cats represent different types because they have certain combinations of attributes which are invariant within the type but decidedly different across types. It is at least logically possible that within a single species there are different personality types which represent just such patterns of characteristics.

Typologies were very popular in European character psychology of the last century, and even today they are more respected in Europe than in the United States. Jaensch, Kretschmer, and Viola come to mind in this connection. Of these, the only one to be influential on this side of the Atlantic is Kretschmer.

Kretschmer's theory of constitutional types has a long history which need not be considered here. Essentially he proposed that there are three fundamental physical types: the asthenic (a frail, linear physique); the athletic (muscular, vigorous physique); and the pyknic (plump, rounded physique). In his psychiatric practice he found a substantial correlation between schizophrenic psychoses and the asthenic-athletic types, while manic-depressives were heavily concentrated in the pyknic category. From this observation he elaborated a theory of cycloid and schizoid personality types which were presumed to be associated with (and perhaps based upon) the individual's physical type.

Kretschmer's theory did not meet with success in this country. Observers who attempted to reproduce his physical typing reported that it was often difficult to decide to which group a given person should be assigned and that there was a tendency for apparent body type to change with age (most of us put on some fat as we grow older, and hence the incidence of "pyknics" increased). Further, there were efforts to develop questionnaire tests or check-lists of the attributes asserted by Kretschmer to define his cycloid and schizoid personalities, and these resulted in normal distributions of scores rather than the discontinuity predicted by his theory. Finally, there was no observable agreement between the personality scores and the body typing.

Sheldon, who was trained first as a psychologist and later as a physician, decided that Kretschmer's ideas had a grain of truth but that they needed a complete restructuring. He propounded (1940) a new concept of physical typing, based upon tendencies toward endomorphy (overdevelopment of the viscera), mesomorphy (overdevelopment of bone and muscle), and ectomorphy (thin, fragile build and perhaps overdevelopment in regard to central nervous system functions).

Parallel to these, he asserted the existence of three temperamental types: viscerotonia (love of comfort, sociability, easygoing disposition); somatotonia (assertiveness, vigor, competitiveness, noisiness); and cerebrotonia (inhibition, love of privacy, hypersensitivity to pain). These traits are rated after interviews and observations, usually by the person who has judged the somatotype. This introduces a contaminating factor which makes many psychologists dubious about the close relationships Sheldon has found between somatotype and temperamental type.

These correlations are astonishingly high. On a group of 200 young men, Sheldon reported correlations of +.79 between endomorphy and viscerotonia, of +.82 between mesomorphy and somatotonia, and of +.83 between ectomorphy and cerebrotonia. Should these be confirmed, it would appear that major components of personality must be determined by constitutional factors. Unfortunately, where other observers have attempted to duplicate Sheldon's work, they have come out with far smaller indices of agreement between physique and temperament.

Several points merit notice in connection with this approach to personality, irrespective of the empirical confirmation of these predicted correlations. One is that Sheldon has successfully devised a way of compromising between the traditional measurement studies, which repeatedly discover normal distributions of human traits on either physical or personality dimensions, and the concept of types. He rates his subjects on a seven-step scale and, as would be expected, gets normal distributions. The type, however, is determined by relative dominance of one of the three components. Thus, an extreme endomorph would be rated 7–1–1 (high on endomorphy, low on mesomorphy and ectomorphy). But a 6–2–2 and even a 5–3–3 would still belong to the same endomorphic type because of the relative dominance of this component over the others. Thus Sheldon depends on the pattern of ratings to establish types, and so he encounters no conflict with the normal distribution of the ratings on separate dimensions.

In a sense, as Hall and Lindzey (1957) have commented, constitutional approaches such as that of Sheldon are more inductive than theoretical. The pattern of temperamental types was arrived at by classifying observations rather than by setting up theoretical postulates. The portion of Sheldon's material which is more theoretical has had more trouble. This is his hypothesis that the three somatotypes correspond to relative overdevelopment of one of the three embryological layers, the endoderm, mesoderm, and ectoderm. Most embryologists seem to find his deductions here contrary to evidence from their own discipline, and since it is not crucial to the psychological implications of his approach, Sheldon has tended to deemphasize this aspect in later writings.

There are two important contributions in the Sheldon approach. One is a revival of concern with temperament as a relatively segregated portion of personality, that relating to the mobilization and discharge of energy. It is correctly assumed that this facet of the total personality will be more closely tied to biological determinants than interpersonal relations and value systems.

The second contribution is his logical solution to the problem of types. From earliest times, observers have shown a strong tendency to invent typological classifications for mankind and to pigeonhole people on arbitrary bases. Sheldon has shown that it is possible to accept the facts of measurement (normal distribution of unidimensional measures) and still have the convenience of types (within which individuals resemble one another more than they resemble persons of other types).

This conclusion has not gone unchallenged. In an important critical article, Humphreys (1957) has charged that some of Sheldon's findings are artifacts of his method rather than logically unbiased results. He notes that Sheldon's "types" are essentially ipsative scales, i.e., scales in which the individual is scored against his own average as a central tendency. Thus, he will automatically have some high and some low scores (he can, of course, be average on all three physical or temperamental scales); ipsative scoring may tell us, for example, that John is better at arithmetic than at history, but it does not tell us whether he is competent in either. Likewise it may say that he is more prone to comfort-seeking than to vigorous exercise, but it does not indicate how strongly, relative to others, he manifests either pattern. "Using relative scores," writes Humphreys, "ensures that everyone will have a high score some place. These characteristics, combined with a presumed high degree of generality in explaining human behavior . . . make type concepts well nigh irresistible for the clinically oriented person" (pp. 224–225). Against this ready acceptance of types, Humphreys argues, as would Cattell and Eysenck, that unidimensional modes of analysis would do a better job and would not produce some of the statistical artifacts found in the Sheldon data.

The Humphreys arguments are not entirely convincing; there is no logical objection to a system in which "everyone will have a high score some place." When the clinician deals with a specific patient, he may need to identify and manipulate this person's strong and weak points, regardless of how the patient compares with a normal population. Sheldon put his case on a very unsatisfactory base by utilizing statistical techniques which were devised for an implicitly assumed unidimensional scaling. There is still a place for a theory of the "personality as a whole," but Humphreys is unquestionably correct in insisting upon rigorous procedures for testing such theories empirically.

Other Physiologically Based Theories

While Sheldon illustrates the most ambitious approach to personality theory based on the extrapolation of physiological principles to psychological data, many others have been proposed. I shall mention here only two of these, which seem to have considerable promise.

First, let us consider the proposal by Eysenck (1957) that relatively broad dimensions of personality may be predicted by (functionally related to) fairly specific physiological attributes. Starting with Pavlov's hypothesis that some individuals manifest relatively strong excitatory tendencies (in the central nervous system) and weak inhibitory tendencies, while other persons reverse this pattern, Eysenck has deduced certain implications for "introversion" and "extroversion," or dysthymia and hysteria, as observable attributes of the total personality.

Eysenck's basic postulate is that human beings differ with respect to the *speed* with which reactive inhibition is produced, the *strength* of the inhibition produced, and the *speed* with which the inhibition is dissipated. He assumes that these are in some way correlated with differences in neural structures, but (probably wisely) he avoids further commitment on this. From this point his logic dictates differences between "introverts" and "extroverts" as follows: Extroverted behavior develops as a consequence of rapid development of inhibition, strong inhibition, and slow dissipation of inhibition. This is coordinated to the fact that extroverts change rapidly from one activity to another, dislike repetitive tasks, etc.

Eysenck has been ingenious in deducing from his basic position various kinds of differences between introverts and extroverts which are open to experimental test. For example, he notes that massed practice generates inhibition and that reminiscence is due to the dissipation of inhibition; therefore, extroverts should show a stronger reminiscence effect than introverts. This has been verified experimentally (Eysenck, 1956).

Eysenck has, not unnaturally, urged that clinicians make use of his scales for the measurement of introversion-extroversion, and he has also endorsed "behavior therapy" based upon learning to replace a symptomatic habit with another habit of greater social desirability and utility. While his success so far seems limited, it would be valuable to have studies made testing his theory for its usefulness as a guide to clinical practice.

Freeman's homeostatic approach. Like Eysenck, Freeman (1948) believes that the clue to understanding the underlying dynamics of personality will be found in physiology. Essentially he is intrigued by the phenomena grouped under the concept of homeostasis, the tendency of living organisms to protect and restore favorable steady states. The analysis of a single adaptive act permits the plotting of a homeostatic response curve, including phases of energy mobilization, phases of discharge of energy in action, and the recovery phase.

Describing data mostly from his own laboratory, and interpolating considerable speculation, Freeman arrives at three basic dimensions of personality variation: (1) Drive arousal, along which individuals can be arranged from those who build up tension rapidly, become angry or excited under relatively slight pressure, or develop strong enthusiasms quickly, to an opposite pole of low arousal, little affective life, and limited effective energy for achieving purposes. (2) Discharge control, a dimension stressing inhibition of energy discharge until suitable outlets can be identified. Freeman cites limited data suggesting that this dimension is completely independent of the first; i.e., individuals may be high on both arousal and control, low on both, or high on one and low on the other. From these combinations he draws some analogies to neurotic and psychotic cases. (3) Discriminative capacity, which seems to be primarily a matter of intelligence, although Freeman tosses in suggestions of homeostatic efficiency at a more biological level as a component of this factor. At the descriptive level it would appear that he refers to the ability to survey the environment and identify the directions in which behavior will lead to optimum tension reduction.

This analysis is primarily dimensional; however, Freeman, like Sheldon, is attracted by typology. He suggests that, even though individuals are distributed along a normal curve for each factor separately, there may be clusterings of particular combinations and that the over-all perceived quality of an individual may be a function of the dominant element in the combination. Thus a person who is relatively higher on discharge control than on the other major variables may give an impression of being very inhibited, calm, or phlegmatic, even though in fact he may show normal energy mobilization. Freeman does not follow through on these suggestions with enough detail to be very helpful; nevertheless, as was indicated in regard to Eysenck, these conceptualizations help to focus our attention on specific ways of categorizing people. Such approaches may thus be useful to the diagnostician in helping him to evaluate the significance of specific observations.

Physiological devices have not become a part of the equipment of the typical psychological clinic; in the future, one may speculate, it will be considered routine to ascertain whether overtly observable lethargy, tension, and fluctuation in energy level reflect physiological processes or discharge control at a higher level. Until that time it may be valuable for the diagnostician to try to assess, by direct observation, the underlying energy mobilization and control mechanisms as well as the overtly manifest activity. This is by no means the same as observing for evidence of unconscious dynamics which may be overlaid by anxiety and repression.

Can Freeman's "energetics" make any contribution to therapy? He has written very little on this point, all of it speculative. He tends to emphasize the successes of shock therapy as evidence for his viewpoint; the general loss of enthusiasm for ECS must therefore count against him in this area. Freeman also offers some ingenious descriptions of analytic psychotherapy in terms of his equilibrium-disturbing and equilibrium-restoring concepts, but these analogies are quite unsupported by data. At most we can say, at this point, that current research on physiological energy phenomena during psychotherapy ought to be analyzed by someone interested in the Freeman hypotheses. However, there seems to be little benefit in restating the procedures of familiar psychotherapies in his physiological vocabulary.

CATTELL'S TRAIT-TYPE APPROACH

At an extreme from the holistic formulations of Lewin, Goldstein, Maslow, et al., there are distinctly molecular or perhaps atomistic approaches to personality. Readers of Cattell's impressively voluminous researches (see Cattell, 1950; Cattell, 1954; Cattell, 1957) may wonder whether it is appropriate to use the term "theory" in relation to his work, which appears to be so doggedly empirical. Theoretical assumptions do crop up in his writings, however, from time to time, and they merit consideration here. Actually Cattell exemplifies a great deal of American research (despite his British origin); our journals are full of studies which take the form: Here is a measurable event; what may be related to it?

Cattell's insistence upon a search for functional unity before descriptive terms are applied to units larger than specific habit patterns is a needed corrective to speculative theorizing which readily postulates global tendencies in personality on the basis of a few dramatic cases. This methodological bias actually conceals a theoretical assumption, namely, that acts which are related positively in one individual will also be related positively in others. This contradicts the assumption by Allport that individuals may show unique traits, organized differently from the common traits identifiable by routine factor analysis. (Cattell has developed a method, called "P technique," for identifying factor structures within a single person, but his major work to date, *Personality and Motivation Structure and Measurement,* gives little space to such studies.) He does recognize that there may be types of personality and that the pattern of functional relations for persons in type A may not correspond to the pattern for those in type B. However, he offers no logical formulation for the determination of types or for the reasons why different regression equations may be needed to predict specific outcomes in such cases. It is obvious, in any event, that such an approach requires determining the type to which an individual belongs *before* attempting to predict his behavior or mode of perceiving a specific stimulus. So far Cattell has offered neither a general theory of types nor a method of determining types in advance of doing correlational analyses of specific actions. He seems, therefore, to be trapped in a logical paradox of no mean dimensions.

An important respect in which Cattell represents an advance over a good deal of trait theory is in his recognition of the importance of "source traits" as opposed to "surface traits." The latter may roughly be defined as uniformities in the observed behavior of a person; the former, as underlying uniformities which may be reflected in somewhat diverse fashion in differing individuals. The source trait, consequently, may include such concepts as unconscious determining tendencies, physiological biasing variables (cf. discussions of Sheldon, Eysenck, and Freeman, above), and other data not superficially related to behavior. One is impressed, further, with the fact that Cattell claims to have identified source traits which resemble superego strength and ego strength, respectively, thus providing convergence with psychoanalytic formulations.

The factor-analytic approach to personality is molecular in the sense that it attempts to deal with personality only as an arrangement (perhaps only the sum) of a large number of S-R units. This is both a strength and a weakness. The strength lies in the added objectivity and the presumed increase in reliability of data based on these carefully specified events. The weakness is found in failure to consider the intrapersonal context within which S-R units occur. Suppose I am asked: "Have you ever crossed the street to avoid meeting someone?" An affirmative answer may mean that I owed the other person money, found him a great bore, thought he might punch me in the nose because I had flirted with his wife the night before, and so on. Thus the functional significance of the act is lost when it is treated as an isolated event.

The supposed statistical advantage of the factor-analytic school is also debatable. The widely cited 16 P.F. Scale developed by Cattell (1957) is based upon repeated factorings, but several scales have reliabilities around +.50, far too low for even most group studies, let alone individual diagnosis. The claim that such measures of common traits, because of their factorial purity, can be generalized more widely is also debated. Wittenborn, himself something of an expert on factorial techniques, criticizes the Cattell 16 P.F. Scale in the following words:

> Inasmuch as the pattern of intercorrelation among items is determined by the habits which the sample of items may represent and by the habits which are present in the sample of subjects employed, factors cannot be claimed to have a significance which transcends time, place and circumstance (1953, p. 88).

This means simply that factorial analyses, like subjective impressions of patients, give us numerical values which reflect the specific items observed in specific subjects under specific circumstances, and generalization from these to other subjects must be made with caution.

The molecularity of the factorial theories results in another kind of weakness. No one can extract from a factor analysis more than he puts in; it is essentially a process for summarizing observed data. Thus, if observations are limited to specific S-R units, nothing can come out which is descriptive of the personality as a whole. I can perhaps best illustrate my point with Thurstone's study of boxes. He measured several dimensions of a large number of boxes, intercorrelated these, and factored the matrix. The result gave him three factors, corresponding to length, width, and depth, which is hardly surprising. Such a system, however, can never give us any information about whether the box is watertight, whether it has inner partitions, how much pressure it will stand, whether it has a delicately etched cover, and so on. In other words, many attributes of the "box as a whole" necessarily get lost in the factoring process. Now it is just such aspects which may be important to a person who deals with boxes professionally. By analogy, we may suggest that the measurable aspects of the personality may be useful but far from comprehensive data about the whole person.

This need not be pushed to the conclusion that subjective impressions are the only kind of usable data on the total personality. There are attributes such as permeability to the environment, degree of internal differentiation, frustration tolerance, etc., which are segmental only in the sense that they can be abstracted and evaluated. It seems at least plausible that personality research will progress more rapidly as attention becomes focused at this level rather than dealing with learning, perception, and motivation.

As our methodological ingenuity improves, we should be able to devise procedures which will enable us to test more rigorously some of the deductions of holistic theory. A single example must serve to illustrate the point. In his attempts to identify significant variables in the therapeutic interaction, Reece devised an operational version of "warm" and "cold" atmospheres which did not depend upon verbal cues (see Reece & Whitman, 1962). Using verbal reinforcement as an indicator of influence upon the subject's behavior, he was able to show that expressive movements do in fact have a marked effect on verbal responses. This points the way to deliberate manipulation of expressive gestures in the actual therapeutic situation, with tape recordings to provide data for a measure of consequences.

We have, of course, many devices already in the literature which could be employed in a study of holistic theories as relevant to clinical situations. These include film and other records of "whole-person" activity, case history material from which certain information is deleted to see whether clinicians can infer it correctly, factor analysis of persons, McQuitty's pattern analysis, and profile studies. It is to be hoped that research in clinical psychology will move more rapidly along these lines in the near future.

Clinical Applications

Cattell has written explicitly about clinical applications of his views—thus differing from most of the authors included in this survey—and I can therefore simply cite some of the points he makes. The following comments are essentially an abstract of his presentation (Cattell, 1957, chap. 16).

Although a holistic approach to diagnosis is reasonable and probably unavoidable in terms of clinical realities, the concept of personality assessment must be erected upon a foundation of sound measurement theory. Reliable and valid measures of factorially pure traits will be more useful to the clinician than impressionistic evaluations contaminated by observer bias, inadequate sampling of situations, etc. Measures should be employed which will provide normative data on both the phenomenal personality (surface traits) and the underlying dynamic structures (source traits). Diagnosis of the unique individual, moreover, requires a consideration of how he stands in a pattern or profile of common traits, as compared with norm populations (cf. the clinical utilization of MMPI profiles), and also a consideration of his identifiable unique traits, attitudes, values, sentiments, fears, and affections. This latter form of diagnosis would require factor-analytic study of each patient; Cattell is undoubtedly overoptimistic in anticipating such a development. In a sense, of course, experienced clinicians do attempt subjectively to find strong and weak motives, emotions, and values in each client. Idealistically it would no doubt be valuable to have this done in an objective fashion (using Cattell's tests if research in other laboratories confirms his findings), but practically I see little likelihood of such a development in the near future.

With regard to therapy, Cattell limits himself mainly to the fairly obvious assertion that studies of therapeutic effectiveness will never be satisfactory until reliable and valid measurement precedes and follows therapeutic intervention. As long as therapists evaluate their own success, no progress in this field can be expected. Evidence for effects of therapy would be particularly convincing if based on Cattell's "objective" tests, i.e., tests of performance as opposed to questionnaire responses. If research should demonstrate changes in time spent on categories of activity, in reactions to controlled suggestion, in speed-accuracy relations, etc., as a consequence of therapy, the arguments on this point would suddenly disappear.

It must be noted, however, that Cattell's theory and his empirical research alike offer no clues with regard to the procedures of therapy. As I have noted above, the Cattell approach is essentially molecular. Nothing is postulated except that certain behaviors can be observed. The universe from which data are gathered is a universe of small segmental functions of organisms. There is no over-all concept of a total personality possessing certain attributes. Further, there is no proposal with regard to the nature of the processes which bring about change. Cattell recognizes that maturation and learning are likely to be involved in personality modification, but he has not incorporated any assertions in his theory with regard to how they operate. At present, therefore, Cattell's contribution in this area of clinical psychology must be restricted to measuring the effectiveness of therapy rather than including guides to its execution.

PSYCHODIAGNOSTICS AND THEORY

Preceding pages have offered numerous comments about possible relevance of specific theories to problems of the diagnostician. Without reviewing and summarizing these, I wish to note some important generalizations about the utility of theory for diagnostic work. These are not offered as original ideas. They are rather to be regarded as my efforts to underline some frequently ignored points.

First, the clinical psychologist often needs to be reminded that his assessment of a client is always relative to a norm. This norm may be implicit, or it may be explicit; it may be numerical, or it may be qualitative. Experts in the area of projective testing seem particularly prone to a fallacy of thinking that they are dealing with observations which do not require comparison with any kind of norm group. Therapists who eschew any formal diagnostic work-up in favor of an understanding which develops as interviews proceed are also subject to this error.

It is important to remind such psychologists that every percept, even those of the physical world, depends for its meaning upon a context of past experience. Such familiar phenomena as size and shape constancy would disappear if every percept had meaning only in relation to the immediately present situation. Similarly, the clinician is not interested in finding a clue to the presence of latent aggression unless he can evaluate this in relation to some kind of norm. He must make judgments as to the relative intensity, frequency, and duration of the states he infers from these cues. Even more importantly, he estimates (often unconsciously) the probability that this finding indicates a deviation from the norm sufficiently great to suggest an abnormal personality.

Some psychologists make better diagnosticians than others. This may be due in part to their greater sensitivity to subtle cues from the patient. But it may also result from a more acute awareness of what kinds of cues fall within a normal range. One value of personality theory is found in the guides offered for such categorizing.

The point may be illustrated by an observation by Maslow (1961) related to his research on a category of persons whom he describes as psychologically healthy, self-actualizing people. He was studying a group of Air Force officers who had many of the attributes he had postulated earlier; but some attributes he expected to find were either missing or drastically modified, and some which he had not predicted were much in evidence. Suddenly he realized that these men were preponderantly mesomorphs, whereas his previous subjects had been almost exclusively ectomorphs. The variation in observed behavior was compatible with Sheldon's theorizing, and Maslow proceeded to modify his hypotheses to allow for variations based on physical type. But if Kretschmer and Sheldon had not written of their speculations about physique and temperament, Maslow might never have spotted the source of his difficulty. I suggest, in other words, that a knowledge of personality theory may make the clinician sensitive to traits, patterns, associations, and relationships which he might otherwise miss.

It is probably necessary to point out the converse of this point. Maslow tended at first to reject certain observations because they ran contrary to his expectations. The psychologist must continually be on guard against seeing only that which his theory predicts. If a theory becomes an orthodoxy, a rigidly structured frame of reference permitting of no deviant observations, it becomes a set of blinders preventing a full view of the reality presented by the patient. Theory, then, can be a help in diagnosis or a hindrance; it should be a guide, not a straitjacket.

THE RELEVANCE OF THEORY TO THERAPY

Clinical psychologists spend a great deal of time doing individual psychotherapy, and they will probably do even more in the future, regardless of critics who find therapy ineffectual (cf. Eysenck, 1952). We must therefore raise the questions: Does personality theory have anything to offer the therapist? Is one theory to be preferred over another in this connection?

In a recent review of selected contributions on psychotherapy, Silverman (1962) concludes with a kind of omnibus definition of psychotherapy as

> . . . the treatment of mental disorders by the use of suggestion, counseling, persuasion, advising, educational direction, occupational techniques, and the like, with the purpose or goal of relieving the patient of distressing neurotic symptoms or discordant personality characteristics which interfere with his satisfactory adaptation to a world of people and events (p. 133).

This is the kind of operational definition which not only avoids but actually defies theoretical analysis. It does, however, serve an important useful purpose in reminding us that theory today has relatively little to do with the stimulus manipulations which constitute psychotherapy.

Logically, therapy attempts to modify certain antecedent variables, predicting that related dependent variables will be modified in the direction desired by the therapist (and, hopefully, by the client). But the relevance of this manipulation and the validity of the prediction depend to a major extent upon the accuracy with which intervening variables are hypothesized. It is as ridiculous to say that all neurotics need manifestations of love and affection as it is to say that all high school pupils need calculus. Much depends on the intervening variables, those which determine how the organism utilizes the stimulus in eliciting a response.

The functions of theory in a scientific enterprise are to arrange empirical data in an orderly fashion, to clarify the investigator's perception of the material under study, and to point the way to further research. Such values clearly inhere in the therapist's utilization of theory. He can benefit by an orderly and interrelated classification of personality events and can achieve insight into the problems of his client more rapidly than without such an aid.

This is not to argue that the exact manipulative procedures in the therapeutic relationship will be significantly different according to the theoretical predilections of the practitioner. In fact, Fiedler (1950) studied therapists of Freudian, Adlerian, and nondirective schools and found that the ideal therapeutic relationship, as experienced individuals described it, was virtually identical across schools. His observations might even be stretched to suggest that theory is a handicap; he found that experienced therapists agreed more with each other (across schools) than they did with inexperienced therapists within their own school of theory. A sounder interpretation, however, is that none of the theories extant could substitute for intimate experience of the therapeutic process.

Also relevant in this connection is the study

by Heine (1953) on therapists of the various schools examined by Fiedler. Heine obtained reports from clients and found that, as we would expect, they described the therapists of all schools as doing very much the same things. It was not possible, from a description of therapist activity, to ascertain to which theoretical school he belonged. When clients were asked about the "fundamental causes" of their troubles, on the other hand, marked differences were found between schools. This suggests that the particular label attached to a personality attribute—Oedipus complex, sibling rivalry, infantile dependency, etc.—has little importance. What is essential to therapeutic success is the modification of the client's percepts and responses, the way he channels his energies, and his tolerance for frustrations.

I do not interpret the Fiedler and Heine studies as deprecating the importance of theory. Theory can still be valuable in giving the practitioner a rationale for his operations and can also be a guide to modifying them as circumstances and personalities vary. The history of medicine reminds us that an incorrect theory may be helpful; keeping windows shut in swampy areas may have kept out mosquitoes as well as "bad air." In the long run, we expect sound theory to guide actions more efficiently than weaker theories, and it is thus worthwhile to focus energy on theoretical questions.

I would propose, for example, that the effect of a specific therapeutic intervention will depend on the total personality structure of the patient. To use Allport's terminology for a moment, modification of a cardinal disposition will undoubtedly ramify to induce far-reaching reorganization of the individual; on the other hand, modification of a secondary pattern will have little significance.

Another approach to the theory-and-therapy problem is to ask how the theorist would conceptualize the therapeutic process and how this might lead to new ways of exploring how personality modifications take place. For a Lewinian, therapy probably should be conceptualized as a process of modifying boundaries between regions within the personality. Dissociated or repressed material is classified as a region surrounded by a relatively impermeable boundary. Such techniques as free association, dream analysis, probing questions, and interpretations may then be conceived as devices which are empirically found to be useful in penetrating this wall and improving communication between the dissociated region and the other portions of the person. Transference and dependency relationships could also be treated as states which modify the permeability of boundaries. It seems likely that expansions of Lewinian theory in the direction of identifying the variables which may be expected to modify boundary properties would be particularly useful to the therapist.

Another problem which is relevant in this connection involves definition of the goals of therapy. It is singularly unfortunate that therapists of the neo-Freudian persuasion, who get outside the biological bias of the Freudians and understand the importance of social role and status in personality breakdowns, have at times seemed to suggest that therapy amounts to helping the client "adjust" to his social milieu. A compromise view, accepting the *biosocial* conceptualization of personality (as formulated by Murphy, for example), would provide a sounder base upon which Fromm and Horney could build their conceptions of therapy. To defend the right of the individual to autonomy, to freedom from the tyranny of the group, we must have some kind of conceptualization which defines the "individual" pole of this individual-environment polarity. A theory which is established solely on the nature of interpersonal interactions cannot do this. It must incorporate some postulates about the biological organism which precedes (logically, if not chronologically) the interaction. This need not be extended to identifying personality with the biological substratum. We can conceive of personality as an interaction event while recognizing the determinant effect of organismic attributes in limiting this interaction. It is difficult to justify a demand for autonomy unless there is a term in this dialectic which is not identified with the interaction itself.

Perhaps the greatest contribution of theory to therapy comes from the emphasis of Lewin, Allport, Murphy, and others on the uniqueness of the individual. Cut-and-dried methods may work some of the time, but the most effective therapist is the one who attempts to consider each patient to be in a class by himself. As a very small illustration of this point, let me cite the study by Whitehorn and Betz (1954), in which seven therapists who had been successful with schizophrenic patients were compared with seven who had not. The former group was found to be characterized by a habit of searching for the personal meanings of events and memories for each individual patient; the latter group seemed to be searching for evidence of developmental stages, symbols, and hypothesized basic conflicts. Thus theory which is held rigidly may be a handicap; theory which points to the unique quality of the individual may be a useful aid to the therapist.

THEORY AND CLINICAL RESEARCH

There are two conclusions that strike me as I consider the area of research done by clinicians and its relation to personality theory. The first is that the relation is pretty remote. Clinicians trying to live up to a graduate school role image have plunged blindly into empirical fact gathering without using theory as a guide. The second is that, in acting thus, they have abandoned their search for an understanding of the whole person and have regressed to such activities as counting the frequency of anxiety attacks or correlating dependency needs with age at weaning.

The problem of the clinician-turned-researcher has been discussed sympathetically by Loevinger (1963), who concedes the difficulties of meeting methodological standards of reliability, independence of errors, and replicability. Loevinger, however, does not offer the clinician a way out of his predicament but seems, rather, to suggest that he learn to live with it. I am reluctant to accept this conclusion. I am inclined to agree with Allport (1961) that there are sound research strategies which are compatible with the clinical commitment and with holistic theory. Some of them are cumbersome; they involve, for example, censoring of case histories to exclude symptoms and judgmental statements about the client and then submitting the material to independent judges for predictions of pathology, etc. Not much has been done with profile analysis; yet this is a device which keeps at least the pattern of major personality attributes as opposed to segmental scores. The construction of synthetic "cases" according to one or another theory, and submission of these to judges of different theoretical persuasions, might help us to conclude that such evaluations are (or are not) projections of an underlying bias on the part of the clinician. Stephenson's Q sort and Cattell's P-type factor analysis are underutilized procedures which offer at least the hope of retaining more of the "total personality." Invariance does not have to be established across individuals; it can also be studied in terms of replicated behavior within the single person.

The concern of the Europeans with expressive movements is appropriate here. It seems peculiar that in the United States, where Watson and his successors have firmly established the tradition of studying overt responses, personality research has almost completely ignored the area of gestures, facial expressions, vocal production, and the like. The intriguing researches by Krout (1935) and Wolff (1943) suggest that data acceptable to clinicians and "holistic" theorists can be obtained from such material. Reece (see Reece & Whitman, 1962) has recently begun some promising experiments using gestures as part of the clinical interaction; although his work is not directly relevant to the kinds of personality theory discussed here, it is probable that the method can be adapted to such investigations.

The use of sound films as stimuli which reproduce pretty much "the whole person" makes it possible to apply invariant stimuli in a clinical context. Similar recordings of an individual's behavior provide response data which can be analyzed independently by various observers, thus meeting one of the important methodological criteria. The ingenious devices developed in the study of social perception can be utilized in this area; personality, after all, is an object of perception and can be studied as such. The development of scales based on theories of Lewin, Allport, and Sheldon, and their application in such judgments, should lead to data on the relative utility and disadvantages of each. Tasks which require judges to make predictions from different types of data may be useful. While the evidence so far favors the statistical as opposed to the global-intuitive basis for prediction, this finding may be reversed by better operational definitions of the holistic personality and by the use of judges versed in specific theoretical approaches.

In short, my view is that clinicians have done poorly in research areas precisely because they have abandoned their holistic orientation and have attempted to do what

Loevinger calls "dissectionist" studies. It is not surprising that so often they have failed to use successfully a methodology which distresses them by its inadequacy Methods derived from holistic theories could well prove both more acceptable to the clinician and more productive of important insights into personality.

THEORY AND CLINICAL PRACTICE

In conclusion, let me assert once more a point I have proposed earlier. This is that the clinician needs to know several personality theories because no single theory seems quite adequate today.

Theories provide ways of organizing and thinking about data. The number of empirical observations which can be made, even about a single person, is almost infinite. The mind of the clinician, no matter how sensitive or how intuitive, cannot possibly grasp, assimilate, manipulate, and interpret such a mass of factual material. There must be categories into which phenomena are grouped; there must be assumptions about developmental sequences and about dependent, intervening, and independent variables; there will inevitably be hypotheses about which items have high predictive value for other important events and which items can be rejected as being of little value. The psychologist simply cannot work without a theory of some kind. Unfortunately, if he is equipped with only a single theory, he will encounter some data which simply do not fit. He will then be tempted to discard these as erroneous or trivial. This does the patient a serious injustice. The theory which is best for Mr. Jones is not necessarily useful in the case of Mr. Brown. The young psychologist therefore needs to become familiar with a variety of theoretical frameworks as part of his preparation for practice.

This is not to deprecate the tendency for most psychologists to prefer, and even to identify with, a particular theory. The beginning clinician will probably find it helpful to accept one viewpoint and use it as his normal guide in thinking about clients. But if he allows this to blind him to the potential usefulness of other theories, he is making a mistake. We do not have access, today, to that universally acceptable theory which can incorporate all the data about all personalities. Training in theory must still provide for diversity, not for orthodoxy.

REFERENCES

Allport, G. W. *Personality: a psychological interpretation.* New York: Holt, 1937.

Allport, G. W. *Becoming: basic considerations for a science of personality.* New Haven, Conn.: Yale Univer. Press, 1955.

Allport, G. W. *Pattern and growth in personality.* New York: Holt, 1961.

Angyal, A. *Foundations for a science of personality.* New York: Commonwealth Fund, 1941.

Barker, R., Dembo, T., & Lewin, K. Frustration and regression. *Univer. Iowa Stud. child Welf.*, 1941, **18**, No. 1.

Cattell, R. B. *Personality: a systematic theoretical and factual study.* New York: McGraw-Hill, 1950.

Cattell, R. B. Personality structures as learning and motivation patterns: a theme for the integration of methodologies. In *Learning theory, personality theory and clinical research.* New York: Wiley, 1954.

Cattell, R. B. *Personality and motivation structure and measurement.* Tarrytown-on-Hudson, N.Y.: World, 1957.

Combs, A. W., & Snygg, D. *Individual behavior.* New York: Harper & Row, 1959.

Dollard, J., & Miller, N. E. *Personality and psychotherapy.* New York: McGraw-Hill, 1950.

Eysenck, H. J. The effects of psychotherapy: an evaluation. *J. consult. Psychol.*, 1952, **16**, 319–324.

Eysenck, H. J. *The dynamics of anxiety and hysteria.* London: Routledge, 1957.

Eysenck, H. J. *The structure of human personality.* (2nd ed.) London: Methuen, 1960.

Fiedler, F. E. A comparison of therapeutic relationships in psychoanalytic, nondirective and Adlerian therapy. *J. consult. Psychol.*, 1950, **14**, 436–445.

Fisher, S., & Cleveland, S. E. An approach to physiological reactivity in terms of a body-image schema. *Psychol. Rev.*, 1957, **64**, 26–37.

Freeman, G. L. *The energetics of human behavior.* Ithaca, N.Y.: Cornell Univer. Press, 1948.

Goldstein, K. *The organism.* New York: American Book, 1939.

Hall, C. S., & Lindzey, G. *Theories of personality.* New York: Wiley, 1957.

Heine, R. W. A comparison of patients' reports on psychotherapeutic experiences with psychoanalytic, nondirective, and Adlerian therapists. *Amer. J. Psychother.*, 1953, **7**, 16–23.

Humphreys, L. G. Characteristics of type concepts with special reference to Sheldon's typology. *Psychol. Bull.*, 1957, **54**, 218–228.

Jaensch, E. R. *Eidetic imagery and typological methods of investigation.* New York: Harcourt, Brace, 1930.

Kent, C. *Man's hidden resources.* Melbourne, Australia: Hawthorn Press, 1961.

Kretschmer, E. *Physique and character.* New York: Harcourt, Brace, 1925.

Krout, M. H. Autistic gestures. *Psychol. Monogr.*, 1935, **46**, No. 208.

Leeper, R. W. Learning and the fields of perception, motivation, and personality. In S. Koch (Ed.), *Psychology: a study of a science.* New York: McGraw-Hill, 1963.

Lersch, P. *Aufbau der Person.* Munich: Barth, 1954.

Lersch, P. Levels of the mind. In H. P. David & H. von Bracken (Eds.), *Perspectives in personality theory.* London: Tavistock, 1957.

Levine, R., Chein, I., & Murphy, G. Relation of the intensity of a need to the amount of perceptual distortion: a preliminary report. *J. Psychol.*, 1942, **13**, 283–293.

Lewin, K. *Dynamic theory of personality.* New York: McGraw-Hill, 1935.

Lewin, K. *Principles of topological psychology.* New York: McGraw-Hill, 1936.

Lewin, K. Conceptual representation and measurement of psychological forces. *Contr. psychol. Theory,* 1938, **1**, No. 4.

Lewin, K. Lippitt, R., & White, R. K. Patterns of aggressive behavior in experimentally created "social climates." *J. soc. Psychol.*, 1939, **10**, 271–300.

Loevinger, Jane. Conflict of commitment in clinical research. *Amer. Psychologist,* 1963, **18**, 241–251.

Maslow, A. H. *Motivation and personality.* New York: Harper & Row, 1954.

Maslow, A. H. Some frontier problems in psychological health. In A. Combs (Ed.), *Personality theory and counseling practice.* Gainesville, Fla.: Univer. of Florida, 1961.

Maslow, A. H. *Toward a psychology of being.* Princeton, N.J.: Van Nostrand, 1962.

May, R., Angel, E., & Ellenberger, H. F. *Existence: a new dimension in psychiatry and psychology.* New York: Basic Books, 1958.

Murphy, G. *Personality: a biosocial approach to origins and structure.* New York: Harper & Row, 1947.

Reece, M. M., & Whitman, R. Expressive movements, warmth, and verbal reinforcement. *J. abnorm. soc. Psychol.*, 1962, **64**, 234–236.

Rogers, C. R. *The clinical treatment of the problem child.* Boston: Houghton Mifflin, 1939.

Rogers, C. R. *Client-centered therapy.* Boston: Houghton Mifflin, 1951.

Schafer, R., & Murphy, G. The role of autism in a visual figure-ground relationship. *J. exp. Psychol.*, 1943, **32**, 335–343.

Sheldon, W. H. *Varieties of human physique.* New York: Harper & Row, 1940.

Sheldon, W. H. *Varieties of temperament.* New York: Harper & Row, 1942.

Silverman, H. L. Psychotherapy: a survey and evaluation. *Psychiat. Quart. Suppl.*, 1962, **36**, 116–135.

Snygg, D., & Combs, A. W. *Individual behavior.* New York: Harper & Row, 1949.

Stagner, R. *Psychology of personality.* (2nd ed.) New York: McGraw-Hill, 1948.

Stephenson, W. *The study of behavior: Q-technique and its methodology.* Chicago: Univer. of Chicago Press, 1953.

Thompson, D. *On growth and form.* (2nd ed.) Cambridge: Cambridge Univer. Press, 1952.

Viola, G. *Le legge de correlazione morfologia dei tipi individuali.* Padova, Italy: Proserpini, 1909.

Whitehorn, J. C., & Betz, B. J. A study of the psychotherapeutic relations between physicians and schizophrenic patients. *Amer. J. Psychiat.*, 1954, **111**, 321–331.

Wittenborn, J. R. Review of Cattell 16 P.F. Scale. In O. K. Buros (Ed.), *Fourth mental measurements yearbook.* Highland Park, N.J.: Gryphon Press, 1953.

Wolff, W. *The expression of personality: experimental depth psychology.* New York: Harper & Row, 1943.

14
Fundamentals of Psychoanalytic Theory

NATHANIEL ROSS AND SAMUEL ABRAMS

Freud was a dedicated research scientist, a skilled clinician, and a bold and imaginative thinker. These assets were the foundations upon which his psychoanalytic theories were erected. To distill out of their complexities the essences which must emerge from so necessarily skeletal an account, one must tread different pathways: those of the evolution of Freud's general psychology, the development of his theory of the neuroses, and the origins of the principles and postulates from which he derived both.

When, after a brief and extraordinarily productive career as a neurologist (Jones, 1953), Freud turned his attention to psychotherapy, he reorganized the existing nosology, adopting a dynamic and humanistic approach to what were then called "nervous" diseases (S. Freud, 1894; S. Freud, 1895; S. Freud, 1896). Views on the etiology of these conditions had been heavily permeated with organicist and hereditoconstitutional hypotheses, from which Freud ultimately liberated himself to an increasing degree, although he never completely relinquished them. By reaching out to disciplines ancillary to psychiatry, he acquired constructs for his psychoanalytic psychology. Under the influences of Herbart and Meynert, he moved toward a psychological frame of reference, dynamic and structural in nature (Hartmann, 1956). Through his neurological and physiological training with Brücke, Meynert, Exner, and Breuer, he discovered a principle—that of constancy—which seemed to underlie certain mental functions, and he also hit upon the idea of applying the concept of energy to the explanation of psychological processes; from Hughlings Jackson the concept of dynamically related hierarchies in the central nervous system (Rapaport, 1960); and from Darwin, a strong tendency to emphasize evolutionary sequences (Rapaport, 1960). From these diverse sources sprang his concepts of the pleasure-unpleasure principle, the primary process, regression, and the unconscious; his idea of the central role of conflict; and his genetic approach to human development. If Freud had been inclined to devote himself purely to research, there was enough here to encompass a lifetime of investigation.

But for Freud, the clinician, neither these postulates nor the implications of Breuer's and Charcot's work concerning technique proved adequate for the treatment of neuroses. Forced to fall back on his own resources, he created his monumental theory of drives, which to this day retains its special rank among classical psychoanalytic clinicians (S. Freud, 1887–1902; S. Freud, 1914; S. Freud, 1915a; S. Freud, 1915b; Jones, 1953).

Such was the impact of this hypothesis that for a period of years it dominated the field of psychoanalysis; indeed, to this day it is synonymous in the minds of the uninformed with all psychoanalytic theory. The integration of the drive theory with numerous of Freud's other germinal ideas, whose statements, if not expositions, can be traced far back in his writings, was to await the advent of the structural point of view (Hartmann, 1950; Hartmann, 1951; Hartmann, 1956; Kris, 1951). This offered not only a unifying principle around which psychoanalytic concepts could be organized but also a conceptual tool of the greatest clinical and theoretical value. Individual psychological functions could now more meaningfully be studied ontogenetically and in their various regressive operations; they could be traced more precisely to their origins, their vicissitudes could be understood more clearly, and the bewildering and seemingly contradictory manifestations of behavior could be correlated with principles more basic than had hitherto been available (Hartmann, 1950; Hartmann & Kris, 1945). In fact, the structural model permitted a more accurate conceptualization of the drives themselves, as well as of the defensive functions of the ego, and made possible the formulation of a new theory of affects. Freud took the latter task on himself (in his seventieth year!), when he brought forth a brilliant new revision of the theory of anxiety (1926). Other classical contributions followed—Nunberg's on the synthetic function of the ego (1931), A. Freud's on the defenses (1936), and Hartmann's on adaptation (1939). There were advances in the investigation of thinking and the affects (Rapaport, 1950; Rapaport, 1951a; Rapaport, 1953); object relations (Panel, 1962a); stimulus thresholds (Bergman & Escalona, 1949); sublimation, autonomous functions, and creativity (Hartmann, 1955; Kris, 1955); the concepts of self and identity (Erikson, 1956; Jacobson, 1954b; Panel, 1958); and the early aspects of psychic development (Benjamin, 1961; Fries & Woolf, 1953; Fries & Woolf, 1961; Greenacre, 1958; Hendrick, 1951; Hoffer, 1950; Kestenberg, 1953; Panel, 1950; Panel, 1951; Panel, 1955a; Panel, 1961; Panel, 1962a; Rangell, 1961; Rubinfine, 1961; Schur, 1955; Spitz, 1954; Spitz, 1955). Attention came to be paid to disciplines allied to psychoanalysis so that new correlations and insights could be discovered. Methods of direct observation, particularly of children (G. Bibring, Dwoyer, Huntington, & Valenstein, 1961; A. Freud, 1951; A. Freud, 1953; Kris, 1950; Spitz, 1950), gave rise to well-organized projects manned by psychoanalytically trained personnel, while experimental methods and close relations with experimental psychologists became integral parts of psychoanalytic research.

On the basis of experimental and clinical studies, Wolman (1960, chap. 15) has suggested that the concept of "cathexis" be expanded to include both the subject who cathects the libido in an object and the recipient of the cathexis and that the term "interindividual cathexis" be introduced to describe this phenomenon.

With all this, the study of psychopathology continued to produce fruitful results. Quite early in his clinical career, Freud had seized upon the Oedipus complex as the nuclear core of neurosis; forty years of psychoanalytic work did not alter his view that this was the bedrock of neurosogenesis. Repeatedly impressed by the universality of this phenomenon, he came to hold the boldly speculative opinion that the Oedipus complex and its ramifications were based upon phylogenetically rooted fantasies (S. Freud, 1915–1917). While certain theoreticians followed this lead and collected evidence to support such a view (Fliess, 1956), many others elected to suspend their judgment and to investigate the largely unexplored territory of the earliest developmental phases of childhood. The accumulating mass of material from child analyses; newer findings derived from broadening the scope of psychoanalytic treatment to include the borderline states, severe character disorders, addictions, and even psychoses; direct child observation; and pressures from divergent groups induced classical theoreticians to pay increasing attention to preoedipal factors and to probe more deeply into the earliest modes of mental functioning. Postoedipal phenomena also came under closer scrutiny (A. Freud, 1951; A. Freud, 1952; Greenacre, 1941; Hartmann, 1950; Hartmann & Kris, 1945; Hoffer, 1950; Spitz, 1950; Spitz, 1955).

At the same time, analytic investigators applied their techniques to exogenous factors as well—the influence of the earliest mother-child relationships, of the parents as carriers of identifications and of mores, and of society itself. (Coleman, Kris, & Provence, 1953; Johnson & Szunek, 1952; Mahler, 1952; Mahler, 1958; Mahler, 1960; Mahler & Gosliner, 1955; Neubauer, 1960; Ritvo & Solnit, 1958). The mental representations of reality, both inner and outer, and the dynamic reactions between them were staked out as legitimate territory for psychoanalytic investigation.

Nevertheless, with all this expansion of psychoanalytic theory and research, encompassing today the most ultimate reaches of the human psyche, one continues to hear the same criticisms of Freudian theory: that it is tied exclusively to sexuality (usually conceived of as adult genital activity); that it is fatalistic and pessimistic and derives behavior only from inherent constitutional factors; that its theoretical constructs are severely limited because it unwittingly takes for granted a code of Victorian mores; that it is a philosophic or religious system organized into a sect of orthodox followers who dare not express critical attitudes for fear of excommunication; that it is so systematized and affectively poverty-stricken that it reduces human behavior to mechanical sterility; that it is based on a mystique of nonexistent instincts and relies on the entirely questionable thesis of phylogenetically transmitted fantasies; and that it reductionistically equates all experience with its origins in early childhood. Freud's theoretical propositions merit evaluations more informed and thoughtful and less polemical than these.

To open the way to a deeper understanding of these propositions, this chapter addresses itself to a broad exposition of the growth and development of psychoanalytic psychology.

FREUD IN THE 1890s

The Original Theory of the Neuroses

By the 1890s, Freud was committed to a predominantly psychotherapeutic practice. It seemed to him that two distinct groups separated themselves from the wide variety of nervous patients with whom he was in contact: those with "actual" neuroses and those with psychoneuroses. He included neurasthenia, anxiety states, and hypochondriasis in the one, and such conditions as hysteria, obsessions, phobias, hallucinatory psychoses, and paranoia in the other. Taking note of the abnormalities in the sexual life of all these diverse patients, Freud was forced to assume that somehow sexuality was etiologic for both groups. He soon arrived at the formula that the actual neuroses were related to physiological tension states secondary to an abnormal current sexual life ("actual" means "current" in German) and that the symptoms of the psychoneuroses reflected forgotten memories of past traumatic sexual experiences (S. Freud, 1894; S. Freud, 1895; S. Freud, 1896; S. Freud, 1898).

A variety of clinical data led Freud to these views. The diagnosis of neurasthenia, for example, rested chiefly upon the complaint of profound weakness. It seemed to Freud that compulsive masturbation was the predominant sexual activity in a neurasthenic's life and that the malaise disappeared following a recommendation to desist from it. Freud reasoned that it was the excessive discharge of energies through masturbation that had left these patients weak and impoverished in the pursuits of their other interests. On the other hand, anxiety neurosis ensued when a complete sexual discharge was hampered, e.g., in the abstinent. For these patients the resumption of normal sexual activity brought discomforts to an end. In this case, Freud thought, the dammed-up somatic sexual tensions which were not released were experienced psychologically as anxiety or as some equivalent of anxiety (1895). Such an admixture of physical and mental concepts was soon to be almost totally discarded in Freud's theorizing—the methodological defect is obvious. It was destined to reappear again in certain areas of psychoanalytic theory, e.g., in the so-called "psychosomatic" states, where physical symptoms themselves are so central. Freud summed up the differences within the actual neuroses in this fashion: "We rather find a kind of antithesis between the symptoms of anxiety neurosis and of neurasthenia, which might be brought out by such labels as 'accumulation of excitation' and 'impoverishment of excitation' " (1895, p. 114).

The psychoneuroses, henceforth to be in the forefront of Freud's interest, were quite differently structured. A purely mental conflict appeared to be the central determinant of discomforts attendant upon them. Freud explained: "Their symptoms arose through the psychical mechanism of (unconscious) defense, that is, in an attempt to repress an incompatible idea . . . in distressing opposition to the patient's ego" (1896, p. 162).

Varying symptoms reflected varying defenses that patients might use to protect themselves from these mental discomforts. It also seemed possible to correlate the specificity of symptoms with the type and the timing of the past traumata. For example, a passively experienced sexual trauma in childhood would usually result in some "bodily form of expression," a process which Freud termed "conversion." On the other hand, an active seduction might predispose the young seducer to obsessional states. In obsessions the defense substituted innocuous ideas for the painful ones; the former then repeated themselves interminably. In another kind of patient the mechanism might constitute a complete "forgetting" of both the idea and the painful associated emotional state. In such a situation a "high degree of pathological predisposition" must be assumed: "The ego breaks away from the incompatible ideas; but the latter is inseparably connected with a piece of reality, so that, in so far as the ego achieves this result, it, too, has detached itself wholly or in part from reality" (S. Freud, 1894, p. 59). In the formation of phobias, Freud postulated a combination of the mechanisms of substitution and displacement, while in paranoia he described as "projection" the attribution of hostile attitudes arising within the patient himself to external objects (1896).

The General Psychology of 1895

Freud's general psychology, upon which his theories of psychopathology rested in part, was originally intended as a psychology for neurologists. In accord with the prevailing scientific ethos, it was an attempt to explain mental processes in neurophysiological terms. At that time such an etiological scheme appeared to be the only possible scientific one (S. Freud, 1887–1902, p. 355).

The significance of "quantities" forced itself early upon Freud's thinking; it is implicit in concepts such as substitution, conversion, displacement, and discharge, which had arisen from his work with Breuer on the hysterias (Breuer & S. Freud, 1893–1895). In accord with his neurological training (Amacher, 1962), Freud assumed that the function of nervous tissue was to reduce the tension states established within it. The reflex arc was a simple example of this concept. He named this tendency the "principle of neuronic inertia" (S. Freud, 1887–1902, p. 356). It became the "pleasure-unpleasure principle," the primary model of psychoanalysis, as soon as Freud accepted the necessity of conceptualizing his theory in purely psychological terms. Neuronic cathexes then became cathexes of mental representations. Since his clinical attention had been drawn to the consequences of external traumata, he at first dealt with the problem of avoiding externally induced unpleasure, unpleasure being regarded as the psychological consequence of the accumulation of cathexes beyond a certain critical point (S. Freud, 1887–1902, p. 358). He was also forced to deal with the effects of such increases secondary to purely endogenous factors, e.g., in the anxiety neuroses, but at this time he thought that endogenous stimuli could cause a psychoneurotic response only if they attached themselves to earlier externally induced traumatic events. With everyone else in 1895, Freud shared the notion that sexuality arose during puberty, but clinical data forced him to assume that infantile traumata could at least "posthumously" be endowed with sexuality. In addition he wrote that some people might suffer from precocious sexuality as a consequence of excessive stimulation in childhood; the inability of a child to deal with such stimuli lent special pathogenicity to this precocity (S. Freud, 1887–1902, pp. 413ff.).

Following Meynert and also modeling his ideas on Hughlings Jackson's concept of neurological hierarchies, Freud wrote that the immature mind contained certain "primary mental processes" which enabled it to effect the requisite cathectic discharge; subsequently these archaic modes were supplanted by more adaptive "secondary processes" (1887–1902, pp. 386–389). An inhibiting structure, an ego, was needed to mediate the more highly evolved latter processes.

This ego which Freud was forced to consider was not yet an elaborate psychological structure. Still conceived originally in neurological terms, it was regarded as an organization, a "group of neurones with a constant cathexis." A host of functions in addition to that of the secondary processes were ascribed to this fairly stable mental structure. It had an inhibiting and a defensive function. The functions of attention and consciousness were effected through it, as well as perception, memory, judgment, organization, reality testing, and thinking (S. Freud, 1887–1902, pp. 387ff.). The ego stood in opposition to the primary processes, but these archaic modes might come to the fore when certain situations impaired the ego's effectiveness, e.g., sleep or pathology. In fact, Freud felt that any intense affective experience, such as severe anxiety, might temporarily impair more complex psychological functions; paralleling Jacksonian neurology, such a situation automatically brought more primitive processes into play. This concept of regression is one of Freud's most significant clinically derived theoretical contributions (1887–1902, p. 414).

Later on, Freud loosely labeled other parts

of the mind "ego" as well, thus weaving a serious semantic confusion into the fabric of his complex theory. The internalization of certain social, ethical, and moral standards also contributed to the formation of the ego, but this part of the ego was soon separated off, first as part of the censorship, then as ego ideal, and finally as superego, although all three are not precisely identical concepts. Freud also called ego a person's concept of himself, the "I" or the "me." His final suggestion was that the ego be regarded only as a specific coherent structure defined by its functions. He continued to use the term "ego" to mean the self ego and also continued to use it in the structural sense. However, even with the relatively recent elaboration by others of the concepts of "self" and "identity" as specific functions or substructures of the ego, usage in this area continues to override definition.

The Fate of the Theories

As they stood, particularly in view of the rapidity of their growth, Freud's general psychology and his theory of neurosis were unique. In postulating quantities of mental energy, they are *economic* theories; in emphasizing the interplay of conflict between forces, they are *dynamic;* in postulating levels of mental functioning, e.g., unconsciousness to consciousness, they are *topographic;* in dividing the mental apparatus into organized groupings of psychological functions, they are oriented in terms of *structure;* in investigating the origin of symptoms and in correlating the timing of traumatic experiences with the development of specific disabilities, they are *genetic;* and, finally, in demonstrating the protective function of symptoms in the psychoneuroses and in emphasizing the individual's relationship to reality, they are *adaptive* theories as well. We call this the "metapsychological" approach. At its beginnings, this included only the first three functions; today, psychoanalysts include under this term all except the topographic (Rapaport & Gill, 1959).

In addition, Freud's early theories were in good part clinically derived, and this is particularly true of the theory of the neuroses. As long as the masturbator's diverse interests returned when he followed the advice to stop; as long as the anxiety of the abstinent abated when he resumed normal sexual intercourse; and as long as the specific early traumata could be unveiled and symptoms relieved with a "cathartic" approach, the theory needed no modification. It could withstand certain important allegedly moral pressures as well as attacks on its internal consistency. But it finally succumbed to the pressures of Freud's own mounting accumulation of clinical data. In 1897, in despair, he wrote to a friend: "Let me tell you straight away the great secret which has slowly been dawning on me in recent months. I no longer believe in my *neurotica*" (1887–1902, p. 215).

Four clinical findings were forcing him to revise his position on etiology. Patients were leaving before their analyses could be concluded, and Freud confessed that these partial successes could be explained in other "familiar" ways. Hysterical patients were constantly claiming that their fathers had performed perverse acts during their childhood. Freud reasoned that since not every sexual trauma could produce a hysteria, perversions would have to be far more frequent than neuroses, and he believed that this was not true. In addition, patients seemed unable to distinguish clearly what had really happened to them in their past from what they had fantasied during childhood. And finally, Freud discovered that in cases of far-reaching psychoses, where access to all sorts of mental depths was possible, the allegedly pathogenic memories were not recovered. How was it possible that they were not accessible in such severely regressed conditions? "I do not know where I am," Freud wrote, and he expressed serious concern about earning his living (1887–1902, pp. 215–218).

Then the solution became clear. In a letter dated November 14, 1897, Freud wrote:

> It was on November 12th, a day under the influence of a left-sided migraine, on the afternoon of which Martin sat down to write a new poem and on the evening of which Oli lost his second tooth, when, after the terrible pains of the last few weeks, a new piece of knowledge was born to me. Truth to tell, it was not entirely new . . . but this time it remained and saw the light of day (1887–1902, p. 230).

This was Freud's "birth announcement"; his theory of the drives, which was now to become the nucleus of his theory of psychopathology, had at last emerged from its gestation (Arlow, 1959; E. Bibring, 1941; E.

Bibring, 1943; Hartmann, 1948; Hartmann, Kris, & Lowenstein, 1949).

THE THEORY OF DRIVES OR INSTINCTS

The Libido Theory

> I have found love of the mother and jealousy of the father in my own case too, and now I believe it to be a general phenomenon of early childhood. . . . If that is the case, the gripping power of the Oedipus Rex . . . becomes intelligible . . . the Greek myth seizes on a compulsion which everyone recognizes because he has felt traces of it in himself. Every member of the audience was once a budding Oedipus in fantasy, and this dream-fulfillment played out in reality causes everyone to recoil in horror, with the full measure of repression which separates his infantile from his present state (S. Freud, 1887–1902, p. 223).

The discovery of infantile longings within himself, independent, as far as he could determine, of specific external stimulation, launched Freud into his bold new formulation, fraught with the most far-reaching theoretical and technical implications, i.e., that sexual urges appear spontaneously in early childhood and develop according to a pattern, progressing through a series of phases designated by the erogenous zones in which they are successively dominant. Thus, a discovery which had first dismayed Freud was turned to the most fruitful account—the perverse acts of seduction ascribed so convincingly by patients to their parents were only fantasies. But whence arose such extraordinary fantasies? Freud concluded that they were rooted deep in the biological matrix of man and that they could exert effects fully as powerful as those of actual experiences. It then became clear why a record of actual events could not be recovered in the far-reaching psychoses; such events had never taken place. With this bold stroke, Freud cleared away the obstacles to the further advance of his theories.

To state it briefly, Freud postulated that the sexual drive (by which, for good clinical reasons, he did not mean simply the desire for sexual intercourse, but the entire gamut of pleasurable experiences associated with somatic activities and their psychic expressions) plays a crucial role in the life of the child from its earliest beginnings. Furthermore, it passes through various phases, finally to culminate in what is designated as genital primacy, which is not achieved until puberty. Freud used the term "libido" to separate the energy invested in this sexual drive from other "cathexes" (energic investments) of the psychic life. Normally, libido originates, together with other energies, in the area of the mouth [later designated by Spitz (1955) as "the primal cavity"]; it is then concentrated in the anal sphincter and its environs and, later in childhood—in what came to be called the "phallic" period—in the penis and clitoris. In addition, certain other organs, such as the eyes, the skin, and the muscular system, can be invested with libido and give rise to certain discharge phenomena. The movement of libido from one organ to another is a mobile and plastic one in childhood, considerably less rigid than later in life; consequently, Freud pictured the child as "polymorphously perverse," although it must be emphasized that he did not in any sense mean that children are normally perverse in the same sense as a pathological adult. Indeed, these polymorphously perverse inner—and at times outwardly expressed—tendencies furnished one of the prime justifications for Freud's insistence on the use of the term "sexual," an insistence which gave rise to the most profound misunderstandings and uninformed rejections of the libido theory (S. Freud, 1905b).

Carefully defining his concepts, now formulated within the framework of a psychological theory, Freud defined an instinct, instinctual drive, or drive—all acceptable English translations of the German word *trieb*—as the mental representation of a continuously flowing endogenous somatic process. A drive can be defined in terms of its "pressure" (or "impetus"), "source," "aim" (internal or external), and "object." By pressure, Freud meant its "motor factor, the amount of force or the measure of demand for work which it represents." The source is the "somatic process which occurs in an organ or part of the body . . . whose stimulus is represented in mental life by an instinct"; the study of sources as such is therefore outside the scope of psychology. The internal aim of the drive was the discharge of cathexes, and the external aim the means by which discharges are effected, e.g., sucking, anal expulsion, penetration, etc. The object is defined as the thing, animate or inanimate, human or nonhuman, by means of which the drive achieves its aims. When the object is the source organ itself, as, for example, the individual's own penis, the activity leading to discharge is called "autoerotic"; if outside the individual, such as a heterosexual partner, the activity is object-libidinal. Thus the libido may move in either direction or, most often, simultaneously in both directions and, in an ontogenetic sense, from oral to anal to phallic sources, aims, and modes of discharge, to culminate finally in the primacy of genital discharge achieved in puberty (S. Freud, 1914; S. Freud, 1915a). Two amendments must be added to this account: (1) The activity directed toward the object is, more strictly speaking, toward its mental representations, since the real external object can never be truly known or understood in all its dimensions; and (2) it is implied that as the individual progresses from pregenital to genital levels of development, his appreciation of the object and feelings for it become successively more oriented toward the interests of the object than of the self.

What, according to Freud, is the fate of the infantile drives? The most favorable outcome is the achievement of genital primacy without the hampering effects of fixations at earlier levels, i.e., of pregenital patternings. To be sure, such patternings are evident in precoital activities and play an important role in preparation for full orgastic discharge, but in a clearly subordinate way. The most complete discharge of libidinal cathexes is in heterosexual love. And it must be added that at no time did Freud define love in terms of its sensual elements in isolation from the tender ones—in fact, he pointed out the pathological results of this dichotomy. In Freud's earlier formulations, perversion was considered "the negative of neuroses"—it represented the simple breakthrough of component sexual impulses, based on intense fixations at pregenital levels. Later this view was profoundly modified by himself and others (Bak, 1953; Bak, 1956; Fenichel, 1945; S. Freud, 1919; Gillespie, 1952; Gillespie, 1956; Greenacre, 1952; Greenacre, 1953; Greenacre, 1955; Greenacre, 1960; Panel, 1960b; Panel, 1962a), but at that time, this hypothesis seemed a plausible one. Neuroses result if the infantile aims and objects meet with severe repression; in such case, the discharge takes place nonetheless, but in a disguised way, through the symptom. Thus, a wish for oral impregnation may underlie the hysterical symptom of vomiting. Certain character traits also bear the impact of these earlier modes of activity, e.g., stubbornness as an expression of an anal fixation (S. Freud, 1908). This mode of behavior then constitutes a partial discharge of the infant's opposition to giving up its feces on demand. In addition, a desexualization of an instinctual drive, together with an alteration of its aim in accord with socially acceptable standards, may lead to the development of a more highly valued cultural activity. This is "sublimation," a concept which has since undergone considerable modification as a result of developments in ego psychology (Panel, 1955b).

At this time Freud categorized a certain group of conditions that were especially amenable to the psychoanalytic procedure as "transference neuroses." Such a classification arose, as did many of his constructs, from clinical considerations. Patients with transference neuroses are able to develop a special kind of relationship to the analyst which makes it possible to proceed with the treatment without the obstacles encountered in other conditions, which were designated as the "narcissistic neuroses," comprising principally the psychoses. Some time after entering analytic treatment, certain patients become so attached to the analyst as to place him at the center of their affective life, with all its neurotic vicissitudes. Freud used the term "transference neuroses" also for this temporary exacerbation or regression, which can be used as a leverage for the most telling interpretations of their neurotic conflicts, rooted as they are in early relationships to the objects of their infantile strivings. The capacity to experience such a therapeutically valuable, if most affectively charged, relationship appears to depend upon the achievement of object relationships at the oedipal level during infancy. Frustrating or disrupting circumstances in adult life or the inception of a heterosexual relationship or other entry into normal adult activities may prove intolerable to individuals fixated at this level and may induce the onset of neurotic symptoms based on taboos, anxieties, guilts, and defenses characteristic of this phase of development. Hysterical and obsessive-compulsive symptoms represent compromise formations between the repressed and repressing forces of the oedipal period, with the latter reflecting a deeper regression—an anal one—in the retreat from the unacceptable incestuous and murderous temptations of the Oedipus complex. In analysis the patient relives the ancient conflicts, through his relationship to the analyst, in such a way that it is possible for the analyst to make unconscious fantasies conscious and to present to him convincing interpretations of the nature of his conflicts (S. Freud, 1915–1917).

The libido theory was a satisfactory integration of the data of psychoanalytic experience then current, and it brought the monumental discovery of infantile sexuality to the forefront of analytic attention. In application, it proved fruitful and illuminating, but ultimately its limitations as a more or less exclusive hypothesis explaining human personality and its development and vicissitudes came to the fore. Characteristically, these led not to a stalemate, but to an increasing expansion of Freud's views on psychopathology as well as to the widening scope of psychoanalysis to encompass a general psychology. Nevertheless, the limitations of the libido theory were among the reasons most frequently advanced by the leaders of dissident movements for their defections (Adler, Horney, Sullivan, Rado, etc.).

Narcissism

To some extent Freud had derived his libido theory from certain phenomenological aspects of various perversions, perversions in which there existed at least some manifest relationships to external objects. Soon, however, he was forced to take note of other types of perversion, whose victims derived gratification not from others, but from themselves. If such a distinction could be made within this particular realm of psychopathology, perhaps it could be used to differentiate various neuroses as well. Consequently, Freud now turned his attention to the current of libidinal interest that was directed to the individual himself.

Before the images of external objects can be cathected, an intermediate step is necessary, one in which the libidinal current is first attracted to the mental representation of the person himself. This process constitutes a state which Freud called the "narcissistic" one. This concept offers some degree of explanation for numerous phenomena: (1) Libidinal cathexes of the ego seem to explain the origins of the degree of self-love required to maintain the "instinct for self-preservation." (2) The schizophrenias, which had heretofore defied psychoanalytic comprehension, are often characterized by features that might plausibly be considered narcissistic: withdrawal of interest in the external world and enhanced, if not grandiose, ideas of self-importance. With the concept of a narcissistic phase, one may hypothesize a regression to this level in the schizophrenias earlier than the fixations attributed to the hysteria and obsessive-compulsive phase. (3) The close relationship clinically observable between hypochondriasis and psychoses might now be brought into the framework of the theory. (4) Children, who so readily believe in the magical power of their thoughts and wishes and who are so patently self-centered, and primitive people, in whom the same tendencies as well as others (such as their forms of social organization) are prominent, can also be understood as illustrating forms of narcissistic behavior. (5) The concept of narcissism was to find its chief application in its great enrichment of the understanding of the most far-reaching subtleties of human relationships. If it is possible to cathect representations of one's own self as well as those of external objects, certain relationships which appear to be object-directed may in reality be externalized narcissistic ones (S. Freud, 1914). Freud first grasped the clinical significance of this phenomenon in his study of Leonardo da Vinci:

> The boy represses his love for his mother; he puts himself in her place, identifies with her, and takes his own person as a model in whose likeness he chooses the new objects of his love. In this way he has become a homosexual. What he has in fact done is step back to auto-erotism: for the boys whom he now loves as he grows up are after all only substitutive figures and résumés of himself in childhood . . . boys whom he loves in the way in which his mother loved *him* when he was a child. He finds the objects of his love along the path of *narcissism,* as we say (S. Freud, 1910, p. 100).

Thus, henceforth the manifest object relationship as well as the manifest dream and symptom required analysis of its latent content for its deepest comprehension as well as for its most effective handling.

Freud made a distinction between two types of narcissism, primary and secondary.

The former is characteristic of the earliest phases of infancy, where there is no self-awareness and where there exists no differentiation between the self and the object world, between external and internal. Here originates the sense of omnipotence, in which the encompassing power of the external world is felt as one's own, and here too is the genesis of the oceanic feeling of mystical states. The other type of narcissism arises in later phases of development, when the differentiation between the self and the object world has been established and when the libido has been invested in objects. When objects have been lost or have proved intolerably disappointing, frustrating, or rejecting, libido is withdrawn from them and reinvested in the self. This is secondary narcissism (S. Freud, 1914; S. Freud, 1915–1917).

What is the fate of infantile narcissism? In part it supplies the energy for the development of the ego as well as for the development of a healthy degree of self-esteem. For the most part, however, infantile narcissism constitutes only an intermediate stage in the maturation of sexuality, to be followed by object love and mature self-regard. Residuals may achieve representation in various ways: in perversions, magical thinking, character types, and disorders in which narcissism plays varying roles and, finally, in the infinite subtleties of object relationships. In addition, it gives rise to one important element in a certain permanent structure of the mental apparatus, the ego ideal, which, in the form of ethical standards and of aspirations, comes to exert a powerful governing force on the functioning of the individual (S. Freud, 1914; S. Freud, 1915–1917; S. Freud, 1916; S. Freud, 1917).

Aggression: the "Dual-instinct" Theory

The next step was the elevation of aggression to full and equal rank with sexuality as an independent instinctual drive, despite certain differences in their conceptualization and modes of operation—chiefly concerning the nature of their organic sources and the greater rigidity of aggressive goals as compared with the plasticity of libidinal ones. Later, Freud wrote, not quite accurately: "I can no longer understand how we can have overlooked the ubiquity of non-erotic aggressivity and destructiveness . . ." (1930, p. 120).

In actuality, he had always paid serious attention to aggression, although he had early rejected Adler's claim that it was an instinctual drive in its own right (Hitchmann, 1947). His earlier view was that it was a necessary component of all instinctual drives and that it played a role in neuroses, in dreams, and in parapraxes; in his early writings on applied psychoanalysis, he also referred to its influence. For example, on May 31, 1897, months before he had established the prime role of infantile sexuality in neurosogenesis and development, he commented thus on the role of hostility in symptom formation:

> Hostile impulses against parents (a wish that they should die) are also an integral part of neuroses. They come to light consciously in the form of obsessional ideas. In paranoia the worst delusions of persecution (pathological distrust of rulers and monarchs) correspond to these impulses. They are repressed at periods in which pity for one's parents is active—at times of their illness or death. One of the manifestations of grief is then to reproach oneself for their death (cf. what are described as "melancholias") or to punish oneself in a hysterical way by putting oneself in their position with an idea of retribution (1887–1902).

With regard to the role of aggression in dreams, Freud devoted an extensive section to death wishes as an active force in the formation of certain dreams, particularly typical dreams (1900, pp. 248ff.). As for parapraxes, Freud wrote in *The Psychopathology of Everyday Life* (1901):

> In healthy people, egoistic, jealous and hostile feelings and impulsions, on which the pressure of moral education weighs heavily, make frequent use of the pathway provided by parapraxes in order to find some expression for their strength, which undeniably exists but is not recognized by higher mental agencies.

In *Jokes and Their Relation to the Unconscious* (1905a), he specifically likened aggressive to libidinal urges. By the time he wrote "Three Essays on the Theory of Sexuality" (1905b), his considerations regarding sadistic and masochistic perversions, as well as the erotized sadomasochistic fantasies which were revealed in the analyses of the transference neuroses, led him to regard aggression as an essential component of the sexual instinct, bearing a particular relationship to the anal phase. Even here, however, in his treatise on sexuality, his earlier view on the independent nature of aggression continued to find expression. He wrote: "It may be assumed that the impulses of cruelty arise from sources which are in fact independent of sexuality, but may become united with it at an early stage owing to an anastomosis near their points of origin" (1905b, p. 193, sec. II).

The research of Abraham, particularly into the depressive illnesses, was decisive in dispelling any doubt about the ubiquity and importance of aggressiveness in man (1911; 1924). But the question of how to place this force within the structure of existing psychoanalytic theory remained.

An early attempt at such integration was to regard aggression as a component of the ego, first associated with an "instinct for self-preservation" and then with an "instinct for mastery" (S. Freud, 1915a). But such hypotheses failed to satisfy Freud. Finally, influenced by certain new clinical discoveries, he formulated a theory in which aggression found its role in the vital stratum of the mind hitherto preempted by the libidinal drives—the realm of the instincts. From his new theory sprang a bold speculation which continues to excite controversy in psychoanalytic thinking (1921).

The clinical data which have been alluded to came from a variety of sources. First of all, Freud became increasingly impressed by the power, especially clear in certain depressive conditions, of the need for self-punishment, which could repeatedly thwart the most dedicated and skillful therapeutic efforts (1917). Suicide itself, whatever the libidinal components involved, furnished weighty evidence for the strength of destructiveness.

The curious responses of certain individuals to the achievement of success—illness, self-destruction—were understandable only as consequences of the ensuing guilt and need for punishment (S. Freud, 1916). The "negative therapeutic reaction" (S. Freud, 1932), the intensification of symptoms upon the attainment of insight, may also be accounted for by acknowledging the power of self-punitive needs. Such patients cannot be deterred from their inexorable drive toward self-immolation. Certain types of delinquency and criminality (S. Freud, 1916) are further evidences of the tremendous power of aggression, while on a vast historical scale, its terrible consequences seem always to be threatening the destruction of the human race itself. Such dramatic phenomena, in the face of which the libidinal forces appeared too often helpless, could no longer be considered to arise from an alloyed libidinal component—aggression could no longer be relegated to a subsidiary position in Freudian instinct theory.

Why did Freud's new "dual-instinct" theory provoke an almost immediate storm of criticism from all sides? Curiously enough, despite the wealth of confirmatory evidence at hand, this was because Freud chose to first present his revision of instinct theory as if it were an outgrowth of purely theoretical and, indeed, highly speculative considerations.

These were as follows: In various clinical conditions, notably the traumatic neuroses, Freud had observed evidence of a *compulsion to repeat*, a previously overlooked psychological principle. He reasoned that if there was such a regulatory law, instinctual drives might themselves contain an essentially conservative tendency—not simply to reduce quantities of energy to a constant level (pleasure principle) but to eliminate them entirely (nirvana principle). What this amounts to, then, is to bring life processes to a halt—to reduce them to an inorganic state. There may then be inherent in mental processes an endogenous movement toward self-destruction. Aggressiveness, curiously enough, would then be the externally directed manifestation of this internally directed force. The two primary polarities ceaselessly operative in all living entities are then the life and death instincts (Eros and Thanatos), corresponding at a biological level to the physiological phenomena of anabolism and catabolism. The libidinal and aggressive drives are the psychological representatives of this biological conflict (S. Freud, 1921).

Why Freud chose to argue for revision of his drive theory on such speculative grounds, with the wealth of clinical evidence at hand, is difficult to understand. His speculations gave rise to many tortured attempts to force clinical data into the procrustean bed of the concept of primary masochism (notably by Bergler) and remain a highly controversial aspect of psychoanalytic theory. It is only fair to point out, however, that to confuse Freud's philosophicobiologic speculations with his psychoanalytic psychology is to surrender one's right to be regarded as a serious critic of his work.

What, according to Freud, is the fate of the aggressive drive? It is parallel to that of the libidinal ones, although, it must be interpolated, it has never proved possible to establish for it a sequential series of phases. Aggression appears prominently in perversions; it achieves discharge in neurotic symptoms and character traits, together with libido; it enters conspicuously into the ontogenesis of one of the three structures of the psychic apparatus, the superego, in the form of self-critical and punitive components; its sublimation is considered particularly significant in impelling man toward "control over nature" (S. Freud, 1930, p. 121); and it fuses with the libido to produce significant developmental and pathological phenomena, etc.

Agreeing with Fenichel's criticism of the death instinct, Wolman has maintained that, since hostility and destructiveness are undeniable empirical facts, hostility should be linked not to a death instinct but to the struggle for survival (1960, chap. 15; 1964).

Shortly before his death, Abraham (1924) attempted to chart as specifically as possible the relationship of the drives to normal phases of maturation and to psychopathology. Such a drive-based nosology dominated clinical psychoanalysis for many years, but its deficiencies became increasingly apparent as the wealth of clinical experience grew and as ego psychology expanded. Today the traditional nosology is considered outmoded by most psychoanalysts (Panel, 1960a). A more modern nosology awaits the integration of drive theory with the most advanced concepts of ego psychology, including the epigenetic formulations of Erikson (1950; 1956).

Despite the complex developments of psychoanalytic theory, far beyond the appearance of Freud's second instinct theory, with its emphasis on aggression, and beyond the earliest statement of structural theory, with its ramifications into ego psychology, the view that psychoanalytic psychology is purely a psychology of sexuality persists in certain clinical and academic circles. If only from the standpoint of drive theory, the cursory historical outline presented above demonstrates the egregiousness of this error. From the frame of reference of Freud's general psychological insights, the drive concept itself represents but one part, however basic that might have been, of psychoanalytic theory.

GENERAL PSYCHOLOGY

The Dream

In the same letter in which Freud wrote in despair: "I no longer believe in my neurotica," he added: "In the general collapse only the psychology has retained its value. The dreams still stand secure, and my beginnings in metapsychology have gone up in my estimation. It is a pity that one cannot live on dream-interpretation . . . " (1887–1902, p. 218).

The repository of Freud's psychology became his classic, *The Interpretation of Dreams* (1900). In all the history of psychology and psychiatry, few treatises rank equally high.

When it became clear to Freud that any attempt to establish a psychology on a neurophysiological base was premature, he committed himself to a psychological approach. Dreams, he explained, were as worthy of investigation as any other mental product. They are, after all, the only means of access to the mind of the sleeper and, for a variety of reasons, are the "royal road" to certain of its areas. Furthermore, the dream is comprehensible. Despite the manifold meanings of its manifest content, the dream has a latent content as well; this latent dream invariably represents a disguised *wish*. A wish is explicitly defined as the mental representation of an internal need seeking discharge. Some mitigation of this need is necessary lest it act as a disturber of sleep—much as any stimulus might—and arouse the dreamer. The fulfillment of such a wish, albeit an illusory gratification, is the achievement of the "dreamwork" accomplished through the reappearance of the percept through which the need had originally achieved satisfaction. The wish obeys the "pleasure principle," the heir to Freud's "principle of neuronic inertia," and hence seeks this perceptual mode, the shortest pathway of discharge. In terms of the existing topography of the mind, the "wish" occupies the deepest layer, the unconscious (*Ucs*); chronologically, it dates from the infantile period of life. Hence, the wish of the dream raises *economic, topographic,* and *genetic* questions.

What makes this wish difficult to perceive as such is the effect of the dreamwork as well as of certain other mechanisms producing distortions to prevent the eruptions of archaic urges; these factors may disrupt sleep as effectively as their total frustration. Freud reduced the distorting mechanisms to four: consideration for plastic representation, the use of certain primitive modes of mental functioning (the dreamwork proper), the influence of the censorship, and the effects of secondary elaboration. These in turn impelled studies of the phenomena of *regression,* of the *primary processes,* and of the *ego* in its inhibiting, prohibiting, and organizing functions. With these considerations, *structural* and *dynamic* questions were raised. In suggesting that the dream serves basic biological functions, i.e., the preservation of sleep and a "safety-valve" activity instrumental in the discharge of painful and even potentially dangerous primitive urges, Freud raised the question of the *adaptive* approach in dream psychology as well.

In short, starting with a clinical approach to a universal mental phenomenon, the dream, Freud produced a number of constructs which subsequently served to clarify psychopathology as well. In addition to his drive theory, which was easily integrated into these discoveries, the psychological concepts that burst forth included those of topography, of the primary and secondary processes, of the pleasure principle and the reality principle, of regression and ontogenesis, and, finally, of structure.

The Topographic Model

Freud's concept that not all determinants of behavior were readily accessible to consciousness was hardly unique. Purely on this descriptive distinction between consciousness and unconsciousness, it would be hard to understand the amount of resistance that this concept aroused. But from the very beginning, Freud's conception of the unconscious comprised a variety of additional features—and it was these which aroused a storm of controversy. Thus, by the term "unconscious" Freud meant not only a quality of mental processes, but also the concept of a locale or system of the mind, *the* unconscious (the system *Ucs*). Freud abandoned this view once his structural model was fully elaborated. Furthermore, he postulated varying levels of unconscious mental processes, determined by their accessibility to the system *Cs* (consciousness); Freud recognized this difference by distinguishing the system or locales of preconsciousness and unconsciousness by their respective abbreviations (*Pcs* and *Ucs*). Before traveling to the *Cs, Pcs,* or *Ucs* locales, Freud cautioned, one ought to be familiar with the regulatory laws that governed each.

In the realm of the *Ucs* there is no concept of time. This system knows only of wishes, and these wishes are exempt from mutual contradictions; their intermingling is determined by no commonly accepted principles of logic and rationality, but by contiguity or similarity in sound or their relationship to a specific drive determinant about which they may cluster. The primary process, i.e., condensation and displacement, operates exclusively there in the service of immediate discharge, and in this system psychic reality is indistinguishable from external reality (S. Freud, 1915b). The *Ucs* is the repository for the drives as well as for the forgotten childhood experiences which congregate about these primitive urges [a condition called the "drive organization of memories" by Rapaport (1951a; 1960)]. As an exclusive determinant of behavior, the *Ucs* is thoroughly maladaptive: no organism could long survive without an ability to discern something more than the "now," without some capacity for delay, without some organization to effect compromises, and without a device for appraising reality. For all this, the system *Cs* has evolved.

As much as the *Ucs* is concerned with pleasure, immediacy, primary process, free cathexes, and the present, the realm of the *Cs* demands a consideration for reality and a capacity for deferring or delaying discharge of cathexes. In addition, this system has a commitment to secondary-process modes of thought organization, i.e., goal-directed associative links using the conceptual organizations of memories (Rapaport, 1951a; Rapaport, 1960); "quiescent," or bound, cathexes abound; regard for the past and anticipations of the future are to be taken into account in any current activity; and discrimination between inner and outer realities and a planned organizational schema are necessary functions. The system *Cs* is as much committed to survival as the system *Ucs* is to pleasure (S. Freud, 1911a).

The preconscious (*Pcs*) is an intermediate realm between these antagonists. Its existence is rooted in the descriptive phrase "accessibility to consciousness." Hence, the most logical, goal-directed, and reality bound transiently suppressed ideas, as well as the most irrational, purely pleasure-bound fantastic images, intermingle freely within it. If the cathexes of the system *Ucs* are highly displaceable or free and if those of the system *Cs* are bound, the energy in the system *Pcs* has a certain fluidity, swinging freely between these poles. Both primary- and secondary-process forms abound. "Primitive" aims, modes, and goals, while achieving representation in dreams and neuroses, may also be electively brought forth in the service of certain creative interests. The sudden inspiration of the artist or scientist may be understood as the final result of a long process of preconscious working-over which may have proceeded totally without significant conscious contribution (Kris, 1950b).

Within the topographic systems that Freud conceptualized, the phenomenon of consciousness itself was considered to be related to the function of *attention*. It was regarded as the functioning of a superordinate sense organ which, Janus-like, might look inward or outward for percepts (S. Freud, 1900). Freud did not pay much attention to *states of consciousness*, a somewhat different concept from that of hierarchical levels of consciousness. Actually, quite early, before psychoanalysis had fully established itself, Breuer had suggested that certain altered states of consciousness, "hypnoid" states, were etiologically significant in the hysterias, a view which Freud himself ignored (Breuer & Freud, 1893–1895). Others have since elaborated upon the significance of such altered states in psychopathology (Gill & Brenman, 1959; Rapaport, 1951a; Rapaport, 1951b). Freud retained permanently within his psychoanalytic theory the concept of varying qualities of mental processes; he turned from the concept of the systems *Cs*, *Pcs*, and *Ucs* in an attempt to organize certain clinical data from another perspective (1938). Still, clinicians, in a kind of psychoanalytic shorthand, often speak of *the Ucs;* the question of the value of this topographic view in a systematic psychoanalytic theory has yet to be fully resolved; attempts to do so have been made recently (Arlow & Brenner, 1964; Gill, 1963).

The Primary Process

Because Breuer had distinguished between different states of energy, "free" versus "tonic" (Breuer & Freud, 1893–1895), Freud credited him, perhaps not justifiably, with originating the concept of the primary process. In Freud's "Project for a Scientific Psychology" (1887–1902), the distinction between the special characteristics of the primary and of the secondary processes had already been made phenomenologically. The former aims for the immediacy of discharge, and the latter involves delay. The chief modes of primary-process discharge are condensation and displacement—for a system committed to rapid and immediate discharge, no other coordinating activities are better suited. The secondary process, on the other hand, uses associative links derived from experience and useful in a goal-directed activity. Freud always emphasized the economic features, i.e., the intimate relationship to cathectic quantities. Thus, the primary process operates with free cathectic energies, or, to state it another way, condensation and displacement function with, and effect discharge of, highly unbound energies. Secondary processes, on the other hand, function with bound or quiescent energies in a highly parsimonious fashion.

It is in the area of thought processes that the concepts of primary and secondary process have received their major application. In the type of psychic structure hypothesized to be present at birth, the drives use their ideational and affective representations in the service of immediate discharge. The free fluidity of these representations appears phenomenologically as displacements, condensations, symbolizations, substitutions, "pars pro toto," and other mechanisms of interchangeability and fusion in accordance with the pleasure principle.

With the evolution of the secondary process accompanying the maturation of the psychic structure, random discharge is inhibited, and associative links are organized around the memories of goals in external reality. Once anticipatory thought has paved the way for appropriate action, discharge may be directed toward the specific goal in reality that will be truly gratifying.

It is possible to conceive of the prospect that goal-directed thinking may in part employ condensed or symbolized fragments, may draw upon earlier modes of thought activity. Artistic creativity, wit, and scientific abstractions may be conceived of as drawing their energies from this "primitive" pool, frequently with striking esthetic results, humor, or illuminating conceptualizations. It is hard, for example, to imagine any great literary work not suffused with subtle displacements and condensations, which play a role in every figure of speech. In these instances the *modes* of primary-process activity (and not its aims) have been utilized in the service of a higher mental organization; the original building blocks which were found to be inadequate as a foundation have been subsequently resurrected, as it were, to add decorative splendor to the resultant superstructure (S. Freud, 1915b; Hartmann, 1939; Kris, 1952).

The Pleasure Principle

The pleasure-unpleasure principle, or simply the pleasure principle, was the concept out of which (in our opinion) grew the economic point of view of psychoanalytic metapsychology. Although the term itself was borrowed from Fechner, Freud's concept of a pleasure principle was substantially different from the former's. Fechner was inclined toward a hedonistic view of mental life. For him this principle was one toward which mature man aspired; for Freud it was one from which the latter had evolved (Ellenberger, 1956).

Simply stated, the pleasure principle suggests that the mental apparatus at first moves in the direction of avoiding increases of tension above certain critical levels—a state experienced as unpleasure—and of discharging this superfluous tension, the resulting state being experienced as pleasure. From this earliest principle evolvea the adaptive "reality principle," under which mental functioning is committed to specific goals rather than merely to random discharge—ultimately pleasure results from this delay of discharge.

Once discharge is delayed—persistent hunger in an infant in the absence of food, for example—the energy retained has a varying fate: some of it is organized into an inhibiting organization; some forms a hallucinatory image of the original object of satisfaction; another part of it is discharged into certain motor and secretory channels; and the rest is discharged into external motor pathways. These hypothetically become, respectively, the models for structure formation, cognition, affect, and conation, each of which may be studied ontogenetically. As Rapaport (1960) suggested, no other psychological system offers such an encompassing concept for a general psychology.

The pleasure principle comes to the fore in sleep, in symptom formation, and in various voluntary regressions in the service of adult pleasures. Freud even suggested that such channels of pleasure were episodically necessary for normal mental functioning.

This principle continues to retain its significant position in psychoanalytic thinking; many analysts view both instinctual drives—sex and aggression—as subordinate to it. Freud himself was led to the view that a more archaic regulatory principle operates in mental life, the *compulsion to repeat,* or the repetition compulsion. This principle suggested a speculative extension, namely, that the return of tension to a constant state through discharge of superfluous energy is a variant of an even more primitive regulatory principle, based on the passive reflex model (Holt, 1962). From this arose the concept of a new duality of instincts—a death instinct struggled with Eros, a life force, rooted in the pleasure principle. It is in the psychological representations of the eternal struggle between these biological forces, Freud thought, that the deepest determinants of the behavior of man are to be discovered (1920).

Ontogenesis and Regression

Two superordinate concepts concerning mental life permeated all Freud's writings, often only implicitly: ontogenesis and regression. Whether one uses the term "ontogeny" or "developmental thrusts" (A. Katan, 1951), "lines of development" (A. Freud, 1936; A. Freud, 1962), "maturational sequences" (Kris, 1950a), or "epigenesis" (Erikson, 1956), the concept of built-in evolving processes is basic to psychoanalytic theory. This automatically raises genetic, structural, and adaptive questions. The process of ontogenesis is implied in such constructs as drive theory, the reality principle, bound energy, and secondary process, for example, and was later applied under differing labels to a comprehension of evolutionary sequences involving other structures, functions, and processes. An increased preoccupation with earlier ontogenetic anlagen became central in analytic work, manifesting itself in the study of certain pathological entities; in unique developmental situations, such as twinning; and, especially, in an enhanced preoccupation with earliest childhood.

In a sense, ontogenesis is the obverse of regression, the process discovered so early by Freud. Briefly stated, regression is described as a reversion to earlier modes of thinking and behavior, goals, objects, etc., in the face of diverse situations. In the study of the dream, for example, Freud's attention was drawn to the predilection for plastic representation of dream elements, usually visual; he demonstrated that this was a reflection of a movement of thought processes from verbalization back to their original perceptions. Commenting on the general significance of regression, he wrote:

> Regression plays a no less important part in the theory of the formation of neurotic symptoms than it does in that of dreams. Three kinds of regression are thus to be distinguished: (a) topographical regression . . . (b) temporal regression . . . (c) formal regression. . . . All of these three kinds of regression are, however, one at bottom and occur together as a rule; for what is older in time is more primitive in form and in psychical topography lies nearer to the perceptual end (1900, p. 548).

Freud recognized that psychoanalysis can construct earlier modes of functioning on the ontogenetic scale by studying such regressive phenomena. Actually, the discovery of infantile sexuality originated in the constructions of childhood events from inferences derived from adult analysis and was not directly confirmed through work with children until six or seven years after it had been formulated.

The potential fallacy of such an investigative method is obvious; i.e., a regressive representation may not necessarily re-create its own earlier mode in precise fashion. A favorite metaphor of Freud's when he described regression was that of troops, who, forced to fall back upon an old garrison position, need not function there in the same fashion as when they first won the position. The core of any criticism of so-called "Kleinian" psychoanalysis, for example, is rooted in such a realization; unfortunately, in this system a fallacious technique of investigation has given rise to claims of scientific validity for its findings.

Freud was alert to the dangers of such a pitfall. When the possibility of the existence of childhood sexuality first appeared to him in a clinical setting, he thought it most likely that he was really confronted with an adolescent experience which had been defensively attributed to earliest childhood. It was only confirmation of the various experiences described by patients by other members of their families and the direct observation of children's behavior that finally eliminated all doubt that just such a methodological error had not crept in.

Ontogenesis and regression involve all structures, all functions, and all processes. The natural "thrusts forward," the factors influencing them, and the subtleties and complexities of selective regressions in mental life constitute the obvious interests of any educator, psychological research scientist, and clinician.

Regression is the process which originally made the science of psychoanalysis a possibility; apparently it is also the process which makes therapeutic psychoanalysis a necessity.

THE STRUCTURAL POINT OF VIEW

Evolution

Studies in dream psychology had laid open for thorough inspection the realm of the *Ucs*, with its peculiar modes of functioning, its highly limited regulatory principle, its economic state, and its single resolve to wish. The dreamwork was examined intensively, and the process of regression continuously scrutinized. But what of the source of those two other distorting mechanisms, the "censorship" and "secondary elaboration"?

In the earlier concept of an ego which Freud had postulated before he conceived of the *Ucs* and the drives, there were contained theoretical constructions into which he could now have placed these two phenomena (1887–1902). To the ego, there had been ascribed an inhibiting and an organizing function. Instead, Freud now viewed these mechanisms predominantly as impediments or resistances to the task of penetrating the depths. The censorship in the dream came from the *resistance*, i.e., to the emergence of the latent content. Obviously this force of resistance is related to the defensive function that Freud had perceived and described so clearly in earlier works (1894; 1896). Apparently he was too preoccupied with his new topography to look back at the project, that old, carefully detailed map of the mind. And so, what had been ego became resistance, repression, censorship, and secondary revision. The system *Pcs-Cs* became the repository of many of the old ego functions, e.g., relationship to reality, secondary process, defense, and prohibition. The dynamic struggle between the systems *Pcs-Cs* and *Ucs*, the economics of both, and the topographic view of the mind became central considerations during the earliest survey of the depths.

Then in 1911 there appeared a paper by Freud in which he began to revive his old ego concept (1911a). As the editors of the standard edition of his work suggest, the contents of this paper "must have struck its readers as bewilderingly full of novelties," since they could have had no access to much of Freud's earlier psychological speculations, which were not to be published until many years later. The unconscious mental processes were reposited in a "pleasure ego," whereas a "reality ego," intending to "strive for what is useful and guard itself against damage," was offered as the pleasure ego's antagonist. This reality ego required certain characteristics to attend to its tasks: the functions of consciousness, judgment, access to motility, thought, and reality testing. For Freud the study of the stages in the development of both the libido and the ego now seemed necessary for a full comprehension of the neuroses.

Gradually at this time, Freud attributed to the ego "instincts" of its own, perhaps one for mastery, perhaps another for self-preservation, but in any event forces in conflict with the unconscious mental processes. Furthermore, there seemed to be a libidinal component attaching itself to the ego as well; thus arose the concept of *narcissism*, which further enhanced the significance of the study of this psychological agency (S. Freud, 1914).

Then more clinical data appeared, particularly surrounding the fate neuroses, certain character disorders, the "negative therapeutic reaction," and the depressive illnesses, all of which suggested that another intrapsychic agency of considerable significance operates within the personality, a compelling and powerful prohibiting force. Freud rediscovered his dream censorship, not as a servant of the repressive forces, but as a determinant of psychopathology in its own right. There was barely enough room in the locale of the system *Pcs-Cs* to accommodate these new discoveries.

Now came a painfully obvious observation: In clinical work the resistances, ostensibly the handmaidens of the system *Pcs-Cs*, are themselves unconscious. The system *Pcs-Cs* thus contained unconscious processes, a paradox which induced Freud to resurrect his structural position. The concept of levels of psychological processes in the mapping of the mind was replaced by that of psychological structures, coherent organizations defined by their functions. The ego, the id, and the superego were established as core concepts in psychoanalytic theory (S. Freud, 1923).

The ego as then conceived was still overshadowed by the unconscious forces. Writing in *The Ego and the Id* (1923), Freud described it in this fashion:

> We see this same ego as a poor creature owing service to three masters. . . . It only too often yields to the temptation to become sycophantic, opportunist and lying, like a politician who sees the truth but wants to keep his place in popular favour (p. 56).

Three years later, however, Freud withdrew from this position concerning the relative strength of the ego. After describing the power and the significance of a variety of ego functions, particularly with respect to symptom formation, he wrote:

> At this point it is relevant to ask how I can reconcile this acknowledgement of the might of the ego with the description of its position which I gave in The Ego and the Id. In that book I drew a picture of its dependent relationship to the id and to the super-ego and revealed how powerless and apprehensive it was in regard to both and with what an effort it maintained its show of superiority over them. This view has been widely echoed in psychoanalytic literature. Many writers have laid much stress on the weakness of the ego in relation to the id and of our rational elements in the face of the daemonic forces within us; and they display a strong tendency to make what I have said into a cornerstone of a psychoanalytic Weltanschauung. Yet surely the psycho-analyst, with his knowledge of the way in which repression works, should, of all people, be restrained from adopting such an extreme and one-sided view (1926, p. 95).

With this Freud turned the psychoanalytic spotlight on the ego.

The Ego

Now that mental structures were to be defined in terms of their functions, the study of functions became a matter of central import. Certain problems in methodology make this appear at times an interminable task. Each function has a developmental history during which it is exposed to arrests, fixations, and distortions and in turn is subject to regression. Furthermore, certain functions are more involved with psychopathology than others; since clinical work still remains the chief research tool of psychoanalysis, functions on the periphery of pathology had not received their due share of analytic attention. On the other hand, others, such as defense, have always been so integral to the formation of pathological states that the intensity devoted to their investigation has tended to distort the concept of the ego altogether.

How to approach even an organization of ego functions? One may describe it historically, detailing the succession in which they were studied—defense, thinking processes, reality appraisal, etc.—or ego functions may be intimately involved with the drives, e.g., binding or defense, as opposed to those that are primarily autonomous from the drives, e.g., memory, perception, access to motility, and certain thresholds. This classification might include functions which may originally have clustered about the drive organization and which have only subsequently become secondarily autonomous from it, e.g., character traits (Hartmann, 1939).

Another possible point of departure is a consideration of the goal of the ego. The ego is ultimately committed to a harmonizing of the needs of its own organization and of the id, the superego, and reality, in the service of adaptation. To be sure, certain of the functions are applicable to various targets. For example, the function of defense operates against the id, the superego, and reality, and there are even intrasystemic defenses; i.e., one defense within the ego may be directed against another, such as introjection versus projection.

Although various attempts have been made to establish catalogues of ego functions and their corresponding disturbances (Bellak, 1958, after Beres, 1956), these have not yet been organized in a sound and logical way. Claims are constantly being advanced for newly discovered functions. This problem remains a task for ultimate elucidation.

One effect of the growth of psychoanalytic ego psychology, with its accent on functions, was to introduce revolutionary alterations into certain conceptual positions. With regard to anxiety and the study of affects, this alteration was to constitute a total reversal (S. Freud, 1926). The concept of defense was viewed from a new perspective; certain other functions, e.g., aspects of reality relationships, the self, or synthesis, could not possibly have been explored in an illuminating way without the structural orientation.

Ego Psychology and the Study of Functions

Anxiety: the psychoanalysis of affects. Freud regarded the problem of anxiety as a nodal point for psychoanalytic theory. His first view, despite some attempts at approaching the problem with a psychological perspective, was the toxic, or "fermentation," theory that anxiety was the transformed result of dammed-up libido, originally developed in his study of the anxiety neuroses (S. Freud, 1895).

By the time of Freud's intensive investigation into unconscious processes around 1915, the anxiety concept had become closely bound to a psychological framework. Certain aspects of neurotic anxiety were contrasted with objective anxiety, serving to illuminate both. Objective fear seems rational, since an external situation of danger exists to provoke it; furthermore, so long as the extent of the reaction is kept within controllable limits, the anxiety in response to a real danger is regarded as adaptive, since it leads to instituting protective measures. On the other hand, Freud considered neurotic anxiety to be purely maladaptive, often paralyzing healthy psychological functions and intensifying the resistances to treatment (1915–1917). For a time, certain educators and clinicians erroneously understood from all this that since repression was the cause of anxiety, allowing children greater freedom in expressing their infantile drives would ensure them against neurosis.

From a developmental point of view, Freud regarded the birth experience as the prototype of anxiety and briefly considered the possibility that this experience might have specific etiologic significance (see Jones, 1957).

The structural model established a new frame of reference for the study of this question. The ego was proclaimed the seat of all affects; it alone could produce and experience anxiety. The ego's main task is to harmonize the demands of the various agencies with which it comes into contact. It is equipped with apparatuses to detect the stimuli emanating from those agencies and to discriminate the limits of its own tolerance to their pressures. Anxiety is a function concerned with the awareness of a danger in the quality or quantity of such stimuli (S. Freud, 1926).

The anxiety reaction itself can be studied ontogenetically. At first it is a total or diffuse reaction involving the primitive somatic and psychological components then available. Gradually the reaction becomes more exclusively a psychological one, more circumscribed and limited, and the energies utilized become more neutralized and desomatized. Furthermore, with maturation of psychic structure, this circumscribed experience of anxiety, now recognized as a signal of danger, can be actively induced by an alerted ego organization, which might then set up the measures necessary to prevent the occurrence of a disabling traumatic situation—the situation of helplessness. This is called the "signal" function of anxiety.

Just as the reaction has a developmental history, so does the danger situation. At first the danger is from flooding by instinctual forces or external stimuli—the stimulus barrier can be overwhelmed. With the gradual maturation of psychological processes and the greater dependence on the mother, the danger becomes the possibility of her loss; after the establishment of object constancy—the ability to internalize the image of the mother and hence tolerate her absence—the key danger becomes the loss of her love. The danger of failure of controls, particularly of drive derivatives and affects, makes its appearance approximately at this phase. At the oedipal stage, the castration threat is the crucial source of anxiety; in the latency phase, conscience and the pressure of morality become predominant (S. Freud, 1926).

Another basic consideration in the development of anxiety is the proximity to the danger situation, whether it is urgent and immediate or only potential or whether it can be anticipated.

Thus, the relationship to the danger situation, as well as the danger itself, has a developmental history; the capacity to deal with these dangers evolves concurrently, varying from early helplessness to the ability to mobilize actively a signal of anticipated danger and do something about it. Conceived of in economic and structural terms, the anxiety reaction develops from a diffuse, truly psychosomatic experience utilizing archaic energy modes to a circumscribed specifically psychological reaction employing more nearly neutral cathexes. Naturally, as with every function, all these aspects of anxiety not only have a developmental history but can be affected selectively by regressive trends (Schur, 1953; Schur, 1955; Schur, 1958).

In terms of therapy it became evident that this new view reversed the relationship heretofore regarded as having existed between anxiety and the repressing forces. Fear mobilizes defenses; repression does not produce anxiety unless it is perceived as a danger situation. In terms of developmental psychology, the anxiety reaction has a natural history and can be observed occurring normally at certain nodal points of a child's life. Even if it were possible, it would be undesirable to rear children free from repression; the absence of fear in an infant during various typical stages is itself indicative of psychopathology.

In its evolution, the psychoanalytic theory of affects followed a somewhat similar pathway to that of the concept of anxiety itself. At first, affect stood for a quantity of energic cathexes, either caught up in the original externally derived traumatic experience in Freud's earliest theory or derived from drive cathexes themselves. Such a theory sufficed for a therapeutic approach oriented about the concept of catharsis, in which affect storms arising with the liberation of memories from repression were indicators to the therapist that he had struck bedrock.

With the development of the concept of the drives, affects, like everything else, were conceived as drive derivatives. The drive was represented in terms of ideational and affective components. Just as anxiety was thought to be transformed libido, affects in general were regarded as transformations of drives. However, this theory already contained the nucleus from which the structural model could grow, since Freud had suggested that the affective representations followed certain spontaneously developing internal motor and secretory pathways. This concept of built-in channels for affect discharge bridged the gap between affect theory purely as a drive-derived concept and as a psychological process which might be studied ontogenetically in a structural and adaptive setting (Rapaport, 1953).

The development of the structural model extended the study of other affects as well, notably depression. E. Bibring, for example, broadened the concept of depressive illness and depressive affects (as well as other clinical entities) in terms of psychoanalytic ego psychology by introducing the concept of ego states (1953). Originally depression had been studied almost exclusively from a drive-derived perspective. Fenichel (1941) and Jacobson (1953) contributed genetic and structural elaborations.

Freud's study of anxiety still remains the model for the investigation of all emotional experiences. Schur's clarifications and metapsychological extensions of this theory have bridged the theoretical, clinical, developmental, and phylogenetic gaps (1953; 1955; 1958). Other contributors have turned their attention to this subject in recent years in an attempt to establish a unitary theory of anxiety. At present the theory must still be considered dualistic, with its division into the traumatic type of anxiety (resulting from instinctual flooding) and the signal type (Rangell, 1955; Zetzel, 1955).

Defense. It is astonishing to realize that Freud's magnum opus, *The Interpretation of Dreams*, contains the term "defense" but once, when only three or four years earlier this concept was for Freud the conceptual basis for the comprehension and classification of all psychoneuroses. Defense, at first conceived of as a protection against the pain of traumatic experiences, became during the period of the survey of the depths more an impediment or resistance to that survey (S. Freud, 1900). During the era of the drive-derived psychology, defenses were defined as "vicissitudes of instinctual drives" or were subsumed under the blanket term "repression" (Brenner, 1957; S. Freud, 1915a).

The considerations which led to the development of psychoanalytic ego psychology, as well as to the structural model itself, served to place the defense concept into a broader perspective, somewhat more in accordance with Freud's earlier constructs, but without disregarding the discoveries of depth psychology. It was plainly apparent that people can be as unaware of their defensive operations as they are of the unconscious mental processes against which these operate. Furthermore, defense seemed to serve certain functions of the total personality; not only could it protect against pain, but, as Freud pointed out in his study of a phobia in a little boy, it could serve the adaptive function of preserving certain significant object relationships as well (1909). With the reexamination of the anxiety concept, defense emerged in a special position, and the maxim that defense analysis must precede the analysis of the drives became a fundamental part of every clinician's therapeutic armamentarium.

A. Freud's book *The Ego and the Mechanisms of Defence* (1936), a useful supplement to Freud's *Inhibitions, Symptoms and Anxiety* (1926), set the concept of defense more firmly into the structural framework.

Before describing Miss Freud's expanded version of the ego's defensive tasks, we briefly detail definitions of the ego defenses as she tabulated them at the time, with ample awareness of the fact that many other defenses have been described in the literature:

1. Repression. This is the basic defense of the ego. It refers to the exclusion from consciousness of both the cognitive and the conative elements of drive derivatives.

2. Regression. This is the return to earlier modes of functioning, at more primitive levels of drive and/or ego manifestations, such as the regression to anal-sadistic levels demonstrable in the obsessive-compulsive states. Properly speaking, regression is not so much a defense as the result of a defense or the failure of defense, though there may be strategic psychic retreats. Further defenses may of course be instituted against regressive modes of functioning.

3. Reaction formation. This is a defense characteristic of the obsessive-compulsive states; it also enters prominently into character formation. It consists in conteracting a drive derivative with measures of an opposing nature, for example, counteracting the urge to soil with excessive cleanliness. It implies the constant expenditure of energy to prevent the emergence of the forbidden impulse.

4. Isolation. Isolation means a splitting off, usually of the affective component of a drive derivative. Thus, an impulse to kill may appear in the form of an obsessive thought devoid of emotional impact.

5. Undoing. Alternating acts or thoughts of an opposing nature are characteristic of this defense. Thus an individual may be compelled to walk around a table three times in one direction and then three times in the reverse direction. Such acts or thoughts are representations of powerfully opposing im-

pulses which arouse guilt. Expiation is expressed in the "undoing" of the urge.

6. Projection. This defense is the attributing of the derivatives of drives (impulses or affects) arising within oneself to external objects. It operates chiefly in the direction of "expelling" unacceptable urges. It is constantly operative in various forms in daily life in a spectrum ranging from relatively normal to extremely pathological manifestations, such as those inherent in paranoid delusions.

7. Introjection. The global "taking in" of the attitudes, affects, or other attributes relating to external objects characterizes this defense. It constitutes the chief anlage of the identification process, plays a basic role in the formation of the superego, and is the crucial defense in depressive states.

8. Turning against the self. This defense is manifested in the reflection of an externally directed impulse upon oneself. Thus, hostile urges which threaten to erupt against an object may be turned back upon the individual, while a similar fate may overtake frustrated love impulses.

9. Reversal. This is the transformation of one instinctual modality into its opposite. Thus an individual tempted by unacceptable loving feelings may instead hate the object of such affects.

10. Sublimation. The defensive aspect of sublimation is based upon the desexualization of the drive and the deflection of the aim to more socially and individually acceptable ones. In current theory (Panel, 1955b), it is generally accepted that sublimation is not simply a defense but that it has neutral and adaptive aspects which may overshadow the defensive ones.

A. Freud went beyond these elementary considerations to describe a variety of other defenses. For example, she studied conflicts with reality as well as with instinctual drives. Nowhere were such conflicts more evident than in the analyses of children. Her father had laid the groundwork for the concepts of "denial" and "splitting of the ego" as defenses against the perception of a painful reality. Miss Freud now proceeded to amplify these concepts, demonstrating with special clarity the operations of "denial in fantasy" and "denial in word and deed." How useful such ego operations may be to a child beset by difficult and even terrifying forces in the external world may easily be imagined. A corollary to such considerations is the extremely valuable deduction that defenses must not be regarded as simply pathological manifestations but play a large role in adaptive behavior (see aso Hartmann, 1939). Therapeutic technique took a leap forward in pointing the way to the more effective handling of severely disturbed people in whom it is necessary to respect the useful, if not essential, protective nature of certain defenses.

Miss Freud further opened the way to the expanded study of the defensive functions of the ego in her descriptions of "identification with the aggressor" (assumption of the attitudes, behavior, etc., of a threatening object in order to combat the danger felt as emanating from it), the defensive nature of restricting ego functions that threaten to lead the individual into anxiety-provoking states and/or situations, the defensive functions of certain identifications, and the defenses of various types appearing in adolescence under the impact of the upsurge of powerful instinctual urges (altruistic surrender, exaggerated idealism, intellectualization, asceticism, etc.).

Considerable research remains to be done in this area of psychoanalytic theory; no aspect of it is as crucial to the development of newer methods of therapeutic technique. Studies of denial, for example, originally defined by Freud as the exclusion of painfully perceived external stimuli, have begun to appear. It is clearly operative in certain character types, in various affective states, and in normal everyday life. In these instances it serves to ward off the perception of an *internally* derived painful affect or stimulus. Attempts have been made to regard denial as a basic defensive process per se and then to study it from purely economic and structural points of view. At the same time, a genetic study of denial and its normal application in the first year of life has been contributed by child-observational studies and psychoanalytic reconstructions (Angel, 1934; Fenichel, 1945; Jacobson, 1957; Lewin, 1950; Waelder, 1951). This trend points to an increasing commitment to the understanding of defense in terms of a broad metapsychology rather than in terms of merely the aims or the objects against which it was to be directed.

What is originally defense and what becomes secondarily involved with it surely constitute another area for research, rooted in the careful distinctions Freud drew in studying the distorting mechanisms in dreams. Some of the distortions are a consequence of mental processes that could be exploited by the censorship, whereas others are primarily intended to conceal the latent dream content. Regression and introjection, for example, are probably processes of primarily nondefensive origin which readily become involved with the aims of self-protection and adaptation. Instinctualization of defensive processes, defense against defense, as well as the study of individual defenses in a thorough metapsychological framework retain, despite the protracted attention to defenses, the special clinical and theoretical interest of virgin soil.

Relationships to reality. A persistent misunderstanding of psychoanalytic theory is that Freudian psychology makes no acknowledgment of the significance of reality.

In part this notion arises from certain unscientific extensions of Freud's concept of psychic determinism. In part it is the precipitate of a host of treatment situations in which the dilemma of what is "real" and what is determined by internal conflict is faced repeatedly; nowhere is this more bewildering than in attempts to perceive the real analyst through the haze of infantile distortions in the height of the transference neurosis. It also arises from consequences attendant upon the psychoanalytic commitment to a purely psychological orientation; with such a stance, the route of access to any reality, internal or external, is restricted to the study of the mental representations of these realities. Thus, the appraisal of reality is limited by the perceptual, differentiating, and organizational capabilities at various phases of life. Despite its undeniable philosophic overtone, this concept has genuine psychological application; in fact, any truly scientific system must recognize the observer as an integral part of the observational data, a principle which has always been self-evident in psychoanalytic research (see, for example, Kanzer, 1955). But, for having recognized the limits of reality assessment, it would be unjust to regard psychoanalysis as having repudiated reality.

An important source of this misunderstanding is probably derived from the period during which the system *Ucs* was a central preoccupation; for a number of years, reality seemed to be simply the circuitous route taken by the pleasure principle to achieve its goal. Even while plumbing the depths, however, Freud recognized that drive derivatives are detectable primarily through their external aims and object relationships, that the pleasure principle evolves into the reality principle as part of normal maturation, and that specific goal-directed thinking emerges from a primary-process orientation. Furthermore, sublimation, the height of defense against instinctual drives, was originally a culturally based concept, a position which later brought upon it justifiable criticism. In addition, from the frame of reference of psychopathology, it was early recognized that the commitment to reality is a basic, distinguishing feature between the neuroses and the psychoses. Identification, so significant in structure building, personality organization, and defensive processes, is obviously an intimate part of reality. Ferenczi's classic contribution on the "sense of reality" dates from the depth period (1913). And even in *Three Essays on the Theory of Sexuality*, Freud's cornerstone of instinctual psychology (1905b), he repeatedly returned to the early familial setting which, in conjunction with the drives, is regarded as etiologic for neuroses and perversions.

Whatever the earliest psychoanalytic concepts and however easily they might have been misconstrued, the structural model offered the foundation for a much broader perspective. The ego now became the organ of adaptation, constructed around the nucleus of "perception-consciousness" and dedicated to harmonizing the various demands of all agencies, the external world included.

At first, reality appeared mainly as the source of outside "dangers": stimulus flooding, object loss, loss of love, threat of castration, and, finally, pressure from the superego, the permanently internalized representative of the infant's view of his personal society.

The concept of identification with real figures was broadly extended. Three ways of representing objects intrapsychically are ultimately discernible: An object can be represented directly as itself; it can be made a part of the person's self-image and therefore be represented through a material change in that individual's personality or character; or it may exist as an introject midway between these positions, not integrated within the self, yet not differentiated as the image of a separate object. The latter process can prove most disruptive (Greenson, 1954; Jacobson, 1954a). Superego identifications are possible as well and are subject to a similarly varying fate (Reich, 1954). Struggles against certain kinds of unacceptable identifications and introjects became the subject of various pathological studies.

The serious effects of real deprivation, highlighting the importance of early object relationships as structural nutriments, have been specifically examined by Spitz, for instance, in his contributions on "hospitalism" and "anaclitic depression" (1945; 1946). Also in recent years, a variety of traumatizing experiences, especially of a seductive nature, have been studied afresh, as, for example, by Greenacre (1952). Freud's revelation about the significance of psychic reality did not turn him away completely from examining the effects of real seductions; he warned repeatedly that they ought not to be ignored. The communication of unconscious wishes by parents to their children, wishes which impelled behavior alien to the conscious standards of the former, has become another area for psychoanalytic pursuit by a variety of workers, especially Johnson (1949).

All these—the dangers, the conflicting identifications, the effects of deprivation and excessive stimulation, and the unconscious demands of parents—tended to push the pathogenic effects of external reality into a position of primary importance.

Still, Freud had committed himself and his science to more than a theory of psychopathology. Beginning in 1939, Hartmann extended the concepts of reality by attempting to depict the adaptive functions of the personality, functions independent of a drive-derived or even a pathology-derived psychology. With his concept of apparatuses of primary autonomy, for example, he recognized inborn "givens," preadapted to an average expectable environment (1939; 1948). Since the instinctual drives in man are more plastic than the instincts of animals, which prepare them for adaptedness, certain other apparatuses must be biologically determined for man to assist him in survival. Such structures appear accessible to study in psychoanalytic terms as functions of the ego which develop so long as certain limits in respect to deprivation or stimulation are not exceeded.

Erikson viewed reality even more broadly. He conceived of man and society as an integral social unit, complementary, as it were; as man matured, society was to offer the necessary supplement to his varying needs, phase for phase. His concept of identity, viewed as part of an epigenetic theory of ego development, illustrated this point clearly. Erikson describes both the differing roles an individual needs and accepts at various times of life and the social modalities that an adequate toal environment must offer his unfolding modes and capacities (1950).

Loewald has pointed out that in certain pathological states, not only are various aspects of reality a danger, but also the loss of a sense of integrated reality itself is feared. During maturation the child struggles to ward off the tendency toward regression to an undifferentiated self-mother state as much as he struggles against dissolving into the drives. Reality has its rewards, and he seeks to retain them (Loewald, 1951; Loewald, 1952). This view stands close to the idea that the individual gradually separates the social and biological matrix of his earliest years from himself and struggles thereafter to retain his autonomy in spite of the pull of both regressive social pressures around him and biological pressures within him. Rapaport emphasized the point that drive and reality may be regarded as units of equal rank, each capable of exerting positive and negative effects on growth and development; the ego's capacity to commit itself to reality guarantees it a relative autonomy from the drives, just as much as the commitment to drive pursuits guarantees it a relative autonomy from reality's demands (Rapaport, 1958).

At this writing it would be premature to attempt an integration of the views of such a variety of workers in this area. Whatever the earlier confusions within and outside of psychoanalytic circles, the significant position of the study of relationships to reality in later times cannot be ignored; no other science has more interest in discerning the real in all its effects upon the psychology of man.

The Id

If the realm of the system *Ucs* had been relatively simple to describe within the topographic framework, that of the other of Freud's "primary" systems, the id, was to present a more difficult challenge. Freud's own use of these concepts reveals numerous ambiguities and contradictions. As long as fifteen years after his presentation of the structural point of view (1923), when he had called the id "the other part of the mind" (i.e. not ego), he was still referring to the id as "obscure" and as "the core of our being," accessible only through other agencies of the mind (1938).

Clearly enough, the id, the psychic structure which contains the instinctual impulses —the libidinal and the aggressive drives—is only part of the unconscious, although, as has been pointed out, it was early conceived of as synonymous with it. From the standpoint of "mode of organization" and "cathectic condition" (Gill, 1963), contents of the id, like those of the *Ucs* in general, are organized according to the primary process and function only with "free" energy. Originally the id was conceived of as a "seething cauldron" of chaotic impulses—instinctual cathexes—seeking discharge through various organs. It was dominated by the regulatory law of the pleasure principle and perhaps by the more archaic nirvana principle as well. This early view postulated that the drives in this structure were undifferentiated at birth and directed toward the interior of the body but that, with maturation, the id was gradually differentiated into the energetic forces which, in varying proportions and fusions, moved toward the body surfaces, particularly toward specific organs. As the "free" energy of the id became "bound" by the pressure of forces subserving the demands of the environment, there gradually emerged the structure called the "ego," which, through maturation and the impact of external influences, developed into a coherent organization of specific functions, such as control and regulation of the drives, perception, defense, motility, etc.

The difficulty seems to be that while the id is conceived of mainly as a structure subserving motivation and discharge, the ego also includes motivations (as well as defensive structures) and discharge structures. The solution appears to be to regard the id and ego as operating along a spectrum of levels of functioning and not as dichotomously differentiated, as is ordinarily conceived. It would seem best to define the id as a structure operating at the more primitive levels of the impulse—defense—discharge hierarchy. From this point of view the id must consequently be conceded a degree of organization which was absent from the older views.

Considerable disagreement exists with regard to the boundaries between the ego and the id. For example, a review of Freud's views on the organization and cathexes of defense has led Gill (1963) to the conclusion that "defenses regulate functioning in a hierarchy from primary to secondary process and from free to inhibited energy." Furthermore, it is clear that while Freud did describe the id as a "seething cauldron," he also included in it memories, symbols, mechanisms, and fantasies. It appears that he made too sharp a distinction between the id and the ego—it seems impossible to deny some kind of ideational activity to the former and to avoid the conclusion that at certain levels the latter follows the laws of the primary process. To solve this dilemma, Gill (1963) has suggested that a redefinition of id and ego is necessary.

The Superego

The superego is the third major subdivision in Freud's structural model. As the "heir to the Oedipus complex," it is constituted of diverse identifications and is endowed with powerful energies derived from the id, but essentially it is a differentiated part of the ego itself. The functions by which it is defined include self-criticism, a moral prohibiting force—the conscience—and the ego ideal, a more or less formulated code of positive ethical and moral standards. Under the best of conditions, the effects of the superego are experienced as variations of mood, self-esteem, pride, and guilt; under more pathological circumstances, it is particularly evident in melancholic states, obsessional neuroses, and delinquent activities. Such an internal structure, originating in childhood and modifiable by external situations, seemed to be a necessary psychological condition for the development of cohesive societies.

The concept of the superego gradually evolved in Freud's writings (Sandler, 1960). In his earliest thinking, Freud (1896) recognized the internalization of social values as significant in symptom formation. He cited the "censor," a guardian against the eruption of objectionable ideas, as an important source of dream distortion (1900). By 1914, Freud had begun to use the term "ego ideal" (which was later displaced by the term "superego") to designate the internalized precipitate of early parental reproaches, admonitions, and threats and the standards of moral and ethical perfection toward which the ego strives. Today, there is a tendency in some circles to separate the ego ideal from the superego, but most analysts continue to speak of the superego as subserving the three functions of self-criticism, conscience, and the setting of ideal standards. Conscience is the force which directs the ego toward attempting to achieve ideals; such an attainment results in the enhancement of self-esteem, which often reaches ecstatic heights. It was an important formulation of Freud's that the formation of the ego ideal is chiefly dependent on its derivation from infantile narcissism. Later (1921) Freud emphasized anew the rewarding aspect of the relationship between ego and ego ideal and cited mania as the extreme pathological example of complete harmonious fusion between the two, just as melancholia reflects their extreme disharmony.

With "The Ego and the Id" (S. Freud, 1923), the definitive structural concept of this agency took shape. It must be emphasized that Freud's view was that the superego is not definitely structuralized until all aspects of the Oedipus complex have been resolved; that this special system within the ego is primarily unconscious; and that, economically, it is linked to the energies of the id more directly than the ego itself seems to be. Freud (1927; 1930) touched on adaptational aspects of the superego later, when he pointed to it as the perpetuator and protector of cultural acquisitions and social organizations, particularly emphasizing its role in the repression of aggressiveness.

The broadening interest in the genetic point of view, and particularly in the preoedipal roots and precursors of various functions, was not to be overlooked in the study of superego functions, despite the special unique relationship which the superego bore to the Oedipus complex. Ferenczi (1925) added that the struggles over the control of impulses characteristic of the anal phase leave their mark on subsequent superego formation, a precursor which he termed "sphincter morality." Early defense mechanisms and particularly preferential styles of defense doubtlessly influence the structural organization of the superego; this seems particularly evident in the defense mechanism of reaction formation (Jacobson, 1954a). Spitz (1957), in an investigation of the "no" response of early childhood, has also made contributions to the understanding of early developmental phenomena decisive in the formation of the superego. In a study chiefly derived from an investigation into affective disturbances, Jacobson has suggested a hierarchy of values, ranging from the striving toward pleasure to that toward the formation of an integrated ethical and moral system in conjunction with the differentiation between the self and the object world (1954b). Hartmann and Loewenstein, taking a cue from Freud, have suggested that the vicissitudes in the development of speech have a significant bearing on superego development (1962).

Antisocial behavior is manifestly a fertile field for the investigation of abnormal superego development. Johnson (1949) and her coworkers, studying the effects of unconscious antisocial attitudes of parents upon their children, have described "lacunae" in superego systems which tended to foster delinquent acts. Freud himself (1916) had once written of a special form of criminality stemming from excessive superego pressures. Reik (1924) also emphasized the manner in which antisocial behavior might result from excessively strong self-punitive tendencies; thus, he demonstrated that when a criminal left a clue and was apprehended, forcing society to administer punishment to him, he thereby gratified his own excessive superego requirements.

In brief, the superego may be regarded as a special substructure of the personality, primarily unconscious, developing out of the resolution of the Oedipus complex. Genetically, many developmental precursors seem particularly significant in its formation: the vicissitudes of narcissism, the development of the differentiating function, the influence of language, the variations of the anal phase, and, finally, the effects of the full impact of the phallic-oedipal period itself. Economically, narcissism and aggression seem particularly worthy of attention in the attempt to understand superego-ego tensions; furthermore, there seems to be a greater fluidity in the energetic system in the superego than, for example, in the ego itself. It is dynamically implicated in a variety of affective disorders, such as the depressions, and it plays a leading role in the obsessional neuroses. In these two sets of conditions, we speak of it as "primitive," "harsh," or "archaic." In antisocial behavior, its functioning is deficient. Structurally, it subserves the three functions described above; the effect of the superego is experienced within the self by alterations in mood, feelings of pride, and experiences of guilt. Adaptationally, by acting as a permanent buffer of the drives and as an internal agent of external reality, the superego permits the development of a coherent social organization and limits regressive destructuralization.

A word of caution is necessary in any discussion of superego development. The superego is *not* a literal representation of parental and social attitudes as appraised by an external observer. It is the structural result of a complex interplay between external forces and internal ones, so that it is entirely conceivable that the superego of a particular individual may be quite different from what might be expected from observation of his cultural and familial milieu.

METAPSYCHOLOGY

The Development of the Concept

"Metapsychology" in psychoanalysis seems to have been somewhat discredited by an arbitrary clang association with metaphysics. Metapsychology merely involves the fundamental points of view and assumptions of psychoanalysis upon which its theory rests. Freud originally wished to emphasize that his psychology, unlike the positions prevalent in the nineteenth century, was a psychology that went beyond consciousness. In a letter in 1897, he clearly enunciated this definition: "Incidentally I am going to ask you seriously whether I should use the term 'metapsychology' for my psychology which leads behind consciousness" (1887–1902, p. 246).

In his dream book (1900), Freud avoided the use of the term, although in his famous chapter on the psychology of the dream processes, he touched upon all the points of view and nearly all the assumptions which were to be catalogued under the term "metapsychology."

By 1915, he had defined it officially: "I propose that where we have succeeded in describing a psychical process in its dynamic topographical and economic aspects, we should speak of it as a *metapsychological* presentation" (1915b, p. 181). Several years later (1920), he restated this definition in almost identical words.

Despite his subsequent development of the structural model (1923), Freud himself never explicitly suggested an alteration of these metapsychological postulates; nevertheless, it is apparent that, particularly with the change in perspective concerning the concept of the *Ucs*, the topographic model ceased to provide, as it might have before, the necessary frame of reference for a thorough understanding of psychological processes from a configurational standpoint (Arlow & Brenner, 1964; Gill, 1963).

Hartmann and Kris (1945) offered the evidence for the significance of the *genetic* point of view in psychoanalysis, a matter previously so self-evident that hardly anyone had bothered to express it so explicitly before. Most clinicians and theoreticians accept this point of view as an essential orienting concept.

The *adaptive* frame of reference in the metapsychological schema owes its origin chiefly to the researches of Hartmann (1939) and Erikson (1950; 1956) as well as to the firm resolve of the prominent psychoanalytic theoretician David Rapaport (Rapaport & Gill, 1959). This is surely the most controversial point of view of all (e.g., see Glover, 1961), in part because it is felt not to be of the same level of abstraction as the others, in part because of the confusion between the concepts "adaptation" and "adjustment," and in part because of the exaggerated, if not exclusive, significance attributed to it by writers such as Rado, Kardiner, Horney, and Sullivan. In fact, Rado has established a school of psychoanalytic theory termed "adaptational psychodynamics."

The Metapsychological Postulates

Definitions are as follows (Rapaport & Gill, 1959).

Dynamic. The dynamic point of view states that forces are involved in any psychological phenomenon. The assumptions underlying this postulate include the view that there are such forces, that they may be defined in terms of their direction and magnitude, and that their effects acting simultaneously are highly variable.

Economic. The economic point of view is based on the concept of psychic energy. The assumptions underlying this postulate are that there are psychological energies, that they follow certain laws, and that they are subject to transformations.

Structural. The structural point of view states that psychological configurations are involved in the operation of any mental phenomenon. The assumptions underlying this postulate are that there are psychological structures, that they are subject to a slow rate of change, that mental processes take place between and within them, and that they are hierarchically ordered.

Genetic. The genetic point of view states that the explanation of a psychological phenomenon requires an understanding of its origin and development. The assumptions underlying this postulate are that mental phenomena do have a history, that there are maturational sequences of psychological processes, that earlier forms may be reactivated at a later time, and that such earlier forms influence subsequent development.

Adaptive. The adaptive point of view implies that a psychological phenomenon must be understood in terms of its relationship to external reality. The assumptions underlying this postulate are that psychological states of adaptedness exist and vary through life; that adaptation, by influencing states of adaptedness, ensures survival; and that man and society adapt themselves to each other.

Metapsychology is the orienting framework for psychoanalysts, fundamental to an understanding of theoretical and clinical considerations in this field. Despite the theoretical controversy and the most extraordinary misunderstandings surrounding the use of this conceptual tool, it offers, when properly applied, the broadest formulation for the development of an all-encompassing systematic psychology. It serves not only to organize existing data around an inclusive conceptual core but also to provide a stimulus to theoretical and clinical research; yet it remains sufficiently open to modification by possible additions and by alterations in definition, in the name of scientific parsimony and as a consequence of the acquisition of new knowledge.

EARLY MENTAL FUNCTIONING

Background

Freud established the Oedipus complex theoretically as the nucleus of the neuroses. He was convinced that this conflict was rooted in phylogeny and brought to fruition and resolution in everyone's psychic development by certain primal fantasies (1913; 1915–1917; Jones, 1957). Although he advocated such phylogenetic constructions, Freud offered ontogenetic data as well; he pursued his investigations backward, beyond the phallic phase to earlier oral and anal ones. He had in fact, from the very beginning, moved in his studies of thought processes, affect, and motility to the earliest stages of life (1900); later he more carefully outlined the evolution of earlier psychic phenomena, as in his study of anxiety (1926). At the same time, although he put forth a phylogenetic explanation of the latency period, Ferenczi (1913) was formulating his classic contribution on the developmental stages of the "sense of reality." Psychoanalysis had been defined as a genetic psychology at its point of origin, and, whatever other explanations might be offered for various phenomena, nothing was more natural for it than to pursue an ontogenetic course.

Clinical data were both the source of, and the stimulus for, the study of early mental processes. The dream, particularly in its demand for a clarification of regressive processes, had been an obvious impetus (S. Freud, 1900). Another appeared in the study of the narcissistic disorders (S. Freud, 1910; S. Freud, 1914; S. Freud, 1915b); interest in developmental aspects of object relationships took root when Freud cited distinctions between narcissistic and object-libidinal attachments. Study of the psychoses became yet another stimulus and source of investigation of early mental processes (Abraham, 1924; Deutsch, 1942; S. Freud, 1911b; Mahler, 1952; Mahler, 1958; Mahler, 1961; Zilboorg, 1941). Reconstructions arrived at in therapeutic situations have provided similar avenues to understandings of earliest mental life, just as they led to the discovery of infantile sexuality. As the psychoanalysis of the neuroses began to bring into focus prephallic and preoedipal influences in etiology, the complexity of infantile psychological development began to be appreciated (Panel, 1957). Then the direct observation of young children began to yield much valuable information, despite certain potentially serious methodological errors, particularly in relation to the difficulty of deducing intrapsychic processes from purely behavioral data (see especially A. Freud's 1960 discussion of Bowlby's 1959 paper). Longitudinal long-range observational studies coupled with subsequent psychoanalytic explorations contain the promise of overcoming such defects. Certain relatively normal conditions and phenomena, such as the presleep states (Isakower, 1938; Lewin, 1950), have shed further light on primitive psychic states, as have certain other not so normal conditions, such as the intoxications and the addictions (Rado, 1926; Rado, 1933). Finally, while the influence cannot be evaluated precisely, another stimulus must surely have been provided by the work of such clinicians as Harry Stack Sullivan, whose interest in the earliest phases of life, particularly concerning the early mother-child relationship, must have been a factor in further inducing psychoanalytic psychologists to fill in developmental gaps.

Recent Studies

Of the many areas in which knowledge has accrued from genetic studies, some of the more important include investigations into constitution and the functions of differentiation, thought, affect, motility, defense, and object relations.

Constitution. Although the development of the structural model and the greater commitment to ontogeny cannot resolve the perennial struggle concerning heredity and environment, they can at least relate the problem to earlier phases and to specific functions. For example, patterns of activity and motility in infants have been assayed in conjunction with predictions as to pathology in a variety of child-observational studies (Fries & Woolf, 1953; Mittelmann, 1958). Others undertook to investigate the question of inherited drive endowment in terms of quantity and distribution, a factor of obvious significance for psychological development (Alpert, Neubauer, & Weil, 1956). Evidence of special sensitivities in children and the early evaluation of stimulus thresholds are other subjects for research with important implications (Bergman & Escalona, 1949).

Differentiation. The differentiating function of the ego has been evaluated in a variety of aspects: ego-id differentiation (Hartmann, Kris, & Loewenstein, 1946); self-object differentiation (Jacobson, 1954b; Mahler, 1952; Mahler, 1958; Mahler, 1961); and the differentiation of libidinal and aggressive instinctual drives from a common drive matrix (Jacobson, 1954b; Rubinfine, 1961). Such studies have influenced theoretical conceptions of psychopathology, understanding of normal development, views of child rearing, and therapeutic orientations. A variety of works emanating from different sources have served to increase psychoanalytic understanding of the function of differentiation and the establishment of separation and individuation in the second and third years of life. Mahler's impressive contributions, resulting from her interest in infantile psychoses, have directly and by extrapolation offered insights into both the normal "autistic" and the normal "symbiotic" phases of childhood as well as the phase of subsequent individuation (1952; 1958; 1961).

A study of twins and the twinning situation offers natural experiments for investigating the conditions for the establishment of circumscribed boundaries of the self (Burlingham, 1952; Panel, 1961). Studying depressive disorders, Jacobson (1954a) has added to the knowledge concerning the differentiation of self and nonself as well as the differentiation of libidinal and aggressive energies from a primary drive source. This theoretical position has an important therapeutic implication: in the situation of the transference neurosis, with its concomitant regression, is it possible to alter the instinctual balance in favor of libido in patients in whom infantile experience has served to swing it in the direction of increased aggression and narcissism? A similar question had years before been approached by Van Ophuijsen (1945) from the standpoint of clinical work with delinquent children. Converging upon the problem of differentiation from yet another direction, A. Freud (1952) described the problem of "emotional surrender," the tendency toward psychological fusion in a therapeutic setting which certain patients resist in the attempt to preserve their individualities. This has particular relevance in the technical handling of adolescence (Fraiberg, 1955).

Finally, the psychoanalytic interest in ethology (Panel, 1960a), particularly with respect to the problem of imprinting, provides an approach through the pathway of comparative psychology to an understanding of the differentiating function in the first years of life as well as of the problem of early object relations.

Thought, affects, and motility. Freud (1900) had offered the conceptual framework for the understanding of the ontogeny of thought, affects, and motility—albeit originally from a drive-derived perspective. His model centered about the infant's original state of hunger in the absence of an object to gratify it. In this situation, Freud hypothesized, the image of the object of satisfaction is hallucinated, and there is some discharge of the rising tensions along internal motor and secretory pathways, together with a diffuse external motor discharge. For Freud, this represented, respectively, the models for the development of thought from ideation, specific signal affects from diffuse affect discharges, and controlled behavior out of passively experienced uncoordinated activity. Fenichel (1945) described the ontogeny of motility and active mastery. Rapaport dealt with the question of a psychoanalytic theory of thinking (1950; 1951a) and one of affects (1953).

Defense. It was natural that psychoanalysis would involve itself in the study of precursors and prototypes of defense. Spitz (1961) has properly suggested that a variety of questions must be answered by research into these areas, specifically what aspects of the early mother-child relationship promote or inhibit different patterns of defense or lead to what has been described as "asymmetric ego development" (Spitz, 1959).

Studies in precursors and prototypes have suggested that the constitutionally guaranteed stimulus barrier may be the prototype of repression (S. Freud, 1920). Hartmann (1950) has offered the idea that closing of the eyelids might bear some relationship to the development of repression as well, while Spitz (1961) suggested that this type of behavior might be more closely related to the defense of denial. Freud thought that projection arose from the tendency to externalize excessive inner stimuli so that the stimulus barrier might be applied against them or so that such externalization might make flight possible—flight from internal danger is obviously impossible. Identification appears to be rooted in the oral process of "taking in"—this has stimulated interest in the relationships between incorporation as an instinctual process, introjection as a more generalized mechanism, and identification as it involves a specific alteration in the representation of the self-image (Hartmann & Loewenstein, 1962). Freud connected the defense of isolation with the process of logical thinking, in which the separation of affect from ideation is necessary. He also related this defense to the taboo against touching (1926). Physical prototypes of subsequent defense mechanisms have been investigated by Hartmann (1939), Greenacre (1958), and Menninger (1954), each from somewhat different perspectives. And Fries (Fries & Woolf, 1961) has offered an experimental study of "protodefenses" based upon assessments of types of activity in infants in response to a variety of stimuli.

Object relationships. From Freud's early insights into the significance of distinguishing between relationships based upon narcissistic attachments from those based on object-libidinal attachments to A. Freud's (1962) emphasis upon the progress from the former to the latter as basis for the evaluation of infant development, there has grown up a considerable literature on the question of object relationships. From the infant's standpoint, the first mother-child unit is undoubtedly primarily narcissistic; the functions of perception, differentiation, and organization have not yet matured to the point where the external object is perceived as much more than being need-satisfying. What are the constitutional and interpersonal activities that contribute to the maturation of the functions which involve relatedness? The effects of the differing aspects of the mother on the differing instinctual phases of childhood, correlated with as much precision as possible, have been of primary interest to analysts (Fries & Woolf, 1961); the early patterns of behavior toward, and fantasies about, the father have been another (Greenacre, 1957; Weissman, 1963). Mahler (1952; 1958; 1961) has been one of many to offer suggestions concerning the differentiation of mother and child. Winnicott (1953) has studied the "transitional object," suggesting its significance in the normal movement from narcissism to object love as well as in separation. Concerning the question of environmental stimulation, the effects of object deprivation have been dramatically documented by Spitz (1945; 1946); such deprivation in institutionalized infants has led to marasmus and death. A more recent study (Coleman & Provence, 1963) has demonstrated the lasting effects of such deprivation, even during just the first year. The study of early relationships, in brief, seems more and more to clarify the significance of the first objects as gratifiers of needs, nutrients for psychological growth, and "organizers" for subsequent structuralization (Panel, 1962a).

Understanding of the earliest phases of development has shed much light on the phenomenology of the psychotic states, if to a much lesser degree on their etiology. In so brief a presentation of psychoanalytic theory as this one, it is impossible to give more than the most sketchy presentation of this subject.

Freud's first studies of the Schreber case led him to his original postulate that psychotic states represent withdrawal of libido from objects to a regression to narcissism of a far-reaching degree. Subsequently, the attempt to restore the object takes the form of the florid secondary symptoms of delusions, hallucinations, etc., reflecting archaic, regressive types of relationship pervaded with hostile, destructive attitudes toward the object. Freud considered paranoia to be derived from the repudiation of powerful homosexual impulses projected upon the object and transferred into sadistic urges attributed to the latter. Although there have been numerous disagreements with Freud's views in this area, and although they have been very much amplified (Bychowski, 1953; Bychowski, 1954; Hartmann, 1953; M. Katan, 1950; M. Katan, 1952; M. Katan, 1953; M. Katan, 1954; Rosenfeld, 1954; Wolman, 1957), most analysts hold the view that psychoses represent the result of a conflict between the ego and the external world, a drastic loss of object cathexes, with a regression to narcissism of varying degree, followed by attempts at restitution of an archaic type, which constitute psychotic symptoms. As for the manic-depressive states, Freud's paper "Mourning and Melancholia" (1917) set the stage for extensive studies of this condition (E. Bibring, 1953; Gero, 1936; Gero, 1953; Jacobson, 1953; Rado, 1928; etc.). Freud's formulation was that depression was essentially a conflict between the ego and the superego. The introjection of an ambivalently regarded object, following an object loss, leads to destructive impulses directed at the ego, so powerful that they may well eventuate in suicide. Mania represents a harmonious fusion beween the two expressed in elation, a sense of omnipotence, etc. In later years, it was pointed out that there were various types of depression essentially characterized by deficiencies in self-esteem, and not necessarily by such vast masses of internalized aggression as described by Freud. (See summary of the subject of psychoanalytic theories of depression by Mendelson, 1960.)

APPLICATIONS OF PSYCHOANALYTIC THEORY

From the earliest years, psychoanalytic concepts have been applied to the understanding of almost every area of human functioning, both individual and social—to such diverse fields as anthropology, archaeology, mythology, folklore and fairy tales, religion, history, sociology, criminology, education, biography, literature, the graphic arts, music, and philosophy and to the origins of science and the problem of creativity and genius. This has been done with varying degrees of validity and with varying success. The general tendency of applied psychoanalysis in methodology and content has represented the progress of psychoanalytic theory from its more narrow preoccupations with psychopathology and the restrictions imposed by the first instinct theory, to the expansion of psychoanalysis into a general psychology, with emphasis upon the factors of aggression, early development, and ego psychology and with increasing attention paid to reality, including cultural and societal influences.

It is impossible to give more than the briefest samplings of applied psychoanalysis. The very designation of the nuclear core of neurosis as the "Oedipus" complex reflected the extrapolation of a constant clinical finding in psychoanalytic treatment to an ancient Greek legend. Freud's *Totem and Taboo* (1913) proposed a hypothesis for the origins of human culture based on speculations proposed by Darwin and Robertson. Freud also attempted to explain group psychology in relation to the leader on the basis of the original subservience to the father (1921), described religion as a universal obsessional neurosis and an illusion (1917), wrote on the inevitable sexual restraints imposed on man by civilization (1930), expressed considerable pessimism about man's ability to control his aggression and hence his *en masse* self-destructive tendencies, made biographical studies of famous artists such as Leonardo da Vinci (1910), and attempted an exposition of the origins of monotheism, proposing the bold thesis that Moses, the leader of the Jews, was originally an Egyptian (1939).

The modern tendency in applying psychoanalytic theory to diverse fields is to employ extensively the concepts derived from ego psychology and to deduce various creative phenomena from early aspects of development, including the loss and restoration of ego boundaries, the varying effects of object loss at different stages of development, the special attributes and endowments of gifted individuals in terms of ego functions, and the manifestations of regression—both pathological and healthy—in the lives and work of creative individuals, etc.

There has been a host of workers in this field: Erikson (1950), Rank (1913), Roheim (1952), Devereux (1951), and Muensterberger (1950) in anthropology; Arlow (1961) and others in mythology; Reik (1931), Bunker (1951), Arlow (1951), Tarachow (1955), and Ross (1958) in religion and ritual; Kris (1952), Eissler (1953; 1963), Tarachow (1948; 1949), Kanzer (1951), Greenacre (1955b), Hitchmann (1956), and many others in biography and the arts; Kardiner (1945; 1951) in sociology; Erikson (1950) in history; Kohut (1951) in the general theory of applied psychoanalysis and in music; Wisdom (1952) in philosophy; Aichhorn (1935), Glover (1960), and Zilboorg (1944; 1950) in the psychology of delinquency and crime; Kanzer (1936; 1955) in the psychology of the scientist; and many of the above-mentioned, especially Kris and Eissler, in problems of creativity and genuis. No psychological discipline has proved as fruitful in its application to diverse aspects of individual or social human behavior as psychoanalysis.

CURRENT TRENDS IN PSYCHOANALYTIC RESEARCH

Within the past few years there has been a considerable ferment of research acitivity in psychoanalysis. Panels held twice a year by the American Psychoanalytic Association and from time to time by the International Psychoanalytic Association are devoted to the examination of basic problems in psychoanalytic theory and practice, summarizing work being done on such topics as the reevaluation of the libido theory; methods of validating psychoanalytic propositions; recent discoveries in early psychic development; the theory of therapy; clarifications of concepts, such as those of defense, identification, narcissism, object relationships, aggression, and the self and problems of identity; and numerous others. The structure of psychoanalytic theory itself was the subject of a monograph by Rapaport (1960), in which he pointed out the achievements of the theory, its shortcomings, and its convergences with other theories. A monograph by Gill subjects the topographic and structural theories to the most searching examination (1963). Another study establishes correlations between psychoanalytic theory and the system of Jean Piaget (Wolf, 1960). At the Hampstead Nursery in London, A. Freud and her coworkers investigated the phenomena of early childhood, with the collaboration of analyzed assistants. Similar studies have been carried on at the Child Study Center at Yale University (Kris, Ritvo, Solnit, Provence, Coleman, et al.). The direct investigations of childhood behavior continue to illuminate early phases of ego development and reveal the varied and complex effects of parental behavior on infants. Experimental studies of sleep and dreams have exploded into prominence within recent years, based upon the pioneer work of Kleitman (followed up by Dement, Fisher, and many others). Fisher (1954; 1956; 1957; Fisher & Paul, 1959) has undertaken a series of studies of subliminal influences of dreams and images, illuminating the nature of perception and the relationships between the primary and secondary processes. There has been an upsurge of interest in the period of adolescence (Blos, 1958; Fraiberg, 1955; et al.) and in the self and problems of identity (Erikson, 1956; Erikson, 1959; Panel, 1958). The relationship of twinning to problems of self-differentiation is studied by direct observation and by means of psychoanalytic treatment itself (Panel, 1960c). Studies combining experimental medicine, hypnosis, and psychoanalysis are concerned with psychosomatic medicine (Margolin, 1953; Schur, 1955) and have already established the fact that many serious organic manifestations can appear at varying periods as a result of vicissitudes in upbringing in the first year of life. The problem of predicting later behavior, both relatively normal and pathological, in children and adults has been investigated by numerous workers (Escalona & Heider, 1959; Murphy et al., 1962) and may furnish material of both theoretical and practical value. Gifted individuals, both alive and dead, have been intensively studied within recent years by Kris (Loomie, Rosen, & Stein, 1953) and Eissler, the latter having produced monumental works on Goethe (1963) and on Leonardo da Vinci (1961), in which he presents the unique point of view that psychopathology in the genuis is not of the same type, order, or significance as in ordinary individuals. More recently, the traditional views on the analyst-patient relationship have been subjected to scrutiny and challenge (Gitelson, 1962; Loewald, 1960; Stone, 1961), so that it certainly appears that the field of psychoanalytic theory remains wide open for investigation of its basic tenets, investigation which its modern protagonists do not in the least hesitate to undertake.

CONCLUSION

This chapter traced the evolution of Freudian metapsychology and (more broadly) of psychoanalytic psychology, demonstrating the dual function of the theory: organization and systematization of existing knowledge and pointing the way to the continuing revision of theoretical structure. That so much was the product of a single mind at times facilitated, but at other times complicated, the development of the theory and its exposition.

In the history of the theory, two vintage years stand out—1897, which witnessed the appearance of the theory of drives, and 1923, when the structural model was expounded by Freud. These two theories brought about the most revolutionary changes in all phases of psychological thought; the metapsychological approach to human behavior furnished an invaluable framework for an ever more inclusive theory of its operations. It is no exaggeration to assert that in the Western world, the concepts of psychoanalytic theory furnish the basis for the psychopathological schemata of most clinical psychologists and psychiatrists, whether acknowledged or not. This is not to say that the basic tenets of psychoanalysis are not subject to constant scrutiny and challenge, from both within and without the established framework of psychoanalytic theorizing, teaching, and practice.

The general tendency in psychoanalytic theory has been to meet challenges concerning the validity of its various concepts with serious examination of the claims. Thus, Freud finally accepted Adler's insistence on the importance of the aggressive drive and recognized it as an instinct in its own right; the discoveries of M. Klein led to further examinations of the role of aggression in early infancy; the challenge of the Horney school stimulated more careful investigations of current reality situations; the Sullivanian approach assisted in focusing more attention on object relationships; and the insistence of the culturalists on the importance of social factors was met by increasing emphasis on these phenomena, while more recently the popularity of studies of the self and identity is in part a result of the views of existentialist psychologists and psychiatrists. But, unlike any of these so-called "deviant" schools, Freudian psychoanalysis has always attempted—usually successfully—to maintain its broad and inclusive scope. The deviant schools seize upon one facet of psychic functioning and inflate it into a central concept of unitary, if not exclusive, etiological significance. The firm insistence of the founder of psychoanalysis upon the close correlation between clinical investigation and theoretical formulation has inevitably slowed down the evolution of psychoanalytical theory, but it has also, by that very token, given it an inclusiveness and solidarity which have thus far defied the dire and wishful predictions of the prophets of its doom.

REFERENCES

Abraham, K. Notes on the psycho-analytical investigation and treatment of manic-depressive insanity and allied conditions (1911). In K. Abraham, *Selected papers on psycho-analysis.* London: Hogarth Press, 1949. Pp. 137–156.

Abraham, K. A short study of the development of the libido, viewed in the light of the mental disorders (1924). In *ibid.* Pp. 418–501.

Aichhorn, A. *Wayward youth.* New York: Viking, 1935.

Alpert, Augusta, Neubauer, P., & Weil, Annemarie. Unusual variations in drive endowment. In *The psychoanalytic study of the child.* Vol. 11. New York: International Universities Press, 1956. Pp. 125–163.

Amacher, P. Introduction to a proposed dissertation on Sigmund Freud's thought. Unpublished manuscript, 1961.

Angel, Any. Einige Bemerkungen über Optimismus. *Int. Z. Psychoanal.,* 1934, **20,** 191–199.

Arlow, J. A psychoanalytic study of a religious initiation rite: barmitzvah. In *The psychoanalytic study of the child.* Vol. 6. New York: International Universities Press, 1951. Pp. 353–374.

Arlow, J. The theory of drives. In M. Levitt (Ed.), *Readings in psychoanalytic psychology.* New York: Appleton-Century-Crofts, 1959.

Arlow, J. Ego psychology and the study of mythology. *J. Amer. psychoanal. Ass.,* 1961, **9**, 371–393.

Arlow, J., & Brenner, C. *Psychological concepts and the structural theory.* New York: International Universities Press, 1964.

Bak, R. Fetishism. *J. Amer. psychoanal. Ass.,* 1953, **1**, 285–298.

Bak, R. Aggression and perversion. In S. Lorand & M. Balint (Eds.), *Perversions: psychodynamics and therapy.* New York: Random House, 1956. Pp. 231–242.

Bellak L., & Benedict, P. K. (Eds.) *Schizophrenia: a review of the syndrome.* New York: Logos Press, 1958. Pp. 7–8.

Benjamin, J. D. Some developmental observations relating to the theory of anxiety. *J. Amer. psychoanal. Ass.,* 1961, **9**, 652–658.

Beres, D. Ego deviation and the concept of schizophrenia. In *The psychoanalytic study of the child.* Vol. 11. New York: International Universities Press, 1956. Pp. 164–235.

Bergman, P., & Escalona, Sybille. Unusual sensitivities in very young children. In *ibid.* Vols. 3, 4. 1949. Pp. 333–352.

Bibring, E. The development and problems of the theory of the instincts. *Int. J. Psychoanal.,* 1941, **22**, 102–131.

Bibring, E. The conception of the repetition compulsion. *Psychoanal. Quart.,* 1943, **12**, 486–519.

Bibring, E. The mechanism of depression. In Phyllis Greenacre (Ed.), *Affective disorders.* New York: International Universities Press, 1953. Pp. 13–48.

Bibring, Greta L., Dwyer, T. F., Hunting, D. S., & Valenstein, A. F. A study of the psychological process in pregnancy and of the earliest mother-child relationship. In *The psychoanalytic study of the child.* Vol. 16. New York: International Universities Press, 1961. Pp. 9–72.

Blos, P. Preadolescent drive organization. *J. Amer. psychoanal. Ass.,* 1958, **6**, 47–56.

Blos, P. *On Adolescence: a psychoanalytic interpretation.* New York: Free Press, 1962.

Bowlby, J. Grief and mourning in infancy and early childhood. In *The psychoanalytic study of the child.* Vol. 15. New York: International Universities Press, 1960. Pp. 9–52.

Brenner, C. The nature and development of the concept of repression in Freud's writings. In *ibid.* 1957. Vol. 12. Pp. 19–46.

Breuer, J., & Freud, S. Studies on hysteria (1893–1895). In *The standard edition of the complete psychological works of Sigmund Freud.* Vol. 2. London: Hogarth Press and the Institute of Psycho-Analysis, 1962.

Bunker, H. A. Psychoanalysis and the study of religion. In I. Roheim (Ed.), *Psychoanalysis and the social sciences.* Vol. III. New York: International Universities Press, 1951. Pp. 7–36.

Burlingham, Dorothy. *Twins: a study of three pairs of identical twins.* New York: International Universities Press, 1952.

Bychowski, G. The problem of latent psychoses. *J. Amer. psychoanal. Ass.,* 1953, **1**, 484–503.

Bychowski, G. On the handling of some schizophrenic defense mechanisms and reaction patterns. *Int. J. Psychoanal.,* 1954, **35**, 147–153.

Coleman, Rose W., Kris, E., & Provence, Sally. The study of variations of early parential attitudes: a preliminary report. In *The psychoanalytic study of the child.* Vol. 8. New York: International Universities Press, 1953. Pp. 20–47.

Deutsch, Helene. Some forms of emotional disturbance and their relationship to schizophrenia. *Psychoanal. Quart.,* 1942, **11**, 301–321.

Devereux, G. *Reality and dream: psychotherapy of a Plains Indian.* New York: International Universities Press, 1951.

Eissler, K. R. On Hamlet. *Samiksa,* 1953, **7**, 85–132.

Eissler, K. R. *Leonardo da Vinci: psychoanalytic notes on the enigma.* New York: International Universities Press, 1961.

Eissler, K. R. *Goethe: a psychoanalytic study.* Detroit, Mich.: Wayne Univer. Press, 1963. 2 vols.

Ellenberger, H. Fechner and Freud. *Bull. Menninger Clin.,* 1956, **20**, 201–214.

Erikson, E. *Childhood and society.* New York: Norton, 1950.

Erikson, E. The problem of ego identity. *J. Amer. psychoanal. Ass.,* 1956, **4**, 56–121.

Erikson, E. Identity and the life cycle. *Psychol. Issues,* 1959, **1**, Monogr. No. 1.

Escalona, Sybille, & Heider, Grace M. *Prediction and outcome.* New York: Basic Books, 1959.

Fenichel, O. The ego and the affects. *Psychoanal. Rev.,* 1941, **28**, 47–60.

Fenichel, O. *The psychoanalytic theory of neurosis.* New York: Norton, 1945.

Ferenczi, S. The psychoanalysis of sexual habits. *Int. J. Psychoanal.*, 1925, **6**, 372–404.

Ferenczi, S. Stages in the development of the sense of reality (1913). In *The selected papers of. . . .* Vol. I. *Sex in Psychoanalyses.* New York: Basic Books, 1950. Pp. 213–239.

Fisher, C. Dreams and perception. *J. Amer. psychoanal. Ass.*, 1954, **2**, 389–445.

Fisher, C. Dreams, images and perceptions: a study of unconscious-preconscious relationships. *J. Amer. psychoanal. Ass.*, 1956, **4**, 5–47.

Fisher, C. A study of the preliminary stages of the construction of dreams and images. *J. Amer. psychoanal. Ass.*, 1957, **5**, 5–60.

Fisher, C., & Paul, I. H. The effect of subliminal visual stimulation on images and dreams: a validation study. *J. Amer. psychoanal. Ass.*, 1959, **7**, 35–83.

Fliess, R. *Erogeneity and libido.* New York: International Universities Press, 1956.

Fraiberg, Selma. Some considerations in the introduction to therapy in puberty. In *The psychoanalytic study of the child.* Vol. 10. New York: International Universities Press, 1955. Pp. 264–286.

Freud, Anna. *The ego and the mechanisms of defence* (1936). New York: International Universities Press, 1946.

Freud, Anna. Observations on child development. In *The psychoanalytic study of the child.* Vol. 6. New York: International Universities Press, 1951. Pp. 18–30.

Freud, Anna. Summary of address of: A connection between the states of negativism and of emotional surrender. *Int. J. Psychoanal.*, 1952, **33**, 265.

Freud, Anna. Some remarks on infant observations. In *ibid.* Vol. 8. 1953. Pp. 9–19.

Freud, Anna. Adolescence. In *ibid.* Vol. 13. 1958. Pp. 255–278.

Freud, Anna. Discussion of Dr. John Bowlby's paper. In *ibid.* Vol. 15. 1960. Pp. 53–62.

Freud, Anna. Assessment of childhood disturbances. In *ibid.* Vol. 17. 1962. Pp. 149–158.

Freud, S. *The origins of psychoanalysis: letters to Wilhelm Fliess, drafts and notes: 1887–1902.* (Marie Bonaparte, Anna Freud, & E. Kris, Eds. Tr. by E. Mosbacher & J. Strachey.) New York: Basic Books, 1954.

Freud, S. The neuro-psychoses of defence (1894). In *The standard edition of the complete psychological works of Sigmund Freud.* Vol. 3. London: Hogarth Press and the Institute of Psycho-Analysis, 1962. Pp. 45–61.

Freud, S. On the grounds for detaching a particular syndrome from neurasthenia under the description, "anxiety neurosis" (1895). In *ibid.* Pp. 90–115.

Freud, S. Further remarks on the neuropsychoses of defence (1896). In *ibid.* Pp. 162–185.

Freud, S. Sexuality in the aetiology of the neuroses (1898). In *ibid.* Pp. 263–286.

Freud, S. *The interpretation of dreams* (1900). In *ibid.* Vol. 4, p. 337. Vol. 5, pp. 339–627.

Freud, S. *The psychopathology of everyday life* (1901). In *ibid.* Vol. 6. P. 309.

Freud, S. *Jokes and their relation to the unconscious* (1905a). In *ibid.* Vol. 8. P. 258.

Freud, S. *Three essays on the theory of sexuality* (1905b). In *ibid.* Vol. 7. Pp. 130–245.

Freud, S. Character and anal erotism (1908). In *ibid.* Vol. 9. Pp. 167–176.

Freud, S. Analysis of a phobia in a five-year-old boy (1909). In *ibid.* Vol. 10. Pp. 5–149.

Freud, S. *Leonardo da Vinci and a memory of his childhood* (1910). In *ibid.* Vol. 11. Pp. 63–137.

Freud, S. Formulations on the two principles of mental functioning (1911a). In *ibid.* Vol. 12. Pp. 218–226.

Freud, S. Psycho-analytic notes on an autobiographical account of a case of paranoia (1911b). In *ibid.* Pp. 9–82.

Freud, S. *Totem and taboo* (1913). In *ibid.* Vol. 13. Pp. 1–162.

Freud, S. On narcissism: an introduction (1914). In *ibid.* Vol. 14. Pp. 73–102.

Freud, S. Instincts and their vicissitudes (1915a). In *ibid.* Pp. 117–145.

Freud, S. The unconscious (1915b). In *ibid.* Pp. 166–204.

Freud, S. *A general introduction to psychoanalysis* (1915–1917). New York: Garden City, 1943.

Freud, S. Some character types met with in psycho-analytic work (1916). In *The standard edition of the complete psychological works of Sigmund Freud.* Vol. 14. London: Hogarth Press and the Institute of Psycho-Analysis, 1962. Pp. 311–333.

Freud, S. Mourning and melancholia (1917). In *ibid.* Pp. 243–258.

Freud, S. A child is being beaten: a contribution to the study of sexual perversion (1919). In *ibid.* Vol. 17. Pp. 179–204.

Freud, S. *Beyond the pleasure principle* (1920). In *ibid.* Vol. 18. Pp. 7–64.

Freud, S. *Group psychology and the analysis of the ego* (1921). In *ibid.* Pp. 69–143.

Freud, S. *The ego and the id* (1923). In *ibid.* Vol. 19. Pp. 12–66.

Freud, S. *Inhibitions, symptoms and anxiety* (1926). In *ibid.* Vol. 20. Pp. 87–174.

Freud, S. *The future of an illusion* (1927). In *ibid.* Vol. 21. Pp. 5–56.

Freud, S. *Civilization and its discontents* (1930). In *ibid.* Vol. 21. Pp. 64–145.

Freud, S. *New introductory lectures on psychoanalysis* (1932). New York: Norton, 1933.

Freud, S. *An outline of psychoanalysis* (1938). New York: Norton, 1949.

Freud, S. *Moses and monotheism* (1939). New York: Knopf, 1939.

Fries, Margaret E., & Woolf, P. J. Some hypotheses on the role of the congenital activity type in personality development. In *The psychoanalytic study of the child.* Vol. 8. New York: International Universities Press, 1953. Pp. 48–62.

Fries, Margaret E. Some factors in the development and significance of early object relationships. *J. Amer. psychoanal. Ass.*, 1961, **9**, 669–683.

Gero, A. The construction of depression. *Int. J. Psychoanal.*, 1963, **117**, 423–461.

Gero, A. An equivalent of depression: anorexia. In Phyllis Greenacre (Ed.), *Affective disorders.* New York: International Universities Press, 1953. Pp. 117–139.

Gill, M. M., & Brenman, Margaret. *Hypnosis and related states.* New York: International Universities Press, 1959.

Gill, M. M. *Topography and systems in psychoanalytic theory. Psychol. Issues*, 1963, 3 (2).

Gillespie, W. H. Notes on the analysis of sexual perversions. *Int. J. Psychoanal.*, 1952, **33**, 397–402.

Gillespie, H. W. The structure and etiology of sexual perversions. In S. Lorand & M. Balint (Eds.), *Perversions: psychodynamics and therapy.* New York: Random House, 1956. Pp. 28–41.

Gitelson, M. The emotional position of the analyst in the psychoanalytic situation. *Int. J. Psychoanal.*, 1952, **33**, 1–10.

Gitelson, M. The first phase of psychoanalysis. *Int. J. Psychoanal.*, 1962, **43**, 194–205.

Glover, E. *The roots of crime: selected papers on psychoanalysis.* Vol. II. New York: International Universities Press, 1960.

Glover, E. Some recent trends in psychoanalytic theory. *Psychoanal. Quart.*, 1961, **30**, 86–107.

Greenacre, Phyllis. The predisposition to anxiety (1941). In Phyllis Greenacre (Ed.), *Trauma, growth and personality.* New York: Norton, 1952. Pp. 27–82.

Greenacre, Phyllis. Pregenital patterning. *Int. J. Psychoanal.*, 1952, **33**, 410–415.

Greenacre, Phyllis. Certain relationships between fetishism and the faulty development of the body image. In *The psychoanalytic study of the child.* Vol. 8. New York: International Universities Press, 1953. Pp. 79–98.

Greenacre, Phyllis. Further considerations regarding fetishism. In *ibid.* Vol. 10. 1955. Pp. 187–194. (a)

Greenacre, Phyllis. *Swift and Carroll: a psychoanalytic study of two lives.* New York: International Universities Press, 1955. (b)

Greenacre, Phyllis. Early physical determinants in the development of the sense of identity. *J. Amer. psychoanal. Ass.*, 1958, **6**, 612–627.

Greenacre, Phyllis. The childhood of the artist. In *The psychoanalytic study of the child.* Vol. 12. New York: International Universities Press, 1959. Pp. 47–72.

Greenacre, Phyllis. Further notes on fetishism. In *The psychoanalytic study of the child.* Vol. 15. New York: International Universities Press, 1960. Pp. 191–207.

Greenson, R. The struggle against identification. *J. Amer. psychoanal. Ass.*, 1954, **2**, 200–217.

Hartmann, H. *Ego psychology and the problem of adaptation* (1939). New York: International Universities Press, 1958.

Hartmann, H. Comments on the psychoanalytic theory of instinctual drives. *Psychoanal. Quart.*, 1948, **17**, 368–388.

Hartmann, H. Comments on the psychoanalytic theory of the ego. In *The psychoanalytic study of the child.* Vol. 5. New York: International Universities Press, 1950. Pp. 74–96.

Hartmann, H. Technical implications of ego psychology. *Psychoanal. Quart.*, 1951, **20**, 31–43.

Hartmann, H. Contribution to the metapsychology of schizophrenia. In *The psychoanalytic study of the child.* Vol. 8. New York: International Universities Press, 1953. Pp. 177–198.

Hartmann, H. Notes on the theory of sublimation. In *ibid.* Vol. 10. 1955. Pp. 9–29.

Hartmann, H. The development of the ego concept in Freud's work. *Int. J. Psychoanal.*, 1956, **37,** 425–438.

Hartmann, H., & Kris, E. The genetic approach in psychoanalysis. In *The psychoanalytic study of the child.* Vol. 1. New York: International Universities Press, 1945. Pp. 11–29.

Hartmann, H., Kris, E., & Loewenstein, R. M. Comments on the formation of psychic structure. In *ibid.* Vol. 2. 1946. Pp. 11–38.

Hartmann, H., Kris, E., & Loewenstein, R. M. Notes on the theory of aggression. In *ibid.* Vols. 3, 4. 1949. Pp. 9–36.

Hartmann, H., & Loewenstein, R. M. Notes on the superego. In *ibid.* Vol. 17. 1962. Pp. 42–81.

Hendrick, I. Early development of the ego: identification in infancy. *Psychoanal. Quart.,* 1951, **20,** 44–61.

Hitchmann, E. The history of an aggression-impulse. *Samiksa,* 1947, **1,** 137–141.

Hitchmann, E. *Great men: psychoanalytic studies.* Edited by S. Margolin, with the assistance of Hannah Gunther. New York: International Universities Press, 1956.

Hoffer, W. Development of the body ego. In *The psychoanalytic study of the child.* Vol. 5. New York: International Universities Press, 1950.

Holt, R. R. A critical examination of Freud's concept of bound versus free cathexis. *J. Amer. Psychoanal. Ass.,* 1962, **10,** 475–525.

Isakower, O. A contribution to the psychopathology of falling asleep. *Int. J. Psychoanal.,* 1938, **19,** 331–345.

Jacobson, Edith. Contribution to the metapsychology of cyclothymic depression. In Phyllis Greenacre (Ed.), *Affective disorders.* New York: International Universities Press, 1953. Pp. 38–66.

Jacobson, Edith. Contribution to the metapsychology of psychotic identification. *J. Amer. psychoanal. Ass.,* 1954, **2,** 239–262. (a)

Jacobson, Edith. The self and the object world. In *The psychoanalytic study of the child.* Vol. 9. New York: International Universities Press, 1954. Pp. 75–127. (b)

Jacobson, Edith. Denial and repression. *J. Amer. psychoanal. Ass.,* 1957, **5,** 61–92.

Johnson, Adelaide. Sanctions for superego lacunae of adolescents. In K. R. Eissler (Ed.), *Searchlights on delinquency.* New York: International Universities Press, 1949. Pp. 225–245.

Johnson, Adelaide, & Szurek, S. A. The genesis of antisocial acting out in children and adults. *Psychoanal. Quart.,* 1952, **21,** 323–343.

Jones, E. *The life and works of Sigmund Freud.* Vol. I. New York: Basic Books, 1953.

Jones, E. *The life and works of Sigmund Freud.* Vol. III. New York: Basic Books, 1957.

Kanzer, M. The personality of the scientist. *Psychoanal. Rev.,* 1936, **23,** 373–382.

Kanzer, M. The passing of the Oedipus complex. *Int. J. Psychoanal.,* 1948, **29,** 131–134.

Kanzer, M. The Oedipus trilogy. *Psychoanal. Quart.,* 1950, **19,** 561–572.

Kanzer, M. The central theme in Shakespeare's works. *Psychoanal. Rev.,* 1951, **38,** 1–16.

Kanzer, M. The vision of Father Zossima from *The Brothers Karamazov. Amer. Imago.,* 1951, **8,** 329–335.

Kanzer, M. The reality-testing of the scientist. *Psychoanal. Rev.,* 1955, **42,** 412–448.

Kardiner, A., Linton, R., DuBois, C., & West, G. *The psychological frontiers of society.* New York: Columbia University Press, 1945.

Kardiner A., Ovesey, L. *The mark of oppression: A psychosocial study of the American Negro.* New York: Norton, 1951.

Katan, Anny. The role of "displacement" in agarophobia. *Int. J. Psychoanal.,* 1951, **32,** 41–50.

Katan, M. Structural aspect of a case of schizophrenia. In *The psychoanalytic study of the child.* Vol. 5. New York: International Universities Press, 1950. Pp. 175–211.

Katan, M. Further remarks about Schreber's hallucinations. *Int. J. Psychoanal.,* 1952, **33,** 429–432.

Katan, M. Schreber's prepsychotic phase. *Int. J. Psychoanal.,* 1953, **34,** 43–51.

Katan, M. The importance of the non-psychotic part of the personality in schizophrenia. *Int. J. Psychoanal.,* 1954, **35,** 119–128.

Kestenberg, Judith. Notes on ego development. *Int. J. Psychoanal.,* 1953, **34,** 111–122.

Kohut, H. The psychological significance of musical activity. *Music Ther.,* 1951, **1,** 151–158.

Kohut, H. Beyond the bounds of the basic rule: some recent contributions to applied psychoanalysis. *J. Amer. psychoanal. Ass.,* 1960, **8,** 567–586.

Kris, E. Notes on the development and on some current problems of psychoanalytic child psychology. In *The psychoanalytic study of the child.* Vol. 5. New York: International Universities Press, 1950. Pp. 24–46. (a)

Kris, E. On preconscious mental processes. *Psychoanal. Quart.,* 1950, **19,** 540–560. (b)

Kris, E. The development of ego psychology. *Samiksa,* 1951, **5,** 153–168.

Kris, E. *Psychoanalytic explorations in art.* New York: International Universities Press, 1952.

Kris, E. Neutralization and sublimation: observations on your children. In *The psychoanalytic study of the child*. Vol. 10. New York: International Universities Press, 1955. Pp. 30–46.

Lewin, B. D. A type of neurotic hypomanic reaction. *Arch. Neurol. Psychol.*, 1937, **37**, 868–873.

Lewin, B. D. *The psychoanalysis of elation*. New York: Norton, 1950.

Loewald, H. Ego and reality. *Int. J. Psychoanal.*, 1951, **32**, 10–18.

Loewald, H. The problem of defence and the neurotic interpretation of reality. *Int. J. Psychoanal.*, 1952, **33**, 444–449.

Loewald, H. On the therapeutic action of psychoanalysis. *Int. J. Psychoanal.*, 1960, **41**, 1–18.

Loomie, L., Rosen, V. R., & Stein, M. H. Ernst Kris and the gifted adolescent project. In *The psychoanalytic study of the child*. Vol. 13. New York: International Universities Press, 1958. Pp. 44–63.

Mahler, Margaret S. On child psychosis and schizophrenia: autistic and symbiotic infantile psychoses. In *ibid*. Vol. 7. 1952. Pp. 286–305.

Mahler, Margaret S. Autism and symbiosis: two extreme disturbances of identity. *Int. J. Psychoanal.*, 1958, **39**, 77–83.

Mahler, Margaret S. On sadness and grief in infancy and childhood: loss and restoration of the symbiotic love object. In *The psychoanalytic study of the child*. Vol. 16. New York: International Universities Press, 1961. Pp. 332–351.

Mahler, Margaret S., & Gosliner, B. J. On symbiotic child psychosis: genetic, dynamic and restitutive aspects. In *ibid*. Vol. 10. 1955. Pp. 195–212.

Margolin, S. A. Genetic and dynamic psychophysiological determinants of pathophysiological process. In F. Deutsch (Ed.), *The psychosomatic concept in psychoanalysis*. New York: International Universities Press, 1953.

Mendelson, M. *Psychoanalytic concepts of depression*. Springfield, Ill.: Charles C Thomas, 1960.

Menninger, Karl. The regulatory devices of the ego under major stress. *Int. J. Psychoanal.*, 1954, **35**, 412–420.

Mittelmann, B. The psychodynamics of motility. *Int. J. Psychoanal.*, 1958, **39**, 196–199.

Muensterberger, W. Oral trauma and taboo: a psychoanalytic study of an Indonesian tribe. In G. Roheim (Ed.), *Psychoanalysis and the social sciences*. Vol. 2. New York: International Universities Press, 1950. Pp. 313–329.

Muensterberger, W. Orality and dependence: characteristics of southern Chinese. In *ibid*. Vol. 3. 1951. Pp. 37–69.

Murphy, Lois M. *The widening world of childhood*. New York: Basic Books, 1962.

Neubauer, P. B. The one-parent child and his oedipal development. *The psychoanalytic study of the child*. Vol. 15. New York: International Universities Press, 1960. Pp. 286–309.

Nunberg, H. The synthetic function of the ego (1931). In *Practice and theory of psychoanalysis*. New York: International Universities Press, 1955. Pp. 120–136.

Panel. Psychoanalysis and developmental psychology. *Bull. Amer. psychoanal. Ass.*, 1950, **6**, 37–42.

Panel. Problems of early ego development. *Bull. Amer. psychoanal. Ass.*, 1951, **7**, 248–252.

Panel. Problems of early infancy. *J. Amer. psychoanal. Ass.*, 1955, **3**, 506–514. (a)

Panel. Sublimation. *J. Amer. psychoanal. Ass.*, 1955, **3**, 515–527. (b)

Panel. Pre-oedipal factors in neurosogenesis. *J. Amer. psychoanal. Ass.*, 1957, **5**, 146–157.

Panel. Problems of identity. *J. Amer. psychoanal. Ass.*, 1958, **6**, 131–142.

Panel. Some theoretical aspects of early psychic functioning. *J. Amer. psychoanal. Ass.*, 1959, **7**, 561–576.

Panel. An examination of nosology according to psychoanalytic concepts. *J. Amer. psychoanal. Ass.*, 1960, **8**, 535–551. (a)

Panel. Psychoanalysis and ethology. *J. Amer. psychoanal. Ass.*, 1960, **8**, 526–534. (b)

Panel. The psychology of twins. *J. Amer. psychoanal. Ass.*, 1960, **8**, 158–166. (c)

Panel. Theoretical and clinical aspects of overt male homosexuality. *J. Amer. psychoanal. Ass.*, 1960, **8**, 552–556. (d)

Panel. Object relations. *J. Amer. psychoanal. Ass.*, 1962, **10**, 102–117. (a)

Panel. Theoretical and clinical aspects of overt female homosexuality. *J. Amer. psychoanal. Ass.*, 1962, **10**, 579–592. (b)

Panel. The concept of the id. *J. Amer. psychoanal. Ass.*, 1963, **11**, 151–160.

Provence, Sally, & Lipton, Rose. *Infants in institutions*. New York: International Universities Press, 1963.

Rado, S. The psychic effects of intoxicants. *Int. J. Psychoanal.*, 1926, **7**, 396–413.

Rado, S. The problem of melancholia. *Int. J. Psychoanal.*, 1928, **9**, 420–438.

Rado, S. The psychoanalysis of pharmacothymia. *Psychoanal. Quart.*, 1933.

Rangell, L. On the psychoanalytic theory of anxiety: a statement of a unitary theory. *J. Amer. psychoanal. Ass.*, 1955, **3**, 389–414.

Rangell, L. The role of early psychic functioning in psychoanalysis. *J. Amer. psychoanal. Ass.*, 1961, **9**, 595–609.

Rank, O. *The myth of the birth of the hero* (1913). New York: Robert Bruner, 1952.

Rapaport, D. The psychoanalytic theory of thinking. *Int. J. Psychoanal.*, 1950, **31**, 161–170.

Rapaport, D. *Organization and pathology of thought.* New York: Columbia Univer. Press, 1951. (a)

Rapaport, D. States of consciousness. In *Contemporary approaches to cognition.* Cambridge, Mass.: Harvard Univer. Press, 1951. (b)

Rapaport, D. On the psychoanalytic theory of affects. *Int. J. Psychoanal.*, 1953, **34**, 177–198.

Rapaport, D. Cognitive structures. In *Contemporary approaches to cognition.* Cambridge, Mass.: Harvard Univer. Press, 1957.

Rapaport, D. The theory of ego autonomy: a generalization. *Bull. Menninger Clin.*, 1958, **22**, 13–35.

Rapaport, D. The structure of psychoanalytic theory. *Psychol. Issues,* 1960, **2** (2).

Rapaport, D., & Gill, M. M. The points of view and assumptions of metapsychology. *Int. J. Psychoanal.*, 1959, **40**, 153–162.

Reich, Annie. Early identifications as archaic elements in the superego. *J. Amer. psychoanal. Ass.*, 1954, **2**, 218–238.

Reik, T. Psychoanalysis of the unconscious sense of guilt. *Int. J. Psychoanal.*, 1924, **5**, 439–450.

Reik, T. *Ritual* (1931). New York: International Universities Press, 1958.

Reik, T. *The unknown murderer.* New York: International Universities Press, 1949.

Reik, T. *Dogma and compulsion: psychoanalytic studies of myth and religion.* New York: International Universities Press, 1951.

Ritvo, S., & Solnit, A. J. Influences of early mother-child interaction on identification processes. In *The psychoanalytic study of the child.* Vol. 13. New York: International Universities Press, 1958. Pp. 64–85.

Roheim, G. *The eternal ones of the dream: a psychoanalytic interpretation of Australian myth and ritual.* New York: International Universities Press, 1945.

Roheim, G. *Psychoanalysis and anthropology: culture, personality and the unconscious.* New York: International Universities Press, 1950.

Roheim, G. *The gates of the dream.* New York: International Universities Press, 1952.

Rosenfeld, H. Considerations regarding the psychoanalytic approach to acute and chronic schizophrenia. *Int. J. Psychoanal.*, 1954, **35**, 135–140.

Ross, N. Psychoanalysis and religion. *J. Amer. psychoanal. Ass.*, 1958, **6**, 519–539.

Rubinfine, D. L. A survey of Freud's writings on early psychic functioning. *J. Amer. psychoanal. Ass.*, 1961, **9**, 610–625.

Sandler, J. On the concept of the superego. In *The psychoanalytic study of the child.* Vol. 15. New York: International Universities Press, 1960. Pp. 128–162.

Schafer, R. The loving and beloved superego in Freud's structural theory. In *ibid.* Pp. 163–188.

Schur, M. The ego in anxiety. In R. M. Loewenstein (Ed.), *Drives, affects, behavior.* New York: International Universities Press, 1953. Pp. 67–103.

Schur, M. Comments on the metapsychology of somatization. In *The psychoanalytic study of the child.* Vol. 10. New York: International Universities Press, 1955. Pp. 119–164.

Schur, M. The ego and the id in anxiety. In *ibid.* Vol. 13. 1958. Pp. 190–220.

Spitz, R. Hospitalism: an inquiry into the genesis of psychiatric conditions in early childhood. In *ibid.* Vol. 1. 1945. Pp. 53–74.

Spitz, R. Anaclitic depression: an inquiry into the genesis of psychiatric conditions in early childhood. In *ibid.* Vol. 2. 1946. Pp. 313–342.

Spitz, R. Relevancy of direct infant observations. In *ibid.* Vol. 5. 1950. Pp. 66–73.

Spitz, R. The primal cavity: a contribution to the genesis of perception and its role for psychoanalytic theory. In *ibid.* Vol. 10. 1955. Pp. 217–240.

Spitz, R. *No and yes: on the beginnings of human communication.* New York: International Universities Press, 1957.

Spitz, R. *A genetic field theory of ego formation.* New York: International Universities Press, 1959.

Stone, L. *The psychoanalytic situation.* New York: International Universities Press, 1961.

Tarachow, S. Totem feast in modern dress. *Amer. Imago.*, 1948, **5**, 65–69.

Tarachow, S. Remarks on the comic process and beauty. *Psychoanal. Quart.*, 1949, **18**, 215–226.

Tarachow, S. St. Paul and early Christianity: a psychoanalytic and historical study. In G. Roheim (Ed.), *Psychoanalysis and the social sciences.* Vol. 4. New York: International Universities Press, 1955. Pp. 223–281.

Van Ophuisen, J. Primary conduct disturbances: Diagnosis and treatment. In N. D. C. Lewis, & B. J. Paceller (Eds.), *Modern trends in child psychiatry*. New York: International Universities Press, 1945.

Waelder, R. The structure of paranoid ideas: a critical survey of various theories. *Int. J. Psychoanal.*, 1951, **32**, 167–177.

Weissman, P. The effects of preoedipal paternal attitudes on development. *Int. J. Psychoanal.*, 1963, **44**, 121–131.

Winnicott, D. W. Transitional objects and transitional phenomena. *Int. J. Psychoanal.*, 1953, **34**, 89–97.

Wisdom, J. O. *Philosophy and psychoanalysis*. Oxford: Blackwell, 1952.

Wolf, P. H. *The developmental psychologies of Jean Piaget and psychoanalysis*. *Psychol. Issues*, 1960, **2** (1).

Wolman, B. B. Explorations in latent schizophrenia. *Amer. J. Psychother.*, 1957, **11**, 560–588.

Wolman, B. B. *Contemporary theories and systems in psychology*. New York: Harper & Row, 1960.

Wolman, B. B. Hostility experiences in group psychotherapy. *Int. J. soc. Psychiat.*, 1964, **10**, 55–61.

Zetzel, Elizabeth R. The concept of anxiety in relation to the development of psychoanalysis. *J. Amer. psychoanal. Ass.*, 1955, **3**, 369–388.

Zilboorg, G. Ambulatory schizophrenia. *Psychiatry*, 1941, **4**, 149–155.

Zilboorg, G. Legal aspects of psychiatry. In J. K. Hall (Ed.), *One hundred years of American psychiatry*. New York: Columbia University Press, 1944. Pp. 507–508.

Zilboorg, G. Psychoanalysis and criminology. In V. C. Branham (Ed.), *Encyclopaedia of criminology*. New York: Philosophical Library, 1950. Pp. 398–405.

15

Non-Freudian Analytic Theories

PATRICK MULLAHY

THE EARLY REVISIONISTS

Alfred Adler

Adler was the first neo-Freudian, and his influence on more recent theorists has been considerable. His contributions to ego psychology were very important. Around 1902 Adler, at the invitation of Freud, joined the latter's group, and although for a time he was an outstanding member, it is doubtful that he ever considered himself an orthodox Freudian. In 1911 he left the Freudian group to found his own. Soon after, Adler and his colleagues began to call their work "individual psychology."

In 1907 he published a monograph on organ inferiority and compensation. He was particularly interested in discovering why people, when they become ill, are afflicted in one area of the body rather than another. His answer to the problem was that a given area that has been afflicted suffers from a defect or basic inferiority due to hereditary or developmental factors. Disease—like health—is relative to the environment. Disease is an outcome of organ inferiority and/or external pressures and demands. Furthermore, even with an inferior organ, a person in a given situation may not suffer a disease. He may compensate for the weakness or inferiority by strengthening the organ through intense and prolonged effort.

Adler soon realized that organ inferiority may lead to pervasive feelings of inferiority, not merely those which arise from the bodily condition. A person—a farmer, for example—who has had a crippled arm from birth may not only feel handicapped because of the objective bodily condition but also experience profound and pervasive feelings of inferiority in almost every sphere of life because of his subjective interpretation of his situation, an attitude going back to his childhood.

This realization led Adler to modify his basic assumption about human nature. The drive to overcome feelings of inferiority was seen as the basic drive in man, not sex, as Freud had for a long time held, along with the drive for self-preservation, not aggression, as Adler himself had once thought. Inferiority feelings in children are a basic fact of human nature. But they may be surmounted, becoming a powerful force toward achievement and superiority. However, abnormal conditions in the home, for example, when the child is pampered or neglected, may lead to, or result in, a lifelong pervasive feeling of inadequacy and inferiority.

Gradually, Adler arrived at a philosophical interpretation of man. Biologically and sociologically, his condition is hazardous. Man is among those weak animals who cannot live alone, and the whole animal kingdom is said to demonstrate the fundamental law that species whose members cannot face the battle for self-preservation gather new strength through group life. Since, from the standpoint of nature, man is an inferior organism, he needs an extensive apparatus to guarantee his existence. Social life helps to provide this. The most notable instrument which man has developed against the rigors of the environment is the soul, whose essence is permeated with the necessity of communal life.

Since man is an inferior organism, his feelings of inferiority and insecurity are constantly present in his consciousness. But, according to Adler, they act as an ever-present stimulus to the discovery of a superior form of adaptation. A "psychic organ" which can effect the processes of adaptation and security is therefore called into being to compensate for man's organic deficiencies. The uninterrupted feeling of inadequacy stimulates the development of foresight and precaution in man, causing his soul to develop to its present state, an organ of thinking, feeling, and acting. The life of the human soul is a *becoming*. Thus, the final purpose or goal of the psychic life is to guarantee man's continued existence on this earth and to enable him to accomplish his development. This psychic life is bound up with the environment. Hence, man's assets and liabilities are relative to the environment. Depending on circumstances, one's inferiorities may be one or the other.

Intrinsic to the concept of adaptation is the fact that the psychic life strives for the achievement of a single goal. The psychic life of man, according to Adler, is determined by his goal. He claimed that all the manifestations of the human soul are directed toward a goal. From the side of the individual, the goal is fashioned in childhood in relation to the environment. Thus, every psychic phenomenon, every psychological activity, can be understood only when regarded as a preparation for some life goal.

The child strives for security and adaptation, but he demands a "coefficient of safety." From this arises a new movement in his soul, a tendency toward domination and superiority. He may become optimistic about achieving his goal, and in such a case courage, frankness, openness, responsibility, industry, etc., will develop. But the child who is not confident of being able to solve his problems will develop timidity, introspectiveness, distrust, etc.

The most significant determinants of the structure of the soul life are developed in the earliest days of childhood. From childhood onward, the goal, the dynamics, and everything which directs the psychic life toward its objective remain constant. Heredity and environment constitute the building blocks from which the child constructs his unique way—his life-style—of adapting himself to the world. At 4 or 5 years of age, the child's life-style is completed.

> His interpretation of what life is, what he is, what others are and what his relationship to others mean, is pretty nearly fixed by that age, and forms his total attitudes to life in all situations. New experiences are, from that time on, interpreted only from the point of view of *his* life style. This results in a biased selection of perceptions, with the exclusion, or at least depreciation, of all those experiences that do not fit his style of life. All thinking, feeling and acting of an individual support his style of life. Thoughts, feelings and actions that would undermine or contradict his life style are largely rejected (Adler, 1963, p. iv).

In this way, and in contradistinction to Freud, Adler arrived at a voluntaristic conception of the creative self. The person's attitude toward life, developed in childhood, "determines" his relationship to the world. The determinism of Freud (or of the recent neo-Freudians) is rejected.

In line with the tradition of German sociology, Adler emphasized the importance of *Gemeinschaft*, of community. Adaptation to the community is the most important function of the psychic life. The child in varying degrees develops and integrates his community feeling or social interest into his life-style. The more successfully he accomplishes this, the more healthy he becomes. Social interest is the feeling for, and cooperation with, people and the experience of belonging and cooperating in the common goal. Through the relationship with the mother, social feelings are developed in the child. A relationship of love fosters the development of such feelings, and this is the mother's most important function: to foster such feelings and encourage their extension to others.

The community is prior to the individual:

> The compulsion toward the community and communal life exists in institutions whose forms we need not entirely understand, as in religion, where the sanctification of communal formulae serves as a bond between members of the community. . . . The communal need regulates all relationships between men. The communal life of man antedates the individual life of man (Adler, 1927b, pp. 26–27).

In man's physical constitution and in his psyche all the means which made community life possible existed or evolved. Thus, because of his weakness, his biological inferiority, man's most precious acquisitions in the course of evolution have developed.

For Adler, the relationship between the individual and his environment is extremely complex. He adopted Vaihinger's notion that man lives by fictional goals. Thus, society creates various fictions, such as that all men are created equal, the meek or the poor or the downtrodden shall inherit the earth, prosperity is gained by hard work, progress is inevitable, etc. Such assumptions enable man to deal more effectively with his environment. Therefore what men believe is as psychologically significant as what actually is, or more so. Whether or not a heaven and a hell exist, if a man believes in them they govern his behavior. In other words, his future expectations motivate him more powerfully than his past experiences. The striving toward a goal is the all-important thing. The history of man is a history of beliefs, ideals, strivings.

Hall and Lindzey have briefly and cogently summarized Adler's contributions vis-à-vis Freud in the following:

> Adler's theory of the person minimized the sexual instinct which in Freud's early theorizing had played an almost exclusive role in the dynamics of behavior. . . . Man is primarily a social and not a sexual creature. He is motivated by social and not by sexual interest. His inferiorities are not limited to the sexual domain, but may extend to all facets of his being, both physical and psychological. He strives to develop a unique style of life in which the sexual drive plays a minor role. In fact, the way in which he satisfies his sexual needs is determined by his style of life and not vice versa. . . .
>
> Adler made consciousness the center of personality. Man is a conscious being; he is ordinarily aware of the reasons for his behavior. He is conscious of his inferiorities and conscious of the goals for which he strives. More than that, he is a self-conscious individual who is capable of planning and guiding his actions with full awareness of their meaning for his own self-realization (1961, p. 118).

After such a generous tribute to Adler by Hall and Lindzey, I may seem churlish when I point out that in almost completely rejecting the theory of unconscious experiences, Adler has neglected one of the basic principles of dynamic psychology. Reacting against Freud, he went too far in the opposite direction. Adler's psychology needs to be supplemented by an adequate recognition of the significance of unconscious forces in human life. And finally, though I have neither the space nor the time to examine them, I believe current claims as to Adler's influence on Horney, Fromm, and Sullivan are grossly exaggerated.

Carl Jung

The theories of Jung are too complex for adequate exposition, short of an entire book. I can only offer a sketchy outline of some of his major concepts. Though in 1906 he began a regular correspondence with Freud, he refused to accept the exclusive importance which Freud attributed to sexuality. For a time the founder of psychoanalysis thought that his brilliant younger colleague and friend would be his successor. But it was not to be. Jung would not accept Freud's "pansexualism." In 1914 Jung resigned his presidency of the International Psychoanalytic Association. The estrangement of the two men was complete and final.

Libidinal energy, or psychic energy, according to Jung, is an undifferentiated energy employed in all the activities of life. Even though Freud eventually redefined libido to include psychic energy in general, he always retained the notion that it has a special qualitative character; it is the energy of Eros. Energy, in the Jungian view, removed from one area, activity, or interest will reappear in another. The redistribution of energy in the various systems of the personality is a basic principle. Thus energy may flow from the unconscious to the conscious, and conversely, depending on the interests, activities, and values of the individual. As a corollary, so to speak, is the principle of entropy, which for Jung means that the distribution of energy in the psyche tends toward an equilibrium. "If one part of the personality is charged with a heavy load of libido and another with a low load, libido will move from the former toward the latter" (Wolman, 1960, p. 302). In general, energy tends to flow from a stronger value or interest to a weaker one until a balance is restored. However, the equilibrium of the various forces or energies of the personality can be and is imperfect. Only in an ideal condition is there a perfect equilibrium of the energies of the human being.

For Jung energy is ultimately governed by a dialectic of opposites, a movement between two extremes. All life depends on forces held in opposition. There must always be present, it is said, height and depth, heat and cold, etc., as it were, in order that the process of equalization can take place.

Culture provides a "psychological machine," the symbol for transforming energy originally required for the essential activities of the organism. Man has a superfluity of energy, and by means of the symbol it can be employed for higher activities, as manifested in mythology, religion, art, science, and so forth. Symbols are born or inherited as predispositions in the unconscious part of the personality. They are never thought out consciously but emerge in the form of so-called "revelation" or "intuition."

One may distinguish three major parts of the psyche: the conscious (the ego), the personal unconscious, and the collective unconscious. But these interdependent systems also have subsystems. Related to these in a bewildering complexity are the attitudes of introversion and extroversion and the functions of thinking, feeling, sensing, and intuiting. Still again there is the self or unified personality which gradually develops.

The conscious and the unconscious are opposites. Jung claims that modern man greatly overemphasizes the conscious mind, with its conscious perceptions, memories, thoughts, and feelings. In harmony with traditional psychology, Jung holds that the conscious mind is responsible for the person's experience of identity. It enables us to adapt to the environment. Since it embodies our conscious attitudes toward the world, we tend to regard the ego as the focal point of our experience.

The personal unconscious contains experiences that have been forgotten, suppressed, or repressed. It contains subliminal perceptions. Attitudes and functions which have been neglected or underdeveloped are to be found in the personal unconscious also. To some extent dreams are manifestations of the personal unconscious, though Jung would tend to seek further for their significance in the collective unconscious.

One subsystem or constellation of thoughts, feelings, perceptions, and memories of the personal unconscious is the complexes. They are more or less autonomous subsystems in the personality, constellating various experiences. The complex has a nucleus which attracts or constellates experiences, for example, the mother complex. Experiences relating to her constellate around the nucleus, forming the mother complex. The nucleus or foundation is derived from the mother archetype, and the complex develops as a result of the child's experiences with his actual mother. The effects of the mother complex on the son may be homosexuality, impotence, or Don Juanism, where a man seeks his mother in every woman he meets. But the effects of the mother complex are not always negative. A man with a mother complex may have a great capacity for friendships, be gifted as a teacher because of his almost feminine insight and tact, be endowed with a wealth of religious feeling, etc.

It is sometimes forgotten that Freud adhered to the notion of a phylogenetic inheritance, which he traced in his book *Totem and Taboo*. Jung's collective unconscious is somewhat similar, though it is of far greater importance in his psychology and is much more elaborate. In one place he explains the collective unconscious as follows:

> In the same way as the individual is not only an isolated and separate, but also a social being, so also the human mind is not only something isolated and absolutely individual, but also a collective function. And just as certain social functions or impulses are, so to speak, opposed to the egocentric interests of the individual, so also the human mind has certain functions or tendencies which, on account of their collective nature, are to some extent opposed to the personal mental functions. This is due to the fact that every human being is born with a highly differentiated brain, which gives him the possibility of attaining a rich mental function that he has neither acquired ontogenetically nor developed. In proportion as human beings are similarly differentiated, the corresponding mental functions are collective and universal. This circumstance explains the fact that the unconscious of far-separated peoples and races possesses a remarkable number of points of agreement (1920, p. 451).

The unanimity of indigenous forms and themes of myths, according to Jung, bears out his contention that there exists a collective psyche. Every individual, he thought, has memories not only of his own unique history but also, by virtue of his membership in the human family, of the "primordial images," that is, inherited potentialities and predispositions of the human imagination, lying latent in the brain. The primordial images are archetypes, representing the memories of a people, a race, a whole epoch.

An archetype is a universal thought form or universal idea which has been inherited, though it is not an innate idea but a *predisposition* toward a primitive mode of thought. Archetypes—which are themselves unconscious—predispose man to experience various critical events common to the human race as his ancestors did: birth, marriage, death, and various other critical periods (such as adolescence) and critical experiences in life. Archetypes are represented in dreams, myths, visions, works of art, certain concepts of science, the symptoms of the mentally ill, fairy stories, fantasies, etc. But their representations in conscious imagery are not the archetypes themselves; the latter are a priori determinants of psychological experiences, just as logical forms are a priori determinants of the reasoning process—except that logical forms may be known directly.

Jung and his followers claim that certain archetypes have been identified. They appear in many sorts of representations: as persons, gods, heroes, geometrical forms, numbers. There are, for example, the archetypes of the mother and the father. The young child, who is not yet a differentiated personality, experiences his mother not as a definite, feminine, unique personality but as a warming, protecting, nourishing entity. She represents an archetype, a composite image of all preexisting mothers, and a "model" of all the protecting, warming, nourishing influences which man has experienced. Thus, traces of certain kinds of experiences of mankind lying dormant in the brain of the child become activated and blend with the nearest and most powerful experience, the child's mother, producing the archetypal experience of the mother.

In human experience, the protecting mother, as an archetypal representation, is also associated with the nourishing earth, the provident field, the warming hearth, the protecting cave, the surrounding vegetation, and the milk-giving cow and the herd. Likewise, the symbol of the mother refers to a place of origin such as nature, to that which passively creates, to matter, and to the unconscious, natural, and instinctive life.

In many ways, the archetype of the father is opposed to that of the mother. It signifies such things as strength, power, authority, the creative breath (or pneuma), and all that is moving, active, and dynamic in the world. According to Jung, the father image is associated with rivers, winds, storms, lightning and thunder, battle and weapons, raging animals such as wild bulls, the violent and changeful phenomena of the world, and the cause of all change.

Jung's formulation of the self is rather obscure. The self is an archetype and represents man's striving for unity. Somehow it integrates the various aspects and systems of the personality, providing equilibrium and stability, though no one ever achieves a complete unification. Jung has formulated the notion of the self as follows:

> If we picture the conscious mind with the ego as its center, as being opposed to the unconscious, and if we now add to our mental picture the process of assimilating the unconscious, we can think of this assimilation as a kind of approximation of conscious and unconscious, where the center of the total personality no longer coincides with the ego, but with a point midway between the conscious and unconscious. This would be the point of a new equilibrium, a new centering of the total personality, a virtual center which, on account of its focal position between conscious and unconscious, ensures for the personality a new and more solid foundation (Wolman, 1960, p. 311).

In essence the self seems to be a principle of unity toward which the individual strives. Hence it is his ultimate goal and thus motivates his behavior. It presupposes the full development and individuation of the various aspects of the personality, an occurrence that does not take place before middle age. In varying degrees it unifies all the conflicting aspects of the personality. A necessary condition of the development of the self is "self-acceptance," since this development requires the person's acceptance of the unconscious as well as the conscious parts of the personality. For Jung, the unconscious, which is a reservoir of collective experience, is a field of experience of unlimited extent. It is an independent, productive force whose essence is an urge toward self-realization.

One of the many things which distinguish Freud from Jung is the latter's insistence that a causal analysis of psychic phenomena is not sufficient. A causal analysis is retrospective, since it seeks the causal conditions of psychological phenomena in what has previously occurred, namely, the person's past experiences. A causal analysis also assumes that psychic phenomena are strictly determined. But this needs to be supplemented by a functional analysis which assumes that the present must also be understood in terms of the future. In other words, psychic activities have a goal, which one must endeavor to understand. Jung believed that both kinds of analysis are necessary.

Another and related point is that Jung believed that the directed, logical thinking of the conscious mind is not adequate for understanding the unconscious. Another kind of thinking is required, namely, one that is spontaneous, nonlogical, imaginative, and largely nonverbal, to grasp the nature of the archaic unconscious processes. I am tempted to call this "intuitive" thinking, though the term can easily be misunderstood. It is not as mysterious as it sounds; I think a great deal of creative activity occurs in such a fashion. In fact I believe many analysts employ both kinds of thinking in their therapeutic work. To put this another way, can most analysts give a logical explanation of their interpretations of patients' dreams and fantasies?

I am not suggesting that analysts generally accept Jung's theories and speculations about archetypes. By definition they are not subject to direct verification. It seems to me that whatever insights can be gained from Jung's formulations do not rest on the acceptance of archetypes. Even so, one does not have to accept his theories literally in order to find them a fertile source for one's own thinking, as indeed has often happened.

Otto Rank

Originally Freud formulated a concept of the birth trauma, but Otto Rank employed it as a central explanatory concept in his *Trauma of Birth*. For him the separation from, or deprivation of, the pleasurable primal situation in the womb is of fundamental significance. Man yearns for the blissful intrauterine state and in one way or another tries to restore it. Physical birth is the most traumatic event in human life, entailing a most painful birth anxiety, which Rank calls the "primal anxiety." Primal anxiety blots out the memory of the original blissful state before birth, setting up an initial primal repression.

It is unnecessary to give a detailed outline of the extreme speculations which Rank created about the birth trauma, so I shall limit my discussion to a few topics.

Every human being is said to need the whole period of childhood to overcome the birth trauma. Because of the birth trauma, the child is prone to anxiety, and the original anxiety is transferable to almost anything. Weaning represents a second trauma, though a great part of its traumatic effect is derived from the trauma of birth. The castration dread hits not only the primal anxiety but the second trauma as well, and that is why it has such a lasting and stupendous effect on the child.

"Neurotics" are people who have not been able to overcome the birth trauma and its subsequent effects.

The intrauterine state of bliss is the prototype of every pleasure, and every pleasure and pleasure-seeking activity aims to reestablish the primal pleasure. The whole problem of infantile sexuality is centered around the question of where babies come from. According to Rank, the child seeks in himself the lost memory of his earlier place of abode. But even when he is able to formulate the question and receives a truthful answer from his parents, he cannot accept the answer because of inner resistances and repressions. But his real interest is to return to the place that he came from.

Both male and female abhor the female sexual organs, which are unconsciously associated with the birth trauma. The little boy clings to the notion that every human being has a phallus primarily because he wants to deny the existence of the female genitals, which tend to remind him of the horror of his birth. The little girl suffers penis envy primarily as a reaction formation against the existence of the female sexual organs and the horror of birth.

The Oedipus complex marks an attempt to transfer the intrauterine pleasure of the primal libido to the anxiety-invested female genitals and there to reopen a former source of pleasure buried by repression.

Rank believed that the sexual act is the sublimest substitution for reunion with the mother, being a partial gratification of the primal wish to return to the womb or a symbolic realization of it. By means of the clitoris libido, the woman is able to identify herself with the penis of the man and thus indirectly to approach the return to the womb. But she has a more far-reaching and normal source of gratification of the primal wish which manifests itself as mother love in her identification with the fruit of her body.

Abhorrence of the female genitals accounts for homosexuality. Homosexuals, unconsciously or consciously, play the mother-child roles, a direct continuance of the asexual but libidinal binding of the primal situation, where there is a physical identity of mother and child.

Without going into further details of the birth trauma and its consequences, I wish to point out that the conception of the birth trauma was a prelude to the conception of the "birth" of individuality and autonomous will, which is often attended by difficult and painful experiences. The concept of the gradual freeing of the individual from dependence through a creative development of personality replaced Rank's earlier "fixation" on the birth trauma. He expressed his later thinking on birth and creativity as follows: the

> . . . whole consequence of evolution from blind impulse through conscious will to self-conscious knowledge, seems still somehow to correspond to a continued result of births, rebirths, and new birth, which reach from the birth of the child from the mother, beyond the birth of the individual from the mass, to the birth of the creative work from the individual and finally to the birth of knowledge from the work. . . . At all events we find in all these phenomena, even at the highest spiritual peak, the struggle and pain of birth, the separation out of the universal, with the pleasure and bliss of procreation, the creation of an individual cosmos, whether it be now physically our own child, creatively our own work or spiritually our own self (1945, pp. 219–220).

Thus, Rank came to see that separation is intrinsic to the developmental process, not only physical separation from the mother but, through the course of time, from various forms of psychological dependence. The embryonic state, in which one is an indivisible whole, though bound inseparably to a greater whole, is a symbol of the condition of wholeness. Birth entails the loss of a feeling of wholeness, and individualization entails further separation. The development of independence is a gradual and conflict-laden process because the child leans on the parents and on the past, which is familiar and provided some security and in which he sees himself personified. The various steps toward independence from birth to death are conceived as continuous separations from previous developmental phases of one's personality.

Rank claims that the separation experience has two opposing dynamic characteristics: (1) a strengthening of the emotional binding to the other, who represents all other ties—biological, social, and moral—because of fear of individuality, and (2) a striving (will) toward freedom and independence from any one person. The fear of individualization, in Rank's view, is the fear of being alone, of loneliness, of the loss of kinship with others and with the "All." The fear of life, of the new, of being alone is poignantly opposed to the fear of destruction, of death in the "neurotic." The fear of life and the fear of death reduce themselves to a fear of loss of connection with a totality.

The development of individuality is an act of will, an initiating power which selects, organizes, modifies, and recreates what the person assimilates in order to live and flourish. Will is "a positive guiding organization and integration of self which utilizes creatively, as well as inhibits and controls the instinctual drives" (Rank, 1945, pp. 111–112, footnote). While I omit a discussion of Rank's theory of the development of will, I wish to mention that at the highest level, when a "truly positive willing" is achieved, we abandon invidious comparisons and cease to measure ourselves by other people's standards. Once we understand the nature of our will, we are able to accept and feel the responsibility "with which our own ethical consciousness has to say 'Yes' or 'No' to our individual willing."

I should like to conclude with a tribute to Rank offered by Salzman in his excellent book *Developments in Psychoanalysis:*

> Rank dignified the status of the neurotic by showing that it was the efforts of the neurotic to overcome his deficiencies and limitations which produced the neurotic symptoms. . . . He saw the neurotic process as one of repair or adaptation and as a striving toward a fuller and more productive existence. . . . His attempts to shorten the process [of therapy] produced novel and exciting experiments. . . . In Rank's hands, therapy became a more active process in which the patient was encouraged to assert himself and strengthen his "will" (1962, p. 43).

Salzman adds that Rank was another forerunner in the growing trend toward an ego psychology.

I surmise that in future years, his contributions to will therapy will gain a wider and more appreciative audience.

NEW DEVELOPMENTS

Karen Horney

Horney's first two books, *The Neurotic Personality of Our Time* and *New Ways in Psychoanalysis,* are major contributions to psychoanalysis. Her subsequent work seems to me to be of much less importance. She is justly called a neo-Freudian because although the content of her theories is very different from the content of Freud's, she adheres by and large to the structure and framework of his thinking. In her earlier work, at least, the syntax and grammar of her psychology are almost identical with Freud's. However, in scope, originality, and daring she is far behind. In my opinion, her most serious theoretical shortcoming lies in her inability to be systematic. This is not so serious in her first two books, where she adheres more or less closely to the Freudian paradigm, but subsequently, when she begins to strike out on her own with no model to serve as a guide or even as a foil, she becomes progressively vague, diffuse, and repetitious in her thinking.

Her critical reevaluation of classical psychoanalytic theories, she says, had its origin in a dissatisfaction with therapeutic results. She claims that almost every one of her patients manifested problems for which traditional psychoanalytic knowledge offered no means of solution.

Since Horney's reformulation of the theory of neurosis—its development, structure, and operation—is her most important contribution, I shall devote most of the space at my disposal to an explication of it. The reader will at once note that Horney has abandoned the libido theory and, in fact, Freud's various instinct theories because she conceives personality to be much more malleable than the founder of psychoanalysis did. Environmental factors are given much greater weight. Thus, while the Oedipus complex, or something resembling it, is important in the etiology of neurosis, it is not, or failure to resolve it is not, the kernel of every neurosis. Nor is the Oedipus complex universal and biologically ordained; it is a response to provocations from emotionally disturbed parents. The social interactions, which are not primarily sexual in character, of child and parents provide the clues to an understanding of the etiology of neurosis, though other factors also have to be taken into account. Horney does not assume that some children have a predisposition to become mentally ill, but she does believe that those children who grow up to be neurotic have parents who are themselves neurotic, emotionally immature, and distorted. Furthermore, the problems of neurotic parents—like those of all parents—and the problems they unconsciously create and foster in their children are born within a social context. The family is the basic social unit of Western society. It embodies various cultural patterns to be found in the society in which any given family exists, and it also in varying degrees reflects the influences of other institutions, economic, religious, educational, etc. Thus the child is born into, and grows up in, a definite sociocultural context. The conventions, the customs, and the cultural patterns which are in varying degrees conveyed to him, first and foremost by the parents, give character and definition to the personality of the growing child and determine whether he is destined to be sick or healthy. His problems cannot, in the main, be understood apart from the social milieu into which he is born and in which he lives. Though a normal adult—or a neurotic adult, for that matter—is by no means a mere carrier of selected sociocultural patterns, these patterns, to an enormous degree, shape the child's thoughts, feelings, motivations, and acts. It is the parents who first begin this shaping, partly unconsciously and partly deliberately. How they accomplish this will profoundly influence or condition the basic structure of the child's personality.

Horney states explicitly that neuroses are generated not only by incidental individual experiences but also by the specific cultural conditions under which we live. Cultural conditions

> . . . not only lend weight and color to the individual experiences but in the last analysis determine their particular form. It is an individual fate, for example, to have a domineering or a "self-sacrificing" mother, but it is only under definite cultural conditions that we find domineering or self-sacrificing mothers, and it is only because of these

existing conditions that such an experience will have an influence on later life (Horney, 1937, p. VIII).

However, though Horney believes that essentially neuroses develop out of early experiences in the family, she does not think that "later reactions" are repetitions of earlier ones, as Freud did. Unfortunate childhood experiences are not the only causes of later difficulties, since, among other reasons, personality development, including maldevelopment, does not cease in childhood.

Theory of neurosis. Leaving aside, for the moment, the question of etiology, I wish to summarize briefly the essential characteristics of the neurotic personality of our time. Horney mentions two generic characteristics in the "manifest picture " of neuroses or, rather, in the behavior of neurotic persons: a certain rigidity in reaction and a discrepancy between potentialities and accomplishments. Rigidity, or lack of flexibility, in meeting life's problems and requirements is indicative of a neurosis only when it deviates significantly from the cultural patterns. Analogously, a discrepancy between potentialities and accomplishments is not an indication of neurosis if the cultural environment is impoverished and harsh as in, say, the Aran Islands. But when a person, despite inherited gifts and favorable external possibilities or opportunities, evinces a (marked) discrepancy between native capacities and accomplishments, then one is justified usually in suspecting he has serious emotional problems or shortcomings.

However, the "manifest picture" does not get to the essence of the problems of neurotics. One must study the dynamics effective in producing neuroses. One, though not the sole, essential factor is anxieties and the defenses built up against them. I shall elaborate on this factor presently. A second factor has to do with the presence of conflicting tendencies, of which the person is not conscious (or at least he is not conscious of their precise contents and manifestations) and for which he automatically attempts to attain certain compromise solutions. I shall elaborate on this point also. These two generic factors are found in every neurosis and, with the qualifications I mentioned, distinguish the neurotic person from the normal.

The common denominator in the childhood histories of a great number of neurotic persons whom Horney studied was a defective home environment possessing certain characteristics in various combinations. "The basic evil," she said, "is invariably a lack of genuine warmth and affection" (1937, p. 80). As a corollary, so to speak, parents have various attitudes and perform many actions which cannot but arouse hostility. These attitudes and actions include preference for other children, unjust reproaches, unpredictable changes between overindulgence and scornful rejection, unfulfilled promises, and, in varying degrees, a thwarting of the child, such as by disturbing his friendships, ridiculing his independent thinking, or spoiling his interest in his own pursuits (Horney, 1937, pp. 80–81). Thus such parents in effect and perhaps unconsciously break the child's will and destroy his integrity.

Nor is this all. In the psychological atmosphere in which the child of such parents grows, destructive and lasting jealousy reactions are artificially generated. Their lack of warmth and their competitiveness contribute to these reactions. Because of their inadequacies, including an inability to have satisfactory emotional and sexual relations, they tend to make children the objects of their (distorted) "love." "They loose their need for affection on the children" (Horney, 1937, p. 83). With terror and tenderness they force the child into those passionate attachments with them which Freud interpreted in terms of the Oedipus complex. Such attachments are characterized by intense possessiveness and jealousy. For various reasons such attachments also arouse hostility in the child.

But the danger for the child's character formation is said to lie not so much in hostile opposition—since there are good reasons for it—but in repressing it. It is not the only danger. There are several dangers, including the likelihood that the child will soon feel he is unworthy of love. In regard to repressed hostility, the danger is that he will develop anxiety and thus start a series of events which culminate in neurosis, from which there may be no road back short of intensive therapy.

Horney claims that there are several "reasons," effective in various degrees and combinations, why a child who grows up in the psychological atmosphere created by neurotic parents will repress hostility, namely, helplessness, fear, love, and feelings of guilt. It will be sufficient for my purposes in this chapter, I think, to summarize only one set of these conditions, helplessness. Too much emphasis has been put on the biological aspect. After the first two or three years, there is said to be a decided change from the prevailingly biological dependence to a kind of dependence that includes the mental, intellectual, and spiritual life of the child. In this, there are great individual differences:

> It all depends on what the parents try to achieve in the education of their offspring: whether the tendency is to make a child strong, courageous, independent, capable of dealing with all sorts of situations, or whether the main tendency is to shelter the child, to make it obedient, to keep it ignorant of life as it is, or in short to infantilize it up to twenty years of age or longer (Horney, 1937, p. 85).

This helplessness is artificially reinforced by the parents of a child growing up in adverse psychological circumstances. They intimidate him; baby him; or force him into, and keep him in, a state of emotional dependence. Therefore his dependence will be prolonged, and his natural tendency to react with hostile opposition perhaps delayed and weakened.

Horney thinks that the infantile anxiety said to follow upon repressed hostility is a necessary but not sufficient condition of the development of neurosis. That is, fortunate circumstances may intervene, such as an early change of surroundings (unspecified), or counteracting influences, coming from teachers, aunts, uncles, cousins, friends, etc., may forestall a definite neurotic outcome. In such circumstances the child's anxiety may be somewhat allayed, and he may learn that it is possible to be liked and trusted.

But these fortunate interventions do not usually occur. Ordinarily, since the family structure is what it is today, the child of neurotic parents is subject to their destructive influence for many years. Hence the consequences of their neurotic attitudes and actions are far-reaching. The parents are the first models. One's expectations about other people and about their attitudes and actions toward oneself are profoundly influenced by one's experiences in the home. And the more difficult the child's experiences in the family are, the more he will tend not only to hate his parents and brothers and sisters but also to develop a distrustful or spiteful attitude toward everyone. The more he is prevented by isolation from others from acquiring corrective experience, the more his attitude of distrust or spite or hate will be fostered. The more he has to conceal his hostile reactions, perhaps by overtly conforming with his parents' attitudes and expectations, the more he projects his anxiety (due to repressed hostility) to the outside world, becoming convinced that the world in general is dangerous and frightening.

Owing to his history of unfortunate and destructive experiences, he will lack self-confidence and will not dare in his relationships with others to be as enterprising or aggressive as they. "He will have lost the blissful certainty of being wanted and will take even a harmless teasing as a cruel rejection" (Horney, 1937, p. 89). He will be painfully vulnerable and less capable of defending himself. Genuinely friendly relationships with others will be almost or quite beyond his reach because he has never known such, never been loved, never been given a fair chance to learn to love. Hence he experiences an insidiously increasing, all-pervading feeling of being lonely and helpless in a hostile world. His acute reactions to "individual provocations" from others crystallize into a character attitude, which is the nutritive soil or matrix out of which a definite neurosis may develop at any time. Horney calls this attitude "basic anxiety," which is inseparably interwoven with a "basic hostility."

Basic anxiety underlies all relationships to people. It will continue to exist night and day, not only in actual interpersonal relations, but also when one is physically alone and even in sleep, as can be shown from an analysis of one's dreams. Basic anxiety is said to be more or less the same "everywhere," in all neurotic people. "It may be roughly described," Horney says, "as a feeling of being small, insignificant, helpless, deserted, endangered, in a world that is out to abuse, cheat, attack, humiliate, betray, envy" (1937, p. 92). A person who feels this way may experience himself as being as helpless as a tiny naked baby or a mouse hiding in his hole from a prowling tomcat. Yet rarely is one conscious of basic anxiety or basic hostility. They can be concealed from oneself in many ways, such as by a superficial conviction that people in general are quite likable or by an indiscriminate readiness to admire others. Basic anxiety may be divested of its personal character, only to appear as a feeling that things and events are dangerous and threatening: thunderstorms, political events, germs, or an overshadowing fate.

In *New Ways in Psychoanalysis,* Horney elaborates her concept of basic anxiety. It differs from Freud's "real" anxiety, which she interprets to mean, primarily, a fear on the part of the child that the environment will punish him with castration or loss of love for any pursuit of satisfaction of forbidden instinctual drives. Basic anxiety, she says, is more comprehensive:

> It contends that the environment is dreaded as a whole because it is felt to be unreliable, mendacious, unappreciative, unfair, unjust, begrudging and merciless. According to this concept the child not only fears punishment or desertion because of forbidden drives, but he feels the environment as a menace to his entire development and to his most legitimate wishes and strivings. He feels in danger of his individuality being obliterated, his freedom taken away, his happiness prevented (1939, p. 75).

According to Horney, this fear is well founded on reality because in an environment in which basic anxiety develops, the child's free use of energies is thwarted, his self-esteem and self-reliance are undermined, fear is instilled by intimidation and isolation, and his expansiveness is warped through brutality, imposition of "standards," or overprotective "love."

Basic anxiety has many destructive consequences. These include emotional isolation combined with a feeling of intrinsic weakness of the self, an underlying lack of self-confidence, and a variety of actual or potential conflicts. Basic anxiety

> . . . carries the germ for a potential conflict between the desire to rely on others, and the impossibility to do so because of deep distrust of and hostility toward them. It means that because of intrinsic weakness the person feels a desire to put all responsibility upon others, to be protected and taken care of, whereas because of the basic hostility there is much too much distrust to carry out this desire. And invariably the consequence is that he has to put the greatest part of his energies into securing reassurance (Horney, 1937, p. 96).

Horney, in *The Neurotic Personality of Our Time,* claims that in our culture there are four principal generic ways in which a person tries to protect himself against basic anxiety. One is by securing affection (or what often passes for affection) in any form and often at considerable cost to one's own sorely diminished integrity so that the other person will not want to hurt one. The second is by being submissive to other persons or to institutions in the hope that one will not be hurt and will be protected because one is compliant. The third is by gaining power—factual power or success, possessions, admiration, or intellectual superiority—in the hope that no one can hurt one. The fourth is by withdrawing emotionally from others, by becoming emotionally detached from them so that no one or nothing will hurt or disappoint one.

These four ways of protecting oneself constitute powerful motivations. Any one of them can be effective in bringing reassurance if one's life situation permits its adoption and pursuit without incurring conflicts. The trouble is that frequently one's social situation does not permit the exclusive pursuit of only one of them. Life is too complex, as a rule, for that. Furthermore, the person is usually driven by more than one of these motivations, and they are in varying degrees incompatible, especially the striving for affection and the striving for power. As a result, existing conflicts and anxieties are greatly intensified, often to the point where one's abilities are gravely undermined.

In several books Horney has analyzed the workings of these incompatible strivings in detail and their consequences for the well-being and happiness of the individual. In *Self-analysis,* for example, she discusses ten such strategies.

So far I have stressed the role of anxiety, which Horney thinks is closely connected with hostility. However, she says that in principle any impulse has the potential power to provoke anxiety provided that its discovery or pursuit would mean a violation of other vital interests or needs, and provided also that it is sufficiently imperative or passionate. In other words, the yielding to any imperative or compelling impulse which would, or which would seem to, entail a catastrophe for the self arouses intense anxiety. Thus the nature of the particular threatening impulse will depend partly on accidental individual experience and partly on the given sociocultural framework. Nevertheless Horney insists that in the neuroses of our time hostile impulses—*repressed* hostile impulses—are the main psychological force promoting anxiety. She also thinks that certain sociological conditions and arrangements foster hostility and anxiety.

It is particularly those hostile impulses, if uncontrolled, which threaten a catastrophe to the self. But why then are they repressed? (The reader will recall that it was Freud who first showed the significance of repression in the etiology of neurosis.) Why are they not retained in consciousness so that one may have an opportunity to control them and perhaps assimilate them into the totality of one's feelings and attitudes, where one could perhaps reduce them to a more realistic perspective or even remove or circumvent their causes? Horney asserts that whether one controls or represses hostility is not a matter of choice because repression is a reflexlike process. If it is unbearable to be aware that one is hostile, repression occurs. The main "reasons" given in *The Neurotic Personality of Our Time* are that one may love or need a person at the same time that one is hostile toward him; that one may not want to see the reasons, such as envy and possessiveness, which have provoked the hostility; and that it may be frightening to recognize hostility within oneself toward anyone. Repression is the shortest and quickest means toward reassurance—however inadequate such a reassurance may turn out to be. The frightening hostility disappears from awareness or, in certain circumstances, is kept from entering awareness.

Of course, hostility does not then cease to be. When repressed it "revolves" within one as an affect which is highly explosive, readily capable of increasing intensity, until it may reach the point of eruption and some sort of discharge. And at some level of awareness, one registers the existence of such an emotion.

Horney's formulation of basic hostility is not too clear. It seems, according to her account of it, to develop in two main stages. In the first stage it becomes repressed and operates without the person's realizing precisely what has happened to him. Then a second, reflexlike process sets in as the individual projects or externalizes his hostile impulses to the outside world. The second stage is required by the first. The individual is compelled to believe that the hostile impulses come not from within himself but from someone or something outside because recognition of their true source would be intolerable. Among other things, the projection serves the need of self-justification. After the second stage has developed, the outside world seems formidable indeed.

Although Horney stresses the capacity of hostility to generate anxiety, she points out that the converse also holds. When based on a feeling of being menaced, anxiety easily provokes a "reactive hostility" in defense of supposed dangers. Reactive hostility can in turn create anxiety, or more anxiety, and thus a "cycle" or vicious circle is built up. "This effect of reciprocity between hostility and anxiety," she says, "one always generating and reinforcing the other, enables us to understand why we find in neuroses such an enormous amount of relentless hostility" (1937, p. 74).

The anxiety experienced by the adult is not the same as that experienced by the child. (This applies to hostility also.) Adult anxiety is not a repetition of childhood anxiety; the former has grown out of the latter, is continuous with it, but is more complex. In *Neurosis and Human Growth,* Horney says:

> What in adult neurotics we identify as basic anxiety is not basic anxiety in its original form but rather modified by the accretions acquired through the years from the intrapsychic processes. It has become a composite attitude toward others which is determined by more complex factors than those involved at first (p. 297).

These complex factors are described at great length in that book.

In her writings subsequent to *The Neurotic Personality of Our Time,* Horney seems to attach less importance to hostility in the etiology of neurosis, but she retains the notion of basic anxiety as fundamental to the evolution of neurosis. In *Our Inner Conflicts,* she modifies her formulation of neurosis as follows: The child's efforts to cope with basic anxiety generate certain trends (ways of trying to deal with the basic anxiety) which together represent a basic attitude toward others and the self and a particular philosophy of life. These trends fall into three categories: moving *toward* people, *against* them, or *away* from them.

When a child moves toward people he accepts his own helplessness and tries to win the affection of others and to lean on them. In this way, and only in this way, can he feel safe with them. By being compliant he gains a feeling of belonging which makes him feel less weak and isolated.

The child who moves against people takes for granted and accepts the hostility around him but consciously or unconsciously determines to fight. He wishes to be stronger than they and defeat them for the sake of his own protection and for revenge. Insofar as opportunity permits, he rebels.

The child who moves away from people wants to stay apart. He believes he has not much in common with others and that they do not understand him. So he builds up a world of his own: nature, dolls, books, animals, dreams.

Horney claims in *Our Inner Conflicts* that in each of the three attitudes an element involved in basic anxiety is overemphasized, that is, helplessness in the first, hostility in the second, and isolation in the third. But owing to the conditions under which the child develops, he cannot accept one of those attitudes to the exclusion of the others, and thus the seeds of lasting conflict are sown. The child who is consistently subjected to the various kinds of destructive experience mentioned above and who fails to encounter or to benefit from corrective experience, tends to develop the various defensive attitudes into rigid patterns. As he grows older he will be driven to comply, to fight, or to be aloof regardless of the objective situation. Should he behave otherwise he would be thrown into a "panic." Thus when all three rigidly molded patterns are present in an intense degree, he is trapped in severe conflict. These attitudes gradually pervade the entire personality, encompassing the person's relation to others, to himself, and to life in general. It is the conflict born of such incompatible attitudes that constitutes the core of every neurosis. Horney calls this conflict "basic." Neurosis is a protective edifice built around the basic conflict.

Therapy. The conflict or conflicts can be resolved only by *changing* those inner (intrapsychic) conditions which created them. The therapeutic goal is to change those conditions. "The neurotic must be helped to retrieve himself, to become aware of his real feelings and wants, to evolve his own set of values, and to relate himself to others on the basis of his feelings and convictions" (Horney, 1945, p. 220).

Psychoanalysis has two main parts or phases. One phase is the analysis in detail of all the unconscious attempts by the patient at solution (not *resolution,* which would entail removal) of the basic conflict and the analysis of the effect those attempts have on his whole personality. The therapist proceeds to analyze all the implications of the patient's predominant attitude, his idealized image (or pattern of self-inflation), his pattern of externalization (the tendency to experience internal processes as if they occurred outside oneself and, usually, to hold them responsible for one's difficulties), etc., *without* overtly taking into account their specific relationship to the underlying conflict. Although these defensive reactions have grown out of the need to reconcile conflicts, they have acquired a life of their own, "carrying their own weight and wielding their own power," or what Allport calls "functional autonomy" (Horney, 1945, p. 221). Horney asserts that it is useless to confront a patient with any major conflict as long as he is bent on pursuing phantoms that to him mean salvation. He must first become aware of (gain insight into) the fact that these pursuits are futile and self-defeating. These defensive reactions have to be worked through in order that one may get to the underlying conflicts.

In the second phase of analysis the therapist helps the patient to become aware of his conflicts, not only of their general outline, but also of their operation in detail. Furthermore, any neurotic attitude or conflict that "crystallizes" during analysis has to be understood in its relation to the entire personality. Such an understanding is directed primarily *not* at a genetic history but at the various ways the attitudes and conflicts are manifested in the patient's present life.

Fundamentals. Horney thought that the most significant of Freud's assumptions and discoveries were those "doctrines" which maintain that psychic processes are strictly determined, that actions and feelings may be determined by unconscious motivations, and that the motivations "driving us" are emotional forces.

Another contribution of Freud's which Horney has adopted is his discovery of defense mechanisms: repression, projection, sublimation, reaction formation, etc. In her theories she makes full use of them.

Also, she has retained and employed Freud's techniques of therapy and most of the concepts, such as transference, resistance, and free association, employed in classical psychoanalysis.

Revision of Freudian psychology. In *New Ways in Psychoanalysis,* Horney attempts a revision of a large part of Freud's psychology. Unfortunately I do not have the space to explicate and discuss her ideas in detail, though I consider them important. For various reasons, she holds that the libido theory is unproved; that, furthermore, it contributes toward a distorted perspective on human relationships, on neurotic phenomena, and on the role of cultural factors in personality; and that it imposes needless limitations on therapy. She regards the Oedipus complex as an abnormal development due to the feelings, attitudes, and actions of parents who suffer various psychological distortions. While childhood experience is enormously important in the evolution of personality, it is by no means definitive. As one grows older, his personality continues to develop in either a healthy or a maladaptive direction.

More generally, Horney, on various grounds, rejects Freud's instinct theories. Therefore, in her view, they do not constitute man's basic motivations. "Man is ruled," she says, "not by the pleasure principle alone but by two guiding principles: safety and satisfaction" (1939, p. 73). In actual fact, the pleasure principle has little significance in her theories. It is *safety* that she stresses:

> People can renounce food, money, attention, affection so long as they are only renouncing satisfaction, but they cannot renounce these things if without them they would be or feel in danger of destitution or starvation or of being helplessly exposed to hostility, in other words, if they would lose their feeling of safety (1939, p. 73).

This statement is poorly formulated and seems self-contradictory. Horney's meaning is, I think, that safety designates not only absence of physical distress and the dread of it, but also absence of various other fears and anxieties. It is the compelling need for emotional security, especially in the "neurotic," that she wants to emphasize.

She has been severely criticized for these assumptions about human motivations. Freudian psychologists have criticized her for slighting libidinal strivings; others, for slighting man's strivings for growth and self-realization. In *Neurosis and Human Growth,* she attempts to overcome the latter criticism. She asserts that there is an inherent tendency in the child toward self-realization, culminating, under favorable conditions, in the development of the "real self" (1950, pp. 13ff.). But owing to a variety of adverse conditions, a child may not be permitted to develop the real self and instead develops an "idealized self," a sort of pseudoself, which "answers all his stringent needs" and becomes a "comprehensive neurotic solution" (Horney, 1950, p. 23). Unfortunately, Horney does not demonstrate how the potential real self, because of adverse circumstances, gives way to the development of an idealized (pseudo) self. Her assumption has no logical force and clarifies little, if anything, about the etiology of neurosis.

Concluding remarks. To my mind, the fundamental theoretical shortcoming in Horney's theories is that she has *no* real theory of personality development and structure. Her criticisms of Freud, however keen and valuable, do not add up to a theory of her own. Her major contribution—and it is a great one—lies in her theories and observations about the neurotic personality. For these, I surmise, almost every psychotherapist is indebted to her.

Erich Fromm

Like Horney, Fromm retains certain theoretical assumptions and discoveries of Freud. But, unlike Horney and others, he strikes out boldly for a theory of history and of the forces governing social life and human nature. Fromm is not, I think, an orthodox Marxist. He is perhaps more accurately called a neo-Marxist who tries to combine various Freudian insights with the Marxian idea of historical materialism and with various ideas of his own. While there are other influences to be found in Fromm's Weltanschauung, Freud and Marx seem to be the most important.

In *Escape from Freedom,* he proclaimed that human nature, though it is the product of biological and historical evolution, has certain inherent mechanisms and laws, whose discovery is the task of psychology. Although man can adapt himself to almost any conceivable condition of life, there are limits to his adaptability. Human nature is not indefinitely malleable. Certain aspects of man's nature are fixed and unchangeable, but others are not. In regard to the latter, strivings and character traits by which men differ from one another manifest a great amount of plasticity and malleability.

Man is governed by two kinds of basic needs. One kind is rooted in the physiological condition of man: physiological needs such as hunger, thirst, the need for sleep and rest, etc. These may be categorized as the need for self-preservation. The other equally compelling generic need may be summed up as the need to be related to the world, or, in other words, the need to avoid aloneness. This need is not rooted in bodily processes but in the very essence of "the human mode and practice of life," in man's mind or spirit. There are many kinds or manifestations of relatedness, some of which may be noble, and some base and degrading, as in the instance of the Nazi storm trooper or the Communist assassin.

The need to be related to the world manifests itself in various passionate strivings, emotions, and character traits. At any given time and place, they are, with a qualification to be noted later, determined by the socioeconomic order. But any social order is itself an outcome of historical evolution; or, more simply, it has a history. Thus, those drives which make for differences in men's characters, such as love and hatred, the lust for power, and the yearning for submission, are said to be products of the social process. "Man's nature, his passions, and anxieties are a cultural product; as a matter of fact, man himself is the most important creation and achievement of the continuous human effort, the record of which we call history" (Fromm, 1941, p. 13).

But although man's energies are thus shaped into specific forms of expression—canalized—they in turn, over a period of time, become productive forces molding the social process. For example, Protestantism caused men in Protestant countries to have a craving to work. This craving, which was itself an outcome of various historical circumstances, became a powerful force in the further development of capitalism.

Within limits, individuals and social groups adapt dynamically to given conditions of life. An individual adapts himself to various external conditions, and in doing so, drives, attitudes, emotions, and character traits which make up a given character structure embodying a certain relatedness to the world are created. Analogously, social groups react dynamically to various sociopsychological and ideological conditions. In doing so they develop a certain type of character embracing a certain constellation of traits—called the "social character"—which they, so to speak, share. It is contrasted with the "individual character," by which people belonging to the same society differ from one another. The individual character is an outcome of the unique hereditary and environmental conditions which influence a person's life, operating in conjunction with those experiences which are common to most people in a given society.

(Critical readers may ask how the traits of the social character are combined with those of the individual character. While Fromm has some suggestive things to say about the interfusion of traits in *Man for Himself*, he has not attempted a detailed analysis. Perhaps a study of Allport's theory of traits in *Pattern and Growth in Personality* would supplement Fromm's characterology.)

The social character has to be understood in terms of its function for a society as a whole. Fromm claims that each society is structuralized and operates in certain ways which are necessitated by a number of objective conditions: methods of economic production and distribution, political and geographical factors, cultural influences, etc. Societies change in the course of historical evolution, but at any given period social structures are relatively fixed; and a society can exist only by functioning within the framework of its particular structure:

> It is the function of the social character to shape the energies of the members of the society in such a way that their behavior is not left to conscious decisions whether or not to follow the social pattern but that *people want to act as they have to act* and at the same time find gratification in acting according to the requirements of the culture (Fromm, 1949, p. 5).

The social character serves the function of molding human energy for the purpose of the functioning of a given society.

Character is no mere agglomeration of traits. It has a definite structure. Character traits form a syndrome which results from a particular organization. Man's character system is said to be the human substitute for the instinctive apparatus of the animal. It enables him to act consistently and more or less efficiently. It is the basis of his adjustment to society. From infancy onward, one's character is molded by the parents—by their feelings, attitudes, and behavior and by their methods of child training. The family is the first and most important educational influence on the child. It is the first psychological agency of society he encounters. Later, when one enters kindergarten, school becomes of great importance. And perhaps still later, mass media of communication in modern society play no small role in conditioning one's character.

So far, the discussion of character has been rather general and abstract. It needs to be supplemented in a more concrete fashion. Because man must eat and drink, sleep and rest, and protect himself in various ways he must work—unless he can exploit others. But one does not work at large. One works in a specific place at a given time under definite social and cultural conditions which one, as an individual, must accept and cannot change. Different societies, owing to their differing social structures, have different kinds of work and different social conditions. The latter require different kinds of personalities, and they make for different kinds of relatedness to the world. So the stage is set for man when he is born. In *Escape from Freedom* Fromm proclaimed that the mode of the individual's life as it is shaped by the peculiarity of an economic system is the primary factor in determining his whole character structure. Subsequently he attributed some weight to other factors, political, religious, etc., but he always stressed the economic.

Emergence of the individual and the problem of freedom. Characterology is a major theme in Fromm's writings, a theme which I shall return to presently. Another is individuation and various related matters, especially the problem of freedom—personal and cultural—with its long evolutionary growth and decline in contemporary society. Since Fromm conceives of freedom as the heart and soul of the phenomenon of individuality, I shall discuss the two concurrently. He conceives of freedom as grounded in the nature of human existence and therefore in some sense ontologically grounded. Freedom, he says, "characterizes human existence as such." But its meaning changes (and enlarges), he adds, according to the degree of man's awareness and conception of himself as an independent and separate being.

Fromm claims that the social history of man began with his emerging from a state of oneness with the natural world to an awareness of himself as an entity separate from surrounding nature and from men. But for a long period of time this awareness remained very dim. He experienced himself largely as one with nature and his tribe or clan, to which he was related by ties of blood. This feeling of oneness with the world, in which one cannot experience himself as a separate and unique individual, is characterized by Fromm as "primary ties." These primary ties are said to block man's full human development, standing in the way of the development of his reason and critical capacities and not permitting him to recognize himself and others except through participation as a member of a clan or social or religious community. They block his development as a free, productive individual with the capacity to live according to the dictates of his reason and will.

But primary ties serve another function. Since man in such a community belongs to a structuralized whole in which he has an unquestionable place and status, he is secure and is not threatened with uncertainty, doubt, isolation, and aloneness. Only over an indefinitely long period of time are those primary ties broken, after man's reason and will have developed beyond a certain point. And then he is faced with a dilemma which I shall discuss in connection with ontogenetic development.

Ontogeny recapitulates phylogeny. Ontogenetically, the process described also occurs. After one is born he becomes a biologically separate entity, but for a period of time he remains functionally one with his mother, partly because he is fed, carried, and taken care of in every vital respect by her. Gradually, as a result of maturation and learning, he slowly begins to experience the world as outside him, as apart from him. Gradually the primary ties are broken. The normal child begins a quest for freedom and independence, though in the main the extent and limits of such a quest are set by social conditions. Even a Socrates is unthinkable in the Homeric era.

This process of increasing, growing individuation also has two incompatible aspects which I have merely brushed so far. In the course of his physical and psychological development, the child grows stronger emotionally, physically, and mentally. Gradually an organized structure guided by the individual's reason and will begins to appear—the self. But this process of individuation has another aspect, namely, growing aloneness. Fromm claims that to the extent to which the child emerges from the world of primary ties, which entailed security and belonging, he becomes aware of being alone, of being an entity separate from all others. Since the world is overwhelmingly powerful in comparison with oneself and one's powers and abilities, and often threatening and dangerous, it, or separation from it, creates a feeling of powerlessness and anxiety. As long as a child or a person in a community where the primary ties have not yet been broken remains an integral part of the world, unaware of the possibilities and responsibilities of individual action, he has no call to be afraid of it. But, according to Fromm, when one becomes an individual, one stands alone and faces the world in all its perilous and overpowering aspects.

Then freedom may become a curse. The person is assailed by doubt, anxiety, feelings of helplessness, and the horror of nothingness. Man cannot stand alone, unrelated to the world, naked and shivering in the long shadow of eternity. Hence the individual is often driven by a desire to abandon his individuality and freedom in order to overcome his experiences of aloneness and powerlessness by submerging himself in the world outside. One may retreat into secondary ties. These new ties, arising from compelling impulses to give up one's individuality, are not identical with primary ties, for the process of individuation is irreversible. As Thomas Wolfe has said, "you can't go home again." Attempts to reverse the process assume the character of submission: to another person or, somewhat later in life, perhaps an institution or the community at large, with its traditional norms and uniformities of behavior.

Thus, for example, when the growing child abandons his individuality by submitting to parents and others, he may consciously feel secure, but unconsciously he knows the price he has paid, a realization that makes him fundamentally more insecure, which in turn results in hostility and rebelliousness. This outcome is all the more frightening since the hostility and rebelliousness are directed against the persons on whom he is dependent. So he feels compelled to engage in further and deeper acts of submission.

The development of freedom and individuality, with its "dialectic" character of incompatible phases, does not necessarily end in submission. Given certain favorable conditions in the family and society, a genuine solution to the problem of freedom may be found. Fromm calls it a "spontaneous" relationship to man and nature, a relationship that unites the individual with the world without depriving him of his individuality. This kind of relationship is realized primarily through the exercise of reason, love, and productive work.

Why then do men abandon their individuality? Why cannot they overcome the dilemma of uniqueness? Fromm's answer is that the growth of the individual self (the "real self") is hampered by a number of individual and social conditions, thus creating a lag between *freedom from* (instinctive determination and the bonds of primary ties) and *freedom to* (develop one's potentialities and preserve one's integrity). In *Escape from Freedom* and *The Sane Society,* he attempts an analysis of the historical and social arrangements and circumstances which he thinks have limited man's freedom and individuality. He is fiercely critical of the economic, political, religious, educational, and other institutions of Western society. While I think his analysis is oversimplified and polemical, I shall leave these matters to the specialists in those fields.

In *Escape from Freedom* and *The Sane Society,* Fromm offers certain suggestions for a revolutionary change in the structure of Western society. These suggestions do not seem to me very promising at the present time, and a discussion of them would exceed the scope of this chapter.

MECHANISMS OF ESCAPE. The lag between *freedom from* and *freedom to* has resulted in several kinds of mechanisms of escape from freedom in order to overcome unbearable feelings of isolation and powerlessness. These mechanisms include maoschism, sadism, destructiveness, and automaton conformity. While they entail the loss of individuality and freedom, they are also ways of relating to the world.

Types of temperament. Fromm distinguishes sharply between temperament and character, the two constituting personality. Temperament is inborn, while character is acquired. *How* one reacts to events depends on one's temperament. A person who reacts quickly and strongly (intensely) may be said to have a choleric temperament; one who reacts quickly and weakly (feebly), a sanguine temperament; one who reacts slowly and strongly, a melancholic temperament; and one who reacts slowly and weakly, a phlegmatic temperament. Thus temperament is a "mode of reaction."

Types of character. *What* one reacts to is in the main governed by one's character. For example, a sadistic person may tend to react quickly and strongly or in any of the other modes, according to his temperament. The loving person will react analogously according to his temperament. But sadism and love are expressions of two different kinds of character. The sadistic person and the loving person respond to quite different situations and objects, or they respond quite differently, as a rule, to similar situations and objects.

In *Man for Himself* Fromm has elaborated a more comprehensive theory of character. It is obviously indebted to Freud and, to a lesser extent, Marx. While Freud's theory is founded on his theory of libido, Fromm's is based on the specific kinds of a person's relatedness to the world. Man is said to relate himself in two ways. One way is by acquiring and assimilating "things," called the "process of assimilation." The other way is by relating himself to people and to himself, called the "process of socialization." There are many ways of acquiring things, just as there are many ways of relating to people. The two "orientations" constitute the core of one's character. Fromm defines character as the relatively permanent form in which human energy is canalized in the processes of assimilation and socialization. A person's behavior is said to be rooted in his character; so are his thoughts, judgments, feelings, attitudes, and perceptions. Although character is acquired, once a person develops a given type of character, it tends to remain fixed and unalterable under normal conditions of life.

Four types of nonproductive orientation in the processes of assimilation and socialization and one type of productive orientation are distinguished. These orientations constitute types of character. The various kinds of character are "ideal types," not the descriptions of the characters of actual people. No one manifests or embodies any character type in pure form. But people do manifest constellations of traits which, according to Fromm, are predominantly those of one or the other of his ideal types. Certain combinations or blends of character traits within the nonproductive orientations and of character traits within the nonproductive orientations with those in the productive are said to be possible, but I omit them because they are not well worked out and are seemingly of no great explanatory importance. The theoretical model is as shown in the accompanying table.

Assimilation	***Socialization***
Nonproductive orientation:	
Receiving	Masochistic
Exploiting	Sadistic
Hoarding	Destructive
Marketing	Indifferent
Productive orientation:	
Working	Loving, reasoning

NONPRODUCTIVE CHARACTER TYPES. Owing to considerations of space at my disposal, I shall not for the most part attempt a detailed explication of the various types of character.

In the receptive orientation the person feels or believes that the only way to get or have what he wants, whether this is material things, ideas, emotional experiences (such as love), or something else, is to *receive* it from an outside source. His attitude toward life is essentially passive, as I shall point out in the discussion of masochism.

While the person who has developed the *exploitative* orientation also feels that the source of all good is found in the outside world, he tries to get what he wants by taking it away from others, either by force (whether physical or moral) or by cunning. He perceives and experiences other people as *things* to use and exploit in all spheres of life experience.

The person who possesses a hoarding orientation has little faith in anything new he might get from the outside world or create himself. His security is derived from saving and hoarding. For him, spending is a threat. In a manner of speaking, he surrounds himself with a protective wall. His main aim in life is to bring in as much as possible and to keep and preserve it within this fortified position. Such a person is miserly about material things, feelings, thoughts, etc. He tends to believe that his stock would be diminished by use and cannot be replenished. In Freudian psychology he is called an "anal character." Thus, for example, for such a person love means possession. In the realm of thought he is sterile and incapable of productive thinking.

The connection between hoarding and destructiveness is obscure. I fail to see it. I can find neither a logical nor an empirical connection between them as they are formulated in Fromm's writings. When I discuss his concept of destructiveness, this problem will perhaps be clearer.

The marketing orientation is said to be an outcome of the phenomenon of the modern economic market. It may be well, at this point, to remind the reader that Fromm leans toward the view that economic factors are the major, though not the sole, determinants of the evolution of social institutions and of the social character as well. Fromm does not attempt to demonstrate the truth of this assumption, though he occasionally offers illustrations of what he thinks the connection is. It would seem, for example, that in the twentieth century, political and ideological factors are at least equally important, but in Fromm's thinking economic determinism looms much larger.

The economic market, he points out, is no longer a meeting place where producers and consumers meet face to face for the purpose of exchanging commodities. In the traditional local market, where goods were exchanged by barter, Fromm seems to imply that use value was a controlling factor, though he is not explicit on this point. In any case, the modern economic market is no longer a meeting place, where the demand is more or less known, but a "mechanism" characterized by abstract and impersonal demand. Though one produces for this market, he does not produce for a known circle of customers. The laws of supply and demand govern this market. Operating according to these laws, it determines whether a commodity can be sold, in what quantity, and at what price. No matter what the use value of a commodity may be, unless it is in demand on the market, its exchange value (or market value) is nil.

The emphasis on market value rather than on use value "has led to" a similar concept of value in interpersonal relations and in the person's attitude toward himself. In other words, people experience themselves as commodities, not *persons,* to be bought and sold on the "personality market." And they value themselves accordingly, in terms of their success on this market. "Clerks and salesmen, business executives and doctors, lawyers and artists all appear on this market" (Fromm, 1947, p. 69). They offer their personalities for sale, being dependent for their material success on a personal acceptance by those who employ them. Hence they must know how to sell their personalities. To be sure, the type of personality required partly depends on the special field in which one works. The personality of a college professor, for example, will be somewhat different from that of a salesman. But in every case, there is one necessary condition: to be in demand.

For this purpose people are "conditioned" in a general way from kindergarten through high school or college. This educational process is implemented by the family. Pictorial magazines, newspapers, pictorial advertising, moving pictures, and television provide specific models for success.

Thus it comes about that more and more people orient their lives toward learning to be a success and acting accordingly. They become passionately concerned, not with developing their powers of reason, imagination, feeling, and will, but with being salable. They subordinate or ignore self-realization for the sake of success. And self-identity is an outcome primarily of self-realization, of the development of what Fromm would call "specifically human powers," such as reason and love. Hence people's human powers become masked from them. Both the powers they have and what they create are estranged, as though different from, or external to, them, to be judged and used by others.

If one's estimation of his own worth or value depends on his success—a success that is dependent on others and largely defined by them—one is in constant need of confirmation by others. A setback in the relentless struggle for success is experienced as a severe threat to one's self-esteem. Insecurity becomes one's constant companion. Moreover, one experiences and judges others as one experiences oneself. That is, not only oneself but also others are experienced as commodities, a state of affairs that is reinforced by the fact that others also present only or chiefly their salable aspect. Hence the relationships between people become superficial and boring. Everyone is "alone, afraid to fail, eager to please."

In addition to the market, the mode of production is another factor, though it is closely related to the market function:

> Enterprises become bigger and bigger; the number of people employed by these enterprises as workers or clerks grows incessantly; ownership is separated from management, and the industrial giants are governed by a professional bureaucracy interested mainly in the smooth functioning and in the expansion of their enterprise rather than in the personal greed for profit per se (Fromm, 1963, p. 97).

In order to function smoothly, our society needs men who cooperate easily in large groups, who wish to consume more and more, and whose tastes are standarized and easily influenced and anticipated. Our society is said to need men who feel free and independent, who are not subject to any authority or principle or individual conscience, and who are yet willing to be commanded, to do what is expected, and to fit into the social machine without friction. Thus our society needs men who can be guided without force, led without leaders, and prompted without an aim, except the aim to be on the move, to function, to go ahead.

This kind of man is the alienated man, whom modern industrial society has produced—the "automaton" (cf. Fromm, 1955, pp. 120ff.). His actions and his own life-forces have become estranged from him. They rule him through the things and institutions into which his life-forces have been transformed.

Before taking up the nonproductive orientations in the process of socialization, I wish to mention that the distinction between assimilation and socialization seems to me artificial and raises otherwise unnecessary problems, such as the relation of the hoarding to the destructive orientation. Furthermore, the marketing orientation seems to pertain more to a way of relating to people than to assimilating things; in other words, logically it seems to come under the heading "socialization." Still again the explanations of the receptive and exploitative orientations are largely repetitious of the explanations of masochism and sadism; the former offer little that is new. In other words, everything that Fromm has to say about character could logically be subsumed under socialization, and nothing of value would be lost, though some revision might be required.

First in the list of orientations under socialization is *masochism*. Masochistic strivings appear most frequently in feelings of inferiority, powerlessness, and individual insignificance. A person in whom such tendencies predominate may consciously complain about them and want to get rid of them, but unconsciously he is driven to feel inferior and insignificant. Sometimes such a person may experience his masochistic strivings as irrational. More often he will rationalize them and conceive of them as love or loyalty or as due to unchangeable circumstances, etc.

The masochistic person escapes unbearable feelings of aloneness and powerlessness by becoming a part of a bigger and more powerful whole outside himself and by submerging himself and participating in it: a person, an institution, the nation, God, conscience, or a psychic compulsion. He gets rid of the individual self because, for him, it entails excruciating conflict and a freedom that has become unbearable. In doing so, he submits and sacrifices his reason, his will, his integrity, and his spontaneity to someone or something more powerful than he.

The person who has a *sadistic* character tries to have complete mastery over another person, to make him a helpless object, to become the absolute ruler over him, and to do with him as he pleases. He may exploit the "object" materially, intellectually, and emotionally. He may make him suffer or want to see him suffer in all sorts of ways. Thus he gains a modicum of conscious security by "swallowing" the other person, and he "enlarges" himself by making the other a part of himself in the hope that he will regain the strength he lost by abandoning his individuality and freedom. For the sadistic person also cannot bear the individual self, since it also entails conflict and the burden of freedom. And while he makes the other person a "part" of himself, he himself becomes a part of the other in a kind of psychological fusion or symbiosis. Still, in a relationship of this sort, one kind of striving, the kind that complements the other, will usually be uppermost in each person in a given situation.

So, while I have written of masochistic and sadistic persons for the sake of ease of exposition, I must point out that the two kinds of strivings are regularly found in the same person, as Freud discovered long ago, and are always blended with each other. Both are outcomes of the same need, and both entail what Fromm calls "symbiosis": "the union of one individual self with another self (or any other power outside the own self) in such a way as to make each lose the integrity of its own self and to make them completely dependent on each other" (1941, p. 158).

There is said to be a constant oscillation between the active and the passive sides of the symbiotic relationship, though at any given time, and depending on various circumstances, one side or the other may appear to be predominant. Hence one speaks of a sadomasochistic character.

Fromm, in *Escape from Freedom,* distinguishes between a normal and a neurotic sadomasochist. The distinction rests on sociocultural considerations. Whether a sadomasochistic person is normal or neurotic largely depends on the particular tasks people in his society have to fulfill and on what patterns of feeling and behavior are current in the particular sociocultural framework. If most people in the society, or in a particular social class within the society, because of their circumstances in life, the tasks they perform, and the sociocultural framework within which they live, share the character structure described as sadomasochistic, then any person in the society or social class who possesses this particular constellation of traits is said to be normal. In other words, the social character of people in that society or social class is typically sadomasochistic as previously outlined. Hence their ways of life are governed by relationships of "dominance-submission."

Fromm has little to say about the neurotic sadomasochist. The neurotic sadomasochist is not able to gain the support from society which the normal sadomasochist can. The latter, to be sure, still suffers from the underlying conflict between desires to be independent and strong and desires to submerge himself in the world outside or to keep himself submerged and dependent, and he also suffers silent unhappiness. Lacking the support of society, the sadomasochist suffers more intensive conflicts and anxieties, for he is not united with millions of others who share such feelings. He will be much less likely to find socially approved outlets for his feelings and strivings. Hence he tends to feel more alone and isolated.

Fromm has a justly famous psychological analysis of authority which I can hardly deal with adequately in a brief space. The sadomasochist, he says, "loves" power over others, while at the same time he is willing to submit to those who are more powerful than he. He despises the powerless, whom he delights in embarrassing, humiliating, dominating, attacking, and hurting. In general, he has great admiration for powerful persons and institutions but is contemptuous of persons or institutions who lack power. His gods are the kings and captains of this world.

A distinction is made between rational and irrational authority. Rational authority rests on competence. One who wields this kind of authority has a specific task to perform, and when it is accomplished the relationship between him and those under his authority ends. Their interests are not antagonistic but complementary.

The "psychological situation" is said to be different in the two kinds of relationships also. Rational authority provokes elements of love, admiration, or gratitude. One may want to identify oneself with it either partially or wholly.

Irrational authority rests on force or cunning. Its purpose is exploitation. Hence the person or group exercising irrational authority wants to perpetuate the relationship with those subjected to it. Their interests are antagonistic.

In this state of affairs, the "subject" resents or hates the authority who exploits him. So, since he is more or less helpless, he has to repress his hostility and cover it up, perhaps with intense and blind conscious feelings of admiration.

Fromm has pointed out that any given authority may in varying degrees contain elements of both rational and irrational authority.

Although sadomasochistic strivings and attitudes are often blended with destructiveness, the latter is said to be an essentially different phenomenon. For the sake of clarity, I must emphasize that the formulation of destructiveness is poorly worked out. The concept seems to be employed in two different senses: as a character type and as a character trait. Thus it is conceived in *Escape from Freedom* variously as a mechanism of escape, as a character type, and as a character trait, which may or may not be dominant in one's character structure and which arises from anxiety and the thwarting of one's life.

A brief discussion will perhaps make these matters clearer. In *Escape from Freedom,* the person with a destructive character is said to aim at destroying the world, for he wishes to eliminate the threatening "object." If he succeeds in removing the threatening object or world (he believes), he will remain alone and isolated. To be sure, he will dwell in "splendid isolation," as Fromm puts it, in which he cannot be crushed by overwhelming external power or force. Destruction of the world is the last desperate attempt to save oneself.

This sort of character structure, it seems to me, may apply to someone overwhelmed by hatred or to some people who are psychotic. The chief difficulty with this formulation is that it is not consistent with one of Fromm's basic assumptions: the need to be related to the world. If one wishes to destroy the world, how can one wish to be related to it?

In *Man for Himself,* destructiveness is said to be the impulse to destroy others following upon the fear of being destroyed by them. But destructiveness is also formulated as the outcome of unlived life, of the thwarting of one's potentialities.

I have already mentioned another difficulty. How is hoarding correlated with desire to destroy the external world? Or, does the hoarding character suffer such severe thwarting that a person who belongs in this category must be destructive? These issues are not too clear.

Fromm makes a very helpful distinction between destructiveness as a trait (character-conditioned hatred) and reactive hostility or hate. Destructiveness is a constantly lingering tendency within a person, a passion which, in a manner of speaking, awaits only a favorable opportunity or situation to be triggered. Reactive hostility (rational hate) is a person's response to a threat to his own or another's life, freedom, or ideas. Its purpose is to preserve life, and it ceases to exist when the factually threatening object or situation has been removed. Character-conditioned hatred may be expressed against others or directed against oneself.

In *Escape from Freedom,* automaton conformity is formulated as a mechanism of escape, an orientation toward the world following upon the abandonment of one's integrity and individuality. It is said to be the particular solution that the majority of normal people in modern society find. One "adopts entirely the kind of personality offered to him by cultural patterns; and he therefore becomes exactly as all others are and as they expect him to be. The discrepancy between 'I' and the world disappears and with it the conscious fear of aloneness and powerlessness" (Fromm, 1941, pp. 185–186).

But why cannot automaton conformity apply equally logically to the authoritarian character? Apparently it can. Hence, on Fromm's assumptions, automaton conformity is the *instrumentality* by which the marketing orientation is acquired.

In *Man for Himself,* automaton conformity as an orientation to the world is replaced by indifference, though very little is said about the latter. It appears to signify an alienation from self and others, often compensated for by a feeling of self-inflation. Logically this notion is compatible with the marketing orientation.

PRODUCTIVE CHARACTER TYPE. The *idea* of productiveness has a long history, which of course Fromm is familiar with. One can find it in one form or another in the Bible, Greek philosophy, medieval philosophy, Renaissance thought, Enlightenment philosophy, and contemporary philosophy, especially in the works of John Dewey. It is surprising, therefore, that Fromm has not formulated his ideas more systematically. Even so there is no psychologist who attaches more significance to it. It is central to his whole psychology.

Productiveness is said to be man's realization of the potentialities characteristic of him, the use of his powers. Although it may be claimed that man has an indefinitely great number of powers, Fromm conceives of certain of these powers as comprising the essence of human nature. But man's specifically human powers can in varying degrees lie dormant or become perverted. It is the task of a science of man to infer the core common to the whole human race from the innumerable manifestations of human nature to be found in different individuals and cultures. Furthermore, while the essence of human nature is everywhere the same, it is never fully realized in any individual in any society at any given time. In the process of history, man gradually realizes or develops his potential, but the potential, the human essence, is always there in every individual.

No exact number of human powers is specified, nor can these powers be enumerated. In Fromm's view, only a science of man—which seems to include a philosophical anthropology as well as empirical science—can discover them. And it is a nice question whether, since the powers of man unfold through time, whose duration cannot be known, even a science of man can ever fully grasp the extent and quality of human nature. This question in turn raises problems of the methodology and philosophy of science.

Although Fromm does not claim that at present one can discover all the human powers which man possesses, his discussion of the productive orientation provides a handle to work with. The productive orientation is characterized mainly in terms of reason, love, and productive work. To a much lesser extent, powers of imagination and sense perception are occasionally discussed. In *The Sane Society,* Fromm indicates how the power of reason operates:

> Although biologically the brain capacity of the human race has remained the same for thousands of generations, it takes a long evolutionary process to arrive at *objectivity,* that is, to acquire the faculty to see the world, nature, other persons and oneself as they are, and not distorted by desires and fears. The more man develops this objectivity, the more he is in touch with reality, the more he matures, the better can he create a human world in which he is at home. Reason is man's faculty for grasping the world by thought, in contradiction to intelligence, which is man's ability to *manipulate* the world with the help of thought (1955, p. 64).

In *The Art of Loving,* Fromm attempts to link up his theory of love with his theory of human nature. The full answer to the "problem of human existence," a problem which Fromm has discussed in several books, "lies in the achievement of interpersonal union, of fusion with another person, in love" (Fromm, 1956, p. 18). The desire for interpersonal fusion is said to be the most powerful striving in man, a passion which keeps the human race together. "Without love humanity could not exist for a day" (Fromm, 1956, p. 18). But not every kind of interpersonal fusion is love. Love is union "under the condition of preserving one's integrity." Love is an activity, which primarily entails giving, not receiving or exploiting. Giving is an expression of potency, the ability to make productive use of one's powers. Normally giving of oneself does *not* mean self-sacrifice, though in some crucial circumstances self-sacrifice, including the sacrifice of the material self (as William James defined that term), may be the supreme expression of love. What then, normally does one give? He gives the other person "of his joy, of his interest, of his understanding, of his knowledge, of his humor, of his sadness." Thus he fosters and enriches the other person and enhances the other person's aliveness—and his own aliveness too. While giving is not for the sake of receiving—love is *not* an exchange—when one gives, he awakens something to life, something that perhaps has been dormant, in the other person, which in turn is reflected back. Thus the other person becomes a giver also, and both share in the joy that has been created.

The ability to love depends on the character development of the participants. One must have developed the ability to love, for one is born only with a potentiality which develops when favorable conditions are present, and not otherwise. The notion that anyone, no matter what his experiences in life may have been, can love is absurd. It is easy to become confused on this matter, for many people equate love with sex, sadism, or dependency.

According to Fromm, there are several basic elements common to all expressions of love. These are care, respect, knowledge, and responsibility. To care is to *care for,* to labor for the growth and happiness of another person, as a mother labors for the well-being and development of her child. Respect is the ability to see a person as he is—to be aware of his unique individuality and to endeavor to foster it, rather than to hinder or denigrate it. A necessary condition of respect for others is self-respect, an experience of one's own worth as a human being with an individual self. In order to respect a person one must know him, and this takes time. Knowledge of this sort requires more than the sheer exercise of reason; it involves direct experience of the other person in all his uniqueness and concreteness. Finallv. to be responsible means to be able to respond to the other person's needs and to be willing to foster and participate in their fulfillment. All four elements are interrelated.

Selfish people cannot love others, for they do not love themselves. For them, only that which is within themselves can be experienced as real. The world outside is experienced only from the viewpoint of its being useful or dangerous.

The theory of love rests on a theory of man. According to Fromm, the unique problem which faces man is separateness. Love overcomes, as nothing else can, this experience of separateness, though there are many other ways in which man seeks interpersonal fusion.

The *practice* of love, like the practice of any art, requires certain general conditions: discipline, concentration, patience, and a supreme concern with the mastery of the art. Since the art of loving is as comprehensive as the art of living, one must practice discipline, concentration, patience, and supreme concern throughout every phase of one's life. They must be practiced voluntarily, not as though they were externally imposed. Hence love presupposes virtue or excellence of character.

Fromm has many penetrating things to say about work in an "alienated society," that is, our capitalistic-managerial society, but it is difficult to formulate his ideas on *productive* work. Work is man's liberator from nature, his creator as a social and independent being, for it is work, production, that enables him to rise above the animal kingdom. "*In the process of work, that is, the molding and changing of nature outside of himself, man molds and changes himself*" (Fromm, 1955, pp. 177–178). Having mastered nature, he emerges from it and develops his powers of cooperation and of reason and his sense of beauty. Having separated himself from the original unity, he reunites himself as nature's master and builder. The more his work develops, the more his individuality is said to develop:

> Whether we think of the beautiful paintings in the caves of Southern France, the ornaments on weapons among primitive people, the statues and temples of Greece, the cathedrals of the Middle Ages, the chairs and tables made by skilled craftsmen, or the cultivation of flowers, trees or corn by peasants—all are expressions of the creative transformation of nature by man's reason and skill (Fromm, 1955, p. 178).

In contemporary industrial society, the worker's role is an essentially passive one. His is a small isolated function in a complicated and highly organized process of production, about which he knows little and cares less. He never encounters his "product" as a whole, save perhaps as a consumer. He is part of the machine which has become his master. His work is meaningless and profoundly boring, toward which he feels, perhaps unconsciously, hostile. Hence he becomes lazy. Thus one's life passes away in the work and pleasure routines, for pleasure too has become highly mechanized.

In order to overcome alienation, Fromm suggests in *The Sane Society* many economic, political, and cultural changes of a rather fundamental nature. The revolutionary's aim would be to create a work situation where man gives his lifetime and energy to something which has meaning for him. Likewise in such a situation, he would know what he is doing, have an influence on what is being done, and feel united with his fellow man. It is not very clear how all this might come about in a society as large and complex as that of the United States, though undoubtedly great changes will occur.

Mental health. The concept of mental health is said to follow from the conditions of human existence. Mental health is the same for man in all times and in all cultures. It

> . . . *is characterized by the ability to love and to create, by the emergence from incestuous ties to clan and soil, by a sense of identity based on one's experience of self as the subject and agent of one's powers, by the grasp of reality inside and outside of ourselves, that is, by the development of objectivity and reason* (Fromm, 1955, p. 69).

Harry Stack Sullivan

Sullivan first began to be known for his work with patients suffering from schizophrenic disorders. As a student of schizophrenia, he was an acknowledged master. During the course of his career, he worked with "neurotics" and became especially interested in obsessional neuroses. Gradually, over a period of about twenty-five years, he worked out a theory of interpersonal relations, for which he is best known, that is meant to apply to the mentally healthy as well as to the mentally ill. It is easy to pay lip service to the idea that there is no radical difference between those who are mentally ill and those who are not, but Sullivan really believed it and put this idea into practice. Thus his theory of interpersonal relations applies equally well in psychiatry and in social psychology, a field in which he has also been profoundly influential.

A second and related theory is of personality development, which he was beginning to work out systematically at the time of his untimely death. It remains rather rudimentary in detail but is still, I think, the best we have, and it has served others well in their researches.

A third is his theory of anxiety, still profoundly misunderstood by many. Perhaps I should add that Sullivan's theory is different from Freud's, though in this, as in many other matters, Sullivan is indebted to the great pioneer in psychiatry.

Even though in his lectures Sullivan lent a peculiar fascination to his interpretations and illustrations of the syndromes of mental disorders, he did not emphasize the neat classifications to be found in textbooks. Even so, he held that for certain purposes classifications are necessary, provided one does not forget that the patient is a person, not a "case." The patient's problems or difficulties (with the partial exception of certain "organic" disorders or inadequacies) have to do with his interpersonal relations, which have become distorted owing to an unfortunate life history. Psychiatric prognosis, Sullivan believed, may best be considered a specialized technique in social psychology.

Quite early in his professional life, he arrived at his interpersonal reorientation, as the following quotation from an article published in 1933 in the *Encyclopedia of the Social Sciences* makes clear:

> This approach [which he worked out] recognizes that the person, psychobiologically conceived, maintains organization, communal existence, and functional activity in and within both the physicochemical and the superorganic cultural universe. The study of the life course of the individual becomes more intelligible when personality is conceived as the hypothetical entity which manifests itself in interpersonal relations, the latter including interactions with other people, real or fancied, primarily or mediately integrated into dynamic complexes; and with traditions, customs, inventions, and institutions produced by man (reprinted in Sullivan, 1962, pp. 301–302).

He goes on to say that along with the elaboration of physicochemical factors, there is a progressive elaboration and differentiation of motives. The latter are acquired from one's experiences with a steadily expanding series of "culture surrogates," such as the mother, the family group, teachers, companions, chums, friends, love objects, enemies, employers, and colleagues. The motives manifest themselves in the integration of total situations involving two or more people, "real or fancied," and a variety of cultural "elements" or patterns. Within these motives there are said to be demands for certain activities, sometimes consciously formulated in terms of a goal and other times not consciously formulated, so that the activity is unnoticed by the participants.

Sullivan's use of the concept of "interpersonal relations" is perhaps not easy to grasp unless one has studied his lectures with care and an open mind. In trying to teach the theories based on this concept, I have often suggested the analogy of a tennis match. Almost everything that one participant does is in relation to what the other one does or is anticipated to do, and conversely. While the analogy is by no means perfect, it suggests the reciprocal interplay of human actions in situations where one is dealing with others.

But Sullivan did not confine his concept of interpersonal relations to actual situations where two or more people are involved. It includes situations where only one of the "participants" is physically present. The other may be physically absent, as, for example, when a diffident adolescent girl rehearses in advance what she will or will not say to her date and what she will or will not do or, subsequently, when she reviews in her mind what she *should* have said or done. Still again the "other" may have no physical existence but be strictly an "imaginary" person, that is, a complex symbolic, personified abstraction of past interpersonal experience. In this connection, novelists and schizophrenics come easily to mind. Finally an individual may perceive another person not as he appears to an objective observer but as a blend of qualities he has with qualities some other person in the individual's past life has had or even with qualities of an imaginary person. In a celebrated article, "Psychiatry: Introduction to the Study of Interpersonal Relations," Sullivan has shown how illusory "me-you" patterns function in interpersonal relations.

Clearly, Sullivan has tried to incorporate "intrapsychic" processes in his theory of interpersonal relations. In other words, following the lead of such men as Charles Horton Cooley and George Herbert Mead, he tried to show how the social world of which one is inextricably a part remains influential even when one is physically alone. This private world may or may not become public. It does become public to the extent that it is communicated.

But why are interpersonal relations, real or fancied or a blend of both, seemingly so all-important? Because man is a sociocultural being, as the quotation I gave suggests. From the time one is born, he has to be cared for by people until the time is reached when he can care for himself. In the meantime, the family, the school, the church, and other institutions and individuals provide for one's education ("acculturation"). From the innumerable interactions (or "transactions," to use Dewey and Bentley's terminology) with others in the home, school, church, playground, and so forth, the individual's personality gradually grows and develops until, under normal circumstances, he reaches adulthood.

What, then, is *personality*? It is *not* the organism, which constitutes for Sullivan the "substrate" of personality. It is not the self or spirit of traditional philosophy. Perhaps I will not lead the reader astray if I say it is a more sophisticated and profound version of William James' empirical self, with the emphasis on James' "social-me." Sullivan defined personality as "the relatively enduring pattern of recurrent interpersonal situations which characterizes a human life" (1953b, pp. 110–111). It is essential to bear in mind the extended sense in which he employs the notion of interpersonal relations. If space permitted, I could demonstrate that Sullivan actually employs *three* different approaches to the study of personality, including what is ordinarily called "intrapersonal" organization.

The "*self-dynamism*" or self-system or self is therefore not the same thing as personality. The latter is the more inclusive structure and includes both the self and dissociated dynamisms.

The psychological importance of self-esteem or self-respect in any person's life was brought home to Sullivan in his work with schizophrenic patients. He wrote in the *American Journal of Psychiatry* (1929–1930):

> In the course of our study it has seemed that in every case of schizophrenic illness there is to be found in the history of the individual a point at which there had occurred what might well be called a disaster to self-esteem. This event is attended subjectively by the state which we identify by the term *panic*. Panic customarily results from the utterly unexpected collapse of something very important in the life process of the individual (reprinted in Sullivan, 1962, p. 198).

Sullivan came to see that the preservation of self-esteem is one of the most powerful determinants of human behavior, with the concomitant necessity of warding off any threats to this preservation, failure of which entails anxiety or, in extreme cases, panic, which results in a grave disorganization of personality structure.

The self-dynamism. Self-esteem is a function of the self-dynamism, which evolves in great part, according to Sullivan, owing to the necessity of warding off anxiety and, as one grows, of protecting self-esteem. But anxiety is induced by "significant people," such as the parents, who embody in their own attitudes, thoughts, and behavior certain limitations and irrationalities of their society. The self is not synonymous with that to which we refer when we say "I" or "me," namely, the personified self. In addition to the personified self, the self-dynamism includes those processes and activities which we fail to attend to or "forget," owing to selective inattention, or which we simply fail to formulate. Briefly, the self is the locus of meaningful organization of life experience. In the main, the self is a product of one's experiences in interpersonal relations, especially those pertaining to the pursuits of satisfaction and security. The self does not include everything that one has lived, undergone, or "prehended." Owing to one's personal history, which is ordinarily closely connected with the social order of which one is a member, he cannot make sense of everything he encounters or "prehends," nor can anyone else. Only, or chiefly, those experiences which have meaning for the person in terms of his life history are incorporated into the self and become material for further enriching or more or less disabling experiences.

The question of why the self operates in this restrictive fashion may still arise. Why must the individual ignore, fail to comprehend, or forget many experiences that might be educating and enriching? Sullivan's answer is that this over-all restriction of awareness is a result of cultural limitations transmitted first and foremost in the home and, more generally, during the process of socialization—education in the broadest sense—which begins at birth or shortly after. Freud has pointed to such limitations in regard to sexual matters, but these are not the only ones or frequently even the most important ones. In his theory of personality development, Sullivan has tried to demonstrate how stage after stage the facilitations and limitations of the "culture complex" are acquired. He has formulated this idea rather succinctly as follows:

> The self-system is struck off in the personality because of the necessity for picking one's way through irrational and ununderstandable prescriptions of behavior laid down by the parents; in other words, the child has to be educated to a very complex social order, long before the reason and the good sense of the whole thing can be digested, long before it becomes understandable—if it ever does. And the self-system comes to be the organization that controls awareness; all the operations that are not primarily of the self go on outside awareness (1956, p. 4).

Usually Sullivan also stresses the irrational and ununderstandable elements of social life which the parents and others embody in their behavior.

Thus, once more, the *self* is not synonymous with *personality*, for some experiences, including motivational factors and behavior patterns, occur outside awareness and cannot ordinarily become conscious. These are the dissociated aspects of personality or, in traditional psychoanalytic language, deeply unconscious systems. They cannot be recognized by the self. One cannot usually assimilate them because they do not make sense in terms of one's past experience and one lacks real foresight as to what they portend. Indeed they are often terrifyingly antipathetic to the individual's self and his values. The therapist has to be aware of this fact and must usually proceed with caution when he explores the manifestations of, and clues to, dissociated dynamisms.

There still remains the question of how the two aspects of personality, the two "systems," remain in balance. One answer is that normally the self-system has sufficient energy at its disposal to keep the forces of the dissociated system functionally isolated. Still another and more specific answer is that the self-system has at its disposal an instrumentality which one unwittingly employs to limit and restrict awareness, namely, selective inattention. I must emphasize that, in Sullivan's view, the major function of selective inattention, operating in the service of the individual's self, is to restrict awareness of experience to what is congenial to it or at least tolerable, that is, not anxiety-provoking. The more one has been exposed to the irrational and ununderstandable prescriptions of behavior laid down by parents and others, the more restrictive the self tends to be, and the more prone to anxiety and conflict one is likely to be. Stated in another way, if in the course of one's upbringing one has been chronically subjected to severe anxiety in connection with one's behavior, selective inattention and dissociation will have to be employed more extensively, sometimes to a point where one's ability to achieve the satisfactions and security one needs is gravely undermined. A neurosis or, in some instances, a psychosis ensues.

In other words, when parents and other significant people, who may have been severely injured themselves by their own life experience, subject the growing child to various kinds of anxiety-provoking and thwarting experiences, he will have difficulty trying to adjust to the requirements of everyday interpersonal relations, frequently with grave consequences to himself and perhaps to "innocent bystanders."

The meaning of anxiety and fear. Unless one is able to recognize instances of anxiety in himself, any explanation of it is likely to be useless. Even a discussion of anxiety seems to provoke anxiety in some people, causing a wonderful display of verbalisms and prestige performances and a beclouding of the whole problem.

To make matters worse, there is often no clear-cut distinction between anxiety and fear in the works of various writers.

In any event, there are two distinct kinds of experience which in some degree apparently every person has. One kind has to do with *the experience of loss of self-esteem*, often associated with loss of status. The other ordinarily has to do with *the experience of great novelty in a situation or of something in a situation that is actually dangerous or at least very unpleasant in the sense of causing pain or severe discomfort*. Anxiety is always related to interpersonal relations. Fear may or may not have to do with people. Sometimes an experience is compounded of both anxiety and fear.

There are several indices of both kinds of experience. Fear is said to cause an increasing alertness and to create changes in the internal economy of the body, such as those Cannon investigated, so that the supply of energy available for muscular action is increased. There are also effects on the contents of consciousness: "namely, the level of consciousness is raised and bent upward, you might say, in the shape of an intense concentration on the fear-provoking situation and on the way to escape it" (Sullivan, 1956, p. 92).

Anxiety in adult life can often be explained as anticipated unfavorable appraisal of one's current activity by someone whose opinion is significant, that is, by someone about whose opinion one cares. This "someone" may include oneself. Anxiety may be considered to be a warning signal that there is "danger" from *within* oneself, that one must do something to ensure that one's security does not sink suddenly "as the result of the action of significant people or significant ideas." By and large, the loss of self-esteem and the loss of security are synonymous occurrences. Apparently the experience of anxiety does not entail the mobilization of energy for action which fear does.

Anxiety is said to be a tension in opposition to (in conflict with) the satisfaction of needs as well as to actions appropriate to their relief. It interferes with observation and alertness to relevant factors in current situations. And since perception and understanding normally tend to regulate behavior, the failure to observe and comprehend relevant factors in situations also interferes with the refinement and precision of action that may be required when dealing with them. For reasons which I shall presently try to make clear, whenever anything happens which would seriously disturb an established pattern of dealing with others, anxiety tends to intervene and arouse actions for its abatement. The more insecure one feels, the more rigidly one tends to adhere to established patterns of relating to others, regardless of the objective demands of the situation. Sullivan called the activities evoked to assuage anxiety "security operations." Thus, from a psychological point of view, anxiety is usually the great force which resists or prevents radical, extensive personal change.

The self-dynamism, a result of the history of the individual, is that aspect of the personality which embodies established and more or less familiar patterns of interpersonal relations. Whenever one encounters a situation which threatens to disturb the organization and functional activity of the self, anxiety tends to intervene. The self employs security operations which will minimize or abolish the anxiety, though at the cost of dealing with situations objectively and rationally.

In this connection, it may be well to point out that the degree of anxiety one suffers from and the extent of one's security operations seemingly depend on two generic factors. These are the level of maturity one has reached (Sullivan, 1953b, p. 310) and the nature of the social order of which one is a member (Sullivan, 1953a, pp. 192–193).

Selective inattention. Attention is selective. One focuses on a given object or situation and ignores or inattends to other things. Unless there are distracting elements, whether external or internal, to impede one's efforts to attend to what one is doing, one concentrates on the relevant factors—relevant to the perception or understanding of the various aspects of the object or situation—and excludes the irrelevant. But the deliberate restriction of perception, thought, and even feeling is not enough. There must also be restriction of recall so that only thoughts and experiences that are relevant to what one is doing come to mind.

These observations are familiar enough, and they are not different from what one ordinarily includes under the heading "attention," though Sullivan chose to include them in his discussion of selective inattention. But "selective inattention" in this sense is not a security operation. However, it may serve to introduce the following significant occurrences.

In certain situations a person may fail to notice clearly and carefully, may fail to attend to significant and relevant aspects of an object or situation, and, furthermore, may begin to recall matters that have no relevance to the business at hand. It seems that people who have serious life problems often overlook highly illuminating aspects of problems and events that occur almost every day because awareness of them would entail severe anxiety and/or some modification of one's personality. But selective inattention in the sense I am now discussing it is by no means confined to the mentally ill. Everyone to some degree employs this device and becomes distressed, anxious if something happens which interferes with the use of this stratagem. Selective inattention is very troublesome in psychotherapy, especially because it hinders the patient's perception and understanding of what he is doing in and out of therapy and also hinders the recall of relevant and useful information. Often the mere hint of anxiety is enough to set off the restrictive "machinery" of the self. In *The Psychiatric Interview* and *Clinical Studies in Psychiatry,* Sullivan has emphatically asserted that the therapist must learn to understand and circumvent the restrictive operations of the self. Otherwise his patient may get "sicker" and more discouraged, or else he may resort to dissociation or have greater and greater difficulty in having a restful sleep.

Selective inattention, according to Sullivan, is *not* another name for suppression or repression. Suppression and repression entail the inhibition of motives. Selective inattention does not, he says, pertain to motives; it pertains to the control of consciousness. Also, in regard to repression, he claimed he never encountered "anything as simple and as comprehensive as the repression of orthodox psychoanalytic theory." Sometimes what has been called "repression," he thought, is actually selective inattention. In some other instances, repression is actually dissociation.

Dissociation. Sullivan conceived of dissociation as a process by which various major "integrative tendencies" or motivational systems are forever denied any clear-cut consciousness. In other words, the person manifests these tendencies but cannot concentrate on these manifestations. In some instances they have always been unconscious; in others, they have been excluded from self-conscious awareness owing to various experiences the person has had during the course of his development or subsequently. To become conscious of such motivational tendencies would ordinarily entail intolerable anxiety and a grave threat to the organization of the self.

In Sullivan's view, everyone to some extent employs dissociation:

> All of us have some dissociated integrative tendencies; all of us have certain impulses which have not been provided with any reasonable channel for development by the culture. In other words, Western culture does not use part of our impulse equipment, if you please, part of our adjustive potentialities. . . . But they are not choked off utterly—it is probably impossible to do so. Like the trees growing at the edge of the Grand Canyon, something happens, however terribly distorted (1956, pp. 65–66).

In some people, because of very unfortunate experience, certain *major* integrative tendencies become considerably elaborated in dissociation. Some of these pertain to the pursuit of satisfactions; others, to the pursuit of security, such as the need for tenderness and affection. The likelihood of an acute disturbance in some interpersonal situation is said to be greatly increased by the presence of an important motivational system in dissociation.

Basic assumptions. Sullivan assumed that everyone is much more "simply human" than otherwise and that anomalous interpersonal relations, insofar as they do not arise from differences in language or custom, are a function of differences in relative maturity of the persons concerned. Partly for this reason and partly also because he thought unique individuality is beyond the grasp of science, he held that a science of interpersonal relations must be based on human identities or "parallels."

He set up certain "ideal constructs" as postulates. Two of these are absolute euphoria and absolute tension, which are inversely related. Absolute euphoria is said to be a state of utter well-being, never closely approximated in life except perhaps by an infant in deep, untroubled sleep. Absolute tension is conceived to be the maximum possible deviation from absolute euphoria. The nearest a person ever comes to absolute tension is thought to be the uncommon and always transient state of terror. In fact, almost all human living is thought to be between these "ideal" limits. They are generic concepts of a high level of abstraction, for there are actually different sorts of euphoria and tension. The state of well-being one is in when one lies on the beach in the summer sun is not the same as when one enjoys a brisk walk on a spring morning. The state of tension one experiences when one is angry is different from the tension of fear or anxiety, which in certain respects is quite different from all other tensions, or of various physiological needs. Sullivan concerned himself mainly, though by no means exclusively, with the tension of needs and the tension of anxiety. The former pertains directly to man's somatic organization; the latter, to his career in interpersonal relations throughout his life. But in the course of anyone's development, the somatic aspect of his nature becomes "invaded" by culture, by his experiences in interpersonal relations, so that many physiological processes and activities become "conditioned" in various ways that are not yet well understood. Thus the sexual drive, to use a familiar example, is a spectacular instance of the close intermingling of somatic and cultural elements.

Anxiety has nothing to do with the "biologically necessary communal existence of the infant." It has to do with interpersonal relations; at first those of the mother (or mothering one) and the infant. Sullivan claims that every human being, before speech is learned, has acquired certain gross patterns of relationships with a parent or with someone who mothers him. These patterns are said to become the utterly buried but quite firm foundations on which a great deal more is built. The mothering one provides the basic patterns of being human. Long before the period one can remember, he catches on to a good deal which is presented to him in the family, first and foremost by the mothering one.

Every infant is said to have the capacity to undergo a very unpleasant experience which will gradually develop into what adults recognize as anxiety. Thus if the mother is anxious or otherwise disturbed she "communicates" or induces a tension state which is thought to be unlike every other kind of tension. According to Sullivan, it is differentiated from all other reductions in euphoria (such as those brought about by the tension of needs) by the absence of anything specific. The infant gradually differentiates "feelings" of hunger or pain, etc., because he catches on to actions appropriate for their relief. For example, breathing begins to define the need for oxygen. But there is no action of the infant that is consistently and frequently associated with the relief of anxiety tension. An anxious mother cannot do anything to help relieve the anxiety she has unwittingly induced in her offspring—except to leave his presence, were she able to understand what is happening. So at an indeterminately early age the need for security, or freedom from anxiety, becomes established. It does not get associated with anything specific, and therefore the infant has no capacity for action toward its relief. Hence anxiety in the infant is not manageable. Since it is in opposition to needs and actions appropriate to its relief, it is in opposition to the tender behavior of the mothering one. For example, it interferes with sucking and swallowing.

Sullivan created a "heuristic classification" of personality development which he formulated as follows: infancy, childhood, the juvenile era, preadolescence, early adolescence, late adolescence, and maturity. Considerations of space restrict me to the barest essentials of Sullivan's formulations.

The developmental eras. INFANCY. The observed activities of the infant arising from the tension of needs are said to induce tension in the mothering one, experienced by her (or him) as tenderness and as an "impulsion" to activities for the relief of the infant's needs. In the course of time, the manifest activity by the mothering one toward the relief of the infant's needs comes to be experienced as the undergoing of tender behavior. And these needs take on the character of a general need for tenderness. According to Sullivan, the need for tenderness is ingrained from the beginning as an interpersonal need because its fulfillment entails a complementary need to manifest appropriate activity on the part of the mothering one, a general need to give tenderness.

When needs are unsatisfied and extremely aggravated, a state called "apathy," in which all the vital processes are slowed down, is said to occur. Sometime in infancy, or later on, an analogous state may occur, called "somnolent detachment," as a response to inescapable and prolonged anxiety.

Although severe anxiety probably contributes no information, less severe anxiety permits a gradual realization of the situation in which it occurs. So from very early in life, there is said to be learning of an inhibitory nature.

Another process of learning is learning from the "anxiety gradient," that is, learning to discriminate increasing from diminishing anxiety and to change activity in the direction of the latter. The infant catches on to the fact that if he tinkers with the region of the genitals or anus when the mother is present his feeling of anxiety increases rapidly and, perhaps, that this experience does not occur in her absence. He may also learn that even when she is present, fiddling with certain areas of the body through a blanket seems not to entail so much anxiety. Gradually there may be manifested a restriction of the areas of the body that are manipulated and/or the times when they are manipulated to perhaps periods of somnolence. In some such way there begins a "long-circuiting" of activities, chiefly those pertaining to zonal needs, to what are socially acceptable, namely, sublimation. Thus before the infant is very many months old, he will have unwittingly hit upon some pattern of activity which partially satisfies a need and at the same time avoids the experience of anxiety.

There are other learning processes which Sullivan discusses and which are also of great importance in the elaboration of the self: trial and success, by rewards and punishments; trial-and-error learning from human example; and the eduction of relations, or what is often called "insight."

These learning processes occur in one of three "modes" of experience: the prototaxic, the parataxic, and the syntaxic modes. They are also "referential processes" in the sense that they designate the ways by which any person "symbolizes" or "abstracts" his experiences of the world.

The prototaxic mode is said to be the "rough basis" of memory, constituting the earliest and possibly the most abundant mode of experience. All that the infant "knows" is momentary states. He does not realize any serial connection between earlier and later states—between past, present, and future—nor has he any awareness of himself as a separate entity. His felt experience is undifferentiated, without definite limits or distinctions. "It is as if everything that is sensitive and centrally represented were an indefinite, but very greatly abundant, luminous switchboard; and the pattern of light which would show on that switchboard in any discrete experience is the basic prototaxic experience itself . . ." (Sullivan, 1953b, p. 29). According to Sullivan, from the beginning to the end of life we undergo a succession of discrete patterns of the momentary state of the "organism." He claimed that this mode of experience was often marked in schizophrenic states.

In the parataxic mode the original undifferentiated wholeness of experience does not occur. Experience is differentiated into various aspects, which are felt as *concomitant*, not yet recognized as connected in an orderly fashion. Connections and relations are not established. There is no logical movement of thought. In other words, the infant gradually learns to associate various elements of his experience with one another before he has the ability to connect them in an orderly way. Perhaps every intelligent adult has experienced the shock of discovering that certain ideas or beliefs he has held have little or no real relationship to fact or logic. The same may apply to some of his observations and perceptions. Thus selective inattention, wherein one does not recognize relevant aspects of situations, is an instance of the parataxic mode.

The first unquestionable organization of experience in the syntaxic mode is said to be in the realm of the "two great genera of communicative behavior," gesture and speech. It usually entails consensually validated symbol activity, which involves an appeal to principles which are accepted as true by the hearer. What distinguishes syntaxic operations from everything else that occurs in the mind "is that they can under appropriate circumstances work quite precisely with other people. And the only reason that they come to work quite precisely with other people is that in actual contact with other people there has been some degree of exploration, analysis and the obtaining of information" (Sullivan, 1953b, pp. 224–225).

By and large, anything that one can talk about or communicate is in either the parataxic or the syntaxic mode. Anything that can be discussed is always "interpenetrated" by elements of the past or by elements of the near future, that is, elements that are anticipated. In infancy, the syntaxic mode is rudimentary or lacking. Recall and foresight are much more rudimentary than in adults, and they lack linguistic formulation. Nevertheless, infantile experience is the foundation on which later experience is built.

The experience of the infant includes a personification of the *good mother* and a personification of the *bad mother*. Analogously the mother has a personification of the infant which may or may not correspond closely to what an objective observer might perceive. A part of what the infant "symbolizes" to her is her recognition of certain social responsibilities she has with respect to him: care and education. More generally, her attitudes and behavior toward him have been "conditioned" by her past experience as well as by her current interpersonal relations and her foresight of the future.

In middle or late infancy, from the experience of rewards and severe anxiety and from experiences connected with the anxiety gradient, there develop three sorts of personifications which will in the course of time be *me* and which are associated with the self-sentient body. These beginning personifications are "good-me," "bad-me," and "not-me." Good-me arises from the experience of satisfactions enhanced by "rewarding increments" of tenderness. Good-me, as it ultimately develops, is said to be the ordinary topic of discussions about "I." Bad-me is the beginning personification resulting from experiences of increasing degrees of anxiety associated with behavior primarily involving the mothering one. These are said to be clearly evident in, and communicated by, the child a year subsequent to the period I have been discussing. Gradually the two personifications are assimilated into a single, more or less consistent perception of the mother.

Not-me, which evolves very gradually, is a personification growing out of experiences (in the parataxic mode) of intense anxiety. The not-me is made up of poorly grasped aspects of living which are presently regarded as dreadful, and still later it is differentiated into incidents which are associated with awe, horror, loathing, or dread. The not-me phase of personality is said to be very emphatically encountered by people undergoing a schizophrenic episode and by a good many people manifesting dissociated behavior. In the life of everyone after childhood, it may appear in nightmares.

The self-system evolves from the personifications of good-me and bad-me. In late infancy and childhood, good-me and bad-me begin to form a unitary system—the self. In other words, the self-dynamism evolves from educative experience in interpersonal relations, part of which is of the character of reward and a very important part of which has the "graded anxiety" element of experience also. It must be emphasized that experience functions in both recall and foresight. Thus the self coheres in terms of the recall and foresight of certain kinds of experience connected with reward from significant others—first and foremost the mothering one—and of certain kinds of experience associated with increasing anxiety. As the self develops stage by stage, it tends to maintain its current organization and functional activity, though in each era there are possibilities for favorable change—for growth—as well as for deterioration. Although I have stressed the restrictive function of the self, I could just as easily have emphasized its constructive features. For example, it is the principal influence which stands in the way of *unfavorable* changes in personality. (For such reasons, clumsy, inept therapeutic "maneuvers" with certain kinds of patients may have very serious consequences.) Probably because of his observations of the markedly restrictive operations of the self-dynamism of patients, Sullivan, it now seems to me, overemphasized his formulations of the self in the direction of its limiting functions, though for some purposes this may be all right.

CHILDHOOD. The acquisition of speech marks the transition to childhood. The first unquestionable organization of experience in the syntaxic mode is said to occur with the help of gesture and speech. From early childhood, the social responsibility felt by the mother to "train" and educate the child brings about an alteration of tender behavior. Some things that were previously tolerated are now forbidden. Probably in the life of every child, disappointments and frustrations are to some degree inevitable. Sullivan's "theorem" of reciprocal motivational patterns seems relevant at this point. "*Integration in an interpersonal situation is a reciprocal process in which* (1) *complementary needs are resolved or aggravated;* (2) *reciprocal patterns of activity are developed or disintegrated; and* (3) *foresight* *of satisfaction, or rebuff of similar needs is facilitated*" (1953b, p. 198).

This "theorem" has very broad applications not only for the course of personality development but for adult behavior as well. In regard to childhood, a need for tenderness may evoke tender behavior by the mothering one or its "denial" or evokes anxiety in the child, which aggravates the need for tenderness. With the increase of pressure on the mother toward socialization of the child, his training entails the thwarting of needs and activities previously acceptable. Since the mothering one now disapproves of various of his actions, they have to be disintegrated or sublimated. Regression in the face of frustration and anxiety is still another possibility. With these qualifications, there may be said to be a steady elaboration and refinement of activities designed to gain satisfactions and security in childhood. Analogously, foresight of satisfactions or of rebuff tends to depend on the "cooperation" of other significant people. In other words, the youngster's developing self-dynamism anticipates satisfactions or forbidding gestures (frowns, certain changes in tone of voice), depending on his previous experience. Subsequently such attitudes may be "transferred" to all significant people.

In childhood, certain youngsters discover that when they need tenderness and do things that once secured tenderness, they are subjected to behavior which brings anxiety and sometimes pain as well; that is, they are made fun of, disadvantaged, etc., and sometimes beaten. And thus it comes about that the "perceived" need for tenderness brings a foresight of anxiety or pain. So the child "shows" something else, namely, a malevolent attitude, an attitude that implies one is surrounded by enemies. Subsequently when such a youngster encounters a person who is potentially kind or tender, he forestalls any kindness or tenderness by his attitudes. Therefore he tends less and less to have experiences which might modify the warp that has been imposed on him by parents or their surrogates who are themselves perhaps seriously warped. The conviction grows on one that he is not worthy and not lovable, and he may acquire costly ways of circumventing anxiety-provoking and fear-provoking situations with authoritative figures.

The transformation toward malevolence is an instance of an arrest of development. The latter does *not* imply that things have become static and, as it were, stay put. An arrest of development signifies, first, *delay* in the manifestation of change which characterizes the "statistically usual" course of behavior and, second, the appearance of eccentricities of interpersonal relations. In general when an arrest of development occurs, one's ability to profit from experience is markedly reduced.

THE JUVENILE ERA. The juvenile era is ushered in by the maturation of the need for "compeers." This era is said to be the actual time for becoming social. Limitations and peculiarities of the home are now for the first time open to remedy. And if they are not remedied, they are apt to survive and color or warp the subsequent course of development. In the United States it is largely the school society that rectifies or modifies previous warp.

There is the learning of *social accommodation*, namely, an "astounding" broadening of one's grasp of how many "slight differences" in living there are; how many of them seem to be all right; and how many do *not* seem to be all right, though an attempt to correct them would be unwise.

There is also the learning of *social subordination*. The juvenile is expected to do things on demand of adult authority figures. And he experiences rewards or punishments in connection with his compliance, noncompliance, or rebellion. Also, the juvenile may perceive the interrelation of the behavior of his compeers to success or failure with the new authority figures. He begins to learn how to subordinate himself to authority figures in a social organization without misery. This development is facilitated or impeded by one's experiences with the parents.

Competition, compromise, and cooperation are outstanding characteristics of the juvenile era. Although competition first appears in childhood, it is much more evident during the school years. Tendencies of juveniles to compete are apparently universal, but in some cultures such tendencies are subjected to "inhibitory influence" by authority figures. In American society competitive tendencies are vigorously encouraged. People who remain "chronically juvenile" adopt competition as a way of life in which nearly everything of real importance entails getting ahead of the other fellow and—if, in addition, they suffered the malevolent transformation—getting the other fellow down.

To compromise is to give up part of what one wants or hopes to obtain in a situation in order to get the rest. Compromise is enforced by the juvenile society and to a certain extent by the school authorities. Like competition, it may become a very troublesome trait. There are some people who go on from the juvenile era perfectly willing to yield almost anything as long as they have what they might call "peace and quiet."

To cooperate is to work with others toward the achievement of a common goal. Cooperation is in general a very rewarding experience, but Sullivan does not seem to have done it the justice it deserves.

In the juvenile era there is normally the beginning differentiation of the childhood authority figures as simply people. Differentiation occurs first as a result of observation of teachers, whom one may or may not discuss in the home, and then as a result of learning from other juveniles about their parents. Failure to make this discrimination may be strikingly manifested later in life.

Also in the juvenile era a great many of the ideas and actions which were acceptable during childhood have to be abandoned. Partly because of the very crude and direct critical reaction to one's behavior of other juveniles and partly because of the relatively formulable and predictable behavior of authority figures, such as teachers, the expanding self-system gains increasing power to control focal awareness. The juvenile learns a great deal about security operations. The ability to employ selective inattention, in both its helpful and its hampering roles, is increased. The sublimatory reformulation of overt behavior and covert processes is of considerable help in coping with needs. It occurs in the parataxic mode. Sublimation is the process by which a behavior pattern which is socially approved and which partially satisfies a need is unwittingly substituted for behavior which might bring optimum satisfaction of the need but which is socially frowned upon or tabooed. The part of the motivational system that is not directly satisfied is discharged in private reverie processes and especially during sleep.

There is one more point about the juvenile era that must be included: the development of supervisory patterns of the self-system. These include a pattern called the "hearer," another called the "spectator," and a third called the "reader." Thus when one is lecturing, a part of his mind, so to speak, "listens" to what he is saying in order to ensure that the lecture is communicable, logically presented, relevant to the topic, etc. Analogously, the spectator diligently pays attention to what one "shows" to others—unless one has had too much alcohol to drink—and if one makes a slip, that is, shows something too revealing, embarrassing, or whatnot, he quickly adds some camouflage, such as a verbalism or a rationalization. Finally, the reader observes what one writes in order to ensure reasonably good grammar, some precision of language, communicability, etc. These supervisory patterns of the self normally persist and become elaborated and refined during the further stages of development.

PREADOLESCENCE. The web of human life is fashioned stage by stage and is not completed until one has reached maturity. Nevertheless, according to Sullivan in his *Conceptions of Modern Psychiatry,* it is during preadolescence that the great controlling power of the cultural forces of society is finally and inescapably woven into the human personality. It is love which reinforces this power; a love which can quickly die and be soon forgotten.

Sullivan writes lyrically but with a note of sadness about this era, believing that "for a great majority of our people, preadolescence is the nearest that they come to untroubled human life—that from then on the stresses of life distort them to inferior caricatures of what they might have been" (1953a, p. 56).

The beginning of preadolescence is marked by a new type of interest in a particular member of the same sex who becomes a chum or a close friend. The chum becomes of practically equal importance in all fields of value as one is to oneself. When fully developed, the integrating tendencies of preadolescence are characterized as love or intimacy. Intimacy is said to be that type of situation involving two people which permits validation of all components of personal worth. It entails clearly formulated adjustments of one's behavior to the expressed needs of the other in the pursuit of increasingly identical satisfactions and in the maintenance of increasingly similar security operations. Thus when the satisfactions and security of the other person are as important to one as one's own, one loves that other person.

The experience of loneliness is another outstanding feature of preadolescence, the period when it first reaches its full significance. Full-blown loneliness is difficult to recall and is more terrible than anxiety. And thus very lonely people may seek companionship even though intensely anxious. In short, loneliness can be an intense "driving force," a powerful integrating tendency.

EARLY ADOLESCENCE. Early adolescence extends from the "eruption" of true genital interest, experienced as lust, to the patterning of sexual behavior, which is the beginning of late adolescence. With the arrival of adolescence, there is normally *change* in the type of object of the need for intimacy, first experienced during preadolescence for a member of one's own sex. The change is manifested as a growing interest in the possibilities of achieving some measure of intimacy with a member of the other sex, a change that is influenced by the concomitant appearance of the genital drive.

During early adolescence several unfortunate developments may appear, only a few of which can be discussed. One unfortunate outcome is a "collision" of lust and one's need for security. This may happen, for example, if the parents have inculcated an attitude that the genital area of the body is disgraceful and disgusting. Any interest in "lustful sports" tends to make one extremely anxious.

The shift in the intimacy need may also collide with the need for security. The family group may bring powerful "repressive influence" to bear on the adolescent. A parent may actively interfere with the adolescent's movement toward a member of the other sex by criticizing him or the object of his interest or by ridiculing him. In extreme cases, a parent may actively threaten suicide.

Still again, there may be a collision of the intimacy need and lust. Embarrassment, diffidence, excessive precautions, and excessive boldness may make the adolescent's movement toward intimacy difficult.

Sullivan claimed that by the time a person has "plunged" into early adolescence, either he will have largely overcome all the crippling handicaps to personality he has suffered or his development in adolescence will be warped. Since lust is outstandingly a part of personality, data on personality warp as manifested in a person's sexual behavior are bound to be useful to the therapist. But, according to Sullivan, it is a profound mistake to think one can remedy personality warp by "tinkering" with the patient's sexual life. He held that patients do *not* go to a psychiatrist for help with their sexual difficulties but that they may *present* them as their problem. And when these sexual difficulties are properly understood, if they are presented, they may indicate what ails the patient concerning his living with people. The "real" problems, the basic problems, concern living with people.

LATE ADOLESCENCE. Late adolescence is said to extend from the patterning of preferred genital activity to the establishment of a fully human or mature repertory of interpersonal relations, as permitted by available opportunity, both personal and cultural. Failure to achieve late adolescence is the "last blow" to a great many warped, immature people. This failure is such an all-absorbing and frustrating experience that it often constitutes the presenting difficulty, though it is by no means the actual difficulty.

Sullivan held that once a person who is not very seriously warped has got the "sex problem" reasonably well straightened out, whatever he does—whether as a university student, a wage earner, an office worker, or an aspiring businessman—is bound to broaden his acquaintance with other people's attitudes toward living, the degree of their interdependence in living, and the ways of handling various kinds of interpersonal problems. Relatively personally limited experience is refined into the "consensually dependable"—insofar as the social order will permit. Hence it is that in late adolescence everyone—or everyone not too seriously warped—is more or less integrated into society as it is.

It is self-system functions which prevent a great many people from getting very far in late adolescence. Insofar as they can communicate their problems, the latter are manifested as inadequate and inappropriate personifications of the self. These people's views of themselves are awry, and they cannot grasp the fact that their personifications of themselves are distorted because any tendency to gain insight into them stirs up anxiety whenever the incongruity and inappropriateness of situations might be evident.

In addition, according to Sullivan, a person cannot personify others with any particular refinement except in terms of his own personification of himself and of imagined critics of himself or, rather, imagined critics of his personification of himself. This of course leads to an inadequate grasp of what others are like. One's personifications of others tend to be stereotypes, embodying prejudices, intolerances, fears, hatreds, aversions, and revulsions.

For all such reasons, and others, many people suffer vast restrictions in freedom of living.

MATURITY. Sullivan claimed that the most mature people are least accessible for study. Hence he had little data on maturity. He "guessed" that each of the outstanding achievements of the developmental eras will be outstandingly manifest in the mature personality. The ability for intimate relations with another person or persons, for example, will be a marked feature of mature living.

Conclusion. I should like to suggest to those who are particularly interested in Sullivanian psychiatry that a study of *The Psychiatric Interview* may be very helpful, partly because it shows how Sullivan applied the ideas I have discussed above. In this connection, also, a paper by M. J. White entitled "Sullivan and Treatment" and included in a symposium I edited, *The Contributions of Harry Stack Sullivan,* is very illuminating.

Finally, in regard to the vexed problem of maturity, I believe that Allport's formulations of the mature personality in *Pattern and Growth in Personality* are unsurpassed.

REFERENCES

Adler, A. *The neurotic constitution.* (Tr. by B. Glueck & J. E. Lind.) New York: Moffatt, Yard, 1917. (a)

Adler, A. A study of organ inferiority and its psychical compensation. (Tr. by S. E. Jelliffe.) *Nerv. ment. Dis. Monogr. Ser.,* 1917, No. 24. (b)

Adler, A. *The practice and theory of individual psychology.* (Tr. by P. Radin.) New York: Harcourt, Brace, 1927. (a)

Adler, A. *Understanding human nature.* (Tr. by B. Wolfe.) New York: Greenberg, 1927. (b)

Adler, A. *Problems of neurosis.* (P. Mainet, Ed.) New York: Cosmopolitan, 1930.

Adler, A. *Social interest: a challenge to mankind.* (Tr. by J. Linton & R. Vaughan.) London: Faber, 1938.

Adler, A. *The problem child.* New York: Capricorn Books, 1963.

Allport, G. W. *Pattern and growth in personality.* New York: Holt, 1961.

Fromm, E. *Escape from freedom.* New York: Holt, 1941.

Fromm, E. *Man for himself.* New York: Holt, 1947.

Fromm, E. Psychoanalytic characterology and its application to the understanding of culture. In S. S. Sargent & Marian W. Smith (Eds.), *Culture and personality.* New York: Viking Fund, 1949.

Fromm, E. *The sane society.* New York: Holt, 1955.

Fromm, E. *The art of loving.* New York: Harper & Row, 1956.

Fromm, E. *The dogma of Christ.* New York: Holt, 1963.

Hall, C. S., & Lindzey, G. *Theories of personality.* New York: Wiley, 1957.

Horney, Karen. *The neurotic personality of our time.* New York: Norton, 1937.

Horney, Karen. *New ways in psychoanalysis.* New York: Norton, 1939.

Horney, Karen. *Self-analysis.* New York: Norton, 1942.

Horney, Karen. *Our inner conflicts.* New York: Norton, 1945.

Horney, Karen. *Neurosis and human growth.* New York: Norton, 1950.

Jung, C. G. The association method. (Tr. by A. A. Brill.) *Amer. J. Psychol.,* 1910, **21** (2).

Jung, C. G. On psychological understanding. *J. abnorm. soc. Psychol.,* 1915, **9,** 385–399. (a)

Jung, C. G. The theory of psychoanalysis. *Nerv. ment. Dis. Monogr. Ser.,* 1915, No. 19 (b)

Jung, C. G. *Collected papers on analytical psychology.* (Tr. by Constance E. Long, Ed.) London: Ballière, 1920.

Jung, C. G. *Psychological types or the psychology of individuation.* (Tr. by H. G. Baynes.) New York: Harcourt, Brace, 1926.

Jung, C. G. *The psychology of the unconscious.* (Tr. by Beatrice M. Hinkle.) New York: Dodd, Mead, 1927.

Jung, C. G. *Contributions to analytical psychology.* (Tr. by H. G. Baynes & C. F. Baynes.) New York: Harcourt, Brace, 1928. (a)

Jung, C. G. *Two essays on analytical psychology.* (Tr. by H. G. Baynes & C. F. Baynes.) New York: Dodd, Mead, 1928. (b)

Jung, C. G. *Modern man in search of a soul.* (Tr. by W. S. Dill & C. F. Baynes.) New York: Harcourt, Brace, 1933.

Jung, C. G. The psychology of dementia praecox. (Tr. by A. A. Brill.) *Nerv. ment. Dis. Monogr. Ser.,* 1936, No. 3.

Jung, C. G. *Psychology and religion.* New Haven, Conn.: Yale Univer. Press, 1938.

Jung, C. G. *The integration of the personality.* (Tr. by S. M. Dill.) New York: Holt, 1939.

Jung, C. G. *The psychology of the spirit.* (Tr. by Hildegard Nagel.) New York: Analytical Club of New York, 1948.

Jung, C. G. *The basic writings of. . . .* (Violet Staub De Laszlo, Ed.) New York: Modern Library, 1959.

Rank, O. *The trauma of birth.* New York: Harcourt, Brace, 1929.

Rank, O. *Art and artist.* (Tr. by C. F. Atkinson.) New York: Knopf, 1932.

Rank, O. *Will therapy and truth and reality.* (Tr. by J. Taft.) New York: Knopf, 1945.

Rank, O. *The myth of the birth of the hero.* (Tr. by F. Robbins & S. E. Jelliffe.) *Nerv. ment. Dis. Monogr. Ser.,* 1914, No. 18.

Salzman, L. *Developments in psychoanalysis.* New York: Grune & Stratton, 1962.

Sullivan, H. S. Psychiatry: introduction to the study of interpersonal relations. In P. Mullahy (Ed.), *A study of interpersonal relations.* New York: Hermitage House, 1949.

Sullivan, H. S. *Conceptions of modern psychiatry.* (2nd ed.) New York: Norton, 1953. (a)

Sullivan, H. S. *The Interpersonal Theory of Psychiatry.* (Helen S. Perry & Mary L. Gawel, Eds.) New York: Norton, 1953. (b)

Sullivan, H. S. *The psychiatric interview.* (Helen S. Perry, Ed.) New York: Norton, 1954.

Sullivan, H. S. *Clinical studies in psychiatry.* (Helen S. Perry, Mary L. Gawel, & Martha Gibson, Eds.) New York: Norton, 1956.

Sullivan, H. S. *Schizophrenia as a human process.* New York: Norton, 1962.

White, Mary J. Sullivan and treatment. In P. Mullahy (Ed.), *The contributions of Harry Stack Sullivan.* New York: Hermitage House, 1952.

Wolman, B. B. *Contemporary theories and systems in psychology.* New York: Harper & Row, 1960.

part 3

Diagnostic Methods

16

Differential Diagnosis

MOLLY HARROWER

Differential diagnosis—as usually understood—is a term borrowed from medicine; its basic purpose is to ensure the proper handling and treatment of the sick and disturbed individual.

Differential diagnosis between brain tumor and cerebral atrophy is required, for example, in order that a lifesaving operation may be performed in the case of the former, and an unnecessary surgical procedure withheld in the latter. With the presenting physical symptoms suggesting either bronchitis or tuberculosis, a differential diagnosis must be made, and the sputum must be examined for the presence of tubercle bacilli. Whether a limb injured in a fall is or is not put in a cast will depend on the differential diagnosis obtained by x-ray pictures, showing that the bone is or is not broken. Of two apparently equally anxious and emotionally distraught individuals, diagnosis of an underlying schizophrenic process in the one and not in the other will lead to a different treatment plan for each. One could multiply such examples indefinitely; what is important is the fact that differential diagnosis never takes place in a vacuum and that it is relevant only insofar as the therapeutic fate of the patient depends on it.

Since 1932, when the second edition of Rorschach's *Psychodiagnostick* was published, differential diagnosis may be said to have included the diagnostic use of psychological tests, a procedure now known as "psychodiagnosis." Perhaps more than any other recently coined term, "psychodiagnostics" may be said to describe activities which are unique to clinical psychologists of the present day. Speaking of the range of the objectives of psychodiagnosis, Thorne (1948) has stated the following:

> In modern clinical science the objective of diagnosis involves more than identifying and naming a psychological syndrome. Recognizing that the personality dynamics in each individual case are different, psychodiagnostics has moved beyond problems of classification to the more mature objective of completely describing the idealogical factors causative of disorder. Among the objectives of psychodiagnostics are:
>
> 1. To demonstrate the etiological factors.
> 2. To differentiate between organic and functional disorders.
> 3. To discover the personality reaction of the organism to the disorder.
> 4. To evaluate the degree of organic and functional disability.
> 5. To estimate the extensity or intensity of the morbid process in relation to actuarial data concerning type and severity.
> 6. To determine a prognosis or probable course.
> 7. To provide a rational basis for specific psychotherapy.
> 8. To provide a rational basis for discussing the case with patient and relatives.
> 9. To provide a scientific basis for classification and statistical analysis of data.
> 10. To formulate a dynamic hypothesis concerning the nature of the pathological process and the mechanisms whereby therapeutic effects are explained.

In the chapters which follow hereafter, it will be shown how each of the various psychodiagnostic devices contributes to the basic problem of patient treatment and patient care. Their peculiar contribution to diagnostic process will be discussed. In this chapter we shall attempt to highlight some of the problems which face the psychodiagnostician in both his service-oriented and his research activities.

In attempting a perspective from a historical point of view, it is possible to trace three stages in the development of psychodiagnosis. There was first an era in which the psychologist accepted the existing psychiatric nosology without question and attempted to give his differential diagnoses within this framework as a matter of course. Next came a period during which psychological evaluation, psychological appraisals, and psychological diagnosis, as described earlier, gradually replaced the rather oversimplified differential judgment. This second stage included a period of interprofessional education, during which it was up to the psychologist—the psychodiagnostician—to demonstrate to the referring physicians the wealth of material which was available from psychodiagnostic testing. We may now be said to be entering a third stage, in which, as a result of the accumulation of material from psychological research and because of the widespread dissatisfaction among psychiatrists and psychologists alike with the established diagnostic categories, the profession of clinical psychology is contributing to a reformulation of the frame of reference according to which individuals are assessed.

THE FIRST STAGE

One must remember, in discussing the problems of the first stage—which occurred during the late thirties and early forties—that a new professional entity, that of the clinical psychologist, was in the process of evolution, giving rise to inevitable problems of status and of rivalry within the multidiscipline team. The clinical psychologist was the newcomer, the stranger, the foreigner in the field of medicine. As such, he axiomatically occupied the low place on the totem pole and accepted the existing frame of reference and the existing methods of formulating problems. He attempted to learn the language and to pattern the information he was asked to give from his own test material in accordance with the established scientific mores of the hospital community or medical environment which he had just entered.

During this early period, much of the research work that was done concentrated on attempts to isolate constellations of responses or "signs," which could be considered characteristic of the Rorschach records of various clinical entities: the schizophrenic, the organic, the neurotic, and so on. Usually this work was prefaced by statements to the effect that such signs could not be expected to describe every member of a given group and that virtually nothing could be considered pathognomonic. It was also accompanied by constant warnings that signs could not tell the whole story. Klopfer & Kelley (1942), for example, stated: "While these signs have been described as pathognomonic, it must again be emphasized that there are no true pathognomonic signs in the Rorschach method."

Nonetheless, signs were the order of the day, and, for its historical interest, Klopfer and Kelley's (1942) table entitled "Occurrence of Certain Rorschach Signs among Schizophrenic Subjects, According to Various Investigators" is included here. Piotrowski's (1937) 10 organic signs and the neurotic signs of Miale and Harrower (1940) follow.

Piotrowski's subjects, from a study of whose Rorschach records he derived his 10 organic signs, included 18 cases with involvement of the brain, 10 cases with noncerebral disturbances of the central nervous system, and 5 cases of conversion hysteria. Proposed in 1937, the signs were as follows:

1. Total number of responses less than fifteen.
2. Response time more than one minute.
3. Only one human movement response.
4. At least one color naming response.
5. Percentage of good form less than 75 per cent.
6. Number of popular responses less than 25 per cent.
7. Repetition of responses.
8. Impotence.
9. Perplexity.
10. Automatic phrases.

His amplification of the last four signs is given as follows, beginning on page 384.

TABLE 1. OCCURRENCE OF CERTAIN RORSCHACH SIGNS AMONG SCHIZOPHRENIC SUBJECTS, ACCORDING TO VARIOUS INVESTIGATORS

	Beck	*Rickers-Ovsiankina*	*Rorschach*	*Kelley and Klopfer*
Manner of approach	Confused; DW most typical	Confused; W-Dd-D	Confused; W-Dd	Confused; W-Dd-D-DW
W	Fewer than normal	Higher than normal; W of poor quality		Crude W or DW
Confabulatory DW	Present	Present	Present	Present
Contamination	Present		Pathognomonic	Usually pathognomonic
Rare detail (Dd)	Scattered; schizophrenics sensitive to them	Qualitatively but not quantitatively important		Frequent; qualitatively and quantitatively important
M	Low	Low	High in paranoids, low in others	High in paranoids, low in others
Color	High C and CF; low FC	Ratio of CF and C to FC important		C and CF high in hebephrenic's low in paranoids and simple schizophrenics
Erlb.	Dominance of C	Dominance of C		Dominance of C
Cn		Present		Occasionally present
F+	Low	Low	Low	Low
P%	Low	Low	Low	Low
Variability in quality (F− to F)	Very important	Very important	Pathognomonic	Very important but not pathognomonic
Blocking	Present	Present	Present	Present
Original responses	Poor quality	Increased number; poor quality; vary in quality	Increased number; presence of 0+ and bizarre 0− together	Increased 0+ and 0−
A%		Relation of A% to 0% important		A% to 0% important
Shading		Present		K and c common; FK, Fc, and C′ rare
Po	Present	Present	Pathognomonic	Present and usually pathognomonic

TABLE 1. OCCURRENCE OF CERTAIN RORSCHACH SIGNS AMONG SCHIZOPHRENIC SUBJECTS, ACCORDING TO VARIOUS INVESTIGATORS (*Continued*)

	Beck	*Rickers-Ovsiankina*	*Rorschach*	*Kelley and Klopfer*
Abstract and personal references	Present	Present	Present	Present
Perseveration	Present	Present	Present	Present
Description of card	Present	Present	Present	Present

"Rpt" stands for repetition or the giving of the same response to several inkblots. This however does not imply meaningless and stereotyped perseveration of one idea. The latter of course can occur also. It appears typical of cortical cases that once stimulated by an inkblot they feel compelled to respond to it even when their imagination fails them and they cannot think of an appropriate response. Rather than keep silent in such a situation they repeat an old response if such repetition seems partly justified. Usually the first of such repetitive responses is a good form response while the following fit their inkblots less well. Normal adults do not perseverate in such a manner.

"Imp" stands for impotence or giving a response in spite of recognition of its inadequacy. This sign means that the patient has realized that at least one of his responses is of poor quality and yet has not withdrawn it. In cortical cases valid self-criticism is disproportionately better than the ability to correct the recognized mistakes. Their intellectual impotence appears to be due, on the one hand, to a paucity of ideas, an inability to think of a new and better response, and on the other hand to a strong tendency to give a definite response to any stimulation, to go through with a process which has once been initiated. Impotence, as defined here, does not occur in the absence of the preceding sign, repetition.

"Plx" means perplexity associated with distrust of one's own ability and quest for reassurance. Patients with mental disorders, especially cortical cases, are frequently disturbed by doubts of their ability. This doubt seems unpleasant to the patients and they try to satisfy their minds by pressing the examiner to decide for them whether their responses have been adequate. Such an attitude implies strong interest in the patient's own achievement. When a patient has taken this attitude, he shows that he is interested in the results he has obtained, that he feels imcompetent to decide by himself whether or not these results are adequate, that he wants some one else to tell him whether he has performed his task well, that he shows satisfaction or frustration according to what he is told about his performance. The patient's perplexity is noticeable in these verbal productions and particularly in the simultaneous general behavior. This type of perplexity has not been reported in Rorschach studies of normal adults. None of our normals exhibited it.

"AP" stands for automatic phrases or the frequent use of a pet phrase in an indiscriminate fashion. Oberholzer observed that many organic cases have pet phrases which they use mechanically without troubling to see whether such a phrase is sensible or not. These phrases may be described as stereotyped reactions to new situations taking place or preceding a more specific and better adjusted reaction to the situation.

The so-called "neurotic" signs of Miale and Harrower (1940) and of Harrower (1943) were first formulated in 1940 and were subsequently modified on the basis of a much larger patient population in 1943. The authors stated:

> While frank psychoneurosis, as distinguished from the normal, on the one hand, and psychosis and organic brain disease on the other, is a reasonably clear clinical entity, classification within the psychoneurotic group presents difficult problems. . . . Clinicians would probably also agree that although diagnosis within the psychoneuroses is based on the predominating symptom, most cases of psychoneurosis present more than one of the afore-mentioned symptoms,

and that pure entities are exceedingly rare. From a clinical point of view the following structural factors may be suggested as common to all cases of psychoneurosis, regardless of the specific features which may occur in any individual type:

1. Lack of inner stability.
2. An infantile adaptation.
3. Inability to adjust to the environment.
4. Excessive anxiety and tension.
5. Stereotypy and restriction of spontaneity, with an attempt to substitute conscious control for genuine adjustment.

It is, however, obvious that borderline psychoneurotics, organics, psychotics, and even so-called normals are frequently most difficult to distinguish clinically, and it was with the hope of finding some specific variance between psychoneurotics and normals that this study was undertaken. In addition, it was felt that such findings would be of value in further studies differentiating the psychoneurotic group as a whole from other types of psychopathy.

Rorschach records were obtained from 43 individuals of varying intellectual levels, aged from 15 to 55, who had been clinically diagnosed as psychoneurotic. The group comprised anxiety neurotics, conversion hysterics, neurasthenics, compulsive-obsessives, and some of mixed type. In addition, however, for the purpose of direct comparison, we obtained records from twenty normal individuals, of intellectual and age levels comparable to those of the experimental group, to serve as a control group.

The neurotic records presented marked differences from the normal ones in a number of ways. The following are the nine signs in the neurotic records which seemed to differentiate them most clearly from the normals:

1. Number of responses to the ten cards not more than 25. Our neurotic group averaged 13 responses to the ten cards. In only three cases (7%) was the total more than 25. The totals in these cases were 26, 27, and 49. The average number of responses from large numbers of normal adults has been reported as between 30 and 40. Our normal group averaged 36, with 30% of them having no more than 25 responses. (Responses under 12, 1943 modification.)
2. Number of M, or human movement responses, not more than one. To produce more than one human movement response a subject must have a considerable degree of maturity and inner stability. 74% of our neurotic cases had fewer than two M responses; their average number was 1.1. All of the controls had more than one M, averaging 5.5.
3. FM, animal movement responses, greater than M, human movement. The FM responses represent a primitive, infantile mode of response, in contrast to the maturity of the M. In 67% of the neurotic records FM was greater than M. In 23% of the cases M and FM were both absent or of equal number, and in only 12% was M greater than FM. 70% of the control group had more M than FM responses; in only 15% of the controls was FM greater than M. (FM twice the number of M and when no FM scores are present, 1943 modification.)
4. Color shock was present in 98% of the neurotic records. Color shock has long been considered a neurotic reaction. In general color shock means that there is evidence of disturbance in reaction to the cards which contain bright color—which represents emotional stimulation from the environment. In accordance with Rorschach practice the following types of reactions to the colored cards were used as the main indicators of color shock:
   a. Significant delay in time prior to the first response to the card.
   b. Comments or exclamations by the subject indicative of newly aroused emotions or anxieties different from those seen in the uncolored cards.
   c. Decline in the quality of the responses, especially when it results in the appearance of F−, poorly perceived form.
   d. Rejection of the card.

While color shock was present in all but one of the neurotic cases, it was found only in 20% of the controls.

5. Shading shock, or reactions to the two strongly shaded cards similar to those evidenced in response to the colored cards in color shock. This is a reaction indicative of considerable anxiety. It was present in 81% of the psychoneurotic records, and in 20% of the normals.
6. Complete refusal to respond to one or more cards is almost never found among normal people, was not found at all in our control group. 47% of the neurotics, however, had refusals, ranging from one to seven of the ten cards.
7. In 51% of the neurotic cases the percentage of pure form responses in the total number of responses was higher than 50.

Only 20% of the normal group had this sign. More than 50% pure form responses represents restriction of spontaneity, with an attempt to substitute intellectual control for genuine adjustment. (F score 10% or less, 1943 modification.)

8. In 58% of the neurotic cases animal figures constituted the content of more than half the responses. 25% of the normals showed this sign. An animal percentage of over 50 is considered an indication of a high degree of mental stereotypy. (To be given also when animal and anatomy responses, together, equal 65% or over, 1943 modification.)
9. The number of FC responses (form-color combinations), indicative of emotional adjustment, was no more than one in 81% of the neurotics, and in only twenty per cent of the normals. The neurotics produced an average of .6 FC responses, while the normal's average was 3.1. 70% of the neurotics produced no FC responses at all, while only 10% of the normals lacked FC's entirely. (Two additional FC responses counting as one main response, 1943 modification.)

The authors conclude:

> It may be emphasized here that the results of the present study are not suggested as a quantitative substitute for the important qualitative elements which a Rorschach examiner uses in diagnosis. It should be emphasized also that the presence of no one sign is diagnostically indicative.

THE TRANSITIONAL PHASE

Several specific problems confronted the clinician during the second, or transitional, phase as he struggled to expand the concept of differential diagnosis and to establish a use for detailed psychological appraisals and true psychodiagnostic evaluations as we now understand them.

There was, for instance, the question of the so-called "blind" diagnosis.[1] In the early days of testing, it was understandable that each referring physician wished to satisfy himself on the relative reliability of this new method, refusing to divulge any information concerning the prospective patient. The psychologist was also on his mettle and was eager to prove that his information was derived exclusively from his test material, so that he accepted this procedure without demur. Yet the refusal by the referring physician to state, in many cases, even what the examination was needed for or why material from another frame of reference would be valuable often put unnecessary burdens on the clinical psychologist and forced him to overextend himself in the hope of coming upon those areas where the problem might be.

We now realize that a far more relevant report can be written if there is a preliminary discussion, between the referring person and the psychologist doing the diagnostic appraisal, about those areas which are least accessible to clinical penetration. Private practitioners and clinical psychologists in hospitals alike feel, at the present time, that a request stating the specific reason why the evaluation is needed is important if a precise and relevant report is to be rendered. Interdisciplinary education was necessary. The physician had to be reminded that, for example, it would be manifestly absurd to refer a patient for x-ray treatment without telling the radiologist which part of the body was to be x-rayed, and it had to be explained that psychologists were frequently faced with equally nonspecific tasks which resulted, on occasion, in their failure to utilize tests which might well have been valuable, had the actual problem been more clearly envisaged.

During this second phase, psychologists became aware of the need to give more balanced reports, that is, reports which included the patient's assets and strengths as well as his weaknesses. Sophistication in report writing seemed, at one time, to equate only with the degree of penetration into all the patient's inadequacies, and only after some years did it become acceptable to turn attention to the all-important personality potential, which, while evidenced in the tests, might well be obscured clinically at the time the patient first seeks help.

Psychologists struggled with problems of placing a given patient within a frame of reference so that his performance before and after treatment could be compared. They faced the problems of relating to the decisions on the scope of diagnostic-evaluative procedures. What was, for instance, a relevant number of tests to use? How many should be employed without extending the examination to a point where it would be too costly for the

[1] The term "blind diagnosis" has come to mean a psychodiagnostic evaluation based upon test protocol only, without any other clinical information or contact with the patient.

patient and unrealistically time-consuming for the psychodiagnostician? During the early days of testing, the Rorschach was apt to be the sole instrument employed. A differential diagnosis or diagnostic report was often synonymous with "to give a Rorschach." However, during this second stage it became accepted as standard practice for the psychologist to base his findings on a battery of tests. It became increasingly clear that the exclusive use of any one test deprives the examiner of valuable material, that is, material which can be obtained only when several diagnostic instruments are used. The wide variety of projective techniques which were coming into being required a clear awareness on the part of the clinician as to what his actual responsibilities were. A reasonable compromise had to be made between a too exhaustive examination, on the one hand, and undue reliance on any single instrument, on the other.

At about this time, another dimension was added to psychodiagnostic testing: the explicit recognition that an understanding of psychoanalytic principles was necessary in order for the fullest and most meaningful use of projective techniques to be made.

True, many of the Rorschach experts were grounded in, and had experienced, personal analysis, but the rank and file of testers had not yet acknowledged the inseparability of analytic experience and psychodiagnosis. With Schafer's (1954) work, it became apparent that in order for depth or three-dimensionality to be given to the description of the patient, the psychodiagnostician must be able to draw freely on psychoanalytic knowledge. As Schafer stated:

> One of our basic needs at this point in the history of Rorschach testing, in particular, and clinical testing, in general, is for a broad treatment of the contribution psychoanalysis has made and can make to test theory and interpretation. We hear so much these days about the influence of the tester on the test results, the symbolic interpretation of response content, the test indications for therapy, and the like, psychoanalytic assumption for almost all is involved in these discussions. Obviously, the more we can specify, amplify, appropriately modify, integrate and concretely illustrate the psychoanalytic assumptions and their applications, the more we may hope to improve our work with tests in practice and research.

Batteries of Tests

Although present-day psychodiagnosticians have, for the most part, incorporated the use of a *battery* of tests into their structured procedure, it may be well to reconsider for a moment why it is important to use a variety of techniques—important, that is, both for differential diagnosis in the strictest sense and for the detailed psychodiagnostic evaluations, which are one of the specific contributions of clinical psychologists to the mental health field.

In the first place, a difference in *level of performance between two tests* can give us information which, axiomatically, a single test cannot provide. This difference in level or in kind of performance may, in itself, be a key to certain diagnostic problems. To give a concrete example, the presence of some organic cerebral pathology may frequently be suspected by virtue of the contrast between the high scores maintained on the Bellevue-Wechsler and the impoverished, restricted, and coarcted performance on the Rorschach. Or let us consider the intact paranoid schizophrenic whose Rorschach record gives no trace of the underlying problems but whose telltale Szondi profile will reveal to the psychodiagnostician, using this as an additional test, the presence of the strong homosexual component and the paranoid hypersensitivity.

This concept of level, or difference, in test performance can be extended beyond the difference between two tests to include differences of performance on a battery of both structured and unstructured tests. Gross discrepancies between tests can be thought of as reflecting the same kind of "scatter" as can occur between the Wechsler subtests. Although we have not yet explored this concept sufficiently, preliminary investigations involving the follow-up of 622 cases subsequent to various forms of psychotherapy indicate that the more uniform the interprojective pattern, the more marked the therapeutic success will be (Harrower, 1965).

A second reason for utilizing more than one technique is that not all our instruments describe or measure the same features of the individual's total makeup. Some reach the relatively unchanging aspects of the person, as opposed to his more fluctuating moods. Some may pick up basic defects or well-established modes of successful adaptation, as opposed to transitory problems and needs.

For example, the emphasis given in an evaluation to an explosive and violent TAT story will be quite different when it is produced by a patient whose Rorschach record shows uncontrollable impulsivity, poor reality testing, and an impoverished inner life from what it will be when it is the product of an individual who shows a rich, ambiequal Rorschach record and whose regressive fantasies may be described as being in the service of the ego.

At this stage, we may well ask the following questions: Are certain tests used more frequently than others for differential diagnosis? Are the same tests used when the differentiation must be made, for example, in regard to schizophrenia, an organic condition, manic-depressive psychosis, or neurotic disturbances? Do those psychologists who have devised tests or whose names are closely associated with any one projective method rely primarily or exclusively on this method for problems of differential diagnosis?

To obtain answers to these three questions, a questionnaire was sent to six experts associated with extensive research in the Rorschach, the Szondi, the Figure Drawing, the Wechsler, the Bender, and the TAT, respectively. Table 2 shows the findings concerning the use of these six projective techniques with respect to four specific problems of differential diagnosis.

The table can be looked at from several angles. One can see, for instance, that for a differential diagnosis involving schizophrenia, all six of the experts would use the Rorschach in order to arrive at their decision. Five of the six would also use the Figure Drawing, four would include the Wechsler, three would find the TAT of additional usefulness, and two would also base their findings on the Szondi and the Bender.

In the case of organic conditions, we find that all six would employ the Wechsler, five would require the Rorschach or would feel it necessary, four would add the Bender to the battery, three would require the Figure Drawing, one would add the TAT, and one would add the Szondi. It can further be seen that for a manic-depressive differentiation, the technique most frequently employed would be the TAT, in all but one case. Finally, in neurotic conditions, there is unanimity about the need for the Rorschach, with the Figure Drawing and the TAT in second place.

The table can also be looked at in another way. The Rorschach appears in 23 out of 24 possible situations, or it receives, shall one say, 23 out of 24 possible votes. In approximately equal second position, one finds the Figure Drawing, the Wechsler, and the TAT, with the Szondi and the Bender definitely less frequently employed where the task is differential diagnosis. Additional assessments, which included the Sentence Completion and the MMPI, showed that they would be used with approximately the same frequency as the Szondi and the Bender.

Organic Disorders

The stages of which we are speaking are not, of course, clearly demarcated on a temporal scale. However, it can be said that, following research which centered on the discovery of specific characteristics in the test records of supposedly homogeneous clinical groups, there occurred a swing of the pendulum. There were misgivings about the danger

TABLE 2. USE OF SIX PROJECTIVE TECHNIQUES

	Rorschach	*Szondi*	*Figure drawing*	*Wechsler*	*Bender*	*Tat*
Schizophrenia	6	2	5	4	2	3
Organic conditions	5	1	3	6	4	1
Manic-depressive psychoses	6	2	3	2	2	5
Neurotic disturbances	6	2	4	2	1	4
Total	23	7	15	14	9	13

of the too sign-oriented approach (from approximately the mid-forties to the mid-fifties).

As early as 1941, Ross pointed out that there was in existence a tendency to expect correlations to occur with groups of disease entities in which psychological factors, however important, could not tell the whole story. Reporting on one of his own studies, he states:

> In an effort to look beyond the search for correlations with diagnostic groups to possible correlations with more general factors relevant to the psychological aspects of disease, a study has been made of the incidence of two sets of signs: those described by Piotrowski as occurring in "organic cerebral disease," and those presented tentatively by Miale and Harrower as suggestive of the presence of a psychoneurosis.

Ross used 236 subjects, 13 to 76 years of age, including hospital patients, Army privates, and members of a university student body. The hospital patients were classified diagnostically as follows: patients with known lesions of the cerebrum, those with other lesions of the nervous system, those with uncomplicated psychoneuroses, those with somatic illness with some neurotic features, those with somatic illness free from neurotic features, those with psychoses of unknown etiology, and those with epilepsy of undetermined cause.

His subjects were also grouped, secondarily, according to other criteria. A group composed of ill individuals could be compared with one composed of healthy individuals. A group composed of all those with some evidence of disturbance of the nervous system, either "organic" or "functional," could be compared with a group of those without nervous disturbance. And, finally, subjects could be grouped according to socioeconomic level. Those with somatic illness free from neurotic features represented the average hospital patient, members of the university student body represented a higher socioeconomic and intellectual level, and the Army privates represented a lower one.

Ross continues:

> Correlations with the primary grouping were not found to be sufficiently specific for diagnostic purposes, when the signs were used by themselves. That is, the Rorschach signs alone were not sufficient to determine in which group the subject belonged. A highly significant correlation was found between Piotrowski's signs and the presence of some dysfunction of the central nervous system. With the criterion of 5 out of 10 of Piotrowski's signs, more than 95 per cent of the cases of nervous dysfunction were correctly classified.
>
> Miale and Harrower signs were found to be present more frequently in psychoneurosis than in either somatic illness with neurotic features or somatic illness without neurotic features. These differences were significant, but the same signs were also correlated with socioeconomic level independent of the presence of manifest neurosis. The factor correlating with low economic and intellectual level, which is more common in individuals who have neurotic symptoms without any associated somatic illness, could well be a basic personality insecurity which would contribute to the development of a neurosis without being its whole explanation. Considered with other information about the physical status and environment of the patient, the detection of this insecurity may become of real value in clinical diagnosis.

Much work continued on the organic patient. Piotrowski's signs have been incorporated into a wider frame of reference by Baker, who gave a thorough account of the status of differential diagnosis and the organic patient in 1954.

Baker (1954) found that Piotrowski's perplexity (Plx) was a reliable sign for all degrees of damage. Impotence (Imp) was found to be good for moderate and severe damage but to occur less often in mild damage. Repetition (Rpt) she found to be again reliable in moderate and severe damage and to occur occasionally in mild damage, while automatic phrasing (AP) she found less reliable than others.

Baker then educes other observations of her own which have been found to be equally helpful. For example, she considers concern over body image to be one of the most dependable signs. Patients may also refer to past experience in order to justify a response. She finds this occurring as an effort to cling to reality in order to combat perplexity and impotence. Poor discrimination between background and foreground, she feels, helps to distinguish the brain-injured patient from the hysteric or simple schizophrenic.

Other observations of Baker's include a

finding of marked discrepancy between the Rorschach and the Wechsler-Bellevue, to the disadvantage of the former, an observation noted by Miale and Harrower (1940). She also finds that the use of shading early in a record is particularly significant for organic cases.

Baker speaks of two signs in conjunction: "pickiness," namely, the patient's referring to small areas which stick up or stick out, and perseveration of an idea content. When these are combined, she feels that there is almost no question but that the diagnosis is brain damage, further differentiating it to suggest that a focal lesion and accompanying seizures could be suspected.

Baker has found a catastrophic reaction (the patient being overwhelmed by anxiety and unable to deal with the blot at all) but states that it has been found by her infrequently, and she raises the question of whether or not it may be the function of the manner in which the impotent feelings of the patient are handled.

Other observations of Baker's include the patient's need to make self-derogatory remarks; mild CF responses on cards VIII, IX, and X; an inability to break down the blot into parts in order to see two or more separate concepts; and the giving of few alternative interpretations for the same area of a blot, even when requested to attempt this.

Baker has also noted the ready use of FC, which she considers a sign of good premorbid adjustment, important in brain damage in that it may aid the differential diagnosis between this condition and schizophrenia.

An interesting sign of Baker's is passive content on the Rorschach accompanied by marked aggression on the TAT. The growing concern of psychodiagnosticians with the comparison of test findings, as opposed to reliance on one test instrument alone for such research observations, parallels the growing use of the differentiated test battery for ordinary psychodiagnostic cases.

NEW DIAGNOSTIC CATEGORIES

Turning now to the third phase—occurring during the late fifties and early sixties—we might describe it as characterized by a growing dissatisfaction with the current diagnostic labels and by an attempt on the part of psychiatrists, sociologists, and psychologists to explore new ways of classification and to search for new and more meaningful frames of reference.

On the social psychiatry side, we have Opler's (1963) plea for new diagnostic categories. As a social psychiatrist, he has begun to emphasize the importance of including cultural factors and social status. He feels that these influence the etiology, dynamics, and epidemiology of mental disorders around the world. He writes:

> In this light, social psychiatry formulated problems of this type which reach beyond the individual patient to social and cultural groups. While the older diagnostic classifications roughly describe, *the newer formulations relate to the processes which are really important in psychiatric illnesses, namely the etiology and dynamics of a more specific illness process in a given group.* When social psychiatry goes in the latter direction of types of illnesses within the older groupings, such as the schizophrenias, it is obviously going beyond categories of symptoms in nomenclature derived from Kraepelin and others to social and cultural roots and redefining dynamic profiles of illness structure and functioning. When this happens, one is pointing beyond static notions of therapy and prognostic estimates as fixed formulas to a more creative approach including social variables that structure the entire communicative process and milieu. Thus, social psychiatry has been thought of not only as a process of redefining illness entities, but as a new adventure in therapy with broader goals in the community than hitherto. Man is a social and cultural animal, and that first and foremost. Whether people function in hospitals or outside, they are functioning in social situations which are structured and predictable. Human responses cannot be adjusted to diagnostic formulations which have already changed both conceptually and in the light of increased clinical and cultural knowledge. Neither are human responses reducible to objectively defined stimuli. Even diagnoses historically have varied with social and cultural factors, as a cross-cultural survey of psychiatry would easily show. As to the symptoms themselves, their actual coloring, affective force and use in the psychic economy have always arisen from experience in a social and cultural milieu or background. Social psychiatry must therefore continue its more precise

definition of these social and cultural variables and their effects on diverse illness forms. This means not only clearer social and cultural classifications of patients, rather than atomistic listings of the symptoms, but more attention to what these differentiations mean in the etiology and dynamics of that half of all illness known as psychiatric disorder.

Wolman also proposes a new classification of mental disorder. His classifications are more specific and have been spelled out in greater detail. They are derived from observation and experimental studies of social behavior as well as from clinical studies based on the psychoanalytic frame of reference. He utilizes these two methods to analyze the same phenomena from diverse points of view. He assumes that all social relations depend upon motivation and perception and that individuals perceive one another in terms of power and acceptance, power being defined as the ability to satisfy needs or to prevent their satisfaction, and acceptance being defined as the willingness or unwillingness to do so.

He further assumes that social relationships can be divided into three categories: (1) instrumental relationships, which occur whenever individuals join others in order to satisfy their own needs; (2) mutual relationships, which occur whenever individuals enter social relations with the purpose of both receiving and giving and whenever their goal is the satisfaction of the needs of both parties; and (3) vectorial relationships, which occur whenever an individual enters into a relationship in order to satisfy the needs of the other person or persons, whether for idealistic or charitable reasons (Wolman, 1956).

Although normal individuals can enter into all these relationships insofar as they are relevant in any given situation, it has been observed in psychotherapeutic work, particularly in a group therapy setting, that one or another of these attitudes may dominate the total pattern of overt behavior of a patient. Wolman finds the psychopath hyperinstrumental; the latent schizophrenic, hypervectorial; and the manic-depressive, paramutual. Thus, in social relations, the psychopath strives to have others serve him, the latent schizophrenic desires his services to be accepted, and the manic-depressive swings from one of these attitudes to the other. The psychopath hates whomever does not serve him; the latent schizophrenic is afraid to hate; and the manic-depressive swings from one of these extremes to the other.

Wolman feels that these findings correspond well to the analytic frame of reference, for the psychopath acts upon an insufficient reality principle; his superego is practically nonexistent, and his ego is primitive. The latent schizophrenic is the opposite: his superego is overdeveloped, domineering, self-righteous, demanding, and moralistic; his ego is overmobilized; and his id is severely controlled. The manic-depressive shows an ego that is disoriented, demoralized, and demobilized and a superego that is inconsistent, sometimes furiously attacking the ego, as in depression, and sometimes embracing it, as in elation (Wolman, 1957; Wolman, 1960).

Table 3 shows Wolman's classification scheme. It will be seen that five levels can be distinguished for each of the three aforementioned types. These levels reflect a transition from neurosis to character disorder, latent psychosis, manifest psychosis, and finally complete disorganization of the personality, as in a demented state. Wolman feels that differential diagnosis must take into consideration both the vertical and the horizontal subdivisions and that an individual can meaningfully be placed in one or another of these 15 subdivisions. This classification, the author contends, is valuable also in predicting the course of a given disorder, provided it is realized, of course, that the continuity indicated here is not a universal phenomenon and that other determinants must always be taken into account.

Test-determined Categories

From the psychodiagnostician's standpoint, a more independent point of view is developing. Take, for instance, such thoughts as expressed by McCully (1962), when considering discrepancies which sometimes occur between clinical and Rorschach data in borderline cases. He states:

> In borderline cases it is not infrequent to find some disparity between behavioral symptoms and the extent of apparent psychopathology in the Rorschach. . . . Not infrequently the Rorschach worker hears "there are no clinical psychotic symptoms;

TABLE 3. WOLMAN'S CLASSIFICATION OF SOCIOGENIC MENTAL DISORDERS

Levels	*Hyper-instrumentalism I*	*Paramutualism M*	*Hypervectorialism V*
Neurosis	Hyperinstrumental neurosis (certain anxiety and depressive reactions)	Paramutual neurosis (dissociative and conversion reactions)	Hypervectorial neurosis (obsessional, phobic, and neurasthenic reactions)
Character neurosis	Hyperinstrumental character neurosis (sociopathic or psychopathic personality	Paramutual character neurosis (cyclothymic and passive-aggressive personality)	Hypervectorial character neurosis (schizoid and compulsive personality)
Latent psychosis	Latent hyperinstrumental psychosis (psychopathic reactions bordering on psychosis)	Latent paramutual psychosis (borderline manic-depressive psychosis)	Latent vectoriasis praecox (borderline and latent schizophrenia)
Manifest psychosis	Hyperinstrumental psychosis (psychotic psychopathy and moral insanity)	Paramutual psychosis (manifest manic-depressive psychosis)	Vectoriasis praecox (manifest schizophrenia)
Dementia	Collapse of personality structure	Collapse of personality structure	Collapse of personality structure

what does it mean when you say the Rorschach picture has schizophrenic features?" Too often, in such a seemingly contradictory context, Rorschach data may be dismissed for one reason or another.

However, he continues: "Rorschach behavior is just as clinical as any other behavior," and he asks: "Must one only make a 'correct' diagnosis when it is based exclusively on relatively well structured sets of stimuli, as in the clinical situation?" Finally, he concludes with the statement: "Psychiatric diagnosis is not always the appropriate standard of comparison or criterion for predictions based on Rorschach's findings."

Klopfer and Spiegelman (1954) voice a generally accepted belief in their statement:

> The new development in Rorschach interpretation has changed the practical value of the Rorschach technique as a diagnostic and prognostic tool profoundly. The old limitation of validating nosological personality characteristics through group comparisons with the help of classificatory signs, was overcome. . . . Even within the diagnostic function of the Rorschach we face a shift of emphasis away from nosological categories per se, towards the descriptions of idiosyncratic thought processes and affective reactions which, in turn, may even make the use of nosological categories more specific and meaningful.

At the same time, they state:

> Rorschach is now more widely used in planning therapy rather than in confirming or modifying clinical diagnostic impressions.

Molish and Beck (1958) have published important material in relation to the schizophrenic group which exemplifies the need of psychologists to produce test-oriented classifications which are better prognosticators of success or failure in treatment.

Their investigations have provided descriptions of the schizophrenic reaction type within a conceptual scheme of personality structure incorporating five theoretical components: (1) defensive organization, (2) associational integration, (3) fantasy activity, (4) emotional state, and (5) social adaptation. In collaboration with colleagues at the Michael Reese Hospital, Beck obtained operational statements which comprise a trait sample of 170 items, which could be applied to all levels of personality integration, extending along a broad continuum from the hypothetical normal to those disruptive ego functions typical of the classic schizophrenic process. Beck and Molish then found Rorschach correlates with each of the 170 items of behavior which had previously been formulated. According to the distribution of scores, Beck (1954) found *six distinct schizophrenic groups* which he has classified as S-1, S-2, S-3, SR-1, SR-2, and SG. These test-determined groups do not necessarily overlap with the clinical diagnostic labels, or, to quote Molish:

> The basic philosophy of the current research and its methodology *deemphasizes the role of nosology* in describing the schizophrenic process. The assumption is that although there are 30 patients described as paranoid schizophrenics in the group, there are sufficient differences within their personality structures to allow for a much finer differentiation by the methodology used. In other words, the most constructive attitude to adopt in relation to this problem is that any paranoid schizophrenic can be placed on a continuum which extends all the way from a less completely systematized disorder to the most severely disorganized syndromes of schizophrenia.

Assessed within this frame of reference, patients can, according to Beck and Molish, be handled *much more effectively therapeutically*. Type S-3 schizophrenics, for instance, while showing few of the gross disturbances in thinking (thinking is purposeful; language productions are orderly; thought is logical as well as coherent), nonetheless respond poorly to treatment. On the other hand, they can maintain their status quo in a relatively benign environment.

Independently, in assessing Rorschach records in a different way, Piotrowski and Levine (1959) have come up with almost identical criteria to describe that group of schizophrenic patients who are somehow impervious to any form of treatment. His alpha type corresponds very closely to Beck's S-3. Piotrowski has also made a fundamental contribution with his long-term prognostic criterion.

Confronted with the request for differential diagnosis, how will the clinician of the future proceed? We have seen that his choice of diagnostic categories is apt to be different; it may well also be expected that, as the years pass, another dimension will be added to his psychodiagnostic work. He will shortly begin to operate on the basis of experimental evidence. A sufficiently large number of cases will have been followed over the years, so that there will be some measure of the accuracy with which diagnosis and prognosis have been made by means of the projective techniques.

Until recently, sufficient time had not elapsed, nor had a sufficient number of cases been followed in a systematic and thorough fashion, to allow the clinical psychologist to give an answer based on fact to such a question as "What is the appropriate type of therapy for this individual?" By means of educated hunches, assessments of ego strength, and general theoretical expectations as to what constituted treatable personality profiles, psychodiagnosticians attempted to answer such queries from therapists. It has been standard practice, for example, to advise against analytic treatment in those cases where primary processes or archaic types of thinking are clearly evidenced in the projective tests. Conversely, the majority of clinicians seem to have operated on the assumption that considerable repression, as exemplified in the test findings, would point to the type of treatment where uncovering techniques were used.

However, as Kubie has pointed out, neither the therapist's questions nor the psychologist's reply could really be taken seriously as long as an adequate method for assessing improvement in treatment was lacking and as long as psychologists had not had the opportunity to follow a sufficient number of patients over a sufficient number of years to discover how correct their predictions were concerning the success or failure of a given case receiving a given kind of treatment.

Harrower's Follow-up Study

This dilemma prompted Harrower (1965) to investigate what could be termed the therapeutic "fate" of over sixteen hundred patients, drawn from a case load of 2,131 psychodiagnostic referrals and seen over an eleven-year period in private practice. While it took four years to accumulate the material, a surprisingly high percentage of therapists finally were able to give information concerning their patients. In all, 1,463 replies were received to a questionnaire which sought information on the following points: the type of treatment the patient had received, the length of time he or she had been in treatment, and the assessed improvement on a four-point scale, ranging from "no improvement" through "slight improvement" and "moderate improvement" to "satisfactory" or "good results."

Since the questionnaire asked that the rating be accompanied by an explanation of why an individual had been so assessed, and since not all the therapists were able to supply sufficiently detailed information, a special group of 622 cases were extracted from the total number of replies because these contained pure evidence that the therapist had followed the patient over a sufficient length of time and knew him sufficiently well to be in a position to assess his progress. Two samples of acceptable evidence are given here for illustrative purposes:

Length of Time in Therapy: Three Years, Seven Months
Type of Therapy: Analytic Psychotherapy
(Moderate Improvement)

> Patient appeared to be an immature dependent personality of above average intelligence and capabilities who was markedly inhibited in all personal relations, and doing very poor work because of rumination, procrastination, and endless preoccupation with unproductive fantasies of a largely sexual nature. He had hysterical symptoms with under-lying homosexual preoccupation. In long analytically oriented therapy he has revealed himself to be a passive dependent personality entirely oriented toward pleasing various father substitutes. His attributes are immense ambivalence, stubbornness, stinginess, fear of emotional involvement (dirt), and unconscious rage.
>
> He has made great strides in his work life where he has become more assertive, independent and creative, as well as financially successful, and has been able to function with more and more awareness of his true feelings. His marriage, however, is without emotional involvement. There are no children or social activities. In therapy he has only recently begun to confront his compulsive defenses. I believe that there is a masculine identification from young childhood; that his present difficulties had their onset with the birth of a younger brother when patient was age 7; and that eventually therapy will have a successful outcome.

Length of Time in Therapy: Four Years
Type of Therapy: Psychoanalytic Psychotherapy
(Good Improvement)

> At the outset this patient appeared to be a borderline schizophrenic college graduate with alcoholism, phobias, and gradual social withdrawal into passivity and depression, marked anxiety in almost every situation and afraid to think her own thoughts or attempt the solution of any problems.
>
> In four years of work, she has developed into a socially active girl who is successful at work, has boy friends and an active social and sex life, and has freed herself from her dependence on her psychotic parents. She continues not to be able to use her fantasies constructively much of the time, but is no longer subject to anxiety about them. She has developed some useful compensations, is increasingly able to give expression to her feelings generally, has been able to stop her former alcoholism and overeating, and has lost about thirty pounds. She now looks and dresses well instead of bizarrely.
>
> She has maintained this improved adjustment for a long time now, although she has distinctly borderline qualities still. Her fantasies are bizarre at times, and at times she is impulsive and impractical in problem-solving. As you might suppose, her continuing real problem is her fear of the close emotional involvements of love, although there is continuing improvement here also. Whether she will be able to marry and have children, I could not predict.

The distribution, in terms of success or failure, in the 622 well-authenticated cases was as follows: maximum improvement, 134; moderate improvement, 212; slight improvement, 129; no improvement, 147.

The investigator then turned to a reexamination of the raw scores from the original test battery in an attempt to classify, on the basis of similarities in total test reactions, the performance on eight projective techniques. Two scales of test-determined categories were established, one scale ranging through seven classifications, from very superior over-all performance to very poor over-all performance. In this scale all tests were reacted to by a subject at approximately the same level of

TABLE 4

*Homogeneous scale**			*Heterogeneous scale†*		
Category	*No. in group*	*Percentage of failure*	*Category*	*No. in group*	*Percentage of failure*
1	5	0	1	45	13
2	17	0	2	67	19
3	71	10	3	13	31
4	73	14	4	51	31
5	83	21	5	46	30
6	74	27	6	42	50
7	35	54	7		
Total	358		Total	264	

* A biserial coefficient of correlation was calculated, using success and failure as criteria. The coefficient was found to be .438, significant beyond the .01 level of confidence.

† The biserial coefficient of correlation was .328. There is some tendency for patients to fail to respond to therapy as their position on the heterogeneous scale worsens. This tendency, however, is not as great as on the homogeneous scale.

achievement; that is, the test production showed an essentially uniform type of performance. This scale was called one of "homogeneous personality endowment."

The second scale included test performances characterized by irregularity. In this scale an individual showed great giftedness or potential on some of the projectives, while on others he might evidence acute problem areas or disturbances. This scale also was based on seven levels of achievement and was referred to as one of "heterogeneous personality endowment." These classifications, it should be emphasized, were made on the basis of only objective test scores. They were in no way related to the accompanying psychiatric diagnosis with which the patient might have been referred.

The relationship of failure to respond to therapeutic intervention increased significantly at the lower end of both scales. A patient falling into the categories homogeneous 1, 2, or 3 had an excellent chance to benefit from psychotherapeutic techniques. Conversely, those falling into test categories homogeneous 6 or 7 or heterogeneous 6 or 7 were shown to profit much less from existing modes of psychotherapy.

Clearly, the projective type as reflected in standardized grouping, based on test scores, is one factor influencing the patient treatability.

The importance of these findings for differential diagnosis would seem to be that they allow, for the first time, empirical evidence to be introduced concerning whether or not a given projective protocol indicates the patient's receptivity to the psychotherapeutic treatment of the present day. Clearly, those at the lower end of the scale are apt to profit much less than those with richer psychological endowments.

SPECIALIZED TRAINING IN DIAGNOSIS

It is becoming increasingly evident that differential diagnosis requires highly specialized training. In order to become a competent psychodiagnostician, capable of mastering the multitude of complex problems described above, one has to have adequate preparation.

It is only fair to say at the outset that there just is no "ready-to-wear" specialized training program in diagnosis for the beginner.

We shall therefore approach the problem by suggesting answers to the following questions rather than by outlining a specific course of professional activity:

1. Just what is specialized training in diagnosis—however come by—meant to achieve?
2. What is the difference between a successful and an unsuccessful handling of a diagnostic task or, rather, between the handling and disposition of a case by an experienced diagnostician and by a novice?
3. What, in the last analysis, constitutes the ability to produce a relevant and meaningful psychological assessment?

If the invidual is clear about the answers to these questions, the chances are that he will have many rewarding and enriching experiences during his "training." They may have a certain idiosyncratic quality, and they cannot necessarily be prescribed for each and every psychodiagnostician in embryo. So to our task.

Breaking up the diagnostic situation into its more obvious elements or units, we have (1) the patient tested; (2) the tools with which the assessment is made, the psychodiagnostic battery; (3) the psychologist himself, who is, of course, a person of many levels; (4) the report, written or verbal, by which information is carried; and (5) the recipient of this report, in some instances an individual with background, experiences, training, and interests somewhat different from those of the psychodiagnostician himself. We may diagram this in the following way:

Patient → Tests → (Psychologist) →
(input)
Report → Recipient
(output)

Let us consider each of these in greater detail.

The Patient Tested

Specialized training for diagnosis must include exposure to as wide a variety of persons as possible. This variety should cover the total spectrum in regard to age, from the youngest children who can participate in a diagnostic situation to persons in their eighties and nineties. It is not sufficient to have read about how the very young or the very old react in test situations; it is not sufficient to know where, in the literature, one may find a collection of adolescent records.

One of the first prerequisites for a well-trained psychodiagnostician is to have his own personally experienced frame of reference from youth to age.

Just as exposure to a wide age range among the normal population is a prerequisite for diagnostic acumen, so is it important to have tested, written reports on, and have available for comparative purposes at least a small cross section of persons from different cultural backgrounds.

It is all too easy to take, as the implicit frame of reference, the psychodiagnostic test data acquired from persons in our culture. Although it is not always possible to make one's own anthropological expedition to acquire records of far-off peoples, it is necessary to have an awareness of such collected records as those of Hallowell (1954), Mead (1949), Abel (1948), and others and, at least, to have sat across the testing table from persons from other lands who speak other languages as their native tongue.

Failure to be aware of the different kinds of test protocols produced by individuals of comparable age but different *socioeconomic status* may also create a blind spot in the psychodiagnostician unless this is tackled explicitly. Startling differences were found, for example, by this author, in a comparison of 100 delinquent adolescents, taken from a children's court and coming from a low socioeconomic group, with a comparable number of adolescents referred as behavior problems from upper- and middle-class homes (Harrower, 1955).

The perspective afforded by records taken under *group conditions* is very important. Regardless of how fast, assiduously, or systematically the psychodiagnostician may attempt to collect records, as long as he is utilizing the individual method of testing, the accumulation of material is relatively slow. One of the great advantages of administering a battery of projectives to groups of subjects at a time is that it is possible to leaf through or scan the test material with certain specific questions in mind and to profit from what might be called the "panorama" seen in this way.

During World War II, this particular experience—of gaining perspective from a large sample of "normal" records—was an unexpected by-product of research being done by this writer on screening techniques (Harrower, 1943).

This experience is recommended as an important step in the specialized training of the would-be psychodiagnostician, since many things come to light in the scanning of a large population at one time which cannot be seen as part of a total pattern if the accumulation of the records is laboriously slow. To give one concrete example, certain basic differences, in terms of personality structure, between the typical student about to enter medicine and the typical student about to enter a theological seminary stand out sharply when several hundred records obtained on each group are contrasted in terms of two basic Rorschach variables M and C (Harrower, 1963).

So far we have spoken of experiences which would tend to acquaint the psychodiagnostician with a sufficiently wide variety of persons tested within the normal population. And while, of course, abnormal records reflecting acute or minor psychological problems will be found in the "normal" population, it is obviously imperative that any kind of specialized training prepare the student to recognize the various forms of psychopathology and to work with disturbed persons of various kinds.

It is important to be able to work and to feel at ease in a situation with a psychotic and deteriorated patient. Therefore, the experience of working in a state hospital and of acquiring records of individuals on the disturbed wards is good to have under one's belt. It is an interesting challenge to attempt to enter the world of the psychotic patient sufficiently to elicit from him the material needed for a diagnostic evaluation. It often requires peculiar tact and imagination to involve the individual, during an acute psychotic episode, to a point where he will participate. Deteriorated patients on the back wards pose a different type of problem, but they afford an opportunity for the trainee to gain self-confidence and to set for himself the goal of keeping the number of those who refuse to be tested at a minimum.

Many psychodiagnosticians do not have the opportunity to acquire records on a group of individuals who are physically ill but who do not necessarily present any kind of psychological problems to their physicians. These individuals may be subdivided into many groups; two contrasting ones are groups of those who must live with chronic disabling diseases and groups of those about to face a specific crisis, for example, a serious operation.

Closely allied to those individuals who are physically ill and who may have to be tested at a hospital bedside are those individuals who are physically handicapped in some way or other. Training in psychodiagnosis must include the opportunity to learn to adapt to the physical handicaps of another in such a way that they will not interfere with the essence of the testing situation. The individual must bring his ingenuity into play frequently in order that the specific handicap may be bypassed. The battery may have to be altered, and the method of administration changed. For example, an individual with a severe speech handicap may respond far more authentically if he is allowed to write his responses than if he is forced to toe the line and make the usual verbal responses. Deaf individuals can also be tested easily through written communication. If the patient happens to have some kind of paralysis or is coping with the tremor of Parkinson's disease, the examiner should already have changed his *modus operandi* so that the cards, for example, are placed before the patient, as a matter of course, and not given into his hand. There are innumerable little details and deviations which must become second nature to the well-trained psychodiagnostician. Therefore, adequate opportunities must be afforded in any kind of specialized training so that the uncertainty goes out of the tester's approach.

A final group of patients may be considered in detail whom we may describe as individuals whose immediate fate may be determined by the evidence educed by the psychodiagnostician. The immediacy is stressed because, by and large, psychodiagnostic reports will contribute to planning in terms of a long-range program rather than a dramatically decisive one. Patients who are suspected of brain tumor fall into this category, for if diagnostic tests support x-ray, electroencephalogram, and neurological examination, the chances are that surgical intervention will be attempted very promptly. As long as all the evidence goes in the same direction—as long as the psychological report merely reinforces other and more time-honored modes of diagnosis—there is no real problem. But the well-trained psychodiagnostician must sometimes face a situation where he alone detects the presence of an organic cerebral condition because the tumor is in a silent area of the brain, giving no clinical evidence of its presence. If the psychodiagnostician's knowledge is a theoretical or secondhand one, he will find it hard to throw the appropriate weight behind his report in favor of his "conflicting" evidence.

One acquires a kind of professional confidence not otherwise easily come by when an exploratory operation demonstrates the presence of a lesion predicted from the psychodiagnostic tests, and from the psychodiagnostic tests alone.

So much, then, for the opportunities which specialized training should provide as far as a variety of patients, subjects, and testees is concerned.

The Diagnostician's Tools: The Test Battery

The chances are that by the time the would-be diagnostic specialist seeks this training, he has a nodding acquaintance with virtually all the tests he will ever employ in his full-time diagnostic work. The chances are that he also will have taken courses—intensive courses—in several of them. It is hard to conceive, for instance, of anyone in the field of clinical psychology reaching the postdoctoral level without being thoroughly well-versed in the Rorschach. The difference between the specialized training which we are considering and the more general training that is available to all is that the former would ensure that one would be able to administer—*facilely, from memory, and without anxiety*—all the tests that he might be called on to use in routine and special examinations.

To this should be added some concentrated training including, perhaps, research or original work in one or two of the better-known projective instruments. It would be valuable, also, in specialized training for the individual to try to detect those clinical situations where he himself feels the usual instruments are inadequate and to try his hand at some form of test construction. Perhaps "test construction" is too formidable a term. He might well be content with trying to make certain special modifications of well-known instruments so that they would more directly meet the needs of a certain patient population with which he is particularly concerned.

Intensive training in the use of tests should also allow the individual to discover his optimum working speed in their administration and the extent to which he can "hold" the average patient within this frame of reference.

An important aspect of training is to allow the individual to discover for himself a group of tests which cover sufficiently different aspects of the patient's personality so that they supplement one another. He should also feel happy and relaxed working with them. There is no getting away from the fact that certain kinds of individuals feel at home with some tests and not with others, regardless of how often they use them or the extent of the training they have had in them.

The Psychologist as a Person

So far we have emphasized that training must provide opportunities for the psychologist to be exposed to a wide spectrum of persons to be tested and to become sufficiently familiar with a variety of tests so that their administration is second nature to him. Looking at our original formulation, we have so far discussed only the intake side of the equation. The psychodiagnostician must now thoroughly digest the information before him, prior to transmitting it in the form of a written report. The third type of training we speak of must, therefore, be directed toward assuring that this process of digestion goes on in as mature an individual as possible, not only so that the correct deductions can be made, but also so that a certain amount of wisdom will be contained in the conclusions.

Some form of personal analysis or insight-giving therapy would seem to be as much a prerequisite for the psychodiagnostician in training as it is for the serious student who expects to be a full-time psychoanalytically oriented therapist. Exactly the same arguments which have been educed in favor of making a training analysis mandatory for the therapist could be used, in this writer's opinion, in the case of the psychodiagnostician. An individual who does not know his own blind spots and biases is vulnerable when working in the field of mental illness or mental health. A person in whom anxiety can be triggered or hostility aroused in certain kinds of interpersonal relationships must, of necessity, be something other than completely neutral or objective when assessing his findings. Specialized training for a psychodiagnostician should include an analytic experience as a patient. There are two other reasons why genuine familiarity with analytic concepts and the psychodynamics of the unconscious is important. The first is, of course, that much of the information concerning an individual tested relates to unconscious motivation. A psychodiagnostic report is known to be superficial insofar as it deals only with a patient's controlled activity. The report is also somewhat superficial, however, if the psychodiagnostician is aware only vicariously, from conscientious reading of the literature, of the meaning of the psychodynamics. Not having grappled with, not being on friendly terms with, his own unconscious, he may become anxious at revelations about his patient which come from the deeper levels.

The second reason why the diagnostician should feel at home in the analytic frame of reference is that many of the referring physicians will have had such training and will expect information slanted in this direction.

Clearly, it is not always necessary or appropriate to emphasize the analytic approach or to write a report couched in psychoanalytic terminology. But specialized training as a psychodiagnostician should prepare one to use this approach when appropriate.

There is another facet of self-knowledge which is much less frequently emphasized but which seems of equal importance in the training of psychodiagnosticians, namely, that he should be aware of his own productions on all the test instruments which he uses and should have had the opportunity to go over a report written on his test production by a thoroughly experienced and wise psychodiagnostic practitioner. Unless this is done, the psychodiagnostician will find himself automatically assuming that somehow or other his own productions constitute a base line of normality. Thus, he will too readily read pathology into test profiles that are dissimilar to his own and, conversely, will find condoning circumstances where there are striking similarities. To give a specific example, a gifted but strongly introverted student in training repeatedly failed to detect the presence of a real schizoid withdrawal in patients whose Rorschach records showed a large number of albeit excellent M responses. To do so would have precipitated considerable anxiety in him, for the similarities of these records to his own were striking. Another trainee constantly overemphasized the "compulsive quality" in records in which there was a reasonably high —but in no way excessive—F per cent. Going over this individual's own Rorschach record with him revealed that he belonged to that small group of individuals whose F per cent is unusually low. Thus, again, to ward off his own anxiety and to avoid having to face this particular personal problem of his own, he envisaged all individuals with a higher F per cent as rigid, overcontrolled, compulsive, and the like.

This type of training should be part of those experiences which were spoken of before as being idiosyncratic. The would-be psychodiagnostician must seek out this kind of experience for himself because opportunities for it do not exist, as a matter of course, in the same way that the opportunities for self-understanding through the analytic techniques do. Yet, seeing oneself in terms of one's test profile, since the diagnostician deals essentially with test profiles and not people, would seem to be as much a "must" for the professional psychodiagnostician as a personal analysis is for the professional psychoanalyst.

Report Writing and Recipient of the Report

The fourth and fifth elements in our initial scheme are the writing of the report and the background, experiences, training, and interests of the recipient. The psychodiagnostician must be trained not only to write the report but also to make it understandable to the person to whom it is addressed. These two aspects are hard to separate. At best, it is a matter of emphasis. A psychodiagnostician needs the opportunity to try his hand at writing reports of all kinds directed toward individuals with various backgrounds. He should have the opportunity to see how a psychological report is spontaneously reacted to by persons in various fields and with various kinds of professional training. He needs to see how he, as a psychologist, fits into their respective frames of reference.

Report writing, it is true, can to some extent be learned. There are chapters in handbooks devoted to it and even some volumes dealing with it exclusively. The ability to know whether or not one's report is actively relevant comes from firsthand experience in the particular field and cannot be acquired by study alone. Is a report actively helpful to the person who has asked for it? Is its full meaning getting across? Are there, perhaps, some visual aids which can be devised or employed to sharpen the recipient's awareness of what the psychologist means? Greening and Bugental (1962) have stated this well in their chapter on psychologists in clinics in *The Profession of Psychology:*

> The optimal use of psychodiagnostic studies depends, in part, on the manner in which the results are communicated to the clinic staff. In addition to a formal written report that is placed in the patient's file, diagnostic findings are usually presented and discussed at a staff meeting. The writing and presentation of meaningful reports is a challenging task, requiring that the psychologist not only formulate his ideas about the patient clearly but also present them in a way that can be understood by nonpsychologists. The use of fancy jargon and far-out abstractions may dazzle his audience but will not increase their understanding of the patient. A balance must be achieved between rote recital

of the scores and speculations that have no apparent relation to observations and test data. Because clinics differ greatly from each other, a psychologist must be able to prepare and present reports in a variety of atmospheres. At one extreme are those staff meetings that are like an informal family Kaffeeklatsch with many siblings struggling for cookies and a part in the discussion. A wide ranging discussion may ensue, requiring the psychologist to document and defend his conclusions against all manner of alternative interpretations. At another extreme are formal courtroom-like proceedings presided over by the clinic director, who allots to each staff member his prescribed role. At these the psychologist is more typically called upon to present a concise, highly organized report, usually stressing a formal diagnostic categorization of the patient.

Perhaps one of the most important training opportunities is that which allows the psychodiagnostician to experiment, to innovate, and to break the established procedure for the purpose of achieving a more relevant service. For example, when working in children's court, where speed in arriving at some kind of psychological evaluation is imperative, it was found that the answering of 10 questions about the raw data from the test battery not only could be done in an extremely short space of time but also actually conveyed more to the judge or the probation officer than the laborious and careful psychodiagnostic evaluation. It was necessary for the psychologist literally to put himself in the position of the judge, a judge faced with the disposition (deciding on the course of action to be adopted). The judge had performed this duty for years, without the "help" of a psychodiagnostic evaluation. A report was unlikely to be read. However, information that could be seen at a glance, in terms of the questions and answers, introduced some meaningful material in a relatively "painless" way. The questions asked and answered (yes and no) in any individual case were as follows:

1. Is this child psychotic?
2. Is there a psychotic potential?
3. Does this child show organic deterioration?
4. Are there unduly strong feelings of rejection?
5. Are sex drives abnormally strong?
6. Is this child unduly aggressive?
7. Is anxiety very great?
8. Is this child retarded intellectually?
9. Is he more retarded than the general population?
10. What are the potential unutilized constructive forces?
11. Does he have a reading disability?
12. How can this child best be reached?
13. Does this child need treatment?
14. Is he treatable?
15. How can we meet his needs realistically in society?

Such a simple and timesaving device could epitomize instantly the different clinical, psychological, and treatment problems involved in a case, for example, of two teen-agers brought before the court for identical misdemeanors, one of whom is psychotic and the other of whom has better than average intellectual and psychological potential.

Such reports had real relevance for nonpsychologically trained personnel who were under pressure to perform their established or routine tasks in a certain amount of time. Thus, if psychodiagnostics is to be helpful, it must fit into and adapt to established schemes and not demand the impossible in terms of psychological sophistication from the recipient of the report.

At the other extreme, there may be highly sophisticated therapists and psychoanalysts who not only can profit from extremely detailed psychodiagnostic evaluations but are also interested in knowing what went into a psychodiagnostician's decision to make each of his evaluative judgments. Samples of such reports have been published by Harrower (1961).

Finally, we may place emphasis implicitly on the *person* to whom the report is to go. To feel at home in the other fellow's world is of paramount importance, and it is up to the psychodiagnostician to be aware of the kind of inevitable distortions and misconceptions to which the terms he uses spontaneously are susceptible. He should actively seek training or experience in places, and among persons, where he is the one who speaks the "foreign" language. He should actively seek to become embedded in another professional world—the strictly medical, the institutional, or the judicial world; the world of business and industry; or the world of the school systems. Any one of these may be alien to him when he first starts, and only by working in it and by absorbing the way in which a psychodiagnostic report is actually envisaged there, will he be able to address himself appropriately to his reader. Furthermore, once he can speak freely in the other fellow's terms, he can set about correcting misconceptions or enlarging a too circumscribed concept of the psychodiagnostician's role which the other fellow may have.

REFERENCES

Abel, Theodora M. The Rorschach test in the study of culture. *J. proj. Tech.*, 1948, **12**, 1–15.

Aita, J. A., Reitan, R. M., & Ruth, J. M. Rorschach test as a diagnostic aid in brain injury. *Amer. J. Psychiat.*, 1947, **103**, 770–779.

Baker, Gertrude. Diagnosis of organic brain damage in the adult. In B. Klopfer et al. (Eds.), *Developments in the Rorschach technique,* New York: Harcourt, Brace & World, 1954.

Beck, S. J. *The six schizophrenias.* New York: American Orthopsychiatric Association, 1954.

Brown, M., et al. Personality factors in duodenal ulcer: a Rorschach study. *Psychosom. Med.*, 1950, **12**, 1–5.

Greening, T., & Bugental, J. F. T. Psychologists in clinics. In W. B. Webb (Ed.), *The profession of psychology.* New York: Holt, 1962.

Hallowell, A. I. The Rorschach technique in personality and culture studies. In B. Klopfer et al. (Eds.), *Developments in the Rorschach technique.* New York: Harcourt, Brace, & World, 1954.

Harrower, Molly. Diagnosis of psychogenic factors in disease by means of the Rorschach method. *Psychiat. Quart.*, 1943, **17**, 57–66.

Harrower, Molly R., & Steiner, M. E. *Large scale Rorschach techniques.* Springfield, Ill.: Charles C Thomas, 1954.

Harrower, Molly. *Medical and psychological team work in the care of the chronically ill.* Springfield, Ill.: Charles C Thomas, 1955.

Harrower, Molly. *Personality change and development as measured by the projective techniques.* New York: Grune & Stratton, 1958.

Harrower, Molly. The contribution of the projective techniques to the problem of diagnosis. In J. H. Masserman & J. L. Moreno (Eds.), *Progress in psychology.* Vol. 5. New York: Grune & Stratton, 1960.

Harrower, Molly. *The practice of clinical psychology.* Springfield, Ill.: Charles C Thomas, 1961.

Harrower, Molly. Psychological tests in the Unitarian Universalist ministry. *J. Relig. Hlth.*, 1963, **2** (2), 129–142.

Harrower, Molly. *Psychodiagnostic testing: an empirical approach based on a follow-up of 2000 cases.* Springfield, Ill.: Charles C. Thomas, 1965.

Harrower, Molly R., & Kraus, J. Psychological studies on patients with multiple sclerosis. *Arch. Neurol. Psychiat.*, 1951, **66**, 44–57.

Klopfer, B., & Kelley, D. McG. *The Rorschach technique.* New York: Harcourt, Brace & World, 1942. Pp. 362–363.

Klopfer, B., & Spiegelman, M. Differential diagnosis. In B. Klopfer et al. (Eds.), *Developments in the Rorschach technique.* New York: Harcourt, Brace & World, 1954.

McCully, R. S. Certain theoretical considerations in relation to borderline schizophrenia and the Rorschach. *J. proj. Tech.*, 1962, **26** (4), 417.

Mead, Margaret. The mountain Arapesh. V. The record of unabelin with Rorschach analysis. *Anthrop. Papers, Amer. Museum nat. Hist.*, 1949.

Miale, F. R., & Harrower, Molly. Personality structure in the psychoneuroses. *Rorschach Res. Exch.*, 1940, **4** (1), 8–25.

Modell, A. H., & Potter, H. W. Human figure drawings of patients with arterial hypertension, peptic ulcer and bronchial asthma. *Psychosom. Med.*, 1949, **11**, 282–292.

Molish, H. B., & Beck, S. J. Further explorations of the "six schizophrenias": type S-3. *Amer. J. Orthopsychiat.*, 1958, **28**, 483.

Opler, M. K. The need for new diagnostic categories in psychiatry. *New Physician,* 1963.

Osborne, R. J., & Sanders, W. B. Rorschach characteristics of duodenal ulcer patients. *J. clin. Psychol.*, 1950, **6**, 258–262.

Peck, H. B., Harrower, Molly, & Beck, Mildred B. *A new pattern for mental health services in a children's court.* Springfield, Ill.: Charles C Thomas, 1958.

Piotrowski, Z. A. The Rorschach inkblot method in organic disturbances of the central nervous system. *J. nerv. ment. Dis.*, 1937.

Piotrowski, Z. A., & Bricklin, B. A long-term prognostic criterion for schizophrenics based on Rorschach data. *Psychiat. Quart. Suppl.*, 1958, **32**, 315, Part 2.

Piotrowski, Z. A., & Levine, D. A case illustrating the concept of the alpha schizophrenic. *J. proj. Tech.*, 1959, **23**, 223.

Rorschach, H. *Psychodiagnostics.* Bern: Hans Huber, 1942. New York: Grune & Stratton, 1942.

Ross, W. D. The incidence of some signs elicited by the Rorschach method. *Bull. of Canad. psychol. Ass.*, 1941.

Schafer, R. *Psychoanalytic interpretation in Rorschach testing: theory and application.* New York: Grune & Stratton, 1954.

Thorne, F. C. Theoretical foundations of directive psychotherapy. *Current Trends clin. Psychol., Ann. N. Y. Acad. Sci.*, 1948, **49**, 867–928.

Wolman, B. B. Leadership and group dynamics. *J. soc. Psychol.*, 1956, **13**, 11–25.

Wolman, B. B. Explorations in latent schizophrenics. *Amer. J. Psychother.*, 1957, **11**, 560–588.

Wolman, B. B. Group psychotherapy with latent schizophrenics. *Int. J. group Psychother.*, 1960, **10**, 301–312.

Wolman, B. B. *Mental disorders: their theory and classification,* in press.

17
The Interview

JOSEPH D. MATARAZZO

HISTORY OF THE INTERVIEW

The interview is a form of conversation wherein two people, and recently more than two, engage in verbal and nonverbal interaction for the purpose of accomplishing a previously defined goal, although for the interviewee and for the novice interviewer it is all too often an ill-defined goal. Since antiquity, the interview has been used professionally by philosophers, physicians, priests, and attorneys. The last century has witnessed the emergence of such new professionals as psychologists, psychiatrists, economists, social workers, sociologists, anthropologists, professional nurses, business executives, salesmen, newspaper reporters, television interviewers, pollsters, motivation researchers, public-opinion takers, college and other educational guidance specialists, vocational rehabilitation and other types of counselors, bank personnel who specialize in loans, finance company interviewers, welfare caseworkers, employment agency specialists, detectives, and, very recently, thought-reform interrogators, to name but a few of the different types of individuals now using the interview as a major technique in their work. There are indications currently (Rioch, 1962) that in the not too distant future, the therapeutic interview, long the trademark of highly trained and skilled professional psychologists and psychiatrists, will be practiced by a new breed of professional counselor (e.g., educated housewives, high school counselors, and other nondoctoral professionals).

Riesman and Benney (1956, p. 3), commenting on the recent developments in uses of the interview, say: "In social research, market research, industry, social work, and therapy interviewing has become in fifty years a major white-collar industry—one of those communications professions which represents the shift of whole cadres into tertiary areas." Quoting from Kephart (1952), Riesman and Benney (1956, p. 3) report that over half the current labor force either changes jobs or takes new employment annually and that all but a few of these 30,000,000 find "an interview the major factor in their new placement."

If one were to add up, worldwide, all the interviews conducted by specialists from all the communications professions in one year, it is conceivable that the sum would approach hundreds of millions, if not billions. In view of these astronomical numbers and the related professional man-hours and moneys of investment that they represent, it is surprising how little is known about the interview in terms of either its historical roots or its present status.

Sociological Interviews

Zubin (1962) points out that according to the *Shorter Oxford English Dictionary,* the word "interview" was first used in the year 1514 to designate a meeting of persons face to face, especially for the purpose of formal conference on some point. In 1869 it was used to designate a meeting between a representative of the press and someone from whom he sought to obtain statements for publication. The two essential elements in both these definitions are that there is a face-to-face meeting and that information is elicited by one person from the other.

Riesman and Benney (1956) have written on the history of the interview from the perspective of sociology. They describe its development from the diplomatic encounters between heads of state during the post-Renaissance period; through its introduction by Horace Greeley as a technique useful to newspaper men; through its use by Mayhew, Booth, LePlay, and Quetelet in understanding the working classes of the newly developing industrial society and, concurrently, by Freud in his then developing psychoanalytic method; and finally to its most recent use by social scientists such as Roethlisberger and Dickson, Lazarsfeld, Merton, and others.

At other points in their paper, Riesman and Benney (1956) add such pithy comments as these: "Interviewing itself is a middle-class profession, in pursuit of middle-class concerns" (p. 12). "We do know that the interview is taking on something of the nature of a *rite de passage* as one moves from one institution to another, from school to army to job to other jobs and finally to the gerontological social worker" (p. 15).

Some of the contributions of Riesman and other social scientists to our understanding of the interview will be reviewed later in this chapter.

Clinical Interviews

The history of the interview as a clinical diagnostic method used in psychology and psychiatry cannot be separated from the history of interviewing techniques in psychotherapy. Since the medium for carrying out most forms of psychotherapy is a two-person interaction, called the "psychotherapeutic interview," the history of interviewing is inextricably wed to the history of psychotherapy as a form of interpersonal influence. Since the early history of diagnostic and psychotherapeutic interviewing is so well known, it will not be repeated here. An excellent introduction to the writings of such men as Hippocrates, Socrates, Aretaeus, Galen, Paracelsus, Pinel, Mesmer, Braid, Kraepelin, and Bleuler, to mention but a few, has been provided by Zilboorg (1941).

May (1953, pp. 19–20) presents an excellent discussion of the manner in which techniques such as interviewing, whether used by educators (as in the time of Socrates), by priests (as in the confessional of the Middle Ages and later), or by psychotherapists (as in modern times), are tied to the *Zeitgeist* of the particular age or cultural period. Recently, Frank (1961, pp. 36–64) has extended this observation and has shown that psychotherapeutic interviewing is not unique but, rather, is only one of many techniques extant now (as well as earlier) in which one person's influence over another human being is used to attain some end (in most instances a therapeutic one). Frank's discussion of the similarities among the shaman (in primitive cultures), the priest, the religious revivalist, the psychotherapist, and the thought-reform interrogator as professionals with a common goal (influence) provides an excellent perspective, albeit a mildly frightening one, for the student of interviewing methods.

A book which surely will become a classic on psychiatric diagnosis is one by Menninger, Mayman, and Pruyser (1963). The authors provide an excellent 70-page history of psychiatric diagnosis from the year 2600 B.C. to 1963. In addition, the rest of their book contains an excellent statement of today's use of the interview in the day-to-day diagnostic study, which these authors call the "essence" of psychotherapy.

A discussion of the interview methods of Freud, Sullivan, and Rogers will be presented below. A later section will review the role of the interview in psychiatric classification and diagnosis.

PERSONALITY THEORY AND INTERVIEW METHODS

Freud's Dynamic Interview Technique

In the last half of the nineteenth century, interest in hypnotic interviewing procedures, introduced by Mesmer in 1778, was revived. Liebeault, in 1864, and later also Charcot and Bernheim, became interested in hypnosis because of its theoretical and clinical therapeutic implications in the understanding of the clinical condition called "hysteria." Before the end of the century, Josef Breuer, a Viennese physician, began to use hypnosis in the treatment of hysteria. Breuer added the innovation of having his patients with hysteria talk about their symptoms. The story of how Freud (1856–1939), then a physician interested in neurology and neurophysiology and later to become the founder of the modern psychoanalytic interview and psychotherapeutic methods, went first to study with Charcot and later to work with Breuer and to experiment with hypnotic interview methods has been well told by Jones in a three-volume biography (1953–1957). Breuer and Freud (1957) published a series of papers in the 1890s in which they describe what they learned about psychopathology as their patients talked freely under hypnosis and *without* hypnosis. However, like physicians and scientists of the earlier (and, for the most part, subsequent) era, Freud, first with Breuer and then alone, abandoned hypnosis in his interview method and merely asked the patient to talk. He found that with a little initial help he could encourage his patients to talk freely. Freud called this innovation in interview procedure the clinical process of "free association."

From this beginning, and at the same time that most of the world's psychiatry was under the influence of Kraepelin's more static descriptive psychiatry, Freud followed with keen intuition the verbalizations of his patients during their free associations. As a result of the insights that Freud believed he derived from these interview glimpses into the "repressed" and "unconscious" memories and impulses which constitute personality, a new era in the history of ideas, which lasted over the next four decades, was born. It is of interest that medicine and psychiatry were slower to accept the insights into the individual and into mankind which Freud felt were being made possible by this new type of interviewing than anthropology, literature, and psychology were. Actually, it was the psychologist G. Stanley Hall who, at Clark University in the early 1900s, gave Freud his first academic hearing and William James, Putnam, and Morton Prince who did so much to popularize and otherwise disseminate Freud's views (Watson, 1953).

Freud's innovations in interview technique are intimately related to his psychotherapeutic technique, which, in turn, is a direct outgrowth of his theory of infantile sexuality and later personality development. The details of these are too well known to repeat here. Suffice it to say that Freud's clinical interview-derived insights led him (1) to reverse the preoccupation of philosophers, physicians, and scientists with the conscious aspects of human behavior and focus their interest on what he called the powerful "unconscious" elements, especially as these were revealed in dreams, free associations, slips of speech, etc.; (2) to introduce such new concepts as the id, ego, and superego for describing psychic structure; (3) to focus attention on the ubiquitous role of anxiety in human behavior and man's employment of a variety of defense mechanisms (repression, projection, rationalization, reaction formation, etc.) for coping with it; and finally (4) to explain how all this knowledge could be used by the interviewer as psychoanalytic interview therapy proceeded and as such predictable interview stages as transference, resistance, and others unfolded.

Freud's interviewing technique was designed to help the patient explore his unconscious and conscious personality to an extent which would permit what Wolberg (1954, p. 8) and others have called a "reconstruction" of his basic personality. The objectives of Freud's insight therapy with reconstructive goals thus were (1) insight into unconscious conflicts, with efforts to achieve extensive alterations of basic character structure, and (2) the expansion of personality growth, with development of new adaptive potentialities. The psychoanalytic interviewing techniques (see Tables 2 and 3) are designed expressly to accomplish these hoped-for goals.

Until almost the middle of the twentieth century, standard textbooks of psychiatry made little mention of Freud or his psychodynamic interview method. Rather, these modern textbooks focused primarily on descriptive psychiatric diagnosis and, in the few conditions where this was known, included some statements about etiology (e.g., paresis and other organic conditions) and treatment (e.g., EST in the depressions). The closest these authors came to mentioning the interview was in a discussion of how to take a psychiatric history or how to perform a mental-status examination. Nevertheless, influenced by the parallel developments in Freudian psychoanalysis, dynamic psychiatry, and clinical psychology, a few psychiatrists began to integrate the insights derived from these new developments into regular psychiatric (in contrast to classical psychoanalytic) interview practice. Notable leaders of this movement of the past twenty years have been Alexander and French (1946); Deutsch and Murphy (1955); Finesinger (1948); Fromm-Reichman (1950); Gill, Newman, and Redlich (1954); Masserman (1946); Menninger (1952); Meyer (1948); Saslow (1952; Saslow & Chapple, 1945); Stevenson (1959); Sullivan (1954); Thorne (1950); and Whitehorn (1944).

In the United States, the actual practice of Freudian psychoanalytic interview techniques could be learned only in the few *nonuniversity* psychoanalytic institutes (especially those in Boston and New York) until almost the middle of the twentieth century. Thus, until such neo-Freudians as Alexander, the Menningers, Sullivan, and others began to change this state of affairs in the 1940s, Freudian dynamic interviewing methods were for the most part not available to clinical psychologists, social workers, and nonpsychoanalytic psychiatrists (the latter then and now constituting an overwhelming majority of America's psychiatrists).

Sullivan's Interpersonal Interview Technique

Adolph Meyer, with his psychobiological approach to the interview and case history, and such neo-Freudians as Franz Alexander, Thomas French, Frieda Fromm-Reichman, Karen Horney, and, especially, Harry Stack Sullivan reversed this exclusive and highly ritualistic interview-learning state of affairs. As a direct effect of the neo-Freudianism introduced by Sullivan in Baltimore, by Alexander and French in Chicago, and by the Menninger brothers (Karl and William) in Topeka, the use of dynamic interviewing procedures by other than highly trained psychoanalytic institute graduates (those with three to ten years of training after medical school graduation) was encouraged, so much so that it is probably fair to say that a large number of today's so-called "dynamic" clinical psychologists, nonpsychoanalytic psychiatrists, and social workers utilize more of Sullivan's interpersonal theory of personality development and its application in psychotherapy interviewing than the techniques or personality theory of Freud or any other modern theorist. (This is not to say that they utilize the interview approach of Sullivan exclusively, for, as will be clear from the later presentation of Carl Rogers's nondirective interviewing approach, the influence during the past twenty years of Rogers on clinical and nonclinical interviewers in all professions has been considerable.)

Up until recently, the writings of Sullivan (1892–1949) were to be found only in journals. Following his death at the age of 56 in 1949, his friends edited his writings and lectures and published several books which present his main ideas. Two of the most important of these for understanding interviewing procedures are *The Interpersonal Theory of Psychiatry* (1953) and *The Psychiatric Interview* (1954).

Sullivan's theory of interpersonal relations lays great stress on the interviewer as a *participant-observer* and gives data obtained about the interviewee by such other methods as reports by others, etc., secondary importance, at most. Unlike Freud, who suggested that the interviewer sit behind the patient, Sullivan recommended that the interview take place face to face. Also unlike Freud's approach, for Sullivan there may be only one interview, or there may be many interviews extending over a long period of time. In Sullivan's approach, the interview is much less one-sided than it initially is in the Freudian framework; in the former, the interview is a system, or series of systems, of *interpersonal processes,* arising from participant observation in which, from the initial interview, the interviewer derives certain conclusions about the interviewee (Sullivan, 1954, p. 128). Sullivan divides the interview into four stages: the formal inception, the reconnaissance, the detailed inquiry, and the termination. The interview is primarily a communication between two people. What the person says as well as how he says it— his rate of speech, intonations, silences, and other expressive behavior—are the chief sources of information for the interviewer. He should be alert to changes in the patient's vocal volume and other patient vocalizations because these often serve as clues regarding the patient's focal problems and attitudinal changes toward the therapist. The interviewer is an expert in interpersonal relations and should utilize his knowledge to the end of helping the patient become more effective in his own interpersonal relations. In order to do this, the interviewer must serve as still another human experience for the patient, albeit in a professional setting. By serving as a highly flexible human-participant-observer, the interviewer can serve as a continually interacting stimulus for the patient's habitual patterns of human interaction, including emotional expression and parataxic distortions

(Sullivan's substitute for Freud's interview transference phenomenon), and for his habitual patterns of behavior, including evidence of the forms taken by his self-system (his core personality) and defensive maneuvers engaged in to protect it.

This presentation of Sullivan's theories is not meant to suggest that Freud conceived the interviewer's role as static or otherwise nonparticipating. It is meant merely to highlight the fact that Sullivan made his interviewer a much more *active* participant than Freud did. It is important to point out that, historically, probably the most significant and unique feature of Freud's view of the interview was that, unlike Bleuler, Kraepelin, and others of his day, he introduced the notion that the interviewer was *not* a neutral participant in the interview. Rather, whether conducting therapy or diagnosis, the interviewer, although *less active* than in Sullivan's approach, is an integral and dynamic catalyst in the interaction which takes place. Thus, reasoning initially from unexpected and hard-to-understand emotional outbursts, distortions, etc., on the part of his patients, Freud was the first, some sixty or more years ago, to see the interviewer himself as an important diagnostic and therapeutic human instrument. The related clinical phenomena Freud called "transference" (and later "countertransference"), "resistance," "abreaction," etc.

Interestingly, even as late as the 1930s Freud gave little thought to the matter of the fidelity or *reliability* of the interviewer's interpretations about transference, interview-observed defense mechanisms, and related phenomena. To this day, most Freudians (and unfortunately neo-Freudians and other so-called "followers" of the dynamic tradition in interviewing) make little or no mention of the effects of potential (and actual) day-by-day biases of the interviewer, as a human instrument, on his tactics and on the inferences he makes from them, despite the fact that Freud (and later Sullivan) early recognized the importance of the interviewer's potential blind spots. To counteract their effects, Freud recommended a personal psychoanalysis for all young psychoanalysts in order to reveal these personal blind spots. A discussion of how important such interviewer biases are will be presented below. This writer has been able to discover no published research which would indicate that such a personal psychoanalysis has the desired effect. In fact, one internationally recognized psychoanalyst, Glover (1951), strongly questions that it does, and there is suggestive research evidence (Bordin, 1959, p. 244; Raines & Rohrer, 1955; Raines & Rohrer, 1960) that Glover was correct. Thus, in the absence of any published evidence for the *reliability* of psychoanalytic interview methods, it is not surprising that, despite its undisputed impact upon interview procedures and upon such fields as art, literature, religion, history, etc., little or nothing has been published on the *validity* (in any of its many accepted forms) of Freudian psychoanalytic interview methods and the data collected by their use. Hopefully, the Menninger group of investigators (Robbins & Wallerstein, 1959), as well as others, may reverse this trend. A group of University of Michigan research psychologists studying psychoanalytic psychotherapy interviews already has made some headway in this area (Bordin, 1959).

Although much the same criticisms could be made of the unvalidated interview techniques of the neo-Freudians, including Sullivan, this writer agrees with Hall and Lindzey (1957, p. 151), who write that, of neo-Freudian theory,

> Sullivan's interpersonal theory has probably been the greatest stimulus to research. One reason for this is that Sullivan employed a more objective language in describing his theory, a language which helped to span the gap between theory and observation. Sullivan kept his conceptual constructions quite closely tied to empirical observation, with the result that he seemed to be describing at close quarters the behavior of real people. In spite of the abstractness of his thought, he did not become so abstruse as to lose touch with concrete, one might almost say everyday, conduct of individuals. Interpersonal theory is a down-to-earth proposition mill which invites and encourages empirical testing.

From the vantage point of the few years that have elapsed since Hall and Lindzey made this observation, this writer believes he sees evidence in the research journals that they were correct. It is hard to predict how much research there will be and what directions it will take. However, because Sullivan's views have so much in common with group dynamics and other phenomena related to social psychology, it is possible that his views and those of other social psychological theorists will fuse and that the resulting research contributions will become hard to dissect regarding their theoretical progenitor(s).

Rogers's Nondirective Interview Technique

The last statements do not apply to the approach to the interview first promulgated by the psychologist Carl Rogers (1942; 1951; Rogers & Dymond, 1954). His approach to the interview stimulated research more than the works of any single writer on the interview before or since.

Research on verbal behavior has had a long history in psychology, and thus it is not surprising that, with this research tradition in psychology behind him, Rogers from the beginning has pursued a vigorous research program in connection with his interview method.

There is evidence that the "free association" technique used by Breuer and Freud in their interviewing was borrowed from the German and English experimental psychology of the day. The first recorded study of the association process was published in England by Galton (1879), while Freud was still in his early twenties. Galton's work provided the German psychologist Wundt with the framework for the first free association experiment, in 1880. In 1885, Galton (pp. 182–203) presented the first systematic research study of association. In the same year, an American, Cattell (1889), turned his attention to association experiments, and several years later, with Bryant, he published frequency tables of associations. Thus the verbal association method began in the earliest psychological laboratories, where it was a respected branch of experimental psychology. However, clinical uses of association grew mainly out of the psychoanalytic method, as was discussed above. Interestingly, in 1892 Kraepelin preceded the psychoanalytic movement with his interest in the bearing of the association method upon the interview diagnosis of clinical states such as schizophrenia. He also analyzed the effects of fatigue, hunger, and drugs upon word association (1892).

During subsequent decades, Jung, Kent and Rosanoff, and other psychologists and psychiatrists continued interest in the research and clinical uses of verbal associations. In the last decade, stimulated by the theoretical formulations regarding verbal behavior of Skinner (1957), interest in the relations between such verbal-behavior experiments and interview procedures has been explosive. Excellent reviews of this research can be found in Greenspoon (1962), Krasner (1958), and Salzinger (1959).

There is little evidence that this line of development had any effect upon the ideas of Carl Rogers (1902–   ), the innovator of a new and intellectually and scientifically practical approach to interviewing. The influence on the development of his nondirective or client-centered approach to the interview of such nonpsychologists as Frederick Allen, Otto Rank, and Jessie Taft (a social worker and psychologist) and of psychologists such as Leta Hollingworth, Goodwin Watson, and E. K. Wickman has been acknowledged (Hall & Lindzey, 1957, pp. 476–478; Rogers, 1942, pp. 27–28; Watson, 1962, p. 21). It is of interest to point out, in view of the strong ethicophenomenological flavor of his approach, that after graduating from college, and before going into psychology, Rogers attended the Union Theological Seminary in New York City. The highly personal element in his philosophical leanings suggested by this fact undoubtedly and quite obviously has had a profound impact upon Rogers's view of the role of the interviewer in the interview relationship.

According to Hall and Lindzey (1957, p. 478):

> Rogers' theory of personality represents a synthesis of phenomenology as represented by Snygg & Combs, of holistic and organismic theory as developed in the writings of Goldstein, Maslow, and Angyal, of Sullivan's interpersonal theory, and of self-theory for which Rogers himself is largely responsible, although he acknowledges a debt to Raimy & Lecky.

To this writer, while acknowledging these influences, the most salient feature of Rogers's approach is the strong ethical, humanitarian, religious, and deeply personal flavor which characterizes it. The point is rarely, if ever, made, but it is clear to this writer that Rogers's approach to the interview, like that of Freud, Sullivan, and all other writers on the subject, is very much a reflection of his (each innovator's) own highly personal philosophy of life. In interviewing, as in all other behavior, the man himself cannot be divorced from his method.

As is the case with Freud and Sullivan,

Rogers's interview procedures cannot be divorced from his own theory of personality. The chief features which make up Rogers's theory are the *organism,* the *phenomenal* field, the *self,* and the basic need of the organism to *actualize* itself (i.e., experience growth).

The self is the central concept in Rogers's theory. [Early research on this variable was published by one of his coworkers, Raimy (1948).] It has, among others, the following properties: It develops out of the organism's interaction with the environment (a view closer to Sullivan's than to Freud's); it may incorporate the values of other people and perceive them in a distorted fashion; it strives for consistency, and experiences that are not consistent with it are perceived as threats; and it may and does change as a result of maturation and learning (including that which takes place in self-exploring client-centered interviews).

While many of these ideas were included in Rogers's early book (1942), they were elaborated and extended in his subsequent one (1951). In the latter book, Rogers speaks less of *nondirective* and more of *client-centered* interviewing. The nondirective or client-centered interviewer is urged to avoid giving information, giving advice, using reassurance and persuasion, asking direct questions, offering his own interpretations, and giving criticism. The major techniques *encouraged* are the recognition and clarification of the *feelings* associated with what the interviewee (client) is saying and a simple, nonjudgmental acceptance of his statements. Occasionally the interviewer explains his own interview role and that of the interviewee. This Rogers calls "structuring," a process whereby the interviewer can communicate his acceptance of the interviewee's thoughts, wishes, and feelings. Structuring does not imply the negative concept of what the interviewer will not do; rather, it is a warm, positive contribution which gives the impression that the interviewer and interviewee will work together to find a solution to the problem.

Rogers has continued to modify his views as his clinical insights have given him new leads. Excellent statements of his more recent views are available (1959; 1961). These changes in his views of the process of interview therapy have been heavily influenced by the writings of Soren Kierkegaard and, more recently, by the new European existentialist phenomenology called "Daseinsanalyse."

One of the early adherents of nondirective interviewing, Porter (1943), did a Ph.D. dissertation in which he analyzed, from 19 phonographically recorded interviews, the interview behavior of directive and nondirective interviewers. The differences were striking, and, following Rogers (1942, p. 123), are presented in Table 1. This table represents but one of many subsequent research publications by Rogers and other client-centered interviewers.

Underlying Rogers's client-centered interview method is the belief that the interviewee is capable of finding his own satisfactory solution to his unique problems. The interviewer consistently makes an effort to accept the interviewee, and this is done largely by responding to the latter's feelings. These feelings are responded to and accepted whether they are positive or negative and whether they involve only the interviewee, his associates, or the interviewer himself. No matter what the interviewee says or communicates, it is accepted.

According to Snyder (1954, p. 532), an early adherent of the client-centered approach (1947a; 1947b) and now a learning theory-oriented therapist who draws heavily on client-centered and psychoanalytic techniques (1961), as a result of the procedures employed by the nondirective interviewer, certain interviewee reactions follow: early catharsis, despair with the method, need for structuring, and expression of negative feelings and then tentative statements of positive feelings and attitudes, further positive feelings and attitudes, insight, a feeling of growth (self-actualization), often a minor relapse, and, if successful, continued growth and satisfactory progress.

Unlike the five interviews per week of classical psychoanalysis (or the one, two, or three of the neo-Freudians), most nondirective interviewers schedule one (or at the most two) interviews per week. Published reports (Rogers, 1942; Rogers & Dymond, 1954; Snyder, 1961) indicate that change in interviewees often is experienced in as few as several interviews, although the length of both nondirective psychotherapy (Rogers & Dymond, 1954, p. 241) and its recent extension by Snyder (1961, p. 352) appears to average about thirty weeks. (This corre-

TABLE 1. TECHNIQUES MOST FREQUENTLY EMPLOYED BY DIRECTIVE AND NONDIRECTIVE INTERVIEWERS*

Directive		*Nondirective*	
Asks highly specific questions, delimiting answers to "yes," "no," or specific information	34.1†	Asks highly specific questions, delimiting answers to "yes," "no," or specific information	4.6
Explains, discusses, or gives information related to the problem or treatment	20.3	Explains, discusses, or gives information related to the problem or treatment	3.9
Indicates topic of conversation but leaves development to interviewee	13.3	Indicates topic of conversation but leaves development to interviewee	6.3
Proposes interviewee activity	9.4	Recognizes in some way the feeling or attitude which the interviewee has just expressed	10.3
Recognizes the subject content of what the interviewee has just said	6.1	Recognizes the subject content of what the interviewee has just said	6.0
Marshals the evidence and persuades the interviewee to undertake the proposed action	5.3	Interprets or recognizes feelings or attitudes expressed by general demeanor, specific behavior, or earlier statements	9.3
Points out a problem or condition needing correction	3.7	Defines the interview situation in terms of the interviewee's responsibility for using it	1.9

* Modified from Rogers, 1942, p. 123.
† These numbers, in order of frequency, represent the number of times per interview, as judged by a group of experts, that each tactic was employed in the two types of interviews.

sponds, not surprisingly, to the nine-month academic year of the university schedules of the bulk of nondirective interviewers. In fairness it should be pointed out that the roughly 250 average interviews of the five-day-per-week psychoanalytic method also correspond to the didactic year of the analyst-in-training!)

Neopsychological Interview Techniques

Although the tactics to be employed by the nondirective interviewer (Rogers, 1942; Rogers, 1951; Snyder, 1961) are no more extensively discussed in appropriate textbooks than the tactics of Freudian and neo-Freudian interviewers (see especially Sullivan, 1954; Wolberg, 1954), followers of the latter interview schools—except for writers such as Bordin (1959); Deutsch and Murphy (1955); and Gill, Newman, and Redlich (1954)—have *published* pitifully little on what an actual interviewer really has done during one or more interview sessions. Several individuals have provided excellent tables for contrasting the interviewer and interviewee responsibilities in the various interview schools of thought. Two of these are sufficiently well done and informative to be reproduced here. The first, Table 2, is adapted from a table given by Wolberg (1954, pp. 90–91). This table enables the reader to see, at a glance, the differences (and similarities) among the nondirective (in this table labeled "insight interviewing with reeducative goals"), Freudian, and neo-Freudian approaches to the interview. It also contains two other approaches, not covered in our discussion: the supportive interview (which includes guidance, reassurance, manipulation of the environment, and related techniques) and the psychoanalytically oriented interview (under which Wolberg includes the views of Alexander and French, Deutsch, and Karpman).

The second table, provided by Snyder (1961) and adapted as shown in Table 3, is more recent and thus provides comparison of the Freudian, Sullivanian, and Rogerian approaches with three others which are products primarily of the last decade. These are Kelly's role therapy (1955), the school of directive interviewing (Thorne, 1950), and the approach which was first identified with Dollard and Miller (1950) and which has now come to be called by Snyder (1961) "learning theory therapy" and by others (Hall & Lindzey, 1957) a "stimulus-response approach." Some of these approaches are discussed in other chapters of the *Handbook*. The original publications of Dollard, Auld, and White (1953); Dollard and Miller (1950); Kelly (1955); and Thorne (1950) or the summaries by Hall and Lindzey (1957) or Snyder (1961) should be consulted by the reader who wishes more information on these new approaches. In the view of this writer, while these three additional approaches have considerable merit, they are utilized currently by only a small percentage of individuals relative to those who utilize the nondirective, Freudian, and neo-Freudian approaches.

Still another newcomer on the scene is Ellis's rational-emotive interviewing technique (1957; 1958; 1961; 1962). Ellis's rational-emotive interview methods have elements more in common with William James and G. A. Kelly's cognitive-emotional approaches than with Freud's or Rogers's phenomenology, although Ellis acknowledges a kinship between his approach and modern existentialism. Employing an approach to interview therapy which to this writer is an interesting blend of the pragmatism of William James and Sullivan, the hardheadedness of Watson, the common sense of Adolph Meyer, and, of course, the uniqueness of Ellis, this approach is so novel and appears so deceptively practical that the writer hopes that, before too long, it too will have its adherents. In this way, it can be predicted, as an interviewing method it too will be examined critically by Ellis's peers.

These examples are merely suggestive and are not meant to be inclusive. The reader interested in an excellent introduction to a much larger number of current interview therapies and a critical comparative study of them is referred to Harper (1959) and to an excellent recent contribution by Ford and Urban (1963).

Dyadic versus Larger-unit Interviewing

All the interview methods described above or shown in Tables 2 and 3 involve only an interviewer and an interviewee; i.e., they constitute a two-person, or dyadic, interaction. During the past decade a number of psychotherapists have been conducting interviews with more than one person alone, e.g., jointly with the patient and his parent(s), spouse, or employer, etc. (Ackerman, Beatman, & Sherman, 1961; Bell, 1961; Gralnick, 1962; Jackson & Satir, 1961; Rabiner, Molinski, & Gralnick, 1962; Saslow & Matarazzo, 1962, p. 14). These investigators, among others, seem to have come to the realization that neither the predominantly one-sided interviewee self-exploration of the psychoanalytic interview[1] nor the nondirective, directive, rational-emotive, learning theory, and other forms of interview therapies take sufficient account of the low generalizability of insights learned during interview therapy to the life of the patient outside the psychotherapy hour.

Every experienced interviewer-therapist has had patient after patient who verbalizes brilliant new insights in the confines of the psychotherapy office but who is completely unable to generalize or otherwise actualize these insights and hopes for new behavior with significant others in his everyday living. For this reason, Rabiner et al. (1962), with schizophrenic patients, and Saslow and Matarazzo (1962), with a variety of psychiatric patients on a psychiatric service in a general hospital, have begun expanding the conventional dyadic interview to three, four, five, and more other significant persons. Saslow recently conducted simultaneous interview therapy conjointly with a mother, father, and five children. As pointed out by Rabiner et al. (1962, p. 629), the interviewer in such conjoint therapy must modify radically his previously learned interview tactics.

> In contrast to the one-to-one psychotherapy model, the therapist must be active. He is forced to regulate verbal traffic in the context of his own value judgments as to what kinds of contributions and by whom will best serve the interests of the process. He is inexorably cast in the role of arbiter, mediator, and judge, carrying the hopes of all participants for acceptance and corroboration under circumstances where the vested interests of all may conflict.

[1] In a personal communication (1962), Prof. Saul Rosenzweig suggested the term "intraview" to describe the self-exploring psychoanalytic interview and the term "interview" for other forms of face-to-face psychotherapy. Therefore, "conjoint interview" or "multiview" might appropriately describe the interview which is larger than two-person.

TABLE 2. A COMPARISON OF INTERVIEW APPROACHES (*Continued*)

			Insight interviewing with reconstructive goals		
	Supportive interviewing	*Insight interviewing with reeducative goals*	*Freudian psychoanalysis*	*Non-Freudian psychoanalysis*	*Psychoanalytically oriented psychotherapy*
Duration of interview therapy	One to several hundred sessions	Several sessions to several hundred sessions	2–5 years	2–5 years	Several sessions to several hundred sessions
Frequency of visits	1–3 times weekly	1–2 times weekly	4–5 times weekly	2–4 times weekly	1–3 times weekly
Detailed history taking	Usually	Often	Rarely	Occasionally	Occasionally
Patient's communications	Interviews focused on symptoms and environmental disturbances	Interviews focused on daily events and interpersonal relationships	Unguided free associations	Interviews focused on current situations, interpersonal relationships, and other conflictual sources. Free associations sometimes used	Interviews focused on current situations, interpersonal relationships, and other conflictual sources
General activity of interviewer	Toward strengthening of existing defenses	Challenging of existing defenses. Activity: directiveness to nondirectiveness	Challenging of existing defenses. Passivity, anonymity, nondirectiveness. Constant analysis of transference and resistance	Challenging of existing defenses. Activity: moderate directiveness to nondirectiveness. Constant analysis of transference and resistance	Challenging of existing defenses. Greater activity: directiveness of moderate sort to nondirectiveness. Constant analysis of transference and resistance
Advice giving to patient	Often	Occasionally	Never	Rarely	Rarely
Transference	Positive transference encouraged and utilized to promote improvement	Positive transference controlled and, if possible, utilized to	Transference encouraged to point of development of a	Transference encouraged to point of awareness of re-	Transference encouraged to point of awareness of repressed attitudes

		promote improvement. Negative transference analyzed as it develops in terms of the reality situation	transference neurosis. Transference analyzed in terms of genetic origins	pressed attitudes and feelings. Transference neurosis avoided by some analysts. Transference analyzed in terms of character structure or genetic origins	and feelings. Transference neurosis avoided as a rule. Transference analyzed in terms of character structure and, occasionally, genetic origins
General relationship of patient to interviewer	Positive relationship fostered and utilized	Positive relationship fostered and utilized	Relationship permitted to develop spontaneously	Relationship permitted to develop spontaneously	Relationship permitted to develop spontaneously. Positive relationship occasionally fostered and utilized
Physical position of patient during interview	Sitting up, face to face	Sitting up, face to face	Recumbent on couch	Sitting up, face to face, or recumbent on couch	Sitting up, face to face. Occasionally recumbent on couch
Dream material	Not utilized	Not utilized	Constantly utilized	Constantly utilized	Constantly utilized
Adjuncts utilized during therapy	Bibliotherapy, art therapy, group therapy, physical therapy, drug therapy, hypnotherapy, occupational therapy	Group therapy; bibliotherapy occasionally used	None	Few or none	Analytic group therapy, hypnoanalysis, narcotherapy, play therapy; art therapy occasionally employed

Modified from Wolberg, 1954, pp. 90–91.

TABLE 3. A COMPARISON OF SIX INTERVIEW SYSTEMS*

Task of the interviewer	*Task of the client*	*Relationship*
Freudian:		
To help patient bring unconscious material into consciousness. Role is ambiguous to aid transference. Emphasis is on the past.	To free-associate until he recovers enough significant repressed material that he loses symptoms and understands himself.	Intense relationship involving transference and countertransference. Emphasis is more on affect than cognition.
Sullivanian:		
To work toward realistic goals based upon adequate knowledge of patient. Emphasis is on personal relationships. Role is ambiguous to avoid having patient assume a role just to please the therapist.	To work toward the goals the therapist has said might reasonably be achieved and particularly to try to understand himself in his relations with others.	Relationship is more cognitive than affective. Therapist is kindly person leading the client by indirect means.
Rogerian:		
To be unreservedly accepting of the client, to try to understand his internal frame of reference, and then to communicate this understanding to him.	To discuss his problems with the therapist until he reaches a condition of self-acceptance which allows him to make full use of his abilities.	Client takes the lead. Attitudes of client toward the therapist are reality-based. Emphasis is on affect more than cognition.
Kelly's role therapy:		
To get the client to form new constructs or to revise old ones. Role is ambiguous to permit client to try different modes of response. Emphasis is on the present	To consider new facts and ideas, to reformulate his concepts, and then to try new methods of action.	Relationship is more cognitive than affective. Therapist is always in control of the situation, pointing out fruitful concepts to be investigated.
Directive:		
To work actively to help the patient achieve better mental health. This involves a case history, diagnosis, treatment plan, and the use of any methods the therapist feels will be of aid to the patient.	To work on finding the reasons for his problems and, as therapy progresses, to assume more responsibility for his actions.	Strong feelings of a dependent type are often developed. Therapist directs therapy. Emphasis more on cognition than affect.
Learning theory therapy:		
To help the patient learn to discriminate and to present the patient with a graded series of learning situations.	To free-associate in order to recover repressed material and, as self-understanding develops, to try new modes of behavior.	Relationship is similar to that in Freudian therapy, but transference and countertransference are not as intense.

* Adapted from Snyder, 1961, p. 8.

Despite this new role for the interviewer, such interview therapy permits him for the first time to really know, for example, how a husband speaks to, or otherwise interacts with, his wife, and vice versa. Since both spouses are interacting before his very eyes, the therapist need worry no longer about the fidelity of each one's report of what they do when they interact. He perceives the human drama with his own eyes and ears. In addition, once a therapist helps such multiple individuals (1) to *identify* the significant aspects of their neurotic or otherwise ineffective interaction and (2) to *practice* constructive alternatives (again in his presence), such newly learned alternatives have a higher probability of being continued (generalized) outside the therapy hour than if only one person were learning, through insight alone, how he might better behave outside the therapy room. It is a well-known fact that the more *similar* the second situation is to the one in which new behavior is learned, the more efficient the generalization of the newly learned behavior is. Thus, having significantly meaningful social units (married pairs, families, supervisee and supervisor, partners, etc.) learn new insights and new behavior together in the psychotherapy conference room will make it considerably easier for such newly learned interpersonal interactions to generalize outside the psychotherapy situation, to the home, office, etc., and thereby to become habitual.

It is too early to speculate on whether or not multiple-person interviewing of this type will find a useful place along with the more traditional two-person psychotherapy or interview model. It is of interest to note that more and more child psychotherapists (and other child guidance specialists) are substituting large-unit conjoint family interviewing for both the dyadic play therapy with a child and the concurrent dyadic interviewing of a parent by a second professional in the team. This writer has been conducting conjoint therapy with married pairs, parents and adolescent or college-age children, and other meaningful groups for the past five years. While he still carries on individual psychotherapy, the numbers of individuals seen only alone has rapidly dwindled. It is his impression that many other psychotherapists are substituting conjoint therapy for individual therapy in increasing numbers of cases. Although individual psychotherapy undoubtedly will continue to be used for persons with intense, generalized problems involving personal anxiety and its many defenses, so many interpersonal problems are *specific* to identifiable social situations and individuals that conjoint therapy appears to be both practical and effective.

RESEARCH ON INTERVIEWER TACTICS

Rogerian Techniques

As mentioned earlier, the tactics presented in Tables 2 and 3 represent, *in theory*, what interviewers from the various schools of interviewing purport to do. It is to Rogers's credit, and it probably played no small part in the adoption of his interview method by individuals from numerous other professions, as well as those in psychology, psychiatry, and social work, that along with publishing an account of his new nondirective method of interviewing, he published (1942, pp. 261–437) the first verbatim transcript of a psychotherapy (although Dr. Earl Zinn, at Worcester State Hospital, a few years earlier had stenographically recorded a psychoanalysis of Ben Wells). The nondirective therapy with "Herbert Bryan" comprised only eight interviews, which were phonographically recorded and transcribed and which, except for minor editing of identifying data, were published by Rogers in their entirety. Thus, after more than half a century of experience with clinical interviewing, other professionals, students, outsiders, and others were given access to a unique human drama: one person's systematic attempt to help another toward greater self-fulfillment.

At the time of publication of Rogers's book, one of his Ph.D. students published the first of a series of papers on studies conducted on and with phonographic recordings of counseling interviews (Covner, 1942a; Covner, 1942b; Covner, 1944a; Covner, 1944b). In these studies, Covner reported, among other things, such findings as the reactions of interviewers to the knowledge that their interviews were being recorded and the accuracy (75 to 95 per cent) and completeness (only 30 per cent) of the interviewers' *reports*, written immediately after an interview, as compared with the typewritten *transcript* of the same recorded interview. It was therefore suggested that if research on interviewing was to be carried out, phonographic recordings and not the biased reports of the interviewers

TABLE 4. PARTIAL LIST OF TECHNIQUES USED BY ROGERIAN NONDIRECTIVE INTERVIEWERS*

	Percentage of responses devoted to tactic	
Tactic	*Snyder, 1945*	*Seeman, 1949*
Clarification of feeling	31.6	63.1
Restatement of content	3.4	15.2
Simple acceptance	27.6	6.7
Structuring	3.6	1.2
Interpretation	8.1	1.2
Nondirective leads	2.2	.8
Direct questions	5.7	.4
Approval and encouragement	4.7	.1
All other directive techniques	4.4	1.65

* Adapted from Snyder, 1954, p. 540, after Seeman, 1949.

should be the raw data of such research. This suggestion seems to have been followed by subsequent investigators representing many different theories and schools. However, Snyder (1945) gave evidence of a type of research in which, for his purpose, there was little difference between stenographic, phonographic, and counselor-recorded material.

Nevertheless, transcripts of whole interviews and series of interviews have been invaluable for research. One study by Snyder (1945) in which 30 out of 48 interviews were phonographically recorded provided, along with Porter's (1943) earlier report, one of the first research investigations of what an interviewer (nondirective) actually did do in his interviewing behavior, in contrast to what he theoretically should do (as this latter is shown in Tables 2 and 3). The results of Snyder's analysis are given in Table 4 (adapted from Snyder, 1954). It is clear from Snyder's 1945 results that an early (1940s) version of the nondirective interviewer did, in fact, devote 59.2 per cent of his responses to the joint techniques of clarification of feeling (31.6 per cent) and simple acceptance of the interviewee (27.6 per cent), while devoting only 5.7 per cent of his utterances to direct questions.

As if to bear out Rogers's view that a decade later (Rogers, 1951) his interview approach had become more "client-centered" than formerly (Rogers, 1942), a study by another of his students (Seeman, 1949) at the University of Chicago, also utilizing phonographic transcriptions, was published. The results of Seeman's study, also presented in Table 4, show a marked increase (from 31.6 to 63.1 per cent) in the use of the interviewer tactic "clarification of feeling" from the Snyder to the Seeman study. There are, of course, many similarities in the results of the earlier Snyder and later Seeman studies. However, how much the difference in the two studies (shown in Table 4) reflects differences in Rogerian *technique* and how much it reflects *individual differences* in the *interviewers* involved in the two studies cannot be answered. That such a research question now could be asked, nevertheless, is a credit to Rogers, Seeman, Snyder, and the whole early nondirective group.

Other Research with Sound Recording

A few psychiatrists, representing other orientations, soon began to utilize sound recordings in their interview practice, teaching, and beginning research. Ruesch and Prestwood (1949) were among the first to publish their results. They were able to show that sound recordings convey *feelings* in a way in which the printed transcript does not, and they concluded that anxiety can be transmitted by sound alone and that the important cues in psychotherapy are primarily acoustic. To learn this they played wire recordings to an audience of psychiatrists and had the latter rate them for anxiety and anger. When only the printed words from the transcriptions were available to these judges, only a few, and these with difficulty, were able to pick up such cues. When the sound track was added, however, the authors report that the resulting timing, intensity, and emphasis, as well as modulation of voice, enabled clear detection of anger and anxiety.

Other investigators who published papers and books on the use of recorded interviews were Bierer and Strom-Olsen (1948); Brody, Newman, and Redlich (1951); Deutsch and Murphy (1955); and Dollard et al. (1953), whose transcripts and editorial comment present an excellent introduction to interviewing from a learning theory orientation; Kogan (1950); Lamb and Mahl (1956); Redlich, Dollard, and Newman (1950); and Will and Cohen (1953).

An interesting innovation was introduced in 1954 by Gill, Newman, and Redlich. To permit students, professional workers, and scientific investigators access to what actually goes on in an initial psychiatric interview, these investigators published both a book containing the verbatim transcripts of three initial interviews (one by each of two experts and one by a beginning interviewer, a medical student) and a long-playing phonographic recording of these same three interviews. Such a contribution has, of course, many research possibilities. As a matter of fact, after what appears to have been several exhausting years of linguistic and psychiatric analysis of merely the first five minutes (!) of one of these initial interviews presented by Gill et al., a group of investigators made up of two psychiatrists and a professor of linguistics (Pittenger, Hockett, & Danehy, 1960) published just such a research study. For their purpose of "microscopic interview analysis," these investigators had to spend twenty-five to thirty hours in merely the faithful *transcription*, from the phonographic recording, of their five-minute sample! They then were able to apply their unique linguistic (phonemes) and paralinguistic (e.g., sighs, drawls, slurs, inhalations, loudness and softness, breathiness, speech coughs, etc.) method of content analysis to the five-minute interview segment. Although obviously a costly research method, the resulting analyses impressed this writer with the potential of such a linguistic approach to content analysis. For accounts of a host of other attempts at content analysis of interview verbal productions, the interested reader should consult Auld & Murray, 1955; Dollard & Auld, 1959; Gottschalk, Springer, & Gleser, 1961; Leary & Gill, 1959; Mahl, 1959a; Mahl, 1959b; Mowrer, 1953; Murray, 1956; Phillips, 1957; and Strupp, 1960. These describe techniques utilizing a "distress-relief" quotient, grammatical analysis, movies with the interviewer's comments delayed, speech dysfunctions, various content-analysis schemata, and many other approaches.

A research innovation which was long overdue has recently been described by Gottschalk (1961). This involved the analysis of the *same* two psychotherapy interviews by investigators representing different approaches and interested in psychophysiological relations between the patient and therapist and a variety of linguistic, psychodynamic, emotional, and other interview dimensions. The participants involved Kanter and DiMascio; Strupp; Jaffe; Mahl; and Gottschalk, Springer, and Gleser.

Research on Single Interview Dimensions

The early 1950s brought still another type of research on the inverview, a detailed analysis of a single dimension (or process) of the interview interaction. Gillespie (summarized in Snyder, 1953, pp. 105–119), studying 218 single interviews from 43 nondirective therapy cases, identified and validated 13 different classifications of *resistance*. These could be grouped under three headings: resistance toward the *interviewer*, resistance to the interview *process*, and resistance within the *interviewee*. Bordin (1955) identified *ambiguity* as another interview variable and reported that an interviewer who provides few cues for an interviewee (i.e., provides primarily ambiguity) tends to increase the interviewee's level of anxiety. This finding was confirmed by Lennard and Bernstein (1960, p. 117). Shortly after Bordin's 1955 study of the ambiguity dimension, Rausch and Bordin (1957) and Bordin (1959) published research on still another interviewer-interviewee interaction variable, the *warmth* of the relationship. Bordin and his University of Michigan Ph.D. students and colleagues, guided by a psychoanalytic theoretical framework, then identified and studied still other dimensions of the dynamic interview relationship: depth of interviewer's *interpretations*, *resistance*, level of interviewee's *anxiety*, degree of interviewer's *commitment*, and other variables. Bordin (1959) has summarized a number of these unpublished studies. In addition to studying these variables singly, Bordin's group has shown a number of interesting, and theoretically important, relationships among the variables of ambiguity, warmth, depth of interpretation, and the others. To his credit, Bordin (1959, p. 244) also reports being troubled because the researches of his group to date have *failed* to demonstrate that personal therapy and greater amounts of professional experience on the part of the observer-judges are associated with greater success in rating such variables as the depth of the interviewer's interpretation. Although Bordin's psychoanalytically oriented group has not as yet published as many studies as the nondirective group, their research to date shows considerable promise for our fuller understanding of the dynamics of the interview.

The Interview in Psychotherapy Research

Probably the single most important research publication on interviewing (as found in psychotherapy) of the decade was published by Rogers and Dymond (1954). Parenthetically—if for no other reason than to demonstrate that authors of chapters in handbooks, like interviewers, are not free of their own preferences and biases—this estimate of the Rogers and Dymond book is not shared by an astute student of interview methods, Eysenck (1961b, p. 707), who writes: "The faults of the experimental design [in the Rogers and Dymond studies] are such, however, that on the grounds of merit alone it is doubtful whether it should have been included [in Eysenck's review]." While granting the merit of some of Eysenck's 1961 criticism, the 1954 publication, coming at a time when interview research appeared barren and tepid, seemed to this writer a work of considerable importance. In that book, Rogers and Dymond and 10 other colleague-adherents of the nondirective school published papers (1) introducing a philosophically sophisticated treatment of a substitute for the traditional success-failure dichotomy for evaluating the effects of interview therapy, (2) showing the use of the then new and promising (but today less so) Q-sort methodology (and questionnaires and ratings by the interviewer, interviewee, and friends of the interviewee) for evaluating changes taking place in the interview, and (3) discussing the use of nonpatient (no-wait group) and patient (wait group) for a similar purpose and a host of other findings, too numerous even to attempt to summarize here.

To his further credit, Rogers (Rogers & Dymond, 1954, pp. 259–409), along with publishing a detailed research analysis of the transcript of a "successful" case (Mrs. Oaks), also published a similar transcript and analysis of a case of "failure" in interview therapy (the case of Mr. Bebb). Few other students of the interview have advanced science as much as Rogers and his colleagues did by publishing such important personal documents.

A discussion of the research vigor of other followers of the nondirective school cannot be included here. Suffice it to say that they have made, and today continue to make, many valuable inroads for our understanding of the complexities of the interview. The recent publication by one of the early Rogerians, Snyder (1961), of his own newly developing interview therapy with 20 different interviewees is another example of a glimpse not only into the therapeutic relationship but also into the private world of another explorer of the interview.

The reader interested in a critical review of numerous other studies utilizing interviews in psychotherapy should read Eysenck's chapter on the effects of psychotherapy in the recently published *Handbook of Abnormal Psychology: An Experimental Approach* (Eysenck, 1961b).

Movies in Interview Research

Another important contribution to the understanding of the dynamics of the interview was made in the 1950s by Strupp. Some of his various papers recently have been integrated into book form (Strupp, 1960). His innovation, potentially as useful as the long-playing record and book combination of Gill et al. (1954), consisted of using specially developed movies in which the comments of the interviewer were *delayed*. Strupp's research approach has been to show the movie to interviewers who adhere to different theoretical schools and, following selected comments of the movie interviewee, to stop the film and have each spectator-interviewer fill in what he would have said or done next, had he been the interviewer in the movie. By this method Strupp has been able to study what interviewers from various of the different schools shown in Tables 2 and 3 do in fact do in their interview interactions (or at least what they say they do under Strupp's conditions). Strupp has been able to discover many things about interviewers of different orientations, from different professions, and of different levels of experience.

Psychophysiology of the Interview

Another important line of research on the interview consists of the *psychophysiological* experiences of the interviewer and interviewee and their relationships to each other and to other dimensions of interview behavior as interviewer and interviewee interact during an interview. Although Grace, Wolf, and Wolff (1951); Holmes, Goodell, Wolf, and Wolff (1950); Wolf and Wolff (1947); and others of their colleagues from the New York Hospital–Cornell Medical School group were among the first to pursue a *program* of research on physiological changes during interviews, several other groups of investigators soon followed them. Notable among these were DiMascio and Greenblatt and their colleagues at the Harvard Medical School (a review is given in Greenblatt, 1959) and Malmo and his coworkers at McGill University (see Malmo, 1957), to mention only two. The work of these investigators, as well as that of dozens of other (laboratory as well as clinical) workers in this area, has been evaluated in an excellent review by Lacey (1959) and should be read by any serious student of the clinical interview. Although Lacey points out that a number of theoretical, methodological, and related questions still need to be answered, his review makes very clear that investigators already have demonstrated interviewee changes in a variety of physiological systems as a function of differences in content of the interview, affect ("anxiety," "hostility," etc.), course in psychotherapy, moment-by-moment changes *within* an interview session, and a number of other variables. Lacey also discusses a paper by Coleman, Greenblatt, and Solomon (1956) in which these investigators studied the *concomitant* physiological changes of one interviewer and one interviewee during 44 successive therapy interviews. This study revealed that the heart rate of the therapist responded in the same way as the heart rate of the patient. Like the patient's, the therapist's heart rate was highest when the patient exhibited a momentary episode of "anxiety" and was lowest in momentary episodes of "depression." Like the patient's, the interviewer's heart rate was intermediate in interview episodes where "intrapunitive hostility" was being expressed. The only difference between therapist and patient was that the patient's heart rate appeared to differentiate anxiety and extrapunitive hostility, while the therapist's heart rate did not. Another study from the same laboratory (DiMascio, Boyd, Greenblatt, & Solomon, 1955) reported the heart rates of three patients interviewed by three different interviewers. Regardless of the order in which the therapists interviewed each of the three patients, one psychiatrist consistently produced a lower heart rate with all three patients!

These and many other studies reviewed by Lacey open up still another very important direction for interview research. Further studies on the relationships between physiologic measures and a host of other interview variables would add much to our understanding of the dynamics of the interview.

THE INTERVIEW IN PSYCHIATRIC DIAGNOSIS

Reliability

Since Kraepelin, in the last century, first introduced his nosological classificatory scheme for diagnosing the varieties of mental illnesses, the interview has been the single most often used procedure for arriving at such a psychiatric diagnosis. Yet from the beginning of the adoption of Kraepelin's nosology, only the rare psychiatrist was concerned with the question of the reliability of the diagnoses reached by the psychiatric interviewer. Writing over forty years ago, Kempf (1920) warned:

> If each important institution can be induced to give, sealed, to a central committee, its actual working system for classifying cases as dementia praecox, manic-depressive, paranoia, hysteria, and neurasthenia, illustrated by cases, the differences would probably be so varied that the whole system would have to be abandoned because the faithful assumption that symptoms are similarly applied and evaluated throughout psychiatry would be brutally discredited.

Some thirty years later, Roe (1949, p. 38), in commenting on research by clinical psychologists at mid-century, echoed a similar concern about the unreliability of psychiatric diagnosis:

> On the other hand, clinicians have managed to take time for research, as witness the papers coming out in such numbers on the use of various psychological devices for making psychiatric diagnoses. I suggest that much of this research is not only a waste of time, and a perpetuation of errors, but is actually preventing advance in the field. There are many reasons why this is true, but one of the most potent is that it involves clinging to a classification which has long since been outlived. I submit that using techniques which are not too precisely validated, if they are validated at all, to place patients in psychiatric categories, the inadequacy of which is admitted by all concerned, is a treadmill procedure guaranteed to keep us moving in circles.

On the other side, Kahn and Cannell (1957, p. 179) write:

> The interview must be considered to be a measurement device which is fallible and which is subject to substantial errors and biases. All this does not suggest, however, that the interview should be discarded. . . . [We] need to learn more about the sources of bias and to develop methods for eliminating them.

In this section we shall examine the utility of the interview in making psychiatric diagnoses. To date, the number of research workers who find diagnostic judgments based on psychiatric interviews unreliable outnumber those who report studies showing that they are reliable. Investigators who believe interviewer-based psychiatric diagnosis to be *unreliable* are Ash (1949); Boisen (1938); Eysenck (1952); Masserman and Carmichael (1938); Mehlman (1952); Pasamanick, Dinitz, and Lefton (1959); and Scott (1958). Arrayed against them are these defenders of the *reliability* of interview-based psychiatric diagnosis: Foulds (1955); Hunt, Wittson, and Hunt (1953); Schmidt and Fonda (1956); Seeman (1953); and Wilson and Meyer (1962). In addition, several authors have contributed excellent *theoretical* and review articles in this general area: Beck (1962); Caveny, Wittson, Hunt, and Herrmann (1955); Eysenck (1961a); and Zigler and Phillips (1961). These last papers do much to clarify the pertinent issues in the reliable-unreliable debate. Rotter (1954, pp. 250–257) outlines steps for improving the reliability of interview-derived judgments.

Evidence for the unreliability of psychiatric diagnosis. One of the first studies on the reliability of psychiatric diagnosis was reported by Masserman and Carmichael (1938). On the basis of a follow-up of 100 psychiatric patients a year after discharge from a mental hospital, these authors reported that in 40 per cent of the cases the original diagnoses required "major revision" a year later. However, how much this change in psychiatric diagnosis one year later was a function of the unreliability of the original diagnosis or of the unreliability of the second diagnosis, or both, and how much it was a function of actual changes in the patients' clinical status during the one-year interval, if at all, cannot be assessed from the Masserman and Carmichael data.

A study which involved several diagnoses arrived at simultaneously, although reasonably independently, was reported by Ash (1949). In his study, 52 white males were evaluated in a government-related clinic in a joint interview by two or three psychiatrists who worked full time in this clinic. Typically one of the psychiatrists conducted a physical examination of each man and then called his colleague(s) in for the psychiatric interview. The psychiatric interview was jointly conducted, each psychiatrist asking whatever questions he wished. However, each psychiatrist recorded his diagnosis independently. Specific diagnoses were not discussed.

Ash presented his results for *pair* combinations of the three psychiatrists for varying combinations (*N*s of 38 to 46) of the 52 cases and jointly for all *three* raters for the 35 out of 52 cases which were seen simultaneously by all three psychiatrists. An earlier, pre-1952 version of the official nomenclature of the American Psychiatric Association (1952) was used for their diagnostic judgments. This involved five *major categories* (mental deficiency, psychosis, psychopathic personality, neurosis, and "normal range" but with "predominant personality characteristic") and some sixty *specific* diagnostic subcategories. Because this study is quoted so often as evidence of the unreliability of psychiatric diagnosis, the results of the agreement levels among the three psychiatrists in the 35 cases examined by all three in simultaneous conference are shown in Table 5. It can be seen that the agreement for all three psychiatrists for the major category diagnosis was 45.7 per cent, while for specific subcategory diagnosis

TABLE 5. AGREEMENT IN DIAGNOSES AMONG THREE PSYCHIATRISTS (35 CASES)*

Type of agreement	*Three psychiatrists agree*	*Two out of three agree*	*None agree*	*Total*
Major category:				
Per cent	45.7	51.4	2.9	100.0
N	(16)	(18)	(1)	35
Specific Diagnosis:				
Per cent	20.0	48.6	31.4	100.0
N	(7)	(17)	(11)	35

*Adapted from Ash, 1949.

it was only 20 per cent. (As might be expected, two out of the three of these psychiatrists, in different combinations of two, showed agreement levels higher than these: 51.4 and 48.6 per cent, respectively.)

In essence these results show that three psychiatrists can agree completely in 45.7 per cent of the cases for five broad categories (where chance expectation would be one in five, or 20 per cent, *if* the base rates of the five conditions were *known* and *equal*—which they certainly are not) and in 20 per cent of the cases in specific categories (where chance expectation would be one in sixty, or 1.7 per cent, *if* the base rates again were known and equal). However, with an *N* as small as 35, such considerations appear overly refined, even if the base rates could be determined.

Ash clearly pointed out the limitation of his study imposed by this small *N*. He also pointed out the possible limitations imposed by the joint conference method and the fact that his 60 (and seemingly only 55 specific) subcategories did not utilize the entire APA diagnostic system. However, what neither Ash nor other reviewers of his study seem to have concerned themselves with is that 104 (75 per cent) out of 139 diagnoses made on the 52 cases by the three psychiatrists were diagnoses of "normal range"; i.e., 75 per cent of Ash's diagnoses were reasonably "normal" with a "predominant personality characteristic" (see Ash, 1949, p. 273, Table 1). This latter included such specific subcategories as aggressive type; unethical; egocentric and selfish type; shiftless; lazy; uninhibited; dull, adynamic type; nomadic type; and balanced personality. It is not surprising to this writer to find that three psychiatrists will agree no more than is shown in Table 5 when so many of their cases (75 per cent) are not frank psychiatric ones. Actually, one can be impressed that they agree as well as they did on what is essentially a study of the reliability of judgment of personality characteristics of a predominantly normal group of 35 men.

Although *not* utilizing two independent clinicians, each examining the *same* patient, the study by Mehlman (1952) did utilize a large sample of Toledo State Hospital patients (*N of* 4,016). His hypothesis was that since assignment of patients to a ward psychiatrist was random, if psychiatric diagnosis were reliable, then the *relative frequencies* of patients in different diagnostic categories would not differ from one admitting psychiatrist to another. Mehlman broke down his data by sex and showed that 16 different psychiatrists on the female services and nine psychiatrists on the male services *did* in fact differ among themselves in the frequency with which they utilized (1) an organic versus a psychogenic diagnosis and (2) a manic-depressive versus a schizophrenic diagnosis. He does not report means, standard deviations, or other data, limiting his results simply to the significance levels of the chi-square values for each of these pair dichotomies.

A similar "relative frequency" study was conducted by Pasamanick et al. (1959) and led them to caution that "psychiatric diagnosis is at present so unreliable as to merit very serious question when classifying, treating and studying patient behavior and outcome" (p. 127). Their study also used only a very indirect method of assessing reliability (relative frequency of six different diagnostic categories assigned to patients on three female wards of the Columbus Psychiatric Institute and Hospital) and thus, while important, is not a conclusive investigation of the reliability of psychiatric diagnosis. As a matter of fact, a recent relative frequency study by Wilson and Meyer (1962), reporting the diagnostic consistency in a psychiatric liaison service at The Johns Hopkins Hospital, reveals the incidence of *almost identical* percentages for various diagnostic categories in samples from two consecutive years—a finding in direct contrast to the two studies just reviewed. Whether the positive, albeit also indirect, findings of Wilson and Meyer are due to differences in (1) patient population, (2) psychiatrists, (3) hospital settings, or (4) the temporal interval or to a host of other factors cannot be evaluated at this time. The study by Boisen (1938), also a relative frequency investigation, revealed that the percentage of patients with the *same* diagnosis was markedly *different* in three states (Illinois, Massachusetts, and New York), thus implicating still other potential factors in the unreliability findings.

Other writers who question the reliability of psychiatric diagnosis are Eysenck (1952, pp. 33–34), Roe (1949, p. 38), and Scott (1958, p. 32). In the characteristic tough-minded manner with which he has served as a critic of other things psychological, Eysenck, after reviewing the studies of Ash and several others, has this to say: "We may then regard it as agreed that psychiatric diagnosis is of doubtful validity and low reliability. . . ." Eysenck continues that since the use, by psychologists, of psychological testing techniques leads to no further improvement in the reliability of diagnosis, ". . . then it is small wonder that so many psychologists have eschewed the Kraepelinian straightjacket in order to indulge in Freudian manic spells which give them at least the illusion of usefulness" (1952, pp. 33–34).

Interview-based personality and related judgments, other than psychiatric diagnosis, also have been reported to show poor reliability and validity. The disappointing results of several all too well-known assessment studies need not be repeated here (Holtzman & Sells, 1954; Kelly & Fiske, 1951; Kelly & Goldberg, 1959; OSS Assessment Staff, 1948).

Evidence for the reliability of psychiatric diagnosis. One of the most vigorous research groups to study the psychiatric interview has been that of Hunt and Wittson and their associates. During hostilities and for the period of a decade following World War II, this group, which had worked together in wartime navy neuropsychiatric screening from 1941 to 1945, published a number of studies and theoretical articles on the reliability and validity of psychiatric diagnosis. References to this work will be found in Hunt (1955) and in many volumes of the *Journal of Clinical Psychology* from 1955 to the present. Whereas the Hunt and Wittson studies of the 1940s and early 1950s were on the reliability and validity of psychiatric diagnosis (and related military selection procedures), the later program of research of Hunt and his other colleagues has been designed around the important premise that psychiatric diagnosis is merely one example of a more general psychological process—clinical judgment—and that the latter human act has much in common with psychophysical and other judgments.

Although only one of the studies of this research group (Hunt et al., 1953) was directed *exclusively* to the question of the reliability of psychiatric diagnosis, a number of their validity studies also bear on the reliability problem—possibly even more than this one reliability study itself. In the Hunt et al. (1953) study, these investigators concerned themselves with "the reliability or consistency of diagnosis, or more specifically with the question of agreement between psychiatrists in a diagnostic situation" (p. 53). However, they were careful to point out two important assumptions: (1) that we mean by the "reliability of diagnosis" whether the same diagnosis will be rendered upon a repeat examination by the same or some other psychiatrist, and (2) that diagnosis is essentially a process of taxonomic categorization with prediction as its function (p. 55). Their many subsequent (predictive) validity reports thus should be understood as intimately related to the reliability question, and validity and reliability should not be clearly distinguished.

The Hunt et al. (1953) study examined the reliability or consistency of the psychiatric diagnoses in a group of 794 naval enlisted men (examined in the psychiatric unit at a naval precommissioning installation) who were found to be unsuitable for service and who were transferred to a naval hospital for medical survey with the neutral, nonbiasing designation "diagnosis unknown, observation." However, a diagnosis had been made of each man and was included in his record and held at the precommissioning station.

TABLE 6. DIAGNOSTIC AGREEMENT BETWEEN PRECOMMISSIONING STATION AND NAVAL HOSPITAL*

	Precommissioning station, no. of cases	*Hospital, no. of cases*	*Agreement, per cent*
Unsuitable for service	794	744	93.7
Agreement within major categories	681	369	54.1
Agreement on specific diagnosis	794	259	32.6

* Adapted from Hunt et al., 1953, p. 59.

Table 6 shows the amount of agreement between the psychiatric diagnoses made on each man in the two installations. The authors point out that since the primary function of a naval neuropsychiatric department is the implicit prediction of unsuitability for military service, their first measure of reliability concerned the number of men considered *unsuitable* by *both* psychiatric staffs. The remarkably high agreement (93.7 per cent) on this category is not invalidated by such relevant considerations as the fact that in receiving the recruit, the hospital unit thereby recognized that the precommissioning station felt something was wrong with him. The personal, administrative, theoretical orientation, and other considerations whereby disagreements among different clinicians abound are too well known to deserve elaboration.

The data on 681 of the 794 men (113 could not be fitted into the three broad categories) were next examined for agreement in the two examining units across three broad, or major diagnostic, categories (including psychosis, psychoneurosis, and personality disorder, as in Ash's 1949 study), and all 794 men were studied for agreement in specific diagnosis (32 subcategories). The reliability values (54.1 and 32.6 per cent, respectively) also shown in Table 6 are not as high as for the unsuitable-for-service diagnosis.

Commenting on the high agreement (93.7 per cent) on the unsuitability diagnosis and the low agreement (32.6 per cent) on the specific diagnosis, the authors raise the validity question when they point out that it may make little *practical* difference in care, treatment, or social implications whether a man is classified as "psychoneurotic: anxiety" or "emotionally unstable." In any event, the study by Hunt et al. is not the best test of the reliability of psychiatric diagnosis since, like Ash's study, it used (young) men who were sufficiently within the *normal* range to have been accepted for military service before being identified at the precommissioning station. This study should be repeated with psychiatric hospital patients, even though the Hunt et al. findings are of considerable interest in that they utilized two *different* clinicians (as Ash did), each seeing the same individual, and not the indirect, relative frequency approach.

Although Hunt et al. caution that their results "may be influenced by factors specific to the naval situation and that broad generalizations to civilian practice are dangerous, if justified at all" (p. 60), the similarity of their results to those of Ash are striking (54.1 versus 45.7 per cent and 32.6 versus 20.0 per cent, for broad and specific categories, respectively).

However, unlike Ash, who interpreted his results solely in a reliability framework, Hunt and Wittson and their coworkers have published a series of follow-up validity studies which demonstrate the validity and thus, indirectly, the reliability of their psychiatric diagnoses (broad and specific categories as well as the very reliable category of unsuitability for military service).

In one such validity study (Hunt, 1951; Raines, Wittson, Hunt, & Herrmann, 1954), these investigators reasoned that if psychiatric diagnostic screening procedures of recruits at the precommissioning training center (boot camp) were efficacious in reducing subsequent psychiatric attrition during later service among the same *groups* screened, then the amount of *subsequent* attrition should be in inverse ratio to the number eliminated during training. That is, the more men discharged for psychiatric reasons during training, the less psychiatric attrition to be expected among the remaining same group of men during subsequent military service.

Fortunately, the peculiar conditions necessary for testing their hypothesis existed in the U.S. Navy during the first part of 1943. At one recruit base, Sampson, the commanding officer was not sympathetic to psychiatric screening, and relatively few discharges were permitted. At Great Lakes, the commanding officer allowed the psychiatric unit to discharge as many men as it saw fit. At Newport, where the investigators worked, the commanding officer asked the psychiatric unit to hold the discharge rate to roughly 4 per cent. According to Hunt et al., in 1943 the three naval training stations were operating under conditions where the quality of the recruit populations, the professional competence of the staffs engaged in psychiatric screening, and the actual psychiatric examination procedures in use were all roughly comparable.

To check their hypothesis, Hunt et al., after the war, knowing the earlier discharge rates for each station, obtained the records of a sample of approximately thirteen hundred men seen in each of the recruit centers during the same month in 1943 in order to see what the discharge rate was for these same men in the 2½ years of *subsequent* naval service. To cross-validate their findings, they repeated the procedure for samples for each of three additional months.

The results, shown in Table 7, are clear-cut: The higher the screening center's rate of diagnosing unsuitability for service, the lower the subsequent psychiatric attrition rate in the same group sample; the lower this training discharge rate (as at Sampson), the higher the subsequent rate of breakdown in this same group under the later military conditions. Hunt et al. also point out that careful inspection of these results indicates that there may be a curve of diminishing returns, since as more men are discharged, there is less and less return in lowered attrition rate. Thus in April, 1943, Great Lakes discharged almost twice as many men as Newport, but its attrition rate was diminished by only one-sixth. Hunt et al. suggest that one may ask whether, beyond an optimal point, the slight improvement in subsequent discharge rate is worth the large manpower loss entailed by the doubled number of training center discharges—a social, economic, and ethical question not answerable by scientists alone.

In commenting on the results shown in Table 7 and the related validity studies of his group, Hunt carefully reminds us of a fact

TABLE 7. PSYCHIATRIC (UNSUITABILITY-FOR-SERVICE) DISCHARGE RATE DURING TRAINING AND SUBSEQUENT PSYCHIATRIC ATTRITION DURING SERVICE*

Training center	*No. of recruits screened*	*Per cent discharged during training*	*Per cent discharged subsequently*
	January, 1943		
Great Lakes	1,310	4.4	2.6
Newport	1,255	5.0	3.7
Sampson	1,350	0.7	4.1
	April, 1943		
Great Lakes	1,525	4.5	1.5
Newport	1,173	2.6	1.8
Sampson	2,823	0.7	3.0
	June, 1943		
Great Lakes	1,347	5.9	3.2
Newport	1,294	4.2	3.0
Sampson	1,284	0.7	3.7
	July, 1943		
Great Lakes	1,350	5.2	3.3
Newport	1,310	3.0	3.6
Sampson	1,354	1.3	5.0

* Adapted from Hunt, 1951.

pertinent here, i.e., that in studying the reliability of psychiatric diagnosis, one need not always be bound by the superficially enticing concept of reliability of diagnosis for single individuals, taken one at a time across a total sample, as, for example, in the studies by Ash (1949), Masserman and Carmichael (1938), and others. Hunt (1955, pp. 201–202) writes:

> The fulfillment of [the clinician's] predictions is often influenced by complex and uncontrolled environmental factors. There are many areas, and many types of behavior, that are not amenable to prediction at present, and some may never be. It must be stressed that the predictions made in psychiatric selection are essentially group predictions rather than individual predictions, since the question of prediction in the individual instance raises many confusing philosophical and mathematical issues in the use of probability data in the clinical sciences. In psychiatric selection we are not making a prediction concerning the future behavior of each and every individual passing through the selection process, but rather making a prediction concerning the total behavior of the group to which the individual belongs on our continuum. We do not hope to be right in each and every individual prediction, but rather to have a high proportion of successes in any group or series of predictions.

Thus it is appropriate to raise a question pertinent to the several studies showing lack of reliability of psychiatric diagnosis, namely, the question of *reliability for what.* As Zigler and Phillips (1961) make clear, and as Caveny et al. (1955) and Hunt et al. (1953) elaborate, the function of psychiatric diagnosis is not a unitary one. Rather, the purpose, or function, of psychiatric diagnosis may be, for example, *administrative, therapeutic, research, preventive,* etc.

Hunt and his coworkers have published numerous additional "historicoexperimental" validity studies, only several of which will be reviewed here. In a study conducted in 1944 (Wittson & Hunt, 1951), 944 cases of naval personnel were sent for interview because of suspected psychiatric symptoms (picked up by enlisted men conducting vocational aptitude placement exams). On the basis of merely a very brief psychiatric interview, these cases were diagnosed and placed into three classes: (1) mild symptoms, treatment not indicated; (2) moderate symptoms, shore duty (but not sea duty) indicated; and (3) severe symptoms, hospitalization indicated. Years later, the subsequent naval careers of 932 of these 944 men were studied for the one-year period after this mild-moderate-severe diagnosis was made, and the psychiatric discharge rates during that one-year period were determined. The results, presented in Table 8, show a remarkable clarity. The subsequent rate of psychiatric discharge (the latter often accomplished far from the scene of the original diagnosis and independent of it) paralleled the original prediction (differential diagnosis): i.e., mild, moderate, and severe ratings had subsequent discharge rates of 6.5, 20.2, and 89.7 per cent, respectively. The normal attrition rate for discharges among *unselected* Navy men during this same period was 1.6 per cent, a figure one-tenth as large as the figure of 15.6 per cent, which obtained for the *total* group of 932 men shown in Table 8.

Although the results shown in this table clearly establish the *validity* of the original diagnostic classificatory process, as Hunt and Wittson interpreted their results, to this writer the results also establish, *ipso facto,* the *practical reliability* of the original crude three-group psychiatric diagnostic system. That is, in the absence of methodological flaws in the research design, to the extent that the three-category differential diagnosis *worked* (predicted) as well as it did in this study, the diagnostic classificatory scheme must be of sufficient reliability to merit serious attention and use. Or, put another way, had the test-retest reliability for the "suitable-for-service–not-suitable-for-service" dichotomy implied by the three classifications shown in Table 8 been only of the order of, for example, .50 to .80, this fact would have to be interpreted within the *context* of the validity results shown in the same table. Granted that the results shown in Table 8 might have been even more striking if the three-category diagnostic scheme shown in this table had better than, for example, a .50 to .80 test-retest reliability across two psychiatrists, the demonstrated validity results attest to not inconsiderable reliability for the original diagnostic classifications. However, *despite* this relatively low hypothetical reliability, the validity results shown in Table 8 cannot be discarded. In most instances, if not all, reliability cannot

TABLE 8. INCIDENCE OF SUBSEQUENT NEUROPSYCHIATRIC DISCHARGES AMONG MEN INTERVIEWED AND DIAGNOSED AS TO SEVERITY OF PSYCHIATRIC CONDITION*

Diagnosis	*Total No.*	*Subsequent NP discharge*	
		No.	*Per cent*
Mild	527	34	6.5
Moderate	367	74	20.2
Severe	38	34	89.7

* Adapted from Wittson & Hunt, 1951.

be divorced from validity. However, few students of the reliability of psychiatric diagnosis have been fortunate enough to be part of a long-range *program* of research which would make possible such a test of reliability through its validity correlates. Pasamanick et al. (1959, p. 130) provide some such validity data in their table showing the results (validity) of EST, drugs, and psychotherapy for different diagnostic categories (reliability).

In a study (Hunt et al., 1952) related to the one shown in Table 8, these investigators determined the subsequent psychiatric discharge rates of three groups of men in whom the initial diagnosis varied as to degree of "certainty" and "severity" as determined by who conducted the psychiatric examination and by the time, energy, and number of professional personnel required to arrive at the diagnosis. The three diagnostic groups used were (1) undiagnosed—despite the presence of some indication of psychiatric difficulty, the clinician concerned was unable to attach a definite diagnostic label; (2) diagnosed—indications of a psychiatric difficulty were present, and a definite psychiatric diagnosis could be made; and (3) board hearing recommended—diagnosed cases each of whom was felt to be possibly unfit for further military service and who were consequently referred by the psychiatrist to the next higher authority, the aptitude board, for final decision, but each of whom nevertheless *was sent to military duty* by the board after careful consideration. The subjects in the diagnosed and undiagnosed groups also were sent to duty, this diagnosis notwithstanding. As a further control group against which to check their hypothesis of differential subsequent psychiatric discharge rates in these three groups, Hunt et al. included a group of false positives, i.e., men referred to the observation ward for psychiatric examination but judged by the examining clinician to be "normal," or free from any positive symptomatology. The study was cross-validated in samples from two successive years. Some twenty clinicians were involved in the study. The original diagnosis was evaluated against a *criterion* of psychiatric discharge by the end of the war (December 31, 1945).

The results shown in Table 9 also are strikingly clear. As the confidence level, or definiteness of severity of condition, of the initial diagnosis increased from none (no NP), through least, moderate, and highest, the subsequent psychiatric discharge rate likewise increased in stepwise fashion. There seems little doubt that this additional "experiment of nature" by these authors adds to the confidence one can have in the reliability, as well as the validity, of the process of psychiatric diagnosis involved in the four classes of judgments shown in Table 9.

In additional studies, Hunt and his coworkers cite evidence to show that despite the lower test-retest correlations found by them and others for such *specific* diagnoses as schizoid personality, psychopath, alchoholic, etc., the validity correlates of these diagnoses as determined by the subsequent military history of each man show remarkable power for them. For example, men diagnosed as psychopaths subsequently show a higher incidence of *disciplinary* infractions and fewer hospitalizations, while neurotics show the reverse, etc. They also cite evidence to show that individuals diagnosed as "low intelligence," "low intelligence plus psychiatric symptoms" (but both groups were still sent to duty), or "normal" controls, all three being evaluated as groups, have markedly contrasting subsequent *differential discharge rates* for psychiatric, medical, and disciplinary reasons. References to these and numerous other validity studies can be found in Hunt, 1955.

One final reliability study should be mentioned. This is the one by Schmidt and Fonda

TABLE 9. INCIDENCE OF SUBSEQUENT NEUROPSYCHIATRIC DISCHARGE AMONG GROUPS DIFFERING IN DEFINITENESS OF INITIAL DIAGNOSIS*

Confidence level of initial diagnosis	*1942* N	*1942* Per cent	*1943* N	*1943* Per cent	*1944* N	*1944* Per cent
Highest (board)	42	21.4	1	0.0	31	32.3
Moderate (diagnosed)	126	15.9	126	15.9	93	29.0
Least (undiagnosed)	126	8.7	126	8.7	93	14.0
Control (no NP)	42	0.0	42	4.8	31	0.0

* Adapted from Hunt et al., 1952.

(1956), conducted at the Norwich State Hospital, and it is one which comes closest to being an adequate experimental test of the reliability of psychiatric diagnosis. This study, although possessing minor methodological shortcomings, used state hospital patients, large samples, the official APA nomenclature, and relatively independent diagnoses between two psychiatrists. Each of 426 patients admitted during a six-month period was diagnosed independently by each of two psychiatrists—one a resident, who made his diagnosis during the patient's first week in the hospital, and the other a chief psychiatrist, who later saw the patient at a formal staff conference. There were eight residents and three chief psychiatrists involved.

Agreement between the two diagnoses for three major categories (organic, psychotic, character) was found in 357 out of the 426 cases (84 per cent), while for 11 specific subtypes, the agreement was 55 per cent (the latter with a range from 6 to 80 per cent).

Table 10 shows the findings on the reliability across the three major categories. The figures in parentheses show the number of cases of agreement between residents and chief psychiatrists for each category. Using the chief psychiatrists as the criterion, the residents' agreement levels were organics, 92 per cent (178 out of 193); psychotics, 80 per cent; and character disorder, 71 per cent. These figures, the lower finding for specific reliability (55 per cent) notwithstanding, show that psychiatric diagnosis possesses a useful degree of reliability. This type of study, utilizing large samples of psychiatric patients, seen *independently* by two psychiatrists, should be repeated many more times, in many settings, by many investigators. If agreement levels of 84 per cent across major categories can be obtained, as in this Schmidt and Fonda study (1956), and 93.7 per cent in "unsuitability-for-service" or other criterion diagnosis, as in the Hunt et al. study (1953), adequate reliability, at least for major psychiatric diagnoses, will have been demonstrated.

That reliability of *specific* diagnoses will be lower is also clear. It appears that one of the major reasons for such lower (specific) reliabilities is the *individual predilections* of different interviewers. This has been clearly demonstrated in the study of Pasamanick et al. (1959, pp. 131–132) and also in the research of Raines and Rohrer (1955; 1960). The work of Raines and Rohrer is of such importance to any discussion of the interview that it will be presented separately.

TABLE 10. MAJOR CATEGORY AGREEMENT: RESIDENT WITH CHIEF PSYCHIATRIST*

	Chief Psychiatrist			
Resident	***Organic***	***Psychotic***	***Character***	***No.***
Organic	(178)	12	12	202
Psychotic	12	(128)	9	149
Character	3	21	(51)	75
N	193	161	72	(426)

*Adapted from Schmidt & Fonda, 1956.

The Raines and Rohrer Studies

In the first of their two studies, Raines and Rohrer (1955) utilized nine experienced Navy psychiatrists, with a range of five to nine clinicians in different phases of the study. The psychiatrists interviewed 886 young Marine Corps officer candidates, and, in one phase of the study, 124 of these candidates were reinterviewed by a second psychiatrist five weeks later. For all Ss, the individual psychiatric interview lasted twenty minutes, the interviewer having available to him during the interview a personal-history form completed by the candidate. The candidates were assigned at random to each psychiatrist. Following each interview, the psychiatrist filled out a standardized psychiatric evaluation form on the man. A two-hour briefing session on the use of this evaluation form was given all the psychiatrists prior to the beginning of the assessment interviews. Thus, in this study, reasonable experimental control was exerted over the following variables: (1) psychiatrists' level of training, (2) their level of experience, (3) diagnostic (personality type) and classificatory nomenclature (definitions) used, (4) length of interview, (5) physical conditions under which the interviews took place, (6) motivation of the client interviewed, and (7) clients interviewed. The seven personality-type categories rated by each psychiatrist were anxiety, hysteria, obsessive, psychopath, cyclothymic, schizoid, and paranoid.

The results of this study, analyzed and presented in a number of different ways, were striking and clear-cut: (1) Two psychiatrists, each interviewing the *same* man, observed *different personality traits* in this man and also reported *different dominant (defense) mechanisms* used by him in his everyday behavior; and (2) any given psychiatrist had a *preferred* personality-type classification which he utilized more frequently than on a chance basis, with different psychiatrists preferring different personality-type categories. Thus, one psychiatrist consistently reported a greater preponderance of anxiety in his candidate types; another, schizoid; another, obsessive; and another, paranoid. Still other psychiatrists "found" a smaller frequency of these and the other categories in their candidates. When five of the psychiatrists reinterviewed 124 of these same candidates five weeks later, with no psychiatrist interviewing a man he had previously seen, these same *predilections* (biases or "projections") of individual psychiatrists obtained, thus showing stability of the individual psychiatrist's bias over time.

To explain these initial findings, Raines and Rohrer postulated what they called a "projection hypothesis"; i.e., a clinical interview serves as a projective device, and the observed differences in ratings of interviewee personality reflect significant aspects of each psychiatrist's own personality. Generalizing from their results, it was hypothesized that each psychiatrist's own life experiences make him more sensitive to certain facets of the patient's intrapsychic dynamics and also result in a greater perceptual distortion of other facets of the patient's personality structure, which is projected in the diagnosis (1960, p. 133). In this way, they would explain the lower reliabilities in specific diagnoses in the studies reviewed above.

In their second paper, Raines and Rohrer (1960) present additional evidence for their projection hypothesis. The subjects used were 116 young, *normal,* enlisted, regular Navy men who were told that the interview was part of an experimental study being carried out for the Navy. The five psychiatrists used were all civilians. All had received three to six years of psychoanalytic training in the *same* institute. The number of years of psychiatric practice each had had ranged from seven to sixteen. The fifth psychiatrist had given personal training analysis and supervision to the other four and thus had become well acquainted with each of them.

One set of data for this study was a written assessment by the senior psychiatrist of the personality structure of each of the four other psychiatrists. A second set of data was supplied from the transcribed (content-analysis) psychiatric assessments of the 116 enlisted men made by the four psychiatrists, immediately following each thirty-minute interview, yielding two sets of data on these four psychiatrists, which would permit evaluation of a projection hypothesis similar to the earlier Raines and Rohrer study.

The results of this second study also were clear-cut: The four civilian psychiatrists rated each of 17 personality traits in their interviewees in *markedly different* relative frequencies (Raines & Rohrer, 1960, p. 135, fig. 1). To evaluate further these idiosyncratic patterns among the four psychiatrists, a comparison was made of the facts revealed in the content-analysis-results profile of each psychiatrist and the independently determined psychodynamic profile of the *same* psychiatrist made by the fifth psychiatrist. A very high degree of agreement was found between these two sets of independent data on each psychiatrist. Raines and Rohrer (1960) conclude: "The high degree of agreement . . . is favorable to the projection hypothesis" (p. 137). They state further:

> Coupled with the findings in our previously reported paper, the argument for the projection hypothesis becomes more convincing, since in the current study we were able to provide a valid independent measure of the psychodynamic structure of the psychiatrists and to demonstrate, with the assessing psychiatrists studied, that the projection hypothesis was substantiated (p. 137).

There is little doubt in the mind of this writer that Raines and Rohrer have identified a major source of error in previous studies of the reliability of psychiatric interviews, namely, the personality-based preferences, biases, or predilections of the interviewer. Their work should do much to clarify further research in this area. Interestingly, Pasamanick et al. (1959) clearly suggest a projection hypothesis when, commenting on the low agreement levels shown in their own study, they write:

> Despite protestations that their point of reference is always the individual patient, clinicians in fact may be so committed to a particular psychiatric school of thought, that the patient's diagnosis and treatment is largely predetermined. Clinicians, as indicated by these data, may be selectively perceiving and emphasizing only those characteristics and attributes of their patients which are relevant to their own preconceived system of thought. As a consequence, they may be overlooking other patient characteristics which would be considered crucial by colleagues who are otherwise committed. This makes it possible for one psychiatrist to diagnose nearly all his patients as schizophrenic while an equally competent clinician diagnoses a comparable group of patients as psychoneurotic (p. 131).

Thus, a decade after the crude initial study by Ash (1949), the seemingly crucial variable in any study of the reliability of clinical judgment—the interviewer himself—has been identified, and beginning investigations have been undertaken.

THE INTERVIEW IN SOCIAL SCIENCE RESEARCH

Reliability of Employer Interviews

The studies just reviewed on the reliability and validity of the psychiatric interviewer's diagnoses should not be construed as the only interest shown by investigators in the possibility of unreliability in interview-based judgments. As a matter of fact, long before the interest of the past two decades in the reliability of psychiatric diagnosis, interview investigators from a number of nonclinical fields had shown interest in the fidelity of interviewer impressions.

Some forty years ago, Hollingworth (1922) reported a study in which 12 experienced sales managers *each* interviewed 57 applicants for positions as salesmen. Each applicant was given a rating from 1 (best) to 57 (poorest) by each of the 12 interviewers. The study provided an excellent opportunity to study the reliability of employment-interviewer judgments. Because they are so illuminating in our evaluation of the interview, part of Hollingworth's results (the ratings by the 12 sales managers of 15 of the 57 applicants) are reproduced in Table 11. The notorious variability and thus unreliability of the interviewer judgments is very clear in this table. For example, applicant C was ranked 1 (best of the 57 applicants) by sales manager 11, but 57 (worst) by sales manager 9! Every experienced employer who utilizes the interview as the sole criterion for selection has had comparable experiences.

This study by Hollingworth is frequently cited as evidence for the unreliability of the interview in employment situations. However, a similar study, involving 20 sales managers and three other interviewers and 24 applicants, reported several years earlier by Scott, Bingham, and Whipple (1916), led these authors to just the opposite conclusion. The results of their study are given in Bingham, Moore, & Gustad (1959, pp. 105–108) from which Table 12 is reproduced. Again the results appear discouraging; e.g., applicant A was assigned rank 1 (best) by interviewer i but was given rank 22 (out of 24) by interviewer r. The last column in Table 12 indicates the range of the ranks received by each applicant, while the next-to-last column gives the average of all the 22 interviewer ranks for each applicant (i.e., the consensus of opinion). It is this consensus, or average rank, which is important in the Scott et al. study. When each interviewer's ranking of each applicant was checked against this consensus (or average rank) for each applicant, the results (when averaged down each column for the 24 applicants) provided an *index of agreement* for each interviewer against this group consensus. These figures (correlations) are shown in the bottom row in Table 12. Thus, interviewer a's rankings on each of the 24 applicants correlated .77 with the consensus of all the judges; interviewer b's rankings correlated .69; etc. Most of the correlations are quite respectable, while many are quite high. The interpretation of Bingham et al. seems apt when they conclude: "A study of this table reveals not merely a wide range of opinion regarding almost every applicant; it shows that in spite of these variations there was a fairly definite agreement among a majority of the interviewers on many of the applicants" (1959, pp. 106–108). It is fair to expect similarly encouraging levels of agreement in psychiatric studies should, for example, 20 psychiatrists or psychologists each interview serially the same 24 patients.

Studies of Interviewer Bias

The fact that, as shown in Table 12, interviewers n and u, for example, correlated only .55 with the consensus nevertheless underscores the fact that personal preferences, biases, and other *individual differences* within interviewers are still a major source of potential error in judgments based on interviews (the Raines and Rohrer effect). Probably the earliest study on this subject best known among social science interviewers, but possibly less well known among clinical interviewers, is one reported by Rice (1929). The study was carried out in 1914, when the New York Commission of Public Charities undertook a study of the mental, physical, and social characteristics of 2,000 consecutive applicants (destitute men) for a night's lodging at the Municipal Lodging House. Twelve trained social workers had the applicants assigned to them in random order; thus each was provided with an unselected (albeit different) sample of the total group. Each interview lasted from twenty to thirty minutes and was guided by a four-page outline of questions having to do with the economic and social history of the man being interviewed.

Upon analyzing the results of these interviews, very definite *differences* in the answers obtained by the different interviewers became clear. For example, one of the interviewers reported that, in his opinion, the downfall of most (62 per cent) of his group of destitute men was caused by liquor. Yet this interviewer was a known ardent prohibition-

TABLE 11. RELIABILITY OF THE INTERVIEW: RATINGS OF THE SAME JOB APPLICANT BY 12 INTERVIEWERS*

	Sales managers											
Applicant	1	2	3	4	5	6	7	8	9	10	11	12
A	33	46	6	56	28	32	12	38	23	22	22	9
B	36	50	43	17	51	47	38	20	38	55	39	9
C	53	10	6	21	16	9	20	2	57	28	1	26
D	44	25	13	48	7	8	43	11	17	12	20	9
E	54	41	33	19	28	48	8	10	56	8	19	26
F	18	13	13	8	11	15	15	31	32	18	25	9
G	33	2	13	16	28	46	19	32	55	4	16	9
H	13	40	6	24	51	49	10	52	54	29	21	53
I	2	36	6	23	11	7	23	17	6	5	6	9
J	43	11	13	11	37	40	36	46	25	15	29	1
K	18	5	55	37	57	16	34	6	46	13	38	26
L	7	20	6	1	1	10	3	7	17	2	2	26
M	18	45	26	9	51	43	33	29	46	32	37	26
N	2	15	6	28	7	45	24	40	40	17	30	48
O	18	42	19	2	16	4	14	51	32	45	31	26

* Adapted from Hollingworth, 1922, p. 269.

TABLE 12. RELIABILITY OF THE INTERVIEW: RATINGS OF THE SAME JOB APPLICANT BY 23 INTERVIEWERS*

Applicant	Interviewers *a*	*b*	*c*	*d*	*e*	*f*	*g*	*h*	*i*	*j*	*k*	*l*	*m*	*n*	*o*	*p*	*q*	*r*	*s*	*t*	*u*	*v*	*w*	*Av.*	*Range*
A	13	14	12	11	18	7	3	19	1	4	4	8	5	5	18	5	16	22	10	11	1	5	19	10	1–22
B	2	8	7	7	12	7	3		6	1	2	2	3	8	7	1	3	2	10	11	4	12	4	2	1–12
C	23	22	17	2	11	20	20	13	12	7	15	12	11	24	23	12	19	11	10	5	24	11	7	15	2–24
D	18	21	8	8	9	9	14		18	2	15	14	17	2	19	15	15	6	5	24	7	10	17	13	2–24
E	22	19	16	24	24	17	23	22	18	22	23	19	20	17	18	19	23	18	23	17	22	15	23	24	15–24
F	20	23	15	23	14	15	9	22	21	24	15	19	23	20	14	21	22	23	16	21	15	20	20	21	9–24
G	11	15	13	16	13	12	18	16	24	12	15	23	22	22	12	22	17	17	16	11	10	18	21	19	10–24
H	15	24	24	20	23	23	23	22	23	23	15	19	24	7	23	10	24	24	10	23	20	24	22	23	7–24
I	16	11	6	18	15	20	23	11	20	9	23	15	13	18	7	20	20	20	16	17	14	19	14	17	6–23
J	12	17	21	19	19	17	14	22	16	15	15	23	15	15	18	24	21	19		17	13	23	9	20	9–24
K	10	9	20	21	21	22	14	14	3		15	5	9	19	3	15	5	21	23	15	17	14	15	14	3–23
L	7	5	9	3	16	11	3	10	8		15	12	8	3	3	19	12	4	10	2	2	9	13	6	2–19
M	14	7	2	9	10	14	18	3		12	15	12	14	9	18	3	9	5	21	7	11	16	5	12	2–21
N	24	12	23	22	21	24	20	19	21	15	23	19	21	22	23	23	13	15	20	21	17	22	24	22	12–24
O	8	6	1	6	3	4	3	16	1	4	4	5	4	12	3	9	9	3	1	5	11	7	11	3	1–16
P	21	13	18	17	16	19	14	12	14	12	15	19	10	16	15	12	14	8	21	17	17	21	18	16	8–21
Q	9	18	3	4	4	1	3	1	15	18	7	2	18	7	11	2	2	7	2	3	6	5	10	5	1–18
R	5	16	11	14	5	6	9	9	9	2	2	19	2	22	12			10	10	1	4	5	8	8	1–22
S	4	4	4	10	7	3	9	7	12	15	15	8	19	10	7	10	9	1	16	14	3	1	3	7	1–19
T	17	20	22	15	21	10	14	16	17	20	7	19	16	13	18	15	9	14	19	21	22	17	6	18	6–22
U	3	1	10	5	6	5	3	2	7	7	2	5	6	1	3	6	1	9	5	11	20	2	2	1	1–20
V	5	2	5	1	1	2	9	5	4	9	15	2	6	13	10	3	3	16	10	7	8	3	1	4	1–16
W	1	3	19	13	2	12	14	4	10	18	15	8	1	10	3	8	9	13	5	4	17	8	12	9	1–18
X	19	10	14		8	17	7	7	5	20	7	8	9	7	9				2		8	13	16	11	2–20
	.77	.69	.70	.82	.76	.78	.81	.76	.76	.59	.69	.83	.72	.55	.69	.74	.81	.67	.63	.60	.55	.85	[illegible]		

* Adapted from Bingham et al., 1959, p. 10.

ist! Another interviewer, a Socialist, was of the opinion that the industrial system and such economic conditions as hard times and layoffs and other industrial conditions were responsible for the misfortune of his group of derelicts; and so on with different interviewer-interviewee group combinations. The results just given represent the *interviewer's own interview-based opinion.* The study called both for this and for a report from the interviewer of the opinions of the *men being interviewed,* as this also purportedly was reported to the interviewer. Here, too, the results were very clear. The prohibitionist interviewer reported that the men in his sample verbalized liquor, primarily, as their downfall; the men interviewed by the Socialist reported primarily industrial conditions as their downfall, and not liquor; etc.

Since the 12 interviewers were well trained and conscientious, Rice interpreted his findings as indicating that the bias of each interviewer was *contagious* and was thus communicated to each of his interviewees. The results of the Raines and Rohrer studies (1955; 1960) utilizing experienced psychiatrist-interviewers, and discussed above, make clear that each interviewer's unique biases (in perception and reporting) would, alone, be sufficient to explain the results of the Rice study.

Sources of Bias in Social Science Interviewing

As a matter of fact, a similar interpretation of Rice's results has been offered by Hyman, a leading research worker in social science interviewing. He writes:

> Rice's findings are undeniable, but there is no support whatever for his particluar explanation of them. The findings reported are perfectly compatible with the notion that the interviewer simply *distorted* the recording of given answers in accordance with his own prejudice, or that he interpreted ambiguous answers in artistic ways (Hyman et al., 1954, pp. 34–35, italics added).

In the fifty years since Rice's 12 interviewers interviewed their sample of destitute men, the opinions of literally millions and millions of persons have been sought out by members of a new profession—the social science opinion interviewers. The Social Science Research Council; the National Research Council; such groups as the National Opinion Research Center and the Survey Research Center of the University of Michigan; as well as groups headed by such well-known figures as Gallup, Roper, and others have all been instrumental in the creation of this new type of interviewer.

Space is being devoted to these developments in this chapter because the results of the research by these groups has a *direct bearing* on clinical interviewing. After decades of social science interviewing, and samples of interviewees numbering hundreds of thousands, the leaders of this addition to the interviewing profession became acutely aware of the presence of *interviewer bias* in the results being obtained. It was for this reason, and with the help of the Rockefeller Foundation, that Hyman et al. (1954) planned and executed a series of studies designed to investigate such factors as determinants of the interview situation; sources of effect deriving from the interviewer (his age, sex, ethnic background, physical characteristics, biases, etc.); reactions of interviewees to interviews; situational determinants of interviewer effects; the role of "rapport" in interviews; conditions under which interviewer errors could be reduced or controlled; and many others. The results, with ample tables, are presented in a 400-page report (Hyman et al., 1954) and deserve serious study by persons interested in clinical interviewing.

A quotation from Hart's remarks in the preface (pp. ix–x) of Hyman's book is pertinent to our study of clinical interviewing:

> In nearly all studies the subjects used were interviewers who were available in research agencies and in colleges and universities where research training is undertaken. Generalization of our conclusions to researchers of greater maturity and sophistication than these subjects has to be made, therefore, with due and proper caution. It would be dangerous, however, though consoling, for the mature and sophisticated interviewer to assume that he is not equally subject to the operation of the same error-producing factors affecting the varied group of interviewers covered by the studies we are here reporting. As a matter of fact, the available evidence suggests that, while the sophisticated interviewer may be less subject to variable errors of a careless sort, he is probably equally subject to certain serious biasing errors.

No one reading the studies of Raines and Rohrer (1955; 1960), which report the astounding biases of expert psychiatrists who had had many years' training and experience in interviewing, can deny Hart's view.

Table 13 presents merely one sample of the type of finding reported by Hyman et al. This table is amended from one given by Benney, Riesman, and Star (1956, p. 146), half of which was first published by Hyman et al. (1954, p. 157).

The results of the political survey, first reported by Hyman et al., involved 1,177 interviewees of both sexes and different ages and also interviewers of both sexes and of widely different ages. At the end of each interview, each interviewer was required to record on a questionnaire his rating of the respondent's (interviewee's) degree of "honesty and frankness" during the interview.

The results of this political survey of the percentage of interviewers, broken down first by sex and then by age, who rated their respondents as "completely frank and honest" on the rating scale completed after the interview are shown in Table 13. Benney et al. (1956) provided the results of a similar study having to do with the attitudes of interviewees on problems related to mental health. These results also are shown in Table 13.

Examination of this table shows a surprising similarity between the results of these two separate surveys. In addition, there are clear sex and age differences in interviewer judgments about the complete frankness and honesty of interviewees. Thus more female interviewers (range of 72 to 79 per cent) thought their interviewees were honest than male interviewers (range of 56 to 68 per cent). In addition, differences in interviewer-reported interviewee candor as a function of interviewer *age* also are shown to be as follows: interviewers under 30, 61 to 69 per cent; 30 to 39, 61 to 74 per cent; and 40 and over, 75 to 81 per cent. In these two studies, then, women interviewers and older interviewers believed their respondents to be more truthful during the interview, in contrast to male interviewers and younger interviewers.

There were many other findings in these two studies, and the original publications should be consulted by the interested reader.

TABLE 13. RELATION OF RESPONDENT CANDOR TO AGE AND SEX OF INTERVIEWER AND RESPONDENT: TWO SURVEYS COMPARED*

Respondent-interviewer combination	*Percentage of interviewers who rated respondents as "completely frank and honest"*		
	Political survey	*Mental health survey*	*Range*
Male interviewers:			
Male respondents	68	60	56–68
Female respondents	56	64	
Female interviewers:			
Male respondents	79	72	72–79
Female respondents	79	76	
Interviewers under 30:			
Respondents under 30	68	66	
Respondents 30–39	69	63	61–69
Respondents 40 and over	68	61	
Interviewers 30–39:			
Respondents under 30	68	70	
Respondents 30–39	66	61	61–74
Respondents 40 and over	74	66	
Interviewers 40 and over:			
Respondents under 30	75	81	
Respondents 30–39	80	76	75–81
Respondents 40 and over	81	77	

*Adapted from Benny et al., 1956, p. 146.

Similar studies showing the effect on interviewees of the age, authority, and presumed status of the interviewer and of related variables have been reported also by Riesman (1958) and by Ehrlich and Riesman (1961).

Although these studies, and those conducted by Hyman et al., did not involve clinical interviews, it is apparent that the results have considerable relevance for understanding such "process" variables as warmth, ambiguity, and the others now being investigated by Bordin, the Rogerians, and others.

An excellent earlier review of the interview as used by social scientists was provided by Maccoby and Maccoby (1954). In addition to reviewing studies having a bearing on methodological questions, these authors also discuss standardized versus unstandardized interviews, depth interviews, the use of open-end versus closed-end questions, sources of interviewer error, recording of interview data, and many other related issues. Two excellent reference sources on the interview also contain reviews of important research on the interview (Bingham et al., 1959; Fenlason, 1952). The reports of the two conferences on research in psychotherapy also should not be missed (Rubinstein & Parloff, 1959; Strupp & Luborsky, 1962).

Social Dyadic Relationships in Therapy Interviews

That sociologists have much they can contribute directly to our understanding of the dynamics of the clinical interview is demonstrated in an important book by a sociologist and a clinical psychologist, Lennard and Bernstein (1960). Their research addressed itself to a description in quantitative terms of the verbal interaction that takes place in interviews in the course of individual psychotherapy. This was done by recording eight therapies (four therapists with two patients each) for a period of eight months. Over 120 of these interview sessions were subjected to an intensive analysis that resulted in the classification of more than forty thousand verbal propositions along several dimensions—dimensions dealing with *structure* and *process* rather than with psychodynamic content, pathology, and psychotherapeutic change. In the introductory words of the authors: "It seems to us . . . that perhaps researchers in the field of psychotherapy and human relations have been overzealous in their pursuit of the more subtle facets and nuances of the therapeutic relation, without having first taken note of the more obvious and gross features" (pp. 9–10). Thus, Lennard and Bernstein suggest that investigation of psychodynamic material, for example, while rich and tantalizing, may have to await considerable refinement in measurement approaches. In the meantime they suggest as alternatives borrowing from theory and methodology already developed by social scientists (i.e., the concepts of action system, role relationships, patient and therapist expectancies, systems in equilibrium, etc., and the measurement approaches exemplified by Bales Interaction Process Analysis and others). Their book represents an application of this theory and methodology to the more than forty thousand verbal statements included in the 120 psychotherapy interview sessions.

While most of the approach is content-oriented, Lennard and Bernstein also present some data on noncontent measures of psychotherapy interaction. For example, statements of their four therapists' prepsychotherapy expectations (assessed by questionnaire) of how verbally active each felt he was in his psychotherapy interviews correlated very highly with how verbally active he was, in fact, during a number of psychotherapy interviews with two different patients. The three measures of therapist verbal activity were (1) the absolute number of interviewer statements in therapy; (2) the proportion of these interviewer verbal statements, i.e., the number of his statements divided by the sum of the therapist and patient statements, and (3) the rate of the interviewer's interaction, i.e., how often he speaks.

In addition, when the ratings given by patients regarding the ease with which each therapy interview had gone for them were correlated with the volume of the interviewers' verbal output, it was found that "the therapists' verbal output during the therapy interviews rated by patients as proceeding 'more easily' was about twice as large as in the sessions rated as proceeding 'about the same' or 'less easily,' while the verbal output of the patients was about 25 per cent higher." In addition:

> The average number of interactions per session was about 50 per cent greater in the

> sessions rated "more easily." The ratio of therapist propositions (verbalizations) to patient propositions (verbalizations) increased on the average from .19 to .29. Evidently, therapeutic communication is rated by patients as proceeding more easily when the therapist's verbal participation reaches a certain level as measured by verbal output and interaction rate. Also, the more symmetrical (perhaps within optimal ratio limits) the quantitative distribution of verbal participation between the patient and the therapist, the greater the satisfaction the patient experiences with the communication process. Increased participation in treatment is not uniquely determined by the specific nature of the content of the communications exchanges, but also appears to be a function of certain formal characteristics of the communication process itself (Lennard & Bernstein, 1960, pp. 183–184).

Probably some of their most provocative findings are contained in the chapter entitled "Equilibrium Processes." In this chapter, Lennard and Bernstein present data which show that (1) there is a definite equilibrium process in psychotherapy such that the relative amounts of therapist and patient speech stabilize at a fixed ratio (which differs for different therapist-patient pairs!) and that this ratio is maintained during the course of many therapy interviews; (2) although therapists differ in the amount of their therapeutic talk, the amount of talk for any given therapist (i.e., his proportion of talk per interview) tends toward a steady state by being relatively stable from interview to interview; (3) nevertheless, within these individual therapist limits, therapists compensate for higher patient output by reducing their own output and compensate for lower patient output by increasing their own output; (4) considering the number of silences (greater than ten seconds) per interview as an index of "session (interview) strain," psychotherapy interviews exhibiting most silences were succeeded by interviews characterized by a higher percentage of therapist evaluative acts and therapist acts of high informational specificity (two content measures); (5) low therapist verbal output was associated with postinterview patient dissatisfaction with communication during that interview; and (6) therapists differ in the degree to which they can vary their ratio of verbal activity, some therapists showing considerable flexibility in their proportion of verbal output from therapy interview to therapy interview, and others showing a constant equilibrium process.

The implications of these findings for the research on interview process being carried on by Bordin, Snyder, Rogers, and others are very clear. Thus, since the publication by Rogers (1942) of the transcript of eight interviews with "Herbert Bryan," research on interviewing has become remarkably more sophisticated. Without the advances in methodology (especially phonographic recording) and personality theory—and, probably more importantly, without the introduction of numerous training centers for nonpsychoanalytically oriented clinical interviewers—our understanding of the dynamics of the interview could hardly have progressed beyond the infant stage it was in prior to World War II.

RESEARCH ON THE ANATOMY OF THE INTERVIEW

In commenting on the low reliabilities of psychiatric diagnoses and other clinical judgments, Pasamanick et al. (1959) write that what is needed is not the elimination of diagnostic and psychodynamic categories. Rather:

> Most important [is] emphasis on the development of objective, measurable and verifiable criteria of classification based not on personal or parochial predilections but on behavioral and other objectively measurable manifestations. Until such time as these criteria are available, research on the incidence and prevalence of the various disorders and their etiology, treatment, and prevention will continue to be hampered and impeded (p. 132).

One might also add that research on many interview "process" variables likewise will be impeded.

The concluding section of this chapter will be devoted to an examination of some highly objective indices of interview behavior which, because of their unusually high reliability and demonstrated validity correlates, may be useful in a variety of studies on the interview. If they serve no other purpose, they will provide "natural-history" or base-line data for other investigators of the interview.

The findings come from a program of re-

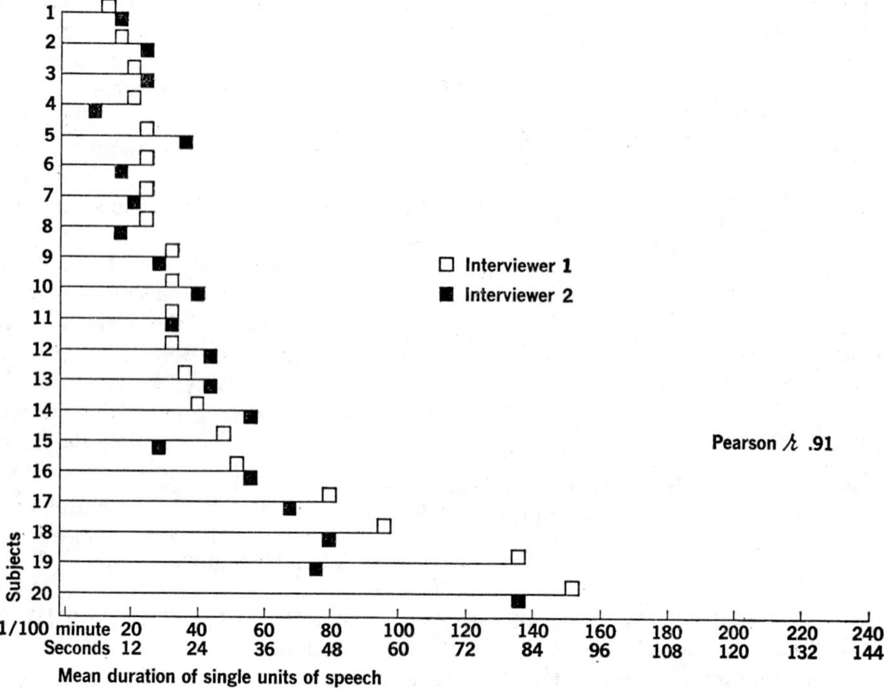

Figure 1. Reliability of 20 interviewees' speech durations: two interviewers, five minutes apart.

search conducted over the past ten years by this writer and George Saslow, in collaboration with a number of colleagues.[2] This research has concerned itself with the reliability and validity of the more formal, structural, or content-free dimensions of the interview, namely, *frequency* and *durations* of single units of *speech* and *silence*.

A review of the studies of a number of other investigators who have studied similar or related content-free or structural dimensions of the interview will be found in Matarazzo, 1962, pp. 495–506. The work of one such investigative team, Lennard and Bernstein (1960), was discussed earlier in this chapter.

Reliability of Interviewee Speech Durations

Five studies were conducted on this problem, and a detailed description of the procedure and results of each study have been summarized in Saslow & Matarazzo (1959). Knowing the low reliability across two independent interviewers of psychiatric description when differential diagnosis was the purpose of the study (see discussion above), it was asked what would be the reliability across two interviewers for a noncontent dimension such as the average duration of each patient's single units of speech during an interview. For the first study, two interviewers were asked to examine the same *new* patient (*N* of 20) in an outpatient psychiatry clinic while an observer, sitting behind a one-way mirror, recorded a variety of formal measures of the interviewer-interviewee interaction. The instrument used for recording these content-free interview dimensions was the Chapple Interaction Chronograph (Matarazzo, Saslow, & Matarazzo, 1956). The two interviewers, one a psychiatrist (GS) and the other an internist (SBG), had no knowledge of the content of each other's interviews. The two interviews, each lasting an average of thirty-three minutes, were conducted *five minutes* apart. Each interviewer talked about whatever content he typically would in such an initial interview. In many cases, analysis of the verbatim audograph recordings made of each interview showed that the content of the two independent interviews had no overlap. Although the interviewer was free to discuss whatever content he wished, he was asked to limit each of his comments throughout the whole inter-

[2] These investigations were supported by research grants M-735, M-1107, and M-1938 from the National Institute of Mental Health, U.S. Public Health Service.

view to approximately five seconds. The importance of this latter five-second "rule" will be shown below.

Figure 1, not previously published in this form, shows the results of this first study. Shown in the figure is the *mean* duration of each patient's single units of speech during the total interview, graphed from the patient with the lowest mean (subject 1) to the one with the highest (subject 20) in order to demonstrate the range of variability of such average patient speech durations. Each individual patient's average speech behavior with the psychiatrist (interviewer 1) is shown by a white square, while the mean of that same patient's duration of speech with the internist (interviewer 2) is shown by a black square. Thus, subject 1's mean duration of single speech units with interviewer 1 was eight seconds, and with interviewer two it was eleven seconds, while subject 20 had mean speech durations with the two interviewers of ninety-two and eighty-two seconds, respectively.

Visual inspection of Figure 1, as well as the Pearson *r* of .91 for the group of 20 Ss across the two interviewers, gives striking evidence that (1) duration of interviewee speech is a highly reliable or stable human characteristic and (2) it shows this stability for each interviewee despite sizable individual differences from one interviewee to the next (a tenfold range between subjects 1 and 20).

In view of the magnitude of this reliability correlation and because speech durations are, in the last analysis, an indispensable dimension for transmitting the all-important diagnostic interview and psychotherapy content, this study was repeated *en toto*. The results of this five-minute-apart (two interviewers) *replication* study were identical. In subsequent studies, the interval between the two interviews was increased to seven days, then to five weeks, and finally to eight months. In each study, the same interviewer (GS) was used for both the test and the retest interviews. Again the reliabilities were unusually high. Figure 2, also not previously published, presents the results of the five-week study. Details of these two and the other three reliability studies can be found in Saslow & Matarazzo (1959). This latter publication also presents data showing comparably high reliabilities for interviewee silence durations and a number of other formal interviewee characteristics.

Figure 2. Reliability of 19 interviewees' speech durations: one interviewer, five weeks apart.

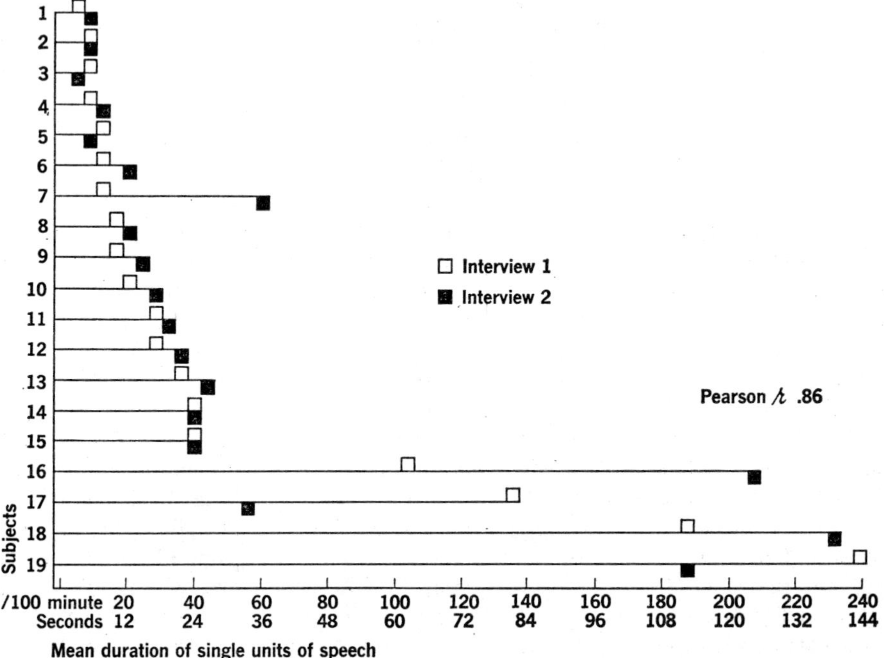

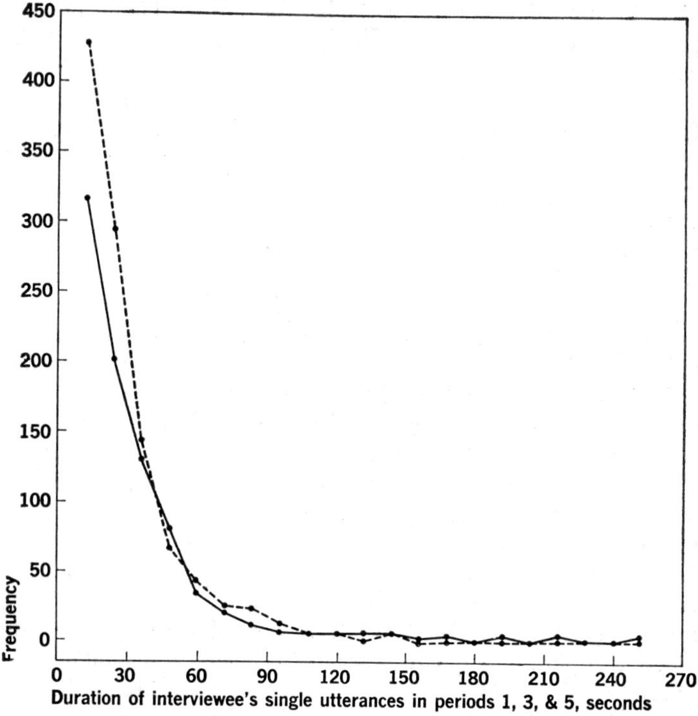

Figure 3. Frequency distribution of single utterances of 20 different interviewees with one interviewer.

Frequency Distribution of Single Units of Interviewee Speech and Silence Durations

Because, as was mentioned above, the very essence of diagnostic interview and psychotherapy material—interview content—is carried by durations of communicative action (utterances) and silence, and because only passing reference to the form (and other normative characteristics) of the distributions of these two highly stable interview variables has been made even by investigators working with these structural dimensions, it was decided to carry out the laborious procedures required for a detailed analysis of them.

In one study (Matarazzo, Hess, & Saslow, 1962) the interviews of a psychologist-interviewer (JDM) with 20 young job applicants undergoing a psychiatric interview and the interviews of 20 additional similar applicants being interviewed by a psychiatrist (GS) were analyzed. In both studies the interviewer again confined himself to five-second comments throughout the interview. The frequency distribution of 815 single units of interviewee speech (durations) contained in the 20 interviews with JDM and the 945 single speech durations making up the interviews with the other group of 20 interviewees seen by GS are shown in Figure 3 (also previously unpublished in this form).

It is clear from this figure that single interviewee speech durations (1) are skewed, (2) take the form of a mirror-image J shape or L shape, and (3) are typically short, with a *mean* of roughly twenty-one to twenty-four seconds (for JDM's twenty Ss, 48 per cent of single interviewee utterances are under eighteen seconds in length, 73.6 per cent are under thirty-six seconds, and 90.6 per cent are under sixty seconds' duration; while, for GS's group, comparable values are 50.1, 77.6, and 90.2 per cent, respectively). The similarity in the distributions of utterances in the two groups of Ss shown in Figure 3 provides a cross-validation of the J-shaped frequency distribution for duration of interviewee utterance as an interview variable.

Although not analyzed in such systematic fashion, the results of single units of interviewee speech duration from interviews with psychiatric patients (for example, the Ss shown in Figures 1 and 2), when compared with the interviews with young normal Ss shown in Figure 3, yield similar mirror-image J-shaped curves.

Figure 4 (not previously published) shows the frequency distribution of the interviewee *latencies* (i.e., silences or reaction times) which preceded the 815 and 945 single units of interviewee speech shown in Figure 3. The results shown in Figure 4, describing the passage of time from the interviewer's termination to the moment the interviewee responded, indicate that, like duration of interviewee speech, duration of this type of interviewee silence also is skewed and yields a J-shaped curve. The means, mode, and medians presented in Figure 4 also indicate that interviewee reaction times to the interviewer's last comment are typically quite short (the mean is under two seconds), even though the range for this latency variable

Figure 4. Frequency distribution of single latencies of 20 different interviewees with one interviewer.

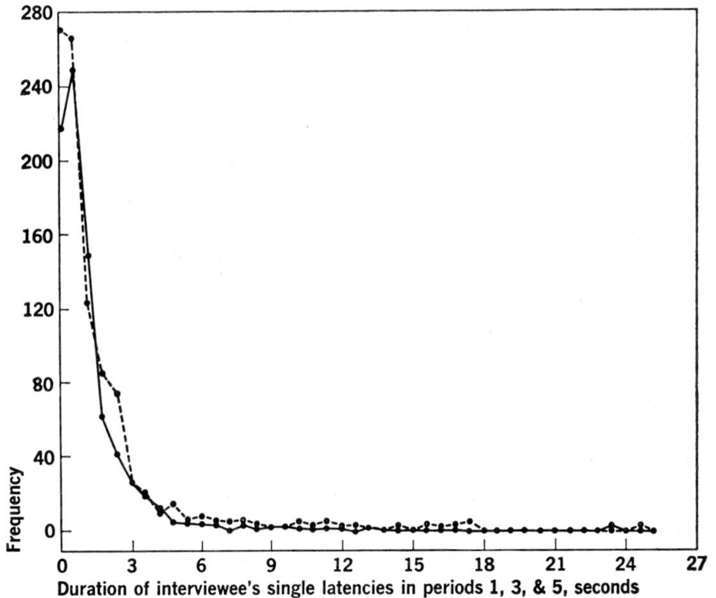

5-MINUTE PERIOD
STANDARDIZED INTERVIEW

•——• Interviewer 1 (J.D.M.)
N = 815 single interviewee actions
Mean = 1.84 seconds
S.D. = 1.27 seconds
Mode = 0.6 seconds
Median = 0.4 seconds

•----• Interviewer 2 (G.S.)
N = 945 single interviewee actions
Mean = 1.57 seconds
S.D. = 2.59 seconds
Mode = 0.6 seconds
Median = 0.4 seconds

reached an upper limit of twenty-five seconds in this population of Ss. The curve yielded by the 20 different Ss seen by GS is identical to the one from the 20 Ss interviewed by JDM, thus providing a cross-validation of one by the other.

Although not shown in Figure 4, analysis of *interviewee* silence or latency data when the interviewer *deliberately* does not respond when the interviewee has just made the last remark (a not unusual tactic in psychotherapy) revealed that the 40 interviewees shown in Figure 4 took the initiative, i.e., *spoke again* following their own last utterances in 64.6 per cent of the available opportunities (approximately 40 times 12, or 480, opportunities) deliberately given them to do so by the interviewer. The interviewer accomplished this by deliberately failing to respond 12 consecutive times in a standardized manner with each interviewee. If, in any of these 12 opportunities, the interviewee failed to speak again in an arbitrarily interviewer-determined upper limit of fifteen seconds, the interviewer himself would then respond. In the 64.6 per cent of the times when the interviewees did speak again following their *own* last utterances, they did so in an average of 4.4 seconds with JDM and 4.5 seconds with GS (this is not shown in Figure 4). The *range* of such initiative silence behavior (what Chapple has called "Quickness") is from one second to the full fifteen seconds, even though the *mean* is 4.4 or 4.5 seconds. For 35.6 per cent of the available opportunities, these same 40 interviewees did not speak again in the fifteen-second period during which the interviewer waited, and thus he spoke again. These results indicate that for the young normals of this study, in two out of every three opportunities, interviewees will react to the interviewer tactic of silence by speaking again themselves following their own last utterances, and they will do so in 4.5 seconds, in contrast to their usual reaction time of 1.5 to 1.8 seconds (to the interviewer's last utterance).

Among patient groups, such interviewee characteristics as age, IQ, socioeconomic status, and level of anxiety (Taylor Anxiety Scale) previously have been shown to correlate with each interviewee's average duration of silence, whether this silence is reaction-time latency or initiative latency (Matarazzo, Matarazzo, Saslow, & Phillips, 1958, p. 332).

Validity Studies of Interviewee Speech Durations

In a preliminary effort to see whether the highly reliable average durations of speech for each interviewee shown in Figures 1 and 2 had promise for differential diagnosis, the average speech durations of five diagnostic groups were examined (Matarazzo & Saslow, 1961). These included 19 state hospital (Rockland) back ward schizophrenic patients, 40 neurotic and acute psychotic inpatients and outpatients from the Massachusetts General Hospital, 60 neurotic outpatients from the Washington University School of Medicine, 40 normal job applicants for sales positions at Boston's Gilchrist's Department Store, and 17 similar applicants from the Carson-Pirie-Scott Department Store in Chicago.

Frequency distributions of the *mean* duration of interview speech for each individual in *each* of these five diagnostic groups are shown in Figure 5. Although the range of individual differences in each diagnostic group is very large, examination of the *median* values (21.0, 26.0, 34.0, 78.0, and 97.0 hundredths of a minute, respectively) shows an interesting *increase* from the presumably sickest group (the back ward schizophrenic patients) through the neurotic and acute psychotic group, then through the outpatient neurotics, and finally to the two presumably healthiest groups (the two normal groups).

Although the variability within each group is large, thus making individual diagnosis by this single variable alone difficult, and although different patient and normal groups might yield different results, the results shown in Figure 5 are a confirmation of the prediction made by Pasamanick et al. (1959, p. 132) that objective indices of behavior, once developed, will materially aid differential diagnosis. In this connection it is interesting to point out that weeks after the interview data shown in Figure 5 were analyzed, a review of the hospital records of the 19 schizophrenics (conducted independently by a person with no knowledge of the interview results) revealed that the only schizophrenic patients from this back ward group who were allowed off-ward privileges were the four Ss with the highest average interview speech durations (shown on the right in Figure 5). Thus, these four Ss had in common with the two normal groups the long interview speech durations, and they were also the most "normal" among the schizophrenic patients in that they were the only

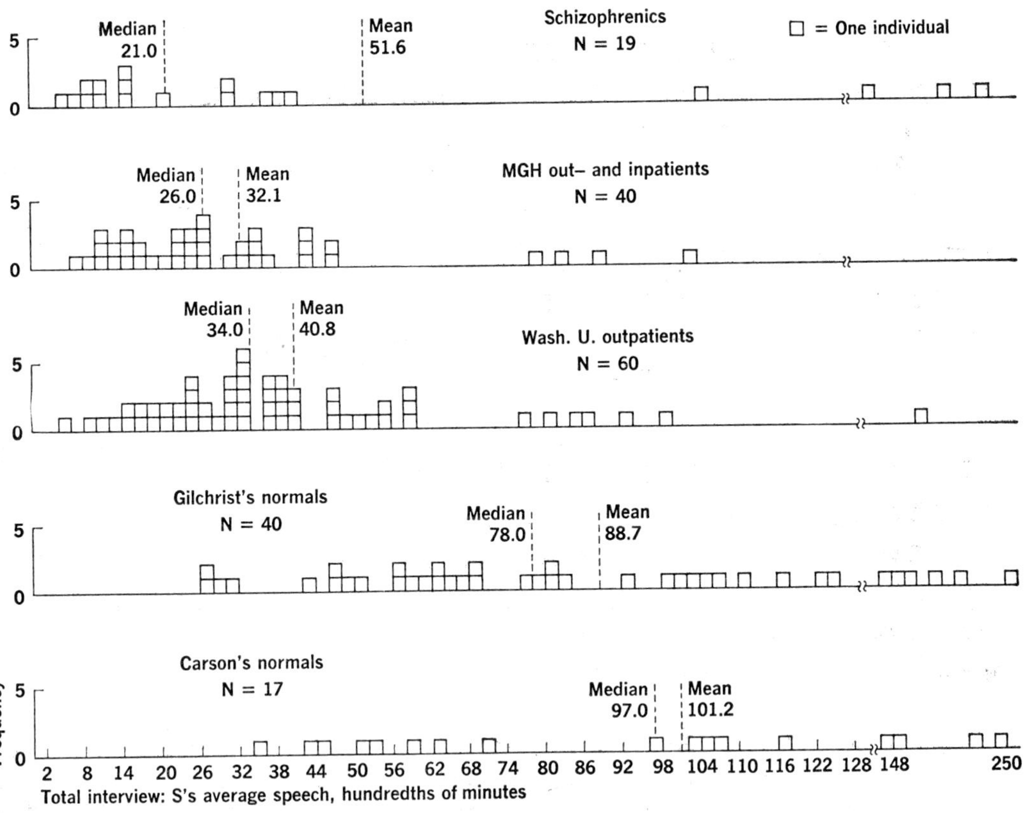

Figure 5. Frequency distributions: S's speech durations.

such patients among the 19 who were allowed to work off the ward (in the kitchen and around the grounds). While this finding is merely suggestive, its implications for a more objective behavioral diagnosis are clear.

Frequency distributions of some eleven other objective interview interaction variables obtained from the same five groups shown in Figure 5 will be found in Matarazzo & Saslow, 1961.

Another validity study on interview speech durations recently was carried out by Matarazzo, Weitman, Saslow, and Wiens (1963). This was a *direct* experimental attempt to influence interviewee speech durations. The interviewees again were 20 young normal applicants for positions as policemen and firemen. [In each of the earlier (Figures 3 and 4) and subsequent (Figures 6 to 8) samples, the characteristics of these young normals are roughly the same: mean age, 25; mean education, thirteen years; WAIS full scale IQ, 114; Taylor Anxiety Scale score, 7. In most respects they resemble the average college graduate of this country.] In the first of these studies of interviewer influence, the method involved a forty-five-minute psychiatric interview which, unknown to the interviewee, was divided into three fifteen-minute periods, during each of which the interviewer (JDM) controlled only the duration of his own speaking times (but *not* the content of what he said). For the first fifteen minutes (period 1), the interviewer spoke in five-second comments, plus or minus slight error variance; in period 2 his speech was always of ten seconds' duration; while for the third fifteen-minute period, each of the interviewer's comments again was always of five seconds' duration. Earlier incidental observations (Matarazzo, 1962) had suggested that such changes in interviewer speech durations would be followed by corresponding increases in interviewee speech durations.

The results (also not previously published in this form) are shown at the top of Figure 6, where it can be seen that interviewer mean speech durations of 5.3, 9.9, and 6.1 seconds (p of .001) during the three fifteen-minute periods elicited corresponding interviewee

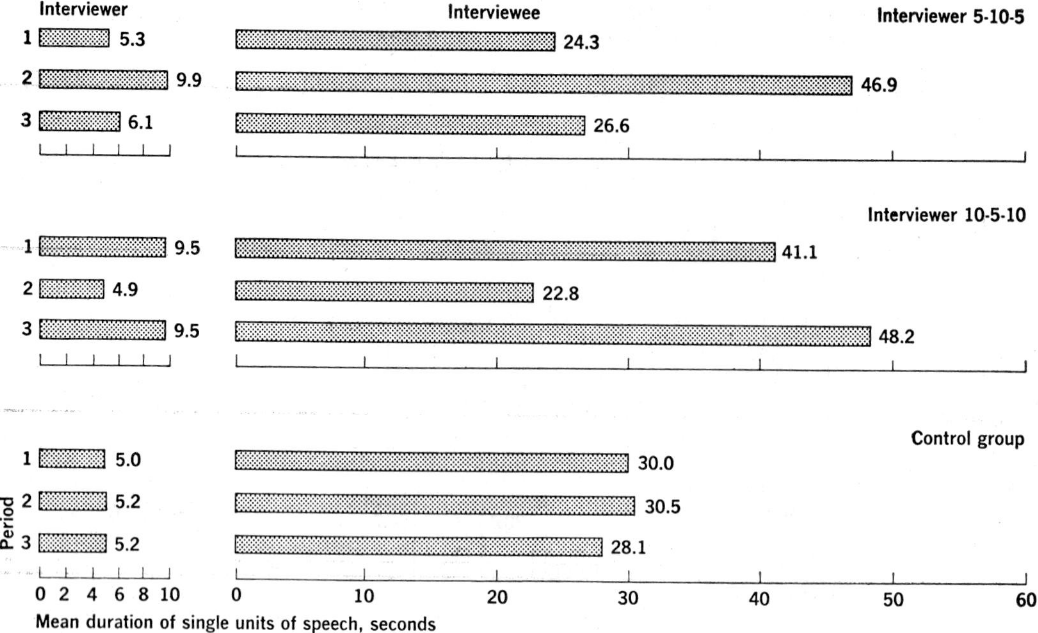

Figure 6. Interviewer influence on duration of interviewee speech.

speech durations of 24.3, 46.9, and 26.6 seconds, respectively (p of .01). Thus, as the interviewer doubled or halved his own speech durations, he "controlled" in like manner the speech durations of the interviewee.

Because this study needed cross-validation and because the *order* or *sequence* of the five- and ten-second periods might introduce a methodological artifact, this study was repeated using 20 additional Ss and having the interviewer use a ten-five-ten-second speech pattern during the three periods in contrast to the earlier five-ten-five-second pattern. The results were identical and are shown in the middle of Figure 6. The values of p for interviewer and interviewees were .001 and .001, respectively.

As a control for these two studies, the interviewer (JDM) interviewed 20 additional Ss using a five-five-five-second speaking-time design. These results, shown at the bottom of Figure 6, were 5.0, 5.2, and 5.2 seconds (p not significant) and 30.0, 30.5, and 28.1 seconds (p not significant).

These three studies reveal clearly that, within the speech-duration limits of this study, an interviewer can increase or decrease an interviewee's speech durations by changes in his own speech durations. Data suggesting that this influence or "control" is also possible with patient groups have been found (Matarazzo, 1962), although schizophrenic patients were not as amenable to this interviewer duration of utterance influence as other patient groups. The implications from Figure 6 for behavior therapy with patients are clear: Psychotherapist-interviewers, for example, conceivably can induce depressed patients to talk in longer utterances by themselves speaking in longer utterances and can influence "manic" or loquacious patients (hysterics) to talk in briefer units by utilizing very brief speaking times with such patients, etc.

Another possibility suggested by the results shown in Figure 6 involves *no* artificial change in the habitual interview speech behavior of psychotherapists; rather, possibly the identification of *individual differences* in such behavior in interviewers and the deliberate pairing of interviewers with known characteristics with patients whose own speech characteristics presumably can best utilize such an interviewer-interviewee combination. Prescribed behavior therapy of this sort appears not far in the future. That interviewers differ widely in the extent to which they speak was discerned twenty years ago by Porter (1943), who found that one *single* interviewer talked twenty-five times as much as another interviewer (Rogers, 1942, p. 122) and that directive counselors, as a *group*, talked more than 2½ times as much as their clients, while nondirective counselors, as a group, talked only one-half as much as their clients, a fivefold difference (Snyder, 1954, p. 539). Examining these and similar interviewer differences fully and investigating the effects of such differences on interviewee behavior would do much to further our knowledge of the elusive *dynamics* of the interview interaction. Lennard and Bernstein (1960), whose research was described earlier, already have made a start in this direction.

Two interview tactics frequently employed by experienced interviewers are (1) head nodding and (2) saying "Mm-hmm mm-hmm" at strategic points throughout an interview. It is believed by most interviewers, although it has never been verified experimentally to this writer's knowledge, that both tactics encourage the interviewee to continue talking (e.g., increase his current speech unit).

Using the same interviewer (JDM) and 20 job applicants from the same population of interviewees, a study was conducted in which a similar three-period forty-five-minute interview was utilized. The interviewer spoke in five-second utterances for each of the three fifteen-minute periods, but, only during period 2, he *nodded* his head each time the interviewee spoke. The results (Figure 7) of his utterance durations in the three periods were 5.1, 5.1, and 5.1 seconds (p not significant), while for the 20 interviewees, the corresponding speech durations were 36.9, 54.7, and 35.4 seconds (p of .001). These results were cross-validated by another interviewer (GS) on a second similar sample of 20 interviewees: 5.1, 5.0, and 5.0 seconds (p not significant) and 25.2, 42.2, and 30.3 seconds (p of .001).

These results and those obtained with the earlier-described control group are shown in Figure 7. It is clear that head nodding, as an interviewer tactic, can profoundly influence duration of interviewee speech.

The effects of the interviewer tactic of saying "Mm-hmm mm-hmm" were shown to be identical in all ways to the effects of head nodding, except that the interviewer (JDM in both studies shown in Figure 8) utilized this *verbal* response in period 2, in contrast to the other study (Figure 7), where head nodding was utilized as the independent variable. The results, shown in Figure 8, are striking. For the interviewer in both groups shown in Figure 8, the p value was not significant, while for both groups the p value for interviewees was .001. Thus, saying "Mm-hmm" also is a powerful tactic which can increase interviewee speech durations.

Similar results were independently re-

Figure 7. Interviewer influence on duration of interviewee speech.

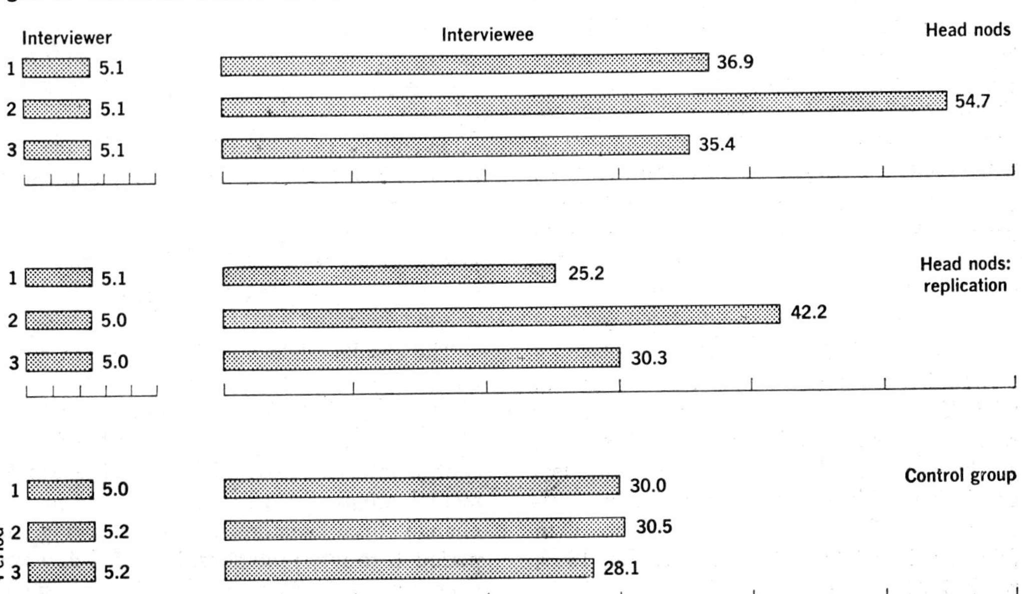

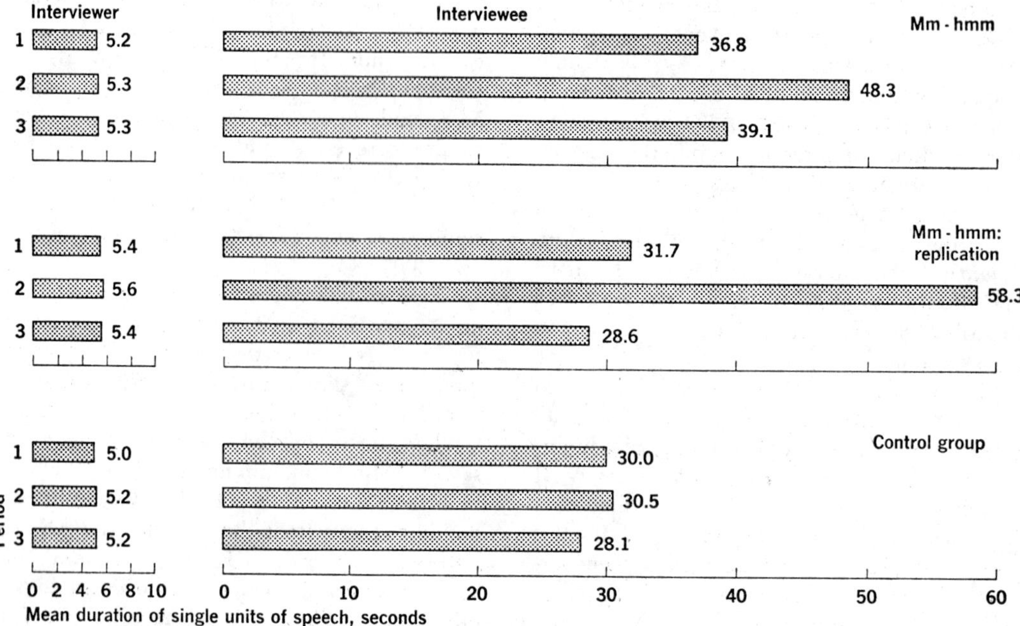

Figure 8. Interviewer influence on duration of interviewee speech.

ported by Kanfer and McBrearty (1962), who, although not controlling as rigorously the interviewer's head nodding and saying "Mm-hmm" as was done in the two above experiments, nevertheless did find that these two tactics, plus interviewer smiling, did increase S's duration of speech whenever they were introduced into a laboratory interview with undergraduate female Ss.

Another tactic frequently employed during interviews by experienced psychotherapists is the use of *interpretations*. Mention was made earlier of the study of this variable by Bordin (1959). Bordin supplies this definition: "Any behavior on the part of the therapist that is an expression of his view of the patient's emotions and motivations—either wholly or in part—is considered an interpretation" (1959, p. 238). Bordin's research approach to this variable is primarily psychodynamic and content-oriented. He quotes the results of a dissertation done at Michigan by Speisman, who "found clear-cut evidence that patient resistance was lowest following interpretations at the moderate level (of depth) and less conclusive evidence that superficial interpretations were followed by less resistance than followed deep interpretations" (Bordin, 1959, pp. 243–244).

The results of a study by Kanfer, Phillips, Matarazzo, and Saslow (1960) of the effect of an interviewer's *interpretations* on duration of interviewee speech may have identified an important additional dimension for measuring Bordin's level of resistance following interpretations. In this study, utilizing nurses as interviewees, the interviewer (FHK), while attempting to keep the durations of his own speaking times roughly to five seconds, employed *nondirective* interviewing throughout the whole of a three-period interview with a control group and *interpretations* during only period 2 with the experimental group. Interpretations were defined as "any statements, often phrased as questions, which analyze; relate several of S's described experiences, attitudes, or feelings; generalize S's statements to suggest a determinant of his behavior; or give a psychological explanation; or a motivational description" (Kanfer et al., 1960, p. 530).

The results, shown in Figure 9, are clear-cut (two nonsignificant p values for the interviewer, a p of .01 for the interpretation interviewees, and a nonsignificant p value for the control interviewees). Thus, with the experimental group, the effect of the interviewer's change from nondirective interviewing, in period 1, to interpretations, in period 2, was a *decrease* in interviewee duration of single speech units from 39.6 to 29.6 seconds, a 25 per cent decrease! When, in period 3, the interviewer discontinued using interpretations, the mean duration of speech returned to its earlier high level (46.4 seconds).

The results of the various studies shown in Figures 1 to 9 indicate both that interviewee speech and silence durations are highly reliable and that these two variables can be investigated in a variety of construct and concurrent (as well as other) validity study designs with surprising and seemingly important validity findings. If they do nothing more, the results shown in Figures 1 to 9 attest to the fact that interview and thus psychotherapy research need not forever be destined to insignificant or barely significant reliability coefficients or, similarly, to low or nonsignificant validity findings. Although duration of interview speech and silence, as variables for study, may appear to lack the glamour of such psychodynamic variables as insight, empathy, transference, etc., the results with them thus far are encouraging. It is this writer's somewhat facetious suspicion that empathy, transference, and other psychodynamic variables may very well turn out to be measured best not by the complicated psychodynamic (content-analysis) scoring schemata we all have used in the past but, rather, by such simpleminded, basic interview measures as frequency and duration of speech, silence, interruptions, initiative, and related formal or structural measures. Or, if not, these latter, in combination with the traditional content-analysis measures, may be more fruitful than the content measures alone. A discussion of the potential usefulness of such noncontent measures in the study of psychotherapy series, as well as a description of additional recent experiments not reviewed here, will be found in a paper by Matarazzo, Wiens, and Saslow (1965). A suggestion that the two-person influence shown in Figure 6 may also apply to astronauts in orbital flight also has been published by Matarazzo, Wiens, Saslow, Dunham, and Voas (1964).

REFERENCES

Ackerman, N. W., Beatman, Frances L., & Sherman, S. N. (Eds.) *Exploring the base for family therapy.* New York: Family Service Association of America, 1961.

Alexander, F., & French, T. M. *Psychoanalytic therapy: principles and application.* New York: Ronald, 1946.

American Psychiatric Association, Mental Hospital Service, Committee on Nomenclature and Statistics of the American Psychiatric Association. *Diagnostic and statistical manual: mental disorders.* Washington, D.C.: 1952.

Ash, P. The reliability of psychiatric diagnosis. *J. abnorm. soc. Psychol.,* 1949, **44,** 272–277.

Auld, F., Jr., & Murray, E. J. Content-analysis studies of psychotherapy. *Psychol. Bull.,* 1955, **52,** 377–395.

Beck, A. T. Reliability of psychiatric diagnoses: a critique of systematic studies. *Amer. J. Psychiat.,* 1962, **119,** 210–216.

Bell, J. E. Family group therapy. *Publ. Hlth. Monogr.,* 1961, No. 64.

Benney, M., Riesman, D., & Star, Shirley A. Age and sex in the interview. *Amer. J. Sociol.,* 1956, **62,** 143–152.

Bierer, J., & Strom-Olsen, R. The recording of psychotherapeutic sessions: its value in teaching,

Figure 9. Interviewer influence on duration of interviewee speech.

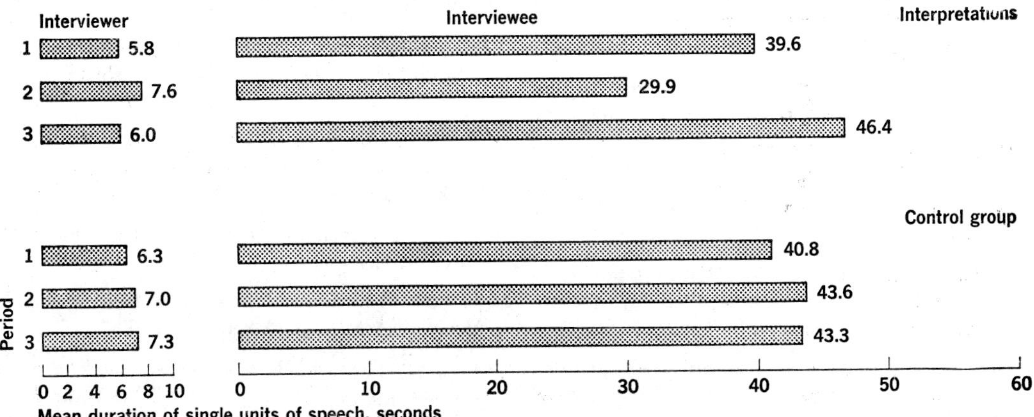

research, and treatment. *Lancet,* 1948, **254,** 957–958.

Bingham, W. V. D., Moore, B. V., & Gustad, J. W. *How to interview.* New York: Harper & Row, 1959.

Boisen, A. Types of dementia praecox: a study in psychiatric classification. *Psychiatry,* 1938, **1,** 233–236.

Bordin, E. S. Ambiguity as a therapeutic variable. *J. consult. Psychol.,* 1955, **19,** 9–15.

Bordin, E. S. Inside the therapeutic hour. In E. A. Rubinstein & M. B. Parloff (Eds.), *Research in psychotherapy.* Vol. 1. Washington, D.C.: American Psychological Association, 1959. Pp. 235–246.

Breuer, J., & Freud, S. *Studies on hysteria.* (Tr. by James Strachey.) New York: Basic Books, 1957.

Brody, E. B., Newman, R., & Redlich, F. C. Sound recording and the problem of evidence in psychiatry. *Science,* 1951, **113,** 379–380.

Cattell, J. M., & Bryant, S. Mental association investigated by experiment. *Mind,* 1889, **14,** 230–250.

Caveny, E. L., Wittson, C. L., Hunt, W. A., & Herrmann, R. S. Psychiatric diagnosis: its nature and function. *J. nerv. ment. Dis.,* 1955, **121,** 367–373.

Coleman, R., Greenblatt, M., & Solomon, H. C. Psychophysiological evidence of rapport during psychotherapeutic interviews. *Dis. nerv. System,* 1956, **17,** 2–8.

Covner, B. J. Studies in phonographic recordings of verbal material. I. The use of phonographic recordings in counseling practice and research. *J. consult. Psychol.,* 1942, **6,** 105–113. (a)

Covner, B. J. Studies in phonographic recordings of verbal material. II. A device for transcribing phonographic recordings of verbal material. *J. consult. Psychol.,* 1942, **6,** 149–153. (b)

Covner, B. J. Studies in phonographic recordings of verbal material. III. The completeness and accuracy of counseling interview reports. *J. gen. Psychol.,* 1944, **30,** 181–203. (a)

Covner, B. J. Studies in phonographic recordings of verbal material. IV. Written reports of interviews. *J. appl. Psychol.,* 1944, **28,** 89–98. (b)

Deutsch, F., & Murphy, W. F. *The clinical interview.* New York: International Universities Press, 1955, 2 vols.

DiMascio, A., Boyd, R. W., Greenblatt, M., & Solomon, H. C. The psychiatric interview: a sociophysiologic study. *Dis. nerv. System,* 1955, **16,** 2–7.

Dollard, J. & Auld, F., Jr. *Scoring human motives: a manual.* New Haven, Conn.: Yale Univer. Press, 1959.

Dollard, J., Auld, F., Jr., & White, Alice. *Steps in psychotherapy.* New York: Macmillan, 1953.

Dollard, J., & Miller, N. E. *Personality and psychotherapy: an analysis in terms of learning, thinking, and culture.* New York: McGraw-Hill, 1950.

Ehrlich, June S., & Riesman, D. Age and authority in the interview. *Publ. Opinion Quart.,* 1961, **25,** 39–56.

Ellis, A. Outcome of employing three techniques of psychotherapy. *J. clin. Psychol.,* 1957, **13,** 344–350.

Ellis, A. Rational psychotherapy. *J. gen. Psychol.,* 1958, **59,** 35–49.

Ellis, A. The treatment of a psychopath with rational psychotherapy. *J. Psychol.,* 1961, **51,** 141–150.

Ellis, A. Rational-emotive psychotherapy. Paper read at Amer. Psychol. Ass., St. Louis, August, 1962.

Eysenck, H. J. *The scientific study of personality.* London: Routledge, 1952.

Eysenck, H. J. Classification and the problem of diagnosis. In H. J. Eysenck (Ed.), *Handbook of abnormal psychology: an experimental approach.* New York: Basic Books, 1961. Pp. 1–31. (a)

Eysenck, H. J. The effects of psychotherapy. In *ibid.* Pp. 697–725. (b)

Fenlason, Anne F. *Essentials in interviewing: for the interviewer offering professional services.* New York: Harper & Row, 1952.

Finesinger, J. E. Psychiatric interviewing: I. Some principles and procedures in insight therapy. *Amer. J. Psychiat.,* 1948, **105,** 187–195.

Ford, D. H., & Urban, H. B. *Systems of psychotherapy: a comparative study.* New York: Wiley, 1963.

Foulds, G. The reliability of psychiatric and validity of psychological diagnosis. *J. ment. Sci.,* 1955, **101,** 851–862.

Frank, J. D. *Persuasion and healing: a comparative study of psychotherapy.* Baltimore: Johns Hopkins, 1961.

Fromm-Reichmann, Frieda. *Principles of intensive psychotherapy.* Chicago: Univer. of Chicago Press, 1950. Chap. 5.

Galton, F. Psychometric experiments. *Brain,* 1879, **2,** 149–162.

Galton, F. *Inquiries into human faculty and its development.* London: Macmillan, 1885.

Gill, M., Newman, R., & Redlich, F. C. *The initial interview in psychiatric practice.* New York: International Universities Press, 1954.

Glover, E. Research methods in psychoanalysis. Paper read at the 17th Int. Psychoanal. Congr., Amsterdam, August, 1951.

Gottschalk, L. A. (Ed.) *Comparative psycholinguistic analysis of two psychotherapeutic interviews.* New York: International Universities Press, 1961.

Gottschalk, L. A., Springer, Kayla J., & Gleser, Goldine C. Experiments with a method of assessing the variations in intensity of certain psychological states occurring during two psychotherapeutic interviews. In L. A. Gottschalk (Ed.), *Comparative psycholinguistic analysis of two psychotherapeutic interviews.* New York: International Universities Press, 1961. Pp. 115–138.

Grace, W. J., Wolf, S., & Wolff, H. G. *The human colon.* New York: Hoeber-Harper, 1951.

Gralnick, A. Family psychotherapy: general and specific considerations. *Amer. J. Orthopsychiat.,* 1962, **32,** 515–526.

Greenblatt, M. Discussion of papers by Saslow & Matarazzo, and Lacey. In E. A. Rubinstein & M. B. Parloff (Eds.), *Research in psychotherapy.* Vol. 1. Washington, D.C.: American Psychological Association, 1959, Pp. 209–220.

Greenspoon, J. Verbal conditioning and clinical psychology. In A. J. Bachrach (Ed.), *Experimental foundations of clinical psychology.* New York: Basic Books, 1962. Pp. 510–553.

Hall, C. S., & Lindzey, G. *Theories of personality.* New York: Wiley, 1957.

Harper, R. A. *Psychoanalysis and psychotherapy: 36 systems.* Englewood Cliffs, N.J.: Prentice-Hall, 1959.

Hollingworth, H. L. *Judging human character.* New York: Appleton, 1922.

Holmes, T. H., Goodell, H., Wolf, S., & Wolff, H. G. *The nose.* Springfield, Ill.: Charles C Thomas, 1950.

Holtzman, W. H., & Sells, S. B. Prediction of flying success by clinical analysis of test protocols. *J. abnorm. soc. Psychol.,* 1954, **49,** 485–490.

Hunt, W. A. An investigation of naval neuropsychiatric screening procedures. In H. Guetzkow (Ed.), *Groups, leadership, and men.* Pittsburgh, Pa.: Carnegie Press, 1951. Pp. 245–256.

Hunt, W. A. A rationale for psychiatric selection. *Amer. Psychol.,* 1955, **10,** 199–204.

Hunt, W. A., Wittson, C. L., & Hunt, Edna B. The relationship between definiteness of psychiatric diagnosis and severity of disability. *J. clin. Psychol.,* 1952, **8,** 314–315.

Hunt, W. A., Wittson, C. L., & Hunt, Edna B. A theoretical and practical analysis of the diagnostic process. In P. H. Hoch & J. Zubin (Eds.), *Current problems in psychiatric diagnosis.* New York: Grune & Stratton, 1953. Pp. 53–65.

Hyman, H. H., et al. *Interviewing in social research.* Chicago: Univer. of Chicago Press, 1954.

Jackson, D. D., & Satir, Virginia. A review of psychiatric developments in family diagnosis and family therapy. In N. W. Ackerman et al. (Eds.), *Exploring the base for family therapy.* New York: Family Service Association of America, 1961. Pp. 29–51.

Jones, E. *The life and work of Sigmund Freud.* New York: Basic Books. Vol. 1, 1953. Vol. 2, 1955. Vol. 3, 1957.

Kahn, R. L., & Cannell, C. F. *The dynamics of interviewing: theory, technique, and cases.* New York: Wiley, 1957.

Kanfer, F. H., & McBrearty, J. F. Minimal social reinforcement and interview content. *J. clin. Psychol.,* 1962, **18,** 210–215.

Kanfer, F. H., Phillips, Jeanne S., Matarazzo, J. D., & Saslow, G. Experimental modification of interviewer content in standardized interviews. *J. consult. Psychol.,* 1960, **24,** 528–536.

Kelly, E. L., & Fiske, D. W. *The prediction of performance in clinical psychology.* Ann Arbor, Mich.: Univer. of Michigan Press, 1951.

Kelly, E. L., & Goldberg, L. R. Correlates of later performance and specialization in psychology: A follow-up study of the trainees assessed in the VA Selection Research Project. *Psychol. Monogr.,* 1959, **73,** No. 12 (Whole No. 482).

Kelly, G. A. *The psychology of personal constructs.* Vols. 1, 2. New York: Norton, 1955.

Kempf, E. J. *Psychopathology.* St. Louis: Mosby, 1920.

Kephart, N. G. *The employment interview in industry.* New York: McGraw-Hill, 1952.

Kogan, L. S. The electrical recording of social casework interviews. *Soc. Casewk.,* 1950, **31,** 371–378.

Kraepelin, E. Ueber die Beeinflussung einfacher psychischer Vorgaenge durch einige Arzneimittel; Experimentelle Untersuchungen. Jena: Fischer, 1892.

Krasner, L. Studies of the conditioning of verbal behavior. *Psychol. Bull.,* 1958, **55,** 148–171.

Lacey, J. I. Psychophysiological approaches to the evaluation of psychotherapeutic process and outcome. In E. A. Rubinstein & M. B. Parloff (Eds.), *Research in psychotherapy.* Vol. 1. Washington,

D.C.: American Psychological Association, 1959. Pp. 160–208.

Lamb, R., & Mahl, G. F. Manifest reactions of patients and interviewers to the use of sound recording in the psychiatric interview. *Amer. J. Psychiat.*, 1956, **112**, 731–737.

Leary, T., & Gill, M. The dimensions and a measure of the process of psychotherapy: a system for the analysis of the content of clinical evaluations and patient-therapist verbalizations. In E. A. Rubinstein & M. B. Parloff (Eds.), *Research in psychotherapy*. Vol. 1. Washington, D.C.: American Psychological Association, 1959. Pp. 62–95.

Lennard, H. L., & Bernstein, A. *The anatomy of psychotherapy: systems of communication and expectation*. New York: Columbia Univer. Press, 1960.

Maccoby, Eleanor E., & Maccoby, N. The interview: a tool of social science. In G. Lindzey (Ed.), *Handbook of social psychology*. Vol. 1. Reading, Mass.: Addison-Wesley, 1954. Pp. 449–487.

Mahl, G. F. Exploring emotional states by content analysis. In I. Pool (Ed.), *Trends in content analysis*. Urbana, Ill.: Univer. of Illinois Press, 1959. Pp. 89–130. (a)

Mahl, G. F. Measuring the patient's anxiety during interviews from "expressive" aspects of his speech. *Trans. N.Y. Acad. Sci.*, 1959, Ser. 2, **21**, 249–259. (b)

Malmo, R. B. Anxiety and behavioral arousal. *Psychol. Rev.*, 1957, **64**, 276–287.

Masserman, J. H. *Principles of dynamic psychiatry*. Philadelphia: Saunders, 1946.

Masserman, J. H., & Carmichael, H. T. Diagnosis and prognosis in psychiatry: with a follow-up study of the results of short-term general hospital therapy in psychiatric cases. *J. ment. Sci.*, 1938, **84**, 893–946.

Matarazzo, J. D. Prescribed behavior therapy: suggestions from interview research. In A. J. Bachrach (Ed.), *Experimental foundations of clinical psychology*. New York: Basic Books, 1962. Pp. 471–509.

Matarazzo, J. D., Hess, H. F., & Saslow, G. Frequency and duration characteristics of speech and silence behavior during interviews. *J. clin. Psychol.*, 1962, **18**, 416–426.

Matarazzo, J. D., & Saslow, G. Differences in interview interaction behavior among normal and deviant groups. In I. A. Berg & B. M. Bass (Eds.), *Conformity and deviation*. New York: Harper & Row, 1961. Pp. 286–327.

Matarazzo, J. D., Saslow, G., & Matarazzo, Ruth G. The Interaction Chronograph as an instrument for objective measurement of interaction patterns during interviews. *J. Psychol.*, 1956, **41**, 347–367.

Matarazzo, J. D., Weitman, M., Saslow, G., & Wiens, A. N. Interviewer influence on durations of interviewee speech. *J. verb. Learning verb. Behav.*, 1963, **1**, 451–458.

Matarazzo, J. D., Wiens, A. N., & Saslow, G. Studies of interview speech behavior. In L. Krasner & L. P. Ullmann (Eds.), *Research in behavior modification: new developments and their clinical implications*. New York: Holt, 1965.

Matarazzo, J. D., Wiens, A. N., Saslow, G., Dunham, R. M., & Voas, R. B. Speech durations of astronaut and ground communicator. *Science*, 1964, **143**, 148–150.

Matarazzo, Ruth G., Matarazzo, J. D., Saslow, G., & Phillips, Jeanne S. Psychological test and organismic correlates of interview interaction behavior. *J. abnorm. soc. Psychol.*, 1958, **56**, 329–338.

May, R. Historical and philosophical presuppositions for understanding therapy. In O. H. Mowrer (Ed.), *Psychotherapy: theory and research*. New York: Ronald, 1953. Pp. 9–43.

Mehlman, B. The reliability of psychiatric diagnosis. *J. abnorm. soc. Psychol.*, 1952, **47**, 577–578.

Menninger, K. A. *A manual for psychiatric case study*. New York: Grune & Stratton, 1952.

Menninger, K., Mayman, M., & Pruyser, P. *The vital balance: the life process in mental health and illness*. New York: Viking, 1963.

Meyer, A. *The commonsense psychiatry of . . . : fifty-two selected papers edited by A. Lief*. New York: McGraw-Hill, 1948.

Mowrer, O. H. *Psychotherapy: theory and research*. New York: Ronald, 1953.

Murray, E. J. A content-analysis method for studying psychotherapy. *Psychol. Monogr.*, 1956, **70**, No. 13 (Whole No. 420).

OSS Assessment Staff. *Assessment of men*. New York: Holt, 1948.

Pasamanick, B., Dintz, S., & Lefton, M. Psychiatric orientation and its relation to diagnosis and treatment in a mental hospital. *Amer. J. Psychiat.*, 1959, **116**, 127–132.

Phillips, Jeanne S. The relationship between two features of interview behavior comparing verbal content and verbal temporal patterns of interaction. Unpublished doctoral dissertation, Washington Univer., St. Louis, 1957.

Pittenger, R. E., Hockett, C. F., & Danehy, J. J. *The first five minutes: a sample of microscopic interview analysis.* Ithaca, N.Y.: Paul Martineau, 1960.

Porter, E. H., Jr. The development and evaluation of a measure of counseling interview procedures. *Educ. psychol. Measmt.*, 1943, **3**, 105–126, 215–238.

Rabiner, E. L., Molinski, H., & Gralnick, A. Conjoint family therapy in the inpatient setting. *Amer. J. Orthopsychiat.*, 1962, **16**, 618–631.

Raimy, V. C. Self-reference in counseling interviews. *J. consult. Psychol.*, 1948, **12**, 153–163.

Raines, G. N., & Rohrer, J. H. The operational matrix of psychiatric practice. I. Consistency and variability in interview impressions of different psychiatrists. *Amer. J. Psychiat.*, 1955, **111**, 721–733.

Raines, G. N., & Rohrer, J. H. The operational matrix of psychiatric practice. II. Variability in psychiatric impressions and the projection hypothesis. *Amer. J. Psychiat.*, 1960, **117**, 133–139.

Raines, G. N., Wittson, C. L., Hunt, W. A., & Herrmann, R. S. Psychiatric selection for military service. *J. Amer. med. Ass.*, 1954, **156**, 817–821.

Raush, H. L., & Bordin, E. S. Warmth in personality development and in psychotherapy. *Psychiatry*, 1957, **20**, 351–363.

Redlich, F. C., Dollard, J., & Newman, R. High fidelity recording of psychotherapeutic interviews. *Amer. J. Psychiat.*, 1950, **107**, 42–48.

Rice, S. Contagious bias in the interview: a methodological note. *Amer. J. Sociol.*, 1929, **35**, 420–423.

Riesman, D. Interviewers, elites, and academic freedom. *Soc. Problems*, 1958, **6**, 115–126.

Riesman, D., & Benney, M. The sociology of the interview. *Midwest. Sociologist*, 1956, **18**, 3–15.

Rioch, Margaret J. Training the mature woman for a professional role. *Amer. Assoc. Univer. Women J.*, 1962, **55**, 236–239.

Robbins, L. L., & Wallerstein, R. S. The research strategy and tactics of the psychotherapy research project of the Menninger Foundation and the problem of controls. In E. A. Rubinstein & M. B. Parloff (Eds.), *Research in psychotherapy.* Vol. 1. Washington, D.C.: American Psychological Association, 1959. Pp. 27–43.

Roe, Anne. Integration of personality theory and clinical practice. *J. abnorm. soc. Psychol.*, 1949, **44**, 36–41.

Rogers, C. R. *Counseling and psychotherapy.* Boston: Houghton Mifflin, 1942.

Rogers, C. R. Client-centered therapy. Boston: Houghton Mifflin, 1951.

Rogers, C. R. A theory of therapy, personality, and interpersonal relationships, as developed in the client-centered framework. In S. Koch. (Ed.), *Psychology: a study of science.* Vol. III. New York: McGraw-Hill, 1959. Pp. 184–256.

Rogers, C. R. *On becoming a person: a therapist's view of psychotherapy.* Boston: Houghton Mifflin, 1961.

Rogers, C. R., & Dymond, Rosalind F. *Psychotherapy and personality change.* Chicago: Univer. of Chicago Press, 1954.

Rotter, J. *Social learning and clinical psychology.* Englewood Cliffs, N.J.: Prentice-Hall, 1954.

Rubinstein, E. A., & Parloff, M. B. (Eds.) *Research in psychotherapy.* Vol. 1. Washington, D.C.: American Psychological Association, 1959.

Ruesch, J., & Prestwood, A. R. Anxiety: its initiation, communication, and interpersonal management. *Arch. Neurol. Psychiat.*, 1949, **62**, 527–550.

Salzinger, K. Experimental manipulation of verbal behavior: a review. *J. gen. Psychol.*, 1959, **61**, 65–94.

Saslow, G. On the concept of comprehensive medicine. *Bull. Menninger Clin.*, 1952, **16**, 57–65.

Saslow, G., & Chapple, E. D. A new life history form, with instructions for its use. *Appl. Anthrop.*, 1945, **4**, 1–18.

Saslow, G., & Matarazzo, J. D. A technique for studying changes in interview behavior. In E. A. Rubinstein & M. B. Parloff (Eds.), *Research in psychotherapy.* Vol. 1. Washington, D.C.: American Psychological Association, 1959. Pp. 125–159.

Saslow, G., & Matarazzo, J. D. A psychiatric service in a general hospital: a setting for social learning. *Int. J. soc. Psychiat.*, 1962, **8**, 5–18.

Schmidt, H., & Fonda, C. The reliability of psychiatric diagnosis: a new look. *J. abnorm. soc. Psychol.*, 1956, **52**, 262–267.

Scott, J. Research definitions of mental health and mental illness. *Psychol. Bull.*, 1958, **55**, 29–45.

Scott, W., Bingham, W., & Whipple, G. Scientific selection of salesmen. *Salesmanship*, 1916, **4**, 106–108.

Seeman, J. A study of the process of nondirective therapy. *J. consult. Psychol.*, 1949, **13**, 157–168.

Seeman, W. P. Psychiatric diagnosis: an investigation of interperson-reliability after didactic instruction. *J. nerv. ment. Dis.*, 1953, **118**, 541–544.

Skinner, B. F. *Verbal behavior.* New York: Appleton-Century-Crofts, 1957.

Snyder, W. U. An investigation of the nature of nondirective psychotherapy. *J. gen. Psychol.*, 1945, **33**, 193–232.

Snyder, W. U. *Casebook of nondirective counseling.* Boston: Houghton Mifflin, 1947. (a)

Snyder, W. U. A comparison of one unsuccessful with four successful nondirectively counseled cases. *J. consult. Psychol.*, 1947, **11**, 38–42. (b)

Snyder, W. U. (Ed.) *Group report of a program of research in psychotherapy.* State College, Pa.: Department of Psychology, Pennsylvania State Univer., 1953.

Snyder, W. U. Client-centered therapy. In L. A. Pennington & I. A. Berg (Eds.), *An introduction to clinical psychology.* New York: Ronald, 1954. Pp. 529–556.

Snyder, W. U. *The psychotherapy relationship.* New York: Macmillan, 1961.

Stevenson, I. The psychiatric interview. In *American handbook of psychiatry.* Vol. 1. New York: Basic Books, 1959. Pp. 197–214.

Strupp, H. H. *Psychotherapists in action: explorations of the therapist's contribution to the treatment process.* New York: Grune & Stratton, 1960.

Strupp, H. H., & Luborsky, L. (Eds.) *Research in psychotherapy.* Vol. 2. Washington, D.C.: American Psychological Association, 1962.

Sullivan, H. S. *The interpersonal theory of psychiatry.* New York: Norton, 1953.

Sullivan, H. S. *The psychiatric interview.* New York: Norton, 1954.

Thorne, F. C. *Principles of personality counseling.* Brandon, Vt.: Journal of Clinical Psychology Press, 1950.

Watson, R. I. A brief history of clinical psychology. *Psychol. Bull.*, 1953, **50**, 321–346.

Watson, R. I. The experimental tradition and clinical psychology. In A. J. Bachrach (Ed.), *Experimental foundations of clinical psychology.* New York: Basic Books, 1962. Pp. 3–25.

Whitehorn, J. C. Guide to interviewing and clinical personality study. *Arch. Neurol. Psychiat.*, 1944, **52**, 197–216.

Will, O. A., & Cohen, R. A. A report of a recorded interview in the course of psychotherapy. *Psychiatry*, 1953, **16**, 263–282.

Wilson, M. S., & Meyer, E. Diagnostic consistency in a psychiatric liaison service. *Amer. J. Psychiat.*, 1962, **119**, 207–209.

Wittson, C. L., & Hunt, W. A. The predictive value of the brief psychiatric interview. *Amer. J. Psychiat.*, 1951, **107**, 582–585.

Wolberg, L. R. *The technique of psychotherapy.* New York: Grune & Stratton, 1954.

Wolf, S., & Wolff, H. G. *Human gastric function.* New York: Oxford Univer. Press, 1947.

Zigler, E., & Phillips, L. Psychiatric diagnosis: a critique. *J. abnorm. soc. Psychol.*, 1961, **63**, 607–618.

Zilboorg, G. *A history of medical psychology.* New York: Norton, 1941.

Zubin, J. Personal communication, October, 1962.

18
Personality Inventories

STARKE R. HATHAWAY

This chapter is not intended as an exhaustive evaluation or description of the current personality inventories. Surveys are abundantly available in routine sources devoted to the systematic collection of such data. Furthermore, it is not particularly useful to the student to read a mass of description and evaluation of a necessarily partial list of tests as seen by one author, who inevitably will be prejudiced. This account will not be strictly historical. History, as expressed here, is full of ambivalent trends and indefinite events. Perhaps this is always true of history, but it is certainly true of the history of personality inventories. Only by quite arbitrary decisions can steps in development be ordered to tell, for example, that a certain device or test was the first of its kind. The rarity of new things in the world, things never before said, thought, or done, seems clearly applicable to the personality test field. Modern inventories are the present stage in a growth which started with back-fence gossip or personal interviews and which developed through the personal information questionnaire.

It is difficult to say whether the slow progress of the psychometrics of personality is due to a lack of a convincing or dominant personality theory that would guide the progress, whether there can never be a good diagnostic or other taxonomic system of personality that is not so arbitrary that the categories are fluid and imperfect criteria, or whether the psychometric methodology necessary for progress to better tests has not yet been developed. One may choose as he wishes among these limitations upon the progress of personality inventories because a good case can be made for each one.

It is this state of affairs that will characterize the selection of material in this chapter. An attempt will be made to bring out the highlights in the practices and development of personality inventories and to emerge with an overview of the area that will support and encourage the obviously needed research and development. The nearly fifty years covered in the account seem rather dramatic when they are condensed into a few pages that create some system out of an often chaotic and wasteful expenditure of research effort. One caution seems appropriate to keep in mind. If this account seems to imply a rather unsatisfactory state of affairs in the development of the personality inventory, the view from the standpoint of other attempts to advance the scientific description and evaluation of clinical features of personality is even less satisfactory. Diagnosis and description from staff conferences, projective data, or even life observation ratings are notably loose and primitive. To deny or disregard this seems a poor position for us to start from in our attempts to make progress in this important area.

Buros (1959) lists 96 nonprojective character and personality devices. Not all these can properly be considered personality inventories, but the number of inventories or scales that have appeared in the literature, as developed or suggested without their becoming significant enough for critical review, must amount to several hundred at least. A very substantial proportion of the pages in almost every professional journal is devoted to work on or with personality inventories. If nothing more can be accomplished in this account that is worth adding to the bales of published material on personality inventories, it may be that a critical presentation will provide better direction to future research. There is no intent in this treatment to generate a hopeless cynicism, although there is little to support optimism. A soft and lenient evaluation does not engender good research by compromising with inadequate data. This field, more than most, seems to be a soft one, where few psychologists require rigorous validity or close experimental control. Perhaps this is because personality measurement comes so close to the complicated human, interpersonal concourse of daily life. We are forced to use our judgment and our imperfect instruments whether they work or not, and it is rather difficult to keep our high morale while being continually reminded that the tools we have to use and the judgments we have to make are so imprecise or at least cannot be shown to be precise.

Although ability and intelligence are usefully conceived as separate from interests and motivation, the separation is arbitrary. We know that one may have great aptitude, and even performance ability, in music and yet lack interest or motivation. Such persons have been shown to be ill-advised to choose a musical field as their vocation. What we usually mean by the word "personality" also is separated from interests and motivation but in even more arbitrary fashion. When we think of the personalities of musicians or shopmen, we think of how they get along with others, how they are evaluated by others, their persistence in tasks, their ambitions, and many other aspects that can greatly influence their success or failure. So one may have great aptitude, great ability, and even great interest in music and yet lack the qualities of persistence, interpersonal responsibility, and ambition or in other ways fail to have the personality that would ensure success in it.

It is difficult to believe that persons with specific interest patterns do not have characteristically different personalities. We tend to think, for further example, that there is a variety of personality differences between persons who are deeply interested and competent in machine shopwork and those who have an intense interest and ability in music. We associate the musical esthete more with introversion and the shopman more with extroversion. Darley and Hagenah have reviewed this area (1956). In summary, it should be apparent that however much we feel that we mean different things by words such as "ability," "interest," and "personality," it will be very difficult to devise psychological tests specific to each arbitrary area. This is most clearly a problem with our attempts to devise personality tests.

Psychological tests, like our conceptions of the psyche, can be broadly grouped into various categories. Cronbach (1960) has a useful table. Everyone is familiar with some intelligence tests. Special aptitude tests are best known as they test for mechanical aptitude (Bennett & Slater, 1945) and clerical aptitude (Andrew, Paterson, & Longstaff, 1946). Achievement tests discover what a subject actually knows. They are illustrated by any subject-matter test to measure progress in a course of study. The interest tests, of which the Strong and Kuder are the dominant examples, are designed to provide classifications of the patterns of interests and dispositions, usually with a vocational slant. Varieties of such classes of tests range from transitional forms, such as tests for measuring prejudice, authoritarian personality, or sex-role identification, to those called "personality" tests. Personality tests, as we usually apply the class term, are directed toward the delineation of categories or scales into which people may fall to express something of the common usage of the complex and elusive concepts that constitute the connotations of the word "personality."

The most widely known and used among the personality tests are those intended as aids in assessment of the nature and strength of those personality qualities that have clinical significance, such as the categories of mental illness. These qualities or variables, such as are illustrated by the word "depression," are very dramatic and important. But more normal qualities of personality, such as feelings of inferiority, self-esteem, ego strength, and dominance, are widely represented in our clinical vocabulary and have daily significance. Many of these ordinary personality qualities can have mental-disorder manifestations and applications, but they are more widely used to differentiate persons who are described by variables in connection with selection for vocational placement, general counseling, and the like.

Almost as soon as psychologists had begun to realize the power and value of intelligence and interest testing as these were developed in applications to vocational and school counseling, it was recognized that aspects of personality might be profitably subjected to the new psychometric methodologies. The attributes of personality are of more general interest and are more meaningful in daily social interaction than any of the other applications of psychometric endeavor.

PERSONALITY AND THE INVENTORY

The general term "personality inventory" can be used for most of the modern objective personality tests, since they tend to sample or inventory elements and qualities of personality. The inventory aspect is represented in the use of numerous and varied questions or statements that permit the subject to respond selectively and by the combination of these elements or items into measures that are more or less properly referred to as "scales."

Personality has had many definitions (Allport, 1937; Murphy, 1947). As a frame of reference in considering the personality inventories, it is helpful to attempt a more specific orientation. A selection of pertinent points from the diversity of concepts about personality will aid in understanding the contrasting and often confused backgrounds that underlie the several widely used personality inventories and their applications.

A first and most troublesome point is that people do not by themselves have personalities (Hathaway, 1961). They must be in contact with others to appear to possess the meaningful interests, dispositions, and attributes that are usually part of what is perceived as personality. A selfish or dominant person is so only as he is evaluated by others. Robinson Crusoe became a personality in relation to his man Friday. When he was alone, he was of no concern to others, and only in his memory of his earlier social life could he see himself as a distinct person. Of course, this view means that even if a person were to remain unchanged, changes in the needs and values of his culture would make us see his personality differently. Daniel Boone, pioneer wanderer and frontiersman, is a valued and fabulous American memory. Daniel Boone in today's world would probably be in real danger of being considered a sociopath or an ambulatory schizophrenic.

Obviously one could expect personality tests to express the cultural-personal double aspect in the scores and profiles they provide. Psychological diagnostic clinical settings, for example, must consider the person and the way his environment relates to him. Rather than being culture-free, such tests should give some idea of how the person will fit into his surroundings. The use of a norm group to provide standard scores is an example. A person differs from his norm by some value. The word "norm" connotes some culturally recognized origin for measures. Again, we aim tests at culturally significant areas rather than at idiosyncratic personal traits that may have little social significance. We test for sociopathy mainly because we wish to predict how much trouble the person may cause. Of course, this in turn leads us to a concern about the causes and consequences of the sociopathy in the person.

One might, from a different angle, expect the tests to express specific and intrinsic personality characteristics. The more abstracted test data showing these personal qualities could then be secondarily evaluated from the cultural points of view. In this case the test profile itself should be relatively culture-free. We might, with such an orientation, measure personality aspects that were interesting only because they showed individual differences and made mathematical sense. This would be a purer conception of the measurement. Despite the fact that we can recognize these contrasting expectations—that personality test profiles should represent both culture and person and that they should be culture-free—practical personality inventories cannot be culture-free, and the cultural value system that contaminates them is not stable. A measure that is significant at one time can become unimportant or even acquire a negative rather than a positive valence as there is evolution of the social values that apply to the assessment of personalities.

Another basic problem for the personality inventory lies in the concept of a developmentally changing or episodic personality in contrast to a stable personality within the individual. The cultural values obviously change, but the person changes also. Here again we cannot make operationally clear distinctions, but the contrasts are clear enough to confuse our assessments of the tests. For example, according to many psychoanalytically based conceptions, determining factors of personality structure are quite stably implanted at an early age. It requires long and intensive psychotherapy to effect changes. Seen in this way, personality tests would seem to have most value when the profiles they provide are stable over time. Tests from this background are often conceived of as measuring personality structure. Test-retest reliability for such tests would be a reasonable criterion for reliability because the basic structure would be stable. But obviously no one expects an absolutely constant structure for personality. To do so would be to deny the value of psychotherapy and the modifying effects of experience and aging.

By contrast, personality can be conceived to be in flux, changing with daily experience and certainly changing as one gets older and is modified by learning. It is easy to hold this view, since daily life impresses us as effecting changes in ourselves and others. There may be days of depression, loneliness, energy, ambition, and many other such states. During these periods we may seem to be quite different persons, and the concept of a stable personality seems inadequate and not helpful. Indeed, the idea of a stable personality would be much too restrictive to satisfy our conception of the adaptability of man to his environment. For many purposes, to those impressed with the way people change, it would seem that the ideal personality inventory should catch these various aspects at different administrations, showing different profiles as we appear changed to ourselves or to others. Personality tests sensitive to changing personalities could not be expected to yield high test-retest reliability. Their validities would have to depend upon ratings by observers whose judgments would catch the same fleeting views as the tests. Clinical diagnoses are understandably frequently used criteria in the development of tests designed to follow variable personality. It should be apparent that the test would need to be administered to the subjects near the time of the diagnostic ratings, since many influences might otherwise change the personality before the test was taken.

But the profiles provided by inventories could conceivably be too sensitive to changes. If the profiles really caught only momentary states, then there could not be many useful applications. Personality profiles chiefly derive their value from the predictions they provide. A too fluid measure of personality would belie our recognition that people do seem to show evidences of some continuity in their personality traits.

These contrasting lines of consideration about personality lead to great difficulty in deciding between error variance and valid variance in personality test data. When we cannot decide how stable we expect personality to be, we have difficulty making a clear distinction between the part of inventory test score variance that can be ascribed to errors of measurement and the part due to valid changes occurring in the personality between tests or between the time the observer makes a criterion rating and the testing time.

In summary, although these contrasting concepts of the stability of personality underlie much of our thinking about all personality tests, we usually accept middle positions. Personality has both intrinsic and social aspects. We measure both what the person is and what we as observers see him to be. Personality also has both stable and transitory aspects. Possibly every separate factor has both properties, or possibly some factors are stable and some variable. At any rate, our tests never provide wholly stable profiles, but they are also not usually so variable that they are of no value.

A fundamental trouble with the field of personality testing lies in the semantic difficulty in the development of numerical criteria to represent adequately the clarity of the variables we perceive in personality. We constantly use descriptive terms with confidence and reasonable success as we evaluate people. These descriptive terms, however, never hang together in a satisfactory way, even when they are used to classify mental illness such as, for example, schizophrenia or sociopathy. As diagnoses these terms can be severely criticized, and despite many calls for a more solidly based conceptualization of the deviant personality, nothing has been successfully established. Challman (1951) summarizes this problem:

> The development of psychodiagnostic methods is hampered by a number of factors. One major problem is that of criteria for validation. Not only are psychiatric diagnoses frequently unreliable, but often they do not furnish a sufficiently homogeneous group in any one category for validational purposes. When one attempts to use characteristics or traits, however, there is no clear lead from personality theory as to which ones to select. Another problem is the lack of statistical methods suitable for use with the results of projective techniques and for the analysis of patterns. Finally, there is the inadequate use of presently available knowledge of experimental design and statistical methods.

Witkin, Dyk, Faterson, Goodenough, and Karp (1962); Phillips and Rabinovitch (1958); and Zigler and Phillips (1960; 1961) are prominent among those trying to establish more meaningful concepts, but so many new conceptualizations have been described and have been abandoned that there is little encouragement to expect much progress. The recent demand emphasizes the need for a less mental illness–oriented system. It is felt that the old mental disorder taxonomy is not appropriate to the present pressure toward prevention in contrast to treatment. Until really new data on the causes, specific treatment, and prognoses of mental illness are available, it is not probable that better description or descriptive generalizations can alone supplant the older diagnostic system.

THE OBJECTIVE METHOD

When treating with personality tests, objective is often put in contrast to projective. Cattell defines an objective test as an "objectively scorable, universally reproducible situation, which is used to predict behavior in *other* situations" (1950). There are, however, numerous angles in the definition of objectivity (Bass & Berg, 1959). Sometimes to use an objective method connotes a value for being scientific. Essential conditions for referring to a test as objective are entailed in the examiner-subject relationship and in the first interpretative step in processing the information from the test.

In the interaction of the examiner and examinee, objective procedures require a standard understanding of what is to be done in the test-taking task. The subject may respond to inkblots, obscurely worded verbal items, or almost any stimulus material as long as the general meaning of the situation restricts some of the variance of behavior that would otherwise affect his responses. For example, the subject may be informed that he is being tested, he may be told to be candid, or he may be told that the task has some other meaning than testing. In all cases there is a definite element of standard administration both in the giving of information to the examinee and in the way he goes about his task. The result permits clearer assumptions about what goes on psychologically in the subject than if there is less guidance. Most inventories, for example, are set up so that it is clear that for each item one answer is to be chosen from among given alternatives.

But even more emphasis in defining objectivity lies with the first treatment of the test data. Again, the conditions require restriction of unknown sources of test score variance, this time by definition of the path that the interpretation will follow. Usually this signifies a constancy of scoring system and a standardization on a sample population that provide for a transformation of raw test scores into some standard form. Nearly all personality inventories meet these conditions. The scoring process does not require professional or even expert decisions, and the raw scores are unequivocally transformed to some variety of standard scores. The product of inventory scoring is usually a profile of standard scores that expresses the standing of the subject on three or more personality scales. The scores of the profile refer to routinely interpreted aspects of personality that determine more or less closely the interpretation of the profile for the subject. To illustrate objectivity the subject's answer sheet for the objective inventories may now be fed to a computer for processing, and the computer can print out a practical description of the salient personality indications as these are inferred from what is known about the test. Obviously no appreciable modifications in test interpretation are contributed by the examiner up to the point of computer readout. There are personality tests to illustrate every degree of objectivity of administration, scoring, or interpretation from this most developed stage of objectivity toward whatever one considers to be a contrasting extreme. Objectivity of test and procedure is clearly a relative, not an absolute, matter.

In the foregoing, one area of requirement for objectivity is related to the stimulus-response situation of the subject as he works at the test. The most objective among personality test items are unequivocal, direct statements such as: "At this moment I am responding to these statements." An extreme contrasting example is the experimental testing situation in which an uninstructed subject is blindfolded and an amorphous plastic lump is placed in his hand. He may, since he is not instructed by either the administrator or the test form, attempt to name its shape, determine its substance, or use it as a tool. Nearly every verbal personality inventory item has ambiguity that leaves the subject some freedom to determine what is meant, as Meehl (1945), Benton (1953), and others have pointed out. An early partial recognition of the significance of item ambiguity occurred as a result of the use of this screening item on war draftees: "Do you wet the bed?" A draftee who was a chronic bed wetter was not wanted, but those who answered "yes" turned out to include many who did not currently do so. For some, a candid response attitude led them to read the item to mean any bed-wetting occasion, even in early childhood. Others read other meanings. All those who answered "yes" had still to be separately interviewed to discover what the apparently definitive response meant. Obviously, as items become more unclear in statement and as they depend more upon introspective judgment, they become less objective if we use criteria of objectivity that require items to mean constantly what they appear to mean.

FACE-VALID ITEMS, SUBTLE ITEMS, AND VALIDITY

Early personality inventory items were all supposed to ask an obvious and unmistakable question that was pertinent to the aspect of personality the scale was designed to measure. We say that such items have face validity; that is, for example, one who knew about neuroticism could recognize from reading them that the items expressed symptoms that were pertinent to neuroticism. Since the items for the early tests came from textbook and case-history symptoms of neuroticism, they were assured of having face validity. The concept that an item might have no face validity and yet make a significant contribution to the validity of a personality scale took years to be recognized as a basic discovery in the development of personality inventories. Items that do not have face validity are often called "subtle." This signifies that the subject being tested or even the sophisticated expert may be unable to recognize the psychometric import of the item. It is, of course, implied that the item has some other kind of validity for the measurement.

Criticism of personality tests often depends upon this face-valid or subtle item concept. Regarding subtle items, the critic protests that he cannot see how the item can be of value, since its content appears so lacking in rational relationship to the test purpose. Regarding face-valid or obvious items, the critic complains that these are so obvious that they invite deliberate dissimulation or other distortions by the subject. Other critics protest that these face-valid items get only at surface traits, that they are little overt symptoms that do not reflect the real personality.

Several types of over-all validity are used for scales of the personality inventories. First there is rational validity. For a scale, this means that the face validities of the individual items appear to be consistently on the subject intended in the scale. Rational validity of scales is a more rigorous concept than face validity of items. It requires that the scale items be meaningful against a conception of dimensions or rational aspects that are presumed to be coherent entities in personality.

Empirical validity is determined in the relationship of the items and test to criterion groups of subjects or to ratings that are applied to persons separately from the application of the test. Validity is suggested in the correlation or overlap statistics that tell how closely the test scores come to the independent criteria. In order to identify them, one would not need to read the items for a scale derived by completely empirical methods. The items may come out to be either face-valid or subtle.

Finally, factorial validity is derived from the factor-analytic method. It is dependent upon the factor loadings of marker tests which themselves have some standing on the other validity criteria. Factorial validity assumes internal consistency of items and factors that are reasonably independent from one another.

THE PERSONAL DATA SHEET

Although the present urgency in their development and application is connected with our acute problems of living in, and adapting to, a complex and populous society, the development of the personality inventories is clearly associated with war. For example, Gideon had collected too large an army, and the Lord saw that the Israelites would give Him scant credit if so many men overran the Midianites camped in the valley. The Lord suggested two screening items for Gideon. The first of these items had face validity: Gideon proclaimed that all who were afraid could go home. More than two of every three did so. The second was subtle: Those who fought the Midianites were the few who drank from their cupped hands instead of lying down to drink. Altogether it was a battle decided by psychological devices, and 300 men literally scared the demoralized Midianites into headlong flight.

During World War I, General Pershing sent the message from France that the "prevalence of mental disorders" suggested that screening methods should be utilized to eliminate unfit draftees. Woodworth and Poffenberger, who were already working with the problems of emotional fitness for warfare, responded with the development of the pioneer Woodworth Personal Data Sheet (Woodworth, 1920).

Although it was not the earliest example, the Woodworth Personal Data Sheet is usually considered to be the prototype of the personality inventories. Under the impetus of the need for a screening device, Woodworth and Poffenberger hit upon the idea of assembling minor neurotic symptoms into a set of questions and tallying up the number of positive answers into a score. Two approaches to an inventory were expressed in the personal data sheet. The score suggested unfitness because of the sheer number of assorted symptoms, but it was also recognized that some single responses alone suggested unfitness. Certain "starred" items were considered so pathognomonic that a "yes" to any one of them was a signal for a psychiatric check by personal interview.

Woodworth collected his symptomatic items by abstracting from the available psychiatric texts every symptom of psychological nervousness that he could find. To this list he added symptoms culled from case histories that had been compiled by psychiatrists recording their observations of neurotic men. Mainly by inspection to eliminate redundancy and unclear wording, a short critical list of 116 items was finally compiled. The items were stated as questions to which an answer "yes" was the neurotic one. The final list was printed on a sheet adapted for group testing by permitting subjects to encircle a "yes" or a "no" answer. These items were, of course, heterogeneous in their import, except for the assumed common relationship to neuroticism. The test items had face validity, but there was not much rational validity. At the time there was no attempt to differentiate subtypes among the neurotic men, although subtypes were used in the psychiatric diagnoses, and even the concept of general neurosis was nebulous and incoherent.

Like Gideon's first item, the items of the Woodworth Personal Data Sheet were obvious. Although it was developed too late to be used much, the face-valid items of the Woodworth would have worked well enough during the war crisis. It was puzzling, however, to those who used the inventories in the war when they found that peacetime use did not provide such dramatic evidence for the sensitivity of the tests. We now recognize that the motivational culture of personality test taking is different in peacetime. Men who were afraid and who considered themselves unfit for war were offered symptoms that permitted them to admit the fact. Under war conditions such face-valid items could be successful in providing a quick screening survey that saved the time of experts who could not adequately interview everyone. There was no time or much inclination to try to identify men who lied to hide their symptoms and qualify for induction.

The successess of psychological testing during World War I encouraged an explosive development of psychometric instruments in America. For peacetime, intelligence and vocational interest tests became a main emphasis. These were directed to school psychometric needs, and a vigorous field of vocational selection and counseling developed. In this period of growth for psychometric applied psychology, the personality inventory was not neglected. From the first, psychologists were intrigued with the problem of developing practical clinical tests that would classify those who were mentally ill or those not fit for special jobs and other tests to show the general structure of personality as viewed from a more rational and normal standpoint.

Until the end of World War II, over two decades later, a steady stream of personality scales flowed into research and practical uses. The majority of these tests showed no real innovation. They were mostly in direct line of descent from the Woodworth Personal Data Sheet. The Bernreuter (1935), Laird's inventories (1925), and the Bell Adjustment Inventory (1934) are examples. But college counselors and other psychologists who wished to differentiate the personalities of normal people pushed the attempt to find more interesting and appropriate personality aspects for the inventories to express. Crude neuroticism seemed an inadequate and limited emphasis for such applications.

The most successful personality test to come out of the period was the Bernreuter Personality Inventory (1935). This inventory, still widely used, incorporates most of the old and some new ideas. It has face-valid item structure and a scale for neuroticism, and it also provides measures of some newer rational constructs such as introversion and dominance. There are standard score equivalents so that the raw scores can be expressed as points on a profile, and the items for the various scales are mixed together so that successive items would count on different scales. The present inventory has 125 questions concerning interests, attitudes, and symptoms. Item responses were objective and used the routine of having the subject encircle his choice as a "yes," "no," or "?" answer. The validity of the scales depended first upon the face validity of the items assigned to the scales and second upon empirical scoring weights derived from contrasting groups of college students that had scored toward the extremes on previously developed scales with similar names. These criterion cases were not verified by interviews or any other validation method independent of the tests.

Devastating critiques of the Bernreuter were published. As early as 1934, Landis and Katz found that several items even appeared to be scored backward. Flanagan, in 1935, factor-analyzed the test and found that the four scales could be represented by only two factors, which he related to self-confidence and sociability. In that same year a revision of the test appeared with the original scales and with Flanagan's two factor scales added to the profile.

In 1942, Super again reviewed the status of the Bernreuter. Despite the meager evidences of its practical validity, he said in summary that it had "considerable validity as a research instrument." He added that it had some value in work with individuals. For the published evaluation studies, validity was usually tested by comparison of the scores of patients with those of college students. It does not seem that it should be difficult to distinguish undifferentiated schizophrenic and neurotic patients from college students, and yet the personality tests could not even separate such groups. Some validity studies did compare clinically identified neurotic or rebellious college students to other students, but the rather obviously deviant students that were used for the criterion cases, like neurotic soldiers, had overt complaints and were ready to proclaim their troubles without dissimulation. Such evidence of validity was not very convincing.

RATIONAL VARIABLES

Although basic methodology of test construction was unchanged, the inventory makers began to use rational personality constructs along with the practical scales of neuroticism. Clinicians such as Jung and Adler were writing their concepts of the deeper springs of motivation and were describing personality types that they felt to be very general. These rational descriptions offered test constructors a source of new face-valid items that were directed to the measurement of interesting variables such as the feeling of inferiority, extroversion-introversion, dominance-submission, and others. The new tests provided scores for several personality dimensions instead of a single neuroticism score. They used standardization groups to develop parameters for standard scores, and one could construct personality profiles that graphically showed the standing of the subject on the several scales.

J. Downey's will-temperament test (1924) provided another intriguing rational interlude shortly after World War I. This test provides a transitional example for the experimentation with rational personality scales. Like others, notably Allport (Allport & Vernon, 1933), Downey felt that analysis of body movements—for example, wide-area-consuming gestures in contrast to cramped movement, the ability to disguise one's handwriting, and the ability to write extremely large and fast or very tiny and slowly—would express personality traits that would have wide applicability. The 12 test tasks that were used had a kind of face-valid relationship to the personality-type concepts they were conceived to measure. Subjects did differ greatly on the scores provided by the Downey test. Some subjects could take an hour to write their names if told to do so as slowly as they could; others could slow down very little. These variations seemed quite significant and rational, but the many ensuing research attempts to relate them to more meaningful measures failed to develop anything like the seeming useful generalizability of the original formulations. This test is also rather unique in that it is an attempt to measure personality with performance testing technique.

Most interesting and persistent among the transitional rational variables that appeared in the war interim years were those that came from two former associates of Freud, Adler and Jung. These men provided beautiful descriptions of personality types that they derived from their studies of patients.

Adler's concept of inferiority offered an appealing rational clinical construct. Seeing the insecurity of every person as inevitable in all societies, Adler conceived that every man, in greater or lesser degree, suffers from fear of inferiority—of being unlovable. To reassure himself, each person engages in compensatory behavior that betrays his inferiority. This compensatory behavior shows in many symptoms that, described from clinical experience, permit the construction of items with rational validity for the inferiority feeling they portray.

Similarly, Jung conceived that some persons turn psychologically inward, living within themselves, and that others turn toward preoccupation with outward events of the social life. These clinically rational personality constructs were an origin for the still popular terms "introversion" and "extroversion," which are applied to persons contrasted at the extremes of a continuum.

Another among the earliest described rational variables was ascendance-submission; the dichotomy femininity-masculinity was also an early rational continuum. As the terms indicate, most of the rational variables were described as bipolar, having rational meanings at both extremes of the test score range. Even neuroticism and inferiority were often considered to be bipolar. These bipolar variables presented a novel problem in contrast to the better-known variables such as tests of intelligence and ability. In these latter measures there was more of a unipolar meaning. Low scores meant a low amount of what another person might have in large amount. In a meaningful sense, such variables as introversion-extroversion had negative scores at one end, and the average represented the zero region. There is still today no real certainty that this bipolar concept is a good paradigm for personality measurement. It is possibly best to think separately of the two extremes and to have separate scales instead of one that reads in both directions. Using the bipolar paradigm, those persons with very few symptoms of neurosis were about as rare as those with many symptoms and were vaguely described as "very normal." There was some early recognition that these supernormal persons might identify a different sort of abnormality. Patients diagnosed as sociopathic were supernormal on such scales (Hathaway, 1939). Most persons got scores somewhere between the contrasted extremes, except that there was usually a skew, with relatively fewer persons getting high scores in the direction of showing undersirable traits.

The Allport-Vernon-Lindzey Study of Values (Allport, Vernon, & Lindzey, 1951; Vernon & Allport, 1931) is another good example of survival of that rational form of test in which validity was based upon the items drawn from personality-type descriptions. The 120 items of this test express the dominant interest value classes assumed to represent Spranger's six ideal types of personality (1928). Six scales that estimate interest dimensions with such names as "theoretical," "religious," and "economic" make the test appealing for research application.

Finally, for a more recent example, the Edwards Personal Preference Schedule (Edwards, 1953a) represents some of the rational factors that developed in the descriptive studies of Murray and associates (Murray,

1938). This schedule or inventory provides standard scores on 15 of the manifest needs that came out of the studies. Again, validity of these scales must depend chiefly upon the personal constructs from which the scales were drawn, and applications thus far have not given much support to practical uses of the inventory. The Edwards test will be further discussed below because of its use of a technique intended as a control for the social-desirability response set.

A series of studies of deceit by Hartshorne and May (1928) was important in modifying the development of personality inventories. The influence of these studies grew out of the fact that Hartshorne and May's various separate tests of deceitfulness were individually so little correlated with the general deceitfulness concept or criterion. A boy who could not be led to steal a nickel might readily be induced to cheat in an examination. Deceit seemed to be identifiable only in numerous specific examples, and the studies produced no really useful general measure. The specificity of the subtests and the generally poor correlations among all the various personality scales meant to measure what appeared to be, or were described as, identical constructs contributed to a deep pessimism about personality testing. Various lines of evidence seemed to show that there was extreme specificity in personality attributes, so that general measures would never have much value. Spearman referred to this condition in the ability field as "anarchic" (1927). The pessimism tended to fix upon the objective inventories, and it now appears that projective tests with their promise of providing personality structure rather than specific measures gained considerable rebound impetus during this period.

Like the Edwards scales, the Hartshorne and May studies made a contribution to later inventory methodology. As a test of honesty they used items of the sort later incorporated into the MMPI L scale and the CPI Gi scale, as examples among others. The items were socially desirable statements, but candid answers for most people required endorsement of the socially undesirable alternative. "Do you ever tell a lie?" is an example. It is socially desirable to be completely truthful, but most persons could not truthfully say that they never tell lies. A scale of such items could be thought to establish the degree to which the subject, in responding to an inventory, is choosing his responses by trying to make a good impression.

OUTCOMES OF THE OPENING PHASE

In the decades of the 1920s and 1930s, innumerable studies were published in which significant correlates of the revised and new personality inventory test variables were sought. These efforts to link the test scores to significant problems in employment or even in the assessment of the mentally ill yielded few useful or interesting relationships. For the most part the validities, while tending to be statistically significant, were too small to be of any practical value. Attempts to improve the scales of the personality inventories by differential weighting of items based upon statistical evidence of their differential power were not rewarding. The differential weights increased the complications of the scoring to a greater extent than they improved the correlations with validity criteria. The tests seemed to be failures partly because they measured such overgeneralized variables as neuroticism and such clinically unused and ungeneralizable or impure variables as ascendancy or introversion but mostly because of the great overlap of scores for groups or individuals among experimentally separated persons who were expected to get deviant scores with scores of persons who were not expected to get deviant scores. High abnormal scores were common among persons who were not very obviously abnormal (false positive), and low scores were too common among obviously ill persons (false negative).

Illustrating some of the futility of over two decades of experimentation with the personality inventory, the Cornell Selectee Index (Weider, Mittleman, Wechsler, & Wolff, 1944) was the personal data sheet of the second war. It came into popularity, like the Woodworth Personal Data Sheet, out of a plea from the war front to find ways to screen out psychologically unfit draftees. It had 92 questions and showed no real change in form, power, or theory over the hundreds of published articles that had appeared during the interwar years. There was still a total score on assorted symptoms, and there were the starred single-item scores, now called "stop items." Again, as use of the Woodworth Personal Data Sheet had suggested, during wartime the inventory was very successful. It required only ten minutes to administer and one minute to score, and the stop items were a signal for the selectee to have a personal interview with the psychological examiner.

The postwar applied psychologists became so disillusioned that when the new clinical psychology training programs were being developed, it was so widely accepted that personality inventories were valueless that some program directors did not feel that any course work in their nature and interpretation was worth the effort. Students dismissed the paper-and-pencil inventories out of hand, without having had any real training in the theory or uses of the available devices.

As late as 1942, a psychologist wishing to make some contribution to the diagnostic evaluation of patients in a psychiatric clinic with the Bernreuter or one of the other available tests was able to announce little more than that persons who were usually obviously neurotic or depressed or schizophrenic had obtained high scores on the tests. He would need to add that an embarrassing number of apparently normal persons would also get high scores. Such test data provided no news to the clinical staff which was in search of more meaningful and differential diagnostic evidence. As for the general screening function, one or two direct items would do the job as well as the tests. One could simply ask, "Are you neurotic, tired, or jittery?" and most all those who scored high on the inventories would speak up. Finally, screening tests are not often used in peacetime applications of personality tests.

The problems with the inventories came partly from the fact that face-valid items could presumably be tampered with by the subject who wished to change his scores and partly from the failure of the rational concepts to hold together. For example, introversion could readily be subdivided into at least two kinds, social and intrapersonal or emotional. Similarly, the other rational variables could be broken down into parts and variations. At first, it appeared that the problems connected with using face-valid or obvious content in items could be easily overcome. A simple cure seemed to lie in subtlety. One might, it was assumed, find items which gave information to the examiner in their contribution to scales but which would seem trivial or seem to be on a different subject to the examinee. He would not be able to influence his scores. But the discovery of subtle items depended upon quite a different approach to personality inventories. It required development of the empirical method of item selection. Identification of subtle items could clearly not depend upon face validity or rational selection, since recognizable item content is inimical to the discovery of subtle items.

THE EMPIRICAL METHOD

Empirical methods of personality inventory scale derivation can be introduced with the Humm-Wadsworth Temperament Scale (1935) as an early representative. This test, providing scales and subscores, was at first released as an aid in psychiatric diagnostic work. Besides being based upon a rational temperament system that was developed by Rosanoff (1938), this test showed two trends that came to dominate work with personality inventories. First, although the items and scales related to temperament were rationally organized by Rosanoff, the items were said to have also been empirically validated by their demonstrated differentiation of cases chosen by psychiatric studies and assigned as criterion cases to the various temperaments. Second, there were intrinsic controls that were designed to give assurance that the test was validly completed. There was, for example, a "no count" which was obtained by counting the "no" responses. Too large a no count invalidated the test because it was assumed that the subject was too guarded. Too small a no count suggested an opposite tendency to accept too many symptomatic statements. Despite the advanced design features, the Humm-Wadsworth did not have good validity, possibly because the items, although they were empirically checked, were based upon criterion groups that were far too small.

It was the sheer frustration of the need for a more practical if not more valid test to use in clinical applications of psychology which led to the development of the first thoroughly empirical personality inventory. Instead of rational studies in the psychology laboratory or the generalized descriptions by leading clinical writers, the MMPI [Minnesota Multiphasic Personality Inventory (Hathaway & McKinley, 1942)] had for its orientation the routine diagnostic and assessment problems of a psychiatric service. The scales, although based generally upon psychometric principles, were devoted to the current taxonomy of mental disorders. Beyond the psychometric features, the inventory was not related to theories about the structure of personality. Subsequent data collection and research have provided systematic and theoretical elements connected with the MMPI, but it still may be criticized for the lack of purity in scale item selection principles and its perpetuation of the Kraepelin-derived nosology.

DEVELOPMENT OF THE MMPI

Research that led to the publication of the MMPI was initiated in 1939. As pointed out above, the impetus came in large part out of practical need. No available personality inventory had much value for application in a routine adult psychiatric setting. The norms and evidence for validity had mostly been drawn from college students as normals, and the patients or prisoners making up the criterion groups were not matched to the students in so many ways that no definite interpretations could be placed on the difference data. Also, the variables that were expressed had little practical application in diagnostic work, even though some of them were widely used in personality description outside of clinical applications. Finally, problems of test dissimulation were recognized but had not been solved or effectively treated; the assumed undesirability of face-valid items had been partly controlled by the discovery of some subtle items; not much validity remained; and when early devices for control, such as the no count, were used, they were either ineffective or, more likely, not validated.

From its inception, an attempt was made to overcome the known defects of personality inventories in the construction of the MMPI:

1. Items were chosen to be intelligible at low reading-ability levels.
2. Items were stated in the first person in an attempt to produce more self-reference in the examinee.
3. All scoring was dependent upon simple item weights of zero or one. Scoring was simplified by various devices. Little skill was required in producing the completed profile. As a further effort, the items were printed on separate cards to be sorted in a box behind index cards clearly indicating the response intended. No pencil was needed.
4. Items were deliberately varied in content; they went far beyond clear face validity. This risked use of many nonfunctioning items, but if the procedure required empirical selection of items for scales, there was no other way to begin.
5. In the hope of breaking the monotony of "true" responses always being associated with bad things, there was an effort to find or state items for which an undesirable implication was associated with a "false" response. The nature of our language limits this effort; it is difficult to find many symptomatic statements to which the undesirable answer is "false." Double negatives had to be the usual device: "I have many fears" became "I do not have many fears." The negative of this item became the confusing, "I do not have many fears—false." Incidentally, some of these awkward items later came to be recognized as possibly good items, since the confusion permitted the expression of less consciously chosen but more valid responses as the examinee sorted the cards and made quick responses.
6. To check further upon the subject's reading ability and to provide a measure of the strength of the tendency to be overly candid, a special scale called "F" was provided. This was arbitrarily composed of items having very infrequent endorsement among the normalizing sample of subjects. Since the mean raw score among the 64 F-scale items was only about 3, inability to read or any other randomizing influence on responses would, with "true" or "false" as the two response offerings, trend upward toward a score of 32, half the items. This would suggest a random score such as a nonreader would get.
7. For measure of too strong a tendency to say good things, the L scale was introduced. These items were an adaptation from the work of Hartshorne and May (1928). They were chosen so that the socially desirable answer would be "true." The items expressed desirable social facts, but the candid subject usually could not endorse them. For example, most persons cannot really say they never lie. One L item is "I never tell a lie." To claim many virtues of this sort makes a high L score. The person appears too good and virtuous.
8. Normative data were obtained from ordinary middle-aged persons more like those who might be tested in the practical situations of clinical work than the normative samples that most inventories had used.

9. All items were validated by reference to empirical frequency differences between the general normal group and various clinically defined deviant groups characterized by internationally known and used categorical terms. Instead of inferiority, ascendancy, introversion, and the like, the variables were tied to schizophrenia, depression, paranoia, hypomania, and other routinely estimated clinical cases.

For the first time, MMPI scales were made up entirely of items selected empirically from among a large and heterogeneous pool. Selection into scales rested upon the actual differences in response frequency between clinical criterion and normal groups. One result of this empirical item-selection method was the discovery of many subtle items. As suggested above, the empirical method is about the only way one can discover such subtle items. But it appears that for some personality scales it is only the obvious items that make a considerable contribution to validity (McCall, 1958). Another outcome of the method was that the resultant scales appeared more heterogeneous in item content. For example, scale 3, derived from criterion cases of conversion hysteria, provides a dramatic illustration of this heterogeneity. Contrary to the current psychometric theory that required internal consistency in a scale, there are at least two strong factors in scale 3. One of these stresses the presence of physical symptoms, and the other stresses denial of mental weakness. These contrasting factors combine to produce the higher scores of the scale.

The MMPI was intended as an objective aid in the routine psychiatric case work-up of adult patients and as a method for determining the severity of the conditions. As a corollary to this, the inventory was expected to provide an objective estimate of psychotherapeutic effect and other changes in the severity of their conditions over time.

For all these tasks the MMPI is only moderately successful. It is probably nearly as good as possible, considering the present state of our taxonomy of personality variables. Something like 60 to 70 per cent of mentally disturbed or handicapped adults will produce profiles judged to be representative of the kind and severity of the disability. Supposedly normal persons will also show such profiles with a rate on the order of 10 to 20 per cent. Very little work has been done that would explicate these seemingly false positive cases. No doubt, many of them would be considered rather maladjusted if they were examined in a clinical setting. There is apparently some factor that is allied to self-dependence or determined independence that prevents the symptoms endorsed by this group from causing so much handicap as is observed among persons who admit to needing professional help.

This problem was recognized in the structure of temperament as advanced by Rosanoff (1938), upon whose ideas the Humm-Wadsworth inventory was based. Rosanoff assumed the existence of a positive personality trait that he called "control," and the Humm-Wadsworth provided a measure of this assumed factor. Meehl, however, was unable to demonstrate a coherent control variable (1945). The measure that has come nearest to meeting the requirements is the K variable of the MMPI (Meehl & Hathaway, 1946; McKinley & Meehl, 1948), which will be further discussed below in the context of response set.

The popularity of the MMPI appears to rest less upon its unusual validity than upon the general structure of the test: the provisions for some control over undesirable response patterns, detection of invalid records such as those from nonreaders, the use of simple language, the simplicity of administration and scoring, and, finally, the general clinical familiarity of the profile variables. It has come to be widely used in many applications not closely related to its original conception. It is used for selection of employees, in counseling of students, in annual health checks, and in many other ways. It appears that the variables that are known in the severe patterns of mental illness are also, in less intensity, important in assessment of rather normal persons; these variables begin to show greater intensity preceding more overt personality breakdown. Some MMPI profiles from high school students are indicative of delinquency (Hathaway & Monachesi, 1953; Hathaway & Monachesi, 1963) and school dropout (Hathaway & Monachesi, 1961; Hathaway & Monachesi, 1963).

For extended validity, the MMPI used a new device. This combines a coding of the test profiles with collections of corresponding case histories of persons who have been studied and described. Coding is a number system that provides a class number for every profile shape. When profiles having similar deviant scores are lumped together under simplified code designations, one can take a profile just obtained and coded and look up the case histories of other persons who received the same code numbers. Reading the case histories will reveal generalities among the descriptions. These similarities among the collected examples of a given code profile suggest that the same may be true of the new person to be assessed. The collections of case histories that are used in this way are called "atlases" (Hathaway & Meehl, 1951; Hathaway & Monachesi, 1961). Since the material of the case histories is not contaminated by knowledge of the test results, the validity derived from specific generalities among the case histories appears to be more completely empirical than that coming from test manuals where the meanings of the scales are described by someone who has depended upon his individual experience to tell what the scale means.

Because, to some psychologists, the MMPI seemed not to be optimal for use with normal populations in guidance and selection, a number of related inventories have appeared. One of these, the California Personality Inventory [CPI (Gough, 1957)], has scales analogous to those of the MMPI and additional ones to make about seventeen in the profile. The wish to get away from the associations with metal illness is manifested in the scales' being oriented to make high scores represent the presumed normal poles of the variables. The CPI is primarily intended for use by counselors and others working with young populations. Variables such as socialization, responsibility, and dominance illustrate the lesser emphasis on mental illness. The Minnesota Counseling Inventory [MCI (Berdie & Layton, 1953–1957)] is similarly related to the MMPI but intended even more explicity than the CPI as an instrument for use in secondary school or college applications.

At present the empirically derived personality inventories dominate the field. It is probable that the code typology of the MMPI profiles now actually has greater heuristic value than the present nosology of mental illness. Code expressions of MMPI profiles such as 27′ . . . , 86′ . . . , 4″ . . . , or 9" . . . appear to identify persons with many predictable similarities, and clinical psychologists familiar with these classes are more and more using the codes to communicate clinical data on persons. A bootstrap phenomenon has operated to preserve some stability in clinical diagnoses, and for some time we may have to use these codes as Stanford IQs came to be used instead of other intelligence constructs.

Although there are many psychologists who are anxious to abandon the old metal illness categories, no one has been able to produce a convincing or popular substitute. If a better nosology of mental disorders could be established, new and better personality tests might be developed. Without such a break, even the best empirical methods cannot produce much improvement.

THE FACTOR APPROACH

Thorne in 1955 stated:

> Due to the fact that objective tests constructed on the basis of face validity, content validity or empirical validity, have been proven to be of limited usefulness and relatively crude measuring instruments, and also because differential aptitude batteries constructed on the basis of factorial validity are still in their infancy, the whole situation of the objective testing of aptitudes and other factors of ability must be regarded as being in a state of developmental flux with existing tests being largely discredited and a bright future on the horizon for entirely new tests constructed on the basis of factorial validity.

These tests that depend upon the statistical methodology and theory of factors are recognizably different in many ways from the empirical inventories. To present this development, we shall again go back to the interwar period.

The development of new statistical tools which provided much more flexible methods for psychometrics than the methodology of psychophysical measurement had led to a flood of research work by psychologists. Central to much of this research, the coefficient of correlation tended to determine the designs of projects. Tests were evaluated by the coefficients of reliability and validity, and item intercorrelations were required to establish internal consistency in measurement. The fields of individual differences that emphasized intelligence, abilities, and interests were clearly advanced by these methods. It is not surprising that this statistically based mold was used for the checking and development of personality inventories. The mathematical assumptions required for proper application of correlations and the associated patterns by which correlations were interpreted were often blatantly used with the implication that when inventories did not fit the mold, the inventories were wrong, not the model. Homoscedasticity, continuity, linearity of regression, and other characteristics necessary to variables where correlation will be appropriate were hypotheses for personality variables. At a more complex level, the statistical paradigms and the associated mathematical tools for solution became a basis for theories of personality structure.

These statistical patterns of thinking did not greatly advance the qualities of the personality inventories, as has been apparent in the foregoing discussion. Perhaps there is really no close relationship between personality variables and their interactions and the mathematical patterns of statistics. For example, it may be that personality concepts cannot be represented in variables that have the properties of measures familiar to us in physical science. They may not be really scalable or continuous in meaning (Hathaway, 1961; Kahneman & Ghiselli, 1962). Temperature, as an example, is a variable that can be, within ordinary ranges, scaled and combined into equations where the contribution makes both mathematical and conceptual sense. High and low values of temperature are all accepted easily as having allied connotations. But it is not clear that personality variables such as prejudice or depression could possibly be fitted to such a scale. If one had a good indicator of depression such that some persons were meaningfully indentified as depressed, it is not certain that any direct meaning at all could be placed on values of the indicator falling below the critical point where other operations such as clinical studies would not produce evidence of depression. To say this another way, we cannot establish nondepression as being a degree of depression. Like physical materials or things, depression may be present, and present in an amount, but there are no degrees of it not being present. This argument is developed as a possible explanation for the failure of the new statistical methodology to lead to more improvement of the personality inventories.

Despite the poor success of the correlational model, the general appeal of the orderly concepts of material science continues to exert a powerful effect upon attempts at the analysis of personality. As new tools of statistical science are developed, they are ever hopefully applied. Factor analysis and the associated theoretical structure have been one such outcome.

Factors are coherent combining variables that result from special statistical methods. They can be very roughly considered analogous to physical dimensions. Like the three-dimensional orthogonal coordinates of our usual space, the factors of personality could provide a number of coordinate test values locating complex variables in a sort of multidimensional psychological space. One might have as many factors or dimensions as are needed to account for the complex variables that we recognize in personality. It was at first hoped that the psychological space might be expressed in the simplest structure using a few pure and orthogonal factors to account for the maximum variety of complexities in psychological qualities.

Thorne (1955) wrote:

> *Factorial validity* is the ultimate available today because it permits a qualitative and quantitative differentiation of the nature of the factor being measured and the efficiency of measurement in terms of the correlation of the test with the factor. Factorial methods are now far enough advanced so that the basic dimensions of ability and personality have been well differentiated in terms of generally accepted lists of factors. The list of generally accepted factors of mind must be regarded as the foundation from which enlightened test construction must spring. Marker tests (items) correlating highest with each factor must be the criteria against which new tests are validated.

This sanguine statement, now nine or ten years old, presents the spirit with which the factor theory was developing.

It must be kept clearly in mind that a factorial approach rests upon a number of assumptions. It assumes that psychological variables have properties of continuity analogous to physical variables such as temperature. It assumes, usually, that the coordinate values can be considered to lie in a linear equation space and that the coordinate factors are at least nearly orthogonal. These assumptions really express a faith that psychological variables will fit the mathematical and physical models of natural science.

Application of factor analysis to the measurement of intelligence, especially as applied to school achievement, was rather successful. Factors of intelligence as introduced by Thurstone and Thurstone (1941) became a prime pattern for some of the most widely known tests. The General Aptitude Test Battery of the United States Employment Service is an example.

It was natural for psychologists to attempt to fit personality inventories into the factor methods and theory. Even before this, a first requisite was applied in an emphasis on the establishment of internal consistency for scales. As stated above, factor theory requires that the items of a scale be consistent; they should be internally consistent, homogenous. There should be good correlations among the items and between items and criterion. Rundquist and Sletto (1936) pushed this requirement as far as they could and ended by criticizing the principle because they found that, for undiscovered reasons, the best scales using this criterion had somewhere lost their validity.

The Bernreuter was factor-analyzed, and only two factors were found to express reasonably well the six scores it provided (Flanagan, 1935). The fact that subsequent editions of the test merely added these factors instead of following the logic and dropping the six old scales shown to have little independent variance presaged much of the future of factor applications to the personality inventory. There has been a perverse tendency for psychologists to disregard the implications of factor work while continuing to accept the principles and some of the scales.

The best known of the early factor-analysis-based inventories was the series with which Guilford has been associated (1945; Guilford & Guilford, 1936; Guilford & Zimmerman, 1949–1955). Using existing items and inventory scales, analysis produced four original factors and others later. The factors of these inventories were given descriptive names, but they were known by letters such as the five STDCR.

Factor scales come almost magically out of the mathematical procedures that in a sense digest numerous input test variables to produce a few that account for most of the variance. Unfortunately the new factor variables did not prove very stable with replication of the process, nor were their validities impressive. The Guilford scales and other factors are of little, if any, more use in prediction and assessment than the less systematically derived scales. Also, factor scales tend to be harder for a user of them to recognize; the measures often had to be given rather unfamiliar names instead of the usual names with which we characterize personality. Finally, the scales tended to change their makeup when different tests were put into the matrix or when new groups of subjects were tested. Modern factor analysts have become aware of this problem. Cattell (1952) and Eysenck have both worked toward stabilization of their factors. Despite these drawbacks, like the Bernreuter, the Guilford scales have persisted and are still used widely.

Eysench (1953) has very actively worked to identify the factors that are most pertinent to clinical application. His introversion-extroversion factor, which is his most pervasive product, is related to neuroticism. By far the most systematic and rigorous attack on the problems of personality measurement is led by Cattell.

THE FACTOR UNIVERSE OF CATTELL

Cattell is engaged in the task of isolating and cataloguing all the factors in life history, personal description, and rating item data. For each factor, he identifies a "trait marker" objective test. The factor scales associated with the trait markers are presented as meaningful alone and in combination to be weighted for the estimation of compound traits.

> The procedure consists in correlating trait elements until one discovers those which correlate positively in every possible internal combination. Such a collection is called a syndrome in abnormal psychology and in normal psychology a surface trait. If the surface trait is very broad we may prefer to call the extremes of it "types." A surface trait is in any case simply a collection of trait-elements, of greater or lesser width of representation, which obviously "go together" in many different individuals and circumstances (Cattell, 1950).

Factors can represent surface traits, but they are more general, more fundamentally explanatory. They are conceivable as the constructs that underlie the correlations that make up a correlation matrix. Cattell sees the program that he and his associates are engaged in as "a search for the dimensions of personality, i.e., for the number of truly independent *directions* in which personality needs to be measured in order completely to describe it" (1950).

The evaluation of this program depends in large part upon the degree to which one accepts the basic postulates and upon one's requirements about the level of verification. The correlations upon which the factors depend are not conclusively large. One needs considerable tolerance for unassigned variances in the statistical logic if the scales are to be adopted for a frame of reference.

The 16 P.F. inventory and allied tests are outcomes of the best of this research from the Cattell program. In the 16 P.F. there are 16 factorial measures which permit the construction of a profile and which can be used in more or less complex regression equations to predict various criteria significant to the practical assessment of personality. Although there are many additional factors and a code-type system for naming them, the 16 P.F. is illustrative.

The 16 factor tests of the P.F. seem to be rather many factors when one considers the central argument for factor tests, the simplification of the personality space. But the manual for the tests states: "A much better multiple correlation is to be obtained by respecting the complexity than by indulging in a fool's paradise of simplification. . . . The questionnaire thus aims *to leave out no important aspect of the total personality*. . . ." (Cattell & Stice, 1949–1950). The 16 factors include abilities, temperament, and dynamic source traits.

When factors are derived, they must be recognized and named arbitrarily from the marker tests with which they are loaded or from some rational estimation of what the items seem to suggest as a personality variable. Some of the names given to the factors of the 16 P.F. will illustrate the point. Factor A is "cyclothymia versus schizothymia." Factor E is given the familiar name "dominance or ascendance versus submission." Factor F is called "surgency versus desurgency or depressive anxiety"; its subtitle is "enthusiastic versus melancholic." Factor Q_1 is "radicalism versus conservatism." A final example, factor Q_3, is called "will control and character stability." The factor scales are arranged on a profile, and standard profiles from various sources help in interpretation.

The characteristic bipolar significance of variables is apparent. Unlike most of the MMPI and similar scales which can be interpreted only when scores vary in one direction from the mean, these scales signify meaningful personality aspects with deviation in either direction from the mean.

Validity studies and applications of the 16 P.F. have also not been much more supportive in demonstrating value for prediction and selection than the validity studies of the empirically derived tests. The field of objective personality inventory use is presently divided between the adherents to the empirically based inventories and the factor-based tests. Both approaches have produced devices which are useful and which are becoming standard procedure for many applications. But it is not difficult to list shortcomings, and the search for better instruments continues.

No absolute establishment of the validity of the factor model has come out of the work. Although primary factors in intelligence were developed and are used, modern intelligence tests where they are most successful are closer relatives of the Binet-Simon than of the scales growing out of factor analysis. Similarly, although many personality scales have been developed by factor-analyzing matrices made up of selections from most current scales and item collections, it is still undecided whether the factor method will be the most powerful or whether the personality scales will depend upon methods for which no clear mathematical model has so far been discovered.

Few definitive studies have been directed to the comparison of the power of factorial scales and empirical scales against the prediction of practical criteria. Marks, Stauffacher, and Lyle (1963) did one such study using the prediction of outcome for patients after discharge. In this study, both types of scale were weak, and neither seemed superior.

It is not surprising that the factors that have resulted from the factor-analytic approach are often recognizable as the variables known routinely in clinical experience which are the criterion determiners of the empirical test variables. Thus neuroticism, schizoid makeup, extroversion-introversion, and other variables originally described as clinical entities are usually among the factors that emerge from clinical test batteries.

It must be appreciated that factor-analytic methods could not produce truly new dimensions. They can isolate only factors that are present in the raw data. The measures used and the subjects to which these measures are applied are the real sources of factors. This establishes an often overlooked circularity. In the light of this fact, it becomes clear why Wittenborn (1955) and others have repeatedly drawn scales from factor-analytic methodology that are so clearly related to the scales found by the empirical methodology. If factors do not "make sense," we cannot use them, and they do not make sense unless we have already recognized them in the people they are to represent.

As new categories of personality are discovered and become useful, factor analysis may clarify their measurement by permitting the discard of scales or items that make no appreciable contribution to the measurement. But this usefulness depends upon the unproved assumption that personality can be usefully represented by continuous variables which permit combination by regression and which order subjects meaningfully both in extreme high and low score ranges and in scores falling near the mean value.

RESPONSE SET AND THE PERSONALITY INVENTORIES

Two allied difficulties had gradually become apparent to those who were working with personality inventories. First, as has been pointed out, face-valid questions worked fine when the respondent was motivated to admit to the way he felt, but it seemed that he could usually recognize and avoid any item that he chose to avoid. The second difficulty was more pervasive. It had become increasingly apparent that some psychological traits or patterns that were not intended by the test constructor were contributing even more variance to test score distributions than the specific personality constructs that the scale was intended to measure were. "Response set" is the general term that has come to be applied to these interloping variables. One of the first recognized among these response sets was the tendency to say "yes" or "no" or "true" or "false." This came out early because almost all the symptom-expressing items were started in the form "Do you have convulsions?" To endorse an item by responding "yes" had face validity as an admission that one had a fault or complaint. Since it had become apparent that subjects interpreted items in unpredictable and various ways, so that few items were absolutely objective, a subject taking a test could readily, and not at all with the intent to lie, find some interpretation of most items so that he could say "no" and deny the symptom. But it has been fairly well established that saying "no" is a set that is partly independent of item content. It is a true response set. The symptom-denial tendency is partly independent of a contrasting tendency or set to say "yes." The acquiescence set probably operated in favor of the validity of draftee screening tests, since endorsement of items meant endorsement of symptoms. In the Woodworth type of inventory, an acquiescence set would tend to lead to endorsement of too many symptoms. This contributed to test validity under the circumstances, since the pressure was greatest in the direction of rejecting the unfit, and it was considered less of an error to obtain a too abnormal test score.

It is apparent that the response-set issue began with worry about the fact that face-valid questions seemed to invite distortion by faking good or bad. Subtle items appeared to be an obvious way to control this, but McCall (1958) concluded from a study of the D scale of the MMPI: "The 60 items of the depression scale of the MMPI were shown to be differentially effective in distinguishing depressive from a matched group of nondepressive psychotics in proportion to their 'face validity,' as determined *a priori*." Such a finding supports the possibility that face validity is a central source of item validity. Wiener (1948) approached the problem by forming separate subscales using the subtle and the obvious items from empirical scales. It will be apparent below that the very reality of many personality variables is tied to face validity. There could not be a subtle scale that would have much value for such a variable.

The Humm-Wadsworth Temperament Scale had adopted a no count as a measure, if not a control, for the "no" response set. The Bennett-Slater test in Britain (Bennett & Slater, 1945) had arranged items so that about half were so worded as to reverse the usual trend and make a "no" response the less desirable one. The first edition of the MMPI provided the L score, which was intended to betray the person who presented himself in what seemed to be a too favorable way, and the F score, which was designed to identify records in which the testee seemed to have endorsed an unduly large number of undesirable items. On the MMPI these scores were called "validity" scores. This terminology was adopted with reference to whether the responses to the inventory appeared to suggest a standard, or valid, test-taking procedure and attitude by the testee.

Experience with the MMPI soon showed that, as with all inventories, there occurred many false negative profiles. These are seemingly normal tests obtained from patients who manifestly should not have normal profiles. There were also the false positive profiles showing abnormal results from nonpatients who, although there was not usually a mental-status examination to prove the fact, appeared normal. It seemed unlikely that some disturbing psychometric influence was operating to produce these seemingly false test profiles.

The first methods of investigation used role playing. Students were asked to take the personality inventory with usual instructions; then, at a different time, they were asked to attempt to produce a more favorable profile (e.g., Gough, 1947). Item-frequency comparisons provided a way to discover the items that would betray the attempt at deception by the frequency with which they were changed from first to second testing. Such studies were not particularly successful in providing scales for dissimulation that were an improvement over the L and F scales or some combination of these, such as the score obtained by subtracting the F score from the L score. Many fake-good profiles could be identified, but many were still not betrayed by any device.

There were two fundamental defects in this methodology. The college students, mostly used for subjects, usually had normal profiles even before being told to fake; also, the routine student test-taking attitude was already one of seeking to make a good impression. The special role-playing instructions could not much change their approach. Few experiments were made with the opposite instruction, to fake a bad profile. Also, few experiments started with people whose natural profile was an abnormal one and asked them to respond while playing the normal role.

One such investigation (Grayson & Olinger, 1957) showed that only about 11 per cent of patients could simulate a normal MMPI profile. Some patients made their profiles more deviant; others merely changed the profile to indicate a different abnormality. The first definitive review of, and contribution to, the problems of test faking or lying, as the response-set problem was still referred to, came with a paper by Meehl and Hathaway (1946). This paper, reviewing the general problem, pointed out that by 1945 very few effective efforts had been made to correct or overcome the distorting effect of test-taking attitudes. This was true despite the considerable number of articles and tests that had recognized the importance of the problem.

Meehl and Hathaway carried out a series of experimental studies of the faking phenomenon. An early discovery of importance was that the items in the MMPI that discriminated the fake-good role were not identical with those that discriminated the fake-bad role but that scales based on either of the two sets of items worked equally well to discriminate those profiles produced under the opposite set. This initiated work toward the development of a single bipolar scale for discrimination of fake good at one pole and fake bad at the other. This scale or factor of test-taking attitude was ultimately made available as the K scale of the MMPI (McKinley & Meehl, 1948).

One of the conclusions of the paper that introduced K was of special significance. It stated:

> On the basis of these findings and study of the relationship of MMPI to certain of the Guilford-Martin scales, it is suggested that perhaps the construction of personality inventories by means of item intercorrelations and factor analytic methods leads to development of tests which are excessively loaded with such test-taking attitudes. The procedure of internal consistency in its various forms is called into question as a profitable method for the construction of personality inventories.

This conclusion suggested the solution to the mystery about the loss of validity as internal consistency was increased, as reported a decade before by Rundquist and Sletto (1936).

The chief purpose of the K studies was the improvement of the validity of MMPI scales for distinguishing persons whose MMPI profiles showed scores near the conventional normal-abnormal borderline value where the score is two standard deviations above the mean. That is to say, the development of K was in the main devoted to the attempt to eliminate the false negative and false positive cases when the test profiles were near the borderline. The derivation of the final K items depended on numerous sources. Meehl (1945) had found what turned out to be the same factor in attempts to discover a scale for normal temperament. Similar items also came out of the item analyses between patients with false negative profiles and nonpatients with false positive profiles. Finally, the factor-analytic method produced nearly the same scale.

Horst (1941) had developed the concept of a suppressor variable in personality inventories. This conceived of a variable which would contribute to clinical scale variance but which had no correlation with the scale criterion variable. Presumably such a variable could be partialed out of a scale measure to remove unwanted variance and leave the scale more purely expressive of the valid variance. The final application of the K factor was determined by this concept. K was used to correct certain scales *on the basis of the empirical effect* it had on profiles of persons whose scores were indicated to need correction for agreement with an independently judged clinical criterion.

Edwards (1953b) showed that the endorsement of an item is more probable as the item is judged more socially desirable. At first he considered two possibilities: "It may be that traits which are judged as desirable are those which are fairly widespread or common among members of a group or culture. That is, if a pattern of behavior is prevalent among members of a group, it will be judged desirable; if it is uncommon, it will be judged undesirable." He also said: "It is also possible that the behavior indicated by an item with a high social desirability scale value is not common, but that the subject is trying, consciously or unconsciously, to give a good impression of himself." In the latter case, it would seem desirable that personality inventory scales be purged of the social-desirability variable.

In another publication, Edwards wrote:

> Under any circumstances, if a statement has high social desirability scale value and if a subject endorses it in self-description, our interpretation of his response is complicated. We have no way of knowing, for example, whether the statement is, in fact, descriptive of the subject or whether he simply says that it is because he regards it as a socially desirable characteristic. Similarly, if a subject fails to endorse a statement with a low social desirability scale value, he may do so because the statement is not, in fact, descriptive of him, or because he does not choose to acknowledge what he may regard as a socially undesirable characterization (1957).

The work of Edwards is typical of a considerable amount of effort directly designed for the study of response sets but more or less indirectly accepting the hypothesis that these sets mostly contribute invalid variance to personality inventory scales. He has applied his principles in the development of an inventory, the Edwards Personal Preference Schedule (1953a). Scales of the PPS are rationally derived, since they assess 15 of Murray's needs. The format was intended to reduce variance of scores from social desirability. After scaling the prospective items for social desirability, the scales of the test were made dependent upon the subjects' making forced choices of preference between pairs of items that were nearly equal in social desirability according to the original scaling. Since the components of the choice had face validity for the needs, the endorsed preferences should relate to the needs rather than to social desirability. Unfortunately, subsequent studies have tended to show that social desirability still influences PPS scores. This may be because the original desirability scaling of the items does not hold constant or because items change in social-desirability value according to context or for some other reason.

One ubiquitous problem arises in this context. As Messick (1960) has shown, it seems that social desirability is not a pure dimension. There appear to be several social-desirability variables that represent the social frame of reference in which the subject makes his response. Following this lead suggests a complicated approach with careful definition and control of the attitude of the subject. Since evidence of multiple meanings to social desirability can be matched by evidence that other response-set variables, such as the MMPI L and K, are also either impure representatives of several sets or merely one representative of a family of closely related sets, the whole area now seems to be in need of a great deal of definitive work. In the meantime, the hypothesis that these various response sets contribute chiefly to error in personality inventory profiles has not been tested adequately, and the response-set literature contains few data like those in the K work, where the chief emphasis was on empirical tests of the scale validity change against clinical criteria as sets are systematically controlled.

Edwards, Wiggins (1959; 1962), Berg (1957), Cronbach (1942; 1946), Jackson and Messick (1961), Fricke (1957), and others have opened up a bewildering variety of possibilities. Beyond the earliest concepts exemplified in the no count, the L and F scales of the MMPI, and the K factor, a number of more or less independent concepts have been named. Cronbach referred to acquiescence, Edwards to social desirability, and Berg to deviation. Recently Couch and Keniston (1960) have added the catching terms "yeasaying" and "naysaying."

There is no doubt that response set is a highly significant area for research and development in the personality inventory field. Although the various sets are of great interest in their own right, the gratuitous assumption that response sets contribute error variance alone to clinical scales should be far more often subjected to empirical proof. One of Horst's requirements for a true suppressor variable was a zero correlation with the criterion. No real evidence has been produced that response-set variance does not make a valid contribution to many clinically useful personality constructs. Obviously if such were the case, the elimination of the effect of set would be undesirable. The work of Meehl and Hathaway did not evaluate the issue, but MMPI scales were known from the first to be correlated with social desirability at least.

The peculiar ambivalence in this area is illustrated by Holtzman, Thorpe, Swartz, & Herron (1961), when they say:

> Unfortunately they [personality inventories] all have the common characteristic of dealing only with the subject's superficial response to items the content of which is often transparent. Although ingenious methods have been developed to disguise this content and force the subject to make choices which can then be scaled and treated psychometrically, the fundamental, superficial nature of such tests still persists. In fairness to the self-inventory approach, it should be pointed out that scales from these tests usually have fairly high reliability and often correlate with socially observable behavior to a higher degree than any projective technique. Such correlations, however, can frequently be traced directly to the fact that the individual has a conscious self-concept that dominates his test responses and is not unrelated to his social behavior as judged by others.

In this passage, it is stated that when a person responds to an item, his responses are too conscious to be valid and that, nevertheless, it must be recognized that people do, in many ways, behave according to their conscious self-concepts, not all of which are jealously kept private. Even if response sets determine portions of the scores on personality scales, these same sets often determine other behavior, and if one had completely subtle items fully corrected for response sets, one would have also eliminated some of the practical aspects of the personality measurement. It seems as though many psychologists have been convinced that all determinates of behavior are unconscious and so cannot accept direct statements; yet we feel we convey useful information about a person if we say he is a "yes man"!

A final summary that is appropriate was written by Christie and Lindauer:

> In short, we believe that individuals do display certain consistencies of behavior over time which permit inferences about their personality structure. However, most of the articles and books we have scanned leave us with the impression of possibly greater inconsistency in the measurements than exist in the subjects investigated. From this point of view, the recently emphasized problems of assessment, involving as they do such matters as response set and social desirability, appear to form a critical area in personality research. Social desirability and response set are important not simply in that they must be eliminated from personality measures as artifacts. Our reading of the literature suggests that these "artifacts" may have as much or more relevance to inferences about personality structure than the manifest content of most measures. A thorough investigation of nonscale behav-

ioral measures as they relate to the manifest content of traditional scales and to the stylistic measures should indicate the extent to which this critical evaluation is justified (1963).

THE PERSONALITY INVENTORY FOR CHILDREN

Possibly because of the lack of any widely accepted classification system for the disorders of childhood and because the developmental stages are too different and too numerous, there has been even less success in the development of personality inventories applicable to the assessment and classification of emotional problems among children. An early inventory, the Test of Personality Adjustment, was constructed by Rogers (Burchinal, Gardner, & Hawkes, 1958; Rogers, 1931). This was followed by, among others, the California Test of Personality (Thorpe, Clark, & Tiegs, 1953). Developed by the usual methodology, the California Test of Personality provided 15 scores on such areas as self-reliance, family relations, and feeling of belonging. Designed for children as young as those in kindergarten, it has been used more as a checklist than as a set of measurements.

Some more recent tests have been designed to apply to at least the late teen-age population. The California Psychological Inventory and the Minnesota Counseling Inventory were adapted to be appropriate for ages from about 14 to adult. These and other inventories have wide popularity in counseling and have been used in a considerable number of research reports, but not many useful clinical applications have been established. The MMPI has also been widely used as far downward as age 14; more importantly, in the ninth grade and beyond it appears to have some value in predicting and understanding such late-teenage outcomes as delinquency and school dropout.

A considerable amount of research has used the Vineland Social Maturity Scale (Doll, 1936). This scale, which is not really a personality inventory, depends upon the reports of an informant as interviewed by the clinician rather than upon the child himself. It provides a general survey of the progress of the child in attaining a degree of social independence and maturity. In the early levels of the scale, the most primitive aspects of social maturity, such as locomotion and the beginnings of language communication, are estimated. Later on, at the higher age levels, the emphasis shifts to more adult aspects of socialization and the growth of occupational independence. The scale's chief value lies in its standardization, which permits the identification of severe retardation in the development of maturity. It is a valuable supplement to the intelligence test at early ages in detecting retardation, although it is also allied to the personality tests.

GENERAL CONCLUSIONS

If the foregoing treatment of the personality inventories does not present a very favorable picture, it is nevertheless a fair estimation. In assessing the situation, at least as much of the difficulty seems to lie with the criteria as with the inventories. In effect, psychologists have been too ready to work with criteria coming from very unreliable clinical judgments, assuming that the failure of the tests was chiefly due to seemingly obvious test inadequacies. This review of some of the chief trends in development has stressed the almost compulsive repetition of unprofitable efforts to produce better inventories. There has been little real effort devoted to the basic problems of classification or other formulation of personality to provide more meaningful and reliable criteria. It is not at all improbable that our inventory development methods are good and have merely not been suitably tested for lack of good criteria.

But there is another area in which progress has been too slow. Impressed with the fact that the inventory scales have low correlations with each other even when they seem to be similarly directed (even the various scales of masculine-femine interest do not correlate highly) and with the false negative and positive scores, it seems that psychologists have not sufficiently studied the predictive and descriptive powers of the better scales among current inventories. There has, for example, been little effort to capitalize upon the code classes or profile types provided by tests such as the 16 P.F. and the various inventories related to the MMPI. Such studies as the MMPI atlases (Hathaway & Meehl, 1951; Hathaway & Monachesi, 1961), the interesting empirical work of Drake and Oetting (1959) for counseling, and the work of Marks and Seeman (1963) for more clinical applications appear to be the most promising evidences. Selecting subgroupings among the profile types, as these methods do, discloses at times a startling similarity among the personality characteristics of the subjects. In effect, these data suggest that the tests may after all provide the inspiration for a new structure of personality. This is in contrast to the presently popular dependence upon clinical observation and experience.

The basic argument for the study of subgroupings provided by closely similar profiles is based upon a simple assumption. If, for example, two persons were to agree perfectly on responses to the hundreds of items on a personality inventory, it would be assumed that these two persons also had high probabilities of similarity in much of their life background and in many behavioral tendencies. Since it is well established that similar culture and similar dispositions produce similar people, it follows that such people will have similar profiles when the profiles represent coherent expressions of significant areas of personality.

Traditional statistical methods and experimental designs in the personality measurement field have not been well adapted to exploit this area for several reasons. A first reason lies in the fact that the argument can apply only to persons with great similarity. For the test data, this means that the argument will apply only to those persons with highly similar profiles. Such persons occur rarely. For example, among thousands of MMPI profiles, even if they are reduced to simple codes, two identical profiles are almost unknown. To identify even small groups of subjects that have close enough similarity so that the argument applies requires that a search be made among hundreds of profiles. Most psychological work with personality inventories has been on far too small a scale to permit the adequate study of this theory.

Second, the argument for similarity embodies a kind of discontinuity. Correlation and many other statistical tools cannot be used because membership in the subgroupings of nearly identical persons will be rapidly tenuous as any significant amount of variation from the group type begins to appear. Once a person has deviated from the group far enough so that errors of measurement are comparable in magnitude to the power of the similarities in predicting group membership, measurement of all relationships to the group becomes meaningless. For example, if one had a good index of profile difference, so that a zero meant identity, a person whose profile dissimilarity to the group type was just large enough so that one could do no better than chance in predicting other similarities or differences from the group would have a meaningless index beyond the fact that it was large enough to indicate that he did not belong. Obviously the differences among all still larger values of the index would also be meaningless, and any statistical device that assumed their rankings had meaning could not be used.

It seems reasonably safe to predict that computers will be the key to progress in this field. These provide the only presently available way in which the vast complexities of individual differences in personality can be coded, stored, and searched to provide interpretive information about a given profile.

In conclusion, there is no field of psychology where research seems more needed and where there is more real opportunity for creative discovery than that of the psychometrics of personality. The mental health manpower shortages, which will become more acute with every year, make our older clinical and individual assessment procedures far too costly in professional time; even if they were better than the personality inventories, their use would not be justified. With the further development of personality inventories and the techniques of their interpretation and use, the clinician will first see his client or patient after he has been provided with an informative collection of psychometric information that will greatly shorten and improve the assessment process.

REFERENCES

Allport, G. W. *Personality: a psychological interpretation.* New York: Holt, 1937.

Allport, G. W., & Vernon, P. E. *Studies in expressive movements.* New York: Macmillan, 1933.

Allport, G. W., Vernon, P. E., & Lindzey, G. *Study of values.* (Rev. ed.) Boston: Houghton Mifflin, 1951.

Andrew, Dorothy M., Paterson, D. G., & Longstaff, H. P. *Minnesota Clerical Test.* New York: Psychological Corporation, 1933. Rev. manual, 1946.

Bass, B. M., & Berg, I. A. (Eds.) *Objective approaches to personality assessment.* Princeton, N.J.: Van Nostrand, 1959.

Bell, H. M. *Adjustment inventory.* Stanford, Calif.: Stanford Univer. Press, 1934.

Bennett, E., & Slater, P. Some tests for the discrimination of neurotic from normal subjects. *Brit. J. Med. Psychol.,* 1945, **20,** 271–282.

Bennett, G. K., Fry, Dinah E., & Owens, W. A. *Test of Mechanical Comprehension.* New York: Psychological Corporation, 1940–1954.

Benton, A. L. The interpretation of questionnaire items in a personality schedule. *Arch. Psychol., N.Y.,* 1935, No. 190.

Berdie, R. F., & Layton, W. L. *Minnesota Counseling Inventory.* New York: Psychological Corporation, 1953–1957.

Berg, I. A. Deviant responses and deviant people: the formation of the deviation hypothesis. *J. consult. Psychol.,* 1957, **4,** 154–161.

Bernreuter, R. G. The theory and construction of the personality inventory. *J. soc. Psychol.,* 1933, **4,** 387–405. (Inventory published by Stanford Univer. Press, Stanford, Calif., 1931, rev. 1935.)

Burchinal, L. G., Gardner, B., & Hawkes, G. R. A suggested revision of norms for the Rogers Test of Personality Adjustment. *Child Developm.,* 1958, **29,** 135–139.

Buros, O. K. (Ed.) *The fifth mental measurements yearbook.* Highland Park, N.J.: Gryphon Press, 1959.

Cattell, R. B. *Personality.* New York: McGraw-Hill, 1950.

Cattell, R. B. *Factor analysis.* New York: Harper & Row, 1952.

Cattell, R. B., & Stice, G. *The Sixteen Personality Factor Questionnaire.* Champaign, Ill.: Institute for Personality and Ability Testing, 1949–1950. Manual, 1950.

Challman, R. C. Clinical methods: psychodiagnostics. In C. P. Stone & D. W. Taylor (Eds.), *Annu. Rev. Psychol.,* 1951, **2,** 239–258.

Christie, R., & Lindauer, Florence. Personality structure. *Annu. Rev. Psychol.,* 1963, **14,** 201–230.

Couch, A., & Keniston, K. Yeasayers and naysayers: agreeing response set as a personality variable. *J. abnorm. soc. Psychol.,* 1960, **60,** 154–174.

Cronbach, L. J. Studies of acquiescence as a factor in the true-false test. *J. educ. Psychol.,* 1942, **33,** 401–415.

Cronbach, L. J. Response sets and test validity. *Educ. psychol. measmt.,* 1946, **6,** 475–494.

Cronbach, L. J. *Essentials of psychological testing.* (2nd ed.) New York: Harper & Row, 1960.

Darley, J. G., & Hagenah, Theda. *Vocational interest measurement: theory and practice.* Minneapolis, Minn.: Univer. of Minnesota Press, 1956.

Doll, E. A. *Vineland Social Maturity Scale.* Vineland, N.J.: Training School, Educational Test Bureau, 1936.

Downey, June E. *The will-temperament and its testing.* Tarrytown-on-Hudson, N.Y.: World, 1924.

Drake, L. E., & Oetting, E. R. *An MMPI codebook for counselors.* Minneapolis, Minn.: Univer. of Minnesota Press, 1959.

Edwards, A. L. *Manual for the Personal Preference Schedule.* New York: Psychological Corporation, 1953. (a)

Edwards, A. L. The relationship between the judged desirability of a trait and the probability that the trait will be endorsed. *J. appl. Psychol.,* 1953, **37,** 90–93. (b)

Edwards, A. L. *The social desirability variable in personality assessment and research.* New York: Holt, 1957.

Eysenck, H. J. *The structure of human personality.* New York: Wiley, 1953.

Flanagan, J. C. *Factor analysis in the study of personality.* Stanford, Calif.: Stanford Univer. Press, 1935.

Fricke, B. G. A response bias (B) scale for the MMPI. *J. consult. Psychol.,* 1957, **4,** 149–153.

Gough, H. G. Simulated patterns on the MMPI. *J. abnorm. soc. Psychol.,* 1947, **42,** 215–225.

Gough, H. G. *California Psychological Inventory manual.* Palo Alto, Calif.: Consulting Psychologists Press, 1957.

Grayson, H. M., & Olinger, L. B. Simulation of "normalcy" by psychiatric patients on the MMPI. *J. consult. Psychol.,* 1957, **21,** 73–77.

Guilford, J. P. The construction of the Guilford-Martin Inventory of Factors G-A-M-I-N. *J. appl. Psychol.,* 1945, **29,** 298–300.

Guilford, J. P., & Guilford, Ruth B. Personality factors S, E, and M, and their measurement. *J. Psychol.,* 1936, **2,** 109–127.

Guilford, J. P., & Zimmerman, W. S. *The Guilford-Zimmerman Temperament Survey.* Beverly Hills, Calif.: Sheridan Supply Co., 1949–1955.

Hartshorne, H., & May, M. A. *Studies in deceit.* New York: Macmillan, 1928.

Hathaway, S. R. The personality inventory as an aid in the diagnosis of psychopathic inferiors. *J. consult. Psychol.,* 1939, 3, 112–117.

Hathaway, S. R. Problems of personality assessment. *Proc. XIV int. Congr. appl. Psychol., Munksgaard, Copenhagen,* 1961.

Hathaway, S. R., & McKinley, J. C. *Minnesota Multiphasic Personality Inventory.* Minneapolis, Minn.: Univer. of Minnesota Press, 1942.

Hathaway, S. R., & Meehl, P. E. *An atlas for the clinical use of the MMPI.* Minneapolis, Minn.: Univer. of Minnesota Press, 1951.

Hathaway, S. R., & Monachesi, E. D. *Analyzing and predicting juvenile delinquency with the MMPI.* Minneapolis, Minn.: Univer. of Minnesota Press, 1953.

Hathaway, S. R., & Monachesi, E. D. *An atlas of juvenile MMPI profiles.* Minneapolis, Minn.: Univer. of Minnesota Press, 1961.

Hathaway, S. R., & Monachesi, E. D. *Adolescent personality and behavior: MMPI patterns of normal, delinquent, drop out and other outcomes.* Minneapolis, Minn.: Univer. of Minnesota Press, 1963.

Holtzman, W. H., Thorpe, J. S., Swartz, J. D., & Herron, E. W. *Inkblot perception and personality.* Austin, Tex.: Univer. of Texas Press, 1961.

Horst, P. The prediction of personal adjustment. *Soc. Sci. Res. Council Bull.,* 1941, No. 48.

Humm, D. G., & Wadsworth, G. W. The Humm-Wadsworth Temperament Scale. *Am. J. Psychiat.,* 1935, **92**, 163–200. (Scale published by Humm Personnel Service, Los Angeles, Calif., 1940.)

Jackson, D. N., & Messick, S. Acquiescence and desirability as response determinants on the MMPI. *Educ. psychol. Measmt.,* 1961, **22**, 771–790.

Kahneman, D., & Ghiselli, E. E. Validity of nonlinear heteroscedastic models. *Personnel Psychol.,* 1962, **15**, 1–12.

Laird, D. A. Detecting abnormal behavior. *J. abnorm. soc. Psychol.,* 1925, **20**, 128–141. (Inventories published by The Hamilton Republican, Hamilton, N.J., 1925.)

Landis, C., & Katz, S. E. The validity of certain questions which purport to measure neurotic tendencies. *J. appl. Psychol.,* 1934, **18**, 343–356.

McCall, R. J. Face validity in the D scale of the MMPI. *J. clin. Psychol.,* 1958, **14**, 77–80.

McKinley, J. C., & Meehl, P. E. The MMPI. VI. The K scale. *J. consult. Psychol.,* 1948, **12**, 20–31.

Marks, J., Stauffacher, J. C., & Lyle, C. Predicting outcome in schizophrenia. *J. abnorm. soc. Psychol.,* 1963, **66**, 117–127.

Marks, P., & Seeman, W. The actuarial description of abnormal personality. Baltimore, Md.: The Williams and Wilkins Co., 1963.

Meehl, P. E. The dynamics of "structured" personality tests. *J. clin. Psychol.,* 1945, **1**, 296–303. (a)

Meehl, P. E. An investigation of a general normality or control factor in personality testing. *Psychol. Monogr.,* 1945, **59**, No. 4. (b)

Meehl, P. E., & Hathaway, S. R. The K factor as a suppressor variable in the MMPI. *J. appl. Psychol.,* 1946, **30**, 525–564.

Messick, S. Dimensions of social desirability. *J. consult. Psychol.,* 1960, **24**, 279–287.

Murphy, G. *Personality.* New York: Harper & Row, 1947.

Murray, H. A. *Explorations in personality.* New York: Oxford Univer. Press, 1938.

Phillips, L., & Rabinovitch, M. S. Social role and patterns of symptomatic behaviors. *J. abnorm. soc. Psychol.,* 1958, **57**, 181–186.

Rogers, C. *Measuring personality adjustment in children nine to thirteen years of age.* New York: Teachers College, Columbia Univer., 1931.

Rosanoff, A. J. *Manual of psychiatry and mental hygiene.* (7th ed.) New York: Wiley, 1938.

Rundquist, E. A., & Sletto, R. F. *Personality in depression.* Minneapolis, Minn.: Univer. of Minnesota Press, 1936.

Spearman, C. *The abilities of men.* London: Macmillan, 1927.

Spranger, E. *Types of men.* Halle, Niemeyer, 1928.

Super, D. E. The Bernreuter Personality Inventory. *Psychol. Bull.,* 1942, **39**, 94–125.

Thorne, F. C. *Principles of psychological examining.* Brandon, Vt.: Journal of Clinical Psychology Press, 1955.

Thorpe, L. P., Clark, W. W., & Tiegs, E. W. *California Test of Personality: 1953 revision.* Monterey, Calif.: California Test Bureau, 1953.

Thurstone, L. L., & Thurstone, Thelma G. Factorial studies of intelligence. *Psychometr. Monogr.,* 1941, No. 2.

Vernon, P. E., & Allport, G. W. A test for personal values. *J. abnorm. soc. Psychol.*, 1931, **26**, 231–248.

Weider, A., Mittlemann, B., Wechsler, D., & Wolff, H. G. The Cornell Selectee Index: a method for quick testing of selectees for the armed forces, *J. Amer. med. Ass.*, 1944, **124**, 224–228. (Test published by Psychological Corporation, New York, 1948.)

Wiener, D. N. Subtle and obvious keys for the MMPI. *J. consult. Psychol.*, 1948, **12**, 164–170.

Wiggins, J. S. Interrelationships among MMPI measures of dissimulation under standard and social desirability instructions. *J. consult. Psychol.*, 1959, **23**, 419–427.

Wiggins, J. S. Strategic method and stylistic variance in the MMPI. *Psychol. Bull.*, 1962, **59**, 224–242.

Witkin, H. A., Dyk, R. B., Faterson, H. F., Goodenough, D. R., & Karp, S. A. *Psychological differentiation.* New York: Wiley, 1962.

Wittenborn, J. R. *Wittenborn psychiatric rating scales.* New York: Psychological Corporation, 1955.

Woodworth, R. S. *Personal Data Sheet.* Chicago: Stoelting, 1920.

Zigler, E., & Phillips, L. Social effectiveness and symptomatic behaviors. *J. abnorm. soc. Psychol.*, 1960, **61**, 231–238.

Zigler, E., & Phillips, L. Case-history data and psychiatric diagnosis. *J. consult. Psychol.*, 1961, **25**, 458.

19
Diagnostic Use of Intelligence Tests

ALBERT I. RABIN

Intelligence testing is a twentieth-century development. Historians of psychology justifiably consider it an outgrowth of the interest in individual differences, which is attributed to such nineteenth-century figures as Galton, Cattell, and others. In a sense this movement of, and concern with, individual differences were not in harmony with the budding scientific psychology, whose interest was centered upon the study of man in general—the psychological characteristics held in common by all Homo sapiens. It was James McKeen Cattell who first used the term "mental test" in 1890 (Anastasi, 1954). The mental tests of that period and of the beginning of the twentieth century were primarily experiments involving specific sensory, motor, and perceptual tasks; some included experiments of memory as well. However, it was not until the labors of Alfred Binet and his coworkers, which culminated in the publication of a full-fledged intelligence test in 1908 (a revision of a cruder form which originated in 1905), that a standard instrument for the assessment of intelligence as such became available to the psychologists of that time.

Undoubtedly Binet's test filled an important social need and met with a receptive *Zeitgeist* in psychology and education. The test became rapidly domesticated in the United States; several translations appeared almost simultaneously, and studies with large groups of feebleminded abounded. The reception was generally positive, although some criticisms of the test's diagnostic validity with the feebleminded were also raised. By the beginning of the year 1914, Kohs had compiled a 254-item bibliography of studies based on the new method for assessing intelligence (Terman, 1916).

Although several versions of Binet's test became available in the United States shortly after its publication, the "Binet era" was not fully launched until the publication of the Stanford-Binet test, standardized on a sizable sample of American children in 1916, under the authorship of Lewis Terman. The Stanford-Binet initiated a movement of diagnostic application of individual intelligence tests and research in the intellectual functioning of various groups, which has not lost any of its vigor and momentum nearly half a century later.

THE STANFORD-BINET ERA

For about a quarter of a century, the Stanford-Binet (SB) was a major tool of clinical psychology. Its applications went beyond the schools, where it originated, and the institutions for the defectives. The clinic and the mental hospital became additional territories within the SB domain. In the following sections we shall deal with several developments in the application of intelligence tests which went considerably beyond the original intent of their authors.

Early Diagnostic Uses of the SB; MA and IQ

Essentially, the early application of Binet's test reflected the original purpose of the author, which consisted of rather modest and limited diagnostic aims. Major concern was with the evaluation of intellectual level as a guide for school placement. Related to this diagnostic application of the mental age and IQ (suggested by Wilhelm Stern) was the identification of the scholastically unfit and their designation as feebleminded. A further refinement of this procedure was the diagnostic labeling of defective subgroups based on their performance on the intelligence tests (i.e., morons, imbeciles, idiots). In other words, it became an aid for the classification of inmates within the institutions for the feebleminded and a guide in their training programs.

In the original manual of the SB, Terman (1916) considers the use of intelligence tests with the gifted, with delinquents, and in situations requiring decisions regarding "vocational fitness," in addition to the applications mentioned above. Worthy of special note is Terman's concern with the problem of discrepancy between school achievement and level of "native ability" as determined by his test.

Thus, the early use of the SB and of other intelligence tests was primarily confined to the comparison of the standing of the testee (with respect to his performance) with that of his age group represented in the standardization sample. It is a useful piece of information which remains so to date. However, psychologists soon began to go beyond the single psychometric index in their analysis of test data.

Studies of Intratest Variability with Psychiatric Patients

Even before the publication of the Stanford revision of Binet's test, interest in the application of mental tests in psychosis had already begun. One of the earliest examples of this trend is reported in an article by Hart and Spearman on mental tests of dementia (1914). However, subsequent to the publication of Terman's standardized version of the Binet, a small trickle of researches on the application of intelligence tests to a variety of psychopathological conditions had expanded into a fairly broad stream by the twenties and thirties. At first some interest centered upon the study of the "effects" of mental disorder on the MA and IQ, despite the fact that the SB had not been standardized on adults. Implicit in this approach was the notion of deterioration, especially in brain damage and in what was called in those days "dementia praecox." Essentially it was a quest for objective psychometric substantiation of the clinical psychiatric impressions regarding the inefficiency and deficit of mental functioning in the psychoses. Also, psychiatrists and psychologists began to have some doubts about the irreversibility of deterioration in the Kraepelinian category of dementia praecox. New, objective measures for the assessment of intellectual functioning and its breakdown were welcome.

Scatter. An early observation by Binet (Wells, 1927) that psychotic individuals and, especially, chronic alcoholics "scatter" their passes and failures on the SB over a larger number of year levels than feebleminded subjects has stimulated a considerable amount of systematic study and observation. This "unevenness in mental functioning" in mental disorder and deterioration has intrigued and interested psychologists for the past half century. A number of studies have, in fact, shown that the performance of patients with the SB spreads over a wide range of mental age levels. This phenomenon was quite consistent with extant notions about deterioration in mental disorder and selective effects of psychosis on different mental function. Pressey and Cole (1918) were among the first to devise quantitative indices of scatter, beyond the mere counting of the number of age levels passed, based on a weighting system of passes and failures relative to the distance of an individual's computed mental age. Wells (1927), however, in his pioneering volume *Mental Tests in Clinical Practice,* is rather cautious about the use of scatter diagnostically: "The scatter is a minor symptom only and must be taken with reference to other facts in the case." He also observes that scatter is frequently noted in normal children and, therefore, is questionable as a sign of pathology. According to him, the situation with psychotic adults is different: "Scattering over five or more years levels . . . may fairly raise the question of organic or toxic involvement." Yet Wells admonishes: "Don't think that 'scatter' is always pathological."

In one section of his extensive review of experimental studies with disordered persons, J. McV. Hunt (1936) has discussed some thirty publications (more than twenty on scatter) which were concerned with scatter and psychometric evaluation of mental patients. The conclusions of the reviewer are that, in general, psychoses involve some loss of intellectual efficiency, with the greatest loss noted in cases with damage to the central nervous system. Moreover, the studies with the intelligence tests also show what appears to be a selective deficit in function, especially on tasks involving "the most self-government or control, in the so-called functional disorders." Vocabulary emerges as relatively invulnerable to the effect of mental disorder and is defended as a base level for measuring functioning loss or inefficiency. Intelligence tests are severely criticized by Hunt as being "exceedingly blunt instruments" for the purpose of research and as being dependent upon the vague concept of intelligence. Finally, he also raises the issue of the representativeness of patients' performance on the tests and the possible interference or involvement of a number of extratest factors. Thus, although Hunt does not support scatter explicitly as an index of psychosis, the general conclusions seem to be consonant with the empirical notion which is implicit in scatter, i.e., that of selective effects of mental disorder upon intellectual functions.

Two rather critical studies of the same period (Harris & Shakow, 1937; Harris & Shakow, 1938) have dealt a rather severe blow to the scatter hypothesis. The first of these publications, a review concerned with different measures of scatter, closes with predominantly negative conclusions. Scatter does not distinguish significantly between feebleminded, delinquent, neurotic, and normal children. Furthermore, scatter varies with age. This finding explained away some of the positive findings and ran counter to the prematurely optimistic statements regarding the diagnostic usefulness of indices of scatter. Another important criticism of scatter involves the failure of these investigations to employ normal adult control groups, especially when inferences with respect to abnormality and pathology are made.

The same authors (Harris & Shakow, 1938) tried to remedy some of the lacunae which they pointed out in the investigations of others. They compared the scatter of 154 schizophrenics, 138 adult delinquents, and 133 normal adults on the SB. The major conclusion is that "only mental age was found to be related in any considerable degree to amount of scatter." All other differences disappeared when mental age was held constant. Thus, scatter in psychopathology appeared to be no longer fact but artifact. The scatter hypothesis was "laid to rest." Subsequently, as we shall note, it arose again and became revived in different reincarnations.

Two large-scale studies of intellectual functioning in mental disorder, which contain relevant data with respect to scatter, have terminated what we called the "Stanford-Binet era." The first is a study of 500 cases of dementia praecox compared with over 300 normals (nurses and hospital employees) and several hundred patients in various nosological categories (Kendig & Richmond, 1940). Several aspects of the study have direct relevance to scatter, although scatter, as traditionally measured, occupies relatively little space in the publication. In the first place, they found that the dementia praecox group does not differ from the normals on scatter scores. The praecox group is more variable; therefore, the authors conclude: "Exceptionally high scores . . . should suggest the possibility of a functional disorder impairing the reliability of the examination, or some organic involvement. . . . " Second, this study involves what Jastak (1949) called an "intuitive factor analysis"—a rather novel approach. Whereas scatter represents a purely empirical approach, Kendig and Richmond dichotomized the SB subtests into "eductive" and "noneductive" categories, roughly following Spearman's "g" and "s" in an attempt to investigate the effects of dementia praecox on intellectual function. Their conclusions, however, indicate that their patients had difficulty with "tests demanding relatively great expenditure of attention and effort" regardless of whether they were classifiable as "g" or "s." This finding is quite similar to one reported by J. McV. Hunt (1936) and mentioned above. Finally, these investigators are impressed by an over-all lower level of intellectual functioning in dementia praecox as compared with normality and with other functional disorders (but not with organics, to whom they are superior). Thus, the selective effects hypothesis is seriously questioned by these results.

The second study (Roe & Shakow, 1942) is not especially centered on dementia praecox but deals with the broad spectrum of mental disorders found in state hospitals. Seventeen diagnostic categories were represented in the sample of 827 patients, whose SB performance was compared with that of the normal sample reported by Weisenburg, Roe, and McBride (1936). The patients were subdivided into "representative" and "nonrepresentative" categories, based on several criteria of cooperativeness during the examination; the over-all test results differed markedly in favor of the former. These investigators have also employed an intuitive factor analysis in the treatment of the SB data in the hope of obtaining some characteristic "profiles" of intellectual functioning in the several nosological categories. The SB items were classified into "learned material" (immediate and remote), "associative thinking" (immediate and sustained), and "conceptual thinking." In addition, a separate analysis on the basis of age (rather than diagnosis) was also made. Although characteristic and unique profiles for the diagnostic categories were not obtained, some generalizations about the effects of mental disorder on intellectual function were warranted. The authors suggest some selectivity in the type of tests affected and postulate a specific sequence of test vulnerability from the most to the least affected. "Essentially it is this: (1) conceptual thinking; (2) immediate learning; (3) sustained associative thinking, immediate associative thinking, vocabulary; (4) old learning." It is worth noting that the authors also conclude that inattention is an important factor in lowering patients' test scores, although it cannot account for the magnitude of intellectual loss apparent in the organotoxic psychoses as well as in unclassified and hebephrenic cases of dementia praecox.

Measures of deterioration: constancy of vocabulary. Since tests of deterioration are a direct outgrowth of intelligence tests and of some of the data obtained with them, some coverage of such diagnostic devices is in order. The findings, though not entirely uncontested, that vocabulary remains relatively intact in mental disorder have led Babcock (1930) to devise a test of mental deterioration based on this principle. Babcock utilized the Stanford-Binet vocabulary to estimate the mental age of her subjects. In addition, a series of short tests including learning, motor, and memory tasks served as a basis for determining a comparable functional level. The discrepancy between the constant and "invulnerable" vocabulary level and the level of functioning based on more than twenty timed subtests allegedly vulnerable to brain damage, toxic disorders, and dementia praecox yielded an efficiency index. Babcock's measure of deterioration is, as Rapaport (1945) pointed out, essentially a form of scatter analysis. High negative indices of efficiency (vocabulary greater than the mean of the other tests) were obtained by the originator of the method (Babcock, 1930), especially with organic brain disorder. These results were confirmed by others. With respect to the functional psychoses, the results are contradictory. Of the two studies mentioned in the previous section, the one by Kendig and Richmond (1940) does not corroborate Babcock's findings regarding deterioration in dementia praecox. The other study (Roe & Shakow, 1942) gives some support to Babcock but raises a number of important questions about the test's rationale. Both these studies compared the SB MA with the vocabulary MA but did not employ the Babcock test itself. A short form of the Babcock test was also administered by Rapaport (1945) as part of his battery. Although he was not interested in the global index of efficiency, but in the patterns of subtests, his results give only partial support to Babcock. Rapaport's data report rather poor efficiency in depression, rather than in schizophrenia, which was considered by Babcock an essentially organic disorder (1933).

A rationale similar to that of Babcock's is involved in the "self-administering scale for measuring mental impairment and deterioration" devised by Shipley (1940). This is a much briefer method which employs the discrepancy between the level of vocabulary performance (multiple choice) and achievement on a concept-formation test as an index of psychological loss or deficit.

Most of the studies on Babcock's and Shipley's tests have been summarized by Hunt and Cofer (1944). They point out some of the weaknesses in this "scatter from vocabulary" rationale. The negative correlation between the "vocabulary SB, MA" discrepancy with mental age, the possibility (to some extent supported by evidence) that vocabulary itself may suffer as a consequence of mental disorder, and the low involvement of "self-direction" in the administration of the vocabulary are all indictments of the application of Babcock's rationale in the assessment of mental deficit or deterioration. We shall return to this topic as it figures in current diagnostic practice with intelligence tests.

Over-all Reduction of Intellectual Functioning

As a by-product of the extensive exploration of various pathological groups with the SB, two additional categories of information that have some relevance to diagnosis have emerged. First, the relative position of the several nosological categories with respect to mean (or median) IQ or MA has become known; second, although adequate SB data on large representative samples of normal adults were lacking, with the possible exception of those reported by Weisenburg et al. (1936), a comparison of the mean IQ of any nosological group with the expected normal average IQ of 100 gave an indication of relative impairment or deterioration. The latter notion carried along the assumption that the premorbid intelligence of the diagnostic groups was normally distributed and that the samples used in the investigations were representative of the particular diagnostic categories.

In general, the data reported in the literature tend to indicate that in the psychoneuroses and in the manic-depressive disorders there is no reduction in intellectual functioning. Over-all indices of intelligence such as IQ, MA, and vocabulary levels show that these groups do about as well as, or better than, the normals (Kendig & Richmond, 1940; Roe & Shakow, 1942). Dementia praecox is consistently reported to achieve levels below those obtained by normals or by the psychotic groups mentioned above. However, there are large differences and great variability among the several subcategories of this broader nosological category. There is pretty general agreement with respect to the hebephrenic subgroup being at the bottom of the intellectual ladder; the other subcategories tend to trade top places within the praecox group, depending on whose study one reads and, by implication, on the diagnostic conventions in the particular hospital from which the material was drawn. Persons with organic brain disorders and toxic disorders and hospitalized epileptics are reported to rate considerably below the praecox group as a whole.

Thus, at that point of development in the testing field some statements regarding over-all mental functioning of diagnostic groups could be made. The relative standing of the groups in terms of functioning level was roughly determined, and all psychotic states (with the possible exception of manic-depressive psychosis and "paranoid condition") were said to show some deficit, i.e., lower than average IQ. Needless to say, although these data were interesting in terms of general trends, they were not very useful in individual diagnosis.

Summary

Some major trends relative to the diagnostic use of intelligence tests (particularly the Stanford-Binet) may be discussed as a result of a quarter of a century of exploration and research:

1. Over-all indices of intelligence (IQ and MA) have proved useful in the classification of school pupils, as an aid in the diagnosis of feeblemindedness and in vocational guidance. They have also been employed with adult psychiatric populations and have shown an over-all intellectual lowering in most psychotic conditions, especially in organic disorders and, to a lesser extent, in dementia praecox.
2. A hypothesis of selective impairment in mental disorder has emerged. Several approaches to its assessment have developed:
   a. A number of measures of scatter did not succeed in differentiating considerably between disordered children and adults and normal ones.
   b. Discrepancy between vocabulary levels and levels of intelligenec based on a variety of other tasks (learning, memory, etc.) was found to be characteristic of many psychotic groups. With some notable exceptions, the evidence points to vocabularly as a function relatively unaffected by mental disorder; it may, therefore, serve as an index of "potential" or premorbid intelligence.
   c. Some promise seems to be reflected in the method of grouping test items logically and in the attempt to evolve characteristic "profiles" of intellectual functioning based on such "intuitive

factor analysis." This goes beyond the purely empirical scatter analysis.

3. "Nonintellective" factors such as attention, motivation, and cooperation become inextricably involved in the testing and, consequently, in the diagnostic process. Some concern with partialing out these elements in an attempt to determine degree of impairment, if any, was evidenced.
4. Most of the studies of this period were limited to an instrument standardized on children (Stanford-Binet), did not employ adequate normal adult control groups, did not take the age factor into consideration, did not deal sufficiently with the representativeness of patient samples, and had to struggle with an omnibus type of test without known functional unities within the multitude of tasks that constitute it.

Although we can point to precious few findings of a positive nature, the accumulated experience of clinicians and investigators and some of the pioneering research efforts gave some direction to the work in the decades that followed and contributed to the vigilance of the workers in this field.

WECHSLER'S TESTS

In a sense, a new era in diagnostic psychological testing was ushered in by the publication of the Wechsler-Bellevue scale (Wechsler, 1939). It filled a need for which the old and the, by then, Revised Stanford-Binet (Terman & Merrill, 1937) were inadequate. The WB was standardized on adults, with separate norms for various age levels, from adolescence to senescence. Its contents are more interesting and appropriate to adults as compared with the SB, and it is a point scale rather than an omnibus test, which permits ready comparison between subjects and within subjects of a number of different functions or abilities. Moreover, from the very start, Wechsler introduced his test not only as a psychometric instrument but as a clinicodiagnostic device as well. Wechsler's volumes (1939; 1944; 1958) are replete with suggestions for more extensive use of the test's results in individual and differential diagnosis.

The original WB acquired a companion, in the shape of an alternative or parallel form, some years later (Wechsler, 1946). Still later, the test was thoroughly revised and restandardized in response to needs and to criticisms expressed of the earlier forms of the test (Wechsler, 1955; Wechsler, 1958). Thus, the most up-to-date form of the test is the Wechsler Adult Intelligence Scale, or the WAIS, as it is popularly called. In addition, a downward extension of the WB, the Wechsler Intelligence Scale for Children (WISC), was published during the same period (1949). The bulk of diagnostic testing with children and especially with adults and most of the research have been done with these instruments for more than twenty years. A brief survey of the accumulated research and practice with these tests is essential for an understanding of present-day diagnostic use of intelligence tests.

Since 1939 extensive reviews of research with the WB (Rabin, 1945; Watson, 1946) and with the other scales for adults (Guertin, Frank, & Rabin, 1956; Guertin, Rabin, Frank, & Ladd, 1962; Rabin & Guertin, 1951) as well as those for children (Littell, 1960) appeared in the literature. They summarize literally hundreds of studies and research reports, some of them trivial and others of greater significance. We shall be particularly concerned, in the following paragraphs, with the research methods and findings that relate to diagnosis and less concerned with the technical and psychometric aspects of the instruments.

The WB and Its Successors as Clinical Instruments

That an intelligence test could produce an index of relative ability, such as the IQ, which can be used in practical, applied situations requiring such assessment, there is no longer any doubt. Nearly a quarter of a century of experience with the SB had prepared the ground for Wechsler's tests (1939). An additional advantage exploited by Wechsler was the attempts at more extended use of intelligence tests in the area of diagnosis of personality and psychopathology that were made during the previous decades. Thus, an early presentation of the WB manual contains a special chapter on diagnostic and clinical features of the test (Wechsler, 1944). In this chapter the author communicates some of his impressions of, and clinical experiences with, the test in different nosological groupings. Essentially he proposes three methods for the diagnostic use of the WB. First is the "verbal-performance discrepancy." He suggests, for example, that organic brain disease, psychoses, and psychoneuroses are the clinical groups which score higher on the verbal tests of the WB. The discrepancy is in the opposite direction in psychopaths and mental defectives. Second, Wechsler suggests a rule of thumb for a crude scatter analysis by indicating that a difference of over two points between any weighted score of a subtest and the mean subtest score is significant. Then he proceeds to tabulate the characteristics of the performance patterns of the five diagnostic groups (organic brain disease, schizophrenia, psychopathic personality, neurotics, and mental deficients) on the WB. Here the analysis is down to the subtest level; e.g., in schizophrenia, Information is "good," Vocabulary is "high," and Arithmetic is "poor." Finally, following some illustrative case material, the author also suggests some qualitative analysis of the responses to individual test items—independently of the classification of correctness and incorrectness. Thus, one may obtain some hints regarding psychopathy from the way the patient handles some Comprehension items or obtain schizophrenic bizarreness in response to the Information questions, etc.

Another issue to which Wechsler addresses himself earlier in his book is the old problem of mental impairment, deficit, or deterioration. Here he assumes that the process of "normal deterioration" due to aging is similar to that found in the more severe psychiatric disorders. Thus, he tentatively suggests a dichotomy, which later becomes converted into a ratio of tests which "hold up with age" and those which do not. Among the former are, of course, Information, Vocabulary, etc.; among the latter are Digits (forward and backward), Digit Symbol, etc. We can readily recognize the "old learning" versus "new learning" in these subtests—echoes of Babcock and others of the earlier Stanford-Binet era.

Needless to say, the clinicoempirical statements about the typical functioning of various diagnostic groups on the WB did not remain unchecked. Many investigators wished to put some of these observations on a much firmer and more objective basis. Results of research with various patterns of test variability such as scatter, deterioration ratios, etc., are dealt with in the next two sections; in closing the present one, however, we shall briefly review a more up-to-date series of suggestions regarding the clinical applications of the WAIS (Wechsler, 1958) which to some degree bear the marks of interim criticisms and research findings.

The space allotted to the nonpsychometric aspects of the WAIS has expanded markedly in the latest edition (1958) of Wechsler's book. Part III of the volume deals entirely with diagnostic and practical applications of the test. Here we have a topical coverage, similar to that in the previous volume, and a reiteration of some of the clinical opinions mentioned above. Thus, in most mental disorders, the performance functions are more impaired than the verbal ones. In young delinquents and adolescent psychopaths, the performance level is higher than the verbal level; moreover, a modification of the rule-of-thumb pattern is again presented for five diagnostic syndromes. With respect to the meaning of discrepancies (e.g., verbal greater than performance) and the relatively elevated or depressed achievement on WAIS individual subtests by the several diagnostic groups, there is a recognition that "greater than" or "high," "low," and similar terms are insufficient unless backed by numbers whose probability of occurrence by chance alone is determined. We find, for example, that a V-P discrepancy of 15 points occurs 13 times out of 100 in a normal population. The diagnostic impulse may be thus tempered by available statistical information.

In addition to the more detailed treatment of clinicodiagnostic issues by Wechsler—a sign of the times—a more extensive presentation of case material illustrating the use of intelligence test materials qualitatively as well as quantitatively is also included. In the instance of qualitative interpretation of test responses, which makes Wechsler somewhat uneasy ("examiner is treading on thin ice"), there is the recognition of a considerable shift in emphasis in intelligence testing, which began in the 1940s, from the *test* to the *tester*, from the "objective" indices which summarize "behavior" to more intuitive and "private" interpretation by the examiner of test responses which are not readily and objectively comparable to available standards. Thus the examiner-interpreter becomes an important instrument for the collection of qualitative data and unique responses, using his accumulated clinical norms as part of this idiographic approach. Essentially, therefore, we note that the trend is away from the strictly nomothetic use of intelligence tests toward a combined approach of nomothetic findings with idiographic data interpretation.

We shall now turn to a brief treatment of the considerable research activity with Wechsler's tests that has been flourishing for nearly a quarter of a century. Our major concern will not be with the studies that test the instruments from the strictly psychometric viewpoint but with the others that attempt to offer a sounder scientific basis for psychodiagnosis via intelligence tests.

The Study of Scatter Revisited

It was quite natural for the waning interest in the scatter and diagnostic use of intelligence to obtain a new lease on life when the WB was published. This test, a points scale which was not subject to the many shortcomings of the omnibus-type Binet tests, standardized on adults and controlled for age, immediately became a popular research as well as a clinical tool. In addition to a purely empirical trend which, in fact, explored "patterns" of mental functioning in a variety of disorders, Wechsler's own impressions and a residue of hypotheses from the Stanford-Binet era came in for detailed study and scrutiny.

More than fifty publications on the new test were covered in the first (Rabin, 1945) and the supplementary (Watson, 1946) reviews. As mentioned earlier, subsequent reviews summarized nearly five hundred additional studies with the several forms of Wechsler's test, bringing the research up to date through 1961.

The study of scatter was facilitated by the very structure of the test. During that period, scatter and "pattern" became undifferentiated as far as common use of the terms is concerned (Rapaport, 1945). The early studies of scatter (or test patterns) with a number of nosological groups have succeeded in obtaining *group* differences; they were, however, inadequate for *individual* diagnosis (Rabin, 1945). Despite a great deal of work during the subsequent years, the utility of scatter did not become greater; its position became weaker because of the array of contradictory findings in the literature.

An important landmark in the development of diagnostic use of intelligence tests was the publication of Rapaport's *Diagnostic Psychological Testing* (1945). Three measures of scatter were used with 217 patients (in 19 categories) and 54 normal controls: vocabulary scatter, which consists of the difference between each subtest score and the weighted score on the Vocabulary, the algebraic sum of these deviations being called "composite vocabulary scatter"; mean scatter, which refers to the "difference between any subtest score and the average of all the subtest scores, excluding the scores of the Digit Span and Arithmetic subtests"; and the modified mean scatter, which refers to the differences between any one verbal or performance subtest and the mean of the remaining subtest scores in the verbal and performance scales, respectively. There are many additional details in these scatter analyses which are not used as sole indices for diagnosis but as additional *aids* in the more complete analysis of the test's findings. These findings include verbal versus performance achievement (special selections within each scale being made on the basis of a "logical" analysis of unity in meaning) and intrasubtest scatter, i.e., the inconsistency of passes and failures in relation to the level of difficulty of items on the test.

The work of Rapaport and his associates (1945), although of great influence in the development of clinical psychology in general and in the diagnostic application of intelligence tests in particular, suffered from many flaws. Some of the published criticisms are summarized elsewhere (Rabin & Guertin, 1951). Suffice it to say that the "control" group of the study was inadequate (there was a failure to control age, sex, socioeconomic status, etc.); the numbers in each clinical group were too small; the measures of scatter could not be used in individual diagnosis; there was no representation of some common diagnostic categories in the patient sample; unusual diagnostic categories were used, which makes replication difficult; and so on. Wittenborn's (1949) statistical reanalysis of the Rapaport test score patterns (scatter) for the different diagnostic groups led him to conclude that the scatter pattern is not any more useful than a simple inspection method of conspicuous successes and failures as a psychometric supplement to diagnosis.

Perhaps the most outstanding contribution of the Menninger research (Rapaport, 1945) is the detailed psychological analysis of the rationale of Wechsler's subtests rather than the production of reliable and valid quantitative psychometric patterns for the purposes of psychodiagnosis. Moreover, the almost simultaneous attempt to relate content to personality structure and dynamics—though not quantified and, perhaps, unquantifiable—has contributed markedly to the clinical, if not to the psychometric, application of intelligence tests to diagnosis (Schafer, 1948). This represents, in part, a shift from the instrument to the clinician, the interpreter and the integrator of information in the diagnostic process.

As sole diagnostic indicators that stand alone, the test patterns and scatter profiles have not been successful. The tremendous amount of research activity with contradictory findings that led nowhere prompted the reviewers (Rabin & Guertin, 1951) to remark rather pessimistically: "The scatter mountain gave birth to a mouse." This remains true as far as individual diagnosis is concerned, although successful group differentiation by means of scatter is possible and will be discussed subsequently. The reviews of later research with the WB, the WB I, and the WAIS (Guertin et al., 1956; Guertin et al., 1962) do not report any marked changes in the utility of scatter as a diagnostic indicator. Research in the area has diminished; yet a few hardy faithfuls are still pursuing the matter doggedly. The troublesome problem of the criterion—the psychiatric syndrome and nosology—remains an important stumbling block on the path of the study of the relationships between cognitive processes and personality.

Relatively few scatter studies with the WISC (Wechsler, 1949) have been reported (Littell, 1960). Perhaps the evidence concerning the dissimilarity of profiles on the WISC to those on the WB (Delattre & Cole, 1952) discouraged investigators from pursuing the matter. Possibly the fact that clear-cut diagnostic categories in children are even harder to come by than those in adults served as a further deterrent.

The Issue of Deterioration

Intellectual impairment which need not have the implications of irreversibility that the term "deterioration" often carries with it may be studied in two ways—from the longitudinal viewpoint and with the cross-sectional–inferential method. The longitudinal approach involves the comparison of indices of intellectual functioning, such as the IQ, obtained before and after the onset of mental disorder, particularly psychosis. Data of this type are hard to come by but are valuable in terms of our understanding of the relationship between mental disorder and intelligence (Rappaport & Webb, 1950).

Most of the studies available, however, are of the second type, involving speculation and inference regarding premorbid intellectual functioning from cross-sectional material which does not extend along the temporal dimension. This approach involves assumptions concerning the representativeness of the pertinent samples or about the relative vulnerability of certain functions to the psychotic process (e.g., vocabulary as a measure of premorbid intelligence).

Most large-scale studies of mental disorder do report a "lowering" of IQ in their samples of psychiatric patients. The studies frequently include normal controls; however, the representativeness of the abnormal as well as of the normal samples is often in doubt. The earlier studies employ hospital personnel for the purposes of normal controls, a procedure of doubtful validity (e.g., Kendig & Richmond, 1940).

In an unpublished study of 1,000 consecutive admissions to a state hospital, this author (Rabin, 1947) reports WB findings on 21 diagnostic categories. The mean IQs for the various categories are quite similar to those reported in earlier studies (Kendig & Richmond, 1940; Roe & Shakow, 1942); the relative positions of the various disorders on the IQ scale are also similar. Our concern at this point, however, is the question of the relationship between IQ and the presence of psychosis.

Since these 1,000 admissions to the hospital, which was the only one in the state, represent *all* the patients admitted during a two-year period, they may be considered a total and, therefore, a representative sample of patients. This patient sample is quite similar, with respect to education and socioeconomic background, to the state's adult population as reported in the United States census figures. The mean WB IQ of the 1,000 patients is 91.4—significantly below an assumed mean IQ of 100 for the entire population. Moreover, the nonpsychotic groups represented (neurosis, psychopathy, alcoholism, etc.) achieved a mean IQ of 94.4; the schizophrenic group (326 cases), a mean IQ of 88.7; and all other psychoses, a mean IQ of 90.6. Thus, it appears that psychosis, and especially schizophrenia, represents a lowering of IQ or impairment of intellectual level. This, of course, depends upon the assumption of the normality of the distribution of intelligence, in this sample, in the premorbid state. To a degree, the educational levels achieved and the socioeconomic backgrounds justify such an assumption. These results are, in general, consonant with the conclusions offered by Payne (1961), who summarized, in his extensive review, a large number of studies published during the past several decades.

The next approach to the problem of impairment or psychological deficit is much more complicated, as we have already seen, for it involves the assumption of differential effects of mental disorder upon intellectual functions. Although the notion of intellectual deficit is related to scatter, the former hypothesizes loss, whereas the latter need not necessarily imply it; it may refer to the uniqueness of the distribution of mental functions that corresponds to different mental disorders. This uniqueness may or may not carry with it the assumption of deficit or loss.

Earlier work (Babcock, 1930; Babcock, 1933) considered vocabulary to be a baseline (original intelligence) to which performance on a variety of other functions was compared; the discrepancy served as an index of deterioration. As noted above, Wechsler suggested a broader base, i.e., the discrepancy (actually the ratio) between tests which "hold up" and those which "do not hold up" (with age). The most recent publication (Wechsler, 1958) offers the same rationale, with the substitution of some subtests. The suggested "deterioration quotient" consists of the ratio of the difference between the "hold" and "don't-hold" subtests to the "hold" tests. The normal ideal score should, of course, approach zero; the data presented by Wechsler actually indicate such mean scores at the different age levels of the standardization population.

Wechsler's (1944) Mental Deterioration Index (MDI), the predecessor of the more recent deterioration quotient, was employed in a sizable number of studies of organic patients. Some of them reported considerable success with the MDI as a diagnostic indicator of organicity; high percentages of patients with organic lesions were identified by means of this index (Rabin & Guertin, 1951). However, the reviewers point to the inadequacy of the MDI in differentiating organics from functional disorders and to the general problem of false negatives and false positives—not unlike the one evident with scatter as well. A more general criticism raised is concerned with the concept of "organicity" as such. This indiscriminate combination of a variety of brain-damaged cases, differing in acuteness, chronicity, localization, and premorbid personality makeup, into a single category is hardly justified. It was not until recently that some headway in the more precise description and identification of organic samples was made (Reitan, 1955; Reitan, 1962).

A later review (Guertin et al., 1956) is even more pessimistic about the MDI as a diagnostic method: "Yet there is uniform agreement that the MDI was not effective with those samples employed." Other attempts at devising new ratios or profiles for the diagnosis of "organicity" have not fared any better. The general discrepancy between the Verbal and Performance scale IQs (in favor of the former) is apparently about as effective a measure for the diagnostic purposes of organicity as the special measures devised. Research findings with the deterioration quotient (Wechsler, 1958) have not contributed to the greater refinement of the diagnosis of deterioration (Guertin et al., 1962) with the possible important exception of Reitan's (1955) results. According to this study, patients with lesions in the left hemisphere do poorly on verbal tests as compared with performance subtests; the opposite is true with those whose right hemisphere is affected. Thus we have a further indication of the necessity for more precise definition of the neuroanatomic damage for which corresponding indices of intellectual deficit are sought.

Summary

1. Wechsler's tests have stimulated a revival of interest in psychometric indices as an aid in differential diagnosis. The research activity is classifiable under two rubrics —scatter and measures of deterioration.
2. A number of test patterns and measures of interest scatter characteristic of a variety of nosological categories have been

proposed. The findings with different measures of scatter are at best contradictory and inconclusive.

3. Indices of deficit or deterioration tend to share a fate similar to that of scatter. Although Wechsler's deterioration ratios or quotients tend to characterize large percentages of "organic" samples, the overlap with groups of functional psychotics is considerable. Some evidence, however, of an over-all reduction in IQ in psychotic samples is available and is supported by a number of studies.
4. There emerged two additional approaches to the interpretation of test data:
   a. The *intratest* scatter which is made possible in the Wechsler type of point scales and the interpretation of the ordinal relationship of passes and fails within the same subtest.
   b. The qualitative and "projective" interpretation of the content of responses, which is not readily quantifiable and which depends greatly upon the clinician-interpreter.
5. There developed a shift in emphasis in diagnostic testing from the psychometric instrument—the test—to the human instrument—the tester.

VARIETIES OF INTELLIGENCE TESTS

In the preceding pages the discussion was focused primarily upon two groups of instruments, the Binet tests and the Wechsler scales. The prominence of the former is determined by history, and the importance of the latter is due to more recent popularity, both in research work and in clinical application. Yet there are numerous other tests (Buros, 1959) of intelligence which are being employed for the purposes of diagnosis. Their detailed treatment, however, must be curtailed, for the extrapsychometric research data available concerning them are rather limited.

Tests of the abilities and development of infants cannot be called intelligence tests, strictly speaking, for their contents are to a large degree unlike the material found in the ordinary intelligence tests. Yet these methods are designed for the appraisal of the development of abilities which presumably underlie intelligence and intellectual development (Gesell & Armatruda 1941). Cattell's test (1940), which is a downward extension of the Stanford-Binet, is considered to be an intelligence test by its author. Similar techniques which depend a good deal upon the detailed observation of infants are concerned more with "developmental analysis." A more recent method for the assessment of the abilities of infants (Griffiths, 1954) yields a "general quotient" which is derived by means of the traditional method, e.g., by dividing the MA by the CA of the child.

Since Griffiths's scale is composed of five different components (locomotor, personal-social, hearing and speech, hand and eye development, and performance), an analysis of "profiles," not unlike that discussed in connection with the WB, is possible. The author sees "clinical implications" in the relative retardation of the child (or advancement) on one of the subscales as compared with the remaining ones. Inspection of the developmental profiles does indeed permit an evaluation of special physical or mental handicaps in early development which is useful to the clinician. No research, however, is available on these clinical implications. Infant scales are generally crude instruments of low predictive potential; their results may be considered of value in describing the current developmental stage of the normal infant or the abnormal infant.

Since the standard intelligence tests are primarily verbal in nature, there is some value, in terms of over-all assessment of intelligence, in the employment of standardized performance tests. Especially with cases from whom verbal responsiveness, because of background, may be a poor indicator of ability potential, the well-standardized performance test is essential. Instruments such as the Arthur Point Scale of Performance Tests (1943) and the Porteus mazes (1959) are good examples of performance tests in frequent use. With the exception of the last-mentioned test, which is concerned with a special aspect of intelligence ("foresight") and with qualitative observation of details of performance, most other tests often used have not been subjected to detailed analysis of a qualitative nature. Their extra-IQ usefulness has not been reported extensively; consequently, their major diagnostic contribution is in terms of indices of "general intelligence" or in terms of discrepancies with other tests of general intelligence which point to some particular "intertest scatter." This inconsistency between different scales of intelligence and the possible meaning of such differences between tests as a diagnostic index will be considered in a later section of this chapter.

CURRENT DIAGNOSTIC USE OF INTELLIGENCE TESTS

Thus far we have been concerned with several lines of research on a few selected tests of intelligence. The selection was determined by two criteria—the popularity, or frequency of use, of those tests in clinical practice and the range of investigation into their usefulness as diagnostic tools in addition to their yielding numerical indices of general intellectual functioning (i.e., IQ and MA). Now an attempt will be made to survey the extent and degrees of involvement of intelligence tests in the diagnostic study of individuals. What the clinician actually *does,* how he *operates* when he applies intelligence tests for diagnostic purposes, is our chief concern in this context.

Intelligence tests present standard situations and make standard demands upon the testee. Most clinicians are interested, in the first place, in the extratest behavior of the individual being tested, in his behavior which is a reaction to the test situation. One may ask to what extent such a situation differs from *any* test situation. The answer would be that in this situation, in which correct or incorrect responses are expected to a structured instrument, the arousal of anxiety and defensiveness may be considerable (Rapaport, 1945). The examiner's job is to evaluate the behavior and assess the anxiety as a possible factor influencing test results. Evidence to this effect, of an objective nature, is currently available (Sarason, Davidson, Lightfall, Waite, & Ruebush, 1960).

In addition to the testing situation itself, tests of intelligence may differ with respect to the potency of their stimuli in arousing emotionally loaded associations. Thus we are told that the Raven matrices, which consist of abstract designs, are less likely than tests such as the WISC or the SB, which contain references to school, family, fighting, etc. (Ross, 1959) to have a disrupting effect on intellectual functioning. Observation of differences in reaction to the stimulus materials offers no inconsequential diagnostic information.

The opportunity to observe a sample of behavior under standard conditions is also offered by tests of functions other than intelligence. The "interaction" with the examiner is characteristic of all individual testing situations. The demands of intelligence tests—"structured, organized responses" (Garner, 1954)—may affect persons in different ways; e.g., some may feel threatened, some may use the opportunity to "exhibit their wares" in an excessively affable and voluble manner, while still others may seriously strive to be precise, accurate, and "task-oriented."

Essentially the foregoing observations are not easily systematized, organized, or, certainly, quantified. The richness of materials of a diagnostic value that are obtained from the interaction depends on the experience, sensitivity, and perspicacity of the clinician and his theoretical orientation and sophistication.

We shall now turn to the types of evidence, to be used for diagnostic purposes, which are produced in response to the tests themselves. Several levels in the application of intelligence tests may be discerned. These levels will be presented more or less in order of increasing demands upon inference and interpretation; i.e., they will demonstrate the shift from the test to the tester. Yet full diagnostic utilization of intelligence tests penetrates through all levels. The test, as well as the tester, is involved in the final product—the interpretation of personality and the shorthand diagnostic inference.

Uses of Numerical Indices of Intellectual Functioning: Level I

Intelligence tests and the numerical index of intelligence, the IQ, became strongly entrenched in applied psychology. The IQ has lost considerable status since the late 1930s, when a good deal of data had begun to accumulate regarding its inconstancy, its susceptibility to environmental changes (McNemar, 1940; Wellman, Skeels, & Skodak, 1940), and its dependency on social and cultural status (Eells, Davis, Havighurst, Herrick, & Tyler, 1951). This "dethronement" of the IQ as an infallible predictor of intelligence did not result in doing away with it altogether. The additional information concerning external effects upon the measured IQ as well as concerning the saltatory aspects of mental growth and development (Bayley, 1955) increased the understanding of its nature and helped qualify and control its application in classification and diagnosis. The IQ, as we shall see, remains a useful index of current mental functioning, though its potency as a predictor may, occasionally, because of special circumstances, be in doubt. Users of intelligence tests for more extensive diagnostic purposes have at times—because of their enthusiasm for, and concern with, the nonintellective factors elicited by them—neglected the index which offers information about the individual's intellectual achievement as compared with that of his peers.

Some of the old applications of the IQ, dating back to the old SB period, are still in force. The discrepancy between the level of intelligence and that of school achievement is one of the important symptoms and diagnostic indicators of emotional disturbance in the school and in the child guidance clinic. Such discrepancies indicate the need for further diagnosis and for remedial work and therapy. Thus, the IQ is often considered the starting point in the diagnostic process—at the first, perhaps most superficial, level.

Another time-honored use of the IQ is in the diagnosis of mental deficiency or retardation. In the earlier years, the IQ was often misused in the diagnosis of mental deficiency, for it was employed as the *sole datum* for the purpose rather than in conjunction with a number of other important etiological and behavioral-personality indices (Sarason, 1959). As noted above, the inconstancy of the IQ and its depression by low socioeconomic status, as well as by inadequate cooperation on the part of the testee, have placed it under considerable jeopardy as a predictor of later mental status. Studies, such as those of Muench (1944), which illustrate dramatically the upward changes in IQ and the adequate social adjustment of adults who eighteen years earlier were diagnosed as defective, on the basis of IQs alone, have clearly demonstrated the need for additional criteria in diagnosis and prognosis. As in the case of recommendations for adoption with infant development scales (Carter & Bowles, 1948), several test administrations which yield adequate consistency over a period of time make the IQ a sounder index and better predictor. Repeated administrations for the purposes of diagnosis of mental retardation would also tend to decrease the possibility of the IQ representing only one of the plateaus (or peaks) (Bayley, 1955) in the child's developmental process.

Still another application of the IQ is in the diagnosis of vocational fitness in counseling, guidance, and rehabilitation. Wechsler (1958) illustrates briefly the application of the IQ in such situations. Available information about the median and ranges of IQs in various occupations and occupational categories (Super, 1949) serves as a framework for the utilization of a global index of abilities represented by the IQ.

Therapeutic processes vary in the degree of verbal ability and general intelligence they require of the patient. Intellectually dull individuals are not very suitable subjects for psychoanalytic or similar types of therapy in which a premium is placed on verbalization, abstraction, and conceptualization. The IQ, therefore, can offer aid in the decision on the therapeutic approach. There are data available (Hiler, 1958) about the relationship between IQ and continuation in therapy. Hiler's findings indicate that patients who remained in therapy (as compared with those who did not) "scored significantly higher in IQ," especially on the Verbal scales of the WB test.

Finally, the IQ has also been found to be a fairly good barometer and predictor of improvement of psychiatric patients. Stotsky (1952) predicted that remitting schizophrenics score higher on the WB than nonremitting ones. This prediction was borne out by the data. Similarly, WB performance of remitting alcoholics turned out to be higher than that of nonremitting alcoholics (Plumeau, Machover, & Puzzo, 1960), and improvement of hospitalized children was reflected in upward changes in IQ (Hiler & Nesvig, 1961). Thus, it would appear that although not diagnostic or predictive in individual cases, fairly high IQs are more compatible with improvement and remission. Although the IQ is, in this instance, a minimal bit of information, it is usable diagnostically and prognostically. Related to the above is some evidence concerning "intelligence test performance and the delay function of the ego" (Spivak, Levine, & Sprigle, 1959). The authors of this study have shown a positive relationship between measures of ego delay functions and IQ. By inference, higher IQs in remitting schizophrenics, alcoholics, and improved children in a psychiatric hospital indicate greater "ego strength," at least as far as the delay function is concerned. The high IQ, therefore, may be indicative of relative intactness of ego and, dynamically speaking, may be of importance in the over-all personality diagnosis.

In summary, then, the IQ is a useful index for diagnostic and prognostic purposes in a number of situations; it is more useful in some instances than in others. Its greatest usefulness is in the diagnosis of retardation and school difficulties as well as with problems of vocational guidance and rehabilitation. Repeated examination in these situations, where a major part of the decisions depend upon the IQ, is highly desirable in view of the quotient's instability. To a lesser extent, as a *first level* of information and as a part of more detailed analysis of additional test information, the IQ is useful in the determination of some aspects of ego functioning, which is, in turn, related to persistence in therapy, improvement, and remission of mental disorder.

Application of Indices of Intertest Variability: Level II

At the second level of the diagnostic use of intelligence tests are the various numerical indices that deal with differential functioning. Historically this was the sort of test analysis that interested clinician-investigators for half a century. Measures of scatter, profiles, deterioration, ratios, and quotients all belong to this category. As we indicated above, the literature is far from reporting unequivocal results with respect to these indices. The findings with various nosological groups are inconsistent, and, at best, group differentiation, rather than individual diagnosis, is made feasible by these measures. Yet if these indices are considered to be but *one component* of the diagnostic process, their usefulness to the clinician is undeniable. The work of Rapaport (1945), Schafer (1948), Wechsler (1958), and others illustrates this point. We shall therefore proceed with a presentation of a series of indices and then consider their occurrence in a variety of diagnostic categories.

Common indices. No attempt will be made to catalogue all combinations and permutations of tests or WB subtests that have been reported in the literature to be effective indices in differential diagnosis. A few of the more common ones or more popular ones, with special reference to Wechsler's tests, will be listed before discussing some specific diagnostic categories.

First, the discrepancy between the verbal and performance scale scores on the WB or WAIS is one of the more useful indices. Discrepancies of moderate size occur in normal people, perhaps in relation to vocational interest or practice. A discrepancy of 20 points, however, would occur only 2 times in 100 (Wechsler, 1958) and should therefore be considered to be a significant deviation. Wechsler suggests 15 points as a useful number diagnostically. The discrepancy, of course, can be in either direction—performance greater than verbal, and vice versa. Each index will be dealt with subsequently in connection with the diagnostic categories.

Second, a most widely used measure of scatter is that of the average deviation score of the subtests from the mean of all the subtests. It is therefore an over-all measure of interest variability. This approach is similar to some of the quantitative measures of scatter on the SB, discussed in an earlier section.

Third, the deterioration quotient or the mental deterioration index (Wechsler, 1944) refers to the ratio of the difference between the "hold" and "don't hold" tests to the "hold." This particular measure of deficit is, as we shall see, applicable to a number of disorders.

Fourth is the inspectional method of profiles of test distribution, including breadth of range of weighted scores. This is not, strictly speaking, a quantitative "index," for calculations are not actually made; it is a variant of scatter, for the "high" and "low" scores are compared with available data on various diagnostic groupings. A tabulation of such data was published by Wechsler (1958). A somewhat thorny question in this connection is what is "high" and what is "low" in the context of a particular profile, since the standardization subjects' performance does not produce a straight-line profile. Information on the sizes of statistically significant differences between pairs of subtests is available (Field, 1960; Wechsler, 1958; and others).

Diagnostic Categories

"A diagnostic conclusion generally involves subscription to a nosological scheme" (Schafer, 1948). Imperfect as the current diagnostic categories, inherited from psychiatry, are, they are the ones with which the psychologist has to deal. Inferences from intelligence tests are drawn via parallelisms between test behavior and perrormance and the symptom clusters and attributed dynamics of the conventional categories.

In most conventional *psychoneurotic* categories, the verbal score is higher than the performance. The obsessive-compulsive is overideational, intellectualizing, and highly verbal; performance achievement tends to be low by comparison. Performance subtests and Digits tend to be most affected in anxiety states; verbal tests appear higher by comparison. In hysteria, however, the reverse seems to be true, especially because of the effects of repression (due to associations) on Information and other verbal tests (Rapaport, 1945; Schafer, 1948). These trends are seriously questioned, however (Gurvitz, 1951).

The diagnosis of *psychopathic personality* has created a good deal of controversy. The performance-greater-than-verbal IQ pattern has been suggested (Wechsler, 1958) and confirmed in several studies and has been rejected by others (Guertin et al., 1962). Since the conflicting results may be due to actual differences in the sampling (e.g., adult prisoners versus adolescent delinquents) and since the "psychopathic" criteria in the sample choices varied markedly, it is not surprising that the findings are inconsistent. Moreover, this is often a "wastebasket" category in psychiatry (Rabin, 1961), and it would therefore be surprising if any kind of consistent and unitary pattern of intellectual functioning were to be actually obtained.

As far as *depressive* states are concerned, one of the major findings reported (Rapaport, 1945) is the relatively low scores on the Performance scales. "We have repeatedly stressed that the severity of depression is closely paralleled by the extent of impairment on the performance subtest scores. . . ."

Gurvitz (1951) shows that Rapaport's conclusions regarding depression are unwarranted by his data. It is interesting to note that the affective disorders seem to be least researched as far as psychological instruments are concerned. The literature in this area is meager. It is "reasonable" that the psychomotor retardation in depression is liable to affect the timed subtests, in particular, of the performance scale.

Schizophrenia, the major diagnostic category, is the most heterogeneous as far as symptomatology is concerned. This state of affairs is also reflected in the inconsistency of the findings resulting from attempts to find diagnostic patterns via intelligence tests. The criteria for the diagnosis of schizophrenia are so diffuse and the test findings so variable that "The past seventeen years of research with the W-B psychometric patterns . . . have produced very little of a positive nature" (Rabin & King, 1958). The Verbal-greater-than-Performance pattern is also noted here (Rapaport, 1945); extreme variability (scatter) in subtests (Schafer, 1948) is another feature noted by clinicians. However, none of these have been satisfactorily confirmed by means of objective studies (Guertin et al., 1956). Cross-validation of signs and patterns, with new samples, rarely succeeded to produce results similar to those obtained with the original groups. Often, *group* differentiations between normals and schizophrenics are adequate; however, the patterns are inadequate for *individual* diagnosis. Clinicians use results of some studies in differential diagnosis, but any one pattern alone is a poor tool, as even Wechsler (1958) indicates. Since schizophrenia is a latter-day descendant of Kraepelin's dementia praecox, investigators and diagnosticians naturally are concerned with the issue of mental loss or intellectual deficit. Thus, the application of the deterioration quotient or index is an additional item of information in schizophrenia. However, attempts to differentiate subgroups within schizophrenia or to differentiate schizophrenics from other clinical groups by means of the deterioration index have not met with great success (Rabin & Guertin, 1951); differentiation from normals seems to fare much better.

The terms "organicity" and "brain damage" are about as vague as "schizophrenia." A variety of disorders of different degrees of chronicity, different localization of cerebral insult, and variable diffuseness of the damage are subsumed under one category (Haynes & Sells, 1963). Reviewers of the plethora of studies with the WB (Rabin & Guertin, 1951) some time ago noted: "Variety of patterns in 'organics' raises the question whether the structural insults of different localizations may produce differential effects upon intellectual functioning." More recently (Reitan, 1962) it has been shown that brain damage is not static; improvement or degeneration may occur. This certainly has important implications for the sampling of patients in the study of patterns, and it explains, in part, inconsistent findings in many studies which have not attended to this issue. Further, Reitan points out: "General agreement . . . exists with respect to impairment of verbal-symbolic functions with damage of the left hemisphere and . . . that lesions of the right cerebral hemisphere have a major effect on visual-spatial perception and problem solving." This summary of the most recent studies in the field tends to give support to the lower performance level on intelligence tests and relatively intact verbal level only in those patients whose right hemisphere is affected. The opposite trend is apparent; i.e., Verbal performance is reduced in left hemisphere damage. Universal indices of deterioration seem to be obviated when these results are taken into account. Some of these new ideas can explain the apparently little intellectual loss noted in the cases of hemispherectomy reviewed by Wechsler (1958). It is not surprising that the most recent results with the WAIS (Guertin et al., 1962) have not been productive of clear-cut relationships between the various ratios and the presence of "organicity." Patients with brain disease, by using some of the previously successful ratios, tend to diagnose large percentages of schizophrenics as organic.

Mental deficiency is another diagnostic category concerning which some patterning has been reported. The IQ, of course, is the major bit of information. Wechsler, however, suggests that not all subtests show a low level of performance; Comprehension and Object Assembly are especially selected as the subtests indicating relatively adequate or high performance. In some instances such information may be useful in the differentiation between retardation and deficit as it might occur in schizophrenia and brain damage. The usually adequate performance, or performance-better-than-verbal, level in mental deficiency has been found effective in differential diagnosis.

Some Issues Regarding the Application of the Indices

That the general indices or patterns mentioned above are based on rather shaky grounds has been emphasized all along. Single patterns may not be useful at all in differential diagnosis. Consequently, Wechsler (1958) proposed the method of *successive sieves*, which consists in the application of several known patterns in succession, thus eliminating false positives and false negatives at each step. This method was successfully employed in his example in which he compared 60 schizophrenics and 60 normals (Wechsler, 1958). This procedure has not yet been studied with a broader range of disorders, perhaps because the number of reported patterns in other disorders is smaller and the number of successive sieves would have to be reduced accordingly.

Consonant with the trend to study the *tester* and not the tests, an investigation of the ability of seven experienced psychologists to arrive at diagnostic formulations on 300 patients (equally divided into neurotics, schizophrenics, and brain-damaged) on the basis of quantitative WB information (subtest scores) turned out to be most damaging to the pattern approach. Presumably these psychologists applied all the quantitative indices of scatter, patterns, etc. Yet only one "correctly diagnosed a significant number of these 300 patients, and only two others had extrachance success in the diagnosis of a single diagnostic group." It would surely seem that quantitative information on levels I (IQ) and II (indices) is insufficient for the purpose of making reliable diagnoses with major psychiatric categories (Cohen, 1955).

The issue of "differential" impairment in schizophrenia has been seriously challenged in a study employing the SRA test (Binder, 1956). Instead, the investigator found an "over-all impairment." The question of whether the lower intellectual functioning is due to impairment other than lower initial premorbid intelligence has been recently raised in the literature. Reported results are contradictory; one study (Miner & Anderson, 1958) reports lower initial intelligence, whereas another one (Mason, 1956) found "no definite relationship . . . between intelligence . . . and maladjustment" with the exception of some groups of schizophrenics. Moreover, some recent findings point to the possibility of a *rise* in intelligence test levels following the onset of schizophrenia (Fitzherbert, 1955; Griffith, Estes, & Zerof, 1962). The patterns used with intelligence tests do not necessarily imply impairment; most of them implicitly consider a uniqueness in the personality organization and development which tends to be reflected in intellectual functions in most disorders, with the possible exception of brain damage. Regardless of the orientation, the empirical fact is that the patterns are not sufficiently clearly demonstrated in order to be useful independently of other findings. Perhaps research on "cognitive style," especially by developmental psychologists (Kagan, Moss, & Sigel, 1963; Sigel, 1963), is the direction for future investigation in the area.

It is also quite obvious that the criterion, i.e., psychiatric nosological classifications, is a source of confusion (King, 1954). It may well be that "Our present labeling devices for disease syndromes and tests seem to have led us into a blind alley" (Shaffer & Lazarus, 1952).

Intratest Scatter: Level III

Much less systematic work has been done with this type of test variability, which involves failures on some easy items of a subtest and passes on some of the more difficult ones. Holzberg and Deane (1950) have devised an "objective measure" of intratest scatter. This "scatter coefficient" consists of the ratio between the number of incorrect items within the range of passed items to the total raw score obtained on the subtests. Some statistically significant differences, on a few subtests, between neurotics, schizophrenics, and organics were obtained by means of this coefficient. Although there has not been much follow-up of research activity on intratest scatter, clinicians use it informally as a part of their test analysis (Burton & Harris, 1955). This use, however, approaches the clinicointuitive or qualitative type of operation, to be discussed in the next section.

Qualitative Analysis of Responses: Level IV

Three levels of the application of intelligence tests in diagnosis have been discussed thus far—the over-all index of intellectual functioning (IQ), the variability of subtests (interest scatter, patterns, profiles), and the variability of performance within subtests (intratest scatter). All these are numerical indices—psychometric procedures which focus on the test or, rather, on the formal responses to the test defined in terms of successes and failures. The content of the responses themselves at these levels is irrelevant. During recent decades, with the shift of the interests of psychologists from "intelligence" as a unitary entity to concern with personality and its description (Rotter, 1963), there developed an emphasis on the less formal products of intelligence tests. W. A. Hunt (1946) expresses it as follows: "The mathematical symbols into which this behavior can be translated are secondary instruments of convenience and should not be allowed to conceal the primary datum, the actual behavior. . . ." With this trend a shift occurs—from the test to the tester, from the automatic compilation of scores defined by the test structure to the evaluation of behavior, responses, and content. Consonant with the projective hypothesis, we find that not only every subtest score but every single response and every part of every response is significant and representative of the subject (Rapaport, 1945).

A good deal has been written, especially in an illustrative fashion, about the interpretation of content obtained in response to intelligence test items (e.g., Anderson, 1951; Mayman, Schafer, & Rapaport, 1951; Schafer, 1948). Schafer, in introducing his book on clinical application of psychological tests, clearly states: "This volume will be a clinical exposition, frequently referring to patterns and interpretations whose validity has been established only by *clinical experience*" (italics added). This is true, in general, about this level of use of intelligence tests (Rotter, 1953); interpretation depends, to a considerable extent, upon the experience (private norms?), dynamics, and theoretical orientation and sophistication of the examiner-interpreter. The kinds of inferences he is going to make about the personality examined strongly depend upon the conceptualization of personality (intervening) variables and dynamics. Next, the relationship between the personality variables and diagnostic labels or a diagnostic schema determines the final formulation, including prediction, which is implicitly—and often explicitly—a part of the diagnostic formulation.

Shaffer (1952), who is concerned with the advance of psychometrics and with a scientific foundation for diagnostic procedures, suggests "quantifying the qualitative." Relatively few attempts have been made in this direction. One study reported results on specific errors on the WAIS picture-completion test (Wolfson & Weltman, 1960) and found that 81 per cent of schizophrenic patients gave more "unique" responses than the normal controls. Of course, the studies concerned with an analysis of responses to vocabulary tests deal with quantification of the qualitative. These investigations (Chodorkoff & Mussen, 1952; Feifel, 1949; Harrington & Ehrmann, 1954; Moran, Moran, & Blake, 1952; Rabin, King, & Ehrmann, 1955) dealt with formal categories of definitions, which are not, however, very useful in dynamic description and diagnosis. The problem posed by Shaffer seems to go beyond the confines of intelligence testing and extend to the entire process of clinical diagnosis.

The Psychoanalytic Ego-psychology Approach

Approaches to intelligence tests have changed. First there was the concern with intelligence per se—whatever it is—and then there was an emphasis on "nonintellective" factors in intelligence tests. In the latter instance, personality factors were considered an adjunct to the main purpose—that of testing intelligence. More recently the view has been promulgated that intelligence *is* part of personality and does not become manifested independently from it (Fromm & Hartman, 1955; Waite, 1961). In a series of publications (Fromm, 1960; Fromm, Hartman, & Marschak, 1957), Fromm and her collaborators have introduced a schema for the classification of intelligence test items. The classification draws upon psychoanalytic ego psychology; its basic tenet is that "since development and intelligence tests investigate ability and learning, they must actually and basically test reality awareness and reality mastery, and therefore ego development." Test items, mostly of children's tests, are categorized into a number of personality variables—id-ego, ego development (ego ideal, anxiety, ego defenses), superego variables, and cultural influences. A total of 700 items from a variety of infants' and children's intelligence tests were thus placed in 41 subcategories of the Freudian tripartite psychic structure. By means of this schema the authors propose a "dynamic" analysis and personality diagnosis. Waite (1963) contrasts intelligence tests with projective techniques by pointing out that the latter "encourage a regressive shift," whereas the former reflect a person's "defensive strategy"—primarily an ego operation. This psychoanalytic approach and the classificatory system of responses, briefly described, have the advantages of integration with theory—the lack of which has plagued the empirically oriented testing movement for a long time. The system suggested by Fromm and associates has not yet been sufficiently applied, nor were results reported on its usefulness for diagnostic purposes. The reliability of the classificatory system is also in need of testing.

The Diagnostic Operation

If IQs, measures of scatter, or other numerical indices were successful in differential diagnosis, the examiner could be entirely eliminated in the interpretation process. This "ideal" state of affairs has certainly not been reached. Moreover, a good deal depends on the meaning of the term "diagnosis." If it means a detailed description and interpretation of a dynamic constellation of personality factors with predictive implications, rather than a mere labeling in the Kraepelinian tradition, then even successful numerical indices will not suffice. Psychologists do not use the *IQ only, patterns only,* or *content analysis only* when they employ intelligence tests for diagnostic purposes. They employ the available material and the accumulated knowledge, *on all four levels,* described above, plus behavioral observations of the patient in a situation that demands his controlled, "secondary process" type of attitude in dealing with the test demands. In applying all four levels of analysis of the obtained material (plus the behavioral observations), the psychologist follows, in a sense, Wechsler's successive sieving procedure. This "sieving," however, is not confined to patterns but extends to all the information obtained for the individual diagnosis and not for group differentiation.

Finally, it must be stressed that, generally, intelligence tests are not employed as a sole basis for personality evaluation and diagnosis. They are usually one component of a battery of psychodiagnostic tools which deal with other areas and "levels of psychic functioning" (Waite, 1961). Thus, it may be asked again whether the investigators utilizing various indices of mental functioning in the quest for individual diagnostic successes have not been expecting too much from their data by searching (as in medicine) for some specific "mental disease organism" to be discovered via statistical manipulation of test data. When knowledge of group trends is combined with behavioral observation and content analysis, then the findings are of practical value (Cronbach, 1957) as an integral part of the battery on which final evaluation, diagnosis, and prognosis are based.

REFERENCES

Anastasi, Anne. *Psychological testing.* New York: Macmillan, 1954.

Anderson, Gladys L. Qualitative aspects of the Stanford-Binet. In H. H. Anderson & Gladys L. Anderson (Eds.), *An introduction to projective techniques.* Englewood Cliffs, N.J.: Prentice-Hall, 1951.

Arthur, Grace. *A point scale of performance tests.* Vol. I. New York: Commonwealth Fund, 1943.

Babcock, Harriet. An experiment in the measurement of mental deterioration. *Arch. Psychol., N.Y.,* No. 117, 1930.

Babcock, Harriet. *Dementia praecox: a psychological study.* Lancaster, Pa.: Science Press, 1933.

Bayley, Nancy. On the growth of intelligence. *Amer. Psychologist,* 1955, **10**, 805–818.

Binder, A. Schizophrenic intellectual impairment: uniform or differential? *J. abnorm. soc. Psychol.,* 1956, **52**, 11–18.

Buros, O. K. (Ed.) *The fifth mental measurements yearbook.* Highland Park, N.Y.: Gryphon Press, 1959.

Burton, A., & Harris, R. E. *Clinical studies of personality.* New York: Harper & Row, 1955.

Carter, J. W., & Bowles, T. W. A manual on qualitative aspects of psychological examining. *J. clin. Psychol.,* 1948, **4**, 110–150.

Cattell, P. *The measurement of intelligence of infants and young children.* New York: Psychological Corporation, 1940.

Chodorkoff, B., & Mussen, P. Qualitative aspects of the vocabulary responses of normals and schizophrenics. *J. consult. Psychol.,* 1952, **16**, 43–48.

Cohen, J. The efficacy of diagnostic pattern analysis with the WB. *J. consult. Psychol.,* 1955, **19**, 303–306.

Cronbach, L. Assessment of individual differences. *Annu. Rev. Psychol.,* 1956, **7**.

Delattre, L., & Cole, D. A comparison of the WISC and the Wechsler-Bellevue. *J. consult. Psychol.,* 1952, **16**, 228–230.

Eells, K., Davis, A., Havighurst, R. J., Herrick, V. E., & Tyler, R. *Intelligence and cultural differences.* Chicago: Univer. of Chicago Press, 1951.

Feifel, H. Qualitative differences in the vocabulary responses of normals and abnormals. *Genet. Psychol. Monogr.,* 1949, **39**, 151–204.

Field, J. G. Two types of tables for use with Wechsler's intelligence scales. *J. clin. Psychol.,* 1960, **16**, 3–7.

Fitzherbert, Joan. Increase in intelligence quotient at onset of schizophrenia: three adolescent cases. *Brit. J. Med. Psychol.,* 1955, **28**, 191–193.

Fromm, Erika. Projective aspects of intelligence testing. In A. I. Rabin & Mary R. Haworth (Eds.), *Projective techniques with children.* New York: Grune & Stratton, 1960.

Fromm, Erika, & Hartman, Lenore D. *Intelligence: a dynamic approach.* Garden City, N.Y.: Doubleday, 1955.

Fromm, Erika, Hartman, Lenore D., & Marschak, Marian. A contribution to a dynamic theory of intelligence testing of children. *J. clin. exp. Psychopath.,* 1954, **15**, 73–95.

Fromm, Erika, Hartman, Lenore D., & Marschak, Marian. Children's intelligence tests as a measure of dynamic personality functioning. *Amer. J. Orthopsychiat.,* 1957, **27**, 134–144.

Garner, Ann M. Intelligence testing and clinical practice. In L. A. Pennington & I. A. Berg (Eds.), *An introduction to clinical psychology.* New York: Ronald, 1954.

Gesell, A., & Armatruda, Catherine S. *Developmental diagnosis.* New York: Hoeber-Harper, 1941.

Griffith, R. M., Estes, Betsy W., & Zerof, S. A. Intellectual impairment in schizophrenia. *J. consult. Psychol.,* 1962, **26**, 336–339.

Griffiths, Ruth. *The abilities of babies.* London: Univer. of London Press, 1954.

Guertin, W. H., Frank, G. H., & Rabin, A. I. Research with the Wechsler-Bellevue Intelligence Scale: 1950–1955. *Psychol. Bull.,* 1956, **53**, 235–257.

Guertin, W. H., Rabin, A. I., Frank, G. H., & Ladd, C. E. Research with the Wechsler intelligence scales for adults: 1955–1960. *Psychol. Bull.,* 1962, **59**, 1–26.

Gurvitz, M. S. *The dynamics of psychological testing.* New York: Grune & Stratton, 1951.

Harrington, R., & Ehrmann, J. C. Complexity of response as a factor in the vocabulary performance of schizophrenics. *J. abnorm. soc. Psychol.,* 1954, **49**, 362–364.

Harris, A. J., & Shakow, D. The clinical significance of numerical measures of scatter on the Stanford-Binet. *Psychol. Bull.*, 1937, **34,** 134–150.

Harris, A. J., & Shakow, D. Scatter on the Stanford-Binet in schizophrenic, normal, and delinquent adults. *J. abnorm. soc. Psychol.*, 1938, **33,** 100–111.

Hart, B., & Spearman, C. Mental tests of dementia. *J. abnorm. Psychol.*, 1914, **9,** 217–264.

Haynes, J. R., & Sells, S. B. Assessment of organic brain damage by psychological tests. *Psychol. Bull.*, 1963, **60,** 316–325.

Hiler, E. W. Wechsler-Bellevue intelligence as a predictor of continuation in psychotherapy. *J. clin. Psychol.*, 1958, **14,** 192–194.

Hiler, W. E., & Nesvig, D. Changes in intellectual functions of children in a psychiatric hospital. *J. consult. Psychol.*, 1961, **25,** 288–293.

Holzberg, J. D., & Dean, M. A. The diagnostic significance of an objective measure of intratest scatter on the Wechsler-Bellevue intelligence scales. *J. consult. Psychol.*, 1950, **14,** 180–188.

Hunt, J. McV. Psychological experiments with disordered persons. *Psychol. Bull.*, 1936, **33,** 1–58.

Hunt, J. McV., & Cofer, C. N. Psychological deficit. In J. McV. Hunt (Ed.), *Personality and the behavior disorders.* Vol. II. New York: Ronald, 1944.

Hunt, W. A. The future of diagnostic testing in clinical psychology. *J. clin. Psychol.*, 1946, **2,** 311–317.

Jastak, J. Problems of psychometric scatter analysis. *Psychol. Bull.*, 1949, **46,** 177–197.

Kagan, J., Moss, H. A., & Siegel, I. E. Psychological significance of styles of conceptualization. In J. Kagan & J. C. Wright (Eds.), Basic cognitive processes in children. *Monogr. soc. Res. Child Develpm.*, 1963, **28,** No. 2.

Kendig, Isabelle, & Richmond, Winifred V. *Psychological studies in dementia praecox.* Ann Arbor, Mich.: Edwards, 1940.

King, G. F. Research with neuropsychiatric samples. *J. Psychol.*, 1954, **38,** 383–387.

Littell, W. M. The Wechsler Intelligence Scale for Children. *Psychol. Bull.*, 1960, **57,** 132–156.

McNemar, Q. A critical examination of the University of Iowa studies of environmental influences upon the IQ. *Psychol. Bull.*, 1940, **37,** 63–92.

Mason, C. F. Pre-illness intelligence of mental hospital patients. *J. consult. Psychol.*, 1956, **20,** 297–300.

Mayman, M., Schafer, R., & Rapaport, D. Interpretation of the Wechsler-Bellevue Intelligence Scale in personality appraisal. In H. H. Anderson & Gladys L. Anderson (Eds.), *An introduction to projective techniques.* Englewood Cliffs, N.J.: Prentice-Hall, 1951. Pp. 541–580.

Miner, J. B., & Anderson, J. K. Intelligence and emotional disturbance: evidence from Army and Veterans Administration records. *J. abnorm. soc. Psychol.*, 1958, **56,** 75–81.

Moran, L. J., Moran, F. A., & Blake, R. R. An investigation of the vocabulary performance of schizophrenics. I. Quantitative level. *J. genet. Psychol.*, 1952, **80,** 97–105.

Muench, G. A. A follow-up of mental defectives after 18 years. *J. abnorm. soc. Psychol.*, 1944, **39,** 407–418.

Payne, R. W. Cognitive abnormalities. In H. Eysenck (Ed.), *Handbook of abnormal psychology.* New York: Basic Books, 1961.

Plumeau, F., Machover, S., & Puzzo, F. Wechsler-Bellevue performances of remitted and unremitted alcoholics, and their normal controls. *J. consult. Psychol.*, 1960, **24,** 240–242.

Porteus, S. D. *The maze test and clinical psychology.* Palo Alto, Calif.: Pacific Books, 1959.

Pressey, S. L., & Cole, L. W. Irregularity in a psychological examination as a measure of mental deterioration. *J. abnorm. Psychol.*, 1918, **13,** 285–294.

Rabin, A. I. The use of the Wechsler-Bellevue scales with normal and abnormal persons. *Psychol. Bull.*, 1945, **42,** 410–422.

Rabin, A. I. Intellectual functioning in mental disorder: a study of 1,000 consecutive state hospital admissions. Paper delivered at AAAS meetings, Chicago, 1947.

Rabin, A. I. Wechsler Intelligence Scale for Children. In O. K. Buros (Ed.), *The fifth mental measurements yearbook.* Highland Park, N.J.: Gryphon Press, 1959. Pp. 560–561.

Rabin, A. I. Psychopathic (sociopathic) personalities. In H. Toch (Ed.), *Legal and criminal psychology.* New York: Holt, 1961.

Rabin, A. I., & Guertin, W. H. Research with the Wechsler-Bellevue test: 1945–1950. *Psychol. Bull.*, 1951, **48,** 211–248.

Rabin, A. I., & King, G. F. In L. Bellak (Ed.), *Schizophrenia: a review of the syndrome.* New York: Logos Press, 1958. Pp. 216–278.

Rabin, A. I., King, G. F., & Ehrmann, J. Vocabulary performance of short-term and long-term schizophrenics. *J. abnorm. soc. Psychol.*, 1955, **50,** 255–258.

Rapaport, D. *Diagnostic psychological testing.* Vol. I. Chicago: Year Book Medical Publishers, 1945.

Rappaport, S. R., & Webb, W. B. An attempt to study intellectual deterioration by premorbid and psychotic testing. *J. consult. Psychol.,* 1950, **14,** 95–98.

Reitan, R. M. Certain differential effects of left and right cerebral lesions in human adults. *J. comp. physiol. Psychol.,* 1955, **48,** 474–477.

Reitan, R. M. Psychological deficit. *Annu. Rev. Psychol.,* 1962, **13,** 415–444.

Roe, Anne, & Shakow D. Intelligence in mental disorder. *Ann. N.Y. Acad. Sci.,* 1942, **42,** 361–490.

Ross, A. O. *The practice of clinical child psychology.* New York: Grune & Stratton, 1959.

Rotter, J. B. Clinical methods: psychodiagnostics. In C. P. Stone (Ed.), *Annu. Rev. Psychol.,* 1953, **4,** 295–316.

Rotter, J. B. A historical and theoretical analysis of some broad trends in clinical psychology. In S. Koch (Ed.), *Psychology: a study of a science.* Vol. 5. New York: McGraw-Hill, 1963.

Sarason, S. B. *Psychological problems in mental deficiency.* New York: Harper & Row, 1959.

Sarason, S. B., Davidson, K. S., Lighthall, F. F., Waite, R. R., & Ruebush, B. K. *Anxiety in elementary school children.* New York: Wiley, 1960.

Schafer, R. *The clinical application of psychological tests.* New York: International Universities Press, 1948.

Shaffer, G. W., & Lazarus, R. S. *Fundamental concepts in clinical psychology.* New York: McGraw-Hill, 1952.

Shaffer, L. F. Theoretical bases for psychometric tests. In P. H. Hoch & J. Zubin (Eds.), *Relation of psychological tests to psychiatry.* New York: Grune & Stratton, 1952.

Shipley, W. C. A self-administering scale for measuring intellectual impairment and deterioration. *J. Psychol.,* 1940, **9,** 371–377.

Sigel, I. E. How intelligence tests limit understanding of intelligence. *Merrill-Palmer Quart.,* 1963, **9,** 39–56.

Spivack, G., Levine, M., & Sprigle, H. Intelligence test performance and the delay function of the ego. *J. consult. Psychol.,* 1959, **23,** 428–431.

Stotsky, B. A. A comparison of remitting and nonremitting schizophrenics on psychological tests. *J. abnorm. soc. Psychol.,* 1952, **47,** 489–496.

Super, D. *Appraising vocational fitness.* New York: Harper & Row, 1949.

Terman, L. M. *The measurement of intelligence.* Boston: Houghton Mifflin, 1916.

Terman, L. M., Merrill, M., & Merrill, A. *Measuring intelligence.* Boston: Houghton Mifflin, 1937.

Terman, L. M., Merrill, M., & Merrill A. *Stanford-Binet Intelligence Scale.* Boston: Houghton Mifflin, 1960.

Waite, R. R. The intelligence test as a psychodiagnostic instrument. *J. proj. Tech.,* 1961, **25,** 90–102.

Watson, R. I. The use of the Wechsler-Bellevue scales: a supplement. *Psychol. Bull.,* 1946, **43,** 61–68.

Wechsler, D. *Measurement of adult intelligence.* Baltimore: Williams & Wilkins, 1939.

Wechsler, D. *Measurement of adult intelligence.* Baltimore: Williams & Wilkins, 1944.

Wechsler, D. *Wechsler-Bellevue Intelligence Scale, Form II.* New York: Psychological Corporation, 1946.

Wechsler, D. *Wechsler Intelligence Scale for Children.* New York: Psychological Corporation, 1949.

Wechsler, D. *Wechsler Adult Intelligence Scale manual.* New York: Psychological Corporation, 1955.

Wechsler, D. *The measurement and appraisal of adult intelligence.* (14th ed.) Baltimore: Williams & Wilkins, 1958.

Weisenburg, T., Roe, Anne, & McBride, Katherine E. *Adult intelligence.* New York: Commonwealth Fund, 1936.

Wellman, Beth L., Skeels, H. M., & Skodak, Marie. Review of McNemar's critical examination of Iowa studies. *Psychol. Bull.,* 1940, **37,** 93–111.

Wells, F. L. *Mental tests in clinical practice.* Tarrytown-on-Hudson, N.Y.: World, 1927.

Wittenborn, J. R. An evaluation of the use of Bellevue-Wechsler subtest scores as an aid in psychiatric diagnosis. *J. consult. Psychol.,* 1949, **13,** 433–439.

Wolfson, W., & Weltman, R. E. Implication of specific WAIS picture completion errors. *J. clin. Psychol.,* 1960, **16,** 9–11.

20
Projective Techniques

EDWIN S. SHNEIDMAN

No contemporary handbook of clinical psychology in America could fail to give a major emphasis to the diagnostic task or, giving that emphasis, could omit focusing on the projective technique approach to the assessment of personality. Any psychologist who attempts an overview or critique of projective techniques in the current scene is faced with the heavy responsibility of choosing—to put the issue in an admittedly oversimplified form—between, on the one hand, simply defining, classifying, and describing various commonly acknowledged projective techniques and, on the other, raising questions about current definitions, discussing the concept and the very designation of these devices, and at least touching upon the whole topic of veridicality (including usefulness, validity, etc.). It would, of course, simplify the writing of this chapter—and considerably ease the reader's task in understanding it—if I could at the outset figuratively look the reader in the eye and say that projective techniques could be defined in such-and-such a way and were made up of such-and-such types and then simply follow this by giving a succinct definition and presenting a short, comprehensive classification scheme. But, of course, I cannot. And this is so primarily because the definition of projective techniques is a complex issue, and, even worse, the very concept and the name itself pose a number of fundamental questions which demand reflection and rethinking. But first—before we become involved in these more complicated issues—let us travel some of the more conventional paths for awhile and examine where they seem to have come from and where they seem to be leading.

Even before we discuss conventional definitions and classifications of projective techniques, let us clear the air by straightforwardly stating that, by common convention in psychology, the ordinarily designated projective techniques usually include the Rorschach and other inkblot techniques, the Thematic Apperception Test (TAT) and other picture-story tests such as the Make-A-Picture-Story (MAPS) Test, sentence-completion and story-completion procedures, word association tests, drawing and drawing-completion tests, mozaic tests, the Picture-Frustration Study, miniature world tests, the Szondi Test, and others of this ilk; and they exclude such commonly used psychological tests of personality and character as the Minnesota Multiphasic Personality Inventory (MMPI), adjustment questionnaires, paper-and-pencil tests of personality, indices, temperament surveys, rating scales, checklists, Q sorts, and others of this ilk. A partial (though not, as we shall see, completely adequate operational) meaning can be given to the phrase "of this ilk" by turning now to some conventional definitions of these techniques.

Let us begin by looking at some definitions of projective techniques which have appeared in general textbooks on personality. We take this tack to see in what manner projective techniques are represented to undergraduate psychology students. With no attempt at systematic sampling, choosing at random four textbooks which appeared during the past several years, we see the following typical statements. The first is from Symonds's text (1946), *The Dynamics of Human Adjustment:*

> A rather recent development in the study of fantasy is through the so-called "projective techniques," a term first used by Frank (241). The use of the term "projective" in this sense is derived from the mechanism *projection* but is a somewhat liberal and inexact use of the term. In projective techniques there is the implication that as a person expresses himself in any kind of constructive or interpretative activity he is acting out inner fantasy. If he is telling a story it is believed that he projects into the characters in the story his own impulses, feelings, and thoughts. That this is true to a degree is beyond doubt, but exploration and experimentation with the method are yet so young that the exact correspondence between the products of expressive material and inner fantasy is not yet known. There is no doubt that if projective techniques are the acting out of inner fantasies, these have been so distorted and disguised by layer upon layer of protective mechanisms that the deeper infantile fantasies are hopelessly hidden. If projective techniques are used in social situations, as in clinics or schools, naturally the stories and productions must also pass the censorship of social acceptability (p. 515).

We note in Symonds's statement a linking of the term "projective" (as used in projective techniques) with the psychoanalytic mechanism of "projection." The obvious similarity in sound between these two words has been a possible source of some high-level theoretical confusion in the entire short history of projective techniques. This issue has been recognized by several writers and was stated in the opening sentence of Bell's early book, *Projective Techniques* (1948), in which he points out the two dominant and confusing possible meanings of projection: the specific psychoanalytic meaning as "a defensive process under the sway of the pleasure principle whereby the Ego thrusts forth on the external world unconscious wishes and ideas, which, if allowed to penetrate into consciousness, would be painful to the Ego" (Healy, Bronner, & Bowers, 1930), and the common-usage, dictionary sense of the word, namely, to cast forward, to project (as a cartographer might project) an almost physical extension of psychological attributes.

In his textbook *Personality,* Murphy (1947) discussed projective methods as follows:

> The term *projective methods* has come into general use in recent years to denote the devices that enable the subject to project himself into a planned situation. He sees in it what he personally is disposed to see, or does with it what he is personally disposed to do. We are interested primarily not in the quantity of production, as in an educational test, but in what he indirectly tells us about himself through his manner of confronting the task. All psychological methods involve some projection in the sense that a person reveals himself in whatever he does. One may put little, or much, of one's self into a production; thus the carpenter projects himself when he makes a doorsill, and to a much greater degree when he makes a boat. The Allport-Vernon methods are in some degree projective, the graphological methods still more so, and the interpretation of ink blots perhaps most projective of all. There is a continuum of self-expression or self-projection, from the slight reflection of individuality in rapid-fire mechanical utterance of the "opposites" to words like black or heavy, up to the identification of one's self with a character in a stage production. Since there is a continuum, the definition is for convenience only. We shall include under projection all those methods in which the individual has full opportunity to live empathetically, that is, in terms of identification with the material presented to him. But we agree that there is *some degree* of empathic self-realization in a much wider variety of methods than we shall describe; that some individuals realize themselves empathically in some materials which are handled rather mechanically by others; and that a method may be exceedingly projective for a person today, but only slightly so tomorrow (p. 669).

We note in Murphy's discussion the emphasis on the *idiosyncratic* and *revelatory* aspects of projective techniques. Further, his concept of a continuum of self-expression, his use of the concept of empathy in terms of identification, is an important one. It is interesting to relate Murphy's remarks on projection to the remarks of the great physicist Percy Bridgman. In discussing the difference between private and public experiences, Bridgman says the following:

> It seems to me that the operation by which I give meaning to your use of "conscious" is a simple one in the sense that everyone uses the operation. I shall call it the operation of "projection." I "project" myself into your position, that is I imagine myself in your position and I ask myself what I would be saying or doing in such a position (1961).

In the sense of Bridgman's definition, he might have, had he addressed his mind to the topic of projective techniques, limited them to those procedures which had human figures as part of their stimulus materials (such as the TAT, the MAPS Test, the Picture-Frustration Study, the Szondi, etc.).

In Guilford's *Personality* (1959), the emphasis seems to be on the unstructured aspect of the stimulus materials:

> Projective techniques are distinguished from other methods of assessment by the use of unstructured tasks and ambiguous materials. The examinee is given a minimum of instruction, and within the limits of the testing situation and the kind of material, he is free to go in his own directions and to give his own unique responses. It is hoped thus to obtain information concerning his personality by the fact that he projects himself into his responses (p. 313).

In a recent text, entitled *Adjustment and Personality,* Lazarus (1961) introduces his discussion of projective tests (as compared to psychometric or objective tests) as follows:

> In contrast with psychometric tests are those designed so that the variability of response between persons is great. The stimuli are usually ambiguous and permit each subject to interpret or structure it in his own way, thus evoking personality characteristics that are somewhat unique to him. These are called *projective tests.* They attempt to obtain more information about the person's unique way of looking at the world, and because of this, the assessor or diagnostician must use his own judgment a great deal in interpreting the responses. The projective tests tend to sacrifice such virtues of the psychometric tests as objectivity, simplicity, and economy in favor of behavior that potentially reflects the subject's unique orientation to the world and his psychodynamics (pp. 403–404).

What one sees in Lazarus's comments is some attention to the issue of unreliability of interpretation and some comment on the "price" by virtue of its not being the other.

In brief summary, we see that the textbook definitions of "projective techniques" have indicated that they are psychological measurement devices which are characterized (1) on the *stimulus* side by *ambiguity* in the stimulus, (2) on the *response* side by the *multiplicity* of responses permitted the subject in an open situation where the responses do not have a right or wrong character, and (3) in the *interpretation* aspect by the interest of the interpreter in the *unconscious* or latent aspects of personality and in their amenability to holistic personality analysis. Under the aegis of a broadened twentieth-century theory of personality which included the concept of unconscious motivation as its keystone, projective techniques were developed (in part) to provide interpreters with instruments which would give their subjects opportunities to demonstrate themselves in ways that they could not verbalize directly.

Lindzey (1961) has done all students of projective techniques a visible service in his recent survey and analysis of these procedures. It is worthwhile to quote his definition—a synthesis and combination of the various elements which appear in the literature. He states:

> A projective technique is an instrument that is considered especially sensitive to covert or unconscious aspects of behavior, it permits or encourages a wide variety of subject responses, is highly multidimensional, and it evokes unusually rich or profuse response data with a minimum of subject awareness concerning the purpose of the test. Further, it is very often true that the stimulus material presented by the projective test is ambiguous, interpreters of the test depend upon holistic analysis, the test evokes fantasy responses, and there are no correct or incorrect responses to the test (p. 45).

Lindzey himself follows his comprehensive definition with the comment: "This relative abstract statement will be unsatisfactory to some readers." Even if one accepts this definition as the most inclusive presently available definition, the fact remains that there are still two topics which need some further discussion: (1) the relationships between projective techniques and "fantasy" and (2) the relationships between projective techniques and "projection." In relation to the topic of fantasy, Holt, in his perspicacious essay (1961), has (after indicating four ways in which general daydream fantasies and TAT stories are similar to each other) developed an impressive series of some fifteen ways in which TAT stories and general daydream fantasies are different from each other. (These differences are along the dimensions of quality of consciousness, spontaneity, imagery, roles of drives and defenses, involvement of affect, relation to action, self-relevance, etc.) Holt concludes that the relationship of daydreams and fantasy to projective test protocols is an important open question.

Apropos of the second concept (projection), there has been, among writers on the topic of projective techniques, interest amounting sometimes to an obsession with the word "projection." In part the confusion which obviously exists on this topic stems from what might be called a "homonymous" error, that is, confusing two words which sound the same but which have different meanings. The most general meaning of projection is in the ordinary sense of projection as extrusion, extension, casting forward, etc. There is still another sense of the term, perhaps one which might be called the "cartographic" sense, in which the projection is either a magnified or minified point-for-point representation of the original object, terrain, or complex.

It seems as though the popularity of the term "projective technique" was in some ways a fortuitous occurrence. It is true that Morgan and Murray, in their original article "A Method for Investigating Fantasies: The Thematic Apperception Test" (1935), did say: "The process involved is that of projection—something well-known to analysts. It is utilized in the Rorschach Test." And, again, in the same article: "For the fantasies being projected may be inwardly disclaimed and thus avoid complete repressions." And again in 1938, in *Explorations in Personality*, Murray discusses the "projection tests," listing the TAT, the Beta Ink Blot Test, the Rorschach test, the Dramatic Productions Test, and others, saying about the TAT: "The test is based on the well-recognized fact that when a person interprets an ambiguous social situation, he is apt to expose his own personality as much of the phenomena to which he is attending" (p. 531).

Frank is ordinarily credited with making the point in print (1939) that there was a new kind of technique with its own rationale and intellectual history which he called "projective," and he is further credited with doing this so effectively that this label has stuck. He says he got this title from a paper by R. Horowitz and L. B. Murphy, but they reciprocally give credit back to Frank for originating the label. But with the statements in *Explorations in Personality* about "projection techniques" in 1938, Lindzey appropriately points out: "The historical priority for linking the concept of projection of these personality measures belongs rightfully to Henry A. Murray" (p. 36).

Frank's conception of projection emphasized the idiosyncratic nature of human perception—we are reminded of the opening line of Rorschach's *Psychodiagnostics* (1921): "The experiment consists in the *interpretation of accidental forms,* that is, non-specific forms"—as well as emphasizing the holistic nature of personality. Frank has continued to be a theoretical leader in the field of projective techniques, especially as he believes that they reflect in the field of personality major trends in twentieth-century science. Others, notably Abt and Bellak (1950), Rapaport (1946), and Schafer (1948), have attempted to develop a projective psychology centered in large part around the psychoanalytic concept of projection.

The confusion that exists between the two main concepts of projection—as a paradigmatic reflection of an inner map of personality structures, on the one hand, and as a psychoanalytically defined defensive process, on the other—may not be amenable to a single synthesis. Perhaps some readers can see their way out of this dilemma by viewing the extension concept of projection as an intervening variable and the psychoanalytic concept of projection as a hypothetical construct—to use the distinction made by MacCorquodale and Meehl (1948).

The fact is that the designation "projective techniques" is not absolutely binding on the tests and procedures that we are discussing in this chapter. This point is illustrated by the fact that they have been given several appellations in their relatively brief history. We have seen that Murray (in 1938) called them "projection techniques," although in 1955 he refers to the "unhappily named 'projective tests'" (Murray, 1955). They have been called "apperceptive distortions" by Bellak (1950); "misperceptive" or "dynaceptive tests" by Cattell (1957); and "imaginative productions" by White (1944). My own present feeling is that a more appropriate label would be "assay" techniques (in the sense that or mineralogist assays the precious ores and slag in any sample)—as opposed to scored quantitative "coinage" (or numismatic) techniques.

Part of the task of defining personologic (or projective) techniques lies in surveying the various *classifications* which these techniques have been given. Something of the variety and scope of these various classifications can be glimpsed if we take just one example, the Rorschach technique, and cite the various ways in which it has been classified by different writers. At least seven designations for the Rorschach method can be found: (1) In 1938, Murray referred to the Rorschach technique as an example of "perceptive projection" (as opposed to apperceptive projection or cognitive projection); (2) in 1939, in his original article, and again in 1948, in his book *Projective Methods,* Frank referred to the Rorschach test as a "constitutive" (as opposed to a constrictive, interpretive, cathartic, or refractive) method; (3) in 1945, H. Sargent, in her classification of projective methods, listed the Rorschach as a "diagnostic" and "experimental" (rather than a therapeutic) technique; (4) Bell, in his *Projective Techniques,* in 1948, discussed the Rorschach technique as a "visual stimulus" (rather than as a word association, expressive movement, or play-drama) technique; (5) Symonds, in 1946, called the Rorschach an "interpretive" (as opposed to an expressive) procedure; (6) in 1957, Donald T. Campbell categorized the Rorschach technique as a "voluntary indirect free-response test (as opposed to an objective, direct, or structured instrument); and (7) most recently Lindzey, in his comprehensive survey of projected techniques, called the Rorschach an "association" (as opposed to a construction, completion, ordering, or expressive) technique. It would thus appear that the Rorschach procedure is a perception constitutive diagnostic experimental visual-stimulus interpretive voluntary indirect free-response associative technique. And what is of equal interest is that the different classifiers made different groupings of the same tests. In all, the most comprehensive survey and discussion of the varieties of projective tests and the varieties of classifications of projective tests are given by Lindzey (1961).

It is assumed that the reader is aware of the generally paradoxical status of projective techniques which has existed almost from the beginning. This paradox lies in the disparity between their equivocal validity status, on one hand, and—in practical and clinical settings especially—their widespread use and the cheerful fealty of their supporters, on the other. What was it in the early days of projective techniques that gave them their great impetus? And what has sustained their great popularity? In this regard, it is instructive to reexamine Sargent's (1945) scholarly and insightful discussion of the theoretical climate in which projective techniques developed. She suggests three main categories: psychoanalysis, global theory, and support from general science. Even today—although the details of her discussion can be modified—it is difficult to improve on her general formulation. In the present context, I shall discuss the factors which seem to have given projective tests their over-all intellectual permissiveness under the following four rubrics.

Psychoanalytic theory. Sargent discussed this category by devoting her discussion entirely to the concept of projection as explicated by Freud. It might be more accurate to say that projective techniques have, in part, gained their *raison d'être* by virtue of the general acceptance of—or at least the inability to ignore—the basic tenets of psychoanalytic theory, especially those parts of the theory which relate to the unconscious motivation. General psychoanalytic theory concerning the possible role of unconscious determinants of human behavior has influenced current American psychological thinking in a way not dissimilar to the impact that Darwin's concept of natural selection had on the general scientific community during the latter half of the last century. When Frank speaks of the individual's projecting his "private world" and when Murray speaks of the individual's relating things about himself that he would not consciously disclose—and, more importantly, does not even know—about himself, they are reflecing this basic concept of unconscious motivation. By and large, although the relationship is not an isomorphic one, psychologists who use projective techniques in clinical settings accept (explicitly or implicitly) the concept of unconscious motivation (and the necessity of another than direct approach to personality), whereas psychologists who adhere solely to paper-and-pencil questionnaires are generally critical of this concept and can eschew it.

Global theory. It seemed obvious that the interest in global, holistic, organismic, or field theory gave conceptual buttressing to the then new projective devices. However, developments in the last fifteen or twenty years indicate that projective techniques are as amenable as other psychological devices to factor-analytic procedures. Further, there are those (Little, 1959) who indicate that if the usefulness of projective techniques is to be increased, they will have to be tailor-made to measure specific attributes of personality and not employ a holistic approach. What seems to be more fundamental is not the holistic atomistic division, but the mathematical-humanistic division to be discussed below. Murray has played a crucial role in America, even to the extent of raising the question of whether or not that model in psychology which demands "mathematically unequivocal results . . . is one of the devil's cunningest contrivances" (1962). The essential feature in the position of the humanist-personologist is that he is more concerned with relevance and completeness than he is with precision. He is less concerned with the intensely precise manipulation of the isolata of human experience and more concerned with the study of the human personality in dyadic relationships. It is Murray and his many colleagues and students (White, 1963) and Maslow (1943) and Frank (1948) who have made the use of projective techniques more permissible because they have made the humanistic approach to the study of man more respectable.

Support from general science. In Sargent's article, she gives appropriate credit to Frank for demonstrating the over-all influence of contemporary scientific methodology on projective techniques. Frank's position was that the projective technique was an application of psychological science in much the same way that Bridgman's operationalism was a conceptual tool for physics. For Bridgman, a concept was defined in terms of the operation by which it was derived. For Frank, personality also was a process, a way of living and feeling, a way of organizing and patterning the life situation. The unstructured techniques tapped the individual's "private world." Today, if one accepts the premise that validity procedures can be viewed as aspects of logic and causality, then there is much that can be added to Sargent's discussion a score of years ago. There has been, as we all know, a revolution in the theoretical foundations of twentieth-century physical science. By the second decade of this century, the theoretical work of Planck, Bohr, Heisenberg, and Einstein (with their principles of indeterminacy, complementarity, and relativity) had thoroughly changed the previous notion of physical causality. It would appear that psychology's task, vis-à-vis physics, is not to emulate their method (inasmuch as their subject matters *are* different) but to reexamine the history of psychology with the purpose to "avoid making some of the methodological errors which beset these earlier movements" (Shneidman, 1959). And in logic, too, the precise craft of mathematics that Whitehead and Russell had attempted to build on a keel laid down by logic was torpedoed by Gödel's theorem, which was, in essence:

> It is impossible to prove that a logical system —at least as complicated as arithmetic— contains no concealed contradictions by using only theorems which are derivable within the system. To prove freedom from potential contradiction, it is necessary to use theorems which can be proved only by going outside the system (Bridgman, 1961, p. 6).

The impact of this notion in psychology was one of "opening up" closed systems of personality in the same way that the impact of Bohr's and Heisenberg's work was to lessen the fetish of certainty and causality. One implication of all this is that we cannot ever know everything and that we cannot ever even know some things with precision.

As a protest movement. In addition to the three points made above—topics touched upon in Sargent's article—it is possible to add a fourth aspect of the *Zeitgeist* which has encouraged the flowering of projective devices. Several critics—for example, Eysenck (1961) and Super (1959)—have severely criticized the projective techniques. There is a statement in the psychological literature to the effect that projective techniques constitute "a scandal in the American psychological scene." It may well be, however, that a persuasive case can be made in the other direction. That is to say, projective techniques represented, among other things, a manifestation—almost a protest movement—based on the felt inadequacies of the objective personality questionnaire instruments, not only in terms of their clinical use but in terms of their providing a *sympatico* understanding of man as well. Thus, amid all the statements relating to the scientific inadequacies of projective techniques, it may be said that the countercharge of the inabilities of objective techniques adequately to reflect the multiform aspects of human personality in a living situation may make more sense.

In his original paper on projective techniques, Frank (1939) concluded his definition of projective techniques by stating:

> It may be emphasized that projective methods are not offered as a substitute for the quantitative statistical procedures, but rather are designed to permit a study of the idiomatic individual which is conceived as a process of organizing experience and so must elude the investigator who relies upon methods that of necessity ignore or obscure the individual and the configural quality of his personality. Finally it should be noted that projective methods of personality study offer possibilities for utilizing the insights into human conduct and personality expression which the prevailing quantitative procedures seem deliberately to ignore.

In his great *Explorations in Personality,* Murray (1938) spoke of "peripheralists" and "centralists." He further identified the peripheralists as resorting to physiological explanations, as being elementaristic, and, in his more recent writings, as being almost exclusively concerned with mathematically unequivocal results. The centralists, on the other hand, were people like psychoanalysts, physicians, and social philosophers who felt no compulsion to count and measure and whose concern was the study of man enmeshed in his intrapsychic and dyadic environments. They were not interested, as a recent article on statistical inference describes the process, in "parading statistical procedures . . . as symbols of respectability pretending to give an imprimatur of mathematical logic to the subjective process of empirical inference" (Edwards, Lindman, & Savage, 1963). On this same point of centralists and peripheralists, philosopher Morris Cohen described two main species of philosophers *and* scientists as follows:

> Among philosophers as among scientists we may roughly distinguish two types that may be called the mathematical and naturalistic. The mathematicians excel in grasping some fruitful idea and elaborating it with such a perfection or finality of form that humanity is compelled, through sheer admiration, to strain the facts to make them fit these perfect forms. The naturalists, on the other hand, are more eager to observe the actual facts in their naked natural state. They love accuracy more than elegance. That philosophers can write with their eye on the object of their observation rather than on the symmetry of their final system, careful readers of Aristotle and Kant know full well. Nevertheless, the prevailing temper among philosophers has been the mathematical one; for all the great men of science whose achievements have stirred the human imagination, from the days of Euclid and Archimedes, down to Copernicus, Galileo, and Newton, have been mathematicians. It was only in the middle of the nineteenth century, and most notably in the case of Darwin, that men of the naturalistic type succeeded in impressing humanity with results of the first magnitude (1944, pp. 197–198).

In the mathematical-naturalistic view of things, whether or not one agrees that one term (either one) is pejorative and the other honorific, it still seems that these two points of view do indeed reflect *different* views of man and are indeed the contemporary counterparts of long-ranging philosophic disputations. There is a current (and enormously successful) trend in psychology today which at its roots can be identified with Democritus, La Mettrie, Descartes, and all the "tough-minded" people who are willing, in order to understand aspects of man precisely and with rigor, to fractionate and to divide the human subject, whom they view in the first place as an essentially mechanistic organism. As far as projective techniques are concerned, it would seem that their historical philosophic alliance (if not always their contemporary allegiance) is to a humanistic notion of man, a notion of man seen globally and sometimes even seen compassionately and poetically. The worst indictment of projective techniques in America is not their lack of rigor or validity—which, as we shall indicate, can be viewed as an irrelevant demand from the "other point of view" —but rather that they themselves have not consistently pursued a global understanding of their human subjects but have been content rigidly to use one or two techniques to which they have oftentimes become cultishly cathected.

An important salvo in the cross fire between the two major points of view was set off by Meehl (1954) in his profoundly stimulating book *Clinical versus Statistical Prediction*. There have been several comments and reactions to Meehl's book, namely by Sarbin and Holt. For my part, I should like to focus the reader's attention to the title of Meehl's book and point out that a more accurate title than *Clinical versus Statistical Prediction* would have been *Clinical-Statistical versus Statistical-Statistical Prediction*, where the second term on both sides of the equation represents the current mathematically oriented psychological *Zeitgeist*. For an over-all commentary on the clinical enterprise (of which projective techniques form an integral part), we are still waiting for a book that might be entitled *Clinical-Clinical versus Statistical-Statistical Diction*. By this title, I mean to imply two points: (1) that there is a need for a treatise written from a *new* point of view and (2) that *prediction* (essentially a correlation with future criteria) does not take account of sometimes useful postdiction (correlation with past criteria), nor does it take account of what I call paridiction (correlation with more or less present criteria). Before we decide whether or not "dictions" (correlation, dialogues, relationships) provide the only paradigm for causality and meaningfulness, let us turn first to a brief discussion of the concept of *validity*.

Since 1954, when the APA committee on test standards, under the chairmanship of Cronbach, published their *Technical Recommendations for Psychological Tests and Diagnostic Techniques* (Cronbach et al., 1954), it has been almost traditional to discuss the concept of validity of psychological tests in terms of the four types or aspects of validity enunciated by the Cronbach committee. These four types, and a brief description of each, are as follows: (1) *content* validity, which has to do with "how well the content of the test samples the class of situations or subject matter about which conclusions are to be drawn. Content validity is especially important in case of achievement and proficiency measures"; (2) *predictive* validity, which "is evaluated by showing how well predictions made from the test are confirmed by evidence gathered at some subsequent time . . . [mostly by] correlating test scores with a subsequent criterion measure"; (3) *concurrent* validity, which "is evaluated by showing how well test scores correspond to measures of concurrent criterion performance or status"; and (4) *construct* validity, which

> is evaluated by investigating what psychological qualities a test measures, i.e., by demonstrating that certain explanatory constructs account to some degree for performance on the test. To examine construct validity requires both logical and empirical attack. Essentially, in studies of construct validity we are validating the theory underlying the test. The validation procedure involves two steps. First, the investigator inquires: From this theory, what predictions would we make regarding the variation of scores from person to person or occasion to occasion? Second, he gathers data to confirm these predictions.

It would appear, at first glance, that individuals attempting to establish the scientific respectability of projective techniques have to deal primarily with the methodological problems attendant to *construct* validity. But, even on this very issue, our second thoughts show that the over-all problem is much more complicated than is implied by a classification of these four types of validity. Our rereflections about construct validity might or might not lead us to reaffirm its crucial role in the projective techniques area (see Bechtoldt, 1959), but as we examine the concept itself we might well conclude that it has at least two shortcomings. The first is that the phrase "construct validity" might turn out to be an interesting contradiction in terms. It is, in effect, like saying "untestable truth," "debatable fact," "transient verity," "unsubstantiated belief," or "unreal reality." That is to say, to conceptualize in terms of construct validity is tantamount to stating that one insists that the phenomena under investigation correlate highly with ideas that one somehow trusts and with taxonomies, usually implicit and unverbalized, whose ordering of the universe into apparent phenomena (implied by the taxonomy) one has unconsciously or uncritically accepted as either optimal or real. Construct validity may contain the usual bedevilments found in any tautology.

A second, and more important, shortcoming latent in the concept of construct validity **is** the possible confusion between validity and a number of other potential types of verifiability, that is, the danger of assuming that an explication of types of validity automatically exhausts the topics of causality, meaningfulness, and "truth." All the propositions within contemporary psychology appear to be amenable to division among a relatively small number of major degrees of confirmation, conceptual buttressing, and/or empirical verification. Thus, within psychology today there appears to be a certain range, containing perhaps no more than three or four more or less similar degrees of precision of prediction and exactness of repeatability—ranging from unprovable to plausible—compared with the larger number of precision-uncertainty positions within the totality of sciences and disciplines. Recognizing this, we should attempt to extend our thoughts about psychological truth not only to include the notions of degrees of certainty, precision, and completeness but also to encompass the concepts of espousal, proof, and maximum potential verifiability, in addition to, and along with, our current ideas of validity. One implication of this is that a classification of types of validity (which might well include something akin to construct validity) would be only one subsection in a larger array of several ways of cognizing our data (Shneidman, 1962).

In the "early days" (roughly, say, in the decade or so before 1940), projective techniques (especially the Rorschach procedure) drifted over America from Europe like a front of cumulus clouds containing the promise of filtered sunshine and welcome precipitation. Concurrently, in our own land, especially in New England, native procedures were being developed. There was a warm breeziness to their style that facilitated empathy with, and understanding of, the individual—in short, attractive ancillae to the psychologist's main task of understanding the person. But today, like many other current psychological endeavors, projective techniques blow like a polar wind, all icicled with frozen tables of formidable numbers, victims to the fetish of particularization and precision. Certainly it was not the fact that the early projective technique proponents lacked courage or conviction that made this depressing outcome a reality, but simply that the moment that projective techniques were integrated with the current American Ph.D. system in psychology, with its essentially mathematical orientation, and became a permissible topic of doctoral dissertations, they were doomed. Their special fragile contribution, point of view, way of life, and philosophy of man were all broken to the mold. Many young American psychologists using projective techniques seem to have been seduced into incorporating (as part of their "criterion image") the standards which accrue to only one side—not necessarily their side—of this pervasive philosophic disputation. By their natures, neither side can probably ever be satisfied with the other's criteria of meaningfulness. The proponents of the humanistic approach will need to develop their own persuasive criteria for meaningfulness and "truth" and be content to be judged on *those* merits. As in *Peter and the Wolf*, in answer to the bird's question, "What kind of a duck are you if you can't fly?" they will need to reply with the duck's counterquestion: "What kind of a bird are you if you can't swim?" Thus, it is my thesis that for a psychologist to consider the topic of projective techniques productively, he must view this field as reflecting a long-standing philosophic (essentially epistemological) issue and, accordingly, come to some personally comfortable philosophic position. Taking this view at the outset may save him from being maneuvered into the position of feeling responsible for providing substantive answers to all sorts of inquiries (stated in conventional validity concepts couched in mathematical terms) which are philosophically irrelevant to his own private professional world.

Projective techniques derive their primary meaning within the purview of a humanistic orientation toward human personalities; otherwise they are just tests routinely administered and routinely interpreted. Projective techniques were never meant, in substance and certainly not in spirit, in either research or clinical practice, as a pictorial substitute for the MMPI or as an unstructured stand-in for the Stanford-Binet. Projective techniques are in essence an expression of a point of view. They are a frame of mind. They reflect the concern of the psychologist whose main interest is the study of man. They are an aspect of the armamentarium of that kind of psychologist who is not content to know some few preselected facts about many people (or even, for that matter, many facts about one person) but rather aspires to investigate with great intensity several people—paranormal, normal, subnormal—looking for what is found in all, present in many, and existent in only one: the ubiquitous, the usual, and the unique. The psychologist who, whatever his professed interest, takes for his primary data the ubiquitous and the usual is what we shall call the "normative" psychologist; the psychologist who is also concerned with the unique and is willing to study a relatively few individuals in depth has been called the "personologist." Projective techniques grew out of personological concerns. The major question seems to be their role in normative science. But, as we have polemicized above, the normative aspirations of projective techniques can also be seen as a clear case of trying to placate the other tribe's totem.

A few words about the "early history" of projective techniques. In most discussions of projective techniques, the names associated with their precursors—projective material or projective-like tests in the preprojective technique period (before the 1930s)—usually include Cattell, Galton, Kraepelin, Jung, Kent, and Rosanoff (in relation to word association); Whipple, Binet, and Stern (in relation to inkblots and cloud pictures); Tendler (in relation to sentence completion); and Brittain, Clark, Libby, and Schwartz (in relation to story construction), all of whom used unstructured stimulus materials or free situations in their investigations of personality (Lindzey, 1961). That their methods did not have the great impact of the Rorschach technique or the TAT may be ascribed largely to the fact that these efforts were not identified with a "movement" or an attitude toward personality or a philosophic point of view. Projective techniques in the current scene, by virtue of a growing sense of self-assurance, self-destiny, and self-identity, stand at the threshold of developing their own criteria of acceptability and giving their techniques and their approach to the human personality what is so rare in practical psychology, a philosophic rationale.

It is interesting to contrast the developments, over the past thirty or so years, of the two most commonly used projective techniques in the United States. The Rorschach technique has, from the time of its introduction, remained relatively sacrosanct. Although there have been important contributions by such pioneers as Klopfer, Beck, Piotrowski, and others, in a [illegible] essentially variations [illegible] theme. It would be po[illegible] course in the inkblot te[illegible] Rorschach's monograph as [illegible] tory of the TAT was very diffe[illegible] —in part because of its Brahmin [illegible] into American society (only one be[illegible] stunning volume of debuts) and, curiou[illegible] flecting in part the well-known gregarious[illegible] of most American psychologists—very early b[illegible] came everybody's favorite adopted baby to change and raise as he wished. For example, in 1951, when a volume called *Thematic Test Analysis* (Shneidman, 1951) appeared, it was possible to demonstrate over twenty different ways of approaching and interpreting that TAT task—not to mention the large number of variations of TAT-like pictorial materials: for Negroes, amputees, children, Indians, and even (during the Korean conflict) pro- and anti-Communists (Shneidman, 1952b).

The interplay and interaction of the special contributions of various projective techniques can be seen in a number of "cases" which have been published. Some examples are the case of Gregor (Bell, 1949), the case of Jay Shneidman, 1952a), the case of El (Shneidman, 1961), and the case of John Doe (Shneidman, 1951). From the last-named case, we see that the Rorschach interpretation seemed to emphasize symptoms and diagnoses, affect, and quality of perception and thought; the TAT interpretations focused more on symptoms and diagnoses, personality defenses and mechanisms, affect, and interpersonal relationships; the Draw-A-Person interpretation concerned itself more with symptoms and diagnoses, motivations and drives, and affect; and the Bender-Gestalt write-up spoke primarily of symptoms and diagnoses and personality defenses.

A listing of the 9 most useful references on projective techniques in general (as contrasted with references to any specific technique or to any specific issue) might very well include the following sources: Abt & Bellak, 1950; Anderson & Anderson, 1951; Frank, 1939; Frank, 1948; Lindzey, 1961; Murray, 1938; Rabin & Haworth, 1960; Sargent, 1948; White, 1944. For a concentrated reading list, Anderson & Anderson, 1951; Lindzey, 1961; and Sargent, 1948, are recommended, to which might usefully be added Gleser, 1963.

This discursive overview of projective tech-

Rorschach Technique

Rorschach's inkblot technique was first published in 1921 (Rorschach, 1921), and after its introduction in America by Beck (1930) and the establishment of the Rorschach Society by Klopfer in 1936, it became the most popular projective technique in both clinical work and personality research. It has been characterized (Beck, 1951) as a multidimensional test of personality.

Rorschach's hypothesis was that an individual's verbal responses to a highly ambiguous visual stimulus situation would, in microcosm, reflect that individual's idiosyncratic ways of perceiving his world and thus provide a sort of x ray of his personality structure.

The test consists of 10 inkblots (on 6- by 9-inch cards) which are symmetrical in shape. Half are achromatic, and the other five have one or more colors. The subject is handed the cards one at a time and is asked to report on what he sees and what it looks like to him. After the subject has responded to all 10 cards, he is (in the usual Klopfer inquiry) asked about the determinants of his perceptions. The most generally used scoring system is Klopfer's (1956). However, other systems (Beck, 1944; Beck, 1945; Beck, 1952; Piotrowski, 1957; Rorschach, 1921) are widely utilized. The scoring systems revolve around the *location* of the blot in which the percept was seen (whole, detail, etc.); the *qualitative aspects* of the perception (called "determinants"), which include shape, color, shading, and vista; and *content* of what was perceived.

In addition to the Rorschach technique, there are other inkblot tests, such as the Beta Ink Blot Test (Wheeler, 1938), Harrower Blots (Harrower, 1945), Levy Blots (Zubin, 1948), Behn-Rorschach Cards (Zulliger, 1952), Howard Blots (Howard, 1953), and the Holtzman Ink Blot Technique (Holtzman, 1961). A method of group administration for the Rorschach technique was developed by Harrower and Steiner (1945). There is a complete discussion of the Rorschach technique in "The Rorschach Inkblot Method," Chap. 21.

Thematic Apperception Test

The Thematic Apperception Test was developed by Henry Murray and his co-worker, Christiana Morgan, as part of their explorations in personality at the Harvard Psychological Clinic (Morgan & Murray, 1935). The TAT consists of 30 achromatic pictures, typically showing one or two individuals; where there are two or more individuals, they are depicted as interacting with one another in some fashion. Murray says: "The test is based on the well-recognized fact that when a person interprets an ambiguous social situation, he is apt to expose his own personality as much of the phenomena to which he is attending."

The 30 picture cards are divided so that the examiner can make up separate sets for males and females and for children, adolescents, and adults. Murray's (1943) instructions are generally followed. The cards are presented, one at a time, and the subject is asked to tell a story for each card. He is asked to tell what led up to the events described, what is happening, and how it will turn out. He is also invited to relate what the characters in his story are doing, thinking, and feeling.

Many different scoring and interpretation schemes have been devised for TAT. Murray's approach is in terms of pervasive thema, from which inferences about the subject's needs and press are drawn and, from them, further inferences about the salient dynamics of the subject's personality (1938; 1943).

Other scoring systems include those of Bel-

[1] It should be noted that although the word "test" is used as part of the title of most of the instruments described below, none of them is a test in the usual psychometric sense of the word; rather they constitute different sets of materials and might better be referred to as "techniques," or "methods," or "procedures." Within the context of this chapter, the word "test" is used as a shorthand device to convey this very thought.

[2] The most useful sources in preparing these précis were Buros's *Fifth Mental Measurements Yearbook* (1959) and Lindzey's *Projective Techniques and Cross-cultural Research*. The assistance of Dr. Charles Neuringer, of the University of Kansas, is gratefully acknowledged.

lak (1947), Henry (1947), Tomkins (1947), Wyatt (1947), Stein (1948), Aron (1949), and Fine (1955). Shneidman (1951) published a study bringing together various scoring systems demonstrated in terms of the same TAT protocol.

Several modifications or specific sets of the TAT have been developed for different types of subjects, such as TAT sets for Negroes (Thompson, 1949), for children (Bellak, 1954), for adolescents (Symonds, 1949; Hartwell et al., 1941), and for several exotic groups, including American Indians, South African natives, Pacific Islanders, etc. A symposium on recent theoretical issues concerned with Thematic Apperception Tests has been edited by Kagan and Lesser (1961). A comprehensive discussion of the TAT is given in "Thematic Apperceptive Methods," Chap. 22.

Draw-A-Person Test

The DAP was developed by K. Machover (1948; 1951) from F. Goodenough's (1926) technique of assessing intellectual levels of children from their drawings of a person. Machover believes that this technique can be used projectively to assess especially those aspects of psychodynamics involved with the self-image and with body images. The test is easy to administer. The subject is given a blank sheet of paper and is asked to "draw a person." After the first figure is drawn, the subject is then asked to draw a person of the opposite sex.

After the drawing session, the subject may be asked to tell a story about each of the persons. Two lists of questions concerning the figures (one for children and one for adults) have been developed by Machover (1951). This includes questions concerning the age, schooling, ambition, marital status, etc., of the drawn figures.

There are several variations of the DAP. Wagner and Schubert (1955) have developed a Draw-A-Person Quality Scale in which the drawing is assessed along an artistic scale running from zero to 8. Caligor's (1957) Eight Card Redrawing Test calls for eight drawings for each sex. Hammer has edited a book on the clinical application of projective drawings (1958). Other drawing techniques are the Drawing Completion Test (Kinget, 1952) and the Mira Myokinetic Test (Mira, 1940).

Bender Visual-Motor Gestalt Test

The Bender Visual-Motor Gestalt Test was introduced by L. Bender (1938; 1946) as a test of visual-motor coordination. The test is based on gestalt perceptional principles; the figures are, appropriately, taken from Wertheimer. The test consists of nine somewhat complex geometrical figures, each on a card, presented to the subject one at a time. The subject is asked to draw or make a copy of each figure. Sometimes the subject has the pattern before him, and sometimes it is taken away; or the subject may be asked to reproduce as many figures as possible from memory.

Even though the test was developed primarily to study visual-motor coordination and has been used as an instrument to test for the presence of organic brain damage and intellectual maturational development, it has come to be used as a projective technique. The style of the drawings, it has been claimed, reveals personality trends (e.g., collisions of figures imply disorganization, heavy lines indicate aggression and hostility, exact duplication suggests compulsive personality, etc.). A recent review of the literature on the Bender test has been completed by Billingslea (1963).

House-Tree-Person Test

Introduced by Buck in 1948, the House-Tree-Person Test requires the subject to draw a house, a tree, and a person, the examiner meanwhile noting the subject's sequence, tempo, behavior, etc. After the drawings are completed, the examiner conducts an extensive interview.

The test thus has a relatively nonverbal unstructured phase, followed by a somewhat more structured verbal period. Buck chose these specific items of house, tree, and person because of their familiarity, their general acceptance, and their apparent proclivity for stimulating free verbalizations. Buck believes that each drawing is a "self-portrait" and that the details of the drawings have personal significance. In addition to the claim that the H-T-P Test is a test for personality (affect, psychosexual level, needs, etc.), he believes that is assesses intellectual features as well. Buck (1948a; 1949) and Hammer (1960) have written about the H-T-P technique.

Sentence-completion Technique

The sentence-completion technique seems to have evolved as a development from word association techniques. Tendler (1930) was the first to use the technique, and it was soon modified by Rohde and Hildreth (Rohde, 1946). Proponents generally believe that SCT responses reflect attitudes, motives, and conflicts (Lindzey, 1961).

Sentence-completion tests are easy to administer and consist of a series of sentence stubs or stems of one or more words which the subject is asked to complete with words of his own choosing. The number of items, as well as the instructions to subjects, varies among the different tests. Subjects are sometimes asked to respond with the very first "thought" that comes into their minds or to take their time and complete the sentence as it applies to them.

There are several sentence-completion tests. Among the best known is the Rotter Incomplete Sentence Blank (Rotter & Rafferty, 1950), which deals with the single variable of personality stability. The Forer Structured Sentence Completion Test (Forer, 1950) is a 100-item inventory that was designed to help in therapy planning. These are separate forms for males and females. The items are grouped to tap certain key areas, such as interpersonal involvements, wishes, aggression, anxieties, etc.

Among the other sentence-completion tests available are the Sachs Sentence Completion Test (Sachs & Levy, 1950), the Sentence Completion Test (Rohde, 1946; Rohde, 1947), the Curtis Completion Test (cf. Buros, 1959), the Forer Vocational Survey (cf. Buros, 1959), the Incomplete Sentence Test for Industrial Use (cf. Buros, 1959). Other forms of the test have also been developed and utilized (Hanfmann & Getzels, 1953; Sanford et al., 1943; Stein, 1947; etc.).

Picture-Frustration Study

The Picture-Frustration Study grew out of Rosenzweig's theoretical interest in the psychoanalytic concept of repression (1945, 1949). He considers the PF Study a controlled projective technique and focuses on the individual's pattern of reactions to frustration.

The subject is given a booklet containing 24 cartoonlike drawings. Each cartoon shows two people in a situation where one is frustrated by the actions of the other. The verbal comments of the frustrator are printed in the cartoon, and the subject is asked to write in the first appropriate reply that comes to mind, from the point of view of the frustrated person.

The test is scored in terms of the direction of the response (intropunitive, extrapunitive, or impunitive) and the type of response (obstacle-dominant, ego-defensive, or need-persistive).

Combinations of type and direction yield nine different possible scores. There is also an over-all group conformity rating which is an index of how conventional the responses are. Norms are available. The PF is easy to administer and can be used with groups and has objective scoring criteria. However, it is primarily focused on dealing with frustration variables.

There is available a PF form for children (Rosenzweig, Fleming, & Rosenzweig, 1948) and a form developed for the study of attitude toward minority groups (Brown, 1947).

Make-A-Picture-Story Test

The MAPS Test, introduced in 1947 by Shneidman, is essentially a variation of the TAT principle in which the backgrounds and the human figures are separated so that the subject can be asked to populate a background picture and then to respond, in TAT fashion, to a situation which he has in part created. The test materials consist of 22 background pictures (such as a living room, street scene, bathroom, bedroom, cave, attic, desert scene, etc.) and 67 appropriately scaled figures. The figures include adults, children, legendary figures, animals, etc. The backgrounds are presented one at a time; all 67 figures are visible to the subject. The subject's choice and placement of the figures for each background—the dramatis personae of his fantasy drama—are recorded on a figure location sheet. The opportunity thus exists not only for the interpretation of the subject's story, as one might interpret a TAT story, but also for the quantitative analysis of the choice and placement of the figures. References to the MAPS Test include work with children and adolescents (Bindou, 1957; Joel, 1948; Shneidman, 1960; Spiegelman, 1956), as well as multiple interpretations of a single case (Shneidman, 1951).

Auditory Apperception Test

The AAT appeared in 1953. It is an auditory projective technique, and its developer, Stone (1950), feels that its basic rationale is the same as that of the TAT. The materials consist of five 45-rpm records which have a variety of sounds (typewriter, windstorm, foghorn, etc.). There are 10 sets of three sounds each. After hearing a set, the subject is asked to make up a story using the sounds. He is asked to tell what led up to it, what is happening now, and how it will end. The test is recommended for use with groups and for blind subjects.

There are some other auditory methods available. The American Foundation for the Blind has an auditory projective test (Buros, 1959). K. L. Bean is at present developing a sound apperception test (Buros, 1959). Notable among auditory techniques is the tautaphone method (Shakow & Rosenzweig, 1940), based on Skinner's (1936) verbal summator. The tautaphone is a record of a series of random vowel sounds. The S is asked to tell what different things the man on the record is saying.

Blacky Pictures

The Blacky Pictures were developed by Blum (1949; 1950; Blum & Hunt, 1952) and utilize the TAT technique of having subjects give spontaneous stories to pictures. Blum originally developed his test as a method of evaluating psychoanalytic concepts, specifically those regarding psychosexual development. The test is composed of twelve cartoon drawings concerning the adventures of a small dog named "Blacky." For male subjects, Blacky is introduced as a male, and for female subjects, Blacky is described as a female. Other cartoon characters are Blacky's mother, father, and undeterminantly sexed sibling called "Tippy." Animals are used because Blum feels that remoteness from realistic figures and events stimulates fantasy production. The cards are designed to relate to the psychoanalytic areas of oral eroticism, oral sadism, anal sadism, oedipal intensity, masturbation guilt, castration fear, penis envy, etc.

The administration of the test is similar to that of the TAT except for special introductory remarks made for each card [e.g., "Here is Blacky and his (her) mamma"]. After the subject tells his (her) story, he is asked to answer a series of standardized questions aimed at eliciting psychoanalytic evidence.

Düss (Despert) Fables

The Düss Fables were introduced (in French) in 1940 (Düss, 1940; cf. Wursten, 1960) and were later translated by Despert (1946; 1949) into English. They have become generally known as the Despert Fables. The fables were designed to tap emotional conflict areas in children. The fables consist of 10 short anecdotes in each of which a problem is posed for the child. The fables are read to the child, and he is asked to solve the problem posed. The particular fables are designed to evaluate certain areas such as weaning complex, castration fears, possessiveness, etc.

One such fable, which deals with the child's separation anxieties about the parents, goes as follows:

> A daddy and mommy bird and their little baby bird are sleeping in a nest on a branch of a tree. All of a sudden a big wind comes along and shakes the tree, and the nest falls to the ground. The three birds wake up quickly. The daddy flies to a pine tree, the mother to another pine tree. What is the little bird going to do? He already knows how to fly a bit (Wursten, 1960)

Other story-completion methods available for children are the Madeleine Thomas Stories (Thomas, 1937) and Raven's Controlled Projection Method (Raven, 1951).

Finger Painting

The use of finger painting as a recreational medium was revived by Ruth Shaw in 1932. Napoli (1946; 1947) further developed and refined the technique so that it can be used as a diagnostic and therapeutic device. Finger painting has several characteristics. As it is one of the least structured of the testing situations, it lends itself well to the stimulation of free associative processes and thus reduces content-derived blocking and resistance. It is readily adaptable to either individual or group situations, and it is applicable for most persons because the directions and procedure are quite simple.

In practice, the subject is presented with a wet piece of paper and is allowed to select the desired colors of paint. He is instructed to "cover the whole sheet of paper and to go off the sides of the paper." Throughout the painting session as well as during the clean-up period, the subject is encouraged to offer verbalizations regarding the painting process or the "finished product." The desirability and value of collecting a series of such "free expression" paintings over a relatively long period of time are stressed. The four commonly used diagnostic indicators are motor behavior, paint preference, formal and symbolic characteristics of the design, and the subject's verbalizations.

Four Picture Test

The FPT was first published in 1948 by Van Lennep (1948; 1951), although he worked on it for several years before that. The stated rationale is that stories given for the FPT reflect the subject's general attitudes toward life very quickly. The author feels that these attitudes are determined by the person's personality dynamics and their interactive effect indication of the person's abilities, of his feelings about himself, and of his interpersonal social milieu. The test consists of four separate small colored pictures. Each of the pictures is vaguely drawn. Picture I represents being with one person; picture II, being personally alone; picture III, being socially alone; and picture IV, being with many others in a group. In giving the FPT, the four pictures are placed in front of the subject in order. The subject then is asked to make a single story in which all four pictures are incorporated. He may use any sequence and is often asked to make up as many integrated stories as possible. Content analyses of the stories, as well as formal analyses of the sequences in which the pictures were used, are employed.

Insight Test

An interesting approach to projective testing has been developed by H. Sargent (1944). She has attempted, in her Insight Test, to evaluate the individual's affective and cognitive reactions by the use of a "paper-and-pencil" projective form. This goal is approached by asking the feelings of a fictional person. One of the 15 situations that is posed to the subject is as follows: "A young man gets the impression that others are discussing him. On several occasions he thinks the conversation has stopped or the subject changed when he entered the room. (A) What did he do and why? (B) How did he feel?" It is from the answers that the subjects writes out that the examiner can make meaningful statements about the person's insights and personality. The various situations tap such areas as family adjustments, attitudes toward the opposite sex, religion, vocational feelings, etc. The responses are analyzed into three areas with respect to the types of emotional expressions used, various cognitive expressions employed, and the type of conflict solution arrived at.

Mosaic Test

The Mosaic Test was developed by Lowenfeld (1952; 1954) and consists of over four hundred small tile or plastic chips of varying designs (squares, diamonds, and triangles) and varying colors. The subject is given the chips and is told to make anything he wants to out of them. The test has been studied by Diamond and Schmale (1944) and has been used more for diagnostic purposes than for the evaluation of personality dynamics. Mosaic patterns are graded from normal mosaics (a pattern demonstrating that the subject has spontaneously developed and executed a pattern utilizing forms and colors to make a recognized and balanced design) to severely defective mosaics (patterns showing little or no inner coherence and organization).

Picture Arrangement Test

The Tomkins-Horn PAT (Tomkins, 1957; Tomkins, 1959) is of special interest because it attempts to unite both the qualitative-intuitive features of the usual projective methods and the quantitative exactness of the psychometric tradition. The two foundations for the PAT are the TAT, with its thematic content materials, and the picture arrangement subject of the Wechsler-Bellevue Intelligence Scale. The PAT consists of 25 plates, each with three drawings depicting the activities of a person. The subject is asked to arrange the drawings in a sequence and to tell what is going on in the pictures. The sources of interpretative data are the ordering of the pictures and the verbal comments of the subject. The latter source utilizes clinical wisdom, while the former source is the heart of the PAT method. The authors have developed norms from normal and disturbed subjects dealing with frequencies of arrangements. The test is easy to administer and can be used with groups.

Psychodrama

Psychodrama as a projective technique was developed by Moreno (1946) from previous work in sociometry and sociodrama. The subject is asked actually to act out situations which are personally meaningful to him and situations in which he interacts with others. There is no standard procedure that is followed, although Hass and Moreno (1951) have produced a general script, in which "auxiliary egos" (trained actors) confront subjects with basic stimulus conditions. The way that the subject handles his acting role is compared with other performances. Sometimes the subject is asked to create an imaginary person and then build a relationship. Observations concerning what kind of relationship is constructed and how the subject communicates are noted.

Moreno feels that only in psychodrama is the subject able to express highly personalized affect material in a situation that is close to ordinary life. He feels that spontaneity and the ability to role-play are of prime importance in uncovering and understanding conflict dynamics.

Interpretation is wholly qualitative. The method has been used profitably as a training device, but its general use as a projective tool is limited because it is relatively time-consuming and elaborate.

Puppetry

The utilization of puppets as a projective technique dates from work within the last decade (Haworth, 1957; Woltman, 1951; Woltman, 1955; Woltman, 1958). To date, the technique has not conspicuously developed any standard procedures, scoring systems, or interpretative hypotheses but relies on the insights and creativity of the puppeteer. Often the puppeteer will make use of the puppets in ingenious ways (e.g., using them with children who are willing to talk with a puppet but not with adult human beings) and for special circumstances (e.g., having the child play out a sibling rivalry incident).

The various puppetry techniques vary and depend on the ingenuity of the examiner. He may stage a puppet show and watch the child's reactions, or he may have the puppets talk to the child. Children are also asked to put on their own puppet shows and act out home situations with a mamma, papa, and baby puppet. Often the children are told to direct a puppet show that is being put on by the examiner. The child thus has a chance to tell the puppets what to do.

There is also the technique of group puppetry, where several children put on a spontaneous puppet show. The interactions among the puppets are noted (e.g., which puppet is afraid of other puppets, whose puppet is aggressed against, etc.).

It is felt that puppetry works well with children because they lose themselves in fantasy and thus produce rich materials. However, the technique does require having a number of varied puppets on hand. Haworth (1957) has tried to solve this problem by producing a filmed puppet show which she hopes to use as a standard stimulus.

Symbol Arrangement Test

The Symbol Arrangement Test was introduced by Kahn in 1955 (Kahn, 1955). It consists of 16 plastic geometrical shapes (such as hearts, stars, dogs, an anchor, a circle, a cross, etc.). The subject is shown a strip of felt that is divided into 15 numbered parts, and he is asked to group the objects into rectangles denoted as "love," "hate," "bad," "good," "living," "dead," "small," and "large." Kahn (1956; 1957) has developed a scoring system which he feels yields objective scoring criteria about the subject's unconscious symbolization processes.

After each trial, the subject is requested to free-associate to the symbolic meaning of each of the objects. After the five trials, the subject is asked to group the objects into rectangles denoted as "love," "hate," "bad," "good," "living," "dead," "small," and "large." Kahn (1956; 1957) has developed a scoring system which he feels yields objective scoring criteria about the subject's unconscious symbolization processes.

Szondi Test

The Szondi Test was developed in Hungary (Szondi, 1947a; Szondi, 1947b) and was brought to this country by one of Szondi's students, S. K. Deri (1949a; 1949b). Szondi's philosophical background is one colored by the concept of genetic determinism. His test was developed to measure families of unconscious traits associated with recessive gene organizations. However, the test can be utilized independently of Szondi's elaborate theories.

The test is composed of 48 cards on which there are portraits of faces. These are portraits of mental patients, representing eight diagnostic categories (homosexuality, sadism, epilepsy, hysteria, catatonic schizophrenia, paranoid schizophrenia, depression, and mania). The 48 cards are divided into six sets of eight cards apiece. Each set contains one card from each of the eight diagnostic categories. The examiner spreads out each set of cards one at a time and asks the subject to choose the two he likes best and the two he likes least from each set.

The interpretation is made from the analysis of cards chosen and rejected through a profile analysis method which accounts for the number of selected and rejected cards occurring in any of the eight diagnostic categories. If four or more pictures occur in a diagnostic category either favorably or unfavorably, that diagnostic area is said to be "loaded" (i.e., there is tension within that area). If most of the card selections are positive for a certain diagnostic area, it is felt that the subject identifies with that group. If the cards are negative, then it is believed that the person denies, rejects, and is alienated from those feelings. Equal distribution indicates ambivalence, whereas a lack of selections or rejections for a particular diagnostic category indicates that tension is absent in that area. Szondi has developed a series of drive vectors which he uses to interpret the protocols further. It is recommended that the test be administered at least six times to get a stable personality picture.

Three Dimensional Apperception Test

The Three Dimensional Apperception Test was published by D. Twitchell-Allen in 1947 (1947; 1948). The test uses small amorphous three-dimensional objects. Twitchell-Allen feels that the test is useful for diagnosis and therapy. She also points out that the use of the tactile, kinesthetic, and haptic dimensions, over and above the usual visual and auditory dimensions found in projective testing techniques, adds ambiguity and areas for projection.

The test is composed of 28 ambiguous plastic forms which vary from geometric (block, ball, cylinder, etc.) to generalized organic forms and more concrete human and animal forms. There are two parts to the administration. Part I is known as the "psychodramatic test." Here, the 28 pieces are laid down on a table in a prescribed order. The subject is asked to choose some forms and make up a story about them. The subject takes the forms he has chosen and utilizes them in his storytelling. He may add additional forms if so desired. The handling of the objects is recorded along with the story. Part II is known as the "naming test." The examiner holds up each figure, and the subject is asked to name it and describe what it is. An inquiry concerning the responses can be given. The subject is then asked to tell another story. The Three Dimensional Apperception Test can be used with blind subjects and with blindfolded subjects as an added evaluation technique. A book by Fein (1960) contains much useful information about this test.

Word Association Test

The word association technique has a long history in experimental psychology; e.g., Wundt used it. Kraepelin learned about it in Wundt's laboratory in Leipzig, and in 1892 he used it with neuropsychiatric patients. Jung (1918) was much interested in it and developed it for the purposes of studying "complexes." Kent and Rosanoff (1910), using a list of 100 words, established population norms for different responses. Luria (1932) added measurements of associated physicomotoric responses to the word association responses.

The word association technique consists of a list of words which is read by the examiner to the subject one at a time. The subject is asked to respond with the first word, image, idea, or percept that occurs to him. He is asked not to reflect or reason but to give his most immediate response. The verbal associations are recorded as well as hesitations, reflections, blockings, etc., of responses.

The word association data can be analyzed in several ways. A response can be compared with norm frequency tables in order to establish whether it is common or idiosyncratic. Norm frequency of response tables for different diagnostic groups are available (Kent & Rosanoff, 1910). The hesitations, blocks, confusions, etc., can be analyzed along content lines in order to identify tension and conflict areas. Rapaport, Gill, and Schafer (1946) have developed a series of signs and clues for use by clinicians in studying word association responses.

The technique is used mostly for assessing general adjustment and neuroticism. It is easy to administer and score, and there are many normative data available. Special lists can, of course, be constructed to explore specific problems.

World Test

There are several versions of the World Test. The prototype seems to have been developed by Lowenfeld (1939), although miniature toys and objects had been used by Erikson in his Dramatic Productions Test (1938). Other forms of the technique have been developed by Bolgar and Fischer (1947) and by Buhler (Buhler, Lumry, & Carrol, 1951). In the world test, subjects are given numerous miniature objects such as houses, trees, soldiers, automobiles, etc., and are told to do what they like with them. Subjects usually construct panoramas. The examiner then discusses the constructions with the subjects, inquiring about the meanings, events, etc., accompanying the world-building activity.

The technique seems to be highly applicable to children, but it has been used with adults as well. Interpretation is qualitative, with few objective norms. Buhler et al. (1951) feel that there are five kinds of symptom worlds (aggressive, in which killing, accidents, etc., occur; empty, in which few objects are used; closed, in which many fences and enclosures are used; chaotic, in which the pieces are scattered without coherent organization; and rigid, in which the constructions are oversymmetrical). Buhler feels that the construction of two or more symptom worlds is indicative of psychopathology. In scoring and evaluating such things as choice of objects, form, and content, the subject's behavior and verbalizations are of importance.

Recently Buhler and Manson (1956) have developed a world test technique in which several pictures are pasted onto large sheets and the subject can draw in objects.

REFERENCES

General References

Abt, L. E., & Bellak, L. (Eds.) *Projective psychology.* New York: Knopf, 1950.

Anderson, H. H., & Anderson, Gladys L. (Eds.) *An introduction to projective techniques.* Englewood Cliffs, N.J.: Prentice-Hall, 1951.

Bechtoldt, H. P. Construct validity: a critique. *Amer. Psychologist,* 1959, **14,** 619–629.

Bell, J. E. *Projective techniques.* New York: Longmans, 1948.

Bell, J. E. The case of Gregor. *J. proj. Tech.,* 1949, **13,** 155–205, 433–468.

Bellak, L. Thematic apperception: failures and the defenses. *Trans. New York Acad. Sci.,* 1950, **12,** 122–126.

Blatt, S. J. The objective and subjective modes: some considerations in the teaching of clinical skills. *J. proj. Tech. Pers. Assessment,* 1963, **27,** 151–157.

Bridgman, P. W. *The way things are.* New York: Viking, 1961.

Buros, O. K. *The fifth mental measurements yearbook.* Highland Park, N.J.: Gryphon Press, 1959.

Campbell, D. T. A typology of testing, projective and otherwise. *J. consult. Psychol.,* 1957, **21,** 207–210.

Carr, A. C., Forer, B. R., Henry, W. E., Hooker, Evelyn, Hutt, M. L., & Piotrowski, Z. A. *The prediction of overt behavior through the use of projective techniques.* Springfield Ill.: Charles C Thomas, 1960.

Cattell, R. B. *Personality and motivation structure and measurement.* Yonkers, N.Y.: World Book, 1957.

Cohen, M. R. *Preface to logic.* New York: Holt, 1944. Pp. 197–198. (Originally published in *New Republic,* 1916, **8,** 118.)

Crombie, A. C. (Ed.) *Turning points in physics.* New York: Harper Torchbooks, 1961.

Cronbach, L. J. *Essentials of psychological testing.* (2nd ed.) New York: Harper & Row, 1960.

Cronbach, L. J., et al. Technical recommendations for psychological tests and diagnostic techniques. *Psychol. Bull. Suppl.,* 1954, **51** (2), Part 2, 1–38.

Cronbach, L. J., & Meehl, P. E. Construct validity in psychological tests. *Psychol. Bull.,* 1955, **52,** 281–302.

Edwards, W., Lindman, H., & Savage, L. J. Bayesian statistical inference for psychological research. *Psychol. Rev.,* 1963, **70,** 193–242.

Einstein, A., & Infeld, L. *The evolution of physics.* New York: Simon and Schuster, 1938.

Eysenck, H. J. The effects of psychotherapy. In H. J. Eysenck (Ed.), *Handbook of abnormal psychology.* New York: Basic Books, 1961.

Frank, L. K. Projective methods for the study of personality. *J. Psychol.,* 1939, **8,** 389–413. (Also in *Trans. N.Y. Acad. Sci.,* 1939, **1,** 129–132.)

Frank, L. K. *Projective methods.* Springfield, Ill.: Charles C Thomas, 1948.

Gleser, Goldine C. Projective methodologies. In P. R. Farnsworth (Ed.), *Annu. Rev. Psychol.,* 1963, **14,** 391–422.

Guilford, J. P. *Personality.* New York: McGraw-Hill, 1959.

Hanfmann, Eugenia. William Stern on "projective techniques." *J. Pers.,* 1952, **21,** 1–21.

Harrower, Molly. *Appraising personality: an introduction to the projective techniques.* New York: F. Watts, 1964.

Healy, W., Bronner, A., & Bowers, A. M. *The structure and meaning of psychoanalysis.* New York: Knopf, 1930.

Holt, R. R. The nature of TAT stories as cognitive products: a psychoanalytic approach. In J. Kagan & G. Lesser (Eds.), *Contemporary issues in thematic apperceptive methods.* Springfield, Ill.: Charles C Thomas, 1961.

Lazarus, R. S. *Adjustment and personality.* New York: McGraw-Hill, 1961.

Lesser, G. S. Custom making projective techniques for research. *J. proj. Tech.*, 1961, **25,** 21–31.

Lindzey, G. On the classification of projective techniques. *Psychol. Bull.*, 1959, **56,** 158–168.

Lindzey, G. *Projective techniques and cross-cultural research.* New York: Appleton-Century-Crofts, 1961.

Little, K. B. Problems in the validation of projective techniques. *J. proj. Tech.*, 1959, **23,** 287–290.

Little, K. B., & Shneidman, E. S. Congruencies among interpretations of psychological test and anamnestic data. *Psychol. Monogr.*, 1959, **73,** 1–42.

MacCorquodale, K., & Meehl, P. E. On a distinction between hypothetical constructs and intervening variables. *Psychol. Rev.*, 1948, **55,** 95–107.

Maslow, A. H. Dynamics of personality organization. *Psychol. Rev.*, 1943, **50,** 514–539, 541–558.

Meehl, P. E. *Clinical versus statistical prediction.* Minneapolis, Minn.: Univer. of Minnesota Press, 1954.

Morgan, Christiana, & Murray, H. A. A method for investigating fantasies: the Thematic Apperception Test. *Arch. Neurol. Psychiat.*, 1935, **34,** 289–306.

Murphy, G. *Personality.* New York: Harper & Row, 1947.

Murray, H. A. *American Icarus.* In A. Burton & R. E. Harris (Eds.), *Clinical studies of personality.* New York: Harper & Row, 1955.

Murray, H. A. The personality and career of Satan. *J. Soc. Issues,* 1962, **18,** 36–54.

Murray, H. A. *Explorations in personality.* New York: Science Editions, 1962. (a)

Rabin, A. I., & Haworth, Mary R. (Eds.) *Projective techniques with children.* New York: Grune & Stratton, 1960.

Rapaport, D., Gill, M., & Schafer, R. *Diagnostic psychological testing.* Vol. II. Chicago: Year Book Publishers, 1946.

Rorschach, H. *Psychodiagnostics.* Berne: Verlag Hans Huber, 1921. New York: Grune & Stratton, 1942.

Sargent, Helen. Projective methods: their origins, theory, and application in personality research. *Psychol. Bull.*, 1945, **42,** 257–293.

Schafer, R. *The clinical application of psychological tests.* New York: International Universities Press, 1948.

Shneidman, E. S. (Ed.) *Thematic test analysis.* New York: Grune & Stratton, 1951.

Shneidman, E. S. The case of Jay. *J. proj. Tech.*, 1952, **16,** 297–345, 444–475. (a)

Shneidman, E. S. The TAT newsletter. *J. proj. Tech.*, 1952, **16,** 378–382. (b)

Shneidman, E. S. Current aspects of the problem of validity: suggestions for the delineation of validational studies. *J. proj. Tech.*, 1959, **23,** 259–262.

Shneidman, E. S. The case of El. *J. proj. Tech.*, 1961, **25,** 131–154, 390–403.

Shneidman, E. S. Projections on a triptych: or a hagiology for our time. *J. proj. Tech.*, 1962, **26,** 379–387.

Sundberg, N. D. The practice of psychological testing in clinical services in the United States. *Amer. Psychologist,* 1961, **16,** 79–83.

Super, D. E. Theories and assumptions underlying approaches to personality assessment. In B. Bass & I. Berg (Eds.), *Objective approaches to personality assessment.* Princeton, N.J.: Van Nostrand, 1959.

Symonds, P. M. *The dynamics of human adjustment.* New York: Appleton-Century-Crofts, 1946.

White, R. W. Interpretation of imaginative productions. In J. McV. Hunt (Ed.), *Personality and the behavior disorders.* New York: Ronald, 1944.

White, R. W. (Ed.) *The study of lives: essays in honor of Henry A. Murray.* New York: Atherton Press, 1963.

References to Specific Projective Techniques

Rorschach and other inkblot techniques

Beck, S. J. *Rorschach's test.* Vol. I. *Basic processes.* New York: Grune & Stratton, 1944.

Beck, S. J. *Rorschach's test.* Vol. II. *A variety of personality pictures.* New York: Grune & Stratton, 1945.

Beck, S. J. *Rorschach's test.* Vol. III. *Advances in interpretation.* New York: Grune & Stratton, 1952.

Beck, S. J. The Rorschach test: a multidimensional test of personality. In H. H. Anderson & Gladys L. Anderson (Eds.), *An introduction to projective techniques.* Englewood Cliffs, N.J.: Prentice-Hall, 1951.

Bochner, Ruth, & Halpern, Florence. *The clinical application of the Rorschach test.* (Rev. ed.) New York: Grune & Stratton, 1945.

Harrower, Molly R. *Psychodiagnostic inkblots.* New York: Grune & Stratton, 1945.

Harrower, Molly, & Steiner, M. Elisabeth. *Large-scale Rorschach techniques.* Springfield, Ill.: Charles C Thomas, 1945.

Harrower, Molly R., and Steiner, M. Elisabeth. *Manual for Harrower inkblots: individual, group and self-administered methods.* (Rev. ed.) New York: Grune & Stratton, 1960.

Holtzman, W. H. *Inkblot perception and personality: Holtzman inkblot technique.* Austin, Tex.: Univer. of Texas Press, 1961.

Howard, J. W. The Howard Ink Blot Test. *J. clin. Psychol.*, 1953, **9**, 209–255.

Klopfer, B., Ainsworth, Mary D., Klopfer, W. G., & Holt, R. R. *Developments in the Rorschach technique.* Vol. I. *Technique and theory.* New York: Harcourt, Brace & World, 1954.

Klopfer, B., & Kelley, D. M. *The Rorschach technique.* New York: Harcourt, Brace & World, 1946.

Klopfer, B., et al. *Developments in the Rorschach technique.* Vol. II. *Fields of application.* New York: Harcourt, Brace & World, 1956.

Piotrowski, Z. A. *Perceptanalysis.* New York: Macmillan, 1957.

Rabin, A. I. Validating the experimental studies with the Rorschach method. In H. H. Anderson & Gradys L. Anderson (Eds.), *An introduction to projective techniques.* Englewood Cliffs, N.J.: Prentice-Hall, 1951.

Rorschach, H. *Psychodiagnostics.* Bern: Verlag Hans Huber, 1921. New York: Grune & Stratton, 1942. (2nd ed.)

Schafer, R. *Psychoanalytic interpretation in Rorschach testing.* New York: Grune & Stratton, 1954.

Wheeler, D. R. Imaginal productivity tests: Beta Ink Blot Test. In H. A. Murray (Ed.), *Explorations in personality.* New York: Oxford Univer. Press, 1938.

Zubin, J., & Young, K. M. *Manual of projective and cognate techniques.* Madison, Wis.: College Typing Co., 1948.

Zulliger, H. *Der Behn-Rorschach Test.* Bern: Verlag Hans Huber, 1952.

Thematic Apperception Test

Aron, Betty. *A manual for analysis of the Thematic Apperception Test.* Berkeley, Calif.: Willis E. Berg, 1949.

Bellak, L. *A guide to the interpretation of the Thematic Apperception Test.* New York: Psychological Corporation, 1947.

Bellak, L. *The Thematic Apperception Test and Children's Apperception Test in clinical use.* New York: Grune & Stratton, 1954.

Bellak, L., & Adelman, Crusa. The Children's Apperception Test (CAT). In A. I. Rabin & M. R. Haworth (Eds.), *Projective techniques with children.* New York: Grune & Stratton, 1960.

Fine, R. A scoring scheme and manual for the TAT and other verbal projective techniques. *J. proj. Tech.*, 1955, **19**, 306–309.

Hartwell, S. W., et al. The Michigan Picture Test: diagnostic and therapeutic possibilities of a new projective test for children. *Amer. J. Orthopsychiat.*, 1951, **21**, 124–127.

Henry, W. E. The Thematic-Apperception technique in the study of culture-personality relations. *Genet. Psychol. Monogr.*, 1947, **35**, 3–315.

Henry, W. E. The thematic apperception technique in the study of group and cultural problems. In H. H. Anderson & Gladys L. Anderson (Eds.), *An introduction to projective techniques.* Englewood Cliffs, N.J.: Prentice-Hall, 1951.

Henry, W. E. *The analysis of fantasy.* New York: Wiley, 1956.

Holt, R. R. The Thematic Apperception Test. In H. H. Anderson & Gladys L. Anderson (Eds.), *An introduction to projective techniques.* Englewood Cliffs, N.J.: Prentice-Hall, 1951.

Kagan, J., & Lesser, G. (Eds.), *Contemporary issues in thematic apperception methods.* Springfield, Ill.: Charles C Thomas, 1961.

Lindzey, G. Thematic Apperception Test: interpretative assumptions and related empirical evidence. *Psychol. Bull.*, 1952, **49**, 1–25.

Mayman, M. Review of the literature on the Thematic Apperception Test. In D. Rapaport (Ed.), *Diagnostic psychological testing.* Vol. II. Chicago: Year Book Medical Publishers, 1948.

Morgan, Christiana D., & Murray, H. A. A method for investigating fantasies: the Thematic Apperception Test. *Arch. Neurol. Psychiat.*, 1935, **34**, 289–306.

Murray, H. A. *Explorations in personality.* New York: Oxford Univer. Press, 1938.

Murray, H. A. *Thematic Apperception Test manual.* Cambridge, Mass.: Harvard Univer. Press, 1943.

Rapaport, D. The Thematic Apperception Test. In *Diagnostic psychological testing.* Vol. II. Chicago: Year Book Medical Publishers, 1946. Chap. 4.

Shneidman, E. S. (Ed.) *Thematic test analysis.* New York: Grune & Stratton, 1951.

Stein, M. I. *The Thematic Apperception Test.* Reading, Mass.: Addison-Wesley, 1948.

Symonds, P. M. *Adolescent fantasy: an investigation of the picture-story method of personality study.* New York: Columbia Univer. Press, 1949.

Thompson, C. E. The Thompson modification of the Thematic Apperception Test. *J. proj. Tech.,* 1949, **13,** 469–478.

Tomkins, S. S. *The Thematic Apperception Test.* New York: Grune & Stratton, 1947.

Wyatt, F. The scoring and analyses of the Thematic Apperception Test. *J. Psychol.,* 1947, **24,** 319–330.

Draw-A-Person Test

Caligor, L. *A new approach to figure drawing: based upon an interrelated series of drawings.* Springfield, Ill.: Charles C Thomas, 1957.

Goodenough, F. L. *Measurement of intelligence by drawings.* Tarrytown-on-Hudson, N.Y.: World, 1926.

Hammer, E. F. (Ed.) *The clinical application of projective drawings.* Springfield, Ill.: Charles C Thomas, 1958.

Kinget, Marian G. *The Drawing-Completion Test: a projective technique for the investigation of personality based on the Wartegg test blank.* New York: Grune & Stratton, 1952.

Levy, S. Figure drawing as a projective test. In L. E. Abt & L. Bellak (Eds.), *Projective psychology.* New York: Knopf, 1950.

Machover, Karen. *Personality projection in the drawing of the human figure.* Springfield, Ill.: Charles C Thomas, 1948.

Machover, Karen. Drawing of the human figure: a method of personality investigation. In H. H. Anderson & Gladys L. Anderson (Eds.), *An introduction to projective techniques.* Englewood Cliffs, N.J.: Prentice-Hall, 1951.

Mira, E. Myokinetic psychodiagnosis: a new technique for exploring the conative trends of personality. *Proc. roy. Soc. Med.,* 1940, **33,** 173–194.

Wagner, Mazie E., & Schubert, H. J. P. Figure drawing norms: reliability and validity indices for normal late adolescents. II. Development of a pictorial scale of draw-a-person quality. *Amer. Psychologist,* 1955, **30,** 321.

Bender Visual-Motor Gestalt Test

Bender, Lauretta. *A visual motor gestalt test and its clinical use. Res. Monogr.* No. 3. New York: American Orthopsychiatric Association, 1938.

Bender, Lauretta. *Instructions for the use of the Visual Motor Gestalt Test.* New York: American Orthopsychiatric Association, 1946.

Billingslea, F. Y. The Bender gestalt: a review and a perspective. *Psychol. Bull.,* 1963, **60,** 233–251.

Halpern, Florence. The Bender Visual Motor Gestalt Test. In H. H. Anderson & Gladys L. Anderson (Eds.), *An introduction to projective techniques.* Englewood Cliffs, N.J.: Prentice-Hall, 1951.

Hutt, M. L. Revised Bender Visual Motor Gestalt Test. In A. Weider (Ed.), *Contributions toward medical psychology.* New York: Ronald, 1953.

Hutt, M. L. The revised Bender-Gestalt Visual Motor Test. In A. C. Carr et al., *The prediction of overt behavior through the use of projective techniques.* Springfield, Ill.: Charles C Thomas, 1960.

Woltmann, A. G. The Bender Visual-Motor Gestalt Test. In L. E. Abt & L. Bellak (Eds.), *Projective psychology.* New York: Knopf, 1950.

House-Tree-Person Test

Buck, J. N. The H-T-P technique: a qualitative and quantitative scoring manual. I. *J. clin. Psychol.,* 1948, **4,** 319–396. (a)

Buck, J. N. The H-T-P Test. *J. clin. Psychol.,* 1948, **4,** 151–159. (b)

Buck, J. N. The H-T-P technique: a qualitative and quantitative scoring manual. II. *J. clin. Psychol.,* 1949, **5,** 37–76.

Hammer, E. F. The House-Tree-Person (H-T-P) drawings as a projective technique with children. In A. I. Rabin & Mary R. Haworth (Eds.), *Projective techniques with children.* New York: Grune & Stratton, 1960.

Sentence-completion techniques

Forer, B. R. A structured sentence completion test. *J. proj. Tech.,* 1950, **14,** 15–30.

Forer, B. R. Sentence completions. In A. C. Carr et al., *The prediction of overt behavior through the use of projective techniques.* Springfield, Ill.: Charles C Thomas, 1960.

Hanfmann, Eugenia, & Getzels, J. W. Studies of the sentence completion test. *J. proj. Tech.,* 1953, **17,** 280–294.

Rohde, Amanda R. Explorations in personality by the sentence completion method. *J. appl. Psychol.,* 1946, **30,** 169–181.

Rohde, Armand R. *Sentence completion method: its diagnostic and clinical application to mental disorders.* New York: Ronald, 1951.

Rotter, J. B. Word association and sentence completion methods. In H. H. Anderson & Gladys L. Anderson (Eds.), *An introduction to projective techniques.* Englewood Cliffs, N.J.: Prentice-Hall, 1951.

Rotter, J. B., & Rafferty, Janet E. *Manual for the Rotter incomplete sentences blank, college form.* New York: Psychological Corporation, 1950.

Sachs, J. M., & Levy, S. The sentence completion test. In L. E. Abt & L. Bellak (Eds.), *Projective psychology.* New York: Knopf, 1950.

Sanford, R. N., et al. Physique, personality and scholarship. *Monogr. soc. Res. Child Develpm.*, 1943, **8**, No. 1.

Stein, M. I. The use of a sentence completion test for the diagnosis of personality. *J. clin. Psychol.*, 1947, **3**, 47–56.

Tendler, A. D. A preliminary report on a test for emotional insight. *J. appl. Psychol.*, 1930, **14**, 123–136.

Picture Frustration Study

Brown, J. F. A modification of the Rosenzweig picture frustration test to study hostile inter-racial attitudes. *J. Psychol.*, 1947, **24**, 247–272.

Clarke, Helen J. The Rosenzweig Picture-Frustration Study. In H. H. Anderson & Gladys L. Anderson (Eds.), *An introduction to projective techniques.* Englewood Cliffs, N.J.: Prentice-Hall, 1951.

Rosenzweig, S. The picture-association method and its application in a study of reactions to frustration. *J. Pers.*, 1945, **14**, 3–23.

Rosenzweig, S., Fleming, E. E., & Rosenzweig, L. The children's form of the Rosenzweig Picture-Frustration Study. *J. Psychol.*, 1948, **26**, 141–191.

Rosenzweig, S. *Psychodiagnosis.* New York: Grune & Stratton, 1949.

Rosenzweig, S. Rosenzweig Picture-Frustration Study. In A. Weider (Ed.), *Contributions toward medical psychology.* New York: Ronald, 1953.

Rosenzweig, S. The Rosenzweig Picture-Frustration Study, Children's Form. In A. I. Rabin & Mary R. Haworth (Eds.), *Projective techniques with children.* New York: Grune & Stratton, 1960.

Make-A-Picture-Story Test

Bindon, D. Marjorie. MAPS tests findings for rubella deaf children. *J. abnorm. soc. Psychol.*, 1957, **55**, 38–42.

Joel, W. The use of the MAPS test with disturbed adolescents. *Rorschach Res. Exch. & J. Proj. Tech.*, 1948, **12**, 1–10.

Shneidman, E. S. The Make a Picture Story (MAPS) projective personality test: a preliminary report. *J. consult. Psychol.*, 1947, **11**, 315–325.

Shneidman, E. S. Schizophrenia and the MAPS Test. *Genet. Psychol. Monogr.*, 1948, **38**, 145–224.

Shneidman, E. S. (Ed.) *Thematic test analysis.* New York: Grune & Stratton, 1951.

Shneidman, E. S. Manual for the MAPS Test. *Proj. Tech. Monogr.*, 1952, **1**, No. 2, 1–92.

Shneidman, E. S. The MAPS Test with children. In A. I. Rabin & Mary R. Haworth (Eds.), *Projective techniques with children.* New York: Grune & Stratton, 1960.

Spiegelman, J. M. A note on the use of Fine's scoring system with the MAPS tests of children. *J. proj. Tech.*, 1956, **20**, 442–444.

Other projective techniques

Anthony, E. J., & Bene, Eva. A technique for the objective assessment of the child's family relationships. *J. ment. Sci.*, 1957, **103**, 541–555.

Barker, R. G., Dembo, T., & Lewin, K. Frustration and regression: an experiment with young children. *Univer. Iowa Stud. Child Welf.*, 1941, **18**, No. 1.

Bender, L., & Woltmann, A. G. The use of puppet shows as a psychotherapeutic method for behavior problems in children. *Amer. J. Orthopsychiat.*, 1936, **6**, 341–354.

Blum, G. S. A study of the psychoanalytic theory of psychosexual development. *Genet. Psychol. Monogr.*, 1949, **39**, 3–99.

Blum, G. S. *The Blacky Pictures : a technique for the exploration of personality dynamics.* New York: Psychological Corporation, 1950.

Blum, G. S., & Hunt, H. F. The validity of the Blacky Pictures. *Psychol. Bull.*, 1952, **49**, 238–250.

Bolgar, H., & Fischer, L. Personality projection in the World Test. *Amer. J. Orthopsychiat.*, 1947, **17**, 117–128.

Borstelmann, L. J., & Klopfer, W. G. The Szondi Test: a review and critical evaluation. *Psychol. Bull.*, 1953, **50**, 112–132.

Buhler, C., Lumry, G. K., & Carrol, H. S. World Test standardization studies. *J. child Psychiat.*, 1951, **2**, 1–81.

Buhler, C., & Manson, M. P. *The Picture World Test.* Los Angeles, Calif.: Western Psychological Services, 1956.

Deri, Susan K. *Introduction to the Szondi Test: theory and practise.* New York: Grune & Stratton, 1949. (a)

Deri, Susan K. The Szondi Test. *Amer. J. Orthopsychiat.*, 1949, **19**, 447–454. (b)

Despert, Louise J. Psychosomatic study of fifty

stuttering children. *Amer. J. Orthopsychiat.*, 1946, **16**, 100–113.

Despert, Louise J. Dreams in children of preschool age. *Psychoanal. Stud. Child,* 1949, **34**, 141–180.

Diamond, B. L., & Schmale, H. T. The Mosaic Test. I. An evaluation of its clinical application. *Amer. J. Orthopsychiat.*, 1944, **14**, 237–250.

Düss, L. La méthode des fables en psychoanalyse. *Arch. Psychol., Genève,* 1940, **28**, 1–51.

Erikson, E. H. Dramatic Productions Test. In H. A. Murray et al., *Explorations in personality.* New York: Oxford Univer. Press, 1938.

Erikson, E. H. Studies in the interpretation of play. I. Clinical observation of play disruption in young children. *Genet. Psychol. Monogr.*, 1940, 22, 557–671.

Fein, Leah G. *The three-dimensional personality test.* New York: International Univer. Press, 1960.

Gehl, R. H., & Kutash, S. B. Psychiatric aspects of a graphomotor projection technique. *Psychiat. Quart.*, 1949, **23**, 539–547.

Haas, R. B., & Moreno, J. L. Psychodrama as a projective technique. In H. H. Anderson & Gladys L. Anderson (Eds.), *An introduction to projective techniques.* Englewood Cliffs, N.J.: Prentice-Hall, 1951.

Harrower, Molly R. The most unpleasant concept test: a graphic projective technique for diagnostic and therapeutic use. In E. F. Hammer, et al. (Eds.), *The clinical application of projective drawings.* Springfield, Ill.: Charles C Thomas, 1958.

Haworth, Mary R. The use of a filmed puppet show as a group projective technique for children. *Genet. Psychol. Monogr.*, 1957, **56**, 257–296.

Jackson, Lydia. Emotional attitudes towards the family of normal, neurotic and delinquent children. *Brit. J. Psychol.*, 1950, **41**, 35–51.

Jung, C. G. *Studies in word association.* New York: Dodd, Mead, 1918.

Kahn, T. C. Personality projection on culturally structured symbols. *J. proj. Tech.*, 1955, **19**, 431–442.

Kahn, T. C. Test of symbol arrangement: administration and scoring. *Percept. mot. Skills Monogr. Suppl.*, 1956, **6**, No. 4.

Kahn, T. C. The Kahn Test of Symbol Arrangement: clinical manual. *Percept. mot. Skills Monogr. Suppl.*, 1957, **7**, No. 1.

Kent, Grace H., & Rosanoff, A. J. A study of association in insanity. *Amer. J. Insanity,* 1910, **67,** 37–96, 317–390.

Krout, Johanna. Symbol Elaboration Test (S.E.T.): the reliability and validity of a new projective technique. *Psychol. Monogr.*, 1950, **64**, 1–67.

Levy, D. M. Use of play technique as an experimental procedure. Amer. *J. Orthopsychiat.*, 1933, 3, 266–277.

Levy, D. M. Hostility patterns in sibling rivalry experiments. *Amer. J. Orthopsychiat.*, 1936, **6**, 183–257.

Levy, D. M. Studies in sibling rivalry. *Res. Monogr. Amer. Orthopsychiat. Ass.*, 1937, No. 2.

Lowenfeld, Margaret. The world pictures of children. *Brit. J. med. Psychol.*, 1939, **18**, 65–101.

Lowenfeld, Margaret. The Lowenfeld Mosaic Test. *J. proj. Tech.*, 1952, **16**, 200–202.

Lowenfeld, Margaret. The Lowenfeld Mosaic Test. London: Newman Neame, 1954.

Luria, A. R. *The nature of human conflicts, or emotions, conflict and will.* New York: Liveright, 1932.

Moreno, J. L. *Psychodrama.* New York: Beacon House, 1946.

Moreno, J. L. *The theater of spontaneity: an introduction to psychodrama.* New York: Beacon House, 1947.

Napoli, P. J. Finger painting and personality diagnosis. *Genet. Psychol. Monogr.*, 1946, **34**, 129–231.

Napoli, P. J. Interpretative aspects of finger painting. *J. Psychol.*, 1947, **23**, 93–132.

Napoli, P. J. Finger painting. In H. H. Anderson & Gladys L. Anderson (Eds.), *An introduction to projective techniques.* Englewood Cliffs, N.J.: Prentice-Hall, 1951.

Rabin, A. I. The Szondi Test. In *ibid.*

Raven, J. C. *Controlled projection for children.* (2nd ed.) London: H. K. Lewis, 1951.

Sargent, Helen. An experimental application of projective principles to a paper and pencil personality test. *Psychol. Monogr.*, 1944, **57**, 1–57.

Sargent, Helen. *The Insight Test: a verbal projective test for personality study.* New York: Grune & Stratton, 1953.

Shakow, D., & Rosenzweig, S. The use of the tautaphone ("verbal summator") as an auditory test for the study of personality. *Charact. & Pers.*, 1940, 8, 216–226.

Shaw, Ruth. *Finger painting.* Boston: Little, Brown, 1934.

Skinner, B. F. The verbal summator and a method for the study of latent speech. *J. Psychol.,* 1936, **2,** 71–107.

Stone, D. R. A recorded auditory apperception test as a new projective technique. *J. Psychol.,* 1950, **29,** 349–353.

Szondi, L. *Experimentelle Triebdiagnostik.* Bern: Verlag Hans Huber, 1947. (a)

Szondi, L. *Szondi Test.* Bern: Verlag Hans Huber, 1947. (b)

Thomas, Madeleine. Méthode des histoires a completer pous le depistage des complexes et des conflits affectifs enfantins. *Arch. Psychol., Genève,* 1937, **26,** 209–284.

Tomkins, S. S. *The Tomkins-Horn Picture Arrangement Test.* New York: Springer, 1957.

Tomkins, S. S. *P.A.T. interpretation.* New York: Springer, 1959.

Twitchell-Allen, Doris. A three-dimensional apperception test: a new projective technique. *Amer. Psychologist,* 1947, **2,** 271–272.

Twitchell-Allen, Doris. *A three dimensional apperception test.* New York: Psychological Corporation, 1948.

Van Lennep, D. J. *Four Picture Test.* The Hague: Marinus Nijhoff, 1948.

Van Lennep, D. J. The Four Picture Test. In H. H. Anderson & Gladys L. Anderson (Eds.), *An introduction to projective techniques.* Englewood Cliffs, N.J.: Prentice-Hall, 1951.

Woltmann, A. G. The use of puppets in understanding children. *Ment. Hygiene,* 1940, **24,** 445–458.

Woltmann, A. G. The use of puppetry as a projective method in therapy. In H. H. Anderson & Gladys L. Anderson (Eds.), *An introduction to projective techniques.* Englewood Cliffs, N.J.: Prentice-Hall, 1951. Pp. 606–638.

Woltmann, A. G. Concepts of play therapy techniques. *Amer. J. Orthopsychiat.,* 1955, **25,** 771–783.

Woltmann, A. G. Play therapy and related techniques. In D. Brower & L. A. Abt (Eds.), *Progress in clinical psychology.* Vol. 3. New York: Grune & Stratton, 1958. Pp. 184–196.

Wursten, H. Story completions: Madeleine Thomas Stories and similar methods. In A. I. Rabin & Mary R. Haworth (Eds.), *Projective techniques with children.* New York: Grune & Stratton, 1960.

21

The Rorschach Inkblot Method[1]

ZYGMUNT A. PIOTROWSKI

Rorschach (1921) stated that he developed his inkblot test for an exclusively theoretical purpose, to study perception and its "three processes," sensation, memory, and association. He added that the test's diagnostic power was "an empirical finding" which had not been anticipated, and he warned that it was impossible to furnish instructions on how to reach a diagnosis from the test data alone or to provide simple diagnostic tables. These words of caution and restraint did not stop him and a host of others from trying to shape the Rorschach Inkblot Test into an objective diagnostic procedure that would be at least as good as the x ray or the electroencephalogram.

Since the world literature on the diagnostic capacity of the test is vast, an attempt was made to limit this review to large-scale investigations that used control groups. As in every field of science, the findings of different investigators tend to be disparate, usually because of the differences introduced into the administration of the test, which undermine the reliability of "scores," "signs," or any other specific test reactions and the validity of the neuropsychiatric diagnoses themselves. The diagnostic test results cannot be more reliable and valid than the independent criterion. Follow-up diagnoses after at least three years are much more valid than diagnoses made after brief periods of observation. The influence of the questionable clinical diagnosis, the independent criterion, is hardly ever raised, and yet it is one of the most important factors determining the value of the inkblot test as a diagnostic aid. Moreover, patients in some diagnostic categories, e.g., schizophrenia, vary so much, depending on the severity and duration of the disease and the pattern of onset and recurrences of the manifest psychosis, that statistically significant results, incompatible with equally significant results of other investigations, can be obtained even in well-designed studies when the number of patients studied is not large. No wonder then that there is so much criticism of the test.

Rorschach's *Psychodiagnostics* and his five blind analyses contain differential diagnostic discussions which are unique. The longest one is appended to the *Psychodiagnostics* (1921). Three appeared in the *Journal of Projective Techniques* (Rorschach, 1954), and one in the *Review of Diagnostic Psychology* (Schneider, 1955). Other introductory texts are Beck's three volume *Rorschach's Test* (1945; 1952; Beck, Levitt, & Molish, 1961) and *The Rorschach Experiment: Ventures in Blind Diagnosis* (Beck, 1960); the two volumes of *Developments in the Rorschach Technique* by Klopfer and associates (Klopfer, Ainsworth, Klopfer, & Holt, 1954; Klopfer & Spiegelman, 1956); Bohm's *Textbook of Rorschach's Psychodiagnostics* (1951); chap. 3 of the second volume of *Diagnostic Psychological Testing*, by Rapaport, Gill, and Schafer (1946); *Rorschach Interpretation: Advanced Technique*, by Phillips and Smith (1953); Halpern's *Clinical Ap-*

[1] The preparation of this chapter was supported, in part, by a grant from the Research Committee of the Supreme Council, 33°, Scottish Rite Free Masonry, Northern Masonic Jurisdiction.

proach to Children's Rorschachs (1953); and Piotrowski's *Perceptanalysis* (1957).

Ames and her collaborators published three volumes with norms and many qualitative remarks about normal children (Ames, Learned, Metraux, & Walker, 1952), adolescents (Ames, Metraux, & Walker, 1959), and old people, aged 70 and more (Ames, Learned, Metraux, & Walker, 1954). *Rorschach Psychology*, edited by Rickers-Ovsiankina (1960), is not a manual but a presentation, by 17 research clinicians, of the major working principles and theoretical assumptions and problems of the Rorschach method. Among other things, it contains a comparison of six systems of scoring symbols in tabular form.

When using the Rorschach test as a tool of neuropsychiatric diagnosis, I find it invaluable to keep in mind several assumptions and hypotheses. In the first place, the test is psychological, not physiological or sociological. The aspects of personality that it reveals pertain not to the physiology of the body or the structure of society but to the manner in which the individual behaves in interhuman relationships that are vital to him. Furthermore, it must be remembered that the test reveals the individual's inner attitudes much more directly and fully than it does his specific overt actions. Specific behavior, including psychopathological symptoms, can be inferred from the test findings alone only with difficulty, if at all.

Most clinical neuropsychiatric diagnoses rely on observation of the patient's overt behavior, while the independent Rorschach diagnostic conclusions rely chiefly on the patient's inner attitudes, which the test makes rather easily accessible to inspection. Therefore, disagreements between these two types of diagnostic conclusions are inevitable. One way out of the difficulty is to delay setting up a criterion until a trustworthy clinical diagnosis is established, based on long observation, knowledge of the patient's temporal changes over the years, and objective laboratory tests. One should wait at least three years and rediagnose the patient at the end of a long follow-up period. Using short-term clinical diagnoses as an independent criterion for Rorschach test diagnoses is unsound because of the low reliability of the clinical diagnoses (Piotrowski & Lewis, 1950b).

The Rorschach test functions like a microscope. It makes individuals appear less integrated and more pathological than they do under other circumstances, and it often reveals a degree of personality disorganization that observation had failed to detect. This is the test's greatest asset as a diagnostic aid. At the same time, it presents a serious problem in clinical use.

The test findings can be interpreted blind, that is, without any knowledge of the patient except his age and sex, in which case the conclusions inferred are not contaminated by extraneous information. Blind analysis is particularly useful for research purposes, while the nonblind use of the test is more appropriate for clinical use when it can be one of a number of sources of diagnosis and personality description. When conditions permit, I find it best to divide the analysis of a Rorschach test record, including diagnostic conclusions, into two phases, blind and nonblind. First a noncontaminated, blind description of personality dynamics and diagnosis should be written, and then the test record should be complemented and, when necessary, reinterpreted in the light of all information available about the patient. The test can add to an understanding of the etiology or of the meaning to the patient of symptoms, even when these symptoms were not or could not be inferred from the test findings.

As a diagnostic tool, the test findings have four different uses, which are not mutually exclusive: pathognomonic, statistically descriptive, systematic, and comprehensive.

The pathognomonic use consists of a search for test reactions that are unique and specific to one category of patients. The advantage of a pathognomonic approach is the high degree of validity of the diagnostic conclusions if the signs are present. Its disadvantage stems from the fact that only a minority of patients in a given disease category produce the pathognomonic signs. Another difficulty is that most pathognomonic signs discovered with the Rorschach test require training to use with assurance and thus have a low degree of reliability.

The statistically descriptive use of the test for diagnostic purposes has received by far the greatest attention. This approach consists in calculating the frequencies and distribution of test components in each diagnostic category singly, disregarding the mutual relations of the components among themselves. Rorschach himself set up the first norms. He ran into difficulties, however, as is indicated by the fact that he set up four different sets of norms for schizophrenics alone. Moreover, one of these is indistinguishable from the norms for healthy subjects published in the same table. This approach fails because it violates the important principle of the interdependence of test components.

A second important point is that the variation in single test components is affected far more by the severity of the neuropsychiatric disorder than by the specific psychological features of the disorder itself. For example, acute schizophrenic patients differ much more from mild and chronic schizophrenic patients in many respects than the latter differ from anxiety neurotics or obsessive-compulsive psychoneurotics. Thus, although the amount and intensity of single test components—particularly of the important ones, such as the whole, movement, color, and shading responses and the percentage of sharply perceived forms—are pertinent in determining the severity of the illness, they throw no direct light upon the nature of the mental illness itself. Factor analyses of the conventional scores have failed to differentiate mental patients from normals (Murstein, 1960). Tetrachoric intercorrelations of 22 different signs were factored by Hughes (1950). Though they yielded eight factors, only one diagnostic group, the cerebral organic, was clearly defined because of the degree of striking impoverishment of test production.

The systematic approach is based on a pattern analysis of test components and a theory concerning mental disorders. Pattern analysis joins various test components or test reactions into a dynamic relationship (Piotrowski, 1945; Piotrowski & Lewis, 1950b). Proportions or ratios between test components, and not single components and their arithmetical sums, are the basis for drawing diagnostic conclusions.

The comprehensive approach consists of two stages. First, the test record is used to reconstruct the personality of the patient with his assets and liabilities and without reference to any diagnostic indices, obtaining as detailed a personality description as possible. Then, and only then, is an effort made to determine the most likely neuropsychiatric diagnosis for a patient with such a personality. This last approach is by far the soundest and the most desirable. Its drawbacks are that it is the most difficult of the four, that it has not been systematically developed, and that it has barely been written about (Beck, 1960).

PSYCHONEUROSIS

Rorschach (1921) believed that there was one outstanding pathognomonic sign of psychoneurosis—color shock. Rorschach defined color shock as a transient associative or intellectual stupor caused by the sudden sight of a chromatic color, most frequently red. "The subjects suddenly become helpless though previously they had been interpreting very well. They find the color plates more difficult to interpret than the black plates and they react with astonishment or vexation." However, contrary to Rorschach's belief that it is pathognomonic of pure psychoneurosis, color shock also appears in organic patients and in schizophrenics. The concept of color shock implies a temporary state of mental creative paralysis. In keeping with this definition, color shock should be measured by a shock reaction caused by the "first" sight of the chromatic colors: either plate II or plate VIII, since the latter follows four gray plates. It seems inadvisable to speak of color shock when the shock appears only in plate IX, X, or III, because these follow II and VIII. Rorschach made a distinction between major and minor color shocks. When the shock reduced productivity, with pauses in the process of interpretation, he classified it as a sign of emotional repression. Minor shock consists only of a diminution in the number of responses to the chromatic color plates, with no significant disturbance in the pace at which responses are produced; Rorschach felt this indicated a deliberate control over the outward manifestations of emotions.

The concept of color shock as shock in the true physiological sense of stupor was experimentally supported by Rockwell, Welch, Kubis, and Fisichelli (1947). They found no sudden marked lowering of skin resistance to an electric current analogous to a startle pattern for any of the plates in subjects who had distinct color shocks on the Rorschach. On the other hand, the emotional and mental stupor was indicated by the gradual psychogalvanic skin reflex deflections indicating lowered resistance, particularly to plate VIII. This was a well-controlled experiment.

My own interpretation is that color shock indicates ambivalence due to unconscious doubt about the advisability of acting out a genuine emotional impulse. The individual does not control the appearance of the anxiety or the anxious shock reaction.

Miale and Harrower (1940) found color shock in 98 per cent of 43 psychoneurotic patients. Piotrowski and Schreiber (1952) noted that color shock decreased in frequency and intensity when measured by the length of the initial reaction times and by the degree of variability of the initial reactions to the 10 plates. Siipola (1950) and Siipola and Taylor (1952) used Rorschach blots in their original chromatic version and in an achromatic form. Measuring shock chiefly by variations in reaction time but also by the content of the response, she found that in some cases color had a disturbing influence upon the pace and content of responses but that in other cases color facilitated productivity; in the latter case, the shape and color of the area were appropriate to the realistic physical features of the image projected onto the respective blot. This finding suggests that even if an achromatic version of a plate elicits a shock, the shocks elicited by the colored and noncolored versions are not necessarily the same in psychological character or significance.

Patients who improve in psychotherapy and who feel less inhibited, freer, and more spontaneous, with less sense of guilt and less anxiety, also have less color shock, and any previously severe color shock decreases. The examination of patients during an acute and nonacute condition is perhaps the best way of measuring the significance of the color shock (Piotrowski & Schreiber, 1952). One important significance of color shock, I believe, is that individuals who show a specific and definite color shock, with no other shock of comparable intensity, are inclined to blame others for their personal difficulties.

Shading shock is another common type of shock, though it is less frequent than color shock. This is measured by the same criteria as color shock, namely, prolonged initial reaction time and/or decreased productivity with or without verbalized or motor signs of discomfort and insecurity. The plate used to measure shading shock is plate IV, the most shaded of all the 10 plates. According to Oberholzer (1931), it is a sign of "fear of fear." It can be described as indicating anxiety associated with feelings of personal inadequacy (Piotrowski, 1957). Individuals who have shading shock tend to attribute their difficulties to their own ineffectiveness. This interpretation of shading shock is indirectly supported by the frequent occurrence of conspicuous shading shock in the early phases of psychosis, both schizophrenic and organic (Piotrowski & Berg, 1955). Shading shock usually occurs with color shock. The individual who has both is more disturbed than the person who has only one of these shocks. However, occasionally shading shock occurs without any color shock. Persons with such records are characterized by prominent mood variations and mood disturbances rather than by emotional inhibitions.

Klopfer et al. (1956, p. 315) found that Rorschach records of patients with fast-growing cancers showed maximum discomfort in dealing with the color and shading stimuli, combined with minimum deficiencies in reality testing. On the other hand, Rorschach records which were exceptionally tension-free or which showed a typically psychotic fragmentation of mental functions were produced by those cancer patients in whom the cancer was slow-growing. However, it must be recognized that color and shading shocks indicating anxiety concerning the advisability of acting out one's own spontaneous impulses are not always a matter of severe illness but may be an expression of personal dissatisfaction with one's achievements. They may occur in somewhat emotionally disturbed people who seek to find peace through their work, or they may occur in people who want to achieve more and at a faster pace than hitherto. Roe (1949), for example, found a high incidence of both shading and color shocks among 188 well-functioning biologists. Both types of shock are specific instances of an uneven pace of interpretation. Any marked unevenness in the pace of interpretation or in the number of responses indicates uneven mental functioning, often associated with anxiety or a sensed loss of control over one's situation in life and with dread of the unknown (Piotrowski, 1957, p. 297).

In the Rorschach, the typical psychoneurotic hallmark of being at cross-purposes with oneself is shown also in the quality of many of the responses. One of the most striking findings in psychoneurotics is the large percentage of negative color responses, e.g., "blood" in plate II in anxiety neurotics (Rapaport et al., 1946; Rorschach, 1921). A negative color response is one which contains an object in a state of disintegration or a destructive process (Piotrowski, 1957, p. 225). The more severe the neurosis, the more numerous are the negative color responses (Piotrowski, Rock, & Grela, 1963; Piotrowski & Schreiber, 1952). This is said to indicate a fear of close emotional ties, which frequently increases to dislike and hatred. During a successful psychotherapy of psychoneurotics, the proportion of negative color responses decreases, while there is an increase in the proportion of positive color responses (color responses in which wholesome objects or life-furthering processes appear) presumably because the emotional fear of others decreases with successful psychotherapy (Piotrowski & Schreiber, 1952).

The classic sign of obsessive-compulsive indecision is spontaneous criticism of one's own responses, specifically, of the degree of fit between the shape of the area onto which the image of an object was "projected" and the realistic shape of the projected object. Milder degrees of obsessiveness are indicated by numerous qualifications spontaneously offered by the subject while interpreting the plate. The production of high percentages (over 10) of small detail or rare detail interpretations indicates the sort of obsessiveness which is manifested by paying a great deal of attention to trivial matters.

According to Rorschach (1921), an obsessive-compulsive psychoneurosis can be inferred from a record which contains no signs of psychosis but which includes a color and/or shading shock with about the same number of human movement and color responses. Obsessive-compulsives also produce white space responses more frequently than other kinds of psychoneurotics. A counterargument against an obsessional neurosis is a normal distribution of whole, detail, and small detail responses and the presence of pure color responses (Kaila, 1949).

It is extremely difficult to infer the exact symptoms from a Rorschach record. However, it is possible to infer the general type of symptom. According to Rorschach, a prevalence of color over human movement responses with signs of psychoneurosis strongly suggests that the main symptoms are motor; if human movement responses dominate color responses, the symptoms tend to be mental or ideational. Rorschach believed that when both movement and color responses are of about equal strength, the patient with neurotic anxiety is indecisive and incapable of forceful, unhesitant action.

A checklist for a rapid and standardized evaluation of the severity of psychoneurotic personality difficulties was offered by Miale and Harrower (1940). It consists of nine signs, which include the conventional scoring categories as well as the color and shading shocks. The checklist differentiated very well between 43 neurotics and 20 normals. It was later applied to 459 records obtained from neurotics and a number of control groups. Eighty per cent of neurotics and 15 per cent of controls produced at least five of the nine neurotic signs. Among neurotics who were also physically ill, 65 per cent had the critical number of signs; among neurotics who had no physical illness, 85 per cent had it. Moreover, only 15 per cent of physically ill but mentally well subjects had five or more of the neurotic signs (Harrower-Erickson, 1942). Another checklist for the same purpose of rapidly evaluating the test and assessing degrees of maladjustment was set up by Munroe (1941). She validated it on a group of 101 female college freshmen.

PSYCHOSOMATIC ILLNESSES

The term "psychosomatic" denotes a physical symptom or syndrome resulting at least in part from chronic emotional stress or constituting its somatic expression.

The underlying psychological factor is believed to be a slowly acting chronic tension or anxiety whose relationship to the physical illness is neither conspicuous nor readily detectable. Such emotional stress is different from a sudden surge of strong emotion which leads to an outburst of anger, to quick escape, or to the overt manifestation of positive affect. A good example of a psychosomatic illness is psychogenic secondary amenorrhea, with no evidence of organic pathology, which seems to have been reliably traced to repressed resentment of a strong and real dependence on the mother that hampers the woman's emotional and, at times, even physical freedom. Proof of the psychogenic origin is provided by successful psychotherapy, which removes the secondary amenorrhea permanently or for long periods of time, sometimes even in cases which have failed to respond to medication (Rakoff, Piotrowski, & Loftus, 1962).

Patients who suffer from an arrested, intermittent, or mild form of psychosomatic illness which is not associated with irreversible tissue pathology (secondary amenorrhea, conversion-hysterical sensorimotor disturbances) display less psychological pathology than patients with a severe or chronic form of the same illness. Organogenic cases of secondary amenorrhea display still greater anxiety, as well as reduction in psychological potentialities, despite similar intellectual levels and life opportunities (Rakoff et al., 1962). Arrested cases of pulmonary tuberculosis, i.e., the milder cases, also have Rorschach records indicative of greater inner freedom and greater psychological potentialities than the more seriously ill chronic tubercular patients (Korkes & Lewis, 1955).

A comparison of 11 married women with cancer of the breast and 11 with uterine cervical cancer with 11 married women without cancer, examined by clinical and laboratory techniques, revealed a significantly higher degree of repression and anxiety in the cancer group (Tarlan & Smalheiser, 1951). The latter's percentage of original responses was lower, their color and shading shocks were more frequent and pronounced, and one-half failed to give a meaningful reaction to at least one plate, while none of the normal women failed to do so. The authors concluded that the personality pattern is not a function of the cancer but may be related to the localization of the disease process. They based this conclusion on the significant difference between the 11 cervix and the 11 breast cancer cases. The latter were psychologically more impoverished than the former; this conclusion was based mainly on the fact that the breast cancer group, matched for intelligence with the other groups, produced only one-half as many human movement and color responses as the cervix group and fewer inanimate movement and shading responses than the cervix patients. The number of whole responses did not discriminate and was about normal. The authors noted that both cancer groups differed from the normal women in that the male figures in their 27 human movement responses were weak, while the female figures were violent. If this finding is interpreted in the light of the theory that same-sex figures, in this case female, express subjectively more acceptable action tendencies in personally vital interhuman relations than other-sex figures (Piotrowski, 1957, pp. 183–184), we can infer that the cancer patients find their weakness unacceptable and do not seem to mind their tendency to hostile actions.

Another study of groups of 20 women each —with breast cancer, uterine or cervical cancer, and no cancer (Wheeler & Caldwell, 1955)—differed from the preceding one in not confirming the relatively greater degree of repression in the breast cancer group. Such desirable test reactions as the form-color responses which are closely associated with the ability to make an easy and adequate adjustment to conventional social situations were more numerous in the breast cancer group than in the controls. Nevertheless, the number of human movement responses followed the previously described pattern in that the normal women produced the largest number of human movements, the cervix group the next largest, and the breast group the smallest. The light shading responses were roughly the same in all groups, but the sum of weighted chromatic color responses was significantly higher ($p<.01$) in the cervix group than in the other two. A tabular summary of five Rorschach studies of cancer patients, including the authors' own 12-patient group (Bahnson & Bahnson, 1963), reveals complete agreement that —compared with a noncancer, normal population—the cancer patients produce fewer total numbers of R, M, ΣC, original, and light and dark shading responses and smaller percentages of responses with human content but larger W per cent, numbers of failures (rejections), and animal percentages.

As inkblot test instances of body barrier or impenetrability, Fisher and Cleveland (1956) used responses in which the body surface or any other object was protected by a definite boundary which would make penetration more difficult. Examples are images of living human bodies, mummies, or manikins wrapped in clothes or otherwise protected; men in armor; animals with specific mention of their skins; turtles with a shell; and even caves with rocky walls, etc. Absence or inadequacy of an outside protective layer was considered an indicator of penetrability. Penetration responses are x rays, broken legs, broken bodies, torn coats, persons bleeding, animals run over by a car, squashed bugs, etc., that is, objects whose external surface has been penetrated. The authors compared 50 patients with cancers on the exterior of the body with 30 with cancer within the body. These two groups differed significantly in Rorschach indicators of their body images. Patients with external cancers saw their bodies as enclosed by an impenetrable boundary, while the internal cancer patients viewed the human body as permeable to external influences. The criterion worked so reliably that one psychologist was able to identify 10 cases correctly, five of one type and five of the other. Two other psychologists misclassified only two of the 10 test records.

Fisher and Cleveland (1956) report that subjects with high barrier and low penetration scores were found clinically to be independent, greatly interested in friendly social relations, and of good ego strength. On the other hand, subjects with high penetration and low barrier scores manifested weakness in direct social confrontation, ego weakness, and pathology. This interpretation is not incompatible with the following opinions. Inkblot test responses in which clothed or covered figures appear reveal fear of social sanctions, a desire to conform to conventions, and respect for high social positions; they may also be associated with concern over certain sexual difficulties (Phillips & Smith, 1953). Responses in which an object is seen in a state of disintegration, partial or complete, in which the capacity for adequate functioning is reduced disclose a sadomasochistic orientation (Schafer, 1954). Examples are responses erupting, inflamed, gangrenous, torn, eroded, bombed, ruined, etc.

The difference in meaning between barrier and penetration scores seems to be essentially that between a high percentage of sharply perceived forms in which wholesome objects appear and a lower percentage of sharply perceived forms, lowered because of ambiguous form responses containing disintegrated objects.

Fisher and Cleveland (1958) found that normals and neurotics have high barrier and low penetration scores, while schizophrenics have low barrier and high penetration scores. Schizophrenics produce significantly more penetration responses in the acute phases of their psychosis than in their calmer chronic states (Cleveland, 1960).

The important contribution of the Fisher and Cleveland studies is the inkblot test differentiation between illnesses of the body surface and interior, which in most cases discriminates between milder and more severe illnesses. Cleveland and Fisher (1960) and Fisher and Cleveland (1960) showed that rheumatoid arthritics and ulcer patients produced different amounts of barrier and penetration responses. Davis (1960) selected 25 men with very high barrier scores and 25 men with very low barrier scores and then made many physiological as well as psychological measurements. His study supports the idea that persons obtaining low and high barrier scores respond differently to stress in terms of changes in blood pressure, electrical skin potentials, heart rate, etc. The women examined by McConnell and Daston (1961) were tested twice during the eighth or ninth month of pregnancy and again several days after delivery. The authors found a positive association between barrier scores and the attitude, favorable or unfavorable, of the women toward their pregnancies. The high barrier scores were associated with the more favorable attitude; the penetration scores declined after delivery.

Eigenbrode and Shipman (1960) failed to corroborate the barrier and penetration concept when they analyzed the Rorschach records of 29 patients with diseases in the body interior—stomach ulcers, ulcerative colitis, and genitourinary disease—and of 54 patients with skin diseases. We do not know whether this is a genuine contradiction of the Fisher and Cleveland finding or whether the difference in results might not possibly be explained by the difference in the patients' degree of concern about their diseases. Sufferers of Parkinson's disease referred to emotional causative factors as influencing their condition and made more frequent negative statements about themselves when their test records contained human movement responses than when they produced no or few human movements (Diller & Riklan, 1957). Both groups, high and low human movement, were alike in the degree of overtly exhibited motor inhibition.

Light shading responses (Rorschach's F (FC), Beck's FY and Y, Klopfer's Fc, and Piotrowski's Fc and c) apparently are positively associated with automatic and self-regulating control over one's overt motor behavior, and chromatic color responses with the amount of energy available for interhuman relationships (Piotrowski, 1957, pp. 224–229, 262–266). The scoring of light shading requires training and skill and can be unreliable. This unreliability can be remedied by the use of special modifications of the Rorschach plates in which shading, as well as color and figure-background contrast, is varied systematically but in which the forms of the original blots are unchanged (Baughman, 1959b). The subject is requested to compare these modified blots and to select from among them the one which, in his opinion, looks most like the image of the object he has in mind. This makes the scoring of shading reactions more objective and reliable. The Rorschach was administered to two groups of adult subjects equated for intelligence, education, age, and sex. Shading and color scores were determined for one group by the standard inquiry method and for the second group by the paired-comparison technique. Color scores for the two groups were not significantly different, but shading scores were significantly more frequent ($p=<.001$) with the paired-comparison technique (Baughman, 1959a). The light shading responses seem to indicate the most desirable form of control over the overt manifestation of emotional impulses. A hypothesis (Piotrowski, 1957) states that this control is desirable because it functions automatically and thus is not enervating, as are positive controls requiring conscious effort (F+ per cent) or negative controls based on inhibition (color and other shocks, impeded movements, etc.). The control measured by the light shading responses is a result of training and socialization. The other controls require more effort and take much more out of the organism. Thus, fear of overtly acting out emotional impulses would, in the absence of adequate and effortless self-control, cause unrelieved tension and create the emotional stress invariably found in psychosomatic illnesses.

Psychosomatic patients regularly produce more color than light shading responses (Piotrowski, 1950; Piotrowski, 1957, p. 289), although they are not the only ones to do so; most psychotics do too (Binswanger, 1944; Rickers-Ovsiankina, 1938; Rorschach, 1921; Tschudin, 1944). The point is rarely made explicitly, but it is evident from the statistics. It was made very clear in a study of 50 patients with psychogenic neurodermatitis and 50 patients with industrial skin burns and chemical irritations. The neurodermatitis group used shading to a lesser degree than color, while the exogenous skin disorder group produced more shading than color ($p<.01$) (R. J. Levy, 1952). Moreover, the former group revealed much less hostility in their movement responses than the latter group but exceeded the latter in white space responses given after a delay.

Duodenal ulcer cases' light shading responses increased after successful psychotherapy which reduced emotional stress and alleviated the somatic symptoms (Ruesch et al., 1948).

Fisher and Cleveland (1956) compared 25 male neurodermatitis patients with 25 patients with skin lesions caused by accidents. The neurodermatitics produced a significantly larger number of responses which contained expressions of self-depreciation, fear, and tendencies to hide and more objects with soft insides and hard exteriors. Also the difference between movement and color responses is important in contact dermatitis (Brown, 1959). Only when college students with contact dermatitis were divided according to whether color or movement dominated their test records was it possible to separate the dermatitis cases from the healthy controls with statistical significance ($p<.01$). The dermatitis cases revealed greater constriction, rigidity, ungratified emotional needs, and anxiety than the controls. The majority of 50 patients with abnormally thick skins and/or morbid blushing produced color and shading shocks, while a significantly smaller number of the 50 controls did so (Plesch, 1951).

The finding of greater immaturity in psychosomatic patients and an inadequate control over the outward manifestation of emotional impulses is one consistent and recurrent finding. In the Rorschach tests of 20 consecutive cases of chronic duodenal ulcer, with a mean age of 42, no common pattern was detected, except shocks, uneven pace of interpretation, significantly more CF than Fc, and immaturity as inferred from content (Kaldegg & O'Neil, 1950). Another study of duodenal ulcer cases ended with the same general conclusion (Brown, Bresnahan, Chalke, Peters, Poser, & Tougas, 1950). In this study, 25 duodenal ulcer patients were compared with 25 patients with no gastrointestinal disease. To check whether different groups could be differentiated from one another as well as from psychiatric and healthy control groups by means of the Rorschach test, Krasner and Kornreich (1954) obtained test records from 25 duodenal ulcer patients, 25 ulcerative colitis cases, 25 anxiety neurotics, and 15 nonpsychosomatic hospitalized controls. The duodenal ulcer groups stood out as being relatively most homogeneous and more clearly differentiated from the other groups in terms of test scores.

In the test records of 15 male veterans with duodenal ulcers, Osborne and Sanders (1950) found an average intellectual level and an average number of whole responses (seven). A study of 25 duodenal ulcer patients and 25 nongastrointestinal controls, matched for socioeconomic level, intelligence, and marital status, led Poser (1951) to conclude that the test supports the theory that ulcer patients suffer from strong inner tensions and inadequate outlets and from ambivalence concerning strong dependency needs. He found the test records of the ulcer group more homogeneous than those of the controls. Low numbers of color responses (even fewer than the human movements, which were exceeded by the animal movements); relatively more color-form responses; and an adequate number of whole responses characterized the ulcer group.

Raifman (1957) compared 15 peptic ulcer patients, 15 psychoneurotics, and 15 normals. Statistically, the most striking and highly significant difference ($p<.01$) was the frequency of flexor animal movements, the normals averaging 1.7 and the neurotics only 0.7; the ulcer cases averaged 1.1 flexor animal movements. If we compute from the author's data the sums of weighted color responses and divide them by the total number of weighted shading responses, we obtain the following quotients: 1.6 in the ulcer group, 0.9 in the neurotic group, and 1.3 in the normal group. The psychoneurotics produced twice as many light shading responses as the ulcer group.

Children with psychosomatic illnesses seem to differ from normal children in about the same way that psychosomatic adults differ from normal adults. Neuhaus (1958) tested asthmatic, cardiac, and normal children, as well as siblings of the psychosomatic cases (a total of 169 children in the 8-to-14 age range), with the Rorschach and a variety of personality inventories. The asthmatics gave significantly fewer assertive human movements, and both cardiacs and asthmatics were more maladjusted according to the Ames et al. (1952) sign list than the normal, nonsibling controls. Yet there were no statistically significant differences between the asthmatics and cardiacs, on the one hand, and their siblings, on the other. The scores used failed to differentiate between asthmatics and cardiacs. The symptom-free siblings of the psychosomatics differed from the normal controls in being more constricted and in producing fewer responses other than pure forms and fewer animal movement responses. Like their sick siblings, the symptom-free children expressed more feelings of insecurity and obtained higher neurotic scores on personality inventories. There were no significant sex differences, but age was a factor in that the younger psychosomatic children manifested more intense anxiety than the older ones. Earlier investigation also revealed a higher incidence of psychoneurotic anxiety in the psychosomatic than in normal children (Schatia, 1941; Vres & Groen, 1951). Bruce and Thomas (1953) have also shown that certain personality traits are more prevalent among the offspring of parents with coronary artery disease or hypertension than among those born of healthy parents.

Shatin (1952) noted that asthmatics had a higher average number of form-color responses than other psychosomatic groups, or psychoneurotics, and also produced more responses with a hostile content. Barendregt (1961) confirmed the asthmatics' higher incidence of hostility by counting the expressions of hostility in the movement and form responses. However, the asthmatics' relatively larger number of responses in which humans or animals were either confined in closed spaces or limited in their movement by crippled wings, cut feet, or tied hands suggests that overt motor expressions of hostility are seriously inhibited. Barendregt found that even when compared with ulcer patients, another psychosomatic group, the asthmatics still produced a larger number of responses with enclosed spaces capable of containing people or animals and responses in which movement is impeded or stopped.

A note of dissent and caution was introduced by Miles, Waldfogel, Barrabee, and Cobb (1954). They could not find any significant differences between Rorschach records of 46 young men with coronary artery disease and those of their 49 carefully matched healthy controls. After consolidating the information gathered by psychiatric interviews, a detailed social inventory, and a battery of psychological tests, the authors compared the two groups in terms of personality factors as well as in other ways, including family incidence of cardiovascular disease, history of stress and strain, somatotype, and blood lipid levels. The coronary patients had tended to work harder, under more stress and strain, although their work was not necessarily physically strenuous. Only a few more coronary patients than controls showed a consistent tendency toward compulsive striving and ascetic self-discipline and a great need to "get to the top" in their chosen work.

Few statistically significant differences were found in the comparison of 25 obese women with 25 women of normal weight (Kotkov & Murawski, 1952). The obese women produced more test indicators of anxiety and tension, fewer self-assertive human movements, and a more meager content of responses.

Bell, Trosman, and Ross (1952) published a summary of 45 Rorschach investigations dealing with the emotional aspects of general medical disorders. Commenting on the very great methodological variability from study to study—some investigations being conducted with great exactness and thought, and others very carelessly and yet culminating in astounding conclusions based on a superficial inspection of test scores—the authors conclude that very few studies help to shed light upon the problem of whether or not specific personality characteristics antedate the development of a particular disease. Booth (1939), a pioneer in the use of the Rorschach with psychosomatic cases, was one of the very few who presented evidence indicating that personality traits believed to be relevant to the development of arthritis and manifested in the Rorschach antedated the onset of arthritis.

Booth (1937) studied 29 patients with chronic arthritis, both rheumatoid and osteoarthritic. There was no control group, but statistics published for the average normal population were used as a standard for comparison. The 43 arthritic patients averaged a ΣC of 2.0 and a sum of shading responses of 1.1, while whole and movement responses were average in number. In a later study, Booth (1946) compared 30 patients having chronic arthritis with 60 cases of hypertension and 30 cases of Parkinson's disease. The hypertensive cases were classified as vascular, and the other two groups as locomotor. The locomotor group produced more human movement responses in which only one figure appeared in the vertical center of the blots. The vascular cases, on the other hand, produced more human movements in which two figures appeared in the lateral areas of the inkblots. The former type of movement was interpreted by Booth as indicating a desire to be self-motivated and individualistic, while the latter was seen as collectivistic, revealing a tendency to give in to the pressure of social norms.

In one of the largest and earliest studies, Ross and McNaughton (1945) studied 50 migraine cases and compared them with 149 controls. The test signs which were found to be significantly frequent among the migraine patients included perseveration and persistence in approach to the task, very few instances of failure to give a meaningful response to a plate, long initial reaction times or other difficulties with plate VI, and a tendency to give exclusively or almost exclusively whole responses. The findings were interpreted as showing rigid persistence in the presence of emotional stress, sexual difficulties, and a tendency to be overly systematic and perfectionistic. Ross (1945) published a study of 50 patients with neurocirculatory asthenia, as compared with 249 controls. The neurocirculatory asthenia cases tended to give only one response per plate, frequently failing to offer any response to some plates, and they produced weak and few whole responses. This group shared an inability to persist in the face of difficulties.

Phillips and Smith (1953) believe that human movement and anatomy responses are typical of psychosomatic cases. They classify as "static" human movements in which the figures are exerting some effort but are not moving through space: "reaching," "standing," "arms upraised." Shatin (1952) also found significantly more anatomy in the records of psychosomatics than in those of psychoneurotic patients. The Phillips and Smith norms for psychosomatics are as follows: a sum of weighted color responses of from three to five with color-form and pure color responses greatly out-weighing the form-colors; a reduced number of human movement responses, one or none; and a high percentage of sharply perceived form responses.

According to Fisher and Cleveland (1960), rheumatics, in contrast to low-back-pain cases, are voyeurs. They emphasize such body parts as waist, bust, and behind; deliberate as to whether the figures perceived by them are clothed or not; "see" transparent dresses, short skirts, etc.; and "see" human or animal figures in unusual poses or with peculiar details—strutting peacocks, women with a ring through the nose, etc.

Kohlmann (1954) computed averages of 140 "vegetative neurotics" and compared them to Tschudin's (1944) norms of 997 subjects, who included 268 normals, 143 brain-damage cases, and 160 epileptics. The smallest difference was between the psychosomatic and the cerebral organic cases, and the largest was between the normal adults, the paranoid schizophrenics, and the psychosomatics.

The following group averages were found, the first figure pertaining to the psychosomatics, the second to the normal adults, and the third to the paranoid schizophrenics: number of responses—17.7, 27.9, 33.2; ΣW—7.2, 8.3, 6.8; ΣM—.8, 2.2, 2.0; ΣC—1.4, 2.4, 2.8; shading responses—1.3, 1.7, 1.4; detail responses—2.0, 4.8, 6.9; white space responses—0.3, 1.8, 2.2; failures—1.4, 0.2, 0.5; animal percentage—52, 47, 40; blood responses—0.1, 0.1, 0.4; anatomy responses—2.0, 1.9, 4.0.

SUICIDE

The act of suicide takes many different physical and psychological forms. We would then hardly expect suicides to have the same or even similar personalities. But they do share one trait. They seem to see no alternative to death, choosing a very radical and irreversible solution of all problems. One must feel extremely frustrated to reject life deliberately.

The first set of test signs successfully discriminating between suicidal and nonsuicidal subjects was developed by Hertz as a result of a careful and extensive investigation, in which she used all available test indicators of suicide, including many of her own. She developed her 14 suicidal "configurations," comparing 113 suicidal patients with 212 nonsuicidal patients and normals (1948) and later checked her signs on 178 consecutive clinical cases (1949).

Hertz's term "configuration" denotes a number of specific test component patterns, one or all of which are viewed as measures of the psychological attitude indicated by the name of the configuration, e.g., depressive states, anxiety, agitation, etc. Fisher (1951b), using Hertz's suicidal configurations, failed to find a significant difference between 20 suicidal and 20 nonsuicidal schizophrenics. The two groups were well matched in age, sex, and intelligence as well as in diagnosis. Fisher included only those patients among his suicides who had actually attempted suicide not earlier than three months before taking the Rorschach test. The sample was rather small, and of a large number of test components, only two discriminated between the groups, the number of form-color responses and the average initial reaction time. Limiting his suicidal patients to those who had recently attempted suicide may have partly contributed to Fisher's largely negative results. A suicidal attempt of a schizophrenic leading to hospitalization is frequently cathartic, and thus the postsuicidal test record may not contain indicators of suicide.

Sakheim's (1955) suicidal group consisted of 40 patients (among whom were 16 schizophrenics), with a mean normal intellectual level, 30 of whom were also tested after a serious attempt to end their lives, having been saved from death only by an accidental discovery of their act and immediate medical intervention. The interval between suicidal attempt and testing averaged two months. When the wish to die did not appear deep and genuine, the patient was not included in the study. Most of the patients injured themselves severely. Ten patients were included because they made a serious suicidal attempt an average of six months *after* the testing. Seven of these patients actually died. The nonsuicidal group of 40 mental patients was matched with the suicides for age, intelligence, educational level, and sex. The frequency of nearly 40 test components was examined. Five or more of Hertz's suicidal configurations were noted in 88 per cent of the suicidal and in only 28 per cent of the nonsuicidal group. The following signs differentiated at the 1 per cent significance level: "depressed states" and "resignation." Several signs differentiated at the 5 per cent significance level: "marked anxiety," "withdrawal," "agitation," plate IV shock, and human movements with animal content. M in animals occurred in 28 per cent of the suicides and in 10 per cent of the nonsuicides. It was suggested that this kind of human movement is produced by disillusioned idealists who develop an attitude of mild cynicism, who are predisposed to prolonged depressive moods

(Piotrowski, 1947; Piotrowski, 1957, pp. 153–154), and who are afraid to grow up because of the threatening nature of the real world (Phillips & Smith, 1953). Inanimate movements, black or dark color, and white space responses did not discriminate, nor did morbid content, blood, and other gory ideas.

Costello (1958) matched 30 patients who had attempted suicide shortly before admission to the hospital with 30 nonsuicidal patients for age, intellectual level, diagnosis, and sex. The mean intellectual capacity was normal, and the average age was 35 years. Humans engaged in vigorous action were imagined on plate III by 20 per cent of the suicides and by 40 per cent of the nonsuicides. However, passive postures were projected onto plate III by 43 per cent of the suicides and by only 20 per cent of the controls. The author validated his signs on a new group of 28 patients who had attempted suicide and 100 nonsuicidal patients. He found that 78 per cent of the suicides and only 30 per cent of the nonsuicides produced the suicidal test pattern.

A significant association between suicide and a specific test response—the shaded color response, in which both the chromatic and the achromatic colors are meaningfully combined—was clinically noted by Michael Dunn and confirmed by Appelbaum and Holzman (1962). One-third of their 330 subjects produced at least one shaded color response. Following are the percentages of subjects with at least one shaded color response in each of the seven groups into which they were divided: 90 per cent among patients who killed themselves, 82 per cent among patients who survived a suicidal attempt, 19 per cent among mental patients who had never attempted suicide, 17 per cent among women with thyroid gland dysfunction, 9 per cent among highway patrolmen, 24 per cent among psychiatric residents, and 35 per cent among college women. The shaded color response was found also in 44 per cent of 25 idiopathic epileptics and in 20 per cent of conversion hysterics matched with the epileptics for age and intelligence with a mean age of 24 years (Piotrowski, 1947).

Six or more of seventeen signs consisting of conventional scores were found in 83 per cent of successful suicides, 72 per cent of attempted suicides, and 17 per cent of controls, who were mental patients without suicidal attempts. The number of subjects in each group was 36. One sign, producing less than three popular responses along with a percentage of sharply perceived forms of above 60, significantly discriminated even between successful and attempted suicides, being more frequent among the former, but not between the controls and either suicide group (Daston & Sakheim, 1960). Another validation study also confirmed the value of the Martin list including the importance of the $p<3$ as well as F+ per cent >60 sign (Weiner, 1961a). Age, sex, and hospital status were not correlated with the discriminatory power of the sign list.

Rorschach studies of suicides have revealed in them significantly stronger indications of depression, agitation, and withdrawal from positive and close emotional ties with others than in nonsuicidal subjects. However, it has been impossible to differentiate between successful and attempted suicides. This is not surprising, since it is very much easier to infer from inkblot test data potential actions and subjective feelings than specific overt actions.

HYSTERIA AND CONVERSION HYSTERIA

The outstanding feature of the hysteric is psychological blindness, that is, unawareness of what one is doing, what one intends to do, and what one would like to do and of the consequences of one's action. In the hysteric, the acting out of an undesirable impulse is frustrated by repression of the awareness of the impulse, while he vicariously experiences the feelings appropriate to the repressed impulse. But because consistency in the face of anxiety is difficult to maintain, the defense against anxiety is rarely limited to a single type and is likely to be variable. Consequently, the most frequent form of psychoneurosis is the mixed one, in which obsessions, compulsions, phobias, depressions, anxieties, and hysterical reactions occur at different times and in varying intensities.

Rorschach used the ratio of human movement to color responses as a basis of differentiation among the forms of psychoneurosis (1921). According to him, hysterics produce more color than human movement responses. Such a patient would be expected to display reproductive rather than creative thinking, labile affectivity, a tendency to manipulate his immediate human environment with some skill, and a tendency to establish superficial emotional relations with many people rather than intensive ones with a few people. On the other hand, psychoneurotics who produce more human movement than color responses would be said to be creative rather than reproductive intellectually, with a well-developed inner fantasy life but with a limited adaptability to the immediate environment and a preference for intensive emotional ties with a few selected people rather than superficial relations with many; these patients would be expected to manifest phobias and neurasthenic symptoms. The obsessive-compulsive psychoneurotic would produce about as many color as human movement responses.

Since it is not easy to measure reliably the degrees of depression, anxiety, hysteria, and effects of phobias, we have no absolutely valid independent criterion for our test findings. This fact as well as the great frequency of the "mixed neurosis" may explain the scarcity of Rorscharch studies of groups of various types of psychoneurotics. The most extensive and careful attempt at qualitatively differentiating among these types can be found in Schafer's book (1954).

The statement that neurotics with conversion symptoms produce high percentages of anatomy responses has not been confirmed (S. Fisher, 1951a; Piotrowski & Bricklin, 1964). Even the average sum of "impulsive" or "loose" color responses was low in 20 female conversion hysterics; the averages were 0.95 CF and 0.30 C. The conclusion was that these patients' test records were not unique and overlapped those of other patient groups (S. Fisher, 1951).

Piotrowski and Bricklin (1964) compared 30 nonpsychotic conversion hysterics, male and female, with 30 psychoneurotics without conversion symptoms, matched for age, intelligence, and sex. The conversion cases had serious symptoms for which they were hospitalized on a neurological floor with a suspicion of an organic central nervous system lesion, which was ruled out after many tests and long clinical observation. The controls were patients with mixed neuroses, some of whom had pronounced obsessive-compulsive symptoms. None of the conventional scoring categories differentiated between these two groups at a confidence level lower than .05 except the total number of responses, which averaged 19 in the conversion and 36 in the nonconversion group. This difference was due solely to the lower number of detail and small detail responses among the conversion cases, as the average number of whole responses was average and practically the same in both groups. When the conversion cases were divided into the most seriously handicapped and the less seriously handicapped, the three noteworthy differences (with p below .05) between these subgroups were animal movement responses, inanimate movement responses, and dark shading responses, all of which were more numerous in the records of the most handicapped. All the conversion hysterics differed strikingly from the nonconversion psychoneurotics in the frequency with which they produced responses referring to death, closed eyes, sleeping, inability to see, decapitations (headlessness), etc., that is, to a condition in which it is impossible to observe and to notice. While only 10 per cent of the nonconversion neurotics produced a response of this kind, 73 per cent of the conversion records contained at least one such response. On the other hand, responses which contained masks, silhouettes, and shadowy figures—that is, objects which hide more than they reveal but which do not imply a lowered human capacity for seeing—did not discriminate and were rather rare, occurring in 11 of the 60 test records. Only 10 per cent of the nonconversion but 67 per cent of the conversion neurotics produced at least one Mp or "movement projection," a response in which no human movement is "seen" but nevertheless is mentioned. It seems to indicate basic action tendencies which are in the process of developing or vanishing as motives determining the patient's role in vital interhuman relationships (Piotrowski, 1957, pp. 170–171). A good example is the following: "These are stones. You could pick them up and throw them." Only the stones were "seen." Although nothing in the blot represented a potential thrower, the idea was accompanied by kinesthetic innervation. Most of the conversion cases' movement projections expressed aggression.

SCHIZOPHRENIA: PATHOGNOMONIC SIGNS

Opinions differ a great deal as to whether there are any truly pathognomonic signs of schizophrenia. Rorschach (1921) himself suggested three: contamination, number or position responses, and sudden drop in form quality. Of these, contamination occurs most frequently. Beck (1945) doubts their pathognomonic status. The conclusion as to whether or not there are any pathognomonic signs of schizophrenia depends largely on how the signs are defined. I found contamination in 14 of 100 followed-up schizophrenics, that is, in patients about whose diagnoses there was practically no doubt because the average follow-up period was nearly six years. The contamination occurred in the prefollow-up test record. Since Rorschach did not fully define the signs, more precise definitions have been developed. I define contamination as the fusing of two or more different percepts, both of which pertain to the same blot area, into one unintelligible percept without the patient's being able to disentangle the resulting percept (Piotrowski & Lewis, 1950a). This definition excludes artificially constructed creatures—part animal and part human, such as a sphinx—because the animal and human parts of the creature do not overlap, although they constitute a functional unit. A genuine contamination contains four pertinent elements. First, the patient spontaneously produces the response. Second, he combines visual images of two different objects into an artificial new object to which nothing in reality corresponds. Third, he produces the contamination not deliberately, but with ease and spontaneity. Fourth, he is unable to disentangle the response into its constituent parts when he is asked to do so. All four elements must be present to constitute a genuine contamination. One has to be on guard against pseudocontaminations, such as the punning of a healthy adult in a humorous mood. Verbally and formally, puns resemble the verbal contaminations of the schizophrenic. The separate constituents of the contamination are usually satisfactory percepts; that is, the imagined forms are fairly well conceived, and they fit adequately the shape of the blot area onto which they are projected (Bohm, 1958). It is the fusing of the different images into one which makes the resulting percept unrealistic and unintelligible. If less exacting definitions are used, then a complex response ceases to be pathognomonic (Beck, 1945; Bohm, 1958; Rapaport et al., 1946).

It is difficult to study contaminations because patients are usually extremely sensitive about them. When asked to explain their responses, either they do not understand what is requested of them, or they deny that they have produced the response, usually claiming that they have been misunderstood. Withdrawing a contaminated response on the grounds of alleged misunderstanding or improving it by removing the illogical and unrealistic aspects of it does not argue against the genuineness of the contaminated response but only against a severe degree of psychosis. Mildly schizophrenic patients are capable of correcting the contaminated responses, just as they are capable of correcting many undesirable reactions when their attention is drawn to them.

Some children produce pseudocontaminations between the ages of 6 and 8. Pseudocontaminations involve the unrealistic fusion of color and form rather than of two forms. Moreover, the object that constitutes the content of a child's pseudocontamination is essentially realistic and usually pleasant. Thus, the responses "two blue flags fluttering in the sky" referring to the middle blue in plate VIII and "bear lying on the grass" in reference to the top green of plate X contaminate a color and a form, but they indicate objects which exist. Normal young children between the ages of 4 and 6 occasionally produce genuine contaminations (Ames et al., 1952). Genuine contaminations produced by subjects who have reached puberty can be interpreted as valid signs of schizophrenia.

Other pathognomonic reactions discovered by Rorschach are the number or position responses, that is, explaining a percept of realistic objects by invoking nonspecific and irrelevant formal (mathematical or geometric) detail. As an example of a number response, a schizophrenic claimed that the small middle angular brown form in plate X looked like his family because there were three parts to it, just as there were three persons in the family. Another schizophrenic interpreted a tiny area at the center top of plate IV as a human head because of its position. Genuine number and position responses are very rare. To be genuine, they must be taken seriously by the patient.

A third Rorschach pathognomonic sign of schizophrenia is a sudden and unexpected drop in the form quality of a response (Rorschach, 1921). Since Rorschach gave no detailed definition, the following one is suggested: A sudden drop in the form quality of the response is pathognomonic of schizophrenia if it contains an indefinite or vague image of an object, the shape of which cannot be clearly and intelligibly inferred from the content of the patient's response. The pathognomonic form response is characterized by the indefiniteness of the shape of the imagined object itself. An extreme example is this: "A prehistoric animal which never existed and about which nobody knows anything." This reaction is not synonymous with a poor form response, in which there is an unsatisfactory correspondence between the shape of the blot area onto which a response is projected and the standard, definite shape of the imagined object. Schizophrenics do, of course, give responses with poor form level, but so also do other patient groups, notably organics (Piotrowski, 1937a).

Another rather frequent pathognomonic sign of schizophrenia involves inconstant percepts of variable dimness (Piotrowski, 1945). The reaction is characterized by the following features: The patient is not certain of the exact meaning of his percept; that is, he is not quite sure of what he is "seeing." Some parts of the percept are visualized by him clearly, and others dimly; the dimness varies in intensity, parts of the percept at times being excluded from the responses and at times clearly focused. The patient's interpretation of what he "sees" varies according to the included blot areas. A good example is the response to the right red area of the reversed plate X: "Here is another face again. A child's face or something [moves finger over upper half of red area and covers the lower half with her hand], but I'm not sure. [Takes hand away and moves eyes over the entire red area, up and down.] Maybe a woman's face, I don't know. [Covers bottom half.] Is it a child's face?"

Pathognomonic signs are more likely to occur when the patient has emotionally charged associations. A patient may give the pathognomonic response with signs of obvious anxiety; he may produce a content which seems to be a symbolic expression of his problems; or he may deny the response in the inquiry. I do not believe these signs of emotional involvement argue against the validity of the signs as reflecting primary, nonpsychogenic thought disturbances. That is, these behaviors do not argue against schizophrenia, but only against a schizophrenia with marked deterioration. With advancing deterioration, both the Rorschach signs of schizophrenic thought disorder and clinical manifestations of the psychosis increase in frequency and gradually become independent of inner stress or environmental pressure.

Schizophrenic ambivalence and inappropriate affect can also be inferred from Rorschach responses. Plate II sometimes elicits responses which epitomize the schizophrenic's emotional ambivalence, the simultaneous feelings of love and hate: "Two friends who are toasting one another. They have been fighting and have bloody knees and faces." Inappropriate affect is manifested by associating boredom or indifference with grave and emotionally charged events or matters. On plate I, a schizophrenic, with no trace of humor, gave the response: "A death mask. Very dull, I'm afraid." Affectless obscenity, another manifestation of inappropriate affect, occurs in test records not only of schizophrenics but also of demented seniles (Ames, 1960).

There are some responses which occur in schizophrenia more frequently than in other patient groups and in normals but which are not pathological in themselves and might be looked upon as idiosyncrasies. These include edging, i.e., tilting the plates and looking at them from the edge. Some authors (Beck, 1945; Kendig, 1949) believe edging to be pathognomonic of schizophrenia (no statistics available). Armitage (1946) found edging in organics, as he did also numerals and geometric shapes; edging occurred in 40 per cent of 69 brain-injured patients and in 17 per cent of 100 control patients who included psychoneurotics.

Rorschach warned that diagnosis of schizophrenia is difficult and that it is not possible to provide specific instructions on how to reach diagnoses from test findings (1921). References to schizophrenia are interspersed throughout his book and case studies; Bohm (1958) presents Rorschach's ideas more systematically. Rorschach's caution is justified, since schizophrenics as a group manifest the greatest imaginable variation of responses both under clinical observation and during the Rorschach test examination. Many test reactions are not easy to quantify but are readily noted because of their peculiarity. Most authors agree rather well on what they see in the test records of schizophrenics but differ as to the use of terms and the way to classify what they see. As the number of qualitative test reactions described by the authors increases, the differences among the test reactions they describe become subtler, less perceptible, and less reliable in scoring. The fact that differences among the authors are in terminology rather than in substance becomes apparent when one reads Rorschach (1921); Muller (1929); Beck (1945; 1960); Rapaport et al. 1946); Kendig (1949); Bohm (1951; 1957; 1958); Watkins and Stauffacher (1952); Gurvitz and Miller (1952); H. Friedman (1953); Phillips and Smith (1953); Schafer (1954); Holt (1956); Klopfer and Spiegelman (1956); Pope and Jensen (1957); Piotrowski and Bricklin (1958); Holt and Havel (1960); Quirk, Quarrington, Neiger, and Slemon (1962); and others.

STATISTICS OF TEST COMPONENTS IN SCHIZOPHRENIA

As distinguished from the "sign" approach discussed in the previous section, the largest number of diagnostic investigations of schizophrenia are statistically descriptive, i.e., establish the frequency with which each conventional scoring category and a few others occur in various diagnostic groups. In my experience this approach is inadequate in cases of incipient schizophrenia and other borderline cases where differential diagnosis is difficult. The reason is that scoring categories in a patient's record are much more closely related to the degree of severity of the illness than to the nature (diagnosis) of the illness. Rorschach's (1921) own statistics show that the difference between the group averages of normals and those of schizophrenic subtypes increases as the psychosocial functioning of the psychotics becomes more abnormal. The same is true of the subgroups of patients with demonstrable brain damage (Aita, Reitan, & Ruth, 1947) and even psychoneurosis.

Skalweit (1934) compared 90 chronic hospitalized schizophrenics with 23 acute schizophrenics; 20 of his patients were retested a number of times. The main conclusion was that deterioration in schizophrenia manifests itself by a gradual decrease in the number of human movement responses and a less marked decrease in the number of color responses, while form-color responses disappear, resulting in a relative increase in color-form and pure color responses. At the first testing, the $\Sigma M:\Sigma C$ ratio of the 20 deteriorating patients was 2.3:4.2; at the last testing, it was 1.3:3.3. However, a more important unfavorable change was the gradual drop of the F+ per cent and the increasing irregularity or confusion of "succession" (the order in which whole, normal detail, and rare detail responses are produced).

Rickers-Ovsiankina (1938) matched 35 schizophrenics with 20 normals for sex, age, and educational and intellectual levels. The most significant single difference was found in the percentage of sharply perceived forms. The numbers of movement and color responses were practically equal in the normal group, while in the schizophrenic group, color dominated over movement because of the paucity of movement responses. In comparison with normals, the psychotics produced more shading responses, about the same number of color responses, fewer popular responses, and more original responses. While schizophrenics gave more original responses than normals, their originals were less likely to show good form (31 per cent of originals given by psychotics had good form, compared with 71 per cent of originals given by normals, a difference significant beyond the 1 per cent level). The coexistence of few populars with many poor-quality originals measured the patients' poor sense of reality. The W+ per cent also was significantly lower in the patient group.

Beck (1938) compared 81 schizophrenics with 64 nonpsychotic patients without brain damage, mental deficiency, or psychopathic traits. The schizophrenics included many paranoids. Seven components significantly differentiated between the groups. As in studies cited above, the most striking difference was provided by the F+ per cent, and again schizophrenics produced more responses in which color dominated over form (more CF and C than Fc). The schizophrenics also produced fewer popular responses, more confabulated whole responses, and more small or rare detail responses.

Tschudin (1944) published statistics on 901 subjects, including 268 normals, 170 chronic schizophrenics, 64 epileptics, 143 organics, and 256 psychopathic personalities. The most striking finding again was the schizophrenics' very low F+ per cent; the number of popular responses was also low, 3.2 on the average. Tschudin also found that chronic psychotics produced fewer white space responses than the acute cases. This finding is consistent with Piotrowski's (1957, p. 95) view that schizophrenics with more than two white space responses tend to deteriorate less than those with few or none.

Binswanger (1944) obtained 74 records from 31 schizophrenics first seen in their original acute episode. Patients showed one of two characteristic patterns of change after the acute attack, patterns which presumably have implications for prognosis, although Binswanger gave no prognostic speculations in reporting his data. For one group of patients there was a sharp drop after the attack in total number of responses, in number of human movement responses, and in percentage of responses to the last three colored cards; the quality of responses (F+ per cent and especially W+ per cent) also dropped significantly. This group gave an average number of W and rarely gave small detail responses. The second group responded quite differently, increasing the number of responses, not by increasing W, which remained at an average level, but by adding small details (up to 20 per cent of responses). In this second group, the quality of response (F+ per cent) improved, responsiveness to the last three colored cards increased, and, as patients improved, color shock appeared.

To summarize, statistical findings of various authors concerning chronic and acute schizophrenics agree rather well if the number of cases is large. When small samples are used, disagreement can be striking. Schizophrenics differ a great deal among themselves, and therefore a sample of them must be large to be representative.

CONTENT

One of the earliest observations on peculiarities of language in which Rorschach responses are expressed was made by Minkowski (Laignel-Lavastine, Minkowska, Bouvet, & Neveu, 1943). She assumed that one of the basic psychological features of schizophrenia, fragmentation, would be reflected also in the Rorschach test performance, and she defined test manifestations of fragmentation as the use of verbs implying the isolation of parts of the blots from one another or the fragmenting of a whole blot or one of its parts. Examples are "cut off," "separate," "divide," "dissolve," "detach," "slit," "find something in an incomplete state," "miss something," etc. In my experience, fragmentation is not pathognomonic of schizophrenia, but it occurs in about two-thirds of schizophrenic test records and is much more rare in records of normals or other mental patients. Sometimes fragmentation occurs with the idea of "connection" (the use of verbs implying any form of putting things together or in touch with one another). Minkowska (1946) found connection to be typical of epileptics.

What might be called "irrelevant overabstraction" was also mentioned by Minkowska (Laignel-Lavastine et al., 1943) as an occasional tendency of schizophrenics. For example, a schizophrenic conveyed the idea that two persons on plate III were doing something with an object in the middle by saying "the idea of central action in a boy frame."

Content alone does not give a valid indication of overt behavior. Schafer (1954) has said that psychologists tend to underestimate degree of adjustment when they rely on content analysis and neglect formal test components. In my experience, even peculiar or morbid content is compatible with adequate social responsibility and efficiency in handling reality problems, provided the formal test components are good: F+ per cent, W+ per cent, ΣW, $\Sigma c/\Sigma C$ ratio, positive color responses, M, R, Irt. In fact, the likelihood of producing peculiar, asocial, or antisocial content increases as the control over the outward manifestation of motor impulses increases (Piotrowski, 1953). This explains why some schizophrenics produce more morbid content when they are in good remission than when they are manifestly psychotic. Bizarre content associated with schizophrenia usually appears in indeterminate form responses and expresses emotionally negative attitudes toward others. Strikingly morbid color responses, such as "gangrenous wound" and "blood mixed with dirt" (Phillips & Smith, 1953) are very rare. "Squashed animal" and similar destruction responses not only are not schizophrenic but may occur even in successfully functioning adults (Piotrowski et al., 1963).

Kuhn (1963), reporting on the Munsterlingen collection of 10,000 Rorschach records, found 1,416 records (or 14 per cent) with at least one blood response. However, blood responses were produced by about 20 per cent of records of schizophrenics, epileptics, and children below age 11. The presence of blood responses was not related to the degree of adjustment or to diagnosis, nor did it differentiate between mental patients and normals. In another study, very successful top business executives and failing top executives gave blood responses with the same frequency (Piotrowski et al., 1963). Kuhn further reported that when 100 of the persons who produced blood responses were asked what blood meant to them, most associated it with fear. Blood responses occurred in records of some individuals whose energetic and externally fearless behavior may have been counterphobic. Responses of blood alone were given more frequently by mental patients, while normals gave more specific responses, i.e., wounded or bloody human or animal bodies.

In the same collection (Kuhn, 1963), there was an average of two anatomy responses (6.76 per cent) in 6,582 records, with 78 per cent of normals giving at least one anatomy response. Children and adult mental patients produced more anatomy than normal adults. The percentage of test records with anatomy was nearly twice as high in schizophrenics as in normals. As the percentage of anatomy responses increased, the average number of M tended to decrease, and the averages for color and shading responses tended to increase. Object, nature, and landscape responses were practically absent in records in which the anatomy percentage was above 30. The total number of responses averaged 30.

Orme (1962) reviewed records of 1,010 mental patients of all categories to ascertain the frequency of sex responses. The percentages of patients with at least one sex response in the various patient groups were 14.4 per cent in schizophrenics, 7.5 per cent in alcoholics, 3.5 per cent in neurotics and psychopaths, and 2 per cent in the brain-damage and mental deficiency group. Young (1950), deVos (1952), and Beck (1954) also found that schizophrenics produce more genital responses than other groups. Men and women did not differ in the number and type of sex responses, confirming previous surveys by Shaw (1948) and Phillips and Smith (1953). Orme found no relationship between sex responses and diagnosis, age, or intelligence; however, Piotrowski (1938) found a positive association between genital responses and good prognosis in schizophrenia.

PARANOIA AND PARANOID SCHIZOPHRENIA

The test recognition of psychosis in paranoids can be extremely difficult. Paranoids with mild clinical symptoms but well-organized delusional systems constitute the majority of schizophrenics undetected by the Rorschach test. However, when it is known that schizophrenia exists, it is much easier to infer paranoid symptoms. Specific test indices of paranoia in a schizophrenic test record are eye responses (DuBrin, 1962) and homosexual responses, using the complete or partial Wheeler list of homosexual signs (Aronson, 1952; Chapman & Reese, 1953; Cutter, 1957; Davids, Joelson, & McArthur, 1956; Wheeler, 1949; Zeichner, 1955). When W are numerous (revealing concern over the future and preoccupation with leaving as little as possible to chance) but at the same time W+ per cent and F+ per cent are low, it can be inferred that the delusional system is ineffective and that the paranoid psychotic will appear confused (Piotrowski, 1957, p. 81). Rare detail responses with original content or unusual locations inside the blot occur more often in the paranoid than in other forms of schizophrenia. A megalomanic tendency, e.g., identification with the world, is typically paranoid. "This looks like the end of the world. I'm ready to die"; "this is all of me at the age of 18" (Zucker, 1958).

A sudden and marked shift in level of imagination, in degree of perseveration, in complexity or unusualness of content, and in proportion of W, D, and dr responses—the shift being maintained until the end of the performance proper—is characteristic of paranoia. In extreme cases, the two parts of the test record, before and after the shift, are so different that they seem to have been produced by two different individuals.

SETS OF SCHIZOPHRENIC SIGNS

Kataguchi (1959) developed the Kataguchi Rorschach Schizophrenic Score by assigning corrected positive and negative weights to formal scoring categories, the Buhler Basic Rorschach Score (1949) and the Watkins & Stauffacher Delta Values (1952). Kataguchi's scores classified as schizophrenic 77 per cent of 30 schizophrenics, 13 per cent of 30 psychoneurotics, and none of the 30 normals. An analysis and quantification of the differences in the organizational pattern of percepts resulted in significant differentiation between 35 male paranoid schizophrenics and 35 male neurotics (Hertz & Paolino, 1960). With the aid of signs, among which were some which occur more frequently in brain-damage cases, it was possible to differentiate significantly between 10 normals and 10 schizophrenics, placing only 3 of the 20 subjects in the wrong category (Vinson, 1960). Weiner (1961b) relied on only three "schizophrenic indicators": (1) presence of one or two CF responses, (2) sum of weighted color responses more than 1.0 but less than 3.5, and (3) presence of at least one CF or C but no c′, i.e., no dark or black color responses. Weiner used a sample of 141 patients with an age range from 15 to 62 and equal sex distribution, including 49 schizophrenics, 49 character neurotics, and 43 psychoneurotics. He found that at least two of his indicators were produced by 78 per cent of the schizophrenics, 29 per cent of the character disorders, and 16 per cent of the psychoneurotics.

Quirk et al. (1962) separated acute psychotics from normals and neurotics as well as from chronic psychotics, using a 10-sign list. The sign list was then cross-validated on 80 new cases, equally divided among the four groups, with 50 per cent of acute psychotics above the cutoff point, compared with 5 per cent of chronic psychotics, 5 per cent of neurotics, and 5 per cent of normals. Most of the signs were derived from an analysis of the verbal content of the patients' responses. Bower, Testin, and Roberts (1960), relying on content analysis in order to estimate the patient's level of maturity in interpersonal relationships, were able to differentiate between 30 cases each of paranoid schizophrenia, catatonic schizophrenia, psychotic depression, obsessive-compulsive neurosis, and personality disorders.

Wittenborn and Mettler (1951) estimated lack of perceptual control by the percentage of responses without definite good form. Patients who received psychosurgery had poorer perceptual control than the nonoperated patients.

Some investigators have tried to enhance the diagnostic power of the Rorschach by introducing techniques designed to measure intellectual flexibility. For example, Lothrop (1960) showed that schizophrenics display their intellectual impoverishment most on tasks, such as the Rorschach, which call for creative thinking; next on well-structured, though unfamiliar, tasks; and least on familiar tasks the solution of which depends chiefly on memory. Bloom and Arkoff (1961) stimulated schizophrenics to give nondeviate responses. Patients who subsequently showed rapid improvement responded positively and thus reduced their schizophrenic disorganization scores, while the slightly improved and unimproved schizophrenics were incapable of improving their responses. Watkins and Deabler (1957) demonstrated that most chronic schizophrenics have one-track minds, being unable to shift or alter their frame of reference to perceive real differences in environmental stimuli. Time of exposure to the blots did not much affect the quality of responses. The most extensive experimental study of the influence of exposure time upon Rorschach test responses is that of Stein (1949). Its most important conclusion was that testing with brief exposure times, .01″ and .10″, reveals covert personality traits and inner inhibition more adequately than testing under normal conditions without time limits. Short exposure times not only increased stress but also reduced the amount of perceived sensory cues. With decreasing exposure time, perception and meaningful interpretation of form greatly decreased. As exposure time was increased, the F+ per cent rose from 45 at .01″ to 80 at full exposure. The FC increased with time in relative numbers and particularly in absolute numbers. Although absolute and relative numbers of normal and rare detail as well as white space responses increased with exposure time, the absolute number of whole responses did not change significantly. However, group averages were not a dependable basis for prediction in individual cases which showed marked differences.

GENETIC LEVELS IN SCHIZOPHRENIA

Dworetzki (1939) examined the structuralization of percepts of 210 adult mental patients, defectives, normals of high and low educational levels, and children between ages 2½ and 15. By "percept" is meant the visual image projected on a particular blot area. She noted the similarities between the children and schizophrenics, particularly in vague syncretistic whole responses suggested by the dark gray shades, in perseveration in content, and in formless or unrealistic color responses. However, schizophrenics differed from children in reaching higher perceptual levels of complexity and in displaying a greater wealth of association. Color disturbed a great many psychotics, reducing the form quality of responses elicited by the colored plates. Children, on the other hand, liked color and were stimulated by it to give more, and more interesting, responses. Schizophrenics revealed their instinctual drives in their contaminations and condensations, while children did not do so. Color and dark shading responses appeared earlier than human movement and light shading responses.

The genetic approach to the Rorschach was developed and formalized by Werner (1948; 1957) and his followers (S. Friedman, 1953; Hemmendinger, 1953; Lane, 1955; Levine, 1959; Pena, 1953; Phillips & Smith, 1953; Rosenblatt & Solomon, 1954; Siegel, 1953; Wilensky, 1959). A scale was constructed to measure such test reactions as lability, diffuseness, rigidity, differentiation, hierarchic integration of the visual material, etc. The genetic-level scale significantly differentiates between normals and conspicuously ineffectual psychotics but does not discriminate between borderline psychotics and normals. Brooks and Phillips (1958) found no consistent relationship between the degree of difficulty of cognitive tasks and Rorschach genetic scores. In a study of 113 schizophrenics, Levine and Cohen (1962) found genetic-level scores to be positively correlated with cooperation and absence of apathy.

Since the child's Rorschach test responses become increasingly differentiated with age, both in perceptual structure and in imagination and variety of content, it is possible to rate test responses in terms of degrees of psychological maturity. There is then a basis for the application of the concept of genetic levels. Mental illness and immaturity (being a child) have similar but by no means identical deteriorating effects upon test performance. Another explanation of the impoverished quality of patients' responses appears more adequate and is more parsimonious than a regression hypothesis. This is the simple assumption that the approach to the blots parallels the approach to life: he who has the energy to organize the visual imagery elicited by the blots in a meaningful manner and thereby achieve a higher genetic-level score also has the initiative and energy to organize and control his life (Levine, 1960).

In the Rorschach, initiative, energy, and drive for personal achievement (or lack of apathy) in normals and patients are estimated primarily by the whole response. Large numbers of whole responses indicate active ambition and a desire to leave as little to chance as possible. The quality of active planning depends on the form quality and the degree of differentiation of the whole response. Kuhn (1953) discriminated between wholes with dependent and with independent parts. An example of the latter is a coal heap, since each part is still a coal heap. On the other hand, the human organism and any form of organized teamwork are examples of wholes with dependent parts, for no part can function in the manner of the whole to which it belongs.

Good-form constructive wholes have at least three dependent parts; they are rare and are produced by individuals of superior intelligence who have the capacity and drive for outstanding achievement (Piotrowski et al., 1963). In general, the number of wholes appears to vary independently of the other area components, D, d, and S; therefore, the percentage of W responses is less useful than the absolute number of W, which varies much less from examination to examination than the D, d, and S (Kuhn, 1953).

SPECIAL TECHNIQUES OF ADMINISTRATION

It is desirable to have as reliable a scoring of the test responses as possible. Beside Baughman's (1959a) technique of showing a number of modified stimuli in order to ascertain more objectively how shading, color, etc., contribute to a response, there is the Grassi (1942) "graphic Rorschach," which greatly helps to determine the perceptual structure and form quality of responses. In the Grassi technique, after the usual examination the subject is asked to draw his responses on plain paper; he is allowed to alter or add to his original percept. It is not necessary to have all the percepts sketched; the graphic technique should be applied to selected percepts of which the structure and form of quality are not clear to the examiner. The technique is especially useful in discriminating between neurotics and psychotics, but it also helps differentiate schizophrenics from organics (Brussel, Grassi, & Melniker, 1942; Grassi, 1942). Extremely blot-dominated drawings, that is, copying of the blot stimulus instead of sketching the image of the object projected visually on the blot, is highly associated with the presence of hallucinations.

SYSTEMATIC DIAGNOSTIC PROCEDURE: NEUROSES VERSUS PSYCHOSES

The systematic or pattern analysis diagnostic approach grew out of the observation that in records of schizophrenics, bizarre content is associated with other test components which are negatively correlated with F+ per cent. Test components were then classified as F+ per cent–depressing components and F+ per cent–raising components. It was assumed that increased inner stress would be accompanied by more F+ per cent–depressing components, and decreased inner stress by more F+ per cent–raising components. "Raising" components are assumed to be related to energy control, while "depressing" components are assumed to be related to energy output. Further, it was assumed that depressing and raising components are of about equal strength; i.e., in homeostasis, in normals and neurotics, energy output and energy control are in relative balance. However, in psychotics and others having mental conditions partially caused by anatomical lesions or serious neurophysiological disorders of the central nervous system, a serious disproportion between components indicating energy control and energy output can be expected. In cases "more serious than a mere neurosis," there can be two different kinds of imbalance between energy output and energy control. In one instance, the Rorschach may show much greater control than appears necessary, since energy output is relatively low. The alpha formula applies to these cases, which are "underactive and overcontrolled" (Piotrowski, 1945; Piotrowski, 1955; Piotrowski & Lewis, 1950b). The alpha case resembles the S3 psychotic of Beck (1954) and the A1 type of Molish (1956).

In the Rorschach, the three major measures of potential energy output are large numbers of W, large ΣC, and the positive difference obtained when the sum of weighted light shading responses is subtracted from the weighted sum of color responses. Energy control or chances against overacting out increase with positive difference between Σc and ΣC ($\Sigma c - \Sigma C$), decrease in number of W, and decrease in ΣC. Obsessiveness also functions as a desirable positive control in psychotics. The alpha formula designed to provide a quantitative measure of chances of acting out was revised slightly several times.

It applies fully only to cases with a ΣW below 7 and a $\Sigma c \geqq \Sigma C$. It was derived from test data of 180 patients in a large metropolis, psychotics and neurotics, whose mean intelligence was above average and none of whom was below average intellectually (Piotrowski & Lewis, 1950b); 50 of these patients were reexamined psychiatrically more than five years after the original testing. During the validation of the formula on a new group of 145 similar patients, the qualification was made that the patient should have an average or even a superior intelligence; the formula identified 83 per cent of psychotics and neurotics (Piotrowski & Berg, 1955).

To study the effect of intelligence, the formula was applied to test records of 26 male veterans with average normal intelligence; there was a follow-up of at least three years in each case who met both formal conditions, $\Sigma W < 7$ and $\Sigma c \geqq \Sigma C$. Since the alpha scores classified the patients correctly into a psychotic or a nonpsychotic group in 85 per cent of the cases, it was concluded that the IQ did not seem to matter (Calabresi, Piotrowski, & Simkin, 1958). The patients came from the same metropolitan area as those described in previous investigations. The Calabresi et al. study (1958), however, did not corroborate, on 34 patients, the suggested positive association between alpha scores and clinical status (Piotrowski, 1955); it was not confirmed that a rise or drop in alpha score is associated with clinical improvement or worsening of the schizophrenic's status. An alpha score of three or more points is considered indicative of a psychotic condition, "more serious than a mere neurosis."

Ballard and Winter (1964) compared two male outpatient veteran groups, 17 with a WAIS IQ of above 110 and 30 with IQs of 110 and less; the average IQs were 117 and 95, respectively. The authors included only those cases on whose alpha scores both agreed. Their independent scoring provided a reliability measure of the formula. Altogether 63 records were scored. In 51 per cent there was complete agreement; in 37 per cent the scores differed by one point; and in 12 per cent they differed by more than one. Eighty-three per cent of the psychotics and 80 per cent of neurotics had the expected alpha scores in the high IQ group, but in the lower IQ group only

TABLE 1. ALPHA FORMULA*

Weighted score	*W*	ΣC	$\Sigma c - \Sigma C$	*F+ per cent*	*c′ shock*
4	0		>4.0		
3	1	0	3.5–4.0		
2	2	0.5	2.5–3.0	<60	
1	3–4	1.0–1.5	1.5–2.0	60–69	present
0	>4	2.0–2.5	0–1.0	>69	absent
−1		3.0–4.0			
−2		>4.0			

* Modified from Piotrowski, 1955.

60 per cent of the psychotics had high scores, and only 11 per cent of the neurotics had low scores.

The very large percentage of false positives among the neurotics was striking in the lower IQ group. It is necessary to provide separate norms for the intellectually average and below-average patients. The great majority of false positives are due to absence of color responses. Absence of shocks, even initial reaction times, raises the probability of psychosis, provided the subject has emotional problems.

Delay, Pichot, and Perse (1958) observed and treated for at last one year 30 ambulatory schizophrenics and 30 neurotics of average ages 24 and 25, with an equal number of men and women in both groups. The alpha formula was applicable to 13 schizophrenic and 16 neurotic records. Only one case, a neurotic with a score of three points, had an alpha score contrary to the formula principle. At least one of the Thiesen (1952) patterns was found in 11 of the schizophrenics and in one neurotic. As expected, a high and significant negative association was found between high alpha scores and the presence of the Thiesen patterns and the authors' 10 pathognomonic and near-pathognomonic signs. No neurotics and 57 per cent of schizophrenics produced at least one of the latter. The 13 high alpha psychotics averaged only 0.4 of the Delay et al. 10 signs, while the 11 with at least one Thiesen pattern averaged 1.9, and the remaining six averaged 1.3.

The 10 schizophrenic signs of Delay et al. (1958) included Rorschach's three pathognomonic signs and the following: color naming; dissociation, or "seeing" a number of disconnected objects but failing to interconnect them in a functional pattern; morbid rationalization consisting of needless secondary associations to which nothing corresponds on the blots but which are not irrelevant ("an Egyptian animal"); symbolic responses ("a lion on each side symbolizing force"); obstetrical content, such as "fetus," "embryo," and "delivery," but excluding metaphors ("birth of spring"); and symmetrical dissociations, or interpreting two corresponding symmetrical details differently ("liver and spleen"). Thiesen (1952) compared records of 60 schizophrenics with those of 157 gainfully employed adult normals. He constructed five patterns in which nine components appear. These components are a high number of anatomy responses, apparently more than two; a low animal percentage, below 34; DW above zero; a low F+ per cent, below 69; no FC+; no M; less than five of Beck's populars; a high number of sex responses, apparently more than one; and a Beck Z score less than 8. At least one of the patterns occurred in 48 per cent of the schizophrenics and in 3 per cent of the normals. The 10-sign list of Delay et al. combined with the alpha formula identified correctly 93 per cent of the 60 patients.

Beck (1954) drew up a list of 170 traits to be used as an aid in differentiating types of schizophrenia. Rorschach records were the criterion for the evaluation of the traits which were Q-sorted (Stephenson, 1953). In this way, Beck described six types. Molish (1956) developed this approach further and confirmed the stability of the Beck S3 and the Molish B and A1 types, describing them as the most expedient way of establishing homeostasis in a muted phase. Frequently this type does not change despite insulin treatment and lobotomy (Molish, Hanlon, & Kurland, 1957).

PROGNOSIS

It seems that prognosis varies directly with the patient's subjective discomfort and inefficiency caused by this inner tension and varies inversely with the degree of primary thought disorders (Greenblatt & Solomon, 1953; Piotrowski, 1941). If the mental patient feels comfortable and is not anxious, hypokinetic, or hyperkinetic, it is not possible to help him. In other words, if he makes an efficient use of his mental abilities, whatever they are, he does not benefit from treatment (Piotrowski, 1939). All the available treatment methods of schizophrenia help only the secondary reactions to the psychosis; that is, they alleviate the emotional disturbance associated with the patient's anxious awareness that he is mentally ill. The patient's thought disorders are primary when they are independent of emotional tension.

A comparison of pretreatment Rorschach records of improved and unimproved schizophrenics who had insulin coma treatment revealed the prognostically favorable significance of M+ and W+ and, to a lesser degree, of the meaningful color response and F+ per cent (Piotrowski, 1938; Piotrowski, 1941). It was noted that even before treatment the schizophrenics who later improved functioned on a higher intellectual and emotional level than the patients who remained unimproved and that the pretreatment test records of many unimproved patients resembled records of patients with confirmed brain pathology (Graham, 1940; Halpern, 1940; Piotrowski, 1938). A subsequent study of 104 insulin-treated schizophrenics confirmed these conclusions and pointed to the importance of discriminating between intellectual regression or primary thought defects and emotional regression or drop in over-all efficiency caused by the patient's fear that his attempts to adjust may fail (Piotrowski, 1941). The procedure of discriminating between the two regressions was illustrated on pretreatment and posttreatment records of one unimproved and one improved schizophrenic (Piotrowski, 1939).

A long-term criterion was developed based on two different kinds of test components, the conventional scoring categories and the manner in which the patients handled their responses, and was limited to schizophrenics whose diagnosis was based on pre- and post-follow-up psychiatric examinations [with an interval of at least three years (Piotrowski & Lewis, 1952)]. To improve the reliability of the criterion signs, the criterion has been revised and simplified (Piotrowski & Bricklin, 1958) and then validated on a new and in many respects different group of 103 schizophrenics (Piotrowski & Bricklin, 1961). The two groups of followed-up schizophrenics were differentiated with a $p < .01$.

Pretreatment and posttreatment testing of 17 paranoid schizophrenics (Lipton, Tamarin, & Lotesta, 1951) confirmed conclusions regarding the traits which are associated with varying degrees of improvement. Even when specific prognostic indices were not confirmed in some studies, the higher level of psychological functioning and the higher degree of neurotic anxiety in the schizophrenic who later improved, whether he was paranoid or not, were confirmed (Grauer, 1953). Rickers-Ovsiankina (1954) followed and retested 38 schizophrenics, divided equally into improved and static ones; she found the improved cases to have more affect and anxiety in their pre-follow-up test records than the unimproved ones. In technical test terms, the improved cases exceeded the static ones in average color, shading, and tension scores. Grassi (1942) predicted the outcome of treatment correctly in 23 of 28 schizophrenics on the basis of his "graphic Rorschach." Of 13 patients whose drawings were completely "lot-dominated" and showed no trace of the patient's imagination, 12 were hallucinated. However, delusional ideas could not be inferred.

The movement responses were found to be of crucial importance in the psychotherapy of neurotics (Piotrowski & Schreiber, 1952). Sheehan, Frederick, Rosevear, and Spiegelman (1954) found that each type of movement response—human, animal, and inanimate—discriminated well, with p at .02, between 19 neurotic stutterers who improved most and 16 who improved least; the total number of responses did not discriminate at all, and form level, shading, and color discriminated insignificantly. Barclay and Hilden (1961) noted that the neurotic's "remaining longer in individual psychotherapy," which is not synonymous with improvement, was relatively most closely associated with the number of human movement, color-form, and total responses and the sum of weighted color responses; the number of individual psychotherapy sessions of 353 male neurotics served as a criterion. This large study is in essential agreement with a number of previous studies of the same problem to which it refers (including Gibby, Stotsky, Miller, & Hiler, 1953).

BRAIN DAMAGE

Brain-damage cases face the danger of intellectual deterioration, sensorimotor defects, and disturbances of consciousness (unawareness of what one is doing at the time and amnesia). It is much easier to obtain reliable and valid medical diagnoses of brain pathology than of schizophrenia. Of the reviews of Rorschach literature dealing with brain-damage cases, Baker's (1956) is long, detailed, highly informative, and critical enough to serve as a handbook. Baker stresses the differences among various types of organic brain disorders. The second longest general survey is that of Delay, Pichot, Lemperiere, and Perse (1957). It contains 223 references from the world literature. The article by Birch and Diller (1959) covers 20 investigations in a succinct manner. The Klebanoff, Singer, and Wilensky (1954) survey of 307 articles is not limited to the Rorschach but includes all psychological methods used in the study of brain-damage cases. However, there is a section devoted to the Rorschach, which gives the reader a good opportunity to compare the Rorschach test results with those obtained with other techniques. Readers interested in geriatrics will want to consult Orme's (1958) statistics, in which he summarizes his own as well as others' findings concerning the normal depression of old age and senile dementia cases, and the volume of Ames and her collaborators (1954). Last, but not least, Bohm (1957) has a chapter on the so-called "organic Rorschach syndrome."

Rorschach (1921) divided his statistics according to the degree of mental deterioration and offered six sets of norms, separating epileptics from the other brain disorder cases. He studied 46 cases. Rorschach suggested that there probably is a positive association between degrees of perseveration and memory defects. He noted that in some cases there is a striking contrast between the superior quality of human movement responses and the inferior quality of form responses.

Oberholzer (1931) noted the drop in human movement responses and increase in CF and C responses, the difficulty in distinguishing the essential parts within a larger whole, the slow pace of interpretation, the rise in DW, and the drop in the percentage of sharply perceived forms and perseveration.

In order to be able to use the Rorschach as a diagnostic aid in the detection of mental changes contingent upon organic brain damage, it was necessary to set up more precise and exacting criteria than those provided by verbal generalizations.

Piotrowski (1937a) studied 18 patients with confirmed lesions of the cortical and subcortical brain areas, i.e., of the gray matter of the cerebral cortex and of the subjacent white matter; 10 patients with spinal central nervous system diseases; and 5 conversion hysterics. The patients with the cortical and subcortical lesions were chronic patients. The control groups were taken from the same neurological wards; brain pathology had been suspected but was ruled out after laboratory tests and a long period of observation. This study resulted in the setting up of 10 signs for the detection of mental changes caused by organic brain disorders. A survey of the literature reveals that 3 of the 10 signs—impotence, perplexity, and color naming—which must meet two very different requirements, seem to be applied sometimes without paying attention to the second requirement.

There are no pathognomonic signs of brain damage. However, "impotence," "perplexity," and "automatic phrases" are near-pathognomonic (Piotrowski, 1937a). Schenk (1938) stated that the presence of impotence or perplexity is sufficient to infer an organic brain disorder. He studied 11 normals, 27 neurotics, and 20 patients with brain disorders. None of his neurotics and normals produced five of the 1937 signs, while 9 of his 20 organics produced at least five of the signs. Four additional patients who produced fewer than five signs had either impotence or perplexity. Schenk suggested two additional signs—namely, W+ per cent below 70 and original plus responses below 50—as aiding in a sharper differentiation. He set up his own group of seven signs: percentage of good form originals below 50, F+ per cent below 70, color naming, no human movement response, repetition, impotence, and perplexity. Impotence and perplexity are consistently found to be the most discriminating of all the test components suggested for the differentiation between organic and nonorganic patients. (Aita et al., 1947; Baker, 1956; Basaglia & Dalla Barba, 1957; Birch & Diller, 1959; Hertz & Loehrke, 1954; Hughes, 1948; Hughes, 1950; Reitan, 1955; Sanders, Schenk, & Van Veen, 1939; Schenk, 1938). Of 51 psychoneurotics, 4 manifested impotence, and 1 perplexity (Piotrowski, 1940).

In brain-damage cases, there is a disproportion between the ability to describe details verbally and the ability to localize them visually. This suggests a malfunctioning of the sensorimotor orientation (Piotrowski, 1937a). Kelley (1941) made a separate sign out of it, "impairment of abstract behavior." Aita et al. (1947) called it "unclear definition of response," and this is the most discriminating of their nine signs; it was found in 70 per cent of the organic and in only 15 per cent of the nonorganic patients' records.

The percentage of brain cases producing at least 5 of the 10 signs (Piotrowski, 1940) varies with the age of the patient and the apparent severity of the damage. Rorschach records of 102 organic cerebral patients were divided according to the age of the patients into four groups: below 12 years, 12 to 18 years, 18 to 50 years, and over 50 years of age. The percentages of patients with the critical number of signs increased with age, being 42 per cent, 50 per cent, 61 per cent, and 89 per cent, respectively. In the largest group of organic patients on whom Rorschach findings were published, Fisher, Gonda, and Little (1955) found at least five of the 1937 signs in 38 per cent of 84 of their organic cerebral cases but in only 6 per cent of 34 controls who had been treated and diagnosed in the neurology department also because of the probability of brain damage on admission. The duration of the primary symptoms was less than three years in over one-half of these cases. The conclusion was then drawn that if the critical signs are present in the record, they are helpful in the detection of mental changes caused by brain damage, but the signs cannot be used to rule out the possibility of brain damage. Only the positive test responses are meaningful; the negative are not (Piotrowski, 1940).

The 1937 signs compared very favorably with the lumbar puncture and skull x rays in terms of screening efficiency. The article is unique in giving statistics on the diagnostic power of neurological laboratory tests, the electroencephalogram, the pneumoencephalogram, skull x rays, lumbar punctures, and clinical neurological examinations administered to the same large group of patients. This study differs from most others in that many varieties of brain pathology are represented in the cases, yielding a wide range from extreme brain pathology through borderline to no brain pathology. Furthermore, all patients were hospital cases who were intensively worked up neurologically because the probability of neurological disease seemed high in all. The final diagnosis was based on the consensus of neurologists who relied on laboratory tests and on psychiatric, neurological, and psychological tests, but not on the Rorschach (Fisher & Gonda, 1955).

Ross (1940) noticed that some patients give a spuriously large number of the 1937 Piotrowski signs by perseverating with anatomical responses. Ross defined as an anatomical perseveration record one in which no more than three responses were nonanatomical. There were 18 such records in a collection of 216, or an incidence of 8 per cent. Ross asked the patients to repeat the test and not give answers which repesented parts of the body. Those unable to make the shift were known clinically to be suffering from anatomical lesions of the central nervous system or from toxic or endocrine disorders. Ross's corrective procedure should be applied in every case of marked perseveration to exclude spurious false positives.

Ross (1941) tested the 1937 signs on 236 subjects. There were two normal groups, soldiers and superior normals, and seven different groups of neuropsychiatric patients with different diagnoses. He found the critical number of signs in 55 per cent of the 18 cases with confirmed cerebral lesions, in 37 per cent of the 19 epileptics, in 30 per cent of cases with central nervous system lesions that were not cortical or subcortical, in 20 per cent of the 15 psychotics, and in 14 per cent of the psychoneurotics. One of the 53 soldiers and no superior normal produced five or more signs. Ross concluded that the presence of five or more of the 1937 signs was an indication not specifically of a cerebral anatomical lesion but of some dysfunction in the nervous system, either "organic" or "functional." He added that such a conclusion was wrong in less than 5 per cent of his 236 cases. The absence of five or more signs was not significant. The scoring of perplexity may have influenced the statistical data, since 29 per cent of the psychoneurotics were credited with this sign. Ross set up his own set of signs (Ross & Ross, 1944).

Aita et al. (1947) examined 60 brain-injured soldiers three to six months after the head injury and compared the records with those of 100 controls from the same hospital ward. These controls included cases with minor closed head injuries, idiopathic headaches, and convulsions of unknown etiology in whom the possibility of a neurological disease was eliminated by the definite opinion of the neurologists. The relative frequency of each of the 1937 signs differed in the experimental and control groups, the most discriminating being impotence, perplexity, automatic phrases, and repetition. Impotence and perplexity were the two most closely associated with the severity of the mental effects of brain injury. The percentages of patients in each of these three groups—severe, moderate, and mild—decreased in the following order: for impotence, 73 per cent, 48 per cent, and 25 per cent; for perplexity, 74 per cent, 48 per cent, and 46 per cent. Edging occurred in 17 per cent of the controls and in 42 per cent of the organics, occurring in 64 per cent of the severe, in 33 per cent of the moderate, and in 39 per cent of the mild cases. Thus while it is not pathognomonic of organicity and certainly not of schizophrenia, it seems to be associated with the severity of the consequences of brain pathology. The authors isolated and defined nine additional signs which differentiate organics from nonorganics with statistical significance.

Hughes (1950) added color and shading shocks to the list of the 1937 signs in order to isolate psychoneurotics from the organics and used contamination and confabulated whole responses to separate schizophrenics from the organics. Hughes was able correctly to identify 82 per cent of the organics and all his nonorganics. However, Hertz and Loehrke (1954) and Fisher et al. (1955) could not obtain quite as good results with the Hughes scale.

Dörken and Kral (1952) set up signs in which they expected the organic patients to be deficient. This set of signs differentiated well between organics and nonorganics (normals, psychoneurotics, and schizophrenics) when these two groups differed greatly in clinical symptoms, but it did not discriminate well when the organics and the controls resembled each other clinically.

Hertz and Loehrke (1954) analyzed Rorschach records of 50 male veterans with head injury, 50 schizophrenics, and 50 neurotics. They tested the reliability of the signs (Piotrowski, 1937a; Hughes, 1950). The agreement between independent scoring of the records by the two authors was very high, indicating that they were scoring the same test reactions in the same way (p=.98). The emphasis is rightly placed on the need for training in the application of these signs. Twenty-six per cent of the organics, 8 per cent of the schizophrenics, and none of the neurotics produced five or more of the 1937 signs. The differentiation between organics and neurotics was at below the .001 confidence level; between organics and schizophrenics, at below the .02 level; and between schizophrenics and neurotics, at below the .05 level of confidence. Taking the three patient groups in the order organic, schizophrenic, and neurotic, impotence occurred in 26 per cent, 4 per cent, and 2 per cent of the groups, respectively; perplexity in 26 per cent, 0 per cent, and 2 per cent; and automatic phrases in 16 per cent, 0 per cent, and 2 per cent. On the other hand, when the record contained an F+ per cent of above 70 and a percentage of popular responses (Beck's list) above 25 and there was no repetition (perseveration), the chances that the patient was organic or schizophrenic were practically nil. Of the 1937 signs, five or more were produced by 25 per cent of the organics and by 8 per cent of the schizophrenics; no neurotic produced five or more of the signs. Hughes's thesis that a score of below three points on his scale eliminated the possibility of organicity was not sustained in this investigation, for 62 per cent of the organics scored that low, as did 78 per cent of the schizophrenics and 78 per cent of the neurotics. On the other hand, when the scores were high, meaning possible organicity (in the case of scores of three to six points) and definite organicity (scores of seven points or higher), 38 per cent of the organics, 22 per cent of the schizophrenics, and 22 per cent of the psychoneurotics scored that high. However, only organics obtained scores of seven points and above. The authors concluded that the Hughes signs were not valid when applied to their posttraumatic group and that the 1937 signs "may reflect organicity" but that they occurred in a small proportion of the patients, and their absence did not preclude organic pathology, in accordance with the principle underlying the set of signs.

Using 118 patients, Fisher et al. (1955) cross-validated four Rorschach sets of signs devised for the detection of brain pathology: the Piotrowski (1937a), the Hughes (1950), the Dörken-Kral (1952), and the Ross and Ross (1944) sets of signs. The Piotrowski, the Ross and Ross, and the Hughes sign systems yielded 6 per cent, 18 per cent, and 9 per cent. The Dörken and Kral set of signs resulted in 76 per cent false positives. Only one of the four systems, the 1937 signs, maintained a validity level comparable to that obtained in previous studies.

Kral & Dörken (1951) made the discovery that persons with lesions in the diencephalon produce no color responses. This finding agrees well with the apathy characteristic of these patients. Of nine cases with diencephalic lesions, eight gave at least five of the 1937 signs. There were other differences between the nine diencephalic patients and the 19 other organics, but the absence of color was the most striking one.

Birch and Diller (1959) not only summarized 20 different investigations of the 1937 signs but also proceeded to explain the significance of the difference between known organic cerebral cases who do produce five or more signs and those who do not have the critical number of these signs. To explain this, they divided the effects of brain pathology into two different types. When brain damage or a lesion causes the disappearance of a function, for example, bringing about defective vision, it is called "subtractive." The other one is called "additive" and "active" in that the lesion causes additional psychological dimensions, thus adding to the behavioral disturbances. For example, a blood clot, though very small, may cause a great many secondary irritations and thus add to the behavioral disturbances. The authors suggest that the 1937 signs are valid indicators of disturbance in those individuals in whom cerebral damage involves active additive physiological changes and that they do not reflect the behavior of patients with lesions which produce a primarily subtractive effect. According to them, the set of signs is not sensitive to brain damage per se but reveals "organicity," or one of the behavioral consequences of brain damage. They view this "organicity" primarily as an impairment in the organization of perceptions.

To test this hypothesis, they divided 10 paraplegic patients into two equal groups, according to whether or not they had five or more of the 1937 signs, and then divided 10 other paraplegics according to whether they did or did not have active additive disturbances, such as sensory disturbances, reflex disturbances, convulsive phenomena, autonomic disturbances, etc. When the 20 patients were lumped into one group, there was a high positive association between the number of additive medical signs and the number of the Piotrowski 1937 signs; the correlation was .77. Organicity can be considered a result of neurophysiological rather than neuroanatomic disturbances, and it is by means of this idea that the authors explained the contradictory results obtained with the 1937 signs, that is, the varying percentages of true positive and false negatives. The additive lesion and the subtractive lesion groups showed the greatest difference in the most important signs—perplexity, impotence, automatic phrases, and repetition (perseveration). Perplexity and impotence are also measures of great intellectual and perceptual insecurity.

LOCALIZED BRAIN PATHOLOGY

It is almost impossible to infer the location of a focal brain lesion from the Rorschach test at the present time. The test seems more helpful in detecting diffuse pathology of the cerebral cortex than subcortical tumors, which is compatible with the test's sensitivity to deinhibition. Delay et al. (1956) concluded that the test is particularly sensitive in spotting the organic mental syndrome of memory difficulties, wandering attention, and "emotional incontinence."

Findings involving frontal lobe lesions were summarized by Yacorzynski and Davis (1945) and by Petrie (1952). The main effect of frontal lobe pathology in the dominant hemisphere (no pathology is usually seen in the Rorschach when the pathology is limited to the nondominant frontal lobe) is the inability to evaluate one's own thinking critically, associated with a markedly reduced capacity for voluntary or deliberate conscious attention (Piotrowski, 1937b). Nadel (1938) compared 15 cases having damage of the left lobe or of both frontal lobes and showing evidence of some mental deterioration with 15 matched controls whose brain pathology seemingly did not involve the frontal lobes and who showed no deterioration. He concluded that the 1937 signs were particularly sensitive to frontal lobe damage.

Hunt (1940), obtaining prelobotomy and postlobotomy test records from 40 schizophrenics in whom postoperative brain damage was slight, found only one patient with six of the 1937 signs. Kisker (1944) reviewed the literature and examined 20 lobotomized psychotics before and after interruption of the thalamocortical projections. He inferred that the 1937 signs were indicative of the psychosis rather than of the lobotomy. Kisker offered as an indicator of memory loss, inattention, and poor concentration the simultaneous presence in the test record of a low F+ per cent, low Pop per cent, increased average time per response, and decreased number of responses. Subsequent lobotomy studies differ somewhat in detail but agree in general conclusions with the early investigations (Atwell, 1953; McFie, Piercy, & Zangwill, 1951; McReynolds & Weide, 1960). According to Spreen (1955), there is a great difference between dorsal and basal injuries of the frontal lobes. He published statistics on 100 frontal lobe injury cases (51 dorsal, 49 basal), 70 brain-damage cases not involving the frontal lobes, and 70 psychoneurotics, comparing the averages with those of 100 normals. The main conclusion is that there can be no single Rorschach syndrome for all frontal lobe cases. Though the frontal lobe cases produce a larger percentage of mutilated anatomy ("a bleeding chest"), Loftus (1947) discovered that this kind of response occurred frequently in records of servicemen who had experienced a severe battle trauma. In 30 cases, Loftus found an average of 14.5 per cent, while Gardner (1936) found only a percentage of 1.2 in 100 nurses who did not see the war at close range, although the nurses' average for all anatomy responses, 10, was high.

Basaglia and Dalla Barba (1957) found five or more of the 1937 signs in 18 of 21 cases of postencephalitic Parkinsonism. Machover (1957) compared 15 persons with Parkinsonism who had been ill from six months to five years with 15 Parkinson's disease cases whose duration of illness ranged from 14 to 38 years. No evidence of a consistent aggressive drive toward activity, independence, and mastery was found in these patients. Diller and Riklan (1957) divided 42 patients with Parkinson's disease into two numerically equal groups, a high and a low human movement group, on the basis of Rorschach administered prior to neurosurgery. The high M group gave significantly more personal psychological rather than impersonal or objective causes for their illness. They also made significantly more negative statements about themselves than the low M group.

A very high positive correlation was found between the usual Rorschach and the graphic technique diagnostic conclusions in identifying brain-trauma cases with mental impairment (Brussel et al., 1942). Armitage (1946) subjected 44 patients with brain injuries to a number of different psychological tests and concluded that counting the number of signs was not sufficient and that it was necessary to consider the intensity and frequency with which each of the 1937 signs occurred in the record as well as the patient's intellectual level. Several pronounced signs were as valid diagnostically as a larger number of less pronounced signs. Koff (1946) tested 185 patients with cerebral concussions. The 1937 signs indicated organic pathology in 67 of the 75 cases whose spinal fluid protein level also indicated organic pathology, and they indicated psychoneurosis in 89 of 100 cases whose spinal fluid protein level was below the critical level for organic pathology. A. Friedman (1956) found five or more of the organic signs in 22 of 30 patients with intracranial pathology following an accident. He noted that the eight who failed to produce the critical number of the 1937 signs were intellectually and educationally superior to the remaining 22.

Zimmerman and Oetzel (1955) followed up and reexamined, after a period of seven years, 100 servicemen who had sustained a head injury. Eleven of these were found to show no evidence of brain damage, while the remaining 89 showed various degrees of subsequent brain and mental damage. All the 11 without brain damage produced less than five of the 1937 signs. On the other hand, 14 of the 89 with brain damage produced at least one of the nearly pathognomonic signs, and 15 of them produced five or more of the 1937 signs. The number of these signs was correlated with the severity of the injury and with the clinical injury score. The authors also examined 48 servicemen with neurosyphilis. Following treatment, which presumably reduced the severity of the infection, the symptomatic cases improved most, and the number of the 1937 signs dropped by at least one-third. The authors concluded that the sign approach to the Rorschach is a rough check of the adequacy of adjustment when intellectual functioning and self-sufficiency are considered.

Hertz and Loehrke (1955) set up a list of 34 "configurations," e.g., "intellectual deterioration," "vagueness of perception," "intellectual rigidity," etc., which were found to have a high degree of scoring reliability. The authors separated significantly ($p<.01$) 50 posttraumatic brain-injury cases from 50 schizophrenics and 50 neurotics.

EPILEPSY

The Rorschach literature on epilepsy is vast, and it was summarized by Delay et al. (1958). Not only did the authors give a comprehensive, critical, and detailed survey of practically the entire world literature, but they also evaluated the methodological approaches of the investigators, their assets, and limitations; moreover, they presented data on 50 of their own epileptics, dividing them into four etiological groups.

Bovet (1936) examined 120 epileptics and 20 head-trauma cases without epileptic seizures. He was impressed by the epileptics' inability to produce human movement responses. Half of his epileptics gave none, and only six of them, all being clinically atypical, gave more than two.

Piotrowski (1947) compared 25 idiopathic epileptics with 25 psychoneurotics who had no indication of brain pathology but who had at first been suspected of genuine epilepsy. All these patients were ambulatory. None was psychotic, hospitalized, or demonstrably deteriorated. The averages and ranges of ages and intelligence quotients and the sex ratios were almost the same in the two groups. It was found that 6 of the 10 original 1937 signs were useful as diagnostic aids and were incorporated in the set of 1947 signs for detection of the epileptic personality disorder. Eight new signs were added: emphasis on symmetry, large or small deviant numbers of whole responses, long average initial reaction time, dark shading shock, frank expression of hostility, meticulousness, "description" or shaded color responses, and comment on degree of difficulty of task. Of the 50 epileptics of Delay et al. (1958), 17 spoke of "joining" (Minkowska, 1946), 48 per cent produced at least seven of the fourteen Piotrowski 1947 signs, and 80 per cent produced at least five of them; 68 per cent of these patients produced also five or more of the 1937 signs.

MENTAL DEFICIENCY

Rorschach test findings with mental defectives are well summarized by Bohm (1958). The degree of emotional stability as well as deficiency can be read not only from the F+ per cent, color responses, and shading responses, but, as Rorschach (1921) pointed out, also from the manner of reasoning as revealed by the structure of the whole responses. Beck's (1932) extensive study confirmed Rorschach's conclusions as well and extended our knowledge. The manner of organizing the visual clues picked from the blots by the defectives was studied by Dworetzki (1939). Abel (1945) investigated degrees of mental and social efficiency in mental defectives.

ALCOHOLISM

A detailed study of alcoholics was made by Buhler and Lefever (1947). The problem was reexamined by Button (1956). Water responses do not indicate alcoholism (Shereshevski-Shere & Lasser, 1952). "Bottle" and "drinking" responses, on the other hand, are nearly always valid indicators of alcoholism, especially if there is much anxiety.

CHARACTERISTIC REACTIONS OF ORGANICS

The cerebral organic's mental stress revealed by the characteristic mobilization of mental strength can be used as a diagnostic aid, provided the diagnostic problem is limited to a choice between brain pathology and schizophrenia. Schizophrenics hardly ever manifest the "mobilization-of-mental-strength syndrome," and when they do, they display it at most in one response. The brain-damage cases manifest it frequently and usually in several responses. The syndrome is divisible into four successive phases. During the first, the patient gropes for an idea, wondering what a blot area, usually the whole plate, might represent. He then makes a decision and names the object he thinks the blot area looks like. The next, or third, phase is the most characteristic; the patient mobilizes his knowledge about the object, the image of which was elicited in his mind by the plate. He proceeds to enumerate the parts which the imagined object normally possesses, as if to clarify the image. The last and fourth phase is sometimes omitted by the patient, but he can be prompted to enter it. This phase consists of visually ascertaining whether the details, enumerated in the third phase, have their equivalents in the proper places on the inkblot. One patient had a vague notion that plate I looked like some flying creature. He then expressed the thought that it might be a bat. Next, he named the parts of a bat: body, wings, feelers, claws, etc. Finally, but with insecurity and hesitation, he moved his finger across the plate to verify whether the enumerated parts could be seen on the plate. Practically no schizophrenic goes through these distinct phases spontaneously and systematically. The schizophrenic is too quick (when productive) and too uninterested in supporting the relevance of his responses by analyzing the fit between his images and the inkblots. He may elaborate on his idea when questioned about it by the examiner during the inquiry, but he is not likely to do it on his own. The diagnosis of organicity—provided the problem consists in choosing between schizophrenia and brain pathology—is strengthened when the patient displays the mobilization-of-mental-strength syndrome in several plates, perseverates with the same content, and refuses to consider the possibility of more than one interpretation per plate.

The two most general differences between brain pathology and schizophrenia—again provided that the differential diagnostic problem is limited to a choice between one or the other psychosis—are shown in the degree of evenness of performance level and the psychological contact with the plates (Piotrowski, 1947). The cerebral case does not show during the same examination marked variations in the level of imagination—usualness of content and ontological variety (real and familiar versus imaginary and unique, present versus distant past, static and solid versus dynamic and abstract). The schizophrenic, on the other hand, makes at least one interesting flight into imagination which contrasts with the drabness of his other responses. It must be pointed out, however, that frequently an inquiry is needed to detect this excursion into the imaginative when the schizophrenic is not sufficiently interested in verbalizing everything he "sees." The other attitude which is typical of brain pathology but not of schizophrenia is the preoccupation with the problem of fit, the correspondence between the shape and color of the imagined response object and the respective blot areas. A persistent concern with adequacy of fit is not schizophrenic. The schizophrenic may, in one or several responses, show this concern, but he will show a complete disregard for adequate fit in other responses. The mobilization-of-mental-strength syndrome is a special variant of the preoccupation with fit.

TEST SIGNS OF ORGANICITY IN SCHIZOPHRENIA

Since the 1937 signs were designed to detect organic brain damage, it is disturbing to find five and more of them in 20 per cent (Ross, 1941) and even in 50 per cent (Eckhardt, 1961) of schizophrenics. A wide statistical survey of Eckhardt's (1961) demonstrated that a state hospital patient's chances of being diagnosed schizophrenic are significantly much higher, and of being diagnosed an organic brain case significantly much lower, in a Southern than in a Northern state. These geographical differences in neuropsychiatric diagnosis may account for the unexpected frequencies of the 1937 signs among Southern state hospital schizophrenics. The influence of geography on diagnosis emphasizes the importance of follow-up diagnoses by well-trained and experienced neuropsychiatrists. Nevertheless, the unreliability of clinical diagnosis does not fully explain the matter. Neiger, Slemon, and Quirk (1962), in Canada, also found critical sums of the signs in nearly one-half of their hospitalized chronic schizophrenics, although six or more signs were produced by only 15 per cent of the same patients. These authors give statistics regarding the incidence of each of the 1937 signs in the various patient groups, and they discuss the reliability of the signs. They conclude that the 1937 signs identify regression rather than anatomical brain damage. In passing, they mention the possibility that some forms of schizophrenia may have organic roots.

Many schizophrenics may suffer from brain pathology. Not only do test records of schizophrenics who remain unimproved resemble those of brain-damage cases, but the most discriminating unfavorable long-term prognostic test criteria seem to pertain to primary thought disorders (Piotrowski & Bricklin, 1958). Pneumoencephalographic investigations point in the same direction. Having reviewed the literature on this subject, Haug (1962) presented his own results. Sixty-one per cent of his 137 chronic schizophrenics had abnormal pneumoencephalograms with definite dilation of the ventricles or marked atrophy of the cerebral cortex. Haug added that the encephalogram is a prognostic aid and helps to predict deterioration and level of adaptation.

There is a remarkable correlation between the percentage of schizophrenics who eventually improve or do not improve, regardless of treatment received, and the decade and country in which the statistics were collected and the theoretical orientation of the investigators. Appel, Myers, and Scheflen (1953) summarized many studies of tens of thousands of patients and showed that the percentage of improved schizophrenics varies between 25 and 30. Special long-term follow-ups result in similar percentages of improved and unimproved schizophrenics (Denker, 1947; Errera, 1957; Holt & Holt, 1962; Rennie, 1939). The great majority of these psychotics have permanent mental scars which affect their thinking as well as their interhuman relations. This observation and the high reliability of the large percentage of the unimproved suggest some chronic brain dysfunction. Therefore, the hypothesis that some brain pathology is involved in chronic unimproved schizophrenics cannot be easily dismissed.

MANIC-DEPRESSIVE PSYCHOSIS

Rorschach (1921) computed his averages on data from records of 14 manic-depressives. These figures are almost the same as the averages he gives for the simple form of schizophrenia. Indeed, they cannot be used as dependable diagnostic aids. The averages for the manics are even less reliable. A true manic who later does not develop schizophrenia is a rarity, and any psychologist would have a hard time collecting a number of cases with verified follow-up diagnoses sufficient to compute reliable statistics.

The first large Rorschach study of manic-depressive psychotics, by Levy and Beck (1931), centered on the formal test components. The diagnosis is a difficult one and appears relatively rarely nowadays.

The first attempt to diagnose a manic-depressive depression by means of a Rorschach formula was by Guirdham (1936) but this formula has not been checked on a large followed-up group of psychotic depressives. Genuine manics are very rare and are practically not testable because of their restless distractibility and continuous physical activity.

SPECIAL SYMPTOMS

Lists of homosexual signs vary greatly in length, from long (Wheeler, 1949) to short (Piotrowski, 1957, pp. 359–363), affecting the percentages of subjects identified as "homosexual," i.e., as heterosexually inadequate, and thus modifying the meaning of the term (Chapman & Reese, 1953; Cutter, 1957; Davids et al., 1956). The literature relating specific test components to specific mental traits or to specific overt acts is very large but suffers from reliance on small population samples and a small number of control groups. Samples of it are Elizur's (1949) anxiety and hostility scales, Rioch and Lubin's (1959) scale of social adjustment for hospitalized patients, Schafer's (1960) investigation of the meaning of "bodies" in schizophrenic records, Wagner's (1961) study of the significance of human movement and anatomy responses for interaction with others, and Rychlak and Gunouard's (1961) correlation of various content categories with behavioral traits.

Freud's psychosexual symbolism seems to be almost directly applicable to the Rorschach test. Other types of symbols require modification. Samples of results obtained from the application of Freud's symbolism to the Rorschach test can be found in Lindner (1947); Brown (1953); Schafer (1954); Holt (1956); Holt & Havel (1960); Zeichner (1955; 1956); Piotrowski (1957, pp. 179–186, 324–332, 363–389); Molish & Beck (1958); Silverman, Lapkin, & Rosenbaum (1962); Holt, Sengstake, Sonoda, & Draper (1960); and Zelin & Sechrest (1963).

OVERT BEHAVIOR PREDICTIONS

Samples of studies investigating rules of predicting overt behavior in various situations include Kuhn (1940); Piotrowski (1943); Holtzman (1950); Orchinik, Koch, Wycis, Freed, & Spiegel (1950); Finney (1955); and Piotrowski (1957, pp. 390–413). The evaluation of intelligence seems relatively most successful when based on the subject's vocabulary, and intelligence may be easily underestimated in withdrawn individuals. If visual imagination alone is taken as a measure of intelligence and if the goodness of fit is disregarded, the subject's intellectual capacity is usually overestimated. The intelligence of emotionally stable subjects is more easily assessed (Ogdon & Allee, 1959; Trier, 1958; Wysocki, 1957).

The Rorschach stimuli constitute a specific experimental technique which has its own laws of eliciting visual imagery differing in many respects from that elicited by other stimuli under different physical and psychosocial conditions. Even a relatively small change in the stimulus blots influences the responses. The removal of shading from the chromatic colors reduces the number of color-form and pure color responses, showing the dependence of the psychologist on the physical properties of his instrument (Canter, 1958). This finding agrees with Baughman's (1959a) experiment showing that meaningful responses to light shading in the regular Rorschach plates are more frequent than is reported in a normal hurried inquiry. Both the color and the shading responses are of paramount importance in evaluating personality and particularly the form and intensity of the overtly manifested emotions.

REFERENCES

Abel, T. M. The relationship between academic success and personality organization among subnormal girls. *Amer. J. ment. Def.*, 1945, **50**, 251–256.

Aita, J. A., Reitan, R. M., & Ruth, J. M. Rorschach's test as a diagnostic aid in brain injury. *Amer. J. Psychiat.*, 1947, **103**, 770–779.

Ames, L. B. Age changes in the Rorschach responses of individual elderly subjects. *J. genet. Psychol.*, 1960, **97**, 287–315.

Ames, L. B., Learned, J., Metraux, R. W., & Walker, R. N. Child Rorschach responses. *J. proj. Tech.*, 1952, **17**, 495–597.

Ames, L. B., Learned, J., Metraux, R. W., & Walker, R. N. *Rorschach responses in old age.* New York: Hoeber-Harper, 1954.

Ames, L. B., Metraux, R. W., & Walker, R. N. *Adolescent Rorschach responses: developmental trends from ten to sixteen years.* New York: Hoeber-Harper, 1959.

Appel, K. E., Myers, J. M., & Scheflen, A. E. Prognosis in psychiatry: results of psychiatric treatment. *Arch. Neurol. Psychiat.*, 1953, **70**, 459–468.

Appelbaum, S. A., & Holzman, P. S. The color-shading response and suicide. *J. proj. Tech.*, 1962, **26**, 155–161.

Armitage, S. G. An analysis of certain psychological tests used for the evaluation of brain injury. *Psychol. Monogr.*, 1946, **60**, No. 1.

Aronson, M. L. A study of the Freudian theory of paranoia by means of the Rorschach test. *J. proj. Tech.*, 1952, **16**, 397–411.

Atwell, C. Rorschach studies: pre- and post-lobotomy. In M. Greenblatt & H. C. Solomon (Eds.), *Frontal lobes and schizophrenia.* New York: Springer, 1953. Pp. 214–216.

Bahnson, C. B., & Bahnson, M. B. Denial and regression of primitive impulses in patients with malignant neoplasm. *Proc. 3rd Int. Congr. psychosoma. Factors Malignant Dis.* London: Pitman's Medical Publishers, 1963.

Baker, G. Diagnosis of organic brain damage in the adult. In B. Klopfer et al. (Eds.), *Developments in the Rorschach technique.* Vol. II. New York: Harcourt, Brace & World, 1956. Pp. 318–428.

Ballard, R., & Winter, G. *The discriminatory power of the alpha score in a specific clinical setting.* Philadelphia: VARO, 1964.

Barclay, A., & Hilden, A. H. Variables related to duration of individual psychotherapy. *J. proj. Tech.*, 1961, **25**, 268–271.

Barendregt, J. T. *Psychological studies: research in psychodiagnostics.* Vol. 1. The Hague: Mouton, 1961.

Basaglia, F., & Dalla Barba, G. Il rifiuto alla V tavola di Rorschach. *Arch. Psicol. Neur. Psich.*, 1957, **18**, 17–24.

Baughman, E. E. The effect of inquiry method on Rorschach color and shading scores. *J. proj. Tech.*, 1959, **23**, 3–7 (a)

Baughman, E. E. An experimental analysis of the relationship between stimulus structure and behavior on the Rorschach. *J. proj. Tech.*, 1959, **23**, 134–183. (b)

Beck, S. J. The Rorschach test as applied to a feeble-minded group. *Arch. Psychol., N.Y.*, 1932, No. 136.

Beck, S. J. Personality structure in schizophrenia: a Rorschach investigation in eighty-one patients and sixty-four controls. *Nerv. ment. Dis. Monogr.*, 1938, No. 63.

Beck, S. J. *Rorschach's test.* Vol. 2. *A variety of personality pictures.* New York: Grune & Stratton, 1945.

Beck, S. J. *Ibid.* Vol. 3. *Advances in interpretation.* New York: Grune & Stratton, 1952.

Beck, S. J. The six schizophrenias. *Res. Monogr. Amer. Orthopsychiat. Ass.*, 1954, **10**, 6.

Beck, S. J. *The Rorschach experiment: ventures in blind diagnosis.* New York: Grune & Stratton, 1960.

Beck, S. J., Beck, A. G., Levitt, E. E., & Molish, H. B. *Rorschach's test.* (3rd ed.) Vol. 1. *Basic processes.* New York: Grune & Stratton, 1961.

Bell, A., Trosman, H., & Ross, D. The use of projective techniques in the investigation of emotional aspects of general medical disorders. I. The Rorschach method. *J. proj. Tech.*, 1952, **16**, 428–443.

Binswanger, W. Uber den Rorschachschen formdeuteversuch bei akuten schizophrenien. *Schweiz. Arch. Neurol. Psychiat.*, 1944, **53**, 101–121.

Birch, H. G., & Diller, L. Rorschach signs of "organicity": a physiological basis for perceptual disturbances. *J. proj. Tech.*, 1959, **23**, 184–197.

Bloom, B. L., & Arkoff, A. Role playing in acute and chronic schizophrenia. *J. consult. Psychol.*, 1961, **25**, 24–28.

Bohm, E. *Lehrbuch der Rorschach-Psychodiagnostik fuer Psychologen, Aerzte und Paedogogen.* Bern: Verlag Hans Huber, 1951.

Bohm, E. *Lehrbuch der Rorschach-Psychodiagnostik.* (2nd ed.) Bern: Verlag Hans Huber, 1957.

Bohm, E. *A textbook in Rorschach test diagnosis.* (Tr. by A. Beck & S. J. Beck.) New York: Grune & Stratton, 1958.

Booth, G. C. Personality and chronic arthritis. *J. nerv. ment. Dis.*, 1937, **85**, 637–662.

Booth, G. C. Objective techniques in personality testing. *Arch. Neurol. Psychiat.*, 1939, **42**, 514–530.

Booth, G. C. Organ function and form perception: Use of the Rorschach method with cases of chronic arthritis, Parkinsonism, and arterial hypertension. *Psychosom. Med.*, 1946, **8**, 367–385.

Bovet, T. Der Rorschach Versuch bei verschiedenen Formen von Epilepsie. *Schweiz. Arch. Neurol. Psychiat.*, 1936, **37**, 156–157.

Bower, P. A., Testin, R., & Roberts, A. Rorschach diagnosis by a systematic combining of scales, thought process, and determinant scales. *Genet. Psychol. Monogr.*, 1960, **62**, 105–183.

Brooks, M. O., & Phillips, L. The cognitive significance of Rorschach developmental scores. *J. Pers.*, 1958, **26**, 268–290.

Brown, D. G. Psychosomatic correlates in contact dermatitis: a pilot study. *J. Psychosom. Res.*, 1959, **4**, 132–139.

Brown, F. An exploratory study of dynamic factors in the content of the Rorschach protocol. *J. proj. Tech.*, 1953, **17**, 251–279.

Brown, M., Bresnahan, T. J., Chalke, F. C. R., Peters, B., Poser, E. G., & Tougas, R. V. Personality factors in duodenal ulcer: a Rorschach study. *Psychosom. Med.*, 1950, **12**, 1–5.

Bruce, J. M., Jr., & Thomas, C. B. A method of rating certain personality factors as determined by the Rorschach test for use in a study of the precursors of hypertension and coronary artery disease. *Psychiat. Quart.*, 1953, **27**, 207–238.

Brussel, J. A., Grassi, J. R., & Melniker, A. A. The Rorschach method and post-concussion syndrome. *Psychiat. Quart.*, 1942, **16**, 707–743.

Buhler, C., & Lefever, D. W. A Rorschach study on the psychological characteristics of alcoholics. *Quart. J. Stud. Alcohol,* 1947, **8**, 197–260.

Buhler, C., Lefever, D. W., Wheeler, W. M., Grayson H. M., Meyer, M. M., & Wesley, S. M. Symposium on a "basic Rorschach score." *J. proj. Tech.*, 1949, **13**, 6–24.

Button, A. D. A Rorschach study of 67 alcoholics. *Quart. J. Stud. Alcohol,* 1956, **17**, 35–52.

Calabresi, R. A., Piotrowski, Z. A., & Simkin, J. S. Further verification of the Rorschach alpha diagnostic formula with a Veterans Administration population. *VA Out-Patient Newsltr.*, 1958.

Canter, A. The effect of unshaded bright colors in the Rorschach upon the form-color response balance of psychotic patients. *J. proj. Tech.*, 1958, **22**, 390–393.

Chapman, A. J., & Reese, D. G. Homosexual signs in Rorschachs of early schizophrenics. *J. clin. Psychol.*, 1953, **9**, 30–32.

Cleveland, S. E. Body image changes associated with personality reorganization. *J. consult. Psychol.*, 1960, **23**, 256–261.

Cleveland, S. E., & Fisher, S. A comparison of psychological characteristics and physiological reactivity in ulcer and rheumatoid arthritis groups. I. Psychological measures. *Psychosom. Med.*, 1960, **22**, 283–289.

Costello, C. G. The Rorschach records of suicidal patients: an application of a comparative matching technique. *J. proj. Tech.*, 1958, **22**, 272–275.

Cutter, F. Rorschach sex responses and overt deviations. *J. clin. Psychol.*, 1957, **13**, 83–86.

Daston, P. G., & Sakheim, G. A. Prediction of successful suicide from the Rorschach test, using a sign approach. *J. proj. Tech.*, 1960, **25**, 355–361.

Davids, A., Joelson, M., & McArthur, C. Rorschach and TAT indices of homosexuality in overt homosexuals, neurotics and normal males. *J. abnorm. soc. Psychol.*, 1956, **53**, 161–172.

Davis, A. D. Some physiological correlates of Rorschach body image productions. *J. abnorm. soc. Psychol.*, 1960, **60**, 432–436.

Delay, J., Pichot, P., Lemperiere, T., & Perse, J. Le Test de Rorschach dans le psycho-syndrome organique. *Rev. Psychol. appl.*, 1956, **6**, 247–287.

Delay, J., Pichot, P., Lemperiere, T., & Perse, J. El test de Rorschach en los enfermos con lesiones organicas cerebrales. *Rev. Psicol. gen. apl.*, 1957, **12**, 393–535.

Delay, J., Pichot, P., Lemperiere, T., & Perse, J. *The Rorschach and the epileptic personality.* (Tr. by R. Benton & A. L. Benton.) New York: Logos Press, 1958.

Delay, J., Pichot, P., & Perse, J. Le test de Rorschach et le diagnostic de la schizophrénie. *Beih. Schweiz. Z. Psychol. Anwend. Suppl.*, 1958, No. 35, 66–83.

Denker, P. G. Results of treatment of psychoneuroses by the general practitioner: a follow-up study of 500 patients. *Arch. Neurol. Psychiat.*, 1947, **57**, 504–505.

deVos, G. A quantitative approach to affective symbolism in Rorschach responses. *J. proj. Tech.*, 1952, **16**, 133–150.

Diller, L., & Riklan, M. Rorschach correlates in Parkinson's disease: M, motor inhibition perceived cause of illness, self-attitudes. *Psychosom. Med.*, 1957, **19**, 120–126.

Dörken, H., & Kral, V. A. The psychological differentiation of organic brain lesions and their localization by means of the Rorschach test. *Amer. J. Psychiat.*, 1952, **108**, 764–769.

DuBrin, A. J. The Rorschach "eyes" hypothesis and paranoid schizophrenia. *J. clin. Psychol.*, 1962, **18**, 468–471.

Dworetzki, G. Le test de Rorschach et l'evolution de la perception. *Arch. Psychol., Genève*, 1939, **27**, 233–396.

Eckhardt, W. Piotrowski's signs: organic or functional? *J. clin. Psychol.*, 1961, **17**, 36–38.

Eigenbrode, C. R., & Shipman, W. G. The body image barrier concept. *J. abnorm. soc. Psychol.*, 1960, **60**, 450–452.

Elizur, A. Content analysis of the Rorschach with regard to anxiety and hostility. *Rorschach Res. Exch.*, 1949, **13**, 247–284.

Errera, P. A 16-year follow-up of schizophrenic patients seen in an out-patient clinic. *Arch. Neurol. Psychiat.*, 1957, **78**, 84–88.

Finney, B. C. Rorschach test correlates of assaultive behavior. *J. proj. Tech.*, 1955, **19**, 6–16.

Fisher, J., & Gonda, T. A. Neurological techniques and Rorschach test in detecting brain pathology. *Arch. Neurol. Psychiat.*, 1955, **74**, 117–124.

Fisher, J., Gonda, T. A., & Little, K. B. The Rorschach and central nervous system pathology: a cross-validation study. *Amer. J. Psychiat.*, 1955, **111**, 487–492.

Fisher, S. Rorschach patterns in conversion hysteria. *J. proj. Tech.*, 1951, **15**, 98–108. (a)

Fisher, S. The value of the Rorschach for detecting suicidal trends. *J. proj. Tech.*, 1951, **15**, 250–254. (b)

Fisher, S., & Cleveland, S. E. Relationship of body image to site of cancer. *Psychosom. Med.*, 1956, **18**, 304–309.

Fisher, S., & Cleveland, S. E. Body image boundaries and sexual behavior. *J. Psychol.*, 1958, **45**, 207–211.

Fisher, S., & Cleveland, S. E. A comparison of psychological characteristics and physiological reactivity in ulcer and rheumatoid arthritis groups. II. Differences in physiological reactivity. *J. Psychosom. Med.*, 1960, **22**, 290–293.

Friedman, A. Psychological diagnosis of intracranial pathology after accident. *Acta Psychother. Psychosom. Orthopaedag.*, 1956, **4**, 352–357.

Friedman, H. Perceptual regression in schizophrenia: an hypothesis suggested by the use of the Rorschach test. *J. proj. Tech.*, 1953, **17**, 171–185.

Gardner, G. E. Rorschach test replies and results in 100 normal adults of average IQ. *Amer. J. Orthopsychiat.*, 1936, **6**, 32–60.

Gibby, R. G., Stotsky, B. A., Miller, D. R., & Hiler, E. Prediction of duration of therapy from the Rorschach test. *J. consult. Psychol.*, 1953, **17**, 348–354.

Graham, V. T. Psychological studies of hypoglycemia therapy. *J. Psychol.*, 1940, **10**, 327–358.

Grassi, J. R. Contrasting schizophrenic patterns in the graphic Rorschach. *Psychiat. Quart.*, 1942, **16**, 646–659.

Greenblatt, M., & Solomon, H. D. *Frontal lobes and schizophrenia.* New York: Springer, 1953.

Guirdham, A. Simple psychological data in melancholia. *J. ment. Sci.* 1936, **82**, 649–653.

Gurvitz, M. S., & Miller, J. S. Some theoretical and practical aspects of the diagnosis of early and latent schizophrenia by means of psychological testing. In P. H. Hoch & J. Zubin (Eds.), *Relation of psychological tests to psychiatry.* New York: Grune & Stratton, 1952. Pp. 189–207.

Halpern, F. Rorschach interpretation of the personality structure of schizophrenics who benefit from insulin therapy. *Psychiat. Quart.*, 1940, **14**, 826–833.

Halpern, F. *A clinical approach to children's Rorschachs.* New York: Grune & Stratton, 1953.

Harrower-Erickson, M. R. The value and limitations of the so-called "neurotic signs." *Rorschach Res. Exch.*, 1942, **6**, 109–114.

Haug, J. O. Pneumoencephalographic studies in mental disease. *Acta Psychiat. Scand.*, 1962, **38**, 1–104.

Hemmendinger, L. Perceptual organization and development as reflected in the structure of the Rorschach test response. *J. proj. Tech.*, 1953, **17**, 162–170.

Hertz, Marguerite R. Suicidal configurations in Rorschach records. *Rorschach Res. Exch.*, 1948, **12**, 3–58.

Hertz, Marguerite R. Further studies of "suicidal" configurations in Rorschach records. *Rorschach Res. Exch.*, 1949, **13**, 44–73.

Hertz, Marguerite R., & Loehrke, L. M. Application of the Piotrowski and the Hughes signs of organic defect to a group of patients suffering from post-traumatic encephalopathy. *J. proj. Tech.*, 1954, **18**, 183–196.

Hertz, Marguerite R., & Loehrke, L. M. An evaluation of the Rorschach method for the study of brain injury. *J. proj. Tech.*, 1955, **19**, 416–430.

Hertz, Marguerite R., & Paolino, A. F. Rorschach indices of perceptual and conceptual disorganization. *J. proj. Tech.*, 1960, **24**, 370–388.

Holt, H. W., Jr., Sengstake, C. B., Sonoda, B. C., & Draper, W. A. Orality, image fusions and concept-formation. *J. proj. Tech.*, 1960, **24**, 194–198.

Holt, R. R. Gauging primary and secondary processes in Rorschach responses. *J. proj. Tech.*, 1956, **20**, 14–25.

Holt, R. R., & Havel, J. A method for assessing primary and secondary process in the Rorschach. In M. A. Rickers-Ovsiankina (Ed.), *Rorschach psychology*. New York: Wiley, 1960. Pp. 263–315.

Holt, W. L., & Holt, W. M. After 30 years, 35% of dementia praecox recovered. *Amer. J. Psychiat.*, 1962, **118**, 737–739.

Holtzman, W. H. Validation studies of the Rorschach test: shyness and gregariousness in the normal superior adult. *J. clin. Psychol.*, 1950, **6**, 343–347.

Hughes, R. M. Rorschach signs for the diagnosis of organic pathology. *J. proj. Tech.*, 1948, **12**, 165–167.

Hughes, R. M. A factor analysis of Rorschach diagnostic signs. *J. gen. Psychol.*, 1950, **43**, 85–103.

Hunt, T. The application of the Rorschach test and a word-association test to patients undergoing prefrontal lobotomy. *Psychol. Bull.*, 1940, **37**, 546.

Kaila, K. K. Ueber den zwangsneurotischen Symptomcomplex (the compulsion neurosis symptom complex). *Acta psychiat. Kbh. Suppl.*, 1949, **57**, 227.

Kaldegg, A., & O'Neill, D. Rorschach pattern in duodenal ulcer. *J. ment. Sci.*, 1950, **96**, 190–198.

Kataguchi, Y. Rorschach schizophrenic score (RSS). *J. proj. Tech.*, 1959, **23**, 214–223.

Kelley, D. M. The Rorschach method as a means for the determination of the impairment of abstract behavior. *Rorschach Res. Exch.*, 1941, **5**, 85–88.

Kendig, I. V. Rorschach indications for the diagnosis of schizophrenia. *J. proj. Tech.*, 1949, **13**, 142–149.

Kisker, G. W. The Rorschach analysis of psychotics subjected to neurosurgical interruption of the thalamo-cortical projections. *Psychiat. Quart.*, 1944, **18**, 43–52.

Klebanoff, S. G., Singer, J. L., & Wilensky, H. Psychological consequences of brain lesions and ablations. *Psychol. Bull.*, 1954, **51**, 1–62.

Klopfer, B., Ainsworth, M., Klopfer, W., & Holt, R. *Developments in the Rorschach technique.* Vol. I. *Technique and theory.* New York: Harcourt, Brace & World, 1954.

Klopfer, B., & Spiegelman, M. Differential diagnosis. In *ibid.* Vol. II. *Fields of application.* 1956. Pp. 281–317.

Klopfer, B., et al. *Ibid.*

Koff, S. A. The Rorschach test in the differential diagnosis of cerebral concussion and psychoneurosis. *Bull. U.S. Army med. Dep.*, 1946, **5**, 170–173.

Kohlmann, T. Psychologische Untersuchungen mit Rorschach-und Kraepelin-Versuch an vegetativen Neurosen. *Rev. Diagn. Psychol. Pers. Explor.*, 1954, **2**, 101–126.

Korkes, L., & Lewis, N. D. C. An analysis of the relationship between psychological patterns and outcome in pulmonary tuberculosis. *J. nerv. ment. Dis.*, 1955, **122**, 524–563.

Kotkov, B., & Murawski, B. A Rorschach study of the personality structure of obese women. *J. clin. Psychol.*, 1952, **8**, 391–396.

Kral, V. A., & Dörken, H. The influence of subcortical brain lesions on emotionality as reflected in the Rorschach color responses. *Amer. J. Psychiat.*, 1951, **107**, 839–843.

Krasner, L., & Kornreich, M. Psychosomatic illness and projective tests: the Rorschach test. *J. proj. Tech.*, 1954, **18**, 355–367.

Kuhn, R. Der Rorschachsche Formdeutversuch in der Psychiatrie. *Mschr. Psychiat. Neurol.*, 1940, **103**, 59–128.

Kuhn, R. Grundlegende statistische und psychologische Aspekte des Rorschachschen Formdeutversuches. *Rorschachiana*, 1953, **1**, 320–333.

Kuhn, R. Ueber kritische Rorschach-Forschung und einige ihrer Ergebnisse. In *Rorschachiana VIII.* Bern: Hans Huber, 1963. Pp. 105–115.

Laignel-Lavastine, Mme., Minkowska, F., Bouvet, M., & Neveu. Le test de Rorschach et la psychopathologie de la schizophrénie. *Ann. Med. Psychol.*, 1943, **1**, 481.

Lane, J. E. Social effectiveness and developmental level. *J. Pers.*, 1955, **23**, 274–284.

Levine, D. Rorschach genetic level and mental disorder. *J. proj. Tech.*, 1959, **23**, 436–439.

Levine, D. Rorschach genetic level and psychotic symptomatology. *J. clin. Psychol.*, 1960, **16**, 164–167.

Levine, D., & Cohen, J. Symptoms and ego strength measures as predictors of the outcome of hospitalization in functional psychoses. *J. consult. Psychol.*, 1962, **26**, 246–250.

Levy, D., & Beck, S. J. The Rorschach test in manic-depressive psychosis. *Res. Publ. Ass. Res. nerv. ment. Dis.* 1931, **11**, 167–181.

Levy, R. J. The Rorschach pattern in neurodermatitis. *Psychosom. Med.*, 1952, **14**, 41–49.

Lindner, R. M. Analysis of the Rorschach test by content. *J. clin. Psychopath.*, 1947, **8**, 707–719.

Lipton, M. B., Tamarin, S., & Lotesta, P. Test evidence of personality change and prognosis by means of the Rorschach and Wechsler-Bellevue tests on 17 insulin-treated paranoid schizophrenics. *Psychiat. Quart.*, 1951, **25**, 434–444.

Loftus, T. A. The Rorschach test in traumatic neuroses. In: A. Kardiner & H. Spiegel, *War stress and neurotic illness.* New York: Hoeber-Harper, 1947. Pp. 401–404.

Lothrop, W. W. Psychological test covariates of conceptual deficit in schizophrenia. *J. consult. Psychol.*, 1960, **24**, 496–499.

Machover, S. Rorschach study on the nature and origin of common factors in the personalities of Parkinsonians. *J. psychosom. Med.*, 1957, **19**, 332–338.

McConnell, O. L., & Daston, P. J. Body image changes in pregnancy. *J. proj. Tech.*, 1961, **25**, 451–456.

McFie, J., Piercy, M. F., & Zangwill, O. L. The Rorschach test in obsessional neurosis with special reference to the effects of prefrontal leucotomy. *Brit. J. med. Psychol.*, 1951, **24**, 162–179.

McReynolds, P., & Weide, M. Psychological measures as used to predict psychiatric improvement and to assess behavioral changes following prefrontal lobotomy. *J. ment. Sci.*, 1960, **106**, 256–273.

Miale, F. R., & Harrower, Molly R. Personality structures in the psychoneuroses. *Rorschach Res. Exch.*, 1940, **4**, 71–74.

Miles, H. W., Waldfogel, S., Barrabee, E. L., & Cobb, S. Psychosomatic study of 46 young men with coronary artery disease. *Psychosom. Med.*, 1954, **16**, 455–477.

Minkowska, F. L'epilepsie essentielle: sa psychopathologie et le test de Rorschach. *Ann. med. psychol.*, 1946, **104**, 321–355.

Molish, H. B. *Schizophrenic reaction types in a Naval hospital population as evaluated by the Rorschach test.* Washington, D.C.: Government Printing Office, 1956.

Molish, H. B., & Beck, S. J. Psychoanalytic concepts and principles discernible in projective personality tests. III. Mechanisms of defense in schizophrenic reaction types as evaluated by the Rorschach test. *Amer. J. Orthopsychiat.*, 1958, **28**, 47–60.

Molish, H. B., Hanlon, M. A., & Kurland, A. A. A prognostic indicator of treatment failure in schizophrenia. *Arch. Neurol. Psychiat.*, 1957, **78**, 177–193.

Muller, M. Der Rorschachsche Formdeutversuch, seine Schwierigkeiten und Ergebnisse. *Z. ges. Neurol. Psychiat.*, 1929, **118**, 598–620.

Munroe, R. Inspection technique: a modification of the Rorschach method of personality diagnosis for large scale application. *Rorschach Res. Exch.* 1941, **5**, 166–191.

Murstein, B. I. Factor analysis of the Rorschach. *J. consult. Psychol.*, 1960, **24**, 262–275.

Nadel, A. B. A qualitative analysis of behavior following cerebral lesions. *Arch. Psychol., N.Y.*, 1938, No. 224, 1–60.

Neiger S., Slemon, A. G., & Quirk, D. A. The performance of "chronic schizophrenic" patients on Piotrowski's Rorschach sign list for organic CNS pathology. *J. proj. Tech.*, 1962, **26**, 419–428.

Neuhaus, V. A personality study of asthmatic and cardiac children. *Psychosom. Med.*, 1958, **20**, 181–186.

Oberholzer, E. Zur Differentialdiagnose psychischer Folgezustände nach Schadelträumen mittels des Rorschachschen Formdeutversuchs. *Z. ges. Neurol. Psychiat.*, 1931, **136**, 596–629.

Ogdon, D. P., & Allee, R. Rorschach relationships with intelligence among familial mental defectives. *Amer. J. ment. Def.*, 1959, **63**, 889–896.

Orchinik, C., Koch, R., Wycis, H. T., Freed, H., & Spiegel, E. A. The effect of thalamic lesions upon the emotional reactivity: Rorschach and behavior studies. *Ass. Res. nerv. ment. Dis.*, 1950, **29**, 172–207.

Orme, J. E. Rorschach performances in normal old age, elderly depression and senile dementia. *Rev. diagn. Psychol.*, 1958, **6**, 132–142.

Orme, J. E. The Rorschach sex response in a psychiatric population: 1,010 Rorschach records surveyed. *J. clin. Psychol.*, 1962, **18**, 303.

Osborne, T. R., & Sanders, W. B. Rorschach characteristics of duodenal ulcer patients. *J. clin. Psychol.*, 1950, **6**, 258–262.

Pena, C. D. A genetic evaluation of perceptual structurization in cerebral pathology: an investigation by means of the Rorschach test. *J. proj. Tech.*, 1953, **17**, 186–199.

Petrie, A. *Personality and the frontal lobes.* New York: Blakiston, 1952. P. 188.

Phillips, L., & Smith, J. G. *Rorschach interpretation: advanced technique.* New York: Grune & Stratton, 1953.

Piotrowski, Z. A. The Rorschach inkblot method in organic disturbances of the central nervous system. *J. nerv. ment. Dis.*, 1937, **86**, 525–537. (a)

Piotrowski, Z. A. Rorschach studies of cases with lesions of the frontal lobes. *Brit. J. med. Psychol.*, 1937, **17**, 105–118. (b)

Piotrowski, Z. A. The prognostic possibilities of the Rorschach method in insulin treatment. *Psychiat. Quart.*, 1938, **12**, 679–689.

Piotrowski, Z. A. Rorschach manifestations of improvement in insulin treated schizophrenics. *Psychosom. Med.*, 1939, **1**, 508–526.

Piotrowski, Z. A. Positive and negative Rorschach organic reactions. *Rorschach Res. Exch.*, 1940, **4**, 147–151.

Piotrowski, Z. A. The Rorschach method as a prognostic aid in the insulin shock treatment of schizophrenics. *Psychiat. Quart.*, 1941, **15**, 807–822.

Piotrowski, Z. A. Tentative Rorschach formulae for educational and vocational guidance in adolescence. *Rorschach Res. Exch.*, 1943, **7**, 16–27.

Piotrowski, Z. A. Experimental psychological diagnosis of mild forms of schizophrenia. *Rorschach Res. Exch.*, 1945, **9**, 189–200.

Piotrowski, Z. A. The personality of the epileptic: the concept of the epileptic personality. In P. H. Hoch & R. P. Knight (Eds.), *Epilepsy.* New York: Grune & Stratton, 1947. Pp. 89–108.

Piotrowski, Z. A. A Rorschach compendium—revised and enlarged. *Psychiat. Quart.*, 1950, **24**, 543–596.

Piotrowski, Z. A. Comments on the Rorschach test and its relation to the psychotherapeutic use of graphic art. In M. Naumburg (Ed.), *Psychoneurotic art: its function in psychotherapy.* New York: Grune & Stratton, 1953. Pp. 108–118.

Piotrowski, Z. A. A defense attitude associated with improvement in schizophrenia and measurable with a modified Rorschach test. *J. nerv. ment. Dis.*, 1955, **122**, 36–41.

Piotrowski, Z. A. *Perceptanalysis: a fundamentally reworked, expanded and systematized Rorschach method.* New York: Macmillan, 1957.

Piotrowski, Z. A., & Berg, D. A. Verification of the Rorschach alpha diagnostic formula for underactive schizophrenics. *Amer. J. Psychiat.*, 1955, **112**, 443–450.

Piotrowski, Z. A., & Bricklin, B. A long-term prognostic criterion for schizophrenics based on Rorschach data. *Psychiat. Quart. Suppl.*, 1958, **32**, 315–329.

Piotrowski, Z. A., & Bricklin, B. A second validation of a long-term Rorschach prognostic index for schizophrenic patients. *J. consult. Psychol.*, 1961, **25**, 123–218.

Piotrowski, Z. A., & Bricklin, B. Psychoneurosis with conversion hysteria: a Rorschach study, 1964 (in press).

Piotrowski, Z. A., & Lewis, N. D. C. A case of stationary schizophrenia beginning in early childhood with remarks on certain aspects of children's Rorschach records. *Quart. J. child Behav.*, 1950, **2**, 115–139. (a)

Piotrowski, Z. A., & Lewis, N. D. C. An experimental Rorschach diagnostic aid for some forms of schizophrenia. *Amer. J. Psychiat.*, 1950, **107**, 360–366. (b)

Piotrowski, Z. A., & Lewis, N. D. C. An experimental criterion for the prognostication of the status of schizophrenics after a three-year-interval based on Rorschach data. In P. H. Hoch & J. Zubin

(Eds.), *Relation of psychological tests to psychiatry.* New York: Grune & Stratton, 1952. Pp. 51–72.

Piotrowski, Z. A., Rock, M., & Grela, J. *The perceptanalytic executive scale: a tool for the selection of top managers.* New York: Grune & Stratton, 1963.

Piotrowski, Z. A., & Schreiber, M. Rorschach perceptanalytic measurement of personality changes during and after intensive psychoanalytically oriented psychotherapy. In G. Bychowski & J. L. Despert (Eds.), *Specialized techniques in psychotherapy.* New York: Basic Books, 1952. Pp. 337–361.

Plesch, E. A Rorschach study of rosacea and morbid blushing. *Brit. J. med. Psychol.*, 1951, **24**, 202–205.

Pope, B., & Jensen, A. R. The Rorschach as an index of pathological thinking. *J. proj. Tech.*, 1957, **21**, 54–62.

Poser, E. G. Personality factors in patients with duodenal ulcer: a Rorschach study. *J. proj. Tech.*, 1951, **15**, 131–143.

Quirk, D. A., Quarrington, M., Neiger, S., & Slemon, A. G. The performance of acute psychotic patients on the index of pathological thinking and on selected signs of idiosyncrasy on the Rorschach. *J. proj. Tech.*, 1962, **26**, 431–441.

Raifman, I. Rorschach findings in a group of peptic ulcer patients and two control groups. *J. proj. Tech.*, 1957, **21**, 307–312.

Rakoff, A. E., Piotrowski, Z. A., & Loftus, T. A. Psychogenic factors in anovulatory women. *Fertil. & Steril.*, 1962, **13**, 1–28.

Rapaport, D., Gill, M., & Schafer, R. *Diagnostic psychological testing: the theory, statistical evaluation, and diagnostic application of a battery of tests.* Vol. II. Chicago: The Year Book Medical Publishers, 1946. Pp. xi, 516.

Reitan, R. M. Validity of Rorschach test as measure of psychological effect of brain damage. *Arch. Neurol. Psychiat.*, 1955, **73**, 445–451.

Rennie, T. A. C. Follow-up study of 500 patients with schizophrenia admitted to hospital from 1913 to 1923. *Arch. Neurol. Psychiat.*, 1939, **42**, 877.

Rickers-Ovsiankina, M. The Rorschach test as applied to normal and schizophrenic subjects. *Brit. J. Med. Psychol.*, 1938, **17**, 227–257.

Rickers-Ovsiankina, M. Longitudinal approach to schizophrenia through the Rorschach method. *J. clin. exp. Psychopath.*, 1954, **15**, 107–118.

Rickers-Ovsiankina, M. (Ed.) *Rorschach psychology.* New York: Wiley, 1960. Pp. xvi, 483.

Rioch, M. J., & Lubin, A. Prognosis of social adjustment for mental hospital patients under psychotherapy. *J. consult. Psychol.*, 1959, **23**, 313–318.

Rockwell, F. V., Welch, L., Kubis, J., & Fisichelli, V. Changes in palmar skin resistance during the Rorschach test. I. Color shock and psychoneurotic reactions. *Mschr. Rev. Psychiat. Neurol.*, 1947, **113**, 129–153.

Roe, A. Analysis of group Rorschachs of biologists. *J. proj. Tech.*, 1949, **13**, 25–43.

Rorschach, H. *Psychodiagnostics: a diagnostic test based on perception.* (Tr. by P. Lemkau & B. Kronenberg.) Bern: Verlag Hans Huber, 1921. New York: Grune & Stratton, 1942.

Rorschach, H. Three Rorschach interpretations. *J. proj. Tech.*, 1954, **18**, 482–495.

Rorschach, H. Blind analysis. (See Schneider, 1955.)

Rosenblatt, B., & Solomon, P. Structural and genetic aspects of the Rorschach responses in mental deficiency. *J. proj. Tech.*, 1954, **18**, 496–506.

Ross, W. D. Anatomical perseveration in Rorschach records. *Rorschach Res. Exch.*, 1940, **4**, 138–145.

Ross, W. D. The contribution of the Rorschach method to clinical diagnosis. *J. ment. Sci.*, 1941, **87**, 331–348.

Ross, W. D. The Rorschach performance with neurocirculatory asthenia. *Psychosom. Med.*, 1945, **7**, 80–84.

Ross, W. D., & McNaughton, D. L. Objective personality studies in migraine by means of the Rorschach method. *Psychosom. Med.*, 1945, **7**, 73–79.

Ross, W. D., & Ross, S. Some Rorschach ratings of clinical value. *Rorschach Res. Exch.*, 1944, **8**, 1–9.

Ruesch, J., Christiansen, C., Harris, R. *Duodenal ulcer: a socio-psychological study of Naval enlisted personnel and civilians.* Berkeley, Calif.: Univer. of California Press, 1948.

Rychlak, J. F., & Gunouard, D. E. Symbolic interpretation of Rorschach content. *J. consult. Psychol.*, 1961, **25**, 37.

Sakheim, G. A. Suicidal responses on the Rorschach test: a validation study. *J. nerv. ment. Dis.*, 1955, **122**, 332–344.

Sanders, J., Schenk, V. W. D., & Van Veen, P. *A family with Pick's disease.* Amsterdam: N. V. Noord-Hollandsche Uitgevers-Maatschappij 1939. Pp. i, 124.

Schafer, R. *Psychoanalytic interpretation in Rorschach testing: theory and application.* New York: Grune & Stratton, 1954.

Schafer, R. Bodies in schizophrenic Rorschach responses. *J. proj. Tech.*, 1960, **24**, 267–281.

Schatia, V. The incidental neurosis in cases of bronchial asthma as determined by the Rorschach test with psychiatric examination. *Psychosom. Med.*, 1941, **3**, 156–169.

Schenk, V. W. D. Der Formdeutversuch /Rorschach/ bei organischen Hirnerkrankungen, *Psychiat. Neurol. Bladen*, 1938, **42**, 350–372.

Schneider, E. (Ed.) Ausarbeitung eines Versuchsprotokolls durch Hermann Rorschach. *Z. Diagn. Psychol. Pers.*, 1955, **3**, 62–72.

Shatin, L. Psychoneurosis and psychosomatic reaction: a Rorschach contrast. *J. consult. Psychol.*, 1952, **16**, 220.

Shaw, B. Sex populars in the Rorschach test. *J. abnorm. soc. Psychol.*, 1948, **43**, 466–470.

Sheehan, J. G., Frederick, C. J., Rosevear, W. H., & Spiegelman, M. A validity study of the Rorschach prognostic rating scale. *J. proj. Tech.*, 1954, **18**, 233–239.

Shereshevski-Shere, E., & Lasser, L. M. An evaluation of water responses in the Rorschach of alcoholics. *J. proj. Tech.*, 1952, **16**, 489–495.

Siegel, E. I. Genetic parallels of perceptual structuralization in paranoid schizophrenia: an analysis by means of the Rorschach technique. *J. proj. Tech.*, 1953, **17**, 151–161.

Siipola, E. M. The influence of color on reaction to inkblots, *J. Pers.*, 1950, **18**, 358–382.

Siipola, E., & Taylor, V. Reactions to inkblots under free and pressure conditions. *J. Pers.*, 1952, **21**, 22–47.

Silverman, L. H., Lapkin, B., & Rosenbaum, I. S. Manifestations of primary process thinking in schizophrenia. *J. proj. Tech.*, 1962, **26**, 117–127.

Skalweit, W. Z. Konstitution und Prozess in der Schizophrenie. Leipzig: Georg Thieme, 1934. P. 88.

Spreen, O. Stirnhirnverletzte im Rorschach-Versuch (Zur Frage eines "typischen Syndroms"). *Rev. Diagn. Psychol. Pers. Explor.*, 1955, **3**, 3–23.

Stein, M. I. Personality factors involved in the temporal development of Rorschach responses. *J. proj. Tech.*, 1949, **13**, 355–414.

Stephenson, W. *The study of behavior: Q-technique and its methodology.* Chicago: Univer. of Chicago Press, 1953.

Tarlan, M., & Smalheiser, I. Personality patterns in patients with malignant tumors of the breast and cervix. *Psychosom. Med.*, 1951, **13**, 117–121.

Thiesen, J. W. A pattern analysis of structural characteristics of the Rorschach test in schizophrenia. *J. consult. Psychol.*, 1952, **16**, 365–370.

Trier, T. R. Vocabulary as a basis for estimating intelligence from the Rorschach. *J. consult. Psychol.*, 1958, **22**, 289–291.

Tschudin, A. Chronische Schizophrenien im Rorschach'schen Versuch. *Schweiz. Arch. Neurol. Psychiat.*, 1944, **53**, 79–100.

Vinson, D. B. Responses to the Rorschach test that identify schizophrenic thinking, feeling, and behavior. *J. clin. exp. Psychopath.*, 1960, **21**, 34–40.

Vres, S. J., & Groen, J. Investigation into the personality structure of a group of juvenile asthmatic patients by the use of the Behn-Rorschach test. *Med. Tijdscher Psychol.*, 1951, **6**, 23–41.

Wagner, E. E. The interaction of aggressive movement responses and anatomy responses on the Rorschach in producing anxiety. *J. proj. Tech.*, 1961, **25**, 212–215.

Watkins, J. G., & Deabler, H. L. Responses of chronic schizophrenic patients to tachistoscopic presentation of Rorschach figures. *J. proj. Tech.*, 1957, **21**, 404–409.

Watkins, J. G., & Stauffacher, J. C. An index of pathological thinking in the Rorschach. *J. proj. Tech.*, 1952, **16**, 276–286.

Wedemeyer, B. Rorschach statistics on a group of 136 normal men. *J. Psychol.*, 1954, **37**, 51–58.

Weiner, I. B. Cross-validation of a Rorschach checklist associated with suicidal tendencies. *J. consult. Psychol.*, 1961, **25**, 312–315. (a)

Weiner, I. B. Three Rorschach scores indicative of schizophrenia. *J. consult. Psychol.*, 1961, **25**, 436–439. (b)

Werner, H. *Comparative psychology of mental development.* (Rev. ed.) Chicago: Follett, 1948.

Werner, H. The concept of development from a comparative and organismic point of view. In D. B. Harris (Ed.), *The concept of development: an issue in the study of human behavior.* Minneapolis, Minn.: Univer. of Minnesota Press, 1957.

Wheeler, J. I., & Caldwell, B. M. Psychological evaluation of women with cancer of the breast and of the cervix. *Psychosom. Med.*, 1955, **17**, 256–268.

Wheeler, W. M. An analysis of Rorschach indices of male homosexuality. *Rorschach Res. Exch.*, 1949, **13**, 97–126.

Wilensky, H. Rorschach developmental level and social participation of chronic schizophrenics. *J. proj. Tech.*, 1959, **23**, 87–92.

Wittenborn, J. R., & Mettler, F. A. A lack of perceptual control score for the Rorschach test. *J. clin. Psychol.*, 1951, **7**, 331–334.

Wysocki, B. A. Assessment of intelligence level by the Rorschach test as compared with objective tests. *J. educ. Psychol.*, 1957, **48**, 113–117.

Yacorzynski, G. K., & Davis, L. An experimental study of the frontal lobes in man. *Psychosom. Med.*, 1945, **7**, 97–107.

Young, R. J. The Rorschach diagnosis and interpretation of involutional melancholia. *Amer. J. Psychiat.*, 1950, **106**, 748–749.

Zeichner, A. M. Psychosexual identification in paranoid schizophrenics. *J. proj. Tech.*, 1955, **19**, 67–77.

Zeichner, A. M. Conception of masculine a[illegible] feminine roles in paranoid schizophrenia. *J. proj. Tech.*, 1956, **20**, 348–354.

Zelin, M., & Sechrest, L. The validity of the "Mother" and "Father" cards of the Rorschach. *J. proj. Tech.*, 1963, **27**, 114–121.

Zimmerman, I. L., & Oetzel, J. L. A comparison of infectious and traumatic brain damage utilizing Rorschach "signs" of adjustment and mental deterioration. *Amer. Psychologist*, 1955, **10**, 338.

Zucker, L. J. *Ego structure in paranoid schizophrenia.* Springfield, Ill. Charles C Thomas, 1958.

Thematic Apperceptive Methods

ROSS HARRISON

The Thematic Apperception Test, more commonly referred to as the TAT, was introduced in 1935 in the context of psychoanalytic therapy as a promising method for investigating unrecognized fantasies (C. Morgan & Murray, 1935). Later H. A. Murray (1943), in the manual to the current edition, somewhat enlarged the scope and spoke of the TAT as "a method for revealing to the trained interpreter some of the dominant drives, emotions, sentiments, complexes and conflicts of a personality." In practice the TAT has on occasion served even broader purposes by describing personality traits, determining intellectual level, diagnosing mental pathology, revealing social attitudes, helping establish therapeutic rapport, analyzing small group interaction, exploring modal personalities in other cultures, measuring the effects of psychiatric treatment, aiding in vocational counseling, predicting school achievement, and evaluating executives. Recently Holt (1961) has given cogent reasons why TAT stories should not be regarded as fantasies. But while some such term as "imaginative product" may be more pleasing to the logical purist, "fantasy" probably slips off the tongue too conveniently to be completely abandoned.

The test has had antecedents in the history of psychology. Having children react to pictures as a way of studying individual differences goes back at least as far as Binet (Binet & Henri, 1896). Some of the older manuals in experimental psychology included exercises with ambiguous pictures to illustrate principles of apperception and sometimes stressed the significance of personal determinants (Sen, 1953). Early in the century, Brittain (1907) and Libby (1908) employed the storytelling technique for studying imagination in adolescents. These pioneer studies, which all dealt with such general facets of mental life as intelligence, apperception, and imagination, were not concerned with the picture-story method as an index to the individual personality.

A more direct precursor was the set of pictures L. A. Schwartz (1932) used as an adjunct in the psychiatric interviewing of delinquents. Van Lennep devised his Four Picture Test in 1930 but did not publish for eighteen years (1948). The principal credit for the innovation still belongs to H. A. Murray, who in the 1930s was the moving spirit in developing new projective techniques at the Harvard Psychological Clinic for the systematic appraisal of college students. Of these techniques, most of which have fallen into disuse, initially the most promising and eventually the most far-reaching in influence was the Thematic Apperception Test.

The test did not immediately gain widespread popularity. There were only a handful of publications during the next several years. Some favorable results on the clinical validity and utility of the TAT obtained at Worcester State Hospital just before World War II (Harrison, 1940a; Harrison, 1940b; Rotter, 1940) may have given impetus to the test, for during the next decade it was increasingly adopted in clinical practice, and after 1940 the number of publications began to climb rapidly, rising in geometrical proportion during the latter half of the decade and reaching a peak and then leveling off during the 1950s. The test was accepted first by clinical psychologists and gradually became a research tool in developmental psychology, social psychology, personality, and culture-personality studies in anthropology. Paralleling these developments, the TAT in its practical applications has spread out into the neighboring field of counseling and into industrial psychology.

In clinics and institutions it is one of the most frequently used of all tests (Bloom, 1952; Burton, 1949; Louttit & Browne, 1947; Sundberg, 1961). While it has a very voluminous literature and is usually considered second only to the Rorschach among projective tests, a recent survey of clinical facilities found that the Machover Draw-a-Picture Test equals it in popularity (Sundberg, 1961). Although American in origin, the TAT is now used internationally. It has made appearances, usually in local adaptations, in most of the non-Communist world, especially in European countries, such as England, France, Germany, and Italy, and also in India and Japan and to a lesser degree in the Spanish-speaking nations.

Several times in the theory-cathected climate of American psychology it has been pointed out that projective techniques in general, and the TAT in particular, lack a solid formal theoretical foundation. The TAT shares, of course, the basic projective hypothesis of other tests of its type that Frank (1939) brilliantly outlined a quarter of a century ago. He compared projective techniques to the physicist's spectroscopic and diffraction methods, which by indirect means elicit the pattern or internal organization of substances without the distortion of the older analytical procedures. Similarly personality reveals some of its organization and ways of organizing experience when the person is given more or less ambiguous stimuli to interpret and in the process projects his own idiosyncratic feelings, meanings, and ideas. As an addendum it should be noted that in the case of the TAT not everything is projection in the narrow sense of the word; some of the inferences from stories are derived from direct expression or reflection of personality.

Not much has been added subsequently to Frank's formulations. From the very beginning the principal inspiration and theoretical framework have been psychoanalytic, although it is possible for eclectics and others not committed to psychoanalysis to work effectively with the test. The most that has been done by way of a rationale has been the rudimentary elaboration of Freudian concepts and application to the TAT by writers such as Rapaport (1946) and Bellak (1954a; 1954b). The latter, who initially felt that ego psychology was an appropriate foundation for the TAT, now holds that the entire Freudian apparatus of id, ego, and superego may be involved in thematic production (1956). Holt (1951a), also working from a psychoanalytic orientation, has elaborated on the principal determinants of TAT narratives.

The apperception method is amenable to other theoretical approaches. Kadis, Greene, and Freedman (1953) interpret according to Adlerian principles. Spiegelman (1955) shows that Jungian theory can be projected into protocols as readily as Freudian. There are even attempts to conceptualize the test in behavioristic terms (Auld, 1954; Goss & Brownell, 1957). Translating projective concepts into "behaviorese" may be an entertaining tour de force but does not contribute to a clarification of the test or to an enlargement of its possibilities, nor is it conceivable that theories which ignore both experience and unconscious determinants of behavior would have generated the TAT or any other projective technique.

The experiences of psychologists with the TAT are so diversified and the literature so extensive and variegated that it is possible to find precisely opposite opinions being expressed on a broad range of topics. The TAT has been said to be valid and not valid, reliable and not reliable, predictive of overt behavior and not predictive of overt behavior, useful in research and not useful in research, easily faked and not easily faked, good for diagnosis and not good for diagnosis, economical and not economical, capable of plumbing the unconscious depths and shallower than other projectives. There is also radical disagreement between the subjective, or qualitative, approach on the one hand and the objective, or quantitative, approach on the other. Furthermore, it is possible for some writers to prove to their own satisfaction either side of an antinomic proposition by presenting what amounts to a lawyer's brief through either insufficient exposure to the relevant literature or careful selection of evidence.

Some of the reasons for the contradictions, aside from bias, are different kinds and degrees of experience with the test, different scoring and analytical methods, and widely divergent approaches and research methods. It is fallacious to approach the TAT indiscriminately, as many test academicians do, as if it were a standard test, comparable to machine-made ability and personality tests—to consider it a homogeneous psychometric instrument with set conditions of administration, scoring, tabular norms, and reliabilities—and if such requirements are not met, then to decide that it does not measure up to scientific standards.

The TAT is in no sense standardized—in the number or kind of pictures, in the mode of administration or the instructions, in the method of analysis, or in the uses to which it is put. Although it is convenient to speak of it as a test, for lack of a better term, properly speaking TAT should stand not for Thematic Apperception Test but for Thematic Apperception Technique. It is not really a test in any usual sense of the word but, like the clinical interview, is more a personality probing or an evaluative method.

The TAT is protean. It has so many facets and is so polyvariant and multidimensional, so broad and flexible, that it contains almost inexhaustible potentialities for analysis, extending from the most molecular to the most molar. Thus it can function as either a wide-band or a narrow-band instrument. The yield is sufficiently rich that it can be used to assess almost any personality variable in which the experimenter may be interested, although sometimes it taxes the skill and inventiveness of the investigator, for it is often difficult to code stories without distorting the phenomena being studied. Lack of standardization has in some ways been fortunate because it has prevented premature formalization of the technique and the consequent loss of flexibility and versatility. The price of this diversity is lack of uniformity and comparability in research. In clinical practice the lack of a generally accepted cut-and-dried scoring procedure, comparable to that of the Rorschach, has discouraged many psychologists. Some clinicians appear to need the support of an authoritatively sanctioned, clearly defined and patterned scoring and interpretive procedure before they can proceed with confidence.

The enormous literature on the TAT and related methods now consists of well over eleven hundred bibliographic items. It is also a favorite of graduate students, for there are over one hundred doctoral dissertations which either are focused on the TAT or employ it as an instrument in research. Unfortunately, the degree of clarification is not in proportion to the volume of publication. Many studies treat minor problems with elaborate statistical design superimposed on inadequate basic procedures that leave them open to Maslow's strictures on the means-centering and triviality of much contemporary behavioral research (1946). Even when the problems are significant, the means are often arbitrary, truncated, and oblique, sacrificing quality and sound procedure to the Procrustean bed of quantification.

The only complete reviews go back fifteen years or more (Bell, 1948; Mayman, 1946; Symonds, 1949; Tomkins, 1947), since which time the literature has burgeoned. More recent publications containing review material either have been selective and incomplete (Bellak, 1950; Bellak & Ort, 1952; Eron, 1959; Jensen, 1959; Watson, 1951; Wyatt & Veroff, 1956) or have dealt with special topics (Kagan, 1960; Murstein, 1959; Murstein, 1961). The conclusions in this chapter are based on a comprehensive review of the literature through 1962, but space restrictions will preclude complete documentation as well as the kind of detailed critical evaluation that many of the studies invite.

The topics to be covered are, in sequence, the effect of stimulus conditions; TAT correlates, such as age and sex; methods of scoring and interpretation; practical applications; the role of the TAT in research; reliability; validity; and other picture-story tests.

ADMINISTRATION AND STIMULUS CONDITIONS

Story protocols are affected by a number of conditions which collectively may be called the "stimulus complex." Studies on the possible influence of methods of administration, variations in instructions, examiner effects, and specific properties of the pictures will be considered.

Administration

Traditionally, stories have been transcribed by the examiner from the dictation of the subject. This arrangement, while time-consuming and burdensome for the examiner, has several advantages over the written method. It allows the examiner to draw out nonproductive subjects, and it makes possible valuable behavioral observations—pauses, hesitancies, voice fluctuations, smiling, laughing, exclamations and ejaculations, and other indications of affective states in relation to particular topics and aspects of the stories. All this is lost in the written method, whether the writing is done individually or in a group with the pictures projected on a screen. The question is whether for most research projects or for the more indolent clinicians enough additional information is gained in the oral method to justify the inconvenience. The oral method is usually regarded as the method of choice for individual work; for research, the advantages of group administration outweigh the disadvantages.

Most of the research shows little or no difference between the oral and written methods for the variables studied (Bernstein, 1956; R. M. Clark, 1944; Eron & Ritter, 1951; Lindzey & Heinemann, 1955; Lindzey & Silverman, 1959; Winchester, 1948). College students gave sadder stories for group administration (B. R. Sarason & Sarason, 1958), while Terry (1952) found greater personal involvement for the oral method. There is no appreciable difference for screen projection or individual handling of cards in group administration (Lindzey & Silverman, 1959) or for single or double sessions (Garfield, Blek, & Melker, 1952).

The presence of a known recording device does not affect the clinical significance of the stories (Sauer & Marcuse, 1957; West, 1953). It lengthens stories and increases reaction time and speech rate for anxious subjects but has less of an effect on nonanxious subjects. Order of presentation of the cards makes little or no measurable difference (Bellak, 1944; Kannenberg, 1948; Lowe, 1952; N. M. Lubin, 1955; Mason, 1952), although there is a position effect for happiness-unhappiness ratings of the pictures (Dollin & Sakoda, 1962).

Set

Instructions which encourage or discourage imagination (B. Lubin, 1960), which involve praise or criticism of the cards (Lowe, 1952), or which present the test as a measure of either intelligence or personality (Sumerwell, Campbell, & Sarason, 1958) or intelligence and leadership (McClelland, Atkinson, Clark, & Lowell, 1953) have been shown to have an effect on responses. With college students, instructions to write in the first person increased initial reaction time, number of pauses, and story length, but only reaction time was increased significantly for psychiatric patients (Solkoff, 1960).

Besides special instructions, the experimental manipulation of either the pretest situation or the conditions concurrent with the test is also reflected in thematic content. An experiment by Bellak (1944) may serve as an illustration. His sharp criticism of the quality of subjects' stories increased the hostile content of subsequent stories. A later section will document the influence on stories of other kinds of experimental manipulation as well as the effects of organismic conditions such as hunger, sex, and sleep deprivation. Not every attempt to show the effects of recent experience has been successful, however. Having psychiatric patients submit to a gynecological examination, which was intended as an embarrassing and stressful experience, did not influence story ratings for hostility, optimism, attitudes toward men, or degree of involvement (Fisher, 1958), but there may be some question as to whether the examination was embarrassing or stressful to most of the women. Even granting that the procedure may have been effective, some of the rated variables do not seem germane. Coleman (1947) likewise found that an innocuous movie short did not affect the stories of institutionalized children. The same objections apply to this study, since there was no evidence of psychological engagement by the children.

Examiner Effects

The presence or absence of an examiner may have some effect, according to Bernstein (1956). Analysis of variance showed that when the examiner was absent there was more involvement and the stories were sadder. When comparisons are made on the effects of different examiners, the studies are in conflict. Turner and Coleman (1962), who have done the most systematic work, concluded that there were only slight effects produced by examiners with different personal characteristics, different amounts of test experience, and different attitudes toward the test. Similar results were obtained by Sumerwell et al. (1958), while Garfield et al. (1952) reported that the sex of the examiner exerted no influence on the plot level, activity of the hero, mood, or outcome. Veroff (1961), in a nationwide survey, found slight examiner effects on certain variables and referred to an unpublished study by Birney, who showed that having instructor and student administrators produced differences in need-achievement scores of college students.

Under certain conditions, examiner effects can be demonstrated unequivocally. Kenny and Bijou (1953) concluded that interpersonal relations between examiner and subject were important, since one of their three examiners consistently obtained longer and richer stories despite strict control over the method of administration. More systematically, Milam (1954) was able to show an isomorphic relation between friendly, unfriendly, and neutral conditions of administration and protocols.

Physical Conditions

There are minimal exposure times below which productivity suffers when measured by the "transcendence index" (mean number of responses that go beyond picture description) developed by Weisskopf (1950b). TI, which has become a widely used measure of TAT productivity, correlates above .60 with judgments of clinical psychologists for the degree of personal projection (Kenny, 1954) and .85 with the number of emotional words (Gurel & Ullmann, 1958). Higher TIs were reported for five-second exposures than for exposures of 0.2 second (Weisskopf, 1950a) and for two-minute exposures than for five-second exposures (Kenny, 1954). For a number of other TAT variables there were little differences between brief and continuous exposures during group administration (Lindzey & Silverman, 1959).

J. E. Bradley and Lysaker (1959), using a TAT-type domestic picture with housewives, varied the illumination from normal to several successively darker and lighter stages. There was no difference in productivity, but there was a positive relationship between degree of darkness and pleasantness of association. In an unusual study on body posture, Beigel (1952) found that interpretations of card 8BM were more vigorous and active and less contemplative when subjects were standing than when they were lying down; responses while seated were intermediate.

Color, Brightness, Background

When chromatic and achromatic versions of the same pictures were compared, it was found that color tended to produce longer and generally more pleasant stories for college students (C. E. Thompson & Bachrach, 1951). Color stimulated mentally defective subjects to relate longer stories with more themes (N. M. Lubin, 1955). A slight increase in productivity for both normals and neurotics was obtained by Brackbill (1951), with neurotics also giving more depressed stories to color pictures.

Reducing brightness of pictures by photographic underexposure had no effect on TI (Weisskopf, 1950a), nor did changing the background alter productivity when the figure remained constant (J. E. Bradley & Lysaker, 1959).

Picture Differences

From the beginning it has been assumed that there are individual differences in the prepotencies of the pictures. There is ample evidence that each picture has its own "pull" in terms of the psychological data it is most likely to yield. This is one of the few TAT topics about which there is unanimity. A large number of studies show card differences for productivity, degree of involvement, emotional tone, nature of stories, interpersonal relations, outcome, and expression of needs (e.g., Bijou & Kenny, 1951; Coleman, 1947; Eron, 1948; Eron, 1950; Eron, 1953; Eron, Terry, & Callahan, 1950; Gurel & Ullmann, 1958; Kutash, 1943; Lindzey & Goldberg, 1953; Lowe, 1952; B. Lubin, 1960: Murstein, 1958a; Newbigging, 1955; B. R. Sarason & Sarason, 1958; Starr, 1961; Terry, 1952; Ullmann, 1957).

Ambiguity

Originally it was thought that considerable ambiguity in a picture was essential for projective purposes and, as a corollary, the greater the ambiguity, the greater the likelihood of personal projection. The assumption that the more ambiguous the stimulus, the greater the apperceptive distortion, and hence the more the personality is revealed has not been confirmed empirically. There can be too little as well as too much structuring of a picture.

In considering research on ambiguity, a distinction must be made between physical ambiguity, or the lack of definiteness in the objective features of the picture, and psychological ambiguity, or the number of possible interpretations. Physical ambiguity has been achieved by distorting contour lines and reducing exposure time and through various photographic techniques; psychological ambiguity has been determined by ratings.

The difficulty of deciding what a picture is about is not correlated with the number of possible interpretations (Brayer, Craig, & Teichner, 1961). Pictures with the most physical ambiguity are the least productive (Kenny, 1954; Veroff, 1961; Weisskopf, 1950a; Weisskopf-Joelson & Lynn, 1953). The psychological ambiguity of pictures has an inverted U-shaped curvilinear relationship with productivity and projective significance, with the moderately ambiguous pictures giving the best results (Kenny, 1954; Kenny & Bijou, 1953; Murstein, 1958b). Murstein (1958a) has presented evidence that for the Murray pictures the more clearly structured the picture the more unpleasant the emotional tone of the story.

Similarity of Subject and Figure

Frequently the plausible assumption has been made that similitude of narrator and central figure encourages ready identification, even though clinical experience has shown that subjects may make identifications across age and sex lines. The desirability of close physical similarity between subject and picture was not supported by the investigation of Weisskopf and Dunlevy (1952), who found that converting the Murray figures into crippled or obese figures did not increase productivity for persons with these handicaps. Similarly, replacing the face of the central figure with a photograph of the subject did not increase productivity (Weisskopf-Joelson & Money, 1953). In working with nuns, Lasaga y Travieso and Martinez-Arango (1946) did not find that using figures of nuns improved the diagnostic value of the test. McIntyre (1954) obtained the same kind of results for similarity of age and sex to subject population in his investigation of short filmstrips as a projective medium. Also relevant is the research, which will be reported later, that shows that the Thompson TAT, with Negro figures, has no superiority over the regular TAT for Negro subjects.

Specially Designed Pictures

Some believe that for many research purposes it is desirable to replace the standard set with specially designed pictures that are more relevant to the need, affect, or problem under study (Kagan, 1959; Kagan, 1960; Lesser, 1961). Custom-made pictures which have been structured for a particular problem area have often produced more data and more reliable and useful information (Eiserer, 1949; Kagan, 1956; Kagan, 1959; McClelland et al., 1953; E. J. Murray, 1959; H. Stone, 1956; Weatherley, 1962). By means of Guttman's scalogram method pictures have been scaled for measuring sex drive (Auld, Eron, & Laffal, 1955) and aggression (Lesser, 1958a) as unidimensional variables. By scaling methods it was hoped to approach more closely the goal of making quantitative interindividual comparisons of motive strength.

Structured pictures, because of anxiety or other inhibitory mechanisms, sometimes produce fewer need-oriented responses. A well-known example is E. J. Murray's experiment with sleep-deprived subjects (1959). Also overtly hostile patients gave more aggressive stories than nonhostile patients to hostile-ambiguous and nonhostile pictures but not to pictures which were obviously hostile in nature (Starr, 1961). Pictures of low sexual relevance best reflected sex drive as measured by orgasm rate, while pictures of high sexual relevance best measured guilt (Leiman & Epstein, 1961). Weisskopf-Joelson, Asher, Albrecht, and Hoffman (1957) found partial support for their hypothesis that repressed father antagonism was less likely to be expressed for appropriate than for inappropriate pictures. But Epstein and Smith (1956) were probably not justified in resorting to an approach-avoidance paradigm to explain their negative results with the hunger motive. Since their control group had eaten one hour before the test and the hungry group only four hours before the test, a more parsimonious explanation for the lack of difference in food imagery for the two groups was that the "hungry" group was not really hungry.

Most of the foregoing indicates how sensitive an instrument the TAT is and points up the need for caution on the part of the examiner. The examiner should be aware of the prepotencies of the cards and of common responses before undertaking an interpretation. Thus, perception of hostility on the part of figures in one picture may indicate projection, while on another it may indicate only respect for the obvious qualities of the stimulus. While the examiner should develop sophistication about stimulus effects, there is a tendency in some quarters to overstate the role of the stimulus and underestimate the role of personality projection. Under ordinary conditions of administration, more story variance is accounted for by projection or expression of personality than by the stimulus complex. Most of the administrative and stimulus variations demonstrated in the laboratory are mainly of academic interest and are not of primary importance in the usual testing situation. Ordinarily an examinee is not presented with a 0.2-second exposure of pictures in color while standing in semidarkness listening to an alluring female administrator who is deliberately creating a hostile atmosphere by making sharply critical remarks.

The consistency with which the individual personality comes through the stories despite the varying stimulus properties of the pictures has been demonstrated in a matching experiment by Palmer (1952). On the basis of a contingency coefficient of .70 he concluded: "The idiosyncratic contribution of the storyteller can be identified from card to card, even by untrained judges." If personality projection were secondary to stimulus conditions, the extensive validation the TAT has received would be improbable.

CORRELATIONAL STUDIES

Under this heading will be considered research which relates the TAT to such extrinsic variables as occupation, social class, and ethnic and national affiliation as well as correlations with age, sex, and intelligence. Education has not been singled out for study as such, but it correlates significantly with intelligence and social class. Veroff (1961) in his national sample survey noted that the less educated segment of the population was more likely to give incomplete and inadequate stories and that the test was less appropriate with this group.

Age

All agree that individual differences loom large at every age, and almost all agree that there are modal age differences. A salient picture of what these differences are does not readily emerge from the research reports. The problem is not so much one of contradictory results but of the noncomparability of populations sampled and the great variety of ways in which TAT protocols have been treated.

Amen (1941) presented preschool children from ages 2 to 4 with pictures appropriate to their age. Their responses to specific questions showed self-identification and projection. The younger ones made concrete and literal interpretations with unanalyzed wholes or reacted to details in place of the whole. The older children ascribed more activity, including inner activity, to their characters and reacted to the whole picture with more tendency to incorporate the details into a gestalt. Suesholtz (1948) studied the age group from 4 to 10. The younger members of the group told short, simple, enumerative stories and were more spontaneous than the older children, who were more productive and interpretive but also more defensive.

Disturbed children under 10 tended to enumerate picture details; even with prodding their responses were fragmentary (Balken & Vander Veer, 1944). For children over 10, the stories became more coherent and contained involved situations with *dramatis personae;* they approached the stories of adult neurotics. Generally with the progression from early childhood to late adolescence the narratives become more productive and more imaginative in quality (Amen, 1941; Balken & Vander Veer, 1944; Harrison, 1953; Sanford, 1943; Suesholtz, 1948). If young children are more imaginative, it is not reflected in this medium.

Aggression, often in the form of melodramatic violence, is very common in the stories of adolescents (Harrison, 1953; McDowell, 1952; Sanford, 1943; Symonds, 1949), including the stories of adolescent girls in India (Ghosh, 1958). Stories with direct sexual reference are rare (Harrison, 1953; Symonds, 1949). Middle and older adolescents show increasing preoccupation with moral problems

(Sanford, 1943; Symonds, 1949), while there is a rise in intellectual control and ego strength and a curbing of primitive affect from preschool to the late teen period (Balken & Vander Veer, 1944; Harrison, 1953; Suesholtz, 1948).

Sanford (1943) did a needs-press analysis with children between the ages of 6 and 14. He found that the stories of the youngest children emphasized sensation and were unconcerned with self-assertion and self-defense. The middle range of children stressed self-forwarding tendencies to the neglect of social feelings and showed a moderate concern with moral issues. Guilt and inferiority feelings were most conspicuous in the oldest group.

Symonds (1949) tallied themes for 40 boys and girls from 12 to 18. The younger adolescents gave stories of adventure with themes of excitement and altruism. Endings were usually happy. They gave freer expression to their impulses than the older adolescents. The stories of the older group contained more anxiety and aggression and showed more concern with moral problems. In a follow-up study thirteen years later, Symonds and Jensen (1961) found that themes characteristic of the adolescents tended to persist. The changes were in the direction of less tendency to reform the world, more depression and wishful thinking, and less aggression and punishment.

In a different kind of study, descriptive rather than statistical in nature, Harrison (1953) analyzed the TATs of prepubescent, postpubescent, and late-adolescent girls, 100 in each group. The stories of the younger groups centered in the home and in parent-child relations. Maternal characters occurred much more frequently than father figures, but by late adolescence indications of maternal dependency had declined. The violent melodrama of the younger groups was largely missing from the narratives of the older girls. With more age and experience a greater degree of psychic differentiation was achieved with more varied themes, greater impulse control, and increasing realism. A wide disparity separated the older group from the girls near the menarche. At puberty there was no sudden psychological change or maturing; instead, the development was continuous and gradual. With the older adolescents domestic preoccupation was superseded by an accelerated interest in heterosexual relations and an increasing identification with the maternal role. The conception of femininity was found to be quite variable with attitudes toward love and marriage, ranging from the realistic-descriptive to the romantic-idealistic.

Several papers have dealt with the adult period. The stories of younger and older Japanese men differ markedly (Marui, 1960). Brackbill (1951), comparing young and middle aged veterans, observed no difference in productivity and little motivational difference except for greater achievement need in younger men and more succorance need in middle age. In contrast Veroff (1961) found, except for the professional and managerial groups, more achievement need in the middle years than for the younger or older men.

J. L. Rosen and Neugarten (1960) studied 144 persons from ages 40 to 71. The older men and women were less able to integrate wide ranges of stimuli or to perceive and deal with complicated or conflict situations, and they tended toward passive rather than active, assertive forms of behavior. These results were interpreted in terms of energy decrease and ego constriction. Older people in Aron's experience were also much less expressive (1949).

Sex Differences

The systematic investigation of sex differences has been neglected except for a couple of studies by Lindzey and collaborators (Lindzey & Goldberg, 1953; Lindzey & Silverman, 1959), who obtained significant differences; but, except for the greater verbal responsiveness of women, the differences were not consistent from one college population to another.

Almost all writers agree on the fact of TAT sex differences, but again because of the specificity of scoring and interpretive methods and because of population sampling, establishing firm trends presents some difficulty. A few writers have not been able to report any real differences (B. Cox & Sargent, 1948; Myers, 1958; J. L. Rosen & Neugarten, 1960); the most likely explanation is to be found in their scoring procedures. That TAT sex differences exist is indicated by Shneidman and Farberow (1958), whose judges could determine sex with significant accuracy from the protocols of adult subjects in 75 per cent of the cases.

There is agreement that girls and young women are more productive and fluent and show more imagination and psychological involvement than males of comparable age (Abel, 1945; Aron, 1949; Ericson, 1947; Lindzey & Goldberg, 1953; Lindzey & Silverman, 1959; Roquebrune, 1959; Weisskopf, 1950b), with only Foulds (1953) dissenting. Except by Kagan (1959), males are reported to show more themes of aggression (McDowell, 1952; Sanford, 1943; S. B. Sarason, 1943b; Symonds, 1949; Whitehouse, 1949). Females show more affect (Aron, 1949; Kagan, 1961; S. B. Sarason, 1943b), relate sadder stories (Eron et al., 1950; Newbigging, 1955), and are more concerned with nurturance (Kagan, 1959; Lindzey & Goldberg, 1953). Usually their stories reflect a greater interest in affiliation and personal relations (Sanford, 1943; Webster, 1953; Whitehouse, 1949; but not Lindzey & Silverman, 1959). In the case of institutionalized defectives, themes of loneliness were more prevalent in the stories of girls (Abel, 1945; S. B. Sarason, 1943b). Sanford (1943) found that girls manifested greater needs for curiosity, deference, exhibition, and avoidance of blame and humiliation than boys.

Intelligence

Productivity and the clinical usefulness of stories are of course very much affected by the level of verbal intelligence. Working with disturbed children, Balken and Vander Veer (1944) reported the stories of high-IQ children to be rich in creative inventiveness, while the low-IQ children gave material that was sterile and naïve. S. B. Sarason (1943a; 1943b), on the other hand, found the TATs of institutionalized morons clinically revealing.

In the stories of normal children the progression from MA 6 to MA 10 is marked by less enumeration and more relationships among the figures; more thought, feeling, and action; less perceptual distortion; more enriching detail in the development of themes and more spontaneity in the narrative; more antecedent and consequent conditions; more coherence and logic; and an increase in sentences and a corresponding decline in phrases (Horowitz, 1952).

Estimates of intelligence can be made from vocabulary, productivity, grammar, logic, range of interests, general knowledge, organization, originality, perceptiveness, and sensitivity. That intelligence can be determined with some accuracy from TAT protocols has been demonstrated (Edelstein, 1956; Graham, 1947; Harrison, 1940a; Harrison, 1940b; Rotter, 1940; Webb & Hilden, 1953). Simple word count correlates .40 with Wechsler-Bellevue and .50 with Thurstone PMA (Webb & Hilden, 1953). From a composite formula based on several formal characteristics Edelstein (1956) obtained a high correlation with Stanford-Binet for a small group of normal children, but with another small group of disturbed children the correlation dropped to insignificance.

Global analyses have generally predicted better. The correlation between TAT IQ estimates and Stanford-Binet IQs for psychiatric patients was .76 when the interpreter administered the TAT and .73 when another psychologist was the administrator (each $p < .01$) (Harrison, 1940a; Harrison, 1940b). Rotter (1940) obtained comparable results with a smaller sample drawn from the same hospital population. Graham (1947) got correlations of .87 with Stanford Binet, .74 with Otis, and .67 with PMA verbal score and Wechsler-Bellevue performance IQ from TAT protocols of 36 high school students. The Rorschach estimates correlated .60 with Stanford-Binet in the same study. These coefficients are as high as those usually obtained between different intelligence tests.

Social Class

Socioeconomic class distinctions have been observed either incidentally or as the main focus of study by Harrison (1953), Mason and Ammons (1956), H. E. Mitchell (1950; 1951), Ruess (1958), and Singer (1954) but were not found by J. L. Rosen and Neugarten (1960). Compared with the middle-class respondents, the lower-class respondents not only tell shorter stories (Korchin, Mitchell, & Meltzoff, 1950), which reflect differences in language usages (Mason & Ammons, 1956), but also reveal greater violence (Harrison, 1953; Ruess, 1958). Harrison's most underprivileged group showed the greatest incidence of mental pathology (1953). H. E. Mitchell (1950; 1951) delineated differences in family life of adult males drawn from lower- and middle-class backgrounds. Family relations were more cohesive in the stories of the middle-class subjects, with middle-class fathers particularly showing more closeness and warmth. The heroes of the middle class were motivated more by their families, while the lower-class heroes were more self-propelled. These results have been confirmed for a group of lower- and middle-class schizophrenics (Singer, 1954).

McArthur (1955) tested hypotheses derived from the writings of social anthropologists on differences between upper and middle classes, using the TATs of Harvard freshmen who had attended either public or private schools. Significant differences confirming the predictions were obtained. The middle-class students were more influenced by their mothers, were more ambitious and work-involved, had greater autonomy needs, and were oriented toward action and the future. Fathers were the exemplars for the upper-class students, who showed less work involvement, sought to maintain the status quo, and were more oriented to the past and to family values.

S. Fisher and Fisher (1960) studied subcultural differences by comparing TAT themes of members of old Texas families with those of members of Jewish families who had not lived in the state more than one generation and in the country more than three generations. After differences were identified—the native Texas families were occupied with issues of responsibility and wanderlust, the Jewish families with superiority-inferiority status—judges were able to sort the two sets of protocols at a .001 level of confidence. The contrasting themes were common to three generations of a family.

Ethnic and National Differences

That other manifestations of cultural background should be considered in making idiographic interpretations is suggested by TAT studies on Negro and white subjects. Among college women, whites gave longer stories than Negroes (Riess, Schwartz, & Cottingham, 1950), but the longer stories did not contain a greater number of ideas (Schwartz, Riess, & Cottingham, 1951). White and Negro morons, however, showed no difference in number of themes (Abel, 1945).

A dissertation on the influence of social class and race on family image presented evidence that social class accounted for more of the obtained differences than race (H. E. Mitchell, 1950; H. E. Mitchell, 1951). The main ethnic difference was that in the stories of the Negro men the mothers were portrayed as more affectionate and comforting.

In a comparison of the TATs of Negro and white boys, the Negro boys perceived their environment as more hostile and their heroes as more indifferent to their surroundings (Mussen, 1953). The heroes of the white boys were more sensitive to family rejection, more often expressed extreme hostility, had greater desire to achieve, and were more responsive to a more favorable environment.

Former Soviet citizens, now displaced persons, were compared with an American sample and were found to be similar in many ways, but the Russian records showed more loss, deprivation, and threat (D. Rosenblatt, 1960). The Russians were more deeply involved in the content of their stories and displayed a wider range of motives, emotions, and relationships.

A large group of West German men, examined on TAT-type pictures by Rainwater (1960), showed as their principal trends feelings of depression and isolation and in general were preoccupied with the more negative potentialities of human relations. Findings were said to be congruent with other studies on German character structure.

The stories of Japanese-Americans were studied to illuminate psychological aspects of the acculturation process (Caudill, 1952; Caudill & De Vos, 1956). Several modes of adjustment for first- and second-generation Japanese-Americans were described, and comparisons were made with the stories of lower- and middle-class white Americans. De Ridder (1961) has recently published a book in which he describes, based on the analyses of 2,500 TATs, common personality characteristics of urban South African men in relationship to their social and cultural milieu. A smaller study by Singer and Opler (1956) found a higher TI among Italian-American schizophrenics than among schizophrenics of Irish extraction.

Occupations

The TAT has been used, often in conjunction with other techniques, to elicit the modal character structures and value systems for men in various occupations. The principal contributor has been Roe, who is best known for her studies on eminent scientists (1949; 1951; 1953). Research has also been reported on artists and nonartists (Eiduson, 1958; Munsterberg & Mussen, 1953), painters (Roe, 1946a; Roe, 1946b), jazz musicians (Tristano, 1953), poets (Wilson, 1958), engineers (Harrison, Tomblen, & Jackson, 1955; Moore & Levy, 1951), chemists and mathematicians (Clifford, 1958), and academic scientists (Eiduson, 1962).

The main conclusions from the TATs of eminent biologists, based on both statistical treatment and qualitative analysis, were that these men had a strong preference for concrete reality and a distaste for imaginative flights, were unaggressive and avoided strong emotional involvement, and showed evidence of a somewhat retarded psychosexual development but attached considerable value to the security that marriage represented (Roe, 1949). The findings for the prominent physicists from Rorschachs, TATs, and interviews were similar (Row, 1951). They were shown to be independent and to lack warmth in personal relations, and they gave indication of impersonal but conflictless parent-child relations and combined sexual evasiveness with conventional morality. Using the same techniques, Eiduson (1962), in a recent book on academic researchers in the physical and biological sciences, came up with a similar picture. The scientists came from homes with lukewarm emotional climate, showed ambivalence to mothers and lack of attachment to fathers, and achieved an adjustment through great investment in intellectual work, to the neglect of close relations with other human beings.

Eminent psychologists and anthropologists were entirely different (Roe, 1953). The social scientists were greatly interested in people, free in describing heterosexual situations, dependent on parental figures, and more liberal, but they seemed to have undergone more emotional turmoil.

A quite different profile was presented by mechanical engineers (Harrison et al., 1955). Their stories were short, uncomplicated, matter-of-fact, commonplace, and lacking in dramatic values. They gave a number of popular responses, were intolerant of ambiguity, and sometimes expressed barbed humor at the expense of the pictures. There was an almost total absence of fantasy or inner life on the part of their characters. The stories were peopled by individuals who never introspect. Feelings were expressed but were closely related to external events. From similar thematical material and from personal histories Moore and Levy (1951) concluded that their successful engineers were concrete-minded, practical, orderly, and independent; reacted positively to authority; preferred objects and processes to people and ideas; and maintained casual, impersonal but friendly relations at work.

Eiduson (1958) did Rorschach and TAT comparisons of people in the contrasting worlds of art and business. Writers, musicians, actors, and artists, not unexpectedly, gave more unusual, original, and imaginative responses, had greater responsiveness to the needs of others, and valued the theoretical and abstract over the practical and realistic. Parallel findings came out of another TAT study on art students and students in other fields (Munsterberg & Mussen, 1953). On the basis of their Rorschachs and TATs successful painters were described as bright, sensitive, unaggressive, emotionally passive, industrious, and self-disciplined (Roe, 1946a; Roe, 1946b).

TAT-like pictures in color were presented to a number of recognized poets and, for comparative reasons, to a group of undergraduates (Wilson, 1958). The poets rejected many of the cards, and they did not usually follow instructions to relate stories but instead indulged in free associations with much self-reference and self-analysis. When they did choose to give stories, their narratives were characterized by fluency and by a rich vein of humor. Their stories contained more conflict than those of the students, while their heroes were less successful in resolving problems.

METHODS OF ANALYSIS

Sometimes stories are scored, sometimes they are evaluated without scoring, and sometimes they are subjected to both procedures, with one designed to complement the other. The same schisms that cut across many regions of psychology—the experimental versus the clinical, the nomothetic versus the idiographic, the atomistic versus the holistic—plague thematic apperceptive endeavors. One school of thought favors detailed scoring methods that are relatively objective, statistical, and psychometric in nature. The opposite orientation does not score but depends on interpretive judgment and is clinical, global, holistic, and gestaltist. Referring to this method as "intuitive" or "impressionistic" is pejorative and, when the method is seriously applied, inaccurate. It should therefore be avoided as prejudicial rather than descriptive. The two approaches will hereafter in this chapter be called the "quantitative" (psychometric) and the "qualitative" (holistic).

The quantitative method is used primarily in research, the qualitative method in both research and practice. Scoring methods are not feasible in clinical work because their substantial yield is minimal in proportion to time expended and because their quantitative entities are frequently irrelevant for clinical purposes. Some clinicians feel that TAT scoring methods are not only cumbersome but also atomistic and unsound in principle and that attempts to reduce the complex configurations of the narratives to discrete measurable elements often succeed only in reducing them to artifacts. The popularity of scoring procedures in research is understandable, however, because of the desirability of quantification. The psychological mores in the United States render suspect any research which does not employ statistics, and scored variables are more readily accessible to statistical treatment than clinical judgments.

There is no one best method for analyzing the TAT under all circumstances, nor would it be desirable for a single method ever to become universally sanctioned. The demand sometimes heard for one consensual method of analysis in unwarranted, for the special merit of the TAT and its outstanding superiority over other test methods consist in its versatility and cornucopian profusion, which defy the bondage that one formalized system would engender. TAT records can be subjected to almost as many kinds of analysis as there are theoretical propositions about personality; there can be as many scoring procedures and interpretive methods as there are variables for researchers and clinicians to conceptualize (Holt, 1958).

Lindzey (1952), in a helpful article, has examined some of the principal assumptions commonly made in TAT interpretation as well as the empirical evidence that bears on these assumptions. Where research evidence is available, it is generally affirmative for the 10 basic assumptions:

1. In completing or structuring an incomplete or unstructured situation, the individual may reveal his own strivings, dispositions, and conflicts.
2. In the process of creating a story the story-teller ordinarily identifies with one person in the drama, and the wishes, strivings, and conflicts of this imaginary person may reflect those of the story-teller.
3. The story-teller's dispositions, strivings, and conflicts are sometimes represented indirectly or symbolically.
4. All of the stories that the subject creates are not of equal importance as diagnostic of his impulses and conflicts. Certain crucial stories may provide a very large amount of valid diagnostic material while others may supply little or none.
5. Themes or story-elements that appear to have arisen directly out of the stimulus material are less apt to be significant than those that do not appear to have been directly determined by the stimulus material.
6. Themes that are recurrent in a series of stories are particularly apt to mirror the impulses and conflicts of the story-teller.
7. The stories may reflect not only the enduring dispositions and conflicts of the subject, but also conflicts and impulses that are momentarily aroused by some force in the immediate present.
8. The stories may reflect events from the past of the subject that he has not himself actively experienced, but rather has witnessed or observed, e.g., street scene, story, motion picture.
9. The stories may reflect group-membership or socio-cultural determinants in addition to individual or personal determinants.
10. The dispositions and conflicts that may be inferred from the story-teller's creations are not always reflected directly in overt behavior or consciousness (Lindzey, 1952).

Lindzey found some evidence for all the postulates except the fourth and the sixth. Subsequently, Lindzey and Kalnins (1958) further substantiated the hero assumption, while Fitzgerald (1958) has given some support to the undernourished assumption that conflicts may be indicated by recurrent themes. Miller and Scodel (1955), however, in finding that unusual stories have no diagnostic advantage over usual stories, indirectly strike at the belief that themes arising directly from stimulus material are less apt to be significant. In this chapter ample evidence either has been or will be cited for the assumptions regarding the effect of momentary influences, group membership, and relationship to overt behavior.

Space restrictions will permit only a quick overview of some of the available scoring systems and interpretive approaches. For a somewhat fuller treatment of several of the major methods, the reader is referred to Watson (1951). For the application of many of these methods to a single case Shneidman's book may be consulted (1951).

Quantitative Methods

The division of methods of analysis into those which are quantitative and those which are qualitative is somewhat arbitrary, since the approaches of some writers partake of both methods. In such a case the quantitative is likely to precede the qualitative and serve as a partial base for interpretation. Within the ranks of psychologists with a scoring, rating, or checklist approach, there are also variations; the system of Aron, for example, is much more psychometric and molecular than those of Wyatt and Bellak.

The original conceptual schema applied by H. A. Murray to TAT analysis derives from the personality theory outlined in his book *Explorations in Personality* (1938). His system, which is primarily an analysis of content, takes the hero or principal character as the point of departure (H. A. Murray, 1943; H. A. Murray, 1953). Each successive narrative event is analyzed into forces emanating from the hero, primarily *needs* but also *emotions* and other inner states, and forces emanating from the environment, called *press*. There are long lists of needs (such as *n* Abasement, *n* Achievement, and *n* Aggression) and press (such as *p* Affiliation, *p* Dominance, and *p* Physical Danger) and several other inner states (such as Conflict, Dejection, and Superego). Each is rated on a five-point scale for strength. Tentative norms are given for a male college population. *Outcomes* of stories are also considered. The interaction of need, press, and outcome constitutes a *thema* (hence, thematic apperception), and a combination of thema makes up complex thema. Murray also notes interests and sentiments manifested by the hero, particularly positive and negative cathexes of maternal, paternal, and sibling figures. The scores are than subjected to interpretation based on several principles which represent the fruit of the author's experience.

The length of time for scoring has been given as three hours (Carlile, 1952) and for complete interpretation from four to five hours (Bellak, 1954b). The Murray scoring is, in a sense, the "official" system, for it is the only one found in the manual that comes with the pictures. This fact has probably dampened initial curiosity and discouraged further exploration for some potential users because the method is too formidable and unwieldy for practical purposes. Other objections are that the system depends on a preconceived personality theory that many will not find acceptable, that it is too static, that the scores are enumerated out of context, that relationships are minimized, and that it allows too much valuable material to slip through its meshes because of the concentration on needs and press. While the Murray method has rarely been used clinically, aspects of it in abbreviated or modified form have often been employed in research. Several authors of other systems have been students of Murray, whose influence on their thinking is apparent.

Aron (1949) has revised and elaborated upon Murray's method with the expressed aim of scoring variables in context. A shorthand notation system has been developed for need, press, and outcome as well as for benefits and deprivations (attributes with which persons are endowed or deprived). Scoring variables are rated for intensity. Although more differentiated than the Murray system, most of the same objections can be leveled against her method.

Tomkins (1947), in his book on TAT analysis, distinguishes four major scoring categories:

1. *Vectors* or the psychological direction of behavior or impulse (on, from, toward, with, against, etc.).
2. *Levels* or the plane of psychological functioning involved (perception, behavior, thought, wish, etc.).
3. *Conditions* or any psychological, social, or physical state which is not itself behavior or impulse (lack, danger, abundance, etc.).
4. *Qualifiers* or more specific aspects of either vectors, levels, or conditions (intensity, negation, contingency, causality, etc.).

After scoring each story in categorical terms, interpretation is accomplished by utilizing three main approaches: Mill's *canons of inference*, such as the methods of agreement, difference, and concomitant variation plus additional methods made necessary by the complex nature of thematic material; *level analysis* (degree of variance, relative frequency, cause-

and-effect relationships between overt and covert needs, degree of awareness, and conflicts between wish and behavior); and *diagnosis of personality* in separate areas like the family, love and sex, social relationships, and work. Most of the volume is devoted to principles of diagnosis in the separate areas. In the numerous illustrations formal scoring is ignored in making interpretations, so the reader is likely to gain the impression that the scoring is not an integral part of the approach.

Wyatt (1947) has developed a system of formal analysis influenced by the Rorschach scoring categories. Fifteen variables are considered for each story:

1. *Story—description*—whether picture description or story.
2. *Stimulus perception*—whether examinee departs from common modes of perception.
3. *Deviations from typical response*—whether common or uncommon plots are given.
4. *Deviation from self*—inconsistencies to be noted only after all stories have been analyzed.
5. *Time trend*—whether responses refer to past, present, or future.
6. *Level of interpretation*—whether factual, subjective, symbolic, etc.
7. *Tone of story*—feeling tone (detached, serene, tense, etc.).
8. *Quality of telling*—language usage and style.
9. *Focal figure*—the hero and his characteristics.
10. *Other figures*—description of other important characters.
11. *Personal relationships*—description of formal and emotional relations with others.
12. *Strivings, avoidances*—positive and negative goals.
13. *Presses*—Murray's environmental forces.
14. *Outcome*—success or failure of the focal figure.
15. *Thema*—abstraction of the main story trends.

Check marks are tallied for these variables where tallying is possible; other variables are inspected for trends. Interpretation is then made from this basis. Special attention is given to deviations of the examinee from the norm and from his own trends.

Bellak (1954b) is difficult to classify as either quantitative or qualitative because he has characteristics of both approaches. Although he is systematic and uses a checklist, his method is hardly psychometric. Interpretive observations are made for each story in different areas, using the language of Freudian psychodynamics. The 10 areas are:

1. *Main theme*—story synopsis
2. *Main hero*—characteristics
3. *Main needs of hero*—overt and latent motives
4. *Conception of environment*—similar to Murray's press
5. *Perception of figures and subject's reaction*—parental, contemporary, and other characters
6. *Significant conflicts*—nature of conflicts and defenses
7. *Nature of anxieties*—sources of tensions and defenses
8. *Main defenses against conflicts and fears*—repression, regression, denial, introjection, etc.
9. *Severity of superego*—punishments and inhibitions
10. *Integration of the hero*—capacity for effective functioning as shown by hero and plot structure

Rudimentary quantification is achieved for some of the areas by placing one to three check marks opposite suggestive subheadings. After analyzing each story for the different areas, the examiner reviews them and writes a summary in the appropriate space on the TAT blank which Bellak has designed to facilitate analysis and interpretation. Following this, the examiner makes a final report on the cover of the blank, using the original analyses and summaries as guides.

Fine's system is more mosaic (1955a; 1955b). He uses a checklist for scoring the presence or absence of many *feelings* (affection, anger, anxiety, etc.), *interpersonal relations* (moving toward, moving against, moving away from) between specific types of persons (mother-child, man-woman, etc.), and *outcomes* (favorable, unfavorable, indeterminate). Feelings are counted, whether they are expressed by the hero or by someone else. The resulting psychogram is regarded as a schematized picture of the personality which forms the core for any further interpretations.

Eron offers a strictly normative, statistical approach in which he determines how the responses of the individual in question differ from the responses of other individuals of similar age, sex, and background (1948; 1950; 1953; Eron & Hake, 1950; Eron et al., 1950). Stories are rated for *emotional tone* (happy-sad) and for *outcome* (success-failure) on a five-point scale. Each story is checked against a long list of *themes* classified as interpersonal, intrapersonal, or impersonal and as showing either equilibrium or disequilibrium (tension). Deviations from the task of making up stories, perceptual distortions, and certain other formal characteristics are noted. The basic data for this system are the degree to which responses are frequent or infrequent and usual or unusual when compared with norms. How any TAT analyst uses these data for interpretation will depend on information available from other sources and on his theoretical orientation.

Shorr (1948) has a checklist of four manifest content variables—*predominant mood, chief worries, presses,* and *endings.* Under each of these categories are a number of subheadings for checking. Ratios of the frequency of each content variable to the total number of stories are calculated. The record sheet also provides space for notations about reaction time, rejected ideas, story sources, added characters, etiology, and bizarre elements.

Other quantitative methods have been reported by Chapin (1953), Combs (1946a), Fry (1953a; 1953b), and Vorhaus (1952b) as well as by several participants in the symposium of TAT specialists who did a blind analysis of the stories of a single patient, as recorded in *Thematic Test Analysis* (Shneidman, 1951). This volume, which is an excellent source for comparing the major methods of thematic analysis in action, also contains the psychiatric record and other test data on the case, so that the individual analyses may be compared with other information. As pointed out by Murray in the foreword and by Kutash (1952) in a review, the more clinical the method the richer the yield, while the more formalized and statistical the method the more removed from the target. Too often with the psychometric group it was a case of the mountain laboring and bringing forth the proverbial mouse.

The psychometric methods have made little mark on the practical use of the TAT. Their lack of popularity is understandable, for the various systems are idiosyncratic in that they reflect the propensities of the individual author and, while each system may have worked to the satisfaction of its originator, are not likely to be found congenial for others unwilling to settle for any particular arbitrary set of variables. Moreover, they have not been validated; they are cumbersome and time-consuming in proportion to yield; they involve the application of nomothetic methods to a technique which is essentially idiographic; and by their molecular nature, they obscure significant molar configurations on which personality diagnosis depends. Tallying discrete items out of context and out of relation to one another results inevitably in some loss of psychological meaning; relationships and gestalts are either distorted or destroyed. The same psychologist who would not think of atomizing an interview by tallying minutiae applies the same inappropriate methods to the TAT because it is reputedly a test, and tests are supposedly scorable. The psychogogic urge to count and be quasi-objective may be satisfied, but in the process the main value of the technique is lost.

There is more reason for employing molecular methods for the more circumscribed objectives of research, providing it can be done without undue distortion and without losing the problem in the process. Something like this in fact has happened in the research use of TAT, although the various formal systems, except for modified versions of the Murray needs, have usually been ignored in favor of a number of *ad hoc* scoring, rating, and ranking devices designed to quantify whatever motives, affects, traits, defenses, or other psychological dimensions the investigator may be pursuing. Some of the more distinctive methods have been the transcendence index (Weisskopf, 1950a), Guttman's scalograms (Auld et al., 1955), level of response (Terry, 1952), semantic differential (Reeves, 1954), motivation index (Arnold, 1962), perceptual scores (Dana, 1955), number of emotional words (Ullmann, 1957), differentiated scoring of needs (Atkinson, 1958), and various multiple-choice procedures (Horrall, 1957; Johnston, 1955).

Qualitative Methods

It is sometimes assumed that if quantitative methods are not utilized the only alternative is to resort to impression and intuition. There are some casual TAT users who do just this—read over the protocols and, without any systematic analysis, form impressions and intuit. The practice is to be condemned; if one does not command a technique, one should not practice it. S. B. Sarason (1948) has argued convincingly (and has illustrated his thesis with case material) that qualitative thematic analysis is not a magical, unscientific, unreasoning process.

A qualitative analysis, properly done, is methodical and involves close reasoning which draws heavily on the resources of the analyst. The analyst functions in a manner analogous to that of a detective working with clues, who by common logic and specialized experience combines the clues to reach his conclusions. The principles for the interpretation of the personal significance of stories are similar to principles that are used by everyone in everyday life with varying degrees of skill when mannerisms and the form and content of verbalizations are examined for the light they may throw on the feelings and motives of others. Two broad working principles utilized by most TAT analysts in one form or another have to do with the frequency of motifs and the degree to which picture associations and narrative development are usual or unusual for interindividual and intraindividual comparisons. Subsidiary principles of intensity and vividness may be subsumed under the principle of unusualness.

Since personal significance usually attaches to unusual story interpretations, to themes which are foreign to picture content, and to uncommon plot developments, a base-line knowledge of what are popular picture associations and plot developments is essential. In addition to subjective norms which each examiner develops out of his own experience, some normative data are now available (Eron, 1950; Rosenzweig & Fleming, 1949; Wittenborn, 1949). Some may find the "interpretive norms" in the manuals of Henry (1956) and Stein (1955) more helpful.

A working arrangement this writer has found convenient is to proceed in two major steps: (1) After reading the stories, write down capsule synopses, rate outcomes, tally motifs, note all unusual and recurrent characteristics, and set up tentative hypotheses to be tested against the internal evidence. (2) Systematically bring together all TAT data relevant to a particular topical heading (such as parent-child relations, psychosexual relations, adjustment and diagnostic status, intellect, affect, goals, general traits and attitudes), and proceed to draw conclusions inductively from the evidence.

A recurrent issue is the relative emphasis to be given to the form and content of stories. The distinction usually made is that content refers to *what* is told, and form to *how* it is told. Content is narrative substance; form is style. There has been some disagreement about the boundaries that divide content and form, and the distinction is not as clear in practice as it may appear on the surface. The two may perhaps best be regarded as integral parts of a single organic unity. Hartman (1949) found that the distinction between content and form variables did not distinguish unique personality areas and that both were equally diagnostic in all the areas studied.

Early in the history of projective techniques the joint clinical use of the TAT and the Rorschach was urged on the grounds that the tests were complementary, the TAT providing mostly psychological content, such as conflicts and complexes, and the Rorschach contributing most heavily to personality structure (Harrison, 1943). It was recognized that there is usually a region of overlapping information, so that to some extent one test may act as a check on the other. Further developments have shown that almost any type of material can be extracted from either instrument, although not with equal facility. Not only is the Rorschach today often analyzed for content as well as scored formally, but several, such as Henry (1956), Holt (1958), and Schafer (1958), have shown the desirability of analyzing the often neglected formal qualities of narratives. Even so, the TAT will probably continue to be a test more for eliciting conclusions in terms of psychological content than for determining diagnosis or describing traits and syndromes. The converse emphases hold for the Rorschach.

There are several hazards inherent in subjective interpretation. Projective tests have sometimes been projective in the sense of projecting one's own traits or theoretical predilections. Pathologizing is a common error among clinicians in making personality evaluations, including projective appraisals. Freudianizing and pathologizing simultaneously are endemic with many clinicians. Both veteran and novice TAT examiners sometimes indulge in the pleasures of excessive interpretation and incautious conclusions.

Statistical studies on the semantic habits of TAT clinicians confirm the operation of the pathologist's fallacy (Cowden, Deabler, & Feamster, 1955; B. Cox & Sargent, 1950; Davenport, 1952; Little & Shneidman, 1955; Little & Shneidman, 1959; Soskin, 1954). Some of the same studies indicate preference for psychoanalytical concepts and terminology (Davenport, 1952; Little & Shneidman, 1955). Filer (1952) has given some evidence that examiners emphasize in their reports personality dimensions which are characteristic of themselves.

Marked individual differences in the proficiency of TAT analysts as measured by external criteria are indicated in the reports of Little and Shneidman (1955; 1959), Samuels (1952), and Ullmann and McFarland (1957). There is no question but that there is an aptitude for thematic analysis independent of general ability and professional qualifications; some have the talent, and some do not. The TAT not only is not a test in the usual sense but, paradoxically, also is a test of its user—of his skill, sensitivity, and soundness as either clinical examiner or laboratory investigator. One can scarcely come away from a survey of the literature without reaching the conclusion that the TAT contains a wealth of riches but that not everybody knows how to exploit its potential. Since the interpreter is very much a part of the technique, negative results may reveal as much about the examiner as they do about the technique. Allowances for individual differences with the instrument must be considered in evaluating validation studies and most other research.

Representatives of the qualitative approach include Arnold (1949; 1962), Harrison (1943), Henry (1956), Holt (1951a; 1951b; 1958), Lasaga y Travieso and Martinez-Arango (1946), Piotrowski (1950), Rapaport (1946), Rosenzweig (1949), Rotter (1946), S. B. Sarason (1948), R. Schafer (1948; 1958), Stein (1955), and Wallen (1956). The best brief introduction to practical problems of administration and interpretation is the article by Rotter (1946). Among more extensive treatments that may be recommended are the manuals by Arnold (1949), Henry (1956), and Stein (1955). Tomkins (1947) may be recommended except for his scoring system. An excellent example of the analysis of form is provided by R. Schafer (1958).

The qualitative approach is not unitary but represents a diversity of viewpoints. However, as Wyatt (1947) has indicated, much of the diversity is a matter of semantics and of emphasis rather than of flat contradiction. Listed below are extremely skeletonized versions of several of these positions. Since a technical publication cannot be summarized in a paragraph, the reader is referred to the original sources.

Rotter's approach may be termed "eclectic" (1946; Rotter & Jessor, 1951). It is dynamic but is not obviously indebted to any one psychoanalytic school. He proceeds in five steps:

1. The entire protocol is read for suggestive leads and for the formulation of tentative interpretations and hypotheses to be investigated further.
2. Each story is analyzed for basic ideas and for structural characteristics. Reference is made to plot norms for each picture.
3. Each story is considered as a unit to identify the characters, conflicts, and relationships in order to decide whether the material is wishful, autobiographical, or superficial and to select hypotheses on the basis of consistency with other stories.
4. All the stories are considered as one organized unit.
5. The tentative conclusions are integrated into a final summary under several categories: family, social, sexual, and general attitudes; personality characteristics; and etiological implications.

There is heavy dependence on the frequency and unusualness postulates. Unusualness includes any deviant choice and development of plot, misrecognitions and distortions, and peculiar word choice. Principles are also given for locating the character with whom the narrator is identifying, selecting among alternative interpretations, making diagnostic inferences, determining problems and complexes, and identifying clichés.

Henry (1956) attributes about equal significance to form and content. For him form includes length of stories, introduced content, richness of imagery, originality or commonness, rhythm, interruptions to story production, level of organization, coherence and logic, whole concepts, manner of approach to the central concept of the narrative, acuity of concepts, and language usage. Content is divided into the rubrics of positive and negative content. Positive content is concerned with what the narrator has actually said. Negative content is concerned with what the narrator might have been expected to say but failed to say. Under positive content are considered such features as emotional tone, basic plot, the characteristics of the hero and other figures, reactions to environment, interpicture variations, interpersonal relations, symbolic content, associative interpretation, best- and least-liked pictures, and story sequence. Broad working concepts for interpreting form and content are given and illustrated.

The five case records are subjected to elaborate and subtle analyses. For each case the TAT data are organized around several life sectors or areas: mental approach, imaginative processes, family dynamics, inner adjustment, emotional reactivity, sexual adjustment, overt behavior with others, and a final descriptive and integrative summary.

Stein (1955) approaches TAT interpretation from the standpoint of Murray's needs-press theory but does not score. The features with which he works are the hero, environmental stimuli, the behavior of the hero, positive and negative cathexes, inner states, the level at which behavior is expressed, and outcomes. Needs are brought under the behavior of the hero, press under environmental stimuli. These various aspects of the stories are explained in detail, and instructions for their interpretation are presented.

Under formal analysis Stein considers test behavior, how the subject complies with instructions, the use of objective features of the pictures, how details are handled in relation to the whole picture, language, and symbolism. "Syndrome or cluster analysis" is concerned with the context of need, press, and sentiment and their interrelationships. Eight cases were fully analyzed to illustrate the interpretive principles.

An invigorating wave of fresh air has come into thematic analysis with the recent publication of the book *Story Sequence Analysis* (Arnold, 1962). Not only are there some appealing novelties in Arnold's approach, but she and her doctoral students have reported some strikingly successful scholastic and vocational predictions and discriminations. Rarely have such criterion groups as achieving and nonachieving high school and college students (Brown, 1953; Garvin, 1960; McCandlish, 1958; Snider, 1954) and more and less successful teachers (Burkard, 1958), seminarians (Quinn, 1961), Federal administrators (Steggert, 1961), and Navy enlisted personnel (Petrauskas, 1959) been distinguished so sharply as they are reported to be by these methods.

Arnold's methods have gone through a gradual evolution since the publication of an earlier article (1949). At that time the procedure involved five steps: (1) brief story synopsis, (2) situational analysis (of such areas as parent-child and heterosexual relations), (3) analysis of attitudes from the situational analysis, (4) sequential analysis to determine whether there is a consistent development of a central theme in different stories, and (5) final integration. Sequence analysis, which is concerned with generalized statements about the narrator's basic outlook as revealed by successive stories, has become increasingly important in the most recent publication.

The method is strictly one of content analysis. Each story is regarded as an imaginative exploration of various problems and their possible solutions. What the narrator says about each picture reveals his deep-seated, but sometimes not fully articulated, convictions, or what may be called the "moral" of the story. When the moral is applied to the narrator's subjective circumstances, the psychologist can arrive at the import or significance of the story. The sequence of imports in successive stories reveals his trend of thought, the way he evaluates human action, what he regards as right and wrong, what will lead to success or failure—in short, his motivational pattern. The configurational principle is explicitly stated. "It is most desirable, therefore, that the stories be treated as a connected whole in which every motif may throw light on every other theme presented." For research purposes the import of each story may be rated on a five-point scale for the degree to which the basic attitude is positive or negative, constructive or destructive. The transformation and summation of these ratings are called the "motivation index."

Arnold also has a static system of content classification which is not particularly helpful. The statement of imports, the analysis of their sequence, and the motivation index are the core of her contribution. If after trial they are found by others to be useful and valid, they could readily be incorporated into most qualitative approaches. The motivation index could fit into quantitative approaches. Her occasional ethico-religious tone, which is distracting in scientific discourse and is likely to repel more secular psychologists, is not an essential or necessary part of the method and should not become a barrier to the acceptance of her contribution.

In summary, the qualitative procedures are the method of choice for clinical and most other practical purposes. For research, the literature shows that both quantitative and qualitative methods have their place. In using quantitative methods the investigator must exercise ingenuity to discover scoring categories that are not so arbitrary and truncated that they relate only tangentially to the problem. Even when the main reliance in research is placed on scored variables, they may profitably be complemented by holistic interpretation for greater understanding and appreciation of the phenomena under study. An alternative to scoring and piecemeal rating which has too seldom been employed in research applications of the TAT is the conversion of conclusions based on qualitative evaluation into numerical form by global ratings or Q sorts. In order to remove some of the onus of subjectivity, more than one judge could be used so that interjudge reliability could be calculated.

PRACTICAL USES AND APPLIED RESEARCH

The first association of most psychologists to the Thematic Apperception Test is with the diagnostic testing activities of clinical psychologists. In clinical testing the TAT is mainly relied on for the delineation of dynamics, but it may also contribute to the description of structural characteristics and sometimes, in conjunction with other tests, to differential diagnosis. It has sometimes been employed as an adjunct to therapy and has become part of the test armamentarium of some vocational and personal counselors, particularly when they are faced with difficult problems. Some clinically oriented industrial psychologists use the TAT in appraisals of key personnel for selection and promotion and in personnel audits. There has been considerable applied research concerned with predicting scholastic or vocational success which has used the TAT as one of the possible predictors. It has occasionally been a tool of motivation research in advertising and marketing (G. H. Smith, 1954). Among its rarer and less expected uses, the TAT has been an adjunct to the interview (Heppell & Raimy, 1951), a teaching aid in a personality-oriented psychology course (Bettelheim, 1947), and even in one instance a lie detector (E. Stern, 1951–1952).

Some have questioned the clinical value of the TAT on the basis of claims that it is time consuming and uneconomical (Sanford, 1949; Michael & Buhler, 1945), does not add substantially to the psychiatric interview (Knehr, Vickery, & Guy, 1953), is lacking in clinical validity (Jensen, 1959) and, in general, that its clinical usefulness has not been demonstrated (Eron, 1959). These statements are contrary to the majority opinion of clinicians who have had considerable experience with the technique, and they may be attributed, where the conclusions are based on selective reviews, to incomplete coverage of the clinical literature and, where they are based on direct experience, to the use of time-consuming and inappropriate psychometric methods. In the one relevant study bearing on its clinical usefulness Winch and More (1956) did not find an appreciable statistical increment of the TAT over interviews and case histories where the evaluation was limited mainly to needs, but they did find that when biographical information was added to blind TAT analysis in the final conference, the altered interpretation added considerable understanding beyond that which it is possible to obtain from the interviews alone.

A larger number of authors have testified to the clinical value of the TAT from their experience (Abel, 1945; Balken & Vander Veer, 1942; Bellak, 1954b; Bergman & Fisher, 1953; Chapin, 1953; Chipman, 1946; Deabler, 1947; Deutscher, 1944; Ericson, 1947; Freed & Eccker, 1946; Garfield, 1946; Hackbusch & Klopfer, 1946; Harrison, 1943; Hutt, 1945; Jaques, 1945; Kamman & Kram, 1955; Kendig, 1944; Kutash, 1943; Lasaga y Travieso & Martinez-Arango, 1948; Leitch & Schafer, 1947; Leunbach & Flachs, 1950; Masserman & Balken, 1938; Reichard, 1951; Rotter, 1940; S. B. Sarason, 1943a; S. B. Sarason, 1943b; Schneck, 1951; Slutz, 1941; J. A. Smith, Brown, & Thrower, 1951; E. Stern, 1950; Watson, 1951). Some have specifically remarked that the TAT is economical when expenditure of time is related to yield (e.g., Chapin, 1953; Rotter, 1940), while others have observed that it often adds information to clinical interviews and case histories (Balken & Vander Veer, 1942; Kendig, 1944; Lasaga y Travieso & Martinez-Arango, 1948; Leunbach & Flachs, 1950; Marui, 1957; Masserman & Balken, 1938; Schneck, 1951; Slutz, 1941). Several have found the method effective with mental defectives, a group that is usually thought of as too inarticulate for any verbal personality test (Abel, 1945; Bergman & Fisher, 1953; Hackbusch & Klopfer, 1946; S. B. Sarason, 1943a; S. B. Sarason, 1943b).

Differential Diagnosis

Although it is conventional to discount the diagnostic function of the TAT, an opinion which gets repeated with a minimum of independent appraisal, and to regard it as diagnostically inferior to the Rorschach, occasionally and for certain diagnostic purposes the picture-story test has been found to be more discriminating (e.g., Canter, 1953; Hooker, 1957). At the present time, the Rorschach is no doubt the superior instrument for differential diagnosis in the hands of most clinicians, but this may be because more diagnostic research has been done with it.

Lindzey, Bradford, Tejessy, and Davids (1959) have assembled in the form of an interpretive lexicon the conclusions of clinicians regarding the TAT characteristics of patients with various psychiatric diagnoses. These *obiter dicta* represent empirical generalizations which are rarely supported by data and which are likely to be affected by perceptual biases and sampling errors. They should not be considered more than a potentially valuable pool of hypotheses for empirical testing. When the conclusions of the clinicians were occasionally exposed to testing, they were often not confirmed (e.g., Eron, 1950; Lindzey & Newburg, 1954).

A survey of 50 articles dealing with TAT characteristics of different nosological groups showed an approximate ratio of 7:1 for articles with positive or group typical findings. Most studies report data but do not usually have control groups, while some are purely descriptive. Several have reported TAT differences between normals and various abnormal groups (N. Bills, 1953; Dana, 1955; Dana, 1956; Eron, 1950; Park, 1952; Ritter & Eron, 1952; S. Schafer & Leitch, 1948; Singer, 1954), but Carlile (1952) could find only slight differences between normal and disturbed adolescent girls from a needs-press analysis.

Distinctive TAT qualities in the stories of neurotics have been described (Balken & Masserman, 1940; Dana, 1955; Dana, 1956; Davison, 1953; Eron, 1950; Foulds, 1953; Goodman, 1952; Lindzey & Newburg, 1954; Masserman & Balken, 1938; Ritter & Eron, 1952; R. Schafer, 1948). Story characteristics that set off disturbed children from normal children (S. Schafer & Leitch, 1948) and from psychotic children (Leitch & Schafer, 1947) have been noted.

The characteristics of schizophrenics have been described many times (Balken, 1943; N. Bills, 1953; Davison, 1953; Eron, 1950; Masserman & Balken, 1938; Nagge, 1951; Park, 1952; Ritter & Eron, 1952; R. Schafer, 1948; Singer, 1954; Valentine & Robin, 1950b). Depressives were studied by Davison (1953), Masserman and Balken (1938), R. Schafer (1948), and Valentine and Robin (1950a), while manic and depressive patients were compared by Welch, Schafer, and Dember (1961). The TATs of defectives have been described by Beier, Gorlow, and Stacey (1951); Bergman and Fisher (1953); Ruess (1958); S. B. Sarason (1943a; 1943b); and Slack (1950). Distinctive stories were given by psychopaths (Foulds, 1953; R. Schafer, 1948), psychopathic defectives (Kutash, 1943), and delinquents (Lyle & Gilchrist, 1958; Nishimura, 1958; Young, 1956).

Typical alcoholic patterns were reported by N. Bills (1953), Klebanoff (1947), and R. Schafer (1948), but working with a psychometric system, Knehr et al. (1953) were not able to distinguish alcoholic from nonalcoholic psychiatric patients. Psychometric scoring also did not differentiate stutterers from nonstutterers (La V. H. Richardson, 1944). In a comparative study brain-diseased, head-injured, and neurotic patients showed poor discrimination, but the variables chosen and the treatment of data left much to be desired (Renaud, 1946). Canter (1953), Landisberg (1947), Richards (1952), and Wentworth-Rohr (1950) found that epileptics had salient TAT characteristics.

Male homosexuals have been studied at length and, except for inconclusive results in a study with poorly defined criterion groups (Wayne, Adams, & Rowe, 1947), show characteristic reactions (N. Bills, 1953; Davids, Joelson, & McArthur, 1956; Hooker, 1957; Lindzey, Tejessy, & Zamansky, 1958). In the Lindzey research, a psychologist from global appraisal of the stories was able to distinguish homosexuals from heterosexuals with 95 per cent accuracy, which was superior to the accuracy obtained by the sign approach. Attempts to discriminate between the stories of suicidals and nonsuicidals have so far been unsuccessful (Broida, 1954; Shneidman & Farberow, 1958), although Crasilneck (1954) found some differences between suicidals and what he termed "pseudosuicidals."

Psychotherapy

In the very first TAT paper published, C. Morgan and Murray (1935) told how in one case "the thematic apperceptions adumbrated all the chief trends which five months of analysis were able to reveal." Bellak (1954b), an experienced analyst, reports that the TAT has been known to bring out material that had not been revealed in almost a year of analysis. All who have published on the therapeutic use of the TAT have been unanimous about its value (Bellak, 1954b; Bellak, Pasquarelli, & Braverman, 1949; Deabler, 1947; Höhn, 1951; Jaques, 1945; Kafka, 1957; Lasaga y Travieso & Martinez-Arango, 1946; Martinez-Arango & Lasaga y Travieso, 1947; Masserman & Balken, 1938; H. A. Murray, 1951; Schneck, 1951; Tomkins, 1947; Watson, 1951; Woolley, 1945). The TAT is not partial to any school of therapy; it has been used in both directive and nondirective therapy, in hypnoanalysis, as a form of play therapy, and in group therapy.

The capacity of the technique to uncover dynamic content material makes it a ready adjunct to psychotherapy where it may be employed either to elicit fresh information for fuller understanding of the patient or directly in interaction with the patient during the therapy hour. Different therapists at different times have used it for the following:

1. To give an overview of the patient's problems and characteristics which may be put to strategic use in planning a treatment program.
2. To assess attitudes toward therapy and toward the therapist, both initially and during the course of treatment.
3. To break the ice with noncommunicative patients or, if the therapy is marking time, to circumvent defenses that are impeding progress.
4. To identify conflicts and defenses or, more generally, to encourage ventilation.
5. To help the patient become more insightful by having him discuss and interpret his own stories or by having him engage in joint interpretation with the therapist.
6. To serve, like dreams, as a point of departure for free associations.
7. To find leads for active interpretation and direct intervention by the therapist.

Counseling

Hire (1951) and Wittenborn (1949) report that in working with college students, the introduction of picture stories quickens insight and enhances the counseling process. The TAT has been used to explore emotional factors in reading and other learning disabilities (Harris & Roswell, 1953; Monroe, 1949; Vorhaus, 1952a) and in vocational guidance (Carlson & Vandever, 1951; Hire, 1951; Kline, 1953; Levine, 1954). Ammons (1950) has tried to tap personality factors in relation to vocational attitudes in the Vocational Apperception Test, which pictures common vocational situations.

Academic Prediction

The TAT has been so uniformly successful in predicting school and college grades and in discriminating between overachievers and underachievers that one wonders why the work has not been replicated with larger populations with the eventual aim of practical application.

The most impressive results come from the Magda Arnold group with the use of the motivation index or equivalent. Brown (1953), Snider (1954), and McCandlish (1958) clearly distinguished high- and low-achieving high school students of equivalent IQs. Arnold (1962) predicted seventh-grade marks with an r of .75, while Garvin (1960) reported the amazingly high coefficients of .83 and .85 with grade-point averages for two colleges. These were higher than the ACE predictions. With an entirely different approach, rating school attitudes from pictures dealing with classroom situations, Malpass (1953) got an r of .45 with grade averages for eighth-grade pupils.

There have been several studies of college students of different levels of achievement. Burgess (1956) confirmed his hypothesis that overachievers and underachievers would differ in personality with a variety of tests. The TAT seemed to be the most productive test in the battery and discriminated better than the Rorschach. In their stories the high achievers showed more need for achievement, aggression, and improvement and less dependency need, and they gave happier endings. With a multiple-choice TAT Horrall (1957) distinguished between high- and low-achieving college freshmen of equated intelligence. Rochlin (1952) found significant attitudinal and trait differences between overachievers and underachievers in mathematics. G. G. Stern (1952) verified his personality model about the characteristics of high- and low-achieving professional school students by means of a projective battery which included the TAT.

In an exploratory study whose conclusions are only suggestive because of the small numbers involved, Hammer (1961) discriminated between creative and facile art students using a combined Rorscharch-TAT. With a larger *N*, G. O. Freed (1961) obtained motivational differences on the TAT between three groups of art students rated for degree of creativity.

Personnel Research

The TAT has sometimes been part of a battery, usually used in conjunction with an interview, for evaluating middle- and upper-echelon personnel in business and industry (e.g., Brower & Weider, 1950; De Ridder, 1961; Harrison & Jackson, 1952; Phelan, 1962).

Henry and Gardner (1949) reported that conclusions derived from the TAT and a personal history form were in agreement with supervisor and peer opinion but failed to give supporting figures. Growing out of this work came a list of distinctive characteristics of successful and unsuccessful executives for which there were again no data, although the traits made psychological sense (Gardner, 1948). In a study on selecting administrative personnel Phelan (1962) got a correlation of .41 between independent TAT and company promotability rankings. After research had been carried out on the determinants of job success, Johannesburg bus drivers were selected from the TAT with 87 per cent success against objective accident and disciplinary criteria (De Ridder, 1961). Arnold's motivation index discriminated between more and less ambitious and successful Federal administrators (Steggert, 1961). A special group TAT, in which members of the group arrived at a story consensus, and in which a sociometric questionnaire was used, successfully selected leaders of an industrial evaluation committee (Rock & Hay, 1953).

The technique has been unsuccessful in predicting for clinical personnel. After some initially encouraging results with psychiatric residents from TAT formal categories and self-interpretation (Luborsky, Holt, & Morrow, 1950), the eventual outcome was a string of insignificant coefficients when TAT variables were correlated with ratings by supervising psychiatrists (Holt, 1958; Holt & Luborsky, 1952; Holt & Luborsky, 1958). The poor showing of projectives, including the TAT, in the VA study on the selection of clinical psychologists is well known (Kelly & Fiske, 1951). Also more a failure than a success was the attempt to predict acceptability of candidates for British Civil Service administrative training (Sen, 1953). The somewhat dubious criterion was agreement with selection board ratings. On the basis of some significant but low correlations Sen felt that the technique showed promise.

Studies on teachers have fared better. From previous research on story characteristics of high- and low-rated teaching sisters in Catholic elementary and secondary schools and by the use of Arnold's sequence analysis, Burkard (1958) secured such nearly perfect separation of the criterion groups as to strain the credibility of skeptical psychologists. The work should be repeated in a more secular setting, not only because of the results obtained, but because of differences in atmosphere and teaching staff in parochial and public schools. With classroom-centered pictures Johnson (1957) and Oelke (1956) obtained favorable results in forecasting teacher proficiency when classroom observation ratings served as the criterion. Significant agreement was found between TAT prediction of classroom behavior of elementary teachers and actual behavior in the classroom (Alexander, 1950). Blind analyses by a TAT specialist did not clearly distinguish adjustment levels of best- and poorest-rated teachers (Ohlsen & Schulz, 1955). The interpreter, however, had not been asked to predict for teaching proficiency. A later content analysis brought out a number of differences between the stories of the two groups. This study seems to have been done backward. Armed with the results of the content analysis, the TAT specialist should have been asked to predict in a cross-validation study.

Research in the social service fields has been generally successful. Quinn (1961) used sequence analysis to predict the adaptability of seminarians to monastic life, as judged by superiors and peers. Correlations were in the neighborhood of .60. In an investigation of camp counselors TAT aggression scores were found to be inversely related to popularity with fellow counselors and competence in handling conflict incidences (McNeil & Cohler, 1958). The personality traits of social service fieldworkers as deduced from TAT were significantly related to ratings for fieldwork competence (S. A. Richardson, 1954). Finally, Semeonoff (1958) found the test promising for selecting marriage counselors; several Wyatt scoring categories significantly discriminated between accepted and rejected candidates.

Military Applications

The TAT was sometimes included in assessment batteries for the screening of officer candidates in the British Army (Vernon & Parry, 1949) and was occasionally employed for difficult cases in OSS (Hanfmann, 1948) during World War II. Probably the earliest military application was the study of men in ROTC whose leadership rankings, based on needs that had previously been shown to relate to leadership, gave a rho of .65 with rankings by superior officers (H. A. Murray & Stein, 1943). In a cross-validation research Newman (1954) obtained significant relationships between TAT authority attitudes and adjustment of airmen in basic training. From the reactions of airmen to combat-relevant pictures Harrower and Grinker (1946) were able to discriminate between men who had suffered from combat fatigue and men who had not.

In another series of cross-validation studies Silverman, Cohen, Zuiderna, and Lazar (1957) predicted with considerable accuracy the reaction of Air Force and student populations to physiological stress (centrifugal force) on the basis of TAT aggressive and dependency responses. This, one of the better personnel predictive studies, was cited by Cronbach (1960) as an example of focused research, inasmuch as the original hypothesis led to the design of aggression-loaded pictures that depicted Air Force situations. In research with Navy personnel the TAT differentiated between submarine school graduates and dropouts (King, 1958) and between offenders and nonoffenders (Petrauskas, 1959).

There are almost as many studies where the results were relatively unproductive. Ossorio and Rigby (1957) could not predict success-failure for Marine officer candidates from TAT conformity responses. In a large-scale research employing many test and assessment techniques with Air Force officers, MacKinnon (1958) obtained significant but low correlations between TAT originality and job proficiency ratings. In this study no test or assessment method did well or could have been expected to do well, since the criteria were highly unreliable. Combat fighters in the Korean conflict with excellent records could not be distinguished from nonfighters who had collapsed under stress on a multiple-choice TAT, but it was possible to sort protocols into two groups on the basis of global evaluation significantly better than chance (Cline, Egbert, Forgy, & Meeland, 1957). Success in the Army Air Forces pilot training program during World War II was not predicted from either scoring or qualitative evaluation of the test (Cerf, 1947). It was pointed out in extenuation that the TAT interpreters were inexperienced and that combat performance would have been more suitable than a training criterion; moreover, none of the needed information about the aspects of personality that were requisite was available.

Examination of the methodology of studies with negative results indicates that the likely cause of failure is some combination of inexperienced examiners, inappropriate scoring, unreliable or ambiguous criteria, and absence of preliminary research on the characteristics of the criterion groups. To be successful personnel research should be focused on target to the extent that the characteristics of the more and less proficient members of an occupation have been determined before deciding on the mode of attack for such a plastic evaluative instrument as the TAT. Where this has been done, the results are more likely to be successful (Burkard, 1958; H. A. Murray & Stein, 1943; Newman, 1954; Silverman et al., 1957). Whether personnel research produces positive or negative results depends mainly on how the research is conducted.

RESEARCH APPLICATIONS

The Thematic Apperception Test has probably made more contributions to academic than to applied research. Often the technique is used in combination with other tests or evaluative methods as a tool of investigation; sometimes it carries the whole burden of the research. There are studies on such diverse topics as the familial inheritance of neurotic patterns (S. Fisher & Mendell, 1956), the need-reduction function of fantasy (Feshbach, 1955), creativity (Pine & Holt, 1960), clothing awareness (Rosencranz, 1960), empathy (Dymond, 1948), personality influences on IQ changes (Kagan, Sontag, Baker, & Nelson, 1958), the attitudes of pregnant women (Fitzpatrick, 1956), the personality of weight lifters (Harlow, 1951), and the adjustment of bilinguals (Spoerl, 1943). The array of studies is too great for comprehensive review; representative examples will be given to indicate the main areas of utilization.

Need Achievement

For more than a decade, a popular field of investigation has been the concern of Atkinson, McClelland, and associates with the conditions of achievement motivation. A severely modified thematic apperceptive method is employed to measure the motive. Subjects in groups write out narrative answers to specific questions about special sets of pictures under instructional conditions which present the test as a measure of intelligence and leadership (McClelland et al., 1953). The need-achievement score (*n* Ach) is a composite of subscores of the achievement imagery shown by story characters—achievement need, goal anticipation, goal-oriented instrumental activity, obstacles, nurturant press, and subjective reactions to success and failure. Need achievement is scored only if there is achievement imagery, which is defined as the presence in stories of the possibility of success in competition with some standard of excellence. Most of the work has been summarized in three volumes—*The Achievement Motive* (McClelland et al., 1953), *Motives in Fantasy, Action, and Society* (Atkinson, 1958), and *The Achieving Society* (McClelland, 1961). In *The Achieving Society* McClelland cites comparative studies which show the operation and importance of *n* Ach in different parts of the world and erects an ambitious theoretical superstructure which on the basis of variations in the achievement motive would explain nothing less than the waxing and waning of nations and civilizations.

A considerable body of empirical data has been gathered which significantly relates *n* Ach to scholastic achievement (Applezweig, Moeller, & Burdick, 1956; McClelland et al., 1953; H. H. Morgan, 1952; H. H. Morgan, 1953; Pierce & Bowman, 1960), learning (Atkinson & Reitman, 1956; Karolchuck & Worrell, 1956; Lowell, 1952), color preference (Knapp, 1958), self-concept (Martire, 1958), memory for incompleted tasks (Atkinson, 1955), risk-taking behavior (Atkinson, 1957), resistance to social pressures (Samuelson, 1958), and linguistic usage (McClelland et al., 1953). It has been correlated also with age (Kagan & Moss, 1959; Veroff et al., 1960), intelligence (McClelland et al., 1953; H. H. Morgan, 1953), education (Veroff, Atkinson, Feld, & Gurin, 1960), social class (Douvan, 1956; B. C. Rosen, 1958; B. C. Rosen, 1959), religion (B. C. Rosen, 1959), occupation (Veroff, 1961; Veroff et al., 1960), race (B. C. Rosen, 1959; Veroff et al., 1960), nationality (McClelland, Sturr, Knapp, & Wendt, 1958; B. C. Rosen, 1959), and physique (Cortés, in McClelland, 1961).

Almost all the research has been performed with male subjects. Female subjects do not usually show an increase in *n* Ach scores under achievement-arousal conditions which stress intelligence and leadership ability as compared with neutral and relaxed conditions of administration (Field, 1951; Lesser, Krawitz, & Packard, 1963; Pierce & Bowman, 1960; Veroff, Wilcox, & Atkinson, 1953). One exception was college women in Brazil (Angelini, 1955), where selective factors operated to make them more competitive than their American counterparts. College women do show an increase in *n* Ach scores when conditions are experimentally manipulated to arouse concern with social acceptance (Field, 1951). High-achieving, bright high school girls showed score increases under achievement-oriented conditions for pictures depicting females, while underachieving girls displayed increased scores only when pictures depicting males were presented (Lesser et al., 1963). The explanations offered for these differences have been in terms of the different social roles assigned to the sexes.

The accomplishments in the need-achievement literature are somewhat offset by several lines of criticism:

1. Many of the correlations of *n* Ach with other forms of behavior are modest.

2. There are also several contradictions in the work of the original or source group (McClelland, 1961; McClelland et al., 1953), which McClelland has tried to dispose of with somewhat elaborate ratiocinations. There is available contrary evidence, for example, on the association of *n* Ach with learning (Birney, 1956; Reitman, 1960) and scholastic achievement (Krumboltz & Farquar, 1957; J. V. Mitchell, 1961; Parrish & Rethlingshafer, 1954). Moreover, many of the conclusions are based on single studies that have never been replicated.

3. There is some problem about reliability. Interscorer reliability and rescorer reliability are usually high (Feld & Smith, 1958; McClelland et al., 1953); split-half reliability gives moderate coefficients (H. H. Morgan, 1953); but retest reliability is unsatisfactory (Krumboltz & Farquar, 1957; McClelland et al., 1953; H. H. Morgan, 1953). McClelland (1958) has given plausible reasons, however, why retest reliability is inappropriate for thematic methods.

4. There is evidence that the *n* Ach score is not a one-dimensional variable but is a conglomerate of two vectors: approach tendencies (hope of success) and avoidance tendencies (fear of failure) (Clark, Teevan, & Ricciuti, 1956; McClelland et al., 1953). Certainly the subscores for negative goal anticipation, negative instrumental acts, and negative affective states should not be part of a measure of a positive, goal-oriented motive. If *n* Ach were purified or stripped of its negative components, possibly correlations with external behavior would rise.

5. Need achievement has little or no relationship with other attempts at measuring or evaluating the achievement motive, such as the Edwards Personal Preference Schedule achievement score, the French Insight Test, self-ratings, clinicians' ratings, sociometry, and various questionnaires and checklists (Bendig, 1957; De Charms, Morrison, Reitman, & McClelland, 1955; Himelstein, Eschenbach, & Carp, 1955; McClelland et al., 1953; Marlowe, 1959; Melikian, 1958; J. V. Mitchell, 1961). This makes it likely, unless all the other measures are invalid, that at best *n* Ach is not more than one aspect of achievement motivation.

Similar approaches have led to the development of scores and validation of such motives as *n* Affiliation (Veroff, 1958a; Veroff, 1958b) and *n* Power (Atkinson, Heyns, & Veroff, 1954; Heyns, Veroff, & Atkinson, 1958; Shipley & Veroff, 1952).

Relation to Overt Behavior

A persistent problem has been the nature of the relationship between the TAT and public or overt behavior. Writers such as Arnold (1962), Bellak (1954b), Feshbach (1961), Kagan (1960), Lazarus (1961), Piotrowski (1950), Sanford (1943), Symonds (1949), and Tomkins (1947) have struggled with the problem and have come up with opinions that are partly in agreement, partly divergent, and partly complementary. There is no question but that under certain circumstances the TAT will be in accord with, or even predictive of, public behavior. The question is rather one of what are the conditions under which we may expect positive relationships, inverse relationships, or no relationships. There is general agreement that if there are cultural prohibitions against the acting out of certain motivational dispositions, they may be expressed in story form but not in overt behavior. What is less clear is whether an overtly satisfied need will be expressed thematically. Apparently sometimes it will, and sometimes not, depending on conditions that are mostly unknown.

While the TAT is rich in personological data, it still is a limited behavioral sample and cannot be expected to reveal a personality in its entirety. Sometimes needs, feelings, and problems are not elicited by the stimuli in the pictures; occasionally a subject who is acutely conscious of antisocial tendencies in himself will deliberately censor their narrative expression. TAT variables that seem to have little correspondence with overt behavior in isolation will often be found congruent with external reality if the stories are evaluated in all their intricate interrelationships, if needs are balanced against defenses, and if motifs are related to context and both are related to outcome. For practical, workaday purposes, biographical and clinical information, even occasionally physiological data (Lazarus, 1961), will help clarify which TAT needs are overt and which are covert.

The earlier information available on the relationship between TAT needs and behavioral expression suggested that the relationship varies with the particular need (H. A. Murray, 1943; Sanford, 1943), is sometimes moderately positive (H. A. Murray, 1943), but is often low (McDowell, 1952; H. A. Murray, 1943; Sanford, 1943; Symonds, 1949). The theory postulated to explain the degree and direction of the correlation was that needs which are socially approved and hence likely to be satisfied will have positive correlations with behavior, while covert needs which are socially disapproved will show zero or negative correlations. The early work is somewhat limited because of its dependence on out-of-context psychometric scoring of needs and is sometimes contradicted by the results of more recent studies which have taken into account anxiety and other defensive inhibitory factors.

Most of the *n* Ach studies that we have reviewed showed significant correlation with achieving behavior. Those students with high dependency imagery on TAT were the most yielding in the Asch conformity situation (Kagan & Mussen, 1956). Patients' reactions to authority figures in stories showed suggestive trends but no significant correlation with cooperative behavior on the ward (Bialick, 1951). Experimentally produced sexual stimulation of male undergraduates increased sexual imagery under the disinhibitory effects of alcohol but decreased sexual imagery under ordinary conditions, presumably because of guilt or other inhibitory influences (R. A. Clark, 1952). Under arousal conditions without benefit of alcohol there was an increase in sexual symbolism (R. A. Clark & Sensibar, 1955). In studies that did not involve experimental manipulation of the drive, TAT manifest sexuality was found directly related to orgasm rate in young men (Epstein & Smith, 1957; Leiman & Epstein, 1961).

The majority of the studies on overt and covert needs have centered around aggression, with most research finding significant, although often complex and sometimes inverse, relationships between aggression in stories and aggression in behavior (Buehler, 1952; Davids, Henry, McArthur, & McNamara, 1955; Goodrich, 1954; Gottfried & Horrocks, 1962; Jensen, 1957; Kagan, 1956; Lesser, 1957; Lesser, 1958b; Mussen & Naylor, 1954; Pittluck, 1950; Purcell, 1956; Starr, 1961; H. Stone, 1956; Tristano, 1953). In a number of investigations on aggression, however, the results have been essentially negative (Gluck, 1955; Heymann, 1956; Holzberg & Posner, 1951; Lindzey & Tejessy, 1956; Scodel & Lipetz, 1957; Takahashi, 1960). Findings are more likely to be positive when measures of thematic aggression stress not frequency of aggression in stories alone but its freedom from such inhibitory influences as guilt and anxiety (Lesser, 1958b; Mussen & Naylor, 1954; Pittluck, 1950; Purcell, 1956) or when the subjects have been reared in environments where aggression is not discouraged (Kagan, 1956; Lesser, 1957; Mussen & Naylor, 1954; H. Stone, 1956). While there has been some enlightenment about the differentials affecting the relationship, there are still unexplained contradictions, and the current state of research does not permit an adequate formulation of why overt aggression and covert aggression are sometimes directly related, sometimes inversely related, and sometimes not related at all.

The whole problem of the relationship of the TAT to external behavior has curiously turned pretty much on the relation of needs to behavior. The TAT is reflective as well as projective, and needs are only a small part of the psychological data that can be extracted from stories. The issue is much broader and relates to traits, abilities, affects, problems, and interests as well as to motives. This chapter is saturated with evidence of correspondence between TAT and extratest behavior in areas other than needs.

Personality Research

The TAT has been used as a tool in research on the personality correlates of perceptual processes (Miner, 1956; Witkin, Dyak, Faterson, Goodenough, & Karp, 1962; Witkin, Lewis, Hertzmann, Machover, Meissner, & Wapner, 1954) and in demonstrating affective influences on perception (Alexander, 1951; Kohn, 1960). Examples of other personological research are studies on the personalities of early- and late-maturing adolescents (M. C. Jones & Mussen, 1958; Mussen & Jones, 1957), the dynamics of aggression

(Holzberg, Bursten, & Santiccioli, 1955), parent-child relations (Gellerman, 1951; Kagan, 1958; Koppitz, 1957; Liccione, 1955), social acceptance (Mill, 1953), self-concept (Faith, 1961; I. Friedman, 1955), and personality determinants of occupational choice (Small, 1953).

The TAT has often been either a part or the focus of research devoted to testing psychoanalytic theories about instinctual drives, complexes, and defenses (e.g., R. A. Clark & Sensibar, 1955; S. M. Friedman, 1952; Groh, 1956; Holzberg et al., 1955; Judson & Wernert, 1958; Kragh, 1959; Mussen & Scodel, 1955; Thurston & Mussen, 1951; Zeichner, 1955; Zeichner, 1956). A curious but not altogether atypical study was the investigation by Scodel (1957) on TAT dependency and somatic preference. Undergraduate males, after taking the TAT, were presented with slides of large and small breasts previously equated for attractiveness. The finding, somewhat disconcerting for the theory, was that dependent males preferred small breasts.

Psychopathology and Medicine

The effects of both individual and group psychotherapy have been evaluated by means of the TAT, which has usually found discernible improvement in the patients (Barr, 1952; F. N. Cox, 1953; Dymond, 1954; Greenwald, 1959; Grummon & John, 1954; Henry & Shlien, 1958). The TAT has also been used to assess the effects of electroshock treatment (Brower & Oppenheim, 1951; Deri, 1947) and prefrontal lobotomy (Ruja, 1951) and to distinguish between improved and unimproved patients after residence in a psychiatric hospital (Goldman & Greenblatt, 1955). The hypnosis card has successfully predicted hypnotizability (S. Sarason & Rosenzweig, 1942; White, 1937), but attempts to foretell the outcome of psychotherapy have led to inconclusive results (Leary, 1957; Levin, 1953).

The picture-story technique has been applied to the determination of personality patterns of patients suffering from orthopedic handicap (Broida, Izard, & Cruickshank, 1950), neurodermatitis (Cleveland & Fisher, 1956), coronary disease and tuberculosis (Cleveland & Johnson, 1962), spastic colitis (Fest & Seward, 1949; Seward, Morrison, & Fest, 1951), asthma (Goodwin, 1949), peptic ulcers (Goodwin, 1949; Marquis, Sinnett, & Winter, 1952), arthritis (Klehr, 1952), poliomyelitis and muscular dystrophy (McCully, 1961), allergies (Saltzman, 1953), and hypertension (Schweers, 1950). Distinctive characteristics were described for each group except the arthritics. Psychogenic invalidism following radical mastectomy could not be predicted from TAT dependency rankings (Bard, 1955), nor could patients diagnosed as suffering from physical disease be separated from psychosomatic patients (Waxenberg, 1955). But in a study using qualitative and quantitative analysis to good effect, Lakin (1957) showed that mothers of colicky infants could be distinguished thematically from mothers of healthy babies.

Several pieces of research have been done around the topic of tuberculosis. Not only have the personalities of tubercular patients been described (Cleveland & Johnson, 1962), but recovery rates (Moran et al., 1956) and ward behavior (S. Fisher & Morton, 1957b) have been predicted from the TAT with some success; and from the thematically expressed attitudes of ward personnel it was possible to tell something about the psychological atmosphere of the wards (S. Fisher & Morton, 1957a). Whether patients would leave the hospital with or without medical approval could not be prognosticated from needs-press scoring (Vernier et al., 1955).

Social Psychology

In social psychology the TAT has contributed to the study, *inter alia,* of the authoritarian personality (Aron, 1950; Frenkel-Brunswik & Sanford, 1945), prejudice (Mussen, 1950; Radke-Yarrow & Lande, 1951), religious and philosophical beliefs (Dreger, 1950; French, 1947), conformity (Mussen, 1958), group dynamics (McPherson, 1952), the effects of war on children (Rautman & Brower, 1945; Rautman & Brower, 1951), the influence of kibbutz and nonkibbutz environments on Israeli adolescents (Rabin, 1961), the psychological aspects of such social institutions as the radio serial (Warner & Henry, 1948) and greeting cards (Henry, 1947a), and the measurement of labor attitudes (Proshansky, 1943).

In addition to the reviewed research on social class, which falls under the heading of either social psychology or sociology, there is a beginning literature concerned with the testing of sociological hypotheses by means of thematic analysis (De Vos, 1960; De Vos & Wagatsuma, 1961; Rose, 1949).

Anthropology

One of the special areas of anthropology—culture and personality—has been invaded by TAT methods. Projective techniques, especially the Rorschach and the TAT, have played a major role in the considerable body of research that has accumulated on the comparison of modal personalities in various, mostly nonliterate, societies. An excellent summary and critique of this work is now available in a recent book by Lindzey (1961). Although both Lindzey and Kaplan (1961) have pointed out a number of difficulties that have been encountered in applying projective techniques to other cultures, including insufficient objectivity and possible contamination effects, these methods have proved fruitful and have established a high degree of agreement between personality descriptions derived from stories told to TAT-like pictures and appraisals from ethnological sources for various American Indian and South Sea Island groups. Projectives were employed to give more depth to intrapsychic description than was possible from the behavioral observations of anthropologists. There have been reports, usually in the form of books and monographs, on the Trukese (Gladwin, 1953; Gladwin & Sarason, 1953), the Navahos (Henry, 1947b; Leighton & Kluckhohn, 1947), the Ojibwa (Caudill, 1949), the Hopi (Henry, 1947b; L. Thompson & Joseph, 1944), the Papago Indians (Joseph, Spicer, & Chesky, 1949), the Ulithians (Lessa & Spiegelman, 1954), and the Pine Ridge Sioux (MacGregor, Hassrick, & Henry, 1946). TAT protocols were usually interpreted independently by psychologists familiar with the test. Where Rorschachs were available, their findings were in agreement with TAT descriptions.

A modified TAT was among the many techniques used in studies on the acculturation of African tribes, as reported in a recent book by Doob (1960). Microcard TAT records are now available for comparative research on peoples of a number of different nationalities and from various nonliterate societies in all parts of the world (Kaplan, 1956–1957).

RELIABILITY

The conventional reliability methods that have been evolved for psychometric tests, such as measures of ability and achievement, cannot be applied in unmodified form to projective techniques like the TAT which are based on entirely different principles. Thus split-half reliability is not suited because, unlike psychometric items, the pictures were designed to yield psychologically different, not equivalent, data. Not only can the pictures not be made to fit into psychologically equivalent pairs, but there are not now available, and are not likely to be available in the future, equivalent sets which could be expected to give the same kind of material.

Regarding the retest method of gauging temporal stability, clinical concern is not with whether the individual over a period of time relates the same narratives but with the significant material that emerges from story analysis. Giving the same pictures to subjects after a short interval creates difficulties in motivation; also, the pictures are not phenomenally the same. McClelland (1958) called attention to the demonstration years ago by Telford (1931) that making an associative response tends to induce resistance to making the same response immediately a second time. Tomkins (1947) must have had something like this in mind when he pointed out that if a person does not appreciate a joke as much when it is told a second time, this does not indicate that the original response was meaningless or was a poor basis for making inferences about the laugher. So if a subject is shown the pictures a day later with instructions to relate the same stories, story consistency will probably be high but will be a test of memory only; if the instructions are to give different stories, story consistency will be much less; and if the instructions are left open, the results will depend on the subject's interpretation of what is expected of him. In neither event is anything meaningful demonstrated about the reliability of the instrument. Moreover, if retesting is done after a considerable interval, the psychological state of the subject is likely to have changed, and what comes out in the form of stories should reflect these changes without being considered unreliable. Moods and feelings, problems and preoccupations, it must be apparent, are subject to more fluctuation than knowledge or abilities. The degree to which these methods are irrelevant will depend on whether the researcher or clinician is employing the TAT as a psychometric instrument or for global analysis. If he scores stories and tries to use the TAT as a psychometric test, then to some extent he must be judged by psychometric standards, even though the split-half and retest methods are not as meaningful as with statistically constructed tests.

Undoubtedly the reliability method that is most applicable to the TAT is interjudge consistency, whether the objects of study are microscopic scores, ratings, or rankings or globally derived macroscopic ratings (Harrison & Rotter, 1945). Interscorer and interrater reliabilities are considered the *sine qua non* for most research purposes. The consistency between different global interpreters is a matter of interest, and agreement among judges is certainly preferable to disagreement, but in the realm of projective techniques low interjudge agreement does not preclude validity. The agreement between two judges may be low because one is accomplished in the art of thematic analysis and the other is not; the inferences of the skillful interpreter may have a high degree of agreement with a validity criterion, while those of the less skilled interpreter do not. There could also be little correspondence between the conclusions of two interpreters with both being correct in their different interpretations, each sampling different aspects of a personality. Something like this has been demonstrated for the clinical case history (Cartwright & French, 1939) and more recently for the TAT (Henry & Farley, 1959). In the TAT study Henry and Farley found only moderate interjudge agreement but a higher degree of agreement between the individual assessments of the several judges and the validating criteria.

Interjudge Reliability

Under this heading will be subsumed studies that compare scores, ratings, and rankings, regardless of whether the judges are operating macroscopically or microscopically. The number of articles is too great for complete documentation.

A survey was undertaken of 62 references that reported interjudge reliability in terms of correlation coefficients. Precise figures cannot be given because many of the reports gave a range of correlations without any indication of central tendency. Approximately four-fifths of all correlations were .70 or above, with most in the .80s and .90s. There was a sprinkling of low coefficients, and one study on the ranking of needs reported an average correlation of .14 (Howard, 1962). Representative figures have been reported by Bard (1955); Bialick (1951); R. E. Bills, Leiman, and Thomas (1950); B. Cox and Sargent (1950); Crandall (1951); Dymond (1954); Eron et al., (1950); Fine (1955b); S. Fisher and Morton (1957b); Fitzgerald (1958); I. Friedman (1955); M. C. Jones and Mussen (1958); Lindzey and Heinemann (1955); B. Lubin (1960); Milam (1954); Sanford (1943); Sarason and Sarason (1958); Scodel (1957); Sen (1953); Waxenberg (1955); Weisskopf and Dunlevy (1952); and Welch (1961).

Thirty-five studies were unearthed which gave results in percentage of agreement between scorers or raters. The agreement was usually between 80 and 90 per cent. Representative reports are those of Aron (1949), Beier (1951), Combs (1946b), Dana (1955), Davids et al. (1956), Epstein and Smith (1956), Garfield et al. (1952), Grummon and John (1954), Jensen (1957), Kagan and Mussen (1956), Liccione (1955), Lindzey et al. (1958), Mussen and Jones (1957), Pittluck (1950), Scodel (1957), and H. Stone (1956).

There is less information available on interjudge reliabilities based on global analyses, and what little there is indicates generally lower consistency (Davenport, 1952; I. Friedman, 1957; Harrison & Rotter, 1945; Kass & Ekstein, 1948; Kelly & Fiske, 1951; Little & Shneidman, 1959; Lyle, Gilchrist, & Groh, 1958). The range is wide—from rs in the .20s (Kelly & Fiske, 1951) to rs in the .70s (I. Friedman, 1957; Harrison & Rotter, 1945). The lower reliabilities might have been anticipated because of semantic difficulties and because greater judgmental demands are made in holistic interpretation than when discrete aspects of stories are singled out for enumeration. Many of the problems of communication could probably be worked out through conferences if we may judge from the experience of the Murray group in raising needs-press scoring reliability to the .90s (Tomkins, 1947).

Intrajudge reliability, or the consistency of rescoring or rerating by the same individual, usually gives agreement between 70 and 95 per cent (Combs, 1946b; Henry & Shlien, 1958; Liccione, 1955; Weisskopf & Dunlevy, 1952). Correlations ran between .60 and .90 (Child, Frank, & Storm, 1956; Feld & Smith, 1958; Greenwald, 1959; Grummon & John, 1954; Sen, 1953), with one exception where a range of .35 to .59 was reported (Little & Shneidman, 1959).

Split-half Reliability

Possibly because of the common recognition that internal consistency as usually calculated is not appropriate for the TAT, there have been relatively few split-half coefficients reported (Bialick, 1951; Calogeras, 1958; Child et al., 1956; Lesser, 1957; Lindzey & Herman, 1955; Sanford, 1943). With the exception of the Child study, which had a range from −.10 to .44, the resulting coefficients fell between .40 and .85. Most of the results were obtained from varying numbers of the Murray cards with needs and press as the usual measure. More pertinent for the problem of internal consistency was the demonstration by Palmer (1952) that persons can be identified from their stories regardless of picture.

Retest Reliability

Five days a week, over a period of ten months, Tomkins (1942) administered a new picture to a single subject. He also gave the entire test three times at three-month intervals and once when the subject was under the influence of alcohol. He found that the main themes all appeared on the first full administration of the test and that in spite of attempts to make the stories different, they reoccurred on subsequent administrations. Other reports, where observations on temporal stability were incidental, have indicated consistency over time but do not give statistical data (R. L. Fisher, 1958; Greenwald, 1959; Symonds & Jensen, 1961).

Where statistics are available, they more often report moderate to high correlations (Lindzey & Herman, 1955; H. H. Morgan, 1953; Tomkins, 1947; Weisskopf & Dunlevy, 1952), but sometimes the consistency is poor (M. O. Bradley, 1957; Krumboltz & Farquar, 1957). The time intervals have usually been weeks, sometimes months, whereas in psychometric studies retesting is usually done a few days apart.

In summary, while generalizations are tenuous because of the overriding importance of the specific conditions in the studies, the more appropriate reliability methods give better results than the less appropriate methods. Interjudge and intrajudge reliabilities are usually fairly satisfactory, while split-half and retest reliabilities are more variable and generally less satisfactory.

VALIDITY

There is no lack of contradictory opinion and evidence on the validity of the TAT. In a recent textbook on testing by Freeman (1962) all the empirical evidence quoted that bears on TAT validity is favorable. In marked contrast, in the fifth edition of *Mental Measurements Yearbook,* one reviewer, after surveying a handful of exclusively negative but atypical studies, writes that "the validity of the TAT is practically nil" and concludes that the test has "low reliability and negligible validity" (Jensen, 1959). These flatly contradictory views are made possible, of course, by judicious selection of evidence and, in the case of the *Yearbook* reviewer, by selecting evidence within articles as well, for in some of his examples the original authors arrived at conclusions at variance with those of the reviewer.

Negative validity results on projective tests like the TAT do not necessarily constitute damaging evidence, for the researchers may have employed improper methods of analysis in confounded designs against unreliable or otherwise inadequate criteria. An analogy may be drawn to a biochemist who successfully synthesizes a drug after others, professionally as qualified, have failed because their methods were not appropriate to the solution of the problem. Another investigator who goes about the task with more finesse and who employs more wisdom in choosing criteria may show clearly that under the specific conditions of his experiment the technique has a specified level of validity. Positive results do demonstrate something, assuming that the work has been done honestly and that grievous errors have not been introduced into the design, but the positive results cannot be generalized from the individual interpreter and the other specific conditions of the study. TAT validity can be discussed meaningfully only when defined operationally in terms of a particular interpreter using particular evaluative procedures with a particular population in a particular design against specified criteria.

The major studies reporting negative results are those of Child et al. (1956), Gilhooly (1952), Little and Shneidman (1959), Meyer and Tolman (1955a), and Samuels (1952). Researches that contain serious negative results intermingled with positive findings are those of Saxe (1950) and Hartman (1949). The latter states his conclusions in terms that are more favorably disposed to the test than examination of his tables would suggest. In all these studies there are serious flaws in the research. They suffer from such multiple defects as inappropriate, usually atomistic, analytical methods (Child et al., 1956; Meyer & Tolman, 1955a); criteria which were unreliable or which otherwise left much to be desired (Child et al., 1956; Gilhooly, 1952; Hartman, 1949; Little & Shneidman, 1959; Meyer & Tolman, 1955a); interpreters who were often inexperienced and unsure of their TAT abilities (Gilhooly, 1952; Samuels, 1952); semantic difficulties and lack of communication between interpreters and criterion judges (Saxe, 1950); contaminated design and artificialities in the procedures which made the full cooperation of the interpreters doubtful (Gilhooly, 1952); and requiring judgments of interpreters when the interpreters did not have adequate TAT data upon which to render judgments (Hartman, 1949; Little & Shneidman, 1959; Samuels, 1952).

The problem of securing adequate validation standards for personality tests is well known. One way of circumventing some of the difficulty is to employ a number of approaches, none of which is fully adequate in itself, and in so doing build up, if the results are uniformly positive, impressive cumulative evidence which will also help define what the test is capable of assessing. In formal terms TAT validity, while it has sometimes involved prediction, is more often of the concurrent and construct types.

Much of the research already reviewed is pertinent to the validity issue and will be referred to only in passing. The studies constitute a form of indirect validation and may be considered a species of construct validity where the construct is the rather broad one of the projection of personality in its many facets through the medium of storytelling. Some examples of indirect validation that have already been documented are the following:

1. TAT findings of sex, age, social class, occupation, and national and racial affiliation are generally similar to what is known from other sources of information.

2. Significant differences have been found between different diagnostic groups.

3. Differential descriptions have been obtained for patients suffering from a wide range of psychosomatic and other medical conditions.

4. Thematic expression of achievement, aggression, and other motives under suitable conditions has been significantly related to behavioral manifestations of these needs.

5. There is concordance with other personality measures in large-scale group research (e.g., Rogers's client-centered therapy evaluation, Witkin's studies on perception and personality, and the California authoritarian personality research).

6. There is demonstration of the psychological effects of psychotherapy and other forms of treatment.

Clinical Criteria

Possibly because of the clinical origins and common usage of the TAT, clinical validation has been most frequently attempted. TAT inferences have been compared with diagnoses, psychiatric hospital case records, and clinical ratings by psychologists, psychiatrists, psychoanalysts, and in some instances diagnostic councils that use several sources of information such as biographical data, interviews, observations, and other tests.

The first quantitative validation was a series of researches carried out at a state hospital in the late 1930s. In one study 40 patients were administered the TAT without prior knowledge on the part of the experimenter. Itemized statements about diagnosis, etiology, intelligence, life history, traits, problems, and interests derived from qualitative story analysis were checked by a collaborator against hospital case records. Eighty-three per cent of the deductions were in agreement, which was significantly better than an empirically determined approximation of chance (Harrison, 1940a). In a second study with 15 patients, where there was no contact of interpreter with patients, accuracy dropped to 75 per cent, which was significantly above chance and marginally different from the figure obtained in the first experiment (Harrison, 1940b). In what was intended to be an exploratory study of clinical usefulness, which aimed at dynamic interpretations in depth, Rotter (1940) found striking agreement when his TAT conclusions were compared with the case records and the opinions of the attending psychiatrists.

Matching methods have often been employed in TAT validation. In the most sophisticated of these investigations Henry and Farley (1959) used a complex matching design recommended by Cronbach (1948) to obviate the usual limitations of matching methods. Nine skilled clinicians were able to do differentiated matching well beyond the .01 level of confidence against an unusually complete multiple criterion based on observations, interviews, and tests. The experiment was the more impressive in that the 36 adolescent subjects were a relatively homogeneous group. In an earlier and simpler matching experiment, staff members who had observed children in their homes, at play, and in interviews were able to identify them from TAT records (Slutz, 1941). Judges were able to match the stories of patients against psychotherapy records far above chance expectations (Miller & Scodel, 1955). Combined Rorschach-TAT appraisals were also matched considerably above chance with counselors' personality sketches (Hire, 1951).

Moderate to high correlations have been obtained between the TAT and improvement rates of schizophrenics (Goldman & Greenblatt, 1955), posthospital adjustment of psychiatric patients (Cowden et al., 1955), psychiatric adjustment ratings of college students (R. D. Cox, 1956), clinicians' ratings of the "alienation syndrome" in students (Davids & Rosenblatt, 1958), adequacy of interpersonal relations as measured by a group therapy scale (Ullmann & McFarland, 1957), and clinicians' personality ratings of scientists (Clifford, 1958). Tumen (1951) obtained 76 per cent agreement between the TAT and a psychoanalyst's findings, but there was internal evidence of a shared Freudian orientation which could have accounted for much of the commonality.

Moving to strictly diagnostic studies, Leunbach and Flachs (1950) obtained predominant agreement with clinical findings in 21 out of 22 psychiatric cases, while the test under conditions of blind analysis effectively separated delinquents from nondelinquents (Lyle & Gilchrist, 1958), mothers of colicky babies from mothers of healthy babies (Lakin, 1957), assaultive from nonassaultive prisoners (H. Stone, 1956), and homosexuals from heterosexuals (Lindzey et al., 1958).

There are many case studies, usually involving single cases, showing agreement with clinical findings (e.g., Baughman, Shands, & Hawkins, 1959; Kass & Ekstein, 1948; Little & Shneidman, 1955; Lyle et al., 1958; D. P. Mitchell, 1949), which obviously carry little weight as scientific evidence. One of the case studies, however, was research-oriented (Little & Shneidman, 1955). From the TAT and MAPS stories of a patient 17 TAT specialists Q-sorted a number of personality items which were also sorted by clinical judges who had access to all the clinical data on the patient. The consensus of judgment by the latter group served as criterion. Validity coefficients ran from .22 to .76, with .61 as the median.

In the majority of investigations reporting positive results, the experimenters have depended on qualitative analysis. When this approach has been used in clinical validation, the ratio of positive to negative results is in the neighborhood of 5:1. Psychometric methods may also be productive of positive results, but the ratio is less favorable. In the case of the best-known of the psychometric procedures, Murray's needs-press scoring and closely related methods, the results when not negative are mixed or indeterminate (R. E. Bills et al., 1950; Calvin & Ward, 1950; Carlile, 1952; Child et al., 1956; Gordon, 1953; Sanford, 1943; Symonds, 1949; Vernier et al., 1955). It is probably asking too much to expect high correlations between complex variables, such as trait ratings from diverse behaviors, and unidimensional thematic scores.

In addition to the clearly negative clinical studies already mentioned (Gilhooly, 1952; Little & Shneidman, 1959; Meyer & Tolman, 1955a; Samuels, 1952),[1] there are several

[1] Samuels's data are from the Michigan VA research project on clinical psychology in which this writer participated. Some of the staff members assigned to TAT assessment were by their own statement relatively inexperienced with the test and performed their duties without confidence. Some of these were later replaced, but not before their appraisals had been incorporated into the permanent pool of records. Moreover, all interpreters were required to fill out ratings for 31 personality traits on all examinees, even though in most instances there were little or no relevant TAT data. Under these conditions it is not surprising that the individual correlations against the criterion (pooled judgment of staff members with access to all information) ran between .21 and .40. Write-ups in which the interpreters could state their conclusions in their own

studies which are ambitendent, being positive in one area and negative in another. Symonds (1949) was not able to show much relationship between psychological and environmental themes (analogous to needs and press) and ratings of adolescents by psychologists and teachers, but in a follow-up study thirteen years later the adolescent themes showed some correspondence with adult behavior (Symonds & Jensen, 1961). Saxe (1950) obtained significant agreement in 10 and nonsignificant agreement in 6 out of 20 cases between TAT evaluation and the opinion of the therapist; conferences between interpreter and therapist showed that disagreement in some cases had been semantic. Hartman (1949) reported low but significant agreement between blind TAT diagnoses and psychologists' and psychiatrists' ratings based on test and interview data for delinquent boys; interjudge reliability of the criterion was only around .40, however. In another part of the same research TAT variables (thematic and formal characteristics) showed higher correlations with personality variables. This promising empirical method of determining extratest correlates of specific TAT characteristics unfortunately has not been sufficiently followed up in subsequent research. It does provide one avenue to removing some of the art in TAT interpretation and introducing more objectivity.

Self-rating Criteria

Autobiography as a criterion will also be considered here. TAT needs correlated as high as .74 with needs rated from autobiographies, according to Combs (1947). Autobiographies may also be matched with TAT analyses considerably better than chance (Holsopple & Phelan, 1954).

Perhaps the most thoroughgoing approach to a comparison of TAT ratings and self-ratings was made by Dymond (1948), who got an average agreement of 83 per cent with the personality self-evaluation of college students. Suggestibility as well as self-knowledge have to be considered in evaluating this study. Forer (1949) showed that undergraduates accepted as characteristic of themselves certain vague, overgeneralized statements, applicable to almost anyone, under the impression that they were their own personality sketches. This study, while intended as a demonstration of human gullibility, is in a sense a study in redundancy because statements that are applicable to everybody would also apply to the students, who should therefore be expected to agree with them. More pertinent is the research by Sundberg (1955), who found that students could not distinguish between their own and faked MMPI personality analyses. There may be some question as to whether MMPI is an ideal test for deriving personality descriptions for college students. Nevertheless, despite these reservations, suggestibility has to be borne firmly in mind in considering self-report studies.

Significant positive results have been obtained between TAT ratings and self-ratings for family attitudes (Calogeras, 1958), self-image (Dymond, 1954), aggression (Lindzey & Tejessy, 1956), and conflict areas (Shulman, 1955). Negative results have been reported by Lindzey and Heinemann (1955) and Child et al. (1956); in both studies, stories were analyzed into discrete motivational and affective categories.

Situational Validity

Situational validity may be construed as a form of construct validity. Various lines of evidence have clearly shown that the TAT is capable of reflecting stable dispositions. The sensitivity of the instrument is further demonstrated if temporary psychological states may also be reflected. In practical testing the disentanglement of what is fleeting from what is stable can create problems for the interpreter, which is one of the reasons why clinicians prefer not to interpret *in vacuo*.

The experimental induction of temporary changes has been carried out by manipulating physiological or social conditions just prior to, or occasionally during, the test administration to produce effects on TAT content for hunger (Atkinson & McClelland, 1948; Sanford, 1936), sex (R. A. Clark, 1952; R. A. Clark &

---

terms were also required but, presumably because of the difficulty of handling them quantitatively, were thereafter disregarded. If the TAT write-ups had been matched against composite write-ups based on all other information on the examinees, more favorable results might have been obtained. This example illustrates not only how validity results depend on the methods employed but also how published accounts of research may be misleading because of the omission of crucial details.

Sensibar, 1955; Mussen & Scodel, 1955), sleep deprivation (E. J. Murray, 1959), achievement (McClelland et al., 1953), affiliation (Atkinson et al., 1954; Shipley & Veroff, 1952), fear (E. L. Walker & Atkinson, 1953), aggression (Bellak, 1944; Crandall, 1951; Lindzey & Kalnins, 1958; MacBrayer, 1959; Matarazzo, 1954; Rodnick, Rubin, & Freeman, 1943), and cumulative frustration (Lindzey & Herman, 1955). Only Epstein and Smith (1956) were unable to demonstrate a thematic effect from food deprivation, but this was because the induced food need was too weak. In some of the studies control and defensive mechanisms operated to produce less rather than more expression of the need (R. A. Clark, 1952; Matarazzo, 1954; E. J. Murray, 1959).

Cross-cultural Criteria

Projective techniques are regarded by some anthropologists as tools for exploring personality structures in other societies in depth. The relationship is also reciprocal; anthropological field data may serve as validating criteria for blind analyses of projective tests when the analyses are performed by psychologists without extensive knowledge of the culture. The approach may be considered another form of concurrent validity.

Henry's early work with Hopi and Navaho children is most frequently quoted and by now may be considered an almost classical example of the method (1947b). Ethnological fieldworkers familiar with the two groups found that the general psychological descriptions of these children deduced from TAT stories as blindly analyzed by Henry were in essential agreement with their knowledge of the societies. In a series of loosely designed small studies the traits of individual children were validated by a matching technique. A high degree of agreement was obtained by judges between blindly analyzed TATs and the ethnologists' personal knowledge of the children, their life histories, and the findings of other projective tests. Henry found, as others have subsequently, that new information was contributed by story analysis.

This was the experience of Gladwin and Sarason (Gladwin, 1953; Gladwin & Sarason, 1953) in their study of the inhabitants of the island of Truk in Micronesia. TATs done independently by the psychologists were congruent with ethnographic and life-history data. Where discrepancies seemed to exist, further investigation confirmed the test and was revealing of new insights. Similar confirmation and accord between TAT and anthropological data were found for the Ojibwa children (Caudill, 1949), children of the Pine Ridge Sioux (MacGregor et al., 1946), and the peoples of Ulithi Atoll in the Caroline Islands (Lessa & Spiegelman, 1954).

Other Criteria

There remains to be considered a miscellaneous collection of criteria involving predictive, concurrent, and construct validity. These include such criteria as school achievement, occupational success, dreams, peer ratings, experiments testing specific TAT hypotheses, and the prediction of specific behaviors. Many of these have been reported before.

One approach involves prediction. Among successful predictions are those for hypnotizability (S. Sarason & Rosenzweig, 1942; White, 1937), classroom behavior of teachers (Alexander, 1950), and, in the case of TB patients, ward behavior (S. Fisher & Morton, 1957b) and the psychological climate of the ward (S. Fisher & Morton, 1957a).

Respectable correlations have been obtained for the prediction of school and college marks (Arnold, 1962; Garvin, 1960; Malpass, 1953), and high and low achievers have been separated by the test (Brown, 1953; Burgess, 1956; Horrall, 1957; McCandlish, 1958; Rochlin, 1952; Snider, 1954; G. G. Stern, 1952).

Abegglen (1958) confirmed his hypotheses about the TAT differences between men who had improved their occupational status over their fathers as compared with men who had shown no upward mobility. The TAT has successfully discriminated between different levels of proficiency in vocations, ranging from teacher to bus driver (Burkard, 1958; De Ridder, 1961; Henry & Gardner, 1949; Johnson, 1957; Oelke, 1956; S. A. Richardson, 1954; Steggert, 1961). There have also been failures, notably with professional clinical personnel (Holt & Luborsky, 1952; Kelly & Fiske, 1951). The attempts at military application, which have already been reviewed, have produced a mixed bag of successes and failures and in general have been plagued by methodological difficulties.

The methods of experimental psychology have been utilized to test hypotheses about the relation of TAT variables to behavior in the laboratory setting. Manifestations of affect and motive on the TAT were significantly related to perceptual thresholds for relevant words or drawings (Alexander, 1951; Ericksen, 1951; Kohn, 1960). Confident behavior on a laboratory task and several TAT variables showed some, but not a highly significant, degree of relationship (Calvin & Ward, 1950).

Dreams and stories are complementary and usually show concordance (Gordon, 1953; Grotz, 1950; S. B. Sarason, 1944; Shulman, 1955). Socially unacceptable problems were revealed more in dreams than in stories (Shulman, 1955); stories showed more the operation of defense mechanisms (Gordon, 1953).

In a matching experiment no success was obtained in matching handwriting with TAT stories (Secord, 1949). Meaningful conclusions about graphology and TAT analysis cannot be drawn from this study because the judges were naïve and both the stories and the handwriting were unanalyzed.

How counselors in a camp for disturbed children handled aggression in their stories was significantly related to sociometric ratings by fellow counselors and to their management of problem behavior of their charges (McNeil & Cohler, 1958). Assessments of constriction by stories and from peer ratings were unrelated for college students (Wohl, 1957).

Tests

Correlation with other personality tests could be considered concurrent validity if there were available any really well-validated personality tests. It is not so considered here because almost no personality test that has been exposed to the fire of empirical validation has come away unburnt. Correlations between TAT and other tests, however, will be summarized in highly condensed form as a matter of minor interest.

TAT needs have consistently showed a lack of relationship with Edwards Personal Preference Schedule needs (Dilworth, 1958; Marlowe, 1959; Silverstein, 1959). Significant correlations, on the other hand, have been reported for other inventories, including the MMPI (Broida, 1954), Kuder Preference (Robbins, 1953), Bell Inventory (Spoerl, 1943), Taylor Manifest Anxiety (Davids & Pildner, 1958; Phares, 1961), and the McFarland-Seitz Psychosomatic Inventory (Davids & Pildner, 1958).

Turning to other projective tests, the TAT does not give findings consistent with the Bender-Gestalt (Samuels, 1952; Wohl, 1957) but does with the Machover Draw-a-Picture Test (Davids & DeVault, 1960; Gallese, 1954; Spoerl, 1943) and usually does with the Rosenzweig Picture-Frustration Study (Lindzey, 1950; Lindzey & Heinemann, 1955; Lindzey & Tejessy, 1956; Petrauskas, 1959; Rosenzweig, 1945). Sometimes there is considerable overlapping with the findings of sentence-completion tests (Carr, 1954; Davids & Pildner, 1958; McGreevey, 1962; Robbins, 1953), and sometimes not (Howard, 1962; Meyer & Tolman, 1955b; Samuels, 1952).

The test that the TAT is compared with most frequently is the Rorschach. Congruence or significant correlation has been reported approximately five times as often as lack of agreement. When the TAT and the Rorschach are treated as a whole, they are more often in agreement than when discrete aspects of the tests are pinched off from the rest. Among the positive and more typical reports are those of Bonner (1949), Carr (1954), Caudill (1949), Davids et al. (1956), Gladwin (1953), Henry (1947b), Hire (1951), Kagan (1961), Murstein (1959), Roe (1949), Shatin (1953; 1955; 1958), and Valentine and Robin (1950a). The most comprehensive and systematic work is that of Shatin. The chief negative reports have come from Dreger (1960), Howard (1962), and Samuels (1952).

Faking

One of the special merits attributed to projective techniques is their relative immunity to deliberate misrepresentation, which is the bane of personality inventories. On the TAT a sophisticated person who is fully aware of a particular problem or conflict may keep it out of his stories by conscious intent but will often reveal his defensive handling of the conflict, and many times during the course of a full-scale test he will be unable to sustain his defenses sufficiently to keep the problem from finding at least indirect expression.

Weisskopf and Dieppa (1951) showed that hospitalized veterans could influence their stories in a favorable or unfavorable direction, so that the diagnostic conclusions of TAT interpreters were affected on some but not on all personality dimensions. Only three pictures were used, so there is some question as to whether the subjects could have consistently faked for a full test.

Dunlevy (1953) obtained the same results when examiners were unaware of the purpose of the experiment. When they were forewarned that some subjects were trying to make more, and others less, favorable impressions, they were able to detect stories told under the different instructions with some success. These conditions are closer to those in practical testing, where test behavior and circumstances surrounding the test, as well as biographical data, all combine to alert the examiner to possibilities of misrepresentation.

Davids and Pildner (1958) administered inventories and self-rating scales as well as projectives to two groups of college students. One group was taking tests as part of an actual job application, the other as participants in a research project. The job applicants obtained significantly better adjustment scores than the research subjects on self-reporting devices but not on the TAT and other projective tests. The real question is whether persons in naturalistic situations often attempt to fake projectives and whether they succeed rather than whether faking can be done under artificial laboratory conditions.

Ni (1959) was able to detect attempts at concealment for six college students from blind analysis. Reznikoff (1961) showed that social desirability does not determine frequency of TAT themes. Tomkins's marathon storyteller, even when he tried to relate different stories, still came out with similar psychological material (1942).

A conservative conclusion at this stage would seem to be that while some faking is possible under laboratory conditions, it is less likely to occur and is more difficult to execute under ordinary testing conditions.

To summarize TAT validity, there is impressive evidence that the technique possesses intrinsic validity. When on occasion empirical findings suggest otherwise, the explanation is usually to be found in methods of analysis, criteria, or experimental conditions that are inappropriate. The clinician or experimenter is and probably will continue to be an inseparable part of what is not too aptly called the Thematic Apperception Test. The "test" is still a test of the tester.

OTHER PICTURE-STORY TESTS

The variations of the present TAT pictures have proliferated too extensively for complete enumeration. While many of the variations are justified by the requirements of particular research, a bandwagon psychology has also operated, so that some of the modifications introduced for general consumption appear to be exercises in novelty for the sake of novelty.

Over sixty sets of pictures have been published or referred to in research articles. These include pictures structured for use in vocational guidance (Ammons, 1950) and executive appraisal (Henry & Moore, 1956); in measuring aggression (Lesser, 1958a) and achievement need (McClelland et al., 1953); in studying attitudes toward school (Malpass, 1953) and toward authority (Newman, 1954); and in exploring adult-child relations (Alexander, 1952), Freudian complexes (S. M. Friedman, 1952), patient-therapist relations (Lebo & Harrigan, 1957), prejudice (Johnson, 1950), and small group interaction (Henry & Guetzkow, 1951). Also there is a sound moving-picture TAT (McIntyre, 1954); a color TAT (C. E. Thompson & Bachrach, 1951); a clothing TAT (Rosencranz, 1960); a verbal TAT, where word descriptions are substituted for pictures (Lebo & Harrington, 1957); an auditory TAT, where stories are related to a miscellany of sounds (D. R. Stone, 1950); and even a negative TAT, where the subject is required to make up the most unlikely stories possible for the pictures (R. M. Jones, 1956). Special pictures have been developed for preschool children (Amen, 1941), older children (Andrew, Hartwell, Hutt, & Walton, 1953), crippled children (Bachrach & Thompson, 1949), Mexican rural children (Shore, 1954), adolescents (Symonds, 1949), Negroes (C. E. Thompson, 1949a), Navy enlisted men (Briggs, 1954), American Indians (Henry, 1947b), South Sea Islanders (Lessa & Spiegelman, 1954), Asiatic Indians (Chowdhury, 1960), and the Japanese (Marui, 1960).

Several of the modifications are distinct tests and require separate mention. The only ones that have any appreciable literature or popularity are the MAPS and the CAT (Sundberg, 1961). For fuller treatment of the individual tests the reader is referred to the fourth and fifth editions of *Mental Measurements Yearbook* (Buros, 1953; Buros, 1959).

Make-a-Picture-Story

This do-it-yourself version of the TAT (Shneidman, 1952; Shneidman, 1960) is the next most popular among the picture-story tests. The subject not only relates stories in the usual way but helps construct his own pictures by selecting one or more of 67 cutout (human and animal) figures and placing them on background pictures selected by the examiner. For clinical purposes 10 background pictures are recommended. A figure location sheet is provided to record choice and placement of figures. There is some evidence that figures are more important in influencing stories than backgrounds (Charen, 1954). Proponents claim that the MAPS has more subject appeal than the TAT and adds a new dimension to storytelling with additional possibilities for formal analysis.

The author is eclectic about scoring and interpretation, although he suggests proceeding in three stages: story-by-story analysis, area-by-area analysis, and finally a synthesis of the two into an integrated summary report. There are as many ways of interpreting the MAPS as there are in interpreting the TAT, for almost any TAT method is applicable. In addition there are many possible formal categories relating to the selection of figures. Standardization is difficult because of the nature of the task, but some preliminary data have been accumulated on differences in choice and placement of figures (Conant, 1950; Farberow, 1950; Fine, 1948; Joel, 1948).

The formal features attendant upon choice and placement of figures offer possibilities for differential diagnosis that are not present in the TAT. Thus on the case that was blindly analyzed by a number of specialists the schizophrenic thinking disorder was more apparent on the MAPS (Shneidman, 1951). When put to the test, however, the formal categories produced only fair discrimination between schizophrenics and normals (Shneidman, 1948). Clinical studies have been carried out with neurotics, schizophrenics, and normals (Conant, 1950); female homosexuals (Ferracuti & Rizzo, 1958); disturbed adolescents (Joel, 1948); deaf children (Bindon, 1957); asthmatic children (Fine, 1948); suicidal mental hospital patients (Farberow, 1950); and children in a guidance clinic (Spiegelman, 1956).

The manual reports no data on reliability or validity. The Little and Shneidman study (1959) gave distressing figures on reliability and validity, but there were serious methodological difficulties with this study, so that the findings cannot be accepted at face value. Results from the single case in the Shneidman symposium were more favorable (Little & Shneidman, 1955). Encouraging agreement was reported when comparisons were made with classroom behavior (Smith & Coleman, 1956) and therapists' opinions (Walker, 1951).

Children's Apperception Test

This test, intended for children from ages 3 to 10, consists of pictures in which all the characters are animals (Bellak, 1954b; Bellak & Bellak, 1952). The pictures show the animal characters in very humanlike situations. They are supposed to evoke reactions to what Freudian theory considers universal problems in early development—orality, oedipal complex, primal scene, masturbation, toilet training, sibling rivalry, aggression, and the like. Possibly as a reaction to criticisms that such common childhood situations as school and play had been overlooked, a supplement to the Children's Apperception Test (CAT-S) is now on the market. The interpretation follows roughly the dynamic principles utilized by Bellak for the TAT. The same manual is available as a practical guide (Bellak, 1954b). A survey of research on the test has recently been published (Bellak & Adelman, 1960).

There are some tentative normative data on preschool children (Byrd & Witherspoon, 1954) and on children ages 6 to 9 (Ginsparg, 1957) and 3 to 10 (Rosenblatt, 1958). Developmental and sex differences have been noted. Socio-economic class influences are said to be negligible (Lehman, 1959). The test has been used in studying twin differences (Magnusson, 1960) and children who are emotionally disturbed (Kanehira, 1958), schizophrenic (Gurevitz & Klapper, 1951), cerebral-palsied (Gurevitz & Klapper, 1951; Holden, 1956), or speech-handicapped (FitzSimons, 1958). Except for one small study which gave inconclusive results (R. E. Bills et al., 1950), there is practically no information available on validity or reliability.

Bellak's assumption that young children identify readily with animals and would be less defensive and hence more productive on animal than on human pictures has been more or less disproved. Only R. E. Bills (1950) reported confirmation of the notion, but his animal and human pictures were not equated for situation. Other research has found either no difference in productivity (Biersdorf & Marcuse, 1953; Boyd & Mandler, 1955; Ouchi, 1957) or superiority of the human pictures (Armstrong, 1954; Budoff, 1955; Furuya, 1957; Light, 1954; Mainord & Marcuse, 1954). Although this would seem to undermine the main reason for the test's existence, not only is it used in the United States, but it has gained popularity in Europe and Japan. Lehman (1959) has criticized the CAT because the pictures give an undue number of oral themes and do not elicit the dynamics that they are supposed to elicit.

Michigan Picture Test

Influenced by reports that the TAT was not entirely suitable for children, the Michigan Department of Mental Health undertook a careful and systematic attempt at selecting and standardizing a set of pictures for evaluating emotional adjustment in children between the ages of 8 and 14 (Andrew et al., 1953; Hartwell, Hutt, Andrew, & Walton, 1951). Each child is given 12 common and four sex-specific pictures. Interscorer and normative data are available. The scoring system, which is concerned with such variables as psychological needs, verb tense, personal pronouns, activity-passivity of the hero, psychosexual level, and interpersonal relations, has thus far showed only partial and, in proportion to the effort expended, somewhat disappointing discrimination between well-adjusted and poorly adjusted children.

The stories are of course amenable to analytical procedures other than those proposed by the authors. The pictures, which are realistic and cover many important aspects of children's lives, are rather good and are vastly superior to the Symonds set. They should be given more of a trial than they have so far received—perhaps divorced from the Michigan scoring system.

Thompson Thematic Apperception Test

C. E. Thompson (1949b) adduced some evidence that Negroes identify more and are more productive when Negro figures are substituted on the Murray cards. In his modification (C. E. Thompson, 1949a) the pictures were changed by giving the figures dark skins and negroid features, but they differ from other modifications designed for cross-cultural studies in that Thompson did not create situations and activities that are appropriate to the group.

Later studies with both Northern and Southern Negroes and with white subjects have failed to show any significant difference between the T-TAT and the standard TAT on measures of productivity and ego defensiveness (Cook, 1953; Klein, 1956; Light, 1955; Riess, Schwartz, & Cottingham, 1950; Schwartz, Riess, & Cottingham, 1951). Subjective reports indicate that Negroes are more inclined to identify with white figures than whites are to identify with Negro figures (Cook, 1953). There is suggestive evidence that the T-TAT can be used with whites as an indication of attitudes toward Negroes, but where Negro prejudice exists idiosyncratic projection is impaired (Light, 1955). Research interest in the test has died down in recent years.

Symonds Picture-Story Test

This set of 20 pictures is designed for use with adolescent boys and girls (Symonds, 1948). The cards depict a wide variety of situations and interpersonal relationships common to the age group. The wash drawings are the work of the same artist and show great uniformity not only of style but unfortunately of tone and facial expression as well. They are almost all gloomy, morose, and mournful. There is no evidence that they produce richer stories than the Murray set.

Symonds analyzed stories told to his set of pictures in terms of psychological and environmental themes (such as needs and press), but they are susceptible to other modes of interpretation. The author employed the test as the mainspring of a full-scale investigation of 40 adolescent boys and girls (Symonds, 1949), some of whom were followed into maturity (Symonds & Jensen, 1961). These two books account for almost all the publication available on the test.

Four Picture Test

The Four Picture Test consists of four ambiguous colored pictures which show figures both alone and in groups (Van Lennep, 1948; Van Lennep, 1951). The task is to relate, either orally or in writing, one continuous story integrating the separate pictures. Analysis is done on both content and form, with the content analysis following that of the TAT. There are certain formal dimensions, especially in the use of time and space, which either are not possible on the TAT or are generally ignored. Because there is only one story and much is lost by way of repetitive patterns, it gives less information than a full TAT. No norms or statistical validation has yet been published in English, but validation and norms are promised for a definitive publication in the future. The author is said to have spent many years in developing the test before publishing.

Object-relations Technique

This test consists of three sets of four pictures and a blank card (Phillipson, 1955). It is based on the theories of the British object-relations psychoanalytic school but may be used by those of other theoretical persuasions. The four pictures of each series are designed to elicit characteristic modes of reaction to one person or to two, three, or a group of persons. One series is done in charcoal shading and is highly ambiguous; another contains heavy shading like a silhouette; and the third uses pastel colors and is more structured. Theoretical significance is said to attach to the way each series is done.

Except for frequency of response norms for small atypical groups, the test is strictly clinical in approach. The author does not face up to problems of reliability and validity. Although the test met with a rather favorable reception when it first appeared, it has subsequently attracted little attention and has almost no literature.

REFERENCES

Abegglen, J. C. Personality factors in social mobility: a study of occupationally mobile businessmen. *Genet. Psychol. Monogr.*, 1958, **58**, 101–159.

Abel, Theodora M. Responses of the Negro and white morons to the Thematic Apperception Test. *Amer. J. ment. Def.*, 1945, **49**, 463–468.

Alexander, T. The prediction of teacher-pupil interaction with a projective test. *J. clin. Psychol.*, 1950, **6**, 273–276.

Alexander, T. A study of perception as influenced by conflict. *Amer. Psychologist*, 1951, **6**, 312.

Alexander, T. The adult-child interaction test. *Monogr. soc. Res. Child Develpm.*, 1952, **17**, No. 17 (2) (Ser. No. 55).

Amen, Elizabeth W. Individual differences in apperceptive reaction: a study of the response of preschool children to pictures. *Genet. Psychol. Monogr.*, 1941, **23**, 319–385.

Ammons, R. B. A projective test for vocational research and guidance at the college level. *J. appl. Psychol.*, 1950, **34**, 198–205.

Andrew, Gwen, Hartwell, S. W., Hutt, M. L., & Walton, R. E. *Michigan Picture Test.* Chicago: Science Research Associates, 1953.

Angelini, A. L. Un novo método para avaliar a motivação humano. *Bol. Fac. Filos. Cienc. S. Paulo*, 1955, No. 207. Cited by Lesser, Krawitz, & Packard, 1963.

Applezweig, M. H., Moeller, G., & Burdick, H. Multi-motive prediction of academic success. *Psychol. Rep.*, 1956, **2**, 489–496.

Armstrong, Mary A. S. Children's responses to animal and human figures in thematic pictures. *J. consult. Psychol.*, 1954, **18**, 67–70.

Arnold, Magda B. A demonstration analysis of the TAT in a clinical setting. *J. abnorm soc. Psychol.*, 1949, **44**, 97–111.

Arnold, Magda B. *Story sequence analysis.* New York: Columbia Univer. Press, 1962.

Aron, Betty. *A manual for analysis of the Thematic Apperception Test: a method and technique for personality research.* Berkeley, Calif.: Willis E. Berg, 1949.

Aron, Betty. The Thematic Apperception Test in the study of prejudiced and unprejudiced individuals. In T. W. Adorno, Else Frenkel-Brunswik, D. J. Levinson, & R. N. Sanford. *The authoritarian personality.* New York: Harper & Row, 1950. Pp. 489–544.

Atkinson, J. W. The achievement motive and recall of interrupted and completed tasks. In D. C. McClelland (Ed.), *Studies in motivation.* New York: Appleton-Century-Crofts, 1955. Pp. 494–506.

Atkinson, J. W. Motivational determinants of risk-taking behavior. *Psychol. Rev.*, 1957, **64**, 359–372.

Atkinson, J. W. (Ed.) *Motives in fantasy, action, and society.* Princeton, N.J.: Van Nostrand, 1958.

Atkinson, J. W., Heyns, R. W., & Veroff, J. The effect of experimental arousal of the affiliation motive on thematic apperception. *J. abnorm. soc. Psychol.*, 1954, **49**, 405–410.

Atkinson, J. W., & McClelland, D. C. The projective expression of needs. II. The effect of different intensities of the hunger drive on thematic apperception. *J. exp. Psychol.*, 1948, **38**, 643–658.

Atkinson, J. W., & Reitman, W. R. Performance as a function of motive strength and expectancy of goal-attainment. *J. abnorm. soc. Psychol.*, 1956, **53**, 361–366.

Auld, F., Jr. Contributions of behavior theory to projective testing. *J. proj. Tech.*, 1954, **18**, 421–426.

Auld, F., Jr., Eron, L. D., & Laffal, J. Application of Guttman's scaling method to the T.A.T. *Educ. psychol. Measmt.*, 1955, **15**, 422–435.

Bachrach, A. J., & Thompson, C. E. *Thematic Apperception Test: modification for the handicapped (experimental set)*. Cleveland: Society for Crippled Children, 1949.

Balken, Eva R. A delineation of schizophrenic language and thought in a test of imagination. *J. Psychol.*, 1943, **16**, 239–271.

Balken, Eva R., & Masserman, J. H. The language of phantasy. III. The language of the phantasies of patients with conversion hysteria, anxiety state, and obsessive-compulsive neuroses. *J. Psychol.*, 1940, **10**, 75–86.

Balken, Eva R., & Vander Veer, Adrian. The clinical application of a test of imagination to neurotic children. *Amer. J. Orthopsychiat.*, 1942, **12**, 68–80.

Balken, Eva R., & Vander Veer, Adrian. Clinical application of the Thematic Apperception Test to neurotic children. *Amer. J. Orthopsychiat.*, 1944, **14**, 421–440.

Bard, M. The use of dependence for predicting psychogenic invalidism following radical mastectomy. *J. nerv. ment. Dis.*, 1955, **122**, 152–160.

Barr, L. Changes in personality measures resulting from participation of college students in group-centered psychotherapy. *Amer. Psychologist,* 1952, **7**, 529–530.

Baughman, E. E., Shands, H. C., & Hawkins, D. R. Intensive psychotherapy and personality change: psychological test evaluation of a single case. *Psychiatry,* 1959, **22**, 296–301.

Beier, E. G., Gorlow, L., & Stacey, C. L. The fantasy life of the mental defective. *Amer. J. ment. Def.*, 1951, **55**, 582–589.

Beigel, H. G. The influence of body position on mental processes. *J. clin. Psychol.*, 1952, **8**, 193–199.

Bell, J. E. *Projective techniques: a dynamic approach to the study of personality.* New York: Longman, Green, 1948.

Bellak, L. The concept of projection: an experimental investigation and study of the concept. *Psychiatry,* 1944, **7**, 353–370.

Bellak, L. The Thematic Apperception Test in clinical use. In L. E. Abt & L. Bellak (Eds.), *Projective psychology: clinical approaches to the total personality.* New York: Knopf, 1950. Pp. 185–229.

Bellak, L. A study of limitations and "failures": toward an ego psychology of projective techniques. *J. proj. Tech.*, 1954, **18**, 279–293. (a)

Bellak, L. *The Thematic Apperception Test and the Children's Apperception Test in clinical use.* New York: Grune & Stratton, 1954. (b)

Bellak, L. Freud and projective techniques. *J. proj. Tech.*, 1956, **20**, 5–13.

Bellak, L., & Adelman, Crusa. The Children's Apperception Test (CAT). In A. I. Rabin & Mary R. Haworth (Eds.), *Projective techniques with children.* New York: Grune & Stratton, 1960. Pp. 62–94.

Bellak, L., & Bellak, Sonya S. *Children's Apperception Test.* New York: C.P.S. Co., 1952.

Bellak, L., & Ort, Eileen. The Thematic Apperception Test and other apperceptive methods. In D. Brower & L. E. Abt (Eds.), *Progress in clinical psychology.* Vol. 1. New York: Grune & Stratton, 1952. Pp. 149–172.

Bellak, L., Pasquarelli, B. A., & Braverman, S. The use of the Thematic Apperception Test in psychotherapy. *J. nerv. ment. Dis.*, 1949, **110**, 51–65.

Bendig, A. W. Manifest anxiety and projective and objective measures of need achievement. *J. consult. Psychol.*, 1957, **21**, 354.

Bergman, M., & Fisher, Louise A. The value of the Thematic Apperception Test in mental deficiency. *Psychiat. Quart. Suppl.*, 1953, **27**, 22–42.

Bernstein, L. The examiner as an inhibiting factor in clinical testing. *J. consult. Psychol.*, 1956, **20**, 287–290.

Bettelheim, B. Self-interpretation of fantasy: the Thematic Apperception Test as an educational and therapeutic device. *Amer. J. Orthopsychiat.*, 1947, **17**, 80–100.

Bialick, I. The relationship between reactions to authority figures on the T.A.T. and overt behavior in an authority situation by hospital patients. Unpublished doctoral dissertation, Univer. of Pittsburgh, 1951.

Biersdorf, Kathryn R., & Marcuse, F. L. Responses of children to human and to animal pictures. *J. proj. Tech.*, 1953, **17**, 455–459.

Bijou, S. W., & Kenny, D. T. The ambiguity values of TAT cards. *J. consult. Psychol.*, 1951, **15**, 203–209.

Bills, N. The personality structure of alcoholics, homosexuals, and paranoids as revealed by their responses to the Thematic Apperception Test. Unpublished doctoral dissertation. Western Reserve Univer., 1953.

Bills, R. E. Animal pictures for obtaining children's projections. *J. clin. Psychol.*, 1950, 6, 291–293.

Bills, R. E., Leiman, C. J., & Thomas, R. W. A study of the validity of the TAT and a set of animal pictures. *J. clin. Psychol.*, 1950, **6**, 293–295.

Bindon, D. Marjorie. Make-a-Picture Story (MAPS) Test findings for rubella deaf children. *J. abnorm. soc. Psychol.*, 1957, **55**, 38–42.

Binet, A., & Henri, V. Psychologie individuelle. *Année psychol.*, 1896, **3**, 296–332.

Birney, R. C. Experimenter effect on the achievement motive. Unpublished paper, Amherst College, 1956. Cited by Reitman, 1960.

Bloom, B. L. Psychological services and professional problems in the field of mental deficiency. *J. consult. Psychol.*, 1952, **16**, 187–192.

Bonner, Barbara H. A comparison of fantasy on the Rorschach and the TAT. Unpublished master's thesis, Purdue Univer., 1949.

Boyd, Nancy A., & Mandler, G. Children's responses to human and animal stories and pictures. *J. consult. Psychol.*, 1955, **19**, 367–371.

Brackbill, G. A. Some effects of color on thematic fantasy. *J. consult. Psychol.*, 1951, **15**, 412–418.

Brackbill, G. A., & Brackbill, Betty J. Some effects of age on TAT stories. *Amer. Psychologist*, 1951, **6**, 351.

Bradley, J. E., & Lysaker, R. L. *Ambiguity as a variable in the use of a projective technique.* Minneapolis, Minn.: Pillsbury Mills. Cited by Murstein, 1959. (Mimeographed)

Bradley, Mary O. The test-retest reliability of the Thematic Apperception Test. Unpublished master's thesis, Fordham Univer., 1957.

Brayer, R., Craig, Grace, & Teichner, W. Scaling difficulty values of TAT cards. *J. proj. Tech.*, 1961, **25**, 272–276.

Briggs, D. L. A modification of the Thematic Apperception Test for Naval enlisted personnel. *J. Psychol.*, 1954, **37**, 233–241.

Brittain, H. L. A study in imagination. *Ped. Sem.*, 1907, **14**, 137–207.

Broida, D. C. An investigation of certain psychodiagnostic indications of suicidal tendencies and depression in mental hospital patients. *Psychiat. Quart.*, 1954, **28**, 453–464.

Broida, D. C., Izard, C. E., & Cruickshank, W. M. Thematic apperception reactions of crippled children. *J. clin. Psychol.*, 1950, **6**, 243–248.

Brower, D., & Oppenheim, Sadi. The effects of electroshock therapy on mental functions as revealed by psychological tests. *J. gen. Psychol.*, 1951, **45**, 171–188.

Brower, D., & Weider, A. Projective techniques in business and industry. In L. E. Abt & L. Bellak (Eds.), *Projective psychology: clinical approaches to the total personality*. New York: Knopf, 1950. Pp. 437–461.

Brown, J. E. Personality dynamics of high and low academic achievers in high school; a modified Thematic Apperception Test reliability study. Unpublished master's thesis, St. Louis Univer., 1953. Cited by Arnold, 1962.

Budoff, M. An investigation of the relative usefulness of animals and persons in a picture-story test for children. Unpublished master's thesis, Univer. of Chicago, 1955. Cited by W. E. Henry, Projective techniques. In P. H. Mussen (Ed.), *Handbook of research methods in child development.* New York: Wiley, 1960.

Buehler, R. E. An investigation of relationships between motivation and interaction behavior in small groups. *Amer. Psychologist*, 1952, **7**, 314.

Burgess, Elva. Personality factors of over- and under-achievers in engineering. *J. educ. Psychol.*, 1956, **47**, 89–99.

Burkard, Mary I. Characteristic differences determined by TAT sequential analysis between teachers rated by their pupils at the extremes in teaching efficiency. Unpublished doctoral dissertation, Loyola Univer., Chicago, 1958. Cited by Arnold, 1962.

Buros, O. K. (Ed.) *Fourth mental measurements yearbook.* Highland Park, N.J.: Gryphon Press, 1953.

Buros, O. K. (Ed.) *Fifth mental measurements yearbook.* Highland Park, N.J.: Gryphon Press, 1959.

Burton, A. The use of psychometric and projective tests in clinical psychology. *J. Psychol.*, 1949, **28**, 451–456.

Byrd, E., & Witherspoon, L. Responses of preschool children to the Children's Apperception Test. *Child Develpm.*, 1954, **25**, 35–44.

Calogeras, R. C. Some relationships between fantasy and self-report behavior. *Genet. Psychol. Monogr.*, 1958, **58**, 273–325.

Calvin, J. S., & Ward, L. C. An attempted experimental validation of the Thematic Apperception Test. *J. clin. Psychol.*, 1950, **6**, 377–381.

Canter, F. M. Personality factors in seizure states with reference to the Rosenzweig triadic hypothesis. *J. consult. Psychol.*, 1953, **17**, 429–435.

Carlile, J. S. The Thematic Apperception Test applied to neurotic and normal adolescent girls. *Brit. J. med. Psychol.*, 1952, **25**, 244–248.

Carlson, H. B., & Vandever, Marguerite. The effectiveness of directive and non-directive counseling in vocational problems as measured by the T.A.T. test. *Educ. psychol. Measmt*, 1951, **11**, 212–223.

Carr, A. C. Intra-individual consistency in response to tests of varying degrees of ambiguity. *J. consult. Psychol.*, 1954, **18**, 251–258.

Cartwright, D., & French, J. R. P., Jr. The reliability of life-history studies. *Charact. & Pers.*, 1939, **8**, 110–119.

Caudill, W. Psychological characteristics of acculturated Wisconsin Ojibwa children. *Amer. Anthropologist*, 1949, **51**, 409–427.

Caudill, W. Japanese-American personality and acculturation. *Genet. Psychol. Monogr.*, 1952, **45**, 61–102.

Caudill, W., & De Vos, G. Achievement, culture and personality: the case of the Japanese American. *Amer. Anthropologist*, 1956, **58**, 1102–1126.

Cerf, A. Z. The Thematic Apperception Test, CE 706A. In J. P. Guilford (Ed.), *Printed classification tests.* Washington, D.C.: U.S. Government Printing Office, 1947. Pp. 637–645.

Chapin, N. A dynamic approach to the TAT. *Psychiat. Quart. Suppl.*, 1953, **27**, 62–89.

Charen, S. The interaction of background and characters in picture test story telling. *J. clin. Psychol.*, 1954, **10**, 290–292.

Child, I. L., Frank, Kitty F., & Storm, T. Self-ratings and TAT: their relations to each other and to childhood background. *J. Pers.*, 1956, **25**, 96–114.

Chipman, Catherine E. Psychological variation within a homogeneous psychometric group. *Amer. J. ment. Def.*, 1946, **51**, 195–205.

Chowdhury, U. An Indian modification of the Thematic Apperception Test. *J. soc. Psychol.*, 1960, **51**, 245–263.

Clark, R. A. The projective measurement of experimentally induced levels of sexual motivation. *J. exp. Psychol.*, 1952, **44**, 391–399.

Clark, R. A., & Sensibar, Minda R. The relationship between symbolic and manifest projections of sexuality with some incidental correlates. *J. abnorm. soc. Psychol.*, 1955, **50**, 327–334.

Clark, R. A., Teevan, R., & Ricciuti, H. N. Hope of success and fear of failure as aspects of need for achievement. *J. abnorm. soc. Psychol.*, 1956, **53**, 182–186.

Clark, Ruth M. A method of administering and evaluating the Thematic Apperception Test in group situations. *Genet. Psychol. Monogr.*, 1944, **30**, 3–55.

Cleveland, S. E., & Fisher, S. Psychological factors in the neurodermatoses. *Psychosom. Med.*, 1956, **18**, 209–220.

Cleveland, S. E., & Johnson, D. L. Personality patterns in young males with coronary disease. *Psychosom. Med.*, 1962, **24**, 600–610.

Clifford, P. I. Emotional contacts with the external world manifested by a selected group of highly creative chemists and mathematicians. *Percept. mot. Skills*, 1958, **8**, 3–26.

Cline, V. B., Egbert, R., Forgy, E., & Meeland, T. Reactions of men under stress to a picture projective test. *J. clin. Psychol.*, 1957, **13**, 141–144.

Coleman, W. The Thematic Apperception Test. I. Effects of recent experience. II. Some quantitative observations. *J. clin. Psychol.*, 1947, **3**, 257–264.

Combs, A. W. A method of analysis for the Thematic Apperception Test and autobiography. *J. clin. Psychol.*, 1946, **2**, 167–174. (a)

Combs, A. W. The validity and reliability of interpretation from autobiography and Thematic Apperception Test. *J. clin. Psychol.*, 1946, **2**, 240–247. (b)

Combs, A. W. A comparative study of motivations as revealed in thematic apperception stories and autobiography. *J. clin. Psychol.*, 1947, **3**, 65–75.

Conant, J. C. A comparison of thematic fantasy among normals, neurotics, and schizophrenics. Unpublished doctoral dissertation, Univer. of Southern California, 1950.

Cook, R. A. Identification and ego defensiveness in thematic apperception. *J. proj. Tech.*, 1953, **17**, 312–319.

Cowden, R. C., Deabler, H. L., & Feamster, J. H. The prognostic value of the Bender-Gestalt, H-T-P, TAT, and sentence completion test. *J. clin. Psychol.*, 1955, **11**, 271–275.

Cox, Beverly, & Sargent, Helen D. The common responses of normal children to ten pictures of the Thematic Apperception Test series. *Amer. Psychologist*, 1948, **3**, 363.

Cox, Beverly, & Sargent, Helen D. TAT responses of emotionally disturbed and emotionally stable children: clinical judgment versus normative data. *J. proj. Tech.*, 1950, **14**, 61–74.

Cox, F. N. Sociometric status and individual adjustment before and after play therapy. *J. abnorm. soc. Psychol.*, 1953, **48**, 354–356.

Cox, Rachel D. The normal personality: an analysis of Rorschach and Thematic Analysis Test responses of a group of college students. *J. proj. Tech.*, 1956, **20**, 70–77.

Crandall, V. J. Induced frustration and punishment-reward expectancy in thematic apperception stories. *J. consult. Psychol.*, 1951, **15**, 400–404.

Crasilneck, H. B. An analysis of differences between suicidal and pseudo-suicidal patients through the use of projective techniques. Unpublished doctoral dissertation, Univer. of Houston, 1954. Cited by Shneidman & Farberow, 1958.

Cronbach, L. J. A validation design for qualitative studies of personality. *J. consult. Psychol.*, 1948, **12**, 365–376.

Cronbach, L. J. *Essentials of psychological testing.* (2nd ed.). New York: Harper & Row, 1960.

Dana, R. H. Clinical diagnosis and objective TAT scoring. *J. abnorm. soc. Psychol.*, 1955, **50**, 19–24.

Dana, R. H. Cross validation of objective TAT scoring. *J. consult. Psychol.*, 1956, **20**, 33–36.

Davenport, Beverly F. The semantic validity of TAT interpretations. *J. consult. Psychol.*, 1952, **16**, 171–175.

Davids, A., & DeVault, S. Use of the TAT and human figure drawings in research on personality, pregnancy, and perception. *J. proj. Tech.*, 1960, **24**, 362–365.

Davids, A., Henry, A. F., McArthur, C. C., & McNamara, L. F. Projection, self evaluation, and clinical evaluation of aggression. *J. consult. Psychol.*, 1955, **19**, 437–440.

Davids, A., Joelson, M., & McArthur, C. Rorschach and TAT indices of homosexuality in overt homosexuals, neurotics, and normal males. *J. abnorm. soc. Psychol.*, 1956, **53**, 161–172.

Davids, A., & Pildner, H., Jr. Comparison of direct and projective methods of personality assessment under different conditions of motivation. *Psychol. Monogr.*, 1958, **72**, No. 11 (Whole No. 464).

Davids, A., & Rosenblatt, D. Use of the TAT in assessment of the personality syndrome of alienation. *J. proj. Tech.*, 1958, **22**, 145–152.

Davison, A. H. A comparison of the fantasy productions on the Thematic Apperception Test of sixty hospitalized psychoneurotic and psychotic patients. *J. proj. Tech.*, 1953, **17**, 20–33.

Deabler, H. L. The psychotherapeutic use of the Thematic Apperception Test. *J. clin. Psychol.*, 1947, **3**, 246–252.

De Charms, R., Morrison, H. W., Reitman, W., & McClelland, D. C. Behavioral correlates of directly and indirectly measured achievement motivation. In D. C. McClelland (Ed.), *Studies in motivation.* New York: Appleton-Century-Crofts, 1955. Pp. 414–423.

Deri, Susan K. Effects of electric shock treatment on depressed patients. *Amer. Psychologist*, 1947, **2**, 286.

De Ridder, J. C. *The personality of the urban African in South Africa: a Thematic Apperception Test study.* London: Routledge, 1961.

Deutscher, M. The clinical psychologist in an AAF mental hygiene unit. *Psychol. Bull.*, 1944, **41**, 543–547.

De Vos, G. The relation of guilt toward parents to achievement and arranged marriage among the Japanese. *Psychiatry*, 1960, **23**, 287–301.

De Vos, G., & Wagatsuma, H. Value attitudes toward role behavior of women in two Japanese villages. *Amer. Anthropologist*, 1961, **63**, 1204–1230.

Dilworth, T., IV. A comparison of the Edwards PPS variables with some aspects of the TAT. *J. consult. Psychol.*, 1958, **22**, 486.

Dollin, Adelaide, & Sakoda, J. M. The effect of order of presentation on perception of TAT pictures. *J. consult. Psychol.*, 1962, **26**, 340–344.

Doob, L. W. *Becoming more civilized: a psychological exploration.* New Haven, Conn.: Yale Univer. Press, 1960.

Douvan, Elizabeth. Social status and success strivings. *J. abnorm. soc. Psychol.*, 1956, **52**, 219–223.

Dreger, R. M. Some personality correlates of religious attitudes, as determined by projective techniques. *Psychol. Monogr.*, 1952, **66**, No. 3 (Whole No. 335).

Dreger, R. M. The relation between Rorschach M and TAT content categories as measures of creative productivity in a representative high-level intelligence population. *J. gen. Psychol.*, 1960, **63**, 29–33.

Dunlevy, G. P., Jr. Intentional modification of Thematic Apperception Test stories as a function of adjustment. Unpublished doctoral dissertation, Purdue Univer., 1953.

Dymond, Rosalind F. A preliminary investigation of the relation of insight and empathy. *J. consult. Psychol.*, 1948, **12**, 228–233.

Dymond, Rosalind F. Adjustment changes over therapy from Thematic Apperception Test ratings. In C. R. Rogers & Rosalind F. Dymond, *Psychotherapy and personality change.* Chicago: Univer. of Chicago Press, 1954. Pp. 109–120.

Edelstein, Ruth R. The evaluation of intelligence from TAT protocols. Unpublished master's thesis, City Coll. of New York, 1956.

Eiduson, Bernice T. Artist and nonartist: a comparative study. *J. Pers.*, 1958, **26**, 13–28.

Eiduson, Bernice T. *Scientists: their psychological* world. New York: Basic Books, 1962.

Eiserer, P. E. The relative effectiveness of motion and still pictures as stimuli for eliciting fantasy stories about adolescent-parent relationships. *Genet. Psychol. Monogr.*, 1949, **39**, 205–278.

Epstein, S., & Smith, R. Thematic apperception as a measure of the hunger drive. *J. proj. Tech.*, 1956, **20**, 372–384.

Epstein, S., & Smith, R. Thematic apperception, Rorschach content, and ratings of sexual attractiveness of women as measures of the sex drive. *J. consult. Psychol.*, 1957, **21**, 473–478.

Ericson, Martha. A study of the Thematic Apperception Test as applied to a group of disturbed children. *Amer. Psychologist,* 1947, **2**, 272.

Eriksen, C. W. Some implications for TAT interpretation arising from need and perception experiments. *J. Pers.*, 1951, **19**, 282–288.

Eron, L. D. Frequencies of themes and identifications in the stories of schizophrenic patients and non-hospitalized college students. *J. consult. Psychol.*, 1948, **12**, 387–395.

Eron, L. D. A normative study of the Thematic Apperception Test. *Psychol. Monogr.*, 1950, **64**, No. 9 (Whole No. 315).

Eron, L. D. Responses of women to the Thematic Apperception Test. *J. consult. Psychol.*, 1953, **17**, 269–282.

Eron, L. D. Thematic Apperception Test. In O. K. Buros (Ed.), *Fifth mental measurements yearbook.* Highland Park, N.J.: Gryphon Press, 1959. Pp. 306–310.

Eron, L. D., & Hake, Dorothy T. Psychometric approach to the evaluation of the Thematic Apperception Test. In J. Zubin, *Quantitative techniques and methods in abnormal psychology*. New York: Columbia Univer. Bookstore, 1950. Pp. 1–14.

Eron, L. D., & Ritter, Anne M. A comparison of two methods of administration of the Thematic Apperception Test. *J. consult. Psychol.*, 1951, **15**, 55–61.

Eron, L. D., Terry, Dorothy, & Callahan, R. The use of rating scales for emotional tone of TAT stories. *J. consult. Psychol.*, 1950, **14**, 473–478.

Faith, H. W., Jr. The discrepancy between self–ideal self concepts as needs projected to thematic apperception pictures. Unpublished doctoral dissertation, Purdue Univer., 1961. (*Dissert. Abstr.*, **21**, 1999.)

Farberow, N. L. Personality patterns of suicidal mental hospital patients. *Genet. Psychol. Monogr.*, 1950, **42**, 3–79.

Feld, Sheila, & Smith, C. P. An evaluation of the objectivity of the method of content analysis. In J. W. Atkinson (Ed.), *Motives in fantasy, action, and society*. Princeton, N.J.: Van Nostrand, 1958. Pp. 234–241.

Ferracuti, F., & Rizzo, G. B. Signos sobresalientes de homosexualidad en una poblaction penitenciaria feminina, obtenidos mediante la aplicacion de tecnicas de proyeccion. *Rev. Ci. soc.*, 1958, **2**, 467–479. (*Psychol. Abstr.*, **35**, 2239.)

Feshbach, S. The drive-reducing function of fantasy behavior. *J. abnorm. soc. Psychol.*, 1955, **50**, 3–11.

Feshbach, S. The influence of drive arousal and conflict upon fantasy behavior. In J. Kagan & G. S. Lesser (Eds.), *Contemporary issues in thematic apperception methods*. Springfield, Ill.: Charles C Thomas, 1961. Pp. 119–140.

Fest, Beverly, & Seward, Georgene. A further analysis of personality in spastic colitis patients. *Amer. Psychologist,* 1949, **4**, 387–388.

Field, W. F. The effects on thematic apperception of certain experimentally aroused needs. Unpublished doctoral dissertation, Univer. of Maryland, 1951. Cited by McClelland et al., 1953.

Filer, R. N. The clinician's personality and his case reports. Unpublished doctoral dissertation, Univer. of Michigan, 1952.

Fine, R. The personality of the asthmatic child. Unpublished doctoral dissertation, Univer. of Southern California, 1948.

Fine, R. Manual for a scoring scheme for verbal projective techniques (TAT, MAPS, stories and the like). *J. proj. Tech.*, 1955, **19**, 310–316. (a)

Fine, R. A scoring scheme for the TAT and other verbal projective techniques. *J. proj. Tech.*, 1955, **19**, 306–309. (b)

Fisher, Rhoda L. The effect of a disturbing situation upon the stability of various projective tests. *Psychol. Monogr.*, 1958, **72**, No. 14 (Whole No. 467).

Fisher, S., & Fisher, Rhoda L. A projective test analysis of ethnic subculture themes in families. *J. proj. Tech.*, 1960, **24**, 366–369.

Fisher, S., & Mendell, D. Communication of neurotic patterns over two and three generations. *Psychiatry,* 1956, **19**, 41–46.

Fisher, S., & Morton, R. B. An exploratory study of some relationships between hospital ward atmospheres and attitudes of ward personnel. *J. Psychol.*, 1957, **44**, 155–164. (a)

Fisher, S., & Morton, R. B. Levels of prediction from the TAT. *J. consult. Psychol.*, 1957, **21**, 115–120. (b)

Fitzgerald, B. J. Some relationships among projective test, interview, and sociometric measures of dependent behavior. *J. abnorm. soc. Psychol.*, 1958, **56**, 199–203.

Fitzpatrick, G. E. Antepartum and postpartum responses to the Thematic Apperception Test by primigravidoris women. Unpublished master's thesis, City Coll. of New York, 1956.

FitzSimons, Ruth. Developmental, psychosocial, and educational factors in children with nonorganic articulation problems. *Child Develpm.*, 1958, **24**, 481–489.

Forer, B. R. The fallacy of personal validation: a classroom demonstration of gullibility. *J. abnorm. soc. Psychol.*, 1949, **44**, 118–123.

Foulds, G. A method of scoring the T.A.T. applied to psychoneurotics. *J. ment. Sci.*, 1953, **99**, 235–246.

Frank, L. K. Projective methods for the study of personality. *J. Psychol.*, 1939, **8**, 343–389.

Freed, G. O. A projective test study of creativity in college students in visual arts. Unpublished doctoral dissertation, Univer. of Michigan, 1961. (*Dissert. Abstr.*, **22**, 640.)

Freed, H., & Eccker, W. F. The Thematic Apperception Test: its value in routine psychiatric practice. *Dis. nerv. System*, 1946, **7**, 146–151.

Freeman, F. S. *The theory and practice of psychological testing.* (3rd ed.). New York: Holt, 1962.

French, Vera V. The structure of sentiments. II. A preliminary study of sentiments. *J. Pers.*, 1947, **16**, 78–108.

Frenkel-Brunswik, Else, & Sanford, R. N. Some personality factors in anti-Semitism. *J. Psychol.*, 1945, **20**, 271–291.

Friedman, I. Phenomenal, ideal, and projected conceptions of self. *J. abnorm. soc. Psychol.*, 1955, **51**, 611–615.

Friedman, I. Objectifying the subjective: a methodological approach to the TAT. *J. proj. Tech.*, 1957, **21**, 243–247.

Friedman, S. M. An empirical study of the castration and oedipus complexes. *Genet. Psychol. Monogr.*, 1952, **46**, 61–130.

Fry, F. D. Manual for scoring the Thematic Apperception Test. *J. Psychol.*, 1953, **35**, 181–195. (a)

Fry, F. D. TAT scoring blank. *J. Psychol.*, 1953, **35**, 197–200. (b)

Furuya, K. Responses of school children to human and animal pictures. *J. proj. Tech.*, 1957, **21**, 248–252.

Gallese, A. J., Jr., & Spoerl, Dorothy T. A comparison of Machover and Thematic Apperception Test interpretation. *J. soc. Psychol.*, 1954, **40**, 73–77.

Gardner, B. B. What makes successful and unsuccessful executives? *Advanc. Mgmt*, 1948, **13**, 116–125.

Garfield, S. Clinical values of projective techniques in an Army hospital. *J. clin. Psychol.*, 1946, **2**, 88–91.

Garfield, S. L., Blek, L., & Melker, F. The influence of method of administration and sex differences on selected aspects of TAT stories. *J. consult. Psychol.*, 1952, **16**, 140–144.

Garvin, J. A. A Thematic Apperception Test study of non-intellective factors related to academic success on the college level. Unpublished doctoral dissertation, Loyola Univer., Chicago, 1960. Cited by Arnold, 1962.

Gellerman, S. W. The relation between social attitudes and a projected thema of frustration by parents. *J. soc. Psychol.*, 1951, **34**, 183–190.

Ghosh, Molina. Fantasy life of girls at the preadolescent and adolescent stages. *U. Rajasthan Stud.* (*Educ.*), 1958, **3**, 54–82.

Gilhooly, F. M. The validity and reliability of the Rorschach and the Thematic Apperception Tests when these tests are interpreted by the method of blind analysis. Unpublished doctoral dissertation, Fordham Univer., 1952.

Ginsparg, H. T. A study of the Children's Apperception Test. Unpublished doctoral dissertation, Washington Univer., St. Louis, 1957. (*Dissert. Abstr.*, **17**, 3082.)

Gladwin, T. The role of man and woman on Truk: a problem in personality and culture. *Trans. N.Y. Acad. Sci.*, 1953, **15**, 305–309.

Gladwin, T., & Sarason, S. B. *Truk: man in paradise.* New York: Wenner-Gren Foundation, 1953.

Gluck, M. R. The relationship between hostility in the TAT and behavioral hostility. *J. proj. Tech.*, 1955, **19**, 21–26.

Goldman, Rosaline, & Greenblatt, M. Changes in Thematic Apperception Test stories paralleling changes in clinical status of schizophrenic patients. *J. nerv. ment. Dis.*, 1955, **121**, 243–249.

Goodman, M. An indirect validity of a Thematic Apperception Test scoring manual. *J. clin. Psychol.,* 1952, **8,** 149–154.

Goodrich, D. C. Aggression in the projective tests and group behavior of authoritarian and equalitarian subjects. *Amer. Psychologist,* 1954, **9,** 380.

Goodwin, P. A. A comparative study of hostility patterns in cases of bronchial asthma and peptic ulcer. Unpublished doctoral dissertation, Univer. of Southern California, 1949. Cited by Alice Bell, H. Trosman, & D. Ross, The use of projective techniques in the investigation of emotional aspects of general medical disorders. II. Other projective techniques and suggestions for experimental design. *J. proj. Tech.,* 1953, **17,** 51–60.

Gordon, H. L. A comparative study of dreams and responses to the Thematic Apperception Test. I. A need-press analysis. *J. Pers.,* 1953, **22,** 234–253.

Goss, A. E., & Brownell, M. H. Stimulus-response concepts and principles applied to projective test behavior. *J. Pers.,* 1957, **25,** 505–523.

Gottfried, N. W., & Horrocks, J. E. Psychological needs and verbally expressed aggression of adolescent delinquent boys. *J. soc. Psychol.,* in press. by J. E. Horrocks, *The psychology of adolescence.* (2nd ed.) Boston: Houghton Mifflin, 1962.

Graham, Elaine. A comparison between estimates of intelligence from projective and standard tests. Unpublished master's thesis, Univer. of Chicago, 1947.

Greenwald, A. F. Affective complexity and psychotherapy. *J. proj. Tech.,* 1959, **23,** 429–435.

Groh, L. S. A study of ego integration by means of an index of identification derived from six TAT cards. *J. proj. Tech.,* 1956, **20,** 387–397.

Grotz, R. C. A comparison of Thematic Apperception Test stories and manifest dream narratives. Unpublished master's thesis, Western Reserve Univer., 1950.

Grummon, D. L., & John, Eve S. Changes over client-centered therapy evaluated on psychoanalytically based Thematic Apperception Test scales. In C. Rogers & Rosalind F. Dymond, *Psychotherapy and personality change.* Chicago: Univer. of Chicago Press, 1954. Pp. 121–144.

Gurel, L., & Ullmann, L. P. Quantitative differences in response to TAT cards: the relationship between transcendence score and number of emotional words. *J. proj. Tech.,* 1958, **22,** 399–401.

Gurevitz, S., & Klapper, Zelda S. Techniques for and evaluation of the responses of schizophrenic and cerebral palsied children to the Children's Apperception Test (C.A.T.). *Quart. J. Child Behav.,* 1951, **3,** 38–65.

Hackbusch, Florentine, & Klopfer, B. The contribution of projective techniques to the understanding and treatment of children psychometrically diagnosed as feebleminded. *Amer. J. ment. Def.,* 1946, **51,** 15–34.

Hammer, E. F. Emotional instability and creativity. *Percept. mot. Skills,* 1961, **12,** 102.

Hanfmann, Eugenia. Projective techniques in the assessment program of the Office of Strategic Services. In American Council on Education, *Exploring individual differences.* Washington, D.C., 1948.

Harlow, R. G. Masculine inadequacy and compensatory development of physique. *J. Pers.,* 1951, **19,** 312–323.

Harris, A. J., & Roswell, Florence. Clinical diagnosis of reading disability. *J. Psychol.,* 1953, **36,** 323–340.

Harrison, R. Studies in the use and validity of the Thematic Apperception Test with mentally disordered patients. II. A quantitative validity study. *Charact. & Pers.,* 1940, **9,** 122–133. (a)

Harrison, R. Studies in the use and validity of the Thematic Apperception Test with mentally disordered patients. III. Validation by the method of "blind analysis." *Charact. & Pers.,* 1940, **9,** 134–138. (b)

Harrison, R. The thematic apperception and Rorschach methods of personality investigation in clinical practice. *J. Psychol.,* 1943, **15,** 49–74.

Harrison, R. The Thematic Apperception Test. In L. K. Frank, R. Harrison, E. Hellersberg, K. Machover, & M. Steiner, Personality development in adolescent girls. *Monogr. soc. Res. Child Develpm.,* 1953, **16,** 60–88 (Ser. No. 53).

Harrison, R., & Jackson, T. A. Validation of a clinical approach to the placement of engineers. *J. appl. Psychol.,* 1952, **36,** 373–376.

Harrison, R., & Rotter, J. B. A note on the reliability of the Thematic Apperception Test. *J. abnorm. soc. Psychol.,* 1945, **40,** 97–99.

Harrison, R., Tomblen, D. T., & Jackson, T. A. Profile of the mechanical engineer. III. Personality. *Personnel Psychol.,* 1955, **8,** 469–490.

Harrower, Molly R., & Grinker, R. R. The stress tolerance test. *Psychosom. Med.,* 1946, **8,** 3–15.

Hartman, A. A. An experimental examination of the thematic apperception technique in clinical diagnosis. *Psychol. Monogr.,* 1949, **63,** No. 8 (Whole No. 303).

Hartwell, S. W., Hutt, M. L., Andrew, Gwen, & Walton, R. E. The Michigan Picture Test: diagnostic and therapeutic possibilities of a new projective test in child guidance. *Amer. J. Orthopsychiat.*, 1951, **21**, 124–137.

Henry, W. E. Art and cultural symbolism: a psychological study of greeting cards. *J. Aesthet. art Crit.*, 1947, **6**, 36–44. (a)

Henry, W. E. The thematic apperception technique in the study of culture-personality relations. *Genet. Psychol. Monogr.*, 1947, **35**, 3–135. (b)

Henry, W. E. *The analysis of fantasy: the thematic apperception technique in the study of personality.* New York: Wiley, 1956.

Henry, W. E., & Farley, Jane. The validity of the Thematic Apperception Test in the study of adolescent personality. *Psychol. Monogr.*, 1959, **73**, No. 17 (Whole No. 487).

Henry, W. E., & Gardner, B. B. Personality evaluation in the selection of executive personnel. *Publ. Personnel Rev.*, 1949, **10**, 67–71.

Henry, W. E., & Guetzkow, H. Group projection sketches for the study of small groups. *J. soc. Psychol.*, 1951, **33**, 77–102.

Henry, W. E., & Moore, Harriet. *Executive personality evaluation: the Henry-Moore test for thematic production.* Chicago: Social Research, 1956.

Henry, W. E., & Shlien, J. M. Affective complexity and psychotherapy: some comparisons of time-limited and unlimited treatment. *J. proj. Tech.*, 1958, **22**, 153–162.

Heppell, H. K., & Raimy, V. C. Projective pictures as interview devices. *J. consult. Psychol.*, 1951, **15**, 405–411.

Heymann, G. M. Some relationships among hostility, fantasy aggression, and aggressive behavior. *Amer. Psychologist*, 1956, **11**, 391.

Heyns, R. W., Veroff, J., & Atkinson, J. W. A scoring manual for the affiliation motive. In J. W. Atkinson (Ed.), *Motives in fantasy, action, and society.* Princeton, N.J.: Van Nostrand, 1958. Pp. 205–218.

Himelstein, P., Eschenbach, A. E., & Carp, A. Interrelationships among three measures of need achievement. *J. consult. Psychol.*, 1958, **22**, 451–452.

Hire, A. W. Use of the Rorschach and Thematic Apperception Tests in the counseling and guidance of college students. *Harv. educ. Rev.*, 1951, **21**, 65–68.

Höhn, Elfriede. Der Thematische Apperzeptionstest als diagnostisches Hilfsmittel in der Psychotherapie. *Z. Psychother. med. Psychol.*, 1951, **1**, 192–205. (*Psychol. Abstr.*, **26**, 5618.)

Holden, R. H. The Children's Apperception Test with cerebral palsied and normal children. *Child Develpm.*, 1956, **27**, 3–8.

Holsopple, J. Q., & Phelan, J. G. The skills of clinicians in analysis of projective tests. *J. clin. Psychol.*, 1954, **10**, 307–320.

Holt, R. R. The Thematic Apperception Test. In H. H. Anderson & G. L. Anderson (Eds.), *An introduction to projective techniques.* Englewood Cliffs, N.J.: Prentice-Hall, 1951. Pp. 181–229. (a)

Holt, R. R. In E. S. Shneidman, *Thematic test analysis.* New York: Grune & Stratton, 1951. Pp. 101–118. (b)

Holt, R. R. Formal aspects of the TAT: a neglected resource. *J. proj. Tech.*, 1958, **22**, 163–172.

Holt, R. R. The nature of TAT stories as cognitive products: a psychoanalytic approach. In J. Kagan & G. S. Lesser (Eds.), *Contemporary issues in thematic apperceptive methods.* Springfield, Ill.: Charles C Thomas, 1961. Pp. 3–43.

Holt, R. R., & Luborsky, L. Research in the selection of psychiatrists: a second interim report. *Bull. Menninger Clin.*, 1952, **16**, 125–135.

Holt, R. R., & Luborsky, L. *Personality patterns of psychiatrists: a study of methods for selecting residents.* New York: Basic Books, 1958. 2 vols.

Holzberg, J. D., Bursten, B., & Santiccioli, A. The reporting of aggression as an indication of aggressive tension. *J. abnorm. soc. Psychol.*, 1955, **50**, 12–18.

Holzberg, J. D., & Posner, Rita. The relationship of extrapunitiveness on the Rosenzweig Picture-Frustration Study to aggression in overt behavior and fantasy. *Amer. J. Orthopsychiat.*, 1951, **21**, 767–779.

Hooker, Evelyn. The adjustment of the male overt homosexual. *J. proj. Tech.*, 1957, **21**, 18–31.

Horowitz, M. J. Developmental changes in Rorschach test and Thematic Apperception Test performance of children, six through nine years of age: an exploratory study. Unpublished doctoral dissertation, Kansas Univer., 1952.

Horrall, Bernice M. Academic performance and personality adjustment of highly intelligent college students. *Genet. Psychol. Monogr.*, 1957, **55**, 3–83.

Howard, K. I. The convergent and discriminant validation of ipsative ratings from three projective instruments. *J. clin. Psychol.*, 1962, **18**, 183–188.

Hutt, M. L. The use of projective methods of personality measurement in army medical installations. *J. clin. Psychol.*, 1945, **1**, 134–140.

Jaques, E. The clinical use of the Thematic Apperception Test with soldiers. *J. abnorm. soc. Psychol.*, 1945, **40**, 363–375.

Jensen, A. R. Aggression in fantasy and overt behavior. *Psychol. Monogr.*, 1957, **71**, No. 16 (Whole No. 445).

Jensen, A. R. Thematic Apperception Test. In O. K. Buros (Ed.), *Fifth mental measurements yearbook.* Highland Park, N.J.: Gryphon Press, 1959. Pp. 310–313.

Joel, W. The use of the Make-a-Picture-Story (MAPS) with disturbed adolescents. *Rorschach Res. Exch. & J. proj. Tech.*, 1948, **12**, 155–164.

Johnson, G. B., Jr. An experimental projective technique for the analysis of racial attitudes. *J. educ. Psychol.*, 1950, **41**, 257–278.

Johnson, G. B., Jr. An experimental technique for the prediction of teacher effectiveness. *J. educ. Psychol.*, 1957, **50**, 680–685.

Johnston, R. A. The effects of achievement imagery on maze-learning performance. *J. Pers.*, 1955, **24**, 145–152.

Jones, Mary C., & Mussen, P. H. Self-conceptions, motivations, and interpersonal attitudes of early- and late-maturing girls. *Child Develpm.*, 1958, **29**, 491–501.

Jones, R. M. The negation TAT: a projective method for eliciting repressive thought content. *J. proj. Tech.*, 1956, **20**, 297–303.

Joseph, Alice, Spicer, Rosamond, & Chesky, Jane. *The desert people: a study of the Papago Indians.* Chicago: Univer. of Chicago Press, 1949.

Judson, A. J., & Wernert, Claire. Need affiliation, orality, and the perception of aggression. *Psychiat. Quart. Suppl.*, 1958, **32**, 76–81.

Kadis, Asya, Greene, Janet S., & Freedman, N. Early childhood recollections: an integrative technique of personality test data. *Amer. J. Indiv. Psychol.*, 1953, **10**, 31–42.

Kafka, J. S. A note on the therapeutic and teaching use of projective techniques with groups. *Amer. J. Orthopsychiat.*, 1957, **11**, 839–840.

Kagan, J. The measurement of overt aggression from fantasy. *J. abnorm. soc. Psychol.*, 1956, **52**, 390–393.

Kagan, J. Socialization of aggression and the perception of parents in fantasy. *Child Develpm.*, 1958, **29**, 311–320.

Kagan, J. The stability of TAT fantasy and stimulus ambiguity. *J. consult. Psychol.*, 1959, **23**, 266–271.

Kagan, J. Thematic apperception techniques with children. In A. I. Rabin & Mary R. Haworth (Eds.), *Projective techniques with children.* New York: Grune & Stratton, 1960. Pp. 105–148.

Kagan, J. Stylistic variables in fantasy behavior: the ascription of affect states to social stimuli. In J. Kagan & G. S. Lesser (Eds.), *Contemporary issues in thematic apperceptive methods.* Springfield, Ill.: Charles C Thomas, 1961. Pp. 196–220.

Kagan, J., & Moss, H. A. The stability and validity of achievement fantasy. *J. abnorm. soc. Psychol.*, 1959, **58**, 357–364.

Kagan, J., & Mussen, P. H. Dependency themes on the TAT and group conformity. *J. consult. Psychol.*, 1956, **20**, 29–32.

Kagan, J., Sontag, L. W., Baker, C. T., & Nelson, Virginia L. Personality and IQ change. *J. abnorm. soc. Psychol.*, 1958, **56**, 261–266.

Kamman, G. R., & Kram, C. Value of psychometric examinations in medical diagnosis and treatment. *J. Amer. med. Ass.*, 1955, **158**, 555–560.

Kanehira, T. Diagnosis of parent-child relationship by CAT. *Jap. J. case Stud.*, 1958, **3**, 49–63.

Kannenberg, Katherine M. A comparison of results obtained from the Thematic Apperception Test under two conditions of administration. *Amer. Psychologist*, 1948, **3**, 363.

Kaplan, B. (Ed.) *Primary records in culture and personality.* Madison, Wis.: Microcard Foundation, 1956–1957. 2 vols. (*Psychol. Abstr.*, **31**, 7849; **33**, 3622.)

Kaplan, B. Cross-cultural use of projective techniques. In F. L. Hsu (Ed.), *Psychological anthropology: approaches to culture and personality.* Homewood, Ill.: Dorsey Press, 1961. Pp. 235–254.

Karolchuck, P. A., & Worell, L. Achievement motivation and learning. *J. abnorm. soc. Psychol.*, 1956, **53**, 255–257.

Kass, W., & Ekstein, R. Thematic Apperception Test diagnosis of a Nazi war criminal: anonymous post-mortem evaluation by a group of graduate clinical psychology students: problems of interjudge consistency. *Trans. Kans. Acad. Sci.*, 1948, **51**, 344–350. (*Psychol. Abstr.*, **23**, 2055.)

Kelly, E. L., & Fiske, D. W. *The prediction of performance in clinical psychology.* Ann Arbor, Mich.: Univer. of Michigan Press, 1951.

Kendig, Isabelle. Projective techniques as a psychological tool in diagnosis. *J. clin. Psychopath.*, 1944, **6**, 101–110.

Kenny, D. T. Transcendence indices, extent of personality factors in fantasy responses, and the ambiguity of TAT cards. *J. consult. Psychol.*, 1954, **18**, 345–348.

Kenny, D. T., & Bijou, S. W. Ambiguity of pictures and extent of personality factors in fantasy responses. *J. consult. Psychol.*, 1953, **17**, 283–288.

King, B. T. Relationships between submarine school performance and scores on the Navy Thematic Apperception Test. *USN med. res. Lab. Rep.*, 1958, **17**, No. 8 (Whole No. 301).

Klebanoff, S. G. Personality factors in symptomatic chronic alcoholism as indicated by the Thematic Apperception Test. *J. consult. Psychol.*, 1947, **11**, 111–119.

Klehr, H. An investigation of some personality factors in women with rheumatoid arthritis. *Amer. Psychologist*, 1952, **7**, 344–345.

Klein, A., Jr. The influence of stimulus material and geographical region on responses to a thematic test. Unpublished doctoral dissertation, Columbia Univer., 1956. (*Dissert. Abstr.*, **16**, 1284.)

Kline, M. V. An hypnotic experimental approach to the genesis of occupational interests and choice. II. The Thematic Apperception Test (a case report). *J. gen. Psychol.*, 1953, **48**, 79–82.

Knapp, A. H. *N* achievement and aesthetic preference. In J. W. Atkinson (Ed.), *Motives in fantasy, action, and society*. Princeton, N.J.: Van Nostrand, 1958. Pp. 367–372.

Knehr, C. A., Vickery, A., & Guy, M. Problem-action responses and emotions in Thematic Apperception Test stories recounted by alcoholic patients. *J. Psychol.*, 1953, **35**, 201–226.

Kohn, H. Some personality variables associated with binocular rivalry. *Psychol. Rec.*, 1960, **10**, 9–13.

Koppitz, Elizabeth M. Relationships between some background factors and children's interpersonal attitudes. *J. genet. Psychol.*, 1957, **91**, 119–129.

Korchin, S. J., Mitchell, H. E., & Meltzoff, J. A critical evaluation of the Thompson Thematic Apperception Test. *J. proj. Tech.*, 1950, **14**, 445–452.

Kragh, U. Types of pre-cognitive defensive organization in a tachistoscopic experiment. *J. proj. Tech.*, 1959, **23**, 315–322.

Krumboltz, J. D., & Farquar, W. W. Reliability and validity of the n-achievement test. *J. consult. Psychol.*, 1957, **21**, 226–227.

Kutash, S. B. Performance of psychopathic defective criminals on the Thematic Apperception Test. *J. crim. Psychopath.*, 1943, **5**, 319–340.

Lakin, M. Assessment of significant role attitudes in primiparous mothers by means of a modification of the TAT. *Psychosom. Med.*, 1957, **19**, 50–60.

Landisberg, Selma. A personality study of institutionalized epileptics. *Amer. J. ment. Def.*, 1947, **52**, 16–22.

Lasaga y Travieso, J. I., & Martinez-Arango, C. Some suggestions concerning the administration and interpretation of the T.A.T. *J. Psychol.*, 1946, **22**, 117–163.

Lasaga y Travieso, J. I., & Martinez-Arango, C. Four detailed examples of how mental conflicts of psychoneurotic and psychotic patients may be discovered by means of the TAT. *J. Psychol.*, 1948, **26**, 299–345.

Lazarus, R. S. A substitutive-defensive conception of apperceptive fantasy. In J. Kagan & G. S. Lesser (Eds.), *Contemporary issues in thematic apperceptive methods*. Springfield, Ill.: Charles C Thomas, 1961. Pp. 51–71.

Leary, T. *Interpersonal diagnosis of personality: a functional theory and methodology for personality evaluation*. New York: Ronald, 1957.

Lebo, Dell, & Harrigan, Margaret. Visual and verbal presentation of TAT stimuli. *J. consult. Psychol.*, 1957, **21**, 339–342.

Lee, S. G. *Manual of a Thematic Apperception Test for African subjects*. Pietermaritzburg, South Africa: Univer. of Natal Press, 1953. Cited by M. D. Ainsworth, Thematic Apperception Test for African subjects. In O. K. Buros (Ed.), *Fifth mental measurements yearbook*. Highland Park, N.J.: Gryphon Press, 1959.

Lehman, I. J. Responses of kindergarten children to the Children's Apperception Test. *J. clin. Psychol.*, 1959, **15**, 60–63.

Leighton, Dorothea, & Kluckhohn, C. *Children of the people*. Cambridge, Mass.: Harvard Univer. Press, 1947.

Leiman, A. H., & Epstein, S. Thematic sexual responses as related to sexual drive and guilt. *J. abnorm. soc. Psychol.*, 1961, **63**, 169–175.

Leitch, Mary, & Schafer, Sarah. A study of the Thematic Apperception Tests of psychotic children. *Amer. J. Orthopsychiat.*, 1947, **17**, 337–342.

Lessa, W. A., & Spiegelman, M. Ulithian personality as seen through ethnological materials and Thematic Apperception Test analysis. *Univer. Calif. Publ. Culture Soc.*, 1954, **2**, 243–301.

Lesser, G. S. The relationship between overt and fantasy aggression as a function of maternal response to aggression. *J. abnorm. soc. Psychol.*, 1957, **55**, 218–221.

Lesser, G. S. Application of Guttman's scaling method to aggressive fantasy in children. *Educ. psychol. Measmt*, 1958, **18**, 543–552. (a)

Lesser, G. S. Conflict analysis of fantasy aggression. *J. Pers.*, 1958, **26**, 29–41. (b)

Lesser, G. S. Custom-making projective tests for research. *J. proj. Tech.*, 1961, **25**, 21–31.

Lesser, G. S., Krawitz, Rhoda, & Packard, Rita. Experimental arousal of achievement motivation in adolescent girls. *J. abnorm. soc. Psychol.*, 1963, **66**, 59–66.

Leunbach, B., & Flachs, A. Clinical validity of the TAT. (In Swedish.) *Nord. Med.*, 1950, **44**, 1665–1668.

Levin, B. M. Predicting progress in psychotherapy: a comparison of Thematic Apperception Test results and psychiatric judgments. Unpublished doctoral dissertation, Univer. of Pittsburgh, 1953.

Levine, Phyllis R. Projective tests in a vocational guidance setting. *J. counsel. Psychol.*, 1954, **1**, 209–214.

Libby, W. The imagination of adolescents. *Amer. J. Psychol.*, 1908, **19**, 249–252.

Liccione, J. V. The changing family relationships of adolescent girls. *J. abnorm. soc. Psychol.*, 1955, **51**, 421–426.

Light, B. H. Comparative study of a series of TAT and CAT cards. *J. clin. Psychol.*, 1954, **10**, 179–181.

Light, B. H. A further test of the Thompson TAT rationale. *J. abnorm. soc. Psychol.*, 1955, **51**, 148–150.

Lindzey, G. An experimental test of the validity of the Rosenzweig Picture-Frustration Study. *J. Pers.*, 1950, **18**, 315–320.

Lindzey, G. The Thematic Apperception Test: interpretive assumptions and related empirical evidence. *Psychol. Bull.*, 1952, **49**, 1–25.

Lindzey, G. *Projective techniques and cross cultural research.* New York: Appleton-Century-Crofts, 1961.

Lindzey, G., Bradford, Jean, Tejessy, Charlotte, & Davids, A. Thematic Apperception Test: an interpretive lexicon. *J. clin., Psychol. Monogr. Suppl.*, 1959, No. 12.

Lindzey, G., & Goldberg, M. Motivational differences between male and female as measured by the Thematic Apperception Test. *J. Pers.*, 1953, **22**, 101–117.

Lindzey, G., & Heinemann, Shirley H. Thematic Apperception Test: individual and group administration. *J. Pers.*, 1955, **24**, 34–55.

Lindzey, G., & Herman, P. S. Thematic Apperception Test: a note on reliability and situational validity. *J. proj. Tech.*, 1955, **19**, 36–42.

Lindzey, G., & Kalnins, Dagney. Thematic Apperception Test: some evidence bearing on the "hero assumption." *J. abnorm. soc. Psychol.*, 1958, **57**, 76–83.

Lindzey, G., & Newburg, A. S. Thematic Apperception Test: a tentative appraisal of some "signs" of anxiety. *J. consult. Psychol.*, 1954, **18**, 389–395.

Lindzey, G., & Silverman, M. Thematic Apperception Test: techniques of group administration, sex differences, and the role of verbal productivity. *J. Pers.*, 1959, **27**, 311–323.

Lindzey, G., & Tejessy, Charlotte. Thematic Apperception Test: indices of aggression in relation to measures of overt and covert behavior. *Amer. J. Orthopsychiat.*, 1956, **26**, 567–576.

Lindzey, G., Tejessy, Charlotte, & Zamansky, H. S. Thematic Apperception Test: an empirical examination of some indices of homosexuality. *J. abnorm. soc. Psychol.*, 1958, **57**, 67–75.

Little, K. B., & Shneidman, E. S. The validity of thematic projective technique interpretations. *J. Pers.*, 1955, **23**, 285–294.

Little, K. B., & Shneidman, E. S. Congruences among interpretations of psychological test and anamnestic data. *Psychol. Monogr.*, 1959, **73**, No. 6 (Whole No. 476).

Louttit, C. M., & Browne, C. G. The use of psychometric instruments in psychological clinics. *J. consult. Psychol.*, 1947, **11**, 49–54.

Lowe, W. F. Effect of controlling the immediate environment of responses to the Thematic Apperception Test. *Percept. mot. Skills*, 1952, **4**, 98.

Lowell, E. L. The effect of need for achievement on learning and performance. *J. Psychol.*, 1952, **33**, 31–40.

Lubin, B. Some effects of set and stimulus properties on TAT stories. *J. proj. Tech.*, 1960, **24**, 11–16.

Lubin, N. M. The effect of color in the TAT on productions of mentally retarded subjects. *Amer. J. ment. Def.*, 1955, **60**, 366–370.

Luborsky, L. B., Holt, R. R., & Morrow, W. Interim report of the research project on the selection of medical men for psychiatric training. *Bull. Menninger Clin.*, 1950, **14**, 92–101.

Lyle, J. G., & Gilchrist, A. A. Problems of T.A.T. interpretation and the diagnosis of delinquent trends. *Brit. J. med. Psychol.*, 1958, **31**, 51–59.

Lyle, J., Gilchrist, A., & Groh, L. Three blind interpretations of a TAT record. *J. proj. Tech.*, 1958, **22**, 82–96.

McArthur, C. Personality differences between middle and upper classes. *J. abnorm. soc. Psychol.*, 1955, **50**, 247–254.

MacBrayer, Caroline T. Relationship between story length and situational validity of the TAT. *J. proj. Tech.*, 1959, **23**, 345–350.

McCandlish, L. A. An investigation of a new method of T.A.T. analysis. Unpublished doctoral dissertation, Loyola Univer., Chicago, 1958.

McClelland, D. C. Methods of measuring human motivation. In J. W. Atkinson (Ed.), *Motives in fantasy, action, and society*. Princeton, N.J.: Van Nostrand, 1958. Pp. 7–42.

McClelland, D. C. *The achieving society*. Princeton, N.J.: Van Nostrand, 1961.

McClelland, D. C., Atkinson, J. W., Clark, R. A., & Lowell, E. L. *The achievement motive*. New York: Appleton-Century-Crofts, 1953.

McClelland, D. C., Sturr, J. F., Knapp, R. H., & Wendt, H. W. Obligations to self and society in the United States and Germany. *J. abnorm. soc. Psychol.*, 1958, **56**, 245–255.

McCully, R. S. Fantasy productions of children with a progressively crippling and fatal illness. Unpublished doctoral dissertation, Columbia Univer., 1961. (*Dissert. Abstr.*, **22**, 643.)

McDowell, J. V. Developmental aspects of phantasy production on the Thematic Apperception Test. Unpublished doctoral dissertation, Ohio State Univer., 1952.

McGreevey, J. C. Interlevel disparity and predictive efficiency. *J. proj. Tech.*, 1962, **26**, 80–87.

MacGregor, G., Hassrick, R. B., & Henry, W. E. *Warriors without weapons: a study of the society and personality development of the Pine Ridge Sioux*. Chicago: Univer. of Chicago Press, 1946.

McIntyre, C. J. Sex, age, and iconicity as factors in projective film tests. *J. consult. Psychol.*, 1954, **18**, 337–343.

MacKinnon, D. W. An assessment study of Air Force officers. V. Summary and applications. *USAF WADC tech. Rep.*, 58–91, 1958.

McNeil, E. B., & Cohler, J. R., Jr. Adult aggression in the management of disturbed children. *Child Develpm.*, 1958, **29**, 451–461.

McPherson, J. H. A method of describing the emotional life of a group and the emotional needs of group members. *Amer. Psychologist*, 1952, **7**, 305–306.

Magnusson, D. Some personality tests applied on identical twins. *Scand. J. Psychol.*, 1960, **1**, 55–61. (*Psychol. Abstr.*, **35**, 6424.)

Mainord, Florence R., & Marcuse, F. L. Responses of disturbed children to human and to animal pictures. *J. proj. Tech.*, 1954, **18**, 475–477.

Malpass, L. F. Some relationships between students' perceptions of school and their achievement. *J. educ. Psychol.*, 1953, **44**, 475–482.

Marlowe, D. Relationships among direct and indirect measures of the achievement motive and overt behavior. *J. consult. Psychol.*, 1959, **23**, 329–332.

Marquis, Dorothy P., Sinnett, E. R., & Winter, W. D. A psychological study of peptic ulcer patients. *J. clin. Psychol.*, 1952, **8**, 266–272.

Martinez-Arango, C., & Lasaga y Travieso, J. I. Psychotherapy based on the Thematic Apperception Test. *Quart. Rev. Psychiat. Neurol.*, 1947, **2**, 271–287.

Martire, J. G. Relationships between the self concept and differences in the strength and generality of achievement motivation. In J. W. Atkinson (Ed.), *Motives in fantasy, action, and society*. Princeton, N.J.: Van Nostrand, 1958. Pp. 373–382.

Marui, F. A method of diagnosing the interrelations in the members of a family. *Bull. Fac. Educ., Nagoya*, 1957, 3, 399. (*Psychol. Abstr.*, **34**, 1265.)

Marui, F. A normative study of the TAT: chiefly on emotional tone, outcome, and shift. *Jap. J. Psychol.*, 1960, **31**, 83–92.

Maslow, A. H. Problem-centering vs means-centering in science. *Phil. Sci.*, 1946, **13**, 326–331.

Mason, Beth B. An experimental investigation of repetition and variation in administration upon the Thematic Apperception Test. *Percept. mot. Skills*, 1952, **4**, 98.

Mason, Beth, & Ammons, R. B. Note on social class and the Thematic Apperception Test. *Percept. mot. Skills*, 1956, **6**, 88.

Masserman, J. H., & Balken, Eva R. The clinical application of phantasy studies. *J. Psychol.*, 1938, **6**, 81–88.

Matarazzo, J. D. An experimental study of aggression in the hypertensive patient. *J. Pers.*, 1954, **22**, 423–447.

Mayman, M. Review of the literature of the Thematic Apperception Test. In D. Rapaport, *Diagnostic psychological testing: the theory, statistical evaluation, and diagnostic application of a battery of tests*. Vol. 2. Chicago: Year Book Medical Publishers, 1946. Pp. 496–506.

Melikian, L. H. The relationship between Edwards' and McClelland's measures of achievement motivation. *J. consult. Psychol.*, 1958, **22**, 296–298.

Meyer, M. M., & Tolman, Ruth S. Correspondence between attitudes and images of parental figures in TAT stories and in therapeutic interviews. *J. consult. Psychol.*, 1955, **19**, 79–82. (a)

Meyer, M. M., & Tolman, Ruth S. Parental figures in sentence completion test, in TAT, and in therapeutic interviews. *J. consult. Psychol.*, 1955, **19**, 170. (b)

Michael, J. C., & Buhler, C. Experiences with personality testing in a neuropsychiatric department of a public general hospital. *Dis. nerv. System*, 1945, **6**, 205–211.

Milam, J. R. Examiner influences on Thematic Apperception Test stories. *J. proj. Tech.*, 1954, **18**, 221–226.

Mill, C. R. Personality patterns of sociometrically selected and sociometrically rejected male college students. *Sociometry*, 1953, **16**, 151–167.

Miller, J. S., & Scodel, A. The diagnostic significance of usual and unusual TAT stories. *J. consult. Psychol.*, 1955, **19**, 91–95.

Miner, J. B. Motion perception, time perspective, and creativity. *J. proj. Tech.*, 1956, **20**, 405–413.

Mitchell, Dorothy P. The validity of the Thematic Apperception Test and its implications for group therapy. Unpublished master's thesis, Univer. of Oklahoma, 1949.

Mitchell, H. E. Social class and race as factors affecting the role of the family in Thematic Apperception Test stories. *Amer. Psychologist*, 1950, **5**, 299–300.

Mitchell, H. E. Social class and race as factors affecting the role of the family in Thematic Apperception Test stories of males. Unpublished doctoral dissertation, Univer. of Pennsylvania, 1951. (*Microfilm Abstr.*, **11**, 428.)

Mitchell, J. V., Jr. An analysis of the factorial dimensions of the achievement motivation construct. *J. educ. Psychol.*, 1961, **52**, 179–187.

Monroe, Ruth L. Diagnosis of learning disabilities through a projective technique. *J. consult. Psychol.*, 1949, **13**, 390–395.

Moore, Harriet B., & Levy, S. J. Artful contrivers: a study of engineers. *Personnel*, 1951, **28**, 148–153.

Moran, L. J., Fairweather, G. W., Fisher, S., & Morton, R. B. Psychological concomitants to rate of recovery from tuberculosis. *J. consult. Psychol.*, 1956, **20**, 199–203.

Morgan, Christina, & Murray, H. A. A method for investigating phantasies: the Thematic Apperception Test. *Arch. Neurol. Psychiat.*, 1935, **34**, 289–306.

Morgan, H. H. A psychometric comparison of achieving and nonachieving college students of high ability. *J. consult. Psychol.*, 1952, **16**, 292–298.

Morgan, H. H. Measuring achievement motivation with "picture interpretations." *J. consult. Psychol.*, 1953, **17**, 289–292.

Munsterberg, Elizabeth, & Mussen, P. H. The personality structures of art students. *J. Pers.*, 1953, **21**, 457–466.

Murray, E. J. Conflict and repression during sleep deprivation. *J. abnorm. soc. Psychol.*, 1959, **59**, 95–101.

Murray, H. A. *Explorations in personality.* New York: Oxford Univer. Press, 1938.

Murray, H. A. *Thematic Apperception Test manual.* Cambridge, Mass.: Harvard Univer. Press, 1943.

Murray, H. A. Uses of the Thematic Apperception Test. *Amer. J. Psychiat.*, 1951, **107**, 577–581.

Murray, H. A. Thematic Apperception Test. In A. Weider (Ed.), *Contributions toward medical psychology: theory and psychodiagnostic methods.* Vol. 2. New York: Ronald, 1953. Pp. 636–649.

Murray, H. A., & Stein, M. Note on the selection of combat officers. *Psychosom. Med.*, 1943, **5**, 386–391.

Murstein, B. I. Nonprojective determinants of perception on the TAT. *J. consult. Psychol.*, 1958, **22**, 195–198. (a)

Murstein, B. I. The relationship of stimulus ambiguity on the TAT to the productivity of themes. *J. consult. Psychol.*, 1958, **22**, 348. (b)

Murstein, B. I. A conceptual model of projective techniques applied to stimulus variables with thematic techniques. *J. consult. Psychol.*, 1959, **23**, 3–14.

Murstein, B. I. The role of the stimulus in the manifestation of fantasy. In J. Kagan & G. S. Lesser (Eds.), *Contemporary issues in thematic apperceptive methods.* Springfield, Ill.: Charles C Thomas, 1961. Pp. 229–273.

Murstein, B. I., & Wheeler, J. I. The projection of hostility on the Rorschach and thematic stories test. *J. clin. Psychol.*, 1959, **15**, 316–319.

Mussen, P. H. Some personality and social factors related to changes in children's attitudes toward Negroes. *J. abnorm. soc. Psychol.*, 1950, **45**, 423–441.

Mussen, P. H. Differences between the TAT responses of Negro and white boys. *J. consult. Psychol.*, 1953, **17**, 373–376.

Mussen, P. H., & Jones, Mary C. Self-conceptions, motivations, and interpersonal attitudes of late- and early-maturing boys. *Child Develpm.*, 1957, **28**, 243–256.

Mussen, P. H., & Kagan, J. Group conformity and perceptions of parents. *Child Develpm.*, 1958, **29**, 57–60.

Mussen, P. H., & Naylor, H. K. The relationships between overt and fantasy aggression. *J. abnorm. soc. Psychol.*, 1954, **49**, 235–240.

Mussen, P. H., & Scodel, A. The effects of sexual stimulation under varying conditions on TAT sexual responsiveness. *J. consult. Psychol.*, 1955, **19**, 90.

Myers, R. L. An analysis of sex differences in verbalizations and content of responses to the Rorschach and to the Thematic Apperception Test. Unpublished doctoral dissertation, Temple Univer., 1958. (*Dissert. Abstr.*, **19**, 365.)

Nagge, W. W. A study of the behavior of paranoid schizophrenics on the Thematic Apperception Test. Unpublished doctoral dissertation, Univer. of Kentucky, 1951. (*Dissert. Abstr.*, **20**, 3838.)

Newbigging, P. L. Influences of a stimulus variable on stories told to certain TAT pictures. *Canad. J. Psychol.*, 1955, **9**, 195–206.

Newman, C. A study of the relationship between attitudes toward certain authority figures and adjustment to the military source. Unpublished doctoral dissertation, New York Univer., 1954. (*Dissert. Abstr.*, **14**, 2402.)

Ni, L. Study on concealment of the subjects in telling stories on TAT pictures. Taiwan, Formosa: National Taiwan Univer., 1959. (*Psychol. Abstr.*, **34**, 1406.)

Nishimura, H. Characteristics of delinquents in TAT. *Jap. J. case Stud.*, 1958, **3**, 29–48. (*Psychol. Abstr.*, **34**, 4654.)

Oelke, M. C. A study of student teachers' attitudes toward children. *J. educ. Psychol.*, 1956, **47**, 193–198.

Ohlsen, M. M., & Schulz, R. E. Projective test response patterns for best and poorest student teachers. *Educ. psychol. Measmt*, 1955, **15**, 18–27.

Ossorio, Elizabeth D., & Rigby, Marilyn K. Thematic Apperception Test response patterns in the prediction of officer success. *St. Louis Univer. Dept. Psychol. tech. Rep.*, 1957, No. 7. (*Psychol. Abstr.*, **33**, 4830.)

Ouchi, G. A study on CAT. II. A comparison with TAT. (In Japanese.) *Bunka*, 1957, **21**, 194–207, 264–265. (*Psychol. Abstr.*, **34**, 6042.)

Palmer, J. O. A note on the intercard reliability of the Thematic Apperception Test. *J. consult. Psychol.*, 1952, **16**, 473–474.

Park, P. D. The performance of normal and schizophrenic adult males on the Thematic Apperception Test in terms of: transcendent reactions; categorized affectivity; and verbal enumeration. Unpublished doctoral dissertation, Yeshiva Univer., 1952. (*Dissert. Abstr.*, **13**, 1262.)

Parrish, J., & Rethlingshafer, Dorothy. A study of the need to achieve in college achievers and non-achievers. *J. gen. Psychol.*, 1954, **50**, 209–226.

Petrauskas, F. B. A TAT and picture-frustration study of naval offenders and non-offenders. Unpublished doctoral dissertation, Loyola Univer., Chicago, 1959. Cited by Arnold, 1962.

Phares, E. J. TAT performance as a function of anxiety and coping-avoiding behavior. *J. consult. Psychol.*, 1961, **25**, 257–259.

Phelan, J. G. Projective techniques in the selection of management. *J. proj. Tech.*, 1962, **26**, 102–104.

Phillipson, H. *The object relations technique.* New York: Free Press, 1955.

Pierce, J. V., & Bowman, P. H. Motivation patterns of superior high school students. *Coop. res. Monogr.*, 1960, No. 2, 33–66. (*U.S. Dep. Hlth Educ. Welf. Publ.*, No. OE-35016.)

Pine, F., & Holt, R. R. Creativity and primary process: a study of adaptive regression. *J. abnorm. soc. Psychol.*, 1960, **61**, 370–379.

Piotrowski, Z. A new evaluation of the Thematic Apperception Test. *Psychoanal. Rev.*, 1950, **37**, 101–127.

Pittluck, Patricia. The relation between aggressive fantasy and overt behavior. Unpublished doctoral dissertation, Yale Univer., 1950.

Proshansky, H. M. A projective method for the study of attitudes. *J. abnorm. soc. Psychol.*, 1943, **38**, 393–395.

Purcell, K. The TAT and antisocial behavior. *J. consult. Psychol.*, 1956, **20**, 449–456.

Quinn, T. L. Differences in motivational patterns of college student brothers as revealed in the TAT, the ratings of their peers and the ratings of their superiors: a validation study. Unpublished doctoral dissertation, Loyola Univer., Chicago, 1961. Cited by Arnold, 1962.

Rabin, A. I. Culture components as a significant factor in child development: symposium, 1960. 2. Kibbutz adolescents. *Amer. J. Orthopsychiat.*, 1961, **31**, 493–504.

Radke-Yarrow, Marian, & Lande, B. Personality variables and reactions to minority group belonging. *Amer. Psychologist*, 1951, **6**, 329–330.

Rainwater, L. Some themes in the personalities of German men. *Genet. Psychol. Monogr.*, 1960, **61**, 167–195.

Rapaport, D. The Thematic Apperception Test. In D. Rapaport, *Diagnostic psychological testing: the theory, statistical evaluation, and diagnostic application of a battery of tests.* Vol. 2. Chicago: Year Book Medical Publishers, 1946. Pp. 395–459.

Rautman, A. L., & Brower, Edna. War themes in children's stories. *J. Psychol.*, 1945, **19**, 191–202.

Rautman, A. L., & Brower, Edna. War themes in children's stories. II. Six years later. *J. abnorm. soc. Psychol.*, 1951, **31**, 263–270.

Reeves, Margaret P. An application of the semantic differential to Thematic Apperception Test material. Unpublished doctoral dissertation, Univer. of Illinois, 1954. (*Dissert. Abstr.*, **14**, 2121.)

Reichard, Suzanne. Some contributions of psychological tests to therapeutic planning. *Amer. J. Orthopsychiat.*, 1951, **21**, 532–541.

Reitman, W. R. Motivational induction and the behavior correlates of the achievement and affiliation motives. *J. abnorm. soc. Psychol.*, 1960, **60**, 8–13.

Renaud, H. Group differences in fantasies: head injuries, psychoneurotics, and brain diseases. *J. Psychol.*, 1946, **21**, 327–346.

Reznikoff, M. Social desirability in TAT themes. *J. proj. Tech.*, 1961, **25**, 87–89.

Richards, T. W. Personality of the convulsive patient in military service. *Psychol. Monogr.*, 1952, **66**, No. 14 (Whole No. 346).

Richardson, La Vange H. The personality of stutterers. *Psychol. Monogr.*, 1944, **56**, No. 7 (Whole No. 260).

Richardson, S. A. A study of selected personality characteristics of social science field workers. Unpublished doctoral dissertation, Cornell Univer., 1954. (*Dissert. Abstr.*, **14**, 2403.)

Riess, B. F., Schwartz, E. K., & Cottingham, Alice. An experimental critique of assumptions underlying the Negro version of the TAT. *J. abnorm. soc. Psychol.*, 1950, **45**, 700–709.

Ritter, Anne M., & Eron, L. D. The use of the Thematic Apperception Test to differentiate normal from abnormal groups. *J. abnorm. soc. Psychol.*, 1952, **47**, 147–158.

Robbins, A. An experimental study of the relationship between needs as manifested on the Thematic Apperception Test and the Kuder Preference Record scales of adolescent boys. Unpublished doctoral dissertation, Columbia Univer., 1953.

Rochlin, I. The investigation, through the use of projective techniques, of non-intellectual factors in the learning of mathematics. *Amer. Psychologist*, 1952, **7**, 368.

Rock, M. L., & Hay, E. N. Investigation of the use of tests as a predictor of leadership and group effectiveness in a job evaluation situation. *J. soc. Psychol.*, 1953, **38**, 109–119.

Rodnick, E. H., Rubin, M. A., & Freeman, H. Related studies on adjustment: reactions to experimentally induced stress. *Amer. J. Psychiat.*, 1943, **99**, 872–880.

Roe, Anne. Artists and their work. *J. Pers.*, 1946, **15**, 1–40. (b)

Roe, Anne. Painting and personality. *Rorschach Res. Exch.*, 1946, **10**, 86–100. (a)

Roe, Anne. Psychological examination of eminent biologists. *J. consult. Psychol.*, 1949, **13**, 225–246.

Roe, Anne. A psychological study of physical scientists. *Genet. Psychol. Monogr.*, 1951, **43**, 121–235.

Roe, Anne. A psychological study of eminent psychologists and anthropologists, and a comparison with biological and physical scientists. *Psychol. Monogr.*, 1953, **67**, No. 2 (Whole No. 352).

Roquebrune, G. Aspects genétiques et typologiques des résultats obtenus à une épreuve projective. *Enfance*, 1959, No. 1, 29–47. (*Psychol. Abstr.*, **34**, 4352.)

Rose, A. W. Projective techniques in sociological research. *Soc. Forces*, 1949, **28**, 175–183.

Rosen, B. C. The achievement syndrome: a psychocultural dimension of social stratification. In J. W. Atkinson (Ed.), *Motives in fantasy, action, and society*. Princeton, N.J.: Van Nostrand, 1958. Pp. 495–509.

Rosen, B. C. Race, ethnicity and the achievement syndrome. *Amer. sociol. Rev.*, 1959, **24**, 47–60.

Rosen, J. L., & Neugarten, Bernice L. Ego functions in the middle and later years: a thematic apperception study of normal adults. *J. Geront.*, 1960, **15**, 62–67.

Rosenblatt, D. Responses of former Soviet citizens to selected TAT cards. *J. gen. Psychol.*, 1960, **62**, 273–284.

Rosenblatt, M. S. The development of norms for the Children's Apperception Test. Unpublished doctoral dissertation, Florida State Univer., 1958. (*Dissert. Abstr.*, **19**, 2150.)

Rosencranz, Mary L. L. The application of a projective technique for analyzing clothing awareness, clothing symbols, and the range of themes associated with clothing behavior. Unpublished doctoral dissertation, Michigan State Univer., 1960. (*Dissert. Abstr.*, **21**, 2392.)

Rosenzweig, S. The picture-association method and its application in a study of reactions to frustration. *J. Pers.*, 1945, **14**, 3–23.

Rosenzweig, S. (In collaboration with Kate L. Kogan.) *Psychodiagnosis: an introduction to tests in the clinical practice of psychodynamics.* New York: Grune & Stratton, 1949.

Rosenzweig, S., & Fleming, Edith E. Apperceptive norms for the Thematic Apperception Test. II. An empirical investigation. *J. Pers.*, 1949, **17**, 483–503.

Rotter, J. B. Studies in the use and validity of the Thematic Apperception Test with mentally disordered patients. I. Methods of analysis and clinical problems. *Charact. & Pers.*, 1940, **9**, 18–34.

Rotter, J. B. Thematic Apperception Tests: suggestions for administration and interpretation. *J. Pers.*, 1946, **15**, 70–92.

Rotter, J. B., & Jessor, Shirley. In E. S. Shneidman, *Thematic test analysis.* New York: Grune & Stratton, 1951. Pp. 163–179.

Ruess, Aubrey L. Some cultural and personality aspects of mental retardation. *Amer. J. ment. Def.*, 1958, **63**, 50–59.

Ruja, D. H. Personality changes following prefrontal lobotomy in twenty-five schizophrenic patients. *Amer. Psychologist,* 1951, **6**, 499.

Saltzman, S. S. An investigation of certain psychological aspects of personality in three allergic groups. Unpublished doctoral dissertation, New York Univer., 1953.

Samuels, H. The validity of personality-trait ratings based on projective techniques. *Psychol. Monogr.*, 1952, **66**, No. 5 (Whole No. 337).

Samuelson, F. The relation of achievement and affiliation motives to conforming behavior in two conditions of conflict with a majority. In J. W. Atkinson (Ed.), *Motives in fantasy, action, and society.* Princeton, N.J.: Van Nostrand, 1958. Pp. 421–433.

Sanford, R. N. The effect of abstinence from food upon imaginal processes: a preliminary experiment. *J. Psychol.*, 1936, **2**, 129–136.

Sanford, R. N. Thematic Apperception Test. In R. N. Sanford et al., Physique, personality and scholarship. *Monogr. soc. Res. Child Develpm.*, 1943, **8**, No. 1 (Ser. No. 34), 258–301.

Sanford, R. N. In Betty Aron, *A manual for analysis of the Thematic Apperception Test: a method and technique.* Berkeley, Calif.: Willis E. Berg, 1949. Foreword.

Sarason, Barbara R., & Sarason, I. G. The effect of type of administration and sex of subject on emotional tone and outcome ratings of TAT stories. *J. proj. Tech.*, 1958, **22**, 333–337.

Sarason, S. B. The use of the Thematic Apperception Test with mentally deficient children. I. A study of high grade girls. *Amer. J. ment. Def.*, 1943, **47**, 414–421. (a)

Sarason, S. B. The use of the Thematic Apperception Test with mentally deficient children. II. A study of high grade boys. *Amer. J. ment. Def.*, 1943, **48**, 169–173. (b)

Sarason, S. B. Dreams and Thematic Apperception Test stories. *J. abnorm. soc. Psychol.*, 1944, **39**, 486–492.

Sarason, S. B. The TAT and subjective interpretation. *J. consult. Psychol.*, 1948, **12**, 285–299.

Sarason, S., & Rosenzweig, S. An experimental study of the triadic hypothesis: reaction to frustration, ego-defense, and hypnotizability. II. Thematic apperception approach. *Charact. & Pers.*, 1942, **11**, 150–165.

Sauer, R. E., & Marcuse, F. L. Overt and covert recording. *J. proj. Tech.*, 1957, **21**, 391–395.

Saxe, C. H. A quantitative comparison of psychodiagnostic formulations from the TAT and therapeutic contacts. *J. consult. Psychol.*, 1950, **14**, 116–127.

Schafer, R. *The clinical application of psychological tests: diagnostic summaries and case studies.* New York: International Universities Press, 1948.

Schafer, R. How was this story told? *J. proj. Tech.*, 1958, **22**, 181–210.

Schafer, Sarah, & Leitch, Mary. An exploratory study of the usefulness of a battery of psychological tests with nursery school children. *Amer. J. Psychiat.*, 1948, **104**, 647–652.

Schneck, J. M. Hypnoanalysis, hypnotherapy, and card 12M of the Thematic Apperception Test. *J. gen. Psychol.*, 1951, **44**, 293–301.

Schwartz, E. K., Riess, B. F., & Cottingham, Alice. Further critical evaluation of the Negro version of the TAT. *J. proj. Tech.*, 1951, **15**, 394–400.

Schwartz, L. A. Social-situation pictures in the psychiatric interview. *Amer. J. Orthopsychiat.*, 1932, **2**, 124–133.

Schweers, R. Some personality correlates of essential hypertension. Unpublished master's thesis, Univer. of California, 1950.

Scodel, A. Heterosexual somatic preference and fantasy dependency. *J. consult. Psychol.*, 1957, **21**, 371–374.

Scodel, A., Lipetz, M. E. TAT hostility and psychopathology. *J. proj. Tech.*, 1957, **21**, 161–165.

Secord, P. F. Studies of the relationship of handwriting to personality. *J. Pers.*, 1949, **17**, 430–448.

Semeonoff, B. Projective techniques in selection for counseling. *Hum. Relat.*, 1958, **11**, 113–122.

Sen, Amya. A preliminary study of the Thematic Apperception Test. *Brit. J. statist. Psychol.*, 1953, **6**, 91–100.

Seward, Georgene H., Morrison, L. M., & Fest, Beverly. Personality structure in a common form of colitis. *Psychol. Monogr.*, 1951, **65**, No. 1.

Shatin, L. Rorschach adjustment and the Thematic Apperception Test. *J. proj. Tech.*, 1953, **17**, 92–101.

Shatin, L. Relationships between the Rorschach Test and the Thematic Apperception Test. *J. proj. Tech.*, 1955, **19**, 317–331.

Shatin, L. The constriction-dilation dimension in Rorschach and TAT. *J. clin. Psychol.*, 1958, **14**, 150–154.

Shipley, T. E., Jr., & Veroff, J. A projective measure of need for affiliation. *J. exp. Psychol.*, 1952, **43**, 349–356.

Shneidman, E. S. Schizophrenia and the *MAPS* Test: a study of certain formal psycho-social aspects of fantasy production in schizophrenia as revealed by performance on the Make a Picture Story (*MAPS*) Test. *Genet. Psychol. Monogr.*, 1948, **38**, 145–223.

Shneidman, E. S. *Thematic test analysis.* New York: Grune & Stratton, 1951.

Shneidman, E. S. *The Make a Picture Story Test.* New York: Psychological Corporation, 1952.

Shneidman, E. S. The MAPS Test with children. In A. I. Rabin & Mary R. Haworth (Eds.), *Projective techniques with children.* New York: Grune & Stratton, 1960. Pp. 130–148.

Shneidman, E. S., & Farberow, N. L. TAT heroes of suicidal and non-suicidal subjects. *J. proj. Tech.*, 1958, **22**, 211–228.

Shore, A. *Autoritarismo y agresion en una aldea Mexicana. Mexico,* D. F., 1954. Cited by F. Riessman & S. M. Miller, Social class and projective tests. *J. proj. Tech.*, 1958, **22**, 432–439.

Shorr, J. E. A proposed system for scoring the TAT. *J. clin. Psychol.*, 1948, **4**, 189–194.

Shulman, H. S. Congruences of personality expression in self-conceptions, the Thematic Apperception Test, and dreams. Unpublished doctoral dissertation, Western Reserve Univer., 1955.

Silverman, A. J., Cohen, S. I., Zuiderna, G. D., & Lazar, C. S. Prediction of physiological stress tolerance from projective tests: the focused thematic test. *J. proj. Tech.*, 1957, **21**, 189–193.

Silverstein, A. B. Identification with same-sex and opposite-sex figures in thematic apperception. *J. proj. Tech.*, 1959, **23**, 73–75.

Singer, J. L. Projected familial attitudes as a function of socioeconomic status and psychopathology. *J. consult. Psychol.*, 1954, **18**, 99–104.

Singer, J. L., & Opler, M. R. Contrasting patterns of fantasy and motility in Irish and Italian schizophrenics. *J. abnorm. soc. Psychol.*, 1956, **53**, 42–47.

Slack, C. W. Some intellective functions in the Thematic Apperception Test and their use in differentiating endogenous feeble-mindedness. *Train. Sch. Bull.*, 1950, **47**, 156–169.

Slutz, Margaret. The unique contributions of the Thematic Apperception Test to a developmental study. *Psychol. Bull.*, 1941, **38**, 704.

Small, L. Personality determinants of vocational choice. *Psychol. Monogr.*, 1953, **67**, No. 1 (Whole No. 351).

Smith, G. H. *Motivation research in advertising and marketing.* New York: McGraw-Hill, 1954.

Smith, J. A., Brown, W. T., & Thrower, Florence L. The use of a modified Thematic Apperception Test in a neuropsychiatric clinic in a general hospital. *Amer. J. Psychiat.*, 1951, **107**, 498–500.

Smith, J. R., & Coleman, J. C. The relationship between manifestations of hostility in projective tests and overt behavior. *J. proj. Tech.*, 1956, **20**, 326–334.

Snider, L. B. A research method validating self-determination. In Magda Arnold & J. A. Gasson (Eds.), *The human person.* New York: Ronald, 1954. Pp. 222–263.

Solkoff, N. Effects of a variation in instructions on responses to TAT cards. *J. proj. Tech.*, 1960, **24**, 67–70.

Soskin, W. F. Bias in postdiction from projective tests. *J. abnorm. soc. Psychol.*, 1954, **49**, 69–74.

Spiegelman, M. Jungian theory and the analysis of thematic tests. *J. proj. Tech.*, 1955, **19**, 253–263.

Spiegelman, M. A note on the use of Fine's scoring system with the MAPS tests of children. *J. proj. Tech.*, 1956, **20**, 442–444.

Spoerl, Dorothy T. Bilinguality and emotional adjustment. *J. abnorm. soc. Psychol.*, 1943, **38**, 37–57.

Starr, S. The relationship between hostility-ambiguity of the TAT cards, hostility fantasy, and hostile behavior. Unpublished doctoral dissertation, Washington State Univer., 1961. (*Dissert. Abstr.*, **21**, 2372.)

Steggert, F. X. An analysis of some personal and executive characteristics of participants in a university program of executive development for federal personnel. Unpublished doctoral dissertation, Loyola Univer., Chicago, 1961. Cited by Arnold, 1962.

Stein, M. I. *Thematic Apperception Test: an introductory manual for its clinical use with adults.* (2nd ed.) Reading, Mass.: Addison-Wesley, 1955.

Stern, E. Minderwertigleitskomplex und Kompensationen in den Geschicten zu Murrays "Thematic Apperception Test." *Int. Z. Indiv.-Psychol.*, 1950, **19**, 109–121. (*Psychol. Abstr.*, **26**, 1503.)

Stern, E. Analyse d'un cas d'un jeune délinquent à l'aide du "Thematic Apperception Test" de Murray. *Crianca portug.*, 1951–1952, **11**, 209–222. (*Psychol. Abstr.*, **27**, 7922.)

Stern, G. G. Personality assessment and the prediction of academic success. *Amer. Psychologist,* 1952, **7**, 324.

Stone, D. R. A recorded auditory apperception test as a new projection technique. *J. Psychol.*, 1950, **29**, 349–353.

Stone, H. The TAT aggressive content scale. *J. proj. Tech.*, 1956, **20**, 445–452.

Suesholtz, Zeborah. Formal characteristics of children's fantasies as measured by the Thematic Apperception Test. Unpublished master's thesis, City Coll. of New York, 1948.

Sumerwell, Harriet C., Campbell, Mary M., & Sarason, I. G. The effect of differential motivating instructions on the emotional tone and outcome of TAT stories. *J. consult. Psychol.*, 1958, **22**, 385–388.

Sundberg, N. D. The acceptability of "fake" versus "bona fide" personality interpretations. *J. abnorm. soc. Psychol.*, 1955, **50**, 145–147.

Sundberg, N. D. The practice of psychological testing in clinical services in the United States. *Amer. Psychologist,* 1961, **16**, 79–83.

Symonds, P. M. *Symonds Picture Story Test.* New York: Bureau of Publications, Teachers College, Columbia Univer., 1948.

Symonds, P. M. *Adolescent fantasy: an investigation of the picture-story method of personality study.* New York: Columbia Univer. Press, 1949.

Symonds, P. M., & Jensen, A. R. *From adolescent to adult.* New York: Columbia Univer. Press, 1961.

Takahashi, S. An investigation into aggressive behavior of children as seen through projective tests. (In Japanese.) *Jap. J. educ. Psychol.*, 1960, **8**, 85–91. (*Psychol. Abstr.*, **35**, 2232.)

Telford, C. W. The refractory phase of voluntary and associative processes. *J. exp. Psychol.*, 1931, **14**, 1–36.

Terry, Dorothy. The use of a rating scale of level of response in TAT stories. *J. abnorm. soc. Psychol.*, 1952, **47**, 507–511.

Thompson, C. E. *Thematic Apperception Test: Thompson modification.* Cambridge, Mass.: Harvard Univer. Press, 1949. (a)

Thompson, C. E. The Thompson modification of the Thematic Apperception Test. *Rorschach Res. Exch. & J. proj. Tech.*, 1949, **13**, 469–478. (b)

Thompson, C. E., & Bachrach, A. J. The use of color in the Thematic Apperception Test. *J. proj. Tech.*, 1951, **15**, 173–184.

Thompson, Laura, & Joseph, Alice. *The Hopi way.* Chicago: Univer. of Chicago Press, 1944.

Thurston, J. R., & Mussen, P. H. Infant feeding gratification and adult personality. *J. Pers.*, 1951, **19**, 449–458.

Tompkins, S. S. The limits of material obtainable in the single case study by daily administration of the Thematic Apperception Test. *Psychol. Bull.*, 1942, **39**, 490.

Tomkins, S. S. *The Thematic Apperception Test: the theory and technique of interpretation.* New York: Grune & Stratton, 1947.

Tristano, M. TAT patterns of professional jazz musicians. Unpublished master's thesis, Loyola Univer., Chicago, 1953.

Tumen, Ethel D. A comparison of TAT personality findings with psychoanalytic findings. Unpublished master's thesis, City Coll. of New York, 1951.

Turner, G. C., & Coleman, J. C. Examiner influence on Thematic Apperception Test responses. *J. proj. Tech.*, 1962, **26**, 478–486.

Ullmann, L. P. Productivity and the clinical use of TAT cards. *J. proj. Tech.*, 1957, **21**, 399–403.

Ullmann, L. P., & McFarland, R. L. Productivity as a variable in TAT protocols: a methodological study. *J. proj. Tech.*, 1957, **21**, 80–87.

Valentine, M., & Robin, A. A. Aspects of thematic apperception testing: depression. *J. ment. Sci.*, 1950, **96**, 435–447. (a)

Valentine, M., & Robin, A. A. Aspects of thematic apperception testing: paranoid schizophrenia. *J. ment. Sci.*, 1950, **96**, 869–888. (b)

Van Lennep, D. J. *The Four-Picture Test.* The Hague, Netherlands: Martinus Nijhoff, 1948.

Van Lennep, D. J. The Four-Picture Test. In H. H. Anderson & Gladys Anderson (Eds.), *An introduc-*

tion to projective techniques. Englewood Cliffs, N.J.: Prentice-Hall, 1951. Pp. 149–180.

Vernier, Claire M., Whiting, J. F., & Meltzer, M. L. Differential prediction of a specific behavior from three projective techniques. *J. consult. Psychol.*, 1955, **19**, 175–182.

Vernon, P. E., & Parry, J. B. *Personnel selection in the British forces.* London: Univer. of London Press, 1949.

Veroff, J. Development and validation of a projective measure of power motivation. In J. W. Atkinson (Ed.), *Motives in fantasy, action, and society.* Princeton, N.J.: Van Nostrand, 1958. Pp. 105–116. (a)

Veroff, J. A scoring manual for the power motive. In *ibid.* Pp. 219–233. (b)

Veroff, J. Thematic apperception in a nationwide sample survey. In J. Kagan & G. S. Lesser (Eds.), *Contemporary issues in thematic apperceptive methods.* Springfield, Ill.: Charles C Thomas, 1961. Pp. 83–111.

Veroff, J., Atkinson, J. W., Feld, Sheila C., & Gurin, G. The use of thematic apperception to assess motivation in a nationwide interview study. *Psychol. Monogr.*, 1960, **74**, No. 12 (Whole No. 499).

Veroff, J., Wilcox, Sue, & Atkinson, J. W. The achievement motive in high school and college age women. *J. abnorm. soc. Psychol.*, 1953, **48**, 108–119.

Vorhaus, Pauline G. Case study of an adolescent boy with reading disability. *J. proj. Tech.*, 1952, **16**, 20–41. (a)

Vorhaus, Pauline G. *TAT summary record blank.* New York: Harcourt, Brace & World, 1952. (b)

Walker, E. L., & Atkinson, J. W. The expression of fear-related motivation in thematic apperception as a function of proximity to an atomic explosion. In J. W. Atkinson (Ed.), *Motives in fantasy, action, and society.* Princeton, N.J.: Van Nostrand, 1958.

Walker, R. G. A comparison of clinical manifestations of hostility with Rorschach and MAPS test performances. *J. proj. Tech.*, 1951, **15**, 444–460.

Wallen, R. W. The Thematic Apperception Test. In R. W. Wallen, *Clinical psychology: the study of persons.* New York: McGraw-Hill, 1956. Pp. 221–255.

Warner, W. L., & Henry, W. E. The radio day time serial: a symbolic analysis. *Genet. Psychol. Monogr.*, 1948, **37**, 3–71.

Watson, R. I. The Thematic Apperception Test. In R. I. Watson, *The clinical method in psychology.* New York: Harper & Row, 1951. Pp. 436–523.

Waxenberg, S. E. Psychosomatic patients and other physically ill persons: a comparative study. *J. consult. Psychol.*, 1955, **19**, 163–169.

Wayne, D. M., Adams, M., & Rowe, Lillian. A study of military prisoners at a disciplinary barracks suspected of homosexual activities. *Milit. Surg.*, 1947, **101**, 499–504.

Weatherley, D. Maternal permissiveness toward aggression and subsequent TAT aggression. *J. abnorm. soc. Psychol.*, 1962, **65**, 1–5.

Webb, W. B., & Hilden, A. H. Verbal and intellectual ability as factors in projective test results. *J. proj. Tech.*, 1953, **17**, 102–103.

Webster, H. Derivation and use of the masculinity-femininity variable. *J. clin. Psychol.*, 1953, **9**, 33–36.

Weisskopf, Edith A. An experimental study of the effect of brightness and ambiguity on projection in the Thematic Apperception Test. *J. Psychol.*, 1950, **29**, 407–416. (a)

Weisskopf, Edith A. A transcendence index as a proposed measure in the TAT. *J. Psychol.*, 1950, **29**, 379–390. (b)

Weisskopf, Edith A., & Dieppa, J. J. Experimentally induced faking of TAT responses. *J. consult. Psychol.*, 1951, **15**, 469–474.

Weisskopf, Edith A., & Dunlevy, G. P., Jr. Bodily similarity between subject and central figure in the TAT as an influence on projection. *J. abnorm. soc. Psychol.*, 1952, **47**, 441–445.

Weisskopf-Joelson, Edith A., Asher, E. J., Albrecht, K. J., & Hoffman, M. L. An experimental investigation of "label-avoidance" as a manifestation of repression. *J. proj. Tech.*, 1957, **21**, 88–93.

Weisskopf-Joelson, Edith A., & Lynn, D. B. The effect of variations in ambiguity on projection in the Children's Apperception Test. *J. consult. Psychol.*, 1953, **17**, 67–70.

Weisskopf-Joelson, Edith A., & Money, L., Jr. Facial similarity between subject and central figure in the TAT as an influence on projection. *J. abnorm. soc. Psychol.*, 1953, **48**, 341–344.

Welch, B., Schafer, R., & Dember, Cynthia. TAT stories of hypomanic and depressed patients. *J. proj. Tech.*, 1961, **25**, 221–232.

Wentworth-Rohr, I. A study in the differential diagnosis of idiopathic and symptomatic epilepsy through psychological tests. Unpublished doctoral dissertation, New York Univer., 1950. (*Microfilm Abstr.*, **11**, 180.)

West, E. P. The effects of procedure on productivity of the TAT. Unpublished master's thesis, Washington State College, 1953. Cited by Sauer & Marcuse, 1957.

White, R. W. Prediction of hypnotic suggestibility from a knowledge of subjects' attitudes. *J. Psychol.*, 1937, **3**, 265–277.

Whitehouse, Elizabeth. Norms for certain aspects of the Thematic Apperception Test on a group of nine and ten year old children. *Persona,* 1949, **1,** 12–15. (*Psychol. Abstr.*, **24,** 1210.)

Wilson, R. N. The poet and the projective test. *J. Aesthet. art Crit.*, 1958, **16,** 319–327.

Winch, R. F., & More, D. M. Does TAT add information to interviews? Statistical analysis of the increment. *J. clin. Psychol.,* 1956, **12,** 316–321.

Winchester, T. H. A study of differences between written and oral protocols from the Thematic Apperception Test. Unpublished master's thesis, Univer. of Denver, 1948.

Witkin, H. A., Dyak, R. B., Faterson, H. F., Goodenough, D. R., & Karp, S. A. *Psychological differentiation: studies of development.* New York: Wiley, 1962.

Witkin, H. A., Lewis, H. B., Hertzman, M., Machover, K., Meissner, P. B., & Wapner, S. *Personality through perception: an experimental and clinical study.* New York: Harper & Row, 1954.

Wittenborn, J. R. Some Thematic Apperception Test norms and a note on the use of the test cards in the guidance of college students. *J. clin. Psychol.*, 1949, **5**, 157–161.

Wohl, J. A note on the generality of constriction. *J. proj. Tech.*, 1957, **21,** 410–413.

Woolley, L. F. New approaches to understanding the alcoholic. A. Introduction. *Alcohol Hyg.*, 1945, **1,** 3–8. Cited by H. G. Gough, The frame of reference of the Thematic Apperception Test, *J. clin. Psychol.*, 1948, **4,** 90–92.

Wyatt, F. The scoring and analysis of the Thematic Apperception Test. *J. Psychol.,* 1947, **24,** 319–330.

Wyatt, F., & Veroff, Joanne B. Thematic apperception and fantasy tests. In D. Brower & L. E. Abt (Eds.), *Progress in clinical psychology.* Vol. 2. New York: Grune & Stratton, 1956. Pp. 32–57.

Young, Florence M. Responses of juvenile delinquents to the Thematic Apperception Test: *J. genet. Psychol.*, 1956, **88,** 251–259.

Zeichner, A. M. Psychosexual identification in paranoid schizophrenia. *J. proj. Tech.*, 1955, **19,** 67–77.

Zeichner, A. M. Conception of masculine and feminine roles in paranoid schizophrenia. *J. proj. Tech.*, 1956, **20,** 348–354.

23

Diagnostic Methods in Childhood Disorders

FLORENCE HALPERN

Like the adult, the child is a dynamic entity, engaged in activity geared toward the reduction of whatever tension he is experiencing. However, just as the needs, interests, activities, and usual, accepted form of behavior of the child differ in many respects from those of the adult, so too do his efforts at coping with discomfort and anxiety. Correspondingly, any evaluation of a child's adjustment, of the adequacy of his functioning, whether or not he is suffering from a "disorder," must take into account the fact that he is still a developing organism that has not yet reached complete physical, mental, or emotional status. Diagnostic procedures with children must be predicated on a thorough knowledge of the problems typical for each age and the ways in which most children at any given age view these problems and respond to them. Normative studies, plus a grasp of what is involved in the growth process in all areas, are the foundation stones for effective clinical diagnostic work with children.

For the infant, "anxiety" stems primarily from bodily discomfort caused most frequently by pain and hunger, although other factors, such as a sensing of changes in the environment or of aloneness, also contribute to his distress. Once there is even a rudimentary awareness of self, the causes of tension and anxiety include not only bodily discomfort but also psychic distress. However, what causes such distress, how meaningful it is to the child, and how he attempts to cope with it, vary markedly from age to age. For instance, a 3½-year-old who is experiencing severe separation anxiety the first day he is taken to nursery school is very likely to react to this anxiety by clinging to his mother in a desperate fashion as he pleads and cries. The 10-year-old boy going to sleep-away camp for the first time may also be suffering from separation anxiety, but he will probably use very different techniques from those of the 3-year-old as he attempts to reduce that anxiety.

The differences in adjustive efforts at different ages are of course due mainly to the differences in ego strength that the child can be expected to possess. Ego development is an ongoing, unfolding process, based initially on innate factors but very strongly influenced by the environmental forces that come to bear on it from the moment of birth and even before birth. The organism strives to effect a resolution between his innate tendencies and external pressures. When the child is not impaired by constitutional weakness or early trauma (mental deficiency; innate vulnerability; brain injury before, during, or after birth), reasonably satisfying resolution can be achieved, provided the environment is of an adequately understanding and supporting order.

For Freud the innate factors are of prime importance. Thus in "Analysis, Terminable and Interminable" (1938), he says: "It does not imply a mystical over-estimation of heredity if we think it credible that, even before the ego exists, its subsequent lines of developmental tendencies and reactions are already determined." For others, particularly some of the neo-Freudians, environmental factors are all-important. Apparently then we are still struggling with the old nature-nurture problem. The significant fact for the clinician who is attempting to evaluate the child's ego strength is the awareness of the importance of both innate and environmental forces in influencing the child's development and adjustment. In particular it must be borne in mind that in the very earliest period of his life, the child is totally dependent upon his environment and can only gradually separate himself from it, physically and psychologically. Even in the later stages of childhood, this dependence, while not as extreme as in infancy, remains a most important factor with which to reckon. Consequently, the reasons why the child has chosen a particular style of life and the adequacy of his particular adjustive efforts can be effectively evaluated only if the nature of the environment—its potential for facilitating, hindering, or actually impairing the child's development—is fully understood.

Less important than an appreciation of the reality of the child's dependence on the outside world, but a factor which nevertheless plays a part in the total diagnostic picture, is the child's understanding of, and attitude toward, the diagnostic experience. In the majority of instances the adult comes for diagnostic evaluation because he recognizes that he has a problem, that he needs help. This is seldom so with the child. It is the rare child who realizes he is maladjusted or who requests help in dealing with his problems. He comes for diagnosis and treatment because others feel he needs it. In fact questioning often reveals that the child does not know why he has come for interview, examination, and observation. When he is somewhat aware of what the procedures are intended to achieve, it is usually because "My mother thinks I have a problem," "I get bad marks in school," "I fight with my sister," etc. The way this information is communicated certainly suggests that in the majority of instances, the child sees the problem as someone else's, not his, concern, and hence his attitude toward the diagnostic relationship may be rather different from that of the adult, at least during the initial contact. His reactions to whatever explanations are offered him by the psychologist and any change in his attitude during the examination procedures can have some diagnostic and predictive value. Certainly the child who comes to recognize his problem and his involvement in it probably has a far better prognosis where therapy is concerned than the child who persists in his denial of any problems, who keeps on reiterating that he does not know and cannot possibly imagine why he is being seen by the diagnostician.

DIAGNOSTIC METHODS

While there are then differences in the diagnostic approach to the behavior and productions of children and adults, these differences consist mainly in the way behavior and test reactions are interpreted rather than in the actual methods employed to evoke such behavior and communications. What is being primarily sought is a measure of ego strength as it manifests itself in the child's functioning in different areas. From a thorough diagnostic evaluation, the nature of the child's adjustment—positive or negative—the dynamic reasons that led to his particular form of adjustment, and the best ways for modifying that adjustment when need for this is indicated can all be ascertained. The term "diagnosis" is being used here in the fullest sense of the word. This includes not only a clinical classification but also an appreciation of etiological and dynamic factors, an evaluation of resources, prognosis, and recommendations for treatment.

Hartmann (1958) states that no one has ever presented a complete list of ego functions. Among those he cites as particularly important are the individual's relation to reality, the effectiveness of his reality testing, the organization and control of motility and perception, and the development of a protective barrier between external and internal stimulation. From a purely practical and operational point of view, it might be said that "ego" is the term used to cover all those functions of the organism which enable it to experience itself and act in self-fulfilling yet environmentally acceptable fashion, thus attaining a state of equilibrium that satisfies inner needs and outer pressures, without producing lasting, pervasive, and crippling anxiety.

Lois Murphy (1962) discusses the developmental problem under the general heading of "coping" styles. For her, these are the "ways of talking about and thinking about what we see when children confront new situations and challenges calling for responses not previously crystallized." Coping is seen as the process, while "adaptation" is the end result.

To assess the adequacy of the child's ego development or coping methods, the clinician evaluates his intellectual functioning, including his verbal ability, his reasoning capacity, his organizing and integrative level, his learning and memory, etc. The nature of his perceptual processes and the richness of his emotional and fantasy life are all part of such an evaluation. Even the child's capacity for regression when this facilitates adjustment should be ascertained. While regression in the very young child (the 2- to 3-year-old) is likely to result in disorganization, in somewhat older children this adjustive effort may have the same positive significance that it does for the adult.

The ways in which the clinician seeks to obtain the measures that are essential for diagnostic purposes are much the same as those employed in the diagnostic process with adults, primarily observation, interviewing, testing, and therapy.

Observation includes observation of the subject, the environment, and the interaction between the subject and his environment. In the early stages of life, this means the immediate members of the family, and as the child's world expands, this takes in peers, teachers, etc. Such observation is most rewarding when it can be extended over a period of time, rather than when it is limited to one or two sessions, and when it can encompass different kinds of situations, formal and informal.

Interviewing (see "The Interview," above) also involves the subject and the significant others in his life. In the case of the infant, interviewing is of course impossible. Interviewing the mother, and possibly also the father, the nurse, and the pediatrician, is most important. When the child is old enough to understand what is being said to him and has sufficient verbal skill to be able to respond, interviewing becomes a most important way of evaluating his perception of himself and his world and how he is trying to present himself to the environment. The interviewing procedure must, of course, be modified to conform to the child's interests and level of comprehension. In this connection informal conversation which the diagnostician can direct into specific channels is likely to be far more rewarding than direct questioning.

Testing (see "Diagnostic Use of Intelligence Tests," above) includes not only intelligence and achievement testing but also the use of "tests" geared to reveal the total personality picture. The former are practically always administered to the child, the only exception being when such testing has been done in the very recent past and the clinician has access to the results. The personality tests, on the other hand, are used not only with the child but also, at least in some instances, with the mother, father, sibling, etc.

The inclusion of *therapy* in the category of diagnostic methods is justified on a number of counts. For one thing, therapy validates or invalidates the diagnostic prediction and in that sense is an extension of the diagnostic process. In addition, there are instances when therapy, either as it is usually conceived of or in the form of an extended "initial interview," can actually clarify the diagnosis in all its ramifications.

In the following pages an attempt will be made to indicate in some detail how these various methods can be best employed in diagnosing children. In most instances, at least observation, interview, and testing should be employed in order to obtain the most valid results. While it is true that an experienced, sensitive clinician may arrive at a correct diagnosis on the basis of just one diagnostic assessment—that is, through observation, interview, or testing, particularly in instances where the deviations are extreme and therefore readily detected—the picture becomes richer and more reliable when all approaches are employed. Actually they cannot be separated, for no testing takes place without observation and probably some interviewing, no interviewing can be done without observation and some modified testing, etc.

Although the title of this chapter stresses "methods," surely the focal points of interest are the child and his environment. Hence, following the formula used in writing diagnostic reports and in carrying out any evaluative procedure, emphasis will primarily be not on the technique or "method," but on the subject to whom the method is applied.

THE INFANT

As was noted above, in the very earliest stages of life there is no ego, only an organism with bodily needs which produce a state of tension when they are not adequately met. Any evaluation of the infant's place on the sickness-health, adjusted-maladjusted continuum, any attempt to prognosticate whether or not he will fall into the group designated as having "childhood disorders," depends largely then on an evaluation of the biological and neurological equipment he possesses and his rate of maturation.

Observation of the infant at various times, asleep and awake, with the mother and without the mother; interviewing of the mother or mother surrogate; possible interviews with the father and the pediatrician; and "testing" are the major ways that the infant is assessed by the clinical psychologist. Occasionally counseling of the mother, which may be construed as a form of "diagnostic therapy" if the term is stretched broadly enough, also facilitates diagnosis and prognosis. For example, a newborn infant cried each time he was diapered, although observation indicated that the mother handled him with gentleness and consideration. Other aspects of the child's behavior suggested that he might be a potential schizophrenic and that his crying when diapered was due to the excessive sensitivity to temperature changes often seen in these infants. The mother was advised to throw a blanket over the child while changing his diapers, and when she did this the crying ceased. While of course any prediction about this child (who became clearly psychotic at the age of 3) on the basis of just one such manifestation would be completely unwarranted, it did constitute an effective way of validating at least one hypothesis about this child, namely, that he was overly sensitive to certain changes in his environment and therefore experienced easy and frequent disturbances of his equilibrium.

Although as yet there is no ego, trained and untrained observers who study the newborn recognize that there are striking differences among infants in the first days, even in the first hours, of life. However, except in cases of gross and fairly obvious anomalies (caused by severe cogenital deficiency or brain damage), it is only recently that any efforts have been made to evaluate and understand these differences in terms of the developmental process and the capacity for ultimate adjustment.

The scales developed by Gesell (Gesell & Amatruda, 1941) and his coworkers are probably the ones most widely used in this country for obtaining an estimate of the infant's rate of development and ultimate potential. They are not simply intelligence tests in the usual sense of the word, and it is significant that what results from this "testing" is described not as an intelligence quotient but as a developmental quotient. The scales evaluate the child's development in four areas: language, motor, adaptive, and personal-social. These functions are viewed as ongoing processes, with specific skills and correlated behaviors appearing at certain ages. Emphasis is on the concept of a "behavior pattern" involving all four functions, and these behavior patterns are described as "the end products of development."

Although Gesell stresses the concept of "behavior patterns," he bases his conclusions almost entirely on the speed and effectiveness of physical maturation. More recently, investigators have focused on other factors, innate and environmental, which might have an impact on the infant's development and eventual adjustment. For example, the infant's predisposition toward indulgence in physical activity, the extent and nature of this, and the effect such behavior has on the subject's environment constitute one such area of investigation (see Friess & Woolf, 1953).

Based on Bender's (1947; Bender & Freedman, 1952) formulation that "childhood schizophrenia represents a lag in maturation within the embryonic level of development," Barbara Fish (1957; 1959; 1960) observed a small number of infants and indicated which ones she felt were vulnerable and might well become schizophrenic. Subsequent follow-up studies, including psychological testing, confirmed the accuracy of her predictions.[1] Her conclusions are based mainly on the hypersensitivity these infants manifested in response to certain forms of stimuli and on the uneven, erratic way their development proceeded. As

[1] Paper to be published.

she described them, these infants showed marked retardation in some areas and precocious functioning in others. Regression of a severe order also occurred as the infant lost skills and strengths that he once definitely possessed.

Using careful, detailed observations of infants, Sibylle Escalona and Grace Heider (1959) also made predictions about the nature of the infant's future adjustment. In some respects the predictions proved quite accurate, and in others less so. The lack of greater predictive success does not in any way imply that such predictions cannot eventually be achieved with a high degree of accuracy as our understanding of the personality traits under examination and our knowledge of what specifically influences such traits improve. At present, we are just beginning to break ground where prognosis of infant adjustment, based on observation of the infant and his environment, is concerned.

Sibylle Escalona (Bergman & Escalona, 1949; Escalona, 1950; Escalona, 1953; Escalona & Leitch, 1953), like Fish, talks about uneven development as an indicator of future difficulties. In fact, in analyzing the functioning of the infants she studied, she uses the term "scatter" in much the same way that clinicians employ it in describing the intellectual performance of older subjects on intelligence tests.

For Sibylle Escalona and Grace Heider (1959), the factor that stood up best as a prognostic indicator was the infant's early response to space. The child who had difficulty in coping with space, in relating to space, was also the one who later manifested a disturbance in his adjustment. This finding ties in with what is so frequently seen in schizophrenic children. They often show severe disturbances in spatial orientation and seem far more easily confused and lost when left in unfamiliar places than other children. On tests which involve spatial relations, such as the Object Assembly test of the Wechsler Intelligence Scale for Children or the Bender-Gestalt test, this weakness is also apparent.

Margaret Friess and Paul Woolf's observations of infants led them to formulate the concept of "congenital activity type." This was based on the amount of activity the infant manifested during the first three months of life in response to certain stimuli. They classify these infants according to whether they are quiet, moderately active, active, hypoactive, or hyperactive. The infants in the two latter groups they regard as vulnerable to disturbance, whereas those in the three other groups are seen as much less vulnerable and therefore far less likely to present disorders later.

All the investigators cited so far in this chapter agree that excessive sensitivity to certain stimuli marks a child as "vulnerable." In addition, uneven development in the infant is also noted as forecasting possible disturbance. Early recognition of such vulnerability is highly significant for both prevention and treatment. The mother who is prepared in advance for her child's oversensitivity and uneven development will be less disturbed when deviations occur than she would otherwise be; and furthermore, with support and guidance, she may be able to shield the child from some sources of tension and also lend him some of the ego strength that he so desperately needs.

The studies reported above focus mainly on constitutional factors as sources of infant and, later, childhood disturbance. However, severe and lasting disturbance stemming from adverse experiences with the environment have also been noted. Spitz (1947)observed the behavior of very young children who had been separated from their mothers. He noted that if the relationship between the child and the mother was a gratifying one for the child, grief resulting from lasting separation became so severe as to result in a generally poor prognosis, including intellectual retardation and even loss of life as the child withdraws completely from interaction with his environment.

Goldfarb (1943; 1945) evaluated the effects of early institutionalization and found that in those instances where the child was placed in a "home" during the first few months of life, where environmental stimulation was minimal and no consistent mother figure was available, the effect on the child's development and adjustment in all areas—intellectual, emotional, and social—was a poor one. Regardless of what the child's potentialities may have been, his mental functioning, as reflected in his intelligence test score, was poor, verbal ability underdeveloped, and affect infantile. From the predictive point of view, this kind of early history offers a very poor prognosis. Lack of love and adequate stimulation in the early, crucial years results in what seems like an irreversible defect in the total personality.

Less severe and pervasive disturbances may arise from the interaction of the child and the mother even during the first few days and weeks of life. The child who cries all night, who is tense and does not eat, who later becomes a head banger, etc., may be responding to what for him is the unsatisfactory nature of his immediate world. The mother's uneasiness in handling him, her sense of pressure because she has so much to do, her distaste for his messiness and the sour smell of his regurgitated food, all may be conveyed to him in the way she holds him and responds to him. Sometimes just temperamental differences lead to difficulty. The very quick, active mother may find her quiet, placid child disappointing, uninteresting; or the quiet mother may be distressed by the behavior of her "active" child. Observation of the child will indicate whether his activity or placidity is within the normal range, while observation of the mother should point up some of her needs and feelings in this respect. Prevention of continued unhappiness on the part of both mother and child can then be effected if, after observing the mother and child together, the nature of the problem is pointed out to her and modifications in her own reactions are suggested.

THE CHILD

Once the period of infancy is passed, diagnosis, prediction, and recommendation must take into account a multiplicity of factors that previously did not obtain. Now the child's world has grown enormously. He can move around and manipulate objects; he can assert himself and express his needs and feelings. Objects other than the mother play a meaningful part in his life, and their impact on him must also be evaluated.

Most significant is the emergence of the sense of self, the "me." In the developmental process, the first ego to emerge is the "body ego," as the child becomes aware of the separation of his body from the body of the mother. Following this comes the concept of "me" as opposed to "not-me" in areas other than the body. Mastery of the self and the environment now becomes an important objective as he constantly expands his horizons, physical and psychological.

In a heterogeneous culture such as ours, it is impossible to recognize and enumerate all the possible combinations of defensive and adaptive techniques that different children develop once the period of infancy is passed. Such a discussion would have to take into account the appropiateness of these different techniques at different age levels, and this would fill a volume in itself. The customary division of childhood into the preschool and school-age periods does not in any way help to solve this issue. The preschool period is from about age 3 to age 5 or 6, and surely what is appropriate for the 3-year-old is not appropriate for the 5- or 6-year-old. Similarly, in the school-age group, the 6-year-old is a very different person from the 10-year-old. All that can be attempted here is a presentation of the types of disturbances characteristic of childhood at all ages, with indications of how they can be recognized and evaluated by the clinician.

For the purposes of this chapter, childhood disorders will be divided into two groups: those caused primarily by organic impairment and those resulting from adverse experiences with the environment. The former group comprises mentally defective, brain-damaged, and most probably schizophrenic children. The latter includes neurotic children, those suffering from nightmares and school phobias, the stutterers, etc.; the children with learning difficulties arising from causes other than limited intelligence; and the acting-out, behavior-problem children.

Assessment of *mental deficiency* depends in good part on intelligence testing (usually the Stanford-Binet, the Wechsler Intelligence Scale for Children, or the progressive matrices, plus achievement tests). In addition, a developmental history, observation of the child, and interview with the mother are all indicated.

Typical of the intellectual functioning of the mentally defective child is his limited understanding of much that he encounters and his inability to deal effectively with much that he is asked to do. He cannot make the correct associations to the stimuli presented to him unless these are of a very simple and familiar order, and he is grossly lacking when required to analyze, organize, and conceptualize. His limitations will be apparent in all areas of functioning; that is, there will be no sudden, unexpected indications of better than defective ability, no flashes of insight that suggest potentialities of a better order than his tests scores indicate. Furthermore, his defects will become increasingly apparent as the situations he is called on to meet become more complex and as higher levels of intellectual functioning are required.

The mental defective's way of meeting his limitations will vary, depending upon the extent of his developmental lag and the attitude of his environment toward him and his deficiencies. Thus, he may be passive and dependent, in this way eliciting from those about him the support and security he needs; he may withdraw from his environment because his contacts with the outside world have netted him only unhappiness, confusion, and frustration; or he may attempt to deny his limitations and act as though there was nothing wrong with him (and indeed he may not appreciate that there is) and correspondingly act in an uncriticial, impulsive fashion which is likely to get him into difficulties.

Diagnosis and prediction regarding the defective's future adjustment depend not only on his performance on the intelligence test—on the IQ he attains—but also on his emotional stability, his capacity for going along in simple routines in a way which suggests that he may eventually be able to be profitably employed, and the willingness and the ability of his environment to provide him with the support and guidance that he requires. Evaluation of all these factors involves observation of, and interviews with, the child and his parents and also the use of personality testing (Rorschach, TAT or CAT, Figure Drawing) of the child.

A group of *brain-injured* children will show less consistent findings than defective subjects. Functioning and adjustment in the brain-injured child vary markedly, depending upon such factors as the location and extent of the damage; the age at which the injury occurred (that is, before there was an ego, before any skills had been developed, or after most basic functions had been well established); the actual nature of the difficulty, whether or not it is progressive, etc.; the attitude of the child and the family toward his handicap; as well as the premorbid personality of the child.

In a review of current research and criteria for evaluating brain injury in the infant and the preschool child, Frances Graham and Berman (1961) conclude: "It remains an important and virtually untested question whether or not injury early in life has a pattern of impairment similar to that seen in older children and adults." Certainly studies of the functioning of brain-damaged children will not be particularly meaningful or helpful if all different kinds of brain damage, as well as damage occurring at different ages, are grouped together as though they constituted a single syndrome.

When injury occurs before, during, or very shortly after birth and the damage is considerable, the picture may be very like that seen in the defective child. In fact, sometimes only medical and family history can make the distinction, and even then the differential may not be a firm one. On the other hand, mild damage even in the early days of life may go unobserved and be only suspected, but never definitely established in later life, when the child shows some difficulty in motor coordination or exhibits explosive behavior or other reactions associated with organic impairment.

Where the damage is not pervasive, it is possible to distinguish the organic child with the low IQ from the defective child because there will be some areas in which he performs above the defective level. As important as a knowledge of the intellectual functioning in these cases is a complete, detailed account of the child's medical history. Sometimes in the course of giving this account the mother will suddenly remember, but without any appreciation of its significance, that there was a period when the child ran a high fever for some time. She herself does not know what caused this fever or what the diagnosis was. Sometimes it is possible to contact the physician who cared for the child during this illness or to obtain hospital records. At other times one can only speculate on what may have been wrong, but certainly the possibility of some form of encephalopathy suggests itself.

In some instances of brain damage the child will present a picture of impaired intellectual functioning that is very similar to that classically described as characteristic of the adult "organic" patient (see Part 4, "Clinical Patterns"); that is, his scores on the performance items of the intelligence scale will be lower than the verbal ones, and he will have particular difficulty with tests involving visual-motor coordination, abstract reasoning, and so on. Impulse control will be weak, with resulting explosive outbursts. While such pictures do occur, there are also many others which bear little or no resemblance to this so-called "typical" one. For example, there is the child who in his efforts to control his impulses resorts to extreme blocking, repression, and constriction and thus presents a picture not unlike that seen in severe obsessive-compulsives. When a subject resorts to such exaggerated forms of defense, and particularly if there does not seem to be a dynamic reason for such modes of adjustment, then some underlying pathology, generally either organicity or schizophrenia, comes into consideration. In such cases the history, the observations, and the test productions must all be minutely scrutinized in order to learn why the child feels so threatened, where his weaknesses lie, and what has caused them.

Current approaches to the organic patient stress the nature of the individual's perception of, and adjustment to, his illness. In the case of the child, the family's attitude toward him and his impairment will go a long way toward determining his concept of it and what it means to him. He may resent his difficulty because it subjects him to restraints and overprotection that he finds most irksome, preventing him from doing many of the things he sees other children doing. He may resent it because he experiences himself as a burden to his family, unwanted and rejected because of the trouble and expense he causes them. On the other hand, it may be that because of his difficulty, he is permitted to be infantile and demanding and is given far more attention and is far more indulged than he would otherwise be. In such a case his impairment is most valuable to him, and he will use it for his own purposes, exaggerating his dependency if he feels this is necessary.

Observation of the child's general behavior, especially in his contacts with the mother and other significant adult figures, and of her response to him becomes crucial in these cases. This is particularly important if the damage the child has suffered is neurologically slight and intellectual impairment minimal or seemingly nonexistent. In all these cases, then, projective testing (Rorschach, CAT or TAT, Figure Drawing, Bender-Gestalt) in conjunction with intelligence testing, medical reports, and observation and interview of the mother and child is the only way the complete picture can be obtained.

As is the case with the organic child, the *schizophrenic child* shows a variety of pictures, ranging from extreme autism to relatively mild yet characteristic schizophrenic departures from normal concepts and normal functioning. In other words, schizophrenia, like any other illness, can run the gamut from slight to very severe. Again as in the organic child, the severity will depend in part at least on the age at which the disturbance became manifest, the innate resources the child can mobilize in his adjustive efforts, and the attitude of the environment toward him and his illness. The common factors in all these cases, severe or mild, is the child's inability to perceive and experience himself in a stable, integrated fashion; to set firm ego boundaries; and to come to terms with reality in an organized, meaningful fashion. Instead, because of the vague, fluid nature of his ego, he experiences both himself and his environment in a diffuse, disorganized manner. Lacking inner stability and organization, he cannot cope constructively with inner or outer pressures. In his case, the ego has erected no "protective barrier," and consequently he is being perpetually flooded by his own primitive, autistic needs and feelings. Correspondingly his reactions are frequently of a deviant, inappropriate, even bizarre order. At the mercy of his impulses, he can perceive the world only as a wild, confusing, dangerous, threatening place, and he reacts to it accordingly, defending himself against it either by withdrawing or by striking back against the objects that he thinks will destroy him.

In contrast to the neurotic child or the child who acts out his disturbances in ways which result in the diagnosis of "primary behavior disorder" (see below), the schizophrenic's deviant functioning and adjustment tend to be pervasive, manifesting themselves in one way or another in all areas—intellectual, emotional, and social—as well as in biological and physiological development. Most conspicuous is the erratic, unpredictable nature of his development and his use of his abilities, very similar to what was noted by the observers of infants. Thus lags and deviations occur along with precocity, and consequently no consistent sense of self or others is possible.

In the intellectual sphere, this highly uneven way of performing is often reflected in the extreme scatter that the subject shows on the intelligence test. For instance, on the Stanford-Binet a 7- or 8-year-old child may base at year V and continue to have successes through year XIV. Similarly, on the WISC, there may be as much as a 12-point or more difference between the low and high score that the schizophrenic child attains. Possibly even more typical for the schizophrenic is the unevenness that characterizes his functioning on any one subtest. He is very likely to fail some easy items, then pass more difficult ones, and continue in this fashion. There is no correlation between the difficulty of the task and his handling of it. Variable effort and attention at the time of testing, as well as very scattered, fragmented observations of the environment and what the environment offers him, seem largely responsible for this rather characteristic way of reacting.

In the social and emotional sphere, the schizophrenic child also shows a wide variety of pictures. There is the autistic child for whom the environment does not really exist. Observation of these children suggests that they know the outside world is there but refuse to permit it to intrude on them, to have any impact on them. Hence they pay no attention to what is said to them, and only when strong efforts are made to force attention do they react to those about them, and then usually in a negative fashion, turning away, expressing their resentment at outside interference through their posture and the release of angry sounds.

At the other end of the continuum there is the schizophrenic child who very much wants to relate to his world but who, because of his inability to control his impulses and feelings and because his concepts are often deviant, even bizarre, has difficulty getting along in his contacts with others. He is then very likely to be criticized by adults and rejected by his peers, thus reinforcing his concept of the world as an unpleasant, possibly dangerous place.

Very often the schizophrenic child manifests certain physical anomalies. According to Bender (1947), he is likely to be too tall or too short, too fat or too thin. Certainly many of the children diagnosed as schizophrenic present such a picture.

In addition to observation of the schizophrenic's behavior in the home, in school, on the playground, etc., personality testing can add a great deal to the understanding of the child's disturbance and his reaction to that disturbance. For example, the unstructured nature of the Rorschach can evoke highly disorganized reactions from the schizophrenic child who is constantly being overwhelmed by every kind of stimulus. In such cases all the indications of "primary-process behavior," lack of reality testing, primitivity, and confusion are rampant. The child simply uses the test stimulus as a springboard for his own highly idiosyncratic associations and makes no effort to bring these in line with more usual concepts. At such times the excessive concreteness and inadequate organizing and integrative abilities of the schizophrenic also become apparent. Thus he can give such interpretations as "A man with three legs and his tail is coming out of his nose and he has two eyes in his tail and he's coming right at me," etc. On the other hand, there are the schizophrenic children who are trying to make order out of inner and outer chaos and who do this by resorting to the commonly employed defenses, particularly withdrawal, denial, repression, blocking, and projection. The picture that emerges from such a child's test protocol will then have many neuroticlike features, but despite all his attempts to adjust, his innate weaknesses will result in occasional breaks of a kind not seen in the neurotic or organic child. However, the fact that the child is trying to adjust, is using his assets in a reasonably positive fashion, certainly points to somewhat more positive ultimate adjustment, provided the environment appreciates and supports his efforts, than is likely to be found in the case of the child who does not have enough resource or desire to make such efforts.

Just as the Rorschach serves as a kind of green light for a release of the child's autistic concepts, so too the CAT or TAT often produces a similar reaction. The child is very likely to start off his story in a way which indicates that he has recognized what the stimulus is, but he then proceeds to move away quickly from that stimulus, and at the end of his story there is little, if any, relation between the stimulus, the child's initial perception and concept, and the end product. What is more, the child's productions are so confused, illogical, and irrelevant that it is often difficult, at times even impossible, to follow him.

Just as such a child's behavior in various life situations is quite different from that of other children, so his behavior in the diagnostic setting, whether it is for interview, observation, testing, or therapy, is of a deviant order. Most children, when invited into an office by a stranger, show an initial hesitance about accepting this invitation. However, with parental reassurance and urging they generally overcome their reluctance. In the case of the schizophrenic child, the response to this particular experience takes a number of forms. The extremely autistic child who ignores the environment may accept or reject the suggestion that he come into the office simply on the basis of whatever inner activity is going on at the moment. The acceptance of this experience, the separation from the mother, does not seem to enter into the picture. Other schizophrenic children may relate too quickly and easily to the interviewer or tester because their relationships are empty and fluid, and they can therefore go readily from one object to another. There are also schizophrenic children who cling desperately to the mother, and it is futile even to try to see such a child unless the mother is also in the room. In fact, in some instances the child refuses to move an inch from the mother's side and may even insist on sitting in her lap.

Interview with the schizophrenic child also carries with it its own unique flavor. To a far greater degree than is typical of other children his age, the schizophrenic child responds to interview in a highly subjective fashion. The questions put to him and the verbal exchange initiated by the interviewer are more likely to be more or less ignored by the child, as he goes along talking only about those matters that concern him at the moment. If the interviewer persists in trying to steer the situation in the direction he would like it to take, the end result is likely to resemble an interplanetary conversation.

Other ways in which the schizophrenic child's productions are likely to differ from those of less disturbed children are his frank expressions of excessive hostility toward the significant figures in his life, particularly parents and siblings; references to excretory and sexual activity; and sudden bizarre comments relevant to whatever issues are currently in the papers or on TV or possibly are being discussed by the parents in the home, the teacher in the school, etc.

Very frequently, observation and "interview" with a schizophrenic child are sufficient to establish the diagnosis. However, intelligence testing not only substantiates the diagnostic impression but also gives a measure of the degree to which the child's illness has interfered with his intellectual functioning and learning ability, and it also points out the areas in which impairment is greatest. It likewise points out those areas in which he may be functioning in highly accelerated fashion, all of which can be useful in arranging an educational program for the child. Personality testing gives a picture of the way in which the child perceives himself and his world; how he is trying to meet the problems that every child, schizophrenic and nonschizophrenic, must face; and what his defensive operations are and where they can be strengthened and where they must be changed. For example, the schizophrenic child who, with the aid of obsessive-compulsive techniques, manages to stay in the environment and function with some degree of effectiveness can be helped in these efforts, whereas the child who resorts only to denial and projection presents a very different picture in terms of educational planning and possible therapy.

In contrast to the various disorders discussed above, there are the *children whose difficulties derive largely from the unsatisfactory nature of their relationships with the environment.* While some constitutional factors, such as a low threshold for emotional stimulation, easy emotional arousal, an innate tendency toward activity, etc., undoubtedly contribute to their problems, the disturbances would probably not have arisen had the environment been of a different order. In evaluating these children, the reasons for their referral and their acceptance of such referral must be evaluated. This is especially important because the symptoms and/or behavior manifested by some of these children is not different from that of children who never come for help. In most instances coming for help for the children of this group, and possibly other groups, depends upon the psychological sophistication of the parents or teachers and their recognition of behavior which signals distress. It also depends upon whether or not the parents are concerned enough about the child to invest the time and money that getting help generally entails and upon what going for help means to the adults in the child's life—whether they regard this as an indication of their own failure, whether it is perceived as a disgrace, or whether it is recognized as a constructive step for the child and his future. Sometimes the only reason a child is brought for diagnosis and treatment is that the school refuses to keep him unless this is done or the court insists upon such a course of action.

The number of personality pictures presented by the children in this group is astronomical. The common factor is the difficulty they have in adjusting to their world, inner and outer, and their inability to bring their own impulses and feelings in line with environmental expectations without feeling frustrated, anxious, or angry. To reduce these feelings and effect some adjustment, they resort to neurotic types of defense or act out their problems directly in their contacts with others. However, although their difficulties cause them to function less adequately than they otherwise might, in certain areas and under certain circumstances, and although they tend at times to be quite self-defeating, the deviations and distortions they manifest are not of a bizarre order and can generally be related dynamically to the child's life experiences. Just why the child chooses a particular form of adjustment or manifests a particular symptom seems in part to be a result of the specific nature of his disturbance and in part a result of the character of his environment. Many far more subtle factors have an impact on this matter of choice of symptom. It is the function of the clinican to try to isolate and understand as many of these factors as possible, the better to appreciate what the symptom is communicating and thus acquire a better understanding of the child.

Observation of the children in this group can shed considerable light on the over-all picture. The child who reacts in a timid, frightened fashion in his contacts with his parents and who strives to present himself to them as a "good," conforming boy while manifesting aggressive, even bullying, behavior with his peers is certainly telling one kind of a story, in contrast to the child who shows just the opposite picture, who is timid with his peers and avoids being alone with them but who is quite assertive and demanding with his parents.

Interview with these children also varies, running the gamut from the shy, inhibited child who responds in monosyllables to the overtalkative child who uses verbal channels as one way of releasing tension, as a means of getting attention, or possibly as a way of controlling the situations in which he finds himself. If he talks, he does not have to hear what others might say to him, and he can determine the direction that the conversation will take.

Many of these children are physically quite restless, seemingly unable to keep their hands off the objects in their vicinity or to sit quietly in their chairs. Many of them show small, ticlike movements; others have very obvious tics.

The way the child perceives and reacts to the interviewing and/or testing situation sheds considerable light on his attitudes toward adults, especially those he perceives as authority figures, and also on the way he would like others to perceive him. Some of these children are made quite anxious by the experience, fearful that they may not perform as well as they think they are expected to or that they may say something they should not say, something that would not be acceptable. Hence they respond hesitantly and cautiously, and their very concern about themselves and the impression they are making tends to handicap them, to reduce their efficiency. These are the children who are dependent on the environment to the point where they will do almost anything to win environmental approval. Their efforts in this connection often take a considerable toll insofar as self-realization and the capacity for happiness are concerned. They are different from those children who constantly ask whether what they have done or what they have said is "right," "smart," "good," etc. Such children also want to impress others and surely have doubts about their adequacy and acceptability, but they are responding to their doubts with attention-getting, assertive forms of behavior, in contrast to the overly anxious, doubt-ridden reactions of the child who produces slowly and tentatively and who is obviously devoting all his effort and energy toward pleasing those about him who are important to him.

Some children reduce the concern the particular situation mobilizes by the adoption of an indifferent attitude. Anything that seems at all difficult to them, that requires any real effort on their part, is likely to be met with a shrug or an "I don't know." They allay whatever sense of discomfort their limitations might evoke by refusing to get involved, refusing to expose themselves to possible frustration or failure. Still other children go to the opposite extreme, never admitting that any experience or any task is too much for them. Thus when a question on the intelligence test is well beyond them, they sit as if considering it, and nothing happens until the examiner suggests they try something else. When admission of failure is inevitable, they find justification for their shortcomings or put the blame for them onto the environment. Thus instead of "I don't know" they say: "We didn't learn that yet," "My mother didn't tell me," "There aren't enough pieces so nobody could do it," etc. Then there are the talkers, the jokers, the laughers, who either are unconcerned or try to convince themselves and others that they are not troubled by the experience, even when it is obviously anxiety-evoking to them.

One important observation that can be made during the course of the interview or the test is of the change that frequently takes place during the time that the child is being studied. The child who can overcome his anxiety and then respond more freely and easily, the child who can stop talking and joking excessively because sooner or later he begins to feel more comfortable, has a degree of flexibility, a capacity for modifying inappropriate forms of behavior, that points to certain strengths.

In actual "interview" with these children, a great deal can be learned about what talking actually means to them. For some, talking is a way of avoiding their own feelings and also of pushing away the feelings of others. For some, talking has a kind of magical quality which they hope may somehow relieve whatever distress they are experiencing. For others, words are mysterious, threatening forces that can expose them, get them into difficulties, and cause them embarrassment. Yet unlike the schizophrenic child, whose recourse to words often reflects only confusion and disorganization, and unlike the organic child, who may have difficulty finding the words to express his ideas, the child with an emotional "problem" generally talks in a reasonably coherent and appropriate manner. While he may express anger at his parents and others for whatever frustrations and unhappiness he is experiencing, he is unlikely to do this in extreme and violent terms, as the psychotic child might.

It is of course not only the way in which the child communicates but also what he communicates that is important in the total diagnostic effort. Again the child who is probably best described as emotionally disturbed but not psychotic or organic will talk about his difficulties as he sees them, but he will also, particularly as he gets older, exercise restraint and display a certain degree of reticence about what he tells and does not tell. Once a good relationship with him has been established, the young child, the preschool child, is likely to talk quite freely about himself—what he is doing, thinking, and feeling at the moment or what he did, thought, or felt during some recent experience that was important to him. He is much less likely to respond to direct questioning, although in the course of his running commentary about himself, occasional questions can of course be introduced.

Without any direct questioning, many 5-, 6-, and 7-year-olds are quite ready to tell anyone who shows the slightest interest all they know about their family and family activities. Their interest in what is going on in their homes seems to lead them to the conclusion that others share equally in this interest. The fact that much that they say is likely to be listened to with avidity by neighbors and also produce some kind of emotional reaction from the members of their own family is probably another reason why children of this age are so willing to share what they have heard and observed in the home with others.

Around the age of 8, the child becomes more maturely identified with his family and no longer wants to share with others all the details of family arguments, family finances, or what have you. The child is no longer naïve about what he is communicating and therefore is less ready to share with others all the information he may have. Interview with these older children must therefore be handled carefully. Yet as is so frequently the case, conversation geared for one purpose may end up fulfilling another. For example, in the first therapy hour with an 8-year-old boy, the therapist asked him whether he knew why he was coming to see her. When he responded negatively, she explained to him that he was coming because his mother thought he was not very happy and that the therapist might be able to find out why this was so and help alter the situation. The child's response was: "My mother knows I'm unhappy! My mother cares I'm unhappy!" Hours of talking and questioning could not have given greater insight into the way this boy experienced his relation to his mother.

What the child consciously and deliberately communicates and what he withholds should be evaluated in terms of what other children at any given age are ready to reveal and also in terms of what we know about personality dynamics. What the subject is ready to talk about is not usually the core of his problem. The child chooses to talk about certain experiences and certain relationships for a variety of reasons. One child may tell things about his parents that other children hesitate to express because in desperation he is looking for an understanding adult who hopefully can change the unhappy situation in which he finds himself. Hence, although he does so with reluctance, such a child will eventually confess that his father frightens him because he shouts all the time, hits him and his mother, etc. On the other hand, a child might relate such matters quite freely because his identification with, and feeling for, the parents is so weak and limited that he is more concerned with exposing, embarrassing, or getting even with them than he is in shielding them from external criticism.

Interview with the child is of course not confined simply to verbal interchange. Other factors, such as the way the child separates himself from the mother and the way he relates to the examiner, are all diagnostically important (see above). The child who is not psychotic but who nevertheless cannot tolerate the separation is a most insecure child, seriously disturbed by every new experience, often because of the threat of his own primitive unacceptable impulses and his need for the concrete presence of the controlling authority figure. The child who has been threatened with separation or who has actually experienced separation will of course also find any effort to part him from the mother a fulfillment of his worst fears. Again, the child who is engaged in an intensive, persistent power struggle with authority, constantly testing out authority, will use the attempt to separate him from the mother as still one more way in which he can assert himself. Which of these reasons obtains in any individual case can generally be determined from the way in which the child carries out his resistance movement, along with careful observation of the mother's response to the child's unwillingness to leave her.

Testing with this group of children serves many important functions. Because of the very important part that school and formal intellectual functioning play in the child's life, intelligence testing (unless of course there is a full, reliable report of recent testing available) should always be undertaken. Although the intertest patterns obtained from this group of subjects will vary greatly and although differential diagnosis based on the findings of the intelligence scale is not as feasible as in the case of organic and schizophrenic children, the test results can indicate whether the child is being subjected to too much or too little pressure where intellectual achievement is concerned and whether his anxieties and his efforts at dealing with these anxieties are interfering somewhat with the effectiveness of his functioning. For example, the overly tense or preoccupied child will have difficulty in concentrating, and the rebellious child may show a marked inability to deal as adequately as he might with tasks requiring disciplined effort, such as arithmetical reasoning.

The content of some of the child's responses on the intelligence test also helps to round out the over-all personality picture. For example, on the comprehension test of the WISC, the very dependent child is likely to give repeated indication of this. When he cuts his finger he "would tell my mother." Similarly, when a smaller child starts to fight with him, he would again turn to his mother. Then there are the children who, in response to questions involving fighting or breaking things, cannot remain objective but keep insisting "I don't fight," "I never did that." Conversely there is the boy who, in response to the question "what is the thing to do if a fellow much smaller than yourself starts to fight with you?" promptly answers: "Beat him up."

Where there are specific school problems, achievement tests in addition to intelligence tests are indicated. Specific subject disabilities can cause a child to feel most unhappy about school and may lead to withdrawal, to truanting, and to other forms of maladjustment.

The choice of projective tests depends, as it does in the adult, on what particular facets of the personality are to be explored, what particular problems need special investigation. The Rorschach is almost always indicated as the instrument best able to give a picture of personality structure and functioning, including the kinds of experiences that are most threatening to the child, the defensive techniques employed, and the effectiveness of these techniques. There are normative (Ames, Learned, Metraux, & Walker, 1952) and clinical (Halpern, 1953) studies dealing with the child's Rorschach responses at different age levels, normal and abnormal.

The CAT or TAT (Rabin & Haworth, 1960) fills in the picture obtained from the Rorschach, offering evidence of the way the child feels about many of his relationships and experiences and what he feels he can do about the disturbances that these relationships and experiences produce. The Make-a-Picture-Story Test by Schneidman (1960) is a test that older children enjoy, and the fact that they have a free choice of characters and can bring into, and leave out of, the situation whomever they please has certain distinct advantages in evaluating their ways of perceiving and structuring their experiences.

For most children, drawing a person is a much less upsetting kind of experience than it is for adults. The majority of children enjoy this task, and it often proves a good way of starting the testing session. It provides one way of evaluating the level of maturity that the child has obtained where his own body image is concerned. The 10-year-old who still produces little more than a round head set upon an egg-shaped body with no intervening neck and who indicates arms and legs simply by drawing sticklike projections from this egg-shaped body has a self-concept that is more in line with that of a 5-year-old child than a boy of his age. If his intellectual functioning is that of a 10-year-old, this disparity becomes all the more meaningful. Assessment of the drawing can be made by use of Goodenough's (1926) scoring technique and clinical evaluation (Hammer, 1958; Machover, 1949). In addition to a determination of the level of maturity reflected in the drawing, specific areas of disturbance often find expression in the emphasis or deemphasis of certain aspects of the figure. For instance, oral aggression is often revealed by a large mouth filled with enormous teeth, feelings of inadequacy by the absence of arms, and depression by the small size of the figure and its placement at the very bottom of the paper. Some investigators have noted that anxious children draw figures that are more rigid and more "mutilated" than less anxious children.

For the investigation of special aspects of the personality, such tests as the Rosenzweig Picture-Frustration Study (Rosenzweig, 1960), a children's form of the Taylor Manifest Anxiety Scale (Castaneca, McCandless, & Palermo, 1956), the Blacky Pictures (Blum, 1960), story-completion tests, and Despert Fables (Rabin & Haworth, 1960) are available.

As is the case in all diagnostic procedures, neither the findings of one test nor testing alone gives the full picture. However, when the information obtained from all the diagnostic approaches is studied and organized so as to give a consistent picture that fits all the known facts, then a full, valid picture of the individual—including his assets and weaknesses and his adjustive efforts, successful and unsuccessful—is available and can provide the means for identifying the nature of his disturbance and what can be done about it.

THE ENVIRONMENT

In order to see the child's behavior in proper perspective and to understand the particular problems he has to face, knowledge of his own strengths and weaknesses, however complete, is not sufficient. It follows then that in addition to an evaluation of the child, there must also be an evaluation of the world in which he operates, the world to which he must adjust. It is therefore necessary to understand the significant objects in the child's life, their needs, attitudes, and behaviors. For example, the neglected and abused child of indifferent, alcoholic parents who makes his adjustment by recourse to evasion, withdrawal, and "weaseling" types of behavior is probably using his resources in the best possible way he can, in the only way that enables him to survive under his particular set of circumstances. Certainly his reactions must be evaluated differently from the way similar modes of adjustment in a child whose environment is essentially of a positive order would be evaluated. Similarly, the functioning of a 6-year-old girl who lived alone with a psychotic mother who boarded up the windows, allowed no one to enter the house, and went down on the street only when it was dark gave indication of deviation and retardation. However, the nature of such limitations and deviations has a different significance, diagnostically and prognostically, from that of similar ones seen in a child who has had the benefit of a reasonably normal, supporting environment.

The Mother

In most cases the mother-child relationship is such a basic one, and the child's development and adjustment so dependent upon the nature of this relationship, that any evaluation of the child without a corresponding assessment of the mother and of what goes on between the child and the mother is of relatively little value. Assessing the nature of this relationship involves observation, interviewing, and sometimes testing of, and therapy with, the mother, plus observation of the mother and child together in a variety of situations, if this is at all possible. Sometimes interviewing of the mother and child simultaneously, and even therapy with the mother and child and possibly also with others—"family therapy"—is indicated.

The therapist seeks to learn the following from his contacts with the mother:

1. The level of her own ego development. Is she a mature person, or is she still dominated by unsatisfied childish needs, so that in her contacts with others she experiences herself more as a child—dependent or rebellious, as the case may be—than as an adult?

2. If she is a disturbed person, what is the exact nature of her disturbance? Is she neurotic, psychotic, or organically or intellectually impaired? Is she physically ill?

3. What dynamics underlie her disturbance, and what impact are her needs and disturbances likely to have on the child?

4. How great is the disparity between her conscious, expressed attitudes toward herself and her child and her real feelings about herself and the child?

5. What resources does the mother possess? Will she be responsive to suggestion, counseling, or therapy, or is she so rigid that no changes in the immediate environment can be anticipated?

Initial contact with the mother is usually in the form of an interview in which she explains why she has brought the child for evaluation, why she or other figures in the environment—those in the school or the court or the family physician—are concerned about the child. Her acceptance or rejection of the child's need for help; the way she formulates the problem; whether she accepts responsibility for the child's difficulties or displaces them onto others or, contrariwise, whether she expresses too much guilt are all of value in the attempt to assess her part in the development of the child's maladjustment, and they also give some indication of whether or not she is likely to be a positive or a negative force in any attempt to help the child overcome conflicts and problems.

Many psychologists working with children have reported that on initial contact, the majority of mothers of schizophrenic children go to great lengths to minimize or deny the extent and nature of the child's difficulties. Asked what concerns then about the child, they are very likely to say: "Oh, he's a very nice little boy. There's really nothing wrong with him. We just thought it would be a good idea to have him checked over." Sometimes the mother will admit that there is one small problem but nothing more. Yet as the interview progresses and the picture becomes clearer, the child's difficulties in practically every area become manifest. Thus, "He doesn't go out and play much with the other boys," is often quickly followed by "But you can't blame him. They're rough and he's sensitive." Although the child is perhaps described as getting along well with others, gradually it develops that he recently broke a neighbor's window or attacked a neighbor's child. Indication of intense hostility toward his own siblings creeps into the account. When all these facts are assembled and fed back to the mother, she may then be ready to concede that there is a problem; she may even be willing to admit that she realized that there was a severe problem but was so threatened by it that she could not face it. The mother who realizes this is more likely to be helpful in the eventual treatment process than the mother who continues to insist that there is no problem and that any issues that have arisen are the fault of a hostile environment rather than due to any defects in her child.

While the mothers of children diagnosed as behavior problems or neurotic may also try to minimize the child's deviations, the disparity between the realities of the situation and the picture they present is rarely as great as in the case of the schizophrenic. These mothers can generally accept the fact that there is a problem because the problem is not so severe, so threatening, or so strange as it is in the case of the psychotic child.

In addition to exploring the mother's perception of the nature and severity of the child's problem, the early contacts with her can be used to obtain important factual data.

Matters pertaining to the nature of the pregnancy and the birth, the early medical history, toilet training, school record, etc., can all be learned. The way this information is communicated also has considerable value. The mother who wallows in self-pity because of the difficulty she had giving birth to the child probably manages to convey to him what she "suffered" on his account. At the same time, how she wants the child and others to see her in the maternal role also becomes evident.

Because there are definite stereotypes of motherhood, ways that are considered correct for a mother where her feelings and attitudes toward her child are involved, mothers can often give what they consider the "correct" answers to interview questions. Depending on the mother's degree of sophistication about child-rearing practices, she may know that overprotection is considered just as detrimental as rejection, and so she can frame her answers accordingly. It is important, therefore, to know just how much "psychology" the mother has imbibed; what, if anything, she reads about mother-child relationships; and what school of thought she espouses. Actually, then, in evaluating what she says, it is the uncensored, inadvertent comment and the affect that accompanies her statements that must be emphasized.

In order to get the answers to the questions that seem essential for any understanding of the mother and her relationship with, and impact on, her child, her attitude toward herself as a woman—what it means to her to be a woman—is perhaps the most crucial. The answer to this involves her girlhood concepts and feelings about womanhood and motherhood, the nature of her doll play, her fantasies about what she would be and do as a grown-up, her reactions when she learned she was pregnant, her feelings when she first saw her baby, and her feelings and attitude toward her husband and toward the role of homemaker. If this was a first child and she was not aware of all the disturbances and discomforts motherhood involves, it is important to know how she reacted when her nights were interrupted by crying and feedings, whether dirty diapers disgusted her, and whether her husband shared some of these tasks with her or whether she had the entire responsibility for the newborn.

Even more important than the mother's attitudes, conscious and unconscious, is the degree of congruence that exists between what she professes to feel, what she says to the child, what she asks of him, and what she really feels and wants. Bateson and his associates (Bateson, Jackson, Haley, & Weakland, 1956) suggest that when the child is caught in what they call the "double bind," when what the mother or some other important person in the child's life says to him is in contradiction to what the child senses is the person's underlying, unexpressed wish or command and when there is no way of resolving this dilemma, schizophrenia will result. In view of the findings that point up the "vulnerability" of the infant who becomes the schizophrenic child, such an explanation hardly seems feasible. However, it may well be that when the potentially schizophrenic child is placed in a double-bind situation, it is far more threatening to him than to a less sensitive child and may well prove to be the precipitating factor in the development of his illness. Whether or not it produces schizophrenia, the situation described as the "double bind" is certainly one which seriously interferes with the child's ability to find himself and develop in a stable, comfortable, constructive fashion.

Current studies of the mother-child relationship stress the importance of behavior rather than attitudes. Among the most thorough and significant researches in this connection, insofar as the mother-infant relationship is concerned, are those reported by Brody (1956) and Escalona and Leitch (1953). Here the stress is largely on the mother's behavior during the course of those activities which are especially important to the infant, such as feeding, and of which he is aware mainly through observation.

In addition to observation and interview, the use of tests may be indicated. Very occasionally, when there seems to be a marked disparity between the intellectual levels of the mother and the child or where gross retardation in the mother is suspected, intelligence testing may be employed. In the main, however, testing the mother generally consists of personality testing, usually the Rorschach and the TAT, and sometimes such paper-and-pencil tests as the Parental Attitude Research Instrument (Schaefer & Bell, 1958), an incomplete-sentence test, etc.

Significant Others

Although no other figure occupies the place with the child that the mother does, there are many others who influence his development and adjustment. In some instances it may even be one of these others who is primarily responsible for the child's difficulties. If such is the case, the disturbing figure is most likely to be the father. In such circumstances, the procedures described above should be employed with him. In fact, even if the father is not necessarily the main cause of disturbance in the child's life, the more that is known about him, the better. Sometimes the strength of the father can offset, to some extent at least, the deleterious impact of the mother.

Fathers as a group seem less anxious to get involved in any diagnostic or therapeutic procedure than mothers. There is apparently a feeling among fathers that child rearing is a woman's function, and only certain fathers, those with a genuine feeling of fatherhood and those who are sufficiently sophisticated to recognize and accept their responsibilities even though their feelings may not be of the most positive order, seem willing to accept interview and/or testing.

Siblings generally also play an important role in the life of the disturbed child. It is therefore important to learn as much as possible about the siblings, how they feel and act toward the patient and whether the patient's perception of them as friend or enemy, as preferred by the parents, as brighter than he, or as infantile and demanding, etc., is realistic or a distortion arising from his particular needs.

Where the problem expresses itself in the school life of the child, contact with the teacher is certainly advisable. If the child is the only one who cannot adjust in a particular class, then the difficulty would seem more peculiarly his. Nevertheless it is important to know something of the personality of the teacher—as much as can be learned from observation and conversation—in order to determine what it is in her personality structure that is so disruptive to the child. Contact with the teacher can sometimes add new dimensions to the reports of school adjustment obtained from the child and the mother.

The family physician is often the first person to whom the family turns when problems of a psychological nature arise. The way he has handled these, what advice he has given the parents, and how they have responded to it also come into the total assessment. Again, in some instances, the physician has knowledge, psychological and medical, of the child and the family that helps round out the picture. Sometimes the same is true of the clergyman.

SUMMARY

Perhaps the most significant fact that emerges from this discussion of diagnostic methods in childhood disorders is the complexity of the problem and the absence of any easily recognized "diagnostic" signs. The multiplicity of factors, innate and environmental, that go into the making of the end product—the child—renders any simple, "cookbook" approach to diagnostic problems impossible. A reliable and constructive diagnostic job, using the term "diagnostic" in the broadest sense, depends on a thorough knowledge of child psychology, child development, the principles of dynamic psychology, methods of intelligence and projective testing, adult psychology, and parent-child relations. It also requires an appreciation of what is involved in the therapeutic experience, having information about community resources, and the ability to use all this knowledge in a discriminating and well-integrated fashion.

REFERENCES

Ames, L. G., Learned, J., Metraux, R. W., & Walker, R. N. *Childhood Rorschach responses: developmental trends from two to ten years.* New York: Hoeber-Harper, 1952.

Bateson, G., Jackson, D. D., Haley, J., & Weakland, J. H. Toward a theory of schizophrenia. *Behav. Sci.*, 1956, **1**, 251–264.

Bender, Linda. Childhood schizophrenia. *Amer. J. Orthopsychiat.*, 1947, **17**, 40–56.

Bender, Linda, & Freedman, A. M. A study of the first three years in the maturation of schizophrenic children. *Quart. J. Child Behav.*, 1952, **1**, 245–272.

Bergman, P., & Escalona, S. Unusual sensitivities in very young children. In the *psychoanalytic study of the child.* Vols. III, IV. New York: International Universities Press, 1949. Pp. 333–352.

Blum, G. S. The Blacky Pictures with children. In A. Rabin & M. Haworth (Eds.), *Projective techniques with children.* New York: Grune & Stratton, 1960. Pp. 95–104.

Brody, S. *Patterns of mothering.* New York: International Universities Press, 1956.

Casteneda, A., McCandless, B. R., & Palmermo, D. S. The children's form of the Manifest Anxiety Scale. *Child Develpm.*, 1956, **27**, 317–326.

Escalona, Sibylle. The use of infant tests for predictive purposes. *Bull. Menninger Clin.*, 1950, **14,** 117–128.

Escalona, Sibylle. Emotional development in the first year. In M. Senn (Ed.), *Transaction of the sixth conference on problems of infancy and childhood.* New York: Josiah Macy, 1953. Pp. 11–92.

Escalona, Sibylle, & Heider, Grace. *Prediction and outcome.* New York: Basic Books, 1959.

Escalona, Sibylle, & Leitch, M. *Early phases of personality development: a non-normative study of infant behavior.* Evanston, Ill.: Child Development Publications, 1953.

Fish, Barbara. The detection of schizophrenia in infancy. *J. nerv. ment. Dis.*, 1957, **125,** 1–24.

Fish, Barbara. Longitudinal observations of biological deviations in a schizophrenic infant. *Amer. J. Psychiat.*, 1959, **116,** 25–31.

Fish, Barbara. Involvement of the central nervous system in infants with schizophrenia. *Arch. Neurol.*, 1960, **2,** 115–121.

Fox, C., Davidson, K., Lighthall, F., Waite, R., & Sarason, S. B. Human figure drawings of high and low anxious children. *Child Develpm.*, 1958, **29,** 297–301.

Freud, S. Analysis, terminable and interminable. *Int. J. Psychoanal.*, 1938, **XVIII,** 373–405.

Friess, M., & Woolf, P. J. Some hypotheses on the role of the congenital activity type in personality development. In *The psychoanalytic study of the child.* Vol. 8, New York: International Universities Press, 1953. Pp. 48–62.

Gesell, A., & Amatruda, C. *Developmental diagnosis.* New York: Hoeber-Harper, 1941.

Goldfarb, W. Infant rearing and problem behavior. *Amer. J. Orthopsychiat.*, 1943, **13,** 249–265.

Goldfarb, W. Effects of psychological deprivation in infancy and subsequent stimulation. *Amer. J. Psychiat.*, 1945, **102,** 18–33.

Goldfarb, W. The mutual impact of mother and child in childhood schizophrenia. *Amer. J. Orthopsychiat.*, 1961, **31,** 738–747.

Goodenough, F. L. *Measurement of intelligence by drawing.* Tarrytown-on-Hudson, N.Y.: World, 1926.

Graham, Frances, & Berman, P. Current status of behavior tests for brain damage in infants and preschool children. *Amer. J. Orthopsychiat.*, 1961, **31,** 713–727.

Halpern, Florence. *A clinical approach to children's Rorschachs.* New York: Grune & Stratton, 1953.

Hammer, E. F. *The clinical application of projective drawings.* Springfield, Ill.: Charles C Thomas, 1958.

Hartmann, H. *Ego psychology and the problem of adaptation.* New York: International Universities Press, 1958.

Machover, K. *Personality projection in the drawing of the human figure.* Springfield, Ill.: Charles C Thomas, 1949.

Murphy, Lois. *The widening world of childhood.* New York: Basic Books, 1962.

Rabin, A., & Haworth, M. *Projective techniques with children.* New York: Grune & Stratton, 1960.

Rosenzweig, S. Rosenzweig Picture Frustration Study: children's form. In *ibid.* Pp. 149–176.

Schaefer, E. S., & Bell, R. Q. Development of the Parent Attitude Research Instrument. *Child Develpm.*, 1958, **29,** 339–362.

Schneidman, E. S. The MAPS Test with children. In A. Rabin & M. Haworth (Eds.), *Projective techniques with children.* New York: Grune & Stratton, 1960. Pp. 130–148.

Spitz, R. Hospitalism: an inquiry into the genesis of psychiatric conditions in early childhood. In *The psychoanalytic study of the child.* Vol. 1. New York: International Universities Press, 1947. Pp. 53–74.

24

Psychiatric Diagnosis, Nomenclature, and Classification

HENRY BRILL

Within recent years, it has become customary to decry psychiatric classifications in general; this includes the various national systems as well as the international one. Yet classification is a part of ordinary human thought—names used in everyday language are products of a process of classification, most of it primitive and long forgotten. Technical and scientific classification fulfills a similar need for abstraction and generalization and reduces, in a way, the bewildering multiplicity of the subject matter and permits further manipulation of data on successively higher levels of abstraction. It cannot usually progress further than the level of knowledge on which it is based, but by facilitating the examination of existing data and by creating the possibility of communication, it promotes the advance of human knowledge. In fact, Pearson (1951) gives classification a central place in his classic work, *The Grammar of Science*. Any body of material may be classified in many different ways, depending on the motives and interests of the classifier; for example, men may be considered as souls, as lovers, as workers, or as "cannon fodder." Scientific and medical data are similarly subject to many possible arrangements, but some arrangement of data is essential, and this becomes more important as the level of thinking becomes more abstract and more scientific. Purely personal classifications of data are quite common and form the basis of much scientific work, but if a classification is to be used for communication, its value will be contingent on, among other things, the degree of general acceptance, the accuracy with which its terms are defined, and the susceptibility of the system itself to higher degrees of abstraction, statistical operations being one of the most important from the public health point of view.

This chapter will be concerned almost entirely with the kinds of psychiatric classification which serve as a type of language for large numbers of workers in the field, centering on the system of the American Psychiatric Association (1952). It will explore the question of the need for such a system and will present some material regarding the theory of classification. The history of classification will be discussed in order to explain the present status of *psychiatric diagnosis* and to support the thesis that this is not a static, sterile activity but a changing, dynamic one which has improved steadily and which promises to continue to do so as an essential element in the total process of psychiatric advance.

THEORIES AND DEFINITIONS

In theory, a distinction is made between psychiatric classification and psychiatric nomenclature (Moriyama, 1960; World Health Organization, 1957), but although unclassified nomenclatures did exist at one time, nomenclature and classification have been combined for so long that it is easy to forget the fundamental difference between the two halves of the term "classified nomenclature."

For our purposes, psychiatric nomenclature may be defined as the total of names, diagnoses, or other designations applied to individuals or to collections of classes of individuals to indicate that they share some important attributes relevant to their illnesses. Just as in biological taxonomy (*Encyclopaedia Britannica;* Gray, 1961), after which much of our procedure is patterned, standardized definitions or descriptions of each psychiatric term are an implicit and important part of the nomenclature which covers symptoms and symptom complexes, disorders assumed to be entities, and the various higher groupings of such disorders (organic disorders, functional disorders, etc.).

Classification is described as a process of discovering or creating order in the world by noting similarities among individuals and among classes and thinking of them as a unit, to that extent reducing the unmanageable multiplicity of nature. Nomenclature is thus a collection of terms and their definitions; classification is a process of distributing individuals or groupings of individuals among these terms and is also a name given to arrangements of nomenclature into certain meaningful patterns. Two of the most important requirements of nomenclature are accuracy and standardization of definitions. Ordinary everyday thinking and communication are successful to the degree that we have some clear and firm definition of words and word combinations. This is even more important in science and medicine because the material is more complex and is especially so in psychiatry, where there is less opportunity for correction and where accuracy of definition is more difficult.

Once having achieved standardization and uniformity of definition, we are in a position to move toward scientific classification which seeks to formulate a scheme of "mutually exclusive and collectively exhaustive" (Pearson, 1951) categories based on the most important characteristics of the things concerned and the actual relations between them.

A natural classification approaches this ideal, and an artificial one is defined as one which deviates from it and which may indeed be purely a convention, as in the case of a classification of plants according to their medical values (*Encyclopaedia Britannica;* Gray, 1961).

In the philosophy of science, this process is accorded a very fundamental place. Pearson (1951) states: "The classification of facts, [and] the recognition of their sequence and relative significance is the function of science. . . . " He adds, perhaps for those who maintain that this has nothing to do with clinical practice: "Scientific method is applicable to social as well as physical problems and we must carefully guard ourselves against supposing that the scientific frame of mind is a peculiarity of the professional scientist."

Moriyama (1960) brings this discussion directly to the classification of disease: "Basic to the study of the natural history of disease is the process of classification. The orderly arrangement of facts so as to bring out the relationships among them . . . is the essence of classification and underlines the clinician's concern with the problems of diagnosis and prognosis. . . ."

The World Health Organization *International Classification of Diseases* (1957) quotes Farr to the effect that statistical classification has the object of bringing together in groups diseases that have considerable affinity in order to facilitate the deduction of general principles.

Obviously all the above discussions assume that all sources of the information to be collated will be talking about the same thing when they use the same term or at least that the designation used by one will be directly convertible into some common term. If schizophrenia means something entirely different in New York from what it does in Paris or London, and if the French diagnose some of these cases as manic-depressive or psychoneurotic, no degree of statistical rearrangement or reclassification will be able to make the data fully comparable.

ADVANCES IN CLASSIFICATION AND NOMENCLATURE SINCE 1800

Classification in psychiatry is often represented as a static or sterile activity, whether this has to do with the diagnosis of the individual or with the statistical manipulations built upon higher orders of classificatory abstraction, which seek relationships among groups of diagnoses.

Actually, progress has been slow but far

from negligible. This becomes obvious when we compare our present status with what has occurred during the last 150 years. In the early 1800s the field abounded with numerous synthetic systems inspired by the success of Linnaeus in biology and patterned after his work in that field. These included a classification by Linnaeus himself, another by Erasmus Darwin, and numerous others long since forgotten except in such entertaining historical accounts as that of Zilboorg and Henry (1941). Yet, progress was made.

At the opening of the century, there was profound confusion between organic and functional psychoses and between them and the mental deficiencies, especially when it was a question of regression or deterioration. The neuroses were not clearly demarcated from the neurological or internal medical disorders, and the depressions and schizophrenias were hopelessly entangled with each other and with most of the foregoing. The very idea of a psychodynamic axis of classification was unthought of, and while there were some foreshadowings of the specific entities, these were almost lost in a welter of competing nomenclatures in a world where almost everyone had his own system. There was, however, a general tendency to follow one or another great authority, such as Cullen or Sauvages.

By the middle of the century, there were already signs of clarification in the writings of such authorities as Griesinger; the work of Kraepelin, toward the close of the century, was often presented as a lifeless system but was in reality a masterful synthesis and an advance over what had gone before. His work commanded more general agreement than had ever previously been achieved in psychiatry. Further progress has taken place since his time and still continues with such regularity that since 1917, there has been need to recast the psychiatric classification in America approximately every ten years. We are even now in the process of another review of this type, as will be described later in this chapter.

OBJECTIONS, THEORETICAL LIMITATIONS, AND PRACTICAL REQUIREMENTS

Many valid criticisms have been directed against the basic theory and practice underlying the various systems now in use throughout the world. These criticisms deserve careful consideration, although it may be said at the outset that in the opinion of this writer, none of them justify two main conclusions that are often drawn from them: (1) that no system of diagnosis or nomenclature is useful and that we should accept the fact that psychiatric disorder is a completely individual matter and that meaningful groupings among patients and among disease entities are to be ruled out a priori, and (2) that because the present generally accepted system has defects, we should abandon it and replace it for general use with another based perhaps on some single axis of classification (a single theory consistent within itself).

Some form of ordering our data seems to be inescapable, and as Stengel maintains in his masterly review (1960), this is true even if the system is largely one of conventions. It must not be forgotten that the original classification of Linnaeus was at its inception a completely synthetic or artificial one, and only much later did the evolutionary and genetic advances of succeeding times give it the natural values which it has today.

In this connection we might inquire whether ours is in any sense a natural classification, as outlined above (under Theories and Definitions), or whether it is partly or largely an artificial one. Actually, we cannot fully resolve this, nor indeed can we resolve the question of whether mental illness is a single or a multiple entity. In this area lie some of the most fundamental questions in psychiatry. Jaspers (1963) states:

> From ancient times the question of disease entity has been answered along two different lines. The one involved the theory of unitary psychosis, that is, there are no disease entities but only varieties of madness with fluid boundaries . . . which merge into each other everywhere. . . . The other involved the theory that the main task of psychiatry is to find natural disease entities which are different from each other in principle . . . in which there are no transitions.

To this day, especially among some of the psychodynamically oriented, there is a leaning toward a unitary theory. From their point of view, the mental disorder is the same whether released by syphilis, brain injury, alcohol, or psychogenetic factors.

It must be admitted that even where the existence of a somatic factor is clearly defined, as in the case of syphilis, we have no understanding of by what process and according to what laws the brain disease might be transformed into psychic symptoms. This would seem to be a part of the larger unsolved problem of the entire relation between brain and mind. However, for practical and for scientific purposes, it is necessary to know something about the frequency of mental diseases as related to the coexistence of noxious agents, if only to expose such facts as the connection between mental defect and maternal German measles or between myxedema and psychiatric symptoms. Moreover, there is a strong body of opinion which holds that there is a clear differential response to various kinds of therapy among three classes of functional cases—namely, the neuroses, the depressions, and the schizophrenias—especially as regards shock therapy, tranquilizers, and deep analytical psychotherapy. It remains to be seen whether this is related to some natural relationship among the cases, but for the present the differential diagnosis does serve to identify patients with a similar treatment response and permits a search for other meaningful relationships and differences among them. The statement that one does not need to know about diagnosis in order to treat may have had some validity when there was virtually no treatment; it is now an anachronistic echo of the past.

Another often-repeated objection, especially from outpatient services, is that many diagnoses convey stigma and, when based on insecure grounds, are doubly unjustified. Unfortunately, the avoidance of stigma is virtually impossible, as has been experienced repeatedly. Stigma attaches itself to anything which designates or marks out the existence of major psychiatric disorder, whether this is a legal procedure, the fact of hospital residence, an administrative procedure such as the famous Section VIII of the Army, or the bizarre behavior of the patient himself. It is often forgotten that the fact of significant mental illness is all too apparent to most laymen; only its designation usually remains in doubt, and the sole security against stigma resides in the most profound secrecy and isolation from observation (once an accepted procedure). A better alternative seems to be the more modern tactic of adequate public education and complete frankness; diagnostic circumlocutions serve feebly and temporarily, and they hardly seem worth the confusion they cause.

A more serious objection to all the diagnostic systems so far available is that they regularly lack the statistical stability which would result from unanimity of opinion and which should characterize a set of scientifically usable data. It has long been known that the boundaries of each nosological entity tend to expand or contract with time and that the expansions, especially, tend to destroy the credibility of the category. This happened with Charcot's hysterias, Beard's neurasthenias, the monomanias of Esquirol, Meynert's amentia, and the paranoia of the 1880s; in the opinion of many European observers, it is now taking place in the American concept of schizophrenia. Even in the organic states where there is a well-defined neuropathology it must be confessed that the statistics are too variable, and indeed the type and intensity of the clinical syndrome are little correlated with the pattern of the organic pathology (Jaspers 1963; Kaplan, 1956) or with its extent. Those interested in finding if not an answer to these vexing problems at least a well-balanced and thoroughly rewarding discussion are referred to Jaspers' *General Psychopathology* (1963).

The fluidity of boundaries is taken to mean that there actually are no boundaries or real natural differences at all. Experience shows that this does not necessarily follow. In the case of general paresis, frequency of diagnosis varied greatly, ranging up to 30 per cent of admissions in one clinic (Jaspers, 1963), before the Wassermann; afterward it became a stable 8 per cent. Most observers would agree that paresis is a natural category. However, even admittedly artificial categories within the limits set by Stengel promote progress, as compared with no method of systematizing information at all.

Another objection to the existing classifications is likely to be heard from persons with special interests in classification as a science. They point out that our existing systems are set up on multiple axes and that as a result, they violate a fundamental rule. Thus some diagnoses are based on etiology (paresis and psychosis due to encephalitides of various types); some are classified according to the underlying neuropathology (cerebral arteriosclerosis, etc.); some are linked to age (senile psychosis, childhood schizophrenia, and involutional psychosis); in some, behavior is the decisive factor (the personality disorders); in some, constellations of inner experiences constitute the foundation for diagnosis (functional disorders); and, finally, in some, age of onset and degree of mental capacity control the diagnosis of defect or retardation. Any one case may fall on several axes, and in this sense the categories overlap and are not mutually exclusive. Cases are found showing almost all possible permutations of these axes of classification; brain damage can coexist with schizophrenic symptomatology or with conduct disorder, mental defect with psychosis, etc. There are conventions by which one can establish one diagnosis and rule out others along competing axes, but this is an arbitrary element in the structure of the classification, a weakness in underlying theory which waits for correction. Ideally we should diagnose along one axis, that of etiology or perhaps by location of the pathology or some other consistent single measure. While the defect of multiple axes reduces the reliability of procedure, it does not destroy its usefulness, for reasons which have already been pointed out (values of an "artificial" system). Actually the situation in medicine generally differs only in degree from that in psychiatry, and it is a source of some comfort to know that classification of somatic disease is by etiology, location of damage, pathological nature of the lesion, age of patient, or one of a number of other axes (World Health Organization, 1957).

THE POSITIVE SIDE

When carried out by experienced clinicians, the process of psychiatric classification, with all its defects, is not a haphazard or a random one. For each patient, it involves a careful examination and weighing of a wide variety of data; it takes time and effort and has demonstrated and acknowledged value in the treatment of the individual and in the study and comparison of groups.

The mastery of any system of classification is no minor matter but demands theoretical training and practical experience. Such mastery facilitates translation of other systems; yet it is still not an easy process, nor is it completely reliable, and this should be kept in mind as we review the systems of the past and those now in use elsewhere in the world. At best we can do no more than examine them in a superficial way. Much that is significant will remain hidden from us.

In spite of all possible objections, for purposes of this discussion it may be accepted that the practice of psychiatric diagnosis and classification is one of the realities of life, based on centuries of tradition and experience. This is so even though these modern classifications are largely artificial and though the categories are fluid and variable in their boundaries from one time to another and from one place to another, are developed along multiple axes, and require considerable skill, experience, and effort if they are to produce useful results.

Actually, in spite of all the defects that are so easy to demonstrate and the flaws in logic and in practice, the fact is that there is a certain degree of consensus about major issues, and this appears to be growing rather than decreasing. Recent international discussions reveal again that there is little question about the general fivefold division of mental illness into the organic mental states, functional psychoses, neuroses, personality disorders, and states of mental defect. The schizophrenias are also generally recognized within the psychoses, as are the depressions, although their relative place is a topic of active debate. In addition, there is little difference of opinion about the subdivisions of the organic states and relatively little about the states of mental defect. Much of the present agreement is due to the fact that all systems have a common history and are derived from a common scientific experience which they share to this day, in spite of defects of communication. Everyone agrees on the desirability of drawing these bonds closer and of developing toward a generally accepted international system through which all national systems will be easily comparable.

HISTORY

It has been said that writing a review of the history of psychiatric classification would be almost tantamount to writing a history of psychiatry (Stengel, 1960). This seems to be quite true, and this writer will present only a few comments in this field, sufficient to supply some background for the discussion, and will add certain detailed data which seem particularly relevant.

Psychiatry up to the end of the eighteenth century, with some notable exceptions, tended to remain within the structure of general medicine, and the classifications which can be reconstructed from the works of Hippocrates, Galen, Aurelianus (1950), and Paracelsus (Pachter, 1951) all are consistent with the medicine of their time. Of historical interest are observations regarding the effects of alcohol, the picture of the depressions, the furors, the dementias, and the various supernatural explanations. Of equal interest is the total lack of a psychodynamic or true introspective psychology, in spite of extensive exploration of human thought. Much of man's interest was directed inward, but it seemed to remain fixed on the mind as a tool of logic, philosophy, and theology and did not stray to examine the self as a subject of objective study and analysis. Perhaps the earliest work to give evidence of an awakening of some critical self-analysis centering on psychopathology was the curious work of the compulsive gambler-physician Cardano (1962), written at the age of 75 in the year 1575. The book is liberally interspersed with psychopathology of the most diverse nature, all reported in a modern spirit of dispassionate self-observation.

In order to understand modern diagnosis and classification, we must turn back only to the time of Pinel (1745–1826) and Esquirol (1772–1840). The success of Linnaeus (1707–1778) had stimulated a profusion of synthetic systems, but these proved to be of no permanent value, remained on an academic level only, and had little or no influence on subsequent developments except perhaps to create a bias against such systems.

Pinel and Esquirol for the first time brought an extensive asylum experience to bear on the problem, and for a long time it was this type of experience which dominated the field. At first Pinel allowed only a fourfold classification—mania, melancholia, dementia, and idiocy—but by mid-century, complexity had returned. The lead in psychiatry had passed from France to Germany, and Griesinger, in 1845, presented an elaborate system which had an extensive influence and which helped reduce diversity of psychiatric classification in various countries. His orientation was strongly organicist, and he viewed mental illness as brain disorder; his work, like that of his French predecessors, was based on mental hospital cases. The somatic interests of psychiatry found constructive expression in, and were in turn reinforced by, a series of advances in study of such conditions as paresis, geriatric brain disease, and alcoholism. Alzheimer, Nissl, Wernicke, Korsakoff, and many others made psychiatric history in these fields. The contributions of Karl Bonhoeffer in the exogenous psychoses (due to poisons or infections) lie in this same area, although on the border of the functional conditions.

Meanwhile, as other areas were clarified, the concepts about schizophrenia and manic-depressive psychoses began to emerge more clearly (Meyer, 1928). This was further facilitated by advances in the understanding of mental defect, which, following the work of Itard and Seguin, had resulted in the creation of specialized institutions by the 1850s. As these other conditions were more clearly delineated, the way was opened up for the development of clearer concepts of functional psychoses.

The development of mental incapacity in previously normal children had already been noted by Thomas Willis in the seventeenth century, but it was not until the 1850s that the term "dementia praecox" appeared, the credit going to a French psychiatrist, Morel. His delineation, however, was clouded with concern about degeneracy (the fate of successive generations) and was still involved with the "vesania" of Cullen and Sauvages, i.e., a total insanity moving through a fixed sequence of phases—first melancholia, then mania, then confusion or paranoia, and finally dementia. (Morel also recognized primary mania and primary melancholia.) The next step which is ordinarily mentioned is that of Kahlbaum, who, although he was concerned with vesania, also came to recognize a series of age-bound psychoses (neophrenia of infancy, hebephrenia, presbyophrenia, etc.). It was his assistant, Hecker, in 1870 who described hebephrenia, a syndrome which was to become a part of our present psychiatry. Four years later, Kahlbaum described catatonia, which he considered to be a part of vesania with predominantly motor symptoms. This too was destined to survive in our present system.

At the close of the century, Kraepelin finally pulled together the hebephrenia and catatonia of Hecker and Kahlbaum. Using the classical criteria of symptoms and course, he added certain dementias, vesanias, and "degenerative" psychoses and created a new concept of dementia praecox which, with some modification, was later to become "schizophrenia" and our present "schizophrenic reaction." The adequacy of the description has never been seriously questioned, but Kraepelin's criterion of outcome has been a matter of controversy, although it is often forgotten that he was doubtful about the universality of this aspect.

Meanwhile, the personality disorders had come to be recognized and described (by Pritchard), and a long experience with mesmerism and hypnosis prepared the ground for work with the psychoneuroses. These were studied extensively by Janet, who began to lay the foundation for a psychodynamics, and finally by Freud, who in 1896 published his first account of psychological mechanisms in a case of hallucinatory paranoia. However, it was not until the 1952 revision of the American Psychiatric Association manual, that his views came to play a role in diagnostic classification.

With some additions, especially those of Bleuler in relation to the use of the term "schizophrenia," this completes a hasty review of the historical sources from which current concepts have been derived to a very large extent.

Organizational and Administrative Measures

During the entire period which we are discussing, psychiatric diagnosis and, indeed, all medical diagnosis and classification remained largely a local or even a personal matter. Each hospital was a law unto itself, and each medical school influenced its graduates. The statistical study of public health data can be traced to the days of John Graunt and the London Bills of Mortality during the Great Plague (Pearson, 1951), but in 1837, William Farr became the first medical statistician of the British General Register Office, and he found that the classification of Cullen used in the public service was unsatisfactory and outdated and that diagnoses in medical practice generally and in hospitals everywhere were haphazard, vague, and irregular. Florence Nightingale (Smith, 1951) joined him in the long battle for uniformity and comparability of public health figures, which she used as a powerful weapon in her battle for improving hospital services. The First International Congress, in 1853, commissioned Farr and Espigne (World Health Organization, 1957) to draft a uniform nomenclature, but though a number of drafts and congresses followed, the work was taken over by other international bodies. The desired standardization was not to be achieved for a long time; in fact, it still remains incomplete.

A list of causes of death was first authorized at the international congress in 1853. This list has since gone through a steady process of revision and development, and during the course of time, it has come to be the list of causes of death which is now internationally accepted (ICD).

The causes of morbidity, however, received little attention until 1900, but since then the classification has been developed in this direction. The manual *International Classification of Diseases, Injuries, and Causes of Death* (World Health Organization, 1957) is a comprehensive list dealing with both morbidity and mortality, where the psychiatric disorders occupy a position analogous to that of the diseases of the psychobiologic unit in the Standard of the AMA (discussed below).

The American Medical Association first moved to adopt a plan for a standard nomenclature of morbidity and death in 1928. Eleven years earlier, the American Medical Psychological Association (now the APA) had adopted a classification of mental disease which was "primarily a statistical classification but usable in a limited way as a nomenclature." Organized psychiatry was therefore well prepared to play its role in the preparation of the AMA's section on psychiatric disorders, and through subsequent revisions of the standard of the AMA, the psychiatric section remained in complete alignment with the manual of the APA (1952), revisions of the two documents being carried out simultaneously and in cooperation. The AMA manual was revised in 1934 and in 1942 (State of New York, Department of Mental Hygiene, 1943) as well as in 1952.

The 1952 revision was the most extensive of the series and sought to incorporate nonmental hospital experience for the first time, drawing on the military data of World War II and on data of clinics and private psychiatric practice, which had been expanding rapidly for some time. The intent was to meet the need for this new kind of practice, since it was felt that hospital-based classifications of the past did not fit extramural needs. The 1952 edition dropped much of the previous terminology which stemmed from classical European psychiatry; it moved away from concepts of constitutional and assumed organic factors and concepts of disease entities, stressing instead the idea that the functional disorders were reactions with decisive social and psychogenic components and that many were classifiable as acute and transitory in nature. It emphasized the adaptational aspects, and organic factors were seen as the direct cause of only the basic impairments of memory, orientation, judgment, and emotion and as the indirect cause of such symptoms as hallucinations, delusions, depression, and specific behavior disorders, releasing previously existing tendencies. Psychosomatic problems were given a new prominence under the new designation "psychophysiologic reactions," and psychodynamic concepts entered into the classification of the psychoneurotic reactions. Throughout the 1952 revision, there was a conscious effort to reduce stigma by dropping such terms as "psychopathic personality," "deterioration," "hysteria," "pathologic," "disease," and "psychosis." The old term "mental deficiency" was retained with the apology that no better name could be found.

The manual (American Psychiatric Association, Committee on Nomenclature and Statistics, 1952) achieved a high degree of success, and although figures are lacking, it seems probable that it has had a wider use than ever was achieved by any previous system of psychiatric classification and nomenclature.

THE NEXT REVISION OF THE MANUAL ON STATISTICS AND NOMENCLATURE

A little over ten years has now gone by since the 1952 revision, and a new one is again called for, partly because decennial revisions have long been a tradition with respect to medical classifications generally and partly because professional criticisms and discontent have accumulated during the practical operation of the system and provide the background for certain organizational developments which are moving toward a complete review by 1965.

Among the professional criticisms, one of the most frequent is that the system as it now stands is unduly complicated and that the qualifying phrases, once seen as a method permitting better descriptions and more flexibility, now appear to be little used, merely adding complexity.

Again, one often hears the comment that certain categories are not really mutually exclusive and that many cases can be placed equally well under any one of a number of different titles. For example, critics question the value of routinely distinguishing between acute and chronic brain syndromes, since chronic brain syndromes often begin as acute disorders or have periods of exacerbation where acute symptoms are mixed with chronic ones.

The mental deficiency section is considered completely inadequate, and the device of scattering the organic types among the brain syndromes has met with serious objections. Classification of the involutional psychotic reaction under "disturbances of metabolism, growth, nutrition, or endocrine function" has been attacked as being arbitrary and without adequate scientific foundation. The division of the undifferentiated type of schizophrenia into acute and chronic has been questioned on the grounds that the usual acute case is merely an exacerbation of a chronic state and that it is illogical to provide for acute and chronic divisions of undifferentiated schizophrenia but not of the other varieties. The designation "paranoia" is now rarely used, although it has historical associations and although many feel that the so-called "psychophysiological" autonomic and visceral disorders are given a prominence beyond what actual usage would justify. The criticism is that this group of disorders is actually best classified under the psychoneuroses or with other functional disorders; yet in some European countries, the psychosomatic concept seems to be actually gaining ground. The distinctions between the personality-pattern disturbances and the personality-trait disturbances seem to have little support, and classification of sexual deviation with addiction and of antisocial reaction with the group of sociopathic personality disturbances has generated opposition on the grounds that these are not all sociopathic states and have nothing in common with one another.

Among other criticisms is the assertion that the term "reaction" is based on pure assumption about the genesis of psychiatric disorders and that terminology should be free of such theoretical preconceptions, the proposal being to use neutral terms such as "schizophrenia," "affective disorder," etc.

Another problem which has been raised repeatedly is that the diagnosis of "brain syndrome" is very often made without any qualifying phrase, thus omitting essential information, and that the classification should not permit such unspecified diagnoses.

The fact that some find the classification too redundant and detailed and others find it too restrictive (for example, child psychiatry, alcoholism, and mental deficiency) can be looked upon as an indication that no classification can be satisfactory to everyone. In addition, the problems discussed lie to a considerable degree with nomenclature rather than with classification; nevertheless, the professional pressure for a full reconsideration is considerable, and the opposition seems small.

From the experience we have had with preliminary efforts so far, it would seem that in essence the final outcome will be conservative, with simplification in some areas and an arrangement which will permit an orderly expansion in others. There will be a greater flexibility in the use of synonyms, with an attempt to remove overlapping categories as far as possible and to clarify the personality disorders; perhaps there will be a return to some of the classical terms such as "hysteria." Agreement is general that any major changes should be made only if based on major advances in knowledge.

A main purpose of the revision would be to forestall development of changes in procedure resulting from professional discontent; failure to use the classification as it was intended; introduction of wide local variations in which some categories are abandoned and others overused or even expanded by the introduction of special subdivisions; and local modifications of definition, which, if unchecked, can distort the classification beyond recognition. This may seem to be a matter of small concern from a short-term, individual point of view, but from the long-term public health standpoint, it constitutes retrogression and a return to the chaotic conditions of the nineteenth century.

Organizational Developments

The need to correct for such drifts and to create and maintain a standard, up-to-date classification and nomenclature of maximum usefulness and general acceptability has led to the development of organizational procedures briefly mentioned under History. At the present time, these are operating to produce an updating and revision of the APA manual.

In 1962, the American Medical Association, in its regular decennial revision (the fifth) of its standard (Thompson & Hayden, 1961), made enough changes in the new section on diseases of the psychobiologic unit to require extensive rearrangements in the manual of the American Psychiatric Association (1952) if the two are to remain in complete alignment. The new items are of a relatively minor nature but are sufficiently numerous and so dispersed and interrelated with the text that nothing less than a complete reworking of the manual would be possible. Ordinarily some immediate move to reconcile these differences would be required, but this is being held in abeyance by common consent between the AMA and the APA because other developments are taking place which promise to require still other changes in the manual within a very short time. It is desirable to avoid the disruptive effect of multiple short-lived revisions.

Perhaps the most important of the moves bearing on this question is the fact that the World Health Organization is now occupied with a seventh revision of its international classification (1957) and has established national committees in various countries to serve as local liaisons for this purpose. The United States subcommittee on psychiatry for the WHO is working with the APA committee on a proposed classification which will serve the needs of the United States and which will be more completely compatible with systems of other countries. Soon all the various national proposals will be submitted for the 1965 ICD, but it is as yet uncertain how the final international classification will relate to the American Medical Association's standard and to the APA manual.

Another important event, of which the ultimate impact remains to be seen, was the publication by the AMA of the first edition of *Current Medical Terminology: 1963* (CMT) (Gordon & Talbott, 1963). It is provided with cross-reference code numbers to the ICD and to the AMA standard and has "stylized definitions." The terminology will be brought up to date, and it will be reissued at frequent intervals, in order to keep abreast of actual practice, rather than being limited to the traditional decennial editions. The continuous selection of new terms will, in essence, be based on authoritative current usage and practice. It seems likely that the CMT (Gordon & Talbott, 1963) will strongly influence nomenclature, but there are still uncertainties with respect to this and about classification, which is the chief interest of the WHO, and concerning interrelationships between the WHO, the AMA, and the APA. In any event, it seems certain that the next APA manual will be much closer to the psychiatric section of the upcoming seventh revision of the ICD than the current APA manual is to the ICD of 1955.

PROMISES FOR THE FUTURE

The CMT opens vistas toward a more flexible use of continuously current terminology of an authoritative and standardized nature. In addition, there are reasons to believe that psychiatric diagnosis and classification may become a part of a larger picture of intercorrelated public health studies on a national and international level. The recently discovered relation between maternal German measles and mental deficiency may prove to be but one of a number of discoveries concerning kinds of maternal infection or other insult which can lead to brain damage in the fetus and subsequent mental defect or behavior disorder in the child. Changing patterns of life in various countries may be reflected in psychiatric morbidity, and such interrelations among somatic and psychiatric morbidity remain to be worked out. Until recently it would have been quite impractical to think of handling the sheer mass of data which analyses of this type might call for, but today, with electronic data-processing devices, volume is virtually no longer a problem. Obviously machines have their limits, but they do extend our horizons vastly.

It should be emphasized that two factors are involved in this increase of potential in the field of public health. The development of electronic devices came second; the first was the long-term advance of organization in medicine and the development of public health techniques, which has at last brought us to the point of considering the possibility of a psychiatric nomenclature and classification which will be like a convertible international intellectual currency. However, it seems unlikely that it will replace the national systems now in use, and perhaps it is undesirable that it do so.

THE NATIONAL SYSTEMS

Internationally, psychiatric classification is still in a relatively heterogeneous state, and much remains to be done before we can hope to bring it into reasonably adequate alignment with any common single international standard. The survey by Stengel (1960) gives some idea of the present status of the question and lists 11 official, semiofficial, or national classifications and 27 others. The French classification introduced in 1943 is considered obsolete, and there is no official German classification, although much of our modern psychiatric thinking came from Germany. The Scandinavian countries differ among themselves, and the Russian system is strongly influenced by Pavlovian theory but still follows classical European nosology. There are many points in common among all systems; yet there are enough differences to create problems in communication and comparison of data. None of the proponents of any system whom this writer knows claim more than a mediocre success for its operation, and all seem to encounter similar problems. Statistical variations remain embarrassingly great, and there are wide differences in judgment as to their application. All these classifications and their predecessors are artificial to a large degree, but history shows that they have nevertheless produced useful results and have been able to anticipate delineations of natural and valid disease entities, as in the case of paresis, cretinism and mongolism, Jacksonian epilepsy, and many others. The importance of classifying similar syndromes close to one another under a common head is to be seen in the statistical history of encephalitis lethargica, where a temporary upswing in the psychopathic states and behavior disorders preceded by several years the statistical appearance of encephalitis lethargica in the annual reports of the New York State Department of Mental Hygiene (1917–1930) of the time (Brill, Unpublished manuscript, 1953). One can trace the inflow of cases quite reliably even before they were specifically recognized because of the fact that they were placed in related categories.

Room for Individuality Remains

It should not be taken from the above discussion that national and international systems have reached such a stage of predominance as to render it impossible to create any individual special-purpose systems or to exercise individual ingenuity and creative thought. Once one turns away from the field of large-scale public health level statistics, which require communication and comparisons of cases over space and time and where uniformity is of overriding importance, one can consider another source of medical advance—the original thinker who seeks to develop new insights into the multiplicity of the psychiatric world by creating new ways of classifying his data.

On a formal or informal level, almost every experienced worker in the field has some personal classification of his own or some important modification of a standard classification on which he may base important judgments. Sometimes these systems are unformulated and not easily put into words and are nothing more than the intuitive part of professional experience which, for better or worse, is an essential element in the armamentarium of each professional. A few workers go further, and a considerable number of ingenious classifications have been developed as a result. Stengel discusses a number of illustrative examples (1960). An interesting one is that of Wolman (in press), who writes in his *Mental Disorders: Their Theory and Classification:* "The present volume is an effort to combine the organic, the psychological, and the sociological. The underlying philosophy is . . . continuity . . . unity despite empirical diversity, and in a gradual process of transition, phylogenetic and ontogenetic . . . monistic transitionalism. . . ."

Wolman sees mental disorders as a failure of certain organisms to perform vital functions in an adequate manner:

> From Pavlov I have learned the theory of conditioned reflexes in their neurological frame of reference . . . [including] the processes of excitation, and inhibition, irradiation, concentration and induction of nervous energy.
>
> The novelty of the proposed system is derived from my sociopsychological theory of power and acceptance. This . . . deals with observable phenomena of overt interaction.

Wolman divides all mental disorders into genosomatogenic, ecosomatogenic, and sociogenic, with the last as the largest group, where distortions of social attitudes dominate the total pattern of overt behavior. The terminology is devised to express this. Psychopathic individuals are hyperinstrumental (self-cathected); well-retained and latent schizophrenics are hypervectorial (object-hyper-cathected); and manic-depressives are paramutual, with inconsistency and exaggeration in human relations. The disorders are discussed in relation to power and acceptance, and they are seen as a product of disbalanced libido and destrudo cathexes resulting in three types and five levels of mental disorders aside from the organic (cf. "Mental Health and Mental Disorders," in Part 4).

From such individual adventures into original thinking may come some new principles of synthesis which could open the way for advances in psychiatry. It has been claimed that we already have enough data to permit vastly better interpretations and that our situation is analogous to that of the biological sciences before Linnaeus and the formulations of Darwin or the field of physics and atomic structure before Mendeleev classified the elements.

The future will have to decide to what extent advance will depend on new information and to what extent it will come from more effective thinking about existing data. Whether classification will remain in the humbler role of ordering data according to some eclectic system like the present ones or whether, through a flash of insight, some new synthesis will open fresh leads will remain to be seen; one thing is certain—classification, formal and standardized, is an integral part of the mechanism of psychiatric advance, and indications are that it will remain so. The fact seems certain; only the terms must be settled by the future.

REFERENCES

American Psychiatric Association, Committee on Nomenclature and Statistics. *Diagnostic and statistical manual of mental disorders.* Washington, D.C.: Author, 1952.

Aurelianus, C. (Ed. by I. E. Drabkin.) *On acute diseases and chronic diseases.* Chicago: Univer. of Chicago Press, 1950.

Brill, H. Unpublished manuscript, 1953.

Cardano, J. *De vita propria liber*. New York: Dover, 1962.

Encyclopaedia Brittanica. Taxonomy.

Freud, S. Weitere Bemerkungen über die Abwehrneuropsychosen. *Neurol. Centralblat.*, 1896, **10**, 434.

Gordon, B. L., & Talbott, J. H. *Current medical terminology:* 1963. Chicago: American Medical Association, 1963.

Gray, P. *Encyclopedia of biological sciences*. Taxonomy. New York: Reinhold, 1961.

Jaspers, K. *General psychopathology*. Chicago: Univer. of Chicago Press, 1963.

Kaplan, O. *Mental disorders in later life*. Stanford, Calif.: Stanford Univer. Press, 1956.

A manual on terminology and classification in mental retardation. Monograph Suppl. to *Amer. J. men. Def.*, 1959, **64** (2).

Meyer, A. The evolution of the dementia praecox concept. *Nerv. ment. Dis. Monogr.*, 1928, V, 3–15.

Moriyama, I. M. The classification of disease: a fundamental problem. *J. chron. Dis.*, 1960, **II**, 462–470.

New York State Department of Mental Hygiene. *Annu. Rep.*, 1917–1930.

Pachter, H. M. *Paracelsus*. New York: Abelard-Schuman, 1951.

Pearson, K. *The grammar of science*. London: Dent, 1951.

Smith, C. W. *Florence Nightingale*. New York: Avon, 1951.

State of New York, Department of Mental Hygiene. *Statistical guide*. Utica, N.Y.: State Hospitals Press, 1943.

Stengel, E. *Classification of mental disorders*. Geneva: World Health Organization, 1960.

Thompson, E. T., & Hayden, Adaline C. (Eds.) *AMA handbook on standard nomenclature of diseases and operations*. (5th ed.) New York: McGraw-Hill, 1961.

Wolman, B. B. *Mental disorders: their theory and classification*, in press.

World Health Organization. *International classification of diseases, injuries, and causes of death*. Geneva: Author, 1957.

Zilboorg, G., & Henry, G. W. *History of medical psychology*. New York: Norton, 1941.

part **4**

Clinical Patterns

25

Organic Mental Disorders

GEORGE K. YACORZYNSKI

HISTORICAL BACKGROUND

In the midst of this happiness, news arrived from the schoolmaster, that from some unexplained cause, the elder boy had begun to exercise a very unreasonable and tyrannical authority over the younger. . . .

A repetition of severe punishment—long incarceration and a rejection by all his relatives—had no effect in changing his disposition—his dislike to his brother became fixed animosity, and from animosity degenerated into the most deadly hatred. . . . Still the boy was not insane; on every topic but one he was reasonable, but torpid. It was only at the sight of his brother, or the sound of his name, that he was roused to madness.

The youth now advanced towards manhood. When about the age of fifteen, he was taken with a violent but Platonic passion for a lady more than forty years of age, and the mother of five children, the eldest older than himself. His paroxysms of fury now became frightful; he made several attempts to destroy himself; but, in the very torrent and whirlwind of his rage, if this lady would allow him to sit down at her feet, and lay his head on her knee, he would burst into tears, go off into a sound sleep, and wake up perfectly calm and composed, and, looking up into her face with lack-lustre eye, would say—*"Pity me—I can't help it!"*

Soon after this he began to squint, and was rapidly passing on into hopeless idiotcy, when he was once more taken to *Mr. Cline,* a surgeon long since dead. . . . A day was fixed for the operation, a circular piece of the skull was removed by the *trephine,* and, on examination, there was found to be a specula of bone, growing from under its surface, and piercing the brain. Here was the hatred to his brother at once explained. He soon recovered, became strongly attached to his brother, and felt no other sentiment towards Mrs. M. than gratitude for the kindness which she had shown him in his illness, and of which he retained but a faint remembrance.

But now listen to the explanation. . . . The disease which led to these horrible results took its rise from the blow of a round ruler, in one of the *gentle* reprimands then so common with schoolmasters; so that the boy's schoolmaster was himself the originator of all the suffering and misery that ensued . . . and, of course, every time that the point of the specula pressed against the brain, the irritability resulting from the portion of the brain against which it pressed, and which was the organ of Destructiveness, led to the frightful results described (Goyder, 1857, pp. 40–42).

It is of interest that the modern antecedents of the development of knowledge regarding brain functions are ideas propounded by what is now considered to be a pseudoscience. Gall early became interested in the personalities of his brothers, sisters, and schoolmates, noting that each one differed from the others. At school he had difficulty competing with those students who could learn more readily than he did. Later he realized that the students who could learn rapidly had prominent eyes, and he concluded that if memory could be recognized by external signs, the same thing might be true for other intellectual powers. He then turned his attention to the head for signs of other faculties. He was soon led to believe that each individual possessed faculties in different degrees and amounts, that these faculties could be localized in different areas of the brain, and that their presence could be gauged by the contours of the skull. The impact of these postulates was great. Societies, journals, and professorships were established and flourished during the next half-century, before the movement gradually began to die down.

Craniology, as developed by Gall (or "phrenology," a term later introduced by Spurzheim) made an important contribution, not in terms of its postulates, but because it raised questions concerning the functions of the brain and set the stage for the tenor of thinking on brain functions which, to some extent, is still prevalent. This idea is that the functions can be localized in a rather definitive manner in different parts of the brain. It is with this orientation and purpose that many investigators have worked in the field of brain functions. The quotation given above indicates that if the theoretical constructs of phrenology are disregarded, the outcome of the surgical procedure could be accepted within the modern frame of reference.

The advent of phrenology was a stimulus to explore the functions of the brain by those individuals who could accept its tenets only on factual grounds. The work of Flourens (1824) and others, who extirpated different parts of the brains of animals and observed their behavior, soon made it evident that the theory of faculty psychology, as proposed by phrenology, was untenable. Many of Flourens's findings smack of the concepts which others who question strict localization advanced in the present century. He concluded that certain parts of the brain have functions of a rather specific nature but that, at the same time, the brain functions in a unitary manner as a single system. Gall (1835) presented some very cogent arguments against Flourens and others who questioned his position because of the results which they obtained with animal experiments. One of them was: "It must, however, be remarked, that my objections or observations against the lesions and mutilations, are particularly directed against those who, by this means, wish to learn the animal functions of the cerebellum and the brain" (p. 160). Another was that behavior observed in animals may be due to a multitude of factors other than brain lesions. Finally, he pointed out that one is unable to study in animals "the mechanical aptitudes, instincts, propensities, and intellectual faculties" (p. 160), or those factors which in the present-day vocabulary would be placed in the categories of higher mental functions and affective states.

If Flourens's speculations had been followed, many of the ideas which have only recently been advanced might have been developed sooner. Soon after 1850, two discoveries were made which led to a different orientation. In 1861 Broca (cf. Head, 1926) was able to make a postmortem examination of two patients with aphasia and to localize the injury in the left third frontal convolution. Ten years later, Fritsch and Hitzig (1870) discovered the precentral motor area of the cortex. Mild electrical stimulation of this area produced relatively discrete motor movements of different parts of the body. Following these discoveries the brain was explored not only for motor but also for sensory areas. Areas for different kinds of aphasic symptoms were sought. It was the era of the "diagram makers," as Head (1926) refers to this period in dealing with aphasia.

Even during this time there were individuals who could not subscribe to a theory based upon localization of function. The foremost among them was Hughlings Jackson (cf. Taylor, 1931–1932). He could not accept strict localization of aphasia, pointing out that speech and related disorders were complex phenomena. Speech did not consist of discrete words and was not based upon the images of these words. It depended upon the ability to "propositionize," or in other words, to express complex relationships. Such relationships could not be localized in any one area of the brain. He did postulate that within limits, some localization is evident. The left frontal area may be more involved in the voluntary expression of the propositionizing, and the right hemispheres in the reception of the proposition, so "that in the former process there is usually actual utterance and in the latter usually only internal revival of words" (Taylor, 1932, quoted from Jackson, footnote on p. 132). He recognized the areas involved in producing some epileptic seizures and postulated three levels of nervous system functioning. At the same time, he emphasized the complexities involved in the interactive processes of the nervous system.

Much that had been done before began to be seriously questioned at the turn of this century. The four men whose contributions can be considered of major importance are Franz (1907; 1915), Lashley (1929), Goldstein (1939), and Head (1926). Franz introduced methods used before in animal experiments, such as the puzzle box, to study brain functions. Lashley followed this procedure with his well-known work on learning in rats. Goldstein and Head worked with human subjects, the former in the field of general brain functions, and the latter on aphasia.

Franz questioned the whole field of localization, even to the extent of proposing that motor areas of the precentral gyrus did not yield specific localizable points, as had been assumed before. He showed that an acquired response did not depend upon specific areas of the cortex and that a response, lost after extirpation of a part of the brain, could be relearned. Lashley, who originally collaborated with Franz, reached the ultimate in this direction in postulating mass action and equipotentiality. In mass action the brain acts as a whole, and the degree of the deficit is dependent upon the amount of the brain tissue destroyed. In equipotentiality an area of the brain can take over the functions of another area, within certain limits. Goldstein, in many respects, was not in agreement with Lashley. For one thing, he was not orientated toward a stimulus-response viewpoint to as great an extent as Lashley. For another, he believed that the brain is not equipotential but that different methods can be utilized by the organism to obtain the same end results. But his general orientation reflects the tenor of the times. The organism responds to the demands of the environment in terms of its internal organization. Specific acts reflect this organizational potential of the organism, but they can be understood only in terms of the unitary functional whole. Much of the behavior of the organism depends upon the ability to organize complex relationships involving the organismic needs. The ability for abstraction is primary to this process. Brain lesions undermine this ability, so that the organism must fall back upon more concrete responses to his environment. Head demonstrated that many of the symptoms associated with aphasia do not depend completely upon lesions of the dominant cerebral hemisphere. He agreed with Jackson that aphasia cannot be considered specifically related to speech, but he substituted the term "symbolic formulation and expression" for "propositionizing." The important over-all function of the brain is vigilance. Vigilance is the reactive potential of the brain which yields high-grade adaptive responses, and it should not be confused with heightened excitability of the nervous system. It is specific and adaptive and can be evident in the intact animal as well as on the spinal level. Lesions of the nervous system as well as toxic conditions, ill health, and sedation can reduce vigilance.

On the question of localization, the present trend is to assume that different parts of the brain may be more involved in some function than in others but that no function has a specific local of its own, unrelated to the total activity of the brain. Some processes have no specific loci but involve the whole brain. This is the position, as a matter of fact, which Lashley in general later accepted. But psychological functions and the localization of them should not be confounded. One deals with a process, and the other with a locus. It is of interest that so much attention has been focused upon localization. Such an interest can labor only under the explicit or implicit assumption that psychological functions consist of separate entities which can be placed in separate compartments of the brain. Maybe this interest reflects the need to cast aside the yoke which was imposed upon psychological thought by faculty psychology. Localization may have an appeal because concrete entities which can be placed in compartments are easy for anyone to understand and because it is not difficult to attack experimentally the problems it raises. Localization may have a practical value for neurological diagnosis, but it yields little information on brain processes.

The present trend is an interdisciplinary research orientation toward understanding how the activity of the nervous system acts as a substratum for behavioral manifestations. Interdisciplinary conferences on brain functions have been frequently held (Sheer, 1961a). So-called "brain institutes" have been established in some centers (French, 1962). A recent trend is to give more attention to the biochemical processes of the brain as they affect psychological functions (Wortis, 1962, parts III, V). As can be expected in this age of threat of extermination by atomic energy, ionizing radiation on the brain has received some attention both in the developing organism and in the adult (Furchtgott, 1963; Haley & Snider, 1962; Piontkovskii & Kotlyarevskii, 1962).

METHODS OF CORRELATING BRAIN FUNCTIONS WITH PSYCHOLOGICAL PHENOMENA

There are a number of methods available for studying the brain in a direct way in order to correlate its functions with psychological phenomena. Some of these can be placed into the category of incursive techniques, in that some direct manipulation of the brain is necessary. One of the oldest methods is to extirpate parts of the brain and then to study the effects upon behavioral and other manifestations of the organism. A more recent method is to embed electrodes in the brain in order either to stimulate electrically a given area or to record electrical potentials from it. Drugs can be used to assault the brain. One method is to place a drug such as strychnine or novocaine upon an exterior area of the brain so as to alter the function of that part. Drugs have also been introduced directly into parts of the brain or into one of the ventricles, either to destroy an area or to produce biochemical changes in it. Two nonincursive methods are available to correlate brain functions with behavioral data. One of these is to use the electroencephalograph, and the other is to introduce into the bloodstream, by injection or ingestion, drugs which are considered to have an effect upon certain functions or areas of the brain.

The incursive methods used on the brain present many problems. In ablation experiments the destruction may be greater than is obviously apparent. This may be due to damage to the circulatory systems and to the necrotic processes which may be initiated. The area destroyed by the application of a drug to the surface of the brain or by injection into its tissue also cannot be accurately localized. Placement of electrodes in the brain can be fairly well localized, but only if the brain is available for histological examinations later on. In such experiments with stimulation, there is no certainty that adjacent areas are not also stimulated. Injection of a drug into the brain can produce local biochemical effects, but physiologically the effects can be much different from those obtained if the drug is conveyed by the bloodstream. Its locus of action is also difficult to evaluate. Nonincursive methods, in many respects, would appear to be superior to the incursive techniques, but such is not the case with the methods now available. There is no exact agreement as to just exactly what the electroencephalograph measures. Presumably many things which happen simultaneously in the brain, or subsidiary activity unrelated to the electrical activity of the brain, are recorded at the same time. As far as drugs are concerned, the specific nature of their action and of their biochemical effects on neural structures and functions is still usually a matter of speculation.

One approach which has proved profitable to the study of the behavioral correlates of brain functions is to deduce the functions from the behavioral data; this method is used extensively in psychological investigations. The experimental situation is structured in such a way as to reflect, in terms of the theoretical orientation of the individual, the processes of the brain. The functions of the brain are deduced indirectly through the experimental variables. This method has been used extensively by gestalt psychologists and learning theorists, especially in the field of conditioning. It does not allow a direct correlation between the psychological and the neurological processes, but it does allow one to deduce the latter from the former.

The difficulties encountered in studying brain functions are compounded when human subjects are used. In any incursive method, a part of the brain must be exposed, and in human beings this is done only if there is a good reason for it. With animals, controlled experiments are possible, using whatever incursive methods on the brain one may deem necessary. Nature must provide human material of this kind for the investigator. The exact delimitation of the lesion is often completely impossible to determine, except under some conditions of surgery. Premorbid information of a meaningful nature is usually lacking, so that exactly what happens following the pathology is difficult to evaluate. In the various kinds of planned topectomies, such as used in the Columbia-Greystone Associates study (Mettler, 1949), preoperative testing and examinations are possible, but the patient is already psychopathologically involved, or otherwise the operation would not be performed. In such cases many functions may be altered or may be difficult to measure because of factors relating to the psychopathology.

Difficulties of a general nature are encountered which are determined by the way the brain functions and are not essentially related to any specific technique. An interactive process among the various areas is present, as is evident in the projection and association fibers. Areas representing the afferent and efferent components are present. Regulatory functions of a complex nature exist. These are found to be present between the cortex and the other brain structures and within the cortex itself. They can be measured by the way one area inhibits or releases the functions of another area. Areas are present in the frontal lobes which regulate the responsiveness of the motor cortex (Dusser De Barenne, Garol, & McCulloch, 1942; Fulton & Kennard, 1934; Hines, 1937). Similar regulation of motor responses is exerted by the cortex over the noncortical areas, such as, for example, the cerebellum (cf. Brookhart, 1960). Bruner (1958), Pribram (1960a), and others suggest that such regulation and control can also be expected to be present in sensory functions, but these may be more difficult to measure than motor responses. There is some evidence that tickle, which has both sensory and motor components, may be regulated by the frontal lobes acting upon an area in the parietal region.

These aspects lead to the following considerations, which must be taken into account in dealing with the brain functions. In the first place, a positive symptom following brain destruction cannot be assigned to the injured area. As Hughlings Jackson pointed out, a response occurring after cerebral insult cannot be assigned to the destroyed tissue. The aphasic symptom of jargon in speech (syntactical defects), which a patient with a left cerebral injury may show, is not a function of the injured area. The jargon is present because of the function of other areas. The injured area interfered with some regulatory process but did not produce the jargon. The response obtained by stimulating the brain with embedded electrodes cannot be assigned to the area under stimulation. Processes of a regulatory nature of other areas are also involved. The second point follows from the first. A process cannot be studied by eliminating factors which are involved in it. An animal with an ablated cortex but an intact hypothalamus will show sham rage to adventitious stimuli which would otherwise not have this effect. The hypothalamus cannot be considered a center for emotions; these lie in other areas which exert their influence on this center. The hypothalamus can be considered simply an energizer, much the same as an amplifier in an electrical circuit. Livingston (1959) marshals much evidence to conclude that brain mechanisms cannot be appropriately studied in an anesthetized animal. Anesthesia eliminates or suppresses many processes which are involved in the response under observation. In the third place, the disappearance of an activity following any manipulation of the brain does not reveal the neural processes which are involved. Such results can be obtained by interfering with the sensory or motor components, the projection or association fibers, or other interactive functions of the brain. In learning experiments, for example, one of the criticisms raised by Hunter (1930) against Lashley's work was that the greater the mass of the brain which was destroyed, the greater would be the interference with the sensory processes involved in learning. This would explain mass action. Equipotentiality could be explained by the ability of an animal to learn a problem after cerebral injury on the bases of sensory components still intact.

THE BRAIN FUNCTIONS: PRESENT STATUS

Some present-day reviewers on the functions of the brain are likely to point to the disorganization of the knowledge in the field and the contradictory results obtained by many investigators working on the same material and sometimes using similar techniques. Many factors may account for this state of affairs, but one is of major importance.

Within the psychological field, one deals with the so-called "higher" mental functions. The main problem with which one is faced is the question of just exactly what these functions are. When reflexive motor behavior and sensations are explored, the problem becomes easier to investigate. That which one is looking for is more readily defined and measured. Such is not the case when higher functions are considered.

The usual method for dealing with brain functions is to use concepts which are primarily derived from the present-day psychological orientations and theories. Learning, conditioning, reasoning, perception, emotions, drives, motives, and personality have been some of the areas which have provided ideas for theory and investigation. One may subscribe to a broad theoretical orientation which would determine the individual's ideas and how he investigates them. At the present time, associationism and field theory are two of the major theoretical viewpoints of this nature. A person may want to divest himself of any special orientation or theory in his research. The operational approach states that only what is done and can be recorded is the proper subject matter for observation. Even if an investigator focuses his attention upon the recording of the behavioral manifestations, his methods and interpretations are predetermined by the present-day orientation.

The brain functions as it does, and not the way that we expect it to function in terms of our conceptualizations. We impose our own ideas of what we are looking for. This approach is not too dissimilar to the postulations of faculties. It is a problem which will be perpetually present because one cannot investigate in a vacuum; certain ideas must be present to begin with, accurate or inaccurate as they may be in terms of how the brain functions. Even if the individual's approach is operational, the method he uses will be determined by the system of thought in which he operates. Learning is of a certain nature, and there are certain ways to explore it. The same holds true for perception. It is of interest that in the Vigotsky test for reasoning, the examiner determines which concept is correct and not which ones the patient can use.

Investigators on brain functions must work within the theoretical orientation and biases of the time with techniques which remain largely inadequate. Improvement of techniques is not the solution. The most important contribution to our knowledge of brain functions can be expected to come from more meaningful theoretical orientations than have been evident in the past. As Jasper (1961) states: "More than new techniques, new concepts are needed" (p. 562). It is in this direction that researchers and theorists must strive to bring order out of what superficially appears to be chaos. The brain does not function in a chaotic manner, but our thinking and methods may impose chaos where order is present.

In the following, the intellectual and affective functions will be discussed from their experimental and theoretical standpoints. Sensory processes, nerve and cord conduction, and synaptic functions, important as they may be, rightfully belong to another area of endeavor. Pathological functions ascribed to specific areas of the brain are covered in "Neuropsychological Analysis of Focal Brain Lesions" in the following chapter. If need be, some of these may be mentioned in what follows, but the emphasis will not be placed in this direction. The material will be oriented toward the understanding of functions which can be used in a meaningful manner in work with human beings. Clinical observations and materials will be introduced wherever appropriate. The final section of this chapter will be devoted to clinical considerations.

EXPERIMENTAL AND THEORETICAL CONSIDERATIONS

The nervous system maintains rapid communication among all parts of the body and serves to integrate its functions. Only by abstraction can it be considered an isolated part of the body. In complex processes, and even in those considered to be simple, the whole body is involved. We relegate to the brain such functions as thinking and reasoning or, on less complex levels, perception sensation, but in all these processes the total organism is involved. No process can be completely understood by abstracting it from the whole. The nervous system is a signaling, integrating, and reacting organ involving all the interactions of the individual with his outside environment.

Chemical, physiological, and physical changes occur in the nervous system during these integrative processes. We may study as directly as possible what occurs in the nervous system and correlate these processes with behavior and feelings. In this way we can formulate hypotheses as to how the brain functions. The processes occurring in the brain are only a substratum for the psychological manifestation of how the individual feels, thinks, and acts. The error of attribution can be easily made in this field and is often implied. What occurs in the brain is not what happens in feelings, thinking, acting, and **so** on. The two kinds of phenomena can be correlated, but one is not the other.

The two statements above, in respect to isolation and attribution, are made to obviate any misunderstanding that might arise when the theoretical approaches to brain functions are considered, for, of necessity, a theory must be delimiting. The data and the ideas are selected. In actuality the nervous system is involved in everything the individual does, as is the rest of the body. Any act, thought, or feeling reflects the functions of the nervous system. The question is not whether the nervous system is involved in any given function, since it is involved in everything, but rather whether the material under observation and study yields generalizations that promote the understanding of much of what man does, thinks, and feels.

Acquisition and Retention Processes

Conditioning. Sherrington (1906) conceptualized the reflex arc in order to rationalize the data which he collected on the spinal animal. He also initially postulated the processes of inhibition and facilitation as well as higher-order reflex-arc dominance. The scratch reflex obtained by tickling the dog's flank was inhibited if, at the same time, the extensor reflex was elicited by administering a noxious stimulus to the plantar surface of the same foot.

The well-known experiments of Pavlov (1927) extended these general ideas to the study of conditioned reflexes. A stimulus which originally does not elicit a response may eventually do so by itself if paired with a stimulus which does produce the reaction. The substitute stimulus is referred to as the "conditioned" stimulus, and the original stimulus as the "unconditioned" stimulus. In the same sequence, the responses are referred to as "conditioned" and "unconditioned." A vast amount of literature has accumulated in this field. The nature and intensity of the conditioned and the unconditioned stimuli have been varied. The time sequence of application of the stimuli has been explored. Many different kinds of responses have been conditioned. Conditioning under various experimental situations of stress, deprivation, lesions of the brain, relationship to psychological states, and so on has been explored.

Of major importance for the understanding of higher mental functions are the concepts of generalization, or irradiation of excitation and inhibition, and higher-order conditioning. A reflex may be conditioned to a stimulus, producing in this instance an excitatory state. A conditioned reflex may be extinguished, producing an inhibitory state. The excitatory or inhibitory states will be generalized to stimuli similar in nature. An excitatory or inhibitory state produced by a tone of a frequency of 1,000 vibrations may be generalized to frequencies close to the original stimulus. The inhibition or excitation produced by a tactual stimulus applied to one spot on the flank of the dog will be generalized to tactual stimuli applied near the area of the skin originally stimulated. The explanation of these phenomena is that the neural processes of excitation or inhibition produced in a specific locality of the brain irradiate to adjacent areas. Stimuli of a similar nature to the conditioned stimulus, whose impulses enter this field, can elicit the response. In this way processes produced in specific areas may affect many functions of the brain.

In higher-order conditioning, a response is progressively associated from one conditioned stimulus to another. A response may be conditioned to a tone. A light paired with a tone may then act by itself as a substitute stimulus. A tactual stimulus may then be paired with the light, eventually producing the response, and so on. Complex interactions in the brain would be established, and these could account for complex acts and for higher mental processes.

Reflexology originated in Russia and finds its greatest adherence in that country (cf. Razran, 1957). Certainly, many variations in the experiments have been introduced, but as near as can be determined by the studies appearing in the Josiah Macy, Jr., Foundation and National Science Foundation (1959–1960) publications, the fundamental tenets are similar to those originally introduced. Voronin (1962), for example, states that inhibition, excitation, and chain reactions are some of the most important areas of investigation in conditioning. As Yakovlev (1961) points out, this generalization does not characterize the approaches of all reflexologists.

A conditioned reflex can be established in animals with an ablated cortex. Shurrager and Culler (1940) originally reported conditioning in a spinal animal, but these results have not been later verified by others. Evidently, subcortical structures are necessary for conditioning (cf. Galambos & Morgan, 1960). Only if conditioning is of a complex nature would some of the higher centers be involved.

Learning. Learning can be considered nothing more than conditioning. In this case no postulates would be necessary to explain learning other than those applicable to conditioning. The sophistication and exploration in this field have gone far beyond Ebbinghaus's original use of nonsense syllables, Thorndike's puzzle box with cats, and Pavlovian conditioning. Theorists in the field such as Mowrer (1950; 1960) and Skinner (1938) have pointed out that even if a generic term such as "learning" is used, there are different kinds of learning which may need postulates of a different nature from one another for their understanding. The insistence of the gestalt psychologist on insight in the acquisition of a response as different from associative learning is well known. Hilgard (1956) discusses theories of learning from some ten different schools of psychology, some of which bear little resemblance to one another.

Within this welter of theories and possibilities, investigators have heroically attempted to determine the area of the brain involved in learning and/or how the brain functions to make learning possible. On the question of localization, Lashley maintained, as has been pointed out, that learning is a function of the whole brain. His dictum probably still holds true. One can interfere with learning without essentially involving the process itself. Lesions affecting motor, sensory, or association neurones involved in a given act may retard its acquisition. Disturbing functions necessary to acquire some kinds of materials, such as the ability for abstract thinking, the vigilance proposed by Head, and other conditions, may have a similar effect.

In respect to theory, associationism is one proposal. Another proposal is advanced by Hebb (1949; 1963). He bases his theory upon the reverberating arcs of Lorente de Nó (1938a), who showed that a neural process initiated in the brain can be self-propagating. For example, nystagmus initiated by vestibular stimulation will continue for some time after the vestibular organs have ceased to discharge impulses. A chain of neurones is involved in this process, forming a self-perpetuating system. One neurone fires another, etc., until the original neurone is fired again, and the process continues. Even with little imagination, infinite and complex systems of this nature can be diagramed, considering the number of available neurones. Hebb considers that many semiautonomous cell-assemblies of this nature exist. They are self-propagating reverberating arcs. They are interlinked so that the semiautonomous cell-assemblies can interact. The semiautonomous cell-assemblies thrown into function could be expected to acquire some permanency if growth or some biochemical change took place at the synapses of the neurones. The pattern of neural connections would acquire some degree of permanency, as would be demanded for learning to take place.

Memory. Many investigators and theorists have focused their attention upon how the brain is capable of reproducing material after it has been acquired. Loci or mechanisms for storing memory have been sought. Either the brain must be able to store memories, which under appropriate conditions can be reproduced, or some processes can be reinstated which have occurred before.

Associationism and semiautonomous cell-assemblies of Hebb would subscribe to the latter view. In the conditioned response, a direct relationship would be assumed to be established between the afferent and efferent impulses, presumably through changes in the synapses, which would be of a fairly permanent nature. By the process of generalization and higher-order conditioning, many different stimuli could reintroduce the response. In the cell-assembly concept, the semiautonomous interacting assemblies would also acquire some permanency. Since the cell-assemblies are interconnected, any one of them would be available to reinstate the original pattern of neural activity.

On the other hand, one may seek an engram of memory with localization in specific areas. Much attention recently has been placed upon the temporal lobes and adjacent areas. Extirpation of some parts of this organ can affect memory for recent events. Electrical stimulation may revive either early memories of the kind that the patient can recall consciously or those he could not previously recall (Roberts, 1961). In some instances, stimulation can produce temporary retrograde amnesia. Brain (1962), after reviewing some of the results on the temporal lobes and adjacent areas, concludes that these structures do not deal with memory because only recall for recent events is usually affected. They may be involved "with the passage of memory to those parts of the brain where they are stored and possibly to some extent with recall" (p. 49). He further concludes, "That the equivalents of different regions of the cortex for retention of memories point to multiple representation" (p. 50). Pribram (1960a) points out that after occipital lobe surgery, memory prior to surgery is not affected and that the material forgotten following surgery can be recalled under emotional duress; the only persistent symptom is an inability to remember the elements in the execution of a sequential act. He thus feels that the occipital lobes are primarily involved in the execution of complex sequences of acts.

The past experiences which the individual can recall may be regarded as facts. They can also be regarded as fantasies. Past experiences are not recalled in their entirety; they are recalled, not as specific incidents, but as fragments relating to the individual's needs and attitudes or to those conditions which have an effect on his life, as anyone working with individual patients can testify. They are interpretive material and are not factual in nature. The reports of vivid recall of visual and auditory material (sometimes they are reported as a dreamlike state) with stimulation of the occipital lobes may appear as if they are taken from the individual's past, although, in some instances, the individual cannot relate these to his past experiences. What these results show is that fantasies of various kinds do occur which the individual can relate to past experiences, but how exactly they relate to his needs, attitudes, desires, and so on would necessitate further exploration.

The delayed response is affected by frontal lobectomy. For the first time, a definite function, reported originally by Jacobsen (cf. Jacobsen, Wolfe, and Jackson, 1935), could be assigned to the frontal lobes and has been verified by others. In a delayed response the animal is made to select an appropriate stimulus, not on the basis of external sensory cues, but on the basis of spatial or temporal factors. The food may be placed in one of five identical receptacles while the animal watches. After a short period of time, the animal must select the appropriate receptacle on the basis of its spatial position. A temporal sequence may be used, such as making three left turns and two right turns, in the absence of any other cues in order to solve the problem. A monkey with frontal lobe lesions is incapable of delaying his response to identical spatial stimuli. In the delayed response, memory is not involved, as this function is understood. It is not something which is acquired and recalled later. It brings into play perceptual processes in the ability to respond correctly to a spatial distribution of identical stimuli or to make a sequence of appropriate moves in a temporal order in the absence of any other cues.

Summary of brain functions in acquisition and retention. There is general agreement that the properties of the nervous system underlie the processes of learning. There is no such agreement concerning the nature or loci of these properties.

In the acquisition of a response, a direct connection may be considered to be formed at the synapse between the sensory and motor neurones. A simple process of association would be involved. If learning is considered to occur only at this level, then no further assumptions are necessary. Subcortical structures, although not on the spinal level, would be sufficient for this process to occur.

Learning is complex, and many different kinds of learning have been proposed. Often the only common element among them is that modification of behavior has occurred as a consequence of experience. Some of these systems would ascribe to learning much of what man does, feels, and thinks. At this level of conceptualization of learning, the cortex would be involved. The association formed at the synapse of incoming and outgoing neural impulses sufficient for the explanation of the conditioned reflex would not be tenable. One may resort to the reverberating semiautonomous cell-assemblies of Hebb as explanatory principles. The nativistic theory of modification of behavior as contrasted with learning theories is discussed in the sections which follow.

The associationism of conditioned reflexology or the semiautonomous reverberating arcs can be used to explain memory. Changes in the synapses occur which allow a response to be reinstated under appropriate conditions.

On the other hand, one can postulate engrams of memory stored in the brain. No one site for memory has been found to be present in the brain. Frontal lobe lesions do interfere with the delayed response. However, the delayed response does not involve memory. It is not acquired and then recalled; it is a perceptual function involving the patterning of stimuli. Much emphasis has been placed recently upon the occipital lobes in memory. Stimulation of this organ can produce vivid recall of past experiences as well as fantasies unrelated to the individual's past. Such feelings may depend not so much upon the recall of memories but upon the individual's present needs, attitudes, and desires. Memory has been reported to be affected by occipital lobe lesions. It may be that memory for past events is not impaired; rather, the individual may display an inability to remember elements in the execution of a sequential act. He does not forget his past. He forgets some of the elements involved in a complex act he is in the process of carrying out. Considerations of this nature lead to the assumption that the whole cortex, and possibly subcortical areas, are involved in memory.

Evaluation of acquisition and retention in organic states. Organic conditions in human beings can produce deficit in learning, but only if there is a diminution of all functions. Mental deficiency can often be attributed to brain damage, especially in children. In such conditions the learning process is affected only to the extent that all functions are diminished. Many functions can be differentially disturbed in the organic. In children this is often evident on individual intelligence tests, such as the Stanford-Binet and the Wechsler Intelligence Scale for Children. In the majority of such instances, the visual-motor items suffer to the greatest extent. On rare occasions verbal items can be found to suffer as a result of brain injury if the processes related to speech are involved. It is instructive that learning is not differentially affected. Tests found to be most diagnostic in organic children, such as those developed by Bender (1938) and Strauss and Lehtinen (1947), do not involve learning. The same condition holds true for the adult. Methods developed by psychologists to diagnose organic states usually do not include learning tasks. If such are present they are used only as secondary methods for the study of some other function. It is true that, for example, the immediate repetition of digits, and especially repeating them backward, is likely to suffer in the organic, but this is also likely to occur as frequently in disturbed emotional states such as the psychoneuroses. Furthermore, the repetition of digits deals with immediate recall and is likely to depend upon the relationships perceived among the numbers.

Memory also cannot be used as a diagnostic yardstick in organic patients. If memory suffers, it usually involves some other process related to it. The writer has had occasion to examine over five thousand patients, many of whom complained of loss of memory. The complaint is found most frequently in patients without an organic involvement and infrequently in patients who have brain damage. Memory measured objectively is actually not found to be selectively impaired in such patients. Other factors interfere with memory. The individual may feel alienated from his environment—as if he does not belong to it or is not a part of it. He may be so involved with his internal emotional turmoil that concrete events are difficult to recall. He may be faced with problems with which he is unable to cope. He reverts to the past and disregards the present.

Memory is usually found to suffer in senile states. In such conditions there is a general deterioration of function, not only of memory. The aging individual without gross senile changes will often show a clearer memory for past events than for recent events. Psychological factors play an important part in this situation. The aging individual often feels that he faces a bleak future, as indeed he does in our culture. He reverts to the past so that he need not face that which is to come.

Electroshock treatment produces, with few exceptions, a progressive diminution of memory. It affects the brain, but in a manner not yet known. Recent events are likely to suffer first, but the individual may eventually reach the stage where he has difficulty recalling his name. The progressive change does not involve memory alone; there is a generalized diminution of all intellectual functions. The sequelae of the treatment, of course, are reversible, although the patient some months later may still report difficulties in remembering certain things.

Psychologists involved in the area of brain

Figure 1. Illustration of figure and ground. Either a vase or two profiles can be seen. Looking at the center, the figure-ground relationships will fluctuate. *After Rubin,* 1921.

functions have been thoroughly exposed to, and even incubated on, the learning theory in the same manner as the experimentalist. They can report only what they observe in spite of theory, although they may not be devoid of theoretical speculations. That learning has played such a minor part in their findings can be viewed with some surprise. A number of possibilities can be considered. One of them is to cast doubt on the whole theoretical structure of learning of modern-day psychology, a thesis which will be further explored in another section.

Perceptual and Conceptual Factors

Three concepts from the gestalt view of perception have received a good deal of attention in brain functions. The first deals with the phenomena which, in terms of the older terminology, have been placed in the category of attention. A person can attend to only a limited aspect of the environment at any one time, and his attention is constantly changing. For these phenomena gestalt psychology has used the term "figure and ground" with a somewhat different connotation than is implied in attention. Within a given perceptual field, that which is clearly perceived is the figure, and that which is not perceived is the ground. It is not that attention fluctuates but that the perception of figure and ground changes. The second concept comes from the fact that stimulus situations are perceived in their totality, even though in most instances only a part of the whole is apprehended. A scene, a person, an object, or any other configurational stimulus can yield only a few cues, and yet the person will perceive the whole. The stimulus pattern is completed, and closure is said to have occurred. The third concept comes from a fact which has puzzled psychologists and philosophers, i.e., that constancy is perceived in an ever-changing environment. An object is perceived as being the same, or as having the same characteristics, no matter what stimulus pattern it produces. Equivalence is perceived in patterns of stimulation which, from any conceivable physical aspects, are never similar to each other.

Figure and ground. One of the methods of studying figure and ground is to use the fluctuating figures of which Rubin's modification is a classical example, as illustrated in Figure 1. The individual will originally see either the vase in the white area or the profiles in the black areas, but each one of these distinctly by itself. If he keeps his gaze fixated about the center of the card, the perception of the vase and the profiles will fluctuate. The fluctuations of the figure and the ground occur without any conscious effort on the part of the perceiver. They are so dramatic that a physicist with a highly developed engineering background, who was for the first time administered the test, looked at the examiner in astonishment and demanded what methods he used to make the stimulus change in this fashion. Figures which are difficult to distinguish because they are embedded in a background which can confuse the observer probably deal with the same phenomena. Gottschaldt (1926) has provided a number of figures of this nature, illustrated in Figure 2.

Cortical lesions will interfere with the figure and the ground. The individual with cerebral lesions will not be able to perceive as readily figures embedded in their background. For the Gottschaldt figures, this has been shown to be true by Teuber, Battersby, and Bender (1951); Zaks, Lachman, Yacorzynski, and Boshes (1960); and others. Harrower (1939) was among the first to report this result with the fluctuating figures. The

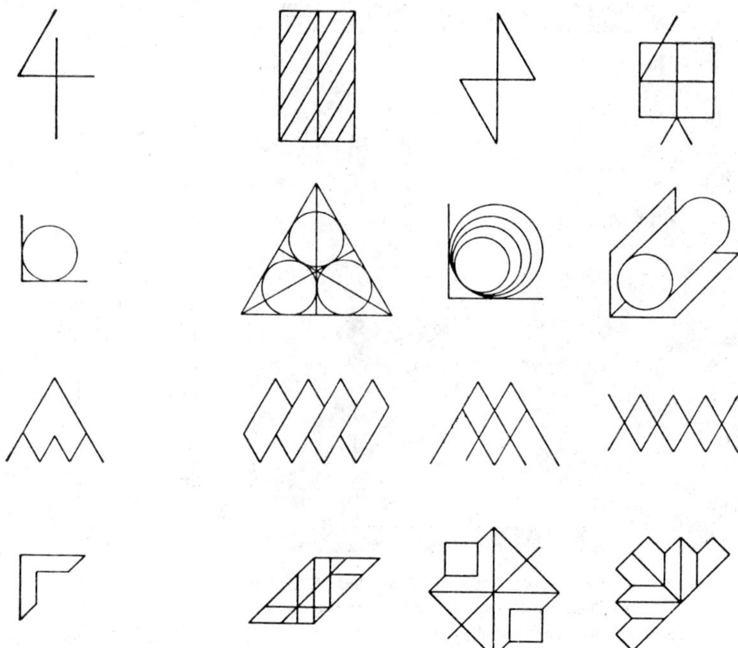

Figure 2. Embedded figures. The figures in the left column are present in the figures to the right. *From Thurstone, 1949, after Gottschaldt, 1926.*

effect appears to be greatest when the lesions are in the frontal areas. Yacorzynski and Davis (1945) showed that the number of fluctuations decreased in patients with unilateral lesions of the frontal lobes. L. Cohen (1959) reports that unilateral lesions of the frontal lobes produce a diminution of the reversals, whereas bilateral frontal lesions increase the rate of fluctuations.

The gestalt psychologists (cf. Köhler, 1940) have advanced theoretical explanations of how the brain functions in perception, including the phenomena of figure and ground. The brain responds as a dynamic unit to stimulus patterns producing an electrodynamic state. This condition is built up to a point of satiation. When the critical point is reached, the electrodynamic state is dissipated, and a new state is established. In the figure and ground phenomena, the electrical field of the brain is built up to the figure until it discharges, and the figure then becomes the ground. A similar process occurs to the new figure. In this way the figure and the ground keep alternating within the conscious perception of the individual.

Closure. The tendency to complete stimulus patterns in everyday life can be illustrated by simple experimental methods. An incomplete isosceles triangle—in which the angles are drawn but the sides are not touching—exposed rapidly may be perceived as a complete triangle if approximately 70 per cent of the lines are present (Bobbitt, 1942). Probably many visual illusions are perceived as such because of their lack of completeness. They have played a prominent part in gestalt theorizing, even though many explanations have been advanced for them.

Yacorzynski and Davis (1945) have shown that unilateral lesions of the frontal lobes may interfere with the illusory effects of many of the commonly known visual illusions. More recently, Price and Deabler (1955); Davids, Goldenberg, and Laufer (1957); Philbrick (1959); and others have obtained similar results with the spiral aftereffects illusion in patients with organic brain pathology.

Closure can be rationalized by the gestalt view of brain functions. Incompleted figures produce an electrodynamic state with lines of force that, under appropriate conditions, merge to yield a complete pattern. Illusory effects are perceived because the electrical forces interact in such a way as to produce a percept which is not compatible with the physical measurement of the external stimulus. Yacorzynski (1963a; 1965), using the general orientation of field theory and data, such as those of Gibson (1937) and Werner and Wapner (1952), has advanced postulates dealing more explicitly with the resolution of forces involved in illusory phenomena. He considers that perception is produced by interacting forces and not by a stimulus pattern on the outside conveying impulses which impinge on the nervous system as the present-day orientation maintains. The interaction of the forces characteristic of the brain and of the forces conveyed to it is responsible for perception in general and specifically for the illusory phenomena. Visual illusions and reversible figures can be rationalized under the hypotheses advanced governing these perceptual forces.

Equivalence—conceptual thinking. The individual may perceive constancy in an ever-changing world because stimulus patterns may have common elements. Things or conditions are recognized as similar or the same because of some identity which exists among them. The situation may differ, but certain elements are still common, and it is on the basis of these cues that similarity is perceived. Generalization in conditioning would use such an explanation. The conditioned reflex or the conditioned inhibition of the reflex is generalized to those stimuli which are similar.

Real as these possibilities may be, they do not explain why constancy is perceived in a changing world. Stimulus patterns which have no identity to one another in the physical sense may produce equivalent feelings and behavior. Actually, similarity is perceived, not because common elements are present, but because some process is built up which leads to identity between physically disparate situations. Klüver (1933) has explored this phenomenon with much care. For example, he has shown that a concept, such as "heavier than," of a relational nature may be responsible for appropriate behavior of the organism in relation to his environment. If a monkey is trained to pull in the heavier of two objects A and B, and then if weights B and C are substituted, the animal will pull in weight C, which is heavier than weight B, and not weight B, which is identical to the stimulus which the animal was originally trained to pull in. Lashley (1938) has shown that rats will respond to physically dissimilar patterns on the basis of factors other than the identity of elements. It is obvious that the organism perceives similarity because of factors which relate together phenomena that are physically completely dissimilar. The law of gravitation fulfills this function. It explains the falling apple as well as the movements of bodies, not only of the planetary system, but of the astronauts. Concepts relate these phenomena—diverse as they may be.

One method of studying concept formation is to present the individual with a task which requires the use of concepts such as color, shape, height, area, and volume, as illustrated in Figure 3. Goldstein and Scheerer (1941) have included the Weigl test in their battery for organic diagnosis. Hanfmann and Kasanin (1937) have popularized the Vigotsky test. Altrocchi and Rosenberg (1958) have used the Yacorzynski block test. Meaningful objects which introduce additional categories of a pragmatic nature, such as the categories of use, function, etc., may be used for this purpose, as was done by Halstead and Settlage (1943). Even drawing a straight line may involve an abstraction of verticality or horizontality. Reproduction of simple or complex figures may also involve abstractions of roundness, squareness, juxtaposition, and so on. Many tests may tap this function, but some to a lesser and some to a greater degree. This is why a clear-cut distinction as to what functions a test may measure is often difficult to make.

Conceptual thinking appears to depend upon the interactive processes of the cortex. It will suffer if the projection and association fibers are destroyed so as to interfere with the interaction among the various areas of the brain. In all the experiments on concept formation, localization of this function in any particular area has not been reported, although concept formation is found to suffer in patients with organic brain pathology. Some hemispheric dominance may be present, depending upon the kind of tasks which are involved. Teuber (1962) reports that the concept of a shape of a block experienced tactually cannot be transferred to similar objects, even with much practice, if the lesion is on the side opposite the hand used in performing the task. This is not true for the hand on the same side as the brain injury. The lack of improvement is not due to sensory defects or related to a specific area of the brain but points to the possibility of equipotentiality within a given hemisphere.

Different areas of the brain have been

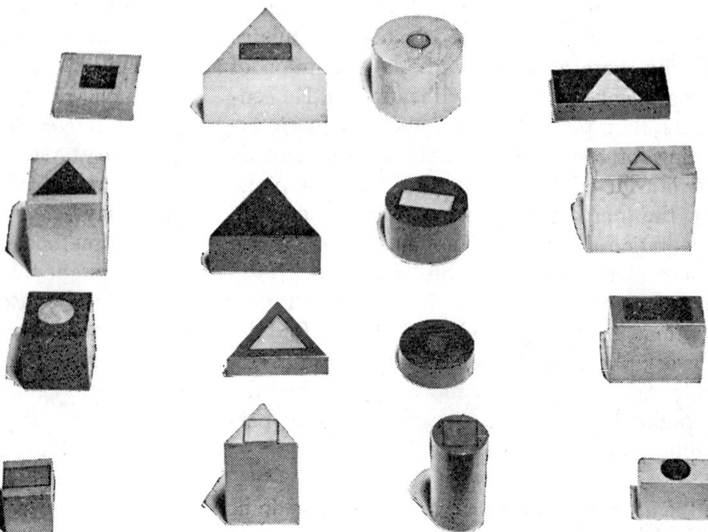

Figure 3. Concept-formation test. The blocks can be divided into four groups, with four blocks in each group, on the bases of color of block, color of figure on block, shape of blocks, shape of figures, height of blocks, volume, area of top of blocks, and area of figure. Testing is continued until the subject exhausts all the concepts he can use.

excised in studying the effects of lobotomies on patients with psychopathological conditions and intractable pain. Two such methods were specifically oriented toward the destruction of projection fibers in order to eliminate the connections between the frontal lobes and the thalamic regions considered to be involved in emotional responses. One of these is the method introduced by Freeman and Watts (1942), and the other is the Second Lobotomy Project (Greenblatt & Solomon, 1953), as illustrated in Figure 4. Greenblatt and Solomon (1958) state without reservation that the bilateral and bifrontal lobotomies do interfere with conceptual processes. This would be expected if associations between this area and other areas of the brain were destroyed. Such deteriorating effects are ordinarily not present in patients with frontal lobectomies, even if these are performed bilaterally (Hebb & Penfield, 1940). Only if the associative processes are affected would such be the case.

In lobotomies, major disturbing psychological symptoms may be reduced, but at the same time conceptual thinking may suffer. The contradictory reports of the effects of lobotomy may depend upon what criteria are used to evaluate its effects. That is probably why in the follow-up studies of patients after a number of years, some individuals report improvement (Paul, Fitzgerald, & Greenblatt, 1956a; 1956b), whereas others report consistent deteriorating effects (A. Smith & Kinder, 1959).

The postulates of the field theory could account for conceptual processes. Electrodynamic states of the brain produced by phenomena of a diverse nature may give rise to similar physical effects in the brain. The diverse phenomena would then be experienced by the individual as equivalent.

Evaluation of perceptual and conceptual factors in organic states. The field theory is a nativistic theory. From the standpoint of the gestalt, perceptual processes occur at the time that a given phenomenon is observed. Perception is not something that is acquired from the past to be reproduced at present or acquired at present to be reproduced in the future. The nervous system responds in a predetermined manner at all times because of its dynamic properties. As the nervous system is brought into function by the external forces, some maturation may occur without, however, producing a different kind of process from that which is already present. Learning is a developmental theory. The nervous system can be altered by incoming impulses; it has the property of change. The theory orients its endeavors toward discovering the possible

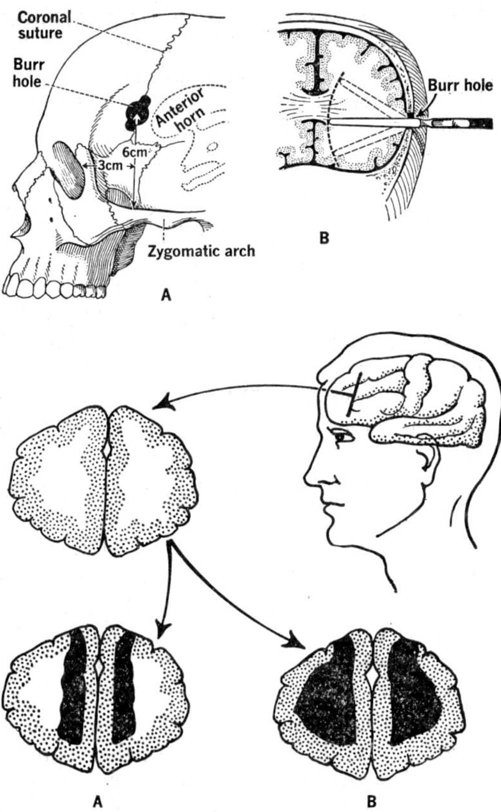

Figure 4. *Top:* Lobotomy as developed by Freeman and Watts (1942). Position of burr hole (*A*) and incision of white matter (*B*). *Bottom:* Bimedial (*A*) and bilateral (*B*) lobotomies used in the Second Lobotomy Project. The white matter is removed (represented by the black areas in *A* and *B*). *After Greenblatt & Solomon,* 1953.

limits of change, under what conditions it occurs, and what laws govern it. Gestalt and learning theories have one thing in common. The nervous system responds to external stimulus situations and is governed by it. Internal states are involved, but these are secondary to what comes from the outside. They form the background for that which is relayed from the outside.

Learning theory can deny that the properties proposed by the field theory exist. A perception is not an outcome of the way the nervous system functions; it is the outcome of the way the nervous system functions in learning. A direct connection between the afferent and efferent impulses of a relatively permanent nature can be established with repetitive stimulation so that perception finally evolves. An intermediate process within the nervous system can be hypothesized. Hebb (1949) does the latter. He would consider that a perception of a geometric object, such as a square, is gradually built up. Many semiautonomous systems would be involved; some of these would involve the angles, and others the lines, or parts of the lines, of the square. The interaction between these systems with experience would produce the conscious percept of a square. Concepts would be formed if unrelated semiautonomous systems already present became associated. Hebb (1963) recognizes that some of the phenomena in perception, such as closure, present difficulties in this theoretical system.

The anatomy of the brain also yields little discriminating insight into these theories. It is true that the brain is composed of literally millions of neurones of different sizes and lengths and with many different shapes of cells. They can convey impulses of a complex nature to all parts of the brain. Learning would require such a system. The objection to the field theory can be made that anatomical and physiological counterparts for the functions which it postulates are not available. One must not overlook the fact, however, that the brain also consists of layers of many different kinds of cells whose functions remain unknown.

One of the problems that a field theory must resolve is that functionally the brain is not bilaterally symmetrical (cf. Mountcastle, 1962). The right and left hemispheres of the cortex do not duplicate each other. Some processes are more dominant in one hemisphere than in the other (Reitan, 1955; Teuber, 1962; Weinstein, 1962). Conceptual processes may have a greater representation in the right hemisphere, and speech functions, at least in their expressive aspects, may be represented to a greater extent in the left hemisphere. Some of these possibilities were early suggested by Hughlings Jackson (cf. Taylor, 1931–1932). The incoming neural patterns do not produce a similar dynamic distribution in each hemisphere. Electrodynamic field differs for each hemisphere, and it is the interaction of these fields which determines perception. These data to some extent may favor the interpretation that semiautonomous systems determine perception.

Perception is affected in a number of ways by pathological involvement of the brain, as has been indicated. Without theory these become unrelated phenomena. One can subscribe exclusively either to a field or to a learning theory, or one can attempt an integration of these viewpoints. Clinical studies on brain functions cannot make a discrimination between these two approaches. Either one is possible. It is true that individuals involved in this area of endeavor have found more changes in perception associated with brain functions than in learning. If perception is interpreted as due to learning, then such a distinction becomes meaningless. Many individuals working in this field will use such terms as "perceptual learning," thus obliterating any distinction between field and learning theories.

Cybernetics

A number of years ago, Wiener (1948) with foresight predicted the use of machines to perform many mental tasks relegated to the domain of man in the past. He rightfully stated that a new era is being introduced similar to that of the Industrial Revolution, when machines displaced much of man's physical labor. He also stated that computers can perform functions similar to those carried out by the nervous system. He did not introduce new psychological concepts, but he pointed out that many processes of learning and perception could be duplicated by machines. "Cybernetics" was the term applied to this movement.

Cannon's (1939) idea of homeostasis postulated self-regulatory systems involving the functions of the whole body. Cybernetics would apply this process primarily to the nervous and endocrine systems. A servomechanism belongs in this category. The mechanism will perform regulatory functions if it is set to do so. Thus a thermostat set at an appropriate reading will maintain a certain room temperature by signaling to the mechanism of the furnace when it is to go on or off. Mechanisms have been built to simulate many of the tasks performed by the living organism. Walter (1953) and Ashby (1960) can be cited as forerunners in this field. These models, and more recent ones, have indeed demonstrated that machines can be devised which resemble in their action much of the intelligent behavior of living organisms. The use of models to simulate psychological processes underlying behavioral data is not a recent innovation. Such models, for example, have been built to demonstrate the various theories proposed for hearing (Hartridge, 1934).

Ingenious and insightful as the postulations and demonstrations of cybernetics may be, those who propound them are likely to overlook a fundamental premise under which they labor. The original idea advanced by Wiener (1948) that computers illustrate nervous system functions has often been reversed by psychologists either directly or by implication. Cybernetics does not illustrate but reveals how the brain functions. The argument advanced is that since computers act in a manner similar to the nervous system, the functions of the nervous system will be revealed by the study of computers. This kind of reasoning is based upon an analogy. In science, analogy is not accepted as proof; it does nothing more than emphasize or illustrate. To demonstrate that data from two different sources are similar is acceptable. To conclude that they are the same is not. One cannot assume that the data collected from one source pertain to another area. To obviate this fallacy the term "model" has been used. The computer is a model of the nervous system. Such a distinction is acceptable provided that the theories derived from the model are not then applied to the functions of the nervous system, unless the nervous system is independently shown to function in the same way.

These statements are not made to imply that important insights on nervous system functions may not be forthcoming from cybernetics. Rather, the statements are made in order to militate against the possibility that an analogy may become the primary subject matter for theorizing, as often appears to be the case.

Dynamisms of Nervous System Functions

Emotions, motives, and drives. By progressively removing the upper layers of the brain, Bard (1934) was able to demonstrate that rage responses, even to slight sources of stimulation, occurred in the animal if the hypothalamus was intact. Ranson and his students (cf. Ranson & Magoun, 1939) studied the functions of the hypothalamus in detail. In the realm of emotional reactions, their results agreed with those of Bard. They were able to obtain responses characteristic of rage by electrical stimulation of parts of this structure. Lesions placed in the hypothalamus of monkeys would make the animals lethargic and unresponsive to the exigencies of the environment. In the alarm reaction of Selye (1950), various biochemical and biological interactions occur in the organism exposed to sudden and intense stimuli. The thalamus and the adrenal gland complex play a major role in these reactions. The changes are multitudinous, involving the total body. A total reaction pattern of this nature has been placed in the category of emotions.

Within certain limits, the lower or noncortical centers appear to function to maintain physiological processes of the body such as food intake, water balance, body temperature, and so on (cf. Field, 1959–1960, vol. 2). These needs of the organism have been placed in the category of drives or motives. Their presence produces an unsatisfactory state which impels the organism to carry out activity of a nature which might produce their relief. Such behavior is considered to be tension-reducing. N. E. Miller (1961a; 1961b), by stimulating different areas of the thalamus, has shown that behavior may be initiated to reduce some of these tensions in the absence of the physiological need of the organism. An animal, upon stimulation, may initiate an act which he has learned before, such as opening the lid of a box to obtain food or running a maze.

General energic factor. Many individuals have postulated a generalized state of reactivity of the nervous system which maintains an appropriate level of integration underlying all functions. Its exact nature has been difficult to define, but even individuals dealing with discrete intellectual factors have been led to the belief of an over-all process. Spearman's G factor is of this nature. A dynamic state of this kind is emphasized by Goldstein (1939). Head's (1926) vigilance, discussed in a previous section, belongs in this category. Halstead (1947), in his four-factor analysis of brain functions, gives prominence to such a process.

One of the consistent results obtained on patients with involvement of the brain is their inability to shift rapidly from one situation to another. The more complex such situations are, the greater is the difficulty. The task may be performed, but not with alacrity. Perseveration may be present. A percept on one card of the Rorschach may be carried over to other cards. Material presented tachistoscopically may take a longer time than usual to be apprehended. The ability to shift readily from one situation to another and to comprehend material rapidly is affected. Specific processes may be responsible for these results; however, the difficulty permeates everything the individual does. Some vigilant state of the nervous system appears to be affected.

Interest—new experiences. Any person in a situation which requires him to work with individual people is aware of the fact that an interest in one's environment, activities, intellectual opportunities, and self-expression is very necessary for the individual. A person will seek new experiences. A child, for example, must have freedom of activity, and one way of upsetting him is to constrain this activity either by verbal command or by physical restraint. Such a child may respond to the demands of the environment, but he is more likely to become destructively active when the restraints are removed. Incarceration can be one of the most severe punishments meted out to an individual. Animals will learn a maze or other series of acts simply as a result of a need to explore, in the absence of any other reward.

In reducing these phenomena to neurological functions, two factors have been pointed out. The first one is that the nervous system is always active, even in the resting organism. Incoming impulses do not act upon an inactive organ; they interact with the activity constantly present. Constant activity is one of the fundamental properties of the nervous system. The other factor is that adaptation takes place. The impulses produced by a repetitive stimulus will gradually decrease; experientially, the individual will adapt to the stimulus. A change of stimulation is necessary to maintain the neural activity fundamental to the functions of the nervous system. The organism seeks new experiences of stimulation to maintain these processes. This can be observed in everyday behavior. Olds (1961) has shown that a rat may seek stimulation delivered directly to parts of the nervous system. He embedded electrodes in various parts of the brain in a situation which allowed the animal to press a lever to administer an electric current. Rats did this with electrodes placed in some areas of the thalamus, the occipital lobe, and adjoining structures.

Evaluation of energic factors in organic states. The loci of drives and motives have been sought by ablation and stimulation methods.

Such assaultive methods point to noncortical centers for these processes. They do not, however, localize the functions. They deal with structures which may be energic centers. The control and integration of the process mediated by these centers are functions of the cerebral cortex, since, if the cortex is removed, the hypothalamic animal will respond only to adventitious and inappropriate stimuli, but if the cortex is intact and the lower centers are stimulated, the animal will carry out complex acts in an appropriate fashion, as if to satisfy the drive triggered by the subcortical stimulation.

Many of the findings on animals may not be applicable to human beings. The stimulation of the reticular formation which in animals produces arousal and alertness (Lindsley, 1960; Moruzzi & Magoun, 1949) does not do so in the human being but is likely to result in an impairment of awareness (Feindel, 1961). Stimulation of the temporal lobe of a person may produce a variety of different kinds of feelings. However, contrary to the findings in Olds's experiment—which leads to the conclusion that rats obtain pleasure from such stimulation—these feelings are unpleasant. Roberts (1961) reports that in only one instance did an individual experience a pleasurable feeling.

Some energic force is present to propel the individual to carry out activities. Emphasis has been placed upon specific drives. These can be studied in lower animals by depriving them of food, water, a mate, or a litter of young or by introducing painful or noxious stimuli. The animal may do something in such situations which may remove the unsatisfactory condition, but a reduction of a drive may not be necessary to impel the organism to activity. The organism may perform and learn simply as an expression of what has been called "exploratory behavior." He may perform acts which will deliver stimulation to specific areas of the brain. This would imply that a need for stimulation and activity is present simply as a natural function of the organism and unrelated to any specific drives. What these results illustrate is that the organism must maintain an optimum level of stimulation. If the stimulation becomes too intense, there is a need to relieve the source of stimulation. If appropriate stimulation is not present, the organism may seek it. In either case, the sources of stimulation sought or avoided may be of various kinds. The fundamental property, however, appears to be the maintenance of a homeostatic balance.

The human being must have sources of stimulation to maintain an appropriate level of self-integration. Interfering with these needs can be disturbing in the same way that untoward sources of stimulation are. The striving for or toward something—the need for self-expression—appears fundamental to the individual. He will seek the opportunities for self-expression. In actuality, this appears to be the fundamental aspect of the self. Goals which the individual sets up and attempts to attain are expressions of the striving; they are secondary to it. The opportunities and rewards provided by a given social milieu determine the goals, and these can be very different from one ethnic group to another. Striving is present, but that toward which an individual strives is determined by the mores of the people around him. Systems of psychology, especially those placed in the dynamic category, have postulated a generalized drive unrelated to any specific goals. It is true that if food or other immediate necessities are not available, the striving may be oriented chiefly toward their attainment. Even under such circumstances the individual strives to obtain something beyond the immediate needs of the satisfaction of the appetite. The general conception is held at present that social needs of the human being develop ontogenetically from the biological needs. Present-day psychological thought emphasizes the historical past as a determiner of the individual's present behavior. As a consequence, a sequential development from biological needs to social needs is a logical assumption within this orientation. The hypothesis is accepted, not on fact, but because of theory. Theory holds this to be true, but evidence for it is lacking.

The nervous system acts as an integrative dynamic unit which initiates and directs to appropriate channels the fundamental needs of the individual for self-expression. Invariably, individuals working with human beings with brain pathology have been led to the postulation of some over-all function maintaining an integrative and directional process. These have been described in various terms. In experimental situations, they are evident in the person's inability to shift readily from one act to another or to apprehend rapidly complex situations. Phenomenologically, they cover every activity in which the individual participates in such a way as to be difficult to describe specifically. Wolff (1962) emphasizes the role of the cortex in the adaptations to the pressures of life situations. He is further led to believe that its capacity to deal with the exigencies of life is not affected by localized lesions but by the amount of cortical tissue destroyed.

Personality

Clinical psychologists are rightfully more oriented toward an evaluation of an individual's personality than toward other aspects of the human being, but these are not necessarily disregarded. Personality can be considered to be divisible into different categories; it can also be regarded in its totality as a psychodynamic process incapable of subdivision. Some attempts have been made to describe personality changes in relation to brain functions using the former approach. They have been sporadic, descriptive, and incomplete.

Holistic approaches to the study of personality dynamics in organic brain conditions are in general lacking. One would expect that by the use of projective tests, these objectives might be attained. However, these tests have been used largely to determine the signs or to evaluate the symptoms of organic conditions (Piotrowski, 1940). The objectives of prefrontal lobotomy (Figure 4) have been to reduce symptoms and, as a long-range goal, to alter the personality to produce better adjustment. Changes in patients following lobotomy have been reported. Symptoms of a severe nature may be reduced. This may be due to factors other than changes in personality. A reduction of conceptual thinking may produce less anxiety in an individual because all those things which he perceives as threatening may no longer have this import. It is one thing to alter personalities, and another to reduce the individual to a more concrete state of thinking. At times, one of the classifications of personality has been applied to organic patients. Willett (1961) believes that organic lesions make an individual in general more extroverted. Whether this alteration is one involving personality or whether it is due to the loss of inhibition is an open question. There is a general tendency for a patient with brain lesions, and especially if the frontal lobes are involved, to become more talkative but somewhat redundant in what he says. In the German literature, this has become known as *Witelsucht*. He may also become more irritable and in this way more expressive.

There is general agreement that brain lesions are likely to release features of personality which are already present but which the individual could adequately manage before. The individual was able either to repress many of his tendencies or to integrate them in a more meaningful or acceptable manner in relation to the demands of the environment. Removing the inhibitory influences or interfering with conceptual thinking may have the result that the patient can no longer exert the controls which were available previously. The case of the patient who had a lobotomy to reduce an obsession that he might kill his wife and who subsequently carried out the act is well known. The personality changes which are usually noted, as would be expected, are those which make for a poorer adjustment.

In aging, there may be many causes of changes in the brain. Aging individuals may show no marked alteration of personality which produces a poor adjustment, and in instances where this does happen, the general consensus is that certain features of personality which the individual could manage are no longer under adequate control. Even minimal organic changes of the brain may produce such symptoms, for the older individual has to face stresses in our culture that reflect the general attitude toward aging. This would mean, as Wolff (1962) points out, that patients with personality problems may present greater difficulties following injury to the brain than they would if such problems were not originally present. This statement essentially contradicts the idea that lobotomies produce an improvement in some patients because psychopathological states are already present which should be released following the operation. The improvement in such instances may consist not so much in a change involving personality but, rather, in a reduction of symptoms.

Feelings

In modern-day psychology, feelings are considered an epiphenomenon secondary to acts and to processes which occur within the individual. Feelings are also relegated to affective states. They are considered personal to the individual, difficult to measure, and usually not appropriate data for psychological experimentation. Some of these questions will be discussed in another context in a subsequent section.

For these reasons, feelings in the study of individuals with organic involvement may be mentioned but never explored thoroughly or systematically. Richards (1958) believes that the difficulties experienced by individuals with brain involvement are due to the feelings which are engendered as a consequence of the threat that the pathology represents to them. Anxiety and other feelings can be disruptive to good performance. This idea is in opposition to the observations that brain lesions reduce anxiety. It may be, however, that the individual with an organic involvement can maintain his integration only by rejecting completely a threat of such proportions that he would be unable to manage it. He defends himself against the anxiety by a complete rejection of the threatening situation.

Psychoprocess

A recent viewpoint developed by Bruner (1958), Livingston (1959), Pribram (1960a; 1961a), and others and belonging outside the categories of the more orthodox theories will be referred to as the "psychoprocess."

It points to a body of facts indicating that afferent and efferent impulses and the interactive processes of the brain (or "transaction," a term proposed by Livingston, Haugen, and Brookhart, 1954) are centrally controlled. It discards the reflexology parameters of behavior. The orthodox stimulus response (S-R) formulation is untenable. Adding the organism to the S-R formula (S-O-R) contributes nothing new to the orthodox reflexology theory, except to state that much which impinges on the organism is affected by what is happening internally. The organism is involved in the response, but he is still under the control of incoming stimuli. The present viewpoint is not that the organism is controlled by those things that are external rather but that a central psychoprocess controls those stimuli that are allowed to affect the organism. Livingston (1959) summarizes evidence from various sources to show how afferent impulses from touch, vision, hearing, and smell are centrally controlled, as well as the various transactive processes occurring in different parts of the nervous system. The control is exerted not only over the neural processes but also over the sense organs. It is due to some mechanism which through an afferent sensory system modifies the amplitude of input and the number of units which will respond.

Dramatic illustrations of the psychoprocess come from the clinical observations of the so-called "hysterical" patients. The patient may be unable to see or hear or to feel touch, pain, or other sensations in various parts of the body, and yet the nervous system and sense organs are intact. The individual actually does not experience sensations within a given sensory field; it is not a matter of denial of the experience, as would be true in malingering. Clinically a distinction is present between hysteria and malingering. Similar dramatic results can be obtained under hypnotism, and the performance of major surgery without pain under hypnosis is well documented. How the control of the psychoprocess is exerted in such instances is a matter of speculation. Past explanations would subscribe to a denial by the patient of the feelings. Another explanation may consider the suppression of the impulses after they enter the nervous system so that they are not consciously experienced. More recent information may indicate that the intensity and the frequency of the impulses of the responding sensory receptors are decreased. The psychoprocess is exerted, not only centrally, but also over the sensory receptors.

Magoun (1958), Lindsley (1961), and others have emphasized the reticular formation in the psychoprocess. Undoubtedly other areas of the brain participate, not only in this manner, but possibly also in other ways difficult to explore experimentally. Pointing to the undifferentiated area of the reticular formation or to any other structure is an oversimplification. It may be that the neural action is funneled through certain structures whose function is either to impede or to facilitate patterns initiated by the psychoprocess.

If higher brain centers exert a control over neural processes, including the way the sense organs will respond to that which impinges upon them, then one must ask an additional question: What determines the controls which the higher centers exert? Psychoprocess can be considered a homeostatic mechanism which acts as an automaton with automatic controls, or there may be some determining conditions which remain relatively unexplored in present-day theoretical orientations. Pribram would tend to favor the former viewpoint. Livingston considers other possibilities. He states:

> Briefly, this sensory control mechanism appears to provide the perceptual processes with an active organizing principle, including an element of purpose, which tends to select and modify sensory messages within the earliest stages of their trajectory. If overt behavior may be assumed to provide a cogent index for the interpretation of *telos*, then this sensory control mechanism is designed to diminish the engagement of higher centers with those signals that have the least significance to the individual (1959, p. 757).

Suggestions for Experimental and Theoretical Integration in Organic States

Investigations of the brain have for their purpose the correlation of psychological states of the organism with the neurophysiological processes. Theoretical formulations attempt to describe how these processes pertain to an understanding of the functions of the individual. Unfortunately, that which is known or speculated about brain functions does not attain its objectives. A clinician working with individual cases, as well as the theoretician dealing with human activities, can well remain baffled. In this state they can do one of two things. Either they can disregard data on brain functions with the expressed and perpetual hope that in time, as more data accumulate, such integration may be possible, or they can rationalize that the neurophysiological correlates of psychological processes are not necessary for the understanding of man and thus formulate theories without the benefit of psychoneurological data. The latter approach is common.

Certainly there is no lack of investigations, in either the clinic or the laboratory, on brain functions. At the present state of our knowledge, the theoretical orientation needs scrutiny, and it is toward the theoretical formulation that the present discussion will turn. An orientation will be proposed in an attempt to give some integrative direction to the manifold things which man does in relation to the neural processes. To do this, concepts already discussed will be examined. A direction for research in this area will be suggested. Only a brief summary is possible. A more extended treatment of the proposed approach is given by Yacorzynski (1963b).

All systems of psychology postulate an energic factor which impels the organism to do certain things, whether this is called "emotions," "drives," "id," "motives," "*élan vital,*" or something else. The individual is a striving organism; the striving cannot be considered to be separate from the individual—something superimposed upon him—but must be considered basic to him. It can be considered a primordial characteristic necessary for survival. The striving is a need of the individual for self-expression—a need to be able to carry out activities within the range of his abilities and environmental opportunities. Psychologists have turned to the study of specific drives and motives, but within the present context the goals and motives are secondary to the striving. They are established by the individual because striving is present. Others have pointed out that brain damage undermines a vigilant state of the individual involving striving that is not directed toward specific goals.

Modifications of the individual are constantly occurring. Our experience dictates to us that somehow or other, one acquires states, conditions, feelings, information, and so on which one did not possess before. This inconstancy is one of the most constant phenomena present in man. If it is not due to maturational factors, then it is placed in the category of learning.

All theories of learning consider that stimuli impinging on the organism produce the modifications. This assumption has been seriously questioned. A selective process, which has been referred to above as the psychoprocess, is present which allows only certain stimuli to affect the individual. Obviously the psychoprocess would be involved in all areas, including the modifications of the individual which are constantly taking place.

External stimuli, or their patterns, determine perceptions. This idea is held whether a nativistic or a learning theory is used to explain perception. Serious doubts have been raised about this possibility. Gibson (1963) points out that specific sensations or patterns of sensations do not determine perception. Constancy is perceived in stimulus patterns which are never alike, and the individual acts to assert and to maintain this constancy. This is the invariant in perception which needs to be understood. It is not determined by sensations (although the senses are necessary) but is an inherent aspect of the self. Sensitivity, and not sensations, determines perception. Perception is dependent upon an active internal system and is independent of specific kinds of sensory inputs or sense organs. In this context, Gibson calls the senses an "esthesic" system. He states:

> Moreover, the theory will have to explain all the observations and experiments of past generations which seem to make it physically evident that the observer *contributes* meaning to his experience, that he *supplements* the data and that significance *accrues* to sensation (1963, p. 11, italics in original).

He further states:

> Every esthesic system is an attentional system. Attention is not an intervening process, therefore, but one that starts at the periphery. It also continues to select and filter the already selected inputs at nerve centers, as we know both from introspection and from the evidence obtained by microelectrode recording (1963, p. 12).

The individual can be considered to project internal states, or feelings, to that which is external to him. In this way he determines that which will affect him, not only experientially, but also in respect to the input of the sensory mechanism. Such selection would mean that the individual is receptive to that which affects him. This receptivity can best be described as a process of introjection. The introjections modify an already receptive state which in turn determines the projections. The term "I-P-I" has been used as a shorthand method to name this process of introjection, projection, introjection, etc. The individual does not learn in the usual sense of acquiring something external to him or perceiving those things which are external, but he is a part of, and is in the process of becoming a part of, those things considered to be external. He introjects those things external to him as part of himself and projects these introjections in interpreting and assigning qualities and values to those things which he considers to be external. In this way he develops a system of values which guides much of what he does, feels, and thinks. As a matter of fact, that which has been considered external is a most meaningful part of the self and exists only as an aspect of the self.

The arguments for this position are manifold. They can be reduced to neurological functions in the postulates of the psychoprocess. They can be substantiated behaviorally by many lines of evidence. Here only the question of imitation will be raised. Psychologists have been baffled by the fact that one behaves like others and does things similar to what others do, and yet specific acts are not imitated. The individual does not learn to imitate others. He becomes a part of others—especially those with whom he is in intimate contact—and thus does as they do.

In the I-P-I process, the individual strives to become a part of those things considered to be external to him. Allport (1955) has used the term "becoming" to describe that which one strives to do and acquire. In a somewhat different context, G. A. Miller, Galanter, and Pribram (1960) point out that the individual proceeds in his everyday activity according to a plan. They liken this to the plan established for a computer in programming data. To the plan should be added the values which an individual holds which select the plan to be put into execution. These values require self-expression as a reflection of the individual's striving.

Underlying the projections and the introjections are the feeling states of the individual. In this context, feelings would be considered to consist of all experiential states of the individual. They would involve ideas, beliefs, logical constructs, affects, and so on. Feelings have often been relegated to the category of affective states, so that if an individual reports an idea, it is not considered to be in the same category as a feeling of love, hate, jealousy, elation, sadness, and so on. In the former instance, the feelings are deduced from data considered to be objective and acceptable in this way by others, so that on this premise others consider that the person who reports an idea is not giving a subjective report. But even if the individual follows a logical line of thinking based upon good evidence, that which he has absorbed and that which he consequently expresses are reflections of his feelings. In this context, feelings would pertain to ideas, to an intent to do or not to do something, and to affective states.

The individual experiences and acts. It is toward the act that modern-day research is oriented. Feelings are secondary or disregarded. The idea is advanced that feelings control the psychoprocess; behaviorally, this standpoint cannot be denied. The individual who feels depressed will see everything in this light; the one who is elated does the opposite. The individual who is fearful may see everything as threatening, and in paranoia he views his environment, not as others see it, but the way he allows it to be seen. Experimental evidence is also not lacking, as has been emphasized by gestalt psychology. A coin appears larger to a child who is poor than to one who is rich. A pattern of dots, stars, or objects can be protective or threatening or can be seen as determining certain spatial patterns, depending upon how the individual interprets these objects. What the individual is essentially doing is projecting his feelings, or those things which have become a part of him, to those objects considered to be external. These are well-known and indisputable facts. The present proposal simply points out that such is the case. It postulates that feelings mediating their effect through the higher centers control the neural processes which are allowed to impinge upon the nervous structures.

The proposal is made that feelings should be investigated in relation to brain function. Such feelings, of course, reflect the values which an individual holds. One may even suggest that values be investigated in relation to brain functions, but the threat inherent in even mentioning such a course of action may at this time be too great for experimental psychologists to tolerate. At least there is precedence for the suggestion that feelings be investigated. As a matter of fact, at the inception of experimental psychology, they were to be the primary subject matter under investigation, unique to psychology as a science (Titchner, 1910; Wundt, 1912).

Since that time, methods of investigation in psychology have controlled the subject matter to be explored and the theories to be proposed. The present proposal does not suggest that the atomistic approach of the Wundtian psychology in the analyses of sensations be reinstated. It does suggest that the general orientation of exploring feelings may lead not only to a better understanding of man but also to a better understanding of man in relation to brain functions.

Obviously, this approach can present difficulties. One of the major criticisms of such an orientation is that a rigid vocabulary for, and means of measurement of, feelings are not available. In animal studies this approach would require great ingenuity. Granted that such is the case, and difficult as this approach may be, it should not be disregarded. Some attempts have already been made to study brain functions from this perspective (King, 1961). The proposal is made to suggest a possible meeting ground for that which the experimentalist observes and that which the clinician observes. Both may be correct in their observations, but the fact that one has contributed little to the other may be due to the general orientation which each one harbors. Feelings in one case need not and cannot be explored, and in the other instance they may be the most important data under observation.

CLINICAL CONSIDERATIONS

Organicity

The term "organicity" is reserved for those clinical observations which lead to the conclusion that they are due to an organic condition of the brain involving higher mental processes. Sometimes the term is used to indicate that the symptoms are such as to make the individual act as if he had an organic involvement without an actual impairment being present. Such a broad meaning of the term loses its value because it may include any behavioral manifestation simulating that of an organic patient. In a neurosis or a psychosis, many behavioral characteristics and performance on organic tests resemble those of a patient with an organic involvement of the brain. Such patients cannot be placed in the category of the organic unless data are available from other sources and previous observations indicating that such indeed is the case. It is best to reserve the term "organicity" for patients in whom an organic involvement of the brain is indicated to be present.

Organicity may be permanent or temporary. In both instances, changes in the brain of an organic nature would be present. Organicity of a permanent nature would be due to an actual destruction of parts of the brain. Intoxicants, virus and bacterial infections, drugs, and other agents may produce a temporary and reversible state of organicity without leaving any permanent residue.

Organicity is a class name. Any pathology of the brain involving higher mental functions would be placed under this classification. The locus and the nature of the destruction and the causative factors may not be known. Definite localized signs may be absent. The diagnosis is made from the results of the available armamentaria for measuring higher mental functions.

The term "cerebral palsy" has often been applied to children with neurological involvement of the higher centers. Cerebral palsy is sometimes taken to mean that the impairment is of such a nature as to produce motor dysfunction. This definition has been abandoned. Other terms besides "cerebral palsy" have at times been introduced. Denhoff and Robinault (1960) use the term "syndromes of cerebral dysfunction." "Perceptual handicap" has been recently introduced. This term emphasizes that perceptual processes are involved in brain damage, whether they deal with the narrower definition applied to specific factors relating to perception or to the perceptual organization of the individual in his environment. "Cerebral palsy," "brain-injured," "brain-damaged," "syndromes of cerebral dysfunction," "perceptual handicap," and other terms of like nature would fall under the general classification of organicity, provided that higher mental functions were involved.

There are many neurological conditions which do not affect higher processes. In such instances, the term organicity would not apply. According to the National Committee for Research in Neurological Disorders (Baker), approximately one out of eight individuals is affected by neurological and related disorders. One child out of sixteen is born with some sort of neurological condition. These numbers would include not only organicity but also spinal cord, receptor, and sensory and motor neurone involvement. One individual out of twenty representing these groups is disabled by brain or spinal cord disorders.

Organicity in children and adults. The suggestion has sometimes been made that organicity in children, especially at a young age, may have more deleterious sequelae than if the same condition occurred in an adult. There is no clear evidence that such is the case. Brain injury, however, produces different effects in children and in adults.

Organicity in children produces behavioral manifestations with sufficient commonality to be identifiable in many cases. The most common behavior, although not necessarily evident in every child, is a hyperactivity with a consequent lack of attention and an inability to direct activity for any length of time toward productive ends. The child may start a task and immediately be distracted by something else. The hyperactivity in more pronounced states may lead to destructive and unmanageable behavior. In an older child this may take the form of simulating sociopathic behavior.

Another common characteristic is that the child may perform very well in some areas but be very deficient on other tasks. On intelligence tests, one may obtain an average or above average intelligence quotient, but the discrepancies among the items may range as much as 10 mental-age years. The child may, for example, pass some items at the 14-year level on the Stanford-Binet but fail some items at the 6-year level. The usual finding is that the visual-motor perceptual tasks may suffer, whereas the verbal items may hold up fairly well. On the other hand, but to a lesser extent, the reverse may be true if areas are affected which involve the functions of speech.

The sequelae following brain injury of adults are different from those observed in children. A generalized, diffused, and unmanageable condition in the adult is seldom present. One may observe a general confusional state in the adult organic patient even if the pathological condition is fairly well localized. Such states can be considered to be due to a fairly extensive involvement of the whole brain, due to pressures exerted on it by a tumor, interference with the circulatory system, or infectious processes which affect the whole brain. If these conditions are alleviated—such as by surgery, if pressure is exerted by a tumor—the confusion clears up and is replaced by more specific symptoms. An individual may show defects in the perceptual fields. Concept formation may suffer. Aphasic symptoms may be present, especially if the pathology involves the left cerebral hemisphere. In children such specificity is the exception rather than the rule.

Unlike the child, the adult patient with an organic brain involvement will usually be most cooperative. This may not be true at the initial inception of organicity with minimal signs of dysfunction. Evidently at this stage the patient is still able to recognize his debility and is disturbed by it. This does not appear to be the case in more severe states. Behaviorally, anxiety may be absent. The patient will attempt any task assigned to him and work at it without resistance, even though he is incapable of performing it at even a relatively low level of competence. There may be overt changes in personality of an adult following brain pathology. As has been pointed out, the consensus is that in such cases, the organicity has released and allowed to come to the surface personality characteristics which were already present but which the patient could adequately manage before.

There may be two reasons for the differential effects of organicity in children and in adults. The brain of the child is in the process of development, whereas an adult brain is already structured. Brain injury in children interferes with the potential development which a given organ may have or with the way in which the organ can be modified through maturational changes, stimulation, and so on. In the adult, the functions which are already present are affected, not those which may develop. In the second place, a child lives in an environment of pressures different from that of an adult. The adult has a job, a way of living, and responsibilities which are already present and to which he has adjusted. The child lives in a world of conformity with his peers and in an environment of adults who place demands upon him to keep modifying his behavior in terms of the norms established by them. He is under pressure for achievement different from that experienced by the adult, who is accomplishing, working, or attempting to maintain his status.

These two factors may be responsible for the different behavioral and feeling patterns of children and adults, even if they stem from similar injuries. But the field is further complicated by the fact that a lesion in an adult in many instances can be well localized. The surgeon removes a necrotic area of recent origin. In children such localization is usually impossible. This is especially true if the injury occurs prior to, or at, birth or if it is due to infections which occur later on. Direct comparisons of the nature of injury of children and adults become well-nigh impossible.

The wide discrepancies of performance on different kinds of tasks by children would mean that some functions remain intact, whereas others are affected to a marked degree by the brain pathology. The unruly and often unmanageable behavior can be considered to be either a direct outcome of the organicity or secondary to it. It is possible that a child who early in life shows marked abilities in certain areas is put under pressure to perform this well at home and/or at school in all fields, especially if the organicity is not recognized at any early age, as it frequently is not. Demands are made on the child to perform tasks which he is incapable of carrying out. Unmanageable and distractible behavior may follow as a consequence of these pressures.

One of the questions often raised is the etiology and symptomatology of schizophrenia and autism in children. Bender (1953) and others believe that a distinction between schizophrenia and autism cannot be made and that in many instances the pathology is due to an organic impairment of the brain. There is good evidence to believe that childhood schizophrenia and autism have different symptomatologies (Cappon, 1953). The causative factors may be different for each condition. Schizophrenia is usually considered to develop as a consequence of an environment conducive to this state (Wolman, 1957; 1960; 1961), although one cannot rule out the possibility of organic brain pathology in some instances. Autism may also be due to factors within the early environment (Kanner, 1948; 1949). Rimland (1963) suggests that autism may be due to hyperoxygenation, such as may occur, for example, in premature birth, which damages the reticular formation. An argument against this viewpoint is that some autistic children later in life show spontaneous recovery. In adults there is no good evidence that permanent damage to the brain, or biochemical changes in the body which leave such a residue, can account for the psychoses, except in a few conditions, such as paresis.

The question has been raised whether the syndrome of the brain-injured child persists later in life. In some instances institutional care is necessary, especially if mental deficiency is present, so that some attrition occurs in this way. In other instances there is general agreement that the hyperkinetic behavior becomes ameliorated as the individual grows older. This may be due in part to the maturational changes occurring in the brain and in part to the psychological adjustment which the individual makes later in life.

There appears to be a good deal of agreement that children with organic conditions are most likely to benefit from specialized instruction not usually present in most educational systems in the country. Strauss and Lehtinen (1947) have outlined procedures for teaching these children. In 1951 an experiment was set up to determine whether children with organic involvement would benefit to a greater extent from the instructions recommended by Strauss and Lehtinen in comparison with the usual methods of pedagogy. In circles dealing with the education of children with organicity, this research has become known as the "Joliet experiment," since it was conducted in this city. The results were favorable enough so that the Department of Public Instruction of the state of Illinois provides teaching facilities for these children in any community with an expressed need for them. A few states have begun to do the same, although at the present time this is an exception rather than the rule.

The adult does not benefit from any general form of training, as is true of children. This can be expected since no generalized behavioral pattern emerges in the adult after an organic involvement. Specific factors may be involved. Training which has been developed and instituted is aimed toward these purposes. Speech training in aphasia has received much attention, and specialized forms of training in this field have been outlined by Wepman (1951) and others. Many different methods have also been introduced to retrain individuals with various kinds of motor dysfunctions such as paraplegia, hemiplegia, and spasticity due to brain injury.

Individuals with organic brain involvement can often benefit from psychotherapy. A diagnosis of organicity often defeats such an approach, if it is indicated, by the attitudes maintained by many individuals. If organicity is found to be present, then all symptoms are likely to be ascribed to it. In parents of organic children, this belief is sometimes firmly held, not only because it "explains" the condition, but also because it absolves the parents of guilt feelings. Modern-day psychology emphasizes the parent-child relationships, and any aberration of behavior of a child is assumed to stem from what the parents have done. If the child gets into difficulties, the parents are likely to feel guilty. Such guilt need not be held if organicity will explain all the untoward behavioral manifestations of the child. The adult may also use organicity as an explanation and as a defense for his condition and actions, and this attitude may be encouraged by professional people whose major emphasis is on organic dysfunctions. Consequently, the clinician must be adroit to militate against the possibility of overemphasizing the organic picture if psychological conditions are also present which will respond to psychotherapy.

Prognosis for socioeconomic adjustment of adults depends upon the nature of the organicity. In frontal lobe involvement, there is general agreement that intelligence, as measured by the standard intelligence tests, remains relatively unaffected. The patient can often go back to work and perform as well as he had done before. This is true even if the job requires rather complex skills in a profession or in business. The changes most frequently found in patients with organicity of the frontal lobes involve figure and ground relationships and closure, as has been pointed out. Evidently alterations in these functions do not produce debilitating effects in pursuits which the individual had been accustomed to handle before. The situation is different in organicity which affects concept formation. As has been stated, conceptual thinking appears to involve an interactive process among the various parts of the brain and is probably dependent upon intact association and projection pathways. These can be affected by a large variety of lesions but are most likely to be destroyed by a generalized deteriorating condition which affects various parts of the brain. The prognosis for any kind of an adequate vocational adjustment for such patients is poor. Even relatively simple tasks may require conceptual thinking which proves too difficult for them.

Causes of organicity. The specific causes of organicity receive comprehensive treatment in neurology texts (cf. Ford, 1960; Merritt, 1963). In this section only general causative factors will be outlined.

Conditions at, and prior to, birth may be present which produce brain damage. The intrauterine period and one month following birth is referred to as the perinatal period. This can be divided into the prenatal period, or the intrauterine life from conception until birth, and the natal period, or the period of birth. The causative factors of organicity are different during the prenatal and natal periods.

In the prenatal period the defects leading to organicity may be present in the germ cell at conception, or they may occur during the embryonic development of the first few months after conception or during the fetal stages of growth later on. A defect leading to organic involvement of the brain present in the germ cell may be inherited, or it may be due to abnormalities occurring at conception and not necessarily passed from one generation to the next. Many instances of mongolism probably belong in the latter category, although the causative factors for this condition have not been completely isolated (Penrose, 1961). It appears to be due to an altered distribution of the chromosomes. Conditions which are inherited may show their effects immediately after birth or later in life. Phenylketonuria, a metabolic condition due to a deficiency of an enzyme which allows high amounts of phenylpyruvic acid to be built up, produces its effect soon after birth. On the other hand, Huntington's chorea will produce its degenerative effects on the brain late in the individual's life. The fetus may suffer damage due to the interchange which occurs between it and the mother through the placenta. One such condition is cretinism. A depletion of the thyroid hormone can occur in the fetus if the mother has a hypothyroid condition. Rh incompatibility of the blood of the parents may produce kernicterus (jaundice of the newborn), although this condition may be caused by other factors, such as premature birth.

Some of the causes of organicity during the natal period are premature birth, prolonged birth with instrumentation, precipitate birth, and anoxia, or the lack of oxygen. A vast amount of literature on these and other conditions of birth is summarized by Montagu (1962). All of them are conducive to brain damage in a certain percentage of births. On the other hand, these conditions do not necessarily produce deleterious effects, and there is some evidence to suggest that they may have been present in more individuals of superior ability than in the general population (Yacorzynski & Tucker, 1960).

Throughout life many conditions may produce organicity. One of the most common causes is the microorganisms, and many virus diseases are known to affect the brain. External conditions such as trauma or piercing wounds of the head are other sources producing brain damage. Pathological conditions of various systems of the body can affect the brain adversely. The endocrine and cardiovascular systems may, through either biochemical factors in the former or physical changes in the latter, affect the brain. Strokes, in reference to cardiovascular pathology, are common causes of organicity, especially in the later periods of life. Various kinds of tumors developing in the nervous tissue or in the structures in or around the brain are other sources of brain pathology.

Problems of diagnosis. The field of psychodiagnosis is covered in another part of the *Handbook*. In this section only certain questions peculiar to the field of organicity will be raised.

At this time any sophisticated individual in the field of organicity could make up tests with an a priori prediction that they would be diagnostic. This was not true a number of years ago. In generalized brain involvement, concept formation is affected. Conceptual tests with increasing difficulty of solution would tap this function. Some of the methods which can be used for more specific delimitation of functions are the perceptual tests involving figure and ground and closure, verbal tests for speech dysfunction, sequential tasks involving the ability to shift readily from one situation to another, and the presentation of stimulus patterns for rapid comprehension.

Psychodiagnosis of organicity still presents many problems difficult of solution. One of these involves children as contrasted with adults. Whereas with adults there are many adequate tests available for an appropriate diagnosis, such is not the case with children. Most of the tests with children rely to a great extent on visual-motor performance such as the Bender-Gestalt (Bender, 1938), but in large measure most diagnosticians make use of signs appearing on items of various tests. Different and unrelated signs of the total psychological profile must be taken into consideration with a qualitative rather than a quantitative approach. The difficulty experienced with children may be due to the lack of specificity of any function present in a brain which is still in the process of development. It may also be due to the lack of localization of the site of the injury, which makes a concerted effort to determine how a particular part of the brain functions impossible.

Another difficulty in the psychodiagnosis of organicity is that differential diagnosis must be made between the organic and the mentally disturbed patients and not between the organic and nonclinical population. Psychoneurotic, depressed, manic, and schizophrenic patients may give results on tests of organicity similar to those found with patients with brain pathology. The underlying causes are, however, different. A psychoneurotic may harbor many anxieties, be easily distracted, and be unable to focus his attention in a concerted effort, and, as a consequence, his performance on some of the tests may suffer. In depression, psychomotor retardation may affect the results on some of the timed tests. A depression may mask many other psychopathological conditions which can affect the results on various tests. If this is not the case, the patient's performance may remain unaffected, provided that he is responsive to some extent and that sufficient time is allowed to complete a task. The manic may approach a task in a euphoric manner in the absence of any plan or purpose directed toward the test material. He may respond in a random fashion and fail on a test, not because of lack of ability to carry out the task, but because he is too preoccupied by his euphoric state and is directed by it. The most difficult differential diagnosis to make is between the organic and the schizophrenic. In some instances this is due to the unresponsiveness of the patient, lack of cooperation, or overt hostility. Even in a cooperative schizophrenic patient, difficulties are likely to be evident on some of the tests. The reason for this is that the patient has a system of thought personal to himself, unrelated to external reality, and in this context the thinking is bizarre. As a consequence, logical thought processes may suffer. He may be unable to use abstract concepts to the same extent as the organic, but for different reasons. The schizophrenic is likely to perseverate on the concept used originally; he is likely to use the material for his own meaningful purposes, such as arranging ships in battle formation, making buildings, etc.; he does not approach the task with an initial exploratory behavior and forethought characteristic of other individuals.

A problem often posed in psychodiagnosis is to determine to what extent the symptoms are due to organic factors and to what extent psychological factors may account for them. A patient may show various psychological states **not** directly related to the organic brain pathology but exacerbated by it. These possibilities must be evaluated for the purposes of prognosis and management of the patient.

Because of these and other factors, organic tests used by themselves are not sufficient for differential diagnosis in clinical practice. Projective tests, and other methods and information, are as important for the diagnosis of organicity as the specific tests standardized for this purpose.

CONCLUDING REMARKS

A wide interest in the functions of the brain has characterized the last few decades. An interdisciplinary approach has gained momentum. In the last decade, brain institutes involving many disciplines have been established, and symposia representing different fields of endeavor have been held.

Much progress has been made from the pragmatic standpoint. The recording of electrical potentials, either from the surface of the skull or by embedding the electrodes in specific areas of the brain, has been developed. The electrical stimulation of the brain, inherited from the last century, has been refined. The field of biochemistry of the brain is being investigated. Ingenious methods of studying complex psychological functions such as learning, perception, and concept formation have been devised, and the older methods have been refined. In the applied clinical field, psychodiagnostic methods have been developed and improved. As was not true some years ago, a skilled clinician can now devise tests with an a priori prediction that they will be diagnostic of brain pathology.

Concepts from learning, perception, drives, emotions, and personality have dominated the present-day approach in the study of brain functions. Techniques developed in these areas have been applied to the exploration of brain processes. The application and the refinement of methods have been the objectives, rather than the examination of the basic ideas underlying the methods. Methods and not theory have dictated the ideas used in the study of brain functions. Most of these ideas are not of recent origin but a product of the thinking initiated at the beginning of this century. Faculty psychology, which had dominated the thinking of the last century, has in general been discarded. It still has its influence in the attempts to localize functions in different areas of the brain.

A new orientation has been recently introduced on brain functions in the postulates of the psychoprocess. The individual is not controlled by stimuli impinging upon him, but the sensory input is controlled internally. This approach questions the stimulus-response formulations fundamental to all psychological thought, whether this deals with learning, perception, thinking, acting, feeling, or any other function. The psychoprocess points to the possibility that internal states, or those which can be rationalized under the category of "feelings" in the broad sense of this term, determine not only what man does but also that which affects him from the external environment. The suggestion is made that this orientation may produce data which will initiate an integration of meaningful aspects of man's activity and brain functions.

The data on brain functions are impressive. The integration of the facts under a theoretical system, meaningful to the understanding of man, has been most difficult. The refinement of approaches so far used can yield more information in an area where such information is already present. This approach should not be discouraged because replication in science and improvement of methods already available are necessary. However, the multitudinous multiplication of minutiae does not appear to lead the way to an understanding of brain functions. Unfortunately, the present-day orientation is in this direction. Its general tone can be best expressed in the following:

Last night I met upon the stair
A little man who was not there.
He was not there again today.
Oh God! I wish he'd go away.
(After Hughes Mearns)

REFERENCES

Abt, L. E., & Riess, B. F. *Progress in clinical psychology.* Vol. 5. New York: Grune & Stratton, 1963.

Ackerly, S. Instinctive, emotional and mental changes following prefrontal lobe extirpation. *Amer. J. Psychiat.*, 1935, **92**, 717–729.

Allen, R. M. & Jefferson, T. W. *Psychological evaluation of the cerebral palsied person: intellectual, personality, and vocational applications.* Springfield, Ill.: Charles C Thomas, 1962.

Allison, R. S. *The senile brain: a clinical study.* Baltimore: Williams & Wilkins, 1962.

Allport, G. W. *Personality: a psychological interpretation.* New York: Holt, 1937.

Allport, G. W. *Becoming.* New Haven, Conn.: Yale Univer. Press, 1955.

Altrocchi, J., & Rosenberg, B. G. A new sorting technique for diagnosing brain damage. *J. clin. Psychol.*, 1958, **14**, 36–40.

Ashby, W. R. *Design for a brain.* New York: Wiley, 1960.

Baker, A. B. *Exploring the brain of man.* Minneapolis, Minn.: Univer. of Minnesota, National Committee for Research in Neurological Disorders.

Bakwin, H. Early infantile autism. *J. Pediat.*, 1954, **45**, 492–497.

Bard, P. Emotion. I. The neuro-humoral basis of emotional reactions. In C. Murchison (Ed.), *Handbook of general experimental psychology.* Worcester, Mass.: Clark Univer. Press, 1934. Pp. 264–311.

Barthol, R. P. Cortical conductivity: age differences and other findings. *Psychol. Rec.*, 1959, **9**, 153–158.

Benda, C. E., & Melchior, J. C. Childhood schizophrenia, childhood autism, and Heller's disease. *Int. Rec. Med.*, 1959, **172**, 137–154.

Bender, Lauretta. *A visual motor gestalt test and its clinical use.* New York: American Orthopsychiatric Association, 1938.

Bender, Lauretta. Psychological problems of children with organic brain disease. *Amer. J. Orthopsychiat.*, 1949, **19**, 404–415.

Bender, Lauretta. Childhood schizophrenia. *Psychiat. Quart.*, 1953, **27**, 663–681.

Bender, Lauretta. Childhood schizophrenia. 2. Schizophrenia in childhood: its recognition, description and treatment. *Amer. J. Orthopsychiat.*, 1956, **26**, 499–506.

Bender, Lauretta. The brain and child behavior. *Arch. gen. Psychiat.*, 1961, **4**, 531–547.

Bobbitt, J. M. An experimental study of the phenomenon of closure as a threshold function. *J. exp. Psychol.*, 1942, **30**, 273–294.

Boring, E. G. *A history of experimental psychology.* New York: Appleton-Century-Crofts, 1950.

Boydston, E. H. (Ed.) *Neurologically handicapping conditions in children: implications for maternal and child health and crippled children's programs.* Berkeley, Calif.: Univer. of California Press, 1961.

Brain, L. (Ed.) *Recent advances in neurology and neuropsychiatry.* London: J. & A. Churchill, 1962.

Brazier, Mary A. B. *The central nervous system and behavior.* Washington, D.C.: Josiah Macy and National Science Foundation, 1959.

Brazier, Mary A. B. (Ed.) *Brain and behavior.* Washington, D.C.: American Institute of Biological Sciences, 1961. (a)

Brazier, Mary A. B. *A history of the electrical activity of the brain: the first half-century.* New York: Macmillan, 1961. (b)

Brickner, R. M. *The intellectual functions of the frontal lobes.* New York: Macmillan, 1936.

Broca, P. Anatomie comparée des circonvolutions cérébrales. *Rev. Anthrop.*, 1878, Ser. 2, **1**, 385–498.

Brookhart, J. M. The cerebellum. In J. Field (Ed.), *Handbook of neurophysiology.* Vol. 2. Washington, D.C.: American Physiological Society, 1960. Pp. 1245–1280.

Brookhart, J. M., Moruzzi, G., & Snider, R. S. Origin of cerebellar waves. *J. Neurophysiol.*, 1951, **14,** 181–190.

Bruner, J. S. The neural basis of perception. *Psychol. Rev.*, 1957, **64,** 340–358.

Bruner, J. S. Neural mechanisms in perception. In H. C. Solomon, S. Cobb, & W. Penfield (Eds.), *The brain and human behavior.* Baltimore: Williams & Wilkins, 1958. Pp. 118–143.

Bucy, P. C. The neural mechanisms of athetosis and tremor. *J. Neuropath. Exp. Neurol.*, 1942, **1,** 224–239.

Cannon, W. B. *The wisdom of the body.* New York: Norton, 1939.

Cappon, D. Clinical manifestations of autism and schizophrenia in childhood. *Canad. med. Ass. J.*, 1953, **69,** 44–49.

Cappon, D., & Andrews, E. Autism and schizophrenia in a child guidance clinic. *Canad. psychiat. Ass. J.*, 1957, **2,** 1–25.

Chapman, L. F., Thetford, W. N, Berlin, L., Guthrie, T. C., & Wolff, H. G. Highest integrative functions in man during stress. In H. Solomon, S. Cobb, & W. Penfield (Eds.), *The brain and human behavior.* Baltimore: Williams & Wilkins, 1958.

Chow, K. L. Brain functions. In P. R. Farnsworth, O. McNemar, & Q. McNemar (Eds.), *Annu. Rev. Psychol.*, 1961, **12,** 281–310.

Cohen, J., Boshes, L. D., & Snider, R. S. Electroencephalographic changes following retrolental fibroplasia. *EEG Clin. Neurophysiol.*, 1961, **13,** 914–922.

Cohen, L. Perception of reversible figures after brain injury. *Arch. Neurol. Psychiat.*, 1959, **81,** 119–129.

Cohn, R. *The person symbol in clinical medicine: a correlation of picture drawings with structural lesions of the brain.* Springfield, Ill.: Charles C Thomas, 1960.

Dandy, W. E. Physiological studies following extirpation of the right cerebral hemisphere in man. *Bull. Johns Hopkins Hosp.*, 1933, **53,** 31–51.

Davids, A., Goldenberg, L., & Laufer, M. The relation of the Archimedes spiral aftereffect and the trail making test to brain damage in children. *J. consult. Psychol.*, 1957, **21,** 429–433.

Denhoff, E., & Robinault, I. P. *Cerebral palsy and related disorders.* New York: McGraw-Hill, 1960.

Donath, J. The significance of the frontal brain with respect to the higher psychic functions. *J. nerv. ment. Dis.*, 1925, **61,** 113–141.

Doty, R. W. Conditioned reflexes formed and evoked by brain stimulation. In D. E. Sheer (Ed.), *Electrical stimulation of the brain.* Austin, Tex.: Univer. of Texas Press, 1961. Pp. 397–412.

Dusser de Barenne, J. G. Experimental researches on sensory localizations in the cerebral cortex. *Quart. J. exp. Physiol.*, 1916, **9,** 355–390.

Dusser de Barenne, J. G. The labyrinthine and postural mechanisms. In C. Murchison (Ed.), *Handbook of general experimental psychology.* Worcester, Mass.: Clark Univer. Press, 1934. Pp. 204–246.

Dusser de Barenne, J. G., Garol, H. W., & McCulloch, W. S. Physiological neuronography of the cortico-striatal connections. *Ass. Res. nerv. ment. Dis. Proc.*, 1942, **21,** 246–266.

Ellingson, R. J. Brain waves and problems of psychology. *Psychol. Bull.*, 1956, **53,** 1–34.

Feindel, W. Response patterns elicited from the amygdala and deep temporoinsular cortex. In D. E. Sheer (Ed.), *Electrical stimulation of the brain.* Austin, Tex.: Univer. of Texas Press, 1961. Pp. 519–532.

Field, J. (Ed.) *Handbook of neurophysiology.* Washington, D.C.: American Physiological Society, 1959–1960. 3 vols.

Florey, E. *Nervous inhibition: proceedings of the second Friday Harbor symposium.* New York: Pergamon Press, 1961.

Flourens, M. J. P. *Recherches expérimentales sur les propriétés et les fonctions du système nerveux dans les animaux vertébrés.* Paris: Crevot, 1824.

Ford, F. R. *Diseases of the nervous system.* (4th ed.) Springfield, Ill.: Charles C Thomas, 1960.

Franz, S. I. On the functions of the cerebrum: the frontal lobes. *Arch. Psychol., N.Y.*, 1907, **1,** No. 2.

Franz, S. I. Variations in distribution of the motor centers. *Psychol. Rev. Monogr.*, 1915, **19**, No. 1.

Freeman, W. J., & Watts, J. W. An interpretation of the functions of the frontal lobes. *Yale J. Biol. Med.*, 1939, **11**, 527–539.

Freeman, W. J., & Watts, J. W. *Psychosurgery.* Springfield, Ill.: Charles C Thomas, 1942.

French, J. D. *Frontiers in brain research.* New York: Columbia Univer. Press, 1962.

Fritsch, G., & Hitzig, E. Ueber die elektrische Erregbarkeit des Grosshirns. *Arch. Anat. Physiol., Leipzig,* 1870, **1**, 300–332.

Fulton, J. F., & Kennard, M. A. A study of flaccid and spastic paralyses produced by lesions of the cerebral cortex in primates. *Ass. Res. nerv. ment. Dis.*, 1934, **13**, 158–210.

Fulton, J. F., Ranson, S. W., & Frantz, A. M. (Eds.) *The hypothalamus and central levels of autonomic function.* Baltimore: Williams & Wilkins, 1940.

Furchtgott, E. Behavioral effects of ionizing radiations: 1955–61. *Psychol. Bull.*, 1963, **60**, 157–199.

Galambos, R., & Morgan, C. T. The neural basis of learning. In J. Field (Ed.), *Handbook of neurophysiology.* Vol. 3. Washington, D.C.: American Physiological Society, 1960. Pp. 1471–1499.

Gall, F. J. *Critical review of some anatomico-physiological works, with an explanation of a new philosophy of the moral qualities and intellectual faculties.* Vol 6. Boston: Marsh Capen & Lyon, 1835.

Gallager, J. J. *The tutoring of brain-injured mentally retarded children.* Springfield, Ill.: Charles C Thomas, 1960.

Gelb, A., & Goldstein, K. Ueber Farbennamenamnesie. *Psychol. Forsch.*, 1925, **6**, 127–186.

Gerard, R. W. Brains and behavior. *Biology,* 1959, **31**, 14–20.

Gerstein, G. L. Analysis of firing patterns in single neurons. *Science,* 1960, **131**, 1811–1812.

Gesell, A., & Amatruda, C. S. *Developmental diagnosis.* New York: Hoeber-Harper, 1960.

Gibson, J. J. Adaptation, after-effect, and contrast in the perception of tilted lines. II. Simultaneous contrast and the areal restriction of the after-effect. *J. exp. Psychol.*, 1937, **20**, 553–569. (a)

Gibson, J. J. Adaptation with negative after-effect. *Psychol. Rev.*, 1937, **44**, 222–243. (b)

Gibson, J. J. The useful dimensions of sensitivity. *Amer. Psychologist,* 1963, **18**, 1–15.

Goldstein, K. The problem of the meaning of words based upon observations of aphasic patients. *J. Psychol.*, 1936, **2**, 301–316.

Goldstein, K. *The organism.* New York: American Book, 1939.

Goldstein, K. *Human nature in the light of psychopathology.* Cambridge, Mass.: Harvard Univer. Press, 1940.

Goldstein, K. The mental changes due to frontal lobe damage. *J. Psychol.*, 1944, **17**, 187–208.

Goldstein, K., & Scheerer, M. Abstract and concrete behavior: an experimental study with special tests. *Psychol. Monogr.*, 1941, **53**, No. 239.

Gottschaldt, K. Über den Einfluss der Erfahrung auf die Wahrnehmung von Figuren. I. Über den Einfluss gehäufter Einprägung von Figuren auf ihre Sichtbarkeit in unfassenden Konfigurationen. *Psychol. Forsch.*, 1926, **8**, 261–317.

Goyder, D. G. The autobiography of a phrenologist. London: Simpkin, Marshall, 1857.

Greenblatt, M., & Solomon, H. C. *Frontal lobes and schizophrenia.* New York: Springer, 1953.

Greenblatt, M., & Solomon, H. C. Studies in lobotomy. In *The brain and human behavior. Res. Publ. Ass. Res. Nerv. Ment. Dis. Proc.*, 1958, **36**, 19–34.

Haley, T. J., & Snider, R. S. (Eds.) *Responses of the nervous system to ionizing radiation.* New York: Academic Press, 1962.

Halstead, W. C. Preliminary analysis of grouping behavior in patients with cerebral injury by the method of equivalent and non-equivalent stimuli. *Amer. J. Psychiat.*, 1940, **96**, 1263–1294.

Halstead, W. C. *Brain and intelligence.* Chicago: Univer. of Chicago Press, 1947.

Halstead, W. C. Thinking, imagery, memory. In H. W. Magoun (Ed.), *Handbook of neurophysiology.* Vol. 3. Washington, D.C.: American Physiological Society, 1959. Pp. 1669–1678. (See especially sec. 1.)

Halstead, W. C., & Settlage, P. H. Grouping behavior of normal persons and of persons with lesions of the brain. *Arch. Neurol. Psychiat.*, 1943, **49**, 489–506.

Hampson, J. L. Relationships between cat cerebral and cerebellar cortices. *J. Neurophysiol.*, 1949, **12**, 37–50.

Hanfmann, E., & Kasanin, J. A method for the study of concept formation. *J. Psychol.*, 1937, **3**, 521–540.

Harlow, H. F., & Bromer, J. A. Acquisition of new responses during inactivation of the motor, premotor, and somesthetic cortex in the monkey. *J. gen. Psychol.*, 1942, **26**, 299–313.

Harlow, H. F., & Settlage, P. H. The effect of application of anesthetic agents on circumscribed motor and sensory areas of the cortex. *J. Psychol.*, 1936, **2**, 193–200.

Harlow, H. F., & Woolsey, C. N. *Biological and biochemical bases of behavior.* Madison, Wis.: Univer. of Wisconsin Press, 1958.

Harrower, Molly R. Changes in figure and ground perception in patients with cortical lesions. *Brit. J. Psychol.*, 1939, **30**, 47–51.

Harrower-Erickson, Molly R. Personality changes accompanying cerebral lesions. I. Rorschach studies of patients with cerebral tumors. *Arch. Neurol. Psychiat.*, 1940, **43**, 859–890.

Hartridge, H. Audition. II. Theories of hearing. In C. Murchison (Ed.), *Handbook of general experimental psychology.* Worcester, Mass.: Clark Univer. Press, 1934. Pp. 924–961.

Head, H. *Aphasia and kindred disorders of speech.* New York: Macmillan, 1926. 2 vols.

Hebb, D. O. Intelligence in man after large removals of cerebral tissue: report of four left frontal lobe cases. *J. gen. Psychol.*, 1939, **21**, 73–87.

Hebb, D. O. Human intelligence after removal of cerebral tissue from the right frontal lobe. *J. gen. Psychol.*, 1941, **25**, 257–265.

Hebb, D. O. *The organization of behavior.* New York: Wiley, 1949.

Hebb, D. O. *A textbook of psychology.* Philadelphia: Saunders, 1958.

Hebb, D. O. Intelligence, brain function and the theory of mind. *Brain,* 1959, **82**, 260–275.

Hebb, D. O. The semiautonomous process: its nature and nurture. *Amer. Psychologist,* 1963, **18**, 16–27.

Hebb, D. O., & Penfield, W. Human behavior after extensive bilateral removal from the frontal lobes. *Arch. Neurol. Psychiat.*, 1940, **44**, 421–438.

Hilgard, E. R. *Theories of learning.* (2nd ed.) New York: Appleton-Century-Crofts, 1956.

Hilgard, E. R., & Marquis, D. G. *Conditioning and learning.* (2nd ed.) New York: Appleton-Century-Crofts, 1961.

Hines, M. The "motor" cortex. *Bull. Johns Hopkins Hosp.*, 1937, **60**, 313–336.

Hunter, W. S. A consideration of Lashley's theory of equipotentiality of cerebral action. *J. gen. Psychol.*, 1930, **3**, 455–468.

Jacobsen, C. F., Wolfe, J. B., & Jackson, T. A. An experimental analysis of the functions of the frontal association area in primates. *J. nerv. ment. Dis.*, 1935, **82**, 1–14.

Jasper, H. H. Reticular-cortical systems and theories of the integrative action of the brain. In H. F. Harlow & C. N. Woolsey (Eds.), *Biological and biochemical bases of behavior.* Madison, Wis.: Univer. of Wisconsin Press, 1958. Pp. 37–61.

Jasper, H. H. Implications for the neurological sciences. In D. E. Sheer (Ed.), *Electrical stimulation of the brain.* Austin, Tex.: Univer. of Texas Press, 1961. Pp. 557–562.

Jefferson, G. Removal of right or left frontal lobes in man. *Brit. med. J.*, 1937, **2**, 199–206.

Jeffress, L. A. (Ed.) *Cerebral mechanisms in behavior: the Hixon symposium.* New York: Wiley, 1951.

Jones, F. A. *Clinical aspects of genetics.* London: Pitman Medical Publ., 1961.

Josiah Macy, Jr., Foundation and National Science Foundation. *The central nervous system and behavior.* Bethesda, Md.: U.S. Department of Health, Education, and Welfare, 1959–1960. 2 vols.

Kahn, E., & Cohen, L. H. Organic drivenness: a brain stem syndrome and an experience. *New Engl. J. Med.*, 1934, **210**, 748–756.

Kanner, L. *Child psychiatry.* Springfield, Ill.: Charles C Thomas, 1948.

Kanner, L. Problems of nosology and psychodynamics of early infantile autism. *Amer. J. Orthopsychiat.*, 1949, **19**, 416–426.

Kanner, L., & Lesser, L. I. Early infantile autism. *Pediat. Clin. N. Amer.*, 1958, 711–730.

King, H. E. Psychological effects of excitation in the limbic system. In D. E. Sheer (Ed.), *Electrical stimulation of the brain.* Austin, Tex.: Univer. of Texas Press, 1961. Pp. 477–486.

Klüver, H. *Behavior mechanisms in monkeys.* Chicago: Univer. of Chicago Press, 1933.

Köhler, W. *Dynamics in psychology.* New York: Liveright, 1940.

Lashley, K. S. *Brain mechanisms and intelligence.* Chicago: Univer. of Chicago Press, 1929.

Lashley, K. S. Integrative functions of the cerebral cortex. *Physiol. Rev.*, 1933, **13**, 1–42.

Lashley, K. S. Learning. III. Nervous mechanisms in learning. In C. Murchison (Ed.), *Handbook of general experimental psychology.* Worcester, Mass.: Clark Univer. Press, 1934. Pp. 456–496.

Lashley, K. S. The mechanism of vision. XV. Preliminary studies of the rat's capacity for detail vision. *J. gen. Psychol.*, 1938, **18**, 123–193.

Lashley, K. S. Structural variation in the central nervous system in relation to behavior. *Psychol. Rev.*, 1947, **54**, 325–334.

Lindsley, D. B. Attention, consciousness, sleep and wakefulness. In J. Field (Ed.), *Handbook of neurophysiology*. Vol. 3. Washington, D.C.: American Physiological Society, 1960. Pp. 1553–1593.

Lindsley, D. B. The reticular activating system and perceptual integration. In D. E. Sheer (Ed.), *Electrical stimulation of the brain*. Austin, Tex.: Univer. of Texas Press, 1961. Pp. 331–349.

Livingston, R. B. Central control of receptors and sensory transmission systems. In J. Field (Ed.), *Handbook of physiology*. Vol. I. Neurophysiology. Washington, D.C.: American Physiological Society, 1959. Pp. 741–760.

Livingston, W. K., Haugen, F. P., & Brookhart, J. M. Functional organization of the central nervous system. *Neurology*, 1954, **4**, 485–496.

Lorente de Nó, R. Analysis of the activity of the chains of internuncial neurons. *J. Neurophysiol.*, 1938, **1**, 207–244. (a)

Lorente de Nó, R. Synaptic stimulation of motoneurons as a local process. *J. Neurophysiol.*, 1938, **1**, 195–206. (b)

Magoun, H. W. An ascending reticular activating system in the brain stem. *Arch. Neurol. Psychiat.*, 1952, **67**, 145–154.

Magoun, H. W. The ascending reticular system and wakefulness. In J. F. Delafresnaye (Ed.), *Brain mechanisms and consciousness*. Springfield, Ill.: Charles C Thomas, 1954. Pp. 1–20.

Magoun, H. W. Non-specific brain mechanisms. In H. F. Harlow & C. N. Woolsey (Eds.), *Biological and biochemical bases of behavior*. Madison, Wis.: Univer. of Wisconsin Press, 1958. Pp. 25–36.

Maslow, A. H. *Motivation and personality*. New York: Harper & Row, 1954.

Masserman, J. H., & Pechtel, C. How brain lesions affect normal and neurotic behavior: an experimental approach. *Amer. J. Psychiat.*, 1956, **112**, 865–872.

Merritt, H. H. *A textbook of neurology*. (3rd ed.) Philadelphia: Lea & Febiger, 1963.

Mettler, F. A. (Ed.) *Selective partial ablation of the frontal cortex*. New York: Hoeber-Harper, 1949.

Meyer, D. R., & Meyer, P. M. Brain functions. In P. R. Farnsworth, O. McNemar, & Q. McNemar (Eds.), *Annu. Rev. Psychol.*, 1963, **14**, 155–174.

Meyer, V. Psychological effects of brain damage. In H. J. Eysenck (Ed.), *Handbook of abnormal psychology*. New York: Basic Books, 1961. Pp. 529–565.

Miller, G. A., Galanter, E., & Pribram, K. H. *Plans and the structure of behavior*. New York: Holt, 1960.

Miller, N. E. Implications for theories of reinforcement. In D. E. Sheer (Ed.), *Electrical stimulation of the brain*. Austin, Tex.: Univer. of Texas Press, 1961. Pp. 575–581. (a)

Miller, N. E. Learning and performance motivated by direct stimulation of the brain. In *ibid*. Pp. 387–396. (b)

Montagu, A. *Prenatal influences*. Springfield, Ill.: Charles C Thomas, 1962.

Morgan, C. T. The psychophysiology of learning. In S. S. Stevens (Ed.), *Handbook of experimental psychology*. New York: Wiley, 1951. Pp. 758–788.

Moruzzi, G., & Magoun, H. W. Brain stem reticular formation and activation of the EEG. *EEG. clin. Neurophysiol.*, 1949, **1**, 455–473.

Mountcastle, V. B. *Interhemispheric relations and cerebral dominance*. Baltimore: Johns Hopkins Press, 1962.

Mowrer, O. H. *Learning theory and personality dynamics*. New York: Ronald, 1950.

Mowrer, O. H. *Learning theory and behavior*. New York: Wiley, 1960.

Nadel, A. B. A qualitative analysis of behavior following cerebral lesions. *Arch. Psychol., N.Y.*, 1938, **32**, No. 224.

Nafe, J. P. A quantitative theory of feeling. *J. gen. Psychol.*, 1929, **2**, 199–211.

Nafe, J. P. The pressure, pain, and temperature senses. In C. Murchison (Ed.), *Handbook of general experimental psychology*. Worcester, Mass.: Clark Univer. Press, 1934. Pp. 1037–1087.

Neff, W. D., & Goldberg, J. M. Higher functions of the central nervous system. *Annu. Rev. Physiol.*, 1960, **22**, 499–524.

Olds, J. Differential effects of drives and drugs on self-stimulation at different brain sites. In D. E. Sheer (Ed.), *Electrical stimulation of the brain*. Austin, Tex.: Univer. of Texas Press, 1961. Pp. 350–366.

Orbach, J., Ehrlich, D., & Heath, Helen A. Reversibility of the Necker cube: I. An examination of the concept of "satiation of orientation." *Perceptual Motor Skills*, 1963, **17**, 439–458.

Page, H. A., Rakita, G., Kaplan, H. K., & Smith, N. B. Another application of the spiral aftereffect in the determination of brain damage. *J. consult. Psychol.*, 1957, **21**, 89–92.

Paul, N. L., Fitzgerald, E., & Greenblatt, M. Bimedial lobotomy: five year evaluation. *J. nerv. ment. Dis.*, 1956, **124**, 49–52. (a)

Paul, N. L., Fitzgerald, E., & Greenblatt, M. Five-year follow-up of patients subjected to three different lobotomy procedures. *J. Amer. med. Ass.*, 1956, **161**, 815–819. (b)

Pavlov, I. P. *Conditioned reflexes.* London: Oxford Univer. Press, 1927.

Pechtel, C., & Masserman, J. H. Cerebral localization: not where but in whom? *Amer. J. Psychiat.*, 1959, **116**, 51–54.

Penfield, W. The interpretive cortex. *Science*, 1959, **129**, 1719–1725.

Penfield, W., & Roberts, L. *Speech and brain mechanisms.* Princeton, N.J.: Princeton Univer. Press, 1959.

Penrose, L. S. Mongolism. In F. A. Jones (Ed.), *Clinical aspects of genetics.* London: Pitman Medical Publ., 1961. Pp. 86–97.

Philbrick, E. The validity of the spiral aftereffect as a clinical tool for diagnosis of organic brain pathology. *J. consult. Psychol.*, 1959, **23**, 39–44.

Piontkovskii, I. A., & Kotlyarevskii, L. I. (Eds.) *Works of the institute of higher nervous activity: experimental study of the effect of ionizing radiation on the higher parts of the central nervous system.* Washington, D.C.: National Science Foundation, 1962.

Piotrowski, Z. The Rorschach inkblot method in organic disturbances of the central nervous system. *J. nerv. ment. Dis.*, 1937, **86**, 525–537.

Piotrowski, Z. Positive and negative Rorschach organic reactions. *Rorschach Res. Exch.*, 1940, **4**, 147–151.

Podolsky, E. The genius and his brain. *Med. Rec.*, 1946, **179**, 162–163.

Pribram, K. H. The intrinsic systems of the forebrain. In J. Field (Ed.), *Handbook of neurophysiology.* Vol. 2. Washington, D.C.: American Physiological Society, 1960. Pp. 1323–1344. (a)

Pribram, K. H. A review of theory in physiological psychology. In P. R. Farnsworth & Q. McNemar (Eds.), *Annu. Rev. Psychol.*, 1960, **11**, 1–40. (b)

Pribram, K. H. Implications for systematic studies of behavior. In D. E. Sheer (Ed.), *Electrical stimulation of the brain.* Austin, Tex.: Univer. of Texas Press, 1961. Pp. 564–574. (a)

Pribram, K. H. Limbic system. In *ibid.* Pp. 311–320. (b)

Price, A. C., & Deabler, H. L. Diagnosis of organicity by means of spiral aftereffects. *J. consult. Psychol.*, 1955, **19**, 299–302.

Ranson, S. W. Somnolence caused by hypothalamic lesions in the monkey. *Arch. Neurol. Psychiat.*, 1939, **41**, 1–23.

Ranson, W. W., & Magoun, H. W. The hypothalamus. *Ergebn. Physiol.*, 1939, **41**, 56–163.

Razran, G. Soviet psychology since 1950. *Science*, 1957, **126**, 1100–1107.

Reed, H. B. C., & Reitan, R. M. A comparison of the effects of normal aging process with the effects of organic brain-damage on adaptive abilities. *J. Geront.*, 1963, **18**, 177–179.

Reitan, R. M. Certain differential effects of left and right cerebral lesions in human adults. *J. comp. physiol. Psychol.*, 1955, **48**, 474–477.

Richards, T. W. Movement in the fantasy of brain-injured (cerebral palsy) children. *J. clin. Psychol.*, 1958, **14**, 67–68.

Richards, T. W., & Hooper, S. Brain-injury at birth (cerebral palsy) and perceptual responses during childhood and adolescence. *J. nerv. ment. Dis.*, 1956, **123**, 117–124.

Rimland, B. *Infantile autism: the syndrome and its implications for a neural theory of behavior.* New York: Appleton-Century-Crofts, 1963.

Roberts, L. Activation and interference of cortical functions. In D. E. Sheer (Ed.), *Electrical stimulation of the brain.* Austin, Tex.: Univer. of Texas Press, 1961. Pp. 533–553.

Roessler, R., & Greenfield, R. S. (Eds.) *Physiological correlates of psychological disorder.* Madison, Wis.: Univer. of Wisconsin Press, 1962.

Rosenberg, B. G., & Altrocchi, J. The Yacorzynski block technique: a cross-validation study. *J. consult. Psychol.*, 1958, **22**, 122.

Rubin, E. *Visuell wahrgenommene Figuren.* Copenhagen: Gyldendolske Boghandel, 1921.

Rusinov, V. S. *Works of the institute of higher nervous activity: experimental studies of higher nervous activity in man and animals.* Washington, D.C.: National Science Foundation, 1962.

Russell, G. V. Interrelationships within the limbic and centrencephalic systems. In D. E. Sheer (Ed.), *Electrical stimulation of the brain.* Austin, Tex.: Univer. of Texas Press, 1961. Pp. 167–181.

Russell, W. R. *Brain, memory, learning.* London: Oxford Univer. Press, 1959.

Rylander, G. *Personality changes after operations on the frontal lobes: a clinical study of 32 cases.* London: Oxford Univer. Press, 1939.

Saucer, R. T., & Deabler, H. L. Perception of apparent motion in organic and schizophrenics. *J. consult. Psychol.*, 1956, **20**, 385–389.

Schlesinger, B. *Higher cerebral functions and their clinical disorders: the organic basis of psychology and psychiatry.* New York: Grune & Stratton, 1962.

Selye, H. *The physiology and pathology of exposure to stress: a treatise based on the concepts of the general-adaptation-syndrome and the diseases of adaptation.* Montreal: Acta, 1950.

Semmes, J., Weinstein, S., Ghent, L., & Teuber, H. *Somatosensory changes after penetrating brain wounds in man.* Cambridge, Mass.: Harvard Univer. Press, 1960.

Sheer, D. E. Brain and behavior: the background of interdisciplinary research. In D. E. Sheer (Ed.), *Electrical stimulation of the brain.* Austin, Tex.: Univer. of Texas Press, 1961. Pp. 3–21. (a)

Sheer, D. E. (Ed.) *Electrical stimulation of the brain.* Austin, Tex.: Univer. of Texas Press, 1961. (b)

Sheer, D. E. Emotional facilitation in learning situations with subcortical stimulation. In D. E. Sheer (Ed.), *Electrical stimulation of the brain.* Austin, Tex.: Univer. of Texas Press, 1961. Pp. 431–464. (c)

Sherrington, C. S. *The integrative action of the nervous system.* New Haven, Conn.: Yale Univer. Press, 1906.

Shurrager, P. S., & Culler, E. Conditioning in the spinal dog. *J. exp. Psychol.*, 1940, **26**, 133–159.

Singer, R. D. Organization as a unifying concept in schizophrenia. *Arch. gen. Psychiat.*, 1960, **2**, 61–74.

Skinner, B. F. *The behavior of the organism.* New York: Appleton-Century-Crofts, 1938.

Smith, A., & Kinder, E. F. Changes in psychological test performance of brain-operated schizophrenics after 8 years. *Science*, 1959, **129**, 149–150.

Smith, O. A., Jr. Food intake and hypothalamic stimulation. In D. E. Sheer (Ed.), *Electrical stimulation of the brain.* Austin, Tex.: Univer. of Texas Press, 1961. Pp. 367–370.

Snider, R. S., & Eldred, E. Cerebro-cerebellar relationships in the monkey. *J. Neurophysiol.*, 1952, **15**, 27–40.

Solomon, H. C., Cobb, S., & Penfield, W. (Eds.) *The brain and human behavior.* Baltimore: Williams & Wilkins, 1958.

Solomon, P., Kubzansky, P. E., Leiderman, P. H., Mendelson, J. H., Trumbull, R., & Wexler, D. (Eds.) *Sensory deprivation: a symposium held at Harvard Medical School.* Cambridge, Mass.: Harvard Univer. Press, 1961.

Spurzheim, J. G. *The physiognomical system of Drs. Gall and Spurzheim.* London: Baldwin, Cradock, & Joy, 1815.

Stevens, S. S. (Ed.) *Handbook of experimental psychology.* New York: Wiley, 1951.

Stilson, D., Gynther, D., & Gertz, B. Base rates and the Archimedes spiral illusion. *J. consult. Psychol.*, 1957, **21**, 435–437.

Strauss, A. A. Aphasia in children. *Amer. J. phys. Med.*, 1954, **33**, 93–99.

Strauss, A. A., & Kephart, N. C. *Psychopathology and education of the brain-injured child.* Vol. II. *Progress in theory and clinic.* New York: Grune & Stratton, 1955.

Strauss, A. A., & Lehtinen, L. E. *Psychopathology and education of the brain-injured child.* New York: Grune & Stratton, 1947.

Taylor, J. *Selected writings of John Hughlings Jackson.* London: Hodder, 1931–1932. 2 vols.

Teuber, H. Effects of brain wounds implicating right or left hemisphere in man: hemisphere differences and hemisphere interaction in vision, audition, and somesthesis. In V. B. Mountcastle (Ed.), *Interhemispheric relations and cerebral dominance.* Baltimore: Johns Hopkins Press, 1962. Pp. 131–157.

Teuber, H., Battersby, W. S., & Bender, M. B. Performance of complex visual tasks after cerebral lesions. *J. nerv. ment. Dis.*, 1951, **114**, 413–429.

Thomas, G. J. Neurophysiology of learning. In P. R. Farnsworth, O. McNemar, & Q. McNemar (Eds.), *Annu. Rev. Psychol.*, 1962, **13**, 71–106.

Thurstone, L. L. *A factorial study of perception.* Chicago: Univer. of Chicago Press, 1949.

Titchener, E. B. *A text-book of psychology.* New York: Macmillan, 1910.

Voronin, L. G. Some results of comparative-physiological investigations of higher nervous activity. *Psychol. Bull.*, 1962, **59**, 161–195.

Walter, W. G. *The living brain.* New York: Norton, 1953.

Walter, W. G. Intrinsic rhythms of the brain. In J. Field (Ed.), *Handbook of neurophysiology.* Washington, D.C.: American Physiological Society, 1959. Pp. 279–298.

Wapner, S., & Werner, H. Gestalt laws of organization and organismic theory of perception: effect of asymmetry induced by the factor of similarity on the position of the apparent median plane and apparent horizon. *Amer. J. Psychol.*, 1955, **68**, 258–265.

Weigl, E. (Tr. by M. J. Rioch.) On the psychology of so-called processes of abstraction. *J. abnorm. soc. Psychol.*, 1941, **36**, 3–33.

Weinstein, S. Differences in effects of brain wounds implicating right or left hemispheres: differential effects on certain intellectual and complex perceptual functions. In V. B. Mountcastle (Ed.), *Interhemispheric relations and cerebral dominance.* Baltimore: Johns Hopkins Press, 1962. Pp. 159–176.

Weisenberg, T., & McBride, D. E. *Aphasia.* New York: Oxford Univer. Press, 1935.

Wepman, J. M. *Recovery from aphasia.* New York: Ronald, 1951.

Werboff, J., & Dembicki, E. L. Toxic effects of tranquilizers administered to gravid rats. *J. Neuropsychiat.*, 1962, **4**, 87–91.

Werner, H., & Wapner, S. Experiments on sensory-tonic field theory of perception. IV. Effect of initial position of a rod on apparent verticality. *J. exp. Psychol.*, 1952, **44**, 68–74. (a)

Werner, H., & Wapner, S. Toward a general theory of perception. *Psychol. Rev.*, 1952, **59**, 324–338. (b)

Wiener, N. *Cybernetics.* New York: Wiley, 1948.

Willett, R. A. The effects of psychosurgical procedures on behaviour. In H. J. Eysenck (Ed.), *Handbook of abnormal psychology.* New York: Basic Books, 1961. Pp. 566–610.

Wolff, H. G. Discussion: laterality effects in audition. (Milner, B.). In V. B. Mountcastle (Ed.), *Interhemispheric relations and cerebral dominance.* Baltimore: Johns Hopkins Press, 1962. Pp. 199–203.

Wolman, B. B. Explorations in latent schizophrenia. *Amer. J. Psychother.*, 1957, **11**, 560–588.

Wolman, B. B. Differential diagnosis in schizophrenia. Paper read at East. Psychol. Ass., 1960.

Wolman, B. B. Fathers of schizophrenic patients. *Acta Psychother.*, 1961, **9**, 193–210.

Woodworth, R. S. *Experimental psychology.* New York: Holt, 1938.

Wortis, J. (Ed.) *Recent advances in biological psychiatry.* New York: Plenum Press, 1962.

Wundt, W. M. *An introduction to psychology.* (Tr. by R. Pintner.) London: G. Allen, 1912.

Yacorzynski, G. K. Differential modification of post-rotational nystagmus of pigeons with cerebral lesions. *Comp. Psychol. Monogr.*, 1946, **19**, No. 2 (Whole No. 99).

Yacorzynski, G. K. *Medical psychology.* New York: Ronald, 1951.

Yacorzynski, G. K. Brain dynamism as reflected in illusions. *Genet. Psychol. Monogr.*, 1963, **68**, 3–47. (a)

Yacorzynski, G. K. *Frontiers of psychology.* New York: Philosophical Library, 1963. (b)

Yacorzynski, G. K. Brain dynamism in perception of reversible figures. *Genet. Psychol. Monogr.*, 1965 (in press).

Yacorzynski, G. K., & Davis, L. An experimental study of the functions of the frontal lobes in man. *Psychosom. Med.*, 1945, **7**, 97–107. (a)

Yacorzynski, G. K., & Davis, L. Studies of the sensation of vibration. III. Evidence for cortical areas in inhibition and mediation of tickle. *Arch. Neurol. Psychiat.*, 1945, **53**, 355–357. (b)

Yacorzynski, G. K., & Guthrie, E. R. A comparative study of involuntary and voluntary conditioned responses. *J. gen. Psychol.*, 1937, **16**, 235–257.

Yacorzynski, G. K., & Tucker, Beatrice E. What price intelligence? *Amer. Psychol.*, 1960, **15**, 201–203.

Yakovlev, P. I. The traditional and the new in Pavlov's theory of "higher nervous activity." In J. Wortis (Ed.), *Recent Advances in biol. Psychiat.*, 1961, **4**, 24–28.

Yaroshevskiy, M. G. Psychology and the concept of the reflex. In Josiah Macy, Jr., Foundation and National Science Foundation, *The central nervous system and behavior.* Bethesda, Md.: U.S. Department of Health, Education, and Welfare, 1960. Pp. 989–1004.

Zaks, M. S. Longitudinal research studies of effects of heart disease and cardiac surgery on psychologic and neurologic functioning. In T. T. Tourlentes, S. L. Pollack, & H. E. Himwich (Eds.), *Research Approaches to Psychiatric Problems.* New York: Grune & Stratton, 1962. Pp. 164–178.

Zaks, M. S., Lachman, J., Yacorzynski, G. K., & Boshes, B. The neuropsychiatric and psychologic significance of cerebrovascular damage (strokes) following rheumatic heart surgery. *Amer. J. Cardiol.*, 1960, **5**, 768–776.

26

Neuropsychological Analysis of Focal Brain Lesions[1]

ALEXANDER R. LURIA

ORGANIZATION OF CEREBRAL FUNCTIONS

The investigation of higher cortical functions and their changes is an important part of the neurological examination. The importance of investigating such complex functions as gnosis and praxis, speech, reading and writing, computation, and simple intellectual functions is greatest in cases involving small, well-defined lesions within those portions of the cortex which exhibit the greatest complexity of organization. This is particularly true of areas in the left, or dominant, hemisphere. Here the usual techniques of neurological investigation, such as tests of sensation, motor activity, and reflexes, may not indicate the precise site of the lesion. If the examination is limited to common neurological tests, these areas may appear to be "silent," and damage to them may appear to be "asymptomatic."

Different results are obtained, however, if, in addition to the usual description of neurological symptomatology, one applies techniques specifically designed for the study of higher cortical functions. Under these conditions it becomes apparent that even damage to the most complex cortical areas gives rise to an extremely varied symptomatology. Subtle disturbances of visual and auditory perception; disturbances of complex motor activity; impairment of expressive and receptive speech; and disorders of reading, writing, computation, and simple intellectual functions not only indicate the presence of cortical dysfunction but, in many cases, also indicate the site of injury.

The testing of higher cortical functions (mental functions) can help in localizing cortical lesions, however, only if one avoids the pitfalls of false prescientific views regarding the localization of mental functions. This can be done only if one keeps in mind all that is presently known about the structure and functional organization of the cerebral cortex. The neurological examination must be based upon present-day knowledge regarding the anatomy and physiology of the brain and upon a proper understanding of the principles of scientific analysis which are applied in the study of symptoms and syndromes arising from focal lesions of the brain. We shall present a very condensed historical review of the study of localization of brain function, for from that starting point it will be possible to convey the modern conception of cortical processes and their functional organization. Finally we shall discuss how these conceptions can contribute to the diagnosis of brain lesions.

The study of the cerebral localization of higher mental functions goes back several hundred years. It originally grew out of primitive "psychomorphological," or "parallelist," conceptions, according to which it was believed that the basic units of mental experience corresponded to particular structures in the cerebral cortex. In the absence of any

1 Translated from the Russian by Douglas Bowden.

physiological form of analysis, early investigators attempted to match directly functions to structures; i.e., they looked for cortical areas which could be considered the "organs" for various mental processes. In other words, they attempted to find "centers" in which complex forms of mental activity were "localized."

In their attempts to localize mental functions, early investigators often took one of two contradictory positions. Some of them believed that the material substrate of complex forms of mental activity was the *brain as a whole* and that, for all practical purposes, the various parts of the brain all carried out one and the same function. These authors claimed that damage to any part of the brain leads to a general "decrement" in mental activity and that the degree of disturbance depends more upon the *total mass* of brain tissue destroyed than upon the site of destruction. This conception, which received the name "antilocalization" or the "theory of equipotentiality," was first formulated early in the nineteenth century by the French physiologist Flourens (1825) and was revived at the beginning of the twentieth century by the American psychologist Lashley (1929). It, quite correctly, drew attention to the importance of the brain as a whole for the execution of complex mental processes, but it failed to recognize the fact that there are indisputable differences in the morphology and function of various cortical areas.

The opposite view was held by a large number of investigators, for the most part clinicians, who developed strict theories of localization functions. These authors proceeded from the assumption that complex mental functions are always performed by specific, highly localized areas of the brain; thus they believed that the cortex could be divided up into a number of centers, each responsible for a specific mental function. Such conceptions were first set forth in ancient times and during the Middle Ages, when certain philosophers attributed such "functions" as perception, memory, and intellect to the "posterior," "middle," and "anterior" ventricles of the brain. They were popular even in the time of Vezali and achieved their most detailed expression in the famous phrenology of Gall, who felt that he could locate even such "faculties" as honesty, love for parents, and greed in limited areas of the cortex.

Despite the naïveté of these psychomorphological conceptions, they did not disappear for a long time. Their popularity during the nineteenth century was associated with the discovery by the physiologists Fritsch and Hitzig (1871) that stimulation of certain areas of the cortex evoked movements of particular parts of the body. Shortly thereafter other authors described cortical areas associated with visual, auditory, and cutaneous sensations. These discoveries were taken as confirmation of the psychomorphological theories, so that psychiatric investigators and neurologists alike began to frame their observations in a psychomorphological terminology. Thus, for instance, Broca's discovery in 1861 that a lesion of the inferoposterior third of the left frontal lobe produced a disturbance of motor speech was interpreted as a demonstration that the "center for the motor images of words" was located at this site. Wernicke's observations, in 1874, of a sensory aphasia arising with damage to the posterior third of the left superior temporal gyrus were considered proof that this area was a "center for the sensory images of words." Following these reports, there appeared descriptions of numerous centers for the most varied types of mental function. By the end of the nineteenth century, handbooks of neurophysiology and psychiatry were full of such centers as Exner's "writing center," Henschen's "calculation center," Broadbent's "ideation center," etc. The psychomorphological conception by which complex mental functions were related to specific cortical areas was so firmly entrenched that even in a relatively recent handbook of neurology (Nielsen, 1946), one finds statements to the effect that "perception of animate objects" and "perception of inanimate objects" take place in different parts of the occipital cortex.

Basic to this kind of conception was the idea that both elementary and complex mental functions are "localized" in limited areas of the human cortex, i.e., that different cell populations in the brain have their own "mental functions." It is based upon the undeniable fact that there is a differentiation of structure and function among the different areas, and in this sense, it is more accurate than the views of the antilocalizationists. On the other hand, the attributing of complex mental functions directly to specific areas with no preliminary physiological analysis of such functions eventually opened these conceptions to grave dispute.

The crisis for psychomorphological conceptions of this strict localization arose both as the result of new findings regarding the extreme degree of complexity and integrated character of central nervous system functions and as the result of a basic change in old conceptions of the mental processes which investigators were attempting to localize. Physiological investigations indicated that the principle of a strict localization was inadequate to account for some relatively elementary phenomena. Experiments showed, for instance, that even such a seemingly simple physiological process as respiration could not be conceived of as being controlled by one particular group of cells constituting a center for this function. In order to explain respiration, it was necessary to take into account considerably more complex neural systems. In reviewing such findings, Pavlov formulated his position as follows:

> From the beginning it was thought that it [the respiratory center] was a point the size of a pin head in the medulla oblongata. But now it has become extraordinarily drawn out; it has stretched upward into the brain and down into the spinal cord, so that now no one can tell where its boundaries lie.[2]

Even greater difficulties arose when attempts were made to localize complex mental functions to limited cortical areas. Clinical investigations showed that when a certain localized area of the cortex was damaged, the result was not loss of a single isolated function, but disturbances of many, sometimes quite heterogeneous, processes. Thus, as we shall see below, damage to the left temporal area could lead to impaired speech comprehension, a writing disorder, difficulty in finding words, etc.; damage to the parieto-occipital area could produce disturbances of stereognosis, computation, logicogrammatical operations, etc. Further, one and the same complex "function" might be disturbed by lesions in many different parts of the cortex. For instance, writing could be disturbed by damage to the temporal area, the parieto-occipital area, or posterior portions of the frontal cortical area of the left hemisphere; impairment of calculation ability could arise with lesions of the parieto-occipital, temporal, or frontal cortical area, etc. Consequently, the old psychomorphological attempts to localize particular functions to strictly limited portions of the cortex lost their claim to factual basis and had to be fundamentally reexamined.

[2] I. P. Pavlov. *Compl. Works*, 1949, III, Part 1, 127.

The final defeat of the psychomorphological concepts of brain function has been dealt by the great increase in our knowledge of the complex functional organization of the cerebral cortex. This increase in basic knowledge, plus the emergence of new concepts to replace prescientific conceptions regarding the structure of higher mental processes, has brought us to a more adequate understanding of cortical function and its pathology. We shall discuss these two factors separately.

Higher Mental Processes as Functional Systems

The psychomorphological conception of precisely localizable mental functions was based upon the old assumption that all mental phenomena may be considered either innate "capacities," which are immutable characteristics of the human psyche, or complex associations of such capacities. At the time Gall and his followers were laying the basis for a strict or direct localization, such complex processes as speech, writing, and calculation and complex drives and emotions were considered basic "capacities" of the human soul. At the time Broca and Wernicke made their discoveries, these ideas were still in vogue, and psychologists generally believed it possible to reduce all complex mental processes to relatively simple "concepts" or "images," each of which had its own "seat" in some isolated area of the cortex. Many authors looked upon different cortical areas as individual "depots" for the storage of simple mental phenomena.

Beginning with Broca and Wernicke, however, psychology took a great step forward; with the advent of modern neurophysiology, there came a fundamental change in views regarding the structure of mental processes. Basic to present-day conceptions of mental processes are two intimately related ideas: The first of these is the concept of the *reflex structure of mental activity;* the second is the idea of the *social origin and systemic*[3] *or-*

[3] Higher mental functions are "systemically organized" in the sense that every "function" is really a dynamic system, and that different groups or "systems" of cortical areas participate in different functions, such as speaking, reading, etc. (Tr.)

ganization of higher mental functions in man.

Since the time of Sechenov, the famous Russian physiologist, even such mental phenomena as sensation or perception and movement or action have come to be considered reflex processes, each having its own afferent and efferent limbs, and each developed as the result of constant interaction between the organism and its environment. According to this conception, sensation cannot be looked upon as a purely passive, subjective phenomenon arising solely as the result of the action of external stimuli on the sensory organs. In actuality, sensory processes are reflex responses involving efferent influences, which constantly tune the sensory organ, giving it a selective character (Granit, 1956; Sokolov, 1958; and others). Voluntary movements and actions, likewise, are not "independent capacities" for "mental activity." They are always determined by a system of afferent impulses which follow a long path, possess different degrees of complexity, and, at higher levels, involve complex orienting activity, the system of speech associations, etc. (Bernstein, 1936; Bernstein, 1947; Luria, 1956; Luria, 1958; Luria, 1959; Zaporozhetz, 1960; and others). The infinitely greater complexity of the reflex processes underlying other mental functions precludes their being looked upon as primary irreductible "characteristics" or "capacities" of the psyche (Leontiev, 1959). Thus it is altogether impossible to conceive of such processes as being localizable to one or another cortical area. The complexity of the reflex processes involved forces one to replace the question of "localization of function" with another question: "*What is the dynamic organization of those reflex processes which are carried out at different levels by the integrated activity of functional systems involving different cerebral structures?*"

The second principle mentioned above is, however, as significant as the first. Human mental processes, particularly the higher mental functions, are not simply the natural derivatives of elementary forms of animal behavior. They represent altogether *new functional systems which are social in origin and which are mediated by the second signaling system.*

Investigations by a number of authors (Janet, 1928; Leontiev, 1959; Wallon, 1942; Vygotsky, 1934; Vygotsky, 1958; Vygotsky, 1960; and others) have shown that basic to all such complex forms of mental activity as meaningful perception, selective memorization, active attention, and voluntary behavior is the *communication among individuals in a social setting.* Such complex processes could come about only as a result of the social division of labor and the human use of tools. These cultural developments were intimately related to the development of language, since they both required communication among individuals. Each individual must master a body of knowledge accumulated in the social history and in the other people's experience. Without the formative influence of social relations and language, it would be impossible to imagine that any of the specifically human activities could have arisen. The intelligent use of tools, for instance, is closely tied up with the verbal analysis of perceived situations and their synthesis[4] on the basis of previously accumulated knowledge. Active attention involves the selection of significant impressions from a mass of irrelevant impressions; processes of logical memory require the systematization of experiences and involve speech to a very great extent. Finally, voluntary action is based upon extremely complex motives which are formulated within the framework of community life and on the basis of the second signaling system. Recent studies have shown, in fact, that even such an apparently simple process as the auditory estimation of pitch is mediated in man by his language and, thus, is social in origin and extremely complex in organization (Leontiev, 1960).

The complex character of higher mental functions and their mediation by the second signaling system are revealed most clearly in studies of their *ontogenetic development.* A number of investigations in recent decades (Galperin, 1959; Leontiev, 1959; Vygotsky, 1960; Zaporozhetz, 1960; and others) have dealt with this question. They show that the development of every higher mental process, whether it is selective memorization, concept

[4] The term "synthesis" as used here and in subsequent pages has several related meanings and connotations which are not always associated with the English word. The sensory analyzers "analyze" their input by extracting significant features or cues. The perceptual process is not completed, however, until these cues have been "synthesized," i.e., regrouped in a meaningful way, integrated into a meaningful pattern, and recoded in terms of past experience. Although there is no good one-word English translation for this, substitution of one of these phrases for the word "synthesis" should clarify its meaning in a given context. (Tr.)

formation, or learning to write and calculate, begins with an *externalized form of activity* requiring the presence of a large number of auxiliary cues. Only later does it gradually become abbreviated. It may depend for some time upon simultaneous speaking aloud and later be guided by inner speech. Only in the final stage does it represent an "inner action" which is a characteristic feature of mental activity in the adult human.

In other words, and this is of critical significance for obtaining accurate answers to questions regarding the cortical organization of complex mental functions, *such functions are generated by different systems of neurophysiological processes at different stages in their development.* Thus, whereas in the early stages of learning to write, the pupil relies heavily upon the analysis of the acoustical components of words and the labored determination of each individual letter so that his writing is made up of a whole series of individual motor acts, the experienced writer loses these characteristics, and his writing becomes automatic; it is guided by firmly entrenched auditory-motor stereotypes. The same can be said for the processes of computation, which, in the beginning, depend upon concrete experience with material objects but which later can be performed by speaking aloud and finally can be performed silently. Eventually it takes on the character of a self-contained automatic process, a "mental activity" based upon entirely different psychological mechanisms from those necessary at the outset.

Thus we see that whereas one and the same outcome is attained at all stages in the development of a given mental function, at these different stages *it involves the activity of different dynamic systems involving different cortical structures.* These are the principles which must provide the basis for our investigation of higher mental functions. As *complex functional systems,* social in origin, systemic in structure, and progressing through several stages in their development, their study demands an approach in which the primary question to be answered concerns their organization within the brain. It is clear that such a conception precludes any kind of psychomorphological attempt to localize complex mental functions to limited areas of the brain and implies a much more complex understanding of their cerebral organization.

Structure and Functional Organization of the Cerebral Cortex

If the cortex is not to be conceived of as consisting of individual centers in which various complex mental functions are localized, what can we say about its structure and functional organization? Here we shall attempt to set down the most important findings regarding the structure and functional organization of the cerebral cortex which have been made possible by modern advances in neuroanatomy and neurophysiology.

The brain is responsible for the analysis and synthesis of external and internal signals, for the formation of temporary associations, and for the equilibration of the organism with its environment. Recent investigations in neuroanatomy and neurophysiology strongly support the view that the brain consists of two morphologically distinct but functionally integrated systems. One is concerned with the reception of information from the external world, while the other regulates the general level of excitation of nervous tissue and makes possible the maintenance of internal homeostasis; by taking into account the results of actions carried out by the organism, it provides a stable background for processes which are constantly being performed within the organism.

As a result of recent successes in neurophysiological investigation, we know quite a bit about structures in the first group. Pavlov suggested many years ago that the cerebral cortex comprises the central portions of the various analyzers which receive signals from the external and internal environments of the organism, submit them to fine analysis and complex synthesis, and make possible the formation of temporary connections. The structure of the central portions of the analyzers is well known, thanks to progress in neuroanatomy and neurophysiology. It is known, for instance, that the cortex can be broken down into a number of different cytoarchitectural fields, as was first done by Campbell (1905) and a short time later by Brodmann (1909). The characterization of different cortical areas by their cytoarchitecture was made more precise by anatomists of the Moscow Brain Institute. In Figure 1 we present a cortical map showing the various areas which have been differentiated on the basis of their cytoarchitecture.

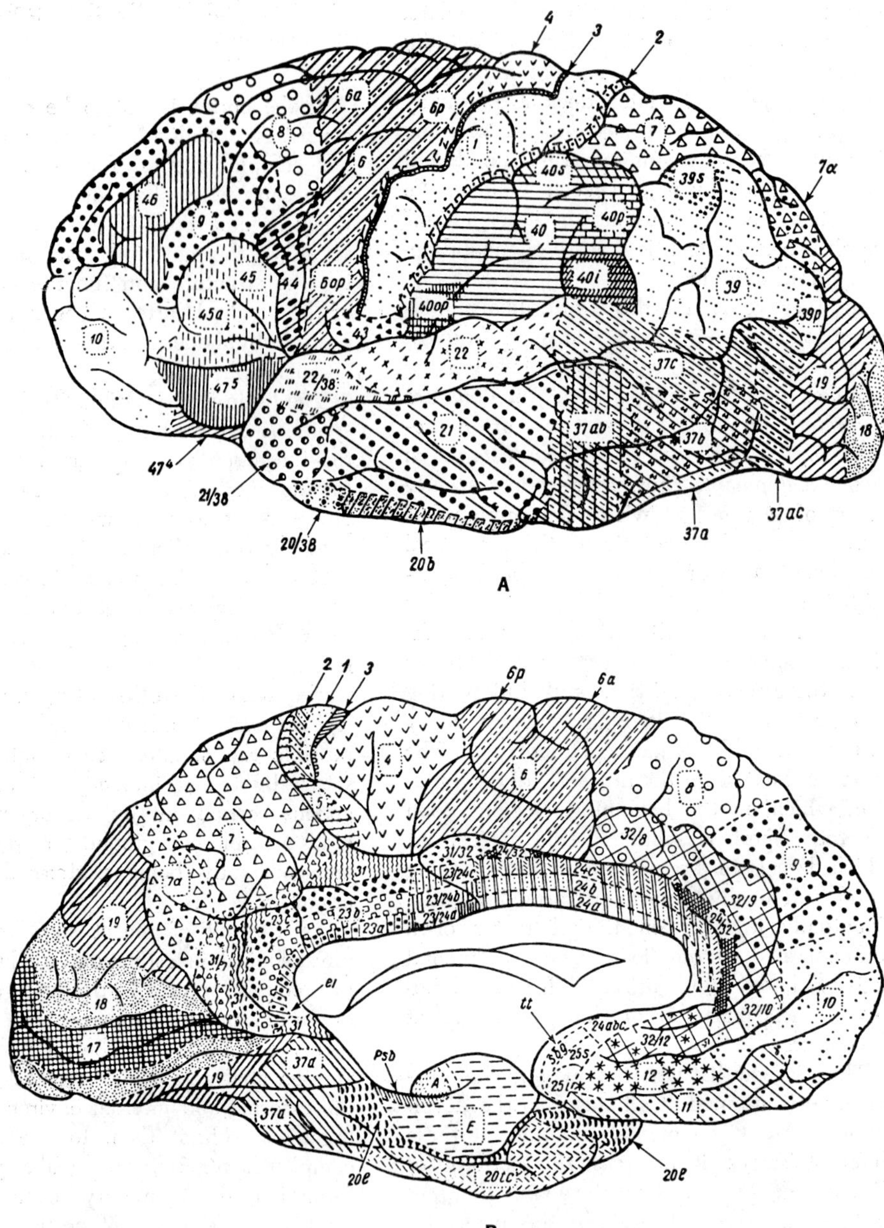

Figure 1. The cytoarchitectural fields. (*A*) Lateral surface. (*B*) Medical surface of the left hemisphere. *Moscow Brain Institute.*

Although various cortical areas vary greatly in their cytoarchitecture, they are united into definite functional units. We shall give here a very short and general account of what is presently known about the structure of the functional units which are composed of cortical structures responsible for the analysis and synthesis of signals to which the organism reacts in everyday life.

Excitation arising in peripheral receptors passes via primary afferent neurons to end in subcortical relay nuclei such as certain thalamic nuclei, the geniculate bodies, etc. From there it is transmitted to new neurons which enter the cortical areas referred to by Pavlov as the "cortical nuclei" of the various analyzers. The cortical nucleus of the visual analyzer is located in the occipital lobe, that of the auditory analyzer in the superior temporal area, and that of cutaneous sensation and kinesthesis in the postcentral gyrus in close association with the nucleus of the motor analyzer in the precentral gyrus.

In man the cortical nuclei or nuclear zones of the various analyzers can generally be broken down into two groups of areas. The first group are referred to as "primary," "projection," or "extrinsic" areas. These include area 17 of the visual analyzer, area 41 of the auditory analyzer, and area 3 of the cutaneous analyzer, which receive fibers directly from the corresponding peripheral receptors. It also includes area 4 of the motor analyzer, from which fibers arise and pass directly to peripheral muscle groups. In the primary projection areas of the visual, auditory, and cutaneous analyzers, the fourth afferent layer of the cortex is more fully developed than in other areas; this is the layer which receives fibers transmitting excitation from peripheral receptors. In the primary motor area, the fifth, or efferent, layer is similarly well developed; here are located the giant Betz pyramidal cells which give rise to the primary motor pathway.

The structure of the primary or "extrinsic" areas is further distinguished by their strict somatotopic organization; i.e., different points within a given area correspond to specific points in the peripheral receptor organ or, in the case of the motor analyzer, to specific muscle groups. As a result, damage to different parts of these areas produces loss of sensation in strictly localized areas of the receptive field or loss of particular movements. As we shall show below, the greater the functional significance of an organ, the greater its representation in the primary cortical field.

The second general group of cortical nuclei comprises the "secondary," "projection-association," or "extrinsic" areas which lie adjacent to the primary areas just described. These areas differ markedly from the primary areas both in structure and in function. The afferent fibers to these areas do not connect them directly with the peripheral receptors. The diagram in Figure 2 shows pathways proposed by Polyakov to connect the different cortical areas with the periphery and with one another. As this diagram shows, fibers which arise in the peripheral receptors synapse with the neurons entering the thalamic nuclei; thus the latter have no direct connection with the

Figure 2. Connections of the primary, secondary, and tertiary areas with the receptors. (1) Receptor; (2) effector; (3) sensory ganglion cell; (4) motor neuron; (5 and 6) interneurons of the spinal cord and brainstem; (7 to 10) interneurons of the subcortical structures; (11, 14) afferent fibers from subcortical structures; (13) pyramidal cell of fifth cortical layer; (16) pyramidal cell of sublayer III^3; (18) pyramidal cells of sublayers III^2 and III^3; (12, 15, and 17) stellate cells of the cortex. G. *I. Polyakov.*

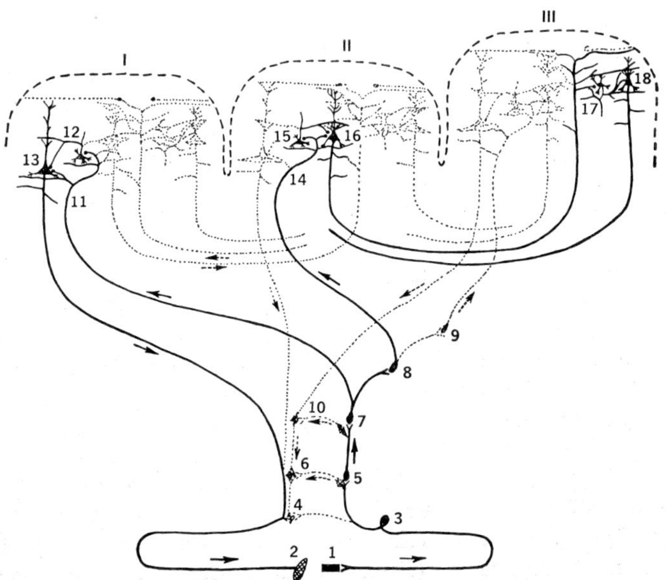

periphery. These thalamic nuclei send fibers to the secondary or extrinsic cortical zones of the appropriate analyzers and, it must be assumed, conduct to the cortex information which has already been processed at lower levels. The fact that the secondary areas are only indirectly connected with the peripheral receptor organs led Rose and Woolsey (1949) and Rose (1950) to classify them as "intrinsic" structures of the cortex to distinguish them from the primary projection areas, or "extrinsic" structures.

The secondary cortical areas belonging to the different analyzers receive fibers other than those from subcortical nuclei, however. Each receives fibers from the primary intrinsic cortical area of the same analyzer (Figure 2). Thus, it is in a position to consolidate the excitations received from different structures, it makes possible the establishment of reverberating circuits, and it can transmit excitation to other cortical areas. In connection with this, the cytoarchitecture of the secondary areas differs from that of other areas. The fourth (afferent) and fifth (efferent) layers are less prominent than in the primary areas; here the predominant layers are the more superficial second and third, or associative, cell layers.

The physiological characteristics of the secondary areas are directly related to their structure. A special technique of neuronography, in which small strychnine-soaked paper disks are applied to the cortical surface and potential changes recorded from surrounding areas, has revealed important differences between the primary and secondary areas. Whereas excitation initiated by the application of strychnine to points within a primary area does not spread far beyond the site of application, excitation initiated within a secondary area spreads to a number of other cortical areas, some of which may lie quite distant from the focus of stimulation (Dusser de Barenne, Carol, & McCulloch, 1942; McCulloch, 1943; and others).

This physiological characteristic of the secondary area of the cortical nucleus of an analyzer makes possible its integrative function. It is able to synthesize the excitations transmitted from many areas into whole dynamic structures, to facilitate the initiation of complex patterns of excitation, and to provide the basis for those *functional systems* which are composed of the most diverse combinations of cortical areas and which are necessary for complex perceptual and motor processes.

As we shall see below, such a broad and, at the same time, selective spread of excitation makes it possible for the secondary cortical areas to carry out the *functional organization of excitations entering the primary extrinsic areas from the periphery. They are responsible for transforming the fine and discrete excitations received from the periphery into complex and flexible dynamic units.* In later sections, as we analyze the syndromes which arise as the result of lesions in these different areas, we shall give special attention to this process. We shall give particular attention to related findings obtained by direct cortical stimulation in patients undergoing brain operations and clinical observations of cases involving definite cortical lesions.

Thorough investigations of cortical areas other than the cortical nuclei of the various analyzers have been carried out by numerous investigators, including a group at the Moscow Brain Institute (Polyakov, 1956; Polyakov, 1959). Between the cortical areas which are related to specific analyzers lie *areas which receive their input from two or more analyzers* and which are quite justifiably referred to as "zones of overlap" between the different analyzers. These "tertiary areas" receive impulses which have been transmitted through a number of different structures. They receive information both from the subcortical "intrinsic" system (Rose, 1950) and, via a rich supply of transcortical fibers, from neighboring cortical areas (Figure 2).

Thus, these intermediate areas are in a position to carry out extremely complex forms of reflex activity involving several analyzers simultaneously. An impression of the variety and complexity of possible reflex systems which may center around these areas may be gained by consideration of Figure 3. This diagram, taken from work of Polyakov, clearly indicates that there are different levels of organization of neural structures at which reflex processes may be carried out and that the integration of activity from a great variety of structures may be accomplished by participation of the tertiary cortical areas.

These structures have become most highly developed in man, concomitant with the development of the second signaling system (Pavlov, 1949). Comparative phylogenetic

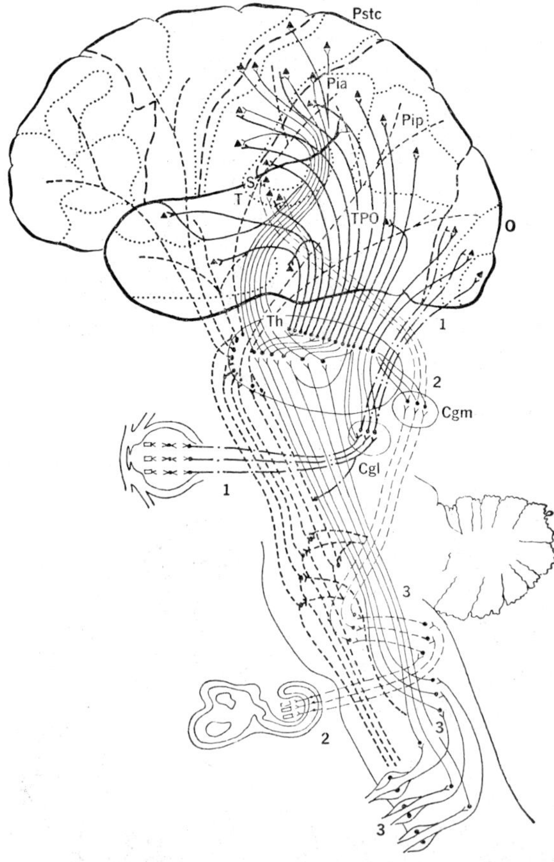

Figure 3. Cortical-subcortical relationships of the primary, secondary, and tertiary areas. Heavy lines indicate the analyzer systems and their subcortical connections. (1) Visual analyzer; (2) auditory analyzer; (3) cutaneous-kinesthetic analyzer; (*T*) temporal area; (*O*) occipital area; (*Pip*) area 39; (*Pia*) area 40; (*Pstc*) postcentral area; (*TPO*) temporo-parieto-occipital area; (*Th*) thalamus; (*Cgm*) medial geniculate; (*Cgl*) lateral geniculate. G. I. Polyakov.

studies have shown that the intermediate cortical areas are absent in lower mammals, that they first appear in the higher apes, and that they reach their full development only in the human brain, where they occupy 40 per cent of the total cortical area.

In Figure 4 we present a diagram developed by Polyakov which shows the relationships among the three types of cortical areas described above. Here we see that, in the human brain, the primary projection areas belonging to the cortical nuclei of the various analyzers occupy a relatively small area. The secondary areas cover more of the cortical surface, but by far the greatest area is occupied by the tertiary or "intermediate zones," which unite pairs or groups of analyzers into complex systems. These areas include the temporo-parieto-occipital area (areas 39, 40, and 37), which unites the visual, auditory, and kinesthetic analyzers; the middle temporal and temporo-occipital area (areas 22 and 37), which unites the auditory and visual analyzers; and the prefrontal area (areas 9, 46, and 10), which is directly associated with the motor analyzer and a wide range of other cortical and subcortical structures. The latter area can justifiably be looked upon as a complex "zone of overlap" which plays a most important role in organization of the complicated forms of human behavior.

It should be noted that these zones of overlap not only are phylogenetically the newest and functionally the most complex

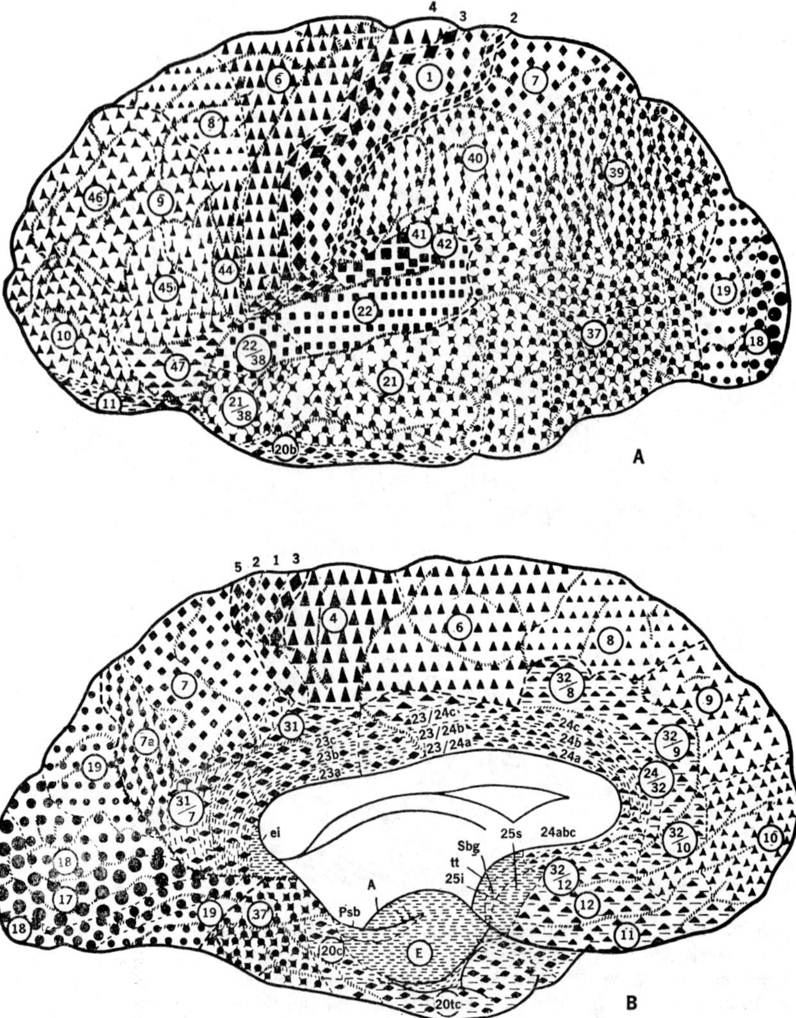

Figure 4. **Nuclear and paranuclear zones of the cerebral cortex. (*A*) Lateral surface. (*B*) Medial surface. Nuclear zones are represented by circles (visual area), squares (auditory area), rhomboids (general sensory area), and triangles (motor area); the central areas are represented by large symbols. Zones of overlap between analyzers in the posterior portion of the hemisphere (parieto-temporo-occipital and infero-parietal areas) are designated by the mixing of symbols, and in the anterior portions of the hemisphere (frontal area) by modified triangles; the limbic and phylogenetically old areas are represented by dashes. *G. I. Polyakov.***

cortical areas but also are the last to mature in the growing child. The myelinization chart presented in Figure 5 shows which cortical areas are first and which last to become myelinated. Comparison of this chart with that in Figure 4 shows clearly that the primary, secondary, and tertiary cortical areas mature at different rates.

All the morphological characteristics of the zones of overlap described above ideally suit them for the flexible execution of those complex neural processes which are necessary for complex forms of instrumental activity and for functions involving the second signaling system. Both the second signaling system and the effective use of tools require the combined function of several analyzers, which is made possible by the intermediate cortical areas. Thus there is every reason to think of these areas as the morphological representation of the highly complex "cortical systems" which underlie the highest forms of human activity, for it is these areas which find their fullest development in the human brain.

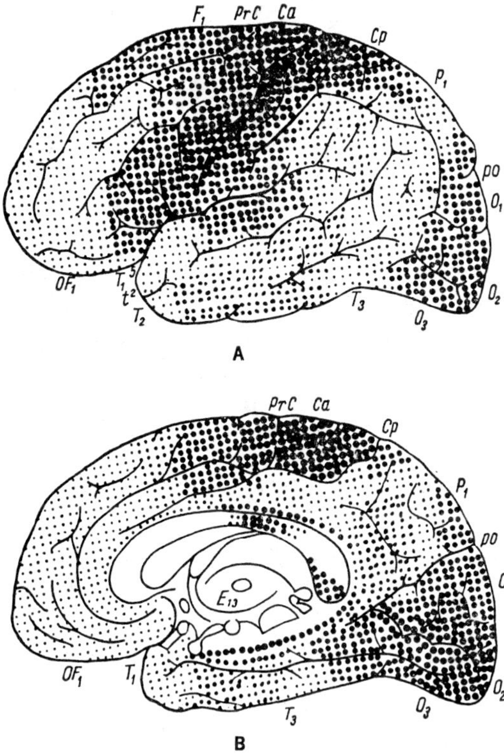

Figure 5. Myelogenetic map. Heavy dots represent the cortical areas which mature first. Light dots represent the last areas to mature. (*A*) Lateral surface. (*B*) Medial surface. Vogts.

So far we have discussed the functional organization of that part of the brain which is best understood at the present time, namely, the systems responsible for the analysis and synthesis of signals reaching the organism and for the formation of temporary connections. It remains for us to mention a second system which has begun to be studied intensively only in recent years. Here we are speaking of the *reticular formation* of the brainstem and the mediobasal cortical areas, which appear to be closely associated with it, as well as the frontal areas, which are concerned with higher levels of organization of brain processes (the latter will be considered in greater detail below, under Structure and Organization of the Frontal Lobes). These areas differ greatly from the systems described so far in that they are primarily concerned with maintaining the *level of excitability of other cerebral structures.* They also take part in homeostatic processes within the organism by permitting the animal to *take account of the effects of its own actions.* Thus, while in lower animals, where the major forms of activity are instinctive, these functions are organized at the brainstem level, in man, where behavior is highly organized and social in nature, they involve cortical mechanisms, particularly frontal lobe mechanisms.

The more elementary structures in this second group are located in the *medial portion of the brainstem* along the cerebral aqueduct and ventricles; the more complex portions are situated in the medial and basal portions of the hemispheres, the so-called "limbic system," and in the hippocampus, as well as in other structures which are frequently referred to as structures of the "central core." Structurally this system differs from the first in that a part of it is composed of neurons which are arranged in a netlike pattern and which are suited not so much for rapid conduction of individual all-or-none impulses as for slow and gradual shifts in excitable state. In contradistinction to the first system described above, this system transmits information which is not modality-specific; i.e., it is not composed of structures which respond only to tactile, visual, or auditory stimuli. For the most part, its neurons conduct generalized nonspecific shifts in excitation. Fibers of this system accompany the specific tracts to all areas of the cortex and constitute the ascending, activating reticular system (Figure 6). Besides these connections, the brainstem reticular formation has close connections with the basal and medial portions of the hemispheres, in particular with the ancient and transitional cortical formations which comprise the limbic area, the hippocampus, and related structures.

Until recently very little was known about the function of the mediobasal cortical areas. Some of them were once thought to be part of the ancient "rhinencephalon," but the results of later investigations made it necessary to reconsider and greatly broaden the early concepts [a summary of these concepts is to be found in a series of works by Pribram (1959; 1960a) as well as in a long series of publications of the last few years].

Experiments involving recordings from electrodes implanted in the hippocampal and limbic systems of animals in free movement situations have been carried out by members of the Magoun school (Adey, 1958; Adey, 1959) and have indicated that any goal-directed activity on the part of the animal is accompanied by powerful bursts of electrical

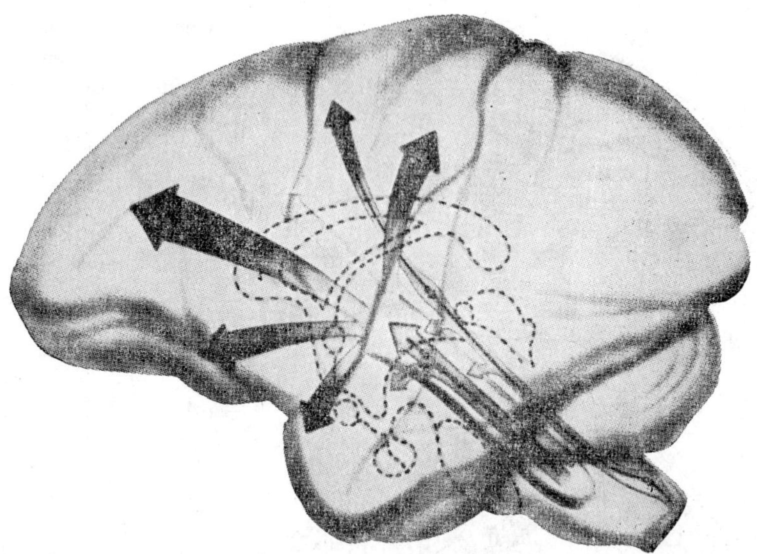

Figure 6. Lateral view of monkey's brain, showing the ascending reticular system in the central part of the brainstem with collaterals from the ascending afferent pathways. Also shown are the corticofugal connections to the central part of the brainstem. *From H. W. Magoun,* The Waking Brain, *2d ed.,* 1964. *Courtesy Charles C Thomas, Publisher, Springfield, Ill.*

activity arising in these areas and spreading to activate the entire nervous system. This form of discharge becomes more intense as long as the animal's actions fail to obtain the goal, e.g., food, and disappears abruptly once the goal has been obtained. Thus, not only are these systems concerned with regulating the excitability of other areas, but they also do this taking into account the results of the animal's own actions; i.e., they play a role in maintaining the homeostasis of the organism by means of feedback. If these areas are stimulated directly or if the animal's activity continues after its needs have been satisfied, the normal regulation of instinctive behavior is disrupted (Delgado, 1955; Delgado & Rosvold, 1956; Hess, 1954; Olds, 1955; and others). Lesions in these areas cause similar behavioral changes (MacLean, 1959; Pribram et al., 1957–1959; and others).

In lower mammals these areas play an independent role in regulating the state of excitability of the central nervous system by registering the results of the animal's actions and by permitting homeostatic maintenance of the organism. In man, on the other hand, higher structures have been superimposed on these systems. The frontal lobes, in particular, are justifiably considered by a number of authors (Pribram, 1959; Pribram, 1960b; and others) to be "tertiary" cortical areas which supersede not only the cortical portions of the exteriorly oriented motor analyzer but also those mechanisms which regulate the state of the organism. These areas are especially adapted not only to programmize the flexible forms of behavior, but to take account of the effects of actions directed by complex motives which are closely associated with the system of inner speech. They collate the results of an action with the intention which evoked it and, on the basis of the comparison, either discontinue the action (if the results match the intention) or continue it (if the action has not achieved the desired effect).

According to this conception of the frontal lobes (and we shall return to it in a later section), they have an important role in the regulation of movements and actions of the organism. These functions arise not only as the result of impulses arising in analyzers of the external environment but also as the result of feedback loops which signal the success or failure of the organism's own actions.

DISTURBANCE OF HIGHER CORTICAL FUNCTIONS BY FOCAL BRAIN DAMAGE

Everything that we have said in the previous two sections permits us, now, to take up the question of how higher mental functions are disturbed by focal brain lesions and to formulate the basic principle by which the resulting symptoms are to be analyzed. Since, fundamentally, we conceive of the higher mental functions as being reflex in nature, social in origin, and, to a large extent, mediated by the second signaling system, we are forced to discard outright any idea that they may be localized in limited areas of the cortex. Instead, we must propose that each of them is accomplished by physiological processes *involving the entire brain as a whole* and that each depends upon the *dynamically interrelated functions of a number of simultaneously acting cortical zones.*

Recent findings regarding the complex functional organization of the cortical systems have served to clarify this position. As a result, we are now able to develop more precise conceptions of exactly how the higher cortical functions are organized and of what roles the various cortical areas play. Thus we are able to achieve a more precise understanding of how these functions may be disturbed by damage to various areas of the brain.

Data accumulated by contemporary neuroanatomists and neurophysiologists give us every reason to suppose that higher cortical functions are performed by *systems of cortical zones which operate conjointly but which are functionally highly differentiated.* These zones represent the cortical parts of the various analyzers and their corresponding zones of overlap. Each of the higher cortical functions depends upon that system of cortical zones whose individual functions are necessary for its execution; zones having other functions are not included. We shall take *writing* as an example of such a complex function.

Writing requires the extraction of significant sounds (phonemes) from the flow of continuous speech, the transformation of these sounds into the corresponding spatial characters (graphemes), and, finally, the initiation of highly specific, smoothly changing patterns of impulses to the peripheral muscle groups responsible for the movements by which written symbols are formed. Thus, it is clear that the cortical portions of the different analyzers participating in this complex activity must be intact if writing is to take place. If the act of writing has not become highly automatic, all these cortical areas play a large role in its execution. On the other hand, if the process has become so automatic as to not require all three of the functional components mentioned above, as in the case of signing one's name, the corresponding cortical areas drop out of the functional system, and writing is carried out without their participation. In a person of a culture with a language which can be written without the auditory analysis of words, writing may be carried out by a different system of cortical areas from that in a person whose language is written phonetically (Luria, 1947; Luria, 1950).

An altogether different system is also seen if one considers the cerebral organization of such a process as *calculation,* for this function depends upon a different group of conjointly operating cortical areas. Written calculation involves less auditory analysis and synthesis than writing; instead, it depends to an extraordinary degree upon the spatial organization of symbols. In this case it is natural to expect that the role of cortical portions of the auditory analyzer should be considerably less, whereas the role of the visuospatial analyzer should be considerably greater than in writing. It is also natural to expect that the cortical mechanisms of computation should change as it becomes more automatic.

This conception of the *systemic localization of higher cortical functions* (see Grashchenkov & Luria, 1945; Luria, 1962) must guide the approach we take in analyzing the *disturbances which arise as the result of focal brain damage.* Having denied the possibility that complex functions might be localized in limited areas of the brain, we should not expect to find that damage to a particular area would result in the total *loss* of some function supposed to be localized in that area. We must, however, guard equally strongly against the assumption that any such limited brain lesion might lead to equal "reduction" in the effectiveness of all brain functions. We have every reason to propose that any brain lesion involving damage to a limited cortical area will produce a *primary disturbance in the function of one or another analyzer;* by weakening the functional status of cells in a given area, it will reduce the stability and flexibility of function. It will disturb the differentiation of processes associated with that area and thus reduce the range and complexity of excitatory patterns to which it can give rise. In addition to this, such a focal lesion will evoke *secondary disturbances in all the functional systems which require the participation of the damaged area, while leaving untouched any functional system in which it is not involved.*

Thus damage to the left temporal area, which constitutes a part of the cortical nucleus of the auditory analyzer, must inevitably lead to impaired word comprehension. Similarly, it may produce a writing disorder and impaired ability to recall words or name objects. But it does not affect the visual recognition of objects, spatial orientation, written calculation, etc. Conversely lesions of the cortical portions of the visual and visuospatial analyzers inevitably produce impairment of visual perception, disturbed spatial orientation, and impairment of the ability to calculate, but they have absolutely no effect on oral speech.

In accordance with the principles set forth in the previous section, it is clear that lesions restricted to the primary extrinsic areas of separate analyzer are less likely to disturb the higher cortical functions than lesions in the secondary areas or zones of overlap, which comprise the rich and varied system of central connections between the different analyzers. The fact that damage to a limited cortical area can interrupt the function of a number of different cortical systems means that any focal lesion will produce a whole *syndrome,* or *complex of symptoms,* all of which share a common feature traceable to the primary underlying disturbance.

The conception of a dynamic, systemic representation of functions in the cerebral cortex leads, also, to another important principle; namely, disturbance of any given function, e.g., reading, writing, or calculation, may result from lesions of a wide variety of cortical areas, though the structure and *severity* of such disturbances will vary greatly, depending upon the site of lesion.

Thus, returning to the previous example, *writing* may be disturbed by lesions of the temporal, occipital, postcentral, or premotor cortical areas. Damage to the temporal areas, the cortical nucleus of the auditory analyzer, however, disturbs the processes of auditory analysis and synthesis necessary for writing, whereas damage to the occipitoparietal area, the cortical nucleus of the visuospatial analyzer, produces a defect in spatial organization of the graphemes. Damage to the postcentral area, the cortical nucleus of the kinesthetic analyzer, produces a writing defect associated with a disturbance of the articulation of speech sounds. Finally, damage to the premotor areas produces a writing disorder due to loss of the motor habits necessary for the smooth execution of writing movements.

It is clear that in every case the *structure of the functional disturbance is different and that by analysis of the structure of the defect it is possible to conclude which aspect of the writing process has been disturbed and, consequently, which area of the cortex is damaged.* Just such *qualitative (or structural) analysis* should underlie the clinical and psychophysiological investigation of the disturbances of higher cortical function which arise as the result of focal brain damage. We shall be concerned with this type of analysis in subsequent sections, as we describe the various syndromes that arise following damage to different cortical areas. As a rule we shall be dealing primarily with disturbances which arise in right-handed individuals as the result of damage to different areas in the *dominant, left hemisphere.* These disorders are intimately related to speech and thus give rise to very distinct disturbances of the higher cortical functions. Unfortunately, we still know disappointingly little about the symptoms of damage to the subdominant, right hemisphere; thus, consideration of that topic lies beyond the scope of this chapter.

LESIONS OF THE OCCIPITOPARIETAL CORTEX AND VISUAL DISTURBANCES

We shall begin our discussion of the disturbances of higher cortical functions arising from focal brain lesions with a consideration of the *visual analyzer.*

As early as 1855, Panizza described a severe form of blindness which follows extirpation of the occipital cortex in dogs. In 1881, Munk supplemented this work by observing that, although such dogs lose the ability to perceive objects standing before them, they retain some aspects of vision. At the beginning of the twentieth century, Pavlov and his students studied this disturbance of "visual recognition" in detail and, further, succeeded in explaining it on a scientific basis. According to Pavlov, the occipital areas of the cortex constitute the central portion of the *visual* analyzer. Damage to this area either prevents the excitation produced by light impinging on the retina from reaching the cortex or prevents the analysis and integration of such excitation at the cortical level. As a result, any kind of complex visual discrimination becomes impossible. Thus, Munk's observation that the animal with occipital area damage "sees but does not recognize" received a physiological explanation.

Further investigation has shown that the higher an animal stands on the evolutionary ladder, the more its visually oriented behavior depends upon the occipital areas of the great hemispheres. Thus a pigeon is able to select and go to a given square painted on the floor, even after total ablation of the occipital areas. After a similar operation, a rat retains the ability to respond selectively to a "general level of illumination" but is unable to discriminate form (Lashley, 1960). A monkey lacking the visual cortex is totally blind (Klüver, 1937).

Analogous data concerning the relation of the occipital lobes to visual function have been collected for man. Willbrandt (1887) and Henschen (1920–22) noted that damage to the occipital pole in man produces a central blindness; thus they concluded that this portion of the occipital cortex may be considered the primary visual area. Other disturbances of visual perception may arise, however, following damage to any part of the occipital lobe, even areas lying outside the pole region itself. Hughlings Jackson noted as early as 1896 that lesions in these adjacent areas could lead to a visual disturbance, "imperception," in which the patient was able to see but unable to recognize what he saw. Finkelburg (1870) referred to this phenomenon as "visual asymbolia"; Charcot (1887) explained it as a loss of memory for visual images. Lissauer (1889) named it "mental blindness" or "optical agnosia" and differentiated two forms: "apperceptive" mental blindness, in which the patient is unable clearly to differentiate visual forms or to unite individual elements into conceptual wholes, and "associative" mental blindness, in which the patient easily differentiates one form from another but is unable to recognize the object it represents. In later works, the "visual agnosia" phenomenon was described by Stauffenberg (1914), Gelb and Goldstein (1920), Lange (1936), and others.

Clinical neurologists have described in detail the type of visual disorders which arise as the result of damage to the occipital areas of the cortex. These may take the form of agnosia for visual figures (visual agnosia), sharply reduced visual attention, or partial or total "central blindness." The physiological mechanisms underlying these disturbances, however, are just beginning to become clear as the result of information collected in the fields of neuroanatomy, psychophysiology, and clinical neurology during the last few decades.

Structure and Functional Organization of the Visual Cortex

It is well known that visual fibers arise in the retina and pass through the optic nerves to the lateral geniculate body (Figure 7). Some cross through the optic chiasma, and some branch off to the superior colliculus, where excitation can be directly transmitted back to efferent pathways controlling the pupillary reflex and simple eye movements. Those reaching the lateral geniculate synapse with fibers which immediately fan out to form the so-called "optic radiation," which ends in the pole and lingula of the occipital cortex (Brodmann's area 17). This zone can be looked upon as the central or primary portion of the cortical nucleus of the visual analyzer.

Cytoarchitecturally, this area is distinguished by its highly developed fourth (afferent) layer, which receives fibers carrying visual impulses (Figure 8). Here are located nerve cells capable of transmitting excitation to closely surrounding cortical areas. Characteristically, fibers coming from the retina are not distributed randomly to various parts of the primary visual cortex but have an orderly distribution, so that every portion of the retinal field is represented by a specific area of the visual cortex (Figure 9). This is the basis for referring to area 17 as the "projection area for the visual field." As a result of this specific somatotopic structure, direct electrical stimulation of any point in this area will produce a *localized visual sensation* in a specific part of the visual field. Similarly, the presence of scar tissue or brain softening at a particular site in this area may lead to epileptic seizures which begin with a visual aura localized to the corresponding portion of the visual field. The strict somatotopic organization of the primary visual cortex also explains the fact that damage to a portion of this area leads to *loss of vision in the corresponding part of the visual field,* a so-called "scotoma" or "hemianopsia." Depending upon the extent of the lesion, the hemianopsia may be either complete or partial; i.e., it involves precisely that part of the visual field which corresponds to the damaged area.

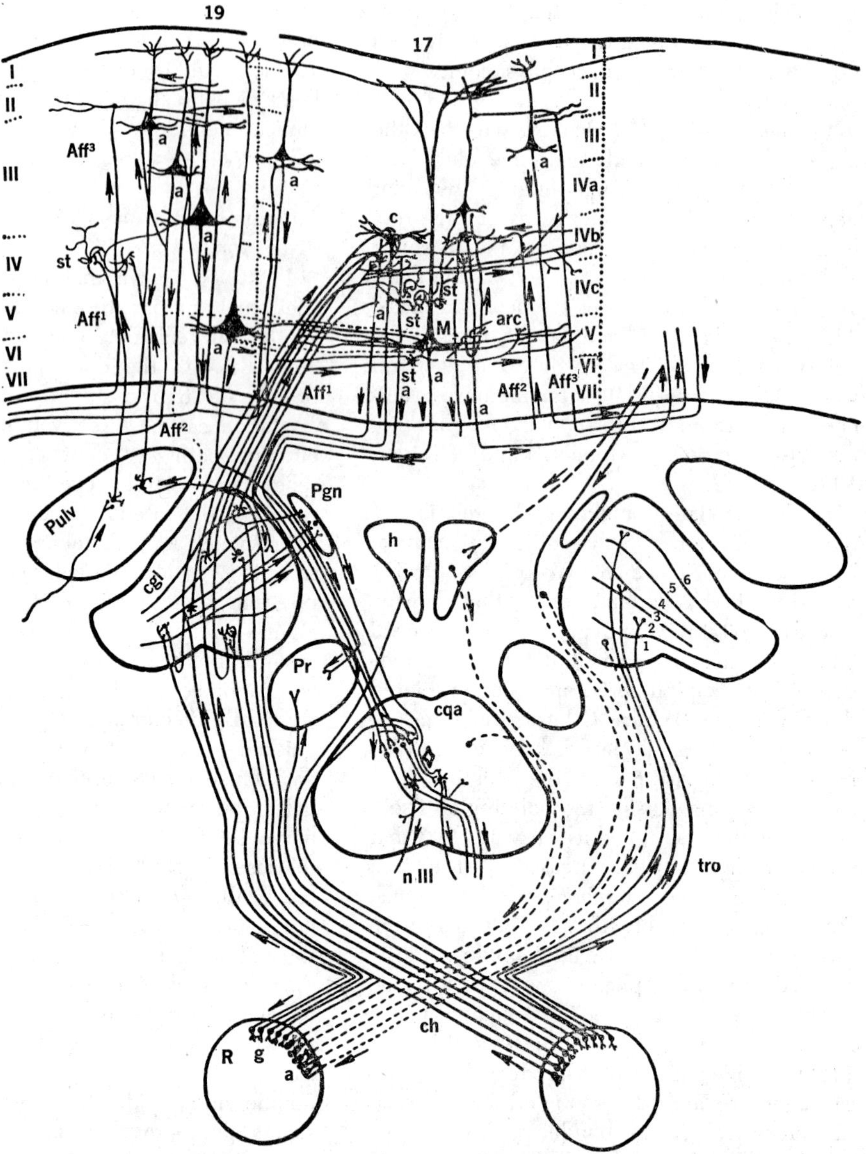

Figure 7. Relays and connections of the visual analyzer. *Above:* Schematic diagram representing areas 17 and 19; Roman numerals represent cortical layers, left, of area 19 and, right, of area 17; area 18, which lies between areas 17 and 19, is not represented. *Center:* Subcortical structures. *Below:* The retinas. Solid lines represent afferent pathways, and dotted lines represent efferent pathways between the retinas and the cortex. (*Pulv*) Pulvinar; (*Cgl*) lateral geniculate; (*Pgn*) pregeniculate nucleus; (*h*) hypothalamus; (*Pr*) pretectal nucleus; (*cqa*) superior colliculus; (*nl II*) oculomotor nerve; (*ch*) chiasma; (*R*) retina; (*g*) retinal ganglion cells; (*a*) retinal bipolar cells; (*tro*) visual tract. Arrows represent the direction of impulse transmission. This diagram is based upon data derived from our own studies and those of other authors (Minkovsky, Le Gros Clark, Polyak, Cajal, Novokhatsky, Chow, and others). *E. G. Shkolnik-Yarros.*

It may involve simply the superior or inferior portion of the contralateral visual field (indicating a lesion of the inferior or superior portion of the visual projection area), or it may be limited to a small blind spot (scotoma) (Teuber, 1960).

Sometimes the hemianopsia resulting from a visual cortical lesion may go unnoticed by the patient. This is especially common if the right hemisphere is damaged giving rise to a left hemianopsia. Such a hemianopsia is "fixated" in character; i.e., the patient does not

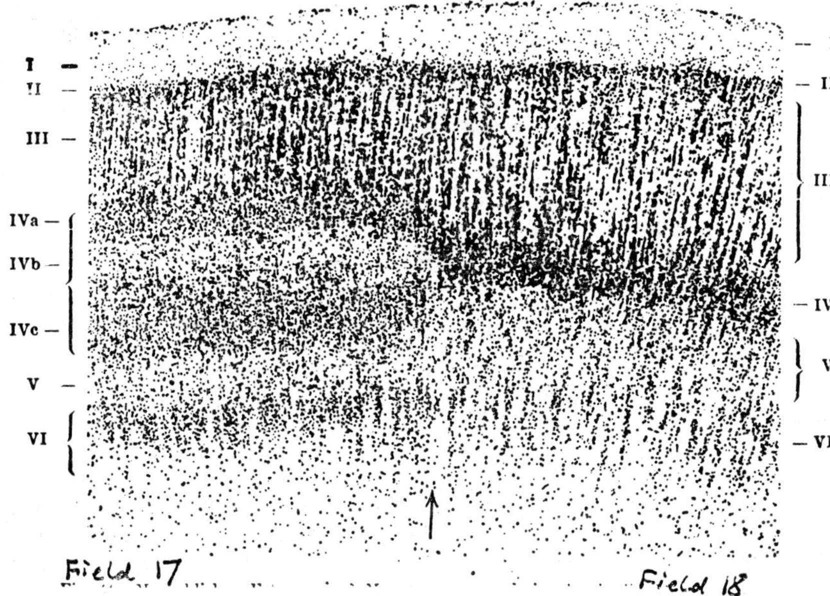

Figure 8. Architectonics of the visual cortex. *Brodmann.*

compensate for it by moving his eyes (Luria & Skorodumova, 1947).

The cortical part of the visual analyzer is not limited to the primary projection area. Directly adjacent to this area lie the *secondary zones of the cortical part of the visual analyzer.* These zones function in conjunction with the primary visual area, but they differ considerably from it in their structure and functional organization. Figure 8 shows the great difference in structure of these two areas. In the secondary area, area 18, the second and third layers are much thicker; these are known to consist of associative neurons which, thanks to their highly arborized dendrites and long axons, are capable of transmitting excitation to both nearby and distant cortical areas. Thus they make possible the establishment of reverberating circuits over large cortical distances. In addition to this, a number of investi-

Figure 9. Cortical representation of the retina. The relationships of various parts of the primary visual cortex (Brodmann's area 17) to the visual field are shown above. (*A*) Visual field. (*B*) Visual area of the cortex. (1) Inferior lip of the calcarine fissure; (2) superior lip of the calcarine fissure. *G. Holmes.*

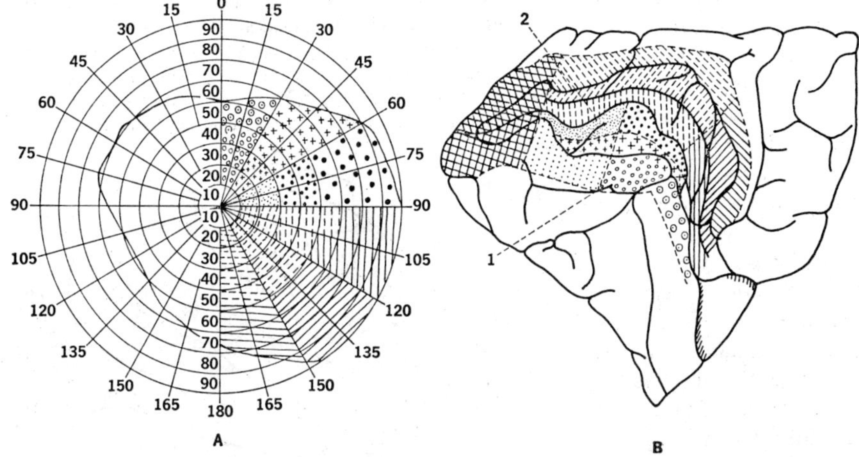

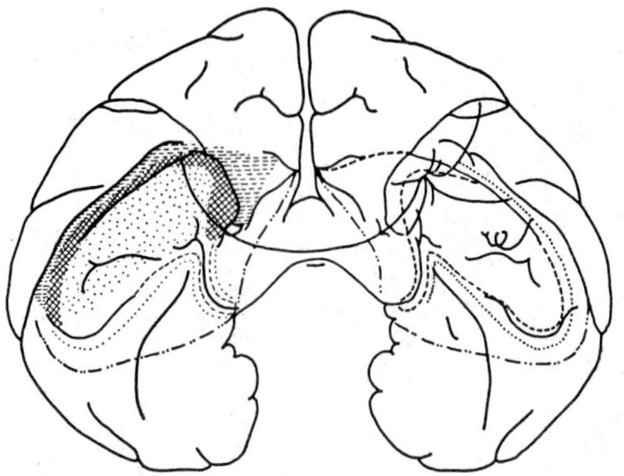

One hemisphere			Contralateral hemisphere		
17	18	19	19	18	17
ΔY	Y				
Y	YΔY	Y		Y	
		YΔ			

Δ Stimulus
Y Response

Figure 10. Spread of cortical excitation with stimulation of primary and secondary portions of the occipital area. ***McCulloch.***

gators (Rose, 1950; Poliak, 1957; and others) have shown that these areas also receive fibers arising in thalamic nuclei which have no direct connections with the periphery. Thus, they receive information which has already been processed at subcortical levels. The anatomical structure of these areas makes possible a new form of functional organization which makes them appropriately referred to as *secondary areas of the cortical part of the visual analyzer.*

Neuronographic studies have indicated that excitation arising in the primary projection area of the visual cortex does not spread far beyond the site at which it is initiated (Figure 10). In contrast to this, excitation initiated in the secondary visual area, area 18, spreads much further. Excitation arising within area 19 inhibits excitation in the first two areas (McCulloch, 1943). The secondary areas of the visual cortex are capable both of initiating excitation which spreads to distant areas and of inhibiting adjacent areas. Thus, the physiological conditions are met for the complex analysis and synthesis of visual signals which enter these areas of the cortex. They also provide for the preservation of stable traces of such excitation and flexible changes in the combinations of these traces. In short, the conditions are met for the most complex forms of visual perception.

The physiological principles underlying the organization of the secondary visual areas manifest themselves also in experiments involving direct electrical stimulation. Investigators such as Foerster, Pötzl, Hoff and Penfield have performed such experiments at the operating table during neurosurgical operations. Figure 11 presents the characteristic results of a sample investigation carried out by these authors to determine the effects of stimulating the *primary* visual area directly. Stimulation in this area evokes elementary visual sensations (phosphene, colored lights, colored spots, etc.). In contrast to this, stimulation of the *secondary* visual areas produces *complex visual hallucinations* (the patient may see people, animals, flowers, different surroundings, etc.). Such hallucinations may be extremely complex in nature, indicating that the secondary areas of the visual cortex play an important role in the synthesis of individual forms of visual stimulation into conceptual entities and in storing the generalized traces of visual experience. Both functions are necessary for the visual perception of objects.

Figure 11. Points of the occipital cortex, stimulation of which produces visual hallucinations. The numbers represent those areas of the cortex of which stimulation gave rise to the following visual hallucinations: (1) "Balls of light"; (2) "colored lights"; (3) "white light"; (4) "a blue disk"; (5) "flames"; (6) "a blue mist"; (7) "faces, sounds coming from below"; (8) "a person walking off to the side"; (9) "faces"; (10) "animals"; (11) "faces and butterflies." ***Pötzl, Hoff, and others.***

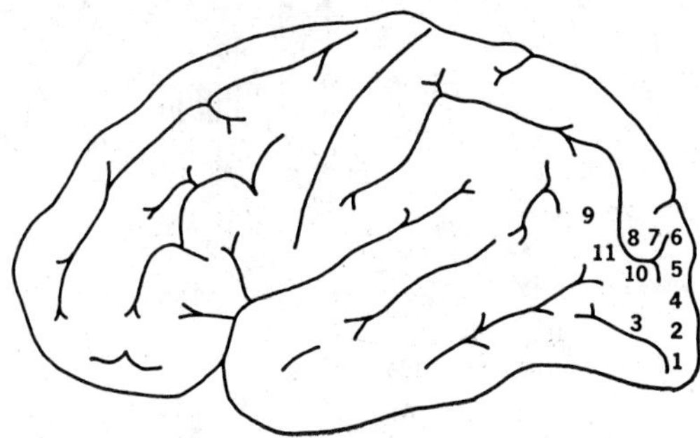

All this brings us to a discussion of those phenomena which are known to the clinician as "visual agnosias" and which are of primary importance in syndromes arising as the result of lesions located in the occipital area.

Lesions of the Visual Cortex and Visual Agnosia

As we indicated earlier, a lesion within the *primary* projection area of the visual cortex produces a partial loss of vision, i.e., central blindness, hemianopsia, and scotoma. During recovery from such a lesion, the initial partial or total blindness may give way to another form of disturbance, so that the patient comes to complain that the edges of objects appear vague, as though "seem through defective or smoked glass." Gradually even these symptoms may disappear, leaving only a slight fatiguability of visual processes, visual adaption difficulties, and the kinds of "visual asthenic" phenomena described by Poppelreuter (1917–1918), Bay (1950), and Chlenov (1948).

Damage to the secondary visual areas gives rise to an entirely different type of disturbance. When a lesion involves area 18 or 19, sometimes referred to as the "broad visual sphere," it may leave visual acuity, color discrimination, and the visual fields undisturbed; but the neurodynamic processes underlying more complex forms of visual analysis and synthesis may be severely deranged, so that visual perception, on the whole, is impaired. These disturbances of visual perception arising as the result of lesions in the secondary visual cortex are seen clinically as various forms of *visual agnosia*. They may arise as the result of lesions in the dominant hemisphere, usually the left hemisphere; but, in the majority of cases, they result from bilateral lesions.

As a rule, a patient with such a lesion is able to perceive the details of a figure which is presented to him, but he is unable to *recognize the object it represents.* He catches individual details, on the basis of which he tries to guess what the object is. Thus a picture of eyeglasses may be characterized as follows: "A circle . . . and another circle . . . and a crosspiece . . . probably a bicycle!" Similarly, a picture of a divan may be identified as a briefcase (by the color of the leather) or as an automobile (the two arms ending in disks similar to headlights); a rooster may be identified as a bonfire (by the plumage of the tail, which is similar to tongues of flame); etc. Sometimes a patient with visual agnosia identifies objects in terms which are too general. It becomes clear that he is basing his conclusion as to the meaning of the total picture on individual cues, as though he were unable to unite them into one total image. As a result he may identify a picture of a monkey as a bear (by the fur), as a man (by the eyes), or, in general terms, as an animal.

This kind of symptom appears most clearly if the figure presented is crisscrossed by extraneous lines having no relation to the figure itself (Figure 12). In this case visual "extraction" of the figure from its complicated background becomes completely impossible. Similar difficulties are met in the identification of visually presented objects. In this case, however, feeling the object permits immediate recognition.

This form of visual agnosia for objects most nearly approximates Lissauer's "apperceptive visual agnosia." All the data indicate that it is based upon a *disturbance of the visual synthesis of individual cues* which the patient perceives separately but which he is unable to unite into a single complex image. He is unable to perceive the component parts simultaneously as a whole. This interpretation is confirmed by obervations that, in contrast to the normal subject, the patient with visual agnosia perceives a figure in the same way whether it is presented all at once or part by part (Birenbaum, 1948); in either case, he catches only isolated cues. The same defect is revealed in pictures drawn by patients with visual agnosia. They consist of disorderly "graphical enumerations" of various elements with no sign of organization into whole figures (Figure 13).

Lissauer's second type of visual agnosia, "associative visual agnosia," is seen considerably less frequently. Patients with this syndrome perceive the outlines of figures but are unable to recognize their meaning. A good example of such a disturbance is loss of the ability to recognize the faces of close friends, even though the ability to recognize them by their voices is retained. This disorder may be so severe as to prevent the patient from distinguishing visually between men and women (Chlenov & Bein, 1958; Hécaen, Ajuziaguerra, Magis, & Angelergues, 1957; Hoff, & Pötzl, 1937; and others). Sometimes this disturbance goes with impaired recognition

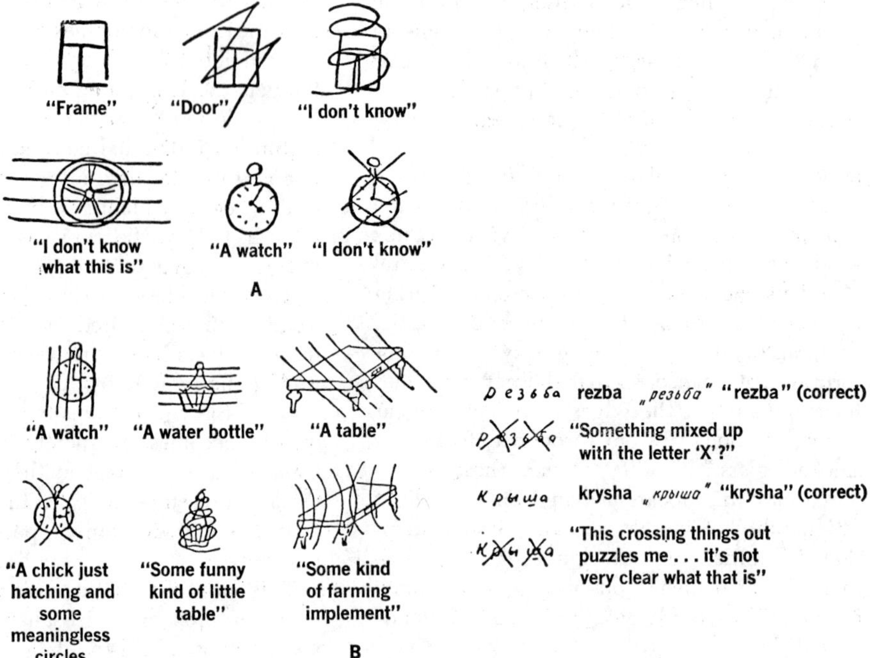

Figure 12. Perceptual disturbance for masked figures in patients with visual agnosia. (*A*) Patient Kon.: extracerebral tumor in the occipital area. (*B*) Patient Eng.: encephalomalacia deep in the left parieto-occipital area.

Figure 13. Drawings by patients with visual agnosia. (*A*) Copying. (*B*) Drawing of a man in response to verbal instructions. (*C*) Picture completion (the heavy lines represent the incomplete outline of a camel presented to the patient; the remaining lines represent his completion of the drawing).

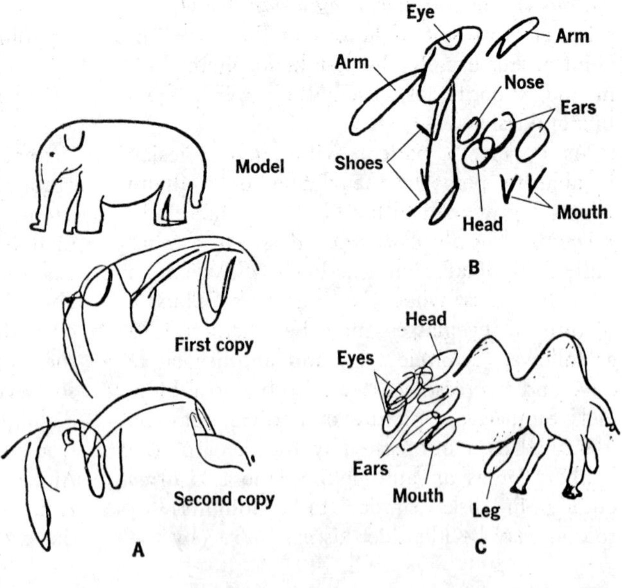

of concrete objects which were earlier quite familiar to the patient: "I see a red kerchief, but I don't know whose it is," says such a patient looking at her own kerchief. This form of visual agnosia is similar to a series of disorders of recognition known to the clinic as being associated with "alienation" of the meaning of objects and is more commonly seen following damage to the visual cortex of the right hemisphere. At the present time it is difficult to judge what might be its pathophysiological basis.

Some light has been thrown on the pathophysiological mechanisms of the visuognostic disturbances described above by a disturbance described by Bálint (1909); Holmes (1919); Wolpert (1924); Etteinger, Warrington, & Zangwill (1959); Luria (1959b); Luria, Vinarskaya, and Yarbuss (1961); and others. This disturbance, referred to as "simultaneous agnosia," is associated with a *disturbance of visual fixation or gaze.* It arises most commonly as the result of bilateral damage to the anterior portion of the occipital cortex at its parietal border. A patient with this lesion is *able to see only one object at a time,* regardless of its size. When he shifts his gaze from one object to another, the first disappears. The same difficulty arises when he examines a picture representing a complex object or scene. A pathological constriction of the "perceptual field," or, as it is often called, a restriction of "visual attention," prevents systematic shifting of gaze from one object to another or from one point in a geometrical figure to another. No matter what he does, the patient is able to see only individual points. Instead of producing systematic eye movements to compensate for the constriction in his visual field, the patient makes ataxic irregular shifts in gaze. Examples of disturbances in gaze seen in such patients are shown in Figure 14, which presents a tracing of eye movements as they are registered on photographic paper by Yarbus's method. Similar difficulties arise when such a patient is asked to trace out a figure, place a point in its center, etc. (Figure 15).

Pavlov, having analyzed one such case described by Pierre Janet, suggested that the patient's symptoms resulted from a pathological weakness of nerve cells in the occipital area of the cortex. Consequently, at any given time, all its activity is concentrated on a single point, while other points appear nonexistent.

The suggestion that this is a physiological mechanism has great significance; it is possible that the mechanism by which an excited area inhibits other areas underlies a much wider range of phenomena, e.g., those defects of visual synthesis giving rise to the visual agnosia for objects which was described above.

Lesions of the Parieto-occipital Areas of the Cortex and Apractagnosia

So far, we have been considering the pathological changes in *visual perception* which arise following damage to the primary and

Figure 14*A*. Eye movements accompanying the inspection of a given object by a normal subject. *Left:* Portrait examined. *Right:* Recording of eye movements.

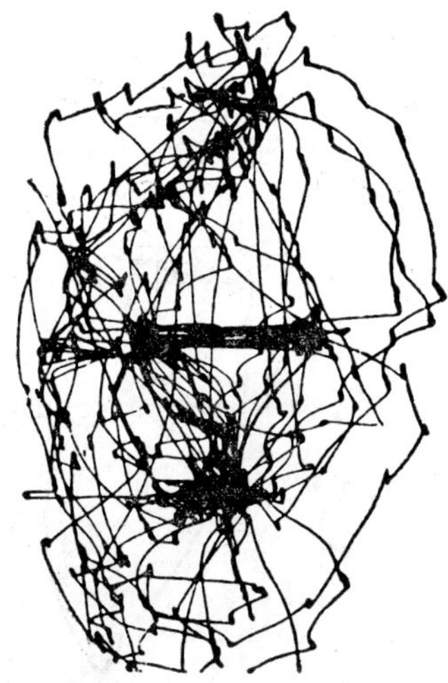

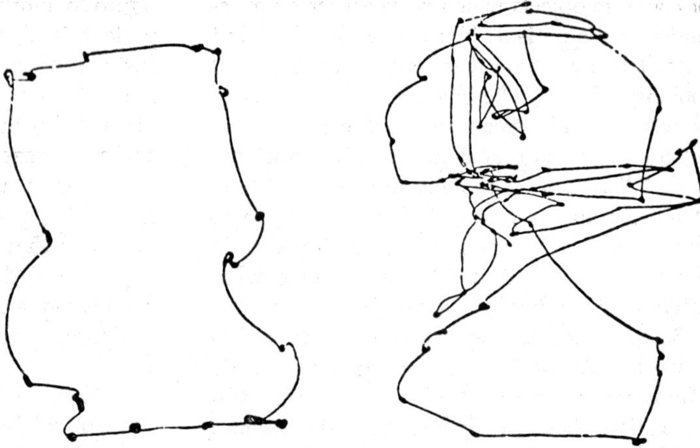

Figure 14*B*. Recordings of eye movements accompanying the inspection of two objects by a patient with peripheral constriction of the visual field. *Left:* A rectangle. *Right:* A statue.

secondary cortical areas of the visual analyzer, i.e., lesions of the occipital cortex. Perception does not involve only visual analysis and synthesis, however. It also involves the *tactile, kinesthetic* analysis of signals reaching the perceiver. The role of tactile and motor analysis emerges most clearly in *spatial perception* and is accomplished by joint activity of the *occipital and parietal areas of the cortex.*

The perception of spatial relations is based upon the integrated neural representation of numerous stimuli conveyed by several sensory modalities. It involves vestibular, tactile, and kinesthetic as well as visual analysis. As Sechenov rightly pointed out, the synthesis of individual stimuli into *unitary patterns or groups* is a characteristic of visuospatial perception. Auditory perception, on the other hand, is characterized predominantly by the synthesis of serially occurring stimuli into *sequential patterns.* Of particular importance for visuospatial perception is the emergence of one hand, usually the right, as dominant, so that the perception of space is asymmetrical and it becomes possible to differentiate right and left.

The complex integrative function underlying spatial perception and the movements

Figure 14*C*. Recordings of eye movements accompanying the inspection of two objects by a patient with "simultaneous agnosia." *Left:* A rectangle. *Right:* A face.

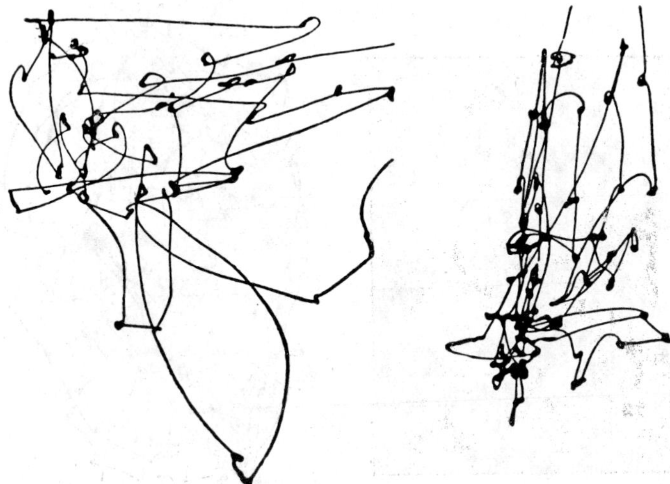

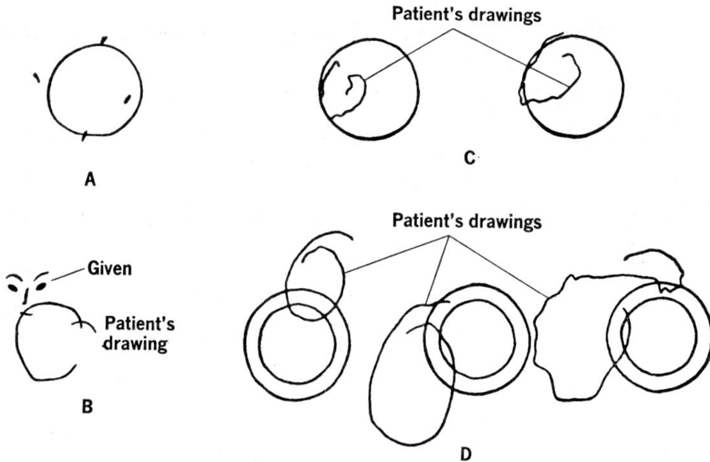

Figure 15. Signs of visual ataxia in a patient with simultaneous agnosia (bilateral lesions of the occipital and parietal lobes). (*A*) Attempts to place a dot in the center of a circle. (*B*) Attempts to complete a face. (*C*) Attempts to outline a circle. (*D*) Attempts to draw circles inside of rings.

which are based upon it are accomplished in man by coordinated activity of the parietal and occipital cortical areas. The areas particularly involved are those which contribute to both the visual cutaneous-kinesthetic and vestibular analyzers. As was pointed out above, these areas constitute the zones of overlap between the cortical portions of the two analyzers and are part of the most complex and phylogenetically most recently developed cortical structures. Damage to areas 39 and 40 (the lower parietal area) and areas 18 and 19 (anterior occipital area), especially of the left, dominant hemisphere, leads to characteristic disturbances which have been described by a number of authors as "visuospatial agnosia" (Kleist, 1934; Lange, 1936; and others).

Patients with this form of disturbance experience no noticeable difficulty in the perception of objects or pictures of objects. They are totally unable, however, to analyze the spatial relationships represented in pictures or diagrams. Thus, such a patient is unable to identify the right and left sides of an object or to analyze the positions of hands on a clock (confusing the symmetrically arranged numbers IV and VI, IX and XI, etc.); he is similarly unable to orient himself in reading a map, since he tends to confuse east and west. Figure 16 shows typical attempts of such patients to draw a simple geographical map.

The disorders which arise from lesions of the lower parietal and parieto-occipital areas of the left hemisphere are not restricted to disturbances in the perception of spatial relations and memory for organized spatial schemata. There are also inevitably disorders of *movements and action* which depend upon

Figure 16. Geographical disorientation in patients with lesions of the occipital and parieto-occipital areas. (*A*) Patient G.: lesion of left parieto-occipital area. (*B*) Patient M.: lesion of the right occipital area.

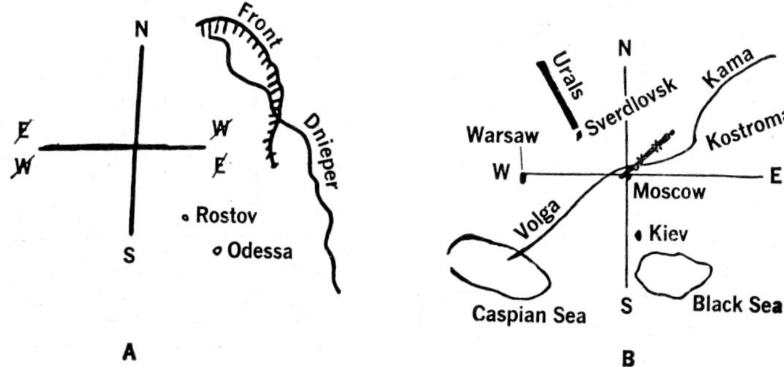

integrative spatial perception. In fact, patients with these disorders so frequently show disruption of the spatial organization of movement that the syndrome has been referred to as "spatial apraxagnosia" (Lange, 1936) or "constructive apraxia" (Kleist, 1934; Kroll, 1933). Having lost the ability to orient himself in relation to other objects, the patient begins to have difficulty with those forms of movement which require the integrity of processes underlying the perceptual integration of spatial areas. He begins to show confusion in practical activities. Thus he may go right when he should go left; in making his bed, he may spread the blankets crosswise instead of lengthwise; in putting on a coat, he may put his arm in the wrong sleeve; in eating soup, he may hold the spoon at such an angle that the soup spills out; in attempting to strike a match, he may touch it to the wrong end of the box or strike in the wrong direction. If such a patient is asked to bring his hands together at a certain angle, he is unable to do so; he is similarly unable to imitate the arrangement of matchsticks in spatial patterns. Such a patient experiences the greatest difficulty in tasks which require that he remember and mentally transform the spatial relations of objects or symbols. This kind of problem arises if he is asked to construct in front of himself the same matchstick pattern as the examiner sitting opposite him has constructed. Figure 17 shows an example of the errors which arise in such a situation as this. It is easily seen that the fundamental disorder is a loss of visuospatial integration. In a later section we shall take up this question again, as we consider the effects which disturbances of simultaneous spatial synthesis have upon processes involving the second signaling system.

Reading and Writing Disorders Arising from Lesions of the Occipitoparietal Areas: Visual Alexia and Agraphia

Not only do the visuognostic disturbances just described manifest themselves in the perception of figures and movements based upon this process, but they can also lead to impaired recognition of symbols (e.g., letters, words, and numerals) as manifested in various forms of visual alexia and agraphia.

The visual perception of letters and numbers involves a complex process of visual analysis and synthesis by which the attributes which distinguish the symbols from one another and which give them special meaning are selected out. Such attributes usually include combinations of straight and curved lines arranged in various configurations. Sometimes the distinguishing characteristic is a relatively small feature; consider, for example, the differences between H and K, d and b, or 6 and 9.

It is easy to understand how a disturbance of visual or visuospatial analysis and synthesis might affect reading and writing. Indeed, it is true that with incomplete development or damage of the left visual area, one may find syndromes involving visual alexia and visual agraphia. They take the form of nonrecognition of individual letters or numerals and are related to a disturbance of visual analysis and synthesis of the elements making up such symbols ("literal alexia"). In such cases patients confuse similar letters, e.g., handwritten d and b, and are unable to recognize letters written in unfamiliar stylized letters. Sometimes they may be unable to perceive whole words at once ("verbal alexia"). They may find it necessary to spell words out letter by letter and combine aloud the letters which they have read. Characteristically, such patients are even unable to recognize immediately such common letter combinations as USA, USSR, etc., which for a normal reader become essentially "visual ideograms." Whereas literal alexia is a special kind of visual agnosia which is so severe as to affect the recognition of individual symbols, verbal alexia can be

Figure 17. Tests of constructive activity as performed by patients with constructive apraxia.

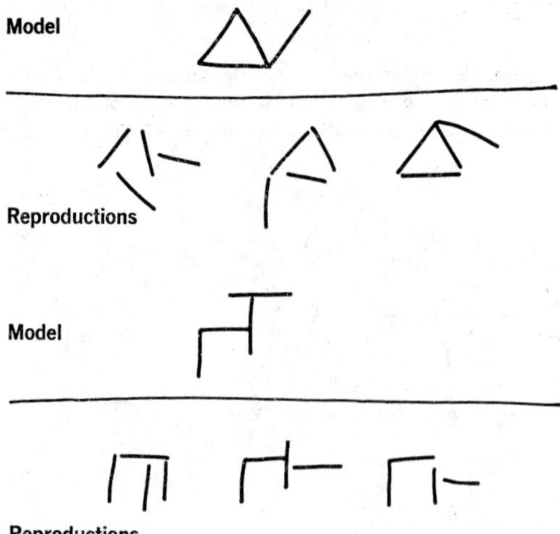

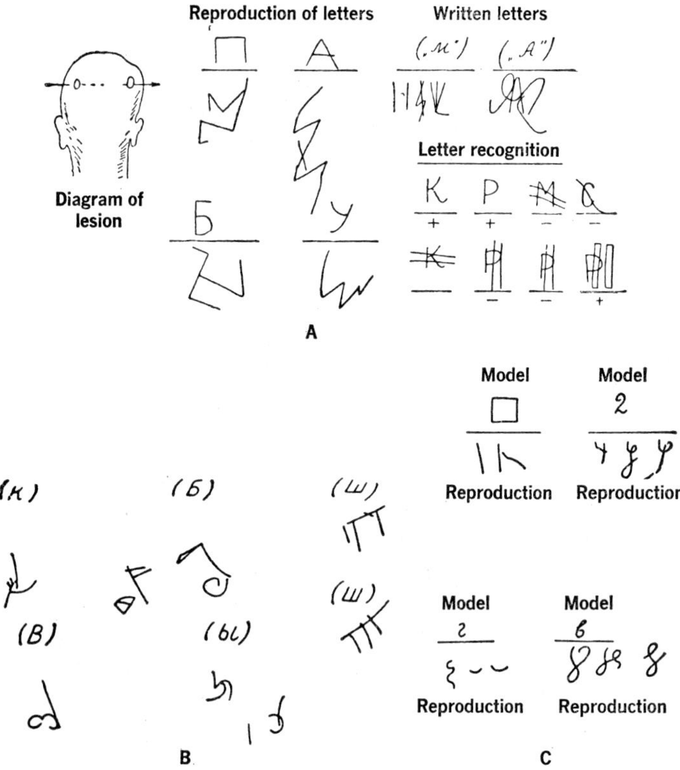

Figure 18. Visuospatial disturbances of writing to dictation and copying in patients with lesions of the parietotemporal areas of the cortex. (*A*) Patient Bul.: bilateral lesion of the occipital area. (*B*) Patient Erol.: lesion of the left parieto-occipital area. (*C*) Patient M.: lesion of the left parieto-occipital area.

considered a pure case of simultaneous agnosia.

A special form of visual alexia and agraphia is seen in the visuospatial disturbance of reading and writing. These syndromes usually arise as the result of lesions in the parieto-occipital portion of the left hemisphere. Patients with such lesions confuse letters which differ from one another by the spatial arrangement of common components and, in writing, are unable to remember the correct configuration of individual letters. Thus they may write letters backward. Figure 18 illustrates various forms of visual agraphia.

Disturbances of Symbolic Processes with Lesions of the Occipitoparietal Areas: Semantic Aphasia and Acalculia

The disturbances of simultaneous and, for the most part, spatial modes of synthesis described above are not restricted to visual perception and the associated processes of reading and writing. If a lesion is located at the border between the left parieto-occipital area and the temporal area (area 39 or 37), the disturbance which arises may involve the cognitive sphere and lead to significant disturbance of symbolic level of mental processes which require spatial (or quasi-spatial) organization. Thus, there may arise the kinds of symptoms which have received the clinical name "semantic aphasia" or "acalculia."

Patients with semantic aphasia show no signs whatever of impairment in the auditory organization of speech (to be discussed in the following section). They easily understand individual words, talk without difficulty, and speak perfectly grammatically. Sometimes they show signs of disturbance in remembering the names of objects, "amnesic aphasia." They sometimes have to give up trying to remember the names of things and substitute descriptive phrases instead. Thus the examiner may hear such expressions as: "Well, what is it . . . well, here, it's for fixing your hair!" or "Well . . . now . . . well . . . what is it . . . it's to eat. . . ." Sometimes the patient is able to recall the name by recalling a familiar context within which it is embedded, e.g., "Well now . . . well . . . how do you say . . . well, you eat soup with a spoon!" Often prompting, though so slight as to be virtually imperceptible, helps the patient to remember the word he is seeking; this characteristic differentiates such patients from the group to be described in the next section and indicates that their defect arises from disturbance of that complex simultaneous system of relations which is necessary for the rapid and accurate recall of names.

The central feature of the whole syndrome, however, is a characteristic *impairment of the ability to comprehend any complex logicogrammatical construction.* Such comprehension cannot be achieved without the cognitive synthesis of individual components into a simultaneous whole. A typical example of such a construction is an instruction which involves a preposition, e.g., "Draw a circle under a square," "Draw a cross under a circle," "Draw a circle to the right of a cross," or "Draw a triangle to the left of a square." Clearer examples are to be seen in more complex constructions of the type "Draw a circle to the right of a square and to the left of a triangle" or a sentence such as "Mary is more blond than Helen but darker than Kate." It is clear that in order to catch the meanings of such logicogrammatical constructions, one must carry out a complex "spatial-organized" operation. Individual elements must be shifted and united into single simultaneous systems. This kind of operation is impossible for a patient with a lesion of the parieto-occipital area of the left hemisphere. Such a patient easily perceives the words "circle," "under," and "cross," but he is unable to unite them cognitively and imagine to himself the relationship which is expressed by this logical formula. As a result, when such a patient is instructed to "draw a circle under a cross," he will usually miss the grammatical significance of the preposition and will draw the two figures in the reverse position, starting at the top and drawing them in the same sequence as they occur in the instruction.

The patient exhibits the same semantic aphasia when he is asked to explain the relationship "brother's father" or "father's brother" for this also requires simultaneous (quasi-spatial) synthesis of the individual words. The same is true of logicogrammatical questions of the type "Peter was walking in front of John. Who was walking behind?" or "Michael hit Paul. Who was hit?" Both require quasi-spatial organization and inversion of the relation expressed in the sentence as it stands.

The disturbance of complex simultaneous synthesis of logicogrammatical constructions and of cognitive operations with normal comprehension of separate words is the basic symptom of so-called "semantic aphasia" and results from the disturbance of simultaneous, primarily spatial synthesis. This results directly from damage to the parieto-occipital areas of the left hemisphere.

Another sign of the same syndrome is the familiar clinical entity "acalculia." Patients with semantic aphasia and acalculia easily perceive simple whole numbers and know their significance. If one presents compound numbers or asks that the patient carry out simple mathematical operations on any kind of number, however, clear evidence of the disturbance emerges. The patient lacks the simultaneous quasi-spatial organization which is necessary for comprehension of compound numbers, for converting fractions into decimals, or for carrying out mental calculations. These processes require the full preservation of simultaneous spatial synthesis.

It is known that mathematical operations grow out of graphic geometrical operations and that even advanced forms of abstract calculation continue to bear certain signs of their origin in their quasi-spatial organization. The preservation of certain spatial relations is necessary even for such elementary operations as comparison of the magnitude of numbers. It is all the more necessary for maintaining the correct order in numbers comprising several digits and is absolutely necessary for performing such operations as addition, subtraction, multiplication, and division. All these require not only attention to whether a given digit represents units, tens, hundreds, etc., but also the internal execution of arithmetical operations.

Thus it is clear why the disturbances of simultaneous spatial synthesis which arise following lesions of the occipitoparietal areas of the left hemisphere prevent patients from being able to understand numbers of more than one digit, i.e., from being able to point out which digits in a four-digit number represent thousands, hundreds, tens, or units. (Sometimes they confuse the meanings of the digits or name them off in reverse order.) We see why mental calculations which involve decimal transitions and so-called "tabular calculations" involving the conceptual rearrangement of number groups are impossible for these patients. Both primary acalculia, which is related to the primary disturbance of simultaneous spatial synthesis, and semantic aphasia are pathognomonic of such lesions.

LESIONS OF THE TEMPORAL CORTICAL AREA AND DISTURBANCES OF AUDITORY GNOSIS: SENSORY APHASIA

Whereas lesions of the occipital area and adjacent portions of the lower parietal area lead to various forms of defects in vision and visuospatial perception, lesions of the temporal area lead to impairment of auditory perception and, in some cases, to speech disturbances which are widely referred to clinically as "sensory aphasia." The essential difference between these two types of disturbance lies in the fact that, whereas the visuognostic disturbances described above are usually the result of bilateral lesions with only a slight preponderance of left hemisphere lesions, clear symptoms of auditory agnosia and sensory aphasia arise, as a rule, only as the result of damage to the *dominant hemisphere*. This means that, in right-handed persons, such symptoms appear with lesions of the left hemisphere and not with lesions of the right, subdominant hemisphere. Thus, *lateralization of function* is one of the most important features of the superior temporal area and of the so-called "speech areas" which lie adjacent to it.

The history of investigation of disturbances which arise as the result of damage to the left temporal area is, in some ways, similar to that characterizing the study of visual agnosias. In 1874, Wernicke described a case which led him to suggest that damage to the posterior third of the left superior temporal gyrus produces a characteristic disturbance. A patient with such a lesion continues to hear individual sounds, but he loses the ability to understand speech; he hears speech as an undifferentiated flow of sounds. Wernicke referred to this syndrome as "sensory aphasia" and pointed out that when it is present, the patient is unable to perceive the sound structure of words. In further attempting to explain this unique phenomenon, he suggested that the posterior third of the superior temporal gyrus receives those auditory fibers which permit one to hear the range of frequencies which are involved in oral speech (*Sprachseite*). Thus, he believed, lesions of this area produce a partial deafness which is the primary disturbance underlying sensory aphasia.

Wernicke's hypothesis was refuted, however, with the further accumulation of knowledge in this field. Subsequent investigations showed that the primary auditory tracts do not end in the primary temporal gyrus; instead, they end in the transverse gyrus of Heschl. On the other hand, the observations of a number of authors (Bonvichini, 1929; Frankfurter & Theile, 1912; and others) indicated that patients with sensory aphasia show no partial loss of hearing whatever and easily respond to tones from that part of the scale which, in Wernicke's opinion, must be missing.

As a result of these findings, the loss of auditory speech comprehension in sensory aphasia ceased to be thought of as a "partial deafness," and some authors began to consider sensory aphasia a complex disturbance of "understanding," one of a group of disturbances of "symbolic activity." In 1905 Pierre Marie set forth the idea that sensory aphasia is actually a result not of an auditory defect but of an intellectual disturbance. In his conception speech was separated from its sensory basis, and Wernicke's aphasia came to be considered a form of dementia.

Further investigations, however, forced a retreat from this position. It was shown that a patient with sensory aphasia is by no means demented; many intellectual processes involving abstraction and generalization remain intact. As a result of such findings, sensory aphasia came more and more to be thought of as a *disturbance of the complex "elaborated" audition* which is a fundamental condition for the comprehension of speech sounds. It is this kind of audition that has since become the central object of investigation.

Thus, we see that clinical neurologists have described an important syndrome, namely, the disturbance of discriminative receptive speech, of "auditory speech," which arises as the result of damage to the posterior third of the superior temporal gyrus of the left hemisphere. They have had to reject the view that this disturbance is basically a partial deafness or a general sign of intellectual impairment. Instead they have introduced the idea that the disturbance of auditory speech and the closely related phenomenon of sensory aphasia represent a special disturbance of highly organized auditory function and have set themselves the task of determining the physiological mechanisms of this disturbance. The advances which have been made in this field result from intensified investigation by morphologists, physiologists, psycholinguists, and clinical neurologists and we have to review the result of their findings shortly.

Structure and Functional Organization of the Auditory Cortex

As is well known, auditory fibers arising in the peripheral auditory receptor, the organ of Corti, pass within the auditory nerve from the cochlea to the brainstem. The tracts partially cross through the trapezoid body, give off branches to the inferior colliculi (to complete the afferent limb of the most elementary auditory reflexes), synapse in the medial geniculate body, and project to Heschl's gyrus, hidden in the superior surface of the temporal lobe.

The auditory pathway differs from the visual pathway in that the nerve fibers arising in each organ of Corti are equally represented in the two hemispheres. Thus damage to the "auditory centers" of one hemisphere does not lead to a marked loss of hearing in the contralateral ear. Heschl's gyrus is similar to the visual projection area in that its fourth (afferent) layer is well developed and the cochlea is somatotopically represented.

Investigations by Pfeiffer (1936), Bremer and Dow (1939), and others have shown that the medial portion of Heschl's gyrus receives auditory fibers responding to high frequencies, whereas the lateral portion receives fibers responsive to the lower end of the tone scale. Thus, there is every justification for considering Heschl's gyrus the primary projection area of the extrinsic cortical part of the auditory analyzer.

The superior temporal gyrus (Brodmann's area 22) is altogether different in structure from Heschl's gyrus. In some ways it is analogous to area 18 of the visual area, which we considered above. Its second and third cortical layers are well developed. The predominant nerve cell type in these layers is the small pyramidal and stellar cell, which may send its axon to other areas both near and far. The fibers which end here arise from that group of thalamic nuclei which have no direct connection with the periphery. They transmit impulses that have already been processed at lower levels and are related to the "intrinsic portion" of vertically arranged connections (Rose, 1950; Rose & Woolsey, 1949). Finally, it is important to note that the posterior third of the superior temporal gyrus receives fiber tracts which connect it with the anterior portion of the "speech area," Broca's area (Blinkov, 1955) and include this zone in the cortical mechanisms of articulatory processes. (See Figure 19.)

These observations make it possible to consider the superior temporal gyrus a *secondary area within the cortical part of the auditory analyzer.* In conjunction with the primary area, it is adapted to carry out the finest forms of analysis and synthesis of auditory stimulation into functionally oriented patterns.

The position we have outlined is supported

Figure 19. Connections between the temporal and inferofrontal areas. Summary diagram of arcuate bundles joining the two areas. The two ends of a given bundle are indicated by the same number appearing at the two sites where it terminates. (*A*) Connections between the temporal and inferior frontal gyrus. (*B*) Connections between the temporal lobe and precentral gyrus. *S. M. Blinkov.*

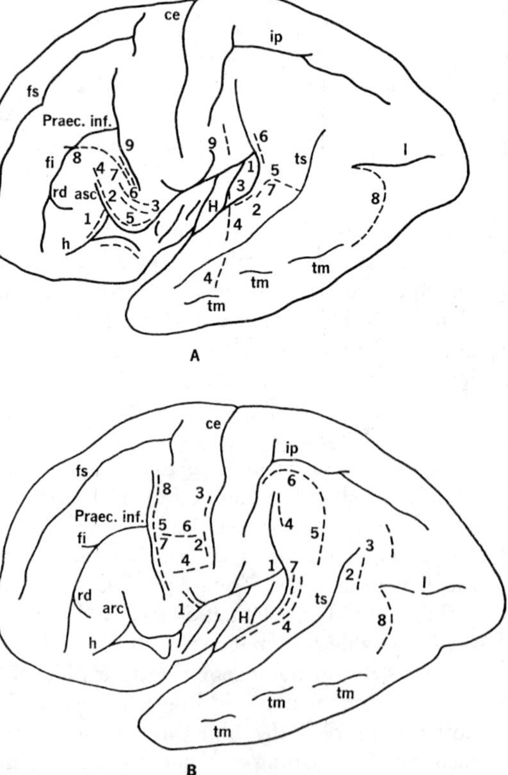

by a number of physiological investigations which have issued primarily from work of the Pavlovian school. Pavlov and his coworkers showed that ablation of the temporal area in dogs does not produce a central deafness but leads instead to severe impairment of the ability to differentiate sounds and sound complexes (Babkin, 1910; and others); as a result, it disrupts normal auditory analysis and synthesis. Similar findings were obtained by Babenkova (1954), Kabelyanskaya (1957), and Shmidt and Sukhovskaya (1954) in studies of patients with damage to superior portions of the left temporal lobe. Thus, it is well established that *while damage to the secondary cortical areas does not lead to a reduction in auditory acuity, it considerably impairs the ability to analyze and synthesize auditory stimuli.*

Other experiments indicating the functional complexity of these areas have involved direct electrical stimulation during neurosurgical operations by such investigators as Pötzl, Hoff, and, especially, Penfield. It was shown that, stimulation of points in the primary auditory area elicit only elementary auditory hallucinations, e.g., tones or noises, whereas stimulation of the secondary areas of the cortical nucleus of the auditory analyzer leads to complex auditory hallucinations, e.g., the hearing of music, words, or sentences. This fact again confirms the view that the superior temporal gyrus plays a special role in the complex functional organization of audition and leads one to expect that damage to these areas would produce important defects in this function.

Figure 19A. Hellwag's "vowel triangle."

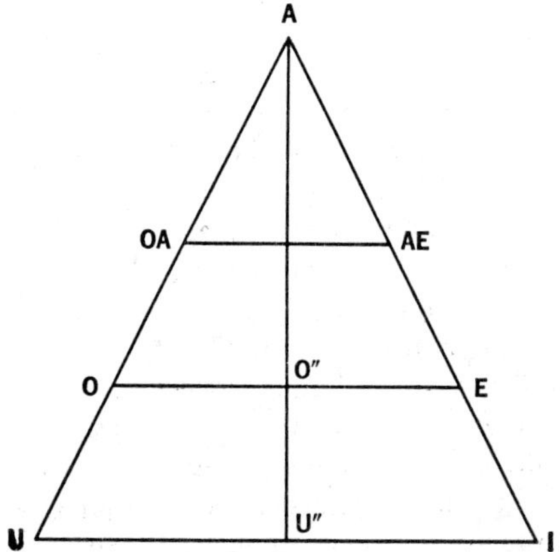

Lesions of the Auditory Speech Areas of the Cortex and Sensory Aphasia

Damage to the superior temporal gyrus of the left hemisphere, and especially a lesion located in the posterior third of that area, leads to impairment of special forms of auditory analysis and synthesis. The central feature of this disturbance is the *impairment of discriminative speech audition,* i.e., the loss of fine discrimination of the units, *phonemic groups,* of sounds and consequent loss of speech comprehension.

To describe this phenomenon and analyze its physiological mechanism, it is necessary to consider what constitutes the essential difference between speech sounds and other sounds and, thus, what distinguishes speech perception from other forms of auditory perception.

In physical terms oral speech is composed of sounds which are broadly classified as vowels and consonants. These sounds flow together in an uninterrupted stream with no specification of the points at which one sound gives way to another. Thus there is no precise boundary between the sounds *u* and *o; o* in turn merges with *a;* a soft *a* may be indistinguishable from *e; e* is easily transformed to *i,* and *i* again merges with *u* (see Hellwag's "vowel triangle," Figure 19*A*). An analogous situation holds with regard to physical characteristics of the consonants. In Russian, the hard *t* of such a word as "Tania" (name) changes to a soft *t* in such words as "tien" (shadow) or "tina" (mud); there is a similarly gradual transition from the soft *t* to *ts,* as in the word "tsirk" (circus). The sound *ts* merges with *s,* as in "Sima" (name), which in turn is easily transformed to *z,* as in "zima" (winter).

Although physically the speech sounds merge with one another in a continuous series, linguistically they are found to represent *discrete groups;* e.g., the sound *t* is sharply differentiated from the sound *"c," ts,* or the sound *d,* so that the substitution of one of these sounds for another changes the meaning of the word in which it is used. Compare, for example, "dome" and "tome" or "drain" and "train." The same can be said of the physically similar but linguistically different sounds *b* and *p* (compare, for example, "bear" and "pear" or *s* and *z* (compare "cease" and "seize").

It is characteristic of a speech sound that it possesses specific *signal* or *phonemic* attributes, alteration of any one of which changes the meaning of the word in which it appears.

In the Russian language, such cues or features include phonation (as in the distinctions between *d* and *t* or *b* and *p*) and hardness-softness (as in the difference between "mat" spelled with a hard *t* to mean "mat" or spelled with a soft *t* to signify "mother"). Another distinctive feature is accent (differentiating the words "zamók" and "zámok"—"lock" and "castle," respectively). Such features distinguish the sound units of a language which, as a result of work by Trubetskoi (1939), Jakobson (1956), and others, have come to be called "phonemes." *Thus, not only does the perception of speech sounds depend upon auditory acuity, but it is also a complex process of analysis and synthesis of the flow of sounds which constitute speech. It requires the extraction of phonemic cues, the generalization of variations on a given sound to make them categorizable as a particular phoneme, and the differentiation of acoustically similar sounds which possess different phonemic features identifying them with different phonemes.*

Different languages make use of different sets of distinctive features. Thus, in German, the length of the sound is a distinctive feature, whereas in Russian it is not (compare "Stadt" and "Staat," "Hütte" and "Hüte"). In English, there is a distinction between fricatives and nonfricatives, e.g., "wine" and "vine"; in French, there is a distinction between open and closed vowels, e.g., "le," "les," "laid," etc.; in Chinese or Vietnamese, tonality is a distinctive feature, e.g., "mā˥" (to buy) and "ma˩" (to sell), etc. In close conjunction with the articulatory process, our auditory system carries out the analysis and synthesis of speech sounds. It permits us to distinguish with utmost clarity the fine differences between phonemes of our own language but does not permit us to discriminate between the phonemes of a foreign language, and thus it prevents us from breaking down the flow of speech produced by a person speaking a language unfamiliar to us. This is why in listening to spoken Chinese or Abkhazian, *we not only fail to comprehend what is said but also fail to hear the individual sounds which are unfamiliar to us and which are derived from an entirely different phonemic system.*

What we have said above indicates that the perception of speech sounds is a process involving complex auditory analysis and synthesis and that it depends upon the phonemic system of a given language. Since this process of analysis and synthesis is carried out by structures including the secondary areas of the auditory cortex in close conjunction with the cortical articulatory structures, we know what kinds of defects to expect as a result of damage to these areas. Careful investigation of the changes which occur following damage to the anterior third of the superior temporal gyrus of the left hemisphere indicates that such an injury does not produce a loss of hearing acuity but a loss of the analysis and synthesis of complex sounds in general and of speech sounds in particular.

Soviet investigators (Babenkova, 1954; Kabelyanskaya, 1957; Shmidt & Sukhovskaya, 1954; and others) have shown that patients with such lesions easily perceive individual sounds but that it is difficult and sometimes impossible for them to react differentially to sounds, to simultaneous sound patterns, or to series of sounds which differ only in the order in which the sound components are presented. The most obvious symptom in these patients is the loss of phonemic hearing. Observations by Luria (1940; 1947) indicate that the overwhelming majority of patients with firearm injuries or tumors of the areas in question are unable to distinguish clearly between so-called "correlative" or "oppositional" phonemes, i.e., phonemes which differ from one another by a single distinctive feature. It is this feature which distinguishes the phonemes *d* and *t*, *b* and *p*, and *z* and *s*. When a patient is asked to repeat such a pair of phonemes as *ba-pa*, he may say *ba-ba*, *pa-pa*, or *pa-ba*. Similarly, such a pair as *da-ta* may be repeated *da-da*, *ta-ta*, or *ta-da*. Figure 20 gives a diagrammatic representation of the frequencies with which this type of disturbance is observed following injuries to the superoposterior portions of the left temporal area and adjacent areas. With massive lesions of the superior portion of the left temporal lobe, these disturbances may be extremely severe. The patient may even be unable to distinguish phonemes which are very different from one another, and he may become totally incapable of breaking down the speech which he hears into individual phonemes. As a result it is impossible for him to form differential conditioned reflexes to different speech sounds, especially to pairs of correlative phonemes.

It is possible for severe disturbances of phonemic hearing to be accompanied by preservation of musical perception. Thus patients

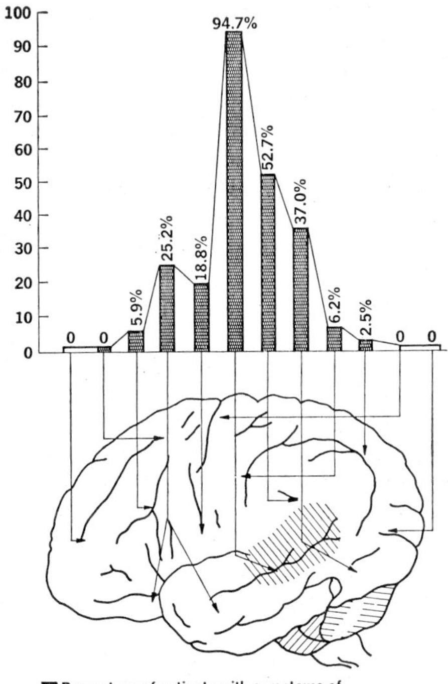

Figure 20. Disruption of phonemic hearing connected with bullet wounds in the left hemisphere. ***Luria.***

with severe forms of sensory aphasia are often able to recognize and reproduce familiar melodies. On the other hand, in a number of cases involving right hemisphere lesions or lesions of the temporal pole, one sees the syndrome of "amusia," which is not accompanied by disturbances of phonemic hearing. The dissociation of these two functions, which would appear superficially to be closely related, serves as an example of the great difference in underlying brain mechanisms of processes which psychologically appear to be essentially identical.

"Speech agnosia," or the disturbance of phonemic hearing, is consequently the primary symptom of damage to the posterosuperior portion of the left temporal lobe.

This primary disturbance gives rise to the symptoms which make up the syndrome of sensory, or auditory, aphasia. Here we shall describe only the most important symptoms of this syndrome. The patient with a disturbance of phonemic hearing not only is incapable of distinguishing different speech sounds and words but also is unable to *repeat* them. Although he may easily repeat sounds which he has heard correctly and words which can be pronounced on the basis of established motor stereotypes, e.g., "well . . ." "oh you . . ." "you see . . ." he may be unable to repeat other sounds and words which appear equally simple. He may substitute some sounds for others and be unable to differentiate individual sounds from the flow of speech; thus he may alter the order of sounds in a given word. Only by carefully following the articulation of the words he is saying, for instance, by observing the movement of his lips and tongue in a mirror or by feeling his larynx, is he able to reproduce words correctly. By substituting visual and kinesthetic cues for auditory ones, he may succeed in repeating words spoken by the examiner. Such means may compensate for his hearing defect.

It is to be expected that such a patient might be largely deprived of *spontaneous speech*. As we indicated earlier, such familiar expressions as "well . . ." "oh you . . ." "well you might say . . ." etc., which are more or less automatic and do not require auditory feedback, may be preserved in these patients so as to be uttered relatively rapidly and clearly. On the other hand, words which the patient cannot pronounce without analyzing their auditory content are impossible for him. The inability to pronounce words smoothly, especially nouns, prevents the patient from speaking normally. Characteristically, the intonational or melodious aspect of speech is preserved in these patients. Thus, even though their speech may be composed largely of simple and habitual expressions, it may be entirely comprehensible. For instance, such a patient may describe the course of his difficulty as follows: "Well, you see . . . well, it was so . . . well, from the beginning . . . and then worse . . . but now . . . I can't." It may be possible to understand such speech even though concrete nouns are few and far between, for the intonational patterns are preserved.

These patients also have difficulty in *naming objects*. The presentation of an object does not directly evoke its name; instead, it leads to a series of attempts and variations on the true pronunciation. In some cases the patient may give up and substitute an associated word or phrase for the correct name. The first type of response is referred to as a "literal aphasia"; for example, in attempting to pronounce the word "kolos" (ear of grain), the patient may say: "glos . . . glosh . . . kors . . . klos

. . . gors," etc., all of which are meaningless. The second type of response is referred to as a "verbal paraphasia" and may be represented by such a response as: "Well . . . in the field. . . ." Characteristically, *prompting* does not help these patients. Sometimes the examiner can utter almost the entire word and it does not help.

All the disturbances which we have described so far possess a common symptom, i.e., a *disturbance of word comprehension*. If, as the result of a phonemic hearing disturbance, all sounds come to be indifferentiable for the patient, he is unable to comprehend them. If sometimes "kolos" (ear of grain) sounds like "golos" (voice), other times like "koros" (meaningless), and still other times like "kholost" (bachelor), its meaning becomes very confused for him, and his comprehension becomes very unreliable. This can be demonstrated by a very simple test. The patient is asked to point out different parts of his face as they are named, for instance, "eye, nose, ear, nose, ear, eye, etc." It becomes obvious after several words have been presented that the words begin to lose their meaning; they become "alien," and the patient may repeat "nos [nose] . . . nosh . . . nozh . . . [meaningless]." Eventually he may stop and ask: "What is a nosh?" By this time he has ceased to be able to carry out the instructions. Such patients soon begin to substitute conjecture for genuine speech comprehension. They come to rely heavily upon context. In such cases one need only present questions out of context in order to reveal the loss of word meanings which has occurred.

The disturbances which are seen in these patients are not restricted to oral speech; reading and writing are also affected. *Reading* may remain relatively well preserved, but, more often than not, it is restricted to the recognition of very simple or familiar words such as USSR, USA, Moscow, etc., the patient's last name, etc. Sometimes the patient is able to recognize such words as "Black Sea," "Crimea," "London," or "Leo Tolstoy" but is unable to pronounce them and can indicate his comprehension only by describing their meanings. Any attempt to identify letters, to read nonsense syllables, or to spell out words ends in failure.

As a rule these patients have great difficulty in *writing*. Although the ability to copy written material and to write highly familiar words is often preserved, writing to dictation and spontaneous writing are very severely disturbed. The patient may try desperately to determine the sounds which are to be symbolized and yet still substitute similar sounds or write down only the most prominent syllables. It is as though he were unable to perform the preliminary auditory analysis of words, to delineate the necessary phonemes, or to preserve the correct order of sounds. As a result his writing assumes a very disorganized character. (See Figure 21.)

Whereas, contrary to P. Marie's view, these patients may retain abstract concepts, they are still unable to carry out complex intellectual functions, such as discursive thought and reasoning, because they have lost the words to represent such concepts. Words easily lose their meanings, and the continuity of the speech process which is necessary for thought cannot be maintained. Thus while patients can easily solve visual problems, such as arranging assortments of cards in proper order or solving simple constructional problems, they are unable to carry out such functions "mentally," i.e., according to a verbal plan. Such a patient may be able to carry out written calculations which do not depend upon auditory analysis, but he is severely limited in his ability to carry out calculations orally or to do them "in his head."

Thus we see that the primary disturbance in patients in this group is impairment of the *analysis and synthesis of speech sounds,* which leads secondarily to a severe disturbance of speech functions which depend in any way upon this primary function.

DISTURBANCES OF ACOUSTICO-MNESTIC PROCESSES AND THE SYNDROME OF ACOUSTICO-MNESTIC APHASIA

We have described those disturbances which arise as a result of lesions of the secondary portions of the cortical nucleus of the auditory analyzer, located in the superior portions of the left temporal area. Lesions giving rise to disturbances of higher cortical functions are not limited to these areas, however. Definite disturbances arise also with lesions of central portions of the left temporal area or with lesions involving deep portions of the temporal cortex. As a result of these lesions, one may see a so-called "acoustico-mnestic" or "transcortical sensory aphasia," which de-

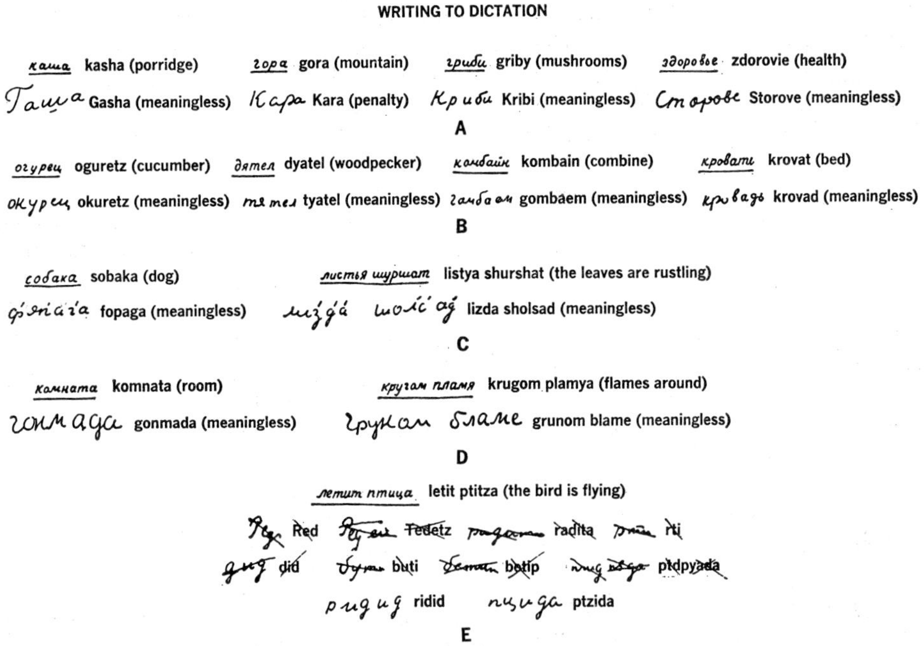

WRITING TO DICTATION

каша kasha (porridge) гора gora (mountain) грибы griby (mushrooms) здоровье zdorovie (health)

Gasha (meaningless) Kara (penalty) Kribi (meaningless) Storove (meaningless)

A

огурец oguretz (cucumber) дятел dyatel (woodpecker) комбайн kombain (combine) кровать krovat (bed)

okuretz (meaningless) tyatel (meaningless) gombaem (meaningless) krovad (meaningless)

B

собака sobaka (dog) листья шуршат listya shurshat (the leaves are rustling)

fopaga (meaningless) lizda sholsad (meaningless)

C

комната komnata (room) кругом пламя krugom plamya (flames around)

gonmada (meaningless) grunom blame (meaningless)

D

летит птица letit ptitza (the bird is flying)

Red ~~Fedetz~~ radita rti

did buti botip ptdpyada

ridid ptzida

E

Figure 21. The disturbance of writing in temporal (auditory) aphasia. (*A*) Patient Strat.: lesion of the left temporal area (seven years schooling). (*B*) Patient Os.: lesion of the left temporal area (seven years schooling). (*C, E*) Patient Pavl.: lesion of the left temporal area (ten years schooling). (*D*) Patient Zvor.: lesion of the left temporal area (seven years schooling). *Luria.*

serves special description and pathophysiological analysis.

The central portion of the temporal area comprises Brodmann's areas 22 and 37. As indicated in Figure 4, these areas are complex in structure and are partially related to the zones of overlap between the cortical portions of the auditory and visual analyzers. In these areas the associative cell layers are especially well developed, thus making possible a wide spread of excitation which is necessary for the functional integration of these two areas. Impulses reaching these areas arise from the "intrinsic portion" of the thalamus. Thus they receive information which has already been processed at lower levels.

The few physiological observations which have been made regarding the functional characteristics of this area fit well with its complex structure. Brenda Milner (1958) observed that extirpation of this area produced a severe disturbance of memory. She was inclined to explain this disturbance on the basis of the close proximity of these structures to structures directly involved in the regulation of cortical tone. Penfield reports that stimulation of this area evokes complex "scene-like hallucinations which may be visual, auditory, or mixed in character." Both these observations point to the functional complexity of this area. Especially interesting are the disturbances which arise as a result of damage to these areas and which, in contrast to those described above, still await physiological explanation.

As a rule, lesions of the central portions of the temporal lobe do not produce severe disturbances of phonemic hearing. Symptoms of the phonemic hearing syndrome may arise under conditions of fatigue or stress, but they can usually be interpreted as the result of a secondary effect on function of the superior temporal gyrus. Schmidt and his coworkers (1954) found such patients to have no difficulty in differentiating the sound stimuli which are confused by patients with lesions of superior portions of the temporal area. The ability to repeat individual words is equally well preserved in these patients. They can read and write individual letters and words. The fluent speech of these patients remains better preserved than that of patients with sensory ("acousticognostic") aphasia. Here the only signs of speech impairment may be frequent searching for words and infrequent use of nouns.

These patients suffer considerable difficulty

in *remembering word lists and in comprehending and reproducing long sentences.* The first of these symptoms is revealed by the fact that whereas the patient is easily able to repeat individual words, he may be incapable of repeating two or three words at a time. As he repeats the first word he forgets the second and third. Even though he may be able to repeat a sequence of three words immediately upon presentation, he forgets it very rapidly. After a short pause he is unable to repeat it, especially if the pause is taken up by nonrelated conversation. In a less severe case, the acousticomnestic disturbance may be seen in the fact that the patient is able to repeat a list of three, four, or even five words but is unable to preserve their order. Thus he may repeat the same group of words several times in different orders and not recognize his mistakes (Luria & Rapoport, 1962). The most severe defects are seen, however, in attempts to repeat long sentences. As a rule the reproduction of such sentences is disorganized and punctuated by perseveration and the interjection of word fragments. The weakness of auditory traces, the ease with which they are suppressed by external inhibition, and the persistence of stereotypes once established constitute the distinguishing characteristics of functional weakness in these cortical auditory areas.

Similar difficulties are encountered in the *comprehension* of words. In contrast to the syndrome described earlier, the comprehension of individual words is relatively intact in these patients. But if two or three words are presented at once, comprehension of the individual words is immediately disturbed. Thus if such a patient is asked to point out three objects which are named for him, he may point out the first but forget the names of the other two, or he may continue to repeat the names of the other two but point to inappropriate objects.

In these patients one sees similar impairment of the ability *to name objects.* It is this symptom which has given rise to the term "amnesia," or more precisely, "acoustico-mnestic aphasia." The systems of auditory and visual associations which lie back of the verbal representation of objects appear to be most severely affected here, and, as a rule, patients in this group experience difficulty in finding the names of objects. Prompting is of as little help to them as it is to patients in the previous group. This, again, indicates a pathological condition of auditory speech traces. Even in cases where the naming of familiar objects is preserved, it is usually possible to demonstrate the disturbance by asking the patient to name two or three objects at once. In this case the defect described above emerges. In producing the first word, the traces of the subsequent words may be so inhibited that it is impossible to utter them.

The physiological explanation of this syndrome remains unknown, but the defect in the auditory speech cortex which gives rise to these phenomena will undoubtedly be studied by contemporary investigators (Luria, Klimkovsky, & Sokolov, unpublished). Eventually it will be possible to explain this syndrome of acoustico-mnestic, or "transcortical sensory," aphasia in pathophysiological terms.

LESIONS OF THE POSTCENTRAL (PARIETAL) CORTEX AND SYNDROMES OF AFFERENT (KINESTHETIC) APRAXIA AND APHASIA

Having considered higher cortical functions of the postcentral (kinesthetic) area, we come to the cortical part of the sensorimotor analyzer and the syndromes which arise when it is damaged.

In early stages of evolution the sensorimotor cortex was a single structure representing both afferent (kinesthetic) and efferent (kinetic) functions. Only at a later stage, in carnivores, did this morphological unity disappear (Kuküev, 1940). In subsequent stages the sensorimotor cortex was differentiated into two groups of areas. The more posterior group, comprising fields 2, 1, 3, and 5, became the cortical part of the cutaneous and kinesthetic analyzer, while the anterior group, comprising fields 4, 6, and 8, became the cortical part of the motor (kinetic) analyzer (in the narrow sense of the term). These two groups of cortical areas continued to share a functional unity. Motor functions (in the broad sense of the term) continued to be carried out through coordinated activity of these so-called "paired centers," one of which is located in the postcentral gyrus and the other in the premotor gyrus. Since these two structures have their own functions, however, it is possible to consider the disturbances related to them separately.

Lesions of the postcentral (parietal) cortical areas have always been associated with

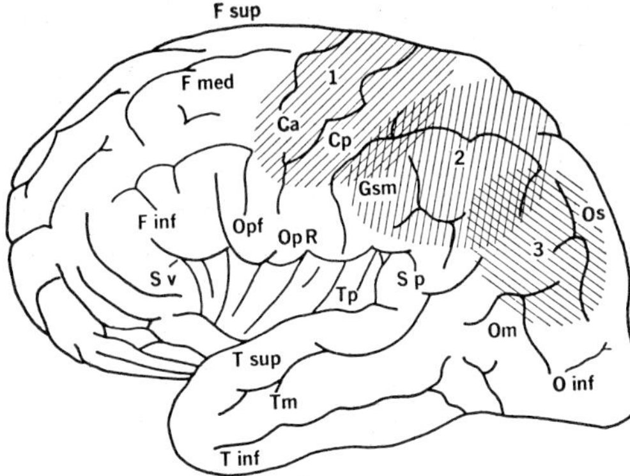

Figure 22. The localization of apraxias. (1) Motor apraxia (apraxias of individual parts; (2) ideokinetic apraxias; (3) ideational apraxias. ***Liepmann.***

both sensory and motor disturbances. A characteristic feature of both forms of disturbance is that they may occur at any level of complexity. The most simple disturbances may involve purely a loss of kinesthetic sensitivity, whereas the most complex forms of disturbance appear far removed from any form of sensory loss or simple motor loss and may be interpreted as disturbances of higher forms of gnosis or praxis.

Here we shall present a short historical account of the investigation of these two forms of disturbances. In 1883, Hofman described disturbances of tactile perception which arose following lesions of the parietal cortex. The disturbances which he described occurred with no loss of cutaneous sensitivity and came to be called "astereognosis." In 1895, Wernicke reported similar observations indicating that lesions of the parietal cortex may prevent tactile recognition of objects. He suggested that this defect was related to a loss of "tactile images." Pointing out that these disturbances involved no defect whatsoever of primary sensitivity, he divided them into "primary" and "secondary" tactile agnosias. The primary group of disturbances resulted from a loss of tactile images; the second group was related to the phenomenon of "asymbolia," in which tactile images are preserved but cease to be associated with the visual representation of objects. The "mental" disturbance supposed to underlie tactile agnosia was thus contrasted with the "cortical" sensory disturbances. As might be expected, this dualist approach did not result in physiological explanations of the phenomena observed.

The study of apraxias arose considerably later than the study of agnosias and aphasias, but once initiated, it followed much the same path of development. In 1900, Liepmann described a case of loss of control of movement and set forth the idea that the basic loss was a disturbance of internal motor schemata or of the structural representations of motor acts. The absence of any signs of paresis or dystonia led him to consider this a disturbance of a "higher order." He equated it with a group of disturbances which Finkelburg (1870) had designated as asymbolic defects and with disturbances which had been interpreted by Meynert (1867–1868) as motor asymbolia.

Distinguishing the two stages in the performance of a motor act, "intention" and "execution," Liepmann described two correspondingly different forms of apraxia: "ideational apraxia," a disturbance of the image of the desired act, and "motor apraxia," a defect in the paths by which it is carried out. He further divided the motor apraxias into two subgroups: "ideokinetic apraxias," involving dissociation of the images of movements from their corresponding innervational patterns, and "acrokinetic apraxias" (*Gliedkynetische Apraxie*), involving the abbreviated engrams which underlie the movements of different organs. Although he described in detail the localization of lesions producing these forms of apraxia (Figure 22), Liepmann's interpretation was couched in subjective and psychological terms. By dissociating apraxia from the more elementary phenomena of paresis, ataxia, and dystonia, he was unable to analyze it from a pathophysiological point of view. A similar position was taken by Kleist (1907; 1908; 1909; 1911; 1935), who made an even more detailed study of the different forms of apraxia. Though these authors contributed detailed descriptions of the clinical syndromes, their tendency to consider tactile agnosia and apraxia apart from more elementary sensorimotor disturbances and to omit attempts at physiological analysis eventually led them into some degree of difficulty. Although their clinical observations have not been challenged even to the present day, a number of authors over the years have maintained that tactile agnosia cannot be considered apart from more elementary forms of sensory deficit and that apraxia cannot be altogether dissociated from more elementary motor disturbances. Thus Dejérine (1914) noted that "pure tactile agnosia does not exist" and declared that underlying every case of tactile agnosia there are concealed other, more elementary sensory defects. He maintained that in many cases these complex "mental forms of disturbance" could be reduced to much more elementary forms of disturbance. The same kind of reaction to the dualistic conception of apraxia was expressed by v. Monakov (1914), who formulated the position that only a complete re-evaluation of the relationship between apraxia and more elementary motor disturbances would make possible a physiological analysis of apraxia and permit an understanding of its underlying mechanisms.

More recent investigations have been concerned with relating the phenomena of tactile agnosia with more elementary sensory disturbances, and the phenomena of apraxia with more elementary motor disturbances. Thus Stein and Weizsäcker (1926) and later Bay (1944) suggested that tactile agnosia arises from a fluctuating sensitivity and a disturbance of sensory adaptation. Similarly, Brun (1921), Sittig (1931), Meier-Gross (1936), Denny-Brown (1958), and others have attempted to analyze the apraxias in terms of more elementary motor disturbances. Such studies have pointed up the shortcomings of earlier concepts regarding the disturbances of higher cortical functions which arise following lesions of the parietal areas and have indicated the path to be followed in further investigations.

Clinical neurologists have noted the important fact that disturbances of tactile recognition and the voluntary control of movements may arise without apparent signs of dystonia or ataxia. According to classical neurology, these disturbances most commonly arise following lesions of the parietal area of the cortex and take different forms, depending on the site of the lesion within that area. The establishment of this fact in itself constituted a great contribution to clinical neurology. But, while the clinical pictures were described with great accuracy, their physiological mechanisms remained unclear, and the complete dissociation of some of them from more elementary forms of motor disturbance was of doubtful value. For this reason great attention should be given to the possibility of interpreting these disturbances in light of our present-day knowledge, especially as regards the fine anatomical structure of the postcentral cortex and the physiological functions of the motor analyzer.

Structure and Functional Organization of the Postcentral Cortex

As we indicated above, the postcentral cortex may be considered the cortical part of the cutaneous-kinesthetic analyzer, which in latest stages of evolution has differentiated out of the combined sensorimotor cortex. In man it represents an independent anatomical structure, but it retains its functional unity with the anterior portion of the sensorimotor area. It was first shown by Betz that this area, Brodmann's areas 3, 1, 2, and 5, differs from the primary motor area by its granular structure. In addition to this, the primary areas of this zone, Brodmann's areas 3 and 1, possess a well-developed fourth afferent cell layer. This area is similar to the primary extrinsic areas of the cortical part of the other analyzers in that they also possess a clear somatotopic organization. They differ from the primary areas of the visual and auditory analyzers, however, in that here the principle of one-to-one "geometrical" projection gives way to the principle of functional representation; i.e., the greater the functional significance of a given area or organ, the greater its area of representation in the primary cortical projection area. Thus, experiments involving direct electrical stimulation of this cortical area carried out by Penfield and Rasmussen (1950) have shown that sensations of touch to the face, lips, and thumb and index finger of the hand are elicited by stimulation of a considerably greater cortical area than sensations in the trunk, lower leg, etc. (Figure 23). Adjacent to the primary projection areas of the kinesthetic analyzer lie secondary areas (areas 2, 5, and 7), in which the superficial associative layers predominate. Here end fibers arising from the secondary, "intrinsic" nuclei of the thalamus (Pribram, 1959; Rose, 1950). The inferior parietal cortex (areas 40 and 39) is made up of the zones of overlap of cortical portions of the cutaneous-kinesthetic and visual analyzers. These areas are seen only in man and constitute one of the most complex and most specifically human structures of the cerebral cortex. Their cytoarchitecture is represented graphically in Figure 4. Both histological studies and certain clinical information to which we shall turn attention below clearly implicate the postcentral cortical areas in the

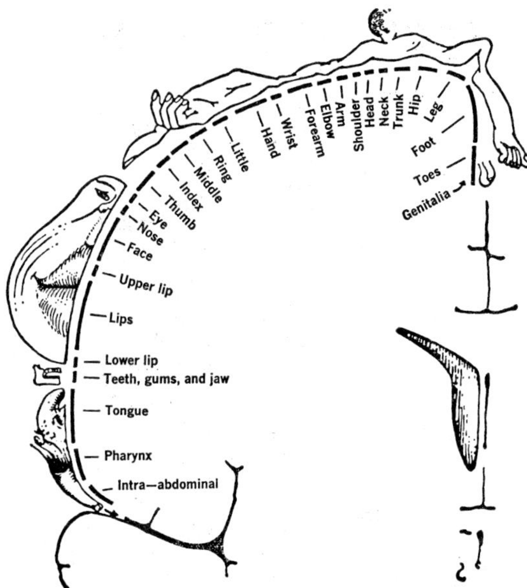

Figure 23. Representation of sensory areas in the cerebral cortex. *Penfield.*

analysis of signals received by cutaneous and kinesthetic sensory pathways.

The cytoarchitectonic findings constitute only one aspect of the study of these cortical areas. A second aspect is their intimate association with the motor areas of the cortex, which has been noted by a number of authors. Thus Lassek (1954) showed that only 40 per cent of the fibers in the pyramidal pathway originate in the precentral gyrus, while 10 to 20 per cent arise from the postcentral cortical areas. McCulloch (1943) showed that strychninization of postcentral cortical areas gives rise to excitation which can affect the motor area (Figure 24). Penfield and Rasmussen (1950), by stimulating the postcentral cortex of patients undergoing brain surgery, produced movements clearly indicating the close relationship of these areas to the cortical motor mechanisms (Figure 25). Finally, experiments on animals and observations of human patients have shown that this area of the cortex is important for discrimination based upon deep pressure sensitivity. Extirpation of these areas (Ruch, 1935) abolishes the ability to make weight discriminations.

All these findings indicate the postcentral cortical area to be the cortical part of the kinesthetic analyzer. It plays an important role in providing the kinesthetic basis of motor activity; thus we have every reason to expect that damage to this area will lead to significant changes in movement.

Lesions of the Postcentral Cortical Areas and the Syndrome of Tactile Agnosia

The study of disturbances arising as a result of lesions to the postcentral (parietal) cortical areas has usually taken one of two directions: the study of tactile agnosia or the study of apraxia. As a rule, these two features have been studied separately, but they have every reason to be considered closely related to one

Figure 24. Neuronographic experiments involving stimulation of the postcentral and precentral cortical areas. The diagram and accompanying table indicate how far excitation spreads following strychnine stimulation at various sites in the cortex of the chimpanzee. Areas 6, 4, 3, 1, 5, and 7 are portions of the sensorimotor cortex. The shaded areas constitute the so-called "suppressor areas." *McCulloch.*

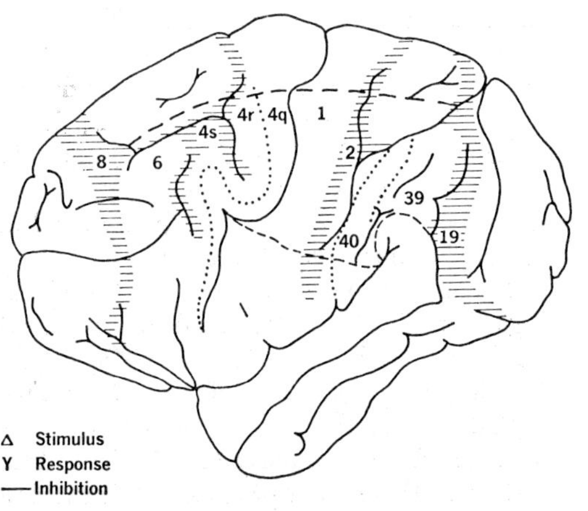

8	6	4s	4r	4q	1	2	5	40	39	19
Y Δ	—	—	—	—	—	—	—	—	—	—
Y	Y Δ	Y	Y	Y	Y	•	Y		Y	
—	—	Y Δ	—	—	—	—	—	—	—	—
		Y	Y Δ	Y						
				Y Δ	Y		Y			
		Y	Y	Y	Y Δ	•	Y		Y	
—	—	—	—	—	—	Y Δ	—	—	—	—
				Y	Y	? Y	Y Δ			
			Y		Y		? Y	Y Δ		
		Y						? Y	Y Δ	Y
—	—	—	—	—	—	—	—	—	—	Δ Y

another. In accordance with neurological tradition, we shall consider them separately, keeping in mind, however, the very close bond which unites them.

It is well known that lesions of the postcentral cortical area disturb primarily superficial (cutaneous) and deep (kinesthetic) sensitivity. In cases involving damage to the primary (and partially to the secondary) fields of the cortical part of the cutaneous-kinesthetic analyzer, the functional disturbances manifest themselves in the contralateral parts of the body. They may involve either total or partial loss of these forms of sensation. A loss may be limited to the part of the body represented in the damaged area. The disturbance is of an entirely different character, however, if the lesion is located more posteriorly so as to involve the secondary areas of the cutaneous-kinesthetic analyzer and adjacent zones of overlap, which are concerned with both the cutaneous-kinesthetic and the visual analyzers. In this case the disturbance of superficial and deep sensitivity may be so mild that it may be considered insignificant. Against a background of what would appear to be completely intact sensory function, one sees the fundamental symptom of this disturbance which has been called "tactile agnosia" or "astereognosis." The patient easily responds to pinpricks, and muscle and joint sensations are relatively well preserved. But he shows *noticeable difficulty in the tacticle recognition of objects.* The attempt to recognize objects by touch loses its systematic character in such a patient. It becomes difficult for him to synthesize the individual tactile cues, and he has difficulty in picking out the most important features of the object. As a result he gives very fragmentary and often erroneous guesses as to what the object might be. Visual perception of objects remains intact, so that the patient is still capable of recognizing objects at a single glance. Tactile agnosias are like the visual agnosias in that they may be broken down into two forms. In one form—primary tactile agnosia, or "Wernicke's agnosia"—the source of difficulty lies in synthesizing tactile cues and thus in the "primary identification of objects." In the other form—secondary tactile agnosia, or asymbolia—the synthesis of tactile cues remains intact, but the visual evaluation of tactile cues is difficult. There is reason to believe that the first form of tactile agnosia is produced by lesions located closer to the secondary areas of the cortical nucleus of the cutaneous-kinesthetic analyzer (Figure 26). The second form of disturbance, on the other hand, is usually associated with lesions located more posteriorly and involving the zones of overlap of the cortical parts of the cutaneous-kinesthetic and visual analyzers. Despite the fact that tactile agnosia and astereognosis have been well described in the literature, their underlying mechanisms remain far from clear. Some investigators (Wernicke, 1895) have felt it possible to dissociate these disturbances from sensory deficits and to consider them as a group of asymbolias. Other authors (Dejérine, 1914; Bay, 1944) feel that the tactile agnosias arise from fine sensory disturbances (fluctuating sensory thresholds, defects in fine tactile discrimination, etc.) and that there exists a strict parallelism between the degree of these primary disturbances and the severity of the tactile agnosia.

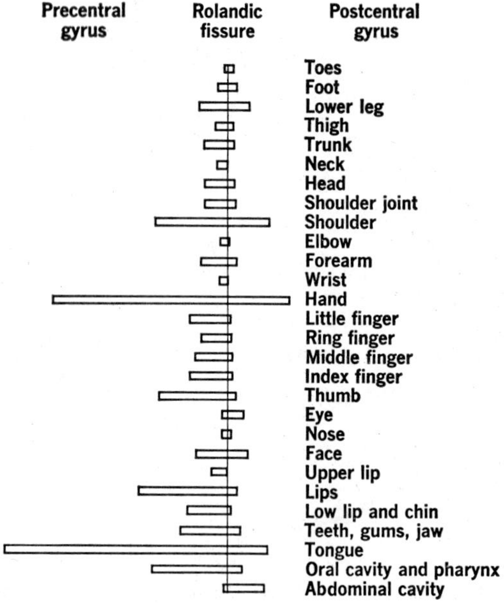

Figure 25. Motor reactions with stimulation of the precentral and postcentral cortical areas. ***Adapted from Penfield & Rasmussen,*** **The Cerebral Cortex of Man,** ***by T. L. Peele in*** **The Neuroanatomic Basis for Clinical Neurology, 1961.** ***McGraw-Hill Book Company. Used by permission.***

It is reasonable to assume that the physiological mechanisms of these disturbances will be discovered by investigation of the ways in which this special form of *analytic-synthetic activity* is disturbed when postcentral cortical areas are damaged. Delay (1935) showed that lesions in these areas produce not so much an

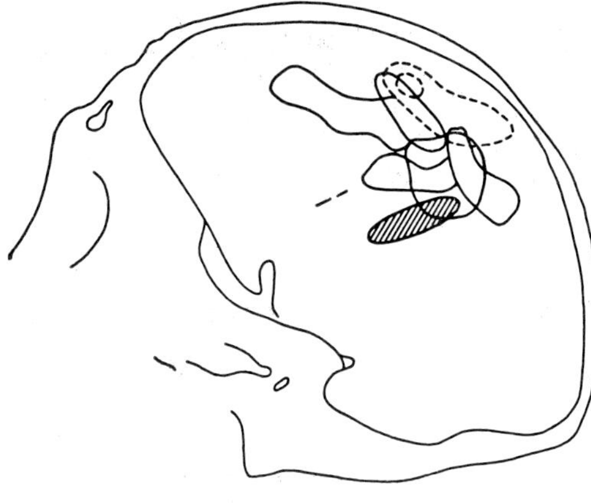

——— Localization of lesions related to astereognosis involving the hand (Bay)

------ Localization of lesions leading to astereognosis involving the hand (Hecaen and David)

▨ Localization of lesions related to astereognosis involving the hand (Gross and Weiser)

Figure 26. The localization of lesions giving rise to tactile agnosia. ***Ajuziagerra and Hécaen.***

absolute reduction of tactile and kinesthetic sensitivity as a disturbance of the analysis and synthesis of tactile and kinesthetic stimuli. As a result these patients cannot utilize the cues which are ordinarily picked up by manipulation and touch, e.g., weight and spatial relationships. It is clear that a functional weakness of cells within the damaged cortical nucleus of the tactile analyzer and adjacent zones should prevent the weaving of tactile cues into comprehensive patterns. Different points within these areas come to inhibit each other, so that, according to Pavlov's conceptions, the defective cortex "is only able to deal with one site of excitation at a time." Other sites remain "effectively nonexistent," and the synthesis of tactile excitations becomes impossible.

It is also understandable that these disturbances should influence the sequence of motions a patient goes through in examining objects by touch. Such activity is the motor expression of the processes by which tactile images are synthesized and is the means by which tactile images are made more precise. Disturbances of this complex form of reflex activity lead to symptoms of tactile agnosia, for, as Sechenov first pointed out, it involves the interaction of tactile-kinesthetic as well as motor factors. Sometimes one sees direct evidence of the disturbance of tactile synthesis; other times there are more complex disturbances involving a dissociation of tactile and visual engrams, so that objects which are not recognizable by touch are still recognized visually.

Lesions of the Postcentral Cortex and the Syndrome of Afferent (Kinesthetic) Apraxia

Consideration of tactile agnosia leads us directly to an analysis of the *motor* disturbances which arise following lesions of the postcentral (parietal) cortical areas. As we indicated above, Liepmann employed the word "apraxia" to indicate that lesions of the postcentral (parietal) cortical areas may impair the control of limb movements, even though there may be no weakness or loss of muscle tone.

Clinical investigations have, indeed, shown that damage to the postcentral cortical areas produces disturbances of the voluntary control of complex movements and that these disturbances are associated with defective *kinesthetic feedback from the motor acts.* As early as 1935, Bernstein (1935; 1947) pointed out that the control of precise movement depends upon constant feedback of impulses from the extremity to the cerebral cortex. These impulses carry information regarding changes in muscular tension and the position of the limb in space; they are a necessary condition for the execution of planned motor activity.

Experimental investigations have shown that it is precisely this constant kinesthetic feedback which is disturbed by lesions of the cortical portions of the kinesthetic analyzer. As a result of such disturbances, impulses are no longer channeled to the appropriate groups of muscles. Inappropriate muscle groups are innervated, and the selective character of the motor act is lost. Figure 27 presents electromyograms recorded from the flexor and extensor muscles of the hands of normal subjects and of patients with lesions of the postcentral portions of the left hemisphere. This figure illustrates the loss of the selectivity of motor impulses which arises following damage to this area. In this case the damage resulted from a meningioma. The disturbance of selective kinesthetic afferentation which leads to the loss of fine motor activity underlies that form of apraxia which Liepmann designated "motor apraxia" but which is more properly referred to as "afferent" or "kinesthetic apraxia."

Very severe lesions of the postcentral area lead to a characteristic form of disturbance

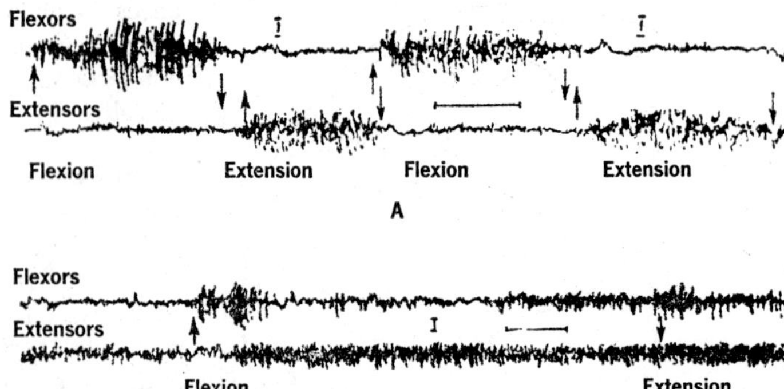

Figure 27. (*A*) Normal subject. (*B*) Changes in the electromyogram of hand flexing appearing with lesions of the postcentral cortical areas. *I. Zambran.*

which Foerster (1936) referred to as "afferent paresis." Although the patient retains strength in his muscles, he is unable to carry out movements because impulses are channeled simultaneously to both agonist and antagonist muscle groups. Since both groups of muscles are contracted simultaneously, no movement results. In less severe cases, the defect may consist in an inability to place the hand in a desired position or to accomplish the selective innervation of fine muscle groups so as to produce a desired act of manipulation. The patient with this type of disturbance attempts to pick up a needle with the same movements by which he grasps large objects. He exhibits the syndrome of "spade hand" described by Foerster (1936). Figure 28 illustrates the kind of disturbances of differentiated movements which are characteristic of patients with afferent (kinesthetic) apraxia. Similar disturbances in the execution of movements are revealed by asking the patient with a lesion of the postcentral area to close his eyes and place his hand in a given position, for instance, to extend the second and third fingers or to flex the third and fourth fingers and extend the second and fifth to form "horns." Such movements are impaired because the impulses generated lose their selectivity, are channeled to inappropriate muscle groups, and prevent the patient from placing his hand in the desired position.

These kinds of disturbance emerge most clearly in cases involving lesions of the postcentral areas of the left (dominant) hemisphere. In these cases both the contralateral (right) and ipsilateral (left) limbs may be involved. If a lesion of the left hemisphere is located in the lower portions of the postcentral area, it may produce analogous disturbances of oral movements. Patients with such lesions may be unable to control movements of the lips or tongue either in response to instructions or by imitation. They are unable to produce symbolic movements such as kissing, spitting, or whistling. Such movements, which were previously easy for the patient to carry out, become impossible due to the "apraxia of pose" which results from his cortical lesion.

The disturbances which were described by Liepmann as "ideational" apraxias and which arise primarily as a result of lesions in the zones of overlap between the kinesthetic and visual analyzers are more complex than those which we have just described. They frequently involve both visuokinesthetic disturbances and the spatial apraxia which was described above.

Disturbance of the Kinesthetic Basis of Speech and the Syndrome of Afferent (Kinesthetic) Motor Aphasia

The disturbance of fine oral movements is associated with a loss of precise kinesthetic feedback. Thus, we come to a discussion of the form of motor aphasia which arises following lesions of inferior portions of the post-central area and which is appropriately referred to as "afferent-kinesthetic motor aphasia." Early in the study of aphasia, Broca (1861) pointed out that a lesion of the posterior portion of the third frontal gyrus of the left hemisphere produced an inability to articulate words. He believed that the underlying defect was a "loss of the ability to express words by means of the coordinated movements which had been established and maintained by long practice."

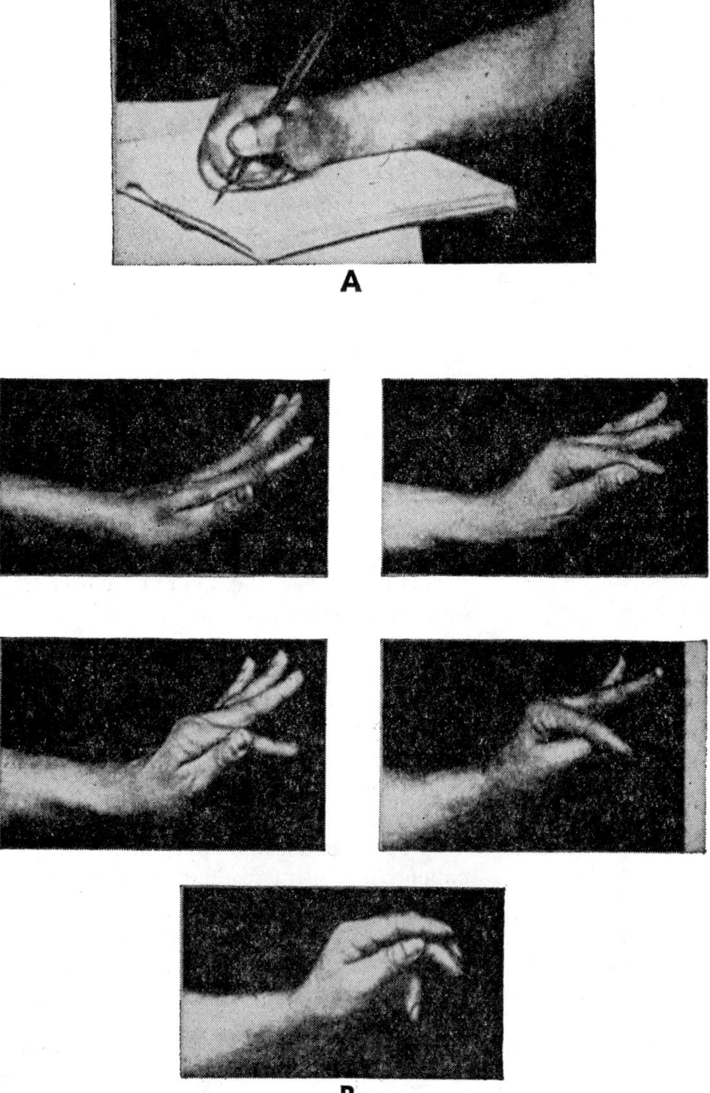

Figure 28. The disturbance of differentiated hand movements in patients with lesions of the postcentral cortical areas. (*A*) Impairment of fine writing movements. (*B*) Signs of static ataxia with a lesion of the postcentral area. *Foerster.*

Subsequent investigation showed, however, that even in the cases described by Broca himself, damage was not limited to the area that he described. It extended considerably further back to involve inferior portions of the postcentral area (operculum rolandi) as well. Detailed studies carried out by Liepmann (1913), Nissl von Meyendorf (1930), and others indicated that a lesion in this area could produce a characteristic *apraxia of the speech apparatus* and a motor aphasia based upon disturbance of the kinesthetic aspect of articulation. As we pointed out above, the articulation of speech sounds requires the precise differentation of the phonemes which constitute the basis of auditory speech. Auditory analysis and synthesis are clearly not all that is required, however. The articulation of speech sounds requires the recoding of phonemes into precise movements of the articulatory apparatus. The theory of phonemic articulation has been worked out in recent years by

R. Jakobson (1942; 1956) and others. It distinguishes groups of sounds on the basis of whether they are articulated quite differently (labials, anteropalatine-linguals, posterior linguals, etc.) or similarly to one another (differing by a single distinctive feature). The latter group includes such sounds as the labials *m, p,* and *b* or the anteropalatine linguals *l, n, t,* and *d.* The pronunciation of these sounds, of course, requires extremely fine differentiation of oral movements which can be made only on the basis of intact kinesthetic feedback. Thus it is understandable that lesions of the lower portions of the left postcentral area should affect speech. The ability to make fine articulatory differentiations disappears, and the precise articulation of speech sounds becomes impossible.

In addition to impairing the articulation of individual phonemes, loss of the kinesthetic basis of articulation may give rise to the full syndrome of afferent motor aphasia. In severe cases, patients are unable to articulate even the most basic and easily differentiable sounds. They are unable to categorize sounds, and, to the extent that articulation participates in the sharpening of phonemic auditory discrimination, one may observe *quasisensory* disturbances of auditory and speech perception.

In less severe cases, the disturbance takes more subtle forms, and the patient demonstrates an inability to differentiate between sounds which are similar in pronunciation, even though they may sound quite different from one another. Thus he may confuse the articulemes *l, n,* and *d* or *m* and *p.* These disturbances are seen in both the *spontaneous* and the *imitative* speech of the patient. The fact that in this form of aphasia the ability to differentiate and accurately repeat speech sounds suffers more than the spontaneous pronunciation of words (which does not demand such precise auditory-articulatory analysis) provides the basis for classifying it according to older terminology as "conduction aphasia."

These patients show similar defects in the *naming* of objects, but here again the primary articulatory difficulties are no more severe than in imitative speech. The clearest signs of afferent-kinesthetic motor aphasia emerge in the patient's *writing.* As a rule, the major difficulties arise in the formation of individual letters, and the patient who may be perfectly able to perceive the number of letters making up a word is usually unable to categorize the sounds and either leaves out certain letters or substitutes their "homorgans." Such substitutions as *l* or *d* or *n* or *b* for *m* constitute a distinguishing characteristic of the writing of such patients. In Figure 29 we present examples of the writing of patients with afferent (kinesthetic) motor aphasia.

The *reading* of these patients is disturbed in a similar manner. It is commonly interupted by pronunciation difficulties. Thus such patients find silent reading (or recognition of words) is preserved better.

Characteristically, these patients are able to recover their speech by substituting visual analysis of oral movements for the defective

Figure 29. Writing disturbances with afferent motor aphasia. (A) Patient Gur.: lesion of the left parietal area (seven years schooling). (B) Patient Vas.: lesion of the left parietal area (seven years schooling). (C) Patient Lev.: lesion of the left parietotemporal area (seven years schooling).

WRITING TO DICTATION

м m — л l — халат khalat (smock) — большой bolshoi (big)

л l — н n — ханат khanat (meaningless) — боньшой bonishoi (meaningless)

хадат khadat (meaningless) — боньш bonish (meaningless)

A

вагон vagod (coach) — стол stol (table) — парта parta (desk)

Вагосу Vagosu (meaningless) — слон slon (elephant) — парна parna (meaningless)

слол slol (meaningless)

B

стол stol (table) — слон slon (elephant) — палата palata (chamber)

стот stot (meaningless) — снот snot (meaningless) — патата patata (meaningless)

C

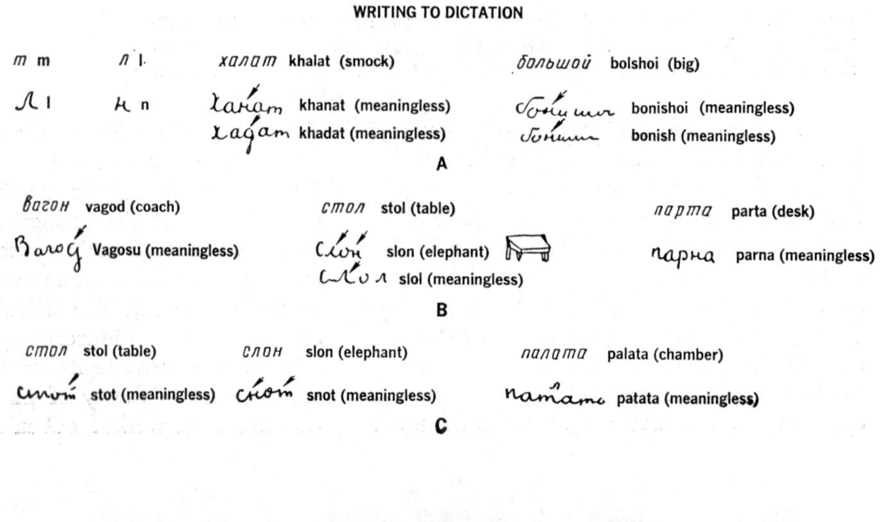

DICTATED		WRITING WITHOUT VISUAL CONTROL OF ARTICULATION		WRITING WITH VISUAL CONTROL OF ARTICULATION, I.E., WITH MIRROR	
муха	mookha (flour)	му а	mua	муха	mookha
оса	osa (wasp)	н	n	оса	osa
сани	sani (sleigh)	сао	sao	сани	sani
ус	us (mustache)	с	s	ус	us
шум	shum (noise)	д... уа	d . . . ua	шум	shum
мост	most (bridge)	о *(отказ)*	o (gives up)	мост	most

Figure 30. Changes in the writing of a patient with afferent motor aphasia with visual analysis of oral position. Patient Nas.: lesion of the left postcentral area; afferent motor aphasia.

kinesthetic feedback. Sometimes one need only provide such a patient with a mirror by which to observe his articulatory movements or diagrams of the articulatory positions to produce a great improvement in his speech and writing. Figure 30 shows an example of the change in writing which may occur when he begins to observe his own articulatory movements in a mirror.

LESIONS OF THE PREMOTOR CORTEX AND THE SYNDROMES OF EFFERENT (KINETIC) APRAXIA AND APHASIA

In describing how motor function is impaired when its afferent (kinesthetic) component is disturbed, we have considered one of the disturbances of voluntary activity which gives rise to inappropriate channeling of motor impulses and disruption of the schemata of movements. There is, however, another aspect of the motor act, namely, the *execution of successive motor units in time.* Any complex movement consists of a chain of individual motor units, each of which must be inhibited (denervated) before the succeeding unit can be executed. In the early stages of habit formation, this process of transition from one link in the motor act to the next requires individual isolated impulses. At later stages it becomes automatic and is governed by a complex pattern of impulses. With time the movement comes to be executed as a single motor sterotype or smooth "kinetic melody."

One of the most significant contributions to neurology has been establishment of the fact that the transformation of a sequence of distinct motor units into a smooth kinetic melody involves cortical zones other than the postcentral areas described above. It has become quite clear that, in addition to the posterior afferent (kinesthetic) cortical centers, we must consider the *anterior efferent* (*kinetic*) *areas* part of the motor analyzer.

Relatively little careful clinical investigation has been done regarding the syndrome which arises as a result of damage to the premotor cortical areas. In 1907, Kleist observed that lesions of the anterior cortical areas gave rise to a characteristic impairment of sequential movements and that the smooth kinetic melody gave way to a series of individual isolated motions. Similar disturbances of skilled activity following damage to the anterior cortical areas were described by Sittig (1931). The first demonstration of the role of the premotor cortical areas in the organization of sequential activity came from the investigations of Fulton (1937), who confirmed the conception of premotor function set forth earlier by Sechenov (Sechenov distinguished two types of synthesis: the synthesis of simultaneous *groups* and the synthesis of sequential *series*). The clinical investigation of disturbances arising as the result of local damage to the premotor cortex has been given detailed attention by Soviet investigators (Luria, 1943, published in Luria, 1963; Luria, 1947; Luria, 1948; Shkolnik-Yarros, 1945; and others).

Structure and Functional Organization of the Premoter Cortex

The premotor zone constitutes a portion of the cortical part of the motor analyzer (in its narrow sense). As we indicated earlier, the sensorimotor cortex in lower mammals is a morphological as well as a functional unit, whereas in man the processes of motor analysis and synthesis are carried out by the coordinated activity of the posterior kinesthetic areas and anterior motor areas. The anterior motor areas differ sharply from the posterior kinesthetic areas even in early stages of ontogenesis; they possess a characteristic cytoarchitecture (Polyakov, 1938–1948) and show a predominance of pyramidal cells.

The primary portion of the cortical nucleus of the motor analyzer is the pyramidal field (Brodmann's area 4), characterized by a well-developed fifth efferent layer which contains the giant Betz pyramidal cells and by a definite somatotopic representation. The work of a number of investigators has shown that the somatotopic character of this area is similar to that of the postcentral area in that the size of the area representing a given structure is proportional to its functional significance. The greater the control a given structure requires, the greater its representation in area 4 (Figure 31). Thus, it is possible to consider this portion of the cortex the *primary projection area of the cortical nucleus of the motor analyzer*.

Superimposed upon this projection area are *secondary areas* of the cortical nucleus of the motor analyzer (Brodmann's areas 6 and 8). These areas make up the *premotor zone* and differ from the primary area by predominance of the superficial association cell layers (the second and third layers). They also differ by their closer connection with the basal ganglia and with the thalamus. The thalamocortical tracts entering the premotor area arise from the "intrinsic" nuclei of the thalamus. These nuclei also receive fibers from the premotor area; they have no direct connection with the periphery and transmit to the cortex information which has already been processed at lower subcortical levels (Figure 32).

The neurophysiological nature of the premotor zone corresponds to its anatomical characteristics. Studies by McCulloch (1943) showed that whereas strychnine-induced excitation in area 4 does not spread very far, excitation induced by strychnine in the premotor area may be traced to adjacent areas and even to areas relatively distant from the site of application (Figure 24).

On the basis of the above it is understandable that the premotor cortical area should possess certain functional characteristics which distinguish it from the primary portion of the cortical nucleus of the motor analyzer. Whereas direct electrical stimulation of area 4 evokes only a response in the muscle groups corresponding to the site stimulated, focal

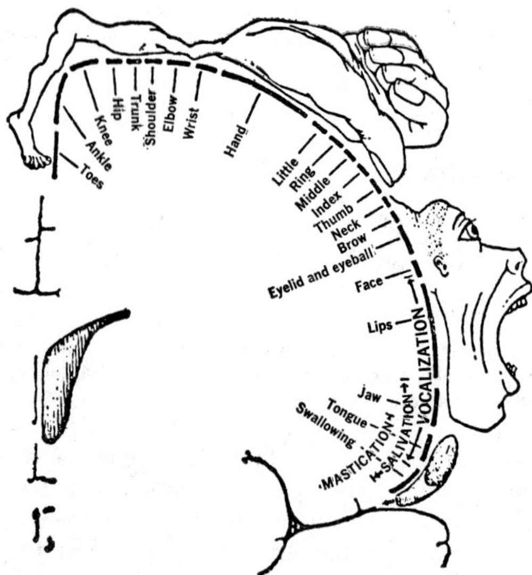

Figure 31. Representation of motor areas in the cerebral cortex. *Penfield.*

stimulation of the premotor cortical area evokes complex movements such as turning of the head and eyes to the contralateral side and grasping movements of the hand (Fulton, 1935; Wyss & Ombrador, 1937; and others). These same complex movements constitute the motor aura of so-called "adversive" epileptic seizures which sometimes arise as the result of pathological foci located in the premotor areas.

All these findings force us to conclude that the premotor area takes part in the analysis and synthesis of movements. It forms an essential secondary component of the cortical part of the motor analyzer and combines the somatotopic projection of muscle groups into functional patterns.

Lesions of the Premotor Cortex and the Syndrome of Dynamic Apraxia

Those characteristics of the premotor cortical area which we have described above make it possible to understand the disturbances of motor processes which arise as a result of lesions in this area. Fulton (1937) showed that extirpation of the premotor area in monkeys did not produce a severe paralysis but greatly impaired the ability of animals to make skilled movements. Similar data were obtained by Foerster (1936) and Kleist (1934), who examined cases of premotor lesions in humans. These authors found no signs of paresis or of apraxia described by Liepmann. Instead they found that the control of fine movements

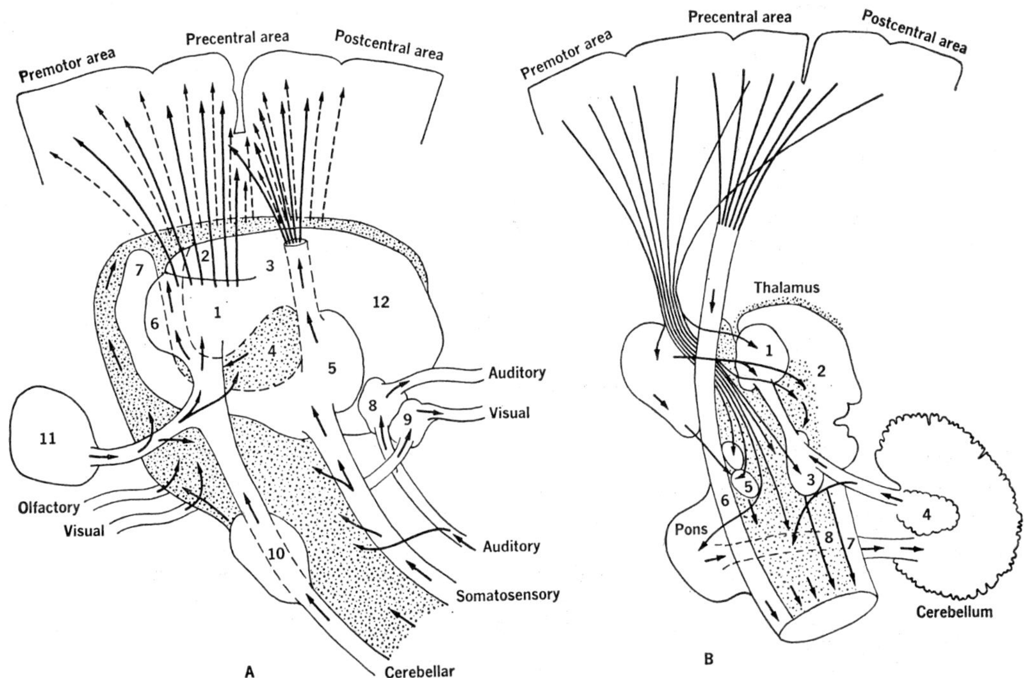

Figure 32. Subcortical connections of the sensorimotor and premotor cortical areas. (*A*) Afferent pathways. (1) Ventrolateral thalamic nucleus; (2) anterolateral nucleus; (3) posterolateral nucleus; (4) centrum medianum; (5) ventroposterior nucleus; (6) ventroanterior nucleus; (7) anterior nucleus; (8) medial geniculate; (9) lateral geniculate; (10) red nucleus; (11) corpus striatum; (12) pulvinar. Dotted area represents reticular formation. (*B*) Efferent pathways. (1) Ventrolateral nucleus; (2) centrum medianum; (3) red nucleus; (4) dentate nucleus; (5) substantia nigra; (6) direct corticobulbospinal pathway; (7) tectospinal pathway; (8) rubrospinal pathway. Dotted area represents reticular formation. *Adapted from Penfield & Rasmussen,* The Cerebral Cortex of Man, *by T. L. Peele in* The Neuroanatomic Basis for Clinical Neurology, 1961. *McGraw-Hill Book Company. Used by permission.*

was disturbed, that kinetic melodies were disrupted.

Data accumulated in recent decades (Luria, 1943; Luria, 1947; Luria, 1948; Shkolnik-Yarros, 1951; and others) have made it possible to describe the syndrome arising as a result of premotor area lesions in considerable detail. These observations have indicated that lesions of the premotor area (especially of the dominant, left hemisphere) produce neither severe paretic disturbances nor the inappropriate channeling of motor impulses which are characteristic of lesions of the postcentral cortical areas. Thus they do not produce the symptoms described above as characteristic of postural apraxia. The primary change observed in these cases is *loss of the continuity of movement,* of the smooth transition from one link in the kinetic chain to another, and a loss of complex motor habits. In view of this, the premotor syndrome might be appropriately referred to as a "dynamic apraxia."

The premotor syndrome in its earliest stages of development, for instance, that arising as a result of a small slowly expanding tumor, is characterized by complaints of the loss of skilled movements. Highly skilled voluntary movements are lost, and individual movements once initiated are extremely persistent, so that the transition from one motion to another requires a special effort. A patient may complain of a change in his handwriting, a typist may note a "loss of smoothness," or a musician may complain that he has "lost his touch."

As the premotor syndrome becomes more severe, the patient may be unable to reproduce rhythms. His attempts to tap out a given rhythm may be interrupted by long pauses or by the insertion of superfluous taps which are difficult to inhibit. He is unable to carry out tasks involving "reciprocal coordination"; for instance, beginning with one hand pronated and the other hand clenched in a fist, the patient is instructed to reverse the positions of

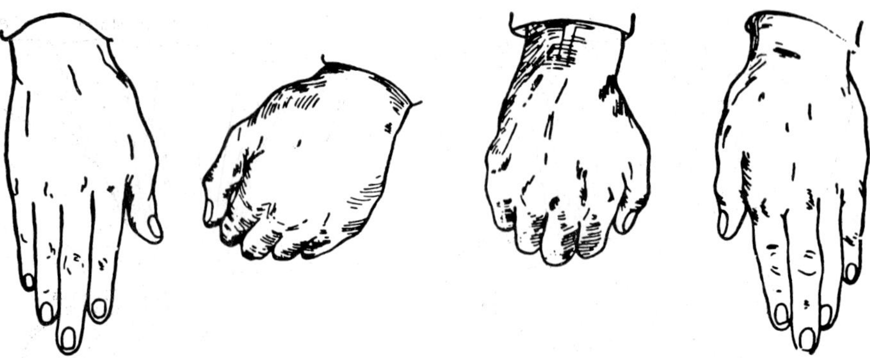

Figure 33. Test of reciprocal coordination.

his hands repeatedly (Figure 33); if his lesion is in the premotor area, he is unable to do so. He may change the positions of both hands, but each is changed separately; as he repeats the changes, the movements may lose their reciprocal character, so that he performs every movement separately or performs the same movement with both hands simultaneously. Such a patient is unable to draw a simple figure composed of two alternating components. He carries out such a task slowly, and his performance lacks continuity. He may repeat one component over and over in a perseverative fashion (Figure 34). In the most severe premotor lesions, which may be so deep as to involve the basal ganglia, the disturbance of smooth kinetic melodies is complicated by the perseveration of motor stereotypes once they are initiated, and complex movements become virtually impossible. In Figure 35 we present examples of the pathological persistence of motor acts, which impairs such a patient's ability to write and to draw.

The dynamic apraxic phenomena which are a primary feature of the premotor syndrome and which are most obvious in the motor sphere also leave their mark on the overall mental activity of the patient (Luria, 1943).

Disturbance of the Dynamic Basis of Speech and the Syndrome of Efferent (Kinetic) Motor Aphasia

The disturbance of skilled motor habits which arises as a result of lesions in the premotor cortical area is not limited to the impairment of fine hand movements. When the lesion is located in the *lower portion of the left premotor area,* it may produce a pathological change in the area known as "Broca's area." Such a lesion produces changes in the patient's *speech* which are familiar to the clinician as the syndrome of motor aphasia. Again, this syndrome can be differentiated from the kinesthetic speech disturbance described in the previous section. This syndrome might be referred to as "efferent (kinetic) motor aphasia." At first glance, the symptoms of efferent motor aphasia may appear to differ little from the kinesthetic disturbances described above. In both cases the primary defect involves the motor (expressive) speech of the patient. Careful analysis, however, reveals an essential difference between the two syndromes.

The primary defect in afferent (kinesthetic) motor aphasia is loss of the precise channeling of motor impulses, which results from kinesthetic apraxia of the speech apparatus. In cases of efferent (kinetic) motor apraxia, on the other hand, the articulation of individual sounds is retained. The difficulty here is not so much in the pronunciation of individual sounds as in the *transition from one sound to another.* As a result, one finds a disturbance of the *smooth execution of the articulatory sequences* characteristic of normal speech.

Figure 34. Graphic test of dynamic coordination. (The arrows indicate errors.)

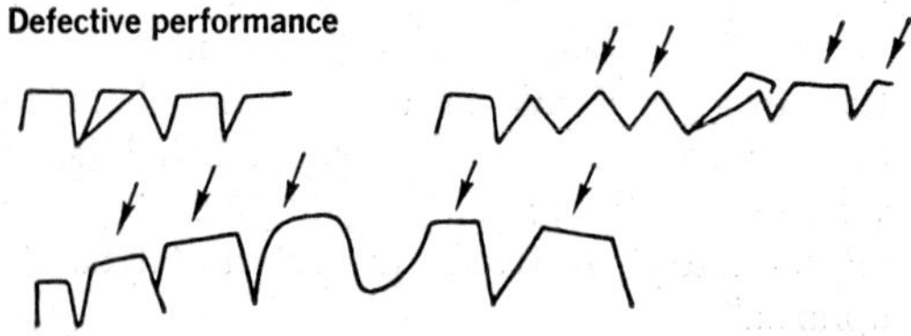

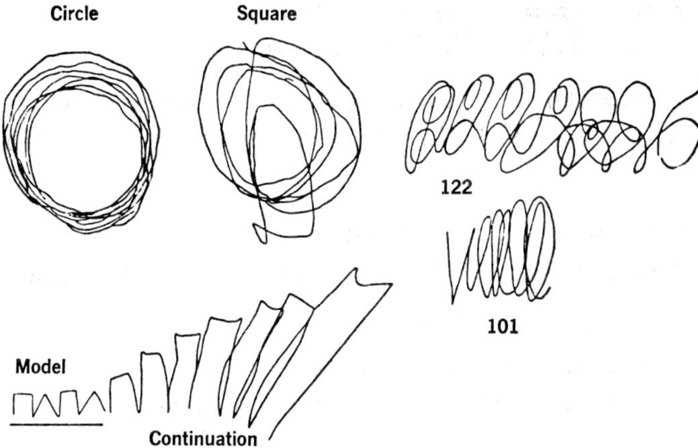

Figure 35. Pathological persistence of movement in a patient with premotor-subcortical syndrome.

In severe efferent motor aphasia, the disturbance of kinetic melodies and the pathological perseveration of motor elements may be so great as to prevent the pronunciation of simple words, since even this requires the smooth transition from one articulation to another. A patient attempting to pronounce the word "mukha" (fly) perseverates on the first syllable, "mu-," as though he were unable to make the transition to the next syllable. Thus, a kind of pathological inertia of the speech system is met by vain attempts to denervate the first articulatory movement, and he may utter something like "mu . . . ma." Only by special methods, such as the incorporation of the two syllables into different contexts by the examiner ("'moo' says the cow; 'kha' laughs the man"), can such a patient be helped to overcome the pathological inertia and articulate the two syllables "mu-kha."

Patients with less severe forms of efferent aphasia do not show such great difficulty in uttering individual words, but they may be unable to utter phrases or sentences composed of several words. As Jackson pointed out, the sentence can be considered the basic unit of connected speech. In these patients the dynamic patterns underlying sentences are profoundly disturbed. They tend to perseverate on individual words in a sentence; the smooth transition from one word to another is impossible for them.

The disturbance of dynamic patterns underlying sentences may characterize the speech of patients in this group for a very long time. Even in late stages of recovery, one may observe that their speech lacks the complex syntactic structure which is characteristic of normal speech. One finds that the verbs and conjunctions which contribute greatly to the smoothness of normal speech disappear and that a whole "sentence" may be made up entirely of nouns. This so-called "telegraph style" is well known to the clinic. Such a "sentence" might be: "It's . . . head . . . and it's . . . speech . . . it's . . . I can't . . . and it's . . . operation!" While this kind of speech is considerably different from that of patients with sensory aphasia, it is extremely common among patients in this group.

A characteristic of patients with efferent motor aphasia is that both *complex spontaneous speech* and the *repetition* of long sentences are extremely difficult for them. The *naming* of individual objects presents no problem. If special difficulty exists, it is restricted to the kinds of impairment of motor speech which were indicated earlier. It is important to note, however, that even though the ability to name objects may be little affected, such patients may have difficulty finding the words they want when they are speaking spontaneously.

Although speech comprehension is not affected directly in these patients, it may suffer great impairment secondary to the speech disturbances described above. These patients also experience *writing* difficulties which, upon careful analysis, prove to be radically different from the disturbances observed in the writing of patients with afferent (kinesthetic) motor aphasia. Whereas pa-

пи pi — мy mu — са sa — ре re — му mu — ва va

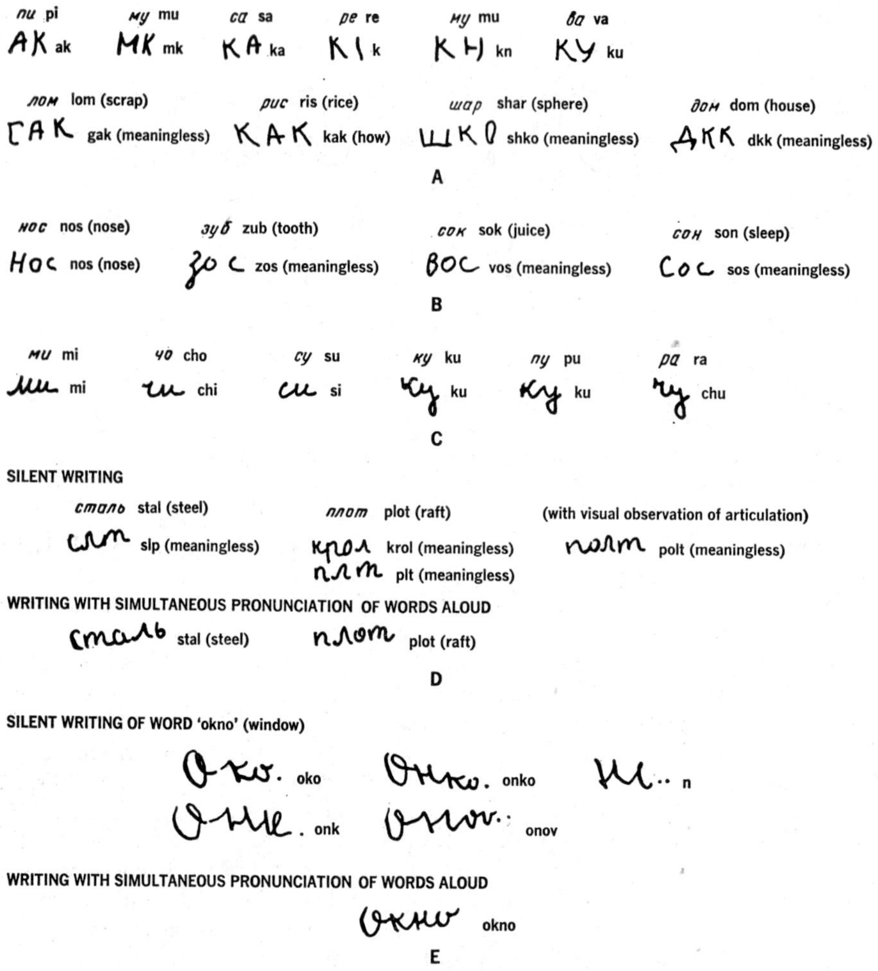

ak — mk — ka — k — kn — ku

лом lom (scrap) — рис ris (rice) — шар shar (sphere) — дом dom (house)

gak (meaningless) — kak (how) — shko (meaningless) — dkk (meaningless)

A

нос nos (nose) — зуб zub (tooth) — сок sok (juice) — сон son (sleep)

nos (nose) — zos (meaningless) — vos (meaningless) — sos (meaningless)

B

ми mi — чо cho — су su — ку ku — пу pu — ра ra

mi — chi — si — ku — ku — chu

C

SILENT WRITING

сталь stal (steel) — плот plot (raft) — (with visual observation of articulation)

slp (meaningless) — krol (meaningless) — plt (meaningless) — polt (meaningless)

WRITING WITH SIMULTANEOUS PRONUNCIATION OF WORDS ALOUD

stal (steel) — plot (raft)

D

SILENT WRITING OF WORD 'okno' (window)

oko — onko — n

onk — onov

WRITING WITH SIMULTANEOUS PRONUNCIATION OF WORDS ALOUD

okno

E

Figure 36. Writing of patients with "efferent" kinetic motor aphasia. (*A*) Patient Vav.: lesion of the left frontotemporal area, two months after injury. (*B*) Patient Dim.: lesion of the anterior speech area, two months after injury. (C) Patient Plotn.: lesion of the left frontotemporal area, two months after injury. (*D*) Patient Is.: lesion in Broca's area; motor aphasia (ten years schooling). (*E*) Patient Min.: lesion of right speech area (left-hander); motor aphasia (engineer).

tients in the afferent aphasia group have difficulty in the evaluation of individual speech sounds and in writing them down, patients with efferent motor aphasia have no difficulty in writing down individual letters. Their difficulty arises in preserving the sequence of sounds, in making the transition from one letter to another, and in inhibiting the further expression of letters once they have been written, i.e., in preventing the perseveration of motor stereotypes invoked for the writing of preceding sequences of letters. These features are characteristic of the writing of patients with efferent motor aphasia and can thus assist in the diagnosis of lesions in the inferior portions of the premotor area. Examples of the writing of patients in this group are presented in Figure 36.

LESIONS OF THE FRONTAL LOBES AND THE DISTURBANCE OF COMPLEX FORMS OF BEHAVIOR

The significance of the frontal lobes for higher mental processes and the symptomatology of lesions in these areas have always been among the most complex and confusing problems of neurology. On the one hand, lesions of the frontal—or, as they are often called, prefrontal—areas of the brain produce no loss of sensitivity and no paralysis or paresis. There are usually no signs of visual, auditory, apraxic, or aphasic disturbances. Thus the frontal lobes, which make up more than one-quarter of the entire mass of the hemispheres, have often been referred to as the "silent areas." On the other hand, it has been clear to neurologists and psychiatrists for a long time that lesions of the frontal lobes can produce extremely severe disturbances of complex behavior. These disturbances have been referred to by various authors as the "impairment of abstract thought or initiative," "the disintegration of complex purposive behavior," etc. Thus, Hughlings Jackson (1884) considered the frontal lobes to be responsible for the highest level of the organization of behavior.

Pavlov, in summarizing his cortical ablation investigations, associated the frontal lobes with the organization of movements "directed toward specific goals." He wrote:

> If you cut out the entire posterior portions of the great hemispheres you obtain an animal which is in general completely normal. He wags his tail when you pet him. He is able to recognize you and his food and all kinds of objects by sniffing and touching them. He will, likewise, express to you his joy at having recognized you by means of his nose, etc. But such an animal will not respond to you if you stand far away, since he is unable to make full use of his eyes; or if you call him by name, again, he will not respond. You can say that such a dog makes very little use of his eyes and ears. But beyond that he is altogether normal.
>
> On the other hand, if you cut out the entire anterior portions of the great hemispheres, starting from the line demarcating the limit of the posterior ablation, you will find that you have apparently an extremely abnormal animal. He will show no appropriate relationship either to you or to his canine comrades. He will seek neither food nor any other object in his environment. This is a thoroughly deteriorated animal, in whom there remains no apparent sign of purposeful behavior. Thus there is a tremendous difference between the two animals, one lacking the anterior the other the posterior portion of the hemispheres. Of one you will say that he is blind or deaf, but otherwise normal; of the other, that he is a total invalid, a helpless idiot.

Just as investigators studying the symptomatology of lesions in the posterior cortical areas tended to dissociate the disturbances of higher cortical function (agnosias, apraxias, and aphasias) from the elementary defects of sensation and movement, investigators studying the disturbances of mental activity which arise following lesions of the frontal cortex have very often limited themselves to the description of mental disturbances with no attempt to determine their physiological mechanisms. Thus, in summarizing investigations of the functions of the frontal lobes, a leading American neurophysiologist, John Fulton, stated: "When we consider the functions of the frontal association areas we come face to face with forms of activity which are extremely difficult to describe in physiological terms" (1943). This theme runs as a red thread through the entire history of the study of frontal lobe functions both in animals and in man.

Investigators observing animals from whom the frontal lobes had been ablated witnessed the same picture as that described by Pavlov in the passage quoted above. They observed that the animal deprived of its frontal lobes lost all forms of purposeful behavior. In general, however, they drew different conclusions from those expressed by Pavlov. They considered the frontal lobes to be the site of such higher mental functions as "abstract thought" (Hitzig, 1874) or "apperception" (Wundt, 1873–1874) and felt that they should be thought of as the morphological substrate for "rational control" or as the "supreme organ of the brain" (Gratiolet, 1861).

Investigators who refused to localize such subtle mental functions in narrow cortical zones took a different position. While not denying the experimental facts, they tended more to the conclusion that the disturbances of complex purposeful behavior resulted not so much from damage to the frontal lobes per se as from a *generalized disorder of brain function* which was associated with such lesions. This position was set forth by Goltz (1887). Other authors who challenged the concept of the localization of higher mental functions were Loeb (1902), V. Monakov (1914), Luciani (1913), and others.

Only a few authors suggested that the gradual development of reflex activity had led to the need at higher phylogenetic stages for special cerebral structures; they thought of the frontal lobes as a "highly complex system of centers" and as "making possible the coordination of a wider range of sensory and motor mechanisms." Such authors included Hughlings Jackson (1884), Bechterev (1907), Bianchi (1921), and others.

Investigation of frontal lobe functions in man followed a similar course of development. It was carried out, for the most part, by psychiatrists. As early as 1868, Harlow described a case in which a heavy iron crowbar penetrated the anterior cranial fossa, creating massive damage to the frontal lobes and an extraordinary change in the man's personality and behavior. Observations similar to these were published by Welt (1888) and Jastrovitz (1888), who described a loss of emotional inhibition, a disturbance of critical faculties, and a tendency to indulge in low forms of humor as a result of frontal lobe lesions. Severe disturbances of rational purposeful behavior and deterioration of planned activity and critical judgment were described by Khoroshko (1912; 1935), Feuchtwanger (1923), Baruk (1926), Kleist (1934), Brickner (1936), Goldstein (1936), Rylander (1939), Freeman and Watts (1942), Shmaryan (1949), Kartzovnik (1949), and others.

Even these descriptions, however, did not go uncriticized. A number of authors (LeBeau & Petrie, 1953; Mettler, 1949; Scoville, 1953; Tizard, 1958) were not inclined to attribute these disturbances simply to frontal lobe damage. They took the position that such severe symptoms as those described by the authors above were more likely to be the result of general disturbances of brain function associated with damage to the frontal lobes.

All the contradictory reports regarding the function of the frontal lobes and the disturbances which arise as a result of frontal lesions arise from one basic difficulty: the difficulty of visualizing the neurophysiological mechanisms upon which frontal lobe functions are based and the consequent difficulty in analyzing physiologically the disturbances which arise as a result of frontal lesions. This obstacle has still not been overcome to any great degree. The investigations begun by Pavlov and recent findings in the field of neuroanatomy, however, point out the path which such investigations will undoubtedly follow in the future.

Structural and Functional Organization of the Frontal Lobes

The frontal—or, more precisely, the prefrontal—portions of the brain (Brodmann's areas 9, 46, 10, and 11) are the most recent product of evolution. They are virtually nonexistent in the lower mammals. Only in primates are they developed to any great degree, and they reach their full development only in man, where, as we mentioned above, they constitute more than one-fourth of the total cerebral mass. In addition to this, investigations at the Moscow Brain Institute (Kononova, 1940; Kononova, 1948) have shown that they have an especially large degree of ontogenetic development after birth. Their growth greatly outstrips that of the other cortical areas during the first seven or eight years of life (Figure 37). Even before these studies were carried out, Flechsig (1920) showed that the myelinization of fibers and development of dendrites are completed later in these areas than in other portions of the brain.

The frontal areas have their own characteris-

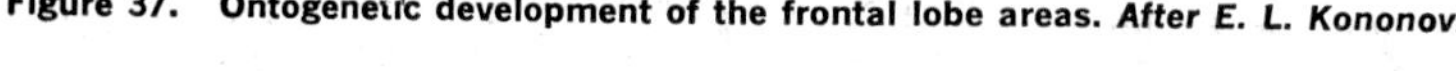
Figure 37. Ontogenetic development of the frontal lobe areas. *After E. L. Kononov.*

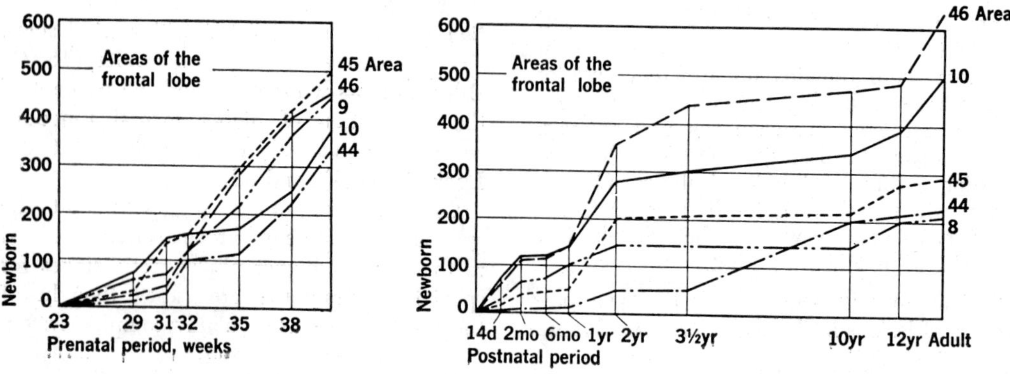

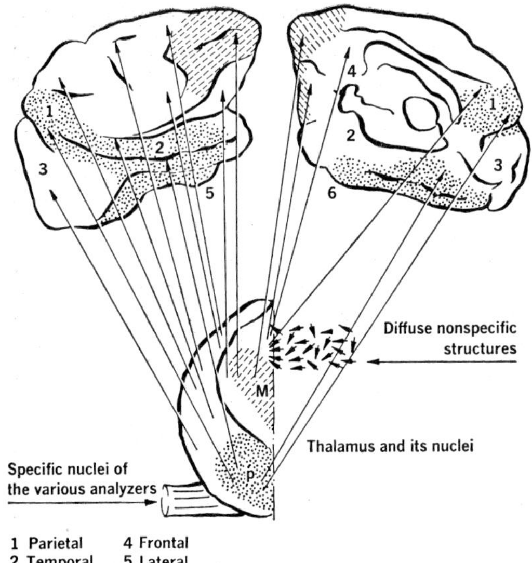

Figure 38. Subcortical connections of the frontal lobes. ***Pribram*, 1960a.**

tic cytoarchitecture and connections. Polyakov (1938–1948) showed that even at the earliest stages of ontogenetic development, the frontal cortical area shows a cytoarchitecture which distinguishes it from surrounding areas and which identifies it with such areas of the cortical nucleus of the motor analyzer as zones 4, 6, and 8. The major difference between it and these latter areas is the predominance of the superficial associative layers and the presence of large fiber tracts which connect it with other areas; it has direct connections both with other cortical areas and with those thalamic nuclei which have no direct connection with the periphery—in particular, with the dorsal medial nucleus. By means of these tracts, the frontal lobes receive information which has already been processed at subcortical levels (Figure 38).

A final important characteristic of the frontal lobes, especially of the mediobasal portions, is their intimate relationship to structures of the limbic system. The limbic system, in turn, receives massive input from the nonspecific structures in the structures of the cerebral stem surrounding the third ventricle and the cerebrospinal canal. These structures comprise the most important activating system within the central nervous system and play a direct role in the regulation of internal homeostasis of the organism.

The results of neurophysiological investigations correlate well with this anatomical picture of the frontal lobes. Data obtained by means of McCulloch's neuronographic method are presented in Table 1.

The frontal areas possess intimate afferent and efferent connections with a great number of other cortical areas. Thus stimulation of the frontal areas gives rise to electrical discharges in many other parts of the brain, and, conversely, stimulation of many other areas such as the premotor, temporal, inferior parietal, and occipital areas (including the cortical speech areas) gives rise to electrical discharges in the frontal cortex. As a result it is reasonable to consider the prefrontal cortical areas one of the highly complex zones of overlap between the cortical portions of different analyzers. In this case the overlap is between the cortical part of the *motor analyzer* and the cortical areas representing all the other analyzers. As a result of these connections, the frontal areas are able to influence not only movement, but the "over-all activity of the brain."

The anatomical and neuronographic data presented above also suggest that the frontal areas, though they comprise a part of the cortical portion of the motor analyzer, are not restricted to dealing with purely efferent impulses. They also handle a wide range of both afferent impulses from other analyzers (including, in man, the cortical speech areas) and feedback from their own motor output.

TABLE 1. RESULTS OF NEURONOGRAPHIC STUDIES OF AREAS IN THE PREFRONTAL CORTEX

Afferent connections	*Efferent connections*
8←18,22,37,41,42	
9←23	8→18
10←22,37,38	10→22
44←41,42,22	46→6,37,39
45←21,22,23,37,41,42	47→38
47←36,38	24→31,32

Thus they make possible extremely complex control of purposeful behavior patterns on the basis of speech associations.

Finally, the extremely close association of the prefrontal cortical areas with the limbic areas and with the subcortical structures governing the general level of cerebral excitation and maintaining the homeostasis of the organism bestows great potentiality for activities of a high degree of complexity. The control of such activities need not be based purely on the reception of signals from the environment but also can take into account the effects of actions taken by the organism.

A number of investigators (Anokhin, 1949; Pribram, 1959; Pribram, 1960; and others) have suggested that the frontal lobes play an important role in synthesizing the complex programs of action which are expressed as "intentions" and which precede the organism's actions. These authors suggest that the frontal lobes are important for collating the results of actions with preceding intentions, a process referred to by Anokhin as the "acceptor of action." In this way they take an important part in the regulation of selective, purposeful activity. These conceptions are supported by a number of observations drawn from experiments on animals.

Anokhin and Shumilina (1949) have observed that extirpation of the frontal lobes sharply alters the motor behavior of dogs. In experiments involving the secretory-motor method, they have found that frontal lobectomized dogs do not develop differential behavior patterns appropriate to the experimental situation. Instead of running to the food pan associated with reinforcement, such a dog does not take into account the effects of its own action and continues to carry out senseless stereotyped approach behavior, going from one food pan to the other. This activity has a perseverative character and clearly is not appropriate to the environmental situation. Similar data regarding the loss of selective adaptive behavior in animals deprived of their frontal lobes have been obtained by Shustin (1958).

Observations of a similar nature were also obtained in experiments carried out by Pribram (1959; 1960). He found that after resection of the frontal lobes, monkeys lost the ability to take account of the effects of previous actions, i.e., of the reinforcement of a given response; they repeated the same actions over and over in a perseverative fashion. The behavior of these monkeys lacked the appropriate adaptive characteristics. In other experiments, Pribram observed that these animals lost the ability to perform delayed-response tasks. They were unable to postpone a selective response and to maintain their attention during the period of time separating the signal from the delayed reinforcement. Observations by Bianchi (1921), Jacobsen (1935), Konorsky (1957), Brutkowsky and Konorsky (1956; 1957), and others also fall into this category. Extirpation of the frontal lobes leads to a disturbance of complex forms of internal inhibition and transforms the organized behavior of the animal into a random sequence of impulsive fragmentary reactions. (See also Warren & Akert, 1964.)

All the studies cited above indicate the important role of the frontal lobes in the regulation of complex behavior. These areas constitute a part of the cortical portion of the motor analyzer, are intimately associated with the complex synthetic (preliminary) organization or programming of selective activity, and participate in matching the results of the action with the preliminary intention and the modification of activity, depending upon its effectiveness. These same studies show also that lesions of the frontal lobes destroy the selective, purposeful character of behavior and, consequently, produce a characteristic syndrome of disturbances of programs of behavior whose neurophysiological mechanisms still await careful investigation.

Lesions of the Frontal Cortical Areas and Disturbances of Behavior Programs

Human behavior is not limited to single manipulatory acts or to the kinds of motor habits which were found to be disturbed in the various forms of apraxia described earlier. Numerous psychological investigations (Leontiev, 1959; Zaporozhetz, 1960; Wallon, 1942; and many others) have shown that human behavior can assume a very complex character and is determined by complex motives which have developed in the course of social history. Human behavior is further directed by the evaluation of situations on the basis of orienting, investigative activity which, itself, passes through a series of successively more complex stages in the course of ontogenesis. All that is the basis of complex programs underlying human behavior.

Not only is complex, conscious, voluntary activity carried out on the basis of direct empirical experience, but it is also largely regulated by systems of verbal influences (overt or inner verbal control), which make it possible to analyze a situation, extract the most important cues, synthesize them into a single pattern, and formulate intentions which will guide the further plan of behavior. Human speech permits a comparison of the effects of a completed act with the expected effect which was formulated as an intention. After evaluation of the effect of an action a given activity may be continued (if the actual effect matches the expected effect), or it may be discontinued (if the desired effect is different from the actual effect). In other words, man's system of speech associations plays an important role in the "acceptor of action" (Anokhin) or T-O-T-E (Pribram) mechanism and in error correction, which occurs in lower animals only at a more elementary level.

All these complex forms of behavior are disturbed by massive frontal lobe lesions. In these cases, patients may shown no signs of paresis, ataxia, or dystonia; there may be no apparent apraxic or agnostic disturbances. Speech, reading, and writing abilities may show no signs of impairment; yet even in the early stages of frontal lobe injury, e.g., in the early development of a tumor, patients may show noticeable disturbances of complex programs of behavior. Such disturbances may manifest themselves as diminution in range of interests or loss of initiative. Occasionally one may observe a disturbance of complex purposeful, intentional behavior, so that the patient unexpectedly falls under the influence of whatever stimuli happen to be acting on him at a given time. He may commit senseless impulsive actions which he has no inclination to correct. For instance, the button which one pushes in order to call a nurse may catch the attention of such a patient; he may reach out and press the button but, when the nurse arrives, be unable to say why he rang for her. This same type of behavior is seen in a patient who, upon arriving at a station in order to travel in a certain direction, impulsively takes a seat on a train which is to travel in the opposite direction. He does this not because he is disoriented in space but because he is unable to inhibit the impulse which destroys his unstable intention. Similar observations on the behavior of "frontal syndrome" patients in domestic and occupational settings have been described by a number of authors (Brickner, 1936; Feuchtwanger, 1923; Rylander, 1937; and others). Not infrequently the instability of a patient's intentions and the inability to submit his behavior to a plan formulated in verbal terms prove to be the primary factors preventing total recovery. It is difficult for such a patient to adapt himself to a steady job (Luria, 1948; Rubinstein, 1944; and others).

Disturbances of stable behavior patterns are seen most clearly in cases involving severe frontal lesions, for instance, massive frontal lobe tumors associated with generalized cerebral hypertension. In these cases purposeful activity may be replaced by one of two types of behavior (Filippycheva, 1952; Luria, 1945b; Spirin, 1951; Zeigarnik, 1949). Either one may see single fragments of stereotyped activity, or one may observe repeated execution of a single action. An example of the first case is the patient who, when asked to strike a match and light a candle, strikes the match and then either blows it out or places it in his mouth as though it were a cigarette. In the latter case, the perseveration of actions indicates a pathological stagnation in the system of afferent connections which evoke behavior or in the cortical nucleus of the motor analyzer itself. Perseveration is most pronounced in cases involving localized lesions of the frontal lobes which sharply reduce the tonus of the cerebral cortex and affect the basal ganglia. Such phenomena may appear in their most distinct form if the patient is requested to carry out some form of graphical act, e.g., to draw a circle, a square, or a cross or to draw a series of figures all named at once. In such cases, the inability to make the transition from one motion to another, the persistent execution of one and the same motion over and over, may emerge with great clarity. In Figure 39 we present examples of perseveration in a patient with a tumor involving the frontal lobes and, in Figure 40, an example of motor perseveration arising in a patient with edema following an operation to remove a tumor in a posterior frontal area.

As a rule, patients with lesions in the posterior portions of the frontal lobes are aware of their motor defects but are unable to correct them. In contrast to this, patients with massive lesions of the prefrontal areas show a severe disturbance of the ability to maintain their intentions; they are unable to collate the

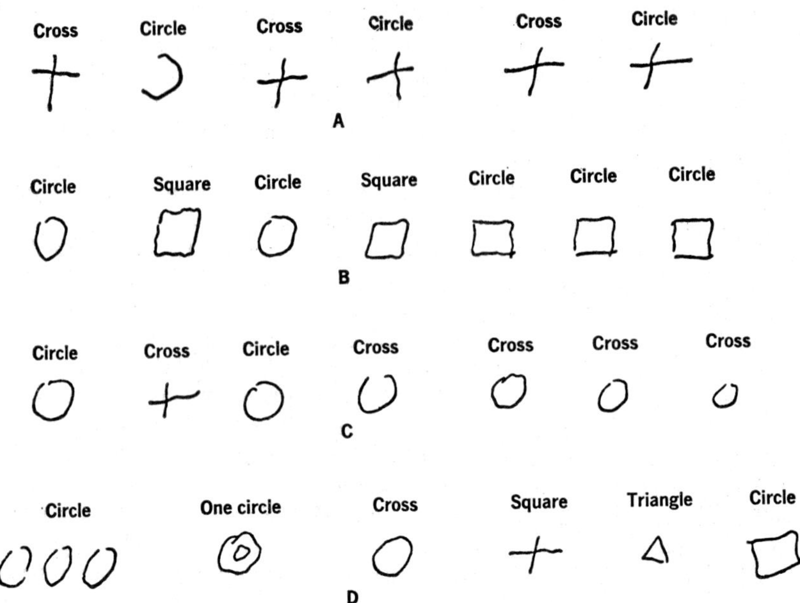

(a)

Figure 39a. Disturbances of performance in individual tasks resulting from pathological persistence of action in patients with massive frontal lobe lesions. (*A*) Patient Kryl.: intracerebral tumor of the left frontal lobe. (*B*) Patient Giash.: intracerebral tumor of the left frontal lobe. (*C*) Patient Pas.: abscess of the right frontal lobe. (*D*) Patient Step.: intracerebral tumor of the left frontal lobe.

Figure 39*b*. Systemic perseveration in patients with massive frontal lobe lesions (see text for explanation). (*A*) Patient Giash.: tumor of left frontal lobe. (*B*) Patient Fes.: tumor of right frontal lobe.

3 122 12 12 12 12 2 2 3 circles 5 lines 10 dots 12 crosses

Model Model Model

Rejection ("not right") 3 circles 3 circles

A

Model

"Oh, not like that . . ."

(1) Fesenko (patient's surname) (2) „окно" okno (window)

(3) „стул" stul (chair)

Saying "ok-no, ok-no . . ."

B

(*b*)

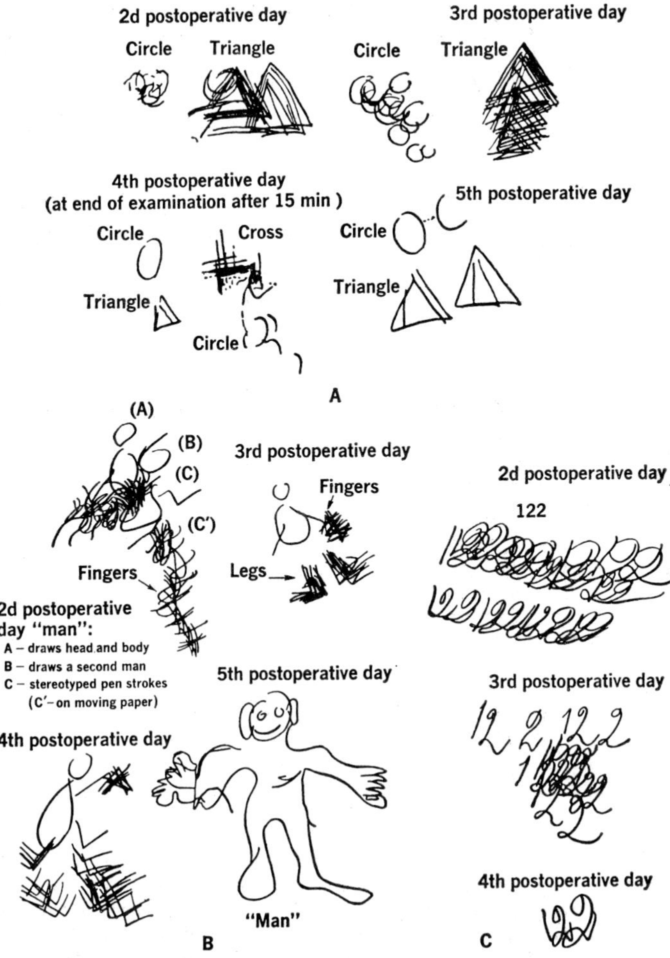

Figure 40. Intensification of activity in drawing and writing of a patient after removal of an arachnoid epithelioma from left premotor region. Patient Ivanov (5180). (*A*) Drawings of simple figures during the period of postoperative edema. (*B*) Drawings of a man during the period of postoperative edema. (*C*) Writing of numbers in the period of postoperative edema.

results of their actions with the instructions which they have received and are unaware of the defects in their behavior. In mild forms of the frontal syndrome, the disturbances of selective actions and their replacement by impulsive behavior or by perseveration may be less pronounced, but the basic type of disturbance is always the same.

The mechanisms underlying the disturbances which we have described have been clarified as a result of investigations carried out in recent years by Meshcheryakov (1953), Ivanova (1953), Homskaya (1959; 1960), Marushevsky (1959), and others. Such studies have revealed a characteristic change in the regulatory function of speech which occurs in patients with lesions of the frontal lobes. Even patients with massive frontal lesions are capable of following step-by-step instructions leading to the completion of a particular task. For instance, they are able to press a rubber bulb in response to a red signal and to withhold the response in response to a green signal or to press firmly in response to a white signal and less strongly in response to a yellow signal. Often they are able to repeat the verbal instructions even after a long-time interval. But, in some cases, after such an interval they may be unable to follow the instruction. They begin to press the bulb haphazardly, to press it in response to all signals, or to squeeze always with the same pressure. Characteristically, they are unaware of their erroneous responses. They do not

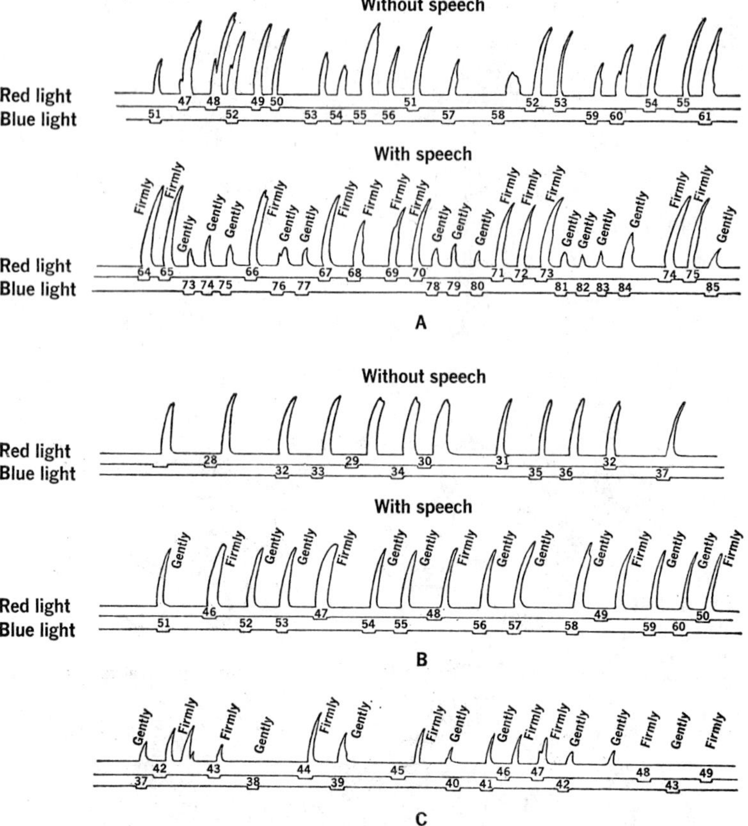

Figure 41. Different degrees of verbal control of motor reactions in patients with lesions of the parietal and frontal cortical areas. Instructions: "On red, press firmly; on blue, press gently." Words written above mechanogram responses represent verbal responses of the patients. (*A*) Patient Kiselev: tumor of the left upper parietal area. Positive effect of speech on the motor reactions of Patient Kis. (*B*) Patient Vid.: intracerebral tumor of the right frontal lobe. Absence of influence of speech on the motor reactions of patient Vid. (*C*) Patient Krut.: tumor of the right frontal lobe. Absence of influence of speech on the motor reactions of patient Vid. *E. D. Homskaya.*

evaluate their errors. Although the speech of such patients retains its nominative and grammatical characteristics, it *loses its regulatory role.* The second signaling system appears to be dissociated from the motor system. In Figure 41, we compare the normal protocol of an experiment with patients having lesions in the parietal areas with the protocol of a frontal lobe patient in whom the regulatory function of speech has been severely impaired.

Impairment of the regulatory function of the second signaling system characteristically expresses itself not only in the motor responses of the patients with frontal lobe lesions but also in their vegetative responses. It is well known that any signal (meaningful) stimulus elicits in the normal person an orienting reaction composed of a vascular response (peripheral vascular constriction), the galvanic skin response, etc. A number of investigations (Sokolov, 1958; Sokolov, 1959; Vinogradova, 1959) have shown that these vegetative components of the orienting reflex easily extinguish with repeated stimulus presentation but that they acquire great stability if, by means of verbal instruction, the stimuli are given some meaning, e.g., if they become signals for clenching the fist or if they are to be counted. It has been found that patients with lesions in the posterior cortical areas react similarly to normal subjects in such experiments Homskaya, 1960; Klimkovsky, 1960). The same result does not hold, however, if one carries out such experiments on patients with frontal lobe lesions. Patients with frontal lobe lesions, while showing no loss

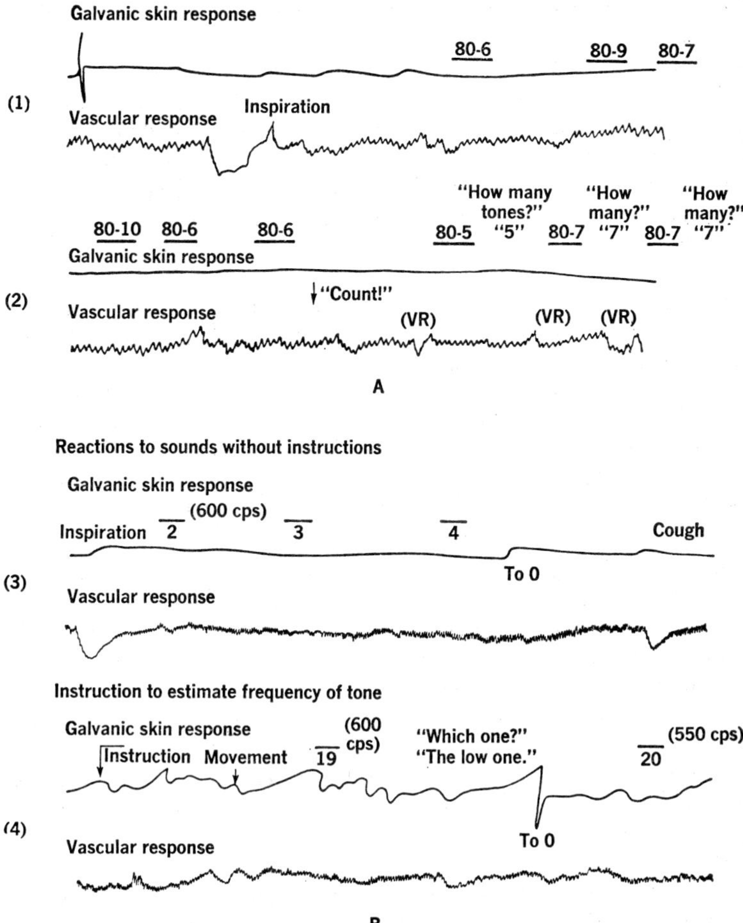

Figure 42. Disturbance of the effect of verbal instructions on vegetative components of the orienting reflex in patients with frontal lobe lesions. (*A*) Absence of influence of verbal instructions on vegetative components of the orienting reflex in patient Sh. (resection of left frontal pole). (1) Habituation of vegetative components of the orienting reflex to an intermittent sound stimulus (80 decibels). Numbers represent sound intensity (in decibels) and the number per group. (2) Failure of vegetative components of the orienting reflex to reappear after the instruction to count the number of sounds. (*VR*) Verbal response. (*B*) Diffuse influence of verbal instructions on vegetative components of the orienting reflex in patient N. (tumor of the right frontal lobe). (3) Habituation of vegetative components of the orienting reflex to sounds of different frequencies (600 and 550 cycles per second). Numbers represent serial numbers of stimuli. (4) Diffuse influence of the verbal instruction to estimate the frequencies of the sounds on vegetative components of the orienting reflex. *E D. Homskaya.*

of the unconditioned vegetative orienting reactions, are unable to prevent rapid extinction of the orienting response following the verbal instructions which give signal value to the stimuli. In Figure 42, we present examples of the protocols from such experiments.

All these findings indicate the extent to which the regulatory role of speech is disturbed, i.e., the dissociation between speech and motor activity and between speech and the tonus of cortical processes in patients with frontal lobe lesions.

Disturbances of Gnostic and Intellectual Processes with Lesions of the Frontal Lobes

The disturbances of functions which arise as a result of frontal lobe lesions are not restricted to the motor sphere. Similar changes of gnostic and intellectual functions occur. As we indicated earlier, lesions of the frontal lobes do not produce visual agnosia of the type observed following lesions of the occipital or parieto-occipital areas. If, however, the tasks a frontal lobe patient is required to perform are greatly complicated, one may observe disturbances of gnostic processes which are quite similar to those disturbances which we have just described as characterizing his motor activity.

Thus, a patient with frontal lobe damage may be capable of perceiving fine visual details of a "thematic" picture, but if he is required to integrate these details, to synthesize them into a conceptual whole by selecting out those elements which are of greater significance, he may be quite unable to do so. He is unable to extract the important cues from among superflous ancillary details and may base his entire judgment as to the general meaning of the picture on a single striking but irrelevant detail. For instance, in studying a picture which shows a man being dragged under the ice of a frozen river, such a patient may turn his attention to a building with many towers appearing in the background and say: "It's a kremlin." Or he may see a "caution" sign standing at the edge of the pond and say: "There's a high power line here," "This is a wild animal reserve, and there are dangerous animals around," etc. The synthesis of a general meaning for a picture develops in the normal subject as a result of well-structured analytical-synthetic activity; in the patient with the frontal syndrome, this complex investigatory activity may be disturbed by uncontrollable ancillary associations evoked by fragmentary observations.

Similar disturbances may arise in the *comprehension of written text.* Although frontal patients may understand the individual words and have no difficulty in perceiving the overall grammatical constructions, they may experience overwhelming difficulty when required to explain the meaning of complex material. They are unable to integrate different elements and extract the general meaning of the paragraph. The patient with a severe frontal syndrome, unable to treat the material in a genuine analytical-synthetic manner, seizes upon individual fragments and makes impulsive judgments as to the meaning of the material on the basis of single, randomly selected details. Any form of material involving figurative speech, such as metaphors or proverbs, offers especial difficulty for such a patient. The direct and concrete meaning of such material so dominates his attention that it is often impossible for him to consider its hidden underlying meaning (Goldstein, 1944; Zeigarnik, 1961; and others).

Finally, in problem-solving situations, patients with frontal lobe lesions show pronounced disturbances of the selective organization of mental activity. In order to solve any problem, whether it involves arithmetic, logic, or complex calculation, a person must first orient himself with regard to the conditions stated, establish the most important factors to be considered, create appropriate hypotheses and programs, and break down the over-all problem into "subproblems." Only after these steps have been taken is he in a position to carry out those operations which are usually thought of as the major aspect of problem-solving activity. It is precisely the complex processes which precede final solution of the problem which make the greatest demands on the accuracy of intellectual processes and which are most severely disturbed in patients with frontal lobe lesions. The preliminary analysis of conditions set by the problem and the elaboration of a general plan for its solution are lost in such patients, or these processes may be so unstable as to be disrupted by any incidental factor and thus give way to impulsive or perseverative activity. Thus, even though a general plan of solution may be established, it is not followed through. A patient with the frontal syndrome, in attempting to solve an arithmetic problem, easily shifts from a rational program of operations to a purely random and mechanical application of arithmetic operations. He may add, subtract, or multiply various numbers appearing in the problem with no regard to the conditions set by the problem.

As a result of this tendency, frontal lobe patients find it almost impossible to carry out such a relatively simple operation as "successive subtractions of 7 from 100" (a problem widely employed in clinical investigations). Such patients show no noticeable primary disturbance of the ability to perform simple calculations, but they easily shift from the appropriate operation to one which is more simple. Thus, they can repeat one and the same operation, but it may be the wrong operation; e.g., they may give the sequence "100 minus 7 equals 93, 83, 73 . . . 63," etc.

Disturbance of the selective quality of complex forms of intellectual activity with the preservation of individual intellectual operations is one of the distinguishing characteristics of patients with massive lesions of the frontal lobes.

Major Variants of the Frontal Syndrome

It would be incorrect to assume that the disturbances of higher cortical functions with lesions of the frontal cortex are restricted to those defects of selective activity which we have just described. Actually there exist a number of variations of the frontal syndrome which depend upon the *size* of the lesion and upon its precise *location* within the frontal lobes. In the great majority of cases fitting the pattern described above, the lesions are *massive, involve primarily the convex surfaces of the frontal lobes, and are complicated by secondary generalized disorders* such as cerebral intoxication or hypertension. Thus we see these forms of disturbance in cases involving large frontal lobe tumors, compound skull fractures with brain lesions, and large hematomas which lead to the destruction and fibrotic replacement of cortical tissue.

Since the frontal area is phylogenetically the youngest of all cortical areas, it is also the "least specialized." The lateralization of function is less pronounced than in structures concerned with speech functions, and the ability to compensate for relatively small lesions is considerably greater in the frontal area than in other areas of the cortex. Thus, while massive frontal-area lesions produce very definite syndromes, less severe injuries, unaccompanied by secondary generalized cerebral disorders, may give rise to extremely mild disturbances and are sometimes virtually asymptomatic. On the basis of this fact, a number of authors (Hebb, 1942; Hebb, 1959; Penfield & Evans, 1935; and others) have suggested that the resection of large areas of the frontal cortex may be carried out with no noticeable consequences. There is every reason to suppose, however, that even in these cases detailed psychophysiological analysis would succeed in establishing the presence of such (perhaps latent) neurodynamic disturbances as those described above.

As we mentioned, the characteristics of the frontal syndrome described so far are associated primarily with lesions in the superior and convex portions of the frontal lobes. There may be important deviations from this picture, however, in cases involving the *mediobasal portions of the frontal lobes*. The first descriptions of this syndrome were published by Welt (1888) and by Jastrovitz (1888), who reported that the kind of disturbances described above were of only secondary importance and sometimes failed to appear altogether. In the place of such disturbances, they observed predominantly affective disturbances.

In experiments performed on animals (Pribram, 1959; Pribram, 1960), it was shown that extirpation of the basal portions of the frontal lobes does not produce the same disturbances of selective motor activity and of the ability to evaluate the effects of such activity as occurs in animals with lesions of the convex portions of the frontal lobes. Instead, extirpation of the basal areas in monkeys leads to a disinhibition of certain forms of behavior, e.g., to increased oral behavior, sexual activity, etc.

Similar data have been collected regarding lesions of the basal areas in man. Patients with the basal frontal syndrome, resulting most often from tumors in the anterior cranial fossa and occasionally from tumors in the hypophysis or perichiasmal meninges, show gross personality changes, lack of restraint, heightened primitive inclinations, and a disturbance in the ability to communicate (Shmaryan, 1949). Such patients exhibit a disturbance of selective forms of motor activity and intellectual processes described above only when the tumor is so large as to cause pathological changes in the frontal lobes as a whole.

It should be noted that the syndrome described above is most clearly seen in cases involving bilateral lesions of the convex portions of the frontal lobes. Lesions of the left frontal lobe, especially of its posteroinferior portion, may produce a characteristic syndrome comprising lack of spontaneity and a loss of initiative which affects primarily speech activity. This disturbance of active speech has justifiably been referred to as "frontal aphasia." Characteristic of this syndrome is the preservation of imitative speech and of the ability to name objects with a severe disturbance of spontaneous speech, narrative speech, and "constructive thought." Patients with this syndrome may be completely unable to develop or elaborate upon verbal statements.

Finally, it should be pointed out that combined lesions of the frontal lobes and of anterior portions of the left temporal area may give rise to a characteristic *frontotemporal syndrome*. Here again, one observes a disturbance of the regulatory role of speech. The loss of selective actions is combined with an impairment of auditory speech and with the "alienation of word meanings," symptoms which are characteristic of the sensory aphasia syndrome of temporal lobe lesions. Such compound syndromes arise quite frequently as the result of large tumors in the cerebral cortex.

REFERENCES

Russian

Anokhin, P. K. *Problems of higher nervous activity*. Moscow: Press of the Academy of Medical Sciences of the USSR, 1949.

Anokhin, P. K. New findings regarding characteristics of the afferent mechanisms of the conditioned reflex. *Questions of Psychol.*, 1955, No. 6.

Anokhin, P. K. General principles underlying compensation for functional disturbances and their physiological mechanisms. *Questions of Psychol.*, 1956.

Babenkova, S. V. On the relation of two signaling systems in speech recovery with different forms of aphasia. VII Session of the Institute of Neurology, Acad: Med. Sci., Moscow, 1954.

Babkin, B. P. Characteristics of the auditory analyzer in dogs. *Proc. Soc. Russ. Physicians*, Petersburg, 1910, **77**.

Bechterev, V. M. *Fundamental principles of brain function*. Vols. 1–7. Petersburg: 1905–1907.

Bein, E. S. A psychological analysis of sensory aphasia. Unpublished doctoral dissertation, Acad. Med. Sci. USSR, 1947.

Bernstein, N. A. Problems of the relationship between coordination and localization. *Arch. biol. Sci.*, 1935, **38** (7).

Bernstein, N. A. *The organization of movements*. Moscow: Medgiz, 1947.

Bernstein, N. A. Some urgent problems regarding the control of motor acts. *Questions of Psychol.*, 1958, No. 6.

Betz, V. A. *Two centers in the cerebral cortex: anatomical and histological investigations* (1879). Moscow: Medgiz, 1950.

Birenbaum, G. V. The relationship between conceptual and structural components of perception. Investigations in the psychology of perception. Moscow: 1948.

Blinkov, S. M. *Structural characteristics of the human brain*. Moscow: Medgiz, 1955.

Chlenov, L. G. The pathology of three dimensional vision. In *Clinical and therapeutic problems of psychic disorders*. Moscow: 1938.

Chlenov, L. G. Inactivity as a manifestation of physiological weakness. *Proc. Moscow Univer.*, 1948, No. 3.

Chlenov, L. G., Bein, E. S. Agnosias for faces. *Neuropath. & Psychiat.*, 1958, 58–68.

Davidenkov, S. N. *Materials for the study of aphasia*. Kharkov: 1915.

Filimonov, I. N. The functional significance of the architechtonic structures of the cerebral cortex. *Neuropath. & Psychiat.*, 1945, No. 1.

Filippycheva, N. A. Perseveration of higher cortical processes with focal lesions of the great hemispheres. Dissertation, Acad. Med. Sci. USSR, 1952.

Galperin, P. Y. The development of investigations into the formation of intellectual activity. *Psychol. Sci. USSR*, 1959.

Grashchenkov, N. A., & Luria, A. R. The systemic principle of the localization of function in the cerebral cortex. *Neuropath. & Psychiat.*, 1945, No. 1.

Grindel, O. M., & Filippycheva, N. A. The reduced plasticity of excitation in the motor analyzer of a patient with a focal lesion of the frontal lobe. *J. higher nerv. Activity*, 1959, **9** (4).

Grinstein, A. M. *Paths and centers of the nervous system*. Moscow: Medgiz, 1946.

Homskaya, E. D. An investigation of the influence of speech reactions on motor behavior in cerebroasthenic children. In *Problems of higher nervous activity of the normal and abnormal child*. Vol. 2. Moscow: Press of the Academy of Pedagogical Sciences of the RSFSR, 1958.

Homskaya, E. D. *Mechanisms for compensation of defects arising from focal brain lesions*. Paper read at First Conf. psychol. Soc., Moscow, 1959.

Homskaya, E. D. The influence of verbal instructions on vascular and galvanic skin response components of the orienting reflex with focal brain damage in different areas. *Trans. Acad. pedag. Sci. RSFSR*, 1960.

Ivanova, M. P. Disturbance of the relationship between the two signaling systems in the formulation of complex motor reactions as the result of brain lesions. Candidate's dissertation, Moscow Univer., 1953.

Ivanov-Smolensky, A. G. *Basic problems in the pathophysiology of higher nervous activity*. Moscow: Medgiz, 1933.

Ivanov-Smolensky, A. G. *Essays on the pathophysiology of higher nervous activity.* Moscow: Medgiz, 1949.

Kabelyanskaya, L. G. The state of the auditory analyzer in sensory aphasia. *J. Neurol. Psychiat.,* 1957, **57** (6).

Kartzovnik, I. I. *The frontal syndrome and its clinical variations with penetrating brain lesions.* Novosibirsk: 1949.

Khoroshko, V. K. *The relationship of the frontal lobes to psychology and psychopathology.* Moscow: 1912.

Khoroshko, V. K. Clinical observations of wartime injuries involving the frontal lobes. *Med. J.,* 1921, 5–6, 6–7.

Khoroshko, V. K. Information about the frontal lobes accumulated in thirty years of personal investigation. *Clin. Med.,* 1935, **13** (10).

Kok, E. P. A study of abstraction and generalization in aphasic patients. Candidate's dissertation, Pavlov Inst. Physiol., 1957.

Kononova, E. P. Development of the frontal area after birth. *Trans. Brain Inst.,* 1940, **5.**

Kononova, E. P. Prenatal development of the frontal lobes in man. *Trans. Brain Inst.,* 1948, **6.**

Konorsky, J. M. The effects of frontal lobectomy on higher nervous activity. In *Problems of contemporary physiology in the nervous and muscular systems.* Leningrad: 1957. (a)

Konorsky, J. M. Hyperactivity after frontal lobectomy. In *Problems of central nervous system physiology.* Leningrad: 1957. (b)

Kroll, M. B. *Neurological syndromes.* Kharkov-Kiev: Ukrainian Medical Press, 1933.

Kroll, M. B. *Aphasia, apraxia, and agnosia.* Moscow: Medgiz, 1934.

Kuküev, L. A. The relationship of the cortical portion of the motor analyzer and the subcortex in human development. Doctoral dissertation, Acad. Med. Sci., Moscow, 1958.

Kyküev, A. A. The relationship of the motor cortex and striopallidum in mammalian phylogenesis. Candidate's dissertation, Univer. of Moscow, 1940.

Lebedinsky, M. S. *Aphasia, apraxia, and agnosia.* Kharkov: 1941.

Leontiev, A. N. *Problems of mental development.* Moscow: Press of the Academy of Pedagogical Sciences of the RSFSR, 1959.

Leontiev, A. N. The social and biological formation of mental processes. *Questions of Phil.,* 1960, No. 12.

Luria, A. R. The study of aphasia in the light of brain pathology: temporal aphasia. Doctoral dissertation, Univer. of Moscow, 1940.

Luria, A. R. The disturbance of grammatical operations with brain lesions. *News Acad. pedag. Sci. USSR,* 1945, No. 3. (a)

Luria, A. R. Disturbances of set and action resulting from brain lesions. *Trans. psychol. Div. Acad. Sci. Georgia, Tbilessi,* 1945. (b)

Luria, A. R. The pathology of numbers and computation. *Trans. psychol. Div. Acad. Pedag. Sci. Moscow,* 1945. (c)

Luria, A. R. *Traumatic aphasia.* Moscow: Press of the Academy of Medical Sciences of the USSR, 1947.

Luria, A. R. *The restoration of brain functions following war trauma.* Moscow: Press of the Academy of Medical Sciences of the USSR, 1948. (English Tr. London: Pergamon Press, 1963.)

Luria, A. R. *Essays on the psychophysiology of writing.* Moscow: Press of the Academy of Pedagogical Sciences, 1950.

Luria, A. R. (Ed.). *Problems of higher nervous activity in the normal and abnormal child.* Vols. 1, 2. Moscow: Press of the Academy of Pedagogical Sciences of the RSFSR, 1956–1958.

Luria, A. R. *Higher cortical functions of man.* Moscow: Moscow Univer. Press, 1962. (English Tr. New York: Basic Books, in press.)

Luria, A. R., & Rapoport, M. Y. Regional symptoms of disturbances of higher cortical functions in intracerebral tumors of the left hemisphere. *Questions of Neurosurgery,* 1962, **4.**

Luria, A. R., & Skorodumova, A. V. Right fixed hemianopsia. In *Collection in memorium of S. V. Kravkov.* Moscow: 1947.

Marushevsky, M. Characteristics of the organization of movements with focal brain lesions. Paper read at First Conf. psychol. Soc., Moscow, 1959.

Meshcheryakov, A. I. Disturbances of the interaction of the two signalling systems in the formation of simple motor reactions with focal brain lesions. Candidate's dissertation, Inst. of Psychology, Moscow, 1953.

Pavlov, I. P. *Complete collected works.* Moscow: Press of the Academy of Sciences of the USSR, 1949.

Polyakov, G. I. Ontogenesis of isocortex in man. *Trans. Moscow Brain Institute,* 1938–1948, **1–6.**

Polyakov, G. I. Interrelations of the basic types of neurones in the human cortex. *J. higher nerv. Activity,* 1956, **6** (3).

Polyakov, G. I. Structural organization of the *cortical representation of different analyzers in* man. *Trans. Acad. med. Sci. USSR,* 1959, No. 9.

Rozinsky, Y. B. *Mental changes with lesions of the frontal lobes.* Moscow: Medgiz, 1948.

Rubinstein, S. Y. Recovery of the ability to work after wartime brain injuries. Dissertation, Inst. of Psychology, Moscow, 1944.

Rudenko, Z. Y. Disturbances of calculation with brain lesions. Dissertation, Acad. Med. Sci. USSR, Moscow, 1953.

Schmidt, E. V., & Sukhovskaya, N. A. The pathophysiology of sensory aphasia. *J. Neuropath. Psychiat.,* 1954, **54** (12).

Sechenov, I. M. *Selected works.* Vol. 1. Moscow: Press of the Academy of Medical Sciences of the USSR, 1947.

Shkolnik-Yarros, E. G. Disturbances of movements following lesions of the premotor areas. Dissertation, Acad. Med. Sci. USSR, Moscow, 1945.

Shmaryan, A. S. *Brain pathology and psychiatry.* Moscow: Medgiz, 1949.

Shumilina, A. I. The functional significance of the frontal lobes for conditioned reflex activity in dogs. In *Problems of higher nervous activity.* Moscow: Press of the Academy of Medical Sciences of the USSR, 1949.

Shustin, N. A. *Physiology of the frontal lobes.* Moscow: Medgiz, 1958.

Sokolov, E. N. *Perception and the conditioned reflex.* Moscow: Moscow Univer. Press, 1958.

Sokolov, E. N. The orienting reflex. In *The orienting reflex and questions of higher nervous activity,* Moscow: Press of the Academy of Pedagogical Sciences of the RSFSR, 1959.

Spirin, B. G. Disturbance of the mobility of nervous processes following brain operations. Dissertation, Acad. of Medical Sciences of the USSR, Moscow, 1951.

Vinogradova, O. S. A plethysmographic study of the orienting reflex in oligophrenic children. In *The orienting reflex and questions of higher nervous activity.* Moscow: Press of the Academy of Pedagogical Sciences, 1959. (a)

Vinogradova, O. S. The role of the orienting reflex in the formation of temporary connections. In *The orienting reflex and questions of higher nervous activity.* Moscow: Press of the Academy of Pedagogical Sciences, 1959. (b)

Vygotski, L. S. *Selected psychological studies.* Moscow: Press of the Academy of the Pedagogical Sciences, 1956.

Vygotski, L. S. *Development of higher mental functions.* Moscow: Press of the Academy of Pedagogical Sciences, 1960.

Zaporozhetz, A. V. *The development of voluntary movements in the child.* Moscow: Press of the Academy of Pedagogical Sciences, 1960.

Zavarzin, A. A. *Notes on evolutionary histology.* Moscow: Press of the Academy of Medical Sciences of the USSR, 1941.

Zeigarnik, B. V. Disturbances of spontaneity resulting from wartime frontal lobe injuries. In *The Neurology of wartime.* Moscow: Press of the Academy of Medical Science of the USSR, 1949.

Zeigarnik, B. V. Disturbances of thought in mental patients. Doctoral dissertation, Inst. of Psychology, Moscow, 1959.

Zeigarnik, B. V. *The pathology of thought.* Moscow: Moscow Univer. Press, 1961.

Non-Russian

Adey, W. R. *Organization of the rhinencephalon reticular formation of the brain.* Boston: Little, Brown, 1958.

Adey, W. R. Paper read at Amer. Acad. Neurol. *Sympos. Rhinencephalon,* 1959, **17**.

Adey, W. R., Sunderland, S., & Dunlap, C. B. The entorhinal area: electrophysiological studies of its inter-relations with rhinencephalic structures and the brain stem. *J. clin. Neurophysiol.,* 1957.

Ajuziaguerra, J. de, Hécaen, H. *Le cortex cérébrale,* Paris: Masson, 1960.

Bailey, R., & Bonin, G., *The isocortex of man,* Urbana, Ill.: Univer. of Illinois Press, 1951.

Bálint, R. Seelenlähmung des Schauens. *Mschr. Psychiat. Neurol.,* 1909, **25**.

Baruk, H. *Les trubles menteaux dans les tumeurs cérébrales.* Paris: 1926.

Bay, E. Zum Problem der taktilen Agnosie. *Dtsch. Z. Nervenheilk.,* 1944, **73**.

Bay, E. Agnosie und Funktionswandel. *Monogr. ges. Neurol. Psychiat.,* 1950, **73**.

Bianchi, L. *La méchanique du cerveau et la fonction des lobes frontaux.* Paris: Arnette, 1921.

Bolton, J. S. *The cortical localization of cerebral function.* Edinburg and London: Oliver and Boyd, 1933.

Bremer, F., & Dow, R. S. The cerebral acoustic area of the cat. *J. Neurophys.,* 1939, **2**.

Brickner, R. M. *The intellectual functions of the frontal lobes.* New York: Macmillan, 1936.

Broadbent, W. H. On the cerebral mechanisms of speech and thought. *Med. Chir. Trans.*, 1872, **55**, 145.

Broca, P. Sur la faculté du langage articulé. *Bull. Soc. Anthrop., Paris,* 1861, **6**, 493.

Brodmann, K. *Vegleichende Lokalisationslehre der Grosshirnrinde.* Leipzig: 1909.

Brouwer, B. Chiasma, Tractus Opticus, Sehstrahlung und Sehrinde. *Bumke-Foerster Handb. Neurol.*, 1936, **6**.

Brun, R. Klinische und anatomishe Studien über Apraxia. *Schweiz. Arch. Neurol. Psychiat.*, 1921, **42**, 350.

Brutkowsky, S. The effect of prefrontal lobectomies on salivary conditioned reflexes in dogs. *Acta Biol. exp., Lodz,* 1957, **17**.

Brutkowsky, S., Konorsky, J., Lawicka, W., & Stephen, I. L. The effect of the removal of the frontal poles of the cerebral cortex on motor conditioned reflexes. *Acta Biol. exp., Lodz,* 1951.

Bucy, P. C. (Ed.) *The precentral motor cortex.* Urbana, Ill.: Univer. of Illinois Press, 1944.

Campbell, A. W. *Histological studies on the localisation of cerebral functions.* London: Cambridge Univer. Press, 1905.

Charcot, P. *Oeuvres completes.* Paris: 1887.

Chritchley, M. *The parietal lobes.* London: Arkola, 1953.

Dejérine, J. *Semiologie des affections du système nerveux.* Paris: Masson, 1914.

Delay, J. *Les astereognosies.* Paris: Masson, 1935.

Delgado, J. M. R. Evaluations of permanent implantation of electrodes in the brain. *EEG clin. Neurol.*, 1955, **7**.

Delgado, J. M. R., Rodwold, H. E., et al. Evoking conditioned fear by electrical stimulation of subcortical structures in the monkey brain. *J. comp. Physiol. Psychol.*, 1956, **49**.

Denny-Brown, D. The nature of apraxia. *J. nerv. ment. Dis.*, 1958, **126**.

Denny-Brown, D. The frontal lobes and their functions. In *Modern trends in neurology.* London: St. George's Hospital, 1951. Chap. 2.

Dusser de Barenne, I., Carol, H. W., & McCulloch, W. S. Physiological neuronography of the cortico-strial connections. *Res. Publ. Ass. nerv. ment. Dis.*, 1942, **21**.

Feuchtwanger E. Die Funktionen des Stirnhirns. *Monogr. Ges. Neurol. Psychiat.*, 1923, **38**.

Finkelburg, P. Asymbolie. *Berlin klin. Wschr.*, 1870, **7**.

Finkelburg, P. *Anatomie des menschlichen Gehirns auf myelogenetische Grundlage.* Leipzig: 1920.

Flechsig, P. *Anatomie des menschlichen Gehirns auf myelogenetischer Grundlage.* Leipzig: 1920.

Flourens, P. J. M. Recherches expérimentalles sur les propriétés et les functions des système nerveux dans les animaux vertébrés. Paris: 1824.

Foerster, O. Symptomatologie der Erkrankungen des Gehirns. Motorische Felder und Bahnen: Sensorische Felder und Bahnen. *Bumke-Foerster Handb. Neurol.*, 1936, **6**.

Frankfurter & Thiele, R. Experimentelle Untersuchungen zur Beezoldschen Sprachsext. *Zeitschr. f. Sinnesphys.*, **47**, 1912.

Freeman, W. Frontal lobes. *Res. Publ. Ass. nerv. ment. Dis.*, 1948, **27**.

Freeman, W., & Watts. I. W. *Psychosurgery: intelligence, emotion and social behavior following prefrontal lobotomy.* Springfield, Ill.: Charles C Thomas, 1942.

Fritisch, G., & Hitzig, E. Über die elektrische Erregbarkeit des Grosshirns. *Arch. Anat., Phys., Wiss. Med.*, 1870, **3** and **37**.

Fulton, J. F. *Functional localization in relation to frontal lobotomy.* New York: Oxford Univer. Press, 1949. (a)

Fulton, J. F. *Physiology of the nervous system.* (3rd ed.) New York: Oxford Univer. Press, 1949. (b)

Fulton, J. F. A note on definition of the "motor" and "premotor" areas. *Brain*, 1935, **58**.

Fulton, J. F. Forced grasping and groping in relation to the syndrome of the premotor areas. *Arch. Neurol. Psychiat.*, 1937, **31**.

Gelb, A., & Goldstein, K. *Psychologische Analysen hirnpathologischen Fälle.* Leipzig: Barth, 1920.

Goldstein, K. Das Symptom, seine Entstehung u. Bedeutung. *Arch. Psychiat. Neurol.*, 1925, **76**.

Goldstein, K. Die Lokalisation in der Grosshirnrinde. *Bethe's Handb. norm. pathol. Physiol.*, 1927, **10**.

Goldstein, K. The significance of the frontal lobes for mental performance. *J. Neurol. Psychopath.*, 1936, **11**, 17.

Goldstein, K. *Aftereffects of brain injuries in war.* New York: Grune & Stratton, 1947. (a)

Goldstein, K. *Language and language disorders.* New York: Grune & Stratton, 1947. (b)

Goldstein, K., & Scheerer M. Abstract and concrete behavior. *Psychol. Monogr.*, 1941, **53.**

Goltz, L. Über die Verrichtungen des Grosshirn. *Arch. ges. Phys.*, 1887, **34.**

Granit, R. *Receptors and sensory perceptions.* New Haven, Conn.: Yale Univer. Press, 1956.

Gratiolet. *Observations sur la forme et le poid ducerveau.* Paris: 1861.

Head, H. *Studies in neurology.* Vols. I, II. London: Oxford Univer. Press, 1920.

Head, H. *Aphasia and kindred disorders of speech.* New York: Macmillan, 1926. 2 vols.

Hebb, D. O. The effect of early and late brain injury upon test scores. *Proc. Amer. phil. Soc.*, 1942, **85.**

Hebb, D. O. Man's frontal lobes. *Arch. Neurol. Psychiat.*, 1945, **54.**

Hebb, D. O. Intelligence, brain functions and the theory of mind. *Brain,* 1959, **82.**

Hécaen, H., Ajuziaguerra, J., Magis, C., & Angelerques, R. Le problème de l'agnosie des physiognomies. *Encephale,* 1952, **4.**

Henschen, S. E. *Klinische und anatomische Beiträge zur Pathologie des Gehirns.* Stockholm: 1920–22.

Hess, W. R. *Diencephalon.* New York: Grune & Stratton, 1954.

Hitzig, F. *Untersuchungen über das Gehirn.* Leipzig: 1874.

Holmes, G. Disturbances of vision by cerebral lesions. *Brit. J. Ophthalmol.*, 1918, **2,** 353.

Holmes, G. Cerebral integration of ocular movements. *Brit. med. J.*, 1938, **2,** 107.

Holmes, G., & Horrax, G. Disturbances in spatial orientation. *Arch. Neurol. Psychiat.*, 1919, **1,** 385.

Horlow, J. Recovery after severe injury of the head. *Publ. Messagh. neurol. Soc.*, 1868, **2.**

Isserlin, H. Die Aphasie. *Bumke-Foerster Handb. Neurol.*, 1936.

Jackson, J. H. *Selected papers.* Vols. I, II. London: 1952.

Jacobsen, C. F. Function of frontal association areas in primates. *Arch. Neurol. Psychiat.*, 1935, **33,** 558.

Jakobson, R. *Kindersprache, Aphasie und allgemeine Lautgesetze.* Uppsala: 1942.

Jakobson, R., & Halle, M. *Fundamentals of language.* The Hague: Mouton, 1956.

Janet, P. Beiträge zur Lokalisation im Grosshirn und über deren praktischen Verwertung. *Dtsch. med. Wschr.*, 1888, **14.**

Janet, P. *L'evolution de la memoire et de notion du temps.* Paris: Maloine, 1928.

Jastrovitz, M. Beiträge zur Lokalisation im Grosshirn und über deren praktische Verwendung. *Dtsch. med. Wschr.*, 1888, **V14.**

Kleist, K. Corticale (innervatorische) Apraxie. *J. Psychiat.*, 1907.

Kleist, K. Die alogischen Denkstörungen. *Arch. Psychiat.*, 1930, **90.**

Kleist, K. *Gehirnpathologie.* Leipzig: Barth, 1934.

Klüver, H., & Bucy, P. C. Psychic blindness and other symptoms following bilateral temporal lobectomy in rhesus monkey. *J. Psychol.*, 1938, **119,** 352.

Klüver, H. An analysis of the effects of the removal of the occipital lobes in monkeys. *J. Psych.*, 1937, **2.**

Lange, J. Agnosien und Apraxien. *Bumke-Foerster Handb. Neurol.*, 1936, **2.**

Lashley, K. S. *Brain mechanisms and intelligence.* Chicago: Univer. of Chicago Press, 1929.

Lashley, K. S. *The neurophysiology.* New York: McGraw-Hill, 1960.

Lassek, A. M. The pyramidal tract. *J. nerv. ment. Dis.*, 1954, **95,** 721.

LeBeau, J., & Petrie, A. A comparison of the personality changes after prefrontal selective surgery, etc. *J. ment. Sci.*, 1953, **99.**

Liepmann, H. Das Krankheitsbild der Apraxie ("Motorische Asymbolic"). *Mschr. Psychiat.*, 1900, 8.

Liepmann, H. *Die Störungen des Handelns bei Gehirnkranken.* Berlin: 1905.

Liepmann, H. Motorische Aphasie u. Apraxie. *Mschr. Psychiat.*, 1913, **34.**

Lissauer, H. Ein Fall von Seelenblindheit. *Archiv. Psychiat. Neurol.*, 1889, **21.**

Loeb, J. *Comparative physiology of the brain and comparative psychology.* London: Murray, 1902.

Luciani, L. On the sensory localization in cortex cerebri. *Brain,* 1884, **7.**

Luciani, L. *Trattato di fisiologia.* Firenze: 1913.

Luria, A. R. Brain disorders and language analysis. *Language & Speech,* 1958, **1.**

Luria, A. R. The directive role of speech in development and dissolution. *Word,* 1959, **15.** (a)

Luria, A. R. Disorders of "simultaneous perception" in a case of bilateral occipitoparietal brain injury. *Brain*, 1959, **82.** (b)

Luria, A. R. Differences between disturbance of speech and writing in Russian and in French. *Int. J. Slav. Linguist. Poet.*, 1960, **3.**

Luria, A. R. Factors and forms of aphasia. CIBA Symposium. *Disorders of language.* London: 1963.

Luria, A. R. *Human Brain and Mental Processes.* Academy of Pedagog. Sciences Press, 1963. (English Tr. New York: Harper & Row, in press.)

McCulloch, W. S. Interareal interactions of the cerebral cortex. *Physiol. Rev.*, 1943, **3.**

McCulloch, W. S. Some connections of the lobe established by physiological neuronography. *Res. Publ. Ass. Nerv. ment. Dis.*, 1948, **27.**

McLean, P. D. *The limbic system with respect to two life principles.* Vol. 2. New York: Josiah Macy, 1959.

Magoun, H. W. *The waking brain.* Springfield, Ill.: Charles C Thomas, 1958.

Marie, P. Revision de la question de l'aphasie. *Semaine Med.*, 1906.

Mettler, F. (Ed.) Selective partial ablation of the frontal cortex. New York: B. Hoeber, 1949.

Meynert, T. *Der Bau der Grosshirnrinde.* Vienna: 1867–1868.

Milner, Brenda. Psychological defects produced by temporal excision: the brain and human behavior. *Res. Publ. Ass. nerv. ment. Dis.*, 1958.

Monakow, von C. *Die Lokalisation im Grosshirn und der Abbau der Funktionen durch corticale Herde.* Wiesbaden: Bergmann, 1914.

Munk, H. *Über die Funktionen der Grosshirnrinde.* Berlin: Hirschwald, 1881.

Nielsen, J. M. *A textbook of clinical neurology.* 2nd ed. New York: Hoeber-Harper, 1946.

Nissl von Meyendorff, E. *Vom Lokalisationsproblem der artikulierten Sprache.* Leipzig: Barth, 1930.

Olds, J. *Physiological mechanisms of reward.* Nebraska Press, 1955.

Olds, J. Higher function of the nervous system. *Annu. Rev. Physiol.*, 1959, **21.**

Ombredane, A. *L'aphasie et l'elaboration de la pensée explicite.* Paris: Presses Universitaires, 1951.

Panizza, R. Osservazioni sul nervo ottico. *G.J.R. Int. Lomb.*, 1855, **7.**

Penfield, W., & Ericson, T. C. *Epilepsy and cerebral localisation.* Springfield, Ill.: Charles C Thomas, 1941.

Penfield, W., & Evans, J. The frontal lobe in man: a clinical study with maximum removals. *Brain*, 1935, **58.**

Penfield, W., & Jasper, H. *Epilepsy and the functional anatomy of the human brain.* Boston: Little, Brown, 1954.

Penfield, W., & Rasmussen, T. *The cerebral cortex of man.* New York: Macmillan, 1950.

Pfeiffer, R. A. Pathologie der Hörstrahlung und der corticalen Hörsphaere. *Monatbuch. Neurol.*, 1936, **6.**

Piaget, J. *La psychologie de l'intelligence.* Paris: 1947.

Pick, A. *Die agrammatischen Sprachstörungen.* Berlin: Springer, 1913.

Pick, A. Aphasie. *Bethe's Handb. Neurol. Pathol. Physiol.*, 1931, **15** (1).

Poliak, S. *The vertebrate visual system.* Chicago: Univer. of Chicago Press, 1957.

Poppelreuter, W. *Die psychischen Schädigungen durch Kopfschuss.* Vols. I, II. Leipzig: Voss, 1917–1918.

Pötzl, O. *Die Aphasielehre vom Standpunkt der klinischen Psychiatrie.* Leipzig: Deutike, 1920.

Pribram, K. H. Comparative neurology and evolution of behavior. In *Behavior and evolution.* New Haven, Conn.: Yale Univer. Press, 1958. (a)

Pribram, K. H. Nocortical functions in behavior. In H. F. Harlow & C. N. Woolsey (Eds.), *Biological and biochemical bases of behavior.* Onsin University Press, 1958. (b)

Pribram, K. H. The neurology of thinking. *Behavioral Science*, 1959, **4**, 265–287.

Pribram, K. H. The intrinsic systems of the forebrain. In *Handbook of Physiology.* Vol. 2. New York: McGraw-Hill, 1960. (a)

Pribram, K. H. A review of theory in physiological psychology. *Annu. Rev. Psychol.*, 1960, **11**, 1–40. (b)

Rose, J. E. Cortical connection of the reticular complex of the thalamus. *Ass. Res. nerv. ment. Dis. Proc.*, 1950, **30.**

Rose, J. E., & Woolsey, C. N. Organisation of the mammalian thalamus and its relationships to the cerebral cortex. *EEG clin. Neurol.*, 1949.

Ruch, T. C. Cortical localization of somatic sensibility. *Res. Publ. Ass. nerv. ment. Dis.*, 1953, **15.**

Rylander, C. *Personality changes after operations on the frontal lobes.* London: 1939.

Scoville, W. B., et al. Observation on medical temporal lobotomy. *Res. Publ. Ass. nerv. ment. Dis.,* 1953, **31.**

Sittig, O. *Apraxie.* Berlin: Karger, 1931.

Stauffenberg, W. Über Seelenblindheit. *Arb. Hirn-Anat. Inst. Zürlich,* 1914.

Stein, H., & Weizsäcker, V. Über Sensibilitätsprüfungen. *Dtsch. Z. klin. Med., Heidelberg,* 1926, **151.**

Sugar, O., French, J. D., & Ghusid, J. B. Cortico-cortical connections of the superior surface of temporaloperculum in monkey. *J. Neurophys.,* 1948, **2.**

Sugar, O., Peter, R., Amadoz, L. V., & Criponissiotes, B. Cortico-cortical connections of the cortex buried in interparietal and principal sulci of monkey. *J. Neuropath. exp. Neurol.,* 1950, **9.**

Teuber, H. L. Physiological psychology. *Annu. Rev. Psychol.,* 1955, **6.**

Teuber, H. L. *Visual field defects after penetrating wounds of the brain.* Cambridge, Mass.: Harvard Univer. Press, 1960.

Tizard, B. The psychological effects of frontal lesions. *Acta Psychiat. Neurol.,* 1958, **33.**

Troubezkoi, S. *Grundzüge der Phonologie.* Pragise: 1939.

Vogt, C., et al. Allgemeine Ergebnisse unserer Hirnforschung. *J. Psychol. Neurol.,* 1919–1920, **25.**

Wallon, H. *De l'acte à la pensée.* Paris: Flammarion, 1942.

Ward, A. A., Pedan, J. K., & Sugar, O. Cortico-cortical connections in monkey with special reference of area 6. *J. Neurophys.,* 1946, **9.**

Warren, J. M. & Akert R. (Eds.). *The Frontal Granular Cortex and Behavior.* New York: McGraw-Hill, 1964.

Weisenburg, T. H., & McBride, K. E. *Aphasia.* New York: Oxford Univer. Press, 1935.

Weiskrantz, L. Behavioral changes associated with ablation of the amygdaloid complex in monkeys. *J. comp. phys. psych.,* 1956, **1.**

Welt, L. Über Characterveränderungen des Menschen in Folge der Läsionen des Stirnhirns. *Dtsch. Arch. klin. Med.,* 1888, **42.**

Wernicke, S. *Der aphasische Symptomenkomplex.* Breslau: 1874.

Wernicke, S. Zwei Fälle von Rindläsionen. *Arb. Psychiat. Klin.,* 1885, **2.**

Willbrandt, H. *Die Seelenblindheit als Herdenerscheinung.* Wiesbaden: 1887.

Wolpert, J. Die Simultanagnosie. *Z. ges. Neurol. Psychiat.,* 1924, **193.**

Wundt, W. *Grundzüge der physiologischen Psychologie.* Leipzig: 1873–1874.

Wyss, O. A. M., & Obrador, S. Adequate shape and rate of stimuli in electrical stimulation of the cerebral motor cortex. *Amer. J. Physiol.,* 1937, **120.**

Zangwill, O. L. *Cerebral dominance and its relation to psychological functions.* Edinburgh: Oliver & Boyd, 1960.

27

Seizures and Convulsive Disorders

ELI S. GOLDENSOHN

HISTORY

Convulsive disorders are recurrent disturbances in mental function or movements of the body or both which result from overactivity of irritated brain cells. The terms "convulsive disorder" and "epilepsy" are synonymous. The recurrent psychic and physical symptoms which constitute epilepsy were recognized and excellently described by Hippocrates in about 400 B.C. (Temkin, 1938). Although epilepsy was known as the "sacred disease" and was considered to be caused by the gods by other ancient healers, Hippocrates's work *On the Sacred Disease* (Chadwick & Mann, 1950) appreciated that epilepsy is the result of organic disease of the brain. Nevertheless, over two thousand years elapsed before a considerable part of the medical profession ceased to look for supernatural causes as the origin of epileptic seizures. It was not until the middle of the eighteenth century that a materialistic approach to the understanding of epilepsy became dominant and the supernatural origin of seizures was discarded. A classic history of epilepsy from antiquity until the end of the nineteenth century entitled *The Falling Sickness* was written by Temkin (1945).

In the second half of the nineteenth century, the English neurologist Hughlings Jackson (Taylor, 1958) concluded that epilepsy resulted from excessive discharging of nerve cells in the gray matter of the brain and that partial seizures including "intellectual" symptoms of epilepsy could be attributed to irritation of specific areas of the brain. These conclusions were confirmed and extended by the measurement of electrical activity of the brain through the human scalp (electroencephalography), which was first reported by the German psychiatrist Hans Berger in 1929, and by electrical stimulation and recording directly from the brain of epileptics at the time of surgery (Baldwin, Bailey, Ajmone-Marsan, Klatzo, & Tower, 1958; Penfield & Jasper, 1954). Also, knowledge of etiological factors has increased in recent years, and a specific or presumptive cause for seizures can now be established in more than half of patients with epilepsy.

With this increased understanding of epilepsy, many symptoms which in the past were believed to be functional have been found to be related to abnormal neuronal discharges and therefore to be a part of epilepsy (Goldensohn & Gold, 1960; Landolt, 1960). The manifold symptomatology encountered in epilepsy depends, in great part, on the numerous sites of origin of these abnormal discharges and on the way their effects spread to other areas of the brain. Just as motor and sensory changes indicate the area of the brain from which the abnormal discharges arise, so often do mental symptoms, such as psychical illusions, hallucinations, other alterations in thinking, arrest or modifications of speech, and clouding of consciousness. For this reason, the analysis of any seizure disorder rests on a thorough understanding of the anatomy and physiology of the brain as well as on the pathological factors which affect cerebral function.

Knowledge of the pathophysiological and chemical changes involved in creating epileptogenic tissue is incomplete. Studies on the basic mechanisms of the epileptic discharge by neurophysiological techniques have recently entered the era of recording electrical activity from single cells in the living brain with microelectrodes (Goldensohn & Purpura, 1963; Kandel & Spencer, 1961; Li, 1959). Investigations of the biochemical abnormalities of epileptogenic tissue (Tower, 1961) and the recognition of genetically determined abnormalities of cellular metabolism in diseases in which seizures occur, such as phenylketonuria (Centerwall, Centerwall, Acosta, & Chinnock, 1961) and galactosemia (Dormandy & Porter, 1961), are opening new areas for the recognition, prevention, and treatment of disorders which cause epilepsy.

The first effective treatment of epilepsy was introduced in 1857 by Locock, who described the use of bromides (1857). Bromides are still occasionally used in the treatment of convulsive disorders. Phenobarbital was introduced by Hauptmann in 1912 (Hauptmann, 1912) and has remained one of the most effective and useful of the anticonvulsants. The next significant advance in the medical treatment of epilepsy occurred in 1937, when the first nonsedative anticonvulsant, phenytoin sodium (Dilantin), was introduced by Merritt and Putnam (1938). Since that time, a number of other effective compounds have been introduced, and it is estimated that about 85 per cent of patients with recurrent seizures can obtain complete or nearly complete control with medicine (Yahr & Merritt, 1956). The surgical removal of abnormal brain tissue responsible for epilepsy was attempted for many centuries with poor results. The era of modern neurosurgery began in 1886, when Sir Victor Horsley successfully operated on the brain of a patient for the relief of focal seizures. In the past few decades, the most notable advances in surgical treatment have come from Penfield and his colleagues (Penfield & Jasper, 1954).

INCIDENCE

Epilepsy is a relatively common disorder. It is more frequent than tuberculosis and about as prevalent as diabetes. There are no precise statistics on the number of epileptics in the United States. Roughly, 1 in every 200 people has recurrent seizures. The epidemiologist Kurland estimates that there are a minimum of 640,000 individuals in the United States subject to recurrent convulsive disorders (1959). Other estimates range up to 1.5 million, based on draft-board figures of World Wars I and II. There is a slight preponderance of male patients over females, and according to Lennox, more than 70 per cent of patients have their first attack before the age of 20 years (1960). There is no good evidence for significant differences in the incidence of epilepsy among national groups, races, or religions. There are no studies concerning the effect of rural versus urban living or of economic status on the incidence of epilepsy.

ETIOLOGY

In every case of epilepsy, the search for the cause of the seizures is a most important consideration. Life-threatening conditions such as brain tumors and conditions which can result in permanent intellectual deficit must be recognized and treated promptly. The seizures themselves are symptoms which indicate to the examiner that an underlying disease process is responsible for them. There are almost as many causes for seizures as there are diseases which directly or indirectly damage the brain. Among the causes are brain injury during birth or in later life, congenital defects, infectious diseases of childhood, meningitis, encephalitis, brain abscess, parasitic infestations, progressive degenerative diseases such as cerebral lipoidosis, Schilder's disease, diffuse sclerosis, cerebral vascular accidents, and brain tumors. Other causes include endocrine disorders such as hypoparathyroidism and hyperinsulinism and inborn errors of metabolism due to imbalance or abnormality in cellular enzyme function, which includes such entities as phenylketonuria and galactosemia. Each of these entities is discussed in such standard texts as Merritt's *Textbook of Neurology* (1963) or Ford's *Diseases of the Nervous System in Infancy, Childhood and Adolescence* (1960).

Since convulsive disorders may precede other symptoms of an underlying disease of the nervous system by many years, repeated evaluations are necessary. Psychological factors appear to be relatively unimportant in the etiology of seizures. There is no good evidence to substantiate the assumption that psychological factors can either cause epilepsy or lead to complete control of seizures. Psychological factors can, however, precipitate and either increase or reduce the frequency of seizures (Efron, 1957). Although most epilepsy is not hereditary, there is a predisposition toward seizures that is familial. The incidence of recurrent seizures in near relatives of patients with epilepsy is about 3.2 times the rate in the general population (Lennox & Jolly, 1954). Whether these familial incidence figures reflect mainly the contribution of both known and as yet unrecognized diseases in which inborn errors of metabolism exist upon the larger number of individuals in which there are no significant genetic influences is not known. As was previously mentioned, a definite or presumptive cause for epilepsy can be found in more than half of patients with recurrent seizures. However, the majority of patients in whom a cause for the epilepsy is found do not have remedial lesions.

In children, the most frequent causes of seizures are congenital defects, trauma, inborn errors of metabolism, infections, and unknown genetic influences. Trauma plays a large role in seizures beginning in young adults. Brain tumor is a cause of seizures at all ages but becomes a frequent cause after age 30. Both cerebrovascular disease and tumors are frequent causes of seizures which begin after the age of 50 (Penfield & Jasper, 1954; Raynor, Paine, & Carmichael, 1959).

THEORETICAL INTERPRETATION

Some of the theoretical considerations which are important in the understanding of epilepsy are (1) the nature of the abnormal discharges which initiate the seizures, including electrical and chemical aspects; (2) the degree of functional localization existing in the brain which may be correlated with the clinical aspects of the seizures; (3) the mode of spread of abnormal discharges from one part of the brain to another; (4) the influence of genetic factors; and (5) the interrelationships between epilepsy and personality disorder.

Both clinical (Earle, Baldwin, & Penfield, 1953) and experimental (Morrell & Baker, 1961; Smith & Purpura, 1960) evidence indicates that injury to the cerebral cortex capable of producing some degree of cellular destruction is capable of initiating recurrent paroxysmal electrical discharges from the periphery of the damaged zone which can result in seizures. Seizure discharges from a freezing lesion placed on the cortex of an experimental animal tend to discharge about once every two seconds for many hours, with waxing and waning in amplitude of discharge and recurring episodes of slowing of the discharge rate from time to time (Smith & Purpura, 1960). The basis for this periodic activity, which is also characteristic of the human being with seizures, is unknown and apparently resides in the basic organization of gray-matter aggregates in the brain as it can be developed in neuronally isolated slabs of cortex. The discharges from the brain when limited in frequency and confined to a small area usually produce no clinical seizure phenomena. The electrical discharges which are recorded by electroencephalography are postsynaptic potentials which represent overactivity and hypersynchronization of electrical activity of both cell bodies and dendrites of cortical neurons (Goldensohn & Purpura, 1963). The postsynaptic potentials themselves are only indirectly related to nerve impulses, which are the actual means of effecting influences over long distances along axons, but rather represent changes in the excitability of the nerve cells which inhibit or facilitate impulse transmission (Purpura, 1959). The abnormal discharging has been related to a number of chemical and ionic changes involving substances normally found in the brain such as gamma-aminobutyric acid acetylcholine and sodium (Tower, 1961). Seizure discharges from injured areas are reflected in the opposite hemisphere (Morrell & Baker, 1961) and remain for some time after the original discharging lesion has ceased to be active. Discharges from a single cortical area if sufficiently intensive spread and cause synchronous discharges from all areas of the brain, resulting in generalized seizures. The reason that a seizure terminates is not understood, nor is the reason that seizures recur at intervals. The mechanism of inhibition of attacks by psychic influences is also obscure (Efron, 1957).

Although any human being is capable of manifesting seizures, the hereditary influence on seizure manifestations is a real although not prepotent one. Of monozygotic twins with epilepsy, 37 per cent showed concordance, while only 1.8 per cent of dizygotic siblings showed concordance (Marshall, Hutchinson, & Honisett, 1962). If an abnormal EEG is equated with a tendency toward convulsions, the concordance of monozygotic twins is considerably higher (Lennox & Jolly, 1954).

SYMPTOMATOLOGY

The manifestations of epilepsy are so varied that a classification according to clinical patterns is possible only in broad descriptive terms. Classification according to clinical seizure patterns takes no consideration of the cause of the seizures or of the part of the brain that is initially involved. It is, however, the most frequently used single classification for seizures. Classification according to the cause of the convulsive disorder is unwieldy because of the great number of diseases and etiological agents which are responsible for recurrent seizures, and it is inadequate because the basis for nearly half of the instances of recurrent seizures is never determined. Classification of convulsive disorders on the basis of the area of the brain in which the abnormal discharges begin is particularly helpful in the localization of potentially remedial lesions, but this is also inadequate because in a great many instances the area from which the seizures originate cannot be ascertained. Because each of these methods of classification is extremely useful but individually inadequate, it is necessary for clinical understanding and rational treatment that each individual convulsive disorder be classified according to all three: (1) clinical pattern or patterns, (2) location in the brain where it originates, and (3) the cause of the disorder in brain function. The most satisfactory classifications encompassing the above concepts are those of Penfield (Penfield & Jasper, 1954) and Symonds (1955). Table 1 shows a general classification.

In recent years there has been a tendency, not yet generally accepted, to bring the descriptive classification in to a degree of compatibility with anatomical localization. The use of the electroencephalogram in finding the area of the brain from which abnormal function originates has been of considerable importance in this regard (Jasper & Kershman, 1949). Generally, the origin of the seizure is referred to as being "primary generalized" or "centrencephalic" (Penfield & Jasper, 1954) if the symptoms and the electrical activity appear to involve the entire brain at once and as being "focal" if the symptoms and the electrical activity originate in one part of the brain. All local or focal seizures are capable of spreading to involve the entire brain and therefore of giving clinical secondary generalized major seizures which appear identical to those which begin in the entire brain at once. The forms of epilepsy which appear to involve all or most of the brain at once are the primary generalized major attack (grand mal), short absence (petit mal), massive spasms, generalized myoclonic jerks, and akinetic attacks. Among the seizure types which appear to originate in a local area of the brain are focal motor, focal sensory, psychomotor, aphasic, visceral, and emotional seizures.

The Generalized Major Attack (Grand Mal)

This seizure, which involves the entire brain, either begins as a focal attack which spreads and becomes generalized or may involve the entire brain at once. In 60 per cent of patients with generalized major attacks, there is some evidence of a focal beginning for the generalized attacks, but in many of these instances the exact area of the focal beginning is not found. In some patients who have evidence of focal onset for their seizures, there may be prodromal symptoms which last for hours or days, the patient undergoing a change in mood or experiencing unusual sensations or sensory distortions. An aura or warning lasting for a fraction of a second to a few seconds occurs in the majority of patients and is actually the first symptom of the seizure. The aura may consist of an illusion, such as a feeling that the environment is hauntingly strange or familiar, of a sensation of floating, or of an auditory or visual hallucination. Other auras are visceral sensations such as feelings of movement in the abdomen or rising epigastric sensations, sensations of numbness of a part of the face or an extremity, ringing in the ears, and movements such as the twitching of a finger or the pulling of the mouth to one side. All these symptoms, although part of the seizure, are also considered warnings because complete consciousness is not lost until after they occur, and they frequently last long enough to enable the patient to remove himself to an area of relative safety before the seizure advances to become a generalized major attack.

The generalized major convulsion, or grand

TABLE 1. CLASSIFICATION OF CEREBRAL SEIZURES

A. Clinical patterns	*B. Localization—general areas (under each general area give specific gyrus or area when possible)*	*C. Etiology—general categories (under each general category indicate the specific cause when possible)*
1. Generalized major (grand mal)	1. Frontal lobe	1. Congenital
2. Short absence (petit mal)	2. Parietal lobe	2. Infections
3. Focal motor (Jacksonian, adversive, postural)	3. Supplementary motor area	3. Intoxications
4. Somatosensory	4. Temporal lobe (*a*) medial (*b*) lateral	4. Trauma—birth and later
5. Special sensory (auditory, vertiginous, olfactory, gustatory)	5. Occipital lobe	5. Neoplasm
6. Psychical (illusions, hallucinations, fear, anxiety)	6. Diencephalon	6. Vascular
7. Automatisms (affective, gestural, ambulatory, verbal)	7. Brain generally	7. Metabolic
8. Psychomotor—combinations of 5 and/or 6 with 7	8. Site undetermined	8. Hereditary
9. Aphasia (or loss of articulation)		9. Cause undetermined
10. Myoclonic (bilateral symmetrical)		
11. Myoclonus (random, asymmetrical)		
12. Akinetic		
13. Infantile or massive spasms		
14. Autonomic (abdominal, respiratory, cardiac)		

* Each of the three categories (A, B, and C) listed should be represented when classifying an individual's seizure disorder

mal attack, is characterized by complete loss of consciousness and falling to the ground. The fall is sometimes preceded by a cry or scream due to forcible expiration resulting from involuntary contraction of the muscles of respiration. Following the fall, the patient stiffens because of generalized tonic contraction of his muscles. If the attack was preceded by an aura, i.e., if it had a focal beginning, the initial contractions may not be symmetrical; the head may turn to one side, and one arm may be raised above the head. If there has been no focal beginning, the contractions are usually symmetrical. The lower limbs are usually extended, and the upper limbs flexed. During the tonic phase, which usually lasts less than a minute, respiration is stopped, and pallor or cyanosis occurs. Following the tonic stage, jerking or clonic movements occur in all four extremities. The tongue may be bitten during involuntary contraction of the masticatory muscles, and urinary incontinence often occurs. Following the clonic phase, the seizure proper terminates as excessive abnormal discharging from the brain ceases, but the patient is usually confused and sleepy and may have a headache. In the confused postseizure state, he may perform complex acts such as undressing or walking into the street. The patient has no recollection of the seizure proper nor of the complex automatic activity which he may perform in the immediate postseizure state. Usually the entire generalized major seizure is over in less than five minutes.

The Short Absence (Petit Mal)

Originally the term "petit mal" was used to describe all small seizures; later it was limited to the description of three types of small seizures (Lennox, 1960): (1) a short absence or simple loss of awareness for a few seconds, (2) generalized myoclonic jerking, and (3) akinetic attacks or the abrupt loss of muscle tone, causing the patient suddenly to collapse to the floor. The term "petit mal" in recent years has become even more restricted (Yahr & Merritt, 1956) and is now used to describe short absences without focal beginning which are accompanied by three spike and wave discharges per second on the electroencephalogram and generalized myoclonic jerks which show similar electroencephalographic patterns. Typical petit mal absences are characterized by short episodes of unresponsiveness which generally last less than fifteen seconds each and which usually occur many times per day, sometimes as many as several hundred. There is no involuntary movement or falling. Following the short interruption of consciousness, the individual is mentally clear and is able to continue what he was doing before the attack. The petit mal absence occurs mainly in children; it does not appear for the first time after the age of 20 and usually disappears by early adult life. At times, petit mal absences become practically continuous, and the patient experiences cloudy states which last for several minutes or, rarely, as long as seventy-two hours (Goldensohn & Gold, 1960). There may be amnesia for all behavior during this period.

Focal Seizures

Focal seizures have already been referred to in the discussion of generalized major seizures in which the auras are, in actuality, focal seizures which then spread to become generalized major attacks.

Focal motor and focal sensory seizures. In these attacks the onset or the entire episode involves one specific part of the body, such as a limb or part of a limb or the face. Focal sensory attacks involve primarily sensations such as numbness or tingling. Focal motor attacks primarily involve movement. Focal sensory seizures beginning in the postrolandic sensory cortex may spread to the prerolandic motor area of the frontal lobe, resulting in localized movements, and vice versa. Seizure discharging from either of these areas often spreads to involve the remainder of the brain, resulting in generalized major seizures (grand mal). Other types of focal seizures include adversive attacks with head and eyes turning to one side. Such seizures often originate in the contralateral frontal lobe. Vertiginous attacks characterized by a feeling of spinning and loss of balance are usually due to brainstem or more peripheral vestibular disturbances but are sometimes focal seizures originating in the temporal lobe Penfield & Jasper, 1954).

Psychomotor Seizures

These are a common type of attack and take a large variety of forms (Baldwin et al., 1958; Gastaut, Toga, Roger, & Gibson, 1959; Penfield & Jasper, 1954). The typical attack begins as a sensory, intellectual, or affective experience which is followed by a depression of awareness or clouding of consciousness and by automatic behavior. The onset or aura of the psychomotor seizure may be an unidentifiable but unpleasant smell or taste or an illusion in which objects or people seem unreal or in which things being experienced for the first time seem to have happened before. Also identifiable or unidentifiable voices or sounds or vivid complex experiences involving objects or people occur. The onset may also be intense fear, a feeling of warmth or cold in the upper part of the body and head, sensation of movement in the abdomen, or consciousness of increased respiration or of the heartbeat. The form of the onset is usually very much the same from attack to attack. Following such an onset or aura, the patient becomes unresponsive to verbal stimuli but may pick at his clothes or examine objects about him. Often he actively resists efforts to prevent his free movement in his confused state. Upon recovery from the attack, which usually lasts from one to three minutes, the patient is completely amnesic to all the attack except the onset or aura. The psychomotor attack is one of the commonest types of the cerebral seizures and most frequently has its origin in the temporal lobe. The hallucinations most frequently originate in the lateral temporal lobe, and the automatic activity in the medial temporal structures including the amygdala nucleus and the overlying cerebral cortex (Baldwin et al., 1958) The attacks do not always have a temporal lobe origin, however, and lesions on the posterior inferior surface of the frontal lobe, the lateral aspect of the frontal lobe, and the insula of the frontal lobe may also initiate this type of attack (Gastaut et al., 1959). For this reason, the term "psychomotor" is reserved for the clinical description of the seizure type and should not be used interchangeably with the term "temporal lobe seizures" (DeJong, 1957).

PERSONALITY DISORDER

The association of personality disorder with cerebral seizures and particularly with psychomotor epilepsy is frequent. Various studies show that between 30 and 75 per cent of patients with frequent seizures have significant personality disorder (Gibbs, 1951; Pond & Bidwell, 1960; Small, Millstein, & Stevens, 1962). Episodic as well as chronic behavioral disturbances are encountered. Recurrent behavioral changes are sometimes associated with electroencephalographic changes considered characteristic of seizures (Goldensohn & Gold, 1960), but usually they are not seen. There is no similar evidence, however, that chronic personality changes are directly related to continuous subclinical interference with perception and thinking by paroxysmal activity within the brain, but this has been hypothesized (Glaser, Newman, & Schafer, 1963).

The concept that there is an epileptic personality has generally been discarded (Guerrant, Anderson, Fischer, Weinstein, Jaros, & Deskins, 1962; Hill et al., 1957; Landolt, 1960). A comparison of epileptic patients with seizures arising from the temporal lobe and those with other forms of chronic disease revealed marked similarity between the two groups, and it has been suggested that "chronic disease personality" might be a better term (Anderson, Guerrant, Weinstein, & Fisher, 1962). Nevertheless, the personality disorders encountered are generally believed to be particularly frequent and characteristic in patients with temporal lobe epilepsy (Bingley, 1958; Gibbs, 1951). These characteristics include adhesiveness, concrete thinking, and egocentricity (Bingley, 1958; Landolt, 1960). However, in a recent study on a group of clinic patients having both frequent seizures and severe personality disorders, the group with temporal lobe epilepsy could not be separated from those having other types of seizures on the basis of their personality characteristics (Small et al., 1962). If patients with recognized progressive neurological disorder are excluded, mental deterioration in epilepsy is infrequent. Studies on patients with apparent mental deterioration which could be reversed raised the question of whether subclinical epilepsy might be responsible for the apparent reversible deterioration (Chaudry & Pond, 1961; Putnam & Merritt, 1941; Yeager & Guerrant, 1957). Although it is a common objective and subjective experience that there is lethargy associated with the therapeutic amounts of some anticonvulsants, these have not been found to change mental capacity appreciably as a result of long-term use (Wapner, Thurstan, & Holowach, 1962).

DIAGNOSIS

A person with recurrent seizures, regardless of the cause, is generally considered to have epilepsy. The diagnosis is in the greatest part dependent upon the description given by the patient or his family of transitory disturbances of functions of the brain which appear episodically. Typically, these are characterized by recurrent episodes of loss of consciousness and involuntary movements. In the many less typical seizures, difficulty in differential diagnosis with functional disorders and syncope is common. The electroencephalogram is of great diagnostic value in such problems (Gastaut, 1954).

Because the term "epilepsy" does not refer to a disease entity but to a symptom complex, it is essential whenever possible to detect the nature of the underlying disease process responsible for the seizures. Because the convulsive disorder can precede other symptoms by years, repeated examinations are necessary. When seizures appear for the first time in an adult, a thorough neurological examination, x ray of the skull, and electroencephalogram constitute the minimal preliminary study. Other examinations including spinal-fluid studies, scanning the brain for unusual uptake of radioactive material, pneumoencephalograms, and arteriograms may also be indicated. Such studies in adults are used to discover or rule out the possibility of a brain tumor, which is one of the principal causes of seizures in the adult.

In children, tumors are seldom the cause of seizures. However, in more than half of all children who have the onset of recurrent seizures in the first two years of life, a contributing cause of the seizures can be found. A list of some of the illnesses responsible for seizures in childhood was given in a previous section of the chapter. A thorough historical review and general neurological examination is indicated for all children with seizures. The minimal laboratory work-up includes a complete blood count, urine analysis including examination for phenylketonuria, x ray of the skull, electroencephalogram, blood sugar, and serum calcium and phosphorus. Additional studies, such as spinal-fluid examination, pneumoencephalography, arteriography, and radioactive brain scanning, are done as indicated. An evaluation of the intellectual capacity of each child is needed, and complete psychological evaluations may be indicated both as aids in differential diagnosis and for the recognition and evaluation of psychiatric disturbances, which so frequently accompany convulsive disorders (Anderson et al., 1962; Guerrant et al., 1962; Small et al., 1962).

TREATMENT

Recurrent seizures, regardless of the cause, always require the long-term use of anticonvulsant medication, and treatment is begun as soon as the presence of recurrent seizures is established. Simultaneously, the search for, and treatment of, any underlying disease process begins. Anticonvulsants are usually needed for many years and are generally continued for at least two to three years after the last seizure has occurred. Reduction of dosage is then done slowly. The principle for the use of anticonvulsant medication is to start with an estimated therapeutic dose and gradually increase it until either the seizures are controlled or bothersome side reactions related to the dose develop. If full control is not obtained, the drug is continued and an additional compound is added. As many as three or four different drugs can be effectively combined and tolerated, and combinations of anticonvulsants are generally more effective than single drugs.

Some correctable causes of unsuccessful treatment are the following: (1) failure to administer sufficient dosage—this is the most common cause; (2) improper classification of seizure type, with resulting failure to use the most effective drugs; (3) failure to recognize progressive neurological disease; (4) frequent shifting of drugs; (5) premature withdrawal of drugs; and (6) poor indoctrination of patients concerning methods of administration of drugs and the psychological and social problems the patient must meet. Anticonvulsants can produce serious toxic effects requiring prompt discontinuation of the offending compound and the substitution of another. For this reason, as well as for adjustment for maximal therapeutic effect, it is necessary that all patients receiving anticonvulsant therapy be seen regularly by the physician and that periodic appropriate laboratory studies be done as indicated.

The solution of psychological, educational, social, and family problems favorably influences not only the adjustment of the patient to his illness but also the frequency of attacks. Patients with seizures still encounter much difficulty in obtaining acceptance in school, community, and social activities. It is not unusual for participation in social activities to be terminated by the occurrence of a seizure in public. If accurate information about the disorder is supplied, most families accept the epileptic member as an individual in need of personal support and make the necessary adjustments without disrupting the family unit. The problems of overprotection of the patient must also be met. It is desirable that the patient be allowed to engage in as much normal activity as possible, but climbing to dangerous heights and working with dangerous machinery should be avoided. It is important that swimming always be very carefully supervised.

About 85 per cent of patients are completely or nearly completely free of seizures on anticonvulsant medication (Yahr & Merritt, 1956). Of those whose seizures cannot be controlled by medication, a relatively small number have areas of damaged epileptogenic brain tissue which are suitable for surgical removal. Relief of seizures by operation is achieved in about 56 per cent of this limited group (Baldwin et al., 1958; Penfield & Jasper, 1954).

REFERENCES

Anderson, W. W., Guerrant, J. S., Weinstein, M., & Fisher, A. The epileptic personality: does it exist? *Neurology*, 1962, **12**, 301.

Baldwin, M., Bailey, P., Ajmone-Marsan, C., Klatzo, I., & Tower, D. (Eds.) *Temporal lobe epilepsy*. Springfield, Ill.: Charles C Thomas, 1958.

Berger, H. Ueber das Elektronkephalogramm des Menschen. *Arch. Psychiat. Nervenkr.*, 1929, **87**, 527.

Bingley, T. Mental symptoms in temporal lobe gliomas. *Acta Psychiat. Neurol. Scand. Suppl.*, 1958, **33** (120), 1–151.

Centerwall, W. R., Centerwall, S. A., Acosta, P. B., & Chinnock, R. F. Phenylketonuria. I. Dietary management of infants and young children. *J. Pediat.*, 1961, **59**, 93–101.

Chadwick, J., & Mann, W. N. (Trs.) The medical works of Hippocrates. *Blackwell Sci. Publ.*, 1950, 301.

Chaudhry, M. R., & Pond, D. A. Mental deterioration in epileptic children. *J. Neurol. Neurosurg. Psychiat.*, 1961, **24**, 213.

DeJong, R. N. Psychomotor or temporal lobe epilepsy: a review of the development of our present concepts. *Neurology*, 1957, **7**, 1–14.

Dormandy, T. L., & Porter, R. J. Familial fructose and galactose intolerance. *Lancet*, 1961, **1**, 1189–1194.

Earle, K., Baldwin, M., & Penfield, W. Incisural sclerosis and temporal lobe seizures produced by hippocampal herniation at birth. *Arch. Neurol. Psychiat.*, 1953, **69**, 27.

Efron, R. The conditioned inhibition of uncinate fits. *Brain*, 1957, **80**, 251–262.

Epstein, A. W., & Ervin, F. Psychodynamic significance of seizure content in psychomotor epilepsy. *Psychosom. Med.*, 1956, **18**, 43–55.

Ford, F. R. *Diseases of the nervous system in infancy, childhood and adolescence.* (4th ed.) Springfield, Ill.: Charles C Thomas, 1960.

Gastaut, H. *The epilepsies: electro-clinical correlations.* Springfield, Ill.: Charles C Thomas, 1954.

Gastaut, H., Toga, M., Roger, J., & Gibson, W. C. A correlation of clinical, electroencephalographic and anatomical findings in nine autopsied cases of "temporal lobe epilepsy." *Epilepsia*, 1959, **1**, 56.

Gibbs, F. A. Ictal and non-ictal psychiatric disorders in temporal lobe epilepsy. *J. nerv. ment. Dis.*, 1951, **113**, 522–528.

Glaser, G. H., Newman, R. J., & Schafer, R. Interictal psychosis in psychomotor temporal lobe epilepsy: an EEG-psychological study. In G. H. Glaser (Ed.), *E.E.G. and behavior.* New York: Basic Books, 1963. Chap. 14.

Goldensohn, E. S., & Gold, A. P. Prolonged behavioral disturbances as ictal phenomena. *Neurology*, 1960, **10**, 19.

Goldensohn, E. S., & Purpura, D. P. Intracellular potentials of cortical neurons during focal epileptogenic discharges. *Science*, 1963, **139**, 840–842.

Guerrant, J., Anderson, W. W., Fisher, A., Weinstein, M. R., Jaros, R. M., & Deskins, A. *Personality in epilepsy.* Springfield, Ill.: Charles C Thomas, 1962.

Hauptmann, A. Luminal bei Epilepsie. *München Med. Wschr.*, 1912, **54**, 1907–1909.

Hill, D., Pond, D. A., Mitchell, W., & Falconer, M. A. Personality changes following temporal lobectomy for epilepsy. *J. ment. Sci.*, 1957, **103**, 18–27.

Jasper, H. H., & Kershman, J. Classification of the E.E.G. in epilepsy. *EEG clin. Neurophysiol. Suppl.*, 1949, **2**, 123–131.

Kandel, E. R., & Spencer, W. A. Excitation and inhibition of single pyramidal cells during hippocampal seizure. *Exp. Neurol.*, 1961, **4**, 162–179.

Kurland, L. T. The incidence and prevalence of convulsive disorders in a small urban community. *Epilepsia*, 1959, **1**, 143–161.

Landolt, H. *Die Temporallappenepilepsie und ihre Psychopathologie.* Basel: S. Karger, 1960.

Lennox, W. G. (In collaboration with Margaret A. Lennox.) *Epilepsy and related disorders.* Boston: Little, Brown, 1960.

Lennox, W. G., & Jolly, D. H. Seizures, brain waves and intelligence tests of epileptic twins. *Ass. Res. nerv. ment. Dis.*, 1954, **33**, 325–345.

Li, C. L. Cortical intracellular potentials and their responses to strychnine. *J. Neurophysiol.*, 1959, **22**, 436–450.

Locock, C. Discussion of paper by Edward Sieveking, M.D., FRCP, at meeting of Royal Medical and Chirurgical Society on May 11, 1857. *Lancet* 1857, **1**, 527.

Lorentz de Haas, A. M. Social aspects of epilepsy in childhood. *Epilepsia*, 1962, **3**, 44.

Marshall, A. G., Hutchinson, E. O., & Honisett, J. Heredity in common diseases. A retrospective survey of twins in a hospital population. *Brit. Med. J.*, 1962, **1**, 1–6.

Merritt, H. H. *Textbook of neurology.* (3rd ed.) Philadelphia: Lea & Febiger, 1963.

Merritt, H. H., & Putnam, T. J. Sodium diphenylhydantoinate in treatment of convulsive disorders. *J. Amer. Med. Ass.*, 1938, **3**, 1068–1073.

Morrell, F., & Baker, L. Effects of drugs on secondary epileptogenic lesions. *Neurology*, 1961, **11**, 651–664.

Penfield, W., & Jasper, H. *Epilepsy and the functional anatomy of the human brain.* Boston: Little, Brown, 1954.

Pond, D. A., & Bidwell, B. H. A survey of epilepsy in 14 general practices. II. Social and psychological aspects. *Epilepsia*, 1960, **1**, 285.

Purpura, D. P. Nature of electrocortical potentials and synaptic organizations in cerebral and cerebellar cortex. *Int. rev. Neurobiol.*, 1959, **1**, 47–163.

Putnam, T. J., & Merritt, H. H. Dullness as an epileptic equivalent. *Arch. Neurol. Psychiat.*, 1941, **45**, 797.

Raynor, R. B., Paine, R. S., & Carmichael, E. A. Epilepsy of late onset. *Neurology*, 1959, **9**, 111–117.

Small, J. G., Milstein, V., & Stevens, J. R. Are psychomotor epileptics different? A controlled study. *Arch. Neurol.*, 1962, **7**, 187–194.

Smith, T. G., Jr., & Purpura, D. P. Electrophysiological Studies on Epileptogenic lesions of cat cortex. *EEG clin. Neurophysiol.*, 1960, **12**, 59–82.

Symonds, C. Classification of epilepsies. *Brit. med. J.*, 1955, **1**, 1235–1238.

Taylor, J. (Ed.) *Selected writings of John Hughlings Jackson,* Vol. 1. New York: Basic Books, 1958.

Temkin, O. Review of Ebbell's translations of the Papyrus Ebers. *Isis,* 1938, **28** (1), 126–131.

Temkin, O. *The falling sickness.* Baltimore: Johns Hopkins Press, 1945

Tower, D. B. In J. Folch (Ed.), *The neurochemistry of convulsive states. Chemical pathology of the nervous system.* New York: Pergamon Press, 1961.

Wapner, J., Thurston, D. L., & Holowach, J. Phenobarbital: Its effect on learning in epileptic children. *J. Amer. Med. Ass.*, 1962, **182**, 937.

Yahr, M. D., & Merritt, H. H. Current status of drug therapy of epileptic seizures: report to Council on Pharmacy and Chemistry. *J. Amer. Med. Ass.*, 1956, **161**, 333–338.

Yeager, C. L., & Guerrant, J. S. Subclinical epileptic seizures: impairment of motor performance and derivative difficulties. *Calif. Med.*, 1957, **86**, 242–247.

28

Speech Disorders

JON EISENSON

The field of speech disorders (speech pathology and audiology) has been, fortunately, defined for us at a national conference in graduate education in speech pathology and audiology held in Highland Park, Illinois, from April 29 to May 3, 1963. A resolution by the participants declared: "The field of speech pathology and audiology is concerned distinctively with the processes and disorders of human symbolization and communication, and interacts with the biological, physical, behavioral, and social sciences."

The relationships of speech pathology and audiology as a discipline to the field of clinical psychology are clearly inherent in the quoted definition. Speech pathologists and audiologists, in their clinical, research, and teaching activities, are concerned with normal and deviant speech, voice, language, and hearing processes.

Speech pathologists may also be known as "speech clinicians," "speech correctionists," and "speech therapists." As a rule, the term "speech pathologist" is reserved for those practitioners who have been educated and trained, clinically, beyond the master's level. The term "audiologist" is similarly reserved for clinicians with advanced education and training who are primarily concerned with the nonmedical aspects of the evaluation and treatment of persons with hearing impairments.

NATURE OF SPEECH DISORDERS

Although speech disorders obviously consist in what a listener hears that sounds aberrant when he responds to a speaker, occasionally disorders are covert in that the speaker must exercise excessive and sometimes anxious control to prevent the production of an aberrant evocation. For the most part, we shall be concerned with the more obvious deviations in the manner or content of speech that may be more or less objectively considered speech disorders.[1]

From the point of view of a respondent, any individual who speaks so that attention is distracted from the content of his communicative effort to the manner of production may be considered to have a disorder of speech. The distraction, as in the case of aphasics and possibly of stutterers, may be in the content itself. For the majority of speech disorders, however, it is usually assumed, perhaps ingenuously, that the basic defect is in the manner of production rather than in the content, in the *how* rather than the *what* of the speaker's utterance. Thus, speech sounds may be distorted, or a speaker's voice may be weak, overloud, poorly modulated, or of an unacceptable quality.

Both the "objective" and the "subjective" aspects of disordered speech are incorporated in the following list of characteristics. Specifically, an individual may be said to have a disorder of speech—is speaking defectively—if his overt products or the self-

[1] The following working definitions may be useful: A "speech deviation" refers to any marked and maintained deviation from a pattern accepted as standard in a speech community; a "speech defect" refers to a deviation sufficient to divert attention from the communicating content to the manner of communication (see Milisen, 1957).

evaluations of his products, actual or potential, may be described in one or more of the following ways:

1. They are not easily intelligible because of articulatory distortions.
2. They are not readily audible.
3. They are audible, but vocally unpleasant.
4. They are visibly unpleasant because of the manner of production.
5. They are deviant in regard to conventional speech rhythm, changes in vocal pitch, or stress or are labored in manner of production.
6. They are linguistically deficient (the words or sentence structure is inadequate or unconventional in regard to the verbal habits of the linguistic community).
7. The manner (voice, articulation, language) is inappropriate in terms of the age, sex, and physical appearance of the speaker.
8. The speaker responds to his own communicative efforts or fails to engage in oral communication because he believes that one or more of the above characteristics may be present.

DEVELOPMENTAL ASPECTS OF NORMAL SPEECH

Before undertaking a consideration of the types and incidence of speech defects, we need to appreciate the fact that speech is a developmental process. The assessment of speech to determine whether it is normal or defective requires an awareness that the correlated abilities to vocalize, articulate, verbalize, and combine words into units of meaning develop over a period of many years. From the linguistic point of view, the development ends with the beginning of decline. But even from the articulatory aspect, proficiency is achieved over a number of years. For example, Templin's (1953) findings indicate that not until age 3 do childern produce American English vowels and diphthongs correctly (in the manner of most normally speaking adults in their community) in 90 per cent of their utterances. Proficiency for some of the consonants is not reached by most girls until age 7 and by most boys until about age 8. Voices continue changing until almost puberty for girls and often continue to undergo changes well into adolescence for many boys. The changes in parts of speech in vocabulary continue throughout life; the length and complexity of sentences change rapidly during preschool years, vary somewhat for the sexes, and vary considerably according to factors of individual intelligence, stimulation, and educational and socioeconomic status of parents (Eisenson, Auer, & Irwin, 1963; McCarthy, 1954; Metraux, 1956; Templin, 1957).

TYPES OF SPEECH DEFECTS

Speech defects—the products of speech disorders—are frequently classified into four major groups:

1. Impairments of articulation (deviations in the manner and end products of articulatory efforts)
2. Defects of phonation (voice production)
3. Stuttering
4. Language dysfunctions (delayed language, childhood and adult aphasia

These classifications are probably too broad and too general to be practical for most clinical purposes. Although they are the bases for Milisen's (1957) discussion of the incidence of speech disorders, we shall present an alternative classification based on categories of persons with defective speech rather than on "disembodied" speech defects. In our alternative classification, we indicate awareness that a single disorder such as cleft palate or a cerebral-palsied condition may be the etiological basis for several types of speech defects.

1. Defects of articulation, which include distortions, omissions, and substitutions of recognized speech sounds in a given oral linguistic system
2. Defects of voice, which include aberrant quality, inadequate or poorly controlled loudness, limited and inappropriate pitch, and inadequate duration in light of the needs of a communicative effort
3. Stuttering (stammering)
4. Cluttering—indistinct speech or dysrhythmia, associated with delayed language maturation
5. Cleft-palate speech (hypernasality and distorted articulation)
6. Cerebral-palsied speech (delayed language, defective language and articulation, and vocal inadequacies)
7. Retarded language development, including congenital aphasia

8. Impairments of previously established language function (childhood aphasia and adult aphasia)

9. Speech defects associated with impaired hearing

Later in our discussion we shall expand on some of the individual types of speech defects and their etiological correlates. Our next immediate consideration will be the incidence of speech defects.

INCIDENCE OF SPEECH DEFECTS

Most broad survey studies of the incidence of speech defects have been limited to the school-age population, usually considered to be between the ages of 5 and 21. The most recent wide survey of the incidence of defective speech was conducted in 1959 by the committee on legislation of the American Speech and Hearing Association. This report estimated that in 1960 at least three million children in the United States would be in need of remedial attention for defects of speech or impairments of hearing because of implications of these defects for educational, emotional, and social adjustments. The findings of the report are summarized in Table 1.

Specific studies based on specific school populations tend to show wide variations (Milisen, 1957, p. 249), varying from 3 or 4 per cent to more than 23 per cent. It is likely that definition, degree of severity, differences in criteria, as well as experience of the investigators account for the wide discrepancies. Although we would expect that the older the cases in the sample, the lower the expected incidence, this is by no means the trend of the findings. Carhart (1939, pp. 61–70) has written that high school teachers in 405 Illinois high schools reported that 20.8 per cent of the students were judged to be in need of remedial speech lessons. This is in interesting contrast with another study by Carhart (1945), in which he reported that approximately 1 per cent of World War I draftees were considered to have seriously defective speech.

We may conclude from such surveys either that the quality of speech among Americans deteriorated considerably between 1917 and 1961 or that the criteria for what constitutes normal and deviant speech vary with the purpose of the investigator and the population investigated. The method of investigation is also undoubtedly a factor in determining the supposed incidence of defective speech. Surveys conducted by questionnaire with nonprofessional reporters (the 1939 Carhart study) might well yield a high percentage of speech defects because the reporters might consider that any deviation from a particular standard, including standards of pronunciation, constitutes deviant speech. Thus an Easterner newly arrived in the Midwest might be designated as having defective speech. Variations in pronunciation might, for persons who are not professional speech pathologists, be confused with articulatory impairments and so result in a higher incidence of speech defects for a particular population than a survey of the same population by a speech pathologist would show. In any event, this writer is inclined to accept the 5 per cent finding of the American Speech and Hearing Association committee on legislation. This report, inci-

TABLE 1. ESTIMATED NUMBER OF SCHOOL-AGE CHILDREN PER 10,000 WITH EACH TYPE OF SPEECH OR HEARING PROBLEM

Type of problem	*Percentage of children with serious problem*	*Number of children with serious problem*
Articulation	3.0	300
Stuttering	1.0	100
Voice	.1	110
Cleft-palate speech	.1	10
Cerebral-palsied speech	.1	10
Retarded speech development	.2	20
Speech problem due to impaired hearing	.5	50
Total	5.0	500

dentally, is in fairly close agreement with an ASHA mid-century White House conference report (1952), which estimated that 5 per cent of the school-age population based on an assumed population of 40,000,000 had defective speech.

Sex Distribution

It is widely recognized that boys begin to speak later and arrive at articulatory proficiency about a year later than girls. The incidence of defective speech, whether on a functional or an organic basis, is also higher among males than among females. Studies on this point have been reviewed by Berry and Eisenson (1956) and Milisen (1957). Apparently, the proportion of males with defective speech continues to be greater than that for females throughout the school grades and through the college years. In one representative study, Morley (1952) found in a survey taken during the World War II period at the University of Michigan that the incidence and proportion of speech-defective students were consistently higher among male than among female students. The ratios ranged from 1.6 males to 1 female to as high as 3.4 males to 1 female.

We shall return to the matter of sex distribution when we consider the individual speech-defect classifications.

CAUSES OF DEFECTIVE SPEECH

We need to be ever mindful that there are no disembodied speech defects. They exist in persons and are incorporated in the expression of personalities. A condition, even an obvious organic anomaly, may be the basis of a major speech defect in one individual and yet seem to have minor implications, at least as far as deviant speech is concerned, for another. Cleft-palate conditions that seem alike tend to be associated with common defects of voice and articulation. In individual instances, however, there is considerable variation. On the other hand, some children and occasional adults with relatively minor organic anomalies, such as poor dental occlusions, seem to have seriously defective articulation. In the final analysis, the individual must be studied to determine not only what may be a basic etiological correlate for his aberrant speech or aberrant language but also what the aberration means to him in the maintenance of his disorder. This is so whether the initiating factor is organic, psychogenic, or imitative. Individually it often seems that what may be cause for defective speech in one person constitutes cause for effective, if not superior, speech in another.

Organic Causes

Some speech defects are obviously organic in origin. Severe hearing impairments, especially if they are congenital or acquired during the first two years of life, are associated with recognized defects of voice and articulation. The voice and articulatory defects of children with oral clefts are, at least at the outset, directly attributable to the physical condition. Severe dental irregularities, especially when they are associated with malocclusions, are likely to be associated with defective articulation. Paralysis of the organs of the speech mechanism or the vocal mechanism is almost invariably associated with defective articulation and vocalization. Cerebral-palsied conditions that involve the speech mechanism are also directly associated with defects of articulation and vocalization and, often less directly, with impairment of language function. Aphasic involvements as well as dysarthrias (articulatory dysfunctions) in adults are clearly associated with neuropathologies. The course of the latter involvements, however, seems subject to factors that are more individually determined. (See Eisenson, 1963b, pp. 20–24, for a discussion of differential diagnosis of language disorders in children, and Eisenson, 1963a, pp. 503–506, for a consideration of some factors related to the maintenance of aphasic involvements in adults.)

Functional Causes

Children with normal sensory intake learn to speak for the most part by ear and to a lesser degree through what they see. If what they hear, or what they see that is associated with what they hear, is defective in acoustic end result or manner, their own speech (language, articulation, voice) is likely to be defective. Such defects are established by identification and imitation. Despite the end product, the speech produced results from normal adaptive behavior. Essentially, imitative speech defects are caused by the older person, usually a parent but occasionally an older sibling or playmate, who is serving as the model for the child. Some children who learn to speak "normally but defectively" change their patterns as they change their identifications. Similarly, some children who learn to speak quite normally change to deviant patterns as the result of later identifications.

Psychogenic Causes

Our discussion will assume that a psychogenic cause for defective speech is arrived at by positive evidence and is not to be presupposed on the basis of the absence of organic or imitative factors. There are some adequate and apparently well-adjusted individuals with defective speech. There is, however, considerable evidence that in many instances speech defects, as either initiating or maintaining causes, are psychogenic. Not infrequently they seem to be the fault of the parents; more especially, they are maternally centered. Wood (1946, pp. 255–275), for example, studied a group of 50 children with articulatory defects and their parents for indications of maladjustments. The inventories used included the California Test of Personality for the parents and the Thematic Apperception Test for the children. Wood's findings indicated that both mothers and fathers had poor adjustment scores, with the mothers, as a group, significantly less well-adjusted than the fathers. A finding of particular importance was that the social standards of the mothers were very high in comparison with other adjustment scores. Wood concluded ". . . on the basis of this study that functional articulatory defects of children are definitely and significantly associated with maladjustments and undesirable traits on the parts of the parents and that such factors are usually maternally centered."

Though the children, according to Wood, showed better over-all adjustment than their parents (the basis for this comparison is not altogether clear), the TAT findings for about half the children revealed dynamisms which suggested frustration, withdrawing tendencies, and a sense of lack of affection.

Peckarsky (1952) studied a group of 26 mothers of children with "psychogenic" (no determined organic cause) delayed speech and a control group of 26 mothers of children with normal speech development. Peckarsky describes the mothers, as a group, to be "overprotective, rigid individuals who are restrictive in their demands upon their children." The home environment was found to be characterized by "confusion, tension, and a lack of organization in the performing of routine tasks." To be sure, some of the same characteristics were found by Peckarsky to be present in the homes of children with normal speech, but the degree to which they were present was considerably more moderate than in the homes of the children who were delayed in speech development.

Findings along the same line were found by Moncur (1952, pp. 155–164) when he compared groups of mothers of stuttering and of nonstuttering children by means of an especially prepared questionnaire. Moncur's questionnaire was designed to reveal tendencies toward parental dominance and the holding of children to excessively high standards of conduct. Moncur concluded from his findings that the mothers of stutterers tended to reveal a variety of dominating behavior that included ". . . domination by disciplinary action, domination by oversupervising and overprotecting the child, domination by holding the child to excessively high standards, and domination by adverse parental criticism."

We may note that the general findings of Wood, Peckarsky, and Moncur are consistent with those of this writer in the studies he has conducted at the speech and hearing clinics with which he has been associated. We may also note, in anticipation, that comparable observations are reported by Johnson (1956, p. 197; 1961, p. 95) for the parents of young stutterers. One wonders, then, if parents of speech-defective children tend to be so much alike, why the children have different speech defects—some (superficially at least) having delayed speech onset, others speaking with articulatory defects, and still others becoming stutterers.

LEVEL OF INTELLIGENCE AND SPEECH DEFECTS

Although speech defects may be found among persons on all levels of intelligence, the consensus of the evidence leaves little question that the lower the intellectual level, the greater the incidence of defective speech. This in no way suggests that a genius may not lisp, that stutterers as a group or as individuals are likely to fall within the normal to above ranges of intelligence, or that a person with a voice disorder should be expected to be a bit dull. The evidence, when analyzed, does strongly suggest that there are several interrelated factors, possibly with a common cause, that include populations with defective speech. Often the representatives of the population will have multiple disorders that include delayed language, defective articulation, as well as defective voice production. Many persons born cerebral-palsied would be included in this multiple handicapped group. Another group with a high incidence of speech and language defects is the severely mentally retarded. A third group is the deaf *and* mentally retarded.

It might well be pointed out, however, that among children who are initially delayed in language development, and so in normal ability to communicate and relate, tests of intelligence tend to exaggerate the degree of intellectual retardation. Certainly early tests of preschool children with delayed language development, even when those tests minimize the need for oral language, are often very poor assessments of intellectual status. When communicative behavior is established, retests often show significant increments in intelligence quotients.

Surveys of the range of intelligence and averages for speech-defective schoolchildren are reviewed by Berry and Eisenson (1956, pp. 7–8). The results indicate that as a selected population, speech-defective schoolchildren, as a group, fall below the average of the population from which they are drawn. Those speech-defective children with physical handicaps include a higher proportion of ones with below average intelligence than the nonhandicapped schoolchildren. Wolfe (1950, pp. 234–251), in a study of 50 cerebral-palsied children, found that 26 per cent of his subjects were so limited in intelligence as to be considered uneducable. Taylor (1959, pp. 25–30), reporting on the intellectual competence of 187 cerebral-palsied adult patients, found that the incidence of mental deficiency was about 50 per cent. These patients had all been examined when they were children. Taylor observes: "The general impression was that earlier estimates on patients with severe physical handicaps stood up surprisingly well. In many instances their constancy was greater than that of some of the medical findings" (1959, p. 27). Although intellectual deficits are not as striking among other groups of physically handicapped children with speech defects, except for stutterers and those with "fuctional" articulatory defects, the general findings indicate that compared with the population at large, a greater proportion of speech defectives will be found on the lower end of the intellectual range.

If we switch the point of departure and consider the incidence of speech defects among mental retardates, we find general consensus that it is considerably higher than in the population at large. Furthermore, we are likely to find that the lower the intelligence of the group studied, the greater the incidence of defective speech and language production. (See Eisenson, 1963c, pp. 192–225, for a review of older studies.) Some specific more recent investigations will be briefly considered. Sachs (1951) studied the incidence of speech defects in a group of 210 mental defectives ranging between 10 and 20 years of age. He found that 57 per cent had defective speech. Gens (1950, pp. 32–36) found that from 70 to 75 per cent of institutionalized mentally defective children had disorders of speech. Smith (1962, pp. 111–124) reviewed the literature on the relationship between speech defects and mental retardation and found that the incidence ranged from 8 to 79 per cent, depending upon the intellectual range of the group studied. With the severely retarded, ". . . language development was delayed, articulation problems were more prevalent, and voice problems occurred commonly."

READING ABILITY AND SPEECH DEFECTS

A review of some of the literature that appeared between 1940 and 1960 on the relationship between reading difficulties and speech defects may be found in Eisenson, 1963c, pp. 200–201. Although the findings of investigations are by no means unanimous, most indicate that difficulties in reading and defects in speech are somehow related. That is, among the speech-defective population, even with the mentally retarded eliminated from consideration, we are likely to find a higher incidence of reading difficulties than in the population at large. Similarly, we are likely to find a higher incidence of speech defects among children with reading difficulties than among children without reading difficulties. Hildreth (1946, pp. 326–332) points to a number of language and speech factors that may be common to reading and speech difficulties. These include indistinct, inaccurate articulation; poor discrimination of speech sounds; and bilingual background. In a more recent study, Weaver, Furbee, and Everhart (1960, pp. 174–180) found that in a population of 638 first-grade children, there was a steady decrease in reading readiness as the number of articulatory faults increased.

EDUCATIONAL ACHIEVEMENT AND SPEECH DEFECTS

With important individual exceptions, the consensus of the evidence suggests that in the school-age population, including older children attending college, those with defective speech are somewhat retarded in school progress compared with those with normal speech (Berry & Eisenson, 1956, p. 9). When children with physical handicaps are included, the incidence of educational retardation is increased. For example, Kodman (1963) found that a group of 100 hard-of-hearing children (average hearing loss of 40 decibels) had a grade placement more than a year below what would be expected, considering their ages (average of 11 years), and a grade achievement a full year below their grade placement.

The questions of intelligence and other psychological factors associated with speech defects will be considered again in our separate discussions of some of the subgroups of the speech-defective population. Space limitations will not permit a discussion of all subgroups.

ARTICULATION DEFECTS

As indicated earlier, defects of articulation—the distortion, omission, or substitution of the appropriate sound in contextual speech—are found in 3 per cent of the speech-defective population. Recent advances in the assessment of articulation proficiency as well as in testing for articulatory defects have enabled clinicians to be considerably more objective in their findings than would have been possible before the 1940s.

Articulation Testing

Several tests for the assessment of articulatory proficiency have been in fairly wide use among speech clinicians since the 1930s. Test inventories such as the Bryngelson-Glaspey (Bryngelson & Glaspey, 1941) and the Hejna (Hejna, 1959) consist of pictures as stimuli selected on the basis of the judgments of the test authors as likely to elicit verbal responses that will include the individual sound in initial, medial, and final position and in sound clusters. Instructions for older tests were not rigid, and generally an examiner was advised to ask an examinee to repeat or imitate a stimulus word, especially those which are difficult to depict. The Templin-Darley (Templin & Darley, 1960) test is a more recent inventory and, for the most part, is one that was standardized for stimulus pictures, words, and administrative procedure according to recognized psychometric approaches.

There are several assumptions inherent in articulation testing: (1) Articulatory proficiency is correlated with maturation and is complete for most children by age 8. (2) Most children show proficiency in vowel production considerably earlier (by age 5) than they show over-all consonant proficiency. (3) Some consonants, e.g., *p, b, k,* and *g,* are proficiently produced much earlier than others, e.g., *s, z, l,* and *r.* The basic investigations for the development of articulatory proficiency include those by Poole (1934, pp. 159–161); Wellman, Case, Mengert, and Bradbury (1931); Templin (1957); Irwin (1952); and Metraux (1950).

The matters of the selection of words to elicit the articulatory response and the manner of presenting the words (spontaneous versus imitative) have been the subjects of controversy in the literature on articulatory testing. The literature and the controversy are briefly reviewed in an article presenting the results of the investigation by Siegel, Winitz, and Conkey (1963). These investigators found that the specific stimulus word used to evoke a response made little difference in the quality of the response. On the positive side, they found that the imitative method (presenting the word and the stimulus picture) elicited more correct responses than the spontaneous method (presenting the stimulus picture alone to evoke the anticipated word).

SPEECH-SOUND DISCRIMINATION

It is generally accepted that there is a relationship between speech-sound discrimination and articulatory ability. Kronvall and Diehl (1954) found a reliable relationship between discrimination and articulation measures in children with no known organic impairments. In a more recent study, Cohen and Diehl (1963, pp. 187–190) found that children with functional articulation defects in the first three grades of elementary school showed significantly more errors in speech-sound discrimination than a matched control group of children free of defective articulation. Both groups showed improvement in sound discrimination as they matured, but the defective group continued to show more errors than the normal controls.

Earlier studies on the relationship of speech-sound discrimination and articulatory defects showed variable and varying results, possibly because the instruments used were relatively crude and the measures employed were not comparable. Textbooks dealing with the correction of articulatory defects nevertheless assumed that poor discrimination of speech sounds was etiologically related to the presence of defective articulation, and so the authors included techniques for improving sound discrimination as part of the therapy for those with defective articulation (Curtis, 1948, p. 113; Van Riper, 1954, pp. 221–234).

Van Riper and Irwin (1958, pp. 22–26), aware of the inconsistent findings, point out that the concept as well as the techniques for measuring sound discrimination may explain the variation in results. They consider the ability for speech-sound (phonetic) discrimination to be a complex of several factors, including auditory memory span and phonetic analysis as well as the ability of an individual to monitor his own sound production so that he is actually producing a product comparable to the model in his mind.

STUTTERING

The limitations of this chapter do not permit either a survey or an evaluation of the theories of the etiology of stuttering. The literature on stutterers and stuttering (or stammering) is old, extensive, contradictory, and inconclusive. Any person with a bias may readily find in the literature considerable "evidence" to support his bias or substantiate his point of view.

Before beginning our general exposition on stuttering, we should like to list a few established findings relative to persons who stutter (Berry & Eisenson, 1956, pp. 250–254):

1. Stuttering occurs in about .7 to 1 per cent of the school-age population.

2. There are more male than female—approximate ratio of 3:1 or 4:1—stutterers.

3. Most stuttering begins in early childhood, about the age when children in the United States and in most Western countries are likely to begin their school careers. A second peak period for stuttering is early adolescence. Stuttering rarely has its initial onset during adulthood.

4. As a group, stutterers are normal or above in intelligence. In this respect they tend to be different from most other groups of speech-defective children.

5. There is a greater evidence of stuttering among twins than among single-born children.

Although many authorities would be inclined to lengthen their lists of established findings in regard to stutterers, the ones we have listed are likely to be included regardless of the bias or theoretical position of the authority.

In the monograph edited by Eisenson (1958), six contemporary authorities present their viewpoints on the essential cause or causes of stuttering and therapeutic approaches for stutterers. The viewpoints on stuttering in this monograph and in general can be classified into three major but not altogether discrete groups, along the following lines:

1. The stutterer has difficulty in speaking—he blocks, hesitates, repeats, grimaces, etc.—because of an unconscious (repressed) need to do so. The stutterer is viewed as essentially a neurotic individual who expresses his neuroticism in part through his aberrant speech.

2. Stuttering constitutes a breakdown or failure in functioning of the complex of neuromuscular and intellectual activity required for communicative speaking. This breakdown may occur temporarily for any speaker, but it is likely to be relatively chronic for those who are either emotionally or constitutionally predisposed to such dysfunction.

3. Stuttering is a learned mode of verbal behavior characterized by "anticipatory struggle" manifestations. It thus becomes an avoidance reaction that is associated with apprehension in regard to hesitations in speech and generally speaking in a manner the individual has learned to regard as stuttering.

In our present discussion, we shall not attempt to support or to refute any of these theoretic positions. Our emphasis shall be on an evaluation of some of the recent literature especially relative to the psychological implications for the individual who is a stutterer. We shall be especially concerned with studies that seek to discover (1) how the psychological environment of stutterers is different from that of normally speaking persons and (2) how the adolescent and young adult stutterers differ psychologically from adolescents and young adults who do not stutter.

Environmental Influences on the Young Stutterer

Johnson (1956), an eminent and diligent researcher on stuttering and stutterers, believes: "So-called stuttering children are not different from children not so diagnosed, with respect to birth injuries, other injuries, diseases, and general development. . . . They are not different with regard to intelligence. In general they are normal children."

Despite this, Johnson holds that a critical difference between the child who begins to stutter and the child who does not may be found in the reaction of his parents to the way he speaks. The parents of the young child who becomes a stutterer feel anxious about the child's speech. They are inclined also to generalize their anxieties so that they become worried not only about his speech but also about his conduct in general. The young child is looked upon as being nervous, unstable, or "defective in some way." The implication made by Johnson is that the crucial difference between the young child who becomes a stutterer and the child who does not is in the way his parents respond to him. This is characterized by a specific anxiety in regard to the child's speech, a generalized anxiety in regard to his total behavior, and an unrealistic expectation as to what normal speech and normal behavior in general should be.

> In all my years of counseling parents who have been concerned about their children's speech. the one thing about them that has impressed me most has been their degree of perfectionism. They differ among themselves, of course . . . but in general they have appeared, as a group, to be inclined to demand a little more of their children in the way of growth and development than would seem to be realistic (Johnson, 1961, p. 95).

Unreasonable expectation of speech performance was also found by Bloodstein, Jaeger, and Tureen (1952, pp. 308–315). They asked 24 parents of young stutterers and 24 parents of young nonstutterers to evaluate (as stuttering or normal) the recorded spontaneous speech of six stuttering and six nonstuttering children. They found that the parents of the stuttering children exceeded parents of the nonstutterers in the extent to which they diagnosed both the stuttering and the nonstuttering children as stutterers.

Glasner (1949, pp. 135–138) investigated the background of 70 stuttering children under the age of 5. Although he believes that young children who stutter are frequently and initially different in personality type from children who do not stutter, he found that on the whole the stuttering children had a background significant for overprotection and pampering, by overanxious, excessively perfectionist parents.

Adolescent and Young Adult Stutterers

Home influences. Glauber (1951, pp. 160–161) reported on a clinical study of mothers of stutterers. According to his report, the stutterer is an inadequate male who identifies himself almost completely, but defectively, with the mother. The basic fault, and the cause of the stuttering, is to be found in the personality of the mother, in her ambivalent attitudes toward the stuttering child, in particular, and in general toward other members of her family, including her own mother. Glauber holds that the nuclear etiological factors in the stuttering syndrome lie in specific elements in the personality structure of the mother. In a later writing, Glauber (1958, p. 99) characterized the mother as suffering from maternal anxieties:

> Birth, nursing, weaning, and onset of speech were felt by the mother as anxious experiences, with a special quality compounded of both separation and clutching. Also the child's taking control of his own locomotion, elimination, the development of his will in its negative and positive aspects, and of his intellect—all these landmarks of his ego development—were felt by the mother as the child's provocative acts of moving away.

Glauber came to his conclusions in regard to stutterers and their mothers on the basis of "an extensive study of the family constellation of stutterers and material from psychoanalyses of stutterers and their mothers." Some of

Glauber's observations differ in at least a few important respects from those previously considered.

Sheehan (1958, pp. 18–25) reviewed studies that employed projective techniques as the instruments of investigation in an assessment of personality aspects of stutterers. He concluded after an evaluation of the results that (1) findings based upon projective studies are inconsistent, (2) stutterers as a population fail to show a definite personality pattern, and (3) there is very meager evidence "to show that stutterers are different from anyone else." In keeping with some of his own studies, Sheehan did find that lower levels of aspiration existed among stutterers than among control subjects who were nonstutterers.

Social adjustments. Except for the subjective opinions in the psychoanalytic literature, in which stutterers tend to be characterized as severely neurotic individuals, there is considerably less unanimity as to their over-all social adjustment. It is, of course, possible that psychoanalysts are correct in their judgments in regard to the limited number of stutterers they treat who may also be severely neurotic. Objective studies, for the most part, do not support the generalized judgments of the psychoanalysts. On the other hand, we should appreciate the fact that most studies of adolescent and young adult stutterers are made using college students as subjects. These students may be a selected group of comparatively well-adjusted stutterers who are able to attend college and accept therapy because they have succeeded in making social adjustments despite their speech impediment. With these reservations in mind, some of the objective studies will now be reviewed.

Fiedler and Wepman (1951, pp. 110–114) investigated the self-concept of stutterers by comparing a group of 10 adult male stutterers and a control group of six nonstutterers in their responses to 76 statements descriptive of personality traits taken from Murray. They concluded that the stutterer's self-concept showed no characteristic difference from that of the nonstutterer.

Spriestersbach (1951, pp. 250–257) compared the verbal evaluation of a group of 50 male stutterers enrolled at the State University of Iowa with that of 183 normally speaking male students and 20 male psychotic patients at an Iowa state hospital. The evaluations were made to a series of pictures which were to be rated to the degree to which they fitted such words as "fun," "undesirable," and "worthwhile." Spriestersbach concluded that the stutterers differed somewhat from the nonstutterers in a way which suggested relatively mild degrees of social maladjustment. The stutterers differed markedly from the psychotic patients in their evaluations.

Murphy and Fitz Simons (1960), based partly on their own studies and partly on an extensive review of the literature, consider that the stutterer's self-concept is dominated by feelings of inadequacy and insecurity, both developed as a result of parent-related anxiety. They concluded that the stutterer's speech as well as his over-all adjustment problems are characterized by an underlying lower self-concept—lower in comparison with that of ideal self—than we are likely to find among peer nonstutterers. Their observations differ appreciably from those made by Fiedler and Wepman, cited earlier.

Our own observations relative to the personality and adjustment problems of stutterers permit of no firm conclusions that would hold for all persons who regard themselves or are regarded as stutterers. Many stutterers seem to be well-adjusted and well-adjusting persons whose adjustments include their inclinations to deviant speech. Some stutterers, we believe, would have greater difficulty, for an appreciable time, if they were suddenly free of their stuttering. Certainly, we would be surprised if adult stutterers—or any other adult—could be insensitive to the reactions of members of their environment who regarded them as not quite normal. Perhaps these adult stutterers are as normal as they want or need to be, despite their overhesitant, repetitive, and otherwise more than normally dysfluent speech. Stuttering too can become a way of life, with secondary gains that outweigh initial or maintained liabilities.

RETARDED LANGUAGE DEVELOPMENT

The child with *delayed* or *retarded language development* is one whose language proficiency is significantly below the norms on the bases of age and intelligence. In a related sense, the term "delayed speech" is used to characterize any significant retardation in language development or articulatory proficiency based on age expectancy alone. It should be understood that mental deficiency, either alone or associated with organic involvement, is the chief cause of retarded language development.

Parental Influences

In our earlier discussion of some factors associated with defective speech, reference was made to several studies concerned with the parents of speech-defective children. These studies tended to indicate that parents, and especially the mothers, of young speech-defective children were less well adjusted than parents of non-speech-defective children. Among the undesirable traits and attitudes found to exist to a greater degree among the test group parents were increased neurotic tendency, lower self-adjustment and social adjustment, greater over-all emotional instability, rigidity, perfectionism, overprotectiveness, and restrictiveness. In addition, many of the mothers had unrealistically high expectations for language performance in their children. In many instances, when a child who is physically and intellectually normal fails to develop speech, the basis of the retardation may be found in his reaction to his parents' expectations and anxieties. The language delay may often be both a reaction to the psychological environment and a manifestation of the child's own difficulties in adjustment.

Rejection. It is our belief that much of the attitude of the parents considered in the studies previously cited probably constitutes an unconscious rejection of the children. A child who senses such rejection and who cannot identify himself with his parent, and especially with his mother, is likely to be delayed in language development. Mowrer (1960, pp. 79–86) points out that a child must first identify himself with his parent with respect to verbal behavior before he can begin to wish to speak. He must, of course, be physically and intellectually mature and ready before the identification will motivate and evoke true speech. The rejected child either may make no such initial identification or may lose the identification once rejection is sensed.

Parental rejection which assumes the form of continuous disapproval and criticism—of language as well as of other forms of behavior—may lead the child to stop talking or may discourage the development of much talking. Where the rejection takes the form of apparent indifference, the ordinary rewards which strengthen speech behavior and which stimulate renewed efforts at speaking are absent. Speech may continue, but on an infantile level.

Goldfarb (1961, p. 200), discussing the schizophrenic child and the influence of his parents, observes:

> The speech model presented by a pathologically perplexed parent may be diminished in phonatory and rhythmic range. Further, in the face of unstructured emotional communication by this kind of parent, the child responds with confusion and unawareness of what is expected of him, so that he never achieves the complicated techniques required for connotative expression.

Ruesch (1957, p. 133), in his discussion of autistic, withdrawn, or frankly schizophrenic children and their disturbances in communication or their failure to develop conventional communicative skills, also considers the behavior of the parents to be the fundamental cause. Says Ruesch: "The parents' unresponsiveness in nonverbal terms prevents the child in the early years of life from learning how to relate through *movement and action.* The absence of early appropriate and gratifying communication through action, gesture, and object leaves traces." Some of the residual impressions and effects are shown in speech that is inadequate both for the expression of feeling and for the development of normal relationships through conventional communicative behavior.

CONGENITAL APHASIA AND LANGUAGE RETARDATION

An aphasic child is one who, as a result of cerebral damage or cerebral dysfunction, presents a syndrome of linguistic and nonverbal behavioral manifestations that distinguish him from other children, both normal and deviant, in the following respects:

1. Developmentally, the child shows specific or generalized perceptual differences, if not dysfunction; auditory inefficiency beyond any audiometrically determined hearing loss; and intellectual inefficiency over and above any "measurable" intellectual deficit.
2. Specific behavioral manifestations in-

clude morbidity of attention, perseveration, inconsistency of response, emotional lability, and frequently general hyperactivity.[2]

3. Linguistically, the child shows a marked amount of retardation in both the understanding and the production of language and a *disproportion and unevenness in the anticipated comprehension/production linguistic ratio.* Developmentally, the child does not show expected or normal increments or the "ordered" pattern by which most children increase their over-all linguistic proficiency.

The aphasic child is distinguished from other nonverbal children by the likelihood that his behavioral manifestations, such as perseveration and over-all lability of performance, as well as his sensory, perceptual, and intellectual inefficiency increase as he is confronted with linguistic situations and as he realizes that a linguistic response is expected of him.

Clinical Picture of the Congenitally Aphasic Child

In our experience, children who are properly designated as congenitally aphasic have, in their clinical backgrounds, established brain damage, atypical cerebral development or atypical developmental history, and behavioral manifestations and general intellectual functioning comparable to those of the child with cerebral pathology. These features include:

1. Perceptual dysfunction in one or more (not necessarily all) avenues.
2. Laterality confusion, often associated with difficulty in spatial orientation.
3. Inconsistency of responses to sounds, and especially to speech.
4. Specific defects in linguistic symbol behavior; developmental unevenness and disparity in the comprehension of auditory, visual, and motor experiences; marked disparity between intake and output of language; and productive language not on the level of expectancy in light of established receptive ability.
5. Morbidity of attention.
6. Morbidity of response. (This difficulty sometimes approaches an inability to change a response once one has been made.) This is frequently associated with difficulty or inability to change an initial frame of reference.
7. Auditory inefficiency. The child's functional hearing (proficiency of hearing) is appreciably below what would be expected from audiometric results.
8. Lability of nonverbal expressive behavior, with lability increasing as verbal behavior is normally expected.

Developmental Background: Out-of-phase Development and the Aphasic Child

Congenitally aphasic children are frequently found to be out of phase in their general sensory, motor, and perceptual development. In regard to these early developmental functions, they are literally "a-phasic" in that their development does not follow anticipated patterns in the establishment of sensorimotor skills and the behavior that is associated with such skills. The pattern and sequence of their development are more highly individualized than "established" norms lead us to expect. Developmental manifestations which usually go together—which correlate and are *in phase* for most normal children—show a lack of such correlation or phasing in children with known brain damage who are congenitally aphasic.

Clinicians are often confronted with the task of assessing nonverbal children for whom brain damage or atypical cerebral maturation cannot be clearly demonstrated by either clinical history or neurological diagnosis. We consider the diagnosis of congenital aphasia to be appropriate only if the developmental history and psychological evaluation of the child show the predominant features of the one with established brain damage.

In making the assessment, the clinician needs to determine if mental retardation and/or hearing deficiency may be basic to the language delay. Beyond this, the clinician needs to be mindful that some authorities consider such children to be schizophrenic. From our point of view, it might be of some comfort to appreciate the fact that the term "childhood schizophrenia" is really an omnibus designation that in some important respects overlaps our criteria for congenital aphasia. Goldfarb (1961, p. 7) acknowledges this in describing the setting of his research on childhood schizophrenia. Says Goldfarb: "The staff was impressed with the great variation among the children in the single diagnostic category 'childhood schizophrenia.' The children

[2] For a detailed consideration of the hyperactive brain-damaged child, including approaches to diagnosis and treatment, see the study by Cruickshank, Bentzen, Ratzeburg, and Tannhauser (1961).

differed markedly with respect to symptoms, defenses, and general level of ego development. They also differed in responsiveness to treatment." With all due awareness, as well as with concern for the fact that diagnosis deterfinal analysis the proof of the diagnosis of mines treatment, we may conclude that in the congenital aphasia is in the individual's responsiveness to a program of treatment.[3]

ACQUIRED APHASIA

Aphasia Defined

The literature in the field of aphasia affords a variety of definitions in keeping with the theoretic bias of the aphasiologist. We shall present two definitions, both of which we believe have the virtue of being relatively simple. Possibly both are brief explanations rather than definitions of aphasia. If we wish, they may be considered operational definitions.

Penfield and Roberts (1959, p. 92) define aphasia as

> that state in which one has difficulty in speech, comprehension of speech, naming, reading, and writing, or any one or more of them; and it is associated with misuse and/or perseveration of words, but is not due to disturbance in the mechanism of articulation (as in pseudo-bulbar palsy) or involvement of peripheral nerves, nor due to general mental insufficiency.

We believe that impairment in the use of *gesture* should be added, along with impairment in the comprehension and production of oral and written language. We also believe that psychotic language disturbances should be differentiated from aphasic linguistic impairment.

According to Eisenson, aphasic impairments result in a reduced likelihood that a given linguistic reaction, involving the comprehension and/or production of language, will take place, of the kind and in the manner most appropriate to the situation. In general, the more abstract and intellectual the required or expected linguistic reaction, the less likely it is that the reaction will occur. In general also, responses that are expected to be *externalized* are likely to be more impaired than those which are personal and not intended for externalization—for reaction by a second individual. Put into simple language, aphasics can be expected to perform more appropriately than they can talk about their performance. It may be assumed, therefore, that the thinking associated with an individual or "private" symbol system is significantly less impaired than the externalized, productive language required to communicate thinking to another person.

As a concluding note of definition or exposition, the clinician would do well to remember that primarily the aphasic is a brain-damaged person who is therefore likely to manifest one or more components of the syndrome of organicity. Secondarily, the aphasic is an individual with impaired communicative ability who temporarily or chronically is suffering from disability even in the conventional expression of his organicity. For example, not only does the aphasic have difficulty in attending and in recalling, but he also is *unlikely to be able to communicate that he cannot attend* for normal time periods or to communicate what he has attended to (recalled) in language appropriate to the situation. The aphasic has the anxieties of the brain-damaged and added anxiety about the communication of linguistic content.

Aphasia in Children

Nature and causes. A child may become aphasic if he suffers an insult to the brain after language (verbal behavior) has been established. Such linguistic impairment is most frequently associated with disease, frequently accompanied by high fever and often by a convulsive episode. The most frequent pathologies include measles, encephalitis, cerebromeningeal involvements, and in general any encephalopathy that may result in brain damage to the "higher" centers.

The immediate manifestations of aphasic involvements vary considerably with the age

[3] Two significant articles can be recommended that stress the subtle deviations in behavior that heretofore have been attributed to psychogenetic influences but that may well be attributed instead to genetic factors, perinatal brain damage, and injuries to the central nervous system in the early years of life. These have come to be referred to, perhaps euphemistically, as "minimal brain dysfunctions." Though the term "minimal brain dysfunction" has not yet been clearly defined, the author thinks of it as maximal behavioral deviation with minimal clearly established neuropathology. For a discussion of the "syndrome" of minimal brain dysfunction, the reader is referred to Clemmens, R. L. Minimal brain damage in children. *Children*, 1961, **8**, 179–183; Clements, S. D., and Peters, J. E. Minimal brain dysfunctions in the school-age child. *Arch. Gen. Psychiat.*, 1962, **6**, 185–197.

and the level of linguistic proficiency reached by the child. A 2- or 3-year-old child may become nonverbal for a time or may regress to a lower level of verbal behavior or to prelingual behavior. A grade school child may suffer impairment of all established symbol functions, including reading, writing, and arithmetic ability, as well as speaking.

Prognosis. The prognosis for the young aphasic child is good providing he has not incurred bilateral and widespread brain damage. If the child has been spared one cerebral hemisphere, the likelihood is that he will recover language and intellectual functioning to a normal or near normal premorbid level. Penfield (1959, p. 240) observes: "Examples of completely successful transfer of speech mechanisms from the left to the right hemisphere in children under three or four years of age are numerous." Our experience with young aphasic children tends to support Penfield's general conclusion. We would, however, not wish to go on record as implying that the transfer of language function is complete and that a child may mature and, relative to language functioning and symbol behavior in general, get along as well with one cerebral hemisphere as he might have with both hemispheres intact.

Children who suffer aphasic involvements in their adolescent years are likely to present pictures comparable to those of adult aphasics. By and large, the prognosis for linguistic recovery for an older adolescent or a young adult is likely to be better than for an older adult. A good prognosis, however, always includes the suppositions that the child will make a physical recovery and have one cerebral hemisphere intact or relatively intact and that no factors will develop that will produce motor impairments of the speech mechanism. Another necessary condition, especially for older adolescents and young adults, is that no secondary gains resulting from the immediate communicative disruption get in the way of the reestablishment of language function.

Aphasia in Adults

Historical notes. In his analysis of the literature on aphasia, Roberts (1959, p. 56) observes: "In 1861 there was considerable argument between those who believed that the cerebral hemispheres function as a whole and those who contended that there is localization of function in the cerebrum." At this writing, more than a century since 1861, the differences in point of view persist. In regard to aphasia, the consensus of recent evidence supports at least one conclusion relative to locus of cerebral pathology. The conclusion is that for almost all right-handed persons and for a clear majority of left-handed persons, the left hemisphere is the one involved when a person becomes aphasic following cerebral insult (Roberts, 1959, p. 137; Russell & Espir, 1961, p. 170). Beyond this, there is no general agreement on localization of function except along the broad, general lines that posterior cerebral lesions are more likely to be associated with impairments of language comprehension (auditory language comprehension and reading), and anterior lesions with the production of language (speaking and writing). There are, of course, many authorities who are quite certain of the relationship between specific disabilities and site of lesion, but these are matched by at least as many who fail to find support that there are any tenable correlations.[4] Reviews of varying points of view may be found in studies by Penfield and Roberts (1959), Eisenson (1957, chap. 13), Wepman (1951), and Schuell, Jenkins, and Pabon (1964). A comprehensive review of the literature up to the end of the first quarter of the twentieth century may be found in volume I of Head's monumental work *Aphasia and Kindred Disorders of Speech* (1926).

The nature of aphasic involvements. The vast literature on aphasia permits of no conclusion (unless one looks for evidence to support a personal bias) regarding the nature and essence of aphasia. One may find support in the literature for any of the following positions:

1. Aphasia is a disturbance of previously established language function.
2. Aphasia is a disturbance of symbol behavior and therefore is a disturbance of language function.
3. Aphasia is an impairment of intellectual functioning and therefore is expressed in language dysfunction.
4. Aphasia is a disturbance in the ability to deal with the abstract and therefore is reflected in language functioning.

[4] An interesting position supported by considerable investigation is presented by A. A. Luria in Part IV.

Eisenson holds that aphasic language disorders are so interrelated with intellect and personality that it is best to view aphasia as a syndrome of involvements that are manifest in (1) symbolic-language disturbances (speaking, writing, reading) and related disturbances in symbol functioning (arithmetic, mathematics, etc.); (2) intellectual modifications in the general direction of reduced intellectual proficiency and, in some instances, more specifically an impairment of ability to deal with abstract concepts; and (3) personality modifications in the direction of increased egocentric behavior, probably associated with premorbid inclinations in this direction. Other modifications result from the intellectual, sensory, and motor deficits and the reactions of the individual to these impairments. Further, Eisenson believes that to understand the aphasic patient and his behavior—verbal and otherwise—we must have information about his premorbid personality and his ways of adjusting to the members of the environments in which he functioned. We must also distinguish between the disturbances that immediately accompany and follow the cerebral insult and those which are maintained after a period of one year or more following the onset, especially when the patient's physical condition has become relatively stabilized. Aphasia, according to Eisenson (1963a), may best be viewed first as a disruption of established verbal behavior and of all intellectual functions associated with such behavior. The disruption of the patterns of verbal behavior impairs the ability of the patient (1) to integrate conventional linguistic symbols produced by others (speakers and writers) into his own pattern of private symbolization and (2) to translate his own "private" system of symbols into the conventional formulations of his culture. Most aphasics have both forms of these difficulties at the outset of their involvements. Aphasics who recover well and rapidly are those who are able to readjust to cultural needs, including cultural verbal habits. Those who make poor linguistic recoveries but who improve well physically fail to make the necessary adjustments as they reorganize their verbal behavior patterns. Their reorganization is characterized by egocentricity and often, as Goldstein (1948) has pointed out, by a marked degree of concretism. These persons become chronic aphasics. Eisenson believes that premorbid inclinations predominate and determine the directions and limitations of their recovery.

Assessment of aphasia. Approaches to the assessment of aphasic involvements tend to reveal the theoretical bias of the author of the inventory or procedure. Thus Goldstein (1948, chap. 4), who views aphasic disturbances as a manifestation of the patient's underlying impairment of abstract attitude, tests for such impairment. The Goldstein-Scheerer (Goldstein & Scheerer, 1941; Goldstein & Scheerer, 1951) test battery for assessing abstract and concrete behavior is then their approach and the instrument of choice.

The clinician who views aphasia as an impairment of one or more language modalities, or of functions underlying language ability, would use an instrument such as the Wepman and Jones Language Modalities Test for Aphasia (Wepman & Jones, 1961). Wepman and Jones believe that their test battery yields differences in the performance of aphasics, in kind as well as in degree. They believe that their test provides information, through separate scores, which represents the possible transmission channels which mediate language behavior as well as scores for the comprehension of language function.

Schuell's aphasia inventory, the Minnesota Test for Aphasia, is based on an assumption that aphasic disturbances represent "a single dimension of deficit crossing all language modalities" (Schuell & Jenkins, 1961, p. 295). The Minnesota test is a research and experimental battery. A preliminary short form is available, A Short Examination for Aphasia (Schuell, 1957). The Schuell-Jenkins approach is to sample breakdowns of performance by providing a variety of linguistic tasks that require the formulation of oral and written responses. Specific tests include serial counting (1 to 20), answering simple questions, defining low-frequency words, expressing ideas, explaining similarities, writing sentences that incorporate given words, and writing a paragraph to describe a picture.

Eisenson's *Examining for Aphasia* (1954) was designed to provide the clinician with a guided approach for evaluating aphasic language disturbances and impairments related to language and symbol functioning. A number of the subtests were taken directly or were adapted from standardized educational achievement tests and are intended to reveal the linguistic assets and liabilities of the aphasic patient at the time of the testing. Special subtests are included for the assessment of agnosias (recognition disturbances) and apraxias (impairment of intentional motor functioning) as well as of dysarthria (articulatory disturbances that may be related to aphasic involvements). Through this approach the clinician should be able to obtain information about the present linguistic abilities and disabilities of the patient, as well as about impairments that may underlie the evaluation (comprehension) and production of oral and written language content. Some of the specific subtests for the assessment of the comprehension of language include auditory verbal comprehension (sentences and paragraphs), silent reading (sentences and paragraphs), recognition of common objects, recognition of nonverbal and verbal sounds, and recognition of high-frequency words and of sentences incorporating high-frequency words. Tests for the production of language include serial counting; recitation of the days of the week and months of the year; writing of numbers, letters, and high- and low-frequency words; writing of sentences; naming of parts of the body; word finding as answers to questions; arithmetic computation and calculation; and oral reading.

Many contemporary tests for aphasia include items of a nature that were originally parts of Henry Head's Serial Tests (1926, chap. 1). This battery is in a very real sense the ancestor of many recent inventories. Head designed his tests to enable the clinician to make a direct study of the various categories of language disturbances that he believed were expressed in aphasic involvements. Several screening tests for aphasia, such as the Chesher Test (Chesher, 1937) and the Wells-Ruesch Examination (Wells & Ruesch, 1945), were directly derived from Head's approach to the examination of aphasic patients.

Therapeutic considerations. In concluding this necessarily brief discussion of aphasia, we shall present several basic considerations evolved from our therapeutic experience with aphasic patients. We believe that these should afford the clinician added insight into the nature of aphasia in general and of aphasics as personalities in particular.

1. Most aphasics, especially those with temporoparietal damage, suffer from some degree of impairment of intellectual efficiency.

2. Most aphasics suffer from some degree of functional hearing loss; this frequently, but *not* invariably, can be discovered by standard audiometric examination. Practical hearing is often more impaired than the results of audiometric results would ordinarily imply.

3. Most aphasics manifest neural time lag. In severe form and under stress, this time lag is expressed in perseveration.

4. Most aphasics usually suffer from a degree of receptive (evaluative) involvement greater than can ordinarily be determined by the usual instruments and inventories for the assessment of aphasic involvements or in casual conversational situations.

5. Anxiety, feelings of inadequacy, and rapidly changing situations are frequently productive of perseveration, catastrophic behavior, and withdrawal behavior.

6. Many aphasics strive too hard and aspire too high at the outset of their training. They often avoid simple language available to them because of a desire to behave with premorbid linguistic proficiency.

7. Most aphasics suffer from some degree of ego involvement. Because of this, indirect therapy is frequently more effective than direct therapy. Group therapy as well as individual therapy can be set up on an "indirect" basis. In group therapy, a task intended for patient A is directed to patient B in the presence of A. The latter can then respond without putting his ego at stake.

8. *The essence of aphasia therapy* for content involving linguistic production is to make content which is somehow not readily available to the patient more readily available. Any technique that does not violate the ego and personality of the patient is acceptable. If a technique produces positive results, the clinician should seek to understand the principle or dynamic that helped with the results. Such a principle or specific dynamic may become basic to other procedures used with the aphasic patient.

HEARING DYSFUNCTIONS

Language delay and defects of voice and articulation are common among children who have significant degrees of hearing loss. The American Speech and Hearing Association's committee on legislation found impaired hearing to constitute the third largest category of the causes of defective speech. Estimates of the incidence of impaired hearing in the school population vary from about 3 to as much as 10 per cent. Glorig (1959, pp. 24–33) reported that 3 per cent of a male population between the ages of 10 and 19 was found to have a hearing loss of 15 decibels or more. This figure is based on a sample of approximately 400,000 persons. Davis and Silverman (1960, p. 416) indicate awareness that there is considerable variability in estimates of hearing loss. They say: "Our best estimate is that 5 per cent of school-age children have hearing levels outside the range of normal . . . and that from one to two of every ten in this group require special educational attention." These estimates refer to hearing impairments of such degree that the individual is likely to think of himself as an acoustically handicapped person. In the speech-defective population as a whole, smaller amounts of hearing loss may have an influence on the quality of speech, even though the speaker may not recognize that he is impaired in hearing.

Among the acoustically handicapped, the specific form of defective speech varies considerably with the type, degree, and age of onset of hearing loss. Children with severe congenital hearing loss are almost always delayed in beginning to speak and continue to be slow in language development. Beyond this, the oral speech they are able to develop is generally characterized by articulatory distortion, faulty rhythm, and often vocal inadequacy. When the hearing loss is acquired after the normal onset of speech, speech defects are likely to become part of the over-all habilitation problem. We accept the observation of Davis and Silverman (1960):

> If the ear can no longer serve as a monitor when one talks, slow degeneration of speech results. The sharpness and precision of enunciation disintegrate. The melodies of speech become monotonous. Intonations lose their life. The quality of the voice becomes rigid. Finally, control over the loudness of the voice suffers.

For a more detailed consideration than is here present of the relationship between hearing loss and speech, the reader is invited to consult Berry and Eisenson (1956, chap. 19).

Auditory Memory and Sequencing

Auditory memory span has been a subject of psychological study for many years, going back to the initial investigations of Ebbinghaus (1913). Most contemporary studies of auditory memory span have used series of digits or of nonsense syllables as basic units for measurement. The assumption that auditory memory is a factor in intelligence is expressed in the frequent inclusion of memory-span tests employing digits forward and digits backward (digit series to be recalled in reverse order of presentation) and in the recall of meaningful material, as in the reproduction of sentences and of units of meaning after the oral presentation of a contextual material. There is considerable evidence to support the assumption that memory span as measured by recall is positively related to intelligence and to mental development. Many speech pathologists believe that poor auditory memory is related to defective speech, though the results of research are by no means consistent. An excellent brief review of the subject may be found in the book by Van Riper and Irwin (1958, pp. 26–29).

Despite the inconsistent results of controlled investigations, many speech pathologists, including this writer, maintain their clinical impression that speech-defective children with retarded language development and articulatory defects are definitely defective in auditory memory. Perhaps the reason for the difference in findings lies in the nature of the experimental designs. Immediate recall when an examinee is not concerned with meaning requires a different mode of investigation from that used for recall of meaningful material. Even more crucial, we believe, is the need to distinguish between recall of material to be imitated (immediately reproduced) and the more complex ability to produce a sequence or series of sounds as a *phonetic and meaningful unit*. Most young children who are just beginning to develop verbal habits often transpose sounds and syllables and may say "hist" for "hits" or "pest" for "pets." Van Riper and Irwin (1958, p. 29) observe that children with defective articulation are often lacking in their ability to combine and analyze sequences of speech sounds. Because of this difficulty, "The articulation case can understand the word spoken by another, can recognize it as correct, yet cannot say it correctly himself. . . . When we find cases with marked deficiencies in phonetic ability of either the analytic or synthesizing type, we can expect difficulty in articulation therapy." Children who are retarded in language development may, we suspect, be lacking in a fundamental ability to analyze any but the shortest auditory sequences, that is, to identify and recall an aurally received event and to hold this and succeeding items in mind until a series (auditory sequence) is recognized as having been completed. Beyond this, the child must be able to synthesize the series of auditory items into an event appropriate to the demands of a speaking situation.

We need to appreciate the fact that auditory events, unlike visual ones, do not "stay put." Impressions received aurally can be reproduced only by a process of adequate feedback. Such feedback must include both the total number of items that can be recalled and the specific sequence in which they need to be recalled for acceptable verbal behavior. When recalled, the items must be organized into recognizable verbal events and must be reproduced (uttered) so that they are intelligible to another listener. For this function, the ability for auditory discrimination and production must also be adequate. For many young children and especially for those with brain damage, the demands for this complex ability seem to be excessive. As a result, these children are slow in the onset of their speech and often are defective and retarded after they begin to talk.

REFERENCES

American Speech and Hearing Association, Committee on the Mid-Century White House Conference. Speech disorders and speech correction. *J. speech hearing Disorders,* 1952, **17** (2), 129–137.

American Speech and Hearing Association, Committee on Legislation. Need for speech pathologists. *ASHA,* 1959, **1,** 138–139.

Berry, M. F., & Eisenson, J. *Speech disorders.* New York: Appleton-Century-Crofts, 1956.

Bloodstein, O., Jaeger, W., & Tureen, J. A study of the diagnosis of stuttering by parents of stutterers and non-stutterers. *J. speech hearing Disorders,* 1952, **17,** 308–315.

Bryngelson, B., & Glaspey, E. *Speech improvement cards.* Chicago: Scott, Foresman, 1941.

Carhart, R. A survey of speech defects in Illinois high schools. *J. speech Disorders,* 1939, **4,** 61–70.

Carhart, R. Some notes on official statistics of speech disorders encountered during World War I. *J. speech Disorders,* 1945, **8,** 91–107.

Chesher, E. C. Technique for clinical examination in aphasia. *Bull. neurol. Inst.,* 1937, **6,** 134–144.

Clements, S. D., & Peters, J. E. Minimal brain dysfunctions in the school-age child. *Archives of General Psychiatry,* 1962, **6,** 185–197.

Clemmens, R. L. Minimal brain damage in children. *Children,* 1961, **8,** 179–183.

Cohen, J. H., & Diehl, C. F. Relationship of speech-sound discrimination ability to articulation-type speech defects. *J. speech hearing Disorders,* 1963, **28,** 187–190.

Cruickshank, W. W., Bentzen, R. A., Ratzeburg, F. H., & Tannhauser, M. T. *A teaching method for brain injured and hyperactive children.* Syracuse, N.Y.: Syracuse Univer. Press, 1961. Pp. 182–183.

Curtis, J. F. Disorders of articulation. In W. Johnson (Ed.), *Speech handicapped school children.* New York: Harper & Row, 1948. P. 113.

Davis, H., & Silverman, S. R. *Hearing and deafness.* (Rev. ed.) New York: Holt, 1960. P. 4.

Ebbinghaus, H. *Memory, a contribution to experimental psychology.* New York: Columbia Univer. Press, 1913.

Eisenson, J. *Examining for aphasia.* New York: Psychological Corporation, 1954.

Eisenson, J. In Travis, L. E. (Ed.), *Handbook of speech pathology.* New York: Appleton-Century-Crofts, 1957. Chap. 130.

Eisenson, J. (Ed.) *Stuttering: a symposium.* New York: Harper & Row, 1958.

Eisenson, J. Aphasic language modifications as a disruption of cultural verbal habits. *ASHA,* 1963, **5,** 503–506. (a)

Eisenson, J. Disorders of language in children. *J. Pediat.,* 1963, **62,** 20–24. (b)

Eisenson, J. In W. Cruickshank (Ed.), *Psychology of exceptional children and youth.* (2nd ed.) Englewood Cliffs, N.J.: Prentice-Hall, 1963. (c)

Eisenson, J., Auer, J., & Irwin, J. V. *Psychology of communication.* New York: Appleton-Century-Crofts, 1963. Chaps. 12, 13.

Fiedler, F. E., & Wepman, J. An exploratory study of the self-concept of stutterers. *J. speech hearing Disorders,* 1951, **16,** 110–114.

Gens, G. W. Speech retardation in the normal and subnormal child. *Train. Sch. Bull.,* 1950, **48,** 32–36.

Glasner, P. J. Personality characteristics and emotional problems in stutterers under the age of five. *J. speech hearing Disorders,* 1949, **14,** 135–138.

Glauber, I. P. The mother in the etiology of stuttering. *Psychoanal. Quart.,* 1951, **20,** 160–161. (Abstract)

Glauber, I. P. The psychoanalysis of stuttering. In J. Eisenson (Ed.), *Stuttering: a symposium.* New York: Harper & Row, 1958.

Glorig, A. Hearing conservation: past and future. *Proc. working Conf. hlth Aspects hearing Conservation, Suppl. Trans. Amer. Acad. Ophthalmol. Otolaryngol.,* 1959, 24–33.

Goldfarb, W. *Childhood schizophrenia,* Cambridge, Mass.: Harvard Univer. Press, 1961.

Goldstein, K. *Language and language disturbances.* New York: Grune & Stratton, 1948.

Goldstein, K., & Scheerer, M. Abstract and concrete behavior: an experimental study with special tests. *Psychol. Monogr.,* 1941, **25** (2), No. 239.

Goldstein, K., & Scheerer, M. *Tests for abstract and concrete thinking.* New York: Psychological Corporation, 1951.

Head, H. *Aphasia and kindred disorders of speech.* London: Cambridge Univer. Press, 1926. New York: Hafner, 1963.

Hejna, R. F. *Developmental Articulation Test.* (Rev. ed.) Madison, Wis.: College Typing Co., 1959.

Hildreth, G. Speech defects and reading disability. *Elementary Sch. J.,* 1946, **46,** 326–332.

Irwin, O. C. Speech development in the young child. *J. speech hearing Disorders,* 1952, **17** (3), 269–279.

Johnson, W. (Ed.) Stuttering. In *Speech handicapped school children.* New York: Harper & Row, 1956. Chap. V, p. 197.

Johnson, W. *Stuttering and what you can do about it.* Minneapolis, Minn.: Univer. of Minnesota Press, 1961. P. 95.

Johnson, W., Curtis, J., Edney, C. W., & Keaster, J. In *Speech handicapped school children.* New York: Harper & Row, 1956. Pp. 59–60.

Kodman, F., Jr. Educational placement of hard of hearing children in the classroom. *J. speech hearing Disorders,* 1963, **28** (3), 297–299.

Kronvall, E. L., & Diehl, C. F. The relationship of auditory discrimination to articulatory defects of children with no known organic impairments. *J. speech hearing Disorders,* 1954, **19,** 335–338.

McCarthy, D. Language development in children. In L. Carmichael (Ed.), *Manual of child psychology.* (Rev. ed.) New York: Wiley, 1954. Pp. 492–630.

Metraux, Ruth W. Speech profiles of the preschool child: 18 to 54 months. *J. speech hearing Disorders,* 1950, **15,** 37–53.

Milisen, R. The incidence of speech disorders. In L. E. Travis (Ed.), *Handbook of speech pathology.* New York: Appleton-Century-Crofts, 1957. Chap. 7.

Moncur, J. P. Parental domination in stuttering. *J. speech hearing Disorders,* 1952, **17,** 155–164.

Morley, D. E. A ten year study of speech disorders among university students. *J. speech hearing Disorders,* 1952, **17** (1), 25–31.

Mowrer, O. H. *Learning theory and the symbolic process.* New York: Wiley, 1960. Pp. 79–86.

Murphy, A. T., & Fitz Simons, R. W. *Stuttering and personality dynamics.* New York: Ronald, 1960. Chap. 6.

Peckarsky, A. Maternal attitudes towards children with psychogenically delayed speech. Unpublished doctoral dissertation, New York Univer., 1952.

Penfield, W., & Roberts, L. *Speech and brain mechanisms.* Princeton, N.J.: Princeton Univer. Press, 1959.

Poole, I. Genetic development of articulation of consonant sounds in speech. *Elementary English Rev.,* 1934, **2,** 159–161.

Roberts, L. In W. Penfield & L. Roberts, *Speech and brain mechanisms.* Princeton, N.J.: Princeton Univer. Press, 1959.

Ruesch, J. *Disturbed communication.* New York: Norton, 1957.

Russell, W. R., & Espir, M. L. E. *Traumatic aphasia.* Fair Lawn, N.J.: Oxford Univer. Press, 1961.

Sachs, M. H. A survey and evaluation of the existing interrelationships between speech and mental deficiencies. Unpublished master's thesis, Univer. of Virginia, 1951.

Schuell, Hildred. A short examination for aphasia. *Neurology,* 1957, **7,** 625–634.

Schuell, Hildred, & Jenkins, J. J. Comment on dimensions of language performance in aphasia. *J. speech hearing Res.,* 1961, **4** (3), 295–299.

Schuell, Hildred, Jenkins, J. J., & Pabon, E. J. *Aphasia in adults.* New York: Hoeber Medical Division, Harper & Row, 1964. Chaps. 1–3.

Sheehan, J. Projective studies of stutterers. *J. speech hearing Disorders,* 1958, **23,** 18–25.

Siegel, G. M., Winitz, H., & Conkey, H. The Influence of testing instruments on articulatory responses of children. *J. speech hearing Disorders,* 1963, **28** (1), 67–76.

Smith, J. O. Speech and language of the retarded. *Train. Sch. Bull.,* 1962, **58,** 111–124.

Spriestersbach, D. C. An objective approach to the investigation of social adjustment of male stutterers. *J. speech hearing Disorders,* 1951, **16,** 250–257.

Taylor, E. M. *Psychological appraisal of children with cerebral defects.* Cambridge, Mass.: Harvard Univer. Press, 1959. Pp. 25–30.

Templin, M. C. Norms on a screening test for articulation for ages three through eight. *J. speech hearing Disorders,* 1953, **18** (4), 323–331.

Templin, M. C. Certain language skills in children. *Inst. child Welf. Monogr.,* 1957, **26.** (a)

Templin, M. C. *Certain language skills in children: their development and interrelationships.* Minneapolis, Minn.: Univer. of Minnesota Press, 1957. (b)

Templin, M. C., & Darley, F. L. *The Templin-Darley tests of articulation.* Iowa City, Iowa: Bureau of Educational Research and Service Extension Division, 1960.

Van Riper, C. *Speech correction.* (3rd ed.) Englewood Cliffs, N.J.: Prentice-Hall, 1954. Pp. 221–234.

Van Riper, C., & Irwin, J. V. *Voice and articulation.* Englewood Cliffs, N.J.: Prentice-Hall, 1958. 1931, **2.**

Weaver, C. H., Furbee, C., & Everhart, R. W. Articulatory competency and reading readiness. *J. speech hearing Res.,* 1960, 3, 174–180.

Wellman, B. L., Case, I. M., Mengert, I. G., & Bradbury, D. E. Speech sounds of young children. *Univer. Iowa Stud., Child Welf. Monogr.,* 1931, **2.**

Wells, F. L., & Ruesch, J. *Mental examiners' handbook.* (2nd ed.) New York: Psychological Corporation, 1945.

Wepman, J. *Recovery from aphasia.* New York: Ronald, 1951.

Wepman, J., & Jones, L. V. *The language modalities test for aphasia.* Chicago: Education Industry Service, 1961.

Wolfe, W. G. A comprehensive evaluation of fifty cases of cerebral palsy. *J. speech hearing Disorders,* 1950, **15,** 234–251.

Wood, K. S. Parental maladjustment and functional articulatory defects in children. *J. speech Disorders,* 1946, **2,** 255–275.

29

Psychological Aspects of Disability

WALTER S. NEFF AND SAMUEL A. WEISS

The scope of the problem[1]

In recent years, a series of events have created a situation in which an increasingly diverse variety of kinds of professionals have begun to devote themselves to the problems of the disabled person. Undoubtedly, the most prominent of these events was World War II itself, which not only mobilized and trained huge human and technical resources but also left as its aftermath—in most of the developed countries of Western Europe and America—a marked concern for new issues of human welfare. In the United States, the last twenty years have seen an enormous increase in the availability of public funds for the solution of a number of human problems. The involvement of the Federal government in these matters was made manifest by the setting up, in 1953, of the U.S. Department of Health, Education, and Welfare, with a secretary of Cabinet rank. The great broadening of the scope of services to the disabled is largely attributable to the work of one of the sections of the department, the Office of Vocational Rehabilitation.[2] A great deal of what we now know or are trying to discover about disability is attributable to the service, research, and training activities supported by this Federal agency, and, as a consequence, the field of psychological interest that we are to describe in this chapter has become identified as the field of rehabilitation. We shall have more to say later on what is meant by this term.

Although greatly increased public interest and Federal financial support have been the direct underpinning of the great expansion of both services to the disabled and research on disability, we must recognize that certain more subtle shifts in both community and professional outlook have provided the social atmosphere which made these changes possible. One of these shifts has to do with a quite serendipitous consequence of World War II: the greatly increased public and professional interest in psychological and psychiatric matters. The surprisingly large number of draftees rejected for psychiatric reasons; the proportionately high frequency of psychiatric casualties in the armed forces; and the massive efforts during the war, and by the Veterans Administration after the war, to train mental health personnel were major factors in drawing both lay and professional attention to the pervasiveness of the problems of emotional disorder. One of the side effects of this greatly expanded interest in psychological and psychiatric issues was the invasion of traditional fields of medicine by notions that hitherto were quite alien. Thus, we had the sudden appearance of what came to be called

[1] The first part of this chapter, pp. 785–800, was written by Dr. Neff. This work was aided in part by a grant to New York University from the Easter Seal Foundation.

[2] In 1963, the office was retitled the Vocational Rehabilitation Administration (VRA), in recognition of the greatly increased scope of its activities. Miss Mary Switzer, who has directed the office for many years, continues in this function with the title of Commissioner.

"psychosomatic medicine,"[3] which, with some excesses at times, began to put forward the claim that many traditionally somatic diseases—tuberculosis, cardiac conditions, stomach ulcer, etc., and especially diseases of a chronic or long-term nature—had powerful psychological factors not only in their sequelae but also in their etiology. Similarly, there has been a hyperdevelopment of psychiatry as a major specialty, a development which not only has included the production of an increased number of medically trained psychiatrists but also has marked a rather massive involvement in direct patient care (not without friction) of a variety of nonmedical specialists, e.g., psychologists, social workers, vocational specialists, and even sociologists and anthropologists. This greatly broadened and deepened public and professional concern with what is increasingly being called "mental health" has become manifest within the framework of a radical transformation of the theory and, to some extent, the practice of patient care.[4]

The combination of these two sets of events—our greatly increased concern for the health and welfare of our citizenry and a coincident enormous expansion of interest in psychiatric and psychological issues—has been a major factor in the development and refinement of "comprehensive rehabilitation."[5] What this latter conception has come to mean involves recognition that the disabled person faces a very wide range of problems, the solution of which requires an extremely broad spectrum of professional experts. Whether the disability in question is a physical limitation or trauma, a variety of the types of mental retardation, an emotional disorder, or some combination of these three coarse classifications, it has become evident that medical treatment is only one facet of what has become a many-sided process. To return the patient to some desired and improved level of functioning now necessitates the services of an almost bewildering variety of experts, ranging from the orthopedic surgeon at one end, to the vocational counselor and special educator at the other. Although Rusk (Rusk et al., 1958, preface) has summed up the entire process as the "third phase of medicine," many experts feel that a great many of the problems of the disabled individual are not medical at all but involve meeting and coping with an entire new set of psychosocial barriers to a life adjustment. But, whatever is felt to be the core of the process, the rehabilitation of a disabled person is now considered to be truly a *comprehensive* affair, involving the professional cooperation of an extremely diverse rehabilitation "team" (an overworked but very necessary word). It is only within the last decade or so that psychologists have been playing an increasingly important role as members of this congeries of specialists in disability.

If treatment of the patient with a traumatic physical impairment is multidimensional, then this applies with as much, or greater, force to the mentally retarded client or to the individual who is recovering from a long-term emotional disorder. Modern methods of patient care are resulting in the discharge from institutions and mental hospitals of tens of thousands of such persons annually,[6] and increasingly large numbers are being referred to rehabilitation agencies and facilities for assistance in maintaining themselves in the community. For such persons, the requirement for medical care (other than that provided by psychiatry) is minimal. On the other hand, these clients need very heavy doses of professional assistance in adjusting or readjusting to their families, in managing some kind of effec-

[3] Typical of the works which exemplify this kind of approach are those of Wittkower and Cleghorn (1954) and Dunbar (1954).

[4] We are referring here to the current strenuous efforts to alter the mental hospital from a custodial institution to what has been described as a "therapeutic community," with the objective of bringing about thoroughgoing changes in internal organization, treatment practices, and discharge policies. Important books and monographs which provide material on the aims and content of this movement are those by Jones (1953); Stanton and Schwartz (1954); Greenblatt, Levinson, and Williams (1957); Caudill (1958); and, in relation to some of the implications for rehabilitation practice, Neff, Gellman, Friedman, Gendel, and Glaser (1957).

[5] This term has come into use comparatively recently to describe the functioning of the multidisciplinary rehabilitation facility, in which the patient can simultaneously receive services crossing a spectrum of medical, psychological, social, and vocational areas. See papers by Redkey (1956; 1959) and Gorthy (1957) and the proceedings of conferences and associations active in the field.

[6] The most recent and comprehensive study of the vicissitudes encountered by the discharged mental patient is found in Freeman and Simmons's book *The Mental Patient Comes Home* (1963). Various aspects of the problems posed for the rehabilitation movement by this vast efflux of discharged mental patients have been discussed by Schwartz (1953), Brooks et al. (1961), Gelb (1959), and Neff (1962a). Since the middle 1950s, the Vocational Rehabilitation Administration has become very heavily involved with support of projects which have the aim of rehabilitation of the mental patient; the extent of this involvement is illustrated by a current listing of the projects receiving support from the VRA (1962).

tive social existence, and in achieving some measure of economic independence. There are, consequently, very urgent demands for all varieties of psychotherapy and psychological retraining, for family casework and social group work, and for all kinds of vocational expertise.[7] The influx into rehabilitation agencies of increasingly large numbers of patients needing these various types of assistance has sharpened the awareness of the rehabilitation expert that many components of the rehabilitation process involve problems of general life adjustment. It is with the psychological aspects of these problems—especially their unique flavor as related to disability—that this chapter will attempt to deal.

DEFINITIONS

Before proceeding further, it will be well to specify what we are talking about. We shall therefore briefly define certain necessary terms.

Rehabilitation

It must be conceded that there is no precise way of defining the term which has become associated with the entire field we are considering. The associations supplied by Webster denote the concepts of restoration and reinstatement. As the term is used in relation to disability, however, there are certain important connotations. The first of these has to do with the fact that there are many kinds of physical, mental, or emotional disorders which, in the present state of medical science, leave behind them some kind of chronic or long-term residual impairment. In this sense, the most frequent objective of rehabilitative procedures is not so much "curative," in the sense of complete elimination of the impairment in question, but rather "ameliorative," in the sense of bringing the person to a maximal level of functioning *within the limits of a continuing deficiency of some kind.* Rusk and Taylor (1953) state the problem as follows: "Lacking specific measures in the cure of many of the chronic diseases, medicine must look to rehabilitation to teach those afflicted by disability to live and work as effectively as possible."

The second connotation of the term has to do with restoration of the ability to work, to find gainful employment. The tremendous—perhaps one-sided—emphasis on vocational objectives which has permeated the field of rehabilitation presents one of its clearest distinctions from the therapeutic objectives typical of the other helping professions. A third important connotation of the term has to do with professional recognition of the fact that the disabled person in our society appears to face many of the problems encountered by rejected minority groups. Thus, the rehabilitative process must also concern itself with the overcoming of powerful psychosocial barriers, related to both the attitudes of others to the disabled person and the attitudes of the disabled person to himself. For all these reasons, the term "rehabilitation" has come to imply a many-sided and multidisciplinary process which follows *after* the acute state of an illness or disorder, the objectives of which are essentially ameliorative or adjustive, and which focuses on an optimal life adjustment.

Disability versus Handicap

In popular usage, these terms tend to be confounded. In the field of rehabilitation, however, it is vital to distinguish clearly between them. By and large, the term "disability" is reserved to refer to some sort of medically diagnosable condition, whether the condition in question is physical, mental, or emotional.[8] On the other hand, the term "handicap" implies that the individual is somehow disadvantaged in relation to some desired life objective.[9] It is obvious that not all disabilities, nor all levels of intensity of a given disability, are handicapping. Similarly, individuals may be disadvantaged with respect to some vital life objective without being

7 See the final report of the Joint Commission on Mental Illness (1961).

8 Cf. Hamilton (1950) and a discussion on this point by Wright in her recent book on physical disability (1960).

9 English and English (1958) define "handicap" in terms of a *reduced "aptitude* [italics added] in performing the ordinary tasks of life, or a particular vocation or avocation," thus distinguishing a handicap from a crippling condition, which they associate with *inability* to perform a certain kind of task. Their distinction (which they correctly state is not always observed) is in the same direction as ours but is somewhat less comprehensive. We wish to include the implication that many disabled persons may be handicapped vis-à-vis some important life objective, not because there is a reduction in any aptitude or ability at all, but simply because people with disabilities tend to suffer social derogation. Thus, a person who has suffered an amputation and who has been provided with an adequate prosthetic device which he uses with skill may be able to perform many work tasks with "normal aptitude," but he may have difficulty securing suitable employment because of employer prejudices. In this sense, he is certainly handicapped, but he cannot be described as having "less than normal aptitude."

disabled, in the technical sense of the latter term. Whether a disability is, in fact, handicapping tends to be something of an idiosyncratic issue, related in part to the manner in which the person perceives himself and in part to the manner in which society deals with him. Of course, the rehabilitation agency will tend to see people who are *both* disabled and handicapped, but the agency must choose among a wide range of strategies, depending upon the individual case. In the typical case, however, the client has reached, or is approaching, a plateau of medical restoration which will leave some residual limitation, and the rehabilitative task is conceived as of helping the person to live with his disability *at maximum effectiveness.* From this point of view, a disability is a permanent residual limitation of some kind which may or may not interfere with an optimal life adjustment. The objective of the rehabilitative process is to assist the individual to overcome or ameliorate the possible handicapping effects of the disabling condition.

THE SCOPE OF THE CHAPTER

The kinds of problems encountered in rehabilitation practice are, of course, extremely diverse, and it is quite impossible to consider all their psychological implications within the scope of a single chapter. Entire volumes have been written upon such single disability groupings as cerebral palsy, blindness, and deafness. Another complication is that psychologists have become interested in the psychological aspects of disability only within the last decade or two, so that there is still a rather meager body of theory and fact. For these reasons, we have simply made our own idiosyncratic choice of what we believe to be the most significant issues in the field, given the present stage of knowledge and practice.

Our plan for the chapter is as follows: First, we shall attempt to consider to what degree and in what specific ways a disabling condition presents the person with unique psychological problems. Second, we shall present a section which is essentially theoretical, dealing with the quite differing theoretical structures within which the psychological problems of the disabled have been conceptualized. Finally, we shall consider some of the more important problems related to techniques of assessment and psychotherapy, insofar as these techniques require unique adjustment to the problems of the disabled.

Disability as a special psychological problem

As Wright puts it (1960), it is more meaningful to speak of a "person with a disability" than to use the shorter and less awkward term "a disabled person." This distinction involves much more than the kind of semantic hairsplitting so frequently involved in professional expertise. Actually, a great deal is involved! In the first place, it is extremely rare to encounter a patient whose disability influences all, or even many, aspects of his total psychological functioning. For example, an individual may have severe problems of gait but be perfectly adequate manually. Similarly, a person may be in only a partial state of remission from a prolonged schizophrenic episode, but his ability to master a complex technical task may be entirely adequate. The point here is that a single ability or aptitude, or even a few abilities and aptitudes, may be impaired as a direct function of a given disability, but it is rare that there are not other important assets upon which to build a rehabilitation program. Second, it has become abundantly clear that it is not permissible to speak of any kind of one-to-one relation between a given disability and any related type of personality structure, e.g., the "cardiac personality," "the epileptic personality," etc.[10] The range of cognitive, affective, and behavioral response patterns in the repertoire of the disabled appears to be as diverse as that displayed by nondisabled individuals. Disability is no respecter of persons

10 When physicians and psychologists first began to think about the psychological implications of physical disease, the notion that there might be a close association between certain kinds of disease and certain personality types appeared quite seductive. We still hear a good deal about efforts, for example, to define the "ulcer personality" or even to make more subtle distinctions between personality formations associated with peptic ulcer, on the one hand, and gastritis, on the other. Rorschach investigators (Piotrowski, 1957) have sought for patterns characteristic of the convulsive disorders. Nevertheless, evidence for these associations continues to be elusive. Garrett and Levine (1962), in summarizing one of the chief outcomes of a collection of monographs on a wide range of disability groups, conclude that the similarities in the psychological problems and reactions common to persons with different disabilities are far more striking than the differences.

and may afflict the highly intelligent as well as the quite dull, the emotionally stable as well as the emotionally inadequate, the outgoing as well as the withdrawn. What is at issue is the "style" of coping behavior which the individual has developed and with which he confronts any of life's tragedies and problems.

If, as appears likely, there are no characteristically unique personality patterns related to disability, to what degree and in what way does a disabling condition present the individual with unique psychological problems? To put this question more sharply, is there anything the rehabilitation psychologist needs to know with which he is not already quite familiar from his training in general psychology and the various areas of psychological specialization?

PROBLEMS PECULIAR TO DISABILITY

In seeking some sort of intelligible answer to this basic question, one encounters several problems which tend to be peculiar to disability. First, we must distinguish between the consequences of a congenital impairment or one that takes place in early childhood (e.g., cerebral palsy, idiopathic epilepsy, mental retardation, and childhood schizophrenia), and a disability which makes itself manifest after the individual is an adult. In the one case, we are dealing with a set of factors which may powerfully affect the developmental process, so that the individual may grow into a very different sort of person from what he otherwise might have been. In the second case, we are dealing with the sudden, or gradual, disruption of what may already be a stable set of intrapersonal and interpersonal arrangements. This distinction between the possibly quite differing consequences of early and later traumata is one that needs to be kept continously in mind in our endeavor to conceptualize the psychological aspects of disability.

A second issue has to do with the essential nature of disability. One of the more important meanings of disability has to do with some kind of *loss*—of a part of the body, of a sensory capacity, of an ability or competency taken for granted by others, of a cherished person, or even of an expected or established place in society. Since the loss of a cherished object may be universally regarded as a grave misfortune, arousing the associated emotions of pity and fear, we might conceive that the central core of the psychological aspects of disability has to do with the psychodynamics of loss. As a matter of fact, this is how Dembo (see below, p. 804) has treated the consequences of severe traumatic injury in adults, with her useful and provocative ideas of mourning and bereavement.

A third aspect of disability which gives it something of a special character has to do with the complexities of the psychosocial situation. The disabled person is typically perceived as different from others—he generally perceives *himself* as different—and the difference relates to a species of unique social status. The shadings related to the social status of being disabled are extremely complex, but it can be argued that the person with a disability presents—to himself and to others—something of a special problem in social perception. In fact, if anything is unique about disability, it may well relate to the special kinds of sociopsychological problems faced by persons with readily perceivable impairments. A significant proportion of the psychologists interested in the field of disability have focused on the psychosocial implications and consequences of chronic or long-term impairment, including Barker and his associates (Barker, 1948; Barker & Wright, 1952; Barker, Wright, Meyerson, & Gonick, 1953), Wright (1960), Dembo, Leviton, & Wright (1956), Heider and Heider (1941), Gellman (1953; 1955; 1956; 1959), Meyerson (1948), and Neff (1959; 1960; 1961; 1962a; 1962b; 1963). A very wide range of problems has interested these writers. We shall have more to say on these matters in a later section of this chapter.

A fourth aspect of disability which suggests special problems for the psychologists has to do with issues related to psychological assessment. Even a minimal acquaintance with the psychological testing of clients who have marked disabilities indicates that often rather massive alteration of standardized testing techniques is required, with subsequent problems in the interpretation of the resultant data. One begins to appreciate the degree to which the fabricators of psychological tests make an implicit assumption of some kind of "normal, average environment,"[11] a condition

[11] Compare quite similar language used by Hartmann (1958), in his discussion of the theoretical requirements for psychoanalytic ego psychology. An early monograph by Neff (1938) makes this point in relation to the social variables involved in intelligence testing.

which cannot be assumed in the case of disability without considerable risk. We shall, in a later section of this chapter, consider some ways in which clinicians confronted with the task of assessing the disabled have attempted to solve some of these problems.

A fifth set of issues concerning which disability creates certain unique problems for the psychologist has to do with the techniques and objectives of psychotherapy. Where the dyadic therapies have been utilized for the disabled, and we should stress that this has not been too frequent an occurrence, the therapist confronts some rather special problems in therapeutic strategy. In the first place, the disturbed person with a disability has a great many insistent reality problems which are not matters of concern to the nondisabled. An individual who has been forced to undergo amputation of an upper extremity is, *in fact,* at a disadvantage in relation to a wide variety of important life situations, and no amount of verbal therapy can change the reality factors involved. In this sense, the psychotherapist working with a disabled person may be compelled to adopt quite different goals from those appropriate for a neurotic who is free from a disability. The optimal therapeutic objective may be to help such a person to appraise his disability realistically so that he will not exaggerate its negative consequences and see rejection where none exists, deny its existence and attempt tasks only achievable by a whole man, or engage in any other defense which is inappropriate and ineffective. Somehow the patient must be induced to accept his disability, to live with it, but of course not in the sense of using it to give up the struggle to live as fully and normally as possible. Looked at in this way, the therapeutic task may be peculiarly delicate and difficult to accomplish. We shall have more to say on this subject in a later section of this chapter.

A sixth element of uniqueness related to the psychological aspects of disability has to do with a matter of emphasis rather than a difference in kind. It may be phrased, somewhat loosely, by saying that the psychologist who is to work with the disabled must have his eye on possible positives (assets) rather than possible negatives (liabilities). The fact is, however, that most of us are better equipped to spot a liability than to discern an asset, as a quick perusal of the chapter titles of the *Handbook* will abundantly suggest. This problem becomes all the more insistent when, as is often the case, nothing whatever can be done about the disability per se and what is wanted is the pinpointing of *other* things about the patient upon which some kind of positive rehabilitation plan can be built. Unfortunately, in the present state of knowledge, this kind of competency cannot be taught in the didactic sense but is best acquired on the job in a rehabilitation setting.

A seventh consideration, which involves rather specialized activities on the part of the rehabilitation psychologist, arises from the nature of the setting in which he performs his service. Typically, he is a staff member of a rehabilitation facility. As such, he is responsible to, and must work with, an extraordinarily great diversity of other kinds of professionals and technicians. In this sense, his position is somewhat akin to that which he occupies in a modern mental hospital, with certain important differences. In the first place, the rehabilitation center is primarily conceived as a transitional facility—from the hospital or the sickbed to the community. In the second place, the modern rehabilitation center has an increasingly heavy investment in matters related to facilitating a work adjustment for the disabled person. The psychologist is often called upon, therefore, to make judgments about matters concerning which his conventional training and experience have not prepared him too well. The medical department may want to know, perhaps, whether a specific amputee will tolerate and learn to use an uncomfortable, or even initially painful, prosthetic device. The vocational department may ask whether the client has the potential to profit from a certain type of training program. He is constantly being asked embarrassing questions about the patient's "motivation." Further, he will find that his services to patients—whether diagnostic, therapeutic, or in the name of research—will most often be rather strictly subordinated to some rather specific rehabilitation goal, a goal which he may play a part in setting but which is set also in relation to many considerations which are remote from his area of professional competence. A compensating aspect of these dilemmas is the fact that the psychologist in the rehabilitation center is often much freer—professionally speaking—than he is in the typical hospital or psychiatric clinic. On the other hand, rather strong reality limitations will tend to limit the amount of individual psychotherapy that can be practically offered to a rehabilitation client, and psychologists who have a strong investment in the more intensive varieties of dyadic therapy may be happier elsewhere.

SUMMARY

In considering the degree to which a disability presents to both the patient and the psychologist an array of unique psychological problems, we have briefly discussed the following:

1. The issue of time of onset
2. The conception of disability as a loss or bereavement
3. The importance of the psychosocial situation
4. The special problems of psychological assessment
5. The special problems of psychotherapy
6. The emphasis on the search for assets
7. The uniqueness of the treatment setting

We should hasten to add that we are not emphasizing the magic number seven! There are other issues of somewhat less significance, but their introduction would entail some risk of belaboring the point. Suffice it to say that there is enough that is specialized about the problems of the person with a disability so that we have the right to speak of disability as involving, to some degree at least, an area of specialization in psychology.

Theory

As is the case in other areas of interest, psychologists have brought with them into the field of rehabilitation a variety of theoretical viewpoints. Since the psychological aspects of disability represent a rather new concern, much of what is theoretical in this field was developed elsewhere and in connection with other phenomena. The term "brought with them" is used advisedly, since the theoretical viewpoints extant in rehabilitation have been largely imported from elsewhere rather than indigenously developed. If a psychologist happens to enter the field whose training and temperament are such that he is strongly committed to classical psychoanalysis, then it is inevitable that he will interpret rehabilitation phenomena from this conceptual framework. Similarly, if an individual has been influenced by Lewinian field theory, it is likely that we will find him talking in terms of psychological differentiation and social locomotion. Thus, as increasing numbers of senior psychologists (and their students) enter the field, we find elements of almost every theoretical position extant in psychology as a discipline. There are Freudians, neo-Freudians, Sullivanians, and Rogerians. There are gestalters and Skinnerians. And, of course, there are many eclectics, who draw upon whatever component of any theoretical position which seems plausible and useful to them in accounting for a particular observation or finding.

Nevertheless, certain features of disability, combined with the special manner in which rehabilitation happened to develop as a field, have tended to accentuate certain theoretical concepts at the expense of others. In the first place, the psychosocial implications of disability are so insistent—as we emphasize in the preceding section—that some writers think of handicapping conditions almost wholly in sociopsychological terms. In the second place, the powerful vocational emphasis in the field made it likely that more people were attracted to disability who received training as counseling psychologists than as clinicians, since the former receive more exposure to material involving careers, vocations, and occupational choice than the latter. Because the influence of the ideas of Carl Rogers (1951) has been very strong in counseling psychology training programs, it is no accident that self-concept theory is fairly widely encountered in the theorizing of rehabilitation psychologists.[12]

[12] In this connection, we are not sure which is the chicken and which the egg. Many disabled persons are found to be highly preoccupied with their self-image as damaged people and the manner in which others perceive them as less than acceptable. It would seem plausible that psychologists who are attempting to deal with this problem would turn to the ideas of a writer (Carl Rogers) who makes the self-concept the core of both his theory of personality and his treatment methods. On the other hand, it is also true that many of the prominent figures in counseling psychology (and in the forty-odd university programs for the training of rehabilitation counselors) are Rogerians in their basic approach. The point is moot!

A third feature of rehabilitation which has tended to make for selective theorizing has to do with conception of disability as *loss*. Here, two trends are manifest. One involves a straightforward application of the psychoanalytic theory of castration anxiety, with all its implications of regression, unconscious fantasy, and the mobilization of repressed infantile material. Another (Dembo) prefers to deal with the implication of loss in terms of the concepts of mourning and bereavement.[13] A fourth aspect of disability which has facilitated the employment of certain familiar theoretical concepts has to do with the chronic or permanent nature of the impairment. Some observers have been struck by the degree to which the chronically or permanently impaired tend to resort to particular kinds of defensive maneuvers, namely, denial of illness. Finally, since disability so frequently involves interference with, or maldevelopment of, the individual's perception of his own body, there has been a good deal of interest in body-image theory.

In the pages to follow, we shall consider these theoretical issues in somewhat more detail. Our objective will be not so much to formulate a general theoretical viewpoint vis-à-vis disability—there are good reasons for believing that such an effort would be highly premature—but rather to indicate some of the ways in which the problems of disabled persons have been conceptualized. The order in which we deal with the various theoretical approaches is not to be understood as saying anything about the relative importance or soundness of the respective positions. It is simply a matter of convenience.

THE SOCIAL PSYCHOLOGY OF DISABILITY

For many writers (Barker, 1948; Dembo et al., 1956; Gellman, 1953; Neff, 1959; Wright, 1960) the chief problems of disability are essentially interpersonal in character. From this point of view, the primary factors in disability have to do with a relative inability to meet certain social standards, both in terms of those prescribed by society at large and in terms of the disabled person's own social goals. In a sense, however, this assertion says both too much and too little. Man is, above all, a social animal, and almost everything he does, feels, or thinks is influenced by social interactions, past or present. We should therefore direct our attention to a somewhat more specific question: What kinds of psychosocial problems appear to be peculiar to disability or, at least, bulk larger in the case of disability than in relation to other kinds of human dilemmas? Since space considerations force us to be selective, we shall discuss three issues which appear to us to be decisive. These are (1) disability as a status position, (2) the role of the family, and (3) the social content of the rehabilitation process.

Disability as a Status Position

We need not here belabor the point that most human beings have a strong tendency to classify others (and themselves) in terms of some overriding characteristic. The characteristic in question may, in reality, be relatively meaningless in connection with the actual qualities of the person concerned, but it serves the heuristic purpose of pigeonholing people, which, for many, is a convenient substitute for thought. We are, of course, in the domain of the social stereotype and the issues involved in the social psychology of prejudice.

Barker and Wright (1952), Wright (1960), and, most directly, Gellman (1959) have drawn a pertinent analogy between the entire social position of the disabled and that of members of underprivileged minority groups. Like the member of a disfavored religious or ethnic minority, the person with a manifest disability faces the task of overcoming many social barriers in order to live the kind of life enjoyed by the favored majority. He suffers, for example, severe restriction of employment opportunities, not only because of employer prejudice but also because of what are frequently negative attitudes on the part of potential coworkers. He frequently encounters considerable difficulty in carrying on a normal "social" or recreational life, including even rejection by desired love or marital partners. Similarly, he may discover that certain qualities are attributed to him because "this is what crippled people are like," that he is being treated and perceived not as a unique individual but as a member of a derogated class.

[13] These two trends might be contrasted by saying that one is more interested in what psychoanalytic ego psychologists (see Rapaport, 1950, and Holt, 1956, for example) would call "primary process," whereas Dembo's interest in mourning would imply more of a concern with "secondary-process" phenomena.

Like all analogies, however, that between disability and minority-group status glosses over some important differences at the same time that it points to similarities. On the similarity side, we have such studies as that of Cowen, Underberg, and Verillo (1958), who found that Ss who showed negative attitudes toward the blind were also prejudiced against Negroes and other minority groups and had high scores on authoritarianism scales. This sort of result, however, tells us more about the dynamics of prejudice than about the social situation of the disabled. It will be instructive to consider some of the more important differences between the situation of being disabled and that of being a member of an ethnic or religious minority group. First, there are clear differences in the reality factors at work in the two cases. Whereas expert opinion, at least, fairly unanimously agrees by this time that racial and religious groupings do not actually differ in basic human capacities and potentials, it cannot be denied that there are many disabling conditions which result in genuine losses of functional capacity. While the extent and significance of such functional losses are easily exaggerated, some disabled persons may not be able to function as well *in certain areas* as the nondisabled. Whereas no one in his right mind would advocate the establishment of sheltered workshops for Negroes as a group, it is publicly and professionally recognized that *some* disabled persons can function productively only in a sheltered work environment. Thus, the disabled person—and the professionals who deal with him—may have to cope with the fact that there are real limitations of function and ability, in addition to the many difficulties placed in his path by social biases and stereotypes.

Other differences between the lot of the disabled and that of persons of minority-group status arise from the special kind of social isolation from which the disabled person suffers. Identification with other disabled persons does not carry with it the kind of group sanction and inner compensations that often arise in connection with minority-group status. There are no cultural traditions that will give a disabled person the feeling that he is at least a member of something, of a persecuted minority, if nothing else. It is not common for a disabled child to have parents and siblings who share the same disability. As Wright (1960) and others have pointed out, there is a special quality about the social isolation of many disabled people, such that they may not even be aware that there are others who are in the same boat. Thus, unlike members of minority groups, the disabled person is not able to avail himself even of the dubious joys attendant to affiliation with a "subculture" but must bear the burden of being "different," with none of the rational or irrational compensations of counteridentification.

It should be noted that not all the social dilemmas of the disabled individual are responses to derogation, whether by others or by himself. He may also be faced with social problems because he is *not* derogated, because others may simply be unaware of certain handicapping features of the disability, or even because others may find some supernormal connotations in disability. When the disabled individual himself does not recognize the limits imposed by his conditions, we speak of "denial of illness" (see pages 805 to 806). Where others do not perceive that a disability may restrict certain behaviors, e.g., getting out of a car, carrying a food tray, or shaking hands, the situation may involve sudden frustrations of normal expectations which provoke embarrassment at the minimum and outright rejection at the extreme. There are also people who, with the best of intentions and because of the weight of certain legends, may endow the disabled person with mystical qualities that transcend actual human capabilities. Wright (1960) labels this process "anormalization" and defines it as the attribution to the disabled person of "certain unusual characteristics, even supernatural ones, so that ordinary expectations do not apply." An example is the very common attribution to the blind of supernormal hearing or the possession of some "sixth sense" of spatial localization, like the radarlike senses of bats and porpoises.[14] De-

[14] After surveying all the available evidence on this issue, Axelrod (1959) concludes that it has not been possible to demonstrate that blind persons have any special auditory or tactual abilities, adding the sober thought that people blind since birth frequently display serious cognitive limitations rather than supernormal capacities. Perhaps the basis of some of the wilder notions comes from the fact that many of the early blind display what Raskin (1962) calls "obstacle perception"; that is, they appear to be able to detect a large obstacle (say, a wall) before blundering into it. A series of investigators cited by Raskin have demonstrated that this ability rests on the use of aural cues related to pitch changes in sound reflected from the obstacle. Not all blind persons show this ability, but presumably most can learn it.

spite the fact that the existence of these special powers cannot be demonstrated, these half-legendary misconceptions are very tenacious and may be very widely held. In developed Western societies, systematic elaborations of these notions have largely been confined to creative writers (compare Dostoevsky's thesis in *The Idiot* that the epileptic has a special kind of mystical sensitivity and insight or the impression conveyed in Mann's *Magic Mountain* that the tuberculous have unusually heightened sexual powers), although of course Adler has developed an entire theory of personality in connection with the related idea of compensation for organ inferiority.[15] In other cultures, however, the disabled person may be treated with a special kind of awe and reverence and may even enjoy a special status in connection with religious ritual. In Greek mythology, prophets and sibyls are frequently described as blind, and this was regarded as the basis for their clairvoyance (Hentig, 1948). Maisel (1953) points out that this belief has persisted to modern times in certain countries. Similarly, Devereux (1956) presents interesting evidence that the shaman in the Plains Indian tribes of North America is a culturally accepted schizophrenic, whose talent for hallucination is conceived as providing a special channel to the spirit world. In many cultures it would almost appear that a condition for spiritual leadership is the display of some kind of striking physical, mental, or emotional abnormality, although we follow Devereux in insisting that not any abnormality will serve but that the deviant behavior must somehow be culturally consonant. It may be gratuitous and even offensive to argue that religious leadership in some societies places a premium on "visions" and prophecy, so that many cult initiators may have been frankly psychotic, and it seems obvious that the individuals concerned must have been only "mad north-by-northwest," since there are a great many responsibilities involved in any kind of leadership which require realistic perception and action. In general, however, to the degree that—in other societies or our own—the disabled are endowed with supernormal qualities, there is always the risk of a discrepancy between expectation and reality. In our own culture, the survivals of the attribution of mythical powers to the disabled may lead to another variant of the social isolation which is one of the chief social consequences of the condition of disability.

Finally, we should like to consider the implications of the application to disability of a number of interesting sociopsychological conceptions which are currently enjoying much research interest. We are referring to such concepts as "comparison level" (Thibaut & Kelley, 1959), "social comparison processes" (Schachter, 1959), "cognitive dissonance" (Festinger, 1957), "person perception and social empathy" (Tagiuri & Petrullo, 1958), and a number of considerations related to "social power" (Heider, 1958; Horwitz, 1963; Thibaut & Riecken, 1955). In recent years, there has been a burst of activity in the experimental social psychology of small-group interactions. The concepts briefly listed and the experimental situations from which they arose should be of extreme interest to rehabilitation psychologists since they relate to the manner in which the individual reacts while under the strong influence of his perception of the roles and expectations of other persons. As we have indicated above, the perception (or misperception) by the disabled of the reactions to him of significant others may be a major issue in the special psychology of disability. It seems unfortunate, therefore, that the chief experimental animal utilized in most of this interesting sociopsychological research has been the college sophomore. It is rare that disabled clients have been the subjects of these ingenious experimental manipulations. The work of Dembo et al. (1956) is in this tradition, although it is not based on the experimental method. Festinger, Gerard, Hymovitch, Kelley, & Raven (1952) have set up experimental situations to examine the reactions of normal persons to extreme deviants, and Hastorf (1959) has utilized these conceptions in working in a camp for handicapped children. Richardson's work (Richardson, Goodman, Hastorf, & Dornbusch, 1961; Richardson et al., 1963), in studying the perception of disability by handicapped and normal children, should also be mentioned,

[15] It seems somewhat odd that Adler's ideas and clinical illustrations have not been more influential in the field of physical disability than they have been, since there would seem to be such a close logical tie. Perhaps the answer is found in the overwhelmingly powerful influence of Freud on American clinical psychology, so that whenever a rehabilitation psychologist sought a psychodynamic explanation of some event, the conceptions of classical psychoanalysis were both better known and more satisfying.

although his techniques are closer to those used in clinical assessment than to those used in experimental social psychology. On the whole, however, application to the disabled of the concepts and techniques of experimental social psychology has hardly been initiated, although it is our belief that such an effort would be very rewarding. A good survey of the implications of modern social psychology for work with the handicapped has been written by Kelley, Hastorf, Jones, Thibaut, and Usdane (1960) as one of the reports of the discussion at a recent conference on psychological research and rehabilitation (Lofquist, 1963).

Although we have not been able to write in detail concerning disability as a status position, we believe enough has been said to indicate the extreme importance of these issues for the rehabilitation movement. The social implications of the situation of being disabled appear to be so profound that to ignore them can only result in misapprehension of the problems of the handicapped and, perhaps, in grave errors in treatment. At the same time, we must wait for the accumulation of a great deal more experience and research before we can be at all definite about the actual pervasiveness of some of the observed phenomena. While some of these conceptions appear quite plausible in theory and have been reported frequently in clinical observation, it is also quite striking to note the frequency with which observers have reported that many handicapped persons are quite free of any special feelings or behaviors related to the status of being disabled. We cannot permit ourselves to tire of repeating that human behavior appears almost infinitely malleable. A great many disabled persons with marked handicapping conditions appear to be so successful in achieving their objective of "being like everyone else" that there appear no traces of feelings or behaviors related to a special social status. For example, Levine's work (1960b; 1962) suggests that there are surprising numbers of congenitally deaf children who are "well adjusted," and the same kind of finding has been suggested for the congenitally blind. While such findings are welcome corrections of certain prevailing misconceptions (e.g., "deaf children tend to become paranoid"), it is nevertheless quite true that handicapped persons must deal with many real consequences of inferior social status. Those interested in the social psychology of disability have a considerable contribution to make in teasing out the dynamics of the process of coping.

The Role of the Family in Disability

The second set of issues we wish to discuss in relation to the social consequences of disability has to do with intrafamilial variables. Although it seems embarrassingly obvious to state that the parents of a disabled child are likely to be decisive in the socialization process, that the pattern in which they relate to the child may well influence the bulk of his future social interactions, we have quite meager factual knowledge of the ways in which this pattern develops. Rehabilitation agencies tend to form only slight relationships to the parents of their disabled clients, despite the rather wide suspicion that the parents may be playing key roles in hindering or aiding the rehabilitation process. In part, this may be due to the fact that family casework, as a rehabilitation specialty, is rather poorly developed, even in those facilities in which such professionals are members of the rehabilitation staff. In part, also, this situation may arise from the fact that many parents of disabled children appear to be so conscious of their inadequacy in solving the problems of such children that they tend to avoid involvement in the rehabilitation process. Whatever the circumstances, many of the most important aspects of the role of a disabled member in a "normal" family remain to be worked out. Only a few, rather heavily overworked concepts are encountered in the available literature. The first of these has to do with parental overprotection and its consequences for conflicts over dependence-independence. A second issue has to do with the psychodynamics of rejection, including the psychoanalytically oriented position that overprotection is simply one of the chief defenses against allowing deep conscious feelings of rejection to come to the surface.

Authorities in this field tend to agree that overprotection is the most frequently displayed parental attitude toward children who have an impairing disability. The work of Shere (1954) on children with cerebral palsy, of Kammerer (1940) on children with other crippling disabilities, and of Sommers (1944) on the blind are examples of this finding. Shere's work is particularly suggestive. He was able to study 30 pairs of twins of which one member of each pair was cerebral-palsied. Of these 30 pairs, 13 children with cerebral palsy were deemed to be overprotected, while none of the nondisabled twins fell in this category. In passing, we note that 13 is not an absolute majority of 30, so that overprotection is by no means the only attitude displayed by these parents. But the contrast with the nondisabled member of each pair is sufficiently striking so that the result deserves to be followed up. If we are interested in the behavioral consequences of parental overprotection, however, we enter shakier ground. By definition, overprotection is something "bad"; its most unfavorable connotation is that the child is infantalized, that more normal development toward adult independence is being blocked. On the other hand, even a minimal acquaintance with family dynamics will make one wonder whether infantalization and underdevelopment can be so neatly related to a single form of parental behavior. Infantile behavior—whether of the disabled or of persons free of a crippling disability—is an outcome of very complex sets of conditions, including outright parental rejection as well as the more benign form of inappropriate behavior we designate as overprotection. Recognizing that the psychodynamics are complex, Shere (1954) is careful to specify that the overprotective parent may be either "acceptant" or "rejectant," or both by turns. In our opinion, however, this promotes semantic confusion. It is true that both highly benign and highly malevolent parents may so overcontrol their children that the result is a passive, dependent, and underdeveloped adult, but we are dealing with quite differential motivational situations, and it is hard to believe that the character structures of the children in the two different situations will not turn out to be quite discrepant. The kernel of truth in this is that both the "accepting" and the "rejecting" parent may prevent the child from growing up, the one because of excessive fear of the dangers and accidents which inevitably accompany the growth process, and the other because of simple indifference or the wish to punish. Shere's usage, which Wright appears to support (1960), appears to us to involve a misreading of Freud's conception of the interdependent polarity of love and hate. While it might be argued that the overprotective parent is merely defending himself (reaction formation) against acknowledgment of his deep hatred and guilt, the very complexity of the defense has significance for parent-child relations and the resulting character structure of the disabled child. It seems more plausible to infer that an openly rejecting parent is more likely to produce a psychotic child than merely a dependent one. An illustration of the manner in which this distinction plays itself out in rehabilitation practice has to do with goal-setting behavior. The overly accepting parent frequently sets goals for the child that are too low; the rejecting or ambivalent parent may be able to display only affection for the child if the child strives for goals that are too high. We are perhaps on safer ground if we conclude that the psychodynamics of the acceptance-rejection dimension are rather poorly understood. Complicating this issue is the probable social fact that parents who trouble to bring their children to rehabilitative agencies are more likely to be "overprotective" in the straightforward sense of this term, in the sense that they are deeply involved—often overinvolved—with the child's problems. Rejecting parents may be so indifferent to the child's problems that they do not seek much in the way of professional assistance or simply solve the problem by abandonment or institutionalization. Clearly, much more, and better controlled, investigation is required before we can say that we know very much about parental attitudes toward their disabled children.

It seems evident that a great unmet need in the field of parent-child relationships involves the provision of intensive family counseling to parents of disabled children—not only to those who manage to find their way to rehabilitation agencies but also to those who have not (or refuse to) become involved with such agencies. Of course, this is easier to ask for than to achieve! The advent in a family of a disabled or impaired child is an extremely traumatic event for *any* parents, and it is quite unreasonable to expect that very many such parents will develop, unaided, as appropriately realistic attitudes as we would wish. Even otherwise quite stable people may be so disturbed by such an occurrence that they cannot refrain from dealing with a disabled child in self-defeating ways. Unfortunately, family counseling is the least developed of all the forms of professional assistance available in the rehabilitation field. An equally unfortunate consequence of this deficiency is that we know less about the actual dynamics of family reactions to disability than about any other aspect of the problems of handicapped persons. Even the highly competent group of writers assembled by Garrett and Levine (1962), each of whom is an expert in one or another kind of disability and many of whom are leading figures in the field of rehabilitation generally, say almost nothing about this very important subject. We can only conclude that here is an entire area of the psychological aspects of disability which remains almost untapped.

The Social Content of the Rehabilitation Process

Although there are a great many other sociopsychological aspects of the situation of being disabled on which we should comment, space permits consideration of only one further set of issues. These have to do with certain social aspects of the rehabilitation effort per se. We shall focus on two issues: the rehabilitation facility as a treatment milieu and the special meanings attached to work both by the rehabilitation movement and by the disabled person himself.

The very nature of its task, which is so frequently defined as helping the patient to live with his disability in an optimal manner, has induced the typical rehabilitation agencies to be vitally concerned with issues of psychosocial adjustment. As Garrett and Levine state in the preface to their recently edited collection of monographs on disability (1962): "A point of great significance that emerges is the degree to which successful rehabilitation can be hampered [we would add "facilitated"] by such factors of practical reality as sociocultural milieu and attitudes. . . ."

In many respects, rehabilitation is seen by its practitioners as a socialization or resocialization process. This is clearly the heart of the process when we are confronted with the rehabilitation of the institutionalized mentally retarded or the ex-mental patient with a history of prolonged hospitalization (cf. Neff et al., 1957). But it is evident also that the focuses of much of the rehabilitation efforts with the physically disabled are on psychosocial matters. An illustration of the force of this trend is afforded by the monographs in the Garrett and Levine collection. Each is a chapter on a specific disability grouping (amputation, arthritis and rheumatism, cardiovascular disability, etc.), and each chapter includes a section on the special rehabilitation problems of the disability in question. There is remarkable unanimity in the manner in which the same issues reappear across diverse disability groupings, i.e., the problems of employment, the problems of maintaining or acquiring some kind of "social" or recreational life, and the problems of family adjustment. Fishman, for example, in searching for an appropriate success criterion in relation to the rehabilitation of amputees (1962), sums up the over-all objective as follows:

> As the ability to use the prosthesis more automatically or subconsciously increases, as the client's awareness of being physically limited and different becomes less threatening, and as the amputation becomes a minimal source of interference in his *familial, vocational* and *social activities*, the elements of successful rehabilitation have been approached (italics added).

In rehabilitation practice, the key element in this social-adjustment triad has been the vocational component. Its great emphasis on vocational objectives is one of the chief sources of strength of the rehabilitation field, but also from this concentration have arisen certain weaknesses and limitations. We shall comment briefly on both aspects.

There is little doubt that the rehabilitation movement is strongly work-oriented. In part, this situation is statutory, since the Federal agency which has supported much of the development of the field (the Vocational Rehabilitation Administration) is obligated by law to spend its money in the service of the vocational adjustment of the handicapped. In part, however, we are close to the nature of the beast when we note that a core problem (if not *the* core problem) of the disabled person is the problem of leading some kind of independent, or quasi-independent, economic life. In a highly work-oriented society such as ours, the status of being chronically unemployed has so many unfavorable consequences that it frequently overrides and complicates any other serious problems the individual may have. For these reasons, the rehabilitation movement has invested a very large portion of its professional time in developing techniques of work evaluation and work adjustment that are particularly suitable for the disabled. In many leading rehabilitation agencies, vocational procedures are the core of the rehabilitation process, and in some agencies this is virtually the only service the rehabilitee receives. Because of this concentration, the rehabilitation movement has been quite inventive in developing novel vocational procedures. Illustrations are the TOWER[16] system of work evaluation, developed at the Institute of the Crippled and Disabled of New York City, and the rehabilitative workshop procedure for the emotionally disturbed originated by the Jewish Vocational Service of Chicago (Neff et al., 1957). One of the most striking features of the rehabilitation movement in the United States has been what amounts almost to a hyperdevelopment of the use of sheltered workshops as *transitional* facilities, with intensive short-term programs designed to equip the rehabilitee with appropriate work habits and work roles. This is in sharp distinction to the continued use of sheltered workshops for the provision of a long-term or terminal protected work environment for disabled persons who cannot compete for employment in the open labor market.[17]

This concentration on vocational objectives has both its positive and its negative side. On the one hand, this focus on work has compelled the rehabilitation movement to become enmeshed with highly practical, reality-oriented objectives. The obtaining of some kind of stable employment has become the basic criterion of success with which to assess the outcome of rehabilitation efforts. This has become so much the case that the Federal agency (VRA) and the many centers which are strongly influenced by this trend report their annual statistics simply in terms of the proportion of clients who were able to enter the labor force. As the field has become more sophisticated, however, a certain amount of discomfort has developed regarding the degree to which this total commitment to work is appropriate for all the clients who enter a rehabilitation process. It is being increasingly recognized that the goal of entry into the unprotected labor market may be highly unrealistic for many clients who are currently being served and that a variety of other, more modest goals need to be explicitly adopted.[18] Rigid adherence to vocational objectives may well have resulted in denial of service to many clients who might have benefited from rehabilitation efforts in important ways. There is in process a widely supported effort to amend present Federal statutes so that VRA funds can be explicitly used for other than vocational objectives,[19] and there is some interest in rehabilitation research which would provide outcome criteria unrelated to the issues of employment.

Even though total adherence to vocational goals is frequently violated or evaded in practice and although we can expect public recognition of the acceptance of other kinds of objectives, one of the signal virtues of the rehabilitation movement has been its commit-

16 TOWER is an acronymic term (testing, orientation, and work evaluation in rehabilitation) for a system of work evaluation through the use of standardized work samples, developed at the Institute for the Crippled and Disabled of New York City. TOWER is in no sense comparable to a mental test but is a series of structured and semistandardized work situations to which the disabled client is exposed over a period of three to seven weeks, on a five-day-per-week, 9 A.M. to 4 P.M. schedule. Its primary objective is to find areas of vocational potential in which the client will profit by extended training, but there is also heavy emphasis on assessment of the work habits and work motivation of the potential trainee. An encapsulated account of this procedure will be found in a publication of the Institute for the Crippled and Disabled (1959). Since 1957, this procedure has been the basis of a VRA-supported training program at the institute which has resulted in applications of this method of work evaluation in over one hundred rehabilitation agencies in this country and abroad.

17 For an indication of the changes made in traditional sheltered workshop procedures, see Black (1959), Gellman (1956), and Neff et al. (1957).

18 Wherever follow-up studies have been conducted, we find that only a portion of clients who are accepted for service in programs of vocational rehabilitation (50 to 75 per cent) are able to meet the rather strict criteria of competitive employment. This may be considered a highly laudable result, in the face of employer resistance and other social factors which are not under the control of the rehabilitation facility. But there is, nevertheless, a strong impression that the remaining 25 to 50 per cent have made gains in certain aspects of personal and social adjustment, despite the fact that they are listed as "failures" according to the standard of employment. The problem is to devise reliable and valid measurements of these more subtle benefits. The virtue of the employment criterion is that it is both objective and comparatively easy to ascertain. Its vice is not only that it may be truly unrealistic for many clients but also that it is confounded with variables unrelated to client characteristics, e.g., employer practices and the vagaries of the labor market.

19 We are referring here to what has been called the "independent living," bills which are designed to amend the present rehabilitation statutes so that VRA can use funds to train the severely disabled to take care of certain personal needs (dress, food, household activities, etc.) where there is no expectation that the individual may become economically self-sufficient. The reasoning here is that such training will result in the freeing of *others,* now tied down by the excessive dependency of some disabled person, for more productive activity.

ment to so vital a reality issue as the ability to work. This commitment has also been one of the chief factors which has given so marked a sociopsychological flavor to the rehabilitation movement. It has become abundantly clear that the barriers which stand between the disabled person and employment are by no means a simple function of his alleged physical or intellectual limitations. Elaborate research is hardly necessary to demonstrate that most of the impediments that block employment of the handicapped arise from attitudes and expectations—conscious and unconscious—of the disabled person himself, or prospective employers, and of potential or actual work peers. Gellman (1953) has argued that the work capacity and performance of any individual—whether disabled or not—are characterized by what he calls the "vocational pattern." It should be noted that most of the components of the vocational pattern, as Gellman describes it, are unrelated to capacity or ability but are heavily psychosocial in content, namely, the person's attitudes and reactions to authority figures, how he handles his relations to work peers, the meanings placed on work and achievement, his ability to play a productive role, etc. Neff (1959; 1961; 1962b; 1963) has written a series of papers on the social meanings attached to work and has concentrated his attention on research designed to demonstrate (as he hypothesizes) that the vocationally handicapped attach special meanings to work which are not manifested by people who take their ability to work for granted (Neff and Helfand, 1963). There have, of course, been efforts to investigate employer attitudes toward the hiring of disabled persons[20] and the beginnings of study of the attitudes of the nondisabled to the disabled (Yuker, Block, & Campbell, 1960; Siller, 1963, 1964).

One of the more interesting implications for theory, which has come from this preoccupation with work, derives from the finding that many rehabilitation clients—the marginal mental retardate, the psychotic in partial remission, the physically disabled client with a disfiguring but nonlimiting impairment—are "physically" capable of working but appear unable to meet certain psychological demands which arise from work as a *social* situation. As a consequence, we find that most rehabilitation programs place heavy emphasis not so much on the acquisition of work skills but on the development of appropriate work habits and work attitudes. This is not to say that skill is irrelevant in the sense that the client is not required to meet minimal output standards. But there is considerable evidence that a great many dismissals and forced resignations occur—not to mention inability to secure employment in the first place—because the individual is perceived by his employers or associates as socially disruptive or inappropriate.

An important by-product of this interest in the factors influencing work adjustment is that some of us have become sensitized to an issue which should be of considerable theoretical interest: the psychodynamics and psychopathology of work. Freud is reported as having stated that the two chief competencies which any human being must somehow display are the ability to love and the ability to work. Unfortunately, as one of us has hitherto commented (Neff, 1961), the psychoanalytic movement has concerned itself almost wholly with the ability to love and has virtually ignored the psychodynamics of work. An examination of Grunstein's index (1960) has failed to yield more than a half-dozen titles related to work among the thousands of books and papers listed. Two of these were written by Hendrick (1943a; 1943b), who develops the conception that the drive to work is a basic human instinct and who speculates about the implications of this notion from the point of view of classical psychoanalytic theory. Lantos has written a suggestive paper (1952) in which she attempts to apply the concepts of psychoanalytic ego psychology to the problems of work adjustment. Menninger (1942) has considered the dynamic and motivational aspects of the inability to work. Beyond this, there is very little! The deeper psychological variables related to competency and achievement (McClelland, 1961; McClelland, Atkinson, Clark, & Lowell, 1953; White, 1959) remain largely to be worked out.

In reviewing the material we have presented on the social psychology of disability, it is obvious that there is room for a massive investigative effort. Nevertheless, there is enough already available, from research and

[20] The Federation Employment and Guidance Service of New York City is an agency that has carried through significant studies of employer practices in hiring the handicapped. For general findings and impressions in this field, see the reports and statements of the President's Committee on Employment of the Handicapped.

practice, to convince us that the strong concentration of rehabilitation staffs on psychosocial matters is not misplaced. Unfortunately, the rehabilitation field has not yet attracted, or is not aware that it *should* attract, more than a handful of psychologists who have training in social psychological theory and technique. The bulk of the psychologists who have become involved with disability have been trained in clinical or counseling psychology, and they are, typically, not very well prepared to deal with the myriad psychosocial problems faced by their disabled clients. It is to be hoped that social psychologists as well as clinicans will be attracted to the developing university training programs in the psychological aspects of disability. At present, the relatively few psychologists who have a professional stake in the development of social psychology are largely unaware of the potentials of the rehabilitation field for research and service.

THE PSYCHODYNAMICS OF PHYSICAL DISABILITY[21]

Reality Factors

Although the good personality resources of one severely handicapped individual offset major insults to the body, while the inadequate personality of another facilitates a psychological exacerbation of a relatively minor disability, certain reality factors cannot be overlooked. Clinical experience demonstrates the profound effects of the frustration of certain basic needs on an individual's functioning and on his view of himself. That is, while the self-image and meaning of the loss, as influenced by the premorbid personality, loom large as major determinants in rehabilitation, one must not lose sight of the concrete reality factors which play a role in shaping or modifying a disabled person's self-image.

Physical function. Disability prevents or hinders performances which were originally comparatively effortless because they were inherent in the repertoire of life activities. Ambulation with crutches, braces, or prostheses is, at best, only an approximation of premorbid function. The complex maneuvers an arm amputee must execute in order to hold a glass of water are a constant reminder of physical decrement (Fishman, 1959). The additional time necessary to perform even simple acts is particularly irritating to one previously accustomed to rapid movement. The losses or limitations in some physical functions affect virtually all disabled persons.

Energy costs. EFFECTS OF PHYSICAL LOSS. It has been estimated that ambulation on the part of an above-knee amputee requires two to three times as much energy as that expended by a nonamputee in the same activity. Some above-knee amputees have described their exertion when walking on a level plane as equivalent to a normal person's climbing a stairway. Artificial limbs and braces, often heavy and cumbersome, tax an individual's resources, especially in warm weather. Considerable fatigue is usually the aftermath of a day's work because of the additional need for continuous attention to the control, use, and activation of the assistive devices. In amputees and persons with other orthopedic disabilities, the loss of the limb or its function introduces problems of body asymmetry with concomitant problems in balance.

EFFECTS OF DISTURBANCE IN METABOLISM. Metabolic problems also ensue because the loss of skin surface interferes with the elimination of waste products in perspiration. These factors make energy costs a significant problem.

Comfort. Some rehabilitants are overoptimistic as regards the restitutive powers of assistive devices. While the considerable measure of function that can often be restored is ample compensation for the patient's efforts, discomfort is a ubiquitous problem. It is not ordinarily pointed out that assistive devices are inherently uncomfortable appendages. As a result of extensive experience with amputees, rehabilitation experts agree that a comfortable prosthesis is simply one that offers a minimum and tolerable degree of discomfort.

Assistive devices such as braces and prostheses involve weight bearing, which strains

[21] The remaining part of this chapter, pp. 800–819, was written by Dr. Weiss. Some of the investigations at New York University discussed below were supported in part by a Research Special Project grant from the Vocational Rehabilitation Administration, U.S. Department of Health, Education, and Welfare. The writer appreciates the cooperation of Miss Harriet Berg for her aid with the manuscript and Dr. Maurice Schweizer, Project Librarian. The cooperation of the New York City offices of the State Division of Vocational Rehabilitation is also acknowledged.

and bruises the tissues, or require use of the musculature in unusual body and limb movements. The confinement of the stump in relatively rigid and impermeable materials, such as metals, wood, and plastics, is a source of discomfort due to heat, perspiration, disabling skin disorders, and the increased metabolic demands to which an amputee is subject.

INDIVIDUAL DIFFERENCES. The great variability among individuals regarding reaction to pain has been studied in terms of the dimensions of pain thresholds and pain tolerance; physiological, cognitive, affective, and attitudinal variables have also been investigated. On the basis of their own work and an evaluation of the studies by Hardy, Wolff, and Goodell (1952), Clark and Bindra (1956) conclude that the *attitudinal* variables are responsible for a large part of the individual differences in both pain threshold and pain tolerance levels and that these attitudinal factors are primarily affective rather than cognitive in nature. After a review of the literature, Barber (1959) concludes that the experience of pain involves two major factors: (1) the feeling of pain itself and (2) the attention paid to it. By removing attention from the pain sensation, by means of training, hypnosis, suggestibility, and religious devotion, the actual feeling of pain may be considerably minimized or totally eliminated. An individual's preoccupation with his body can be a *cause* of aggravated pain experience as well as a result of illness.

AGE DIFFERENCES. Older or geriatric amputees, in particular, suffer from discomfort problems. A study (S. A. Weiss, 1961) of 70 male unilateral lower-extremity prosthesis wearers at the Prosthetic and Orthotic Studies of New York University involved a comparison of an older group, ages 56 to 75, with a younger one, ages 18 to 35. The older group showed more somatic preoccupation on an association test, a revised form of the Secord Body Cathexis Test (Secord, 1953), as well as more marked passivity and constriction, as reflected on the masculinity and occupational scores of the Wechsler Work Interest Inventory (see A. J. Weiss, 1959).

CULTURAL AND SEX DIFFERENCES. Sanua (1960), Zborowski (1952), and Kramer, (1964) found that members of different ethnic groups revealed different attitudes toward their problems in rehabilitation and toward suffering. In our own experience with amputees, we have consistently found that women as a group show more somatic preoccupation on our revised form of the Secord test.

Economic security. Unskilled workers and skilled technicians, whose earning capacity is primarily dependent on physical power or manual dexterity, are more subject to serious industrial accidents which destroy, or seriously limit, future vocational choices and which shake their economic security. Individuals high on the socioeconomic scale whose income depends mainly on education and personality are less subject to traumatic accidents.

After injury, the former group is usually dependent on governmental care centers and social agencies for treatment and rehabilitation, while individuals with greater financial resources can often accelerate the rehabilitation process. The important need to be economically self-sufficient is more apt to be frustrated in the former group.

Psychosocial insecurities. SUCCESS FACTOR. The emphasis on success and achievement in American life has led to a "spread" of the fear of failure from basic areas, such as the financial and interpersonal, to less significant ones. Even minor failures experienced in public places cause embarrassment because of the great fear of "appearing ridiculous." Assistive aids, such as machines with movable parts, sometimes fail because of fitting problems, inadequacies in design or fabrication, and the occasionally imperfect control of the apparatus by a fallible human being. Failures in simple acts of prehension with an artificial hand or hook or a fall in a crowded place by a brace wearer or lower-extremity amputee is a source of embarrassment, especially to women, who are unprotected sartorially. Ample testimony by some rehabilitants affirms that the first mental reaction during and immediately after a fall is a concern about embarrassment, exposure, and failure. These feelings may temporarily mask the pain even of a severe bruise.

SYMBOLIC FACTOR. The fear of falling has also become symbolically associated with a *moral* fall in the minds of some phobic clients who require special prostheses (for example, the "Bock" knee) to ensure knee stability, even in the absence of physical body weakness. Two such phobic female above-knee amputees, who were provided with psychotherapy under the auspices of the New York State Division of Vocational Rehabilitation[22] (S. A. Weiss, 1964), were unable to venture from their homes or to use public transportation for many years until they realized that their fear of falling stemmed from the fear of becoming "fallen women." Their phobias protected them from being exposed to temptation away from home. The symbolic meaning of falling was completely obscured by its displacement into a fear of physical injury and embarrassment at possible public display.

Cosmetic needs. In American society, cosmesis has been elevated to a major need by public communication media such as television, the cinema, and the elaborately embellished popular magazines. The reduced cosmesis in disablement arouses anxiety about possible rejection or avoidance by the nondisabled. These feelings are often reality-based and not solely the fears of a neurotic disposition. Some normal individuals readily admit to an extreme intolerance for maimed individuals. While some studies (Ray, 1946) have found normal individuals expressing positive attitudes toward the disabled, others suggest that unverbalized and unconscious feelings of rejection are operative.

THEORIES IMPLYING INNATE OR INGRAINED TENDENCIES. Winkler (1931, in Barker et al., 1953) offers evidence that the unusual postures and movements of the crippled, even when they are not consciously recognized as crippled, limit physically normal individuals in the establishment of an empathic relationship with them. The work of Wolff (1943) and Huntley (1940) suggests that Winkler's assumptions are correct. Hebb and Thompson (1954) report that chimpanzees react negatively to the unusual postures of sick or disabled peers. The latter investigators suggest, and not merely obliquely, that innate tendencies predispose these reactions to visual stimuli (see also Hebb, 1958).

Although not all normal individuals react aversely to disability and although acclimation to a hospital environment by the nondisabled often leads to more positive acceptance of the disabled, it is evident from the clinical behavior of many patients that they expect aversive or negative reactions. This is evident in the attempts of many individuals to hide their disabilities, e.g., by keeping their hand prostheses in their pockets, even in a rehabilitation setting.

The cosmetic aspects of physical restoration are especially important in America. Certain restorative operations, commonly performed on war amputees in Germany during World War II because of their effectiveness in improving function, were generally rejected by those American servicemen who were not coerced by their captors or made subject to extreme pressure. For example, the Krukenberg operation was especially adapted for long forearm stumps. The forearm is split into two long "fingers," which work against each other, thus permitting grasp but also retaining sensation in the top of each "finger." Another technique (cineplasty) utilized the remaining muscles in the amputation stump by making tunnels through them, lining the muscles with skin, and then attaching them by means of ivory pegs through a yoke to an artificial hand. The prosthesis is activated by the same muscle which normally activated the fingers of the natural hand. The cineplastic operation was ideal in bilateral above-elbow amputations (Kessler, 1949). These operative procedures were unpopular in America, the Krukenberg because of the uncosmetic "claw" effect, and cineplasty because of the deformation and "mechanization" of the residual stump and the difficulty in maintaining cleanliness in the tunnels. Amputees were willing to forego improved function in order to avoid undesirable appearance.

FAMILY INFLUENCES. Rehabilitation of a child or infant with a congenital or traumatic amputation usually brings the cosmesis versus function dilemma into prominence, since a choice must be made between the relative advantages and limitations of active versus passive artificial hands or of a hand versus the more functional, but uncosmetic, hook (New York University, 1964). Many parents prefer a passive, cosmetic limb for their child or no prosthesis at all because they are intent on denying or hiding their child's disability, even when confronted with the imperatives of functional restoration if the child is to gain better control over his environment. Parents may be

[22] The cooperation of Harry Katz, Dr. Daniel S. Sanford, Israel E. Weissfeld, and Dr. David Guralnick, of the New York City offices of the Division of Vocational Rehabilitation, is appreciated.

more interested in the defensive behavior of negating their own irrational guilt feelings than in helping facilitate the best adjustment of the child. The clinic often becomes a battleground between parents and rehabilitation personnel, where defensive and camouflaged needs collide with reality needs. The recent development of arm prostheses for children is an attempt at compromise: the retention of useful, though not maximum, function with acceptable cosmesis (Fishman & Kay, 1964).

SEX DIFFERENCES. Women are less hesitant in expressing discontent regarding cosmesis, while men supposedly profess a matter-of-fact interest in function in order to assert their masculine uninterest in "prettiness." Extensive experience with orthopedic aids has demonstrated, however, the covert eagerness for improved appearance, which emerges as an important factor in the acceptance or rejection of an appliance (S. A. Weiss, 1958).

Another example of the potent influence cosmetic needs exert on the male rehabilitant is the experience with cosmetic gloves. Cosmetic gloves (fitted over the hand mechanism) have been developed which are remarkable in their duplication of the skin color, texture, fingernails, and "natural irregularities" and idiosyncrasies of the human hand. An older study (Cattell, Dembo, Koppel, Tane-Baskin, & Weinstock, 1949) had shown that in casual contacts, 80 per cent of the salesmen exposed to a cosmetic hand were completely unaware that it was not the natural limb. Evidently, the region of its *visual presence* was not identical with the region of the observer's *visual concern.* Yet, a recent study (Army Prosthetics Research Laboratory, 1956) of improved cosmetic gloves showed how concerned even male subjects were about slight and almost unnoticeable deviations in the gloves. These are often the very same amputees who will consciously underscore the need for function while assigning little importance to cosmesis.

Auditory cosmesis is also of great concern to disabled individuals who are sensitive about the "unsocial noise" produced by prostheses, orthopedic aids, and braces in the form of clicks, squeaks, and the sound of escaping air.

Thus, reality factors must always be considered in the evaluation of rehabilitation plans.

Concepts Invoked to Account for Behavioral Phenomena Associated with Disability

Some concepts specifically associated with disability or neurotic defense mechanisms are often invoked to account for the behavior of disabled individuals. These concepts refer mainly to the individual's *perception* of his state, the resultant self-feelings, and his reactions to the environment.[23]

Perception of body resources. A disabled individual's perception and feelings about his body exert a considerable influence on his rehabilitation. A patient who is tremulous about his physical resources hesitates to undergo rehabilitation procedures which require exertion and pain tolerance. The undue concern that some patients feel about their physical adequacy is often at variance with the objective and positive evaluation by the professional rehabilitation personnel. Clinic personnel constantly encounter such individuals whose flesh is willing to undergo rehabilitation but whose spirit is weak. These persons remain ensconced in a wheelchair, which they view as a throne and from which they attempt to dominate their families by evoking guilt and concern.

Meaning of loss to person. A self-image is sketched in dark or rosy hues in accordance with the *meaning* a particular disability has

[23] In addition to furnishing valuable knowledge, compendia, as products of scholars who are fallible, often perpetuate dogmatic errors or misinterpretations (see Dreikurs, 1948). The discussion of biblical themes in relation to disability is one example.

While some writers have stressed the positive influence of religion in helping the disabled (Garrett, 1955; Palmer, 1962), others have attributed to religion a predominantly negative influence as regards disablement. A careful perusal of the Bible, which purportedly derogates the maimed, discounts the validity of these conclusions. Some citations are taken out of context from obscure passages, and the conclusions reflect more the bias of the writer than the clarity of the passage. While, in admonitions to the nation, disease and sickness are mentioned as punishment for sin, so are poverty and exile. There is, however, no exclusive association of disability with sin. The exclusion of the maimed from the priesthood (Lev. 21) is not due to their sinfulness. (The disabled priests enjoyed complete equality as regards economic support.) When it is considered that the pagans often indulged in maiming (I Kings 18:28) and self-castration (Goldberg, 1958) as an outcome of their religious frenzy, the exclusion of maimed individuals from the temple service is readily understood as an attempt to wean the people from these sadomasochistic practices of self-mutilation and other mutilation.

for an individual. The extent of disability, whether extreme or minor, is often not as crucial as the individual's perception of it.

The greater the inaccuracy of perception, the greater is the degree of frustration because the subjective, phenomenological experience conflicts with reality and leads to ineffective coping mechanisms. These may be attempts to reach an unattainable degree of physical restoration, at one extreme, or at the other, the perceiving of the impairment as of such cataclysmic proportions as to foster withdrawal or resignation.

As an example, some above-knee amputees regard their disability as a misfortune because it limits their activities, but not as a catastrophe which converts them to helpless cripples. Other individuals who incur only an ankle-disarticulation amputation and who can walk without a noticeable limp regard the loss of the foot as catastrophic and as a severe blow to their narcissism. A brace wearer may learn to integrate his orthotic device (brace) into his body image almost as readily as the average person accepts spectacles, or he may regard the supportive aid as a parasitic, artificial monstrosity. In brief, it is the *meaning* assigned to the disability that often determines the role it plays in the person's life. Health may be seen as a *comparative* value, without which one is socially inferior, or it may be seen as a valuable *asset,* the absence of which will not destroy one's feeling of value and integrity as a person (Dembo et al., 1956).

Premorbid personality and postmorbid adjustment. An individual incurring a disability must often revise his body image drastically and realistically so as to adjust to the new demands placed on him by his environment. In the clinical judgment of most rehabilitation personnel, the degree of flexibility and readiness to face the demands of reality depends on the patient's premorbid personality. If the body has been the main source of an individual's satisfaction, while the intangibles of personality have been deemphasized, the loss of body intactness will be devastating. If the premorbid personality was rooted in more enduring values, readjustment will be more readily accomplished.

Frustration and conflict. In virtually all cases of disability, frustration and conflict are prominent and retain their potency in causing dysphoric feelings until an effective adjustment to the disability, or the erection of psychological defenses against anxiety, reduces the magnitude of suffering. An important contribution to suffering is the difficulty in reaching one goal without sacrificing an equally important one. The incompatibility of achieving maximum restoration in both cosmesis and function is an example of the "donkey with the two bales of hay" dilemma that is always present in the coping process.

Frustration and conflict cause only unpleasant emotional reactions, and the frequent thwarting of goals leads to a reduction in self-regard. In intrapunitive individuals, the tensions arising from frustration lead to withdrawal tendencies, where such mechanisms as encapsulation or constriction, phobic reactions, feelings of depression, pessimism and somatic preoccupation, or somatization play a prominent role. In extrapunitive persons, the feelings of inadequacy are projected or displaced on others, and the more prevalent reactions may be in the form of sociopathic or neurotic impulsivity and other aggressive reactions. Some patients shuttle ambivalently between withdrawal and aggressive defenses and are characterized by uneven functioning and the inadequate control of anxiety.

Guilt. Guilt feelings among the disabled and their relatives are pervasive in some cultures. Whiting and Child (1953) found that (1) those areas of child development which are severely socialized (oral, anal or genital, etc.) are also invoked to account for illness in that society; (2) societies using loss of love as a threat in discipline also induce acceptance by the patient of the responsibility for illness; and (3) those societies with the severest socialization practices create the most anxiety and guilt, which lead the patient to accept responsibility for illness.

Experience shows that guilt feelings often play a considerable role in negative attitudes toward the injured. Parents often experience intense guilt feelings for producing a congenitally imperfect child. When a child is injured, parents may regard this as retribution for their own crimes. While some parents may attempt to atone with self-sacrifice and overprotection, others reject the child in an effort to dissociate themselves from this reminder of their own supposed guilt or imperfection. These negative self-attitudes also characterize some disabled individuals. If guilt is accepted *intrapunitively*, it may lead to depression and withdrawal because the disabled person desires to hide his shame; if the guilt is not accepted but repressed, it may be projected on others, in a paranoid mechanism. If a sense of justice precludes the luxury of *extrapunitive* defenses but allows a deep repression of guilt feelings (an attempt at an *impunitive* defense), these feelings may emerge in disguised form in phobias, where the guilt is displaced on animals, places, or inanimate objects such as the person's own braces, prosthesis, or other assistive aids (S. A. Weiss, 1960).

Maladaptive neurotic defenses bring the individual in conflict with either himself or others. In the former case, the dysphoric feelings and anxiety lead to self-deprecation as a malfunctioning or "sick" person. Conflicts with others bring retribution from them, which in turn mobilizes more aggression or maladaptive defenses, which lead to defective socialization.

Mourning and bereavement. Loss of limb or function is usually followed by the experience of psychological shock, which has been compared to bereavement for a beloved. The individual is unable to reconcile himself to his loss and to the personal and social satisfactions which are now denied to him (Dembo et al., 1956). He continually compares his present condition with his former state. The shock reaction is regarded as an emergency defense against the overwhelmingly painful emotions, which are allowed to emerge only in discrete quanta that can be handled by the ego (Blank, 1957). Following a period of extreme shock, the mourning state pervades all areas of life, with no differentiation between the life areas directly linked with the disability and the intact areas still capable of providing satisfactions. There may be a need to make a public display of grief, fulfill the form requirements of propriety, make a bid for sympathy, and indulge in self-pity (see the biblical Book of Job). In loss due to combat, mourning may be attenuated in the early shock period by the feeling of "luck" at having escaped death, a feeling not characteristic of noncombat injuries. Later, shame and self-pity increase, while depression and the sense of "luck" decrease (Randall, Ewalt, & Blair, 1945). In time, a satiation factor enters, and the individual becomes involved again in life activities. Dembo et al. (1956) trace the process of the acceptance of physical loss through the stages of containing the effects of disability, enlarging the scope of values so that physique is subordinated to them, and transforming comparative values, wherein the injured person devalues himself completely, into asset values, where he can elevate his worth as a person above the loss of assets.

Experience has shown the absence of mourning to be *negatively* related to recovery. Absence of mourning may arise from the patient's strong dependency needs, which the loss sanctions, and may presage long-term dependency. In others, absence of mourning represents an unnatural stifling of intense emotion which should be released cathartically. The feelings are bound to explode later with an ego-destructive violence.

Denial of illness. *Denial* is regarded as a very primitive psychodynamic mechanism in comparison with other defenses. In neurological cases, denial may be so thorough as to constitute a blatant perceptual obliteration of reality. In these people, a blindness resulting from a lesion in the retina (and not in the occipital lobe) may be denied with such rationalizations as "being in a dark cellar," "tears in my eyes," etc. (Anton's syndrome). In patients with paraplegia, hemiplegia, amputations, etc., who also have brain damage, denial may be verbally *explicit* or only indirectly *implicit*. Weinstein and Kahn (1955) found that the mechanism of denial itself (anosognosia) and the particular disability denied were not traceable to defects in the body scheme related to specific lesions in any brain area. These investigators regard denial as a mode of adaptation to stress that is based on premorbid personality. Patients who verbally denied their disability *explicitly* had, premorbidly, regarded ill health as an imperfection, weakness, or disgrace (Weinstein & Kahn, 1955, p. 73). The effect of brain damage is to provide the milieu of altered function in which the patient may deny anything that he feels is wrong with him. The denial and misnaming of objects (paraphasia) are clearly related to certain traumatic environmental conditions while judgment in other areas might be excellent, thus pointing to the motivational aspect so important in denial. Denial operates in an hedonic system or belief where what gives relief or satisfaction is "true" and what causes unhappiness is "false" (Weinstein & Kahn, 1955, p. 128).

Denial also operates as a neurotic mechanism, an ego-protective apparatus, in non-brain-damaged people. Denial in disability may be emphatically complete in a child who refuses to recognize the existence of any disability. Denial may function more selectively in a sophisticated adult who, while admitting the existence of an impairment, will deny those implications of its presence that are evident to others.

Body image. The body-image concept is defined as "the picture or mental representation one has of his own body at rest or in motion at any moment. It is derived from internal sensations, postural changes, contact with outside objects and people, emotional experiences and fantasies" (English & English, 1958, p. 70). This concept is more delimited than the self-concept or self-image, which is "the self one *thinks* oneself to be. This is not a directly observed self-object but a complex concept: of one's personality, character, studies, body and bodily appearance. It may differ greatly from objective fact" (English & English, 1958, p. 487).

The body-image conceptualization was accorded treatment by Pick (1915), Head and Holmes (1911), and Schilder (1950). The learning factor, emphasized in this concept of central nervous system function, traced establishment of the body image to the impingement on the brain of tactile, postural, and other stimuli. The illusory experience of a "phantom" limb following amputation was explained by Schilder as the reactivation of the given perceptive pattern established premorbidly. Simmel (1962) has recently emphasized the postural component and *use* of the limb in the establishment of the limb image. In the experience of professional personnel in rehabilitation, cogenital amputees and children amputated at a very early age do not experience phantom sensation because they had no premorbid use of the limb. Weinstein and Sersen (1961) claim, however, to have elicited reports of phantom sensation in congenital *child* amputees by means of careful interrogation, although the reported incidence is lower than in traumatic amputations. These investigators claim that the body scheme is "given" or innate, although it is strengthened by the experiential factors. They interpret a similar report by Pick of a phantom in a congenital amputee as an indication of a genuine sensation rather than a suggested "illusion."

The perplexing phenomenon of the shrinking, foreshortened, or telescoped phantom, wherein the distal part of the limb, hand, or foot is perceived near the stump rather than in the appropriate premorbid anatomical position, has received considerable attention. Personality and psychophysiological measures were employed by Haber (1956) in studying tactile sensation in above-elbow amputees and their choice of prostheses.

S. A. Weiss and Fishman (1963) presented a theory of phantom telescoping which takes into account the relationship between limb image and stump cues. Phantom telescoping is seen as a result of an interaction between established limb image and the cues arising from stump sensitivity. If the stump cues are more potent than the intensity or affective tone of the limb image, the phantom will be perceived as shortened, rather than in the appropriate anatomical position. The factors of central-cortical representation, cephalocaudad gradient, learning, amputation type and etiology, and psychogenic experiences contribute to the conflict between limb image and stump cues. Thus, above-elbow amputees have a high amputation and are also high on the gradient. They have the greatest incidence of shortened phantoms. Below-knee amputees are low on the gradient with less limb missing. They have the smallest incidence of shortened phantoms. Racial factors also play a role. It seems to us that skin pigmentation might also affect stump cues (see Johnson & Corah, 1963).

Developmental factors, as related both to phantom limb experiences and to thalidomide-induced phocomelia, have been recently discussed (S. A. Weiss, 1963a, b). A recent paper from Poland by Stepien (1963) has given additional information on the role of the post-central gyrus in the cortex and its relationship to phantom phenomena.

The body-image concept has been given extensive treatment by Fisher and Cleveland (1958). These investigators have developed a scoring system based on the boundary regions of Rorschach percepts. Boundary definiteness, expressed in "barrier" scores, is regarded as equivalent to the degree of definite structure, substance, and surface qualities assigned to the percept (for example, "cave with rocky walls," "man in armor"). "Penetration" responses, in contrast, emphasize weakness, lack of substance, and penetrability (for example, "mashed bug," "person bleeding"). These responses are regarded as projections of the respondent's feelings about himself. Fisher and Cleveland have postulated that the differential expression of psychosomatic illness, externally or internally, such as in rheumatoid arthritis or ulcers, respectively, is related to the subject's feelings about his body boundaries. Although Eigenbrode and Shipman (1960) and Blatt (1963) could not replicate Fisher and Cleveland's original findings on the disease groups, Fisher (1963) has presented an impressive review of many other significant findings based on barrier-penetration conceptualization.

Since the body is the main protagonist in physical disability, further work, utilizing other body-image theories, may provide productive and useful concepts in the assessment and treatment of the physically disabled.

Physical Disability in the Light of Personality Theory

Classical psychoanalytic theory. NARCISSISM. Freud (1959) maintained that the hypochondriac or ill person withdraws his libidinal cathexes or "charges" back upon his own ego and sends them forth again when he recovers. The realization of impotence, of one's inability to love because of mental or physical disability, has an exceedingly lowering effect on self-regard. Freud thus underscores the personal rather than the psychosocial effects of disability or illness. The state of the injured person during the mourning period, when he is preoccupied with his loss, exemplifies Freud's concept of the withdrawal of libidinal energies by the disabled person back upon himself. When the individual accepts his disability and becomes involved in life activities again, the libido is again sent forth toward others. Nevertheless, the residual disability and castration feelings may limit the extent of further libidinal investment in others.

An example of a positive effect of libido invested in oneself is the self-preoccupied "professional amputee," the very dextrous prosthesis wearer who serves an extremely useful function as a demonstrator to rehabilitants of the potentialities of physical restoration. In this case the narcissistic investment benefits others. In other cases, however, the increase in narcissism leads to defective socialization rather than to the sharing of experiences.

HYPOCHONDRIA. Even when disability is real, the internalization of the libido cathexes may lead to the exaggeration of the illness in the form of somatic complaints not intrinsically associated with the physical damage. A hysterical reaction may thus be mixed with an organic illness or may exacerbate it. Among tuberculosis patients, a psychosomatic effect was discerned in the form of a definite relationship between psychological attitudes and onset of disease and also in the form of a marked relationship between attitudes and relapse (Derner, 1953).

MOURNING OF LOSS. In Freudian theory, the feeling of depression is often the consequence of the turning of aggression *inward*. Mourning for loss of limb or function therefore represents the internalization of aggressive feelings. The injured person is depressed, not merely because of his loss, but also because of the *guilt*, generated by the superego, which the loss implies and which compels the victim to turn the aggression inward. In the Book of Job, Job initially accepts his misfortune and disfigurement. ("The Lord hath given and the Lord hath taken. Blessed be the name of the Lord.") This internalization of guilt evidently depresses him and prevents him from uttering a sound for the first seven days in the presence of his friends. Only when his own innocence becomes manifest to him is he able to *externalize* his aggression and demand from God and his friends a reason for his suffering.

AVOIDANCE OF THE DISABLED BY THE NONDISABLED. Meng (in Barker et al., 1953, p. 76) concluded, on the basis of his psychoanalytic studies, that three deep, unconscious mechanisms are responsible for the fear and avoidance of the physically disabled by the normal person: (1) the belief that physical distortion is a punishment for evil and hence that a disabled person is evil and dangerous, (2) the belief that a disabled person is dangerous because he is under pressure to commit an evil act in order to balance his unjust punishment, and (3) the projection of one's own unacceptable desires upon the disabled and hence the belief that he is evil and dangerous.

Some normal individuals admit to an extreme emotional intolerance for maimed persons. The sight of the disability is abhorrent to them. This reaction could be interpreted as the activation of the observer's castration fears at the sight of the injured (Chevigny & Braverman, 1950).

CASTRATION ANXIETY. In classical psychoanalytic theory, injury and disability have been regarded as extensions of castration. The Oedipus myth, which plays a central role in Freud's system, is a prime example of displaced punishment, from the genitals to a different body area. Oedipus Rex inflicts self-punishment for his inadvertent murder of his father and incestuous marriage to his mother by blinding himself. This enucleation is regarded by Freud as a symbolic representation of genital castration.

By extension, injuries to the body and threats appearing in the fantasies and dreams of patients are interpreted as castration since the body *in toto* can be regarded as a phallic symbol. Amputation of a limb is particularly reminiscent of the oft-fantasied father's retaliatory revenge of cutting off the child's penis because of the latter's incestuous wishes for his mother.

Meng claims (Barker et al., 1953) that he found no indication that physical disability increases the castration complex. This claim that the physically disabled do not fear castration since they have already experienced it is surprising. The traumatic amputee who has lost a limb has been castrated mainly in a *symbolic* fashion, and the loss may activate fears of more decisive *genital* castration, especially in the light of the amputation phenomena we shall now consider. In any case, Freudian theory emphasizes castration feelings even in women who believed, in childhood, that they had been castrated.

Medical problems and castration feelings. Medical problems, aside from psychosocial factors, may also contribute to feelings of inadequacy which engender feelings of castration in some disabled persons. Many amputations today are the inexorable aftermath of diabetes and peripheral vascular diseases. In these conditions, especially diabetes, neuropathy (Lawrence & Locke, 1961) tends to impair sexual potency. Disability in these people is therefore not merely a neurotic problem or a symbolic representation of castration but also entails medical factors which interfere with sexual functioning.

Another condition devastating to the sex role of males is paraplegia, which involves transection or severe injury to the spinal cord (Berger, in Garrett, 1952). In high spinal injuries (often the aftermath of missile wounds or accidents to the neck when diving into a pool, individuals may incur paralysis below the neck and lose the use of all four limbs (quadriplegia). In paraplegia, where only the lower extremities are involved, total impotence frequently occurs as a result of injury to the sensory and motor nerves of the spine. Where only partial injury has occurred, or with the impairment of sensory functions only, some paraplegics are capable of maintaining an erection, without obtaining, however, any sensory feedback. They may retain the ability to "perform" in sexual intercourse and satisfy their wives, with only altruistic pleasure to themselves. This is a condition of "sensory castration," in which physical function remains intact.

Psychophysiological factors and the castration syndrome. In amputation the shape of the scarred stump itself is a reminder of a mutilated penis. An interesting and striking phenomenon among numerous lower-extremity amputees is the sensation, during urination, of the stump, rather than the phallus, as the source of the stream (see illustrations in "Studies Relating to Pain in the Amputee"). We may conjecture that physiological factors also play an important role in this experience. The sensitized amputation stump, involving also the severed sciatic nerve, may more readily be perceptually associated with the stream during the release of tension, and the illusion of the stump as the source of the stream is thus facilitated (as is the case in the phenomenon of phantom telescoping, discussed above). One can imagine the effect of this experience on a naïve amputee. The analytic concepts of castration and the symbolic substitution of the above-knee stump with the penis do not seem so conjectural in the light of these sexual and physiological experiences.

Psychosocial experiences and castration feelings. Certain experiences of the disabled tend to reinforce the association of disablement with castration. The smaller incidence of marriage among the severely disabled (Lowman & Seidenfeld, in Barker et al., 1953, pp. 130–131), due to both real as well as anticipated rejection by the nondisabled, probably reflects feelings about the disabled person's helplessness or weakness. Aside from any medical limitations, sexual relations often involve difficulties because of awkwardness, limited movement, and the insecurities aroused by feelings of diminished attractiveness. Phallic potency or adequate sexual response is often impaired by anxiety, as attested in clinical interviews with amputees and other disabled individuals.

Adlerian theory. In Adlerian theory, the concepts of "organ inferiority" "compensation," and "overcompensation" assume central positions. In his early writings, Adler assumed an unknown, direct, neurological connection between inferior organs and central nervous compensation. In his later theoretical elaborations, although the reference to the organic basis remains, it is more tenuous, and a purely psychological drive for mastery or protest against inferiority assumes more central importance. We may conjecture that the original assumption of a neurological link between organ inferiority and compensation probably led some writers to perpetuate the notion of a "mechanistic" relationship between inferior organs and compensation, even when the psychological factor was later emphasized by Adler. Dreikurs (1948) insists that Adler did not posit a "mechanistic" connection between inferiority and compensation, since the variables of "courage," "social interest," and "life-style" intervene between inferiority and outcome. The effects of inferiority depend on these variables and the meaning inferiority has for the subject. The condition of inferiority may characterize any objective function without, however, its being perceived or realized by the subject. Inferiority feelings, on the other hand, may exist without any real inferiority. Only inferiority *feelings* can stimulate a compensation or overcompensation, depending on the intervening variables and the meaning the disability has for the individual. The term "inferiority complex" implies a deadlock against any further development and is the defense assumed by a discouraged individual for a real or assumed deficiency. Its purpose is to obtain special consideration ("the secondary gains" of disability) or to gain an excuse for nonparticipation and withdrawal.

As regards inferiority feelings, an individual with courage *compensates* for the inferiority feelings that are invariably aroused by physical defects. He achieves a good measure of adjustment or a superior measure of achievement because of the drive to compensate. *Overcompensation,* however, is indicative of maladjustment; the individual has gone too far in compensating for his inferiority feelings.

Interpersonal theory: Sullivan. Some of the chief distinguishing structural features of Sullivan's interpersonal theory (Hall & Lindzey, 1958) are applicable to physical disability.

SELF-SYSTEM. Sullivan views the self-system in a negative light. The pattern of behavior which develops as a result of anxiety is the "dynamism of the self" or the "self-system." Anxiety is a product of interpersonal relations transmitted from mother to infant and, later in life, generated by threats to one's security. The individual employs various protective measures in order to avoid or reduce the unpleasant experience of anxiety. Conformity to parental standards is an example of a security measure forming the self-system which sanctions certain forms of behavior (the "good-me" self) and forbids other forms (the "bad-me" self). The self-system also operates to exclude even useful information which initially arouses anxiety and threatens the security system. The self-system thereby tends to become isolated from the rest of the personality, and, by the exclusion of important information that is incongruous with its present organization, it prevents the individual's profiting from experience.

A self-system originally based on the need for perfection of somatic integrity may, in subsequent disablement, lead to the exclusion from awareness of the limitations imposed by physical impairment. The finding (Weinstein & Kahn, 1955) that such individuals do tend to deny their illness attests to the maladaptive role that can be played by the self-system.

Sullivan's threefold classification of cognitive experience is also applicable to disability. The *"prototaxic"* mode, similar to James's "stream of consciousness," refers to the experience of raw sensations, images, and feelings flowing through the mind that have no interconnections and no meaning for the infant. The experience of shock in sudden trauma seems to be a temporary regression to the prototaxic mode. The "parataxic" mode, that of seeing causal, although not logical, relationships between events that occur together in time, seems to characterize the oversensitive, disabled person who, in a paranoid manner, connects unrelated actions into a fable concerning his rejection by the nondisabled. Similarly, the superstitions entertained toward the disabled by the normal are in the parataxic mode, such as the association of ugly deeds with a disfigured countenance. The "syntaxic" mode consists of consensually validated symbol activity, the symbols that have a standard meaning to a group of people. This mode characterizes the realistic images or personifications entertained by well-adjusted rehabilitants.

Sullivan emphasizes the powerful role of anxiety in inducing the parataxic mode. If a disabled person cannot deal with his problems, he may regress to "somnolent detachment," the withdrawal characteristic of the injured individual who isolates himself from the society which he has *malevolently transformed* into an enemy.

Fromm. Fromm claims that "the understanding of man's psyche must be based on the analysis of man's needs stemming from the conditions of his existence" (1955, p. 25). These needs are five: relatedness, transcendence, rootedness, identity, and frame of orientation. They are readily applicable to the situation of the disabled in society.

1. To satisfy the need for relatedness, *productive love,* which implies *mutual* care, responsibility, respect, and understanding, is necessary. The proper balance of reciprocity or mutuality can be disturbed in disability when dependency, especially in the early stages of illness, makes the patient an oral-receptive rather than a productive individual.

2. If man's need for transcendence—his need to rise above his animal nature and become a creative person—is frustrated, he becomes a destroyer. In disablement, the frustrations arising from thwarted goals may mobilize intense aggression.

3. The need for rootedness and identity is also disturbed if the meaning of his disability to the injured person invests him with the feeling that he is no longer rooted in "normal" society.

4. The loss of identity as a normal person may drive him to become totally rooted in a nondisabled society and to create a psychological ghetto for himself.

5. The shake-up resulting from traumatic disability may dislocate the patient's frame of reference—a stable and consistent way of understanding and perceiving the world. In this situation the impaired individual becomes a marginal man with no roots in either normal or disabled groups but with ambivalence toward both.

Rogerian self-concept. In Rogerian theory (Rogers, 1951), the individual, or organism, is involved in a totality of conscious or unconscious experience, which is termed the "phenomenal field." The "self" is a differentiated portion of the phenomenal field and consists of a pattern of perceptions and values that are experienced as "I" or "me." The self develops as a result of the organism's interaction with the environment, and it may either truly assimilate the values of other people or—consciously, but erroneously—refer to these values as "I" or "me." The self strives for consistency. Experiences not consistent with the true self-structure are perceived as threats, and an erroneous or incomplete assimilation of introjected values may therefore lead to conflict.

The organism tends and strives to actualize, maintain, and enhance itself. It reacts as a whole to its experiences or phenomenal field. If a concept of oneself is in conflict with reality, it will mislead one, and self-actualization is impeded.

A perceived experience may be handled in any of the following ways:

1. It may be ignored because no relationship to the self-structure is perceived.

2. It may be symbolized, perceived, and organized into a relationship to the self.

3. It may be distorted or denied symbolization because the experience is inconsistent with the self-structure. The experience may then be neutralized by a defense mechanism such as projection. Since the individual is unaware of the experience, the chance for conflict with reality is increased.

The organism is in need of the positive regard of others and self. In general, a person seeks *conditions of worth* whereby he avoids experiences that destroy, and seeks those that enhance, self-regard.

In disability, disfigurement of the organism may preclude acceptance by others. The introjection of these valuations may lead to negative self-regard. The realities of injury, magnified by feelings of shame, may inhibit the organism from seeking available conditions of worth. In disablement, the previously established self-concept may be inflexible and incapable of reorganization in terms of present reality needs. Denial may be used as a defense, and the proper symbolization of the experience is therefore precluded. Relegation of the conflict to the unconscious usually leads to maladjustment.

Problems in psychological assessment

Three problems will be considered: the assessment of cognitive skills, affective structures and personality, and attitudes toward disability.

PROBLEMS AND SPECIAL TECHNIQUES IN THE ASSESSMENT OF COGNITIVE SKILLS

It is obvious that a perceptual motor task (such as the WAIS Digit Symbol) cannot be routinely given to a person with a disability of the dominant hand, even if the subject is convinced that he can substitute his nondominant hand (Briggs, 1960). Unless caution is exercised, a misleading estimate of the subject's cognitive or perceptual functioning will be obtained, since many such individuals fail to call the examiner's attention to this substitution.

Certain physical disabilities are the inexorable aftermath of infectious, metabolic, circulatory, or malignant diseases which may lead to amputation, paraplegia, or deformation. These conditions may also debilitate cortical functions in a subtle, if not dramatic, fashion. The patient may seem to be intellectually intact unless special assessment efforts are made (Weinstein & Kahn, 1955). Thus, figure drawings and Bender-Gestalt productions of elderly amputees and diabetics reveal marked deviations from those of the nondisabled, although intellectual deficit may not be apparent in the interview (S. A. Weiss, 1961). In a study of children, Worden (1961) found an intellectual deficit in boys with pseudohypertrophic muscular dystrophy (PMD) but not in those with other muscular and metabolic diseases. These illustrations suggest how intellectual deficit may be restricted to certain diseases and age levels. The evaluation instruments employed in such studies are often the conventional Wechsler and Binet scales, perceptual-motor tasks and achievement tests. While these conventional instruments sometimes prove to be valuable, they are not tailor-made to the specific functioning and needs of different disability groups.

With these problems in mind, the examiner must carefully consider the subject's unique problem in terms of his particular disability if the assessment of cognitive skills is to be at least reasonably accurate.

Time Factor

In disabilities where fatigue fluctuates in intensity (for example, an above-knee amputee who has ambulated all day on his prosthesis), the time schedule for testing must be adjusted accordingly. Similar considerations apply to patients subject to periodic pain exacerbation or nervous irritability, such as occurs in osteoarthritis, poliomyelitis, etc.

Position Factor

The seated position of the subject merits special consideration where body deformation or imbalance is a vital factor. Information obtained in clinical interviews with amputees and from experimental work (Comalli, 1963; Teuber, Krieger, & Bender, 1949) has shown that even in lower-extremity amputees, the *manual* performance, as well as visual and kinesthetic perception, is affected by laterality of amputation and the wearing or removal of the prosthesis. Dissimilarity between the subject's posture during testing and the position that he will maintain on the job may result in a distorted estimate of cognitive and perceptual-motion performance.

Mood Factor

The mood of the subject must be accurately gauged because intense feelings of mourning, depression, elation, or hostility or nervous irritability, arising from specific experiences before testing, will obscure assessment results.

These examples can be merely illustrative. The examiner must always be alert to the persistent and fluctuating factors in his unique setting in order to accomplish a reliable evaluation.

Evaluation and Ultimate Employability

Another important consideration is the relationship between cognitive performance in a sheltered hospital setting and the productive utilization of these abilities in a *stress* situation. Some individuals cannot function under stress, despite superior cognitive abilities, and the "sheltered" assessment in the hospital or clinic therefore bears little relation to vocational outcome. Experience with the disabled fosters the conviction that more successful and valid prediction might be possible if more measures of stress and frustration tolerance were included in the psychologist's battery (see Davis, 1955). Of course, in the induction of stress the ethical implications involved must remain paramount if the patient's human integrity is to be preserved (American Psychological Association, 1953).

PROBLEMS AND SPECIAL TECHNIQUES IN THE ASSESSMENT OF AFFECTIVE STRUCTURES AND PERSONALITY

The assessment of affective structures and personality traits is impeded by numerous factors.

The value of standard clinical instruments such as the Rorschach, the Thematic Apperception Test, figure drawings, the Bender-Gestalt, and subtest configurations on the Wechsler scales is still hotly debated. While there is a growing feeling and substantial evidence that experienced and competent clinicians can obtain very useful information with these tests, attempts to objectify the nosological and predictive signs have not met with consistent success.

Utilization of these standard instruments with the physically disabled involves additional limitations. The impairment of cognitive functions in some disability groups (discussed above) confounds personality evaluation since it may be uncertain whether the deficit is traceable to cognitive impairment specifically related to the disease entity, primarily to emotional reactions that arise from neurotic mechanisms, or to increased emotional irritability found in certain diseases such as poliomyelitis (Seidenfeld, in Garrett, 1952).

In physical disability, temporal factors are relevant. If the patient is tested immediately after trauma, the prevailing shock reaction may obscure performance. The mourning period, which is variable in different individuals, may also depress and obscure the patient's performance.

When the emotional reactions to disability have seemingly been stabilized, the question of tailor-made instrumentation is again pertinent. Concepts imported from clinical areas with minimum alteration and employed as predictive indices in personal and vocational areas do not generally give gratifying results. Arnholter's (1962) conclusions are illustrative of negative results in prediction. She found that neither Rorschach rigidity nor maladjustment scales were predictive of ultimate employability. Staff ratings based on *several* variables were more likely to be valid.

The attempt to obtain a valid assessment of the physically disabled by means of figure drawings is another problem area illustrative of the difficulties inherent in personality evaluation. Controversy has raged over the validity of perceptual-motor productions such as the Bender-Gestalt (Billingslea, 1963) or figure drawings in reflecting the degree of maladjustment among the emotionally or physically disabled. Silverstein and Robinson's study (1956) of the human figure drawings of different disability groups produced negative results, while Schmidt and McGowan (1959) found that success depended on the affective, rather than the cognitive, orientation of the raters. The Silverstein and Robinson study may have been weighted against success because *diverse* disabilities were grouped together, a procedure that may obscure differences. Artistic talent also plays a role in figure drawings and may obscure or magnify the image which the subject attempts to project on paper. Levi (1961) controlled the talent factor by employing a selection of Sarbin's (1954) standard stick figures in her study of hand and orthopedic disabilities, with considerable success.

In any assessment of personality, the classic question is: "Are we dealing with a *core trait*, or are the tests effective only in eliciting and reflecting *defenses against* the core traits?" This question stems from the Freudian mechanism of reaction formation, where, for example, a behavior pattern seemingly indicative of love may represent the very opposite.

Frenkel-Brunswik, in a different context (1940), repeatedly emphasized the importance of this problem. In papers dealing with Fisher and Cleveland's barrier and penetration scores (1958), Eigenbrode and Shipman (1960) and Blatt (1963) could not replicate Fisher and Cleveland's original findings on disease groups, although the latter investigators (Fisher, 1963; Fisher & Cleveland, 1958) present an impressive review of many other significant findings based on the scoring system they developed. The importance of the classic difficulty, "Are we dealing with the core or the defense?" is evident. Does a person depict his disability in his drawing, or does reaction formation lead to repression or idealization? In Weinstein and Kahn's (1955) study of neurological patients, individuals who denied their disability *explicitly* tended to depict themselves as nondisabled in their drawings, while *implicit* denial of illness was associated with drawings that revealed the loss. The results are less clear in studies of physically disabled individuals without severe neurological involvement, as is attested in the literature.

Holden's (1962) study is an approach that seems to sidestep the core versus defense dilemma. Holden was successful in utilizing figure drawings to assess changes in body image of physically handicapped children after a summer camp experience. It should be noted that he did not attempt to find *specific* depictions of disabled limbs, as was attempted in the cited studies. We may conjecture that underlying Holden's global approach was the implicit hypothesis that significant positive experiences lead to a reduction in anxiety, with the liberation of the child's resources, which in turn make him less guarded or constricted in his later behavior as well as in his drawings. This global approach does not depend on specific depiction or nondepiction of the disability and thereby sidesteps the core versus defense dilemma.

In summary, a consideration of the conflicting results in the area of personality assessment of the disabled fosters the feeling that a wholesale importation of concepts and techniques from different areas will not improve the reliability and validity of the assessment and predictor instruments. Even well-defined and clearly conceptualized variables must be adapted to the specific disability group studied. This procedure requires a careful consideration of the personality variables that extended clinical experience has shown to be consistently relevant and salient to the disability entity under consideration. When these variables are isolated clinically, it may then be possible to modify conventional instruments or devise original measures in order to develop norms on the specific disability groups.

A study oriented in this direction is the Amputee Psychology Project (New York University Post-Graduate Medical School, 1960b) at New York University Prosthetic and Orthotic Studies. The psychodynamic variables and the related measures are based on extensive clinical experiences with 250 amputees. It is hoped that these measures, rooted and proved in experience, will be more predictive than instruments based only on abstract concepts derived from less salient areas.

The purpose of the study is the development of a psychological test battery to predict success or failure in the prosthetic and vocational rehabilitation of lower-extremity amputees. The specific goal is to determine which amputees are psychologically ready to withstand the stresses associated with rehabilitation and to identify those individuals who require psychological assistance in order to benefit from the rehabilitation process.

The prediction instrument is designed to evaluate personality from numerous vantage points, a global approach which evolved from a theory which attempts to explain behavior shown by maladjusted or "neurotic" individuals (S. A. Weiss 1959; S. A. Weiss, 1960). It is felt that the degree of adjustment or maladjustment characterizing an individual depends on his ability to deal with *anxiety* and *insecurities.* Although anxiety is usually a limiting influence, it also can be used constructively. If channeled into appropriate behavior, anxiety may serve as energy which an amputee can utilize to help him overcome obstacles in his environment. When directed into maladaptive defense mechanisms, however, anxiety impedes physical and psychological rehabilitation. In brief, the potentially successful rehabilitant "budgets" his anxiety by repressing some of it successfully and channeling the remainder into productive, compensatory activity. The inadequately adjusted amputee "packages" his anxiety in maladaptive mechanisms.

At the time of this writing, the sample of 100 lower-extremity amputees has just completed the psychological battery, but criterion information on all of them is yet to be obtained.

The following findings emerged from a preliminary analysis of the relationships among some of the variables: Constricted or encapsulated amputees magnified painful experiences depicted pictorially, admitted to more neurotic problems, and showed lower pain thresholds. Amputees who magnified painful experiences were more constricted and pessimistic about prosthetic restoration. The admission of neurotic problems was also associated with less frustration on a performance test (S. A. Weiss, Fishman, & Krause, 1964).

PROBLEMS AND SPECIAL TECHNIQUES IN THE ASSESSMENT OF ATTITUDES TOWARD DISABILITY

Aside from the general problems of personality evaluation, discussed above and in the various sections of the *Handbook*, assessment of attitudes toward disability presents a unique problem. This is the *difference in salience and ego involvement between the disabled and the nondisabled.*

To the disabled individual his problem is vital. His entire self or ego is so immersed in ruminating on, and coping with, his problems that his feelings and attitudes probably reflect crystallized personality traits or defenses. To the nondisabled respondent, however, the problems of the disabled are primarily academic. His responses are not based on crystallized core feelings and probably reflect superficial, half-baked generalizations. Moreover, the disturbing conflicts within a person may prompt him to reveal himself in order to obtain cathartic relief, while the normal individual has no such motives. His feelings toward the disabled individual are probably less salient than his attitudes toward the ethnic and racial problems that occupy the stage in current events. Support for this distinction is found in a study by Bell (1962). A group of 30 hospital employees with disabled relatives or friends scored significantly higher on Yuker's (Yuker et al., 1960) Attitude Toward Disabled Persons Scale (ATDP), indicating greater acceptance than was shown by two groups without close personal ties to disabled persons. Of Ss without personal ties, a group of 40 rehabilitation workers did not differ in the ATDP scores from a group of 40 hospital employees not engaged in therapeutic work.

This study suggests the importance of ego involvement as a factor in attitudes toward disability. A study by Ladieu, Adler, and Dembo (1948) illustrates, even more clearly, how intensive interviews of the ego-involved disabled can elicit nuances of feeling which would be beyond the ken of emotionally uninvolved normal subjects.

These investigators studied the perceptions, on the part of visibly injured individuals, of attitudes entertained toward them by the noninjured. Their findings may be summarized as follows:

The injured can appreciate realistic limitations on their nonparticipation in some activities but object to (1) total devaluation or nonacceptance; (2) overestimation by the noninjured of the extent of disability or its unsightliness, with the consequent extension of nonparticipation to areas unaffected by injury; (3) the rationalization of the exclusion of the injured on the grounds of the fear of "hurting" him, instead of respecting the latter's ego strength; (4) emphasis by the noninjured of the inconvenience they must endure when participating with the injured; and (5) the apparent but ungenuine acceptance of the injured on the basis of duty or pity, in contrast to the genuine acceptance the latter seeks.

If the salience distinction is valid, the instruments which have proved to be of value in the majority-minority studies and which have been imported virtually unchanged into assessment of disability require considerable modification if they are to be more profitably applied to the study of disability.

With these distinctions in mind, different assessment techniques may be considered.

Depth Studies

Depth studies of an individual undoubtedly enable a perceptive therapist or analyst to gain, in the course of time, a very deep and intimate understanding of his client's personality patterns. Experience demonstrates that core personality traits recur thematically in the course of treatment, and the internal consistency of the patterns in defense maneuvers, behavior style, and dreams provides the insightful therapist with reliable hypotheses that have predictive value as to his client's reactions. Depth interviews may also be profitably employed in the elicitation of valuable information, as indicated in the previous section. While depth assessment is impractical in obtaining attitudes from large samples, this difficulty might possibly be overcome if many rehabilitation workers were to pool their results. Even if this goal is not readily attained, the insights that can be gained from even a limited case load may be translated into items for more objective group questionnaires.

Questionnaire Methods

Although group questionnaire methods permit greater response and scoring objectivity, they are, as a rule, less ego-involving than depth assessments where personal interaction with the respondent facilitates more emotional expression. Moreover, in depth studies the actual behavior, and not merely the opinions, of the respondent can be scrutinized for its relationships to professed attitudes.

Group questionnaires are also subject to conscious and unconscious distortion and fabrication. Professed positive attitudes do not often determine actual behavior since they often reflect defensive reactions or socially desirable responses, rather than true feelings. This conclusion may be made about the finding that nondisabled respondents attributed many positive traits to the disabled as a group (Barker, et al., 1953; Ray, 1946). Respondents may feel uncomfortable or uneasy in the presence of the disabled but compensate for this feeling by "giving them a break" on an attitude scale, while others displaying the same feelings may less be inclined to do so. In a factor-analytic study of attitudes toward the disabled, Siller and Chipman (1963) conclude that there has been an overevaluation of the effects of response-set factors in self-report studies, but, nevertheless, the positive relationship between measures of ego strength and acceptance of the disabled is low, though significant (in large samples).

The most vital question is the nature of the translation of attitudes into practice. Attitude scales can merely suggest, not define. It seems that more of the *situational* observations and experiments, such as those employed by Schoggen (1963) on disabled children, might provide information about actual behavior.

The major approach in work dealing with attitudes toward disability has centered on the personality traits of the normal, as related to their feelings and attitudes toward the disabled. Some research has suggested a relationship between negative attitudes and authoritarianism (Cowen et al., 1958) and indices of maladjustment (Siller, 1962; Steingisser, 1954). The more pertinent (and probably repressed) question can be posed as to the influence of the disabled person's personality on his rejection by the nondisabled. Winkler's study and the supporting evidence (discussed above) suggest that either innate tendencies or subtle social indoctrination may make certain physical postures unesthetic. Perhaps a closer investigation of this esthetic factor is warranted so that corrective education might help modify such tendencies which cause the rejection of so many humans. Certainly, a cultural factor is also operative, as indicated in the discussion on cosmesis in a previous section.

It seems that aside from general problems of evaluation techniques, some considerations must receive special emphasis in regard to the disabled:

1. Is the instrument or situation ego-involving?

2. In terms of previous experience, are the variables related to disability, or are they wholesale importations from different areas?

3. Is the instrument or situation disguised? Oscar Wilde's aphorism conveys a great truth: "Give a man a mask and he will tell you the truth."

Rehabilitation and the treatment process

The role of the clinical psychologist in the treatment process of the disabled is many-sided and cannot be confined to the traditional dyadic therapies. While individual therapy or counseling may be required, the treatment process is at least as much involved with the provision of an appropriate psychological environment which will assist the patient to overcome his feelings of deprivation, loss, and self-derogation. Thus, interactions with other persons important to the patient (his spouse, his family, his physical therapists, his friends, his employers) may be as vital to the treatment process as direct verbal interaction with the patient himself. In the following sections, we shall deal with some of the more important considerations related to this total treatment process.

ESTABLISHING A RELATIONSHIP

The first task is the establishment of a human-professional relationship with the disabled individual as soon as he becomes a patient. The initial interpersonal experiences, in a hospital or clinic, often remain vivid to the patient, thereby contributing to the image he has of the professional personnel. A traumatic experience may exert a negative influence on his perceptual interpretation of the therapeutic procedures to which he is subsequently subjected. (The vividness of sudden, traumatic incidents can be illustrated, paradigmatically, by soldiers who lose an arm in a premature hand-grenade explosion. Some amputees thereafter "feel" their lost hand, the "phantom," in the position it was held during the trauma (see illustrations in S. A. Weiss, 1963b).

The attitude of the professional personnel who first establish a relationship with the patient is therefore of prime importance. This involves more than a superficial "bedside" manner (although even this is occasionally lacking); it is necessary to communicate a feeling of real concern and respect for the patient as an individual rather than as a "case." Experience demonstrates that an explicit verbal affirmation to the patient that he is seen as a human in need of aid rather than as a "case," a "cripple," or a limb attached to a body produces a visible, positive reaction. Wherever possible the patient should be prepared for surgical or medical intervention by kindly conveying to him the relevant information that he can constructively assimilate so that he will be reassured. The *repetitious* communication of respect, concern, and reassurance is necessary to maintain a high motivational level throughout the rehabilitation regimen, since disease and disability precipitate the narcissistic regression to more dependent and immature behavior because the patient's ground support is shaken by illness (Freud, 1959).

An obstacle to the maintenance of mutual respect is the use of the prevailing nomenclature that emphasizes "crippling" and misfortune. Rehabilitation centers bear such names because of the efficacy of these terms in eliciting sympathy in the fund-raising activities, but rehabilitants find it difficult to reconcile the respect conveyed by enlightened personnel with the woebegone pictures of the disabled in the various posters in trains and buses and in murals of the major rehabilitation centers in which they are treated. Conflicting self-images fostered by conflicting pragmatic needs do not help in rehabilitation.[24]

The distinction between the terms "sympathy" and "empathy" illuminates two contrasting perceptions of the patient by the professional. Sympathy implies a *vertical* attitude toward the patient, connoting an emphasis of the latter's helplessness, inadequacy, and consequent inferiority. This perception may easily lead to a benign-authoritarian role toward the rehabilitant which fosters irrational dependency feelings as well as resentment. Empathy, however, implies a *horizontal* perception, a "feeling with" (*mitleid*) the subject. In this relationship, authority by the professional must be human and rational (Fromm, 1947) and is contingent on the personal needs, as well as the disability needs, of the rehabilitant. The disability needs are ordinarily met in the course of rehabilitation and decline in salience, while the human relationship improves. In a vertical perception, however, the satisfaction of patient needs often proceeds in isolation from the human relationship.

Some rehabilitants will unconsciously test their therapists by means of periodic regressions to previous, low-level performance, thereby determining whether they are accepted for themselves, as persons, or only because they are "successful" cases that enhance the ego and reputation of the therapist. This process resembles one that occurs in psychotherapy or psychoanalyses when, after considerable improvement has occurred, the patient has periodic regressions in order to test the therapist's human feelings.

In brief, people are eager to be accepted for what they believe themselves to be, for their negative as well as their positive traits. Geniuses may often resent their acceptance by society solely in terms of their talent. Certainly, a self-respecting disabled individual does not desire an enlarged focus on his

24 One recent poster is a move in a corrective direction. It depicts a staff sergeant vociferously ordering the audience to hire disabled persons as workers. A private corrects him by emphasizing the good business aspects of employing the disabled.

disability while his personal and human needs are ignored.

These considerations may not be so important where the rehabilitation period is brief and is restricted to relatively peripheral treatment. Physical, psychological, and vocational rehabilitation is, however, a prolonged procedure, and human feelings emerge with an éclat, a cacophony or a symphony, depending on the nature of the interpersonal relationship established.

FACILITATION OF GOAL ACHIEVEMENT

With the establishment and maintenance of a good relationship between therapist and client, physical restitution and psychological restitution proceed more optimally. Physical restitution will help in modifying the patient's self-image as a "shattered body" or "half a man" and will help him meet personal and vocational goals.

Physical Restoration

The integrity of the soma concerns some amputees, and they will oppose the surgeon's recommendation of shortening an overlong stump so as to facilitate subsequent prosthetic restoration. One amputee stated: "I told the surgeon I want to hold on to as much of myself as I can." He stated that he preferred a poorer gait to the sacrifice of a few additional inches of his healthy stump. He admitted a great narcissistic investment in his *corporal substance,* which he regarded as of greater importance than the improved and more natural gait that a shorter, but more optimal, stump length would promote. Other instances of attempts to maintain physical integrity at the expense of improved function are the reactions to the Krukenberg and cineplasty procedures previously discussed.

Psychological Restoration

The need for physical restitution often spills over into psychological areas. Some rehabilitants vocalize a need to incorporate and assimilate a prosthetic device into their body scheme. It is not uncommon to hear an amputee state explicitly that he regards his artificial limb as "my leg." The total-contact socket (New York University, 1962) for above-knee amputees and the patellar tendon-bearing prosthesis (*Manual for Below Knee Prosthetics*) for below-knee amputees eliminate auxiliary suspension systems such as thigh lacers, shoulder straps, and waist belts. Aside from the advantages of improved comfort, gait, cosmesis, etc., some subjects claim that the absence of these appendages invests them with the feeling that these prostheses are more "natural."

Experience with early models of a radically new prosthesis at New York University and the Veterans Administration (see Bernstock, 1963; Stone, 1963), a hydraulic above-knee artificial limb, also sheds light on the subjective, psychological factors that influence the rehabilitation process. It had been conjectured (S. A. Weiss, 1958, pp. 28–29) that this mechanically sophisticated and complex prosthesis, which has some of the complexity of a natural limb, would be integrated more readily into the body concept of an amputee than a relatively simple and conventional wooden or plastic limb. The hydraulic mechanism "substitutes" for the lost muscles and facilitates a more natural gait while, at the same time, requiring less effort and energy on the part of the subject than is the case with a conventional prosthesis. In practice, the hydraulic leg was accepted by the subjects despite recurring mechanical problems. The engineering group was surprised, however, when the amputees refused to relinquish the leg even when the mechanism became defective and no longer fulfilled its function. They concluded that it was indeed the posited psychological, rather than the engineering, factor that was responsible for the acceptance of these experimental hydraulic legs. In subsequent studies, mechanically superior models were developed.

The "coalescing" phantom limb is another illustration of a *symbolic* substitution for physical restoration. Some amputees experience phantom limbs which vary in length (S. A. Weiss & Fishman, 1963). Donning the prosthesis may cause the telescoped phantom to become extended and to fit the contours of the prosthetic hand or leg. Removal of the prosthesis allows the phantom to shrink to its telescoped position. Some amputees state that the "fusion" of the phantom with their prosthesis is so complete that they experience the prosthesis as a natural limb! A similar experience is that of some paraplegics who insist that they experience sensation in the truly insensitive legs. Bors (1951) found this to be the case for paraplegics whose phantom occupies the same space as the physical and paralyzed leg, a phenomenon that fosters the illusion.

These examples illustrate how underlying psychological feelings, aside from psychophysiological factors, influence the meaning that physical restitution and body integrity have for a rehabilitant. Physical restitution is so intertwined with emotional significance that goal achievement depends on the satisfaction of psychological as well as physical needs.

Purposeful Activity

The rehabilitant is immersed in purposeful activities at the earliest possible time in order to (1) minimize brooding about the irreversible past, (2) reduce boredom by giving him a structured and well-organized day, and (3) prepare him—physically, emotionally, and vocationally—for rehabilitation. In the course of these planned activities, the client should be constantly provided with realistic encouragement and repeated reassurance. As the program of activities becomes an integral part of the patient's existence, he is in the position, with guidance, to evaluate his resources and to affirm or modify his life goals as he learns more about his actual functioning. The emphasis should be on *purposeful* activity if the client is to become ego-involved and well motivated.

Therapy and Counseling

Since some patients become very dependent in the period following disability, programs have been developed to decrease dependency feelings gradually as the patient's performance and ego become equal to the task. Neff (1959), in his discussion of rehabilitation workshops, describes the planned changes in professional role which are introduced to coincide with the development of the client's ego abilities and resources. The analysis provides insight into the degree of growth that can be developed in the patient when the role assumed by the professional is attuned to his changing potential. In some situations, two contrasting roles must be assumed by work supervisors and counselors in order to elicit appropriately adaptive behavior. Another example is the prevocational therapeutic situation. The patient's psychotherapist provides the warmth and support that are expected of a mother figure, while the vocational counselor may assume the more realistic role of the father in urging the client to utilize the resources that are liberated in therapy in the latter's daily confrontation with reality. Experience shows that less resentment and less intense resistance are elicited in this dual approach. The client cannot easily develop resentment against the psychotherapist because the latter maintains a warm, accepting mother role, although the psychotherapist may modify it cautiously to attune it to the position taken by the vocational counselor.[25] The latter has structured his agency's role to the patient before sending him for psychotherapy, and the patient readily accepts the confines of the agency's rules as he develops in the "psychotherapeutic womb." This mother-father tandem, in relation to the patient-client tandem, sometimes facilitates more rapid progress because the role division minimizes the intensification of resistance (S. A. Weiss, 1964).

Association with Other Rehabilitants

A group therapeutic approach in rehabilitation involves the placement of the rehabilitant with others who have conquered some of the serious obstacles. Individuals with clashing personalities should not be placed in the same group. Embittered or unsuccessful amputees exert a negative influence on the new arrival. On the other hand, individuals with extraordinary skill cannot serve as realistic models for identification since the new group member may feel unequal to exceptionally endowed individuals who represent unattainable levels of accomplishment. Considerable skill and experience are required to make a proper blend of personalities in a group rehabilitation setting.

While other successful rehabilitants can serve as good models for the new arrival, the latter must be prepared for the final goal of functioning as a member in a nondisabled society, if this is possible. Rehabilitation is not entirely successful if the disabled person creates a psychological ghetto because of his physical limitations.

Education of the Rehabilitant's Family

An often neglected aspect is the education of the rehabilitant's family, both following the trauma and during rehabilitation. Family

[25] We appreciate the cooperation of Dr. Daniel S. Sanford, of the New York City office of the Division of Vocational Rehabilitation.

members may infect the rehabilitant with the negative attitudes toward disability so prevalent in society [see, for example, the negative stereotypes of the amputee in a recent best seller (Wallace, 1963, pp. 35–36)]. Unless the family is educated to deal realistically and supportively with the patient, a "Penelope" (Homer's *Odyssey*) pattern may ensue. The hard-earned gains of the rehabilitation center can be completely unraveled during one weekend or one visit.

Common examples of the operation of the "Penelope" pattern are the following:

1. Mindful of the suffering of the patient, an oversolicitous mother or wife may encourage a diabetic to "cheat a little" on sugar or starch consumption in order to compensate for the rigorous hospital regimen.
2. Improperly indoctrinated family members may shower the rehabilitant with pity and such "passionate compassion" as to undo gains in independent living achieved by the patient in the hospital setting.
3. Guilt-ridden family members may encourage dependency to assuage their conscience.
4. Unvoiced resentments against hospital personnel may be aired at home and destroy the faith of the client in his therapists.
5. Insurance litigation may be overemphasized so that the client begins to feel that he has become a cash asset rather than an individual in need of rehabilitation.

Other occurrences, too numerous to mention, are constantly operative in undoing the strenuous efforts of the rehabilitation team if the family members are not educated as to their important roles in implementing the rehabilitation regimen.

Criteria for Successful Rehabilitation

Although physical restoration is an important goal, not all clients are able to reach the maximum goals envisioned for them by sincere and idealistic personnel. Nevertheless, experience leads to the following conclusions:

1. Successful rehabilitation does not necessarily mean the achievement of maximum goals.
2. If the patient's brooding over, and preoccupation with, the unattainable are eliminated and if attention is focused on achievable goals, a measure of rehabilitation has been achieved.
3. The restoration of the integrity of the self-image, concomitant with a respect for oneself as a person, despite physical limitations, is a major achievement.

REFERENCES

Abt, L. E., & Riess, B. F. (Eds.) *Progress in clinical psychology.* Vol. V. New York: Grune & Stratton, 1963.

American Psychological Association. *Ethical standards of psychologists,* 1953.

Army Prosthetics Research Laboratory. Progress report of coloring program. *Tech. Rep.,* 1956, No. 5643.

Arnholter, Ethelwyne G. The validity of Fisher's maladjustment and rigidity scales as an indication of rehabilitation. *Personnel Guidance J.,* 1962, **40,** 634–637.

Axelrod, S. *Effects of early blindness: performance of blind and sighted children in tactile and auditory tasks.* New York: American Foundation for the Blind, 1959.

Barber, T. X. Toward a theory of pain: relief of chronic pain by prefrontal leucotomy, opiates, placebos, and hypnosis. *Psychol. Bull.,* 1959, **56,** 430–460.

Barker, R. G. The social psychology of physical disability. *J. soc. Issues,* 1948, **4,** 28–38.

Barker, R. G., & Wright, Beatrice A. The social psychology of adjustment to physical disability. In J. F. Garrett (Ed.), *Psychological aspects of physical disability.* Washington, D.C.: U.S. Department of Health, Education, and Welfare, Office of Vocational Rehabilitation, Rehabilitation Service Series 53, No. 210, 1952. Pp. 18–32.

Barker, R. G., Wright, Beatrice A., Meyerson, L., & Gonick, Mollie R. Adjustment to physical handicap and illness: a survey of the social psychology of physique and disability. *Soc. Sci. Res. Council Bull.,* 1953, No. 55.

Bell, A. H. Attitudes of selected rehabilitation workers and other hospital employees toward the physically disabled. *Psychol. Rep.,* 1962, **10** (1), 183–186.

Berger, S. Paraplegia. In J. F. Garrett (Ed.), *Psychological aspects of physical disability.* Washington, D.C.: U.S. Department of Health, Education, and Welfare, Office of Vocational Rehabilitation, Rehabilitation Service Series 53, No. 210, 1952. P. 53.

Bernstock, W. M. *Clinical application study of the hydra-cadence above-knee prosthesis: a technical report.* Washington, D.C.: Veterans Administration, Research and Development Division, Prosthetic and Sensory Aids Service, 1963.

Billingslea, F. Y. The Bender-Gestalt: a review and a perspective. *Psychol. Bull.*, 1963, **60**, 233–251.

Black, B. J. The protected workshop. In M. Greenblatt et al., *Rehabilitation of the mentally ill.* Washington, D.C.: American Association for the Advancement of Science, 1959.

Blank, H. R. Psychoanalysis and blindness. *Psychoanal. Quart.*, 1957, **26**, 1–24.

Blatt, Eva F. Body image and psychosomatic illness. *Amer. Psychol. Abstr.*, 1963, **18**, 401–402.

Bors, E. Phantom limbs of patients with spinal cord injury. *Arch. Neurol. Psychiat.*, 1951, **66**, 610–631.

Briggs, P. F. The validity of WAIS performance subtests with one hand. *J. clin. Psychol.*, 1960, **16**, 318–320.

Brooks, G. W., Chittick, R. A., Deane, W. N., & Irons, F. S. *The Vermont story.* Washington, D.C.: U.S. Department of Health, Education, and Welfare, Vocational Rehabilitation Administration, 1961.

Cattell, E., Dembo, Tamara, Koppel, S., Tane-Baskin, E., & Weinstock, S. *Social usefulness of the cosmetic glove.* New York: New York University College of Engineering, Research Division, 1955.

Caudill, W. *The psychiatric hospital as a small society.* Cambridge, Mass.: Harvard Univer. Press, 1958.

Chenven, H., & Somers, B. J. A rehabilitation center program for mental patients. *Ment. Hyg., N.Y.*, 1963, **47**, 228–238.

Chevigny, H., & Braverman, S. *The adjustment of the blind.* New Haven, Conn.: Yale Univer. Press, 1950.

Clark, J. W., & Bindra, D. Individual differences in pain thresholds. *Canad. J. Psychol.*, 1956, **10** (2), 69–76.

Comalli, P. H., Jr. *Effect of unilateral above-the-knee amputation on perception of verticality.* Paper read at Eastern Psychological Association, New York City, 1963.

Cowen, E. L., Underberg, R. P., & Verrillo, R. T. The development and testing of an attitude to blindness scale. *J. soc. Psychol.*, 1958, **48**, 297–304.

Davis, D. S. An investigation of the relationship of frustration tolerance in paraplegics and degree and rate of success in rehabilitation. Unpublished doctoral dissertation, New York Univer., 1955.

Dembo, Tamara, Leviton, G. L., & Wright, Beatrice A. Adjustment to misfortune: a problem of social psychological rehabilitation. *Artificial Limbs*, 1956, **3**, 4–62.

Derner, G. F. *Aspects of the psychology of the tuberculous.* New York: Hoeber-Harper, 1953.

Devereux, G. Normal and abnormal: the key problem of psychiatric anthropology. In J. Casagrande & T. Gladwin (Eds.), *Some uses of anthropology.* Washington, D.C.: Anthropological Society of Washington, 1956. Pp. 23–48.

Dreikurs, R. The socio-psychological dynamics of physical disability: a review of the Adlerian concept. *J. soc. Issues*, 1948, **4** (4), 39–54.

Dunbar, F. *Emotions and bodily changes.* New York: Columbia Univer. Press, 1954.

Eigenbrode, C. R., & Shipman, W. G. The body image barrier concept. *J. abnorm. soc. Psychol.*, 1960, **60**, 450–452.

English, H. B., & English, A. C. *A comprehensive dictionary of psychological and psychoanalytical terms.* New York: McKay, 1958.

Festinger, L. *A theory of cognitive dissonance.* New York: Harper & Row, 1957.

Festinger, L., Gerard, H. B., Hymovitch, B., Kelley, H. H., & Raven, B. The influence process in the presence of extreme deviates. *Hum. Rela.*, 1952, **5**, 327–346.

Fisher, S. A further appraisal of the body boundary concept. *J. consult. Psychol.*, 1963, **27**, 62–74.

Fisher, S., & Cleveland, S. *Body image and personality.* Princeton, N.J.: Van Nostrand, 1958.

Fishman, S. Self-concept and adjustment to leg prostheses. Unpublished doctoral dissertation, Columbia Univer., 1949.

Fishman, S. Amputee needs, frustrations, and behavior. *Rehabilit. Lit.*, 1959, **20**, 322–328.

Fishman, S. Amputation. In J. F. Garrett & Edna S. Levine (Eds.), *Psychological practices with the disabled.* New York: Columbia Univer. Press, 1962.

Fishman, S. & Kay, H. W. Acceptability of a functional-cosmetic artificial hand for children. *Orthoped. prosthet. appliance J.*, 1964, **18** (1), 28–35.

Foort, J. *Adjustable brim fitting of the total contact above knee socket.* Berkeley, Calif.: University of California, Biomechanics Laboratory, 1963.

Freeman, H. E., & Simmons, O. G. *The mental patient comes home.* New York: Wiley, 1963.

Frenkel-Brunswik, Else. Psychoanalysis and personality research. *J. abnorm. soc. Psychol.*, 1940, **35**, 176–197.

Freud, S. On narcissism. In *Collected papers*. Vol. IV. London: Hogarth Press, 1959.

Fromm, E. *Man for himself*. New York: Holt, 1947.

Fromm, E. *The sane society*. New York: Holt, 1955.

Furman, Bess. *Progress in prosthetics*. Washington, D.C.: National Research Council, Prosthetics Research Board, 1962.

Garrett, J. F. Psychological aspects of disability. *Education*, 1955, **76**, 119–122.

Garrett, J. F. (Ed.) *Psychological aspects of physical disability*. Washington, D.C.: U.S. Department of Health, Education, and Welfare, Office of Vocational Rehabilitation, Rehabilitation Service Series 53, No. 210, 1952.

Garrett, J. F., & Levine, Edna S. *Psychological practices with the physically disabled*. New York: Columbia Univer. Press, 1962.

Gelb, L. A. Rehabilitation of mental patients in a comprehensive rehabilitation center. *N.Y. State J. Med.*, 1959, **60**, 12 pp.

Gellman, W. G. Components of vocational adjustment. *Pers. Guidance J.*, 1953, **31**, 536–539.

Gellman, W. G. Interpersonal orientation and vocational adjustment of the occupationally handicapped. Unpublished doctoral dissertation, Univer. of Chicago, 1955.

Gellman, W. Job adjustment of "apparent unemployables" through a vocational adjustment workshop. In E. L. Chouinard & J. F. Garrett, *Workshop for the disabled*. Washington, D.C.: U.S. Department of Health, Education, and Welfare, Vocational Rehabilitation Administration, 1956. Pp. 113–128.

Gellman, W. Roots of prejudice against the handicapped. *J. Rehabilit.*, 1959, **25**, 4–6.

Goldberg, B. Z. *The sacred fire: the story of sex in religion*. Vol. II. New York: Grove Press, 1958. Chap. 2.

Gorthy, W. C. Organization and administration in the center. In *Proceedings of the Institute on Rehabilitation Center Planning, Chicago, Feb.-Mar., 1957*. Washington, D.C.: U.S. Department of Health, Education, and Welfare, Vocational Rehabilitation Administration, 1957. Pp. 172–187.

Greenblatt, M., Levinson, D. J., & Williams, R. H. *The patient and the mental hospital*. New York: Free Press, 1957.

Grunstein, A. *The index of psychoanalytic writings*. Vols. 1–5. New York: International Universities Press, 1960.

Guralnick, D. The relationship of personal characteristics and educational experience of mentally retarded persons to their successful utilization of a vocational rehabilitation program. Unpublished doctoral dissertation, New York Univer., 1963.

Haber, W. B. Observations on phantom-limb phenomena. *Arch. Neurol. Psychiat.*, 1956, **75**, 624–636.

Hall, C. S., & Lindzey, G. *Theories of Personality*. New York: Wiley, 1958.

Hamilton, K. W. *Counseling the handicapped in the rehabilitation process*. New York: Ronald, 1950.

Hardy, J. D., Wolff, H. G., & Goodell, H. *Pain sensations and reactions*. Baltimore: Williams & Wilkins, 1952.

Hartmann, H. *Ego psychology and the problem of adaptation*. New York: International Universities Press, 1958.

Hastorf, A. H. The handicapped: as perceiver and perceived. Paper read at Midwest. Psychol. Ass., Chicago, 1959.

Head, H., & Holmes, G. Sensory disturbances from cerebral lesions. *Brain*, 1911, **34**, 187–189.

Hebb, D. O. *Text of psychology*. Philadelphia: Saunders, 1958.

Hebb, D. O., & Thompson, W. R. The social significance of animal studies. In *Handbook of social psychology*. Vol. I. Reading, Mass.: Addison-Wesley, 1954. Pp. 532–563.

Heider, F. *The psychology of interpersonal relations*. New York: Wiley, 1958.

Heider F., & Heider, G. M. Studies in the psychology of the deaf. *Psychol. Monogr.*, 1941, **53**, No. 5.

Hendrick, I. The discussion of the instinct to master. *Psychoanal. Quart.*, 1943, **12**, 561–565. (a)

Hendrick, I. Work and the pleasure principle. *Psychoanal. Quart.*, 1943, **12**, 311–329. (b)

Hentig, H. von. Physical disability, mental conflict and social crisis, *J. soc. Issues*, 1948, **4**, 21–27.

Holden, R. H. Changes in body image of physically handicapped children due to summer camp experience. *Merrill-Palmer Quart.*, 1962, **8** (1), 19–26.

Holt, R. R. Gauging primary and secondary process in Rorschach responses. *J. proj. Tech.*, 1956, **20**, 14–25.

Horwitz, M. Hostility and its management in the classroom. In W. W. Charters, Jr., & N. L. Gage (Eds.), *Readings in the social psychology of education.* Boston: Allyn and Bacon, 1963.

Huntley, C. W. Judgments of self based upon records of expressive behavior. *J. abnorm. soc. Psychol.,* 1940, **35**, 398–427.

Institute for the Crippled and Disabled. *Tower: testing, orientation and work evaluation in rehabilitation.* New York: Author, 1959.

Johnson, E. W., & Wayloris, G. W. Conduction latency of the facial nerve in diabetes mellitus. *Arch. Phys. Med. Rehabilit.,* 1962, **43**, 357–358.

Johnson, L. C., & Corah, N. L. Racial differences in skin resistance. *Science,* 1963, **139**, 766–767.

Joint Commission on Mental Illness and Health. *Action for mental health.* New York: Basic Books, 1953.

Jones, M. *The therapeutic community.* New York: Basis Books, 1953.

Jorgensen, M. B., & Buck, N. H. Studies on inner ear function and cranial nerves in diabetes. *Acta Otolaryngol.,* 1961, **53**, 350–364.

J. soc. Issues, 1948, **4**, 14.

Kammerer, R. C. An exploratory study of crippled children. *Psychol. Rec.,* 1940, **4**, 47–100.

Kelley, H. H., Hastorf, A. H., Jones, E. E., Thibaut, J. W., & Usdane, W. M. Some implications of social psychological theory for research on the handicapped. In L. H. Lofquist (Ed.), *Psychological research and rehabilitation.* Washington, D.C.: American Psychological Association, 1960.

Kessler, H. H. Rehabilitation of the amputee. In W. H. Soden (Ed.), *Rehabilitation of the handicapped.* New York: Ronald, 1949. Pp. 82–94.

Klein, G. S. On inhibition, disinhibition and primary process in thinking. *Proc. XIV Int. Congr. appl. Psychol.* 1961, 179–198.

Kramer, H. E. Report on a tour of European Prosthetic Centers. *Orthoped. prosthet. Appliance J.,* March, 1964, **18** (1), 36–39.

Ladieu, Gloria, Adler, D. L., & Dembo, Tamara. Studies in adjustment to visible injuries: social acceptance of the injured. *J. soc. Issues,* 1948, **4** (4), 55–67.

Lantos, Barbara. Metaphysical considerations on the concept of work. *Int. J. Psychoanal.,* 1952, **33**, 439–443.

Lawrence, D. G., & Locke, S. Motor nerve conduction velocity in diabetes. *Arch. Neurol.,* 1961, **5**, 483–489.

Levi, Aurelia L. Orthopedic disability as a factor in human-figure perception. *J. consult. Psychol.,* 1961, **25**, 243–246.

Levine, Edna S. Auditory disability. In J. F. Garrett & Edna S. Levine, *Psychological practices with the physically disabled.* New York: Columbia Univer. Press, 1960. (a)

Levine, Edna S. *The psychology of deafness.* New York: Columbia Univer. Press, 1960. (b)

McClelland, D. C. *The achieving society.* Princeton, N.J.: Van Nostrand, 1961.

McClelland, D. C., Atkinson, J. W., Clark, R. A., & Lowell, E. L. *The achievement motive.* New York: Appleton-Century-Crofts, 1953.

McCully, R. S. Human movement in the Rorschach materials of a group of pre-adolescent boys suffering from progressive muscular loss. *J. proj. Tech.,* 1961, **25**, 205–211.

Maisel, E. *Meet a body.* Unpublished manuscript. New York: Institute for the Crippled and Disabled, 1953.

Manual of below knee prosthetics. Berkeley, Calif.: University of California, Biochemics Laboratory, 1959.

Menninger, K. Work as a sublimation. *Bull. Menninger Clin.,* 1942, **6**, 170–182.

Meyerson, L. Physical disability as a social psychological problem. *J. soc. Issues,* 1948, **4**, 2–10.

Morrow, R. S., & Morrow, S. Psychological aspects of disability. In L. E. Abt & B. F. Riess (Eds.), *Progress in clinical psychology.* Vol. V, Chap. 2. New York: Grune & Stratton, 1963. Pp. 16–37.

Neff, W. S. Socio-economic status and intelligence: a critical survey. *Psychol. Bull.,* 1938, **35**, 727–757.

Neff, W. S. The rehabilitation workshop as a therapeutic medium. *J. Jewish communal Serv.,* 1959, **36**, 225–231.

Neff, W. S. *The success of a rehabilitation program.* Washington, D.C.: U.S. Department of Health, Education, and Welfare, Office of Vocational Rehabilitation, 1960.

Neff, W. S. Work: its value and meaning to the handicapped. *Proc. fifth annu. N.Y. State Inst. on sheltered Workshops,* 1961.

Neff, W. S. A study of the factors involved in the rehabilitation of vocationally disadvantaged mental patients: a research proposal submitted to the Vocational Rehabilitation Administration. New

York: Institute for the Crippled and Disabled, 1962. (a)

Neff, W. S. Work: its meaning to society and the individual. *Rehabilit. Rec.*, 1962, **3** (2), 3–6. (b)

Neff, W. S. Automation and rehabilitation. *Rehabilit. Rec.*, 1963, **4**, 14–17.

Neff, W. S., Gellman, W. G., Friedman, S. B., Gendel, H., & Glaser, N. M. *Adjusting people to work.* (2nd ed.) Chicago: Jewish Vocational Service, 1957.

Neff, W. S., & Helfand, A. A Q-sort instrument to assess the meaning of work. *J. counsel. Psychol.*, 1963, **10**, 139–145.

New York University Child Prosthetic Studies. *Acceptability of a functional-cosmetic artificial hand for young children.* New York: Author, 1964.

New York University Post-Graduate Medical School. *Narrative progress report for vocational rehabilitation administration.* New York: Author, 1960. (a)

New York University Post-Graduate Medical School. *Development of a psychological test battery for predicting success in prosthetic rehabilitation (narrative progress report to vocational rehabilitation Administration).* New York: Author, 1960. (b)

New York University Prosthetic Devices Study. *Report on amputee acceptance of the APRL Nielson glove.* New York: New York University, Research Division, College of Engineering, 1955.

New York University. *Evaluation of the UCB total contact above-knee socket fabrication technique (interim report).* New York: New York University, Research Division, College of Engineering, 1962.

Palmer, C. E. The role of religion in rehabilitation. I. *Rehabilit. Lit.* 1962, **23**. II. 1963, **24**.

Pick, A. Zur pathologie des bewusstseins vom eigenen korper. *Neurol. Zbl.*, 1915, **34**, 257–265.

Piotrowski, Z. A. *Perceptanalysis.* New York: Macmillan, 1957.

Randall, G. C., Ewalt, J. R., & Blair, H. Psychiatric reaction to amputation. *J. Amer. med. Ass.*, 1945, **128**, 645–652.

Rapaport, D. The psychoanalytic theory of thinking. *Int. J. Psychoanal.*, 1950, **30**, 1–10.

Raskin, N. J. Visual disability. In J. F. Garrett & E. S. Levine, *Psychological practices with the physically disabled.* New York: Columbia Univer. Press, 1962.

Ray, M. H. The effect of crippled appearance on personality judgment. Unpublished master's thesis, Stanford Univer., 1946.

Redkey, H. Components of a rehabilitation center. *Int. Arch. phys. Med. Rehabilit.*, 1956, **37**, 627–628.

Redkey, H. *Rehabilitation centers today.* Washington, D.C.: U.S. Department of Health, Education, and Welfare, Vocational Rehabilitation Administration, Rehabilitation Service Series, No. 490, 1959.

Research and demonstration projects: an Annotated Listing. Washington, D.C.: U.S. Department of Health, Education, and Welfare, Vocational Rehabilitation Administration, Rehabilitation Service Series, Nos. 56–62, 1962.

Richardson, S. A., Goodman, H., Hastorf, A. H., & Dornbusch, S. M. Cultural uniformity in reaction to physical disabilities. *Amer. sociol. Rev.*, 1961, **26**, 241–247.

Richardson, S. A., Goodman, H., Hastorf, A. H., & Dornbusch, S. M. Variant reactions to physical disabilities. *Amer. sociol. Rev.*, 1963, **28**, 429–435.

Rogers, C. R. *Client-centered therapy.* Boston: Houghton Mifflin, 1951.

Rusk, H. A., & Taylor, E. J. *Living with a disability.* New York: Blakiston, 1953.

Rusk, H. A., et al. *Rehabilitation medicine.* St. Louis: Mosby, 1958.

Sanua, V. D. Sociocultural factors in responses to stressful life situations: the behavior of aged amputees as an example. *J. Hlth hum. Behav.*, 1960, **1**, 17–24.

Sarbin, T. H. Role theory. In *Handbook of social psychology.* Vol. I. Reading, Mass.: Addison-Wesley, 1954. Pp. 223–258.

Schachter, S. *The psychology of affiliation.* Stanford, Calif.: Stanford Univer. Press, 1959.

Schilder, P. *The image and appearance of the human body.* New York: International Universities Press, 1950.

Schmidt, L. D., & McGowan, J. F. The differentiation of human figure drawings. *J. consult. Psychol.*, 1959, **23**, 129–133.

Schoggen, P. Environmental forces in the lives of children with and without physical disability. Paper read at Amer. Psychol. Ass., Philadelphia, 1963.

Schwartz, Charlotte G. *Rehabilitation of mental hospital patients.* Washington, D.C.: U.S. Government Printing Office, Public Health Service Publication, No. 297, 1953.

Secord, P. F. Objectification of word association procedures by the use of homonyms: a measure of body-cathexis. *J. Pers.*, 1953, **21**, 479–495.

Secord, P. F., & Vourard, S. M. The appraisal of body-cathexis: body-cathexis and the self. *J. consult. Psychol.*, 1953, **17**, 343–347.

Shere, M. O. An evaluation of the social and emotional development of the cerebral palsied twin. Unpublished doctoral dissertation, Columbia Univer., 1954.

Siller, J. Reactions to physical disability. *Rehab. counsel. Bull.*, 1963, **7**, 12–16.

Siller, J. Personality factors influencing reactions to the physically disabled. (*In preparation*, 1964.)

Siller, J., & Chipman, S. Response set paralysis: implications for measurement and control. *J. consult. Psychol.*, 1963, **27**, 432–438.

Silverstein, A. B., & Robinson, H. A. The representation of orthopedic disability in children's figure drawings. *J. consult. Psychol.*, 1956, **20**, 333–341.

Simmel, Marianne L. Phantom experiences following amputation in childhood. *J. Neurol. Neurosurg. Psychiat.*, 1962, **25**, 69–78.

Sommers, V. S. *The influence of parental attitudes and social environment on the personality development of the adolescent blind.* New York: American Foundation for the Blind, 1944.

Stanton, A. H., & Schwartz, M. S. *The mental hospital.* New York: Basic Books, 1954.

Steingisser, E. R. The influence of set upon attitudes toward the blind as related to self-concept. Unpublished master's thesis, Univer. of New Hampshire, 1954.

Stepien, L. *The importance of the cerebral cortex for the sensation of pain.* Warsaw: 1963. Pp. 215–251. (Published for the National Science Foundation and the U.S. Department of Health, Education, and Welfare.)

Stone, G. Some considerations in the design of externally powered upper extremity prostheses. In E. Bennett, J. Degan, & J. Spiegel (Eds.), *Human factors in technology.* New York: McGraw-Hill, 1963. Pp. 411–424.

Studies relating to pain in the amputee. *Progr. Rep. prosthet. Devices Res. Proj. Univer. Calif.*, 1952.

Tagiuri, R., & Petrullo, L. (Eds.) *Person perception and interpersonal behavior.* Stanford, Calif.: Stanford Univer. Press, 1958.

Teuber, H. L., Krieger, H. P., & Bender, M. B. *Organization of sensorimotor functions following loss of limb.* 1948. (mimeographed)

Thibaut, J. W., & Kelley, H. H. *The social psychology of groups.* New York: Wiley, 1959.

Thibaut, J. W., & Riecken, H. W. Some determinants and consequences of the perception of causality. *J. Pers.*, 1955, **24**, 113–133.

Ventur, P. A. Some effects of upper extremity prosthetic restoration. Unpublished doctoral dissertation, Columbia Univer., 1961.

Wagman, M. Attitude change and authoritarian personality. *J. Psychol.*, 1955, **40**, 3–24.

Wallace, I. *The prize.* New York: Signet Books, 1963. Pp. 35–36.

Weinstein, E. A., & Kahn, R. L. *Denial of illness.* Springfield, Ill.: Charles C. Thomas, 1955.

Weinstein, S., & Sersen, E. A. Phantoms in cases of congenital absence of limbs. *Neurology*, 1961, **11**, 905–911.

Weiss, A. J. Differential responses of young adolescents to four measures of masculinity-femininity and the relationship between test scores. Unpublished doctoral dissertation, New York Univer., 1959.

Weiss, S. A. The body image as related to phantom sensation: a hypothetical conceptualization of seemingly isolated findings. *Ann. N.Y. Acad. Sci.*, 1958, **74**, 25–29.

Weiss, S. A. The relationship between personality traits and acceptance of prosthesis. *Amer. Psychologist*, 1959, **14**, 351 (abstract). Paper read at Amer. Psychol. Ass., Cleveland, 1959.

Weiss, S. A. The problem of predicting success in prosthetic rehabilitation. *Orthoped. prosthet. Appliance J.*, 1960, **14** (3), 53–61.

Weiss, S. A. The geriatric amputee: psycho-social and therapeutic aspects. *Geriat. Amputee, Natl Acad. Sci. Natl Res. Council Publ.*, 1961, No. 919, 218–229.

Weiss, S. A. Foreshortened phantom limbs and phocomelia. *J. Amer. Med. Ass.*, 1963, **183**, 1053. (a)

Weiss, S. A. Phocomelia and foreshortened (telescoped) phantom limbs. *Inter-clin. Information Bull., res. Div. Coll. Engng N.Y. Univer.*, 1963, **3** (1), 11–16. (b)

Weiss, S. A. *Treatment of phobic amputee women: a case report.* New York State Division of Vocational Rehabilitation, 1964.

Weiss, S. A., & Fishman, S. Extended and telescoped phantom limbs in unilateral amputees. *J. abnorm. soc. Psychol.,* 1963, **66,** 489–497.

Weiss, S. A., Fishman, S., & Krause, F. Consistency of neurotic mechanisms following amputation trauma. *Amer. Psychol.,* 1964, **19,** 566 (abstract). Paper read at Amer. Psychol. Ass., Los Angeles, 1964.

Weiss, S. A., Fishman, S., & Krause, F. *The Psychological evaluation of lower extremity amputees.* New York: New York University, Research Division, College of Engineering, 1965.

White, R. W. Motivation reconsidered: the concept of competence. *Psychol. Rev.,* 1959, **60,** 297–333.

Whiting, J. W. K., & Child, I. L. *Child training and personality.* New Haven, Conn.: Yale Univer. Press, 1953.

Wittkower, E. D., & Cleghorn, R. A. (Eds.) *Recent developments in psychosomatic medicine.* Philadelphia: Lippincott, 1954.

Wolff, W. *Expression of personality: experimental depth psychology.* New York: Harper & Row, 1943.

Worden, D. K. The intelligence of boys with muscular dystrophy. *J. consult. Psychol.,* 1961, **25** (4), 369.

Wright, Beatrice A. *Physical disability: a psychological approach.* New York: Harper & Row, 1960.

Wylie, R. C. *The self-concept.* Lincoln, Nebr.: Univer. of Nebraska Press, 1961.

Yuker, H. E., Block, J. R., & Campbell, W. J. *Hum. Resources Stud.,* 1960, No. 5. 14 pp.

Zborowski, M. Cultural components in responses to pain. *J. soc. Issues,* 1952, **8** (4), 16–30.

30

Clinical Patterns of Aging

WALTER G. KLOPFER

HISTORY OF THE PROBLEM

The attitudes of modern philosophers and scientists toward the aged may well appear unique. However, as reviewed by Birren (1959), the viewpoints of the ancient Greek and Roman philosophers do not differ radically from contemporary thinking. Even then the aged were considered peculiar, eccentric, and hoary. Aristotle is said to have described them in a very negative fashion as persons having little remaining to them. In contrast, Plato took the more hopeful position that old age brings "profound repose and freedom from love and other passions." Both Plato and Cicero emphasized that the foundation for old-age adjustment is laid in youth; thus a person who found ways of having his intrapersonal and interpersonal needs met satisfactorily during youth and middle years could be expected to reap the benefits during his decline.

The first therapeutic suggestion for clinical problems of the aged was made by Ulysses, who advised the old man Laertes to have "warm baths, good food, soft sleep, and generous wine."

What constitutes the aged period has, of course, changed with the increasing longevity of man. During the Iron and Bronze Ages, men were expected to live until the age of 20 to 30 years. The Mongols hoped to achieve the age of 40, and the Romans were expected to live at least that long. A man was not eligible for the Roman Senate until he was 40 years old, by which time it was assumed that his father would no longer be living. An interesting precursor of the theories later developed by Freud was the Romans' belief that a position of public trust and responsibility, such as senator, could be adequately filled only by a person who was in every sense the head of his household.

Interest in the period of aging among psychologists and other behavioral scientists is of relatively recent vintage. The first compendium on the subject was published in 1939 by Cowdrey and was entitled *Problems of Aging*. Serious research on the subject began in 1930 under the direction of Walter Miles and his associates. After World War II, interest in the organization of professional services for the aged began to grow with the establishment of the U.S. Federal Security Agency in 1951. Traditionally, youth has always been a preferred age for study, and this is true even at the present time. To explore fully the reasons for this preference is beyond the scope of this chapter. However, a few of the major hypotheses might be mentioned: (1) In contrast to other societies, our Western European society has always tended to worship youth. Attractiveness, productiveness, progressive attitudes, and other socially desirable characteristics are associated with the early part of life, the explicit assumption being that these characteristics tend to fade with the encroachment of old age. (2) Beginning with middle age, the dominant generation has always tended to hide its negative feelings toward younger persons, while emphasizing its positive feelings. The threat that youth represents to those who have passed the physical prime is evident to any psychologist but has not been explicitly incorporated by the mores of our society. (3) In a culture such as ours, which fosters ambition and power, the declining years are a threat to the morale of scientists who might otherwise be tempted to conduct investigations in this area. Time and again professional colleagues insist that they will become interested in geriatric research when they themselves become older but that they do not want to become involved in it for the present.

Psychologists are relatively new in the field. One of the first articles describing clinical work in geriatrics by a psychologist was published little more than a decade ago (Klopfer, 1951). It suggested that all the traditional activities of the clinical psychologists, such as psychodiagnosis, psychotherapy, and clinical research, could make important contributions in a home for the aged. Since that time the situation has become more favorable for geriatric research. The investigator has more facts, better methods, and the beginnings of a theory, as will be elucidated later in this chapter. Research problems that remain include such dilemmas as the use of the cross-sectional versus the longitudinal approach, the difficulties of cross-cultural comparisons, and the conflict between representative and experimental design.

BASE LINE

Since psychologists know so little about what is to be normally expected among the aged, it seems highly desirable at this point to devote some space to the discussion of this topic, with special emphasis on the available research in the area.

According to Birren (1959), most studies point to a gradual decline in intellectual efficiency during the aged period. Typically, retained learning (information and vocabulary tests) exceeds the learning of a new task (Knox cubes, block design, etc.), as exemplified in Heston and Cannell's study (1941). However, as shown by Feifel (1949), the quality of definitions in a vocabulary test may deteriorate without any alteration of the score. Among the changes between middle and old age that may result in modifications of intellectual performance are the following:

1. Motivational changes. The younger person administered a psychological test often perceives the test within the context of some particularly desired goal. This may be educational or vocational advancement, the demonstration of mental well-being, or a change in status in some other area. On the other hand, an older person taking the test may not be inclined to do his best because of a lack of interest in such goals.

2. Sensory changes. With the encroachment of old age, vision, hearing, and other sensory modalities obviously undergo changes in the direction of lesser efficiency. Unless an intellectual task has been especially selected to deemphasize skills based on sensory acumen, lower scores are likely to be the result.

3. Educational differences. In the last few generations, there has been a gradual upgrading of typical educational requirements for most people. The middle-aged person of today is likely to have had more years of school than the middle-aged of the last generation. Insofar as many of our intelligence tests are influenced by the extent of information supplied during school years, scores will be lowered.

4. Cultural differences. Attitudes toward intellectual achievement vary from generation to generation. If a person is a member of the anti-intellectual group which crops up in our society from time to time, he may well be unskilled in certain areas as they emerge on the intelligence tests. Certain other subcultural groups that place unusual emphasis on intellectual achievement may produce results that equally diverge from the mainstream of the aged population.

5. Miscellaneous factors. In addition to the above, innumerable factors may come into play, including test practice, speed, and memory. Unless all the foregoing are taken into account, it will be difficult to justify any general conclusions about intellectual changes during the period of old age.

The question of changes due to organic brain damage has received considerable attention. The most tangible influence in this area has probably been the famous monograph by Goldstein and Scheerer (1941), which presented many interesting methods for evaluating this concept, even though no particular research findings were presented. The impairment score based on the test by Halstead (1947) varies directly with age. This fact really begs the question of what value such an index might have in distinguishing between normal and abnormal aging. According to Thaler (1956), performance on the Weigl sorting task is correlated significantly with performance on the Wechsler-Bellevue. A low number of responses on the Rorschach test correlated at better than the .01 level of significance with concreteness on the Weigl, and increasing age correlated at better than the .001 level of significance, with lower performance scores on the Wechsler-Bellevue. Thus one might infer that aging produces a general lowering of efficiency in problem-solving tasks. According to Dorken and Greenbloom (1953), the discrepancy between intellectual functions is likely to be greater for abnormal aged than normal aged. They state that for subjects over 64, an efficiency quotient is a better index of efficiency than an intelligence quotient.

Many authors have addressed themselves to a general question of what constitutes adjustment among the aged. Among the few investigators who have actually suggested methods for measuring adjustment is Davis (1962). Most writers have contented themselves with presenting theoretical positions. It is suggested by Kuhlen (1959) that sources of satisfaction may differ from one age to the next. In the younger and middle years, sources of satisfaction include achievement in school, the development of relationships within the family, vocational and avocational achievements, and the broadening of the social milieu. In the later years, according to Kuhlen, satisfactions are most easily derived from religion, philosophy, or some other form of sedentary navel contemplation. If some such interest does not exist, there is likely to be bleak isolation. Simmons (1952) states that old people are inclined to project and conserve their gains. General thinking about old-age adjustment seems to revolve around the nature of interests and motives and whether these are appropriate to the physical and intellectual limitations imposed upon the organism by the process of aging. Pressey and Kuhlen (1957) contend that even though existing evidence justifies describing the typical older person as rigid, conservative, and dogmatic, there is no reason to infer poor adjustment from the syndrome. Friedsam (1961) performed an extremely interesting study of reaction to stress which suggested that the older person is less able to involve himself, that objects and significant others become less replaceable, and that loss is felt more keenly. Dunn (1961) argues that the adjustment difficulties of the older person are the result of disintegrated communication and lack of creative imagination. The same author in another paper (1957) contends that old age will seem depressing if regarded merely as a negative condition which lacks the qualities and attitudes characteristic of younger ages. A more hopeful view of old age is to regard it as the "crowning consummation" of life. From Dunn it may be inferred that adjustment in old age can be managed by the creative expression of maturity on the part of those who are no longer bothered by the itch to compete and keep up with the Joneses, who no longer feel threatened by youth and strength, and who have given up thinking of themselves as inadequate middle-aged people and think of themselves as first-class oldsters.

The adjustment problem of old age has been described as a narcissistic trauma in a study by this author (Klopfer, 1958). According to his theoretical formulation, all emotional problems are due to a basic threat to self-esteem, which in turn produces anxiety, which then must lead to the development of new adaptive techniques by the older persons in order that they may retain good adjustment. These adaptive techniques include compartmentalization, or the avoidance of over-all fear and anxiety by limiting concern to small manageable hunks of life; identification with younger persons so that the future can be viewed through their eyes with hope; and increased interest in religion and life beyond. Those elderly persons in the study who were identified as well-adjusted tended to be involved in useful activities within their own or someone else's frame of reference. Compatible with these conclusions is Havighurst's (1950) definition of adjustment in old age in terms of (1) the quantity of interpersonal relationships, (2) the gradual tapering off of interpersonal relationships as aging progresses, (3) a degree of congruence between interpersonal relationships and current personal vigor, (4) the retention of basic family ties, and (5) the ability to recover from stress and illness with due speed.

Finally, the adjustment of the aged has not been particularly aided by professionals in the mental health field. Those who have spent many years working in institutional settings containing older as well as younger patients cannot have helped but witness how a new staff member or intern typically expresses preference for not working with the aged. They are often considered hopeless and uninteresting, and a lack of opportunity for valuable experience is anticipated by the initiate in clinical psychology. According to a study by Tuckman and Lorge (1952), mental health professionals believe many negative stereotypes about the aged, and 24 per cent of them agree with the statement: "The aged are a burden on society."

INCIDENCE

In 1900, 4.1 per cent of the population of the United States was over 65, totaling 3,030,000 persons. By 1950, the number had risen to 8.2 per cent, or a total of 12,300,000 older persons, and by 1959 it was 8.6 per cent, or 14,400,000. At present, approximately one thousand persons reach the age of 65 every day. In 1956, according to the Metropolitan Life Insurance Company (1956), the expected age of men and women was 70 years. Probably this estimate would have to be revised upward today. Moffatt (1959) reports a life expectancy of 79 at age 65 in New Jersey, while Davidson and Kruglov (1952) reveal that the number of persons over 65 increased 37 per cent in the decade from 1940 to 1950.

The above figures refer to "official" old age, which is the typical retirement age of 65. Actual old age, as operationally defined by illness, inability to work, or total dependency, is usually not in force until the age of 70 (Birren, 1959). Organic conditions of old age are said to occur in approximately 22 persons out of 100,000, as of 1953. Their greater frequency in males is defined by a ratio of 4:1, according to Brain (1954). Cerebral arteriosclerosis, with an average onset between the years 50 and 65, occurs three times as often in males as in females. Of first admissions to mental hospitals, Kallman (1950) noted that 33 per cent are sufferers from senile psychosis or cerebral arteriosclerosis. Senile dementia is considered more common among women by a ratio of 2:1. Generally, the organic psychosis of the elderly is associated with areas of poverty, according to Dunham (1955). Alzheimer's disease is the most common of the presenile dementias, being found in 4 per cent of patients subjected to autopsy in psychiatric institutions. It occurs more frequently in women by a ratio of 3:2. Similarly, Pick's disease is found in women more than men by a ratio of 2:1. Involutional psychotic reactions constituted 4.4 per cent of first admissions in mental hospitals in 1953, according to the National Committee against Mental Illness (1957). The illnesses of old age tend to take a paranoid form in women more than in men, according to Mayer-Gross, Slater, and Roth (1955).

The above figures speak for themselves. The enormity of the problem is impossible to exaggerate. Evidently, the number of the aged population and the number of the maladjusted among it are currently on the increase.

ETIOLOGY

Birren's source book (1959) states: "No disease is so specific as to be found exclusively in late maturity." Fuller investigation of this area underscores the point that specification of biological, sociological, and psychological factors in the etiology of mental diseases of old age is a uniquely difficult and challenging task. Among the types of etiology described in most standard textbooks on the subject are the following.

1. Disorders caused by, or associated with, an impairment of brain-tissue function. Under this heading are two major divisions, namely, the acute and the chronic disorders. Acute disorders are thought to be caused by infection (either intracranial or systemic); intoxication; trauma; circulatory disease; or disturbances of metabolism, growth, or nutrition. Chronic disorders are considered to have been caused by infection (the most common of which is syphilis of the brain); intoxication; trauma; circulatory disease; disturbances of metabolism, growth, or nutrition; or hereditary factors. There is some question of whether Alzheimer's disease is caused by heredity, but it seems definitely established that Pick's disease is.

2. Psychogenic disorders. This classification occurs mainly by default and is not clearly defined. Usually conditions regarded as being of psychogenic origin show no discernible or definitive clinical cause and are not accompanied by any specific or microscopically visible structural change. Included among these disorders is the involutional psychotic reaction, to which psychologists have given considerable attention and to which they have attempted to assign some specific psychogenic

causes. For example, it is felt that women have specific fears which are aroused by the onset of the menopause. They are afraid of obesity, insanity, cancer, hirsutism, and a cessation of sexual activity. More tangible environmental changes that may have etiological significance are the necessity for giving up the mother role and the visible signs of aging, with their concomitant implications of loss of attractiveness to the opposite sex.

Men who show adjustment difficulties during the involutional period also are thought to have specific psychological problems. These include loss of sexual potency, increasing obesity, a tendency to be attracted to respecting younger females, and jealousy of younger males. An analogy might be made to the elephant herd in the jungle. Such a herd usually consists of an older male who is the leader of the herd, a number of females, and young of both sexes. If one of the younger male animals wishes to challenge the leader of the herd to combat, the older male has everything to lose and nothing to gain. If he should win, the younger bull elephant can lick his wounds and submerge himself once more in the herd to await a better time for resuming the struggle. Someday he will win. But the older elephant, if he should lose, has no choice but to crawl off into the jungle to die. Members of our human species may experience the same fear in symbolic form during the involutional period.

Another of the psychogenic disorders is the affective reaction sometimes occurring during the later years. This is usually thought to occur in persons whose personality has been basically cyclothymic in nature throughout their life-span and who hitherto have been able to deal with it through activity, involvement in vocational and family affairs, and the like. As these defenses or adaptive devices become less available, the basic mood swings may become more permanent in the behavior of the individual. There are also psychotic depressive reactions, difficult to distinguish from the above but usually characterized by an extreme form of situational reaction to loss. During old age there are many possibilities for loss of job, of significant others, and of tangible worldly possessions, any of which may produce such a reaction. Finally, there are the paranoid reactions of old age, usually thought to occur in those who have always been somewhat suspicious and inclined to take offense easily. With the loss of sensory efficiency and other marks of vigor, paranoid tendencies that were heretofore latent may become manifest.

3. Psychophysiological reactions. This group of reactions may or may not include structural change. These are disorders with unknown combinations of physiological and psychological etiology that result in symptom formations that are usually exacerbated by psychological stress. They include arthritis, low-back pain, constipation, and similar disorders.

4. Psychoneurotic disorders. These are considered purely functional, and they closely parallel similar disorders to be found among younger persons. Since they are described in detail elsewhere in the *Handbook*, they will receive only passing mention here. The anxiety state among the aged is commonly associated with the actual loss of functional efficiency and self-esteem. Adaptive devices such as conversion, compulsion, and phobia may be exaggerated and thereby result in acute neurotic disturbances. Depressions of a neurotic sort often occur during the aged period. These may not be associated with guilt (Birren, 1959), as is the case with younger persons, but with loneliness, feelings of isolation, and so forth. Hypochondriac symptoms commonly occur and may, if no discernible cause for the symptom is found, be due to exaggerated needs for attention and other psychological desires. Hypochondriac symptoms may become substitutes for larger concerns and may serve the function of compartmentalizing general feelings of inferiority and incompetence. Finally, there are traumatic reactions so typical of the aged period. These are illustrated in the study by Friedsam (1961), in which older persons were examined under conditions of catastrophe. They seemed to react to loss of tangible and personal objects with a "higher sense of deprivation." To them not only houses, trees, and tables are being destroyed, but even time itself. This is something they cannot afford to be without.

At the end as well as at the beginning of this section, it is necessary to point out the difficulty of assigning specific organic or functional causes to the disorders cited above. Malamud (1950) has pointed out that many senile psychotics show neuropathological changes such as atrophy of the brain, senile plaques, specific cell changes, areas of devastation, and vascular pathology. However, as he goes on to explain, these changes also occur among the old-age group who are not psychotic. There are even many psychotics who do not show these changes. Where this leaves us in regard to the basic question of etiology the reader must decide for himself.

SYMPTOMATOLOGY

In pinpointing the symptoms descriptive of geriatric disorders, it is again necessary to recall the base-line picture. If the younger or middle-aged are to serve as a standard for comparison, old people are likely to fall short. A typical interpretation by Light and Amick (1956) refers to old people as being generally suspicious, anxious, and evasive in their approach to the Rorschach and as having a somewhat immature, introversive inner life colored by fantasy and unreality; difficulties in interpersonal relationships; little awareness of affectional needs; and many signs of inflexibility, stereotypy, and intellectual impotence. Such conclusions as the foregoing confront the reader with the difficult question of whether to use the middle-age criterion and find all old persons severely maladjusted or whether to use the old-age norm itself and perhaps radically reduce the number of persons considered maladjusted.

How many maladjusted persons are to be found probably depends on many variables such as the locale (urban or rural?), the setting (institutional or community?), and the general degree of visibility (exposure to general public view) of the person in question. According to Morgan (1937), 33 per cent of the time of persons over 70 is spent mainly in housekeeping activities, 32 per cent in hobbies and recreation, and only 4 per cent in paid employment. Probably those oldsters who are employed need more than any others to be impeccable in regard to their symptoms.

From a symptomatic viewpoint, there are generally considered to be two broad diagnostic categories, the organic and the functional disorders. Organic conditions are characterized by intellectual impairment (difficulties in comprehension, calculation, problem solving, learning, and judgment); spotty memory; and labile, even inappropriate, emotionality. It is difficult to distinguish acute from chronic conditions on the basis of symptoms. Acute organic conditions include paranoid and hallucinatory phenomena, but so do some chronic ones. In all probability, diagnostic distinctions could be most easily effected by tying up each set of symptoms with the supposed etiological factor. Thus, conditions attributed to infection are characterized by a general slowdown of functioning, poor judgment, unstable memory, behavioral changes, and deterioration. Conditions due to intoxication are characterized by depression, irritability, and weakness. Conditions due to circulatory disturbances, such as cerebral arteriosclerosis, are characterized in their early stages by poor memory and judgment and then later on by irritability and quarrelsomeness. Senile brain disease in its mild form is typified by a self-centered attitude and mild lability; further deterioration produces a severity of condition characterized by depression, agitation, paranoid reactions, and schizophrenic type of thinking.

One of the most difficult diagnostic distinctions, of course, is that between cerebral arteriosclerosis and senile dementia. Most writers believe that the deterioration in cerebral arteriosclerosis is less profound—that persons suffering from this condition tend to have headaches, dizziness, lability, and spotty and fluctuating memory. Seniles, on the other hand, tend to have diffuse memory defect as well as moral and sexual problems, which often bring them to the attention of a psychologist or psychiatrist. Senile dementia in itself has been broken down into subcategories on the basis of the most typical symptoms. These categories are the simple type, the delirious (confused) type, the depressed and agitated type, the paranoid type, and the presbophrenic type, which is characterized mainly by loss of memory. The two main presenile conditions are Alzheimer's and Pick's disease, the former being accompanied by poor memory, a lack of logical thinking, and partial insight, which often causes considerable distress. Pick's disease produces less activity than Alzheimer's disease, has aphasia as a common symptom, and sometimes comes into the picture a little earlier.

The second large category consists of the functional disorders, among which the most common is involutional psychosis. Concomitant physical reactions include headache, vertigo, fatigue, nervousness, and irritability; the psychological manifestations are insomnia, suspiciousness, doubt and indecision, hypochondriac trends, misinterpretations, delusions, and feelings of physical decline and unforgivable sin. The symptom of "forgetting" is considered by Kaufman (1940) to be an adaptive reaction to some of these unpleasant thoughts. Other affective reactions of old age belonging under this heading are manifested primarily by cyclical mood swings, psychotic depressive reactions, and specific depression without accompanying symptoms; paranoid reactions are manifested by predisposing traits and a preservation of intellectual efficiency, as contrasted with the other symptoms mentioned above. A paranoid reaction is often associated with specific memory loss, such as deafness or poor vision. Such physical handicaps always leave much to the individual's imagination, so that if he already tends to have a rather jaundiced view of the world, having minimal feedback is likely to make him assume the worst. Finally, there are the psychophysiological reactions and the psychoneurotic reactions. Anxiety in old age is often experienced in connection with imminent death (Klopfer, 1947) and is usually accompanied by hypochrondriac symptoms and depression. Other common psychoneurotic symptoms during the period of old age are insomnia and a general loss of smooth social techniques.

THEORETICAL INTERPRETATIONS

There are, of course, many theoretical interpretations of what occurs to make adjustment difficult in old age. Not so many years ago, fantastically naïve statements were current in psychological textbooks; the period of old age was regarded as closely analogous to the period of early childhood, and the elderly were considered to be free of all but the most elementary needs. Today theoretical opinion has become considerably more sophisticated.

Among the most prolific writers on this topic have been the psychoanalysts. Weinberg (1956) believes that the older person is likely to withdraw his attention from the various details of daily life which have no intensive bearing on his personal situation while becoming more introverted. Hamilton (1942) describes in sexual terms what he calls "regression" in old age. All problems of old age are due to the forbidden sex impulses. According to Hamilton, the psychosexual development simply reverses itself from genital maturity back to primitive receptive orality. He interprets the empirical work of Kinsey and his coworkers on various age groups as a verification for his hypotheses. Adler (1920) attributes all the aged person's difficulties to impotence of a general sort, due to both real and imaginary factors. Lewinian attitudes toward aging focus around the concept of rigidity. Thus a study by Kounin (1941) is typical of many in demonstrating that the elderly find it difficult to shift; they are inclined to rely unduly upon past behaviors to guide them in making present and future decisions. Such findings are in turn subjected to analytic interpretation as a reaction to lack of heterosexual energy, which is thought to be the source of all energy. Grotjahn (1940) attributes the narcissistic trauma of old age to castration anxiety. He says that transference to the analyst by the older person is a mixed one, wherein the analyst is regarded as both father and son. He suggested the concept of the "inverted Oedipus" (described by Kaufman, 1940), a conflict in which the middle-aged adult regards his aged parent as a child and retaliates for the lack of power granted him during his own childhood by overwhelming and controlling the parent as he himself once felt overwhelmed and controlled. Most analysts contend that improvement as a result of psychotherapy among the aged can be only symptomatic since orgiastic potency cannot be restored. Because they deem this the only real sign of good adjustment, they must therefore accept a highly limited goal for their aged patients.

Birren (1959) describes a deterministic concept of aging in which the process is thought to be the result of intrinsic or environmental influences. In this he infers that experiments should be possible in which later stages are predictable from antecedent ones. This author and his colleagues talk about aging within three separate frames of reference: psychological aging, social aging, and biological aging. Biological aging is defined as the capacity for survival; psychological aging is measured by the achievements and potentialities of the person; and social aging refers to the person's acquired habits and status.

An interesting study by Davis (1962) describes a method whereby social aging can be a function of self-concept. He found that aged persons regarding themselves as happy, satisfied, and worthy tend to be preferred by their peers. Such oldsters are better able to express themselves and voice more concern about physical well-being and social harmony. They tend to be less ambiguous about describing their own concept of being aged or youthful in reference to their own status in the institution. They were also considered to be generally better adjusted. For psychological purposes, a person is regarded as socially "old" if he is so perceived by his contemporaries. It remains to be seen only whether he accepts this role or not. A lag evidently exists between official aging, which our society has defined as taking place at the age of 65, and functional aging, which may occur considerably later. Different segments of society have greater or lesser tolerance for the eccentricities of older people, and what begins to be called a "mental disorder" in old age is rather vague. Social workers trying to move elderly patients out of mental hospitals and into nursing homes often have difficulty convincing the patient's relatives of the desirability of such a move. Comfort (1956) explains that readjustment during old age is a breakdown of "programs" fundamental to growth and based upon selective survival pressures. Frank (1950) regards aging as a lowering of homeostatic capacity and a lessening of drives.

Havighurst (1961), a prolific writer in this area, specifies two different theories of successful aging, the "activity" and the "disengagement" theories. The activity theory maintains that the middle-aged model is the only criterion for success. Consequently, the degree to which the aged person can maintain himself according to this model is a measure of the success of his adjustment to the period of old age. The disengagement theory (described in detail by Cumming & Henry, 1961), which he tends to favor, focuses upon adjustment to the specific characteristics of old age, the giving up of the middle-aged model, and the enjoyment of lack of pressure. Havighurst has attempted to present methods for measuring successful aging and for solving the question of how to decide between these two theories. Behavioral characteristics of successful aging include a way of life socially desirable for the aged group in a particular subculture and the maintenance of enjoyable and desirable activity. Subjective characteristics of this successful aging include feelings of satisfaction with present status and activity as well as happiness and contentment with life generally. An instrument developed by Havighurst for measuring adjustment in these terms includes tests for zest versus apathy, resolution and fortitude, goodness of fit between desired and achieved goals, the presence of a positive self-concept, and appropriate mood tones. This instrument has a reliability of .73, when compared to its alternative form, and a validity of .73, using the Chicago Attitude Inventory as a criterion.

It is widely felt, besides being demonstrated by the study of Reichard, Livson, and Peterson (1961), that there are many ways to adjust in aging. These include passive ways, active ways, and those which are most mature and which take into account the specific capacities and limitations of the individual. Indeed there are many ways of maladjusting during this period if the environmental pressure is in the opposite direction from the habitual ones. It will be difficult even for theoreticians to wax enthusiastic about the potentialities of these later years for adjustment unless they believe it possible in their hearts.

DIAGNOSTIC, PROGNOSTIC, AND THERAPEUTIC METHODS

How do clinical patterns of aging manifest themselves on psychological tests? One study (Williams, 1956) indicated that patients suffering from senile dementia demonstrate spatial disorientation on a visual maze task. Dorken and Greenbloom (1953) examined 67 seniles and contrasted them with 20 normals on the Wechsler-Bellevue Intelligence Scale. They conclude that senile dementia is unrelated to the normal aging process and that the organization of abilities is different from that in normal adulthood. They recommend as the best short form for evaluating intellectual efficiency among aged persons in this category the use of the Information, Vocabulary, Digit Span, and Picture Completion subtests. Hopkins and Roth (1953) found seniles lowest on the W-B Vocabulary and Information subtests and on the short form Raven Matrices. Scoring slightly higher were sufferers from arteriosclerosis, while highest were patients diagnosed as having affective psychoses of old age. Lakin (1956), studying aged persons with the Bender, discovered that partial rotations are most valuable in detecting the effects of general aging. Other useful signs are perseverance of line and dots, fragmentation, and overlapping.

This author (Klopfer, 1946) found that the

Rorschach test did not discriminate between institutionalized and noninstitutionalized aged. Davidson and Kruglov (1952), however, contend that it does. But all three tend to agree that the Rorschachs of aged persons are characterized by inferred lower intellectual efficiency, less projection of movement, lower content spread, less use of color and shading, and more signs of insecurity, impotence, and perplexity. There are few illustrative protocols cited in the literature. Burgemeister (1962) gives illustrative protocols of two patients suffering from Parkinson's syndrome and of one cerebral arteriosclerotic. Klopfer (1946) presents protocols of a senile maladjustment reaction, a cerebral arteriosclerotic, a neurotic depression of old age, and a senile dementia case.

Davidson and Kruglov administered a Rorschach to 46 subjects over 60, with an average age of 76. All subjects were of the Jewish religion. Compared with young adults, these subjects had a low number of responses, high F per cent, high F– per cent, low M and FM, low color, and a low range of interests. Also found were concreteness, aphasia, and negativism. Women were considered more labile, more energetic, and better adjusted. Prados and Fried (1947) studied normals, comparing them with the subjects cited in Davidson and Kruglov's study. Their sample had more responses, more W, lower F per cent, and more color. Their inference was that aged persons living outside of institutions are more like young adults than those living in institutions, which is interpreted as being "psychologically less aged." They studied three different groups: one aged 50 to 60, one aged 61 to 70, and one aged 71 to 80. A further interesting finding was that persons over 71 generally look better because they have given up the struggle to keep up with the middle-aged. They seem more subjectively relaxed but more intellectually disabled. This author (Klopfer, 1954) discussed special problems of administering Rorschachs to the aged, such as poor vision, slow reaction time, and excessive garrulousness, that would make it difficult to get down to the job at hand. However, he went on to say further that oldsters are so extremely eager to engage themselves, at least with younger persons, that getting their attention and establishing rapport are really not such difficult problems. The Rorschach norms for the aged generally seem to be low M; FM greater than M, with m, k, K, and FK negligible; shading low; and color absent or CF plus C greater than FC. Only three of the ten Klopfer populars are given more than 50 per cent of the time; W is generally greater than D; and animal per cent is over 50, with the total responses being 14 or 15. This material, plus other accompanying qualitative data, suggests the following interpretations: (1) Old persons tend to be intellectually slow, inefficient, and unproductive; (2) they are more efficient in dealing with practical than theoretical problems; (3) they feel inferior and react well to support; (4) they have restricted thought content; and (5) they tend emotionally to be either inhibited or egocentric. Giedt and Lehner (1951) contend that the Draw-A-Person Test can be used to gauge age preference (subjective age identity). However, this is both highly inferential and of doubtful reliability. Two studies on aged persons involved the use of the TAT. One such (Klopfer, 1947) revealed that "active" old persons have more self-esteem, more positive concepts of the future, and more identification with children or child surrogates. A study by Whiteley and McArthur (in press) involved the administration of TATs and Rorschachs to a number of aged deaf persons, all of whom were considered psychogenically deaf. Not only was the group extremely bright (average IQs in the superior range), but the design was rather poor. The results were interpreted as indicating that the psychogenetic deafness was due to repressed anger leading to focalized anxiety.

In addition to the above, old people are, of course, subject to all the special symptom pictures characterizing other age groups. Yet none of these seem to be a particular problem. Alcoholism, according to Jelliuik (1946), is a minor problem among the aged since drinking decreases after the age of 45. This author was unable to find any work done on drug addiction among the aged, suggesting that this must also be a relatively insignificant problem. Suicide, on the other hand, is quite common (Gruhle, 1941), often being due to real psychological and social factors rather than to unrealistic, psychotic motivations.

The United States government advises: "For the older person a fully integrated family life can spell the difference between loneliness and fulfillment—between frustration and independence. It's up to you to make the three-generation family flourish and succeed" (U.S. Department of Health, Education, and Welfare, 1957). Thus our government has taken an official position on what is essential in reducing maladjustment in old age. This position, however, is not necessarily the consensus of the professional workers in this field, who have generally been extremely silent on constructive suggestions for easing the lot of the older person, whether he is adjusted or maladjusted. But what of those attempts that have been made to evaluate and treat the elderly?

According to both Birren (1959) and this author (Klopfer, 1958), patients with organic conditions of old age are said to respond to a carefully regulated pattern of life and to the assignment of tasks at which they can succeed. The study by Klopfer demonstrated definite differences in adjustment among the population of a home for the aged, depending on the availability of tasks which could make them feel useful and necessary. For most deteriorative organic diseases, such as Alzheimer's disease, Pick's disease, and senile brain disease, no known treatment exists at the present time.

Somewhat more enthusiasm has been expressed concerning functional disorders. Most authors seem to feel that involutional cases can be treated by psychotherapeutic means. This usually consists of two simultaneous approaches. On the one hand, the individual is relieved of his loneliness by the presence of the therapist, is given an opportunity to express his feelings in the session, and is largely absolved of any guilt feelings he may have concerning persons who have died. On the other hand, some attempt is made to manipulate his environment by creating new interests and sources of enthusiasm. Distinctions between involutional cases and those with a lifelong history of manic-depressive disorders can be made only with the use of anamnestic information. Diagnostic distinction does not necessarily have any therapeutic implication. Paranoid individuals have a high survival value, but they do not obtain easy release from state hospitals since their difficulties tend to be annoying to other members of society. Thus many old paranoids who could well function outside an institutional setting remain there, mainly because of the reluctance of society to put up with their eccentricities and antagonisms. Neurotic oldsters, according to Clow and Allen (1949), improve from psychotherapy 80 per cent of the time.

It would appear that psychotherapeutic techniques as applied to the aged population have never really had a fair test. The elderly are not usually in an economic position to benefit from private services, and when in institutions they are often overlooked in favor of younger and seemingly more interesting patients. The fact is that social and recreational approaches to the aged have usually had astounding results, so that in all likelihood much of the current pessimism in this field is not warranted.

CONCLUSIONS AND RECOMMENDATIONS

The need for a complete reorientation in thinking concerning old persons is evident from this review. Only a decade ago most writers attributed functional maladjustment in old age primarily to impotence and inadequacy, using the middle-age model as the base-line criterion. They were inclined to feel that an inevitable loss of self-esteem results from sensory impairment and that abnormality in old age is to be expected and is hardly a legitimate subject for research or treatment. However, the definition of old age as the "crowning achievement" of life has interesting implications. Perhaps a new way of defining adjustment in old age might be in terms of a realistic acceptance of both the limitations and the assets of this period of life. Studies involving self-concept and level of aspiration might shed further light on the directions in which society should move to facilitate adjustment for the aged.

The present lag between medical research, which keeps people alive longer, and psychological research, which deals substantially with the bases for adjustment during this period, can and should be attacked. A paper by Havighurst (1952) suggests that a longitudinal research approach is vastly preferable to a cross-sectional one. He points out that we cannot really judge what aging does to people unless we follow them along the life-span. The suggestions for research he made more than a decade ago deserve repetition, for they have by no means been exhausted. They include discovery of proper tests for assessing modifications in abilities with age; the development of methods for evaluating a shift from work to play, which characterizes compulsory retirement; the evaluation of changing values during the period of aging and how they affect adjustment; differing reactions to stress among the aged, whether they tend to withdraw and capitulate more and thereby lose the ability to attack; and the clarification of social roles among aged persons. Tools to be used in the above kinds of research include not only standard personality inventories but also situational tests, sociometric procedures, and intensive interviews. At this stage the field of geriatrics can be likened to a veritable gold mine in which no one has as yet struck the mother lode.

REFERENCES

Adler, A. *Praxis und Theorie der Individualspsychologie*. Munich: Bergmann, 1920.

Birren, J. E. (Ed.) *Handbook of aging and the individual.* Chicago: Univer. of Chicago Press, 1959.

Brain, W. Neurological disorders after age 60. In *Old age in the modern world.* London: E. S. Livingstone, 1954.

Burgemeister, Bessie. *Psychological techniques in neurological diagnosis.* New York: Harper & Row, 1962.

Chesrow, E. J., Woskia, P. H., & Reinitz, A. H. A psychometric evaluation of aged white males. *Geriatrics,* 1949, 4, 169–177.

Clow, H. E., & Allen, E. G. Study of depressive states in aging. *Geriatrics,* 1949, **4,** 11–17.

Comfort, A. *The biology of senescence.* London: Routledge, 1956.

Cowdrey, E. V. (Ed.) *Problems of aging.* Baltimore: Williams & Wilkins, 1939.

Cumming, Elaine, & Henry, W. F. *Growing old. The process of disengagement.* New York: Basic Books, 1961.

Davidson, Helen, & Kruglov, L. Personality characteristics of institutionalized aged. *J. consult. Psychol.,* 1952, **16,** 5–12.

Davis, R. The relationship of social preferability to self-concept in an aged population. *J. Geront.,* 1962, **17,** 431–436.

Dorken, H. J., & Greenbloom, G. C. Psychologic investigation of senile dementia: Wechsler-Bellevue Adult Intelligence Scale. *Geriatrics,* 1953, **8,** 324–333.

Dunham, H. W. Current status of ecological research in mental disorders. In A. Rose (Ed.), *Mental health and mental disorders.* New York: Norton, 1955.

Dunn, H. L. *Significance of levels of wellness in aging.* Washington, D.C.: U.S. Department of Health, Education, and Welfare, 1957.

Dunn, H. L. Communication and purpose-ingredients for longevity. *J. speech hearing Disorders,* 1961, **26,** 109–117.

Feifel, H. Qualitative differences in the vocabulary responses of normals and abnormals. *Genet. Psychol. Monogr.,* 1949, **39,** 151–204.

Frank, L. K. Intrapersonal aspects of gerontology. *Trans. twelfth Conf. Problems Aging,* 1950.

Friedsam, H. J. Reactions of older persons to disaster-caused losses: an hypothesis of relative deprivation. *Gerontologist,* 1961, **1,** 34–37.

Giedt, F. H., & Lehner, G. F. J. Assignment of ages on the DAP by male neuropsychiatric patients. *J. Pers.,* 1951, **19,** 440–448.

Goldstein, K., & Sheerer, M. Abstract and concrete behavior: an experimental study with special tests. *Psychol. Monogr.,* 1941, **53,** 1–151.

Gredt, F., & Fechner, G. F. Assignment of ages on the Draw-a-person test by male neuropsychiatric patients. *J. Bers.,* 1951, **19,** 440–448.

Grotjahn, M. Psychoanalytic investigation of a 71-year-old man with senile dementia. *Psychoanal. Quart.,* 1940, **9,** 39–47.

Gruhle, H. W. Suicide in old age. *Ztschr. Alternforsch.,* 1941, **3,** 21–502.

Halstead, W. C. *Brain and intelligence.* Chicago: Univer. of Chicago Press, 1947.

Hamilton, G. V. Changes in personality and psychosexual phenomena with age. In E. V. Cowdry (Ed.), *Problems of aging.* Baltimore: Williams & Wilkins, 1942.

Havighurst, R. J. *Interpersonal aspects of gerontology.* Transactions of the Twelfth Conference on Problems of Aging. New York: Josiah Macy, Jr., Foundation, 1950.

Havighurst, R. J. Sociology, psychology, education and religion. *Trans. fourteenth Conf. Problems Aging,* 1952.

Havighurst, R. J. Successful aging. *Gerontologist,* 1961, **1,** 8–13.

Heston, J. C., & Cannell, C. F. A note on the relation between age and performance of adult subjects on four familiar psychometric tests. *J. appl. Psychol.*, 1941, **25**, 415–419.

Hopkins, B., & Roth, M. Psychological test performance in patients over sixty. *J. ment. Sci.*, 1953, **99**, 451–463.

Jelliuik, E. M. Phases in the drinking history of alcoholics. *Quart. J. Stud. Alcohol*, 1946.

Kallman, F. J. *Genetic aspects of psychosis in biology of mental health and diseases.* New York: Hoeber-Harper, 1950.

Kaplan, O. J. (Ed.) *Mental disorders in later life.* (2nd ed.) Stanford, Calif.: Stanford Univer. Press, 1956.

Kaufman, M. R. Old age and aging: the psychoanalytic point of view. *Amer. J. Orthopsychiat.*, 1940, **19**, 73–79.

Klopfer, W. G. Personality patterns of old age. *Rorschach Res. Exch.*, 1946, **10**, 145–166.

Klopfer, W. G. Attitudes toward death in the aged. Unpublished master's thesis, Coll. of the City of New York, 1947.

Klopfer, W. G. The role of a clinical psychologist in a home for the aged. *Geriatrics,* 1951, **6**, 404–406.

Klopfer, W. G. The application of the Rorschach technique to geriatrics. In B. Klopfer et al., *Developments in the Rorschach technique.* Vol. II. New York: Harcourt, Brace & World, 1954.

Klopfer, W. G. Psychological stresses of old age. *Geriatrics,* 1958, **XIII**, 529–531.

Kounin, J. S. Experimental studies of rigidity. *Charact. & Pers.*, 1941, **9**, 251–282.

Kuhlen, R. G. Aging and life-adjustment. In J. E. Birren (Ed.), *Handbook of aging and the individual.* Chicago: Univer. of Chicago Press, 1959.

Lakin, M. Clinical use of the Bender Visual Motor Test in psychological assessment of the aged. *J. Amer. geriat. Soc.*, 1956, **4**, 909–919.

Light, B. H., & Amick, J. H. Rorschach responses of normal aged. *J. proj. Tech.*, 1956, **20**, 185–195.

Malamud, W. Problems of aging: psychopathological aspects. *Trans. twelfth Conf. Problems Aging.* 1950.

Mayer-Gross, W., Slater, E., & Roth, M. *Clinical psychiatry.* Baltimore: Williams & Wilkins, 1955.

Metropolitan Life Insurance Company. Longevity reaches three score and 10. *Statist. Bull.*, 1956, **37**, 1–3.

Moffatt, M. P. The aging in our contemporary culture. *J. educ. Soc.*, 1959, **33**, 28–34.

Morgan, M. The attitudes and adjustments of recipients of old age assistance in upstate and metropolitan New York. *Arch. Psychol.,* 1937, **30**, 131.

National Committee against Mental Illness, Inc. *What are the facts about mental illness?* Washington, D.C., 1957.

Prados, M., & Fried, Edrita. Personality structure in the older age groups. *J. clin. Psychol.*, 1947, **3**, 113–120.

Pressey, S. L., & Kuhlen, R. G. *Psychological development through the life span.* New York: Harper & Row, 1957.

Reichard, Suzanne, Livson, Florine, & Peterson, P. Personality and aging. New York, Wiley, 1961.

Shock, N. W. The role of research in solving the problems of the aged. *Gerontologist,* 1961, **1**, 13–16.

Simmons, L. W. Social participation of the aged in different cultures. *Ann. Am. Acad. Political Social Sci.*, 1952, **279**, 43–51.

Thaler, M. Relationships among Wechsler, Weigl, Rorschach, EEG findings and abstract-concrete behavior in a group of normal aged subjects. *J. Geront.*, 1956, **11**, 404–409.

Tuckman, J., & Lorge, I. Attitudes toward the aged. *Science,* 1952, **115**, 685–687.

Tuckman, J., & Lorge, I. The projection of personal symptoms into stereotypes about aging. *J. Geront.*, 1958, **13**, 70–73.

U.S. Department of Health, Education, and Welfare, Public Health Service, National Office of Vital Statistics. The older person in the home. *Publ. Hlth Serv. Publ.*, 1957, No. 542.

Weinberg, J. Personal and social adjustment. In J. Anderson (Ed.), *Psychological aspects of aging.* Washington, D.C.: American Psychological Association, 1956. Pp. 17–20.

Whiteley, J. M., & McArthur, C. C. A study of psychogenic deafness. *J. proj. Tech.* (in press).

Williams, M. Spatial disorientation in senile dementia: the psychological mechanisms disturbed and some methods of compensation. *J. ment. Sci.*, 1956, **102**, 291–299.

31

Mental Deficiencies

KARL F. HEISER AND BENJAMIN B. WOLMAN

This chapter is entitled "Mental Deficiencies" (accent on the plural) to emphasize the fact that we are not dealing with a distinct clinical entity. Mental deficiency as a term covers a field which includes a great variety of conditions differing widely from each other in etiology, clinical patterns, and possible pathologic lesions. These conditions are grouped together because of a characteristic which is thought to be common to all: that is, a significant deficit in intellectual development. Intellectual development is frequently estimated by rate of maturation of mental activities and development of learning capacities and certain aspects of emotional adjustment and adaptation to the social environment. Accordingly, the field of mental deficiency is concerned with individuals whose adjustments, achievements, and happiness are thwarted or rendered inadequate by conditions or influences which produce a level of intellectual development markedly below normal or average.

Many terms are in popular use to denote mental deficiency. In this country "mental retardation," "mental deficiency," "mental subnormality," "mental handicap," and "feeblemindedness" are often used synonymously. In England "amentia" is widely used to denote mental deficiency. "Oligophrenia" and "hypophrenia" are not so widely employed, although they have much to recommend them.

HISTORY

In the history of man, there have always been individuals with a limited capacity for comprehending and reasoning, who fell behind intellectually and could not participate successfully in the economic, cultural, and social life. These individuals were "labeled as dumb, stupid, imbeciles and idiots and were utterly neglected, often ridiculed and exploited but never helped" (Wolman, unpublished).

Efforts to help mentally defective human beings are loosely correlated with the rise of democratic ideals. Prior to the nineteenth century, persons suffering from pronounced mental defects were considered to be absolutely and hopelessly beyond any possibility of amelioration, and no attempts were made to treat them (Tredgold, 1952). The first recorded study of the problem of helping the mentally retarded from what we might call the psychological point of view was the work of the French educationist Itard (1801), who undertook to train the "wild boy of Aveyron" found in the forest in 1798 living much as an animal. Pinel, the famous physician who examined the child, described the boy as an idiot and did not believe in the possibility of educational success. Itard, however, made some progress with the lad. The "wild boy of Aveyron" learned to communicate with speech rather than grunts and gestures, but he failed to develop adequate self-controls and was unable to adapt himself socially and emotionally to civilized living. After great efforts, Itard concluded that the boy was not only a victim of neglect but also congenitally defective.

Itard's published account directed the attention of Voisin, Esquirol, and others to the area of mental deficiency about the same time

Saegert of Berlin and Güggenbohl of Switzerland began the treatment and training of defectives. In 1842 Édouard Seguin, who had been a pupil of Itard and had already attempted to educate a defective child, was appointed to carry out his methods on the defective children of the Bicêtre. Seguin's account of his work (Seguin, 1846) showed that improvement was possible in many of these children. His patient and systematic training marks the beginning of our modern methods in this field. Thereafter the training of mental defectives began to occupy a more or less definite place in the social system of many civilized countries. Tredgold (1952) observed that the history of institutional care of retarded individuals has demonstrated two points: First, relatively few persons are so defective they cannot be improved to some extent, even if only in habits of cleanliness and the curtailing of destructive tendencies. Second, no case of true retardation (primary amentia) was ever cured. Some defect, however mild, will always remain, rendering competition on an equal footing with the normal population impossible.

In the present century, the field of mental deficiency has belonged largely to psychology and education because of the work of Binet, Goddard, and Terman. The history of intelligence tests and their significance in the diagnosis of mental deficiency will be discussed later in the chapter.

Until very recently, research and public concern with prevention and treatment of mental deficiency have been very meager indeed. Actually in the United States relatively little attention was paid to this pressing problem until the last decade (Mayo, 1962). There was hardly a state with a fully developed service or training program in mental retardation as a part of its regular maternal and child health program.

In later years, however, the climate has changed. Starting in 1954, state programs began to improve and expand. Today nearly every state has special projects in mental retardation in its maternal and child health program. Medical research relating to mental retardation has begun in a number of leading universities. More funds are constantly being made available. In 1961, the National Institute of Mental Health alone spent over 2.5 million dollars on research, technical assistance, and grants for studies in mental retardation (Mayo, 1962).

INCIDENCE

Considerable variations may be noted in the estimates of investigators regarding the incidence of mental deficiency in the general population. Since different criteria are used for diagnosis—social adjustment, academic achievement, intelligence-test scores, and institutionalization—it is inevitable that the resulting figures will disagree. Figures will also vary according to samples and conditions. The more advanced or mechanized or complex and educated populations surveyed have given larger percentages. Urban communities have had a higher incidence than rural environments. Also in depressed areas of low employment, poor standards of living, malnutrition, inferior educational facilities, and high mobility we find a greater incidence of mental deficiency.

According to a recent survey sponsored by the National Association for Retarded Children, where the criterion of disability was the inability to obtain gainful employment, it was estimated that

> with the possible exception of mental illness, mental subnormality is the most significant handicap of our present society. Of the 4,200,000 children born annually in the United States, 3 per cent (126,000) will never achieve the intellect of a 12-year-old child, 0.3 per cent (12,600) will remain below the seven year intellectual level and 0.1 per cent (4200), if they survive, will spend their lives as completely helpless imbeciles, unable even to care for their own creature needs (Masland, Sarason, & Gladwin, 1958, p. 3).

Mayo, who was chairman of President Kennedy's Panel on Mental Retardation, reports (1962) that some five million people in the United States are mentally retarded to some degree.

On the basis of the data available at present, it may be assumed that the estimated frequency of mental deficiency in the population of Western civilization is about 2 per cent. Within a mentally defective population, it is estimated that about 75 per cent show mild defect (morons), 20 per cent moderate defect, and not more than 5 per cent severe defect (idiots) (Jervis, 1959).

CLASSIFICATION

Before the era of intelligence testing it was customary to classify mentally defective people in three categories, based upon the observable degree of the defect. According to this scheme, an individual would be called a high-grade defective or feeble-minded if he were in the most able of the three categories, an imbecile if he were in the middle category, and an idiot if in a most defective group.

Today we have a great variety of classification schemes depending upon the field or discipline from which the classification is approached. The chief systems are as follows.

According to Mental Ability

This system dates back to 1884, when Galton established the Anthropometric Laboratory. Galton's work was carried on by James Sully and by students, of whom many became well-known psychologists, including Sir Cyril Burt, J. M. Cattell, and Karl Pearson. Galton's clinical laboratory was set up for the purpose of testing the mental, sensory, and physical capacities and abilities of children, who were graded according to these tests. It was Cattell who brought the new ideas and methods to the University of Pennsylvania, resulting in the organization there of the first American psychological clinic under Lightner Wittmer.

In 1905 Binet and Simon published the first scale for measuring intelligence by means of tests. The purpose of Binet's work was to give Paris school officials a method by which they could predict academic achievement and thus devote more effort to those with the greatest promise, shunting inferior scholars to training of a less intellectual sort. In 1906 Elizabeth S. Kite of the research department of The Training School at Vineland was in Paris and learned about Binet's work. She translated Binet's scale into English and persuaded Goddard, the head of her department, of the tests' utility in classifying the feeble-minded. Thus the Vineland Revision of the Binet scale came into being and was announced publicly in 1910 at the meeting of heads of institutions for the feeble-minded (Goddard, 1910). This Vineland Revision was gradually accepted by teachers and psychologists in institutions and training schools. Goddard suggested the Greek term "moron" to represent the classification hitherto called high-grade feeble-minded, so that "feeble-minded" now became the generic term. Goddard used Binet's concept of mental age according to the level of success in tests of progressive difficulty.

William Stern in Germany suggested in 1912 the concept of relating mental age, its acceleration or retardation, to the child's chronological age. Mental age divided by chronological age and multiplied by 100 became known as the intellience quotient, or IQ. Whenever mental development keeps pace with the child's age, the IQ is average or 100. Whenever mental development is ahead of the chronological age, the IQ is above average and more than 100. Whenever mental development lags behind, the IQ is below average, below 100.

Next, Lewis M. Terman, who, like Goddard, received his psychological training under G. Stanley Hall at Clark University, embarked upon the task of standardizing the Binet scale of age-level tests for the American population. His first revision, called the Stanford-Binet, was published in 1916. A new revision with improved standardization and two comparable forms, L and M, was published in 1937. A new, one-form L-M revised version of the Stanford-Binet tests was published in 1960.

The most popular definition of mental deficiency hinged on intellectual efficiency as measured by standardized psychological tests of intelligence. Within the range of IQ from 0 to 70 three categories have been distinguished: idiot, imbecile, and moron. The simplicity of this psychometric definition has had some unfortunate results. It imputes a totally unreasonable omniscience to the intelligence test, a power which has been seldom, if ever, claimed by test constructors. This definition assumes, also, a greater constancy in the IQ than has ever been demonstrated, and it neglects the broad practical problems in such areas as the physical, medical, social, and personality development and functions. Although the psychometric approach has been of considerable value in regard to such problems as classification, administration, and education, it has serious limitations as the sole criterion for mental deficiency (Heiser, 1952; Wolman, 1938; 1943; 1957).

The psychometric criterion has been concerned with the individual's rank in the population in regard to performance on intelligence tests. The IQ range of 70 to 80 is usually accepted as the area which separates mental deficiency from normality. There is no particular reason for choosing the IQ of 70 as the absolute lower limit of normality; it is merely an arbitrary figure. There is no assurance that an IQ of 70 from one test is comparable with an IQ of 70 from some other scale since, among other things, standard deviations may vary from test to test. It seems reasonable to believe that a statistical definition of mental deficiency and a standard deviation to be used for tests of intelligence will be generally accepted. Such a system would permit us to measure the level of mental deficiency by standard deviations (Heiser, 1952). In fact, such a system was introduced by Heber (1959).

Another imperfection of intelligence tests is that they are not culture-free. Like any other test, they measure performance, and all performance is influenced by learning opportunities and experience. Children of newly arrived migrants, of slum areas, of underprivileged minority groups, of broken homes, etc., may obtain lower IQ scores although there is no reason to believe that they are necessarily defective or pathological (see Goodenough & Morris, 1950; Klineberg, 1935; Garth, 1935; Wolman, 1949).

Finally, emotionally disturbed children sometimes fail intelligence tests because they cannot concentrate or are easily distracted or preoccupied or worried or afraid of the test or examiner. One investigator found that the IQ of schizophrenic children "would range from moron to normal, depending on who did the testing" (Kaufman, 1962, p. 274).

According to Social Criteria

The social criteria are concerned chiefly with adjustment and self-direction. In England the legal concept of mental deficiency is based on social incapacity (Tredgold, 1952). In this country also it is quite common for the maladjusted or delinquent individual who exhibits faulty social judgment to be called mentally defective even if his IQ is in the dull normal range between 80 and 90. This confusion of social and intellectual deficiency is partly due to the tendency to find a diagnosis which will enable one to give a particular individual the most beneficial treatment. According to this social definition, an individual with IQ of 65 would almost inevitably be called mentally deficient in a modern, urban environment, whereas he might not be thought defective if he seemed to make a satisfactory social adjustment in an environment in which the social and vocational demands were limited and simple (see Kanner, 1948, p. 71).

The psychometric and social definitions or criteria illustrate two major areas of concern with the problem of mental deficiency. The former is the natural outgrowth of the work of educators and their psychological collaborators whose objectives have been measurement of intellectual performance in relationship to education. The latter definition illustrates society's concern with management of a serious social problem in a complex competitive society. In considering the criteria for mental deficiency, it is well to remember, as McCulloch (1947) points out, that the term "mental deficiency" often represents an administrative grouping that changes as social standards and requirements change. The association between intellectual and social competence is low among the higher-grade defectives, and prognoses vary widely. Tredgold strongly favors the social criteria. He states:

> The essential purpose of mind is that of enabling the individual to make a satisfactory and independent adaptation to the ordinary environment of his fellows; it would be intolerable if a person able to do this, to earn his living and to manage himself and his affairs with reasonable prudence and efficiency, were to be stigmatized as defective, and subject to control, merely on the ground of illiteracy and poor scholastic attainments, or because he failed to come up to some arbitrarily fixed intelligence quotient. Hence I regard the social as not only the most logical and scientific concept of mental deficiency, but as the only criterion which the community can justly impose (Tredgold, 1952, p. 5).

According to Etiology

Several systems have been suggested. Ideally an etiologic classification should be recommended; it is, however, difficult to apply it in several cases where etiologic data are insufficient or contradictory. Furthermore, there are several types of mental defect in which the etiology is largely unknown. In addition, more than one etiologic factor may be responsible for the defect in some individuals. Nevertheless, it is only from a grouping of patients according to etiologic factors, even though the grouping may be imperfect, that one can hope for a better understanding of the nature of mental deficiency and a rational guide to preventive and therapeutic measures (Jervis, 1959).

An early etiological classification system still used is that of Tredgold (1908), who advanced a system with four main groups:

1. Primary amentia, in which the deficiency is due to germinal or endogenous factors or simply to heredity.
2. Secondary amentia in which the deficiency is due to exogenous factors, to causes from the environment.
3. Amentia due to mixed or combined, or both hereditary and environmental, causes.
4. Amentia with unknown cause.

Prenatal. In the early years of research on mental deficiency it was assumed by most investigators that primary amentia—mental deficiency due to poor heredity—accounted for 90 per cent of the cases. This seems to have been based on what we would now call a sampling error; that is, the early investigators thought that the people whom they examined were typical of all mental defectives. Goddard's (1912) book *The Kallikak Family* did much to foster this erroneous belief. It seems strange to us now that the early researchers would make the error of thinking that the institutionalized defectives, on whom most research was done, were typical of all such children. Obviously, people with severe intellectual handicaps are not able to compete successfully in our society and thus support their families. It is natural that their children should be preponderantly represented in public institutions.

As investigations progressed, the estimates of the proportion of mental deficiency due to heredity steadily decreased. The percentages have almost reversed in the last fifty years. Instead of the 90 per cent due to heredity and 10 per cent to all other causes, we might estimate now that 10 per cent are due to heredity and 90 per cent to other causes. What are some of the other causes of secondary amentia, and how do we classify them?

Sometimes they are classified according to their time of operation. Thus, we have prenatal exogenous factors, which include all sorts of infections; metabolic, nutritive, or poisonous agents; and physical or mechanical accidents and interventions occurring between the time of conception and birth. Then, we have paranatal causes, which include all the same kinds of factors operating immediately before, during, and soon after birth. Finally, there are postnatal causes, including the same sort of factors but operating any time after birth.

Of late there has been much interest in the role of blood types and the Rh factor. Yannet and Lieberman (1948) discovered the possibility that A and B isoimmunization or maternal ABO incompatibility is a significant factor in the etiology of the undifferentiated cases of deficiency. Despite some negative findings, several investigators have found evidence for the Rh factor as one of the agencies contributing to mental deficiency.

Birth injuries. The significance of birth injuries or paranatal factors as causes of mental deficiency has been stressed by several research workers. A broad and still significant discussion of birth injuries, infections, toxic process, prematurity, asphyxia, hemorrhages, and trauma of the skull is given by Alpers (1949).

Certain conditions such as prolonged labor and eclampsia are associated with lower IQs in children, according to Battle (1949), who studied the birth records of 453 high school pupils. However, normal delivery at full term does not preclude serious intracranial birth injury (DeLange, 1950). Furthermore, it cannot be assumed that birth injury always means mental deficiency or retardation. More attention has been given recently to the development of methods to determine to what extent the organic defects of the brain-injured result in mental deficiency (Krout, 1949).

In reference to birth injuries, there is no doubt that accidents during the delivery do account for some cases of mental deficiency. Sometimes hospital nurses delay or impede delivery until the obstetrician arrives, thus causing prolonged labor dangerous for the child's mental development. If the child turns out later to be mentally defective, it is sometimes assumed that the forceps and the physical injuries caused the mental deficiency. However, the evidence for mental deficiency due to damage by obstetricians at delivery is rather inadequate. Great stresses and strains occur in what is called cephalopelvic dystocia when the infant's head is too large for the opening between the mother's pelvic bones.

Even from such a condition there is little evidence of permanently impairing the child's intelligence. The greatest likelihood of such damage at birth seems to occur from asphyxia or anoxia. Considerable damage may be caused when the child's head is pounded against the pelvic bones during labor, and the rapid and great changes of external pressures upon the head may cause a rupture of cerebral arterioles. Severe damage may be caused when the child is suffocated by lack of oxygen or strangled by the umbilical cord or injured by the use of analgesic drugs to relieve the mother's suffering.

Although birth injury due to mechanical means is probably less frequent than was formerly thought, it seems likely that premature birth may be responsible for a great amount of damage to the child's mental development. For example, Masland, Sarason, and Gladwin (1958) found in follow-up studies of infants born prematurely an increased incidence of mental retardation, especially in the cases of very premature births. Prematurity may be defined as an unusually light weight at birth (in the United States, less than 5 pounds) as well as birth before the normal term of nine months. But it must be pointed out that prematurity of birth in a child who is later found to be mentally defective does not establish a causal relationship between the two phenomena. Prematurity may be a result of the prenatal pathologies that cause mental deficiency, and it may be also the cause of deficiency. It is more probable that difficult deliveries are a product of prenatal pathologies that often cause mental deficiency than that the mental deficiencies are the result of birth injuries. Neonatal jaundice or kernicterus is one paranatal etiologic agent which accounts for a significant number of cases of mental deficiency.

Postnatal causes. The postnatal causes or conditions that prevent normal intellectual development are many and complex. Here the influence of environment becomes especially apparent, although from the time of conception until birth environmental factors are certainly as significant as any other. The postnatal factors may be thought of as falling into two groups: (1) physical injuries to the organism, especially to the central nervous system, such as cerebral vascular pathologies, diseases of the nervous system (especially the encephalitidies which attack the tissues covering the brain and nerves), and the convulsive disorders; and (2) psychological noxious factors. Emotional deprivation, poverty of environmental, cultural, and intellectual stimulation, and sensory deprivation rate high among the psychological factors.

Combined causes. It is evident, of course, that anyone may be classified according to more than one cause by this system. There may be many instances in which both heredity and disease or environmental conditions are jointly responsible for the mental deficiency. And, finally, Tredgold's system has a category for those of unknown etiology. Many writers have called these latter cases pseudo feeble-minded, but it is likely that the cause would fall into one of the categories if more were known about the history of the case.

From the clinical point of view, most mental defectives are to be classified according to physical symptoms, disease processes, and the causes of the condition. Thus, it is of more significance to call an individual a mongoloid or a microcephalic than to say that his IQ is 45 and his capacity for social adjustment is defective (Heiser, 1952). The clinical view is represented by Yannet (1945), who recommends the following twelve etiologic categories, said to encompass 70 per cent of institutionalized mental defectives: (1) familial defective, (2) cerebral palsy, (3) mongolism, (4) epilepsy, (5) infection, (6) trauma, (7) craniofacial defects, (8) phenylpyruvic amentia, (9) cerebral lipidosis, (10) cretinism, (11) muscular dystrophy, and (12) congenital ectodermosis.

Organic versus functional. Another system of classification closely related to Tredgold's and based upon etiologic factors has only two main headings: (1) organic and (2) functional. Other terms which may be substituted are (1) causes which operate through the direct impairment of the physical organism and its physiology so that normal intellectual powers and efficiency do not develop and (2) psychologic causes which impair the functioning of the organism through disturbances in the sensory field.

Hereditary impairment or genic defects responsible for Tredgold's primary amentia and familial deficiency are classified under group 1. Psychogenic factors such as environmental poverty and emotional deprivation would be subsumed under group 2.

This kind of system was proposed by Lewis (1933), who suggested the terms "pathological" and "subcultural." The etiologies of the "pathological" group could be organic or genic or environmental in the sense of disease or accidental injury. The latter group is, thus, psychogenic in origin.

Although this classification system fits our conventional patterns of dichotomous thinking in terms of things being either physical, organic, and tangible on one hand or conceptual, functional, and psychologic on the other, we should not think of these categories as being mutually exclusive (Wolman, 1964). They are not. There is probably no physical handicap which does not have its psychological effects on behavior, and there is very likely to be one or another physical concomitant of any strong psychological force or reaction. Certainly the typical familial defective child has psychological barriers to growth and the lack of intellectual stimulus in his early development as a result of the cultural poverty in his environment, and it seems quite possible that any emotional reaction sufficiently deep and serious to disturb intellectual capacity would have its effects upon the individual's physical and organic health.

Wolman classification. Another variation of an etiologic classification has recently been proposed by Wolman (1964). As a central part of his system, Wolman suggests the omission of three distinct categories of individuals who receive low IQ scores, yet are not mentally abnormal. To the first category belong otherwise normal individuals whose IQs occupy the end of the normal curve of distribution. It is fairly well established that the distribution of intelligence approximates a normal curve. At the low end of the scale the distribution is skewed, apparently because of the presence in this sector of pathological mental defectives. However, the bulk of this sector consists of the "normal low IQ" population. These individuals form an integral part of the general population, just as much as individuals of superior intelligence with an IQ of 130 or above. From the basis of the normal curve, it is evident that the largest number of these people will be in the moron classification and a very small number at the low level of intelligence. According to Wolman, children with a low IQ but no other problems are normal although, unfortunately, not too bright. Educators may worry what to do about them, but clinicians need not. In fact, several studies (Benda, 1954) have shown that individuals within three standard deviations (IQ 67 to 52) can become self-supporting, raise a family, and participate in the life of their community. The low IQ per se is not necessarily detrimental to their adjustment; whenever it is, this is because, as Kanner has put it (1948), their shortcomings "appear as soon as scholastic curricula demand competition."

Educationally retarded children belong to the second category, improperly classified as mentally deficient. These are the children who fail intelligence tests primarily because the tests are not culture-free and, as a rule, favor urban middle- and upper-class populations. Furthermore, the results obtained on intelligence tests are frequently influenced by learning opportunities and experience. Studies conducted in Israel (Wolman, 1946, 1949) found that children of immigrants from Asia and Africa scored lower on intelligence tests than children from European-American stock. Cultural factors appeared to determine the outcome of mental measurements.

The third group that Wolman suggests to exclude from genuine mental deficiency comprises those whose apparent deficiency is actually related to neuroses or psychoses. These are individuals who obtain low scores for intelligence but whose IQ changes with each testing to such an extent that all efforts to assess their intelligence are rendered useless. Potter (1927) found in schizophrenic and schizoid children loss of interest in their immediate environment, dereistic thinking, bizarre associations, symbolization, condensation, perseveration, and incoherence. Obviously such children are often erroneously classified as mentally defective. Psychotic children have a short span of attention, are easily distracted, fear failure, and often give the impression of being mentally defective (Wolman, 1938). One investigator (Richards, 1957) found 22 schizophrenic children in an institution for the mentally defective.

Neurotic conflict, also, can lead to an inadequate performance on a mental test. Some neurotic children fail aptitude and achievement tests because they lack self-confidence and are afraid that they may be wrong in their answers. Obsessive-compulsive individuals who are overconscientious and pedantic may be so slow and persevering that they fail on tests. Anxious and insecure children often have speech and reading difficulties that may lead to an over-all failure in scholastic achievements.

In Wolman's classificatory system of mental disorders mental deficiency is not a clinical entity. It is merely a syndrome that accompanies several organic disorders, such as the cases of Down syndrome (mongolism), cretinism, phenylketonuria, and other *organic* conditions. Jervis (1959) has described these conditions as "pathological mental deficiency."

The classification system of choice depends upon the uses to which it is to be put. If one wishes to measure potentials or academic achievement or education, it is likely that a classification based upon IQ will be the most useful. If one wishes the classification system to aid in the development of research which might lead to prevention and treatment, it is obvious that one based upon etiology would be preferable. And if we are interested in classification in connection with vocational training and placement, we are likely to need two systems, one based upon intellectual efficiency and another based upon physical and social skills or competence.

CLINICAL PATTERNS

Mental deficiency which has alternately been called oligophrenia, pathological mental deficiency, and clinical mental deficiency is primarily a biological failure, an organic inadequacy which, in turn, leads to a failure in social adjustment. In many cases the social and educational neglect makes the failure even more severe; on the other hand, the best social and educational care can only alleviate the situation but cannot remedy it. Mental deficiency, much like the organic mental disorders, cannot be cured with psychological and educational methods. It is a serious impairment of the total personality structure with most pronounced inability to grow intellectually or with cessation of or deterioration in the intellectual development (Wolman, in press).

A major category in oligophrenia, or true mental deficiency, is deficiency due to inheritance. In this grouping the cause of the defect is completely, or for the most part, germinal. It is therefore termed idiopathic, endogenous, or primary oligophrenia.

The primary oligophrenia, called "oligoencephaly" by Benda (1954, p. 1130), is frequently accompanied by physical anomalies. The oligophrenics who belong to this group show definite asymmetries in their physical development. Frequently there are noticable differences between the right and left parts of the body; the joints display unusual flexibility; the extremities are cold and moist; and there are noticeable irregularities in the nervous system. Delay in ossification, as shown by x-ray examination of the wrists in children, is frequently present. Abnormal conditions of the skeleton are of common occurrence, the cranium, palate, jaws, and teeth being most frequently affected. The most important anomalies of the circulatory and respiratory systems are stenosis of the pulmonary artery and defects of the auricular and ventricular septa. The heart is usually smaller than that of a normal person of corresponding weight (Tredgold, 1952). Benda's (1954) anatomical studies found the brains to be much below the average size and weight. Nerve cells are smaller than average and irregular. Circulation is poor; the heat-regulating mechanism is imperfect; digestion is often so defective that in spite of abundance of wholesome food, they remain small and stunted. While there are many individual exceptions, it may be said of primary oligophrenics in general that their resistance to disease is decidedly low. Thus disease is easily contracted and often proves fatal. In fact, as Tredgold pointed out (1952, p. 141), the life history of many of them may be stated in two words: "defective vitality" of both brain and mind.

Clinical Varieties of Primary Oligophrenia

While primary oligophrenics differ widely among themselves and while many of them, especially those of low grade, suffer from various anatomical abnormalities and pathological lesions, in the majority of cases there is no reason to regard them as special clinical types. They may be considered the simple or undifferentiated variety of primary oligophrenia. A small proportion, however, do possess certain anatomical, pathological, or physiognomic features which are sufficiently pronounced to be placed in special clinical categories, as described below. It is likely that further research will enable the placement of all of them in specific categories.

Microcephaly. This term is applied to a mentally defective person whose skull, on completion of development, is less than 17 inches in its greatest circumference. Microcephalics are generally of small stature, with an extremely small head. Their number is not large: probably not more than about 5 per cent of all defective children under ten years of age (Tredgold, 1952). Some microcephalics die in childhood. Microcephaly can be either produced by genetic factors (true microcephaly) or developed in the intrauterine life as a result of a disease of the cerebrum. The occurrence of the intrauterine microcephaly has been related to infectious diseases and even to overdose of x rays (Murphy, 1928). The true or primary microcephaly is probably a recessive genetic disorder (Jervis, 1959).

Although many microcephalics are on the level of idiots or imbeciles, some morons have been reported. The microcephalics on the moron level are usually very active; they may learn to read and write and become partially self-supporting. Those on the level of idiocy are mute. Most microcephalics are well developed physically with muscular ability well preserved. A greatly reduced sensitivity to pain has been found in many of the cases.

Macrocephaly. The brain of the macrocephalic infant weighs more than the normal neonate brain and continues to grow disproportionately to his body. Convulsions are a frequent symptom; also vision is often impaired. Macrocephaly is usually associated with a very low IQ.

Macrocephaly is believed to be caused by a neoplasm or growth in the brain tissues. Too few cases have been reported to warrant a definite conclusion as to the exact nature of the genetic mechanism.

Hydrocephaly. Hydrocephaly is a result of an accumulation of the spinal fluid in the ventricular system. In this disorder, the head becomes enlarged by the progressive accumulation of fluid within the ventricular cavities and the brain is damaged by the continuous pressure. Hydrocephaly can be either produced by genetic factors or developed by various infections. Hydrocephaly may be a result of a lack of development of the cortical fluid or the hyperproduction of the spinal fluid caused by certain infections, particularly syphilis, tuberculosis, and tumors. Meningitis and perineuritis are other infectious diseases which may prevent or substantially reduce normal absorption of the spinal fluid. Operative procedure aimed at reestablishing fluid circulation is sometimes effective in controlling the progression of the disease.

As a result of the pressure of the spinal fluid, a more or less severe atrophy of the cortex takes place and the ability for mental functioning is badly impaired, if not completely destroyed. There are, however, mild cases of hydrocephaly with little mental impairment. Motor coordination in hydrocephalics is poor, and some of them have convulsions. Most hydrocephalics are low-grade defectives, but their IQ has been known to vary from the level of idiots up to that of morons. Tredgold (1952) hypothesized that both macrocephaly and hydrocephaly are complications of microcephaly.

Phenylketonuria or amino acid oligophrenia. Phenylketonuria is a disease characterized by mental defect and urinary excretion of phenylpyruvic acid. Phenylalanine, an essential amino acid present in all proteins, is normally catalyzed by a specific enzyme, phenylalinase. In phenylketonuria, the enzyme is missing, and the unmetabolized phenylalanine accumulates in the body fluids. However, at this time the relationship of the biochemical error to the mental deficiency is not well understood (Jervis, 1959). Electroencephalograms indicate atrophy of the frontal lobe of the cortex. The degree of mental deficiency is almost always very severe, mostly below the IQ of 25.

There is no doubt that phenylketonuria is caused by an abnormality of the germ. Penrose (1935) is of the opinion that it is due to a single recessive gene, and Munro (1941) shares his view. Treatment by low phenylalanine diets in phenylketonuric infants has been apparently successful in preventing the development of mental deficiency (Jervis, 1959).

Tuberous sclerosis. The three major symptoms are mental defect, epilepsy, and adenoma sebaceum. Where this combination is present it is practically certain that the patient has tuberous sclerosis of the brain. In the absence of adenoma sebaceum or other skin anomalies, it is rather difficult to make a positive diagnosis while the patient is alive. However, postmortem examination may subsequently reveal the presence of tuberous sclerosis of the brain and tumors of the various internal organs.

Tuberous sclerosis, also known as epiloia, is a characteristic form of neuroectodermic mental deficiency. The adenoma sebaceum consists of a nodular rash covering the nose and the cheeks in a butterfly shape. Tredgold (1952) estimated that the number of cases of tuberous sclerosis was not more than 0.5 per cent of all mental defectives. Mental defect is usually pronounced in degree and often increases with advancing age. Psychotic manifestations are frequent. Convulsions are usually severe and of the grand mal type. They may start in the patient's first year and continue throughout life. Genetic causation is apparent in about a third of the cases, the pedigree being consistent with the hypothesis of a single dominant gene (Borberg, 1951). There is no known effective treatment for this disease. Life expectancy is shortened by frequent occurrences of malignant tumors.

Cerebral lipidoses. This is the name given to a group of rare diseases characterized by the storage of certain complex lipids in the central nervous system (Van Creveld, 1953). These diseases are associated with an enlarged liver and spleen. Mental defect is an outstanding feature, and familial incidence is typical. Each condition is characterized by the accumulation of a different lipid substance.

The best-known disorder of this group is amaurotic idiocy or Tay-Sachs disease. It usually starts before the tenth month of life and leads gradually to severe intellectual deterioration, blindness, seizures, and motor impairment. When the disease starts before the end of the first year of life, death usually occurs before the end of the third year of life.

Several studies describe cases of "juvenile" amaurotic idiocy that started later in life and were protracted (Jervis, 1939; Marburg, 1942). Here the onset is at 5 to 6 years, and death occurs between 15 and 18 years. The pathological picture is similar to but less conspicuous than that seen in "infantile" amaurotic idiocy. Amaurotic idiocy is believed to be a recessively inherited disorder.

Another well-known type of cerebral lipidosis is known as gargoylism or Hurler's syndrome. An enlargement of the liver has been observed, as well as an accumulation of fat and glycogen in the liver, spleen, and lungs. The physical characteristics include stunted growth, enlarged head, coarse grotesque face (hence the term "gargoyle"), a short neck, and thick nose and lips. According to Jervis (1959), the disease can be transmitted in two different manners: as an autosomal recessive character and as a sex-linked recessive with only males affected.

Mongolism. Mongolism, or congenital acromicria (Benda, 1949), is a frequent type of oligophrenia. It occurs about four times per thousand births in the United States and comprises close to 10 per cent of all mentally defective individuals.

The physical symptoms associated with mongolism are easily recognizable. The skin is milk-white-rosy and delicate, the belly is protruding, the extremities are smaller than normal, the genital organs are small and rudimentary, and speech is retarded or completely missing. Other characteristics include a broad, flattened, depressed face with a short, wide nose having a sunken bridge. The eyes of the mongoloid tend to slant upward and outward owing to the formation of an internal epicanthus. Also noticeable are the mongoloid's short, stumpy hands with the characteristic shortenings and depression of the middle phalanx of the fifth finger. Instead of the whorls found in the fingerprints of other types of mental defectives and of normal people, the mongoloid shows a series of loops (MacGillvray, 1959). Congenital defects of the heart are present in about one-fifth of the cases. Other malformations include anal atresia, pyloric stenosis, megacolon, and syndactylia (Jervis, 1959).

The etiologic factors responsible for mongolism are not completely known. Benda (1949; 1960), Ingalls (1952), and Beidelman (1955) believe that the difficulty lies in maternal inner secretory responses. The mother's condition, either at the beginning of pregnancy or shortly thereafter, is regarded by Benda (1960) as the significant factor. He dismisses the possibility of the cause lying with the father, for no consistent anomalies have ever been found on the paternal side.

Eighty per cent of the mothers of mongoloids are between 30 and 45 years of age, the average age being 41 at the time of birth of the defective child (Goldstein, 1954). More than 50 per cent of women bearing mongoloid children were beyond the age of 35 when the mongoloid child was born. Menopausal imbalance is believed to be an important factor in the etiology of mongolism.

The mother's specific physical condition at the time of pregnancy is stressed by Goldstein (1954), who found that very often a mongoloid child is born when she is on the threshold of sterility. There is a high incidence of interrupted pregnancies among these mothers just prior to the conception resulting in the defective child. These interruptions take the form of abortions, both induced and spontaneous, miscarriages, bleeding, etc. These terminated pregnancies may also be due in part to nutritional deficiencies in the mother. According to Goldstein, the intake of protein in those mothers fell below the average during their pregnancies.

The genetic mechanism seems to be of great significance in the causation of mongolism. The incidence of the disease in the same family is of the order of 4 per cent, or 20 times greater than in the general population (Böök & Reed, 1950). A study of twins shows that monozygotic twins are always concordant and dizygotic twins, with few exceptions, discordant (Jervis, 1959). According to Penrose (1954), minor defects are present in the relatives of patients with the overt disorder. He hypothesized that mongolism is due to a recessive mechanism, the responsible gene being quite common but with a manifestation hindered by protective factors which are inherent in younger women but decrease with advancing age.

A new and most important discovery in the field of genetocytology came with the study of Lejeune, Gautier, and Turpin (1959) on the human chromosome in tissue culture. They reported finding a supernumerary (extra) chromosome in mongoloids. Until recently it has been believed that man had 48 chromosomes. It is presently known that normal human beings have only 46 chromosomes, whereas the mongoloid defective has 47.

It has not yet been demonstrated whether the accessory chromosome in mongolism is genetically active (Benda, 1960). The way the extra chromosome produces mongolism is also a controversial issue (Rowley, 1962). The supernumerary chromosome is the same size as the Y chromosome. Some investigators think there may be a relationship between mongolism and the Y chromosome, since sex anomalies are extremely frequent in this condition (Benda, 1960). Jacobs et al. suggest that there is a cytoplasmic dysfunction which impairs the life of the cell in the mongoloid, including the cellular life of all the organ systems.

SECONDARY OLIGOPHRENIA AND ITS CLINICAL VARIETIES

In secondary oligophrenia, the potentiality of the germ cell is normal. However, arrest or impairment of brain development has been brought about by some adverse environmental influence acting directly upon the child either before, during, or at some period after birth. Secondary oligophrenia can be divided into types according to the agent—infectious, toxic, traumatic, or endocrine in nature—causing the defect (Jervis, 1959). Unlike primary oligophrenia, in most cases of the secondary form the family history is normal. Furthermore, there is usually fairly clear evidence of the operation of some adequate external cause, and the child's appearance and physical development, apart from conditions consequent on the cerebral lesion, do not differ significantly from those of the ordinary child.

Secondary Oligophrenia Due to Infections

This group includes all those cases of mental defect in which the arrest of development has been brought about by some infection of the nervous system. According to Tredgold (1952) these comprise approximately 11 per cent of all oligophrenics. In the majority of cases in this grouping, the infection causes an inflammation of the brain or its membranes. The amount of brain damage varies considerably, according to the particular type of infectious agent, the severity of the acute process, and the age of the patient at the time of infection (Jervis, 1959).

Syphilitic oligophrenia. Syphilitic infection (by *Treponema pallidum*) may be transmitted during pregnancy from the infected mother to the fetus. If this happens early, miscarriage is produced. If it occurs later in pregnancy, the child may be born with signs of congenital syphilis, and diffuse or localized meningovascular lesions may result. In a considerable number of cases where syphilis is acquired *in utero* the child is born dead. Some of those born alive present no abnormality of mental development beyond being small, anemic, and underweight. Others are intellectually dull, and a proportion are mentally defective. Previously, the incidence of this type of mental deficiency was estimated at 2 to 5 per cent of the defective population. However, this has been reduced to a fraction of 1 per cent by the adoption of routine serological tests of pregnant women and consequent treatment of infected mothers (Jervis, 1959).

Oligophrenia Due to Encephalitis in Infancy or Childhood

Encephalitis is not particularly rare in infancy and childhood. Many patients make a complete recovery; others die during the acute phase of the disease; but a small number recover with sequelae, among which mental defect is one of the most common (Brain, Hunter, & Turnbull, 1929; Jervis, 1959). Cerebrospinal meningitis, encephalitis lethargica, and encephalitis complicating acute infectious diseases, such as measles, chicken pox, whooping cough, and scarlet fever, have also been known to produce mental deficiency as aftereffects (Penrose, 1954a). The increased use of antibiotics during the acute phase of the disease has resulted in a decrease of death rate and in a noticeable increase of defective patients. Postencephalitic children often undergo a complete alteration of character. The individual who has previously been well behaved now has episodes of overactivity, restlessness, impulsiveness, assaultiveness, and wantom destruction. It is estimated that encephalitis is responsible for about 5 per cent of all institutionalized defectives (Jervis, 1959).

Oligophrenia Due to Rubella in the Mother

In recent years attention has been drawn to the harmful effects of maternal rubella, or German measles, in the first three months of pregnancy. In an Australian epidemic reported by Gregg (1941), several mothers were affected and those who caught the disease during the first three months of pregnancy gave birth to defective infants. The children showed a variety of abnormalities, including deafness, blindness due to cataract or retinitis, heart malformation, and mental deficiency. Since that time physicians have been on the alert to discover similar cases, and a great many have been found (Penrose, 1954a). Other virus diseases besides rubella that have been demonstrated as causes of prenatal brain damage are cytomegalic inclusion disease, equine encephalitis, and mumps (Jervis, 1959).

Toxic Oligophrenia Due to Radiation or X-ray Therapy

Exposure to radiation or x-ray therapy is injurious to fetal growth. D. P. Murphy (1928) found several cases of various developmental abnormalities in children of mothers subjected to pelvic irradiation during pregnancy. Most frequently these were cases of arrested cerebral development, particularly microcephaly. A few similar microcephalic children were born in Japan to pregnant women who had received a large amount of radiation from atomic explosions (Jervis, 1959).

Oligophrenia Due to Lead Poisoning

Lead poisoning is a cause of retardation of intellectual development. Cases of lead poisoning are seen in very young children when the tendency to put things in the mouth is prevalent. Poisoning may follow a single ingestion of large amounts or the repeated ingestion of very small amounts of lead. In lead-poisoning cases, mental deficiency is usually severe, with convulsions being frequently observed.

Oligophrenia Due to Rh Blood Factor Incompatibility

Another cause of mental defect which may act while the child is *in utero* is hemolysis of the blood and damage to the brain cells by Rh blood factor incompatibility. At birth these patients characteristically develop jaundice, anemia, paralysis, and convulsions, and later mental deficiency and spasticity with choreoathetosis (Jervis, 1959). Pathological lesions are found mainly in the basal ganglia (hence the term "kernicterus"). Only a small proportion of Rh-positive children from Rh-negative mothers develop the disease.

Traumatic Oligophrenia

Cerebral trauma resulting in brain damage and mental deficiency may occur before birth, at birth, or after birth. In the large majority of cases the injury is inflicted during birth. Cases of oligophrenia due to trauma before or after birth do not present any essential clinical differences. See previous discussion of birth injuries.

Oligophrenia Due to Endocrine Disturbance

It is now established that certain endocrine secretions are essential for normal brain development. However, although minor endocrine disturbances are quite common in a substantial number of defectives, in only a small proportion can there be an established etiological relationship between endocrine disorder and mental defect.

Cretinism

Cretinism is one of the severe types of secondary oligophrenia. It occurs in two forms, sporadic and endemic. Although they are both due to absence or insufficiency of the secretion of the thyroid gland, the chief difference between the endemic and sporadic cretin is that in the sporadic condition a goiter is present, although this is practically functionless.

The cretin child usually appears normal at birth, and not until the second half of the first year does his condition begin to attract attention. It becomes noticeable that he is apathetic and slow in all his movements. He fails to respond to a smile and may be so lethargic as to refuse to suck. The growth is stunted, and the head is large and disproportionate to the entire body. In the fully developed condition, the legs are extremely short and bowed, the feet and hands stumpy and malformed. The neck is short and thick, and the skin is dry, pale, and rough. The face is characteristic, with its broad, flat nose, eyes wide apart, thick lips, and large protruding tongue. The ossification of the bones is delayed considerably beyond the normal period. There is often defective hearing. The external genitals often retain an infantile appearance until past mature age, and many cretins are sterile.

Most cretins have IQs below 25, but some of them, often called "semicretins," can learn to feed and dress themselves and even to communicate verbally (Wolman, 1938; 1943). The most advanced group, the so-called "cretinoids," can attend a special school, learn simple academic skills, and even acquire a simple occupation. Children of all three types of cretinism are usually placid, quiet, good-tempered, and affectionate. According to Tredgold (1952) they are among the least troublesome of all oligophrenics.

The cause of cretinism has been shown to be insufficient iodine intake. It is frequent in mountainous areas where the soil and water contain little iodine, the main element of thyroxine. Cretinism is endemic in certain places in the Alps of Europe, the Himalayas of India, and the Andes and Rocky Mountains of America.

Administration of desiccated thyroid is the specific treatment for cretinism. In the case of very young children, only a comparatively short time is necessary to remove all the physical signs. Where the child is several years old before the treatment is initiated, the change is slower, and in those cases who have not been treated until adult life, comparatively little change takes place (Tredgold, 1952). In many cases there is also a marked improvement in intelligence. However, treatment must be begun in the early months of life if the child is to reach normal mental development.

Froelich's Syndrome

Early impairment of the pituitary gland produces dwarfism and, in a few cases, mental defect. However, the relationship is inconsistent and poorly understood.

Administration of pituitary extract has not produced any beneficial effect.

DIAGNOSIS

For a detailed description of diagnostic methods, consult the various chapters in Part 3 of the *Handbook*.

The diagnosis of mental deficiency involves all the consideration necessary for the diagnosis of any mental patient. The history is of paramount importance and should include as much as can be learned about the physical, genetic, medical, social, educational, and vocational background of the family. It should be as accurate as possible in regard to the mother's experiences in pregnancies and deliveries. The child's early physical development may give important clues, particularly his motor coordination and language development. He should be examined very carefully for sensory and muscular defects as well as peculiarities in form or stature. In the diagnosis of milder forms of deficiency, social adjustment, general behavior, educational achievement, emotional maturity, and personality traits deserve careful consideration. Individually administered intelligence tests are indispensable tools for determining the level of intellectual functioning.

Diagnostic classification of the different types of pathological mental deficiency is often dependent on the use of standard medical methodology. In earlier days it was often considered sufficient to wait until the patient was dead before attempting to discover etiological factors. However, today there are numerous special techniques particularly adapted to the study of defectives, such as opthalmoscopic examinations, skull x rays, the techniques of pneumoencephalography, the techniques of serology, tests for the excretion of hormones, etc. (Penrose, 1954a). In many cases an understanding of the formal principles of genetics and a knowledge of the analytical methods which are used in human genetics to evaluate family data are essential.

PROGNOSIS

Many authorities have written that the prognosis for mental deficiency is poor or hopeless. In fact, they have said that improvement in intellectual functioning means, *ipso facto,* that the diagnosis of mental deficiency was in error and that it must have been a case of pseudomental deficiency. The only "pseudo" is the diagnosis itself (Wolman, 1964). Actually, there is no problem about prognosis; the problem is with the definition of the pathology with which we are concerned. If we are concerned primarily with IQs below 75, we can say with some degree of confidence that under such and such circumstances the IQ may be raised or lowered so many points or will remain much at the same level. If we are concerned with difficulties of occupational adjustment or with education, we can say that the prognosis is good or poor, according to certain specified conditions in the demands of the environment and the person's life situation. If we are concerned with the physical and organic conditions which are responsible for the intellectual limitations, we can say that some kinds of damage to the central nervous system are irreversible and the results of some diseases permanent.

To some, prognosis means life expectancy; the prognosis is thought to be good if the mentally defective individual has normal life expectancy and poor if he has not. We do not have good data from which to predict longevity, but we may be clear and unequivocal in saying that there is no demonstrable *causal* relationship between intelligence per se and life expectancy. As a rough generalization for Western civilization, more intelligent people have better education and economic circumstances, take better care of their physical health and nutrition, and can often secure better medical attention. However, intelligence does not seem to prevent death from lung cancer or from strontium 90. Longevity, then, appears to be causally related to the physical health of the organism, its nutrition, and its protection from physical and other harm.

In any one instance of mental deficiency, the prognosis should be specifically indicated in terms of the questions under consideration: whether they are based upon physical factors, disease states, emotional stresses and reactions, or the stability of the intellectual performances and potentials.

TREATMENT

The treatment of the mentally defective individual today comprises three important areas. First, there is the medical treatment of physical conditions. Second, there is the appropriate education and training of the defective person. Third, treatment should include psychotherapy through one or more channels.

Medical Treatment

Since there is no pathological condition in mental deficiency based on the expression of normal variation in the intellectual capacities, to speak of a medical cure would be absurd. However, when mental deficiency is intimately connected with physical disease, as is so frequently the case with oligophrenics, it has been naturally hoped, perhaps, that some drug, hormone, or vitamin might be found to cure such a disease, on the assumption that in its absence the normal mental level would appear. In fact, in the past many drugs have been tried and many have failed, partly because, in the attempt to raise the intelligence level, no consideration was given to the particular nature of the defect. For example, efforts to increase mental capacity by feeding with thiamine or other vitamins such as riboflavin (Stevenson & Strauss, 1943) have proved fruitless. Similarly, administration of stimulant drugs, such as caffeine and benzedrine, has been shown to have little value (Penrose, 1954a).

As previously discussed, the therapeutic use of thyroid extract in cases of cretinism has yielded remarkable results, occasionally obtaining an average level of intelligence. Treatment of pituitary disorders by attempting to replace the missing hormones has not been successfully applied to cases of mental deficiency. The possibility of improving low-grade cases suffering from rudimentary gonads by supplying them with sex hormone substitutes has not yet been fully explored (Penrose, 1954a).

In 1944 it was claimed by Zimmerman and Rose that white rats which had been fed with glutamic acid had an increased ability to learn. In 1946 Albert, Hoch, and Waelsch reported that in seven out of eight defective patients to whom the drug had been given there was a rise of IQ. Later, Zimmerman, Burgmeister, and Putnam (1948) reported that the average gain of 6 to 8 points in Binet IQ is achieved in six months and that thereafter no further improvement is obtained. However, other investigators, among them McCulloch (1950), were unable to find any evidence of improvement in mental ability as the result of administration of glutamic acid.

Education and Training

The defective individual is in need of appropriate education and training so that he may be able to gain skills which enable him to contribute to his own support. Also, keeping him productively engaged builds up his ego strength in addition to lifting him out of trouble and despondency. Training of the mentally defective requires unlimited patience, good will, and common sense. In most cases, academic improvement is considered secondary to the patient's personal adjustment to social life. Among idiots and imbeciles, instruction still tends to follow lines laid down by Seguin and Montessori.

What kinds of training facilities are now available to the mentally defective? Communities vary in these respects, just as they do in education, sanitation, and other services. In some parts of the United States there are literally no provisions aside from custodial care in institutions. In others, there is a good variety of facilities, beginning with specialized diagnostic services and including visiting teachers, visiting nurses, sheltered workshops for training and remunerative employment, vocational guidance, and personal counseling for the mentally handicapped person himself as well as for parents and guardians. Many of the state institutions have begun to live up to their name of "training schools." While a very few private schools can give more in the way of effective training and treatment to some of their residents than the best of the state schools, their cost is much higher, and it is no longer true that the private school for the "retarded" is *ipso facto* better than the available state schools. There are some private schools which are very weak in program, although they may have impressive façades and reputations for their work in the past. Some of them depend upon the unpaid labor of their paying "children" and do little or nothing to prepare them for return to the community. Many of the state schools now do an excellent job of training for useful employment and give follow-up counseling. In the case of institutions, there is gradually developing a general acceptance among the well informed that money spent on training and education saves even more money that would have been spent by the public indirectly because of these mentally handicapped individuals (see literature on education).

Psychotherapy

Over the years the attitude of many therapists regarding the effectiveness of psychotherapy with the mentally defective has been quite negative. However, in the past decade the work of Abel (1953), Sarason (1952, 1953), and Thorne (1948), among others, has brought home the fact that pessimism concerning the beneficial results of psychotherapy with retarded children has been based upon theoretical deductions rather than upon actual practice and specific research considerations. For example, Heiser (1954) studied 14 mentally retarded children who were given psychotherapy. They ranged in IQ score from 44 to 75. The diagnosis varied; one was diagnosed as familial, six as organic; and seven were mentally defective children with moderate to severe emotional problems. Each child had from 11 to 58 hours of psychotherapy. Twelve children improved in social and environmental behavior; only one of organic and one of psychogenic origin did not improve. Dichter (1962) feels that the most important aspect of psychotherapy with the mentally retarded is the opportunity provided for such a child to identify with the therapist. This process of identification with the therapist seems, to the child, to make external conditions safer and eventually enables him to strengthen his grasp of reality.

Individual psychotherapy, despite its proved benefits, is a limited form of treatment because of the scarcity of well-trained therapists and the great expense involved. psychotherapy for mental defectives can also be undertaken through handling the environment, the social stimulation and relationships, and the recreational and occupational program of the individual. The parents or guardians and institutional employees are crucial figures in the milieu therapy.

REFERENCES

Abel, Theodora M., Resistance and difficulties in psychotherapy of mental retardates. *J. clin. Psychol.*, 1953, **9**, 107–109.

Albert, K., Hoch, P., and Waelsch, H. Preliminary report on the effect of glutamic acid administration in mentally retarded subjects. *J. nerv. ment. Dis.*, 1946, **104**, 263.

Alpers, B. J. Cerebral birth injuries. In S. Brock (Ed.), *Injuries of the brain and spinal cord and their coverings.* Baltimore: Williams & Wilkins, 1949.

Battle, Margaret. Effect of birth on mentality. *Amer. J. Obstet. Gynaec.*, 1949, **58**, 110–116.

Beidelman, B. Mongolism: A selective review including an analysis of 42 cases from the records of the Boston Lying in Hospital. *Amer. J. ment. Defic.*, 1955, **50**, 35–52.

Benda, C. E. *Mongolism and cretinism.* (2nd ed.) New York: Grune & Stratton, 1949.

Benda, C. E. Psychopathology of childhood. In R. Carmichael (Ed.), *Manual of child psychology.* New York: Wiley, 1954.

Benda, C. E. *The child with mongolism.* New York: Grune & Stratton, 1960.

Böök, J. A., & Reed, S. C. Empiric risk figures in mongolism. *J. Amer. med. Ass.* 1950, **143**, 730.

Borberg, A. Clinical and genetic investigation into tuberosclerosis, Copenhagen: Munksgaard, 1951.

Brain, W. R., Hunter, D., & Turnbull, H. M. Acute meningoencephalomyelitis. *Lancet,* 1929, 221.

DeLange, Cornelia. On serious birth injuries of the brain after normal delivery at term. *Acta paediat.* 1950, **39**, 179–191.

Dichter, A. Psychotherapy for the mentally retarded. *Pathways child Guid.*, 1962, **4**, 2–3.

Garth, T. R. A study of the foster Indian child in the white home. *Psychol. Bull.*, 1935, **32**, 708–709.

Goddard, H. H. A measuring scale of intelligence. *Train. Sch.*, 1910, **6**, 146–155.

Goddard, H. H. *The Kallikak Family.* New York: Macmillan, 1912.

Goldstein, S. A study of mongolism and nonmongoloid mental retardation in children. *Arch. Pediat.*, 1954, **71**, 11–28.

Goodenough, F. L. & Morris, D. B. Studies in the psychology of children's drawings. *Psychol. Bull.*, 1950, **47**, 369–433.

Gregg, N. McA. Congenital cataract following German measles. *Trans. opth. Soc. Aust.* 1941, **3**, 35.

Heber, R. Manual on terminology and classification of mental disorders. *Amer. J. ment. Defic. Monogr. Suppl.*, 1959, **64**, No. 2.

Heiser, K. F. Applications of clinical psychology to mental deficiency. In (Eds.), *Progress in clinical psychology.* New York: Grune & Stratton, 1952.

Heiser, K. F. Psychotherapy in a residential school for mentally retarded children. *Train. Sch. Bull.*, 1954, **50**, 211–218.

Ingalls, T. H. Pathogenesis of mongolism. *Amer. J. Dis. Child.*, 1947, **73**, 279–292.

Ingalls, T. H., Mongolism. *Scientif. Amer., 1952,* 60–67.

Itard, J. M. G. *De l'éducation d'un homme sauvage.* Paris: 1801.

Jervis, G. A. Phenylpyruvic oligophrenia. *J. ment. Sci.*, 1939, **85**, 719.

Jervis, G. A. The mental deficiencies. In S. Ariet (Ed.), *American handbook of psychiatry.* New York: Basic Books, 1959.

Kanner, L. *Child psychiatry.* (2nd ed.) Springfield, Ill.: Charles C Thomas, 1948.

Kaufman, I. Crimes of violence and delinquency in schizophrenic children. *Amer. J. Psychiat.*, 1962, **118**, 909.

Klineberg, O. *Negro intelligence and selective migration.* New York: Columbia Univer. Press, 1935.

Krout, M. H. Is the brain-injured a mental defective? *Amer. J. ment. Defic.*, 1949, **54**, 81–85.

Lejeune, J., Turpin, R., & Gautier, M. Le mongolisme, premier example d'aberration autosomique humaine. *Ann. Génétique*, 1959, **2**, 41–49.

Lewis, E. O. Types of mental deficiency and their social significance. *J. ment. Sci.*, 1933, **79**, 298.

McCulloch, T. L. Reformulation of the problem of mental deficiency. *Amer. J. ment. Defic.*, 1947, **52**, 130–136.

McCulloch, T. L. The effects of glutamic acid feeding on cognitive abilities of institution-mental defectives. *Amer. J. ment. Def.*, 1950, 55 July.

MacGillvray, R. C. Mongolism in both of monozygote twins. *Amer. J. ment. Defic.*, 1959, **64**, 450–454.

Marburg, O. Studies in the pathology and pathogenesis of amaurotic family idiocy. *Amer. J. ment. Defic.*, 1942, **46**, 312–322.

Masland, R. L., Sarason, S. B., & Gladwin, T. *Mental subnormality*. New York: Basic Books, 1958.

Mayo, L. W. The nation mobilizes. *Pathways in Child Guid.*, 1962, **4**, 2–3.

Munro, T. A. The genetics of phenylketonuria, Cambridge Univer. Press, 1941.

Murphy, D. P. Ovarian irradiation: Its effect on the health of subsequent children. *Surg. Gynec. Obstet.*, 1928, **47**, 201–215.

Penrose, L. S. Two cases of phenylpyruvic amentia. *Lancet*, 1935, **223**, 23–24.

Penrose, L. S. *The biology of mental defect*. London: Sidgwick & Jackson, 1954. (a)

Penrose, L. S. Observations of the etiology of mongolism. *Lancet*, 1954, **2**, 505–509. (b)

Potter, H. W. Mental deficiency and the psychiatrist. *Amer. J. Psychiat.*, 1927, **6**, 691–700.

Richards, B. W. Childhood schizophrenia and mental deficiency. *J. ment. Sci.*, 1957, **97**, 290–312.

Rowley, Janet. A review of recent studies of chromosomes in mongolism. *Amer. J. ment. Defic.*, 1962, **66**, 529–532.

Sarason, S. B. Individual psychotherapy with mentally defective individuals. *Amer. J. ment. Defic.*, 1952, **56**, 803–805.

Sarason, S. B. *Psychological problems in mental deficiency*. New York: Harper, 1953.

Seguin, É. *Traitement moral, hygiène des idiots*. Paris, 1846.

Stevenson, I., & Strauss, A. A. The effects of an enriched vitamin B² (riboflavin) diet on a group of mentally defective children with retardation in physical growth. *Am. J. ment. Defic.*, 1943, **48**, 153.

Throne, F. C. Counseling and psychotherapy with mental defectives. *Amer. J. ment. Defic.*, 1948, **52**, 263–271.

Tredgold, A. F. *Mental deficiency*. London: Bailliere, 1908.

Tredgold, A. F. *A textbook of mental deficiency*. (8th ed.) Baltimore: Williams & Wilkins, 1952.

Van Creveld, S. The lipidoses. *Advances Pediat.*, 1953, **6**, 190–242.

Wolman, B. B. Medicine and therapeutic education. (Polish.) *Szkola Specjalna*, 1938, **14**, 18–25.

Wolman, B. B. Diagnosis in clinical psychology. (Hebrew.) *Hed Hachinuch*, 1943, **18**, 17–21.

Wolman, B. B. Juvenile delinquents in Palestine. (Hebrew.) *Hachinuch Quart.*, 1946, **17**, 50–79.

Wolman, B. B. Disturbances in acculturation. *Amer. J. Psychother.*, 1949, **3**, 601–605.

Wolman, B. B. The Jewish adolescent. *Jew. soc. Studies*, 1951, **13**, 333–334.

Wolman, B. B. Intelligence and its measurement. (Yiddish.) *Encyclopedia Dertziung*, 1957, **1**, 206–230.

Wolman, B. B. The nature of mental deficiency, 1964 (in press).

Yannet, H. Diagnostic classification of patients with mental deficiency. *Amer. J. Dis. Child.*, 1945, **70**, 83–88.

Yannet, H., and Lieberman, Rose. Further studies of ABO isoimmunization, secraton status and mental deficiency. *Amer. J. ment. Defic.*, 1948, **52**, 314–317.

Zimmerman, F. T., Burgmeister, B. B., & Putnam, T. H. The ceiling effect of glutamic acid upon intelligence in children and adolescents. *Amer. J. Psychiat.*, 1948, **104**, 593.

Zimmerman, F. T., and Ross, S. Effect of glutamic acid and other amino acids on maze learning in white rat. *Archiv. Neurol. and Psychiat.*, 1944, **51**.

32

The Psychosomatic Approach

FRANZ ALEXANDER AND GLENN W. FLAGG[1]

Historical remarks

The oldest approach in medicine was psychosomatic. Primitive man explained all physical phenomena psychologically. Thunder and lightning were expressions of the wrath of supernatural spirits; rain was the gift of the gods. Also, physical disease was inflicted by evil spirits. Primitive man did not know anatomy or the laws of physics and chemistry; however, he possessed a primitive knowledge from awareness of his own emotional processes. Accordingly, he extrapolated this introspective knowledge to all phenomena of nature. He animated nature with beings which —although more powerful than he—were similar to him and his fellow men, and he tried to influence them by appealing to the goodwill of the spirits or by bribing or intimidating them. Exorcism was based on psychological theory and methods.

The first attempt to explain natural events from natural causes was made by the Greek cosmological philosophers of the seventh and sixth centuries B.C. Their rationalistic approach was applied systematically to biological phenomena by Hippocrates and his school. Hippocrates's approach was not psychosomatic but pronouncedly somatopsychic. Mental disease was the result of physical causes, of the disharmony in the distribution of the four basic bodily humors, which he took over from Empedocles's four-element theory. His influence on medicine was all-pervasive; psychology became relegated to the philosophers. Originally, the Sophists (in particular, Protagoras) introduced interest in psychological phenomena which culminated in the philosophy of Socrates, Plato, and Aristotle. Their psychology, however, was no longer magical, and it lost its previous demonological components; it was a rational psychology based primarily on introspective knowledge. Plato and Aristotle believed in the supremacy of the mind, which rules over the body. The entity of the organism was explained from the principle of a central government—the soul—which is responsible for the coordination of all bodily processes. This principle of goal-directedness, which Aristotle called "entelechia," survived until the modern era in the concept of the animal spirits and, later, in the "vital force" of the vitalists and in Bergson's philosophy. Nevertheless, in Greco-Roman medicine the Hipprocratic mechanistic, materialistic tradition continued to prevail, and the soul remained the subject matter of the clergy and the phi-

[1] Franz Alexander was an intuitive clinician as well as a creative thinker, possessing the ability for both broad and detailed conceptions of a problem. His intellectual curiosity, his ability as a teacher, and his enthusiasm for scientific investigation were great and formative influences upon all who worked with him. Franz Alexander is remembered for his double-blind studies on the "seven psychosomatic diseases" at the Chicago Psychoanalytic Institute and, later, for his remarkable approach to the study of the influence of emotions on chronic diseases. The study of chronic disease using motion pictures to create stressful and lifelike situations was Dr. Alexander's greatest area of interest in the later years of his life. Our science has lost a great leader, and I personally have lost a great teacher and friend. *Glenn W. Flagg*

losophers. This strict division, however, was mainly in theory. The physician dealt with an indivisible human being and could not fully disregard the patient as a feeling person. To make the patient comfortable became a focal interest of the practically oriented Roman physicians. The psychological approach to the suffering human became an explicit topic, not of theory, but of the practice of medicine. Soranus and Caelius Aurelianus, in Rome, became the first psychotherapists. It is perhaps not an accident that the first explicit statement of the psychosomatic approach came not from a physician but from Cicero, when he asked:

> Why for the cure or maintenance of the body there has been devised an art. . . . Whilst on the other hand the need of an art of healing for the soul has not been felt so deeply . . . nor has it been studied so closely. . . .
>
> What we call frenzy they call melancholia, just as if the truth were that the mind is influenced by black bile and not in many instances by . . . wrath or fear or pain . . . (*Tusculan Disputations*).

He stated that bodily ailments may be the results of emotional factors. He might be called the first psychosomaticist.

With the collapse of the Roman Empire, demonology reentered the cultural scene. In a society which had lost its moral foundations, the bewildered masses, ravaged by pestilence and hunger, turned toward faith. They needed more than cold reason to face a world which was anything but hospitable. Christian faith gave to the people a substitute for Greco-Roman rationalism, a substitute which was most suited to their emotional needs. It took more than fifteen centuries for European man to become ready to absorb the rationalistic tradition of the ancients. Aristotle and Hippocrates were rediscovered, the latter mainly through his codifier, Galen. The Renaissance humanists and artists restored to man his faith in his own reasoning powers, and the stage was set for the "scientific era." It continued just at the point where the Greeks and the Romans left it.

The principal accomplishment of the last 300 years was the consistently progressing deanimation of nature, the rediscovery of physical causality, and the substitution of "natural causes" for evil and benign spirits. During the nineteenth century, biology and medicine also came completely under the sway of the natural sciences. Scientists hoped that eventually all mysteries of life, just as those of inanimate nature, could be solved by applying to them the laws of physics and chemistry. Increasingly, the modern physician thought of himself as a mechanic, a glorified and specialized repairman of that complex physiochemical apparatus, the human organism. It is this orientation to which modern medicine owes its great advancements. Western man, however, went to the opposite extreme. After he thoroughly eliminated supernatural, spiritual forces from his view of the inanimate world, he attempted to deanimate man himself. He reduced human personality to something which does not need to be considered in the scientific study of man.

The psyche, however, could not be completely removed from medicine. During the seventeenth century, when astronomy, physics, anatomy, and physiology made spectacular advances, two of the greatest clinicians explicitly recognized emotional influences in normal and pathological bodily processes. Thomas Sydenham gave an amazingly lucid description of hysterical conversion symptoms, which he attributed to the "commotions of the mind." William Harvey, in his *Do Motu Cordis,* called attention to the influence of emotions upon heart action and heart failure. He presaged the coming of the psychoanalytic era when he wrote:

> And what indeed is more serving of attention than the fact that in almost every affection, appetite, hope, or fear, our body suffers, the countenance changes, and the blood appears to course hither and thither? In anger the eyes are fiery and the pupils contracted; in modesty the cheeks are suffused with blushes; in fear, and under the sense of infamy and of shame, the face is pale, but the ears burn as if for the evil they heard or were to hear; in lust how quickly the member [penis] is distended with blood and erected! . . . Such is the force of the blood pent up and such are the effects of its impulse.

These were, however, sporadic exceptions. During the eighteenth century, the mechanistic orientation steadily progressed, and the philosophers as well as the medical men of the era of the Enlightenment considered it only a question of time before the body and all its diseases, including the mental ones, would be fully understood on the basis of mechanistic, materialistic principles—those of anatomy, physiology, physics, and chemistry. This materialistic orientation was interrupted at the beginning of the nineteenth century for about fifty years. The high hopes of the French Revolution for the eventual rule of reason, which would make the world a better place to live in, collapsed after Napoleon's defeat. Under Metternich's police state, people withdrew from participation in great public events of the world and retreated into the daily occurrences of their personal lives. Political and social oppression blocked the open vistas of the Enlightenment, and the mind turned inward to the only remaining free outlet, the depths of the inner life. This "romantic reaction" was short-lived but was of outstanding significance for the history of psychiatry.

In 1803 the first systematic treatise on psychiatry was written by a German, Christian Reil, who insisted that mental diseases should be cured by psychological treatment methods. Another German romantic psychiatrist, Johann Christian Heinroth, followed the same path and used, for the first time, the expression "psychosomatic" in referring to the somatic effects of psychological conflict. In about the middle of the nineteenth century, Carus, a German obstetrician, in his book *Psyche*, postulated the concept of the unconscious and considered, as did also George Groddeck later, all physical and mental ailments to be the result of unconscious mental processes.

In the second half of the nineteenth century, under the influence of Wilhelm Griesinger in Germany and Henry Maudsley in England, a strong reaction arose against the psychological theories of the romantic psychiatrists. Both these leaders in psychiatry demanded that psychiatry be purified of philosophical and psychological speculations and that mental disturbances be understood on the basis of organic pathology.

At the end of the nineteenth century, Charcot, a most hardheaded and scrupulous observer and the leading neurologist of the era, experimentally demonstrated the influence of ideas upon bodily disturbances in hysterics. It was Charcot who inspired Freud in his explorations of unconscious mental phenomena.

Neurophysiology, however, continued its spectacular advances. Freud's work remained at first an alien body in medical thought. Under his influence, the rift in psychiatry between the psychological and the organic orientation broadened, and the psychiatric world became divided into two camps: the organicists versus the psychologically minded followers of Freud. From this historical perspective, the current psychosomatic approach appears to be an effort to find a synthesis between these two orientations.

The psychosomatic approach

The psychosomatic approach is based upon certain basic postulates: (1) Psychological processes must be subjected to the same scientific scrutiny as is customary in the study of physiological processes. Therefore, instead of referring to emotions in such general terms as "anxiety" or "tension," the actual psychological content of an emotion must be defined so that it may then be studied with the advanced methods of dynamic psychology and correlated with bodily responses. (2) Psychological processes are fundamentally not different from other processes which take place in the organism. They are at the same time physiological processes and differ from other bodily processes only in that they are perceived subjectively and can be communicated verbally and nonverbally to others. Therefore, they can be studied by psychological methods, verbal communication being the principal one. Bodily processes are directly or indirectly influenced by psychological stimuli because the whole organism constitutes a unit in which all the parts are directly or indirectly connected with the seat of psychological processes, the highest integrating center of the nervous system (the brain). The psychosomatic approach therefore can be applied to most phenomena which take place in the living organism. (3) Psychological observations should be correlated with their physiological concomitants whenever possible by standardized objective methods. (4) Some psychophysiological interactions can be best studied according to a psychosomatic model, and others according to a somatopsychic model. The influence of grief, for example, upon gastrointestinal or circulatory functions requires the psychosomatic model; the influence of alcohol upon ideation requires the somatopsychic model. This does not imply that they are two fundamentally different processes, for psychologically induced elation or grief, as well as alcohol-induced elation or grief, has its physiological correlate. The two models, the somatopsychic and the psychosomatic, are but methodological choices of approach dictated by the specific phenomenon under investigation.

The psychosomatic approach in therapy is basically an attempt to place medical art or the psychological effect of the physician upon the patient on a scientific basis and to make it an integral part of treatment. The modern psychosomatic approach in medicine tries to span the gulf which until the present time separated psychiatry, the "art of medicine," from scientific medicine. This separation occurred as a result of the rapid advancements which medicine made by successfully applying the principles of physics and chemistry during the nineteenth century. A psychosomatic approach in medicine based on sound scientific principles rather than intuition would have been impossible without the discovery of the psychoanalytic method of Freud, which gave clinicians the first reliable method for the systematic study of the human personality. Personality research or motivational psychology as a science began with Freud. He was the first to apply consistently the postulate of strict determinism of psychological processes (psychological causality).

By discovering that a great part of human behavior is determined by unconscious motivation and by developing a technique by which unconscious motivations could be made conscious, Freud was able to demonstrate for the first time the psychogenic factors in psychopathological processes. The view emerged that the personality is an expression of the unity of the organism. Just as a machine can be understood only from its function and purpose, the synthetic unit which we call the "living organism" can be fully understood only from the point of view of the personality, the needs of which are served, in the last analysis, by all parts of the body in an intelligible coordination.

Psychoanalysis, then, enabled the synthetic point of view to gain acceptance in clinical medicine. The "scientific approach" of the late nineteenth and early twentieth centuries had divided the organism into a number of organs and systems which were studied by various specialists without integration of the details into a whole. Other parallel trends toward synthesis in medicine and psychology became apparent at the start of the century. After the introduction into psychology of the experimental method by Fechner and Weber, there developed a psychology of vision, hearing, memory, etc., with no attempt by these experimental psychologists to understand the interrelationship of all these mental faculties and the integration into what we call the "human personality." Gestalt psychology emerged as a reaction against these fragmented analytic orientations, and its most important contribution was the clear formulation of the thesis that the whole is not the sum total of its parts but something different from them and that from the study of the parts alone, the whole system could never be understood. In fact, just the opposite is true—the parts can be thoroughly understood only after the meaning of the whole has been discovered.

The work of Hughlings Jackson and Sherrington in neurology demonstrated the hierarchical organization of the central nervous system. Thus the unity of the organism is clearly expressed in the function of the central nervous system, which regulates the internal vegetative processes in the organism (internal affairs of the organism), and its interaction with the environment (external affairs). The central government is represented by the highest center of the nervous system, the psychological aspects of which in human beings are called the "personality." In fact, it became obvious that psychological studies of the highest centers of the central nervous system and psychological studies of the personality deal with different aspects of one and the same thing. As physiology approaches the functions of the central nervous system in terms of space and time, psychology approaches them in terms of the various subjective phenomena which are the *subjective reflections of physiological processes.*

An added stimulus for the synthetic point of view came from the discovery of the ductless (endocrine) glands; this furthered the understanding of the many complicated interactions between the different vegetative functions of the organism with one another and with the environment. The endocrine glands also were found to be arranged in a hierarchical order, with the anterior pituitary functioning as the master gland. Present-day research findings indicate that the regulation of the ductless glands is ultimately subjected to the highest level of brain function, that is, to psychological stimuli. Thus the mechanisms of how "the mind rules the body" and of how peripheral functions of the body in turn influence the central functions of the nervous system became established on anatomical, neurophysiological, and endocrinological principles. Our whole life consists in carrying out voluntary movements aimed at the realization of ideas and wishes and the satisfactions of subjective feelings and needs, such as anxiety, love, hate, thirst, hunger, etc., which are all accompanied by physiological processes.

The application of all these considerations to certain morbid processes of the body gradually led to the psychosomatic approach, which involved a new and more sophisticated multidisciplinary study of the causation of disease. Knowledge of the influence of acute emotions on body functions belongs to everyday experience. However, the specific syndrome of physical change corresponding to a particular emotional situation, that is, the specific psychosomatic response (for example, laughter and weeping), was considered of little medical interest since these bodily reactions to acute emotions were felt to be of passing nature. However, psychoanalytic studies of hysterical patients by Freud revealed unmistakably that the influence of prolonged emotional conflicts could contribute to chronic physical disturbances of the body (conversion hysteria). These changes were noted in muscles, controlled by the will, and in sense perceptions. Thus Freud demonstrated that ego-alien emotions which become repressed and which cannot be expressed and relieved through normal channels by voluntary activity may become the source of chronic psychic and physical dysfunction. Physiologically viewed, hysterical conversion symptoms resemble any usual voluntary or expressive innervations or perceptions, but in hysteria the motivating psychological impulse is unconscious. In a conversion symptom the leap from the psychic to the somatic is similar to that which takes place in any common voluntary motor innervation except that the motivating psychological content is unconscious, and hysterical symptoms are to a high degree individual, sometimes unique, creations of the patient, invented by him to express his particular repressed psychological content. Expressive movements like laughter are, in contrast, standardized and universal.

A fundamentally different group of psychogenic bodily disturbances are those of the internal vegetative organs innervated by the autonomic nervous system. Early psychoanalytic investigators repeatedly erred in attempting to extend the original concept of hysterical conversion to all forms of psychogenic disturbances of the body, including even those occurring in the visceral organs. They ignored the fact that the vegetative organs, since they are controlled by the autonomic nervous system (and thus are not directly connected with ideational processes), could not express ideational content. Such symbolic expression of psychological content exists only in the field of voluntary innervations, such as speech, and expressive innervations (a possible exception is blushing). Though several organs, such as the liver and the kidney, cannot express ideas, they can be influenced by emotional tensions which are conducted to any part of the body via corticothalamic and autonomic pathways. This type of chronic emotional stimulation or inhibition of a vegetative function, once it becomes chronic and excessive, has been called an "organ neurosis" or a "vegetative disturbance of psychogenic origin." These are disturbances of the vegetative organs which are caused, at least partially, by nervous impulses, originating in the cortical and subcortical areas of the brain.

The difference between a conversion symptom and a vegetative neurosis (organ neurosis) can be defined as follows: A conversion symptom is a symbolic expression of an emotionally charged psychological conflict which attempts to find discharge for the emotional tension which led to the conflict. Thus conversion symptoms occur in voluntary, neuromuscular, or sensory perceptive systems whose original functions are to register, express, and relieve emotional tension. In contrast, a vegetative neurosis is not an attempt to express an *emotion* but is a physiological *adaptive response* of the vegetative organs to constant or periodically recurring emotional states. Elevation of blood pressure, for example, under the influence of rage does not relieve the rage but is a physiological component of the total phenomena of rage. Thus the only similarity between hysterical conversion symptoms and vegetative responses to emotions is that both are responses to psychological stimuli.

With the recognition that functional disturbances are due to emotional factors, psychotherapy gained a legitimate entrance into medicine proper. In functional disturbances of vegetative processes, the personality of the patient became one important object of therapy, and the emotional influence of the doctor upon the patient (medical art) was recognized in scientific medicine as a most important therapeutic factor. However, the role of psychotherapy still remained restricted to mild functional disturbances, as opposed to genuine organic disorders based on demonstrable tissue changes. Although the emotional state of the patient (psychic factor) was recognized as an important influence on the course of a genuine organic disturbance, the causal connection between psychological conflict and chronic disease was not recognized. This strict and artificial distinction between the functional and the organic disappeared as evidence accumulated to show that functional disorders of long duration gradually led to serious organic disorders associated with definite and distinct morphological changes; e.g., a hysterical paralysis of a limb might lead to degenerative changes in the muscles and joints, or emotional conflicts causing continued fluctuations of blood pressure sooner or later could result in chronic elevated blood pressure, with vascular changes and irreversible forms of kidney damage.

Finally, the concept of "psychogenic organic disorder" was formulated; this recognized two phases in the development of these disorders: first, a functional disturbance of a vegetative organ, caused by chronic and excessive emotional stimulation, and second, the gradual transition from a chronic functional disorder to tissue changes and finally to an irreversible organic disease.

Thus etiological concepts were expanded when it was recognized that disturbed function might be the *cause* of altered structure. This was a most basic revision of medical thinking since it opposed the medical dictum based on Virchow's principle that disease is caused by disturbed structure. The concept that disturbed function can cause disturbed structure met with strong resistance because the classical concept of pathology considered disturbed function as always resulting from disturbed structure. It appears, however, that many chronic diseases of unknown origin will be proved ultimately to be instances of diseases in which prolonged disturbed function led to structural changes. An outstanding example is toxic goiter, the onset of which is often due to emotional trauma followed eventually by pronounced structural changes within the thyroid and the cardiovascular system. The functional theory of organic disorders essentially amounts to the recognition of the existence not only of acute *external* causative factors but also of chronic *internal* causes of disease. Stated more simply, many chronic disturbances are not caused primarily by external mechanical or chemical factors or bacteria but by the continuous functional stress arising during the everyday life of the individual in his struggle for existence. Fear, aggression, guilt, and sexual tension, if repressed, result in permanent chronic emotional tensions which disturb the functions of the vegetative organs. Just as certain bacteria have special affinity for certain organs, so also there is strong evidence that certain specific emotional conflicts tend to afflict certain internal organs. Inhibited rage, for example, seems to have a specific relationship to the cardiovascular system. Dependent, help-seeking tendencies seem to have a specific relationship to the functions of nutrition. A conflict pertaining to communication with others seems to have a specific influence upon respiratory functions. The psychosomatic approach brings internal physiological processes into synthesis with the individual's relations to his social environment.

The term "psychosomatic" does not imply a dichotomy between mind and body. It should be understood that psychic phenomena are the subjective aspect of certain physiological or central nervous system processes. The term "psychosomatic" designates merely *a method of approach both in research and in therapy* which is aimed toward the simultaneous and coordinated use of somatic and psychological methods and concepts. Some scientists view the psychosomatic approach as a transitory phase in medicine which will be abandoned when improved physiological or electronic techniques are developed to study those processes which today yield only to psychological methods (for example, grief). This contention is often held by those who interpret psychological processes as merely "epiphenomena." It is indeed possible that in the future a biochemical or electronic formula might be used to describe a receptive longing which takes place somewhere in the cortex, but such a formula could describe only the processes within the organism itself. It could never explain or describe satisfactorily the transactional aspects of the organism with its environment, that is, its social or interpersonal relationships.

Another controversial issue pertains to the diagnostic concept of "psychosomatic disease" as proposed by Halliday (1943; 1948), which is based on the assumption that in these diseases, the primary etiological factor is psychological. Others such as F. Alexander (1946) always questioned the appropriateness of this term and concept. His view is illustrated by the following excerpt from his book *Psychosomatic Medicine* (1950):

> All evidence, however, points to multicausal explanations in all branches of medicine. We are no longer satisfied to say that tuberculosis is caused by the exposure to the bacillus of Koch but recognize that specific and nonspecific immunity, the resistance of the organism to infection, is a complex phenomenon which may depend partly on emotional factors. Accordingly, tuberculosis is a psychosomatic disease. And conversely, the merely psychogenic explanation of such diseases as peptic ulcer cannot be depended upon in view of the fact that the typical emotional constellations found in patients suffering from ulcer are also observed in large numbers of patients who do not suffer from ulcers. Local or general somatic factors, as yet ill defined, must be assumed, and only the coexistence of both kinds of factors, emotional and somatic, can account for ulcer formation. Equally important is the fact that in different cases the relative importance of somatic and emotional factors varies to a high degree. Multicausality and the varying distribution of psychological and nonpsychological factors from case to case invalidates the concept of "psychosomatic disease" as a specific diagnostic group. Theoretically every disease is psychosomatic since emotional factors influence all body processes through nervous and humoral pathways. The following factors may be of etological importance in disease:
>
> D (disease) f (function of) a, b, c, d, e, g, h, i, j . . . n
>
> a—hereditary constitution
>
> b—birth injuries
>
> c—organic diseases of infancy which increase the vulnerability of certain organs
>
> d—nature of infant care (weaning habits, toilet training, sleeping arrangements, etc.)
>
> e—accidental physical traumatic experiences of infancy and childhood
>
> g—accidental emotional traumatic experiences of infancy and childhood
>
> h—emotional climate of family and specific personality traits of parents and siblings
>
> i—later physical injuries
>
> j—later emotional experiences in intimate personal and occupational relations
>
> These factors in different proportions are of etiological significance in all diseases. The psychosomatic point of view added the factors d, g, h, and j, to the other factors, which have long been given attention in medicine. Only the consideration of all these categories and their interaction can give a complete etiological picture.

BASIC CONCEPTS OF THE PSYCHOSOMATIC APPROACH

Psychogenesis

Since psychological and somatic phenomena take place in the same organism and are merely two aspects of the same process, the term "psychogenesis" must be clearly defined. Psychogenesis does not mean that in acute hyperthyroidism, for instance, the overactivity of the thyroid gland is effected by some nonsomatic mechanism. Sustained fear, which in itself is accompanied by an increase in body metabolism, in turn stimulates the central nervous system, and the thyroid secretion is increased via corticohypothalamic-pituitary pathways. Thus, hyperthyroidism due to sustained fear is the end result of a chain of events in which every link can be described at least theoretically in physiological terms. Psychogenic factors such as emotions or ideas and fantasies are distinguished by the fact that they *can also* be studied psychologically through introspection or by verbal communication. Verbal communication is therefore the most potent instrument of psychology and by the same token, of psychosomatic research. When we speak of psychogenesis, we refer to physiological processes consisting of central excitations in the nervous system which can be studied by psychological methods because they are perceived subjectively in the form of emotions, ideas, or wishes.

Physiological Functions Affected by Psychological Influences

These can be divided into three main categories: (1) coordinated voluntary behavior, (2) expressive innervations, and (3) vegetative responses to emotional states.

Coordinated voluntary behavior. Voluntary behavior is under the influence of psychological motivations and is consciously willed. When one is hungry, one makes certain coordinated movements to obtain food, which involve the initiation of certain psychological processes; for instance, one remembers where food is stored and then makes the movements to get it. The dynamic system of psychological forces whose function is to carry out complicated tasks of voluntary coordination is called the "ego." Failure of its function gives rise to different forms of psychoneurosis and psychoses.

Expressive innervations. These are physiological processes such as weeping and sighing, etc., which take place under the influence of a specific emotional tension and which, by complex movements, relieve the specific emotional tension, such as sadness, self-pity, etc. These expressive innervations have as their only function the relief of emotional tension. If the normal discharge of emotional tensions by these expressive processes is blocked because of emotional conflict, a neurotic symptom results. Here the patient invents his own individual expressive innervations in the form of conversion symptoms which serve both to discharge the repressed emotions and to defend against their expression. Although a discharge may take place through the usual appropriate expressive processes, such as occurs in cases of hysterical weeping and laughter, the underlying emotions are repressed, and the patient does not know why he weeps or laughs, the discharge of the emotional tension is not complete, and the weeping or laughing is prolonged and uncontrollable.

Vegetative responses to emotional states. Visceral reactions to emotional stimuli are of special importance since the psychosomatic approach originated in the study of vegetative disturbances which developed under certain emotional states. Normally, the total functioning of the nervous system can be understood as maintenance of homeostasis, that is, maintaining conditions within the organism in a constant state. The voluntary central nervous system is concerned with the regulation of the organism's relations to the external world, whereas the autonomic nervous system controls the internal affairs of the organism, that is, the internal vegetative processes. The parasympathetic division of the autonomic nervous system is more explicitly concerned with conservation and upbuilding, that is, anabolic processes such as digestion and reflex protective actions (contraction of the pupil against light).

The main function of the sympathetic portion of the nervous system is the regulation of internal vegetative functions in relation to external activity, particularly emergency situations, i.e., the preparation of the organism for fight or flight (Cannon, 1920). During the preparation for, and performance of, such activities, it inhibits anabolic processes, such as gastrointestinal activity, and it stimulates heart and lung action and changes the distribution of the blood. To a high degree, the sympathetic and parasympathetic actions are antagonistic. The generalization may be made that under parasympathetic preponderance, the individual withdraws from his external problems into a merely vegetative existence, whereas under sympathetic stimulation, he neglects or inhibits the peaceful functions of upbuilding and growth and turns all his attentions toward facing his problems in relation to the external environment. Usually there is a harmony between parasympathetic and sympathetic systems. In neurotic disturbances of the vegetative functions, this harmony between the external situation and internal vegetative processes is disturbed.

Inhibition or repression of self-assertive hostile impulses blocks appropriate adaptive behavor (fight or flight), and if this inhibition is chronic, the organism remains in a constant state of physiological preparedness, which is normally needed only in emergency situations. In a normal individual, these bodily changes are only temporary, lasting only as long as the need for increased effort persists and rapidly returning to a normal base line on cessation of action. However, when activation of the vegetative processes involves no action and when repeated stimulation of these adaptative physiological responses occurs, they eventually become chronically elevated. For example, in essential hypertension, the blood pressure is sustained under pent-up and never fully relieved anger. Other neurotic persons may react to the necessity for concentrated self-assertive behavior with an emotional withdrawal from action into a dependent state. Instead of facing the emergency, they retreat from taking action and turn for help as they did when they were children (vegetative retreat). If a man develops diarrhea when in danger instead of acting in an appropriate manner, he is manifesting a vegetative retreat. The functional disturbances of the gastrointestinal tract due to emotional stress are of this type since they involve a regression to body responses characteristic of the infant. All forms of nervous indigestion, nervous diarrhea, cardiospasm, and mucous colitis; certain forms of constipation and certain fatigue states associated with disturbance of carbohydrate metabolism; and the psychological component in bronchial asthma illustrate a retreat from action into a dependent, help-seeking attitude.

One is inclined to assume in the first category of vegetative responses a sympathetic preponderance, and in the latter group a parasympathetic preponderance in autonomic balance. However, every displacement of autonomic equilibrium produces instantaneous compensatory or counterregulatory reactions to maintain homeostatic equilibrium. Thus only at the onset can the disturbing stimulus be identified with the sympathetic or the parasympathetic division of the autonomic nervous system.

To summarize, every neurosis consists, to a certain degree, of withdrawal from action, that is, the substitution of autoplastic processes for action. In psychoneuroses without physical symptoms, motor activity is replaced by psychological activity, by acting in fantasy instead of in reality. The division of labor in the central nervous system, however, is not disturbed because psychoneurotic symptoms are based on the activity of the central nervous system, the function of which is to control external relationships. This holds true for conversion hysteria because here, too, the symptoms are localized in the voluntary and sensory perceptive system, which deals with the external affairs of the organism. Every neurotic disturbance of vegetative function, however, consists in a disturbance of the division of labor within the nervous system; outward-directed action is omitted, and the unrelieved emotional tension induces chronic internal vegetative changes. If sympathetic preponderance occurs, the disturbance of the division of labor is not so thoroughgoing as is the case when a parasympathetic excitation prevails since sympathetic functions are in an intermediary position between internal vegetative functions and outwardly directed actions (sympathetic function tunes up and charges the vegetative functions toward active solution of external problems). Hence in disturbances where there is a sympathetic hyperactivity, the organism does not go into action, although it undergoes all the preparatory changes necessary for action. In those disorders which develop under parasympathetic preponderance, a more complete withdrawal from the solution of problems occurs. Here the unconscious psychological material which is connected with the symptom corresponds to a withdrawal to an early vegetative dependence on the mother organism rather than to a preparation for action. Thus the patient with a gastrointestinal symptom prepares himself to be fed instead of to fight.

The division of vegetative symptoms into these two general categories of response to emotional conflict is helpful in understanding the activation of a particular division of the autonomic nervous system. However, those specific factors which could account for the choice of the particular organ function which will be affected by parasympathetic or sympathetic activation are still unknown. Why do repressed aggressive tendencies, for example, lead in some cases to chronic hypertension and in other cases to palpitation or to a disturbance in carbohydrate metabolism or to chronic constipation, and why do passive regressive tendencies lead to gastric symptoms in some instances and to diarrhea and asthma in others? A correlation between symptoms and unconscious attitudes cannot be extended directly to a correlation between overt personality features and symptoms. Moreover, a combination of both types of reactions may be observed in the same person at different periods in his life and in some cases even simultaneously.

Specificity of Emotional Factors in Somatic Disturbances

The theory of specificity states that both normal and morbid physiological responses to emotional stimuli vary according to the nature of the precipitating emotional state. Thus laughter is a response to merriment, and weeping is a response to sorrow. The vegetative responses to different emotional stimuli vary also according to the quality of emotions, and every emotional state has its own physiological syndrome. For example, increased blood pressure and accelerated heart action are constituent parts of rage and fear. The degree of specificity of physiological responses to various emotional stimuli is still the subject of intensive psychosomatic research. However, the theory differentiates principally between the two attitudes mentioned above: (1) a preparation to deal with the anxiety-producing situation by meeting it actively, and (2) a retreat from it to a dependent, childlike appeal for help. In accord with Cannon's concepts, the first type of emotional attitude goes with increased sympathetic, and the second with increased parasympathetic, excitation. Many investigators still adhere to an older view that no specific correlation exists between the nature of the emotional stress and its physical sequelae. This concept maintains that any emotion may contribute to any organic disturbance and that the local vulnerability of the affected organ is wholly responsible for the localization of the disease. The theory of emotional specificity, however, does not imply that nonemotional factors such as the constitution and history of the organ system involved are unimportant influences in its specific susceptibility to emotional stimuli. The controversy concerning the specificity of psychodynamic factors operative in vegetative disturbances is obscured by the fact that the significant psychological influences such as anxiety, repressed hostile and erotic impulses, frustration of dependent cravings, and inferiority and guilt feelings are present in all these disorders. It is not the presence of any one or more of these psychological factors that is specific, but the presence of the dynamic configuration in which they appear. Furthermore, the physiological response depends upon the manner in which the psychological motivating force may express itself; for instance, hostility can be expressed in physical attack, whether this is via the extremities, by spitting, by verbal invectives, by destructive fantasies, or by other less direct modes of attack. The physiological responses will vary accordingly. Thus the psychological content, together with the dynamic configuration of these motivating forces, determines at least partially the physiological functions that will be activated or inhibited.

Personality Type and Disease

The concept that certain personality types are predisposed to certain diseases is not new, and the relationship between certain emotions and certain organs has been noted by Alvarez (1931) and Draper (1924, 1935, 1942). However, the first systematic studies of the correlation between personality types and certain organic diseases were done by Dunbar (1943). Using the method of modern psychiatric diagnosis, she established statistical correlations between disease and personality type. However, she concentrated on external personality patterns, and these varied to such an extent among different patients suffering from the same disease that they were hardly significant. The most valid of her profiles was that of the coronary patient as opposed to the impulse-ridden character or the accident-prone person. A more reliable kind of correlation between personality factors and disease is that certain disturbances of vegetative functions can directly be correlated with specific emotional states. Although the personality profile of two ulcer patients may be very different (one may be hard-driving and responsibility-loving, and the other openly dependent and demanding), the significant correlation is between the wish to receive love and help and the activity of the stomach, no matter whether this wish is thwarted by external circumstances or by pride which prevents the person from accepting external help. A mysterious and vague correlation between personality and disease does not exist, but there is a distinct correlation between certain emotional constellations and certain vegetative innervations.

Relation of Nervous and Hormonal Mechanisms

Generally, the longer a disturbance prevails, the more complex the autonomic participation becomes. Further, in such chronic disturbances, the neurogenic mechanisms become less important, and hormonal regulations come to the foreground. The theory of specificity obtains only in regard to the factors which initiate disequilibrations and not to their secondary result. The precise relation of the neurogenic and hormonal regulations in normal and morbid conditions is still problematical. However, the studies of Selye (1946) and many others represent definite steps toward the elucidation of such mechanisms. This is discussed later in this chapter.

Emotional factors in various acute and chronic diseases

Intuitive observations between emotional turmoil and the onset and exacerbation of various illnesses have been made by poets, physicians, and philosophers for centuries. The "family doctor," being a friend of his patients as well as their physician, knew their life situations and their intrapsychic and interpersonal conflicts, and he recognized these factors as influencing his patients' susceptibility to physical as well as emotional illness and took them into account as part of the "art" of medicine. As the physician became more "scientific," he hesitated to admit openly to his colleagues his impressions of the effect or precipitating aspects of emotions in organic diseases lest he be criticized for being an "unscientific philosopher" or a "moralist."

However, as "scientific medicine" proved disappointing in the discovery of specific "organic" causes in a number of chronic diseases, systematic surveys of the existent medical literature dealing with the effects of emotions on the general resistance of patients to illness began to appear. Dunbar (1943; 1947a & b), and Weiss & English (1949) summarized observations by various internists and psychiatrists on the correlations between emotions and somatic disturbances. Other studies dealt with the effects of specific kinds of emotional stress on the onset and course of particular diseases. These efforts progressed to the investigation of "incidence" of "psychosomatic" diseases, which in turn led to such confusing concepts as "psychosomatic versus somatopsychic" (actually, the two terms were classifications replacing such operationally meaningless terms as "functional" and "organic").

Regardless of the confusion, consistent progress has been made toward outlining and clarifying the specific nature, content, and mechanism of action of emotional stress in many acute and chronic diseases by controlled clinical, laboratory, and sociological studies.

Engel (1961), for example, considers grief as important as bacteria in the production of disease since it precedes the onset of so many serious psychological and somatic illnesses. Grief reactions resulting from an actual or threatened important object loss are powerful agents in the total adjustment of the organism through their influence via the limbic and reticular activating systems. Schmale (1958) reported that 41 out of 42 patients hospitalized on a medical service reported that they had suffered an object loss immediately prior to their illness and that they had at that time experienced feelings of helplessness and hopelessness. Hinkle, Ostfeld, Benjamin, Christenson, Richter, Kane, Gittinger, Goldberger, Thetford, Leichter, Pinsky, and Wolff (1958) conducted detailed studies on the relationship between life experience, personality characteristics, and general susceptibility to illness in matched social groups and concluded that although the life experiences of groups might be the same,

> The more frequently ill appeared to be more predictively oriented towards goals, duties and responsibilities and showed more concern and reaction to events and situations they encountered. They also tended to view their lives as difficult, demanding and unsatisfactory. They were also more self-absorbed and highly aware of interpersonal problems. The well group showed opposite tendencies.

Ittelson, Seidenberg, and Kutash (1961) reported that perceptual differences (as indicated by a trapezoid score) between somatizing and nonsomatizing patients exist. They viewed somatization reactions as a way of binding anxiety and minimizing the distortion of reality by internalizing conflict. The resultant somatic complaints with or without organic basis are perceived as coming from within the patient's body, thereby enabling him to perceive the external perceptual stimulus in his usual way without altering his perceptual rigidity and allowing him to maintain a familiar reality. The nonsomatizer, on the other hand, undergoes perceptual change too readily and distorts the perceptual stimulus which produces anxiety reactions without somatic complaints, neuroses, or distortions of psychotic proportion.

Erfman (1962), in a recent large series, reaffirmed the impression that psychosomatic disorders appear earlier as a rule than the "great psychoneuroses" which occur toward middle age. The earlier appearance of psychosomatic disorders may be due to constitutional factors.

EMOTIONAL FACTORS IN GASTROINTESTINAL DISTURBANCES

In early infancy the alimentary process is the center of the child's universe. The strongest emotions of displeasure and gratification become associated with various aspects of these functions. In general, extroverted interests, particularly intense rage or fear, inhibit the functions of the alimentary tract, whereas hunger, the sight and smell of food, the desire to be fed, and the wish to be helped stimulate alimentary functions. In gastrointestinal disorders, the harmonious adaptation of gastrointestinal activity to the general state of the organism is disturbed.

Disturbances of Appetite and Eating

Psychology of the nutritional process. Since the infant's emotional security is intimately associated with being fed, the satisfaction of hunger is vital, not only to physical existence, but also to normal emotional development. To be fed is to be loved, worthwhile, and secure. The nucleus of insecurity is fear of starvation (fear of the future), which may be openly expressed in pronounced depressive states. The biological dependency of the child and his feeling of utter dependence on adults for food (and security) thus become linked with eating and hunger and produce greed, jealousy, and envy. To the child, possession is equivalent to bodily (oral) incorporation. Frustration of this possessive, passive receptive tendency leads to intense aggressive impulses to take by force that which is denied. Thus biting (oral aggression) becomes the first manifestation of hostility, and these possessive, aggressive impulses centering on oral incorporation are the origins of the first guilt feelings, as the primitive conscience develops. Evidence of the strength of this early conscience are neurotic disorders of eating in adults which are caused by repressed guilt feelings reactivated in later life.

The significance of possessiveness, greed, jealousy, envy, and the striving for security in disorders of the alimentary function is easily understood since these emotions are closely linked with oral incorporation. Commonly such emotions become repressed because of their aggressive asocial nature and thus are blocked from expression through voluntary behavior, and a chronic disturbing influence on different phases of the alimentary process is created. The pleasurable physical sensations connected with the early forms of nutrition (sucking) explain the frequency of the emotional disturbance of the nutritional function when the mature genital functions are inhibited by conflicts. Then a regression to an early pregenital phase takes place.

Eating inhibitions. ANOREXIA NERVOSA. Periodic or chronic loss of appetite is a common occurrence, particularly in reactive depressions, during the depressive phase of manic-depressive psychosis, and occasionally in schizophrenia and psychosomatic disorders. However, if the loss of appetite is the outstanding symptom and no overt psychosis exists, the syndrome is called "anorexia nervosa." It is much more common in women, especially in girls after puberty. Occasionally it is difficult to differentiate it from Simmond's disease.

King (1963), studied 21 cases and differentiated a primary from a secondary syndrome of anorexia nervosa. In the primary form, the abstinence from food was a positive pleasure and a primary gain. In secondary cases, it was due to phobic dread, delusions, or depression. The primary group showed the classic personality traits and family backgrounds often described for anorexia nervosa, and the secondary group did not. King views primary anorexia nervosa as a basic organic disorder which is influenced secondarily by psychological factors. In severe anorexia, secondary manifestations of impaired endocrine function appear, such as loss of axillary hair, cessation of menstruation, disappearance of sexual desire, and cessation of growth. Abnormalities in behavior which resemble anorexia nervosa can be produced by starvation, even in emotionally healthy individuals. Although anorexia nervosa develops as a consequence of psychological conflict, once the anorexia is established, a vicious circle may ensue because of diminished activity of the endocrine glands and an increase in blood ketones, which reinforce the loss of appetite on an organic basis.

Psychoanalytic studies of anorexia nervosa patients reveal unconscious conflicts over aggressive impulses such as envy and jealousy as outstanding factors. The patient inhibits these aggressive impulses because of guilt and expiates the guilt by denying himself the pleasure of eating. The anorexia is an unconscious spite reaction in which the patient, like an angry, pouting child, coerces attention and special favor from his environment. If the oral aggressive and receptive tendencies become eroticized and connected with fantasies of sexual practice, such as fellatio, cunnilingus, or a forbidden oral-impregnation fantasy, the association of the hunger drive with such ego-alien sexual impulses may also lead to eating difficulties. Unconscious pregnancy wishes and a fearful rejection of such desires constitute a common psychodynamic background of eating difficulties among young girls.

Jessner and Abse (1960) emphasized that the patient communicates with the action pattern of refusing food, and they noted the extent of the regressive flight of these patients, as did Blitzer, Rollins, and Blackwell (1961). They felt that the failure to eat was caused as much by anxiety and guilt as by anorexia. They noted that regression was as important in anorexia nervosa as depression. Jessner and Abse found that the anorexia patients had experienced a period of oral deprivation followed by a period of closeness and gratification, leading to an ambivalence toward the mother. By displacing their anal defiance onto the father, they renounced oedipal aims in order to maintain the closeness with the mother. A preverbal oral fixation lays the groundwork for the later nonverbal action patterns.

Bruch (1962) outlined three areas of functionally disordered psychological experience in anorexia patients:

1. A disturbance of body image of delusional proportions. (What is pathognomonic of anorexia nervosa is the stubborn lack of concern over emaciation.)

2. A disturbance in the perception of stimuli arising in the body which causes an inability accurately to perceive nutritional needs. Coddington, Dean, Bruch, and Keller (1963) tested the ability to perceive gastric stimuli in patients with eating disorders and normal persons by administering known amounts of fluid to their stomachs. They found that the lower the subject's ability to perceive the gastric stimuli, the greater was his weight abnormality.

3. An all-pervasive sense of ineffectiveness due to a lack of spontaneous behavior. Bruch maintains that traditional insight therapy not only is useless but also reinforces a basic personality defect, namely, "not knowing how they felt but being told by mother." Therapy should be "fact-finding," and the therapist should listen to what the *patients* have to say, so that they may become aware of their own impulses.

BULIMIA AND OBESITY. Bulimia, or voracious eating, is almost never a result of an organic condition, with the exception of hyperthyroidism as a result of the increased metabolism.

In bulimia of psychogenic origin, eating usually results from an intense craving for love mixed with aggressive tendencies to devour or possess the love object. Unconscious feminine sexual fantasies, pregnancy fantasies, and castrative wishes may play an important role. In two cases analyzed by one of the authors (Flagg), the obesity was a defense against the feminine role, literally a "protective coat" covering the feminine body, which both patients rejected because of its masochistic connotation. Anorexia nervosa may subsequently develop in a patient with bulimia. Gottsfeld (1962) compared the body cathexes of "superobese" patients and neurotic patients using a questionnaire and body drawings. The superobese group had a more negative body cathexis than the neurotic group, but not a more negative self-cathexis. The obese patients tended to deny personality difficulties on a conscious level; such patients are thus often poorly motivated for psychotherapy.

Plesset and Shipman (1963) studied the problem of the effect of dieting in provoking anxiety or depression in obese people. Obese persons with high scores in anxiety and depression were unsuccessful dieters, suggesting that high anxiety and depression in the obese person were signs of an inability to overcome unconscious factors against weight maintenance.

Stunkard (1959) studied gastric motility of obese women and found that they denied feelings of hunger even when their stomachs showed hunger contractions. He suggested that the denial of hunger occurred in persons who had conflicts over eating and who were also subjected to strong social pressures in this regard.

A recent approach to the problem of intractable obesity has been by total fasting for periods of ten to fourteen days. Weight loss may be as much as 2.5 pounds per day. Anorexia and a feeling of well-being occur after the first day of fasting and parallel the degree of hyperketonemia (the rationale of this therapy is that ketones which result from the breakdown of fatty tissue produce a secondary anorexia).

OTHER FORMS OF EATING INHIBITIONS. Sometimes the patient experiences no loss of appetite but cannot eat in the presence of certain persons. Young girls particularly, although they are quite hungry, may be unable to eat in the presence of men to whom they have an emotional attachment. The eating inhibition and their embarrassment and fear may be based on unconscious sexual fantasies with an oral aggressive connotation (oral castrative wishes). The meaning of the symptom to the individual patient must be determined before forced feeding, etc., is started since the symptom is an attempt to relieve deep-seated guilt feelings. The breaking of a symptom without adequate psychotherapy may provoke violent self-destructive tendencies leading to suicide. Such patients when forced to eat may induce vomiting or may excessively consume laxatives to "give back" what they have unconsciously stolen. This has been observed in cases of colitis.

NERVOUS VOMITING. While in anorexia the incorporative function is inhibited, in patients with nervous vomiting the incorporated food is expelled because of emotional conflict usually due to intense feelings of guilt, motivated by aggressive, grabbing, incorporating tendencies. The patient feels he must give back or return that which he took because of guilt. In addition, vomiting is caused by an unconscious fear of retaliation from the incorporated object, which was incorporated in an aggressive, destructive manner. He fears that the object (food) inside him will turn on him and attack him, so he must expel it.

Disturbances of the Swallowing Act

Esophageal neuroses. In esophageal neuroses, the patient may choke on food because he cannot swallow, again as a result of the rejection of incorporation based on unconscious aggressive impulses. Others have a constant subjective sensation of a foreign body in the upper part of the esophagus (globus hystericus). Kronfeld (1934), on the basis of psychiatric studies, distinguished two forms of esophageal neurosis, a sensory hyperalgetic form and a reflectory spastic form.

The sensory hyperalgetic form may be superimposed on a local disturbance. This does not occur in the spastic form. Kronfeld tried to differentiate between the emotional backgrounds of patients with anorexia, esophageal neurosis, and hysterical vomiting. He compared the esophageal neurotic to the gambler in that both dared to incorporate or take things and expose themselves to an imagined danger. The patient with anorexia simply refuses to eat, and in hysterical vomiting the reaction comes only after the crime symbolized by eating has been committed. Disgust, he felt, played an important role in this disturbance, for he defined disgust as a combination of temptation and rejection with an ambivalent attitude toward incorporation.

Cardiospasm. Cardiospasm is a disturbance of swallowing characterized by a contraction of the lower end of the esophagus, leading to a dilation of the proximal portion. Weiss (1944) concluded that cardiospasm was a disorder with a somatic predisposition but that it was a conversion hysteria which expressed the unconscious symbolic idea, "I can't swallow the situation." The symptom appeared when the patient was in a situation of emotional impasse in regard to some external affair.

Rubin, Nagler, Spiro, and Pilot (1962) recorded esophageal motility with a pressure transducer on five normal subjects during psychiatric interviews and found a significant association between nonpropulsive esophageal activity and affectively charged periods which continued as long as the affectively charged material was discussed.

Disturbances of the Digestive Function

Gastric neuroses. The secretory and motor functions of the stomach and the duodenum are influenced in a complex manner by central and organic (local) factors. Faulty eating habits which may be based on emotional conflicts can produce local organic disturbances, although the primary causes of the faulty eating habits, such as incomplete mastication, rapid eating, immoderation, and poor food selection, are emotional in origin. Complaints may range from slight heartburn to intractable vomiting or to a chronic gastric neurosis, such as "rejection dyspepsia" (Robertson, 1963), which occurs in women who complain of abdominal distension, chronic eructation of air, and small amounts of gastric juice, and who are found to be immature, dependent, and sexually frigid.

Most psychogenic gastric disturbances involve a conflict due to the frustration of help-seeking, dependent tendencies. These infantile dependent fixations often conflict with the adult ego and become repressed because of pride and the wish for independence and self-assertion (F. Alexander, 1934).

Peptic ulcers. Peptic ulcer is one of the most widely recognized conditions where chronic functional disturbance might in time lead to structural (organic) tissue changes. Peptic ulcer may develop after a long history of gastritis, or it may develop acutely with no significant history of gastrointestinal distress. Certain intuitive clinicians have described the ulcer-prone person: the "go-getter" type of Alvarez (1931) and the "man who needs to overcome obstacles" (Hartman, 1933).

Studies conducted at the Chicago Institute for Psychoanalysis have shown that although ulcer occurs more often in one personality type, what is more characteristic is a *typical conflict* situation in which a patient develops an ulcer. Some patients overcompensate for their dependent desires by becoming responsible, but others are openly dependent and demanding, their dependent drives being frustrated not by conscience but by external reality. Thus the critical factor in the pathogenesis of ulcer is the frustration of dependent, help-seeking demands for love. When the wish to receive love is rejected by the adult ego or is frustrated by external circumstances, it is converted regressively into the wish to be fed. This repressed longing to receive love serves as a chronic stimulus which specifically activates gastric hyperfunction. Thus, in response to such emotional needs, the stomach behaves with hypersecretion and hypermotility, as if food were being ingested, and if the added constitutional predisposition is present, an ulcer develops (F. Alexander, 1950).

Many clinical studies have confirmed the pronounced oral receptive trends in ulcer patients which are either overtly expressed or denied. Wiseman (1956) found that the symptoms occurred in six male patients when the "threat of depletion exceeded the promise of replenishment and the angry protest was restrained." Streitfeld (1954) compared the specificity of oral conflict in 20 ulcer patients with that in 20 other psychosomatic patients by means of the Blacky Story score and the Rorschach. He attempted to separate oral aggressive versus dependent tendencies and concluded that oral dependent tendencies were not more common in the ulcer patients (slightly less, in fact) but that oral aggressive tendencies were significantly greater than in the control group.

Garma (1958) believes that a predisposition to ulcer occurs in the early months of life and that when the ulcer patient is later faced with conflict he undergoes an "oral digestive regression," in which the "internalized bad mother aggressively acts in his digestive tract in the form of biting." His concepts are based on Klein's views, which attribute complicated mental processes to young infants. In addition, such symbolization in a truly vegetative adaptive reaction is highly questionable.

Pilot, Lenkowski, Spiro, and Schafer (1957) and Pilot, Rubin, Schafer, and Spiro (1963) described the emotional onset situation of peptic ulcer in identical twins. Both had identical heredity and background and very similar character structures (passive, shy, and dependent), and both had high blood-pepsin levels. A peptic ulcer developed, however, only when each individual found himself in a typical specific precipitating conflict situation. Twin A developed ulcer when his wife had a near psychotic breakdown and threatened violence to her children. The second twin, married to a protective, maternal woman, developed an ulcer later when his wife lost her job and thought she was pregnant.

Taboroff and Brown (1954) studied six male ulcer patients (aged 7 to 15) by psychological tests and interviews and confirmed the specific conflict situation (formulated by F. Alexander) of frustration of dependent, help-seeking demands for love combined with a fear of losing the mother, who was felt to be the sole source of support. Poser and Gilmore (1963) administered five TAT cards to 30 ulcer patients, 30 patients with ulcerative colitis, and 30 controls, and the protocols were subjected to a blind analysis. The significant differences between the three groups were that ulcer patients had high achievement needs, a lack of creative imagination, and a reluctance to relate to their social group and that ulcerative colitis patients exhibited passive, compliant attitudes and an exaggerated tendency to avoid stressful situations. These results added objective validity to the clinical impressions of many other investigators.

Castelnuovo-Tedesco (1962) focused attention on the immediate emotional antecedents in 20 patients who had perforated ulcers of the stomach or duodenum. He suggested that a "perforation syndrome" might be a depressive equivalent of the climax of an emotional conflict in which the patient consciously or unconsciously felt damage to his self-esteem and to which he reacted with impotent rage.

Cleveland and Fisher (1954) obtained the body-image fantasies of ulcer and rheumatoid arthritis patients by the Holzman Blot Test and interviews. The ulcer patients fantasied their body boundaries as weak and vulnerable (low barrier score and high penetration score). In contrast, the arthritis patients conceived of their body boundaries as well-defined "hard shells." Thus the major difference in body image between the groups was that the arthritic's body image was primarily an external part of his body which contained "a fluid substance" (Cleveland & Fisher, 1960). He was athletic and overly friendly, and he condemned exhibitionalism and loud-mouthed behavior. In contrast, the ulcer patient's body boundary was weak and vulnerable, and he felt deprived, manipulated, and maneuvered. By exposing ulcer and arthritis patients to a loud noise and recording heart rate and GSR, they showed that ulcer patients reacted with increased heart rate (penetration). and arthritis patients with a larger GSR reaction (barrier).

Experimental Research on Emotions and Stomach Function

Some of the psychodynamic formulations mentioned above have been tested experimentally. Mittleman and Wolff (1942) subjected 13 normal individuals and 10 patients suffering from ulcers, gastritis, and duodenitis to stress interviews. In all cases, hydrochloric acid, mucous and pepsin secretion, and peristalsis were increased, but the increase was much more pronounced in the pathological group. The ulcer subjects often reacted with pain, increased bile secretion, and bleeding to the experimentally induced anxiety, insecurity, guilt, and frustration. Normal gastric function was reestablished in situations which engendered feelings of emotional security.

Silbermann (1927) sham-fed dogs who had artificial fistulas for periods up to an hour. This caused profound gastric secretion in the empty stomach and regularly produced ulcers.

The findings of Palmer (1933) and Winkelstein (1933) constitute experimental evidence supporting the hypothesis that a causative factor in ulcer is chronic gastric secretion due to psychological conflict. They found increased secretion during the night, and Winkelstein also found high acidity in ulcer patients as a reaction to sham feeding.

H. G. Wolff and Wolf (1942) found hyperemia, hypermotility, and hypersecretion as reactions to insecurity and to inhibited hostile, aggressive feelings in their patient with a gastric fistula. P. Wolff and Levine (1955) analyzed the stomach contents of five ulcer and five nonulcer patients on two successive nights, introducing a stress situation on the second night by suggesting to the subjects that they had stomach pathology. The ulcer patients had much higher acid values than the controls (in volume and in free and total acidity). The acid values of the controls increased markedly the second night, but a similar increase did not occur in the ulcer patients. They proposed that the ulcer patients were already experiencing chronic anxiety, resulting in maximum gastric secretion before the experiment.

Reichsman, Cohen, Colwill, Davis, Kessler, Shepardson, and Engel (1960) correlated states of sleep and wakefulness with hydrochloric acid secretory rates (especially total acid rate) in 28 young, healthy male subjects (two to six nights). They also studied the effect of histamine on parietal cell function during sleep (sleep states were evaluated by EEG and direct observation). Two subcutaneous injections of histamine each night—one during waking and one during sleep—were given. Natural HCL secretion rates varied greatly from subject to subject and in some individuals from night to night. There were no correlations between the states of sleep or waking with HCL secretion rates, either natural or histamine-induced. Their results differed from the studies on the infant Monica (see below), and it was felt that certain methodological difficulties, such as the necessity to use drugs to induce sleep in the adult subjects (or the fact that biological sleep in adults is different from sleep in the depression-withdrawal state in the infant), could have been possible factors. The gastric secretory, psychological, and behavioral studies on the infant Monica, with a gastric fistula (59 experiments during the ages from 15 to 20 months), by Engel, Reichsman, and Segal (1956) had shown that (1) total hydrochloric acid secretion rate was closely related to the total behavioral activity of the infant; (2) outgoing affective states, libidinal or aggressive, were associated with rising rates of hydrochloric acid secretion; (3) the depression-withdrawal reaction, characterized by a sad face, muscular flaccidity, inactivity, and withdrawal, and occasionally progressing into sleep, was correlated with a marked decrease or even cessation of HCL secretion; (4) conversely, the more active transactions with the environment were associated with rising HCL acid secretion rates; (5) histamine was ineffective in stimulating gastric secretion during the depression-withdrawal state but was a potent stimulator of HCL secretion in outgoing states; (6) there was support for the psychoanalytic concept of an oral stage of development with an oral intaking object representation; and (7) the depression-withdrawal reaction in the infant resulted from object loss—a repetition of an earlier depressive pattern which might have represented a regression to the preoral stage of development.

Mahl (1949) studied gastric secretion in dogs and challenged the view that increased gastric secretion was due to a specific emotional conflict. He concluded that only chronic fear produced increased secretion and motility; therefore, Cannon's theory (which relates fear to sympathetic stimulation) was contradicted. F. Alexander (1950) took issue with Mahl's conclusions and explained them by pointing out that what occurred in the dogs was a regressive *parasympathetic* response to fear. In a later study on human subjects (a stress-situation group and reassurance-situation group), Mahl (Mahl & Brody, 1954; Mahl & Karpe, 1953) measured gastric acidity on three successive mornings and reported that acidity of the "chronic anxiety" group was only suggestively greater. However, when pain and pain-anticipation stimulation interacted with sustained pretest anxiety, there was a significant increase in HCL secretion. Mahl again interpreted his results as evidence contradictory to the extension of the emergency theory of emotions to chronic emotional states.

Heller, Levine, and Sohler (1953) studied 10 hospitalized patients, five which upper gastrointestinal complaints and five with no complaints. Their findings were consistent with those of other investigators in demonstrating an increase in gastric acid secretion with anxiety. (Anxiety was induced by indirectly suggesting to the subjects that they had some serious illness.) The elevated acid secretion was sustained over the twelve-hour period of anxiety. The possible effect of spasm and retention of stomach acid and the effect of motor influences on blood supply in the etiology of ulcer are still unclear.

Dale and Feldberg (1934) observed that acetylcholine liberated during parasympathetic stimulation causes anoxemia as well as increased acid secretion. Both Winkelstein and Necheles have commented on the abnormally high parasympathetic irritability of the ulcer patient.

Mirsky and his colleagues (Mirsky, Block, Osher, & Broh-Kahn, 1948) designed one of the first studies for the longitudinal correlation of measurements of gastric secretion with concomitant emotional factors. They largely confirmed the views of F. Alexander and his collaborators. Mirsky used uropepsin levels as an indicator of rates of gastric secretion and related the values to significant daily events. Later papers of Weiner, Thaler, Reiser, and Mirsky (1957) and Mirsky (1958) compared the psychological evaluations with the serum pepsinogen levels of a group of healthy subjects entering the Army (which was traumatic to some subjects). The study was designed to evaluate the *predictive value* of biochemical, psychological, and sociological factors in relation to gastrointestinal activity. The concentration of serum pepsinogen was used as an index of gastric secretion. "Hyposecretors" and "hypersecretors" were studied in terms of their style of interpersonal interaction, which could be inferred from psychoanalytically oriented interviews and derived from projective tests and other psychological techniques.

All the subjects who had or who developed evidence of duodenal ulcer were found to be among those with high pepsinogen values. Independent evaluation of the psychological data revealed that the subjects who developed peptic ulcer had displayed evidence of major unresolved and persistent conflicts with their need for dependent oral gratification. A psychodynamic constellation was formulated on the basis of several of the psychological tests (Blacky test, Saslow questionnaire, Rorschach, etc.). This correlated well with the ratings of the hypersecretors and hyposecretors of pepsinogen. The authors were able to predict the subjects who would develop an ulcer. The study indicated that neither a higher rate of gastric secretion nor a specific psychodynamic constellation alone was responsible for ulcer formation. Together, however, the two parameters constituted essential determinants in the precipitation of an ulcer.

Glass and Wolf (1960) have linked gastrointestinal secretory and motor activity with parasympathetic-sympathetic imbalance (excessive vagal discharge). Well-designed studies by Waddell (1956) showed differences in urinary levels of catechol amines in ulcer and nonulcer patients. These levels may reflect differences in sympatheticoadrenal responsivity. The influences of catechol amines on gastric secretion associated with vasoconstriction of the gastric vessels and the increase in gastric secretion associated with vasodilation have been established. Waddell believes that the rate of gastric secretion is dependent to a large degree on the tonic state of vagal reflex centers, which in turn is maintained by the continuous inflow of afferent impulses from many areas, particularly the mouth and the antral area of the stomach.

Cohen, Bondurant, & Silverman (1960) studied the association of specific emotional states with catechol amine levels and vascular responses. According to the authors, this may be due to the activation of specific hypothalamic areas with the selective release of neurohormones. It has been demonstrated by Folkow and von Euler (1954) that stimulation of specific hypothalamic areas causes the selective release of adrenaline and noradrenaline, and Hillarp (1953) has shown evidence that cells in the adrenal medulla may release adrenaline and noradrenaline independently and that these cells may be innervated by different hypothalamic areas.

The investigations of Chapman, Livingston, Livingston, and Sweet (1950) and Gellhorn (1957) suggest that there may be control mechanisms mediating specific emotional responses and that these mechanisms may be related to neural circuits concerned with the release of catechol amines as well as the activation of specific portions of the autonomic nervous system. Cohen, Silverman, Waddell, and Zuidema (1961) emphasized the need for objective studies on the "interaction of the psychological, gastric, physiological and neurohumoral factors in the development of duodenal ulcer." They hypothesized, on the basis of their previous work, that (1) a consistent relationship might exist between catechol amine levels and the presence or absence of duodenal ulcer, (2) a previously identified relationship between specific psychological characteristics and catechol amine excretory rates might also occur in the subject population, and (3) the psychological characteristics usually associated with various catechol amine levels were not expected in ulcer patients but would be noted only in those who showed characteristic catechol amine levels as well as an ulcer. They did gastric secretory studies and urinary assays for catechol amines on 10 patients with radiologically proved ulcers and on 10 nonulcer patients. A group of psychological tests and a specially constructed interview were administered. The patients whose psychological measures were scored (without any knowledge of clinical diagnosis, gastric secretion, or urinary catechol amine levels) had a high degree of anxiety and a low level of discomfort with the expression of aggressive impulses and were the ones most likely to have a low noradrenaline output and a duodenal ulcer.

The results reconfirmed the correlations previously noted: (1) The levels of adrenaline and noradrenaline excreted in a patient's urine correlated with the degree of aggressivity and anxiety expressed on specific psychological test measures. (2) Specific psychological characteristics can discriminate ulcer and nonulcer patients. (3) The ratio and level of urinary catechol amines might be a reflection of autonomic imbalance and are associated with duodenal ulcers.

A direct experimental attempt to evaluate in monkeys the effect on the stomach and duodenum of chronic stimulation applied to the visceral brainstem was performed by J. P. French, Porter, Cavanaugh, and Longmire (1957). Electric current was applied to the hypothalamus and surrounding regions for thirty to eighty-six days in a test group of 19 animals, as compared with a control group of 20 animals. In the test group, three animals exhibited on autopsy focal leisons in the pyloric antrum, three had "ulcers" in the duodenum, and two showed diffuse changes in the stomach. All the animals in the test group that developed gastroduodenal lesions had received excitation currents to a low midline axis in the hypothalamus. The remaining 11 animals in which visceral changes did not develop had been stimulated outside the central hypothalamic region. These investigators felt it important that focal changes in the gut could be produced by central excitation in animals that do not develop such a disorder spontaneously.

Wenger, Clemens, and Cullen (1962) tested 100 hospitalized patients with chronic disorders during rest and during stimulation (31 ulcer patients, 36 with nonulcerative gastrointestinal disorders, 17 with neurodermatitis, and 16 with other skin disorders) and a normative control sample of 93 university students. A procedure involving fifteen minutes of rest followed by the insertion of the right foot into ice water for one minute was carried out, and autonomic measures were taken. The mean composite score of autonomic balance of each patient group differed significantly from that of the control group. This indicated an apparent relative dominance of sympathetic nervous system activity. Additionally, both the patients with gastrointestinal complaints and those with skin lesions tended to demonstrate more frequently a particular form of mixed physiological pattern, previously reported in other groups, in which certain variables show relative sympathetic dominance, and others relative parasympathetic dominance. No significant differences occurred among the patient groups, but the neurodermatitis and nonulcerative gastrointestinal patients showed significantly less increase in diastolic blood pressure and greater increase in heart rate than the normative subjects. Their results partly supported the hypothesis that different groups of chronic patients differ in autonomic functions and that the greatest differences are demonstrable under controlled resting states.

Studies on stomach function during psychotherapy or psychoanalysis represent an added approach to validate or refute accepted psychodynamic concepts relative to the effects of emotions on the stomach and/or ulcer symptoms.

Margolin (1951) analyzed a 22-year-old Negro woman with a fistulous gastrostomy. He correlated total acid secretion, pepsin, blood flow, and motility with stomach activity with certain specific psychic patterns. He found that when repressed material was about to emerge into consciousness, gastric function was in a state of high activity. If reaction formation was the main psychological defense being used, gastric activity was at a low level. If the ego defenses were in equilibrium, gastric activity was randomized.

Mahl and Karpe (1953) observed the relationship between the intensity of emotion and the degree of HCL secretion in a female analytic patient to evaluate the effect of oral dependency needs (the specificity-nonspecificity concepts) regarding peptic ulcer. They found that all the high acid hours were high anxiety hours and that all the low acid hours were low anxiety hours, although three of the low acid hours were expressions of intense dependency cravings and marked hostility over their frustration. They decided that hydrochloric acid secretion increases with anxiety, whatever its origin (sexual, hostile, or passive dependent), rather than with the needs themselves. They interpreted these results in the same manner as in their earlier studies on dogs and monkeys; i.e., hydrochloric acid secretion plays an etiological part in peptic ulcer. It does not, however, result from an oral dependency, but instead from anxiety.

For 2½ years, Stein, Kaufman, Janowitz, Levy, Hollander, and Winkelstein (1962) studied the gastric secretory functions of a 60-year-old woman with a small gastric fistula (of fifty-two years' duration). Her gastric activity through the fistula was regularly studied while she was receiving, simultaneously although separately, intensive psychotherapy. The hydrochloric acid secretion of the stomach was found to be at persistently high normal levels. She had a severe neurosis with masochistic character traits, and there was clear-cut evidence of intense unconscious oral aggressive conflicts. After eight months of psychotherapy with conscious verbal expression of her previously unconscious oral aggressive drives, HCL secretion dropped abruptly and remained at a low normal level for the next eighteen months. It appeared possible that psychotherapy, by allowing the patient to express the unconscious oral aggressive fantasies, lessened their stimulating effect on the secretory activity of the stomach. A more probable explanation, they felt, was that psychotherapy forced the patient to become aware of anxiety-provoking oral conflicts which led to a "depression-withdrawal" type of reaction, with inhibition of the stimulating oral fantasies and a withdrawal of cathexis from oral objects (like the therapist and one of the physiologists to whom she was closely attached) and with a resultant decrease in the secretory activity of the stomach.

Kehoe and Ironside (1962) used seven healthy volunteer subjects and subjected them to hypnosis. Under hypnosis, five categories of affective response were induced and measured psychologically and physiologically. In hypnotized and nonhypnotized subjects, the total gastric secretory rate was highest with anger and lowest with hopelessness and helplessness.

Therapeutic Considerations

In peptic ulcer, the first therapeutic consideration must be treatment of the local condition with antiacids or antispasmodics or by surgery. Section of the vagus nerve to the stomach is a useful technique in the therapy of peptic ulcer since it decreases the continuous acid secretion. However, psychotherapy is the only treatment which can alter the patient's psychic conflict, which constitutes the primary disturbance in the chain of events causing the ulcer. Szasz (1949) emphasized the fact that vagotomized patients are prone to develop other more or less serious disturbances if no psychotherapy is undertaken. It should be remembered as a general principle that psychotherapy in all disorders of functional nature is not directed at the symptom but at the underlying conflicts. Orgel (1958) reported his results on the psychoanalytic treatment of his 15 patients with peptic ulcer. Follow-up studies undertaken ten to twenty-two years later showed that 10 patients remained symptom-free but that five cases did not benefit. (It was questionable, however, whether these five patients received adequate therapy.)

It appears, as claimed by Alexander and his group at the Chicago Institute for Psychoanalysis, that in carefully chosen ulcer cases, brief active psychoanalytically oriented psychotherapy directed at the patient's specific emotional conflict may produce marked symptomatic improvement as well as a marked personality change toward maturity (F. Alexander, 1946).

Disturbances of the Eliminative Function

The excremental functions play an important role in the emotional life of the infant since bowel function and training have a profound association with emotional attitudes such as possessiveness, pride in achievement, and tendencies to give and to retain. Pleasurable sensations can also be produced by retaining feces, and adult interference with this pleasure is more difficult than with sucking. The child develops a feeling of independence associated with anal function. However, this self-assertive attitude conflicts with toilet training, which "specifies" regular intervals and a certain place for bowel movements. Resistance to toilet training is also based on the child's coprophilic attitude toward his excreta, which become a valued possession. (Feces is thus the child's first real "possession" or money with which he can barter.) This coprophilic attitude is, however, inhibited by educational procedures and changed to its opposite, that of disgust and depreciation, which explains its later sadistic and aggressive (soiling) connotation. Hence, hostile impulses such as attacking and soiling also become associated with elimination.

Chronic diarrhea; spastic colitis; mucous colitis. White, Cobb, and Jones (1939) viewed mucous colitis as a disorder of function of the colon resulting from an overactive parasympathetic nervous system due to neurotic conflicts. Overconscientiousness, dependency, sensitivity, anxiety, guilt, and resentment are the emotional traits most commonly found in patients suffering from mucous as well as other forms of colitis. Patients with chronic diarrhea and spastic or mucous colitis reveal a typical conflict centering around their strong demanding (oral aggressive and receptive) wishes, for which they try to compensate by activity and the urge to give through substituting bowel movements for real accomplishment or giving (Wilson, 1934). They must give compensation for all they want to receive or take from others. They worry and fret about their duties and obligations and appear overconscientious, but they harbor a great reluctance to exert themselves in any systematic or strenuous work. Thus an essential difference is seen between the patient with colitis and the peptic ulcer patient who also overcompensates for dependency but who does so by actual exertion and accomplishment in his external activities.

Ulcerative colitis. Many authors after Murray (1930) and Sullivan (1932) commented on the importance of emotional factors in ulcerative colitis. In spite of many systematized studies, the mechanisms (hormonal, biochemical, neurological) by which psychological conflicts influence the course of the pathological physiological process in the mucous membrane of the colon are not known. Psychosomatic explanations of ulcerative colitis tend to involve the following hypotheses with varying degrees of emphasis: (1) Affects influence the colon via the parasympathetic division of the autonomic nervous system and can produce in predisposed persons a severe and persistent diarrhea which secondarily leads to tissue pathology. (2) Ulcerative colitis is a complex psychophysiological state, with depression as its affective expression and vascular changes in the mucosa and submucosa as its somatic expression.

Grace, Wolf, and Wolff (1951) have called ulcerative colitis part of an ejection-riddance pattern involving the human colon, whereby a subject, when confronted by overwhelming environmental demands, may elaborate a pattern of ejection.

Groen (1947) views ulcerative colitis as the result of chronic anxiety which produces a motility imbalance leading secondarily to ulceration. The anxiety is due to an inability to take action in life.

Lindemann (1945) described 87 patients with the disease and believed that the loss of a key person followed by a "morbid grief" reaction was the important etiologic agent. He was struck with the similarity of the affect of the colitis patients to that of people suffering severe morbid grief reactions.

Prugh (1950) speaks of the "conditioned hypermobile response of the rectosigmoid region of the large bowel to emotional stimuli of a specific type." He sees a basic conflict in which a child who intensely wishes to be loved and accepted by his parents finds in himself unacceptable feelings of anger and resentment toward them as a result of their inconsistent and confused handling of him. The onset of the disease occurs when emotional security is lost and when acute and overwhelming, yet unacceptable, guilt-provoking anger or resentment is aroused in the patient.

Sperling (1946) has described a characteristic mother-child relationship in which the mother manifests a contradictory attitude of unconsciously attempting to maintain the child in a state of lifelong dependency on her in order to satisfy her own needs and simultaneously showing strong unconscious destructive impulses toward the child, which become intensified if the child fails to satisfy her needs or if his attempts to do so mobilize guilt or anxiety in her. Avoidance of illness depends upon the patient's willingness and ability to find a replacement for the unsatisfactory or lost love object. If he is unable to accomplish this, intense frustration ensues, with an acute increase in repressed destructive impulses which are discharged through the symptom of bleeding. Sperling has equated ulcerative colitis with a "somatic dramatization of melancholia" in which "the destruction and elimination of the object through the mucosa of the colon would seem to be the specific mechanism." F. Alexander (1950) has cautioned against the interpretation of psychological findings in ulcerative colitis as causative in nature since organic symptoms such as diarrhea may be utilized by patients symbolically to express fantasies or feelings. The fantasy of eliminating a bad mother, assumed to be a psychogenic factor by Sperling, may well be a secondary utilization of the symptom for unconscious needs rather than the cause of it. This is especially so when one considers that diarrhea is not evident as an initial symptom in many cases. Thus the explanation of the diarrhea as a restitutive giving also has to be reconsidered.

Engel (1954a; 1954b; 1955; 1956; 1958) has emphasized the primary etiologic importance of the impaired vascularity of the mucosa and submucosa of the colon in ulcerative colitis. Psychologically, he stresses the role of the symbiotic nature of the mother-child relationship in the onset of the disease due to real or fantasied loss of this key object, with a consequent atypical depression. Thus the essential psychological condition leading to the onset of ulcerative colitis is an affective state characterized by helplessness and despair. The mother-child relationship is one in which the mother can be warm and succoring only if the child's behavior does not mobilize guilt or anxiety in her. The basic needs of the child such as feeding, bowel activity, and motor activity seemed to evoke anxiety, guilt, or shame in the "colitigenic" mothers. As a result, the child (future patient) relinquishes a considerable amount of autonomy over bodily function to the mother in order to obtain security and love. As a result of this symbiosis, the major part of the ego of the child remains within the mother, producing a state of helplessness. Any separation is then particularly traumatic for the child.

Fullerton, Kollar, and Caldwell (1962) studied 47 ulcerative colitis patients with the following conclusions: (1) Diarrhea is a secondary process and thus not an etiological factor, contrary to motility and symbolization hypotheses. (2) A majority of the cases had premorbid bowel difficulties unrelated to ulcerative colitis. (3) Ninety per cent had histories of other psychosomatic and psychiatric disorders. (4) A consistent pattern existed of weak fathers and controlling, hostile, overprotective, or domineering mothers. (5) A majority suffered feelings of heterosexual inadequacy, and many had homosexual fears without perverse histories. (6) Events precipitating acute episodes could be interpreted as object losses or as the loss of a major source of narcissistic gratification. (7) A passive, inactive depression characterized a majority of the patients both in interviews and on psychological testing, and this depression coincided with or preceded the somatic process, rather than being a result of it. (8) Depression was more preeminent among the colitis patients than in a control group of patients referred for psychiatric evaluation. (9) Ulcerative colitis is a complex psychobiological state which occurs in predisposed individuals as a consequence of real or fantasied object loss. (10) Panpsychopathology is consistently present in these patients and is evidence of their defective ego structure, which predisposed them to a morbid response to object loss. (11) They felt there was no basis for symbolic etiology of the disorder, nor could it be linked to specific difficulties in the mother-child relationship during a circumscribed phase of development.

Mohr, Joselyn, Spurlock, and Barron (1958) studied ulcerative colitis in six children (7 to 11 years of age). All the patients' mothers felt a lack of maternal warmth and care from their own mothers and thus were unable to develop their own effective patterns of mothering. Three aspects of mothers' experience of, and reaction to, maternal care and pregnancy were important: (1) they themselves had minimal gratification from their own mothers; (2) they viewed the world as a dangerous place, in which one survived only as a result of one's efforts; and (3) at the time of the birth of the child who later developed ulcerative colitis, some event either in their external life or relating to their pregnancy disturbed their emotional economy enough so that they were even less capable of maternal giving. A parental inability to meet the needs of the child was found in all cases, and the response of the child was an effort toward independence and self-reliance in order to satisfy those needs not adequately provided for by the parents. This overstriving of the colitis or precolitis child represented a lifesaving maneuver, a reaction to fantasied danger of abandonment to destructive forces, maternal or environmental. When such compensatory efforts of the child to assume parental responsibility for himself fail, a feeling of helplessness develops, accompanied by augmentation of symptoms.

Arthur (1963) tested 19 children with ulcerative colitis (10 boys and 9 girls) with the Thematic Apperception Test to obtain the role perception of the self and various members of the family group in terms of the incidence of three needs, *n* Dominance, *n* Nurturance, and *n* Succorance. Her findings were as follows (1): The boys viewed the mothers as being less dominant than the girls did and as being more in need of succorance. The girls viewed the mother as primarily dominating but as capable of giving nurturance if manipulated into doing so. (2) The boys and the girls did not differ in regard to the ways in which they viewed the father figure when the quantitative analysis was made, but they did differ primarily in regard to the role played by the father in maintaining the hypercathected mother-child relationship. (3) The boys and the girls differed significantly in their views of both same-sexed and heterosexual relationships at the adult level. Both groups regarded adult relationships as a continuation of the relationships which they had in childhood with their parents. (4) The boys and the girls differed in their self-percept, with the boys attributing *n* Succorance to the self-percept more often than *n* Dominance or *n* Nurturance. The girls also projected the *n* Succorance to the self-percept but did so less often, being more inclined than the boys to project *n* Dominance. The girls showed very little *n* Nurturance, while the boys showed more. The family patterns of the children obtained by another technique were in general agreement with the clinical findings of Engel, Sperling, and Prugh.

In a psychophysiological study during psychotherapy, Karush, Hiatt, and Daniels (1955) have shown evidence of organ activity as related to emotional and ideational patterns. They measured the physiological activity of the parotid glands, the peripheral vascular bed, and the distal colon in six patients with ulcerative colitis during psychotherapeutic interviews and demonstrated that (1) the outstanding personality characteristic of their patients was a dependency on a magical and omnipotent authority, (2) the patients had a general personality structure resembling that of paranoid schizophrenics, and (3) the most significant emotion coincident with the appearance of segmental colonic activity was *fear*. When rage toward the parental figures was present, its expression was inhibited by fear of retaliation and was accompanied by persistent autonomic excitation of the colon. Colonic activity was associated with almost complete inhibition of salivary activity during interviews. The vascular bed responses were not specific.

Thus fear related to conflict over dependent attitudes causes frustration or a threat to security and provokes rage leading to intense, usually unconscious, fear of retaliation, which is then equated with death and which must be repressed. Such states of fear and rage produce persistent autonomic excitation. "Activation" of the colon is an outlet for this excitation and may be induced by an infantile fantasy of defecation as a means of expressing the suppressed rage at the frustrating parent or by other equally archaic fantasies of the rectum and its contents, stimulated by the patient's inability to resolve security conflicts on a mature, conscious level. However, after the disorder begins and local symptomatology has developed, subjective experiences are secondarily elaborated in primitive terms of destruction.

Most authors make some reference to the regressive, pregenital (narcissistic) emotional organization of ulcerative colitis patients, their prevailing anal characteristics and their unusually strong ambivalent dependence upon the mother, which results in repressed, sadistic, hostile impulses. The personality organization of patients with ulcerative colitis closely resembles that of patients with other forms of diarrhea, and a psychodynamic differentiation is difficult and may be quantitative rather than qualitative. The integrative capacity of the ego of many ulcerative colitis patients is relatively weak, and consequently there is a tendency toward projection and psychotic episodes. Certainly the authors have been impressed with the vulnerability of the ulcerative colitis patient to object loss (even through sharing) and by their strong desire to maintain a primitive symbiotic relationship. However, F. Alexander (1946; 1950) and F. Alexander and French (1948) have made certain specific observations regarding the conflicts of ulcerative colitis patients and particularly the emotional constellation preceding the onset and exacerbation of the illness. Two emotional factors are conspicuous in the precipitation of the disease and its relapses: (1) the frustration of a need to carry out an obligation, whether it is biological, moral, or material, and (2) the patient's hopeless attitude about his capacity to accomplish something which requires concentrated expenditure of energy. In women this most frequently has to do with conflicts about giving birth to a child or living up to maternal responsibilities, whereas in men the conflict may be over the realization of a financial or professional goal.

Commonly, ulcerative colitis patients have ambitious parents who wished to realize their own goals through their children at an early age. Acceptance and love of the child is based upon performance and living up to high parental standards—often ill-defined and unclear to the child. Since failure in achievement is equated with worthlessness (loss of love), the child strives desperately to please through achieving. When "good is not good enough" and the patient senses failure in spite of all effort, his self-confidence and pseudo-self-reliance are replaced by a feeling of hopelessness, futility, and desperation. A period of depression or flu-like symptoms may develop, followed by the onset of frank colitic symptoms.

All forms of anal regressive emotional stimuli have a specific affinity toward the function of the colon. This is related to the infant's emotional evaluation of the excremental act, which signified the loss of a cherished possession, on the one hand, and an accomplishment or achievement, on the other. If an emotional fixation occurs with an ambivalence conflict, when such a person is expected in later life to "give" or "accomplish" something or to take the initiative on an adult level and when at the same time appropriate external behavior is inhibited, a regression to the anal form of giving or accomplishment ensues. However, since anal regression of this type is very common in all kinds of diarrhea and in psychoneurotics who do not display any somatic symptoms, some unknown somatic factor must be responsible for the fact that in some patients anal regression produces ulceration in the bowel.

Engel (1954a; 1954b), in his review of the literature on the local and systemic physiology of ulcerative colitis, emphasized that bleeding rather than diarrhea or constipation is the first symptom of the illness in 60 per cent of the cases. The somatic manifestations may be the expression of a basic severe psychobiological depressive reaction due to helplessness and object loss. On the other hand, the view that frustrated or inhibited externally directed effort mobilizes bowel activity (peristalsis and/or hyperemia) is strongly supported by clinical observation. Further discussion of the physiological mechanisms of the ulcerative process is beyond the scope of this brief review, but the relationships between psychological, general, and local somatic factors need further clarification.

Engel (1956) has observed that headaches very commonly herald an improvement in the colitis patient and occur during remissions (see the later section on headaches). Psychotherapy of the ulcerative colitis patient, especially during an acute exacerbation of the colitis, is a most difficult task. It is absolutely necessary for the internist and the psychiatrist to coordinate their efforts. The results of short-term psychotherapy (three months) on 70 hospitalized ulcerative colitis patients (Mt. Sinai, New York), with follow-up information on 40 of the patients, were reported by Weinstock (1961). He mentioned the difficulties inherent in evaluating objectively the results of psychotherapy in this illness. He concluded that (1) ulcerative colitis patients improved generally during hospitalization, regardless of the form of treatment, but that psychotherapy seemed to contribute to their physical and emotional improvement; (2) psychotherapy did not, however, prevent recurrences after discharge, nor did it prevent ileostomy; (3) there was nothing specific in the personality or the conflict of the patients; and (4) patients must be selected very carefully and should be treated by experienced analysts.

Earlier, Daniels (1948) had noted the self-destructive component in the ulcerative colitis patient. Later, Daniels, O'Connor, Karush, Moses, Flood, and Lepore (1962) reviewed the results over fifteen years on 57 cases seen at least seven times at the Columbia Psychoanalytic Clinic. Five of the cases had over three hundred analytic hours. Their results were more optimistic than those of Weinstock in that they felt that psychotherapy helped the patients in their interpersonal adjustments and careers. They emphasized two points, which have been recognized by Engel and by the authors' own experiences. First, a crucial factor in the treatment of the ulcerative colitis patient is his feeling of security in a relationship with a physician (or an institution), to whom he can turn in times of stress. This alone is good reason for never formally discharging such a patient from therapy. Under such management many patients may function well physically and emotionally for long periods without relapses, whereas if they were terminated they would soon become depressed and regress into illness.

Second, a basic goal in the psychotherapy of the ulcerative colitis patient is to help him accept more realistic goals instead of urging him to perform beyond his capacity. Also, they must learn to accept failure as a possibility in any human endeavor and to realize that it should not be considered a measuring stick of one's worth. This gradually may lead to considerable increase in self-esteem, a feeling of well-being, and a remission of colitic symptoms.

Chronic psychogenic constipation. Emotional conflict is the most common cause of constipation. Persons with chronic constipation exhibit attitudes of pessimism, defeat, and distrust of, or lack of confidence in, others, accompanied by the feeling of being rejected or actually mistreated. In exaggerated cases, this attitude may become a paranoid delusion resembling those seen in a psychotic depression. A positive correlation between constipation, paranoia, and depression was found in statistical studies conducted by F. Alexander and Menninger (1936).

The emotional psychodynamics of chronic constipation are as follows: "I cannot expect anything from anybody, and therefore I do not need to give anything. I must hold on to what I have." Also, an unconscious aggressive and depreciatory attitude toward others, which is a reaction to the general feeling of being rejected, is found. This attitude is so deeply repressed and inhibited that instead of soiling and attacking, with feces, the person who has angered him, the patient becomes constipated. Constipation is often a spite reaction toward love objects, a refusal to give them love or a means of controlling them. The common identification of feces with a child has been described by several early psychoanalysts as the frequent basis of constipation; the withholding of feces expresses unconscious pregnancy fantasies.

EMOTIONAL FACTORS IN RESPIRATORY DISTURBANCES

Bronchial Asthma

Asthma was originally considered a nervous illness ("asthma nervosa"), but later the recognition of allergic factors came into the foreground. However, recently emotional factors have been reemphasized as contributing to asthmatic attacks (Dunbar, 1943, 1947a, 1947b; T. M. French and F. Alexander, 1941).

The Chicago Institute for Psychoanalysis studied asthma and outlined a nuclear psychodynamic conflict. The asthma patient shows an excessive and repressed dependence on the mother as a constant feature around which different types of character defenses develop. Therefore, the patient may be aggressive and ambitious, or he may be a hypersensitive person. The dependency need of the asthma patient differs from that of the ulcer patient who wishes to be fed. The asthma patient wants to be accepted and protected by the mother or her surrogate. His fantasies and dreams reflect this wish, with a high frequency of intrauterine fantasies expressed in the form of water symbolism of caves and closed places (T. M. French and F. Alexander, 1941). Real or threatened separation from the protective mother image commonly precedes an asthmatic attack. The precipitating factor in the onset and later attacks of the illness are well recognized: (1) In children, it may be the birth of a sibling or the sibling rivalry which develops later. (2) In a girl, it may be the menarche, which because of competition or guilt separates the girl symbolically from her mother since she now sees herself as the mother's competitor instead of her child. (3) In the boy, oedipal wishes may threaten the dependent relationship to the mother, for mothers of asthmatics are aware that they are physically attracted to their sons and, as a defense, react to them with rejection and withdrawal, which the boy perceives as a separation trauma. (4) In adults, sexual temptation or illicit love affairs may precipitate attacks. (5) Thus any aggressive or defiant impulse directed against the mother or any surge of independent behavior may precipitate the onset or an attack of asthma. Maternal rejection in the lives of asthma patients is found as a recurrent motif, and the child who still needs maternal care and acceptance characteristically responds to it with an increase in insecurity and clinging to the mother. A paradoxical situation occurs, however, when some mothers are insistent in pushing the child toward a premature and unacceptable independence. Just the opposite result is achieved, and the child reacts by becoming more insecure and clinging.

Weiss (1922) postulated that the repressed desire for the mother produces spasm of the bronchioles, since the asthmatic attack represents a suppressed cry for the mother. Halliday (1937a) also postulated the same relationship. Asthma patients do spontaneously report that they do not cry easily, and moreover, many observers have repeatedly noted that asthmatic attacks often terminate when the patient releases emotional tension by crying or by freely ventilating his secrets. Immediate improvement in patients after they had confessed something for which they felt guilty and for which they expected rejection was reported by T. M. French (1944). The confession reestablishes the dependent attachment to the parent or to the therapist in the transference relationship. Although speaking (confession) is a more sophisticated use of the respiratory apparatus for communication than the child's crying, the aims of both are the same—to regain the love of the person upon whom the patient depends. The suppression of prolonged crying leads to dyspnea and wheezing, as can be observed in a child who tries to control his urge to cry. This struggle resembles an attack of asthma.

This *inhibition of free communication* with a person on which the patient depends is the most specific psychological factor in the precipitation of asthmatic attacks. The relative etiological importance in asthma of emotional conflict and allergic sensitivity is still uncertain, although if they coexist, as is common, either factor alone may produce an attack. After resolution of their emotional conflict, the attacks of asthma disappear in many patients since they resulted from a combination of the emotional and allergic factors ("summation of stimuli").

The Child Study Center at Mount Sinai Hospital, Los Angeles, has studied eczema and asthma in the preschool child (Mohr, Selesnick, & Augenbraun, 1963; Mohr, Tausend, Selesnick, & Augenbraun, 1963). Based on their observations of the interfamilial dynamics in early eczema and asthma which precipitated and/or reinforced the symptoms, they proposed a developmental communicative scheme in regard to these illnesses. They note that the eczematous child is infantilized by his parents and that the mode by which the child or parent expresses affects is referred to the cutaneous area of the child (a primitive organ of communication). The asthmatic child senses that his mother feels inadequate in attending to his needs, and as a result he develops a pseudo mature character structure, which is perpetuated as long as he has a modicum of support forthcoming from the mother or her surrogate. When he feels that he might alienate his mother by verbally expressing affects of which she disapproves, he fears estrangement from her, and the pseudo mature defense structure collapses, which leads to an asthmatic wheeze (a disturbance in an organ involved in a higher mode of communication). Selesnick (1964) has proposed that the threat of separation may not be from the actual mother but from the internalized concept the child has of his mother as well as from the fantasy relationship to the father or to any strongly cathected object, internalized or externalized.

Knapp and Nemetz (1957a) conducted psychophysiological studies on 40 patients with chronic, active perennial asthma. A certain degree of neuroticism was found in all their subjects, who ranged from mildly neurotic individuals with mild physical incapacity to severely disturbed individuals with crippling respiratory illness. (Seven had psychotic episodes, but there was no simple relationship between asthma and psychosis.) However, they found a high positive correlation between the severity of the pulmonary disturbance and the severity of the personality disturbance, which had often existed years before the development of asthma. No patient with severe asthma was found who did not also have major personality problems. Later (1957b) they studied the sources of tension in asthmatic patients and established that their position in the family did not differ from that of a group of psychoneurotics but that more asthma patients were married than in the psychoneurotic group. A major area of conflict was chronically unsatisfied oral needs leading to depression and shame, which were closely related to nasal and olfactory preoccupation. Concern over crying, concealment, confession, and speech was found, not because of their content, but for their motor and acoustic values. More than half of the patients had been exposed to a respiratory illness of a member of their families, usually of a nonallergic nature. No factor had universal significance. Knapp and Nemetz felt that the oral-nasal-vocal-respiratory apparatus could be sensitized in different ways, such as identification with the respiratory patterns of others.

They found in their psychoanalytic study of 406 attacks in nine severely asthmatic patients that feelings and fantasies of physical illness tended to accompany asthmatic attacks (1960). These fantasies protected them against obvious psychological problems, although after the asthma became established, there were emotional concomitants of a depressive character (sadness, helplessness, hopelessness, and at times ideas of dangerous or poisonous inner substances). Usually within forty-eight hours before an attack, some event caused the arousal and excitement of a drive or impulse, and this state of arousal was then inhibited because of a fear of loss of love. Thus events which led to frustration of powerful impulses and those which seemed to stimulate or eroticize dangerous wishes, although not necessarily specific for asthma, might activate a vulnerable respiratory pattern having both intake and expulsion functions.

In a recent study, Knapp and Bahnson (1963) conceptualized emotions as existing within a field in complex interplay with one another and with ego processes, unconscious drive states, and fantasies of key persons. They studied a severely ill male and a female asthmatic patient from this point of view. Interviews and data from repeated administration of a brief "microbattery" of psychologic assessment procedures were used to quickly and repeatedly tap various levels of the emotional field. They used a blind rating procedure on 21 sessions. The results seemed to prove the relationship between the regressive breakdown of certain defenses, the activation of powerful drives and emotional processes, and the exacerbation of the asthma.

Purcell, Berstein, and Bukantz (1961) studied asthmatic children in the Jewish National Home by making observations on two groups. Group I included those children who dramatically became symptom-free and who remained so when separated from their homes. Group II consisted of those children who required continuous maintenance doses of corticosteroids to remain symptom-free. They explained the differences in the two groups on the basis of the psychological influences. The group who became rapidly symptom-free in the Jewish home were shown to have more neurotic symptoms, but with a later age of onset. However, no significant difference was found in the frequency with which symptoms usually related to asthma (i.e., coughing and nasal discharge) were reported. A parent attitude test showed that the parents of the rapidly remitting children more often practiced certain psychologically undesirable methods of child rearing (e.g., hostile rejection) than the parents of the steroid dependent children. Thus psychological disturbance among the rapidly remitting children and their families was generally more frequent, and they stressed the importance of treating these groups separately in psychological investigations of the asthmatic children.

In isolated observations on sudden death from asthma, Leigh (1955) presented the thesis that such sudden deaths from status asthmaticus may be due to extensive vagal discharge, which produces bronchial constriction and increased bronchial secretion, and it is possible that this could follow excessive emotional discharge during psychiatric interviews.

Stein and Ottenberg (1958) observed that 22 out of 25 asthma patients reported that odors (usually anal derivatives) had precipitated asthmatic attacks. By exposing asthmatic subjects to such odors, they discovered that the subjects had a significant blocking of associations to common odorous substances which were definitely connected with childhood experiences and unresolved conflicts usually of the anal period. Frequently the asthmatic patients showed a "perceptual type" of blocking of association to odors, which was considered an attempt to avoid stimulation of unresolved infantile conflicts. Also, a respiratory reflex with the purpose of denying further access of the odors to the lungs occurred. This led to the hypothesis that the attack of the asthmatic patient is a means of physiologically defending against odors connected with childhood conflicts.

Dekker and Groen (1956) studied the effect of psychological stimuli (on the basis of the patients' individual history) in reproducing asthmatic attacks. Using the vital capacity as a measure of the patient's condition, they found that they reproduced in 6 out of 12 of the subjects attacks indistinguishable from spontaneous attacks. For instance, one patient gave an account of an asthmatic attack starting immediately after viewing a goldfish in a bowl. When the experimenters exposed the patient to a goldfish in a bowl, he developed a severe asthmatic attack with a fall in vital capacity similar to that of a spontaneous attack. After such provocation tests, the patients related traumatic life experiences, disturbing fantasies, and dreams. Often the environmental asthmatogenic stimulus was associatively related to the former traumatic life experiences. They concluded that a high intensity of emotion was not sufficient to produce an attack but also that the emotional setting needed to be more or less specific.

Funkenstein (1953) correlated the cardiovascular responses of asthmatic patients exposed to psychological stress situations with the severity and duration of asthmatic attacks experimentally produced by mecholyl (which precipitates asthma only in asthma patients). Using the cardiovascular system as a measure of response to stress, they found that mecholyl produced severe asthmatic attacks in all asthmatic subjects during the *nonstressful situation. During the stressful situation, however, the drug produced no asthmatic attacks or only mild ones.* This evidence suggests that excessive secretion of norepinephrinelike or epinephrinelike substances during stress in the patient's life could account for the absence or mildness of the asthmatic attack precipitated by mecholyl at that time. These findings confirmed the observations of Grace, Wolf, and Wolff (1951) that the physiologic action of drugs on the autonomic nervous system varies with the emotional state of patients.

Doust, Lovett, and Leigh (1953) studied 25 asthmatic patients by the use of spectroscopic oximetry. They found that emotional tension denied free expression produced anoxemia. In asthma-prone subjects, such emotional tensions may cause asthmatoid symptoms of expiratory dyspnea. This anoxemia could be overcome by the motor expression of emotion or by asthma. They postulated a condition resembling neurogenic shock, existing as an alternative of the asthma attack under intense emotion.

Ottenberg, Stein, Lewis, and Hamilton (1958) by sensitization procedures, produced a respiratory syndrome in young male guinea pigs with a marked resemblance to human asthma. Differences in susceptibility to attacks suggested inherent biological differences. They conditioned the pigs and found that asthma can be learned, for many guinea pigs had several daily attacks in response to the experimental chamber without the presence of allergic substances. Evidence for the validity of the learned response was that extinction of the conditioned reflex was possible. This demonstration that asthma can be learned is important, not only in relation to allergic factors, but also in relation to any agent such as physical irritants, odors, or psychological factors that may produce bronchiolar constriction.

Colds and Respiratory Disorders

Ruddick (1963) maintains that the word "cold," as it is used in many languages, reveals that the term is closely associated with ideas of birth, death, pregnancy, and sexual arousal. In his study he considered only those coryzalike conditions which seemed related predominantly to two emotional-stress situations—separation and loss, either actual or threatened. Separation situations ranged from actual separation of one person from another to separation from one environment to another. The loss situations varied from actual loss of a person, object, job, or income to memorial mourning reactions. In one of his patients, coughing and sniffling were related to unconscious fantasies around oral and anal respiratory incorporation. In an extensively analyzed female patient, the fantasies around intercourse, impregnation, pregnancy, and birth were filled with particularly terrifying ideas. In her case, agoraphobic symptoms associated with separations and losses later changed to severe colds under such circumstances, and later on in the analysis they changed to depression and mourning. The cold symptoms appeared to be related to fantasies of incorporation mobilized by the loss of an object. In other female cases, although the defense mechanisms and the conflict situations differed, the colds showed a relationship to separations and losses. In the male cases, evidence suggested that the colds were related to conflicts over feminine identification, complicated by the arousal of passive oral wishes.

The cases studied could not be called clearly psychosomatic since at times they resembled hysterical conversion symptoms and at times depressive equivalents. The two functions of respiration—breathing and smelling—must be differentiated. The close relationship of the oral (taste) and respiratory (smell) spheres was obvious, but a study of this relationship is needed to clarify the role of the cold in the hierarchy of conflict, symptom, and defense.

EMOTIONAL FACTORS IN CARDIOVASCULAR DISTURBANCES

Disturbances of Heart Action (Bradycardia, Tachycardia, and Arrhythmia)

Functional cardiovascular disturbances (such as tachycardia, nervous palpitation, arrhythmias, and neurocirculatory asthenia) have long been recognized, but only recently have systematic investigations been conducted on the nervous control of heart function because of its complexity and because of technological difficulties. A general correlation between the emotions of anxiety, fear, and rage and heart action; their general vascular hemodynamics; and their relationship to the autonomic nervous system have been studied by Ax (1953). These emotions are chronically sustained in many types of psychoneurosis, particularly in anxiety states. Symptom choice, i.e., the development of an arrythmia rather than a tachycardia, is determined by the interaction of constitutional differences, structural defects, and emotional factors, and any one factor may be decisive (i.e., a slight structural defect exists which forms the nucleus of neurotic symptoms). Chronic free-floating anxiety or repressed hostile impulses are usually involved. Resting heart rate is regulated by the sinoauricular (SA) node, or "pacemaker" (a small bundle of nerve cells). Heart-rate changes are caused by variations in the effect of the vagus nerve on the SA node. An increase in vagal tone will produce slowing of heart rate (bradycardia), and strong increase will produce a transitory complete heart block (Stokes Adams syndrome) characterized by very slow pulse rate (10 to 20 per minute), dizziness leading to fainting, and possibly convulsions. Recently, Meinhardt and Robinson (1962) studied a 28-year-old man with frequent Stokes Adams episodes whose only pathology was conduction abnormalities. Detailed psychiatric study revealed that the episodes of complete heart block which occurred during interviews resulted from the expression of intense grief and resentment over disappointed dependency strivings. Probably these emotions produced intense vagal stimulation leading to the heart block. Premature contractions and irregular heart rate (sinus arrhythmia) also result from variations in vagal tone. Sinus tachycardia (rapid heart rate) and paroxysmal tachycardia (episodes of very fast heart rate) may be due to a sudden decrease in vagal tone. It is emphasized, however, that although arrythymias may be functional, they are often signs of a severe underlying organic disease. It is probable that under chronic emotional tension, a functional disorder may gradually develop into a structural disorder. This explains certain situations where patients with a diagnosis of functional or neurotic heart disorders may suddenly die from coronary occlusion. All this demonstrates the futility of separating organic from functional illness.

Coronary Artery Disease

The layman and the clinician alike have commonly assumed an etiological relationship between emotional tension (especially suppressed anger associated with a feeling of impotence) and angina pectoris, coronary artery disease, hypertension, and stroke (cerebrovascular accident). The common expressions, "Don't have a stroke," "Don't have a coronary," and "Don't get your blood pressure up" are not chance remarks. What is intriguing is the fact that until late 1959, there were only a few studies which dealt with the investigation of this problem (Arlow, 1945; Gildea, 1949).

Warren (1963) studied documented cases of myocardial infarction in a large industrial utility with relation to functional physiologic and laboratory parameters. He found that 79.4 per cent of attacks were experienced in the 46-to-60-year age group and that the place where the coronary occlusion occurred was related to the actual time spent in that specific activity. Cholesterol and uric acid levels appeared to be unimportant. However, hypertension, obesity, diabetes, peptic ulcer, renal disease, and smoking appeared to be related to an increased incidence of myocardial infarction.

Pell and D'Alonzo's (1963) six-year study on 1,356 employed patients from 25 to 64 years of age found that among salaried employees, the risk of infarction appeared to be inversely related to job level. An increase of attacks occurred during waking hours in persons with hypertension and/or diabetes and in overweight men under age 45 (in those over 45, weight had no significance).

In another sixteen-year study, Keys, Taylor, Blackburn, Bruzek, Anderson, and Simonson (1963) investigated the importance of relative weight, body fatness, blood pressure (BP), and serum cholesterol of 281 healthy Minnesota business and professional men. At the first year examination, only the cholesterol level was statistically significantly related to the incidence of coronary disease, although body weight and increased systolic blood pressure increased the susceptibility during later years. However, Dimond (1963) described a study of 527 railway operating employees with high blood pressure. A follow-up analysis, twenty to thirty-five years later, showed that severe high blood pressure was associated with a significantly increased incidence of cerebral vascular accidents, disability, and death. However, the incidence of coronary heart disease was not related to the degree of high blood pressure.

Gildea (1949) described coronary-prone persons as having a "great need for and respect for authority." They often stuck to one occupation or planned career and were often compulsive executives or officials. Dunbar (Dunbar, Wolfe, & Rioch, 1936), in their personality profile of the coronary patient, agreed with Gildea and noted that they had few hobbies or interest in sports but a strong interest in intellectual activities. Both they and Arlow emphasized a history of a childhood conflict with authority. Arlow remarked on their faulty identification with the father, leading to a deep-seated lack of conviction about themselves which stimulated compulsive competitiveness and which made any failure traumatic. To quote Arlow: "The coronary patient thus evades his neurosis but pays the price with a predisposition to this somatic disease."

Miles, Waldfogel, Barrabee, and Cobb (1954) summarized the literature and compared the personality traits of 46 young men with coronary disease to controls, using a detailed inventory battery, psychological tests, and interviews. Miles and his group could not confirm the results of Gildea and Dunbar. They saw the major factors in coronary disease as "maleness," body build, and probably some inherited intrinsic metabolic defect.

Bacon (1954) also studied rare or frequent cardiac pain in eight men and four women undergoing psychoanalysis. Pain appeared when an acute conflict between receptive help-seeking drives and hostile aggression and fear was mobilized as a result, she felt, of a simultaneous stimulation of the sympathetic and the parasympathetic nervous systems which produced ischemia and consequent cardiac pain. Russek (1959), in attempting to evaluate the role of heredity, diet, and stress in coronary disease, observed that a prolonged period of emotional strain associated with occupational responsibility preceded the attack in 91 out of 100 patients with coronary heart disease. In 100 control patients with other diseases, he found that only 20 had undergone such a strain. Russek then constructed ratios for the various factors; thus 91/20 or 4.6 was given to emotional stress, as compared with a ratio of 2.7 for diet, 2.0 for tobacco, 1.7 for heredity, 1.3 for obesity, and 1.0 for exercise.

Minc, Sinclair, and Taft (1963) have related the efficiency of cardiovascular and coronary adaptation to an adequate arousal of the autonomic nervous system. Thus individuals who exercise more intellectual control are more prone to cardiocoronary disturbances. Minc believes that coronary disease may be caused by socially imposed pressures which lead to an intellectually controlled mode of activity and to insufficient integration of emotional with rational activity. He found coronary patients to be more inhibited in both behavior and cerebral cortical functioning. This low level of cortical alertness was felt to be environmentally determined. Minc cited evidence that subjects with high serum cholesterol possess a constitutional temperament which is incompatible with the above inhibited behavior, and thus the assumption of two types of coronary heart disease was necessary, i.e., those in which primarily constitutionally determined factors are prevalent and those in which sociopsychological factors are prevalent.

Cleveland and Johnson (1962) studied 25 young males hospitalized with myocardial infarction by projective tests, paper-and-pencil tests, and brief interviews. As controls, 25 males awaiting serious surgery and 25 males with benign skin disorders were used. TAT data were also collected on 25 males, four to six weeks following hospitalization for skin disorders. As compared with presurgery controls, the coronary patients showed on the Rorschach significantly more mobilized fear and anxiety concerning physical harm, decline, and death as well as more unexpressed hostility. The anxiety level for the group with skin disorders was significantly below that obtained for both the coronary and the presurgery groups because they were in no immediate life-threatening stress. The responses of the coronary patients reflected an unusual self-concern. They felt fragile and shattered, as though their lives hung by a thread. In interviews, however, they overtly behaved quite differently. They were active, had a high self-image, and were confident and unperturbed. At the fantasy level, coronary patients were significantly less achievement-oriented than controls. The coronary TAT stories reflected a hopeless, "what's the use" attitude. They showed nostalgia for the past, and many sought hope through religious salvation. The precoronary behavior of the patients was nearly identical; they were unable to relax and enjoy doing nothing. They wished to behave in a conventional manner and to conform to accepted ethical norms and presented a controlled, cautious front. The TAT results showed a close and conspiratorial relationship between the coronary patient and his father, and the mother was perceived as distant and dissatisfied. It was suggested that the overt ambitious behavior of the patients was an attempt to placate the mother since their fantasy behavior (covert) was the opposite.

Adsett, Schottstaedt, and Wolf (1962) established psychophysiological correlations between stressful interviews (discussion of subjects known to be stressful to each individual patient) and coronary blood flow, blood pressure, pulse rate, cardiac output, and peripheral resistance. It was shown that in anxiety and especially in anger there is increased coronary blood flow. Other attempts to relate overt personality characteristics and biochemical changes to the incidence of coronary artery disease are illustrated by observations of Friedman, St. George, Byers, and Rosenman (1960), who measured the urinary excretion of 17-ketosteroids, 17-hydroxycorticosteroids,

5-hydroxy indole, epinephrine, and norepinephrine in 12 men who exhibited a behavior pattern (pattern A, to be described subsequently) thought to be associated with a high incidence of coronary disease. The nocturnal urinary excretion of these hormones was found to be the same in these men as in the control men exhibiting the converse behavioral pattern. However, when urine formed during working hours was analyzed, it was found that a far greater increase in norepinephrine level occurred in that of the men exhibiting the behavior pattern A than in that of the men in the control group. The authors concluded that this may be related to the development of coronary disease.

In a study in 1963, serum lipids and lipoproteins were determined on 20 men in a "blind study" by Rosenman and associates (Rosenman & Friedman, 1963). Ten of these men exhibited the overt behavior pattern A, which in earlier work was associated with a high prevalence of clinical coronary heart disease, and 10 showed a converse overt behavior pattern (pattern B). The men exhibiting type A behavior pattern were found to have significantly higher serum levels of triglycerides, phospholipides, cholesterol, serum beta and other low-density lipoprotein lipids, and significantly lower a/b lipoprotein cholesterol ratios, which were not ascribable to differences in diet, weight, or physical activity. They outlined a particular overt behavior pattern which was felt to be important in the pathogenesis of clinical coronary heart disease occurring in young and middle-aged subjects, characterized notably by enhanced drive, competitiveness, ambitiousness, and an excessive sense of urgency of time which appeared to stem particularly from habitual immersion in multiple vocational and avocational pursuits subject to "deadline" time pressures. It differs from such reactions as anxiety, fear, worry, and simple neuroses, which are not characteristic of behavior pattern A.

In group B, the persons' occupations demanded neither competitive activity nor preoccupation with deadlines, such as municipal employment in clerical or accounting duties, embalming, and routine bookkeeping.

Oral fat-tolerance tests were given by Freedman and Frajola (1963) to 42 patients under the age of 45 with myocardial infarction and to controls. Blood samples were analyzed for serum cholesterol, total fatty acids, phospholipids, and serum proteins. The results confirmed previous data that a distinct abnormality of fat metabolism exists in the coronary artery disease group, particularly in total esterified fatty acids after nine hours. The reading in most instances surpassed the fasting level in the subject group, a finding which occurred only infrequently in the control group. A close correlation existed between an immediate family history of myocardial infarction and an abnormal fat-tolerance test.

Thomas (1961) is conducting, at present, a long-term investigation on the precursors of hypertension and coronary disease which encompasses genetic, physiological, metabolic, and psychological characteristics in healthy young medical students. She advances a multifactorial hypothesis. Some of her observations are the following: (1) Children of two parents affected with hypertension and/or coronary disease are different in significant ways from children of two unaffected parents. They are, on the average, 10 pounds heavier, have hypercholestermia and higher resting systolic blood pressure, and are likely to be smokers. (2) The children of two obese parents are distinguished by their own excessive weight and higher cholesterol levels. (3) Conversely, the offspring of two parents unaffected by hypertension, coronary artery disease, obesity, or diabetes weigh less and have lower cholesterol levels and lower systolic blood pressure, and fewer of them smoke. (4) When subjects with at least one parent affected by hypertension and/or coronary disease with certain positive individual metabolic and physiologic traits (group I) are compared with subjects of two unaffected parents and with negative individual traits (group IV), certain trends are noted. Subjects in group I, when under situations of stress, react more often with anger and tremulousness. They tend to have an increased urge to eat and an urge to confide and seek advice. In the Rorschach test, a greater proportion were found to have a high number of popular responses, anatomy responses, and pure color responses and a high degree of ego strength. Subjects in group IV showed a significantly greater urge to be alone when under stress, tended to have an increased need to sleep, and showed decreased activity. In the Rorschach test, there were more individuals with a high degree of organizational activity and more with a large number of fantasy responses.

Thomas concludes that the offspring of different kinds of human mating have significantly different physiological, metabolic, and psychological characteristics, and although usually not great, their differences—even when highly contrasting groups of subjects are compared—are compatible with the hypothesis of multifactorial inheritance. Thus the prediction of individual susceptibility to hypertension and/or coronary artery disease probably depends on a constellation of factors.

No studies exist which have combined the psychoanalytic method with physiological and biochemical techniques to outline more precisely the interaction of emotional, endocrine, and psychological factors in coronary disease, as has been done, for example, in hyperthyroidism and hypertension. The same emphasis should be placed on the careful and accurate study of the effects of emotion in the onset and course of coronary disease as in the study of the adrenal cortex.

Essential Hypertension

Essential hypertension is defined as a chronic elevation of blood pressure in the absence of a discernible organic cause. In the early phase of the disease, the blood pressure is labile and fluctuates markedly, but in later stages it becomes stabilized at a high level and produces secondary kidney and heart damage. The elevated arterial pressure is attributed, by most investigators, to a widespread constriction of the arterioles throughout the vascular system. The fact that systemic circulation time remains normal, as does blood flow, in chronic hypertension does not support the concept of a basic vascular lesion as the primary etiologic cause; rather, it indicates that the concletion results from an interaction between the nervous system and the endocrine system and that it involves a disturbance in the homeostatic mechanism. The pressor responses which occur in early hypertension as reactions to many external stimuli, such as immersion of the hand in ice water, physical work, and emotional conflicts aroused by life situations, lend support to such a concept. Probably the increased blood pressure is caused by increased vascular tone which results from an increase in the vasomotor impulses to the smooth muscle of the arterioles, an increase in some circulating pressor substances, or a combination of these and other factors. Goldblatt (1937) demonstrated the effect on blood pressure of renal ischemia. He found that ischemia of the kidney leads to the release of a pressor substance called "renin," which acts on the smooth muscle of the vessels and produces hypertension. Goldblatt's work stimulated efforts to demonstrate lesions in the renal vessels which might induce kidney ischemia and lead to hypertension. Renal lesions which are extensive enough to produce the elevated blood pressure are seldom found, but the renal blood vessels do react very strongly to emotional and physical stimuli, with vasoconstriction which could lead to ischemia.

Blomstrand and Lofgren (1956) recently demonstrated that emotional stress profoundly altered the renal circulation in cats. During the stress, the kidney cortex was shown to become very anemic, whereas the medulla was very hyperemic. No diversion of blood through juxtamedullary glomeruli occurred.

Sancetta (1960) noted that intravenous infusions of angiotensin in normotensive patients significantly increased arterial blood pressure but did not alter the cardiac output, although systemic vascular and total pulmonary resistances were increased greatly. Pulmonary arteriolar resistance, however, was the same. Since angiotensin appeared to produce peripheral arteriolar constriction without concomitant pulmonary arteriolar narrowing, Sancetta viewed his results as evidence that angiotensin could be a causative agent in human essential hypertension. The results of the experiments of Blomstrand and Lofgren and of Sancetta would seem to indicate that pressor agents ought to be considered as a possible factor in the pathogenesis of essential hypertension. Blomstrand and Lofgren felt that they had found in nature a reproduction of Goldblatt's experiments. They concluded that emotional stress acts quite simply as if a number of Goldblatt clamps were placed on the peripheral branches of the renal trunk.

Katz (1962) has said that the involvement of the nervous system in essential hypertension includes (1) afferent nerves from many external and internal sensors and (2) the complex central nervous system cybernetic apparatus (hypothalamus, thalamus, limbic areas, and the cerebral cortex). All such impulses ultimately reach the final common paths in the efferent nerves to the systemic arterioles, the venules, and the heart and, probably by way of efferent nerves, to the kidney vasculature, excretory apparatus, and/or its secretory portion (the juxtaglomerular apparatus), where renin is formed. In addition, some efferent impulses probably act on the endocrine glands, notably the adrenal medulla and cortex and the anterior and posterior pituitary.

People may show either a normal or an excessive blood-pressure elevation in response to a given stressful stimulus in the environment, the response being related to a genetically inherited factor and to the conditioning of the nervous system. In one person, a stimulus may cause a temporary rise in blood pressure for a period which in degree and duration could be considered normal, while in another individual, the same stimulus may cause an excessive rise in blood pressure for an unusually protracted time. If such a stimulus recurred frequently, fluctuating hypertension would occur, as seen in early primary hypertension. Katz assumes that the continuation of these hypertensive episodes can lead to anatomical change in the arterioles, so that the lumen becomes narrower and fixed hypertension develops. He concludes, as have many other investigators, that whatever the mechanisms may be in hypertension, it is obvious that the autonomic nervous system is involved in all of them, as the most effective therapy for hypertension—primary, secondary, or accelerated—consists in influencing or blocking the function of the nervous system, whether by use of tranquilizers, ganglion blockers, or sympathectomy or by the administration of agents that interfere with the action of norepinephrine as an effector substance through which the sympathetic system operates.

Katz concluded that the disease will be better understood from the study of genetic factors and the integrative role of the nervous system than from continued concern with the adrenal electrolyte-renal mechanisms.

Many studies have been conducted which relate psychogenic factors to exacerbations of the hypertensive syndrome. The important role of inhibited hostile tendencies in chronic hypertension has been noted by most investigators—a fact which is in accord with Cannon's (1920) observation that fear and rage produce an increase in blood pressure in animals because of activation of the sympathetic nervous system and secretion of epinephrine.

In an early study, F. Alexander (1939a; 1939b) commented that chronic inhibited aggressive impulses associated with anxiety markedly influenced blood-pressure levels. Binger, Ackerman, Cohn, Schroeder, and Steele (1945) described typical family constellations in patients with hypertension. Studies at the Chicago Institute for Psychoanalysis clearly outlined certain characteristics of the hypertensive patient. They found that hypertensive patients have in common the inability to express aggressive impulses freely and that they maintain a remarkable degree of self-control. Superficially they give the impression of having well-adjusted, mature personalities. They are extremely compliant and attempt to please their associates. Although they may be consciously ambitious, they limit their competition to their fantasy lives. They are compliant toward authority figures, whom they at the same time resent. Their normal self-assertiveness is inhibited, leading to self-accusation and loss of self-confidence. The more they are compliant, the greater their reactive hostility to those to whom they submit. There is pronounced conflict between passive dependent or feminine tendencies and compensatory, aggressive hostile impulses (Saul, 1939; F. Alexander, 1939a). Sexual inhibition is common in them, and illicit relationships produce a great amount of anxiety and guilt since they are felt as a rebellion against internalized authority. Even rebellion against their own submissiveness produces fear and forces a retreat from competition to a passive dependent attitude. A vicious cycle ensues because the passive dependency stirs up more inferiority feelings and hostilities. An emotional paralysis results from the block created by the opposing tendencies of submission and aggression. Many have work histories of keeping badly remunerated and strenuous jobs for years because of the inhibition of their competitive and self-assertive tendencies. They are conscientious plodders ("beasts of burden") who do unpleasant tasks themselves rather than asking subordinates because of a fear of refusal leading to anger which they cannot express. Since they cannot utilize even the legitimate outlets for aggressive impulses provided by society, they are in a chronic state of suppressed hostility.

A hypertensive patient may have been aggressive during early life and later, during puberty, have begun to act in an intimidated, meek manner. Some of these patients make a conscious effort to control their tempers in order not to alienate others.

Draper (1935) observed a fall of the blood pressure of some hypertensives to normal when the dammed-up hostile impulses were released through neurotic symptoms and thus no longer served as a source of chronic excitation of the vasomotor mechanisms. However, again it must be pointed out that many neurotic persons reveal an inhibition of aggressive impulses based on a nuclear conflict similar to that of patients with hypertension but yet do not develop an elevated blood pressure. A basic constitutional factor must therefore be postulated (Alexander's X factor).

Moses, Daniels, and Nickerson (1956) conducted ballistocardiographic studies to determine the stroke volume and cardiac output in early cases of hypertension and used those hemodynamic values to calculate the peripheral resistance. Psychodynamic data were also collected and were analyzed in terms of the predominant affects of anxiety and rage in relationship to the deprivation of basic needs. Hypertensive individuals tended to mobilize excessive and continuous anxiety and rage in response to frustration of basic dependency and security needs. These affects were poorly suppressed, only partly repressed, or minimally bound in specific psychic symptoms and inadequately discharged in verbalization or motor activity.

Three general psychodynamic and hemodynamic correlations were made: (1) Rage and resentment were the predominant psychic concomitants of excessive blood-pressure elevations and were related to an increased peripheral resistance with normal stroke volume and heart rate. (2) Anxiety with minimal overt expression was the predominant psychic concomitant of minor blood-pressure elevations and was related to increased peripheral resistance with normal stroke volume and heart rate. (3) When anxiety was overtly expressed, the minor blood-pressure elevations were related to increased stroke volume and heart rate and a normal peripheral resistance. They felt that psychotherapy of the early hypertensive individual could achieve major reconstructive personality changes and that the arrest of the early hypertensive vascular process was possible.

Schachter (1957) experimentally tested the following three hypotheses relating to pain, fear, and anger in hypertensive and normal subjects: (1) In fear, the predominant cardiovascular response is characterized by increased heart rate and stroke volume and decreased peripheral resistance. In anger and pain, a different kind of cardiovascular responses occurs. (2) Hypertensive subjects show a greater elevation of blood pressure than normotensives during pain, fear, and anger. (3) Hypertensives express less anger psychologically than normotensives. In acute fear, 35 out of his 48 subjects had a predominantly epinephrinelike response, whereas during the pain of the cold pressor test, most of them had a predominantly norepinephrinelike reaction. In anger, 19 showed a norepinephrinelike effect; 22 showed an epinephrinelike effect; and seven had mixed effects. The 18 hypertensives showed an average significantly greater rise in blood pressure during pain, fear, and anger than 15 normotensives. Blood-pressure responses of the hypertensives exceeded those of the normotensives. Face temperature during anger dropped less in hypertensives than in normotensives. However, the peripheral resistance index, cardiac output index, stroke volume index, heart rate, hand temperature, GSR, muscle potential, and other measures failed to show significant differences between the hypertensives and the normotensives. The hypertensives expressed psychologically more fear and anger than the normotensives to the acute emotional stimulation, although the difference did not achieve significance. Also, resting mean blood pressure in 48 subjects showed a significant mean positive correlation with the psychological intensity of acute fear and anger.

Oken (1960) studied the emotional and cardiovascular responses evoked by a stressful interview in a mixed group of 10 normotensive psychiatric patients. He attempted on different days to induce various emotional states. On the first day he attempted to provoke anxiety, and on the second day, anger. On the third day a nonspecific communication blocking technique was used. Affect responses were quantified using rating scales for consciously experienced anxiety, anger, and depression based on continuous observation behind a one-way mirror and an evaluation interview. Continuous blood-pressure and heart-rate measurements indicated a close relation between anger, heart rate, and blood pressure, especially between increased blood pressure and anger.

Subjects tending to suppress anger rather than express it had a higher diastolic and a lower systolic blood pressure at equal levels of anger, compared with those who were more free to express it. This same group was characterized by lower levels of consciously experienced behaviorally expressed anger. The inhibition of anger was associated with physiological differences consistent with an elevated peripheral resistance. These data provide additional support for the hypotheses about the role of inhibited anger in hypertension.

S. N. Kaplan, Gottschalk, Magliocco, Rohovit, and Ross (1961), using verbal sampling and hypnotically induced dreams, demonstrated a quantitative relation between blood pressure and hostile emotions. However, they considered the possibility that the hostile verbal content could be due to the elevation of blood pressure, rather than vice versa, or that both might be dependent variables of a third factor.

Hardyck, Singer, and Harris (1962) presented contradictory results. They observed the relationships between psychological events during an interview and corresponding blood-pressure levels. Life-history interviews were conducted on six female hypertensives while blood pressure and other physiological functions were recorded. Based on his verbatim transcripts only, the interviewer independently rated selected parts of the interview as being associated with high, medium, or low blood-pressure levels. The results indicated that blood-pressure level can be predicted with significant accuracy from interview material. The interviewer's predictions were based on his estimate of the degree of the patient's involvement in communicating information, regardless of its content. An examination of content categories revealed no relationship between type of affect and blood-pressure levels.

H. Weiner, Singer, and Reiser (1962) explored this same problem (content versus interaction) in hypertensive patients and used ulcer patients as controls. They reported that heart-rate and blood-pressure responses appeared to be related to the interaction between the subject and the experimenter, but not to content; i.e., merely looking at the TAT card without having to tell a story coincided with negligible physiological responses. However, if the subject knew he had to tell a story, physiological responses occurred. Although failure to interact with the experimenter was always associated with physiological hyporeactivity, the hypertensive subjects were characterized by a lack of physiological responsiveness which was related to their relationship to the examiner. Hypertensives were superficially cooperative in producing stories of voluminous content, but they dealt primarily with the physical aspect of the card situation and avoided any emotional connotations or fantasies. If the experimenter attempted to press for such material, they remained distant and uninvolved in their attitude. In those cases where this distancing from the experimenter was abandoned for a closer interaction, physiological hyperactivity was observed. In contrast, the controls (the subjects with peptic ulcer) displayed lower heart-rate and blood-pressure responses. The group of subjects with peptic ulcer was divided into those who were clearly depressed and those who were not. The physiological responses of the former were the most attenuated. A group of nondepressed ulcer subjects did not actively comply with the task and dealt with the experimenter in a clinging yet friendly way. Their stories contained fantasies but little affectively colored response. The subgroup of depressed ulcer patients were slow in their responses, apathetic, and uninterested and did not engage in any active dealing with the experimental situation.

Graham and his collaborators developed a specificity of attitude hypothesis for certain psychosomatic diseases which they attempted to test experimentally by hypnotic suggestion of attitudes. In a recent study (D. T. Graham, Kabler, & Graham, 1962), 20 healthy male subjects were given two attitude suggestions on each of two days, with the order of presentation reversed on the second day. Of the two attitudes suggested, one was presumably associated with hives and the other with hypertension. The subject was made to feel that he was being unjustly treated and could do nothing about it. The other suggestion was that he had to be on guard against bodily assault. Predictions that the skin temperatures would rise more with the hives suggestion than with that for hypertension and that the diastolic blood pressure would rise more with the hypertension than with the hives suggestion were confirmed. Changes of skin temperature during the hives suggestion were significantly greater than the corresponding change during the hypertension suggestion. Diastolic blood pressure was significantly greater during the hypertension than during the hives suggestion.

A recent study by Lee and Schneider (1958) lends indirect support to these hypotheses that a specific emotional conflict situation rather than a personality type or particular occupation contributes to the onset and course of essential hypertension. Matched categories including 1,171 male executives, 460 male nonexecutives, and 563 female nonexecutives were studied by periodic complete medical history, physical examinations, and routine laboratory procedures for an average of five years. The executive groups showed less arteriosclerotic disease than the nonexecutive group, and they showed no increase in cardiovascular disease, compared with less demanding business positions. Possible explanations are that (1) career attainment goes hand in hand with good health, (2) with greater financial income, a person can afford a high standard of living and better medical care, and (3) perhaps the more successful executives had developed outside avenues of expression and were less frustrated.

A multidisciplinary team (Alexander, Flagg, Selesnick, Clemens, and Michael) is conducting a pilot study at Mt. Sinai Hospital in Los Angeles, as part of a program in which the subject's psychophysiological and behavioral responses upon exposure to certain "stressor motion-picture films" are recorded. (The developmental history and rationale of this research methodology will be presented in more detail in the section on hyperthyroidism.) To date, 21 hypertensive patients have been studied with a variety of observational techniques before, during, and after viewing a stressor film, *On the Waterfront*. On the day before the film viewing, patients and controls are given a perceptual test consisting of a word association test in which emotionally threatening and neutral words are selected for each subject. Both threatening and neutral words are then presented tachistoscopically to the subject, who perceives either the threatening words (sensitization) or matched neutral words (avoidance). This test provides clues as to whether a given person will attempt to deal with or avoid environmental situations. A Rorschach, a TAT, and a brief intelligence test are also given and are rated independently and are compared with the psychiatric evaluations. On the second, or experimental, day, an observer views the subjects before, during, and immediately after the stressor film by means of a one-way mirror and rates behavioral changes during selected tranquil and stressful scenes of the stressor film. During the film, measures of heart rate, respiration rate, peripheral blood volume flow, skin resistance, and systolic blood pressure are continuously and simultaneously recorded. Psychiatric interviews are conducted after the film to collect data regarding the subject's mood state before coming to the laboratory and before, during, and after the movie as well as his verbal reaction to specific scenes in the movie. A second anamnestic interview is usually conducted the next day to obtain information about the infantile conflicts and the history of the onset situation.

Only trends can be established at this time since complete data are available on only nine subjects. It appears that if a relative deficit in internal ego functions exists as independently rated by both psychiatric and psychological evaluations, these results are also reflected in (1) greater overt behavioral disturbance during film viewing, (2) greater systolic blood-pressure reactions, and (3) greater than normal perceptual avoidance.

Superficially, most of the patients appeared well integrated and relaxed, but the utilization of evasion, denial, suppression, and repression during psychological and psychiatric interviews was easily detected. Perceptually, they were relatively sensitive to threatening stimuli on a nonverbal level and showed little or no tendency to decompensate in systolic blood pressure during the entire stressor movie. Although six patients responded vigorously during film viewing (systolic blood-pressure lability) and three showed little reaction (systolic blood-pressure stability), all, on the average, were able to return to their high initial systolic blood-pressure levels by the end of the film. Unfortunately, the experimenters were not able to monitor diastolic blood pressure on most persons, which may have produced quite different results. [It may well have confirmed Oken's (1960) finding that the suppression of anger is associated with a higher diastolic pressure and a lower systolic pressure. These experimenters' findings tend to confirm his observation that more conscious anger and more motoric release are associated with an increased systolic blood pressure (epinephrine life effect).]

Of particular interest is the fact that the

average autonomic nervous system scores (which included SBP readings) were nearly identical to those of untreated and treated hyperthyroid patients and control subjects combined. In view of the higher systolic blood-pressure reaction, one could tentatively assume that autonomic nervous system reactions were somewhat truncated and that organ specificity of response to a particular conflict situation in the stressor film might be experimentally demonstrated. However, at this point these are only tentative suggestions.

Role of Emotions in Cardiovascular Accidents and Congestive Heart Failure

The theory that intense emotional stress can lead to cardiac decompensation or that emotions can cause severe spasm of cerebral vessels of such intensity or duration that permanent brain damage can result from ischemia or thrombosis (or hemorrhage from a vessel already arteriosclerotic) is commonly assumed, but few systematic studies exist to establish a definite relationship. The effect of emotional stress on the precipitation of congestive heart failure was reported on 25 patients by Chambers and Reiser (1953), who established that in 76 per cent of cases the decompensation was precipitated by emotional tension. In 12 patients, these episodes occurred in combination with other events which stirred up intense feelings of rage and frustration.

The following year, Ecker (1954) demonstrated in a study of 20 cases of stroke (cardiovascular accident) that overwhelming emotional upset had often occurred immediately before the stroke. He found that such persons had great difficulty in dealing with their hostile feelings and that the women rejected their femininity and competed with men. In comparing the angiographs of the stroke victims with those of patients with suspected brain tumor, he found severe spasm in 90 per cent of the stroke subjects and only a 10 per cent occurrence of it in brain tumor suspects. He concluded that the threshold for the production of spasm was lower than average, that the arteries of stroke or stroke-prone subjects contracted excessively, and that this could be a result of emotional disturbance. Ischemia due to severe and prolonged spasm may contribute to the pathological changes in the brain, ultimately leading to a catastrophic alteration of cerebral blood flow.

Later, Seidenberg and Ecker (1954) presented their findings on six patients who had died of stroke. On autopsy they showed no structural changes in the vascular system such as arteriosclerosis, aneurysm, etc. They assumed that emotional disturbance had an etiological significance.

Disturbance of Tone in the Peripheral Vascular System

Acute disturbance of cardiovascular hemostasis (vasodepressor syncope). This is the most common type of fainting, even in healthy individuals, and is a transitory, homeostatic disturbance of the cardiovascular hemodynamics. It has been studied by Romano & coworkers (Romano & Engel, 1945; Romano, Engel, Webb, Ferris, Ryder, & Blankenharn, 1943). It is thought to occur when one is faced with an overwhelming danger, particularly in a situation where the expression of fear must be suppressed. Fainting occurs because of a sudden drop in blood pressure. Engel (1950) believes that if emotional factors interfere with appropriate muscular discharge, the circulatory preparation for effort consisting in vasodilation in the muscles as a part of the normal adaptative response for flight results in a kind of internal bleeding into the muscular system. The blood pressure drops, and if it falls below a critical level, loss of consciousness occurs. The person must be in an erect position for this type of fainting to occur, and this makes the differential diagnosis from hysterical fainting quite easy. In addition, hysterical fainting is a symbolic expression of an emotional conflict, and there are no changes in the cardiovascular system in hysterical fainting. Thus vasodepressor syncope is a typical example of a vegetative neurosis. The normal physiological response to fear is initiated, but an inhibition interferes with the normal voluntary motoric behavior (the flight reaction is never consummated by action).

D. T. Graham, Kabler, and Lunsford (1961), however, consider vasovagal fainting a diphasic response. They studied vasovagal (vasodepressor) fainting in three different situations: (1) in persons donating blood, (2) in persons having a simple venipuncture, and (3) in patients undergoing pneumoencephalography. Fainting occurred most often during the donation of blood. The fainting is the result of low blood pressure and bradycardia, which they thought was the second phase of a diphasic response. The first phase was characterized by rapid or rising heart rate and by rising diastolic blood pressure. These results are compatible with the view that the first (hyperdynamic) phase is a reflection of anxiety, while the second phase begins with the cessation of anxiety. They believe that fainting is based on a reflex mechanism activated by the first phase and then left suddenly unopposed. Graham and his group refute the usual psychobiological interpretations of fainting because they feel that such interpretations do not recognize its diphasic nature. They argue that fainting and dying are physiological states which bear close resemblances.

An investigation carried out by Silverman and Cohen (1960) on pilot blackout has relevance to those factors which effect the stability or lability of the cardiovascular system. It is well known that a pilot in a steep turn or pullout from a dive may "black out" as a result of downward acceleration acting against the ability of his cardiovascular system to maintain an adequate blood supply to the head and eyes. If cardiovascular reflexes fail, a progression from loss of peripheral vision, to complete loss of vision, to unconsciousness occurs. Relying on the work of previous investigators, such as Goodall (1951); Von Euler, Gemzell, Levi, and Strom (1959); and many others, and on interviews with experienced pilots, they formed the following general hypotheses: (1) Anxiety was associated with lowered g tolerance, whereas aggression and sense of control or mastery were related to a higher tolerance against fainting. (2) A given subject withstood the effect of gravitational forces best when he felt in control of the situation or was aggressive or angry. (3) The emotional factors were associated with specific neurohormonal and cardiovascular response modalities. (4) The specific emotional factor increasing g tolerance was of an aggressive nature.

It should be apparent to the reader that the same psychological conflict and physiological response were postulated as being responsible for vasodepressor syncope (see illustrative case at the end of this section).

This and other research projects, such as the psychophysiological studies being done at Mt. Sinai Hospital, in Los Angeles, suggest that specific emotions or conflicts stimulate the selective release of neurohormonal substances which influence the organ-system response (see the section on thyroid disorders). Such hormonal and physiologic response patterns and their fluctuations within an individual are not a function of a basic organic or physiological predisposition, but they are expressions of a person's ever-changing psychophysiological state.

Carotid sinus syndrome. Many cases of so-called "carotid sinus syndrome" are actually cases of hysterical fainting. In other instances, an actual carotid sinus syndrome has assumed a secondary and symbolic meaning to the patient. One of the authors (Flagg) recently saw a 50-year-old man with a clinically confirmed carotid sinus syndrome. Pressure from a tight shirt collar or any pressure applied over the carotid sinus would produce weakness, slowing of the heart, and decreased blood pressure. He had fainted at work on several occasions. The patient was referred for a reactive depression with psychomotor retardation, self-depreciatory ideas, and hypochondriasis. During his depressive phase, he had no syncopal attacks, nor did he fear them. After electroshock therapy, as he recovered from his partial amnesia, he became conscious of a chronic murderous rage against his wife and his employer; most of all, he became conscious of his childhood rage against a strict grandmother. He was a shy, passive, mild-mannered man with disguised paranoid tendencies. He did not remain in therapy long but returned to work. He functioned well in spite of a hostile, competitive relationship with his fellow workers and his superior. At times he would leave the store because he felt weak, but his carotid sinus syncopal attacks never recurred. This man probably had a tendency to vasodepressor (carotid sinus) syncope which then was reinforced by emotional conflict and which had taken on a symbolic meaning. (The carotid plexus sends fibers to the carotid sinus nerve and to the glossopharyngeal nerve, and it also has CNS connections.) It is probable that suppressed or repressed rage which is excluded from conscious awareness because of guilt stimuates hypothalamic autonomic (sympathetic) pathways as an adaptive reaction for fight. A parasympathetic overcompensatory reaction occurs, and the blood pressure and heart rate drop below critical levels. As a result, vasodepressor syncope may follow. When this particular patient was depressed, he had submitted to his superego masochistically, and he did not need to take "flight from the internal danger of his own sadistic impulses." Brief psychotherapy provided a "corrective emotional experience" since the therapist's attitude was more permissive than that of the parents.

Orthostatic hypotension and psychoneurosis. A brief account of a newly described syndrome is presented here as a warning to clinicians against the occasional temptation to arrive at a psychiatric diagnosis because of no demonstrable structural or organic etiology, rather than basing such a diagnosis on positive psychodynamic evidence. This requires a thorough psychiatric anamnestic study.

Schatz (1963) called attention to a condition which is now being recognized more frequently. The patient presents a picture of urinary incontinence, impotence, and anhydrosis. Either he may be manifesting chronic idiopathic orthostatic hypotension, or the orthostatic hypotension may be a side effect produced by an antihypertensive or tranquilizing drug, which his physician fails to recognize. Schatz feels that orthostatic hypotension secondarily resulting from these compounds is much more common than the primary cases caused by organic diseases, i.e., diabetes, multiple sclerosis, and adrenal malfunctions. Many secondary cases show neurologic findings months before the low blood pressure develops, which is support for the thesis that the basic defect is of central nervous system origin and not secondary to hypoxia.

Headaches. Headache is a very common symptom and is most often caused by emotional conflict. There are many different types of headaches, and it should not be considered a disease entity. Headaches may be classed according to etiology [reflex neuromuscular, migraine, migranoid, histamine (allergic), focal infection, hypertensive, or increased intracranial pressure] or according to the type of pain experienced by the patient and its distribution (pulsating, bursting, bandlike, continuous, etc., or frontal, occipital, unilateral, bilateral, etc.).

CONVERSION HEADACHE. Some headaches of emotional etiology are conversion symptoms (hysterical) which may result from repressed hostile or sexual impulses and have a symbolic meaning to the patient. Whether any underlying physiological changes are present in such conversion reactions is difficult to determine. Many individual cases have been reported in detail by psychoanalysts.

MIGRAINE HEADACHE. Migraine headache constitutes a well-defined and definite clinical entity with respect to symptomatology and physiology, although the etiology is still doubtful. The attacks are characterized by their periodic nature, prodromal disturbances (scotomata, occasional paresthesias, speech difficulties), and pain. The pain is unilateral in classic cases and is associated with photophobia, and the attack often terminates with vomiting, which may be followed by a euphoric state. The physiological mechanism of the pain has usually been explained on the basis of vascular stretching of the cerebral and cranial arteries as a result of vasodilatation (J. R. Graham & Wolff, 1938; Clark, Hough, & Wolff, 1935). This explains why ergot and its derivatives give such dramatic relief from attacks because of their vasoconstricitive effects. The actual migraine attack (pain), however, is preceded by an initial phase of vasoconstriction which produces the prodromata. Wolff considered the vasodilatation an overcompensatory reaction to the vasoconstriction. Later, Wolff and his associates (1957) found experimental evidence for the existence of a locally noxious agent or agents acting during migraine headaches, which were felt to be damaging to tissues and which lowered the pain threshold. F. Alexander (1950) considered the vasodilatation to have an independent origin. Dalessio (1962) recently proposed that the headache phase of migraine headache results from unstable central vasomotor centers which evolve as a part of a learned inappropriate pattern of response. These aberrations in central vasomotor functions are associated with excessive cranial vascular reactivity which characterize the migraine headache attack. The prophylactic value of methysergide (a lysergic acid derivative) is due to its effect on vasomotor functions, potentiating the vasoconstrictor responses of the cranial blood vessels to endogenous or exogenous catechol amines. The antiserotonin activity of methysergide may be responsible for its capacity to modulate central vasomotor functions.

Further evidence of the role of central vasomotor regulatory centers and serotonin in "migraine-type" headaches was gathered by Abbott (1962), who reported on 172 patients with frequent and often excruciating headaches who received methysergide prophylactically over a two-year period. It was of little or no value in neuromuscular tension headaches. While methysergide was of conspicuous benefit in postconcussion headache of the migraine type, it was of no benefit in other forms of headache. It seems that methysergide is effective in preventing migraine and histamine headache or any other type of vascular headache which is based on central vasomotor regulatory disturbances and serotonin effects.

Touraine and Draper (1934) have described a "constitutional personality type" characteristic of the migraine individual who shows some physical acromegaloid traits accompanied by a retarded emotional development and superior intelligence. According to these authors, migraine appears when these individuals lose the protection of home, particularly maternal dependency, which has helped them avoid facing the responsibilities of living alone. Fromm-Reichman (1937) treated eight patients with migraine by intensive psychotherapy and found that all showed hostile, envious impulses originally directed against intellectually brilliant persons and that these impulses were turned against the self because of guilt. Knopf (1935) commented on the "goody goody nature of these ambitious but reserved, relaxed, and dignified 'proper' ladies with no sense of humor." H. G. Wolff (1937), in addition to his contributions on the physiology of migraine attacks, outlined the personalities of persons with migraine as compulsive, perfectionistic, ambitious, excessively competitive, and rigid and characterized by an inability to delegate responsibility. A chronic resentful attitude results from their lack of success in handling compulsively assumed responsibilities and perfectionistic ambitions. An attitude of tension and fatigue develops, and finally some external event further increases the ever-present resentfulness and triggers a migraine attack. Selinsky (1939) also commented on the importance of "struggle, resentment and anxiety" in migraine. Patients with migraine headaches show surface attitudes which are characteristic of the so-called "compulsive" character. The precipitating emotional factors which lead to an attack are even better documented than the general personality traits (Fromm-Reichman, 1937; H. G. Wolff, 1937).

Lippman (1954) studied the recurrent dreams of patients with migraine and described different dream patterns which occurred, according to him, only in persons with migraine or in migrainoid individuals (the latter are direct descendants or siblings of individuals with recurrent classic migraine headaches). He found that the dream patterns helped to make an accurate diagnosis. The dream patterns were characterized by (1) recurrence, (2) brilliant colors, (3) their appearance at specific times in the life-span of the patient, (4) certain emotional tones which usually carry over into the waking state, and (5) persistence of the hallucination after the patient is awake. Repressed rage is most responsible for the migraine attack, and it is common for an attack to terminate abruptly if the patient becomes conscious of the rage and gives expression to it in abusive words. This observation establishes a specific and direct correlation between repressed rage and migraine.

HYPERTENSIVE HEADACHE. Some interesting observations have been made by Moser, Wish, and Freidman (1962) in a three-year study of 54 patients with headache and hypertension. Frontal or occipital early-morning headache occurred most frequently, but the type of headache could not be clearly defined. *Headaches frequently antedated the onset of hypertension.* Over 50 per cent of patients experienced either relief from headache or a significant fall in blood pressure after antihypertensive drug therapy. Less than 30 per cent, however, noted relief of headache and a satisfactory blood-pressure response. Of 1,296 patients, only 20.5 per cent of those with hypertension had migraine headaches. Only 35.4 per cent of those with migraine had hypertension. Many of the headaches followed emotional upset.

Schottstaedt (1956) studied the renal excretion of fluid and electrolytes in association with vascular headache, since H. G. Wolff (1948) had noted changes in fluid balance and body metabolism in such patients (increased body weight, localized edema of the face and scalp, puffy lids, and swelling of ankles and fingers). Schottstaedt found in an extensive study of five patients and a total of 27 headache episodes that (1) the vascular headache may be preceded, accompanied, or followed by an increase, decrease, or no significant change in renal excretion of water, sodium, and potassium; (2) the alternations in renal excretion correspond to the situation, behavior, attitudes, and emotions of the subjects rather than to the phase of the headache; and (3) the alternations in renal excretion are not etiological in the genesis of the headache.

Raynaud's Disease. Millet, Lief, and Mittlemann (1953) reported that in the four cases of Raynaud's disease they studied, the onset of the illness and the subsequent attacks appeared to be a symbolic expression of anxiety. The anxiety appeared to result from guilt feelings and fears of retaliation associated with self-blame for the death of some close family member. The authors felt that the blanching of the hands was a symbolic identification with the dead person, that it was an attempt by the patient to expiate guilt, and that it expressed the desire to be forgiven and loved. The attacks, which usually occurred after some threatening experience, diminished in frequency and severity after the patients gained insight during psychoanalysis.

D. T. Graham (1955) described two patterns of vascular response: One is seen characteristically in persons with Raynaud's disease but also in other individuals in states of anxiety or hostility, and the other is found in individuals in states of depression. The pattern in Raynaud's disease was that of vasoconstrictive changes in both arterioles and minute vessels. In the depressive individuals, there was constriction of the arterioles, but this was accompanied by a *decreased* tone of the minute vessels. Graham specifically associated attacks of Raynaud's disease with the wish to carry out some hostile action. He postulated that since anxiety produces the same vascular changes, it would seem probable that anxiety would increase the severity of Raynaud's phenomena. Graham, in challenging the symbolic interpretations of Millet, correctly pointed out that Raynaud's phenomenon has been described by some authors as being limited to the hands, when in actuality it is a general characteristic of the skin of these patients.

Thromboangitis obliterans (Buerger's Disease). Thromboangitis obliterans is a disease of the peripheral nerves, arteries, and veins with associated venous and arterial thromboses, frequently leading to gangrene. It is of unknown etiology.

Millet and Dyde (1957) reported two cases of successful psychotherapy in this syndrome and observed a striking parallel in the psychodynamic patterns of their two patients. Both had strong ambivalent, passive dependent ties to their mothers, who dominated the families, and both suffered marked inhibition of any sexual or hostile behavior and had contracted marriage in defiance of maternal standards. Both cases had complete remission after psychotherapy which provided sufficient insight and support to enable them to get divorced. No claim for specificity of personality structure was made.

Cohen, Bondurant, and Silverman (1960) designed a study to observe the effect of psychogenic stimuli on venomotor tone by measuring changes in 10 volunteer subjects exposed to auditory stimuli which consisted of exciting words and phrases, as compared with exposure to bland words or silence. In addition, four silent periods were introduced. Pulse rates, skin resistance, and EEG measures were carried out to evaluate the level of arousal of the subjects. Post-run psychiatric interviews evaluated the specific meaning of the experimental procedure to the subject. Venous pressure changes were significantly greater following the introduction of the charged words and phrases than following bland expressions. Furthermore, the changes following bland expressions were considerably higher than during silent periods. The decreases in skin resistance specifically associated with the presentation of words were significantly greater after charged than after neutral expressions. The pre-skin-resistance and post-skin-resistance records indicated a more intense level of arousal in the poststimulus period following charged words, an equivalent level after bland words, and a decreased level after the silent period. Individual reactions not only were related to the type of stimulation but also were closely related to the personal meaning the stimulus had for the subject. Venous pressure changes resulting from emotional stimuli are probably due to an increased level of central nervous system arousal, which leads to an increase in sympathetic nervous system excitation and then to venoconstriction. Thus vascular changes occur in the venous system as well as in the arterial system or in cardiac function as a result of emotional stress.

The question of why a person with inhibited hostility develops hypertension instead of arthritis, migraine, or a peripheral vascular disorder, such as Raynaud's disease, is still enigmatic. The choice of psychosomatic symptom is most likely determined both by the specific psychodynamic constellation and by the early acquired hereditary or somatic predisposition. Migraine, hypertension, and epilepsy, for example, all involve pent-up destructive, hostile impulses, and the coincidence of migraine and hypertension or epilepsy is fairly common. F. Alexander (1950) has commented that in the above disorders, the specificity of the precipitating psychodynamic factors, i.e., the nature of the hostile impulses, must be considered. A fully consummated aggressive attack has three phases: First, there is the preparation of the attack in fantasy (conceptual phase). Second, there are the circulatory and metabolic changes which prepare the body for concentrated activity (vegetative phase). Third, there is the consummation of the aggressive act through muscular activity (neuromuscular phase).

The nature of the physical symptoms may depend on the phase in which the expression of aggression is inhibited. If the inhibition occurs during the conceptual phase of preparation for the aggressive attack, a migraine, epileptic, or narcoleptic state may develop. After the second phase, or vegetative preparation for the attack, an inhibition may result in hypertension, Raynaud's phenomenon, or Buerger's disease. Finally if the third, or voluntary, act is inhibited, arthritic symptoms may result. This hypothesis is favored by the observation that migrainous and narcoleptic persons are primarily thinkers rather than doers, while arthritics and catatonics have a strong inclination toward muscular activity. The catatonic schizophrenic patient demonstrates the extremes of conflict between action (catatonic excitement) and nonaction (catatonic stupor).

Strongly supporting a specific relation between the nature of an emotional conflict and the particular organ system involved are Engel's (1956) observations on headache in ulcerative colitis patients. He found that the headaches in 20 out of 23 consecutive ulcerative colitis patients could be classified as migraine, muscle tension, or hysterical in type. In 12 patients, these headaches always occurred when a remission was beginning in the colitis or when colitis was not present. A striking difference in their emotional states existed between the bleeding periods and the headache periods. Headaches occurred when the patients felt in control, had taken an active or aggressive stand, or had made a decision which produced conscious or unconscious guilt but which did not produce the threat of significant object loss. In contrast, bowel bleeding occurred when the patient felt helpless or hopeless in relation to a real or fantasied object loss.

EMOTIONAL FACTORS IN SKIN DISEASES

Klauder (1935) remarked that the psyche exerted a greater influence on the skin than on any other organ and that only the eye was more important than the skin in expressing emotions—for example, blushing of the skin as an expression of shame or itching as sign of impatience. The body surface is also the somatic locus of exhibitionism. Reflex changes in the skin such as pallor, flushing, and so forth are constituent parts of emotional states of rage and fear. The skin functions as an important sensory organ and is affected by conversion symptoms such as anesthesia and parasthesia. In the psychology of the skin, pain has a central place, and masochistic tendencies may therefore have a close affinity to the skin. Many clinical studies of skin manifestations as a part of neurotic symptomatology have been conducted on neurodermatitis, eczema, angioneurotic edema, urticaria, and pruritis. Psoriasis has also been connected with exhibitionism by some authors. In eczema and neurodermatitis, sadomasochistic and exhibitionistic trends have been claimed to be correlated to the skin symptoms. According to Miller (1948), the body is exhibited in order to obtain attention, love, and favor, but because this involves a hostile competition with rivals (siblings), it arouses guilt feelings. According to the talion principle (the punishment should be equal to the crime), the skin which serves as a tool of exhibitionism becomes the place of a painful and disfiguring affliction. Some authors also emphasized narcissistic exhibitionistic traits. Scratching is of great etiological significance in these diseases, and psychoanalytic studies reveal that the scratching is due to inhibited hostile impulses which, because of guilt feelings, are deflected from their original target and are turned against the self. Craving for physical expression of affection, such as being held, cuddled, stroked, and soothed, is involved in skin reactions. This desire becomes highly eroticized and often creates guilt, particularly because of its competitive aspects.

Cleveland and Fisher (1956) compared 25 male patients suffering from neurodermatitis with a group of 22 males with industrial and accidental skin lesions. Further comparisons were made with 25 rheumatoid arthritis patients and 20 patients with low back pain. The dermatitis patients showed a higher degree of masochism than the control group and a highly depreciated self-concept. The dermatitis patients unconsciously conceive of their bodies in terms of dirt and repulsion and make masochistic pleas to those in authority. They also tended to defend against exhibitionism by covering and hiding the body because of its negative image. Although repressed hostility toward both parental figures was found, they showed an "armor plate" defense, in common with rheumatoid arthritics, in that their bodies were conceived of as being surrounded by an impermeable barrier which protected them against internal disruption. They viewed their fathers as powerful and distant and attempted to placate them in a masochistic manner. Even more anxiety and conflict existed in their relationships with their mothers, toward whom they held great resentment because of never receiving adequate love and attention.

Mohr et al. (1963), in detailed studies, related infantile eczema to a parent-child relationship where "contact hunger" is fostered by inconsistency in providing gratifying bodily contact, for example, deprivation in this respect by one parent and overindulgence by the other. A restrictive, overprotective atmosphere compensatory for destructive attitudes of the mother was commonly observed which was conducive to infantilization of the child. The eczematous child is involved in intense infantile relationship with the mother. Sexual impulses occurring in the oedipal situation threaten the child with estrangement from the infantilizing mother, now experienced as a sexualized mother. Initial attacks of asthma in some eczematous children occur when they are confronted with the conflicts characteristic of the anal or the oedipal (phallic) developmental phase.

The studies on body cathexis of Anderson and Cross (1963) indicate that the face and the genitals are commonly the most highly cathected parts of the body. The hands are not highly cathected because of a strong countercathexis from the superego (the hands are the executive agents in sexual and aggressive acts). Since neurodermatitis patients produce inflammation of the skin by repeated rubbing and scratching, these authors emphasized that treatment must be directed at both the emotional problem and the resulting cutaneous lesion. Primary neurodermatitis is usually localized, circumscribed, and symmetrical and has a poorer prognosis than secondary neurodermatitis. In a study of 195 patients who had had primary neurodermatitis for over five years, they found a close relationship between the severity of the dermatitis, the degree of emotional disturbance, and the distribution of the skin lesions. The most disturbed patients attacked the most highly cathected areas (face), and the least disturbed patients attacked the least highly cathected areas (hands).

Bergman and Aldrich (1963) conducted a follow-up study on 28 adolescent subjects who had been treated for infantile eczema between 1940 and 1946. Interviews, which usually included parents and which covered psychiatric and medical histories and appraised the subjects' current adaptation, were conducted. Fourteen subjects still suffered from active atopic eczema; 6 of the 14 who had no evidence of active eczema had asthma or hay fever. The severity of the eczema at the time of follow-up did not seem to be related to the severity in infancy. Eighteen of the subjects had a definite psychosis or personality-trait disturbance. Eleven of the eighteen subjects with specific psychiatric disorders still had eczema. This group included all three of the subjects with the most severe eczema and most of those with severe psychiatric disturbance. Sixteen mothers showed marked evidence of rejection or overprotection. Eight of the fourteen girls were tomboys; nine of the thirteen boys were athletes. Evidence of passivity, latent exhibitionistic tendencies, and pronounced skin cathexis was frequently found. Exacerbations of eczema were often associated with threats to the patient's dependent relationships, and remissions with evidence of increased security.

Seitz (1953) evaluated the efficiency of brief psychotherapy in 12 out of 13 patients who completed a 12-session course of treatment, as compared with 12 of the 25 who did not complete treatment and who derived no benefit. Thus in Seitz's group, the major factor related to a remission seemed to be the brief psychotherapy.

Schoenberg and Carr (1963) attempted to determine predictive criteria for selecting patients capable of tolerating the anxiety inherent in the treatment method. Their 26 neurodermatitis patients received short-term psychotherapy which specifically encouraged and reinforced the expression of hostility toward their present life situations. They commented that (1) certain neurodermatitis patients experienced a remission of their skin disorder by the specific type of short-term psychotherapy, and (2) those who did not improve or who discontinued psychotherapy differed significantly from those who completed it successfully. Those whose treatment was successful showed more overt hostility in interviews and in Rorschach responses. Hostility was felt to be a significant factor in the etiology of neurodermatitis.

Kepecs, Robin, and Munro (1960) developed a tickle test utilizing the subjective response of subjects as an indicator of their reactions and defenses against a mildly irritating stimulus. The responses ranged from "irritation" (associated with emotional volatility and lability), to "adaptation," to mixed reactions. Kepecs considered the tendency to react to stress with the skin (dermal fixation) to be a combination of (1) constitutional predisposition; (2) delayed, impaired, or only partial development of the dermal stimulus barrier against irritation; (3) premature learning to localize and scratch the irritant; and (4) some sort of central registration and retention of these experiences available for activation under stress.

Urticaria has been correlated with suppressed weeping by Saul and Bernstein (1941) and in several cases observed by F. Alexander (1950). Kepecs, Robin, and Brunner's (1951) demonstration, however, that exudation into the skin increases *during* weeping as well as when weeping is inhibited contradicted the assumption that psychogenic exudation into the skin is merely a weeping into the skin. Nevertheless, in patients with urticaria, as in those with asthma, to which urticaria has an intrinsic relationship, inhibited dependent longings for a parental object are a conspicuous finding. The fact that in many urticaria patients who inhibit weeping the urticarial attacks are often terminated by weeping indicates an intimate relationship between weeping and urticaria.

Wittkower (1953), in his personality studies of urticaria patients, defined the following psychopathological mechanisms: repressed aggressiveness, masochism, repressed exhibitionism, and a regressive revival of infantile skin eroticism. He saw urticarial wheals as a result of infantile fury. Instead of hurting, scratching, and attacking others, these individuals scratched themselves. Revival of infantile skin eroticism in emotionally starved individuals may well account for the pleasurable sensation often experienced by patients on rubbing and scratching.

Recently Shoemaker (1963) studied the affective determinants of chronic urticaria. He evaluated 40 cases to determine whether they manifested any psychosomatic specificity (his group excluded patients in whom allergic and physical agents were factors). Their method compared cross-sectional psychiatric studies of patients suffering from hives with longitudinal studies (biographical studies). Without exception, the patients were more active prior to the onset of urticaria, and they experienced events and circumstances that caused a breakdown of various activities which had served as defenses. There was also a consistent history of some form of parental rejection. Physical violence seemed important in the psychodynamics of chronic urticaria. Anxiety was consistently present, and hostility appeared to be an important factor in the urticaria complex. Saul's conclusions about the essential dependency of his urticaria patients seem to be verified by this study. At the time the urticarial reaction occurs, the patient appears to be caught between abject dependency and destructive rage.

In the different forms of pruritis, particularly pruritis ani and pruritis vulvi, inhibited sexual excitement is an important psychodynamic factor. In these cases scratching is a source of conscious erotic pleasure and is clearly a masturbatory equivalent. This is also a feature in neurodermatitis.

Macalpine (1953) found that male patients with pruritis ani showed extreme exhibitionism in their eagerness to be examined, as a manifestation of a need for reassurance about their sex. Deeper anxieties caused by archaic pregnancy fantasies occurred in both sexes, which in the male implied homosexuality. No specific personality type was noted, but all of them were obsessed with cleanliness and feared something becoming lodged inside them, and all had sexual disturbances and feared that something was tearing away at them, leading to constipation. The fantasy that children grow in the stomach was reactivated in the current life situation, but the specific precipitating factors were not clear.

S. I. Greenberg (1961) maintains that pruritis is a symptom of depression which resists treatment until the cause for depression is removed. The pruritis may occur without any objective evidence of cutaneous disturbance, so-called "idiopathic" pruritis, or it may appear as an exacerbation of the itch that regularly accompanies many dermatologic conditions. Other observers have also noted depression in patients with chronic pruritic dermatoses who failed to respond to treatment until their depression was relieved. It is not surprising that pruritis is a common manifestation of depression, for excessive itching and scratching are related to self-punitive attitudes, as is the case in depression. Since the itching and scratching have a defensive value in maintaining the emotional balance, too rapid removal of the symptoms, as by hypnotic suggestion, may precipitate a frank psychosis. Greenberg noted that most of the patients are middle-aged or elderly, the very age groups in which depression is most frequent. In his five cases, the degree of the patients' depressions ranged from neurotic to psychotic. Occasionally, antidepressant drugs or electroconvulsive treatment is indicated.

Isolated studies of the effects of emotional stress in lupus erythematosis and other collagen diseases such as scleroderma exist. Mufson (1953) studied seven cases of scleroderma and proposed that scleroderma was an extension of Raynaud's disease. He described the patients as susceptible to threats of death and indigence or loss of a significant protective love object. When the threat to security became real, it was promptly followed by onset and persistence of vasospasm and its sequelae. As long as this life situation continued, the disease process persisted, and when the life situation improved, the complicating thrombotic manifestations became amenable to vasodilating therapy.

EMOTIONAL FACTORS IN ENDOCRINE AND METABOLIC DISTURBANCES

Thyrotoxicosis

Clinical observations confirmed the importance of emotional factors in precipitating thyrotoxicosis, after Caleb Parry, in 1803, noted its acute onset following a severe fright in a 21-year-old girl. The onset of the illness following an acute emotional trauma, e.g., a war experience or the witnessing of the accidental death of a loved one, is called "shock Basedow." From psychodynamic studies, certain personality features common to hyperthyroid patients have been outlined (Brown & Gildea, 1937; Conrad, 1934; Lewis, 1925; Lidz, 1954; Mandelbrote & Wittkower, 1955; Mittleman, 1933).

Kracht (1952) demonstrated a "fright thyrotoxicosis" in wild rabbits which occurred when they were exposed to a barking dog. The hyperthyroid response which occurred in all the rabbits was so marked that the animals died in a "thyroid crisis" (extreme hyperthyroidism) if they were left in the presence of the dogs, unless they received thyroid treatment. Kracht viewed the phenomenon as a specific thyroidal stress reaction based on histological findings of marked hyperactivity in the thyroid glands and normal cytology in all other endocrine glands in the animals at autopsy. The same authors showed that in tame as well as in wild rabbits, the elimination of thyroid-stored hormone began ten to thirty minutes after the beginning of the stress, showing that the thyroid can react in a matter of minutes.

Hetzel, De La Nabe, and Hinkle (1952), by use of stress interviews, produced changes in the protein-bound iodine blood levels in euthyroid and hyperthyroid subjects. Their hyperthyroid subjects showed little PBI-level change when they were relaxed, and they observed a drop in the PBI value in two patients after the patients had verbally expressed their emotional conflicts, especially resentment. The authors believed that the rapid rises of PBI were similar to those obtained with TSH and that the thyroid was not a sluggish organ concerned only with long-term adaptation. Starr, Petit, Chaney, Rollman, Aiken, Jamieson, & Kling (1950) found normal PBI levels in patients with psychoneurosis and psychosis and concluded that anxiety alone was not sufficient to stimulate thyroid activity. Similarly, Brody (1949) found that emotional tension did not alter the PBI levels in psychiatric patients, which he found were essentially normal. Eranko and Muittari (1957) produced an experimental anxiety neurosis in rats by alternating gratification (eating) with frustration and pain. Except for behavioral and physiological signs of anxiety, the rats seemed normal. However, at autopsy all the neurotic rats showed a *relative* and an *absolute* increase in thyroid weight caused by twice the amount of stored hormone. The authors felt that they experimentally demonstrated that psychic conflict may produce change in endocrine glands.

Many other conflicting studies have been reported concerning thyroid activity in psychiatric patients. Much of the disagreement was due to the unreliability of laboratory techniques such as the basal metabolic rate and protein-bound iodine determination. Because of more accurate biochemical techniques and the introduction of radioactive tracer methods, recent studies are more reliable. Recently, Board, Hamburg, and Persky (1956) determined 17-hydroxycorticosterone and plasma PBI levels in 30 patients, twenty-four hours after admission to a psychiatric hospital, and found that 17-OH and plasma PBI levels were distinctly higher than in controls but that the difference was proportionately less for PBI than for 17-OH. High levels of the hormones were associated with very intense distress (especially depressive affect with retarded behavior and disintegration of personality). Fourteen days later, the 17-OH levels had dropped, but PBI was still elevated at a level that was near that of the initial day. Doniger, Wittkower, Stephens-Newsham, and Hoffman (1956) conducted stress interviews with 28 subjects. Radioactive iodine neck counts and the PBI-131 levels in the plasma were determined before the interview and were repeated immediately and then one to two hours after the interview was terminated. For measuring long-term thyroid secretion, they used the biological decay curve. The rate of disappearance of I-131 from the gland is a sensitive index of hormonal secretion, and thus a shorter half-life is evidence for an overactive thyroid gland. The biological decay curves of 27 professional people were used as controls. Of their 27 subjects with anxiety, five had a family history of thyrotoxicosis, five had a past history of thyrotoxicosis, and 17 had no family history. Anxiety experienced on a conscious level by the subject was the only criterion for selection apart from those subjects especially referred because of a personal or family history of thyrotoxicosis. No patients with thyrotoxicosis were studied. No significant rise in plasma PBI-131 resulted from the stress interviews, and no correlation between the degree of anxiety and activity of the gland was found. However, a correlation between the type of biological decay curve in the first group of 27 patients and the psychodynamic formulation was noted. Therefore, they selected 44 additional subjects, and on the basis of psychiatric interviews, they predicted the type of biological decay curve for each subject. Their prediction proved correct in 34 out of 44 cases. These correct predictions indicated the validity of previous psychosomatic studies as to the personality conflicts in hyperthyroidism.

In 1949, Ham, Alexander, and Carmichael presented an analysis of anamnestic interviews of 23 patients and prolonged psychoanalytic treatment of one patient from which they formed the hypothesis that hyperthyroid patients exhibited a specific psychological gestalt and that the activation of a specific emotional conflict by a current life situation was etiologically significant in the precipitation of the illness.

The personality features were characterized by a premature need for self-sufficiency and maturity through taking care of self, siblings, and parents, as a consequence of inadequate parental support, resulting in frustrated dependency needs. There had been instances of death, divorce, or separation of parents; other forms of parental rejection; continued or excessive economic stress; and traumatic exposure to significant death episodes. Many patients had multiple siblings, with a significantly high incidence of the patient being the oldest child. They showed an inability to express hostility, and they defended themselves against fear by denial and repression and, most characteristically, by counterphobic attitudes.

They were ambitious, long-term planners and were prone to assume excessive obligations. The women had a strong urge to bear many children. Finally, they had frequent affect-laden dreams of death and caskets.

The dynamic nucleus was found to be fear of death. Although childhood insecurity is found in both neurotic and healthy individuals, the hyperthyroid patients have a characteristic manner of handling their insecurity. Because of their anxiety over the frustration of their dependent needs, they make a desperate attempt to identify themselves prematurely with one of the parents, usually the mother ("If I cannot have her, I must become like her so that I can dispense with her").

Such a precocious identification is beyond their physiological and psychological capacity and results in a persistent struggle to master anxiety and insecurity by a pseudo self-reliance. Other investigators, too, noticed different aspects of this constellation (Ruesch, Christiansen, Patterson, Dewees, & Jacobson 1947). The struggle against anxiety is manifested by denial, and a counterphobic attitude of a compulsive urge to undertake just those activities which are most feared. For example, a woman may show a compulsive urge to become pregnant, in spite of her fear of pregnancy. Likewise, the feared loss of the mother is combated by becoming a mother. The high incidence of phobias in the life history of hyperthyroid patients was noted by Ficarra and Nelson (1947). The hyperthyroid patients' excessive urge to become self-sufficient is explained by the fact that they could not alleviate their early childhood insecurities by depending on the adults. The histories of hyperthyroid patients reveal that many of them, as children, actually experienced starvation, deprivation, or loss of a parent through death or divorce or had been subjected to or witnessed physical violence. Since the original publication of Ham et al. (1949), the above-described specific emotional conflict in thyrotoxicosis has been validated by a multiple blind specificity study carried out by Alexander and a research team of internists and psychoanalysts at the Chicago Institute for Psychoanalysis. These investigators maintain that emotional patterns in different chronic diseases are characteristic of the various disease entities. In other words, the chronic diseases they have studied have not only a characteristic pathophysiology but also a characteristic psychopathology Different types of emotional stress situations have specific affinity to certain types of organic function or dysfunction.

Emotional and physiological changes characteristic of hyperthyroidism can be induced by the administration of excessive amounts of thyroid hormone to normal subjects and are the direct results of increased thyroxin levels. However, the administration of excessive thyroid hormone does not produce the striking personality characteristics which are so typical of the hyperthyroid patient. Burwell and Eppinger (1955), Hamburger and Lev (1930), and others have reported apathetic, nonactive, or masked hyperthyroidism. Bursten (1961) found that although the incidence of hyperthyroidism in a psychotic population was low, sufficient cases of psychosis in populations of thyrotoxic patients existed to suggest a functional relationship between the two disease processes. No type of psychosis was characteristic, but some manifested a "manic veneer." Sometimes the course of the illness suggested that the thyrotoxicosis had precipitated the psychosis, and sometimes it seemed that the anxieties and activity associated with psychotic decompensation had precipitated the thyrotoxicosis or that both processes had developed simultaneously as a consequence of psychodynamic shifts and that the two disease processes were synergistic.

Bennett and Cambor (1961) confirmed the personality patterns in hyperthyroid patients as outlined above.

Alexander observed a patient with *hypothyroidism* (myxedema) who revealed a character structure indistinguishable from that found in *hyperthyroid* patients (marked counterphobic attitudes). Possibly such as case represents a "burned-out" hyperthyroid patient. The psychodynamic pattern, it seems, is not specific for a particular disease but for the dysfunction of an organ or organ system. The growth-stimulating function of the thyroid gland and the conspicuous urge of the hyperthyroid patient to become mature at an accelerated tempo may be interrelated. If so, the patient's constant efforts to maintain his pseudo maturity might overstimulate the thyroid gland. As the counterphobic defense mechanisms used to deny unconscious dependency needs become inadequate and the phobic anxieties and the dependent needs begin to emerge into consciousness, this seems to precipitate hyperthyroidism. Certainly thyroxin (thyroid hormone) stimulates cell metabolism and therefore favors intellectual growth and performance; increases sensitivity and alertness (and, if levels are excessive, produces anxiety); and stimulates growth and the procreative processes. Compared with adrenaline, the stimulating effects of thyroxin are directed toward situations in which the body is called upon to perform long-term accomplishments, although recent studies have established that stress may result in increased thyroid secretion in a matter of minutes. Why hyperthyroid patients react to insecurity with a progressive effort toward maturation rather than with regressive symptoms, as is found in many other persons, is unknown. Possibly early infantile emotional experiences discouraging dependency are a factor. Because of the familial nature of the disease, hereditary factors must also be considered. Certainly thyrotoxicosis is not the result of a local condition of the thyroid gland. Thyroid secretion is an effector link in a chain of physiological processes. It is regulated by the release of thyrotrophic hormone from the anterior pituitary, which in turn is influenced by the central nervous system via the hypothalamus. Thoughts and emotions exert their influences on the hypothalamus, pituitary, autonomic nervous system, and other endocrine glands by complicated connections between the cerebral cortex and the "visceral brain" or limbic system, as outlined by the early studies of MacLean (1949), Papez (1937), and others.

We have not yet been successful in establishing precisely the physiological mechanisms through which emotions can produce bodily changes. Most neurophysiological and psychophysiological investigations today are based on Cannon's concept of homeostasis and on Selye's (1946) formulation of the general adaptation syndrome. The study of the influence of emotional stress in the etiology or recurrence of a disease entity began with isolated individual case reports, only to progress more recently to multidisciplinary experimental studies which attempt to establish correlations between well-defined emotional conflict situations with specific organ responses and to identify the specific neurophysiological and neuroendocrine pathways through which the emotional stress exerts its influence.

An example of the latter approach is the work of Shizume, Matsuda, Irie, Lino, Ishii, Nagataki, Matsuzaki, and Okiaka (1962), at the University of Tokyo. They reported that the thyroidal response which occurs after stimulation of the anterior hypothalamus or median eminence appears to result from increased secretion of thyroid-stimulating hormone by the pituitary gland. Upon electric stimulation of the anterior hypothalamus or the median eminence of normal dogs, the concentration of protein-bound radioiodine (PBI-131) in the thyroid venous blood increases significantly. The response appears within fifteen minutes and is most pronounced after thirty to sixty minutes.

Over the past five years, a research team (Alexander, Flagg, Foster, Clemens, & Blahd, 1961) at the Psychiatric and Psychosomatic Research Institute of Mt. Sinai Hospital, Los Angeles, has been investigating the psychological, autonomic, and thyroid responses in treated and acute untreated hyperthyroid patients and control subjects before, during, and after exposure to a stressor film (*Wages of Fear*) or to a series of nonstressor films (travelogues) within a laboratory setting. A series of psychological tests are administered before and after film viewing, and behavioral observations, continuous radioactive count over the thyroid gland, continuous measures of autonomic nervous system reactions during film presentation, as well as protein-bound iodine 131 and chemical PBI determinations (before, and at hourly intervals after, the stressor films) are carried out. A psychiatric interview follows the stressor and nonstressor films. A total of 44 acute untreated and 15 treated hyperthyroid patients and 27 control subjects have been exposed to this experimental procedure. The results indicate the following:

1. The thyroid gland in acute untreated hyperthyroid patients is a highly reactive organ, capable of responding to emotional stimulation within a period of less than two minutes. This was shown by *decreases* in the radioactive count over the thyroid gland, especially during the more exciting portions of the stressor film, and by *increases* in circulating PBI-131 during and after film viewing. The subjective impact and content of the stimuli, as well as the emotional state of the patients at the time of the experiment, were correlated with these thyroid reactions. In general, the more psychologically disturbed untreated hyperthyroid patients showed greater thyroid response. Quite apart from the degree of mainfest psychological disturbance, patients who saw the stressor film had significantly greater thyroid reactions than those who viewed the travelogues.

Determinations of the chemical PBI (as contrasted with the PBI-131 and the radioactive count over the thyroid gland) did *not* show significant changes, which strongly suggests that this measure is not a sensitive indicator of thyroid response. There was very little change in thyroid output in control subjects and treated hyperthyroid patients.

2. Continuous and simultaneous recording of autonomic nervous system functions also revealed that acute untreated hyperthyroid patients had greater reactions to the stressor

film than to the nonstressor films. However, untreated patients who were rated as being emotionally more disturbed than others in that group showed greater ANS response, regardless of the content of the films which were shown. Control subjects and treated hyperthyroid patients had nearly identical average composite measures of ANS reactivity during film viewing.

3. In comparing relatively more disturbed with nondisturbed acute untreated hyperthyroid patients, the results supported a "response specificity" hypothesis to the extent that the disturbed group tended to overreact in thyroid and ANS activity, regardless of the over-all content of the film material which was presented. However, there were many indications within the same stressor film that content such as rejection and the loss of affection engendered very little psychophysiological reaction in untreated hyperthyroid patients, whereas in scenes where physical danger and threatened loss of life were prevalent, frequent and marked psychophysiological responses occurred. In most instances, idiosyncratic reactions to the film content could be related to specific life experiences of the individual subjects. These results tended to support a "stimulus specificity" hypothesis, although further investigation is necessary. These studies support the hypothesis that repetitive stimuli have a cumulative effect on the organism and its psychophysiological processes which may be of etiological significance in predisposed individuals in the development of chronic organic diseases.

For the creation of emotional stress situations in the laboratory, three types of experimental studies have been undertaken: (1) those which study the physiological effects of stress interviews; (2) those which take advantage of recurring stress situations as they occur in real life, e.g., by studying psychophysiological changes in students before examinations, exposing the experimental subjects to the sight of injuries in a hospital emergency room, etc.; (3) those which take advantage of surgical opportunities—for example, gastric fistulas—to observe directly stomach activity under various emotional influences; and (4) those in which there is alteration of psysiological functions by means of hypnotic suggestions.

A major advantage of using dramatic films is not only that they can introduce into the laboratory different types of lifelike situations but also that they can reproduce them with high authenticity and with a great sense of reality. Many experimental studies use too simple stimuli or stress situations, which appear too artificial to the subjects and which therefore rarely involve the ego of the subject sufficiently to resemble any of the true vicissitudes of life. In contrast, the emotional involvement in movies often approaches that of real life.

Such rigorous and objective psychophysiological studies conducted by multidisciplinary research teams illustrate the natural evolution from the astute, intuitive observations of Caleb Parry, who first described hyperthyroidism, to well-controlled experimental investigations.

Fatigue States

Fatigue, like pain, is largely a subjective response to excessive and prolonged physical or mental activity. It has, however, physiological concomitants. Emotional participation, interest, and zest are important factors in the feeling of fatigue. If a person is bored or resents a certain activity, he may feel fatigued quickly, whereas a keen interest in a strenuous task may prevent fatigue for a long time. One special type of fatigue is due to a low blood sugar resulting from functional causes (nonorganic). It is characterized by acute attacks of extreme fatigue, lightheadedness, cold perspiration, fear of fainting, and/or free-floating anxiety.

The psychological manifestations have been described by both internists and psychiatrists, such as Wilder (1943), Rennie and Howard (1942), and Himwich (1944). Wilder emphasized the characteristic psychological concomitants (dullness of consciousness, weakness of concentration, and a depressive or anxious state of mind) of the bodily symptoms. In very severe attacks, mannerisms, changes of speech, double vision, and ataxia occur as different areas of the brain are affected.

In the first psychosomatic study of such cases, Szondi and Lax (1929) demonstrated an abnormal (flat) glucose-tolerance curve associated with the physical and psychological symptoms. Many of these individuals had previously been diagnosed as "neurasthenic." Later, both Rennie and Howard (1942) ("tension depression") and Portis and Zitman (1943) explained the flat glucose-tolerance curves in patients complaining of excessive fatigue as being due to hyperinsulinism caused by overactivity of the right vagus nerve. They found that the glucose tolerance returned to normal if the patient's emotional difficulties were resolved or if the vagus nerve was blocked by atropine and if sugar was eliminated from the diet. F. Alexander and Portis (1944) correlated the psychodynamic situation with the state of carbohydrate metabolism in nine patients. They found that the attacks of fatigue consistently related to a complete lack of initiative in the subject for an activity in which he was engaged (whether the routine activities in the office, school, or home, or even social activity). Acute fatigue usually developed in the patient after he was forced to abandon a cherished goal and had resigned himself to continue with some distasteful routine against which he revolted in turn. Alexander and Portis explained these fatigue states as an emotional sit-down strike. When the subjects were frustrated in their genuine desires and proclivities and were forced into routine activities, because of external pressure or their consciences, they developed their own form of protest, which was often accompanied by regressive fantasies and daydreams involving self-indulgent wishful imagery. They found the flat glucose-tolerance curve and assumed that this was the physiological parallel of the patient's emotional state and that there was a causal relationship between the psychological situation and the disturbance of the carbohydrate-regulating mechanism. In accordance with Cannon's views, preparation for outwardly directed activity stimulated by fear or anger is mainly a sympathetic nervous system effect. They extended Cannon's view by postulating that enthusiasm, zest, and continuous purposeful striving, like anger and fear, exerted a tuning-up effect upon the sympathetic adrenal system. In their fatigue cases, not only was sympathetic stimulation lacking, but the regressive emotional protest produced a state of passivity and relaxation characterized by a preponderance of parasympathetic stimulation. Physiologically, this manifests itself in an increased parasympathetic tonus and increased insulin secretion. Thus the organism while engaged in effort behaves vegetatively as if it were resting, a state which Alexander called a "vegetative retreat."

In another study, Carlson, McCulloch, and Alexander (1949) found that in the fatigue group, the fasting blood-sugar level was significantly lower at the end of the experiment than in the normal group. In this fatigue state, they found the following psychodynamic situations: (1) There was a lack of hope of achieving some cherished goal or a frustrating struggle against insuperable odds. (2) There was no genuine incentive involving routine activities or occupations, which were nevertheless carried out because of external pressure or conscience. (3) In certain instances, a feminine identification was conspicuous and opposed aggressive ambitious attitudes. (4) At times, anxiety was an important factor since prolonged frustration created a compensatory hostile aggressiveness which produced anxiety, which in turn contributed to a regressive retreat from activity.

Shands and Finesinger (1952) maintain that fatigue may be understood as a danger signal closely related to anxiety. Fatigue is seen as a signal which causes the person to desist from aggressive behavior. Anxiety says to the individual: "Something must be done," whereas fatigue says: "Something must be stopped."

Narcolepsy and Epilepsy

In more severe disturbances of subjective mood such as narcolepsy, cataplexy, and epilepsy, the role of emotional conflict has been recognized. Pond, of Maudsley Hospital (1952), observed eight cases of narcolepsy and describes it as a disturbance of vigilance. Sexual maladjustment was present in all subjects, and the men identified with passive mothers, taking their part against strict fathers, who were violent or alcoholic. However, Levin (1953) saw narcolepsy more as a direct inhibition of a wish to attack. The psychophysiological studies of Vogel (1960) are convincing evidence of the influence of emotion in the etiology of idiopathic narcolepsy. He noted that since the external situations in which narcoleptic attacks occur do not differ from those which make normal individuals sleepy or bored, the difference between narcoleptic and normal individuals may be one of degree. Militating against the theory that narcolepsy is a convulsive disorder is the absence of EEG abnormalities, its rare association with epilepsy, and the cure of some cases by psychotherapy. Vogel's hypothesis was that pathological sleep functions as a psychological defense against anxiety or as a defense against intense sexual or aggressive impulses. In one case which he studied intensively, the narcoleptic attack provided hallucinatory gratification of forbidden fantasies by the specific mechanism of wish fulfillment through dreaming. Thus the narcoleptic attack had the specific function of producing a dream which provided hallucinatory gratification of the sleep-provoking unacceptable fantasy. Vogel tested his hypothesis by making EEG recordings of his patient after he rapidly went to sleep. Repeatedly, his subject was dreaming within four minutes after the onset of sleep. If the patient went to sleep a number of times, the interval between the onset of sleep and dreaming lengthened. The early appearance of dreaming in narcoleptic patients, as contrasted with the absence of dreaming in the early phase of normal sleep, supports the proposition that the narcoleptic patient makes use of his sleep for fantasy gratifications which are unacceptable during waking life.

Epstein and Ervin (1956) studied two patents with psychomotor epilepsy who were receiving intensive psychotherapy and concluded that the seizures were highly organized discharges of dynamic conflictual material. The content and structure of the seizure could be understood in the same fashion as a dream since it had meaning for the individual in terms of wish fulfillment and/or riddance. As motivated behavior, it dispelled mounting psychological tension. Such seizures, they felt, represented *nonreported* thought.

Bandler, Kausman, Dykens, Schleiser, Shapiro, and Arico (1958) reported two analyzed cases of epilepsy and described the nuclear dynamic conflict leading to seizures as sexual and not involving aggressive impulses, as outlined by other investigators. The seizures occurred in relationship to current sexual conflicts and to the sexual transference. Past seizures occurred in relationship to past sexual conflicts which were similar to the current ones.

An 18-year-old girl who had petit mal and grand mal seizures was observed by one of the authors (Flagg) during four years of intensive psychotherapy. The conflict which produced the grand mal seizures was always that of frustrated oral receptive tendencies, with an unconscious inhibited rage reaction resulting in a motor discharge of the psychological tension. The conscious content of the seizure was often eroticized with fantasies of sexual activity with the analyst or her father. However, the seizures decreased markedly when the rage was relieved. It also became clear that the patient used the grand mal seizures secondarily to express affects and ideas through hysterical symbolization. Of no less clinical importance was the fact that the patient often unconsciously forgot to take her anticonvulsant medication in order to precipitate a seizure. The petit mal seizures usually occurred when the patient wanted to escape from ego-alien thoughts of an unconscious sadistic nature. The petit mal attacks could be produced in the interviews if such material was stimulated.

Diabetes Mellitus

The effect of psychological stress on the course of diabetes is presently well established. That emotional conflict can be of etiological significance is not yet demonstrated, but there is evidence that in an individual who is genetically susceptible to diabetes, the onset of the illness may be precipitated by emotional conflict. Cannon (1920) demonstrated that fear and anxiety can produce glycosuria even in normal human subjects. Although this "emotional glycosuria" (sugar in the urine) may be produced in nondiabetic subjects, a significant rise in their *blood-sugar* concentration does not occur (Mirsky, 1946; Mirsky, 1948). In the diabetic person, the regulatory mechanisms of carbohydrate metabolism are disturbed, leading to a vulnerability to stress of any kind (trauma, infection, exposure). Emotional upheavals also aggravate the existing metabolic disturbance in the diabetic by an increased breakdown of liver glycogen due to the activation of the autonomic nervous system and the secretion of epinephrine (Cannon's emergency concept).

Dunbar (1943) proposed that diabetic patients had great difficulty in giving up infantile dependency needs and were prone to substitute words for action. Bruch and Hewelett (1947) maintained that in one-third of the children they studied, the diabetes appeared after a separation experience. These children had a tendency toward compulsive behavior or submissiveness, or they used passive resistance. Benedek and Mirsky, of the Chicago Psychoanalytic Institute, in 1950 described the diabetic patient as having some basic conflict related to the acquisition of food which was reflected in exaggerated aggressive oral incorporative tendencies manifested in a variety of ways. For instance, a tendency to reject food may be followed by an increased need for replenishment, expressed as an insatiable desire to be fed, or by an excessive demand for receptive gratification in interpersonal relationships. The incorporative impulses lead to an exaggerated identification with the mother, which may impair psychosexual development. In men, the maternal identification may lead to conflicts concerning bisexuality, while in women, the hostile identification activates marked defenses against the feminine role.

Obesity is a factor in the onset of diabetes (75 per cent of cases), but since only 5 per cent of obese persons develop diabetes, a yet unknown vulnerability exists. Since very often obesity is due to emotional conflict, it is possible that the increased incorporative tendencies of diabetics originate in an inherited physiological tendency which makes the satisfaction of their biological needs impossible and which produces a struggle over excessive infantile oral needs. The recent work of Gwinup (1963) is revealing as to the etiologic role of the eating habits, especially gorging, which is so common in obese patients. Four hospitalized subjects on a metabolic ward were compared as to the effects of periodicity of food intake on carbohydrate metabolism, as reflected by the glucose-tolerance curve over a two-week period. The same *amount* of food was given in the following manner: (1) three meals daily, (2) nibbling—10 equal feedings over a nineteen-hour period—and (3) gorging—all the food for one day given in one hour in the evening. Nibbling produced a normal glucose-tolerance curve, while gorging produced a "diabetic" type.

Meyer, Bollmeier, and Alexander (1945) related the increased glycosuria of the diabetic to the conflict between infantile wishes to receive and demands to give and take care of others. A regressive withdrawal into passivity was associated with a decrease in glycosuria.

One of the gravest situations is diabetic acidosis and coma. Mirsky (1942; Mirsky et al., 1948) and Rosen and Lidz (1949) reported that often such a condition was a result of the patient's willfully neglecting to regulate his diet or to take insulin. Some patients with recurrent acidosis used their illness to escape into the shelter of the hospital or to attempt suicide. However, Hinkle and Wolf (1949; 1952) and Hinkle, Conger, and Wolf (1949), in a study on 50 acidotic states, showed that emotional tension could induce ketosis even though the patient was faithful to his diabetic regime. They found that stress interviews could rapidly produce ketosis in severe diabetics even though they adhered to proper diet. If the stress persisted, a true clinical acidosis resulted.

In 1963 Slawson, Flynn, and Kollar (1963) reported on the psychological and environmental setting in which diabetes mellitus developed. They reviewed the literature as far back as the seventeenth century on the influence of emotional conflict in precipitating diabetes. Their bibliography included observations by Thomas Willis, Savage, Maudsley, Allen, Neilson, Masson, and Cowie and the first systematic studies by Menninger (1935) and others. They believe that object loss, grief, or depression is particularly important in the precipitation of diabetes. As evidence, they cited the work of S. M. Kaplan, Mass, Pixley, and Ross (1960), who reported the diminution of glycosuria in depressed diabetics receiving the antidepressant impramine hydrochloride (Tofranil). Glycosuria increased to preexperimental levels when the drug was withdrawn.

Slawson and his group studied 25 adult new diabetics by a psychiatric evaluation and a standard personality profile (MMPI). They obtained the following results: (1) 14 gave a history of definite object loss, and in six, loss could be reasonably inferred; (2) 10 presented findings suggestive or unresolved grief, and seven were clinically depressed; and (3) 14 were living in an emotionally deprived environment. Slawson and his group felt that diabetic patients might be subject to a type of specific stress in that their response to emotional deprivation might represent a type of metabolism characteristic of starvation. Their patients exhibited the mechanisms of "separation depression," as described by Schmale (1958). Their findings did not support the psychophysiological hypothesis of Mirsky or Alexander (see above), which views the illness as a depletion exhaustion state secondary to an intense prolonged psychophysiological state of excitation. In fact, they believe that diabetics can cope with anxiety-producing stresses. They proposed a hypothesis to explain why intense stressful situations, such as prolonged combat, have not been cited as having etiological importance. Their results agreed with the views of Hinkle and Wolf, which conceive of diabetes as an inappropriate metabolic adaptive mechanism where an emotionally deprived individual responds metabolically as though he were being starved. The starving individual has many of the metabolic characteristics of the diabetic. The metabolism shifts from carbohydrates to fats, with a marked ketosis in both, and the starving individual also has a diabetic glucose-tolerance curve. Diabetics are said to tolerate starvation as well as nondiabetics and may even be controlled on a starvation-level diet. This may be an important reason why individuals subjected to simultaneous food and emotional deprivation do not seem to have an increased incidence of diabetes. Both the study of Hinkle and Wolf and that of Slawson on the metabolic shifts in both normals and diabetics during stress interviews indicate stress specificity. When the interviews were centered about topics which produced despair and hopelessness, the subjects responded with ketosis. The differences between diabetics and normals were quantitative, suggesting that the metabolic derangement is an accentuation of normal adaptive mechanisms. Slawson did not postulate psychological stress as a necessary etiological factor in diabetes; rather, he maintained that such a stress might trigger the existing metabolic imbalance in predisposed individuals.

Management of the diabetic patient is very important for his rehabilitation. The physician must evaluate the individual needs and psychological conflicts of the patient so that a hostile, ambivalent, mutually frustrating and punitive struggle does not ensue.

Addison's Disease (Adrenocortical Insufficiency)

Addison's disease is an insidious and usually progressive endocrine disorder due to adrenocortical hypofunction (characterized by increasing weakness, abnormal pigmentation of the skin and mucous membranes, weight loss, hypotension, dehydration, hypoglycemia, and gastrointestinal upsets). It has been related to psychic stress by Maranon and Wallerstein. That emotional factors should be thoroughly investigated is indicated by the fact that in 70 per cent of the cases, the cause of the depletion of the adrenal cortex, which produces Addison's disease, is unknown. Maranon (1929) commented that just as the thyrotoxic state represents the structuralized duplication of the psychic syndrome of acute terror, so Addison's symptom complex duplicates the manifestations of a prolonged emotionally depressed state. Wallerstein, Sutherland, and Lyons (1954) presented a detailed anamnestic case study of a man with Addison's disease. Their patient had manifested unrecognized clinical symptoms of Addison's disease for a long time, and there was evidence that the development of the frank physiological manifestations of adrenal insufficiency was preceded by a long period of psychological disturbance. Evidence is constantly accumulating which objectively demonstrates the fallacy of viewing any illness as purely "organic," "functional," "psychosomatic," or "somatopsychic." For example, Fowler and Zechel (1953), after studying patients with Meniere's syndrome, concluded that the patients have a fundamental emotional predisposition toward the development of the illness. The first acute attack of vertigo and most subsequent attacks follow either an emotional outburst or a damming up of tension in response to an intolerable situation. They found that the red blood cells in the labyrinthian vessels of these patients before and immediately after the attacks resembled those seen in cats subjected to intravenous epinephrine or cervical sympathetic stimulation. Blood clumps stick in the tiny vessels of the labyrinth and produce local disturbances which sooner or later produce the structural changes characteristic of the advanced disease. The above examples illustrate the intricate interrelationships between the cerebral cortex, the autonomic nervous system, and the endocrine glands.

DISTURBANCES OF THE JOINTS AND MUSCULAR SYSTEM

Rheumatoid Arthritis

Dunbar (1947a), in her book *Emotions and Bodily Changes*, reviewed the work which considered emotional conflict to be partially etiological in rheumatoid arthritis. The studies of Booth (1939) and Halliday (1937b; 1942) agreed with the conclusions of the group at the Chicago Institute for Psychoanalysis (Johnson, Shapiro, & Alexander, 1947). They all noted, especially in women, a great tendency toward bodily activity and a predilection for outdoor activities and competitive sports.

In adolescence, such women show decidely tomboyish behavior, and later, as adults, they tend to control all emotional expression. In addition to their self-control, they attempt to control those persons close to them, such as their husbands and children. They may be demanding and exacting toward their children but at the same time may overprotect and indulge them. This domineering solicitude is a mixture of a tendency to dominate and a masochistic need to serve other people. Thus they may be called "benevolent tyrants," in that although they serve and sacrifice themselve, they also dominate and control. Most of the women overtly reject the feminine role and develop a strong masculine protest reaction. They compete with men and view the female role as submissive, humiliating, or injurious. Consequently, they are prone to choose compliant, passive men as mates, sometimes even those with an obvious physical defect. F. Alexander (1950) feels that the precipitating emotional factor in the onset or exacerbation of the illness can be related to a few significant factors: (1) The disease begins when the unconscious hostility toward, and rebellion against, men has been increased because of certain situations and threatens to erupt, e.g., when a patient is abandoned by a man with whom she had felt safe or if he begins to assert himself instead of being compliant. (2) Any event which tends to increase hostility and guilt feelings previously latent and successfully repressed can also precipitate the illness (sibling rivalry). In addition, guilt over aggressive attitudes may be mobilized when the patient cannot masochistically expiate it by serving others. (3) If a woman is forced to accept the feminine role, against which she reacts with an increased masculine protest, she is liable to develop arthritis.

The emotional background consists of a chronic inhibited, hostile, aggressive attitude which represents a chronic rebellion against any form of outer or inner pressure toward being controlled (by other persons or even by the patient's own very strict conscience).

Although the masculine protest reaction is the most conspicuous rebellion against being dominated, the central chronic, inhibited, hostile state can be traced back usually to a highly characteristic early family constellation consisting of a strong, domineering, demanding mother and a dependent, compliant father. In such an atmosphere, the little girl develops a dependence upon, and a fear of, the cold, aggressive mother but at the same time harbors strong rebelliousness which she does not dare to express even through normal channels because of fear of rejection. Such inhibited rebellion against the mother forms the nucleus of the hostile impulses of such women and is later transferred to men and everyone within the family. When they become mothers, *they reverse the situation and control their children as they were controlled in the past.*

In summary, a disposing personality factor results from restrictive parental influences which prohibit the free expression of frustration of the child by random motor discharge. When, because of punitive measures, this discharge becomes associated with fear and guilt, a "psychological straightjacket" results, which persists into adult life. Such patients try to achieve an equilibrium between aggressive impulses and control. They attempt to discharge aggression through muscular activity in acceptable channels (exercise, sports, etc.) and to relieve the restrictive influences of strict conscience by serving others. If this equilibrium is disturbed by anything that blocks the discharge of hostility and the simultaneous guilt-relieving behavior patterns (helping and controlling others at the same time), chronic inhibited aggression leading to increased muscle tonus may aggravate or precipitate the arthritic process, which, in itself, appears to be fundamentally a metabolic disorder.

In the patient with far-advanced arthritis who is physically crippled, a stoical and optimistic attitude is seen.

Much less is known about male arthritic patients, although Alexander and his Chicago collaborators found the same chronic inhibited, rebellious state but saw it to be more a reaction against unconscious passive dependent or feminine trends, for which such patients overcompensate with aggressiveness. The inhibition of these aggressive impulses creates a psychodynamic picture similar to that seen in female patients.

Cleveland and Fisher (1954) studied the behavior and unconscious fantasies of 25 white male patients with rheumatoid arthritis using clinical interviews, the Rorschach, the TAT, and the Draw-a-Person Test. Their control group consisted of 20 patients with low back pain. Their results revealed that the arthritic sees himself as a hollow chamber filled with soft material. This soft material, they believe, represents fluid, angry impulses which the hard exterior prevents from escaping. Thus the arthritic dramatizes in his body scheme a conflict about expressing anger. According to the authors, this body image resulted from inconsistent parents; the fathers were ordinarily calm but occasionally burst forth in anger, and the mothers were self-sacrificing but on projective tests appeared as prohibiting and seductive figures. Arthritis patients attach unusual significance to their bodies and are unconsciously desirous of exhibiting them, but they overtly deny this desire and complain of shyness and inadequacy.

Blom and Nichols (1954) studied 28 children (23 girls and 5 boys) with rheumatoid arthritis ranging in age from 2 to 6 years and observed an unusually close and intense mother-child relationship which predated the illness but which was also reinforced by it. The mothers were found to have the following characteristics in common: (1) deep deprivation in childhood, (2) a marked tendency to depression, (3) a slavish devotion to the arthritic child as well as in other areas of their lives, and (4) a marked difficulty in expression of feelings, either positive or negative. The authors reported psychotherapy with these children as slow and gradual because of their difficulty in developing a proper relationship. Relieving the mother of her depression may be of help. The arthritic child has basically an infantile personality and is incapable of achieving separateness from the mother.

T. M. French and Shapiro (1949) confirmed the tendency of arthritis patients to express repressed tendencies through the skeletal system by studying their dreams. One of the writers (Flagg) treated a patient with arthritis who initially perceived "feeling states" in motoric terms. When her affect began to emerge, she "would see and feel herself dancing."

A detailed psychophysiological study on rheumatoid arthritis is now in the pilot phase at the Psychiatric and Psychosomatic Research Institute at Mt. Sinai Hospital, Los Angeles.

Psychogenic Back Disorders

Backache of emotional origin is very common and may be purely hysterical (to express the feeling, "I don't want to shoulder my responsibilities" or "Oh, my aching back"), or it may be an actual fibromyositis due to increased muscle tension resulting from a chronically suppressed emotional state.

Seaman and Reder (1963) have described three major types of psychogenic back disabilities and two lesser types. The first of the lesser types is the backache which occurs in overworked women and asthenic men. The symptoms resemble those of low back pain due to disk damage and are relieved by a decrease in the work load, the use of a corset, and exercises to increase abdominal strength. Another lesser type of backache is found in psychoneurotic patients with multiple complaints who frequent outpatient clinics and who go from one physician to another. Here the only approach is psychotherapy.

Of the major types of psychogenic back disability, the most common one occurs in a setting of unresolved litigation. It almost invariably follows an injury, usually involving a direct blow to the back rather than a falling or lifting injury. The patient may sit in a relaxed position while being interviewed and yet claim to be in severe pain. He has a poor work record, for which he blames others. Paranoid trends are common. Seaman and Reder list as the second major type of psychogenic back disability that which occurs in intelligent young women following exposure to cold air, following stress to the back, and/or following an emotional upset. They point out that the pain may be so severe as to prevent movement but is of short duration. In these cases one can demonstrate extreme muscle spasm, with relief of pain in extension and hyperextension and increase in pain in flexion of the back.

The third type of psychogenic back disability follows surgery for herniated disk. The authors believe that the diagnosis of psychogenic back disability or proneness to it should be made before operation since such a patient may use his actual mild organic disability for emotional gratification.

Dorpat and Holmes (1963) studied the pain and muscle activity patterns in 65 subjects ranging from ages 14 to 56 by using needle electrodes and EMG recordings. They found that backache symptoms or increased muscle tension appeared in situations in which the individuals were unable to take positive measures to resolve their difficulties for fear their action might add to insecurity and frustration. Fear of retaliation for angry feelings inhibited their action. The contrasting forces are reflected in rigid posture and increased muscle tension. They were able to illustrate, during stress interviews, the waxing and waning of muscular tension related to the abovementioned emotional conflict. They found that all their backache patients had a tendency to vigorous muscle activity as their major satisfaction and that the women were all tomboys, usually interested in vigorous and competitive play. They felt that although there is no specific personality configuration, there are specific attitudes to the stressful circumstances which precipitate the backache. All such patients wanted to perform action involving body musculature such as running or fighting, but all of them were unable to act. Their actions are inhibited by either their own guilt or fear of retaliation.

The Accident-prone Person

The great majority of accidents are not really accidents but are the result of the individual's "acting out" and discharge of a forbidden and unconscious impulse. Usually the sufferer from an accident has some active part in its causation, and thus it is not a true accident. Such accidents include industrial and home accidents, traffic accidents, and those "accidental pregnancies" which occur quite often in single and married women with an impulsive and masochistic character structure. Careful and detailed investigation reveals that most accidents are not simply due to fatigue or chance but are caused by repressed emotions. Some people indeed appear to be prone to accidents.

More than thirty years ago, Marbe (1926) discovered that an individual who has had one accident is more likely to have another one than the person who has never suffered an accident is likely to have a first. Dunbar (1943; 1947a & b) described the accident-prone person as being decisive or even impulsive, concentrating on immediate pleasures and satisfactions and acting on the spur of the moment. He is a lover of excitement and adventure and does not like to plan or prepare for the future. Many accident-prone subjects are the products of a strict upbringing and have developed an unusual amount of resentment against persons in authority. By their impetuous behavior they rebel against the restrictions of authority and all forms of external coercion. In fact, the accident-prone person is such a rebel that he cannot even tolerate self-discipline and rebels against even his own judgment and self-control. The emotional state of the person immediately before his accident is a significant factor. Studies by Dunbar (1943; 1947a & b), have shown that in most accidents there is an element of unconscious guilt which the victim tries to expiate by self-punishment. A combination of revenge and guilt is commonly found, since there is a strong ingrained attitude in our civilization that suffering expiates guilt—that the suffering person regains the love of his parents or of his own superego. The most common cause of guilt feelings is hostile rebellion against the parent. The accident-prone person retains his childhood rebellion against persons in authority, and he also retains the guilt reactions originally felt toward parents. The combination of these two, resentment and guilt, is a common factor in accidents.

SEXUAL FUNCTIONS AND THEIR DYSFUNCTIONS

Sexual maturation in the human which leads to procreation is influenced by gonadal hormones, but the initiation or pattern of sexual behavior is not. Sexual hormones influence the threshold of arousal in the sex organs, but cultural factors determine the nature of effective sexual stimuli as well as the response of the individual. To separate the psychological from the hormonal factors in man is very difficult.

Lief, Dingman, and Bishop (1962) reported the case history of a man with cyclic alteration of feeling and acting as a male and as a female for eleven years prior to his entering therapy at age 23. Soon after the beginning of therapy, the alternating phases ceased. No other such cases are reported in the literature. Accompanying this cessation of periodicity was a striking increase in urinary 17-ketosteroids. The deficiency of adequate levels of male hormone probably contributed to and accentuated an already existent effeminate childhood pattern (identification with women).

Gerard (1939) showed that enuresis was a manifestation of a bisexual tendency. Both boys and girls suffer nightmares the content of which is fear of being attacked by an adult of the opposite sex. This fear mobilizes sadomasochistic excitation, which is discharged by urination. In such cases, the behavior of the boy is regressive, passive, and self-depreciatory, while the behavior of the girl is overcompensatingly active and motivated by masculine identification. The emotional vicissitudes of the oedipal phase culminating in superego formation have a profound influence upon psychosexual development. After a period of latency (reduced sexual awareness), at puberty the gonadotrophic hormones of the pituitary gland stimulate the production of both androgens and ovarian hormones, causing in both sexes the gradual appearance of the secondary sex characteristics and influencing the emotional attitudes of the adolescent. During this period, the physiological pressure of the sexual drive threatens sexual repression and produces conflict. *During adolescence, sexuality changes from a general pleasurable excitation to an essential need.* In addition, conflicts and anxieties from the oedipal period are rekindled, and the resultant deep-rooted anxiety contributes to the typical insecurity of the adolescent. The degree of adolescent conflict is determined by the strength of the instinctual need and the fear of punishment following sexual gratification (castration fear or fear of loss of love). Sexual maturity or genital sexuality means that the individual is able to gratify his instinctual needs without inherent conflicts. Fixation of the instinctual drives on pregenital patterns of gratification may block the progression to sexual maturity and favor development of different forms of perversion. Fenichel (1945) assumed that "every fixation necessarily changes the hormonal status" (a most dubious assumption). However, an intrapsychic conflict, if intense enough, may alter the external expression of sexual interest and prevent normal gratifications. The male sexual function is performed in the act of coitus, and this single function is reflected by the fact that the male is influenced by only one sexual hormone (androgen). In all adults there is a correlation between gonadal hormone production and the urgency of the sexual impulse, but no cyclical pattern occurs, as in women. In women the cycle of gonadal hormone production and its interaction with psychodynamic processes have been studied thoroughly. Benedek and Rubenstein (1942) studied the psychosexual manifestations of ovarian functions by comparing vaginal smears and temperature charts with psychoanalytic material of women in analysis. From the psychological material alone, particularly from the nature of the patients' dreams, they could predict the phase of the menstrual cycle of the women. Primary sexual urges in women, particularly, are disguised and modified by cultural patterns and by individual developmental processes which mold sexual expression. Benedek and Rubenstein established that (1) the emotional manifestations of the sexual drive, like the reproductive function itself, are stimulated by gonadal hormones; (2) the production of estrogen, an active extroverted heterosexual tendency, motivates the behavior; (3) parallel with the progestin phase, the psychosexual energy is directed inwardly as a passive receptive and retentive tendency; and (4) parallel with the hormonal cycle, an emotional cycle evolves.

The sexual cycle begins with the follicular ripening phase, characterized by (1) an increasing estrogen level, (2) active heterosexual tendencies, expressed overtly or disguised in dreams and fantasies, and (3) stimulation by estrogens to a higher ego integration and coordination of its activities in other than sexual areas. However, in those women who are inhibited in sexuality, an increase in defenses occurs, such as anxiety or hostility toward men, which may cover up strong heterosexual tendencies. Ovulation is characterized by (1) estrogen production at its peak, (2) the beginning of progesterin production, and (3) a psychobiological state accompanied by the highest psychosexual integration, reflecting an increasing biological and emotional readiness for conception. Subjectively, the woman is approaching, during this phase, the highest state of libidinal readiness for receiving her mate, and if she is frustrated she experiences increasing emotional tension. The postovulation period is characterized by the following: (1) There is a sudden relief of heterosexual tension and a period of relaxation. (2) Psychosexual energy is directed and concentrated upon the woman's body and its welfare. (3) Generalized readiness for a sexual partner is usually conscious, but the desire for impregnation is revealed only in dreams and fantasies. (4) The psychological material shows a preparation for motherhood which is expressed as a wish for pregnancy or, if conflict about it exists, a fear of it or hostile defensiveness against it. (5) Analytic material reveals that the woman repeats her childhood conflicts, which she may unconsciously still maintain with her mother. There is a striving for resolution of those conflicts and for a reconciliation with the mother, especially in the acceptance of, and the desire for, motherhood. Fantasies about having children and concern for child care are prevalent. Conversely, if this level of psychosexual maturation is not achieved, the woman's regressive wish to be a child herself and to be taken care of is now expressed, accompanied by a depressive mood. There is a progestin decline if impregnation does not occur, and an early premenstrual phase ensues with (1) a low hormonal level, characterizing the premenstrual phase of the cycle, (2) a partial regression of the psychosexual integration, and with pregenital, usually anal sadistic and eliminative, tendencies apparent in analytic material, and (3) increased irritability of the sympathetic nervous system, probably explaining why the premenstrual phase is called a "recurrent neurosis of women" (Chadwick, 1932). Also, anxiety and fear of bleeding revive the idea that menstruation is connected with castration; infantile sexual concepts may return in anxiety dreams, and the woman may be irritable and/or depressed. The late premenstrual phase reveals low hormonal levels of both progestin and estrogen, but with estrogen production beginning to increase, and a state of emotional tension leading to a driving quality in activities and a sense of urgency, productivity, and accomplishment. The sexual desire may show an urgency which the same woman may not experience in other phases of her cycle. There appears to be a regression of the ego leading to a partial loss of some integrative capacity, a decrease in frustration tolerance, and a resultant emotional lability, which is the most marked feature of the whole cycle. The menstrual flow marks the end of the cycle with a sudden decrease in hormone production, a relaxation of the tense mood after the flow is established, and an acceptance of the menstrual flow in the adult woman. A depressive attitude may continue from the premenstrual period into the period of flow, possibly because of hormonal changes, but the corresponding psychological material reveals regret over the failure of pregnancy.

Remorse about previous abortions and depreciation of the female genitals are common. The menstrual flow may be equated with feces, and the genitals are considered dirty. When the follicular function of the new cycle begins, a state of well-being is reinstated, and sexual stimulation reoccurs.

The opposite effect, or the influence of the emotions on the gonads, thereby affecting the course of the menstrual cycle and the time and amount of menstrual flow, is well established. For example, there is evidence that gratifying or exciting heterosexual intercourse may facilitate ovulation, while frustration or fear may inhibit or change the ovulation time.

Progestin is a hormone specific to the female, and its level determines the length of the menstrual cycle and its variations. A short progestin phase or low level, as found in puerile individuals, causes a short cycle. A woman with infantile fixations (oral receptive retentive tendencies) will have a long phase and a long cycle. If the psychosexual development is even more inhibited, long low hormone periods characterize the cycle, and the menstrual flow may occur with irregularities within the normal range.

The two female sexual functions are accompanied by two tendencies: an active tendency, which secures the sexual act, and a passive (receptive-retentive) tendency, which accompanies the functions of pregnancy. According to Deutsch (1944, 1945): "A tendency towards introversion and a deep rooted passivity are the specific qualities of the female psyche."

Pregnancy

Pregnancy interrupts the cyclic function of the ovaries, and the normal rhythm is not reestablished until after lactation ceases or is suppressed. The woman's emotional state is an intensification of the psychological state every normal woman feels during the progestin phase except that the "turning in of her emotional energy" is more pronounced and prolonged. As Benedek (1949) has pointed out, after conception a symbiosis begins between the mother and the fetus. The mother normally experiences a feeling of well-being and may indulge herself in many ways that she would not permit in the nonpregnant state. Such intensification of receptive tendencies is a manifestation of the increased biological process of growth. The woman is free of guilt or shame about regressive indulgence because when she indulges or loves herself she is indulging or loving the baby. Any severe deprivation of her dependency needs during the period of pregnancy may block the development of the maternal attitudes which are necessary for a proper postpartum mother-infant relationship.

There are many factors about the psychophysiology of pregnancy which are not understood. Many neurotic women become more disturbed during pregnancy, while others become symptom-free and almost euphoric. Such formulations, baby-breast-penis-feces, etc., although applicable in many cases, are oversimplifications. Common food idiosyncrasies, false labor pains, and nausea and vomiting of pregnancy are still not completely understood. For instance, it is commonly assumed that morning vomiting of pregnancy beyond the third month on a "functional" basis is the expression of the rejection of pregnancy. A purely physiological explanation of morning vomiting is questionable because pregnant animals do not vomit.

Chertok, Mondzain, and Bonnaud (1963) recently evaluated 100 primiparous women (of whom 68 suffered from vomiting) by means of verbally expressed attitudes. Although this study did not obtain data about deep-seated attitudes toward the unborn child, the authors concluded that vomiting of pregnancy is based on an *ambivalent* attitude toward the child, of rejection conflicting with joy and expectation. They referred to Sendral's (1915–1916) observation that in France unmarried expectant mothers who undoubtedly reject motherhood *seldom* vomit, whereas in Switzerland unmarried pregnant women *do* vomit. The difference might be related to the ease in obtaining abortion for health reasons in Switzerland. In Nordmeyer's (1908) series of 85 women who sought abortion, not a single one suffered from vomiting.

Parturition

The influence of emotions, particularly pain and fear, on the course of labor and the effect of emotional trauma during childbirth on the mother's relationship to her child have been the subject of lively debate. Some clinicians feel that the pains of childbirth are always traumatic, whereas others maintain that normally the pains of childbirth enhance the mother's love for her child. Certainly the birth process interrupts the biological symbiosis between the mother and child and involves abrupt and gross adaptive changes for both.

Normally, immediately after the delivery the mother recovers from her physical discomfort, her concern over her own body disfiguration decreases, and she invests a great quantity of the love she has previously felt toward her own body in her newborn child. This psychological transfer of emotion (narcissistic love to object love) is aided by the hormone prolactin, which stimulates lactation. Lactation and nursing partially reestablish the mother-child symbiosis, but on an extrauterine level. Both the mother and the child experience erotic pleasure from the nursing experience. The mother unconsciously feels reunited with her own mother by identification with her baby, which permits her a regression to the fantasy of being replenished while actually giving. Normal maternal attitudes develop as a result of the repetition of this pleasurable and mutually gratifying interaction.

Emotional conflict in the mother may produce psychosomatic disturbances in the mother-child unit such as suppression of lactation in the mother, irritability and colic in the child, and even autistic withdrawal or marasmus. The normal intensification of passive dependent (oral receptive) tendencies provides a proclivity for severe depressive reactions in those women whose oral conflicts with their own mothers are remobilized during their postpartum period. Feelings of worthlessness, futility, and hopelessness and occasionally frank separation anxiety producing disorders of psychotic intensity are possible sequelae. These women, particularly, are overly sensitive in regard to their ability to be good mothers. Because of their unconscious protest, "I cannot give what I never received," they view even the normal frustration and irritation of the infant as signs of their failure and become easily anxious and depressed because of guilt and shame. Such patients may be unable to nurse, reject the child in some subtle way, or, occasionally, frankly take to their beds—"a literal emotional laying down on the job." Such a reaction is common in women who want children in order to deny their own dependency strivings. After the child is born and demands attention, the defense may break down.

Menopause

The menopause (cessation of the menstrual flow) takes place during the climacterum ("change of life"). It is the authors' opinion that the various psychosomatic complaints of many menopausal women often result from anxiety and depression. They often are treated with hormones causing a fixation of symptoms believed by the patient and physician to be purely organic. This approach is as prevalent today as "tonics" for anemia (a euphemism for depression and boredom) were twenty years ago. There is no doubt, however, that decline of ovarian function causes vasomotor instability, which is reflected in a more labile emotional state. Yet a mature woman can find compensation for her loss of reproductive power. Such a woman's identity, status, or self-esteem is not totally dependent on her physical attractiveness or upon retaining her youth. In other words, she is prepared for the normal decline by cultivating other or sublimated creative activities. A highly positive correlation exists between the woman with a long history of premenstrual depression, dysmenorrhea, etc., and menopausal emotional crises. These women have character structures dominated by a still unresolved confustion of sexual identity stemming from childhood (masculine identification) which has prevented the development of true femininity. Much of their psychic energy has been used to maintain repressions by compulsive devotion to family and children. Such a rigid character pattern makes it difficult for these women to expand their emotional vistas. They see in the growing independence of their children a desertion, and they react with suppressed rage and depression. The flexible, normal menopausal woman develops many new creative interests and finds that the climacterum, in the psychological sense, is a new phase in her development (Benedek, 1942).

Psychosexual Dysfunctions

Sexual inhibitions, impotence, frigidity, and enuresis are essentially based on conversion hysterical mechanisms, and the reader is referred to the extensive literature on psychopathology.

In dysmenorrhea (painful menstruation) without obvious organic disease, both somatic and psychogenic factors must be considered. The most common emotional factor is ambivalence about the feminine role.

Boyd and Valentine (1953) tested 21 patients suffering from dysmenorrhea and 11 control subjects with a word association test designed to detect emotional conflicts in sexual and personal relationships, while at the same time recording their galvanic skin responses. The subjects with dysmenorrhea showed anxiety about bodily functions in their responses to the word association test as well as by their psychogalvanic responses. Their attitudes toward sex were characterized by anxiety, and their social history suggested a high proportion of disturbed home situations. This study supports the psychoanalytic view that "menstrual colic" is an autonomic discharge mobilized by anxiety and is an attempt to get rid of the "dirty" products of menstruation. Conditioning due to expected repetitions of painful periods is also important. The cause of functional dysmenorrhea is more likely to be such autonomic discharges than any hormonal imbalance.

Oligomenorrhea, or scanty menstruation at long intervals, sometimes is a secondary result of psychic regression, for example, in cases of bulemia or anorexia nervosa. In these syndromes the woman responds to the female sexual function, not with masculine identification, but with depression and regression to the oral phase of development.

Amenorrhea (the absence of menstruation) may result from emotional conflict situations where suppression of menstruation in young women is a defense against sexuality and where a rich heterosexual fantasy life substitutes for all the unacceptable, painful, and disagreeable parts of femininity. When such women can allow heterosexual stimulation, the amenorrhea usually disappears. Amenorrhea also occurs as a part of the syndrome of pseudocyesis, "false pregnancy," which is a form of conversion hysteria. Here the patient develops objective signs of pregnancy without actually being pregnant, representing the wish for, and the fear of, pregnancy. Often it occurs in sterile women who are unconsciously afraid of pregnancy and guilty about hostility to children based on sibling rivalry but who deny this and demand the privilege of motherhood. Emotional disturbances related to pregnancy result from ambivalence toward pregnancy. Hypochondric symptoms may result from the fear the woman has of motherhood. Emotional conflict may affect the hormonal and metabolic balance of pregnancy. Fear and hostility toward the process of pregnancy may sufficiently alter the metabolic and hormonal state to produce abortion or premature birth, although the woman may have no conscious conflict about her pregnancy. The expression of the emotional ambivalence concerning pregnancy through such hormonal and metabolic disturbances as habitual abortion, premature birth, and difficult labor many times goes unrecognized by the nonpsychiatrically oriented physician.

Sterility may result from emotional conflicts which suppress the desire for intercourse during the fertile period or which shift the time of ovulation to the menstrual period, when intercourse does not occur (Rubenstein, 1939). Sterility may be due to spasm and closure of the fallopian tubes which prevent the ovum from reaching the upper portion of the uterus, where conception normally occurs. As mentioned above, emotional conflict may actually suppress ovulation in the woman. Whether a significant number of women with functional sterility become pregnant and give birth to their own children after adoption of an infant is still unknown. Several studies recently have reported that the incidence of pregnancy in sterile women following adoption was not greater than chance.

Dunbar (1963) has claimed that spontaneous abortions are due primarily to neurogenic impulses and that a decreased progesterone output is secondary. Tupper (1963) has recently demonstrated pathological changes in the placentas of habitual aborters resembling those found in collagen diseases (known to be in part due to stress). The uterus in habitual aborters is known to be unusually hypersensitive to emotional stimuli; in fact, the autonomic instability is so marked that a minimal stimulus produces an extreme response. A woman who all her life dislikes being a female and who finds herself in conflict with men and fearful of motherhood may be particularly abortion-prone. In the presence of such emotional conflicts, a sudden fright or shock may disturb uterine circulation sufficiently to bring about detachment of the placenta, causing abortion. Tupper, by using psychotherapy as the only method of treatment in a recent experimental study, reported that 24 out of 25 habitual aborters produced viable babies. He believes that the common denominator in the success of the many diverse methods of treatment (hormones, etc.) is psychotherapy. Tupper has also discovered that the agglutinating factor (the collagen antibody) in the serum of aborting women, which is also absorbed by the placenta, seemed to be the same as that found in patients with rheumatoid arthritis. Unmarried women and normal pregnant women in the first three months do not show these antibodies. Mann and Grimm (1963) report that psychological aborters do not appear to be sick in a psychiatric sense but that they are inveterate psychosomatic reactors. They react to stress with diarrhea, vomiting, and headaches, although in some the psychosomatic tendency is more specific and confined primarily to the reproductive system.

Blau, Slaff, Easton, Welkowitz, Springarn, and Cohen (1963) compared 30 mothers with premature babies with 30 control mothers of full-term babies by means of a quantitative psychological rating scale after cues as to prematurity had been excluded. Both the clinical and the statistical findings showed the following distinctive differences between the premature and the term mothers: (1) The premature mothers had negative attitudes to the pregnancy exceeding the normal ambivalence of most pregnant women. (2) Many became pregnant unwillingly and reacted to the pregnancy with conscious feelings of hostility and rejection, and some attempted to induce abortion. (3) The mothers of the premature babies were more emotionally immature, had more body narcissism, and had inadequately resolved their familial problems. Generally, the control mothers either desired the pregnancy or were ambivalent in that they both wanted and rejected the pregnancy.

McDonald, Gynthe, and Christakos (1963) studied the relationship of obstetric complications, total labor times, and birth weights to maternal anxiety. The Kent EGY intelligence scale and the IPAT Anxiety Scale were administered to 86 white gravid patients at the beginning of the third trimester, and MMPI protocols were scored for the repression-sensitization scale. They found an abnormal group which obtained significantly higher composite anxiety scores than a normal group. The abnormal group was found to have less ego strength and less self-sentiment development and more ergic tension and guilt proneness. The abnormal group on the repression-sensitization scale indicated that they responded to threatening situations, such as pregnancy, with intellectual and obsessional defenses. No significant differences were found for mean birth weights or total labor times, but significant positive correlations were observed between maternal anxiety and both birth weights and labor times.

Bressler, Nyhus, and Magunssen (1958) maintain that pregnancy fantasies are the cause of many psychosomatic symptoms in women. According to them, the difficulties in these women on superficial examinations seem to be in their relations with men. On an oedipal level, their conversion reactions may be looked upon as protecting them from an awareness of forbidden incestuous wishes to have a child by the father. However, usually the basic conflict is oral in origin and stems from their unsatisfactory relationship to the mother.

SENSORY DEPRIVATION, SLEEP DEPRIVATION, AND DREAM DEPRIVATION

Sensory Deprivation

Sensory deprivation involves the removal of perceptual experiences with which the person is most familiar and on which he is, in varying degrees, dependent for his body image (kinesthetic, tactile, thermal, etc., stimuli) and those on which he depends for his social identity or environmental familiarity (background noise, hearing other people, etc.).

Studies on sensory deprivation were begun at McGill University about ten years ago, and at present there are close to two hundred papers on the subject. Techniques to reduce sensory input have varied with the interest and purpose of the investigation and have ranged from the submersion of the subject in water to the simulated isolation of space flight. Certain theoretical formulations have been tested in relation to psychotic withdrawal states as well as the recognition that conditions of sensory isolation do occur naturally and may probably be more frequent in the coming space age. There is no doubt that experimental manipulation of the environment to reduce sensory cues and patterns can produce behavioral and cognitive abnormalities, including hallucinatory experiences occurring in normal subjects. Generally, the more complete the sensory deprivation, the more quickly thinking and affective disturbances develop.

However, as Vosburg, Fraser, and Guehl (1960) observed, while psychoticlike quality of behavior under sensory deprivation was evidently recognized, there was no general formulation of the content and sequence of thoughts experienced by subjects while under conditions of sensory deprivation. In the same paper they described the transition from adaptive to breakdown behavior as follows:

> Behavior in sensory deprivation, (1) begins with an attempt at adaption characterized by cycles of successive excursions into memories starting from available external stimuli and ending in sleep, (2) breakdown from adaptive behavior by development of classic neurotic behavior, characterized by reduced exploratory facility and (3) ends in either flight or panic. The time axis for these developments is proportional to the severity of sensory deprivation and varies from subject to subject.

As would be expected, both epinephrine and norepinephrine excretion rates increase during the stress of sensory isolation (Mendelson, Kubzansky, Leederman, Wexler, Dutoit, & Solomon, 1960). However, there were no clear categories of epinephrine responders (fear) versus norepinephrine responders (anger). In experiments conducted by Davis, McCourt, and Solomon (1961) on five pairs of male strangers and on a later occasion on 11 married couples, it was shown that in spite of the effects of social contact (the pairs could not see one another but could talk), some of the effects of sensory deprivation occurred. Some subjects hallucinated, and some experienced delusions and pseudosomatic subjective symptoms, mental clouding, and intellectual impairment. Thus it seemed that social isolation in itself produces none of the effects of sensory deprivation and that social contact does not eliminate the mental disturbances in sensory deprivation but does ameliorate it. Subjects who rely more on external than internal cues react differently to a sensory deprivation experience. Silverman, Cohen, Shmavonian, and Greenberg (1961) found that the field-dependent subjects performed more poorly on pre-experimental and postexperimental discrimination and letter identification tests, remained more aroused (GSR, EEG), and tended to show more motor restlessness during a two-hour period spent in low sensory environment. Postexperimentally they expressed more discomfort about the experiment, struggled more with feelings and fantasies (or denied them), were more suspicious, and projected more.

Jackson, Wesley, Pollard, and Kansky

(1962) reasoned that if the unusual experiences of subjects during experimental sensory deprivation resulted from decreased external stimulation, then it would follow as a plausible hypothesis that a rational approach to the psychotic episodes seemingly due to clinical sensory deprivation (such as those following cataract operations. poliomyelitis, etc.) would be to increase the outside stimulation of the subject. However, they were unable to establish a simple positive correlation between the psychotic episodes and the degree of sensory deprivation.

Gibby, Adams, and Carrera (1960); Harris (1959); and Azima and Cramer (1956) were among the first investigators to report improvement in schizophrenics and other psychiatric patients in a sensory deprivation environment rather than a deepening of pathology, as occurs in normal humans. However, Gibby did not utilize any controls in his study, and the validity of the results was questioned by Cleveland, Reitman, and Bentinck (1963) on the basis of a placebo effect. Cleveland and his coworkers isolated a group of 20 schizophrenic patients and a group of 20 nonpsychotic patients and utilized a control group of 20, which went through all the procedures except the four-hour sensory isolation period. All their subjects were rated by psychological tests and psychiatric interviews before and after. All their schizophrenics had reported hallucinatory experiences prior to the sensory deprivation exposure, and none of them were relieved of the hallucinations, as had been reported by Gibby and Harris, each in separate studies. In fact, patients had an increase in hallucinatory activity. Cleveland found no consistent changes in behavior or psychological test performance between his two schizophrenic groups when only one was subjected to sensory deprivation. Cooper, Adams, and Gibby (1962) later reported a study in which they found an increase in ego strength resulting from sensory deprivation. They chose 30 male VA psychiatric inpatients and subjected them to six hours of perceptual and social isolation. (Again no controls were used.) They assessed the patients' ego strength by clinical interviews the day before and immediately after isolation, and at the same time the Cartwright modification of the Klopfer Rorschach Prognostic Rating Scale was given. They found that exposure to sensory deprivation produced significant and different affects in individual subjects. Subjects who functioned least effectively before deprivation showed the most improvement following exposure to deprivation. Sensory deprivation techniques, they felt, could have considerable therapeutic utility for certain classes of psychiatric patients.

The assumption that an decrease in sensory input will facilitate the attainment of a hypnotic state has been made by Gill and Brenman (1959).

Levitt, Brady, Ottinger, and Hinesley (1962) attempted to test the Gill-Brenman hypothesis by trying to hypnotize, following sensory restriction, three individuals who had previously been found refractory to hypnosis. The three individuals were "isolated" together for four hours with standard deprivation procedures. At the end of the procedure, an attempt was made to hynotize them with the help of a tape recording. None of the three subjects who had previously been resistant to hypnosis were hypnotized. They concluded that within the limitations imposed by their sample size, their results suggested that while sensory restriction may influence suggestibility or even hypnotizability in a random group. there is a definite limit to its potential effect on the later. It did not appear that sensory restriction was sufficient to overcome refractoriness to hypnotic induction. In fact, it was conceivable that the experimental procedure may have enhanced the tendency to resist.

Charny (1963) reported on five seriously disturbed children at a residential treatment center who were subjected to isolation, each in his own room, away from all peer contacts and play objects. The only contacts permitted were with staff and family. The isolation represented a last-stage effort to eliminate acting-out crises. The period of isolation ranged from 2 to 5½ months and was designed in each case to cut the patient off from any stimulus which might serve as a cue for him to enlist the help of his pathological defenses. At the end of isolation, three children showed favorable responses. The other two did so later. Charny noted the following sequence of regression and reorganization: (1) a period of intense anxiety during which some of the patients asked to be removed from the isolation situation; (2) attempts to orient habitual defenses around such stimuli as footsteps and the timing of meals; (3) extensive loosening of personality organization in the wake of failure of the child's defenses (at this time each child began the process of externalizing the mother introject); (4) a prolonged period of intensified resistance in which the child defended himself by transforming the isolation into a fusion experience with the mother; and (5) the final period of significant therapeutic interventions involving both staff and parents. The author points out that a considerable degree of ego strength is a prerequisite for isolation therapy. For many patients, the experience might induce panic and further decompensation.

Pollard, Uhr, and Jackson (1963) designed an experiment of sensory deprivation to compare the effects of repeated sensory deprivation with the effects of tranquilizing or stimulating drugs. Results revealed that most of the subjects adapted to the isolation. During the second eight hours of isolation, much less bizarre experiences were reported than during the first eight hours. The effect of suggestion on the intensity of bizarre experiences was discovered in that the subjects felt that they were participating primarily in a drug study, as they had been told they might receive drugs. Therefore, the emphasis was not on sensory deprivation in the first experiment. When the investigators emphasized the sensory deprivation aspects of the experiment, the results were much more bizarre.

Sleep Deprivation

Although there is great interest today in sleep deprivation and related states, there are still large gaps in the understanding of the neurophysiology of sleep. Is there a true sleep center? Is there rhythmicity? What determines the sleep threshold of sleeping as opposed to waking? The relationships between the great afferent system, the reticular activating system, the midbrain, and the cerebral cortex are only beginning to be understood.

Interest in the effects of sleep deprivation was stimulated by the revelation that the confessions of war crimes they did not actually commit made by American soldiers during the Korean conflict were probably due to a large extent to chronic sleep deprivation which produced mental disturbance. West, Hanszen, Lester, and Cornelisoon (1962), who interviewed many such soldiers, concluded that the chronic lack of sleep had produced a psychotic disturbance with an ego disintegration which did not disappear simply after normal periods of sleep were allowed. West confirmed his hypothesis in later studies. The intuitive physician has always recognized the harmful effects of lack of sleep of endogenous origin, as seen in depressive, manic, or acute emotional crises. Sedation is given in an attempt to prevent a further disintegration from lack of sleep in an ego overburdened with the stress of internal psychological conflict or some external calamity.

By sleep deprivation, it seemed possible to produce a "model psychosis" which could be studied to further the understanding of schizophrenia. Systematic studies of the psychophysiological effects of chronic sleep deprivation, however, have not been attempted until recently, partly because interest in the psychophysiology and psychopathology of sleep disorders was lacking; in addition, electronic and biochemical techniques had not been sufficiently perfected to give reliable measures.

In states of chronic sleep deprivation, deficits or defects in psychological test performance, psychotic behavior, and a decrease in EEG alpha activity occur. Williams, Lubin, and Goodnow (1959) attributed both the deterioration in psychological test performance and the perceptual disturbances to periodic partial or total blocking of sensory input due to somnolence. This theory, based on a gradually decreasing level of activation, is supported by a disappearance of EEG alpha activity during the periods of unresponsiveness. Malmo (1958) has taken an opposite view based on Hullian theory, which maintains that sleep deprivation produces a high state of arousal or activation. To support his view, he made continuous autonomic recordings which demonstrated an upward shift in physiology when his subjects were stimulated by a tracking test. Ax and Luby (1961) measured the autonomic changes in five subjects who were kept awake for 123 hours and who were given daily psychophysiological examinations. Their results were opposite to those of Malmo. They found that prolonged wakefulness produced a marked decline in arousal state as shown by (1) decreasing palmar sweating and frontalis muscle tension and (2) diminishing galvanic skin response and a paradoxical fall in diastolic blood pressure in response to a pain stimulus. Ax explained such responses as a result of profound fatigue of the central sympathetic centers after about one hundred hours of no sleep, leading to a parasympathetic predominance. The behavioral observations, the fall in EEG alpha activity, and deterioration in psychological test performance were all consistent with the autonomic findings.

Ax recognized the possibility that different investigators might obtain contradictory results because of differences in the length of the deprivation period, in testing alertness, or in certain unrecognized changes in metabolism and circulation due to fatigue. Luby, Froman, Grisell, Lenzo, and Gottlieb (1960) had previously made an intensive study on a single subject who remained awake for 220 hours. An important observation was that the enzyme systems associated with intermediary carbohydrate metabolism responded on the fourth day with an increase of specific activities which represented an emergency energy mobilization, but by the seventh day these emergency activities began to fail. The energy transfer system apparently responded to a stressor similarly to the pituitary adrenal axis and passed through stages of alarm, resistance, and exhaustion. They concluded that such a mobilization of adaptational energy was crucial to the organism's ability to master stress of any kind and that impairment of this adaptational response might have a genetic basis or might result from certain stressful life experiences.

Dream Deprivation

The effects of dream deprivation have been studied by Berger and Oswald (1962); Fisher (1962); Fisher and Dement (1963); Snyder (1963); Roffwarg, Dement, Muzio, and Fisher (1962); and many others. In 1960, Dement studied the amount of dreaming in eight male subjects by recording eye movements along with the low-voltage nonspindling electroencephalographic pattern. His results indicated that a certain amount of dreaming each night was necessary and that if it did not occur, a need to dream built up, and the deficit was made up on following nights. The fact that the increased compensatory dreaming could be maintained over four or more recovery nights suggested more or less quantitative compensation. It appeared to Dement that a suppression of dreams over a long enough period would result in serious disturbance of the personality.

Berger and Oswald (1962) studied six male subjects on four base-line nights and four recovery nights after 108 hours of sleep deprivation. Their recordings of EEG and eye movements during the first recovery night revealed a significant increase in the mean percentage of total sleep time during which EEG signs of deep sleep were present, associated with a significant decrease in the mean percentage of total sleep time spent in dreaming compared with the base-line nights. On the second recovery night, there was a significant increase in mean dream percentage, compared with that on the base-line nights.

Roffwarg et al. (1962) studied dream imagery and its relationship to eye movements and demonstrated that a dream is both a physiological and a mental process. They found that the ongoing dream imagery corresponded with the rapid eye movement and also with the ocular quiescent gaps between rapid eye movements. It would appear that a dream is a continuous phenomenon, not merely a series of interrupted "packets" of imagery. Further, the dreamer is deeply involved, as a participant-observer in the experience, almost as if he were awake.

Snyder (1963) proposed the thesis that dreaming was a facet of a substantial, predictable, universal, and basic biological function. Snyder maintained the following: (1) In humans, that form of consciousness which we call "dreaming" is a concomitant of a pervasive and distinct physiological state. (2) This organismic state recurs with greatest regularity as an extensive and integral part of normal sleep in all the mammalian forms yet studied. (3) The regular recurrence of this state is determined by an intrinsic physiological mechanism involving primitive cerebral structures and is probably neurohumorally mediated. (4) The conditions of "dream deprivation experiments" impede this mechanism in its normal progression, and the ensuing effects should be interpreted on a purely physiological basis. (5) Chronic disturbance of this basic biological function may lead to anomalies of waking experience and behavior having characteristics of dreaming and could be implicated in the "waking dream" of psychosis.

Aserinsky and Kleitman (1953) also reported regularly recurring periods of sleep which were physiologically different from other periods and which were characterized by a low-voltage EEG pattern together with bursts of rapid conjugate eye movements. This physiological pattern was highly correlated with sleepers' recall of detailed dream experiences. In addition, Snyder points out that in dreaming, changes in respiration, pulse rate, basal skin resistance, blood pressure, and muscular activity occur. Therefore, he suggests that if the psychological experience of dreaming is accompanied by such distinctive physiological events, "dreaming sleep" should be considered a separate organismic state, different from both "nondreaming sleep" and the waking state. Snyder's observations indicate that a normal person dreams about 20 per cent of his total sleeping time during precisely demarcated periods and at intervals of about ninety minutes from the onset of one period to the next. Thus he challenges the time-honored assumption that dreaming is a response to a disturbance of sleep (that is, a phenomenon of partial arousal). Rather, he says that the disturbance of sleep facilitates the remembering of dreams, since dreaming which is not followed by a period of waking is forgotten within about ten minutes. Snyder emphasizes the marked similarities between episodes of dreaming during normal sleep and studies where after five days of sleep deprivation, normal subjects exhibit psychotic behavior which is more marked at night and which tends to occur with a periodicity of from 90 to 120 minutes. He considers that the behavior of sleep-deprived subjects reflects the same neurobiological rhythm that is seen in dreaming. Snyder concludes that dreaming may not even be dependent upon sleep, per se, but rather upon a relative absence of environmental stimulation; that dreaming tends to supervene the regular periodicity throughout the twenty-four-hour cycle; but that the extent of its manifestions is inversely related to the level of reticular arousal at any given time. Thus "day-dreaming" may be more than a figure of speech.

Fisher and Dement (1963) recently have studied the nature, meaning, and function of the dream-sleep cycle to determine whether dreaming is a necessary psychobiological function. They used two approaches: (1) experimental manipulation of the cycle in an effort to suppress it and investigation of the behavioral and other consequences of this suppression and (2) study of the natural and spontaneous fluctuations in the cycle in total dream time during the recovery nights. Forced awakening was carried out on 20 subjects, ranging in age from 20 to 30 years, for periods of from 1 to 16 nights. A progressively increasing number of awakenings was required to suppress dreaming in the course of consecutive nights. During subsequent "recovery" nights, when the subjects were not disturbed, there were marked increases in the amount of dreaming. Extensive control experiments during nondreaming phases of sleep did not cause the dream deprivation effect. They concluded that dreaming was a necessary psychobiological function and that more or less complete suppression of it might have serious psychic consequences. Then Fisher and Dement examined their data in terms of the psychoanalytic theory of dreaming. They assumed that instinctual drives, if prevented from discharge in nocturnal dreaming, would show themselves in the daytime in various kinds of disturbed behavior. During dream deprivation, but not during the period of control awakenings, the subjects showed disturbances in a number of ego functions. They developed greater or lesser degrees of tension and anxiety, difficulty in concentration, irritability, motor incoordination, and disturbances in time sense and in memory. Thus if dream deprivation were carried out intensively enough and for a long period of time, a dream deficit would increase the pressure of instinctual drives toward discharge, which could theoretically cause an eruption of the dream cycle into the waking state, with a resultant psychotic disturbance.

EMOTIONAL FACTORS IN MALIGNANT DISEASES

The essential etiology of neoplastic disease is still unknown. It is most probable that there are several types of malignant growths. Evidence is strong that some malignancies are the result of irritants (tar, soot, etc.), but epidemiological studies indicate that certain intracellular viruses probably can cause tumors with malignant potential. Failure of homeostatic mechanisms is probably importantly involved in the process whereby a localized lesion begins to spread. The concept of "host resistance" (the ability of the organism to defend itself against noxious external and internal stimuli) is undoubtedly important. It is feasible that certain cancers result when a normal defense mechanism of the organism gets out of control from the regulatory influences of the enzyme systems, hormones, or the central nervous system.

Emotional factors in the etiology of neoplasms have been sporadically studied, and any evidence for an etiological relationship between emotions and cancer is most circumstantial. Probably more meaningful for the practitioner is an understanding of the emotional interaction between the cancer patient, his relatives, and the physician. Humans react to any disease in which the cause and particularly the cure are unknown with fear. This fear, if conscious, may lead to acute anxiety in the patient or the relatives. Usually, however, the main defense against free-floating anxiety is denial. An intelligent patient may, in spite of all evidence to the contrary (x-ray treatment, radical surgical procedures), believe that his lesion is noncancerous and appear in good spirits or even mildly euphoric. This attitude in the patient is often reinforced by those about him, including his physician. Though there are some advantages to such an approach, unfortunately too often the patient cannot maintain his denial, even if the family and physician wish him to do so, and as a result he must deal with his plight alone and is deprived of important sources of support and comfort. Sometimes when such a patient is finally told the truth he reacts with a sense of relief and initially uses the word "cancer" frequently in conversation, as if he had finally been permitted to use a tabooed word. Patients who have mutilating surgical procedures —particularly women who have radical mastectomies for breast cancer—are apt to be more concerned about their altered body image than about the fact that they suffer from a malignant tumor. Depressive reactions following surgery for cancer are often mourning reactions for a lost part of the body, especially if the organ is highly cathected. This is common after hysterectomy in women past the childbearing age who have uterine tumors in which the prognosis for cure is excellent. Certainly these grief reactions are not based merely on the fear of death or on the fact that they must give up a realistic wish for children but are due to the emotional meaning the patient ascribes to the loss of the organ and to her altered internal image. Often it is felt that the operation is a punishment for some previous sinful act. The study of psychological factors in the occurrences of cancer consists of anamnestic interviews, psychoanalytic studies of cancer patients, and the administration of psychological tests. The object of all these investigations is to establish personality patterns or conflicts which might be characteristic.

Perrin and Pierce (1959), in a review of all the literature on the psychological aspects of cancer, made the following generalizations: (1) A slightly higher cancer death rate occurs in hospitalized psychotic patients than in the normal population, although the reason is obscure. Faulty statistical data might account for this finding. (2) The psychological reactions and defenses of cancer patients are reported to be similar to those of neurotic patients. Particularly prominent are depressions and a sense of guilt. (3) Some investigators report the development of cancer secondary to emotional trauma and believe that cancer appears in patients of a specific immature type of personality. (4) One group of investigators believes that the growth of cancer is slower in less inhibited persons. Perrin and Pierce commented that the methods used in cancer studies were (1) ancedotal, (2) interview and case history, (3) sociological and demographic analysis, and (4) psychological testing. Most of the studies were poorly designed, and the findings were questionable.

Data collected on the personality development and psychotherapy of five women with cancer of the breast were intensively studied by Renneker, Curler, Hora, Bacon, Bradley, Kearney, and Cutler (1963). They thought that the sudden failure of a previous neurotic structure at an age when the patient was susceptible to cancer might be a factor. The critical psychological situations observed in the patients with breast cancer were (1) depressive reactions stemming from disruption of a security-invested object relationship which produce a decrease in host resistance, (2) disturbance of heterosexual impulses in women with strong oral fixation, and (3) disturbed immature maternal impulses.

Among the most comprehensive investigations of the role of psychological factors in neoplastic diseases are the longitudinal studies of patients with lymphomas and leukemias by Greene (1954; 1958; 1959; Greene & Miller, 1958; Greene, Young, & Swisher, 1956). He studied patients with leukemia and lymphomas (lymphocytic leukemia, myelocytic leukemia, lymphosarcoma, Hodgkin's disease, reticulum cell sarcoma, and reticuloendotheliosis). No characteristic personality pattern was found, but all the patients were reacting to the loss of a significant object relationship at a time when no replacement of the object was available. In most cases, this object loss was concurrent with other threatening traumas, such as injury, aging, and retirement. Greene suggested that psychological stresses may have been a factor which contributed to the abnormal reaction of the reticuloendothelial system. He offered three hypotheses to explain the reaction. The first involved anxiety and fight or flight responses; the second concerned a mechanism to deal with noxious agents, including psychic stress within the organism; and the third suggested that alteration in this system might occur as a nonspecific response to changes in the organism more specifically related to psychological stress.

Patients with leukemia and lymphoma reacted to the early loss of a significant person with other than usual processes, such as mourning, melancholia, or hypochrondriasis. The processes of adaptation involved two phases. In the first phase, the individual preserved his own personality but also assumed the role of the lost object. In the second phase, he used someone in the environment who had also usually suffered the same type of object loss as a vicarious object. Such a mechanism of adjustment to object loss was utilized successfully by many of the patients on a general medical service, and only upon its dissolution did they develop manifest somatic disease. In children with leukemia, Greene found that most had been vicarious objects for their mothers. Later, the mother gave up the child as a vicarious object and usually became depressed. It was under these circumstances that the child developed manifest leukemia. In his study of 32 women (19 with leukemia and 13 with lymphoma), he noted again that separation from a key object was followed by depression. The symptoms of the patients during the weeks or months prior to the onset of illness were fatigue, weakness, sadness, anorexia, and nausea. Particularly the affect of sadness or hopelessness was apparent for weeks or months prior to the onset of the physical illness. Exacerbations of the lymphoma or leukemia process often occurred during times of separations. Thus Greene relates the development of the disease to disturbances of the mother-child unit. Of 33 leukemic children and adolescents below the age of 20, 31 had experienced one or more of the following losses: birth of a sibling, change of school or home, and loss or threat of loss of a significant person, such as the father or maternal grandparents through death or illness. Half of the separations or losses occurred during the six months prior to the onset of the disease. In addition, 27 of the 33 mothers were depressed and/or anxious for weeks or months before evident symptoms developed in the child. From these findings in children and in adults, Greene suggested that an involvement in a vicarious object relation is one common precursor of leukemia and "other psychosomatic diseases." Disruption of the vicarious object relation for such persons determines the time when the psychosomatic symptoms will develop, but he felt that the disease is determined mainly by biological rather than psychological characteristics of the individual.

EMOTIONAL FACTORS IN MISCELLANEOUS DISEASES

Blood Dyscrasias

Browne, Mally, and Kane (1960) have studied, over a three-year period, the social and medical histories of 28 hemophilic children (average age of 7 years) and their families, focusing on (1) the patient's conflict about physical activity and movement and its relation to bleeding episodes and (2) the source and perpetuation of this conflict in the mother-child relationship. Twenty-six mothers and fourteen fathers were interviewed, and each child was evaluated in one or more psychiatric interviews or play sessions. Twenty-one of the children had Rorschach studies, and three were followed weekly for two years. Emotional factors appeared to contribute to the timing of spontaneous bleeding episodes in hemophilia, and the theme most commonly associated with the episodes was the anticipation of increased activity or independence. The specific psychic conflict involved was between the desire to be active and aggressive and the inhibition of this wish. The patient's inhibition of his activity was a reflection of the mother's anxiety about the harm she felt it might produce. Thus being passive was equated with being good and pleasing mother, and bleeding brings about passivity. Passivity is further encouraged in the child by the mother's overprotective attitude toward him due to guilt which she feels as the transmitter of the disease. Since she assumes such a full responsibility for the care and management of her child, the child may show strikingly little concern for his own welfare. The symbiotic relationship of the mother and child estranges them from the father, who then often reacts with resentment toward, and criticism of, the mother.

Benedict (1954) described the relationship between psychogenic factors and hemolytic crises in two cases of familial spherocytosis, five cases of sickle-cell anemia, and eight cases of thrombocytopenic purpura. She found the onset or recurrence of the disorder to be related to a situation which followed a prolonged period of psychic stress involving the loss or alienation from the mother or mother figure due to unexpressed hostility.

A pilot study by Lewin (1959) consisting of interviews of 10 patients with pernicious anemia revealed no specific personality traits. However, depression and recent object loss prior to the onset of illness were found. Contrary to the classical description, there was no evidence of a paranoid core in the personalities of these patients. The theory that a depressive state might be an etiological factor in the production of pernicious anemic by reducing the intrinsic factor in the stomach below the critical level was considered, but Lewin was not able to correlate positively the severity of the blood disorder with the severity of the patient's depression. A genetic factor leaves certain people prone to such events. He noted that Mirsky had shown duodenal ulcer to be more common in pepsinogen hypersecretors, whereas pernicious anemia is more common in hyposecretors. Also, Engel's studies have shown that depression reduces gastric secretion. Macht (1952) showed that anxiety in blood donors affects the coagulation time. In the most anxious subjects, coagulation required one to three minutes, in the moderately anxious subjects it was three minutes, and in the relaxed subjects eight to twelve minutes was required.

Agle and Ratnoff (1962) studied psychiatrically nine patients with autoerythrocyte sensitization. All patients had hysterical conversion reactions. Seven had dissociative episodes with frequent syncope, and eight patients admitted to severe family problems and other maladjustments. A masochistic trend was a prominent characterological finding. Their episodes of purpura were related to the activation of this masochistic trend.

RESEARCH ON THE EFFECTS OF EMOTIONAL STRESS ON THE AUTONOMIC NERVOUS SYSTEM AND THE ADRENAL GLAND

In the vegetative disorders which constitute the largest field of interest in psychosomatic medicine, the understanding of the function of the atonomic nervous system in terms of its effects on target organs, of the interaction between its parasympathetic and sympathetic divisions, of the relationship of the autonomic nervous system to the endocrine glands, and of the reciprocal relationships and interactions of both the endocrine and the autonomic systems with the higher brain centers is of importance.

Luby (1963), in a review on psychosomatic disorders, described the interactions between the limbic system (visceral brain), the hypothalamus, and the reticular activating system. Within these systems are motivational subsystems concerned with reward or punishment. For example, self-stimulation by a rat of the posterior hypothalamus produces avoidance behavior, and self-stimulation of anterior and lateral hypothalamic zones causes a pleasurable state. Punishment areas powerfully stimulate the pituitary-adrenal axis. Prolonged neuroendocrine responses may eventually lead to cardiovascular and renal damage and finally to death, and they may be elicited by fear and rage. Responses to stressor stimuli also include sympathetic activation which increases the release of neurokinin and hence increases the inflammatory response. Psychosomatic reactions occur as the result of profound autonomic and neuroendocrine changes which come about from prolonged fear and rage which are not followed by flight or attack. If the patient is unable to master his affects by neurotic or psychotic defenses and cannot withdraw from the stress situation or respond to it effectively, he remains in a chronically stressed state which eventually leads to structural tissue changes.

The damaging physiological effects of stress and the opposite effect of emotional security are suggested by an experiment which compared two group of rats. One group was stroked for ten minutes a day for three weeks immediately following weaning, while another group received no such attention; all other conditions were the same. Later, when exposed to a stress situation the gentled rats performed better. Physically, the gentled rats weighed more and had higher body temperatures, and on autopsy they showed less cardiovascular damage and smaller adrenal glands, probably because they secreted less ACTH in the stress situation than the scared rats (Weininger, 1954).

The adrenal gland is of major importance in maintaining the internal environment of man, particularly in regulating the metabolic, vascular, and electrolyte changes in response to stress. The adrenal medulla secretes adrenaline and noradrenaline needed in emergency situations. The adrenal cortex secretes steroid compounds which mediate the adaptation to prolonged stress (general adaptation syndrome of Selye). The adrenal medulla is actually an extension of the sympathetic nervous system and therefore is regulated in large measure through sympathetic fibers. The regulatory control of the secretory activity of the adrenal cortex is mainly hormonal.

Sontag (1963) has conducted longitudinal psychological and physiological studies on individuals since 1920. He demonstrated that the more active the individual was as a fetus, the more likely he was to show social apprehension in nursery school. There was a significant negative relationship between quick fetal activity and peer aggression in nursery school. The children who had shown quick fetal activity tended to avoid conflict. Furthermore, social apprehension in the 2½-year-old was predictive of social apprehension at ages 22 to 25.

In regard to autonomic nervous system function, Sontag found that the cardiac response of individuals did not vary from stress to stress but did vary from individual to individual. Strong cardiac reactors were inclined to perceive situations imaginatively. When fetuses were startled by noises close to the mothers' abdomens, some reacted strongly and some weakly. A study is currently being conducted to determine whether the degree of response to stress during pregnancy is predictive of what it will be in later life. If such a relationship is found, it will suggest relationships between fetal autonomic behavior, young adult autonomic behavior, and young adult cognitive and perceptual behavior.

Studies on the autonomic functions by Richmond and Lustman (1955) indicated qualitative and quantitative individual differences in autonomic functions apparent within the first few days of life. Constitutional autonomic endowment might therefore predispose an individual to specific disease.

Grossman and Greenberg (1957) confirmed that individual differences in autonomic function existed in newborns and emphasized that several autonomic functions, and not a specific one, should be used as an index of the level of autonomic homeostasis. They refuted the concept that uniformly deficient homeostatic regulations are characteristic of the newborn. An infant may have one "vulnerable component" of the autonomic nervous system which responds to environmental stimulation with greater lability. Their position was that the lability or stability of the autonomic nervous system might be constitutionally characteristic for only a single autonomic nervous system component or for a few of them and that it requires the fortuitous coincidence of an available "vulnerable" segment with the "proper" psychopathology for a psychosomatic disorder to occur.

N. H. Greenberg, Cepan, and Loesch (1963) observed that when an infant sucked, the heart rate regularly and consistently increased, following a characteristic curve, and that between sucking periods the heart rate decreased.

Sternbach (1962) utilized the dramatic film methodology developed at Mt. Sinai Hospital, Los Angeles, by Alexander, Flagg, and Clemens for the systematic comparison of psychological, autonomic, and endocrine responses to different lifelike emotional states under controlled conditions. Sternbach used a dramatic film to induce sadness, fearfulness, and gladness in sequence in a group of eight boys and girls while such variables as palmar skin resistance, gastric motility, respiration rate, heart rate, eyeblink rate, and finger pulse volume were recorded. In postviewing interviews, all the children agreed that the death of "Bambi's" mother was the saddest scene. Their skin resistance and lacrimation during this scene increased significantly, suggesting an inhibition of sympathetic nervous system activity in sadness, whereas there was a significant decrease in gastric peristaltic rate during happy sequences, suggesting a decrease in vagal activity. They confirmed that the showing of selected films to produce specific and authentic emotional states in the laboratory was a reliable procedure.

Autonomic response specificity as defined

by Lacey, Bateman, and Van Lehn (1953) means that (1) for a given set of autonomic functions, individuals tend to show a pattern of autonomic response in which the activation occurs in the same physiological function, no matter what the stress may be, and (2) for a given set of autonomic functions, there exists a quantitative variation among individuals of such a degree that a pattern of response is stereotyped.

Wenger, Clemens, Coleman, Cullen, and Engel (1961) studied eight autonomic variables in 30 male college students under four stimulus conditions to determine each individual's response specificity and stereotypy. Eight of the subjects showed complete response specificity by response-level scoring (that is, maximal activation occurred in the same variable under the four stimulus conditions). Only two showed complete specificity by reactivity scoring (near chance). A tendency toward response stereotypy (that is, a stable hierarchy in autonomic response patterns to different stimuli) was demonstrated in 22 of the subjects using the response-level scoring. For reactivity scoring, only four satisfied their criteria. From their data they concluded that response specificity and stereotypy, when they are reported, are due in part to the method of measurement and in part to significant individual differences in resting autonomic nervous system functions.

Ax (1953) presented experimental evidence that differences between fear and anger could be shown by autonomic measurements. He reported that four autonomic variables showed a greater average reaction during anger: the diastolic blood pressure rises, the heart rate falls, galvanic skin responses are greater, and muscle tension increases. Three variables showed greater responses for fear: skin conduction, muscle tension, and an increase in respiration rate. Anger represents a state of greater physiological integration with response patterns which resemble those produced by injections of epinephrine and norepinephrine. Response patterns of fear resembled the results of injections of epinephrine. This work stimulated Funkenstein to study the effects of epinephrine and epinephrinelike substances. Funkenstein assumed that psychiatric patients and healthy normotensives under stress would show two types of elevated blood pressure (one resulting from excessive secretion of epinephrine and the other from excessive secretion of norepinephrine) and that this could be determined by blood-pressure reaction to mecholyl. If the elevated blood pressure was due to epinephrine, the administration of mecholyl would cause a sustained fall in the blood pressure, whereas if it was being caused by norepinephrine, no sustained drop would follow. In an extension of his hypothesis, Funkenstein, King, and Drolette (1954) and Funkenstein and Mead (1954) stated that changes in physiological patterns obtained during stress would differ in subjects reporting subjective feelings of anger toward other persons and in those whose anger is directed toward themselves. The hypotheses were substantiated by data on 69 college students with blood-pressure and ballistocardiographic readings. It was hoped that the Funkenstein test would serve as a reliable and simple means of selecting the most effective type of treatment for psychoneurotic and psychotic patients.

Gellhorn (1956; 1957) attempted to explain the neurophysiology of the Funkenstein test, while L. Alexander (1955) found it a valuable guide in the choice of those patients who would respond well to electroshock therapy. Gellhorn maintained that the methacholine-induced fall of blood pressure activated the hypothalamus, which in turn stimulated a sympathetic discharge. The sympathetic discharge caused the blood pressure to rise again to the initial level. He believed that the measurement of blood-pressure changes following methacholine was an indirect measure of hypothalamic excitability.

Pasquarelli, Campbell, Polatin, and Horwitz (1956) evaluated the Funkenstein test in terms of its general prognostic value for therapeutic response (to electroshock as compared with psychotherapy). They believed that a high percentage of patients with a high basal blood pressure who responded to mecholyl with a marked and prolonged hypotensive effect improved with electroshock treatments, as contrasted with the poor results in those with a hypertensive or a minimal response to mecholyl. They found that those who showed a hypotensive response to mecholyl had more adequate and appropriate affects than the hypertensive groups (80 per cent of the hypotensive responders had adequate affect, as compared with 48 per cent of the hypertensive group). Also, they found that the hypotensive responders had a significantly higher improvement rate (78 per cent) than the hypertensive group (48 per cent) in psychotherapy.

Clemens (1957a; 1957b) studied autonomic nervous system response as related to the Funkenstein test and determined that the magnitude of systolic blood-pressure rise to epinephrine was a fairly reliable index of sympathetic reactivity. He showed that the predictive validity of a number of autonomic measures was greater than that of a single measure.

The concept of autonomic imbalance caused by a predominance of the parasympathetic nervous system (vagotonia) as the cause of psychosomatic disorders was originally introduced by Eppinger and Hess (1910). They reported that patients in such vagotonic states reacted strongly to pilocarpine and atropine but were relatively insensitive to adrenaline. However, Kuntz (1945; 1951) cited clinical situations where people with increased parasympathetic tonus, such as in gastric ulcer, also reacted strongly to pilocarpine, thus suggesting heightened reactivity of both divisions of the autonomic nervous system. Wenger (1941) investigated a number of autonomic variables in children and adults and argued that either division of the autonomic nervous system could manifest a dominant influence over the other. Clemens observed that most of the studies of the autonomic nervous system had been conducted on subjects under resting conditions (a lack of *external* stimulation). In his study, Clemens recognized the importance of measuring numerous autonomic variables after external stimulation. Autonomic responses to mecholyl of 46 male patients with malignancies were studied in the resting state by Clemens (1957) with the conclusions that (1) the drop in systolic blood pressure induced by mecholyl activated sympathetic compensatory mechanisms, especially increased heart rate and peripheral vasoconstriction, which tended to counteract the hypotensive state; (2) with increasing age, an apparent decrease in sympathetic excitability occurs; (3) the systolic blood-pressure response to mecholyl is only partially indicative of the total autonomic nervous system reactivity and does not provide a valid index of autonomic reactivity; and (4) neither resting levels nor initial reaction appeared to be related to a secondary overcompensatory systolic blood-pressure response to mecholyl.

Possibly some of the contradictory observations of various investigators as to the validity and reliability of the Funkenstein test are explained by the findings of Clemens. For instance, Lotsof and Yobst (1957a; 1957b) tested 30 patients and 15 medical students with mecholyl and epinephrine on separate occasions and recorded only systolic blood-pressure readings. They questioned the response to mecholyl as an indicator of either autonomic responsivity or response to electroshock treatment. They used the mecholyl test as a predictor of response to electroshock therapy and found that there was no consistent relationship between groupings, based on the mecholyl test, and recovery following EST.

Blumberg (1960) commented that the reproducibility of mecholyl test on serial testing was fairly reliable if the interpretation of the test results was limited to the blood-pressure curve. However, the test was not reproducible on serial testing to any useful or significant degree when the conventional methods of classification of Funkenstein and Gellhorn were used.

S. D. Kaplan (1960) has developed a visual analogue of the Funkenstein test and has validated the visual test against the blood-pressure test of hypothalamic excitability. The visual test is based on the finding that sympathetic arousal increases sensitivity to short spectral wavelengths and decreases sensitivity to long wavelengths. Parasympathetic arousal has an opposite effect. The visual changes were thought analogous to the blood-pressure changes of the Funkenstein test in that in each case, the autonomic balance of sympathetic versus parasympathetic predominance was "tuned." The Funkenstein test tuned the autonomic balance reflected in blood-pressure response to sinoaortic pressures. The visual test tuned the autonomic balance of image intensity to spectral wavelengths. The blood-pressure test involved a "downward" hypothalamic discharge, while the visual test was to represent an "upward" discharge. The difference between the two tests in the direction of hypothalamic discharge was the reason for calling the visual test an "analogue" rather than stressing its identity with the Funkenstein test. An advantage was that the visual test required only a mild dose of a parasympathomimetic drug, in contrast to the severe dose required in the Funkenstein test.

Although the Funkenstein test has been disappointing in its prognostic value, it gave the impetus to research on the functions of the autonomic nervous system, the study of autonomic patterns in different emotional states, and its interaction with the endocrine system and the higher central nervous system. This evolved into the experimental investigations of the psychophysiological mechanism of anxiety, fear, and other stress responses. The complexity of such investigations is shown by Gellhorn (1957), who made the following comment on sympathetic excitation:

> It is known that mild degrees of sympathetic excitation involve a neurogenic mechanism whereas stronger stimulation also activates adrenomedullary secretion. However, the adrenomedullary secretion does not reinforce the effects of sympathetic discharges but rather it inhibits them. Such inverse feedback mechanisms automatically prevent any major deviation in homeostatic regulation in a particular part of the body. However in different parts of the body, this inverse feedback mechanism may not work so well since what is a neurogenic stimulus in one part of the body may cause an inhibition in another part.

To explain certain apparent paradoxes, Dykman and Gantt (1958) introduced the concept of schizokinesis, or split development, which states that the usual parallelism of motor and cardiac responses tends to be replaced by a schizokinesis when the stress of the conditioning experiment or the learning problem exceeds the tolerance of the organism. Just as there is some degree of discreteness and even antagonism among autonomic responses, so also in the central nervous system there is no equipotential homogeneity. For example, a central nervous system depressant may depress the cortex more than subcortical areas in a gradient, or it may depress the cortex and release subcortical areas from inhibition. The same depressant, therefore, may have different results in different parts of the same person.

Lacey, Smith, and Green (1955) attempted to correlate, by means of a conditioning procedure, conscious and unconscious anxiety with autonomic functions. Students were conditioned by giving them a shock after presentation of a word. Half of the subjects were shocked after the word "cow" and half after the word "paper." During the experiment, the palmar skin resistance, digital blood flow, and heart rate were recorded. Although the subjects were unaware of the relationship between the word signal and the shock, they very quickly showed unconscious anxiety which was not limited to the specific stimulus itself but which spread to other words meaningfully related to the stimulus words. This response developed very rapidly and was interpreted as revealing the anxiety proneness of humans. In the subjects who were made aware before the experiment that they would be shocked after specific words, the conditioning curves were very different from those of subjects who were unaware. Aware subjects immediately developed a strong emergency response following the designated stimulus words, and this response did not grow as a function of a number of reinforcements but showed a gradual adaptation. Unaware subjects showed typical conditioning curves. The spread of anxiety as seen in the curves of generalization seemed greater at the unconscious level. This conditioning procedure, with its simplicity, objectivity, and possibilty for experimental manipulation and quantification, was one of the finest experimental designs in studying unconscious processes by objective psychophysiological methods.

Wenger, Clemens, Darsie, Engel, Estess, and Sonnenschein (1960), using six of the twelve autonomic variables, demonstrated the differences between maximum responses to epinephrine and norepinephrine. The most important differences were associated with cardiac output (rate and stroke volume) and peripheral vascular activity. A reduction of blood flow to the skin appeared under both drugs, but the vasoconstriction to norepinephrine was less in the skin than to the blood vessels supplying the skeletal musculature. Since only small changes in diastolic blood pressure accompanied skin vasoconstriction in response to epinephrine, they felt that epinephrine produces vasodilation in the muscles.

Oken, Grinker, Heath, Sabshin, and Schwartz (1960) measured the stress responses of 10 patients who manifested chronic and intractable psychiatric illnesses. Although they were a mixed nosological category, they could be best described as "inadequate," and all had depression as their presenting symptom. The stress was a provocative interview on one day, followed by receiving curare the next day. The responses of these chronic patients were distinctive in that they were sharply limited to the stress period, whereas a previously studied group of acute patients came to the situation already aroused and manifested a response that persisted beyond the nuclear stress. The focal nature of the observed response was quite compatible with the characteristics of the defensive structure described. Apparently there was no interference with the capacity to respond, but rather an extraordinarily efficient exclusion of stimuli which might excite response. This hyperconstricted type of defensive organization represents an opposite pole of the "too open" and overgeneralized responses of the acute group and is equally seriously maladaptive.

Speisman, Osborn, and Lazarus (1961) have attempted to obtain systematic information about the structure of autonomic reactivity under neutral and stressor conditions. Thirty-five male and thirty-five female undergraduate students participated in their experimental procedure, consisting of a personality assessment session, a control session (neutral film on corn farming), and an experimental session (seventeen-minute stressor film on primitive subincision surgical rites on the penis and scrotum of adolescents). During the control and experimental sessions, continuous recordings of heart rate and skin resistance were made. Thus, they compared autonomic response in four experimental conditions: (1) *control base,* (2) *control film,* (3) *stress base,* and (4) *stress film.* The autonomic scores were followed across the four experimental conditions, and this provided a correlation matrix of 63 variables for skin resistance and 53 variables for heart rate. Their conclusions were the following: (1) Certain types of autonomic measures are independent of one another. (2) The structure of the autonomic measurement varies with the specific channel (heart rate or skin resistance) being studied and with the experimental conditions under which the experiments are made. (3) Some measurements of autonomic nervous system activity, often employed in research of personality dynamics, were inadequate. The measurements of level and variability appear to be particularly meaningful, since they often either define independent dimensions themselves or load heavily on other cluster dimensions. Other classes, such as recovery or response, appear less useful, although the concepts which define them are much better known. (4) From the standpoint of methodology, they feel that their research showed that a great many redundancies exist among the many possible measurements.

Two main conclusions concerning the effects of the stressor films on autonomic activity were that (1) their experimental condition was successful in producing stress, and (2) there was little relationship between heart rate and skin resistance activity. They remarked that this lack of correlation across the two autonomic channels was consistent with the findings of other investigators.

Oken, Grinker, Heath, Korchin, Herz, and Schwartz (1962) tested the hypothesis that inhibition of affect discharge under stress would heighten physiological responses. Oken selected 18 normal college students and divided them into two groups of nine each on the basis of interview ratings to represent opposite ends of a continuum of affective lability, range, and threshold. Measurements of nine physiological variables and ratings of six psychiatric response categories (three affective and three defensive) were made during three experimental sessions. The initial psychologically stressful day consisted of the alleged administration of a dangerous psychoactive drug and the viewing of a film about mutilative surgery. The second day's stress was exposure to a room temperature of 95° F and humidity of 50 per cent. Control measures were obtained on the third day. The psychological stress produced the greatest affective and defensive stimulations, and there was little arousal on the control day. Physiological responses differed on the two days and were related to the nature of the stimuli: The affectively expressive ("high") group had significantly greater psychological response than the more constrained ("low") group. However, the hypothesis that affectively less expressive subjects would manifest greater physiological responses was not generally substantiated. For heart rate, systolic blood pressure, skin resistance, calf-muscle blood flow, and respiratory rate, the trend was actually in the opposite direction, although the differences were quite small except for the respiratory rate, which was statistically significant. The variables which did show differences between the groups were GSR and three independent measures of vascular tone: diastolic blood pressure, finger blood flow, and skin (finger) temperature. Although none of the differences were great enough to be statistically significant, their consistency was interpreted as supporting the view that essential hypertension is linked to suppression of feelings. The effect of anger suppression could not be determined in their study. In terms of autonomic response specificity (the pattern of response of several variables in a particular subject in the different experimental situations), the level of physiological variables did have a distinct tendency to remain in a consistent order over the three days, but the specific variable exhibiting maximum levels showed but slight constancy.

Thus it appeared that while autonomic response specificity does seem to characterize individuals, it largely characterizes their tendency to maintain a stable hierarchy of level rather than a consistent pattern of change. Therefore, a subject's response to stress is a function of several factors, including stimulus-specific changes as well as individual characteristics.

In a later paper, Lazarus, Speisman, and Mardkoff (1963) again took issue with the traditional interindividual (across subjects) procedure for correlating the responses of different autonomic nervous system indicators of psychological stress. Their position was that only a number of intraindividual correlational methods were logical and appropriate. They presented data obtained and analyzed from an extensive study of the effects of a benign and a stressor motion picture (recordings of heart rate and skin resistance of 50 subjects viewing the film). They maintained that when intraindividual correlational methods were applied, substantial correlations were found between heart rate and skin conductance. For example, one method yielded a correlation of plus .545 under the stressor-film conditions. A curvilinear correlation method also produced substantial correlations. In addition, the magnitude of the intraindividual correlation between heart rate and skin conductance rose significantly from the benign control film to the stressor film. They confirmed the hypothesis that different autonomic indicators of stress rise and fall with the degree of stress. They felt that this phenomenon could not be shown by interindividual statistics but requires opportunity for study within subjects of the changes of stress reactions over the various stimulus conditions over time. They pointed out, in addition, the advisability of employing a small number of autonomic or behavioral response variables (possibly even one) in inferring the presence of psychological stress.

The autonomic reactions of medical students to tones and to emotional and nonemotional questions were studied in two test situations spaced one year apart by Dykman, Ackerman, Galbercht, and Reese (1963). They found the important determinants of physiological reactivity to be (1) level of functioning at the time the stimulus was presented, (2) level of stress as defined by the nature of the experimental conditions, (3) response consistency measured by the tendency of subjects to maintain their group position across different stimuli or stressors, (4) group conformity measured by the tendency of subjects to show concordant patterns of reaction when the level of stress becomes sufficiently high, (5) serial position of stimuli measured by the tendency of an individual to give responses of increasingly smaller magnitude as a function of the repetitions of any stimulus of a particular type (extinction), and (6) personality variables of defensiveness, anxiety, intelligence, and achievement. Contrary to some past work, they did not find subjective emotional reactions of anger and fear associated with autonomic functioning, nor were the subjects' own evaluations of stress level reliably related to physiological functioning.

Obrist (1963) found cardiovascular sympathetic-type effects during conceptual activity and during noxious stimulation, while heart-rate deceleration was found during stimulation where the subjects' attention was centered on environmental inputs. Twenty-eight undergraduate male subjects were exposed to six different stimulus conditions: two noxious stimuli, a conceptual task, and three conditions requiring close attention to environmental inputs. Changes in heart rate, systolic blood pressure, peripheral blood flow, skin resistance, and respiration were obtained beween a basal period just prior to stimulation and during the stimulus. Their results confirmed their previously reported findings and were consistent with a theoretical scheme relating cardiovascular activity to central mechanisms. With one exception, noxious stimuli and the conceptual task resulted in sympathetic-type responses in all measures. On the other hand, stimuli which required attention to environmental inputs decelerated the heart rate consistently for all individuals. Systolic blood pressure and pulse pressure showed either no change or some decrease. Skin resistance revealed increase in sympathetic tonus or no change. There was no evidence to suggest that the heart-rate deceleration could result from a general decrease in sympathetic tonus, increased vagal effects resulting from respiratory changes, or baroreceptor-medullary reflexes. Their results support a hypothesis of individual autonomic response specificity.

L. A. Graham, Sanford, Shmavonian, and Kirshner (1963) studied the relationship between independent behavioral dimensions and patterns of autonomic and neuroendocrine activity by a conditioning experiment which involved 32 male college students. Subjects who were informed of the experimental designs were compared with those who were not. Adrenaline levels in the resting period differed with behavioral groups. Adrenaline values for uninformed subjects rose during the first session and fell during the second. Informed subjects had very high resting levels which fell sharply.

The systematic study of the relationship between physiological activity and ego strength has been difficult because of the lack of objective and reliable methods to assess ego strength. Roessler, Alexander, and Greenfield (1963) designed an experiment to test the hypothesis that groups of individuals differing in ego strength (Es), as defined by scores on the Es scale of the Minnesota Multiphasic Personality Inventory (MMPI), would differ in their physiological responses. Their subjects (Ss) were drawn from patients admitted to a psychiatric inpatient service who were not on medication and who could cooperate. Controls were subjected to the same procedure.

It was hypothesized that a high ego-strength group would show a greater magnitude of response to various intensities of sound on measures of skin resistance, heart rate, finger blood volume, and muscle potential than a middle and low Es group. When each physiological variable was considered separately, the differences in the predicted direction were significant for skin resistance, finger blood volume, and muscle potential; the heart-rate measure showed differences in the predicted direction which were not statistically significant. When all measures were considered together, the correlations were significant.

A secondary hypothesis, that the greater differences in responsible magnitudes among ego-strength groups would occur at stimulus intensities near threshold, rather than near the stimulus of maximum intensity, was partially confirmed. A further hypothesis that the responses of all groups taken together would show an approximately linear relationship to stimulus intensity was confirmed for all four physiological measures employed. On the other hand, a prediction that higher ego-strength groups would show a different adaptation than lower ego-strength groups could not be confirmed for any of the four physiological measures employed.

Subsequent reports by Roessler's group (1963) dealt with the temporal and recovery characteristics of the physiological responses as related to ego strength. The findings did not allow generalizations across physiological measures or across scores, unlike the previously reported finding that the magnitude of response on all four measures was directly related to Es grouping. Moreover, the effects of stimulus intensity upon these measures and scores were also complex and did not allow generalizations. Among the physiological measures employed (skin resistance, heart rate, finger blood volume, and muscle potential), there were no group differences on the latency score.

Their general hypothesis that ego strength and the amount of physiological periodicity a subject demonstrates were related was supported on two of the three parameters of periodicity.

The Adrenal Cortex

Much investigative work has been centered on the effects of various emotional stresses on the secretion of adrenocortical hormones.

Blood levels of adrenocortical and thyroid hormones in acutely disturbed patients were studied by Board, Persky, and Hamburg (1956). The 30 patients showed a significantly higher plasma 17-OH over the control subjects, and their diurnal fall was less than that of controls. The patients' protein-bound iodine levels were distinctly higher than those of controls, but the difference was proportionately less than that observed for 17-OH (17-hydroxycorticosteroids).

Subgroups were established on the basis of psychiatric criteria according to (1) quality and intensity of emotional distress and (2) diagnostic categories. Analysis of hormone level of the patients in these subgroups suggested that exceptionally high hormone levels are associated with (1) very intense stress (especially of a depressive affect in the presence of retarded behavior) and (2) the development of extensive personality disintegration (especially psychotic depressive reactions). Fourteen of the patients were retested seventeen days later and were found to have lower mean 17-OH levels than on the day of admission, but still slightly above the controls. The PBI levels were unchanged. When the patients who received electroconvulsive therapy were compared with those who did not, they differed notably in mean levels of 17-OH and PBI. The more disturbed patients who had received the EST had relatively high levels, while the less disturbed patients who had not received EST manifested normal levels. Schwartz and Shields (1956) conducted a somewhat similar study but utilized the urinary excretion of formaldehydogenic steroids (FS) and creatinine levels in medical students under the stress of a final examination. The FS levels rose significantly during, and fell following, the examination period. FS excretion paralleled the student's estimate of emotional tension. A similar pattern of rise and fall was noted in creatinine excretion, but the correlation with tension was poor. Urinary volume and creatine excretion were not clearly related to the stress of taking the examination. However, one individual studied over a long period showed a definitely negative correlation between daily tension and the level of corticoid excretion. The adrenocortical reactions of subjects under two real-life situations were studied by Bliss, Migeon, and Branch (1956). They measured the level of 17-hydroxycorticosteroids in the peripheral blood and in the urine of relatives of patients seen in acute situations in an emergency room and of medical students during examinations. These emotional disturbances caused consistent but modest increases in the 17-OH compounds in the blood and in the urine. Plasma steroid values remained within normal physiological range under the influence of emotional upset. The changes were smaller than those observed following intravenous administration of ACTH, electroshock, and physical exercise. Twenty-two anxiety-prone patients were subjected to stressful interviews while being observed by two nonparticipant-observers who rated their emotional response (Persky, Hamburg, Basowitz, Grinker, Sabshin, Korchin, Heig, Board, & Heath, 1958). The plasma level of hydrocortisone was simultaneously studied. The degrees of increase in anxiety, anger, and depression and a combined effect were found to be significantly and linearly related to the change in plasma hydrocortisone levels.

Curtis, Cleghorn, and Sourkes (1960) investigated the relationship between noradrenaline, adrenaline, and 17-hydroxycorticosteroids in the urine of psychiatric patients and of normal human subjects. A second objective was to learn whether affective states of differing quality influenced the excretion of any of the three hormones. Patients were classified according to whether the major affective content characterizing the illness was anxiety or depression.

The results suggested that in affective states of depression, noradrenaline is excreted preferentially in comparison with adrenaline and corticoids, while corticoids are excreted preferentially in states of anxiety. In states of mixed affect, there was a preferential excretion of adrenaline and corticoids. In subjects whose principal difficulties were disorders of thinking or behavior, there was preferential excretion of adrenaline and noradrenaline. The authors cautioned against generalizing from their findings or from the literature cited in their study, but it would seem that various qualities of "emotional stress" are specific if one relates the affective state to the balance between hormones rather than to a single hormone.

Persky, Maroc, Conrad, and den Breeijen (1959) noted that anxious and normal subjects differ markedly in their ability to produce and metabolize hydrocortisone (one of the two principal hormones of the adrenal cortex). Anxious subjects produce more hydrocortisone than the normal subjects and metabolize it differently. This increase in production of hydrocortisone by the anxious individual has been demonstrated by such criteria as elevated plasma hydrocortisone level, elevated urinary hydroxycorticoid and 17-ketosteroid excretion, greater urinary hydroxycorticoid output in response to exogenous corticotrophin, and increased turnover of radioactively tagged hydrocortisone. They suggested three possible explanations for the increased production of hydrocortisone by the anxious subjects: (1) The hypercorticoidism may result from an over-response by the adrenal cortex to the stimulus supplied by the corticotrophin, as occurs in patients with adrenal hyperplasia. (2) It may have resulted from a prolongation of the action of corticotrophin on the adrenal cortex, possibly because of an inhibition of the enzyme system which inactivates the pituitary hormone. (3) It may have resulted from an absolute increase in the circulating level of corticotrophin. They felt that the most likely reason was that the plasma corticotrophin level of the anxious patient is already elevated because there is little response to injection of exogenous corticotrophin and it is unrelated to dosage. Because of this, the investigators decided to determine the level of circulating corticotrophin in anxious and normal subjects. There are two corticotrophins: the adrenal weight maintenance factor (AWMF) and ACTH, or ascorbic acid depletion factor (AADF). A group of anxious hypercorticoid patients were shown to have a mean plasma level of AWMF which was more than twice that of the control group of normal subjects. The mean blood level of AADF (the conventional corticotrophin) was higher in the anxious group but not significantly so. The levels of both AWMF and AADF were shown to be significantly correlated with clinical anxiety rating. It is suggested that a critical anxiety level exists below which neither AWMF nor AADF was present in the blood.

Fictional and documentary movies of murders, fights, torture, executions, and cruelty to animals were shown to medical students by Von Euler, Levi, and Strom (1959) for seventy minutes. During the showing, the urinary excretion rates of 17-ketosteroids, pregnenediol, and noradrenaline showed a slight increase, and that of adrenaline a more pronounced increase. After short intermission and immediately after the end of the experiment, both arterial blood pressure and pulse rate were lower than just before the beginning of the films. Eight of the subjects reacted emotionally to the viewings by discomfort; one reacted by pronounced discomfort; and one was indifferent. The results indicated to the researchers that moderate emotional stress of relatively short duration may activate both the adrenal medulla and the adrenal cortex.

An attempt to correlate adrenal steroid excretion patterns with the personality of 18 healthy subjects was conducted by Fox, Murawski, Bartholomay, Gifford, and Sandford (1961). The results suggested that (1) excretion rates of 17-hydroxycorticosteroids and 17-ketosteroids are relatively constant in healthy individuals over a period of time, (2) individuals maintain the same relative position throughout this period in regard to the others within the group studied, according to an identifiable steroid excretion pattern, and (3) the output of 17-hydroxycorticosteroids is related to certain aspects of personality. The data suggested the tentative hypothesis that the more a person reacts emotionally, the higher will be the level of 17-hydroxycorticosteroids. The more guarded the individual (the more control is exercised over feelings), the lower is the level of the 17-hydroxycorticosteroids. At one extreme of a psychophysiological continuum are the individuals with vivid personal feelings who experience a sense of emotional urgency, and at the other extreme are those who are relatively guarded and withdrawn.

Korchin and Herz (1960) tried to delineate what specific aspects of the total psychological situation (involving stress, affect, defense, etc.) were most importantly involved in determining adrenal activity and whether response might not be more particularly related to some, rather than other, types of psychological threat or emotional behavior. It was usually assumed that the amount of corticoid response was roughly proportionate to the extent of emotional involvement, which is triggered off by the psychological stress. Stated schematically, a novel, taxing, or threatening event ("stress") evokes some degree of psychological disturbance (grossly defined and measured as "anxiety" or "emotional involvement"), which leads to adrenal activation. Other psychological factors, residing in the larger social situation in the subject's personality, or ego defenses, may be considered to be secondary factors which are of importance only insofar as they determine the effectiveness of the stress for arousing emotional disturbance.

Although some authors had suggested that adrenocortical responses might be more specifically related to certain qualities of the anxiety state, usually they were viewed as nonspecific responses to the over-all level rather than to the type of emotional involvement. Some investigators had related increased adrenocortical response to dread, apprehension, or exhilaration. Patients awaiting surgery have elevated plasma hydrocortisone levels. However, on the basis of careful interviews and Rorschach studies, Price, Thaler, and Mason (1957) concluded:

> The response of the pituitary-adrenocortical system was related to emotional processes, and further . . . it was probably not associated with a single specific emotional state, such as anxiety or fear, but, rather . . . with a number of emotional states that have the relatively undifferentiated component of distress-involvement.

In their study, Korchin and Herz (1960) exposed 20 paid volunteer subjects, divided into two groups, to an experimental task intended as a shame threat (scrambled sentences) and another designed as a disintegrative threat (picture description) on the second of two experimental days. Plasma hydrocortisone levels were found to be significantly elevated at the time of the first measurement, yielding further evidence for the impact of a novel situation on adrenocortical activity, even in the absence of intended stress. Measures taken before and after the tasks on the stress day indicate both adrenocortical and emotional responses to both experimental conditions. However, there are important differences between the two conditions: Subjects exposed to the disintegrative procedure showed proportionately more corticoid and proportionately less affective response, while those in the shame condition had relatively less corticoid and relatively more affective response. The findings were taken as evidence of the need for distinguishing the various aspects of the stress experience—the threatening situation, the affective response, and physiological or behavioral change—and for considering the precise way in which they are interrelated, rather than assuming any simple or direct relations among them.

Levi (1963) has devised a stress-tolerance test with simultaneous study of physiological and psycological variables. It consists of the sorting of steel balls of nearly the same size in the presence of disagreeable noise and variations in intensity of light. Nineteen essentially normal subjects were divided into two groups thought to have high stress tolerance and low stress tolerance. Significant differences were found between these groups with regard to working efficiency and urinary output of adrenaline and noradrenaline. The low-stress-tolerance group put out the higher levels and worked less efficiently. No differences in 17-ketosteroids and corticosteroids in the urine were found.

Suwa and his group (Suwa, Yamashita, Owada, Shinohara, & Nakazawa, 1962), at Hokkaido University, have been studying for the past seven years the adrenocortical function of mental patients as a part of their research program on emotions. They have used two procedures: (1) testing subjects suffering from various mental disorders or psychic manifestations in order to uncover differences of statistical significance between the groups examined and (2) longitudinal, serial, long-term, day-by-day measurement of test samples obtained from the same subjects under close clinical observation. Daily estimates were made of circulating eosinophil count and of excretion of urinary 17-hydroxycorticoids (17-OHCS) and uropepsin in 44 patients. In normal controls, eosinophil count and urinary excretion of 17-OHCS and uropepsin were usually constant from day to day. In psychoneurotics, fluctuations in these biologic indices were synchronous with changes in emotional state. Schizophrenics who for some time had seemed calm and whose personality patterns had shown only slight regression showed a stability in the daily values of these indices. Schizophrenics whose clinical state alternated between remission and collapse revealed adrenocortical hyperactivity during psychic aggravation. Those in an extreme state of schizophrenic deterioration had fluctuations which were irregular and of much wider range. In the manic-depressives, findings indicated that when emotional disturbance is at its height, or shortly after it abates, daily fluctuations in eosinophil count and uropepsin excretion are quite irregular and of wide range and appear not to correlate with other clinical changes; sometimes after complete recovery, however, biologic indices such as blood eosinophil counts will begin to show daily values constant within a very small range of fluctuation.

From these findings, the authors postulate that the function of the adrenal cortex is the same in neurotics (except during an anxiety attack) as in a normal subject. In advanced schizophrenics and other psychotics the function is qualitatively different, probably because of a defect in the maintenance of homeostasis of the entire body. However, they emphasized that such findings were tentative.

Fiorica and Muehl (1962) studied two groups of nonstressed nonhospitalized subjects who were designated as either low-anxious or high-anxious on the basis of extreme performance of the Taylor Manifest Anxiety Scale. Blood samples were taken from all subjects and were assayed for free 17-OH corticosteroids. A significant positive relationship was found between plasma levels of these steroids and the anxiety scale scores. It is suggested that adrenocortical function may be normally susceptible to psychic influence.

Plasma and urinary 17-hydroxycorticosterone (17-OHCS) levels were measured by Wadeson, Mason, Hamburg, and Handlon (1963) before and after the viewing of commercial moving pictures in three small groups of young adults. Significant elevations in plasma 17-OHCS levels were observed during a war movie in one group. Marked decreases in plasma 17-OHCS levels occurred rather consistently during viewing of Disney nature films. These findings suggest a remarkable sensitivity of the pituitary-adrenocortical system to psychological influences and support the notion of a continuous tonus exerted by the brain upon neuroendocrine systems.

Bunney, Mason, and Hamburg (1963) attempted to determine whether urinary corticosteroid values would correlate positively with specific behavioral changes during the course of a depressive illness. Behavioral and biochemical data on 17 depressed patients were collected independently on a continuous longitudinal basis throughout each patient's hospitalization. A reliable observational system was developed which included the completion of daily behavioral ratings by a nursing research team. Measurements of urinary 17-hydroxycorticosteroids were used as an index of pituitary-adrenocortical activity at regular time intervals. The best and worst days in terms of symptom fluctuations were selected for comparison of 17-hydroxycorticosteroids.

It was found that patients could be subdivided into two groups: those whose illness fluctuated little and those with marked fluctuations. In the subgroup of patients with marked behavioral fluctuations, 17-hydroxycorticosteroid values fluctuated also and correlated positively (at the $p=.0001$ level) with changes in ratings of depression and anxiety. Elevations in corticosteroids up to five times the normal were found in this subgroup of depressed patients. Fewer significant correlations occurred in the patients who had a stable clinical course.

Urinary 17-hydroxycorticosteroid (17-OHCS) excretion rates were determined by S. B. Friedman, Mason, and Hamburg (1963) in 43 subjects, representing one or both parents of 26 children with neoplastic disease. Twenty-nine of the parents were admitted to a National Institute of Mental Health ward for study while their children were hospitalized. The remaining 14 parents lived at home and were studied on an "outpatient" basis. A slight, but statistically significant, elevation was found at the time the parents were first admitted to the ward. A statistically significant sex difference was observed, with mean values for all fathers and mothers of 7.1 milligrams per twenty-four hours and 5.0 milligrams per twenty-four hours, respectively. In this situation of chronic psychological stress, repeated 17-OHCS determinations showed that levels in each parent tended to remain within a relatively constricted range, even when the parent was exposed to severe superimposed acute stresses, and that the subjects could be ranked according to their 17-OHCS excretion rates. It is suggested that the level and pattern of corticosteroid excretion may be related to the effectiveness of the coping behavior in minimizing distress, regardless of the means through which this is accomplished.

Parents of children with fatal malignancies are exposed to the prolonged threat of loss. Each parent had a relatively stable and characteristic rate of 17-hydroxycorticosteroid excretion during this stressful experience. Individual parents have mean excretion rates that fall on a continuum; they can be empirically placed into three groups: "low," "middle," and "high" excretors (Wolff, Mason, Friedman, & Hofer, 1963). The hypothesis was derived that individuals whose psychological defenses were effective in keeping psychic tension at low levels would have lower corticosteroid excretion rates. The less effectively a parent can modify the immediate impact of the threat of loss, the higher would be his mean excretion rate.

To test this hypothesis, each available parent was interviewed for three to four hours by one experimenter, who made a blind prediction of the mean excretion rate. This prediction was based on the effectiveness of the subject's defenses, both during the interview and as reported during the course of his child's illness.

Twenty-one of the thirty-one subjects were predicted correctly to belong in the high, middle, or low group.

Kling (1963) has designed a study to observe the effects of surgical lesion in certain brain areas on the regulation of ACTH secretion. Monkeys were presented with tasks involving (1) reward, in which the monkey was required to depress a lever in response to a light signal in order to receive a pellet of food, and (2) punishment, in which a mild electric shock to the buttocks was given if the lever was not depressed in response to the light signal.

In the normal monkeys, reward produced a small drop in the plasma 17-OHCS level. In the operated group, both small rises and drops occurred. With punishment, the normals, as well as five with small amygdala plus frontal or cingulate ablations or frontal lesions alone, showed consistent elevations. In contrast, three monkeys having large amygdala lesions with or without frontal granular cortex ablations showed small decreases in their plasma 17-OHCS levels. When subjected to a physical stress, normals and operated monkeys showed a decrease in adrenal ascorbic acid content, indicating a capacity to release ACTH.

The results of this study indicate that large amygdala lesions may block ACTH release to emotional "stress," while lesions of frontal granular cortex or cingulate gyrus are ineffective.

In a variation of the usual experimental procedure of measuring levels of hormone after a stress, Persky (1962) compared the *production* and *removal* rates of hydrocortisone for a group of normal subjects and a group of hospitalized anxious patients. The rates for anxious patients were 50 per cent higher than those for normals. Although the subjects of this study exceeded the controls by only about 50 per cent, the anxious patients exhibited only modest quantities of affect, a condition essential to the execution of the experiment. It is highly probable that patients rated higher on an anxiety scale would have exhibited considerably higher values, but such patients usually are unable to cooperate in the tests required for these hormone measurements.

Handlon, Wadeson, Fishman, Hamburg, and Mason (1962) have published research findings on these conditions which might *lower* the levels of 17-hydroxycorticosteroid concentration (17-OHCS). They used 19 normal young adult males viewing Disney nature films. It was discovered that levels of plasma 17-hydroxycorticosteroid (17-OHCS) were lowered to significant degrees in comparison with levels during a control period when no films were shown and during a showing of emotionally arousing films. The difference between plasma 17-OHCS response to arousing and to bland films suggested that the adrenal cortex responds to events of emotional significance within the range of mildly stressful ordinary experience and that the central nervous system regulation of adrenocortical function consists in both lowering and raising plasma 17-OHCS concentration.

In order to assess the effect of the plasma hydrocortisone level on anxiety, Weiner, Dorman, Persky, Stack, Norton, and Levit (1963) gave hydrocortisone and a placebo on separate occasions to a group of 32 normal men. The hydrocortisone *did not* increase the mean Affect Adjective Check List score but did raise the Institute for Personality and Ability Testing Anxiety Scale scores and sum C of the Rorschach test. The object of this study was to establish whether *anxiety proneness* rather than *current anxiety* was elevated by the administration of the hormone.

The effects of hydrocortisone on hypnotically induced anxiety were studied by Levitt, Persky, Brady, and Fitzgerald (1963) in a double-blind study. Sixteen student-nurse subjects were infused with heavy loads of plasma hydrocortisone, while 16 control subjects received an appropriate placebo. Anxiety was then induced in all subjects by means of hypnotic suggestion. No differences between the two groups were found on three psychological measures of anxiety (Affect Adjective Check List, IPAT Anxiety Scale, and psychiatric rating). The data suggest that anxiety tended to persist after its hypnotic relief in the subjects receiving the hormone infusion and was more rapidly dispelled in placebo subjects.

REFERENCES

Abbott, K. H. Clinical studies on the treatment of vascular headaches. *Bull. Los Angeles neurol. Soc.*, 1962, **27**, 137.

Adsett, C. A., Schottstaedt, W. W., & Wolf, S. G. Changes in coronary blood flow and other hemodynamic indicators induced by stressful interviews. *Psychosom. Med.*, 1962, **24** (4), 331–336.

Agle, D. P., & Ratnoff, O. D., Purpura as a pyschosomatic entity: a psychiatric study of autoerythrocyte sensitization. *Arch. intern. Med.*, 1962, **109**, 685–694.

Alexander, F. The influence of psychologic factors upon gastrointestinal disturbances: a symposium. I. General principles, objectives and preliminary results. *Psychoanal. Quart.*, 1934, **3**, 501.

Alexander, F. *The medical value of psychoanalysis.* New York: Norton, 1936.

Alexander, F. Emotional factors in essential hypertension. *Psychosom. Med.*, 1939, **1**, 173. (a)

Alexander, F. Psychoanalytic study of a case of essential hypertension. *Psychosom. Med.*, 1939, **1**, 139. (b)

Alexander, F. Training principles in psychosomatic medicine. *Amer. J. Orthopsychiat.*, 1946, **16**, 410.

Alexander, F. Treatment of a case of peptic ulcer and personality disorders. *Psychosom. Med.*, 1947, **9**, 320.

Alexander, F. *Fundamentals of psychoanalysis.* New York: Norton, 1948.

Alexander, F. *Psychosomatic medicine.* New York: Norton, 1950.

Alexander, F., Flagg, G., Foster, Susan, Clemens, T., & Blahd, W. Experimental studies of emotional stress. I. Hyperthyroidism. *Psychosom. Med.*, 1961, **23** (2).

Alexander, F., & French, T. *Psychoanalytic therapy: principles and application.* New York: Ronald, 1946.

Alexander, F., & French, T. *Studies in psychosomatic medicine.* New York: Ronald, 1948.

Alexander, F., & Menninger, W. C. Relation of persecutory delusions to the functioning of the gastrointestinal tract. *J. nerv. ment. Dis.*, 1936, **84**, 541.

Alexander, F., & Portis, S. A. A psychosomatic study of hypoglycaemic fatigue. *Psychosom. Med.*, 1944, **6**, 191.

Alexander, L. Epinephrine-mecholyl test (Funkenstein test): its value in determining the recovery potential of patients with mental disease. *Arch. Neurol. Psychiat.*, 1955, **73**, 496.

Alvarez, W. C. *Nervous indigestion.* New York: P. Hoeber, 1931.

Anderson, P. C., and Cross, T. N. Body cathexis and neurodermatitis. *Comp. Psychiat.*, 1963, **4**, 40–46.

Arlow, J. A. Identification mechanisms in coronary occlusion. *Psychosom. Med.*, 1945, **7**, 195.

Arthur, Bettie. Role perceptions of children with ulcerative colitis. *Arch. gen. Psychiat.*, 1963, **8** (6), 536–545.

Aserinsky, E., & Kleitman, N. Regularly occurring period of eye motility and concomitant phenomena during sleep. *Science*, 1953, **118**, 273–274.

Aserinsky, E., & Kleitman, N. Two types of ocular motility occurring in sleep. *J. appl. Physiol.*, 1955, **8**, 1–10.

Ax, A. The physiological differentiation between fear and anger in humans. *Psychosom. Med.*, 1953, **15**, 433–442.

Ax, A., & Luby, E. D. Autonomic responses to sleep deprivation. *Gen. Psychiat.*, 1961, **4** (1), 55–59.

Azima, H., & Cramer, F. J. Effects of partial perceptual isolation in mentally disturbed individuals. *Dis. nerv. System*, 1956, **17**, 117–122.

Bacon, Catherine L. Psychoanalytic observations of cardiac pain. *Psychoanal. Quart.*, 1954, **23**, 7–19.

Bandler, B., Karesman, Charles I., Dykens, James W., Schleiser, Maxwell, Shapiro, Leon N., & Arico, Joseph F. The role of sexuality in epilepsy: hypothesis, analysis of two cases. *Psychosom. Med.*, 1958, **20** (3).

Benedek, Theresa. The psychosomatic implications of the primary unit: mother-child. *Amer. J. Orthopsychiat.*, 1949, **19**, 642.

Benedek, Theresa, & Rubenstein, B. B. The sexual cycle in women. *Psychosom. Med. Monogr.*, 1942, **3**, Nos. 1, 2.

Benedict, Ruth B. Psychosomatic correlations in certain blood dyscrasias. *Psychosom. Med.*, 1954, **16** (1), 41–46.

Bennett, A. W., & Cambor, C. G. Clinical studies of hyperthyroidism. *Arch. gen. Psychiat.*, 1961, **4** (2), 160–165.

Berger, R. J., & Oswald, I. Effects of sleep deprivation on behavior, subsequent sleep and dreaming. *J. Ment. Sci.*, 1962, **108**, 457–465.

Bergman, R., & Aldrich, C. K. The natural history of infantile eczema: a follow-up study. *Psychosom. Med.*, 1963, **25**, 495. (Abstract)

Binger, C. A. L., Ackerman, N. W., Cohn, A. E., Schroeder, H. A., & Steele, J. H. *Personality in arterial hypertension.* New York: American Society for Research in Psychosomatic Problems, 1945.

Blau, M. D., Slaff, B., Easton, K., Welkowitz, Joan, Springarn, J., & Cohen, J. The psychogenic etiology of premature births. *Psychosom. Med.*, 1963, **25**, 201–211.

Bliss, E. L., Migeon, C., Branch, C. H., & Samuels, L. T. Reaction of the adrenal cortex to emotional stress. *Psychosom. Med.*, 1956, **18** (1).

Blitzer, J. R., Rollins, Nancy, & Blackwell, Amelia. Children who starve themselves: anorexia nervosa. *Psychosom. Med.*, 1961, **23.**

Blom, G. E., & Nichols, Grace. Emotional factors in children with rheumatoid arthritis. *Amer. J. Orthopsychiat.*, 1954, **24**, 588–601.

Blomstrand, R., & Lofgren, F. The influence of emotional stress on the renal circulation. *Psychosom. Med.*, 1956, **18** (5).

Blumberg, A. Reproducibility of the mecholyl test. *Psychosom. Med.*, 1960, **22** (1).

Board, Frances, Persky, H., & Hamburg, D. Psychological stress and endocrine function: blood levels of adrenolcortical and thyroid hormones in acutely disturbed patients. *Psychosom. Med.*, 1956, **18** (4).

Booth, G. C. The psychological approach in therapy of chronic arthritis. *Rheumatism,* 1939, **1** (3), 48.

Boyd, P. S., & Valentine, M. Word association tests in dysmenorrhea: a polygraph investigation. *Brit. J. Med. Psychol.*, 1953, **26**, 58–63.

Bressler, B., Nyhus, P., & Magunssen, F. Pregnancy fantasies in psychosomatic illness and symptom formation: a clinical study. *Psychosom. Med.*, 1958, **20** (3).

Brody, E. B. Psychologic tension and serum iodine levels in psychiatric patients without evidence of thyroid disease. *Psychosom. Med.*, 1949, **11**, 70.

Brown, W. T., & Gildea, E. A. Hyperthyroidism and personality. *Amer. J. Psychiat.*, 1937, **94**, 59.

Browne, W. J., Mally, Mary, & Kane, Ruth P. Psychosocial aspects of hemophilia: a study of twenty-eight hemophilic children and their families. *Amer. J. Orthopsychiat.*, 1960, **30**, 730–740.

Bruch, Hilde. Perceptual and conceptual disturbances in anorexia nervosa. *Psychosom. Med.*, 1962, **24** (2).

Bruch, Hilde, & Hewelett, E. Psychologic aspects of the medical management of diabetes in children. *Psychosom. Med.*, 1947, **9**, 205.

Bunney, W. E., Mason, J. W., & Hamburg, D. A. Correlations between behavioral variables and urinary 17-hydroxycorticosteroids in depressed patients. *Psychosom. Med.*, 1963, **25** (5).

Bursten, B. Psychoses associated with thyrotoxicosis. *Arch. gen. Psychiat.*, 1961, **4.**

Burwell, D. S., & Eppinger, E. C. In S. C. Werner (Ed.), New York: Hoeber-Harper, 1955. Pp. 507–510.

Cannon, W. B., *Bodily changes in pain, hunger, fear and rage.* (2nd ed.) New York: Appleton, 1920.

Carlson, H. B., McCulloch, W., & Alexander, F. Effects of zest on blood sugar regulation. Paper read at Ass. Res. nerv. ment. Dis., New York, 1949.

Castelnuovo-Tedesco, P. Emotional antecedents of perforation of ulcers of the stomach and duodenum. *Psychosom. Med.*, 1962, **24**, 398–416.

Chadwick, M. The psychological effects of menstruation. *Nerv. ment. Dis. Monogr. Ser.*, 1932, No. 6.

Chambers, W. N., & Reiser, M. F. Emotional stress and the precipitation of congestive heart failure. *Psychosom. Med.*, 1953, **15**, 38–60.

Chapman, L. F., Ramos, A. O., Goodell, H., Silverman, G., & Wolff, H. G. A humoral agent implicated in vascular headache of the migraine type. *Arch. Neurol.*, 1960, **3**, 223.

Chapman, W., Livingston, R., Livingston, K., & Sweet, W. Possible cortical areas involved in arterial hypertension. *Proc. Ass. Res. nerv. Dis.*, 1950, **29**, 775–798.

Charny, I. W. Regression and reorganization in the "isolation treatment" of children: a clinical contribution to sensory deprivation research. *J. Child Psychol. Psychiat.*, 1963, **4**, 47–60.

Chertok, L., Mondzain, M. D., & Bonnaud, M. Vomiting and the wish to have a child. *Psychosom. Med.*, 1963, **25** (1).

Clark, D., Hough, H., & Wolff, H. G. Experimental studies on headache: observations on histamine headache. *Ass. Res. nerv. ment. Dis. Proc.*, 1935, **15**, 417.

Clemens, T. L. Autonomic nervous system responses related to the Funkenstein test. II. Mecholyl. *Psychosom. Med.*, 1957, **21** (5). (a)

Clemens, T. L. Autonomic nervous system responses related to the Funkenstein test. I. To epinephrine. *Psychosom. Med.*, 1957, **19** (4). (b)

Cleveland, S. E., & Fisher, F. Behavior and unconscious fantasies of patients with rheumatoid arthritis. *Psychosom. Med.*, 1954, **16**, 327–333.

Cleveland, S. E., & Fisher, S. Psychological factors in the neurodermatoses. *Psychosom. Med.*, 1956, **18** (3).

Cleveland, S. E., & Fisher, S. Comparison of psychological characteristics and physiological reactivity in ulcer and rheumatoid arthritis groups. *Psychosom. Med.*, 1960, **22** (4).

Cleveland, S. E., & Johnson, D. L. Personality patterns in young males with coronary disease. *Psychosom. Med.*, 1962, **26** (6).

Cleveland, S. E., Reitman, E. E., & Bentinck, Catherine. Therapeutic effectiveness in sensory deprivation. *Arch. gen. Psychiat.*, 1963, **8** (5).

Coddington, R. D., Bruch, Hilde, & Keller, Jean. Gastric perceptivity in normal, obese and schizophrenic subjects. Paper read at Amer. Psychosom. Soc., 1963, Atlantic City, Apr. 27–28.

Cohen, S. I., Bondurant, S., & Silverman, A. Psychophysiological influences on peripheral venous tone. *Psychosom. Med.*, 1960, **22** (2).

Cohen, S. I., Silverman, A. J., Waddell, W., & Zuidema, G. D. Urinary catechol amine levels, gastric secretion and specific psychological factors in ulcer and non-ulcer patients. *J. psychosom. Res.*, 1961, **5** (2), 90–115.

Conrad, A. The psychiatric study of hyperthyroid patients. *J. nerv. ment. Dis.*, 1934, **79**, 505.

Cooper, G. D., Adams, H. B., & Gibby, R. G. Ego strength changes following perceptual deprivation. *Arch. gen. Psychiat.*, 1962, **7** (3).

Curtis, G. C., Cleghorn, R. A., & Sourkes, T. L. The relationship between affect and the excretion of adrenaline, noradrenaline, and 17-hydroxycorticosteroids. *J. psychosom. Res.*, 1960, **4**, 176–184.

Dale, H. H., & Feldberg, W. Chemical transmitter of vagus effects to stomach. *J. Physiol.*, 1934, **81**, 320.

Dalessio, D. J. On migraine headache serotonin and serotonin antagonism. *J. Amer. med. Ass.*, 1962, **181** (4).

Daniels, G. E. Psychiatric factors in ulcerative colitis. *Gastroenterology*, 1948, **10**, 59.

Daniels, G. E., O'Connor, J. F., Karush, A., Moses, L., Flood, C. A., & Lepore, M. Three decades in the observation and treatment of ulcerative colitis. *Psychosom. Med.*, 1962, **24** (1).

Davis, J. M., McCourt, W. F., & Solomon, P. Sensory deprivation. *Arch. gen. Psychiat.*, 1961, **5** (1).

Dekker, E., & Groen, J. Reproducible psychogenic attacks of asthma. *J. psychosom. Res.*, 1956, **1** (58).

Dement, W. The effects of dream deprivation. *Science*, 1960, **131**, 1705.

Deutsch, H. *The psychology of women.* Vols. I and II. New York: Grune & Stratton, 1944, 1945.

Dimond, G. B. Coronary disease. *Arch. intern. Med.*, 1963, **112**, 550.

Doniger, M., Wittkower, E. D., Stephens-Newsham, L., & Hoffman, M. M. Psychophysiological studies in thyroid function. *Psychosom. Med.*, 1956, **18** (4), 310–323.

Dorpat, T. L., & Holmes, T. H. Backache of muscle tension origin. In *Psychosomatic obstetrics, gynecology and endocrinology.* Springfield, Ill.: Charles C Thomas, 1963.

Draper, G. *Human constitution: a consideration of its relationship to disease.* Philadelphia: Saunders, 1924.

Draper, G. The common denominator of disease. *Amer. J. med., Sci.*, 1935, **190**, 545.

Draper, G. The emotional component of the ulcer susceptible constitution. *Ann. intern. Med.*, 1942, **16**, 633.

Dunbar, Flanders. Physical mental relationships in illness: trends in modern medicine and research as related to psychiatry. *Amer. J. Psychiat.*, 1934, **91**, 541.

Dunbar, Flanders. *Psychosomatic diagnosis.* New York: Hoeber-Harper, 1943.

Dunbar, Flanders. *Emotions and bodily changes.* (3rd ed.) New York: Columbia Univer. Press, 1947. (a)

Dunbar, Flanders. *Mind and body: psychosomatic medicine.* New York: Random House, 1947. (b)

Dunbar, Flanders. Emotional factors in spontaneous abortion. In *Psychosomatic obstetrics, gynecology and endocrinology.* Springfield, Ill.: Charles C Thomas, 1963.

Dunbar, J. F., Wolfe, T. P., & Rioch, J. M. Psychiatric aspects of medical problems: psychic component of disease process (including convalescence) in cardiac, diabetic and fracture patients. *Amer. J. Psychiat.*, 1936, **93**, 649.

Dykman, R. A., Ackerman, Peggy T., Galbercht, C., & Reese, W. G. Physiological reactivity to different stressors and methods of evaluation. *Psychosom. Med.*, 1963, **25** (1).

Dykman, R. A., & Gantt, H. W. *Cardiovascular conditioning in dogs and in humans: Physiological bases of psychiatry.* Springfield, Ill.: Charles C Thomas, 1958.

Ecker, A. Emotional stress before a stroke: a preliminary report of 20 cases. *Ann. Intern. Med.*, 1954, **40**, 49–56.

Engel, G. L. *Fainting: physiological and psycho-*

logical considerations. Springfield, Ill.: Charles C Thomas, 1950.

Engel, G. L. Studies of ulcerative colitis. I. Clinical data bearing on the nature of the somatic process. *Psychosom. Med.*, 1954, **16**, 496–501. (a)

Engel, G. L. Studies of ulcerative colitis. II. The nature of the somatic processes and the adequacy of psychosomatic hypotheses. *Amer. J. Med.*, 1954, **16**, 416. (b)

Engel, G. L. Studies of ulcerative colitis. III. The nature of the psychological processes. *Amer. J. Med.*, 1955, **19**, 231.

Engel, G. L. Studies of ulcerative colitis. IV. The significance of headaches. *Psychosom. Med.*, 1956, **18** (4).

Engel, G. L. Studies of ulcerative colitis. V. Psychological aspects and their implications for treatment. *Amer. J. digestive Dis.*, 1958, 3, 315.

Engel, G. L. Is grief a disease? *Psychosom. Med.*, 1961, **23** (1).

Engel, G. L., Reichsman, F., & Segal, H. L. A study of an infant with a gastric fistula. I. Behavior and rate of total hydrochloric acid secretion. *Psychosom. Med.*, 1956, **18** (5).

Eppinger, H., & Hess, L. *Die Vagotonie.* Berlin: 1940.

Epstein, A., & Ervin, F. Psychodynamic significance of seizure content in psychomotor epilepsy. *Psychosom. Med.*, 1956, **18** (1).

Eranko, M. A. Effects of experimental neurosis on the thyroid and adrenal gland of the rat. *Acta Endocrinol.*, 1957, **26**, 109.

Erfman, Irmgard. Age and manifestation of psychosomatic disorders. *Bita Hum.*, 1962, **5**, 161, 166.

Fenichel, O. *The psychoanalytic theory of neurosis.* New York: W. W. Norton, 1945.

Ficarra, B. J., & Nelson, R. A. Phobia as a symptom in hyperthyroidism. *Amer. J. Psychiat.*, 1947, **103**, 831.

Fiorica, V., & Muehl, S. Relationship between plasma levels of 17-hydroxycorticosteroids (17-OHCS) and a psychological measure of manifest anxiety. *Psychosom. Med.*, 1962, **26** (6).

Fisher, C. The use of psychoanalytic method and theory in psychiatric research. Paper read at Joint Meeting, Amer. psychoanal. Psychiat. Soc., 1962.

Fisher, C., & Dement, W. C. Studies on the psychopathology of sleep and dreams. *Amer. J. Psychiat.*, 1963, **119**, 1160–1168.

Folkow, B., & von Euler, U. S. Selective activation of noradrenaline and adrenaline producing cells in the cat's adrenal gland by hypothalamic stimulation. *Circulation Res.*, 1954, **2**, 3.

Fowler, E. P., Jr., & Zeckel, A. Psychophysiological factors in Meniere's disease. *Psychosom. Med.*, 1953, **15**, 127–139.

Fox, H. M., Murawski, B., Bartholomay, A., Gifford, S. D., & Sandford, M. D. Adrenal steroid excretion patterns in eighteen healthy subjects. *Psychosom. Med.*, 1961, **23** (1).

Freedman, M. J., & Frajola, W. J. Serum lipid patterns in men under 45 years with myocardial infarction. *Amer. J. med. Sci.*, 1963, **246**, 277.

French, J. P., Porter, R. W., Cavanaugh, E. B., & Longmire, R. L. Experimental gastroduodenal lesions induced by stimulation of the brain. *Psychosom. Med.*, 1957, **19** (3).

French, T. M. Physiology of behavior and choice of neurosis. *Psychoanal. Quart.*, 1941, **10**, 561.

French, T. M. (In collaboration with A. M. Johnson.) Brief psychotherapy in bronchial asthma. *Proc. second brief Psychother. Council, Chicago Inst. Psychoanal.*, 1944.

French, T. M., & Alexander, F., Psychogenic factors in bronchial asthma. I, II. *Psychosom. Med. Monogr.* 1941, **2**, **4**, Nos. 1, 2.

French, T. M., & Shapiro, L. B. The use of dream analysis in psychosomatic research. *Psychosom. Med.*, 1949, **11**, 110.

Friedman, M., St. George, S., Byers, S. O., & Rosenman, R. H. Excretion of cathechol amines, 17-ketosteroids, 17-hydroxycorticoids and 5-hydroxyindole in man exhibiting a particular behavioral pattern associated with a high incidence of clinical coronary artery disease. *J. Clin. Invest.*, 1960, **39**, 758.

Friedman, S. B., Mason, J. W., & Hamburg, D. A. Urinary 17-hydroxycorticosteroid levels in parents of children with neoplastic diseases. *Psychosom. Med.*, 1963, **25** (4).

Fromm-Reichmann, F. Contribution to the psychogenesis of migraine. *Psychoanal. Rev.*, 1937, **24**, 26.

Fullerton, D. T., Kollar, E. J., & Caldwell, A. B. A clinical study of ulcerative colitis. *J. Amer. med. Ass.*, 1962, **181** (6).

Funkenstein, D. H. The relationship of experimentally produced asthmatic attack to certain acute life stresses. *J. Allergy*, 1953, **24**, 11–17.

Funkenstein, D. H., King, S. H., & Drolette, Margaret. The direction of anger during a laboratory stress induced situation. *Psychosom. Med.*, 1954, **16**, 403–413.

Funkenstein, D. H., & Meade, Lydia W. Norepinephrine-like and epinephrine-like substances and the elevation of the blood pressure during acute stress. *J. nerv. ment. Dis.*, 1954, **119**, 380–397.

Garma, Angel. *Peptic ulcer and psychoanalysis.* Baltimore: Williams & Wilkins, 1958.

Gellhorn, E. Analysis of autonomic hypothalamic functions in the intact organism. *Neurology,* 1956, **6**, 335.

Gellhorn, E. Autonomic imbalance and the hypothalamus: implications for physiology, medicine, psychology, and neuropsychiatry. Minneapolis, Minn.: Univer. of Minnesota Press, 1957.

Gerard, Margaret. Enuresis: a study in etiology. *Amer. J. Orthopsychiat.*, 1939, **9**, 48.

Gibby, R. Z., Adams, H. D., & Carrera, R. N. Therapeutic changes in psychiatric patients following partial sensory deprivation. *Arch. gen. Psychiat.*, 1960, **3**, 33–42.

Gildea, F. F. Special features of personality which are common to certain psychosomatic disorders. *Psychosom. Med.*, 1949, **11**, 273.

Gill, M. M., & Brenman, M. *Hypnosis and related states.* New York: International Universities Press, 1959.

Glass, G. B. J., & Wolf, S. Hormonal mechanisms in nervous mechanism of gastric acid secretion in humans. *Proc. Soc. exp. Biol. Med.*, 1960, **73**, 535.

Goldberg, M. Comments on "cancer mortality rate." *Arch. gen. Psychiat.*, 1963, **9**, 179.

Goldblatt, H. Studies on experimental hypertension. V. The pathogenesis of experimental hypertension due to renal ischemia. *Ann. intern. Med.*, 1937, **11**, 69.

Goodall, McH. Studies in adrenalin and noradrenalin in mammalian heart and suprarenals. *Acta Physiol. Scand. Suppl.* **85**, 1951.

Gottsfeld, H. Body and self-cathexis of super-obese patients. *J. psychosom. Res.*, 1962, **6**, 177–183.

Grace, W. J., Wolf, S. G., Jr., & Wolff, H. G. *The human colon.* London: Heinemann, 1951.

Grace, W. J., Pinsky, R. H., & Wolff, H. G. The treatment of ulcerative colitis. II. *Gastroenterology,* 1954, **26**, 462.

Graham, D. T. Cutaneous vascular reactions in Raynaud's disease and in states of hostility, anxiety and depression. *Psychosom. Med.*, 1955, **17**, 200–207.

Graham, D. T., Kabler, J. D., & Graham, Frances. Physiological response to the suggestion of attitudes specific for hives and hypertension. *Psychosom. Med.*, 1962, **24** (2).

Graham, D. T., Kabler, J. D., & Lunsford, L., Jr. Vasovagal fainting: a diphasic response. *Psychosom. Med.*, 1961, **23** (6).

Graham, J. R., & Wolff, H. G. Mechanism of migraine headache and action of ergotamine tartrate. *Arch. Neurol. Psychiat.*, 1938, **39**, 737.

Graham, L. A., Sanford, I., Shmavonian, B., & Kirshner, N. Sympathetico-adrenal correlates of avoidance and escape behavior in human conditioning studies. *Psychosom. Med.*, 1963, **25** (5).

Greenberg, N. H., Cepan, P., & Loesch, J. G. Some cardiac rate and behavioral characteristics of sucking in the neonate. *Psychosom. Med.*, 1963, **25** (5).

Greenberg, S. I. Pruritus: a symptom of depression. *Psychosomatics,* 1961, **2**, 109–111.

Greene, W. A., Jr. Psychological factors and reticuloendothelial disease. *Psychosom. Med.*, 1954, **16**, 220–230.

Greene, W. A., Jr. Role of a vicarious object in the adaptation to object loss. I. Use of a vicarious object as a means of adjustment to separation from a significant person. *Psychosom. Med.*, 1958, **20** (5).

Green, W. A., Jr. Role of a vicarious object in the adaptation to object loss. II. Vicissitudes in the role of the vicarious object. *Psychosom. Med.*, 1959, **21** (6).

Greene, W. A., Jr., & Miller, G. Psychological factors and reticuloendothelial disease. No. 4. Observation on a group of children and adolescents with leukemia: an interpretation of disease development in terms of the mother-child unit. *Psychosom. Med.*, 1958, **20** (2).

Greene, W. A., Jr., Young, L. E., & Swisher, S. M. Psychological factors in reticuloendothelial disease. II. Observations on a group of women with lymphomas and leukemias. *Psychosom. Med.*, 1956, **18** (4).

Greenfield, N. S., Alexander, A. A., & Roessler, R. Ego strength and physiological responsivity. II. The relationship of the Barron Ego Strength Scale to the temporal and recovery characteristics of skin resistance, finger blood volume, heart rate, and muscle potential responses to sound. *Arch. gen. Psychiat.*, 1963, **9** (2).

Groen, J. Psychogenesis and psychotherapy of ulcerative colitis. *Psychosom. Med.*, 1947, **9**, 151.

Grossman, H. J., & Greenberg, N. H. Psychosomatic differentiation in infancy. I. Autonomic Activity in the newborn. *Psychosom. Med.*, 1957, **19** (4).

Gwinup, G., Byron, R. C., Roush, W. H., Kruger, F., & Hamwi, G. J. Effect of nibbling versus gorging on glucose tolerance. *Lancet,* 1963, **2**, 165.

Halliday, J. L. Approach to asthma. *Brit. J. med. Psychol.*, 1937, **17**, 1.

Halliday, J. L. Psychological factors in rheumatism: preliminary study. *Brit. med. J.*, 1937, **1**, 213–264. (b)

Halliday, J. L. "Psychological aspects of rheumatoid arthritis. *Proc. roy. Soc. Med.*, 1942, **35**, 455.

Halliday, J. L. Concept of a psychosomatic affection. *Lancet*, 1943, **2**, 692.

Halliday, J. L. The incidence of psychosomatic affections in Britain. *Psychosom. Med.*, 1945, **7**, 135.

Halliday, J. L. Epidemiology and the psychosomatic affections: a study in social medicine. *Lancet*, 1946, **2**, 185.

Halliday, J. L. *Psychosocial medicine: a study of the sick society*. New York: Norton, 1948.

Ham, G. C., Alexander, F., & Carmichael, H. T. Dynamic aspects of personality features and reactions characteristic of patients with Graves' disease. Paper read at Ass. Res. nerv. ment. Dis., New York, 1949.

Hamburger, W. W., & Lev, M. W. Masked hyperthyroidism. *J. Amer. med. Ass.*, 1930, **94**, 2050–2056.

Handlon, J., Wadeson, R. W., Fishman, J. R., Hamburg, D. A., & Mason, J. W. Psychological factors lowering plasma 17-hydroxycorticosteroid concentration. *Psychosom. Med.*, 1962, **24** (6).

Hardyck, C. D., Singer, M. T., & Harris, R. E. Affective involvement and blood pressure. *Arch. gen. Psychiat.*, 1962, **7**, 15.

Harris, A. Sensory deprivation in schizophrenia. *J. ment. Sci.*, 1959, **105**, 235–236.

Hartman, H. R. Neurogenic factors in peptic ulcer. *Medical Clin. North Amer.*, 1933, **16**, 1357.

Heller, M. H., Levine, J., & Sohler, T. P. Gastric acidity and normally produced anxiety. *Psychosom. Med.*, 1953, **15**, 509–512.

Hetzel, B. S., De La Nabe, D. S., & Hinkle, L. Rapid changes in plasma PBI in euthyroid and hyperthyroid subjects. *Trans. Amer. Goiter Ass.*, 1952.

Hillarp, N. Evidence of adrenaline/noradrenaline in separate medullary cells. *Acta. Physiol. Scand.*, 1953, **30**, 55–68.

Himwich, H. E. A review of hypoglycemia: its physiology and pathology, symptomatology and treatment. *Amer. J. digestive Dis.*, 1944, **11**, 1.

Hinkle, L. E., Conger, G. A., & Wolf, S. Experimental evidence on the mechanism of diabetic ketosis. *J. clin. Invest.*, 1949, **28**, 788.

Hinkle, L. E., Jr., Ostfeld, A., Benjamin, B., Christenson, W. N., Richter, P., Kane, F. D., Gittinger, J. W., Goldberger, L., Thetford, W. N., Leichter, H., Pinsky, R., & Wolff, H. G. An investigation of the relation between life experience, personality characteristics and general susceptibility to illness. *Psychosom. Med.*, 1958, **20**, 278.

Hinkle, L. E., & Wolf, S. Experimental study of life situations, emotions, and the occurrence of acidosis in a juvenile diabetic. *Amer. J. med. Sci.*, 1949, **217**, 130.

Hinkle, L. E., Jr., & Wolf, S. Summary of experimental evidence relating life stress to diabetes mellitus. *J. Mt. Sinai Hosp.*, 1952, **19**, 537.

Ittelson, W. H., Seidenberg, B., & Kutash, S. Some perceptual differences in somatizing and nonsomatizing neuropsychiatric patients. *Psychosom. Med.*, 1961, **23** (3).

Jackson, C. W., Jr., Pollard, J. C., & Kansky, E. W. The application of findings from experimental sensory deprivation to cases of clinical sensory deprivation. *Amer. J. med. Sci.*, 1962, **243**, 558–563.

Jessner, Lucie, & Abse, W. D. Regressive forces in anorexia nervosa. *Brit. J. med. Psychol.*, 1960, **33**, 301–312.

Johnson, A. M., Shapiro, L. B., & Alexander, F. A preliminary report on a psychosomatic study of rheumatoid arthritis. *Psychosom. Med.*, 1947, **9**, 295.

Kaplan, S. D. (With the technical assistance of Beverly Kaplan & J. Schraider.) A visual analog of the Funkenstein test. *Arch. gen. Psychiat.*, 1960, **3** (4).

Kaplan, S. M., Mass, J. W., Dixley, J. M., & Ross, W. D. Use of imipramine in diabetics. *J. Amer. med. Ass.*, 1960, **174**, 511.

Kaplan, S. N., Gottschalk, L. A., Magliocco, B. E., Rohovit, D., & Ross, D. Hostility and verbal productions and hypnotic dreams in hypertensive patients. *Psychosom. Med.*, 1961, **23** (4).

Karush, A., Hiatt, R. B., & Daniels, G. E. Psychophysiological correlation in ulcerative colitis. *Psychosom. Med.*, 1955, **17**, 36–56.

Katz, L. N. Newer concepts in relation to hypertension. *Calif. med. Ass. J.*, 1962, **97** (4).

Kehoe, M., & Ironside, W. Studies on the experimental induction of depressive responses upon the secretion of gastric acid. *Psychosom. Med.*, 1962, **25** (5).

Kepecs, J., Robin, M., & Brunner, M. J. The relationship of certain emotional states and transudation into the skin. *Psychosom. Med.*, 1951, **13** (1).

Kepecs, J. G., Robin, M., & Munro, Clare. Tickle in atopic dermatitis. *Arch. gen. Psychiat.*, 1960, **3**.

Keys, A., Taylor, H. L., Blackburn, H., Brozek, J., Anderson, J. T., & Simonson, E. Coronary heart disease among Minnesota business and professional men followed fifteen years. *Circulation*, 1963, **28**, 381.

King, A. Primary and secondary anorexia nervosa syndromes. *Brit. J. Psychiat.*, 1963, **109**, 470–479.

Klauder, J. V. Psychogenic aspects of diseases of the skin. *Arch. Neurol. Psychiat.*, 1935, **33**, 221.

Kling, A. Plasma 17-hydroxycorticosteroid in relation to reward and punishment in the brain-operated monkey. *Psychosom. Med.*, 1963, **25** (5).

Knapp, P. H., & Bahnson, C. B. The emotional field: a sequented study of mood and fantasy in two asthmatic patients. *Psychosom. Med.*, 1963, **25** (5).

Knapp, P. H., & Nemetz, J. Personality variations in bronchial asthma. *Psychosom. Med.*, 1957, **19** (6). (a)

Knapp, P. H., & Nemetz, J. Sources of tension in bronchial asthma. *Psychosom. Med.*, 1957, **19**, (6). (b)

Knapp, P. H., & Nemetz, J. Acute bronchial Asthma. I. Concomitant depression and excitement and varied antecedent patterns in 406 attacks. *Psychosom. Med.*, 1960, **22** (1).

Knopf, O. Preliminary report on personality studies in 30 migraine patients. *J. nerv. ment. dis.*, 1935, **82**, 270, 400.

Korchin, S. J., & Herz, M. Differential effects of "shame" and "disintegrative" threats of emotional and adrenocortical functioning. *Arch. Gen. Psychiat.*, 1960, **2**, 640–651.

Kracht, J., & Kracht, V. Histopathology and therapy of the shock thyrotoxicosis in the wild rabbit, virchows. *Arch. path. Anat.*, 1952, **321**, 238–274.

Kronfeld, A. Oesophagus-neurosen. *Psychother. Praxis*, 1934, **1**, 31.

Kuntz, A. *The autonomic nervous system.* Philadelphia: Lea & Febiger, 1945.

Kuntz, A. *Visceral innervation and its relation to personality.* Springfield, Ill.: Charles C Thomas, 1951.

Lacey, J., Bateman, Dorothy, & VanLehn, Ruth. Autonomic response specificity. *Psychosom. Med.*, 1953, **13**, 8–21.

Lacey, J., Smith, R., & Green, A. Use of conditioned autonomic responses in the study of anxiety. *Psychosom. Med.*, 1955, **17**, 208–217.

Lazarus, R. S., Speisman, J., & Mardkoff, A. The relationship between autonomic indicators of psychological stress: heartrate and skin conductance. *Psychosom. Med.*, 1963, **25** (1).

Lee, R. E., & Schneider, R. L. Hypertension and arteriosclerosis in executive and non-executive personnel. *J. Amer. med. Ass.*, 1958, **167**, 1447.

Leigh, D. Sudden deaths from asthma. *Psychosom. Med.*, 1955, **17**, 232–239.

Leonsins, A. J., & Waddell, W. R. The inhibiting effect of norepinephrine on gastric secretions in human subjects. *J. appl. Psysiol.*, 1958, **12**, 334.

Levi, L. New stress tolerance with simultaneous study of psychological variables: a preliminary study. *Psychosom Med.*, 1963, **25**, 392. (Abstract)

Levin, M. M. O. Aggression, guilt and cataplexy. *Arch. Neurol. Psychiat.*, 1953, **69**, 224–235.

Levitt, E. E., Brady, J. P., Ottinger, D., & Hinesley, R. Effect of sensory restriction on hypnotizability. *Arch. gen. Psychiat.*, 1962, **7** (5).

Levitt, E. E., Perksy, H., Brady, J. P., & Fitzgerald, J. The effect of hydrocortisone infusion on hypnotically induced anxiety. *Psychosom. Med.*, 1963, **16** (2).

Lewin, K. K. Role of depression in the production of illness in pernicious anemia. *Psychosom. Med.*, 1959, **21** (1).

Lewis, N. D. C. Psychological factors in hyperthyroidism. *Med. J. Rec.*, 1925, **122**, 121.

Lidz, T. The thyroid. In E. D. Witthower & R. Cleghorn (Eds.), *Recent developments in psychosomatic medicine.* Philadelphia: Lippincott, 1954.

Lief, H. I., Dingman, J., & Bishop, M. T. Psychoendocrinologic studies in a male with cyclic changes in sexuality. *Psychosom. Med.*, 1962, **26**, (4).

Lindemann, E. Psychiatric problems in conservative treatment of ulcerative colitis. *Arch. Neurol. Psychiat.*, 1945, **53**, 322.

Lippman, C. W. Recurrent dreams in migraine: an aid to diagnosis. *J. nerv. ment. Dis.*, 1954, **120**, 273–276.

Lipton, E. L., Steinschneider, A., & Richmond, J. B. Auditory discrimination in the newborn. *Psychosom. Med.*, 1963, **25** (5).

Lotsof, E. J., & Yobst, J. Electric shock therapy and the mecholyl test. *Psychosom. Med.*, 1957, **19** (5). (a)

Lotsof, E. J., & Yobst, J. The reliability of the mecholyl test. *Psychosom. Med.*, 1957, **19** (5). (b)

Lovett Doust, J. W., & Leigh, D. Studies on the physiology of awareness. The interrelationships of emotions, life situations, and anoxemia in patients with bronchial asthma. *Psychosom. Med.*, 1953, **4** (15), 292–311.

Luby, E. D. An overview of psychosomatic disease. *Psychosomatics*, 1963, **4**, 1–8.

Luby, E. D., Frohman, C. E., Grisell, J. L., Lenzo, J. E., & Gottlieb, J. S. Sleep deprivation: effects on behavior, thinking, motor performance and biological energy transfer stystems. *Psychosom. Med.*, 1960, **22**, 182–192.

Macalpine, Ida. Pruritis ani. *Psychosom. Med.*, 1953, **15**, 499–508.

McDonald, R. L. Gynthe, M. O., & Christakos, A. C. Relations between maternal anxiety and obstetric complications. *Psychosom. Med.*, 1963, **25** (4).

Macht, D. R. Influence of some drugs and of emotions on blood coagulation, *J. Amer. med. Ass.*, 1952, **141** (4).

MacLean, P. D. Psychosomatic disease and visceral brain. *Psychosom. Med.*, 1949, **11**, 338–353.

Mahl, G. F. Effect of chronic fear on the gastric secretion of HCL in dogs. *Psychosom. Med.*, 1949, **11**, 30.

Mahl, G. F., & Brody, E. B. Chronic anxiety symptomatology, experimental stress and HCL secretion. *Arch. Neurol. Psychiat.*, 1954, **71**, 314–325.

Mahl, G. F., & Karpe, R. Emotions and hydrochloric acid secretion during psychoanalytic hours. *Psychosom. Med.*, 1953, **15**, 312–327.

Malmo, R. B. Measurement of drive: an unsolved problem in psychology. In M. R. Jones (Ed.), *Nebraska symposium on motivation*. 1958. Pp. 229–265.

Mandelbrote, B. M., & Wittkower E. D. Emotional factors in Grave's disease. *Psychosom. Med.*, 1955, **17**, 109.

Mann, E. C., & Grimm, Elaine R. Habitual abortion. In *Psychosomatic obstetrics, gynecology and endocrinology*. Springfield, Ill.: Charles C Thomas, 1963.

Maranon, G. Sobrela etiologia eamocional de la enfermedad de Addison. *Siglo Med.*, 1929, **8**, 30.

Marbe, K. *Praktische Psychologie der Unfälle und Betriebsschäden*. Muenchen-Berlin: R. Oldenbourg, 1926.

Margolin, S. G. The behavior of the stomach during psychoanalysis: a contribution to a theory of verifying psychoanalytic data. *Psychoanal. Quart.*, 1951, **20**, 349.

Meinhardt, K., & Robinson, H. A. Stokes-Adams syndrome precipitated by emotional stress (report of a case). *Psychosom. Med.*, 1962, **24** (4).

Mendelson, J., Kubzansky, P., Leederman, P. H., Wexler, D., DuToit, C., & Solomon, P. Catechol amine excretion and behavior during sensory deprivation. *Arch. gen. Psychiat.*, 1960, **2**, 147.

Meyer, A., Bollmeier, L. N., & Alexander, F. Correlation between emotions and carbohydrate metabolism in two cases of diabetes mellitus. *Psychosom. Med.*, 1945, **7**, 335.

Miles, H. H. W., Waldfogel, S., Barrabee Edna L., & Cobb, S. Psychosomatic study of 46 young men with coronary artery disease. *Psychosom. Med.*, 1954, **16** (6).

Miller, M. L. Psychodynamic mechanisms in a case of neurodermatitis. *Psychosom. Med.*, 1948, **10**, 309.

Millet, J. A. P., & Dyde, J. F. Psychoanalytical observations in two cases of thrombophlebitis migrans. *Psychosom. Med.*, 1957, **19**, 275.

Millet, J. A. P., Lief, H., & Mittelman, B. Raynaud's disease: psychogenic factors and psychotherapy. *Psychosom. Med.*, 1953, **15**, 61–65.

Minc, Salep, Sinclair, G., & Taft, R. Some psychological factors in coronary heart disease. *Psychosom. Med.*, 1963, **25** (2).

Mirsky, I. A. The etiology of diabetic acidosis. *J. Amer. med. Ass.*, 1942, **118**, 690.

Mirsky, I. A. Some considerations of the etiology of diabetes mellitus in man. *Proc. Amer. Diabetes Ass.*, 1945, **5**, 117.

Mirsky, I. A. Emotional hyperglycemia. *Proc. central Soc. clin. Res.*, 1946, **19**, 74.

Mirsky, I. A. Emotional factors in the patient with diabetes mellitus. *Bull. Menninger Clin.*, 1948, **12**, 187.

Mirsky, I. A. Physiologic, psychologic and social determinants in the etiology of duodenal ulcer. *Amer. J. digestive Dis.*, 1958, **3**, 285–314.

Mirsky, I. A., Block, S., Osher, S., & Broh-Kahn, R. H. Uropepsin excretion by man. I. The source, properties and assay of uropepsin. *J. clin. Invest.*, 1948, **27**, 818.

Mittelman, B. Psychogenic factors and psychotherapy in hyperthyreosis and rapid heart imbalance. *J. nerv. ment. Dis.*, 1933, **77**, 465.

Mittelman, B., & Wolff, H. G. Emotions and gastro-duodenal function: experimental studies on patients with gastritis, duodenitis and peptic ulcer. *Psychosom. Med.*, 1942, **4**, 5.

Mohr, G. J., Selesnick, S., & Augenbraun, Bernice. Family dynamics in childhood asthma: some mental considerations. In H. Schreer (Ed.), *Asthmatic child*. New York: Harper & Row, 1963. Chap. 8.

Mohr, G., Joselyn, I. M., Spurlock, H., & Barron, S. N. Studies in ulcerative colitis. *Amer. J. Psychiat.*, 1958, **114**, 1067.

Mohr, G., Tausend, Helen, Selesnick, S., & Augenbraun, Bernice. Studies of eczema and asthma in the pre-school child. *J. Amer. Acad. Child Psychiat.*, 1963, **2** (2).

Moschcowitz, E. Biology of disease. *Mt. Sinai Hosp. Monogr.*, 1948, No. 1.

Moser, M., Wish, Helen, & Friedman, A. P. Headache and hypertension. *J. Amer. med. Ass.*, 1962, **180** (4), 301.

Moses, L., Daniels, G. D., & Nickerson, J. L. The psychogenic factors in essential hypertension: methodology and preliminary report. *Psychosom. Med.*, 1956, **18** (6).

Mufson, I. FACP: an etiology of scleroderma. *Ann. intern. Med.*, 1953, **39**, 1219–1227.

Murray, C. D. Psychogenic factors in the etiology of ulcerative colitis and bloody diarrhea. *Amer. J. med. Sci.*, 1930, **180**, 239.

Nordmeyer, K. Zur Aetiologie der Hypesernesis gravidarum. *Psychiat. neurol. Wschr.*, 1908, **10**, 102, 125, 134, 149, 156, 164, 190.

Obrist, P. Cardiovascular differentiation of sensory stimuli. *Psychosom. Med.*, 1963, **25** (5).

Oken, D. An experimental study of suppressed anger and blood pressure. *Arch. gen. Psychiat.*, 1960, **2** (4).

Oken, D., Grinker, R. R., Heath, Helen A., Korchin, S. J., Herz, M., & Schwartz, N. B. Relation of physiological response to affect expressions including studies of autonomic response specificity. *Arch. gen. Psychiat.*, 1962, **6** (5).

Oken, D., Grinker, R. R., Heath, Helen A., Sabshin, M., & Schwartz, Neena. Stress response in a group of psychiatric patients: special reference to the use of curare on a stressful stimulus. *Arch. gen. Psychiat.*, 1960, **3** (4).

Orgel, S. Z. Effect of psychoanalysis on the course of peptic ulcer. *Psychosom. Med.*, 1958, **20** (2).

Ottenberg, P., Stein, M., Lewis, J., & Hamilton, C. Learned asthma in the guinea pig. *Psychosom. Med.*, 1958, **20**, 395.

Palmer, W. L. Fundamental difficulties in the treatment of peptic ulcer. *J. Amer. med. Ass.*, 1933, **101**, 1604.

Papez, J. W. A proposed mechanism of emotion. *Arch. Neurol. Psychiat.*, 1937, **38**.

Pasquarelli, B., Campbell, R. J., Polatin, P., & Horwitz, W. Further appraisal of the adrenalin-mecholyl test (Funkenstein test). *Psychosom. Med.*, 1956, **18** (2).

Pell, S., & D'Alonzo, C. A. Acute myocardial infarction in a large industrial population. *J. Amer. med. Ass.*, 1963, **185** (11).

Perrin, G., & Pierce, Irene R. Psychosomatic aspects of cancer: a review. *Psychosom. Med.*, 1959, **21** (5).

Persky, H. Introduction and removal of hydrocortisone from plasma. *Arch. gen. Psychiat.*, 1962, **7** (2).

Persky, H., Hamburg, D. A., Basowitz, H., Grinker, R. R., Sabshin, M., Corchin, S. J., Heig, M., Board, F. A., & Heath, H. D. Relation of emotional responses and changes in plasma hydrocortisone level after stressful interview. *Arch. Neurol. Psychiat.*, 1958, **79**, 434.

Persky, H., Maroc, J., Conrad, E., & den Breeijen, A. Blood corticotropin and adrenal weight-maintenance factor levels of anxious and normal subjects. *Psychosom. Med.*, 1959, **5.** (Abstract)

Pilot, M. L., Lenkowki, L., Spiro, H. M., & Schafer, R. Duodenal ulcer in one of identical twins. *Psychosom. Med.*, 1957, **21** (3).

Pilot, M. L., Rubin, J., Schafer, R., & Spiro, H. M. Duodenal ulcer in one of identical twins: a follow-up study. *Psychosom. Med.*, 1963, **25** (3).

Plesset, M. R., & Shipman, W. G. Anxiety and depression in obese dieters. *Arch. gen. Psychiat.*, 1963, **8**, 530–535.

Podore, C. J., Broh-Kahn, R. H., & Mirsky, I. A. Uropepsin excretion by man. III. Uropepsin excretion by patients with peptic ulcer and other lesions of the stomach. *J. clin. Invest.*, 1948, **27**, 834.

Pollard, J. C., Uhr, L., & Jackson, C. W., Jr. Studies in sensory deprivation. *Arch. gen. Psychiat.*, 1963, **8** (5).

Pond, D. A. Narcolepsy: a brief critical review and study of eight cases. *J. ment. Sci.* 1952, 98, 595–604.

Portis, S. A., & Zitman, I. H. A mechanism of fatigue in neuro-psychiatric patients. *J. Amer. med. Ass.*, 1943, **121**, 569.

Poser, E. G., Lee, S. G. Thematic content associated with two gastro-intestinal disorders. *Psychosom. Med.*, 1963, **25**, 162–173.

Price, D. B., Thaler, M., & Mason, J. W. Preoperative emotional states and adrenal cortical activity: studies on cardiac and pulmonary surgery patients. *Arch. Neurol. Psychiat.*, 1957, **77**, 646.

Prugh, D. G. Variations in attitudes, behavior and feeling states as exhibited in the play of children during modifications in the course of ulcerative colitis. *Res. Publ. Ass. Res. nerv. ment. Dis.*, 1950, **29**, 692.

Purcell, K. The TAT and anti-social behavior. *J. consult. Psychol.*, 1956, **20**, 449.

Purcell, K., Berstein, L., & Bukantz, S. C. A preliminary comparison of rapidly remitting and persistently "steroid-dependent" asthmatic children. *Psychosom. Med.*, 1961, **23** (4).

Reichsman, F., Cohen, J., Colwill, J., Davis, Nancy, Kessler, W., Shepardson, C. R., & Engel, G. L. Natural and histamine induced gastric secretion during waking and sleeping states. *Psychosom. Med.*, 1960, **22** (1).

Renneker, R., Curler, R., Hora, J., Bacon, Catherine, Bradley, G., Kearney, J., & Cutler, M. Psychoanalytic explorations of emotional correlates of cancer of the breast. *Psychosom. Med.*, 1963, **25** (2).

Rennie, T. A. C., & Howard, J. E. Hypoglycemia and tension-depression. *Psychosom. Med.*, 1942, **4**, 273.

Richmond, J. B., & Lustman, S. L. Autonomic function in the neonate. I. Implications for psychosomatic theory. *Psychosom. Med.*, 1955, **17**, 269–275.

Robertson, G., & Gladstone, G. Rejection dyspepsia. *Lancet*, 1963, **1**, 63–66.

Roessler, R., Alexander, A. A., & Greenfield, N. Ego strength and physiological responsivity. I. The relationship of the Barron ES Scale to skin resistance, finger blood volume, heart rate and muscle potential responses to sound. *Arch. gen. Psychiat.*, 1963, **8**, 142–154.

Roffwarg, H. P., Dement, W. C., Muzio, J. M., & Fisher, C. Dream imagery: relationship to rapid eye movements of sleep. *Arch. gen. Psychiat.*, 1962, **7** (4).

Romano, J., & Engel, G. L. Studies of syncope. III. The differentiation between vasodepressor syncope and hysterical fainting. *Psychosom. Med.*, 1945, **7**, 3.

Romano, J., Engel, G. L., Webb, J. P., Ferris, E. B., Ryder, H. W., & Blankenhorn, M. A. Syncopal reactions during simulated exposure to high altitude in decompression chamber. *War Med.*, 1943, **4**, 475.

Rosen, H., & Lidz, T. Emotional factors in the precipitation of recurrent diabetic acidosis. *Psychosom. Med.*, 1949, **11**, 211.

Rosenman, R. H., & Friedman, M. Behavior patterns, blood lipoids and coronary heart. *J. Amer. med. Ass.*, 1963, **184** (12).

Rubenstein, B. B. Functional sterility in women. *Ohio State med. J.*, 1939, **35**, 1066.

Rubenstein, B. B. The vaginal smear–basal body temperature technic and its application to the study of functional sterility in women. *Endocrinology*, 1940, **27**, 843.

Rubin, J., Nagler, R., Spiro, H. M., & Pilot, M. L. Measuring the effect of emotions on esophageal motility. *Psychosom. Med.*, 1962, **24** (2).

Ruddick, B. Colds and respiratory introjection. *Int. J. Psychoanal.*, 1963, **44**, 178–190.

Ruesch, J., Christiansen, C., Patterson, L. C., Dewees, S., & Jacobson, A. (In cooperation with M. H. Soley.) Psychological invalidism in thyroidectomized patients. *Psychosom. Med.*, 1947, **9**, 77.

Russek, H. I. Role of heredity, diet and emotional stress in coronary heart disease. *J. Amer. med. Ass.*, 1959, **171**, 503.

Sancetta, S. M. General and pulmonary hemodynamic effects of pure decapeptide angiotensin in normotensive man. *Circulation Res.*, 1960, **8**, 616–621.

Saul, L. J. Hostility in cases of essential hypertension. *Psychosom. Med.*, 1939, **1**, 153.

Saul, L. J., & Bernstein, C. The emotional settings of some attacks of urticaria. *Psychosom. Med.*, 1941, **3**, 349.

Schachter, J. Pain, fear, and anger in hypertensives and normotensives. *Psychosom. Med.*, 1957, **21** (1).

Schatz, I. Orthostatic hypotension and psychoneurosis. *J. Amer. med. Ass.*, 1963, **185** (2).

Schmale, A. H., Jr. Relationship of separation and depression to disease. I. A report on a hospitalized medical population. *Psychosom. Med.*, 1958, **20** (4).

Schoenberg, B., & Carr, A. C. An investigation of criteria for brief psychotherapy of neurodermatitis. *Psychosom. Med.*, 1963, **25**, 253–263.

Schottstald, W. W. Renal excretions of fluid and electrolytes in association with vascular headache. *Psychosom. Med.*, 1956, **18** (3).

Schwartz, T. B., & Shields, D. R. Urinary excretion of formaldehydogenic steroids and creatinine: a reflection of emotional tension. *Psychosom. Med.*, 1956, **18** (2).

Seaman, G. J., & Reder, E. L. Psychogenic back disorders. *Psychosom. Med.*, 1954, **16**, 374–392.

Seidenberg, R., & Ecker, A. Psychodynamic and arteriographic studies of acute cerebral vascular disorders. *Psychosomatics*, 1963, **4**, 15–21.

Seitz, P. F. D. An experiment in dynamically oriented brief-psychotherapy: psycho-cutaneous excoriation syndromes. *Psychosom. Med.*, 1953, **15**, 200.

Selesnick, S. Separation anxiety and asthmatic attacks related to shifts in object cathexis. In *The Asthmatic child: psychoanalysis and current bio-*

logical thought. Madison, Wis.: Univer. of Wisconsin Press. Chap. 12. New York: Harper & Roe, 1963.

Selinsky, H. Psychological study of the migrainous syndrome. *Bull. N.Y. Acad. Med.*, 1939, **15**, 757.

Selye, H. The general adaptation syndrome and the diseases of adaptation. *J. clin. Endocrinol.*, 1946, **6**, 117.

Sendral, L. Sur les vomissents gravidiques; celles qui vomissent celles qui ne vomissent pas. *Thèse Montpettier*, 1915–1916, No. 14.

Shands, H. C., & Finesinger, J. A note on the significance of fatigue. *Psychosom. Med.*, 1952, **16**, (4).

Shizume, K., Matsuda, J., Irie, M., Lino, S., Ishii, J., Nagataki, S., Matsuzaki, F., & Okinaka, S. Hypothalamic stimulation and thyroid. *Endocrinology*, 1962, **70**, 298–302.

Shoemaker, R. J. A search for the affective determinants of chronic urticaria. *Psychosomatics*, 1963, **4**, 125–132.

Silbermann, I. S. Experimentelle Magen-Duodenalulcus-erzengung durch Scheinfuettern nach Pavlov. *Zbl. Chir.*, 1927, **54**, 2385.

Silverman, A. J., & Cohen, S. Affect and vascular correlates to catechol amines. *Psychol. Res. Rep.*, 1960, **12**.

Silverman, A. J., Cohen, S. I., Shmavonian, B. M., & Greenberg, G. Psychological investigations in sensory deprivation: The body field dimension. *Psychosom. Med.*, 1961, **23** (1).

Slawson, P. F., Flynn, W. R., & Kollar, E. J. Psychological factors associated with the onset of diabetes mellitus. *J. Amer. med. Ass.*, 1963, **185** (3).

Snyder, F. New biology of dreaming. *Arch. gen. Psychiat.*, 1963, **8** (4).

Sontag, L. W. Somatopsychics of personality and body function. *Vita Hum.*, 1963, **6**, 1–10.

Speisman, J. C., Osborn, Janet, & Lazarus, R. Cluster analysis of skin resistance and heartrate at rest and under stress. *Psychosom. Med.*, 1961, **23** (4).

Sperling, M. Psychoanalytic study of ulcerative colitis in children. *Psychoanal. Quart.*, 1946, **15**, 302.

Starr, P., Petit, D. W., Chaney, A. L., Rollman, H., Aiken, J. B., Jamieson, B., & Kling, I. Clinical experience with the blood protein bound iodine determination as a routine procedure. *J. clin. Endocrinol.*, 1950, **10**, 1237.

Stein, A., Kaufman, M. R., Janowitz, H. D., Levy, M. H., Hollander, F., & Winkelstein, A. Changes of hydrochloric secretion in a patient with gastric fistula during intensive psychotherapy. *Psychosom. Med.*, 1962, **24** (5).

Stein, M., & Ottenberg, P. Role of odors in asthma. *Psychosom. Med.*, 1958, **20** (1).

Sternbach, R. A. Assessing differential autonomic patterns in emotions. *J. psychosom. Res.*, 1962, **6**, 87.

Streitfeld, H. S. The specificity of peptic ulcer to intense oral conflict. *Psychosom. Med.*, 1954, **16**, 315–326.

Stunkard, A. Obesity and the denial of hunger. *Psychosom. Med.*, 1959, **21** (4).

Sullivan, A. J., & Chandler, C. A. Ulcerative colitis of psychogenic origin. *Yale J. Biol. Med.*, 1932, **4**, 779.

Suwa, N., Yamashita, I., Owada, H., Shinohara, S., & Nakazawa, A. Psychic state and adrenocortical function: a psychophysiologic study of emotion. *J. nerv. ment. Dis.*, 1962, **134**, 268–276.

Szasz, T. S. Psychiatric aspects of vagotomy. II. A psychiatric study of vagotomized ulcer patients with comments on prognosis. *Psychosom. Med.*, 1949, **11**, 187.

Szondi, L., & Lax, H. Über die Alimentarre Glykamische Reaktion bei Neurasthenie. *Z. ges. exp. Med.*, 1929, **64**, 274.

Taboroff, L. H., & Brown, W. H. Study of the personality patterns of children and adolescents with a peptic ulcer syndrome. *Amer. J. Orthopsychiat.*, 1954, **24**, 602–610.

Thomas, Caroline B. Pathogenetic interrelations in hypertension and coronary artery disease. *Dis. nerv. System. Monogr. Suppl.*, 1961, **22**, 39–45.

Touraine, G. A., & Draper, G. The migrainous patient. *J. nerv. ment. Dis.*, 1934, **80**, 1, 183.

Tupper, W. R. C. Psychosomatic aspects of spontaneous and habitual abortion. In *Psychosomatic obstetrics, gynecology and endocrinology.* Springfield, Ill.: Charles C Thomas, 1963.

Vogel, G. Studies in psychophysiology of dreams. III. The dream of narcolepsy. *Arch. gen. Psychiat.*, 1960, **3** (4).

Von Euler, G. U. S., Levi, C. A., & Strom, G. Cortical and medullary adrenal activity in an emotional stress. *Acta Endocrinol.*, 1959, **30**, 567.

Vosburg, R., Fraser, N., & Guehl, J., Jr. Imagery sequence in sensory deprivation. *Arch. gen. Psychiat.*, 1960, **2**, 134–356.

Waddell, W. R. The physiologic significance of retained antral tissue after partial gastrectomy. *Ann. Surgery*, 1956, **143**, 520–553.

Wadeson, R. W., Mason, J. W., Hamburg, D. A., & Handlon, J. H. Plasma and urinary 17-OHCS responses to motion pictures. *Arch. gen. Psychiat.*, 1963, **9** (2).

Wallerstein, R. S., Sutherland, R. L., & Lyons, J. Psychosomatic considerations in Addison's Disease. *Psychosom. Med.*, 1954, **16** (1).

Warren, J. E. Myocardial infarction in an industrial population. *Arch. Environ. Hlth*, 1963, **7**, 210.

Weiner, H., Singer, Margaret T., & Reiser, M. F. Cardio-vascular responses and their psychological correlates. I. A. study in healthy young adults and patients with peptic ulcer and hypertension. *Psychosom. Med.*, 1962, **24** (5).

Weiner, H., Thaler, Margaret, Reiser, M. F., & Mirsky, A. I. The etiology of duodenal ulcer. I. Relation of specific psychological characteristics to rate of gastric secretion (serum pepsinogen). *Psychosom. Med.*, 1957, **21** (1).

Weiner, S., Dorman, D., Persky, H., Stack, T. W., Norton, J., & Levitt, E. Effect of anxiety of increasing the plasma hydrocortisone level. *Psychosom. Med.*, 1963, **25** (1).

Weininger, O. Physiological damage under emotional stress as a function of early experience. *Science*, 1954, **119**, 285–286.

Weinstock, H. I. Psychotherapy in severe ulcerative colitis: its ineffectiveness in preventing surgical measures and recurrences. *Arch. Gen. Psychiat.* (Chicago), 1961, **4**, 509–512.

Weiss, E. Psychoanlyse eines Falles von nervoesem Asthma. *Int. Z. Psychoanal.*, 1922, **8**, 440.

Weiss, E. Cardiospasm: a psychosomatic disorder. *Psychosom. Med.*, 1944, **6**, 58.

Weiss, E., & English, O. S. *Psychosomatic medicine.* (2nd ed.) Philadelphia: Saunders, 1949.

Wenger, M. A. The measurement of individual differences in autonomic balances. *Psychosom. Med.*, 1941, **3**, 427.

Wenger, M. A., Clemens, T. L., Coleman, D. R., Cullen, T. D., & Engel, B. T. Autonomic response specificity. *Psychosom. Med.*, 1961, **33** (3).

Wenger, M. A., Clemens, T. L., & Cullen, T. D. Autonomic functions in patients with gastrointestinal and dermatological disorders. *Psychosom. Med.*, 1962, **24** (3).

Wenger, M. A., Clemens, T. L., Darsie, M. L., Engel, B. T., Estess, F. M., & Sonnenschein, R. I. Autonomic response patterns during intravenous infusion of epinephrine and norepinephrine. *Psychosom. Med.*, 1960, **22** (4).

West, L. J., Hanszen, H. H., Lester, B. K., & Cornelisoon, F. S., Jr. The psychosis of sleep deprivation. *Ann. N.Y. Acad. Sci.*, 1962, **96**, 66–70.

White, B. V., Cobb, S., & Jones, C. M. Mucous colitis. *Psychosom. Med.*, 1939, **1**.

Wilder, J. Psychological problems in hypoglycemia. *Amer. J. digestive Dis.*, 1943, **10**, 428.

Williams, H. L., Lubin, A., & Goodnow, J. J. Impaired performance with acute sleep loss. *Psychol. Monogr.*, 1959, **73**, No. 484.

Wilson, G. W. The influence of psychologic factors upon gastro-intestinal disturbances: A symposium. III. Typical personality trends and conflicts in cases of spastic colitis. *Psychoanal. Quart.*, 1934, **3**, 558.

Winkelstein, A. A new therapy of peptic ulcer. *Amer. J. med. Sci.*, 1933, **185**, 695.

Wiseman, A. D. A study of psychodynamics of duodenal ulcer exacerbations with special reference to treatment and the problem of specificity. *Psychosom. Med.*, 1956, **28** (1).

Wittkower, E. D. Studies on the influence of emotions on the functions of the organs including observations in normals and neurotics. *J. ment. Sci.*, 1935, **81**, 533.

Wittkower, E. D. Studies of the personalities of the patients suffering from urticaria. *Psychosom. Med.*, 1953, **15**, 116–126.

Wolff, C. T., Mason, J. W., Friedman, S. B., & Hofer, M. A. The relationship between ego defenses and the adrenal response to the prolonged threat of loss: a predictive study. *Psychosom. Med.*, 1963, **25** (5). (Abstract)

Wolff, H. G. Personality features and reactions of subjects with migraine. *Arch. Neurol. Psychiat.*, 1937, **34**, 895.

Wolff, H. G. *Headache and other head pain.* New York: Oxford Univer. Press, 1948. Pp. 255–261.

Wolff, H. G., & Wolf, S. Studies on a subject with a large gastric fistula: changes in the function of the stomach in association with varying emotional states. *Trans. Ass. Amer. Physicians*, 1942, **57**, 115.

Wolff, P., & Levine, J. Nocturnal gastric secretions of ulcer and non-ulcer patients under stress. *Psychosom. Med.*, 1955, **17**, 218–226.

33 Psychoneuroses

SAMUEL B. KUTASH

The psychoneuroses occupy a place of central importance in the field of *clinical psychology* because of the concept of psychogenicity with which they are associated. As clinical psychology emerged from the intelligence, achievement, and *psychometric* testing stage of its development, which was at its height in the era between the two World Wars, and entered its mature, more professional state, now reaching full adulthood, it broadened its functions in the areas of psychodiagnosis, psychotherapy, research, training, and theory building, making important contributions, through projective techniques and other refined methods of diagnosis, to the careful delineation of the psychodynamics of neurosis, and, through analytic and nonanalytic methods of psychotherapy, to the treatment of neuroses. Of particular significance have been the contributions of the clinical psychological researcher to the understanding and description of the psychoneuroses and the research into the nature of anxiety, the psychology of conflict behavior, the study of character structures and reaction patterns, as well as the problems of so-called symptoms in relation to depth psychology. Clinical psychologists and nonmedical psychoanalysts with thorough training and background in clinical psychology have raised serious questions about the concept of disease in the medical sense as it relates to psychoneurosis, although the neuroses certainly have great importance in the medical field as clear-cut examples of syndromes of symptoms with wide variability in clinical pictures for which no demonstrable organic causes or anatomical changes have been demonstrated.

It is now recognized that psychoneurotic overlay, or the concept of a psychoneurosis superimposed upon an organic illness or upon social pathology originating from a pathogenic culture, is a frequent occurrence and must be distinguished from the organic or social pathology and often treated over and above the strictly medical or socioeconomic measures. The intensive study of the psychoneuroses has contributed to our understanding of the so-called normal personality as well as the functional psychoses, all the organic illnesses, and group and social behavior.

In reference to the functional psychoses, Rosen (1953, p. 78), for example, believes in a linear development from neurosis through the manic-depressive disorder toward schizophrenia. Arieti (1955, p. 70) also believes that among the factors which may delay or completely avert psychosis is the ability of the patient to resort to additional neurotic defenses.

The development of theories of neurosis and of psychoanalysis such as those of Freud, Adler, Jung, Rank, Reich, Stekel, Horney, Fromm, Sullivan, and others has contributed much to the advancement of human thought and culture—in science, philosophy, art, literature, and religion. The entire discipline of psychoanalysis, with its infusion of new ideas into the understanding of human behavior, may be said to have arisen out of attempts to understand the neuroses. The widespread prevalence of neuroses and the need to understand them better has led to the development of many if not most of the more refined clinical psychodiagnostic tools, such as the projective techniques, situational and stress techniques, and the many other methods and tests described in other chapters of this volume. They have also served as an impetus to the development of most of the major psychotherapeutic methods and many of the most widely accepted personality theories. Clinical psychology is thus intimately concerned with the study, differential diagnosis, treatment, and understanding of the psychoneuroses.

The psychoneuroses include a large variety of heterogeneous clinical manifestations and syndromes of psychogenic origin which usually have four elements in common: (1) *anxiety,* which may be overt and expressed more directly or covert and hidden, in which case it is controlled unconsciously, in part or in full, by psychological defense mechanisms; (2) *conflict* between unconscious and conscious motivations or between contradictory desires, needs, or drives that are either unresolved or poorly resolved; (3) *symptoms* that result in unhappiness, inefficiency, problems in interpersonal relationships, or illness; and (4) a *character structure* or *reaction pattern,* including character defenses which have become part of the individual's neurotic life style.

According to Malamud (1946) the term "psychoneurosis" was first introduced by Dubois (1904) when the full variety of neurotic disturbances was as yet undescribed and when much less was known about their inherent complexity. Thus, while it is convenient and informative to group the psychoneuroses together, there is serious difference of opinion as to whether they represent or should be regarded as a disease entity or even as one kind of life style or reaction pattern. As mentioned previously, there is some question as to whether they represent disease in the medical sense or behavioral maladjustment in the psychological sense. The problem is further complicated by such interrelated considerations as value systems, cultural norms, favorable versus unfavorable neurotic patterns, philosophical considerations, and the variety of personality theories and schools of psychology and psychiatry.

Those authorities and writers on the subject who regard psychoneurosis as a mental disorder stipulate that the illness "does not involve gross falsification of external reality in the sense of delusions or hallucinations" and that it is "not likely to cause" its victims "to engage in violent behavior with respect either to society or to themselves" (Coleman, 1950, pp. 160–161). Psychoneurotics are considered to be individuals who need psychotherapeutic help by reason of unhappiness, anxiety, inefficiency, or other associated symptoms which do not ordinarily require hospitalization except in extreme instances. On the other hand, those authorities who consider psychoneurosis a "mode of life" or "a difficulty in living happily and effectively" stress the social and interpersonal concomitants and the behavioral reaction patterns of the individual (Thompson, 1950). Some authors, such as Wolman (1964), explain all mental disorders as maladjustive patterns of behavior.

INCIDENCE

Psychoneurotic disturbances undoubtedly have a higher incidence than any other form of mental, emotional, or maladjustive disturbance. An estimate of the number of people whose adjustment is affected by the various forms of psychoneurosis depends largely on the definition of what constitutes neurotic personality and neurotic reactions. For example, if there are included all the pure psychoneurotic syndromes or reaction patterns and the various neurotic character structures and neuroses superimposed upon somatic diseases, a very high percentage of the general population could be said to be psychoneurotic. One could also include the so-called psychosomatic disorders. Many persons who have neurotic symptoms or even lifelong neurotic patterns rarely or never consult a psychiatrist, psychologist, or physician. Psychoneurosis, because of its prevalence alone, is a problem of the highest magnitude not only in the fields of medicine, psychiatry, clinical psychology, social work, and education but in all living in today's world. Actual estimates of the incidence of psychoneuroses in the United States alone include as a realistic and conservative figure about ten million people, but as suggested the estimate could be increased to as many as twenty-five million or more. Cobb (1952) estimated only 2,500,000 psychoneurotics.

J. F. Brown wrote, "When these other problems which have recently been recognized as psychiatric are added to the psychoses and psychoneuroses, it is easy to see that probably everyone needs psychiatric care at some time or other in his life" (1940, p. 367). By "these other problems" are meant such conditions as alcoholism, delinquency, behavioral acting out, psychosomatic disorders, etc. However, for psychoneurotics this is often a matter of choice, and this depends largely upon how the neurosis fits into the individual's life situation. In some types of life situations the neurotic reaction pattern itself serves a purpose which may obviate the urgent need for therapy, and it is only when the neurotic pattern is no longer sufficient to enable the individual to control his anxiety and he is not flexible enough to change without professional assistance that he may need therapy. What brings most psychoneurotic persons to seek treatment and to be identified as neurotics is the emergence of *symptoms* which may be regarded as inadequate attempts to resolve intrapsychic or other conflicts through compromises.

In spite of all that has been written about psychoneurosis, it is almost impossible to get exact statistics on the frequency of its occurrence. Perhaps the easiest way to secure an accurate estimate is to take a random sampling of a few thousand people, diagnose them, and multiply by a multiple derived from the ratio between the sample and the total population. To complicate things further, the varieties of neurosis are such and its mildness or severity covers such a wide range that some kinds merge into the so-called normal reaction patterns on the one hand and the psychoses on the other. Medical doctors assert that as many as 60 per cent of their patients are neurotic. Many authors believe with J. F. Brown that "the individual who never suffers neurotic disturbance is quite as rare as the individual who never has had colds" (1940). In spite of the high incidence of psychoneuroses, only about 4 per cent of all first admissions to hospitals for mental disorders in the United States were diagnosed as psychoneurotics. This is related, of course, to the introduction of medical measures such as tranquilizing drugs for controlling anxiety and the availability of improved preventive mental hygiene practices and psychotherapeutic treatments.

CLASSIFICATION

Since it is necessary for the clinical psychologist to be cognizant of the most prevalent systems of classification of the neuroses, these will be presented as background, and then our attention will be directed to some of the newer psychodynamic formulations and the attempts at genotypical as contrasted with phenotypical classification. The most widely used nosology for the psychoneuroses is that promulgated by the American Psychiatric Association (1960), which attempts to deal with reaction patterns and to take into account the psychodynamic considerations in terms of neurosis as a means of controlling or attempting to control anxiety. According to this system, anxiety is viewed as a common element in all varieties of psychoneurosis and the specific psychoneurotic reactions are understood in terms of the patterns of reaction that are developed in order to cope with the anxiety or to channel its expression or control. The role that the anxiety plays in the total picture is given primary emphasis.

The *Diagnostic and Statistical Manual* of the American Psychiatric Association states: "Longitudinal (lifelong) studies of individuals with such disorders usually present evidence of periodic or constant maladjustment of varying degree from early life. Special stress may bring about acute symptomatic expression of such disorders" (1960). It goes on to say that

> anxiety in psychoneurotic disorders is a danger signal felt and perceived by the conscious portion of the personality. It is produced by a threat from within the personality (e.g. by supercharged repressed emotions, including such aggressive impulses as hostility and resentment) with or without stimulation from such external situations as loss of love, loss of prestige, or threat of injury.

The anxiety may be expressed and experienced directly, as in the *anxiety reaction,* which is characterized mainly by diffuse, often severe "free-floating" anxiety, not related (at least on the surface) to any specific situation or threat. Attempts to cope with specific threat from within or without or stress situations give rise to a variety of neurotic patterns which represent defenses against the basic anxiety. These defenses—depression, conversion, rationalization, isolation of affect, etc.—emerge as the symptoms of the particular variety of neurosis. It must be recognized, however, that often neurotic reaction patterns appear as *mixed neuroses.* These become psychodiagnostic problems because of the difficulty in distinguishing them from borderline or ambulatory or pseudoneurotic schizophrenia.

In the *asthenic reaction,* which is not given separate status in the current *Manual,* the anxiety is dealt with by inhibition of involvement and the development of such symptoms as feelings of weakness, fatigue, and malaise, lack of enthusiasm, and various somatic preoccupations and complaints. In school populations this reaction often manifests itself in the pattern of the underachiever who fails to get involved in his studies sufficiently to make full use of his potentialities. Among the adult working population this pattern is associated with inefficiency and difficulties in being productive.

Some anxiety-ridden individuals show the so-called *hypochondriacal reaction* (also not currently given separate status in the American Psychiatric Association *Manual*), characterized by morbid and obsessive concern about their health when there is no detectable serious organic disease. Chrzanowski (1959) sees the dynamic nature of the asthenic reaction and the hypochondriacal reaction as more of a difference in degree than in kind with hypochondriasis usually seen as the more ominous condition. The common descriptive denominator of both is the somatic preoccupation. The *conversion reaction* or hysteria converts the anxiety into various symptoms of physical illness, such as the paralysis of a leg or loss of sight, again in the absence of actual underlying organic pathology. In the *dissociative reaction* the impulses giving rise to the anxiety are discharged or deflected into such symptomatic expressions as amnesia, fugue states, somnambulism, "blackouts" and losses of consciousness, as well as multiple personality.

Some neurotic individuals show as their major symptoms the persistence of irrational fears even when the person recognizes their irrationality. This is called a *phobic reaction.* A phobia may be defined as a morbid dread of an object, act, or situation. By the employment of the phobic reaction, the neurotic individual attempts to handle his anxiety by focusing upon a single external object or situation. This restores the possibility of constructive action, even if it consists of no more than keeping away from the threat. In the *obsessive-compulsive* reaction, irrational thoughts, impulses, and acts persist despite the fact that the individual is aware that they are irrational. In the obsessive-compulsive reaction anxiety is associated with preoccupation with unwanted ideas (obsessions) and with persistent impulses to repeat certain acts over and over (compulsions).

When anxiety is specifically focused on a traumatic event such as loss of a loved person, a severe environmental setback such as a serious financial reverse, the loss of an organ or limb, or the suffering of any disagreeable deprivation through illness or otherwise, a *neurotic-depressive* reaction may ensue which is characterized by severe dejection. The anxiety in this reaction may be relieved partially by the depression and self-depreciation.

In some cases the neurotic pattern of reaction is mostly the concomitant or the outcome of the struggle between the anxiety and the individual's ego defenses. The experiencing of the anxiety is then channeled through the autonomic nervous system, resulting in a variety of visceral symptoms and psychophysiologic complaints. This is called a *somatization reaction.* There is a great variety of somatization reaction patterns and a tendency for individuals to channel these through particular organ systems or glandular channels. Any of the organ systems, such as the gastrointestinal (duodenal or peptic ulcer), the genitourinary (psychic impotence), the cardiovascular system (essential hypertension), and the skeletal system (arthritis, low back pain, etc.), may be affected. The psychosomatic disorders in themselves constitute a major medical, psychiatric, and clinical psychological problem.

Since the psychosomatic disorders are covered in "The Psychosomatic Approach" and the depressive states in "Depression" while the classification of mental disorders is dealt with in "Mental Health and Mental Disorders," the present chapter will omit further detailed discussion of these.

EGO BOUNDARIES AND THE PSYCHONEUROSES

The various types of neurotic reactions described above may be understood in terms of Federn's (1952) concept of ego boundaries as further developed and applied specifically to the neuroses by Gutheil (1958) and others, such as Zucker (1959), Ivey (1959), and Kutash (1963). In addition to the primary *anxiety state* or *reaction* exacerbated by external or internal threat or stress, the two basic types of psychoneurosis, considered from the point of view of the ego boundaries in neurosis, can be designated as anxiety hysteria with or without phobic symptoms and obsessive-compulsive neurosis.

The ego is thought of as having two major boundaries; one between itself and the outside world of reality and the other between itself and the inner world of the unconscious or id. In the psychologically, well-functioning individual, these boundaries are optimally cathected and flexible so that the ego functions are properly exercised, including suitable repression and selective admittance into consciousness of primordial and instinctual drives from within and adequate reality testing and cognitive, perceptual experiencing of the external world. The major task of the ego is the successful integration of these pleasure drives and needs from within with the reality considerations and requirements of the external world.

The normal state of the ego boundaries in the well-functioning personality may be represented diagrammatically in Figure 1.

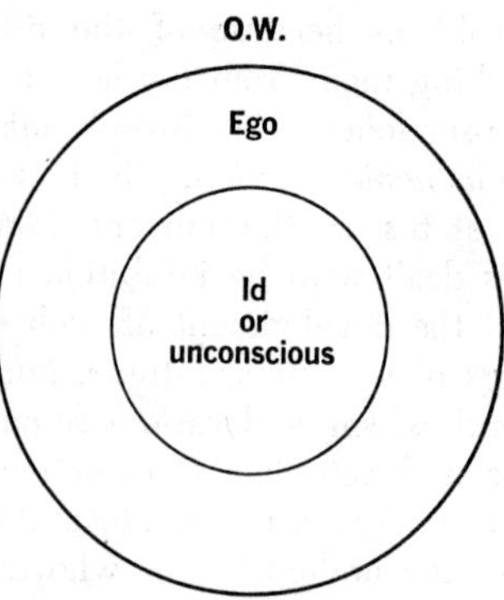

Figure 1

In the hysterical personality structure the ego-id boundary is too rigid or overcathected, reflecting massive repression of instinctual drive in varying degree and the damming up of libido (see Figure 2). This may have resulted from early specific trauma or a chronically traumatic or neurotic early childhood situation in which the major defense of repression was developed and much of the unpleasant, painful material was rendered unconscious. A good share of the libidinal or psychic energy became tied up in maintaining the repressions, leaving an inadequate cathexis of the ego–outer world boundary, which remains too permeable, resulting in such symptoms as extreme suggestibility, histrionic acting out, problems of identity, tendencies toward dissociation reactions, emotional displays, and the usual kaleidoscopic array of hysterical symptoms which are acted out. The rigidity of the inner boundary results in sexual naïveté, belle indifférence, lack of drive, etc. Thus, the various psychoneurotic reactions like the *asthenic, hypochondriacal, conversion, dissociative,* and *phobic* reactions may be thought of as varieties of hysterical personality structure. Phobias may be regarded as symbolic representations of the repressed intrapsychic sources of the original anxiety, which are projected outward or displaced to less threatening objects in the outside world and perceived as external threats. This is possible only when there is too fluid or permeable a boundary between the ego and the outer world and too rigid a boundary between the ego and the id. For example, the repression of incestuous wishes and drives may be experienced in anxiety hysteria as a phobic reaction manifested by fear of enclosed places or of tunnels.

With this type of patient, the therapist in the outside world makes ready contact with the patient's ego through the poorly cathected, loose outer boundary, and an intense positive transference may be formed which can be utilized in therapy to help bring unconscious material into consciousness through release of repressions. This is the classical type of neurosis prevalent in Freud's day as conversion, asthenic, dissociative, and hypochondriacal reactions and in relation to which he developed his epoch-making theory and practice of classical psychoanalysis which was aimed at bringing the repressed unconscious material into consciousness, thus releas-

Figure 2

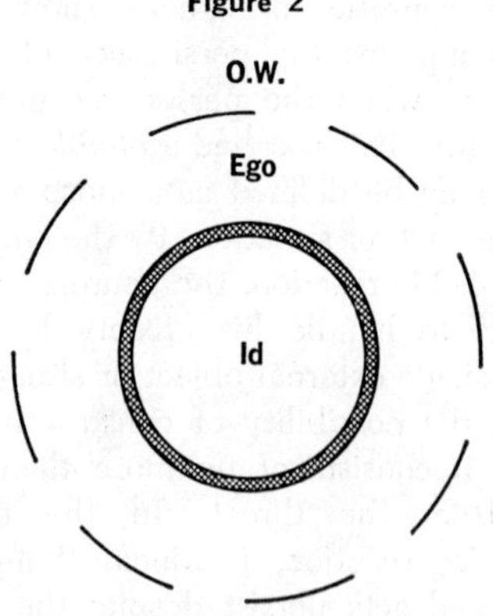

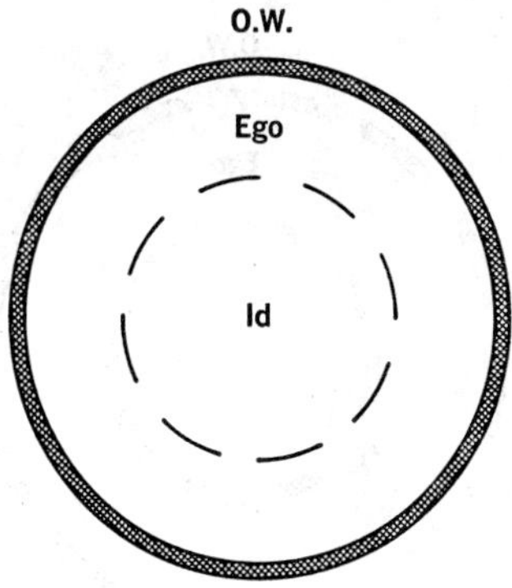

Figure 3

ing libido cathexis from the inner ego boundary and making it available for more optimal cathexis of the outer ego boundary.

In the obsessive-compulsive personality structure it is the ego–outer world or outer boundary that is too rigid, not permeable enough, or overcathected (see Figure 3). The individual has erected a barrier between himself and the outside world, bolstered by such character defenses as intellectualization, rationalization, isolation of affect, and compulsions. The inner boundary, by contrast, is too permeable, so that sexual thoughts, unacceptable ideas, and promptings from within continually enter consciousness in the form of obsessions. These are prevented from being acted out in the environment by the relatively impermeable outer boundary. This neurotic arrangement sets up the typical symptomatology of the obsessive-compulsive reaction in which "the anxiety is associated with the persistence of unwanted ideas and of repetitive impulses to perform acts which may be considered morbid by the patient" (American Psychiatric Association, 1960, p. 33). The individual is compelled by pushes from within to carry out his rituals. He is often aware of his antimoral and antisocial trends. As Gutheil indicated,

> Although the repressive effectiveness of their ego is reduced, they still must deal with their destructive anti-moral and anti-social tendencies. They are forced to use other means of defense to protect the integrity of the ego, means different from repression or sublimation. In the forefront of the new strategic approach stands magic. From the outset their situation seems desperate. The "enemy forces," coming from the id, have overrun the weak barricades of repression and have penetrated into the center of the ego fortress. Unable to deal with the enemy at peripheral points, the ego is forced to invoke defenses it has used in its past, such as wishful thinking, feelings of omnipotence, magic formulas, symbolic gestures and compulsive rituals. It resorts to the mechanisms of denial and negation, to various oaths, clauses and invocations, to ward off the dangers of the id invasion (Gutheil, 1958, p. 351).

The reality-testing capacity of the obsessive-compulsive is preserved at the expense of rigid defenses around the ego–outer world boundary and its overcathexis. "Preoccupied as he is with warding off the instinctual forces, he is loath to deal with any influences from the outside world. He is rigid, incapable of absorbing much that impinges upon him from his environment. His views are extremely conservative since, above all, he is anxious to maintain the existing order" (*ibid.*, p. 343).

The obsessive-compulsive patient needs to undergo character analysis of the defenses and the rigid character structure since the symptoms are part of the character structure and the defenses of rationalization, isolation of affect, etc., need to be penetrated and dissolved, relieving the rigidity of the outer boundary so that the inner boundary can be properly cathected. The obsessions would not be focused on nor would there be a heavy emphasis on bringing more unconscious material into consciousness since the inner boundary is already too vulnerable. The therapist faced by the rigid outer boundary may be confronted with a negative transference, hostility, and a host of defenses before he can get through to the patient's ego. The denial mechanisms and attempts at negation will be strong. Treatment not only would not necessarily involve an uncomplicated approach of bringing unconscious material into consciousness but rather would be directed more toward analyzing the relationships with the outside world and people in it, as in Sullivanian interpersonal therapy (1953) and other neo-Freudian methods (Fromm-Reichman, 1950; Fromm, 1947).

In the ambulatory schizophrenic or *pseudoneurotic* schizophrenic, both ego boundaries are damaged and there is a danger of schizophrenic decompensation, but there are islands of defense in terms of pseudoneurotic symptoms and rigidities in both boundaries, side by side with breaks in the boundaries (see Figure 4). In the neurotic *depressive reaction* the attempt is made to preserve a homeostatic equilibrium in the boundaries by distributing the cathexis evenly through constricting the ego or contracting it (see Figure 5). The depressive reaction in this sense may be understood as a defense against the development of actual defect in one of the ego boundaries and obviating the need for compensating in the other boundary in order to preserve equilibrium. In the depressive reaction the circumferences of the two boundaries—particularly the outer boundary—become smaller through contraction of the ego, resulting in preservation of accuracy of perception, keen awareness of bodily processes, some hypochondriasis, and preserved and sharpened reality sense. Rather than allow the ego to become impaired, the depressive chooses to depreciate or squelch it until it can be expanded again when the stress or threat is lessened.

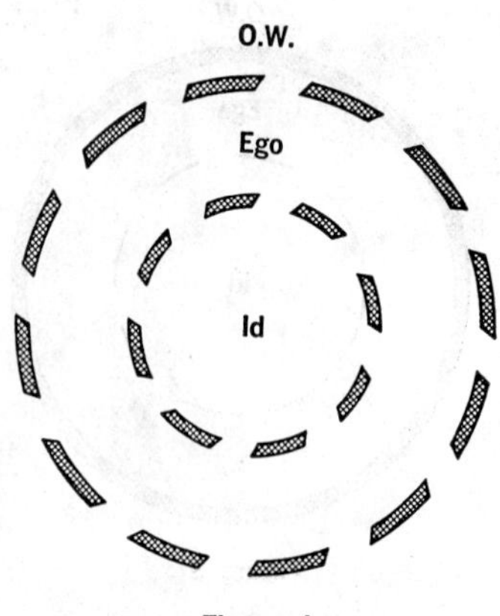

Figure 4

Wolman (1959, 1964) has proposed a classification of psychogenic mental disorders based on different types of social maladjustment. In this scheme, all human relations are divided according to the *aims* of their participants, depending on whether their main purpose is the satisfaction of their own needs (Instrumental) or their partners' needs (Vectorial) or both (Mutual or Mutual Acceptance). A normal or well-adjusted individual is seen as balanced in his social interactions. That is, he is instrumental in the struggle for survival, mutual in relationships with friends and family, and vectorial in regard to children and to those who need help. He is reasonably selfish (instrumental), reasonably mutual, and reasonably vectorial.

Mentally disturbed individuals cannot preserve this balance. Either they are *hyperinstrumental*, displaying infantile selfishness and parasitism as their major mode of relatedness, or they neglect themselves and worry constantly about others in a morbid *hypervectorialism*, or they exaggerate in giving and taking in shifting moods of *paramutualism*. According to Wolman's analysis, certain types of neurosis, expecially anxiety and neurotic-depressive reactions, can be classified under Hyperinstrumental neurosis; obsessional, phobic, and neurasthenic reactions, under Hypervectorial neurosis; while dissociative and conversion reactions can be classified under Paramutual neurosis (see "Mental Health and Mental Disorders," below).

ETIOLOGY

More possible causes have been proposed for the psychoneuroses than for any other mental disorder or emotional condition. During the era in psychiatry and clinical psychology ushered in by Freud (1948), determinism became a cornerstone of the great psychodynamic theories of neurosis beginning with Freud's own hypothesis. He originally proposed a traumatic theory which attributed the origin of neurosis to early trauma mostly prior to the age of six, resulting in massive repression, damming up of libido, and development of neurotic symptoms. This theory was built upon firsthand, intensive analytic experience with hysterical cases and fits very well the model for the anxiety-hysteric described above in terms of a rigid, overcathected inner ego boundary (repression) and a weak, undercathected outer ego boundary. After a while, Freud began to stress the importance of

Figure 5

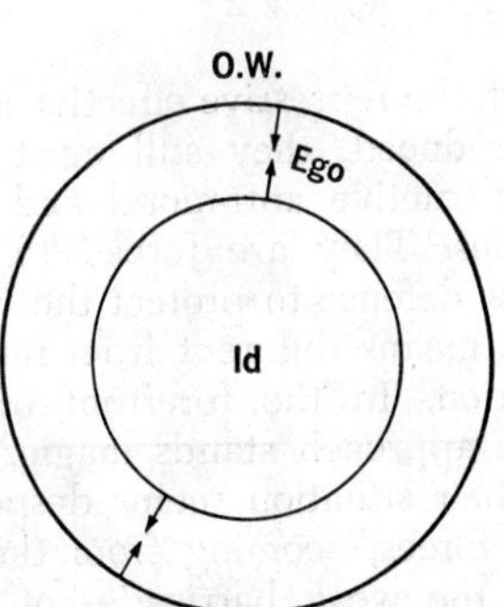

innate tendencies and predispositions as important in the etiology of neurosis, postulating that the traumatic events or traumatic neurogenic environment must fall on the soil of an innate predisposition. Freud's libido theory is a biologically oriented theory (see Part 2, "Fundamentals of Psychoanalytic Theory") which attributes a sexual origin to the neuroses, combining a hereditary predisposition with external trauma, causing repression or damming up of libidinal energy which is channeled into symptom formation. Around 1910 Freud (1953) added to his sexual theory of neurosis the factor of aggression, the frustration of which could also lead to neurosis or neurotic character structure. Prior to 1920 anxiety was given little stress by Freud and his followers as an important contributing factor in the development of neurosis. In his original formulations in 1894 Freud considered anxiety as resulting physiologically as a reaction to frustration of the sexual orgasm. While it was present in neurotics, it was not seen as a possible etiological factor in neurosis. However, in 1923, in his book *The Problem of Anxiety* (1936), Freud accorded anxiety a higher position as a causative factor in neurosis. More recent authorities regard the various forms of neurotic behavior as different reaction patterns developed as attempts to cope with anxiety (see section on classification, above in this chapter). Since Freud's earlier formulations the clearest, most extensive, and detailed Freudian psychoanalytic explanation of neurosis can be found in the classical work of Fenichel (1945), which individualizes and explains the kaleidoscopic mechanisms and forms of neurosis and neurotic symptomatology by Freudian theory. Freud's system of character structure, making use of the concept of fixation at one or more of the stages of libidinal development—*oral, urethral, anal,* and *phallic*—must also be mentioned in terms of the etiology of the neurotic character structure. The importance of the resolution of the Oedipus complex in producing maturity also became an important etiological factor.

While Freud hinged his explanation of neurosis on the libido theory, also according a place to anxiety, frustration, and other phenomena derived from libidinal malfunctioning, *Adler* (1932) postulated that the basic cause of neurosis stems from *feelings of inferiority*. Starting with emphasis on actual organ inferiority, either functional or morphological, he postulated that the individual compensated either organically through overdevelopment of the *inferior* or other functions or organs or in his psychological functioning and personality development. Later it was assumed that inferiority feelings were universal and stem from the smallness and helplessness of the child in comparison to the adult. Adler enlarged his theory to postulate the development of compensative neurotic goals, or guiding fictions. His corollary theories of "masculine protest," drive for power, were offered as the major determinants of neurosis instead of sex. For sexual drive he substituted the will to power as the guiding force in human behavior, and in emphasizing the pursuit of goals he minimized the importance of the initial cause (see "Non-Freudian Analytic Theories" in Part 2). As Thompson points out, Adler's theory began to ascribe importance "to the role of the ego in producing neurosis and to show that the direction in which a person is going, that is his goals, significantly contribute to his neurotic difficulties" (1950). A complete exposition of Adler's theory of neurosis can be found in the recent book by H. L. Ansbacher and R. R. Ansbacher (1956).

Jung, in 1909, attributed neurosis or other difficulties to the neurotic difficulties of the parents as decisive influences. Among these he mentioned concealed discord between the parents, their repressed hidden wishes, and their secret anxieties. He also stressed the importance of the maternal influence and repression as an important neurotic craving. Jung (1915) eventually modified the libido theory, considering sexual libido as only one form of "primal" libido or undifferentiated energy, which he referred to as psychical energy. While Jung placed great importance on early childhood in producing neurosis, he denied that sexuality was an important factor in that period. Jung's greatest contribution to the understanding of the etiology of neurosis is perhaps his postulate that man not only tends to repress his unacceptable aspects but also represses some of his positive potentialities, so that some neurotic patterns take the form of difficulty in realizing one's actual capabilities; thus the treatment of neurosis is not only an attempt to overcome and eliminate what is undesirable but also—and even more important—to bring out the undeveloped aspects of the patient's personality, or what Jung called the *inferior functions*. His idea of the persona, his theory of extroversion-introversion, etc., all contributed to further understanding of neurosis. Jung's theory of personality is summarized and discussed fully in Jacobi's book (1943).

Rank (1945) postulated that all neurotic problems stem from the trauma of birth instead of from the Oedipus complex and its resolution. He saw birth as a profound shock physiologically and psychologically and felt that this produced the primal anxiety within the person, portions of which were released in all later anxiety-producing situations. He stressed the psychological importance of separation from the mother and postulated that all later experiences involving a separation acquired a traumatic quality, such as weaning, castration anxiety, loss of loved ones, etc. His theory led to greater consideration of the analytic situation in therapy and the relationship between patient and therapist. Rank saw neurotics as reacting to the threat of separation and felt that they remained dependent, frightened at the prospect of independence, and willing to give up leadership of their own lives because of this fear. He emphasized the assertion of the patient's own will as a goal for therapy to overcome the sense of guilt that he had whenever he asserted himself (1945). Thus, according to Rank, the neurotic cannot postively identify himself with the group, nor can he stand alone, for this would produce guilt and inferiority feelings. A full exposition of Rank's contribution to the theory of neuroses can be found in the work by Karpf (1953).

Ferenczi (1955) stressed the idea that neurotics were people who had never been accepted or loved as children and that therapy should provide a corrective emotional experience with a "good" parent. The neurotic had a craving for love which caused him to feel frustrated, unhappy, and unfulfilled. His attempts to win love resulted in the development of neurotic mechanisms.

Reich (1945) went further than Freud in emphasizing a sexual theory of neurosis and hypothesized that failure to achieve orgastic potency was the basic cause and symptom of neurosis. While he subscribed later to unsubstantiated, questionable, nonanalytic, unverifiable hypotheses concerning the so-called "orgone," his earlier contribution to character analysis of neurosis merits careful attention. He implied that the character structure of the neurotic was created by the social order, thus emphasizing the role of cultural factors in neurotic difficulty. The type of patient he worked with, among the most resistive to the Freudian approach of bringing unconscious material into consciousness, needed analysis of the character defenses and resistances and in terms of ego boundary theory would be more like the model presented in this chapter for the obsessive-compulsive.

Stekel (1950), another early follower of Freud, placed great emphasis on the role of intrapsychic conflict in the etiology of neurosis and developed an active analytic technique for uncovering and treating these unconscious conflicts. He postulated that all neurosis resulted from emotional conflict. Later, all the theories of neurosis made room for the idea of intrapsychic conflict as a major etiological factor, although they differed about what the important conflicts were. Stekel's emphasis on the bipolarity of the personality made conflict the primary determinant of anxiety and neurosis. Some of the conflicts involved as the antagonistic trends were heterosexuality versus homosexuality, id versus superego, sadomasochistic conflict, and conflict between the ego and external requirements.

Thus far we have given examples of theories of neurosis which emphasized inner causes, the libidinal or biological factor, and conflicts between inner drives and channels of expression for them. We turn now to some examples of theories that place greater emphasis on cultural and interpersonal causes of psychoneurosis.

Horney, in 1937, published an extensive cultural interpretation of neurosis (1937) and in a later book (1939) took issue with Freud's libido theory. While Adler substituted the will to power for Freud's sexual etiology of neurosis, he did not postulate it as a primary neurotic force but rather as a basic problem in people. Horney (1963) definitely saw the will to power as a neurotic mechanism, but only as one of several. Thus, she included a hierarchy of etiological trends like the neurotic need for love. She took into account also the development of emotional conflicts, which she referred to as "psychological vicious circles within the person." These vicious circles grew out of the neurotic defenses developed at first to circumvent difficulties. As Thompson stated it,

> Neurotic defenses produced in reaction to difficulties, in turn produce new difficulties which in turn produce new defenses, so that by the time the patient comes for treatment, a complicated defensive system must be unwound, beginning with the patient's present life situation (Thompson, 1950).

Horney also agreed with Adler that the patient is neurotic not only because of what has happened to him but because, in coping with it, he has established goals which, among other things, lead him to pursue false values. An example of this is the *idealized image,* the defense of having a false or faulty picture of oneself and one's virtues or assets. Horney spoke of neurotic goals as a potential source of anxiety, and of conflicting neurotic goals that clash with each other. The pursuit of one threatens the other. Thus, the need to be admired, clashing with the need to assert oneself, may produce acute conflict. The production of secondary anxiety as a perpetuating factor of neurosis became substituted for Freud's theory of the *repetition compulsion.* Horney described neurosis primarily as due to the effects of cultural pressures.

Fromm regarded neurosis as an outgrowth of the "specific kind of relatedness of the individual towards the world and to himself" (1955). He took issue with Freud's theory of the relation of man to society in that Fromm did not consider the satisfaction of instinct as the central problem in human nature. According to Fromm,

> Man gets into neurotic difficulties as a result of the new needs created in him by his culture as well as because of deprivations and frustration of his potentialities forced upon him by it. Man's lust for power and his yearning for submission, for example, are not basic biological needs, but attitudes developed out of the raw material of human nature by a specific culture (Thompson, 1950, p. 206).

A full exposition of Fromm's views, including his explanation of the "mechanisms of escape," the "destructive personality," "automation conformity," etc., may be found in his *Escape from Freedom* (1941) and other works. In *Man for Himself* (1947) he develops his theory of character structure—the *receptive, exploitative, hoarding, marketing,* and *productive* characters, of which the first four are neurotic. This is further developed in *The Art of Loving* (1956).

Sullivan, in his theory of interpersonal relations, attributes two important goals to the human being: the pursuit of security and the pursuit of satisfaction. The latter deals with biological needs, while the former is concerned mostly with and results from the cultural processes. He postulates that most neurotic disorders result from "difficulties encountered in the formation of security operations." He conceives of anxiety as orginating from unfavorable interaction with the parents and other significant figures and that this anxiety in turn produces lack of awareness of the anxiety-producing situations: repression, dissociation, or isolation of affect, for example. Sullivan's views have been published in detail (1953). He replaces Freud's concept of transference with the concept of *parataxic distortion.* Sullivan's method of treatment aimed at gradually bringing to the awareness of the patient, and to his understanding, the truth of what is going on between himself and others, especially pointing out the parataxic (or neurotic) aspects.

In addition to the psychodynamic or psychodynamically derived theories of the etiology of neurosis, a variety of nonanalytic explanations have been developed and offered. An etiological theory which may be considered a bridge between the psychodynamic and nonanalytic is that of Carl Rogers, who states that "in the typical neurosis, the organism is satisfying a need which is not recognized in consciousness, by behavioral means which are consistent with the concept of self and hence can be consciously accepted" (1951, p. 508). Thus, neurosis is tied in with the self-concept. One form would be where the behavior is inconsistent with the self, another where the desires are unacceptable to the self and hence modified neurotically, and lastly where the self-esteem is lowered to conform to the behavior.

The widespread entry in the past two decades of clinical psychologists into the field of diagnosing and giving therapy to people suffering from psychoneurosis has led to the application of established psychological theories of personality as explanations for neurotic behavior. This has been added to by the burgeoning extent of experimental and clinical psychological research. The conditioning theory of neurosis stems from the psychological principles of conditioning originating largely in the work of Thorndike[1] (1898) and of Pavlov (1927) (1849–1936) in Moscow and continued in the United States by Watson (1914), Dunlap (1928), Hilgard and Marquis (1940), Hilgard (1948), and many others (Mowrer, 1960). The most recent representatives of this approach, such as Eysenck (1957), Wolpe (1958), Skinner (1938), Festinger (1957), and others, regard neurosis, as did their predecessors, as a form of behavior to which the individual has been "conditioned" by repetitive reinforced experiences throughout his life. They regard the symptoms of neurosis as the illness itself and assert or imply that symptomatic treatment by "favorable conditioning" or learning techniques is all that is necessary or effective in treating neurotic complaints. From their point of view, underlying depth causes in the psychodynamic sense would be of lesser importance, possibly irrelevant, but not necessarily ruled out. The work of Hull (1943) ushered in the revival of interest in the behavioral approach.

Noteworthy in this connection is the production of experimental neuroses in animals. Pavlov, who first showed the possibility of producing neurosis experimentally in dogs, produced the neurotic behavior by

> establishing conditioned responses to two signals, one always reinforced and the other never reinforced by food. The two signals were then gradually made so similar that the animals could no longer discriminate between them, with the result that ordered behavior broke down (Pavlov, 1927).

In his work entitled "Conditioned Reflex Method and Experimental Neurosis," Liddell (1944) summarized all the research along these lines: his own with sheep, pigs, and goats; Gantt's (1944) with dogs; Maier and Schneirla's (1942) with rats; Hebb's (1946) with chimpanzees; and Masserman's (1943) with cats.

Whether the breakdowns produced experimentally in animals can be regarded as the same order of phenomenon as human neurosis is, of course, questionable. The experimenters themselves differ as to what is happening. Masserman's method seems to involve producing an anxiety state through frustration of the hunger drive created by conflict between the urge to eat and the urge to escape. Liddell uses a traumatizing procedure producing fright, while Pavlov induces a state of severe shock. Whether these behavioral breakdowns are neuroses in the true sense of the word is open to question.

One way of conceptualizing neurosis is in terms of a learning process. Psychotherapy can also be understood as a learning process. A major segment of American psychologists, including many clinical psychologists, regard psychoneurosis as a form of learned maladaptive behavior which can be unlearned through psychotherapy or through such procedures as operant conditioning, reciprocal reinforcement, and cognitive dissonance, or other methods based on learning theory.

Mowrer (1953) and Dollard and Miller (1950) both took psychoanalysis as a point of departure in applying learning theory to problems of neurotic behavior. Mowrer (1953) postulated that neurotics had "learned" social taboos but not assimilated them and that this was the major problem in psychoneurosis rather than conflict stemming from a hypertrophied or too strict superego leading to massive repression. Dollard and Miller (1950) borrowed from Hullian learning theory and reinterpreted psychoanalysis in learning terms, again explaining neurosis as a learned reaction. Other attempts to apply learning-theory approaches have been developed by Rotter (1954), Phillips (1956), Shaffer (1947), Shoben (1953), Shaw (1948), and Pepinsky and Pepinsky (1954).

Other nonanalytic but phenomenological approaches which have implications for the neuroses are the *personal construct* theory of G. A. Kelly (1955), which regards neurosis as a product of the personal constructs or verbal and preverbal abstractions which the person has built up. He then attempts to fit all new experiences into the "Procrustean bed" of his rigidly adhered to personal constructs. Ellis (1962), in his *rational-emotive* method, regards neurosis as the product of "what the individual tells himself" about his experience and his distortions and unfounded beliefs.

One of the recent conceptualizations of neurosis in terms of perceptual theory resulted from collaboration between a representative of the transactional school of perception and a dynamically oriented, analytically trained clinical psychologist. Kutash (1961),

[1] Pavlov acknowledged Thorndike's priority: 1898 compared to 1902 (see R. S. Woodworth, *Contemporary Schools of Psychology*, p. 61).

as a result of his joint work with Ittelson and others in a long-term study of perceptual changes in psychopathology, put forth the idea that mental health can be defined in positive terms as optimal perceptual flexibility. Ittelson and Kutash postulated that

> neither the content of perception nor the perceptual process itself are static characteristics of an individual, but rather change continually as the individual changes. This capacity to change one's perception, or perceptual flexibility, is the overriding process which may give us the clue to a workable operational definition of mental health (Ittelson & Kutash, 1961).

In their experiments Ittelson and Kutash and their collaborators utilized some of the Ames Demonstrations in Perception to devise measures of perceptual flexibility. They hypothesized that there was an optimal range of perceptual flexibility which went along with mental health and good prognosis. By the same token, too much perceptual rigidity would go along with psychoneurosis. This concept can be harmonized with psychoanalytic theory, learning theory, gestalt theory, and most of the other theories that have been applied to explain neurotic behavior.

For example, one of the Ames Demonstrations consists of the so-called distorted room (Ittelson, 1952). The walls are not parallel, and the floor and ceiling are not parallel to each other. The optical cues are so arranged that when the subject looks into the room monocularly a conflict of cues is set up, which the subject resolves in terms of his past experiences by seeing the room as a rectangular "normal" room. Once he has made this basic unconscious assumption that it is a rectangular room (which it is not), he will distort everything in the room in size in order to carry out the original visual perceptual assumption. Thus, if two equally sized dolls, one wearing a pink dress and the other a blue dress, are placed in the room, one in each corner, one doll will appear large and the other small in size, carrying out the original assumption that it is a rectangular room. If now the dolls are exchanged, the pink one being placed in the corner previously occupied by the blue one and vice versa, the large one will now be seen as small and vice versa. This occurs in spite of the conscious knowledge that the dolls are of equal size and the room is *not* rectangular.

If the subject is put through a learning experiment in which he uses a pointer to become aware of the slope of the floor, ceiling, and walls, he gradually learns that the room is distorted and will see it as a distorted room, at which time the dolls "return" to normal size, as does everything else in the room, which is now perceived accurately. The rapidity with which this can be "learned" is an index of the person's perceptual flexibility. The measurement of this is made by a selsyn apparatus attached to a rod mounted in the room. The subject is instructed to align the rod parallel to the floor or the right wall, etc.; a reading on the apparatus scale informs the experimenter when the subject is seeing the room accurately.

This method can be used as a basis for building a theoretical model of what happens in psychoneurosis. It is postulated that as a result of a situation or situations in which there were conflicting cues in childhood, the individual formed a perceptual assumption concerning the situation and the people involved, such as mother and father, which became his characteristic *perceptual distortion.* Subsequently, any occurrence or experience involving any elements in common with the original pathogenic conflict and the perceptual distortion resulting therefrom is distorted secondarily (as the doll's size is distorted) to make the new experience fit the previous assumption. This becomes a neurotic pattern based on *perceptual rigidity* which can be likened to what Freud referred to as the repetition compulsion or, in the case of distortion of persons, the *transference;* Adler called it the *life style,* and Sullivan referred to it as *parataxic distortion.* A general theory of psychoneurosis would then postulate that it consists of the formation of rigid neurotic patterns based on perceptual distortion and proliferated into varied symptom clusters by secondary distortions designed to carry out the original wrong assumption. The secondary distortions constitute the defenses and symptoms which cover up the original distortion. Most often the early conflicts involve interpersonal interactions with the mother, and later the father, resulting in basic perceptual distortion of these figures and of subsequent mother, father, and sibling figures. This results in disturbed interpersonal relations and the development of the varied phenomena seen in the different types and cases of psychoneuroses.

Practically all authorities on neurosis agree that rigidity or lack of flexibility is a definitely identifiable characteristic of psychoneurosis: that the neurotic tends to repeat his difficulties over and over, seemingly not learning by experience. The *perceptual theory of neurosis* can also be related to the explanation of neurosis in terms of ego boundaries. Rigidity in one of the ego boundaries is present in all types of neurosis and is related to the ego defenses built up to "protect" the original primary distortion or distortions.

From this point of view, psychotherapy for neurosis consists in uncovering, reviving, abreacting, and reperceiving in a new light the original distorting situations or pathogenic conflicts and thus eventually eliminating all the secondary distortions which have been formed on the basis of the original perceptual distortion. It is quite possible that the original distortion takes place under the influence of strong or overwhelming anxiety, as in a traumatic event or a series of repetitive chronic traumata. The handling of subsequent anxiety requires the repetition of the same mechanism of defense or the development of additional defenses, which in turn bring on secondary anxiety.

It is evident that all systems of psychoanalysis and personality theories have emphasized important, probably correct, elements or aspects of the etiological background of psychoneurosis. Currently there is a movement away from determinism or cause-effect theories of neurosis. Psychoneurosis is being seen more and more by the dynamic schools as a gestalt in which the interrelationship between the elements of the gestalt provides the characteristics of the neurotic picture and the description of the picture provides the understanding of the neurosis. From this point of view each of the schools of thought has contributed something of importance, depending also on the kinds of cases and facets of behavior they have focused on in arriving at their conceptualizations. Fromm and Sullivan worked with different kinds of neurotics than Freud, while Adler, Jung, Horney, Stekel, Mowrer, Rogers, and all the others each worked with different samplings of psychoneurotics.

The gestalt school of psychology, whose major representatives are Wertheimer (1923), Koffka (1935), Kohler (1929), and Lewin (1936), views neurosis from a *holistic* point of view, adhering to the principle that behavior can be understood only as a whole and that atomistic methods result in misleading or distorted principles. Thus, any one of the phenomena of neurosis, anxiety, emotional conflict, defense mechanisms, rigidity, transference, parataxis, symptoms, cannot be understood truly or fully by themselves because they are in continual interaction with and modify each other. This is also the view of the transactional theory (Kilpatrick, 1952).

SYMPTOMATOLOGY

In addition to the general phenomena of anxiety, conflict, ego defenses, impairment of efficiency, and unhappiness to be found in all the neurotic reaction patterns, each *type* of neurotic reaction has its specific symptomatology. It is, of course, understood that symptoms can be viewed either as the end result of a cause-and-effect relationship or more often as part of a personality structure or gestalt in which the personality organization includes the symptoms as inadequate attempts to keep the structure in homeostatic equilibrium. Two diametrically opposed viewpoints with reference to symptom treatment in the neuroses dominate the scene in the field of psychotherapy today. On the one hand are the various dynamic analytically oriented schools which share the view of Freud and his followers that symptoms are the outward clinical manifestations of underlying causes and intrapsychic conflicts and hence cannot or should not be treated directly with the hope of cure or significant personality reorganization. By contrast, an increasingly influential group side with Eysenck, Wolpe, Skinner, Festinger, and others who assert or imply that symptomatic treatment is all that is necessary or effective and that the underlying causes are irrelevant.

Perhaps the most practical approach is one which takes into account the holistic nature of personality and the unique qualities of the individual case. In some personality structures or kinds of personality organizations symptom removal results in the most profound personality reorganization and virtual cure of the patient, while in others it makes little difference in the total personality configuration or in the eventual outcome of the therapy. In certain kinds of fragile, vulnerable structures, removal of the symptom can even precipitate more serious personality decompensation or psychotic breakdown.

Adler (Ansbacher and Ansbacher, 1956) always asked what purpose the symptom served in the personality economy of the individual and what it prevented the person from doing. Freud (1953) regarded the symptom as a manifestation of deep, unconscious motivations which had to be brought back into consciousness to effect cure. Theories concerning symptoms and their significance in psychotherapy abound, depending upon the kinds of patients from whom the clinician researcher's experiences and data were derived. Thus, Freud's theoretical model of psychoanalysis was based mostly on painstaking work with hysterics and related kinds of personality structure, while some of the neoanalytic models such as the Sullivanian were derived more from obsessive-compulsive and borderline schizophrenic patients. Rogers has recently pointed out that in surveying the dozens of approaches to psychotherapy there is no agreement on

> whether the goal is removal of symptoms, reorganization of personality, curing of a disease, or adjustment to the culture. . . . An experience which is seen by one therapist as healing, growth-promoting, helpful, is seen by another as none of these things (Rogers, 1963).

In deciding whether psychotherapy or treatment should be focused on symptoms, character structure, or the total personality in a particular case, consideration must be given to the personality organization or structure of the patient and the role or place of the symptom or symptoms in that structure. Of particular importance in evaluating this is the degree of flexibility or rigidity of the patient's ego boundaries. The principles of individualizing the place of the symptom or symptoms in the total personality configuration can be conceptualized through any of the systematic theories of personality. In terms of psychoanalytic theory, symptomatic complaints represent "ineffective compromises arrived at by the ego in its effort to re-establish psychological equilibrium" (Hollon & Zolik, 1962). In terms of perceptual theory the relevant concept is perceptual flexibility or the capacity to change one's perception of persons, objects, situations, and events. In accordance with this criterion, those symptoms which increase or decrease perceptual flexibility or rigidity have profound effects on personality change, while those that do not are of superficial importance.

Specific neurotic reaction patterns will now be discussed in terms of symptomatology and psychodynamics.

ANXIETY REACTION

The cardinal symptom of the anxiety reaction is *diffuse anxiety,* often referred to as free-floating anxiety, which can be understood as a kind of danger signal and takes the form of fear of impending disaster, vague apprehension, general excitement, severe feelings of insecurity, and fear of dying. The bodily changes designed to meet normal stress situations are mobilized, resulting in such somatic complaints as heart palpitations, rapid pulse and other cardiac symptoms, pains of one kind or another, giddiness, and headaches. Many of the patients develop feelings of fatigue, insomnia, low mood, emotional instability, and inferiority feelings. Gastrointestinal upsets and breathing difficulties may also be present in acute attacks. Some patients develop panic states, indecisiveness, intolerance, suicidal ideas, subjective disturbing thoughts, loss of interest and motivation, and difficulties in focusing attention on the tasks at hand. The symptoms vary in intensity day by day, with acute attacks punctuating the milder chronic states. Many patients are relatively free of symptoms between attacks.

In this syndrome the symptoms represent the anxiety reaction itself with a minimum of defensive process. The attempt is made to ward off the anxiety by mobilizing to overcome the internal or external stress that brought it into the picture. The anxiety reaction may be explained in terms of the subject's feeling that the world is a threatening place and that he will be unable to meet the demands upon him. He is insecure and has acute feelings of inadequacy. Probably the most important predisposing factor for anxiety neurosis is a history of emotional insecurity. Somehow the patient has formed the unconscious assumption, on the basis of emotionally charged conflict experiences, that he is inadequate and will be unable to cope with the problems of life as they arise. Such an evaluation becomes self-perpetuating, and the individual is acutely and unrealistically sensitive to the slightest setback.

The acute anxiety reactions are most often precipitated by stress situations which mirror the ones that led to the faulty self-perception and perception of the world as a dangerous place. Among such stresses may be threats to security of status, livelihood, goals, or position, threatened break-through of forbidden or tabooed instinctual drives or of dangerous desires, and the stress of an unsatisfactory life situation in which the person sees no readily available way out or no satisfactory resolution of his conflict or little hope of achieving his goals.

DISSOCIATIVE REACTION

In this reaction the repressed impulse which is the source of the anxiety is deflected into or discharged by various symptomatic expressions such as depersonalization, dissociated or multiple personality, stupor, amnesia, fugue, dream state, and somnambulism. These conditions are, of course, dynamically related to the conversion reactions, but the expression is on the behavioral level rather than in terms of somatic compliance, and this merits consideration as a separate reaction

DEPERSONALIZATION

This is a state in which a person loses the feeling of his own reality. Everything seems dreamlike, and actions of oneself or others are watched with indifferent detachment. This results from the too great permeability or weakness in the boundary between the ego and the outer world and a consequent confusion about what comes from the ego and what stems from the outside world. The feeling of unreality, like loss of identity, may occur in organic conditions such as delirium, head injury, or diseases of the nervous system as well as in psychosis or psychoneurosis. Any condition in which there is weakness or obliteration of the outer ego boundary results in difficulty in distinguishing ego from outer world; but in the psychosis and organic states both ego boundaries may be impaired, in contrast to neurosis, in which one is impaired while the other is compensated with defenses and extra cathexis.

AMNESIA

Along with depersonalization there may be amnesia or an inability, partial or total, to recall or identify past experience. In organic brain pathology there is an actual failure of retention and registration so that the material cannot be recovered. Amnesia of psychogenic origin, by contrast, is ordinarily limited to a failure to recall. The forgotten material is still in the preconscious or unconscious and can be elicited by hypnosis. A frequent precipitant of amnesia is a severe psychological shock or trauma.

In *amnesia* the individual often cannot recall identifying facts: his name, who he is, where he lives, or any other such information. He is usually aware of this inability and often expresses the desire to recall the forgotten material. The amnesia may be partial or complete. It may cover an entire period of time, or it may be restricted and apply to only a single person, locale, or event. A related problem is the misidentification of people, attributing the wrong name to a remembered face. Such a faulty identification is called a *paramnesia.*

FUGUE

In the so-called fugue state the individual may go on for quite a while functioning as an adequate new person, even perhaps assuming a new name and complete identity. He forgets altogether his previous history and takes on new patterns of living without any recall of his former life. This state may last for a short time or for years. The person reveals no concern about his previous life history and activities. When these do suddenly come back into consciousness, the neurotic may have no recollection of the fugue phase of his life, remembering only up to the point of the development of the fugue. He forgets completely his former life during the period of the fugue.

MULTIPLE PERSONALITY

The multiple personality may be considered a more extreme form of the type of dissociation seen in amnesias and fugues. Dual or multiple personalities are rare in clinical practice but do occur. Multiple personality is a dissociative reaction to stress in which two or more complete personalities are developed. Each personality has distinct, well-developed emotional and thought processes and is unique and relatively stable. The patient may shift from one personality to another at intervals varying in time. The personalities are often very different from each other, and each has no memory of what the other has done or thought. In some individuals one personality is dominant and functions on a conscious level while the other continues to function subconsciously. Here we have a *coconscious* personality. The coconscious personality is aware of the thoughts of the conscious one and of the realities in the outside world, but this is indicated only through some roundabout way like automatic writing. By contrast, the conscious personality usually is totally unaware of the coconscious personality.

SOMNAMBULISM

In somnambulism, the patient walks and carries out other motor activities while asleep. This is another type of hysterical dissociation and may occur nightly or irregularly. The varieties of dissociative reactions are made possible by the combination of repression and extreme suggestibility which we find in the hysterical personality structure and which are related to the conversion reactions, except that the patient avoids the stress, conflict, or unpleasant situation by forgetting or dissociating certain things instead of by developing an illness such as a hysterical paralysis.

A usual conflict in amnesia is the desire to get away from the stress situation opposed by a strict conscience that makes this solution unacceptable. The stress situation eventually becomes so unbearable that whole components of the personality and even the stress situation itself are repressed while a more pleasant pattern of life is substituted and lived out in the fugue state. In the multiple personality, which is an extreme development, the conflicting parts of the personality develop a high degree of autonomy and function almost as separate personalities in their own right.

CONVERSION REACTION

Laughlin defines conversion as

> the name for the unconscious process by which intrapsychic conflicts, which would otherwise give rise to anxiety, instead secure symbolic external expression. The consciously disowned ideas, plus the psychologic defenses against them, are transmuted or converted into a variety of physical, physiologic and psychologic symptoms (Laughlin, 1956, p. 241).

He outlines three types of conversions. The somatic conversion is defined as

> an emotional illness in which the consciously disowned impulses and/or other elements of the unconscious conflict over them are transmuted into symbolic somatic expression. The body symptoms which result serve to allay anxiety by maintaining repression and by seeking resolution of unconscious conflicts (*ibid.*, p. 242).

The physiologic conversions are

> a large group of psychogenic manifestations or illnesses in which the consciously disowned impulses and/or other elements of the unconscious conflict over them, are transmuted into *symbolic physiologic expression.* The functional symptoms which result serve to allay anxiety by maintaining repression and by seeking resolution, or some relief from the pressure, of the unconscious conflicts (*ibid.*).

Laughlin defines psychologic conversions as

> a large group of psychogenic manifestations or illnesses, in which the consciously disowned impulses, and/or other elements of the unconscious conflicts over them, are transmuted into *symbolic psychologic expression.* The psychologic symptoms which result serve to allay anxiety by maintaining repression and by seeking resolution, or some relief from the pressure, of the unconscious conflicts (*ibid.*).

In the conversion reactions the repressed material finds its outlet somatically in physical symptoms. This results in a bodily expression or language. Conversion reactions may simulate a wide range of organic illnesses, and the specific symptoms that occur are numerous and varied. The reaction may be understood as a neurotic defense in which symptoms of some organic impairment appear without actual organic pathology. The symptoms include loss of sensory and motor functions, disturbances of movement and activity, visceral symptoms, and a number of gross and occasionally bizarre expressions. Laughlin reports:

> Herein are included instances of motor paralysis in which the reflexes are active and the innervation remains demonstrably intact. Large areas of sensory loss are seen which may not conform to anatomic distribution,

e.g., glove or stocking types of anesthesia. Impairment or loss of function of the special senses is seen on a hysterical basis. Dyskinesias are seen, with various movement and coordination disturbances, tics, convulsions, and fainting. Often symptoms are less gross and dramatic, however, and instead of a paralyzed arm, the arm may be weak. Aphonia is not uncommon, and hysterical pain in various bodily areas is frequent. Hysterical vomiting, dysphagia, and globus hystericus are encountered. Instead of symptoms, or in addition to them, certain rather typical hysterical character traits may be observed (Laughlin, 1956).

Among the sensory conversion symptoms are *anesthesias* or losses of sensitivity, *hypoesthesias* or partial losses of sensitivity, *hyperesthesias* or excessive sensitivity, and *paresthesias* or exceptional sensations such as tingling. Blindness, deafness, loss of touch, and pain sensitivity in various parts of the body, as well as occasional loss of the sense of smell, are examples of the anesthesias that may occur. Loss of pain sensitivity is referred to as an *analgesia*. A wide range of sensory symptoms may occur on a conversion basis.

The motor symptoms of a conversion hysterical nature are so varied and numerous that they will not be covered in detail here. Loss or disturbances in motor ability of various muscles may occur, although actual paralyses usually involve a single limb, such as a leg or an arm. Occasionally a *hemiplegia* is seen in which the entire left or right side of the body is affected. The loss of function may be selective and related to the patient's occupation, as in *aphonia* in a singer. Among the most numerous motor symptoms are tremors or shaking and trembling of muscles and *tics* or unconscious muscular twitches. *Contractures* may also occur, involving the flexion and extension of fingers and/or toes or rigidity of the knee and/or elbow joints. The contractures and paralyses may result in walking disturbances. An example is *astasia-abasia,* a disorganized walk with the legs wobbling about in every direction.

Some patients show disturbances in expressive speech, such as *aphonia* or diminution of speech to a whisper and *mutism* or complete inability to speak. Occasionally one sees cases of hysterical *convulsions* or *fits* resembling epileptic seizures but distinguishable from them by the fact that the patient does not usually bite his tongue, injure himself, or suffer incontinence. His pupillary reflex to light remains unaffected. The convulsions in the hysterics usually occur in the presence of other people.

Among the visceral symptoms are headache, globus hystericus, sensations of choking, breathing difficulties, cold and clammy extremities, nausea, vomiting, belching, and a kaleidoscopic array of assorted vague pains and aches. Such things as persistent hiccoughing and sneezing occur in some patients. In *anorexia nervosa,* the patient loses the appetite for food, cannot keep food down, may not be able to swallow food, and thus becomes emaciated through limitation of nourishment.

Hysterics have been known to simulate a large variety of illnesses such as tuberculosis, appendicitis, surgical illnesses, etc. It is important to distinguish between hysterical and organic disturbances. Some of the criteria to be used are the *belle indifférence* of the hysteric in relation to his symptom, the frequent failure of the dysfunction to follow a correct anatomical or nerve distribution pattern, contradictions such as the person who is hysterically blind but avoids bumping into persons or objects, and the susceptibility of the symptoms to removal by hypnosis or suggestion.

There is almost always a secondary gain in the conversion reaction so that the patient's illness enables him to avoid or solve some problem or conflict. The symptoms prevent him from having to face the traumatic situation, bring him sympathy, and enable him to control others. More specifically the symptoms may serve any or all of the following purposes: (1) removal of the patient from an unpleasant or traumatic situation; (2) regaining of attention, concern, or status or the patient's lost position as the center of attention and affection; (3) self-punishment to alleviate guilt; (4) punishment of others, making them feel that their inconsiderate treatment made the patient sick; (5) perpetuation of actual physical or organic illness hysterically after the organic condition has cleared up to exploit the illness for unconscious gains; (6) receipt of monetary compensation when covered by insurance; and (7) iatrogenically induced or symptomatology discussed by the physician which is absorbed due to the suggestibility of the hysteric.

Conversion hysterical reactions sometimes

occur in "epidemic" form, with many suggestible patients participating in the outbreak of symptoms.

PHOBIC REACTION

This is persistent, morbid, and unreasonable fear exaggerated out of proportion to the danger of the dreaded object or situation. The apparent stimulus for the phobia or the object feared pathologically may be and usually is symbolic of some unconscious underlying dread for which it has been substituted in order to channel the anxiety into less traumatic directions. Phobias may be developed in relation to a large variety of situations and objects. The technical term designating each phobia is formed by adding an appropriate prefix to the stem "phobia" as in *claustrophobia* (fear of small or enclosed places), *agorophobia* (fear of open spaces), *acrophobia* (fear of heights), *algophobia* (fear of pain), *cardiophobia* (fear of heart attack), *hematophobia* (fear of blood), *pyrophobia* (fear of fire), *cancerophobia* (fear of cancer), *thanatophobia* (fear of death), and a host of others.

The phobia serves as a means of circumscribing anxiety in that as long as the individual avoids the dreaded situation or object he is relatively free of anxiety. He must confine his reactions to the restrictions and limitations imposed by the phobia; then no emotional symptoms are aroused. When he is, however, exposed to the object or situation which he fears, he experiences an acute emotional reaction or panic syndrome including such symptoms as rapid heartbeat, tremor, cold perspiration, dyspnea, and faintness or feelings of weakness. Thus, a patient suffering from acrophobia usually goes to great effort to avoid heights even when it is essential for him to take an elevator, for example. The patient usually admits the irrationality of his fear but cannot overcome it.

Patients suffering from specific phobias most often suffer additional neurotic symptoms such as dizzy spells, feelings of inadequacy, gastrointestinal upsets, back pains, headaches, hysterical faintness, etc. Phobias have been recognized as a frequent part of the symptomatology of anxiety hysteria (Gutheil, 1959), in contrast to obsessions which occur in the obsessive-compulsive personality.

While a phobia could develop out of a simple conditioned fear reaction, and Wolpe (1958) has stated that phobias can be eliminated by reciprocal inhibition, most phobic reactions represent an actual displacement of the anxiety to some symbolic object or idea so that the patient remains completely unaware of the real source of his anxiety and fear. Phobias often serve a protective function by keeping the patient from situations in which his repressed impulses, sexual or aggressive, might become dangerous. The anxiety is displaced. The thing feared consciously is not the basic or the original cause of his anxiety or fear. Some patients have a variety of phobias. Often phobias are related to guilt feelings and fear of punishment. As Coleman states, "It is not uncommon for certain types of predisposed personalities who have been rigidly trained in sex morals to develop syphilophobia and mysophobia after engaging in what is to them completely unacceptable sexual behavior" (1950, p. 196). Friedman emphasizes that phobias "are par excellence the neuroses of childhood" (1959, p. 309) and that separation anxiety seems to be responsible for a variety of phobic reactions which in recent years have received a great deal of attention under the general heading of "school phobia." According to Fenichel (1945), phobias may lead to various secondary gains, such as increased attention, sympathy, and assistance or being able to dominate the behavior of others.

OBSESSIVE-COMPULSIVE REACTION

The obsessive-compulsive neurosis involves the concomitant presence of both *obsessions* reflecting too permeable an ego-id boundary and *compulsions* resulting from too rigid an ego–outer world boundary. Where obsessions predominate, compulsive behavior is almost always present; and when compulsions are most marked, obsessional fears and doubts are always found. In those cases in which the obsessions are the major manifestations, the neurosis is usually more severe, more regressive, and closer to possible psychosis, while in those with more compulsive behavior (compensatory defenses) the condition is milder but more fixed in the character structure. This results from the differing cathexes of the ego boundaries as described in the model for obsessive-compulsive neurosis presented earlier in this chapter.

The *obsessions*, which are most troublesome to the individual afflicted by them, are persistent, unwelcome ideas which the patient recognizes as morbid but which continue to enter consciousness and to disturb him. These ideas may be self-accusatory and accusatory to others and sometimes border on paranoid delusions. Obsessions may be sexual in nature, representing unacceptable sexual ideas and drives that keep entering consciousness and invading the ego without being "acted out." Obsessions of aggression occur with some frequency, such as the recurrent idea that a mother might have about killing or poisoning her child. A patient may have the obsessive idea that someone is trying to or will attempt to kill him. Sometimes obsessions take a metaphysical turn and involve preoccupations with death and burning in hell. Most often the obsessions center around unacceptable promptings from within which enter consciousness as persistent ideas.

The compulsions which usually accompany obsessions protect the patient against the acting out of the obsessive idea. The patient experiences much conscious anxiety about the obsessions and has fears that he will not be able to control them. Often he is overcome with feelings of helplessness, inadequacy, and self-doubts. At times the obsessional neurotic may feel unreal or wonder whether this could be happening to him, that he should have such terrible thoughts. Besides the secondary anxiety the individual develops compulsive doubting, particularly with regard to the fact of the obsession but also in reference to many everyday decisions.

This neurotic syndrome may be *mild* in form, consisting of obsessional preoccupations which are slightly disabling or of increasing severity up to completely disabling obsessional neurosis. If the condition increases in severity and continues unchecked, a decompensation into a psychosis such as paranoid schizophrenia may result.

Compulsions are irresistible and persistent tendencies to engage in senseless or meaningless motor acts or behaviors. They may range from simple reactions like stepping over the cracks in sidewalks or doodling while listening to a lecture to complex integrated forms of behavior like *kleptomania* (the irresistible impulse to steal) or *pyromania* (the irresistible impulse to set fires) and the like. The obsessional idea connected with the compulsion may be carried over or forced back onto the unconscious by the compulsion.

Most commonly, the compulsion to perform an act which appears senseless or even ridiculous to others is very strong, and the failure to carry it out creates anxiety. An example would be a compulsion to wash one's hands repeatedly because of the underlying obsession of sexual guilt or symbolic contamination with dirt or germs. The compulsion, like the obsession, isolates the affect of the unconscious conflict by displacing it to an indifferent act or object. For example, the hand-washing compulsion, like the compulsion to count money or the compulsion to touch every round object, becomes an act through which the energy connected with the repressed and forbidden acts of looking and touching is discharged with less anxiety. *Isolation of affect* and the attendant defense mechanisms of *rationalization*, *intellectualization*, *magical thinking*, and *denial* are common mechanisms in the obsessive-compulsive reaction.

Compulsions, like obsessions, tend to become chronic and to be connected with some anxiety and much doubting. The chronic cases gradually become structured more rigidly into the obsessive-compulsive character structure, while acute decompensations merge into borderline schizophrenia.

The psychodynamics involved in obsessive and compulsive reactions are quite intricate, as shown in the excellent explanations offered by Fenichel (1945). In obsessional reactions the affect connected with a repressed emotional experience is disconnected or isolated and transferred or displaced to some less embarrassing or relatively harmless object. This object, however, is still related symbolically or otherwise to the more elemental or primal emotional experience. Thus, the source of the individual's obsession of being infected by touching doorknobs may go back to masturbation guilt. An obsession may be a transformed self-derogation for some tabooed yet wished-for aggressive or sexual act. Freud has demonstrated how isolation of affect from its original significance reduces anxiety. According to Freud (1953), the severe obsessive doubting is derived from the late anal period when ambivalence is quite prevalent. During the late anal period the bipolar struggles between hostility and libido and between homosexuality and heterosexuality are quite marked. Conflict between anal-sadistic id urges and superego in the obsessional neurotic is constantly being held in tenuous balance. On the *Rorschach* test the obsessive-compulsive usually shows an *ambiequal experience* balance between human movement responses, representative of the inner life, and color responses, representative of the external stimuli or environmental pressures. The compulsive acts which accompany or follow the obsessive thoughts serve to counteract or neutralize the guilt which the obsession arouses and are an example of a magical defense in which the ritual absolves one of the guilt.

According to Rado, in the etiology of obsessive-compulsive behavior the ultimate psychodynamically ascertainable factor is rage. He states:

> Obsessive behavior is based on a predisposition which is acquired in childhood and includes five clearly discernible factors: (1) overstrong rage; (2) guilty fear made stronger by retroflexion of the larger part of repressed rage; (3) stronger-than-average residues of primordial omnipotence that make rage strong and its paradoxical retroflexion possible; (4) relative pleasure deficiency in the area of genital orgasm, with its consequent enfeeblement of genital love and affection—a deficiency that makes it imperative to control rage by retroflexion; (5) intelligent foresight leading to realistic fears (Rado, 1959, p. 338).

The conflict between good and evil is prominent in the psychodynamics of the obsessive-compulsive who, as the condition progresses, becomes more repressed and concerned with the typical conflict of childhood between the wish to be naughty and the need to be good. An important mechanism is the phenomenon of *undoing* or the performance of compulsive acts which neutralize the effect of forbidden wishes. This enables the person to reduce some of the anxiety which the threatened rearousal of the conflict awakens. Compulsive acts protect against the anxiety aroused by the obsessions and preserve the ego in a more intact condition.

Some examples of the undoing quality of compulsions are compulsions to cleanliness which protect against the guilt feelings connected with infantile sexuality and especially masturbation.

DEPRESSIVE REACTION (NEUROTIC)

Since "Depression" (below) deals exclusively with the depressive reactions, the present chapter will cover very briefly the neurotic depressions in which the anxiety is partially relieved and soothed down by self-depreciation and depression. The neurotic-depressive reaction is also known as a situational depression or reactive depression because it is often ushered in by a current situation such as a loss sustained by the patient. The condition is frequently associated with deep-seated guilt feelings involving remorse over past failures or wrongdoing. The severity of the depression is often proportionate to the extent of the patient's ambivalence in relating to the lost object or person as well as to the extent of the loss itself and its realistic proportions. In the neurotic form of depression the prognosis for recovery is generally good.

The neurotically depressed individual gives the outward general appearance of being dejected, discouraged, and sad. He may have an extremely sorrowful expression on his face or a dull, masklike one. He seems to see only the dark side of everything, may stay by himself, seems uninterested in any pleasurable activities, and may just sit and stare. Although his thinking is not slowed up, he may complain of difficulties in concentrating. He may have trouble sleeping, feelings of restlessness, irritability, and inward tension. Vague hostile feelings may be detected.

The person subject to neurotic-depressive reactions usually has marked feelings of inadequacy and sees the world as a frightening, threatening place even before the event precipitating the depression. Such events may involve the death of a loved person, *loss of a sex object, loss of prestige,* loss of a bodily function through illness or accident, a work setback, or other failure involving guilt feelings. *One often finds that the particular event has a traumatic effect because of a prior conspicuous psychic overcharge (overcathexis) of certain objective values, such as money, prestige, or the like.* The vulnerable person, whose reaction to such losses or disappointments is exaggerated so that the depressive feelings last longer and are more severe, is usually hypersensitive to ordinary mood swings.

Dynamically the neurotic depression is related to underlying or repressed hostility, highly ambivalent feelings, and guilt. The expiation of the guilt or the covering over and repression of the hostility may be accomplished by the depressive reaction. The patient often uses his symptoms unconsciously to elicit sympathy and favorable reactions from others.

OTHER PSYCHONEUROTIC REACTIONS

Under this heading we shall discuss briefly the asthenic, hypochondriacal, and somatization reactions which are not now considered as major classifications in the current *Diagnostic and Statistical Manual* of the American Psychiatric Association (1960, 13th printing). A complete coverage of the *psychosomatic disorders* is given in "The Psychosomatic Approach" (above).

In the *asthenic reaction* the major symptoms are various aches and pains in a context of chronic physical and mental fatigue. It usually occurs in young adults and particularly in overburdened individuals such as "the frustrated housewife." There seems to be a lack of energy to carry out ordinary and even minor tasks. There is difficulty in concentrating, and therefore tendencies toward distraction before an activity can be successfully completed. Although much time is spent sleeping in the effort to feel more rested and refreshed, the patient wakes up fatigued, and this gets worse as the day proceeds. In spite of the general malaise and weariness, many neurasthenics selectively show a vigorous amount of energy and endurance in activities they really enjoy, like tennis, golf, or other games. Their lack of enthusiasm and "tiredness" is almost always manifested in relation to vocational pursuits or routine work duties. Accompanying the fatigue symptoms may be a variety of somatic complaints such as headaches, digestive disturbances, etc.

Neurasthenia or the asthenic reaction rarely occurs without some marked obsessional or hysterical content. However, everything seems to be clustered around the feeling of fatigue and diminished capacity to work. The asthenic reaction and the anxiety neurosis were referred to by Freud as the "true neuroses" because of the directness of the symptomatology, and he attributed the syndrome to sexual frustration as the underlying cause. Today the prevalent point of view is that it results from sustained emotional stress which the person has been unable to cope with adequately.

Related to the asthenic reaction is the so-called *hypochondriacal reaction* in which the major symptom is morbid concern about one's body or the state of one's health. It occurs most often in the fourth and fifth decades of life. The patients may complain of somatic discomfort of one kind or another in the stomach area, the chest, the head, or any other bodily region, but often they have trouble giving an accurate description of symptoms such as to enable a physician to make an adequate medical diagnosis. The symptomatology may keep shifting, and the patient is constantly discovering new and additional manifestations of disease. The hypochondriac often attempts his own diagnoses, which may be very unusual in terms of the facts of medical pathology, and he will be searching constantly for new treatments or cures mentioned in newspapers or magazines.

In the hypochondriac the normal interest shown by most people in their bodily functioning is exaggerated to a pathological concern and preoccupation. Like the asthenic patient, the hypochondriacal patient is reacting to disappointing life experiences and situations. The reaction protects the patient from his feelings of failure. The secondary gain element is strong in this reaction. Hypochondriacs often control the behavior of the other people around them. Often the neurosis develops in a background of having been brought up by hypochondriacal parents, a history of early illness or injury, and parental overconcern about the child's health.

Dynamically hypochondria may be viewed as a psychological defense used by the patient unconsciously to avoid responsibilities. If he is considered ill, he need not work hard nor attempt to solve his own problems. He receives sympathy instead of blame. He may be cared for and given special privileges.

In some instances, a hypochondriacal reaction may be superimposed upon an actual illness or injury of an organic nature which the patient uses as a core around which to develop the "additional" or exaggerated symptoms which serve him as a defense against feelings of failure or as an escape from responsibility. He evades the challenge of life by giving up and resigning himself to his seemingly incurable ailment.

In the *somatization reaction* the individual actually experiences somatic symptoms or complaints on a psychogenic basis as in the *psychogenic gastrointestinal reaction, psychogenic cardiovascular reaction, psychogenic genitourinary reaction, psychogenic respiratory reaction,* and *psychogenic skin reaction* (see "The Psychosomatic Approach," above). In these reactions the anxiety is relieved by channeling the original impulse through the autonomic nervous system into organ symptoms and complaints. The *Diagnostic and Statistical Manual: Mental Disorders* indicates, "These disorders are here given a separate grouping between psychotic and psychoneurotic reactions, to allow more accurate accumulation of data concerning their etiology, course, and relation to other mental disorders" (American Psychiatric Association, 1960, p. 29). The *Manual* states further,

> Differentiation is made from conversion reactions by (1) involvement of organs and viscera innervated by the autonomic nervous system, hence not under full voluntary control or perception; (2) failure to alleviate anxiety; (3) physiological rather than symbolic origin of symptoms; (4) frequent production of structural changes which may threaten life.

DIAGNOSIS

Since all of Part 3 of this *Handbook* deals with diagnostic methods, we shall confine this section to the specific problems in differential diagnosis presented by the psychoneuroses, including: diagnostic methods of differentiating some neurotic from borderline psychotic reactions, organic disorders, and normal reaction to stress; diagnostic differentiations within the psychoneuroses themselves; methods of delineating diagnostically the psychodynamics of neurosis in each specific case as a preparation for therapy.

The choice of the proper therapy or treatment for a particular neurosis and the individualization of the treatment require an accurate and psychodynamic identification and description of each particular patient's neurotic reaction pattern. To secure this it is generally advocated that a complete psychodiagnostic work-up be instituted, including a personal interview, a full case history (physical, mental, social), the administration of a battery of psychological tests (including projective techniques and an intelligence scale), a physical and neurological examination, and such other specialized additional diagnostic procedures as seem indicated.

Since, as has been pointed out, the hysterical neurotic shows damage in the ego–outside world or outer ego boundary while the obsessive-compulsive shows weakness in the ego-id or inner boundary and the ambulatory or borderline schizophrenic shows damage in both boundaries, there is often some overlapping symptomatology attributable to the weak boundary. The possibility of the obsessive-compulsive neurotic decompensating, in some cases, through a crumbling of the defenses in the compensated outer boundary presents an urgent problem of differentiating diagnostically between the severe obsessive-compulsive reaction and the early paranoid schizophrenic. Are the obsessions likely to be "acted out" as delusions because the defensive compulsions are losing their strength as defenses? For this differentiation the Rorschach examination and a variety of other projective techniques have been found helpful in addition to the other diagnostic methods.

Another difficult and frequent differentiation that often needs diagnostic clarification is that between the anxiety hysteric with phobic symptoms and the ambulatory or borderline schizophrenic. Both may show histrionic displays of superficial and shallow emotions, feelings of unreality, depersonalization, dissociative phenomena, extreme suggestibility, loss of identity, and other symptoms related to the weak outer boundary. The strength of the repressive defense and of the inner ego boundary has to be assessed diagnostically as well as the availability of other defenses. Here again a complete diagnostic work-up by or with the aid of a clinical psychologist is necessary, utilizing interview, case history, and particularly projective techniques, including the Rorschach.

In the examples above, a mistake in diagnosis or a failure to differentiate the conditions could result in attempting an uncovering deep psychoanalysis with a vulnerable borderline psychotic with consequent danger of a complete or open psychotic breakdown.

Thus, one important function in differential diagnosis in the neuroses (see Part 3 "Differential Diagnosis") is that of ruling out the presence of psychosis. This usually involves the utilization of specialized diagnostic procedures and techniques, including interview, for detecting *paralogical thinking* (Kutash, 1957). Another problem in the diagnosis of psychoneurosis is the differentiation of organic from psychogenic conditions showing similar symptoms. For example, a patient may show symptoms of severe headache, "blackouts," visual disturbances, tics, and losses of sensation in the lower extremities. There may be a history of a fall resulting in a closed head injury with a short period of loss of consciousness. Some of the questions that arise may be: Is the patient suffering from epilepsy, and did the fall result originally from an epileptic seizure during which a secondary injury to the head occurrred? Was it a hysterical blackout? Was the fall due to accidental causes, and do the symptoms arise from the head injury or concussion? Are we dealing with a *conversion reaction*, an *organic brain disorder*, an *epileptic disorder*, or a case of *vascular disturbance?* It is apparent that a complete diagnostic work-up is needed, including—in addition to the routine procedures like interview, case history, physical and neurological examination, psychodiagnostic testing, and intellectual appraisal—such specialized procedures as electroencephalographic studies, cardiovascular and other tests for circulatory disturbances, and the like. To establish a positive psychogenic diagnosis it is not enough to rule out organic findings but in addition the Rorschach, other projective techniques, and other psychological results must show definite evidence of psychoneurosis with a psychodynamic picture that fits in. A study of the defenses, in the case of hysteria, must show evidence of severe repression and rigidity in the ego-id boundary, while the ego–outer world boundary must be poorly cathected.

The differentiations diagnostically within the psychoneuroses themselves must deal with the symptomatology and the syndrome presented by the symptom picture, the defensive system, and the defense mechanisms in relation to the handling of anxiety, the identification of the repetitive rigidity or neurotic pattern, the characteristic perceptual distortion, the estimate of the range of perceptual flexibility, the condition of the ego boundaries, and the psychodynamic conflicts involved. The different kinds of psychoneurotic reactions, such as the dissociative reaction or the obsessive-compulsive reaction, when they are clear-cut, can be readily detected by a complete psychodiagnostic study which should include the symptomatology, history, test findings, and psychodynamics. The differentiation of the neurotic reactions on the Rorschach, TAT, and Wechsler-Bellevue are well presented in Schafer's book (1948).

When there seem to be admixtures of neurotic features reflecting what appears to be a mixed neurosis it is important to differentiate in terms of whether this is a *pan neurosis* or *pseudoneurotic schizophrenia.* Some other challenging problems are *decompensating* psychoneurotic structures and the so-called *pseudopsychopathic neurotic states* and *superimposed neuroses* on other preexisting conditions such as organic disorders.

In the psychoneuroses the most important diagnostic step is not necessarily the labeling of the specific type of neurosis but the living psychodynamic description of the neurotic personality of the particular individual under study with all of its uniqueness and characteristics. Each neurotic is an individual different from all other neurotics in important respects, even when they are classified together. Some neurotics are more flexible than others, some are better defended, some are of higher intelligence, and some are more motivated toward improvement. These features should be stressed in individual diagnosis.

The unique and particularly important contribution of the clinical psychologist to the diagnosis and psychodynamic study of the psychoneuroses is in the skillful use of psychological tests and techniques (Part 3, this *Handbook*). The central problem in the use of psychological testing is in aiding the choice of psychotherapeutic approach and prognosticating results. The Rorschach examination has proved particularly useful (Kutash, 1951). A more recent method of aiding in the estimation of severity of psychoneurosis consists of a *Perceptual Flexibility Battery* (Kutash, 1961). Another important aspect of diagnosis consists of the estimation of motivation for treatment or psychotherapy (Dengrove & Kutash, 1950). The psychologist's role in clinical practice in terms of the diagnostic, prognostic, and therapeutic functions, particularly in relation to the psychoneuroses, began to be emphasized after World War II and was given widespread recognition in the Veterans Administration (Kutash, 1947).

While a great deal of clinical research has

been done and is in progress, there is still need for refinement of diagnostic techniques to help match therapeutic methods to psychoneurotic patterns and individual patients so as to bring about better psychotherapeutic results.

PROGNOSIS

While prognosis is an individual matter and must be estimated or evaluated for each patient individually, some general statements may be made on the prognosis for psychoneurosis as distinguished from psychosis, character disorders, and organic brain syndromes. In general, the psychoneuroses have the best prognoses of all the emotional disorders and by many authorities are considered to be behavioral difficulties in living happily rather than diseases. In the psychoneuroses the ego is intact, although one of the major boundaries may be weakly cathected while the other is overcompensated with defenses. In this sense it is an effective protection against more severe personality disorganization.

In estimating prognosis in an individual case, the following factors must be taken into account: severity of symptomatology, duration of the neurosis, manner of onset, condition of the ego boundaries, rigidity and/or flexibility of the personality structure, age and intelligence of the patient, his life situation, motivation for treatment, capacity for insight, the type of neurotic reaction, the variety and strength of defenses, the handling of anxiety, and the general health of the person.

All the psychoneuroses are considered curable and amenable to treatment or psychotherapy, and some clear up or improve spontaneously with changes in the patient's life situation. Severity of symptomatology as a predictor of outcome has some value but needs further research in controlled studies. However, if severity of symptomatology is defined in terms of duration and chronicity one might generalize that the longer the duration of the symptoms and the more chronic, the poorer the prognosis, while the shorter the duration of the symptoms and the more acute, the better the prognosis. Acute, dramatic symptomatology, as in the amnesias and hysterical states, does not necessarily portend a poor prognosis but on the contrary often reflects a good outcome, particularly with treatment. Duration of the neurotic reaction is one of the best prognosticative indexes and usually goes along with rigidity of the personality structure and the defenses. Even conversion reactions, which generally have a relatively favorable prognosis in treatment, have a poor prognosis if of long duration. If the patient shows an optimal range of perceptual flexibility the prognosis with any kind of treatment is good. A measure for this is the *perceptual flexibility* index, or PFI, which has been devised by Ittelson and Kutash and their collaborators (1961) and is still in process of fuller evaluation. The condition of the ego boundaries is also closely related to prognosis. In considering whether the neurotic reaction or character neurosis will yield to treatment, motivation, degree of anxiety, age, intelligence, etc., are of the utmost importance. In general, neurotic cases that have been permitted to become chronic have a poor prognosis.

As Kardiner has said concerning the traumatic war neuroses, the reason for the poor prognosis in chronic cases is that

> the subject develops a pattern of existence suitable to his reduced resources. The longer this consolidation is permitted to go on, the harder it is to dissolve. New patterns of gratification become organized and are difficult to break up. The chief obstacle in these chronic cases is the complete collapse of self-esteem. These subjects no longer have any pride in themselves or in their accomplishments. Hence, without being criminal, they expect nothing from themselves, and take from society quite ruthlessly (Kardiner, 1959, p. 254).

Conversion reactions have a generally favorable prognosis, although some cases of conversion reaction have a less favorable prognosis, such as those in which the secondary gain is so great that the patient cannot give up the symptom, which may be the sole possible emotional answer to a real-life situation for which better solutions are not available. The existence and depth of dependency needs must be taken into consideration. The factors of chronicity and dependency needs also enter into the prognosis of phobic patients, who vary widely in response to treatment. The anxiety reactions are among those with the most favorable prognoses when psychotherapy is instituted.

Obsessive-compulsive reactions and patients who have rigid character defenses designed to protect the ego from the threatening world or the so-called character neuroses have a poorer prognosis and require longer-term therapy.

TREATMENT

The psychoneuroses are the most treatable of the emotional disorders by analytical psychotherapy and/or psychoanalysis, which are still the treatments of choice. Recent progress in the development of newer and more streamlined variants of the classical model of psychoanalysis and the integration of analytic knowledge with many other kinds of therapeutic procedures have resulted in the availability of new varieties of individual and group psychotherapy which have become increasingly effective with psychoneurotic patients. A great deal of clinical and laboratory research is in progress designed to fit the particular therapeutic approaches to the individual case or type of psychoneurotic reaction. More refinement is needed in choice of method of psychotherapy. Since Part 5 of this *Handbook* gives a full exposition of methods of treatment of all varieties, we might state here that all the methods described in the first nine chapters have been applied with good effect in the treatment of the psychoneuroses.

In the anxiety reactions treatment can be aimed either at relief of the anxiety or at the more long-term goal of fundamental personality reorganization. For the relief of anxiety a host of methods are currently in use; examples are various tranquilizers and drug therapies; somatic treatments of one kind or another, such as shock treatment and carbon dioxide inhalation; and a great many suggestive and supportive techniques, including hypnosis and conditioning. However, their use is advocated only on an emergency basis, such as in acute anxiety and panic states. The symptomatic measures may be used as adjuvants by psychotherapists in conjunction with more fundamental psychotherapy.

In insightful analytical therapy which aims at fundamental personality reorganization the anxiety level must be watched and controlled by the therapist much as the physician watches and controls the fever in the management of an infectious illness. He must quickly become aware of the occurrences and factors that precipitate anxiety in a particular patient and what measures relieve the anxiety so that he can control this while the deeper uncovering therapy or character-analytic therapy is in process. For some patients, relief of the anxiety may permit deeper personality reorganization so that repetitive anxiety attacks may be avoided, but for most a therapy of greater depth is needed.

The various hysterical patterns, such as dissociative, hypochondriacal, asthenic, phobic, and conversion reactions, are all amenable to psychoanalytic therapy, including classical psychoanalysis. In fact, the classical model of psychoanalysis was developed by Freud for the hysterical type of neurosis and has as its major aim the uncovering and bringing into consciousness of the repressed material from the unconscious, thus relieving the rigidity of the ego-id boundary and improving the efficiency of the ego functions attributable to the ego–outer world boundary. The classical model may be streamlined for some patients, as in hypnoanalysis and short-term psychotherapy. The obsessive-compulsive reaction requires a character-analytic technique as developed by Reich and others with a dearmoring of the ego–outer world boundary. In the neurotic-depressive reaction, relationship therapy, in which the therapist's empathy, sincerity, and permissiveness play a prominent role, offers excellent chances of success. The overstrict superego of the patient must be counteracted by the therapist as a superego substitute that permits the incorporation of more palatable standards by which to evaluate guilt. The therapist must conduct himself with strength and kindness in a context of active psychotherapy. In acute dangerous depressions, drugs, shock, and other measures may need to be used in the initial phases of treatment.

In the treatment of the neuroses, flexibility in the psychotherapeutic approach is of the utmost importance. While training in a particular system or school of psychoanalysis is certainly a necessary prerequisite, as well as personal and control analyses, the therapist must also develop flexibility of approach and expose himself to all available variants of analytic method to ensure maximum effectiveness in individual cases. The therapist in training often perceives therapy in a certain prescribed way as a result of his first supervised experiences with it from a particular school of therapy and then could conceivably attempt to fit all subsequent patients into this perceptual model of therapy. Fortunately, well-analyzed therapists will modify their perception of the therapeutic process with each patient instead of distorting the patient to fit the original assumptions about therapy. Thus, experimentation with new techniques and methods of treatment, innovations in methodology and approach, should be encouraged in the well-trained therapist. Group therapy has proved particularly valuable in the treatment of neuroses.

The psychoneuroses are the most prevalent and the most treatable of human problems, and with the current burgeoning of varieties of approach to therapy greater numbers of psychoneurotic individuals are being benefited. The study of the individual case and the gearing of the therapeutic strategy to the individual is still the most effective approach.

REFERENCES

Adler, A. *Individual psychology and its results in the practice and theory of individual psychology.* New York: Harcourt Brace, 1932.

American Psychiatric Association. *Diagnostic and statistical manual: mental disorders.* (13th printing.) 1960.

Ansbacher, H. L., & Ansbacher, R. R. *The individual psychology of Alfred Adler.* New York: Basic Books, 1956.

Arieti, S. *Interpretation of schizophrenia.* New York: Robert Brunner, 1955.

Brown, J. F. *Psychodynamics of abnormal behavior.* New York: McGraw-Hill, 1940.

Chrzanowski, G. Neurasthenia and hypochondriasis. In S. Arieti (Ed.), *American Handbook of Psychiatry.* New York: Basic Books, 1959. Chap. 13.

Cobb, S. *Foundations of neuropsychiatry.* (5th ed.) Baltimore: 1952.

Coleman, J. D. *Abnormal psychology and modern life.* New York: Scott, Foresman, 1950.

Dengrove, E., & Kutash, S. B. Why patients discontinue treatment in a mental hygiene clinic. *Amer. J. Psychother.*, 1950, **4**, 457–472.

Dollard, J., & Miller, N. E. *Personality and psychotherapy: An Analysis in Terms of Learning, Thinking and Culture.* New York: McGraw-Hill, 1950.

Dubois, C. *Les psychoneuroses et leur traitement moral.* Paris: Masson et Cie, 1904.

Dunlap, K. A revision of the fundamental law of habit. *Science,* 1928, **67**, 360.

Ellis, A. *Reason and emotion in psychotherapy.* New York: Lyle Stuart, 1962.

Eysenck, H. J. *Dynamics of anxiety and hysteria.* New York: Praeger, 1957.

Federn, P. *Ego psychology and the psychoses.* New York: Basic Books, 1952.

Fenichel, O. *The psychoanalytic theory of neurosis.* New York: Norton, 1945.

Ferenczi, S. *The problems and methods of psychoanalysis.* (M. Balint, Ed.) New York: Basic Books, 1955.

Festinger, L. *A theory of cognitive dissonance.* Evanston, Ill.: Row, Peterson, 1957.

Freud, S. *The problem of anxiety.* New York: Norton, 1936.

Freud, S. *Collected papers.* London: Hogarth Press, 1948.

Freud, S. *The complete psychological works of Sigmund Freud.* (Standard Ed.) London: Hogarth Press, 1953.

Friedman, P. The phobias. In S. Arieti (Ed.), *American handbook of psychiatry.* New York: Basic Books, 1959.

Fromm, E. *Escape from freedom.* New York: Farrar & Rinehart, Inc., 1941.

Fromm, E. *Man for himself.* New York: Rinehart, 1947.

Fromm, E. *The sane society.* New York: Rinehart, 1955.

Fromm, E. *The art of loving.* New York: Harper, 1956.

Fromm-Reichmann, F. *Principles of intensive psychotherapy.* Chicago: Univer. of Chicago Press, 1950.

Gantt, W. H. *Experimental basis for neurotic behavior.* New York: Hoeber-Harper, 1944.

Gutheil, E. A. Dreams as an aid in evaluating ego strength. *Amer. J. Psychother.*, 1958, **12**, 338–355.

Gutheil, E. A. Problems of therapy in obsessive-compulsive neurosis. *Amer. J. Psychother.*, 1959, **13**, 793–808.

Hebb, D. O. *The organization of behavior.* New York: Wiley, 1949.

Hilgard, E. R. *Theories of learning.* New York: Appleton-Century-Crofts, 1948.

Hilgard, E. R., & Marquis, D. G. *Conditioning and*

learning. New York: Appleton-Century-Crofts, 1940.

Hollon, T. H., & Zolik, E. S. Self-esteem and symptomatic complaints in the initial phase of psychoanalytically oriented psychotherapy. *Amer. J. Psychother.*, 1962, **16**, 83–93.

Horney, Karen. *The neurotic personality of our time*. New York: Norton, 1937.

Horney, Karen. *New ways in psychoanalysis*. New York: Norton, 1939.

Horney, Karen. *The collected works of. . . .* New York: Norton, 1963.

Hull, C. L. *Principles of behavior*. New York: Appleton-Century-Crofts, 1943.

Ittleson, W. H. *The Ames demonstrations in perception*. Princeton, N.J.: Princeton Univer. Press, 1952.

Ittelson, W. H. *The Ames demonstrations in perchanges in psychopathology*. New Brunswick, N.J.: Rutgers Univer. Press, 1961.

Ivey, E. P. Recent advances in diagnosis and treatment of phobias. *Amer. J. Psychother.*, 1959, **13**, 35–50.

Jacobi, J. *The psychology of Jung*. (Tr. K. W. Bash.) New Haven: Yale Univer. Press, 1943.

Jung, C. G. *The theory of psychoanalysis*. J. nerv. ment. Dis. Publishing Co., 1915.

Jung, C. G. *Collected papers on analytical psychology*. (Tr. Constance E. Long.) London: Moffat, Yard & Co., 1917.

Kardiner, A. Traumatic neuroses of war. In S. Arieti (Ed.), *American Handbook of Psychiatry*. New York: Basic Books, 1959, Chap. 12.

Karpf, F. B. *The psychology and psychotherapy of Otto Rank*. New York: Philosophical Library, 1953.

Kelly, G. A. *The psychology of personal constructs*. New York: Norton, 1955.

Kilpatrick, F. P. (Ed.) *Human behavior from the transactional point of view*. Hanover, N.H.: Institute for Associated Research, 1952.

Koffka, K. *Principles of gestalt psychology*. New York: Harcourt, Brace, 1935.

Kohler, W. *Gestalt psychology*. New York: Liveright, 1929.

Kutash, S. B. The psychologist's role in clinical practice. *J. clin. Psychol.*, 1947, **3**, 321–329.

Kutash, S. B. The Rorschach examination and psychotherapy. *Amer. J. Psychother.*, 1951, **5**, 405–410.

Kutash, S. B. Ambulatory (borderline) schizophrenia: psychodiagnostics and implications from psychological data. *Amer. J. Orthopsychiat.*, 1957, **27**, 667–676.

Kutash, S. B. Perceptual flexibility and mental health. In Ittelson, W. H., & Kutash, S. B. (Eds.), *Perceptual changes in psychopathology*. New Brunswick, N.J.: Rutgers Univer. Press, 1961, Ch. 2.

Kutash, S. B. Treatment of symptoms, perceptual flexibility, and ego boundaries. Paper read at Eastern Psychol. Ass., 1963.

Laughlin, H. P. *The neuroses in clinical practice*. Philadelphia: Saunders, 1956.

Lewin, K. *Principles of topological psychology*. New York: McGraw-Hill, 1936.

Liddell, A. S. Conditioned reflex method and experimental neurosis. In J. McV. Hunt (Ed.), *Personality and the behavior disorders*. New York: Ronald Press, 1944.

Maier, N. R. F., & Schneirla, T. C. Merchanisms in conditioning. *Psychological Review*, 1942, **49**, 117–134.

Malamud, W. Psychoneuroses. In *Encyclopedia of psychology*. New York: Philosophical Library, 1946. Pp. 608–620.

Masserman, J. H. *Behavior and neurosis*. Chicago: Univer. of Chicago Press, 1943.

Mowrer, O. H. *Psychotherapy theory and research*. New York: Ronald Press, 1953.

Mowrer, O. H. *Learning theory and behavior*. New York: Wiley, 1960.

Pavlov, I. P. *Lectures on conditioned reflexes* (Tr. G. V. Anrep.) London: Oxford Univer. Press, 1927.

Pepinsky, H. B., & Pepinsky, P. N. *Counseling theory and practice*. New York: Ronald Press, 1954.

Phillips, E. L. *Psychotherapy: a modern theory and practice*. Englewood Cliffs, N.J.: Prentice-Hall, 1956.

Rado, S. Obsessive behavior, so called obsessive-compulsive neurosis. In S. Arieti (Ed.), *American handbook of psychiatry*. New York: Basic Books, 1959.

Rank, O. *Will therapy; and truth and reality*. New York: Knopf, 1945.

Reich, W. *Character analysis*. New York: Orgone Institute Press, 1945.

Rogers, C. *Client-centered therapy*. New York: Houghton Mifflin, 1951.

Rogers, C. R. Psychotherapy today. *Amer. J. Psychother.*, 1963, **17**, 5–16.

Rosen, J. N. *Direct analysis.* New York: Grune & Stratton, 1953.

Rotter, J. B. *Social learning and clinical psychology.* Englewood Cliffs, N.J.: Prentice-Hall, 1954.

Schafer, R. *The clinical application of psychological tests: diagnostic summaries and case studies.* New York: International Universities Press, 1948.

Shaffer, L. F. The problem of psychotherapy. *Amer. Psychologist,* 1947, **2**, 459–467.

Shaw, F. J. Some postulates concerning psychotherapy. *J. consult. Psychol.,* 1948, **12**, 426–431.

Shoben, E. J. Some observations on psychotherapy and the learning process. In Mowrer, O. H. (Ed.), *Psychotherapy: theory and research.* New York: Ronald Press, 1953.

Skinner, B. F. *The behavior of organisms.* New York: Appleton-Century-Crofts, 1938.

Stekel, W. *Conditions of nervous anxiety and their treatment.* London: Routledge & Kegan Paul, 1950.

Sullivan, H. S. *The interpersonal theory of psychiatry.* (Helen S. Perry & Mary L. Gawel, Eds.) New York: Norton, 1953.

Thompson, C. *Psychoanalysis: evolution and development.* New York: Hermitage House, 1950.

Thorndike, E. L. Animal intelligence: an experimental study of the associative processes in animals. *Psychol. Rev. Monogr. Suppl.,* 1898, **2**, No. 8.

Watson, J. B. *Behavior: an introduction to comparative psychology.* New York: Holt, 1914.

Wertheimer, M. Untersuchungen zur Lehre von der Gestalt. *Psychol. Forsch.,* **4**, 301–350, 1923.

Wolman, B. B. The continuum hypothesis in neurosis and psychosis and the classification of mental disorders. Paper read at Eastern Psychol. Ass., 1959.

Wolman, B. B. *Mental disorders, their theory and classification* (in press), 1964.

Wolpe, J. *Psychotherapy of reciprocal inhibition.* Stanford: Stanford Univer. Press, 1958.

Woodworth, R. S. *Contemporary Schools of Psychology.* New York: Ronald Press, 1948.

Zucker, L. J. Ego weakness, ego defenses and ego strengthening techniques. *Amer. J. Psychother.,* 1959, **13**, 614–634.

34

Schizophrenia and Related Disorders

BENJAMIN B. WOLMAN

HISTORICAL REMARKS

Kraepelin and Bleuler

As early as 1674, a British brain anatomist described children who "passed into obtuseness and hebetude during adolescence." Esquirol believed that this "acquired idiocy" developed as a result of masturbation, head injury, etc.

Morel, in 1857, coined the name *démence précoce* and emphasized the arrest in mental development and "degeneration" that inevitably led to a state of dementia.

In 1863, K. L. Kahlbaum described mental deterioration in adolescence, calling it *paraphrenia hebetica.* Eleven years later (1874) he described a case of catatonia and called it *Spannungs-Irrsinn* (insanity of tension). Kahlbaum believed that catatonia was a brain disease leading to disturbances in motility. The states of melancholia, mania, stupor, and confusion follow, and finally dementia takes place. In 1871, Kahlbaum's disciple and friend, E. Hecker, described hebephrenia in detail as a progressive disease of adolescence that starts with depressive moods, leads into a stage of wild excitement, and ends in a progressive mental decline.

Kraepelin introduced a systematic classification of mental disorders in 1893. He distinguished two major psychoses, namely, the manic-depressive psychosis and dementia praecox. Dementia praecox, the name reintroduced after Morel, included Kahlbaum's and Hecker's catatonia and hebephrenia.

In 1896, in the fifth edition of his classic work, Kraepelin elaborated his system in detail. He distinguished three types of dementia praecox: (1) catatonia (Kahlbaum), (2) hebephrenia (Hecker), and (3) vesania typica (Kahlbaum) characterized by delusions of persecution and auditory hallucinations and later called the paranoid type of dementia praecox. Later Kraepelin added the simple type of dementia praecox.

Kraepelin penetrated beyond the diversity of observable phenomena and combined the various types of symptoms into one nosological entity. The common denominator of this entity was the mental decline ending in dementia, i.e., complete dilapidation of mental capacities. Kraepelin subordinated to the dementive process all other symptoms such as bizarre behavior, asocial and antisocial actions, loss of emotional control, delusions and hallucinations, stereotypical conduct, etc. He believed that the intellectual decline was the core and essence of this disease and that schizophrenia was related to disturbances in metabolism (Kraepelin, 1919).

In 1911, P. E. Bleuler published his now classic monograph entitled *Dementia Praecox, or the Group of Schizophrenias* (first published in English in 1950). Bleuler accepted

Kraepelin's idea of the nosological entity of this disorder. He observed that the majority of cases were the mild patients who did not need hospitalization, the so-called latent schizophrenics.

Moreover, Bleuler was opposed to the emphasis on intellectual decline. "As the disease need not progress as far as dementia, and does not always appear praecociter, i.e. during puberty or soon after, I prefer the name schizophrenia," he wrote.

Bleuler regarded emotional and associative disturbances as the core features of schizophrenia. He emphasized the disturbance of affectivity expressed in indifference on the one hand and uncontrolled affects on the other.

Bleuler shifted the emphasis from dementia, the eventual outcome of the process, to the morbid process itself. He introduced the concept of autism that indicated withdrawal from reality into a private world of one's own thoughts and emotions not related to other individuals. With this concept Bleuler paved the road for future studies that emphasized social relations as determinants of schizophrenia.

Bleuler believed that the outstanding features of the illness were the loosening of the associative function and the disruption in the continuity of personality. Accordingly, schizophrenia seemed to be the proper name for this split (schism) in the patient's mind (phrenos).

S. Freud

S. Freud described a paranoid type of schizophrenia in 1896. In this, Freud's first paper on schizophrenia, the mechanism of projection was described. Early childhood experiences, especially those of sexual nature, were believed to be represented in the delusions. The resulting guilt feeling and self-criticism were projected on the environment and experienced by the schizophrenic as ideas of reference and auditory hallucinations.

In 1907 K. Abraham, one of Freud's brilliant disciples, discussed the etiological importance of early sexual traumata. He wrote:

> Experiences of sexual nature, whether they have the true value of a trauma, or produce a less severe impression upon infantile sexuality, are not the causes of illness, but merely determine its symptoms. They are not the cause of delusions and hallucinations; they merely give them their particular content. They are not responsible for the appearance of stereotyped words and postures; they merely determine the form which such manifestations take in an individual case (Abraham, 1955).

In 1911, Freud analyzed the famous Schreber case. Schreber's paranoid delusions of persecution were related to repressed homosexuality. Freud believed that the conflict around the negative Oedipus complex and homosexuality leads to a paranoid delusional system. In schizophrenia the libido regresses from object love to autoeroticism, and at the same time it struggles to regain contact with the objects in restitution symptoms. Hence, loss of object and efforts for restitution are the content of the schizophrenic disorder.

In further studies (1914 and 1915) Freud explained the narcissistic regression in schizophrenia and the nature of its mental processes. The primary processes of displacement and condensation, which usually take place in dreams, occur in schizophrenics in the waking state. The libido withdraws from objects, but the retention of cathexis "of the verbal idea is not part of the act of repression (the withdrawal phase of the illness) but represents the first attempt at recovery or cure which so conspicuously dominates the clinical picture of schizophrenia" (Freud, 1915, *Collected Papers*, 1924–1950, vol. 4, p. 98).

A clear presentation of Freud's ideas on schizophrenia was given by Fenichel. He wrote:

> The infant starts out in a state of "primary narcissism" in which the systems of the mental apparatus are not yet differentiated from each other, and in which no objects exist as yet. The differentiation of the ego coincides with the discovery of objects. An ego exists in so far as it is differentiated from objects that are not ego. . . . The schizophrenic has regressed to narcissism; the schizophrenic has lost his objects; the schizophrenic has parted with reality; the schizophrenic's ego has broken down. In schizophrenia the collapse of reality testing, the fundamental function of the ego, and the symptoms of "disintegration of the ego" which amount to a severe disruption of the continuity of the personality, likewise can be interpreted as a return to the time when the ego was not yet established or had just

begun to be established" (Fenichel, 1945, pp. 414–416).

STATISTICS

Incidence

Statistical studies related to the incidence of schizophrenia face several difficulties. Only hospitalized schizophrenics have been, as a rule, included in the official reports. Hospitalized schizophrenics usually represent the most severe cases of manifest schizophrenia. There are, however, many schizophrenics whose disorder is quite manifest and who are not hospitalized. Many of them do not need to be hospitalized but attend outpatient clinics and offices of private practitioners. Often they are called "ambulatory schizophrenics." The name ambulatory merely indicates that they are not confined in mental hospitals.

Some statistics include those ambulatory schizophrenics who attend outpatient departments in hospitals, but do not cover the patients seen in private practice. Besides, there are many schizophrenics whose overt behavior is not especially offensive nor openly aggressive, and they are neither recognized nor treated. In addition, there are quite a number of untreated, neglected cases of an obvious schizophrenic behavior and probably latent ones, too, who are not included in any count and statistics.

Lemkau, Tietze, and Cooper (1941) believe that the number of psychotics at large in the community was approximately one-third of the number in mental hospitals. Although this estimate is given by highly competent workers, one may still doubt whether it includes the large category of latent schizophrenics (Lemkau, 1955).

Additional difficulty stems from the looseness of diagnostic classification. For instance, in 1940–1941, 7,558 schizophrenic patients (called at that time "suffering from dementia praecox") were admitted to mental hospitals in New York City. In 1952 their number was about 14,200, and in 1955–1956 about 16,000. The increase is probably a result of a change in classification in the direction of a greater inclusiveness of the term "schizophrenia."

Faris and Dunham (1939) reported the incidence of schizophrenia in various parts of Chicago as low as 111 per 100,000 population and as high as 1,115 per 100,000. They related the high incidence ratio to social disorganization, social mobility, and "hobohemia." Lemkau and Crocetti (1958, p. 72) believed that in a Western European type of society the incidence of schizophrenia was between 50 and 290 cases per 100,000 population per year. In 1955 there were approximately 160 cases of hospitalized schizophrenics per 100,000 population in the United States.

Schizophrenics form approximatey 25 per cent of all new admissions to mental hospitals in the United States. However, their stay in hospitals is prolonged, averaging about 13.1 years. Hence schizophrenics form approximately 50 per cent of patients at any time in the mental hospitals (Lemkau & Crocetti, 1958, p. 80). Some authors, however (Noyes & Kolb, 1958, p. 391), maintain that 60 per cent of the population in state mental hospitals is made up of schizophrenics.

It is still a controversial issue whether there has been any increase in the ratio of schizophrenics in the population. Goldhamer and Marshall's (1949) studies did not support such a belief.

One should distinguish between *incidence,* or the "number of cases occurring in a given population in a given period of time," and *prevalence,* or the "number of cases presently existing in any given population at a particular time" (Lemkau and Crocetti, 1958, p. 67). Obviously an estimate of prevalence is less reliable than an estimate of incidence.

Sociocultural Variables

Hollingshead and Redlich (1958) found in their Yale study that severity of mental disorder was inversely related to social-economic class. The prevalent rate of schizophrenia in the lowest class was about eight times higher than in the highest class. Also Hare (1955) found a positive correlation between schizophrenia and low socioeconomic status in England. Goldhamer (1959), however, questioned the reliability of the Hollingshead and Redlich study because of their small number of cases.

Stein (1957), in her study of mental disorders in London, found higher incidence of schizophrenia in two boroughs. While there was a lower rate of schizophrenia in the more wealthy borough, a higher rate was found in the lowest economic class of each borough.

Morris (1959) remarked that although the incidence of schizophrenia is highest in the lowest socioeconomic class, the fathers of schizophrenics represent all socioeconomic classes. This could mean that schizophrenia is not related to socioeconomic status. The low socioeconomic status of schizophrenics may therefore be not a cause but a *result* of schizophrenia. Kanner (1948), for example, found that most parents of schizophrenic children belong to the middle and upper social class. It seems that schizophrenics in private practice belong to the middle and upper social classes, while schizophrenics in public hospitals belong mostly to lower socioeconomic classes (Wolman, 1957; 1961a; 1965b). Schizophrenia is, therefore, not a class privilege. Families of wealthy schizophrenics, as a rule, seek help from private practitioners, but poor schizophrenics are most frequently committed to mental institutions.

Faris and Dunham (1939) found a high concentration of schizophrenia in the center of Chicago, with rates much lower in the peripheries. This report gave rise to a great many empirical studies and speculations in regard to social mobility and schizophrenia. The findings of Tietze, Lemkau, and Cooper in Baltimore (1942) supported such a relationship (Lemkau, 1955).

About twenty years later Dunham (n.d., p. 9) stated that residence may not be a criterion of one's social life, which, in urban communities, may be more related to one's occupation and job mates than to one's place of residence. However, A. R. Mangus (quoted after E. Leacock, 1957, p. 318) found more mental disorders in the open country and among farmers than in cities.

In a review of pertinent literature Lemkau and Crocetti concluded "there is a great deal of evidence justifying the speculation that there is an etiological relationship between schizophrenia and urbanization. However, the nature of the relationship or even its unchallenged existence has not yet been completely demonstrated" (1958, p. 73).

While mobility has been frequently related to schizophrenia, R. Freedman (1950) failed to find positive correlation between high mobility and high hospital admission rates of schizophrenics.

Migration is believed to correlate with schizophrenia. Malzberg and Lea (1956) found that psychosis rates were twice as high for migrants as for nonmigrants, but it was not clearly evident that rates of schizophrenia were especially high.

Perhaps this question could be best solved by analysis of the studies of migration to the United States (O. Ødegaard, 1932; 1945) and to Israel (Wolman, 1946; 1949). In Ødegaard's study in 1932, the rates of first admissions of Norwegian-born immigrants in Minnesota were much higher than those of native-born Americans in Minnesota and of Norwegians in Norway. Thus migration was a definite cause of mental disorder. But thirteen years later Ødegaard found (1945) in the internal migration in Norway that migrants had rather a lower rate of admission to mental hospitals than the nonmigratory population. In a study of delinquency in Israel (Wolman, 1946) I have found that the ratio of juvenile delinquency for children of immigrants from the Middle East, compared with children of parents of European stock, was four to one. However, there was no difference between Israeli-born and those whose parents immigrated from Central Europe. The conclusion was that not the migration but the *acculturation* created emotional conflict (Wolman, 1949).

Internal migration does not create problems of acculturation. When people move from substandard areas into better neighborhoods, whether it is in Norway, the United States, or any other place, there is no reason to expect deterioration in their mental health. Loosing one's cultural frame of reference and acquiring another is a great challenge to one's mental resources. The migrants coming to Israel from Europe did not have to give up their cultural values. Those Jews, however, who came to Israel from the Middle East and Africa were in a position similar to that of many migratory groups in the United States. Most of them hurriedly renounced their cultural values and endeavored to embrace in haste the cultural values of European Jewry. This in itself overtaxed the mental resources of many. Moreover, the father, as the representative of the "old" country, lost a great deal of prestige. The lowering of his social status and decline of his authority have been related to the increase of mental disorder, especially schizophrenia (Wolman, 1965b).

Similar data and conclusions were reported by Beaglehole in New Zealand (1939a) and Hawaii (1939b). The ratio of schizophrenia to all other mental disorders in the Hawaiian population was 30.3 to 43.4 per cent, while in migrants it was 51 to 58 per cent.

The overall correlations between schizophrenia and national cultures are rather inconclusive. One may or may not agree with Gold (1951), who says that there are fewer schizophrenics than manic-depressives in Ireland, Israel, Morocco, Portugal, and Tunisia.

Adeoye (1955) compared rural members of the Yoruba tribe in Nigeria with urbanized Yorubians and with those Yorubians who studied in Europe. Westernization apparently led to an increase in schizophrenia. In all those cases, westernization means a decline in paternal authority. The study of Eaton and Weil (1955) of the Hutterites in North America discloses a low incidence of schizophrenia; the Hutterites preserved patriarchal, conservative family patterns.

As far as clinical patterns are concerned, Tooth concluded that the main clinical patterns of schizophrenia "are the same in Africa as in other races" (1950, p. 6).

ETIOLOGY

Genetics

Several research workers believe schizophrenia is an inherited disorder. According to Kallmann's findings (1938; 1946; 1948; 1953) children with one schizophrenic parent have 16.4 per cent probability of developing schizophrenia, while children with two schizophrenic parents have a 68.1 per cent probability. Even more impressive are the data obtained by comparison of fraternal and identical twins. Where one fraternal twin has developed schizophrenia, there is a 16.4 per cent probability that the other will develop it also; in identical twins the chances are 86.2 per cent. In Kallmann's study of 691 twins, dizygotic twins have shown concordance with schizophrenia in 14.7 per cent of cases, as compared to 77.6 to 81.5 per cent in monozygotic twins. The higher percentage applies to twins who have been together for five years prior to breakdown. Thus, Kallmann concluded, "Inheritance of schizophrenia follows a biological genetic pattern" (1946, p. 318).

Kallmann did not exclude environmental factors. He believed the outcome of schizophrenia to be "the result of intricate interaction of varying genetic and environmental influences."

A summary of Kallmann's studies of expectancy of schizophrenia is represented below (see Kallmann, 1962):

	Per cent
One-egg twins	86.20
Two-egg twins	14.50
Siblings	14.20
Half siblings	7.10
General population	0.85

Altshuler (1957) confirmed Kallmann's findings and stressed the fact that expectancy rates for relatives of schizophrenics are much higher than for the general population. Vorster (1960) found 17 per cent incidence of schizophrenia in two-egg twins, as compared with 70 per cent of incidence in one-egg twins.

Kallmann's and other research data show that the incidence of schizophrenia correlates highly with consanguinity. According to Kallmann it is very improbable that this could be a dominant type of heredity; thus schizophrenia is most probably caused by a recessive gene.

The idea of recessive heredity was strongly criticized by Böök (1960) and Slater (1953; 1958). Since the corrected risk figures of schizophrenia "do not differ to a significant degree between parents, siblings, and children with one or no affected parent" (Böök, 1960, p. 29), the hypothesis of a recessive heredity becomes untenable. Also Gregory (1960) noticed that the incidence of schizophrenia in various classes of relatives does not follow a simple dominant or simple recessive pattern.

Böök hypothesized that schizophrenia could be caused by gene differences expressed in homozygotes in a recessive and, occasionally, in heterozygotes in a dominant, manner. This hypothesis is based on the concept of "reduced penetrance," i.e., on the assumption that the presence of a genetic factor may not affect the person carrying it. Böök admitted (1960, p. 31) that the principle of penetrance has been questioned in regard to mankind. However, Garrone (1962) applied the penetrance hypothesis to a study of the Geneva population and maintained that schizophrenia was inherited in a simple recessive mode with 67 per cent of homozygous penetrance.

Also Loretta Bender (1956) favors a genetic theory of schizophrenia. She believes schizophrenia to be a process of dysmaturation and arrest of development on the embryonic level, determined by genetic factors. Resultingly, the child is born with a sort of primitive *plasticity*. The entire neurological system bears witness to the organic lag of development. The infant's sleep, respiration, blood circulation, muscular tone, and metabolic processes are disturbed. The trauma of birth activates certain defense mechanisms which develop into the well-known behavioral patterns of schizophrenia. Thus schizophrenia is a sort of *encephalopathy*.

While some workers seem to support Bender's hypothesis, others are critical of it. Fish (1959) reported that a child diagnosed at the age of 5½ as schizophrenic has shown neurological and physiological disturbances as early as one month of age. However, Goldfarb (1961) found no significant differences in physical appearance between normal and schizophrenic children. Also Eisenberg (1957) questioned the anatomical evidence of Bender's theory of encephalopathy. On the other hand, Bergman and Escalona (1949) reported unusual sensitivity in infants later diagnosed as psychotic. These data are based on parental observation; there is no evidence in regard to these sensitivities being inherited or acquired.

Roth remarked that "no simple genetic hypothesis accords with all the facts" (1957). D. Rosenthal, while in favor of a genetic interpretation of schizophrenia, stated that the question of what is actually inherited would remain unclear "until the specific metabolic error can be located or the specific patterns of influence defined or established" (1960).

D. Jackson (1960) has critically examined the literature pertaining to genetics in schizophrenia. Schizophrenia apparently does not follow the rules of dominant heredity; were schizophrenia a product of recessive heredity, as Kallmann maintains, the rate of expectancy for monozygotic twins should be 100 per cent; it would also be 100 per cent for children of two schizophrenic parents. Since Kallmann's rates are substantially lower, the hypothesis of recessive heredity is also excluded (Jackson, 1960, p. 46). Thus one may doubt whether schizophrenia is an inherited disorder, for it does not follow either a dominant or a recessive pattern.

Heredity in schizophrenia is far from being a closed issue, and intensive research in the genetics of schizophrenia is being conducted at the present time in several scientific centers the world over.

Physique

The etiology of schizophrenia has been often related to bodily structure. In 1921 E. Kretschmer published his work entitled *Körperbau und Charakter,* translated into English in 1925, reprinted and published since in several languages. Kretschmer introduced a new version of the ancient Hippocratic theory of relationship between bodily structure and personality type and applied it to mental disorders. The Hippocratic theory of four fluids has influenced the thinking of several generations and undergone several modifications. Instead of the Hippocratic four bodily fluids or "humors," Galen introduced in the second century a theory of nine temperaments resulting from combinations of the basic fluids. In modern times Esquirol ascribed monomanic states, corresponding to what is presently called schizophrenia, to the *lymphatic* type. The *lypemanic* states, corresponding to what is presently called affect psychosis, have been related by Esquirol to the *sanguine* temperament.

The body-temperament tradition has been much pronounced and is still very much alive in European psychology and psychopathology. Kretschmer distinguished three physical types, the leptosomatic, athletic, and pyknic. The first two types were highly correlated to schizophrenia.

Kretschmer's study went beyond the walls of a mental hospital. He found the three physical types applicable to the general population and correlated to normal personality traits. Normal individuals with leptosomatic or athletic bodily structure were classified as normal schizothymics. Should they ever deteriorate mentally and become mental patients, their disorder would be schizophrenia.

Kretschmer's studies have had a great impact on the theory of mental disorders for several reasons. First, Kretschmer implied a normalcy-abnormalcy continuum. Second, he related mental disorders to tangible physical characteristics.

Kretschmer's theories have been modified by W. H. Sheldon (1940) and B. Lindegarde (1953). Although there has been, since then, a great deal of theorizing on schizophrenia based on the three constitutional theories (to be discussed later in this chapter), empirical research has lent little if any support to these theories. M. Bleuler (1955), Rees (1957), and others failed to find a definite relationship between schizophrenia and somatic types, while other workers (Bellak & Holt, 1948) tried to relate certain schizophrenic syndromes to bodily types. In a review of research in this area, Rees wrote, "The proportion of individuals with the pyknic type of body-build was similar in the schizophrenic and the normal group" (1957). Furthermore, research workers found a "considerable overlapping in the distribution of physical types between the manic-depressive and the schizophrenic group" (*ibid.*, pp. 8–9). Rees did not reject Kretschmer's ideas; yet he stated clearly, "Modern methods of analyzing and classifying variations in body-build have indicated the existence of a continuous variation rather than the existence of physical types as discrete and independent entities" (*ibid.*).

Biochemical and Other Factors

Several research workers relate schizophrenia to biochemical factors, with or without a clear genetic explanation. Baruk (1949) believed that schizophrenia is caused by "cerebral anemia." One can artifically impair cerebral blood circulation by injecting mescaline, adrenaline, and other toxic elements. These injections can produce symptoms similar to those of catatonic schizophrenia, especially an inhibition of volition processes. However, Kety et al. (1948) found that the over-all blood circulation in schizophrenics was normal.

Several workers (see H. Freeman's review of literature, 1958) related schizophrenia to the alleged increase in cerebrospinal protein level. Katzenelbogen (1935) did not find evidence of a higher cerebrospinal protein in schizophrenics, as compared to normals. Davidson (1960) and Hyden (1961) did not find any evidence in regard to the role of RNA and protein in the etiology of schizophrenia.

Several research workers, among them R. Gjessing (1938), R. G. Hoskins (1946), Hoagland (1952), Reiss (1954), and others, believed hormonal disbalance to be the cause of schizophrenia. There has been a wide range of disagreement among the abovementioned workers as to whether it was thyroid or adrenaline or any other endocrine disorder that served as a cause. M. Bleuler (1954), H. Freeman (1958), and others stated, however, that at that time no connection had been established between schizophrenia and endocrine factors.

Hendrickson believes schizophrenia to be "an organic abnormality of the nervous system, really a complex and subtle type of neurological disorder" (1952, p. 10). However, most detailed research in brain activity (Davidson, 1960; Hyden, 1961) has not reached the point where one could safely say schizophrenic behavior *is* caused by a lesser amount of RNA in the ganglion cells, as compared with normal.

As mentioned before, L. Bender also believes in organic determinants of schizophrenia. "Childhood schizophrenia involves a maturational lag at the embryonic level . . . characterized by a primitive plasticity in all areas from which subsequent behavior results" (Bender, 1956, p. 499). Similar views have been expressed by A. M. Freedman (1954).

Kety expressed serious doubts as to whether "a generalized defect in energy metabolism . . . could be responsible for the highly specialized features of schizophrenia" (1960). Also Böök (1960, p. 32) found the toxicity data rather controversial. Richter (1957), in a review of his own studies as well as of research conducted by R. Fisher, H. H. DeJong, H. Hoagland, I. Munkvad, and others, concluded that no evidence was found of free aminos or any specific toxic compounds or abnormal metabolites in the blood of schizophrenics.

Recently Heath brought out the hypothesis that "schizophrenia is a disease characterized by alterations in the metabolic pathways for the breakdown of certain endogenously occurring compounds" (1960, p. 146). The presence of taraxein in the blood stream causes a toxic compound that alters the activities of certain parts of the brain and leads to schizophrenic behavior. Kety reported (1960) that injection of taraxein caused symptoms resembling schizophrenia, but there is no evidence that taraxein causes schizophrenia. Nor is there evidence for the amino acid metabolism hypothesis. "The chromatographic search for supportive evidence is interesting and valuable,'" wrote Kety, but "the preliminary indications of differences that are characteristic of even a segment of the disease rather than artifactual or incidental has not yet been obtained" (1960, p. 127). The presence of phenolic acids in the urine of schizophrenics has been, according to the study of T. D. Mann and E. H. Lambrosse, "better correlated with the ingestion of this beverage [coffee] than with schizophrenia" (*ibid.*). Also Kline (1958) pointed out that the alleged link between biochemical deviations and psychosis is often a product of a peculiar food intake by institutionalized patients.

As research in biochemical determinants of schizophrenia goes on, old hypotheses are tested and new ones are formed. For example, Woolley's hypothesis (1958) in regard to the role played by the serotonin enzyme has been put to a test in the so-called "model psychoses." However, studies reported by Kety (1960), Szára (1958), and others failed to find significant differences between normal controls and schizophrenia.

It has been stated by several workers (Kety, 1960; Kline, 1958; and others) that various biochemical deviations reported in scientific literature turned out to be an artifact of hospital diet and its metabolic consequences rather than causal determinants of schizophrenia.

Reviews of research by H. Freeman (1958), W. Overholser and S. L. Werkman (1958), S. L. Werkman (1959) and S. Kety (1960) did not disclose any clearly determined causal relationship between organic factors and schizophrenia. On the other hand, one may get the impression that "everyone is right," for several biochemical abnormalities have been discovered in some schizophrenics.

Psychosomatics

The question is of the causal order. Is schizophrenia a *result* of biochemical defects, or does it cause them? The somatopsychological theories stress somatic factors, but, as Richter pointed out, "It is always difficult to distinguish between cause and effect" (1957, p. 68).

On the other hand, several workers (Arieti, 1955; Wolman, 1964b) pointed to the possibility of a reverse causal order and viewed schizophrenia as a psychosomatic or rather sociopsychosomatic disorder.

The fact that social interaction can produce lasting biochemical changes has been proved by Chitty (1955), Krech et al. (1960), Hyden (1961), and many others. Krech concluded the study of cholinesterase activity by saying, "We have now shown that cerebral ChE activity . . . can in turn be modified by behavioral and environmental circumstances."

Hoskins (1946), Shattock (1950), Doust (1952), and others observed several pathological phenomena in schizophrenics, including cyanosis or bluing of feet and hands caused by venous stasis and other defects in their vasomotor system such as decrease in systematic blood pressure, decrease in the volume of flow of blood, and a tendency to vasoconstriction. Yet Kety and his associates (1948) could not find significant differences between the oxygen consumption and the flow of blood in brains of schizophrenics and normal controls. There was no evidence for a cerebral anoxemia; yet the disturbances in the circulatory system of schizophrenics are well-established facts.

A psychosomatic interpretation of these phenomena seems to be plausible. According to Arieti, vasoconstriction in schizophrenics is a compensatory mechanism that prevents dissipation of bodily heat. The bizarre postures of catatonics activate antigravity vasoconstrictor mechanisms. "Without these mechanisms, edema due to blood stasis would be very frequent" (Arieti, 1955, p. 395).

Several physiological peculiarities have been observed in schizophrenics, such as little reactivity to stimuli; reduced senstivity to pain, combined with an increased fear of anticipated pain; strong inclination to skin diseases; frequent colds and an increased sensitivity to colds; sharpening of olfactory sensitivity; lowered body temperature; etc. (Arieti, 1955; E. Bleuler, 1950; Buck, Carscallen, & Hobbs, 1950; Wolman, 1957; 1964b; and others).

In the interpretation of all these symptoms one can invoke the experimental studies in interoceptive conditioning (see Bykov, 1957; Ivanov-Smolensky, 1954; Pavlov, 1941). The magnitude of general metabolism can be changed by conditioning or even by second-order conditioning through word signals. In Shatenstein's experiment reported by Bykov (1957, p. 179), a man who remained lying quietly on a couch showed a definite increase in metabolic rate when it was suggested to him that he had just finished an exerting, hard physical effort. Thus neuropathological changes can be interpreted as a result rather than a cause of schizophrenia.

Psychogenic Factors

In 1896 Freud related schizophrenia to an early repression of libido. However, in 1907 he shifted the emphasis from sexual traumata to more general concepts of libido development. In the same year Abraham (1955) elaborated this point as follows: "Experiences of a sexual nature, whether they have the true value of a trauma or produce a less severe impression upon infantile sexuality, are not the causes of illness, but merely determine its symptoms."

In 1908 Abraham hypothesized that schizophrenia was caused by a regression of libido from object relationship into the autoerotic stage. According to the Freud-Abraham timetable, mental disorders are a product of fixation and/or regression. More severe disorders are a product of earlier fixations.

"The psychosexual characteristic of dementia praecox is the return of the patient to autoeroticism, and the symptoms of this illness are a form of autoerotic activity," wrote Abraham in 1908. "The autoeroticism is the source not only of delusions of persecution but of megalomania" (Abraham, 1955, pp. 74–75). "The psychosexual constitution of dementia praecox is based, therefore, on an inhibition in development." It is "an abnormal fixation to an erotogenic zone—a typical autoerotic phenomenon" (*ibid.*, p. 77). In dementia praecox "a person who has never passed out of the primary stage of his psychosexual development is thrown back more and more into the autoerotic stage as the disease progresses" (*ibid.*, p. 78).

Freud (in 1911 and 1912) accepted Abraham's ideas regarding pathogenesis of schizophrenia and saw in schizophrenia a struggle between the regression of libido and its withdrawal from object relations and its efforts to recapture or restitute the object relations.

Later in this chapter the theoretical explanations of schizophrenia given by Freud and other psychoanalysts will be discussed.

It is worth while to mention here that Freud left open several questions in regard to the etiology of schizophrenia. Freud's theory includes the biologically determined developmental stages and the socioculturally determined human interactions (see Wolman, 1960a, chap 6). Assuming that all human beings go through the Freudian stages, the way they go through depends upon interactional patterns. Whether a child will pass safely through an oral or anal stage or remain fixated or regress eventually depends on the amount and quality of satisfaction and frustration received by the child in the *interaction* with his close environment. According to Freud, "Owing to the general tendency to variation in biological processes it must necessarily happen that not all these preparatory phases will be passed through and completely outgrown with the same degree of success; some parts of the function will be permanently arrested." The development can be "disturbed and altered by current impressions from without" (1949b, pp. 297ff.).

These "impressions from without" have been studied by H. S. Sullivan. Sullivan pointed to peculiarities in the personalities of parents of schizophrenics and related the origins of schizophrenia to a state of panic disastrous to the patient's self-esteem (1931). Parent-child relationships that prevent the establishment of the "self-system," and especially panic states producing dissociation (the not-me feeling), have been perceived by Sullivan as causes of schizophrenia (1947, 1953).

Several workers, accepting or rejecting Sullivan's theory of interpersonal relations, began to study the peculiar parent-child relationship. Whether these relationships caused schizophrenia as interpreted by a Freudian withdrawal of libido or Sullivanian dissociation or any other theory, the nature of these relationships became a major topic in research in schizophrenia.

Interactional Determinants

The data pertaining to the incidence of schizophrenia do not indicate clearly that schizophrenia is related to any peculiar country or type of civilization (see Linton, 1956). Also the hypothesis that certain personality types of parents or certain intrafamilial interactional patterns produce schizophrenia still lacks evidence.

A review of research seems to indicate that parents of schizophrenics are not necessarily schizophrenics, nor do they form a clear-cut pathological group. Kanner (1948), Kanner and Eisenberg (1955), J. L. Despert (1951), B. Rank (1955), Nuffield (1954), Rosen (1953), and others found the parents of schizophrenics, and especially the mothers, highly disturbed, narcissistic, cold, etc. Some have used the term "schizogenic mother," but there has been no agreement in regard to the personality traits that make a mother "schizogenic."

Research workers failed to find any definite pathology in the parents of schizophrenics. One worker (Alanen, 1958) found 10 per cent of the parents of schizophrenics to be disturbed and slightly over 5 per cent schizophrenic. I have found (Wolman, 1957; 1961a; 1964b) about 40 per cent of fathers and 50 per cent of mothers of schizophrenics displaying a great variety of pathological conditions, but it was impossible to state that schizophrenia in offspring is caused by any peculiar mental type of parents.

The main body of research has turned lately into the study of the intrafamilial interaction.

Kanner and Eisenberg, in a follow-up study of 105 cases, wrote about both parents as follows: "The majority of parents . . . were cold, detached, humorless perfectionists" (1955). Arieti found most frequently among the parents of schizophrenics "a domineering, nagging and hostile mother, who gives the child no chance to assert himself, is married to a dependent, weak man, too weak to help the child" (1955, p. 52).

The peculiar patterns of mother-child communication, called the "double bind," were studied by Bateson, Jackson, Haley, and Weakland (1956). Hill described the parents of schizophrenics as follows: "These mothers were ill. They needed their sons and daughters to give them a reason for existence. . . . These mothers are devastatingly, possessively all-loving of their child who is to be schizophrenic." The father was often aggressive, but this "belligerence was that of a very unwilling agent of his wife" (1955, pp. 106–107).

Lidz and his associates (1957; 1958; 1960) found lack of mutual understanding and cooperation between the parents of schizophrenics.

> We realized soon, that the intrapsychic disturbances of the mothers were not nearly as relevant to what happened to one or more children in the family (especially to the child who became schizophrenic), as was the fact that these women were paired with husbands who would either acquiesce to the many irrational and bizarre notions of how the family should be run or who would constantly battle with and undermine an already anxious and insecure mother (Fleck, 1960, p. 335).

Similar findings have been reported by Wolman (1957; 1961a), Lu (1961; 1962), and many others.

Apparently the etiology of schizophrenia "requires . . . the failure of the father to assume his masculine controlling function. . . . To produce schizophrenia it appears necessary for the mother to assume the father role" (Whitaker, 1958, p. 108). "The parents follow a pattern very much like divorced parents who share their children. The mother, the overadequate one in relation to the inadequate child, is in charge of the child. . . . The father is then in the functioning position of a substitute mother" (Bowen, 1960, p. 363).

All these studies point to peculiarities in intrafamilial relationships. The reported data may differ in detail, yet show an almost uniform pattern of interaction. Thus a sociopsychological theory has been proposed that could link all the data into one coherent system.

Three types of social relationship, depending upon the objectives of the participants, have been distinguished. Whenever an individual enters a relationship with the objective of receiving, it is an *instrumental* type, for the partner or partners are used for the satisfaction of the individual's needs. The infant-mother relationship is the prototype of instrumentalism. The infant is weak, the mother is strong; the infant must receive, yet cannot give. Whenever an individual enters a relationship with the objective of satisfying his own needs and also the needs of others, it is a *mutual* relationship. Friendship and marriage represent mutualism. Sexual intercourse is probably the prototype of mutualism. Whenever an individual's objective is to satisfy the needs of others, it is a vectorial relationship. Parenthood is the prototype of *vectorialism*; parents are strong, infants are weak; parents give love and support and protect their children.

Normal adults are capable of interacting in all three ways. In business they are instrumental; in friendship and marriage, mutual; and in parenthood and in their ideals, vectorial (Wolman, 1956; 1958a; 1960b).

Schizogenic Families

In normal families parents are perceived by their children as strong and friendly adults who relate to each other in a *mutual*, give-and-get manner and have a *vectorial* attitude toward the child, irrespective of what the child may be or do. Parental love is unconditional; the smaller and weaker the child, the more vectorial the parental attitude.

This vectorial protecting attitude of the parents enables the instrumentally minded infant to progress toward higher levels of interindividual relations. At the anal stage the child graciously accepts toilet training, with its demands to give something away. The growing child "generalizes" this give-and-take or mutual acceptance attitude and learns reciprocity in relations with his peers. This social development, brought about by both maturation and learning processes, helps the child to grow toward a future vectorial attitude toward his children. The child who had a normal family background develops into an adult capable of instrumental, mutual, and vectorial relationships.

Detailed case studies and interviews show that it is not the "weak father and strong mother" that produce schizophrenia in their offspring. If this were so, *all* siblings of a schizophrenic would be schizophrenic also. The empirical evidence is to the contrary. Also observations of families of manic-depressives point to several cases of domineering mothers and submissive fathers. Accordingly, *frustrated instrumentalism in the interparental relationship is the main cause of schizophrenia* (Wolman 1957; 1961a; 1964b). A woman who expected to find a father in her husband hates the man she married and seeks the child's attention instead. The man who hoped his wife would become his mother may try to compete with or seduce his own child.

This intrafamilial relationship does not fall into the usual descriptive categories of rejection, overprotection, overindulgence, etc. The schizogenic family relationship represents a *reversal* of *social positions* and, resultingly, causes in the mind of the child who will become schizophrenic a *confusion in social roles of age, sex, family position, etc.*

Mother confuses the child by presenting herself as a martyr. She appears to be strong, for she controls the entire family and imposes her will on all in the household. She does it in a protective-hostile manner with the child: she tells the child that he is weak, sick, stupid, or ugly and that she must protect him and do things for him. Yet she presents herself as a self-sacrificing, suffering, almost dying person.

This tyrant-martyr attitude with constant accusations of ingratitude and the incessant demands for appreciation is, as far as the content of communication goes, a "double bind" (Bateson et al., 1956). But the issue is more than a matter of communication.

The mothers cannot tolerate any independence, any growth of the child, any success not brought about by mother. These mothers are possessive, control their child's life, and demand from the child an unlimited love, gratitude, and self-sacrifice for the self-sacrificing tyrant-martyr mother (see Davis, 1961; Foudraine, 1961; Lu, 1961; 1962; Weakland, 1960; Wolman, 1961a; 1965b; Wynne et al., 1958; and many others).

The normal reaction to this extortion would be hate, but the avenues of hate toward those who hurt are obstructed in the preschizophrenic child. The normal reaction of the sheep to the wolf is fight or flight. But when the wolf succeeds in convincing the sheep that he keeps the sheep in his cave to protect it, the helpless sheep may become utterly confused. Soon the sheep will hate itself for having hostile feelings toward the kind, self-sacrificing wolf. And this seems to be the origin of schizophrenia (Wolman, 1957). The frightened child is forced to hypercathect his love objects at the expense of self-cathexis (Federn, 1952).

The future schizophrenic starts his life in the same way as any other child. He is helpless and depends upon aid from outside. His attitude is instrumental, and he depends upon "narcissistic supplies." Soon he cannot fail to realize that there is something wrong with his parents. The child lives under the threat of loss of his martyr-type mother and nonparticipant baby-father. All schizophrenics, as Sullivan amply observed (1953), are panic-stricken. The child begins to worry about his parents and takes on a premature and much too costly protective hypervectorial attitude toward them. In order to survive, he must protect his protectors. *Vectoriasis-praecox* (the new name for schizophrenia) sometimes comes very early and uses up the child's mental resources (Wolman, 1957; 1958b; 1959b; 1961a; 1962; 1965b).

Certainly no woman could destroy her child without an active or tacit approval of her husband, and all fathers of schizophrenics participate in the development of schizophrenia in offspring. The father-mother relationship causes the woman to demand from the child what she failed to get from her husband. When the "mutual" interparental relationship fails, chances are that mother will develop an instrumental, exploitative attitude toward the child.

It seems that fathers trigger the tragic involvement. They expect the child to give them what they failed to get from their wives. Most of these fathers are seductive to children of both sexes, spreading confusion in regard to age and sex identification. Some of them fight against their own wife and child. Many schizophrenic families live under father's terror.

Manic-depressive and other paramutual patients wish to be sick or dying to elicit mother's love. Their mother is perceived as a strong and hostile person whose sympathy and favors can be won only by weakness or illness. Schizophrenics and other hypervectorial types cannot expect anything in sickness. They will be blamed for getting sick and for imposing a burden on their martyr-type mother.

Thus their fantasies take an opposite direction. They wish to be God, creator, Messiah, savior; they would like to become superfathers and supermothers. They often dream of how to wreck the entire world and put an end to their misery. They dream about power, while manic-depressives dream about weakness. When they hallucinate, they hallucinate a superparental power (Fenichel, 1945).

THEORETICAL INTERPRETATIONS

Psychoanalytic theories

Whenever behavior is disturbed, disorganized, or abnormal, the first question to be asked is, Why? Causation is not an observable fact; what is observable is merely a temporal sequence of events. Yet the causal principle is an exceedingly useful and methodologically necessary postulate that helps to relate events in a coherent and intelligible manner (see Wolman, 1960a, pp. 523ff.). All psychopathological theories endeavor to relate observable phenomena to the underlying causes and deal with explanation of past causes and prediction of future results.

Kraepelin saw in schizophrenia an incurable process of deterioration. In 1898, in a paper on "The diagnosis and prognosis of *dementia praecox*," he explained that dementia praecox (later called schizophrenia by E. Bleuler) was an endogenous, deterioriating, and incurable disease of organic origin. At first, Kraepelin believed schizophrenia was related to brain pathology, but later he favored a metabolic explanation. He believed that catatonic symptoms may end in the death of the patient (1919).

E. Bleuler shared the organic view of the etiology of schizophrenia but refuted Kraepelin's ideas of deterioration, incurability, and lack of affect. He reported several cases of recovery in schizophrenia, with or without specific treatment. He saw the core of schizophrenia in dereistic and autistic thinking, disturbances in associations, emotional ambivalence, withdrawal from reality into a world of fantasy (1950).

Bleuler's theory was influenced by the above-mentioned Freud-Abraham studies. Freud assumed that the fixation point of schizophrenia lies in the transition from the autoerotic stage toward the beginning of object relations. Schizophrenia belongs to "narcissistic neuroses" because the patient is unable to develop object relations. The origins of the ego are related to "the differentions from objects that are not ego." Schizophrenia is a regression to narcissism, i.e., loss of objects, loss of contact with reality, and breakdown of the ego. As a result, schizophrenics are incapable of transference (see Fenichel, 1945, pp. 415ff.).

In the period 1911 to 1914 Freud stressed the inner struggle that takes place in schizophrenia. On one hand schizophrenia is a process of regression and withdrawal of libido from objects, but at the same time it is a restitutive struggle to repair object relations. This recathexis of objects with libido, wrote Freud in 1915, "represents the first of the attempts at recovery or cure which so conspicuously dominate the clinical picture of schizophrenia" (1925, vol. 4, p. 136).

Freud related delusions of persecution to repressed homosexual impulses. In the famous Schreber case (1911) the patient tried to fight off a homosexual urge by reaction formation and by projecting his hate onto his love object. Schizophrenic ideas of reference and "influencing machine" have been interpreted by Tausk (1933) as projection; at the preego and preobject relations stage there is no clear dividing line between the organism and the outer world. Thus the schizophrenic may perceive his own sensations as if they were coming from without.

In the later development of psychoanalytic thinking, Abraham in 1916 (1955) and Nunberg in 1921 (1948) related schizophrenia to the oral stage where introjection was the only possible object relationship. At this stage there are no definite boundaries between the organism and the outer world; therefore incorporation and projection take place easily. In 1924 Abraham concluded that introjection may be also anal (see Abraham, 1955). In the same year Freud introduced the concept of tripartite personality structure composed of id, ego, and superego. Psychosis has been characterized by ego's loss of contact with reality and surrender to the id.

Later Developments

Orthodox Freudians such as Back, Fenichel, Federn, Hartmann, Katan, Roheim, and others elaborated, with some deviations, the Freud-Abraham interpretation of schizophrenia. Hartmann (1955) hypothesized that the schizophrenic ego is unable to "neutralize" aggressive energy. Katan (1954) stressed the importance of homosexual conflict. Federn and Roheim have introduced new ideas on schizophrenia. Roheim (1955) believed that oral trauma, such as loss of mother, was the core of schizophrenia. Schizophrenia is a regression to the infantile fantasy of the internalized mother.

Federn made the important contribution to the understanding of schizophrenia. In his successful treatment of schizophrenics he discovered that they do develop transference. Schizophrenia is not a withdrawal of object cathexes but a hypercathexis of objects. It is not a loss of the love object; rather, the patient's ego has lost the cathexes. The ego of schizophrenics is impoverished, inadequately cathected, and unable to test reality (1952).

Federn introduced the concept of "ego boundaries," a sort of center of perception of the "ego feeling." This feeling distinguished "everything that belongs to the ego" from everything else. In schizophrenics the poorly cathected ego boundary breaks down; consequently there is no correct perception of reality.

Melaine Klein and her school represent an independent point of view and a substantial deviation from Freud. M. Klein (1946) rejected the concept of primary narcissism and hypothesized very early object relationships. The earliest objects, breast and later penis, are perceived as good or bad. Early projection and introjection of the bad breast typifies the "paranoid position," ascribed by Klein to infants in their third month of life. Under the pressure of threats of dissolution, ego may fall apart. This "falling of ego to pieces" underlies the "states of disintegration in schizophrenics," wrote Klein. The infant identifies the object with hated parts of himself. This hateful introjection and projection is, according to Klein, the essence of schizophrenia.

Another British psychoanalyst, Rosenfeld (1952), followed M. Klein in some of her ideas in regard to early introjection. He believed that schizophrenics were afraid they might destroy their love objects by introjection; therefore they withdrew from objects. Rosenfeld (1953) stressed the preponderance of aggressive impulses in schizophrenics and the fear of them.

Non-Freudian Psychoanalytic Views

Schizophrenia, being the most frequent and most severe psychosis, has attracted the attention of several non-Freudian analysts. Some of their views will be described below.

As early as 1906 C. G. Jung took exception to Kraepelin's interpretation of schizophrenia and stressed emotional overinvolvement which leaves little energy for facing real problems. Jung wrote:

> The separation of the schizophrenic patient from reality, the loss of interest in objective happenings, (all this) is not difficult to explain when we consider that he persistently stands under the ban of an invincible complex. . . . He dreams with open eyes and psychologically no longer adapts himself to his surroundings (Jung, 1936, p. 89).

The schizophrenic complex, Jung believed, is rooted in collective unconscious; unconscious archaic, atavistic material may be the essence of schizophrenia.

An important contribution toward the understanding of schizophrenia was made by H. S. Sullivan, who traced its roots to *disastrous interpersonal relations* between the schizophrenic and his parents and/or other significant adults. Severe anxieties experienced in childhood led to parataxic distortions, resembling Bleuler's autistic thinking, and dissociation, analogous to Freud's repression. Thus schizophrenia is basically a "regressive preponderance" associated with a profound loss of self-esteem, panic states, and regression to the uncanny, weird, prototaxic mode.

Sullivan's idea of "regressive preponderance" and Von Domarus' (1944) principle of "paleological thinking" have been further developed by S. Arieti. Arieti's monograph on schizophrenia (1955) is a detailed and elaborate exposition of his principle of "teleologic regression." Arieti believes that schizophrenia is a regression "because less advanced levels of mental integration are used." It is a teleologic regression because "the regression seems to have a purpose, namely to avoid anxiety by bringing about the wanted results" (1955, p. 192).

It is worth while to notice that Freudians and non-Freudians alike stress regression, aggression, unconscious processes, and loss of contact with reality.

Kretschmer

The intricate puzzle of schizophrenia has been explained by a great variety of concepts and theories. As mentioned before, Kraepelin believed in an organic, chemogenic, or endocrinogenic origin of schizophrenia, and several workers have supported the organic interpretation (see this chapter, section on etiology).

A full-fledged theory of schizophrenia was developed by Kretschmer (1925), who associated schizophrenia with the asthenic (leptosomic), athletic, and often dysplastic bodily structures. Kretschmer's theory, in addition to its constitutional ideas, presented all mental disorders, inclusive of schizophrenia, on a continuum starting with normal schizothymics. Accordingly, any individual of the abovementioned three types of physique could be normal introvert with some tendency to abstraction and fantasy life. Should the normal schizothymic individual deteriorate and become psychotic, his psychosis must be schizophrenia. Critical questions in regard to Kretschmer and Sheldon have been raised above in the section on etiology.

"Model Psychoses"

Experiments with mescaline and LSD 25 have aroused considerable interest and a great deal of speculation concerning the nature of schizophrenia. The symptoms produced in these experiments resemble schizophrenia; the volunteering subjects experienced disturbance in thought processes, severe states of anxiety, general confusion, and delusions (see Baruk, 1949; Savage & Cholden, 1956; Linton & Langs, 1962). Some workers interpreted these findings as indicative of the chemogenic nature of schizophrenia (Osmond & Smythies, 1952).

The fact that mescaline and lysergic acid produce symptoms resembling schizophrenia cannot serve as evidence that schizophrenia is a chemogenic disorder. For example, boldness can be produced by electric current; yet this is not the way men usually get bold. Furthermore, symptoms produced by mescaline and lysergic acid are not specific; nonschizophrenics may display some of these symptoms, and schizophrenia may occur without most of them. Criticism has been raised also in regard to the use of volunteers and validity of results in general (see Esecover, Malitz, & Wilkens, 1961; Wolman, 1962; and others).

While the experiments with model psychosis have shed light on the relationship between chemical agents and human behavior, one may doubt whether they have contributed much to the understanding of schizophrenia. Since most schizophrenics have been incurable, or at least not cured, the experimenters had to be fairly sure that what they produced was merely a state of transient mental confusion.

Pavlov's Theory

Pavlov (1928; 1941) suggested a neurophysiological theory of schizophrenia. He hypothesized that schizophrenia is a protective reaction of weak cortical centers. Schizophrenics are easily excitable and overreact to strong stimuli. When overstimulated, they may burst out in a raging fury. Thus schizophrenia is interpreted by a general *protective inhibition* of the cortex to protect overstimulation of nerve cells. In catatonia the protective inhibition spreads to subcortical and autonomic nerve centers. Outbursts of violence have been interpreted by Pavlov as a lack of control of the weak cortex over subcortical centers.

A great deal of research has been conducted in the Soviet Union on Pavlovian lines. Pavlov's theory operates with several hypothetical constructs. The fact that these constructs are neurophysiological makes them neither more nor less hypothetical than any other constructs. Several empirical studies (see the section on symptomatology) offer impressive support to Pavlov's general ideas.

Learning Theory

There have been efforts to interpret schizophrenia in terms of Hull's learning theory. Mednick (1958) believes that acute schizophrenics are in a state of "heightened drive" which tends to increase the strength of responses. Accordingly, a high-drive group should display faster conditioning than a low-drive group. The studies by Taylor and Spence (1954) and Spence and Taylor (1953) have shown faster eye-blink conditioning in schizophrenics, as compared to normals.

Garmezy (1952) and Mednick (1957), in experiments of generalization of pitch and of space dimensions, respectively found higher generalization in schizophrenics than in normals. However, contrary to Hull's theory, Dunn (1954) found that normal controls generalize better than schizophrenics do with social materials.

According to Hull's theory, organisms in high drive turn to irrelevant and incorrect responses. The fact that schizophrenics perform poorly on complex tests (Hall & Crookes, 1951; Hunt & Coffer, 1944; Mednick, 1957) has been explained by Mednick in a Hullian fashion as follows: "The schizophrenic performance has been retarded by irrelevant, incorrect response."

Other Theories

A multiple-factor theory of schizophrenia was proposed by Bellak. Bellak doubts whether there is one principal cause for schizophrenia. He compares schizophrenia to "fever" as diagnosed in early studies of medicine. Schizophrenia can be produced by LSD 25, by perceptual isolation, and by several other physicochemical or psychological factors. "Schizophrenia lies at the low end of the continuum of ego strength," wrote Bellak (1958, p. 53). "Schizophrenia was designated as a syndrome characterized by a final common path of disturbances of the ego, with a primary etiology of chemogenic, histogenic, genogenic or psychogenic nature and a combination thereof, different in each individual case, but probably identifiable as clusters in subgroups" (*ibid.*, pp. 61–62).

A comparative-developmental theory of schizophrenia based on H. Werner's work has been introduced by A. E. Goldman. Goldman views schizophrenia as a "regression," meaning by that "the structural re-emergence of developmentally lower levels of functioning as the more advanced and more recently developed levels are disorganized" (1962). Thus, emotions become uncontrolled, aggressive and impulsive feelings are fused, and the emotional experience of an acute schizophrenic becomes similar to that of a young child, labile and unpredictable. There is regression in perception, and attention is shifting. Schizophrenics perform poorly on complex tests, and their total behavior is indicative of a low-level performance.

Adolf Meyer (see Lief, 1948) stressed the gradual deterioration in mental life. Schizophrenia may start as a series of "trivial and harmless subterfuges" such as decline in interest in the outside world, gradual withdrawal into fantasy life, moodiness that may eventually lead into a schizophrenic reaction.

Existentialist psychology has interpreted schizophrenia chiefly as a "hypotonia of consciousness." Schizophrenic sense of reality has been affected. The schizophrenic experiences himself "as so limited in his full humanity that he can no longer feel himself as really 'existent'" (Frankl, 1955).

Sociopsychosomatic Theory

An effort has been made to bring together all the relevant factual data and present schizophrenia in a sociopsychosomatic continuum. Such a continuum reverses Pavlov's somapsychological continuum. While Pavlov started from the "weak cortex" and went to behavior, my starting point has been behavior.

The psychological frame of reference of this theory is a modified Freudian personality model. While Sullivan's emphasis on interpersonal relations has influenced most workers dealing with schizophrenia, there seems to be no need to abandon Freud's superior personality model. However, some modifications of Freud's theory seem to be advisable. A new theoretical construct—namely, "interindividual cathexis"—a revision of Freud's pleasure and pain theory, and finally a new interpretation of the role of hate and destructive impulses in mental disorders have been introduced (Wolman, 1960a, chap. 15).

The study of manifest social relations has been conducted experimentally in the framework of the power and acceptance theory. Power has been defined as the ability to satisfy needs; acceptance, as willingness to do so. Furthermore, a distinction has been made into instrumental (take), mutual (give and take), and vectorial (give) types of interaction (Wolman, 1955; 1958a; 1960b).

As mentioned in the section on etiology, in schizogenic families the parent versus parent relationship is hostile-instrumental. Mother versus child relationship is pseudovectorial, actually exploitative-instrumental. Father versus child relationship is frankly instrumental, either seductive or competitive. The child is forced to worry about his parents instead of their worrying about him. In this reversal of social roles the child becomes the "protector of his protectors."

This noxious social relationship represents in a modified Freudian framework a disbalance of interindividual cathexes. The child who is normally a "taker" (instrumental) is forced prematurely into a precocious giving (hypervectorial) relationship. Hence *vectoriasis praecox,* the proposed new name for schizophrenia. This abundant, premature object cathexis inevitably leads to an inadequate self-cathexis. Whatever exists, exists in some quantity; thus an abundant object cathexis of libido adversely affects self-cathexis of libido (see Federn, 1952). Hence the lowered vitality and general decline in behavior proficiency.

All living organisms struggle for survival. The preschizophrenic sacrifices himself, as it were, to protect those who are supposed to protect him. When he reaches an exceedingly low level of libido self-cathexis, destrudo (the hostile impulse) takes over. A wounded animal either flees in mortal fear or attacks everyone in terror. Paranoid and catatonic hostility resemble the rage of a wounded animal.

Thus schizophrenia can be interpreted as a process of downward adjustment in an irrational struggle for survival. In the "hebephrenic" type there is less fight and more regression; the "simple" type represents resignation and surrender.

Schizophrenia starts as a paradoxical action of an organism that abandons its own protection to protect those who should protect the organism. It is a severe disbalance of libido and destrudo cathexes; in its milder, latent stages it represents a struggle against its own hostile impulses and fear they may break through. In psychoanalytic terms, the superego is overgrown, demanding, and dictatorial and the ego struggles to prevent the outburst of id impulses. As long as the struggle goes on, it is a neurotic, character neurotic, or latent psychotic stage. When the ego fails and the unconscious impulses and primary processes disrupt the conscious control, it is a manifest psychosis. In some cases the destroyed personality structure lies in shambles in a dementive state.

Obviously these profound psychological changes must affect the function of the central and autonomous nervous system and usually affect also endocrine and other organic processes. Somatic symptoms in schizophrenia are, therefore, interpreted as psychosomatic ones (Arieti, 1955). These symptoms could be interpreted as a result of an inadequate libido self-cathexis; the hypocathected organs are affected first (Wolman, 1964b, chap. 3).

SYMPTOMATOLOGY

Mental Deterioration

While Kraepelin stressed the over-all dementia in schizophrenics, E. Bleuler believed that the disturbances in association and thought processes are the main symptoms. According to Bleuler, associations in schizophrenia are disrupted, and in acute cases "one often finds so complete a fragmentation of the thinking processes that they cannot result in a complete idea or action" (1950, p. 350).

Several workers, among them C. G. Jung (1936), Von Domarus (1944), K. Goldstein (1946), and others, stressed the impairment of thinking in schizophrenics. Hanfmann and Kasanin (1942), Goldman (1962), and others found in schizophrenics substantial decline in the ability of conceptual thinking.

Shakow, in several studies (1946, 1962), pointed to the inability of schizophrenics to keep a "set." It is not to be confused with a general mental decline; schizophrenic mental processes are not dementive but peculiarly fragmentary, disjointed, and discontinuous.

It has been noticed (Wolman, 1958b) that schizophrenics misplace objects, make errors in writing or typing, worry about their own health and the well-being of family and friends. They often forget what they have to do and worry about their forgetfulness.

Often schizophrenics regress to prelogical ways of thinking, and their reasoning becomes fallacious (Arieti, 1955). Anne Roe and D. Shakow (1942), using the 1916 Stanford-Binet Scale, found that the mean in months of mental age for normal controls was 164, for catatonics 165, for simple schizophrenics 156, for paranoids 155, for unclassified 144, and for hebephrenics 129. E. Harper (1950) used Form I of the Wechsler-Bellevue Scale. On the verbal IQ scores the undifferentiated cases of schizophrenia scored 95, paranoid schizophrenics 92, simple schizophrenics 87, catatonics 86, hebephrenics 84.

Rapaport and Webb (1950) compared the IQ scores of schizophrenics in their premorbid high school years to the scores they obtained when hospitalized. The decline of 33.7 points was largely related to negativism and lack of attention.

Hall and Crookes (1951) administered verbal learning lists to normal, organic, and schizophrenic subjects. Chronic schizophrenics scored lowest. They frequently used stereotyped response patterns. Schizophrenics were easily discouraged; whenever they failed in their efforts, they turned to stereotyped, purposeless movements.

Shakow (1946) found a .56 correlation coefficient between cooperation rates of schizophrenics and their performance on the Stanford-Binet. The correlation coefficient between cooperation and performance on the Army Alpha was .61.

Binder (1956) applied Thurstone's Test of Primary Mental Abilities to 120 schizophrenics and 107 controls. The over-all performance of schizophrenics was poorer than that of normals.

The vocabulary performance of schizophrenics is a controversial issue. Shakow (1946) found that schizophrenics obtained better scores on vocabulary tests than on any other item in intelligence tests. However, Yacorzynski (1941) and Feifel (1949) found significant differences in verbal definitions between schizophrenics and normals. Rabin, King, and Erhman (1955) studied two groups of schizophrenics, one of a recent onset and the other chronic. No significant differences were found between the short-term schizophrenics and the normal controls, but chronic schizophrenics scored lower than both the normal controls and the short-term schizophrenic cases. Intellectual impairment was "not noted in catatonic and paranoid types" (Rabin & King, 1958).

Mason (1956) studied 368 inducted men diagnosed as schizophrenics. The catatonic and paranoid schizophrenics obtained normal IQs. Simple and hebephrenic schizophrenics obtained lower IQs than the normal controls and other psychopathological recruits.

Garmezy (1952) shed additional light on this problem. He trained acute but cooperative schizophrenics and normal controls in auditory perception involving the ability to discriminate tones. In one test reward was given for a proper discrimination of tones; in another test reward was given for correct answers and a mild punishment administered for incorrect ones. In the first set of experiments there were but minor differences between acute schizophrenics and normals. When exposed to mild punishment, schizophrenics failed on the test and gave up efforts to improve.

A threat of failure may impair the intellectual functioning of schizophrenics. However, if the threat does not come directly from the supposedly friendly figure, be it a therapist, a parent, or an experimenter, but is an external threat, schizophrenics may work better (Wolman, 1957; 1958b). In an experiment conducted by Pascal and Swensen (1952), schizophrenics attained the same level of performance when exposed to a loud, threatening, and distracting noise. My interpretation is that an external threat helps to shift mental energies from the superego to the ego. When a threat comes from an emotionally neutral source such as inanimate nature, animals, or strangers, this threat forces a flow of energies into the protective apparatus, the ego. When the ego becomes libido-cathected, the performance on the task improves.

The fact that motivation greatly influences the level of intellectual functioning of schizophrenics was demonstrated by Huston and Shakow (1946). Schizophrenic performance on motor learning was less efficient than the performance of normal controls. However, when an experimental group of schizophrenics was encouraged and prodded, their performance reached about the normal level.

Performance on a test depends largely on the attention of the experimental subject. Apparently most schizophrenics are overattentive to detail and underattentive to the over-all task.

Impairment of attention has been the subject of extensive studies in the U.S.S.R. Hamburg (in Russian, Gamburg) reported experiments with auditory stimuli and mild electric shock on 69 schizophrenics. Normal individuals respond with alertness, called by the Russians "orientation reaction"; that is, increase in muscular, autonomic activity and electroencephalic frequency. Paranoid schizophrenics reacted defensively to the stimuli; simple schizophrenics did not react at all. While this behavior can be interpreted in terms of Pavlov's "protective inhibition" (see Malis, 1961), it can also be interpreted as an unconscious fear to do anything that might be an invitation to criticism (Wolman, 1957; 1958b).

Schizophrenics are "children of mood"; in a happy mood, when they feel accepted—i.e., when they receive libido cathexes—they are at their best. When they feel rejected, especially by those whom they love or respect, their performance may go down. This is probably the reason why research workers cannot agree as to whether there is any substantial decline in mental functions in schizophrenia.

While over-all mental decline in schizophrenia can be doubted, peculiarities in the intellectual functioning of schizophrenics have been noticed. Z. Piotrowski (1937; 1946) and other research workers noticed that schizophrenic children perceive on Rorschach minute details with great precision and then proceed to elaborate while overlooking larger details (see also Part 3, "The Rorschach Inkblot Method").

This overattention to detail is not necessarily a product of an impairment in cognitive processes; it may also represent a peculiar manner of relating oneself to the world. The tendency to hypercathect certain objects must lead to hypocathecting of others. A schizophrenic may become attached to a minute detail and overlook everything else.

The hypothesis of an over-all perceptual regression in schizophrenia has been forwarded by H. Friedman (1953) and E. L. Siegel (1953). Both studies are based on analysis of Rorschach data. The Rorschach responses of adult schizophrenics were considerably less mature than those of normal adults; most of the responses resembled children's Rorschach responses. Siegel observed that the responses of paranoid schizophrenics were on the perceptual level of age 6 to 10 and the responses of catatonics and hebephrenics were on the age level of 3 to 5 years.

K. Goldstein, however, noticed that a schizophrenic is not always schizophrenic.

> Under some conditions the patient behaves abstractly, logically, particularly in situations where his *personal relationship is not concerned*. . . . The withdrawn child, who later may become schizophrenic, often develops his intellectual capacities very well. . . . The abnormal concreteness of the schizophrenic is not an effect of a damage of abstraction, does not represent a deterioration of the mind, is not a defect in thinking. It represents an expression of the restriction in the use of the highest mental capacity in a special realm of life because in this way the individual is protected against the dangers of the anxiety which arise from this realm as an after-effect of the events in infancy. (Goldstein, 1946).

Federn (1952) and several other research workers confirmed Goldstein's ideas. I came across several children who scored poorly on mental tests but improved rapidly when put into a friendly and encouraging environment. I am inclined to believe that the impairment of cognitive and reasoning functions in schizophrenia is not a product of a genuine mental impairment as in organic disorders and deficiency. Intellectual impairment in schizophrenics is a product of a loss of contact with reality and the unconscious flooding the conscious.

C. L. Winder wrote that the

> current utility of the vague clinical concept "intellectual deterioration" seems small indeed. That individual patients show deficit in the area of intellectual functioning is certain both from clinical observation and from psychometric research. One must conclude that this topic is in an infant stage of conceptualization and investigation. (Winder, 1960, p. 205).

I am inclined to believe that the irrational thinking and acting of schizophrenics is produced to some extent by the *situation* in which the schizophrenic finds himself *here and now*. Schizophrenia is an escape into a lower level of functioning (downward adjustment). When the ego fails, some sort of morbid adjustment is made. Schizophrenia is a morbid way of living adopted when every other way seems to have failed.

Conditioning

Research in conditioning of schizophrenics has brought controversial results. Russian studies (see Malis, 1961; Lynn, 1963) have reported various degrees of impairment in conditioning, most in catatonics, less in paranoiacs. Soviet scientists interpret this impairment by invoking Pavlov's theory of general protective inhibition of the cerebral cortex. Also Skinner (1954), B. D. Cohen (1956), and other workers found learning performance in schizophrenics inferior in comparison to normal controls.

Huston and Shakow (1948) found that motivation is an important factor in learning of schizophrenics. The same schizophrenics who initially performed poorly attained a normal level after a period of prodding.

Hull's school of learning claims different results. In contradistinction to all the above-mentioned studies, Taylor and Spence (1954) and Mednick (1958) found that schizophrenics conditioned *better* than normals. Their superior learning performance, as mentioned before, has been interpreted by an intensification of anxiety that affects the increase in the strength of the conditioned response. According to Hull, heightened drive state always causes an increase in response; accordingly the tense schizophrenics should perform better.

Also stimulus generalization was found higher in schizophrenics than in normal controls with the same intelligence (Garmezy 1952). Mednick (1958) found schizophrenics exceeding on simple tasks and failing on complex ones. He interpreted this phenomenon by Hull's theory. However, King (1954) found chronic schizophrenics inferior in speed of tapping, finger dexterity, and simple reaction time. Stotsky (1957) found that chronic and remitted cases improve reaction time in repeated trials. Venables (1961) failed to find significant difference between schizophrenics and normals in regard to delayed or accelerated reaction time. Huston and Shahow (1946) found no differences between cooperative schizophrenics and normals in regard to eye-hand coordination. The factor of social motivation in reaction time was stressed by Rosenbaum et al. (1957). Other motivational factors were studied by Fedio, Mirsky, Smith, and Parry (1961) and Cavanaugh, Cohen, and Lang (1960).

In brief, motivational factors and social interaction seem to play an important role in determining the level of schizophrenic performance.

Unconscious

All schizophrenics, whether on a prepsychotic or manifestly psychotic level, have unusual recollections from their early childhood. They recall events that happened years before and talk about them as if they took place only yesterday. They can give a detailed description of minute events that happened twenty or thirty years ago and relate precisely the feelings they experienced in early childhood.

Normally, preconscious is easily accessible and unconscious warded off. In schizophrenics the barrier between unconscious and preconscious gradually or rapidly disappears.

As long as the ego somehow controls the mental apparatus, the preschizophrenics may display unusual abilities. The access to unconscious resources enriches one's mental life, and many schizophrenics have a past history of brilliant performance at the elementary, high school, or college level. Not all schizophrenics are gifted, and most probably there is no causal relationship between the incidence of schizophrenia and IQ; schizogenic families are not a class or educational or intellectual privilege. Some preschizophrenic children perform below their ability and are sometimes diagnosed as mentally retarded; other preschizophrenics perform at their best. As long as the ego exercises its control over unconscious resources, the latent schizophrenic may be as creative and productive as his innate abilities warrant.

When the unconscious breaks through the barriers, the continuity of conscious processes is disrupted. The unconscious floods the conscious; overt, manifest psychosis starts.

Once the unconscious breaks through, the schizophrenic may believe he is a most important person. He may imagine he is an inventor, a king, a great and dangerous person, a prophet, or a monster, but always the omnipotent superparental figure, always the protector of protectors. He may believe others try to steal his ideas, fear his power, and hate him. Certainly his enemies read his mind. Hence paranoid accusations of persecution, ideas of reference, delusions and hallucinations of grandeur, and world-saving or world-destroying wishes.

The drama of the schizophrenic personality

overdevoted to his parents evolves in delusions and hallucinations. What is carefully hidden and desperately repressed in the prepsychotic stages breaks through with an irresistible clarity in the display of unconscious in manifest schizophrenia. Schizophrenics are not the rejected children; they are the "overdemanded," overcriticized, and overinvolved. When rational controls break down, the conflict between the demand for perfection and the failure to meet this demand may take on delusory forms (Wolman, 1964b).

Depression and Elation

Practically all schizophrenics go through frequent and prolonged periods of depression, of which two types may be distinguished. When one is exposed to overwhelming odds that make him feel defeated and helpless, it is an *exogenous* depression. Whenever depression is caused by inner strife, it is *endogenous.* The latter can be interpreted as a self-directed aggression, mainly an aggression of the superego directed against the ego. In schizophrenia the superego, representing the overdemanding parents, is always directed against the ego. Hence profound feelings of guilt and depression.

Schizophrenics often harbor hostile feelings toward others and toward themselves. Whenever they display hostility to others (object destrudo) they feel guilty and depressed. This phenomenon has been interpreted as a retaliation of the primitive superego against the ego that failed to control destructive impulses (see Bychowski, 1952; Federn, 1952; Wolman, 1958b).

Endogenous depression can be fostered and perpetuated by an exogenous depression. Life histories of most schizophrenics contain several bitter disappointments, for their irrational behavior is not conducive to success. Failures in study and occupation and severe frustrations in interindividual relations cause an objectively determined exogenous depression. Thus schizophrenics cannot help seeing their past experiences as a history of defeat.

Schizophrenics can be in a good mood, especially when people pay attention to them or genuinely like them. This interindividual libido cathexis coming from within seems to improve their balance of intraindividual cathexes.

Schizophrenics are greatly elated when they hallucinate power and omnipotence. A sharp distinction has to be made between the schizophrenic exultation and the manic bliss. The manic-depressive elation stems from mother's love toward him. The schizophrenic is elated when *he* feels capable of loving and protecting his mother, when *he* acts as a *superparent.*

Self-neglect

Schizophrenia is a regression to a lower degree of functioning in accordance with the principle of downward adjustment. Lack of personal care counts among the most outstanding symptoms. Most schizophrenics neglect their looks and health and do not act in a rational, self-protective manner as other people do. Some schizophrenics, if not taken care of, will die out.

Practically all schizophrenics are highly irregular in their sleeping habits and in the intake of food and water; they often overdo in the intake of food or neglect it altogether. Neglect of physical appearance and personal neatness is another symptom of schizophrenic deterioration. Schizophrenics often fail to comb their hair, to wash, to brush their teeth, to change linen, and to keep themselves neat and tidy. They neglect their physical well-being and fail to take care of themselves when ill.

Sexual Disturbances

When a constricted, bashful, self-restrained latent schizophrenic becomes highly promiscuous, one may suspect a severe decline in the ego controls and apparatus. Among manifest schizophrenics premarital and extramarital sexual relations run exceedingly high. Most women "can not resist" or "want to please," "do not care to resist" or feel "it just does not matter," or they simply "get involved." Men either practice sex indiscriminately with girls of a significantly lower social class or marry, against their own judgment, aggressive women who lead them to the altar. Sexual violence and acts of rape may take place. Once the barriers fall, the raw, unbound, unneutralized impulses break loose (see Hartmann, 1955; Kris, 1955).

The inability to control impulses applies also to homosexuality. Obviously not all homosexuals are schizophrenics, nor are all schizophrenics necessarily homosexual, for sexual perversions and anarchy are not an infrequent phenomenon among the deteriorated types of all mental disorders who lack self-restraint and inhibitions.

Freud noticed in 1911 (the Schreber case) the peculiar connection between homosexual tendencies and paranoid projections (1924–1950, vol. III, pp. 387ff.). Freud admitted that these phenomena are found also in psychoneuroses and not in schizophrenia only. Some workers (Katan, 1954) stressed the importance of fear of homosexuality in the etiology of schizophrenia. It seems, however, that the *reversal of age and sex roles* in the schizogenic families confuses the preschizophrenics. This confusion prevents proper sex identification and leads in many cases to definite homosexual patterns. Some schizophrenics, especially hebephrenics, practice homosexuality without apparent anxiety; in paranoid schizophrenics, however, the homosexual impulses seem to create a profound anxiety. In the paranoid persecution delusion the individual denies his homosexual impulses and ascribes them to his parent of the same sex or to a parental substitute. In order to deny the parental true or imaginary homosexual advances, he assumes that the parent hates him. A reaction formation that makes the patient feel "I hate him" instead of admitting "I love him" completes the maneuver (see Fenichel, 1945, chap. 18).

This paranoid maneuver applies probably also to heterosexual incestuous fears. Several male and female patients reported alleged parental seductions and rapes that were later disproved (Wolman 1965a). Paranoid delusions may relate to any threat stemming from the superego and projected on true or imaginary objects.

Withdrawal

Schizophrenia, being produced probably by morbid interindividual relations, certainly disrupts normal human relations. The hurt schizophrenic fears, distrusts, and avoids people. He fears to become overinvolved, as he has been with his mother. He fears competition, punishment, and/or rejection, as experienced so often in his childhood. He fears the criticism and ostracism that have usually been found in school and among children. Preschizophrenics are, as a rule, shy and insecure and rarely become popular with their agemates. The less faith they have had in themselves, the less they have had courage to enter social relations, and most of them were social isolates in childhood.

Loneliness is one of the most outstanding symptoms of schizophrenia. Yet whenever a schizophrenic breaks through the wall of fear he becomes overinvolved in an intense relationship. Schizophrenics know no moderation in interindividual relationships; they are either shallow, cold, and withdrawn or intensely involved. When involved, they become possessive, jealous, despotic-protective, and overdemanding.

Depersonalization

Schizophrenics often feel that something is missing in them. When reality testing fails, they may experience delusions and hallucinations. Somatic sensations play a significant role in these processes. A schizophrenic may feel that his hand turns into glass or his body is full of bugs. He may complain about his poor vision or poor motor coordination or not being self any more. Loss of ego control over the perceptory and motor apparatus is experienced as a loss of identity. Unconscious images coming from within, hallucinations, and delusions deepen the feeling of not being oneself.

THE MAIN SYNDROMES

Process and Reactive Types

Bleuler's distinction between deteriorating and recovering cases gave rise to a division of schizophrenia into process and reactive types. Kant (1948) believed the malignant *process schizophrenia* to be characterized by a gradual decline of activity, dullness, autism, ideas of reference, and thought disturbances. Oscillation between excitement and stuporous depression, and periods of almost normal functioning alternating with states of confusion, are characteristics of the benign, *reactive schizophrenic*.

Chase and Silverman (1943) studied recovery rates in Metrazol and insulin shock therapy. Pyknic body type, acute onset, short duration of severe symptoms, premorbid good adjustment, and extrovert personality type have been related to a good prognosis. Asthenic body type, apathy, introversion, insidious onset of severe symptoms, dissociation, awareness of personality disintegration, have been related to poor prognosis. The Metrazol and insulin shock therapies have produced satisfactory results in the good-prognostic cases only. Apparently all these cases belong to the reactive type.

According to Kantor, Wallner, and Winder (1953) reactive schizophrenics have good premorbid adjustment, good physical health, adequate adjustment at home and in school, extroversion, no somatic delusions, etc. The process schizophrenics have a prolonged history of maladjustment, poor physical health, difficulties at home and in school, abnormal family relationships, insidious onset of psychosis, somatic delusions, etc. However, Rorschach administered to patients diagnosed as process and reactive schizophrenics failed to prove psychosis in most of the process schizophrenics. Thus serious doubts have been voiced as to whether the so-called process schizophrenics are schizophrenics (Herron, 1962) and, if so, whether the distinction of two types is justified. King (1958) found, according to the above-mentioned Kantor et al., that reactive schizophrenics reacted to mecholyl with a substantially greater drop in blood pressure than the process schizophrenics. Research conducted by Zuckerman and Gross (1959) contradicted King's findings.

Brackbill and Fine (1956), McDonough (1960), and others hypothesized that process schizophrenia is related to organic factors. No definite evidence has been adduced. Arieti (1955), Becker (1956), Wolman (1957), and other workers did not find clear indications for a reactive versus process distinction. On the other hand, Herron (1962) stated in a recent review that it is possible to demonstrate differences between these two groups. Phillips (1953), Garmezy and Rodnick (1959), and others have seemed to believe that such a distinction has some prognostic value; however, the premorbid history of each patient is determined to a great extent by his environment.

The schizophrenic personality is exceedingly labile and easily influenced by interaction with other individuals. A schizophrenic is not always schizophrenic; the fact is that even the so-called chronic schizophrenics respond to human warmth and kindness and show surprising improvement (see Freeman, Cameron, & McGhie, 1958; Rosen, 1953; Schwing, 1954; Wolman, 1964b). Thus prognosis in schizophrenia depends not only upon past experiences but also upon future interaction.

Some research workers divide all schizophrenics into high- and low-reacting patterns (Gellhorn, 1958; and others). Venables (1960), in a similar vein, distinguished between a high and a low level of arousal in schizophrenic behavior. Mednick (1958) found substantial differences between high- and low-level anxiety types in schizophrenia.

Freud, as mentioned above, stressed the loss of objects and efforts to regain them. Accordingly, Fenichel divided schizophrenic symptoms into two categories. *Regressive* symptoms are

> direct expressions of a regressive breakdown of the ego and an undoing of differentiations acquired through mental development (a primitivation). Other symptoms represent various attempts at restitution. The first category of symptoms embraces phenomena such as fantasies of world destruction, physical sensations, depersonalization, delusion of grandeur, archaic ways of thinking and speaking, hebephrenic and certain catatonic symptoms. The second category embraces hallucinations, delusions, most of the schizophrenic social and speech peculiarities, and other catatonic symptoms (Fenichel, 1945, p. 417).

Division of symptoms related to ego strength has been proposed (Wolman, 1958b; 1964b). The *ego-protective* symptoms indicate the struggle of the ego to retain the control over the unconscious impulses. All "defense mechanisms" and varieties of neurotic symptoms belong to this category. The preschizophrenic has been called pseudoneurotic by Hoch and Polatin (1949); most probably he is a schizo-type neurotic before he becomes a schizophrenic psychotic (Wolman, 1958b; 1958c). The main ego-protective symptom of this hypervectorial or preschizophrenic neurotic is the overmobilization of the ego reflected in his constricted, introvert, high-strung, tense personality. The preschizophrenic neurotic is overconscientious, moralistic, and dogmatic. He often develops phobias, obsessive-compulsive behavior, and partial withdrawal from social contacts. All these *ego-protective* symptoms may postpone and even prevent psychotic breakdown.

Whether the ego-protective symptoms will prevent the onset of manifest psychosis depends on a variety of benign and noxious factors (see Arieti, 1955; Hill, 1955; Bychowski, 1952). When these symptoms fail, a series of ego-deficiency symptoms start, indicating an insidious or sudden collapse of the ego. Loss of contact with reality, paranoid delusions, hallucinations, inability to control unconscious impulses, violence, stupor, depersonalization, as well as motor and speech disturbances belong to the ego-deficiency symptoms.

No schizophrenic has lost contact with reality completely and irreversibly. The therapeutic work of P. Federn (1952), F. Fromm-Reichmann (1950; 1952; 1959), J. N. Rosen (1953), S. Arieti (1955), G. Schwing (1954), Sechekaye (1956), Eissler (1947; 1952), H. S. Sullivan (1947; 1953), Wolman (1957; 1964b) and scores of other workers indicates that even severely deteriorated schizophrenics are accessible and responsive to treatment. Whether this "treatment" is a planned therapeutic interaction or a result of an unplanned but exceedingly helpful interaction with a friend is an open question. There is, however, no doubt that schizophrenics in remission develop *ego-compensation* symptoms, as if going back from psychosis toward normalcy. How far back they can go is still a controversial issue (see Arieti, 1955; Brody & Redlich, 1952; Dawson, Stone, & Dellis, 1961; English, Hanupe, Badon, & Settlage, 1961; Knight, 1953; Riemer, 1950; Rifkin, 1957; Scher & Davis, 1960; Wolman, 1959a; 1964b).

Continuum Theory

It seems possible to present preschizophrenic and schizophrenic syndromes in a continuum starting from an almost normal behavior toward the most severe disorder. Kretschmer's theory (1925) represents such a continuum leading from a normal schizothymic behavior toward a fully developed manifest schizophrenia. Physique was the uniting factor in the variety of symptoms of Kretschmer's schizothymic type.

One can present schizophrenia and related disorders in a continuum using sociopsychological determinants as the uniting factor. According to the above-mentioned sociopsychosomatic theory (Wolman, 1964b), schizophrenia, in a broad sense of the word, starts with the peculiar disbalance of libido cathexes. Precocious object hypercathexis and resulting self-hypocathexis or, in terms of overt social behavior, a precocious hypervectorialism is the core of the group of schizothymic or hypervectorial disorders.

One may distinguish five *levels* of mental disorders; namely, neurosis, character neurosis, latent psychosis, manifest psychosis, and dementive stage (see "Mental Health and Mental Disorders," below). In hypervectorial or schizo-type disorders the neurotic step includes phobic, neurasthenic, and obsessive-compulsive patterns. The schizoid character neurosis corresponds to what is usually called the schizoid personality. The next step in schizophrenic deterioration is latent schizophrenia. Next comes manifest schizophrenia, called *vectoriasis praecox* (Wolman, 1957). The manifest psychotic level may come in four syndromes; namely, the paranoid, catatonic, hebephrenic, and simple deterioration. The last, dementive level is the end of decline and a complete collapse of personality structure. All five levels represent an ever-growing disbalance of cathexes of sexual and hostile impulses. The decline of the controlling force of the ego is the most significant determinant of each level. As long as the ego exercises control, it is neurosis. When ego comes to terms with the symptoms, it is character neurosis. When ego is on the verge of collapse, it is latent psychosis. When ego fails, it is manifest psychosis, or the full-blown schizophrenia in one of its four syndromes. A complete dilapidation of the ego and behavior on the id level is typical for the severely deteriorated, dementive stage.

The Neurotic Level

Freud, in a paper on "Neurosis and Psychosis" published in 1924, wrote, "Neurosis is the result of a conflict between the ego and its id, whereas psychosis is the analogous outcome of a similar disturbance in relation between the ego and its environment (outer world)" (1924–1950). In *An Outline of Psychoanalysis* (first published in 1940) he wrote, "The precipitating cause of the outbreak of psychosis is either that reality has become intolerably painful or that the instincts have become extraordinarily intensified" (1949a, p. 114).

One may say, therefore, that as long as the ego somehow preserves its contact with the external world and controls the id, it is neurosis. Whenever the ego loses contact with reality and the id impulses take over, it is a full, manifest psychosis. Psychosis is most often a neurosis that failed (Wolman, 1957; 1959b).

Not all psychotics were neurotics prior to becoming psychotics. Psychosis may start in childhood when a failing or underdeveloped ego was never capable of developing neurotic ego-protective symptoms. There are cases, however, in which schizophrenia was temporarily or entirely prevented by the neurotic mechanisms. In hypervectorial disorders the main mechanisms are compulsions, phobias, and rigidity.

This similarity in personality between preschizophrenia and the psychasthenic (obsessive-compulsive) neurosis has been stressed by several workers.

> It is important to emphasize the fact that one usually finds the psychasthenic syndrome developing in a certain type of personality. Long before the actual outbreak of the fully developed symptom we find these persons exhibiting such characteristics as rigid pedantry, scrupulousness, tendency to hair splitting, stubbornness in their convictions. . . . The personality makeup of such an individual is very likely to be that of the introverted, self-centered, daydreaming type (Malamud, 1944, p. 852).

The obsessional patient's "way of dealing with his symptoms, or rather concealing them, is not inherently different from that which is practiced by some paranoid and paraphrenic patients, or even by those in the early stages of schizophrenia" (Skottowe, 1954, p. 308).

Several research workers found exactly the same phenomenon in psychasthenics and schizophrenics, namely lack of inductive thinking, preference to W and Dd responses on Rorschach with neglect of D responses, perseveration, and rigidity. Preoccupation with minor aspects of life is typical for both obsessive-compulsive neurosis, schizoid character, and latent schizophrenia (see Parts 3, 6, of this *Handbook*).

Rorschach investigators had difficulties in differentiating between mild and latent schizophrenics on one side and neurotics on the other (Mace, Koff, Chelnek, & Garfield, 1949; Piotrowski & Lewis, 1950). Their diagnostic difficulties seem to be sometimes insurmountable. Perseveration, rigidity, preoccupation with minute detail, compulsive accuracy, were found in several cases of neurotics classified as obsessive-compulsives, neurasthenics, etc., and in milder cases of schizophrenics. Research in Rorschach points to identical elements in personality structure of the obsessive-compulsive neurosis and schizophrenia:

> Exaggerated emphasis upon the accuracy of the match between blot form and object form is frequently found in compulsive neurotics. . . . Their reality testing, correspondingly, is rigid and inflexible. . . . In its inflexibility, the reality testing reveals its origin in a reaction formation against distortions of reality. However, we see the impairment of reality testing in two other ways. . . . Life situations in general do not require such rigid delineations of what is "real." It is a result of inner compulsion, not of outer need. It is at this point that the compulsive individual is almost a caricature of accuracy. In order to be so exact, he chooses smaller and smaller blot areas to match with his percepts. . . . The reality testing part of the extremely compulsive individual is so taken up by preoccupation with the minor aspects of life that he fails to come to terms with the broad issues (B. Klopfer et al., 1956, vol. 11, p. 288).

Freud's analysis of the obsessive neurosis (often called psychasthenia or obsessive-compulsive) pointed to the peculiar relationship between the ego and superego. While the superego is very exacting, the ego rebels against the guilt feeling imposed by the superego (Freud, 1927). This "rebellion" is, I believe, nothing but the dependence-independence syndrome of schizophrenia reflecting the internalized maternal demands, the child's hostile rebellion, and the child's fear that his hostile rebellion may kill mother. Hence ritualistic compulsions to ward off the threat of doing something wrong. Practically every obsessive-compulsive neurotic, in a striking similarity to schizophrenics, is tormented by recurring thoughts that he may hurt his relatives, commit a sacrilege, eliminate in public, or practice incest or homosexuality. There is invariably the feeling of "being pushed to do something wrong and pulled back from doing it." "Do" and "don't" are indispensable elements of this neurosis. The impulses

> consist of something terrifying such as temptations to commit serious crimes, so that the patient not only repudiates them as alien

> but flees from them in horror and guards himself by prohibitions, precautions, and restrictions against the possibility of carrying them out (Freud, 1949b, p. 229).

The main defense mechanisms in the obsessive neurosis are repression, displacement, undoing, and reaction formation. The obsessive actions "are mostly repetitions and ceremonial elaborations of ordinary everyday performances, making these common necessary actions—going to bed, washing, dressing for walks, etc.—into highly laborious tasks of almost insuperable difficulty" (*ibid.*, pp. 229–230).

Phobias are probably as frequent in this neurosis as compulsions. Phobias apply the mechanism of displacement (Anna Freud, 1946). Fear of becoming a rapist was displaced in one patient into a fear of going out, of being in the open space, or *agoraphobia*. A fear of hurting his father turned into a fear of cutting bread; with a female patient, a fear of penis turned into a fear of roosters.

Phobias can change into compulsive actions, and obsessive thoughts can turn into phobias. The psychoanalytic theory offers an ample explanation of these phenomena. The obsessive-compulsive neurotic who is

> threatened by the rebellion of his (regressively distorted) sensual and hostile demands feels protected as long as he behaves in an "orderly" manner. . . . The unconscious anal-sadistic drives, however, usually sabotage orderliness. . . . Any disturbance of "routine" unconsciously means murder and incest. . . . Compulsion ensures against the menace of dangerous spontaneity. . . . The compulsion neurotic is aware that he has instincts nevertheless. He can never achieve the satisfying feeling that he is actually following the rules, that enough rules are provided to govern all possibilities, and that he knows all the rules sufficiently (Fenichel, 1945, pp. 284–285).

Many schizophrenics in remission develop symptoms (ego-compensation) of the neurotic stage of the hypervectorial type.

> We have observed that without exception every psychotic patient we have had has passed through a phase of his illness which was characterized by a preponderance of paranoid ideas. Many patients remain at this stage which the colleagues agree to call paranoid; some go on for one reason or another to levels of deeper regression, namely hebephrenia and catatonia, and others even improve back to a severe form of neurosis, particularly of the obsessive-compulsive type (Rosen, 1953, p. 97).

E. Bleuler, as early as 1911, stressed the connection between catatonic automatisms, hallucinations and obsessive ideas, and compulsive acts. He wrote, "When compulsive ideas occur in conjunction with schizophrenia, the symptoms of the latter disease become manifest very early in the course of the illness and . . . assume a prominent position (1950, pp. 449ff.).

In 1894 Freud explained that repressed ideas lead to obsessive-compulsive symptoms. In some cases, however,

> the ego rejects the unbearable idea together with its associated affect and behaves as if the idea never occurred to the person at all. But, as soon as this process has been successfully carried through, the person in question will have developed a psychosis, and his state can only be described as one of "hallucinatory confusion" (Freud, 1924–1950, vol. 1, pp. 72–73).

My interpretation of the transition of an obsession into hallucination is somewhat different; it is the victory of the repressed impulse that breaks through the defense mechanisms.

The phobic and compulsive symptoms need not be regarded as a clinical entity. One may develop phobias or compulsions and not be a hypervectorial or an obsessive-compulsive neurotic. It is highly improbable that a single symptom can serve as an adequate diagnostic clue.

On the neurotic level of the hypervectorial disorder, compulsive and phobic symptoms can be grouped into a cluster or syndrome. The ego protects itself against the onslaught of the superego, using displacements and repressions. When the ego-protective symptoms fail, compulsions may turn into catatonic automatisms and phobias into delusions; for example, a phobic fear of bacteria may turn into delusions of being destroyed by them or being full of them.

Obsessive-compulsive symptoms and phobias are two chief ego-protective symptoms. However, some neurotic schizophrenics manifest other symptoms, such as apathy, excessive fatigue, irritability, inactivity, lack of interest, passivity, sensitivity, and difficulties in social relations. A great many of them were diagnosed as "neurasthenics" prior to becoming schizophrenic.

Neurasthenia was believed to be caused by an exhaustion of nerve cells. No evidence was ever given to that effect, but even today a profound feeling of general fatigue and tension is still frequently put under the name neurasthenia. The causes of this disorder are now believed to be psychological.

> Sometimes repressed hostility or other anxiety-exciting factors produce the reaction. In other instances the asthenic reaction seems to arise from constant failure, frustration, and disappointment. . . . The premorbid personality of the patient . . . has been usually characterized by dissatisfaction and by a sense of being thwarted and rejected. . . . Any exertion, either mental or physical, seems too great. . . . Many patients are shy, awkward, irritable, lack confidence, exhibit irresolution, indecision, and irascibility. They are pessimistic and lack initiative and ambition. . . . Sometimes it is difficult to distinguish early schizophrenia from the asthenic reaction (Noyes & Kolb, 1958, pp. 481–482).

Neurasthenics typically experience a feeling of inadequacy, of inferior performance, guilt feelings, and inability to make decisions. They are chronic worriers who anticipate the worst, experiencing hypochondrial fears and feelings of defeat and worthlessness.

> Some of them feel simultaneously the paralysing fatigue due to impoverishment and the tension and restlessness originating in the warded-off impulses that demand discharge. . . . They want to be told what to do . . . and they reject all suggestions (Fenichel, 1945, p. 185).

They are often submissive, well-behaved, model children who hide their fear of their own hostility.

A closer scrutiny of the so-called neurasthenics discloses the same etiological factors of schizogenic families (Wolman, 1964b). The hypervectorial neurotics are individuals whose basic emotional conflict stems from the peculiar family situation where intraparental relationships are instrumental to one another, the mother-child relationship is pseudo-vectorial (actually parasitic-instrumental), the father-child relationship is overtly instrumental, and the child's attitude to its parents is hypervectorial. The same type of relationship has been observed in obsessive-compulsive neurotics, in cases usually denoted as neurasthenics, and others (Wolman, 1957; 1959b). The typical schizophrenic personality structure has been observed in all the hypervectorial neurotics whose superego is overdemanding and whose ego is overmobilized in fear of the outbursts of id impulses.

Fear of his own impulses, fear of doing something wrong, fear of hurting parents whom he (so he believes) is supposed to protect, is the core conflict in a schizophrenic. As long as the ego exercises a stern control over these impulses, it is a neurosis. It is a continuous struggle in which the ego uses defense mechanisms of repression, displacement, reaction formation, isolation, and undoing. On the neurotic level it is a struggle symptomatically expressed in obsessive thoughts and compulsive actions, in phobias, hypochondrial fears, rigidity of personality, guilt feelings, general irritability, excessive fatigue, and escapes into fantasy. Psychasthenia and neurasthenia are the most frequent syndromes on the neurotic level.

SCHIZOID CHARACTER

Character Neurosis

The idea of continuity does not imply that all individuals must go through all steps and levels of regression. Some cases of hypervectorial disorder become arrested on a neurotic level with a prevalence of psychoasthenic or neurasthenic or other symptoms. Some develop powerful, rigid defenses of a character neurosis. The term "character" indicates the way the ego functions or "how the ego acquires the qualities by which it habitually adjusts itself to the demands of instinctual drives and of the external world, and later also of the superego" (Fenichel, 1945, p. 467).

Freud distinguished between the cathectic and the anticathectic or reactive manner in which the ego handles the id impulses. In well-adjusted individuals instinctual demands become cathected. They are either successfully repressed or sublimated by the ego.

When the ego is unable to act in a cathected manner, it develops anticathected, reactive, or defensive patterns. These reactive patterns or reactive character traits are characterized by avoidance mechanisms such as phobias and reaction formations.

The reactive character, being unable to satisfy or sublimate his instinctual demands, erects rigid barriers. A sort of "armor" is established against one's own impulses (Reich, 1949). Rigid avoidance patterns (phobias) and reaction formations form the "character defenses."

One of the outstanding symptoms in the schizoid character neurosis is social withdrawal. The schizoid character neurotics crave to be with people, to talk, and to be talked to. They are lonely and afraid of seclusion, but even more they are afraid of being with other people, for they believe others may not like them. Thus a wall of suspicion and estrangement grows between the schizoid character neurotic and his environment. This social withdrawal is covered up by rationalizations. Also compulsions are rationalized better than on the neurotic level. A neurotic may be aware of the irrationality of his compulsive acts, yet unable to stop them. A character neurotic rationalizes his compulsions. Thus, his stinginess may become a virtue that helps national economy, and obstinacy seems an evidence of lofty moral principles.

A schizoid character may invest his libido in a certain person or goal and have no compassion toward other people. It is exceedingly easy for a schizoid character neurotic to become ruthless and cruel. When his love has been given away in a fanatical frenzy to a religious, political, or other abstract goal, he acts out his hostile impulses with a self-righteous cruelty.

Latent Schizophrenia

Fenichel defined latent schizophrenia as schizophrenics who have not yet broken with reality and who "under unfavorable circumstances of life, may develop into psychotics" (1945, p. 443).

The superego of the schizophrenic does not prevent reality testing but impairs it. The cognitive processes are affected in certain areas only; consequently there is a considerable unevenness in the mental functioning of all latent schizophrenics. Outside emotionally loaded areas and in nonthreatening situations they may function comparatively well with some degree of rigidity.

The ego of the latent schizophrenic (i.e., latent hypervectorial psychotic) develops in an atmosphere of constant emergency. The ego tries to keep the id impulses under strict control. Even pain and pleasure is put under rigid restraint. A latent schizophrenic may know a great deal of his unconscious life. This access to the unconscious may produce esthetic sensitivity and even artistic creativity. The empathy of latent schizophrenics is usually far better than average.

Latent schizophrenics often give the impression of being cold, shallow, and unattached. Actually all schizophrenics are "object addicts," and their love is generously invested in some objects, usually mother and father. Once they love someone or something, they are affectionate, devoted, and loyal (see Fenichel, 1945; Federn, 1952; Kretschmer, 1925; Wolman, 1957).

Latent schizophrenics have difficulty in accepting friendship and love. In most cases they avoid love relationships and are exceedingly reluctant in developing new emotional attachments. The fear of being hurt prevents them from entering into give-and-take relationships.

In latent schizophrenia ego-deficiency symptoms start, including the inability to take frustration, irritability, impatience, and flaring up at a slight provocation. Bychowski (1952) called them signs of a weak ego. The weak ego is unable to control sexual and hostile impulses. On a hypervectorial neurotic level the ego wards off the fear of the id-originated object hostility. Compulsions, phobias, and over-all rigidity are choice defense mechanisms. Severe guilt feelings are experienced as a result of the superego's hostility. In the hypervectorial character neurosis, the ego acts out the object hostility under disguise of righteousness. The neurotic guilt feelings, stemming from the superego's accusations, are alleviated by the character-neurotic maneuver. In the latent psychotic stage of hypervectorial disorder (latent schizophrenia), the ego struggles desperately against both the id and superego. The ego uses projection, ascribing its own hostility to others.

Whenever a latent schizophrenic "acts out" hostility, a merciless superego attack follows. The superego repeats mother's "double-bind" accusation (Bateson, 1956). The individual blames himself, no matter what he does.

Hypervectorial neurotics and character neurotics, as a rule, overcontrol their sexual impulses. Latent schizophrenics overdo this in the sexual self-restraint. When they loosen this self-restraint, they go into impulsive promiscuity.

The inability to control emotions and impulses is an apparent ego-deficiency symptom. Some latent schizophrenics are unable to restrain appetite and rapidly gain weight; others cannot govern sexual impulses; some have difficulty in bladder control. Many of them have crying spells, and some become drunkards and drug addicts.

Latent schizophrenics' defense mechanisms begin to fail. While some of them still prevail as neurotic ego-protective symptoms, ego-deficiency symptoms develop. A latent schizophrenic may stay latent for years. A slight provocation or a gradual deterioration may destroy the last barriers and start a manifest schizophrenia.

Psychotic Breakdown

In some schizophrenics the onset of manifest schizophrenia is highly dramatic.

> The acute schizophrenic cataclysm is usually described as something which has happened to the person involved, something visited upon him from outside the boundaries of his ego. It is beyond his volition or control. Patients having this experience, or speaking about it in retrospect, refer to influences, uncanny and strange events, weird sensations, and indescribable confusion. . . . The patient endures unbelievable mental pain and anxiety. It appears to him that all this is part of a cataclysm or a cosmic catastrophe. In some magical way the patient is the central figure in this world crisis. Something which he must do will determine the outcome for good or bad. What this something is he does not clearly know. He is to be a Messiah, a Savior; he is to be miraculously saved, or he is to be eternally lost (Hill, 1955, pp. 28–29).

A dramatic breakdown is believed to be prognostically more favorable then an insidious onset. Fenichel wrote:

> All acute cases are more hopeful than chronic cases that have developed slowly; cases with intense anxiety at the start seem to be better than cases which "surrender" to the schizophrenic process without much protest. . . . Sometimes cases that seem much worse have a better prognosis than a slowly developing apathy (Fenichel, 1945, p. 447).

A dramatic breakdown usually bears witness to an inner struggle. The ego, even defeated, regresses into archaic forms and keeps alive. However, should the ego give up the fight, hope may be lost forever. My hypothesis is that in paranoid and catatonic syndromes the ego has not yet surrendered. In the less vehement hebephrenic and simple deterioration syndromes, the ego has lost the battle already.

Manifest Schizophrenia

The diagnostic and statistical *Manual of Mental Disorders of the American Psychiatric Association* (1952) describes schizophrenia as follows (pp. 26–28).

Schizophrenic Reactions

> This term is synonymous with the formerly used term dementia praecox. It represents a group of psychotic reactions characterized by fundamental disturbances in reality relationships and concept formations, with affective, behavioral, and intellectual disturbances in varying degrees and mixtures. The disorders are marked by strong tendency to retreat from reality, by emotional disharmony, unpredictable disturbances in stream of thought, regressive behavior, and in some, by a tendency to "deterioration." The predominant symptomatology will be the determining factor in classifying such patients into types.
>
> ***Schizophrenic reaction, simple type.*** This type of reaction is characterized chiefly by reduction in external attachments and interests and by impoverishment of human relationships. It often involves adjustment on a lower psychobiological level of functioning, usually accompanied by apathy and indifference but rarely by conspicuous delusions or hallucinations. The simple type of schizophrenic reaction characteristically manifests an increase in the severity of symptoms over long periods, usually with apparent mental deterioration, in contrast to the schizoid personality, in which there is little if any change.
>
> ***Schizophrenic reaction, hebephrenic type.*** These reactions are characterized by shallow, inappropriate affect, unpredictable giggling, silly behavior and mannerisms, delusions, often of a somatic nature, hallucinations, and regressive behavior.
>
> ***Schizophrenic reaction, catatonic type.*** These reactions are characterized by con-

spicuous motor behavior, exhibiting either marked generalized inhibition (stupor, mutism, negativism and waxy flexibility) or excessive motor activity and excitement. The individual may regress to a state of vegetation.

Schizophrenic reaction, paranoid type. This type of reaction is characterized by autistic, unrealistic thinking, with mental content composed chiefly of delusions of persecution, and/or of grandeur, ideas of reference, and often hallucinations. It is often characterized by unpredictable behavior, with a fairly constant attitude of hostility and aggression. Excessive religiosity may be present with or without delusions of persecution. There may be an expansive delusional system of omnipotence, genius, or special ability. The systematized paranoid hypochondriacal states are included in this group.

Schizophrenic reaction, acute undifferentiated type. This reaction includes cases exhibiting a wide variety of schizophrenic symptomatology, such as confusion of thinking and turmoil of emotion, manifested by perplexity, ideas of reference, fear and dream states, and dissociative phenomena. These symptoms appear acutely, often without apparent precipitating stress, but exhibiting historical evidence of prodromal symptoms. Very often the reaction is accompanied by a pronounced affective coloring of either excitement or depression. The symptoms often clear in a matter of weeks, although there is a tendency for them to recur. Cases usually are grouped here in the first, in an early, attack. If the reaction subsequently progresses, it ordinarily crystallizes into one of the other definable reaction types.

Schizophrenic reaction, chronic undifferentiated type. The chronic schizophrenic reactions exhibit a mixed symptomatology, and when the reaction cannot be classified in any of the more clearly defined types, it will be placed in this group. Patients presenting definite schizophrenic thought, affect and behavior beyond that of the schizoid personality, but not classifiable as any other type of schizophrenic reaction, will also be placed in this group. This includes the so-called "latent," "incipient," and "pre-psychotic" schizophrenic reactions.

Schizophrenic reaction, schizo-affective type. This category is intended for those cases showing significant admixtures of schizophrenic and affective reactions. The mental content may be predominantly schizophrenic, with pronounced elation or depression. Cases may show predominantly affective changes with schizophrenic-like thinking or bizarre behavior. The prepsychotic personality may be at variance, or inconsistent, with expectations based on the presenting psychotic symptomatology. On prolonged observation, such cases usually prove to be basically schizophrenic in nature.

Schizophrenic reaction, childhood type. Here will be classified those schizophrenic reactions occurring before puberty. The clinical picture may differ from schizophrenic reactions occurring in other age periods because of the immaturity and plasticity of the patient at the time of onset of the reaction. Psychotic reactions in children, manifesting primarily autism, will be classified here. Special symptomatology may be added to the diagnosis as manifestations.

Schizophrenic reaction, residual type. This term is to be applied to those patients who, after a definite psychotic, schizophrenic reaction, have improved sufficiently to be able to get along in the community, but who continue to show recognizable residual disturbance of thinking, affectivity, and/or behavior.

According to the sociopsychosomatic theory of schizophrenia (Wolman, 1965a), four syndromes can be distinguished. The first syndrome roughly corresponds to what has usually been described as *paranoid schizophrenia* and is characterized by the ego losing contact with reality and leaving it to the superego. In the second syndrome, the *catatonic*, the superego takes over control also of the motor apparatus. In the *hebephrenic* syndrome the ego yields to the id; the superego is defeated and the id takes over. In the *simple deterioration* there is a process of losing life itself.

The four syndromes are not discrete nosological entities. They are merely descriptive categories roughly corresponding to observable behavioral patterns. A great deal of overlapping and transition from one type to another has been observed (see Kraepelin, 1919; E. Bleuler, 1950). There have been several other proposals of classification of schizophrenic syndromes (Kleist, 1947; Schwab, 1949; Cloutier, 1953; and others).

Paranoid Schizophrenia

Paranoid schizophrenia is prognostically probably the best syndrome. In paranoid schizophrenia projection serves the purpose of alleviating the superego's pressure and guilt feeling. This projection is unconscious, impairing reality testing, wholly irrational, and thus it is psychotic. It is an ego-deficiency symptom. Paranoid schizophrenics deny their impulses and ascribe them to others in a gross violation of reality testing.

Paranoid schizophrenics represent a variety of symptoms (Guertin & Zilaitis, 1953). Some of them develop somatic delusions. Others are prone to develop delusions of being persecuted. Psychoanalytic literature knows of many cases where jealousy is actually a projection by which the individual tries to ward off his own impulse toward infidelity and homosexuality (Freud, 1924–1950, vol. II). In schizophrenia one may expect both acting out of one's own impulses and "justification" of them by projection. A highly promiscuous schizophrenic lady was constantly accusing her passive and probably innocent husband of infidelity, to justify her own sexual escapades.

Paranoid ideas of reference relate to the fear that this maneuver may be discovered. The fear has often started in childhood when the preschizophrenic began to believe his mother always knew about his intended misbehavior. His conclusion was that he was bad and mother was reading his thoughts. She knew that he had "bad thoughts." The feeling that mother knew his bad intentions and tried to control them has become externalized in the superego and projected on other people. "They" know how bad he was and want to punish him.

Paranoid schizophrenics often come out with accusations that reflect their own sexual and destructive impulses. They may act out their delusions. Many of them attack maliciously, and some of them even murder their alleged enemies.

Catatonic Schizophrenia

The paranoid schizophrenia represents a compromise between the ego and superego. In catatonic schizophrenia the superego takes over the control also of the motor apparatus. Rigid passivity and complete submissiveness are imposed on the organism. The individual renounces his own will and wishes.

> In compulsion neurosis it is not uncommon for the patient to smile in a friendly manner for purposes of defense, if he meets situations that remind him of something that threatens to arouse anxiety; in a similar way, many instances of "dull smiling" in catatonic patients . . . are intended to deny and repudiate certain gloomy, fearful emotions (Fenichel, 1945, p. 424).

In catatonia the "dull smile" is a renunciation of one's own anxiety-producing wishes.

Compulsive neurotics are, as a rule, docile, obedient, and conforming. They repress their own rebellious feelings against tyrannical mothers and ward off the fear of their own hostility, using ego-protective symptoms such as compulsions and phobias.

Catatonia is frequently accompanied by somatic symptoms such as leukocytosis, cyanosis, various metabolic changes, etc. (Gjessing, 1938).

Catatonic symptoms could be interpreted as struggle between the fear of one's own hostility and breaking through of that hostility (Wolman, 1964b). Echolalia, echopraxia, mutism, stupor, and many other symptoms reflect the patient's desperate efforts not to be hostile. When these defenses fail, anger and fear burst out. Catatonics may go into a furious rage and attack everything and everyone. On that level of regression destrudo is not directed to any particular object. A hurt organism responds with a disorganized, wild, uncontrollable fury.

One may hypothesize that in catatonia the ego has abdicated to the superego, renounced its contact with reality, and given up the control of motor activities. Stupor is a tenuous dictatorship of superego that can be easily disrupted by id violence.

The choice of symptoms in schizophrenia, as in any other mental disorder, is determined by the totality of interactional patterns in the individual's life history. Arieti believes that

> in cases of catatonia . . . the parents not only have imposed their will . . . but have also prevented the children from developing the capacity to will and, therefore, to a certain extent, the capacity to act according to their own wishes. . . . If these patients make their own decisions, they feel that the mother will be angry, or that the action will turn out to be wrong, and they will feel responsible for their failure. One of the fre-

> quent methods by which they try to solve their difficulties is by giving up their will and putting themselves completely at the dependency of another person, a symbolic omnipotent mother. . . .
>
> If these solutions cannot be found . . . the patients will try to protect themselves from anxiety in any possible way; one frequent method . . . is to resort to violence (Arieti, 1955, pp. 125–126).

Catatonics may have periods of remission. These so-called "spontaneous remissions" are not so coincidental as they seem to be. I have had the opportunity to check the causes and circumstances of some of them. In several months that I spent in a closed ward as a "nonparticipant observer" (Wolman, 1964b), I noticed that some of these allegedly spontaneous remissions were a product of therapeutic work of dedicated resident psychiatrists. On a few occasions remissions have been caused by a friendly, affectionate attitude of the nurses or attendants. I participated in the meetings of the nurses' aides, most of whom were unskilled and even primitive women. In several cases an attitude of an attendant who was sympathetic and attached to a patient brought about a spectacular remission.

In remission some catatonics resemble latent schizophrenics; some, severe obsessive-compulsives; the wealth of ego-compensation symptoms suggest that in catatonia the ego is, so to say, "pushed aside" but not completely destroyed.

Hebephrenic Schizophrenia

> [In hebephrenia] the ego undertakes no activity for the purpose of defending itself but, beset by conflicts, "lets itself go." If the present is unpleasant, the ego drops back to the past; if newer types of adaptation fail, it takes refuge in older ones, in the infantile ones of passive receptivity and even, perhaps, in intrauterine ones. If a more differentiated type of living becomes too difficult, it is given up in favor of a more or less vegetative existence. Campbell called it "schizophrenic surrender" (Fenichel, 1945, p. 423).

In paranoid and catatonic syndromes the ego has surrendered to the superego. In hebephrenia it is *surrender of the ego to the id,* a surrender for survival. Ego and superego yield to the id. It is a full regression to an infantile behavior.

Yet psychotic regression of an adult is never a regression to a true infancy, and in hebephrenia infantile elements are mixed with adult experiences and primary processes are mixed with secondary ones. Adult vocabulary and adult patterns of behavior determined by heredity, maturation, conditioning, and cathexis are mixed with regressive elements.

Hebephrenic behavioral patterns indicate a confusion of developmental strata, learned patterns, and early schizophrenic elements. Hebephrenics can be as suspicious as paranoids and as vehement as catatonics. They lack, however, the ego-protective symptoms of partial reality testing of paranoid schizophrenics and the stuporous defenses of catatonics. They may easily burst out in uncontrollable rage directed against self or others.

Hebephrenics are unable to control love or hate. When sexually aroused, they masturbate publicly or try to make love to others. Homosexuality no longer frightens them, nor do they show any restraint in regard to incestuous hetero- or homosexual impulses. Most hebephrenics are insulting, abusive, hostile, provocative, and aggressive sexually and destructively.

The disturbances in reality testing, cognitive functions, reasoning, and thought processes are most pronounced. Hebephrenics experience delusions of grandeur, hallucinate frequently, have ideas of reference and paranoid fears. They regress to primary prelogical, irrational ways of thinking. Their reasoning lacks purpose and consistency, is full of condensations and distortions. Their associative processes follow verbal, phonetic, or other irrelevant clues. Their giggling, laughing, anger, and apprehension bear witness to a lack of contact with reality and reflect their unconscious, irrational modes of reaction. Hebephrenics' neologisms and autistic talk are often distortions of socially approved symbols. When a hebephrenic said "soldiriver," she meant that her doctor sold her down the river (Wolman, 1964b).

Shakow (1946) pointed to the utter lack of initiative, purpose, and effort in hebephrenics. Other investigators pointed to "silliness," infantile regression, incoherent speech, and frequent hallucinations. Langfeldt (1953) believed hebephrenia to be the most typical form of schizophrenia. Yet even in hebephrenia some elements of the ego seem to be preserved and the "silly" talk and behavior may convey some message.

I believe the simple deterioration and hebephrenic types are more severe than the paranoid and catatonic ones. In hebephrenia there is a gradually growing confusion about who is who and what means what. There is an ever-increasing inability in goal-directed reasoning. On a prepsychotic or latent psychotic level the patient is irritable, easily annoyed, shows poor self-control, and occasionally acts and talks silly. Neglect in personal care, lack of interest, and decline in ability to concentrate become apparent.

As the disorder progresses, inner controls give up and deficiency symptoms multiply. The ego loses control over the motor apparatus; speech becomes incomprehensible, bowel and bladder control are impaired, table manners are lost altogether. The unconscious floods the conscious, and primary processes mix with secondary ones. Mental confusion, loss of goal and purpose, lack of interest, occasional agitation, and hallucination complete the picture (E. Bleuler, 1950; Freeman et al., 1958; Wolman, 1958b; 1964b).

Simple Deterioration Schizophrenia

The "simple deterioration" type, often called just "simple," is frequently regarded as a mild type. This is, however, not the case. The onset is usually insidious, gradual, and slow. The origins may go far back to early childhood. Most simple deterioration cases have a long history of maladjustment, social withdrawal, and daydreaming; in their earliest years they display autistic features, shyness, inability to do things on their own, lack of interest, lack of initiative, depressive moods, and a peculiar type of docile, passive, overdependent behavior, with occasional crying spells and periods of excessive irritability.

In many cases "neurasthenic" symptoms develop, combined with an exceeding sensitivity toward the environment. On the prepsychotic level they daydream of greatness and intend to protect their parents and all those who suffer. Their true life history is, as a rule, a series of failures and frustrations.

It seems that in simple deterioration schizophrenia the object hypercathexis has been very excessive, reducing the libido resources and substantially lowering the vitality of the organism.

This renunciation of one's own narcissistic pleasures and sacrifice for the parents is perhaps the purest form of *vectoriasis praecox*. In all other forms of schizophrenia there is an inner fight between the normal self-preservation drive and the desire to protect the protectors. In the simple deterioration form there is very little fight, if any. The individual seems to have given away all his desires and displays no interest, no ambition, no will to live. The profound decline of sensitivity to pain makes one less capable of survival, for he is less inclined to avoid injury. Thus I believe that the simple deterioration cases are the most typical schizophrenics.

Kant (1948), too, in a study of 64 simple deterioration cases, arrived at the conclusion that they are the most typical schizophrenics. Kant found in 62.5 per cent of cases, family disorganization; in 98 per cent, poor sexual adjustment; in 87 per cent, lack of assertiveness. Delusions, hallucinations, and antisocial behavior were frequent.

Unless properly treated, simple deterioration cases are likely to deteriorate further. Gradually they lose self-control, decline intellectually, act out impulses, and end up in a dementia. Some of them try to commit suicide; others die out. More lives than minds of the simple deterioration cases are saved in hospitals; left alone, they would perish. Simple deterioration cases need desperately someone to lean on, to care for them and take care of them (see Whitaker, 1958, pp. 19–20). M. L. Hayward described some cases (*ibid.*, pp. 28–29) as "thanatotic schizophrenia" or "some form of biological self-destruction." Simple deterioration schizophrenics are unable to fight for survival.

In the paranoid syndrome the failing ego yields reality testing to the superego; hence delusions, hallucinations, and self-righteous hostility. In catatonia the superego takes over the motility also; hence stupor and obedient posture. When the id breaks through, "terror"-type hostility pours out. In hebephrenia both the ego and the superego are defeated; the irrational, infantile, impulsive id floods the system. In simple deterioration there is not enough energy even for an infantile, regressed life (Wolman 1957; 1964b).

Dementive Schizophrenia

The severe deterioration of some schizophrenics is often a product of isolation, neglect, and hospital routine. In the "back wards" of mental hospitals one may find

> the chronic, unemployable schizophrenic patients, some mutely vegetating on benches, others oddly attired, standing in a corner or pacing automatically to and fro, grimacing and absorbed in their delusions, bursting forth occasionally into spasms of hostility and aggression. Undoubtedly this "deterioration" is to a considerable degree often a hospital artifact and would not occur if the institution offered a more intensive therapeutically oriented program (Noyes & Kolb, 1958, p. 419).

It is quite possible that the dementive behavioral pattern is a continuation of the "downward adjustment process" that permits survival on the lowest possible level in the custodial hospital environment (see Stanton & Schwartz, 1954).

Not all schizophrenics deteriorate. E. Bleuler (1950, p. 257) told about patients who, after years of schizophrenic disorder, made names for themselves as scientists and artists. Many schizophrenics adjust to a lower level of living.

Those who deteriorate do not show a uniform dementive picture after a lapse of years. A study of hospitalized schizophrenics showed that after 25 years 65 per cent still experienced delusions. Fifty per cent of paranoid schizophrenics still preserved their paranoid hostile delusions after 25 years of illness (Riemer, 1950).

The duration of illness does not necessarily correspond to severity of regression. Freeman et al. reported their work with severely deteriorated schizophrenics with an average duration of 8 to 9 years of illness, a minimum of 4½ years, and a maximum of 19 years. One of them, 11½ years ill, was "pale, withdrawn, and untidy, with smeared food and feces on her clothing. At times she masturbated publicly and washed her hair in W.C." (1958). Another patient, duration of illness 6 years, "presented a picture of a restless, grossly demented patient." On the other hand, a patient with 19 years of illness was still actively suspicious and aggressive.

Kraepelin (1919) distinguished nine end states in schizophrenia: (1) cure, (2) cure with defect, (3) simple dementia, (4) imbecility, (5) hallucinatory deterioration, (6) hallucinatory insanity, (7) paranoid dementia, (8) silly dementia, (9) apathetic dementia. The last two stages were believed to be "distinct and terminal states," the end of the "progressive deterioration."

Arieti (1955, pp. 350ff.) distinguished five steps. He noticed that 5 to 15 years after the onset of schizophrenia "primitive habits" appeared. This stage, called by Arieti "preterminal," occurred in all nosological categories, but the different types converged. At this stage it may be difficult to distinguish a catatonic from a paranoid. Hebephrenics and catatonics tend to deteriorate further. In this stage hallucinations and delusions subside almost completely. Arieti found a general deterioration of thought processes in all patients. Most patients developed peculiar habits such as rhythmic, monotonous movements, picking their own skin, pulling hair, hoarding useless items such as old newspapers, broken pieces of wood, cardboard, stones, leaves, etc., and self-decorating.

Arieti (1955, pp. 360ff.) distinguished also a "terminal stage" in schizophrenia. This stage usually started after 7 to 40 years from the onset of illness. There was an increase in activity, and patients became more aggressive, impulsive, and destructive. They were unable to experience delusions or hallucinations, and their verbal expressions were either absent or reduced to a limited incoherent speech. The patients developed "voracious appetite." They grabbed food, ate fast, and placed inedible things in their mouths. Arieti compared their behavior to "what is generally observed in cats, dogs, monkeys, and other animals. The animal is coerced to react to the food, at the sight of it" (*ibid.*, p. 365). Similar observations were made by K. Goldstein (1939) on human beings with severe cerebral defects, whose actions have been "forced by the stimulus."

Severely regressed schizophrenics show very little sensitivity to temperature, pain, and taste. They swallow inedible food, hurt themselves badly, and expose themselves to very high temperatures. One is reminded that Pavlov's dogs became conditioned to food despite skin burns (Pavlov, 1928). Pavlov interpreted it as the superiority of the food center. The question is still open as to whether mankind in general could salivate while their skin is burnt. Severe, dementive schizophrenics apparently do it. Hunger becomes more powerful than pain. Lower animals may not experience pain, but all animals eat. One is reminded here of the principle of downward adjustment in schizophrenia.

Dementia represents decay and destruction of personality structure. Apparently in the fifth or dementive level of schizophrenia there is just id. Movements, aimless activity, mannerisms, lack of bowel and bladder control, resemble severe mental deficiency.

DIAGNOSTIC METHODS IN SCHIZOPHRENIA

Sociopsychological Diagnostics

One can search for diagnostic clues in three ways: the organism, personality, and patterns of social interaction.

Research in neurology, biochemistry, and other organic factors in schizophrenia has been directed mainly at the search for etiologic determinants (Bellak, 1958; Hoskins, 1946; Jackson, 1960; Richter, 1957). Perhaps the acceptance of the psychosomatic interpretation of somatic changes in schizophrenia (Arieti, 1955) will enable research workers to discover adequate somatic diagnostic clues.

Physchological diagnostic tools have been in use for several decades, and the literature dealing with projective techniques and other psychological methods amounts to thousands of titles; there is no need to summarize it here. Nine chapters of Part 3 of this *Handbook* are devoted to diagnostic methods.

It is suggested here to add a third diagnostic method based on clues derived from direct observation of overt behavior and especially overt interaction patterns and analysis of communication (Wolman, 1961b). No claims are made as to the superiority of the proposed psychosocial diagnostic methods in comparison to neurological examinations, psychiatric interviews, and projective techniques or any other diagnostic methods. The psychosocial diagnostic methods proposed here, far from being in their final form of elaboration, introduce an additional avenue of diagnostic work based on overt behavioral patterns.

Two sociopsychological methods of diagnostic procedure are suggested, the first based on direct observation of patients, the second on interviews with the patients and members of their families.

This diagnostic method has been derived from the statogram and statometric technique (Wolman, 1949; 1955; 1956; 1958a; 1960b). Members of small experimental groups have been requested to rate one another in terms of "power" (ability to satisfy needs) and "acceptance" (willingness to do so). Their ratings have been graphically presented on quasi-Cartesian ordinates of the statogram, and statometric quotients of power and acceptance have been computed.

The sociodiagnostic methods are based on the same rationale of evaluating behavior on the power and acceptance dimensions. The advantage of the proposed sociopsychological diagnostic methods to be explained below lies chiefly in the fact that they (1) deal with *observable* phenomena of the individual's behavior, interaction, and communication with others, (2) are based on a systematic classification of the mental disorders, (3) are related to etiology and dynamics and not only to changing patterns and symptoms, and (4) may be of help in determining the strategy of therapeutic interaction.

The Socio-Psychological-Diagnostic Inventory of Observation and the Socio-psychological-Diagnostic Interview roughly correspond to the techniques of statogram and self-statogram, respectively. In the Inventory of Observations the observer or observers record carefully the overt patterns of behavior of the subject and categorize them in terms of power and acceptance. The observers register empirical data, record them carefully, and tabulate. To increase the objectivity of observations one can employ several observers, as reported in one experimental study (Wolman, 1956), and correlate their ratings. This observation includes actions (eating, sleeping, working, entertainment) and interaction and communication with other individuals.

The Socio-Psychological-Diagnostic Interview reflects the subject's perception of himself and his environment in terms of power and acceptance. The interviewer conducts an open-end, focused-type interview (Merton & Kendall, 1964). The subject is requested to tell his life history, dwell on his childhood memories, describe his achievements and failures, describe his past experiences, etc. The interviewer avoids asking any direct questions; he encourages a free flow of communication and whenever necessary tries to bring out a point by asking a question such as "And what happened next? What have you done? How did you feel about it? And what was the reaction of others?" etc.

The foremost diagnostic problem is to find out the *type* of disorder; the problem of *level* of disorder comes next. The following description of sociodiagnostic clues is devoted mainly to the types, especially in the neurotic and latent psychotic levels.

Behavioral Clues

The diagnostic clues described below are not precise, rigid patterns but descriptive hints not to be taken literally. They are meaningful only in the context of a total personality picture.

1. Observations in terms of *power* may start with a general *activity and vitality*. Hypervectorials (schizophrenic type) display as a rule less vitality, less energy, and an overall reduced initiative and activity as compared to average normal subjects. They are more precise and pay more attention to detail but are usually much slower than other people are. The hyperinstrumentals (psychopathic type) are active whenever it serves the satisfaction of their needs; otherwise they do not make much effort. The paramutuals (manic-depressive type) are either senselessly hyperactive, doing things no one needs and being loud, verbose, and full of energy, or senselessly passive even when passivity jeopardizes their well-being.

2. In intellectual functioning the hypervectorials display certain peculiarities. While they may be especially keen, attentive, and alert in one area, they often display lack of interest and apathy in many others. When involved in something, they are exceptionally perceptive, their judgment sharp and logical. The hyperinstrumentals seldom show such an acuity of mind; rarely are they seriously involved in anything outside their own immediate, usually material or sexual, needs. The paramutuals can be exceedingly alert in one moment and go entirely blank and oblivious in another.

3. The three types differ also in the patterns of *thinking*. Intelligence is not correlated with mental disorder, and one may find mental disorders associated with any degree of innate intellectual abilities; there are intellectually inferior and superior individuals in all three types. However, certain peculiarities in the thought process are distinguishable by psychological tests and, in extreme cases, even in a simple observation. The hypervectorials overlook gross detail; they are logical (unless deteriorated) but not empirically minded. They are prone to indulge in abstract thinking and deep speculation with little regard to reality and overemphasis on minute detail. Their fantasy is rich but often unrealistic, leading to autistic thinking and bizarre reasoning.

The hyperinstrumentals with a high IQ are more shrewd than wise, more cunning than planning, more plagiarists than inventors. Their thinking lacks depth, and their ideas are narrow. The paramutuals are rarely as shrewd as hyperinstrumentals or as deep as hypervectorials; they are, as a rule, more practical than the hypervectorials and more profound than the hyperinstrumentals. When deteriorated, their mind goes blank and dull as in the hyperinstrumentals.

4. The three types differ also in the *intake of food*. Food is highly important to hyperinstrumentals, who can barely stand any food deprivation. Hypervectorials are usually finicky eaters; eating is a problem to many schizophrenics. They either refuse to eat or overeat (to reduce anxiety) or toy with food. Paramutuals eat quickly and often overeat. At meals in the hospital, schizophrenics are usually the slowest and manic-depressives the fastest eaters.

5. The rhythm of *waking* and *sleeping* states is frequently disturbed in hypervectorials. Whenever disturbed, they have difficulties in falling asleep and cannot sleep the night through. On the neurotic level, sleep difficulties are often the outstanding symptom that brings the patient to the consultation room. In latent and manifest schizophrenics sleep disorders may become tantamount to the inability to fall asleep.

The hyperinstrumentals sleep well and like to sleep many hours, unless under threat. Paramutuals are either sleepy, falling asleep whenever perturbed by inner or outer threats, or unable to sleep when excited. In manifest, manic-depressive psychosis, they frequently go to bed early, being unable to stay up late in the evening. In depressive moods they wake up very early in the morning hating themselves and the world; in these the danger of suicide is quite high.

6. *Personal care* offers another clue in differential diagnosis. Hypervectorials do not care much for themselves but worry what other people will think about them. On the neurotic, character neurotic, and latent psy-

chotic levels they are meticulously neat. Neglect in personal cleanliness and appearance is usually a sign of serious deterioration. On manifest, and even more on dementive, levels all personal care may disappear entirely.

The hyperinstrumentals take good care of themselves but are not too particular about cleanliness. They are quite concerned with their external appearance whenever they meet strangers whom they would like to impress. The paramutuals swing from an extreme show-off care to a complete self-neglect.

7. There are definite differences between the three types in regard to *property* and *money*. Hyperinstrumentals are greedy and acquisitive, hypervectorials are retentive, paramutuals are inconsistent. Hyperinstrumentals grab what they can and are unwilling to share. Hypervectorials cannot part with their possessions and sometimes would rather spend money on others than on themselves.

8. At *work*, hyperinstrumentals are inclined to work hard only when driven by fear or reward; they cheat whenever they can. The hypervectorials are, as a rule, highly conscientious workers. Paramutuals depend on their fluctuating moods.

9. In *success*, hypervectorials tend to worry; in *failure* they blame themselves. Hyperinstrumentals in success act as victorious beasts, greedy and triumphant; in defeat they become subservient. Paramutuals exaggerate in a joyful self-praise at a slight success and exaggerate in blaming themselves and others whenever defeated.

10. In regard to *pain* one can say that hypervectorials are usually masochistically inclined, hyperinstrumentals sadistically, and paramutuals sadomasochistically. Hypervectorials frequently neglect their own health, notwithstanding pain. Hyperinstrumentals are highly sensitive to pain and overdo in demanding medical care. Paramutuals go from one extreme to the other.

11. The hypervectorials *fear* mostly their own hostile impulses that will prove to the world how bad they are. Hyperinstrumentals distrust and fear people. Paramutuals in elation have no fear, in depression fear everything.

12. *Self-esteem* is usually low in all three types. Feelings of inadequacy and dissatisfaction with oneself accompanies all mental disorders. Yet the hypervectorials feel most dissatisfied with themselves because they believe they are bad. They perceive themselves as hostile and worry lest others may feel the same way and blame them. The hyperinstrumentals are little concerned with what others think about their moral standards. They themselves worry about their own power only—power to get what they need and destroy whatever is in their way. As one psychopathic patient put it, "I feel either as a tiger that can tear the world apart or as a vegetable, anyone can step over me." Their self-esteem depends on tangible achievements.

Manic-depressives combine the power and acceptance dimensions. They swing, in their own eyes, from giants to dwarfs. When they feel accepted, they feel strong and friendly; when rejected, they feel weak and hostile to themselves and the outer world. Self-esteem in hypervectorials depends on whether their love has been accepted, that is, whether parental figures or another significant person whom they love has accepted the love. Paramutuals need to receive love from everywhere and are never satiated; occasionally they may believe they are loved and enjoy short periods of elation.

Interactional Clues

There are distinct differences in the way the three types relate to and interact with other people.

1. Hypervectorials display a great deal of *empathy;* i.e., they sense the feelings of others. Instrumentals have very little empathy, if any. Paramutuals have less empathy than hypervectorials and more than hyperinstrumentals. Schizophrenics are not always friendly, but they are usually understanding; psychopaths do not care about others; manic-depressives go from one extreme to the other.

2. Hypervectorials excel also in *sympathy*. Hyperinstrumentals have no sympathy and no mercy, but they expect sympathy from others. Paramutuals go to extremes; occasionally they are hypersympathetic and self-sacrificing and swing back to an almost psychopathic cruelty. Hypervectorials are cruel when furious; hyperinstrumentals are cruel when it pays to be; paramutuals are cruel when agitated.

3. Hypervectorials in neurotic, latent psychotic, and remissive phases are usually *tactful* and *considerate;* they are often cold and cruel in schizo-type character neuroses and manifest schizophrenia. Psychopathic hyperinstrumentals are tactful toward those they per-

ceive as strong and tactless and brutal toward those they perceive as weak. Paramutuals are oversentimental toward those whose love they wish to get and brutal toward those they do not care for; they are rarely tactful.

4. *Moral* rigidity characterizes hypervectorials; lack of morality is typical of hyperinstrumentals; moral inconsistency is the sign of paramutualism. Hypervectorials cling to principles, are dogmatic and self-righteous. Hyperinstrumentals have no moral principles whatsoever; they are radical opportunists. Paramutuals are highly idealistic and moralistic in one situation and the reverse in another. Hyperinstrumentals try very hard to be God-like angels and fear they are devils; when defenses fail, their destrudo erupts in a wild violence. Hyperinstrumentals are overtly selfish and unfair and believe they are within their rights. The whole world seems to be one *Lebensraum* for their ever-hungry wolf jaws, while they believe themselves to be innocent sheep. Paramutuals are Dr. Jekyll and Mr. Hyde. When they feel rejected they become brutal and aggressive.

5. Hypervectorials tend to *blame* themselves; hyperinstrumentals blame others; paramutuals do both.

6. All disturbed individuals are prone to tell *lies.* Hyperinstrumentals lie whenever it is profitable. Hypervectorials rarely lie but may do so if their self-esteem is in jeopardy; they lie when they are afraid people will think they are bad or stupid. Paramutuals lie frequently, usually for self-aggrandizement. Their lies are fantastic, often nonsensical; sometimes they say things that do not make sense even to themselves. Paramutuals often sound insincere even when they are sincere.

7. The picture that hypervectorials have of other people is highly confused. They usually *perceive* others as better, stronger, smarter, than themselves and the members of their family. Their feeling of inferiority spreads to those for whom they feel responsible.

Hyperinstrumentals divide the world into those to fear and those to exploit. Paramutuals divide the world into those who love and those who reject.

8. Hypervectorials are slow to form *friendship,* get lastingly overinvolved, and are unable to break off an attachment. Hyperinstrumentals have no friends on a give-and-take basis; a friend to them is someone to be exploited. Their friendships are formed for practical reasons and accordingly are either dropped or conveniently preserved. Paramutuals easily develop profound attachments, but their feelings are rarely lasting.

9. Hypervectorials are most persistent and involved in *love.* When their love is not accepted, it turns into *hate.* Paramutuals are never deeply in love, but they hate those who refuse to give love to them. Paramutuals are "love addicts," constantly in search of new love objects. Their love is always ambivalent, and when it is not returned, it becomes hate.

10. *Sexual deviations* accompany all mental disorders. Psychopaths are most frequently *polymorphous perverts,* capable of and willing to participate in any type of sexual activity. Schizophrenics are frequently torn by the conflict of sex identification and fear of homosexuality. Manic-depressives frequently display impotence, frigidity, and other sexual disturbances.

11. The hypervectorials try to control hostility; they display *hostility* whenever rejected, offended, or unable to bear inner hostility and when their defense mechanisms fail. Hyperinstrumentals are hostile whenever their needs are frustrated; that is, whenever their victims protest or anyone gets in their way. Their basic attitude is the defensive-aggressive hostility. The paramutuals frequently show ambivalent hostility, hating friends who do not love them enough. A schizophrenic fights because he cannot control his hostile impulses; a psychopath fights to win; the manic-depressive vents his hostility whenever he is not loved. While the hypervectorial schizophrenics are often hostile, they *cannot take hostility.* Blame or criticism sets off hostile reactions in hypervectorials. Hyperinstrumentals will accept criticism from those they perceive as strong and retaliate for criticism coming from weak individuals. Paramutuals are not very sensitive to criticism coming from strangers but become aggressive-depressive (i.e., hostile toward others and themselves) when criticized by those who are expected to love.

In deep regression the hyperinstrumental psychopaths wish to bite and regress to bestiality, cannibalism, and ruthless murder. The paramutual manic-depressives wish to sleep and regress into a sleepy, intrauterine, parasitic life. The hypervectorial schizophrenics do not wish anything. They withdraw from life and, if not taken care of, will die.

The Interview

Similar diagnostic clues can be obtained from the Psycho-Socio-Diagnostic Interview. The main difference between the Interview and the Observation Inventory is the observer. In the Inventory the descriptive data are obtained by one or more observers, while in the Interview the interviewed individual reports his observations.

The observations of the interviewed subject, whether patient or a member of his family, contain facts as seen by an interested and interesting party. The *evaluation* of the observed facts by the one being interviewed has great psychological significance. What actually happened can be found by interviewing several members of the same family unit, but how they *see* and *evaluate* what happened offers highly important sociopsychological clues.

While the interviewed subjects describe themselves and others, these descriptions can be tabulated in accordance with the power and acceptance categories. What does the subject think of himself? Does he perceive himself as being "strong" or "weak" in regard to (for example) what has been described above as "behavioral clues"? Does he believe himself to be active, alert, efficient? Or, outside these clues, does he believe himself to be intelligent, good-looking, successful, etc.?

These self-ratings are not objective measurements of personality. They are merely patterns of self-rating that will go up in hyperinstrumentals whenever they experience tangible success, will fluctuate rapidly in paramutuals, and will be persistently low in hypervectorials.

In describing others, hyperinstrumentals will give scanty, rather mechanized descriptions such as "the girl in the office," "the supervisor," etc., while hypervectorials will spend a great deal of time talking about others and describing their feelings. Paramutuals will most often resemble the hyperinstrumentals in their egocentric talk but will pay more attention to the feelings of others.

In the dimension of acceptance the differences are even more pronounced. Hypervectorials criticize themselves and avoid criticizing others; when they hate, they tend to develop projective mechanisms and claim that others hate them. When they talk about parents and other relatives, they use a great deal of caution.

Hyperinstrumentals speak frankly and critically about all whom they dislike. They find their hostility justified and give a frank though often distorted picture of interaction with others.

Paramutuals are more critical than the other two types. They blame everyone, including themselves, are highly opinionated, and label others. They either praise or condemn, and their story is full of value judgment. When they repeat the same detail in a subsequent interview, the two accounts rarely resemble each other.

The data obtained by both methods can be tabulated. Content analysis is possible in regard to recorded interviews and, to some extent, to the content of recorded observations, especially when related to interindividual communication.

METHODS OF TREATMENT

Psychotherapeutic Methods

Methods of treatment have been described in detail in the respective chapters of Part 5 of this *Handbook*. Thus, a brief analysis of a few methods most frequently used with schizophrenics will suffice here.

Classic Freudian psychoanalysis does not seem to be the choice method for schizophrenia. The reclining position and the psychoanalyst's passivity seem to increase anxiety and foster regression. Even Freudians such as Bychowski (1952), Brody (in Brody & Redlich, 1952), Eissler (1947; 1952), Federn (1952), Knight (1953), Rosen (1947; 1953), Wolman (1959a), and others had to deviate from Freud's techniques whenever they treated schizophrenics. Thus the differences between Freudians and non-Freudians such as Sullivan (1953), Fromm-Reichmann (1950; 1952; 1959), Arieti (1955), and others have been reduced, for both groups have strongly emphasized the importance of face-to-face interpersonal relations as a prerequisite of successful treatment.

It is worth mentioning that several therapists claim good results using a great many methods, most of them representing variations of Freudian and non-Freudian approaches (see Bellak, 1958; Bettelheim, 1950; 1955; Hill, 1955; Karon, 1963; and many others). Apparently there is no general agreement as to how schizophrenics should be treated. For example, some psychoanalysts, especially followers of Melanie Klein, believe in the necessity of interpretation of unconscious processes as is done with neurotics (Pichon-Rivière, 1952; Rosenfeld, 1953; Winnicot, 1955). Other experts feel that "encouraging psychotic patients to associate freely is strictly contraindicated," for free association induces and increases disintegrated thinking (Fromm-Reichmann, 1950). Eissler, in a discussion of Rosen's direct interpretation, expressed the belief that "another set of interpretations might have achieved a similar result" (1952, p. 143).

All psychotherapists seem to agree on the necessity to spare the emotional resources of schizophrenics, on cautious handling of transference phenomena (see Rifkin, 1957), on the importance of neutralization and sublimation of hostile impulses (Fromm-Reichmann, 1952; Bychowski, 1952; Wolman, 1959a), and on stressing reality testing.

A patient is believed to be helped when (1) he becomes capable of correct perception of reality, (2) his emotions are balanced, (3) he is socially adjusted. (For criteria of mental health see Part 4, Chapter 39, of this *Handbook.*)

According to the sociopsychosomatic theory (Wolman, 1964b) the core of schizophrenia is a severe disbalance of libido and destrudo interindividual cathexes. This disbalance can be corrected by an unconditionally vectorial attitude on the part of the therapist.

In fact, all successful therapists act in a similar way, notwithstanding semantic differences in their reports. Federn (1952, pp. 323ff.) was most successful with patients he took into his home. J. N. Rosen described his work as follows:

> In order to treat the schizophrenic, the physician must have such a degree of inner security that he is able to function independently, whether he is loved by the patient or not. . . . He must make up for the tremendous deficit of love experienced in the patient's life. Some people have this capacity for loving as a divine gift (Rosen, 1953, p. 73).

Arieti stressed the necessity of giving the patient the feeling "that he has been given something" and that no demands were being made on him (1955, p. 439). Redlich wrote in a review of Eissler's (1947), Federn's (1952), Ferenczi's (1926), Fromm-Reichmann's (1950), Knight's (1946), and Schwing's (1954) therapeutic techniques that all these methods reflect the "eternal common sense methods of love and patience" (Brody & Redlich, 1952, p. 30).

This common denominator of practically all successful techniques, irrespective of the assumed theoretical differences, permitted the formulation of the principles of *vectorial psychotherapy* (Wolman, 1957; 1959a; 1960a; 1964b). The unconditional vectorial attitude of the therapist has been viewed as the prerequisite of therapeutic success.

Vectorial psychotherapy includes five principles: (1) supportive attitude; (2) emphasis on conscious elements (ego therapy) with selective and cautious interpretation of unconscious processes; (3) prevention of further regression; (4) pragmatic and flexible therapeutic strategy (while the main task of psychotherapy with schizophrenics is the strengthening of the ego, in severe cases a temporary strategy with the superego may be advisable); (5) individualization, depending on the present and past of the individual patient and on the emotional resources of the individual psychotherapist.

Whitehorn and Betz found that successful psychiatrists "expressed personal attitudes more freely on problems being talked about and set limits on the kind and degree of obnoxious behavior" (1960). The successful psychiatrists "have a problem-solving, not a purely regulative or coercive approach." However, there seems to be no way to predict when a certain therapist will be successful with a certain patient (see Benedetti & Mueller, 1957; Scher & Davis, 1960). It has also been questioned whether the satisfactory results obtained by a good therapist are permanent (English et al., 1961).

Prognosis

Since Kraepelin's statement that about 13 per cent of schizophrenics recovered quickly and 4 per cent of them lastingly (Kraepelin, 1919), there has been a great deal of controversy around the problem of prognosis. The fact that the admission rate for schizophrenics is about 25 per cent of the total mental hospital admissions, while close to 50 per cent of beds are occupied by schizophrenics (Lemkau, 1955), points to a poor prognosis in schizophrenia.

A summary of the literature (Bellak, 1958) showed the great differences in evaluation of recovery rates, ranging from 22 to 54 per cent. The rate of discharges is not necessarily identical with the rate of recovery; many patients are readmitted later, and those who are not, are not necessarily cured. Hospitals tend to discharge patients whenever there is some improvement and if there is no need for inpatient treatment.

A study reported by Kramer and his associates (1956) described a slow increase in discharge rates in the Warren State Hospital, starting with 49 per cent in the years 1926 to 1935 and rising to 70 per cent in the period 1946 to 1953. The question is still open as to what caused this increase. Kramer's studies imply a connection between the improvements in treatment and prognosis. Several other workers (Freyhan, 1955; Schofield, Hathaway, Hastings, & Bell, 1954; and others) related the acuteness of onset with good prognosis.

Phillips (1953) related good prognosis to good interindividual relations and satisfactory sexual adjustment in the past. Hollingshead and Redlich (1954) related poor prognosis with lower socioeconomic status.

Research workers, including the abovementioned Phillips, Schofield, Redlich, and others, related good prognosis to a great many diversified symptoms. It seems that the presence of affective life was a better prognostic symptom than the lack of it. This supports the hypothesis that severe schizophrenia is associated with resignation, giving up of fight, and decline in vitality. As long as the inner struggle goes on (as in paranoid and catatonic syndromes), the prognosis is somewhat better.

Actually there is no clear-cut evidence that the type of schizophrenia or the age of onset or any other factor or symptom gives a definite indication of a better prognosis. Studies by Kramer and many other workers point to one fact only: the better the treatment, the better the prognosis. The spectacular results obtained by Rosen, Schwing, and Fromm-Reichmann and the cases reported in the works of Whitaker (1958), Freeman et al. (1958), Brody and Redlich (1952), Bellak (1958), and Dawson et al. (1961) seem to confirm the hypothesis that schizophrenia is par excellence a sociogenic disorder; thus prognostic judgment must include also the social environment and therapeutic interaction.

Thus my conviction is that a *schizophrenic becomes incurable only when there is no one willing and able to cure him. A schizophrenic becomes curable when there is some willing person capable of using all his resources to help the schizophrenic.* Each schizophrenic requires an unlimited amount of consideration, care, patience, understanding, and a prolonged vectorial relationship. Each schizophrenic is a new challenge, no matter how gifted and experienced the therapist may be. The amount of emotional investment and skill necessary for the cure of one schizophrenic is enormous. No wonder most schizophrenics are neglected.

In hospitals those schizophrenics who attract the attention and sympathy of the therapeutic staff have better chances than their less fortunate hospital mates. The alleged "spontaneous recovery" cases are patients who evoked interest and sympathy in someone and received a better or worse, scientific or intuitive, planned or unplanned, psychotherapy given to them by a vectorially minded individual. Whether the remission was partial or almost complete, short-lived or lasting, depended on both the severity of the disorder and the nature of the psychotherapeutic relationship.

The therapeutic interaction with schizophrenics is full of hardships. The schizophrenic was the "overdemanded" child who was expected to give love more than he could afford. Schizophrenic symptoms include also his exaggerated demand for love and attention to compensate for early loss of libido. Regression is a regression to infancy and a desperate call to receive love. A schizophrenic may be so hurt in early years that he may fear to ask for love or be frightened whenever affection is expressed toward him. If he is still capable of accepting affection, he may cling to the giver and become possessive, jealous, and overdemanding, as if trying to compensate for the years of emotional starvation.

No wonder therapists may not be able and willing to give so much. Some therapists feel exhausted and unduly impoverished after each therapeutic hour with a schizophrenic. The schizophrenic onslaught of vehement love and hate represents a serious challenge even to a well-trained and well-balanced psychotherapist. Schizophrenics may put exaggerated demands on the time and work of their therapists. One patient used to telephone the therapist several times a day and at odd hours of the night. Another patient refused to eat unless "her doctor" would feed her. Still another insisted on seeing his doctor any time he felt the need to see him, irrespective of the doctor's obligations toward other patients. Some psychotherapists manage to preserve a friendly, therapeutic relationship and help the patient to grow into adulthood. Some of them get involved or impatient or disappointed.

With all this in mind, I doubt the possibility of a valid prognosis in regard to an individual case. The single greatest factor is the therapist, and even he is not entirely predictable. The attitude of the therapist to the patient is not the only prognostic factor but certainly the most important one. Its importance could be reduced to a minimum in classic psychoanalysis with neurotics. In dealing with psychotic hypervectorial disorders an emotional detachment on the part of the therapist is tantamount to giving up treatment. Even orthodox analysts (Bak, Bychowski, Eissler, Federn, and others) did not practice classic psychoanalysis with schizophrenics.

The other important prognostic factors are the *severity* of the disorder, the *level* of regression, the *degree* of damage done to the personality structure, etc. As in any other disorder, the longer the duration and the more severe the deterioration, the lesser the chances for recovery. Last, but not least, is the *environment* in which the patient has to live.

Group, Family, and Milieu Therapy

The belief that schizophrenia is a product of faulty interindividual relations (Bateson, Lidz, Wolman, Wynne, and others) has given strong support to new and unorthodox methods of treatment. Even the traditional mental hospital is undergoing changes. The new ideas of social psychiatry (Leighton, 1960; Stanton & Schwartz, 1954; and others) have introduced substantial changes in the approach to mental disorders (see Chapters 34 and 36 of the *Handbook*).

It was certainly a great leap forward to change the mental asylum into a mental hospital. The developing concepts of mental disorder have led to a great many innovations in methods of treatment. The idea of the group-centered hospital and therapeutic community (Jones, 1956; Barnard, 1952) is symptomatic of this development. Open wards, day-care centers, community-oriented mental care, reorganization of nurses' services, and other reforms bear witness to the growing awareness that most mental disorders, and especially schizophrenia, are a result of *mismanagement of men (children) by men (parents)* and that therapeutic *interaction* is the choice method to right the wrongs (see Bowen, 1960; Eissler, 1947; Knight, 1953; Brody, 1956; Midelfort, 1957; Slavson, 1950; Whitaker, 1958; Wolman, 1957; 1964b).

Several therapists have embarked on treatment of the family as a whole. The underlying rationale is the assumption that schizophrenia is a product of a "sick family"; thus the family is the true patient (Ackerman, 1958; Bowen, 1960; Haley, 1962).

Group psychotherapy is another application of the sociopsychological approach to treatment of schizophrenics. One of the advantages of group psychotherapy is moderation in transference phenomena (Hulse, 1958; Slavson, 1950; Wolman, 1960c). Schizophrenics are prone to develop profound and often vehement transference; the "sharing" of the therapist with several other people and seeing him interacting with others may mollify transference. The group permits multiple transferences, facilitates corrective social experience, and enables its members to restore the balance of libido and destrudo cathexis (Alikalos, Starer, & Winick, 1956; Hulse, 1958; Wolman, 1964a). The group setting helps in "consensual validation" of experiences, thus forcing the schizophrenic to keep contact with reality. Although it is perhaps too early for an evaluation of results obtained by group psychotherapy with schizophrenics, the method appears to hold great promise.

Physicochemical Methods

The use of physical methods of treatment is as old as mankind. When a mother strikes a child, she inflicts pain and fear of future pain; she expects that pain and the fear of pain will act as deterrents and produce a modification in the child's behavior. Similar results have been expected in flogging, cold packs, refrigeration therapy, fever therapy; but the results obtained by all these methods have been rather unimpressive (Bellak, 1958, chaps. 9–13).

M. Sakel, the inventor of the insulin shock treatment (ICT), is believed to have obtained 70 per cent remissions and about 18 per cent partial remissions (1950). These results are high above the usual one-third improvement in a nonspecific, routine type of treatment.

In a review of the ICT treatment, Hoch and Pennes (1958) quoted three studies that compared the rates of recovery and improvement in nonspecific hospital routine to results obtained by ICT treatment. In L. Alexander's (1953) 9,483 cases treated by Sakel's method (Sakel, 1954), significant improvement was obtained in 61.3 per cent of the cases, i.e., more than twice the 29.3 per cent rate of improvement in controls not treated by ICT. The patients treated by ICT had 21 per cent of complete recovery, as compared to 5 per cent in the nontreated controls. The study by Appel and associates (1953) reported that the rate of improvement in the ICT-treated patients was 44±11, as compared to 29±10 in controls. The Staudt and Zubin study (1957) has shown 58 per cent improvement in the ICT-treated patients, as compared to 30 to 40 per cent improvement in the preshock-era controls and 25 per cent in the shock-era controls. The last group of controls was probably composed of more deteriorated cases (Hoch & Pennes, 1958, p. 416).

Two questions have been raised. First, what does this "improvement" mean? What are the psychological changes obtained by this method? Does the ICT merely remove the symptoms, or does it produce personality changes? Hoch and Pennes believe that a "true alteration of the pre-psychotic personality following successful ICT is rare. In our opinion the subtle schizophrenogenic matrix remains as indicated by clinical examination and the occurrence of relapses" (1958, p. 420). Unfortunately, this seems to be the general impression. Although the improvement and/or remission is often spectacular, in an adverse situation such as hardship or disappointment most ICT-treated patients relapse. No such relapses have been witnessed in successful psychotherapy.

This leads to the second question in regard to the longevity of the effects. Unfortunately, even the most favorable results obtained in insulin shock treatment are not lasting. One investigator (Salzman, 1947) found 17 out of 44 insulin-treated patients readmitted to a hospital after one year, as compared to 6 out of 45 patients treated by other methods. Appel and associates (1953) found that after five years the rate of relapse was the same in the ICT-treated and nontreated schizophrenics. Similar results have been stated by Staudt and Zubin (1957). A follow-up study of ICT treatment (West et al., 1955) has shown that while about two-thirds of ICT-treated patients improved immediately, after twelve years there was no difference between them and the preshock controls; both groups had the rate of 26 per cent remissions.

In regard to children the efficacy of shock therapy seems to be even more dubious. Bender stated, "Shock treatment did not appear to have been beneficial for this group of children" (1961, p. 4). Kanner wrote that "shock treatment (insulin, metrazol, electroshock) disappoints those who tried them with children" (1948, p. 728).

Lately convulsive treatment, and especially electric convulsive treatment, has been applied to schizophrenics. The metrazol convulsive treatment was introduced in 1936 by Von Meduna, who believed that schizophrenia and epilepsy were opposites and hoped that convulsions might cure schizophrenia. Cerletti and Bini introduced the electric convulsive treatment two years later. The effects obtained on ECT do not differ substantially from those on ICT. Follow-up studies after ECT indicate that "the five-year result does not convincingly exceed that of spontaneous remission or so-called non-specific treatment" (Hoch and Pennes, 1958, p. 446). Staudt and Zubin (1957) found 39 per cent of patients improved five years after ECT treatment, as compared with 42 per cent improved after five years of nonspecific treatment in the preshock era and 25 per cent improved in the shock era. The last low percentage, as mentioned before, could be explained by the selection of more deteriorated cases as controls. In G. M. Alexander's study (1953) 28 per cent of schizophrenics have been improved five years after ECT.

No explanation or theory of shock therapies has gained general or even wide approval. One author counted fifty different theories (Gordon, 1948). Hoch and Pennes summarized their authoritative review by stating that "neither a single psychological (nor organic) theory can explain all the actually observed clinical phenomena. . . . The shock therapies at the present time must be limited to nonspecific, empirical and quantitative methods of action" (1958, p. 455).

Roth (1957) has stressed the nonspecific

nature of the action of ECT. The clinical facts are that

> ECT influences depression and mania, stupor and hyperactivity. . . . ECT has a therapeutic effect on schizophrenia, affective disorders, confusional states with clouding, epileptic fugues and twilight states, and acute psychotic symptoms in paresis. A similar case may be made out for the nonspecificity of ICT, both with regard to the variety of symptoms altered and the diagnostic categories that respond favorably (Hoch and Pennes, 1958, p. 453).

If ECT or ICT had been related in any way to the factors that produce schizophrenia, their application would have given more lasting results and have been more specific. No wonder Von Meduna himself has compared shock treatment to "kicking of a Swiss watch" (Redlich, 1952, p. 28). Redlich remarked that "in contrast to the crudely empirical approach of the organic therapies, the psychotherapeutic approach is at least rationally directed against the outstanding symptoms" (*ibid.*, pp. 28–29).

Thus, one must conclude that all shock therapies are nonspecific treatment methods. Although the various shock methods are still widely used, no one really knows why they do help and why they fail in the long run. Even the type of "metabolic change taking place and being responsible for a therapeutic effect in the nervous system during such comas, however, remains unknown. The purely empirical nature of convulsive therapy cannot be denied" (Kalinowski, 1959, p. 1516).

Psychosurgery

Psychosurgery, introduced by Egas Moniz in 1933, was first practiced by A. Lima in 1935, and its theory was developed by W. Freeman, J. W. Watts, and many others. Freeman believed the results with schizophrenics to be "usually quite good especially from the administrative point of view. Disturbed patients often become friendly, quiet, and cooperative. They retain their basic psychotic dissociation and often their delusional ideas, but they no longer react to them so vigorously" (1959, p. 1528).

However, the reviews of literature (Freeman, 1958; Paul & Greenblatt, 1958; etc.) seem to indicate that the only advantage of psychosurgery with schizophrenics is the administrative one. Patients become less violent, less offensive, and easier to handle. As pointed out by several workers, psychosurgery transforms a potentially curable functional disorder into an organic, incurable defect. In the U.S.S.R., lobotomy is forbidden by law. The various theoretical interpretations of the effects of psychosurgery are highly controversial, its therapeutic results dubious, and its physical damage beyond repair.

In Bellak's collective volume on schizophrenia (1958) the bibliography of papers dealing with the tranquilizing drugs has 184 titles. In another chapter describing various somatic treatments and dealing with barbiturates, amphetamines, other pharmacological and hormone therapies, the bibliography includes 258 titles.

There is no doubt that pharmacotherapy has enabled hospital staffs to work under less stress. Tranquilizing drugs, especially *reserpine,* derived from *Rauwolfia serpentina,* and *chlorpromazine,* manufactured under the name of lactargil and thorazine, have increased the rate of discharge from mental hospitals.

The fact that these two drugs are chemically so different (reserpine is an alkaloid extract, while chlorpromazine is a hydrochloride) militates against their specificity. Although most investigators believe in the superiority of reserpine and chlorpromazine over placebos and are supported in their beliefs by impressive statistical data, some workers found no significant advantage in tranquilizers (Penman and Dredge, 1956; Sommerness et al., 1955).

How much "cure" has been obtained from drugs? There is no agreement on this point; there is also no agreement in regard to the duration of the improvement, but there is a literature pointing to negative aftereffects. Cattell (1959) reported on the degree of toxicity and side reactions of the various drugs, compared to their effectuality. His report should serve as a memento and call for utmost caution in the use of drugs.

Tentative Interpretation

It has been frequently observed that acute physical illness brings about considerable improvement in schizophrenia (Mayer-Gross, 1954; Freeman et al, 1958; and many others). My interpretation of these often miraculous changes is similar to the interpretation of shock treatment. A serious physical threat to the organism may reverse the libido cathexes, i.e., increase the self-cathexis and decrease object cathexis. The attacked organism usually mobilizes its resources for self-defense.

When the attack comes from without in the form of a hostile action from parents or friends, the elicited fear paralyzes the organism or leads to a diffuse hostile reaction of "terror." But when the threat comes from within in the form of a violent metabolic upheaval caused by shock treatment or an acute febrile infection, probably the deep layers of the id are stimulated and a great amount of energy is invested in self, in the jeopardized ego. However, when the ego has not yet been formed, such a process is not likely to occur, as corroborated by Bender's (1961) and Kanner's (1948) studies on schizophrenic children.

The fact that patients with a short duration of manifest psychosis and acute onset and also paranoid and catatonic schizophrenics respond better to ICT (and, for that matter, to any shock treatment), as compared to chronic hebephrenics and simple deterioration cases who respond poorly (Kalinowski & Hoch, 1952), supports our hypotheses both in regard to the degree of severity of personality damage in schizophrenia (see Part 5, "Perspectives in Client-centered Therapy") and in regard to the lack of specificity in the shock treatment. *Any threat to the organism may help the organism to mobilize its resources, if the organism is still capable of such a mobilization.* Such a threat, be it a shock, physical disease, or social disaster (I saw schizophrenics improving in bombed areas in wartime), forces the organism to reverse the balance of cathexes by withdrawing its object cathexes and reinvesting libido in itself. The friendly, caring attitude of the physicians who administer the shock does the rest.

Let us not forget that even physicochemical treatment is an interindividual relationship. The doctor and the nurse are usually perceived by the patient as friendly persons, and their actions as vectorial. If the patient does not see things this way all the time, he sees it in his lucid moments. Should the therapists be perceived as enemies, the treatment would become almost impossible, resembling flogging and medieval tortures conducted allegedly for the well-being of the victims against their wishes.

All of us undergo voluntarily minor and major surgical operations with or without analgesics and anethetics. We agree to be punctured and cut by physicians in whom we have faith; that is, we perceive them as strong (competent) and friendly (honest) individuals who will do everything within their power to help us. Although we are used to paying for all services, we firmly believe that the doctor and the nurse who take care of the sick have a vectorial motivation. People do not trust doctors who are concerned with their income only, although everyone understands that they must have some income to survive.

This is our tentative interpretation of the high relapse rate in all shock treatments. Shock treatment mobilizes the self-cathexes by a threat (shock), and vectorialism (care) makes the schizophrenic momentarily less schizophrenic. Unless followed by a thorough modification of personality, the improvement may be soon lost.

As far as drugs are concerned, "It is undoubtedly true that some proportion of the improvement from drugs is due to the increased interest and attention of the hospital personnel," wrote H. Freeman (1958, p. 499). Some experts (Hoch, 1959) recommend a combination of drugs and psychotherapy.

There is no doubt that human moods can be changed by chemical factors. Consider alcohol, benzedrine, and scores of tranquilizers and stimulants. Yet it is questionable whether profound and lasting personality changes could be obtained by this method. Even the nature of the changes is not really understood.

Further research in somatic methods of treatment may bring new ideas and discoveries. The reader is reminded that the schizophrenic process starts as a product of environmental pressures communicated to and influencing the psychological apparatus of the individual and ultimately causing somatic aftereffects. This sociopsychosomatic causal chain seems to justify our emphasis on interindividual relationships in the treatment of schizophrenia.

The question arises whether a complete or partial cure could be obtained by starting from the somatic end of the chain. If the sociopsychosomatic theory is right and psychological factors effect somatic changes, it may be, per contra, that somatic factors could produce psychological changes. In this light we should encourage research in physico- and chemotherapies.

PREVENTIVE METHODS

Can we prevent schizophrenia?

> Its etiology is unsettled, its pathology unknown, and its clinical limits in dispute and yet it is a more serious problem than either tuberculosis or cancer. Each year not less than 30,000 to 40,000 individuals soon after adolescence or in the first flush of manhood or womanhood fall victim to this condition. They are condemned to a living death, devoid of emotional life as others savour it, and barred from participating in the normal activities and affairs of the living (Strecker & Ebaugh, 1940, chap. 7).

This does not need to be true. As the evidence shows, schizophrenia is a schizogenic disorder, a *product of mismanagement of men by men, of children by their parents.* It is not inherited; it is a man-made disaster.

Cannot men correct and prevent the wrong they are doing? They cannot change the laws of nature, but the understanding of those laws may give them the power to change themselves and their actions and prevent the harm they are causing. Perhaps schizophrenia could be prevented if we had a better understanding of the human relations that create this disorder.

The problem of prevention of schizophrenia transcends the traditional borders of psychiatry and clinical psychology. It is a problem of totality of human relations; it is a problem of social philosophy and human morality. There is no evidence that instrumental, materialistic societies produce more schizophrenics, but there is a great deal of evidence that instrumentalism, selfishness, and hostility *inside* a family produce schizophrenia in the children. And families do not live in a vacuum. The patterns of intrafamilial interaction are influenced to a great extent by social, economic, and cultural factors.

The only common denominator in personalities of all the fathers and mothers of schizophrenic patients was their parasitic, demanding, exploitative attitude to the marital partner and to the child. This attitude may be a product of a great variety of factors.

Perhaps the terms "sickness," "therapy," "cure," and so on are inexact words borrowed from physical health and hygiene and introduced in a loose way into the area of mental disorders. If schizophrenia is a mental "disease," then the sick patient is a part and a product of the *sick family* and the "treatment" should be perceived as a *corrective social interaction.*

But why start the corrective action *after* damage has been done to social relations and consequently to psychological structure and eventually to somatic processes? Why not start with a large-scale social reform of the family unit? Why not prevent *social diseases of family life?*

Despite the apparently growing interest in social aspects of mental disorder and research in the family (see Ackerman, 1958; Argell, 1936; Bateson, 1956; Bowen, 1960; Cavan, 1955; Jackson, 1960; Leighton et al., 1957; Lidz et al., 1958; Myers & Roberts, 1959; and many others), we do not know enough about factors that influence family life and eventually produce mental disorder. The only thing that we are pretty sure about is that "sick" family relations produce mental disorders.

Perhaps the whole idea of psychotherapy, as a one-to-one relationship, is a costly and obsolete error. Perhaps the problem is not how to help one individual. Perhaps *sociotherapy* is a better name and a better method. Mentally disturbed people are greatly influenced by interindividual relations. Their improvement or deterioration depends largely on their interaction with the environment.

Thus, the idea of group therapy is an important step forward. Family therapy is another step. Therapeutic community is another major step. But perhaps the time is ripe for more? Why "cure"? Why not prevent?

Perhaps the future task of the mental-health workers, psychiatrists, psychologists, social workers, nurses, hospital staff, etc. will be directed toward "friendly parenthood" or "rational parenthood" or "humanitarian society." Horney (1937), Fromm (1955), and many others pointed to the sociological and sociopsychological roots of mental disorder. Opler (1956; 1959), Leighton et al. (1957), Kardiner and Ovesey (1951), Hollingshead and Redlich (1958), Myers and Roberts (1959), and scores of workers examined thoroughly the cultural factors of mental disorder. Leighton, in a recently published volume (1960), calls for a new approach to the problem of social psychiatry. We are witnessing and participating in a third revolution in this area. The first revolution started with Pinel, who declared that the insane are *sick people* who deserve consideration and not punishment. The second revolution started with Freud, who proved that most mental disorders are not somatogenic. Presently we are amassing evidence of the sociogenic nature of most mental disorders.

Can we prevent schizophrenia? The only thing I know is that love helps normal growth and hate poisons it. Children brought up in homes full of love, where parents love each other and love their children with a vectorial type of love, grow and blossom like flowers basking in the sun. Children who are brought up in an atmosphere of dissension, where parents hate each other and involve the children in their problems, cannot grow but wither away like flowers in the dark. Their childhood is poisoned, their joy robbed, their happiness destroyed. They are forced prematurely into a morbid, hypervectorial attitude toward their parents. This is the core of schizophrenia—*vectoriasis praecox.* In order to prevent schizophrenia we obviously need to enhance the moral standards of society. We must revive the desire to be of service to men. We must educate youth to perceive society, not as an oil field to be exploited, but as a treasury to be protected. The power that man has accumulated must be used for the promotion of life, for helping oneself and others, in a balance of cathexes. Perhaps we have too many schizophrenics because we are too selfish.

Unconditional love coming from parents whose emotional needs are mutually satisfied will help the children to grow normally and pass safely the developmental stages progressing from infantile instrumentalism into mutualism and vectorialism. Mutual respect among parents will increase the child's respect for them ("Thou shalt honor!") and the child's feeling of security. A child who feels loved and sees love around him in his home cannot become schizophrenic. When parents love and control the child, when they are *strong* and *friendly,* the child can identify with them and become a normal adult.

A thorough reform of educational values may be necessary. One cannot educate for freedom and democracy by renouncing discipline and granting freedom and equal rights to children. Education is the will of society imposed on its children, taught to them, and instilled in their hearts. Education should use liberal and kind methods; but children must accept discipline from without until they develop their inner controls by a rational identification and by reality testing (Wolman, 1949). Teacher-training programs must be revamped and reorganized, educational philosophies rewritten, educational practices reformed, so as to make the teachers the true standard-bearers of our cultural values. We are not poor; we possess immense treasures in our Western civilization, and we must bequeath them to our children—the parents of the future. Teachers should represent the vectorial attitude, the moral standards, the cultural values, and no school should turn into a blackboard jungle.

Schizophrenia and other sociogenic mental disorders cannot be eradicated by drugs, nor can injections prevent them with immunity. The theory of the sociogenic origin of schizophrenia points to the possibilities of cure and prevention. Although a preventive program will inevitably face most serious problems in social structure, family relations, and moral and educational standards, the stakes are high, and the effort is worth making.

REFERENCES

Abraham, K. *Selected papers on psychoanalysis.* New York: Basic Books, 1955.

Ackerman, N. W. *The psychodynamics of family life.* New York: Basic Books, 1958.

Adeoye, L. T. The role of cultural factors in paranoid psychosis among the Yoruba Tribe. *J. ment. Sci.,* 1955, **101,** 239–266.

Alanen, Y. O. The mothers of schizophrenic patients. *Acta psychiat. et neurol. scandinav.,* 1958, **33,** Suppl. 724.

Alexander, L. *Treatment of mental disorders.* Philadelphia: W. B. Saunders, 1953.

Alikalos, L. C., Starer, E., & Winick, W. Observations on the meaning of behavior in groups of chronic schizophrenia. *Int. J. group Psychother.,* 1956, **6,** 180–192.

Altshuler, K. Z. Genetic elements in schizophrenia. *Eugen. Quart.,* 1957, **4,** 92–98.

American Psychiatric Association. *Diagnostic and statistical manual of mental disorders.* Washington, D.C.: Am. Psychiat. Ass., 1952.

Appel, K. E., Myers, J. M., & Scheflen, A. E. Prognosis in psychiatry. Results of psychiatric treatment. *A.M.A. Arch. Neurol. Psychiat.*, 1953, **70**, 459–468.

Arieti, S. *Interpretation of schizophrenia.* New York: Brunner, 1955.

Barnard, R. I., et al. The day hospital as an extension of psychiatric treatment. *Bull. Menninger Clin.*, 1952, **16**, 50.

Baruk, H. Experimental catatonia and the problem of will and personality. *J. nerv. ment. Dis.*, 1949, **110**, 218–235.

Bateson, G., Jackson, D. D., Haley, J., & Weakland, J. Toward a theory of schizophrenia. *Behav. Sci.*, 1956, **1**, 251–264.

Beaglehole, E. Some modern Hawaiians. *Univer. Hawaii res. Publ.*, 1939, No. 19. (a)

Beaglehole, E. Culture and psychosis in New Zealand. *J. Polynes. Soc.*, 1939, **48**, 144. (b)

Becker, W. A genetic approach to the interpretation and evaluation of the process reactive distinction in schizophrenia. *J. abnorm. soc. Psychol.*, 1956, **53**, 229–236.

Bellak, L. (Ed.) *Schizophrenia: A review of the syndrome.* New York: Logos, 1958.

Bellak, L., & Holt, R. R. Somatotypes in relation to dementia praecox. *Amer. J. Psychiat.*, 1948, **104**, 713–724.

Bender, Loretta. Schizophrenia in childhood: Its recognition, description, and treatment. *Amer. J. Orthopsychiat.*, 1956, **26**, 499–506.

Benedetti, G., & Mueller, C. (Eds.) *Symposium internationale sur la psychothérapie de la schizophrénie.* Basel: Karger, 1957.

Bergman, P., & Escalona, S. K. Unusual sensitivities in very young children. *Psychoanal. Stud. Child,* 1949, 3–4.

Bettelheim, B. *Love is not enough.* Glencoe, Ill.: Free Press, 1950.

Bettelheim, B. *Truants from life.* Glencoe, Ill.: Free Press, 1955.

Binder, A. Schizophrenic intellectual impairment: uniform or differential? *J. abnorm. soc. Psychol.*, 1956, **52**, 11–18.

Bleuler, E. *Das autistisch-undisziplinierte Denken in der Medizin und seine Überwindung.* Berlin: Springer, 1919.

Bleuler, E. *Dementia praecox or the group of schizophrenias.* New York: International Universities Press, 1950.

Bleuler, M. *Endokrinologische Psychiatrie.* Stuttgart: Thieme, 1954.

Bleuler, M. Research and changes in concepts in the study of schizophrenia. *Bull. Isase Ray med. Lib.*, **3**, 1955.

Böök, J. A. Genetical aspects of schizophrenic psychoses. In D. D. Jackson (Ed.), *The etiology of schizophrenia.* New York: Basic Books, 1960.

Bour, P. Schizophrénie et dissociation familiale. *Evolut. psychiat.*, 1958, **1**, 85–104.

Bowen, M. A family concept in schizophrenia. In D. D. Jackson (Ed.), *The etiology of schizophrenia.* New York: Basic Books, 1960.

Brackbill, G., & Fine, H. Schizophrenia and central nervous system pathology. *J. abnorm. soc. Psychol.*, 1956, **52**, 310–313.

Brody, E. B. Modification of family interaction patterns by a group interview technique. *Int. J. group Psychother.*, 1956, **6**, 38–46.

Brody, E. B., & Redlich, F. C. (Eds.), *Psychotherapy with schizophrenics: A symposium.* New York: International Universities Press, 1952.

Buck, C. W., Carscallen, H. B., & Hobbs, G. E. Temperature regulation in schizophrenia. *AMA Arch. Neurol. Psychiat.*, 1950, **64**, 828–842.

Bychowski, G. *Psychotherapy of psychosis.* New York: Grune & Stratton, 1952.

Bykov, K. *The cerebral cortex and the inner organs.* New York: Chemic. Publ., 1957.

Campbell, R. J. The schizophrenias—current views: A report on second international congress for psychiatry. *Psychiat. Quart.*, 1958, **32**, 318–334.

Cavanaugh, D. K., Cohen, W., & Lang, P. J. The effect of "social censure" and "social approval" on psychomotor performance of schizophrenics. *J. abnorm. soc. Psychol.*, 1960, **60**, 213–218.

Chase, L. S., & Silverman, S. Prognosis in schizophrenia. *J. nerv. ment. Dis.*, 1943, **98**, 464–473.

Cloutier, F. The development of the concept of schizophrenia. *Union med. Canada,* 1953, **82**, 1236.

Cobb, S. *Foundations of neuropsychiatry.* Baltimore; Williams & Wilkins, 1958.

Cohen, B. D. Motivation and performance in schizophrenia. *J. abnorm. soc. Psychol.*, 1956, **52**, 186–190.

Davis, D. R. The family triangle in schizophrenia. *Brit. J. med. Psychol.*, 1961, **34**, 53–63.

Dawson, J. G., Stone, H. K., & Dellis, N. T. (Eds.) *Psychotherapy with schizophrenics.* Baton Rouge: Louisiana State Univer., 1961.

Despert, J. L. Some considerations relating to the genesis of autistic behavior in children. *Amer. J. Orthopsychiat.,* 1951, **21,** 335–350.

Doust, J. W. I. Spectroscopic and photoelectric oximetry in schizophrenia and other psychiatric states. *J. ment. Sci.,* 1952, **98,** 143–160.

Dunham, H. W. Some remarks on the sociology of schizophrenia. In S. A. Mednick & J. Higgins (Eds.), *Current research in schizophrenia.* (n.d.)

Dunn, W. L. Visual discrimination of schizophrenic subjects as a function of stimulus meaning. *J. Pers.,* 1954, **23,** 48–64.

Eaton, J. W., & Weil, R. J. *Culture and mental disorders.* Glencoe, Ill.: Free Press, 1955.

Eisenberg, L. The fathers of autistic children. *Am. J. Orthopsychiat.,* 1957, **27,** 715–724.

Eissler, K. R. Dementia praecox therapy—psychiatric ward management of the acute schizophrenic patient. *J. nerv. ment. Dis.,* 1947, **105,** 397–402.

Eissler, K. R. Remarks on the psychoanalysis of schizophrenia. In E. B. Brody & F. C. Redlich (Eds.), *Psychotherapy with schizophrenics: A symposium.* New York: International Universities Press, 1952.

English, O. S., Hanupe, W. W., Bacon, C. L., & Settlage, C. F. *Direct analysis and schizophrenia.* New York: Grune & Stratton, 1961.

Esecover, H., Malitz, S., & Wilkens, B. Clinical profiles of paid normal subjects volunteering for hallucinogen drug studies. *Amer. J. Psychiat.,* 1961, **117,** 910–915.

Faris, R. E. L., & Dunham, H. W. *Mental disorders in urban areas.* Chicago: Univer. Chicago Press, 1939.

Federn, P. *Ego psychology and the psychoses.* New York: Basic Books, 1952.

Fedio, P., Mirsky, A. F., Smith, W. J., & Parry, D. Reaction time and EEG activation in normal and schizophrenic subjects. *Electroenceph. clin. Neuropsychol.,* 1961, **13,** 923–926.

Feifel, H. Qualitative differences in the vocabulary responses of normals and abnormals. *Genet. psychol. Monogr.,* 1949, **39,** 151–204.

Fenichel, O. *The psychoanalytic theory of neurosis.* New York: Norton, 1945.

Ferenczi, S. *Further contributions to the theory and technique of psychoanalysis.* London: Hogarth Press, 1926.

Fish, Barbara. The detection of schizophrenia in infancy. *J. nerv. ment. Dis.,* 1957, **125,** 1–24.

Fleck, S. Family dynamics and origin of schizophrenia. *Psychosom. Med.,* 1960, **22,** 333–344.

Fleck, S., Lidz, T., Cornelison, A., Schafer, S., & Terry, D. The intrafamilial environment of the schizophrenic patient. In J. H. Masserman (Ed.), *Individual and family dynamics.* New York: Grune & Stratton, 1959.

Foudraine, J. Schizophrenia and the family: A survey of the literature 1956–1960 on the etiology of schizophrenia. *Acta Psychother.,* 1961, **9,** 82–110.

Frankl, V. E. *The doctor and the soul.* New York: Knopf, 1955.

Freedman, A. M. Maturation and its relation to the dynamics of childhood schizophrenia. *Amer. J. Orthopsychiat.,* 1954, **24,** 487–491.

Freedman, R. *Recent migration to Chicago.* Chicago: Univer. Chicago Press, 1950.

Freeman, H. Physiological studies. In L. Bellak (Ed.), *Schizophrenia: A review of the syndrome.* New York: Logos, 1958.

Freeman, H. The tranquilizing drugs. In *ibid.*

Freeman, T., Cameron, J. L., & McGhie, A. *Chronic schizophrenia.* New York: International Universities Press, 1958.

Freud, Anna. *The ego and the mechanisms of defense.* New York: International Universities Press, 1946.

Freud, S. *Collected papers.* London: Hogarth Press and the Institute of Psychoanalysis, 1924–50. 5 vols.

Freud, S. *The ego and the id.* London: Hogarth, 1927.

Freud, S. *An outline of psychoanalysis.* New York: Norton, 1949. (a)

Freud, S. *A general introduction to psychoanalysis.* New York: Perma Giants, 1949. (b)

Freyhan, F. A. Course and outcome in schizophrenia. *Amer. J. Psychiat.,* 1955, **112,** 181–196.

Friedman, H. Perceptual regression in schizophrenia. *J. proj. Tech. pers. Assess.,* 1953, **17,** 171–185.

Fromm, Erich. *The sane society.* New York: Holt, Rinehart & Winston, 1955.

Fromm-Reichmann, F. *Principles of intensive psychotherapy.* Chicago: Univer. Chicago Press, 1950.

Fromm-Reichmann, F. Some aspects of psychoanalytic psychotherapy with schizophrenics. In

E. B. Brody & F. C. Redlich (Eds.), *Psychotherapy with schizophrenics. A symposium.* New York: International Universities Press, 1952.

Fromm-Reichmann, F. *Psychoanalysis and psychotherapy.* Chicago: Univer. Chicago Press, 1959.

Gantt, W. H. *Physiological basis of psychiatry.* Springfield, Ill.: Charles C Thomas, 1958.

Garmezy, N. Stimulus differentiation by schizophrenic and normal subjects under conditions of reward and punishment. *J. Pers.*, 1952, **20**, 253–276.

Garmezy, N., & Rodnick, E. H. Premorbid adjustment and performance in schizophrenia. *J. nerv. ment. Dis.*, 1959, **129**, 450–466.

Garrone, G. Statistical genetic study of schizophrenia in the Geneva population between 1901–1950. *J. genet. Psychol.*, 1962, 89–219.

Gellhorn, E. *Autonomic imbalance and the hypothalamus.* Minneapolis: Univer. Minnesota Press, 1958.

Gjessing, R. Distribution of somatic function in catatonia with a periodic course and their compensation. *J. ment. Sci.*, 1938, **84**, 608.

Gold, H. R. Observations on cultural psychiatry during a world tour of mental hospitals. *Amer. J. Psychiat.*, 1951, **108**, 462–468.

Goldfarb, W. *Childhood schizophrenia.* Cambridge, Mass.: Harvard Univer. Press, 1961.

Goldhamer, H., & Marshall, A. W. *Psychosis and Civilization.* New York: Basic Books, 1949.

Goldman, A. E. A comparative-developmental approach to schizophrenia. *Psychol. Bull.*, 1962, **59**, 57–69.

Goldstein, K. The significance of special mental tests for diagnosis and prognosis in schizophrenia. *Amer. J. Psychiat.*, 1939, **96**, 575–588.

Goldstein, K. Methodological approach to the study of schizophrenic thought disorder. In J. S. Kasanin (Ed.), *Language and thought in schizophrenia.* Berkeley: Univer. Calif. Press, 1946.

Gordon, H. L. Fifty shock therapy theories. *Milit. Surgeon*, 1948, **103**, 397.

Gregory, I. Genetic factors in schizophrenia. *Amer. J. Psychiat.*, 1960, **116**, 961–972.

Guertin, W. H., & Zilaitis, V. A. A transposed factor analysis of paranoid schizoprenics. *J. consult. Psychol.*, 1953, **17**, 455–458.

Gutheil, E. *The handbook of dream analysis.* New York: Liveright, 1951.

Haley, J. Whither family therapy. *Family Process*, 1962, **1**, 69–100.

Hall, K. R. L., & Crookes, T. G. Studies in learning impairment: I. Schizophrenic and organic patients. *J. ment. Sci.*, 1951, **97**, 725–737.

Hamburg, A. L. Orientation and defense reaction in simple and paranoid types of schizophrenia. In L. G. Voronin (Ed.), *The orientation reflex and orientating-inquisitive behavior.* (Russ.) Moscow: Acad. Ped. Nauk, 1958.

Hanfmann, E., & Kasanin, J. Conceptual thinking in schizophrenia. *Nerv. ment. dis. Monogr.*, 1942, No. 67.

Hare, E. H. Mental illness and social class in Bristol. *Brit. J. soc. Med.*, 1955, **9**, 191–195.

Harper, E. A. Discrimination between matched schizophrenics and normals by the Wechsler-Bellevue Scale. *J. consult. Psychol.*, 1950, **14**, 351–357.

Hartmann, H. Notes on the theory of sublimation. *Psychoanal. Stud. Child*, 1955, **10**, 9–29.

Hartmann, H., Kris, E., & Loewenstein, R. M. Comments on the formation of psychic structure. *Psychoanal. Stud. Child*, 1946, **2**, 11–38.

Hayward, M. L. In Whitaker (Ed.), *Psychotherapy of chronic schizophrenic patients.* Boston: Little, Brown, 1958.

Heath, R. G. A biochemical hypothesis on the etiology of schizophrenia. In D. D. Jackson (Ed.), *The etiology of schizophrenia.* New York: Basic Books, 1960.

Hendrickson, W. J. Etiology in childhood schizophrenia: An evaluation of current views. *Nerv. Child*, 1952, **10**, 9–18.

Herron, W. G. The process-reactive classification of schizophrenia. *Psychol. Bull.*, 1962, **59**, 329.

Hill, L. B. *Psychotherapeutic intervention in schizophrenia.* Chicago: Univer. Chicago Press, 1955.

Hoagland, H. Metabolic and physiologic disturbances in the psychoses. In S. S. Cobb (Ed.), *The biology of mental health and disease.* New York: Hoeber, 1952.

Hoch, P. H., & Pennes, H. H. Electric convulsive treatment and its modifications. In L. Bellak (Ed.), *Schizophrenia: A review of a syndrome.* New York: Logos, 1958.

Hoch, P. H., & Pennes, H. H. Insulin shock treatment. In *ibid.*

Hoch, P. H., & Polatin, P. Pseudoneurotic forms of schizophrenia. *Psychiat. Quart.*, 1949, **23**, 248.

Hollingshead, A. B., & Redlich, F. C. Schizophrenia and social structure. *Amer. J. Psychiat.*, 1954, **110**, 695–701.

Hollingshead, A. B., & Redlich, F. C. *Social class and mental illness.* New York: Wiley, 1958.

Horney, Karen. *The neurotic personality of our time.* New York: Norton, 1937.

Hoskins, R. G. *The biology of schizophrenia.* New York: Norton, 1946.

Hulse, W. C. Psychotherapy with ambulatory schizophrenic patients in mixed analytic groups. *AMA Arch. Neurol. Psychiat.*, 1958, **79**, 681–687.

Hunt, McV., & Coffer, C. N. Psychological deficit. In McV. Hunt (Ed.), *Personality and the behavior disorders.* New York: Ronald Press, 1944.

Huston, P. E., & Shakow, D. Studies of motor function in schizophrenia. III. Steadiness. *J. genet. Psychol.*, 1946, **34**, 119–126.

Huston, P. E., & Shakow, D. Learning in schizophrenia. I. Pursuit learning. *J. Pers.*, 1948, **17**, 52–74.

Ivanov-Smolensky, A. G. *Essays on the pathophysiology of higher nervous activity.* Moscow: Foreign Language Publ., 1954.

Jackson, D. D. (Ed.) *The etiology of schizophrenia.* New York: Basic Books, 1960.

Jackson, D. D., & Weakland, J. H. Conjoint family therapy. *Psychiatry,* 1961, **24**, 30–45.

Jones, M. The concept of a therapeutic community. *Amer. J. Psychiat.*, 1956, **112**, 647–650.

Jung, C. G. *The psychology of dementia praecox.* New York: J. nerv. ment. Dis. Publishing Co., 1936.

Kalinowsky, L. B. Convulsive shock treatment. In S. Arieti (Ed.), *American Handbook of Psychiatry.* New York: Basic Books, 1959.

Kalinowsky, L. B. & Hoch, P. H. *Shock treatments, psychosurgery, and other somatic treatments in psychiatry.* (2nd ed.) New York: Grune & Stratton, 1952.

Kallmann, F. J. *The genetics of schizophrenia.* New York: Augustin, 1938.

Kallmann, F. J. Genetic theory of schizophrenia: Analysis of 691 twin index families. *Amer. J. Psychiat.*, 1946, **103**, 309–322.

Kallmann, F. J. Genetics in relation to mental disorders. *J. ment. Sci.*, 1948, **94**, 250.

Kallmann, F. J. *Heredity in health and mental disorders,* New York: Norton, 1953.

Kanner, L. *Child psychiatry.* Springfield, Ill.: Charles C Thomas, 1948.

Kanner, L., & Eisenberg, L. Notes on the follow-up studies of autistic children. In P. H. Hoch and J. Zubin (Eds.), *Psychopathology of childhood.* New York: Grune & Stratton, 1955.

Kant, O. Clinical investigation of simple schizophrenia. *Psychiat. Quart.*, 1948, **22**, 141.

Kantor, R., Wallner, J., & Winder, C. Process and reactive schizophrenia. *J. consult. Psychol.*, 1953, **17**, 157–162.

Karon, B. P. The resolution of acute schizophrenic reactions. *Psychotherapy,* 1963, **1**, 27–43.

Katan, M. The importance of the nonpsychotic part of the personality in schizophrenia. *Int. J. Psychoanal.*, 1954, **35**, 119.

Kety, S. S. Recent biochemical theories of schizophrenia. In D. D. Jackson (Ed.), *The etiology of schizophrenia.* New York: Basic Books, 1960.

Kety, S. S., et al. Cerebral blood flow and metabolism in schizophrenia: Effects of barbiturate seminarcosis, insulin coma. *Amer. J. Psychiat.*, 1948, **104**, 765–770.

King, H. E. *Psychomotor aspects of mental disease.* Cambridge: Harvard Univer. Press, 1954.

Klein, Melanie. *Contributions to psychoanalysis.* London: Hogarth, 1946.

Kleist, K. The paranoid schizophrenias. *Nervenarzt,* 1947, **18**, 481; 544.

Klopfer, B., et al. *Developments in the Rorschach technique.* Yonkers, N.Y.: World Book Co., 1956. 2 vols.

Knight, R. P. Management and psychotherapy of the borderline schizophrenic patient. *Bull. Menninger Clin.*, 1953, **17**, 139.

Kohn, M. L., & Clausen, J. A. Parental authority behavior and schizophrenia. *Amer. J. Orthopsychiat.*, 1956, **26**, 297–313.

Kraepelin, E. *Dementia praecox and paraphrenia.* Chicago: Chicago Med. Book, 1919.

Kramer, M., et al. Application of life table methodology to the study of mental hospital population. *Psychiat. res. Rep. APA,* 1956, No. 5.

Krech, et al. Interhemispheric effects of cortical lesions on brain biochemistry. *Science,* 1960, **132**, 352–353.

Kretschmer, E. *Physique and character.* London: Kegan Paul, 1925.

Kris, E. Neutralization and sublimation: Observations on young children. *Psychoanal. Stud. Child,* 1955, **10**, 30–46.

Langfeldt, G. Some points regarding the symptomatology and diagnosis of schizophrenia. *Acta psychiat. et neurol. Scand. Suppl.*, 1953, **80**, **7**.

Leacock, Eleanor. Three social variables and the occurrence of mental disorder. In A. H. Leighton, J. A. Clausen, & R. N. Wilson (Eds.), *Explorations in social psychiatry*. New York: Basic Books, 1957.

Leighton, A. H. *Introduction to social psychiatry*. Springfield: Charles C Thomas, 1960.

Lemkau, P. V. *Mental hygiene in public health*. New York: McGraw-Hill, 1955.

Lemkau, P. V., & Crocetti, G. M. Vital statistics of schizophrenia. In L. Bellak (Ed.), *Schizophrenia: A review of the syndrome*. New York: Logos, 1958.

Lidz, T., et al. The intrafamilial environment of schizophrenic patients: II. Marital schism and marital skew. *Amer. J. Psychiat.*, 1957, **114**, 241–248.

Lidz, T., et al. The intrafamilial environment of schizophrenic patients; IV. Parental personalities and family interaction. *Amer. J. Orthopsychiat.*, 1958, **28**, 764–776.

Lidz, T., & Fleck, S. Schizophrenia, human integration, and the role of the family. In D. D. Jackson (Ed.), *The etiology of Schizophrenia*. New York: Basic Books, 1960.

Lief, A. *The commonsense psychiatry of Dr. Adolf Meyer*. New York: McGraw-Hill, 1948.

Lindegarde, B. *Variations in human body build*. Copenhagen: Munksgaard, 1953.

Linton H. B., & Langs, R. J. Subjective reactions to lysergic acid and diethylamide (LSD-25). *Arch. gen. Psychiat.*, 1962, **6**, 352–368.

Linton, R. *Culture and mental disorders*. Springfield, Ill.: Charles C Thomas, 1956.

Lu, Y. C. Mother-child role relations in schizophrenia. *Psychiatry*, 1961, **24**, 133–142.

Lu, Y. C. Contradictory parental expectations in schizophrenia. *Arch. gen. Psychiat.*, 1962, **6**, 219–234.

Lynn, R. Russian theory and research in schizophrenia. *Psychol. Bull.*, 1963, **60**, 486–498.

Mace, N. C., Koff, S. A., Chelnek, I., & Garfield, S. L. Diagnostic problems in early schizophrenia. *J. nerv. ment. Dis.*, 1949, **110**, 336–346.

Malamud, W. The psychoneuroses. In J. McV. Hunt (Ed.), *Personality and the behavior disorders*. Vol. II. New York: Ronald, 1944.

Malis, G. Y. *Research on the etiology of schizophrenia*. New York: Consultants Bureau, 1961.

Mason, C. F. Pre-illness intelligence of mental hospital patients. *J. consult. Psychol.*, 1956. **20**, 297–300.

Mednick, S. A. Generalization as a function of manifest anxiety and adaptation to psychological experiments. *J. Consult. Psychol.*, 1957, **21**, 491–494.

Mednick, S. A learning theory approach to research in schizophrenia. *Psychol. Bull.*, 1958, **55**, 316–327.

Merton, R., & Kendall, P. L. The focused interview. *Amer. J. Sociol.*, 1964, **51**, 541–557.

Midelfort, C. F. *The family in psychotherapy*. New York: McGraw-Hill, 1957.

Myers, J. K., & Roberts, B. A. *Family and class dynamics in mental illness*. New York: Wiley, 1959.

Noyes, A. P., & Kolb, L. C. *Modern clinical psychiatry*. (5th ed.) Philadelphia: Saunders, 1958.

Nuffield, E. J. A. The schizogenic mother. *Med. J. Australia*, 1954, **2**, 283–286.

Nunberg, H. Practice and theory in psychoanalysis. New York: J. nerv. ment. Dis. Publishing Co., 1948.

Ødegaard, O. Emigration and insanity. *Acta Psychiat. Neurol.*, 1932, **4**.

Ødegaard, O. The distribution of mental diseases in Norway. *Acta Psychiat. Neurol.*, 1945, **20**, 247–284.

Opler, M. K. *Culture, psychiatry and human values: The methods and values of a social psychiatry*. Springfield, Ill.: Charles C Thomas, 1956.

Osmond, H., & Smythies, J. J. Schizophrenia: A new approach. *J. ment. Sci.*, 1952, **98**, 309–315.

Overholser, W., & Werkman, S. L. Etiology, pathogenesis, and pathology. In L. Bellak (Ed.), *Schizophrenia: A review of the syndrome*. New York: Logos, 1958.

Pascal, G. R., Swenson, C. H., et al. Prognostic criteria in the case histories of hospitalized mental patients. *J. consult. Psychol.*, 1953, **17**, 163–171.

Pavlov, I. P. *Lectures on conditioned reflexes*. New York: Liveright, 1928.

Pavlov, I. P. *Conditioned reflexes and psychiatry*. New York: International Publishers, 1941.

Penman, A. S. & Dredge, T. E. Effect of reserpine and open-ward privileges on chronic schizophrenics. *A.M.A. Arch. Neurol. Psychiat.*, 1956, **76**, 42–49.

Phillips, L. Case history data and progress in schizophrenia. *J. nerv. ment. Dis.*, 1953, **117**, 515–535.

Pichon-Rivière, de E. Quelques observations sur le transfert chez des patients psychotiques. *Rev. Franc. Psychoanal.*, 1952, **16**, 254–262.

Piotrowski, Z. A. A comparison of congenitally defective children with schizophrenic children in regard to personality structure and intelligence type. *Proc. Am. Assn. Ment. Def.*, 1937, **42**, 78–90.

Piotrowski, Z A. Experimental psychological diagnosis of mild forms of schizophrenia. *Rorschach res. Exch.*, 1945, **9**, 189–200.

Piotrowski, Z. A., & Lewis, N. D. A case of stationary schizophrenia beginning in early childhood with remarks on certain aspects of children's Rorschach records. *Quart. J. Child Behavior*, 1950, **2**, 115–139.

Prout, C. T., & White, M. A. The schizophrenic's sibling. *J. nerv. ment. Dis.*, 1956, **123**, 162–170.

Rabin, A. I., & King, G. F. Psychological studies. In L. Bellak (Ed.), *Schizophrenia: A review of the syndrome*. New York: Logos, 1958.

Rabin, A. I., King, G. F., & Ehrman, J. C. Vocabulary performance of short term and long term schizophrenics. *J. abnorm. soc. Psychol.*, 1955, **50**, 255–258.

Rank, B. Adaptation of the psychoanalytic technique for the treatment of young children with atypical development. *Amer. J. Orthopsychiat.*, 1949, **19**, 130–139.

Rank, B. Intensive study of preschool children who show marked personality deviations or "atypical development" and their parents. In J. Caplan (Ed.), *Emotional problems of early childhood*. New York: Basic Books, 1955.

Rapaport, D., & Webb, W. B. An attempt to study intellectual deterioration by premorbid and psychotic testing. *J. clin. Psychol.*, 1950, **14**, 95–98.

Rees, L. Physical characteristics of the schizophrenic patient. In D. Richter (Ed.), *Schizophrenia: Somatic aspects*. New York: Macmillan, 1957.

Reich, W. *Character analysis*. (3rd ed.) New York: Noonday, 1949.

Reiss, M. Correlations between changes in mental states and thyroid activity after different forms of treatment. *J. ment. Sci.*, 1954, **100**, 687–703.

Richter (Ed.), *Schizophrenia: Somatic aspects*. New York: Macmillan, 1957.

Riemer, M. D. Mental status of schizophrenics hospitalized for over 25 years into their senium. *Psychiat. Quart.*, 1950, **24**, 309.

Rifkin, A. H. *Schizophrenia in psychoanalytic office practice*. New York: Grune & Stratton, 1957.

Roe, Anne, & Shakow, D. Intelligence in mental disorder. *Ann. New York Acad. Sci.*, 1942, **42**, 361–390.

Roheim, G. *Magic and schizophrenia*. New York: International Universities Press, 1955.

Rosen, J. N. The treatment of schizophrenic psychosis by direct analytic therapy. *Psychiat. Quart.*, 1947, **21**, 117–119.

Rosen, J. N. *Direct Analysis*. New York: Grune & Stratton, 1953.

Rosenbaum, G., et al. Effects of biological and social motivation on schizophrenic reaction time. *J. abnorm. soc. Psychol.*, 1957, **54**, 364–368.

Rosenfeld, H. Notes on the psychoanalysis of the superego conflict of an acute schizophrenic patient. *Int. J. Psychoanal.*, 1952, **33**, 111–131.

Rosenfeld, H. Considerations regarding the psychoanalytic approach to acute and chronic schizophrenia. *Int. J. Psychoanal.*, 1953, **35**, 135.

Rosenthal, D. Confusion of identity and the frequency of schizophrenia in twins. *Arch. gen. Psychiat.*, 1960, 3, 297–304.

Roth, M. Interaction of genetic and environmental factors in the causation of schizophrenia. In D. Richter, D. (Ed.) *Schizophrenia: Somatic aspects*. New York: Macmillan, 1957.

Sakel, M. The classical Sakel shock treatment; a reappraisal. *J. clin. exp. Psychopath.*, 1945, **15**, 255–316.

Salzman, L. An evaluation of shock therapy. *Amer. J. Psychiat.*, 1947, **103**, 669.

Savage, C., & Cholden, L. Schizophrenia and model psychoses. *J. clin. exp. Psychopathol.*, 1956, **17**, 405–413.

Scher, S. C., & Davis, H. A. *The out-patient treatment of schizophrenia*. New York: Grune & Stratton, 1960.

Schofield, W., Hathaway, S. R., Hastings, D. W., & Bell, D. M. Prognostic factors in schizophrenia. *J. consult. Psychol.*, 1954, **18**, 155–166.

Schwab, H. Confused schizophrenics on basis of catamnestic studies: schizophasia. *A.M.A. Arch. Neurol. Psychiat.*, 1949, **182**, 333–399.

Schwing, G. *A way to the soul of the mentally ill*. New York: International Universities Press, 1954.

Sechekaye, M. A. *New psychotherapy in schizophrenia*. Transl. G. Ruben-Rabson. N.Y.: Grune & Stratton, 1956.

Shakow, D. The nature of deterioration in schizophrenic condition. *Nerv. ment. dis. Monogr.*, 1946, No.70.

Shakow, D. Segmental set. *Arch. gen. Psychiat.*, 1962, **6**, 1–17.

Shattock, M. F. The somatic manifestations of schizophrenia: a clinical study of their significance. *J. ment. Sci.*, 1950, **96**, 32.

Sheldon, W. H. The varieties of human physique. New York: Harper, 1940.

Siegel, E. L. Genetic parallels of perceptual structuralization in paranoid schizophrenia. *J. proj. Tech.*, 1953, **17**, 151–161.

Skinner, B. F. A new method for the experimental analyses of the behavior of psychotic patients. *J. nerv. ment. Dis.*, 1954, **120**, 403–404.

Skottowe, I. *Clinical psychiatry.* New York: McGraw-Hill, 1954.

Slater, E. Psychotic and neurotic illnesses in twins. *Med. res. council, Special Report no.* 278, London: H. M. Stationery office, 1953.

Slater, E. The monogenic theory of schizophrenia. *Acta Genet.*, 1958, **8**, 50–56.

Slavson, S. R. *Analytic group psychotherapy.* New York: Columbia Univer. Press, 1950.

Sommerness, M. D., Lucero, R. J., Hamlon, J. S., Erickson, J. L., & Mathews, R. A. Controlled study of reserpine on chronically disturbed patients. *A.M.A. Arch. Neurol. Psychiat.*, 1955, **74**, 316–319.

Spence, V. W., & Taylor, J. A. The relation of conditioned response strength to anxiety in normal, neurotic, and psychotic subjects. *J. exp. Psychol.*, 1953, **45**, 265–272.

Stanton, A. H., & Schwartz, M. S. *The mental hospital.* New York: Basic Books, 1954.

Staudt, V. M. & Zubin, J. A. Biometric evaluation of the somato-therapies in schizophrenia—a critical review. *Psychol. Bull.*, 1957, **54**, 171–196.

Stotsky, B. A. Motivation and task complexity as factors in the psychomotor responses of schizophrenics. *J. Pers.*, 1957, **25**, 327–347.

Sullivan, H. S. Sociopsychiatric research: Its implications for the schizophrenia problem and for mental hygiene. *Amer. J. Psychiat.*, 1931, **10**, 77–91.

Sullivan, H. S. *Conceptions of modern psychiatry.* Washington, D.C.: W. A. White, 1947.

Sullivan, H. S. *The interpersonal theory of psychiatry.* New York: Norton, 1953.

Szára, S. The comparison of the psychotic effect of tryptamine derivatives with the effects of mescaline and LSD-25 in self-experiments. In S. Garattini & V. Ghetti (Eds.), *Psychotropic Drugs.* London: Cleaver-Hume Press, 1958.

Tausk, V. On the origin of the influencing machine in schizophrenia. *Psychoanal. Quart.*, 1933, **2**, 263.

Taylor, J. A., & Spence, K. W. Conditioning level in the behavior disorders. *J. abnorm. soc. Psychol.*, 1954, **49**, 497–503.

Tooth, G. Studies in mental illness in the Gold Coast. *Research Publications no.* 6, London: H. M. Stationery Office., 1950.

Venables, P. H. The effect of auditory and visual stimulation on skin potential response of schizophrenics. *Brain*, 1961, **80**, 77–92.

Von Domarus, E. The specific laws of logic in schizophrenia. In J. S. Kasanin (Ed.), *Language and thought in schizophrenia.* California: Univer. Calif. Press, 1944.

Vorster, D. An investigation into the part played by organic factors in childhood schizophrenia. *J. ment. Sci.*, 1960, **106**, 494–522.

Wahl, C. W. Some antecedent factors in the family histories of 568 male schizophrenics in the U.S. Navy. *Amer. J. Psychiat.*, 1956, **113**, 201–210.

Weakland, J. H. The double-bind hypothesis of schizophrenia and three party interaction. In D. D. Jackson (Ed.), *The etiology of schizophrenia.* New York: Basic Books, 1960.

Werkman, S. L. Present trends in schizophrenic research. *Am. J. Orthopsychiat.*, 1959, **29**, 473–480.

West, F. H., Bond, E. D., Shurley, J. T. & Meyers, C. D. Insulin coma therapy in schizophrenia. A fourteen-year follow-up study. *Amer. J. Psychiat.*, 1955, **111**, 583–589.

Whitaker, C. A. (Ed.), *Psychotherapy of chronic schizophrenic patients.* Boston: Little, Brown, 1958.

Whitehorn, J. C. Psychodynamic approach to the study of psychosis. In F. Alexander and H. Ross (Eds.), *Dynamic psychiatry.* Chicago: Univer. Chicago Press, 1952.

Whitehorn, J. C., & Betz, B. J. Further studies of the doctor as a crucial variable in the outcome of treatment with schizophrenic patients. *Amer. J. Psychiat.*, 1960, 215–223.

Winder, C. L. Some psychological studies of schizophrenics. In D. D. Jackson (Ed.), *The etiology of schizophrenia.* New York: Basic Books, 1960.

Winnicot, D. W. Régression et repli. *Rev. franç. Psychoanal.*, 1955, **19**, 323–330.

Wolman, B. B. Juvenile delinquents in Palestine (Hebrew). *Hachinuch Quart.*, 1946, **17**, 50–79.

Wolman, B. B. Friendship (Hebrew). *Hachinuch Quart.*, 1947, **18**, 1–21.

Wolman, B. B. Disturbances in acculturation. *Amer. J. Psychother.*, 1949, **3**, 601–615.

Wolman, B. B. Social relations as a function of power and acceptance. Paper presented at *Annu. Convention Amer. sociol. Soc.*, 1955.

Wolman, B. B. Leadership and group dynamics. *J. soc. Psychol.*, 1956, **43**, 11–25.

Wolman, B. B. Explorations in latent schizophrenia. *Amer. J. Psychother.*, 1957, **11**, 560–588.

Wolman, B. B. Instrumental, mutual acceptance, and vectorial groups. *Acta Sociologica*, 1958, **3**, 19–29. (a)

Wolman, B. B. The deterioration of the ego in schizophrenia. Paper presented at *East. psychol. Ass.*, 1958. (b)

Wolman, B. B. Libido and destrudo in pseudoneurotic symptoms in schizophrenia. Paper presented at *Amer. psychol. Ass.*, 1958. (c)

Wolman, B. B. Psychotherapy with latent schizophrenics. *Amer. J. Psychother.*, 1959, **13**, 343–359. (a)

Wolman, B. B. Continuum hypothesis in neurosis and psychosis and the classification of the mental disorder. Paper presented at *East. psychol. Ass.*, 1959. (b)

Wolman, B. B. *Contemporary theories and systems in psychology*. New York: Harper, 1960. (a)

Wolman, B. B. Impact of failure on group cohesiveness. *J. soc. Psychol.*, 1960, **51**, 409–418. (b)

Wolman, B. B. Group psychotherapy with latent schizophrenics. *Int. J. Group Psychother.*, 1960, **10**, 301–312. (c)

Wolman, B. B. The fathers of schizophrenic patients. *Acta Psychother.*, 1961, **9**, 193–210. (a)

Wolman, B. B Differential diagnosis in schizophrenia. Paper presented at *East. psychol. Ass.*, 1961. (b)

Wolman, B. B Research in etiology of schizophrenia. Paper presented at *East. psychol. Ass.*, 1962.

Wolman, B. B. Hostility experiences in group psychotherapy. *Int. J. soc. Psychiat.*, 1964, **10**, 57–63. (a)

Wolman, B. B. Non-participant observation on a closed ward. *Acta Psychother.*, 1964, **12**, 61–71. (b)

Wolman, B. B. *Vectoriasis praecox or the group of schizophrenias*. 1965. (a)

Wolman, B. B. Family dynamics and schizophrenia. *J. Hlth. hum. Behav.*, 1965. (b)

Woolley, D. W. Serotonin in mental disorders. *Res. Publ. Ass. nerv. ment. Dis.*, 1958, **36**, 381–400.

Wynne, L. C., et al. Pseudo-mutuality in the family relations in schizophrenics. *Psychiatry*, 1958, **21**, 205–220.

Yacorzynski, G. K. An evaluation of the postulates underlying the Babcock deterioration test. *Psychol. Rev.*, 1941, **48**, 261–267.

Zilboorg, G., & Henry, G. W. *A history of medical psychology*. New York: Norton, 1941.

35

Depression

J. RICHARD WITTENBORN

Among the well-known accounts of depressive disorders, the earliest may be found in the story of Job, an able, conscientious man who reacted to misfortune with persisting despair, self-condemnation, inertia, and somatic complaints, but whose eventual remission of all symptoms was complete. The Biblical explanation is in terms of God's willingness to test Job's faith by subjecting him to torment.

Although the disfavor of the gods was the supernatural explanation often employed in the classical literature, possession by an evil spirit has been claimed by some depressed patients in more recent times. This is currently characteristic of certain simple Africans who explain their feelings of worthlessness by claiming that they have become witches (Field, 1960). These people who charge themselves with witchcraft are members of a community which believes that witches do indeed exist. In such communities charging oneself with witchery is an effective way of concretizing and making specific the irrational guilt and self-condemnation which are so characteristic of the depressive illness. It is possible that some of the many confessions of witchcraft at different periods, particularly the inquisitional period of Western Europe and the witchcraft trials of New England, were the product of persons who were susceptible to strongly depressive reactions and, when falsely accused, would respond with a depressive episode generating delusions of guilt and false confessions.

For at least two thousand years, however, the primary explanations of depressive disorders have been in terms of some specified physical basis, usually constitutional in nature and sometimes hereditary in origin. Hippocrates and Plato refer to depressions as due to a disturbance of body juices, and the term "melancholia" may have originated with Hippocrates' emphasis on the preponderance of black bile in those persons afflicted with depressions.

The fact that the classical period knew depressions in much the same form that we observe them today is amply documented, and according to the indications gleaned by Zilboorg (1941) concerning the observations of Aretaeus, some of the most stable and distinguishing views which we have concerning depressions were expressed as early as the first century. These would include the principle that mania and depression may be different manifestations of the same underlying disorder, that depressive disorders occur later in life than schizophrenia, that such disorders are not malignant and may be intermittent in their appearance. He observed that the intellectual functions are less affected than the emotions and noted that some persons were prone to develop a depressive manifestation as merely an extension or an exaggeration of their normal personality.

Depressed states of moderate duration which were an understandable consequence of trauma or deprivation were doubtless always recognized as such. For some persons, however, such depressive reactions persist and may be confused with the pervasive and irrational depressions which are considered to be pathological. Nevertheless, it is not apparent that the concept of a reactive depression was generally employed by medical writers of the classical period. The explicitly recorded medical recognition of a reactive depression may be found in the literature of the early part of the seventeenth century, e.g., Ferrand, Bonet, and Denis (Zilboorg, 1941), and a reactive significance of depression is implicit in Cullen's (1777) eighteenth-century concept of depression as a collapse. Despite the importance of reactive states, the ancient notion that depressions were somehow endogenously determined persisted strongly though the centuries and continued to be pivotal in the approach of many of the writers through the first half of the twentieth century.

Since the time of Hippocrates and probably before him, there have appeared statements associating body type with temperamental traits and with disease susceptibility. These claims appear to have a meandering, inconsistent quality, and it is possible that presumptions of association between body type and mental disease reached their zenith in the writings of Kretschmer (1925), who concluded that a pyknic or mixed pyknic body type was characteristic of approximately 67 per cent of the manic-depressives but was apparent in only 13 per cent of the schizophrenics. Kretschmer's pyknic type, reminiscent of Hippocrates' *habitus apoplecticus*, was distinguished by a stocky build with a large trunk and relatively short limbs. Attempts to reproduce Kretschmer's findings have not always been successful (Garvey, 1933), and it is possible that some of the body-type differences which have been reported in comparisons of schizophrenics and manic-depressives could be explained by such factors as the relatively advanced age and possibly the accompanying obesity of many depressed patients. Certainly depressions have not been a traditional disorder of youth, while many cases of schizophrenia may be truly described as a dementia praecox (Gregory, 1962). Although this problem has been brought up to date by Sheldon and Stevens (1942), recent attempts to correlate his indexes of physique with relevant personality variables have also been discouraging (Hood, 1963).

During the first half of the twentieth century, it was commonly assumed that depressions, particularly disorders which followed the manic-depressive pattern, were not only constitutional in nature but a result of hereditary determination. Nevertheless, the exact nature of the genetically determined characteristics which implement the development of manic-depressive psychosis remained a matter of paradoxical uncertainty. Symonds (1941) comments:

> Apart from heredity there is little known of cause. What is important, perhaps, is that precipitating cause when definite may be so various—emotional disturbance, infective or toxic illness, fatigue, or head injury. . . . What perhaps is even more noteworthy is that the affective disorder can persist so long and yet be so completely reversible. There can, therefore, be no structural alteration of a kind we should call lesion, and it is possible, if not probable, that there is a cause outside the brain itself—physical or chemical (quoted by Cobb, 1944, p. 577).

The genetic explanation for manic-depressive psychosis was advanced emphatically by Cobb (1944; 1962), who endorsed and extended Symonds' comments in the following remarkably unqualified quotation:

> The sorrows caused by manic-depressive psychosis are common and great. Mild depressions cause much unhappiness and inefficiency, while mild manic states disrupt social relationships to an extraordinary degree. I agree with Symonds entirely, but would like to underline, for emphasis, the words "*of a kind we should call a lesion.*" I *do* believe that there is "structural alteration" in every case of manic-depressive psychosis. I have not discussed it above, in the main body of the chapter, because the structural alteration may not be in the brain. Nevertheless, the disease is strongly inherited, and to carry this taint the gene must have structural abnormality; function is action and cannot be inherited. The defect in the gene has not as yet been microscopically detected, but it must be there. No abnormality of any organ is regularly discovered in the bodies of persons suffering from this psychosis. Perhaps the lesion escapes notice because it consists of the imbalance of two or more organs no one of which shows enough abnormality to be recognized by our present methods. Such a deviation from the normal would coincide with Symonds' conception. Another possibility is that a lesion (defined as visible structural change) will be found in the diencephalon when methods are improved.

> In that case manic-depressive symptoms will form a large chapter in the discussion of lesions that affect the personality. One thing is certain, and that is that the term "functional" cannot reasonably be applied to this disease. Etiologically speaking, manic-depressive psychosis is strongly genogenic, a large chemogenic factor is probable and psychogenic precipitants are known to occur in some cases (Cobb, 1944, p. 577).

Since numerous investigators have observed that depressive disorders, particularly those of a cyclical nature which may be called manic-depressive, characterize some families much more than others, it has been frequently concluded that manic-depressive disorders are not only inherited but inherited according to a dominant pattern (Rüdin, 1916). Most conspicuous among current investigators of this persuasion is Kallmann (1954), who examined data from many sources and found consistent indication that manic-depressive kinship was appreciably more characteristic of manic-depressive patients than it was of other patients. Such findings as these are not compelling, however; common inheritance usually implies common environmental influences, and in the study of familial resemblances any trends must be examined from the standpoint of confounding environmental influences.

Regardless of the ultimate validity of various suppositions concerning the hereditary basis for depressive disorders, many clinicians and possibly most students of depressions do not currently require a hereditary hypothesis to account for their observations of depressive patients, and perhaps even fewer find such a hypothesis clinically useful. Concurrent with the diminished emphasis on a hereditary viewpoint, there has arisen an increasingly large body of data concerned with the epidemiology of mental disease, particularly depressions. Most of these data are of such a nature as to encourage the formulation of explanations which emphasize psychogenic factors and place no strong claim on genogenic explanations.

INCIDENCE

In consequence of certain consistencies in the environment, attitudes and reaction patterns may come to characterize individuals in ways which make them susceptible to depressive disorders. Such a viewpoint is, however, primarily a contribution of the twentieth century. The kinds of evidence which would favor an environmental point of view have come from many sources. Not the least of these have been certain studies of an ecological nature. Several investigators had indicated that schizophrenic patients were most prevalent in those areas of the city which had the lowest economic status, while depressive disorders were most frequent in the areas of relatively high socio-economic status (Dunham, 1959).

Although such findings as these raise numerous methodological questions concerning such matters as changes in diagnostic criteria from one economic region within the city to another or changes in referral rate or commitment criteria from region to region, the challenge to traditional etiological concepts was a solid one, and the influence of the milieu on the development, adaptive significance, and custodial requirement of mental patients has come to receive an increasingly serious consideration. Such considerations appear to be particularly pertinent to the study of depressive disorders. For example, during the ten-year period 1940 to 1950, the rate of first admissions to mental hospitals rose from 28 per 100,000 to 31. During this same period, however, the first-admission rate for manic-depressive psychosis dropped from 7.6 to 4.7 (Kramer, Pollack, & Redick, 1961). Such a drop could reflect changes in diagnostic criteria, an increased capacity of the community to care for depressed patients without resorting to hospitalization, or perhaps a diminution of those factors which generate depressive personalities and precipitate depressive reactions. Certainly such a marked reduction in admission rate would be difficult to explain if depressive disorders were expected to emerge at a characteristic rate merely in consequence of the genetic constitution of the population.

The implications of the epidemiological considerations become elaborated when one considers reports that in the hospitals of the northeastern part of the United States, at least, depressive illnesses are much less frequent among Negroes than among whites. In view of the work of Field (1960), it seems improbable that a susceptibility to depression is in some manner lacking among Negroes. Accordingly, the fact that depressive disorders are relatively less prevalent among the economically underprivileged (Dunham, 1959) and in technologically backward areas (Wittkower & Fried, 1959) may be applied as a partial explanation of what at first glance may appear to be a racial difference. Eventually, however, the question must be posed: What are the differences between the class strata which would appear to make depressions less prevalent among the lower classes than among the middle class?

The incidence of depressive disorders shows various trends which are provocative of further study. As noted (1961), the nationwide first-admission rate of depressive disorders to public mental hospitals had been characterized by a substantial reduction during a period when mental hospital first admissions in general had markedly increased. There are interesting regional exceptions to this general reduction in rate of depressive admissions. In New Hampshire and Vermont, and in Rhode Island as well, the rate of depressive admissions increased markedly from 1940 to 1950. A similar increase was recorded for Nevada. It is possible that these notable exceptions to the general pattern reflect the use of different diagnostic criteria in the hospitals of these states. It is possible also that the kinds of deprivations that appear to be conducive to the precipitation of a depression were particularly prevalent in those regions. For example, there may have been a significant deterioration in the economic climate in those regions during this era. Although no published analyses have come to the writer's attention concerning regional variations in the intensity of depressions, current impressions verbalized by responsible observers indicate that severe depressions during the last decade have become less frequent in the East, while in some of the Middle Western states, particularly Wisconsin and Minnesota, depressions of marked severity are still encountered in great numbers.

SYMPTOMATOLOGY

There has long been a tendency to categorize individuals into types as if there were indeed disjunctive patterns or classes of personality. As methods for the quantitative summarization of descriptive data have improved during the last fifty years, it has become increasingly evident that there is no behavioral basis for the disjunctive classification of individuals. It would appear that regardless of the nature of the behavioral manifestation or combination of manifestations, individuals differ from each other by degree, and there are very few, if any, abrupt disjunctions which require such arbitrary typological classifications as those implicit in descriptive diagnoses. Since no concrete evidence has been adduced to identify an underlying metabolic, morphologic, toxologic, or constitutional basis to distinguish a depressive disease, the investigator is left with only individual differences in depressive symptoms and individual differences in relevant personality characteristics. Accordingly, in the study of psychopathology, particularly depressions, an increasing reliance has been placed on both overt symptomatological manifestations and background circumstances as a basis for inferring underlying predispositions. An increasingly large group of investigators tends to see depressions as disorders which may be described in terms of kind and degree of symptomatic manifestation only.

The symptomatic variation within a group of patients diagnosed manic-depressive psychosis, depressed type, is illustrated in a report by Wittenborn, Holzberg, and Simon (1953). As illustrated in Table 1, patients bearing this diagnosis, far from being highly similar to each other, showed appreciable individual variation from the standpoint of any one of a standard set of symptomatic characteristics. From this table, it is apparent that a diagnostic formulation need not imply a distinctive symptom pattern and that a neat diagnostic disjunction does not represent a neat behavioral distinction.

The cluster scores used in order to measure the individual differences which are the point of interest in Table 1 have a pertinence to the present discourse and may be examined from that standpoint. Specifically, a large group of psychiatrists had been interviewed with the request that they indicate the symptomatic characteristics which they considered important in the assessment and diagnosis of mental illness (Wittenborn, 1951). These symptomatic characteristics, which were presumably a good sample of pertinent symptoms, were expressed in the form of rating scales. After suitable pretesting and refinement, a standard set of 55 scales was used by psychiatrists in rating the symptoms of a series of new admissions at Connecticut State Hospital at Middletown (Wittenborn & Holzberg, 1951). The

TABLE 1. PATIENTS DIAGNOSED MANIC-DEPRESSIVE PSYCHOSIS, DEPRESSED TYPE (N = 36) (SCORE DISTRIBUTION FOR EACH CLUSTER WITH MEDIAN CLUSTER SCORE ITALICIZED)

Cluster name	*Cluster score*									
	1	*2*	*3*	*4*	*5*	*6*	*7*	*8*	*9*	*10*
1. Acute anxiety	5	2	*11*	5	4	3	2	0	4	0
2. Conversion hysteria	*22*	3	4	2	2	1	2	0	0	0
3. Manic state	*21*	6	4	3	0	2	0	0	0	0
4. Depressed state	4	5	8	*3*	5	4	3	2	1	1
5. Schizophrenic excitement	8	9	*9*	3	3	2	2	0	0	0
6. Paranoid condition	17	*9*	5	4	0	0	1	0	0	0
7. Paranoid schizophrenic	10	*9*	4	4	2	2	2	2	1	0
8. Hebephrenic schizophrenic	15	*4*	8	5	1	2	1	0	0	0
9. Phobic compulsive	14	*10*	2	5	1	2	0	1	1	0

symptom ratings for the newly admitted patients were intercorrelated and factor-analyzed by the centroid method, and the resulting factors were rotated orthogonally according to the criteria of simple structure. These factors comprise clusters of symptoms which were then used as a basis for cluster scores, such as those employed in Table 1.

It is important to observe that these factors and the resulting cluster scores do not refer to types of patients but to independent dimensions which permit one to distinguish among the patients. The dimensions which are defined on the basis of this factor-analytic procedure provide two important features which distinguish depressions from other severe emotional disorders. The first is the bipolar dimension of mania-depression, the depressive pole of which includes such specific symptoms as "gives in easily to the opinions of others," "avoids people," "all activities at a minimum," "cannot make decisions," and "failures of affective response." The second is the dimension of anxiety which includes such symptoms as "delusion of guilt," "fear of impending doom," "feeling of intolerable anxious distress." A recent study of chronic patients (Wittenborn, 1963) reveals useful distinctions within these general dimensions of depression.

The question of heterogeneity within an illustrative diagnostic group has been examined somewhat differently by Wittenborn and Bailey (1952) in a scrutiny of symptomatic similarities and dissimilarities among patients who have the diagnosis of involutional psychosis. Specifically, twenty patients bearing this diagnosis were rated with a standard set of 55 rating scales. On the basis of these rating scales, each patient was correlated with every other one, and these intercorrelations were factor-analyzed by the centroid method. The factors were orthogonally rotated to simple structure, and it was apparent that there were several distinguishable patterns of symptom manifestations among the patients comprising this diagnostic group. For example, there was one pattern identifying individuals with high scores on the paranoid schizophrenic cluster and without conspicuously high scores on any other symptom cluster, while a second pattern was distinguishable on the basis of relatively high cluster scores for somatic conversions and anxiety but without appreciable pathological indications from other cluster scores.

The diversity of ways in which depressions may be manifested by different individuals becomes increasingly apparent and should be considered when one wishes to assess the state of a depressed patient or make distinctions among depressed patients. In a recently completed study (Wittenborn, unpublished), a set of 82 pertinent variables was factor-analyzed by the method of principle components for a sample of 180 newly admitted mental hospital patients. The patients were females not yet in the climacteric, and their disorder was essentially a depression without apparent schizophrenic features. The 82 variables were selected for the analysis because earlier investigations had indicated that they or similar variables either characterized patients suffering from a depression or changed with the degree of depression. On the basis of the factor analysis, it was found that twelve independent dimensions were required in order to summarize the 82 descriptive variables; i.e., there were twelve different ways in which these patients differed from each other. Presumably, therefore, these dimensions should be considered if a comprehensive assessment of the state of depressed patients is desired at the time of admission to the hospital.

These twelve descriptive characteristics which may be used to indicate differences between patients with a diagnosis of a depression may be summarized as follows:

1. Ratings by the ward nurse indicating a low order of narcissistic involvement with no interest in one's appearance, pleasures, or companions.

2. An obsessive, anxious, fear-ridden hopelessness, which is characterized by a delusional intensity and incapacity for action.

3. Hesitancy and slowing in interpersonal situations, such as the Standard Interview.

4. Dysphoric and negative self-evaluations as indicated by scores from the MMPI and the Clyde Mood Scale.

5. Reduced pressure for self-expression as indicated by brief duration of responses in the Standard Interview.

6. A manic-depressive symptom complex as indicated by the items drawn from the manic and the depressive cluster scores for the WPRS.

7. Somatic complaints as indicated by items comprising the Conversion Hysteria cluster score of the WPRS.

8. Psychomotor slowing as indicated by impaired reaction time and reduction of perceptual reversals to the Necker cube.

9. Impaired cognitive performance indicated by subtests on the WAIS and the DAT series.

10. Impaired appetite as indicated by low caloric intake on various occasions.

11. An elevation of blood pressure and pulse rate accompanied by obsessive-compulsive symptoms.

12. Motivational impairment as indicated by high Ego Defense and low Need Persistence scores on the Rosenzweig test which, curiously enough, are accompanied by an increased CO_2 combining power of the blood.

Some of these behavioral characteristics of depressed patients are associated with somatic distinctions, i.e., blood pressure, liver-function tests, and CO_2 combining power of the blood. This brings us to a reconsideration of the ancient and persisting notion that primarily depressive disorders have an endogenous nature and a somatic basis. Other relevant aspects include the findings that the serum of depressed patients slows the maze behavior of dogs (Poliakova, 1961) and that symptoms suggestive of depression have been found to accompany both hypo- (Coirault, Descles-de-la-Fonchais, Ramel, & Neiger, 1959) and hyper- (Mandel, 1960) calcemic states. It would be premature, however, to draw causal inferences on the basis of such association. It is quite possible that the correlations between somatic and behavioral manifestations are as pertinent to the argument that the behavioral and motivational inertia of a depression have their metabolic consequences as to the argument that metabolic states generate these psychological manifestations.

The literature describes other factor analyses of samples of depressed patients. Because of the use of unconventional or little-known methods, because of limitations in the variety of variables, or because of a heterogeneous ill-defined sample, it is difficult to be certain of the implications of these analyses for the task of identifying the major dimensions of a depressive disorder. For example, the study by Overall (1963), although based on a sufficiently large sample ($N = 204$), includes involutional and schizo-affective patients and is limited to a set of 31 symptom-rating scales. Nevertheless, the general implications of this study are in substantial agreement with the foregoing account based on the writer's recent study. The Overall report does, however, show factoral distinctions within the general group of depressive symptoms in a manner reminiscent of other published analyses based on a heterogeneous patient sample. Grinker, Miller, Sabshin, Nunn, and Nunnally (1961) provided two factor analyses for a sample of 96 depressed patients. One analysis was based on a set of 57 feelings and concerns; the other was based on a check list of 84 behavioral items. The method of analysis used by Grinker and his associates is unconventional and resulted in some factors which are rather highly intercorrelated. The uncertainty in comparing the results of this analysis with those of other studies is heightened by the fact that the behavior check-list analysis included almost as many items (84) as subjects (96), and this fact, combined with the dichotomous nature of the data, may possibly mean that the results cannot all be reproduced. Nevertheless, the dysphoric affect, the anxiety, the isolative withdrawal, the use of somatic symptoms, and other dimensions correspond with the writer's study and contribute to the conclusion that the disorders of depressive patients may be expressed in many different ways. The importance of making distinctions within the depressive entity is emphasized by British investigators Kiloh and Garside (1963), who extracted two factors from a symptom matrix in order to show that it is appropriate to distinguish between a symptom cluster which they called endogenous and another which they described as neurotic. Hamilton and White (1959) have also contributed to the definition of the symptomatic diversities that may be found among the depressions.

THE DIAGNOSTIC PROBLEM

At the beginning of the twentieth century, the study of mental disorders was primarily classificatory in its emphasis, with a Continental enthusiasm for diagnostic labeling epitomized in the classical writing of Kraepelin (1921) and with an English search for hereditary taints or stigmata of degeneracy which could be used to identify the disorder and predict its course. It was in this atmosphere that Adolf Meyer in America assumed an identity by insisting that biological considerations alone could not provide a sufficient study of mental illness. Without repudiating or disregarding biological considerations, Meyer encouraged the dynamic individual meaning of mental illness and insisted that arbitrary classifications often obscured more than they revealed.

> Since there *are* cases in which we cannot find any precipitating factors we are apt to spread ourselves on a statement of heredity and possibly degeneracy of make-up, of possible lesions, etc., and to overemphasize these issues. What we actually know is that this patient is apt to react with a peculiar depressive reaction where others get along with fair balance. The etiology thus involves (1) constitutional make-up and (2) a precipitating factor; and in our eagerness we cut out the latter and only speak of the heredity or constitutional make-up. It is my contention that we must use *both* facts and that of the two, for *prevention* and for the special characterization of the make-up, the precipitating factor is of the greater importance because it alone gives us an idea of the actual defect and a suggestion as to how to strengthen the person that he may become resistive (Meyer, 1908, pp. 169–170).

Thus it would appear that Meyer prepared the ground for a reaction which has not yet run its course. The primary emphasis on intrapersonal considerations which characterize the psychoanalytic movement and the related emphasis on interpersonal considerations continue to gain momentum in the orientation and efforts of those who are interested in depressive disorders. This contemporary reaction had been suppressed somewhat because until recently the treatment of choice for depressions—electroconvulsive therapy—was grossly physical in nature and primarily neurological in its implications. Since 1960, however, there have been mounting indications that energizing treatment based on the new antidepressant drugs is as effective as, and in some pertinent respects possibly more effective than, electroconvulsive therapy (Oltman & Friedman, 1961; Wittenborn, 1961).

Despite the promise of new approaches, the essential nature of the depressive disease is yet to be defined, and indeed it cannot yet be stated with confidence whether there are several depressive diseases or no disease at all. Because of this uncertainty about the essential nature of the depressive disorder or disorders, an abandonment of classificatory interests and standard descriptions is premature. Currently there are three approaches to the classification or description of mental disorders. Of the greatest practical interest are those distinctions which represent general clinical practices (Cameron and Magaret, 1951). In addition, however, there are those diagnostic categories which are traditional for official records and the maintenance of continued mental-health statistics, and there are also the symptom-cluster scores based on factor-analytic studies which measure patients descriptively instead of classifying them and are commonly employed in researches for evaluating the effects of treatment.

The clinician's description of the patient will vary substantially according to his own theoretical orientation and according to his purposes in preparing a description. The current literature on psychoactive drugs emphasizes a distinction between endogenous and reactive depressions. This distinction is not always easy to apply or to defend (Lehmann,

1959). As one becomes increasingly aware of the individual patient's motivational *requirements*, the possibility that the depressive episode may have indeed been a reaction to some unverbalized if not unrecognized deprivation becomes acceptably plausible. There are, however, several descriptive concepts which have appeared with sufficient frequency to justify distinguishing among them at this time. Cameron (Cameron & Magaret, 1951) offered four major clinically distinguishable groups: the retarded depressions, the agitated depressions, the involutional melancholias, and the manic-depressive cycles. These labels are almost self-explanatory. A retarded depression is distinguishable by a quality of psychomotor retardation and general apathy which accompany the depressive dysphoria, while an agitated depression is marked with intense, intractable anxiety which is expressed in motoric restlessness and phobic reactions and may lead to exhaustion. The involutional depression is best identified by the fact that it occurs during the involutional period of life and has not been preceded by other depressive episodes. As a group, involutionals are more inclined to irritability and paranoia than other patients of the depressive group. The manic-depressive psychosis is ordinarily identified by a history of one or more manic periods having intervened between depressive episodes.

The symptoms of depression alone are not sufficient for diagnostic purposes, and the identification of an essentially depressive disorder requires the elimination of other diagnoses. For example, debility from a wasting disease could be mistaken for a depressive illness, or a metabolic deficit due to hypothyroidism could produce a state of inertia and indecision reminiscent of mild depressive retardation. The most serious errors in descriptive diagnosis lie in overlooking schizophrenic features. Depressive episodes have an intermittent, self-limiting nature, and although the susceptibility to depressions tends to continue as a characteristic of the personality, the remission of symptoms is usually complete. In contrast, although the schizophrenic may sometimes present the appearance of depression, he has a somber prognosis, and the distinctive features of schizoid thought and feeling are often identifiable, even during periods of relative freedom from symptoms (Lewis & Piotrowski, 1954). In consequence, the identification of a depressive disorder is contingent on an ability to eliminate appreciable schizophrenic features. The skill with which schizophrenia may be detected and the criteria by which it may be identified no doubt vary, and it is possible that the diagnosis of a depressive disorder may have a substantially different meaning from clinic to clinic, from hospital to hospital, or from period to period. Perhaps in the past significant schizophrenic features were overlooked and depressed schizophrenics were misclassified as patients suffering from a depression. These possibilities may account for the apparent reduction in the recorded number of depressive disorders in recent years.

As may be seen, the distinction between some depressed schizophrenics and patients in whom the depression is so severe that the patient may be described as psychotic may become one of expert judgment. In such cases, the principal guiding criterion may be whether the delusional and hallucinatory material is expressive only of the patient's dissatisfaction with himself or whether it is more general in nature and may involve a deterioration of all aspects of the personality.

A distinction between psychotic and neurotic depressions is commonly claimed, but the differences implied are relative rather than absolute. All depressions, whether severe or mild, involve systems of fantasies, both conscious and unconscious, which can become sufficiently specific to be delusional in nature. Hallucinatory experiences expressive of the patient's guilt and self-condemnation may occur during certain phases of a psychotic depression. Unless a comprehensive history or personality study is available, it may be very difficult on the basis of symptoms alone to anticipate correctly whether a neurotic person with depressive tendencies will show psychotic features when his depression is severe. Despite the commonly observed distinctions between neurotic and psychotic depressions, the writer has found them to be of value only in distinguishing between the possible states of the patient and of little continuing value in distinguishing between patients.

As may be inferred from the earlier section of this article on symptomatology, there are numerous distinguishable qualities among the characteristics of depressed patients. The problem of diagnostic classification is correspondingly complicated in a way which can be appreciated only by a review of the various diagnostic entities which involve depressive features. The distinction between neurotic and psychotic depressions is maintained in the *Diagnostic and Statistical Manual, Mental Disorders,* published by the American Psychiatric Association (1952). Under a section entitled "Disorders of Psychogenic Origin or Without Clearly Defined Physical Cause or Structural Change in the Brain," several major headings, such as Psychotic Disorders, Psychoneurotic Disorders, and Personality Disorders, all include subheadings describing essentially depressive states or predispositions. The following excerpted definitions provide the standard documentary distinctions for mental hospital records of depressed patients and emphasize that the symptom of depression may be found in many diagnostic syndromes. They provide official definition for the various diagnostic terms that are commonly involved in the description of a depressive state.

Disorders of Psychogenic Origin or without Clearly Defined Physical Cause or Structural Change in the Brain

Psychotic Disorders

000–796 INVOLUTIONAL PSYCHOTIC REACTION. In this category may be included psychotic reactions characterized most commonly by depression occurring in the involutional period, without previous history of manic depressive reaction, and usually in individuals of compulsive personality type. The reaction tends to have a prolonged course and may be manifested by worry, intractable insomnia, guilt, anxiety, agitation, delusional ideas, and somatic concerns. Some cases are characterized chiefly by depression and others chiefly by paranoid ideas. Often there are somatic preoccupations to a delusional degree.

Differentiation may be most difficult from other psychotic reactions with onset in the involutional period; reactions will not be included in this category merely because of their occurrence in this age group.

000–x10 AFFECTIVE REACTIONS. These psychotic reactions are characterized by a primary, severe, disorder of mood, and with resultant disturbance of thought and behavior, in consonance with the affect.

000–x11—000–x13. These groups comprise the psychotic reactions which fundamentally are marked by severe mood swings, and a tendency to remission and recurrence. Various accessory symptoms such as illusions, delusions, and hallucinations may be added to the fundamental affective alteration.

Manic depressive reaction is synonymous with the term manic depressive psychosis. The reaction will be further classified into the appropriate one of the following types: manic, depressed, or other.

000–x11 MANIC DEPRESSIVE REACTION, MANIC TYPE. This group is characterized by elation or irritability, with overtalkativeness, flight of ideas, and increased motor activity. Transitory, often momentary, episodes of depression may occur, but will not change the classification from the manic type of reaction.

000–x12 MANIC DEPRESSIVE REACTION, DEPRESSED TYPE. Here will be classified those cases with outstanding depression of mood and with mental and motor retardation and inhibition; in some cases there is much uneasiness and apprehension. Perplexity, stupor or agitation may be prominent symptoms, and may be added to the diagnosis as manifestations.

000–x13 MANIC DEPRESSIVE REACTION, OTHER. Here will be classified only those cases with marked mixtures of the cardinal manifestations of the above two phases (mixed type), of those cases where continuous alternation of the two phases occurs (circular type). Other specified varieties of manic depressive reaction (manic stupor or unproductive mania) will also be included here.

000–x14 PSYCHOTIC DEPRESSIVE REACTION. These patients are severely depressed and manifest evidence of gross misinterpretation of reality, including, at times, delusions and hallucinations. This reaction differs from the manic depressive reaction, depressed type, principally in (1) absence of history of repeated depressions or of marked cyclothymic mood swings, (2) frequent presence of environmental precipitating factors. This diagnostic category will be used when a "reactive depression" is of such quality as to place it in the group of psychoses (see 000–x06 Depressive reaction).

000–x27 SCHIZOPHRENIC REACTION, SCHIZO-AFFECTIVE TYPE. This category is intended for those cases showing significant admixtures of schizophrenic and affective reactions. The mental content may be predominantly schizophrenic, with pronounced elation or depression. Cases may show predominantly affective changes with schizophrenic-like thinking or bizarre behavior. The prepsychotic personality may be at variance, or inconsistent, with expectations based on the presenting psychotic symptomatology. On prolonged observation, such cases usually prove to be basically schizophrenic in nature.

Psychoneurotic Disorders[1]

The chief characteristic of these disorders is "anxiety" which may be directly felt and expressed or which may be unconsciously and automatically controlled by the utilization of various psychological defense mechanisms (depression, conversion, displacement, etc.). In contrast to those with psychoses, patients with psychoneurotic disorders do not exhibit gross distortion or falsification of external reality (delusions, hallucinations, illusions) and they do not present gross disorganization of the personality. Longitudinal (lifelong) studies of individuals with such disorders usually present evidence of periodic or constant maladjustment of varying degree from early life. Special stress may bring about acute symptomatic expression of such disorders.

"Anxiety" in psychoneurotic disorders is a danger signal felt and perceived by the conscious portion of the personality. It is produced by a threat from within the personality (e.g., by supercharged repressed emotions, including such aggressive impulses as hostility and resentment), with or without stimulation from such external situations as loss of love, loss of prestige, or threat of injury. The various ways in which the patient attempts to handle this anxiety results in the various types of reactions listed below.

In recording such reactions the terms "traumatic neurosis," or "traumatic reaction" will not be used; instead, the particular psychiatric reaction will be specified. Likewise, the term "mixed reaction" will not be used; instead, the predominant type of reaction will be recorded, qualified by reference to other types of reactions as part of the symptomatology.

000–x04 PHOBIC REACTION. The anxiety of these patients becomes detached from a specific idea, object, or situation in the daily life and is displaced to some symbolic idea or situation in the form of a specific neurotic fear. The commonly observed forms of phobic reaction include fear of syphilis, dirt, close places, high places, open places, animals, etc. The patient attempts to control his anxiety by avoiding the phobic object or situation.

In recording this diagnosis the manifestations will be indicated. The term is synonymous with the former term "phobia" and includes some of the cases formerly classified as "anxiety hysteria."

000–x06 DEPRESSIVE REACTION. The anxiety in this reaction is allayed, and hence partially relieved, by depression and self-depreciation. The reaction is precipitated by a current situation, frequently by some loss sustained by the patient, and is often associated with a feeling of guilt for past failures or deeds. The degree of the reaction in such cases is dependent upon the intensity of the patient's ambivalent feeling toward his loss (love, possession) as well as upon the realistic circumstances of the loss.

The term is synonymous with "reactive depression" and is to be differentiated from the corresponding psychotic reaction. In this differentiation, points to be considered are (1) life history of patient, with special reference to mood swings (suggestive of psychotic reaction), to the personality structure (neurotic or cyclothymic) and to precipitating environmental factors and (2) absence of malignant symptoms (hypochondriacal preoccupation, agitation, delusions, particularly somatic, hallucinations, severe guilt feelings, intractable insomnia, suicidal ruminations, severe psychomotor retardation, profound retardation of thought, stupor).

Personality Disorders

These disorders are characterized by developmental defects or pathological trends in the personality structure, with minimal subjective anxiety, and little or no sense of distress. In most instances, the disorder is manifested by a lifelong pattern of action or behavior, rather than by mental or emotional symptoms.

000–x43 CYCLOTHYMIC PERSONALITY. Such individuals are characterized by an extratensive and outgoing adjustment to life situations, an apparent personal warmth, friendliness and superficial generosity, an emotional reaching out to the environment, and a ready enthusiasm for competition. Characteristic are frequently alternating moods of elation and sadness, stimulated apparently by internal factors rather than by external events. The individual may occasionally be either persistently euphoric or depressed, without falsification or distortion of reality. The diagnosis in such cases should specify, if possible, whether hypomanic, depressed or alternating.

Thus it is apparent that a depression is not any given formal diagnosis. Among young

[1] See "Psychoneuroses," above.

patients, at least, it refers to states or conditions which tend to characterize individuals with certain types of personality dynamics, background circumstances, and psychiatric histories. It may be cogent, as some writers have maintained (Pare et al., 1962), to emphasize a distinction between neurotic and endogenous depressions. Certainly such a distinction would be justifiable if this distinction implies both a differentiating history and a differential response to treatment. The identification of an endogenous depression is not always easy and usually involves consideration of advancing age.

The diagnostic assessment of a depressive disorder in women who have reached the climacteric is complicated by the fact that there is considerable uncertainty concerning the contribution of physiological changes to the depressive development. In some cases the life history reveals a depressive personality with a history of earlier depressive episodes. For these patients one may wonder whether the climacteric has any relevance to the appearance of the depression, and it may be useful to disentangle two sets of interacting symptom manifestations: those symptoms characteristic of the patient's depressive episodes and those symptoms generated by the changes in the patient's hormone metabolism per se and not necessarily directly related to the depression.

There are other female patients in whom a depression of the involutional period appears to be, at least in part, a reaction to the loss of childbearing potential, the correlated loss of a nurturant role as children mature and begin to be emancipated, and other real or imagined losses, such as employability and sexual attractiveness.

In many patients the depressive features of the involutional mental illness appear to be secondary; much of the behavior assumes an irrationally imprudent quality, and the disorders of thought are characterized by systematic delusions, including grandiose and persecutory ideas. For most such individuals, a diagnosis of schizophrenia would have been given unhesitatingly, despite the depressive features, had the patient been younger.

In virtually all the depressions of the involutional period somatic features are conspicuous. As previously indicated, however, somatic complaints—particularly fatigue, aching muscles, dizziness, and palpitations—are common among depressions of all ages and are not distinctive to the involutional patients.

For the purposes of the present discussion, depressions of the involutional period will not be emphasized as a distinct type. It must be recognized, nevertheless, that during this period of life depressive disorders may appear concurrently with, be augmented by, or be precipitated by both the social and physiological changes.

In general the nature of a depressive disorder involves a reversible dysphoria which may be accompanied by psychomotor retardation or an anxiety which finds its expression in agitation. The identification of a depression involves three considerations: the appearance of at least part of a characteristic symptom pattern, the exclusion of characteristics which would identify a schizophrenic process, and a developmental course which, during the present episode or at least in previous episodes, includes eventual remission of symptoms.

As is the case in most episodes of mental disorder, the diagnosis of a depression is always tentative and becomes most conclusive on the basis of *ex post facto* considerations. If the dysphoria is short-lived, it may be suspected that the depression was a single reaction to situational factors. If the depression persists with a development of depersonalization or intellectual deterioration or if the depression is interrupted with excited outbursts of a disorganized nature, one may be inclined to suspect that the disorder is schizophrenic in nature. The diagnosis of a depression becomes most conclusive when, after a few weeks or months, the dysphoria lifts, the remission of symptoms is complete, and the patient returns to his former level of adjustment.

Because of a depression's episodic, intermittent quality, susceptibility to depressive disorders, other than involutional, becomes a *de facto* characteristic of the personality. For this reason a proper diagnostic inquiry should emphasize both the presenting symptomatic picture of the patient and a search for a history which includes prior dysphoric episodes exceeding the obvious affective demands of the situation, but which excludes schizophrenic reactions. Thus current concepts of depression all involve both cross-sectional and longitudinal considerations.

No review of a mental-health problem which is prepared for a handbook of clinical psychology can be complete without explicit acknowledgment of the important role of psychological tests and measurements. As the preceding sections indicate, a depressive disorder can manifest itself in many ways. As a matter of fact, it is so pervasive that there are few aspects of human behavior which are unaffected. For this reason, a comprehensive survey of all the ways in which tests and measurements are pertinent to the topic would comprise no less than an exhaustive review of the entire field of psychodiagnostic testing. Accordingly, the present paragraphs must be limited to comments on the *ways* in which tests and measurements lend themselves to the study of depressions and refer the reader to the standard textbooks and periodical literature for a description of the exact *nature* of this application.

There are three major ways in which psychological tests and measurements have been employed in the study of depressions.

Traditionally, psychological tests have been used in the *diagnostic identification* of a depressive disorder. In this application, tests have had their greatest use in the task of separating the varieties of patients who present a depressive façade. For most youthful patients, the principal problem is one of identifying those individuals who have schizophrenic features in their thought and feeling. For this purpose, the writer would prefer the Rorschach. For some other youthful patients, however, the depressive constellation of motivational characteristics may not be complete, and the episode appears to be a dysphoric reaction to an adverse situation growing out of irresponsible or antisocial behavior. For individuals where a character disorder is suspected, such projective devices as the Thematic Apperception Test and the Sentence Completion Test may be of particular value, and doubtless there are some who are content to rely on the Rorschach for this purpose.

In patients of all ages, particularly those in their middle and later years, it is always possible that the depressive episode may be an accompaniment of some physical trauma or deterioration, particularly of a neurological nature. Fortunately, the psychologist's armamentarium for detecting perceptual, conceptual, and memory losses of an organic nature is quite sufficient for the requirements of most of these cases and should be resorted to freely on a precautionary basis.

With the recent emphasis on *evaluating the efficacy of treatments,* particularly psychotropic agents, almost every kind of psychological device has been brought to bear, and many of these have proved to be useful (Wittenborn et al., 1961). Since depressions can affect almost any aspect of behavior, the kinds of psychological tests which can be employed advantageously in the evaluation of any given treatment will vary with the nature of the treatment. At present, however, the useful devices which have been reported in the periodical literature include such measures of cognitive functioning as the subtests of the WAIS and the DAT, such psychomotor procedures as reaction time, perceptual reversal, and copying numbers, and such motivational indicators as the Rorschach and the Rosenzweig. In addition, devices for revealing the subjective state of the patient—for example, the MMPI and the Clyde Mood Scale—have also been found to be expressive of changes in consequence of treatment. Special situational procedures, such as standard interviews, have been employed advantageously from the standpoint of either temporal considerations or the content of spontaneous verbalization. Beyond this, a wide variety of check lists and rating scales descriptive of a patient in an interview, on the ward as perceived by nurses or as perceived by physicians, have all been fruitfully applied to show changes in depressive patients in response to treatment. There are promising indications, moreover, that some of these or other devices may prove useful eventually in identifying those patients who will be particularly susceptible to or resistant to the treatment under consideration.

With the growing confidence in the efficacy of psychotherapy and the general acknowledgment that at least some somatic treatments, particularly ECT, may at best provide only symptomatic relief, *understanding* the dynamic motivational significance of a depressive disorder becomes a subject of increasing interest. Although traditional projective devices may be used to expedite the therapist's understanding of the motivational significance of a depressive episode, it is quite possible that the demand for systematic research into the dynamic significance of depressions and their relevance to characterizing personality attributes will generate new devices for the standard assessment of personality.

The main tide of new developments appears to be elaborative in nature and in recognition of the diversity of depressive manifestations accepts the necessity of a many-faceted approach; nevertheless, there are countertrends. Among these are tendencies to develop omnibus scales and measures for depressive states. This counterdevelopment seems to be more in tune with the rather impersonal but nevertheless practical interest in whether the patient improves than acceptant of the fact that since different patients manifest their depressions in different ways, their recovery can be gauged only in terms of a suitable variety of different indexes.

DYNAMIC CONSIDERATIONS

Among those students of depression who appear to have accepted the validity of a constitutional predisposition, there are some who have presumably concluded that the somatic aberration should be the primary focus of treatment and that psychotherapy is but a palliative and is, therefore, secondary (Alexander, 1954; Campbell, 1953). Others, however, after making deference to the constitutional predisposition, address themselves to the underlying motivational structures and the varieties of coping mechanisms which tend to characterize the patient who is subject to depressive disorders. Students of this persuasion—and among them could be included many of the important writers of the psychoanalytic tradition—have further concerned themselves with the manner in which adventitious features of the environment, particularly the background and familial interaction, have contributed to the development of a depressive character disorder. The treatment orientation of this group is primarily psychotherapeutic and principally psychoanalytic. A useful review of the beliefs of those who have written in the psychoanalytic tradition has been prepared by Mendelson (1960), and its comparative spectrum ranges from the classical teaching of Freud (1917) and Abraham (1911) to the writings of Cohen and her collaborators (1954). A dynamic formulation of contemporary significance has been prepared by Wolman (1964), whose many distinctive and original insights could be a useful source of hypotheses for clinical research.

In Mendelson's opinion (1960), the psychoanalytic literature on depressions begins in 1911 with a contribution by Abraham. At that time Abraham emphasized the importance of repressed hostility which could be projectively ascribed to others. As a secondary consequence their misperceived dislike of others was introjected by the patient. On this basis Abraham began to explain the delusional guilt and self-condemnation which are so characteristic of the severely depressed patient. The assumption of repressed hostility was further elaborated in a way to explain the depressive's obsessional rumination about real or imagined hurts, the accompanying inability to forgive, and the desire for revenge (which is often expressed directly by obstructionistic maneuvers or indirectly by self-punishing reaction formations which deny the vengeful impulse). The intrinsic inability to love others was used by Abraham in order to explain the feeling of barrenness and impoverishment which contributes to the anguish of the depressive personality.

In a later contribution (1916), Abraham continued his deductions from the depressed patient's incapacity to love and suggested that in response to the loss felt in consequence of their incapacity to love, the depressive personalities regress to oral levels of gratification. Because of an impaired ability to find gratification at mature levels, regressive oral requirements are intensified but become guilt-laden, and in this way ambivalence about food is generated. Abraham's formulation, with its emphasis on repressed hostility and subsequent orality, is useful in understanding some of the more important symptomatic characteristics of the depressed patient.

In Abraham's early analyses, the etiological basis for this dynamic constellation was not a distinguishing emphasis, but in 1924 he refers with particular cogency to two kinds of etiological considerations. First, a constitutional predisposition to oral eroticism is postulated, thereby accounting for the regression to oral levels in response to interrupted object gratifications. Second, the inability of the depressive to find satisfying object relationships at a mature level is ascribed to childhood disappointments in his love relationships. Subsequent depressive episodes are seen to be associated with disappointments (by the mother) which may be regarded as representations of early disappointment before the resolution of his Oedipal wishes. It is interest ing to note that Abraham sees the paradoxical humility of the depressive patient as but a simple mask for a latent grandiosity which, in most patients, expresses itself implicity in their delusions of injustice or misfortune and in some may erupt in the form of manic episodes.

In 1917, Freud observed that melancholia, although similar to mourning in its manifestations, is distinguishable because the loss is intrapsychic and not external. For this reason the patient may be unaware of the nature of his loss and therefore may feel the loss without knowing its significance. In Freud's formulation it is not the world that becomes poor in the eyes of the melancholic patient, but the patient himself. On this basis the self-abasement of the depressive patient receives partial illumination. Freud explains this situation by suggesting that the inadequacy which the patient further ascribes to himself may be found to bear some descriptive validity for someone else in the patient's environment. The essential mechanism in generating the depressive constellation seems to be an introjection of the disappointing love object. The phenomenon is interpreted as a narcissistic regression which assumes the form of a primitive identification with the love object and results in an inability to make distinctions between the characteristics of the introjected object and the self. Thus, the patient comes to hate himself as (he would) the one who is objectively responsible for his frustrations and deprivations.

Freud did not restrict his etiological thinking to a regressive introjection of a love object which had been particularly disappointing. He suspected that a susceptibility to this type of introjection would be most characteristic of persons whose object choices were of a most narcissistic kind. He reserved the possibility of explaining such narcissistic characteristics in terms of predisposing somatic factors, including a weakening of the ego at a physiological level, e.g., in consequence of trauma or toxins.

When the origins and significance of depressive conditions are under consideration, there are variety and diversity to be found in the views of the psychoanalytic writers. Among the more recent contributors, however, the point of view of Jacobson is of particular interest because she emphasizes the centrality of loss of self-esteem and finds meaning of depressive reaction in terms of attempts to regain self-esteem. In addition to the loss of self-esteem which characterizes all depressives, she distinguishes the psychotic depressions as further subject to severe regressions. This regressive defect in psychotic depression is seen to have its origins in severe disappointments in early life, with a devaluation of love objects occurring before the child has had opportunity to distinguish between itself and its parents.

In the neurotic depressions, the love object is excessively idealized, and any failure of the love object is a source of great distress to the patient because the patient has no conviction of his own intrinsic worth. Thus, he may tend defensively to conceal or deny the defects of his idealized love object, but unfortunately such denial of limitation in object tends further to conceal the patient's own intrinsic strength.

Jacobson (1953), like Abraham and Freud, writes illuminatingly about the dynamic qualities involved in the form of depressive manifestations and in this way provides some clues concerning possible symptom shifts and the nature of circumstances which may precipitate a depressive episode. All these writers rely to some extent on a sensitivity or vulnerability to hurt which they assume is to some substantial degree, at least, somatically determined and constitutional in nature.

The observations of Mabel Blake Cohen and her associates (1954) are of particular interest to the psychologist because they describe patterns of interactions within the family which appear to account for the vulnerability within the personality. This reduces the importance of pointing to the soma as the locus for psychic tenderness and ego inadequacy in explicit expression of love and hate.

Although the formulation of Cohen and her associates (1954) is based on a study of but twelve cases, it illuminates the depressive personality in the light of status strivings. Usually it was the mother who was most ambitious and perhaps contemptuous of the father, who often was lovable but unable to protect the patient from exploitation by the aggrandizing mother. In this family constellation the patient was unable to acquire any conviction of a right to fulfill his own capacity for a meaningful independent existence. The difficulty of the depressive patient in ordinary give-and-take was explained in terms of the paradoxical position of the child in the family where she or he was not only the object of great interest but also the subject of a great deal of criticism. Thus the patients found nothing casual in their relations with others and were inclined to force all experiences into an acceptable or unacceptable category, just as in their developmental years most of their own behavior was so dichotomized.

Wolman views the manic-depressive disorders in the framework of his socio-psychological and modified psychoanalytic theory (1960, chap. 15). Accordingly, he distinguishes (1) hyperinstrumental, i.e., psychopathic disorders, (2) hypervectorial, i.e., schizophrenias and related states, and (3) paramutual or manic-depressive and other cyclic disorders.

The outstanding feature of the paramutual or manic-depressive disorders is the rapid transition back and forth from self-love to object love, from love to hate, from elation to depression, from feelings of power to feelings of worthlessness. Manic-depressives are masters of inconsistency, torn by contradictory and often dramatic changes. They are Dr. Jekyll and Mr. Hyde; energetic and constructive up to a certain point, they destroy whatever they build. Their main driving force is the desire to be loved. They seem to hope to attain their goal through self-defeat.

Wolman related the manic-depressive disorders to rejection in early childhood, hence their insatiable craving to be loved ("love addiction"). The manic-depressive believes he has been the rejected Cinderella, and he hopes that someday, when he reaches the depths of despair, he will be rewarded for all his true or imaginary sufferings. Thus depression, interpreted by Wolman as self-directed aggression, is the core of this disorder. Elation is merely one of the defenses against an unbearable depression. Wolman distinguishes four syndromes of the manic-depressive or paramutual psychosis, namely, mania, paranoia, agitated depression, and simple deterioration (Wolman 1959; 1965).

In recent analyses, the writer identified items of background information which distinguished depressed patients from other groups. A factor analysis of 82 items revealed ten interpretable factors. Some of the factors refer to premorbid personality characteristics, such as a rebellious disposition, an unsympathetic self-centered orientation, a tendency to criticize one's self, a confiding dependence on others, and an obsessive-compulsive disposition. Other factors describe background circumstances, such as a happy mother, a critical mother, recent reverses with reactive implications, and a stigmatizing family background. It is apparent that different kinds of backgrounds and premorbid dispositions may be identified within a sample of depressive patients.

In the course of the writer's observations, virtually all depressed patients have appeared to be characterized by an extraordinarily high order of two motivational predispositions: competitiveness and dependency. In our society an individual who has excessive requirements for both a competitive role and a dependent role is subject to many disappointments and defeats. When one dares to compete in an assertive manner, one must relinquish dependency expectations, particularly from one's competitors. If, however, one wishes to enjoy a dependent relationship, one must be content with what is freely given and renounce the rewards that may be gained through self-assertion.

A frustration of dependency expectations is seen as the most likely precipitant of a depressive episode. Such frustration can occur where passive dependent expectations have been excited but not fulfilled, for example, when a person has permitted himself to dream of a reward or a recognition or an expression of appreciation or love which was not forthcoming, or after the birth of a child when a woman's fantasies of a sweeter, more cherished role fade in the light of new responsibilities. A similar frustration of dependency requirements may occur when a person has been enticed or provoked into an assertive move and then found that love, commendation, or reassurance is withheld. This can occur also when the demands of the environment become stern and experiences which in the past were a guarantee of dependency are withdrawn. In females, this may occur when there are financial reverses, when purchasing privileges are restricted, or when the family moves from one dwelling to another.

The home background of virtually all depressive patients was found to have been organized in such a way as to develop an extraordinarily high order of both competitive and dependent requirements. The competitive predisposition is understandable when it is found that the parental figure with whom the patient appears to identify was an envious, insecure person much more concerned about "what other people thought" than about what he or she truly desired; in consequence of identification, this exaggerated concern with "what other people think" appears in the make-up of the depressed patient. Often this dissatisfied parent had either directly or indirectly maneuvered the patient into perceiving himself as the one who would be the salvation of the family and would confound and overwhelm those whose opinion was regarded with such concern. In addition, in the families of most depressives, there is real or imagined stigma from which the family must be redeemed. The stigma may be in the form of poverty, of delinquent or ne'er-do-well relatives, or of a feeble-minded or a psychotic relative.

Usually the parent of the depressive patient is unable to give unstinted praise or reassurance. This may be because the parent has seen failure in himself and is, therefore, most intolerant of it in his child. Certainly he is more disposed to draw the child's attention to his shortcomings or ways in which he could improve his performance than to give the child the feeling of assurance, competence, and satisfactory performance. In this way the depressed patient may have learned to view his attainments, regardless of their nature, as unequal to his obligations and not a proper basis for satisfaction in his own existence. Thus he may learn to envy in others the self-satisfaction and love-worthiness for which he hungers.

Some of the circumstances which contributed to the depressive's competitive orientation contribute also to his unusual dependency needs, particularly the great concern for the approval of others and the imperative someday to wring an expression of unqualified approval from the obsessively faultfinding or calamity-fearing parent. Beyond this, however, many parents of depressive patients have tended to live vicariously through the patient by setting goals, controlling dress and friendships, intervening with teachers or employers, closely regulating recreations, and exactly prescribing methods of work. Thus the individual never learns to see himself as a self-sufficient organism capable of dealing directly with his environment; instead he acquires the expectations of supervision, support, and control which are the essence of dependency. These persons look to others to provide the definition of the significance of their existence and are terrified when others refuse to play this role. They regard such refusal on the part of others as a total rejection and an absolute loss of love in the most infantile sense. Attempts to find their own significance and deny their dependence have usually been unsuccessful. In the parental home the nonexploitative parent, usually the parent of opposite sex, is either absent or weak, in the sense that this parent has not been disposed to back up the patient's attempts to gain freedom from the exploitative parent and to assert his own capacity for self-fulfilling existence.

It has been observed that depressions are more frequent among females than among males. It is possible that this is an accident of the fact that in our society women are encouraged to expect a dependent role, and in some ways, at least, they may gauge their success in terms of the degree to which their dependency requirements are gratified. Presumably the usual child-rearing practices for male children and the general social environment tend not to favor the development of excessively strong dependent needs, and therefore dependency requirements of an intensity sufficient to predispose an individual to depressive reaction are less prevalent among males than among females.

The relative prevalence of depressive disorders among the middle class may be partly explainable in terms of a characteristic striving for achievement or social and economic advancement (Rosen, 1958). Certainly the literature characterizes the middle-class homes in terms of a strong achievement orientation with child-rearing practices wherein concern for the child's future achievement is explicit and reservations about the adequacy of his current performance are implicit, if not explicit. Thus, the strongly competitive point of view which is hypothesized here as an essential component in the depressive personality is a major component of middle-class life and may contribute to the relative prevalence of depression in the middle class.

It is quite possible that some societies are more favorable to the development of depressive disposition than others (Burton, 1867), and it is possible to perceive the characters who populate the historical accounts of certain past eras as manifesting a combination of attributes which would lead to defeat and depressive reactions. During the classical period, for example, there are numerous characters, such as Seneca, the poet Lucan, and perhaps Nero, who were most strivingly competitive in their outlook, often attempting to outdo their contemporaries and their predecessors in their deeds. Nevertheless, they remained acutely sensitive to the manner in which they were regarded by the very persons they sought to outdo or discomfort, and the ultimate test to which they submitted themselves was the acceptance and esteem of those who would surely reject them. In turn, these characters responded to this rejection with a suicidal despair in which they punished themselves for limitations which other personalities would have been able to overlook, and by their own destruction they sought to shame those who withheld approval. Personalities not susceptible to depression might have found it possible to disregard those who could not love them.

It is often useful to regard a depression as a state of ambivalence, wherein the victim is neither free to assert his competitive impulses nor ready to capitulate so that he may enjoy his dependency. In such a state of ambivalence purposeful effective activity cannot long be sustained, and the behavior tends to deteriorate in the form of vacillating indecision or apathetic inactivity. An individual with obsessive characteristics may be increasingly preoccupied with futile ruminations at this time, and other individuals with a hysterical disposition may be disposed to explain their inactivity in terms of somatic complaints. In addition to manifesting profound and pervasive conflict, the patient may, according to his disposition and circumstances, manifest other symptoms. The hostility which he feels toward others may be turned inward on himself, and the dependency requirements which paralyze him may be projectively ascribed to others. Nevertheless, his dependency continues to find expression, and it may often be useful to regard it as a secondary gain from the incapacity of his illness; by making himself a burden on others and obstructing their normal enjoyments, he may also use his illness as a device for his hostile competitive motives. In this light a depression may be viewed not only as an ambivalent position but as an adaptation which is at least partly successful in the sense that some gratification may be provided to both the aggressive and dependent motives.

The research literature includes very few formal investigations which describe the background of depressed patients with sufficient diversity of data to provide solid confirmation of the various clinical observations and inferences which are described here. One fact of substantial significance has been confirmed by several independent investigations (Brown, 1961; Beck, Sethi, & Tuthill, 1963). Specifically, childhood bereavement and orphanhood are particularly characteristic of the background of depressed patients.

It is well known that suicidal attempts are especially characteristic of depressed patients. Ayd (1961) has reported that more suicidal patients may be found among those who have a depressive illness than among those bearing any other diagnosis. In the writer's series of depressed female patients, approximately 55 per cent had made a definite suicide attempt. An analysis of the literature could be organized about two questions: (1) how do patients who complete suicide differ from other patients (Dorpat & Boswell, 1963; Stengel, 1960), and (2) how do patients who make suicidal attempts differ from those who do not (Rubenstein, Moses, & Lidz, 1958)? The characteristics of patients who complete suicide appear not to have been described in a manner which is acceptable to the majority of investigators. Although the impulse to destroy one's self can be understood, the theoretical paradox lies in the failure of the anxiety which accompanies the approach of an anticipatable death. It is argued, therefore, that the mental patient who succeeds in committing suicide is probably sufficiently disturbed that the ordinary defenses are no longer effective. For this reason it is often supposed that most patients who complete a suicide were schizophrenic (Balser & Masterson, 1959; Ayd, 1961). There are several studies which examine the background of depressed patients who make suicidal attempts. Virtually all of these studies agree that the depressed patient who makes a suicidal attempt is different from the one who does not in two respects (Bruhn, 1962; Hendin, 1960): (1) the background of those who make the attempt usually reveals early abandonment (actual or symbolic) by the mother or some kind of impairment of parent-child relationship and (2) a recent frustration of dependency requirements which could be construed as symbolic reenactment of the original abandonment (Tabachnick, 1961). The problem of suicide and suicidal attempts has been the subject of lively interest, and many excellent investigations and reviews are now available (Shneidman & Farberow, 1957; Farberow and Shneidman, 1961). Because of its religious and legal significance, however, suicidal behavior, whether complete or incomplete, is often concealed and not subject to proper investigation. The one area which appears to be particularly subject to concealment but may, nevertheless, require our most urgent attention is suicidal behavior among children and adolescents (Toolan, 1962).

SOMATIC TREATMENT OF DEPRESSIVE DISORDERS

The belief that many depressions have an endogenous origin and that manic-depressive disorders are inherited keeps pace with the advancing knowledge of the neurochemical correlates of behavior. A representative discussion is provided by Campbell, who examines manic-depressive disease comprehensively from the standpoint of its presumptive somatic origins. He postulates an "inherently sensitive autonomic nervous system" (1953, p. 168), and he reasons that this weakness makes the control of ordinary stresses fatiguingly difficult and that unless persons with a manic-depressive disposition are protected from aggravating factors there is an eventual "complete disorganization of autonomic function, a condition synonymous with psychosis" (*ibid.*, p. 169). Campbell identifies many of the symptoms of a depression with stimulation of the sympathetic nervous system and postulates from an examination of the various indications of autonomic disturbance that

> disorders of sleep, peripheral autonomic disturbances, mood disorders, anxiety, crying for no cause or an inability to cry, distortions in sensory impressions and many other symptoms of manic-depressive psychosis stem from disordered physiology in the diencephalic area. . . . The depressed patient, for instance, complains, "I cry but I have nothing to cry about," or "I feel like I want to cry but I can't," or, "I feel like if I could cry I would feel better." Symptom after symptom, time after time, the observer is impressed with the fact, from the patient's own descriptive terms, that in this disease there is an endogenous disturbance in central autonomic functions, some of which deviate one way, some another (Campbell, 1953, pp. 169–170).

Campbell uses this diencephalic postulate in order to account for the efficacy of electroconvulsive therapy in the control of the symptoms of a manic-depressive psychosis.

> The patient with dilated pupils, excessive perspiration, pylorospasm, anorexia, insomnia, depressed spirits and impaired libido, more-or-less suddenly, after four or five ECT's, appears more relaxed and rested, can now eat and enjoy food, can sleep better, is capable of smiling normally for the first time in weeks or months, and develops erotic tendencies that have for a long time been dormant. Looking upon this change from the physiologic viewpoint, as the researcher would view such a change in a laboratory animal, how else could these findings be recorded except as a swing from sympathetic to parasympathetic dominance? Thus, even in the recovery process, one observes evidence that manic-depressive psychosis is a diencephalic disease (*ibid.*, p. 191).

Ten years later Gellhorn and Loofbourrow are concerned with the same scientific terms, but they appear to use them "the other way round."

> In a depressed patient the hypothalamic sympathetic reactivity is low (indicated, as previously emphasized, by the type III reaction to Mecholyl), whereas in the normal (young) person and also in the aggressive psychopathic personality it is high. In view of the sympathetic excitation produced by electroshock, we believe that the autonomic balance is shifted from a relative preponderance of the parasympathetic division to one of the sympathetic division. Physiologically this range covers sleep and wakefulness, whereas under pathological conditions the range expands to include depressive states on the one side and manic behavior on the other (Gellhorn & Loofbourrow, 1963, p. 321).

Although most of the somatic treatments for depression can be discussed from the standpoint of their possible influence on a hypothesized autonomic imbalance, it should be observed that the various somatic treatments—that is, convulsive treatments, such as electroconvulsive therapy or insulin coma, or pharmacological treatments, such as amine oxidase inhibitors or adrenaline metabolites—were not generated deductively from an assumption of autonomic imbalance as the critical somatic defect. As the history of these treatments all too eloquently testifies, they are the result of serendipitous *ex post facto* deductions, and the rationalization for their efficacy seems at times to place a heavy burden on the data at hand.

Thus we see that the nature of a depressive disorder remains in dispute. The preferred somatic treatments have been stumbled on by accident; their hypothesized mode of action, although scientifically impeccable in its referents, is frankly speculative in its nature; and a suitably *comprehensive* survey of the manner in which these treatments affect an explicitly defined, relatively homogeneous patient population is not available.

Since 1957, there has been an increasingly accelerated interest in antidepressant drugs. Although the literature describing the effects of the various treatments is now hugely voluminous by almost any standard, the number of suitably controlled studies which use a comprehensive set of criteria and are concerned with a sufficiently homogeneous sample to permit meaningful generalizations is still quite small. So far as the writer is aware, the most comprehensive study has been conducted by the Rutgers Interdisciplinary Research Center in collaboration with the state hospital system of the New Jersey State Department of Institutions and Agencies. Since this is also the study which the writer knows best, it will be reviewed here both from the standpoint of the methodological problems which characterize such inquiry and from the standpoint of its substantive significance for the use of somatic methods of treatment, particularly certain antidepressant drugs.

In the Rutgers–New Jersey studies, the primary inquiry was based on newly admitted female patients who were not yet in the climacteric, who were free from appreciable schizophrenic features, and whose condition was not complicated by any metabolic or other organic disorder which would contraindicate the use of any one of the treatments under consideration. Females were selected because they were most plentiful, and schizophrenic, involutional, and organic patients were excluded because it was feared that their response might obscure the effects due to the largest homogeneous group of depressed patients, i.e., young females. The research plan involved a comparison of treatment groups with a placebo group and employed a design which required the use of criteria which were gathered on a pretreatment and a posttreatment basis.

Specifically, newly admitted patients who were accepted for study were pretested and assigned at random to one of the available treatments. The treatments were administered according to the clinical discretion of the hospital physicians, and as soon as the patient recovered sufficiently to leave the hospital or after a maximal period of ten weeks, the treatment was suspended and a posttreatment period of evaluation was conducted in a manner identical with the pretreatment evaluation.

The inquiry was based on the use of four treatment groups: a placebo group ($N = 50$), an iproniazid group ($N = 32$), an ECT group ($N = 47$), and an imipramine group ($N = 51$). Iproniazid was the most promising of the early antidepressant drugs. Although it is apparently a truly effective treatment, it has been considered too dangerous for ordinary use and was withdrawn from the market in 1961. The danger inheres in the possibility of creating an irreversible jaundice among patients who are susceptible because of liver pathology. Iproniazid is classified as a monoamineoxidase inhibitor, and other drugs of this type remain on the market because they are presumably less dangerous (but are apparently less efficacious). Imipramine, too, appears to be an efficacious drug, and it has an important place in the market. Nevertheless, the market includes other drugs about which less is known. Thus the two most generally used classes of drugs in the treatment of depressive disorders are monoamineoxidase inhibitors whose mode of action may in some way be related to the metabolism of serotonin and imipramine-like substances which may represent adrenaline metabolites or their analogues.

From the standpoint of the psychological investigator, a most critical problem in the evaluation of treatment lies in the selection of criteria. If too few criteria are selected, it is possible that some important effects may be overlooked. If many criteria are employed, the possibility is increased that a practical significance could be mistakenly ascribed to several selected effects which are misleadingly inflated by chance. That is, when numerous criteria are involved in a comparison between two or more groups, the sampling errors will be correlated from criterion to criterion, and there is consequent probability that the levels of significance for testing the various criteria will be confounded with each other. It is obviously desirable, therefore, to reduce the number of criteria without sacrificing desirable variables.

In the Rutgers study, the pretreatment-posttreatment assessment, which required several days, comprised many pieces of information selected to include such facets of a depressive disorder as cognitive, motivational, subjective, interpersonal, psychomotor, somatic, and symptomatological. Because of the fallibility of behavioral measurements, it is desirable to represent each class of variable by several different tests or rating scales. For that reason, the original list of data comprised 150 items. These were reduced on the basis of preliminary considerations to 82. The 82 were intercorrelated and submitted to the factor analysis which was summarized in the section (above) on symptomatology.

On this basis, it was possible for the attention of the investigators to be focused on a set of criteria which represented the major factors found in the analysis of the pretreatment data and a few clinical laboratory tests of somatic functions as well.

It is possible that the variables representative of the various facets of the depressive disorder could respond concurrently and in a mutually consistent fashion to therapy. In this case, a patient's response to treatment could be described in terms of any one or some combination of the patient's changes in the criteria. It is also possible, however, that different patients may show a different kind of therapeutic response. If this were true, no one criterion of change would be sufficient to describe treatment effect for all patients, although some general or composite criterion might be a suitable indication of the therapist's satisfaction with the patient's progress. In the Rutgers inquiry, the emphasis was on the *patient's response*, and the analysis of the *therapist's feeling* about the patient's response cannot be described at this writing.

From the standpoint of any one criterion, response to treatment was expressed in terms of a posttreatment score which had been adjusted for individual differences in pretreatment effects. Specifically, for each of the selected criteria separately, the regression of the posttreatment scores on pretreatment scores was computed. The regressed posttreatment score was then subtracted from the observed posttreatment score, leaving a residual or adjusted posttreatment score which was independent of correlated pretreatment differences. It then became possible to examine the patterns of interrelationships among these adjusted posttreatment scores for each treatment group separately. This was accomplished by a series of factor analyses. Specifically, a selected set of adjusted posttreatment scores was intercorrelated and factor-analyzed for the 50 placebo patients. Identical analyses were conducted separately for the 32 iproniazid patients, for the 47 ECT patients, and for the 51 imipramine patients. For each of these treatment groups, it was apparent that the pattern of response was represented by several different factors. It was further apparent that the factors generated by one treatment group varied appreciably from those generated by another treatment group, particularly in the case of the ECT group. This is not surprising, in view of the nature of ECT. Thus, the concept of over-all improvement is of little value in assessing the response of patients to these treatments, and the various modes of treatment response must be represented in any attempt to gauge the efficacy of one treatment relative to another or relative to placebo.

Since it is obviously desirable to use several different criteria for evaluating treatment effects, one must find a way of reducing the risk of ascribing differential treatment effects to a criterion difference which is an accident of sampling. The most desirable way of obviating this hazard requires replicating the entire study for an independent sample. This is both time-consuming and expensive, and support for such replication was not available. Accordingly, a multivariate discriminant analysis was conducted to provide an over-all test of the discriminating power of the criteria as a set.

Specifically, a multivariate discriminant analysis was conducted to show which of 19 behavioral criteria could provide significant distinctions among the four treatment groups. The over-all discrimination was significant at the 1 per cent level, and the extent to which each of the various behavioral criteria contributed to this over-all discrimination was subsequently examined. A similar analysis showed that the physical criteria were also effective as a set in discriminating among the treatment groups, and the relative contribution of each of these various criteria was examined. It was apparent that iproniazid is more effective than placebo, particularly from the standpoint of interpersonal response as indicated by reduced latency in the Standard Interview, mental alacrity as indicated by improved arithmetic performance on the DAT, increased perceptual fluidity as indicated by the Necker cube, general subjective improvement as indicated by greater friendliness and less jitteriness on the Clyde Mood Scale, and better ability to mobilize and sustain self-assertion as indicated by the ego defense score on the Rosenzweig. If one were to use a one-tailed test of significance, which could be defended because it was anticipated that iproniazid would reduce depressive characteristics, other criteria would appear as significant, particularly symptom ratings of anxiety and depression.

Imipramine also appeared to be efficacious, but in somewhat different respects. It is clear that the patients in this group were symptomatically less anxious, less depressed, and less phobic than the placebo group. It is interesting to observe, however, that the nurses did not see the imipramine group as improved in their interpersonal behavior. It may be noted that the imipramine patients do not show the mental, psychomotor, and motivational improvement which appeared for the iproniazid group.

ECT is also superior to placebo, particularly from the standpoint of subjective considerations as indicated by symptom ratings for anxiety, the two subtests of the MMPI (depression and psychasthenia), and the Friendly score on the Clyde Mood Scale.

On the basis of these data, it appears that iproniazid is a particularly efficacious treatment, and it is regrettable that the apparent hazard for susceptible patients necessitated its becoming unavailable for others.

It was particularly interesting to examine the comparisons between the iproniazid group and the placebo group from the standpoint of the physical criteria. Specifically, iproniazid appeared to be distinctive in its effect of lowering serum cholesterol and blood pressure. There appeared to be some salt retention, however, as inferred from an increase in the sodium ion concentration in the serum and an increase in weight without a significant increase in the ingestion of food.

Thus, it is apparent that drugs, such as iproniazid and imipramine, are effective in relieving some of the features of a depressive state. Nevertheless, their mode of action remains unknown at this writing, and there is no *rational* basis for deciding when one of the available treatments is preferable to another. Nevertheless, some preliminary empirical studies have been undertaken for the purpose of identifying pretreatment characteristics of patients who will respond in various ways (Blair, 1960; Rothman, Grayson, & Ferguson, 1961).

The most comprehensive investigation of this type has been undertaken as a part of the Rutgers–New Jersey study and may be summarized in the following paragraphs.

It was believed that the pretreatment information which might be useful in anticipating the individual's response to treatment would fall into two classes: (1) the kind of material that could be gathered directly from the patient and (2) the kind of material that could be descriptive of the patient's background and should be gathered from family informants.

The predictive potential of a limited body of information which could be gathered from the patient in the clinical setting will be described first. The selected pretreatment characteristics to be explored as predictors included age, whether there was a history of suicidal attempts, number of previous hospitalizations, education, and two important symptomatic features—the extent to which the patient was excited as indicated by the manic-state score on the Wittenborn Psychiatric Rating Scales (WPRS) and the extent to which the patient was projecting hostility as indicated by the paranoid schizophrenic score from the WPRS.

One of these clinical predictors was found to be particularly important for predicting responses in the iproniazid treatment group. It appears that even the slightest indication of paranoid thinking with its rigidity and ideas of reference is likely to be accompanied by no change or even an adversive change if the patient is treated with iproniazid. For example, the partial correlations between the paranoid score (WPRS) and treatment response in terms of the anxiety-symptom cluster score, the depression-symptom cluster score, the depression score on the MMPI, and the Friendly and the Jittery scores on the Clyde Mood Scale were found to be .49, .54, .66, −.45, and .47, respectively.

The exploration of the predictive value of background information was somewhat complicated in its development. The study provided for a family visit by the social-worker member of the investigating team. On the basis of her visit, which usually involved several hours, she filled out a standard inventory comprising several hundred items which at the time the investigation was begun were considered to be relevant to the development of a depressive personality, descriptive of the premorbid characteristics of depressive patients, or indicative of precipitating circumstances. It was obviously necessary to reduce these many items to a manageable number. As a first step, comparable information was gathered for a sample of schizophrenic females; items which did not distinguish between the depressed and the schizophrenic women were eliminated from further consideration. As a second step, the background data were gathered for a sample of women who had no psychiatric history but had a physical illness; items which failed to distinguish between these women and the depressed women were also eliminated from consideration. As a result of these two steps and other a priori reductions, there were 82 items which were considered suitable for more intensive scrutiny. These items were factor-analyzed, and the resulting 10 factors were used for a system of background factor scores.

When these background factor scores were correlated with the patient's response to treatment, several of them revealed significant relationships. In the sample treated with imipramine, for example, it was found that those patients with a dependent, self-critical premorbid personality were inclined to become more depressed, anxious, and phobic as indicated by the WPRS scores and more jittery as indicated by the Clyde Mood Scale. It is apparent from these relationships that background characteristics can be used to anticipate the nature of the patient's response to treatment. It is obvious that all this work is in its most primitive stages. Nevertheless, it is of interest not only because some gradual refinements in the selection of treatment seem to be possible but also because relationships of this type may eventually generate better insights into the general nature of various depressive reactions and the mode of action whereby some of the treatments are efficacious.

Although antidepressant drugs, such as iproniazid and imipramine, appear to compare favorably with ECT when various factors, such as changes in symptom ratings, psychological test results, and duration of remissions, are considered, it is known that some patients whose symptoms resist drug treatment respond to ECT and that some chronic patients, resistant to ECT, respond to monoamineoxidase inhibitors (Blair, 1960; Bates & Douglas, 1961). It is apparent that not all patients are equally responsive to any one of the available treatments, and it is probable, therefore, that the relative efficacy of the treatments involved in any one comparison may be in part a consequence of the composition of the sample of patients. For example, in 1962, Greenblatt, Grosser, and Wechsler reported that ECT appeared to be more efficacious than drugs for a heterogeneous sample of depressed patients, many of whom were either schizophrenic or elderly. It would be useful to know the characteristics of the patients who responded favorably to the various treatments. Freyhan (1959) and Kiloh, Child, and Latner (1960) reported that patients treated with ECT tended to relapse at a relatively high rate, and the characteristics of such relapsing patients could be of obvious value in those instances where the therapist may choose between drugs and ECT. The tendency to relapse may be a result of other factors which are confounded with the effect of the drug or ECT. For example, Oltman and Friedman (1961), in reporting that the ECT patients were more likely to relapse than drug-treated patients, observed that the drug-treated patients tended to receive more continuing care of a follow-up nature than did the ECT patients. Upon discontinuing ECT, these investigators have reported (Oltman & Friedman, 1962) that durations of hospitalization were shorter than they had been during the prior period when ECT was in use. Although this result may be subject to alternative interpretations, it is interesting to observe that it has been possible to discontinue ECT without any prolongation of hospital care.

Although the importance of pretreatment identification of persons who have various response potential has been emphasized (Cole, Jones, & Klerman, 1961; Bay's discussion of a paper by Turner, O'Neill, & Merlis, 1962), the studies which have been undertaken for imipramine, as well as other drugs, are mostly either conflicting or inconclusive, and it may be that the familiar symptomatic and diagnostic distinctions within depressed groups do not provide the required guides. For example, many of the articles which offer to distinguish between patients who do or do not respond to a given treatment require a further distinction between endogenous and reactive depressions. Thus, there are several reports claiming that endogenous depressions respond more favorably to imipramine than do reactive depressions (Cole et al., 1961). Unfortunately, such a distinction is not always useful because as one becomes more intimately acquainted with the patient the possible reactive significance of the depressive episode becomes increasingly apparent.

The fact that the efficacy of somatic treatment appears to be qualified by characteristics of the patient emphasizes the potential importance of careful pretreatment evaluation and draws our attention to the possibility that psychological testing may eventually be most practical for this purpose. At present there are several ways in which psychological testing may contribute to diagnostic refinements in the study of a depressive disorder. Although it has not been indicated in the present discussion, there are some instances when cerebral pathology is accompanied by symptoms similar to those of a depressive episode. The patient may become withdrawn, distrustful, uncertain, irritable, and, in a manner suggestive of a depressive episode, unhappy without apparent cause. Nevertheless, psychological testing can often reveal characteristic indications of brain dysfunction and result in diverting the inquiry from psychodynamic assessment to an identification of specific brain pathology. In addition, psychological testing—particularly projective testing—can be most sensitive to the disorders of thought and feeling which characterize the paranoid process. As one of the writer's recent analyses has suggested, patients with paranoid tendencies may not respond particularly well to monoamineoxidase inhibitors. It may prove prudent, therefore, for patients to be examined from the standpoint of paranoid qualities if the use of monoamineoxidase inhibitors in treatment is under consideration. Other reports (Fleminger & Groden, 1962; Wortis, 1963) give various preliminary indications that the effects of the different somatic treatments for depression are qualified by characteristics of the patients, and it is probable in many cases that a careful psychological assessment, particularly for the identification of schizophrenia, may prove to be pertinent in the selection of treatment. The psychodiagnostic literature is rich in studies of mental test characteristics which distinguish different kinds of patients, and many devices are available for this purpose.

PSYCHOTHERAPY

The management of the depressed patient in the psychotherapeutic situation places certain rather special demands on the therapist. Specifically, in order to retain the patient's confidence, it is important for the therapist to perceive the affective experiences of the patient with complete sensitivity and to permit the patient to know that his affective state is appreciated. As many writers, including psychoanalytic authorities such as Edith Jacobson (1953) and Mabel Balke Cohen (1954), have observed, however, the depressive patient is particularly manipulative, and he often attempts to control the therapist by luring him into taking the responsibility for the patient's affective condition. This the therapist must avoid at all costs. Accordingly, the therapist must remain one who is empathically perceptive of the patient's feelings but acknowledges no explicit responsibility for managing them.

Instead the therapist seeks to establish with the patient a shared recognition of hopes and sources of despair so that particular vulnerabilities to hurt, characteristically defeating modes of reaction, and false goals (based on reaction formation and denials) may be identified. In this way the therapist establishes in the mind of the patient not only that the patient has things to learn but that he can learn them. Thus the patient begins to lose the illusion that there is something special about him whereby he must in some situations pay more than others, while in other situations he can use credits which others do not possess; instead, the patient learns, usually with great reluctance, that the terms under which he negotiates with life are no better, yet no worse, than the terms available to others and that he, too, can operate satisfactorily under such terms.

The manipulative character of the depressive patient and his need for unqualified control of himself and his environment have been described repeatedly in the literature. The motivational predisposition for this reaction to life is emphasized in the following quotation from Fenichel.

> Depression is based on the same predisposition as addiction and pathological impulses. A person who is fixated on the state where his self-esteem is regulated by external supplies or a person whose guilt feelings motivate him to regress to this state vitally needs these supplies. He goes through this world in a condition of perpetual greediness. If his narcissistic needs are not satisfied, his self-esteem diminishes to a danger point. He is ready to do anything to avoid this. He will try every means to induce others to let him participate in their supposed power. On the one hand the pregenital fixation of such persons manifests itself in a tendency to react to frustrations with violence; on the other hand their oral dependence impels them to try to get what they need by ingratiation and submissiveness. The conflict between these contradictory devices is characteristic for persons with this predisposition (Fenichel, 1945, p. 387).

These essential features of the depressive disposition are drawn to the psychotherapist's attention by Whitehorn.

> In searching clinically for a basis of mutual understanding with depressed patients—some way of appreciating the patient's experience of his psychosis and of establishing communication—an appreciation that the patient has demanded of himself and of others a very extreme degree of self-control has frequently provided the key to otherwise unintelligible self-accusations and self-recriminations. Many of these patients demand of themselves a control of themselves or of events amounting almost to omnipotence, failing which they feel guilty and insecure. When one perceives this point and comments upon it, these patients do not usually agree—they do not usually quite agree with anything one says—but subsequent conversations are often less inhibited, as if the patient, although constrained not to agree, feels relieved that the other fellow is looking into that aspect of the guilt feeling (Whitehorn, 1952, pp. 275–276).

Wolberg, too, has noted this quality and has emphasized its pivotal significance in successful psychotherapy.

> Psychotherapy is also very difficult in depressed patients because their demands for help and love are insatiable. No matter how painstaking the therapist may be in supplying their demands, they will respond with rage and aggression, often accusing the therapist of incompetence or ill-will. . . .
>
> One of the ways of maintaining the relationship on a positive level is by communicating empathy, by avoiding differences in opinion, by trying to see his point of view and sympathizing with it (Wolberg, 1954, pp. 628, 629).

Not all therapists are optimistic about effecting a sufficient change in the basic personality of the depressive patient (Sullivan, 1953). As early as 1911, however, Abraham declared that psychoanalysis was the only rational therapy for manic-depressive disorders. The optimal conditions for initiating psychotherapy remain a matter of some uncertainty, with Wolberg (1954) commenting that psychotherapy is usually ineffective during extremely depressed phases, while Diethelm (1953) states that patients who have recovered from a manic-depressive illness are usually highly inaccessible to penetrating analysis. From this it could be inferred that an optimal time for initiating therapy would be during the period of considerable discomfort on the part of the patient but not at a time of extreme apathy and retardation.

Since most depressed patients (probably because of their dependency) tend also to be quite suggestible, an initial positive transference is readily established and provides a basis whereon a therapeutic interaction may be developed. For the extremely withdrawn, apathetic patient, however, it is probable that the therapist's personality must be most resonant if the quality of the patient's despairing apathy may be correctly empathized on the basis of the very few available cues, and many therapists may feel that when the depressed patient is not sufficiently accessible attempts at psychotherapy should be postponed until symptomatic remission occurs spontaneously or in consequence of drug therapy or ECT. Certainly this is a possible alternative because most patients eventually go into symptomatic remission spontaneously or on placebo; Rothman states, "There are so many different types of depression that it is almost impossible to generalize about psychotherapy. . . . We found that 60 per cent of the patients responded to the placebo. . . . Some patients clear up when you just close the door on them and leave them in the hospital" (Ayd, 1962, p. 704). Currently the consensus appears to be that most neurotic and reactive depressions are best treated by immediate psychotherapy and that antidepressant drugs may prove upsetting to the patient, while the severely depressed individual who may be in a withdrawn or weakened condition can profit from symptomatic relief by the use of drugs.

The writer has formulated a program of psychotherapy which appears at this point to be effective. In the broadest sense the program comprises three phases. Although these phases are overlapping and may be so intermittent in their emphasis that they really represent strategic considerations, there is some general order in their appearance. During the first phase, aggressive motives are stimulated and their expression is encouraged. Much of this takes the form of abreactive counteraggression against the initially exploitative parent and continues with a recognition of a hostile, competitive disposition toward others. A second phase is concerned with the despairing feelings of insufficiency which engulf the patient as he begins to assert his independence and fears that even minimal dependent requirements are in jeopardy. In this phase the goal is to help the patient discover that his fear of being rejected in consequence of asserting his own interests competitively is not well founded and that his conviction that these roles are mutually exclusive alternatives was appropriate only in his relationship with an exploitative parent and is not necessarily congruent with the requirements of the world in which he now lives. He learns also in this phase that he can tolerate some delay and deprivation in the gratification of dependency requirements and that he can learn ways of securing the desired response from others without sacrificing his needs for self-assertion. As a third phase the therapy is designed to assist the individual in learning that he can express affection and esteem for others without jeopardizing his own need to be esteemed. In this phase the patient learns that his ability to stimulate and support others is an important source of power, self-sufficiency, and esteem.

SUMMARY

Severe affective depressions are an ancient and continuing scourge of mankind. Traditionally they have been considered to be of endogenous origin and merely provoked or exacerbated by the conditions of life. During the twentieth century, however, a steadily increasing interest has been shown in the personality make-up of individuals who are susceptible to depressive experiences, and the question implicit in such findings is now being expressed explicitly. Is it possible that a depression is merely an expression of the dismay and indecision of a person who, in orderly response to recognizable features in his formative environment, has developed a personality which involves him in successive defeats? With the growing emphasis on the role of the personality, there has been a concomitant development of optimism concerning the possibilities of psychotherapeutic remediation.

For many reasons appropriate psychotherapy is not available for most of the myriad individuals who suffer depressive episodes. Because of the obvious misery of these victims and the concern of their families, the search for symptomatic relief is so desperate that even such drastic procedures as electroconvulsive therapy are accepted. The use of antidepressant drugs brightens the picture appreciably, but there is still much systematic research required before these procedures can be used to proper advantage.

In the writer's opinion, the ultimate mastery of the problem of depressive disorders can best be advanced by investigations which seek to illuminate the nature, genesis, and practical modification of personalities which develop depressive episodes.

REFERENCES

Abraham, K. Notes on the psychoanalytic investigation and treatment of manic-depressive insanity and allied conditions. In *Selected Papers on Psychoanalysis*. London: The Hogarth Press and the Institute of Psychoanalysis, 1911.

Abraham, K. The first pregenital stage of the libido. In *ibid.*, 1916.

Alexander, L. The influence of physical treatment methods in mental disease upon the defensive operations of the ego. In P. H. Hoch & J. Zubin (Eds.), *Depression.* New York: Grune & Stratton, 1954, pp. 210–233.

American Psychiatric Association. *Diagnostic and statistical manual, mental disorders.* Washington: Amer. psychiat. Ass., 1952.

Ayd, F. J. *Recognizing the depressed patient.* New York: Grune & Stratton, 1961.

Ayd, F. J. Toxicology of antidepressants. In J. H. Nodine & J. H. Moyer (Eds.), *Psychosomatic medicine.* Philadelphia: Lea & Febiger, 1962.

Azima, H., & Vispo, R. H. Imipramine: a potent new anti-depressant compound. *Amer. J. Psychiat.,* 1958, **115,** 245–246.

Balser, B. H., & Masterson, J. F. Suicide in adolescents. *Amer. J. Psychiat.,* 1959, **116,** 400–404.

Bates, T. J. N., & Douglas, A. D. McL. A comparative trial of four mono-amine oxidase inhibitors on chronic depressives. *J. ment. Sci.,* 1961, **107,** 538–546.

Beck, A. T., Sethi, B. B., & Tuthill, R. W. Childhood bereavement and adult depression. *Arch. gen. Psychiat.,* 1963, **9,** 295–302.

Blair, D. Treatment of severe depression by imipramine (Tofranil). *J. ment. Sci.,* 1960, **106,** 891–905.

Brown, F. Depression and childhood bereavement. *J. ment. Sci.,* 1961, **107,** 754–777.

Bruhn, J. Broken homes among attempted suicides and psychotic out-patients: a comparative study. *J. ment. Sci.,* 1962, **108,** 772–779.

Burton, R. *Anatomy of melancholy.* New York: W. J. Widdleton, 1867.

Cameron, N., & Magaret, A. *Behavior pathology.* Boston: Houghton Mifflin, 1951.

Campbell, J. D. *Manic-depressive disease.* Philadelphia: Lippincott, 1953.

Cobb, S. Personality as affected by lesions of the brain. In J. McV. Hunt (Ed.), *Personality and the behavior disorders.* New York: Ronald Press, 1944. Pp. 550–581.

Cobb, S. Psychosomatic medicine today. *J. nerv. ment. Dis.,* 1962, **134,** 299–304.

Cohen, Mabel B., Baker, Grace, Cohen, R. A., Fromm-Reichmann, Freida, & Weigert, Edith. An intensive study of twelve cases of manic-depressive psychosis. *Psychiatry,* 1954, **17,** 103–137.

Coirault, R., Descles-de-la-Fonchais, S., Ramel, R., & Neiger, R. Variations in total blood calcium, ionized blood calcium, and urinary calcium in 24-hour urine in the course of electroshock therapy and chemotherapy for control of anxiety (imipramine and nialamide). *Med. Exp.,* 1959, **1,** 178–186.

Cole, J. O., Jones, R. T., & Klerman, G. L. A critical review of the recent clinical literature on psychopharmacologic agents currently used in treatment of psychiatric depressions. In E. J. Spiegel (Ed.), *Progress in neurology and psychiatry,* New York: Grune & Stratton, 1961.

Cullen, W. *First lines of the practice of physic.* London, 1777.

Diethelm, O. The fallacy of the concept: psychosis. In P. H. Hoch & J. Zubin (Eds.), *Current problems in psychiatric diagnosis.* New York: Grune & Stratton, 1953.

Dorpat, T. L., & Boswell, J. An evaluation of suicide intent in suicide attempts. *Comprehensive Psychiat.,* 1963, **4,** 117–125.

Dunham, H. W. *Sociological theory and mental disorder.* Detroit. Wayne State Univer. Press, 1959.

Farberow, N. L., & Shneidman, E. *The cry for help.* New York. McGraw-Hill, 1961.

Fenichel, O. *The psychoanalytic theory of neurosis.* New York. Norton, 1945.

Field, M. J. *Search for security.* London. Faber & Faber, 1960.

Fleminger, J. J., & Groden, B. M. Clinical features of depression and the response to imipramine ("Tofranil"). *J. ment. Sci.,* 1962, **108,** 101–104.

Freud, S. Mourning and melancholia. In *Collected Papers.* Vol. IV. London: The Hogarth Press and the Institute of Psychoanalysis, 1917.

Freyhan, F. A. Clinical effectiveness of Tofranil in the treatment of depressive psychoses. *Canadian psychiat. Ass. J. Spec. Suppl.,* 1959, **4,** S86–S99.

Garvey, C. R. Comparative body build of manic-depressive and schizophrenic patients. *Psychol. Bull.,* 1933, **30,** 567–568.

Gellhorn, E., & Loofbourrow, G. N. *Emotions and emotional disorders.* New York: Harper & Row, 1963.

Greenblatt, M., Grosser, G. H., & Wechsler, H. A comparative study of selected antidepressant medications and EST. *Amer. J. Psychiat.,* 1962, **119,** 144–153.

Gregory, I. Selected personal and family data on 400 psychiatric inpatients. *Amer. J. Psychiat.,* 1962, **119,** 397–403.

Grinker, R. R., Miller, J., Sabshin, M., Nunn, R., & Nunnally, J. C. *The phenomena of depressions.* New York: Hoeber, 1961.

Hamilton, M., and White, J. M. Clinical syndromes in depressive states. *J. ment. Sci.*, 1959, **105**, 985–998.

Hamilton, Max. A rating scale for depression *J. neurol. neurosurg. Psychiat.*, 1960, 23, 56–61.

Hendin, H. Suicide in Denmark. *Psychiat. Quart.*, 1960, **34**, 443–460.

Hood, A. B. A study of the relationship between physique and personality variables measured by the MMPI. *J. Pers.*, 1963, **31**, 97–107.

Jacobson, Edith. The affects and their pleasure-unpleasure qualities in relation to the psychic discharge processes. In R. M. Loewenstein (Ed.), *Drives, affects, behavior*. New York: International Universities Press, 1953.

Kallmann, F. J. Genetic principles in manic-depressive psychosis. In P. H. Hoch & J. Zubin (Ed.), *Depression*. New York: Grune & Stratton, 1954. Pp. 1–24.

Kiloh, L. G., Child, J. P., & Latner, G. Endogenous depression treated with iproniazid—a follow-up study. *J. ment. Sci.*, 1960, **106**, 1425–1428.

Kiloh, L. G., & Garside, R. F. The independence of neurotic depression and endogenous depression. *Br. J. Psychiat.*, 1963, **109**, 451–463.

Kraepelin, E. *Manic-depressive insanity and paranoia*. Edinburgh: E. & S. Livingston, 1921.

Kramer, M., Pollack, E. S., & Redick, R. W. Studies of the incidence and prevalence of hospitalized mental disorders in the United States: current status and future goals. In P. H. Hoch & J. Zubin (Eds.), *Comparative epidemiology of the mental disorders*. New York: Grune & Stratton, 1961. Pp. 56–100.

Kretschmer, E. *Physique and character* (Tr. from 2nd ed. by W. J. H. Sprott). New York: Harcourt, Brace, 1925.

Lehmann, H. E. Psychiatric concepts of depression: nomenclature and classification. *Canadian psychiat. Ass. J. Spec. Suppl.*, 1959, **4**, S1–S12.

Lewis, N. D. C., & Piotrowski, Z. A. Clinical diagnosis of manic-depressive psychosis. In P. H. Hoch & J. Zubin (Eds.), *Depression*. New York: Grune & Stratton, 1954. Pp. 25–38.

Mandel, M. M. Recurrent psychotic depression associated with hypercalcemia and parathyroid adenoma. *Amer. J. Psychiat.*, 1960, **117**, 234–235.

Mendelson, M. *Psychoanalytic concepts of depression*. Springfield, Ill.: Charles C Thomas, 1960.

Meyer, A. Mental factors in psychiatry. From "The Role of the Mental Factors in Psychiatry," read at the annual meeting of the American Medico-Psychological Association, Cincinnati, May, 1908. In A. Lief (Ed.), *The commonsense psychiatry of Dr. Adolf Meyer*. New York: McGraw-Hill, 1948

Oltman, Jane E., & Friedman, S. Comparison of EST and antidepressant drugs in affective disorders. *Amer. J. Psychiat.*, 1961, **118**, 355–357.

Oltman, Jane E., & Friedman, S. Comparison of temporal factors in depressive psychoses treated by EST and antidepressant drugs. *Amer. J. Psychiat.*, 1962, **119**, 579–580.

Overall, J. E. Dimensions of manifest depression. *J. psychiat. Res.*, 1963, **1**, 239–246.

Pare, C. M. B., Rees, Linford, & Sainsbury, M. J. Differentiation of two genetically specific types of depression by the response to anti-depressants. *Lancet*, Dec. 29, 1962, 1340–1343.

Poliakova, M. la. The effect of blood from patients with manic depressive psychoses on the higher nervous activity (behavior) of dogs. *Zhurnal Nevropatologii i Psikkiatrii imeni S. S. Korsakova*, 1961, **1**, 104–108.

Rees, L., Brown, A. C., & Benaim, S. A controlled trial of imipramine ("Tofranil") in the treatment of severe depressive states. *J. ment. Sci.*, 1961, **107**, 552–559.

Rosen, B. C. The achievement syndrome: a psychocultural dimension of social stratification. In J. W. Atkinson (Ed.), *Motives in action, fantasy, and society*. Princeton: D. Van Nostrand, 1958.

Rothman, T., Grayson, H., & Ferguson, J. A comparative investigation of isocarboxazid and imipramine in depressive syndromes. *J. Neuropsychiat.*, 1961, **2**, 158–162.

Roulet, N., Alvarez, R. R., Duffy, J. P., Lenkoski, L. D., & Bidder, T. G. Imipramine in depressions: a controlled study. *Am. J. Psychiat.*, 1962, **119**, 427–431.

Rubenstein, Robert, Moses, R., & Lidz, T. On attempted suicide. *Arch. Neurol. Psychiat.*, 1958, **79**, 103–112.

Rudin, E. *Zur Vererbung und Neuentstehung der Dëmentia Praecox*. Berlin: J. Springer, 1916.

Sheldon, W. H., & Stevens, S. S. *The varieties of temperament*. New York: Harper, 1942.

Shneidman, Edwin S., & Farberow, Norman L. *Clues to suicide*. New York: McGraw-Hill, 1957.

Stengel, E. The complexity of motivations to suicidal attempts. *J. ment. Sci.*, 1960, **106**, 1388–1393.

Sullivan, H. S. *The interpersonal theory of psychiatry*. New York: Norton, 1953.

Symonds, C. P. The neurological approach to mental disorder. *Proc. roy. Soc. Med.*, 1941, **34**, 289–302.

Tabachnick, N. Countertransference crisis in suicidal attempts. *Arch. gen. Psychiat.*, 1961, **4**, 572–578.

Toolan, James M. Suicide and suicidal attempts in children and adolescents. *Amer. J. Psychiat.*, 1962, **118**, 719–724.

Turner, W. J., O'Neill, F. J., & Merlis, S. The treatment of depression in hospitalized patients before and since the introduction of antidepressant drugs. *Amer. J. Psychiat.*, 1962, **119**, 421–426.

Whitehorn, J. C. Psychodynamic approach to the study of psychoses. In F. Alexander & Helen Ross (Eds.), *Dynamic psychiatry*. Chicago: Univer. of Chicago Press, 1952.

Wittenborn, J. R. Symptom patterns in a group of mental hospital patients. *J. consult. Psychol.*, 1951, **15**, 290–302.

Wittenborn, J. R. Distinctions within psychotic dimensions: a principal component analysis. *J. nerv. ment. Dis.*, 1963, **137**, 543–547.

Wittenborn, J. R., & Bailey, C. The symptoms of involutional psychosis. *J. consult. Psychol.*, 1952, **16**, 13–17.

Wittenborn, J. R., & Holzberg, J. D. The generality of psychiatric syndromes. *J. consult. Psychol.*, 1951, **15**, 372–380.

Wittenborn, J. R., Holzberg, J. D., & Simon, B. Symptom correlates for descriptive diagnosis. *Genet. psychol. Monogr.*, 1953, **47**, 237–301.

Wittenborn, J. R., & Plante, M. Patterns of response to placebo, iproniazid, and electroconvulsive therapy among young depressed females. *J. nerv. ment. Dis.*, 1963, **137**, 155–161.

Wittenborn, J. R., Plante, M., Burgess, Frances, & Livermore, Nancy. The efficacy of electroconvulsive therapy, iproniazid and placebo in the treatment of young depressed women. *J. nerv. ment. Dis.*, 1961, **133**, 316–332.

Wittenborn, J. R., Plante, M., Burgess, Frances, & Maurer, Helen. A comparison of imipramine, electroconvulsive therapy, and placebo in the treatment of depressions. *J. nerv. ment. Dis.*, 1962, **135**, 131–137.

Wittenborn, J. R., Sgro, F., and Plante, M. Descriptive characteristics of a depressed state. (Submitted for publication.)

Wittkower, E. D., & Fried, J. Some problems of transcultural psychiatry. In M. K. Opler (Ed.), *Culture and mental health*. New York: Macmillan, 1959. Pp. 489–500.

Wolberg, L. R. *The technique of psychotherapy*. New York: Grune & Stratton, 1954.

Wolman, B. B. The continuum hypothesis in neurosis and psychosis and the classification of mental disorders. Paper read at *East. Psychol. Ass.*, 1959.

Wolman, B. B. *Contemporary theories and systems in psychology*. New York: Harper, 1960.

Wolman, B. B. *Mental disorders: Their theory and classification*, in press.

Wortis, J. Psychopharmacology and psychological treatment. *Amer. J. Psychiat.*, 1963, **119**, 621–626.

Zilboorg, G., & Henry, W. *A history of medical psychology*. New York: Norton, 1941.

36

Psychopathic Condition, Addictions, and Sexual Deviations

IVAN N. MENSH[1]

The clinical patterns of psychopathic condition, addictions, and sexual deviations are defined (American Psychiatric Association, 1960) as personality disorders (see also "Mental Disorders in Childhood," below). These

> are characterized by developmental defects or pathological trends in the personality structure, with minimal subjective anxiety, and little or no sense of distress. In most instances, the disorder is manifested by a lifelong pattern of action or behavior, rather than by mental or emotional symptoms.

Although semantics long have been the bane of mental health investigators and although the *Diagnostic and Statistical Manual: Mental Disorders* represents an effort to organize the recent knowledge of psychiatry, even the brief definition just cited may provoke controversy over the description and dynamics of clinical patterns of behavior. For the purposes of this chapter, the manual's nomenclature will be followed, since it represents the single organized, relatively accepted descriptive system extant in the United States.

The diagnostic classifications of personality disorders include sociopathic personality disturbance, antisocial reaction, and dissocial reaction under one main grouping; sexual deviation in a second main grouping; and the addictions—alcoholism and drug addiction—in a third main group of disorders.

Individuals diagnosed as sociopathic personality are

> ill primarily in terms of society and of conformity with the prevailing cultural milieu, and not only in terms of personal discomfort and relations with other individuals. However, sociopathic reactions are very often symptomatic of severe underlying personality disorder, neurosis, or psychosis, or occur as the result of organic brain injury or disease. Before definitive diagnosis in this group is employed, strict attention must be paid to the possibility of the presence of a more primary personality disturbance. . . .
>
> Antisocial reaction . . . refers to chronically antisocial individuals who are always in trouble, profiting neither from experience nor punishment, and maintaining no real loyalties to any person, group, or code. They are frequently callous and hedonistic, showing marked emotional immaturity, with lack of sense of responsibility, lack of judgment, and ability to rationalize their behavior so that it appears warranted, reasonable, and justified. . . . The term includes cases previously classified as "constitutional psychopathic state" and "psychopathic personality." As defined here the term is more limited, as well as more specific in its application. . . .
>
> Dyssocial reaction . . . applies to individuals who manifest disregard for the usual social codes, and often come in conflict with them, as the result of having lived all

[1] Grateful acknowledgment is made to Mrs. Marielle Fuller for her contribution to this chapter through comprehensive search and abstracting of the literature.

their lives in an abnormal moral environment. They may be capable of strong loyalties. These individuals typically do not show significant personality deviations other than those implied by adherence to the values or code of their own predatory, criminal, or other social group. The term includes such diagnoses as "pseudosocial personality" and "psychopathic personality with asocial and amoral trends."

This diagnosis [sexual deviation] is reserved for deviant sexuality which is not symptomatic of more extensive syndromes, such as schizophrenic and obsessional reactions. The term includes most of the cases formerly classed as "psychopathic personality with pathologic sexuality." The diagnosis will specify the type of pathologic behavior, such as homosexuality, transvestism, pedophilia, fetishism and sexual sadism (including rape, sexual assault, mutilation). . . .

Included in this category [addiction and alcoholism] will be cases in which there is well established addiction to alcohol without recognizable underlying disorders. Simple drunkenness and acute poisoning due to alcohol are not included in this category. . . .

Drug addiction is usually symptomatic of a personality disorder, and will be classified here while the individual is actually addicted; the proper personality classification is to be made as an additional diagnosis. Drug addictions symptomatic of organic brain disorders, psychotic disorders, psychophysiologic disorder, and psychoneurotic disorders are classified here as a secondary diagnosis (American Psychiatric Association, 1960).

These, then, represent the formal descriptions of the clinical patterns presently under review.

PSYCHOPATHIC CONDITION

The history of this concept has been traced by a number of writers (Henderson, 1939; Jenkins, 1960; Kahn, 1931; Maughs, 1960; Partridge, 1930; Preu, 1944). Prichard (1835) generally is regarded as the first writer to use the terms "moral insanity" and "moral imbecility," and Maughs (1960) has traced the evolution of this concept to that of psychopathic personality. In 1888, Koch introduced the term "psychopathic inferiority"; Adolf Meyer, in the United States, later introduced the concept of "constitutional inferiority"; and the evolution of psychiatry (Koch, 1891; Kraepelin, 1915) and the accumulation of experience resulted in the term "psychopathic personality" (Davidson, 1956) or "sociopathic personality" (Overholser & Owens, 1961). The term "psychopathic inferiority" is the descriptive label generally in use, in spite of the 1952 APA manual and its 13 editions through 1960 and in spite of the evaluation of the committee on public information of the American Psychiatric Association: "Increasingly considered a poor and inexact term." This comment follows the entry in the psychiatric glossary of the committee (American Psychiatric Association, 1957) describing a psychopath as

> a person whose behavior is predominantly amoral or antisocial and characterized by impulsive, irresponsible actions satisfying only immediate and narcissistic interests without concern for obvious and implicit social consequences, accompanied by minimal outward evidence of anxiety or guilt.

Jenkins (1960) reviews and comments on the difficulties in conceptualization of the various behaviors diagnosed as psychopathic or antisocial personality. Karpman's clinical reports (1951; 1959), derived from his long experience at St. Elizabeth's Hospital in Washington, D.C., with the "criminally insane" and other psychiatrically ill patients, and Davidson's use of the term "oligothymia" (1956) for psychopathy represent other clinical pictures and labeling which at times introduce order and at times produce confusion in variously discriminating or relating psychopathic behavior to delinquency and crime, the addictions, and sexual deviations. For example, Davidson reports that about sixteen variants have been described, adding to the Kraepelinian forms and producing results "which render the concept useless."

Numerous attempts to infer the dynamics of psychopaths have been published, none satisfactory or satisfying except to those readers with identifications similar to those of the particular author. Thus Salzman writes (1960) that masochism and psychopathy are similar adaptive behaviors: "Both . . . feel powerless, and worthless, cheated and abused, and are attempting to obtain compensation for their claims. Both use exploitive methods in their attempts. . . ." Davidson (1956) considers "the poverty of affectivity to be the central fact of psychopathy." He proposed that the disorder "consists on the descriptive level of [the] symptoms . . . of . . . lack of guilt feelings, abnormal aggressiveness and narcissistic self evaluation. . . ." The sought-for etiological and descriptive explanations of psychopathic behavior in the phenomena of masochism and disordered affect appear frequently in the literature, but so do they appear in the literature on etiology of schizophrenia and other disorders. Also, the etiology suggested here is not any more documented than in these other diseases.

In the range of description and suggested etiology, there also are Maudsley's early observation (1896) that psychopathic behavior may be associated with organic brain disease, the more recent studies with the EEG pattern as dependent variable (D. Hill, 1952; D. Hill & Watterson, 1942; Hodge, 1945; Kennard, 1956; Knott & Gottlieb, 1943; Rioch, 1952), related studies of organic brain dysfunction in the psychopath (Chornyak, 1941; Palmer & Rock, 1953; Silverman, 1949), and the typology of the "pure" psychopath (Bender, 1950) and the "aggressive" psychopath (Frosch & Wortis, 1954). Kennard (1956), for example, develops the pragmatism of the rationale for this latter typology "solely because these [the two types of psychopath] correspond to particular EEG patterns." However, this follows immediately on her summary statement that the "EEGs of the adult psychopathic personality have been discussed many times but there has been much confusion, largely as the result of clinical reporting which has used terms and measurements of clinical conditions which varied with the school of psychiatric thought of the investigator." In this forest of confusion, the data summarized by Kennard and others, e.g., Ehrlich and Keogh (1956), suggest a high alpha index (20 to 80 per cent) among "pure" psychopaths and "excessive" quantity (30 to 60 per cent) of theta activity in the EEG patterns of the "aggressive" psychopaths. Silverman's review of six independent studies, totaling nearly seven hundred cases, indicated abnormal EEGs in about half of this number.

A number of writers have attempted to relate or integrate these suggestions of an organic component of psychopathic behavior with dynamic concepts. Thus, Silverman (1949) reported that 80 per cent of his psychopathic patients had "clearly traumatic childhoods involving disturbed parent-child relationships." He offers a formulation relating "inborn or an early acquired defect," reflected in an abnormal EEG pattern, to a dynamic psychiatric view in this statement: "The cerebral defect serves to increase the sensitivity to the emotional trauma of childhood and may even facilitate the psychopathic choice of the neurotic pattern—the tendency to 'act out' rather than internalize the conflict."

The utility of such a formulation as this depends upon the reliability of the data used in support of the hypothesis. Though Silverman argued (1949) that six independent studies (Gottlieb et al.; Hill & Watterson, 1942; Hodge, 1945; Silverman, 1949; Simon et al.; Simons & Diethelm) produced essentially similar findings (approximately 50 per cent of psychopaths with abnormal EEGs and the aggressive type yielding consistently many more abnormal patterns than the inadequate psychopathic personality), Hughes and Ryan noted in their discussion of Silverman's observations that others have reported that EEGs of aggressive, asocial psychopaths are not significantly different from patterns obtained from normals. The usual rationalization for the diversity in the findings is the presence of different diagnostic criteria among the various studies.

Another attempt to make order out of the areas of agreement and disagreement in the definition of the term "psychopathic personality" is represented in the study reported by Albert, Brigante, and Chase (1959). These authors did a content analysis of a sample of 10 articles selected from journal articles and books listed in *Psychological Abstracts* from 1947 to 1953 under the headings "psychopathic personality," "behavior problems," and "psychopath." This analysis yielded a list of 165 statements descriptive of adult psychopathic personality and 45 descriptive of children diagnosed with this condition. Further analysis produced a final list of 75 items. The three investigators analyzed and independently coded the 10 articles for attributes mentioned as *always* characteristic, not characteristic, or as occurring as often in the general population as among psychopaths. Albert and his coworkers reported: "The most striking result . . . is the large agreement shown regarding the concept of psychopathic personality." There was "decided agreement" regarding the psychopath's antisocial aggression, lack of ability to delay satisfaction, lack of insight, inadequacy of superego functioning, deficiency in planning ability, hyperactivity, and callousness; and there was "agreement" with respect to such characteristics as inability to identify with others and disturbed early parent-child relationships. Disagreements were found among writers regarding the presence of conflict and anxiety in the psychopath and his capacity to alter his behavior.

Another interpretation of the psychopathic type was suggested by Wolman (1960; 1965). Wolman divided all mental disorders into three types on the basis of interactional patterns combined with a modified psychoanalytic frame of reference. The first type, the "hypervectorial," includes the obsessive-compulsive neurosis and schizophrenic disorders; the "paramutual" type includes hysteria and manic-depressive disorders; and the "hyperinstrumental" type corresponds to what is usually called "sociopathic" or "psychopathic" disorders.

The hyperinstrumental disorders are characterized by a persistently selfish, exploitative, and narcissistic personality structure and by absence or "hypothrophy" of superego. Wolman distinguishes five levels within each type. Accordingly, psychopaths or hyperinstrumentals can be neurotics, character neurotics, latent psychotics, manifest psychotics, or dementive psychotics. The level of disorder within each type is determined by the degree of damage caused to the ego.

Another look at psychopathic behavior is the phenomenological and descriptive characterization of "impulse disorders." Under this rubric, Frosch and Wortis (1954) diagram two major groups of impulse disorders. The first resembles the classical symptom neurosis with one or many symptoms and contains three subgroups: impulse neuroses (kleptomania, pyromania, addiction); perversion (the impulsive sexual deviations found in exhibitionism, voyeurism, sadism, masochism, and homosexuality); and the controversial so-called "catathymic crisis," an isolated, nonrepetitive violent act stemming from intolerable tension. The second group is that of the character disorders, in which impulsivity is not limited to any symptom but dominates the character structure. Included in this group of persons with impulsive character disorders are those with syndromes apparently caused by, or associated with, an organic component (suggested by behavioral and/or EEG data); the impulsive "actor-outers who tend to shunt off their conflicts into repeated impulsive actions . . ."; those with neurotic character disorders; and those with psychopathic personality. Frosch and Wortis (1954) speculate "as to why the body rather than language is used so much more in impulse disorders as a medium of expression" and seem to prefer Greenacre's theorizing (1950) about early experience and constitutional factors.

As in much of the literature, however, the evidence for this position is not strong. Operations on 12 hospitalized psychopaths on maximum security wards of a state hospital and on six "milder cases" later, with the MMPI as "objective confirmation" and with follow-up for a year or more, constitute the data. The authors conclude: "More than half of the cases operated on are now socially adjusted away from the hospital. Seventeen of the 18 cases have been amenable to retraining; some of these cases will adjust to normal society in the future."

Although this review does not at all exhaust the range of formulation of psychopathic behavior, another attempt to understand this condition is represented in the observations of Glover (1960). He, too, suggested two major categories of psychopath, labeling these "private" and (in the social sense) "benign" psychopathy, in which the condition affects the individual's "private life and character," and ("again socially speaking") "malignant" or "criminal" psychopathy, where the disorder is demonstrated in "serious and persistent antisocial manifestations." As is the case with other writers, Glover offers his dichotomy for this reason:

> It is incidentally psychopathic personality. They do not see either a qualitative or quantitative deficiency in the social interactions of the individual . . . no certain type of environment will cause the psychopathic personality, for psychopaths come from the most diverse types of environment and home conditions.

Darling and Sanddal argue that leucotomy cannot correct a deficiency nor change the environment, and they go on to offer a tenuous rationale:

> The predisposition to psychopathic personality may be found in the parents . . . an inherited tendency . . . rather than a con-

> genital personality deviation. . . . The syndrome develops as the result of environment. The fact that mild psychopaths are successful would indicate that a good environment may modify the basic hereditary predisposition as in other psychoses.

Inadequate sampling, measurement, and follow-up data again are the weaknesses, appearing so often, together with the argument for classification of psychopathic behavior as psychosis. Though validity data are lacking, consensual validation suggests that psychosis may be a misclassification of most psychopathic personality disorders.

Many investigators feel that long-term follow-up studies and adequate reliable and valid predictor and criterion variables are the only solutions to the confusion in the field. This need exists also for other psychiatric disorders, so that psychopathic behavior is not in this sense peculiarly baffling. There have been several follow-up studies, and two are presented here, one from Britain and the other from the United States. Gibbens, Pond, and Stafford-Clark (1959) report a study covering an eight-year follow-up of 72 "severely psychopathic criminals and 59 control prisoners." This group characterized their subjects as inadequate or aggressive and found the expected significantly higher rate of reconviction among the psychopaths but also

> the surprising feature . . . that no less than 24 per cent of the psychopaths had one or no reconvictions. . . . [These] are alive and not in mental hospitals . . . mainly inadequate psychopaths; aggressive psychopaths almost always offend again . . . [but were] much more often convicted of acquisitive than aggressive crimes. . . . Only 18 (committed by 9 individuals) out of 105 subsequent convictions were for (purely) aggressive crimes.

EEGs were more often abnormal in the psychopaths than in the control sample, but this was not prognostic of later adjustment. Relapse rate was similar to that reported for other offenders, with most relapses occurring six to twelve months after release and thereafter in rapidly decreasing frequency. Unusual, however, was the postrelease behavior of the control subjects. These were reconvicted at a relatively even rate throughout the eight years of follow-up. Finally, there was no significant difference in the criminal behavior of those in either sample who had a previous history of four or fewer convictions and who were reconvicted after release. "The authors concluded that the diagnosis of psychopathic personality did not appear to contribute anything to the criminal prognosis."

This latter finding was supported even after a further characterization of the experimental sample as (1) without complication (*N* of 34), (2) with history of epilepsy (*N* of 9), and (3) with history of head injury (*N* of 29). Postrelease behavior did not discriminate these three groups, though preprison records indicated that the third group had the highest proportion, with more than three convictions, and that nearly half of these convictions were for violent offenses. The first group, however, had the heaviest sentences imposed. The reader may infer the logic of the sentencing judges from this observation.

The second follow-up study was more broadly based and involved very different methodology, but it did include individuals evaluated at follow-up as sociopaths. O'Neal and Robins (1958; Robins & O'Neal, 1958) studied a consecutive series of 524 individuals who in the 1920s had been referred to a child guidance clinic, and they compared the histories of these during a thirty-year period with a matched group of normal controls. Psychiatric and sociologic interviews provided the data at follow-up. The subjects who had been referred to the clinic thirty years previously had a high rate of psychiatric illness, compared with the normal controls. Though differing little in the rate of neurotic reactions, the experimental group included many cases of sociopathic personality, psychotic reactions, and alcoholism. The sociopaths at adulthood came primarily from the children whose behavior thirty years earlier was termed "juvenile delinquent." The psychotic group had childhood histories of antisocial behavior but without court hearings. The psychiatrically well adults were those who, as children in the clinic, had neurotic problems (fighting, sex problems, tantrums, and the "classic neurotic traits of childhood"). This group came from families of better socioeconomic background than the children with antisocial problems and delinquency, but social class was not a significant variant among the psychiatrically well adults who presented neurotic problems in childhood. Also, broken homes were more often reported in the patients than in the controls, but this variable was not related to the continuance of psychiatric problems from childhood to the adult years. It is of interest that few members of the patient groups sought psychiatric help, although the rate of psychiatric illness among them was evaluated as high by the investigators.

The data of the O'Neal and Robins study (1958) on an initial sample of 150 subjects may be summarized in the following way: The 35 child delinquents were seen in adulthood as sociopaths (37 per cent), neurotics (14 per cent), psychotics (6 per cent), alcoholics and sufferers from other diseases (12 per cent), and those without psychiatric disease (14 per cent). The other subjects (17 per cent) were undiagnosed. The 47 antisocial children developed equally often (30 per cent in each group) into adults with neurotic reaction or with psychotic reaction, 6 per cent sociopathic, 4 per cent with other diseases, 19 per cent with no psychiatric disease in adulthood, and 11 per cent undiagnosed. The 33 neurotic children later showed 37 per cent with neurotic reaction, 30 per cent without disease, 15 per cent with psychotic reaction, 6 per cent with other diseases, and 12 per cent undiagnosed. The 35 control children showed at adulthood 23 per cent with neurotic reaction, 6 per cent with other diseases, 60 per cent without disease, and 11 per cent undiagnosed. These data "suggest that children who are sufficiently disturbed to be referred to a child guidance clinic grow into adults who . . . contribute a disproportionate share to serious social problems. . . ."

In a very different approach to better understanding of sociopathic behavior are the psychological test studies of several investigators. Wiens, Matarazzo, and Gaver (1959) reviewed five earlier studies of the Wechsler-Bellevue Intelligence Scale with sociopaths. The observation by Wechsler that the test performance of adolescent sociopaths is characterized by subtest scatter was supported by the study of J. H. Clark (1949) but found no support in the data reported in four other studies, those by Strother (1944), J. H. Clark and Moore (1950), Thurston and Calden (1950), and Gurvitz (1950). The Wiens et al. study brought the score to 2 to 4 but excluded subjects who reported no court appearance before age 21. Field (1960) then attempted to test the hypothesis with data from a sample of 65 men whose median age was 39.5. All reported no court appearance before the age of 21, but had 10 or more convictions, were currently serving sentences, and had had no previous testing with the Wechsler-Bellevue. Field's study moved the score to 2 to 5. However, the usual difficulties in comparing studies obtain here. For example, several subjects in the study of Wiens et al. were mentally defective, and Field's subjects were characterized by him as "more extreme" sociopaths.

One more study may suggest still another variant of methodology for investigating psychopathic, sociopathic behavior. Lykken (1957) utilized Cleckley's criteria (1950) to categorize 49 diagnosed psychopaths as "primary" or "neurotic" sociopaths, and with 15 "normals" as controls he investigated the responses of these three samples to tests of "anxiety reactivity or anxiety conditionability." The hypotheses at test related to the discrimination of the first of these samples from the other two. The "primary sociopathic group" were

> (a) clearly defective as compared to normals in their ability to develop (i.e., condition) anxiety, in the sense of an anticipatory emotional response to warning signals previously associated with nociceptive stimulation. Persons with such a defect would also be expected to show (b) abnormally "little manifest anxiety" in life situations normally conducive to this response, and to be (c) relatively incapable of "avoidance learning" under circumstances where such learning can only be effected through the mediation of the anxiety response.

The MMPI booklet form was used and an anxiety index calculated by Welsh's formula (1952). Another index was derived from responses to the Heineman form of the Taylor scale (1953). GSR recording provided the dependent variable data to test hypothesis A, and an electrically operated maze, criterion of 20 trials to learn with electroshock alternations, yielded data designed to test hypothesis C. Analyses of these sets of data showed significantly less anxiety in the questionnaire responses, less GSR reactivity to the conditioned stimulus associated with shock, and less avoidance of punished responses in the maze-learning task for the primary sociopathic subjects, as compared with the normals. The neurotic sociopaths scored significantly higher on the Taylor and Welsh scales. On eight

TABLE 1

Measure	Primary sociopaths	Neurotic sociopaths	Normals
Taylor scale	471	556	462
Anxiety index	472	557	464
Anxiety scale	470	511	529
MMPI Pd scale	532	547	395
Avoidance learning	461	501	558
GSR reactivity	498	494	534
GSR conditioning	478	483	551
Generalization	473	543	490

measures, converted to a scale of mean 500 and S.D. 100, differences were significant at the $p = .01$ to .05 level for all but generalization. In brief, the data were distributed as shown in Table 1.

In summary, investigations of psychopathic conditions have ranged from subjective to objective reports and systematic studies. The problems of definition of these conditions of behavior, understanding of the etiology and dynamics, treatment methods, and prognoses still loom large in an assessment of the present state of knowledge, even though deriving from three-quarters of a century of professional and scientific experience.

ADDICTION TO DRUGS

> Drug addiction is usually symptomatic of a personality disorder, and will be classified here while the individual is actually addicted; the proper personality classification is to be made as an additional diagnosis. Drug addictions symptomatic of organic brain disorders, psychotic disorders, psychophysiologic disorders, and psychoneurotic disorders are classified here as a secondary diagnosis (American Psychiatric Association, 1960).

Thus it is seen that there is an important discrimination to be made that addiction is not a behavior disorder; rather, it is symptomatic of a pattern of personality adjustment. A second discrimination also is made in the understanding of addictive behavior, that between narcotic addiction and addiction of habit-forming drugs (e.g., Armitage & Sim, 1960). For example, a number of states report a decrease in commitments for narcotic addiction during the past decade but an increase in commitments for addiction to habit-forming drugs, the ratios shifting from about 5:1 to 1:1. Also, the age and sex ratios may vary between these two classes of addiction; e.g., in California, two-thirds of the narcotic commitments are in the 21-to-34 age range, and most of these are males, while three out of four commitments for addictions to habit-forming drugs are past 34 years of age and are principally females. Unlike other types of personality disorders, the addictions illustrate a peculiar "contagion" or "infection" in that a special social problem exists which is not found in other disorders. This phenomenon in addiction is the introduction of others to the use of drugs, estimated to number six for the typical adult, and thereby expanding the social network of addiction, with the consequent behaviors necessary to maintain supplies of drugs, often crime and other antisocial behavior. As one addict reported, in his fifteen years of addiction, he increased his needs to the point where he had to steal $500 worth of merchandise regularly in order to obtain $80 from their sale for purchase of the drugs necessary to maintain him.

Another phenomenon of addiction which makes for an acute social problem is the youth of addicts (Ausubel, 1952; Ausubel, 1961) at the time of beginning addiction, so that their potential positive contributions to society do not even see the light of day. Thus, New York City's Riverside Hospital for the treatment of addicts (Gamso & Mason, 1958) was designed entirely for patients under the age of 21. These addicts have used opium and its derivatives, cocaine or marijuana, with the "overwhelming majority . . . addicted to heroin, which seems to be the drug choice of today." As has been the case with other efforts to increase the efficacy of methods for the early identification of addicts and early intervention in the usage and spread of drugs, this hospital was established under a public health rather than a criminal statute to emphasize the disease rather than the criminal characteristics of addiction, with patients rather than delinquents, but in most instances not certifiable to state hospitals. Unfortunately, as with the U.S. Public Health Service Hospital at Lexington, Kentucky, and many other hospitals for addicts, alumni (and alumnae) report that they did not note the discrimination between these two approaches, even for the voluntary admissions. Whether or not these perceptions are objectively reliable is less important than the patients' observations since it is the latter which determine their behavior. It is significant that arrests within one year after hospital release may be as high as 25 per cent of those released "HTC" (hospital treatment completed).

Reflections of the social disorganization in various subcultures of our society are found in the data of hospitals and other drug treatment centers. Gamso and Mason reported for Riverside a bed capacity of 140 and 1,600 first admissions between 1952 and 1958. Mean age at admission was about 18; first addictions began typically at about age 16; white and Puerto Rican admissions rose over the study period, while Negro first admissions dropped; two-thirds of the sample were diagnosed as personality disorders and one-quarter as schizophrenics, though few of the latter had to be transferred to state hospitals; and barely one per cent were diagnosed as mentally defective or as having organic brain disorder. Attendance at an after-care clinic is required, but an important observation is made:

> [the] prevalent custom of discharging patients to the community and their families [is] unsatisfactory as it's realized that patients may not have been sufficiently strengthened by their stay in hospital and therapy to cope any better than before with the strains of unsatisfactory interpersonal relations in a family.

The authors suggest halfway houses as a bridge between hospital and the community. As with psychiatric care for other illnesses, the observation on family and community noted above is not peculiar to treated addicts. Also, the social network and personal satisfactions which obtain for the drug addict tend to attract him in the way that the rewards of personal fantasy activity may be so much greater for the schizophrenic than those of other reactions to stresses.

Since 1925 there have been suggested numerous classifications of the personalities of drug addicts. One of the earliest was that by Kolb (1925), later revised in 1938 (Kolb & Ossenfort), and then modified by Pescor (1939; 1943) and again in 1944 by Felix. This evaluation resulted in a four-way classification—addicts without psychosis but with psychopathic personalities, the psychoneurotic group, addicts with associated psychosis, and normal individuals accidentally addicted. As the discussion in the following pages develops, we shall see how this grouping fares.

The physiological dependence upon drugs has been variously evaluated, together with the psychosocial variables in addiction. Ausubel (1961) argues that this dependence and the avoidance of withdrawal symptoms are not convincing arguments:

> The drug addict has been amazingly successful in deluding both himself and the American Public into believing that [avoidance of withdrawal symptoms] is the primary causal consideration. Physical dependence cannot account convincingly for the surplus dosage and intravenous route habitually taken by the confirmed addict, or for the latter's willingness to risk social ostracism and incarceration just to avoid a moderately severe ten-day illness. Nor does it explain the recurrence of addiction long after dependence is lost nor the strong addictive potential of new opiate-like drugs which give rise to only minimal degrees of physical dependence, nor the ease with which normal persons are able to overcome the physical dependence on narcotics they may inadvertently acquire during the course of a prolonged illness.

Ausubel (1952; 1961) suggests that a discrimination be made between the "experimental" form of addiction, transitory and self-limiting, and the "adjustive . . . true or permanent addicts." In referring to opium, its derivatives such as morphine and codeine, synthetic opiates such as heroin, and the opiumlike Demerol and methadone, Ausubel reports (1952) four "physiological" properties of which two are psychological: tolerance, physiological dependence, euphoria, and psychological habituation. Physiological, pharmacological, and psychosocial variables are integrated into a rationale to support his view of the dominance of psychosocial variables in the etiology of addiction. The adjustive value of narcotics to the addict (internal variables), the "ready availability" of drugs ("the major external and necessary precipitating factor"), and the reinforcing "predisposing environmental factor of high community or cultural tolerance for the practice . . . are sufficient to induce the disorder in individuals who are highly susceptible (for adjustive reasons) to addiction."

Wikler (1953), however, concludes from studies of juvenile addicts at Lexington that most of these boys have physical dependence upon their drugs. This is deduced from observations of the addicts immediately after admission to the Lexington hospital and before medication is given and from "abstinence" responses of boys who had not shown symptoms of "physical dependence" on admission to single doses of *N*-allylnormorphine. "These data constitute strong evidence that the genesis of the opiate abstinence syndrome is in large part related to factors of little or no symbolic significance."

There also are the studies and theoretical formulations designed to integrate what is known about habit formation, learning, personality theory, and drug addiction. This learning and personality dimension approach is related to the studies of Eysenck (1947; 1952; 1959). These suggest that introverted individuals in stress situations would adopt the behavior patterns of their associates, following a classical Pavlovian conditioning model, and would become addicts if this was the pattern of behavior of their associates. Psychopaths who become addicted may do so, in Eysenck's rationale, because of their undersocialization, depending upon the extent of the extroversion factor.

Walton's formulation of the learning approach (1960) offers an alternative hypothesis, arguing instrumental rather than classical conditioning as the model. In his view, introverts are more likely to be anxious, and this emotional response has a central role in their addiction, in terms of drive-reduction theory, together with hyporeactivity to society's concern about their behavior. He concludes:

> Drug addiction may be a learned phenomenon developing as a simple function of the consequences of the drug. . . . Learning does not always increase with an increase in reward and what is equally important, when this increase (in learning) does occur it is not always proportional to the amount of reward. Thus one cannot say with any confidence that the severity of the addiction is a simple function of the severity of the neurosis, though some degree of neuroticism appears necessary to guarantee that the rewards are sufficient to produce the reinforced addictive response.

The relatively infrequent psychotic addict is noted by V. H. Vogel, Isbell, and Chapman (1948). This group at Lexington Hospital also reports that one of the five personality types which they identify among addicts consists of neurotics who take drugs to relieve symptoms such as anxiety. However, they feel that most addicts are psychopaths who developed addiction through association with other addicts. In contrast are the reports of Bromberg (1955) and Mason (1958), which stress early maternal influences in the etiology.

Henderson and Gillespie (1940) also identified most opium addicts as psychopaths or "people originally of psychopathic make-up," and Walton's analysis (1960) of the 968 case histories reported by Hathaway and Meehl (1951) "tentatively confirms" the Henderson and Gillespie inferences. Unfortunately, the Walton analysis rests on the MMPIs of only 28 addicts, and thus sampling and generalizability are much in question. This failing is not peculiar to Walton's report, however, and the literature abounds in reports whose findings do not even merit the description "tentative."

A more adequate attempt at sampling MMPI data is reported by H. E. Hill, Haertgen, and Glaser (1960), using the responses of 270 hospitalized addicts. Teenagers and adults and white and Negro addicts were studied. The one common characteristic was a T score of 70 on the Pd scale, with the adolescents producing as deviant profiles as the adult addicts. About 15 per cent of the total sample, though with deviant profiles, were not classified because the first two high points of their scales did not place them in one of the three differentiable, abnormal, composite profile groups of neurotic, psychopathic, or schizoid. As in other clinical studies which have reported 2 to 4 per cent of addicts with "normal" personalities, the present study identified about 5 per cent as "normal." The investigators concluded:

The adolescent and all adult addict groups exhibited deviant personality characteristics which were associated with psychopathy or which were predominantly psychopathic in nature. The extreme similarity between the teenage and adult addicts supports the belief that personality characteristics do not materially change following addiction, even though the procurement, use and effects of drugs necessarily demand changes in the individual's daily activities.

Treatment of the addictions consists of withdrawal of the addicting drugs, correction of the often observed nutritional deficiencies through proper diet, and psychotherapy, in an attempt to modify the personality response pattern of the addict. Motivation for treatment remains a significant problem, and voluntary behavior has not yet been consistently produced in any significant number of addicts. "Voluntary" admissions often are motivated by threats of court action, and addicts report that they respond to psychotherapy by producing reactions desired by their therapists, the primary motivation for the addict being his anticipation of early release and return to drugs. Therapeutic orientation, as with other psychiatric disorders, varies from psychoanalytic to directive. Even though addicts may be "mainliners," with intravenous intake, the "orality" of addicts frequently is advanced as the basic dynamic interpretation. As in alcoholic addiction, where orality also is interpreted, one of the treatment methods which has developed from the addicts themselves is group interaction. Alcoholics Anonymous (AA) has its counterpart in Synanon (the product of an addict's attempt to say "seminar" and to characterize the group structure for verbal exchange), though the latter group strongly resists any comparison between it and AA. Because of the selective biases among addicts and in the group which they may join, the relatively small numbers involved, and inadequate follow-up data, such treatment directions are difficult to evaluate. It is true, of course, that these methodological criticisms exist also for studies of addicts who arrive at hospitals, clinics, prisons, and reformatories, but at least publication of sampling and methodology in the scientific and professional journals makes available to others the opportunity to evaluate such studies. The enthusiasm of testimonials of apparent successes in Synanon (Winslow, 1961a, b) easily matches the fervor of disciples of the more organized, formal orientations to personality theory, and as with some of these other efforts, the Synanon graduates have experienced the therapy which they advocate. Finally, at the present time (Bier, 1962; Hoch & Zubin, 1958; Kolb, 1962) there does not seem to be any treatment of choice, although the rationale is agreed upon—treatment of the physical state of the individual (withdrawal and nutritional care) and therapy for the psychological adjustment pattern which seems to have produced the addiction.

What has come from these efforts? Several follow-up studies provide some data, but the inconclusive and indeterminate character of these warn against the usual, too easy generalizations offered on every side by governmental agencies, workers in the field of addiction, and addicts themselves. A recent report (J. A. Clark, 1962) reviews the subsequent history of 120 addicts treated between 1949 and 1960 at Crichton Royal Hospital in Britain. As noted previously, sampling variations limit generalizations, and in the Clark study more than half (65 out of 120) of the sample belonged to either the medical or the nursing profession. Of these 65, 50 were followed with sufficient data to warrant reporting. The data frequently came from hospitals to which the addicts had been admitted after discharge from Crichton Royal. The sample characteristics were as follows: 34 males and 16 females, ages 24 to 64, mean drug use about four years, mean hospital stay three months, and median follow-up period over five years. Unlike the 2 to 4 per cent of "normal" adjustment found among addicts, Clark reports that in 60 per cent of the 50 patients followed, "no previous evidence of psychological disorder could be determined." Only one-quarter (*N* 13) of the total were evaluated as sociopaths prior to addiction, and half this number (*N* 7) had evidence of other psychiatric illness, frequencies very different from those found in studies in which patients from the medical and nursing professions were not so frequently represented. In any event, Clark reports that of the 50 patients, 14 "had successfully overcome their addiction."

Pescor's much older study (and again it is important to keep in mind differences in sampling and criteria among various studies) was with addicts discharged from Lexington. In a two-year follow-up period for over one thousand addicts (Pescor, 1943a), about one-third had "recovered," an equal number had relapsed, and nearly the same number could not be traced. In view of the cautions cited previously, generalizations are indeed not very reliable.

The review just concluded suggests the personal and social problems of the addict, hypotheses regarding the etiological formulation and the dynamics of this mode of behavioral adjustment, the seemingly inadequate treatment methods generally available, and the difficulties in generalizing about individuals who are addicted to drug usage due to the sampling biases and the lack of reliable follow-up data.

ALCOHOLISM

The APA's *Diagnostic and Statistical Manual: Mental Disorders* (1960) includes in the category of alcoholism "cases in which there is well established addiction to alcohol without recognizable underlying disorder." This discrimination of the addiction from an underlying disorder seldom is made, however, and many investigators insist that alcoholism is a symptom complex and not a disease, not unlike the drug addictions. As in other addictions, personality and behavior pattern typologies frequently have been suggested as aids to understanding alcoholism and the alcoholic. The types are many, varying from writer to writer and along several dimensions. Other complexities in the picture of the alcoholic addict are the differential sex roles and responses and cultural and subcultural variations. Because of these variations and its recognition of them, and because of its relatively international acceptance, the World Health Organization's description (1952) seems to serve better than the APA's:

> Alcoholics are those excessive drinkers whose dependence upon alcohol has attained such a degree that it shows a noticeable mental disturbance or an interference with their bodily and mental health, their interpersonal relations, and their smooth social and economic functioning, or who show the prodromal signs of such developments.

Although alcoholism is not a new personal and social problem and has been reported in many cultures for centuries, some authorities date the systematic and scientific study of alcoholism as recently as the past quarter-century, specifying the beginning in 1935, with the "Yale Plan on Alcoholism" (Bier, 1962) and the start of the *Quarterly Journal of Studies on Alcohol*. At this time, the Laboratory of Applied Physiology at Yale turned its attention to the effects of alcohol on the human body. It is of interest that 1935 is also the year that the social and psychological focus for alcoholics, Alcoholics Anonymous (AA), was founded by two alcoholics. Much has been written about this organization, and even more has been said; yet it has not been systematically evaluated in terms of either selection (both self-selection and selection by the group after the initial contacts) or follow-up.

Although the "true" number of drug addictions also is in question, the prevalence of alcoholism is even more difficult to ascertain. The far greater number of alcoholics is suggested by the easy availability and lower costs of alcohol; the multitude of scientific and popular journal magazines and of newspaper articles; and the many organizations involved, e.g., police and traffic, scientific and professional, to a much greater degree than is true for drug addiction, even with the recent and current increased attention to the drug addictions. The National Council for Alcoholism reported for the United States an estimate of five million alcoholics and an additional three million "excessive drinkers" (Boyle, 1962). The council also listed the United States as first among nations in its alcoholic problem (4,400 per 100,000 population), ahead of France (3,000 per 100,000), and California as the state with the greatest numbers, ahead of New York's sixth place. The problem of reliability is reflected in comparison of these estimates with other reports; e.g., the Office of the Commission on Alcohol estimated in 1958 that New York was in fourth place and that France was in first place. Reports of the sex ratio of men to women alcoholics include Scandinavia's 23:1, the United States' 6:1, and the 2:1 ratio of the British Isles (Gordon, 1956). One is reminded that social, psychological, and cultural variables obscure such statistics and the reliability of the reporting which constitutes the data. This caution also must apply to the NCA's estimate that 30 per cent of "skid-row" habitués are alcoholics (the layman is convinced that this figure is too low!) and that this 30 per cent constitutes three per cent of the nation's total alcoholic population (Boyle, 1962).

The varieties of classifications of alcoholism are reflected in the following series. Kennedy (1962) finds useful for his understanding the discriminations among the occasional, social, weekend, spree, and plateau classes of drinkers. The latter he defines as the skid-row type, who is constantly "high" or "tight" but not drunk. Boyle (1962) suggests a three-way sort—social, excessive, and addictive or pathological. Campbell (1962) finds the essential, primary, or chronic alcoholic as one type and the "habitual inebriate" as a second type, similar to the reactive class of Knight (1937; Rudie & McCaughran, 1961). Alexander (1956) prefers to view the psychodynamics of alcoholism as an escape mechanism or a second group as orally regressed, and Jellinek (1960) reports that "tissue adaptation" must be considered, as in addictions to drugs. The psychologically adaptive function of alcohol is contrasted with its nonadaptive consequences (Gerard, Saenger, & Wile, 1962), and its potency as a "universal medicament" includes effects on anxiety, depression, loneliness, hostility, and the gamut of emotions and their expressions. Even the other universal medication, aspirin, cannot boast such accomplishment! As Chotlos and Deiter phrase the situation (1959): "The alcoholic may be regarded as a self-medicated anxiety state for whom inebriation is an unhappy coincidence of tension reduction." Society and the individual, however, view "problem drinking" in terms of its disadvantageous consequences, i.e., personal and social disorganization in family, work, and other interactions. Further, attitudes of even professional workers, with respect to prognosis and other variables in alcoholism, adversely affect possible changes in the alcoholic's behavior (Hayman, 1956).

Addiction to drugs often has been associated with cultural differences, as in the stereotype of the Chinese opium addict and the Negro heroin addict, but these variations are nowhere as startling as those among alcoholics of various national origins in the United States. The disproportion in large numbers of Irish and Scandinavians and low numbers of Italians and Jews in this country (Lolli, Serianni, Golder, Luzzatto-Fezig, 1958; Snyder, 1958; Snyder, 1959) who are alcoholic has been studied and interpreted in terms of specific and general personal and social learning and dynamics. Thus psychic tensions and stresses differentially affect individuals within a culture or subculture, and their responses are perceived and reacted to as a function of the social norms of their specific social group. For example, Snyder (1959) summarizes the situation with respect to the Jewish subculture in the United States. He reports that there is much drinking of all types of alcoholic beverages among this group but an extremely low rate of alcoholism, and he interprets this phenomenon against the background of the Jewish "cultural tradition [which] locates the act of drinking squarely in the network of sacred ideas, sentiments and activities . . . primarily of an expressive, communicative and religiously symbolic character." Snyder evaluates drinking in the Irish culture and perceives this behavior to be dissociated from the network of religious ideas, sentiment, and activities and not a part of the family social routine. With the waves of immigration of large numbers of nationals into the United States no longer in the pattern of the generations from the 1850s to the 1920s, and with the acculturation of succeeding generations, there also has developed a blending which has reduced these national differences so that social-class variations rather than national origin now operate within the framework of personal dynamics and social group relations. Lemert (1956) has written a provocative review of studies of alcoholism and the sociocultural situation, summarizing the difficulties in simple explanations of alcoholism among such varied cultures as those of the Jews, Irish, Mexicans, American Indians, Aleuts, Japanese, Chinese, and French.

Personal and social norms also function in the peculiarly linked relations between alcoholism and sex, where the woman alcoholic in many ways differs from her male counterpart, more so than appears to be the case in many other psychological disorders and symptoms. Hirsh (1962) presents six dimensions along which women alcoholics appear to differ from men:

> First, from the onset of moderate social drinking it usually takes far less time for a woman to become an alcoholic. Second, although they may not consume as much as men, they tend to become more intoxicated, more frequently, more quickly and, in the final stages, they become sicker alcoholics. Third, their psycho-sexual life appears to be

more completely involved in their alcoholism. Fourth, they show more "acting out" and impulsive "living out" of underlying personality and instinctual problems when intoxicated than men do. (Few women alcoholics behave much the same drunk as when they are sober, as is the case with many men alcoholics. Their intoxicated behavior is not only different and intrapsychically more intense but much more devastating in effect.) Fifth, they not only make more suicidal attempts but actually more women alcoholics suicide successfully. Sixth, if their alcoholism is checked, they more frequently develop other serious psychopathological states of symptoms, so that they remain chronically ill.

The etiology of alcoholism has been studied in many ways and yet remains confusing. The definition of the condition has somewhat more consensus, though linked to etiological hypotheses—loss of control of drinking; disorganization in one or more spheres of physiological, psychological, familial, and other social interactions and in economic functioning; and dependence upon the universality of the panacea which alcohol seems to offer. This background of definition and presumed etiology offers so little for preventive and therapeutic approaches that empirical methodology generally has been the rule. Thus, withdrawal, abstinence, or "drying out" drugs and psychotherapy have represented attempts at control, with conditionability of alcoholics a subject of importance in a number of studies (e.g., Vogel, 1960). The *Quarterly Journal of Studies on Alcohol* and journals of scientific and professional associations in psychiatry, other medical specialties, sociology, social work, and psychology are replete with reports on innumerable efforts at intervention. Again, the follow-up of patients who have participated in controlled studies may provide the only valid criterion for the effectiveness of various methods. Here, too, sampling biases and incomplete follow-up designs have frustrated efforts to evaluate adequately methods of intervention.

Various state commissions, e.g., those of California, Connecticut, Massachusetts, and New York, have reported follow-up studies. Gerard et al. (1962) followed 50 patients known to the Connecticut Commission on Alcoholism who appeared to have been abstinent for at least a year prior to the follow-up interview. Typically, "only 50 follow-up records had sufficient qualitative data to permit the quantitative analysis. . . ." This small and selected sample was divided among four subgroups—overtly disturbed (54 per cent), "inconspicuously inadequate personalities" (10 per cent), "AA success" (12 per cent), and "independent success" (10 per cent). Half of the 50 patients initiated their abstinence long after their last contact with the commission, and only 17 began abstinence during or shortly after treatment, though the investigators curiously report that "abstinence was rarely initiated or sustained in such a context!" (". . . through an interpersonal interaction in a treatment setting"). Gerard et al. also support the generalization about skid-row patients, and in their report only 2 of 41 such patients were abstinent at follow-up.

In the search for a definition of the alcoholic personality, many psychological studies have employed a wide range of techniques. Reviews of these research efforts have been published by Chotlos and Deiter (1959); Hampton (1951a); Sutherland, Schroeder, and Tordella (1950); and Syme (1957). The investigatory techniques have included laboratory studies (Jellinek & McFarland, 1940), intelligence test performance (Plumeau, Machover, & Puzzo, 1960), questionnaire and personality measures (Brown, 1950; Button, 1956b; Hewitt, 1943; Hampton, 1951a, b; Hampton, 1953; Manson, 1948), and projective techniques (Bühler & Lefever, 1947; Button, 1956a). Studies with lower animals (e.g., Conger, 1951; Masserman & Yum, 1946) will not be reviewed here because of the clinical orientation of this text, although these have provided useful tests of hypotheses about alcoholic addiction.

The pathological sign approach common to analyses of Rorschach response data has not shown validity, although the use of the Rorschach method in understanding individual dynamics has been argued (Button, 1956a, b; Chotlos & Deiter, 1959). The reports of MMPI studies generally characterize the alcoholic profile with a high Pd (psychopathic deviate) scale, and Manson (1948) and Hampton (1951a, b; 1953) have reported successes in differentiating alcoholics from nonalcoholics through their responses to inventories developed around the response characteristic of a high Pd score. As in other personality-pattern studies, no specific alcoholic personality adjustment pattern has been identified, and the only safe generalizations may be about the prevalence of psychoneurotic, psychopathic, and character disorder adjustments among alcoholics. This generalization unfortunately serves little use because of its inability to provide any greater focus; yet it does indicate the need to examine individual adjustments and the specifics of the behaviors by which various individuals come to react to stresses by alcoholism, as others turn to the addictions to drugs or to other adjustments.

The desire for easily administered, scored, and interpreted scales for discriminating various behaviors, reflected in such attempts as reported above, has resulted in more than two hundred scales which have been developed (Dahlstrom & Welsh, 1960) from the MMPI. Of this number, three representing alcoholism scales derived by contrasting responses of diagnosed male alcoholics with responses of nonalcoholics are evaluated by MacAndrew and Geertsma (1963). It is of more than passing significance that most studies have been of the male alcoholic, not of the female, although the numbers of alcoholics among both sexes constitute serious personal and social problems. Here again, the sex differences in society are much more than biological. The MacAndrew-Geertsma study reviewed the work and MMPI-derived scales of Holmes (cf. Button, 1956b), Hampton (1953), and Hoyt and Sedlacek (1958), and they presented their data on MMPI responses of 300 male alcoholic outpatients and 300 nonalcoholic male psychiatric patients. Reanalysis of the data reported by the authors of the first three scales suggested that these scales primarily were measures of general adjustment and maladjustment.

Further, an analysis of the Holmes, Hampton, and Hoyt and Sedlacek scales showed a total of 191 different items among the three scales. Among these 191 items, there were but seven items common to the three scales, though overlap among the scales occurred variously.

> The manifest content of these seven items indicated that, relative to normals, people diagnosed as alcoholics describe their alcohol intake as excessive rather than moderate, they tend to accept the responsibility for their past failures and transgressions, and while less consistent churchgoers, they are more likely to believe in miracles.

The numbers of items specific to the scales are shown in Table 2.

The MacAndrew-Geertsma analyses should themselves be evaluated in terms of sampling variations among both experimental and control subjects of the four sets of studies. These variations are examined, and rationales for the comparisons are suggested by the authors.

Other methods for discriminating responses of alcoholics from those of nonalcoholics are represented in such studies as those of Meer and Amon (1963) and Corotto (1963) and in the screening device developed by members of the Division of Alcoholic Rehabilitation in California's Department of Public Health (1961a). In the first of these studies, 145 males jailed for alcoholism, 67 others hospitalized for alcoholism at a state mental hospital, and 77 normal controls were evaluated from their responses to Meer's Photos Preference Test. The test stimuli were 100 facial photographs of individuals of both sexes and in the 18-to-80-year-age range. Factor analyses of the age-sex preference responses produced four factors and two patterns which differentiated (p .05) the alcoholics and normals but which did not discriminate between the two samples of alcoholics. The authors interpreted the response variations "in terms of the alcoholic's failure to make an adequate masculine identification."

TABLE 2

Scale	*Total N items*	*N items specific to scale*
Hampton	125	92
Holmes	59	22
Hoyt and Sedlacek	68	25
MacAndrew and Geertsma	24	14

Corotto utilized Gough's *California Psychological Inventory* (1957) to study two groups of hospitalized alcoholic patients, a group who volunteered to remain in the hospital for continued treatment (*N* 61) and a second group which did not volunteer to remain beyond the initial thirty-day treatment period (*N* 114). On 7 of the 18 CPI scales, there were significant differences between the two samples, with the volunteer alcoholic patients scoring lower on the Well-being, Socialization, Self-control, Tolerance, Good Impression, Achievement via Conformance, and Psychological-mindedness scales. Generalizations from sampling variations in this study are hazardous since all subjects were state hospital admissions (101 voluntary and 74 involuntary commitments), the end product of a complex selection system and, of a total of 245 admissions, only 175 were able to complete both the volunteer form and the CPI, an attrition of more than 28 per cent, attesting to still other and complex selection variables.

As is the case in many states, California has developed a program of research, treatment, and rehabilitation in alcoholism. The first alcoholism study contract between the State Department of Public Health and the Alcoholic Rehabilitation Commission was designed to follow up treated alcoholics and to investigate variables in causation or epidemiology of alcoholism, later named the Etiology Study. In a series of studies beginning in 1955 (*Alcoholism and California*), community concepts and definitions were gathered from interviews with community leaders, and a screening device was developed for "earlier detection and identification of individuals at risk of alcoholism." The interview data yielded opinions which emphasized frontier, occupational, ethnic, familial, and religious traditions; the number of "rootless" persons; the climate; and the availability of the wine industry as a beverage source. Persons at risk of alcoholism were those under stress from one or more of these personal, social, and other environmental variables.

The screening test derived from the conceptual schema developed from the interview material consisted of 74 items which could be answered, primarily by checking one of several responses, within a ten-minute period. The dimensions of the screening device were identifying and descriptive data, psychosomatic complaints, use of alcoholic beverages, problem situations, reactions to stress, and trait characteristics. Item analyses and scoring methods, whether additive or by another rationale and system, await further trials. In the initial study, 202 persons were selected for interview, of whom 27 refused to participate. As frequently noted previously, future studies will depend upon the sampling bias, i.e., the ways in which respondents and nonrespondents differ on dimensions other than response compliance. In the pilot study, the 175 respondents were categorized, by trait and problem situation scores, into four groups, as shown in Table 3.

The follow-up studies are divided into retrospective and prospective studies, and to date only a report on comparative mortality of treated alcoholics (California Department of Public Health, Division of Alcoholic Rehabilitation, 1961c) is available, summarizing two to five years of follow-up of the populations of both the retrospective and the prospective studies since 1955, totaling 1,692 individuals. For this population, the five-year survival rate of alcoholics was 8 per cent less than that of the general population. Leading causes of death were by violence (24 per cent), heart disease (23 per cent), and cirrhosis of the liver (14 per cent). There were no differences between survivors and those who died, with respect to sex, education, religion, marital status, or occupation. The latter group was older and in poorer health at time of interview and had a higher percentage of white persons.

TABLE 3

Category	*N*	*N problem situations*	*N inadequacy traits*
I	70	Two or more	Three or more
II	27	Two or more	Two or less
III	36	One or less	Three or more
IV	42	Two or less	Two or less

In another effort, the "California Drinking Practices Study" of Cisin, Fink, and Knupfer (1963), the drinking practices of the *general* population were studied, and the 1,600 respondents were categorized as drinkers or abstainers—light, moderate, or heavy drinkers if in the former group, and classified also by the importance of alcohol to the individual. The heavy drinkers were further sorted out by signs of "pathological drinking": the heavy drinkers but without serious involvement in their drinking, a second group with greater involvement but no signs of pathological drinking, and a group of pathological drinkers. The second group was defined as having "high risk" of becoming alcoholic. Following on the study of drinking practices is the second study designed to follow heavy drinkers and to attempt to identify shifts toward problem drinking (Knupfer, 1963).

Study goals similar to those in the California studies have produced various methodological approaches in other states, and a final example is that of the Iowa studies (Mulford & Miller, 1960; Mulford & Miller, 1961). These investigators surveyed the attitudes and drinking practices of nearly twelve hundred respondents chosen to represent the adult Iowan population. One of the results of the study is the Iowa Scale of Preoccupation with Alcohol, a 12-item cumulative scale. Among the 1,185 respondents, 35 with extremely deviant drinking behavior and 671 others who used alcoholic beverages were identified. The authors define as dependent variables drinking versus abstaining, heavy drinking, and alcoholic drinking, and they offer the concept of "definitions of alcohol" as a

> social psychological variable, intervening between the background sociocultural factors and the dependent measures of drinking behavior. . . . The individual, through interaction with others, has learned to think about, or to define, alcohol in terms of its functions. . . . Heavy drinkers tend to define alcohol for personal effects. . . . Other drinkers are inclined to define alcohol, not in these personal terms but, rather, in terms of social effects. . . .

As in addictions to drugs, there are methodological and substantive concerns in the area of sustained research with the diagnosis, treatment, and outcome of alcoholism. These point to the personal and social, and to the lay as well as the professional and scientific, involvement necessary for a better understanding of this class of response to stress in the human organism.

SEXUAL DEVIATIONS

Deviant sexuality may occur as a symptom in many types of disorders, including the psychoses and neuroses. However, the formal diagnosis of sexual deviation is reserved for those sexually deviant behaviors which are not symptomatic of more extensive syndromes, and the type of pathologic behavior is specified, such as homosexuality, transvestism, pedophilia, fetishism, and sexual sadism, the latter including rape, sexual assault, and mutilation.

Since the beginning of recorded history, there have been accounts of sexual deviations, with social acceptance of the behaviors varying with both the specific cultures and the specific times in the development of the cultures, in both the Occident and the Orient. Thus, value judgments characteristically have been placed upon sexual behavior, but whether or not specific behaviors have been classed as deviant has been a function of the culture (Ford & Beach, 1951; Hooker, 1956; Hooker, 1957; Hooker, 1958). Perhaps because of the greater numbers involved, homosexuality has drawn more attention in both subjective and systematic studies of sexual deviation. As would be expected from the earlier sections of this chapter, the issue of the homosexual as a personality type often has been the focus of controversy.

In 1870, less than a century ago, Westphal (H. Ellis, 1944) suggested that homosexuality was neither vice nor insanity and that it was not an acquired but a congenital condition. These observations reflect the picture of the latter nineteenth century, in the Victorian era, but it is not more clear from more recent reports just what the homosexual individual is. For example, Myerson and Neustadt (1942) described the homosexual as a psychopathic personality who also may be either neurotic or psychotic. The constitutional nature of homosexuality, rather than homosexuality on the basis of learned, acquired behavior, has been argued by many investigators since Westphal (Diefendorf, 1923; Greenspan & Campbell, 1944). Perhaps one of the most strongly stated positions is that of Greenspan and Campbell (1944):

> The homosexual . . . is an individual endowed with sex desires directed wholly or in part toward members of the same sex. . . . The manifestations . . . may occur early, via arrested psychosexual development, or late, through . . . regression, and its origin is always constitutional or biological, never environmental or acquired . . . a congenital anomaly rather than a disease.

Greenspan and Campbell (1944), Henry and Galbraith (1934), Henderson and Gillespie (1940), and others argue the biological position from the reported predominance of physical (including hormonal) as well as psychological characteristics among homosexuals which differentiate them from heterosexual individuals. The genetic aspects are emphasized by Kallman (1952). Another school of thought emphasizes the psychological, personal, and social variables which may differentiate the homosexual from the heterosexual more reliably and validly than is possible with a biological theory as the basis for categorization. Thus the studies of Westwood (1960); Allen (1962); Kinsey (1941); Kinsey, Pomeroy, and Martin (1951; 1953); Hooker (1956; 1957; 1958); and others do not support the biological theory approach, finding no systematic data on significant physical or endocrinological differences between homosexuals and heterosexuals. Westwood's study of 100 male homosexuals and their 127 contacts illusrates, for example, the diversity of ages, occupations, family and home structure, conflict over the sexual patterns of behavior, treatment sought and received, and professional opinions. It is revealing that the 1955 memorandum of the British Medical Association, in part dealing with homosexuality (Westwood, 1960), included observations that moral values and even religious conversion were recommended by physicians as cures for homosexuality, while at the same time the Anglican clerics wrote that clinicians generally held the condition to be irreversible and therefore clerics should not hold out the hope of cures through religious experiences!

Psychological theories have ranged from essentially orthodox psychoanalytic interpretations to social learning (Hooker, 1956; Hooker, 1957; Hooker, 1958). In the former group are references to unconscious identifications with the parent (West, 1959), fixations, equating of the breast with the penis or the buttocks or both, and narcissism to an extreme degree, with the sexual practices and the clothes worn (e.g., tight trousers) assumed to offer support of these interpretations (Allen, 1962). Other suggestions have to do with classifications of homosexuals, an exercise which often arouses discussion about bisexuality, a description vigorously rejected by Bergler (1948; 1951; 1959)—"only . . . a flattering description of the homosexual who is at times capable of mechanical heterosexual activity" —and characterized by Bailey (1955) as homosexual acts performed by heterosexual individuals.

Kinsey (1941) developed a six-point rating scale to describe ranges of sexual behavior, from exclusively homosexual to exclusively heterosexual; Hirschfeld (1937) offered a three-way classification; Allen (1962) proposes an inclusive 12-category schema; and most writers relate both description and presumed etiology to therapeutic programs and expected outcomes. The generally held clinical opinion is that homosexuality does not respond to psychotherapeutic efforts, and Allen (1962) remarks: "In spite of the great social importance of the sexually abnormal there is no clinic devoted solely to the treatment of this illness anywhere in the world!" Hooker (1956; 1957; 1958) has studied systematically the relation between individual personality dynamics and group dynamics in determining patterns of behavior of the overt male homosexual, and her studies indicate several possible reasons for the lack of success in modifying homosexual behavior. The findings relate to personal and social motives, adjustments, identifications, and reward systems of the homosexual, his society, and the larger community in which the homosexual society is an isolated group with its own identification and communication patterns.

Most investigators report that the homosexual world is not adequately sampled in studies of deviant sexual behavior and that many homosexuals live in the general community in apparent "normal" adjustment. Several studies have attempted to identify such individuals, but the usual sampling has consisted of psychiatric patients or apprehended and/or convicted sex offenders, the latter often not homosexuals, though these not uncommonly are swept up in the net of law enforcement following a sexual crime (Yamahiro & Griffith,

1960). Marsh, Hilliard, and Liechti (1955) developed an MMPI scale of 100 items, and Wheeler earlier (1949) had reported Rorschach content indices as methods for identifying sex deviants, not specifically homosexuals. The study of Yamahiro and Griffith (1960) suggested that such studies primarily identify the deviant characteristic of the homosexual or other sexual deviate, just as the neurotic or psychotic may also be identified as deviant, but that there is not a specific discrimination of the disorder.

Therapeutic programs for homosexuals have been reported on numerous occasions (Allen, 1962; Bergler, 1959; A. Ellis, 1956; Monroe & Enelow, 1960; Ross & Mendelsohn, 1958), but no generalization appears in the samples studied, the therapeutic methods, or the dynamics of the subjects, unless one reads only the report of a single author and disregards the experiences published by other investigators.

Other sexually deviant behaviors besides homosexuality are represented in fetishism, transvestism, the seeking of sex transformation, exhibitionism, and the range of other behaviors constituting sex offenses (Hirschberg, 1961), i.e., molestation, rape, incest, etc. As in homosexuality, biological theories are suggested as well as psychological interpretations. An example is an analysis of fetishism and transvestism by Epstein (1960; 1961), in which he attempts to relate the psychopathology to brain mechanism disorders in temporal lobe function, involving such psychological mechanisms as identification with the mother; sexual fears and aggressive impulses; and obsessive-compulsive and, occasionally, passive dependent behaviors. An excellent review of the history of transvestism is the survey of Lukianowicz (1959).

Some writers, e.g., Gutheil (1954), see various expressions of disturbed sexuality as related. Gutheil theorizes that transvestism results from the occurrence of several psychopathologic states in the individual—latent or manifest homosexuality with an unresolved castration complex, sadomasochism, narcissism, scoptophilia, exhibitionism, and fetishism.

Grant (1960) also reports transvestism and fetishism as related, and Yalom (1960) reports case studies of voyeurists who committed arson and burglaries to seek gratifications similar to those derived from peeping. The use of case studies without systematic sampling does not, however, promise much. Thus it is not surprising that writers can and do select one or more individuals whose behavior may be interpreted as "evidence" for a theoretical assumption. Reports of therapeutic programs for transvestites have not differed from those of such programs for other disorders, but it may be of interest to note the introduction of aversive conditioning in one instance (Lavin, Thorpe, Barker, Blakemore, & Conway, 1961), where apomorphine effects in conjunction with the presentation of slides of the patient as transvestite resulted in behavioral change at least for a six-month follow-up period.

The seeking of sex transformation presents another complex phenomenon in the study of behavior. Two major groups appear in studies of this class of behavior—individuals who show no signs of true or pseudohermaphroditism (Worden & Marsh, 1955) and those who show such signs, as in the intersexed patients studied by Stoller, Garfinkel, and Rosen (1960; 1962) and Stoller and Rosen (1959). The former group appears to be characterized by men who frequently state that "they are really women with male bodies. . . . The idea of being female represents for all of them the solution to the problem of maintaining a comfortable level of self-esteem." Worden and Marsh conclude that psychological, physiological, endocrine, or chromosomal factors cannot singly account for the condition and that present knowledge is insufficient to delineate the relative contributions of these several classes of variables.

The second group of individuals who seek sex transformation differ significantly from the former subjects in their external appearance, primary and secondary sexual characteristics, and endocrinologic state. Typically, these individuals are reared as one sex into or through adolescence and later seek transformation into the sex whose anatomy and endocrinology now are prominent. The ambiguous and contradictory nature of sexual characteristics (Stoller et al., 1960) in intersexed patients, the complex mixture of their somatic and psychological states, and their sex identifications at various ages all provide variations which differentiate these individuals from those traditionally regarded as sex deviants. Whether primary identification as male or female or predominant somatic state should determine transformation has been debated by investigators, and the significance of the psychology of identification is reflected in such other studies as those of Money, Hampson, and Hampson (1955; 1957).

Finally, studies of the broad spectrum of sex offenders and "sex psychopaths" seldom are evaluated in an appropriate perspective. The significant discriminants marking these individuals are two, their apprehension and their conviction. The intricate and complex variables—personal, social, and situational—which function in the selection of these individuals for public attention (i.e., police, courts, and detention), both temporary and prolonged, are often reported upon but too little understood. The enormous amount of statistical data at Federal, state, and local levels is impressive; yet these data deal only with those individuals who are apprehended or with those victims who report the incidents. Even so, the data represent the best estimate available to the investigator.

An example of the relation of data on convicted sex offenders to popularly held assumptions about them appears in Frisbie's study (1959) of more than eleven hundred discharged sex offenders who had psychiatric treatment and a statement to the court that they had improved and no longer were considered a menace to society (recidivism for this institution in California has varied from 7 to 9 per cent; in New Jersey, it is reported as even lower, second only to homicide). Frisbie reviews the "assumptions that molesters of female children are old men more or less in their dotage, and that incestuous relationships between fathers and daughters seldom occur and also that the molester of male children is . . . a middle-aged tramp or hobo who entices little boys into culverts or vacant buildings. . . ." The data show that 81 per cent of the offenses involved physical contact, and the remainder of offenses primarily were indecent exposure, voyeurism, or transvestism; 60 per cent of the offenders were under 40 years of age, and the median age for the total sample of 1,114 was 37 years; 14 per cent of the offenders had had incestuous relationships with a daughter or stepdaughter; and more girls than boys (2½ times as many) were victims of molesters, and girls were younger (median age under 9 years) than the male victims (median age 12 years).

Finally, the above reference to popular perceptions of sexual offenders suggests an examination of professional perceptions as well. Berman and Freedman (1961) conducted such an investigation of psychiatric descriptions of sex offenders and other offenders (convicted for aggressive and acquisitive acts) in a state prison. Clinical impressions of the offenders were rated by a professional staff as positive, neutral, or negative. The ratings were distributed as shown in Table 4 (percentage of individuals rated).

To further evaluate perceptions of the offenders by trained professional workers (eight psychiatrists in this second part of the study), 200 photographs equally divided between the two groups of offenders were shown the panel, who were asked to rate the photos as handsome, homely, or "atypical." When the offense was known to the raters, a significantly larger percentage of the sex offenders were rated as homely or atypical, indicating that this group of offenders were judged as different in appearance from other offenders and that the judges tended to react negatively to the former.

Because of the history of the taboo nature of discussion of sexual behavior, perceptions of the lay as well as the professional and scientific public are rooted deeply in the value orientations of our culture. The history of past cultures and of other contemporary cultures emphasizes the relative nature of such value systems. The recency of the Victorian era of civilization in the Western world and the continuing influence of social mores and customs relative to sexual behavior have produced the phenomenon of only recent systematic attention to sexually deviant behavior. Social, psychological, psychoanalytic, sociological, and other directions of study have been designed to evaluate and to discriminate these behav-

TABLE 4

	Positive	*Neutral*	*Negative*
Sex offenders	30	18	52
Other offenders	67	14	19

iors. Cultural taboos persist and reduce the efficiency of such research efforts and the possibility of their contributing to an understanding of sexually normal as well as sexually deviant behaviors. The study of the pathological or deviant adjustment may contribute also to knowledge about normally adjustive sexual responses. Both areas of knowledge are significant in the general understanding of human behavior.

REFERENCES

Albert, R. S., Brigante, T. R., & Chase, M. The psychopathic personality: a content analysis of the concept. *J. gen. Psychiat.*, 1959, **60**, 17–28.

Alexander, F. Views on the etiology of alcoholism: the psychodynamic view. In H. D. Kruse (Ed.), *Alcohol as a medical problem.* New York: Hoeber-Harper, 1956.

Allen, C. *A textbook of psychosexual disorders.* London: Oxford Univer. Press, 1962.

American Psychiatric Association, Committee on Nomenclature and Statistics. *Diagnostic and statistical manual: mental disorders.* (13th ed.) Washington, D.C.: Author, 1960.

American Psychiatric Association, Committee on Public Information. *A psychiatric glossary: the meaning of words most frequently used in psychiatry.* Washington, D.C.: Author, 1957.

Armitage, G. H., & Sim, M. Barbiturate addiction and sensitivity. *Brit. J. med. Psychol.*, 1960, **33**, 144–149.

Ausubel, D. P. An evaluation of recent adolescent drug addiction. *Ment. Hyg.*, 1952, **36**, 373–382.

Ausubel, D. P. Causes and types of narcotic addiction: a psychosocial view. *Psychiat. Quart.*, 1961, **35**, 523–531.

Bailey, D. S. *Homosexuality and the Western Christian tradition.* London: Longmans, 1955.

Bender, L. Anxiety in disturbed children. In P. Hoch & J. Zubin (Eds.), *Anxiety.* New York: Grune & Stratton, 1950.

Bergler, E. The myth of a new national disease. *Psychiat. Quart.*, 1948, **22**, 66–88.

Bergler, E. *Neurotic counterfeit sex.* New York: Grune & Stratton, 1951.

Bergler, E. *1000 homosexuals: conspiracy of silence or curing and deglamorizing homosexuals.* Paterson, N.J.: Pageant, 1959.

Berman, L. H., & Freedman, L. Z. Clinical perception of sexual deviates. *J. Psychol.*, 1961, **52**, 157–160.

Bier, W. C. (Ed.) *Problems in addiction: alcohol and drug addiction.* New York: Fordham Univer. Press, 1962.

Boyle, T. J. Social effects. *Ibid.*

Bromberg, N. Maternal influence in the development of moral masochism. *Amer. J. Orthopsychiat.*, 1955, **25**, 802–812.

Brown, M. A. Alcoholic profiles on the Minnesota Multiphasic. *J. clin. Psychol.*, 1950, **6**, 206–269.

Bühler, C., & Lefever, D. A. A Rorchach study on the psychological characteristics of alcoholics. *Quart. J. Stud. Alcohol*, 1947, **8**, 197–260.

Button, A. D. A Rorschach study of 67 alcoholics. *Quart. J. stud. Alcohol*, 1956, **17**, 35–52. (a)

Button, A. D. A study of alcoholics with the MMPI. *Quart. J. Stud. Alcohol*, 1956, **17**, 263–281. (*b*)

California Department of Public Health, Division of Alcoholic Rehabilitation. The development of a screening device for risk populations. *Alcoholism & California*, 1961, No. 7. (a)

California Department of Public Health, Division of Alcoholic Rehabilitation. Follow-up studies of treated alcoholics: description of studies. *Alcoholism & California*, 1961, No. 5. (b)

California Department of Public Health, Division of Alcoholic Rehabilitation. Follow-up studies of treated alcoholics: mortality. *Alcoholism & California*, 1961, No. 6. (c)

California Department of Public Health, Division of Alcoholic Rehabilitation. A study of community concepts and definitions. *Alcoholism & California*, 1961, No. 1, Part 1. (d)

California Department of Public Health, Division of Alcoholic Rehabilitation. Selected aspects of the prospective follow-up study: a preliminary review. *Alcoholism & California*, 1960, No. 2.

Campbell, R. J. The etiology and background. In W. C. Bier (Ed.), *Problems in addiction: alcohol and drug addiction.* New York: Fordham Univer. Press, 1962.

Chornyak, J. Diagnosis of the psychopathic delinquent. *Amer. J. Psychiat.*, 1941, **97**, 1326–1340.

Chotlos, J. W., & Deiter, J. B. Psychological considerations in the etiology of alcoholism. In D. J. Pittman (Ed.), *Alcoholism: an interdisciplinary approach.* Springfield, Ill.: Charles C Thomas, 1959.

Cisin, I., Fink, R., & Knupfer, G. California drinking practices study. *Calif. Alcohol Rev. Treatment Dig.*, 1963, **6**, 1–5.

Clark, J. A. The prognosis in drug addiction. *J. ment. Sci.*, 1962, **108**, 411–418.

Clark, J. H. Subtest variation on the Wechsler-Bellevue for two institutionalized behavior problem groups. *Amer. Psychologist,* 1949, **4**, 395. (Abstract)

Clark, J. H., & Moore, J. H. The relationship of Wechsler-Bellevue patterns to psychiatric diagnoses of Army and Air Force prisoners. *J. consult. Psychol.,* 1950, **14**, 493–495.

Cleckley, H. *The mask of sanity.* (2nd ed.) St. Louis: Mosby, 1950.

Conger, J. J. The effects of alcohol on conflict behavior in the albino rat. *Quart. J. Stud. Alcohol,* 1951, **12**, 1–29.

Corotto, L. V. Personality characteristics of patients who volunteer. *Quart. J. Stud. Alcohol,* 1963, **24**, 432–442.

Dahlstrom, W. G., & Welsh, G. S. *An MMPI handbook.* Minneapolis, Minn.: Univer. of Minnesota Press, 1960.

Darling, H. F., & Sanddal, J. W. A psychopathologic concept of psychopathic personality. *J. clin. exp. Psychopath.,* 1952, **13**, 175–180.

Davidson, G. M. The syndrome of oligothymia (psychopathy). *J. nerv. ment. Dis.,* 1956, **124**, 156–162.

Diefendorf, A. *Clinical psychiatry.* New York: Macmillan, 1923.

Ehrlich, S. K., & Keogh, R. P. The psychopath in a mental institution. *Arch. Neurol. Psychiat.,* 1956, **76**, 286–295.

Ellis, A. The effectiveness of psychotherapy with individuals who have severe homosexual problems. *J. consult. Psychol.,* 1956, **20**, 191–195.

Ellis, A. A homosexual treated with rational psychotherapy. *J. clin. Psychol.,* 1959, **15**, 338–343.

Ellis, H. *Psychology of sex.* (2nd. ed.) New York: Emerson, 1944.

Epstein, A. W. Fetishism: a study of its psychopathology with particular reference to a proposed disorder in brain mechanisms as an etiological factor. *J. nerv. ment. Dis.,* 1960, **130**, 107–119.

Epstein, A. W. Relationship of fetishism and transvestism to brain and particularly to temporal lobe dysfunction. *J. nerv. ment. Dis.,* 1961, **133**, 247–253.

Eysenck, H. J. *Dimensions of personality.* London: Routledge, 1947.

Eysenck, H. J. *The scientific study of personality.* London: Routledge, 1952.

Eysenck, H. J. The differentiation between normal and various neurotic groups on the Maudsley Personality Inventory. *Brit. J. Psychol.,* 1959, **50**, 176–177.

Felix, R. M. An appraisal of the personality types of the addict. *Amer. J. Psychiat.,* 1944, **100**, 462–467.

Field, J. G. The performance-verbal I.Q. discrepancy in a group of sociopaths. *J. clin. Psychol.,* 1960, **16**, 321–322.

Ford, C. S., & Beach, F. A. *Patterns of sexual behavior.* New York: Harper & Row, 1951.

Frisbie, L. V. Treated sex offenders and what they did. *Ment. Hyg.,* 1959, **43**, 262–267.

Frosch, J., & Wortis, B. S. A contribution to the nosology of the impulse disorders. *Amer. J. Psychiat.,* 1954, **111**, 132–138.

Gamso, R. R., & Mason, P. A hospital for adolescent drug addicts. *Psychiat. Quart. Suppl.,* 1958, 32, 99–109.

Gerard, D. L., Saenger, J., & Wile, R. The abstinent alcoholic. *Arch. gen. Psychiat.,* 1962, **6**, 83–95.

Gibbens, T. C. N., Pond, D. A., & Stafford-Clark, D. A follow-up study of criminal psychopaths. *J. ment. Sci.,* 1959, **105**, 108–115.

Glover, E. *The roots of crime.* New York: International Universities Press, 1960.

Gordon, J. E. The epidemiology of alcohol. In H. D. Kruse (Ed.), *Alcohol as a medical problem.* New York: Hoeber-Harper, 1956.

Gough, H. *California Psychological Inventory.* Palo Alto, Calif.: Consulting Psychologists Press, 1957.

Grant, V. W. The cross-dresser: a case study. *J. nerv. ment. Dis.,* 1960, **131**, 149–159.

Greenacre, P. General problems of acting out. *Psychoanal. Quart.,* 1950, **19**, 455–467.

Greenspan, H., & Campbell, J. D. The homosexual as a personality type. *Amer. J. Psychiat.,* 1944, **101**, 682–689.

Gurvitz, M. S. The Wechsler-Bellevue test and the diagnosis of psychopathic personality. *J. clin. Psychol.,* 1950, **6**, 397–401.

Gutheil, E. A. The psychological background of transsexualism and transvestism. In Transsexualism and transvestism: a symposium. *Amer. J. Psychother.,* 1954, 81, 231–239.

Hampton, P. J. A psychometric study of drinkers. *J. consult. Psychol.,* 1951, **15**, 501–594. (a)

Hampton, P. J. Representative studies of alcoholism and personality. I. Naturalistic studies. II. Clinical studies. III. Psychometric studies. *J. soc. Psychol.,* 1951, 34, 203–233. (b)

Hampton, P. J. The development of a personality questionnaire for drinkers. *Genet. Psychol. Monogr.*, 1953, **48**, 55–115.

Hathaway, S. R., & Meehl, P. E. *An atlas for the clinical use of the MMPI.* Minneapolis, Minn.: Univer. of Minnesota Press, 1951.

Hayman, M. Current attitudes to alcoholism of psychiatrists in Southern California. *Amer. J. Psychiat.*, 1956, **112**, 485–493.

Heineman, C. E. A forced-choice form of the Taylor anxiety scale. *J. consult. Psychol.*, 1953, **17**, 447–454.

Henderson, D. K. *Psychopathic states.* New York: Norton, 1939.

Henderson, D. K., & Gillespie, R. D. *A textbook of psychiatry for students and practitioners.* (5th ed.) London: Oxford Univer. Press, 1940.

Henry, G. W., & Galbraith, H. M. Constitutional factors in homosexuality. *Amer. J. Psychiat.*, 1934, **13**, 1249–1270.

Hewitt, C. C. A personality study of alcohol addiction. *Amer. J. Psychiat.*, 1943, **4**, 368–387.

Hill, D. The EEG in episodic psychotic and psychopathic behavior. *EEG clin. Neurophysiol.*, 1952, **4**, 419–442.

Hill, D., & Watterson, D. J. Electroencephalographic studies of psychopathic personalities. *J. Neurol. Psychiat.*, 1942, **5**, 47–65.

Hill, H. E., Haertgen, C. A., & Glaser, R. Personality characteristics of narcotics addicts as indicated by the MMPI. *J. gen. Psychol.*, 1960, **62**, 127–139.

Hirschberg, J. H. *Bibliography on data pertaining to sex offenders.* Ohio: Department of Mental Hygiene and Correction, 1961.

Hirschfeld, M. *Sexual anomalies and perversions.* London: Simpkin, Marshall, 1937.

Hirsh, J. Women and alcoholism. In W. C. Bier (Ed.), *Problems in addiction: alcohol and drug addiction.* New York: Fordham Univer. Press, 1962.

Hoch, P. H., & Zubin, J. (Eds.) *Problems of addiction and habituation.* New York: Grune & Stratton, 1958.

Hodge, R. S. The impulsive psychopath: a clinical and electrophysiological study. *J. ment. Sci.*, 1945, **91**, 472–476.

Hooker, E. A preliminary analysis of group behavior of homosexuals. *J. Psychol.*, 1956, **42**, 217–225.

Hooker, E. The adjustment of the male overt homosexual. *J. proj. Tech.*, 1957, **21**, 18–31.

Hooker, E. Male homosexuality in the Rorschach. *J. proj. Tech.*, 1958, **22**, 33–54.

Hoyt, D. P., & Sedlacek, G. M. Differentiating alcoholics from normals and abnormals with the MMPI. *J. clin. Psychol.*, 1958, **14**, 69–74.

Jellinek, E. M. *The disease concept of alcoholism.* New Haven, Conn.: Hillhouse, 1960.

Jellinek, E. M., & McFarland, R. A. Analysis of psychological experiments on the effects of alcohol. *Quart. J. Stud. Alcohol*, 1940, **1**, 272–371.

Jenkins, R. L. The psychopathic or antisocial personality. *J. nerv. ment. Dis.*, 1960, **131**, 318–334.

Kahn, E. *Psychopathic personalities.* New Haven, Conn.: Yale Univer. Press, 1931.

Kallman, F. J. Comparative twin study on the genetic aspects of male homosexuality. *J. nerv. ment. Dis.*, 1952, **115**, 283–298.

Karpman, B. Psychosis with psychopathic personality: an untenable diagnosis. *Psychiat. Quart.*, 1951, **25**, 618–640.

Karpman, B. Contrasting psychodynamics in two types of symptomatic psychopathy. *Arch. crim. Psychodynam.*, 1959, **3**, 69–152.

Keller, M., & Efron, V. The prevalence of alcoholism. *Quart. J. Stud. Alcohol*, 1955, **16**, 619–644.

Kennard, M. A. The electroencephalogram and disorders of behavior. *J. nerv. ment. Dis.*, 1956, **124**, 103–123.

Kennedy, R. J. H. The forms of drinking. In W. C. Bier (Ed.), *Problems in addiction: alcohol and drug addiction.* New York: Fordham Univer. Press, 1962.

Kinsey, A. C. Homosexuality: criteria for a hormonal explanation of the homosexual. *J. clin. Endocrinol.*, 1941, **5**, 424–428.

Kinsey, A. C., Pomeroy, W. B., & Martin, C. W. *Sexual behavior in the human male.* Philadelphia: Saunders, 1951.

Kinsey, A. C., Pomeroy, W. B., & Martin, C. W. *Sexual behavior in the human female.* Philadelphia: Saunders, 1953.

Knight, R. P. The psychodynamics of chronic alcoholism. *J. nerv. ment. Dis.*, 1937, **86**, 538–548.

Knott, J. R., & Gottlieb, J. S. The electroencephalogram in psychopathic personality. *Psychosom. Med.*, 1943, **5**, 139–142.

Knupfer, G. A longitudinal study of changes in drinking practices. *Calif. Alcohol Rev. Treatment Dig.*, 1963, **6**, 1–5.

Koch, J. L. A. *Die Psychopathischen Mindervertigskeiten.* Ravensburg: Maier, 1891.

Kolb, L. Types and characteristics of drug addicts. *Ment. Hyg.*, 1925, **9**, 300–313.

Kolb, L. *Drug addiction.* Springfield, Ill.: Charles C Thomas, 1962.

Kolb, L., & Ossenfort, W. F. The treatment of drug addicts at the Lexington hospital. *South. med. J.*, 1938, **31**, 914–922.

Kraepelin, E. *Psychiatrie.* Vol. 4, Leipzig: Barth, 1915.

Kruse, H. D. (Ed.) *Alcohol as a medical problem.* New York: Hoeber-Harper, 1956.

Lavin, N. S., Thorpe, J. G., Barker, J. C., Blakemore, C. B., & Conway, C. J. Behavior therapy in a case of transvestism. *J. nerv. ment. Dis.*, 1961, **133**, 346–353.

Lemert, E. M. Alcoholism and the sociocultural situation. *Quart. J. Stud. Alcohol,* 1956, **17**, 306–317.

Lolli, G., Serianni, E., Golder, G., & Luzzatto-Fegiz, P. *Alcohol in Italian culture.* New York: Free Press, 1958.

Lukianowicz, D. P. M. Survey of various aspects of transvestism in the light of our present knowledge. *J. nerv. ment. Dis.*, 1959, **182**, 36–64.

Lykken, D. T. A study of anxiety in the sociopathic personality. *J. abnorm. soc. Psychol.,* 1957, **55**, 6–10.

MacAndrew, C., & Geertsma, R. An analysis of alcoholics' responses to Scale 4 of the MMPI. *Quart. J. Stud. Alcohol.*, 1963, **24**, 23–33.

MacAndrew, C., & Geertsma, R. A critique of alcoholism scales derived from the MMPI. *Quart. J. Stud. Alcohol,* 1964, **25**, 68–76.

Manson, M. P. A psychometric differentiation of alcoholics from nonalcoholics. *Quart. J. Stud. Alcohol.*, 1948, **9**, 175–206.

Marsh, J. T., Hilliard, J., & Liechti, R. A sexual deviation scale for the MMPI. *J. consult. Psychol.*, 1955, **19**, 55–59.

Mason, P. The mother of the addict. *Psychiat. Quart. Suppl.*, 1958, **32**, 189–199.

Masserman, J., & Yum, K. S. An analysis of the influence of alcohol on experimental neuroses in cats. *Psychosom. Med.*, 1946, **8**, 36–52.

Maudsley, H. *Responsibility in mental disease.* London: King, 1896.

Maughs, S. B. Current concepts of psychopathy. *Arch. crim. Psychodynam.*, 1960, **4**, 550–555.

Meer, B., & Amon, A. H. Age-sex preference patterns of alcoholics and normals. *Quart. J. Stud. Alcohol,* 1963.

Money, J. *The psychologic study of man.* Springfield, Ill.: Charles C Thomas, 1957.

Money, J., Hampson, J. G., & Hampson, J. L. An examination of some basic concepts: the evidence of human hermaphroditism. *Bull. Johns Hopkins Hosp.*, 1955, **97**, 301–319.

Money, J., Hampson, J. G., & Hampson, J. L. Imprinting and the establishment of the gender role. *Arch. Neurol. Psychiat.*, 1957, **77**, 333–336.

Monroe, R. R., & Enelow, M. L. The therapeutic motivation in male homosexuals: an adaptational analysis. *Amer. J. Psychother.*, 1960, **14**, 474–490.

Mulford, H. A., & Miller, D. E. Drinking in Iowa. V. Drinking and alcoholic drinking. *Quart. J. Stud. Alcohol,* 1960, **21**, 483–499.

Mulford, H. A., & Miller, D. E. An index of alcoholic drinking behavior related to the meanings of alcohol. *J. Hlth hum. Behav.*, 1961, **2**, 26–31.

Myerson, A., & Neustadt, R. Bisexuality and male homosexuality. *Clinics,* 1942, **1**, 932–957.

O'Neal, P., & Robins, L. N. The relation of childhood behavior problems to adult psychiatric status: a 30-year follow-up study of 150 subjects. *Amer. J. Psychiat.*, 1958, **114**, 961–969.

Overholser, W., & Owens, D. J. The "psychopath": some legal and treatment aspects. *J. soc. Ther.*, 1961, **7**, 127–134.

Palmer, D. M., & Rock, H. A. Brain wave patterns and "crystallized experiences." *Ohio St. med. J.*, 1953, **49**, 804–806.

Partridge, G. E. Current conceptions of psychopathic personality. *Amer. J. Psychiat.*, 1930, **10**, 53–99.

Pescor, M. J. The Kolb classification of drug addicts. *Publ. Hlth Rep. Suppl.* 1939, No. 155.

Pescor, M. J. Follow-up study of treated narcotic drug addicts. *Publ. Hlth Rep. Suppl.*, 1943, No. 170. (a)

Pescor, M. J. A statistical analysis of the clinical records of hospitalized drug addicts. *Publ. Hlth Rep. Suppl.*, 1943, No. 142. (b)

Plumeau, F., Machover, S., & Puzzo, F. Wechsler-Bellevue performances of remitted and unremitted alcoholics, and their normal controls. *J. consult. Psychol.*, 1960, **24**, 240–242.

Preu, P. W. The concept of psychopathic personality. In J. McV. Hunt (Ed.), *Personality and the behavior disorders.* Vol. II. New York: Ronald, 1944.

Prichard, J. C. *Treatise on insanity.* London: Gilbert and Piper, 1835.

Rioch, D. McK. Résumé: the EEG in relation to

psychiatry. *EEG clin. Neurophysiol.*, 1952, **4**, 457–462.

Robins, L. N., & O'Neal, P. Mortality, mobility, and crime: problem children thirty years later. *Amer. Sociol. Rev.*, 1958, **23**, 162–171.

Ross, M., & Mendelsohn, F. Homosexuality in college. *Arch. Neurol. Psychiat.*, 1958, **80**, 253–263.

Rudie, R. R., & McGaughran, L. S. Differences in developmental experience, defensiveness, and personality organization between two classes of problem drinkers. *J. abnorm. soc. Psychol.*, 1961, **62**, 659–665.

Salzman, L. Masochism and psychopathy as adaptive behavior. *J. indiv. Psychol.*, 1960, **16**, 182–188.

Silverman, D. Implications of the electroencephalographic abnormalities in the psychopathic personality. *Arch. Neurol. Psychiat.*, 1949, **62**, 870–873.

Snyder, C. *Alcohol and the Jews.* New York: Free Press, 1958.

Snyder, C. R. A sociological view of the etiology of alcoholism. In D. J. Pittman (Ed.), *Alcoholism: an interdisciplinary approach.* Springfield, Ill.: Charles C Thomas, 1959.

Stoller, R. J., Garfinkel, H., & Rosen, A. C. Passing and the maintenance of sexual identification in an intersexed patient. *Arch. gen. Psychiat.*, 1960, **2**, 379–384.

Stoller, R. J., Garfinkel, H., & Rosen, A. C. Psychiatric management of intersexed patients. *Calif. Med.*, 1962, **96**, 30–34.

Stoller, R. J., & Rosen, A. C. The intersexed patient. *Calif. Med.*, 1959, **91**, 261–265.

Strother, C. R. The performance of psychopaths on the Wechsler-Bellevue test. *Proc. Iowa Acad. Sci.*, 1944, **51**, 397–400.

Sutherland, E. H., Schroeder, A. M., & Tordella, A. B. Personality traits and the alcoholic: a critique of existing studies. *Quart. J. Stud. Alcohol*, 1950, **11**, 548–561.

Syme, L. Personality characteristics and the alcoholic: a critique of current studies. *Quart. J. Stud. Alcohol.*, 1957, **18**, 288–302.

Thurston, J. R., & Calden, G. Intelligence factors in irregular discharge among tuberculosis patients. *J. consult. Psychol.*, 1950, **14**, 493–495.

Vogel, M. D. The relation of personality traits to GSR conditioning of alcoholics. *Canad. J. Psychol.*, 1960, **14**, 275–280.

Vogel, V. H., Isbell, H., & Chapman, K. W. Present status of narcotic addiction. *J. Amer. med. Ass.*, 1948, **138**, 1019–1026.

Walton, D. Drug addiction and habit formation: an attempted integration. *J. ment. Sci.*, 1960, **106**, 1195–1229.

Welsh, G. S. An anxiety index and an internalization ratio for the MMPI. *J. consult. Psychol.*, 1952, **16**, 65–72.

West, J. C. Parental figures in the genesis of male homosexuality. *Int. J. soc. Psychiat.*, 1959, **5**, 85–97.

Westwood, G. (In collaboration with M. J. Schofield.) *A minority: a report on the life of the male homosexual in Great Britain.* London: Longmans, 1960.

Wheeler, W. M. An analysis of Rorschach indices in male homosexuality. *Rorschach res. Exch.*, 1949, **13**, 97–126.

Wiens, A. N., Matarazzo, J. D., & Gaver, K. D. Performance and verbal I.Q. in a group of sociopaths. *J. clin. Psychol.*, 1959, **15**, 191–193.

Wikler, A. *Opiate addiction.* Springfield, Ill.: Charles C Thomas, 1953.

Winslow, W. Experiment for addicts. *Nation*, 1961. (a)

Winslow, W. Synanon revisited. *Manas*, 1961, **14.** (b)

Wolman, B. B. Group psychotherapy with latent schizophrenics. *Int. J. group Psychother.*, 1960, **10**, 301–312.

Wolman, B. B. *Classification of mental disorders.* 1965 (in press).

Worden, F. G., & Marsh, J. T. Psychological factors in men seeking sex transformation: a preliminary report. *J. Amer. med. Ass.*, 1955, **157**, 1292–1298.

World Health Organization. Alcohol and alcoholism. *World Hlth Organization Tech. Rep. Ser.*, 1952, No. 48.

Yalom, I. D. Aggression and forbiddenness in voyeurism. *Arch. gen. Psychiat.*, 1960, **3**, 305–319.

Yamahiro, R. S., & Griffith, R. M. Validity of two indices of sexual deviancy. *J. clin. Psychol.*, 1960, **16**, 21–24,

37
Delinquency

ROBERT M. MACIVER[1]

The rapid increase in the number of programs undertaken by a large variety of organizations concerned with juvenile delinquency has involved calls for several kinds of professional service, not least of which is that of the psychologists. It is generally agreed, except perhaps by budget directors, that these services are still quite inadequate to the need both for clinical tests and for over-all aid and direction in the improvement of these programs. With this point in mind, we shall review the present state of various areas of service to delinquents.

First, there is the essential preliminary function of screening and diagnosis. In the investigation made between 1956 and 1961 by the Juvenile Delinquency Evaluation Project of the City of New York, of which the writer was the director, it was found that throughout, the problem of screening juvenile offenders and diagnosing their various troubles was very inadequately met. Many different types of agencies have to face this problem continually: the school, the child guidance clinic, the court (both in its intake procedure and in the process of adjudication), the detention house, and the institution for the training of delinquents committed by the courts or sent by other agencies. Even the police have an important screening role in deciding which cases coming to their attention should be dealt with through admonitions and reports to parents, which should be referred to social service agencies, and which should be arrested for appearances before the courts.

[1] With the assistance of J. Liblit.

SCHOOLS

Let us consider first the schools. Since virtually all children attend school, the school is in a strategic position to spot potential maladjustment and take appropriate action. Various studies have found delinquents to have a history of classroom misbehavior, reading difficulty, truancy, dropout, and a variety of educational problems. The school comes into contact with a youngster at an early age and is in a position to observe him closely over a long period of time. Very often, it is the first community agency to become aware of a child's difficulties, to take note of a broken home or a disruptive family life. The school can play a vital part in prevention of juvenile delinquency by identifying the children who need special attention and seeing to it that they receive the necessary help.

No intelligent teacher can fail to observe which pupils are troublemakers or are recalcitrant, withdrawn, listless, unresponsive to instruction, or obsessed by some trouble that seriously impedes their educational development. Some of these difficulties can be met by giving discerning guidance, such as teachers should be trained to give, or by calling for guidance specialists. Other cases are more obdurate and complex, and occasionally there is a deeper mental disorder. The teacher may be able to detect such disorders but does not always know where to go or precisely what is needed. Here the psychologist can effectively come to the teacher's aid and discover the nature of the trouble and, where necessary, report the case as calling for specialized therapeutic treatment. A well-run school system offers guidance on two levels. One is educational and vocational guidance, commonly accepted as a normal school function. The other, which is often neglected, is guidance for troubled children, many of whom are beginning to show signs of incipient delinquency. The latter, which might be defined as clinically oriented guidance, calls for the particular skills of the psychologist along with other types of specialized personnel. This kind of special guidance is a proper school function, for many of the difficult children will not be prepared to receive a normal education until some of their underlying problems are dealt with.

The school is not expected to become a psychiatric clinic or to engage in long-term therapy. However, it should be able to spot maladjustment, to make some initial diagnosis, to arrange for clinical treatment where necessary, and to see that the child is placed in the right educational program. These services are particularly important in the lower grades, where attention to seemingly minor problems may prevent serious difficulty at a later stage.

A further role of the psychologist is in the development of the curriculum and school program. The school is responsible for the education of all types of children—the gifted child and the slow learner, the well adjusted and the disturbed. Problem children often require special curriculums, specially trained teachers, and a variety of special school services. A prime illustration is remedial reading. There is a high correlation between severe reading retardation and emotional maladjustment. The remedial reading programs which seem to have the most favorable prospects of success are those which adopt a clinical approach, sometimes combining teaching with therapeutic services. Group therapy experiments which developed reading material based on the interests and experiences of the children themselves have demonstrated unusual advances in reading skills. Under the best circumstances, a remedial reading team may utilize the skills of the teacher, the counselor, the social worker, and the psychologist. The psychologist makes a specific contribution in testing and diagnosis; he provides insights which will be of use in the classroom; and he may be involved in some short-term treatment. Emotional and reading problems are thus handled simultaneously. Where sustained therapy or psychiatric help is indicated, the child is referred to an outside agency. The same kind of team approach has validity for other types of special school programs. The potential school dropout, the educationally retarded, the truant, and the withdrawn or aggressive child may all require services beyond that which is ordinarily provided in the classroom. An additional function of the psychologist is to bring about a mental health atmosphere or awareness in the school and to help train teachers along these lines. He consults with teachers regarding classroom problems and provides assistance in understanding and handling difficult pupils.

In the case of pupils who are simply unmanageable in the regular school, it is usual for the principal to report them as needing to be sent to special schools designed for unruly youngsters. Here again it is quite important that such commitment not be made before careful diagnosis. Obtrusive serious mistakes can be made that may affect the whole future of the child concerned, since commitment to these schools carries a potential stigma and encourages undesirable companionship. The psychologists in the special schools need to be even more deeply involved in diagnosis and curriculum and sometimes in treatment. The progress and adjustment of the youngsters must be constantly evaluated so that they may be returned to the regular classes as soon as this is warranted and so that the effectiveness of the programs may be tested. There is a particular need in these schools for experimentation on the therapeutic possibility of art, music, drama, etc.

While local school districts throughout the country are increasingly employing psychologists, very few maintain even the minimum, and grossly inadequate, number sometimes recommended for the regular schools—one psychologist for every three thousand pupils. There are indications, however, that the need for guidance services for troubled children is being recognized. The National Defense Education Act provides Federal financial assistance and encourages the states to put up matching funds for school guidance programs. State education departments in New York, Indiana, and Delaware offer special incentives, financial reimbursement, and direct services to induce localities to expand their school psychological facilities. Many school systems are beginning to develop such services as part of their normal educational responsibilities.

Recognition that delinquent behavior is so often associated with personality disorder has led to an emphasis on the mental health approach to both prevention and treatment of juvenile delinquency. Authorities agree that early guidance for children who are in need of help holds greatest promise for control of delinquency. The Juvenile Delinquency Evaluation Project of the City of New York reflected the general thinking in the field in calling for

> a directed program of prevention which gets down to the problems and maladjustments of the young, to the young persons who for one reason or another are beginning to get into trouble or are showing quite recognizable signs in the family, in the school, in the streets, which indicate that they are on the verge of danger.

We have already discussed the school's role in this program. In a like manner, the community agency offering diagnostic and treatment services is able to act before a youngster becomes a legal delinquent. Where such agencies come into contact with potentially delinquent children at an early age, they may be considered to be preventive as well as treatment resources.

CLINICS

There has been considerable growth in recent years of community mental health facilities under both public and private auspices. The child guidance clinic is a primary resource. Some family service agencies, day-care centers, and settlement houses have established auxiliary clinical facilities. Traditionally, the clinical team is made up of a psychiatrist, a psychologist, a social worker, and a pediatrician. The actual composition will depend on the nature of the agency involved and on the type of professional help which is available at the time. The clinic tries to carry out an individual case study of the child as well as an appraisal of the family and home environment. Treatment may extend to both the parents and the child.

Increasingly, local and state governments are expanding their community mental health programs specifically to combat delinquency. In Nevada, the Bureau of Mental Health, under its juvenile delinquency program, is developing preventive service in various communities. The state of Washington has established child guidance centers to work with problem children. New York City, through its Community Mental Health Board and its Youth Board, makes substantial grants to voluntary agencies and municipal departments for mental health activities. There is still, however, a severe shortage of clinical facilities and professional personnel to work with problem children. The need for additional resources has been stressed in practically every study.

The mere existence of clinical facilities, however, does not guarantee that they will serve the children in greatest need. Child guidance clinics tend to restrict their intake to those showing the greatest promise of success. It is generally held that personality disorders in children stem from a breakdown in family relationships and can be adjusted when the parents are aware of the problem and are anxious to cooperate. Desirable parental attitudes, however, are not always characteristic of families from which many delinquent children come. Potential delinquents either do not become known early enough or somehow get lost as they move from one agency to another. Problem children not yet in trouble with the law cannot be compelled to accept help. Their parents do not seek assistance and may even resist it. The most disturbed families may not realize that they have a problem at all and may need to be induced to take part in treatment.

An over-all program, therefore, requires a system for discovering, even recruiting, unwilling parents and children. There has been a good deal of emphasis, in recent years, on aggressive casework methods. The so-called "reaching-out approach" is geared to locate those who mistrust outside interference and who do not come forward of their own volition. Community-oriented programs have been quite effective in this task. Working in the high delinquency areas of the city, the neighborhood-based organizations are in a good position to discover young persons just beginning to get into trouble and to ensure effective referral and follow-up. This type of facility can be an important part of a system of directed prevention.

We should also point out that clinical treatment alone, without supportive auxiliary service, may not prevent or reduce the incidence of delinquent behavior. Treatment considered in its broadest sense extends to a wide range of rehabilitative activities which complement the work of the behavioral specialist. If the guidance clinic has been successful in its work, the child may have developed a different outlook toward life, so that he is now motivated toward schooling, employment, or other constructive activity. Opportunities for such activities in his community, however, may be severely limited. His new attitudes may be out of line with those of his companions, and he may be constantly pressured to return to his old ways. Any treatment facility, whether in the community or in a correctional setting, has to consider the need for sustained supervisional aftercare. The child guidance clinic is a valuable resource for both prevention and treatment. It is particularly effective where its services are coordinated with other facilities and when it is a part of a total community strategy for detection, treatment, and follow-up of the most vulnerable youth.

COURTS

The professional services of the clinical psychologist are called for, again, in the courts for juveniles and adolescents. The philosophy of the children's courts is not to punish but to rehabilitate. The court, in taking custody of a child, is theoretically assuming a parental responsibility. A delinquent child is supposed to receive the same care as the neglected or handicapped youngster under the protection of the court. The concern of the juvenile court is not with the offense but with the welfare of the offender—what Roscoe Pound termed "individualized justice." Accordingly, the laws defining "juvenile delinquent" or "wayward minor" are so vague that a wide variety of behaviors could place a youngster under the court's jurisdiction. If the judge is to follow through on a treatment approach, he must understand the child's history, his home environment, and his personality and psychological makeup.

A variety of auxiliary services, therefore, are brought into play. Some screening takes place as part of the initial intake procedure. In some of the juvenile courts, there is reason to believe that more professional and authoritative screening would reduce the number of those who come before the judge. The fact that the number of dismissed cases runs around 25 per cent and that about another 25 per cent are discharged might seem to justify this conclusion. Many cases can be adjusted without formal court action, some by settling the dispute on the spot and others by referral to a community agency. Where there is effective intake screening, the limited facilities of the court are set aside for those who really require them, while youngsters who might not benefit or who could be hurt by a formal court hearing are dealt with in other ways. The major screening, however, is that of the disposition process, where a judge must decide for the great majority of adjudicated delinquents whether to put them on probation or commit them to an institution. In the more complex cases, it would seem highly desirable that before making his decision, the judge refer the problem to a diagnostic clinic. For the determination of such cases, the judge often is not adequately equipped, partly because with crowded calendars he has to dispose of the case too hurriedly, partly because the probation officer report submitted to him is often too scrappy or perfunctory, and partly because in some instances he has no special training for the task.

Few juvenile courts have diagnostic facilities as an integral part of the court. Where clinical services are attached to the court, they are usually so overcrowded that reports may be delayed for months. In most cases the only diagnostic services available to the court come through state or city hospitals; sometimes they come through a detention facility and occasionally through a voluntary clinic. Again, these institutions receive referrals from many other sources as well; they are overtaxed and usually have a large backlog of referrals. As a result, judges do not request clinical evaluations or are unable to obtain psychological studies, even where they are clearly needed. The courts sometimes are forced to remand juveniles to temporary detention, not because detention is warranted, but because the detention home may be the only place where clinical facilities are readily available. This is an improper use of detention, for economic reasons and also from the point of view of the well-being and legal rights of the child. Moreover, this practice crowds detention facilities, which should be held for those who absolutely need them.

Some courts are provided with psychiatric clinics, but these have not been particularly successful in those areas of which we have knowledge. It is hard to get, and harder to retain, a sufficient number of qualified psychiatrists because the competition of private practice or of more flexible private institutions is so strong. Consequently, there is considerable delay between the referral of the case to the clinic and the subsequent evaluation. The psychiatric clinic is necessary for cases where there is evidence of a psychopathic condition, but the great majority of children appearing before the courts do not fall into this group. There seems to be greater advantage to a broad-based diagnostic clinic, representing various professions and giving a prominent role to psychologists, child welfare specialists, and probably a pediatrician. A psychiatrist might be on call for special consultation. The diagnostic clinic would not review all cases appearing before the children's court but would evaluate the more difficult problem cases. It could receive referrals from the judge or directly from the probation department where further study was indicated before final disposition.

Where the need for institutional care is indicated, the court must choose a proper facility. Too often the decision is made by "shopping around" until an empty bed is found. The private institution has its own intake controls, but the state reformatory or training school must accept a commitment whether or not its program is suited to the particular child. Here again, diagnostic services are needed. Commitment to the wrong correctional facility could do serious harm, causing a child to become even more confirmed in his delinquent tendencies. The psychotic or highly disturbed youngster requires one type of institutional setting, the physically disabled delinquent still another, and so on. While an open or minimum security institution may be best for most young offenders, some require a greater degree of watchfulness. Certain children could be helped in a psychiatrically oriented treatment center. Others would do better in a forestry or conservation camp which stresses work experience and vocational training. Still others simply need a short-term residence home within the local community. Institutions under different auspices have developed distinct philosophies and emphases in treatment, but there is still a great need for a wider range of specialized institutional facilities to serve different types of delinquent children. There are many cases of seriously disturbed youngsters who are committed to the large state training schools, which are not prepared to deal with them.

There seems to be a growing trend toward the establishment of centralized structures for screening and diagnosis which are responsible for evaluation of adjudicated cases before commitment to a specified institution. A number of states have established such centers. In New York, the adolescent offender, over 16 years of age, is sent to the Elmira Reception Center before being placed in one of the state's correctional institutions. He is studied intensively, and a tentative treatment plan is drawn up; only then is he committed. He may be sent to a state reformatory or to a more permissive and open work camp. Here again, the variety of institutions is limited, but New York State is moving ahead rapidly in developing new types of facilities with opportunity centers, youth division homes, and short-term training centers. In states where the Youth Authority system has been adopted, commitment is made to the Authority rather than to the institution. The Youth Authority, instead of the court, retains jurisdiction of the child until he has reached 21 or 25 years of age, deciding the length of commitment, the type of care, conditions of parole, release, etc. In Minneapolis and California, the Authority operates diagnostic reception centers as well as institutions and treatment facilities of various kinds. Only after clinical investigation, testing, and observation is the youth placed in a facility suited to his needs. The reception center even returns a youngster to the court when it feels that institutionalization is not warranted.

PROGRAMS AND POLICIES

Over the whole broad range of screening, only part of which we have touched upon, the role of the psychologist is or should be of permanent importance. His field, as social or as clinical psychologist, is largely concerned with social problems and social disorders as they emerge out of the personality in its social relationships. Some of his journals, ranging from the *Journal of Social Issues* to the *Journal of Abnormal Psychology*, are mainly devoted to these subjects. Moreover, he has a special advantage because the area of psychological testing is primarily his. Such tests, carefully supervised and controlled, are a primary tool for effective screening. While in general much more professional aid of various kinds is called for in the prevention and control of delinquency, for the preliminary screening service the psychologist is particularly qualified.

When we turn to the programs and policies of treatment, we find many developing opportunities for the psychologist. Screening and diagnosis are preliminary to the determination of the treatment program, and the counsel of the psychologist is certainly needed in the making of such determinations. The kind of treatment the juvenile offender needs varies greatly with the nature of his trouble. To decide on it properly requires an exploration of his family life and his associational background, his history from the earliest years, and his mental characteristics. Were the probation services really developed—as it rarely is—these considerations would apply here also. In the institutions to which the more confirmed delinquents are committed, such preliminary planning is essential. Here, of course, the psychologist usually has a role, but often—as is the case elsewhere—he is called in for consultation too seldom or too late and does not have a sufficient part in the determination of the appropriate treatment. The diagnostic intake clinic has an excellent opportunity to offer guidance for both prevention and rehabilitation programs and could thus provide new insights for those concerned with problem children, not the least important of whom are the judges of a juvenile court. The commitment of a youngster to an institution is at best a precarious business and should be made only when his being at large is a manifest danger either to the community or to the youngster himself. Too often he leaves the institution, even the better one, more confirmed in his delinquent ways than when he entered. This is particularly true for the large institution containing several hundred young persons who are in a rebellious mood under custody and who form a kind of underground subculture of their own. Small, specialized institutions for different types of delinquents, where more personal relations can be established between the young people and the professional staff, have better chances of success, as some experimental institutions, such as that in Highfields, New Jersey, have shown. The presence of clinical psychologists in city and state commissions on delinquency would be of considerable value in helping the authorities plan their institutional systems. A similar service could be rendered in the planning of probational methods and services, for in the whole treatment of delinquency there is no area to which, in general, less adequate consideration has been given than to the potentials of the probation system.

The comments we have made are based on firsthand experiences and on the findings of many research projects and are in line with the following statement from the chairman of the Senate Subcommittee to Investigate Juvenile Delinquency:[2] "If we are to make headway in the prevention of crime, if we are to succeed in our correctional and rehabilitative efforts, the scientists and the practitioners in this field must first realize their efforts." In this strategic task the clinical psychologists should have a primary role.

The great need for a psychological approach for the education and direction of the workers "at the face" of the delinquency problem has been stressed many times. The majority of those in daily contact with youngsters who get into trouble—probation officers, workers with gangs or street clubs, school attendance officers, police youth officers, counselors in detention homes and shelters, cottage parents in the institutions, and fieldworkers of various kinds—do not have established professional status in the social service field. Conflicts often develop between those in immediate contact with difficult children and the behavioral specialists. A correctional institution may formulate a treatment approach as a matter of policy, but if the cottage parents and the custodial staff do not accept it or if they actively oppose it, not an unusual occurrence, the entire treatment program may fail.

In view of the severe shortage of personnel in social service areas, it is impractical to ask that all those who work with problem children be professionally trained. The subprofessional group, however, should have some knowledge of the treatment approach and at least a sympathetic understanding of problem children. The psychologist is asked to help develop and carry out programs of orientation and education along these lines.

[2] Senator Thomas J. Dodd, in an address given on June 14, 1962, We Know More about Crime Prevention and Control Than We Put into Practice, reproduced in *Federal Probation*, September, 1962.

Various institutes, workshops, inservice training programs, etc., are being established for those below the specialist level working with problem children. The Delinquency Control Institute at the University of Southern California provides a special program primarily for police youth officers. New York State, in cooperation with St. Lawrence University, sponsors a summer institute on delinquency and crime for persons in correction work, law enforcement, and youth work. Police academies frequently include courses in juvenile delinquency, psychology, or "human relations" in their curriculums.

In some institutional settings, there exists some confusion and even a degree of conflict over the respective roles of the various professions involved, the psychologist, the psychiatrist, the social worker, and the child specialist. The psychoanalyst, on the other hand, with his distinctive views on the genesis and etiology of delinquency, is usually to be found either in private practice or in therapeutic programs and institutions under his own control. As for the four categories mentioned above, in the diagnostic process they are all concerned, and there is no problem aside from the differences of viewpoint that may arise wherever scholars of different disciplines seek to arrive at a decision. There is mostly enough consensus for adequate direction, and should it be otherwise, some decision is arrived at anyway. In the treatment process itself, the allocation of function is partly a matter of expediency and partly one of the relative rather than absolute relevance of one or another type of professional training to the particular case.

DELINQUENCY AND MENTAL DISORDERS

It is rather common to speak of delinquents as being "disturbed" in various degrees or according to various descriptive distinctions, such as "emotionally," "mentally," "seriously," or "severely." A good proportion of them, however, are not disturbed in a sense that has special significance for the psychiatrist, and some of them should not be called "disturbed" at all. The two neutral types that call especially for the psychiatrist are those usually designated as "psychopathic" or "psychotic," the latter referring to a more deep-seated mental disorder or to disease probably rooted in congenital defect and involving a mental state characterized by persistent delusions. The psychotic condition does not respond to the therapeutic approaches that have proved in a number of instances to have been effective with psychopaths.

Fortunately, the psychotic condition obtains for a relatively small percentage of our delinquent youth; as for the others, they have been the object of research by social scientists of every kind. The psychiatrists, whether or not we include them as social scientists, have more distinction in the region of therapy than of research. But it is impossible to draw any line of demarcation between the psychologists, whether they are called "clinical" or "social" or whether they remain undifferentiated by any adjective, and their social science brethren, the sociologists, the criminologists, and in some areas the anthropologists. We can draw theoretical lines, assigning each a particular focus, but human problems are complicated and refuse to be pigeonholed in academic compartments. This is easily seen in the researches carried out by members of these various groups. It is often impossible to tell from the content, the approach, or the methods employed whether research has been the work of a sociologist or, say, a psychologist.

If we are then to characterize the role of the psychologist in the study or the treatment of delinquency, we might distinguish between his broader joint or team operation and the type of work in which he usually has the major part to play. In the diagnostic center he should be an important factor, but in conjunction with other types of specialists. In the guidance process, whether in the school or the custodial institution, he is emphatically needed, not only for teamwork but also for consultation on cases appropriately referred to him. For behavior problems in general, and particularly in any clinical setting, his approach and his training give him an expert standing. More than anyone else, the psychologist has been concerned with probing the complex nature of personality. The psychiatrist, it is true, focuses on the individual personality, but with more emphasis on its "sicknesses." The socially oriented psychologist—and here we are unable to draw any line of distinction between him and his sociological colleague—can complement quite significantly the program of the psychiatrist.

An important stimulus to the clinical role of the psychologist was given by Healy and

Bronner in their pathfinding volume *New Light on Delinquency and Its Treatment* (1936). Attention was there focused on the psychology of delinquency, whereas earlier studies had been sociological in a narrower sense, concerned with relating delinquency to the conditions prevailing in high-delinquency urban areas. For Healy and Bronner it was primarily a problem of the social adjustments of youth to familial relationships within the broader context of the high-delinquency environment. These authors maintained that where the parent-child tie was strong, a basis of adjustment to socially acceptable habits and activities would probably be built. Many later investigators, including the Gluecks, took the same approach and some found in it a lead for therapeutic planning. The Gluecks, after comparing 500 institutionalized delinquent boys with a matched group of 500 nondelinquents, attempted to identify the factors which distinguished one from the other. On this basis they have constructed a series of predictive tables designed to discover those children who are in danger of becoming delinquent; the tables cover psychological test factors, personality traits, character structure, and social factors. The social prediction factors, which the authors suggest be used as a guide for treatment as well, measure discipline by father, supervision by mother, affection of father, affection of mother, and family cohesiveness. The Gluecks do not feel that the influence of the neighborhood or of the more inclusive environmental conditions presents a fruitful target for exploration. This approach has been subject to criticism on the grounds that it ignores other factors which should be reckoned with if we are to approach a fuller understanding of why some persons become delinquent and others do not.

Characteristic of the more recent literature on delinquency research is a strong tendency to describe the attitude of the delinquent as a form of mental deviance. The confirmed delinquent is frequently characterized as being "disoriented," "alienated," or "anomic," referring to three not yet clearly differentiated stages of progressive mental deviance. Studies of causation frequently stress the individual delinquent and his emotional makeup. The maladjustments characteristic of delinquent children are often described in terms of psychiatric and psychoanalytic classifications. A number of researchers, however, have become concerned with the interaction of personality factors and environmental factors. One of the earliest works taking this approach is a study by Hewitt and Jenkins, *Fundamental Patterns of Maladjustment* (1946), which classifies behavior types into three groups: the unsocialized aggressive child, the socialized delinquent, and the overinhibited child. The study relates patterns of family and community background to syndromes of behavior symptoms and suggests how environment and personality can produce varying kinds of behavior.

A leading researcher in this field, Albert J. Reiss, Jr., attracted considerable attention as the result of an article in the *American Sociological Review* (December, 1952) entitled "Social Correlates of Psychological Types of Delinquency." Like almost all classifications of delinquency types, his basis for classification is psychological, influenced in this case by psychoanalytic concepts. His three types are the "relatively integrated" delinquent, the delinquent with "weak ego controls," and the "defective superego" delinquent. His classification represents a significant departure from other modes of classification, for he suggests a series of interesting correlations between these psychologically defined delinquent types and environmental factors.

A good deal of the research in the delinquency field now reflects both sociological and psychological thinking, taking into account the maladjustments of the child's personality as well as the effect of local conditions. At a hearing of the New York Temporary Commission on Youth and Delinquency, it was suggested that delinquents may be divided into two broad and overlapping groups:

> those suffering from psychiatric problems and those subject to a variety of social stress, deprivation, rejection, isolation, etc. The first group needs to be broken down into various sub-groups, children with organic brain pathology, epilepsy, schizophrenia, etc., each requiring different therapeutic approaches.

Some authorities distinguish between children with normal personalities reacting to adverse conditions, those with neurotic conflicts, and those with highly disorganized personalities who do not have the same control over their behavior as other children. A distinction is often made between the conscious, or "adaptive," delinquent and the disturbed, or "maladapted," type. The former does not fall into the category of mental illness at all. The youngster may be well adjusted to the patterns of behavior within his own group or community. In the slums, surrounded by congestion and conflict, he may be responding to what has been called a "delinquent subculture." Many delinquents are undoubtedly affected by some combination of cultural and psychological influences.

In the main, it is to the psychological researchers that we must turn for our knowledge of the differential mental characteristics that lie back of delinquent behavior. A good deal of knowledge of the types of malfunction, the nature of disturbances which result in juvenile delinquency, has been derived from the work of Fritz Redl. Psychologists have been particularly concerned with the process of personality growth and with the influences on personality development that have evoked deviant forms of behavior. Some psychologists have given particular attention—as Healy and Bronner did—to the role played by deprivation and frustrations in childhood and to the variant reactions to those conditions that depend on differences of mental or constitutional type. Psychological studies of personality changes at the outset of puberty and through adolescence are useful for the understanding of delinquency that manifests itself in the early teens. Another type of psychological inquiry has been the classification of personality types. However, while it is convenient to make certain broad distinctions here, personality is so complex and many-faceted a totality and there are so many combinations of attributes of varying degrees of strength, as well as so many changes in the course of the life history, that every classification has its problems, and none have become authoritative. This statement is applicable also to the variant classifications of the delinquent personality. We certainly need some simple *ad hoc* classifications for practical purposes, especially for the screening of cases prior to disposition and treatment. In looking through the intake records of certain institutions, the writer was struck by the frequent resort to the term "disturbed," usually qualified by an adjective such as "very," "emotionally," "mentally," or "severely." So vague and inclusive a term has no diagnostic value. It might even be applied to delinquents who are reasonably well adjusted within their delinquent associations though causing considerable disturbance otherwise. It is certainly applied to delinquents who either are chafing under the restraints imposed on them or, on the other hand, are suffering from a deeper-seated mental trouble.

What proportion of delinquents are psychologically maladjusted? A number of researchers have looked into this, but the evidence is not conclusive. Studies have come up with conflicting results, partly because those who study the problem do not always use the same criteria or vocabulary. Any review of case records of children known to the special schools, the courts, or the private agencies reveals a large number who seem to have emotional problems which will require special assistance. Indeed, the records indicate some kind of disturbance among the parents of many of these children as well. It is difficult, however, to place these children into precise categories because comparable data are not available for all of them. Terminology and standards depend on the particular agency or the professional discipline involved. Some agencies, recognizing the inexperience of their diagnostic personnel, prefer a general description and do not attempt to type delinquent behavior. A clarification of the common vocabulary of those who work with delinquents is certainly needed. In the absence of an accepted classification, we frequently type delinquents according to the reason for arrest or referral. While this is the simplest basis for compiling delinquency statistics, it does not tell us much about the youngster, nor does it provide a foundation for developing a treatment program.

With the stress now laid on mental deviance regarded mainly as the responsiveness of youth to situations of tension and pressure, stemming from some conjuncture of environmental conditions, many variant therapeutic programs have been devised and are being pursued with rather promising indications of their value. Practitioners have come to realize that new and flexible techniques are needed to treat the delinquent or potentially delinquent youth. Unlike the conventional middle-class patient, the delinquent child is not motivated to accept psychotherapy. Among the groups from which he comes, there is considerable stigma attached to treatment, and social pressure does not encourage cooperation while in treatment. The youth may be interested in immediate problems and not see the future reward to be derived from long therapeutic sessions. He may not trust the therapist, seeing him as just another repressive force. The delinquent child's capacity for establishing close relationships with adults may have been impaired. He may view the permissive approach with suspicion or regard it as a sign of indifference. His lack of language skills makes it difficult for him to communicate with the therapist, and vice versa.

THERAPEUTIC TECHNIQUES

Modern therapeutic techniques are constantly being developed and tested. Redl's experiments with children in a residential treatment setting yielded a great deal of knowledge on the disturbed and aggressive child. Redl's concept of the "life-space interview" represented a departure from conventional treatment methods in that it called for psychological assistance on the spot when it was needed, as close as possible to the time the child was going through some emotional upset. The therapist was to be available immediately to interpret to the child the meaning of his behavior.

There have been other interesting experiments employing rather unorthodox methods of analysis and treatment, such as setting clearly defined limits to behavior and using authority in the treatment process, providing concrete incentives (even cash payments) as inducements to participate in treatment, showing interest in practical and current problems which trouble the youngster, teaching him new skills at the same time that efforts are made to redirect his personality, etc. There has been greater recognition that children from different ethnic groups and cultural backgrounds respond to different therapeutic techniques.

Aside from individualized treatment, there has been a proliferation of group therapy programs. Some of them are detached from any institutional setting, but the majority are operated within a variety of institutions, schools, residential treatment centers, camps, and custodial and corrective institutions. The Highfields Treatment Center in New Jersey is an outstanding example of an institution utilizing group therapy as the core of its program. A major therapeutic instrument here is the daily "guided group interaction" session, where the boys themselves exert pressure on their peers to join in. Since it has a small population, twenty boys or so, Highfields is able to develop team spirit and create the atmosphere of a sort of therapeutic community.

On a neighborhood level, community centers and settlement houses have begun to experiment with group therapy. Certain children were found to be so hostile and aggressive that they were unable to function in the regular group work or recreational programs, and yet many of the disturbed youngsters could not accept outside referral for individual psychological treatment. Some community agencies have therefore set up their own treatment groups. The Manhattanville Community Center "clinical group program" is a noteworthy experiment along these lines. The clinical group numbers about six boys or girls. Each group is led by a regular member of the settlement staff, already familiar to the youngsters, who works under the supervision of a clinical psychologist. The goals of the program are to help the child understand his behavior and resolve his conflicts so that he can get along with others and return to his own natural groups. The primary technique used is an adaptation of the life-space interview, confronting the youngster with his behavior as it takes place and commenting on and explaining what is happening. The Manhattanville Centers found that most of the boys in the "clinical groups" made sufficient progress after one or two years to enable them to return to the regular group programs.

There are many variations of group therapy. In one type, a group of youngsters, under a leader, are simply encouraged to expose their attitudes and motivations, their discontents and their troubles. A variation takes the form of a drama or "psychodrama," in which the youths in character roles can vent their aggressions and hostilities, a prescription for purging of the emotions that goes back to Aristotle. In another type, a sort of tutorial group therapy, the attempt is made to enlist the cooperative endeavor of the youths to deal with questions that should be of real concern to them, but without touching on aspects that come too close to their own troubles. Another form makes a special effort to create the image of the therapist as a friendly investigator who is interested in personality differences for their own sake, so to speak, and who would like them to tell about their own, hoping in this manner to lead them on to freely given expression of their feelings and motivations. More characteristic forms of group therapy are embodied in programs of instruction in the arts and in music and, for young children, in storytelling, playlet acting, and puppet-show sessions. Remedial reading is also a promising area in which group therapy is being tried experimentally.

Group therapy has more recently been extended to sessions with the parents of delinquents as well as to family groups as wholes. Some researchers and therapists have combined individual treatment with occasional meetings of the whole family. Others have maintained the more traditional pattern of separate therapists working individually with the members of the family but collaborating together. John Elderhorn Bell, of the Public Health Service, has found a treatment technique which he calls "family group therapy" to be particularly effective in working with older children and adolescents. The basis of this method is a series of conferences involving the parents, the older children, and the therapist. The therapist avoids any special relationship or ties to individuals and works only with the family as a group. While the case is initiated through referral of a difficult child, the problem is regarded as a family problem, not that of the child or the parents. The therapist is concerned with the disturbed family unit, with bringing about a greater understanding of the role each member plays, and with the interaction between the different members of the family.

There seems to be no limit to the types of situations to which group therapy is in some sense extended. Accordingly, the term tends to be used rather loosely for all sorts of get-togethers of which the object is to develop mutual understanding in the group regarding the nature of the behavioral troubles that afflict them, as a means of changing their attitudes and thus alleviating or solving the problems that underlie their troubles. The term "psychotherapy" has become professionalized as a name for the science that treats behavioral disorders, but it is used also in a rather free sense.

Finally, there is no more difficult problem for the behavioral treatment specialist than the psychopathic delinquent. The term "psychopathic" has become fairly well defined. One definition of it is offered by William and Joan McCord, as follows: "The psychopath is an asocial, aggressive, highly impulsive person, who feels little or no guilt and is unable to form lasting bonds of affection with other human beings." The typical delinquent psychopath is full of unreasoning hostility; Redl described his psychopathic boys—our appellation and not his—as "the children who hate." The identification of this type (with its several varieties) is well confirmed in such studies as those of Robert Linder, Kate Friedlander, R. D. Rabinowitz, Lauretta Bender, and others. Many of these studies insist on the role of early rejection, emotional starvation, or brutal treatment in evoking the psychopathic features. "In study after study" say the McCords, "emotional deprivation appeared to have precipitated a psychopathic personality structure." This conclusion does not preclude the existence of a congenital or constitutional mental disorder, perhaps of some glandular irregularity, or again of an initial psychic tendency that may have been developed or accentuated as a result of emotional shock, but the cases that have been recorded of successful treatment indicate that a socializing therapy can be applied with rather good prospects of success.

The first promising efforts were made under the auspices of psychoanalysts, but their characteristic line of treatment involved no exclusively psychoanalytic methods. A lead was given by the Viennese psychoanalyst August Aichhorn, who set up his own home for delinquents, finding in the frustrated yearning for love and affection the basis of delinquent behavior and believing that a system of persistent, friendly, permissive care was best calculated to bring about a readjustment. For Aichhorn, a larger part of the problem is the enabling of the delinquent to achieve "identification" with a therapist. He claimed that the results achieved by his institution were excellent.

Aichhorn's lead had considerable influence and has been followed up by various promising experiments in treatment along the lines he pioneered. A notable example of such experiments was Fritz Redl's Pioneer House, where a group of extremely difficult boys were found to respond well to treatment and showed an increased capacity to deal with their problems. In Redl's judgment, however, Pioneer House was closed down before the experiment was completed. In other experiments, less favorable results were reported. A thorough investigation of the conditions under which one experiment succeeds and another fails might prove very revealing.

In view of the great increase in the literature on juvenile delinquency, the numerous public and private agencies that are now directed to its prevention and treatment, and the developing interest in the study of behavioral problems and more especially those of the young, there can be no question that here is an area in which the clinical psychologist has a major and growing contribution to make.

REFERENCES

Ackerman, N. W. *Psychodynamics of family life.* New York: Basic Books, 1958.

Aichhorn, A. *Wayward youth.* New York: Viking, 1935.

Bell, J. E. Family group therapy. *U.S. Dep. Hlth Educ. Welf. Publ. Hlth Monogr.* No. 64, 1963.

Cohen, A. K. *Delinquent boys: the culture of the gang.* New York: Free Press, 1955.

Cook, D., & Rubenfeld, S. The nature of treatment. In *Report to the Congress on juvenile delinquency.* 1960. Appendix II, Chap. 4.

Eissler, K. R. *Searchlights on delinquency: new psychoanalytic studies.* New York: International Universities Press, 1949.

Glueck, S., & Glueck, E. *Predicting delinquency and Crime.* Cambridge, Mass.: Harvard Univer. Press, 1959.

Healy, W., & Bronner, Augusta F. *New light on delinquency and its treatment.* New Haven, Conn.: Yale Univer. Press, 1936.

Hewitt, L. E., & Jenkins, R. L. *Fundamental patterns of maladjustment.* Springfield, Ill.: Department of Public Welfare, 1946.

Houtz, F., & Kosteck, E. Preparation of juvenile delinquents for treatment. *Amer. J. Orthopsychiat.,* 1947, **17**, 143–150.

Juvenile Delinquency Evaluation Project of the City of New York. The institutionalization of young delinquents. *Interim Rep.,* 1958, No. XI.

Juvenile Delinquency Evaluation Project of the City of New York. Delinquency prevention through guidance in the schools. *Final Rep.,* 1961, No. III.

McCord, W., & McCord, J. *Psychopathy and delinquency.* New York: Grune & Stratton, 1956.

McCorkle, L. W., Elias, A., & Bixby, F. l. *Highfields story: an experimental treatment project for youthful offenders.* New York: Holt, 1958.

Manhattanville Community centers, Inc. *Treating disturbed children in a settlement house.*

Morgolin, J. B., Roman, M., & Harari, C. Reading disability in the delinquent child. *Amer. J. Orthopsychiat.,* 1955, **25**, 25–35.

New York State Temporary Commission on Youth and Delinquency. Youth and delinquency. *Rep. Hearings,* 1956.

Peck, H. B., & Bellsmith, V. *Treatment of the delinquent adolescent.* New York: Family Service Association, 1954.

Redl, F., & Wineman, D. *Children who hate.* New York: Free Press, 1951.

Redl, F., & Wineman, D. *The aggressive child.* New York: Free Press, 1957.

Slack, C. W. Experimental-subject psychotherapy: a new method of introducing intensive office treatment for unreachable cases. *Ment. Hyg.,* 1960, **44**, 238–256.

Witmer, H. L., & Kotinsky, R. New perspectives for research on juvenile delinquency. *U.S. Dep. Hlth Educ. Welf. Child. Bureau Publ.,* 1956, No. 356.

Wolman, B. B. Disturbances in acculturation. *Amer. J. Psychother.,* 1949, **3**, 601–615.

38

Mental Disorders in Childhood

HAIM G. GINOTT AND ERNEST HARMS

EMOTIONAL DISORDERS IN CHILDREN[1]

There is considerable controversy over whether or not childhood psychopathology should be considered incomplete manifestations of adult disorders of similar nature. Our position is that childhood disorders should be considered to be separate from adult disorders. Just as a description of the bud does not describe the flower, so childhood psychopathology cannot be properly described in adult psychiatric terms. Certain psychopathological conditions seem to occur only in childhood and only against a background of the still undeveloped nature of the child, and they end before adulthood is reached (Harms, 1953; Harms, 1955).

Independent presentations of childhood psychopathology were made as early as the first quarter of the nineteenth century, when English as well as French doctors—Perfect (1852), for example—described what they called "puberty neuroses." In the middle of the nineteenth century, Greisinger (1845), in Germany, and later Maudsley (1895), in England, held that mental illness in children not only existed in different forms but also should be studied apart from mental illness in adults. A quarter of a century later, Kahlbaum (1890) and Hecker (1877) published monographs on a juvenile form of mental illness which they called "hebephrenia." In 1887, Emminghaus wrote the first complete textbook in this field, entitled *Die psychischen Stoerungen des Kindesalters* (the psychic disturbances of childhood). This book formulated concepts related to the facts of mental abnormalities occurring only in children. The authors of the great modern textbooks on psychiatry, Bleuler (1918) and Kraepelin (1883), were fully aware of the existence of a mental pathology specific for the juvenile, and both, within certain limits, discussed these problems in their works. In the beginning of the present century there was an enormous upsurge in the study of the mental pathologies of childhood. For a history of the development of child psychiatry see Harms, 1962.

The establishing of detailed and objective insight into mental disorders of childhood demands specific diagnostic methods and procedures. How can psychopathological phenomena in childhood be recognized, and what is their scope? And on what basis may these phenomena be distinguished from other psychopathologies? In the past, childhood psychopathologies were seen as deviations or incompletely developed forms of adult psychopathologies. We view childhood psychopathology as a deviation of the corresponding normal form of childhood behavior.

In consequence, attention will first be focused on the normal child. Although there is not yet a satisfactory inventory of the major

[1] The first section of this chapter was written by Dr. Harms.

aspects of the early period of human life, the intensive work of Gesell and Ilg (1945; 1946; 1956), Buehler (1930; 1935), Katz (1937), Garrison (1959), Strang (1940), Hurlock (1953), Watson (1959), and others provides a sound foundation for gaining insight into the first two decades of human life.

Only a start has been made concerning primary observation of abnormality in the infant. It has been proposed that a first step would be an inventory of supposedly abnormal traits or behavior patterns. Up to now there have been attempts to inventorize abnormal adolescent behavior (Ackerson, 1931), but not abnormal behavior in earlier stages of childhood. Some standard categories, however, have been offered (C. Stern & Gould, 1955), for example, that certain so-called "normal" behavior patterns appear too early or too late or not at all. If such conditions appear, they can be taken as symptoms of pathology. The infant whose ability to move, cry, smile, sit, stand, walk, or talk is delayed is showing signs of pathology. So is the infant who moves about excessively, who cries constantly, who does not sleep, and who is a feeding problem. Other signs of pathology are the well-known specific abnormalities of appearance, such as a too large or too small head, the inability to move the eyeballs in the normal way, and the continuous rocking movements and head banging. There is, however, a danger of misjudging slight abnormalities of behavior. Since Gesell and Ilg (1945; 1946; 1956) published their scales of so-called "normal" development, many a parent has hurried to the pediatrician's office, worried that the baby was abnormal because of a delay of a few weeks in achieving a supposedly normal level of development. In attempting to establish abnormality, definite and repeated unusual behavior should be looked for. Only if a child shows continuing lack of response to outside stimuli or continually rocks his head are we justified in suspecting mental abnormality.

This dual aspect of retardation and hyperactivity of a variety of functions seems to be an adequate criterion for a preliminary evaluation of mental pathology during the first decade of life. Recently, attempts were made to establish or circumscribe specific syndromes of psychopathology in infancy; yet it is not until after the third or fourth year of life that the psychopathological behavior pictures justify differential labeling. This, of course, does not apply to general constitutional, organic, or neurological pathology.

Human nature, as we are concerned with it here, does not start with birth but with conception, and perhaps for more thorough insight, it should even be considered to start with the condition of the parents. Montague's (1962) study of prenatal influence has shown that unsound maternal life and behavior and maternal illness can condition the physical as well as the mental health of the child. Major deformities such as imbecility, idiocy, and mongolism, as well as hydrocephalitis and microcephalitis, are conditions that begin in the womb.

There is a difference of opinion about whether the moment of birth is traumatic for the infant. There are other conditions at the moment of birth that can have traumatic effects; for example, impairment may be inflicted on the child delivered with the aid of forceps or other mechanical methods.

The impact of infant physical existence upon mental existence is of greater importance than at any later period of human life. During the first days of his life, a baby sleeps and eats. Only slowly does he step out of the "arms of Morpheus" into waking life. The study of the sleep of infants and what might be called "infants' dreams" has only just begun, and considerable work remains to be done before the necessary facts are established.

Psychoanalysis (A. Freud, 1947; A. Freud, 1948; S. Freud, 1955) and individual psychology (Adler, 1929; Adler, 1930) have shed light on the importance of the earliest episodes of human existence and their influence on the healthy as well as the psychopathological formations of character and personality. A baby is not only a mouth, a stomach, and a colon; from the beginning, he is a sensitive psychic being. Bakwin's (1942) observations of hospitalized babies deprived of maternal contact, in his famous study "The Loneliness of Babies," confirmed this assumption. Evidently even a newborn infant, although almost entirely in a prewaking state of existence, possesses an awareness that has a considerable impact on his health (Harms, 1952). In spite of the amount of information encountered on feeding problems in infants, we still do not have adequate information on this initial phase of human mental life. Up to now we have relied more on observations of neurological and psychosomatic pathology of the first months of life than on the actual psychic behavior. EEG studies of the waking habits of infants, their short episodes of wakefulness, and the process of tiring may become another source of knowledge of the unfolding of infant mental life.

Classification

A system of classification based on a standard nomenclature is a requirement for a scientific discipline; it enables scientists to communicate and to use one another's insights and findings. The formulation and testing of hypotheses about etiology, treatment, and prevention of a syndrome depend on the classification of disorders.

The field of childhood disorders suffers from a plethora of diagnostic terminology. Different schools of thought and training centers, as well as individual clinicians, use diagnostic terms which reflect their specific theoretical orientations. There have been at least a dozen classifications in use. Brown, Pollock, Potter, and Cohen (1937) offered a psychiatric classification of problem children, which was officially approved by the New York State Department of Mental Hygiene. This outline distinguished among 10 "principal groups": (1) mental deficiencies; (2) psychoses; (3) psychoneuroses and neuroses; (4) convulsive disorders, including epilepsy; (5) behavior disorders with somatic disease or defect; (8) primary behavior disorders ("i.e., not secondary to other groups in this classification"); (9) social problems; and (10) other problems. In his famous textbook, Kanner (1935) divided the disorders into three main classes: personality disorders that form (1) sequels of physical illness, (2) involuntary part dysfunctions, and (3) involuntary whole dysfunctions. In the 1948 edition, Kanner gives the following classification: (1) physical illness, (2) psychosomatic problems, and (3) problems of behavior. Problems of eating, sleeping, and speech; jealousy; schizophrenia; hypochondria; and suicide are all found in the third category.

Classifications based on generic terms created even greater confusion. This relates especially to attempts to differentiate between personality problems and behavior and conduct problems (Ackerson, 1931; Louttit, 1936; Payntor & Blanchard, 1929).

Howard and Patry (1935) devised three groups of "reactive disorders on the basis of emotional, situational, habit training and personality maladjustment." The reasons given for such grouping are unconvincing. Pearson's (1949) "classification of psychological illness in children" is an attempt to bring child psychiatry more in line with adult psychiatry. His categories are (1) direct reaction to present environmental areas; (2) acute and chronic anxiety states; (3) anxiety hysteria; (4) conversion hysteria, including conversion hysteria after the phallic step of development is attained and pregenital conversion hysteria; (5) organic neurosis; (6) compulsion neurosis; (7) perversion; (8) psychosis; and (9) character neurosis. Hall (1947), a British psychiatrist, classified childhood disorders from the educational viewpoint. Hutt and Gibby (1957) developed a classification based on relationship problems, environment, and cure.

The standard nomenclature for mental disorders of patients of all ages, issued by the American Psychiatric Association in 1952, is the only diagnostic terminology that has official recognition. Basically, this classification divides mental disorders into those associated with organic brain disturbance and those occurring without it. In each group there are secondary divisions designating the presence of psychotic, neurotic, and behavior disorders. Mental deficiency (without brain damage) is subclassified into mild, moderate, and severe. Under schizophrenic reactions, there is a subcategory of childhood type. The psychophysiologic autonomic and visceral disorders are subclassified according to the organ system in which manifestations appear. The psychoneurotic disorders are subclassified according to how the anxiety is manifested or transformed into symptoms: (1) anxiety reaction, (2) dissociative reaction, (3) conversion reaction, (4) phobic reaction, (5) obsessive-compulsive reaction, (6) depressive reaction, and (7) other reactions. The personality disorders are categorized according to four general reactions, and each of them is further broken down by specific qualifications: (1) personality-pattern disturbance (inadequate, schizoid, cyclothymic, paranoid); (2) personality-trait disturbance (emotionally unstable, passive, aggressive, other); (3) sociopathic personality disturbance (antisocial, dyssocial, sexual deviation, alcoholism, drug addiction); (4) special symptom reactions (learning disturbance, speech disturbance, enuresis, somnambulism, other). Under transient situational personality disorders, specific subgroupings refer to infancy, childhood, adolescence, adulthood, and late life.

The official nomenclature is used mostly for record keeping in formal discharge diagnoses. It is not generally used as a primary source for diagnostic terminology, as it is considered inadequate for the fields of child diagnosis and treatment. There is a pressing need for a better nosology for childhood disorders.

Two recent attempts at classification are noteworthy. Lesser (1964) has devised a classification system that is dynamically oriented. It assumes that since children are in the process of rapid growth, their emotional disturbance cannot be categorized into a rigid system. The familial environment constitutes an integral part of the child's ego, and his emotional difficulties result largely from pathological environmental situations. The exact type of problem exhibited will depend upon two things: (1) the influences to which he is subjected at various ages and (2) his specific reaction to these situations. He may rebel against the environment; he may submit to reality; or he may play passively and deny, ignore, distort, withdraw, or evade realities. The ways in which a child presents his conflicts and his methods of dealing with them constitute the symptomatology of his disorder.

Lesser's classification

I. Disorders associated with CNS dysfunction.

II. Disorders of psychogenic origin without clearly defined physical cause or structural change in the brain.

A. Psychotic disorders: Early autism; symbiotic psychosis; childhood schizophrenia.

B. Psychophysiologic autonomic and visceral disorders: Somatization reactions; hypochondriasis.

C. Adjustment problems: Fixation at, or regression to, less mature modes of behavior. It is important to note that many if not the majority of cases are mixed; that is, they show symptoms as described in many or all of the subheadings below. Subheadings are based on predominant symptomatology into the following:

1. Anxiety reactions that are made up of various manifestations of denial-fear-withdrawal phenomena. Here anxiety and anger cannot be perceived or expressed in a fashion which is acceptable to the patient or others, and consequently anxiety mounts. Reality may be distorted to aid in exclusion of conflictual stimuli. Adjustive techniques for binding the anxiety have not come into play. These are often temporary mechanisms which are later supplanted by others and which are accompanied by poor work or school performance. When the latter symptoms predominate, one may designate the problem as follows:

a. Educational disability: Here the anxiety and/or conflict interferes with concentration and attention and hence with learning. This leads to poor performance and its consequences, which in turn intensify anxiety and guilt. Specific reading and mathematical disabilities may be considered variants of educational disability. They may also represent rebellion against parental pressures for learning and fit into the following category:

2. Conduct disorders (primary behavior disorders): Symptoms are directed toward the environment and include overaggressiveness, "passive resistance," disobedience, lying, stealing, destructiveness, fighting, running away, fire setting, truancy, cruelty, and various sexual activities.

a. Limited social significance.

b. Serious social significance.

3. Personality-trait disorders: Here the symptoms are directed toward the patient, as contrasted with conduct disorders. These include disturbances of sex orientation or preference and subsume previous groupings: habit disturbance, which includes breath holding, nail biting, thumb sucking, enuresis, masturbation, and temper tantrums, and neurotic traits, which are closely related but less pleasurable. These include tics, habit spasms, somnambulism, stammering, overactivity,

and phobias. The latter group continues almost imperceptibly into the following group:

D. Psychoneurosis: Structuralized adult symptomatology including full-blown anxiety and dissociative states, conversion reactions, obsessive-compulsive neurosis, etc. Here the symptoms are inaccessible to awareness and are symbolic of the conflict.

E. Gross stress reactions: Here a child with a heretofore healthy personality and seemingly normal adjustment decompensates because of external events.

F. Deprivation reactions: Spitz, Goldfarb, Bowlby phenomena; anaclitic depression.

III. Mental deficiency: no demonstrable organic basis.

Chess (1959) proposed a simplified diagnostic classification that "may be readily correlated with the standard nomenclature of the American Psychiatric Association": (1) normal, (2) organic brain disturbance, (3) reactive behavior disorders, (4) neurotic behavior disorders, (5) neurotic character disorders, (6) neurosis, (7) childhood psychosis and schizophrenic adjustments, (8) psychopathic personality, and (9) mental retardation. These categories have served well with etiological formulations and therapeutic planning. Discussion of each category will now be presented.

Some normal children come to the attention of psychologists and psychiatrists because of parental misinterpretation of normal behavior or overexaggeration of a minor maturational stress. It is appropriate to diagnose the child as normal. Chess (1959) points out the difficulty of agreeing on a definition of normality and offers the following description: A normal child "gets along reasonably well with parents, siblings, and friends, has few overt manifestations of behavioral disturbance, is using his apparent intellectual potential to a degree close to its estimate, and is contented for a reasonable proportion of the time." The description includes a wide variety of personality patterns, from the somewhat shy and quiet one to the somewhat active and aggressive one.

Organic brain disturbance is discussed in "Organic Mental Disorders," chap. 25.

Reactive Behavior Disorders

This category corresponds to the widely used term "primary behavior disorders," meaning that they are not secondary to an organic process. This category includes behavior patterns developed as defenses against inappropriate restraints or as results of restrictions caused by physical illness or traumatic events; the term "reactive" implies that a change in the stress situation will bring a change in adjustment. Typically, children with such disorders may pose problems at home but not at school, or vice versa. They may misbehave at camp but not in the playground. The circumstances under which the behavior disorder appears may point to its etiology; factors of relationships with parents or siblings, space limitations, lack of privacy, and other irritants should be investigated. Difficulties with a special subject or a special teacher need to be taken seriously, and help offered. The symptoms themselves of fighting, truancy, destructiveness, etc., do not establish the diagnosis; limitation as to the place of acting out and reversibility under environmental manipulation or brief treatment are the essential evidence.

Neurotic Behavior Disorders

This syndrome signifies that the reaction pattern has become the dominant one in all situations. In addition, there may be present the beginning of compulsions, phobias, and hysterical reactions. These disorders are not modifiable by ordinary methods of removing stress. Treatment requires a combined attack on the environment and on the behavioral pattern itself. At times, treatment or guidance of parents alone may be enough to modify the child's behavior. In other cases, the child must be seen in treatment.

Neurotic Character Disorders

This category signifies the further progression toward rigidity of the previous categories. In this phase the child battles constantly with his environment as well as with his drives; his defensive pattern becomes part of his personality structure. While his behavior is adequate in some respects, in others it displays the rigidity of his defense mechanisms.

The character of these children is manifested not by classical symptoms but in their behavior and relationships. They may have poor relations with other children because of too much aggression or passivity, or they may be overdependent and overdemanding or overorderly, stubborn, and miserly. Though a child may feel that there is little wrong in his behavior, the negative response he engenders in others brings consequences that cause him anxiety and further intensification of defenses. Group therapy is the treatment of choice for children with character disorders.

PSYCHONEUROSIS IN CHILDREN

Freud's famous aphorism, "No adult neurosis without an infantile neurosis," succinctly states his discovery of childhood symptoms in the history of his adult patients. By Freud's own definition, however, psychoneurosis is not an infantile disorder. It originates at a later psychosexual developmental stage as a result of unsuccessful resolution of the Oedipus conflict, which occurs in children between the ages of 4 and 7. The nucleus of every neurosis is the child's libidinal drive toward the parent of the opposite sex and his fear of retaliation by the parent of the same sex. When the incestuous drives are not adequately handled, a conflict rages between the id and the superego, with the ego serving as the battleground. When the ego is too weak to repress the incestuous drives and to reconcile the conflict, anxiety is generated. The ego attempts to deal with the incestuous and infantile strivings and the anxiety they generate by erecting defenses, whose function is to keep the impulses unconscious.

The defenses are never sufficient to contain all the anxiety or to repress all the infantile strivings. As a result anxiety reappears, and additional defenses are required to keep the impulse from awareness. The entire psychic structure becomes burdensome. Symptoms appear, which represent a compromise between inner impulses and prohibitions against them. A symptom is the price that the neurotic pays in order to avoid becoming aware of his true conflict. It is a symbolic solution that allows the real problem to remain unsolved. While full-blown neuroses are less frequent in children than behavior disorders, nevertheless anxiety reactions, phobias, and obsessive-compulsive symptoms are not rare in childhood.

Anxiety is fundamental to all neuroses. It is the internal alarm system that warns when forbidden impulses are threatening to break into consciousness. Differentiation among the neuroses is based on the particular method used to handle anxiety.

Anxiety Reaction

In this neurosis, free-floating anxiety is present constantly. In children it is manifested by hyperactivity, fidgeting, tension, and clumsiness. The children are described by their mothers as being always "on the move" and always "doing something with their hands," moving the legs or tapping with the fingers. They have difficulty falling asleep, and they toss and turn during the night. Nightmares or sleepwalking may appear. Although he may not be aggressive or mischievous, such a child is a constant problem to the teacher. His anxiety makes him restless, and the constant fidgeting upsets the class and the teacher. The parents are usually surprised when the school finds these children to be behavior problems because they may be timid or friendly in the neighborhood.

The child with chronic anxiety fears new situations and new people. Though he may not have phobias, he is often afraid of being alone, of starting new ventures, of being in the dark, and of most other ordinary life situations.

In the playroom such a child may appear initially polite, pleasant, and intelligent, but tense. He does everything rapidly. There is quality or commitment in whatever he does. The smallest failure may make him abandon whatever he is doing. He does not seem to enjoy his play, whether it is painting, sewing, or throwing darts. He is constantly on the move for something different.

When anxiety becomes severe, the symptomatology becomes more serious. The child becomes less efficient in school and more fearful at home, and he withdraws even further from friends and social give-and-take.

Phobic Reaction

Phobias have been labeled the "normal neurosis of childhood" (English & Pearson, 1945), as they occur in many children. Typical examples are fears of the dark, animals, heights, and monsters (and of schools). Transient phobias occur in many normal children during the oedipal stage and represent the child's projection on the outer world of his fears of his unconscious inner impulses. These normal phobias diminish or disappear as the oedipal situation is resolved and as the child moves into latency.

The child with a neurotic phobic reaction is one whose phobias are more severe and more exaggerated. Any child may fear a big ferocious dog, especially if once bitten. A phobic child will fear all dogs, regardless of size and nature. The phobia is a symbolic representation of the unacceptable libidinal and aggressive impulses, many of them stemming from an inadequately resolved Oedipus complex.

The content of the phobias sometimes points to the origin of the unconscious difficulty. Fear of witches and monsters probably represents a projection of the hostility toward, and fear of, the mother and father.

It is impossible to reduce all phobias to a categorical system. However, many phobias represent concern with punishment for forbidden impulses toward a significant adult.

Conversion Reaction

This syndrome is characterized by a tendency to convert emotional conflicts into symptoms. The symptoms may involve the voluntary musculature (spastic flaccid paralysis), a special sense (blindness, deafness, anesthesia of an area), or the autonomic system (functions of the gastrointestinal tract and the vascular system, etc.).

Conversion reactions are compromise solutions in the conflict between the unresolved oedipal striving of a libidinous and aggressive nature and the fear of castration. A facilitating condition for the development of conversion reaction is the phenomenon of somatic compliance. This refers to the tendency of the psyche to utilize normal and abnormal body functions as focuses for conversion (Harms, 1945; Harms, 1953). An example is the child who develops a persistent pain in a postoperative scar.

The child with a conversion reaction is emotionally immature and unstable and comes from a background of naïveté and superstition. In modern times, there are fewer cases of special sense conversions such as blindness and deafness. There are, however, conversions involving the autonomic system.

The prognosis for conversion reactions in childhood is considered to be favorable. The children have progressed further in their psychosexual development than other neurotic children. Children with conversion reactions have regressed to the phallic stage, and they fare better with therapy than those with primarily oral and anal difficulties.

Obsessive-compulsive Reaction

The obsessive-compulsive reaction is characterized by the presence of relentless tendencies to think, say, or do something in a particular way; by resistance to such tendencies; and by rising anxiety that leads to indulgence, followed by momentary relief. The thoughts and acts may be trivial, such as saying a phrase, whistling a tune, or snapping the fingers, or they may be more painful and humiliating to the child. The relief from tension achieved by indulgence is always temporary.

Sooner or later tensions begin to mount until the child is again compelled to indulge in order to reduce them. The child may be ashamed and perplexed by the actions and may resent their humiliating nature.

At times the obsessive thoughts have an "undoing" quality; thus the repetitious thought "I hate mother" may immediately be followed by the thought "I love mother." The compulsive acts serve to ward off some unknown danger and catastrophe.

The child may avoid stepping on cracks in the sidewalk ("Step on a crack, break your mother's back"), or he may count stairs, touch telephone poles, or dress and undress in a rigid order. These are some examples of compulsions seen in children especially during latency. The obsessive child is often subject to peculiar throat noises, spitting sounds, blocking on certain words, or placing dirty objects or body secretions in his mouth. He shows excessive interest in bowel movements and other excretory products.

The obsessive-compulsive neurosis affects the personality of the child to a much greater extent than hysteria. In hysterical reaction, unacceptable strivings are repressed. In the obsessive-compulsive reaction, the child's ego tries to avoid recognition of the libidinal and aggressive strivings by regressing from the phallic stage to the anal sadistic stage of development. The mechanisms that the ego uses are numerous: magic ritual, undoing, reaction formation, and isolation. It is the combination of repression and the use of large numbers of defenses that affects the whole personality.

The underlying psychopathology of the compulsive lies in his anality. Unconsciously he returns to the attitudes of an infant: ambivalence, sadomasochism, messiness, obstinacy, and rebelliousness. When it is unacceptable to adults, the child may develop defenses to keep the impulses from becoming conscious. Instead of being messy, he becomes meticulous; instead of being sadistic, he becomes ingratiating; instead of being dirty, he becomes excessively clean. The excessive use of reaction formation puts the child in constant conflict. His unconscious impulse is in the opposite direction from his defense. The inefficiency, from a psychological view, is the waste of energy entailed in such a system.

The obsessive-compulsive child tries to conceal his emotions. Since this cannot be achieved, he is prone to temper tantrums. Sudden storms and sadistic episodes are characteristic.

Special Bothersome Symptoms

There is a group of symptoms that cannot be put in any of the foregoing categories because they occur in almost any childhood disorder.

Enuresis. Nocturnal enuresis is one of the most common symptoms of emotional problems of childhood (Bakwin, 1949). There is some dispute about the earliest age at which a child can be labeled "enuretic." The practice is to postpone making a diagnosis of enuresis until the child is beyond 4 years of age and only after organic cause has been ruled out. Finch (1960) estimates that in only 5 per cent of incontinence the symptom is caused by physical factors such as bladder infections, diabetes, epilepsy, or genitourinary anomalies.

English and Pearson (1945) divided enuresis into several categories:

1. *Revenge enuresis,* an unconscious expression of rebellion against strict parental demands.
2. *Regressive enuresis,* a psychosexual regression as the result of some emotional threat. Gerard (1959) found that more than half of enuretic children have confused sexual identification and that they dream of urinating in the position of the opposite sex.
3. *Enuresis with castration fears.* Some children become enuretic after injury, surgery, illness, or sexual trauma. They become convinced that they have incurred permanent damage to their genitals.
4. *Enuresis* due to hysterical identification with an incontinent parent.
5. *Enuresis due to lack of training.* In some large families, especially of the lower socioeconomic classes, it is accepted as the normal pattern of the family to wet the bed. The younger children, if not instructed to the contrary, will continue in the family tradition.

Encopresis. Most children who soil beyond the age of 3 or 4 suffer from emotional rather than physical problems.

This problem is common among preschoolers, but it is also found among school-age children. The older the child, the more serious the pathology. The symptom itself is very annoying to parents. Their criticism and shaming of the child usually lead him to hide his soiled underwear, which brings further deterioration in the parent-child relationship. Encopresis may serve as a form of revenge and as a continuous rebellion against strict toilet training and against parental authority in general. It may also represent fixation or regression to the anal phase. The symptom then represents a symbolic expression of the conflicts with parents and of forbidden anal fantasies.

The therapeutic approach to encopresis, after medical clearing, must deal with the child's inner conflicts as well as with the relationship between parents and child.

School phobia. This term does not designate a diagnostic category. School phobia can be found as a symptom in almost any emotional disorder, and its presence does not indicate the severity of the disorder. Frequently it represents fear of separation from the mother rather than fear of school per se. The child may be afraid, also, to visit other children or to stay home by himself, or he may insist on going with the mother wherever she goes.

School phobias must be differentiated from nonattendance due to lack of interest, shame of academic failure, or truancy. "A true phobic reaction is an expression of intense anxiety in the school situation from which the child protects himself by withdrawing from school."

Treatment of school phobia, as of any symptom, will depend on the specific nature of the underlying emotional disorder. It is best if the child can continue to attend school and to avoid the secondary gains involved in being home with the mother. Psychotherapy is facilitated when the anxiety-producing situation is not totally removed. During the time of heightened anxiety, demands may be softened and some special privileges granted (such as exemption from gym or assembly).

If the legal exemption from school attendance is arranged, the home regime must minimize secondary gains, and study plans must be introduced and carried out.

OTHER SCHOOL PROBLEMS. Four areas would come under consideration in a survey of psychopathology related to schooling: (1) the general psychopathological problems of the student, (2) the psychopathology of the learning process, (3) the psychopathology of the classroom or educational setting, and (4) the psychopathology of the pupil-teacher relationship (Greiszinger, 1945).

The general psychopathological problems of the student include mental retardation or some form of psychopathology that impairs the child's capacity for classroom participation; this includes the child with physical impairments such as partial deafness or partial blindness and the slow learner, the child with an introverted disposition, or an otherwise slow-to-develop child. In this category are also included the so-called "wonder" children who have a one-sided disposition and who do not want to be bothered with learning the three R's, preferring to occupy themselves entirely with the development of their extraordinary faculties. As Buehler (1930; 1935) has shown, irregularities in general development do not necessarily indicate inferiority. Children who are slow in developing may become more able individuals than some who develop more rapidly. Finally, among general psychopathological problems of the schoolchild there is social impairment such as that resulting from a broken home, orphancy (Harms, 1943), or poverty that hampers scholastic abilities.

Under psychopathology of the learning process, there are children of limited intellectual capacity and children with reading or mathematical disabilities; others with good ability at remembering historical or geographical facts may lack ability in special interest spheres (Hamilton, 1947). It is recognized that there is a difference between the imaginative and the rational learner and that some children are more susceptible to aural than to visual reception.

Classroom psychopathology is another condition that is only partially recognized today. It was the Polish psychologist Hessen (1936) who, several decades ago, called attention to the class as a group with different abilities to comprehend, depending on how it is organized. He wrote a "gestalt psychology" of learning in groups. For the neurotic child, the classroom indeed presents considerable problems of adjustment. Radical rejection of school and truancy are not always "bad-boy" behavior. Most truants are such because of psychopathological factors that prevent them from accepting classroom instruction. The restless child should be studied to determine whether there are psychopathological factors involved before he is punished. Finally, there are the elements of ambition, anxiety, jealousy, and simple nervousness, all of which can play a role in the classroom.

Psychopathology in pupil-teacher relationships (Heuyer, 1951) results from the fact, as someone has ironically said, that "teachers are also human beings." The overcrowded classroom and the close personal relationship between teacher and children of different ages, character structures, and learning abilities are the basis of countless problems and conflicts. The emotional demands of a class of 30 to 40 children can create problems that cannot be handled in the time and space allotted to the present-day classrooms. The superior child presents special problems, especially in pupil-teacher relationships. The more superior the child (Hollinsworth, 1926), the more difficult is the pupil-teacher relationship, and the more susceptible the child is to impairment. It is especially here that the teacher must take on a parental role, since parents are generally unable to cope with the intellectual and emotional demands of the superior child. The child's growth may be endangered if he does not have a superior teacher who can respond to his needs.

PSYCHOPATHOLOGY AS A PROCESS

The discovery that a majority of mental disorders begin in childhood and that the childhood forms of mental disease must be studied if a complete picture of the course of the trauma is to be obtained was considered an important advance in our knowledge of psychopathology. Dynamically, it meant moving backward to childhood. It was the great contribution of Benjamin (1930) to change the direction of the study of childhood psychopathology as a developmental process. It appears, however, that two aspects have still not been properly taken into account. The first is the "dual developmental line" in childhood psychopathology, and the second is the course of cure of childhood psychopathology.

By "dual developmental line" is meant that the child himself is a growing concern. All the child's physical and mental forces are geared to healthy growth. When illness occurs, these healthily growing elements are an essential and primary factor in cure, either as an underlying healthy power or, where severe impairment is present, as a compensatory factor. Where one of the senses has been impaired or lost, the functioning of the healthy forces may be sharpened. Thus children with cerebral palsy caused by prenatal or birth injury show ability to compensate for their impairment.

In many respects we still lack precise information about the actual course of psychopathology in childhood, the aspects involved in improvement, and the duration and the process of "cure." In most cases we lack actual specific knowledge of the inner therapeutic process. The future task of child psychopathology is to gain insight into the dynamics of the major mental disorders of childhood and to establish scientific methods of cure and prevention.

CHILDHOOD PSYCHOSES[2]

Incidence

Psychiatric folklore of the not too distant past entertained the belief that the earliest evidence of psychosis could not be detected before adolescence. A clinical cliché described psychotics as "those who founder on the rocks of puberty." Although insanity in children was not unknown, it was looked upon not as a childhood illness but as a developmental mutation and a clinical oddity. Ekstein, Bryant, and Friedman (1958) attribute the need to deny frank psychotic states in children to the dread of psychoses of adults still fearful of the infantile aspects of their own personalities. Mahler (1955) noted that the reluctance to label a child "psychotic" and to face the severity of his illness brought a host of "softened" diagnostic labels such as "pseudopsychosis," "pre-psychosis," and "incipient" and "borderline" psychosis.

It is of more than historical interest to note the changes that have occurred in the professional approach to childhood psychoses. Once childhood schizophrenia became a legitimate diagnostic category, the apparent rate of incidence increased with each passing decade. The last decade witnessed a plethora of detailed case histories dealing with the many aspects of childhood schizophrenia. In fact, there is now a tendency to overdiagnose and to label any severe disturbance "schizophrenic."

In 1942, Bender stated that many psychiatrists did not accept the diagnosis of childhood schizophrenia because they had never seen a case. In 1963, Milt, of the National Association of Mental Health, reported that there are about four thousand psychotic children in state hospitals and about twenty-five hundred in residential treatment and day-care centers. About three thousand schizophrenic children are seen at outpatient psychiatric clinics. He emphasizes the fact that there are tens of thousands of children suffering from childhood schizophrenia. Some estimates reach as high as half a million.

These figures sadly confirm the fact that childhood schizophrenia is not at all a rare disease. It may be rare only in comparison with the total number of emotionally disturbed children.

Etiology

Psychoses in children, like those in adults, can be classified as (1) organic (the chronic brain syndromes), (2) toxic (the acute brain syndromes), and (3) functional (the disorders of psychogenic origin, without clearly defined physical cause or structural change in the brain). The discussion will be confined to the functional psychoses.

The nosological confusion inherent in the problem of childhood psychoses was cleared up considerably by the contributions of Kanner (1943; 1949; 1955), Mahler (1952; 1954; 1958), and Bender (1947; 1953; 1956). Their "early infantile autism," "symbiotic psychosis," and "childhood schizophrenia," respectively, met the standard of dynamic nosology. Their classification defines the problem, the factors that produced it, and the patient who has it.

EARLY INFANTILE AUTISM

In 1943, Kanner reported about a group of 11 children whose clinical picture appeared to comprise a psychotic illness previously undescribed. Independently in 1944, Asperger, an Austrian psychiatrist, published a lengthy paper entitled "Autistische Psychopathen im Kindersalter." The first reports met with some skepticism, but soon many confirmatory findings were published both in the United States and abroad. Autistic children were studied in the United States by Despert (1951), Eisen-

2 This section of the chapter was written by Dr. Ginott.

berg (1956), Mahler (1952), Rank (1952; 1955), Weil (1953), and others; in Canada by Cappon (1953); in England by Creak (1951); in France by E. Stern and Schachter (1953); and in Holland by van Krevelen (1952), Grewel, Prick, Sunier, Kamp, and Gaudia (1954), and Rimland (1964).

According to Kanner, the syndrome of early infantile autism results from gross deficiencies in the earliest ego development due to (1) a constitutional predisposition of the infant toward faulty ego development and (2) a pathological emotional atmosphere created by the parents. The normal infant is autistic during the first three months of his life. He is relatively unaware of, and unresponsive to, people and objects. This phase has been termed by Mahler the "normal autistic phase" of the mother-infant relationship.

Through the regularly repeated cycle of body tension, relief, and gratification, the infant becomes dimly aware of external reality, as represented by the mother's breast, face, voice, and touch. Between the third and fourth months, he becomes responsive to sights, sounds, caresses, and smiles.

If there is no person to provide the required emotional warmth and physical care, the infant may never grow out of the autistic phase. The typical parents of the autistic children were described by Kanner as cold and obsessional, intelligent and detached, and extremely impersonal and mechanical. In this emotionally refrigerated atmosphere, the infants remain interpersonally unstimulated and unresponsive. The basic psychopathology stems from the failure of the infantile ego to perceive the mother as the first representative of outer reality. For the autistic child, the mother as a person and as a separate entity did not ever become cathected.

A diagnosis of early infantile autism is rarely made during the first two years of life, although the syndrome is manifested almost from birth. During the first year the evidence is hard to recognize because the normal immaturity of all infants masks the deficiencies in ego development of the autistic children. Only in retrospect, as the case history is reviewed, does it become apparent that the severe defects in ego development had always been present. Typically, parents may remark that even as an infant their baby was averse to physical contact and that he was an undemanding baby; he rarely cried, never got angry, and demanded only minimal care and fondling. Each case history reveals the decisive defect: the child's failure to develop any relationships with people.

The significance of this fact is often overlooked by parents. They see it as an idiosyncrasy which the child will outgrow. They become alarmed, however, during the second or third year of the infant's life, when the more obvious signs of autism begin to reveal themselves.

The most common symptom for which parents seek professional help is the child's failure to pay attention to or even to hear the parents' words and warnings. Though there are many other autistic signs, parents usually focus on the child's hearing in the hope that his odd behavior is due to physical deafness rather than emotional disturbance.

Symptoms

Extreme self-insulation. The most telling symptom of the autistic child is his extreme insulation. He is seemingly content to be left alone. He does not demand attention, and he resists any human intrusion. He is described by mothers as being indifferent to their presence or absence, as disliking bodily contact or caresses, and as never making a personal appeal for help.

Similar behavior is also evident when an autistic child is seen by a clinician in the playroom (Ginott, 1961). He separates from his mother with relative ease, and he evinces apathy, as though her person had no meaning to him. Indeed he does not differentiate between one adult and another, and he will follow anyone at all who takes his hand. He seems utterly isolated and unreachable. He does not respond to overtures, friendly or threatening; he does not show signs of fear, nor does he shrink away when the adult approaches; he persistently fails to look up when he is addressed and does not react even when the adult leaves the room. During the session there is barely a change in his expression. There is no smile of pleasure, no sigh of sadness, and no look of interest. He exhibits frozen indifference to persons around him.

The autistic child relates to parts rather than to the whole of people and objects. He will use the adult's hand as though it were a handle; if he wants help in opening a door, he may drag the adult's hand in the direction of the door, never looking at the adult's face to note his reaction. He will not smile at the helping person, even in response to a smile, and he will make no gesture of thanks.

Insistence on sameness. In his efforts to live in an unchanging world of his own, the autistic child shows a relentless insistence on preservation of sameness. Mothers report that such children can play with a few toys for hours on end and that they become enraged at any change in the inanimate surroundings. Kanner (1943) reports that any modification meets with perplexity and discomfort. The children find security in sameness, "a security that is tenuous because changes do occur constantly and the children are therefore threatened perpetually."

In the playroom (Ginott, 1961), the autistic child's behavior may be directed primarily to himself in a stereotyped manner. He may pull his ear, twist his hair, eat nasal mucus, or stick his fingers into a crack in the wall. With monotonous fascination he may spin a wheel, click a switch on and off, turn doorknobs back and forth, or twiddle a piece of string for an entire hour. When seen for several sessions, he wants the very same toys every time, and he may show an uncanny memory for the kind and number of toys present in the playroom. He reacts violently to a broken toy or torn doll clothes, but his tears and tantrums stop abruptly when things are restored to their former condition.

Language disturbance. Language disturbance in the autistic child ranges from failure to develop speech to extreme idiosyncratic use of words. Even when he has speech, he shows no interest in communication. In his talk, he uses phrases that are correct in structure but irrelevant to the situation. When directly questioned, he may respond with parrotlike repetition of the question. Some of the children have normal phonation; others use singsong or talk like Donald Duck. Some of them can recite an amazing number of rhymes, ditties, and prayers as well as the alphabet, lists of animals, and names of presidents. Though they can use such sentences for recitation, they may not be able to use these words for purposes of communication with others. Some of the children speak only to themselves or only to toys and inanimate objects, and some find it difficult ever to stop talking.

Some autistic children never use speech, as though they were deaf and dumb. They make no direct response to sound, regardless of intensity. The lack of response represents denial of perception rather than deafness. When his name is called or when a metal object is dropped near him, the autistic child does not respond with a move or a startle. However, when a record of a familiar tune is played, he may turn in the direction of the sound or move rhythmically with the music. The autistic child remains indifferent when urged to talk, and he never tries to imitate adults' facial expressions or the movement of their lips.

Aberrant reaction to pain. Some autistic children display aberrant reactions to physical pain; they do not communicate feelings of distress through the usual outlets of crying and whining. It appears as though the child is insulated even against his own physiological reactions, since he will occasionally indulge in serious self-injury; for example, he may bang his head, bite his tongue, cut his hand, squeeze his fingers in a door, or sit on a hot radiator. All this occurs without a word of complaint. Any attempts to offer sympathy will go unacknowledged.

The meaning of symptoms. According to Mahler, Furer, and Settlage (1958), childhood psychoses can be understood as psychopathological distortions of the normal phases of ego development which depend on the early mother-child relationship. When a primary love object is functionally nonexistent, autism becomes the primary defense. The defective ego of the child is overtaxed by his inner stimuli and cannot cope with additional stimulation from the outside world. The undifferentiated ego cannot mediate between external and internal stimuli. The outer reality is experienced as a source of constant irritation, so that a barrier is built up against intrusions, especially against stimuli which demand emotional and social responses.

Autistic children are usually toilet-trained at the age of normal children. The relative ease of the training, like their lowered sensitivity to pain, stems from their low body cathexis and insufficient erotization of body surface and orifices. The ease of toileting also reflects their lack of emotional involvement with the mother, whom they do not need to please by defecating or to spite by withholding.

Mahler et al. (1958) sees the self-hurting activities of the autistic child as pathological attempts to feel alive. By banging, biting, and cutting themselves, they get a feeling of their body and its boundaries and thus achieve a sense of "entity if not identity."

SYMBIOTIC PSYCHOSIS

Infantile symbiotic psychosis was first defined by Mahler in 1952. The onset of this syndrome occurs in children aged 1 to 4. The onset is more dramatic, and the clinical picture more complex, than in early infantile autism, since it occurs at a more differentiated ego stage.

The roots of this psychosis lie in the symbiotic phase of development. Under normal conditions, ego development proceeds from a three-month autistic phase to a normal symbiotic phase, which is gradually replaced during the next two years by a separation-individuation phase. The normal child is able to achieve this emotional and physical separation from the mother; the child with symbiotic psychosis is not.

During the symbiotic phase, the infant relies totally on the mother for his physical and emotional nurture. The crucial phase in adaptation or maladaptation to reality is the one in which the mother is gradually recognized as being outside the orbit of the self. Emerging from a mother-infant unit, the toddler separates himself and his image of himself from that of the mother. This is a very vulnerable stage in ego development.

In the second and third years of life, the infant is confronted with the difficult task of coordinating physical maturation and emotional development. The maturation of the central nervous system grants the child a degree of physical autonomy with which his emotional growth must keep pace. Some children lose this race. Because of either constitutional or environmental reasons, their emotional development lags far behind their somatic spurts. Their emotional lag expresses itself in their inability to differentiate from the mother. They cannot separate from her emotionally, even though they are able to do so physically. The discrepancy between maturational and emotional development increases with age. When autonomous ego functions and sexual maturation far exceed the emotional differentiation from the mother, the child's brittle ego structure tends to fragment.

The basic psychopathology, then, involves an early mother-infant symbiotic relationship which does not progress to the next stage of object libidinal cathexis of the mother, so that the image of the mother remains fused with the image of self. Through symbiotic fusion with the mother, the child attempts to maintain the illusion of omnipotence and to ward off the overwhelming panic entailed in separation and individuation. However, inevitable situations develop which threaten the symbiotic unit of mother and child. The crisis may be the birth of a baby, the illness of the mother, or any other sudden change in family constellation or life. The child's brittle ego is unable to tolerate the trauma, and psychosis results.

Mahler emphasizes that symbiotic children are not normal children in whom a psychotic process is induced by a disturbed mother; rather, these children are constitutionally vulnerable and predisposed toward development of a psychosis. The constitutional ego defects in the child help to create the vicious circle of pathogenic mother-child relationship by stimulating the mother to react to the child in ways that prevent his separation and individuation. The ill effects are increased by the mother who tends either to push the child prematurely onto the stage of individuation or to infantilize him by extreme overprotection and engulfment.

The fear of separation from the mother and engulfment by mother form the central conflict of the symbiotic child; the symbiotic solution is thus his defense-protection against overwhelming panic and anxiety.

Symptoms

The case history may indicate that until the traumatic event, the child seemed to have been developing normally. He may have crawled, walked, and talked at the proper times and presented no special problems. Then obvious regression took place, with relentless dependence on the mother as its most prominent feature. As he clings to the mother, the child exhibits a "melting phenomenon." He seems literally to melt into her, as though they were one. Mahler et al. (1959) noted six primary symptoms in symbiotic psychotic children: (1) panic reactions with violent rage, (2) unpredictable outbursts of excitement and apparent pleasure alternating with violent destructiveness, (3) confusion between inner and outer reality, a consequence of the fusion of the self and nonself, (4) inability to differentiate between animate and inanimate reality and use of magical control over external stimuli, (5) a strong but spurious clinging attachment to adults, and (6) conspicuous presence of dereistic thinking, feeling, and acting.

As the psychosis persists, secondary symptoms appear, representing, for the most part, psychotic defense mechanisms and attempts at self-integration. In an attempt to restore the lost cathexis of the body ego, the child endows parts of the body with libido. To counteract the dissolution of ego boundaries, he seeks seclusion and gives up interests appropriate to a child of his age. His contact with reality gradually decreases, and his life becomes extremely limited, as he remains in the home, close to the mother. His thinking begins to show evidence of primary process, and his speech is full of neologism. He may be quite talkative, but his talk is weird and hard to understand. Established sleeping, eating, and toilet habits begin to break down, and enuresis and encopresis may appear. The psychotic child cannot attend a regular nursery school; he is unable to follow directions or to profit from formal instruction, although in some area he may have a surprising fund of knowledge. New situations throw the child into panic, which drives him even further to desperate clinging to the mother. In her absence, he may react with violent bursts of anger and destructiveness. Like his autistic counterpart, the symbiotic psychotic child is disturbed by minor variations in living arrangements, and he too engages in ritualistic routines. In fact, after a year or two of psychosis, the symbiotic child resembles his autistic counterpart. The differential diagnosis will rely heavily on case history and etiology.

Treatment of Autistic and Symbiotic Children

The goals of treatment with psychotic children, according to Mahler (Mahler et al., 1959), are: (1) to establish greater body integrity and a sense of identity, (2) to develop object relationships, and (3) to restore missing or distorted maturational and developmental ego functions. To achieve these goals, the child needs to go through the missed phases of development: the autistic, the symbiotic, and the separation-individuation phases. The therapist's function is substitutive; he provides the children with a readily available substitute ego. The therapist may also have to serve as a substitute stimulus barrier; he protects the children from excessive environmental stimuli while luring them away from threatening inner stimuli and into gratifying common pursuits. At times, the therapist's role is educational; he helps the children understand time realities, body functions, and social relations. An important function of the therapist is to set firm limits on destructive and self-destructive activities. He must be able to convey to the children that he will protect them against their own rage and will not let them harm themselves or others. Limits and boundaries are necessary both in the play situation and in interpersonal relationships. The therapist must be able to understand and to respond with empathy to the primary-process thinking and symbolic behavior of psychotic children. He needs to reassure them verbally about their basic integrity as organisms and about their basic worth as persons.

Mahler (Mahler et al., 1959) points out differences in approach to autistic and to symbiotic children. The treatment of choice for autistic children is individual therapy. The autistic child is intolerant of direct human contact; yet he must be lured out from his withdrawn state with all kinds of devices to which he responds, such as music, rhythmic activities, toys, and materials. By pleasurable stimulation, the autistic child is led to test reality through higher sense organs rather than through licking, biting, and smelling of objects and people. Mahler cautions against any haste in forcing attention, bodily contact, or social relations on autistic children. Even a caress or a touch may throw them into panic.

The symbiotic child, in contrast to the autistic child, can profit from the specialized educational methods of the residential treatment school. He needs diversified relationships to substitute for the parasitic fusion with the mother. However, they must be introduced very gradually so that the child can test reality at his own pace. As he slowly begins to test himself as a separate entity, he needs the constant support of the teachers, therapists, and other adults who represent diversified substitutes for the pathological symbiotic fusion. The symbiotic child may have to live many years on borrowed ego strength. Only thus can he develop ego strength of his own and achieve age-adequate individuation.

The essence of treatment is for the therapist to become a substitute mother figure, a symbiotic partner, who helps the child relive and reexperience in a beneficial way the early phases of psychic life.

Prognosis of Infantile Autism and Symbiotic Psychosis

The prognosis of the child with early infantile autism is extremely guarded. Research (Ribble, 1941; Spitz, 1945; Spitz, 1946) shows that prolonged exposure to a pathological environment in infancy causes almost irreversible damage to the ego. Finch (1960) warns against the tendency to react optimistically when a diagnosis of early infantile autism, instead of mental deficiency, is made: "The prognosis is not necessarily much different especially if the diagnosis is not made until school age."

Although psychotherapists convey optimism about the possibility of helping autistic children, the results of follow-up studies are not too encouraging. Regardless of the kind of treatment given, only one-third appear to be able to achieve at least minimal social adjustment. As Kanner and Lesser (1958) put it: "The future of these children cannot be predicted with certainty at this time. The ultimate evaluation of treatment efforts must await further investigation."

On the basis of her rich experience, Mahler (1952) made the following generalized prognostic statement:

> Establishment of contact and substitution therapy over a long period of time may sometimes give spurts of impressive and gratifying results. But they are usually followed by an insuperable plateau of arrested progress, which usually taxes the patience and frustrates the renewed hopes of the parents. But, if the autistic type is forced too rapidly into social contact . . . he is often thrown into a catatonic state and then into a fulminant psychotic process. . . . If such catastrophic reactions cannot be avoided, it seems that such autistic infants are better off if allowed to remain in their autistic shell, even though in "a daze of restricted orientation" they may drift into a very limited degree of reality adjustment only. Diagnosis of their "original condition," of course, then usually escapes recognition; they are thrown into the category of the feebleminded.

Kanner and Eisenberg (1955) reported that every point of Mahler's statement was borne out by their follow-up studies. They also found that differences in the intensity of autistic aloneness and fragmentation exist from the start and that autistic children are not alike. However, the diagnostic signs common to all autistic children were isolation and insistence on sameness. Speech was found to be the most important prognostic indicator. In one study, 42 autistic children were followed up about nine years after the critical diagnosis was made. Of 19 children who did not talk at about the age of 4, 18 remained in a state of complete isolation. None of the varieties of psychiatric treatment had any noticeable effect on them. Of the 23 speaking children, 13 have improved sufficiently to function in a more or less schizoid manner at home and in the community; the other 10 have become clearly psychotic. The conclusion of the study is that the presence or absence of language function in preschool age may serve as a criterion of the severity of the autistic process.

In another study, Eisenberg (1957) confirmed the above findings. Sixty-three patients were classified into three categories: "good"—those who function well academically and socially; "fair"—those able to attend school at about grade level though deviant in personality; and "poor"—the apparently feebleminded and those with gross psychotic behavior. Of the 63, 3 were classified as "good," 14 as "fair," and 46 as "poor." Thus only about 27 per cent were functioning at a fair to good social level.

Mahler (Mahler et al., 1959) expresses a cautious view on prognosis: "Even though the [symbiotic] child may be able to function on a higher level, he will continue to require a certain degree of anaclitic relationship and infusion of ego-strength, perhaps throughout his life."

CHILDHOOD SCHIZOPHRENIA[3]

Kanner (1943) and Mahler (1952) consider early infantile autism and infantile symbiotic psychosis to be types of childhood schizophrenia. Others (E. Stern, 1952; E. Stern & Schachter, 1953) consider childhood schizophrenia to be a separate entity. The *Psychiatric Dictionary*, by Hinsie and Campbell (1960), defines childhood schizophrenia as "a clinical entity occurring in childhood, usually after the age of one and before the age of 11, characterized by disturbance in the ability to make affective contact with the environment and by autistic thinking."

The criteria for establishing a diagnosis of

[3] See also "Mental Hospitals," in Part 5.

childhood schizophrenia are not well defined, although a multitude of definitions exist. Bender (1953) defines childhood schizophrenia as

> a maturational lag at the embryonic level in all the areas which integrate biological and psychological behavior; an embryonic primitivity or plasticity characterizes the pattern of the behavior disturbance in all areas of personality functioning. It is determined before birth and hereditary factors appear to be important. It may be precipitated by a physiological crisis, which may be birth itself, especially a traumatic birth.

According to Bender, the disorder of maturation involves those basic mechanisms which govern the development of all future behavior: homeostatic mechanisms dealing with the vasovegetative area, tonic-neck-reflex motor patterning muscular tone, respiratory patterns, and sleep and wakefulness. Freedman (1954) and Caplan (1956) and the research of Kallmann (1956) support Bender's view of dysmaturation, a primary cause of childhood schizophrenia. Bergman and Escalona (1949) review the role of basic biological factors in the development of early personality structure leading to future psychosis. Their view is based on psychoanalytic principles. The authors observed unusual sensitivities in infants who later became psychotic. On the basis of Freud's theory regarding the organism's protective barrier against overwhelming external stimuli, they conceptualized the relationship among the following three variables: hypersensitivity to sensory stimulation, excessive vulnerability to emotional hurt, and occurrence of psychosis. The infant who is not sufficiently protected from outer stimuli because of a thin protective barrier or because of maternal nonprotection may react with premature ego formation. When, in consequence of a trauma, this primitive and premature ego breaks down, psychotic manifestations appear.

Bender (1956) contributed systematic clinical descriptions of schizophrenic children and their symptomatology, based on her biologically oriented theoretical framework. In the sphere of vasovegetative functioning, Bender described such disturbances as flushing; perspiring; unpredictable temperature responses in illness; disturbed rhythms of sleeping, eating, and elimination; and disorders of menstruation and pubertal functions without accompanying endocrine disturbance.

In the sphere of motility, there are histories of motor awkwardness and poor muscular control. Primitive reflex-patterned activities, normal in the first months of life, may reappear as residuals in the form of oral mannerisms or in play activities. Head turning and whirling reactions beyond the age of 6 are considered almost pathognomonic of the illness.

In the spheres of perception, thought, and language, Bender describes such incongruities as the simultaneous presence of early and late patterns of maturation, of abstraction and concretism, and of regressive and accelerated drives and the child's use of the infantile third-person pronoun instead of "I," while demonstrating an advanced vocabulary and abilities in painting, dancing, or music.

In the psychological sphere, the schizophrenic child shows preoccupation with, and disturbance in, identity, body image, interpersonal relations, and orientation in time and space. The disturbances in his identification process and in self-others relations are the essential psychological problem.

Bender emphasizes that contrary to expectation, schizophrenic children do not appear withdrawn in their human relations; their contact is pathologically invasive, at least for a period of time. Through their contact with the therapist or parent figure, whom they make part of their personality, they attempt to ward off their endless terror. Contrary to prevalent descriptions, the schizophrenic child may not appear cold, unresponsive, or unappealing. In fact, he may instantly win the therapist's empathy and raise unrealistic prognostic hopes.

Bender classified childhood schizophrenia into the following three clinical pictures based on the child's defenses:

1. The pseudo defective or autistic child, who is characteristically physically labile, with inadequate muscle tonus and homeostasis.

2. The pseudo neurotic child, who displays a picture of panneurosis with anxiety, phobias, obsessive-compulsive symptoms, and hypochondriac or psychosomatic defenses. Such children are greatly concerned about body image, body boundary, identity, and orientation in time and space. They display disturbed thought process and speech, exaggerated introjections and projections, invasive relationships, high verbal and graphic capacity, and superior intelligence.

3. The pseudo psychopathic child, who exhibits paranoid ideation, difficulties in identifying or relating to peers, resentment of authority, impulsiveness, and serious antisocial behavior, such as fire setting.

Prognosis

Bender's view is that regardless of later therapeutic or other relationship experience, schizophrenic patterning will persist in the individual throughout life.

ATYPICAL CHILDREN

Research workers at the James Jackson Putnam Center called their severely disturbed youngsters "children with atypical development" (Putnam, 1955; Rank, 1949; Rank, 1955). The outstanding symptoms of these children are

> withdrawal from people, retreat into a world of fantasy, mutism or the use of language for autistic purposes, bizarre posturing, seemingly meaningless stereotyped gestures, impassivity or violent outbursts of anxiety and rage, identification with inanimate objects or animals, and excessively inhibited or excessively uninhibited expression of impulses (Rank, 1955, pp. 491–492).

The most important etiological factors are considered to be profound disturbance in the early parent-child relationship and traumatic events, especially separation from parents. The child's "fragmented ego" is seen as "the result of the infant's unsuccessful struggle to obtain vital satisfaction from his parents" (Rank, 1955). The category of "atypical children" seems to encompass the entire group of children with varied schizophrenic manifestations. Therefore, Mahler (1958) feels that the term "atypical child" is perhaps both too cautious and too broad.

According to Putnam (1954), treatment with the atypical child goes through two phases. The first phase of therapy aims to make restitution for the frustration of his past and present life. The child's needs are met, with a minimum of frustration and a maximum of gratification. In the second phase of therapy, steps toward socialization are taken. The child learns to postpone immediate gratification, to test reality, and to establish tender relationships with people. Educational and supportive measures play a prominent part in therapy. They enable the child to modify aggressive and libidinal drives and to channel them into play, learning, and activity.

MORE BENIGN PSYCHOSES

Mahler et al. (1959) defined more benign cases of childhood psychosis, in which symptoms develop more insidiously. The children show a lack of emotional differentiation, low frustration tolerance, immaturity, extreme impulsivity, unevenness of development, mood swings, poor judgment, and unstable relationships. They also display many neurotic symptoms and defenses. Because of better ego development, the children are in contact with reality and do not have delusions or hallucinations. However, their tolerance of frustration is so low that they withdraw to a fantasy world at the slightest provocation. In prolonged psychoanalytic therapy, some of these children may show remarkable improvement; others do not weather adolescence without psychotic episodes. The children in this group of benign psychoses resemble cases described by Geleerd (1946) and Weil (1953).

ANACLITIC DEPRESSION

Spitz (1946a) described a severe disturbance in infancy which he named "anaclitic depression." The syndrome, a form of psychosis, develops when an infant who has established a constant cathexis with his mother is separated from her for long periods of time. First, the infant displays distress, but after several months of separation the weepiness subsides, and depressive withdrawal ensues. "These children would sit with wide open, expressionless eyes, frozen immobile face and a far away expression as if in a daze, apparently not perceiving what went on in their environment. . . . Contact with children who arrived at this stage becomes increasingly difficult and finally impossible" (Spitz, 1946a). The main symptoms are dejected expression and posture and relative immobility. The reaction occurs in infants 6 to 8 months of age, when separated for about three months. Interestingly, anaclitic depression occurred in full form in children who were separated from a "good" mother-child relationship; those with a "bad" relationship did not develop the syndrome.

Anaclitic depression is reversible if the

mother is restored to the child within three months. The recovery is complete. If the mother is not restored, the process continues, and the child deteriorates. The picture becomes that of stuporous catatonia or agitated idiocy, and the condition seems irreversible.

Spitz considers anaclitic depression to be the infantile counterpart of later depressive psychosis. He draws a parallel between adult melancholia and anaclitic depression. In the former, the aggression of the superego is directed against the ego; in the latter, sadism of the external love object (which functioned as the infant's superego) is directed against the infant's ego. Mahler (Mahler et al., 1959) conceptualized the relation between anaclitic depression in infancy and other psychotic syndromes. The main difference is that anaclitic depression "is inflicted upon an infant with per se normal ego anlage."

The main common feature is the interference in the libidinization of the body and its boundaries and disturbance of the progress toward "object constancy" or libidinal cathexis of the outer world. In the autistic and symbiotic psychoses, there is an intrinsically defective mother-child unit. In anaclitic depression, there is a damaged mother-child unit. In the former, the deficiency results in a confused orientation between self and outside world; in the latter, the lack of mothering overburdens the primitive ego with unneutralized aggression. However, the ego, with a normal anlage, is able to utilize even minimal opportunities to restore mother-child unity and to build object relationships.

HOSPITALISM

A condition similar to anaclitic depression was described by Bakwin (1942) and Spitz (1946b) as "hospitalism." The term designates a vitiated condition of the infant's body due to long confinement in, or morbid atmosphere of, a hospital or institution. The symptoms are lack of appetite, loss of weight, poor sleep, emaciation, proneness to infections, pallor, listlessness, unresponsiveness, and appearance of unhappiness. This debilitating condition was referred to as "marasmus"—the wasting disease—and was attributed to malnutrition and infection. In 1915 Chapin recognized the need of infants for individual care and affection and suggested changes in their institutional care. Ribble (1944), who studied the reaction of marasmic infants in a ward of a large city hospital, reported that the experimental introduction of a "foster mother" to give personal care to these infants "brought dramatic results in restoring appetite, alertness, and reflex excitability."

Goldfarb (1943; 1944; 1945) compared institution children who were transferred to foster homes at about 3 years of age with children who were in foster homes after a brief period with their own relatives. At adolescence, there were striking differences between the two groups. The institution children showed the following in greater degree: (1) "Concept deficiency"—they found it difficult to learn songs, stories, number concepts, and time and space orientation or to recall the past and anticipate the future. (2) Absence of normal inhibitory patterns—they were overactive, disorganized, enuretic, unmanageable, and given to temper tantrums. (3) Affect hunger—they showed an indiscriminate and insatiable demand for attention and "never had enough." (4) Emotional shallowness and superficiality of relationship—they did not develop strong ties to foster homes even when fully accepted. (5) Absence of visible guilt or anxiety following aggression, cruelty, or failure in school. (6) Social regression—they were inferior in social maturity as compared with children who spent infancy in foster homes. Goldfarb's main conclusions were: "An extensive period of deprivation of babies in an infant institution is profoundly detrimental to their psychological growth. . . . The extreme deprivation experience of the institution children has apparently resulted in a quasi-constitutional fixation on the most primitive levels of conceptual and emotional behavior" (Goldfarb, 1943).

PARENTS AND PATHOLOGY

The literature reflects three points of view on the dynamic interplay between parents and the psychosis of their children: (1) Parents (especially the mother) are the basic source of pathology. A more wholesome mother would have prevented psychosis in the child. (2) The parents' personality has no direct etiological importance. The parents' behavior is a reaction to the peculiarities and bizarreness which existed from the start in the child. (3) Children with innate inability to relate to people are further damaged by emotionally deviant parents and their mismanagement. A sick reciprocal relationship is established in which the parent rejects or "overprotects" the child who was difficult in the first place. Wolman (1960) related schizophrenia in children to peculiar interparental interaction.

Many references have been made in the literature to the so-called "schizophrenogenic" mother, the cold, narcissistic, rejecting or overstimulating, seductive, and shallow woman who causes her infant to turn away from her and from the world (Despert, 1947; Despert, 1951; Fromm-Reichman, 1943; Fromm-Reichman, 1950; Klein, 1932; Rank, 1952; Rank, 1955). On the other hand, there is a concern about the overevaluation of the mother's role in the etiology of childhood psychosis. Bender (1955) emphasizes that there is no typical group of pathological attitudes in mothers which could account for psychogenic childhood schizophrenia. This view is shared by Bettelheim (1950), Bellak (1958), Escalona (1948), Freedman (1954), and Peck, Rabinovitch, and Cramer (1949). Erikson (1950) believes that the role of maternal rejection in the genesis of schizophrenia is still unproved. It is possible that the children's lack of "sending power," their failure to return the mother's glance and smile, blocks an emphatic relationship from the start and leads the mother to withdraw unwittingly from the child. Even the most efficient mothering cannot adequately support the inherently defective tension-regulation apparatus of the child's deficient ego anlage.

Bateson, Jackson, Haley, and Weakland (1956) studied tapes of actual conversations between parents and their schizophrenic children. They discovered that the parents persistently involved their children in "double-bind" situations and communications. Double bind is a situation in which a child is faced with contradictory messages. The situation is not readily visible as such because of concealment or denial or because the messages are on different levels. The child can neither escape from the situation nor comment on the contradiction. Bateson et al. see the double-bind pattern of communication as provoking behavior characteristic of schizophrenia.

Others have underrated the etiologic role of parental attitudes, largely for practical (therapeutic) rather than theoretical consideration. Thus Betz (1947) dispenses with the etiological concept and family history, feeling that they serve only to satisfy the therapist's scientific curiosity. According to Bettelheim (1949), it is best to devote time and therapeutic effort to the child, rather than to the parents, as they cannot be sufficiently changed to be of help to the psychotic child. Mahler (Mahler et al., 1959) holds the opposite view: "During the treatment there may be times when the child needs to be separated from mother because institutional care is indicated. Despite this separation, the mother or substitute for her must be regarded as an essential part of the treatment program at all times." Mahler believes that it is absolutely essential to have a close alliance with the mother or her substitute if the child is in an institution. The child's communications can often be understood only if the therapist has knowledge of current events in his life.

Most psychiatric centers believe in coordinated treatment for parents and child. Slavson (1963) suggests child-centered guidance groups for parents of schizophrenic children. The discussions are focused on, and directed toward, sensitizing parents to the uniqueness of their children. Slavson reports that as a result, parental attitudes have grown more benign and more emphathic. Szurek (1951) feels that it is necessary to work therapeutically with the parents while the child is an inpatient. Bettelheim (1955) rejects this view: "It seems pointless for an institution . . . to attempt therapy of fathers and mothers. Several of the parents of our children underwent extensive psychotherapy or psychoanalysis . . . which failed as far as having a salutary effect on the disturbed child was concerned."

THE SOCIOPSYCHOSOMATIC THEORY OF CHILDHOOD SCHIZOPHRENIA

Wolman (1964) has formulated a systematic sociopsychosomatic theory of childhood schizophrenia and has related it to four types of adult schizophrenia:

1. The pseudo amentive schizophrenia in children, which corresponds to dementive schizophrenia in adults. This is a most severe phase of illness in both children and adults.
2. The autistic schizophrenia in children, which corresponds to simple deterioration and hebephrenia in adults.
3. The symbiotic schizophrenia in children, which corresponds to catatonia in adults.
4. The aretic schizophrenia in children,

which corresponds to adult paranoid schizophrenia.

This classification is based primarily on etiology and personality dynamics rather than on symptomatology. It corresponds to four stages in which the disorder was produced. The pseudo amentive stage is formed on a preverbal, preego formation level in the first months of life. The three other types originate in the first two years of life. Wolman assumes that degree of severity of the illness is related to age of onset—the earlier the start, the more severe the disorder, and the more difficult the therapy. Wolman provides a conceptual rationale for each stage and relates it to the known research and literature.

A STRUCTURAL APPROACH TO CHILDHOOD SCHIZOPHRENIA

A distinct contribution to the conceptualization and treatment of childhood schizophrenia is a recent book by Des Lauriers (1962). His central theme is that the experience of reality constitutes a matter of life and death in the development of the human individual. To the extent that a human being lacks sufficient narcissistic cathexis of his body boundaries, he lacks the necessary psychological structures to experience himself as a reality separated and differentiated from others. This is the condition of schizophrenia. The schizophrenic is not one who has withdrawn from reality to live in a world of his own; rather, he is a person who because of severe diminution of narcissistic cathexis of his body boundaries does not have the capacity to experience himself as differentiated from others. His total behavior can be viewed not as escape from unbearable experience or as defense against a threatening world but as disorganized and frantic efforts at establishing the boundaries of his reality and at discovering himself.

From his view of the nature of schizophrenia, Des Lauriers developed a definite method of treatment. The schizophrenic ego functioning, as Engel (1963) put it, may be likened to the performance of musicians without a score and without a conductor. There is little sense in attempting to discover melody in the cacophony. What is necessary is to provide a conductor and a score; only then can the confusion become a unified melody. Following this analogy, the therapist is the conductor who provides the schizophrenic child with a clear score. He does not explore or interpret primary-process, hallucinatory, and delusional material. He is not trying to understand the id but tries to develop an effective and organized ego in the patient. From the first session on, the therapist establishes himself as a clear-cut intruding force in the life of the patient. This is not a question of rapport, transference, or warm relations (it is taken for granted that a meaningful relationship is impossible at start and that it is the task of the therapist to create conditions for an eventual relationship). It is a matter of a *presence* that is forceful, insistent, and genuine and of *contact* that communicates because it is so total; it is physical, sensual, intellectual, emotional, and motoric.

The assumption is that the schizophrenic wants to know reality but that he does not know how to do it because of basic structural ego deficiencies. Left to himself, the schizophrenic child will not become aware of himself as a unified subject of his experience; his attention must be focused, and he needs to be stimulated and made aware of himself as an experiencer of events. The therapist intrudes and brings to his attention the primary features of reality. He repeats for his patient his height, weight, eye color, name, and age, as differentiated from those of the adult. The communication during therapy is direct, concrete, and physical. It needs little interpretation since its main value is in putting the schizophrenic in contact with another person. What is said is much less important than the act of saying it.

Des Lauriers (1962) states that when a patient "achieves a clear awareness of his own reality, separated and differentiated from what is not himself and when, as subject of his experience, he can relate to others as objects of his interests, at that moment he is no longer schizophrenic." The process of recovery is conceived therefore as "a growth and maturational moment which takes place, not because primarily obstacles are removed, but because . . . nourishment and climate is given."

From the viewpoint of establishment of ego and reality in the children, the process of therapy has several phases: the phases of "imprinting," of "imitation," of acting out, and of identification.

Though the claims of effectiveness for this method are modest, Des Lauriers's theory and practice inspire prognostic optimism.

TREATMENT APPROACHES

Somatic Therapies

Those who view childhood schizophrenia as a basically biological disorder use somatic therapies as the treatment of choice (Bender, 1954; Freedman, Effron, & Bender, 1955). However, there is consensus that somatic treatment should be only one part of a broad therapeutic program (Bakwin, 1950; Bender, 1954; Silver, 1955). A sobering statement to this effect was made by Bellak (1958): "The fond hopes of curing schizophrenia by a single drug are probably as reasonable as the expectation that one may learn a number of foreign languages by intravenous injection."

Three main categories of somatic treatment are used with schizophrenic children: pharmacotherapy, electroshock and insulin therapy, and psychosurgery. An excellent review of the literature by Ekstein, Bryant, and Freedman can be found in Bellak's *Schizophrenia: A Review of the Syndrome* (1958, pp. 631–649).

Psychotherapies

A survey of the literature from 1936 to 1946 (54 items) by Bellak (1948) and a review by Escalona (1948) do not contain even a single reference to analytic psychotherapy with psychotic children. The prevailing pessimism was reflected in Escalona's statement: "Adequate therapeutic measures in cases of childhood psychosis can be developed, if at all, only if the nature and cause of these conditions can be understood much more fully than they are at the present."

A survey of the literature from 1946 to 1956 by Ekstein et al. (1958), consisting of 515 items, has 190 references to treatment, over half of them about psychotherapy. In 1952, Harms devoted an entire issue of *The Nervous Child* to the problems of schizophrenia in childhood.

These facts reflect the increasing therapeutic optimism about the possibilities of progress in the field of mental illness.

Operant Conditioning in the Study and Treatment of Psychotic Children

In 1954, Skinner reported on a new method for experimental analysis of the behavior of psychotic patients. Since then, Skinner and his colleagues have perfected the method of free operant conditioning and have applied it to the study of behavior of chronic and acute psychotic children and adults.

The impetus for studying psychotic children by the operant conditioning method came from Skinner (1953), who eliminated the need for verbal instructions. Skinner demonstrated that cooperation between individuals can be developed solely by manipulating the contingency between reinforcing stimuli and the cooperative response. Reinforcement techniques, which required no verbal instructions, were effective in shaping cooperation responses in normal children (Azrin & Lindsley, 1956), in adult schizophrenics (Ayllon & Haughton, 1962), and in early childhood schizophrenics (Hingtgen, Sanders & DeMyer, 1963).

Ferster (1961) presented a clear conceptualization of infantile autism based on learning theory; he accounts for the manifestation of the disorder and suggests methods of treatment. Ferster and DeMyer (1961; DeMyer & Ferster, 1962) have reported success in controlling and enriching the behavioral range of autistic children in a laboratory setting. The application of their methods was taught to nurses, attendants, and parents so that the desired behavior could be maintained for a longer period of time (DeMyer & Ferster, 1962; Wolf, Mees, & Risley, 1963).

Hingtgen et al. (1963), in their experiment, hypothesized that a schizophrenic child could be led to interact with another child if reinforcement were contingent upon that interaction. By gradually increasing the complexity of this interaction—method of successive approximation (Ferster & Skinner, 1957)—a form of social behavior could be obtained. Thus, six schizophrenics ranging in age from 3 years, 7 months, to 8 years, 3 months, who had been observed to initiate little or no social interaction with their peers, were trained to operate a lever to obtain coins on a fixed-ratio schedule of reinforcement. These coins were used in vending machines to obtain candy, crackers, and cereal. Each child worked daily for thirty minutes in the experimental room until a base line of behavior was achieved. The subjects were then paired on the basis of their length of hospitalization, and both members of a pair were placed together in the room for all following sessions. Using nonverbal operant conditioning techniques, the cooperative response was shaped in succeeding sessions as follows: (1) S 1 and S 2 of each pair were free to operate the coin lever at any time during the session. (2) In order to obtain coins, S 1 and S 2 were required to alternate in using the coin lever. (3) In order to operate the coin lever, a new lever had to be operated first; S 1 and S 2 were required to alternate on this new lever. (4) S 1 was required to operate the new lever to enable S 2 to obtain coins, and vice versa. The results indicated that it was possible to shape cooperative responses in early childhood schizophrenics within an average of 23 sessions. The frequency of physical contacts between subjects, although not directly reinforced, was higher during shaping of the cooperative response than in the ward. The subjects were also observed to make vocal responses and facial expressions which appeared to be directed to their partners. By making reinforcement (previously obtained in a nonsocial situation) contingent upon the emission of cooperative responses, these responses were obtained, and in addition other forms of social interaction were observed to increase in frequency in the experimental room. While there was little evidence of any continuation of social interaction when the subjects were returned to the ward, it was suggested that an extension and a modification of the reinforcement contingencies in a ward situation might produce more permanent changes in behavior.

REFERENCES

Ackerson, L. Children's behavior problems. Chicago: Univer. of Chicago Press, 1931.

Adler, A. *Individual Psychologie in der Schule.* Leipzig: 1929.

Adler, A. *The education of children.* New York: Greenberg, 1930.

American Psychiatric Association. *Diagnostic and statistical manual: mental disorders.* Washington, D.C.: Author, 1952.

Asperger, H. Autistische Psychopathen im Kindesalter. *Arch. Psychiat.,* 1944, **117.**

Ayllon, T., & Haughton, E. Control of the behavior of schizophrenic patients by food. *J. exp. anal. Behav.,* 1962, **5,** 343–352.

Azrin, N. H., & Lindsley, O. R. The reinforcement of cooperation between children. *J. abnorm. soc. Psychol.,* 1956, **52,** 100–102.

Bakwin, H. Loneliness in infants. *Amer. J. Dis. Child,* 1942, **63,** 30–40.

Bakwin, H. Enuresis in children. *J. Pediat.,* 1949, **34.**

Bateson, G., Jackson, D. D., Haley, J., & Weakland, J. H. Toward a theory of schizophrenia. *Behav. Sci.,* 1956, **1,** 251–264.

Bellak, L. *Dementia praecox: the past decade's work and present status: a review and evaluation.* New York: Grune & Stratton, 1948.

Bellak, L. (Ed.) *Schizophrenia: a review of the syndrome.* New York: Logos Press, 1958.

Bender, Lauretta. Childhood schizophrenia. *Nerv. Child,* 1942, **1,** 138.

Bender, Lauretta. Childhood schizophrenia. *Amer. J. Orthopsychiat.,* 1947, **27,** 68–79.

Bender, Lauretta. Childhood schizophrenia. *Psychiat. Quart.,* 1953, **27,** 663–681.

Bender, Lauretta. *A dynamic psychopathology of childhood.* Springfield, Ill.: Charles C Thomas, 1954.

Bender, Lauretta. Twenty years of clinical research on schizophrenic children, with special reference to those under six years of age. In G. Caplan (Ed.), *Emotional problems of early childhood.* New York: Basic Books, 1955.

Bender, Lauretta. Schizophrenia in childhood: its recognition, description and treatment. *Amer. J. Orthopsychiat.,* 1956, 26, 499–506.

Benjamin, E. *Grundlagen und Entwicklungsgeschichte der kindlichen Neurose.* Leipzig: Thieme, 1930.

Bergman, P., & Escalona, Sybil. Unusual sensitivities in very young children. In *The psychoanalytic study of the child.* Vols. 3, 4. New York: International Universities Press, 1949. Pp. 333–352.

Bettelheim, B. A psychiatric school. *Quart. J. Child Behav.,* 1949, **1,** 86–95.

Bettelheim, B. *Love is not enough.* New York: Free Press, 1950.

Bettelheim, B. *Truants from life.* New York: Free Press, 1955.

Betz, B. J. A study of tactics for resolving the autistic barrier in the psychotherapy of the schizophrenic personality. *Amer. J. Psychiat.,* 1947, **104,** 267–273.

Bleuler, E. P. *Lehrbuch der Psychiatrie.* Berlin: Springer, 1918.

Brown, S., Pollock, H. M., Potter, H. W., & Cohen, D. W. *Outline of the psychiatric classification of problem children.* Utica, N.Y.: State Hospitals Press, 1937.

Buehler, Charlotte. *The first years of life.* New York: John Day, 1930.

Buehler, Charlotte. *From birth to maturity.* London: Kegan Paul, Trench, Trubner & Co., 1935.

Caplan, H. The role of deviant maturation in the pathogenesis of anxiety. *Amer. J. Orthopsychiat.,* 1956, **26,** 94–107.

Cappon, D. Clinical manifestations of autism and schizophrenia in childhood. *Canad. med. Ass. J.,* 1953, **69,** 44–49.

Chapin, H. D. Are institutions for infants necessary? *J. Amer. med. Ass.,* 1915, **64,** 1–3.

Chess, Stella. *An introduction to child psychiatry.* New York: Grune & Stratton, 1959.

Creak, Mildred. Discussion: psychoses in childhood. *Proc. roy. Soc. Med.,* 1952, **45,** 797–800.

DeMyer, M. K., & Ferster, C. B. Teaching new social behavior to schizophrenic children. *J. Child Psychiat.,* 1962, **1,** 443–461.

Des Lauriers, A. M. *The experience of reality in childhood schizophrenia.* New York: International Universities Press, 1962.

Despert, J. L. The early recognition of childhood schizophrenia. *Med. Clin. N. Amer.,* 1947, **31,** 680–687.

Despert, J. L. Some considerations relating to the genesis of autistic behavior in children. *Amer. J. Orthopsychiat.,* 1951, **21,** 335–350.

Eisenberg, L. The autistic child in adolescence. *Amer. J. Psychiat.,* 1956, **112,** 607–612.

Eisenberg, L. The course of childhood schizophrenia. *Arch. Neurol. Psychiat.,* 1957, **78,** 69–83.

Eisenberg, L., & Kanner, L. Early infantile autism: 1943–1955. *Amer. J. Orthopsychiat.,* 1956, **26,** 556–566.

Ekstein, R. Vicissitudes of the "internal image" during the recovery process of a borderline schizophrenic adolescent. *Bull. Menninger Clin.,* 1955, **19,** 86–92.

Ekstein, R., Bryant, K., & Friedman, S. Childhood schizophrenia and allied conditions. In L. Bellak (Ed.), *Schizophrenia: a review of the syndrome.* New York: Logos Press, 1958. Pp. 555–693.

Emminghaus, H. *Die psychischen Störungen des Kindesalters.* Tuebingen: Laupp, 1887.

Engel, Mary. To discover the real. *Contemporary Psychol.,* 1963, **8,** 212–213.

English, O. S., & Pearson, G. H. *Emotional problems of living.* New York: Norton, 1945.

Erikson, E. H. *Childhood and society.* New York: Norton, 1950.

Escalona, Sybil. Some considerations regarding psychotherapy with psychotic children. *Bull. Menninger Clin.,* 1948, **12,** 124–126.

Fenichel, C. Educating the severely disturbed child. *Pathways Child Guidance,* 1963, **5** (2, 3).

Ferster, C. B. Positive reinforcement and behavioral deficits of autistic children. *Child Develpm.,* 1961, **32,** 437–456.

Ferster, C. B., & DeMyer, M. K. A method for the experimental analysis of the behavior of autistic children. *Amer. J. Orthopsychiat.,* 1962, **32,** 89–98.

Ferster, C. B., & Skinner, B. F. Schedules of reinforcement. New York: Appleton-Century-Crofts, 1957.

Finch, S. M. *Fundamentals of child psychiatry.* New York: Norton, 1960.

Freedman, A. M. Maturation and its relation to the dynamics of childhood schizophrenia. *Amer. J. Orthopsychiat.,* 1954, **24,** 487–491.

Freedman, A. M., Effron, A. S., & Bender, Lauretta. Pharmacotherapy in children with psychiatric illness. *J. nerv. ment. Dis.,* 1955, **122,** 479–486.

Fromm-Reichmann, Frieda. Psychoanalytic psychotherapy with psychotics. *Psychiatry,* 1943, **6,** 277–279.

Fromm-Reichmann, Frieda. *Principles of intensive psychotherapy.* Chicago: Univer. of Chicago Press, 1950.

Garrison, K. C. *Psychology of the exceptional child.* New York: Ronald, 1959.

Geleerd, E. R. A contribution to the problem of psychoses in Childhood. In *The psychoanalytic study of the child.* Vol. 2. New York: International Universities Press, 1946. Pp. 271–291.

Gerard, Margaret W. *The emotionally disturbed child.* New York: Child Welfare, 1959.

Gesell, A. *An atlas of infant behavior.* New York: Oxford Univer. Press, 1934.

Gesell, A., & Ilg, Frances L. *Embryology of behavior.* New York: Harper & Row, 1945.

Gesell, A., & Ilg, Frances L. *The child from five to ten.* New York: Harper, 1946.

Gesell, A., & Ilg, Frances L. *The child from ten to sixteen.* New York: Harper & Row, 1956.

Ginott, H G. *Group psychotherapy with children: the theory and practice of play-therapy.* New York: McGraw-Hill, 1961.

Goldfarb, H. The effects of early institutional care on adolescent personality. *Child Develpm.,* 1943, **14,** 213, 223.

Goldfarb, H. Infant rearing as a factor in foster home replacement. *Amer. J. Orthopsychiat.*, 1944, **14**, 162–166.

Goldfarb, H. Effects of psychological deprivation in infancy and subsequent stimulation. *Amer. J. Psychiat.*, 1945, **102**, 18–33.

Grewel, F., Prick, J. J., Sunier, A., Kamp, L., & Gaudia, Z. *Infantiel autisme (infantile autism).* Pur mer end: Muusses, 1954.

Griesinger, W. *Die Pathologie und Therapie der psychischen Krankheiten.* Berlin: Hirschwald, 1845.

Hall, Muriel B. *The psychiatric examination of the school child.* London: E. Arnold, 1947.

Hamilton, G. *Psychotherapy in child guidance.* New York: Columbia Univer. Press, 1947.

Harms, E. Childhood schizophrenia and childhood hysteria. *Psychiat. Quart.*, 1945, **19.**

Harms, E. Differential pattern of manic-depressive disease in childhood. *Nerv. Child,* 1951–1952, **9,** 326–356.

Harms, E. (Ed.) Our present knowledge of schizophrenia in childhood. *Nerv. Child,* 1952, **10,** 1–178.

Harms, E. Hysteria in general and in childhood. *Nerv. Child,* 1953, **10.**

Harms, E. Present status of knowledge of abnormal psychology of the child. In Robback (Ed.), *Present day psychology.* New York: Philosophical Library, 1955.

Harms, E. Die Entwickelung der Kinderspsychiatrie. *Praxis Kinderpsychol.*, 1962, **2.**

Hecker, E. *Die Ursachen und Anfaenge der psychischen Krankheiten.* Leipzig: Breitkopf, 1877.

Hessen, S. Totalitaet in paedagogik. *Actes eigth int. Congr. Phil.*, 1936.

Heuyer, G. *Psychiatrie sociale de l'enfant.* Paris: Centre Internationale d'Enfance, 1951.

Hingtgen, J. N., Sanders, B. J., & DeMyer, Marian K. Shaping cooperative responses in early childhood schizophrenics. Paper read at Amer. Psychol. Ass., Philadelphia, August, 1963.

Hinsie, L. E., & Campbell, R. J. *Psychiatric dictionary.* (3rd ed.) New York: Oxford Univ. Press, 1960.

Hollinsworth, Leta S. *Gifted children.* New York: Macmillan, 1926.

Howard, F. E., & Patry, F. L. *Mental health: its principles and practice.* New York: Harper & Row, 1935.

Hurlock, Elizabeth B. *Developmental psychology.* New York: McGraw-Hill, 1953.

Hutt, M., & Gibby, R. G. *Patterns of abnormal behavior.* Boston: Allyn and Bacon, 1957.

Kahlbaum, K. Ueber Hebridophrenie. *Allgem. Z. Psychiat.*, 1890, **46.**

Kallman, F. J., & Roth, B. Genetic aspects of preadolescent schizophrenia. *Amer. J. Psychiat.*, 1956, **112,** 599–606.

Kanner, L. *Child psychiatry.* Springfield, Ill.: Charles C Thomas, 1935.

Kanner, L. Autistic disturbances of affective contact. *Nerv. Child,* 1943, **2,** 217–250.

Kanner, L. Early infantile autism. *Amer. J. Orthopsychiat.*, 1949, **19,** 416–426.

Kanner, L. General concept of schizophrenia at different ages. *Ass. Res. nerv. ment. Dis.*, 1955, **108,** 23–26.

Kanner, L., & Eisenberg, L. Notes on the follow-up studies of autistic children. In P. Hoch et al. (Eds.), *Psychopathology of childhood.* New York: Grune & Stratton, 1955.

Kanner, L., & Lesser, L. I. Early infantile autism. *Ped. Clin. N. Amer.*, 1958, 711–730.

Katz, D. *Animals and men.* London: Longmans, 1937.

Klein, Melanie. *The psycho-analysis of children.* London: Hogarth Press, 1932.

Kraepelin, E. *Compendium der psychiatrie.* Leipzig: Abel, 1883.

League for Emotionally Disturbed Children. *A parent speaks.* New York: Author, nd.

Lesser, L. *The diagnostic process in child psychiatry.* Unpublished manuscript, 1964.

Louttit, C. M. *Clinical psychology: a handbook of children's behavior problems.* New York: Harper & Row, 1936.

Mahler, M. S. Remarks on psychoanalysis with psychotic children. *Quart. J. Child Behav.*, 1949, **18** (1).

Mahler, M. S. On child psychosis and schizophrenia: autistic and symbiotic infantile psychoses. In *The psychoanalytic study of the child.* Vol. 7. New York: International Universities Press, 1952. Pp. 286–305.

Mahler, M. S. Childhood schizophrenia. Round table, 1953. Discussion. *Amer. J. Orthopsychiat.*, 1954, **24,** 523.

Mahler, M. S. Discussion of chaps. 13–16. In P.

Hoch et al. (Eds), *Psychopathology of childhood.* New York: Grune & Stratton, 1955.

Mahler, M. S. Autism and symbiosis: two extreme disturbances of identity. *Int. J. Psychoanal.*, 1958, **39**, 77.

Mahler, M. S., Furer, M., & Settlage, C. F. Severe emotional disturbances in childhood: psychosis. In S. Arieti (Ed.), *American handbook of psychiatry.* New York: Basic Books, 1959.

Maudsley, H. *The pathology of the mind.* London: Macmillan, 1895.

Milt, H. Serious mental illness in children. *Publ. Affairs,* 1963, No. 352.

Montague, M. F. A. *Prenatal influences.* Springfield, Ill.: Charles C Thomas, 1962.

Paynter, R. H., & Blanchard, P. *A study of educational achievement of problem children.* New York: Commonwealth Fund, 1929.

Pearson, G. H. J. *Emotional disorders of children.* New York: Norton, 1949.

Peck, H. B., Rabinovitch, R. D., & Cramer, J. B. A treatment program for parents of schizophrenic children. *Amer. J. Orthopsychiat.*, 1949, **19**, 592–598.

Perfect, W. *Annals of insanity.* London: Cassell, 1852.

Putnam, Marion C. Draft of international preparatory commission's report on childhood psychosis. Paper read at Int. Ass. Child Psychiat., Toronto, 1954.

Putnam, Marion C. Some observations on psychosis in early childhood. In B. Caplan (Ed.), *Emotional problems of early childhood.* New York: Basic Books, 1955.

Rank, B. Adaptation of the psychoanalytic technique for the treatment of young children with a typical development. *Amer. J. Orthopsychiat.*, 1949, **19**, 130–139.

Rank, B. Treatment of young children with a typical development by psychoanalytic technique. In Bychowski et al. (Eds.), *Specialized techniques in psychotherapy.* New York: Basic Books, 1952.

Rank, B. Intensive study and treatment of preschool children who show marked personality deviations, or "atypical development," and their parents. In B. Caplan (Ed.), *Emotional problems of early childhood.* New York: Basic Books, 1955.

Ribble, M. A. Disorganizing factors of infant personality. *Amer. J. Psychiat.*, 1941, **98**, 459–463.

Ribble, M. A. Infantile experience in relation to personality development. In J. Hunt (Ed.), *Personality and the behavior disorders.* New York: Ronald, 1944.

Rimland, B. *Infantile autism.* New York: Appleton-Century-Crofts, 1964.

Silver, A. A. Management of children with schizophrenia. *Amer. J. Psychother.*, 1955, **9**, 196–215.

Skinner, B. F. Some contributions of an experimental analysis of behavior to psychology as a whole. *Amer. Psychologist,* 1953, **8**, 69–78.

Skinner, B. F. A new method for the experimental analysis of the behavior of psychotic patients. *J. nerv. ment. Dis.*, 1954, **120**, 403–406.

Slavson, S. R. Steps in sensitizing parents (couples) in groups toward schizophrenic children. *Int. J. Group Psychother.*, 1963, **13**, 176–186.

Spitz, R. A. Anaclitic depression. In *The psychoanalytic study of the child.* Vol. 2. New York: International Universities Press, 1946. P. 313. (a)

Spitz, R. A. Hospitalism: a follow-up report. In *Ibid.* P. 255. (b)

Stern, Catherine, & Gould, T. *The early years of childhood.* New York: Harper & Row, 1955.

Stern, E. A propos d'un cas d'autisme chez un jeune enfant. *Arch. Franc. Pediat.*, 1952, **9**.

Stern, E., & Schachter, M. Zum Problem des fruehkindlichen Autismus. *Praxis Kinderpsychol. Kinderpsychiat.*, 1953, **2**, 113–119.

Strang, Ruth. *An introduction to child study.* New York: Macmillan, 1940.

Szurek, S. A. The family and the staff in hospital psychiatric therapy of children. *Amer. J. Orthopsychiat.*, 1951, **21**, 597–611.

Van Krevelen, D. A. Een Geval van "Early infantile autism." *Nederl. Tijdschr. Geneesk,* 1952, **96**, 202–205.

Watson, R. J. *Psychology of the child.* New York: Wiley, 1959.

Weil, A. P. Certain severe disturbances of ego development in childhood. In *The psychoanalytic study of the child.* Vol. 8. New York: International Universities Press, 1953.

Wolf, M., Mees, H., & Risley, T. *Application of operant conditioning procedures to the behavior problems of an autistic child.* Western Psychological Association, 1963.

Wolman, B. B. The fathers of schizophrenics. *Acta Psychother.*, 1960, **9**, 193–210.

Wolman, B. B. *Schizophrenia in childhood.* Unpublished manuscript, 1964.

39

Mental Health and Mental Disorders

BENJAMIN B. WOLMAN

SCOPE

The problem of mental health and mental disorders belongs to society as a whole. It is no longer the sole domain of psychiatry, psychology, or social work. It is a national problem. In 1955 the United States Congress passed the Mental Health Study Act. The Congress resolved:

> Sec. 2 (a) It is the sense of Congress that there exists a critical need for such an objective, thorough and nationwide analysis and reevaluation of the human and economic problems of mental illness and the resources, methods, and practices currently utilized in diagnosing, treating, caring for, and rehabilitating the mentally ill, both within and outside of the institutions, as may lead to the development of comprehensive and realistic recommendations for such better utilization of these resources or such improvements on and new developments in methods of diagnosis, treatment, care and rehabilitation as give promise of resulting in a marked reduction in the incidence or duration of mental illness, and in consequence, a lessening of the appalling emotional and financial drain on the families of those afflicted or on the economic resources of the state and the nation.
>
> (b) It is declared to be the policy of the Congress to promote mental health and to help solve the complex and the interrelated problems posed by mental illness by encouraging the undertaking of nongovernmental, multi-disciplinary research into and reevaluation of all aspects of our resources, methods, and practices for diagnosing, treating, caring for, and rehabilitating the mentally ill, including research aimed at the prevention of mental illness. It is the purpose of this joint resolution to implement that policy.

There is no clear-cut evidence that the incidence of mental disorder is growing (Goldhamer & Marshall, 1953). The growth of *awareness* of the problem is, however, evident. More and more people realize what is at stake, and more people are turning for help. At the present time, the taxpayers of the United States spend over 1 billion dollars for the care of mentally disturbed people. Every other bed in the nation's hospitals is occupied by a mental case. Each year, state hospitals, supported by taxes, take care of 1 million mental patients (Fein, 1958; Joint Commission on Mental Illness and Health, 1961).

Yet all this is apparently inadequate. There is no agreement about the number of people who have less or more serious mental problems. The estimates vary from a conservative 10 per cent up to 81.5 per cent (Srole, Langner, Michael, Opler, & Rennie, 1962). A nationwide survey conducted by the Survey Research Center of the University of Michigan disclosed that every seventh adult sought help in mental problems and that one in every four adults admitted the need for psychological help (Gurin, Veroff, & Feld, 1960).

THE SICK ROLE

The problem of mental health and mental disorder goes back to the origins of the human species and probably even further back. In prehistoric and early ancient times, abnormal behavior was recorded (Selling, 1943).

Men who behaved in a strange, disordered, disorganized, offensive way have usually been perceived as a threat to others who could not understand or predict the future actions of such disturbed individuals. In most cases, disturbed people were blamed for their misery and their troubles and were believed to be punished by God; e.g., it was believed that Nebuchadnezzar became insane because he destroyed the Lord's temple. Men frequently decided to add their own punishment to God's, and mentally disturbed individuals have been locked up, flogged, tortured, and even murdered (Linton, 1956; Zilboorg & Henry, 1941).

It was the French Revolution that unlocked the dungeons of mental asylums and broke the chains of enslavement. The slogan *Liberté, égalité, fraternité* has been applied also to disturbed individuals. Dr. Philippe Pinel demanded that the French Revolution grant equal rights also to the inmates of Bicêtre. Pinel believed that the "mentally sick, far from being guilty people deserving of punishment, are sick people whose miserable state deserves all the consideration that is due to suffering humanity" (Zilboorg & Henry, 1941).

This radical change in evaluation of the behavior of mentally disturbed individuals, which raised their status from that of persons doing sinful, evil, and malicious deeds to that of sick persons, was, I believe, one of the greatest steps in the history of human civilization. The names "raving maniac," "lunatic," and "madman" implied threat to others. Society, threatened by the madmen, felt it had to lock them up and inflict severe punishment upon them. Thanks to the French Revolution, the "sick role" was ascribed to the inmates of a mental asylum, and the entire attitude to their problems underwent a most profound change.

True, in medieval times even physically ill people were often exposed to torture. Fever was sometimes taken as a sign of internal fire brought about by sinful behavior. Yet this harsh treatment was not directed against the sick individual. As a rule, the sick person has been perceived not as a threat to others but as a person under a threat of loss of life. The Judeo-Christian tradition, although not always consistent, has favored a charitable attitude toward the sick, the handicapped, invalids, and suffering individuals.

Certainly the sick role easily became overinclusive and encompassed several unrelated ills. It is fashionable today to ascribe the sick role to thieves, swindlers, drunkards, prostitutes, hoodlums, dope peddlers, racketeers, political enemies, radicals, unfaithful husbands and wives, juvenile delinquents, children who fail in school, truants, people who cannot earn a living, new migrants, and whoever for this reason or another does not conform. This overinclusion may put the sick role in disrepute. Some students of this issue, rightly protesting the overinclusion, suggest the abandonment of the application of the sick role to mental disorders altogether (cf. Szasz, 1961).

However, one need not forget that the concept of the sick role has been the most beneficial step toward the solution of the problem. If catatonic schizophrenics are sinful, mean, dishonest individuals who consciously and maliciously set a house on fire, society must defend itself against them. But if they are victims of natural forces beyond their control, society must help them. Actions of an individual call forth reactions from his environment. Presently, civilized societies willingly accept the burden of care of millions of individuals classified as neurotics, psychotics, etc. Were they not "sick" in the sense of being threats to *their* own lives, why care for them?

Unfortunately, the overinclusion in the sick role has often led to moral confusion. Every human society has established certain rules aimed at the protection of human life and well-being. Whether these rules are taboos, religious commandments, or a bill of rights, they reflect what a given social group believes is right or wrong, moral or immoral. All adult members of the society are expected to respect the agreed-upon minimum rules of living together. Without these agreed-upon rules of coexistence, no society could survive. Thus every society establishes sanctions and penalties necessary for its survival and the survival of its members.

Exemption from these rules must be judiciously granted to those who are unable to comply. Not every mentally disturbed individual must be excused. Only in the most severe cases, those persons driven by uncontrollable impulses, can the sick role justify leniency. As Pinel implied, these individuals cannot be held responsible for their deeds even when these deeds harm others. This, however, must not be overextended to include anyone with any psychological problems whatsoever. Such an overinclusion may lead to a lowering of moral responsibility necessary for the survival of everyone. In this light one may view the criticism of Szasz of the term "mental illness" and Mowrer's ideas on neurosis (see "Learning Theory and Behavior Therapy," in Part 2, for further references). Without agreeing with either of them, one must view both standpoints as a reaction against oversimplification of the problem of mental disorder and the overinclusion in the sick role.

THE ORGANIC APPROACH

One may argue whether the "mentally sick" are sick in the same sense that physically sick people are. One may also doubt whether those who take care of the mentally sick must receive the same training as those who take care of the physically sick. One may even question the wisdom of using the term "sickness" in regard to disturbed behavior. While raising questions in regard to the nature of mental disorders, the content of treatment, and the best training for those who treat, one must not forget the importance of the sick role to mental patients, which is analogous to its importance to patients with physical illness.

Pinel's revolution started with the *moral* aspect of the problem. With Pinel, men became their brothers' keepers and assumed responsibility for those who suffer. Other societies (cf. Linton, 1956; Opler, 1959) have tortured or tried to get rid of mental cases.

Those who flogged mental patients did not need to understand them. It has always been easy to punish and hurt, for every ignoramus can use a whip and a knife. But whoever wants to help must know how to do it. In order to do right, one must understand what went wrong.

Physicians, whose job has always been to help the physically ill, had to study mental illness before they could help. In their search for causes of mental disorders, they turned where they were trained to turn—to the organism and its nervous system. Hence mental patients were no longer considered lunatics; they became "nervous" (a term which has survived for centuries and which has outlived any real meaning); deranged and crazy behavior was called from that time on "nervous" or "neurotic."

Certainly the organic stage of research in, and treatment of, mental disorders, originating with the concept of the sick role, has been exceedingly useful. It is sufficient to mention the contributions of Babinsky, Broca, Charcot, Esquirol, Griesinger, Krafft-Ebing, Kraepelin, Morel, and others, as well as the host of present-day neurologists, to point up the tremendous role played by neurophysiological studies in the understanding of mental disorders. (For more details and a review of contemporary research, consult "The Case Study Method," "Experimental Methods in Clinical Psychology," and "Measurement in Clinical Research," in Part 1; and "Psychological Aspects of Disability," "Speech Disorders," "Organic Mental Disorders," and "Neuropsychological Analysis of Focal Brain Lesions," above.)

For awhile, it seemed easy to divide all mental disorders into the "organic" and the "functional." Organic disorders such as dementia paralytica, first described in 1798 by Haslam, were related in 1913 by Noguchi and Moore to syphilis; this is an *organic* mental disorder. (So are brain injuries, familial amanrosis, and many other disorders.) There have been, however, many mental disorders where the most precise histological studies failed to discover neurophysiological or any other organic factors. The term "functional" could have meant that not anatomy but the "function" of the nervous system was impaired, but even such an assumption is unproved as far as the major neuroses and psychoses are concerned.

THE PSYCHOGENIC APPROACH

It took Freud no less moral courage than intellectual genius to embark on psychogenic concept formation and research in regard to mental disorders. Freud was a physician brought up in the best neurophysiological tradition, and it was not easy for him to shift from the somatogenic tradition toward a psychogenic interpretation. In 1894, Freud wrote: "It is scarcely possible to avoid picturing these processes as being in the last resort of chemical nature" (1924–1950, vol. 1). In 1938, Freud wrote that these processes

> are in themselves just as unknownable as those dealt with by the other sciences, by chemistry or physics, for example; but it is possible to establish the laws which those processes obey. . . . This cannot be effected without framing fresh hypotheses and creating fresh concepts. . . . We can claim for them the same value as approximations as belongs to the corresponding intellectual scaffolding found in the other natural sciences. . . . It will be entirely in accordance with our expectations if the basic concepts and principles of the new science (instinct, nervous energy, etc.) remain for a considerable time no less indeterminate than those of the older sciences (force, mass, attraction, etc.) (1949, p. 36).

These "fresh hypotheses and fresh concepts" were nonorganic. The theoretical constructs of Eros and Thanatos, id, ego, and superego are not related, nor can they be reduced to chemistry or neurology. Mental disorders have been interpreted in psychogenic terms. The focus in psychopathology has shifted from the nervous system to repression, fixation, complex, reaction formation, and other "mentalistic" processes.

The concept of mental health has been transformed into one of a *balanced personality*. As a result, a balanced id-ego-superego triad, with the ego holding a firm grip on external reality, is considered to be tantamount to mental health. The ego, wrote Freud, in *New Introductory Lectures on Psychoanalysis*, "has to serve three harsh masters. . . . The three tyrants are the external world, the superego, and the id . . ." (1933, p. 103). When the ego is hard-pressed and is unable to exercise adequate control and/or to reconcile in a reasonably adequate manner the demands of id, superego, and reality, neurosis ensues. Whenever the ego loses contact with reality, a psychosis has started.

THE SOCIOLOGICAL APPROACH

K. Horney accused Freud of neglecting social factors and of being unduly "biological" (1939, p. 39). Good biology, however, has always been ecological. So is Freud's theory. Horney's accusations can be easily refuted (Wolman, 1954), for Freud's developmental stages do not exclude environment. Whether an infant will or will not pass safely from one developmental stage to another largely depends on his interaction with his parents and other people. Certainly Freud's model of personality leaves enough room for interactional factors, though one has to admit that some non-Freudians have stressed these factors more than Freud did.

Adler (1929) was not given the well-deserved credit for his emphasis on parent-child interactional patterns. Horney, Fromm, and Sullivan are as indebted to Adler as they are to Freud. The emphasis of the "sociological school" of psychoanalysis on interactional patterns in mental health and mental disorder coincided with the rapid expansion of sociological studies of mental disorders. Faris and Dunham (1939), in their study of ecological factors, have opened new vistas in sociological research in psychopathology. At the same time, Sullivan (1931) and Horney (1939) analyzed the pathogenic implications of social relations in early childhood. At the present time, we are witnessing a new revolution, this time in the direction of social determinants.

It is worth mentioning that the three consecutive stages in the history of psychopathology, the somatogenic, the psychogenic, and the sociogenic, do not exclude one another. Organism, personality, and society are three mutually complementary factors, and students of mental disorders must not omit any of them. Research workers, whether they follow Freud or Pavlov and whether they pursue studies in conditioning or in psychoanalysis, include all three factors: organism, personality, and society.

CONDITIONING

In the Soviet Union conditioning has been interpreted on a neurological basis, in a strict adherence to Pavlov's theory. Pavlov distinguished three types of reaction to stress related to excitation and inhibition. The prevalence of excitatory reflexes, aggressiveness, and inability to form inhibitory processes has been interpreted by Pavlov as a "neurasthenic" reaction. Prevalence of inhibitory processes characterized by a timid, shy, and submissive behavior has been classified by Pavlov as a "hysterical" reaction, and schizophrenia was classified as severe hysteria. The normal behavior is the "central" or equilibrated; a central personality type can withstand stress well (Pavlov, 1927; Pavlov, 1928).

Pavlov also followed Hippocrates's theory of four temperaments. The sanguinic and phlegmatic types are believed to be normal or central; the sanguinic is energetic and productive, and the phlegmatic is quiet and persistent. Manic-depressives and neurasthenics belong to the choleric, excitable type; hysterics and schizophrenics belong to the melancholic type (Pavlov, 1928, pp. 377ff.). Later on, Pavlov added three more types, namely, the intermediate, the artistic, and the intellectual. A combination of the four Hippocratic types with the three cultural types permitted a greater variability in classification. Thus, for instance, hysteria is a combination of inhibitory, melancholic types with the artistic type, characterized by an abnormal prevalence of the first signal system and the subcortex (Platonov, 1959, pp. 273ff.).

Apparently Pavlov and his disciples have related mental disorders to inherited reaction types and to certain conditioning processes that affect the excitatory and inhibitory processes (cf. Gantt, 1944; Pavlov, 1928; Platonov, 1959; Winn, 1961). However, cultural factors and "second-level" verbal conditioning seem to play an increasing role in the Soviet Union in the interpretation of mental disorders.

LEARNING THEORY

American and European learning theorists seem to agree unanimously that disordered and disturbed behavior is caused by conditioning. Some of them come close to Pavlov's type of experimentation, emphasizing inner conflict as the precipitating and perhaps the total cause of neurosis. In Pavlov's experiments, the dog exposed to conflicting stimuli of excitation and inhibition "presented all the symptoms of a condition of acute neurosis" (Pavlov, 1927, p. 291).

Maier's experimental studies with rats (1949; 1956) followed a similar pattern. Maier intended not only to frustrate the experimental animals but also to put them in a conflict situation. Maier's critics believe that stress itself was a sufficient cause for the seizure states. Gantt (1944), Liddell (1953), and others followed Pavlov's thinking closely and in several studies pointed to the conflict between excitation and inhibition as the crucial pathogenic factor.

Several learning theorists singled out frustration as the causal factor in mental disorders. Following Maier's research with rats (1949), Jenkins (1950; 1952) concluded that continuous and severe frustration in interpersonal relations is the main cause of schizophrenia.

Dollard and Miller (1950) have tried to adapt some Freudian concepts to Hull's learning theory. They have assumed that anxiety is a drive that motivates the organism to act in order to reduce the drive. Hence abnormal behavior can be interpreted in terms of conditioning of maladjusted behavioral patterns.

Many learning theorists interpret mental disorder in terms of Bekhterev's "avoidance learning" (1932). Anxiety-producing situations evoke avoidance reactions. These reactions become reinforced by the repetition of the anxiety-producing situations. A patient, wrote Shoben (1948, p. 139), "is typically ridden by anxieties, that is, his habit structures are characterized by a number of well established S-R bonds between various stimuli and those visceral reactions called fear or anxiety." The patient "has built up a number of defenses . . . against these anxieties." These defenses lead to symptom formation, and they breed further "anxiety, guilt, or insecurity."

Miller (1948) has interpreted the occurrence of neurotic symptoms according to the hypothesis that avoidance behavior is generalized more widely than positive approach behavior. Skinner and Skinnerians have applied operant techniques to the study of abnormal behavior. They seem to assume that aversive stimuli produce avoidance or escape behavior or suppression. Such behavior is believed to be abnormal (cf. Lindsley, 1956; Sidman, 1962; and others).

Neither Skinner and his disciples nor Hull and his school have developed a full-fledged theory of mental health and mental disorders. It seems that at the present time, learning theories have introduced methodological refinement into clinical research but have not yet been able to produce an over-all system of interpretation. However, the facts observed by those who use experimental methods are basically the same as stated by clinicians. As Wilson (1963) put it, both clinical and experimental studies point to intense anxiety, stereotyped and repetitive behavior, and fixation of needs and emotions at an immature level.

There is an undeniable fact that some mental symptoms are a product of conditioning. This fact does not prove that all mental disorders are caused by conditioning, nor does it explain why certain individuals in certain situations develop morbid behavioral patterns.

Rapaport (1959) wrote: "Psychoanalytic theory at present cannot escape this embarrassment, since it has no learning theory of its own to pit against conditioning." I do not see any reason for embarrassment because I see no contradiction between Freud's and Pavlov's teachings. Symptoms can be produced by cathexis, by conditioning, or by both.

Mowrer occupies an independent position among learning theorists and offers an original theory of mental disorders. His point of view is described in "Learning Theory and Behavior Therapy," in Part 2.

SZASZ'S VIEWPOINT

Lately several workers have tried to reconsider the entire issue of mental health. Three major efforts (those of Szasz, Jahoda, and Wolman) will be discussed below.

Szasz, in his book *The Myth of Mental Illness,* stated that the definition of psychiatry as used traditionally places this area next to such sciences as "alchemy and astrology, and commits it to the category of pseudo-science" (1961, p. 1). According to *The Myth of Mental Illness,* "hysteria is nothing other than the 'language of illness,' employed either because another language has not been learned well enough, or because this language happens to be especially useful" (1961, p. 12). According to Szasz, "mental illness is a myth" (1961, p. 296). He feels that an individual with a mental disorder provides professional psychiatric assent to a rationalization, that "problems in human living experienced and expressed in terms of bodily feelings or signs . . . are significantly similar to diseases of the body." He feels that the problem of mental illness must be redefined and included in the usual category of the "science of man." This, Szasz goes on to say, would entail a revision of thought in the areas of psychopathology and psychotherapy. Thus: "The former should be conceived in terms of object relationships, rule-following, social roles, and game playing. As to psychotherapy, it should be systematized as a theory of human relationships, involving special social arrangements and fostering certain values and types of learning" (Szasz, 1961, p. 297).

JAHODA'S REVIEW

Marie Jahoda suggested the six following criteria of mental health based on a thorough review of the pertinent literature.

The first of the six criteria has to do with *attitudes toward oneself,* among them the accessibility of the self to consciousness. On this point Jahoda quotes Mayman (1955), who said:

> An intact sense of selfhood or self-determination indicates a successful synthesis by the individual of all he has been and done, with all that he wants to be and do, with all that he would and is able to be and do, without his disowning any major feelings, impulses, capacities or goals in the interest of inner harmony (Jahoda, 1958, p. 25).

Allport, discussing the objectivity of self-perception, distinguished the mature personality as revealing self-objectification. Thus both Allport and Mayman regard the self-concept as important and desirable "when it contains an image of all important aspects of the person" (Jahoda, 1958, p. 26). Another aspect of the attitudes toward the self as criteria for mental health is the correctness of the self-concept. The more realistically and objectively one sees oneself, the better is his mental health. Distortions of the self-concept in relation to reality may be either negative or positive. In the case of the latter, the ideal self tends to fuse with the real self. "Whatever the direction, such distortion is based on an inability to control rationally the wishes and fears that thus color the perception of the self" (Jahoda, 1958, p. 27). Feelings about one's self-concept are also important in this area, the important idea being that of acceptance of the self with its shortcomings as well as its virtues. A sense of identity is a significant aspect of this and refers to the integrative attribute of the self. "A healthy person knows who he is and does not feel basic doubts about his inner identity" (Jahoda, 1958, p. 29).

Erikson speaks of this sense of identity as an indicator of mental health. He distinguishes five stages in the development of a healthy personality, namely, the stages of basic trust, autonomy, initiative, industry, and finally identity. Ego identity

> is the inner capital accrued from all the experiences of each successive stage, when successful identifications led to a successful alignment of the individual's basic drives with his endowment and his opportunities. . . . The sense of ego identity, then, is the accrued confidence that one's ability to maintain inner sameness and conformity (one's ego in the psychological sense) is matched by the sameness and continuity of one's meaning for others (1950, p. 135).

The second criterion for mental health is *growth, development,* and *self-actualization.* This is based on Goldstein's idea that an organism strives to realize its potentialities. This idea is also present in the thinking of Sullivan, Fromm, Carl Rogers, Allport, and Maslow. To Goldstein, self-actualization is the chief motive of the organism. Fromm seems to share this view, for he says that the healthy person understands that "there is only one meaning to life: the act of living itself" (1941, p. 263). Maslow (1955), in his theory of the hierarchy of motives, distinguishes between deficiency and growth motivation. The deficiency motives are those which lead to tension reduction, such as the need for safety, respect, and love, but which do not foster positive mental health. According to Maslow, the greater the amount of growth motivation, the better the mental health. Allport (1955) agrees with Maslow's ideas and regards the dynamics of the conscience as an example of a growth motive.

The third criterion advanced by Jahoda is *integration,* which refers to the "coherence of personality" as "the relatedness of all processes and attributes in an individual" (1958, p. 36). The emphasis is placed on three areas: The first is a balance of psychic forces in the individual, which refers to the balance of the ego, id, and superego, or the conscious, unconscious, and preconscious psychic levels. Hartmann (1947) suggested a balance in which the ego can accommodate the id and superego and does not deny or exclude their demands. Hartmann (1939) discussed the flexibility or plasticity of the ego as a factor in mental health. Kubie (1954), quoted by Jahoda, believes that mental health is a balance among the conscious, unconscious, and preconscious. He sees a healthy balance resulting in flexibility; therefore flexibility becomes the criterion for normality or mental health.

Allport (1937) introduced the terms "self-extension" and "self-objectification" to distinguish that individual who possesses a unifying philosophy from which he knows his potentialities and goals and his place in the nature of the world. A unifying philosophy of life "results in the individual's feeling that there is purpose and meaning to his life" (Jahoda, 1958, p. 40).

Many authors think of mental health in terms of the individual's resistance to stress. Here we find such terms as "anxiety tolerance," "frustration tolerance," and "ego strength." "All authors who speak about this aspect, agree that tension, anxiety, frustration, or unhappiness occur in normal and in sick persons. The difference lies not in the presence of symptoms but rather these symptoms can seriously unbalance the degree of integration an individual has achieved" (Jahoda, 1958, p. 42).

The fourth criterion of mental health advanced by Jahoda is *autonomy, independence,* or *self-determination.* Foote and Cottrell (1955) speak of autonomy as referring to "the clarity of the individual's conception of self (identity)"; the extent to which he maintains a stable set of criteria for mental health, for "evaluation of actions as sick, or normal, or extraordinary in a positive sense often depends largely on accepted social conventions" (Jahoda, 1958, p. 13). Asch (1952) said that human behavior cannot be understood in terms of symptoms which are isolated but must be looked upon in terms of the norms and values of the particular society in which the symptoms are discovered. Some anthropologists take a strong stand against this idea of cultural relativism; it is Linton's contention that "only with regard to the manifestations of the disease is cultural relativism appropriate" (Jahoda, 1958, p. 13).

The second point made by Jahoda is that normality is not to be taken as a criterion for mental health, for this implies that "whatever exists in the majority of cases is right by virtue of its existence" (1958, p. 15). There are many instances in which majority rule is unsatisfactory; the "majority does many things which we hesitate to call mentally healthy . . ." (Jahoda, 1958, p. 16). Thus, mental health may be, but is not necessarily, the majority status. The third point made by Jahoda is that various states of well-being are not to be used as criteria for mental health. Jones (1942) speaks of mental health in terms of happiness. The term "satisfying" is used by other writers. Boehm states: "Mental health is a condition and level of social functioning which is socially acceptable and personally satisfying" (1955, p. 537). As a general rule, people are happy when what they desire from life is in terms of what life has to offer them. This kind of happiness is a function of external events over which the individual has no control.

Another criterion of normality is related to the concept of self and

> to the extent to which he maintains a stable set of internal standards for his actions; the degree to which he is self-directed and self-controlled in his actions; his confidence and his reliance upon himself; the degree of self-respect he maintains; and the capacity for recognizing real threats to the self and of mobilizing realistic defenses when so threatened (Foote & Cottrell, 1955, p. 55).

The second aspect of autonomy is that of independent behavior, which is described by Jahoda as the outcome of the decision-making process. Maslow (1954) describes the autonomous individual as one who is independent of the environment and dependent upon himself and his resources for continued growth and development.

The fifth criterion of mental health, as discussed by Jahoda, is *perception of reality,* which is free from what she has termed "need-distortion" (1958, p. 49). The mentally healthy individual has a correct perception of the environment. The correct perception of reality is one of Barron's (1955) criteria for mental health. However, a major problem arises here which lies in the use of the word "correct," for who is to say what is and what is not correct? On this point, Jahoda says:

> The point at issue here is that "correctness" of perception cannot mean that there is one and only one right way of looking at the world around us. But whatever the individual, and perhaps peculiar, way of perceiving the world, there must be some objective cues to fit the resulting perception. This is what accuracy or correctness mean when one speaks of mentally healthy perception (1958, p. 51).

Thus, there is a replacement of the word "correct" with the term "relative freedom from need-distortion" (Jahoda, 1958, p. 51). In this sense, then, "mentally healthy perception" means a process of viewing the world so that one is able to take in matters that one wishes were different without distorting them to fit these wishes (Jahoda, 1958, p. 349). Thus, reality testing, in which the individual checks his perceptions with the facts of the environment, is one criterion for mental health. Along this line of reasoning, Jahoda (1958) has suggested empathy or social sensitivity as being very important for mental health. The requirement of the mentally healthy individual in this area of perceiving the emotions and attitudes of others is "that he treat the inner life of other people as a matter worthy of his concern and attention" (Jahoda, 1958, p. 52). His conclusions about others must, like those about himself, be free from distortion.

The sixth and final criterion for mental health suggested by Jahoda is *environmental mastery.* This mastery is subdivided into two general themes of success and adaptation, manifested in six forms, the first of which is the ability to love. The second form of manifestation is stated by Jahoda to be adequacy in love, work, and play, the "three crucial areas of living" (1958, p. 55). Many authors agree on this point. Blau (1954), quoted by Jahoda, speaks of the mentally healthy person as being one who "is able to work adequately and to create within the limitations of his capacities, to relax after work and enjoy recreation . . ." (Blau, 1954, p. 594). The third manifestation of environmental mastery is seen in adequacy in interpersonal relations. This concept is apparent in the work of Sullivan, Horney, and other neo-Freudians. Sullivan contends that the main goal of every human being is security and a feeling of belonging to a group which results from interpersonal relationships. The fourth manifestation in this area is the meeting of situational requirements which must be specifically evaluated in every situation in which there is measurement of mental health. However: "Some situational requirements, if met, can call for behavior that must be deemed unhealthy when viewed in terms of some other criteria . . ." (Jahoda, 1958, p. 59). Thus, the criterion should "be applied only when there is some consensus on the reasonableness of the requirement" (Jahoda, 1958, p. 59). The fifth manifestation is seen in the requirements of adaptation and adjustment. Adaptation implies that an arrangement can be created between reality and the individual by modification of either or both. Thus, the term "adaptation" conveys the idea that the individual can change both the external environment and the inner balance of his psychic forces. Piaget (1952) conceives of adaptation as a balance between the active and passive parts in one's adjustment to the environment. The final manifestation of environmental mastery is found in problem-solving behavior. Jahoda set up three dimensions in this process. The first involves the time sequence of different stages. This includes the awareness of the problem to be solved, a consideration of the means to be followed in its solution, a decision to use one of the previously considered methods, and the implementation of the decision. The second dimension involves the feelings which correspond to and accompany the different stages. In the earlier stages, there is some discontent, which acts as an incentive for progressing to the following stages. The third dimension of this process concerns the directness or indirectness of the approach to the core of the problem. Jahoda feels that "a maximal degree of healthy problem solving combines the three dimensions; a tendency to go through all stages, the maintenance of an appropriate feeling tone, and a direct attack on the problem. Going through this process, rather than finding a successful resolution, is taken as an indication for mental health" (1958, p. 64).

WOLMAN'S SYSTEM

Another system of mental health and mental disorders has been introduced by Wolman (1965). This system stresses the organism-personality-society continuum.

The problem of mental health may be compared with a similar problem in the area of physical health. Health and disease are not irreconcilable opposites, for both describe the state of a living organism. Life and death are the two extreme points on the scale or continuum of physical health, and one's physical state is estimated in terms of his distance from death. Normal or abnormal and healthy or sick are matters of degree, and each individual is more or less normal and healthy. Death is the final point of abnormalcy, deficiency, and disease.

Not all diseases lead to death; some of them severly incapacitate the individual. Mental disorder is not lethal, but severe forms of mental disorder incapacitate the individual and prevent adjustment to his environment. In the extreme forms of mental disorder seen in the back wards of mental hospitals, the impairment of the ability to live becomes apparent. In physical disease, the closer to death, the more serious the disease. In mental disorder, the lesser the ability to live, the more serious the disorder. Thus, my tentative definition of mental disorder points to a generally incapacitating condition that reduces the individual's chances for survival. All the observable behavior of living organisms *aims for survival.* A mentally sick individual is often unable to use his resources in that struggle for survival. He gives up the struggle, defeats himself, tries to destroy his chances for success, or attacks himself. Usually one's achievements are proportional to one's innate potentialities and environmental circumstances, but not if one is a victim of a mental disorder. *The inability to use one's physical and mental resources is one of the outstanding signs of mental disorder.* There are three main areas where this inability is apparent: in cognitive functions, in emotional response, and in social relations.

Cognitive Functions

In order to survive, organisms adjust to their environment through perception. Men act according to what they see, hear, smell, touch, etc. They perceive the situation and adjust to it. Man's abilities to observe and to see things as they really are, to notice similarities and differences, to comprehend relations and to reason, and to learn from experience have been his most valuable weapons in the struggle for survival. In mental disorder, the cognitive capacities are disturbed in a peculiar way. In neurosis and psychosis the mental apparatus is usually well preserved, but the individual is unable to use his capacities to perceive things realistically and to act in a rational manner in accordance with what he sees. Freud called this difficulty a disturbance in reality testing. By this he meant the inability to distinguish one's inner stimuli from the outer stimuli; thus, one's own wishes and the external stimuli become confused.

Infants probably hallucinate, but gradually, by checking their perceptions and manipulating the perceived objects, they learn to "test reality." Sullivan (1953) has suggested another distinction. He conceived of three stages in human life with respect to perceiving one's environment correctly. These are the prototaxic stage, which is the state of unconscious, diffused experiences of the infant; the parataxic stage, in which the individual perceives the world as a series of experiences in a nonlogical order, with himself as the center of the universe; and finally, the syntaxic stage, in which the individual develops the ability to check his perceptions against those of others and validate them through the consensus of the group. In mentally disturbed individuals, this ability for consensual validation is impaired or nonexistent. A mental disorder becomes severe whenever the picture of the outer world does not correspond to reality at all. Whenever an individual distorts or misinterprets reality, he has a delusion. When the perception of reality is not related to any external stimulation and the individual sees ghosts or hears voices, he has a hallucination. In this case the ability for reality testing is completely lost.

The question of cultural influences has been raised in connection with this problem. History and anthropology provide several instances of erroneous perceptions of the world. Myth and truth have been too often confused, and wish and dreams too often taken for reality. It is rather difficult to perform satisfactory reality testing when everyone else accepts delusion. However, reality testing *within* cultural limitations has always been a valid criterion of mental health.

Emotional Response

All living organisms act in accordance with the law of homeostasis. This law states that whenever the human organism is exposed to stimulation which disturbs its equilibrium, a reaction takes place that is aimed at the restoration of the initial equilibrium. This principle applies to all functions of the organism, including emotional life. Human beings respond with pleasure and pain, joy and sorrow, elation and depression to situations in which they find themselves. The normal or mentally healthy individual reacts emotionally to stimuli in proportion to their magnitude (stronger reaction to the stronger stimuli and weaker reaction to the weaker stimuli) so that the best possible adjustment and restoration of emotional balance result. Thus, the emotionally balanced individual acts in a rational manner that enhances his chances for successful living; he reacts to stress in an adjustive manner. The reaction of the mentally sick or emotionally unbalanced individual may be exaggerated and out of proportion to the stimulus. Some individuals are in the throes of despair whenever they meet hardships or suffer a loss. Even when the loss is negligible and can be easily replaced, the disturbed individual is carried away by his emotions and acts in an irrational manner that certainly will not make matters better. One may expect a deterioration in this individual's ability to cope with hardships. Gradually increasing irritability and growing difficulty in restoring the emotional balance bear witness to an aggravation of the mental disorder. Emotionally balanced individuals are "normal"; those who are poorly balanced are less normal. Severe emotional disbalance is one of the indicators of the severity of the disorder.

Social Adjustment

In order to survive, man must satisfy his needs. The better one is equipped to do this, the stronger he is (the more power he possesses), and the better are his chances for survival. One can use his power to satisfy his own needs and the needs of others. Usually people exchange goods and services to help one another. Power can be used for satisfaction of needs or for prevention of their satisfaction, for protection of life or for its destruction. A classification of social relations based on motivation of the participants has been proposed (Wolman, 1956). All human relations can be divided into three classes according to the aims of the participants. When people join a group in order to have their own needs satisfied, it is an *instrumental* group. In such a relationship, the individual regards the other group members as tools or instruments. The infant-mother relationship is the prototype of instrumentalism, for the infant's life begins as a parasitic process; he is dependent on the mother for satisfaction of all his needs. A friendly and supportive attitude on the part of the parents gives the child an increasing feeling of power and enables him to enter the next developmental stage of give-and-take, or *mutual* relationships. Gradually children develop genuine mutuality based on the willingness of each party to be of help to the other. Mutuality achieves its peak in the marriage relationship and in friendship.

Parenthood is the prototype of the third

type, *vectorial* relationships. Parents create life, protect it, and care for it, regardless of any attributes of the child. The weaker the child, the more they protect it. To be an adequate parent one needs to be strong, friendly, and willing to give and to be ready to take care without asking anything in return. To give without asking, without expecting anything in return, is the highest degree of love. This is the essence of vectorialism (Wolman, 1960a).

A mentally normal and well-adjusted individual must balance in his social interactions. He is instrumental in the struggle for survival, mutual in relationships with family and friends, and vectorial in regard to children and those who need help. Mentally disturbed individuals cannot preserve this balance. They are hyperinstrumental, displaying infantile selfishness and parasitism; they neglect themselves and worry constantly about others, thus being *hypervectorial;* or they exaggerate giving and taking in shifting moods of *paramutualism*. Thus, they are socially maladjusted.

Hostility. Men cannot satisfy their needs unless they interact with others in the society, whether through competition or cooperation. Each social group has its share of constructive, life-preserving, and cooperative forces and its share of disruptive, destructive, and antisocial forces. However, when the forces of hate or hostility win, life and society perish. Therefore, no society can afford to tolerate a free play of hostile and disruptive forces.

One can distinguish four types of hostility: defense, aggression, panic, and terror. Civilized societies impose restrictions on hostility, while they usually accept defense provided it serves to protect life, is related to a real threat, and is acted upon in a rational and socially approved manner.

A mentally healthy individual is capable of living on friendly terms with his group. He is capable of cooperating and is willing to help, and he eagerly enters social relations based on mutual respect, agreement, and responsibility. He may occasionally disagree, without becoming disagreeable, and he can understand that others may disagree with him. He may occasionally feel hostile, but his feelings are under rational control and are acted out only in self-defense and in a manner approved by his social group.

Mentally disturbed individuals are usually socially maladjusted. As a rule, they find it difficult to relate to other individuals. In some cases they distrust people, suspect them, and shy away from them and withdraw into seclusion. In some cases the inner hostility may break through. In a psychotic fury, one may attack everything and everybody, including himself. The severity of social maladjustment usually corresponds to the severity of mental disorder, although it is not a simple one-to-one relationship.

Personality Model

The three areas of cognitive functions, emotional response, and social adjustment are based on the over-all principle of the ability to live. They must be ordered to a certain personality structure. My choice has been Freud's theory of personality.

Freud offered a detailed, applicable, and flexible system of hypotheses and developed an elaborate model of personality. This model deals with topography, i.e., the mental strata (conscious, unconscious, and preconscious), economy of the driving forces (libido and destrudo), and mental apparatus (id, ego, and superego). However, Freud's model requires some modification in regard to social relations. The term "cathexis" is merely a logical construct that enables us to distinguish between various types of object relations. Freud's studies dealt with the cathecting individual and omitted the cathected object. Sociologically oriented neoanalysts such as Horney and Sullivan were concerned with this issue. Instead of Freudian love, sexual or aim-inhibited, Horney introduced protection and safety; instead of Freud's active cathexis of libido or need to love, she emphasized the need to be loved (Wolman, 1954, p. 4). Sullivan went even further in his theory of interpersonal relations, for he tied personality directly to interpersonal relations. Without using the term "cathexis," he emphasized empathy, describing it as a kind of "emotional contagion or communion" between the child and parental figures. Freud dealt with the individual who cathects his libido in the object; I suggest including also the cathected object in the study. This enables one to use the important contributions made by the neoanalytic schools without abandoning Freudian personality theory.

This new concept of "interindividual cathexis" is merely a logical construct and has been introduced because of its methodological flexibility and usefulness. Thus, in instrumental relationships, the individual's aim is to receive libido cathexes from others; in mutual relationships, the individual aims at receiving libido cathexes as well as at giving them to those from whom he aims to receive; and in vectorical relationships, the individual aims to object-cathect, to give to others. A well-balanced individual is capable of functioning in all three types of relationships. His libido is reasonably balanced in interindividual relationships and is properly divided between intercathexes and intracathexes. A disbalance in interindividual cathexes, caused by interaction between the individual and his environment, inevitably leads to a disbalance in intraindividual cathexes. In other words, improper social relations must cause personality disorder.

Ares. Another modification of Freud's theory of personality has been suggested (Wolman, 1960a) and pertains to the destructive instincts and the theory of death. Freud suggested the theory of Thanatos as the death instinct, the opposite of Eros, or the life instinct, which serves to protect life. How can this supposed death instinct protect death? No living organism uses instinctual energy to die or to increase or to protect death, nor is it true "that the final aim of the destructive instinct is to reduce living things to an inorganic state" (Freud, 1949, p. 20). Certain organic processes continue after the organism as a whole dies, and so no living organism turns with death into a rock.

Starting with Charles Darwin and continuing with T. Huxley, I. P. Pavlov, T. Schjeldrum-Ebbe, and recently K. Lorentz, biologists pointed to the use of physical force for self-defense as the general law of nature. Lorentz believes that hate is a more general and fundamental pattern than love and that hostility is the primary pattern in the animal kingdom; it is the main drive in the struggle for survival. When man is hungry or hurt or when his energies are low, the available energy is predominantly destructive, and he can be easily provoked to violence. The hostile drive, called "Ares," serves life too. Its emotional energy, called "destrudo," can be cathected analogously to libido (Wolman, 1960a, chap. 15).

Through the developmental stages of life, there is a gradual modification in the intercathexes and intracathexes of libido, usually combined with destrudo. Oral love is a fusion of object libido with an obvious predominance of destrudo. In the anal stage, in "tenderness," object cathexis of libido becomes stronger. At the phallic stage, in possessive-protective love, there is an additional gain of libido over destrudo. In well-adjusted adults, destrudo is partially sublimated, partially aim-inhibited, and partially adequately repressed. Destrudo is primitive and archaic, and there are no developmental stages analogous to those of libido, for there cannot be any progress in destrudo. Destrudo takes over when libido fails. In emergencies, in states of severe deprivation, starvation, lack of sleep, exhaustion, and pain, destrudo takes over. When love cannot help, hate is called in.

Destrudo is the controlling power of the organism only in a state of serious regression. In normal states it is partially fused with libido and partially sublimated, but it never has pure, uncontrolled, savage liberty. An unbound, bursting-out destrudo is symptomatic of severe mental disorder.

DEFINITION OF MENTAL DISORDER

I have approached the problem of mental disorder from two angles: observation of overt behavior and analysis of personality structure. The first approach led to the conclusion that mental disorder is a pattern of maladjustment. Three criteria have been advanced: irrationality in cognitive processes, emotional disbalance, and social maladjustment. Mentally disturbed individuals are apparently unable to keep their behavior balanced in instrumental, mutual, and vectorial relationships, nor are they capable of restraint of hostile attitudes.

These conclusions, derived from observational data and experimental studies, have been related to Freud's theory of personality: (1) Freud's theory has been modified by the application of the concept of cathexis to interindividual relations, and (2) Freud's destructive instinct has been presented not as a death instinct but as a guarding force (Ares).

Normal individuals are balanced in their libido cathexes; they are reasonably selfish (self-cathexis) and reasonably considerate of others (object cathexis). They use destrudo in self-defense with moderation and restraint and in a socially approved manner.

In mentally disturbed individuals, libido cathexes are disbalanced, and destrudo is not too well controlled. The peculiarities in the disbalance of cathexes may serve as good criteria for classification of mental disorders.

PRINCIPLES OF CLASSIFICATION

One may classify objects in many different ways. One may, for instance, classify animals according to the shape of the body, the color of the skin, or the number of legs. One may classify plants in accordance with color, smell, size, etc. Men can be classified as young or old, tall or short, wearing glasses or not wearing glasses, male or female, etc. No classification per se is "better" or more "essential" than the other. For a real estate broker, mankind is divided into those who buy and those who take up his time without buying; for a bridge player, the world is composed of nonplayers, beginners, good players, and masters.

One of the first steps in the history of science was classification (Wolman, 1960a, pp. 507ff.). Classification enables the scientist to form general and abstract concepts. When objects or events are put together into a class or category on the basis of at least one common denominator, one can make generalizations or statements pertaining to the entire class.

There are two requirements in regard to scientific classification, namely, *economy* and *usefulness*. A classification is economical when no object within a given system of classification belongs to more than one class and when every object belongs to a certain class; e.g., if we divide students in a class according to their height and classify those below 5 feet as short and those above 6 feet as tall, we leave many students out. If we classify those below 6 feet as short and those above 5 feet as tall, those between 5 and 6 feet belong to both classes, and our classification is uneconomical.

Classification of mental disorders based merely on symptomatology is usually uneconomical. Autistic patterns of behavior are typical not only of schizophrenic children but also of children after encephalitis or anoxia. Hallucinations may accompany a great many disorders. So do depressions, anxieties, phobias, homosexual impulses, psychosomatic disorders, addictions, antisocial behavior, etc. Most of these symptoms accompany more than one type of mental disorder.

The economical classification of biological species into plants and animals and of animals into vertebrates and invertebrates enables the biologist to make general and truthful statements pertaining to each class. But when the *Diagnostic and Statistical Manual: Mental Disorders*, of the American Psychiatric Association (1952), distinguishes psychophysiologic autonomic and visceral disorders from psychoneurotic disorders, it is guilty of overlapping and of uneconomical classification, for a great many psychoneurotics described in the same manual display psychophysiologic disorders.

When a scientist classifies objects, he keeps in mind his objectives, i.e., prediction and explanation. The business of science is the discovery of truth and the explanation and prediction of the chain of causes and effects. When a chemist or a physicist introduces classificatory systems, he introduces them for the sake of generalization, explanation, and prediction.

This applies also to the area of investigation. Mental disorders can be classified in many ways (cf. Zilboorg & Henry, 1941), but a classification becomes scientifically useful if and when it helps to *explain* the present state (symptoms) by invoking the past causes and when, knowing the past causes, it helps to *predict* their future outcome. Thus a scientifically useful classification must include etiologic factors; the dynamics of personality changes reflected in clusters of symptoms must be put in the same nosological category.

Some mental disorders originate in deficiencies of the organism; they are *somatogenic*. Organic or somatogenic disorders can be either *genosomatogenic*, if inherited, or *ecosomatogenic*, if acquired.

All mental disorders exclusive of the inherited ones are products of interaction between the organism and the environment. If this interaction is physical or chemical, the disorder is *ecosomatogenic*. If it is neither physical nor chemical, it is *sociogenic*. There are obviously no other categories, and all mental disorders are genosomatogenic, ecosomatogenic, or sociogenic. The so-called "functional" or "psychogenic" mental disorders are products of interaction with the social environment; they are caused either by *cathexes* (i.e., they are products of the inherited constitutional factors interacting with the environment) or by *conditioning* (i.e., they are products of environmental factors that modify the constitutional factors by establishing new connections). In both cases, mental disorder is a product of noxious influences of environmental factors that either cause morbid changes in the system of cathexes or condition morbid behavioral patterns. These environmental factors act upon what we may call "mentality," "mental apparatus," "psychological structure," or "personality structure."

However, in the spirit of transitionism (Wolman, 1965b), I believe that psychological processes can and are frequently transformed into physiochemical processes. Sociogenic mental disorders are always sociopsychological and frequently develop psychophysiologic autonomic and visceral symptoms, thus becoming *sociopsychosomatic*.

The sociogenic or sociopsychosomatic disorders can be divided into the following three large categories.

Hyperinstrumental Type

Some disturbed individuals are highly *instrumental* in any situation and in regard to all people. They always ask for something for nothing; they show no consideration for their fellow men, not even for their own parents, marital partners, or children. They seem to believe that the world owes them a living and that they owe nothing to anyone. They treat life as if it were a bank to be robbed or an oil field to be exploited. They have no love for anyone except themselves. They are exploitative, selfish, and brutal. They feel sorry for themselves but have no mercy for anyone else. They never blame themselves but always put the blame on others. They believe themselves to be weak and friendly.

This type of disturbed person is the *hyperinstrumental type*. This name corresponds to what has usually been called the "psychopath" or the "sociopath." Hyperinstrumentals are selfish, dishonest, and disloyal, and yet they believe that they are always right; they believe others are hostile, and they are resentful whenever others refuse to serve them or are in their way. They are very sensitive to their own suffering and deprivations, but they have no empathy or sympathy for anyone else and least of all for their victims. They have no moral restraints, no consideration, no compassion for their fellow men. They may become criminals unless they fear retaliation. Their symptom formation offers both primary and secondary gains; it alleviates their feelings of being weak and helpless and also helps them to win privileges from the environment.

The personality structure of the hyperinstrumental or psychopathic type can be described as follows: His libido is self-hypercathected. The hyperinstrumental has never outgrown the primary narcissism of the infant and is always madly in love with himself. He has no true object love for others; whatever object relations he has are on an exploitative, primitive-instrumental, oral-cannibalistic level. He loves to use people and to destroy them for his own use. People are to be used and not helped. If they resent being used, they must be "liquidated." In hyperinstrumentals, destrudo is highly mobilized, always ready to strike. It is object-directed. The hyperinstrumental type views the world as an enemy that he must devour or it will devour him. Those he perceives as being weak he treats as a wolf treats sheep; toward those he perceives as strong, he acts like a sheep. He perceives himself as weak and friendly, as an innocent, poor, hungry animal who has to defend himself against his enemies. He is a coward, brutal and cruel to those who fear him but obedient and subservient to those he fears.

The hyperinstrumental, or psychopath, has no moral principles, no ethical standards, no human obligations. He has only needs and nothing else. His superego is practically nonexistent. If he is religious, his gods are either cynical masters whom one may bribe or warriors that have to help him to conquer the world. His gods are always on the side of the big battalions. His ego may be weak or strong, but it always sides with the id.

The hyperinstrumental, or psychopathic, type fears people and is suspicious, hostile, greedy, insecure, and never satiated.

Hypervectorial Type

The second group of disturbed individuals are the extreme opposite of the first type. They are hypervectorial even in situations in which people are usually instrumental. They are always ready to give, to protect, to sacrifice themselves. In their childhood they did not act as all other children did, i.e., in a selfish, instrumental way. As children they behaved as if they were the protectors of their parents. They seem to believe that they owe everything to the world and that no one owes them anything. They treat life as an obligation to be honored, as a ritual to be followed, or as a mission to be fulfilled. They have sympathy for everyone except themselves. Once in love they are absolutely loyal, overprotective, and often domineering and despotic in their overprotectiveness. When their exaggerated self-controls fail, they regress into autistic seclusion.

This type of disturbed individual is the *hypervectorial* type. This name covers all that is described under the name "schizophrenia" and related conditions. Symptom formation offers mainly primary gains. The hypervectorials are unselfish and hyperethical, though often self-righteous; they usually believe that they are strong and hostile and fear their own hostility. Their libido is object-hypercathected, and their destrudo overrepressed. The superego is overgrown, dictatorial. A detailed description is given in "Schizophrenia and Related Disorders," Chapter 34.

Paramutual Type

The third type is an epitomy of inconsistency. The paramutual, or cyclic, types overdo in love for others, as the hypervectorials do, or they feel no love for others and are as selfish as the hyperinstrumentals are. When the paramutuals love, they expect their love objects to return even more love, and they shower their love objects with protectiveness and tenderness and are ready for any self-sacrifice. When not repaid with a high interest, their assumedly great unselfish love turns into a selfish, brutal hostility. Not only their object love but also their self-love turns easily into hostility. Usually they love themselves very much, but their self-directed love may turn into hate and lead to suicidal attempts. Their changing, cyclic moods reflect their libido and destrudo disbalance. When they feel loved, they believe themselves to be great, strong, and wonderful, and their mood is elated. When they feel rejected, they believe themselves to be weak, small, destitute, and hostile, and their mood is depressed. These fluctuations of moods give rise to the name *"manic-depressives."* The *paramutual* type is torn by exaggerated feelings of love and hate toward others and himself. In a loving mood, he is Dr. Jekyll; in a hating mood, he is Mr. Hyde. They swing from extreme honesty to dishonesty, from love to hate, from heroism to cowardice.

The paramutual, or cyclothymic, type is a "love addict" who hates because he is not loved. His libido swings from object cathexis to self-cathexis, back and forth, and from libido to destrudo, depending on whether he feels loved or not. When he receives libido cathexes from without, he loves himself and loves those who love him, but he expresses his feeling in a highly exaggerated and most inconsistent manner. He is then in love with himself, and the allegedly "giving" attitude is immediately discontinued if not met with love and praise. On a neurotic level (hysteria and related conditions), the paramutual sounds melodramatic and insincere, rather like a soap-opera actor who actually believes himself to be the hero whose role he is playing. Charcot's patients acted out dramatically this syndrome of swinging moods, dramatization, imaginary illnesses, and a variety of psychosomatic symptoms. Paramutuals are not simulants or conscious liars, but they are easily carried away by their swinging emotions and do and say things that are not true; in calmer moods they would admit that they have been carried away in their pseudologia fantastica and have dramatized their emotional difficulties. On a psychotic level, in the manic-depressive psychosis, they lose contact with reality and are driven by blind libido and destrudo forever.

The ego of the paramutuals still controls to some extent the swinging libido and destrudo cathexes. On latent and manifest psychotic levels, the ego invariably merges with the id, as if regressing to an intrauterine position of merging with mother's body. This hypothesis is supported by the peculiar childhood history of the paramutuals (to be reported elsewhere) and their highly inconsistent superego. When their superego attacks the ego, the depressed moods reflect vehement hate for themselves and for others. When, rarely, the superego approves of the ego, the elated, euphoric, blissful moods express oceanic love for themselves and for the universe. Obviously secondary gain or the winning of social approval is the main objective of symptom formation in paramutual disorders.

NEUROSIS-PSYCHOSIS

The above outlined classification is economical (Wolman, 1959; 1965) and based on the balance of the interindividual and intraindividual cathexes and interindividual relations. The term "economical" implies that the hyperinstrumental, paramutual, and hypervectorial types cover the entire field of the sociogenic mental disorders, that no sociogenic mental syndrome is left out, and that no mental syndrome belongs to two categories.

Traditionally the so-called "functional" mental disorders have been divided into (1) psychoneuroses; (2) functional psychoses; (3) psychopathic conditions, deviations, and addictions; and (4) psychosomatic disorders (Arieti, 1959). The manual published by the American Psychiatric Association (1952) divides the "disorders of psychogenic origin or without clearly defined physical cause or structural change in the brain" into (1) psychotic disorders; (2) psychophysiologic autonomic and visceral disorders; (3) psychoneurotic disorders; (4) personality disorders that include sexual deviations, addictions, etc.; and (5) transient situational personality disorders, such as stress situations, adjustment of late life, etc.

I doubt whether the above classification is economical and useful. The first problem is the relationship between (1) neurosis, (2) character or personality disorders, and (3) psychosis. In my system these three categories do not represent qualitative entities but *levels* or degrees of three *types* of mental disorders. The difference between neurosis, character neurosis, and psychosis is a matter of degree; the difference between the paramutual neurotic (usually hysteric) and the paramutual psychotic (a manic-depressive) is a matter of deterioration in personality structure, of aggravation of inner strife, of decline or loss of ego controls, of topographic changes in the conscious-unconscious distribution, of severity of superego, etc. If and when a hysteric (the quoted manual calls hysteric "dissociative reaction") deteriorates to such an extent that his ego loses control and the unconscious primary processes flood the conscious, he turns into a manic-depressive psychotic. The main elements of manic-depressive psychosis exist already in the neurotic precursor, the hysteria or dissociative disorder. There are basically the same disbalances of libido and destrudo, the same paramutual distortions and exaggerations, the same swings of mood, the same inconsistencies in superego, and the same dramatic dissociations of Dr. Jekyll and Mr. Hyde. On a neurotic level, the ego keeps the libido and destrudo impulses in check; on a psychotic level, the ego has lost the battle. An analogous situation occurs in the hyperinstrumental and hypervectorial types of deterioration.

A normal personality is a balanced personality (cf. Rogers, 1963). Once a disbalance in cathexes is started, the ego, in accordance with Freud's "constancy principle" and its main task of protection of the organism, tries to counteract the maladjustive processes. The struggle of the ego against pressures from within creates profound feelings of anxiety with a great variety of ego-protective symptoms. Although the nature of the symptoms depends on the nature of the threat or damage and is specific in each of the three types of disorder, the common denominator for this level in all three types is anxiety and ego-protective symptoms. As long as the ego is capable of asserting itself, using a galaxy of defense mechanisms, *neurosis* exists. It can be a hyperinstrumental neurosis, a paramutual neurosis, or a hypervectorial neurosis; they are different *types* of neurosis, but they are on the same first level of mental disorder.

When the ego, so to speak, comes to terms with the neurotic symptoms and the neurotic symptoms or attitudes become "included in the ego" or "blended into personality" (Fenichel, 1945, pp. 463ff.), then neurosis becomes *"character neurosis,"* "character disorder," or "personality disorder." These three names describe the same category, the same second level of mental disorder.

Sometimes the defenses are inadequate, and a neurosis or a character neurosis may turn into a latent or manifest psychosis. A neurosis does not have to become first a character neurosis, then a latent psychosis, and later a manifest psychosis. Character neurosis serves as a "protective armor" (Reich, 1949), a rigid set of ego-protective symptoms that prevent further deterioration into psychosis; but sometimes even armor may break. Yet, in some cases, in spite of a severe psychotic deterioration, the individual still is not manifestly psychotic. He somehow continues to function on a slim margin of ego controls; a slight misfortune or insult can throw him into a manifest psychosis. As long as his ego keeps on going and a contact with reality is preserved, it is a *latent* and not a manifest psychosis.

The main difference between neurosis and psychosis lies in the ego. As long as the ego controls the id and preserves the contact with reality, it is neurosis. *Psychosis* is a neurosis

TABLE 1. CLASSIFICATION OF SOCIOGENIC MENTAL DISORDERS

Types or levels	*Hyper-instrumentalism* *I*	*Paramutualism* *M*	*Hypervectorialism* *V*
Neurosis	Hyperinstrumental neurosis (certain anxiety and depressive reactions)	Paramutual neurosis (dissociative and conversion reactions)	Hypervectorial neurosis (obsessional, phobic, and neurasthenic reactions)
Character neurosis	Hyperinstrumental character neurosis (sociopathic or psychopathic personality)	Paramutual character neurosis (cyclothymic and passive-aggressive personality)	Hypervectorial character neurosis (schizoid and compulsive personality)
Latent psychosis	Latent hyper-instrumental psychosis (psychopathic reactions bordering on psychosis)	Latent paramutual psychosis (borderline manic-depressive psychosis	Latent vectoriasis praecox (borderline and latent schizophrenia)
Manifest psychosis	Hyperinstrumental psychosis (psychotic psychopathy and moral insanity)	Paramutual psychosis (manifest manic-depressive psychosis)	Vectoriasis praecox (manifest schizophrenia)
Dementia	Collapse of personality structure		

that failed; it is a defeat of the ego, which lost contact with reality, and a victory of the id.

As a result of either lack of care or further noxious factors, a manifest psychosis can deteriorate into a complete dilapidation of the mental apparatus. This *dementive* state is the lowest, fifth level of deterioration in mental disorders.

The three *types* and five *levels* of mental disorders yield 15 clinical entities, presented in Table 1.

THE PROBLEM OF CONTINUUM

Not every mentally disturbed individual must go through all or any levels or stages of deterioration. As explained in "Mental Disorders in Childhood," above, childhood schizophrenia may start from the lowest stage; the pseudo amentive infantile schizophrenia corresponds to the last, dementive level in adult schizophrenia.

Yet mental disorders represent a continuum of deterioration. When rocks fall down, some roll one level down and come to a stop; some roll down step by step; some skip a step; some roll down all the way through. The fact that some rocks roll only one step down and some skip steps does not contradict the fact that there are five distinct steps on the slope.

These five steps are empirically observable phenomena. What has been added here is the *link* between them, the idea of continuity in mental processes, counterposed to a rigid and untrue assumption voiced by some workers that a neurotic cannot go psychotic.

The idea of a continuum introduces a deterministic outlook on mental disorders. The type level and course of disorder in each individual are not matters of chance but are *fully determined by causative factors*. The type of disorder is determined by pathogenic social factors acting in one's childhood, and especially by the particular pattern of intrafamilial relationship, as it has been explained in detail with regard to the hypervectorial type.

The level and course of mental disorders are determined in each case by seven factors. First come the broadly conceived *predisposing* factors, such as heredity, physical constitution, mental endowment, social class, and cultural background that may play a larger or lesser role in predisposing one or making him more susceptible to a mental disorder. Second are the *precipitating* factors, which include the traumatic and other noxious events in the life of the individual that break up his personality structure, destroy the defenses, and precipitate a manifest onset of the disorder. The third factor involves the *time* and *developmental* stage. The same traumatic factors, such as the death of a parent, have different impacts in the oral, anal, and phallic stages and during adolescence or, let us say, late adulthood. Although the time factor is of great importance, its importance seems to have been somewhat overestimated in Abraham's theory (1953). Abraham explained the origins of mental disorders in terms of fixation at certain developmental stages.

The fourth factor concerns the actual *personality structure* and ability to withstand stress of the organism. Innate and acquired elements should be included here, such as innate abilities and predispositions, talents and inclinations, education, and past experiences. The same adverse conditions act differently on different people, depending on whether they were exposed to compensatory or noxious factors, what the damage to them was, what their ego-building experiences were, etc. In brief, the damage caused by shelling depends not only upon the gunfire but also upon the strength of the walls or protective armor.

The fifth factor is the amount of the *damage*, i.e., its severity. A latent psychotic may almost instantly turn manifestly psychotic when exposed to a malicious attack on his ego that badly damages his precarious inner balance.

The sixth factor involves the *consequent experiences*. Suppose our latent psychotic, after a terrible insult from his parents, flew into a rage, attacking everything and everybody. The consequent experience can be aggravating or soothing, forcing more regression or fostering remission.

The seventh factor has to do with *cultural influences*. Certain behavioral patterns seem to be facilitated in one culture and discouraged in another. Linton remarked that certain forms of neurotic behavior receive cultural encouragement. Neuroses may stem from frustration of any primary drive. For instance, the neurotic problems of the Marquesans have little to do with sex deprivation but, rather, involve food deprivation (Linton, 1956, pp. 97–99). Undoubtedly, patterns of culture exercise certain influences upon the type, level, and course of the disorder and mostly upon the choice of symptoms. Linton remarked (1956, p. 108): "One form of hysteria which has definitely vanished within my own lifetime is that of the fainting lady."

DECLASSIFIED CATEGORIES

The description of the three types divided into five levels omitted several traditional categories, such as alcohol and drug addictions; sexual deviations, such as homosexuality, transvestism, fetishism, and sadism; all psychophysiologic or psychosomatic disorders; paranoia and paranoid states; and all transient and developmental disorders, such as gross stress reactions (traumatic neurosis) and adjustment reactions in infancy, childhood, adolescence, late adulthood, and old age, including involutional melancholia and nonorganic senile reactions (cf. American Psychiatric Association, 1952).

The reason for excluding all these categories is that they are not separate clinical entities but symptoms or clusters of symptoms that accompany various mental disorders; therefore, they have already been included in our 15 clinical patterns. Consider alcoholism or drug addiction. Any hyperinstrumental, paramutual, or hypervectorial individual can become easily addicted to alcohol or drugs. No one ever became an addict unless addiction offered primary or secondary gains or both. Thus no one ever became an addict unless he was a neurotic or a psychotic of one of the three types; addiction has been one of the symptoms of his disorder. It is a well-known fact that one can find alcohol and drug addicts in any clinical type or pattern of disorder and that any mental disorder may lead to drug and alcohol addiction.

The same applies to sexual aberrations. It is empirically unjustified to put sexual deviations into a separate category. It may well be true that the hyperinstrumentals (psychopaths) display more overt sexual perversions than the two other types, but this does not mean that there are no manic-depressive or schizophrenic homosexuals, fetishists, rapists, etc.

The psychophysiologic or psychosomatic disorders do not form a pathologic category either. They are symptoms and products of definite emotional difficulties, brought about by practically any type of mental disorder. Now we know that not only hysteria is accompanied by "conversion" symptoms. Psychophysiologic ailments can accompany any mental disorder, of any type and at any level.

The issue of paranoia and paranoid states is another source of classificatory confusion. The essence of all paranoid reactions is projection, a defense mechanism used in a variety of mental patterns. It is a prevalent symptom in hypervectorial disorders; it comes to the forefront of the clinical picture in the paranoid syndrome of manifest schizophrenia and is less apparent in other clinical patterns of the hypervectorial type. Paranoid tendencies are quite apparent in the entire outlook of the hyperinstrumental type, who views the world as an aggregate of potential and actual enemies. Paranoid ideas loom large also in the paramutual disorders whenever such persons are depressed and hate themselves and others. The classic paranoia is merely a reaction of the paramutual psychotic to the unbearable burden of self-hate. When overwhelmed by terrible depression caused by a vicious, destructive attack of the superego, the paramutual psychotic can react by (1) giving up and committing suicide, (2) surrendering to the superego in the hope that it, as the bad but not yet entirely heartless mother, will embrace the suffering, dying ego and an elated, manic mood will start, or (3) denying the guilt, projecting it on others in a detailed, highly elaborated plot of a full-blown paranoia (Wolman, 1965).

Also, the transient disorders do not form a special category outside the 15 categories of the sociogenic system. The transient disorders caused by an acute stress situation follow the same pattern as any other disorder; the acute stress plays the role of a precipitating factor and nothing else. Not all people who went through war, disaster, or catastrophe developed mental symptoms, transient or lasting. Those who did were predisposed toward these symptoms by their past history. The severity of the traumatic disorders (cf. Kardiner, 1941) depends upon the severity of the blow and the weakness of personality structure. The peculiar pattern of the ensuing neurosis or psychosis depends not so much upon the nature of the trauma as upon pathologic changes caused in the individual's life history brought into the open by the traumatic experience.

Childhood disorders certainly present a problem in classification as well as in diagnosis (see "Diagnostic Methods in Childhood Disorders," in Part 3). Yet there seems to be no logical or empirical advantage to establishing new and independent clinical categories. Developmental disorders should be classified from the developmental angle; their future pattern, the outcome in adulthood, where they lead to—these are the pertinent questions that will help to decide whether, for example, infantile autism is a new clinical category or an early form of schizophrenia (see "Mental Disorders in Childhood," above).

A similar method should be applied in regard to old-age disorders. Old age, per se, is no more conducive to mental disorders than any other age. There have always been a great many men and women who preserved their good minds into very late age. Whenever mental disorders started, either they were caused by organic factors or they were overstayed cases of neuroses or psychoses. The so-called "involutional melancholia" occurs in women who have had a long history of emotional difficulties (Palmer, 1943). Most probably a variety of mental disorders are put into this category.

REFERENCES

Abraham, K. *Selected papers.* New York: Basic Books, 1953.

Adler, A. *Understanding human nature.* New York: Greenberg, 1929.

Allport, G. W. *Personality: A psychological interpretation.* New York: Holt, 1937. (a)

Allport, G. W. *Becoming: Basic considerations for a psychology of personality.* New Haven: Yale Univer. Press, 1955.

American Psychiatric Association. *Diagnostic and statistical manual: mental disorders.* Washington, D.C.: Author, 1952.

Arieti, S. (Ed.) *American handbook of psychiatry.* New York: Basic Books, 1959. 2 vols.

Asch, S. E. *Social psychology.* New York: Prentice-Hall, 1952.

Bekhterev, V. M. *General principles of human reflexology.* New York: International Publishers, 1932.

Boehm, W. W. The role of psychiatric social work in mental health. In A. M. Rose (Ed.), *Mental health and mental disorder.* New York: Norton, 1955.

Dollard, J., & Miller, N. E. *Personality and psychotherapy.* New York: McGraw-Hill, 1950.

Erikson, E. H. Growth and crises of the "healthy personality." In M. J. E. Seen (Ed.), *Symposium on the healthy personality.* New York: Josiah Macy, 1950.

Faris, R. E. L., & Dunham, H. W. *Mental disorders in urban areas.* Chicago: Univer. of Chicago Press, 1939.

Fein, R. *Economics of mental illness.* New York: Basic Books, 1958.

Fenichel, O. *The psychoanalytic theory of neurosis.* New York: Norton, 1945.

Foote, N. N., & Cottrell, L. S., Jr. *Identity and interpersonal competence.* Chicago: Univer. of Chicago Press, 1955.

Freud, S. *Collected papers.* London: Hogarth Press, 1924–1950. 5 vols.

Freud, S. *New introductory lectures on psychoanalysis.* New York: Norton, 1933.

Freud, S. *An outline of psychoanalysis.* New York: Norton, 1949.

Fromm, Erich. *Escape from freedom.* New York: Farrar & Rinehart, 1941.

Fromm, E. *The sane society.* New York: Holt, 1955.

Gantt, W. H. *Experimental basis for neurotic behavior.* New York: Hoeber-Harper, 1944.

Goldhamer H., & Marshall, A. W. *Psychosis and civilization.* New York: Basic Books, 1953.

Gurin, G., Veroff, J., & Feld, Sheila. *Americans view their mental health.* New York: Basic Books, 1960.

Hartmann, H. Psychoanalysis and the concept of health. *Int. J. Psychoanal.,* 1939, **20,** 308–318.

Hartmann, H. On rational and irrational action. In Geza Roheim (Ed.), *Psychoanalysis and the social sciences.* Int. Univ. Press, 1947.

Horney, Karen. *New ways in psychoanalysis.* New York: Norton, 1939.

Jahoda, Marie. *Current concepts of mental health.* New York: Basic Books, 1958.

Jenkins, R. L. The nature of the schizophrenic process. *Arch. Neurol. Psychiat.,* 1950, **64,** 243–262.

Jenkins, R. L. The schizophrenic sequence: withdrawal, disorganization, psychotic reorganization. *Am. J. Orthopsychiat.,* 1952, **27,** 738.

Joint Commission on Mental Illness and Health. *Action for mental health.* New York: Basic Books, 1961.

Jones, E. The concept of a normal mind. *Int. J. Psychoanal.,* 1942, **23,** 1.

Kardiner, A. *The traumatic neuroses of war.* New York: Hoeber-Harper, 1941.

Kubie, L. S. The fundamental nature of distinction between normality and neurosis. *Psychoanal. Quart.,* 1954, **23,** 167–204.

Liddell, H. S. A comparative approach to the dynamics of experimental neurosis. *Ann. N.Y. Acad. Sci.,* 1953, **56,** 164–170.

Lindsley, O. R. Operant conditioning methods applied to research in chronic schizophrenia. *Psychiat. Res. Rep.,* 1956, **5,** 118–139.

Linton, R. *Culture and mental disorders.* Springfield, Ill.: Charles C Thomas, 1956.

Maier, N. R. F. *Frustration: the study of behavior without a goal.* New York: McGraw-Hill, 1949.

Maier, N. R. F. Frustration theory: restatement and extension. *Psychol. Rev.,* 1956, **63,** 370–388.

Maslow, A. H. Deficiency motivation and growth motivation. *Nebraska symposium on motivation.* Lincoln: Univer. of Nebraska Press, 1955.

Miller, N. E. Theory and experiment relating psychoanalytic displacement to stimulus-response generalization. *J. abnorm. soc. Psychol.,* 1948, **43,** 155–178.

Opler, M. K. (Ed.) *Culture and mental health.* New York: Macmillan, 1959.

Pavlov, I. P. *Conditioned reflexes.* London: Oxford Univer. Press, 1927.

Pavlov, I. P. *Lectures in conditioned reflexes.* New York: Liveright, 1928.

Piaget, J. The origins of intelligence in children. New York: Int. Univ. Press, 1952.

Platonov, K. *The word as a physiological and therapeutic factor.* Moscow: Foreign Languages Publishing House, 1959.

Rapaport, D. The structure of psychoanalytic theory: a systematizing attempt. In S. Koch (Ed.), *Psychology: a study of a science*. Vol. 3. New York: McGraw-Hill, 1962.

Reich, W. *Character analysis*. New York: Noonday Press, 1949.

Rogers, C. R. The concept of the fully functioning person. *Psychotherapy*, 1963 **1**, 17–26.

Selling, L. S. *Men against madness*. New York: Garden City, 1943.

Shoben, E. J. A learning theory interpretation of psychotherapy. *Harvard educ. Rev.*, 1948, **18**, 129–145.

Sidman, M. Operant techniques. In A. J. Bachrach (Ed.), *Experimental foundations of clinical psychology*. New York: Basic Books, 1962.

Srole, L., Langner, T. S., Michael, S. T., Opler, M. K., & Rennie, T. A. *Mental health in the metropolis: the midtown Manhattan study*. New York: McGraw-Hill, 1962.

Sullivan, H. S. Sociopsychiatric research: its implications for the schizophrenia problem and for mental hygiene. *Amer. J. Psychiat.*, 1931, **10**, 77–91.

Sullivan, H. S. *Conceptions of modern psychiatry*. (2nd ed.) New York: Norton, 1953.

Szasz, T. *The myth of mental illness*. New York: Harper & Row, 1961.

Thompson, Clara. *Psychoanalysis: evolution and development*. New York: Nelson, 1950.

Wilson, R. S. On behavior pathology. *Psychol. Bull.*, 1963, **60**, 130–146.

Winn, R. B. *Psychotherapy in the Soviet Union*. New York: Philosophical Library, 1961.

Wolman, B. B. Psychoanalysis without libido. *Amer. J. Psychother.*, 1954, **8**, 21–31.

Wolman, B. B. Leadership and group dynamics. *J. soc. Psychol.*, 1956, **43**, 11–25.

Wolman, B. B. Continuum hypothesis in neurosis and psychosis and the classification of the mental disorder. Paper read at Eastern Psychological Association, 1959.

Wolman, B. B. *Contemporary theories and systems in psychology*. New York: Harper & Row, 1960. (a)

Wolman, B. B. Impact of failure on group cohesiveness. *J. soc. Psychol.*, 1960, **51**, 409–418. (b)

Wolman, B. B. *Mental disorders: their theory and classification*. 1965. (a)

Wolman, B. B. Principles of monistic transitionism. In B. B. Wolman & E. Nagel (Eds.), *Scientific psychology: Principles and approaches*. New York: Basic Books, 1965. (b)

Wolpe, J. *Psychotherapy by reciprocal inhibition*. Stanford, Calif.: Stanford Univer. Press, 1958.

Zilboorg, B., & Henry, G. W. *A history of medical psychology*. New York: Norton, 1941.

part **5**

Methods of Treatment

40

Psychotherapeutic Methods

JOHN G. WATKINS

FOUNDATIONS OF PSYCHOTHERAPY

Treatment of human ailments through the relationship effect which one person has on another is as old as the human race. Long before man discovered therapeutic agents in the physical environment, he was aware that the interaction of one individual with another could influence the feeling of well-being and affect the course of disease. In fact, psychotherapy was probably the first form of treatment. It has been pointed out that through the centuries, and in all cultures, more people have been treated by one form of psychotherapy, suggestion, than by all other therapies put together.

Definitions of Psychotherapy

What do we mean by the term "psychotherapy"? Literally speaking, it means "treatment of the mind." Under this definition we would subsume all methods which influence human behavior, including use of ataractic drugs, plastic surgery, and lobotomy. The psychologist, however, prefers to consider measures "psychotherapeutic" if their effect is achieved through their psychological (relationship, behavioral) impact on the one being treated rather than through physiological means. Thus a placebo would be a psychotherapeutic method, but not a tranquilizing or antidepressant drug.

Since psychotherapy has been practiced in many different disciplines, including those of the psychologist, the psychiatrist, the physician, the minister, the social worker, the educator, the attorney, the nurse, and others, definitions often vary, depending upon the point of view of the definer. Most definitions tend to fall under one of four general headings:

1. Those which view the relief of the patient from symptoms, anxiety, and conflict as the chief objective of psychotherapy: "Psychotherapy is a form of treatment for problems of an emotional nature in which a trained person deliberately establishes a professional relationship with a patient with the object of removing, modifying or retarding existing symptoms, of mediating disturbed patterns of behavior, and of promoting positive personality growth and development" (Wolberg, 1954).

2. Those which perceive the objective as the establishing of a feeling of adequacy of the self, self-integration, and personal maturity: "Psychotherapy in the broad sense includes any acceleration in the growth of a human being as a person" (Whitaker & Malone, 1953).

3. Those in which the aim is the improvement of interpersonal relationships, including the ability to give and receive love: "An emotional exchange (process) in an interpersonal relationship which accelerates the growth of one or both participants" (Whitaker & Malone, 1953).

4. Those which seek to achieve an adjustment to society and culture: "To alter the behavior and change the attitudes of a maladjusted person toward a more constructive outcome" (Rogers, 1942).

A few definitions have been so worded as to restrict the procedure to a specific profession: "The art of treating mental diseases or disorders" (Hinsie & Shatzky, 1945). However, these are the exception, and most comprehensive formulations include one or more elements based on the above four main points. The particular school or persuasion of a psychotherapist may determine to which aspect he gives primary emphasis. Legislators and courts of law have found it almost impossible to define "psychotherapy" in such a way as to include, by universal agreement among therapists, that which *is* psychotherapy and to exclude that which *is not* psychotherapy.

Counseling and Psychotherapy

One of the greater difficulties has been in distinguishing between what is called "counseling" and what is called "psychotherapy." Thus the profession of medicine has often fought to define "psychotherapy" as an exclusively medical prerogative, while leaving "counseling" to other disciplines. Some psychologists consider the two terms synonymous. However, in general, there is agreement that although they overlap greatly, the two terms do emphasize different problems treated and goals undertaken.

The counselor, as opposed to the psychotherapist, usually concerns himself with matters of educational and vocational adjustment and with areas of personal behavior such as marital happiness. He usually refers to those he treats as "clients" rather than "patients." He generally thinks of the individuals with whom he deals as being "normal" and not as being mentally or emotionall "ill." The client is usually considered to be one whose disturbance is relatively mild and restricted to some specific area of behavior.

A second difference between counseling and psychotherapy lies in their relation to conscious or unconscious motives and conflicts. As the problem becomes more complex, the disturbance more deep-seated, the area of behavior affected broader, and the subjective discomfort or suffering greater, counseling merges imperceptibly with psychotherapy without any clear line of demarcation. Within the broader conception, counseling represents one general area of psychotherapeutic operation.

Psychotherapeutic Techniques and Approaches

There are so many different methods of psychotherapy that it is difficult even to name or enumerate them. For the sake of convenience, we may divide them into two classes: those which are called "supportive," and those which might be termed "reconstructive."

By supportive methods we mean those whose goals are the alleviation of symptoms without a change in basic personality structure. Following is a list of procedures which could be considered primarily supportive. Some of them may also contain reconstructive elements.

1. Reassurance
   a. Nonreassurance
2. Suggestion
   a. Autosuggestion
3. Advice
4. Reasoning and persuasion
   a. Frankl's "logotherapy"
5. Motivational procedures
   a. Rewards
   b. Punishments
6. Desensitization
7. Ventilation and verbal catharsis
   a. In the face-to-face interview
   b. Through expressive writing
      (1) "Poison-pen" therapy
8. Abreaction
9. Counseling, directive and nondirective
   a. Educational
   b. Vocational
   c. Personal
      (1) Marital
10. Rest
11. Progressive relaxation
    a. Schultz's "autogene training"
    b. Schultz's "nirvana therapy"
12. Hypnotherapy
13. Reeducation
    a. Conditioned-reflex therapy
       (1) Aversion, or conditioned avoidance
14. Environmental manipulation
15. Social service
16. Chemotherapies (as psychotherapies)
17. Remedying physical defects
    a. Plastic surgery
18. Physical therapy and rehabilitation
    a. Physiotherapy
19. Occupational therapy
    a. Manual arts therapy
20. Food therapy
21. Recreational activities (attending and participating)
    a. Games and sports
    b. Plays and shows

22. Dance therapy
23. Music therapy (listening and performing)
24. Art therapy
25. Bibliotherapy (prescribed reading)
26. Group therapy (supportive types and methods)
27. Religious therapies
    a. Confession
    b. Pastoral counseling
    c. Participation in church activities
    d. Christian Science
28. Dynamic supportive approach
    a. The unconscious significance to the patient of various supportive procedures

Reconstructive therapies include those procedures which secure relief of symptoms indirectly by significantly reorganizing the patient's basic attitudes toward himself and his customary modes of personality interaction with others. Such a process occurs in a close interpersonal relationship with the therapist. Some clinicians believe that insight is the cause of such emotional growth. Others consider insight merely a result or indicator of progress in personal development. Most reconstructive therapies also contain supportive elements.

The following systems of reconstructive therapy have been proposed and utilized by various clinicians. Some represent major approaches which are widely used; others are minor variations or unique methods which have received limited attention.

1. Psychoanalysis
2. Modifications and variations of psychoanalytic therapy
    a. The Washington "cultural" school (Sullivan, Fromm)
    b. Horney's "holistic" approach
    c. Stekel's "active analytic" psychotherapy
    d. Ferenczi's experiments with "active" techniques
    e. Brief psychoanalytic therapy (the Chicago school)
    f. Herzberg's "active" psychotherapy
    g. Karpman's "objective" psychotherapy
    h. Deutsch's "sector analysis"
    i. Mowrer's "two-factor learning theory" approach
    j. Reich's "character analysis"
    k. Reich's "character-analytic vegetotherapy"
    l. Federn's "ego psychology"
    m. Wolman's "interactional" psychoanalysis
    n. Berne's "transactional analysis"
    o. Dollard and Miller's integration of psychoanalysis and learning theory
3. Analytical psychology (Jungian analysis)
4. Will therapy (Rankian analysis)
5. Relationship therapy (Taft, Allen)
6. Client-centered (nondirective) therapy (Rogers's approach)
7. Experiential psychotherapy (Whitaker and Malone's approach)
8. Individual psychology (Adlerian analysis)
9. Psychobiology (Meyer's approach)
    a. Distributive analysis, dynamic psychotherapy (Diethelm's approach)
10. Constructive alternativism (Kelly's approach)
11. Hypnoanalysis
12. Hypnoidal psychotherapy (Steger's approach)
13. Therapy under drug-induced narcosis
    a. Narcosynthesis (Grinker and Spiegel's approach)
    b. Narcoanalysis (Horsley's approach)
14. Play therapies
15. Release therapy (Levy's approach)
16. Psychodrama (Moreno's approach)
17. Group therapies, reconstructive
18. Projective psychotherapy
19. Gestalt therapy
20. General semantics (Korzybski's approach)
21. Existential analysis
22. Fate analysis (Szondi's approach)
23. Religious experience
24. Zen psychology

The different systems and techniques of psychotherapy, as outlined above, will be described later by various authors in greater detail, with complete chapters devoted to the major theoretical approaches. We shall be concerned here only with what might be said about psychotherapy in general. In this respect a consideration of the origins of treatment is essential for a proper perspective.

History

Treatment of ills in prehistoric man was a composite of magic, superstition, religion, and pragmatic science. The medicine man was shaman and priest. His remedies included herbs, bits of bone, amulets, charms, incantations, and the prestige which the healer always possesses in the eyes of the sufferer. As the spokesman for the gods, he was endowed by his patients with godlike qualities. This prestige was enhanced through rituals, dances, and costumes. A patient's ailments were alleviated when he identified with the deified, omnipotent medicine man. When one has gods on one's side, why should one be discouraged? The mobilization of constructive inner processes was further enhanced through the giving and receiving of the amulet gifts, which themselves were considered to be endowed with magical healing power.

Somewhere in the course of this process, and through the shrewd observation by the shaman of the effects of various applied substances, the first glimmerings of modern medical science began. Charms made of tea leaves (which contain tannic acid) were found to be more efficacious in healing burns than applications of bone or feathers. Man began the long study of physiology and pharmacology.

Yet the therapeutic effect of relationship and belief in magic could not be gainsaid. The intangibles of human interaction complicated the search for causations in health and recovery, and the effects of substances ingested or applied to the body of a person were so inextricably mixed with these intangibles that the primitive scientist of physical and psychological medicine was often confused and misled—as he is also so often today.

The applying clinician, interested primarily in results, compounded his remedies of chemicals, charms, faith, and human interaction. He was both magician and priest, both physician and psychologist. The concept of the total treatment of a patient, physiologically and psychologically, was never more fully realized than in the prescientific days of the healing arts.

Even the nature of a sickness, whether it was viewed as requiring the letting of blood or the casting out of a demon, called upon both the scientific knowledge and the personal qualities of the healer. Modern medicine can be said to have begun with the appearance of rationalism in treatment, as exemplified by early writings of Egyptian and Babylonian physicians between 2000 and 3000 B.C. (Bromberg, 1954).

The early Egyptian "psychotherapist" thought in terms of possession by spirits. Various sacred animals were believed to be able to defeat evil spirits, and replicas of these (bull, crocodile, etc.) were used on therapeutic amulets for their magical symbolism. These charms protected both individuals and communities from evil. Priest-physicians incorporated such practices into the complicated rituals of worship of animal gods. And indeed, faith and the man of religion have ever since been installed as rightful agents of healing. The hospital chaplain is the most direct descendant of the primitive healer.

During the period of Greek civilization, men made a most significant, although temporary, advance from magic and religion toward more objective science. The writings of Aristotle and of Hippocrates, the "father" of modern medicine, exemplify the application of observation, control, and rational consideration of phenomena.

This "naturalism" did not extend into the understanding of "mental" illness, for the Greeks considered such disturbances to be largely due to possession by spirits and divine interventions. Yet, in spite of an irrational psychopathology, they used many psychotherapeutic techniques that are accepted and respected today. Feasts, sleep, rest, dietetics, baths, massage, and exercise were used on the disturbed sufferer much as they are applied today in "total-push" therapy. The disquieted warrior could repair to the temple, where he would lie on a stone couch, relaxing and listening to words of suggestion and wisdom from the lips of the priest-physician. Dream interpretation was frequently used, and some of the interpretations by temple oracles handed down to us through the plays of Sophocles and other Greek dramatists show a sensitivity to prelogical meanings which were consciously formulated by Freud centuries later.

Hippocrates was instrumental in working to remove religion from medical treatment; yet his influence was only temporary. Supernaturalism returned and prevailed in concepts of etiology throughout the Roman and medieval periods. Plato considered "beautiful" logic (interpretation) to be therapeutic, and the recognition of individual differences and persuasive approaches in handling mental cases was discussed by Aretaeus, the Cappadocian physician of the second century.

It is thus apparent that psychotherapy as an applied methodology had advanced during the Greco-Roman period considerably further than a supporting knowledge or theory of psychopathology. This is partly why, during the subsequent centuries of the Middle Ages, rationalistic approaches to mental treatment gave way again to theories of demoniacal (or angelic) possession and therapy was based on an amalgam of magic and Christian religious theology.

The church assumed the responsibility for social control. It exacted complete obedience and relied on faith as its strongest instrument. Thus church-administered psychotherapy during this period represented a form of rationalized suggestion. Adjustment to church doctrine became the appropriate psychotherapeutic objective. Mental health was equated with such adjustment, and deviations were thought of as emanating from witchcraft, the devil, and heresy. When suggestion through faith was not efficacious, punishment through torture and death was frequently applied. However, the situation was confused in that in certain monastery hospitals, the earlier attitudes of Christian humility and humanitarianism continued to be practiced.

During the later Middle Ages, the cause of psychotherapeutic treatment was set back, when throughout Europe the fear of witchcraft became so pronounced. It has been suggested that this represented the mass externalization of repressed sexual impulses. And indeed, the fantasies with which "witches" and "incubi" (male witches) were supposed to preoccupy themselves consisted of homosexual and other sexually deviant thoughts. It is not without reason that the devil was conceived as possessing a tail and as being engaged primarily in sexual seduction. The breakdown of the compulsive medieval society was reflected in its paranoid absorption with fearful fantasies of sexual inversion and its defensive measures of rigid punishment and suppression. One is reminded here of the decompensation of an obsessive-compulsive structure into a paranoid psychosis within an individual. Treatment, as we now conceive it, was for some three centuries neglected. Man's cruelty in the simultaneous expression and suppression of prelogical impulses held full sway over society.

By the eighteenth century, interest had arisen in the more humane treatment of the insane, and asylums began to become hospitals where serious study was undertaken in trying to understand and treat such conditions. Pinel's introduction of kindness into the hospitals of France in 1780 heralded the beginning of this era. During the early 1800s there arose a struggle over the matter of restraint as a psychotherapeutic technique. Originally grounded in the concept of punishment, restraint was next practiced with a rationale which conceived of it as beneficial and healing, as reconstructive of the normal state. Even the great psychiatrist Benjamin Rush, who was noted for his humanitarian reforms, invented and utilized the tranquilizing chair, a device which held a patient motionless in complete rigidity until his "mania" had subsided.

Reformers such as Dorothea Lynde Dix, a New England schoolteacher, visited mental hospitals protesting the neglect of physical needs and the cruelty commonly practiced. Prior to the period of the early nineteenth century, insanity was regarded as incurable. Under the impact of more humanitarian therapeutic approaches, individuals were found to return to normal functioning, and new hope for the mentally ill arose. Modern-day psychiatry can be said to date from about this period. Revivals in the utilization of hypnotic suggestion appeared in 1780 and again in the 1840s, first in France, then in England and India, and later again in France. The view of mental illness as being of psychological, but rational, origin laid the foundation for the work of Bernheim, Janet, Charcot, and Freud and for the development of a new understanding of mental illness based upon the hypothesis of disturbed unconscious processes.

Once mental illness was conceived as being due to deviant but learned mental processes, the possibilities of unlearning or of relearning opened the whole area of treatment by mind, or psychotherapy. Psychotherapy as we now consider the process originated in the middle and late nineteenth century. For the first time, man seriously, and with preknowledge and planning, used his relationship influence to treat others. Gone was the emphasis on talismans, amulets, magic, symbols, and faith alone. For a time even the efforts to cure by pharmaceutical means yielded the spotlight to psychological approaches and awaited the development of better pharmacological research such as has been appearing in the last two decades.

The approaches to mental healing, based on concepts of unconscious conflicts and developed by Freud and his disciples, including such later dissidents as Adler, Jung, Stekel, and Rank, are described in detail as to their basic theories and techniques in subsequent chapters. After psychotherapy became a psychological approach to the treatment of mental ills, it began to splinter into many different schools, each backed by a body of unique psychological theory and each developing a rationale, a set of therapeutic goals, and a methodology to achieve those goals.

The field of psychotherapy during the twentieth century developed dozens of theories and techniques, each claiming omniscience regarding the etiology and treatment of emotional disturbances. Without evaluating them here, we take the position that each, as in the story of the blind men and the elephant, has a contribution to make. Each views the problem from a certain different perspective, and yet no one has given us the comprehensive rationale and procedures which might bring universal agreement and objective communication among therapists. Psychotherapy may be studied scientifically, but it is practiced as an art, and that which we do not know far exceeds that which we understand in our efforts to alleviate human mental distress.

Goals in Psychotherapy

A person (called a "client" or a "patient") approaches a psychotherapist for the alleviation of some dysfunction. The patient may experience a sense of pain or discomfort, such as might characterize a psychosomatic headache. He may exhibit an observable lesion, such as a neurodermatitis, or an obvious limitation of function, such as a hysterical paralysis, aphonia, stuttering, or sexual impotency. He may be plagued with uncomfortable feelings of anxiety or depression, or he may have unreasonably structured fears (phobias). He may have difficulty reading or studying, in spite of an adequate level of mental ability. He may have marital problems or blocks in his ability to establish constructive love relationships. Perhaps he is unable to carry on his occupation or to hold a job, although this does not seem to come from lack of talent or ability. He may suffer from severe disorders of mental functioning such as delusions or hallucinations, or he may experience pain which is disproportionate to the degree of determinable organic pathology. He may be accident-prone, or he may engage in sexually deviant attacks on others. He may have a compulsion to steal or the tendency to lose control of his emotions and engage in violent behavior. He may be an alcoholic or a drug addict. He may be a potential suicide, or his thought processes may be schizoid or dissociative, characterized by blocks, amnesias, and inconsistency. He may be unable to accept and adjust to a physical disability or the loss of a loved one. He may find no happiness in his existence, no *joie de vivre*. And finally, he may simply seek to improve his efficiency as a person.

He has come to a psychotherapist because someone—he, his physician, his social worker, his attorney, his family, a judge, or a friend—believes that his difficulty is amenable to improvement through psychological intervention and has induced or coerced him to come. This illustrates the wide number of problems for which one may seek psychotherapeutic assistance and the varied conditions under which this aid may be forthcoming.

There may be an equally wide number of goals involved in the psychotherapeutic transaction. First, one must consider those held by the patient himself. The improvement of his symptoms, the relief from discomfort, the loss of a disability, or the increase of abilities is likely to be uppermost in the mind of the person who is the object of the treatment. Thus the depressed client seeks relief from his misery; yet his employer, who has referred this person to a psychologist, may conceive of the goal of treatment as the reviving of more efficient work habits, which have shown recent decline. After an initial evaluation, the psychotherapist may perceive the problem as the education of his client about immature relationship practices in which the client has been engaging and the initiation of improved social interaction with family members. Thus each one concerned with this psychotherapeutic undertaking may view the task of the psychotherapist in a different way. The therapist, while recognizing the validity of the goals of the other two, may subsume them into his own objectives, which he considers a prerequisite for the others. In time, the patient may also come to recognize that greater understanding and improved adjustment in his home relationships must predate relief from his mental anguish. In fact, a most common experience of the patient in psychotherapy is his progressive discovery of the extent to which his emotional relationships with others, past and present, are determining his difficulty. This discovery usually comes as a surprise, and psychotherapists herald such new understanding by the client as the beginning of progress. The patient says: "I suffer. You help me." The therapist replies: "You are not perceiving, feeling, or behaving maturely in your interactions with others. When you do, your sufferings will become less."

The therapist's formulation of the causes of the difficulty is quite often meaningless and unacceptable to the patient, especially in the early stages of the treatment. And indeed, even the therapist's view of the etiology of the patient's problem may differ widely from that which would have been formulated by another therapist. In subsequent chapters, the various theories of origin of mental disability and the divergences of goals and of techniques aimed at reaching such goals will be described. The Freudian, the Adlerian, the Jungian, and the Rogerian conceive of the patient differently and approach him differently. At the present time our body of objective, research-validated fact is not sufficient to determine whether a given patient would respond best if treated from the psychoanalytic point of view or from that of the Jungian theory of analytical psychology, etc.

At this point the field appears to be very confusing. A patient with something which needs changing approaches a psychotherapist because someone believes that the psychotherapist, through psychological intervention, can constructively deal with this need. A relaship between therapist and patient is established, and communication begins. Even the professional source of referral may be confused. A distinguished therapist, who concerns himself primarily with problems of speech and aphasia, once noted that he had received a referral from a neurologist who merely said: "I am sending you a patient. I don't know just what it is you do, but do it."

Let us return to our depressed patient, who was referred to a psychologist by his employer. The goal of improved work adjustment is contingent upon an improved feeling of well-being in the patient, which is itself dependent on an improvement in family relationships. Thus each of these is a goal of the treatment, but each is at a different level. We see that it is not usually possible to formulate one simple, single goal for the therapy. Many different interacting objectives all make legitimate claims upon the process. Yet, in the course of treatment certain goals will be dealt with first and certain others later, and a different emphasis will be placed on each, depending on the theories and techniques used by the therapist.

Let us consider some possible consecutive goals in the case of our depressed patient. The therapist's first objective might be to ensure that the individual is protected from any suicidal attempt due to his depression and to see to it that a continuing relationship with his therapist is established which will bring the man back to his next therapeutic hour. The first emergency goal, that of protecting his patient from suicide, becomes an absolute prerequisite for the next, that of inducing him to return to therapy. The therapist may concentrate on getting his patient to verbalize anger and resentment and to feel that the therapist is a dependable ally. Such a maneuver, if successful, may sufficiently alleviate the severity of the depression so that hospitalization is unnecessary and treatment may be continued on an outpatient basis.

Perhaps his next goal will be to induce a free flowing of verbalizations and communication, especially if the patient is a constricted, uncommunicative individual. Next, the therapist may work to achieve some recognition by his patient that his depression is not due entirely to the rejections or encroachments of others but that his own defective social understanding and ineffective social behavior have contributed significantly to his state of unhappiness. Evidence of understanding this may mark the achievement of another "goal" along the road to better mental health.

Following this, a goal may be established which involves acceptance by the patient of some personal responsibility for his condition and for his therapeutic movement, thus bringing greater self-motivation into a previously passive individual. Examples of spontaneous behavior will constitute evidence to the therapist that such a goal is being approached.

The determination of the extent to which therapeutic goals are achieved becomes a joint responsibility of patient and therapist. When the patient reports that his depression is alleviated, we may mark this as achievement, at least on a temporary basis, of one of the therapeutic goals. The wise therapist, however, mindful of regressions and recognizing that sometimes a temporary loss of symptoms precedes their return with great force, will temper his rejoicing at the apparent gain with caution and will not relax his attention.

The goal of insight or deep emotional understanding may be evidenced by exclamations which reflect thorough intellectual comprehension of some probable cause-and-effect relationships. Yet again the therapist knows that the mere intellectual verbalizing of theoretical formulations about cause and effect without the release of genuine feeling may only serve to mask further resistance. Deeper emotional reorganization has in this case been avoided by a defensive maneuver designed to mislead both patient and doctor. The criteria for the achievement of insight goals are not easy or certain. If the apparent arrival at self-understanding is accompanied by definite and continued behavioral alterations in the direction of improved interpersonal relationships and societal adjustment and if such "insight" was secured after much "working through" and with the release of genuine emotions, then the likelihood that this goal has been truly accomplished is increased.

The patient may be quite pleased when he has reached the goal of relief from his depressive symptoms, while the therapist may still be dissatisfied if this change is not accompanied by signs of greater self-understanding, behavioral changes in the direction of improved interpersonal relationships, societal adjustment, and general evidence of a more "mature" attitude toward life in general. The disappearance of neurotic symptoms without "deeper" personal reorganization may not be permanent. The danger of a relapse remains great.

Some therapists use test techniques (see Part 3) to evaluate or compare pretherapy and posttherapy behavior. Such measurements may increase the validity with which a therapist determines the extent to which therapeutic goals have been achieved. Other therapists, most likely those who operate within psychoanalytic frameworks, may carefully study changes in dream materials as they reflect the continued existence of inner neurotic mechanisms, evidences of progress, or resolution of emotional conflicts. The particular criteria which each therapist uses in measuring the results of his treatment will vary widely, reflecting the many different theoretical views and therapeutic techniques employed by clinicians of different schools.

There comes a time when this unique relationship called "psychotherapy" terminates. Our depressed patient may feel himself "well," or the therapist may believe that a state of diminishing returns has been reached and that further sessions do not promise increased progress. Perhaps the patient has terminated because he did not establish an adequate "psychotherapeutic relationship," a condition about which we shall have more to say. Sometimes economic insufficiency or interference by threatened family members may bring about a cessation of treatment before the goals are achieved. At other times it becomes apparent to either patient or therapist or to both that the established goals were unrealistic or unrealizable. Occasionally, a patient terminates treatment in a fit of resistance anger when his relationship with his doctor is not strong enough to carry him through a period during which he is resentful or has a feeling of not being understood. Many factors may operate in the decision of one or both parties to this transaction to terminate their work. Often the objectives which brought the patient to the therapist have become so modified in the course of the treatment that the patient leaves changed and improved, but not in the way that he envisioned on seeking help. In this respect, he may or may not evince "satisfaction" at what he received. It is quite common for the gains from psychotherapy to come in unexpected ways. One is reminded here of the parable of the father who on his deathbed told his sons that there was a great treasure hidden on their farm. The young men dug and dug but found no treasure. However, there was an exceedingly heavy crop next year on the well-plowed land. All this is in the nature of what might be generally said about psychotherapy which does not tie it to any single school or specific theoretical approach.

The Therapeutic Self

As difficult as it is to define specifically just what the formal training of the psychotherapist should be,[1] the picture becomes even more confusing when we try to describe the *psychotherapeutic personality* or *self*. Most therapists would agree that the healer should reflect a greater degree of maturity and ad-

[1] See Part 6, "Graduate Education in Clinical Psychology" and "Postdoctoral Training in Clinical Psychology."

justment than the one he is treating, although even this cannot be proved to be universally true. One facetious definition of psychotherapy has been offered: "a process of talk between two people, one of whom is less sick than the other." Certainly some psychotherapists have their own personal and emotional problems and yet have been able to benefit at least some of the patients who come to them. However, there is little doubt that the highly disturbed therapist may often be not only of little help but also actually harmful to those he contacts. A stable, well-adjusted personality, acquired either by fortuitous heredity or environment or through successful personal psychotherapy, is still most desirable for success in this field. It is such reasoning which dictates the requirement of personal analysis as part of the training of the psychoanalyst. Some therapists consider this an absolutely mandatory precondition, while others concede only that it is highly desirable.

In general, those same characteristics which make for a likable person also appear to make for a better psychotherapist, such as humaneness, kindness, social sensitivity, personal integrity and honesty, dedication to service, etc. Here again, it should be noted that some therapists who demonstrate these qualities in the therapeutic interaction with their patients do not always show them in other aspects of their living, where they may be viewed as aloof, cold, or socially awkward. We do not play the same role in all phases of our living.

Furthermore, it should be noted that different types of psychotherapy make different demands upon the therapist. Thus the psychoanalyst may do much more listening and less talking than the directive psychotherapist. The degree of activity or passivity, of firmness or mildness, etc., changes with the patient, the technique, and the particular school of thought. However, there is no doubt but that some clinicians possess what can be called a "therapeutic self" more than others. The patients of some therapists get well more rapidly than those of others whose formal training has been quantitatively and qualitatively equal.

The good therapist tries to maintain an effective balance between objectivity and personal involvement in the difficulties of his patient. The Sullivanian school has termed this the role of the "participant-observer," one who objectively evaluates on the one hand and subjectively interacts on the other. This balance is difficult to maintain, for if the therapist is only objective and detached, if he treats his patient only as a "thing" to be observed, then he does not mobilize his own emotional resources and understanding on behalf of his patient. The patient senses this lack of personal commitment to the therapeutic task.

On the other hand, if the therapist overidentifies with his client, he no longer stands on the ground of mature reality to which he hopes to move the one he is treating. Therapy is a joint emotional experience, which in its extreme form becomes a *folie à deux* as the two are "sick" together. Thus the therapeutic self, like the early Mediterranean mariner, must successfully negotiate the dilemma posed by the Scylla-like rock of cold detachment on the one side and the Charybdian whirlpool of overinvolvement on the other.

We see that the job of a therapist involves a complex problem in freedom, interaction, and control. It requires all the affective and intellectual resources the treating one can muster. He must interweave his psychological knowledge and training with his personal skill in interpersonal relationships, his science with art, and his sensitivity in listening with his appropriateness in responding. The therapeutic self stands like a bridge, with one foot planted on the shore of reality and maturity, and the other resonating to the misery and pathology of the patient; the connection between permits the realistic and the pathological to communicate and resolve differences. Truly, the therapeutic self of the treater is confronted with a monumental task. It is not merely a problem of doing; it is a problem of *being*.

Not too much can be said at this time about how the therapeutic self is developed. However, it is a product of the original personality and ego strength of the treater, of his training and experience, of his successes in therapy, and of the rewards which he receives from all aspects of his life. It is affected by those who love or hate him, by his views of himself, by his philosophy of life, and by the satisfactions or lack of satisfactions to be found in his own existence. The rich may not choose to give, but one must first have in order to be able to give. The "have-not" self does not belong as a practitioner of psychotherapy.

This therapeutic self is undoubtedly subject to growth and improvement. The young clinician brings to the treatment situation the enthusiasm which generally characterizes persons who explore new opportunities for the first time. This zest may diminish as through the years he is confronted with untreatable cases or those who retrogress rather than improve. However, the good therapist undertakes each new therapeutic relationship with a recognition that every person is an unexplored land within himself and that no matter how much we may know of psychodynamics and psychopathology, no two people are ever alike. The psychotherapist explores new country with each new case. He must keep from the disillusionment and rigidity which bring staleness to his personality and his manner of approach. Patients soon sense whether or not they are objects of dedicated interest to their doctors.

The enthusiastic fascination with this new modality of interaction, which is common to the beginning therapist, is, however, generally more than offset by the lack of developed sensitivity, the eagerness to accomplish too much too soon, the unwillingness to be patient and to learn, the haste in making suggestions and interpretations, the blind spots in perception in some directions and the overinvestment in others, and the unawareness of his own unconscious personal needs, which may bring those distortions into the therapeutic relationship known as "countertransference." In this latter case, the therapist may be treating his own neurosis projected onto his patient rather than the patient's problem. This is often the case when a beginning therapist has recently been in personal therapy or analysis. One young psychiatrist, just out of analysis, "saw" in almost every patient many evidences of castration anxiety. He was still too close to this problem himself to evaluate the true extent, if any, of this conflict in his patients' illnesses. It is not always easy to distinguish between what is me and what is thee.

Facts and theories about psychotherapy can be learned from books like this one. But reading alone will not make a therapist. The psychotherapist grows from awareness and perception to sensitivity, from skills and knowledge to understanding, and then to wisdom. The good therapist is a product of much knowledge, of many learned techniques, of self-awareness, and of personal maturity, all developed and integrated through the seasoning of time and experience. There is no short-cut to becoming a psychotherapist. He starts from certain positions of science and philosophy and gradually amalgamates these into a highly complex experiential art. He learns to develop and utilize many aspects of his own being, not only intellectual, but also emotional, social, and behavioral. He moves from his early scientific enthusiasm for predicting and controlling toward a true humility in regard to humanity and its foibles as he learns to be tolerant and to recognize that the conflicts of the inner man do not follow simple laws of stimulus and response.

Good basic training in psychology provides a solid scientific heritage which keeps him from abandoning himself to the vagaries of uncontrolled observation. His recognition of the unreliabilities in small-sample theory continues to exert a healthy control on the human tendency to overgeneralize when the patient population equals one. In addition, the frequently reported objective studies by more experimentally minded colleagues which show correlations of low order in the effectiveness of various therapeutic approaches serve to mitigate the all too human tendency in many psychotherapists to "play God." Psychotherapy can become a stage where the treating one can play out his own needs to be omnipotent and omniscient, to receive adulation and approbation, to be needed, to be a "peeker" into the intimate privacies of others, to control, to master, to receive love, or to seduce. All these common human inpulses can be activated within the person of the therapist, since he too is human. It is not possible (or perhaps even desirable) for him to eliminate all such needs. In fact, his ability to experience them within himself makes him more understanding of their impact on others. But the mark of the master psychotherapist is his awareness of their existence, his ability to control them and to utilize them only in the interests of his patient. He becomes not less of a person but more of a *treating person*, whose lifework is the service of humanity.

The Nature of the Psychotherapeutic Relationship

Some aspects of the "self" of the psychotherapist have been discussed. In Part 4 of the *Handbook*, the nature of various types of disturbances in patients has been described. Yet 2 and 2 do not necessarily add up to 4 in the complex relationship we call "psychotherapy." This bipolar situation, through continuous interaction and feedback, is a dynamic, ever-changing process. It needs consideration as a special entity in its own right.

Communication between two people is not itself a relationship; however, it is a prerequisite for relationship, and it constitutes a medium which nourishes, enhances, maintains, or destroys a relationship. Communication in psychotherapy relies heavily, but not exclusively, on verbal techniques. We come to know others not only by what they say but also by the way they say it; by what they do not say; by what they imply; by their posture, their gesture, and their dress; and by every aspect of their behavior, both that which is observable during the psychotherapeutic interview and that which occurs between sessions. The skilled therapist becomes increasingly an interpreter of communications in many "tongues." He learns that a comment made by a patient when the patient is in one posture may not have the same meaning that it does when the patient has assumed a different physical stance. He learns to listen to overtones and undertones to what is being said. At times he recognizes that the patient is talking symbolically with a different latent meaning from that which appears on the surface—just as the dream can be a symbolic communication. A schizophrenic patient who said to his therapist: "We're trying to get a bill through Congress making General Marshall general of the armies" was trying to tell the clinician that he hoped to accept (getting a bill through Congress) the therapist (General Marshall, who overthrew the evil forces and helped the downtrodden countries of Europe to restore themselves) in the role of his father (the name "general of the armies" was first applied to George Washington, the father of our country). Such symbolic communications may not be apparent to the patient or to the therapist until, through a combination of associations, experience, and intuition, the underlying meanings are revealed. Thus in the communications in therapy the clinician learns to listen, as in music, to the harmonies and countermelodies as well as to the main melody. "Listening with the third ear," as the process has been termed by Theodore Reik, is something like what the music lover who hears the voice of the cello as well as that of the violin does.

Different systems of therapy (psychoanalytic, individual psychology, client-centered) have varying theories as to what "voices" are most significant. Communication at all times is on many different levels, as varying aspects of a complex (and conflict-ridden) individual seek release and expression. No therapist can "receive" and respond to all that goes on in this interaction. Even the most sensitive, experienced, and highly trained practitioner probably responds to only a small part of what is actually transpiring during the relationship. The therapist is maintaining a kind of free-floating attention to the stream of communications from his client. He is continually selecting certain of these for concentrated scrutiny, others for (at least temporary) dismissal, some for filing in mind for future reference, and some to which he will make immediate responses.

If the particular school of psychotherapy to which he adheres holds that repressed sexual conflicts are commonly the root of a neurotic illness, then the therapist may be more selectively attentive to communicative cues which tend to reveal the existence and nature of this problem. Such a therapist may consciously or unconsciously pay less attention to communications centered about matters of inferiority-superiority than a therapist trained in the theoretical positions of Adlerian individual psychology (see "Non-Freudian Analytic Methods," below).

This means that no therapist can perceive the patient "as he really is," but only through a personal filtering process which selectively permits certain cues to "get through" and others to be ignored. It seems almost certain that no one therapeutic theory or approach is best for all kinds of patients. Someday we may be able to study this interaction problem with scientific controls. We may then, for example, be able to demonstrate that one patient could benefit more from a therapist trained in the Jungian tradition, while another should be assigned to a Rankian therapist. As yet, psychotherapy has not reached this state of objective science.

Occasionally a disturbed person will say: "I tried psychotherapy, and it failed." Such a statement means nothing. It should be compared with such comments as "I went to a physician once, and he didn't heal me" or "I took a course with a teacher once, but I didn't learn anything." Each therapist-patient relationship is unique. It may even differ from time to time, such that a patient may not find a given therapist able to help him at one time;

then later, some change in himself or his situation (or in the therapist) will cause the renewal of that relationship to become constructive and successful.

Such apparent inconsistency makes us despair of effective prediction in this field. Yet it does leave the way open for hope and continued efforts in the face of past failures. Psychotherapy is not a cure for all mental ills; some patients may fail to respond to the efforts of any practitioner, while others can be helped by many different therapists. We do have certain criteria which appear to prognosticate possible success and others which indicate a poor prognosis. It is not our province to discuss them at this point. Although the prediction of the outcomes of therapy is far from an exact science, it is better than sheer guess.

While the therapist is selectively "receiving" communications from his patient, he is formulating possible constructive responses to be made. These will be in the languages of the patient, which although primarily verbal, may also be postural, gestural, etc. They may include suggestion, reassurance, construction or interpretation, explanation, reiteration, reflection of feeling, clarification, emphasis, or distraction. But the communication back to the patient will represent some bit of leverage, some tactic, some constructive facilitation which the therapist feels will further movement toward the strategic goals of the treatment.

If the therapist's design of the moment is to assist the patient to bring forth material which is below the level of conscious awareness, he may emphasize elements which are closely associated with the repressed content. If he feels that the patient has a faulty perception and his goal is a perceptual reorganization, then his responses may be designed to fill in missing elements or to call attention to connective material which will aid the patient in forming new gestalts of understanding. If he perceives the current problem as relearning or the correction of previous faulty learning, he may then organize his responses, like an effective teacher, and call on everything he knows about learning theory and educational techniques.

Skill in the proper timing and appropriateness of his responses challenges the therapist's training to its utmost. Often it is here that the battles are won or lost. A therapist may have a very good understanding of his patient and the causes of his disorder and yet fail to make responses that will stimulate the client to corrective action. It is here that the years of education, experience, self-growth, sensitivity, and personal maturity join into a creative action which brings forth a "healing" response. Even the appropriateness of response is relative, one reply being mildly facilitative and another much more richly relieving. This applies in all systems of treatment and all theories of psychotherapy.

Psychotherapy, whether viewed as growth, relearning, perceptual reorganization, the realization of self, or any other similar process, becomes a matter of trial and error, of the assembling of bits and pieces, of big steps and little steps, and sometimes, temporarily, of backward steps. Patient and therapist together plan, try, experiment, fumble, fail, and succeed in moving their way closer toward the envisioned goals of their common endeavor.

As there is communication and countercommunication between therapist and patient, their relationship tends to become more meaningful and productive. Each party to this bipolar endeavor invests more of himself. Often what was begun by the patient in a casual and haphazard manner, and only at the suggestion of some referral source, becomes a mighty effort of struggle involving his whole being; absorbing his time between sessions; and influencing all his behavior, work, recreation, and social activities.

Personal change is not secured lightly, and the energy demands on both parties may be high. If the treatment is prolonged, the relationship itself and the various social leverages involved may become more important to the patient than achieving the therapeutic goal. If the therapist does not recognize this, the treatment may become unnecessarily prolonged. It may itself turn into a way of life rather than a preparation for an improved way of life. Passive-dependent "stickiness" often becomes a problem when the patient makes no progress but refuses to be "weaned."

Effective treatment is seldom unemotional. The ability intellectually to parrot back to the therapist interpretations made by him without submitting the self to the painful feelings of true evaluation and reorganization is a resistance which plagues so much of psychotherapy. It is responsible for such jokes as that which describes the patient who banged his head on the floor; after much treatment he still bangs his head, but now he knows why. To convert communications into true behavioral and experiential reorganization constitutes the greatest challenge. Only by the successful surmounting of this common form of difficulty can the practitioner answer the often-asked question: "How can words heal?" For, in truth, words often do not heal; only when they have become effectual cues for genuine personal change can we speak of them as "healing."

Therapy exists in a dimension of time, and time is required for change. But this time must be measured in experiential and not chronological terms. Mere duration is no measure of significance or "depth" of treatment. Some therapist-patient teams achieve significant changes in a fraction of the time that it takes others. Sometimes constructive lifelong reorganizations of behavior occur in certain therapies and with certain therapists in a few sessions, while other relationships are struggling through hundreds of hours of verbal chatter which is expensive, time-consuming, and unrewarding. This need for the shortening of therapeutic time has been verbalized in the comment: "What this country needs is a good 10-cent analysis." While it is doubtful that such a goal can be reached, human nature being as rigid as it is, therapists of all persuasions seek ways to expedite their work without sacrificing the significance of their results. Such methods, to be discussed later, as group therapy ("Group Psychotherapy and Psychodrama," below) and hypnotherapy ("Hypnotherapy," below) are but a few of the attempts to facilitate and speed up the interaction in therapeutic relationships.

There is something about the therapeutic relationship, however intensive, however meaningful, however constructive, which is artificial, not natural. Perhaps it is because these people come together for a limited goal, one which it is hoped will be achieved, before they disengage from each other and go their separate ways. It is not to become a continuing, normal way of life. The disengagement may come after one session wherein the patient was helped in some meaningful way. Perhaps it is after ten hours, or 100, or 500. But there comes a time in every therapy when it is, or should be, terminated. The main goals have been achieved; one or both of the participants recognize that they cannot be achieved; or the patient has given up his original goals and has accepted newer and more realizable ones. The interaction ceases to move forward; a plateau has been reached. It is time for a break.

Practitioner and patient may both find such a break difficult, sometimes even painful. Their relationship has been so significant, so important, and so meaningful that both, especially the patient, are loath to relinquish it. A return of his symptoms at this time often represents an inner protest at the need to leave. Sometimes the relationship has become so important that it is continued on after therapy as a real relationship. While possible, this is also fraught with certain dangers. The wise therapist usually prefers that the relationship be resumed on a *real* basis only after a period of disengagement has given reasonable proof that this is not a product of transference, hero worship, or unrealistic fantasy. Accordingly, most psychotherapists practice the policy of keeping their professional and their personal lives separate. Socializing with patients can become a source of distortion and a pitfall for failure of a treatment. Psychotherapists generally prefer not to treat friends or family members.

Conditions of Treatment

With the more global views of man and his illnesses, a strong tendency is occurring in the medical, psychiatric, and psychological fields toward integration and continuous communication between therapists who treat by different methods. So many presumably organic illnesses have a strong psychogenic overlay and are truly psychosomatic, and so many disturbed psychological conditions can be constructively influenced by drugs, surgery, physiotherapy, and radiological treatment. If a person, in his physical, social, and psychological entirety, is to be the focus of constructive effort by clinicians, then the physician, the psychologist, the social worker, the psychiatrist, the internist, the sociologist, and the penologist may all be called upon to work with any given case. From the practical point of view, it is not possible for all the different specialists who might make constructive contributions to be called in on all cases, but the general principle of intercommunication and collaboration is a sound one. The *Ethical Practices Code* of the American Psychological Association insists that the psychologist who does psychotherapy make provision for the treatment of medical conditions and collaborate with physicians trained to handle borderline problems, such as neurologists, psychiatrists, and pediatricians.

Mental hygiene clinics today often include teams consisting of a psychiatrist, a clinical psychologist, and a psychiatric social worker. At first these had strictly divided functions. The social worker interviewed relatives, oriented the patient, and gathered a "social history"; the psychologist administered psychological tests; and the psychiatrist performed the psychotherapy. In the modern clinic of today, however, each of these people will probably be doing psychotherapy, with assignment based primarily on the skills and specialized approaches which each possesses. The working atmosphere tends to be one between equal, self-respecting colleagues, and the "pecking order" is little in evidence. The complexities of psychopathology and of psychotherapy are such that no single practitioner can be a master in all areas. Mutual consultation becomes the rule, and the group staffing of cases provides for interchange of suggestions.

Not only does the treatment of a given patient often require psychologist, psychiatrist, and social worker, but also physicians of other specialties, such as neurologists, internists, and surgeons, may work in close harmony with the psychologist doing psychotherapy. Sometimes communication must be maintained with courts, police, parole officers, and attorneys as conditions involve socially disapproved behavior symptoms. The psychologist who is a psychotherapist must truly be a master of contacts and communicative processes.

This is true even when he is engaged in private practice, perhaps even more true. He is responsible for seeing that his patient does not die of an undiagnosed brain tumor while he is treating a hysterical symptom. The wise psychologist therefore generally requires medical examinations in all conditions of question and does not hesitate to refer his patient to another specialist at any time during the treatment process when conditions so warrant. It is the mark of maturity in a psychotherapist that he does not try to "play God" and treat all conditions with which his client is plagued.

The physical conditions of treatment deserve careful consideration, not only in terms of whether treatment takes place in an outpatient clinic, a hospital, or a penal institution, but also in terms of whether the therapy is free, subsidized by government, or paid for by the patient, as in private practice. There has been much controversy in this field, some therapists maintaining that unless the patient himself pays, he will not benefit from the treatment. Certainly the continued use of psychotherapists in state and Federal hospitals would indicate that this is not necessarily so. But a good case can also be made that the patient who is not willing to commit his own earnings to support of the treatment may not commit himself to the therapeutic process. The willing patient is generally found to be more easily treated than the one who has come in at the request or appointment of others and whose therapy has been paid for by the efforts of others.

Other factors which influence the therapy include the degree of privacy afforded in the treatment office and the time allocated to the therapy (the fifty-minute hour is most common). Some treatments, such as psychoanalysis, are usually conducted on a basis of three to five sessions a week. Others meet only once a week. The optimum number of sessions per week is a matter of differing opinions. The severity of the treatment, the intensity of the therapy undertaken, the available time of the therapist, and the source of financial support for the treatment may all play a role in the setting of the frequency of the interviews. In the effort to treat more people, the trend (except in the classical forms of psychoanalysis, is toward the less frequent sessions. Research evidence is now available to indicate that infrequent sessions over a longer period of time are generally more efficacious than frequently spaced interviews within a comparatively shorter interval.

Increasingly, the psychologist is being used within a general medical and surgical hospital as a specialized consultant to the physician. Here he takes over some of the functions assumed in the past by the old family doctor. The treatment of pain conditions through such techniques as psychotherapy or hypnotic suggestion in collaboration with physicians and surgeons has become the function of many psychologists. The psychologist as a "psychotherapeutic consultant" may be called in to advise on problems of acute anxiety, presurgical or postsurgical depression, or other unusual fears or difficulties of patient morale. At times he may have to deal in brief therapy with the angry and disturbed patient who has become belligerent and uncooperative on the ward. In this respect he works in close association with ward doctors, nurses, and other ward personnel. The psychotherapeutic psychologist of today finds that there are increasing demands on his time as he learns to be "therapeutic" even within brief, five-minute contacts. The older, more structured situations of psychotherapy seem to be constantly changing.

Research in Psychotherapy

A scientific field cannot remain static. Change, and we hope progress, must characterize it, or it dies. Since so much of psychotherapy has developed as an art, little of it has been subjected to rigorous experimental validation. Although many papers are written in the field, most of these do not report on controlled research studies but rather on individual experiences using one or another approach with varying types of cases.

Rogers and Dymond (1954) and their associates were the first to undertake consistent and large-scale studies on the effects of psychotherapy and the psychotherapeutic process itself. They made many tape recordings of treatment according to the nondirective, or client-centered, approach and subjected these to detailed content analyses aimed at determining factors affecting the treatment process and the effects on the client of different kinds of therapist response.

There has been a reticence on the part of proponents of other theoretical persuasions, notably the psychoanalytic, to subject their therapists to such intensive, objective scrutiny. More recently, Shakow has made sound films of entire psychoanalyses, thus collecting mountains of data material. The overwhelming difficulties of simplifying and analyzing such data seem tremendous. It has been suggested that data of this type should be coded and handled by electronic computers in order to bring out trends and significant factors.

A number of reviews of research studies in the field have been published. Notably, those by Mensh (1956), Rubenstein and Parloff (1959), Strupp and Luborsky (1962), and Worchel (1955) are of significance. In 1958 the Division of Clinical Psychology of the American Psychological Association sponsored a conference on research in psychotherapy which was financed by a grant from the National Institute of Mental Health (Rubenstein & Parloff, 1959). Participants from both psychiatry and psychology who represented a number of different systems of psychotherapy were invited to participate. Topics discussed included the problems of controls, methods of assessment of change, and the therapist-patient relationship. In summarizing the results of this conference, Rubenstein and Parloff (1959) called attention to the first problem, that of communication between therapists whose theoretical bases differ widely. It was interesting to note that initial suspicion, hostility, and defensiveness tended to melt as these people presented their experiences, indicated different approaches to similar objectives, and came to respect the calibre of thinking of those who held different points of view. The problem of language and communication is one of the greatest obstacles to research. As long as psychotherapy is dependent on so many different theories of personality, each with a different terminology to describe mental processes, objective research is severely hampered.

The 1958 conference on research in psychotherapy gave much greater attention to studies on the process of therapy and did not seem to consider studies related to therapeutic outcome to be worthy of as much respectable scientific attention. It was noted that participants tended to divide themselves into "naturalists," those who preferred to observe the process of therapy without any control or interference with its movement, and "experimentalists," who placed greater confidence in the time-honored methods of physical science in which all factors except those being measured are subjected to elimination or control. The naturalists were more associated with "subjective-minded" therapists, and the experimentalists with those who aimed at a high "objectivity" in their studies of human behavior. As one might expect, therapists who emphasized the goals of therapy as related to change of "self" tended to be naturalistic, and those who considered the purpose to be the alteration of observable behavior were inclined to be experimental.

The 1958 conference initiated respect and communication between workers who otherwise would not have ever collaborated. It did define certain crucial problems, and it outlined a number of the obstacles and proposed methodology for overcoming these difficulties.

In 1961 a follow-up conference was held under the same sponsorship and with a personnel which was not identical but which overlapped considerably that of the earlier conference (Strupp & Luborsky, 1962). In this second conference, the earlier disciplinary and school-wise defensiveness had considerably declined. The conference began in an atmosphere of greater amicability and proceeded more directly toward problems of research. Gone also was the earlier heavy emphasis on naturalist versus experimentalist, even though these two centers of emphasis continued to exist. Cross-fertilization from the earlier conference and the intervening years of experience was most evident. Topics were organized under the basic headings of research goals, research methods, and selection of variables. There was much greater agreement on goals. The aim of most of the research contributions was to identify specific interactions between the main sets of variables, such as life situation, patient, therapist, and treatment. Studies on outcome seemed by this time to have a respectability more closely approximating those on process. Scoring systems were being developed which could rate process more objectively.

It was noted that most psychotherapy researchers hoped to make basic contributions to personality theory as well as to an understanding of therapy. The conference spent some time studying the values and snares of clinical inference and indicating the need for reliability studies in this area. Perhaps the greatest emphasis came in discussion of what variables were the crucial ones and should be selected for investigation. Certain ones given attention concerned the nature of therapeutic influence: manipulation versus growth facilitation, therapist activity versus inactivity as a technique of change, and ambiguity versus structure of the therapist.

Much greater attention was given at this conference to the study of the therapist, his personal qualities, his ability to "resonate," and his mental processes. Problems were raised concerning the nature of patient change, the principal patient variables, the need for better measures of outcome of the treatment, and methods of matching patient and therapist.

This by no means exhausts the topics which came under discussion at these two conferences but is representative of the types of problems which received the attention of these researchers—and which are in need of further study. It was pointed out that good scientific studies in psychotherapy require much time and need substantial financing. In psychotherapy, as in other phases of psychology, we unfortunately can measure with greater objectivity and reliability factors of less significance, while matters of great moment become so complex that we are reduced to a low order of objectivity and reliability when we attempt to bring them under systematic observation.

One other conclusion should be noted, namely, that the type of individual needed to do good investigation in this field should be trained both in scientific methods of research methodology and in therapy—that neither the pure experimentalist, who often is unappreciative of the complexities of the situation, nor the pure therapist, who will not submit his observations to the rigors of scientific control, is able, without communication and assistance from the other, to carry through the really needed, significant studies. A trend toward recognition of this leads us to expect an increase during coming years in both the quality and the quantity of good research.

One factor which complicates the work of the investigator is the finding that the results of psychotherapy are not immediately assessable. Not only are many of them intangible, but their effects are delayed. Many a patient has left treatment without apparent change, only to find that later he was more successful in work, love, and recreation. Personal growth continues after blocks have been removed. The therapy was not itself the growth, but it made such growth possible. At the time of disengagement, few therapists or their patients can truly evaluate just what was accomplished or what was not achieved. As time was required for personal growth, so also is time required for its testing.

When successful, the patient leaves, his therapeutic experiences fade from mind, and his relationship with his therapist becomes merely a memory. The therapist, too, disengages himself and, except for some postreflections aimed at improving his future technique, commits himself to new patients and to new therapeutic relationships. Regardless of the extent to which the treatment was successful, each has left a mark on the other. The more intensive the relationship and the more prolonged the experience, the more significant has been the effect on each. If constructive and successful, not only the patient but also the therapist has grown during this interaction. The patient has become a more effective person, and the practitioner a better and more understanding therapist. One tackles life with greater vigor; the other undertakes new therapeutic tasks with increased effectiveness.

The goals of psychotherapy are the goals of living itself, and a constructive interaction is beneficial to both poles of its being, even though its primary aim was the improvement of only one. Growth and maturity, whether occurring naturally or as aided within a psychotherapeutic relationship, mean in essence the preservation and enhancement of "being," as opposed to disintegration and movement toward death. Thus psychotherapy progresses toward meaningful integration both between people and within people. It is a planned assistance of natural growth processes which facilitates the harmonic evolution of life.

OTHER APPROACHES TO PSYCHOTHERAPY

Earlier in the chapter, the various treatment techniques were divided into two major classes: supportive and reconstructive (see also Watkins, 1960). In subsequent chapters, specialists in a number of the major theoretical systems among the reconstructive approaches elaborate in detail the basic tenets and methodologies of these therapies. It remains for us here to consider the various supportive tactics and some of the other reconstructive systems which have not yet received wide understanding and utilization.

Supportive Therapies

The first group of these, *reassurance, suggestion, advice, reasoning, persuasion,* and *motivational procedures,* have been discussed in considerable detail by Thorne (1950). They are included under what is commonly called "directive" methods. In these, the therapist or counselor takes a very active role and, much like the good teacher, attempts to modify patterns of behavior by direct intervention.

Some forms of counseling, particularly of the brief type or those which might involve vocational choice, can be very successfully handled by the therapist who helps the patient analyze an immediately present external problem of relationship. He then offers constructive suggestions for the solving of this problem. Such procedures do not generally consider matters of unconscious conflict. They deal with the here and now. When conflicts are clear and are on, or close to, the conscious surface of thought, directive techniques may alter immature behaviors in a comparatively short period of time.

The sensitive psychotherapist soon finds that when conflicts are deep-seated, his use of such procedures must be guided by considerable understanding of the dynamics of human behavior. For example, the patient who is receiving secondary-gain benefits from his illness does not respond favorably to reassurance which informs him that he really is not ill and has nothing to worry about. His usual reaction to such reassurance is immediately to become more ill. Furthermore, suggestions which are contrary to the motivational needs of the patient, either conscious or unconscious, tend to be rejected. Sometimes what a normal person would consider a punishment turns out to be a reward. Thus, a patient with an underlying layer of guilt may seek and secure self-punishment because of the rewarding effect he receives from relief of such feelings.

The process of *suggestion* has had considerable study, and a number of principles governing its effective utilization have been delineated by Weitzenhoffer (1953) and others. It has been found that a condition of readiness or "set" prepares a client for the acceptance of a suggestion and that suggestions may be better built upon simpler, earlier suggestions than when they are presented directly to the patient without prior preparation. Prestige is an important factor. Both suggestion and advice are accepted better when the doctor is an admired and respected figure.

When the therapist unemotionally discusses matters such as death, sex, and hatred and when he calmly uses terms usually charged with feeling, he lessens their disturbing impact. As he speaks of them in a matter-of-fact way he engenders, through confidence, the discussion by his client of such matters. The emotional stimulus value or "sting" tends to be removed from them. This process is called "desensitization." It enables the client to move closer to the heart of significant problems which he had previously avoided because of fear.

An extension of this process leads naturally to those techniques which are called "ventilation" and "verbal catharsis." The man in the street may describe this merely as "talking it out" or "getting it off your chest." It is effective therapy when a disturbed person is able to verbalize his feelings, to express his conflicts, to describe his life, to air his grievances, and to find in his therapist a sympathetic audience. There is something about the mere talking out of a problem which in itself is therapeutic and which tends to make the difficulty seem less significant. The conflict is brought closer to possible control and mastery. Such verbal catharsis is generally experienced through talking in a face-to-face interview. "Poison-pen" therapy (Watkins, 1949) is a term which has been used to describe the writing of angry letters. These are, however, discussed with the therapist rather than sent to the person toward whom one is enraged.

When the individual who is ventilating his troubles truly reexperiences them, he may so identify with the difficult situation that he throws himself into full participation with bodily, mental, and emotional revivification. For example, a patient with an anxiety neurosis who has been recently removed from a battlefield situation may, with his doctor, relive the experience, accompanied by the same tremendous fear, anxiety, and horror which he was unable to master and which caused his breakdown. This process is termed "abreaction." It involves revivification and reexperiencing within the constructive and supportive relationship offered by the therapist. The patient is enabled to master the situation by release of his repressed anxiety and emotion. The therapeutic effectiveness of this procedure is sometimes directly proportional to the violence and intensity with which the emotion is released. It may be compared in the psychological area to the lancing of a boil or, in the medical field, to the extirpating of a pocket of infection. Abreactive therapy has been most effective with acute, traumatic neuroses.

Passivity, rest, inactivity, and the reduction of tension through *change of environment* or physical manipulation have been found of value. The removal of an anxious, tense soldier from the field of combat for a few days to a rest camp may permit sufficient self-restoration to enable his return to active duty. Exercises of the various muscle groups which teach a patient how to relax his entire body, while ordinarily considered symptomatic rather than etiological treatment, nevertheless can be very beneficial. These approaches, termed "progressive relaxation" (Jacobson, 1938), have been found effective in dealing with neurotic-type disorders which involve considerable anxiety. Schultz and Luthe (1959) have combined such procedures with hypnosis and suggestion into a generalized psychotherapeutic approach known as "autogenic training."

The chapter on *hypnosis* in psychotherapy ("Hypnotherapy," below) describes these procedures with much more detail and sophistication. In general, suggestions administered under hypnosis may be more effective than suggestions administered without hypnosis. Hypnotic suggestion would come under the category of supportive techniques. The enucleation of deep-seated conflicts through analytic techniques under hypnosis, called "hypnoanalysis," should be considered a reconstructive therapy.

The most prominent kind of *reeducative therapy* is the conditioned-reflex method. Notable in this respect is the approach to the alcoholic through aversion, or conditioned avoidance. The patient is permitted to drink, but the liquor contains an emetic and becomes associated with nausea. This approach is often effective in removing the symptom. Critics point out that the basic causes which underlie the alcoholic's problems are untouched. The patient may turn to another type of symptom, one worse than that which he has relinquished. This difficulty can often be resolved by the administration of an insightful, reconstructive therapy simultaneously or subsequently.

Since the individual always functions in an environmental milieu, changes in his living, working, and social setting are often beneficial. Thus the removal of the disturbed relative to some institution or the transferral of an emotionally upset child to a more favorable home climate may make for effective adjustment. This *manipulation of the environment* is a technique widely used in social service and most effectively employed by trained social workers.

The giving of any drug to an ill patient has a *placebo* effect beyond its pharmaceutical properties. The receiving by the patient of a gift from an admired and respected person such as a doctor, especially when he is told that this gift has potent abilities to heal, often helps the patient to mobilize his constructive resources. In this respect, the placebo effect is suggestive. It is closely related to results secured in suggestive treatment, especially in suggestive hypnotherapy. One is reminded of the amulet charm used by the ancient Egyptian priest-therapists.

Other physical methods which have psychotherapeutic effects include the *remedying of physical defects* by plastic surgery. The individual who has been rejected by associates because of a physical defect or facial ugliness may find a great change in his social acceptance when these have been altered surgically. On the other hand, *physical therapy* as utilized in the rehabilitation of individuals suffering from bone or muscle disorders may also give reassurance or suggestion. It aids the patient in believing that something constructive is being done for him, without at the same time challenging his self-view through implying that he is a mental case in need of "psychiatric" treatment.

The removal of depressions, the restoration of morale, and the initiation of motivation to progress often are assisted by *occupational therapy*. This includes practice in utilizing tools and the constructing of art or other worthwhile objects by manual methods. Hobbies, activities, and cooking have all been found valuable in helping to reconstruct a previously demoralized patient.

Participation in the arts, such as dance, music (both listening and performing), painting, and sculpture, is a good sublimating device. On the one hand, it offers an outlet through which the patient can distance himself from his inner disturbance, and on the other hand, the achievements that are consequent to these actions may further bolster the self-confidence level of the inferior-feeling individual.

Some therapists have prescribed reading, or *bibliotherapy*, as a method of initiating understanding into their patients. This may include reading about personality difficulties through selected books on psychology which are within the understanding of the patient or reading novels and short stories which illustrate the overcoming of difficulties. In these the patient can identify with the struggling hero; his eventual success reinforces the patient's own motivation.

All these supportive techniques may be employed in groups as well as with individuals. Group therapy (see "Group Psychotherapy and Psychodrama," below), both the supportive types and the more intensive reconstructive types, is becoming increasingly utilized as a therapeutic approach. It treats more patients by the same method in a given period of time. The group also adds something unique to the therapeutic situation, reinforcing the skills of individual therapy and permitting, through trial and error, the practicing of new social skills upon others before trying them in the outside world.

Finally, it should be mentioned that the various supportive therapies are often encompassed by the activities of churches and their leaders. Included within *religious therapies* are the ventilation and verbal catharsis found in the confessional and the opportunities for help received through pastoral counseling and participation in church activities. The constructive use of suggestion is employed by such religious approaches as that of Christian Science.

Reconstructive Therapies

It is not possible for any text to cover exhaustively all the various systems and approaches to psychological treatment. In other chapters the major theories and techniques of reconstructive treatment are discussed in considerable detail. At this point a few key concepts of some of the less well-known methods will be described, especially those which appear to hold undeveloped possibilities for greater use.

Federn's Ego Psychology

Federn (1952) was an associate of Freud's who developed theories about the nature of the ego and treatment approaches which began as an extension of Freudian psychoanalysis. However, he and his disciple, Edoardo Weiss (1960), extended their concepts into directions which differ markedly from classical psychoanalysis. Because of Federn's difficulty in clear language expression, these are not yet very widely known or understood, by either psychoanalysts or others.

Federn equated the "ego" with ego feeling. He defined this as the feeling of unity in continuity, contiguity, and causality in the experiences of an individual. This he considered to be different from consciousness. Experience represents the investment of continuously changing contents with this unifying, coherent, ego feeling. Ego feeling is the experiential manifestation of an energy which he termed "ego cathexis." That mental content which is "ego-cathected" is felt as "I," hence as subject. Ego cathexis was considered to be composed of varying quantities of integrative energy (libido) and destructive energy (mortido or destrudo).

Federn delineated a mental ego and a bodily ego, depending on whether this mental energy is invested in mental or physical processes. He held that the ego alone is capable of being experienced as both subject and object. Thus "I" can experience "myself."

He believed that the ego is separated from nonego (either the id, within, or the outside world) by a boundary and that the ego itself is broken into various "states," separated from one another by boundaries. Whatever stimulation crosses the ego's external boundary from either the id or the outside world is experienced as object. And, indeed, this sensing of "reality" is one of the main functions of the energized (or egotized) boundary.

When there is little ego cathexis invested in the boundary, the self is not able to distinguish between what is subject and what is object, or between what is part of, and what is alien to, the ego. An estrangement is felt with the outside world. Deficiency in cathexis of the ego nucleus brings about feelings of depersonalization. Therapy becomes a problem of the economic and psychodynamic displacements of ego cathexes.

In the field of therapy, especially of the schizophrenic disorders, Federn felt that the problem was the recathecting of ego boundaries so that the individual could distinguish himself from the outside world and adequately repress primitive, id material. Id material which presses through the boundary into the ego without being cathected with ego energy is experienced by the patient as hallucination. The job of the therapist is to provide for the increase of ego energy and for its proper displacement to permit reality testing and re-repression into the id again of unassimilable material. He described this process as "psychoanalysis in reverse," or the re-repressing of that which had burst through the boundaries and which was overwhelming the weakened ego.

To accomplish this, Federn reversed the usual pattern of interpreting the content of unconscious material. Instead, he would interpret the process which caused the patient to "misperceive" reality and thus help him to increase the appropriate reality-testing function of his ego. He also helped the patient to establish a more sound ego economy which brought into better balance the utilization and expenditure of ego cathexis. Ego cathexis was viewed as being created in the process of body metabolism.

To assist in the ego-conserving process, Federn used "mother-helper" figures, since the mother was the original source of ego support and nurturance for the infant. Gertrud Schwing (1954) describes this process of "mothering," which in association with "psychoanalysis in reverse" aided in restoring sound ego economy to psychotic patients.

Federn's procedures appear to be best adapted for the treatment of schizoid and psychotic conditions, although his theories also hold a wealth of promise for understanding such situations as dissociative reactions, obsessive-compulsive neuroses, and hypnosis.

Interactional Psychoanalytic Psychotherapy

Another modification in psychoanalytic technique has been introduced by Wolman. This *interactional psychotherapeutic technique* is based on a modified psychoanalytic approach (Wolman, 1960, chap. 15), a set of sociopsychological concepts (Wolman, 1958), and a theory of mental disorders (see "Mental Health and Mental Disorders," in Part 4). Wolman assumes that psychotherapeutic process is an interaction or exchange of cathexes. A disturbed individual suffers from a disbalance of intraindividual libido and destrudo cathexes. In the therapeutic interaction, through interindividual cathexes, the emotional balance of the individual (balance of interindividual cathexes) can be restored.

In extensive therapeutic work with psychotics, Wolman (1959) has viewed transference phenomena as true emotional involvements and, as such, has treated with utmost caution. The psychotherapist's giving, "vectorial" attitude, combined with a strict adherence to professional rules, is a prerequisite of a successful psychotherapeutic interaction.

The psychotherapeutic technique must not be applied uniformly to all mental patients but must be carefully adjusted to the level of the disorder (neurosis, latent psychosis, or manifest psychosis) as well as to the type of disorder. Wolman maintains that the classic psychoanalytic technique is applicable to hysterics and manic-depressives only; according to Wolman, all these disorders belong to the paramutual type. The hypervectorial type, which includes obsessive-compulsive and schizophrenic types of disorders, and the hyperinstrumental type, which corresponds to the psychopathic disorders, require specific modifications in psychoanalytic technique (Wolman, 1964).

Transactional Analysis

Berne (1961) has proposed a theoretical system and treatment approach which draws a number of its basic tenets from Federn's ego psychology, especially his concept of ego states. The interactions and communications between people and within a person by various ego states are termed "transactions." Berne italicizes the terms "adult," "parent," and "child" when he wishes to indicate interactions of these ego states within an individual. During therapy these states become personified to the patient as he learns from whence they originated, how they act within him, and how they can become reconciled and integrated.

Experiential Psychotherapy

Whitaker and Malone (1953) have offered a rather comprehensive theory of psychopathology and a treatment approach which, although couched in quite different terms, has much in its execution resembling psychoanalytic methods of treatment. Their *theoretical* position appears to be closer to that of Otto Rank than to that of Sigmund Freud. They considered that the adaptation of the organism to stress is part of the general principle of growth. Pathology was viewed as a disruption of the growth process, and repair of such disruption as an adaptive response aimed at restoring homeostasis. Psychotherapy was defined as catalyzed repair. They held that implicit psychotherapy inheres in all constructive doctor-patient relationships and is practiced as an art.

Whitaker and Malone divided the process of psychotherapy into a "preinterview" segment with a "social" therapist and an "interview" segment with a professional therapist. This latter segment was further broken down into seven stages. During the "presymbolic" phase, stage I consists of anamnesis (history gathering). Stage II is called "symbolic casting," or learning by the therapist and his patient to involve each other in an intrapsychic dynamic relationship. In the "symbolic phase" which follows, stage III is termed "competitive" (the struggle between the symbolic parent and child). This moves to stage IV, "regressive," which consists of the acceptance by the therapist of his role as primordial parent and by the child of his own child-self. In stage V, called "core," the therapist and the patient introject each other and establish a single intrapsychic "society." During the "ending phase," stage VI ("testing"), the patient increasingly rejects the therapist as a symbolic parent and moves toward independence. In stage VII, "withdrawal," the therapist and patient accept the autonomous adult status of each other. This is followed by a "postinterview" segment with the social therapist.

Whitaker and Malone spoke of "patient and therapist vectors," by which they meant the respective feelings the two participants have toward each other. In this regard, they used the term to mean something similar (although not identical) to the psychoanalytic terms "transference" and "countertransference."

This therapeutic approach involves an intense emotional interaction between therapist and patient. It has been criticized by "rational psychotherapists" (Wolf & Schwartz, 1958–1959) as encouraging the doctor's and the patient's joint "pathology" and as abandoning the "reality position" to which the patient should be led.

Psychobiology

Adolf Meyer, who was an eclectic, proposed an approach to the treatment of mental disorders which he called "psychobiology" (1957). Essentially it began from a global concept of integrated sociopsychophysiological functioning. Meyer emphasized a rational, commonsense approach to treatment which tied psychotherapy closely to physical therapies. He held that the therapist should be broadly trained in both the biological and the social sciences and should use whatever psychological or pharmacological therapies prove valuable. His emphasis was on "holistic" functioning of the individual in his environment. He tended to pay little attention to unconscious factors. The psychobiological approach to mental treatment is commonly used by psychiatrists who do not find themselves sympathetic to the psychoanalytic theories.

Therapy under Drug-induced Narcosis

Horsley in England (1943) and Grinker and Spiegel in the American Army (1945) independently developed methods for inducing abreactions in soldiers with acute war neuroses through the releasing effects of certain drugs, notably sodium pentothal and sodium amytal. Techniques were improved for interviewing and stimulating the release of repressed feelings. As previously described in the discussion of abreactions (page 1160), the goal was one of securing the patient's mastery over strong feelings of guilt, fear, or hatred which had been suppressed and bound by defense. The relief of such situations often resulted in a dramatic loss of symptoms. The drugs were used as agents to facilitate the abreaction.

Gestalt Therapy

Perls, Goodman, and Hefferline (1951) have turned the gestalt theories on the organization of perceptions into the basis for a view of mental disturbance and an approach toward treatment. They described psychopathology as a disturbance of figure-ground formation. They considered therapy an analyzing of the internal structure of experience and of achieving a "strong gestalt," hence a stable pattern of figure-ground relationships within the psychic economy. Except for the utilization of a different theoretical formulation and the employment of different terms, their actual techniques in treatment seem to be not unlike the more traditional psychoanalytic methods.

General Semantics

Korzybski (1948) has diverged strongly from most other therapeutic theorists by holding that psychopathology is essentially a language disturbance, a problem of distorted meanings and communication. Some of his basic concepts are that vegetable life is "energy-binding," animal life is "space-binding," and humans are "time-binding." He distinguishes "signal" from "symbol" reactions, comparing the latter to solution learning which involves meaning rather than mere perceptual cues such as constitute the signal reactions. Neuroses are viewed as disorders of meaning. Their treatment consists in the correction of improper use of language. He distinguishes "intensional" from "extensional" thinking. By the first, he means the qualities which are possessed by objects bearing the name. By the second, he refers to the objects to which the term may be applied. The therapist seeks to move his patient from an intensional toward an extensional orientation in his thinking and in his word habits.

Korzybski developed a number of word and meaning exercises which became the tactics of the therapy. This approach has not received the attention that it undoubtedly merits, partly because Korzybski himself wrote in a style which is difficult to understand. Others who have been influenced by his thinking, such as Hayakawa (1954), Johnson (1946), and Ruesch and Bateson (1951), are in the process of applying his principles, developing his concepts further, and communicating treatment approaches based on these to present-day psychotherapists.

Existential Analysis

Perhaps the most significant recent movement in the field of psychotherapy has been that which stems from a series of philosophers who have been called "existentialists" (May et al., 1958). Their concern has been with the essence of man's existence, the meaning of his life, his purposes, and the goals of living.

In this respect, the existentialists are more positive in their thinking than the psychoanalysts, for they seek a movement toward greater richness in "beingness" as the goal of therapy, rather than the mere removal of symptoms, the elimination of "pathology," or movement away from negative aspects of living. The questions raised by the existentialists have been a subject of philosophic study since long before the time of Aristotle, and it was disgust with the dilemma of the ideal versus the material, or mind versus matter, into which philosophy had gotten itself which prompted the reexamination of the reasoning process by Immanuel Kant (1934). Similarly, the blind alley of rational materialism at which man had arrived by the middle of the nineteenth century impelled Kierkegaard (1954), a Danish philosopher and theologian, to reexamine the very reason for his own existence. The resulting questions as to why we should even exist, let alone what we should treat, why we should treat, and to where we wish to move the patient in treatment, brought a new view to the entire field of psychological therapy.

Existentialism is not a unified school in the same sense as psychoanalysis or the various modifications of analytic theory. Rather, it is a way of thinking (in its own terms a way of "being") which any therapist, of whatever persuasion, may incorporate in his approach to his patient. It has its "left-wing" movements (Sartre, 1953), its "right-wing" tendencies, (the Catholic Marcel, 1948), its theoreticians (Buber, 1955; Heidegger, 1949), and its applying clinicians (Binswanger, 1963). It is espoused by those whose theoretical backgrounds range from directive therapy and hypnotic therapy to psychoanalysts, and it has developed no body of "therapeutic technique" by which it can be studied, learned, or specifically applied. After all, how one is to "be" toward a patient is not as easy to describe as what one is to "do" to a patient. Existentialists are more concerned with "being-in-the-world," as they term it, than with specific methods of behaving. In this respect, existentialism seems to be quite diametrically opposed in its views to the emphasis placed on behavior by such schools as Adlerian individual psychology and the Sullivanian interpersonal relationship theories. It is definitely an approach committed to attention to the self and the meaning of the self's existence. Behavior is viewed as a corollary to be derived from the establishment of meaningful self-existence.

The various existentialist writers differ widely from one another in the terms they use and the devices by which they hope to achieve their goals, and they even differ concerning whether the goals themselves are fully worthwhile. One of the most prolific of these writers, Sartre, portrays in his stories and plays the apparent meaninglessness of the existence of the common man. Yet these writers are bound by a new search for a way out of the materialism of present-day culture, which has produced the "organization man," the "beatnik," and the thousands of compulsive rigidities by which man defends himself amid the complexities of modern living.

Existentialism thus does not aim merely to improve psychotherapeutic technique; rather, it seeks to formulate new goals for even treating at all, and it hopes to broaden these to include not just the pathology of a person but that of all mankind. In its widest extension it becomes a search for a new way of life for all men which will give to existence such rich meaningfulness as to make unnecessary and infrequent the individual pathologies which so fill our mental hospitals, reformatories, prisons, and divorce courts. In this respect it may be viewed more as a system of mental hygiene for humanity.

The existentialist would hold that the psychotherapist imbued with such attitudes who is willing continually to reexamine his own existence, his "world cast," can bring to his psychotherapeutic approach a freshness which will counteract the staleness and pessimism so characteristic of much of our psychotherapy. A new "seeking to life and love" is transmitted to his patients individually and to society as a whole as such attitudes become widely generalized.

On the critical side it has been pointed out that existential therapy is so idealistic, so general, and so devoid of specific techniques that it is not teachable or transmittable and hence cannot be incorporated into the training programs by which we prepare future psychotherapists. Its subjective uniqueness for each theorist and therapist does not permit the development of a coherent rationale for procedure. It points to a new utopia for mankind but leaves us in a state of confusion as to how to reach this goal.

One doubts that existentialism will develop a specific "school." However, it may be anticipated as continuing its role of catalyst, of leavening agent, in the field of psychotherapy. It has already greatly modified the thinking and attitudes of many workers in this area and will continue to be felt as a strong influential force.

Zen Psychology

One other organized approach to treatment which should be mentioned within this chapter comes from the Orient. It is termed "Zen." A branch of Buddhism, it comes close to being an Eastern version of existentialism. It, too, is concerned with the same questions which the existentialists raise. However, it differs in that there are more specific techniques described. It aims for the attainment of a state of complete role identification with all aspects of the universe, termed "satori."

Zen teaches that one thing is as good as another and that we must seek to be content with what is. The aim is antirational and antifeeling, as it contends that one must eliminate the sensory and the intellectual part of the mind. The experiencing of "oneness" with every subject and object becomes the goal of the student of Zen. This is to be achieved by exercises in "nonstriving," by long training in physical postures, and by many hours of meditation, during which the applicant suppresses his doubts and his worldly drives. The teacher of Zen employs the technique of creating greater conflict in his subjects with the purpose of demonstrating the complete futility of conflict and doubt.

Zen is difficult for the Western mind to comprehend and still more difficult to practice. Its philosophical bases are opposed to those which underlie Western existence and the "American way of life." These latter emphasize conscious, rational effort and goal seeking. Zen's exponents, such as Watts (1957), emphasize that this is the very reason for its significance, since it is needed as the therapeutic antidote to a Western culture and value system which have created much subjective misery and have reached a complete blind alley of purpose. Western psychotherapists have not as yet been able sufficiently to alter their modes of thinking and attitudes to incorporate this approach effectively into their methods of treating. It demands virtually a complete abandonment of all that has in the past constituted Western-style "existence." It is easier for the Oriental man to comprehend and follow. However, like existentialism, it points to a different value system, different goals, and different ways of reaching such goals from those which characterize our present mode of living.

CONCLUDING STATEMENT

This chapter and the others in Part 5 of the *Handbook* attempt to present a definitive overview of the systems and techniques of psychotherapy. If the reader finds himself at this point in a state of confusion, it is because the field itself is still in a state of disorganization. We see that there is no one, right way; that the road to the amelioration of human ills can be approached along many different routes; and that serious-minded men from different learned disciplines, operating from different theoretical positions, have devised different ways of helping their disturbed fellow men. This is good. But progress will be most facilitated as the theoretician, the clinician, and the researcher of the future acquire broad familiarity with all the past thinking and study in this field. For the ability of people to understand and communicate with each other is the nuclear essence of the process of psychotherapy, whether its goal is alleviation of human misery or an improved existence for mankind.

REFERENCES

American Psychological Association. *Ethical standards of psychologists.* Washington, D.C., 1953.

Berne, E. *Transactional analysis in psychotherapy.* New York: Grove Press, 1961.

Binswanger, L. *Being-in-the-world.* New York: Basic Books, 1963.

Bromberg, W. *Man above humanity.* Philadelphia: Lippincott, 1954.

Buber, M. *Between man and man.* Boston: Beacon House, 1955.

Federn, P. *Ego psychology and the psychoses.* (E. Weiss, Ed.) New York: Basic Books, 1952.

Grinker, R. R., & Spiegel, J. P. *War neuroses.* New York: Blakiston, 1945.

Hayakawa, S. I. *Language, meaning and maturity.* New York: Harper & Row, 1954.

Heidegger, M. *Existence and being.* Chicago: Regnery, 1949.

Hinsie, L. E., & Shatzky, J. *Psychiatric dictionary.* New York: Oxford Univer. Press, 1945.

Horsley, J. S. *Narco-analysis.* New York: Oxford Univer. Press, 1943.

Jacobson, E. *Progressive relaxation.* Chicago: Univer. of Chicago Press, 1938.

Johnson, W. *People in quandaries.* New York: Harper & Row, 1946.

Kant, I. *Critique of pure reason.* New York: Dutton, 1934.

Kierkegaard, S. *Fear and trembling and the sickness unto death.* New York: Anchor, 1954.

Korzybski, A. *Science and sanity.* (3rd ed.) Lakeville, Conn.: International Non-Aristotelian Library, 1948.

Marcel, G. *The philosophy of existence.* London: Harvill, 1948.

May, R., Angel, E., Ellenberger, H. F. (Eds.) *Existence: a new dimension in psychiatry and psychology.* New York: Basic Books, 1958.

Mensh, I. N. Research in counseling and psychotherapeutic processes. In Vol. II. (D. Brower & L. E. Abt (Eds.), *Progress in clinical psychology.* New York: Grune & Stratton, 1956.

Meyer, A. *Psychobiology.* (Eunice E. Winters & Anna Mae Bowers, Eds.) Springfield, Ill.: Charles C Thomas, 1957.

Perls, F. S., Goodman, P., & Hefferline, R. *Gestalt therapy: excitement and growth in the human personality.* New York: Julian Press, 1951.

Rogers, C. R. *Counseling and psychotherapy.* Boston: Houghton Mifflin, 1942.

Rogers, C. R., & Dymond, Rosalind F. (Eds.) *Psychotherapy and personality change.* Chicago: Univer. of Chicago Press, 1954.

Rubenstein, E. A., & Parloff, M. B. (Eds.) *Research in psychotherapy.* Washington, D.C.: American Psychological Association, 1959.

Ruesch, J., & Bateson, G. *Communication: the social matrix of psychiatry.* New York: Norton, 1951.

Sartre, J. *Existential psychoanalysis.* New York: Philosophical Library, 1953.

Schultz, J. H., & Luthe, W. *Autogenic training.* New York: Grune & Stratton, 1959.

Schwing, Gertrud. *A way to the soul of the mentally ill.* New York: International Universities Press, 1954.

Strupp, H. H., & Luborsky, L. (Eds.) *Research in psychotherapy.* Washington, D.C.: American Psychological Association, 1962.

Thorne, F. C. *Principles of personality counseling. J. clin. Psychol.,* 1950.

Watkins, J. G. Poison-pen therapy. *Amer. J. Psychother.,* 1949, **3,** 410–418.

Watkins, J. G. *General psychotherapy.* Springfield, Ill.: Charles C Thomas, 1960.

Watts, A. W. *The way of Zen.* New York: Pantheon, 1957.

Weiss, E. *The structure and dynamics of the human mind.* New York: Grune & Stratton, 1960.

Weitzenhoffer, A. *Hypnotism: an objective study in suggestibility.* New York: Wiley, 1953.

Whitaker, C. A., & Malone, T. P. *The roots of psychotherapy.* New York: Blakiston, 1953.

Wolberg, L. R. *The techniques of psychotherapy.* New York: Grune & Stratton, 1954.

Wolf, A., & Schwartz, E. K. Irrational psychotherapy: an appeal to unreason. I. *Amer. J. Psychother.,* 1958, **12,** 300–314. II. 1958, **12,** 508–521. III. 1958, **12,** 744–759. IV. 1959, **13,** 383–400.

Wolman, B. B. Instrumental, mutual acceptance, and vectorial groups. *Acta Sociol.,* 1958, **3,** 19–28.

Wolman, B. B. Psychotherapy with latent schizophrenics. *Amer. J. Psychother.,* 1959, **13,** 343–359.

Wolman, B. B. *Contemporary theories and systems in psychology.* New York: Harper & Row, 1960.

Wolman, B. B. Transference and countertransference as an interindividual cathexis. Paper read at Second Sci. Conf. Psychoanal. Council Psychoanal. Psychother., New York, February, 1964.

Worchel, P. A critique of current trends in psychotherapy research. *J. counsel. Psychol.,* 1955, **2,** 297–303.

41
The Psychoanalytic Technique

ARNOLD BERNSTEIN

THEORY AND PRACTICE

This chapter will deal with developments in the *practice* of psychoanalysis. The *theoretical* foundations of psychoanalysis and the theoretical differences among varying schools of psychoanalysis are covered elsewhere in the *Handbook* ("Fundamentals of Psychoanalytic Theory," in Part 2, Chapter 14). There is, however, a confusing and somewhat tenuous relationship between the theory and the practice of psychoanalysis, for there are really *three* theories that can properly be referred to as "psychoanalysis"; only one of these is a theory of treatment, and even this is not inseparable from practice.

Three Classical Theories

General theory. One theory is a theory of broad and general psychological interest embracing a comprehensive theory of personality and human nature, including the psychoanalytic theory of neurosis. It is historical, developmental, and genetic and includes motivational and structural hypotheses. Typical concepts referable to this schema are those that Freud classified as economic, topographic, and dynamic. They include constructs such as ego, superego, and id; principles such as the pleasure principle and the reality principle; and concepts such as the unconscious, infantile sexuality, libido theory, and the Oedipus complex. Freud's *Three Essays on the Theory of Sexuality* exemplifies such a contribution.

Method. The second psychoanalytic theory is methodological and ahistorical. It provides a set of operations for processing data and drawing inferences; the use of free associations, dreams, and symptomatic acts are elucidated within this frame of psychoanalytic reference, as are psychodynamic processes such as displacement, condensation, projection, and symbolization. The concept of psychic determinism and the technique of interpretation belong here. Freud's *Interpretation of Dreams* is the masterwork in this area.

Treatment. The third theory, called "psychoanalysis," is a theory of treatment. It refers specifically to what happens within the treatment hour between patient and therapist and deals with phenomena such as transference and resistance, the timing and use of interpretation and other therapeutic interventions, countertransference, fees, termination, goals of treatment, and the general management of the interpersonal relations between the two participants in the therapeutic dyad. It is to this latter branch of psychoanalysis that this chapter is devoted.

But, as if matters were not complicated enough, there are two ways of construing a theory of treatment. A theory of treatment may be a theory of therapy and may be addressed to such events as catharsis and abreaction, ego modification, reconstruction of the superego, lifting of the repressions, etc.—inferences that pertain to what happens in the patient to account for cure. On the other hand, a theory of treatment may be a theory of practice and may address itself to problems of technique and principles of procedure (such as interpretation, passivity, use of the couch, etc.) that refer to the behavior of the psychoanalyst. Practices may therefore derive from two different bodies of principles, (1) a theory of therapy or cure and (2) a theory of practice, and these in turn depend on (1) a general theory of human behavior and (2) a general theory of psychotherapy (including therapy and practice).

There has been, and should be, a continuous reciprocal interweaving and feedback among these bodies of knowledge and, in turn, between them and clinical practice. The history of the psychoanalytic movement and the turnings in the ways of psychoanalytic theory and treatment evidence the effects of the clinic upon theory and of theory upon practice.

While psychoanalytic literature describing the vicissitudes of personality development is quite extensive, the literature devoted to the theory of treatment is comparatively small, actual studies of the treatment process itself are rare, and only a small proportion of psychoanalytic writings concern the precise mechanisms by which therapeutic effects are achieved (Strachey, 1934). Psychoanalysts holding the same theoretical convictions often differ quite considerably from one another in the way they conduct their practices, and within those practices they tailor their procedures to meet the exigencies of each of their cases. Nor does the actual practice of psychoanalysis follow directly from the psychoanalytic theory of neurosis. On the contrary, the theory of neurosis derives from practical experience with patients, and many additions and modifications of the main body of psychoanalytic knowledge have followed rather than preceded technical innovations in treatment procedure.

Early formulations consist of the efforts of Breuer and Freud (1895) to account for the peculiar events they observed transpiring between themselves and their patients. Most major psychoanalytic discoveries thereafter and most major psychoanalytic constructs can be viewed as attempts on the part of practicing analysts to rationalize data uncovered in the course of day-to-day work with patients.

As Munroe (1955) observes, the treatment of hysterical patients by hypnosis provided Freud with his first acquaintance with the role of the unconscious in mental life and later suggested to him the basic nature of sexuality in human development. Contacts with obsessional patients required Freud to broaden his concept of psychodynamics beyond repression and also drew his attention to the problem of anxiety. The problem presented by the traumatic neuroses required Freud to add the repetition compulsion to the repertoire of psychoanalytic constructs. The extension of psychoanalytic treatment to the character disorders is partly responsible for the recent emphasis on ego psychology in psychoanalytic theory. And until new therapeutic procedures had been tested, schizophrenia was not considered to be amenable to psychoanalytic treatment.

It is true that the practice of psychoanalysis is governed by a set of general rules of procedure, but it is also a function of experience, the analyst's personality and ingenuity, the nature of the patient's illness, the particular requirements of the individual patient, reality considerations, the personal limitations of the analyst, intuition, inspiration, trial and error, and innumerable semantic, communicational, cultural, and operational factors.

Although there are Freud's fundamental works on technique as well as scattered remarks on technique in many of his writings, and although the works of Ferenczi, Reich, and others have dealt with individual technical problems, on the whole there are just about as many individual techniques as there are individual psychoanalysts. The technical rules laid down by Freud and the others are few when measured against the multitude of problems presented in everyday practice.

Although the general goals of treatment are stated clearly enough (namely, that one has to dissolve resistances or "remove the amnesias" and that one must "handle" the transference), how and when these operations are carried out and what specific actions are called for in different cases and in different situations have never been systematically set forth There are wide differences of opinion with respect to the management of any given problem in analytic practice. When a particular resistance occurs, one analyst will say it calls for one measure, and a second will say it calls for another. And when an analyst, after having received such advice, again approaches his case he discovers innumerable other possibilities, and the issue seems further from solution than before (W. Reich, 1933).

Freud (1913) put it that, like a game of chess, only the opening moves of the game admit of exhaustive systematic description, and the endless variety of the moves that develop after the opening defies description. The exceptional diversity of mental processes and their plasticity and the great number of determining factors prevent the formulation of a stereotyped technique and "also bring it about that a course of action, ordinarily legitimate, may be at times ineffective, while one which is usually erroneous may occasionally lead to the desired end" (S. Freud, 1913).

"I must however, expressly state," Freud (1912c) says, "that this technique has proved to be the only method suited to my individuality; I do not venture to deny that a physician quite differently constituted might feel impelled to adopt a different attitude to his patients and to the task before him." And though Ferenczi and Freud differed hardly at all on major theoretical issues, they were frequently poles apart with reference to their treatment techniques.

It is therefore hardly remarkable that a comprehensive and definitive theory of psychoanalytic treatment has not been forthcoming. The task of classifying and subsuming the details of the therapeutic process into a body of generalized hypotheses and scientific laws applicable to the existential clinic situation has only recently begun, as has the work of forging a general theory of treatment. The question, "How?" has been added to the classical questions, "What?" and "Why?"; and exclusive preoccupation with patients' problems has given way to concern for those of the operating psychoanalyst (see Burchard, 1958; Goldstein, 1962; Lennard & Bernstein, 1960).

Many of the factors that have proved to be therapeutic in professional practice—abreaction, catharsis, insight, persuasion, suggestion, interpretation, emotional support, and transference—also occur in everyday life. "Methodical psychotherapy is, to a large degree, nothing more than the systematic, conscious application of those methods. . . . Psychotherapy becomes a *scientific* practice when it replaces intuitive knowledge with well-established principles" (Alexander & French, 1946).

PSYCHOANALYSIS AND PSYCHOTHERAPY

If one grants, as Menninger (1958), Bernstein (1954), and others maintain, that psychotherapy is a formal treatment of patients distinguished by an exclusive reliance upon psychological and mainly verbal, rather than physical or chemical, agents, then psychoanalysis as a treatment method falls logically within the broader genus of psychotherapy. Freud never hesitated to characterize psychoanalysis as a form of psychotherapy, and in fact he referred to it as "the particular method of psychotherapy that Freud employs" (1904a). Therefore, arguments as to whether a particular treatment approach is psychoanalysis *or* psychotherapy are gratuitous. The issue is not whether an approach is psychotherapy *or* psychoanalysis but rather whether it is psychotherapy *and* psychoanalysis; for while all psychoanalytic treatment is psychotherapy, not all psychotherapeutic endeavors are psychoanalytic.

How then does one distinguish psychoanalytic from nonpsychoanalytic forms of psychotherapy? Knowledge and experience have wrought such great changes in the conception and practice of psychotherapy as a result of Freud's work that many of the early distinctions are no longer apparent and have lost their validity.

General developments in psychotherapeutic theory have brought about changes in psychoanalytic practices, while at the same time developments in psychoanalysis have influenced the development of other dynamic and causal psychotherapies. The traditional psychoanalytic method is only one of the many possible technical procedures currently employed and is not necessarily the most effective in all cases. All modern treatment methods aim at ameliorative change in patients, although they do not all employ psychoanalytic practices. Menninger (1958) believes that psychotherapy can be effective only insofar as it successfully employs the action of such therapeutic factors as support, emotional experience, and insight and that consequently distinctions between different kinds of psychotherapy must rest upon artificial and theoretical grounds. These must refer to differences in the theoretical outlooks of therapists or to their adherence to relatively superficial technical procedures, such as the use of the couch, the number of hours of therapy a week, etc. But it was Freud's conviction that any method of treatment could be considered psychoanalytic if the therapist worked consciously with interpreting transference and undoing resistances.

Fenichel (1945b) maintains "that only psychoanalytic science understands what is going on in neuroses, and that there is but one theory to give a scientific explanation of the effectiveness of *all* psychotherapies." What he undoubtedly means is contained in another observation: "There are many ways to treat neuroses but there is only one way to understand them." Here we see a characteristic confusion between psychoanalysis as a theory and psychoanalysis as a practice. The *theoretical* findings of psychoanalysis can, of course, be applied to many different psychotherapeutic procedures; however, it is also true that psychoanalytic *practices* can be viewed in the light of nonanalytic psychological approaches (see also Jones, 1909).

MODERN VERSUS CLASSICAL PSYCHOANALYTIC TECHNIQUES

In this chapter we shall concern ourselves with elucidating the therapeutic procedures that fall within the framework and rationale of Freudian psychoanalysis. Nonanalytic and neo-Freudian approaches are described elsewhere ("Non-Freudian Analytic Methods," see Chapter 42). But even within the framework of psychoanalytic doctrine, there is a wide range of techniques. Technical or procedural departures from the orthodox or traditional therapeutic technique (the so-called "standard" or "model" technique), however, do not necessarily distinguish the Freudian from the non-Freudian psychoanalyst. Even the most orthodox and doctrinaire Freudian analyst recognizes the need to modify treatment parameters when dealing with special conditions and intractable resistances. Any psychotherapeutic procedure may be considered psychoanalytic if its proponents derive its use from classical psychoanalytic theory. For the purposes of this chapter, we shall distinguish a non-Freudian or a neo-Freudian from a Freudian on the basis of their differences of opinion on basic theoretical matters rather than on the basis of differences in practice and technique. "Whether the patient lies down or sits, whether or not certain rituals of procedure are used does not matter. . . . That procedure is the best which provides the best conditions for the analytic task. A 'non-classical procedure,' when the classical one is not possible, remains psychoanalysis" (Fenichel, 1945b).

Both Ferenczi and Freud anticipated that technical changes would be required if the psychoanalytic method were to be effectively applied to conditions other than anxiety hysteria and obsessional neurosis. Technical improvements were also called for in the analysis of cases which proved refractory to the classical procedure and in which a stagnation in the treatment had occurred. Ferenczi believed that modifications in the standard technique were required to overcome treatment stalemates and to accelerate movement. Although Freud was quite conservative in instituting changes in procedure, he also anticipated their invention. It was Ferenczi who experimented with changes in the classical technique by the introduction of what he called "active therapy." He reported these experiments as early as 1915. His technical inventions were precursors of the character-analytic techniques of Reich and other developments in psychoanalytic practices which represent departures from the classical or model technique. Such departures have recently been characterized by Eissler (1953) as "other parameters." We have chosen to describe the recent developments and departures from classical psychoanalytic technique as "modern" psychoanalytic technique. A distinction between modern and classical psychoanalytic techniques is a useful means of emphasizing differences that have developed in technical procedures, in the conduct of psychoanalytic treatment, within the framework of Freudian psychoanalysis. Modern psychoanalytic techniques are distinct from other departures in treatment method, for they introduce no departure in psychoanalytic theory. They are to be distinguished from the classical or standard psychoanalytic procedure because they may depart from the classical paradigm of passivity, strict adherence to the "fundamental rule," five sessions a week, the use of the couch, and other parameters of treatment which will be described below.

SUGGESTION AND PSYCHOANALYSIS

Before the discovery of the cathartic method of treatment and the development of psychoanalysis, psychotherapy consisted almost entirely in crude and direct suggestion, exhortation, advice giving, and environmental manipulation. Neither the psychotherapist nor his patient understood the etiology of symptoms or knew how to bring about lasting changes in the personality of the patient. Suggestions were commands delivered directly against symptoms, and the struggle was considered to have been brought to a successful conclusion when the therapist succeeded in suppressing the symptomatic manifestations of a neurosis. As hypnosis was extraordinarily useful in rendering the patient more accessible to the therapist's suggestions, it was used, often with quite spectacular results, to bring about remission of symptoms.

The advance made by Breuer and Freud beyond this point consisted in the recognition that one had to get behind the symptom to its cause and remove the cause, and the symptom would disappear spontaneously. Incidentally, it was this advance which, at that time, marked the difference between psychoanalysis and psychotherapy and which constitutes the historical basis for that distinction. Psychoanalysis was regarded as a causal therapy of the neurosis and accordingly eschewed the use of direct suggestion and the other manipulative techniques of what was then known as "psychotherapy." Although psychoanalysts as a rule refrain from giving advice and guidance to patients concerning the conduct of their private lives, this is not always possible or always therapeutically indicated, Freud (1920) says, especially with very young or with very helpless and defenseless persons.

Actually there is an antithesis between the suggestive approach and the analytic technique. For one thing, Freud (1904b) remarks, the technique of suggestion superimposes something new and alien upon the patient, in the expectation that it will suppress the pathogenic process; but analytic treatment seeks to remove something or to bring out something that is already present. Direct suggestion involves forcing upon the patient or demanding unquestioning acceptance of external psychological influences, by intimidation, or psychological seduction. The setting aside of personal reservations and critical faculties on the part of the patient is a precondition for successful suggestion because the operation of suggestion is essentially irrational and unconscious and the element of insight is lacking. Ferenczi (1912) points out that this requires and encourages the patient to assume the position of a helpless child, incapable of contradicting or of independent thinking. He must place the responsibility for his cure and his destiny wholly in the hands of the suggestor.

Of course not everyone can be influenced to the same degree by suggestion. The more independent, mature, and psychically developed an individual is, the less likely it is that he can be forced into the role of an obedient child. But at best the effect of suggestion is only temporary and tends to last only as long as suggestions are made by the suggesting authority or as long as the confidence placed in him remains unshaken.

Freud (1904b) reports:

> I gave up the suggestive technique, and with it hypnosis, so early in my practice because I despaired of making suggestion powerful and enduring enough to effect permanent cures. In all severe cases I saw the suggestions which had been applied crumble away again; and then the disease or some substitute for it returned.

Unlike suggestion, psychoanalysis proposes a form of rational therapy based upon an attempt to understand the etiology of the disorder and proceeds on the principle of strict determinism of psychological events. During psychoanalysis one tries to uncover the forgotten psychic wounds which have become unconscious and which are, presumably, the determinants of the pathological state. While hypnosis and suggestion either deny the causes or bury them more deeply, psychoanalysis searches energetically for the cause of the illness and depends for its therapeutic efficaciousness, at least in part, upon the enlistment of the mature and willing cooperation of the patient as well as his insight and understanding. Ferenczi (1912) points out that in addition to avoiding the use of suggestion, psychoanalysis engages in a constant battle against the operation of suggestive influences: "The technique of analysis uses more protective measures against blind and unquestioning submission than any methods of teaching and enlightenment that have ever been used in the nursery, the university, or the consulting-room."

Freud (1904b) recognized that suggestion may enter as a factor into a psychotherapeutic relationship, in spite of the therapist's efforts to exclude its occurrence, simply because it is a natural unconscious accompaniment of all human interpersonal processes. As one has to control for placebo effects in estimating the therapeutic effect of drugs, so one must factor out the effects of suggestion in evaluating the results of psychological interventions, however rational the consequences may appear. The effects of suggestion may be subtle or obvious, unwitting or intentional, unconscious or conscious, indirect or direct, and whole or partial. As such effects are inevitable, it is incumbent upon a psychotherapist to take cognizance of them in order that they may be controlled and turned toward reliable and rational therapeutic ends. A psychoanalyst may combine a certain amount of suggestive treatment with psychoanalysis in order to accomplish particular psychodynamic results. But when he does so, he does not seek to effect therapeutic consequences in his patient by means of the direct suggestion, as is the case in so-called "suggestive" therapies, but rather to observe and analyze the effects of such suggestions upon the patient's resistances and insights. In other words, it may sometimes appear that a psychoanalyst is telling his patient what to do, but he hardly ever does so with the intention that his patient should act on the basis of such suggestions (see, for example, Ferenczi's Active Technique, above). In these instances one expects the psychoanalyst to be quite conscious of what he is doing and to recognize when his use of suggestion transcends the boundaries of psychoanalytic technique.

Another form of suggestive influence that naturally falls upon the psychoanalyst lies in the inevitable educative role that he must play. It is only natural, Freud (1912c) says, that a psychoanalyst should want to see his patient make the fullest use of new-found capacities as the analysis progresses and frees him from pathological inhibitions. But in pointing out alternative courses of action, the psychoanalyst should use the patient's capacities rather than his own wishes as his standard. Freud cautions against cutting patients off from easier and simpler gratifications by demanding excessive sublimation of their impulses. A psychoanalyst should be tolerant of his patient's limitations and should be content to restore even an increment of the capacity for work and enjoyment in a person of moderate ability. Ambitiousness on the part of the analyst in the educative direction is as undesirable as it is in the therapeutic direction. In those who are capable of a high level of sublimation and achievement, these occur without further intervention as soon as their internal inhibitions have been removed. But it is not to be forgotten that many neurotics would never have fallen ill in the first place if their capacities for sublimation had been great enough to enable them to cope with the demands made upon them. "Efforts to bring about sublimations of the impulses in the course of psychoanalytic treatment are no doubt always praiseworthy but most certainly not in all cases advisable" (Freud, 1912c).

THE CATHARTIC METHOD

It is not to be supposed that psychoanalytic theory, method, and practice sprang simultaneously full-blown from Freud's brow, nor is it strictly true, as is frequently asserted, that psychoanalysis began as a method of treatment. Rather it is an outgrowth of the so-called "cathartic" method, which was Breuer's invention and which was subsequently elaborated and modified by Freud (1904a).

Freud's first psychoanalytic contributions were theoretical constructions designed to account for results obtained by catharsis and explained by abreaction. The changes that Freud introduced into Breuer's method of treatment were at first merely changes in procedure, but these brought about new findings and finally necessitated new explanations and new conceptions. *Studies on Hysteria* deserves a careful reading, and the importance of this contribution should not be underestimated, for in it one finds the precursors of many of the main theoretical and technical innovations of psychoanalysis.

The curative effect of the cathartic method was attributed to the abreaction or discharge of pent-up emotions through the mechanism of catharsis or speech, with simultaneous recall of the associated but forgotten memories that form the basis for the hysterical symptoms. Hysterical symptoms were found to disappear after the memory of the event by which they had been provoked was successfully brought into consciousness, with its accompanying affects, and after the patient had described the event in the greatest possible detail and had put all his feelings into words. Abreaction was considered to be the essential curative experience and continued to be so regarded even after the cathartic procedure had given way to the psychoanalytic one.

Recall of repressed or forgotten events was brought about by the use of suggestion after the patient was hypnotized. The effectiveness of the method was not dependent upon suggestions issued against the symptom by the therapist but upon the discharge of "strangulated affect" that occurred upon recall of the traumatic experiences. But the success of the cathartic method depended upon hysterics who could be hypnotized. Notwithstanding the advantages of the cathartic method over direct suggestion, it was designed to deal only with acute hysterical symptoms and did not endeavor to bring about any basic changes in the patient's personality structure. It therefore offered no protection against the reactivation of the hysteria, and though it presumably provided a permanent protection against the return of old symptoms, it did not prevent them from being replaced by new ones, should the appropriate circumstances arise.

The gradual transformation of the cathartic method into psychoanalysis began with a change in technical procedure that Freud introduced when he found himself unable to hypnotize a patient. In this circumstance Freud was faced with the alternatives of abandoning the cathartic method or attempting to employ the method without inducing a somnambulistic state. He chose the latter alternative and attempted to assist the patient to recover forgotten memories by placing his hand on the patient's forehead and insisting that she remember. So surprisingly successful was this procedure that Freud was soon able to dispense with the use of hypnosis altogether.

Experiences like this convinced Freud that it was possible for pathogenic ideas, which were after all certainly present, to be brought to light by mere insistence; and since this insistence involved effort on his part, it suggested the idea that he was overcoming a resistance on the part of the patient. It then occurred to him that the psychical force he had to overcome in the patient was one opposed to the pathogenic ideas becoming conscious and that such a force was undoubtedly the same force that played a part in generating the neurotic symptom in the first place.

He still believed that the patient could be relieved of neurotic symptoms only by recollecting the ideas that caused them and by giving utterance to them with an expression of emotion. The therapeutic aim consisted solely in helping the patient to do so. But this aim now involved helping the patient to overcome his resistances to remembering and putting his memories into words. From this point on, Freud addressed himself to the problem of recognizing and overcoming resistances in the patient. He saw that the so-called "pressure technique" was no more than a device to overwhelm the patient's resistance to remembering. The task of the therapist now became that of using every means at his command to overcome the patient's resistances. At that time, these means consisted in (besides suggestion, insistence, and the pressure technique) enlisting the patient's cooperation by an appeal to his rational motives and in mobilizing the affective factor through the personal influence of the therapist.

Freud already recognized a "disturbing" influence in treatment which he called "transference" and which, when the patient's relation to the therapist is disturbed, can constitute "the worst obstacle that we can come across" (Breuer & Freud, 1895), and he was about to discover the method of free association and interpretation. The role of abreaction, and with it the cathartic method, was soon to recede into the background.

THE CLASSICAL PSYCHOANALYTIC APPROACH

At first the classical procedure consisted in inviting the patient to recline comfortably on the couch; the analyst was seated in a chair behind him, outside of his field of vision. The psychoanalyst attempted to divine from free associations, symptomatic acts, and dreams what the patient could not remember. The patient's resistances to remembering were circumvented by the work of interpretation and by making its results known to the patient. Though the analyst's interest was still concentrated on uncovering the forgotten events that lay behind the illness, attribution of the therapeutic effect to abreaction seemed to have given way to the effect upon the patient of successfully overcoming the inner resistances that prevented him from associating in accordance with the fundamental rule. This procedure was later modified, and the psychoanalyst ceased to concentrate on uncovering any particular element or problem but instead studied whatever was occupying the patient at the moment. The technique of interpretation was turned toward recognizing the resistances that arose in connection with the patient's associations and was used to make the patient aware of them (S. Freud, 1914). It was Freud's contention that the unconscious complexes would come to light as soon as the resistances had been recognized and removed (1910).

Aim of Treatment

The analyst endeavors to uncover the resistances that oppose self-knowledge and to bring into consciousness the patient's unconscious (repressed) impulses. The work by which this material is brought into the patient's mind and into consciousness constitutes the classical psychoanalytic technique (S. Freud, 1919).

Free Association

The patient is required to say everything that comes to mind, without plan or censorship; this is the so-called "fundamental rule of psychoanalysis." He is to put all his thoughts, memories, and feelings into words. He is told simply to talk, and the choice of subject matter is left to him. However, he is instructed to report everything that passes through his mind, irrespective of whether he thinks it is relevant or important. In fact, he is specifically interdicted from trying to construct a consistent and logical narrative as he might under ordinary circumstances and instead is told to follow his thoughts wherever they may lead him, even if they do not seem to make any sense (S. Freud, 1913).

An individual's thoughts are influenced by four determinants: (1) external stimuli, (2) visceral-somatic stimuli, (3) conscious intentions (for example, what he wants to say, which requires the suppression of other thoughts that might interfere), and (4) unconscious or repressed ideas that seek discharge and interfere with conscious intentions. Since the psychoanalyst is specifically interested in exposing this last group of determinants, he tries to minimize the effects of the other three as much as possible, in order that the latter may become more recognizable. External stimuli during the psychoanalytic hour are therefore reduced to a minimum and are held relatively constant. Internal physical distress cannot be controlled, but when present it interferes with the analytic work. The main object of the fundamental rule is to eliminate the patient's conscious intentions and goals. When these are excluded, presumably what determines the patient's productions are the remaining unconscious and irrational impulses within (Fenichel, 1945b).

Freud (1900) differentiates between the psychological states of *thinking* and self-observation. In both cases there is concentrated attention, but in directed thinking one makes use of the critical faculty and rejects some thoughts while accepting others. In self-observation, however, one attends to all thoughts that enter consciousness and thus obtains material that might otherwise be rejected or escape notice. Thoughts so obtained, because they may be deemed "irrelevant" from the point of view of a set of arbitrary rules of morality, logic, grammar, intentionality, etc., are regarded during the normal process of thinking as "undesired" ideas. But as objects of self-observation, such apparently spontaneously rising undesired ideas become the "desired" ones. It is hardly necessary to draw attention to the fact that it is the aim of psychoanalysis to recover and make conscious undesired ideas that have for so long escaped the neurotic's attention and that by eliminating the patient's resistances to self-observation, the analyst helps him to achieve this goal (see also Reik, 1948).

Use of the Couch

The use of the couch, the hallmark of classical psychoanalysis, is a carryover from the hypnotic method out of which psychoanalysis evolved (Freud, 1913). However, it is a necessary concomitant of the fundamental rule. The kind of communicational transaction and the subject matter discussed from this position are different from those occurring in a face-to-face encounter. With the analyst out of sight, the patient is thrown entirely upon his own inner resources for cues to verbalization. His field of attention is uncontaminated by distracting visual stimuli from the analyst's facial expressions, and his attention may accordingly be directed inward at his own thoughts rather than at the usual feedbacks from normal conversation. While this objective may not be therapeutically indicated in all forms of mental illness and at all times in the course of treatment or for all methods of therapy, it is nevertheless required to accomplish the objectives of the classical psychoanalytic method.

At the same time, the patient's averted gaze permits the analyst the liberty of total relaxation and frees him from the necessity of guarding against transmitting cues to the patient which may influence the patient's communications. This permits the analyst to give his attention over entirely to the control of the inner thoughts provoked in him by the stream of associations emanating from the patient. The reclining position, notwithstanding many patients' protests which are psychologically motivated, is objectively a more comfortable position for accomplishing the analytic work. And it is decidedly more comfortable for an analyst to be free of the physical strain of the constant postural and gestural control that is imposed on him when a patient is seated and watching him.

Attitude of the Psychoanalyst

The psychoanalyst assumes an attitude which is complementary to that of his patient. He makes no effort to concentrate his attention on anything in particular but maintains the same measure of calm attentiveness, "evenly hovering attention," with respect to everything that he hears. He is thus enabled to avoid being a prisoner of his own expectations and thereby losing the advantage gained by the patient's compliance with the fundamental rule. It is essential that he refrain from all conscious effort to criticize or select in order to permit full play to his own free associations. "One has simply to listen and not to keep in mind anything in particular" (S. Freud, 1912c).

Freud (1912c) recommends that an analyst, like a surgeon, put aside his own personal feelings and concentrate on performing the operation as skillfully as possible. Personal involvement of any sort produces a state of mind in the therapist which is unfavorable for performing the work of classical analysis, for an analyst must be free to use everything that he is told without introducing any selective censorship of his own or any projective distortions. The free associations of the patient are raw data fashioned by his unconscious and communicated to the sensitive and receptive mind of the analyst. These communications are a sort of verbal code which, when properly translated or interpreted, reveal the contents of the patient's unconscious to the analyst. They induce in the analyst's mind representations of ideas in the patient's unconscious, and these determinants of the patient's free associations may accordingly be inferred from the associations they lead to in the analyst's mind, when the analyst adopts a self-observing rather than a reflective attitude toward the ideas that they stimulate in him.

Preparation of the Psychoanalyst

A considerable amount of preparation and experience is required of a psychoanalyst before he can be expected to be able to use his mind in this way as the sine qua non for performing the work of analysis (S. Freud, 1912c). He must of necessity be reasonably free of inner resistances that might tempt him to withhold from consciousness what is perceived by his unconscious as a result of the stream of associations directed at him by his patient. "Every analyst's achievement is limited by what his own complexes and resistances permit" (S. Freud, 1910). For this reason, an analyst's training must include a thorough personal psychoanalytic experience, in part to free his mind to perform the task of free association and in part to learn the techniques of psychoanalysis. The only instrument that a psychoanalyst employs in his work is his own mind, and this instrument must be properly fashioned and tuned. To the extent that the psychoanalyst knows himself, he is able to know his patient, for he understands his patient by studying the effects of his patient upon himself. Freed of his own complexes and personal needs in the psychoanalytic situation, he may safely assume that the thoughts and feelings that he experiences therein are induced in him by his patient. The analyst must be able to entertain precisely those thoughts that are withheld from the patient by the latter's resistances. In the end, through the work of interpretation, the patient will use the analyst's freedom to find freedom himself.

It was Freud's (1927) view that "psychoanalysis is not a specialized branch of medicine . . . but simply . . . psychology"; that the danger of overlooking a medical problem in a patient can easily be prevented by a medical examination either before or during treatment, and that medical education was itself not directly relevant to the content of psychoanalytic training. "What is known as medical education appears to me to be an arduous and circuitous way of approaching the profession of analysis" (S. Freud, 1927). Nevertheless, from the beginning, the majority of psychoanalysts have been recruited from among physicians, and it has only lately come about that large numbers of psychologists and caseworkers have qualified themselves to practice psychoanalysis. Although it is generally conceded that medical education plays no direct role in psychoanalysis and that a properly trained nonmedical person is quite as able to conduct a successful analysis as a medically trained one, the question of whether to admit persons other than physicians to psychoanalytic training has been the subject of considerable soul-searching and discussion among physician-analysts (Jones et al., 1927).

Indications and Limitations of Classical Psychoanalysis

The classical procedure seems to work best with reasonably young, intelligent, educated persons suffering from conversion hysteria. The nature of the treatment and its duration make considerable demands upon those who submit to it, and only persons having the requisite traits of character can endure the hardship or possess the qualifications to derive benefit from it (S. Freud, 1904a; S. Freud, 1904b). With slight modifications, the classical technique is also considered to be effective with obsessional neuroses and phobias (S. Freud, 1910), but considerable departures from the classical paradigm are required for the management of character disorders, depressions, perversions, addictions, impulse disorders, and psychoses, in that order (Fenichel, 1945b).

The ideal age for undertaking a classical analysis lies somewhere between 15 and 50 years of age. Persons younger than this still lack the intellectual maturity and reasonableness required, and those older than this have ordinarily lost the elasticity of mental processes upon which success of the treatment depends (S. Freud, 1904b). Moreover, in older people, there is the practical matter of whether the psychological profit to be accrued merits the investment in time and energy required by such a prolonged and intensive treatment effort.

The feasibility of conducting a classical analysis depends upon whether the patient is sufficiently reasonable and cooperative. If a person cannot cooperate or refuses to cooperate, he is manifestly not suitable for classical analysis. For these reasons, feeblemindedness or mental deficiency, psychoses, states of confusion, depressions, and psychopathy militate against the use of the classical procedure. For the same reasons, it is inadvisable to undertake the treatment of persons who are not themselves highly motivated to seek a cure but who are forced into treatment by external pressure.

Because the classical procedure is a prolonged one, it is not suitable as an emergency measure and is contraindicated when the symptoms are acute and dangerous and their expeditious management is called for. The classical approach is also of little assistance when the patient's life situation is too oppressive or when reality problems demand solution.

The Abstinence Rule

It is not to be expected that all forms of psychological disorder can be treated by means of the same technique. Classical psychoanalysis was fashioned as a treatment for hysteria, and it is especially designed to cure this condition. The treatment of phobias calls for modification in the psychoanalytic procedure because a phobia does not ordinarily yield to the classical approach if the psychoanalyst simply waits for the patient to let the analysis influence him to surrender it. Freud (1919) found that phobic patients do not voluntarily submit to the analyst the material required for the resolution of a phobia because a phobic symptom enables the patient to protect himself against anxiety; as long as it is permitted to operate, it will successfully prevent the patient from facing the inner problems from which it springs. It is therefore necessary for the psychoanalyst to intervene, at the strategic point in the treatment of such conditions, and induce the patient to modify his phobic behavior before the associations and memories that will enable the phobia to be resolved will come to the patient's mind. For example, in a severe case of agoraphobia, the patient may have to be forced to go out alone and struggle with the anxiety it produces in him before the treatment can be brought to a successful conclusion. Likewise in obsessional states, active intervention may be required before the obsessional defense against remembering can be resolved.

The manifestations of mental disorder are repugnant to a patient exactly in proportion to the amount of suffering they engender for him. It is suffering that brings the patient into treatment, and relief from suffering is the goal he seeks. The virtue of a neurotic symptom lies in the *epinosic gain* or *secondary gain* that the patient derives from it in the form of substitutive gratification or escape from pain and anxiety. He seeks relief from his symptom only when its negative side effects outweigh its value to his psychic economy.

It is only natural that motivation for achieving a "cure" should be reduced as treatment progresses and suffering diminishes. Premature relief from suffering or too much gratification retards the accomplishment of the ultimate aim of the treatment. Toward the end of maintaining or intensifying the patient's drive toward health and completion of the treatment, the psychoanalyst opposes various of the patient's efforts to find substitutive gratifications. In classical psychoanalytic treatment, insofar as is possible the patient is denied all gratifications that would tend to distract his interest from the psychoanalytic work. Beyond this he is asked to endure a certain amount of frustration by postponing present pleasure for future gain, a step forward along the road of abandoning the pleasure principle for the reality principle. A certain amount of frustration, successfully mastered, in the course of the treatment raises the patient's frustration threshold and enables him the better to endure the frustrations that he must inevitably incur later in life.

The temptation to dally along the pathway to cure visits the patient from two prime sources. Above all the patient looks for his substitutive gratifications in the treatment itself. Needless to say, the patient must not be allowed to get too much gratification out of the treatment, although a certain amount is required to maintain the treatment relationship. Treatment is carried out under conditions of privation, in a state of abstinence (S. Freud, 1919). This constitutes a motivation for the patient, at the end, to abandon treatment in favor of getting his gratifications out of life. The patient may also seek substitutive gratifications outside of the treatment situation through various kinds of activities, pleasures, interests, and habits. Such distractions diminish the patient's interest in the treatment and are accordingly interdicted by the analyst, however harmless they may be.

Interpretation and Construction

The work of psychoanalysis is divided between the psychoanalyst and the patient. The classical psychoanalyst, knowing that the patient's utterances are frequently allusions to other things, endeavors to deduce what lies behind the allusions and at the proper time to impart this information to the patient. This procedure of deducing what the patient actually means and telling it to him is called "interpretation." In this respect, the analyst acts like a translator or an interpreter.

In addition, it is the analyst's task to infer what the patient has forgotten from what the patient tells him and to reconstruct the patient's past. Unlike simple interpretation, which refers to how the analyst handles a single bit of information, reconstruction (or construction, as Freud preferred to call it) refers to the recovery and putting together of whole pieces of the patient's buried past (S. Freud, 1937b). It is the equivalent in the analyst of remembering in the patient. Substantially the same principles govern the use of constructions in analysis that govern the use of interpretations. Both are verbal interventions aimed at making conscious the hidden meanings of behavior patterns and their unconscious determinants. The distinction between construction and interpretation has, however, not found a secure place in psychoanalytic usage, and consequently the term "interpretation," as used, usually includes both meanings.

On the part of the patient, besides the work of free association, the work consists of assimilation or "working through" of the interpretations and constructions as well as the explanations with which the analyst accompanies them. Presumably, a correct interpretation or construction will lead, sooner or later, to the psychoanalytic goal of recollection and the recovery of repressed memories, but unfortunately this is not always the case. Nevertheless, in such cases a construction can often lead to such a conviction of truth that it achieves the same therapeutic result as a recaptured memory (S. Freud, 1937b).

Timing of interpretation. Freud (1913) recommends against communicating interpretations or constructions to a patient as soon as they are perceived by the analyst. He says that it is not difficult for a skillful and experienced analyst to read the patient's hidden wishes plainly between the lines of his complaints, but even in the later stages of analysis one should be careful about communicating the meaning of a symptom or the interpretation of a wish until the patient is close upon it himself, so that he has only a short step to take in order to arrive at the explanation himself. Premature communication of interpretations may be wasted because they are unacceptable to the patient, or they may drive the patient out of treatment because of the resistances they evoke or because of the relief that results from the insight obtained.

Uses and meaning of interpretation. The act of interpreting is a complex and overdetermined therapeutic operation. In purely operational terms, literal or direct interpretation is an act of translation (S. Freud, 1904a). It consists in putting something into words—language—although indirect and virtual interpretations can take the form of demonstrations (M. L. Coleman & Nelson, 1957; Nelson, 1962a). An interpreter ordinarily translates one language into another. If the patient's communication is nonverbal, that is, behavioral, the analyst may translate the patient's behavioral language into verbal language. The analyst applies his interpretive skills to (1) the patient's dreams, (2) his free associations, (3) symptoms and symptomatic acts, (4) behavior within the session, (5) behavior outside the session, (6) behavior in the past, (7) his relationship to the analyst, (8) his interpersonal relationships, past and present, and (9) his life-style and character. These in turn are translated by the analyst internally into the special language of the theoretical system and set of conceptions that he has learned in the course of his experience and training, and they are translated to the patient into their commonsense equivalents or into whatever terms the patient understands best.

Different analysts have different reasons for offering interpretations, and the same analyst may use interpretations for different reasons at different times during the treatment. An interpretation may be "designed to make the unconscious conscious." It may be used to provide the patient with an insight or the solution to a problem. An interpretation may be given to the patient to allay anxiety and as a means of support. It may be used to overcome a resistance and to facilitate free association. It may be used to produce a change in the patient's behavior outside of the treatment or to forestall acting out. It may be used to deepen the transference and the patient's interest in the analysis. It may be motivated by countertransference considerations, namely, the analyst's need to "do something for the patient," to prove himself, etc. Its use may be based upon the therapist's belief that interpretations are, in and of themselves, therapeutic. Interpretations may also be silent; that is, they may occur in the therapist's mind and not be communicated to the patient, and they may form the basis of the therapist's treatment plan and his understanding of the patient's needs in the treatment situation.

Clearly, the form of an interpretation or its level will be determined by the theoretical system of beliefs and the values of the analyst. Insofar as a patient and an analyst are speaking the same language, they can understand each other. Understanding in this sense means the ability to translate one set of words into another set of words that have meaning. A statement may therefore be translated into a variety of different languages, each of which possesses the same meaning. In this sense, one might speak of a particular language as a metaphor vis-à-vis another language. The analyst may therefore speak in the patient's metaphor or language, or he may translate the patient's metaphor or language into his own (see also Paul, 1963).

Mutative interpretations. Those interpretations that succeed in effecting a change in a patient's knowledge and feelings about himself are characterized as *mutative* interpretations by Strachey (1934). Such interpretations appear to him to be the ultimate instrument of psychoanalytic therapy and to be responsible for the therapeutic action of psychoanalysis. The effect of a mutative interpretation is emotionally "immediate;" the patient experiences it as something actual because it is addressed to impulses, feelings, and cognitions that are in operation in the patient at the time the interpretation is offered. Since such interpretations do not represent theoretical constructions or mere analogies but refer to realities present in the treatment situation, their validity can be directly observed and experienced by the patient.

Strachey maintains that only *transference* interpretations can be mutative. According to his conception, an extratransference interpretation cannot set into motion the chain of events that lead to modifications in the ego. In the first place, extratransference interpretations are hardly likely to pertain to the present situation and hence will lack immediacy. They tend to be concerned with experiences that are distant in both time and space and to have the character of what Strachey calls "dictionary interpretations." But in the second place, owing to the fact that the object or situation itself is not actually present as a criterion, it is less possible for the patient to be confronted by the differences between the real object and the fantasy object.

Because mutative interpretations aim at effecting changes in a patient's way of seeing things, they must be administered in minimal doses (Strachey, 1934). A patient can cope with reality only when it is presented to him in small quantities, and sometimes not at all. Each confrontation (Devereux, 1951) and interpretation demands a reorganization and working through within the psyche, for the implications of each new insight must eventually be reconciled with those other convictions with which it may conflict. Nobody can be expected to surrender too great a proportion of his world view without a struggle, no matter how convincing and unimpeachable are the evidences from reality, and some will choose the dignity and pleasure of preserving their ideals and beliefs (and symptoms) or even the martydom of self-destruction rather than yield to a reality that is unacceptable to them (see also Glover, 1931).

Use of dream interpretation. Although the art of interpretation owes much to the study of dreams (S. Freud, 1900), and although dreams offer an especially fruitful form of data for analysis, Freud (1912b) warns the psychoanalyst against displaying too great an interest in his patient's dreams during the conduct of treatment. In general, dreams should be subject to the same technical management as the other material the patient introduces in the session. The analyst should always address himself to the problems the patient is presenting at the moment, and special attention to the patient's dreams must be sacrificed to this criterion.

The Rule against Acting Out

Recollection. This form of recall is a relatively simple mental operation involving the translation of memories from one mental state into another. The action of recollecting the past requires the calling into consciousness of material from the memory traces of previous experiences. Material thus reproduced in consciousness is said to be remembered and is called a "conscious memory." Under normal circumstances, such memories of the past are recognized to be reproductions of earlier experiences and are readily discriminated by the individual from those originating in the present. He can then give an account, in words, of mental processes that have had their origins in past experiences. A recollection, then, is simply a conscious reproduction in the mind of a mental process originating in past experiences, i.e., a memory.

When "forgotten" material is recollected, it is not experienced by a patient as something new but as something that has been known all along and simply not called to mind. The forgetting of impressions, scenes, events, etc., hence nearly always reduces itself to a form of mental "dissociation" (S. Freud, 1914). Dissociated memories, because they are "forgotten" and unavailable, are not corrected or subjected to critical reflection and are not part of, or subject to, the individual's volitional control.

Repetition or acting out. It is not to be thought, however, that the effects of dissociated or forgotten experiences are not present and operative in the patient's mind but rather that the evidence of their existence is to be sought in the patient's behavior, not in his recollections. For it frequently happens that a patient recollects nothing of what is forgotten and repressed but instead expresses it in action. Instead of reproducing his memories by recollection, he acts them out. He repeats a past experience without, of course, knowing that he is repeating it (S. Freud, 1914). To the extent that a patient reproduces in action instead of remembering, his past can be reconstructed by an analyst from inferences drawn from the way he behaves in the present, both within and outside of the treatment hour. Because behavior within the hour is directly observable and occurs within a relatively controlled environment, it lends itself better to interpretation and consensual validation. A patient may not remember the way he behaved as an infant, but he may nevertheless reproduce his infantile behavior in his relationship with the analyst. Having been conditioned to respond in certain ways as a child, he will automatically repeat these old conditioned responses in the treatment setting when they are called forth by the present stimulus situation. Such automatic but often inappropriate repetitions occur in reference not only to the psychoanalyst but also to many other facets of the patient's current life situation, and they in fact form a basis for his having come into treatment. The impulse to remember has been replaced by the compulsion to repeat and consequently colors the patient's conduct in all matters with which he is currently engaged, including love relations, work habits, and projects he may undertake during the treatment.

To substitute recollection for repetition and to free the patient from compulsion are the ultimate goals of the psychoanalyst's therapeutic maneuvers. A psychoanalyst engages in a continuous effort to keep his patient mindful of this goal and directed toward its accomplishment; he instructs his patient not to carry his impulses into action and especially warns him not to make any important decisions affecting his life during the course of treatment but, in any case, to postpone any action until it has been discussed first. He takes advantage of every opportunity to force his patient to replace deeds with words and indeed demands within the limits of the analytic session that the patient refrain from all actions except talking. Every transgression of this prohibition is scrutinized as "grist for the analytic mill."

The rule against acting out serves a number of purposes. As a precautionary measure it sometimes protects a patient from undertaking dangerous or self-destructive actions, which in a more rational frame of mind he may later regret. Since it is not always possible to prevent a patient from carrying out quite undesirable projects during the course of treatment, it is hoped that the patient will profit from the experience and become willing to submit the unhappy incident to analysis afterward. It is a cardinal principle of classical analysis to make the patient conscious of impulses that he is translating into action instead of words and to divert into the work of recollection those he would discharge in action.

The rule against acting out provides the analyst with a lever by which to reveal the patient's resistances, lack of self-control, and infantile behavior. Against the background of this prohibition, each violation exposes the patient's unwillingness or inability to cooperate with the analyst for the achievement of the rational goals of the treatment. Each renunciation of action in favor of thought and words advances the analysis and the patient's progress toward maturity (see also Fenichel, 1945a; Greenacre, 1950).

Transference

Transference refers to the repetitions that take place during analytic treatment in connection with the patient's relationship to the psychoanalyst. It is a form of acting out and refers to the fact that patients must inevitably transfer and repeat in the treatment relationship the characteristic attitudes and expectations which they have developed in the course of their lives and which operate in the present to interfere with their capacity to live a normal and satisfactory life (S. Freud, 1912a). The feelings and expectations that the patient develops toward the analyst are often memories which he lives through as something real and actual attaching to the present situation but which are in actuality revivals or reproductions of past experiences that have yet to be recollected. The psychoanalyst allows such "repetitions" to occur during the analytic treatment because they constitute a conjuring into existence, as a piece of real life, within the treatment situation, of samples of the patient's typical behavior patterns, which may be dealt with as actual forces, active at the moment, and not as events in his past life (S. Freud, 1914). In the course of the treatment, it is expected that a patient will sooner or later exhibit all his inhibitions, disadvantageous attitudes, and pathological traits of character.

According to Freud (1915), the only really serious difficulty that an analyst encounters in the conduct of analysis is the handling of the problems created by the patient's transference. The patient often loses all interest in the treatment and all understanding of the treatment relationship and will not hear or speak of anything but love or hatred for the psychoanalyst. His accusations and demands become irrational and unrealistic, and his expectations clearly transcend those which might reasonably occur in a professional relationship. They are recognizably the kind of accusations and demands one makes of parents, a lover, friends, and siblings and are clearly inappropriate in the patient-therapist situation. Freud warns against any countertransference reactions in the psychoanalyst in response to the patient's protestations. The analyst must not lose sight of his analytic role and objectives in order that he may avoid being provoked into destroying the analytic relationship by responding directly to the patient's demands. While the patient lives out the transference as if it were something real and actual, the analyst observes and treats it as a repetition of the patient's past and continues the therapeutic work of translating it back again into terms of the past (S. Freud, 1914). (See also Fenichel, 1941; Glover, 1949; Greenacre, 1954; Lagache, 1953; Macalpine, 1950; Menninger, 1958; Silverberg, 1948.)

Resistance

The therapeutic effect of classical analysis rests upon the lifting of the patient's repressions and the recovery of the unconscious memories that motivate his behavior. This is accomplished through the analyst's constructions and interpretations. But as long as the patient's resistances are at work, the analyst's interpretations will fall upon deaf ears. For during treatment, as in all the circumstances of his life, the patient's resistances stand in the way of his becoming aware of the significant but unconscious determinants of his own behavior. They are oppositional trends in him which tend to maintain the status quo in his psychic economy and which are called into play whenever his beliefs or attitudes are challenged. It is not to be wondered at that the patient's ego will resist directing its attention to perceptions and ideas that it has, for the better part of a lifetime, made a rule of avoiding (S. Freud, 1926). Had the patient been free of resistances to begin with, his need for treatment would have been replaced by the normal corrective effects of his ordinary life experiences and education, and upon successful conclusion of the treatment, the effect of the elimination of resistances should considerably expand his ability to profit from life's experiences.

The knowledge that is presented to the patient by the analyst, in the form of constructions and interpretations, is the very knowledge about himself against which his repressions are aimed. And when confronted by interpretations in the course of the analysis, the very same mechanisms of defense that operate within the patient to prevent recollection and self-knowledge reappear in the form of resistances, mobilized against the analysis (S. Freud, 1937a). "The main point is that the patient repeats these modes of reaction during the analysis itself, exhibiting them, as it were, before our very eyes; in fact that is the only means we have of learning about them . . ." (S. Freud, 1937a).

Resolving resistances. The patient's resistances, like his repressions, are unconscious, but unlike repressions they are manifest, objective, and observable; indeed, they may be regarded as externalizations of repressions. The first step toward overcoming a resistance is made by the analyst, who must recognize and identify it and draw the patient's attention to it. But merely naming a resistance does not result in its immediate disappearance. The patient must get to know the resistance of which he is ignorant, must work it through and overcome it by continuing the work of the analysis in spite of it. This "working through" of resistances is arduous for the patient and a trial of patience for the analyst, but Freud (1914) says that it is this procedure which effects the greatest changes in the patient and which is the characteristic of psychoanalytic treatment that distinguishes it from every kind of suggestive treatment. Only when a resistance has reached its height, when its manifestations are clear and unmistakable, and only by living through it, will a patient finally be convinced of its existence and power. The handling of resistances calls for the greatest skill and experience, and attention to resistances takes precedence over all other therapeutic maneuvers.

Only during a state of profound hypnosis, when a patient's will, defenses, critical faculties, and ability to oppose the analyst are removed and held in abeyance, is he temporarily free of resistance. But recollections obtained during this state leave the patient's normal defensive repertoire and resistances untouched, and they resume their characteristic operations as soon as the patient's ego regains control.

Manifestations of resistance. As a general rule, any unwillingness or inability on the part of a patient to cooperate with the analyst to accomplish the goals of the treatment, or any violation of the rules, may be regarded as prima-facie evidence of resistance and should be suspect. Silence, tardiness, acting out, broken appointments, projections, displacements, rationalizations, etc., are signs of resistances.

Transference resistance. The transference phenomenon generally provides the source of the strongest resistances to the cure (S. Freud, 1912a). If the transference becomes hostile or unduly intense, the patient is likely to abandon his interest in the work of recollection and in being analyzed and may seek to destroy the treatment. In the case of negative transference, a patient becomes uncooperative and may break off the treatment. In the case of erotic or intense positive transference, the patient demands that the therapist substitute a love relationship for the analytic one. In the throes of the transference resistance, the patient arrogates to himself the freedom to ignore all the resolutions and agreements with which he entered the analysis. He becomes impervious to reason and logic and falls victim to powerful emotions welling up from within him that demand satisfaction (S. Freud, 1915).

The transference repetition is regarded by Freud (1912a) as an unavoidable and necessary consequence of the neurotic's life history. It is a manifestation of repressed unconscious impulses and their derivatives. Part of the work of the analysis is to make such material accessible to consciousness through memory and to reveal to the patient the reality of his infantile attachments and expectations. By studying the patient's transference behavior as repetitions that have been substituted for recollections, the analyst is able to reconstruct the clichés and stereotypes that perpetually repeat and reproduce themselves throughout the patient's life. But any aspect of the patient's unconscious that is transferred onto the person of the psychoanalyst is defended by the patient with the utmost obstinacy and resistance against interpretation (S. Freud, 1912a).

The transference yields if the analyst succeeds in overcoming the patient's resistances to continuing the analytic work and in showing him that his feelings do not originate in the contemporary situation and do not really attach to the person of the analyst but are reproductions of something that happened to him long ago. In this way the transference repetition is transformed into recollection (S. Freud, 1920).

Epinosic- or secondary-gain resistance. Epinosic gain refers to the advantages accruing to a patient as a result of his illness and to the pleasures derived therefrom. For example, the "injustice collector," however much he may suffer from the injuries he unconsciously solicits, experiences the narcissistic satisfaction of being right; and the sick child receives extra consideration and love. The patient is naturally unwilling to renounce and surrender any gratification or relief that he obtains, especially in view of the excessive amount of frustration that, as a neurotic, he is likely to have suffered throughout his history. Often the patient fears to be "cured" of his neurosis because he is afraid that he will be worse off without it. He wishes to remain unchanged but to be spared the suffering. Only after he is convinced of the advantages of health over illness and of the greater pleasures to be achieved from cure will this source of resistance be weakened.

Resistance to the discovery of resistances. As we have seen, resistances are defensive operations of the patient's ego directed against the efforts of the analyst to make him conscious of realities that for one reason or another are unacceptable to him. Their function, as is the case with all defenses, is to protect the patient from pain or injury. Their effect is to preserve the status quo, and accordingly they are obstacles not only to the lifting of the patient's repressions but also to the whole process of analysis and cure (S. Freud, 1937a). "The past is the patient's armory out of which he fetches his weapons for defending himself against the progress of the analysis, weapons which we must wrest from him one by one" (S. Freud, 1914).

These resistances, although apparent and manifest in the patient's behavior, are nevertheless unconscious to him, and he appears to be unaware of their operation. The analyst engages in a campaign to make the patient conscious first *that* he is resisting and then of *how* he is resisting. Only after the patient recognizes and acknowledges the existence of a resistance can an analyst advance various logical arguments against it and point out the advantages and rewards to be derived from its elimination. But it is not to be supposed that this is an easy task. Instead of cooperating with the analyst's efforts to discover and elucidate his typical resistance patterns, the patient regards the analyst's efforts in this direction as a personal attack upon him of a most disagreeable nature, and he greets such attempts at enlightenment with the strongest possible resistance (S. Freud, 1937a). A major portion of the therapeutic work of analysis consists in overcoming the patient's resistances to recognizing his resistances and then, after this, in convincing him to give up his resistances in favor of adopting a cooperative attitude toward his analysis.

Resistance of the unconscious. According to the earlier, classical view, after the patient's resistances have been overcome his repressed memories should become accessible to consciousness, but experience teaches us that unfortunately this is not the case. For even after the resistances on the part of the ego have been relinquished, there still remains the difficulty of undoing the effect of the repressions (S. Freud, 1926). Consequently, upon the resolution of a resistance, there must follow a period of "working through" to overcome what Freud calls the "power of the repetition compulsion." This means, in practice, the necessity of providing what learning theorists call "reinforcement" and amounts to a process of reconditioning or deconditioning. The situation engendered by lifting a repression or resolving a resistance may be viewed as the equivalent of learning a new passage to the extent of one successful repetition. The same resistance and the same repression will recur again and again and will have to be dealt with over and over before the patient finally abandons his old modes of thinking and acquires new ones. The tendency of the patient to repeat his habitual defense patterns and to forget what new insights he may be given has to be overcome by repeatedly working through the same problems until the new solutions are permanently remembered.

Superego resistance. A pathologically strict or hostile superego may lie at the source of a number of resistance manifestations. Guilt, shame, embarrassment, moral prohibitions, categorical imperatives, self-hatred, and self-destructive impulses take on the function of resistances during the course of treatment. Uncomplaining resignation and diminished motivation to achieve a cure are resistances traceable to this source. In fact, one gets the impression that in many neurotics there is a "will to suffer" or a "will to be ill," and they seem to have nothing in view but self-injury and self-destruction. The ego of such a person seems incapable of fulfilling its task of self-preservation because it is inhibited by the strict prohibitions of the superego (S. Freud, 1926; S. Freud, 1940).

The superego resistances do not always stand in the way of the intellectual work of the analysis, but if they are not resolved they can, at the last, defeat all the work of the analysis and render it useless and ineffective. A patient without hope, without lust, and without *joie de vivre* or a patient who feels worthless and despicable cannot and does not take advantage of the insights gained. There often occurs, instead, a negative therapeutic reaction to the analyst's efforts to effect a cure in one who feels the need for punishment.

Other manifestations of resistance. A number of examples of behavior in patients that may be regarded as manifestations of resistance have been reported. For example, Freud (1913) says that it may be regarded as a manifestation of resistance if a patient begins treatment and disclaims having any thoughts to talk about. Other samples of resistances are exemplified by patients who claim that too much occurs to them and that they cannot decide what to talk about (Ferenczi, 1919); patients who prepare material in advance of the session (S. Freud, 1913); patients who discuss material with persons outside of the analysis—the emotional leak (S. Freud, 1913); patients who become preoccupied with the same material and go over it without insight or progress—the "broken record" type of resistance (Menninger, 1958); patients who discuss only reality problems—the "reality resistance" (Menninger, 1958); and patients who are preoccupied with the analyst—"erotization resistance" (Menninger, 1958). Some patients act as though they understood the instruction to recount everything to mean that they should relate *only* senseless things—abuse of free association (Ferenczi, 1919); other patients present an unending supply of long and obscure dreams (S. Freud, 1912b). Fingert (1952) regards it as resistance if a patient forgets or fails to pay fees, demands treatment free of charge, or in other ways fails to deal properly with the economic obligations relating to his treatment. Other examples of resistance are shown by patients who feel sleepy or who fall asleep during the session (Ferenczi, 1914) and patients who are overly compliant and nonresistant—latent resistances (W. Reich, 1933).

FURTHER DEVELOPMENTS IN PSYCHOANALYTIC TECHNIQUE

Ferenczi's Active Technique

Ferenczi (1920) explains that his so-called "active therapy" was not meant to alter the classical method in any essential way but was designed to enable an analyst, "by means of certain artifices," to make a patient comply even more successfully with the fundamental rule of free association. The technique is employed only when it becomes necessary to handle a resistance situation which has resulted in stagnation in an analysis. Once the resistance has been overcome, he recommends that the therapist resume the normal passively receptive attitude that the classical procedure calls for.

The key to understanding Ferenczi's thinking about active therapy is hidden in the meanings of "passivity" and "activity." Passivity and activity are terms that may be applied to either the patient or the therapist with respect to either their thoughts or their conduct. In the classical situation both patient and analyst are required to assume a passive attitude with respect to their mental and physical conduct. Only two forms of activity are permitted to the classical analyst: (1) He may actively *reflect* upon his thoughts and arrive at a construction or an interpretation which he may *decide* to communicate to the patient, and (2) he may actively "interfere" with the patient's psychic activity through the communication of such interpretations and constructions. To the extent that an analyst's communications deflect the direction of a patient's thoughts, they may be considered to be active interferences in the patient's psychic activities. But the patient is required to behave passively toward the analyst's communications.

Classical psychoanalysis demanded no *activity* from the patient except verbal activities in the course of the therapeutic session. He was required to keep his appointments and to pay his fees, but except for the abstinence rule, there was no attempt on the part of the therapist to direct the conduct of his life. The first exception to this procedure was introduced by Freud (1919), when he found it necessary to compel phobic patients to expose themselves experimentally to a situation they had avoided because of its painfulness. The effect of their subjecting themselves to this intense emotional experience was to overcome resistance, and repressed material became conscious and accessible to analysis.

This procedure constitutes a paradigm of what is described by Ferenczi as "active technique." It consists in imposing certain tasks upon a patient in addition to obeying the fundamental rule. In the case of phobia the task may consist in his being asked to carry out the phobic act. In other cases it may consist in requiring the patient to renounce certain pleasurable activities (symptomatic acts) within the hour and outside of it. The goal of requiring such activities of the patient is the overcoming of his resistances so as to enable new memories to become accessible to consciousness so that the progress of an analysis might be accelerated.

Ferenczi (1920) regarded the enforcement of the classical rule of abstinence as a form of active technique. By active therapy he meant the use of prohibitions and commands by an analyst for the purpose of mobilizing the patient's resistances and affects. Such commands and prohibitions are pitted against the operation of the pleasure principle and accordingly force the observing ego to face its own weaknesses and irrational defenses. Unless a strong and enduring transference has been established, however, such tasks, which involve an inevitable amount of suffering and renunciation, may prove too great for a patient, and he may break off the treatment. This very liability of the method during the opening phase of the treatment may be used to advantage during the terminal phase.

Character symptoms. Like Wilhelm Reich, Ferenczi believed that, to some extent, an analyst has to contend with a patient's character in every analysis and that in some cases, abnormal traits of character, rather than neurotic symptoms, are the predominant feature. A character symptom differs from a neurotic symptom in that it is not experienced as ego-alien but as ego-syntonic. It represents an abnormality of the ego itself and manifests itself as a resistance. The patient's ego defends its character symptoms as it would defend itself, so that efforts to modify the patient's character evoke the patient's narcissistic defenses. According to Ferenczi, it is therefore sometimes necessary, before a patient will recognize his character defenses and experience them as symptoms, to draw his attention to them by setting him unpleasant tasks to perform that will mobilize and crystallize his resistances so that they appear in an unmistakable and exaggerated form. Thus traits of character that lie latent and are preconscious will appear full-blown as opposing the will of the conscious ego. The patient's narcissism is thus turned against the frustrating character defense. The analyst's suggestions force the patient to become aware of impulses that he has concealed from himself and cause him to enact them in the analysis. By challenging him to control these impulses consciously, especially when they are simply foolish and infantile, the analyst subjects "the whole process to a revision that was dispatched at some other time in a purposeless fashion by means of repression" (Ferenczi, 1920). The analyst thus enlists the patient's active participation in the process of his therapy and self-education (see also Ferenczi, 1925; Ferenczi, 1931).

Wilhelm Reich and Character Analysis

From a practical point of view, Reich (1933) contributed to a fundamental shift in therapeutic technique. He shifted his emphasis from the unconscious material obtained by free association to the patient's character, that is, to his "characteristic" *behavior* during the analytic session, in particular to the measures the patient uses to defend himself against analytic insight and unconscious material. These changes made psychoanalysis applicable to certain patients who had previously remained inaccessible to it.

While Reich assumed that each definite analytic situation admits of only one optimal technical procedure and that there is one definite procedure in each situation that is better than any other, it seems more likely that for any given situation there are a number of equally probable and equally adequate technical solutions. Nevertheless one must agree with Reich that some set of principles should be laid down to govern the choice of any particular action on the part of a therapist. For example, simply to interpret material in the order of its appearance does not always achieve the desired therapeutic effect. Interpretations are therapeutically effective only under certain conditions. But Reich says that if one is not to give interpretations at random, criteria must be established that enable an analyst to know what to choose from the wealth of material he faces, why and when interpretation should be given, and whether to interpret the unconscious material which has become manifest or the resistance.

When Freud attempted to make patients understand the unconscious meaning of their symptoms by direct interpretation, he discovered that the success of the method depended on whether or not a patient was ready to accept such an interpretation (S. Freud, 1913). In fact, he found that patients often opposed direct interpretations. In the face of resistances it became necessary to alter the technical procedure and to shift from direct interpretations in favor of analysis of resistances. This new approach is probably best called "resistance analysis."

"This fundamental change in theoretical concept and technique was the turning point in the history of analytic therapy at which the therapy of today began to develop" (W. Reich, 1933). But as is the case with abreaction, catharsis, and direct interpretation, resistance analysis assumes that with the elimination of the resistances, the unconscious will be made conscious, and the symptoms will disappear. But Reich says that even after the resistances have been dissolved and the unconscious is made conscious, the symptoms may nevertheless persist, and he asks: "What determines whether or not the lifting of a repression leads to cure?"

The direct application of psychoanalytic theory to the treatment of a patient without a theory of practice leads to what Reich calls a "chaotic situation" in the analysis. The patient continues to bring material, and the analyst continues to analyze, but nothing seems to get worked through; there does not seem to be any movement toward a therapeutic goal. Though the analyst gives many interpretations, these never seem to deepen the analysis in one way or another.

Causes of the chaotic situation. According to Reich (1933), a number of technical errors lead to a chaotic analysis:

1. *Premature interpretations* of the meaning of the symptoms. Such intellectual interpretations are then used in the service of resistance, and the patient remains untouched by the analysis.

2. *Unsystematic interpretations*. Interpretations are offered in the sequence in which the material presents itself, without considera-

tion of the stratification of the material. The error consists in offering an interpretation simply because the material presents itself clearly.

3. *Content interpretation.* The interpretation of the content precedes the interpretation of the resistance.

4. *Latent transference resistances.* These are overlooked by the analyst. The interpretation of the transference resistance is unsystematic and inconsistent. Latent resistances are attitudes of the patient that are not expressed directly and immediately. Examples are extreme compliance or lack of manifest resistances such as doubt, distress, being late, silence, spite, and lack of associations.

Reich's rules for systematic interpretation and resistance analysis

1. View the patient without preconceived ideas.

2. Identify the resistance as it occurs in the particular case.

3. Avoid interpretation as long as the cardinal resistances have not become clear and have not been eliminated, no matter how ample, clear, and interpretable the material may be.

4. Do not interpret content when a resistance interpretation is needed. If one interprets the meaning before dealing with the resistance, the patient either accepts the interpretation for reasons of the transference or tends to reject it.

5. Do not interpret resistances before they have been fully developed.

6. Proceed from the psychic surface. Interpret the most manifest and the most superficial material first. But even when one is confronted with two simultaneous manifest contents, for example, excessive politeness and homosexual fears, particularly at the beginning of treatment, deal with the formal rather than the content aspects of the material, in this case the politeness (which is the resistance) rather than the homosexuality (which is the impulse).

Character resistance. In classical analysis the material upon which the psychoanalyst focuses his attention includes the patient's communications, dreams, associations, slips of the tongue, and, to some extent, symptomatic acts and abnormal behavior. But there is a tendency to underestimate or overlook the character of the patient's normal and usual manner and behavior. It is true that Freud (1913) remarks on the usefulness of observing the patient's behavior during the session, especially at the beginning of treatment, and analysts are generally aware of the significance of behavioral signs, but until Reich, these were treated as incidental rather than central phenomena in the course of the analysis. The interpretation of the patient's character became for Reich what the interpretation of dreams was for classical analysis. He called this new approach to treatment "character analysis."

The patient's character expresses itself in his total behavior pattern, his manner of speech, his facial expressions, his style of dress, his gestures, his handshake, his attitude, etc. The form rather than the content of his behavior presents the most important point of departure for the analysis of character (W. Reich, 1933). During the analysis, the patient's character constitutes a major and ubiquitous resistance. Character resistances remain the same in any given patient throughout the treatment, irrespective of what material is being presented. The patient's character plays the same role in the treatment that it plays in ordinary life, that of a defense mechanism, the patient's peculiar total adaptation to life. The patient is "characterologically armored" against the outer world, as he is against his inner drives. Reich calls this a "narcissistic" defense.

The ego defense (character resistance) in a given patient has a characteristic form that corresponds to his character and personality. This means that the same patient may ward off different impulses using the same defense, and different patients may ward off similar impulses by means of different typical defenses. If the analyst addresses himself to the interpretation of the impulse, he leaves the patient's character untouched. If, on the other hand, the analyst attends to the patient's defense, he includes the patient's character in the analysis. In the first case, the analyst interprets *what* the patient is afraid of. In the second case, the analyst tries to make him conscious *that* he is afraid and then of *how* he reacts defensively. He thus interprets the defense rather than the impulse. Reich says that although classical analysts had begun to know and recognize the principles of resistance analysis, they were in practice still more likely to use the classical method of interpreting the unconscious impulse or content. In part because of the impact of Reich's work, modern psychoanalytic practice places greater emphasis upon the analysis of resistances and character (see also Sterba, 1951).

The goal of the character-analytic technique, though it concerns itself chiefly with present-day modes of behavior, is the same as that which permeates all forms of psychoanalytic treatment, to reduce acting out to remembering. The consistent analysis of character resistance should lead to a spontaneous recollection of infantile material (W. Reich, 1933).

Alexander and French and the Flexible Approach

The use of psychoanalytic technique gradually changed, over the years, as the practical exigencies of the clinical situation demanded new strategies and new conceptions of the therapeutic process. Emphasis was shifted from the interpretation of unconscious impulses to the interpretation of resistances; then from passivity to activity; and finally from dealing exclusively with the patient's free associations and symptomatic acts to examination of the patient's total behavior (character). Recently the whole therapeutic situation and procedure was brought under scrutiny by Alexander and French and their colleagues at the Chicago Institute of Psychoanalysis.

Alexander and French (1946) and others did not question the validity of the principles and goals of classical psychoanalysis so much as recommending considerably more flexibility in applying them to treatment. They experimented by varying the conditions and conduct of treatment, in place of the dogmatic adherence to the highly standardized form in which classical analysis was conducted, in order to develop more economical and effective procedures adjusted to the individual requirements of the great variety of neurotic conditions and patients. Along with their colleagues, they stressed the value of designing a "plan of treatment" based upon a diagnostic appraisal of the patient's personality and his presenting problems and shaped to meet these specific contingencies. This contrasts with the traditional attitude, which is to let the treatment take its own course and to follow the lead of the material produced by the patient.

Among the modifications of the standard procedure proposed by the Chicago school of thought were changing the frequency of visits, giving directives to the patient concerning his daily life, employing interruptions of long or short duration in preparation for the end of the treatment, and making use of real-life experiences as an integral part of the therapy. These changes were made necessary by the desire of the Chicago group of psychoanalysts to treat patients for whom the standard technique did not seem applicable.

Frequency of interview. According to Alexander (1946b), the procedure of requiring daily interviews can sometimes gratify the patient's dependent needs more than is desirable, and in such cases emotional insight and relief from anxiety can be achieved with fewer interviews. A patient whose needs for dependence are continually gratified never becomes aware of them, and in such a situation, if the frequency of visits is reduced the patient is confronted by an awareness of his dependence upon the treatment, and reactive resentments to the frustration of his dependent needs are mobilized.

Alexander points out that daily interviews may pander to the neurotic's regressive as well as procrastinating tendencies. He believes that it should be a general principle in all psychotherapy to check regressive tendencies from the very beginning of the treatment, allowing no more procrastination and regression than are absolutely necessary to minimize panic, anxiety, and despair.

Because daily interviews become routine (and affects are discharged as fast as they accumulate), they tend to attenuate the development and display of intense feelings. He suggests that, in principle, frequent interviews are desirable for patients in whom emotional discharge and the accompanying insight must take place very gradually. This would include patients with so-called "weak" egos. Such individuals cannot tolerate intense emotional participation and therefore require small abreactions in almost daily interviews over a long period of time. But patients with "strong" egos can endure more intense sessions without regression and therefore require relatively less frequent interviews. Interruptions of the treatment may also be useful, to permit working through, reality testing, consolidation of gains, integration of new insights, and time for a general self-inventory by the patient, through experience, of the problems he still retains.

Alexander invokes what he calls the "maxim of economical psychotherapy," which is to allow as little regression as the patient can stand, no more procrastination than is unavoidable, and the minimum corrective dosage of gratification from the treatment.

The corrective emotional experience. Psychotherapy is viewed by Alexander (1946a) as providing a corrective emotional experience in which the patient can learn how to handle emotional situations that he could not handle in the past. He is enabled to do this successfully for a variety of reasons. He is now more mature and more experienced. The therapist is present to guide and help him. The conditions under which the reexposure occurs, within the treatment situation, are controlled and controllable.

Alexander points out that in the classical formulation of the dynamics of treatment, the stress is placed upon transference as merely a repetition of an old conflict. But Alexander draws attention to the therapeutic significance of the differences between the original conflict situation and the present one in respect to the presence of a therapist whose behavior is different from that of the authoritative person in the past. This gives a patient an opportunity to face the old emotional situation under more favorable circumstances and to deal with it in an effective and successful way. By an actual living through of the experience in treatment, in his relationship with the therapist, he is enabled to achieve more than mere intellectual insight (see also Nelson, 1962b). If the transference is used as a corrective experience rather than interpreted as a repetition of the past, it can offer the patient a unique opportunity to work through a great number of problems successfully. This is because the conflict as it appears in the transference situation is less intense than the original one and also because the analyst reacts differently toward the patient than the original object did.

Transference phenomena reconsidered. French (1946) believes it is important to distinguish between transference reactions, which are the patient's reactions to the analyst that repeat his reactions to a person who has at some previous time played an important role in his life, and reactions that are adequate to the present real situation. He says that a patient does not react to a therapist entirely as if the therapist were somebody else but that he sometimes reacts quite naturally to what the therapist actually does or says and to the therapist's actual personality characteristics and behavior. He believes this distinction to be of the greatest practical importance in therapeutic practice because he believes it is one of the important therapeutic tasks to help the patient to distinguish between transference reactions and normal reactions. By helping the patient to make this distinction, the analyst helps him to acquire new ways of reacting that conform more closely to the present situation. French calls this part of therapy "reality testing" within the therapeutic milieu.

Similarly, not all so-called "irrational" reactions of patients in treatment are to be regarded as merely transference reactions. A disturbing interpretation by an analyst is a present reality and constitutes an attempt to interfere with ("attack") defenses which have been, until the present, necessary for the patient's peace of mind.

> When a patient reacts with anger to such an interpretation, therefore, his anger is not based upon a misunderstanding of the present situation as a repetition of a memory from the past. His anger is rather a direct reaction to the therapist as a real and present threat to the patient's peace of mind. Such a reaction is obviously a manifestation of the patient's resistance to treatment, but it cannot be looked upon as a manifestation of the transference neurosis (French, 1946).

The modern attitude. According to French (1946), a therapist should not endeavor to be a "blank screen" upon which the patient simply projects, but, whenever possible, he should try to put the patient at his ease by behaving in a way one would normally expect from one to whom one has come for help and counsel. He proposes that an analyst behave in such a way as to meet the patient's normal expectations and that he treat him as a normal and rational human being and continue to do so until the patient himself, by his own behavior, demonstrates the contrary.

In his opinion, a modern psychoanalyst does not concentrate exclusively upon reconstructing the patient's past history and infantile neurosis but recognizes the importance of repetition and working through in the therapeutic process. He believes an analyst does best to focus his interest upon helping the patient to work through his infantile neurosis in the transference relationship. Accordingly, an analyst's policy should be to strengthen the reality-testing function of the ego by centering the patient's attention upon his real, present problems and to turn his attention to the past only for the purpose of casting light upon the motives for irrational reactions in the present. Several other schools of thought exist today, however, and research data are not available to make it possible to settle the continuing controversies about technique.

Recent advances in ego psychology have also had their impact upon technique and have helped to clarify and assist analysts in more accurate management of the timing of interpretations. The shift in attention to the psychology of the ego has led to a deepened understanding of the role of ego defenses and their resolution during treatment (see Hartmann, 1951; Kris, 1951).

The Paradigmatic Nature of Psychoanalytic Treatment

Throughout the developments in psychoanalytic treatment methods, from classical analysis through character analysis, runs the notion that there occurs within the treatment hour a kind of acting out, a repetition and working through, of unresolved problems that find their expression there. The patient reproduces his problems in the treatment setting, and the analyst tries to help him to find successful solutions. The strategy of treatment is directed toward this end. Were a patient completely rational and an analyst sufficiently wise, a dialogue might ensue in which the analyst would interpret the patient's problems, and the patient, having arrived at reasonable understanding, would embark upon a new course of action based upon his new insights. Unfortunately things do not run so smoothly. In the face of all logic and reason, the patient often behaves in a most obstinate and uncomprehending manner. When in the face of the patient's peculiar and defensive behavior, an analyst persists in the procedure which has shown itself to be unrewarding and futile, the treatment either reaches a stalemate or must be terminated. He has thus merely reproduced or repeated a technique which was not appropriate in that treatment situation and not tailored to meet that patient's needs. Different techniques are required for different kinds of patients, and presumably a sophisticated analyst will possess an array of technical models to choose from.

A repetition or a reproduction is a model or a pattern that possesses an element or a quality that may be described as "meaning" or "significance." That is to say, it is not merely a thing-in-itself but is also a representation of something else. A dream is composed of its manifest content, but in its structure and form it symbolizes another content that can be inferred from its representation in the dream. Repetitions or representations can take the form of the patient's transference neurosis; the form of his resistances, his character, and his symptoms; the form of acting out, in and out of treatment; and the form of the formal characteristics of his role relations with the therapist as well as of his behavior in all therapeutic encounters. The analyst's behavior may also constitute a repetition, either unwitting, as in unconscious countertransference resistances, or conscious and deliberate, as in the carrying out of therapeutic maneuvers designed to achieve specific therapeutic results. Bernstein (1958) suggests that ritualistic and dogmatic conduct of treatment may itself be an unconscious repetition of unresolved transference problems in analysts, relating to their own training analyses.

M. L. Coleman and Nelson (1957) have adopted the term "paradigm" to apply to these phenomena (see also Eissler, 1953). They say that this concept provides a consistent rationale for the various courses of action that take place in all forms of psychotherapy and perhaps in all social behavior. A paradigm is a pattern, a model, or an example. To be paradigmatic means literally "to set forth by example," to demonstrate. Insofar as a patient's behavior and expectations, as they manifest themselves in the treatment situation, are repetitions, they constitute demonstrations or paradigms representing memories. As Freud (1919) says of the patient's compulsion to repeat: "We admit it into the transference as to a playground, in which it is allowed to let itself go in almost complete freedom and is required to display before us all the pathogenic impulses hidden in the depths of the patient's mind." By his behavior the patient "shows" his pathology, and conversely, whether he wills it or not, an analyst's behavior will be interpreted paradigmatically by his patient. For by his behavior, the analyst will demonstrate love and hate, reason and unreason, sickness and health, acceptance and rejection, confidence and insecurity, and a whole gamut of possible postures and roles. The treatment situation becomes a model of the world, a stage on which all possible dramas and roles may be played out.

The transference neurosis is a kind of artificial illness, Freud (1919) says, that falls into an intermediate realm between illness and real life. By working through this artificial illness, the analyst provides the patient by demonstration, as it were, with paradigms for the solution of "real" illnesses. Thus every problem solved within the treatment setting adds to the patient's repertoire of problem-solving paradigms. He even learns (introjects) the techniques that the analyst has employed in dealing with the emotional problems (countertransferences) that the patient has provoked in him. The treatment comes to be a paradigm of life (see Nelson, 1962b).

Not only do solutions to problems constitute paradigms, but also they may themselves have been arrived at paradigmatically. One can learn by being told (the classical paradigm of interpretation), but one can also learn by being shown (the paradigmatic approach). Instead of "telling" a patient that he is resisting, how he is resisting, the unconscious meaning of his behavior, or the solution to his problems, etc., an analyst can deliberately fashion his behavior and verbal responses so that the patient arrives at the insight himself. A number of such paradigmatic maneuvers have been suggested by Nelson (1962a) and others. (See also J. V. Coleman, 1962; Kesten, 1957; Sherman, 1961; Spotnitz & Nagelberg, 1960; Strean, 1959.)

Adaptation of Psychoanalytic Technique to the Analysis of Children

Child analysis originated with the analysis of "Little Hans" (S. Freud, 1909). But until the work of Melanie Klein and Anna Freud, its possibilities were hardly realized. Developments in the field of child analysis have followed the two main lines laid down by these workers. Klein is responsible for the introduction of play technique into the analysis of small children, while Anna Freud applies psychoanalysis to treatment of children during the latency period.

Klein (1932) believes that the psychoanalytic method can be applied directly to the treatment of children without any major modification in the classical procedure, but Anna Freud (1926) holds that owing to the nature of the child and his situation, major differences in method are called for. Klein maintains that children develop a transference neurosis during treatment, while Anna Freud feels that they do not because their original love objects are still real and present. Instead, the analyst enters the arena as a new person rather than as a transference object, and his behavior is quite different from what it is with an adult patient. The educative role of the child analyst results in his child patient knowing very well what the analyst approves of, what seems desirable to him, and what seems to him to be undesirable. Under such circumstances, Anna Freud suggests, he is not a very good object for the projection of transferences. She observes that children do not yet have fully developed inner controls in the form of an adult superego and that consequently the child analyst must "succeed in putting himself in the place of the child's Ego-ideal for the duration of the analysis." On the contrary, Klein employs a method, equivalent to adult analysis, which avoids all educational measures. While Anna Freud has found that the superegos of children are weak and malleable and still inseparably bound to the authoritative adults in their environment, Klein feels that it is very difficult to mitigate the severity of the child's superego, even with deep analysis.

Anna Freud takes note of the reality situation of the child, with respect to its immaturity and dependence upon both its parents and the analyst for protection and guidance. For one thing, she says, as opposed to the situation with adults, the decision to undergo an analysis never comes from the child who is to be the patient but from some other person. Consequently, the usual conditions, i.e., insight into the illness, voluntary decision, and the will toward cure, are absent. Children's analyses therefore require a preparatory period which does not ordinarily occur with adults. These reality considerations with respect to children militate against the proposition that the conditions of child analysis are equivalent to those in the adult situation. Notwithstanding transference phenomena, children are in fact dependent and relatively helpless, and the analyst is an adult with greater knowledge and power. Moreover, instead of relying exclusively upon the patient for a reconstruction of the case history, as is the case with adults, with children one has to put the case history together from information furnished by the family. Successful upbringing, Anna Freud states, requires an affectionate attachment on the part of the child to the person in charge of him. Accordingly, while in adult analyses both positive and negative attitudes toward an analyst are equally useful for transference interpretations, in child analysis negative impulses toward the analyst are essentially inconvenient, however revealing they may be in other respects.

Except that play technique is substituted for the adult free-association technique, Klein conducts child analyses along the lines of the classical model, utilizing for interpretation, besides the things that the child does with the toys, all his actions respecting other objects found in the room and toward her own person. She begins from the premise that the child's actions during play are on a par with an adult's spoken ideas, and she assumes that the play actions of children have the same status as the free associations of adults. Anna Freud concedes that the normal methods of interpretation may readily be applied to the dreams of children, but she does not feel it to be justified to ascribe symbolic significance to everything the child does. For one thing, she says, children are often uninclined to embark upon free association; also, the psychological structure and attitude present in an adult with respect to the method of free association are absent in children.

Some of the differences that appear to apply to the theoretical positions of these two workers are far from irreconcilable but arise in part from a difference in emphasis, in part from attention to different aspects of the therapeutic situation, and in part from differences in practice and patients. Their proposals and theoretical suggestions merit careful scrutiny for their implications regarding the conduct of adult analyses.

Adaptation of Psychoanalysis to the Treatment of Psychoses

It will be recalled that Freud (1920) wrote of psychotics: "They produce no transference, and are, therefore, inaccessible to our efforts, not to be cured by us." For this reason, Freud characterized psychoses as "narcissistic" neuroses. The classical procedure was considered to be suitable only for the treatment of the so-called "transference" neuroses. Recent years have seen the classical treatment paradigm give way to the discovery of many new treatment innovations within the framework of psychoanalytic theory that have led a number of psychoanalysts to hold a more hopeful attitude toward the adaptability of psychoanalysis to the treatment of psychotics and borderlines (Arieti, 1955; Bychowski, 1952; M. L. Coleman & Nelson, 1957; Federn, 1952; Fromm-Reichmann, 1950; Fromm-Reichmann, 1959; Rosen, 1953; Spotnitz, 1961; Spotnitz, 1962; Sullivan, 1931; Wolman, 1959).

According to Federn (1943), Bleuler reported that the Burgholzi Clinic was able to discharge three times as many cases after the clinic staff had begun to act on the basis of its new psychoanalytic insights. The discovery that psychotic patients could profit from psychoanalysis followed upon their having been taken into treatment as a consequence of erroneous diagnosis or with the intention of using analysis for the purpose of investigation, and it was noted that some seemed to profit from the increased clinical interest they received. Though they were not really psychoanalyzed in the classical sense, their psychoanalysts had unwittingly treated them in such a way as to have established good positive transferences.

Federn (1943) reports that the taking of anamneses in psychotic or postpsychotic cases of schizophrenia is contraindicated. He also found that such patients had to be aided and protected and not left to suffer their own tribulations outside of the analytic hours. Psychotics tend to relapse at home or elsewhere when left without the continuous support of the transference. He also asserts, on the basis of his experience, that psychotics have a better chance of recovering when they have a moderate amount of sexual gratification.

For patients with acute psychotic conditions, he proposes that the following treatment principles be applied: (1) Establish and maintain a positive transference; (2) interrupt the treatment in the face of negative transference; (3) provide continuous postpsychotic psychoanalytic support and supervision; and (4) provide a reasonable solution to the sexual problem (see also Wolman, 1959). Other patients with less severe character disorders can also be helped by these procedures but do not require them. But even in such cases, he says, strict adherence to the classical rules is not desirable. Free association tends to encourage manic flights of thought, and recollection of past periods of life leads to depression by making guilt feelings conscious. Though the goal of treatment in neurosis is to lift repressions, in psychosis it is to create or reinforce repressions.

Federn also recommends against the use of the recumbent position with psychotics (see also Fromm-Reichmann, 1959). He says that when a psychotic lies on a couch, he produces associations of a schizophrenic nature, whereas if he sits up, he will make associations in a normal manner; and unlike a neurotic when a psychotic rises from the couch he does not immediately resume his normal behavior in his conscious relationship to the analyst. "I wish to emphasize," Federn (1943) says, "that in manifest and latent psychoses the typical analysis used in neuroses is harmful and must be abandoned, or used only in homeopathic doses." Homeopathic dosage is so small that it does not inhibit any function and provokes only very slow changes (see also Spotnitz, 1963).

Federn (1943) offers a number of recommendations for the modification of the classical procedure which he believes are required for the treatment of psychotic patients:

1. Free association is not to be encouraged because too much material is already being offered by the psychotic process itself.

2. The positive transference should not be analyzed because psychotic patients can be treated only in the presence of the positive transference.

3. The development of the transference neurosis should not be encouraged because it develops into a transference psychosis.

4. Resistances should not be eliminated prematurely because it is not desirable to uncover any more unconscious material.

5. Interpretation should be applied to the material and symptoms rather than to the transference and the resistances.

6. Federn distinguishes between resistances that are directed against recovery and those that are directed against unconscious material. The former are to be resolved, and the latter are to be reinforced (see also Spotnitz, 1962).

Spotnitz (1961) believes that self-hatred is the nuclear problem that has to be resolved in working with schizophrenics. The analyst must therefore be prepared to cope with the therapeutic discharge of destructive hostility and to channel such impulses into verbal behavior. The patient, he says, is suffering from too much stimulation (lack of insulation) and too little discharge (accumulation of "frustration-aggression"). Thus resistances must sometimes be reinforced because of their insulative value in order to prevent the accumulation of more aggressive impulsivity than the patient can release verbally. The aim of the treatment is to build up the insulative capacities of the ego and to enrich its patterns of self-expression (Spotnitz, 1962).

The approach of Rosen (1953), which he characterizes as "direct analysis," has been the subject of considerable controversy. Although Rosen employs classical psychoanalytic formulations, his procedure is dramatically different from the classical psychoanalytic model. Rosen (1950) treats schizophrenic manifestations as though they were a direct display of unconscious processes without interference from resistances and defenses. He regards hallucinations as possessing a survival function for the schizophrenic, recreating, much in the manner of a mirage, certain necessary survival conditions. Rosen actively enters into the patient's delusional system and attempts therein to provide the patient with the support and corrective experience that he requires. The absence of resistances and the appearance of primary-process material enable Rosen to offer direct and almost literal interpretations.

Most workers dealing with psychotic patients recognize the intense and infantile nature of the transference reactions that occur during the treatment of schizophrenics. Eissler (1954) believes that the analyst must help such patients to form new and more adult ego structures under the protection of a well-managed transference. He encourages patients to expose themselves to what may have formerly appeared to them to be unbearable feelings and situations. By so doing, the analyst is able to make the patient aware of his ego defects, and by helping the patient to master such feelings and problems successfully, the analyst stimulates the formation of new ego structure. Bychowski (1954) also encourages reenactment of infantile problems within the therapeutic session. He regards the treatment session as the place for undertaking current reality testing, within the framework of the transference. Because the schizophrenic's ego is so infantile and literal, he requires concrete interpretations and a minute working through of each pathological thought. Bychowski confirms the findings of other workers as to the necessity for massive reassurance and support from the transference during each stage of therapy with psychotic patients.

Wolman has developed a method of psychoanalytic treatment of psychotics with a sociological emphasis. He distinguishes three types of human relationships: (1) instrumental, (2) mutual, and (3) vectorial. The infant's attitude toward his mother is an example of the instrumental (taking) type of relationship; marriage exemplifies the mutual (give-and-take) type of relationship; and the parent-child relationship represents the vectorial (giving) type of relationship. The theory is articulated with a modified Freudian theory through the introduction of the concept of "interindividual cathexes" (Wolman, 1965, chap. 5). Wolman assumes that schizophrenia is generated by a reversal in social positions and roles within the schizophrenic's family. The parent-child relationship becomes instrumental instead of vectorial, and the child is forced to assume an abnormal "hypervectorial" attitude toward his parents (Wolman, 1957; Wolman, 1961). Wolman deals with the transference situation as an interactional process in which transference elements are fused with the "here-and-now reactions," much as Anna Freud manages the transference in the treatment of children. His aim is the restoration or establishment of a normal balance of intraindividual and interindividual cathexes of libido and destrudo. He believes that a vectorial, realistic, and frank attitude on the part of the therapist is required for this purpose (Wolman, 1959; Wolman, 1965).

Other Technical Problems

Brief mention must be made of other important problems that arise in the course of analytic practice, such as the following.

The meanings and uses of the psychoanalyst's countertransference. As first conceived by Freud, countertransference refers to feelings induced in a psychoanalyst by a patient that interfere with the analyst's ability to perform an objective analysis. Such feelings are by definition undesirable and are due to unanalyzed or repressed elements in the psychoanalyst's unconscious against which he must constantly guard and which are to be eliminated whenever possible by self-analysis or through controls. In this sense they are the analogue in an analyst of transference in a patient. More recently, psychoanalysts have begun to acknowledge other feelings induced in them by their patients which may also be regarded as countertransferences but which do not represent projections and which facilitate rather than interfere with their capacity to understand the patient's communications and unconscious. In this latter sense, countertransference refers to objective rather than subjectively induced feelings in a psychoanalyst. In a third sense, countertransference has come to include all the feelings generated in an analyst during the conduct of treatment and embraces the whole of his attitudes toward himself and his patient. The management of countertransference is as crucial for the success of treatment as the management of transference and will be determined by the psychoanalyst's inclination to permit or omit his own feelings during the analytic process (A. Balint & M. Balint, 1939; Benedek, 1953; Berman, 1949; Cohen, 1952; Heimann, 1950; Little, 1951; Racker, 1957; A. Reich, 1951; Spitz, 1956; Spotnitz, 1963; Tauber, 1952; Thompson, 1952; Tower, 1956; Winnicott, 1949).

The problem of termination and cure. Many questions have been raised about a definition of what constitutes a successful analysis and about the criteria that should apply to the termination of treatment. Many analyses seem interminable, while others are brought to a conclusion, by mutual agreement between analyst and patient, when they are still far short of the achievement of any of the ideal theoretical goals of treatment. Reasons for terminating treatment vary with the temperament and aspirations of different analysts as well as with the needs and capacities of different patients.

While some analysts strive for personality reconstruction, others are content to bring about what they feel to be a permanent remission of the painful and incapacitating symptoms that brought the patient into treatment. Still others seek for a removal of infantile amnesia and a lifting of repressions followed by abreaction and insight. Psychoanalysts tend to agree that an analysis may be regarded as successful if, to a reasonable degree, a patient's capacity for working and loving has been raised to within normal limits and if his neurotic misery has been reduced to normal unhappiness (M. Balint, 1950; M. Balint, 1936; Barchilon, 1958; Bridger, 1950; Buxbaum, 1950; S. Freud, 1937a; Hoffer, 1950; Klein, 1950; Menninger, 1958; A. Reich, 1950; Rickman, 1950; Weigert, 1952).

Problems of supervision and training of psychoanalysts. It is generally agreed that the preparation of an analyst requires a personal analysis, specialized training in the theory and practice of psychoanalysis, and a period of control and supervision, by experienced analysts, of his actual contacts with patients. The setting of standards for the fulfillment of each of these requirements has given rise to many theoretical and practical issues. For example, is a training analysis different from a therapeutic analysis? What are the critera for an adequate training analysis? What role should the training analyst play later in the selection procedures and supervision of his analysands? What effect does the role of training analyst have upon the transference-countertransference situation? Where, when, and how shall the candidate receive his formal instruction in psychoanalytic subject matter? Of what formal course contents shall psychoanalytic training consist? How much control and supervision does a candidate require? How does one manage the transference-countertransference reactions in supervisor and supervisee? What are the criteria for selection and approval of candidates and control analysts? Although practical decisions on these matters have been arrived at by training institutes and accrediting associations, no general and satisfactory consensus exists concerning the theoretical issues involved (Ackerman, 1953; M. Balint, 1948; M. Balint, 1954; Benedek, 1954; Benedek, 1955; Bibring, 1954; Ekstein, 1955; Fromm-Reichmann, 1949; Gitelson, 1948; Gitelson, 1954; Grotjahn, 1954; Grotjahn, 1955; Heimann, 1954; Kovacs, 1936; Nacht, 1954; Nielsen, 1954; Searles, 1955; Szasz, 1960; Weigert, 1955; Windholz, 1955).

Evaluation of the results of psychoanalytic treatment. Although several efforts have been undertaken to assess the therapeutic results of psychoanalytic treatment, a number of methodological obstacles have so far made a definitive finding impossible. Reports indicate that roughly 60 per cent of all cases are considered to be recovered or improved. The problem lies in interpreting such findings in a meaningful way, for these findings are based upon cases that are not comparable, on samples from unknown populations, on cases of varying degrees of pathology and of unspecified diagnoses, on purely subjective and unspecified criteria for improvement and recovery, and on treatment procedures of varying degrees of intensity undertaken by psychoanalysts of varying degrees of competence. Moreover, the difficulties of comparing results of psychoanalytic technique with results of other techniques and of evaluating and measuring subtle qualitative changes and improvements due to situational changes have not been solved (Glover, 1937; Hendrick, 1950; Knight, 1941; Nunberg, 1954; Oberndorf, 1942; Oberndorf, Greenacre, & Kubie, 1948).

REFERENCES

Ackerman, N. W. Selected problems in supervised analysis. *Psychiatry,* 1953, **16,** 283–290.

Alexander, F. The principle of corrective emotional experience. In F. Alexander & T. M. French, *Psychoanalytic therapy.* New York: Ronald, 1946. Pp. 66–70. (a)

Alexander, F. The principle of flexibility. In *ibid.* Pp. 25–41. (b)

Alexander, F., & French, T. M. *Psychoanalytic therapy.* New York: Ronald, 1946.

Arieti, S. *Interpretation of schizophrenia.* New York: Brunner, 1955.

Balint, Alice, & Balint, M. On the transference and countertransference. *Int. J. Psychoanal.,* 1939, **20,** 223–230.

Balint, M. The final goal of psycho-analytic treatment. *Int. J. Psychoanal.,* 1936, **17,** 206–216.

Balint, M. On the psychoanalytic training system. *Int. J. Psychoanal.,* 1948, **29,** 163–173.

Balint, M. On the termination of analysis. *Int. J. Psychoanal.,* 1950, **31,** 196–199.

Balint, M. Analytic training and training analysis. *Int. J. Psychoanal.,* 1954, **35,** 157–162.

Barchilon, J. On countertransference "cures." *J. Amer. psychoanal. Ass.,* 1958, **6,** 222–236.

Benedek, Therese. Dynamics of the countertransference. *Bull. Menninger Clin.,* 1953, **17,** 201–208.

Benedek, Therese. Countertransference in the training analyst. *Bull. Menninger Clin.,* 1954, **18,** 12–16.

Benedek, Therese. A contribution to the problem of termination of training analysis. *J. Amer. psychoanal. Ass.*, 1955, **3**, 615–629.

Berman, L. Countertransferences and attitudes of the analyst in the therapeutic process. *Psychiatry*, 1949, **12**, 159–166.

Bernstein, A. On the nature of psychotherapy. *Doubleday Papers Psychol.*, 1954, No. 12.

Bernstein, A. Transference problems among psychoanalysts. *Psychoanal. psychoanal. Rev.*, 1958, **45** (3), 86–91.

Bibring, Grete L. The training analysis and its place in psycho-analytic training. *Int. J. Psychoanal.*, 1954, **35**, 169–173.

Breuer, J., & Freud, S. *Studies on hysteria* (1895). New York: Basic Books, 1957.

Bridger, H. Criteria for the termination of analysis. *Int. J. Psychoanal.*, 1950, **31**, 202–203.

Burchard, E. M. L. The evolution of psychoanalytic tasks and goals. *Psychiatry*, 1958, **21**, 341–357.

Buxbaum, Edith. Technique of terminating analysis. *Int. J. Psychoanal.*, 1950, **31**, 184–190.

Bychowski, G. *Psychotherapy of psychosis.* New York: Grune & Stratton, 1952.

Bychowski, G. On the handling of some schizophrenic defense mechanisms. *Int. J. Psychoanal.*, 1954, **35**, 147–153.

Cohen, Mabel B. Countertransference and anxiety. *Psychiatry*, 1952, **15**, 231–243.

Coleman, J. V. Banter as psychotherapeutic intervention. *Amer. J. Psychoanal.*, 1962, **22**, 69–74.

Coleman, Marie L., & Nelson, B. Paradigmatic psychoanalysis in borderline treatment. *Psychoanalysis*, 1957, **5**, 28–44.

Devereux, G. Some criteria for the timing of confrontations and interpretations. *Int. J. Psychoanal.*, 1951, **32**, 19–24.

Eissler, K. R. The effect of the structure of the ego on psychoanalytic technique. *J. Amer. psychoanal. Ass.*, 1953, **1**, 104–143.

Eissler, K. R. Notes upon defects of ego structure in schizophrenia. *Int. J. Psychoanal.*, 1954, **35**, 141–146.

Ekstein, R. Termination of the training analysis within the framework of present-day institutes. *J. Amer. psychoanal. Ass.*, 1955, **3**, 600–613.

Federn, P. Psychoanalysis of psychoses (1943). In *Ego psychology and the psychoses.* New York: Basic Books, 1952. Pp. 117–165.

Federn, P. *Ego psychology and the psychoses.* (E. Weiss, Ed.) New York: Basic Books, 1952.

Fenichel, O. *Problems of psychoanalytic technique.* Albany, N.Y.: Psychoanalytic Quarterly Press, 1941.

Fenichel, O. Neurotic acting out. *Psychoanal. Rev.*, 1945, **32**, 197–206. (a)

Fenichel, O. *The psychoanalytic theory of neurosis.* New York: Norton, 1945. (b)

Ferenczi, S. Suggestion and psychoanalysis (1912). In *Further contributions to the theory and technique of psycho-analysis.* London: Hogarth Press, 1950. Pp. 55–68.

Ferenczi, S. On falling asleep during analysis (1914). In *ibid.* Pp. 249–250.

Ferenczi, S. On the technique of psychoanalysis (1919). In *ibid.* Pp. 177–197.

Ferenczi, S. The further development of an active therapy in psycho-analysis (1920). In *ibid.* Pp. 198–217.

Ferenczi, S. Contra-indications to the "active" psycho-analytical technique (1925). In *ibid.* Pp. 217–232.

Ferenczi, S. Child analysis in the analysis of adults. *Int. J. Psychoanal.*, 1931, **12**, 468–482.

Fingert, H. H. Comments on the psychoanalytic significance of the fee. *Bull. Menninger Clin.*, 1952, **16**, 98–104.

French, T. M. The transference phenomenon (1946). In F. Alexander & T. M. French, *Psychoanalytic therapy.* New York: Ronald, 1946. Pp. 71–95.

Freud, Anna. *The psycho-analytical treatment of children* (1926). New York: International Universities Press, 1946.

Freud, S. *The interpretation of dreams* (1900). New York: Basic Books, 1955.

Freud, S. Freud's psychoanalytic method (1904). In *Collected papers.* Vol. 1. London: Hogarth Press, 1924. Pp. 264–271. (a)

Freud, S. On psychotherapy (1904). In *ibid.* Pp. 249–263. (b)

Freud, S. *Three essays on the theory of sexuality* (1905). New York: Basic Books, 1962.

Freud, S. Analysis of a phobia in a five-year-old boy (1909). In *Collected papers.* Vol. 3. London: Hogarth Press, 1925. Pp. 149–289.

Freud, S. The future prospects of psychoanalytic therapy (1910). In *ibid.* Vol. 2. 1924. Pp. 285–296.

Freud, S. The dynamics of the transference (1912). In *ibid.* Pp. 312–322. (a)

Freud, S. The employment of dream-interpretations in psycho-analysis (1912). In *ibid.* Pp. 305–311. (b)

Freud, S. Recommendations for physicians on the psychoanalytic method of treatment (1912). In *ibid.* Pp. 323–333. (c)

Freud, S. Further recommendations in the technique of psycho-analysis. On beginning the treatment. The question of the first communication. The dynamics of the cure (1913). In *ibid.* Pp. 342–365.

Freud, S. Further recommendations in the technique of psycho-analysis: recollection, repetition, and working through (1914). In *ibid.* Pp. 366–376.

Freud, S. Further recommendations in the technique of psycho-analysis: observations on transference love (1915). In *ibid.* Pp. 377–391.

Freud, S. Turnings in the ways of psychoanalytic therapy (1919). In *ibid.* Pp. 392–402.

Freud, S. *A general introduction to psychoanalysis* (1920). New York: Garden City, 1938.

Freud, S. *Inhibitions, symptoms and anxiety* (1926). London: Hogarth Press, 1949.

Freud, S. *The question of lay analysis* (1927). New York: Norton, 1950.

Freud, S. Analysis terminable and interminable (1937). In *Collected papers.* Vol. 5. London: Hogarth Press, 1950. Pp. 316–357. (a)

Freud, S. Constructions in analysis (1937). In *ibid.* Pp. 358–371. (b)

Freud, S. *An outline of psychoanalysis.* New York: Norton, 1940.

Fromm-Reichmann, Frieda. Personal and professional requirements of a psychotherapist. *Psychiatry,* 1949, **12,** 361–378.

Fromm-Reichmann, Frieda. *Principles of intensive psychotherapy.* Chicago: Univer. of Chicago Press, 1950.

Fromm-Reichmann, Frieda. *Psychoanalysis and psychotherapy.* (D. M. Bullard, Ed.) Chicago: Univer. of Chicago Press, 1959.

Gitelson, M. Problems of psychoanalytic training. *Psychoanal. Quart.,* 1948, **17,** 198–211.

Gitelson, M. Therapeutic problems in the analysis of the "normal" candidate. *Int. J. Psychoanal.,* 1954, **35,** 174–183.

Glover, E. The therapeutic effect of inexact interpretation. *Int. J. Psychoanal.,* 1931, **12,** 397–413.

Glover, E. Therapeutic results of psychoanalysis. *Int. J. Psychoanal.,* 1937, **18,** 125–132.

Glover, E. *Psychoanalysis.* (2nd ed.) London: Staples, 1949.

Goldstein, A. P. *Therapist-patient expectancies in psychotherapy.* New York: Macmillan, 1962.

Greenacre, Phyllis. General problems of acting out. *Psychoanal. Quart.,* 1950, **19,** 455–467.

Greenacre, Phyllis. The role of transference. *J. Amer. psychoanal. Ass.,* 1954, **2,** 671–684.

Grotjahn, M. About the relation between psychoanalytic training and psycho-analytic therapy. *Int. J. Psychoanal.,* 1954, **35,** 254–262.

Grotjahn, M. Problems and techniques of supervision. *Psychiatry,* 1955, **18,** 9–15.

Hartmann, H. Technical implications of ego psychology. *Psychoanal. Quart.,* 1951, **20,** 31–43.

Heiman, Paula. On countertransference. *Int. J. Psychoanal.,* 1950, **31,** 81–84.

Heiman, Paula. Problems of the training analysis. *Int. J. Psychoanal.,* 1954, **35,** 163–168.

Hendrick, I. *Facts and theories of psychoanalysis.* New York: Knopf, 1950.

Hoffer, W. Three psychological criteria for the termination of treatment. *Int. J. Psychoanal.,* 1950, **31,** 194–195.

Jones, E. Psychoanalysis and psychotherapy (1909). In *Papers on psychoanalysis.* London: Baillière, 1918. Pp. 271–280.

Jones, E., et al. Discussion on lay analysis. *Int. J. Psychoanal.,* 1927, **8,** 174–283.

Kesten, J. Learning for spite. *Psychoanalysis,* 1957, **4** (1), 63–67.

Klein, Melanie. *The psychoanalysis of children.* London: Hogarth Press, 1932.

Klein, Melanie. On the criteria for the termination of an analysis. *Int. J. Psychoanal.,* 1950, **31,** 204.

Knight, R. The evaluation of the results of psychoanalytic therapy. *Amer. J. Psychiat.,* 1941, **98,** 434–446.

Kovacs, Vilma. Training and control-analysis. *Int. J. Psychoanal.,* 1936, **17,** 346–354.

Kris, E. Ego psychology and interpretation in psychoanalytic therapy. *Psychoanal. Quart.,* 1951, **20,** 15–30.

Lagache, D. Some aspects of transference. *Int. J. Psychoanal.*, 1953, **34**, 1–10.

Lennard, H. L., & Bernstein, A. *Anatomy of psychotherapy.* New York: Columbia Univer. Press, 1960.

Little, Margaret. Countertransference and the patient's response to it. *Int. J. Psychoanal.*, 1951, **32**, 32–40.

Macalpine, Ida. The development of the transference. *Psychoanal. Quart.*, 1950, **19**, 501–539.

Menninger, K. *Theory of psychoanalytic technique.* New York: Basic Books, 1958.

Munroe, Ruth. *Schools of psychoanalytic thought.* New York: Basic Books, 1955.

Nacht, S. The difficulties of didactic psycho-analysis in relation to therapeutic psycho-analysis. *Int. J. Psychoanal.*, 1954, **35**, 250–253.

Nelson, Marie C. The effect of paradigmatic techniques on the psychic economy of borderline patients. *Psychiatry,* 1962, **25**, 119–134. (a)

Nelson, Marie C. Role induction: a factor in psychoanalytic therapy. In *Paradigmatic approaches to psychoanalysis: four papers.* New York: Psychology Department, Stuyvesant Polyclinic, 1962. Pp. 51–62. (b)

Nielsen, N. The dynamics of training analysis. *Int. J. Psychoanal.*, 1954, **35**, 247–249.

Nunberg, H. Evaluation of the results of psychoanalytic treatment. *Int. J. Psychoanal.*, 1954, **35**, 2–7.

Oberndorf, C. D. Consideration of results with psychoanalytic therapy. *Amer. J. Psychiat.*, 1942, **99**, 374–381.

Oberndorf, C. D., Greenacre, P., & Kubie, L. Symposium on the evaluation of therapeutic results. *Int. J. Psychoanal.*, 1948, **29**, 7–33.

Paul, L. (Ed.) *Psychoanalytic clinical interpretation.* New York: Free Press, 1963.

Racker, H. The meanings and uses of countertransference. *Psychoanal. Quart.*, 1957, **26**, 303–357.

Reich, Annie. On the termination of analysis. *Int. J. Psychoanal.*, 1950, **31**, 179–183.

Reich, Annie. On countertransference. *Int. J. Psychoanal.*, 1951, **32**, 25–31.

Reich, W. *Character-analysis* (1933). (3rd ed.) New York: Orgone Institute Press, 1949.

Reik, T. *Listening with the third ear.* New York: Farrar, Straus, 1948.

Rickman, J. On the criteria for the termination of an analysis. *Int. J. Psychoanal.*, 1950, **31**, 200–201.

Rosen, J. H. The survival function of schizophrenia. *Bull. Menninger Clin.*, 1950, **14**, 81–91.

Rosen, J. *Direct analysis.* New York: Grune & Stratton, 1953.

Searles, H. F. The informational value of the supervisor's emotional experiences. *Psychiatry,* 1955, **18**, 135–146.

Sherman, M. Siding with the resistance in paradigmatic psychotherapy. *Psychoanal. psychoanal. Rev.*, 1961, **48** (4), 43–59.

Silverberg, W. V. The concept of transference. *Psychoanal. Quart.*, 1948, **17**, 303–321.

Spitz, R. Countertransference: comments on its varying role in the analytic situation. *J. Amer. psychoanal. Ass.*, 1956, **4**, 256–265.

Spotnitz, H. The narcissistic defense in schizophrenia. *Psychoanal. psychoanal. Rev.*, 1961, **48** (4), 24–42.

Spotnitz, H. The need for insulation in the schizophrenic personality. *Psychoanal. psychoanal. Rev.*, 1962, **49** (3), 3–25.

Spotnitz, H. The toxoid response. In *Insulation and immunization in schizophrenia.* New York: Psychology Department, Stuyvesant Polyclinic, 1963. Pp. 26–39.

Spotnitz, H., & Nagelberg, L. A pre-analytic technique for resolving the narcissistic defense. *Psychiatry,* 1960, **23**, 193–197.

Sterba, R. Character and resistance. *Psychoanal. Quart.*, 1951, **20**, 72–76.

Strachey, J. The nature of the therapeutic action of psycho-analysis. *Int. J. Psychoanal.*, 1934, **15**, 127–159.

Strean, H. S. The use of the patient as consultant. *Psychoanal. psychoanal. Rev.*, 1959, **46** (2), 36–44.

Sullivan, H. S. The modified psychoanalytic treatment of schizophrenia. *Amer. J. Psychiat.*, 1931, **11** (3), 519–540.

Szasz, T. S. Three problems in contemporary psychoanalytic training. *Arch. gen. Psychiat.*, 1960, **3**, 82–94.

Tauber, E. S. Observations on countertransference phenomena. *Samiksa,* 1952, **6**, 220–228.

Thompson, Clara. Countertransference and love. *Samiksa,* 1952, **6**, 205–211.

Tower, Lucia E. Countertransference. *J. Amer. psychoanal. Ass.*, 1956, **4**, 224–255.

Weigert, Edith. Contribution to the problem of terminating psychoanalysis. *Psychoanal. Quart.*, 1952, **21**, 465–480.

Weigert, Edith. Special problems in connection with termination of training analyses. *J. Amer. psychoanal. Ass.*, 1955, **3**, 630–640.

Windholz, E. Problems of termination of the training analysis. *J. Amer. psychoanal. Ass.*, 1955, **3**, 641–650.

Winnicott, D. W. Hate in countertransference. *Int. J. Psychoanal.*, 1949, **30**, 69–74.

Wolman, B. B. Explorations in latent schizophrenia. *Amer. J. Psychother.*, 1957, **11**, 560–588.

Wolman, B. B. Psychotherapy with latent schizophrenics. *Amer. J. Psychother.*, 1959, **13**, 343–359.

Wolman, B. B. Fathers of schizophrenic patients. *Acta Psychother.*, 1961, **9**, 193–210.

Wolman, B. B. *Vectoriasis praecox or the group of schizophrenias*. 1965.

42

Non-Freudian Analytic Methods

EMANUEL K. SCHWARTZ

There is a current tendency to use loosely such terms as "psychoanalysis," "analytic treatment," and "analyst." Freudian, neo-Freudian, non-Freudian, Sullivanian, Horneyan, Rankian, Adlerian, existential, Jungian, Zen Buddhist, Buberian, culturalist, and Marxist are descriptive words that practitioners have been using quite irresponsibly. It was Freud's position that at least three factors were central to psychoanalysis: (1) recollection, repression, and resistance; (2) infantile experiences, including infantile sexuality; and (3) unconscious processes, to be understood through the interpretation of dreams, the psychopathological manifestations in everyday life, and so on (Freud, 1949). Although many followers of Horney, for example, have accepted the idea that if one analyzes dreams and transference then one is an analyst, in general the non-Freudians, except perhaps the Jungians, tend to reject the significance of unconscious processes. The question may be raised whether they need be considered analytic schools. In his interesting schematic overview of the history of psychotherapy, Lewis sees the analytic psychology of Jung and the individual psychology of Adler as the only non-Freudian derivatives. The interpersonal psychiatry of Horney, Sullivan, Robbins, Fromm-Reichmann, Thompson, Fromm, and others and the group therapies he sees as parallel developments from psychodynamics (Lewis, 1958, p. 24). The use of the term "psychoanalysis" by all schools of psychotherapy, without systematic orientation concerning the originations of psychoanalytic psychology, is complicating. The high prestige value of the title "psychoanalyst" represents a force for resisting a clarification of present confusions and a breakthrough to improved treatment of patients. But such is the situation.

What is offered here are some generalizations regarding variations in emphasis in techniques of treatment utilized by non-Freudian, that is, nonorthodox, analysts. The central question, "What helps the patient get well?" has still not been answered except in the broadest and most theoretical terms. What is clearly a factor in all methods is to decide where to put the emphasis in the treatment process and outcome. To this end, the patient must be known through and through; he must be thoroughly understood. The primary tools of the analyst are discrimination and selectivity. These are the backbone and mainstay of psychoanalytic procedure. By exquisitely discriminating what is central from what is peripheral, the analyst attempts to undermine the psychodynamic structure of the current adaptation to provide for the possibility of change in a healthier direction (Wolf & Schwartz, 1958–1959). It is largely in the area of what is considered important in life and in treatment that the separation between the Freudian and the non-Freudian analysts can best be seen.

Therapy is tailor-made. How to treat a patient cannot be learned from a book and requires flexibility and ingenuity. In a sense it is a continuous creation that has a quality of uniqueness with each patient. This does not mean that one cannot learn or that one has to rediscover the clinical and theoretical formulations and conceptualizations which have been derived before. Moreover, separation of theory and practice and divergence between theory and practices further complicate our problem. A welter of human data is presented to the analyst. What he chooses to investigate or to modify, to reinforce positively or negatively, identifies his approach to the treatment of the emotionally disturbed person.

Despite the inherent pitfalls, some generalization cannot be avoided. The more classical form of Freudian therapy is characterized by rigidity in the selection of patients, in the structure of the therapeutic situation, and in the setting of goals and the methods for accomplishing these. It stresses the historical, individual developmental originations of current adaptation. It sponsors the remembering of early infantile experiences, including sexual ones, and recognizes the establishment of patterns of behavior based upon the earliest periods of life. The genetic approach to understanding present modes of behavior requires that great attention be paid to the intrapsychic, especially unconscious, mental processes and that in therapy there be an attempt to bring them into consciousness. The manifest is continuously explored for its latent meaning through the processes of free association, dreams, and feeling.

The analysis of resistance and the overcoming of it are two of the main activities in analytic treatment. Changes are brought about through awareness of motivation and multiply determined causation in the present. Reuniting intellectual insight and deep feelings leads to a meaningful basis for coping with repetitive patterns of impulse and compulsion and to a commitment to reality rather than illusion as the basis for behavior. Sex and aggression are seen as primary forces, and activity in either is seen as acting out, as resistance to analysis. Transference, regression, and the transference neurosis represent the matrix for treatment. Interpretation is a primary technical intervention. Working through is the repetitive confrontation of more appropriate alternatives based upon conscious understanding and an awareness of feelings.

The non-Freudians tend to utilize the experiential rather than the historical and stress experiencing in the here and now in treatment as well as in life. Interpersonal transactions become the major focus of therapy, with an exploration of conscious mental processes, long-range attitudes, and value systems. The manifest content is accepted as the basis for work, and the less aware is brought into greater awareness. Less attention is paid to dreams and unconscious mental processes. Rather than resistance being worked with continuously, the cooperative enterprise of patient and therapist becomes the arena of struggle. Stress is laid upon the awareness of consequences of current behavior. Sexuality is seen as an aspect of generalized attitudes with regard to the human situation. The importance of acting out is rejected, and emphasis is placed upon acting of every form. Activity becomes a way of changing modes of thinking, feeling, and doing. The process is one of reconditioning the behavioral patterns through an unlearning of old patterns and new learning. This approach is characteristic of many adherents of Horney, Sullivan, Adler, Fromm, and Rank.

Jungian analysts, along with the followers of Ferenczi and to some extent also the existential and the cultural therapists, tend to pursue a philosophical, phenomenological approach. The culturalists are sociohistorically oriented; they recognize the importance of resistance to understanding the less aware, but they utilize education, that is, activating by providing an experience of striving for greater meaning in life. The Jungians place more value on the deeply historical and the deeply unconscious, and they stress the importance of deep-level drives in current individual behavior. The existentialists are more phenomenological and similarly use inspiration and reeducation rather than interpretation as the premise for change.

TECHNICAL ASPECTS

It is difficult to describe the techniques of psychotherapy used by any one therapist belonging to a particular school. It is even more difficult to know the similarities and differences in actual treatment methods of two therapists from two different schools of thought. These difficulties are in part due to the fact that theory and practice are often not in harmony, but in part they are due also to the fact that detailed reports of what actually transpires in the interaction between therapist and patient are rare. Most of the arguments in the field revolve more about issues of theory, approaches, and values than techniques. It is not unusual that in discussing methods of treatment there is some spillover into questions of theory. This discussion, then, reflects my personal understanding and evaluation of some of the similarities and differences in methods of treating patients by nonclassical analytic methods.

Psychoanalysis, for most, represents a theory, a method of treatment, and a method of research. There are some analysts who go so far as to say that the method of investigation is the method of cure, that the research technique and the treatment technique are one and the same.

For me, psychoanalysis is a way of understanding human behavior. It is a psychology. The psychoanalyst, therefore, is committed to a way of understanding human nature and the techniques of treating a specific personality. The course of a therapeutic exchange will vary from patient to patient, but the commitment of the therapist to analytic psychology will provide the primary modes for viewing and modifying the interaction.

Freudian methods are largely identified with classical psychoanalysis. Sometimes it is called "orthodox" analysis, which is a contradiction in terms. A primary objective of analysis is increased degrees of freedom; an attitude of freedom pervades the analytic relationship, and the goal is greater freedom from impulse and compulsion. Orthodoxy and psychoanalysis seem mutually exclusive, whether fostered by a Freudian or a non-Freudian.

For these and other reasons I prefer to deal with variations in analytic methods along topical lines rather than by personalities. The usual approach is to see how one Titan differed from the other; for example, "Freud or Jung?" This has not proved very fruitful. I am therefore going to deal with central themes of therapeutic practice and shall try to indicate some of the nonclassical modifications affecting these areas.

THE ANALYTIC SETTING

The traditional use of the couch and the air of privacy and anonymity have been changed considerably. Face-to-face therapy becomes commonplace as the focus shifts from the intrapsychic life of the patient and as more emphasis is put upon the encounter between therapist and patient. No longer is the neurotic patient the only one for whom analysis is available.

The tradition of analytic sessions nearly every day is no longer followed. Fromm-Reichmann strongly recommends seeing patients less frequently (1950). Some therapists still differentiate between everyday analysis and psychotherapy one, two, or three times a week, regardless of who the analyst is and what kind of work is being done with the patient.

The attitude of no communication between therapist and patient outside and sometimes inside the office and among patients and of very limited contact between the therapist and other members of the family has been altered considerably. A more realistic view of the therapist-patient relationship has contributed to some of these changes. The development of psychoanalysis in groups, the same therapist seeing more than one member of a family, and a beginning trend to treat an entire family as a group are significant new directions (Ackerman, 1958; Grotjahn, 1949; Lehrman, 1963; Wolf & Schwartz, 1962).

THE ANALYST, THE PATIENT, AND THE RELATIONSHIP

Great change has taken place in this area. All methods emphasize the analyst's potential as the therapeutic agent. The more traditional view that what transpires between analyst and patient is entirely unreal and symbolic is still held by classical analysts. "The relief from the *as if* problem lends approval to the acceptance of the relationship to the therapist as real. In analysis this would be unwelcome; in psychotherapy it might be most helpful" (Tarachow, 1963, p. 15). The nonorthodox no longer see the relationship as purely a one-directed, unilateral set of projections that need to be interpreted and analyzed, but rather as interpersonal transactions in which the appropriate and inappropriate feelings, thoughts, and actions of the therapist are as important as those of the patient in moving him forward to a resolution of his suffering. Horney stressed the bilateral nature of the analytic experience. "The ever-present question is: is what is going on now leading to self-awareness in bringing us closer to self-realization? . . . If the analyst is merely a catalytic agent and nothing has changed in him, how much really could have gone on within the patient" (Cantor, 1959, p. 31).

Rigid adherence to one kind of activity, as in the case of more traditional analysts, seems to result in a limited form of therapy for the many varieties of patients. The less orthodox therapist may play different roles with different patients. It has been suggested that because he is conscious of his activity, there is an absence of sincerity. This depends upon what the therapist is sincere about. He asserts that he plays roles in order to test the patient's reactions and to give him a chance to experience himself. In place of mere reflection, for example, Reich (Munroe, 1955) suggests playing the role of mother or father as the analyst thinks they were for the patient. Alexander warns, of course, against playacting in providing the corrective emotional experience (1961, p. 266).

There is a continuum in self-concept, of therapist role, which may be charted. At one extreme is the therapist who insists that he must be himself under any and all circumstances and that in this way, through his own sincerity, he promotes sincerity and trust in the patient (May, Angel, & Ellenberger, 1958; Wolf & Schwartz, 1958–1959).

There is the middle ground of the traditional analyst who is neutral. Neither is the therapist himself in the sense that he satisfies his own needs or expresses himself, nor does he play a particular role. His function is to be objective, as nonreactive as possible, without providing reality to the patient that he might latch onto in rationalizing his projections (Grinberg, 1962; Tarachow, 1963). There is an apparent humility on the part of Freudians who indicate that the role of the analyst is one of such neutrality that it is quite secondary. It has been suggested that it is possible to conduct an entire analysis without the analyst uttering a single word.

On the other end of the continuum are those who insist that the therapist must play a role, for example, those who employ paradigmatic methods. Whatever the therapist does, he does as part of a consciously determined plan in order to provoke in the patient certain kinds of reactions. If the patient threatens to jump out of the window, such a therapist might say: "Why don't you jump out of the window?" (see "The Psychoanalytic Technique," above, Chapter 41).

In these three different positions, certain questions arise. In whose interests is the particular attitude of the therapist maintained? Is the therapist ostensibly neutral because he wishes to protect himself in his ignorance and impotence? If the therapist wants to be himself, is he doing this for narcissistic gratification of his own ego eccentricities? If the therapist plays a provocative role, is he doing this to vent his sadism upon the patient? Is it possible that these three positions or any variation along the continuum might be maintained in his honest effort to try to help the patient? It may very well be that a discriminating therapist might take any one of these positions with different patients or at different times with the same patient, depending upon the real needs of the patient. In this connection, it is always interesting that the validity of neutrality is so often denied by the successes of the tyro who in his zeal breaks all the rules of the game and yet manages somehow to effect significant changes in the patient (Schwartz, 1965; Schwartz & Wolf, 1964; Wolf & Schwartz, 1958–1959).

Horney rejects the "comparatively passive role the Freudian analysts play." She says: "The analyst should deliberately conduct the analysis" (1939, p. 286). "The quest for happiness becomes one of the foremost forces in the patient to be sponsored." Like Rank (Munroe, 1955), she believes in the mobilization of willpower, that one should bring "certain connections and motivations to the patient's awareness and thereby enable him to judge and to decide." Unlike Freud, she is committed to the analyst's position with regard to "moral problems and value judgments" (1939, pp. 296ff.). Like most analysts, Horney accepts the general position that fear is the underlying corrosive force in the development of all forms of emotional disturbance and that the problem always revolves around how best to help the patient overcome his fear, whether it is called "anxiety," "phobia," "conflict," "tension," or any other name.

It is in the treatment situation that an emotional security is accomplished by the patient in the relationship with his analyst. This facilitates not only regressive but also progressive processes, which in any method must be the ultimate outcome of treatment. Regression is fostered by the nature of the therapeutic relationship, and all schools have an attitude toward it. Some encourage it as far as developing a transference neurosis, and others tend to discourage it, but the relationship and its regressive aspects constitute part of any therapy. The regression must be reversed at the point of working through so that the progressive processes in the patient take precedence. This can be crucially determinative in the therapeutic outcome.

Current non-Freudian techniques seem to be based upon a set of assertions. A corrective emotional experience is all that is necessary. The significant figures of the past are of no importance at the present moment. The new experience with the therapist makes the patient a coparticipant; each becomes more of an object to the other. The present mental contents of the patient are the matrix for the therapeutic transaction. Insight is relatively unimportant. There is a kind of unconscious-to-unconscious sensitivity, a reading in the eyes of the other, such as described by Sullivan (1953), which represents the essential breakthrough in changed behavior.

Again and again, non-Freudian analysts stress the importance of the person of the therapist and how necessary it is that he be experienced by the patient as a real and worthwhile human being and that both contribute to, and participate in, successful treatment. The more orthodox, however, still see the analyst's entrance into the relationship largely in terms of countertransference (Grinberg, 1962).

In the Horney approach, "it is through the analyst's faith and confidence in his patient's constructiveness, predicated on a belief in his own constructiveness, that the patient may begin to feel more hopeful about himself." It is "the total acceptance and mobilizing the constructive" which moves the patient to change (Wassell, 1955, p. 28).

For Ferenczi, the essential characteristics of the analyst are "clear understanding of oneself, depth of feeling and human kindness, humility, high imagination, great patience and endurance, fearlessness, a capability to learn and ability to teach by example rather than by precept" (de Forest, 1954). Small wonder a patient was led to describe his analytic experience with Ferenczi as "redemption by love" (de Forest, 1954, p. 179).

On the basis of experimental work, Strupp hypothesizes that the

> staggering task [of psychoanalytic treatment] cannot be accomplished unless the patient is deeply convinced that the analyst is a reliable partner in the enterprise, and that his attitude encompasses uncompromising personal integrity, dedication, honesty, and faith in the fruitfulness of the task in whose name sacrifices are demanded (1960, p. 31).

Recognition of the importance of the joint fantasy encompassing the therapeutic experience and of the need for the therapist's consciousness of it is reflected in the work of Frank: "The finding that all types of psychotherapy obtain roughly equal improvement rates accords with the likelihood that the patient's state of trust or faith may be more responsible for his improvement than the specific nature of the object of his trust" (1958, p. 38). Moreover, he also suggests that the skill in fostering and utilizing such attitudes may play a larger role in the success of psychotherapy than specific theory or technique. At best, then, the therapist continuously "accommodates his and the patient's expectancies to each other as their relationship develops" (Frank, 1958, p. 41).

The growing awareness on the part of nonclassical analysts of the reality aspects of the therapeutic experience is exemplified by Wolberg, when he points out the inevitable intrusion of intercurrent factors too often treated with neglect, inattention, or denial, to the detriment of the treatment result:

> Adventitious elements enter into all psychotherapies, influencing the process for the good or bad. These elements may enhance or neutralize the activities of the therapist, bringing progress to a halt or expediting it beyond reasonable expectancy. . . . It is doubtful if the therapist can avoid these contaminations; he must instead accept them as inevitable. His skill is related to the advantage he takes of their positive virtues, while reducing the negative influences they may wield (1963, p. 18).

PASSIVITY AND ACTIVITY

One of the key parameters of traditional psychoanalytic treatment is passivity. The entire procedure is dedicated to ensure the passivity of both the analyst and the patient in an atmosphere of quiet isolation. The passivity, however, is not for its own sake but is rationalized systematically in terms of certain understandings about the nature of the roles of analyst and patient.

For the *analyst*, passivity is indicated to accomplish a variety of objectives. It encourages the analyst to listen, to wait, and to see; not to jump at conclusions; and not to be seduced by the manifest content of the patient's communications. It provides him with support for maintaining distance and stresses his objectivity and his interest in discriminating selection of appropriate interventions, the most important of which is interpretation (Alexander, 1961; Freud, 1949; Munroe, 1955). Interpretation is the creative reintegration of the developmental data of the patient's life. It is dedicated to providing insight, that is, a new way of seeing the connection between one series of events and another, between the past and the present, and between conscious and unconscious processes.

Moreover, passivity for the analyst fosters one of the primary qualities of a psychoanalytic relationship, namely, the transference neurosis. The transference neurosis is a major short-range objective and becomes the tool and matrix for change in the patient. It is best accomplished, in the traditional sense, if the analyst does not become an object for the patient. The assumption is that the less real the relationship between analyst and patient, the more *as if* it becomes. The transference neurosis is the acme of the *as if* or symbolic relationship in which symbiotic and infantile attitudes are reexperienced with the analyst. So that the analyst does not become an object, he must remain as passive as possible; he must be inactive and not make a move. The therapist's directive to the patient is: "Know thyself, not me!" It is as if Freud had taken inspiration from Goethe's *Faust*. Faust invokes the earth spirit in order to have access to its power but is rejected by it with the words: "You are like the spirit you understand, not me!" If the analyst permits the patient to know him and becomes object, the difference between reality and illusion is obscured, and they fail in achieving the analytic goal: "Where id is, there let ego be!"

As already indicated, Tarachow (1963) presents the Freudian viewpoint that to the extent that the analyst becomes an object for the patient, treatment is not psychoanalytic. Since it is patently impossible for the patient to remain totally oblivious, totally unaware, and totally unknowing of any reality concerning the analyst, it is futile to hope to attempt ever to achieve such an idealized model for treatment. Analysis in this sense may never occur, may never be experienced. If the analyst utters a single word, he may be thought of as giving up his commitment to psychoanalysis. Yet most non-Freudians of all persuasions, starting with Adler, introduce a large reality factor and stress the educational activity of the therapist.

Freud recognized this dilemma, the contradiction between the ideal and the real, the hoped-for model and the treatment necessity. At one point he suggests that the analyst must never gratify in the least the transference demand of the patient. At another point he says that, of course, this is only a matter of more or less (Freud, 1949; Robbins, 1956b). Nonclassical analysts recognize the reality of the impossibility of accomplishing psychoanalysis in the ideal sense. They seek consciously to modify their relationship to the patient and to utilize the degree and quality of becoming object to the patient for therapy facilitation. Perhaps they have even rationalized this limitation by suggesting that becoming an object to the patient is not always therapy-impeding and that positive therapeutic outcomes may be accomplished with some patients at some time by becoming object to some extent in some specific way to some particular patient. The orally deprived patient, for example, may move forward in his therapy if the therapist offers him a cup of coffee.

For the *patient*, the passivity demanded by the classical analytic approach serves the purpose of giving him an opportunity to come to grips with his inner feelings; to go from object to subject, that is, to himself; to be trained to be introspective; to associate freely; and, most importantly, to stop acting. The assumption was that the neurotic in *all* his acts was acting out because he was neurotic. All his activity had to be frustrated. This led to the general directive to analytic patients that they make no major changes in life situations during the course of the analysis. If the activity of the patient in analysis is indeed acting out, how better to protect the patient from his destructive impulses than to tell him to stop acting, to be passive. It is obviously impossible to adhere to this model and may be inhuman if it were. For example, some early analysts experimented with forbidding patients to have sex during the period of treatment so as to increase frustration and feeling. Some contemporary therapists terminate analysis because the patient gets married or has a baby before the analyst thinks the patient is ready, which is just the time when the patient needs the analyst most.

So long as the patient is alive he will act; total passivity on his part is again unrealistic. To the extent that the patient acts, the analyst will need to be able to discriminate between which acts are acting out, that is, on transference and in resistance, and which may be constructive efforts at living. This has led some non-Freudians to rationalize all activity of the patient as desirable, even to the extent that they have viewed acting out as nonpathological and always constructive (Wolf & Schwartz, 1958–1959). But the pendulum need not swing that far. Acting out is acting out. It is symptomatic and pathological, but it may serve a constructive purpose at this moment in this particular patient's life, such as the breaking of the repetition compulsion and the trying of a new, alternative human experience. Such a piece of acting out can be used constructively in therapy if it becomes subject for study, exploration, and investigation, and a new understanding is achieved by the patient. This is analytic therapy in its truest sense (Wolf & Schwartz, 1962).

> At this point, I would like to offer some opinions which differ from Freud's view of acting-out. In my opinion, the weakening of the neurotic's ego—leading to acting-out—can be attributed to the analyst's *success* in the analysis. Here I am disagreeing with Freud, who seems to maintain that acting-out is indicative of analytic failure. As I see it, one goal of a psychoanalyst, treating a neurotic, is to resolve the patient's resistances. This resolution of the resistance allows the patient's repressed wishes to emerge. When these repressions are lifted, what happens? Impulses and feelings emerge which were orginally directed toward the mother or father. The analyst, as the principal transference-figure during analysis, may become the target for these impulses and feelings as they emerge from repression. Or, some other person may become the target: for instance, the spouse, the siblings, or the patient's own children.
>
> Thus, in my view, acting-out by the patient indicates that the analyst is making progress. I do not share the view of some analysts, including Freud himself, that acting-out indicates an analytic failure. I think that it indicates an analytic success.
>
> I would like to qualify this opinion with some further comments. Hopefully, the analyst is not unprepared for acting-out behavior on the part of his patient. If the analyst knows what he is doing, it seems to me that he is able to judge when the analysis is getting "warm." Therefore, he anticipates that acting out is likely to occur and that it will present certain practical problems in treatment (Rosen, 1963a, p. 393).

Non-Freudian analysts, except perhaps Jung, reject regression and its implied passivity. It can be held that the more inactive the patient is, the closer he approaches death, but one does not need to die in treatment in order to be reborn. Reinforcing the patient's general inactivity may be encouraging isolation, apathy, alienation, and anomie. Horney (1939) rejects the magic of symbols and isolation in the passivity of illusion. Of course, many impulse-ridden patients act without thinking or feeling; the therapist will want to get them to inhibit acting so that time may be devoted to reflection and feeling and so that more appropriate activity may be selected. But there are also many patients who think and do not act, such as the obsessive, the passive character, and the depressed. For these, encouragement to activity may be a necessity.

The question arises whether the analyst needs to wait on insight to get his introspective patients to a point where they may act. Placing a premium on verbalizing rather than demonstrating may lead to talking about others who often are seen as intrapsychic figures without reality. Whether insight precedes activity is largely academic. The chances are that for certain kinds of patients under certain kinds of conditions, certain kinds of actions may precede certain kinds of insights, and certain kinds of insights may precede certain kinds of actions, each leading to the enrichment of the other.

In this connection, Alexander states:

> The corrective emotional experience of the transference alone may produce lasting therapeutic results. A purely intellectual understanding of the neurosis has seldom much therapeutic effect. On the other hand, intellectual insight based on and combined with emotional experiences stablizes emotional gains and paves the way for new emotional experiences. The ego's basic function is mastery of impulses through integration.

> This is the essence of the function we call understanding. Understanding gives the patient a feeling of mastery and this in turn encourages mobilization of repressed material which before could not be mastered by integration with the rest of the conscious personality (1961, p. 271).

The more classical analyst justifies his treatment model by restricting psychoanalysis to neurotic patients, that is, to more or less healthy patients who can tolerate a temporary state of frustration, inhibition, isolation, and passivity without it becoming a way of life for them. To the extent that a person has ego imperfection (and all do), to that degree the puristic approach will need consciously to be "contaminated by reality." The non-Freudians are not so exclusive in the choice of patients, and they treat the more severe neurotic, such as the obsessive, the character-disordered, and the varieties of psychotic patients. Sullivan, like Fromm-Reichmann, saw schizophrenia as a human process to be understood, participated in, and healed.

CONSCIOUS AND UNCONSCIOUS PROCESSES

The so-called "non-Freudians" deviate from the Freudian position in two directions. At one extreme are the Jungian and existential analysts and the followers of Ferenczi, who are more "spiritual." At the other extreme are the cultural analysts, including followers of Adler, Rank, Horney, Sullivan, and Fromm, who are more materialistic. But of all these, currently only the Jungians are committed to an exploration in treatment of the unconscious processes of the individual and his historical development, including a person's prehistory.

Jung may be seen as the originator of most of the inspirational movements in psychotherapy. His approach is quite systematic, with a tight personality theory as the basis for change through treatment. The existential analysts, for example, derive much of their general philosophical and humanistic values from him, but their stress upon phenomenology rather than unconscious processes leads them to a poorer psychology and less clear-cut procedures (Jung, 1933; May et al., 1958; Wolf & Schwartz, 1958–1959).

Jung's emphasis upon the intrapsychic led him to suggest "the possibility of a 'psychology with the psyche'—that is, of a field of study based upon the assumption of an autonomous psyche" (1933, p. 180). His preoccupation with the unconscious led him to the position that "Man's unconscious likewise contains all the patterns of life and behavior inherited from his ancestors, so that every human child, prior to consciousness, is possessed of a potential system of adapted psychic functioning" (1933, p. 184). The unconscious perceives, has purposes and intuitions, feels, and thinks as the conscious mind does. Jung claims that there is sufficient evidence for this from psychopathological or clinical experience as well as from the investigation of dream processes. Consciousness is transient, whereas unconscious processes are transcendental or eternal. Reality is not objective or external but rather internal. He says: "All immediate experience is psychic and . . . immediate reality can only be psychic . . ." (Jung, 1933, p. 191).

In analyzing a particular patient, Jung suggests: "His fundamental error lay in his moral attitude" (1933, p. 193). There is a need to understand the meaning and purpose of life and the spiritual nature of psychic life. The conflict to be worked through with the patient resides in his wish to avoid the spiritual source of his mental contents.

With regard to unconscious processes, Jung's position is atypical of the non-Freudians. Robbins represents the essential Horney line when he states: "We are concerned with the *entire* activity of the patient, and our first task is to try to understand *the nature of her outlook on life*, the kind of person she is, her 'conscious existence'" (1955, p. 15). Individual history and infantile experience are not of much importance.

Consciousness is the central problem of psychiatry, and the therapist's function is predominantly educational (Robbins, 1956a).

> "Our function as psychotherapists is not so much to correct their [patients'] ignorance as to alter their world outlook, to change their consciousness, to replace incorrect or distorted reflections with relatively accurate ones. It is not so much to make conscious that which is unconscious as to replace an irrational outlook with a more rational one. For us, cure is change in the direction of rational consciousness (Robbins, 1956c, p. 294).

For Adler, too, the unconscious was only the "not understood." His emphasis was on the social reality; on education or reeducation of the patient in new social values; on encouragement and responsibility with regard to violence and aggression; on the strengthening of consciously applied controls and values with regard to authority; and finally on the empathic involvement with other human beings ("Annals of Psychotherapy: What Is Psychotherapy?" 1959; Farau, 1962; Munroe, 1955). Education and inspiration are the usual techniques employed by the Adlerians, largely for the purpose of supporting the courage of the patient to take a chance in consciously acting in new directions more appropriate to the social and to his own personal reality. Encouraging the patient consciously to take a chance, to be active, to do, to try, to struggle is one of the central themes in Adlerian treatment. Only by consciously changing his life-style can the patient hope to achieve some sense of a fulfilled life. The therapist supports the patient through the conscious collaborative effort of treatment.

Where dreams are interpreted by the non-Freudians, it is often with regard to the actual life problems of the patient. Use of dream interpretation in avoiding such discussion is viewed as resistance. The manifest content of the dream is worked with, but latent content, personal symbols, and collective symbols are rejected, in the main (Schwartz, 1959). It is fortunate in some ways that most non-Freudians have not yet resolved for themselves in practice this split. On the one hand, they recognize and explore deep-level attitudes, recognizing that "Enough research has been done by social scientists to corroborate many of Freud's ideas about unconscious processes" (Haley, 1958, p. 190). On the other hand, the treatment process, as a consequence, is open to unclarity, inconsistency, and confusion.

REALITY AND EGO PSYCHOLOGY

In any analytic treatment approach, reality is a key factor. There are multiple realities, any one or all of which may be emphasized by different groups of therapists. The nonclassical analysts consider the interpersonal reality to be as important as the intrapsychic, and probably more important, and to include the relationship to the self as well as the relationship to others, the relationship to therapy and to the therapist. The social reality rather than the purely personal is explored. Ego psychology, then, with all its ramifications has been developing among Freudian and non-Freudian analysts. In working with ego psychology, more attention is paid to conscious processes, character structure, and values such as false pride, manipulativeness, competitiveness, and attitudes toward success, failure, money, and death (Farau, 1962; Horney, 1939; Munroe, 1955; Thompson, 1950). As a consequence, techniques are devoted to building ego strength and repressing rather than opening repression and freeing the impluses. This condition is related to the fact that in this culture at this time, therapists are not seeing the kinds of repressed patients seen by earlier analysts in Europe or in this country prior to World War II. Most American analysts, the non-Freudians more so, have been treating patients who are fragmented, acting with little control and little inhibition of sexual or aggessive impulses. For most of these, there is need to reestablish repressive forces. Most patients seem manifestly, at least, to have greater problems with aggression than with repressed sexual feelings. A much more central problem is the one of dependency, hostility, aggression, and violence as the vehicles for coping with authorities and peers. The popular novel and play as well as general clinical experience suggest that the activity of most patients requires the analysis of the linkage of sex and aggression which is so common today. It is insufficient to analyze merely the sexual aspects of a relationship; its aggressive aspects must also be analyzed. The reverse is also true, that the aggressive aspects are insufficiently analyzed if the sexual are not also understood (Wolf & Schwartz, 1962).

> Today, the important theoretical and practical interests of psychoanalysis and dynamic psychiatry are the genesis and function of the ego, the problem of anxiety, conflicts with aggressive and dependency needs and the defense mechanism, and not only what has been referred to as the older "Id psychology," largely preoccupied with the vicissitudes of the sex drive. We might add, however, to our observations that psychoanalysis and dynamic psychiatry are less likely to flourish in a culture which has less guilt over sex, aggression, and the dependency—either because behavior is freer and not under very severe controls, or because there has been a chance for better sublimation for individuals and groups (Redlich, 1958, p. 84).

The use of ego strengthening and ego supportive techniques often involves giving up the couch, the silence and the facelessness of the analyst, and the premium placed on introspection. As a consequence, there is less likelihood of deep regression and an attenuation of the transference neurosis, both of which are rejected by non-Freudians on theoretical and technical grounds.

As already indicated, isolation and anonymity are no longer as significant to the analytic interaction. The passivity engendered by the couch and free association are replaced in Rank, for example, by greater emphasis on ego attitudes, such as will and conscious action, and in Adler by training and courage. The more recent developers of analytic group therapy have followed their leads, to some extent, and have recognized that copatients urge efforts at new alternatives before insight is accomplished. The patient cannot withdraw into fantasy; he is called upon to be participant and interactive (Wolf & Schwartz, 1962).

Although reality and the ego are stressed and regression is minimized, there is a growing interest, especially among some nonclassical analysts, in early childhood experiences and in fantasies with regard to prenatal psychology (Klein, 1960; Monroe, 1955). The existentialists, following somewhat Jung and Klein, have moved the period of time in which the human condition is to be seen in both directions, intrauterine life and death. For them, these two factors begin to play a larger role in the understanding of human psychology. Their treatment, then, includes not only the examination of the here and now, the present encounter, and the current reality—the search for identity in the real world—but also the understanding of the meaning of the essential moment in terms of the earliest beginnings of life as well as the unique separation and change involved in death (May et al., 1958).

DEVELOPMENTAL FACTORS

Nonclassical analysts, like Freudians, recognize the importance of the childhood environment and age crises. The non-Freudian therapists explore the role of the family structure to understand a person's sexual and social development and seem to put greater stress on the significance of pregenital experiences. The role of the mother is investigated deeply (Klein, 1960), and the nursing situation is seen by some as the prototype of adult sexuality (Silverberg, 1952). There is fairly general acceptance that "the early maternal environment . . . [serves] to launch and guide the individual from earliest infancy through the entire span of life." This concept is "the key to our understanding and treatment" of the emotionally disturbed individual (Rosen, 1963b, p. 48). Such a slant coupled with a view that the family is the primary social and humanizing unit easily gives rise to the diagnosis and treatment of the family as a group (Ackerman, 1958).

In addition to the preoccupation with ego processes, as has already been indicated, there is greater emphasis on character structure than on psychodynamics and diagnosis. This seems to be connected to the temporal shift in contemporary technique from the past and future to the present. If the therapist need consider only the here and now, it is claimed, there is no need for genetic reconstruction. The totality is in the moment, and the moment is all. The pursuit of repetitive patterns or early recollections is viewed by such non-Freudian therapists as growth-impeding for the patient.

The classical analysts attempt in treatment to reconstruct the first six years of life. Unlike Klein, who is preoccupied with the preverbal, preoedipal period, they attend to later ego developments. Classical psychoanalysis requires the dissociation of the ego, in which "the analysand is called on 'to answer for himself' and the unconscious, ceasing to be expressed in behavior, becomes articulate in *words*" (Klein, 1960, p. 126). This emphasis upon verbalization seems to be in contrast to the non-Freudian position, with its stress on activity, including nonverbal forms of communication, and its varieties of manifestation. This may be connected to the early relationship to the mother and the preverbal factors involved, especially in the more seriously disturbed patients (Ferenczi, 1930; Klein, 1960; Sechehaye, 1957). On the other hand, Thompson feels that Freudians tend to emphasize nonverbal aspects more than non-Freudians (1950).

For the Adlerian, therapy is a learning process in which the intellectual processes responsible for growth, improvement, and change are brought into the open. It is a kind of training which does not neglect the emotions. The Adlerian analyst is interested somewhat in developmental concepts, in that the family constellation, which is the basis for developing a style of life, is reconstructed by early recollections. This recall, however, is directed toward the patient's understanding of his basic concepts and his basic errors (Farau, 1962; Munroe, 1955).

In understanding the developing personality, Sullivan selected the juvenile era, preadolescence, and adolescence as central. The importance of these age periods leads to the necessity of working out interpersonal anxiety through becoming comfortable in the man-to-man relationship of therapy. It is a means for changing the self-system; because one person draws so close to another, one is newly capable of seeing oneself through the other's eyes. The adolescent phase is especially significant in correcting autistic, fantastic ideas about oneself or others. Experiences at this time are the core of the development of serious mental disorders, and Sullivan almost alone pursues in treatment the investigation of this period (1953, pp. 247ff.). Change based on a reevaluation of the self in relation to others is similar to Horney's objective in reevaluating or altering the patient's idealized image of the self.

One of the important differences between Jung's work; that of the Freudians, who emphasize the first six years of life; and Sullivan's concentration on latency, puberty, and adolescence is that Jung emphasizes the middle and later years of life. This a sharp shift in focus. The self-image is not too remote from Jung's concept of the persona and is related to the problem of identity (a nuclear problem of modern analysts), the problem of "Who am I?" The persona is developmental and largely adaptive on the basis of actual experience. The Jungian self is in the main unconsciously determined by virtue of deep relationships to the symbols of mankind (Jung, 1933; Munroe, 1955).

Rankian analysts accent the understanding of a person's reaction to the birth trauma, which is close to the emphasis on the mother. Rank's work gave rise to many of the later speculations with regard to the role of separation anxiety in the development of the individual and the concepts of the fear of life and the fear of death, which have been further developed by the existential analysts. For the Rankian analyst, the problem of the will is the core issue in treatment, namely, invoking the cooperation or the will of the patient in dealing with his fear and consequent hostility to treatment. The cooperative enterprise seeks to explore how the person functions in terms of an enlarged social reality. The patient is helped to discover why he wants to live his life or the purpose of his existence ("Annals of Psychotherapy: What Is Psychotherapy?" 1959; Munroe, 1955). This is close to some of the philosophical underpinnings of the existential therapists.

ENVIRONMENT, SOCIETY, AND CULTURE

Although psychoanalysis had its origins in Central Europe via Freud, modified psychoanalytic therapies have had their greatest development in the United States, where the ethos is quite different. The United States, with its frontiers, its democracy, its "do-it-yourselfism," and its emphasis on the activity of people, may have created forces against the overevaluation of passivity in the analytic relationship. The non-Freudian emphasis upon the importance of the other persons in one's life, whether these are the analyst, the members of the extended family, or those in the community or the culture, may also be derived, in part, from the American concern with social realities.

Horney developed her deviation and was supported in her rebellion against conformism in the United States. There is greater recognition here that other persons, in addition to the patient, are important in the cause of mental illness and its perpetuation and in the promoting of mental health. The significance of prevailing attitudes in the culture and the role of society was given impetus by Adler, but their formulation as a systematic approach to the cause and treatment of mental health appeared on the American scene. Burrow (1949), who insisted that constructive behavioral modifications are brought about only on the socioindividual level, and Sullivan are native examples. In this context, the unprecedented expansion of group methods needs to be mentioned (Ackerman, 1958; Grotjahn, 1960; Wolf & Schwartz, 1962).

In another and somewhat paradoxical sense, social forces in the United States may also have contributed to the development of non-Freudian analytic procedures. The regard in the United States for the individual, individual differences, and human diversity compels sensitive, seeking psychoanalysts to break away from rigidity and to develop more flexible means of treatment. The oversimplified reductionistic systems of orthodoxy seem unacceptable to the American spirit. To treat all individuals and even all groups of individuals in exactly the same way, with the same techniques, is to deny the reality of individual differences and to create a new illusion rather than to cleave to reality. For some of the Freudian analysts, psychoanalytic concepts and principles do not allow modification in techniques.

Exclusive treatment of a selected group of patients, the neurotics, was also bound to be broadened to include other groups of persons who might benefit from appropriately adapted techniques. Jones saw the American recognition of the necessity for care of the psychotic as well as the neurotic patient as representing an essential unity:

> The problems of social adaptation, or maladaptation, will therefore always stand in the foreground of his attention. It would be tempting to inquire how this broad conception of psychiatry came to be developed only in America. . . . It appears, in fact, to be an expression of the American social conscience (1930, p. 83).

For many non-Freudian analysts, the significance of environment in the development of maladaptation far outweighs that of inner processes. Maladjustments or unusual integrative patterns of the abnormal person are seen largely as consequences of the struggle of the individual to survive under environmental conditions that tend to be pathogenic. Their treatment concentrates on the analysis of interpersonal relations in the context of the pathologic values of society.

Horney, for example, is concerned with problems of alienation and the purposefulness of life. For her, treatment requires an awareness that someone cares, that there is a warm relationship; this is similar to the thinking of Ferenczi, who felt that love and tender feelings were sufficient in therapy. But Horney stresses activity. She tries to invoke the mobilization of resources, to get the patient to do something. The therapist keeps a firmness about the relationship, stressing his authority in moving the patient to attempt to alter the environment. By raising his aspiration level and his accomplishments, the patient's self-esteem is fostered, and his self-hatred diminished. For Horney and others of the more environmental school, the private fantasy of the individual, such as the "search for glory," is to be replaced in treatment by a new kind of fantasy, the search for a meaningful life in terms of vital social values. Jung, too, saw the analyst function as encouraging moral freedom and responsibility by utilizing inspiration techniques to inculcate social and spiritual values (1933).

The importance of the analyst's values is increasingly accented by the non-Freudian analysts. They recognize that the roles of social imitation and of identification represent significant means by which therapy takes place. "Some of the changes observed in the patient's behavior may result, not so much from the intentional interaction between the patient and the therapist but rather from active learning by the patient of the therapist's attitudes and values which the therapist never directly attempted to transmit" (Bandura, 1961, p. 154). The way in which the analyst learns to be an analyst carries with it also this quality of social imitation as explicated by Grotjahn (1949).

In non-Freudian approaches, the responsibility of the analyst as well as that of the patient receives greater attention. The analyst is expected to understand the culture and the social reality as well as the inner life of his patient. He needs to take on new forms of responsibility to make modifications in treatment so as to be more successful in his interventions and to reduce the cost of treatment also by shortening it. He ultimately becomes aware that the culture may sponsor or hinder treatment success. Not only does the culture affect the patient, but it also may be so specific as to determine the analyst's interpretive analytic activity. Devereux states that the level, depth, and timing of the interpretation will be modified contrary to traditional practices by the patient's expectations due to his cultural education (1953). The therapist must come to recognize his share of responsibility for the outcomes of the therapeutic experience (Alexander, 1961; Horney, 1939; Schwartz, 1956; Schwartz & Wolf, 1964; Strupp, 1960a; Strupp, 1960b). Often the analyst's avoidance of responsibility encourages patients to expend much of their energy seeking an answer to the question, "Who's to blame?" But the successful outcome of this form of treasure hunt results in resentment and added guilt. As a consequence, therapeutic progress is made more complicated because this point is not the end of therapy but just the beginning.

Horney, like Adler, was convinced that to analyze a woman as if she were a defective man was obviously going to lead to more problems rather than less. Adler (Farau, 1962; Munroe, 1955) recognized that the social position of women had something to do with the kinds of problems they had, quite apart from biological or psychodynamic factors, but it was Horney who broke through to what she called "feminine psychology." This clear-cut attempt to differentiate the analytic treatment of men from that of women is characteristic of Horney's attempt to derive the bases for psychoanalytic therapy from the real world and the problems of reality and the ego. She says: "In my opinion, one has to look not for biological reasons but for cultural ones," in order to answer the questions, for example, concerning the masochistic trends in women (Farau, 1962, p. 113). Her emphasis upon the importance of the culture in which the human being develops led her to stress reality factors, the ego and the superego, and to gear her treatment technically in accordance with these theoretical observations.

Affirmation of feminine psychology and the distinct role of the woman constitutes a direct shift from a classical analytic view, even with regard to the importance of the mother. This is to be seen in Horney, is even clearer in Ferenczi, and is brought to an impressive height in Klein and in Silverberg, who sees the father's role in the early psychological development of the child as essentially unimportant.

The broader view of mental illness deriving from the non-Freudians has resulted in new diagnostic formulations, the social neurosis (Burrow, 1949), for example; new diagnostic techniques, family diagnosis (Ackerman, 1958; Grotjahn, 1960), for example; and new treatment methods, group therapies (Ackerman, 1958; Grotjahn, 1960; Wolf & Schwartz, 1962), for example. The recognition of social realities encouraged the development of social psychiatry and new formulations concerning the nature of emotional disorders (Szasz, 1961).

In this connection, an interesting paradox should be noted. The American, orthodox, Freudian analysts have rigidly and inappropriately rejected the practice of analytic treatment by nonmedically trained professionals, regardless of their qualifications or the level of their development and training (Schwartz, 1956; Szasz, 1959; Szasz, 1961). "In official [American] Freudian circles the judgment of Sigmund Freud [regarding lay analysis] has been overwhelmingly overridden" (Rosenzweig, 1963, p. 228). Freud (1949, vol. 5. pp. 213f.) condemned the orthodox analysts of the United States for their position, and in this sense they are anti-Freudian.

Many of the non-Freudian schools, on the other hand, recognize and train the nonmedical professional as a psychoanalyst. Along with medical training, most non-Freudian analysts reject also a rigorous experimental approach to the patient in an attitude of silence and replace it with a human and humane offer of more active cooperation.

> It is obvious that absolute cure does not exist. We live in a sick society with which we must make some compromise, and probably no one exists who is so healthy that he can make all the compromises necessary for survival without occasionally resorting to mechanisms of escape, or at least temporary denials of reality. A successful analyst does not offer a person heaven on earth, as many patients hope. It merely makes it possible for the individual to cope with life with a minimum of psychological excess baggage, that is, repressions, feelings of inferiority, of anxiety, and so on (Thompson, 1950, p. 242).

REFERENCES

Ackerman, N. W. *Psychodynamics of family life.* New York: Basic Books, 1958.

Alexander, F. *The scope of psychoanalysis.* New York: Basic Books, 1961.

Annals of psychotherapy: what is psychotherapy? *J. Amer. Acad. Psychother.*, 1959, **1** (1).

Bandura, A. Psychotherapy as a learning process. *Psychol. Bull.*, 1961, **58**, 143–159.

Burrow, T. *The neurosis of man.* New York: Harcourt, Brace & World, 1949.

Cantor, M. B. Karen Horney on psychoanalytic technique: the quality of the analyst's attention. *Amer. J. Psychoanal.*, 1959, **19**, 28–32.

De Forest, Izette. *The leaven of love.* New York: Harper & Row, 1954.

Devereux, G. Cultural factors in psychoanalytic therapy. *J. Amer. psychoanal. Ass.*, 1953, **1**, 629–655.

Farau, A. Fifty years of individual psychology. *Comprehensive Psychiat.*, 1962, **3**, 242–254.

Ferenczi, S. The principle of relaxation and neocatharsis. *Int. J. Psychoanal.*, 1930, **11**, 428–443.

Frank, J. D. Some effects of expectancy and influence in psychotherapy. In J. H. Masserman & J. L. Moreno (Eds.), *Progress in psychotherapy.* Vol. III. New York: Grune & Stratton, 1958.

Freud, S. *Collected papers.* Vol. I. London: Hogarth Press, 1949. P. 297.

Fromm-Reichmann, Frieda. *Principles of intensive psychotherapy.* Chicago: Univer. of Chicago Press, 1950.

Grinberg, L. On a specific aspect of countertransference due to the patient's projective identification. *Int. J. Psychoanal.*, 1962, **43**, 436–440.

Grotjahn, M. The role of identification in psychiatric and psychoanalytic training. *Psychiatry*, 1949, **12**, 141–152.

Grotjahn, M. *Psychoanalysis and the family neurosis.* New York: Norton, 1960.

Haley, J. The art of psychoanalysis. Etc.: *Rev. gen. Semantics*, 1958, **15**, 190–200.

Horney, Karen. *New ways in psychoanalysis.* New York: Norton, 1939.

Jones, E. Psychoanalysis and psychiatry. *Psychiat. Quart.*, 1930, **4**, 81–94.

Jung, C. G. *Modern man in search of a soul.* New York: Harcourt, Brace & World, 1933.

Klein, Melanie. *The psychoanalysis of children.* New York: Grove Press, 1960.

Lehrman, N. S. The joint interview. *Amer. J. Psychother.*, 1963, **17**, 83–93.

Lewis, N. D. C. Historical roots of psychotherapy. In J. H. Masserman & J. L. Moreno (Eds.), *Progress in psychotherapy.* Vol. III. New York: Grune & Stratton, 1958. Pp. 20–26.

May, R., Angel, E., & Ellenberger, H. F. (Eds.) *Existence.* New York: Basic Books, 1958.

Munroe, Ruth L. *Schools of psychoanalytic thought.* New York: Dryden Press, 1955.

Redlich, F. C. Social aspects of psychotherapy in the United States. In J. H. Masserman & J. L. Moreno (Eds.), *Progress in psychotherapy.* Vol. III. New York: Grune & Stratton, 1958. Pp. 79–86.

Robbins, B. S. The myth of latent emotion. *Psychotherapy*, 1955, **1**, 3–29.

Robbins, B. S. Consciousness: the central problem of psychiatry. *Psychotherapy,* 1956, **1**, 150–153. (a)

Robbins, B. S. The nature of femininity. *Psychotherapy*, 1956, **1**, 99–108. (b)

Robbins, B. S. Sigmund Freud: 1856–1939. *Psychotherapy*, 1956, **1**, 289–295. (c)

Rosen, J. N. "Acting-out" and "acting-in." *Amer. J. Psychother.*, 1963, **18**, 390–403. (a)

Rosen, J. N. *The concept of early maternal environment in direct analysis.* Doylestown, Pa.: Doylestown Foundation, 1963. (b)

Rosenzweig, S. Hubbub at the hub: a review of "The birth of an institute: twenty-fifth anniversary of the Boston Psychoanalytic Institute." *Contemporary Psychol.*, 1963, **8**, 225–228.

Schwartz, E. K. Is there need for psychology in psychotherapy? In M. L. Krout, *Psychology, psychiatry and the public interest.* Minneapolis, Minn.: Univer. of Minnesota Press, 1956. Pp. 113–134.

Schwartz, E. K. *Verbal communication in psychotherapy: the meaning and use of dreams.* Los Angeles, Calif.: Univer. of California, Postdoctoral Institute of the Los Angeles Society of Clinical Psychologists in Private Practice and Department of Psychology, 1959. (Mimeographed)

Schwartz, E. K. Leadership and the psychotherapist. In *W. H. Hulse memorial volume.* Basel: Karger, 1965.

Schwartz, E. K., & Wolf, A. Psychoanalysis in groups: resistance to its use. *Amer. J. Psychother.*, 1963, **17**, 457–464.

Schwartz, E. K., & Wolf, A. On countertransference in group psychotherapy. *J. Psychol.*, 1964, **57**, 131–142.

Sechehaye, M. La réalisation symbolique: un catalyseur de la structuration du moi schizophrenique. *Acta Psychother.*, 1957, **5**, 274–296.

Silverberg, W. V. *Childhood experience and personal destiny.* New York: Springer, 1952.

Sterba, R. The fate of the ego in analytic therapy. *Int. J. Psychoanal.*, 1934, **15**, 117–126.

Strupp, H. H. Nature of psychotherapist's contribution to treatment process. *Arch. gen. Psychiat.*, 1960, **3**, 119–231. (a)

Strupp, H. H. *Psychotherapists in action.* New York: Grune & Stratton, 1960. (b)

Sullivan, H. S. *The interpersonal theory of psychiatry.* New York: Norton, 1953.

Szasz, T. S. Psychiatry, psychotherapy, and psychology. *Arch. gen. Psychiat.,* 1959, **1,** 455–463.

Szasz, T. S. *The myth of mental illness.* New York: Hoeber-Harper, 1961.

Tarachow, S. *An introduction to psychotherapy.* New York: International Universities Press, 1963.

Thompson, Clara. *Psychoanalysis: evolution and development.* New York: Nelson, 1950.

Wassell, B. The analytic relationship. *Amer. J. Psychoanal.,* 1955, **15,** 22–30.

Wolberg, L. R. Intercurrent factors in psychotherapy. In J. H. Masserman (Ed.), *Current psychiatric therapies.* New York: Grune & Stratton, 1963. Pp. 8–18.

Wolf, A., & Schwartz, E. K. Irrational psychotherapy: an appeal to unreason. *Amer. J. Psychother.,* 1958, **12,** 300–314, 508–521, 744–759. 1959, **13,** 383–400.

Wolf, A., & Schwartz, E. K. *Psychoanalysis in groups.* New York: Grune & Stratton, 1962.

43

Perspectives in Client-centered Therapy[1]

JULIUS SEEMAN

BEGINNINGS

The purpose of this chapter is to present a description of client-centered therapy. It will be useful in this description to take advantage of the perspective now afforded by history; hence the chapter will be organized with a view to chronology. It will indicate the ways in which current thinking has evolved from earlier formulations.

Client-centered therapy arrived upon the professional scene in a surprisingly provoking fashion. If Rogers's first book on counseling (1942) dwelled on a discovery, it also documented an objection. Rogers had been brought up professionally on intervention in therapy and had found it wanting. Thus he was constrained in the book to say what he *was* doing by making clear also what he was *not* doing. And what he was not doing was interpretative therapy and traditional vocational counseling. The pained and angry response of those who practiced these methods to Rogers's first book has ceased reverberating and belongs to the dialectic of history. It is a dialectic in which views at first rejected out of hand were gradually reexamined and assimilated meaningfully. Vocational psychology at that time had a technology but no interpersonal theory upon which to base its counseling procedures. Rogers's theory had elements needed by vocational psychology; these elements have slowly found their way into theories of vocational development and counseling method.

The enduring process which Rogers set in motion in 1942 was a reexamination of the nature of therapy. It is an examination which continues to this day with no closure. There have been moments during this process of search when one might have assumed that tentativeness was ended and certainty at hand. But this was always an illusion, and the development of client-centered therapy has turned out to be just as much a process as therapy itself.

Rogers began as all clinical theorists have begun. He began inductively, with observation and curiosity but with little theory. He was to put theory together slowly, out of the events he witnessed and helped to shape. In this task, Rogers was always outstanding in devising and synthesizing ideas, but he received incalculable aid from students and colleagues who added to and stimulated his own thinking.

One who seeks perspective on the development of client-centered therapy will find that certain themes have remained central in this development. One of the central questions has concerned the nature of the therapist's function. The answer has spanned a wide band from objectivity and restraint, on the one hand, to subjectivity and involvement, on the other.

In the earliest period, Rogers took particular exception to therapist activity which he regarded as intrusive. He thus emphasized objectivity and restraint for the counselor. In one passage of his 1942 volume, he said: "He

[1] The author acknowledges, with thanks, permission from Eugene Gendlin, Frank Farrelly, and Carl Rogers to quote portions of their work.

[the counselor] will do better to face openly the fact that to some extent he is himself emotionally involved but that this involvement must be strictly limited for the good of the patient" (p. 87).

It was clear that this attitude served no isolated purpose but was integrally related to its corollary, namely, that restraint on the part of the counselor permitted freedom to the client. The autonomy of the client ranked high on the nondirective therapist's scale of values.

Empirical analysis of the early therapy records made it clear that the nondirective therapist was indeed making room for the client to talk. A word count of counselor-client verbalization indicated that the nondirective therapist accounted for about one-third of the total interview verbalization, while the client accounted for two-thirds (Porter, 1943). This proportion contrasted with the greater proportion of talk by the more "directive" counselor.

In this early period, the conception of the counselor's task was that he could best implement the objective of therapy by recognizing and clarifying the client's expressed feelings. The last two words carried the bulk of the weight. It was important to concentrate on the client's feelings rather than on the intellectual content of what he said, and it was important to respond only to feelings which had been expressed. On this point Rogers was unequivocal. He said: "It is always best to deal with attitudes already expressed. To interpret unexpressed attitudes is definitely dangerous" (1942, p. 205).

These descriptions of counselor activity were couched in terms of manifest behavior. It could be no other way because there was as yet no structure of theory to permit abstraction. The same held true for the description of the therapeutic process in the client. This description followed closely the sequence of the client's observed verbal behavior. This sequence consisted of the following major steps: the client released expression, achieved insight, and developed the capacity for choice and action. It was very nearly that simple. There was no theory of personality to mediate this description or to give it nuance and depth. Such theory as had developed was sparse enough to be contained in a bit over four pages (1942, pp. 206–210).

The act of appraising history is a strangely time-bound process. Events already past and settled nevertheless continue to change perspective. It is so with client-centered therapy. If the beginning was a time of innovation and daring, it can now be seen also as a time of caution and constraint. The client was to be made free, but the cost turned out to be high structure and low freedom of movement for the counselor. The counselor could lock himself into a ritual of verbal response which was anything but spontaneous. And in the end, a situation so much structured for the counselor could not be free for the client.

But in this beginning, hesitant and groping as all beginnings are, there was the element which must assure development in any scientific enterprise. That element was an attitude of inquiry and self-searching, an attitude in which the quest for validity was an integral part of the search itself. Such an attitude made change inevitable.

THE SECOND PHASE

During the second period of development in client-centered therapy, several major themes emerged. Of these themes, a dominant one was increasing concentration upon the phenomenological world of the client. The shift in terminology from "nondirective" to "client-centered" had begun almost as soon as the former term was coined. In Rogers's second book on therapy, *Client-centered Therapy* (1951), the term "nondirective" was used only at the beginning of the book. In the index under "nondirective counseling" the only entry was "*See* Client-centered psychotherapy." The transition was complete.

The term "nondirective" had served its purpose in calling attention to contrasts between this therapy and others, but it was a most unsatisfactory term for describing the essence of this therapy. The term "client-centered" more accurately conveyed the message that the subject matter of this therapy was the client's world of immediate experience.

But if the term cleared up old problems, it also created passing misconceptions of its own. Counselors sometimes felt that it must mean caring about the client. In this sense, it was argued, all good therapy was client-centered. This argument missed the technical meaning of "client-centered." The term was intended not as a value term but as a descriptive indication that in this therapy, the focus was on the client's internal frame of reference.

Understood in this way, the term "client-centered" accurately identified the growing phenomenological emphasis of the therapy. Rogers summarized this emphasis thus:

> This formulation would state that it is the counselor's function to assume, in so far as he is able, the internal frame of reference of the client, to perceive the world as the client sees it, to perceive the client himself as he is seen by himself, to lay aside all perceptions from the external frame of reference while doing so, and to communicate something of this empathic understanding to the client (1951, p. 29).

This statement of the counselor's function went hand in hand with a parallel trend which was to have decisive influence in shaping client-centered therapy. That trend was the development of a theory of personality. The theory not only would help explain the structure and development of personality but also would add to the understanding of personality change in therapy. This shift from the theoryless empiricism of the earlier period to an emphasis on conceptual understanding led to increased productivity in therapy-process research. It also set the pattern for continued growth in theory development.

It will be useful to summarize here the key elements of self-theory because they are essential to an understanding of the therapy which accompanied the theory. In client-centered personality theory, the main concepts concerned the way in which the self developed. These concepts undertook to explain the process of normal development, the basis of emotional disturbance, and the way in which integrative personality reorganization could take place. According to the theory, the matrix of an individual's experience led him to develop a relatively consistent and enduring framework of self-regarding attitudes, called "the self-concept." The self-concept was a set of constructs available to awareness, a statement of perceived personal identity. But the self-concept was more than a self-description; it also energized and shaped the person's behavior.

This description leads directly to an understanding of both normal and disturbed behavior. The person who could accept his experiences and bring them into the orbit of his self-concept was an effective person. He was living a process which had its own built-in correctives, for as experience changed, the concept of self could shift in congruence with this new experience.

The disturbed person was one whose self-concept was developed selectively by accepting some experiences and denying others. Somewhere in his development, the person had learned that some experiences were dangerous. Such experiences were systematically denied a place in the person's view of himself. Thus a struggle was set in motion, a struggle in which personal intactness was preserved at the cost of denying part of oneself.

One consequence of such development was tension and anxiety. But there was another consequence, equally disabling. The person learned ultimately to distrust his own experience as a guide to action. The alternative was to scan the environment and find guides which would be safer. Thus the person learned to act upon cues furnished by others. He acted on the basis of someone else's nervous system. He lived by introjected values.

This formulation defined the counselor's task. His task was to help release in the client the integrative potential which prior experience had disturbed. The therapist could do this by creating an environment in which the client dared to face denied feelings. In such an environment the client could come to experience and discover aspects of himself which had previously been too painful to accept. He could become a whole person.

It can be seen from this formulation that the theory placed high priority on the nature of the therapeutic environment. This was so because the theory postulated that the individual's integrative capacity was not destroyed but only disrupted. Hence the main question concerned the conditions under which this capacity could be restored.

Though safety might be a key component in the therapeutic climate, it was not the only component. If the client was to restore integration through self-discovery, the counselor could help by attempting to understand the tentative, emergent feelings for which the client sought expression. It was an understanding rooted in the client's phenomenal world.

In describing the activity of the counselor during this period, Rogers moved sharply away from the earlier accent on therapist technique and began to emphasize counselor attitude as the central force in the therapist's behavior. This behavior was to be no longer a matter of following particular verbal patterns but of implementing an underlying attitude about the nature of a helping relationship.

This shift in emphasis was ultimately to have important consequences for therapy method, but it took a long time really to get under way. The very clarity of technical exposition in the earlier book and the advocacy of its use made unlearning of technique more difficult. Changes in therapy method were slow in coming. A research sidelight in this connection is provocative. A study done during this second period (Seeman, 1949) indicated that 85 per cent of all counselor responses were in the category of "reflection of feeling." This proportion represented a distinct increase in the use of this response mode, as compared with figures given in an earlier study by Snyder (1945). One could argue that such an increase represented sharpening of skill, but it might also indicate a fixed conception about the verbal forms then considered necessary to implement the client-centered hypothesis. We shall see that this conception was to yield as time went by, but the time was not yet ripe for the development of new alternatives.

It is pertinent now to shift our attention from the activity of the counselor and to consider the developing statements about the therapy process in the client. These statements follow directly from the self-theory framework already summarized. An early step in therapy for the client was to begin self-exploration. In this beginning step the client often held his feelings at arm's length, exploring tentatively and sometimes impersonally. The direction of movement, however, was toward exploration of attitudes which were painful or unknown. As the client moved inward, he dared to experience these attitudes more fully and to incorporate them into his view of himself. Thus the experiencing of new attitudes and the modification of the self-concept went hand in hand. Concurrent with this shift came an increasing readiness to trust one's own experience. The client was ready to discard introjection as a guide to behavior and to move toward an internal locus of evaluation.

The three process elements suggested here, then, are (1) experiencing previously denied attitudes, (2) reorganizing the self-concept, and (3) developing an internal locus of evaluation. The following quotations of verbatim passages in counseling will serve to illuminate these concepts. The passages are taken from the counseling experience of a young man in his middle twenties.

C: Well ah, I've been th-thinking about my ag-aggression. I'm beginning to feel more that I might be showing a lot of aggression in my st-stuttering toward other people because I know now ah, the other person suffers even more than I do sometimes. I mean this is something I could never—I could never admit before. I mean, I mean it would —if I just said it, it would just be a lie, but I'm beginning to see now maybe it isn't a lie, maybe I do have a lot of aggression in myself. That's the way I'm showing it toward other people. . . . I rather enjoy talking now. And I can also be quiet and sort of enjoy it. (slightly laughing) But before I didn't want to talk and I didn't want to be quiet either (very loud). Boy, That was terrible! (raising voice) I was completely licked.

T: What a fight you were having about your speech; talking or no talking, it was still a fight.

C: Boy, it was, it was a terrible fight. I never realized it. I guess it was too painful to admit that fight. I mean, it's, I mean, I'm just beginning to feel it, to feel it now. Oh, the terrible pain. I mean it was terrible. I never realized how terrible it was. I'm just beginning to, I just have a little feeling now. I'm now just beginning to sort of get a hold of a small, small bit now, yeah, right now. I'm just trying to feel it now, trying to get hold of it here right now. It was *terrible* to talk, I mean you wanted to talk and then I didn't want to. M-hm.

T: It hurt you so much all these years that you didn't really know that it hurt you that much.

C: That's right. I'm just beginning to feel it *now* after all these years of that. Gee I don't know what to do. I don't know what to do; it's terrible (pause) (sigh). I can hardly, I'm having a time getting my breath now too, just all choked up inside.

T: You've let yourself feel it so much. . . .

C: I'm all *tight* inside, I'm all tight in the lungs. I mean I don't feel like crying, I'm just tight! All this heavy burden I've been bearing. I just feel like I'm crushed. Like I've been hit by a truck. . . . (Pause) Do you know, I just can't realize, I just can't realize that I had a lot of aggression in me. Gee, I mean it's so new yet. (sounds surprised) I mean I have to go back and talk about it again and again. It's just, boy! I'm aggressive. Even now, no, I'm not aggressive. Yes I am. I mean I just said I was, but I just don't want to *quite* accept it yet. I am aggressive—or am I? I'm beginning to doubt. . . . I'm beginning to enjoy this now, I'm getting a big kick out of it. Even about all these old negative things, I don't want to make progress, that I'm aggressive, I'm, I'm, I'm, joyful with my aggression. Sad and mo-mo-mournful, mournful, mournful about it (keeps repeating the word voluntarily). There the third time, why I'll do it, you just give me plenty of time (laughs). That's something I wasn't able to do before; I would have just said mo-mournful once and hurried to something else. But. . . .

T: Now, you're saying to me, "OK, so I'll let you know I have trouble with my speech and I'm going to keep on working, right in front of your face."

C: Right! That's right! I don't care what you think about it. Maybe I'm showing ag-ag-aggression like that. Maybe I am. Maybe I'm, I'm just gonna make you hurt. (leans very close to therapist, voice raising) I'm just gonna hurt you all I can with this stuttering. That's some-hmm. I'm surprised I said that. I'm just going to hurt you all I can with my speech. I'm just gonna st-st-st-stutter all I c-c-c-can (voluntarily imitates stutter). That wasn't an actual block, I imitated those, but I'm able to do it and I'm able to s-s-show ag-ag-aggression (real stutter) towards you like that. Gee! I showed quite a bit of aggression even toward my therapist, toward my therapist. Boy this is surprising.

T: You never knew you felt that?

C: I never knew I could do something like that. I'm surprised you're not klopping me on the head or something. "Mustn't do that, man, mustn't do that." I'm surprised you're not rejecting me, you're not punishing me, I'm surprised.

T: Surprised that I'm not giving. . . .

C: (Talking at the same time) I am, I'm terribly surprised (slightly laughing).

T: Surprised that I'm not coming back at you.

C: Yeah, that you're not. I can't believe it. (softly) I can't (slightly laughing) I can't, I can't believe it . . . (Seeman, 1957).

A later interview

C: You know—this is it, you know, I always used to beg, you know, for their affection. That's it, I used to beg. I'd always—be nice and proper and I'd be a gentleman and you know everything the way you're supposed to do.

T: Please like me.

C: Yea, yea that's it, that's right, that's it by golly that's it; by golly, please like me, please like me, I'll be a good boy, I'll be a good boy if you'll like me. Oh here's, here's something. My masculinity used to depend on whether I had a girl or how successful I was with the opposite sex. If I was su-successful with the girls, if they liked me well then I would assume that I'd be masculine. Hell, if they wouldn't like me that would be a threat to my masculinity. So, in other words my masculinity is not determined by my relationships with the girls. It's something within me. It's the way I look at everything—at the women, at men, kids and everything else. It's the way I look at myself, it's the way I act (Seeman, 1957).

The foregoing excerpts illustrate some central elements in the therapy process. For one thing, the excerpts show Jim in the middle of self-concept modification. He begins by exploring tentatively his view of himself as an aggressive person. He pauses for a bit in ambivalence and then steps past the threshold of this new "self" by experiencing himself directly as an aggressive person through his verbal attack upon the therapist.

The experiencing aspect of therapy comes through not only in the aggression but also in his readiness to experience the pain of his speech difficulty. This pain, suppressed and muted for a long time, comes through strongly enough to make Jim feel "crushed" and as if he had been "hit by a truck."

Finally, in the last excerpt, Jim indicates his own history of introjected attitudes and his readiness to live by his own internal locus of evaluation.

This chapter has identified different periods in the development of client-centered therapy. An attempt has been made for purposes of analysis to differentiate these periods as clearly as possible. It would be a mistake, however, to think of these periods as discrete and self-contained. The reverse was true. Progress was more nearly continuous. Each period initiated trends and developments which foreshadowed newer thinking. The second period of development was particularly fruitful in this regard.

With regard to the therapy process in the client, there was progressive clarification of the close relationship between the process of therapy and the level of personality integration. There were further questions about the nature of experiencing, and there were explorations concerning the meaning of psychosis.

The nature of the counselor's participation in therapy was continuously reexamined. The earlier emphasis on objectivity and detachment had become less and less satisfying. In its place came formulations which moved toward a closer and more subjective involvement. The verbal technical forms were reexamined, and their limitations upon spontaneity were noted. Questions were raised about experiencing in the counselor as well as in the client. All these questions were to show their effect upon newer perceptions of the counselor's task.

THE THIRD PHASE

It may be said that on balance, the second period of development in client-centered therapy saw the greatest progress in clarifying the therapy process in the client. This was the period during which self-theory was developed, the period during which personality theory and psychotherapy were linked.

During the third period of development, sustained attention centered on the counselor's function. Questions here were still very much open, and new conditions prompted new concentration of effort upon these questions. Client-centered therapists had developed their concepts chiefly in clinical work with the upper-middle-class person who could function in the community. Little had been done with the psychotic person. Client-centered therapists began to feel this gap in knowledge. Shlien (1960), at Chicago, sought experience with the psychotic person. Much of the stimulus for Rogers's and Gendlin's move to Wisconsin came about because there were new opportunities at Wisconsin for therapy and research with hospitalized psychotic patients. Answers to questions about the task of the therapist could no longer wait.

The answers came in the form of a marked revision in conceptions of the therapist's function. This revision was not so much a sudden act of invention as it was a process of development. Though the developments were speeded by the urgencies of the new situation, each element in the new formulation already existed. Let us see what these elements were.

As early as 1950, a paper by Raskin (1950) summarized unpublished Chicago Counseling Center memoranda on the counselor's function. A memorandum by Streich suggested: "When the therapist's capacity for awareness is thus functioning freely and fully without limitations imposed by theoretical formulations of his role . . . we have . . . balanced, therapeutic, self-growing, other growth facilitating behavior . . ." (Raskin, 1950).

In a manifest sense, Streich was saying here that the effective therapist had to go beyond technique and use his total organism as the instrument of therapy. Streich was also conveying a less manifest message which could be understood only in the context of contemporary writings. Rogers had just formulated a concept of the posttherapy client which he called the "fully functioning person." Streich's portrait of the "fully functioning therapist" hypothesized that the principles of therapy which applied to the therapist were the very same principles which applied to the client.

A few years later, Seeman (1956) described the emergent views of therapist function through the concept of the "integrated relationship." In the integrated relationship, there was a congruence between the inner state of the therapist and his verbal symbolization to the client. The therapist had to be involved in a real relationship rather than a role relationship. This real relationship came about when the therapist communicated his real self to the client.

Meanwhile, further formulations abandoned the view of the therapist as a detached person and described him as an involved person. Bown articulated this view early when he said: "As therapist I can allow a very strong feeling or emotion of my own to enter the therapeutic relationship and expect that the handling of this feeling from me by the client will be an important part of the process of therapy for him" (Rogers, 1951, p. 160).

These emergent descriptions of the counselor's function had come to view the counselor as a more totally caring and participating person. These views served as a vital reservoir when client-centered therapists began to work with hospitalized psychotic persons. In this new setting the patterns of verbal interaction which had worked in the community counseling center were not enough. The counselor had to reach the patient in other ways. The resources for such communication were found precisely in the developing attitudes of caring and participation. The patient might not be ready to involve himself in a relationship, but the therapist could. Even if the patient could not communicate himself, the therapist could. And though the patient could not offer his experience as a basis for contact, the therapist could.

Gendlin (1961) described this view of the counselor's function as follows:

> The same trend of more expressiveness with less imposition applies not only to our mode of initiating psychotherapy, but also to our whole way of working during psychotherapy. We find that even when we cannot know what the client is thinking and feeling, we can respond to him. If he is silent, I as therapist, may be quite in the dark as to what he is thinking and feeling. I only know what I am thinking and feeling, and how I imagine him. As I express my present feeling and my vague images of what may be happening between us now, a very personal quality enters into my expressions. I am giving words to my ongoing experiencing with him. There is a quality of personal risk and openness in my saying these things. There is a quality of gentle closeness in giving directly of my imaginings and feelings. In expressions I often state also my intention in saying what I say, and my unsureness concerning what is happening in him. I clearly say: "this is what is happening *in me* now" or "this is what *I imagine* is happening between us, but I can't be sure." The client lives in a responsive context made up of my person and my openly expressive inter-action with him. Yet, his side of the inter-action is left tentative, implicit, responded to by me only in a preconceptual, undifferentiated way.

It can be seen from this description that the therapist's task could no longer be defined in terms of verbal patterns but rather in terms of the "experiencing" of the therapist. This experiencing would not represent simply stream-of-consciousness responses by the therapist. Much more often the therapist would be attending to the client's world of experience. Nothing in theory or clinical experience had attenuated the importance of listening to the client's phenomenal world. It was simply that the counselor had learned to use himself more fully as a person.

With the foregoing formulation of the therapist's behavior, one would expect more variability in such behavior. Analysis of therapy records indicates that this is indeed the case. Three excerpts of therapy, each from a different counselor and patient, are presented here to indicate the varied nature of client-centered therapy today:

Excerpt 1: Male Therapist, Female Patient

T: I was just thinking, I'd be responding so differently to you.

C: What do you mean? I don't know what you mean.

T: Well, that I'd wade into the . . . messiness of it, the scariness of it. I'd wade right smack dab into the center of it. . . . I'd say things like, Well, of *course* you're thinking of committing suicide; what the hell do *you* have to live for? *Really!* . . . You're flunking out of school . . . holed up in some you know . . . holed up in X Street. . . . What friends do you have? You don't think anybody likes you—you cordially hate them.

C: Why not kill myself, right?

T: No, I—no, I'm not saying that, but I'm saying it, it makes sense to me that you would think that way. . . . *I'm* not suggesting that you kill yourself, but, of course *you've* suggested it to yourself, you know, how many times during the past several weeks? (Pause—C doesn't answer.)

T: Hmm?

C: (almost inaudible) Oh . . . on some days, not too. . . .

T: You get sulky. Don't ya? . . . Ya did.

C: (with life in her voice) Yeah! I do!

T: (exclaiming in almost a whisper) God, you get sulky! You're one of the sulkiest persons I've ever met.

C: Well, so what? That's what I was reading this morning about how schizophrenics

T: (interrupting) Yeow! You get *bitter,* and *sulky.*

C: I can't help it. Things affect me that much.

T: (interjecting) Yeah.

C: That's how much I'm hurt.

T: Mhm.

C: By little things.

T: Mhm.

C: (hostilely) And so . . . big deal, you tell me . . . that I'm sulky—big deal.

T: Mhm.

C: Fat . . . (she begins to smile) deal.

T: (laughs)

C: (laughs)

Excerpt 2: Male Therapist, Male Patient

T: And I guess your silence is saying to me that either you don't wish to or can't come out right now and that's okay. So I won't pester you but I just want you to know, "I'm here."

(Silence of *17 minutes, 41 seconds* has been eliminated from the tape)

T: I see I'm going to have to stop in a few minutes.

(Silence of 20 seconds has been eliminated from the tape)

T: It's hard for me to know how you've been feeling, but it looks as though part of the time maybe you'd rather I didn't know how you were feeling. Anyway it looks as though part of the time it just feels very good to let down and . . . relax the tension. But as I say I don't really know . . . how you feel. It's just the way it looks to me. Have things been pretty bad lately?

(Silence of 45 seconds has been eliminated from the tape)

T: Maybe this morning you just wish I'd shut up. . . . And maybe I should but I just keep feeling I'd like to, I don't know, be in touch with you in some way.

(Silence of *2 minutes, 21 seconds* has been eliminated from tape)

(Mr. Vac yawns)

T: Sounds discouraged or tired.

(Silence of 41 seconds has been eliminated from tape)

C: No, just lousy.

T: Everything's lousy, huh? You feel lousy?

(Silence of 39 seconds has been eliminated from the tape)

T: Want to come in Friday at twelve at the usual time?

C: (Yawns and mutters something unintelligible)

(Silence of 48 seconds has been eliminated from the tape)

T: Just kind of feel sunk way down deep in these lousy, lousy feelings, huh? Is that something like it?

C: No.

T: No.

(Silence of 20 seconds has been eliminated from tape)

C: No. I just ain't no good to nobody, never was, and never will be.

T: Feeling that now, huh? That you're just no good to yourself, no good to anybody. Never will be any good to anybody. Just that you're completely worthless, huh? . . . Those really are lousy feelings. Just feel that you're no good at *all*, huh?

C: Yeah. That's what this guy I went to town with just the other day told me.

T: This guy that you went to town with really told you that you were no good? Is that what you're saying? Did I get that right?

C: Uh, hum.

T: I guess the meaning of that if I get it right is that here's somebody that . . . meant something to you and what does he think of you? Why, he's told you that he thinks you're no good at all. And that just really knocks the props out from you. (C weeps quietly) It just brings the tears.

(Silence of 20 seconds has been eliminated from tape. Voices from corridor in the background)

C: I don't care though.

T: You tell yourself you don't care at all, but somehow I guess some part of you cares because some part of you weeps over it.

Excerpt 3: Male Therapist, Male Patient

C: A man's way is to turn the power off at the other building. That's the way I feel about it myself, but. . . .

T: What, if I didn't hate you I'd turn it off?

C: Yeah.

T: Boy, if I could turn it off I'd turn it off.

C: Yeah, I know, you said the same story three months ago.

T: Damn right.

C: Don't you think (T: you remember that) what you do to me, what you say, if you were a man and stuck up for me or ever would stick or ever planned on that thing about me, that you would do it though?

T: You damn right. If I could turn it off and I didn't turn it off, I would *really* be a shit. (Pause) From what I know about people that hear voices it's damn uncomfortable.

C: Oh, you bet.

T: And you're pretty damn mad about it too.

C: I don't like guys like you, just stuck up.

T: I'm stuck up?

C: Um-hum. You like to see a guy screw himself.

T: I like to see a guy screw himself? Screw himself? What does it mean?

C: Well, I take you as a (words lost) aged man. You act too cockeyed for a man that age.

It is obvious from these excerpts that verbal response patterns as such can no longer define client-centered therapy. This raises the question as to the touchstones which are now relevant in identifying client-centered therapy. The answer thus far is that the issue is quite ambiguous, and indeed there is not much interest in pursuing the problem in these terms. The attempt has been rather to identify more generically the therapeutic conditions which facilitate personality change. Writers in client-centered therapy have offered various formulations, and Rogers (1957) has synthesized these alternatives in a paper on necessary and sufficient conditions for therapy. These alternatives represent a summary of what has been considered here. Among the six conditions mentioned by Rogers, the three basic characteristics of the therapist are (1) empathic understanding, (2) unconditional positive regard, and (3) congruence.

The first two of these characteristics are historically the more familiar in client-centered therapy. Empathic understanding has meant and still means the process by which the therapist senses accurately the immediate feeling state experienced by the client. Unconditional positive regard refers to the unconditional acceptance of the client as a person; in this there is no connotation of agreement, but simply a nonevaluative willingness to let the client be. In another sense the concept does not connote affective neutrality or detachment, but the kind of caring that is described by Bown earlier in this chapter.

Congruence concerns the quality of the therapist's integration in the relationship. It means that the therapist's internal experience and his symbolization to the client are in harmony with each other. The therapist, for instance, is not verbalizing acceptance when he is experiencing fear or hostility. He is acting as an integrated person in the relationship.

The three therapist characteristics mentioned here have intriguing contingencies. At times they may all be present, but there may also be times when the presence of one precludes the presence of another. For instance, a congruent therapist who is made anxious or angry at the client is hardly likely at that moment to experience unconditional positive regard. The implicit priority system in client-centered therapy suggests that congruence is the most basic precondition of effective therapy.

Up to this point we have described current concepts of the function of the counselor. We may turn now to an analysis of the therapy process from the standpoint of the client. A formulation which has had major impact on theory and research is the paper by Rogers entitled "A Process Conception of Psychotherapy" (1961). Before writing the paper, Rogers spent many hours listening to recorded therapy interviews with a view toward making a fresh appraisal of the therapeutic process. What emerged was a conception of therapy which linked more closely than ever the dual phenomena of therapy process and level of personality integration.

Such a development was far from casual. Indeed in retrospect one might consider that it was inevitable. For Rogers, more than most clinical theorists, had concerned himself with conceptions of the integrated person. Thus it was natural to find him charting the steps leading toward personality integration.

Rogers visualized a continuum of therapy change for which he enumerated seven stages. These stages were not discrete but represented simply seven definable points on the continuum. The first stage of this continuum was characterized by rigidity and by remoteness of experiencing. There was no exploration of self or any self-relevant communication to others. In the second stage there was some verbalization of feeling, but it was guarded and externalized. By the fourth stage, feelings could be readily reported and owned as past events, but present feelings were still removed from direct experiencing of them. The sixth stage was characterized by an ability to experience with directness and immediacy. Feeling as an object began to give way to feeling as a process. In the seventh stage the self was perceived in terms of immediacy and continuity of experiencing. Internal communication went on clearly and with little effort. In Rogers's earlier terms, this stage characterized the emergence of the fully functioning person.

This concept brings us to an issue which has from the beginning been a central one in client-centered therapy. The issue concerns the basic assumptions in client-centered therapy about the nature of man. In Rogers's first book he talks about the individual drive toward growth and health (1942). Often, however, the terms get quite fuzzy and are couched in value terms not readily susceptible to empirical analysis, e.g., terms like "respect for the capacity of the individual."

The issue has come to be progressively clarified, and what emerges is a hypothesis couched not in value terms but in terms of the biopsychological nature of man (Seeman, 1956). The postulation here is that the organism has a tendency to stay within the orbit of effective developmental regularities. When disturbances in development occur, the task of therapy is to provide conditions for the removal or assimilation of these disturbances so that organic order or integration may function again. This formulation places the issue in the realm of biopsychology.

Rogers's concept of the fully functioning person is a natural extension of the foregoing formulation. Through this concept he describes in much greater detail the operational meaning of "organic order or integration" and continues to construe the nature of man in biopsychological terms.

This concept of the fully functioning person has been an important and enduring one in client-centered theory. It has been the hallmark of Rogers's interest in optimal integration, and its ideas have been central to the theory of therapy and personality change. Interestingly enough, the paper was never published as it was originally written in 1952 and was not published at all by Rogers until nine years later (Rogers, 1961).[2] Yet its ideas permeated much of the writing between those years.

For Rogers, the fully functioning person was a person fully open to his own experience, a person who could sense and interpret immediate experience without denial or distortion. Such a person lived "existentially"; he trusted these presently felt data to guide his behavior to a maximal degree.

This brief summary of the concept is not likely to convey much of the real flavor of Rogers's description. From the standpoint of logic, however, one can see that Rogers is describing an "effective" organism, one in which action is based upon a maximum of communication and hence upon a maximum of reality data. Since these conditions are not time-bound but continuous, they represent an ongoing process by which optimal integration remains most likely.

Up to this point in our discussion of the client, we have dealt with descriptions which are at least one step removed from the moment-to-moment interaction in therapy itself. It will be useful now to consider the ways in which this interaction has been described.

[2] The original paper has since been published in *Psychotherapy: Theory, Research, and Practice*, 1963, 1, 17–26.

In this connection one of the key concepts has been that of experiencing. Because the concept is so embedded in client-centered theory, allusions have necessarily been made to it already. Gendlin, in an important work (1962), has treated the idea systematically and has shown logically its explanatory power in subsuming many other concepts in therapy.

Experiencing is the immediately felt process which is perceived by the person at a given moment in time. Immediacy is one of its defining characteristics. Another characteristic is that it is preconceptual. Because it is an immediately felt process, it precedes talking "about" it or symbolizing it. Of course, it may later be symbolized and often is, but that is a step subsequent to initial experiencing.

Experiencing constitutes the most elemental unit of a "living" process. It is for this reason that experiencing becomes crucial in therapy. Because it is the most elemental activation process within the person, it becomes the energy source for learning oneself—not merely learning *about* oneself, but learning oneself in a direct sense. But experiencing is also the precursor to conceptualizing, to thinking about oneself and deriving generalizations. Hence experiencing becomes also the necessary precondition of understanding and reorganizing the structure of the self.

This relationship between experiencing and conceptualization has of course been of longstanding interest in theories of therapy, as far back as Breuer and Freud's first work (1957). The relative importance of experiencing and symbolization is not entirely a settled issue in client-centered therapy. Rogers emphasizes the crucial component of awareness when he says: "In therapy the person adds to ordinary experience the full and undistorted awareness of his experiencing . . ." (1961, p. 104). Gendlin makes the intriguing point that adjustment is not due to the symbolized awareness of the *content* of experience but lies in the "fully functioning" component itself, i.e., the absence of blockage or exclusion. This view seems to make preconceptual experiencing quite focal, though one should not conclude from this that symbolized content is unimportant. Indeed, Gendlin points out that symbolization may act as a spur to further experiencing. Seeman (1956) focuses on the interaction of experiencing and symbolization and defines the integrative act as the achievement of congruence between an inner state and symbolization of that state. Hobbs (1962) tends to consider the conceptual component less important and, indeed, an ex post facto derivative of change.

Whatever differences in emphasis may exist with regard to conceptualization, there is agreement that learning takes place precisely at the point where energy is concentrated in direct experiencing. Hence the counselor focuses on the immediacy of the client's experience. This has been widely misunderstood to mean that the counselor is interested only in the present and not in the past. This is not the meaning of immediacy. What is meant, rather, is that the counselor attends to the energized data of immediate experience, whatever their content may be. There probably never was a client who did not feel impelled to speak of his past. The principle of immediacy suggests that the most fruitful time for the counselor to be at that point is the time when the client is concentrating his energy on experiencing that past.

The concept of immediate experiencing has implications also for a process versus content view of therapy. Let us suppose, for example, that a client is trying to decide whether or not to leave school. The immediacy principle leads to a process view of this issue. The subject matter of therapy for the counselor will not be the decision to leave or stay in school, but the moment-to-moment process which the client is living as he struggles with this issue. Indeed, when the counselor focuses on immediacy, the outcome of the struggle is not even likely to be in his perceptual field.

DEVELOPMENTS IN RESEARCH

At any point in time, research in client-centered therapy has always reflected closely the emergent theoretical formulations of that period. One might in fact trace the development of client-centered therapy quite accurately by studying its research alone. This fact is an index of the persistence with which research has been pursued.

There is another fact that is timely here concerning the place of research in client-centered therapy. Research has always followed practice and has never led it. Innovations in practice have come from direct experience and not from research. This is in striking contrast to much medical research. A new drug or procedure is evolved and then tried out experimentally. If it works, it is used in general practice.

Research in client-centered therapy has never served this discovery function. It has had, rather, the function of clarification and validation. Research has served to quantify the intuitive observations and findings and to check factually the validity of these observations. But research has not led to application; it has always trailed application.

Perhaps the best procedure to follow here is to provide some perspective on the total sweep of the research by describing representative studies from different time periods. On this basis, the early studies by Lewis (1943), Porter (1943), and Snyder (1945) must be noted here. All these studies were descriptive in nature. Porter demonstrated that nondirective therapy had a consistent methodology which could be described and differentiated from other methods. Lewis and Snyder also dealt with counseling method, but their most significant findings concerned the client process through therapy. They found that therapy was characterized by a systematic and orderly progression in client expressions over the course of therapy. Because we have known this now for some time, these findings have lost their initial impact. But it is no small gift to perceive order in the complexity of therapy, and these studies gave us this view.

With all their value, one thing which these studies could not give us was a better understanding of personality change, for the studies were not rooted in personality theory. This is not a complaint, but a commentary on the developmental stage out of which these studies grew. For these studies were a product of the time before such theory was developed, and so they could be only simple descriptive studies.

The first study derived from personality theory was, strangely enough, a product of this otherwise theoryless period. This was the study by Raimy (1948), published long after it was completed. Raimy set forth an extensive formulation of a self-concept theory of personality and studied the ways in which the self-concept changed in psychotherapy. Changes in the self-concept, he argued, constituted an index of change in personality. His study of therapy records supported his hypothesis. Cases judged successful showed positive shifts in self-concept, while cases judged unsuccessful did not.

Raimy's study was the forerunner of what we may consider the second stage of research in client-centered therapy. During this stage, theory formulations were markedly prominent. The self-concept had become a central construct in client-centered theory, and a number of investigators undertook to study various aspects of the theory. A study by Raskin (1949) serves as a good illustration of this period in research. Raskin asserted that one index of effective behavior lay in the valuing processes of a person. An individual could, in varying degrees, rely upon the evidence of his own senses as a basis for action, or he could rely on values and attitudes set by others. Raskin postulated that the more effective valuing mode was an internal locus of evaluation, in which the person anchored his behavior in his own perceptions of events. Raskin then constructed a "locus of evaluation" scale and applied it to the therapy transcripts of 10 clients. He found that over therapy, a significant shift took place in the direction of greater use of self as an evaluator of experience. This was of course in consonance with the theory.

The second phase of research in client-centered therapy had begun with a strong emphasis on research in the therapy process. It culminated with a large-scale study of therapy outcome (Rogers & Dymond, 1954). This study was more massive by far than any which had preceded it. In this study a number of outcome variables were applied to one group of clients so that interrelationship of outcomes could be assessed. Some of the chief outcome measures used were client self-description, counselor judgments, friends' assessment of emotional maturity, and test evaluations (TAT, ethnocentrism scale). Significant change over therapy and one year later was observed in client self-descriptions, counselor judgments, and TAT adjustment ratings.

More complex findings were obtained on friends' ratings of clients' emotional maturity. Over-all changes from pretherapy to posttherapy were not significantly different from those found in the control group. However, when the more successful cases were compared with the less successful ones, striking differences were observed. Friends' ratings of emotional maturity in the clients indicated that the more successful cases received higher maturity ratings by friends after therapy than before. This was not true for less successful cases. Indeed, the correlation between counselor judgment of outcome and judgments by clients' friends was .67. Such a correlation says convincingly that change in psychotherapy is a real phenomenon, observable from highly diverse vantage points.

Two other observations must be made about the Rogers and Dymond book. The first of these comments concerns the struggle to introduce adequate controls into the design. Two methods were used. One was the own-control method, in which some clients were tested and then were asked to wait two months before starting therapy. This two-month no-therapy period could then be used as a baseline to study later changes in therapy. The second control method was the equivalent-control method, in which nontherapy individuals were matched with clients according to age, sex, and educational status. This mode of control gave information on changes over time without therapy.

These control procedures were partial approximations, and they were rather considerably better than nothing. But they were piecemeal controls and could not go to the heart of the matter, which was this: What changes would occur in people who resembled the therapy group in degree of disturbance and motivation for therapy if therapy was withheld for a time period equal to that which was given for therapy? No research study done with an outpatient group has ever answered this question, and no such study is likely to do so. The odds against it are just too great. For one thing, a clinic could not withhold service for that long a time, and even if it could, the clients would go elsewhere for service. Add to this the fact that a nonclient control group ignores the most crucial variables, and we are forced to the conclusion that definitive outcome studies must be done in settings other than outpatient settings. A great many other kinds of therapy studies are of course still open to outpatient settings.

To return now to the final contribution of the Rogers and Dymond book, there is a study by Grummon which deserves far more attention than it has gotten because it speaks of a central control issue in the evaluation of therapy. Grummon analyzed the test results of the two-month no-therapy period for the own-control group. It turned out that 8 of the 23 clients in this group chose not to enter therapy (attrition group), while the other 15 did (continuing group). Grummon then made a comparative analysis of the test changes in the attrition group and the continuing group. He found strong evidence of differential test changes in the two groups. The attrition group showed significant improvement in many of the measures during the no-therapy period, but the continuing group showed no improvement at all.

The significance of this point should not escape our attention. It means that people who remain in therapy are *individuals who are selectively self-chosen and who do not improve without therapy*. Thus any comparison of a therapy group with a spontaneous-remission group is not an appropriate comparison; individuals who show spontaneous remission do not become clients (witness the improvement in the attrition group).

This point is important because the most cogent (and devastating) criticism of psychotherapy has come from men like Eysenck (1952) who use spontaneous-remission groups as the base line for evaluating the outcomes of therapy. Grummon's study casts doubt on the validity of such a procedure.

We now come to the third and most recent research period in client-centered therapy. A significant proportion of this research is now in progress at Wisconsin, where schizophrenic patients are being used as the therapy sample. These studies are unique in many ways. For one thing, they have come fully to terms with the control issue. In an institutional setting one can choose individuals equivalent or randomized on the pertinent variables and then assign them randomly to an experimental or control group. This was the procedure followed, and it led to the formation of truly equivalent therapy and control groups.

There are other features in this study worthy of note here. The study represents a risk and a commitment as far in reach as one can imagine. A research group would have to search far indeed to find more ways to stack the cards against success. Virtually every ingredient of poor prognosis exists: chronic and severe psychosis, low or nonexistent motivation for therapy, and low socioeconomic status. The cumulative impact of these variables is probably geometric in nature.

One important characteristic of the study is that it tries to assess the interaction of process and outcome. Many studies in the past have considered one or the other of these elements, but the Wisconsin project attempts continuously to track both of them. At this writing the results are not yet complete. It is possible, however, to indicate partial results which are still in the draft-writing stage.

At the 1961 APA convention, Truax (1961b) reported on the relation between the level of empathy shown by the counselor and the degree of patient improvement as measured by psychological tests. He found that for the test-improved patients, the level of therapist empathy was consistently higher than that for the nonimproved patients. There was, in fact, very little overlap in degree of empathy for the two groups.

In another unpublished paper, Truax, Liccione, and Rosenberg (1961) considered the relationship between process and outcome measures. They found that patients for whom therapist conditions were high showed significantly higher test outcomes than patients with less optimal therapist conditions.

One very crucial question in research of this kind concerns the nature of the process-outcome contingencies. Rogers's postulates have the character of an "if-then" statement, in which it is assumed that if the specified therapeutic conditions exist, then they are sufficient for personality change. The postulate is thus cast in terms as nearly causal as one can get in science. Postulates of this kind bear very close scrutiny. They demand much more stringent analysis than the ordinary statistical test of association, which hypothesizes only covariation among variables. To put the issue another way, the postulate as stated concerns only the independent variation contributed by the therapist. An adequate test of the postulate requires analysis of the variation due to patient variables and therapist-patient interaction variables as well as of the variation due to therapist variables. Only as all the possible sources of variation are analyzed can we know the relative contributions of each to the total effect of therapy.

There are as yet no studies in therapy, client-centered or otherwise, which have analyzed the sources of variation in quite this way. This is not to say, however, that the problem is a new one or that answers have not yet been attempted. There are indeed a number of studies in client-centered therapy which have dealt with outcome variation associated with both client and counselor variables. One of the earlier studies of this kind sought to predict therapy outcome on the basis of the first interview (Kirtner, 1955; Kirtner & Cartwright, 1958). Kirtner found that there were characteristic client patterns in the first interview which predicted success or failure. The client who was ultimately considered successful began therapy by engaging in exploration of self-relevant feeling, while the client who was later rated less successful began with more distant, more impersonal, and less affective interview behavior. Studies by Cartwright (1958) indicated that a prognostic index based on Rorschach responses predicted significantly the outcome of therapy.

Butler (1963) and his colleagues (Wagstaff, Rice, & Butler, 1960) have made extensive analyses of factors in the interview which are related to outcome. These studies are part of a larger research program which has developed methods of describing objectively the phenomena of therapy. The studies report three distinct typologies of client interview behavior and relate them to outcomes as rated by the counselor. Such counselor judgments have been shown consistently to correlate with other outcome measures (Rogers & Dymond, 1954). The factor-I client explores freely his feeling life and personal experiences and is the client most often rated as successful. The factor-II client discusses self-relevant matters but displays little affect and a low energy level. Persistence of these qualities is usually related to an intermediate success rating. The factor-III client externalizes his problems. He does not discuss self-relevant feeling and does not get personally involved in therapy. As one might expect, the client with this pattern is most often found in the failure group.

The foregoing studies indicate that there are persistent, predictable qualities in the client which exist at the outset and which differentiate success and failure. The Wisconsin studies which were discussed earlier indicated that certain conditions provided by the therapist are also related to variation in success. What is still needed is studies indicating the nature of the interaction of these variables. Even here we do have a provocative study by Truax (1961a), which considered the relative effect of therapist and patient upon the degree of accurate empathy shown by the therapist. Truax was interested in determining whether high empathy was an attribute which resided primarily in the therapist's skill alone or whether it was a quality which was evoked by the patient. The design of the study was such that recorded therapy sessions were obtained and analyzed for eight patients, each of whom saw eight therapists for one interview each. Samples of these interviews were rated for degree of empathy shown by the therapist. The results indicated a significant effect for therapists but not for patients. Thus we can say that in this study the phenomenon of empathy resided in the therapist and was not a condition evoked by particular qualities in the patient.

If we take a long view of the research that has been reported here, we can see that much has been done in two decades. The studies have gone from simple descriptive studies to theory-oriented studies of the therapeutic process. Outcome studies have grown in sophistication, and linkages between process and outcome have been made. The problem of controls, always a stubborn one, is now being met on a satisfactory basis. These are solid and durable gains. In many ways these gains have represented a period of preparation for crucial research which still lies ahead. But one is entitled to some optimism that this preparation will ultimately unfold new answers to questions about how and why therapy works.

REFERENCES

Breuer, J., & Freud, S. *Studies on hysteria.* New York: Basic Books, 1957.

Butler, J. M., Rice, L., Wagstaff, Alice, & Knapp, Sarah. *Quantitative naturalistic research.* Englewood Cliffs, N.J.: Prentice-Hall, 1963.

Cartwright, Rosalind D. Predicting response to client-centered therapy with the Rorschach PR scale. *J. counsel. Psychol.,* 1958, **5,** 11–17.

Eysenck, H. The effects of therapy: an evaluation. *J. consult. Psychol.,* 1952, **16,** 319–324.

Gendlin, E. T. Client-centered developments in psychotherapy with schizophrenics. *Univer. Wis. Psychol. Inst. Bull.,* 1961, **1** (7).

Gendlin, E. T. *Experiencing and the creation of meaning.* New York: Free Press, 1962.

Hobbs, N. Sources of gain in psychotherapy. *Amer. Psychologist,* 1962, **17,** 741–747.

Kirtner, W. L. Success and failure in client-centered therapy as a function of personality variables.

Unpublished master's thesis, Univer. of Chicago, 1955.

Kirtner, W. L., & Cartwright, D. S. Success and failure in client-centered therapy as a function of client personality variables. *J. consult. Psychol.*, 1958, **22**, 259–264.

Lewis, Virginia. Changing the behavior of adolescent girls. *Arch. Psychol.*, 1943, **87** (279).

Porter, E. H. The development and evaluation of a measure of counseling interview procedures. *Educ. psychol. Measmt,* 1943, **3**, 105–126.

Raimy, V. C. Self reference in counseling interviews. *J. consult. Psychol.*, 1948, **12**, 153–163.

Raskin, N. J. An objective study of the locus of evaluation factor in psychotherapy. Unpublished doctoral dissertation, Univer. of Chicago, 1949.

Raskin, N. J. Developments in client-centered therapy. In L. E. Abt & D. Brower (Eds.), *Progress in clinical psychology*. Vol. 1. New York: Grune & Stratton, 1950.

Rogers, C. R. *Counseling and psychotherapy.* Boston: Houghton Mifflin, 1942.

Rogers, C. R. *Client-centered therapy.* Boston: Houghton Mifflin, 1951.

Rogers, C. R. The necessary and sufficient conditions of therapeutic personality change. *J. consult. Psychol.*, 1957, **21**, 95–103.

Rogers, C. R. *On becoming a person.* Boston: Houghton Mifflin, 1961.

Rogers, C. R., & Dymond, Rosalind, F. (Eds.) *Psychotherapy and personality change.* Chicago: Univer. of Chicago Press, 1954.

Seeman, J. A study of the process of nondirective therapy. *J. consult. Psychol.*, 1949, **13**, 157–168.

Seeman, J. Client-centered therapy. In D. Brower & L. E. Abt, *Progress in clinical psychology.* Vol. II. New York: Grune & Stratton, 1956.

Seeman, J. *The case of Jim.* Nashville, Tenn.: Counselor Recordings, 1957.

Shlien, J. M. A client-centered approach to schizophrenia. In A. Burton (Ed.), *Psychotherapy of the psychoses.* New York: Basic Books, 1960.

Snyder, W. U. An investigation of the nature of nondirective psychotherapy. *J. gen. Psychol.*, 1945, **33**, 193–223.

Truax, C. B. Effects of therapists and patients on empathy in psychotherapeutic interaction. Unpublished paper, Univer. of Wisconsin, 1961. (a)

Truax, C. B. Therapeutic conditions. *Univer. Wis. Psychol. Inst. Bull.*, 1961, **1** (10c). (b)

Truax, C. B., Liccione, J., & Rosenberg, M. Psychological test evaluations of personality change. Unpublished paper, Univer. of Wisconsin, 1961.

Wagstaff, Alice K., Rice, Laura N., & Butler, J. M. Factors of client verbal participation in therapy. *Univer. Chicago counsel. Center Discussion Papers,* 1960, **6** (9).

4

Behavior Therapy

HARRY I. KALISH

The recent and effective application of the principles of learning to psychotherapy represents one of those rare occasions which may ultimately effect significant transformations in both the rationale and the techniques of therapy. The development of behavior therapy as an explicit set of rules for practice has been exceedingly slow relative to the amount of time that the principles of learning and conditioning have been in existence. Among the important factors contributing to this delay have been the separation between theory and application, reluctance to use the clinic as a laboratory, and acceptance of the traditional methods as the model for psychotherapy.

The introduction of classical conditioning in the United States and its acceptance by Watson furnished psychologists with a potentially useful method and produced a brief but somewhat aborted attempt to relate conditioning to psychopathology, exemplified by the work of Watson and Rayner (1920) and the early efforts of M. C. Jones (1924), in her study of the elimination of naturally occurring fears in children. A survey of the work during this period reveals a great deal of interest in the relationship between conditioning and the acquisition of pathological behavior (Bagby, 1922; Humphrey, 1922; Smith & Guthrie, 1922) but very few instances of the application of behavioral principles to treatment (Brousseau, 1923). Under the circumstances, it is not difficult to understand why psychoanalysis, with its origins in clinical material, made a far greater impact. With rare exceptions (Guthrie, 1938; Mowrer & Mowrer, 1928), the surge of interest in learning theory brought with it a corresponding retreat to the laboratory. As a measure of self-protection against the encroachment of practical problems, most learning theorists adopted a kind of defensive know-nothingism which promoted the belief that learning theory had little to offer to the analysis and treatment of behavior deviations.

Another important factor responsible for the delay in applying behavioral techniques to the study and practice of psychotherapy derives, paradoxically, from the efforts of psychologists to structure psychotherapy in terms of learning theory (Dollard & Miller, 1950; Shaw, 1946; Shoben, 1948). Instead of adapting psychotherapeutic techniques to the conditions prescribed by learning, the concepts of learning were used to describe the events occurring within the traditional dyadic model. Thus the vaguely defined and ambiguous therapeutic process was translated *pari passu* into a language derived from highly controlled experiments. The results were neither prescriptive in suggesting procedures which might expedite learning in therapy nor helpful in deciding which of the present set of variables were relevant. Bandura (1961; 1963) has pointed out that despite the conceptualization of psychotherapy as a learning process, the practice has remained essentially unchanged.

With the introduction of behavioral techniques, these sequences have been reversed. The procedures in treatment do not begin with the accepted therapeutic model. Instead, the principles of learning define the conditions of therapy, depending upon the characteristics of the response to be changed. In behavior therapy the model for treatment is the experiment, in which it is generally considered good practice to permit the problem to dictate the procedure.

METHODS

The term "behavior therapy" or "behavioristic therapy"[1] designates those techniques which make explicit use of either learning theory or behavior principles to analyze the therapeutic process and establish the *conditions and procedures for therapy*. The principles of behavior are statements of empirical relationships between classes of variables established on the basis of laboratory investigations. Theories of learning, on the other hand, employ the principles as postulates in formal systems for the purpose of deducing new principles. The term "learning" itself is a construct which refers to inferred processes resulting from the effect of such associative variables as rewarded practice, and the results of learning are reflected in performance changes combining both associative and motivational variables. In this chapter, however, the term "learning" will be used synonymously with the term "performance" to indicate observed changes in behavior.

Virtually all the methods in behavior therapy are based on principles derived from two major sources originating in laboratory investigations of animal behavior—*classical conditioning* (Pavlov, 1927) and *instrumental learning* (Thorndike, 1911)—and on the extent to which these principles are expressed in theories of learning (Dollard & Miller, 1950; Hull, 1943; Mowrer, 1960) or descriptive accounts of behavior processes (Guthrie, 1935; Skinner, 1938).

In classical conditioning, the sequence of events is typically arranged so that a stimulus defined as the "conditioned stimulus" (CS) is paired with or precedes a stimulus designated as the "unconditioned stimulus" (UCS), which regularly evokes the unconditioned response (UCR). As a result of pairing, the CS acquires the capacity to elicit a conditioned response (CR) resembling the UCR. The sequence of events is independent of the subject's response, and emphasis is placed on the ability of the CS to acquire control over a specified segment of behavior. Instrumental conditioning, by contrast, deals with response-reinforcement contingencies in which the subject's behavior controls the occurrence or nonoccurrence of stimuli defined as "positive" or "negative" reinforcers. These two basic conditioning situations have been described by Skinner (1938) as "respondent learning" (classical conditioning), characterized by elicited behavior under the control of a stimulus, and "*operant learning*" (instrumental conditioning), in which behavior is emitted in the absence of a demonstrable antecedent or originating stimulus. This does not mean that there are no controlling or originating stimuli in operant learning, but behavior may be successfully shaped without utilizing them—a process which has its counterpart in certain forms of behavior therapy.

The nature and function of the reinforcing event in the two types of learning have prompted the belief that classical and instrumental conditioning represent two basically different learning processes with different underlying principles. Classical conditioning is often regarded as learning by contiguity, while instrumental conditioning is presumed to obey the laws of reinforcement. Several theorists have attempted to reconcile these differences by combining both types of learning into one process. Hull (1943), for example, believed that the association between the CS and the CR was established on the basis of drive reduction due to reinforcement. More recently, Mowrer (1960) proposed a theory in which both stimulus and response become conditioned to internal states of the organism, thereby reducing a two-factor theory to the unitary process represented by classical conditioning.

Kimble (1961) has identified four instrumental conditioning procedures which, in addition to classical conditioning, may provide a suitable arrangement for classifying the process involved in the establishment of deviant behavior and the method employed to modify it. The system originally proposed by Konorski (1948) distinguishes four basic training methods: reward, avoidance, omission, and punish-

[1] "Behavior therapy" (Eysenck, 1960) will probably become the generally accepted term to describe techniques of therapy derived from learning principles. Bandura (1963) has used a variant of this term, "behavioristic psychotherapy," and a quarterly journal entitled *Behaviour Research and Therapy* has recently been established.

ment. As Kimble points out, the classification depends upon whether the subject's behavior generates a positive reinforcer or avoids a negative one.

In instrumental conditioning, *reward training* is exemplified by the early trial-and-error experiments of Thorndike (1911), in which the animal was required to learn a response in order to obtain a reward. Increases in the frequency of the rewarded response or decreases in the latency of performance were regarded as indications of learning. The response the animal was required to learn did not necessarily have a "meaningful relationship" to the appearance of the reward. In some instances such apparently nonfunctional behaviors as scratching, sniffing, bowing, etc., have been elicited and strengthened primarily because they have been associated with reward. Operant conditioning, in which the characteristics of an already existing response (emitted behavior) can be altered by variations in the conditions of reinforcement, is a special case of reward learning (Skinner, 1938). When a specified stimulus is employed to control the instrumental response, the behavior is classified as a "discriminated operant" (Skinner, 1938).

In *avoidance learning*, Bekhterev (1932) extended the classical procedures of escape training by permitting the animal to avoid a CS which had acquired aversive properties through association with a noxious event instead of merely escaping it. Except for the instrumental avoidance response, Bekhterev's procedures, including the use of an exteroceptive stimulus, followed Pavlov's operations very closely. Avoidance learning is especially important because it has long been regarded as the basis for the acquisition of psychoneurotic disturbances (Freud, 1936; Mowrer, 1939).

Omission training is much less frequently used as a laboratory paradigm, but it may serve to explain why certain behaviors are never high in the hierarchy of some individuals despite the absence of punishment. Under the conditions of omission training, "a specified response would lead to the nonoccurrence of a positive reinforcer . . . a situation roughly the same as that in which the parent withholds privileges for undesirable behavior" (Kimble, 1961, p. 70).

Punishment training, in contradistinction to avoidance, is designed so that the occurrence of a response leads to the appearance of a negative reinforcer. This type of training is often used to increase the speed with which responses are abandoned.

The similarity between classical and instrumental conditioning is illustrated by the similarity in basic principles derived from them. Virtually all the experiments involving either of the learning procedures demonstrate fairly uniform *acquisition* and *extinction* functions, indicating that behavior is learned and abandoned in an appreciably similar manner. Phenomena such as *generalization* and *discrimination*, which show that a response conditioned to a particular stimulus may be evoked by similar stimuli or that a subject may learn to differentiate among stimuli, are equally applicable to both methods. Finally, it has also been demonstrated for both types of learning that neutral stimuli can become *secondary reinforcers* or *secondary drive stimuli* through association with reinforcement or motivation. In the former case, a stimulus acquires the capacity to evoke responses associated with reinforcement, while in the latter, responses are elicited by stimuli which have been paired with specific motivational states such as anxiety or hunger.

At present, both classical and instrumental learning, the behavior principles corresponding to them, and the use of anxiety as a motivational state appear to exhaust all the conditions necessary to describe the changes which have been obtained from the use of techniques encompassed by behavior therapy. The use of a specific method in behavior therapy is very largely determined by the characteristics of the response to be changed. Where therapists and research psychologists, dealing with clinical subjects, have sought to associate old responses with new or altered stimuli, as in the case of enuresis training (H. G. Jones, 1960b), or new responses with old stimuli, as in certain forms of desensitization therapy (Wolpe, 1958), classical conditioning procedures have been used effectively with some modification. Instrumental methods have been employed where existing responses are to be altered without any precise knowledge of the maintaining stimuli, as in tics (Barrett, 1962; Yates, 1958a), or delinquency (Schwitzgebel, 1960). In certain instances where it was necessary to arrange the contingencies for a selected response to appear so that it could be associated with a class of stimuli, e.g., treatment of a conversion reaction (Brady & Lind, 1961), both operant and classical techniques were combined.

The review of the methods of therapy to be presented in this chapter is structured in terms of the learning procedures described rather than in terms of the syndrome presented by the patient. This is done to stress the uniformity of techniques used for varying syndromes and to emphasize the *processes* involved in producing behavior change. Some of the methods to be described have demonstrated their effectiveness and are used as standard procedures. Others are still in the exploratory stage.

Classical Conditioning

Therapy by means of classical conditioning involves association by contiguity of an identifiable stimulus with an involuntary or semivoluntary response. Because in certain of the treatment situations to be described attempts are made to associate pleasurable or relaxed responses with stimuli which are already CSs for existing responses, e.g., reciprocal inhibition therapy (Wolpe, 1958) and the method of direct conditioning (M. C. Jones, 1924), the process has often been referred to as "counterconditioning" (Bandura, 1961; Shoben, 1949). In these instances, a given response, such as withdrawal, must be eliminated entirely. In other cases involving classical conditioning, however, e.g., training for control of micturition (H. G. Jones, 1960a; Mowrer & Mowrer, 1928), the *same response* must be conditioned to modifications of the original stimulus (altered threshold values corresponding to increases or decreases in detrusor tension from the bladder).

The control of enuresis first proposed by Mowrer and Mower (1928) is a therapeutic procedure designed to alter the characteristics of the stimuli for urination. To accomplish this, an apparatus was devised consisting of a sensitive electric circuit arranged so that a small amount of urine activated a bell which aroused the subject. It was assumed that awakening the subject at or near the threshold value for micturition would have the effect of conditioning detrusor tension from the bladder to the response of awakening and voiding in the bathroom (H. G. Jones, 1960a). Under these conditions, detrusor stimuli act as the CS as well as the UCS, since they are present prior to urination and are contiguous with the remaining chain of responses, including voiding in the bathroom and cessation of urination. During the first part of the training, the child continues to wake to the sound of the bell; ultimately, stimuli from the bladder become anticipatory, and the child wakes before urination has begun. Hefferline and Perera (1963) have furnished support for such an explanation of the conditioning events by demonstrating that weak proprioceptive stimuli, of which the subject is unaware and which he is unable to control, can be made to acquire discriminative control over other overt or covert responses.

Explanations for the complete inhibition of micturition which eventually occurs without waking are more speculative. H. G. Jones (1960a) accounts for both the waking response and the inhibition of micturition in terms of simultaneous reduction in bladder thresholds required to achieve waking, increases in micturition thresholds through summation of generalized detrusor responses, and an increase in the capacity of the bladder. A less involved explanation is provided by Guthrie's (1935) supposition that the last act in a sequence will be conditioned. If the detrusor stimuli are present from the beginning of the chain of events to the final act of cessation of micturition, these relatively weak stimuli will be conditioned to inhibit voiding at low bladder thresholds.

Despite differences in explanation of the precise conditioning mechanism, the results have been overwhelmingly effective. In a review of the literature, H. G. Jones (1960a) presents results from several studies with children of varying ages (Table 1). These results are not directly comparable because of variations in type of apparatus and techniques employed, severity and complexity of patients' conditions, follow-up period, and criteria of success (H. G. Jones, 1960a, pp. 399–400).

Kahane (1955) reports conflicting results from a study indicating that half of the children of a group in which treatment was intentionally delayed by several months showed spontaneous remission. In addition, 13 members of the original 21 given immediate treatment relapsed. Spontaneous remission of bedwetting is not surprising, since all children, with rare exception, eventually learn to inhibit urination at night. H. G. Jones (1960a) feels, however, that the incidence of relapse is high for the Kahane study probably because the

TABLE 1. SUMMARY OF ENURETIC CASES TREATED BY CONDITIONING*

Author	*No. of cases*	*Age range*	*Percentage cured*	*Percentage markedly improved*	*Percentage of failures*
Mowrer and Mowrer (1938)	30	3–13	100	100	0
Davidson and Douglass (1950)	20	5–15 (plus 2 adults)	75	25	0
Crosby (1950)	35	3½–10½	88	3	9
	23	11–28	83	5	12
Sieger (1952)	106	3–15 (plus 4 adults)	89	7	4
Geppert (1953)	42	5–10	74	16	10
Baller and Schalock (1956)	55	Median 9.5	70	30	30
Wicks (1958)	100	5–17	50	24	26
Gillison and Skinner (1958)	100	3½–21	88	5	7
Freyman (1959)	15	5–14	33	40	27
Murray (1959)	33		75	9	16
Martin and Kubly (1955)	118	3½–18½	56	18	26
Lowe (1959)	322	5–10	88	12	12

* From H. G. Jones, 1960a, p. 377.

children were not given a second course of training to overcome the spontaneous recovery of enuretic behavior which occurs in some cases. One of the important consequences of the use of conditioning methods for the treatment of enuresis is the doubt which has been cast on the supposition that enuretic behavior invariably represents a symptom of more profound disturbance. In some cases enuresis does occur in a constellation of other behavior, but its mere presence is not indicative of pathology. The response of enuresis to conditioning techniques indicates that in most instances, bed-wetting represents a learning inadequacy which does not result in "symptom substitution" when corrected.

The case of a patient treated for frequency of micturition by H. G. Jones (1956) provides a striking illustration of conditioning designed to modify the CS to achieve greater control over an existing response. The patient, a 23-year-old woman, was admitted to the hospital with complaints of frequency of micturition, associated secondary fears, and lack of confidence. On admission to the hospital, she was diagnosed as having anxiety reaction with hysterical urinary frequency and was given a course of psychotherapy lasting five weeks without results. A physical examination prior to conditioning revealed abnormally high bladder pressure at low bladder volume, the urge to urinate at low bladder volume, and sluggish detrusor muscles, which did not respond adequately to changes in bladder volume. The patient reported an urge to urinate at a volume of 300 milliliters. Treatment was designed to increase the patient's ability to retain normal amounts of fluid and to improve the sluggish detrusor muscles. Using a method introduced by Bykov, H. G. Jones (1956) constructed an apparatus which enabled varying amounts of saline solution to be introduced into the bladder. A manometer was also incorporated in the apparatus, and the patient was familiarized with the relationship between volume of urine and increased manometer readings. During initial trials, manometer readings corresponded to actual bladder pressure, and the patient was instructed to relax in order to lower the manometer readings when a pressure of 300 milliliters was reached. Some improvement was attained under these conditions, but on the last trial the manometer reading was lowered by the experimenter, so that a true reading was not recorded. Treatment continued for five days, during which time true readings of the manometer were alternated with contrived readings. After the fifth day, the symptoms disappeared, and the patient was able to retain normal amounts of urine without difficulty. According to the author, additional behavior changes occurred which made it possible for the patient to participate in a program of rehabilitation. The anxiety reaction was treated by desensitization therapy.

Of particular interest in connection with the two conditioning methods presented above is a recent article by Aiba (1963) describing the conditioning of absolute threshold to light. Replicating the work of Russian investigators, the author succeeded in conditioning increases in absolute threshold to light by associating an illuminated panel with pure tone. Subsequent presentation of the tone alone to the subjects raised the dark-adapted threshold. These studies suggest that the association of artifically low manometer readings with stimuli from the bladder may have produced increases in detrusor threshold.

The methods described above were effective in modifying responses by changing the characteristics of the stimuli which control them. In each case, threshold values from the detrusor muscles were altered to achieve greater stimulus control. When a response must be eliminated without altering the characteristics of the stimulus which maintains it, however, the experimenter is confronted with a more difficult training problem. The CS which formerly evoked R1 must now be made to evoke R2, an entirely different, and in some respects directly antagonistic, response. In order to achieve this, the experimenters have temporarily modified certain aspects of the CS—a procedure basically similar to that described in the control of enuresis.

Two of the earliest advocates of conditioning procedures designed to deal with these situations, Guthrie (1935) and M. C. Jones (1924), proposed similar principles for establishing the new response, which involved utilization of the CS in reduced strength. In her exploration of naturally occurring fears in children, M. C. Jones (1924) included a scheme for introducing the phobic stimulus gradually in the context of stimuli evoking pleasurable responses. This method of "direct conditioning" was used to extinguish fear of a rabbit in a 3-year-old boy named Peter. To reduce the effective strength of the CS (rabbit), M. C. Jones utilized the principle of stimulus generalization by presenting the rabbit some distance from Peter, thereby evoking only a fraction of the originally aversive response. Since no reinforced response occurs to the weak aversive stimulus, its presentation constitutes an extinction trial. Moreover, association with the positive reinforcer (candy) enables the aversive CS to acquire secondary reinforcing qualities and, therefore, the ability to evoke pleasurable responses. On subsequent trials, the rabbit was brought closer to Peter until the fear responses were completely eliminated. It is interesting to note that the use of generalized stimuli is in accord with Pavlov's (1927) observation that conditioning will not occur if the CS evokes a more intensive response than the UCS.

Wolpe (1958) extended the paradigm originally proposed by M. C. Jones and devised a system for the treatment of adults with phobic as well as other related behavior disorders. The rationale for his treatment by reciprocal inhibition is based on an elaborate theoretical structure consisting of Hullian learning theory, Sherrington's description of reciprocal inhibition on the neurological level, Watson's and M. C. Jones's experiments with fear, and Jacobson's method for training deep relaxation.

According to Wolpe (1958), neurotic behavior consists in persistent habits learned (conditioned) in anxiety-generating situations, the core of the behavior being anxiety or specifically the responses of the autonomic nervous system.

Using principles derived from animal experiments, Wolpe (1962) asserted that a response inhibitory to anxiety and occurring in the presence of anxiety-evoking stimuli will weaken the connection between the stimuli and the anxiety responses. The justification for this assumption is found in Sherrington's description of the reciprocal relaxation which takes place in one set of muscles (flexors) when the other set (extensors) is activated. Wolpe also found it necessary to postulate the concept of reciprocal inhibition and the accumulation of reactive inhibition to account for reduction in the strength of the aversive stimulus. [It should be noted that an empirical analysis of these events, such as those proposed by M. C. Jones (1924), simply involves a description of the operations whereby the original CS which has been reduced in strength acquires secondary reinforcing properties by virtue of its association with the positive reinforcer.] Regardless of which explanation is used, however, the results are substantially the same, since both are based on identical procedures. The responses which Wolpe found useful to inhibit anxiety are (1) relaxation responses, (2) sexual responses, (3) assertive responses, and (4) respiratory responses [carbon dioxide-oxygen mixtures are sometimes used for cases of pervasive or free-floating anxiety because it is impossible to evoke any of the other responses (Wolpe, 1958, p. 113)].

The principles of reciprocal inhibition described by Wolpe have given rise to a basic therapeutic method known as "psychotherapy by reciprocal inhibition." The use of relaxation as the choice of response to inhibit anxiety is a special case of the basic method and has come to be known as "systematic desensitization." As a form of treatment, systematic desensitization requires the gradual introduction of stimuli which are fear-arousing to the patient at the same time that the patient is given instructions in progressive relaxation either by the Jacobson method (1938) or by light hypnosis. Prior to this, a hierarchy of anxiety-arousing stimuli is constructed for the patient from interviews, and the fear-arousing stimuli, taken from the list, are presented to the patient beginning with the least anxiety-arousing stimulus. The patient is encouraged to visualize the situations portrayed in the fearful themes (height, crowds, rejections, etc.), and reactions are observed. When the anxiety to a particular theme is reduced, the others are presented in successive order until the strongest item is reached. According to Wolpe, it was found at every stage in the process that ". . . freedom from anxiety to an imagined stimulus confers freedom from anxiety upon confrontation with the real equivalent (though sometimes the latter lags behind)" (1962, p. 564). Since Wolpe feels that most neurotic behavior, including the character and personality disturbances, consists of intricate systems of phobias, desensitization therapy is, in principle, applicable to virtually any therapeutic situation in which a clearly defined fear stimulus can be employed. An obverse corroboration of the principles employed in desensitization therapy is found in descriptions of treatment conducted with combat-induced psychiatric casualties during World War II by Menninger (1948) and Ludwig and Ranson (1947). Both studies indicated that the removal of the patient from the zone of combat (300 to 500 miles behind the lines) for treatment invariably prolonged symptoms, resulting in only 10 per cent return to duty. When treatment was conducted in a zone 10 to 20 miles from the front lines, 60 per cent of the men were returned to duty, with the majority adjusting successfully to combat conditions. Presumably, removing the soldiers from the combat zone, far from the front lines, also effectively removed them from the aversive stimuli and the possibility of neutralizing these stimuli through association with some of the anxiety-reducing events in therapy.

The range of patients treated by both reciprocal inhibition and desensitization threapy is considerable. Wolpe (1958) lists 88 patients (1958, pp. 208–213, Table 1) who have benefited from treatment in varying degrees, using a criterion of symptom-free behavior. The cases include inferiority feelings, depression, impotence, claustrophobia, paranoid obsessions, hysterical paresthesias, and others. Wolpe has also been careful to point out that while both forms of treatment have been remarkably successful, it is difficult to separate the effects of the therapeutic interviews from the treatment itself or the relationship which may have been established in therapy. Nevertheless, the results suggest that the method is extremely effective, since 90 per cent of Wolpe's 210 patients were apparently "cured" or much improved after a mean of little over 30 sessions. Approximately 60 per cent of these cases required five or less interviews. In a survey of follow-up studies (Wolpe, 1962), only 4 relapses from among 249 patients were found.

In addition to the two forms of treatment already mentioned, Wolpe (1962) describes several variations which have proved beneficial. The first increases the probability of occurrence of a response antagonistic to anxiety by urging the patient to practice certain responses, e.g., assertiveness in instances where fear of being assertive does not ordinarily occur. The supposition is that constant encouragement from the therapist will gradually change the patient's attitude to evoke the desired response. The second method employs drugs to diminish the level of anxiety as an aid to reciprocal inhibition. The reduction of anxiety following the administration of drugs will often permit other responses to appear. The third procedure involves the acquisition of a dominant motor response. In therapy the patient is given a mild electric shock and is conditioned to produce a well-defined motor response. According to Wolpe, this method has not been too successful. Finally, a stimulus is made to acquire secondary reinforcing properties by pairing with shock reduction. If the patient is required to say "calm" to switch off a shock, the word should acquire "anxiety-relief" characteristics and may be used subsequently as a stimulus for anxiety reduction. Obviously all the additional procedures are intended to encourage the appearance of anxiety-competing responses.

Wolpe's successful development and application of the treatment procedures based on the principles of conditioning have stimulated other investigators, mostly in England and Canada, to duplicate his efforts (Beech, 1960; Bevan, 1960; Bond & Hutchison, 1960; Lazarus, 1958; Lazarus, 1959; Lazarus, 1961; Lazarus, 1962; Lazarus & Rachman, 1957; Meyer, 1957; Meyer & Gelder, 1963; Rachman, 1959). The remarkable uniformity of method in these studies is an indication of the ease with which the basic principles can be communicated.

Among those who have been active in the use of reciprocal inhibition and systematic desensitization, the work of Lazarus has been especially noteworthy. In one particularly important study (Lazarus, 1961), desensitization and interpretative therapy were compared in a group setting. The groups included 11 acrophobics, 15 claustrophobics, five impotent men (treated as sexual phobias), and four mixed phobic disorders (fear of sharp objects, fear of physical violence, fear of moving vehicles, and fear of dogs). All phobias were severe enough to impose a limitation on social mobility and interpersonal relationships. Patients were assigned, at random, to three groups matched in terms of sex, age, and nature and severity of the disorder. Desensitization subjects received "group" therapy as a homogeneous unit organized in terms of similarity of the phobia. A mixed group of patients was also treated as a unit to determine whether desensitization techniques are effective with heterogeneous phobic responses. Initial sessions for the desensitization subjects consisted of instruction in deep relaxation prior to the introduction of the anxiety hierarchy lists, which were constructed separately for each group. Both interpretative groups were treated similarly by a form of insight therapy with reeducative goals (Wolberg, 1954). According to Lazarus, abreactive and cathartic responses emerged from historical data during the interpretative sessions, and violent emotional reaction often accompanied recall of memories. One of the interpretative groups was given relaxation after interpretation to determine the effect of relaxation without desensitization. The criterion of recovery for all patients was ability to perform the previously feared act one month after therapy.

The results of therapy are shown in Table 2. All patients who failed to recover from phobic symptoms in the interpretation group were afforded an opportunity to receive desensitization therapy.

In a follow-up study conducted from 1.5 to 15 months after recovery ($M = 9.05$ months), 10 of the 13 patients given group desensitization maintained their freedom from phobic symptoms. Of the two patients involved in interpretation and relaxation, one relapsed. Eight of the ten patients given postinterpretative desensitization therapy sustained their gains.

In discussing the possibility of contamination due to experimenter bias arising from the use of the same therapist, Lazarus indicates that his personal preference was decidedly in favor of interpretative methods. He adds: "Fortunately the ennui which is generated while applying desensitization procedures is adequately offset by the gratifying results" (1961, p. 509). Commenting on the relative speed of recovery for the postoperative desensitization group, Lazarus maintains that the atmosphere created by the therapist during the initial stages of therapy may, in itself, help to reduce the level of anxiety and thereby increase the probability that the competing relaxation response will appear. Finally, the positive feedback from removal of annoying symptoms leads to changes in the home environment and promotes further improvement in related behavior.

Instrumental Conditioning

The therapeutic methods assigned to the category of instrumental conditioning are aimed at altering existing responses by establishing the following response-reinforcement

TABLE 2. NUMBER OF PATIENTS ASSIGNED TO EACH CONDITION AND THERAPEUTIC OUTCOME*

Patients	*Treated by desensitization*	*Recovered*	*Treated by interpretation*	*Recovered*	*Treated by interpretation and relaxation*	*Recovered*
Acrophobics	5	4	3	0	3	1
Claustrophobics	7	4	3	0	5	1
Impotence	2	2	3	0		
Mixed group	4	3				
Total	18	13	9	0	8	2

* From Lazarus, 1961.

contingencies; avoidance, reward, omission, and punishment. In some instances, identifiable events are used as discriminative stimuli (use of alcohol or fetish object), while in others the behavior is regarded as an emitted response (tics, stuttering). Often two methods are used simultaneously (omission and reward), and assignment to either category is largely arbitrary.

Avoidance learning. Most of therapy which is classified as "avoidance conditioning" begins with a conditioned approach response (which may have been acquired either because of its ability to remove aversive stimuli or because of some intrinsic reward value due to adventitious conditioning) which is to be changed to avoidance. Avoidance conditioning as a therapeutic device has been reasonably successful in cases involving alcoholism (Franks, 1958; Oswald, 1962) and sexually deviant behavior, including fetishism and homosexuality (Freund, 1958; Max, 1935; Oswald, 1962; Raymond, 1956). The area of "aversion" conditioning, in general, has been reviewed by Franks (1958) in an article containing several trenchant observations concerning conditionability as a personality trait, the nature of the unconditioned stimulus, the relationship between stimulus and response in conditioning, and suggestions for further research.

A survey of the vast literature on conditioned-reflex treatment of alcoholism (Voegtlin & Lemere, 1942) discloses that the procedures first established by Kantorovich in 1930, in which shock was used as the UCS, have been adopted as standard in aversion therapy. Treatment of either alcoholism or sexually deviant behavior consists fundamentally in the association of a CS (whiskey or fetish object) with a noxious experience—nausea and violent retching usually induced by such drugs as apomorphine or emetine hydrochloride (UCS) administered in conjunction with a stimulant (benzedrine). The initial conditioning is therefore neither escape nor avoidance and perhaps is more like punishment training, since the subject cannot avoid the painful event. When the CS has finally acquired aversive properties and tends to produce nausea and vomiting (CR), avoidance conditioning is achieved.

Accounts of the effectiveness of avoidance-conditioning therapy with alcoholics vary considerably. The continuing studies of Voegtlin and Lemere (1950) disclose that of 4,096 cases treated over a thirteen-year period, 60 per cent abstained from drinking for one year or longer, 51 per cent for two years or longer, 38 per cent for five years or longer, and 23 per cent for ten years or longer. A more recent study conducted by the Menninger Clinic (Wallerstein, 1957) compared the effectiveness of four different treatment regimes: antabuse, conditioned-reflex therapy (avoidance conditioning), group hypnotherapy, and milieu therapy. The results from this study indicated a much less favorable rate of recovery for avoidance-conditioning therapy, since only 24 per cent of this group improved, compared with 53 per cent with antabuse, 36 per cent with hypnotherapy, and 26 per cent with milieu therapy. The percentage of recovery for most of the studies reviewed (Wallerstein, 1957) appears to vary from a low of 24 to a high of 60. When the procedures established by Voegtlin and Lemere are followed with respect to choice of patients and method, the results usually approximate a 51 per cent overall rate of recovery.

The variability which is found in the reports of treatment with avoidance conditioning is due to a number of factors, not the least of which is the peculiarities inherent in learning initiated and maintained by alcohol or drugs, both of which provide immediate and powerful sources of reinforcement. The successes which have been achieved, however, suggest that certain other factors, such as personality of the subject, nature of the UCS, sequence of events in conditioning, and the basic rationale governing the use of aversion therapy in general, may be equally responsible for the dissimilar findings.

One of the important findings of the Wallerstein study (1957) indicates that, as a group, alcoholics do not reflect any homogeneous personality configurations and that therefore the results of avoidance conditioning will vary accordingly. Aggressive individuals appear to rebel against the punitiveness involved in the treatment, while submissive and guilty patients seem to accept it as welcome punishment. Conditionability also appears to be an important factor, according to Franks (1958). Research conducted by him on both normal subjects and neurotics indicates that introverted subjects condition better than extroverted subjects. Moreover, certain drugs such as amylobarbitone (sodium amytal) and methylpentynol (oblivon), both central depressants, retard the formation of conditioned responses and decrease their resistance to extinction, while dexamphetamine (a central stimulant) has opposite results. If the personality characteristics of the patient undergoing therapy are unknown and if the drug administered as the UCS acts essentially as a depressant, the results of conditioning are likely to be unpredictable.

The sequence of events during aversion treatment is often contrary to the best principles for establishing a conditioned response. Presumably, one of the reasons several studies were able to duplicate the results of Voegtlin and Lemere was that there was rigid adherence to the procedures recommended by Pavlov (1927) for establishing a conditioned response. In some instances the CS was introduced after vomiting was initiated and remained in the patient's presence throughout the course of sickness and after recovery. The argument that such an arrangement is not optimal for avoidance conditioning is supported by experiments with animals demonstrating that a CS preceding a noxious stimulus acquires aversive properties, while that following the cessation of a painful event becomes a secondary reinforcer. The presence of the to-be-conditioned stimulus both during and after vomiting could conceivably negate the results by acting simultaneously as a secondary drive and as a secondary reinforcing stimulus.

Several therapists have attempted to modify the avoidance-conditioning procedure. Oswald (1962) introduced a tape recorder with a continuous loop on which a faint male or female voice (or both) was recorded intoning phrases describing the CS appropriate to the behavior ("whiskey makes him sick") followed by sounds of laughter and vomiting. Apart from the development of unique illusory and hallucinatory experiences, the effect of these variables on the rapidity or strength of conditioning was not noted. Lazarus (1959) reports success in pairing shock with the words "Mother's bed" in the case of a 10-year-old boy who woke in the early hours of the morning with a desire to enter his mother's bed. The boy was also required to say "my bed" in order to terminate shock. The use of a response associated with shock termination is essentially Wolpe's method for conditioning "anxiety-relief" responses and emphasizes the necessity for the inclusion of reward factors in the use of treatment based on avoidance.

If avoidance is to be used as a technique, then some provision should also be made for the patient to derive satisfaction from making a response which does not merely avoid the CS but which, in avoiding it, achieves some other desired result. The success achieved in avoidance conditioning with sexual deviants is probably due to the natural availability of an alternative response which provides a convenient substitute. Franks (1958) has suggested that it might be possible to condition a patient to use stimuli other than alcohol to reduce anxiety by associating the feeling of well-being and tension reduction with these stimuli. In general, the principles of learning would recommend positive reinforcement of socially acceptable behavior at the same time that the reinforcement supporting the deviant response is removed (Bandura, 1963).

Reward learning. It has already been suggested that all instrumental learning can be regarded in terms of two orthogonal dimensions involving behavior and the consequences of the behavior. When the consequences of *responding* or *not responding* produce *positive reinforcement,* the learning procedure is classified, respectively, as "reward" or "omission" training. If the *response* or the *absence of response* results in *negative reinforcement,* the learning procedure is said to be, respectively, "punishment" or "avoidance."

Except for the prevalence of reward as an important but largely unrecognized component in the traditional forms of therapy, treatment methods based explicitly on the manipulation of response-reinforcement contigencies are relatively new. Early, rudimentary attempts to shape behavior by arranging conditions to elicit specific responses were made by M. C. Jones (1924) in the elimination of children's fears. In one of the methods (social imitation), two nonphobic children helped to encourage a phobic child's approach response toward a feared object by reacting favorably to it, while in another (method of distraction), a substituted activity was offered the child. The role of reinforcement in traditional therapy has not been adequately understood, although some efforts have been made to analyze the patient's behavior in terms of the therapist's reinforcement potential. Finesinger (1951), for example, indicated that several classes of response, ranging from vigorous approval to absolute indifference, can be used to direct the patient to talk about certain material. Similar results have been obtained from verbal conditioning studies.

The stimulation for most of the current work in the relationship between deviant behavior and reward learning stems largely from Skinner's (1938) dedication to the operant as a revealing method for the study and control of behavior. In shaping behavior by operant conditioning, the methodological emphasis is on the successive reinforcement of small segments of response which approximate the behavior ultimately to be conditioned. When the behavior is finally established, its control depends upon how often and how much it is reinforced. Thus, for example, if a pigeon is to learn to peck at a disk or if a rat is to learn to press a lever, orientation responses toward the site of the disk or lever are reinforced initially. The final response is produced only after several approximating responses have been rewarded. The frequency with which behavior is subsequently emitted is determined by the availability of reinforcement.

The behavior for which reward learning as a form of treatment has been found suitable falls into two broad categories: behavior which does not appear under appropriate reinforcement conditions (psychosis, hysterical inactivation) and behavior which occurs only under socially inappropriate reinforcement conditions (antisocial behavior). Although reward learning is also an important aspect of interview methods of therapy, any consideration of this area is beyond the scope of this chapter. The subject has been treated by Dollard and Miller (1950), Kanfer (1962), Shoben (1948; 1949), and Phillips (1956).

Among the distinguishing features of schizophrenia are the absence of reality-oriented behavior and the loss of interpersonal relationships. For psychotic patients, events in general and people in particular appear to have lost their ability to elicit and sustain behavior under appropriate reinforcement conditions. Psychoanalytic theory interprets psychotic behavior as a phenomenon exhibiting the dynamics of regression to primary narcissism—a developmental state prior to ego formation (Munroe, 1955). According to the theory, both ego development and the formation of object relationships are consequences of transition from primary-process behavior, characterized by inability to delay gratification (pleasure principle) to the secondary process, where delays of gratification are tolerated (reality principle). In terms of learning, the ability to delay gratification is related to the process whereby objects (people or events) acquire secondary reinforcing properties, a process which may be equivalent to formation of object relationships in psychoanalytic theory. If this process is disrupted either because of maturational inadequacies or because the objects acquire negative reinforcing characteristics, the individual is likely to turn to internal and more basic sources of gratification, reflected in autistic and regressive behavior. Much of the experimentation using operant methods in psychosis appears to be directed toward restoring reinforcement mechanisms which will permit objects in the external world to regain their significance as symbols of reinforcement.

One of the earliest studies in the reorganization of reward systems for psychotic patients was conducted by Peters and Jenkins (Peters & Jenkins, 1954; Peters & Murphee, 1954). The rationale for their study, however, was based on the hypothesis that schizophrenic behavior represents "frozen" maladaptive responses which can be corrected by retraining (Jenkins, 1950). Subshock injections of insulin were administered to deteriorated schizophrenic patients to raise the hunger level. Initially, the patients were given the task of solving a graded selection of simple problems involving mazes and obstructions, with fudge as a reward. Ultimately, they were encouraged to solve more difficult problems in multiple-choice learning and verbal reasoning in which the reward was gradually associated with the experimenter. Insulin injections were discontinued after several weeks, and the patients participated in the solution of interpersonal problems. Social rewards had by this time recovered their effectiveness, and candy was no longer used as a reinforcement. Comparison with a control group to distinguish the effects of insulin and reward from special attention indicated that the patients in the insulin-reward group made a significant improvement in social behavior in the hospital.

King, Armitage, and Tilton (1960) demonstrated similar results in the use of an operant-interpersonal method with chronic schizophrenic males, all of whom had undergone psychotherapy in the past. The group involved in operant-interpersonal therapy was seen three times a week for fifteen weeks in sessions lasting twenty to thirty minutes. The same amount of time was devoted to a verbal therapy group administered both individual and group treatment. One of the remaining groups was given recreation and three to five hours a week of special activities, while the other participated in the usual ward activities with no special attention.

The operant-interpersonal group was encouraged to operate a series of levers on a multiple-operant problem-solving apparatus, individually and in cooperation with another patient. Unlike the situation in the study reported by Peters and Jenkins (1954), primary motivation was not manipulated, although the patients were given cigarettes and candy as rewards for correct performance. In some cases it was necessary to place the candy in the patient's mouth because of his deteriorated condition. Food reinforcement was also followed by verbal reward such as "good" or "very good." In accordance with the principles of successive approximation, every response was rewarded which gradually moved the patient toward verbalization. Ultimately, the patient was required to verbalize the solution of the problem, and conversations not related to the operant task were encouraged. In the final phase, subjects worked cooperatively with one another in mutual solution of problems.

The results of the experiment were assessed by several rating scales of improvement, including a ward observation scale. Five of the twelve subjects in the operant-interpersonal groups were rated as showing considerable improvement (one patient was transferred to an open ward), and three showed minor improvements. In the recreation group, two patients showed considerable improvement, and two showed minor improvement. The patients undergoing verbal therapy became somewhat withdrawn, and the no-attention group showed no change. A six-month follow-up indicated that the operant-interpersonal group continued to retain the gains they had made in such behavior as level of verbalization, motivation to leave the ward, and decreased enuresis. The authors entertain the possibility that the amount of gain obtained is all that can be expected from this particular method with psychotics because of the possibility of organicity in schizophrenic disorders.

In a somewhat different application of operant techniques, Ayllon and Michael (1959) analyzed the ward behavior of hospitalized patients and concluded that the problems presented by the patients in the hospital were due to reinforcement of specific response patterns. They found that such behavior as "failure to eat, dress, bathe, interact socially with other patients, and walk without being led, hoarding various objects, hitting, pinching . . ." (Ayllon & Michael, 1959, p. 323) interfered seriously with the hospital's routine and detracted from time devoted to direct treatment. The authors instituted a program of training for the patients consisting essentially of operant techniques, with the nurses as "behavioral engineers." The customary behavior of the patient designed to attract the nurses' attention was ignored, and the incidence of such behavior was markedly reduced. In two instances where patients were unwilling to feed themselves, the nurses spilled food on their clothes when they insisted on being fed. Since the patients were somewhat meticulous about their appearance, they soon fed themselves.

Sidman (1962) has reviewed the research in application of operant techniques to therapy and diagnosis. Attempts have been made to develop a behavior repertoire in autistic children through a controlled environment using the principles of shaping, reinforcement schedules, extinction, and secondary reinforcement (Ferster & DeMeyer, 1961). Initially, the children learned to manipulate simple devices for which food, candy, and music were given as reinforcement. More complex devices were introduced, and coins were established as generalized reinforcers. After such treatment, the children displayed normal behavior in the laboratory for several hours at a time but still remained autistic in other situations. Apparently one of the chief difficulties in applying operant techniques to psychotic behavior is the inability to transfer the gains to activities outside the laboratory.

Rate of responding and quality of reinforcer are being studied as possible indices to supplement the subclasses of psychosis by identifying syndromes of behavioral deficit (Lindsley, Skinner, & Solomon, 1953–1956). Methods of reinforcement through brain stimulation are also being explored with psychotic patients (Bishop, Elder, & Heath, 1963). Self-stimulation of reinforcement centers through electrode implants in schizophrenic subjects produces highly stable lever-pressing behavior which persists despite hunger and offers of food. Heath and Torkildsen (1960) have obtained temporary therapeutic benefits from stimulation of "pleasure-inducing" centers in chronic schizophrenic patients. The use of brain-stimulation techniques may ultimately provide a highly manipulable source of primary reinforcement which can be used in conjunction with certain response-reinforcement contingencies to restore human relationships as rewarding events for psychotic patients.

Operant procedures have been used in an exceptionally resourceful manner to restore functioning in a case of hysterical blindness (Brady & Lind, 1961). The patient, a 40-year-old veteran, had previously developed difficulty in one eye, reducing vision to 20/80. Complete blindness occurred when his wife and mother-in-law became more demanding. Sodium pentathol treatments were not successful, and the authors decided to explore therapy based on operant methods.

Treatment began by establishing relatively stable behavior from which the effects of visual stimuli could be observed. The patient was required to press a button on a DRL schedule (differential reinforcement of low rate) of eighteen seconds with a limited hold of three seconds. A response which followed the preceding response by less than eighteen seconds or more than twenty-one seconds was not rewarded, and the apparatus was reset. Need for approval supplemented by special trips to the canteen was used as a reinforcer for correct responding. Illumination in the experimental room was increased during the eighteen- to twenty-one-second periods, and the patient could improve his score by making use of these visual cues. Initial introduction of the light produced a large amount of responding outside of the eighteen- to twenty-one-second period, as though the patient was trying to avoid the cues. He also appeared tense and frightened when the light was first introduced and covered his eyes to avoid it. In subsequent sessions, the light was introduced directly in front of him and was gradually increased in illumination. He was also told that it would help him regain his sight. During the forty-fifth session, the patient finally saw light and learned a difficult discrimination pattern. Support and rehabilitation were introduced after the patient had regained his sight, and a follow-up after thirteen months indicated complete adjustment.

An analysis of the result of Brady and Lind's study merely in terms of an increased operant appears inadequate, especially in view of the patient's behavior during the course of treatment. The method used by Brady and Lind has a great deal in common with the classical conditioning techniques used by Wolpe to establish competing responses. The primary purpose of the study was to increase sight by associating it with rewarding instead of aversive consequences. This was accomplished by maximizing the probability of reinforcement when the light was introduced during the eighteen- to twenty-one-second period. It will be recalled that the initial introduction of light evoked tension and avoidance, resulting in a large number of incorrect responses. When the light was subsequently introduced with decreased illumination, however (a situation reminiscent of Wolpe's desensitization), the patient eventually incorporated it as a cue for reward. Thus, light became the CS for behavior associated with pleasurable instead of aversive cues.

Reward learning is being utilized to shift both response and reward hierarchies in behavior occurring under socially inappropriate reinforcement conditions. Bandura (1961) maintains that socially inappropriate or antisocial behavior represents a learning deficit created by failure of the socialization process. He also indicates that psychoanalytic theories of personality and their corresponding therapeutic methods have been developed for the treatment of oversocialized neurotics and, therefore, are ineffective for altering the behavior of antisocial personalities (Bandura, 1961, p. 148). As in psychosis, the treatment of recidivism and delinquency requires the therapist to arrange conditions so that he ultimately becomes an instrument of reward capable of promoting new patterns of behavior. Such a goal may involve radical departures from traditional interview techniques in the initial phases of treatment such as those initiated by Slack (1960) and Schwitzgebel (1960; 1961). These investigators shaped the responses of adolescent delinquents who would ordinarily not accept therapy by reinforcing small segments of behavior which would ultimately lead to reliable and continued attendance. Therapy was construed as an experimental project, and the boys were paid for participating. No effort was made to schedule appointments initially; the subjects were rewarded with food for coming at any time and for any reason. When attendance became dependable, attempts were made to encourage scheduled appointments by rewarding more or less prompt arrival and by giving unexpected bonuses. Gradually a time was set which was more convenient for the experimenter, and after 15 to 30 meetings, appointments were generally kept. The final stage in shaping came when the reinforcement was shifted from payment of money for participation to the establishment of a relationship between the experimenter and the subject.

Omission training. In omission training, the occurrence of a specified response leads to the absence of reward, a condition which most closely approximates the laboratory arrangement for extinction due to nonreinforcement. Omission training has rarely been used as a therapeutic method except in combination with one of the other methods, usually reward, but Walton (1960) reports a case of neurodermatitis which was successfully treated by merely altering the customary response-reinforcement contingencies. A young woman of 20 developed a serious neurodermatitis which was exacerbated by constant scratching and which persisted for two years, despite treatment by medication and x ray. The patient's record disclosed an authoritative father who showed preference for the son and a family situation in which both the mother and the daughter were held in inferior positions. Following the development of dermatitis, the patient received more attention from both her father and her fiancé, who applied the ointment prescribed for her. Walton developed his therapeutic procedure from Hull's postulates governing the acquisition of reactive and conditioned inhibition resulting from nonreinforced responding. (It should be recognized that both reactive inhibition and conditioned inhibition are derived concepts used to explain extinction in the absence of reward.) Members of the patient's family were told to ignore the ailment, and the fiancé was requested to refrain from applying the ointment in order to remove the source of reinforcement sustaining the response. Over a period of two months, the frequency of scratching decreased, resulting in a gradual improvement in the neurodermatitis. After three months the symptoms disappeared completely, and the results of a four-year follow-up revealed that the patient was happily married and gainfully employed.

Similar methods were employed by Williams (1959) to eliminate the tantrum behavior of a 21-month-old child who demanded special care and attention. The boy had been ill for eighteen months and had grown accustomed to the presence of the parents in his bedroom. Whenever the parents attempted to leave the bedroom, the child cried and displayed tantrums; finally they were forced to spend from one to two hours at a time with him. Data presented by Williams indicate that the tantrum showed rapid extinction when the parents were advised to leave the bedroom and not reenter it. After extinction had been achieved, a relative unwittingly reinstituted the tantrums by indulging the child. The same procedure was reintroduced, resulting in complete extinction. Williams emphasizes the fact that no punishment was used and that no substitute behavior was acquired.

Punishment training. It has already been suggested that the difference between avoidance and punishment is in the nature of the stimulus controlling the response and in the consequences of the response itself. Mowrer (1960) has proposed that since the response associated with avoidance and punishment is designed to eliminate fear, the only distinction between both is in the stimuli to which fear becomes attached: "In so-called punishment, these stimuli are produced by (correlated with) the behavior (or response) which we wish to block. . . . In avoidance learning the fear-arousing stimuli are not response-produced" (1960, p. 32). He also points out that avoidance learning is in the imperative mood—"Do this . . . or pain will follow"—whereas in punishment "the mood is conditional. . . . If you do this . . . pain will follow" (1960, p. 33). M. C. Jones (1924) considered the "method of repression" based on punishment for an avoidance response to be the least satisfactory for the elimination of children's fears.

Studies using punishment as a procedure for eliminating undesirable behavior fall into two groups: those which employ external sources of punishment and those which attribute the punishing event to some conceptual state of the organism. The latter studies derive their procedures from the method of negative practice introduced by Dunlap (1932) for reducing the frequency of errors by conscious repetition of responses and their rationale from the concepts of reactive inhibition (Pavlov, 1927) and conditioned inhibition (Hull, 1943).

When first introduced, the method of negative practice was used largely to eliminate errors involved in such skills as typing and piano playing by instructing the subject to repeat these errors deliberately until they disappeared. Later, the method was extended to speech blockage and stuttering and even to enuresis, masturbation, and homosexuality, apparently with very little success. In his review of negative practice as a therapeutic technique, Lehner (1954) points out that Dunlap's failure to provide detailed descriptions of the application of negative practice was one of the contributing factors to its failure to develop as a therapeutic method. Kendrick (1960) also suggests that the absence of any systematic conceptual framework to interpret the results of negative practice limited its expansion. Experimenters who have continued to use deliberate repetition of a response to reduce its frequency explain the results in terms of the accumulation of reactive inhibition and conditioned inhibition, which are interpreted as forms of intrinsic punishment.

The concept of inhibition was first proposed by Pavlov (1927) to describe cessation of responding under conditions of nonreinforcement. Hull (1943) subsequently proposed a two-factor theory of extinction using both reactive inhibition and conditioned inhibition as conceptual variables according to which each response produces an increment of reactive inhibition similar to fatigue. Since reactive inhibition is an aversive state, it encourages resting responses which ultimately become conditioned to stimuli in the situation and which produce a more durable and permanent form of extinction. Continued responding increases the amount of reactive inhibition. The dissipation of reactive inhibition during rest encourages the accumulation of conditioned inhibition.

Yates (1958a) devised a method for treating multiple tics in a 25-year-old woman on the basis of Hull's analysis of the extinction process. The patient had four pronounced tics: a complex stomach-contraction breathing tic, a nasal "explosion" (expiration), a coughing tic, and an eye-blink tic acquired ten years previously when she felt she was being suffocated while undergoing anesthesia. Yates instructed the patient to reproduce each tic as accurately as possible for five one-minute trials with one-minute rest periods between trials. Each session lasted forty-five minutes, and at the end of 100 sessions the tics began to show a significant decline in frequency. Yates also tested several hypotheses concerning the effects of massed and distributed practice in the remaining 25 sessions and reported marked changes in behavior. The nasal tic disappeared almost completely, the eye-blink and throat tics were sharply reduced in frequency, but the stomach tic showed little change. The patient reported that, in general, she felt more relaxed in public, a finding confirmed by her friends and physician. H. G. Jones (1960b) continued treatment with Yates's patient and made considerable gains. He found that her tics were far less noticeable and more easily brought under voluntary control but that they were still exacerbated by illness and social and vocational frustration.

Walton (1958) successfully treated a case of chronic hysterical aphonia of seven years' duration based on the concepts of inhibition and desensitization. The patient's inability to speak was regarded as a conditioned avoidance response which had achieved an autonomous function, and treatment was designed to inhibit the avoidance response. During the first phase the patient was required to read aloud from a book for periods of fifteen minutes. Two extra minutes were added to each session when she failed to show any increase in volume. Improvement, however, was followed by a two-minute reduction in the length of the session. This plan was adopted on the assumption that hysterics should develop reactive and conditioned inhibition rapidly (Eysenck, 1960). The desire to rest and reduce the length of the session was regarded as reinforcement for increases in loudness, and the patient showed rapid improvement. During the second and third phases, the sessions lasted for ½ hour but were interrupted every five minutes to minimize fatigue and encourage rapid development of conditioned inhibition. In addition, a therapist and a friend, with whom the patient had established good relationships, were introduced as part of the audience. This plan had the advantage of approximating the conditions of everyday life in order to increase transfer from the experimental situation. In the final phase, dexedrine was introduced as a stimulant to establish a more introverted behavior pattern and reduce the amount of reactive inhibition. The patient made rapid improvement, was given vocational advice, and helped to make certain changes in living conditions outside of the hospital. Follow-up twenty months after discharge indicated that there was no recurrence of aphonia and that it had not been replaced by any other symptoms.

Using the concept of conditioned inhibition as a rationale for treatment, Walton and Black (1958) also achieved a permanent reduction in stammering which was considered a conditioned avoidance response. Inhibition was created by requiring the subject to shadow the experimenter's voice while speaking into a telephone in the presence of several other people.

The second group of studies is distinguishable by the use of extrinsic punishment and an explanation of the effects of punishment similar to that proposed by Schoenfeld (1950). When a source of punishment is used which is initially independent of the subject's behavior, the proprioceptive stimuli accompanying the punished response acquire aversive properties through association with punishment. Eventually, the subject's intention to respond is preceded by aversive proprioceptive stimuli, and the response tends to be extinguished. Flanagan, Goldiamond, and Azrin (1958; 1959) have shown that chronic stuttering can be reduced or increased by combining external punishment with the rewarding effects of escape from punishment. Each nonfluency was punished by turning on a loud tone (105 decibels), which decreased the frequency of stuttering. Increases in frequency of stuttering were also obtained whenever a nonfluency was successful in avoiding the loud tone. Barrett (1962) was able to reduce the rate of multiple tics in a 38-year-old patient by combining punishment and reward in a free operant procedure. The tics had developed fourteen years previously without any apparent trauma and consisted of complex contractions of neck, shoulder, chest, and abdominal muscles; head nodding; bilateral eye blinking; opening of the mouth; and other mild facial movements. Drugs and psychotherapy had been administered with no effect, and the tics were considered symptomatic of an extrapyramidal system disturbance. An apparatus was devised to program the following contingencies: Each tic produced a 1.5-second interruption in music which the patient was enjoying, while the absence of tics for a period of 1.5 seconds permitted the patient to listen for at least that period. [The schedule is a variation of DRL used by Brady and Lind (see above).] In addition, each tic produced a 1.5-second noise which was interrupted for at least 1.5 seconds when no tics occurred. The procedure effectively reduced the rate of tics from an operant level of 64 to 116 tics per minute to 15 to 30 tics per minute when the music contingency was employed. Although no cure was obtained, the patient exhibited remarkable improvement. The studies by Barrett (1962), Yates (1958a; 1958b), and Jones (1960b) provide interesting contrasts in method. Yates and Jones depended upon intrinsic punishment from the inhibitory state to eliminate the response, while Barrett used both reward and extrinsic punishment. Neither method achieved absolute elimination of tics, but the reduction in rate suggests that some variant may ultimately be successful.

Beech (1960) has advocated a modification in the treatment of writer's cramp and associated motor difficulties, devised by Liversedge and Sylvester (1955; Sylvester & Liversedge, 1960). Their observations of the cramp during writing indicated two principal components: tremors and spasms, which led to the development of several pieces of apparatus designed to "decondition" the response. To control tremors, shock was delivered for improper insertion of a stylus into a series of graduated holes or for failure to negotiate a series of zigzag patterns correctly. The retraining mechanism for spasms consisted of an ordinary pen modified to produce shock when excessive pressure was applied. Of the 39 cases treated by these methods, 29 showed complete freedom from motor difficulties following three to six weeks of therapy. A follow-up period ranging from one month to 4.5 years indicated that five cases had relapsed. The remaining 24 were gainfully employed, some engaged in writing from four to six hours per day (Sylvester & Liversedge, 1960).

Beech's (1960) inability to obtain as good a recovery rate as Sylvester and Liversedge, using their methods, suggested that the patients treated in each of the studies were not equivalent. Beech's sample was predominantly neurotic, while the sample collected by Sylvester and Liversedge appeared to be less anxious. This distinction led Beech to suggest that punishment achieved results in cases with initially low levels of anxiety. For patients with high anxiety levels, a plan of treatment was formulated combining negative practice and desensitization in which the patient was encouraged to imagine the act of writing at the same time that he was given relaxation training. Two cases treated in this manner made successful recoveries.

BEHAVIOR THERAPY AND THE SOVIET UNION

It should be clear from the preceding discussion of the development and practice of behavior therapy that the emphasis in certain psychotherapeutic techniques (classical conditioning) derives largely from the empirical and methodological aspects of Pavlov's and Bekhterev's work rather than from the conceptual nervous system which Pavlov ultimately devised to interpret his experimental findings. In some instances, behavior therapy has been somewhat indirectly related to Pavlovian theory through the concept of inhibition; in others, the concept of excitation and inhibition has been employed as the basis for a theory of personality (Eysenck, 1960). For the most part, however, the method rather than the neurophysiological theory has been of utmost importance. Russian treatment methods, on the other hand, evolved from an interpretation of psychopathology based on Pavlov's (1941) position that all ailments of the nervous system, and hence neuroses, arise from a disturbance of the proper relations between excitatory and inhibitory processes. Gantt (1941) has suggested that these two processes are analogous to the action of acetylcholine, which stimulates certain peripheral nerves, and sympathin, which acts as an inhibitor because it stimulates peripheral nerves, having, in general, opposite effects of those stimulated by acetylcholine. Although Pavlov (1941) stressed the importance of environmental conditions in the production of pathology in animals, he also proposed a constitutional hypothesis to explain differing reactions to the same stimulus conditions. Three types of nervous systems were identified: the strong, in which inhibitory processes are considerably weaker than the excitatory; the weak, in which both processes are insufficient, especially the inhibitory; and the balanced, where inhibitory and excitatory processes begin at the same level. Experimental treatment methods were based on the supposition that most pathology originates in the exhaustion of the inhibitory potential of cortical cells. Successful treatment, according to Pavlov (1941), depended not only on the administration of bromides to achieve ". . . a strengthening of the inhibitory potential of the animal" (Pavlov, 1941) but also on the type of nervous system involved. In weak types the conditioned reflex could be improved and regulated, but no more than this was possible because the problem of pathological inheritance was involved. The strong and balanced types responded more favorably to treatment. It is also interesting to note that Pavlov did not emphasize the methods he derived from his work with the conditioned reflex in order to effect changes in the behavior of the animal. Presumably, this was accomplished through the use of drugs.

Current treatment methods in the Soviet Union are compounded from the three elements introduced by Pavlov: (1) constitutional differences in the nervous system, (2) the conditioned reflex, and (3) prolonged sleep or rest as a method for altering behavior. Each of these is, in turn, based on a neurophysiological model. The prevalence of the constitutional hypothesis is documented by the fact that most case discussions allude to the type of nervous system involved. While neurosis is produced by an individual's specific contact with life, the type of nervous system is exceedingly important in determining not only whether neurosis will occur but also what the specific form of the neurosis will be. Pavlov later elaborated the hypothesis to include three types inherent only in man: the intellectual, the artistic, and the intermediate. Combinations of these types and those described earlier form the basis for most neurotic conditions. For example, according to Platonov:

> Neurasthenia is a morbid form of the weak general and intermediate human type, while hysteria is a manifestation of the weak general type combined with the artistic type and a pathological prevalence of the first signal system and the subcortex. Psychasthenia arises in the weak general type combined with the intellectual type and a pathological predominance of the second signal system. . . . An obsessional neurosis is based on a "trigger point" retained for a long time because the zone of inhibition which isolates it and is formed according to the mechanism of negative induction (1959, p. 274).

The conditioned reflex is the method whereby changes in the neurophysiological substrate occur and is equivalent to the learning process. The chief difference between the use of the term in the Soviet Union and its meaning elsewhere is that in Russia the process of conditioning is primarily related to changes in the cerebral cortex and only secondarily to behavior. Thus, while all conditioning is designed to alter behavior, the methods of conditioning are formulated from an analysis of its effects on the central nervous system. This explains, to some extent, why such variables as reinforcement have never been stressed.

Prolonged sleep or rest induced by hypnosis or drugs has long been the accepted form of treatment in the Soviet Union, in response to Pavlov's conclusions concerning the role of sleep in the restoration of equilibrium in the cortical cells. Apart from serving as a medium in which new conditioning can take place, sleep also acts as a form of internal inhibition, preventing the cells of the cerebral cortex from further functional exhaustion, thus limiting further destruction and aiding in "storing the spent excitable substance" (Lynn, 1963; Platonov, 1959, p. 32). More recently, however, and presumably under the influence of Pavlov and Bekhterev, the importance of language as a method for changing behavior has been stressed. The entire first half of one of the most comprehensive works on therapy in the Soviet Union (Platonov, 1959) is devoted to an analysis of language and its effect on the central nervous system, presumably in order to establish psychotherapy as a legitimate and acceptable form of treatment within the rubric of conditioning methods. Language, the "secondary signal system," acts as a conditioned stimulus for man, and words as conditioned stimuli are "immaterial" until conditioned reflex bonds between them and some unconditioned stimulus or conditioned stimuli of the first signal system are established in the cortex. The exact function of language in therapy is to

> influence the cortical dynamics [by] *explanation, persuasion* or *suggestion* [to] change in the desired direction the consciousness of the patient, his emotional sphere, his endocrine-vegetative activity and other physiological processes. . . . Psychotherapy must, first of all, ensure an optimal relationship between the basic nervous processes of the cortex and subcortex and both signal systems in the activity of the integral organism. By creating in the cerebral cortex new dynamic structures which aid in regulating the general physiological state of the human organism and remove pathological states, psychotherapy thus contributes to the speediest restoration of its normal functioning (Platonov, 1959, p. 222).

The ultimate function of psychotherapy, therefore, is similar to that of prolonged sleep: to restore cortical imbalance. Sometimes sleep or a drowsy state is used as a medium for language because conditioning is more effective under these circumstances.

The methods of therapy which are described by Platonov (1959) and which are contained in the volume by Winn (1961) grow out of the assumed link between language as a conditioned stimulus and its effect on the central nervous system. Both Miassischev (1961) and Platonov (1959) appear to agree that the prevalent techniques can be classified into two broad categories: direct and indirect. The direct method, which incorporates both explanation and persuasion, corresponds to the highest activities of the secondary signal system and makes conscious and critical analysis accessible to the patient (Miassischev, 1961). Under these conditions, psychotherapy takes place on a "conscious level," and the effect of explanation and persuasion is to

> activate the patient's cortex and increase its tone. . . . The physician [aids] in removing the pathological bonds in the cortical dynamic structures and in creating new ones which is accomplished by the patient by means of a critical re-elaboration (under the supervision of the physician in a frank interview with him) of the entire pathogenetic situation which served as the cause of the ailment (Platonov, 1959, p. 226).

In virtually all the cases described by Platonov (1959) and in several contained in the volume by Winn (1961), therapy proceeds by first making an assessment of the factors responsible for the patient's condition (these may be historical) and then by explaining these factors to him. Ultimately, attempts are made to persuade the patient that these factors are no longer important in determining behavior. Platonov divides therapy on a conscious level into three forms: The first, explanatory therapy, is illustrated by the case of a student who was deserted by her husband in the fifth month of pregnancy. She became depressed and complained of severe headaches, drowsiness during the day, and sleeplessness at night. The reason for her condition was explained by the physician, and she was enjoined to forget her husband, since his action indicated he was not worthy of her. She was also advised to concentrate on her studies (Platonov, 1959, p. 228). In the second form of therapy, direct verbal suggestion or persuasion, a pregnant woman who was troubled by prenatal vomiting was told by her physician that she was well and had no reason to vomit any more, in answer to her protest that therapy had not yet begun. According to the author, the patient returned the following day relieved of her symptoms ostensibly because of the strong imperative suggestion given her by the physician. Platonov also observes that in order for these procedures to work effectively, the physician must be a person of authority. The third form of explanation and persuasion involves rest and complete passivity. The patient is placed in a bed or an armchair with weak or diminished lighting. Direct methods are also referred to as "rational therapy" because the patient is given an explanation for his ailment and because his difficulties are discussed in rational terms with the physician. Kantorovich (1961) also prescribes direct methods of treatment to ameliorate symptoms in schizophrenia but adds that it is not possible to cure psychoses merely by psychotherapy.

The rationale for the indirect methods of therapy is similar to that for the direct methods, with the exception that the indirect methods, which include suggestion in states of drowsiness and hypnosis, are prescribed in those instances where indirect methods do not work or where the "neurotic ailment occurred under conditions of a deeper inhibitory state . . . by stronger factors traumatizing the mind" (Platonov, 1959, p. 231). The point is also made that since competing influences are fully excluded in these states, the physician's suggestive words are more influential (Platonov, 1959, p. 231). Schreiber (1961) describes the method as it is used in hysteria. After the patient has been informed that his illness is functional in character and after he has been assured that he will be helped, he is required to wait several days in "expectation" of treatment. Ultimately, he is brought into a room, is requested to lie down on a couch, and is administered "medication" through a special mask. In the meantime, two physicians discuss the effectiveness of the treatment within his hearing. In cases of the treatment of alcoholism through avoidance conditioning, hypnosis is used to establish the effectiveness of some neutral stimulus by first pairing it with apomorphine or antabuse (Gordova & Kovalev, 1961).

With almost no exceptions, Russian therapists agree on the effectiveness of the methods described. A few, however, have attempted to use methods which are less neurophysiologically oriented. In describing psychotherapy with smokers, for example, Povorinsky (1961) contends that hypnosis is not always successful because it places the patient in conflict. Instead, he argues that it is of paramount importance to remove it from the position of a reflex habit. Smoking, according to Povorinsky, compared with other forms of narcomania, has many well-established ties of conditioning and is, in fact, the easiest form of narcomania and the least limited by time, place, income, or other conditions:

> That is why the fight against the automatisms of smoking, against various habitual associations is so significant in the treatment of the habit. When the patient consents to recording every cigarette he smokes, his attention is directed to activities previously performed almost unconsciously. The strength of automatisms is thus sapped and undermined (Povorinsky, 1961, p. 151).

The final stage of treatment involves hypnotic suggestion.

It is extremely difficult to assign the methods of treatment proposed by the Russian therapists to the categories constructed for the description of behavior therapy. Certainly, all therapy is ultimately construed as classical conditioning in the Soviet Union mainly because of the tradition established by Pavlov. But the so-called "newer" methods—those involving direct procedures such as explanation, persuasion, and, to some extent, suggestion—appear to resemble operant procedures because of the attempt to establish response-reward contingencies by the therapist. Except for the neurophysiological speculation involved in the description of the direct methods, the case for classical conditioning is exceedingly difficult to establish. The situation is somewhat the same for the indirect methods of therapy utilizing suggestion under light sleep or hypnosis. It may be possible to construe these methods in terms of Wolpe's reciprocal inhibition therapy, but much closer control of the variables is required to confirm this similarity. If, as Platonov claims, 58 per cent are cured completely, 20 per cent show considerable improvement, 16 per cent show slight improvement, and 6 per cent show no effect as a result of using these methods (1959, p. 224), they certainly merit closer study. In any event, one of the striking features of Soviet therapy is the willingness to explore different procedures.

CONCLUSIONS AND COMMENTS

The distinction between a classical and instrumental conditioning in the description of treatment methods reflects differences in application of behavioral principles rather than important differences in fundamental processes. There are several reasons, however, for the impressive results obtained thus far from the use of classical as opposed to instrumental conditioning. In virtually all instances where classical learning has been used (Mowrer & Mowrer, 1928; Wolpe, 1958), the experimenter had access to specific stimuli which could be manipulated to produce change. In some cases these stimuli were broadly interpreted to include fear of performing an act, e.g., fear of assertion or sexual impotence (Wolpe, 1958). Instrumental techniques, by contrast, are largely exploratory and have been used in instances where discriminative or controlling stimuli are unknown (conversion reactions, recidivism), where behavior is exceedingly resistant to change (chronic psychosis), and where anxiety does not appear to be a major motivational factor in sustaining the response. Treatment using operant methods will continue to demand the kind of resourcefulness and imagination exhibited by Brady and Lind (1961), Slack (1960), and Schwitzgebel (1961) before any general principles can be abstracted which will be appropriate for a large number of cases.

The omission of a discussion of interview methods in this chapter is not intended to suggest a discontinuity in the principles underlying conditioning and the more traditional forms of therapy or to imply that these techniques do not constitute part of the procedures in behavior therapy. The relationship between learning and psychotherapy has already been explored by others (Dollard & Miller, 1950; Kanfer, 1962; Shaw, 1946; Shoben, 1948), and there are many similarities to psychotherapy in the methods used by Wolpe (1958) and Phillips (1956). One of the chief differences between the methods based on learning theory and those derived from the psychodynamic model, however, is related to the role of the therapist. In all traditional therapy, the initial therapeutic objective is the establishment of a patient-therapist "relationship." This makes the explicit, though often unrecognized, assumption that the major source of reinforcement in all therapy should be the therapist. In behavior therapy, the nature of the reinforcing event depends on the type of therapy being conducted. In classical conditioning and certain cases of operant learning, very little direct use is made of the therapist as an instrument of reward, and the response-reinforcement contingencies are placed in the environment or the patient's response. Treatment centers around the extinction and/or facilitation of a response, almost independently of the therapist. In other types of learning (Peters & Jenkins, 1954; Schwitzgebel, 1961), the therapist himself provides the incentive to develop certain patterns of behavior, and he becomes a source of reinforcement when the behavior is finally elicited.

The use of behavior principles has raised several questions concerning the importance of certain commonly accepted beliefs about psychotherapy.

1. In accordance with the medical model of pathology, deviant behavior is regarded as a symptom—an overt manifestation of a more fundamental pathogenic process. Symptom amelioration is said, therefore, to lead to symptom substitution. The results of the follow-up studies conducted by most of the investigators cited above suggest that underlying "psychic" mechanisms need not be assumed in order to secure enduring changes in behavior (Yates, 1958b).

2. Historical and developmental sequences in the patient's life must be explored to achieve behavioral changes in the present. Such an assumption fails to make the distinction between the historical and developmental laws necessary for a comprehensive theory of personality and the ahistorical laws governing learning, which may be sufficient to deal with behavior in the present. Tacit recognition that a consideration of historical variables may not be necessary for therapy has come from the introduction of such psychoanalytic concepts as "secondary autonomy" (Hartmann, 1960) and its psychological equivalent, "functional autonomy" (Allport, 1937). Both stress the independence of behavior from the original sources of motivation.

3. The therapist must treat the "whole" personality. The exact meaning of "whole" is often unclear; however, the studies cited in this chapter have demonstrated that beneficial effects can be derived from dealing with highly circumscribed segments of behavior. Generally, the patient's ability to gain control over specific responses has a pronounced positive effect on other aspects of his functioning.

4. "Learning theory seems to be the academic theoretical backbone of the majority of recent, mass produced clinical psychologists. But since this theory cannot guide their clinical work, they rely increasingly upon psychoanalytical propositions, whose theory they have not studied" (Rapaport, 1959, p. 144). The studies reported in this chapter appear to be an effective answer to this proposition. Moreover, the use of behavior principles in the clinic may serve to bridge the gulf between experimental and clinical psychologists by illuminating their common purposes and common roots (Bachrach, 1962, p. x).

REFERENCES

Aiba, T. S. Can the absolute threshold be conditioned? *J. exp. Psychol.*, 1963, **65**, 233–239.

Allport, G. *Personality*. New York: Holt, 1937.

Ayllon, T., & Michael, J. The psychiatric nurse as a behavioral engineer. *J. exp. Anal. Behav.*, 1959, **2**, 323–334.

Bachrach, A. J. (Ed.) *Experimental foundation of clinical psychology*. New York: Basic Books, 1962.

Bagby, E. The etiology of phobias. *J. abnorm. soc. Psychol.*, 1922, **17**, 16–18.

Bandura, A. Psychotherapy as a learning process. *Psychol. Bull.*, 1961, **2**, 143–157.

Bandura, A. Behavioristic psychotherapy. Unpublished manuscript, 1963.

Barrett, B. H. Reduction in rate of multiple tics by free operant conditioning method. *J. nerv. ment. Dis.*, 1962, **135**, 187–195.

Beech, H. R. The symptomatic treatment of writer's cramp. In H. J. Eysenck (Ed.), *Behaviour therapy and the neuroses*. New York: Pergamon Press, 1960. P. 349.

Bekhterev, V. M. *General principles of human reflexology*. New York: International Universities Press, 1932.

Bevan, J. R. Learning theory applied to the treatment of a patient with obsessional ruminations. In H. J. Eysenck (Ed.), *Behaviour therapy and the neuroses.* New York: Pergamon Press, 1960. P. 165.

Bishop, M. P., Elder, S. T., & Heath, R. G. Intracranial self-stimulation in man. *Science,* 1963, **140,** 394–396.

Bond, J., & Hutchison, H. C. Application of reciprocal inhibition techniques to the treatment of exhibitionism. *Canad. med. Ass. J.,* 1960, **83,** 23–25.

Brady, J. P., & Lind, D. L. Experimental analysis of hysterical blindness. *Arch. gen. Psychiat.,* 1961, **4,** 331–339.

Brousseau, K. Suggestion on a case of traumatic hysteria. *J. abnorm. soc. Psychol.,* 1923, **4,** 346–349.

Dollard, J., & Miller, N. E. *Personality and psychotherapy: an analysis in terms of learning, thinking, and culture.* New York: McGraw-Hill, 1950.

Dunlap, K. *Habits: their making and unmaking.* New York: Liveright, 1932.

Eysenck, H. J. (Ed.) *Behaviour therapy and the neuroses.* New York: Pergamon Press, 1960.

Ferster, C. B., & DeMeyer, M. K. The development of performance in autistic children in an automatically controlled environment. *J. chron. Dis.,* 1961, **13,** 312–345.

Finesinger, J. A discussion of psychotherapy and the doctor-patient relationship. *Neuropsychiatry,* 1951, **1,** 43–63.

Flanagan, B., Goldiamond, I., & Azrin, N. Operant stuttering: the control of stuttering behavior through response-contingent consequences. *J. exp. Anal. Behav.,* 1958, **1,** 173–177.

Flanagan, B., Goldiamond, I., & Azrin, N. H. Instatement of stuttering in normally fluent individuals through operant procedures. *Science,* 1959, **130,** 979–981.

Franks, C. M. Alcohol, alcoholics and conditioning: a review of the literature and some theoretical considerations. *J. ment. Sci.,* 1958, **104,** 14–33.

Freud, S. *The problem of anxiety.* New York: Norton, 1936.

Freund, K. Some problems in the treatment of homosexuality. *Acta Neuropsiquiat. Argentina,* 1958, **4,** 233–247.

Gantt, H. W. Introduction. In I. P. Pavlov, *Lectures on conditioned reflexes.* Vol. II. *Conditioned reflexes and psychiatry.* New York: International Publishers, 1941.

Gordova, T. N., & Kovalev, N. K. Unique factors in the hypnotic treatment of chronic alcoholism. In R. B. Winn (Ed.), *Psychotherapy in the Soviet Union.* New York: Philosophical Library, 1961.

Guthrie, E. R. *The psychology of learning.* New York: Harper & Row, 1935.

Guthrie, E. R. *The psychology of human conflict.* New York: Harper & Row, 1938.

Hartmann, H. Psychoanalysis as a scientific theory. In S. Hook (Ed.), *Psychoanalysis, scientific method and philosophy.* New York: Grove Press, 1960. P. 3.

Heath, R. G., & Torkildsen, A. In E. P. R. Ramey & D. S. O'Doherty (Eds.), *Electrical studies on the unanesthetized brain.* New York: Hoeber-Harper, 1960. P. 144.

Hefferline, R. F., & Perera, T. B. Proprioceptive discrimination of a covert operant without its observation by the subject. *Science,* 1963, **139,** 834–835.

Hull, C. L. *Principles of behavior.* New York: Appleton-Century-Crofts, 1943.

Humphrey, G. The conditional reflex and the elementary social reaction. *J. abnorm. soc. Psychol.,* 1922, **2,** 113–120.

Jacobson, E. *Progressive relaxation.* Chicago: Univer. of Chicago Press, 1938.

Jenkins, R. L. Nature of the schizophrenic process: a working hypothesis for therapy. *Arch. Neurol. Psychiat.,* 1950, **64,** 243–262.

Jones, H. G. The application of conditioning and learning techniques to the treatment of a psychiatric patient. *J. abnorm. soc. Psychol.,* 1956, **52,** 414–419.

Jones, H. G. The behavioral treatment of enuresis nocturna. In H. J. Eysenck (Ed.), *Behaviour therapy and the neuroses.* New York: Pergamon Press, 1960. P. 377. (a)

Jones, H. G. Continuation of Yates' treatment of a tiqueur. In H. J. Eysenck (Ed.), *Behaviour therapy and the neuroses.* New York: Pergamon Press, 1960. P. 250. (b)

Jones, Mary C. The elimination of children's fears. *J. exp. Psychol.,* 1924, **7,** 383–390.

Kahane, M. An experimental investigation of a conditioning treatment and a preliminary study of the psychoanalytic theory of the etiology of nocturnal enuresis. *Amer. Psychologist,* 1955, **10,** 369–370. (Abstract)

Kanfer, F. H. Comments toward conceptualization of psychotherapy as a learning process. Unpublished manuscript, 1962.

Kantorovich, N. V. The role of psychotherapy in the treatment of psychoses. In R. B. Winn (Ed.), *Psychotherapy in the Soviet Union.* New York: Philosophical Library, 1961.

Kendrick, D. C. The theory of conditioned inhibition as an explanation of negative practice effects: an experimental analysis. In H. J. Eysenck (Ed.), *Behaviour therapy and the neuroses.* New York: Pergamon Press, 1960. P. 221.

Kimble, G. A. *Hilgard and Marquis' conditioning and learning.* New York: Appleton-Century-Crofts, 1961.

King, G. F., Armitage, S. G., & Tilton, J. R. A therapeutic approach to schizophrenics of extreme pathology: an operant-interpersonal method. *J. abnorm. soc. Psychol.*, 1960, **61**, 276–286.

Konorski, J. *Conditioned reflexes and neuron organization.* New York: Cambridge Univer. Press, 1948.

Lazarus, A. A. New methods in psychotherapy: a case study. *S. Afr. med. J.*, 1958, **33**, 660–663.

Lazarus, A. A. The elimination of children's phobias by deconditioning. *S. Afr. med. Proc.*, 1959, **5**, 261–265.

Lazarus, A. A. Group therapy of phobic disorders by systematic desensitization. *J. abnorm. soc. Psychol.*, 1961, **63**, 504–510.

Lazarus, A. A., & Abramovitz, A. The use of "emotive imagery" in the treatment of children's phobias. *J. ment. Sci.*, 1962, **108**, 97–105.

Lazarus, A. A., & Rachman, S. The use of systematic desensitization in psychotherapy. *S. Afr. med. J.*, 1957, **32**, 934–937.

Lehner, G. F. J. Negative practice as a psychotherapeutic technique. *J. gen. Psychol.*, 1954, **51**, 69–82.

Lindsley, O. R., Skinner, B. F., & Solomon, H. C. *Periodic project reports.* Waltham, Mass.: Metropolitan State Hospital, June, 1953–August, 1956. Microcard No. FO–57–524–527, L.C. No. Mic. P 57–30.

Liversedge, L. A., & Sylvester, J. D. Conditioning techniques in the treatment of writer's cramp. *Lancet,* June, 1955, 1147–1149.

Ludwig, A. O., & Ranson, S. W. A statistical follow-up of effectiveness of treatment of combat-induced psychiatric casualties. I. Returns to full combat duty. II. Evacuation to the base. *Milit. Surgeon,* 1947, **100**, 51–62, 169–175.

Lynn, R. Russian theory and research on schizophrenia. *Psychol. Bull.*, 1963, **60**, 486–497.

Max, L. W. Breaking up a homosexual fixation by the conditioned reaction technique. *Psychol. Bull.*, 1935, **32**, 374.

Menninger, W. C. *Psychiatry in a troubled world.* New York: Macmillan, 1948.

Meyer, V. Case report: the treatment of two phobic patients on the basis of learning principles. *J. abnorm. soc. Psychol.*, 1957, **55**, 261–267.

Meyer, V., & Gelder, M. G. Behavior therapy and phobic disorders. *Brit. J. Psychiat.*, 1963, **109**, 19–28.

Miassischev, V. N. Certain theoretical questions of psychotherapy. In R. B. Winn (Ed.), *Psychotherapy in the Soviet Union.* New York: Philosophical Library, 1961.

Mowrer, O. H. A stimulus-response analysis of anxiety and its role as a reinforcing agent. *Psychol. Rev.*, 1939, **46**, 553–565.

Mowrer, O. H. *Learning theory and behavior.* New York: Wiley, 1960.

Mowrer, O. H., & Mowrer, W. M. Enuresis: a method for its study and treatment. *Amer. J. Orthopsychiat.*, 1928, **8**, 346–459.

Munroe, R. L. *Schools of psychoanalytic thought.* New York: Holt, 1955.

Oswald, I. Induction of illusory and hallucinatory voices with considerations of behavior therapy. *J. ment. Sci.*, 1962, **108**, 192.

Pavlov, I. P. *Conditioned reflexes.* London: Oxford Univer. Press, 1927.

Pavlov, I. P. *Lectures on conditioned reflexes.* New York: International Universities Press, 1941.

Peters, H. N., & Jenkins, R. L. Improvement of chronic schizophrenic patients with guided problem-solving, motivated by hunger. *Psychiat. Quart. Suppl.*, 1954, **28**, 84–101.

Peters, H. N., & Murphee, O. D. The conditioned reflex in the chronic schizophrenic. *J. clin. Psychol.*, 1954, **10**, 126.

Phillips, E. L. *Psychotherapy: a modern theory and practice.* Englewood Cliffs, N.J.: Prentice-Hall, 1956.

Platonov, K. *The word as a physiological and therapeutic factor: the theory and practice of psychotherapy according to I. P. Pavlov.* Moscow: Foreign Languages Publishing, 1959.

Povorinsky, Y. A. Psychotherapy of smoking. In R. B. Winn (Ed.), *Psychotherapy in the Soviet Union.* New York: Philosophical Library, 1961.

Rachman, S. The treatment of anxiety and phobic reactions by systematic desensitization psychotherapy. *J. abnorm. soc. Psychol.*, 1959, **58**, 259–263.

Rapaport, D. The structure of psychoanalytic theory: a systematizing attempt. In S. Koch (Ed.), *Psychology: a study of a science.* Vol. 3. New York: McGraw-Hill, 1959. Pp. 58–183.

Raymond, N. J. Case of fetishism treated by aversion therapy. *Brit. med. J.*, 1956, **2**, 854–856.

Schoenfeld, W. N. An experimental approach to anxiety, escape, and avoidance behavior. In P. W. Hoch & J. Zubin (Eds.), *Anxiety*. New York: Grune & Stratton, 1950.

Schreiber, Y. L. The method of indirect suggestion as used in hysteria. In R. B. Winn (Ed.), *Psychotherapy in the Soviet Union*. New York: Philosophical Library, 1961.

Schwitzgebel, R. A new approach to understanding delinquency. *Fed. Probation*, 1960, **5**, 31–35.

Schwitzgebel, R. & Schwitzgebel R., Reduction of adolescent crime by research method. *Corrective Psychiat. J. soc. Ther.*, 1961, **7** (4).

Shaw, F. J. A stimulus-response analysis of repression and insight in psychotherapy. *Psychol. Rev.*, 1946, **53**, 36–42.

Shoben, E. J. A learning theory interpretation of psychotherapy. *Harvard educ. Rev.*, 1948, **18**, 129–145.

Shoben, E. J. Psychotherapy as a problem in learning theory. *Psychol. Bull.*, 1949, **46**, 366–392.

Sidman, M. Operant techniques. In A. J. Bachrach (Ed.), *Experimental foundation of clinical psychology*. New York: Basic Books, 1962. P. 170.

Skinner, B. F. *The behavior of organisms*. New York: Appleton-Century-Crofts, 1938.

Slack, C. W. Experimenter-subject psychotherapy: a new method of introducing intensive office treatment for unreachable cases. *Ment. Hyg.*, 1960, **44**, 238–256.

Smith, S., & Guthrie, E. R. Exhibitionism. *J. abnorm. soc. Psychol.*, 1922, **17**, 206–209.

Sylvester, J. D., & Liversedge, L. A. Conditioning and the occupational cramps. In H. J. Eysenck (Ed.), *Behaviour therapy and the neuroses*. New York: Pergamon Press, 1960. P. 334.

Thorndike, E. L. *Animal intelligence*. New York: Macmillan, 1911.

Voegtlin, W. L., & Lemere, F. Treatment of alcoholic addiction: review of the literature. *Quart. J. Stud. Alcohol.* 1942, **11**, 717–803.

Voegtlin, W. L., & Lemere, F. An evaluation of aversion treatment of alcoholism. *Quart. J. Stud. Alcohol.*, 1950, **11**, 199–204.

Wallerstein, R. S. (Ed.) *Hospital treatment of alcoholism*. New York: Basic Books, 1957.

Walton, D. The application of modern learning theory to the treatment of chronic hysterical aphonia. *J. psychosom. Res.*, 1958.

Walton, D. The application of learning theory to the treatment of a case of neuro-dermatitis. In H. J. Eysenck (Ed.), *Behaviour therapy and the neuroses*. New York: Pergamon Press, 1960. P. 273.

Walton, D., & Black, D. A. The application of learning theory to the treatment of stammering. *J. psychosom. Res.*, 1958, **3**, 170–179.

Watson, J. B., & Rayner, R. Conditioned emotional reaction. *J. exp. Psychol.*, 1920, **3**, 1–4.

Williams, C. D. The elimination of tantrum behaviors by extinction procedures. *J. abnorm. soc. Psychol.*, 1959, **59**, 269.

Winn, R. B. *Psychotherapy in the Soviet Union*. New York: Philosophical Library, 1961.

Wolberg, L. R. *The technique of psychotherapy*. New York: Grune & Stratton, 1954.

Wolpe, J. *Psychotherapy by reciprocal inhibition*. Stanford, Calif.: Stanford Univer. Press, 1958.

Wolpe, J. The experimental foundations of some new psychotherapeutic methods. In A. J. Bachrach (Ed.), *Experimental foundations of clinical psychology*. New York: Basic Books, 1962. P. 554.

Yates, A. J. The application of learning theory to the treatment of tics. *J. abnorm. soc. Psychol.*, 1958, **56**, 175–182. (a)

Yates, A. J. Symptoms and symptom substitution. *Psychol. Rev.*, 1958, **65**, 371–374. (b)

45

Group Psychotherapy and Psychodrama

MAX ROSENBAUM

HISTORICAL ROOTS

There are many claims as to who pioneered the method of group therapy, and where (Bach & Illing, 1956; Bierer, 1948a; Corsini, 1955a; Dreikurs, 1950; Dreikurs, 1959; Dreikurs & Corsini, 1954; Gifford & Mackenzie, 1948; Hadden, 1955; Klapman, 1946; Kotkov, 1950; Meiers, 1945; Moreno, 1957; Slavson, 1950; Slavson, 1951; Teirich, 1957; Thomas, 1943). Actually, there are many incidents in the past where some type of therapy group could be noticed. The all-day Greek drama, medieval morality plays, and Anton Mesmer's large groups in the 1700s can be considered forerunners of group therapy. Probably the history of group psychotherapy goes back to the beginning of recorded time. Every religious movement that has reached masses of people might be described as a form of group psychotherapy.

Most observers today credit Joseph Hersey Pratt, an internist who practiced in Boston, as being the founder of contemporary group psychotherapy (Mullan & Rosenbaum, 1962; Rosenbaum & Berger, 1963). Pratt originated the technique in 1905. His technique was empirical. Pratt was treating tubercular patients who were discouraged and disheartened, for tuberculosis was at that time both a social and a physical disease. He put these patients into class-type settings, of no more than 25 patients each. Each patient kept a detailed record of his physical condition. The groups of patients met every week, and during these meetings Pratt lectured to them and inspired them to attempt sound practices of physical hygiene. As Pratt lectured to them and attempted to alleviate their discouragement and pessimism, they found that they were not alone in their suffering, and a spirit of camaraderie developed that overcame ethnic, racial, and religious differences. Pratt himself had a background in medicine, religion, and psychology. At one point he was actively supported in his efforts by a religious group. Later he was criticized for having this support; the organized medical community resented what they felt to be the infringement of clergymen on the area of medical counseling. Pratt did not see clearly what he was doing, but he was pragmatic. It is worth mentioning that group psychotherapy evolved in Boston, the heartland of American democracy. Thus group psychotherapy seems to be related to the evolution of democracy insofar as it continues John Locke's concept of a compact among individuals to carry out a greater enterprise.

By 1913 Pratt seemed to have become a little more sophisticated; he read and spoke to a few psychiatrists, who were too busy fighting their own battle for professional recognition to be concerned with the problems of one busy Boston internist. Pratt had no contact with psychologists. Besides, Pratt felt that most patients with emotional difficulties should be treated by either the internist or the family physician, and he seemed rather reluctant to involve psychiatrists in his work. At this time, Freud's theories were attracting attention, as witnessed by his lecture at Clark University.

None of Freud's theories have been related specifically to the group, although in his later writings he was concerned about the application of individual psychotherapy to larger groups of patients (1948).

Moreno maintains that from 1910 to 1914, he carried on experiments in Vienna with groups of children, displaced persons, and prostitutes. He believes that his work and Pratt's class method were the beginning of group psychotherapy, while at the same time he describes group psychotherapy as an American product.

Dreikurs and Corsini (1954) wrote that from 1900 to 1930, German and Austrian psychotherapists were using a group method called "collective counseling" to treat alcoholics, stammerers, patients suffering from sexual difficulties, and neurotics. There is some evidence also that Russian and Danish psychiatrists were using group methods of psychotherapy. Freud's psychoanalysis was largely confined to patients who were more affluent, but Alfred Adler, who was a socialist, was concerned with bringing psychotherapy to the working class. The group method of treatment seemed to him an excellent solution for the problem. Most European psychoanalysts, bound by their own class and status needs as well as by their adherence to the various sects in psychoanalysis, appeared rather hostile to the concept of group psychotherapy. Therefore those psychiatrists who used group methods worked in relative isolation, ignorant of one another's work. In later years, with the growth of fascism, the group method seemed to be used less and less, since it apparently needed a climate of political freedom in order to flourish. Some students of politics have noted that as the political climate becomes conservative, novel techniques of psychotherapy are frowned upon.

GROUP PSYCHOTHERAPY IN THE UNITED STATES

Before World War I, there were few physicians in the United States besides Pratt who used group methods of counseling. There was, however, some psychotherapy of an inspirational nature, carried on by clergymen. By the end of World War I, Lazell (1921) worked with schizophrenic patients in a government hospital in the Washington, D.C. area. His approach was didactic. While he did not use psychoanalytic interpretation, he appeared relatively sophisticated and aware of the deeper dynamics involved. When he reported on his work, he indicated that he had a good knowledge of the psychoanalytic literature of that time, which in itself would be considered unusual. In 1935, Marsh (1935), a minister who later became a psychiatrist, described his group method. He was essentially an inspirational psychotherapist and was aware of the work of Pratt. Marsh used every technique that he felt would be helpful to the psychological well-being of his patients. In addition to his group lectures, classes, art classes, and dance classes, he encouraged patients to help one another and support one another—a very early version of Alcoholics Anonymous. About the same time that Marsh described his work, Wender (1936) reported on his work with borderline psychotics in a mental hospital where he practiced group psychotherapy using psychoanalytic concepts. This work was begun in 1929 and was reported in 1935. Wender was specific in describing his work as psychoanalytic, differentiating it from other group techniques which he felt were educational and orientative. At that time Wender indicated that group psychotherapy was applicable only to disorders in which some degree of affect was present and in which intellectual impairment was absent. In 1934, Schilder (1939) utilized psychoanalytic concepts as he carried out an experimental project in group psychotherapy with 50 patients in the outpatient division of Bellevue Hospital, in New York City.

Moreno has stated that he used group therapy in 1910 and that he coined the term in 1931 (1911; 1953). While all this has been questioned by some writers, there is no doubt that he used the term in an article published in 1932. He has expressed the view that his pioneering contribution to the field of group psychotherapy has not achieved sufficient recognition. There is therefore an unfortunate tendency on the part of many clinicians to minimize his contribution, since they react to him rather than to his theory. He is primarily identified with psychodrama, which he introduced into the United States in 1925. Moreno has been interested in the individual's relationship to the group and has consistently cooperated with social scientists, unlike many clinicians, who have remained rather isolated from other behavioral scientists. He has at-

tempted to integrate role playing, the capacity of an individual to take another's role, with the group therapy technique of psychodrama. He also developed the concept of sociometry, which is essentially a graphic representation of group membership needs.

Since World War II, Rosenbaum (1963a) has been somewhat successful in extricating the work and concepts of Trigant Burrow from oblivion. Burrow (1927), a physician and psychologist, was one of the first psychoanalysts in the United States, and he used the term "group analysis" as early as 1925. Little attention has been paid to this seminal thinker, who was deeply dissatisfied with the emphasis psychoanalysis placed on the individual, an emphasis that he felt excluded social forces. He believed that behavioral disorders should be traced back to social relationships and that effective research was best carried out in a group setting. Toward the end of his life, Burrow became deeply interested in the biological principles underlying group behavior.

During the 1930s, Slavson, an engineer who later became a group worker and group educator, carried out a program of activity group therapy at the Jewish Board of Guardians, in New York City. Slavson's work blended progressive education, psychoanalysis, and group work. It is primarily a therapy for children up to the age of 15. In 1943 he presented the results of nine years of work with approximately eight hundred children. This work was described again in a book published in that year.

During World War II, many versions of group psychotherapy were used extensively in the American military forces and to some extent in the British Army. The growth of group psychotherapy was largely due to the shortage of trained personnel and the need to treat large numbers of psychiatric patients. The psychiatric climate at that time appeared more receptive to modifications of technique, and every school of analytic theory and psychological counseling was using some technique which was called "group psychotherapy." By then, group psychotherapy ranged from an overtly repressive inspirational method, where the group method was used as a cathartic and supportive device, to the psychoanalytic method, in which group psychotherapy was used reconstructively. It has not been the writer's intention to present the definitive history of group psychotherapy but rather some of the major figures. Many names have been omitted in this rather brief summary, but the interested reader can spend many an hour filling this gap (see Mullan & Rosenbaum, 1962; Rosenbaum & Berger, 1963).

Carl Rogers encouraged his students to apply techniques of "client-centered" psychotherapy to clients who were seen in groups (Hobbs, 1951). Rogers himself apparently viewed group therapy as based on activity group therapy. His students, at least those who have engaged in group psychotherapy with adults since World War II, have stressed a phenomenological point of view which is concerned with the resolution of situational conflicts on conscious levels. A problem that is believed to cause an individual or a group concern is the focus of attention. The therapist is accepting and permissive, since any individual is believed to have a capacity to heal himself if provided with a secure environment where he can discuss his problems in living. The terms "psychotherapy" and "counseling" are not differentiated, since any relationship which permits the client to perceive his needs clearly is therapeutic. There is definitely no effort made to regress the patient emotionally, and present perceptions are stressed and clarified. Since the central problem is believed to be in the area of self-concept, the rationale is that threats to self-concept must be clarified. The approach is strongly intellectual (Bock, 1961; Gorlow, Hoch, & Telschow, 1952).

The entire nondirective approach, even when it appears to look like psychoanalytic therapy, is in marked contrast to a psychoanalytic approach, which is concerned with depth therapy in effecting personality change. Psychotherapy, as a psychoanalytically trained therapist uses the term, refers to a focus on personality change. Counseling, as seen by him, is a method of treatment for troubled individuals whose problems appear to be based on reality or situational conflicts. The rather brief distinction is important and will be emphasized again because the novice in the field of psychotherapy, and particularly group psychotherapy, will become confused. Everything may be considered helpful and therapeutic, from the friendly, accepting counselor, whether he is a recreation worker, a nondirective therapist, or an intensively trained psychoanalyst who works in depth and whether he works individually or in a group. But there are major theoretical differences behind the work of these people. The confusion arises when the reader attempts to equate the work of therapists whose goals are vastly different.

Since World War II, the literature in the field of group psychotherapy has grown tremendously. At the end of 1955, there was a bibliography of 1,700 items. Approximately two hundred items—books, articles, reports, and so on—are issued every year. The novice in the field is overwhelmed generally by the amount of reading required. Unfortunately, many writers in the field of group psychotherapy have not canvassed the field adequately or researched the literature, and there is some degree of duplication. Because of the rapid growth in the field, this section will be devoted to the establishment of some guideposts for evaluating the field of group psychotherapy.

Group psychotherapy is a flexible method and may be used with children (Ginott, 1958), adolescents (Slavson, 1943), adults (Mullan & Rosenbaum, 1962), and the elderly (Ross, in Rosenbaum & Berger, 1963), as well as in settings such as industry-personnel groups. Thus group psychotherapy can be used in a variety of settings, with all age groups and with all degrees of emotional upheaval. Because group psychotherapy is such a flexible method it has been attempted with many kinds of patients. Many times the technique has been misused, so that the biological desire of people to come together has led to easy formation of a group with no clear purpose as to the therapy desired.

Group psychotherapy should be thought of along the continuum repressive-inspirational to regressive-reconstructive. Many groups are formed along more supportive lines. Thus a "mothers' group" may be formed to meet a certain number of times. The emphasis will be on the problems that the mothers face in rearing their children. As a result of this experience, the mother generally gains the feeling that she is not alone in her difficulty. She has learned how other mothers handle children. The group has a closed membership, and the therapist actively controls the group because he perceives the group members as "not knowing." Group members are placed together because they have something in common—a problem. When the group members have learned how to handle the problem, there is no need for the group to continue. The therapist, in the course of leading this group, will be active, directive, inspirational, and advice-giving, and he will emphasize the present reality. This mothers' group will have something of the reparative, inspirational, and constructive aspect of psychotherapy.

A regressive-reconstructive group is formed slowly. Patients are seen individually before being placed in a group, depending upon their particular difficulties in living, their needs, and the therapist's assessment. The goal is deep personality change. A woman may come to therapy because she suffers from feelings of inadequacy and unworthiness. A man may come to therapy because he constantly fears failure, overreacts to what he perceives to be rejection, fears women, or is sexually impotent. The goal here is to direct therapy toward permanent and evolving personality change. Therapy continues over a prolonged period of time. Like life itself, the group is totally heterogeneous and includes men and women and every variety of race, culture, and social class as well as any emotional disturbance which lends itself to a "talking" type of psychotherapy. Group members mature and finally leave the group, and new members are introduced. The group, like life, never ends. Symbolically, there are births—members entering the group—and deaths—actual or those who become discouraged about therapy and settle for an unhappy type of existence. The group leader promotes the expression of affect in this therapy and encourages the reenactment of past historical events—particularly intrafamilial relationships—and he relates this to behavior in the therapy groups. Dreams, fantasies, and delusions are all-important and are discussed and explored. The immediate interaction of group members is analyzed, and the personality mechanisms used in the interaction are explored as well as the recurrent compulsiveness of these mechanisms. This is intensive, depth psychotherapy. Rather than placing the particular type of group psychotherapy to be described in the continuum repressive-inspirational to regressive-reconstructive, the writer encourages the reader to make his own judgment. With increasing knowledge of the field, he will change the points along the continuum where he places a

therapy approach. The field of group psychotherapy is still very new, and the methods vary greatly. There is a great sense of excitement in the field of group psychotherapy, and there is much mobility.

Psychodrama: A Form of Group Psychotherapy

Moreno founded the theater of spontaneity in 1921 in the city of Vienna. He became aware there of the deeper possibilities of spontaneous acting. From this he evolved his theory of psychodrama, which he introduced into this country in 1925. Since then he has developed modifications of this technique—sociodrama, role playing, sociometry, and axiodrama. As Moreno describes psychodrama (1946), five instruments are used: the stage; the patient or subject; the director; the staff of therapeutic aides, or auxiliary egos; and the audience, which is also considered an instrument.

The stage, the first instrument, provides the patient with a space for living which is completely flexible and multidimensional. The stage is an extension of life beyond the reality of life. The therapeutic requirements dictate the architecture of the stage. For example, the circular forms of the stage may be equated with the aspiration levels of the individual on stage as he moves from one circle to another.

The patient or subject, the second instrument, is requested to be himself on stage and to share his own private thoughts. He is instructed *not* to perform but to act freely as things come to his mind. From this freedom Moreno has evolved his theory of spontaneity, freedom of expression. Following this freedom of expression comes the process of enactment, where the patient acts. The form of enactment may be a present problem, anxiety about a future problem, or role playing. Moreno contrasts this with the traditional psychoanalytic experience, where, in its purest form, the analyst remained the mirror of the patient and always attempted to be objective and to have minimum emotional involvement. It is questionable how much this pattern ever existed in practice. However, in psychodrama, a maximum involvement is expected and provoked. Many techniques are used on stage to provoke the patient to be what he is rather than a performer. Among the techniques Moreno mentions are self-presentation, reversal of roles, auxiliary world, double ego, and mirror techniques. As in all forms of psychotherapy, at times it seems as if a new language has been invented when various esoteric terms are used. To the writer, it seems that these terms complicate communication between advocates of different theoretical approaches.

The director is the third instrument. He serves as analyst, producer, and psychotherapist. As the analyst, he interprets and integrates into his interpretation the responses coming from members of the audience watching this psychodrama as well as information from family members, neighbors, and friends. As the producer of this psychodrama, he has to keep the dramatic action moving and must always maintain rapport with the audience, which is an integral part of the psychodrama. The director, serving as therapist, may be passive, letting the patient dominate the session, or he may attack, criticize, laugh, and joke with the patient.

The auxiliary egos are the fourth instrument. They are a staff of people who serve as therapeutic actors. Moreno conceives of them as extensions of the director as well as extensions of the patient, used to portray the real or imagined people in the patient's life. Thus the auxiliary ego aids the director and also helps the patient as he portrays roles needed in the patient's world.

The audience is the fifth instrument. It has a double purpose: First, it serves as a sounding board of the public response. Since it is a heterogeneous group, the responses of the audience are as extemporaneous as the patient's responses. For the very isolated patient whose world is made up of delusions and hallucinations, the accepting and understanding audience is very helpful. On occasion, the patient may help the audience as he reenacts the collective problems of audience members. This is the second purpose of the audience.

What is the purpose of psychodrama? Moreno states that Freud and Breuer were ignorant of the therapeutic implications of the Greek drama. He states that he rediscovered this dramatic technique to effect mental catharsis. He has reversed the drama by stressing the initial phase rather than the end phase. Since every form of human activity is believed to be the source of some form of catharsis, Moreno has attempted to find the different sources of catharsis and what catharsis represents. He has stated that his aim is to define catharsis so that "all forms of influence which have a demonstrable cathartic effect can be shown as positive steps within a single total process of operation" (1946). The common principle which produces catharsis is spontaneity, according to Moreno, who also states:

> The treatment of audiences has become an important alternative to individual treatment. The relationship of the audience to itself in a psychodramatic session, being treated by its own spokesman on the stage, gives us a clue as to the reasons of the cathartic effect of psychodrama.

After briefly noting the history of the Greek drama, Moreno states that he has "put the psyche itself on the stage. The psyche which originally came from the group—after a process of reconversion on the stage—personified by an actor—returns to the group—in the form of the psychodrama" (1946, 1951, 1953).

A recent issue of Moreno's journal contained a report on psychodance (Fine, Daly, & Fine, 1962), in which dance techniques were used in the St. Louis State Hospital so that severely regressed patients might dance out nonverbally, through music and rhythm, their conflicts. Another article described the use of psychodrama in a college classroom (Facos, 1963). Recently, Murray (1962) reported a case where malunion of the femur was caused by emotional problems and where he used psychodrama to effect a recovery.

It is worth noting that although there are marked differences in the various practices of group psychotherapy, there is also much overlap.

The Directive-Didactic Approach

The earliest group procedures in state mental hospitals consisted in organizing patients into didactic groups where the group leader presented material which was used for guided discussion (Klapman, 1946; Klapman, 1950; Klapman & Lundin, 1952; Marsh, 1935). The framework of such a group emphasizes the intellectual and is particularly useful with regressed, hospitalized psychotic patients. It may also be used with patient groups where there is marked social distortion; here an effort is made to define the situation clearly. Such groups might include prisoners, paroled convicts, and juvenile offenders.

Didactic groups rely heavily on pedagogy and conditioning, as opposed to manipulation of instinctual drives and affects. Advocates of the didactic method equate motivated learning with the transference process as it occurs in psychotherapy which is psychoanalytically based (Klapman & Lundin, 1952). The teaching method is used in a variety of ways. The therapist may depend upon the patient's bringing to class a problem for general discussion. At this point the therapist serves as leader and moderator and at times makes active interpretations. Such a technique is important when there are very inarticulate patients who may repress strong aggressive feelings. The therapist sometimes delivers a series of talks or lectures. These lectures are to be well planned and organized so that there is maximum structure for the patients. The best method is to have these materials in printed or in textbook form. The printed material provides a systematic, logical, and planned sequence of material which the group leader wishes to cover. Theoretically it serves to stimulate and at the same time control the patients' associations. The patients are to be encouraged through this method to be active participants in the lectures, as they read aloud from the materials presented, recite, associate, and comment. This is particularly important with the regressed schizophrenic patients. The reader may note the similarity to a Bible-reading class in a religious setting. Since there is organized material presented, there is a continuity of program, and nothing should happen if a therapist leaves the group or is replaced. Another teacher-therapist takes over and continues the presentation. This method is particularly important in a state hospital setting where there is a high turnover of professional staff, as psychologists and psychiatrists complete their psychiatric training and leave the hospital. The organized material serves as a consistent standard for the entire hospital, and theoretically there should be an opportunity to compare the different patient groups. The printed word carries additional authority; note the much-abused expression, "the power of the printed word." Since there is material presented, there are no periods of silence, which is of particular importance with regressed psychotics. Silence with a group of neurotics may not indicate resistance but may be a period of reflection and assessment. This is not generally true with a psychotic population. During the didactic presentation no pressure is exercised, nor is there any effort made to "cover material." At any time, the class may stop at one expression or phrase, and the

leader will encourage discussion, comment, and associations. On occasion the previous material presented will be reviewed. Besides the formal class "text" or materials, patients may be assigned books to read, which constitutes a form of bibliotherapy, which is guidance in the resolution of personal problems through assigned, selected readings. Debates, discussions, and discussion of autobiographical material to be commented upon by the entire patient group, as well as symposia arranged by the group, are all part of the didactic method. A group member may even be encouraged to present a case history based upon himself, which serves as a point of departure for a reading assignment and group discussion. Since there is a structured presentation, this entire process lends itself to easy use in a mental hospital. Until very recently, mental hospitals have been mass boarding facilities with thousands of patients, suffering as well from a marked shortage of psychiatric and ward personnel. Often there is poor communication between ward personnel and the psychiatric staff, so that specific patients never end up in the assigned therapy group. The entire situation seemed to present complete chaos, particularly to the young professional. With the didactic approach, there is an organized program which pulls the patients out of the back wards, where they have been deteriorating for many years. The psychiatric staff gains the satisfaction of doing something besides administrating and dispensing tranquilizers.

Pratt noticed the camaraderie of group members and the members' beneficial influence upon one another. The same may apply as patients gather together for a didactic group. In the early 1900s, Joseph Jules Dejerine, a French physician who pioneered in the treatment of psychoneurosis (Dejerine & Gauckler, 1913), wrote a book which finally came to Pratt's attention (1953). The book stressed persuasion and reeducation. At a time when psychotherapy was largely overshadowed by purely physical treatment, Dejerine stressed a psychotherapeutic approach which contained his basic principle: "Psychotherapy depends wholly and exclusively upon the beneficial influence of one person on another. . . ." The principle was one that Pratt followed in all his work.

In the most current work conducted by some psychoanalysts in mental hospitals, there is great stress on the didactic method. The therapist is encouraged to check unconscious material (Boenheim & Dillon, 1962). The recent work of conditioned-reflex therapists, such as Wolpe (1958) and his students (Lazarus, 1961), emphasizes the importance of treating specific symptoms with a more intellective approach. This appears to fall into the category of the didactic approach. In a most recent application of Wolpe's system of "reciprocal inhibition," a group of patients suffering from phobic disorders were exposed to group desensitization. The therapist (Lazarus, 1961) constructed a group hierarchy of anxiety stimuli. The patients were then trained in intensive muscular relaxation, which they were instructed to practice morning and night. Then desensitization was instituted with progressively stronger anxiety stimuli presented, while at the same time the therapist named the muscle groups to be relaxed. The theory behind all this follows Wolpe (1958):

> If a response incompatible with anxiety can be made to occur in the presence of anxiety-evoking stimuli so that it is accompanied by a complete or partial suppression of the anxiety-responses, the bond between these stimuli and the anxiety-responses will be weakened.

This method incorporates Jacobson's finding that muscular relaxation inhibits anxiety and that their concurrent expression is physiologically impossible (1938). The technique described does not attempt to effect changes in personality or general adaptation. It is devoted to relief of symptoms. One other advocate of the didactic approach has not received much attention. Low (1950) has organized a movement called Recovery, Inc., which is largely based in the Chicago area. He worked with training methods for postpsychotic and psychoneurotic patients in the practice of psychiatric self-help. He rejected the psychoanalytic concepts as both a therapeutic and a philosophical technique and emphasized "will" therapy. The movement was founded in 1937 with a group of 30 patients who had been in Illinois psychiatric hospitals and who had received shock treatment or other physical therapies. The emphasis on the technique is self-help. Here again, there is much use made of the group camaraderie, and while there is heavy emphasis on the didactic, there is also a stress on the repressive-inspirational.

Therapeutic Social Clubs

After World War II, reports came to the United States of the group psychotherapy carried on in England, largely by psychiatrists who, as in the United States, looked for ways of treating large groups of psychiatric patients with limited professional personnel. One of these is Bierer (1944; 1948a). As Bierer was confronted with the population of mental hospitals as well as recently discharged patients, he began, in 1938, to encourage the formation of social clubs made up of these patients. The first club was formed at Runwell Mental Hospital, in England. These clubs were formed along the accepted rules of parliamentary procedure. They elected their own officers, arranged social activities, collected dues, and maintained the premises where they met. The major purpose of therapeutic social clubs is to increase the patients' social skills in social participation. Many have never acquired these skills, and others have sustained such damage to self-esteem that withdrawal has occurred, with consequent loss of whatever social skills were originally present. Bierer has formed an entire social therapy center in England. There is also an industrial rehabilitation unit in Belmont, England, formed along the same principles. The clubs are especially useful for patients who have been recently discharged from mental hospitals because they provide a kind of "half way house"—a point of rest in the transition from the social isolation of the mental hospital to the demands of community life. While Bierer cannot be described as the founder of the day-hospital concept (1962), an idea which has stemmed from many sources, particularly with the emphasis on keeping the patient in the community at least part of the time, his philosophy has certainly made an impact on current psychiatric thinking, especially the concept of the "therapeutic community" (Jones, 1953; Jones 1962). The most promising development in current mental hospital psychiatry in the United States is the development of programs of decentralization. As the massive hospitals are broken down into flexible treatment units, there are serious problems of role changes at all levels, and new treatment cultures are set up. There has to be constant examination of roles and role relationships. The therapeutic community implies the optimal use of the potential within the staff and patient population for the improvement of the patient's condition. Any technique in which there is a social contact and the fostering of a democratic equalitarian structure rather than the more usual hierarchical structure engenders anxiety in the staff because it challenges them. The entire patient population and staff of the hospital finally end up needing therapy, the former for their problems in living, and the latter to cope with the patients' increasing strength and refusal to be led.

Repressive-Inspirational Approach

The formation of patient groups to foster a sense of group identification and the feeling of belonging is easily done with the repressive-inspirational approach (Marsh, 1931; Worcester, McComb, & Coriat, 1908). Obviously such a technique may be used with any population, whether it is made up of neurotics, psychotics, hospitalized psychotics, alcoholics, obese persons, narcotic addicts, criminals, or persons of many other types (Kotkov, 1950; Mullan & Rosenbaum, 1962; Rosenbaum & Berger, 1963; Slavson, 1950). Low's (1950) "will training" is an example of this. The work of Alcoholics Anonymous, as well as that of the Christian Science religious movement, is also repressive-inspirational. Actually, what is set up is a supportive subculture. The leader of the group is vitally important because it is his or her enthusiasm which establishes the original climate of the group. Some of the many mechanisms at work in the repressive-inspirational approach may be isolated. Corsini and Rosenberg (1955) have noted the following: group identification, group status, *esprit de corps,* friendly environment, communal feeling, unification of the group, group socialization, loss of isolation, emotional acceptance of the group, ego support, social approval, realization that others are in the same boat, testimony and example of others, sharing of mutual experiences, and reassurance. Attempting to reduce all group psychotherapy to three major factors, Corsini and Rosenberg have noted the approach which emphasizes the intellect, the approach which emphasizes the emotional, and the approach which emphasizes the actional. The repressive-inspirational strongly emphasizes the emotional and the actional.

Frank (1953) has defined the major types of psychotherapy and has described the major practice of group psychotherapy as "free interaction." This category includes interview

group therapy, intensive group psychotherapy, group-centered psychotherapy, and psychoanalytically oriented group therapy. While it is true that all these types of group psychotherapy encourage interaction in an atmosphere conducive to a free and honest expression of feeling, that is about all they have in common. The theoretical substructures are vastly different.

Nondirective Group Psychotherapy

Group psychotherapy is quite flexible and therefore lends itself well to the theoretical predisposition of the group therapist. The Rogerian school of nondirective psychotherapy has formed a base for one particular type of group therapy (Hobbs, 1951). Here again there are many variations, since of late therapists perceive Rogers's work differently (Gordon, 1955; Lifton, 1961). The techniques espoused by Rogers appear to be easily acquired and have proved very popular with many American psychologists; they follow much of the philosophy of pragmatism. The philosophical root lies in the idea that man is basically good and that he is striving constantly toward a more effective kind of life. The viewpoint describes man as self-actualizing. Every effort is made in therapy to provide opportunities for an individual to recognize his needs and to test ways in which he may obtain satisfaction. Man is perceived as having a positive growth potential. As he tests his needs in a group, he will find that he can get from others the things he wants only when he has developed a relationship with them which will stimulate them to give him what he needs. Many contemporary psychotherapists would accept the concept of man as essentially good and capable of growth, whether they are traditionally trained Freudian psychoanalysts or existential psychotherapists. In today's culture, many people can agree that they are opposed to sin. But here is where nondirective therapists begin to differ from other schools of therapy. The phenomenological or client-centered (nondirective) point of view seems to rely too heavily on the intellect of man to provide the solution to personal difficulties. The reasoning runs as follows: In order to help the individual, one must start with his perception of the problem. The problem that is causing the group (or individual) the most concern should be the focus of immediate concern. Groups (or individuals) have an innate capacity to heal themselves. As the group (or individual) feels more secure or accepted, more and more information is accepted. The egocentric individual resolves his paradox in living as he finds that his needs can be met only through other people. The emphasis through all this is on the client (not patient, since the term "client" emphasizes the positive potential, a good but somewhat overworked point, for it is often an evasion of the patient's feeling that he is "sick"), who is believed to have the inherent capacity to recognize and solve his emotional problems as he develops them with a nondirective, accepting counselor. The nondirective school emphasizes that every individual has a drive toward health, growth, and personality maturation. Change is believed to occur in counseling, which is not seen as a preparation for change. Since the counselor is permissive, the client matures psychologically under "self-scrutiny." The counselor in the nondirective group is not a leader but a catalyst; he aids the client to develop fuller understanding of himself. The counselor will generally say little in the group except to confront, clarify, and guide what the clients are saying and presumably thinking. In one experiment with the use of client-centered group therapy with adult offenders placed on probation by a criminal court, published in 1963, the writers describe the theoretical framework under which the group therapy was conducted, as based on the work of Rogers:

> Within this methodological orientation the therapist tries to convey to the client through gesture, posture, facial expression as well as by verbal means, the therapist's *congruence,* his sense of acceptance and of confidence in the ability of the client, with the help of the group, to resolve his problems. The therapist avoids interpretation and does not engage in statements of a probing nature, evaluative comments or reassuring remarks (Smith, Berlin, & Bassin, 1963).

Further, these writers state that the

> most important function of the client-centered group therapist is to provide an atmosphere in which the group members feel free to explore their feelings and to communicate these reactions to the other group members. The therapist does not interpret, probe, evaluate or reassess, no mat-

ter how attractive the situation may seem for these kinds of explanations.

It is pertinent to question whether nondirective group therapy can be used with acutely troubled individuals who are looking for fundamental personality change. It appears to be primarily a relationship therapy, as opposed to a group therapy of an analytic, insight-developing nature. Among the other types of group therapy which emphasize the intellectual approach is the group therapy developed by Mowrer, based on his work in the field of learning theory (1950; 1953). Several other investigators have recently described work in the field of group psychotherapy based on a learning theory approach. Fundamentally this involves the assumption that patients' symptoms are learned maladjustments, subject to reinforcement, extinction, and new learning (Saslow & Matarazzo, 1962; Small, Matarazzo, & Small, 1963).

Psychoanalytic Group Psychotherapy

Psychoanalysis has made a major contribution to the practice of individual psychotherapy. Therefore it is not surprising to find many advocates of group psychotherapy who are desirous of integrating group psychotherapy and psychoanalysis. Unfortunately, the novice in the field of psychoanalysis will become confused by the wholesale borrowing of terms from the field of individual psychoanalytic therapy and their application to the field of group psychoanalytic therapy.

Although Lazell worked with psychoanalytic concepts (1921) immediately after World War I and although Burrow (1927) worked out an entire theory blending the group process and psychoanalysis, there was no great step made before Wender (1936), in 1929, and Schilder (1939), in the mid-1930s. Both men were trained as psychoanalytic psychiatrists and they actively integrated psychoanalytic theory and methodology with the group process. Both these men were conversant with the concepts of transference, a basic concept of psychoanalytic theory, and they understood its significance and use in the group milieu. Transference is the seeking of the patient, mostly unconscious, to relieve or relive in his relationship to his analyst traumatic and gratifying relationships with significant figures from his earlier years. Schilder was experimental in his desire to use psychoanalytic concepts. He developed ideas in the late 1930s concerning the feasibility of a group therapy approach with criminals. He felt that group discussion of the fundamentals of human life would give the prisoner clearer insight into ideologies, with the "emphasis not merely on the socializing effects of activities, but on the increase of insight into an individual's own problems, from a human point of view" (1940). Since then, group methods in correctional treatment have become an accepted approach. Within the last decade, Rosow (1955) took over almost an entire prison, placing the inmates in a group therapy program. He ended up treating almost seven hundred men, about 65 to 70 per cent of the prison population. The long-range effects of the work of Wender and Schilder are tremendous, for each of these men trained other people who were in a position to carry on the work in different settings. In another instance, Schilder (1939) developed techniques of group psychotherapy on an outpatient level as well as for inpatient psychiatric populations. Today, almost every psychiatric setting which has an outpatient facility carries on some form of group psychotherapy, usually psychoanalytically based.

While there was little published during World War II, there were many variations of the group technique in military services. Most of the practitioners worked in relative isolation from one another, although Wender did permit the United States Army to modify and use his original article on group psychotherapy for the training of neuropsychiatrists. In 1943, Giles Thomas was able to compile a review of the group psychotherapy literature which in retrospect gives the reader some idea of the groundswell of enthusiasm that was to develop for group psychotherapy. By 1943, Slavson had presented a paper on his work with activity group therapy at the annual meeting of the American Orthopsychiatric Association. Ten people present at that meeting, who were apparently deeply interested in the application of group process to psychotherapy, met later to form the American Group Psychotherapy Association. At that time, the chairman of the panel, Lawson Lowrey, noted that he had discussed group therapy approaches at an earlier meeting, in 1939. Slavson's concepts of group therapy were described as stemming from group work, progressive education, and psychoanalysis. At the time the point was made that this was therapy *by* the group

rather than therapy *in* the group. Slavson described his activity group therapy, which has not changed much in the ensuing years. His work was based on nine years of experience with 800 children and 63 distinct groups. He described the treatment as "interpersonal therapy." While noting that the treatment of adults in groups was not new (in 1943), he stressed that his work was with children from the ages of 8 to 15, with the emphasis on activity rather than interview. The general setting for activity group therapy is work in simple arts and crafts for about a 1½-hour period. Following this, the children and the group therapist cook a meal, eat together, and then wash the dishes. After this they clean up the room. At times the group and the leader may have picnics or planned excursions. The group then serves as a substitute family for children who have experienced destructive relationships with other children as well as with adults. The group leader becomes a substitute parent figure, but this time a warm, giving one. Group therapy in the activity setting is situational therapy, as differentiated by Slavson from interview and treatment by interpretation. Insight which develops is incidental to the main focus, which is the human experience of acceptance. Essentially, Slavson's method of activity group therapy was not designed for severely disturbed children. The method encourages the acting out of conflicts and behavior problems in the setting of a play group, a relatively permissive environment. The interaction of the children, as well as their relationship to the activity group therapist, is carefully studied. The activity group is composed of eight children of about the same age and of the same sex. The group is carefully structured to achieve some sort of balance. The withdrawn child would be a balance to the aggressive child. At the time his original paper was published, Slavson stated:

> The opportunity we offer to each child to use environment in accordance with his particular needs is of immense importance. We believe that psychotherapy consists of removing the patient's resistance to the world, his self-encapsulation, as it were. Once this is done, living in a social environment is itself a therapeutic situation. As long as the patient isolates himself either through resistance, active aggression, or withdrawal, the world cannot get at him. He remains in a state of isolation and develops or continues with anti-social attitudes. When we make it possible for our clients to go out into their environment to a degree to which they are ready and in a manner suitable to them, we not only give them release and comfort, but their perception of the world as a hostile destructive force to be feared or attacked changes. It is in this changed attitude that our therapy largely lies.

Slavson was and still remains concerned with proper selection of patients for all types of group psychotherapy. His experience is largely confined to children and adolescents, although he has organized and led parent discussion groups. He has expressed his disbelief that psychoanalysis (psychoanalytic therapy) can be practiced in the group setting. At the present time, group treatment of children and adolescents has achieved wide application in psychiatric clinics, social agencies, and hospitals. Most of this work is patterned on Slavson's activity group therapy. With children of preschool age, a modified form of activity group treatment has evolved (Ginott, 1958). Adolescents seem to respond to discussion groups as adults do.

Play group therapy, the extension of activity group therapy, offers the more infantile, dependent, orally demanding child an opportunity to express these consuming needs for mothering and protection through the medium of play materials and the group. The unique aspect of this, as differentiated from individual play therapy, is that the child cannot have the adult completely to himself. He has to share.

Wolf's System

Alexander Wolf, a psychoanalyst and psychiatrist, published a lengthy paper in 1949 in which he described his work on the "psychoanalysis of groups." Both in 1948 and in 1949, he had reported his work at conferences of the American Group Psychotherapy Association. Wolf has directly applied the principles of individual psychoanalysis to the group setting, using the major tools of the psychoanalytic method, such as transference, free association, dreams, and historic development. He describes his work as the re-creation of the original family, where the patient works through his unresolved problems. This is similar to the primary group that the sociologist is concerned with. Wolf began his work in 1938, stimulated by the reports of Wender and Schilder; within one year he became so enthusiastic and optimistic about his results that he telescoped most of his private practice and by 1940 was working with five groups of eight to ten patients each. His groups meet twice a week for 1½ hours each time. They meet at least once a week on their own without the therapist. This meeting is called the "alternate session" and is designed to encourage the patients to move toward peer experiences as well as to discuss their reactions to one another and the group psychoanalyst when the therapist is not present. Wolf has trained many psychiatrists, psychologists, and social workers in his technique of group psychoanalysis. His original interest was a result of his reluctance to turn away patients of low income who needed sustained psychotherapy. This encouraged him to read in the group psychotherapy literature and fifinally to work out a method that made sense to him.

One of the most valuable aspects of group analysis that Wolf stressed was that it facilitates the replacement of the ideal of a relationship to the single-parent analyst. Instead of the omniscient ego ideal of the single therapist, the patient is presented with a group "with whose common aims he must align himself." The group apparently precludes the evasion of social reality, which may exist in the cloistered one-to-one relationship of individual psychoanalysis. Further, he states:

> Rather than strengthening the entrepreneurial ideal—typified in the neurotic's mind by the notion of the omnipotent therapist—group analysis helps to destroy the false antithesis of the individual versus the mass by helping the patient to become aware that his fulfillment can only be realized in a social or interpersonal setting.

When one reads this passage, it seems rather puzzling to account for Wolf's recent strongly antagonistic position with reference to the inclusion of a group dynamic approach in intensive psychotherapy, but this is his conviction. He states:

> There is as yet no clinical evidence demonstrating that attention to these phenomena [group dynamics] is useful to the understanding and treatment of the patient in a group setting. How do group dynamics achieve a healing objective? (Schwartz & Wolf, 1960).

Wolf stresses that the group qua group cannot become the means by which its members resolve intrapsychic difficulty. The need for such differentiation led Wolf to call his work "psychoanalysis *in* groups" rather than "psychoanalysis *of* groups." He stresses that he does not treat a group but the individual in interaction with other individuals.

Wolf points out that his technique precludes the analyst's having a face-to-face confrontation. The group then forces interaction. He uses the technique of "going around," a procedure, according to Wolf, in which each member takes a turn at free-associating about the next member. Mullan and Rosenbaum (1962) have expanded on this and note that to ask the group members to go around is to ask them to participate fully and spontaneously in what they perceive or conceive to be a single member's problem, dream, fantasy, or interaction either in the group or outside of it. The technique has been called an "icebreaker." The group's impact is felt upon a particular problem, while at the same time group members are forced to become cotherapists. It is ego-strengthening, since for the first time patients do realize that they can contribute to one another's welfare and be really helpful. Through the technique of going around, the therapist, somewhat like the permissive parent, assures the child in the patient that his perceptions are important and even valuable. The total impact of going around is a more accurate discernment than the perception of the individual therapist. This is a major advantage of group over individual psychotherapy. Technically, going around is based on the transference relationship, which is to be found in the one-to-one relationship of individual psychoanalysis. When a patient is asked by a therapist in individual treatment: "How do you see me, or what do I represent for you, or who do I remind you of?" there is the origin of the process of going around. The group enlarges this relationship.

While the patient discusses the here and now in psychoanalytic group psychotherapy, he is also encouraged to regress and to relate his early life experiences. His patterns of relating to other members of the group and the symbolic meaning of these distorted reactions are clarified. For example, a patient might

respond to another member of the group who reminds him of a rejecting father or a dominating sibling. His overreaction will be pointed out, and an effort is made to trace back the historic origin of this transference distortion. Maximum distortion is to be observed during these periods of regression, but after this point there is a move toward reconstruction, where patients see one another as they really are.

At this stage of the development of group psychotherapy, one major point should be remembered. As might be expected in such a vital field, and one that is growing by leaps and bounds, the *practice* of group psychotherapy has been considerably in advance of its *theoretical* understanding and *conceptual* clarity. Since every major school of individual psychotherapy has begun to apply its methods of theory to the treatment of people in groups, a good deal of confusion has ensued. This may seem discouraging to the psychologist-reader who looks for a more "scientific" approach. But the relief of suffering is quite primary for the practitioner who cannot wait for his theory to catch up. The marked discrepancies in the frames of reference as well as in the standards of reporting of even practitioners who profess to adhere to the same "school" can become quite confusing. The majority of practitioners who come from psychoanalytic training attempt to explain group therapy in terms of individual dynamics. Some have struggled beyond Freud's speculations, as expressed in his book *Group Psychology and the Analysis of the Ego* (1948). In writing this book, Freud was highly influenced by the concept of Le Bon, the French sociologist who described the group as a collective entity—a distinct being. Freud noted that the group is held together by a common identification with a leader, and in his book he commented upon the primary group. His speculations, because that is what they were, were often adopted by group therapists and applied as a theoretical rationale for work in group psychotherapy. Freud did note: "The indestructible strength of the family as a natural group formation rests upon the fact that this necessary presupposition of the father's equal love can have a real application in the family." By extension, the therapist's love and the patient's positive transference or feeling for the therapist sustain the individual patient in the move to the psychotherapy group.

GROUP PSYCHOTHERAPY IN BRITAIN

So much attention has been paid in the professional literature to group psychotherapy in the United States that, until recently, there was a certain insularity. But group psychotherapy was practiced in Europe for many years, and after World War II reports came to the United States of the exciting work carried out in England during the war. Taylor surveyed the history of this development in an article published in 1958. During World War II, a few British psychoanalysts became interested in the therapeutic potentialities of group processes. Their interest was aroused because they came to realize that many soldiers became psychiatric casualties as a result of being placed in the wrong jobs. New selection machinery was devised as well as new selection procedures for choosing suitable candidates for training as officers. The procedures made use of situational group tests, specifically the "leaderless group" test devised by Bion, a British psychoanalyst whose influence was to be felt again in the following years. The test was one in which a particular task was given to a group of candidates. Observations were made of the way in which they went about solving the task. The group was unstructured and leaderless at first. Everyone started from the same or equal group status. As the candidates proceeded to carry out the task, it was observed that a hierarchy of status developed. Some men chose leader roles, while others chose to collaborate with the leader or to obstruct him.

In 1934, Bion and John Rickman, another psychoanalyst, were sent to the Northfield Military Hospital to deal with unruly conditions that had developed in one of the sections there. Rickman followed a traditional procedure of group discussions with the men, but Bion tried a more daring procedure. He aimed at changing the traditional authoritarian setting of the military hospital. The men were obviously unhappy with army discipline and wanted a return to civilian life. He aimed at transforming them into a responsible and cooperative community so that a healthy group structure and feeling of belonging would ensue. Bion therefore relinquished the authoritarian role of the doctor and military officer and faced the patients with the following: They had to choose between suffering the discomforts of a chaotically unstructured community life and shouldering the responsibility of organizing communal activities themselves. From this point they could no longer use the Army as a scapegoat but had to cope with their own disruptive and antisocial tendencies.

Bion stayed at the hospital for six weeks and was successful. Later, in the second "Northfield experiment," he worked out a similar technique for a major hospital; these techniques were linked with methods of small-group psychotherapy. The development of therapy group activities in Great Britain can be traced back to these two Northfield experiments. Before this, Bierer, in 1938, had started group treatment in mental hospitals by means of therapeutic social clubs and small discussion groups. His influence was minor, however.

Bion's second experiment led to a reexamination of the administrative structure of mental hospitals, which had grown in size and had begun to look like prisons. The hospitals at this point were segregating patients from society rather than treating them. The stimulus of Bion led to the encouraging of patients to accept more self-determination and responsibility for their activities in the hospital, so that today we have the open-door and open-ward policy, with very few locked wards.

At the Northfield Military Hospital, small-group psychotherapy was widely used. The group membership generally ranged from six to ten in number, similar to the group size of Wolf. They met once a week for 1½ hours. The majority of group therapists in Britain have modeled their work on psychoanalytic practice and generally follow the structure devised at Northfield.

Foulkes's System

Besides Bion, who will be discussed a little later, the outstanding exponent of group therapy in England today is Foulkes, whose work has become well known in the United States (1948; Foulkes & Anthony, 1957). Unlike Wolf, Foulkes, also a psychoanalyst, does not like to apply the term "psychoanalysis" to a multipersonal situation. He uses psychoanalytic concepts in the classical sense, and he states: "Psychoanalysis as a method of treatment may in time lose importance and in its pure form become restricted in application to very special circumstances" (1959). Group analysis as practiced and taught by Foulkes is more than the mere application of psychoanalytic principles in the group. The most significant features, as he describes the process (Foulkes & Anthony, 1957), are the following: Seven or eight members meet together with the group analyst for 1½ hours. They are seated in a circle; no directions are given, so that all contributions arise spontaneously. The group treats all communications as the equivalent of individual free association in individual psychoanalysis. While the therapist clarifies and interprets transference, he notes all communications and relationships, which are seen as part of a total field of interaction—the group matrix. The group analyst is a participant-observer. Foulkes states that the regressive, infantile relationship of individual analysis is discouraged by the presence of the group. The group itself is a "dynamic field of experience." He describes his approach as sharing with other psychoanalytic approaches the indebtedness to the theories of Freud but states that it is nearer to the gestalt school of psychology and to the topological psychology of Kurt Lewin. He describes the group analytic situation as a *T* situation. A *T* situation is one in which therapeutic processes can optimally operate. This is not to be confused with the *T* groups of the group dynamics researchers at the National Training Laboratories in America. He calls the group leader the "conductor" and states that his influence remains decisive from beginning to end. The therapy that goes on is described as being crucially dependent on the therapist's presence. The conductor's task is to accept willingly all material, including fantasy about himself; to refuse to act in any other role but that of a therapist; and to volunteer minimal private information.

Foulkes tries to extend some Freudian assumptions about group psychology, but his effort to integrate field theory and psychoanalysis seems to be forcing the fit. This is not unlike the American psychologist Bach, who has formulated a concept of group psychotherapy based on Lewin's field theory, where he stresses that the "doctor must be group-oriented rather than only patient-oriented. . . . He treats the individual patient by conscientiously creating an atmosphere that stimulates self treatment . . ." (1954). In his

work with groups, Foulkes has developed a theory of group therapy in which he rejects two hypotheses of Freud. The first is the Freudian concept of two basic drives in the individual—Eros (the life instinct) and Thanatos (the death instinct)—which would be expressed in the group as the struggle between constructive and destructive forces. The forces that bring people together to work with one another in a group would be derived from Eros, and the forces that lead to fear and thus to fragmentation of group structure would be derived from Thanatos. Foulkes rejects a second hypothesis of Freud, that an independent social drive or herd instinct leads to the behavior observed in the group. Instead, he postulates that the group is a more fundamental unit than the individual: "Collectively they constitute the very norm, from which, individually, they deviate. . . . The group tends to speak and react to a common theme as if it were a living entity, expressing itself in different ways through various mouths" (1948). The work of Foulkes is by now known to American group therapists, although his concepts have not made an appreciable impact.

The English psychiatrist Bion has attempted, during the last decade, to formulate a relationship between group dynamics and psychotherapy. His work has attracted the interest of American researchers in the field of group dynamics but has in the main been ignored by most group psychotherapists in the United States until very recently. Bion, unlike most group psychotherapists, has concerned himself with an understanding of what the group context is. Most group psychotherapists, in their emphasis on the individual, have neglected the group variables at work in group psychotherapy. Bion, in a series of articles, attempted to set forth a theory of group culture and social structure which would apply to group psychotherapy. His articles have recently been collected and published by him in book form (1961). He states:

> I am impressed, as a practicing psychoanalyst, by the fact that the psychoanalytic approach, through the individual, and the approach these papers describe, through the group, are dealing with different facets of the same phenomena. The two methods provide the practitioner with a rudimentary binocular vision.

Bion's work points toward a synthesis between psychoanalysis and group dynamics.

From his work with therapy groups in England, Bion developed a series of rather complex processes that he believes are present in all groups. The processes are set up as conscious and rational as well as emotional and irrational. His detailed statement of the processes at work may be found in the work cited, but his approach may be summarized without too much violence to his theory.

Bion's System

Bion noticed certain massive emotional reactions in the group setting. Occasionally the group seemed to express a need for the group therapist to provide more direction, or the group members would show a desire to run away from the group. Bion developed the theory that a group can be described as a series of emotional states or basic assumption cultures. Affective need was deeply tied in with the work the group was attempting. As the individuals in the group reacted against the cultures or agreed to accept the cultures, they would contribute to the work of the group. The relationship between the individual and the group culture was grouped by Bion under a series of "valences." The individual is seen as moving along the valence of pairing, dependency, or "fight-flight." The process of group movement can be seen as a series of shifts from one emotional culture to another, based on the valence. At all times the leader is able to ask: "What is the group really doing at this moment? Is it avoiding or attempting to get to the problem?" This would be the emotional culture. Bion dealt with his therapy groups in a unique way. Following upon his military experience in the Northfield experiment, he provided the group with no structure or direction, and the patient's reactions to the lack of structure—his anger or confusion—were the material initially used for exploration. As soon as Bion became aware of the group's emotional state, he gave an interpretation. The interpretation was focused on group behavior rather than on individual behavior.

To evaluate Bion's system it is important to note that he has been trained and influenced in his psychoanalytic development by Melanie Klein, who was an English psychoanalyst whose influence is apparently minimal in America but who carries great weight in Europe and South America. Bion does not specifically advance Klein's theories but states that his work convinces him of the central importance of her thinking. To summarize Klein, we would say that she has modified the orthodox Freudian concept of personality. She believed that the *ego exists from birth.* Good and bad emotions come from the infant's contact with the mother, who represents the external world. The capacity to love and feelings of persecution stem from these early contacts, which in turn are influenced by environment and constitutional forces. As the infantile ego develops, two major processes come to the fore—introjection and projection. The people and situations that the infant encounters are taken up in his inner life—thus introjection. The infant attributes to others different feelings—therefore projection. Basic to the infant's perception of the world is the interplay of these two processes. The ego splits, dividing objects into good and bad. This splitting occurs in the early months of living. Ego growth is accompanied by anxiety and destructive impulses, which Klein called the "paranoid-schizoid position." If the infant develops healthily, there is increasing ability to understand reality. From the sixth to the twelfth month of his life, the infant enters a depressed period related to his guilt and anxiety about his destructive impulses. The infant never fully recovers from this depressive period, and this finally plays a part in the child's perception of social relationships. According to Klein, human relationships can be interpreted in terms of introjection, projection, and splitting, with the individual accepting his good feelings and denying his bad impulses. This is an individual-centered concept of group phenomena.

Thelen's System

Thelen (Stock & Thelen, 1958), an educator and student of group dynamics, has carried out a series of investigations at the Human Dynamics Laboratory of the University of Chicago since World War II. These investigations were concerned with studies of group issues such as composition, subgroup formation, developmental phases, sociometric choice, group culture, and individual learning and change. Appropriate methodology was developed to study sequential group interaction, group-relevant aspects of personality, and member perceptions of self and others. Work groups and training groups, specially composed, were utilized as settings for the research. In the course of its work, the research team under Thelen became interested in the writings of Bion, which seemed to fit their thinking about group interaction as a functional process, the relevance of cognitive and emotional factors in group life, as well as relationships between individual personality and group culture. A theoretical position developed based on Bion's work, and Bion's hypotheses were systematically researched. The work still continues; finally the group dynamics researcher and the practicing group psychotherapist have begun to join hands. While the academic psychologist and sociologist may be uneasy about working with the practicing clinician who does not present problems that are easy to solve, there is an increasing desire on the part of sophisticated group therapists to find out what they are doing. The clinical practitioner cannot take a research point of view toward the patients he is responsible for. Research becomes secondary to his major task —helping the people who come for help.

In 1964, three of Thelen's students (Whitaker, Stock, & Lieberman) published a book entitled *Phychotherapy through the Group Process,* in which the group is emphasized as a social system. The theory presented is the "group focal-conflict theory," derived from the work of Thomas French, a leading Chicago psychoanalyst. In any given session of the group, the focal conflict is defined as the most superficial conflict explaining all or almost all verbalizations and behavior during that period. The therapist preferably interprets the reactive rather than the disturbing motive in any given conflict. French (1952–1954) originally formulated focal-conflict theory as an approach to understanding individual psychoanalysis and dreams. The assumption is that although many diverse and seemingly unrelated elements appear in an analytic hour or in a dream, an underlying coherence and a relatedness are present. All the patient's associations can be seen as relevant to a particular preconscious conflict, which can be considered "focal" for that session. The concept of focal conflict has been applied to understanding group interaction. Here the attempt is made to account for the diverse content of a group therapy session in terms of a slowly emerging and developing conflict situation and varying attempts to solve this conflict.

RECENT TRENDS

During the last decade, many articles have been published describing innovations in the method of group psychotherapy. There is now much use made of multiple therapists, the use of more than one therapist at one time in individual or group psychotherapy. This has been called by many names—"cotherapy," "multiple therapy," "role-divided therapy," "three-cornered therapy," "conjoint therapy," "three-cornered interviews," "joint interviews," "cooperative psychotherapy," and "dual leadership" (Rosenbaum & Berger, 1963; Spitz & Kopp, 1957). While the techniques of multiple therapy are exciting, it is still not known whether the time given by more than one therapist is justified either by a shortened period of treatment or by more successful results.

Until recently, psychoanalytic psychotherapists avoided treatment of members of the same family; they would even avoid contact with members of the patient's family. Today there is treatment of families as units (Midelfort, 1957). Since Ackerman feels that the patient cannot be understood apart from the family, he treats the patient and the patient's family (1958). Grotjahn (1959) points out that Freud treated "Little Hans" in 1909 by using the child's father as a therapist, so there is a precedent for family therapy. By treating the entire family, the therapist is believed to gain a new perspective on family interaction and its impact on each member of the family. Because Grotjahn predicts radical changes in the family structure, he advocates that the family therapist help in the adjustment to these changes. This new kind of therapist will have to combine the wisdom and experience of the old-time family physician with the knowledge and skills of the psychoanalyst.

Grotjahn compares the family to analytic therapy in that he sees both as being based on transference phenomena. The individual does not see the members of his family merely as they really are; he also sees them as representatives of important figures from his own childhood. He transfers images of his inner childhood family to the outer realistic family of adulthood. There exists, then, for the individual his real childhood family, the unconscious image of that family within himself, and the projection of these images onto the family of the next generation. Conflicts that existed between the individual and some other member of his childhood family are reenacted with the member in the family of the next generation onto whom the unconscious image has been projected. In healthy family life, these conflicts are worked through without conscious insight, and a more realistic appraisal of the family is achieved. In neurotic families the conflict continues endlessly. Another factor in family therapy comes from recent studies in communication demonstrating the importance of nonverbal communication (Rosenbaum & Berger, 1963). Such communication, when properly operating in family life, permits smooth and effective family functioning. When communication is disturbed, serious pathology can develop. There is also awareness today, as entire families are treated, that pathological behavior in one member of the family can give gratification to other members of the family. Often the entire family conflict is centered in one individual. The family is able to blame their entire disturbance on this one individual. This is similar to the neurotic wife of an alcoholic who can remain healthy only when her husband is sick. As he becomes healthy and abstinent, she goes into a tailspin. Bell has recently advanced a theory of family therapy in which he applies small-group theory from social psychology to the natural family group (1962). In line with the treatment of families, there is also a trend at this time to treat married couples in groups (Perelman, 1959; Whitaker, 1958).

A review of the literature for 1963 and the early months of 1964 indicates a vitality and excitement in the field of group psychotherapy. Group psychotherapy is being used in the training of marriage counselors and family-life educators (Ormont, 1962). It is being used in high schools and colleges with underachievers—students not living up to their potential (Siegel, 1962). It is used in the training and treatment of clergymen (Holt & Winick, 1962).

Recently, Wolman has introduced some ideas on group psychotherapy based on his modification of the psychoanalytic theory and studies in social psychology. He maintains that group therapy offers certain advantages in comparison with individual psychotherapy, for it permits multiple reality testings, multiple transferences, and correction of the self-cathexes and object-cathexes through multiple patterns of social interaction.

Wolman (1956; 1958) distinguishes three

interactional patterns. When individuals join a group to have needs satisfied, it is an "*instrumental*" relationship; when the aim is to give and receive satisfaction, it is a "mutual" relationship; when the aim is to give, it is a "vectorial" relationship. Normal adults are capable of behavior in all three types of relationships.

Emotionally disturbed individuals are seriously disturbed in their interindividual relations, and this is caused by disbalances in intraindividual and interindividual libido cathexes. Some individuals are "hyperinstrumental" (psychopaths), with abundant self-cathexis and paractically no object cathexis. Others belong to the "hypervectorial" type (obsessive-compulsives and latent and manifest schizophrenics), with an inadequate self-cathexis and a tendency to become overattached to their love objects and to hypercathect them. Still others swing in their moods and their social relations from one extreme to the other; these are the "paramutual" hysterics and manic-depressives. A psychotherapy group is balanced when it includes all three types (Wolman, 1964).

In addition to the horizontal division, there are vertical levels of disorder, such as neurosis, character neurosis, latent psychosis, and manifest psychosis. A group is "vertically" balanced when there is not too much discrepancy in the level of disorder in the group members. A group functions better and offers more therapeutic opportunities when it is heterogeneous and vertically and horizontally balanced. Accordingly, his groups include neurotics and psychotics (Wolman, 1960).

The old arguments continue. Thus one author writes:

> The manifestations of transference interaction among group members constitutes the therapeutic climate in group therapy, and the resolution and understanding of these multiple transference constellations which exist in simultaneous interaction among group members is the unique therapeutic task of the group therapist (Farrell, 1962).

And another writer states: "The question, therefore, becomes not *whether* transference develops in the group, but what form it takes" (Durkin, 1962). Remember that the British group dynamic therapists have stressed the phenomenon of the dynamic totality of the group. They view it from the side of the combined group process rather than in terms of transference to the whole group. They have little use for the concept of transference. Foulkes and Anthony (1957) have summed up their position as follows: "Transference phenomena do occur in the group but they are not of paramount importance for the therapeutic trend of the group." American psychoanlytic group therapists stand in sharp disagreement with such an opinion. Rosenbaum (1963b) points out that there is still the question of deep acceptance of group psychotherapy. How accepted is group psychotherapy by individual therapists who profess to be flexible? Pavlovian concepts dominate group psychotherapy which is currently practiced in Russia and Czechoslovakia. There is still a dearth of training facilities for group therapy (Rosenbaum & Berger, 1963). The inexperienced group therapist is left largely on his own to discover, through trial and error, what special problems may be encountered, how they may be handled, and what the probable effects of different methods of therapeutic leadership are.

To a large extent, there is at present a "hard-sell" campaign for group therapy, and this is dangerous. Group therapy is supposed to help you lose weight, give up smoking (Lawton, 1962), and cope with whatever else ails you. Even the animal kingdom has not escaped. Thus, Harlow, in describing his much-publicized experiments on social deprivation in monkeys, writes: "Group psychotherapy for monkeys raised in isolation in the laboratory was attempted by removing them to the semi-wild conditions of the zoo after they reached maturity" (1962).

Sound conceptualization, organized research, and thorough training, described by Rosenbaum (1962; 1963) in two recent texts on group psychotherapy, are still needed. There are no shortcuts, and enthusiasm is no substitute for thorough training. Rosenbaum notes that the regressive-reconstructive approach centers upon the possibility that the patient will become responsible not only for himself but also for society. The emphasis in the experiential affect approach that he proposes is on the patient's responsibility as a creator of his culture and as a transmitter of patterns of behavior. To achieve this, his personality must continue to change in an evolving way after formal therapy has ended. The stimulus for this comes from a therapy of depth which can occur in the group. Rosen-

Grotjahn, M. *Psychoanalysis and the family neurosis.* New York: Norton, 1959.

Hadden, S. B. Historic background of group psychotherapy. *Int. J. group Psychother.,* 1955, **5,** 162–168.

Harlow, H. F., & Harlow, M. K. Social deprivation in monkeys. *Sci. Amer.,* 1962, 1–11.

Hobbs, N. Group-centered psychotherapy. In C. Rogers, *Clint-centered therapy.* Boston: Houghton Mifflin, 1951.

Holt, H., & Winick, C. Group psychotherapeutic experiences with clergymen. *J. Relig. Hlth,* 1962, **1** (2), 113–126.

Jacobson, E. *Progressive relaxation.* Chicago: Univer. of Chicago Press, 1938.

Jones, M. *The therapeutic community: a new treatment method in psychiatry.* New York: Basic Books, 1953.

Jones, M. Group psychotherapy and the therapeutic community. Paper read at 39th annu. Conf. Amer. Orthopsychiat. Ass., Chicago, March, 1962.

Klapman, J. W. *Group therapy: theory and practice.* New York: Grune & Stratton, 1946.

Klapman, J. W. The case for didactic group psychotherapy. *Dis. nerv. System,* 1950, **11** (2), 35–41.

Klapman, J. W., & Lundin, W. H. Objective appraisal of textbook mediated group psychotherapy with psychotics. *Int. J. group Psychother.,* 1952, **3,** 116–126.

Kotkov, B. Bibliography of group therapy. *J. clin. Psychol.,* 1950, **6,** 77–91.

Lawton, M. P. A group therapeutic approach to giving up smoking. *Appl. Therapeut.,* 1962, **4,** 1025–1028.

Lazarus, A. A. Group therapy of phobic disorders by systematic desensitization. *J. abnorm. soc. Psychol.,* 1961, **63** (4), 504–510.

Lazell, E. W. The group treatment of dementia praecox. *Psychoanal. Rev.,* 1921, **8,** 168–179.

Lifton, W. M. *Working with groups.* New York: Wiley, 1961.

Low, A. A. *Mental health through will-training.* Boston: Christopher, 1950.

Lowrey, L., Slavson, S. R., et al. Group therapy (special section meeting). *Amer. J. Orthopsychiat.,* 1943, **13,** 648–690.

Marsh, L. C. Group therapy of the psychoses by the psychological equivalent of the revival. *Ment. Hyg.,* 1931, **15,** 328–349.

Marsh, L. C. Group therapy and the psychiatric clinic. *J. nerv. ment. Dis.,* 1935, **82,** 381–392.

Meiers, J. I. Origins and developments of group psychotherapy. *Sociometry,* 1945, **8,** 499–534.

Midelfort, C. F. *The family in psychotherapy.* New York: Blakiston, 1957.

Moreno, J. L. *Die Gottheit als Komediart.* Vienna: Anzengruber Verlag, 1911.

Moreno, J. L. *Application of the group method to classification.* National Commission on Prisons and Prison Labor, 1932.

Moreno, J. L. Psychodrama and group psychotherapy. *Sociometry,* 1946, **9,** 249–253.

Moreno, J. L. *Sociometry, experimental method and the science of society.* New York: Beacon House, 1951.

Moreno, J. L. *Who shall survive?* New York: Beacon House, 1953.

Moreno, J. L. *The first book on group psychotherapy.* New York: Beacon House, 1957.

Mowrer, O. H. *Learning theory and personality dynamics.* New York: Ronald, 1950.

Mowrer, O. H. *Psychotherapy theory and research.* New York: Ronald, 1953.

Mullan, H., & Rosenbaum, M. *Group psychotherapy.* New York: Free Press, 1962.

Murray, N. Malunion of the femur treated by group psychotherapy and psychodrama. *Sth. med. J.,* 1962, **55** (9), 926–991.

Ormont, L. The use of group psychotherapy in the training of marriage counselors and family life educators. *Marriage fam. Living,* 1962, **24** (2), 140–150.

Perelman, J. S. Group therapy of married couples. *Int. J. group Psychother.,* 1959, **10,** 136–142.

Pratt, J. H. The use of Dejerine's methods in the treatment of the common neuroses by group psychotherapy. *Bull. New Engl. med. Center,* 1953, **15,** 1–9.

Rosenbaum, M. Current controversies in psychoanalytic group psychotherapy. *Proc. int. Cong. Group Psychother.,* 1963. (a)

Rosenbaum, M. Resistance to group psychotherapy in a community mental health clinic. *Int. J. soc. Psychiat.,* 1963, **9** (3), 1–4. (b)

Rosenbaum, M., & Berger, M. *Group psychotherapy and group function: selected readings.* New York: Basic Books, 1963.

Rosow, H. M. Some observations on group therapy with prison inmates. *Arch. crim. Psychodynam.,* 1955, **1** (4), 866–896.

Saslow, G., & Matarazzo, J. D. A psychiatric service in a general hospital: a setting for social learning. *Ment. Hosp.*, 1962, 13, 217–220.

Schilder, P. Results and problems of group psychotherapy in severe neurosis. *Ment. Hyg.*, 1939, **23**, 87–98.

Schilder, P. The cure of criminals and the prevention of crime. *J. crim. Psychopathol.*, 1940, 149–161.

Schwartz, E., & Wolf, A. Psychoanalysis in groups: the mystique of group dynamics. In *Topical problems of psychotherapy.* Vol. II. *Sources of conflict in contemporary group psychotherapy.* Basel: S. Karger, 1960. Pp. 119–154.

Siegel, M. Group psychotherapy with gifted underachieving college students. Paper read at 19th annu. Conf. Amer. Group Psychother. Ass., January, 1962. (Mimeographed)

Slavson, S. R. *An introduction to group therapy.* New York: Commonwealth Fund, 1943.

Slavson, S. R. *Bibliography on group psychotherapy.* New York: American Group Psychotherapy Association, 1950.

Slavson, S. R. Pioneers in group therapy. *Int. J. group Psychother.*, 1951, **1**, 95–99.

Small, I. F. Matarazzo, R., & Small, J. G. Total ward therapy groups in psychiatric treatment. *Amer. J. Psychother.*, 1963, 254–265.

Smith, A. B., Berlin, L., & Bassin, A. Problems in client-centered group therapy with adult offenders. *Amer. J. Orthopsychiat.*, 1963, **33** (3), 550–553.

Spitz, H. H., & Kopp, S. B. Multiple psychotherapy. *Psychiat. Quart. Suppl.*, 1957, **31**, 295–331.

Stock, D., & Thelen, H. *Emotional dynamics and group culture.* New York: New York Univer. Press, 1958.

Taylor, F. K. A history of the group and administrative therapy in Great Britain. *Brit. J. medical Psychol.*, 1958, **31**, 153–173, Parts 3, 4.

Teirich, H. R. Gruppentherapie und dynamiche gruppenpsychotherapie in Deutschland. *Heilkunst,* 1957, **10**, 1–6.

Thomas, G. W. Group psychotherapy: a review of the recent literature. *Psychosom. Med.*, 1943, **5**, 166–180.

Wender, L. The dynamics of group psychotherapy and its application. *J. nerv. ment. Dis.*, 1936, **84** (1), 54–60.

Whitaker, C. A. Psychotherapy with couples. *Amer. J. Psychother.*, 1958, **12**, 18–23.

Whitaker, C. A., Stock, D., & Lieberman, M. A. *Psychotherapy through the group process.* Englewood Cliffs, N.J.: Prentice-Hall, 1964.

Wolf, A. The psychoanalysis of groups. *Amer. J. Psychother.*, 1949, **4**, 16–50; 1950, **1**, 525–558.

Wolman, B. B. Leadership and group dynamics. *J. soc. Psychol.*, 1956, **13**, 11–25.

Wolman, B. B. Instrumental, mutual acceptance and vectorial groups. *Acta Sociol.*, 1958, **3**, 19–28.

Wolman, B. B. Group psychotherapy with latent schizophrenics. *Int. J. group Psychother.*, 1960, **10**, 301–312.

Wolman, B. B. Hostility experiences in group psychotherapy. *Int. J. soc. Psychiat.*, 1964, **16**, 55–61.

Wolpe, J. *Psychotherapy by reciprocal inhibition.* Stanford Calif.: Stanford Univer. Press, 1958.

Worcester, E., McComb, S., & Coriat, I. H. *Religion and medicine.* London: Methuen, 1908.

46

Hypnotherapy

MILTON V. KLINE

A comprehensive survey of the contemporary status of hypnosis and its therapeutic application must take into account the historical background and psychological evolution of the nature of both hypnosis and the therapeutic milieu within which it has developed (Brenman & Gill, 1947; Breuer & Freud, 1936; Hadfield, 1942; Lindner, 1945a; Platonov, 1959; Sarbin, 1950; Speyer & Stokvis, 1938; Wedge, 1948).

The work of Anton Mesmer (Conn, 1957) is generally considered to mark the dividing point between the prescientific use of hypnosis as a quasi-religious therapeutic modality, which reverts back to all antiquity, and the emergence of modern psychotherapy. With Mesmer we observe the beginnings of a rationale for psychotherapy with definitive recognition of the significance of suggestion and persuasion as well as the meaningfulness of interpersonal relationships in the therapeutic process. Historical accounts which are provocative not only in the descriptive sense but also in the sense that they link psychological functions with affective and ideational constructs are to be found in the works of Braid (1960), Esdaile (1902), and Bramwell (1921), to mention only a few.

The formative years in the development of psycholanalytic theory and practice coincided with more precise clinicoexperimental studies of hypnosis and hypnotic behavior and the emergence of dynamic concepts of psychopathology (Breuer & Freud, 1936; Freud, 1924; Kline, 1958; Schneck, 1960a). Charcot (Conn, 1957), Janet (1907; 1925), Freud (1924; Kline, 1958), Breuer (Breuer & Freud, 1936), Bernheim (1947), Forel (1949), Moll (1890), Liebeault (1892), and Prince (1908; 1914; 1939) are some of the major contributors, and their work marks the beginning of a close relationship between experimental psychology and hypnosis. Schneck's history of psychiatry (1960a), written largely from a clinical perspective, highlights the focus of scientific interest in hypnosis during this period.

The full emergence of psychoanalysis somewhat dampened interest and work with hypnotherapy until the early 1930s and the work of Hull (1933) and his associates. This was followed by the resurgence of interest in hypnotherapy during World War II. Though we are now focusing on the contemporary features of hypnotherapy, its dynamisms and theoretical constructs, the serious student and clinical psychologist cannot avoid familiarity with the historical aspects of hypnosis, the experimental foundations of hypnotic behavior, and the over-all contributions to the nature of the hypnotic process. A few of the comprehensive reviews of this phase of the literature of scientific hypnosis may be found in the works of Wolberg (1945a; 1945b; 1948), Weitzenhoffer (1947), Rosen (1953b), Schneck (1959), Kroger (1963), Watkins (1949), Schilder (Schilder & Kauders, 1927), Dorcus (1956), and Kline (1958; 1962).

Hypnosis can be viewed neither as an instrument of suggestion alone nor as a phenomenon of behavior apart from the mainstream of psychological theory and a general psychology of mental functioning (Brenman,

Gill, & Hacker, 1947; Conn, 1959; Kline, 1959). For it is only through an understanding of the meaningfulness of hypnotic behavior that therapeutic applications can be adequately grasped and utilized in the treatment process (Brenman, Gill, & Knight, 1952; Brickner & Kubie, 1936; Conn, 1960; Erickson, 1939b; Erickson, 1941; Erickson, 1948a; Erickson, 1948b; Erickson & Hill, 1944). It is within this frame of reference and with this knowledge of the technical contributions from the field of experimental hypnosis that the clinical psychologist is prepared to view the contemporary status of hypnotherapy and hypnoanalysis (Arnold, 1959; Bellak, 1955; Brenman & Gill, 1943; Brenman & Knight, 1943; Conn, 1960; Erickson, 1933; Erickson, 1939a; Erickson, 1954; Erickson & Kubie, 1939; Erickson & Kubie, 1941; Farber & Fisher, 1943; Gill, 1951; Haley, 1960; LeCron, 1951).

Shortly after World War II, an increasing number of articles were published dealing with the incorporation of hypnotic techniques in the treatment of emotional disorders.

With the emergence of hypnosis as a rediscovered dynamic tool in psychotherapy, both clinical and experimental papers began to appear in great abundance, beginning in about 1950. Many in the area of psychotherapy could well have been written before the turn of the century and are not consistent with the contemporary utilization of hypnotic techniques as an integral part of present-day psychotherapy. Since such papers tend to perpetuate antiquated notions of the nature of hypnosis and suggestion and its therapeutic applications and since they also tend to reinforce the resistances which in the past have been leveled against hypnosis, they will not be discussed in this chapter.

Many worthwhile papers on hypnotherapeutic application may detail technique which is adequately covered in another paper; however, for the purposes of this chapter, such overlapping references will not be separately considered but will be found in the references to the major literature of this area of psychotherapy.

The clinical psychologist should be aware that psychologists and physicians are now making extensive use of hypnosis in the treatment of organic conditions and particularly in the control of pain. Since such areas of therapeutic application are peripheral to psychotherapy as considered within the framework of this chapter, only passing reference will be made (Dorcus & Kirkner, 1948; Guze, 1953a; Rosen, 1949; Rosen, 1952; Volgyesi, 1950).

The following major trends are to be noted in the clinical literature of hypnotherapy: (1) a significant distinction between the process of hypnotic induction and the hypnotic relationship (Adler & Secunda, 1952; Christenson, 1949; Guze, 1951; Kline, 1953); (2) the increasing use of patient-centered induction procedures and the recognition of the fact that patients may be hypnotized without conscious awareness of the process and with their implied rather than stated consent (Rosen, 1953a; Rosen, 1953b); and (3) the employment of a vast number of a very specialized and, at times, complex hypnotic techniques in addition to the use of hypersuggestibility and abreactive experiences (Brenman & Knight, 1945; Cooper, 1948; Cooper & Erickson, 1950; Erickson, 1938; Erickson, 1944; Erickson, 1955; Erickson & Kubie, 1940; Gill and Menninger, 1946; Hodge, 1959; Klemperer, 1963; Kline, 1952; Lindner, 1945b; Marcuse, 1950; Schneck, 1957).

The major techniques that have been incorporated into current hypnotherapeutic practice include the dynamic use of induced dreams, both hypnotic and posthypnotic; the influencing and elaboration of nocturnal dreaming, age regression, age progression, time distortion, revivification, and fantasy production; the use of imagery and hallucinatory responses; and the extension of acting-out techniques, based upon the elucidation of symbolic material relating to sensory, imagery, and affective mechanisms. The use of hypnotically elucidated painting, modeling, and sculpting has also resulted in meaningful developments in contemporary hypnotherapy (Baron, 1960; Erickson, 1937; Erickson, 1938; Guze, 1953b; Klemperer, 1962; Kline, 1951; Kubie, 1943; Lindner, 1953; Loomis, 1950; MacDowell, 1948; Meares, 1960; Meares, 1960a; Meares, 1960b; Rosen, 1955; Schneck, 1947c; Schneck, 1948a; Schneck, 1956b).

Perhaps the most significant way to summarize the contemporary phase of hypnotherapy would be to point out that hypnotic procedures and the hypnotic process are now being utilized along with special hypnotic methods in all forms of psychotherapy, ranging from formal psychoanalytic treatment to the physical therapies, such as shock therapy and chemotherapy (Kroger, 1963; Schneck, 1959). Clinical problems which are now treated on a hypnotic level include neurotic and psychotic disturbances; psychosomatic illnesses; a variety of psychological problems, such as reading disabilities, speech impairment, and learning blocks; and organic illnesses and the pain resulting from them. The hypnotic process can be integrated into the treatment situation only after thorough patient evaluation, and such integration must be in keeping with the therapeutic competence of the therapist. Hypnosis does not constitute a therapy by itself but rather an exceedingly potent and varied process which can be accommodated meaningfully and productively to a variety of therapeutic procedures. It does, however, pose certain problems, dangers, and contraindications, all of which require specialized training and experience before the therapist can be considered competent to utilize hypnosis as part of his therapeutic armamentarium. Training in hypnosis itself without adequate training in psychodynamics and psychotherapy cannot provide an adequate background for hypnotherapy any more than training in psychotherapy alone can (Bird, 1948; Dribben, 1949; Fox, 1960; Levbarg, 1941; Moreno & Enneis, 1950; Paley, 1952; Raginsky, 1960; Schneck, 1946; Schneck, 1948b; Schneck, 1953a; Secunda, 1948; Spiegel, 1963; Watkins, 1946; Watkins, 1947; Wells, 1944; Wolpe, 1958).

INDUCTION

The induction of hypnosis is a significant part of the therapeutic interaction and in most instances involves observable projective behavior on the part of the patient, which may be used for diagnostic purposes and as part of the therapeutic process (Christenson, 1949; Kline, 1943). Erickson's (1948b) development of the hand-levitation technique and Schneck's (1947b) modification of it, along with the use of ocular-fixation procedures and the development of visual-imagery approaches (Kline, 1958), are among the major methods for the clinical induction of hypnosis. Kroger (1963), in his recent major review of clinical and experimental hypnosis, adequately describes most modifications of induction procedures and particularly details the use of sensory-imagery methods, progressive relaxation, tension-relaxation techniques, hyperventilation, cataleptic devices, the confustional procedure, and mechanical approaches.

While the foregoing techniques cover the major dimensions of induction in clinical practice, the therapist will find that the hypnotic approach to the individual patient requires many modifications of technique which must be adapted to meet the needs of the patient and the circumstances of the particular case (Schneck, 1950a; Schneck, 1961).

Careful appraisal of patient resistances and the symbolic expression of defensive maneuvering will often determine the manner in which induction will be direct or indirect, sensory or imagery, or peripheral or regressive in relation to depth (Conn, 1958; Erickson & Hill, 1944; Guze, 1951; Kline, 1953; Levitt, Lubin, & Brady, 1963; Schneck, 1950b; Schneck, 1950d; Schneck, 1950e; Schneck, 1951a; Schneck, 1953a).

As long as psychological practice has extended itself to hypnosis, the problem of hypnotizability has persisted. The ratio of individuals capable of being induced into a trance state and the ranges for the various "levels" of hypnosis generally have been verified from the older literature (Schilder & Kauders, 1927). Apparently 90 to 95 per cent of all individuals have some degree of hypnotizability. Approximately 10 per cent are capable of a depth state within which such phenomena as complete anesthesia, spontaneous amnesia, positive and negative hallucinations, and posthypnotic behavior are capable of being produced easily and with long-term effectiveness.

Contemporary research with hypnosis in therapy has clearly indicated, with respect to treatment procedures and in relation to the clinical handling of psychodynamic material, that light states of hypnosis not only are useful but often are preferred (Dorcus, 1956; Kline, 1958; Schneck, 1957; Weitzenhoffer, 1962). Although "deep hypnosis" has been associated with gross alterations in behavior generally, it has only recently been recognized that many highly complex and subtle changes in psychological functions can be brought about by extremely light hypnotic states. That deeper states of hypnosis are crucial for experimental work has been emphasized very distinctly by Erickson (1954). However, for much psychotherapeutic work, light states offer many advantages in terms of both time and the ease of handling which the deeper states do not. The major areas within which light hypnotic states have been useful are projection, self-reflection, increased associative functioning, imagery, projective testing, amplification of general psychologic productivity, fantasy evocation, and somatic alterations (Conn, 1959; Klemperer, 1947; Kline, 1960; Kline & Schneck, 1951b; LeCron, 1952; Lindner, 1946; Regardie, 1950; Schneck, 1948c; Schneck, 1951c; Schneck, 1962a; Schneck, 1962b).

The induction phase of hypnotherapy is important in the understanding of the hypnotic transference and cannot be viewed as a simple mechanical step. Frequently there will be some distortion in sensory experience and the elucidation of affective material which require reorganization and incorporation before further productive use can be made of hypnosis.

RECENT ADVANCEMENTS

Recent advancements in hypnotherapy have been based largely upon two distinctive trends: (1) the ability to integrate and manage psychodynamic material and concepts in a more productive and effective manner through the utilization of hypnosis, and (2) the use of specific hypnotic techniques, such as age regression, age progression, scene visualization, imagery activity, fantasy evocation, sensory hypnoplasty, and other modifications of perceptual functioning (Bowers, 1960; Bowers, Brecher-Marer, & Polatin, 1961; Dorcus, 1960; Kartchner & Korner, 1947; Kline, 1952; Kline, 1958; Kline, 1959; Kline & Guze, 1951; Kline & Haggerty, 1953; LeCron, 1952; Meares, 1960a; Meares, 1960c; Rosen & Myers, 1947; Schneck, 1951d; Schneck, 1952).

Although Anton Mesmer's early prominence and notoriety were in connection with his treatment of a child, little concentrated work in child psychotherapy has been reported in relation to the use of hypnosis. Ambrose (1949; 1950; 1951a; 1951b; 1952), in England, has in recent years used hypnotherapy in the treatment of a number of behavior disorders of children. He has reported upon cases of anxiety reactions, asthma, enuresis, epilepsy, stammering, insomnia, and various psychosomatic manifestations.

Recently, psychotherapists and pediatricians have utilized hypnosis in connection with the medical problems of children, and Jacobs (1962) rather clearly points out its particular role in pediatric practice. Betcher[1] has reported on its use in anesthesia with children, and Browning, Quinn, and Crasilneck (1958) have reported on it in connection with the direct treatment of suppression amblyopia.

Buckley (1950), in describing the use of hypnoanalytic methods in the treatment of "posttraumatic syndrome" following head injury, illustrates an effective therapy for many psychological disorders which follow physical injury and which appear to be based upon body-image alterations. Abreaction, ablation of time concepts, and associative methods all play a role in this type of therapy.

Conn (1949), in emphasizing the concept of patient-centered psychotherapy, has employed hypnotherapy as a unifying interpersonal experience. He utilizes the term "hypnosynthesis" to describe an approach in treatment which permits the patient objectively to experience what he is doing and to bring together in his own interpretative frame of reference the motives for his behavior.

Schneck and Kline (1950; 1951; 1952; 1953) have described and utilized visual imagery in the form of scene visualizations for projecting unconscious ideas and feelings through techniques involving the word association test, the TAT, the House-Tree-Person test, and direct associative activity. Visual imagery, as well as hallucinated behavior, has been utilized for purposes of unconscious productivity, clarification, and abreaction (Kline, 1952; Kline, 1958; Schneck, 1950c).

There has been a growing awareness that the hypnotic state is in itself a highly complex gestalt. Schneck, in a series of provocative clinical researches, has emphasized the unconscious aspects of the hypnotic relationship for the patient and has shown how this reaction is descriptive of the patient's personality dynamics and how it may be incorporated into psychotherapy (1950b; 1950d; 1950f; 1951a; 1951d).

From clinical observations in therapy has emerged the recognition that in a state of hypnosis there exists a subtle, though highly complex, alteration of the patient's mode of perception and communication (Bowers & Glasner, 1958; Brenman et al., 1947;

[1] A detailed description of induction and management of the hypnotic process with children is given in A. M. Betcher, Hypno-induction techniques in pediatric anesthesia, *Anesthesiology*, 1958, 19, 279–281.

Ehrenreich, 1951; Kline, 1958; Kline, 1962; Kubie & Margolin, 1944; Luria, 1932; Meares, 1960b). With hypnosis it has been found that psychologic productivity, emotional accessibility, cognitive reflection, and self-reference reactions become not only more understandable but also more manageable.

Brenman and Gill (1947), in their earlier review of the literature, take into account the historical background of contemporary practice and divide the literature of hypnosis, from a therapeutic point of view, into six major areas: (1) prolonged hypnosis without direct suggestion or explanation; (2) direct suggestion of symptom disappearance; (3) direct suggestion of the disappearance of attitudes underlying symptoms; (4) abreaction of traumatic experience; (5) the use of specialized hypnotic techniques, in what might best be described as directive or active psychotherapy; and (6) hypnoanalysis.

At the present time, some use might be made of all these procedures, and, as the gap between psychoanalytic psychotherapy and nonpsychoanalytic psychotherapy has narrowed, we might within the present scope of psychotherapeutic practice either view all these approaches as being meaningful in selective individual cases or, at times, view a variety of such approaches as being selectively integrated and utilized in keeping with patient needs.

It is, therefore, not at all uncommon for the contemporary hypnotherapist to apply analytic procedures along with direct hypnotic suggestions which are designed either to bring about affective states or to produce ideational material underlying attitudes relating either to symbolic or to symptomatic material. This may be utilized in connection with either insight development or the production of behavior designed to clarify a particular underlying symptom or etiological factor.

Erickson (1939a; 1941; 1954), in his classical contributions both to the understanding of the nature of hypnosis and to the development of dynamic hypnotherapy, has emphasized the role of specialized hypnotic procedures, including hallucinatory experiences and the distortions of time, as significant techniques in the treatment of both neurotic and psychotic disturbances. He has made a notable distinction between the process of inducing hypnosis and the nature of the trance state itself, with the particular characteristics that it possesses in relation to therapeutic activity. Among the procedures which he has described in connection with clinical material are the development of automatic writing and the putting of particular stress upon the role of unconscious mental activity during hypnosis.

Along with Kubie, Erickson (Erickson & Kubie, 1941) has described a patient with a hysterical depression who was able to regress under hypnosis to an important aspect of childhood experience. Here the role of dissociative functions and repressive mechanisms is described in relation to therapeutic gain. The use of age-regression techniques and the employment of revivification have been described by a number of other investigators (Kline, 1950; LeCron, 1952; LeCron & Bordeaux, 1947; Leeds, 1949; Lindner, 1944; Rosen, 1955; Sarbin, 1950; Schneck, 1960b).

The use of hypnosis in psychoanalytic treatment has been well documented by Lindner (1953), Schneck (1959), and Wolberg (1945a). Watkins (1949) also has illustrated the use of hypnoanalytic methods and has described their use in the treatment of both war neuroses and emotional illnesses unrelated to such traumatic origins. Klemperer (1947; 1962; 1963) has contributed a number of papers emphasizing the role of recall under hypnosis and revivification as a meaningful step in the resolving of conflicts relating to both obsessional and compulsive features and, especially, to aspects of anxiety. Meares (1960b; Kline, 1962), in recent theoretical and clinical contributions, has described the atavistic elements involved in hypnosis and has developed an approach which utilizes sculpting and modeling and other aspects of nonverbal communication in the therapeutic process. He has also delineated two kinds of hypnoanalysis. He states that in formal psychoanalysis, hypnoanalysis is merely a tool used to overcome specific resistances as they arise. When hypnoanalysis is to be used in this way, it is usual to commence by giving the patient a series of training sessions in hypnosis until he is able to reach a satisfactory depth of hypnosis at short notice. Then formal psychoanalysis is started in the usual way. Hypnoanalysis itself can be used as the main technique in psychotherapy. For convenience it is best to refer to this method as hypnoanalysis proper. Actually, this is an eclectic technique of psychotherapy. It is not just a matter of using hypnosis to overcome resistances in psychoanalysis. Although it is an eclectic technique, it is essentially oriented toward psychoanalytic concepts. Psychotherapy is nondirective, but free association is used only sparingly. The therapist, for the most part, remains passive. This combination of circumstances becomes possible by virtue of the fact that the deeply hypnotized patient either will talk spontaneously or can be led into talking uninhibitedly. Treatment consists of a series of sessions of hypnoanalysis with occasional sessions of waking psychotherapy, but not necessarily any formal psychoanalysis. The waking psychotherapy is used to integrate the material which has been ventilated in hypnotic sessions.

There are a number of meaningful and significant modifications of this approach (Kline, 1958; Kroger, 1963; Moss, 1962; Rosen, 1953b; Schneck, 1959; Schneck, 1962a), but in essence this describes the use of hypnosis as a dynamic means of dealing with both unconscious material and the defenses created against unconscious conflicts within the behavior that either develops spontaneously or is elicited by hypnotic technique.

Rosen (1953a) has reported on the use of fantasy and fantasy evocation as a means of utilizing unconscious and dynamic material in the analytic approach to psychotherapy. Schneck (1959), in describing hypnoanalysis, describes it as psychotherapy with an admixture of hypnotic techniques and psychoanalytic concepts. During the past two decades, Schneck (1947a; 1948a; 1952a; 1952b; 1953b; 1956b; 1957; 1959) has contributed major elements of technique and therapeutic management in this area, including the treatment of phobias, the relief of anxiety episodes, the nature of spontaneous sensory and motor phenomena (1951c) during hypnoanalysis, and the role of dreams and automatic writing during such treatment. There has been much emphasis on the use of hypnosis in the psychotherapy of psychosomatic disturbances by Schneck (1959), Rosen (1953b), Raginsky (1960), Kline (1958), Guze (1953b), Watkins (1949), and Conn (1949), to mention only a few. Schneck (1959; Kline, 1962) and Meares (1960b; Kline, 1962) have also contributed theoretical aspects of hypnosis as viewed within the therapeutic interaction, and Schneck (1950b; 1950f; 1951d) has elaborated this in relation to the equation of hypnosis with death and with homosexuality. Meares (1960c) has related hypnosis to preverbal atavistic mental functioning. Bowers (1960; Bowers et al., 1961) has described the use of hypnotherapy in the treatment of schizophrenia.

Crasilneck and his coworkers (Crasilneck et al., 1955; Crasilneck & Erwin, 1958; Crasilneck & Hall, 1959), in a number of papers, have emphasized the role of hypnosis and hypnotherapy in the treatment of acute pain and its role as an adjunctive procedure in the treatment of servere burns as well as in the treatment of suppression amblyopia in children.

Wright[2] has elaborated on the role of hypnotherapy in the rehabilitation process, and Raginsky (1960), as well as Shapiro and Kline,[3] has reported on the use of hypnosis in the treatment of multiple sclerosis. Such approaches, particularly in relation to organic diseases, illustrate the manner in which both psychotherapy and the employment of hypnotic procedures may be of great value not only to the psychotherapist but also to the internist and other medical specialists as a means of facilitating recovery from organic disease and physical injury.

Schneck's paper on current advances in hypnotherapy (1957) evaluated the status of hypnotherapy at that time, which has not changed radically since then. Circumscribed problems and individual symptoms may be investigated hypnotherapeutically with the goal of understanding and relief. The likelihood of achieving fairly rapid and decisive beneficial results is greatly enhanced if the patient is functioning efficiently in areas other than the presenting difficulty. Pervasive anxiety or anxiety interfering with abilities of patients to gain an adequate start in treatment may very often be effectively eliminated with hypnotic procedures. Also to be noted are the effects of hypnosis in clarifying attitudes toward the self and others, elucidating patterns

[2] In an extremely comprehensive review, Wright outlines the uses of hypnosis and hypnotherapy in the total approach to physical rehabilitation. M. E. Wright, Hypnosis and rehabilitation, *Rehabilit. Lit.*, 1960, **1**, 2–12.

[3] In an experimental treatment situation, one case of multiple sclerosis is described in connection with the use of hypnosis as a direct nonpsychotherapeutic procedure. A. Shapiro & M. V. Kline, The use of hypnosis in evaluating the physiological and psychological components in the functional impairment of the patient with multiple sclerosis, *J. clin. exp. Hypnosis*, 1956, **4**, 69–78.

of behavior in psychological defenses, and evaluating goals and the strivings toward them. Hypnotherapy may involve a significant revision of personality functioning. Contrary to impressions of hypnotherapy as basically delimited and circumscribed, psychological functioning of patients may be explored to varying degrees, based on needs and desires of individual patients and clinical judgments of the therapist.

Among the more recently developed and emphasized approaches in hypnotherapy have been symptom substitution, symptom removal by symptom transformation, and time abstraction.

The use of ideomotor signaling to bring about corrective emotional responses has also been described, along with the use of reciprocal inhibition techniques in psychotherapy enhanced by hypnotic methods (Cheek, 1962; Wolpe, 1958).

There has also been increased use of projective techniques within the framework of hypnoanalysis, particularly such devices as the theater technique, crystal gazing, scene visualization, and the Thematic Apperception Test. Hypnodrama (Moreno & Enneis, 1950) is a method which can be employed when the patient is under hypnosis; the entire conflict situation can be dramatized, and the therapist or professional actor can play one of the roles. Watkins (1947) has made use of yet another interesting technique which he describes as the "affect bridge," in which, after the patient is dehypnotized, previously elicited material is discussed and then, during rehypnosis, is used for further discussion and questioning to ascertain whether his understanding is complete.

The production of experimental conflicts and the use of hypnoplasty and hypnography constitute still further modifications of approach at the present time. Raginsky (1961; 1962) has developed and reported on the use of sensory hypnoplasty. Sensory hypnoplasty is a technique in hypnoanalysis in which the hypnotized patient models clay to which various sensory stimuli have been added to stimulate basic primitive memories, associations, sensations, and conflicts. This procedure allows the patient to give plastic expression to repressed and suppressed material, which is then followed by verbalization of conflicts. The therapist remains passive and silent throughout the session.

Sensory hypnoplasty has been used successfully in the treatment of character disorders, anxiety states, phobic reactions, diverse neurotic symptom complaints, various psychophysiologic reactions, and some phychotic reactions of schizophrenia.

REGRESSIVE EXPERIENCE

Hypnotically induced age regression has been utilized as a technique in psychotherapy within a variety of treatment orientations. Wolberg (1948), Schneck (1959), Kline (1958), and Conn (1958) have described its use within analytic or dynamic psychotherapy, and many others have reported upon its utilization in more direct symptom-oriented hypnotherapy (Kroger, 1963).

For the greater part, clinical studies and experimental reports of hypnotic age regression in psychotherapy have dealt with its value in relation to emotional catharsis, release of hostility, abreaction of traumatic events, and release of repressed material. The handling of material so obtained is generally consistent with prevailing techniques of psychotherapy.

In more direct hypnotherapy, age regression has frequently been utilized to abreact a traumatic event, with therapeutic success reportedly related either to the ventilation process itself or to the rapid insight that has resulted.

In analytic hypnotherapy, spontaneous age regressions are not uncommon and have been described with clarity by Conn (1958), Schneck (1960b), and Kline (1958), as well as by other investigators working with experimental hypnosis (Gidro-Frank & Buch, 1948; Gidro-Frank & Bull, 1950; Mercer & Gibson, 1950; Platonov, 1933; Schneck, 1955; Spiegel, Shor, & Fishman, 1945). The motivation for spontaneous age regression in itself is of considerable interest and frequently relates to long-standing feelings of guilt with a wish to reveal what has been repressed. As such, the spontaneous regression may result from the transference relationship and its management or from other material being dealt with in therapy. The "contagiousness" of associated material within hypnotic states is apparently related both to lowered levels of ego functioning and to the intensification of emotional response to ideas, sensations, and recollections. In this respect, most spontaneous age regressions involve an aspect of revivification as well as of regression and might well be considered, by way of classification, to be of the type that Schneck (1956a) refers to as "dynamic regression."

This type of spontaneous behavioral activity constitutes an advantage when properly utilized within psychotherapy, but it may constitute a basis for contraindication to the use of hypnosis where intensive psychotherapeutic involvement is absent and where the resultant activity may produce only a lowered level of reality contact and more poorly integrated emotional response.

Symptom-oriented hypnotherapy which utilizes age regression in order to relive a traumatic experience and to abreact presumably underlying causative agents in symptom development has, with few exceptions, been inadequately appraised and incompletely reported in the clinical literature. The value of hypnotic abreaction or ventilation per se appears to be more valuable than has generally been considered. It would seem questionable, however, whether the "insight" gained from such experiences functions as insight at all, and thus the question is raised, in view of reported clinical success, as to the *real* reasons for therapeutic gain.

It is reasonably clear that there is lacking at the present time in all psychotherapies an objective correlation between therapeutic technique and therapeutic success. There are, in addition, inadequate follow-ups for many of the briefer utilizations of intensive hypnotherapy, while for those that have been followed up, an inadequate evaluation of everyday living components in addition to the symptoms which may have been treated is provided. That some therapeutic success with brief hypnotherapy may be the result of magical ideas on the part of the patient and/or therapist and the powerful gains of a positive transference process is rather likely and certainly cannot, at this point, be overlooked. Experimentally we know that it is possible to have another investigator eliminate hypnotically induced symptoms with hypnotherapy based upon "insights" and "interpretations" which have no semblance of meaningfulness or validity. It is also evident that similar procedures and techniques can be accomplished on a nonhypnotic level, and while of value within a full concept of treatment procedure, they should be recognized for what they are rather than for what they may appear to be mechanistically. Kline,[4] in evaluating hypnotic age regression as utilized in psychotherapy, states that it may be considered a technique either for catharsis or for uncovering purposes and for the *utilization of regressive experience and of the regressive process for its experiential value.*

One of the primary advantages of age regression appears to be that it makes possible a transference relationship which assumes great importance to the patient and which permits a degree of freedom and spontaneity most characteristic of the preadolescent period. In this respect it is more open, since it lacks the criticalness which is more typical of later psychological development. The lack of critical capacity is, of course, accompanied by a reduction of ego defenses and reality testing. When reinforced through the use of strong supportive and ego-recognizing devices in the therapeutic relationship, this breach in the defenses of the individual does not pose any more of a problem than it would in a nonhypnotic therapeutic situation.

Through the use of relationship experience rather than suggestiveness alone, there develops within the regression a reconstruction of many attitudes and values which go into the creation of the world of reality as we know it. In this basic interaction, the patient makes available aspects of his own self-concept and body image which may now be influenced and directed through the regressive experience, which, while repetitive of earlier developmental experiences, has within it the uniqueness of the therapeutic relationship which was previously lacking (Kline, 1958).

At this level, therapist and patient interact at a point where with such uncritical ego functioning as exists in regression, it is possible to strengthen and initiate drives, affects, and values. As they become more intense, they assume greater reality in the nonhypnotic state and become synthesized into workable and acceptable ideas, feelings, wishes, and desires.

The results point to the use of regression not only as a technique in therapy but also as an intense dynamic experience within which

[4] Detailed studies of age regression with specific reference to clinical material are reported in M. V. Kline (Ed.), *Clinical correlations of experimental hypnosis,* Springfield, Ill., Charles C Thomas, in press; and M. V. Kline, Age regression and psychotherapy: clinical and theoretical observations, *Int. J. clin. exp. Hypnosis,* 1960, **1,** 17–35.

the patient's world of reality may for the first time since his own childhood be touched and influenced both motivationally and reactively.

PROJECTIVE TECHNIQUES IN RELATION TO THERAPY

The use of projective techniques, particularly the Rorschach and the Thematic Apperception Test, warrants mention in a chapter on hypnotherapy because of the relevance of these techniques to the dynamics of the hypnotic transference and because of their diagnostic significance.

Wilkins and Adams (1947) report an investigation of the use of the Rorschach under hypnosis in military psychiatry. They found that such a technique was particularly useful with the inaccessible patient, with cases where there is a paucity of responses, and with the fearful or combat-fatigue patient. They found that the Rorschach record elicited under hypnosis shows an increase in percentage of responses to cards VIII, IX, and X. The total number of rejections is greatly reduced, generally to zero. Sum C generally was noted to decrease, and M and FM to show increases. The findings from a study of this type point not only to a specialized technique for the examination of difficult patients but also to a technique for the further study and validation of projective devices. In this connection Lane reports on a validation test of the Rorschach movement interpretations (1948). The investigation of the validity of M score interpretations involved inducing productivity and introversive mechanisms by suggestions and noting results and changes in the M score and experience type on the Rorschach test. Rorschach tests were administered to a subject in the waking state and in a state of hypnosis per se, as well as in a state of hypnosis with suggestion. The results indicated that hypnosis per se seems to produce a slight increase of the introversive tendencies beyond the normal state, while the gross effects of hypnosis with specific suggestions intensify the introversive tendencies far beyond the level of hypnosis per se.

In Lane's study, the qualitative analysis of the movement responses indicated that the subject was responding with movement interpretations. As a result of hypnotic excitation, in addition to verifying certain constructs of the Rorschach technique, this study points up another aspect of hypnosis which has been a point of serious consideration, that is, the nature of creativity and productivity in personality as a result of hypnosis. Critics of hypnosis (Orne, 1951; Sarbin, 1950) have often labeled hypnotic behavior "acting" and an example of nonproductive psychological activity. Schneck (1951b) contradicts this point of view and describes some distinctly productive and creative aspects of hypnotic behavior with specific reference to psychotherapeutic activity. In Lane's study, the subject engaged in dream activity and verse writing, which was clearly an expression of ideational and affective productivity with pertinent relationship to definitive personality problems which were confronting the subject and which lead to some clarification. In addition to the clinical findings, the quantitative changes in the Rorschach pointed to a much more extensive use of color areas and to improved form level. The implication was one of personal productivity of considerable degree.

Bergman, Graham, and Leavitt (1947), in their study of Rorschach changes during consecutive hypnotic chronological-age-level regressions of one patient, found the test changes to parallel closely the clinical life data of the patient. The appearance of new interpersonal relationships which produced anxiety and unconscious hostility was noted along with the expression (pyschometrically) of defense mechanisms designed to cope with these new developments and conflicts.

The possibility of employing the Rorschach as well as other techniques and instruments in clinical psychology for the longitudinal analysis of personality now exists. As such, psychological procedures of diagnostic design can be incorporated into psychotherapy and, with proper management, can extend both the use of psychological tests and the extent of psychotherapeutic technique. The possibility of further studying the relationship between learning theory and psychotherapy is enhanced because of the longitudinal controls which would now be available to the therapist through hypnometrics.

In a study of ego defense and hypnotizability, Sarason and Rosenzweig (1942) utilized the Thematic Apperception Test. The main conclusions drawn tended to confirm the quantitative findings of the earlier relationship expressed in the triadic hypothesis, which has been stated by Rosenzweig as follows: "Hypnotizability as a personality trait is to be found in positive association with repression as a preferred mechanism of defense, and with impunitiveness as a characteristic type of immediate reaction to frustration." In analyzing the stories projected with regard to hypnosis, the dynamics of ego-defense mechanisms and the needs of the individual became united and conceptualized. On the basis of the stories produced on the TAT, it was possible significantly to differentiate hypnotizable from nonhypnotizable subjects.

In a study designed to investigate the personality correlates of hypnotizability, Rosenzweig and Sarason (1942) used a correlative technique to determine whether or not hypnotizability as a personality trait is to be found related to repression as a selected mechanism of defense and with "impunitiveness" as an immediate reaction to frustration. Their results would seem to validate this hypothesis in positive association, though with certain selective aspects of personality expression altering the characteristic mode of response. The correlations between suggestibility and repression were .25 and .47; between hypnotizability and repression, .66. Findings of this sort have two immediate implications: (1) a practical clinicodiagnostic technique for selecting patients likely to be workable in a hypnotherapeutic setting and (2) a means of evaluating ego defenses and the dynamics of aggression-frustration reactions.

The problem of vocational interests and personality has received considerable attention in clinical psychology and vocational guidance and to some extent in psychoanalysis. Psychologists interested in the problem of vocational choice and personality adjustment have in recent years been placing greater stress upon the role of psychodynamic processes involved in occupational interests and choices.

In a series of clinical investigations of the origins of vocational interests and choice, a hypnotic method has been employed in studying the genesis of occupational interests, and a scene-visualization technique has been described for this purpose (Kline & Schneck, 1950; Kline & Schneck, 1951a). These reports deal with patients who were seen in hypnotherapeutic and vocational analysis settings. The purpose of a technique of the scene-visualization type is to further the study of the underlying personality motives and psychodynamic processes which lead to the development of occupational interests and vocational goals. In clinical application, the results not only proved useful in the therapeutic approach but also afforded insight into the unconscious factors that might become motivating elements in the development of vocational interests generally. It was found that meaningful scene visualization could be obtained from patients in a light nonsomnambulistic trance and that additional hypnotic and therapeutic techniques could be employed in interpreting and analyzing the productions from these visualizations. In many instances it was possible to undercut the conscious motivations for specific vocational plans and goals and to get directly at the unconscious origin of these patterns of behavior. The findings were then utilized in the total treatment plan and led to clarification of the patient's personality difficulties. It was also noted that this hypnotic technique frequently brought to consciousness associated images which were of a nonoccupational nature and which also could be incorporated with meaningfulness into the therapeutic approach. As a technique for therapeutic application and as a psychological method for further investigating the origin of vocational interests and vocational choice, the hypnotic scene-visualization method would appear to have considerable value.

Schneck and Kline (1950; 1951; 1952; 1953) have reported on a technique which utilized the House-Tree-Person test in measuring the effectiveness of psychotherapy. Such a method, since it is dependent upon only a light hypnotic state, can be easily utilized with almost all forms of psychotherapy.

Visual imagery, induced through hypnosis, has been described in a variety of psychotherapeutic approaches. Kline[5] in reporting on spontaneous-regressive phenomena during hypnotherapy, has described sensory and motor reactions as well as the production of drawings and paintings similar to those Naumburg (1963) has obtained in art therapy. She concludes that the tapping of regressive kinesthetic levels of the unconscious speeds up the therapeutic process in the same manner as in hypnosis.

[5] Paper presented at the 1960 meeting of the American Psychological Association, New York City.

EXPERIMENTAL TECHNIQUES

Kupper (1945) describes a patient with a history of classical convulsive seizures of grand mal type with abnormal electrocortical activity on the EEG. His attacks started six years before examination and were precipitated by an emotional upset. Under hypnosis, convulsive seizures were induced by discovering and suggesting the specific psychic conflict. EEG recordings could be altered by suggesting that the patient under hypnosis regress to an age prior to his first convulsion.

Brenman and Gill (1947) report on a case where, using experimental techniques in therapy, a patient some months after being exposed to a particular situation was regressed back to that time hypnotically. This involved principally time rather than age regression, though both are related. The subject spontaneously began to perspire and to complain of the heat. This was rather surprising in view of the fact that this particular phase of the study took place in winter. The experimenters then recalled that the day to which the patient was now regressed had been one of the hottest of the summer.

In considering the phenomena of hypnotically induced changes in age and time orientation, we have in the past been concerned with a regression or a chronologically going-back problem, which involves not only the memories and recalled experiences of that time but also all learned and unlearned experiential activity. The issue of experiential age activity has always been assumed to be the nuclear core in age regression and has in part contributed to the difficulty in ascertaining the validity and the nature of age regression. Recent evidence has pointed to time-age orientation changes in the opposite direction, namely, aging.[6] The term "hypnotic age progression" has been applied to this phenomenon.

Meerloo (1956), in describing emergency psychotherapy, presents material relating to the use of hypnocatharsis combined with techniques of autohypnosis carried on by the patient at home. In describing this technique, the therapist explains the general principle of muscle relaxation and its influence on mental functioning. Then, after an initial relaxation exercise, the patient is put under light hypnosis. At the end of the first treatment, the patient is asked to lie down at home at the same hour every afternoon or evening and to repeat the relaxation exercises by himself. Following this he is to meditate about the different questions that have come up during the treatment situation. The words "hypnosis" and "autohypnosis" are usually not mentioned to the patient because of the possible distorted associations. The patient is asked to recall the images the therapist evoked in him during the period of muscle relaxation. As a result, all conscious imagery sometimes disappears from the patient's mind, and he falls asleep. Clinical sessions, preferably one a week, are used for further psychotherapeutic exploration after the short relaxation session is repeated and finished. According to Meerloo, childhood memories come through more easily, and dream material is more readily remembered.

Although the successful relief of symptoms of various allergic conditions by hypnosis has been widely reported over many years, few details of controls have been published. Mason and Black (1958) describe a case of allergic skin response abolished under treatment by hypnosis, in which the patient's skin reactions were carefully studied under controlled conditions.

A patient with a long history of allergic asthmas and hay fever was relieved of her symptoms by hypnotic treatment. Weekly skin tests showed decreasing sensitivity to the well-known allergens. When finally the patient had no skin reactions, intradermal injection of her serum into a nonallergic volunteer made it possible to demonstrate the passive transfer of skin sensitivity to the original allergens. Treatment procedure consisted in direct suggestion of alteration of symptomatic distress and is of considerable interest to psychologists concerned with both the psychophysiology of psychosomatic disorders and the psychodynamics of the hypnotic relationship, since there was no attempt to deal directly with meaningful emotional material. Nevertheless, rather significant emotional changes seem to have taken place, together with rather profound physiological alterations.

Schneck (1957), in reviewing current advances in hypnotherapy, divided the subject matter into two areas: (1) the use of hyp-

[6] Age progression as an aspect of hypnotic behavior has been investigated experimentally and utilized in psychotherapeutic settings. M. V. Kline (Ed.), *Hypnodynamic psychology*, New York, Julian Press, 1955.

nosis as a psychotherapeutic modality and (2) the problems arising out of the induction process, the postinduction therapeutic phase, and the termination period. In hypnotherapy, hypnosis constitutes an adjunctive procedure; as such, it is a part of the general practice of psychotherapy and cannot be separated from it. As knowledge of psychodynamics grows, understanding and integration of hypnosis in the framework of psychodynamics will take place, and it will become an integral part of the psychotherapeutic approach. There is a place for hypnosis as an adjunctive technique in the treatment of a variety of problems, and it is particularly useful with patients having conversion and phobic reactions and reasonably good ego strength.

Schneck (1959) has also described hypnoanalytic therapy with problems of stuttering, anxiety, asthma, marital conflict, and depression. Such problems are frequently found in routine psychotherapeutic practice. The specific measures incorporated into treatment with patients included hypnotic scene visualization, stimulated identifications, symbol interpretations, free association, transference analysis, and hypnotic suggestion for nocturnal dreaming and recall. He emphasizes how hypnotic techniques, rather than restricting their use to dealing with repressive mechanisms only, are helpful in more subtle fashion, in eliciting the operation of many dynamisms, such as isolation, identification, projection, symbolism, displacement, condensation, and rationalization.

Ikemi[7] and others undertook experimental studies of psychosomatic disorders of the digestive system by studying the influence of emotions induced by hypnotic suggestion. It was found that hypnotic suggestion of apparently the same kind of emotion seems to induce different psychophysiological reactions, depending upon the condition of subjects at the time of the experiment and their personalities and upon the technique of hypnosis.

Conn (1958), in a clinical study of the meanings and motivations associated with spontaneous hypnotic regression, found that the motivational influences and meanings associated with spontaneous regression are of considerable psychodynamic interest. It was postulated that when a patient spontaneously regresses, he has a wish to re-create a previous life situation. Clinical material indicated that patients can be brought out of regression without any attempt to reorient them to the present. During spontaneous regressions, patients can discuss topics which are subsequent to the regressed age levels. The patient does not revive whole memories but "memory romances," which are rationalizations and wish-fulfilling fantasies.

The patient in the hypnotic trance is not passive but is an active agent who uses the therapist as a means of restoring his feeling of mastery and control. In this manner, a painful, baffling life situation which formerly had been the source of conflict, guilt, or self-deprecation is mastered. Conn feels that this is in keeping with Whitehorn's (1954) view:

> Symptoms have meaning in a motivational sense . . . morbid patterns of reactions are part of an adaptation struggle . . . one of the main tasks in psychiatric work is to conduct an individualized study of each patient to point up the main recurrent theme of dissatisfaction and conflict and to assess the individual's currently unused potentialities for dealing with this issue.

Crasilneck and Erwin (1958) studied the effect of general anesthesia on posthypnotic suggestion. Ten patients who were conditioned to respond to posthypnotic suggestions prior to surgery were observed when the suggestions were given following surgery. The main reaction time to respond to the posthypnotic suggestion was one minute and twenty-six seconds following the return of the eyelid reflex. The results indicated that the patients responded prior to entering a state of consciousness. From an empirical standpoint, this study reveals that it is possible to elicit a posthypnotic suggestion following a general anesthesia prior to the patient's return to consciousness. It may therefore be advantageous to use hypnosis in certain conditions following the administration of a general anesthesia to maintain a state of analgesia. The purpose of using hypnosis is to maintain analgesia following a surgical procedure without interference or side effects from narcotics.

Bowers and Glasner (1958), in studying the autohypnotic aspects of the Jewish cabalistic concept of Kavanah, concluded from their ob-

[7] Experimental investigations of psychosomatic disorders by Ikemi and his coworkers have many provocative relationships to current therapeutic procedure. Y. Ikemi et al., Psychosomatic aspects of gastrointestinal disorders, *Int. J. clin. exp. Hypnosis,* 1959, 3, 139–150.

servations that the Jewish mystics, from former times to the present, use autohypnosis as a deliberate technique for the production of religious ecstasy and as a means for obtaining deeper religious insights or revelations. Both the methods by which they induce the autohypnotic trance, or Kavanah, and the ways in which they utilize it parallel many of the modern methods of hypnotic induction and the utilization of the hypnotic trance.

Moss (1961), in a study of therapeutic suggestion and autosuggestion, concludes that clinicians should not ignore certain aspects of patient behavior accessible via hypnosis or autohypnosis. Psychologically effective suggestion is that which is presented to a patient in such a manner that he accepts and acts on it uncritically. It requires an imaginative, skillful approach combined with an intimate knowledge of individual dynamics to avoid arousing strong resistances. In selected cases, the author feels that autohypnosis may be an effective therapeutic technique. In the last analysis he believes there is no successful suggestion without autosuggestion. Sound psychotherapeutic practice places emphasis on helping the patient to help himself, and training in autohypnosis may minimize the dependency aspects of the relationship and increase the possibility of reducing troublesome emotional reactions and symptoms, thereby allowing the patient to adjust to his problems with greater flexibility. This study is of importance in that it highlights the current conflicting opinions and attitudes toward the use of self-hypnotic techniques in psychotherapy. The greater utilization of these techniques would seem to indicate that more exacting studies of indications and contraindications are both desirable and warranted.

Schneck (1959), in discussing the relationship between hypnotist-audience and hypnotist-subject interaction, writes that patients discussing or entering hypnotherapy are frequently influenced in their attitudes by some measure of direct or indirect contact with popular exhibitions of hypnosis. Expectations, interpretations, general behavior, and transference relationships are affected by these contacts. He found that, in most instances, hypnotist-subject interactions are reduced to the simplest essentials. In stage demonstrations, stress is placed on the hypnotist-audience relationship. In some of the demonstrations there were varying degrees of subtle interplay between hypnotist-subject and hypnotist-audience, with the fostering of audience-subject identification and subject-hypnotist identification via coentertainer status.

The hypnotist was capable at times of capitalizing on what he apparently sensed were the needs and the probable reactions of certain subjects in some forms of posthypnotic behavior. The quality of the performance was mixed from an amusement point of view. Errors in technique occurred to a surprising degree, considering the hypnotist's extensive experience.

Wagner (1959), in studying attitudes toward hypnotic induction, found that in spite of the supposed interest in hypnosis, less than one-fourth of psychiatric residents volunteered as subjects in a research project on hypnotic induction. The immediate impression of a general attitude of anxious hesitancy was confirmed through subsequent projective testing, interviews, and hypnotic experiment. Subjects' attitudes, as revealed by the different sources of information, showed considerable consistency.

Hypnosis was frequently fantasied as a controlling, powerful instrument, and the hypnotic induction as a "battle between minds." The underlying conflict-dominance versus submission or independence versus dependence was easily discernible. The subjects' responses to the hypnotic situation varied from strong resistance to consistent cooperation. Mixed responses frequently reflected attempts by the subject to harmonize conflicting motives and fantasies. Some typical examples are described to illustrate the uniqueness of such compromise solutions, characteristic for the individual. The closer the subject's preconceived ideas were to the actual experimental situation, the more successful were his responses. No direct connection between maturity or neuroticism and susceptibility could be demonstrated. No common character trait could be found that related to the subject's ability to follow the suggestions. The responses could, however, be understood in terms of the individual's attempt to gratify or ward off the anxiety aroused in the interpersonal relationship developed by the experimental setting.

Crasilneck and Hall (1959) undertook a comprehensive review of the literature since 1948 on the physiological changes associated with hypnosis. Their material covered hypnotic techniques, the problem of the depth of hypnosis, the types of suggestion utilized in producing changes in physiological function, and the role of accidental or nonverbal communications, as well as antecedent lability of organ systems. They felt that many of the contradictory reports of physiological alteration could be explained by recognition of hypnosis as a psychodynamic relationship rather than a quantitative state.

Raginsky (1959) reported a striking and provocative case of temporary cardiac arrest induced under hypnosis. He described an experiment in which the symptoms of syncopy and temporary complete cardiac arrest were induced under hypnosis in a patient who had been operated on for Adams-Stokes syndrome.

Hodge (1959) described the management of dissociative reactions with hypnosis in the case of a 19-year-old white Marine who had hysterical seizures in which he acted the part of his dog, which had died several years before. The attacks occurred at irregular intervals, but when the patient was first seen they were occurring about twice weekly. During these seizures, which came on without warning, the patient would get down on all fours and bark and growl like a dog, attack ward personnel, paw at the floor, and respond to simple commands like those given to a dog, such as "Down boy" and "Play dead." The really dangerous act which he performed, however, was an attempt to gouge out his eyes with his hands. For this reason, cuff restraints had to be applied during each attack. Hypnotic control proved to be the only successful method. Several hypnotic techniques were used, namely, direct suggestion to control the duration of attacks, building of ego strength to help the patient control his attacks, posthypnotic suggestion, and prediction of the future by means of regulating the environment during the attack and guiding the direction of treatment.

This unusual case is illustrative of many aspects of the psychodynamics of hypnosis and of the utilization of hypnosis as a dynamic therapeutic procedure. Direct suggestion was given essentially as an emergency technique to control the most dangerous symptoms and was effective. Although the suggestions were direct in nature, enlisting the cooperation of the patient in using the symptom to cure itself, the major symptom was never challenged directly, but an explanation of it was diligently sought. Direct communication with the symptom was used to encourage the symptom to "explain" itself and to permit an "acting out" of itself in an autonomous manner which lent greater hypnotic incorporation.

Although the ideational process has distinct limitations as a motivating device, this does not imply a similar limitation of hypnosis itself as a therapeutic procedure and treatment relationship. The hypnotic situation is perhaps uniquely structured for nonverbal communication, and the alteration of perceptual orientation on the part of the patient in psychotherapy may at times require hypnotic intervention on this level if strongly reinforced defenses are to be made more plastic and if newly acquired drives are to be motivated to survive.

Hallucinated alterations in the size and shape of an individual's body image produce not only changes in emotional expression and behavior but also marked changes in social values, intellectual functioning, and personality structure, as measured by psychological tests. When maintained for a few days, subjects adapt to their new body images by changes in personal expression, eating habits, sexual reactions, avocational interests, and the general handling of relationships with others. All these changes represent spontaneous, self-directed, and autonomous reactions, since the only hypnotic suggestion given had to do with specific body size or shape.[8]

SUMMARY

The main body of scientific literature in the area of hypnotherapy has grown at a tremendous rate during the past ten years and is currently one of the most active areas of expansion for clinicians in psychology and psychiatry. To paraphrase the statement of the subcommittee on hypnosis of the Council of Mental Health of the American Medical Association, the validity of hypnosis and its phenomena can no longer be questioned, nor can its therapeutic value be unrecognized. There is, however, a continuing need for high-level research and for the integration of existing knowledge of hypnotic behavior within the

[8] M. V. Kline, paper presented at the fourteenth annual scientific meeting of the Society for Clinical and Experimental Hypnosis, Portland, Oregon, July, 1962.

framework of behavior organization generally.

The review of current advances in hypnosis in relation to psychotherapy presented in this chapter selectively surveys the literature reported in the various journals but does not include an evaluation of experimental research with hypnosis in many areas of psychology. As has already been implied, the greatest progress in connection with the clinical use of hypnosis has been its increasing recognition and employment in a variety of psychological, psychiatric, medical, and surgical settings. Work with hypnosis, since it always involves the psychodynamics of behavior, is meaningful for the clinical psychologist even when it is related to strictly medical and surgical issues. In this sense, the past decade has witnessed an increasing application of hypnosis in the management of behavioral problems of patients, not only the emotional and personality aspects of their adjustment, but also their reactions to pain, stress, and the vicissitudes of physical or psychological illness. This period has witnessed the beginnings of sound educational programs in hypnosis for psychologists in university and institute settings and the establishment of standards for the clinical practice of hypnosis within designated areas of professional competence. The development of the American Board of Clinical Hypnosis,[9] with its subdivision, the American Board of Examiners in Psychological Hypnosis, constitutes an important step in the further recognition and incorporation of hypnosis as a meaningful therapeutic tool in the armamentarium of the clinical psychologist.

With respect to basic progress, one might point, in summary, to the fact that no current advances have been made in fundamental problems of hypnotizability, although the literature has continued to emphasize the facility with which hypnotic states may be brought about through proper manipulation of the transference relationship and through greater skill on the part of the therapist in recognizing many of the subtle nuances which characterize hypnotic involvement and the hypnotic relationship. Rather than the development of new procedures for the induction of hypnosis, of which there are relatively few, there has been an altered spectrum, within which we now can more readily recognize the presence of the hypnotic relationship. Methods for its elucidation, direct or indirect, become more accessible as the therapist's recognition of these elements and the nature of the patient's subjective responses indicate the onset of this particular form of relationship.

At the present time, little work is being done with hypnosis in its historical therapeutic role, namely, suggestive therapy with the utilization of posthypnotic reaction as the major source of behavioral change. Rather, we see the emergence of hypnosis as a dynamic tool for gaining access to many facets of personality and behavioral reactions.

Advances in the theoretical understanding of hypnosis and its significance for personality theory and psychotherapeutic concepts continue to emphasize the regressive qualities of hypnosis. Continuing emphasis is placed upon the alterations in perception and the nature of consciousness as well as upon the overall functions of the ego in relation to vigilance, criticalness, and self-awareness.

Little or no therapy, at the present time, is considered to be done by hypnosis but rather within the framework of the hypnotic relationship. The incorporation of hypnosis into psychotherapy constitutes a movement away from inactive passivity, on the part of both the patient and the therapist, and for the greater part leads to the development of those psychotherapeutic approaches, both analytic and nonanalytic, which emphasize directiveness and intensification of perceptual and affective processes. Hypnotherapy thus attempts to bring about a patient-centered movement, which, through reinforcement, can become more autonomous in nature and less dependent upon treatment procedure.

The current scientific scene in hypnosis is one wherein experimental evidence and investigations, both of a laboratory and of a clinical nature, continue to be meaningful for the investigator and the clinician. In many respects hypnosis, because of its intriguing nature and its paradoxical capacities to reduce critical vigilance and increase psychological productivity, offers a meeting ground for concepts in clinical psychology which emphasize the core of psychodynamic theory. Research with and in hypnosis at the present time continues to emphasize consciousness, perceptual and learning theory, and neurophysiology. The

[9] Evaluated and recognized by the Board of Professional Affairs of the American Psychological Association, *Amer. Psychologist*, 1960, **15**, 68.

applications point up not the use of hypnosis as a circumscribed treatment modality alone but the use of a highly intensified and at the same time regressively structured relationship for the more direct incorporation of stimulating and reinforcing elements in the behavioral process.

REFERENCES

Adler, M. H., & Secunda, L. An indirect technique to induce hypnosis. *J. nerv. ment. Dis.*, 1952, **106**, 190.

Ambrose, G. Hypnosis: its value in child guidance. *Brit. J. Med. Hypnotism*, 1949, **1**, 42.

Ambrose, G. The technique and value of hypnosis in child psychotherapy. *Brit. J. Med. Hypnotism*, 1950, **1**, 8.

Ambrose, G. The hysterical reaction in childhood: treatment by hypnotherapy. *Brit. J. Med. Hypnotism*, 1951. (a)

Ambrose, G. Psychological treatment in a child guidance clinic: with special reference to hypnotherapy. *Brit. J. Med. Hypnotism*, 1951. (b)

Ambrose, G. Hypnotherapy in the treatment of the delinquent child. I. The intelligent delinquent. *Brit. J. Med. Hypnotism*, 1952.

Arnold, M. Brain function in hypnosis. *Int. J. clin. exp. Hypnosis*, 1959, **3**, 109–120.

Baron, S. Levels of insight and ego functioning in relation to hypnoanalysis. *Int. J. clin. exp. Hypnosis*, 1960, **8** (4), 141.

Bellak, L. An ego-psychological theory of hypnosis. *Int. J. Psychoanal.*, 1955, **36**, 1–4.

Bergman, M. S., Graham, H., & Leavitt, H. C. Rorschach exploration of consecutive hypnotic chronological age level regressions. *Psychosom. Med.*, 1947, **14**, 20.

Bernheim, H. *Hypnosis and suggestion in psychotherapy.* New York: University Books, 1964.

Bird, W. H. Varying hypnotizability in a case of Parkinsonism. *Bull. Menninger Clin.*, 1948, **12**, 210.

Bowers, Margaretta K. Theoretical considerations in the use of hypnosis in the treatment of schizophrenia. *Int. J. clin. exp. Hypnosis*, 1960, **9** (4), 39–46.

Bowers, Margaretta K., Brecher-Marer, Sylvia, & Polatin, A. Hypnosis in the study and treatment of schizophrenia: a case report. *Int. J. clin. exp. Hypnosis*, 1961, **3**, 105.

Bowers, Margaretta K., & Glasner, S. Auto-hypnotic aspects of the Jewish cabalistic concept of kavanah. *J. clin. exp. Hypnosis*, 1958, **1**, 50–70.

Braid, J. *Braid on hypnotism.* (Rev. ed.) New York: Julian Press, 1960.

Bramwell, J. M. *Hypnotism: its history, practice and theory.* New York: Rider, 1921.

Brenman, M., & Gill, M. Treatment of a case of anxiety hysteria by hypnotic technique employing psychoanalytic principles. *Bull. Menninger Clin.*, 1943, **7**, 163.

Brenman, M., & Gill, M. *Hypnotherapy.* New York: International Universities Press, 1947.

Brenman, M., Gill, M., & Hacker, F. J. Alterations in the state of the ego in hypnosis. *Bull. Menninger Clin.*, 1943, **7**, 163.

Brenman, M., Gill, & Hacker, F. J. Alterations in the state of the ego in hypnosis. *Bull. Menninger Clin.*, 1947, **11**, 60.

Brenman, M., Gill, M., & Knight, R. P. Spontaneous fluctuations in a depth of hypnosis and their implications for ego-function. *Int. J. Psychoanal.*, 1952, **33**.

Brenman, M., & Knight, R. P. Hypnotherapy for mental illness in the aged: case report of hysterical psychosis in a 71-year old woman. *Bull. Menninger Clin.*, 1943, **7**, 188.

Brenman, M., & Knight, R. P. Self-starvation and compulsive hopping with paradoxical reaction to hypnosis. *Amer. J. Orthopsychiat.*, 1945, **15**, 65.

Breuer, J., & Freud, S. *Studies on Hysteria.* New York: Nervous and Mental Disease Publishing Company, 1936.

Brickner, R. M., & Kubie, L. S. A miniature psychotic storm produced by a superego conflict over simple posthypnotic suggestion. *Psychoanal. Quart.*, 1936, **5**, 467.

Browning, Carrol W., Quinn, L. H., & Crasilneck, H. B. The use of hypnosis in suppression amblyopia of children. *Amer. J. Ophthalmol.*, 1958, **46** (1), Part I.

Buckley, R. W. The treatment of post-traumatic syndrome by hypnotic analysis. *J. nerv. ment. Dis.*, 1950, **111**, 122.

Cheek, D. B. Ideomotor questioning for investigation of subconscious "pain" and target organ vulnerability. *Amer. J. clin. Hypnosis*, 1962, **1**, 30–41.

Christenson, J. A. Dynamics in hypnotic induction. *Psychiatry*, 1949, **12**, 37.

Conn, J. H. Hypnosynthesis: hypnosis as a unifying interpersonal experience. *J. nerv. ment. Dis.*, 1949, **109**, 9–24.

Conn, J. H. Historical aspects of scientific hypnosis. *Int. J. clin. exp. Hypnosis*, 1957, **5**, 17–24.

Conn, J. H. Meanings and motivations associated with spontaneous hypnotic regression. *J. clin exp. Hypnosis,* 1958, **1**, 21–44.

Conn, J. H. Cultural and clinical hypnosis: placebos and aspects of suggestibility. *Int. J. clin. exp. Hypnosis,* 1959, **7**, 175–186.

Conn, J. H. Psychodynamics of recovery under hypnosis. *J. clin. exp. Hypnosis,* 1960, **8**, 3–16.

Cooper, L. F. Time distortion in hypnosis. *Bull. Georgetown Univer. med. Center,* 1948, **1**, 214.

Cooper, L. F., & Erickson, M. H. Time distortion in hypnosis. II. *Bull. Georgetown Univer. med. Center,* 1950, **4**, 50.

Crasilneck, H. B., Stirman, J. A., Wilson, B. G., McCrainie, E. J., & Fogelman, M. J. Use of hypnosis in the management of patients with burns. *J. Amer. mel. Ass.,* 1955, **158**, 103–106.

Crasilneck, H. B., & Erwin, K. W. The effects of general anesthesia on post-hypnotic suggestion. *J. clin. exp. Hypnosis,* 1958, **1**, 45–49.

Crasilneck, H. B., & Hall, J. E. Physiological changes associated with hypnosis: a review of the literature since 1948. *Int. J. clin. exp. Hypnosis,* 1959, **7**, 9–50.

Dorcus, R. M. (Ed.) *Hypnosis and its therapeutic applications.* New York: McGraw-Hill, 1956.

Dorcus, R. M. Recall under hypnosis of amnestic events. *Int. J. clin. exp. Hypnosis,* 1960, **8** (1), 57.

Dorcus, R. M., & Kirkner, F. J. The use of hypnosis in the suppression of intractable pain. *J. abnorm. soc. Psychol.,* 1948.

Dribben, I. S. Psychosis following "amateur hypnosis": a case report. *Milit. Surgeon,* 1949, **104.**

Ehrenreich, G. A. The influence of unconscious factors on hypnotizability. *Bull. Menninger Clin.,* 1951, **19**, 45–57.

Erickson, M. H. The investigation of a specific amnesia. *Brit. J. med. Psychol.,* 1933, **13**, 143.

Erickson, M. H. Development of apparent unconsciousness during hypnotic reliving of a traumatic experience. *Arch. Neurol. Psychiat.,* 1937, **38**, 1282–1288.

Erickson, M. H. The use of automatic drawing in the interpretation and relief of a state of acute obsessional depression. *Psychoanal. Quart.,* 1938, **7**, 443.

Erickson, M. H. The application of hypnosis to psychiatry. *Med. Rec.,* 1939, 60–65. (a)

Erickson, M. H. Experimental demonstration of the psychopathology of everyday life. *Psychoanal. Quart.,* 1939, **8**, 338–353. (b)

Erickson, M. H. Hypnosis: a general review. *Dis. nerv. System,* 1941.

Erickson, M. H. The method employed to formulate a complex story for the induction of an experimental neurosis in a hypnotic subject. *J. gen. Psychol.,* 1944, **31**, 67.

Erickson, M. H. Hypnosis in medicine. *Med. Clin. N. Amer.,* 1948, 571–583. (a)

Erickson, M. H. Hypnotic psychotherapy. *Med. Clin. N. Amer.,* 1948, 571. (b)

Erickson, M. H. Special techniques of brief hypnotherapy. *J. clin. exp. Hypnosis,* 1954, **2**, 109–129.

Erickson, M. H. Self-exploration in the hypnotic state. *J. clin. exp. Hypnosis,* 1955, **3**, 49–57.

Erickson, M. H., & Hill, L. B. Unconscious mental activity in hypnosis: psychoanalytic implications. *Psychoanal. Quart.,* 1944, **13**, 60.

Erickson, M. H., & Kubie, L. S. The permanent relief of an obsessional phobia by means of communications with an unsuspected dual personality. *Psychoanal. Quart.,* 1939, **8**, 471.

Erickson, M. H., & Kubie, L. S. The translation of the cryptic automatic writing of one hypnotic subject by another in a trance-like dissociated state. *Psychoanal. Quart.,* 1940, **9**, 51.

Erickson, M. H., & Kubie, L. S. The successful treatment of a case of acute hysterical depression by a return under hypnosis to a critical phase of childhood. *Psychoanal. Quart.,* 1941, **10**, 583.

Esdaile, J. *Mesmerism in India.* Chicago: Psychic Research, 1902.

Farber, L. H., & Fisher, C. An experimental approach to dream psychology through the use of hypnosis. *Psychoanal. Quart.,* 1943, **12**, 202–215.

Forel, A. *Hypnotism or suggestion and psychotherapy.* New York: Allied, 1949.

Fox, J. The systematic use of hypnosis in individual and group psychotherapy. *Int. J. clin. exp. Hypnosis,* 1960, **8**, (2), 109.

Freud, S. *Group psychology and the analysis of the ego.* New York: Boni & Liveright, 1924.

Gidro-Frank, L., & Buch, M. K. B. A study of the plantar response in hypnotic age regression. *J. nerv. ment. Dis.,* 1948, **107**, 443.

Gidro-Frank, L., & Bull, N. Emotions induced and studied in hypnotic subjects. *J. nerv. ment. Dis.,* 1950, **111**, 91.

Gill, M. Ego psychology and psychotherapy. *Psychoanal. Quart.*, 1951, **20**, 62–71.

Gill, M., & Menninger, K. Techniques of hypnoanalysis illustrated in a case report. *Bull. Menninger Clin.*, 1946, **10**, 110.

Guze, H. Hypnosis as wish fulfillment: a projective approach. *Brit. J. Med. Hypnotism*, 1951, **2**, 6.

Guze, H. Anesthesia and instrumentation trauma as revealed in hypnotherapy. *J. clin. exp. Hypnosis*, 1953, **2**, 71–77. (a)

Guze, H. Posture, postural reintegration and hypnotherapy. *J. clin. exp. Hypnosis*, 1953, **1**, 26–82. (b)

Hadfield, J. A. Treatment by suggestion and hypno-analysis. In E. Miller, *The neuroses in war.* New York: Macmillan, 1942.

Haley, J. The control of fear with hypnosis. *Amer. J. clin. Hypnosis*, 1960, **2**, 109–116.

Hodge, J. R. The management of dissociative reactions with hypnosis. *Int. J. clin. exp. Hypnosis*, 1959, **4**, 217–222.

Hull, C. L. *Hypnosis and suggestiblity.* New York: Appleton-Century, 1933.

Jacobs, L. Hypnosis in clinical pediatrics. *N.Y. State J. Med.*, 1962, **23**, 3781–3787.

Janet, P. *The major symptoms of hysteria.* New York: Macmillan, 1907.

Janet, P. *Psychological healing.* New York: Macmillan, 1925.

Kartchner, F. D., & Korner, I. N. The use of hypnosis in the treatment of acute combat reactions. *Amer. J. Psychiat.*, 1947, **103**, 630.

Klemperer, Edith. Hypnotherapy. *J. nerv. ment. Dis.*, 1947, **106**, 176.

Klemperer, Edith. Projective phenomena in hypnoanalysis. *Int. J. clin. exp. Hypnosis*, 1962, **10** (3), 127.

Klemperer, Edith. Symptom removal by revivification. *Amer. J. clin. Hypnosis*, 1963, **4**, 277–280.

Kline, M. V. Hypnotic age regression and intelligence. *J. genet. Psychol.*, 1950, **77**, 129.

Kline, M. V. The application of hypnosis to nondirective psychotherapy. *J. clin. Psychol.*, 1951, **3**, 283–287.

Kline, M. V. Visual imagery and a case of experimental hypnotherapy. *J. gen. Psychol.*, 1952, **46**, 159–167.

Kline, M. V. Toward a theoretical understanding of the nature of resistance to the induction of hypnosis and depth hypnosis. *J. clin. exp. Hypnosis*, 1953, **2**, 32–41.

Kline, M. V. *Freud and hypnosis.* New York: Julian Press, 1958.

Kline, M. V. Soviet and western trends in hypnosis research. *Int. J. Parapsychol.*, 1959, **1**, 89–100.

Kline, M. V. The value and limitation of hypnosis in psychotherapy: two clinical illustrations. *Int. J. clin. exp. Hypnosis*, 1960, **8** (4), 263.

Kline, M. V. (Ed.) *The nature of hypnosis.* New York: Institute for Research in Hypnosis, 1962.

Kline, M. V., & Guze, H. The use of a projective drawing technique in the investigation of hypnotic age regression and progression. *Brit. J. Med. Hypnotism*, 1951, 10–21.

Kline, M. V., & Haggerty, A. D. An hypnotic experimental approach to the genesis of occupation interest and choice. III. Hypnotic age regression and the TAT: a clinical case study in occupational identification. *J. clin. exp. Hypnosis*, 1953, **3**, 18–31.

Kline, M. V., & Schneck, J. M. An hypnotic experimental approach to the genesis of occupation interests and choice. I. Theoretical orientation and hypnotic scene visualization. *Brit. J. Med. Hypnotism*, 1950, **2**, 2.

Kline, M. V., & Schneck, J. M. A control study relating to H-T-P testing and hypnosis. *Brit. J. Med. Hypnotism*, 1951, **3**, 2–11. (a)

Kline, M. V., & Schneck, J. M. Hypnosis in relation to the word association test. *J. gen. Psychol.*, 1951, **44**, 129. (b)

Kroger, W. S. *Clinical and experimental hypnosis.* Philadelphia: Lippincott, 1963.

Kubie, L. S. Use of induced hypnogogic reveries in the recovery of repressed amnesic data. *Bull. Menninger Clin.*, 1943, **7**, 172.

Kubie, L. S., & Margolin, S. The process of hypnotism and the nature of the hypnotic state. *Amer. J. Psychiat.*, 1944, **100**, 611.

Kupper, H. I. Psychic concomitants in wartime injuries. *Psychosom. Med.*, 1945, **7**, 15–21.

Lane, B. M. A validation test of the Rorschach movement interpretations. *Amer. J. Orthopsychiat.*, 1948, **18**, 292.

LeCron, L. M. Relief of myopia by hypnosis and eye training. *Dis. nerv. System*, 1951, **12**, 1–4.

LeCron, L. M. The loss during hypnotic age regression of an established conditioned reflex. *Psychiat. Quart.*, 1952, **26**, 657–662.

LeCron, L. M., & Bordeaux, J. *Hypnotism today.* New York: Grune & Stratton, 1947.

Leeds, M. An hypnotic regression series. *Persona,* 1949, **1**, 13.

Levbarg, J. J. Hypnosis: treatment used in a stammerer with marked mental disturbances. *Eye, Ear, Nose Throat Mon.*, 1941.

Levitt, E. E., Lubin, B., & Brady, J. P. On the use of TAT card 12M as an indicator of attitude toward hypnosis. *Int. J. clin. exp. Hypnosis,* 1963, **10** (3), 145.

Liebeault, A. Du Sommeil et des Etats. *Analogues,* etc. Vienna: Duetricke, 1892.

Lindner, R. M. *Rebel without a cause.* New York: Grune & Stratton, 1944.

Lindner, R. M. Hypnoanalysis as psychotherapy. *Dis. nerv. System,* 1945, **6**, 371. (a)

Lindner, R. M. Hypnoanalysis in a case of hysterical somnambulism. *Psychoanal. Rev.*, 1945, **32**, 325. (b)

Lindner, R. M. An evaluation of hypnoanalysis. In B. Gluerk et al., *Current therapies of personality disorders.* New York: Grune & Stratton, 1946.

Lindner, R. M. Hypnoanalysis as a psychotherapeutic technique. In *Specialized techniques in psychotherapy.* New York: Basic Books, 1953.

Loomis, E. A. Hypnotic production of visual imagery: a clinical report. *Brit. J. Med. Hypnotism,* 1950, **2**, 22.

Luria, A. R. *The nature of human conflicts.* New York: Liveright, 1932.

McDowell, M. An abrupt cessation of major neurotic symptoms following an hypnotically induced artificial conflict. *Bull. Menninger Clin.*, 1948, **12**, 168.

Marcuse, F. L. Hypnosis and symptom treatment. Paper read at Soc. Clin. Exp. Hypnosis, New York, May, 1950.

Mason, A. M., & Black, S. Allergic skin responses abolished under treatment of asthma and hay fever by hypnosis. *Lancet,* 1958, 877–880.

Meares, A. *Shapes of sanity.* Springfield, Ill.: Charles C Thomas, 1960.

Meares, A. *Hypnography.* Springfield, Ill.: Charles C Thomas, 1960. (a)

Meares, A. *A system of medical hypnosis.* Philadelphia: Saunders, 1960. (b)

Meares, A. The Y-state: an hypnotic variant. *J. clin. exp. Hypnosis,* 1960, **8**, 237–242. (c)

Meerloo, J. A. M. Emergency psychotherapy and mental first aid. *J. nerv. ment. Dis.*, 1956, **6**, 535–545.

Mercer, M., & Gibson, R. W. Rorschach content in hypnosis: chronological age level regression. *J. clin. Psychol.*, 1950, **4**, 352.

Moll, A. *Hypnotism.* London: Walter Scott, 1890.

Moreno, J. L., & Enneis, J. M. Hypnodrama and psychodrama. *Psychodrama Monogr.*, 1950, No. 27.

Moss, C. S. Therapeutic suggestion and autosuggestion. *J. clin. exp. Hypnosis,* 1961, **2**, 109–115.

Moss, C. S. An additional study in hysteria: the case of Alice M. *Int. J. clin. exp. Hypnosis,* 1962, **10** (2), 59.

Naumburg, Margaret. Spontaneous art in psychotherapy. *Progr. clin. Psychol.*, 1963, **5**, 74–87.

Orne, M. T. The mechanisms of hypnotic age regresssion: an experimental study. *J. abnorm. soc. Psychol.*, 1951, **46**, 312.

Paley, A. Hypnotherapy in the treatment of alcoholism. *Bull. Menninger Clin.*, 1952, **16**, 14–19.

Platonov, K. I. On the objective proof of the experimental personality age regression. *J. gen. Psychol.*, 1933, **9**, 190.

Platonov, K. *The word as a physiological and therapeutic factor.* Moscow: Foreign Languages Publishing House, 1959.

Prince, M. *The dissociation of a personality.* New York: Longmans, 1908.

Prince, M. *The unconscious.* New York: Macmillan, 1914.

Prince, M. *Clinical and experimental studies in personality.* (A. A. Roback, Ed.) Cambridge: Sci-Arts, 1939.

Raginsky, B. B. Temporary cardiac arrest induced under hypnosis. *Int. J. clin. exp. Hypnosis,* 1959, **2**, 53–68.

Raginsky, B. B. The use of hypnosis in internal medicine. *Int. J. clin. exp. Hypnosis,* 1960, **4**, 181.

Raginsky, B. B. The sensory use of plasticine in hypnoanalysis (sensory hypnoplasty). *Int. J. clin. exp. Hypnosis,* 1961, **4**, 233.

Raginsky, B. B. Sensory hypnoplasty with case illustrations. *Int. J. clin. exp. Hypnosis,* 1962, **10**, 205.

Regardie, F. I. Experimentally induced dreams as psychotherapeutic aids. *Amer. J. Psychother.*, 1950, **4**, 643.

Rosen, H. The medical use of hypnosis. *Johns Hopkins Nurses Alum. Mag.*, 1949.

Rosen, H. The hypnotic and hypnotherapeutic unmasking: intensification and recognition of an emotion. *Amer. J. Psychiat.*, 1952, **2**, 120–127

Rosen, H. Hypnodiagnostic and hypnotherapeutic fantasy: evocation and acting-out techniques. *J. clin. exp. Hypnosis,* 1953, **1,** 54–66. (a)

Rosen, H. *Hypnotherapy in clinical psychiatry.* New York: Julian Press, 1953. (b)

Rosen, H. Regression hypnotherapeutically induced as an emergency measure in a suicidally depressed patient. *J. clin. exp. Hypnosis,* 1955, **3,** 58–70.

Rosen, H., & Myers, H. J. Abreaction in the military setting. *Arch. Neurol. Psychiat.,* 1947, **57,** 161.

Rosenzweig, S., & Sarason, S. An experimental study of the triadic hypnothesis: reaction to frustrations, ego-defense and hypnotizability. I. Correlational approach. *Charact. & Pers.,* 1942, **12,** 1–19.

Sarason, S., & Rosenzweig, S. An experimental study of the triadic hypnothesis: reaction to frustrations, ego-defense and hypnotizability. II. Thematic apperception approach. *Charact. & Pers.,* 1942, **12,** 150–165.

Sarbin, T. R. Mental age changes in experimental regression. *J. Pers.,* 1950, **19,** 221.

Schilder, P., & Kauders, O. *Hypnosis.* New York: Nervous and Mental Diseases Publishing Company, 1927.

Schneck, J. M. Luckenschadel in a patient with amnesia amenable to hypnotherapy. *J. nerv. ment. Dis.,* 1946, **104,** 249.

Schneck, J. M. A clinical note on electrocardiography under hypnosis. *Milit. Surgeon.,* 1947, **100,** 65. (a)

Schneck, J. M. Modified technique for the induction of hypnosis. *J. nerv. ment. Dis.,* 1947, **106,** 77. (b)

Schneck, J. M. The role of a dream in treatment with hypnosis. *Psychoanal. Rev.,* 1947, **34,** 485. (c)

Schneck, J. M. Audiometry under hypnosis. *Psychosom. Med.,* 1948, **10,** 361. (a)

Schneck, J. M. The hypnotic treatment of a patient with amnesia. *Psychoanal. Rev.,* 1948, **35,** 171. (b)

Schneck, J. M. Psychogenic cardiovascular reaction interpreted and successfully treated with hypnosis. *Psychoanal. Rev.,* 1948, **35,** 14. (c)

Schneck, J. M. Apparatus supplying an auditory stimulus for the induction of hypnosis. *Dis. nerv. System,* 1950, **11,** 26. (a)

Schneck, J. M. Hypnoanalytic elucidation of the hypnosis-death concept. *Psychiat. Quart. Suppl.,* 1950, **24,** 286, Part 2. (b)

Schneck, J. M. A note on spontaneous hallucinations during hypnosis. *Psychiat. Quart.,* 1950, **24,** 492. (c)

Schneck, J. M. Notes on the homosexual component of the hypnotic transference. *Brit. J. Med. Hypnotism,* 1950, **24,** 1. (d)

Schneck, J. M. Psychosomatic reactions to the induction of hypnosis. *Dis. nerv. System,* 1950, **11,** 118. (e)

Schneck, J. M. Some aspects of homosexuality in relation to hypnosis. *Psychoanal. Rev.,* 1950, **37,** 351. (f)

Schneck, J. M. Hypnoanalysis, hypnotherapy, and card 12M of the Thematic Apperception Test. *J. gen. Psychol.,* 1951, **44,** 293. (a)

Schneck, J. M. Hypnosis and the productive orientation. *Dis. nerv. System,* 1951, **12,** 241. (b)

Schneck, J. M. Spontaneous homonymous hemiamopsia in hypnotic imagery. *Brit. J. Med. Hypnotism,* 1951, **2,** 2. (c)

Schneck, J. M. The unconscious relationship between hypnosis and death. *Psychoanal. Rev.,* 1951, **38,** 271. (d)

Schneck, J. M. The hypnoanalysis of phobic reactions. In L. M. LeCron, *Experimental hypnosis.* New York: Macmillan, 1952. (a)

Schneck, J. M. Automatic writing during hypnoanalysis. *J. gen. Psychol.,* 1952, **46,** 233. (b)

Schneck, J. M. Hypnotherapy of a patient with an animal phobia. *J. nerv. ment. Dis.,* 1952, **116,** 48. (c)

Schneck, J. M. Psychogenic gastrointestinal disorder and cephalagia with paradoxical reactions to hypnosis. *J. nerv. ment. Dis.,* 1953, **2,** 130. (a)

Schneck, J. M. Automatic writing and the hypnotic transference. *J. gen. Psychol.,* 1953, **48,** 91. (b)

Schneck, J. M. Spontaneous regression to an infant age level during self-hypnosis. *Gen. Psychol.,* 1955, **86,** 183–185.

Schneck, J. M. Dynamic hypnotic regression. *Amer. J. Psychiat.,* 1956, **113,** 178. (a)

Schneck, J. M. Hypnoanalytic therapy with case illustrations. *Amer. J. Psychother.,* 1956, **10,** 536. (b)

Schneck, J. M. Current advances in hypnotherapy. *Amer. J. Psychother.,* 1957, **2,** 408–421.

Schneck, J. M. *Hypnosis in modern medicine.* (2nd ed.) Springfield, Ill.: Charles C Thomas, 1959.

Schneck, J. M. *A history of psychiatry.* Springfield, Ill.: Charles C Thomas, 1960. (a)

Schneck, J. M. Special aspects of hypnotic regression and revivification. *Int. J. clin. exp. Hypnosis,* 1960, **1**, 37. (b)

Schneck, J. M. Hidden determinants in deceptive requests for hypnoanalysis. *Int. J. clin. exp. Hypnosis,* 1961, **4**, 261.

Schneck, J. M. Hypnoanalysis. *Int. J. clin. exp. Hypnosis,* 1962, **1**, 1. (a)

Schneck, J. M. Hypnoanalysis. *Int. J. clin. exp. Hypnosis,* 1962, **10**, 1–13. (b)

Schneck, J. M., & Kline, M. V. Clinical psychiatric status and psychological test alterations following hypnotherapy. *Brit. J. Med. Hypnotism,* 1950, **2**, 30.

Schneck, J. M., & Kline, M. V. Hypnodiagnosis and evaluation of therapy in psychiatry and clinical psychology: report of a case involving the H-T-P. *Brit. J. Med. Hypnotism,* 1951, **2**, 8.

Schneck, J. M., & Kline, M. V. Hypnotic scene visualization and the word association test. *J. gen. Psychol.,* 1952, **46**, 29.

Schneck, J. M., & Kline, M. V. The H-T-P and TAT in hypnodiagnostic studies, *Brit. J. Med. Hypnotism,* 1953.

Secunda, L. Use of hypnosis in psychotherapy. *Dis. nerv. System,* 1948, **9** (4).

Solovey, G., & Milechnin, A. Hypnosis as the substratum of many different psychotherapies. *Amer. J. clin. Hypnosis,* 1960, **3**, 9.

Speyer, N., & Stokvis, B. The psychoanalytical factor in hypnosis. *Brit. J. Med. Psychol.,* 1938, **17**, 217.

Spiegel, H. Hypnotic intervention as an adjunct for rapid clinical relief. *Int. J. clin. exp. Hypnosis,* 1963, **1**, 23–29.

Speigel, H., Shor, J., & Fishman, S. An hypnotic ablation technique for the study of personality development. *Psychosom. Med.,* 1945, **7**, 273.

Volgyesi, F. A. The recent neuro-psychiatric and bio-morphologic justifications of hypno-therapeutic empiricism. *Brit. J. Med. Hypnotism,* 1950, **2**, 6.

Wagner, F. A. A clinical study of attitudes towards hypnotic induction. *Int. J. clin. exp. Hypnosis,* 1959, **1**, 3–8.

Watkins, J. G. The hypno-analytic location of a lost object. *J. clin. Psychol.,* 1946, **2**, 390.

Watkins, J. G. The hypnoanalytic treatment of a case of impotence. *J. clin. Psychopath.,* 1947, **8**, 453.

Watkins, J. G. *Hypnotherapy of war neuroses.* New York: Ronald, 1949.

Wedge, B. Hypnotism as a practical therapeutic procedure. *Hawaii Med. J.,* 1948, **7**, 305.

Wells, W. R. The hypnotic treatment of the major symptoms of hysteria: a case study. *J. Psychol.,* 1944, **17**, 269.

Weitzenhoffer, A. *General techniques of hypnotism.* New York: Grune & Stratton, 1947.

Weitzenhoffer, A. The significance of hypnotic depth in therapy. *Int. J. clin. exp. Hypnosis,* 1962, **2**, 75.

Whitehorn, J. C. The scope of motivation in psychopathology and psychotherapy. *Amer. J. Psychoanal.,* 1954, **34**, 14–34.

Wilkins, W. L., & Adams, A. J. The use of the Rorschach test under hypnosis and under sodium amytal in military psychiatry. *J. gen. Psychol.,* 1947, **36**, 131.

Wolberg, L. R. *Hypnoanalysis.* Vols. I, II. New York: Grune & Stratton, 1945. (a)

Wolberg, L. R. Mechanism of hysteria elucidated during hypnoanalysis. *Psychoanal. Quart.,* 1945, **14**, 528. (b)

Wolberg, L. R. *Medical hypnosis.* New York: Grune & Stratton, 1948.

Wolpe, J. *Psychotherapy by reciprocal inhibition.* Stanford, Calif.: Stanford Univer. Press, 1958.

47

A Review of Psychopharmacology

AUDREY R. HOLLIDAY

Mental patients occupy one out of every two hospital beds in the United States. Remmen, Cohen, Ditman, and Frantz (1962) place the figure at 54 out of every 100 hospital beds. Remmen et al. indicate that some estimates place the percentage of our population suffering from mental illness at close to 10. The Joint Commission on Mental Illness and Health (1961) estimated that, depending upon the maintenance of the present rate of population increase, there will be 2 million patients requiring treatment for major mental illness alone by 1971. The Joint Commission has made recommendations directed toward increasing to an adequate level the number of psychiatrists, psychologists, social workers, nurses, and other personnel needed for proper patient care. While the Joint Commission has emphasized the need for increases in treatment personnel, it also has recognized that drugs, particularly the tranquilizing drugs to date, have largely supplanted the use of other procedures such as leukotomy and lobotomy, insulin shock, and electroconvulsive therapy. There is further recognition that chemotherapy deserves the larger share of credit for the decrease in state hospital inpatient loads in recent years and has generally revolutionized the management of hospitalized psychotic patients. Objective evidence of these developments has been supplied by Brill and Patton (1957; 1959), who surveyed the population in New York State's mental hospital system, particularly noting the periods from 1954 to 1955, when no chemotherapy was used; 1955 to 1956, when chemotherapy was introduced; and 1956 to 1958, when both chemotherapy and a number of other favorable situational factors were present. They point out that New York's mental hospital population had increased by 400 per cent during the first half of the century and that this trend had continued through 1954, with an increase in 1954 of 2,421 patients. With the introduction for general use of chlorpromazine and reserpine in January, 1955, this trend of increase was halted; further, there was a decrease in patient load of 452 patients. There continued to be a decrease in number of institutionalized patients in 1956, 1957, and 1958. Brill and Patton found that there had been no change in treatments of patients in 1955 and 1956 except that chlorpromazine and reserpine therapy had been instituted. They conclude that the decrease in patient population was attributable to the use of these two tranquilizers. Following the year 1955–1956, the data are confounded by the fact that not only were drugs being used, but also special treatment programs had been instituted, increases in personnel had been gained, and changes had been made in hospital policies. They suggest that the accelerating trend of decrease in hospital population shown in 1958 probably was due both to chemotherapy and to these other changes. However, Brill and Patton also showed in their studies that the discharge rate for drug-treated patients in the year 1957–1958 was double that for non-tranquilizer-treated patients.

The report of Casey and Lindley (1962) is similar in import to that of Brill and Patton. They indicate that a survey made in January, 1957, of 79 of the Veterans Administration hospitals to determine the over-all effects of the use of tranquilizers on the treatment program showed that there had been a significant decrease in the use of both electroshock and insulin coma therapy, an increase in the use of both individual and group psychotherapeutic techniques, and more freedom allowed to patients. While many of the hospitals indicated that it was thought that these changes in therapies were not made possible by the use of tranquilizers alone, there was still a consensus that chemotherapy had aided in rendering the patients more available for increased use of various forms of psychotherapy. Casey and Lindley further report that the decrease in use of shock therapies continued to be shown through 1961.

Whether one argues from the theoretical point of view that some of the psychoses are functional in etiology or from the theoretical point of view that they are all organic in etiology, and whether one argues from the point of view that drugs are adjunctive forms of treatment to psychotherapy or from the point of view that psychotherapy is an adjunctive form of treatment to drug therapy, it would appear to be a fact that drugs are of major therapeutic usefulness. The therapeutic success of chemotherapy in regard to both management and treatment of patients suffering from mental illness has stimulated a marked reawakening of interest in the search for an organic, i.e., structural or biochemical, etiology of mental illness. Even the most violent proponents of functional etiologies of mental illness, with their accompanying insistence upon the efficacy of various forms of psychotherapy and various forms of environmental manipulation in the treatment of mental illness, must join in the hope that this search ultimately will be successful. No one would argue that the need for psychotherapists for patients mentally ill as a consequence of pellagra was not nullified by the introduction of niacin as a means of prevention and treatment. No one would argue that the need for hospital beds for patients suffering from psychosis as a consequence of neurosyphilis was not sharply reduced with the advent of penicillin. No one would argue that psychosis resulting from bromide poisoning cannot be prevented without benefit of psychotherapists.

The challenge to scientists occasioned by the breakthrough in the treatment of the mentally ill with drugs not only has given rise to enormous research activity but also has resulted within the last decade in the evolvement of a new discipline, psychopharmacology. It is intended that psychopharmacology be a science which integrates research findings and hypotheses from such disciplines as pharmacology and neuropharmacology, biochemistry and neurochemistry, physiology and neurophysiology, neurology, psychiatry, and psychology in regard to the study of drugs affecting the behavior of organisms. It is common for reviewers to point out that the field of psychopharmacology is in disarray. It is. This is partly due to the fact that it is a young science and is still in the process of definition; partly due to the unprecedented burgeoning of research effort, some of it of a crash-program nature; and partly due to the fact that so many disciplines are, of necessity, involved. Further, psychopharmacology has emerged as a discipline precisely because of a need for integration. Due to prevailing trends of overspecialization in training, there are few clinicians or scientists now directing attention to psychopharmacologial problems who can, in effect, function as Renaissance men within the field.

None of the foregoing is meant to imply that the clinician or scientist interested in the problems relating to the field of psychopharmacology will not always make his finest contribution in the area of the discipline in which he is fully trained. However, it is meant to imply that, for the present and until such time as training programs extant have provided a new generation of psychopharmacologists, more integration in psychopharmacology ought to take place at the level of the research project itself; perhaps the much-vaunted team approach should be insisted upon to some degree. As it is, the findings in the literature are very difficult to evaluate because, for example, too many psychologists without adequate knowledge of drug variables, too many psychiatrists without adequate knowledge of controlled experimental procedures, and too many pharmacologists without adequate scientific knowledge of human behavior are conducting studies which are well conceived insofar as the variables relating to the scientists' own disciplines are concerned but which are not well conceived insofar as the variables relating to important findings from other disciplines are concerned.

Fortunately, there already has been much in the way of worthwhile response to the need for bringing order into the discipline of psychopharmacology. Recognizing the impact of chemotherapy on mental illness, as indicated by the success of chlorpromazine and reserpine as therapeutic agents, the National Institute of Mental Health, as a consequence of an appropriation by Congress, established in 1956 within the research grants and fellowships branch the Psychopharmacology Service Center. It is the purpose of the center to further and promote a broad research program aimed at increasing knowledge of the mechanisms of action and of the efficacy and the limitations of psychopharmacological agents. In addition to supporting and pointing up the need for research on the pharmacological and psychological mechanisms of drug action and drug efficacy, the program of the center includes research advisory functions.

As part of its coordinating and information function, the Psychopharmacology Service Center began, in January, 1959, publication of the *Psychopharmacology Service Center Bulletin*, which is distributed at irregular intervals to interested physicians and investigators engaged in research in psychopharmacology. While not intended to be a substitute for journal publication, the *Bulletin* provides for a rapid exchange of information between investigators, providing materials such as reference lists, summaries of research reported at scientific meetings, reviews of psychopharmacological research, descriptions of new methodologies and techniques, and summaries of translated articles. The papers applicable to the field of psychopharmacology necessarily are scattered among innumerable journals. Beginning in January, 1961, the center encouraged the publication of *Psychopharmacology Abstracts;* it does not directly publish it. This publication, not available on a subscription basis but available to those investigators who qualify by virtue of research interest and scientific specialty, provides brief noncritical abstracts of the international literature in psychopharmacology. *Psychopharmaca* (Caldwell, 1958) provides a comprehensive list of references to articles published between January, 1952, and December, 1956, concerned with the effects of the psychopharmacological agents on the psychological, behavioral, and encephalographic reactions of human and animal subjects and contains an incomplete listing of references for 1957.

In recognition of the need for psychopharmacology to assume its integrating function, various divisions of the National Institute of Mental Health provide training grants to departments or groups of departments wishing to increase offerings in the field of psychopharmacology and offer fellowships to individuals wishing to receive research training in psychopharmacology. Doubtless, a new generation of psychopharmacologists with more broadly based training will emerge.

Much in the way of integration has also taken place through the medium of the conference. Some of the major conferences and proceedings of conferences which are of particular import for this chapter follow. In 1957, the Collegium Internationale Neuro-Psychopharmacologicum was founded with the purpose of promoting research and stimulating collaboration between the experimental and clinical branches of the neuropsychopharmacological sciences. Thus far, volumes 1 and 2 of the proceedings from these conferences have been published under the title *Neuropsychopharmacology* (Bradley, Deniker, & Radouco-Thomas, 1959; Rothlin, 1961). The American College of Neuropsychopharmacology was organized in October, 1961.

The Society of Biological Psychiatry includes at its meetings special sections devoted to chemotherapy and to general psychopharmacological research. The proceedings of the fourteenth scientific session of the Society of Biological Psychiatry constitute volume I of *Biological Psychiatry* (Masserman, 1959). Since then, the proceedings have been edited by Wortis (1960; 1961; 1962; 1963) and have appeared under the title *Recent Advances in Biological Psychiatry*.

Several conferences relating to the effects of drugs and to basic mechanisms of drug action have been held under the auspices of the New York Academy of Sciences. Issues of the *Annals of the New York Academy of Sciences* which are particularly appropriate to this chapter are those edited by Miner (1954;

1955), Whitelock (1957a; 1957b; 1959; 1960), Furness (1962), and Whipple (1963).

The Josiah Macy, Jr., Foundation has sponsored conferences concerned with the basic mechanisms of drug action. The proceedings of these conferences have been edited by Abramson (1955; 1956; 1957; 1959; 1960a). A Macy conference specifically relating to the use of *d*-lysergic acid diethylamide in psychotherapy is of interest (Abramson, 1960b).

The Veterans Administration, with psychiatric facilities across the nation, held the first of a continuing series of conferences organized around multihospital, cooperative, well-controlled studies of the use of chemotherapy in psychiatry in 1956. The transactions, *Chemotherapy in Psychiatry,* edited by Lindley (n.d.; 1958; 1959; 1960a), reflect primary concern with the effects of certain psychopharmacological agents on mental illness. While the VA Cooperative Research Program was initiated to evaluate the therapeutic efficacy of tranquilizing drugs, it has since been broadened to include research on the causes of mental illness. The proceedings, *Cooperative Chemotherapy Studies in Psychiatry and Research Approaches to Mental Illness* (Lindley, 1960b; Lindley, 1961), reflect this broadened scope. It is to be regretted that the VA no longer publishes the transactions of these annual conferences, for, collectively, their contents not only provide knowledge of the therapeutic effectiveness of the psychopharmacological agents studied, of the toxicity of such agents, and of basic mechanisms of drug effects but also provide a most interesting view of the ironing out of problems relating to a multidiscipline team approach to research, the development of adequate controls, and the development of methodology for clinical research. Representative published reports based upon the VA chemotherapy studies are those by Caffey (1961); Caffey and Klett (1961); Casey, Lasky, Klett, and Hollister (1960); Lorr, McNair, Weinstein, Michaux, and Raskin (1961); and Overall, Hollister, Pokorny, Casey, and Katz (1962).

Representative proceedings from other national and international conferences which have been particularly of value because they show the integrative aspects of psychopharmacology are *Psychotropic Drugs* (Garattini & Ghetti, 1957), *Tranquilizing Drugs* (Himwich, 1957), *Psychopharmacology* (Kline, 1956), *Psychopharmacology Frontiers* (Kline, 1959b), and *Chemical Concepts of Psychosis* (Rinkel & Denber, 1958).

Because they reflect a growing awareness of, and concern with, problems relating to the interactions of drug variables, personality variables, and environmental variables, the following conference proceedings are of particular import for this chapter: *Therapeutic Community* (Denber, 1960), *Control of the Mind: Man and Civilization* (Farber & Wilson, 1961), *Conflict and Creativity: Man and Civilization* (Farber & Wilson, 1963), *A Pharmacologic Approach to the Study of the Mind* (Featherstone & Simon, 1959), *Mental Patients in Transition* (Greenblatt, Levinson, & Klerman, 1961), *Specific and Non-specific Factors in Psychopharmacology* (Rinkel, 1963), and *The Dynamics of Psychiatric Drug Therapy* (Sarwer-Foner, 1960).

While there are many fine journals published within the various fields which contribute to the discipline of psychopharmacology and while there are a number of excellent texts in pharmacology, there are only a few of particular relevance to this chapter. *Psychopharmacologia,* a journal devoted solely to psychopharmacology, was first published in July, 1959. This journal presents original experimental and clinical papers and reviews of recent literature, bringing together under one cover findings from the fields of neurophysiology, neuropharmacology, neurochemistry, neurology, psychiatry, and psychology. *Clinical Pharmacology and Therapeutics,* a journal publishing original articles and reviews dealing with the effects of drugs in man, began publication in January–February, 1960. *Pharmacologic Principles of Medical Practice* (Krantz & Carr, 1961), a textbook, is recommended because it includes a chapter on the use of drugs in treatment of the mentally ill. *Advances in Pharmacology* (Garattini & Shore, 1962) contains an excellent chapter by Shepherd and Wing (1962), who have reviewed the pharmacological aspects of psychiatry and have included in their review a number of studies relating to the effects of psychotropic drugs on human subjects.

Methodological problems in the field of psychopharmacology are particularly complex because of the very large number of variables involved and because of their often peculiar and unforeseen interactions. An awareness of this and an awareness on the part of investigators in the field of psychopharmacology of the methodological inadequacies of many studies published in the literature have led to countless papers and conference discussions on methodology in psychopharmacology. Almost all the proceedings previously cited in this chapter contain references to methodological problems. Cole has made a continuing effort to delineate the methodological problems in psychopharmacological research, particularly those relating to chemotherapy (1959; 1962; Cole & Fisher, 1960; Cole & Gerard, 1959; Cole, Ross, & Bouthilet, 1957).

How much improvement in quality of research has resulted from this information giving in regard to methodological considerations is problematical. Sandifer, Dunham, and Howard (1961) thought not much. Heilizer (1960), after critically reviewing a large number of published experiments with chlorpromazine in human subjects and finding that very few of them met even minimum standards of scientific investigation, concluded that clinical investigators in the field of chemotherapy had not assimilated the requirements for conducting scientific investigations, in spite of the fact that many publications dealing with methodology in the field of psychopharmacology were then available. However, if one takes a rather longer view, it would appear that there has been improvement in the degree of attention paid to methodological considerations in clinical research. Cole (1962) points out that only 60 controlled studies in regard to insulin shock treatment were produced in the first ten years of experience with that clinical procedure but that at least 522 controlled studies of chemotherapy in psychiatric patients had been carried out between 1952 and 1962. Even so, in view of the very large number of psychotropic chemotherapeutic agents extant, one wonders whether the ratio is much better.

Reviews of methodology specifically relating to the study of drug-behavior interactions include those of Beecher (1959a), Hamilton (1957), Lehmann (1959), and Pichot (1961a). Steinberg (1961) provides a review of methods (descriptive, physiological, and those depending upon efficiency of performance) used in measuring changes brought about in emotions and personality by drugs. Uhr and Miller (1960) have edited a text on specific experimental procedures and general methodological considerations that includes chapters written by a large number of investigators working in the area of assessing drug-behavior interactions. Modell (1959) has reviewed a number of the current problems concerning evaluating drug effects in man. In regard to the specious argument pertaining to choice of subjects for investigation, he points out that one would choose as subjects patients evidencing a particular disease state if the purpose of the investigation was to predict the efficacy of the drug for treatment of that disease state. However, if the purpose of the investigation is not to conduct a therapeutic evaluation but is rather to define the pharmacological action of a drug in man, the normal man may be even the more desirable subject.

This chapter is neither the first review of psychopharmacology nor the first review of that aspect of psychopharmacology relating to the interactions of drug variables and personality variables. For example, both Ross and Cole (1960) and Wikler (1957) have undertaken to review the field of psychopharmacology, with Wikler critically reviewing studies falling within the period from 1930 to 1955, and Ross and Cole covering the period from 1954 to 1959. Most of the studies utilizing human subjects that Wikler presents are concerned with the therapeutic evaluation of drugs. His review is particularly notable for a chapter on psychological aspects of theories and mechanisms of drug action, in which he predominantly has presented studies relating to concepts of the conditioned reflex and of psychoanalysis. This chapter may be of particular interest to investigators experimenting with animals because animal studies are heavily emphasized, there being approximately 95 animal studies and approximately seven human studies considered. Ross and Cole discuss primarily human studies, particularly those relating to drug effects on normal human subjects.

Lindemann and von Felsinger (1961) have provided a comprehensive, well-organized, evaluative review of studies relating to drug effects and personality theory. They discuss particularly the need to relate drug effects to dynamic processes of personality, rather than trying to relate them to one personality dimension or trait. They therefore review a number of studies pertaining to the concepts of repression, anxiety, drive, and function of the ego. Their review concerning these concepts includes much material in regard to their own observations and conceptual frames of reference.

Zubin and Katz (1964) review a few studies bearing upon the influence of personality on drug action and the effects of drugs on personality. Generally finding the field of personality measurement in the "doldrums" and concluding that neither the field of psychopharmacology nor the field of "personality change" has reached an adequate level of articulation, Zubin and Katz propose a model for studying drug effects on personality. While the model presented is not sharply delineated, Zubin and Katz perhaps do emphasize more than some others have the possibility of using conceptual changes as a means of studying drug effects. They designate as personality the "conceptual or cognitative component, i.e., memory storage" that is systematically characteristic of an individual.

Citing Burdock, Sutton, and Zubin (1958), Zubin and Katz propose the concept of an "idling state," the ongoing brain activity at the time a stimulus (and the drug might be considered a stimulus) is applied. Interactions between this ongoing brain activity and drug effects would be reflected in changes in ongoing behavior. Zubin and Katz suggest that practiced ongoing behaviors such as conversation or swimming ought to be studied in relation to drug effects upon them. They indicate that these behaviors do not need to be elicited by a controlled external stimulus. They do not give in detail methods of measurement or controls to be applied in this kind of setting. Zubin and Katz would also extend the possibility suggested by R. J. Williams (1956) of classifying people into relatively homogeneous subgroups on the basis of individual biochemical differences to that of attempting to classify people into such subgroups by virtue of measuring changes in their practiced ongoing behaviors after varying doses of chemical substances.

The concept of the idling state sounds very much like the concept argued in favor of by Klein and Krech (1952) of a basal value of cortical conductivity. That is, an individual might have a high or a low general state of excitation or inhibition of the cortex prior to the introduction of any known external stimulus. Eysenck (1963) has pointed out that there are difficulties in delineating the differential existence of such a state due to the confounding of stimulus-produced effects with any side effects which might be present.

The thesis that there are interactions between psychotropic drug effects, physiological-biochemical states, personality, more transient emotional states, and the environment in which the drug is given is a ubiquitous article of faith. Some have directed effort toward trying to separate what is specific and what is nonspecific in regard to drug action. Pichot (1961b) proposes that there ought to be a differentiation between specific and nonspecific drug effects, with those effects that are directly a function of the drug considered specific and those effects that are a function of personality considered nonspecific. Lindemann and von Felsinger (1961) say that reactions determined by personality have confounded the search for patterns of reaction that are drug-specific, and they call for separation of the two aspects of the response by the use of more careful methods. Rinkel (1963) has edited a symposium on the topic of factors of a specific and nonspecific nature in psychopharmacology.

Zubin and Katz (1964) point out that reactions dictated by personality structure may predominate when a drug is given in a low dosage and that physiological and sensory reactions may predominate when the drug is given in a high dosage. Steinberg (1961), pointing out that an investigator is always observing the results of drug-personality-environmental interactions and that the dichotomy posed by speaking of specific and nonspecific drug effects is spurious, calls for investigators to speak in terms of predominant rather than specific drug effects. Like Wikler (1957; 1958), she suggests that the real problem is to specify under what conditions drug effects are likely to be modified.

The foregoing is a general introduction to a basic body of literature in psychopharmacology. The rest of this chapter will be sharply limited in scope. First, it will be confined to studies using human subjects and delineating the interactions between drug, personality, and/or environmental variables. Experiments with animals are, and always will be, an essential first step in the study of any drug effects or drug-behavior interactions; see reports by Brady (1956) and Sidman (1959) for reviews of animal research. This is dictated by considerations of safety, of economics, of the law, and of the fact that there has been considerable successful prediction from the behavior of animals to that of humans. This does not obviate the fact that generalizing from the results of psychotropic drug effects on animal behavior to their effects on human behavior is very frequently unreliable and that in the case of some behavioral parameters it cannot be done. Therefore, it is essential, and required by law, that drugs ultimately be tested both for efficacy and for safety in the human subject. The use of human subjects in psychopharmacological studies does add immeasurably to the complexity of methodological problems, and there is great need not only for more consistent application of known methodological principles and techniques in human studies but also for advances in procedure and techniques. However, it is precisely there that the challenge to the behavioral scientist lies. Consequently, animal studies will not be reviewed, even though eliminating them will eliminate some of the more ingenious and more methodologically sound studies bearing upon the psychological aspects of the effects of drugs on infrahuman behavior.

Second, the rest of this chapter will, wherever possible, be concerned only with studies which at least purport to be controlled experimental studies. Astute clinical observation has frequently led to considerable information in regard to drug effects. A powerful drug with reasonably clear predominant effects applied to an appropriate population may well be clearly described in regard to its effects simply on the basis of clinician observation. Well-controlled, methodologically sound clinical trials which follow may add little new information. As an extreme example, the chemist Hofmann (Stoll & Hofmann, 1943), in what first amounted to an accidental one-subject–one-observer study, both discovered and very well described the dysleptic properties of lysergic acid diethylamide. Nonetheless, the relatively uncontrolled observations often disseminated through the literature ought to be treated as hypotheses or precursors to hypotheses in need of controlled testing, not as facts to be bandied from review to review.

Third and last, the remainder of this chapter will be a critical review in the sense that, wherever indicated, results will be presented in the context of the methods and procedures from which they were derived. This means that, because of considerations of space, only a fraction of the studies in the literature can be considered. However, one ought to be able to judge results for reliability in the context of the methodology employed, whether they are statistically significant or insignificant. Statistical significance of a result tells nothing about the validity or invalidity of an experimental arrangement.

Eysenck (1957a; 1957b; 1963) has propounded a theoretical framework in regard to drugs and personality from which hypotheses have been derived and tested in a number of experiments. He stands alone in behavioral psychopharmacology in respect to the degree to which he has delineated his theory and systematically derived his explicit hypotheses. In what category Eysenck places his own theory is not entirely clear. He has stated (1957a) that it is a rational system allowing predictions and testing of predictions in terms of the hypothetico-deductive methods of science. He has stated (1957b) that such a rational theoretical framework is really not possible in the context of the degree of present knowledge in psychology, and he has therefore described his theory as being one which is based upon a qualitative system of postulates which have been derived in a "nonrigorous way" from data from previous experiments and which have resulted in the possibility of making somewhat rigorous "qualitative" predictions and deductions. Later (1963), he points out that the purpose of a theory is to lead to exploration, and he speaks of his own theory as being a general theory from which some specific theorems and hypotheses have been derived. In any case, there is no question that Eysenck's statements of his theory and his deductions from his theory have led to a considerable body of work bearing upon drug effects and personality.

Eysenck's theory of personality is derived from that of McDougall (1926; 1929). Eysenck (1957a) embraces McDougall's concept of a continuum or dimension of personality, that of introversion-extraversion. Following Jung (1921), as McDougall did (1926; 1929), in the linking of the introversion-extraversion typology with the typology of Janet (1909), who grouped neurotics into two clusters (psychasthenics and hysterics), Eysenck (1957b) proposes that hysterics are identified with extraversion and that dysthymics are identified with introversion.

He has attempted to define operationally the dimension introversion-extraversion in terms of objective tests. As pointed out by Franks (1961), Guilford and Guilford (1934) thought that the factor of impulsiveness accounted for McDougall's statements about the concept of introversion-extraversion and thought that there were probably at least three other factorial aspects really included in the concept. Therefore, Guilford concluded that it was unrealistic to try to mold introversion-extraversion into a single dimension. While Guilford's rhathymia scale has been used to define the dimension of introversion-extraversion, Eysenck latterly has used the Maudsley Personality Inventory (Eysenck, 1959).

Franks (1961) has criticized this self-rating scale on the grounds that, with patient or neurotic groups, he could demonstrate no agreement between self-ratings and the judgments of others. However, Franks had altered the MPI in some respects before subjecting it to a test of validity, and, while his criticism may be correct, he gains no truly relevant support for it from his experimental arrangement. In any case, even if the MPI is deficient in regard to reliability and/or validity, a difficulty it would share in common with many measures, this would not obviate Eysenck's postulate (1957a, p. 124): "Any test which has been shown to differentiate reliably and validly between introverts and extraverts will, when applied to subjects who have been administered a stimulant (or depressant) drug, show shifts in scores in the direction characteristic of greater introversion (or extraversion)."

Actually, one would hardly expect a single dose of either a "stimulant" or a "depressant" drug to produce any basic shift in personality structure. Perhaps the MPI is capable of reflecting transient shifts in mood, affect, or emotion, but probably a better measure for testing such shifts is needed. In any case, Eysenck's general contention is that an individual's position on the behavioral continuum of introversion-extraversion can be ascertained by obtaining either ratings from judges or self-ratings, and that seems fair enough. Recent reviews (Christie & Lindauer, 1963; Gleser, 1963; Tucker, 1963) suggest that there is considerable activity in the field of test measurement, and there ought to be continuing improvement in methods for assessing dimensions of personality and shifts in personality or emotions.

Eysenck (1957a; 1957b; 1960; 1963) has linked concepts from learning theory with the foregoing concepts of personality. Rejecting McDougall's (1929) "substance X" as being, in varying amounts, the causal factor underlying the continuum of introversion-extraversion, Eysenck drew upon the concepts of Pavlov (1927; 1928) and Hull (1935; 1943) and, in the case of the concept of satiation, upon the work of Köhler and Wallach (1944) for explanatory constructs of individual variation and clustering in personality. He postulates that the molar concepts of inhibition and excitation are causally related to the behavior patterns of extraversion and introversion. He says (1957a, p. 122): "Extraverted behaviour patterns are produced by excessively strong reactive inhibition and/or excessively weak excitation, while introverted behaviour patterns are produced by excessively weak reactive inhibition and/or excessively strong excitation."

Both Becker (1960) and Franks (1961) have pointed out that Eysenck has tended to use the terms "reactive inhibition," "satiation," and "cortical inhibition" interchangeably. As Becker has pointed out, Eysenck has modified Hull's concept of reactive inhibition by ruling out muscular effects, and Becker suggests that Eysenck's resulting concept might more appropriately be referred to as "reactive cortical inhibition." Franks has pointed out that it is sometimes not clear whether Eysenck is referring to inhibition as a constitutional property of nervous tissue or as a reaction within the tissue which might or might not be related to the originally present level of inhibition. In any case, while he has not been consistent in his usage of terminology, Eysenck (1957b; 1963) has referred to inhibition as an "interfering process" within the CNS and has specified the type of interference by reference to two types of inhibition, temporal inhibition and spatial inhibition. He relates temporal inhibition to Pavlov's concept of internal inhibition and to Hull's concept of reactive inhibition, specifying that the building up of a performance decrement is a consequence of the performance itself. Spatial inhibition is, Eysenck says, similar to Pavlov's concept of external inhibition and refers to the production of a performance decrement through interference by some other form of activity occurring at the same time or nearly at the same time. Thus, Eysenck (1963) restricts cortical inhibition to stimulus-produced inhibition. However, Eysenck agrees with Klein and Krech (1952), and has often seemed to say himself that there probably is individual variation in basal level of cortical conductivity. Eysenck points out (1963) that the construct of cortical conductivity is unavoidable on a theoretical level if consistent individual differences are postulated in stimulus-produced inhibition. However the terms "inhibition" and "excitation" and the inhibition-excitation balance may ultimately be defined, Eysenck uses them as molar concepts or theoretical constructs without any definite physiological meaning, although it is hoped that ultimately physiological counterparts will be discovered for them. The inhibition-excitation balance is meant to be directly and causally related not only to extraversion-introversion but also to individual differences in the performance of various tasks. Thus, according to Eysenck, the speed with which conditioned responses are acquired and their resistance to extinction are decreased by inhibitory potentials and, conversely, are increased by excitatory potentials.

Eysenck's (1957a, p. 123) drug postulate is as follows: "Depressant drugs increase cortical inhibition, decrease cortical excitation, and thereby produce extraverted behaviour patterns. Stimulant drugs decrease cortical inhibition, increase cortical excitation, and thereby produce introverted behaviour patterns." It is common for reviewers (Lindemann & von Felsinger, 1961; Zubin & Katz, 1964) to criticize Eysenck for his oversimplified use of the terms "depressant" and "stimulant" in reference to drugs. However, Eysenck is not the first, nor will he be the last, investigator to be trapped by the exigencies of pharmacological classification.

Because problems relating to drug classification (Delay, 1959; Kline, 1959a; Lehmann, 1959; Shepherd & Wing, 1962) may partially explain Eysenck's (and others') failure to confirm some of his hypotheses, a statement of a few of those problems follows: Drugs of similar chemical structure may produce disparate effects on behavior, and drugs of disparate chemical structure may produce similar effects on behavior. Individuals displaying the same predominant behavior patterns may react differently to the same drug. Drugs do not have a single action. Even though the predominant effect of two different drugs may be classed as the same, e.g., depressant, this does not mean that the effects need be either quantitatively or qualitatively equal; there are variations in action of any two drugs around the predominant effect. The variation of the two drugs in regard to effect on behaviors other than the one under study must be taken into consideration, not simply relegated to the category of "side effects," there to be ignored.

In Eysenckian experiments there has been a tendency to use ethyl alcohol or amobarbital sodium to test predictions regarding effects of "depressant" drugs (e.g., Eysenck, Casey, & Trouton, 1957; Eysenck, Holland, & Trouton, 1957a; Eysenck, Holland, & Trouton, 1957b; Franks, 1961; Franks, 1963; Franks & Trouton, 1958). It is agreed (Goodman & Gilman, 1956; Hulpieu & Harger, 1958; Krantz & Carr, 1961; Shideman, 1958) that, pharmacologically, both ethyl alcohol and amobarbital sodium are central nervous system depressants. However, it is clear that the predominant behavioral effects of alcohol and amobarbital sodium are very disparate. The predominant effect of amobarbital sodium is one of producing sedation or hypnosis, depending upon the dose given, in the vast majority of individuals ingesting it. By contrast, the predominant effect of alcohol, within reasonable dose limits, is not one of producing sleep but is, in the majority of cases, even one of causing behavior to appear to be stimulated. Krantz and Carr (1961) point out that one of the first effects of alcohol upon the cortex is that of depression of the inhibitory centers. Shideman (1958) indicates that the barbiturates may produce sleep as a consequence of suppression of activity in the hypothalamus or may simply render the central nervous system less responsive to afferent stimuli. In sum, it seems clear that predictions, e.g., depressant drugs will produce a decrease in the rate of conditioning, may well be confirmed or disconfirmed depending largely upon the choice and dose of the depressant drug. Predictions should be couched in terms of *this* depressant or *that* stimulant, not in terms of depressant drugs or stimulant drugs. After all, if all depressants produced precisely the same effects, only one would be needed in the pharmacopoeia.

Considering the well-formulated theoretical framework and explicitly derived hypotheses that Eysenck presents, it is difficult to understand the procedures he has utilized for the systematic testing of the hypotheses. Zubin and Katz (1964) have pointed out that testing of Eysenck's predictions has failed as often as it has succeeded to give significant confirmation of them. In view of his equating of one depressant (or stimulant) with another for purposes of prediction and in view of the very poor experimental procedures often employed for the testing of Eysenck's hypotheses, this fact probably has little significance for Eysenck's theory. Specific examples of shortcomings in Eysenck's experimental arrangements follow.

1. Most frequently, too few subjects from too special a population are used. In disregard of the fact that there may well be sex differences in response to drugs, Eysenck uses both men and women where neither the distribution by sex in the group nor the total number in the group would allow testing for the presence of such sex differences. For example, in one series of experiments, Eysenck and Easterbrook (1960a; 1960b; 1960c; 1960d; 1960e; 1960f) used a total of eight subjects, five men and three women, and drew these subjects from a club where the membership consisted of people who had achieved some measure of excellence on a paper-and-pencil intelligence test. In another series of experiments, Eysenck and Aiba (1957) and Eysenck, Holland, and Trouton (1957a; 1957b) used six subjects, five men and one woman, drawn, with one exception, from a class of postgraduate students in psychology.

2. A second reason for the fact that Eysenck's predictions are confirmed on one occasion and disconfirmed on another (Eysenck & Easterbrook, 1960a; Eysenck, Holland, & Trouton, 1957b) may lie in inadequate methods of measurement. For example, in these two studies a visual aftereffect was induced with a rotating spiral. The subject was instructed to say "now" when the visual aftereffect had ceased. The investigators timed the duration of the visual aftereffect by stopwatch, timing the interval between the moment the experimenter stopped the motor and the moment the subject said "now." The reaction time of the subject was confounded with the reaction time of the experimenter.

Failure to control for practice effects also has resulted in obscuring and confounding of results bearing upon Eysenck's hypotheses. In one study (Eysenck, Casey, & Trouton, 1957) one of the predictions was that ingestion of a depressant drug would result in the showing of a more rapid and marked work decrement than ingestion of a placebo would. The continuous work task consisted of three separated five-minute periods of performance on a pursuit rotor. No previous practice on this demanding motor task was given, with the consequence that all treatment groups (amobarbital sodium, placebo, and two *d*-amphetamine groups) showed an increment in performance from the beginning of the first work period to the end of the third work period. It did appear that the increment was greater for the placebo group than for the depressant group by the third period. The curve of placebo-group performance clearly showed that learning-practice effects were present. One has no way of knowing from this study whether the depressant drug effect as compared with placebo effect was one of belated interference with learning or, because of the dose (approximately 292 milligrams), belated interference with performance of the motor task. The time intervening between the administration of the 292 milligrams of amobarbital sodium and the beginning of the task was not stated in this article. In any case, comparing across trials rather than between groups, the depressant drug "effect" was one of enhancement of performance.

3. While Eysenck generally counterbalances order of drugs in an attempt to control for serial effects, it appears that he does not counterbalance the order of tasks. Serial effects resulting from the presentation of many tasks in a fixed order within a short period of time make it doubtful that confirmation or disconfirmation of a prediction shown by any particular measure can be considered independently of the total series of measures taken. Further, except for the study by Eysenck, Casey, and Trouton (1957), all the studies cited in this section have utilized a crossover design; i.e., each subject serves under every treatment condition. Even assuming that there is no direct influence of one drug on the next due to residual traces of it in the system, there are probably indirect influences resulting from one treatment condition and carried over to another. For example, a subject may form an attitude or set in reaction to the first drug given him and maintain this set, the set interacting with the next drug effect and altering the expected response.

Where a crossover design is used and where neither serial task effects nor practice effects have been controlled, there must be considerable interaction between these effects and the time that a given drug is introduced. If one individual receives a given drug on the first day, he has had no practice on the task before him. A second individual receiving the same drug on the third day of a study not only has had practice on the tasks on two prior days but also probably has built up certain attitudes in regard to the entire experimental arrangement. One would not expect the performances of these two individuals under a given drug necessarily to be very similar. Eysenck and Eysenck (1960) have argued against the use of random, independent groups on the grounds that such an experimental design is "wasteful." One might argue that it is more wasteful to have 50 per cent of one's predictions fail to be confirmed (Zubin & Katz, 1964) without being able to specify the reason for the failure. In psychotropic drug studies utilizing human subjects it is highly doubtful that a crossover design should ever be utilized in view of the complexity of drug effect interactions as well as the complexity of further interactions resulting from such factors as expectations, attitudes, sets, and varying states of affect and mood.

4. Last, with the exception of his apparatus descriptions, which are usually very complete, Eysenck's reporting of his procedures is such as to make his experimental studies very difficult to evaluate. There are remarkable omissions of necessary information. Eysenck and Easterbrook specify nothing in their six articles in regard to such subject facts as age, weight, physical and mental condition, prior experience with drugs, current status in regard to medication, etc. Eysenck, Casey, and Trouton (1957) carefully specify the time intervening between drug ingestion and testing for two treatment groups and give no such information for two other treatment groups.

In neither of the two series of experiments cited does the article specifying the general procedures give either a listing of the tasks or the order of the tasks. One discovers what the tasks were only by looking at each article (generally one per task). One never discovers what the order of tasks was. There is an occasional reference to a task being "the fifth to be carried out" (Eysenck & Easterbrook, 1960c, p. 831). Most frequently, however, the investigators simply state that a task was "only one of several" carried out (Eysenck & Easterbrook, 1960a, p. 842). This can be rather serious. For example, Eysenck, Holland, and Trouton (1957b) report an experiment investigating spiral aftereffects where the stimulus was presented for four separated (by one minute) one-minute trials. In the following experiment (Eysenck, Holland, & Trouton, 1957a), the task consisted of 2 two-minute Necker cube trials, with it being specified that the two trials were separated by a "rest-period" of approximately ten minutes. It is only incidental to a point later raised by the investigators that one learns that the 4 one-minute trials on the rotating spiral were run in the supposed ten-minute "rest period" separating the 2 two-minute Necker cube trials.

In sum, while Eysenck has made a significant contribution in terms of presenting a theory linking drug actions to concepts of learning and personality, there are shortcomings in his actual experimental procedures which make it extremely difficult to evaluate whether a specific prediction has been confirmed or disconfirmed, regardless of the results obtained.

A number of Eysenck's predictions have been well tested. On the basis of his drug postulate, Eysenck has predicted: "Depressant drugs should produce a decrease in the rate of conditioning, while stimulant drugs should produce an increase in the rate of conditioning" (1957a, p. 125). Franks and Trouton (1958) demonstrated that subjects ingesting 10 milligrams of *d*-amphetamine two hours prior to conditioning trials conditioned significantly more readily than subjects ingesting a placebo. Subjects given 4.5 grams of amobarbital sodium forty-five minutes prior to the conditioning trials conditioned significantly less readily than the placebo subjects. Franks and Trouton used random, independent, homogeneous groups of approximately twenty subjects each and employed good experimental controls. Franks and Laverty (1955) also demonstrated that amobarbital sodium reduces the number of acquired conditioned eye-blink responses and increases the rate of extinction.

Using essentially the same conditioning procedure as Franks and Trouton (1958) had in their demonstration, Franks (1961; 1963) failed to demonstrate inhibition of the rate of acquisition of the conditioned eye-blink response by ethyl alcohol. Franks (1963) attributes this failure to the fact that his placebo group may have been exposed to maximal suggestion. He offers the possibility that suggestion may be equal to the physiological properties of alcohol in modification of CR behavior.

However, there are a number of alternative reasons for his failure to show a significant difference between his placebo and ethyl alcohol groups. It is here assumed that, while there are minor differences in reporting, the study presented by Franks (1963) is identical to a study previously reported in the context of a series of experiments (Franks, 1961). That is, the means and standard deviations in regard to conditioned eye-blink responses shown by each group during both acquisition and extinction are identical in the 1961 and 1963 reports. Franks (1961; 1963) administered to the subjects in his alcohol group 90-proof blended whiskey in doses ranging from 4.5 to 6.8 ounces, depending upon the body weight of the subjects (one milliliter per pound). There was considerable variation in amount of time subjects took to complete the drink; the range in drinking time was from three to sixty minutes (Franks, 1961). The range of subjects' percentage by weight of blood alcohol just prior to the conditioning trials was from 0.048 to 0.150 (Franks, 1961). The amount of time intervening between the completion of the drink and the beginning of the conditioning trials ranged from 30 to 180 minutes (Franks, 1961).

Krantz and Carr (1961, p. 430) point out: "The maximal effect of alcohol on the brain is during the time when the curve of blood concentration is in its ascendancy." Further, they say that a given concentration of blood alcohol which results in certain behavioral effects at the beginning of a time-concentration curve may evoke no behavioral effects when it appears in the descending part of the time-concentration curve (approximately one hour later). Half of Franks' (1961, pp. 111–112) subjects were introduced to the conditioning procedure in excess of sixty minutes from the point of completion of ingestion of alcohol.

The foregoing leaves open to question how effective the dose of alcohol might have been at the time of the conditioning procedure and suggests that there was probably considerable variation between subjects within the group. By contrast, Franks and Trouton (1958) probably did have an effective dose (whether for interference with central learning or for interference with performance of the CR not tested) of amobarbital sodium in their study. Approximately 292 milligrams of amobarbital sodium was administered. One hundred to three hundred milligrams of amobarbital sodium is a hypnotic dose (Shideman, 1958).

In sum, Franks' failure to obtain a significant difference between his placebo subjects and ethyl alcohol subjects in regard to either rate of acquisition or rate of extinction of the conditioned eye-blink response, in view of the fact that he obtained such a difference with amobarbital sodium, is not possible to explain definitively. It may have been due to differences in effect between amobarbital sodium and ethyl alcohol. While both are "depressant" drugs, their effects on behavior are not identical. It may have been due to nonequivalence in dose used between ethyl alcohol and amobarbital sodium. It may have been due to shortcomings in his experimental arrangement rather than to any true lack of difference. It is extremely difficult to maintain adequate controls in a study involving ethyl alcohol. This makes it imperative to control well those aspects which can be controlled. Franks (1961; 1963) could have controlled more adequately the amount of drinking time and the amount of time intervening between ingestion of alcohol and the conditioning procedure. He could have taken readings of amount of blood alcohol more frequently and attempted to test his subjects at a time of comparatively equal concentration.

One assumes from his complete report (1961) that he did not do these things because he attempted to get too many data in too short a time, with consequent compromises in maintenance of controls. While Franks (1963) says that the procedures intervening between the time of the ingestion of alcohol and the time of the eye-blink conditioning procedure were of "no relevance," his 1961 report shows that the eye-blink conditioning procedure came approximately midway in a fixed series of several tasks, and serial effects could have been operative. In short, Franks' failure to confirm the hypothesis in regard to the effect of alcohol on rate of acquisition of eye-blink conditioning cannot be considered a crucial or reliable disconfirmation of the hypothesis. The interpretation that the failure to discriminate between the subjects in the placebo and the alcohol groups was due to a factor of suggestion operating in the placebo group would appear to be gratuitous.

For other representative research carried out within an Eysenckian framework, see reports by Choppy and Eysenck (1963), Claridge (1960), Claridge and Herrington (1963), Costello (1963), Holland (1960), Holland and Gomez (1963), Lynn and Eysenck (1963), Martin (1960), Petrie (1960), Rodnight and Gooch (1963), Sylvester (1963), Treadwell (1960), and Willett (1960; 1962).

Any method for reliably dividing samples of people into more homogeneous subgroups has important implications both for research and for therapy. Eysenck's approach of linking drug response to personality typology has been described. Another significant typological approach to the study of drug-personality interactions in shown by the studies of DiMascio, Rinkel, and Leiberman (1961) and Klerman, DiMascio, Greenblatt, and Rinkel (1959). For other references to these same two studies, see reports by DiMascio and Rinkel (1963) and Rinkel, DiMascio, Robey, and Atwell (1961). A general description of the program of the Massachusetts Mental Health Center is given by DiMascio and Klerman (1960).

Reference to the report of DiMascio, Klerman, Rinkel, Greenblatt, and Brown (1958) is essential to an evaluation of the report by Klerman et al. (1959) because it more fully specifies the experimental arrangement. DiMascio et al. (1958) indicate that the 15 healthy, normal, male college student subjects studied were tested on a minimum of 67 dependent variables, i.e., 11 psychophysiological measures representing a total of 15 dependent variables, 41 self-rated items, and 11 psychiatrist-rated behavioral dimensions.

While DiMascio et al. (1958) had described their 15 subjects as constituting a "homogeneous" group, they had noted individual variations in response. Therefore, *post hoc,* Klerman et al. (1959) used the subjects' pretreatment MMPI scores and psychiatric ratings to achieve a separation of the subjects into two groups of contrasting personality types. They found five of the fifteen subjects presenting well-defined common personality characteristics (type A) and five (type B) presenting exactly contrasting personality characteristics, e.g., type-A mesomorphs versus type-B endomorphs; type-A father-identified versus type-B mother-identified; type-A athletic versus type-B nonathletic; type-A considerable alcohol intake versus type-B limited alcohol intake, etc.

Klerman et al. (1959) state that they analyzed the data for "all measurements" (presumably a minimum of 67 dependent variables) but that they report only the statistically significant differences obtaining between type-A and type-B subjects (statistical methods not specified except as being "mainly of the nonparametric type"). Significant differences between the two personality types were shown on from five to six variables under each treatment condition; e.g., under the placebo condition, four type A's versus one type B were rated as showing improved rapport; under the reserpine condition, type A's decreased 5 per cent (in comparison with their predrug performance) in tapping speed versus type B's, who increased 2 per cent; under the phenyltoloxamine condition, type A's decreased 5 per cent in tapping speed versus type B's, who decreased 13 per cent.

Considering that there were only five subjects in each group, that scores were frequently expressed as percentage change, and that the number of significant findings may well be due to chance, these data cannot be regarded as providing firm evidence for a differential response to drugs due to personality. Replication, cross-validation, and a more adequate method of data analysis are required.

In a second study of this type, DiMascio et al. (1961) investigated the differential responses of nine type-A (athletic) and nine type-B (esthetic) subjects, who were selected on the bases of MMPI scores and psychiatric interview data. Each subject served under three dysleptic drug conditions (lysergic acid diethylamide, mescaline, and psilocybin).

The number of dependent variables included in this study cannot be specified. The investigators state only that their subjects were interviewed by a psychiatrist and were administered a test battery consisting of "sixteen individual testing procedures." However, it seems unlikely that the four self-rating questionnaires, the checklist for somatic complaints, and the ratings by a psychiatrist included in the test battery provided only one dependent variable each; e.g., one of the figures presented shows a significant difference between the groups on a single item, postdrug occurrence of seeing colored patterns.

In any case, the report indicates only six statistically significant differences between groups under the three treatment conditions (statistical method not specified): (1) a greater degree of deterioration (difference between number of units completed predrug and 2½ hours postdrug) on the part of the type-B subjects on both the serial addition and the digit symbol tasks under the conditions of both lysergic acid diethylamide and mescaline; (2) a significantly greater number of the type-A subjects reporting the occurrence of colored patterns after the ingestion of mescaline; and (3) a significantly greater number of type-A subjects rating themselves as becoming more anxious under the lysergic acid diethylamide condition.

The investigators conclude that there was a differential response of these two personality types to the three dysleptic drugs administered. They specify that the type-B subjects predominantly showed intellectual changes and that the type-A subjects showed "euphoria and physiological changes." There were absolutely no statistically significant differences between groups indicated in this report either on any physiological parameter or on the euphoria-depression dimension. The same criticisms apply to this study as to the previous study by Klerman et al. (1959).

The conceptualization of these studies is interesting and ought to provide a significant approach to the specifying of drug-personality interactions, but the methodology employed is inadequate. It may well be that type-A and type-B subjects are extant in the population; it may even be that they each comprise one-third of the population (Klerman et al., 1959); it may be that people of differing personality structures respond differentially to the same drug. It is possible that replication of these two studies may produce some of the same results. However, there is no reliable data evidence supplied in these reports to support the interpretations made. This work must be considered exploratory in nature.

Kelly, Miller, Marquis, Gerard, and Uhr (1958a; 1958b), in a complex but carefully controlled study, correlated subjects' personality characteristics with their performance on a wide range of behavioral tasks under three treatment conditions. This report is outstanding for its inclusion of all information necessary to evaluate the study, clear specification of procedure, and absence of interpretations not warranted by the data. The investigators selected (factor analysis) 20 personality variables (out of 69 measured) to correlate with a representative group of 40 (out of 51 measured) behavioral variables. In all, 2,400 correlations were computed (800 for each of the three treatment comparisons) in the search for possible drug-personality relationships. The investigators point out that 24 of the obtained 28 correlations significant beyond the 1 per cent level would be expected by chance. While they discuss the implications of their findings, they sensibly specify that the findings should be regarded only as "potentially fruitful" hypotheses to be further investigated.

Studies undertaking to show significant shifts in subjects' scores on various tests or rating scales of personality or behavior as a consequence of the ingestion of some drug are legion but are not pertinent to this section. Of more interest is the recent trend toward predicting, from his pretreatment scores on objectively rated dimensions of personality and behavior, a drug of choice for an individual. The work of Overall, Hollister, Honigfeld, Kimbell, Meyer, Bennett, and Caffey (1963) represents a preliminary approach to this methodologically and therapeutically important goal. Their initial purpose was to compare perphenazine and acetophenazine in regard to efficacy. Pretreatment ratings of 110 male schizophrenics were obtained on the IMPS (Lorr, Klett, McNair, & Lasky, 1963) and the BPRS (Overall & Gorham, 1962; Overall & Gorham, 1963). The 98 subjects completing six weeks of therapy were then rerated on both scales by a psychiatrist and a psychologist jointly.

Change scores (predrug minus postdrug) computed for both scales reflected signficant improvement within each group. The mean difference in degree of improvement between the two groups was not significant; i.e., the drugs were equally effective. An examination of the total pathology score from the BPRS indicated a statistically significant difference in variance of the change scores for the two groups. The two correlations computed between the predrug and postdrug total pathology scores were significantly different, being .77 in the case of perphenazine and .40 in the case of acetophenazine. A differential response to acetophenazine was indicated, and the problem became one of identifying the specific types of patients most likely to benefit from treatment with this drug.

A computer analysis of the initial ratings on the BPRS classified the patients as either "paranoids" or "core" schizophrenics. A two-way analysis of variance comparison of the effectiveness of the two drugs in these two patient classes was made and revealed a highly significant interaction between drugs and diagnosis. Both paranoid and core schizophrenics responded equally well to perphenazine, while only the paranoids responded well to acetophenazine.

Klett and Caffey (1963) indicate that the staff of the VA Central NP Research Laboratory has developed regression equations derived from data from an earlier study of drug efficacy to predict differential response to the drugs. The method has been cross-validated using data obtained on several hundred other patients. It is expected that a new study shortly will begin, where the intent will be to predict from patients' pretreatment symptomatology (as indicated by rating scales and perhaps other measures) the efficacy of a given drug for a given patient.

A problem both in the specifying of drug-personality interactions and in the separating of humans into homogeneous subgroups is that investigators do not speak the same language. An investigator is bound to discuss behavioral changes he observes in the language of the measuring instrument he uses. Something of a babel has ensued because there is a plethora of instruments available for measuring personality-behavioral changes. Further, an investigator will frequently find existing instruments unsatisfactory for his purpose and may simply "construct" an instrument for the occasion. However, there have been a few approaches which seem particularly promising for the measurement of drug-personality interactions.

Lorr (1960) has reviewed 19 rating scales he considers the best developed and most promising for rating changes in behavior, particularly behavior of hospitalized psychiatric patients. Even so, he points out that less than half of the scales he reviewed provide scoring and interpretation manuals, that many of them do not provide evidence of validity, and that some fail to report any reliability information. Lorr, Klett, and McNair (1963), in a chapter of their book *Syndromes of Psychosis*, critically review types of factor analyses identifying psychotic syndromes from ratings.

The series of psychiatric rating scales (containing items specific to discrete symptoms or behaviors which are combined to yield factor scores) by Lorr and his colleagues is well known (Lorr, Jenkins, & Holsopple, 1953; Lorr, Klett, McNair, & Lasky, 1963; Lorr, O'Connor, & Stafford, 1960; Lorr, Rubinstein, & Jenkins, 1953). Wittenborn's scales (1955; 1962) for rating changes of behavior in mental patients also rest upon considerable normative data. Overall and Gorham (1962; 1963) have developed a psychiatric rating scale containing symptom constructs of a relatively abstract nature, e.g., hostility and anxiety.

Haertzen, Hill, and Belleville (1963) describe the development of a 550-item inventory, the statements in the inventory being similar in format to those used in the MMPI but with the content being selected specifically for investigation of drug effects. Hill, Haertzen, Wolbach, and Miner (1963a; 1963b) list the items of the inventory, indicating those items which discriminate a given drug from the placebo condition (1963a), and give some scale standardization data (1963b).

The adjective checklist described by Nowlis and Nowlis (1956) and Wendt and Cameron (1961) is probably excellent for delineating the effects of psychotropic drugs on the mood of normal humans, providing that the procedures for its use which are well and exactingly described by Wendt and Cameron are followed. The discriminative strength shown by this adjective checklist may lie more in the experimental arrangement in which Wendt and his colleagues have used it than in the checklist itself. Wendt, Cameron, and Specht (1962) have presented data from four experiments where comparable procedures were used, reporting on the use of both a placebo and a dimenhydrinate condition as methodological controls and showing excellent reproducibility of results.

A major criticism of the method of Wendt and his colleagues centers about the method of data analysis. Generally, simple change scores from predrug to postdrug (with the significance of the change being based upon empirically derived estimates) are used. Utilizing 133 adjectives, many of them taken from the list of Wendt and Nowlis, Clyde (1960) demonstrated six factors of mood. It is too early to tell whether this instrument will be any more validly or reliably discriminating than Wendt's original adjective checklist. See reports by Krugman, Ross, Vicino, and Clyde (1960) and Trent (1962) for representative studies using this scale.

In contrast to the approaches and instruments reviewed for dividing people into more homogeneous subgroups in order to study drug-personality interactions, there is the approach of grouping subjects on the basis of their differential responses to drugs. The use of methacholine chloride by Funkenstein, Greenblatt, and Solomon (1949; 1950; 1951) as a measure of gross autonomic reactivity is well known. This test has been used largely to predict differential response to electroshock therapy.

Shagass (1954; 1957a; 1957b; 1960) and his colleagues (Shagass, Azima, & Sangowicz, 1959; Shagass & Kerenyi, 1958; Shagass, Naiman, & Mihalik, 1956) have, working within an Eysenckian theoretical framework, developed and validated the use of a "sedation threshold" to show that differential tolerance to amobarbital sodium reflects individual differences in affect and personality. Briefly, the sedation-threshold test is a clinical neurophysiological test to determine the amount of intravenous amobarbital sodium required to produce slurred speech and concomitant EEG changes.

A representative report of Shagass' use of the sedation threshold to explore for a neurophysiological basis for the introversion-extraversion dimension of behavior is that of Shagass and Kerenyi (1958). Shagass and Kerenyi measured the sedation thresholds of 224 men and women (data not shown to be examined for sex differences) who also had been rated (by two psychiatrists not connected with the sedation-threshold measurements) in regard to degree of hysterical (extraversion) or obsessional (introversion) symptomatology. The correlation between the sedation threshold and the hysterical-obsessional score was .53, a statistically significant positive correlation. A Guilford introversion score was obtained for 36 (study not completed when reported) of these patients. The correlation between degree of introversion and sedation threshold was .60, a statistically significant positive correlation. Shagass and Kerenyi conclude that the sedation threshold is correlated with a personality factor of extraversion-introversion or, extending this to neurotics, a hysterical-obsessional dimension. Shagass' work has been criticized by Bartholomew and Marley (1959), Pampiglione (1958), and Thorpe and Barker (1957).

Goldman (1959; 1962) finds that EEG activation produced by the intravenous injection of thiopental sodium results in effects which will differentiate between certain schizophrenics and patients showing other psychotic states.

Relating susceptibility to methylpentynol to personality variables as measured by the neuroticism-normality and extraversion-introversion scales of the Maudsley Personality Inventory, Bartholomew and Marley (1959) found that a toxic response to this alcohol was related to high neuroticism scores. The relationship obtaining between susceptibility and extraversion-introversion scores was somewhat more equivocal.

Attempts have been made to specify the relationship between personality and drug action with a measure of stimulation threshold (Giberti and Rossi, 1962; Shagass & Lipowski, 1958). Giberti and Rossi showed a significant difference between neurotic depression and psychotic depression groups in regard to the amount of intravenously administered methylamphetamine hydrochloride required to produce certain neurovegetative and behavioral changes.

Lasagna, von Felsinger, and Beecher (1955) noted that there were typical (e.g., euphoric response to amphetamine) and atypical (e.g., dysphoric response to amphetamine) reactors in their group of 20 subjects. The atypical reactors were, of course, the minority. Von Felsinger, Lasagna, and Beecher (1955) examined for differences between the personalities of the atypical and the typical drug reactors by means of psychiatric ratings and Rorschach responses. While this study shares all the usual shortcomings stemming from use of an unstructured interview and an unstructured test as measures, it exemplifies another approach to delineating drug-personality interactions by first separating subjects on the basis of their behavioral responses to the drug.

Lehmann and Knight (1961) attempted to show differential responses between a control group and a group of "alcoholics or drug addicts" to a variety of psychological tasks. While this is an interesting approach to defining operationally subjects' behavior, i.e., addict or nonaddict, the assumption that a person addicted to one drug is like a person addicted to another drug may not hold.

There have been attempts to separate people into relatively homogeneous subgroups on the basis of their respective responses to a placebo. A placebo is an inert substance, and responses occurring upon ingestion of a placebo cannot be directly dictated by a pharmacological variable. Therefore, there is maximum likelihood that events occurring under the placebo condition are dictated by person-milieu variables. Unfortunately, there has been much specious argument in regard to both the concept of placebo "effects" and the concept of placebo "reactors." Hollister (1960), particularly, has pointed out the nonsensical quality of many interpretations in regard to placebo effects.

Beecher (1955; 1959a; 1959b) has presented a list of toxic effects he considers attributable to the placebo. Pogge (1963) also has provided a tabulation of the nature and frequency of toxic effects appearing under the placebo condition. Sensibly, he presents it to indicate that a placebo condition is necessary to evaluate the significance of unwanted effects occurring under the condition of a new drug rather than to indicate that the placebo causes such effects. Because the 3,549 subjects represented in Pogge's data were, in the vast majority, patients suffering from some illness or disorder, the remarkable thing is not that toxic effects occurred under the placebo condition but that so few did. One rather expects patients to complain of symptoms of the type Pogge reports, e.g., drowsiness, headache, nausea, constipation, etc.

Case reports have sometimes been used to substantiate the argument that toxic reactions follow placebo ingestion. Wolf and Pinsky (1954) describe "serious toxic reactions" exhibited by three patients in their study, two of the patients exhibiting reactions under both the drug and the placebo condition. These dramatic descriptions may also be found in reports by Wolf (1953; 1959b; 1959c).

Investigators presenting case reports have begun to look for the multiple determinants of such reactions. Cytryn, Gilbert, and Eisenberg (1960) studied young children presenting diagnoses of hyperkinetic behavior disorder, mental defectiveness, neurosis, and antisocial reaction. In reporting toxic effects of medication, they describe one child said by his mother to be "wild and unmanageable" on two separate courses of placebo (thought by the mother to be active medication). They point out that the mother initially had been hostile to the idea of medication (and apparently still was).

Hankoff (1962) reports the case of a woman with a history of hospitalization for acute delusional episodes who had been receiving medication from a clinic. Her doctor was changed; the new doctor suggested that she ought to change medication. She was hostile to the idea of change of medication (and apparently also hostile to a change of doctors), but she did accept green placebo capsules as a substitute for one of the several medications she had been taking. She then reported that the "green capsules" had caused her to become "sick all over" and to experience symptoms of nausea, blindness, dizziness, and numbness around the mouth. Hankoff points out that such responses may be entirely unrelated to a specific agent, placebo included, when a change in other treatment conditions is concomitant with a change in medication.

In sum, there is no question that toxic effects are exhibited under a placebo condition. However, this fact per se provides no information relevant to either the existence of placebo effects or the existence of placebo reactors. If the purpose of a placebo group in a study is to provide a control for a drug group in the same study, then it is of value for comparison to record the incidence of symptoms occurring under the placebo condition. However, if the purpose is to specify that the psychological-social variables surrounding the giving of a pill in some way result in the occurrence of these symptoms, then not only base rates of symptoms present prior to the administration of the placebo but also base rates of symptoms present in a no-drug group of similar patients in the same study are essential.

Following Jellinek (1946), Beecher (1955; 1959a; 1959b) has been a major proponent of the argument for the existence of a placebo reactor. He argues that the consistency shown from study to study in the percentage of patients satisfactorily relieved of their symptoms under the placebo condition augurs the "power" of a placebo to produce such relief. He chose, at random, 15 studies (seven from his laboratory and eight from others) and tabulated the data from them to exhibit that (over a total of 1,082 patients) placebos showed an "average significant effectiveness of 35.2 ± 2.2 %" (1955, p. 1603). In the absence of data obtained from a no-treatment group of control subjects suffering from the same symptoms to delineate the base rate of spontaneous recovery, these data have no meaning in regard to the "power" of a placebo. Further, in transmitting data from at least one of the original studies (Lasagna, Mosteller, von Felsinger, & Beecher, 1954) to the columns both for number of patients in the study and for percentage of patients whose symptoms were satisfactorily relieved by a placebo, gross errors have been made which, if nothing else, rather destroy the nicety of the "±2.2%."

The study of Lasagna et al. (1954) often has been cited as providing evidence for differential personality characteristics of the placebo reactor and nonreactor. Trouton (1957) has provided an appropriately harsh review of this study. Essentially, the study now is of only historical interest because the procedures utilized were such as to warrant no confidence in the data presented to substantiate the assertions made.

Working along the same conceptual lines as Lasagna et al. (1954) in regard to a definable class of both placebo reactors and placebo nonreactors being extant, Joyce (1959a) took 12 items from the Bernreuter along with certain other information and was able to predict beyond chance level the responses of preclinical medical students to a placebo. This appears to be a rather more sophisticated approach to the problem of discriminating between reactors and nonreactors to placebo (for other references to Joyce's work, see Joyce, 1959b; Joyce, 1961). Morison, Woodmansey, and Young (1961) found their placebo reactors to show introversion and neuroticism on the MPI and found their nonreactors to score significantly higher on the Bernreuter scale of social dominance.

Fisher and Fisher (1963) have demonstrated a relationship between a subject's tendency to acquiesce and his tendency to respond under the placebo condition. They gave the Bass Social Acquiescence Scale (Bass, 1956) to 72 normal college students, all naïve concerning drugs. In the experiment proper, the subjects were all given a placebo but were told that the "drug" given would produce a variety of symptoms and sensations. They found a significant relationship obtaining between subjects' respective degrees of acquiescence and their spontaneous (suggested) reporting of symptoms as well as a significant relationship between acquiescence and number of symptoms indicated on a symptom checklist.

While the foregoing shows that there is some evidence extant for the position that a placebo reactor exists at one end of a continuum and that a placebo nonreactor exists at the other, evidence also has been accumulated and logic has been brought to bear to show that responses under a placebo condition are not particularly of predictive value. Honigfeld (1964a) has reviewed extensively the placebo literature and has concluded that placebo reactors or nonreactors are, for all practical purposes, mythical characters.

Wolf, Doering, Clark, and Hagans (1957) gave subjects seven trials under a placebo condition and found that the placebo responses given showed a pattern of distribution identical to that of a chance distribution achieved by designating coins as subjects and flipping the coins seven times. Wolf (1959a; 1959b; 1959c) points out that the placebo reactor does not remain constant from one situation to another, that responses to a placebo will vary depending upon the situation, and that there are, in general, multiple determinants of a placebo response, e.g., the nature of the test agent, the motivation of both patient and physician, and the life situation of the subject.

Hypotheses regarding multiple determinants of a response frequently have been provided by psychoanalytically oriented investigators in a position to observe the marked interplay obtaining between complex person dynamics and situational variables. For an introduction to this work, see the writings in the book edited by Sarwer-Foner (1960) and Ostow's work (1962). See the report by Cole and Fisher (1960) for a critique.

This chapter concludes with an examination of a few studies bearing upon the problem of the interaction of drug effects with environmental or milieu variables. It is recognized that there are a large number of such variables which probably do interact with drug variables, e.g., the hospital environment. However, most studies here reviewed are concerned with the important variable of physician-milieu. For an extensive but essentially noncritical review of socio-psychological factors as determinants in treatment, see the report by Honigfeld (1964b).

Whitehorn and Betz (1954; 1960) early tested for interactions between psychotherapeutic effects and physician-milieu. They report a distinction between profiles obtained on the Strong Vocational Interest Blank by successful (A) and unsuccessful (B) physicians treating schizophrenics. Betz and Whitehorn (1956) found that a group of schizophrenics showed 82 per cent improvement when treated by A physicians with psychotherapy alone. A group of schizophrenics treated with psychotherapy alone by B physicians showed only 34 per cent improvement. When insulin was combined with psychotherapy, the group of patients treated by A physicians showed no further improvement. However, insulin combined with psychotherapy for the patients treated by B physicians resulted in a rise in success rate from 34 to 82 per cent.

Fisher, Cole, Rickels, and Uhlenhuth (1962) also have studied physician-milieu and therapy effect interactions. They randomly assigned selected neurotic patients to one of four conditions. Half of the subjects received meprobamate, and half received placebo. Half were treated by physicians instructed to provide a therapeutically oriented milieu (T physicians), and half were exposed to physicians instructed to convey an experimentally oriented milieu (E physicians). At the time this interactive-model study was reported, only the dependent variable of dropout rate had been analyzed. For the placebo subjects, the dropout rate was 31.7 per cent, regardless of whether the patient had a T or an E physician. However, for the patients receiving meprobamate, a differential response was shown, depending upon whether the patient had been exposed to a T or an E physician. Of the meprobamate patients with E physicians, 32.1 per cent dropped out, whereas only 16.4 per cent of meprobamate patients with T physicians dropped out.

Kast (1961), in spite of the fact that the study was extremely poorly controlled, took the interesting approach not only of varying the physician-milieu but also of varying the type of patient exposed to the two physicians. In studying the effects of a monoamine oxidase inhibitor on depression, he selected 20 agitated depressives and 20 withdrawn depressives. Half the patients in the withdrawn group and half in the agitated group were exposed to a very positive physician-patient relationship (DP1), whereas the other half in each group were exposed to a negative physician-milieu (DP2). All patients were administered a placebo for four to six weeks prior to being placed on drug; they were then placed on medication for six weeks. For the withdrawn depressive group, the DP1s showed 40 per cent and the DP2s 10 per cent improvement under the placebo condition. For the agitated depressive group, the DP1s showed 20 per cent and the DP2s 50 per cent improvement under the placebo condition.

The DP1 withdrawn depressives showed an increase in improvement rate to 75 per cent and the DP2 withdrawn depressives to 60 per cent when the drug was introduced. The DP1 agitated depressives showed an increase in improvement rate to 45 per cent and the DP2 agitated depressives to 70 per cent under the drug condition.

The results of this study cannot be taken too seriously because the raters not only knew when the drug was introduced but also knew which patients were serving under which physician-milieu condition. Further, the rating of change of mood in only two gross categories, i.e., improved and not improved, allows for maximum bias to enter. Lastly, the investigators probably had expectations derived from their psychiatric concepts concerning the dynamics of withdrawn depressed patients versus the dynamics of agitated depressed patients which provided a source of bias in need of control. Nonetheless, the study is an example of an interesting model for studying the interactions between drug variables, patient variables, and milieu variables.

As suggested by Honigfeld (1964b), it perhaps would be best, methodologically, to separate the functions of treater and rater. Certainly, this would seem to be true where the primary purpose is to delineate the interactions obtaining between drug effects and physician-milieu effects. Sabshin and Ramot (1956) suggested that negative attitudes toward drug therapy on the part of the patients and staff in a certain hospital resulted in chlorpromazine and reserpine being rated as relatively ineffective drugs. Feldman (1956); Eisen, Sabshin, and Heath (1959); and M.

Williams and McGee (1962) (the latter two studies being quite well controlled) all have shown that therapists' attitudes toward the use of drugs significantly affect their evaluations of their patients' improvement or lack of improvement under drug therapy.

Even so, Haefner, Sacks, and Mason (1960), conducting a study for the purpose of investigating the impact of physicians' differential attitudes toward chemotherapy on patients' responses to medication, allowed the treating physicians to serve also as raters of the patients' progress. The investigators concede that there may be some confounding of variables in their study, that the attitude of the participating physicians toward drug therapy may have biased the results relating to patients' progress. However, the concession does not make the confounding go away, and neither does the "incidental evidence" presented by the investigators to show that the attitude of the physician did not bias his rating of patient change.

Citing Fisher (1961), Klerman (1963) has presented a thoughtful series of models for conceptualizing drug-milieu interactions. Perhaps such conceptual models will lead to research more adequately designed to explicate the interactions between drug variables, personality variables, and environmental variables than much of the research presented in this chapter. Generally speaking, this review of the literature has shown that what we all "know" to be true, that such interactions do exist, is certainly not confirmed by any large body of reliable experimental data. Neither, of course, has what we all "know" to be true been particularly disconfirmed. There is obviously a need in this field for more adequately conceptualized, designed, and executed research. Being a Cowardly Lion, the reviewer concludes with a still appropriate statement made by Heilizer (1960, p. 120):

> The most startling finding of this review is that only 37 studies meet certain minimum standards of scientific evaluation. The conclusion seems warranted that clinical chemotherapy investigators have not generally assimilated basic scientific standards. . . . It appears, therefore, that this situation is due to a resistance to the use of scientific methods. Further, in order for such a situation to exist, it must be at least accepted by the domain of interested parties, e.g., research groups, funding foundations, drug houses, journal editors, etc.

REFERENCES

Abramson, H. A. (Ed.) *Neuropharmacology.* Vol. I. New York: Josiah Macy, 1955.

Abramson, H. A. (Ed.) *Neuropharmacology.* Vol. II. New York: Josiah Macy, 1956.

Abramson, H. A. (Ed.) *Neuropharmacology.* Vol. III. New York: Josiah Macy, 1957.

Abramson, H. A. (Ed.) *Neuropharmacology.* Vol. IV. New York: Josiah Macy, 1959.

Abramson, H. A. (Ed.) *Neuropharmacology.* Vol. V. New York: Josiah Macy, 1960. (a)

Abramson, H. A. (Ed.) *The use of LSD in psychotherapy.* New York: Josiah Macy, 1960. (b)

American Medical Association. *Program of the council on mental health.* Chicago: Author, 1963.

Bartholomew, A. A., & Marley, E. Susceptibility to methylpentynol: personality and other variables. *J. ment. Sci.,* 1959, **105,** 957–970.

Bass, B. M. Development and evaluation of a scale for measuring social acquiescence. *J. abnorm. soc. Psychol.,* 1956, **53,** 296–299.

Becker, W. C. Cortical inhibition and extraversion-introversion. *J. abnorm. soc. Psychol.,* 1960, **61,** 52–66.

Beecher, H. K. The powerful placebo. *J. Amer. med. Ass.,* 1955, **159,** 1602–1606.

Beecher, H. K. *Measurement of subjective responses: quantitative effects of drugs.* New York: Oxford Univer. Press, 1959. (a)

Beecher, H. K. Placebos and the evaluation of the subjective response. In S. O. Waife & A. P. Shapiro (Eds.), *The clinical evaluation of new drugs.* New York: Hoeber-Harper, 1959. Pp. 61–75. (b)

Betz, Barbara J., & Whitehorn, J. C. The relationship of the therapist to the outcome of therapy in schizophrenia. *Psychiat. res. Rep.,* 1956, **5,** 89–105.

Bradley, P. B., Deniker, P., & Radouco-Thomas, C. (Eds.) *Neuro-psychopharmacology.* Vol. 1. Amsterdam: Elsevier, 1959.

Brady, J. V. *Comparative psychopharmacology: animal experimental studies on the effects of drugs on behavior.* National Research Council, Washington, D.C., 1956.

Brill, H., & Patton, R. E. Analysis of 1955–1956 population fall in New York State mental hospitals in first year of large-scale use of tranquilizing drugs. *Amer. J. Psychiat.,* 1957, **114,** 509–517.

Brill, H., & Patton, R. E. Analysis of population reduction in New York State mental hospitals during the first four years of large-scale therapy with psychotropic drugs. *Amer. J. Psychiat.*, 1959, **116**, 495–509.

Burdock, E. I., Sutton, S., & Zubin, J. Personality and psychopathology. *J. abnorm. soc. Psychol.*, 1958, **56**, 18–30.

Caffey, E. M., Jr. Experiences with large scale interhospital cooperative research in chemotherapy. *Amer. J. Psychiat.*, 1961, **117**, 713–719.

Caffey, E. M., Jr., & Klett, C. J. Side effects and laboratory findings during combined drug therapy of chronic schizophrenics. *Dis. nerv. System*, 1961, **22**, 370–375.

Caldwell, Anne E. *Psychopharmaca: a bibliography of psychopharmacology, 1952–1957. Publ. Hlth Serv. Publ.*, 1958, No. 581.

Casey, J. F., Lasky, J. J., Klett, C. J., & Hollister, L. E. Treatment of schizophrenic reactions with phenothiazine derivatives: a comparative study of chlorpromazine, triflupromazine, mepazine, prochlorperazine, perphenazine, and phenobarbital. *Amer. J. Psychiat.*, 1960, **117**, 97–105.

Casey, J. F., & Lindley, C. J. Recent advances in Veterans Administration psychiatry. In J. H. Masserman (Ed.), *Current psychiatric therapies*. Vol. 2. New York: Grune & Stratton, 1962. Pp. 233–246.

Choppy, M., & Eysenck, H. J. Brain-damage and depressant drugs: an experimental study of interaction. In H. J. Eysenck (Ed.), *Experiments with drugs*. New York: Macmillan, 1963. Pp. 313–323.

Christie, R., & Lindauer, F. Personality structure. *Annu. Rev. Psychol.*, 1963, **14**, 201–230.

Claridge, G. The excitation-inhibition balance in neurotics. In H. J. Eysenck (Ed.), *Experiments in personality*. Vol. II. *Psychodiagnostics and psychodynamics*. New York: Humanities Press, 1960. Pp. 107–154.

Claridge, G. S., & Herrington, R. N. Excitation-inhibition and the theory of neurosis: a study of the sedation threshold. In H. J. Eysenck (Ed.), *Experiments with drugs*. New York: Macmillan, 1963. Pp. 131–168.

Clyde, D. J. Self-ratings. In L. Uhr & J. G. Miller (Eds.), *Drugs and behavior*. New York: Wiley, 1960. Pp. 583–586.

Cole, J. O. Research problems in clinical psychopharmacology. In J. Masserman (Ed.), *Biological psychiatry*. New York: Grune & Stratton, 1959. Pp. 212–223.

Cole, J. O. Evaluation of drug treatments in psychiatry. *Psychopharmacol. Serv. Center Bull.*, 1962, **2** (3), 28–38.

Cole, J. O., & Fisher, S. Psychopharmacological research in the psychoanalytic setting. In G. J. Sarwer-Foner (Ed.), *The dynamics of psychiatric drug therapy*. Springfield, Ill.: Charles C Thomas, 1960. Pp. 208–218.

Cole, J. O., & Gerard, R. W. (Eds.) Psychopharmacology: problems in evaluation. *Nat. Acad. Sci., Nat. Res. Council Publ.*, 1959, No. 583.

Cole, J. O., Ross, S., & Bouthilet, Lorraine. Recommendations for reporting studies of psychiatric drugs. *Publ. Hlth Rep.*, 1957, **72**, 638–645.

Costello, C. G. The effects of meprobamate on the visual afterimage. In H. J. Eysenck (Ed.), *Experiments with drugs*. New York: Macmillan, 1963. Pp. 197–227.

Cytryn, L., Gilbert, A., & Eisenberg, L. The effectiveness of tranquilizing drugs plus supportive psychotherapy in treating behavior disorders of children: a double-blind study of eighty outpatients. *Amer. J. Orthopsychiat.*, 1960, **30**, 113–128.

Delay, J. Discussion of pharmacological treatment of schizophrenics: classification and terminology. In N. S. Kline (Ed.), *Psychopharmacology frontiers*. Boston: Little, Brown, 1959. Pp. 426–428.

Denber, H. C. B. (Ed.) *Therapeutic community*. Springfield, Ill.: Charles C Thomas, 1960.

DiMascio, A., & Klerman, G. L. Psychophysiological studies of psychoactive drugs. In L. Uhr & J. G. Miller (Eds.), *Drugs and behavior*. New York: Wiley, 1960. Pp. 360–364.

DiMascio, A., Klerman, G. L., Rinkel, M., Greenblatt, M., & Brown, J. Psychophysiologic evaluation of phenyltoloxamine, a new phrenotropic agent. *Amer. J. Psychiat.*, 1958, **115**, 301–317.

DiMascio, A., & Rinkel, M. Personality and drugs: "specific" and "non-specific" influences on drug actions. In M. Rinkel (Ed.), *Specific and non-specific factors in psychopharmacology*. New York: Philosophical Library, 1963. Pp. 130–140.

DiMascio, A., Rinkel, M., & Leiberman, J. Personality and psychotomimetic drugs. In *Third World Congress of Psychiatry: proceedings*. Vol. II. Toronto: Univer. of Toronto Press, 1961. Pp. 933–936.

Eisen, S. B., Sabshin, M., & Heath, H. A comparison of the effects of investigators' and therapists' attitudes in the evaluation of tranquilizers prescribed to hospital patients. *J. nerv. ment. Dis.*, 1959, **128**, 256–261.

Eysenck, H. J. Drugs and personality. I. Theory and methodology. *J. ment. Sci.*, 1957, **103**, 119–131. (a)

Eysenck, H. J. *The dynamics of anxiety and hysteria.* New York: Praeger, 1957. (b)

Eysenck, H. J. *Manual of the Maudsley Personality Inventory.* London: Univer. of London Press, 1959.

Eysenck, H. J. Levels of personality, constitutional factors, and social influences: an experimental approach. *Int. J. soc. Psychiat.*, 1960, **6**, 12–24.

Eysenck, H. J. Personality and drug effects. In H. J. Eysenck (Ed.), *Experiments with drugs.* New York: Macmillan, 1963. Pp. 1–24.

Eysenck, H. J., & Aiba, S. Drugs and personality. V. The effects of stimulant and depressant drugs on the suppression of the primary visual stimulus. *J. ment. Sci.*, 1957, **103**, 661–665.

Eysenck, H. J., Casey, S., & Trouton, D. S. Drugs and personality. II. The effect of stimulant and depressant drugs on continuous work. *J. ment. Sci.*, 1957, **103**, 645–649.

Eysenck, H. J., & Easterbrook, J. A. Drugs and personality. VIII. The effects of stimulant and depressant drugs on visual after-effects of a rotating spiral. *J. ment. Sci.*, 1960, **106**, 842–844. (a)

Eysenck, H. J., & Easterbrook, J. A. Drugs and personality. XI. The effects of stimulant and depressant drugs upon auditory flutter fusion. *J. ment. Sci.*, 1960, **106**, 855–857. (b)

Eysenck, H. J., & Easterbrook, J. A. Drugs and personality. VI. The effects of stimulant and depressant drugs upon body sway (static ataxia). *J. ment. Sci.*, 1960, **106**, 831–834. (c)

Eysenck, H. J., & Easterbrook, J. A. Drugs and personality. X. The effects of stimulant and depressant drugs upon kinaesthetic figural after-effects. *J. ment. Sci.*, 1960, **106**, 852–854. (d)

Eysenck, H. J., & Easterbrook, J. A. Drugs and personality. VII. The effects of stimulant and depressant drugs upon pupillary reactions. *J. ment. Sci.*, 1960, **106**, 835–841. (e)

Eysenck, H. J., & Easterbrook, J. A. Drugs and personality. IX. The effects of stimulant and depressant drugs upon visual figural after-effects. *J. ment. Sci.*, 1960, **106**, 845–851. (f)

Eysenck, H. J., & Eysenck, S. B. G. The classification of drugs according to their behavioral effects: a new method. In H. J. Eysenck (Ed.), *Experiments in personality.* Vol. I. *Psychogenetics and psychopharmacology.* New York: Humanities Press, 1960. Pp. 225–233.

Eysenck, H. J., Holland, H., & Trouton, D. S. Drugs and personality. IV. The effects of stimulant and depressant drugs on the rate of fluctuation of a reversible perspective. *J. ment. Sci.*, 1957, **103**, 656–660. (a)

Eysenck, H. J., Holland, H., & Trouton, D. S. Drugs and personality. III. The effects of stimulant and depressant drugs on visual after-effects. *J. ment. Sci.*, 1957, **103**, 650–655. (b)

Farber, S. M., & Wilson, R. H. L. (Eds.) *Control of the mind: man and civilization.* New York: McGraw-Hill, 1961.

Farber, S. M., & Wilson, R. H. L. (Eds.) *Conflict and creativity: man and civilization.* New York: McGraw-Hill, 1963.

Featherstone, R. M., & Simon, A. *A pharmacologic approach to the study of the mind.* Springfield, Ill.: Charles C Thomas, 1959.

Feldman, P. E. The personal element in psychiatric research. *Amer. J. Psychiat.*, 1956, **113**, 52–54.

Fisher, S. NIMH-PSC outpatient study of drug-set interaction. *Psychopharmacol. Serv. Center Bull.*, January, 1961, 4–7.

Fisher, S., Cole, J. O., Rickels, K., & Uhlenhuth, E. H. *Drug-set interactions: the effect of expectations on drug response in outpatients.* Paper read at Collegium Int. Neuro-psychopharmacol., Munich, 1962.

Fisher, S., & Fisher, Rhoda L. Placebo response and acquiescence. *Psychopharmacologia,* 1963, **4**, 298–301.

Franks, C. M. *The effects of alcohol as related to personality.* Princeton, N.J.: New Jersey Neuro-Psychiatric Institute, Psychological Service and Research Center, 1961.

Franks, C. M. The apparent failure of ethyl alcohol to inhibit the formation of conditioned eyeblink responses in man. *Psychopharmacologia,* 1963, **4**, 433–440.

Franks, C. M., & Laverty, S. G. Sodium amytal and eyelid conditioning. *J. ment. Sci.*, 1955, **101**, 654–663.

Franks, C. M., & Trouton, D. S. Effects of amobarbital sodium and dexamphetamine sulfate on the conditioning of the eyeblink response. *J. comp. physiol. Psychol.*, 1958, **51**, 220–222.

Funkenstein, D. H., Greenblatt, M., & Solomon, H. C. Psychophysiological study of mentally ill patients. I. The status of the peripheral autonomic nervous system as determined by reaction to epinephrine and mecholyl. *Amer. J. Psychiat.*, 1949, **106**, 16–28.

Funkenstein, D. H., Greenblatt, M., & Solomon, H. C. A test which predicts the clinical effects of electric shock treatment on schizophrenic patients. *Amer. J. Psychiat.*, 1950, **106**, 889–901.

Funkenstein, D. H., Greenblatt, M., & Solomon, H. C. Autonomic changes paralleling psychologic changes in mentally ill patients. *J. nerv. ment. Dis.*, 1951, **114**, 1–18.

Furness, F. N. (Ed.) *Some biological aspects of schizophrenic behavior. Ann. N.Y. Acad. Sci.*, 1962, **96**, Art. 1.

Garattini, S., & Ghetti, V. (Eds.) *Psychotropic drugs*. New York: Elsevier, 1957.

Garattini, S., & Shore, P. A. (Eds.) *Advances in pharmacology*. Vol. 1. New York: Academic, 1962.

Giberti, F., & Rossi, R. Proposal of a psychopharmacological test ("stimulation threshold") for differentiating neurotic from psychotic depressions: preliminary report. *Psychopharmacologia*, 1962, **3**, 128–131.

Gleser, G. C. Projective methodologies. *Annu. Rev. Psychol.*, 1963, 391–422.

Goldman, D. Specific electroencephalographic changes with pentothal activation in psychotic states. *EEG clin. Neurophysiol.*, 1959, **11**, 657–667.

Goldman, D. Electroencephalographic changes brought to light under pentothal activation in psychotic (schizophrenic) patients, with particular reference to changes produced by pharmacological agents. *Ann. N.Y. Acad. Sci.*, 1962, **96**, 356–374.

Goodman, L. S., & Gilman, A. *The pharmacological basis of therapeutics*. (2nd ed.) New York: Macmillan, 1956.

Greenblatt, M., Levinson, D. J., & Klerman, G. L. (Eds.) *Mental patients in transition*. Springfield, Ill.: Charles C Thomas, 1961.

Guilford, J. P., & Guilford, Ruth B. Analysis of the factors in a typical test of introversion-extraversion. *J. abnorm. soc. Psychol.*, 1934, **28**, 377–399.

Haefner, D. P., Sacks, J. M., & Mason, A. S. Physicians' attitudes toward chemotherapy as a factor in psychiatric patients' responses to medication. *J. nerv. ment. Dis.*, 1960, **131**, 64–69.

Haertzen, C. A., Hill, H. E., & Belleville, R. E. Development of the addiction research center inventory (ARCI): selection of items that are sensitive to the effects of various drugs. *Psychopharmacologia*, 1963, **4**, 155–166.

Hamilton, M. *Methodological problems in investigating psychotropic drugs: report to study group on ataraxics and hallucinogenics*. World Health Organization, Geneva, Switzerland, 1957.

Hankoff, L. D. Treatment comparison and the placebo effect. *Dis. nerv. System*, 1962, **23**, 39–40.

Heilizer, F. A critical review of some published experiments with chlorpromazine in schizophrenic, neurotic, and normal humans. *J. chron. Dis.*, 1960, **11**, 102–148.

Hill, H. E., Haertzen, C. A., Wolbach, A. B., Jr., & Miner, E. J. The addiction research center inventory: appendix. I. Items comprising empirical scales for seven drugs. II. Items which do not differentiate placebo from any drug condition. *Psychopharmacologia*, 1963, **4**, 184–205. (a)

Hill, H. E., Haertzen, C. A., Wolbach, A. B., Jr., & Miner, E. J. The addiction research center inventory: standardization of scales which evaluate subjective effects of morphine, amphetamine, pentobarbital, alcohol, LSD-25, pyrahexyl and chlorpromazine. *Psychopharmacologia*, 1963, **4**, 167–183. (b)

Himwich, H. E. (Ed.) *Tranquilizing drugs*. Washington, D.C.: American Association for the Advancement of Science, 1957.

Holland, H. C. Drugs and personality. XII. A comparison of several drugs by flicker-fusion method. *J. ment. Sci.*, 1960, **106**, 858–861.

Holland, H. C., & Gomez, B. H. The effects of stimulant and depressant drugs upon visual aftereffects. In H. J. Eysenck (Ed.), *Experiments with drugs*. New York: Macmillan, 1963. Pp. 255–264.

Hollister, L. E. Placebology: sense and nonsense. *Current therap. Res.*, 1960, **2**, 477–483.

Honigfeld, G. Non-specific factors in treatment. I. Review of placebo reactions and placebo reactors. *Dis. nerv. System*, 1964, **25**, 145–156. (a)

Honigfeld, G. Non-specific factors in treatment. II. Review of social-psychological factors. *Dis. nerv. System*, 1964, **25**, 225–239. (b)

Hull, C. L. The influence of caffeine and other factors on certain phenomena of rote learning. *J. gen. Psychol.*, 1935, **13**, 249–264.

Hull, C. L. *Principles of behavior*. New York: Appleton-Century-Crofts, 1943.

Hulpieu, H. R., & Harger, R. N. The alcohols. In V. A. Drill (Ed.), *Pharmacology in medicine*. (2nd ed.) New York: McGraw-Hill, 1958. Pp. 195–214.

Janet, P. *Les nevroses*. Paris: E. Flammarion, 1909.

Jellinek, E. M. Clinical tests on comparative effectiveness of analgesic drugs. *Biometrics*, 1946, **2**, 87–91.

Joint Commission on Mental Illness and Health. *Action for mental health*. New York: Basic Books, 1961.

Joyce, C. R. B. Consistent differences in individual reactions to drugs and dummies. *Brit. J. Pharmacol. Chemotherap.*, 1959, **14**, 512–521. (a)

Joyce, C. R. B. The personality of healthy reactors and non-reactors to dummy treatments. In P. B. Bradley, P. Deniker, & C. Radouco-Thomas (Eds.), *Neuro-psychopharmacology*. New York: Elsevier, 1959. Pp. 448–452. (b)

Joyce, C. R. B. Experiments with control substances. *Ann. rheumat. Dis.*, 1961, **20**, 78–82.

Jung, C. G. *Psychologische typen*. Zürich: Rascher & Cie, 1921.

Kast, E. C. Alpha-ethyltryptamine acetate in the treatment of depression: a study of the methodology of drug evaluation. *J. Neuropsychiat.*, 1961, **2**, Suppl. 1, S114–S118.

Kelly, E. L., Miller, J. G., Marquis, D. G., Gerard, R. W., & Uhr, L. Continued meprobamate and prochlorperazine administration and behavior. *Arch. Neurol. Psychiat.*, 1958, **80**, 247–252. (a)

Kelly, E. L., Miller, J. G., Marquis, D. G., Gerard, R. W., & Uhr, L. Personality differences and continued meprobamate and prochlorperazine administration. *Arch. Neurol. Psychiat.*, 1958, **80**, 241–246. (b)

Klein, G. S., & Krech, D. Cortical conductivity in the brain injured. *J. Pers.*, 1952, **21**, 118–148.

Klerman, G. L. Assessing the influence of the hospital milieu upon the effectiveness of psychiatric drug therapy: problems of conceptualization and of research methodology. *J. nerv. ment. Dis.*, 1963, **137**, 143–154.

Klerman, G. L., DiMascio, A., Greenblatt, M., & Rinkel, M. The influence of specific personality patterns on the reactions to phenotropic agents. In J. H. Masserman (Ed.), *Biological psychiatry*. New York: Grune & Stratton, 1959. Pp. 224–242.

Klett, C. J., & Caffey, E. M. (Eds.) Newsletter. *Cooperative Stud. Psychiat., Central NP Res. Lab., VAH*, 1963, **7** (3).

Kline, N. S. (Ed.) *Psychopharmacology*. Washington, D.C.: American Association for the Advancement of Science, 1956.

Kline, N. S. Discussion of pharmacological treatment of schizophrenics: classification and terminology. In N. S. Kline (Ed.), *Psychopharmacology frontiers*. Boston: Little, Brown, 1959. Pp. 428–429. (a)

Kline, N. S. (Ed.) *Psychopharmacology frontiers*. Boston: Little, Brown, 1959. (b)

Köhler, W., & Wallach, H. Figural after-effects: an investigation of visual processes. *Proc. Amer. phil. Soc.*, 1944, **88**, 269–357.

Krantz, J. C., Jr., & Carr, C. J. *Pharmacologic principles of medical practice*. Baltimore: Williams & Wilkins, 1961.

Krugman, A. D., Ross, S., Vicino, F. L., & Clyde, D. J. A research note: effects of dextro-amphetamine and meprobamate on problem-solving and mood of aged subjects. *J. Geront.*, 1960, **15**, 419–420.

Lasagna, L., Mosteller, F., von Felsinger, J. M., & Beecher, H. K. A study of the placebo response. *Amer. J. Med.*, 1954, **16**, 770–779.

Lasagna, L., von Felsinger, J. M., & Beecher, H. K. Drug-induced mood changes in man. I. Observations on healthy subjects, chronically ill patients, and "postaddicts." *J. Amer. Med. Ass.*, 1955, **157**, 1006–1020.

Lehmann, H. E. Methods of evaluation of drug effects on the human central nervous system. In F. J. Braceland (Ed.), *The effect of pharmacological agents on the nervous system*. Vol. 37. Baltimore: Williams & Wilkins, 1959. Pp. 126–146.

Lehmann, H. E., & Knight, D. A. The psychopharmacological profile: a systematic approach to the interaction of drug effects and personality traits. *Rev. Canad. Biol.*, 1961, **20**, 525–538.

Lindemann, E., & von Felsinger, J. M. Drug effects and personality theory. *Psychopharmacologia*, 1961, **2**, 69–92.

Lindley, C. J. (Ed.) *Chemotherapy in psychiatry*. Vol. I. Washington, D.C.: Veterans Administration, n. d.

Lindley, C. J. (Ed.) *Chemotherapy in psychiatry*. Vol. II. Washington, D.C.: Veterans Administration, 1958.

Lindley, C. J. (Ed.) *Chemotherapy in psychiatry*. Vol. III. Washington, D.C.: Veterans Administration, 1959.

Lindley, C. J. (Ed.) *Chemotherapy in psychiatry*. Vol. IV. Washington, D.C.: Veterans Administration, 1960. (a)

Lindley, C. J. (Ed.) *Chemotherapy studies in psychiatry and research approaches to mental illness*. Vol. V. Washington, D.C.: Veterans Administration, 1960. (b)

Lindley, C. J. (Ed.) *Chemotherapy studies in psychiatry and research approaches to mental illness*. Vol. VI. Washington, D.C.: Veterans Administration, 1961.

Lorr, M. Rating scales, behavior inventories, and drugs. In L. Uhr & J. G. Miller (Eds.), *Drugs and behavior*. New York: Wiley, 1960. Pp. 519–539.

Lorr, M., Jenkins, R. L., & Holsopple, J. Q. Multidimensional scale for rating psychiatric patients: hospital form. *VA tech. Bull.*, 1953, No. 10–507.

Lorr, M., Klett, C. J., & McNair, D. M. *Syndromes of psychosis*. New York: Macmillan, 1963.

Lorr, M., Klett, C. J., McNair, D. M., & Lasky, J. J. *Inpatient multidimensional psychiatric scale: manual*. Palo Alto, Calif.: Psychological Press, 1963.

Lorr, M., McNair, D. M., Weinstein, G. J., Michaux, W. W., & Raskin, A. Meprobamate and chlorpromazine in psychotherapy. *Arch. gen. Psychiat.*, 1961, **4**, 381–389.

Lorr, M., O'Connor, J. P., & Stafford, J. W. The psychotic reaction profile. *J. clin. Psychol.*, 1960, **16**, 241–245.

Lorr, M., Rubinstein, E. A., & Jenkins, R. L. A factor analysis of personality ratings of outpatients in psychotherapy. *J. abnorm. soc. Psychol.*, 1953, **48**, 511–514.

Lynn, R., & Eysenck, H. J. Some effects of carisoprodol on pain reactivity. In H. J. Eysenck (Ed.), *Experiments with drugs*. New York: Macmillan, 1963. Pp. 324–328.

McDougall, W. *Outline of abnormal psychology*. London: Methuen, 1926.

McDougall, W. The chemical theory of temperament applied to introversion and extraversion. *J. abnorm. soc. Psychol.*, 1929, **24**, 293–309.

Martin, I. The effects of depressant drugs on palmar skin resistance and adaptation. In H. J. Eysenck (Ed.), *Experiments in personality*. Vol. I. *Psychogenetics and psychopharmacology*. New York: Humanities Press, 1960. Pp. 197–224.

Masserman, J. H. (Ed.) *Biological psychiatry*. Vol. 1. New York: Grune & Stratton, 1959.

Miner, R. W. (Ed.) Reserpine (Serpasil) and other alkaloids of Rauwolfia serpentina: chemistry, pharmacology, and clinical application. *Ann. N.Y. Acad. Sci.*, 1954, **59**, Art. 1.

Miner, R. W. (Ed.) Reserpine in the treatment of neuropsychiatric, neurological, and related clinical problems. *Ann. N.Y. Acad. Sci.*, 1955, **61**, Art. 1.

Modell, W. Problems in the evaluation of drugs in men. *J. Pharmacy Pharmacol.*, 1959, **11**, 577–594.

Morison, R. A. H., Woodmansey, A., & Young, A. J. Placebo responses in an arthritis trial. *Ann. rheumat. Dis.*, 1961, **20**, 179–185.

Nowlis, V., & Nowlis, H. H. The description and analysis of mood. *Ann. N.Y. Acad. Sci.*, 1956, **65**, 345–355.

Ostow, M. *Drugs in psychoanalysis and psychotherapy*. New York: Basic Books, 1962.

Overall, J. E., & Gorham, D. R. The brief psychiatric rating scale. *Psychol. Rep.*, 1962, **10**, 799–812.

Overall, J. E., & Gorham, D. R. A pattern probability model for the classification of psychiatric patients. *Behav. Sci.*, 1963, **8**, 108–116.

Overall, J. E., Hollister, L. E., Honigfeld, G., Kimbell, I. H., Jr., Meyer, F., Bennett, J. L., & Caffey, E., Jr. Comparison of acetophenazine with perphenazine in schizophrenics: demonstration of differential effects based on computer-derived diagnostic models. *Clin. Parmacol. Therap.*, 1963, **4**, 200–208.

Overall, J. E., Hollister, L. E., Pokorny, A. D., Casey, J. F., & Katz, G. Drug therapy in depressions. *Clin. Pharmacol. Therap.*, 1962, **3**, 16–22.

Pampiglione, G. *Proc. roy. Soc. Med.*, 1958, **51**, 79–81.

Pavlov, I. P. *Conditioned reflexes*. London: Oxford Univer. Press, 1927.

Pavlov, I. P. *Lectures on conditioned reflexes*. (Tr. by W. H. Gantt.) New York: International Publishers, 1928.

Petrie, Asenath. Some psychological aspects of pain and the relief of suffering. *Ann. N.Y. Acad. Sci.*, 1960, **86**, 13–27.

Pichot, P. L'evaluation des modifications du comportement humain sous l'influence des drogues psychotropes. In E. Rothlin (Ed.), *Neuro-psychopharmacology*. Vol. 2. New York: Elsevier, 1961. Pp. 304–318. (a)

Pichot, P. Structure de la personnalité et appréciation des modifications psychologiques produites par les drogues psychotropes. *Rev. Psych. appl.*, 1961. (b)

Pogge, R. C. The toxic placebo. *Med. Times*, 1963, **91**, 773–778.

Remmen, E., Cohen, S., Ditman, K., & Frantz, J. R. *Psychochemotherapy: the physician's manual*. Los Angeles, Calif.: Western Medical Publications, 1962.

Rinkel, M. (Ed.) *Specific and non-specific factors in psychopharmacology*. New York: Philosophical Library, 1963.

Rinkel, M., & Denber, H. C. B. (Eds.) *Chemical concepts of psychosis*. New York: McDowell, Obolensky, 1958.

Rinkel, M., DiMascio, A., Robey, A., & Atwell, C. Personality patterns and reactions to psilocybine. In E. Rothlin (Ed.), *Neuropsychopharmacology*. New York: Elsevier, 1961.

Rodnight, E., & Gooch, R. N. A new method for the determination of individual differences in susceptibility to a depressant drug. In H. J. Eysenck (Ed.), *Experiments with drugs*. New York: Macmillan, 1963. Pp. 169–193.

Ross, S., & Cole, J. O. Psychopharmacology. *Annu. Rev. Psychol.*, 1960, **11**, 415–438.

Rothlin, E. (Ed.) *Neuro-psychopharmacology.* Vol. 2. New York: Elsevier, 1961.

Sabshin, M., & Ramot, J. Pharmacotherapeutic evaluation and the psychiatric setting. *Arch. Neurol. Psychiat.*, 1956, **75**, 362–370.

Sandifer, M. G., Dunham, R. M., & Howard, K. The reporting and design of research on psychiatric drug treatment: a comparison of two years. In C. J. Lindley (Ed.), *Chemotherapy studies in psychiatry and research approaches to mental illness.* Vol. VI. Washington, D.C.: Veterans Administration, 1961.

Sarwer-Foner, G. J. (Ed.) *The dynamics of psychiatric drug therapy.* Springfield, Ill.: Charles C Thomas, 1960.

Shagass, C. The sedation threshold: a method for estimating tension in psychiatric patients. *EEG clin. Neurophysiol.*, 1954, **6**, 221–233.

Shagass, C. A measurable neurophysiological factor of psychiatric significance. *EEG clin. Neurophysiol.*, 1957, **9**, 101–108. (a)

Shagass, C. A neurophysiological study of schizophrenia. *Congr. Rep. 2nd Int. Congr. Psychiat., Zürich*, 1957, **2.** (b)

Shagass, C. Depression: problems in the classification and treatment. *Missouri Med.*, 1960, **57**, 23–29.

Shagass, C., Azima, H., & Sangowicz, J. Effect of meprobamate in sustained high dosage on the electroencephalogram and sedation threshold. *EEG clin. Neurophysiol.*, 1959, **11**, 275–283.

Shagass, C., & Kerenyi, A. B. Neurophysiologic studies of personality. *J. nerv. ment. Dis.*, 1958, **126**, 141–147.

Shagass, C., & Lipowski, Z. J. Effect of methedrine on critical flicker fusion and its relation to personality and affect. *J. nerv. ment. Dis.*, 1958, **127**, 407–416.

Shagass, C., Naiman, J., & Mihalik, J. An objective test which differentiates between neurotic and psychotic depression. *Arch. Neurol. Psychiat.*, 1956, **75**, 461–471.

Shepherd, M., & Wing, Lorna. Pharmacological aspects of psychiatry. In S. Garattini & P. A. Shore (Eds.), *Advances in pharmacology.* Vol. 1. New York: Academic, 1962. Pp. 227–276.

Shideman, F. E. Sedation, hypnosis, and analgesia. In V. A. Drill (Ed.), *Pharmacology in medicine.* (2nd ed.) New York: McGraw-Hill, 1958. Pp. 137–284.

Sidman, M. Behavioral pharmacology. *Psychopharmacologia*, 1959, **1**, 1–19.

Steinberg, Hannah. Methods and problems of measuring drug-induced changes in emotions and personality. *Rev. Psychol. appl.*, 1961, **11** (spec. no.), 361–372.

Stoll, A., & Hofmann, A. Partialsynthese von Alkaloiden vom Typus des Ergobasins. *Helv. Chim. Acta.*, 1943, **26**, 944–965.

Sylvester, J. Depressant-stimulant drugs, inhibition and the visual constancies. In H. J. Eysenck (Ed.), *Experiments with drugs.* New York: Macmillan, 1963. Pp. 284–309.

Thorpe, J. G., & Barker, J. C. Objectivity of the sedation threshold. *Arch. Neurol. Psychiat.*, 1957, **78**, 194–196.

Treadwell, E. The effects of depressant drugs on vigilance and psychomotor performance. In H. J. Eysenck (Ed.), *Experiments in personality.* Vol. I. *Psychogenetics and psychopharmacology.* New York: Humanities Press, 1960. Pp. 159–196.

Trent, C. L. Changes in the Clyde mood scale produced by a sleep threshold dose of amobarbital. *Psychopharmacologia*, 1962, **3**, 468–472.

Trouton, D. S. Placebos and their psychological effects. *J. ment. Sci.*, 1957, **103**, 344–354.

Tucker, L. R. Scaling and test theory. *Annu. Rev. Psychol.*, 1963, **14**, 351–364.

Uhr, L., & Miller, J. G. (Eds.) *Drugs and behavior.* New York: Wiley, 1960.

von Felsinger, J. M., Lasagna, L., & Beecher, H. K. Drug-induced mood changes in man. II. Personality and reactions to drugs. *J. Amer. Med. Ass.*, 1955, **157**, 1113–1119.

Wendt, G. R., & Cameron, J. S. Chemical studies of behavior. V. Procedures in drug experimentation with college students. *J. Psychol.*, 1961, **51**, 173–211.

Wendt, G. R., Cameron, J. S., & Specht, P. G. Chemical studies of behavior. VI. Placebo and dramamine as methodological controls, and effects on moods, emotions and motivations. *J. Psychol.*, 1962, **53**, 257–279.

Whipple, H. E. (Ed.) New reflections on monoamine oxidase inhibition. *Ann. N.Y. Acad. Sci.*, 1963, **107**, Art. 3.

Whitehorn, J. C., & Betz, Barbara J. A study of psychotherapeutic relationships between physicians and schizophrenic patients. *Amer. J. Psychiat.*, 1954, **111**, 321–331.

Whitehorn, J. C., & Betz, Barbara J. Further studies of the doctor as a crucial variable in the outcome of treatment with schizophrenic patients. *Amer. J. Psychiat.*, 1960, **117**, 215–223.

Whitelock, O. von St. (Ed.) Meprobamate and other agents used in mental disturbances. *Ann. N.Y. Acad. Sci.*, 1957, **67**, Art. 10. (a)

Whitelock, O. von St. (Ed.) The pharmacology of psychotomimetic and psychotherapeutic drugs. *Ann. N.Y. Acad. Sci.*, 1957, **66**, Art. 3. (b)

Whitelock, O. von St. (Ed.) Amine oxidase inhibitors. *Ann. N. Y. Acad. Sci.*, 1959, **80**, Art. 3.

Whitelock, O. von St. (Ed.) Nonnarcotic drugs for the relief of pain and their mechanism of action. *Ann. N.Y. Acad. Sci.*, 1960, **86**, Art. 1.

Wikler, A. *The relation of psychiatry to pharmacology.* Baltimore: Williams & Wilkins, 1957.

Wikler, A. Methodology of research in psychological pharmacodynamics. In J. H. Masserman & J. L. Moreno (Eds.), *Progress in psychotherapy.* Vol. III. New York: Grune & Stratton, 1958. Pp. 212–218.

Willett, R. A. The effects of depressant drugs on learning and conditioning. In H. J. Eysenck (Ed.), *Experiments in personality.* Vol. I. *Psychogenetics and psychopharmacology.* New York: Humanities Press, 1960. Pp. 110–137.

Willett, R. A. The effect of a stimulant and a depressant drug on the serial rote learning of nonsense syllables. *Psychopharmacologia,* 1962, **3**, 23–34.

Williams, M., & McGee, T. F. The bias of the drug administrant in judgments of the effects of psychopharmacological agents. *J. nerv. ment. Dis.*, 1962, **135**, 569–573.

Williams, R. J. *Biochemical individuality.* New York: Wiley, 1956.

Wittenborn, J. R. *Psychiatric rating scales.* New York: Psychological Corporation, 1955.

Wittenborn, J. R. The dimensions of psychosis. *J. nerv. ment. Dis.*, 1962, **134**, 117–128.

Wolf, S. Toxic effects of placebo administration. *Clin. Res. Proc.*, 1953, **1**, 117.

Wolf, S. Human beings as experimental subjects. In S. O. Waife & A. P. Shapiro (Eds.), *The clinical evaluation of new drugs.* New York: Hoeber-Harper, 1959. Pp. 85–99. (a)

Wolf, S. Placebos. In F. J. Braceland (Ed.), *The effect of pharmacologic agents on the nervous system.* Baltimore: Williams & Wilkins, 1959. Pp. 147–161. (b)

Wolf, S. The pharmacology of placebos. *Pharmacol. Rev.*, 1959, **11**, 689–704. (c)

Wolf, S. Placebos: problems and pitfalls. *Clin. Pharmacol. Therap.*, 1962, **3**, 254–257, Part IV.

Wolf, S., Doering, C. R., Clark, M. L., & Hagans, J. A. Chance distribution and the placebo "reactor." *J. lab. clin. Med.*, 1957, **49**, 837–841.

Wolf, S., & Pinsky, R. H. Effects of placebo administration and occurrence of toxic reactions. *J. Amer. Med. Ass.*, 1954, **155**, 339–341.

Wortis, J. W. (Ed.) *Recent advances in biological psychiatry.* Vol. 2. New York: Grune & Stratton, 1960.

Wortis, J. W. (Ed.) *Recent advances in biological psychiatry.* Vol. 3. New York: Grune & Stratton, 1961.

Wortis, J. W. (Ed.) *Recent advances in biological psychiatry.* Vol. 4. New York: Plenum Press, 1962.

Wortis, J. W. (Ed.) *Recent advances in biological psychiatry.* Vol. 5. New York: Plenum Press, 1963.

Zubin, J., & Katz, M. M. Psychopharmacology and personality. In P. Worchel & D. Byrne (Eds.), *Personality change.* New York: Wiley, 1964.

48

Treatment of Personality Disorders in Children

AARON H. ESMAN

GENERAL PRINCIPLES OF THERAPY IN CHILDHOOD

The treatment of emotional disorders of childhood, in the sense in which we understand it today, is a product of the twentieth century. Prior to the rise of the social welfare movements in Europe and the United States and to the catalytic stimulus of psychoanalysis, the management of personality disorders in children had been the province of the correctional agencies of the state, the custodial services for the mentally defective, or the church. Indeed, child psychiatry as a descriptive, let alone a therapeutic, discipline did not exist.

But the winds of change that stirred up, in varying parts of the world, such phenomena as the juvenile court movement, progressive education, and Freud's discoveries of infantile sexuality and psychic determinism uncovered the emotional life of the child and exposed him as a proper subject for psychiatric inquiry and, ultimately, psychiatric therapy. Freud's (1909a) epochal exploration of the mental life of "Little Hans," the first recorded case of the rational psychotherapy of a child, paved the way for what has ultimately burgeoned into the child guidance movement and the practice of child therapy.

Freud's inquiries were rapidly followed by those of his coworkers and followers. Melanie Klein (1939) and Anna Freud (1946) developed their conflicting theories of child analysis in the 1920s, while at the same time Aichorn (1935) was applying psychoanalytic views to the practice of residential treatment of delinquents, an area previously left largely to the police. During this period, the American child guidance clinic, devoted primarily to diagnosis and parent guidance in its early years, also appeared on the horizon.

With the advent of Hitler, America and Britain became the beneficiaries of the work of the many European analysts who had been blazing trails in this tangled forest, and the emphasis in the child guidance field began to shift in the direction of direct psychotherapy of the afflicted child—in all cases directly or indirectly influenced by the seminal conceptions of psychoanalysis. Simultaneously, the field of residential treatment of the recently defined group of childhood psychotics as well as of the traditional class of delinquents came under the aegis of psychoanalysts and psychoanalytically trained educators, and new frontiers were opened in the areas of group process and milieu therapies.

Thus it is apparent, and will be amply exemplified below, that whatever the modality of therapy in question, and irrespective of theoretical divergences and fashions of technique, child therapy and psychoanalysis are inseparably linked in their development and their influence. Their foundations both rest, ultimately, on the rock of developmental evaluation and accurate, flexible application of rational interventions into the pathological developmental process.

All therapy, but particularly that of the emotionally disordered child, must be based on accurate, discriminating, and thoroughgoing diagnosis. This is a truism and is one that has traditionally been honored in the assigning to the child, after a diagnostic study, of a classifying label of one of the classical Kraepelinian categories.

It has become increasingly clear, however, that this is an inadequate basis for effective therapeutic intervention; that is, in addition to understanding the structural factors that underlie the manifestations of illness and the contemporary dynamic forces at work, it is essential that the therapist be aware of the timetable of psychosexual and ego development followed by the patient in question; its correspondence with, and/or divergences from, developmental norms; the role of specific traumatic factors and their timing; the presence and phase-specific character of fixations and precocities; and the progressive unfolding of patterns of interaction between the developing child and his human, animate, and inanimate environments.

As Anna Freud (1962) has pointed out, we are somewhat hampered in respect to this kind of diagnosis by our limited knowledge of developmental norms and of the natural history of pathological processes in children. Which phobic pattern in the 5-year-old is part of the normal process of resolution of the Oedipus complex, for instance, and which betokens fixed neurotic pathology is often beyond our capacity to evaluate prognostically. Obviously, further study along the lines marked out by Miss Freud and those pursued by Kris (1957) and her associates will be necessary to permit completely accurate appraisal of developmental potentialities. Nonetheless, in clinical practice a systematic developmental evaluation is an indispensable prerequisite to any rational therapeutic intervention. Practically, of course, such an evaluation will usually be made *pari passu* with the unfolding of the treatment relationship with both parents and child, and it will in itself be a dynamic process. But each intervention must be assessed in terms of its significance in the developmental evolution of the child's personality.

For it is in this context that one must consider the aims of child therapy. These will necessarily vary according to one's evaluation of the pathology in question, and the therapeutic techniques to be applied in a specific case will largely be determined by one's view of the nature of the underlying conflicts and their dynamic and structural consequences (cf. Ross, 1957). But in all cases, the fundamental aim is to permit the freest possible development along normal lines. In some instances this may be achieved by minimal environmental manipulation, while in others a profound, total-push kind of treatment will prove necessary. In each instance, however, the ultimate aim—that of getting the child back on the developmental track and of removing, as far as possible, insuperable obstacles along the way—is the same. This implies, among other things, that one may allow a considerable amount of current symptomatology to go untreated—if it appears that it is part of a transient developmental crisis and that the child's basic capacity for normal development is not impaired. In such situations, other modalities, as described below, may be utilized in preference to direct psychotherapy of the child.

Experienced child therapists have become aware that only rarely can one terminate treatment in a formal and definitive way. Most frequently the therapist is most effective and useful to the child and his family when he remains available on a "standby" basis, accessible for consultation and for intervention in the most appropriate manner in response to any developmental crisis that may occur, even after the child's formal "treatment" has been officially terminated. This concept of continuous care, analogous to the role of the family doctor or pediatrician, may have great value for the prophylaxis of later disturbances.

The judgments needed for such a role presuppose, of course, a high level of sophistication on the part of the therapist. Who shall treat the child is a question that has occupied the attention of the child guidance field for many years, and it is still unresolved. The first child analysts were lay therapists, such as Anna Freud, Melanie Klein, and others, and it has been their understandable tendency to train other nonmedical personnel in their methods. In the United States, however, the predominant trend in the early years of the child guidance movement was to restrict direct child therapy to the psychiatrist, assigning the psychologist to diagnostic testing and the social worker to parent guidance and, occasionally, to parent treatment. This design, which became known as the "clinical" or "orthopsychiatric" team, has tended in recent years to break down, with less rigid differentiation of roles among members of the team, so that in many clinics both psychologists and social workers function as therapists, though at least nominally under the supervision of psychiatrists. The present situation has been well characterized by Anthony (1959), as follows:

> At the risk of appearing old-fashioned, I would have liked to hear a little more doctoring from the doctors, psychologizing from the psychologists, and socializing from the social workers. Somewhere the team idea is in danger of being wholly lost, and I think we ought to do something about it before it is too late. (I get the feeling that it is already too late in America.) Perhaps, with the march of time, it is being swallowed up along with other traditional and much loved dichotomies and trichotomies of male and female (theory of bisexuality), father and mother (concept of the phallic mother) and (if the countertransference movement really gets going), therapist and patient. If it ever comes to this we must be prepared to fight for our therapeutic rights. Which side of the couch do you belong to, brother?

However one views this arrangement of therapeutic responsibilities, certain qualifications are necessary preconditions for the practice of child therapy. Whatever his discipline, the child therapist must have a thorough grounding in child development and experience in observation of normal and deviant children in normal situations. He must also be thoroughly familiar with the psychoanalytic theory of personality development, structure, and function, and he must be conversant with classic and current literature in the field. He must finally have had extensive supervised experience in the treatment of children in a clinical setting, with a varied range of cases and experiences with parents as well as children. Such training must be on a graduate level, presupposing adequate basic training and some practical experience in the basic clinical discipline.

Beyond all these training requirements, however, the person who proposes to venture into the field of child therapy must possess certain personality characteristics as well. He must be of sufficient maturity and poise to be able to empathize without overidentifying, to permit himself a measure of controlled regression without losing his capacity to observe and interpret, and to endure intense affective pressures without loss of control. He must be able to deal with provocation without being provoked, with seduction without being seduced. It is the rare individual who possesses such resources without having had the experience of personal psychoanalysis. Certainly the self-awareness necessary to preclude countertransference reactions is virtually impossible to achieve without such analytic experience.

Above all, however, the child therapist must possess a genuine interest in children, a sensitive curiosity about what makes them tick, and a willingness to subordinate doctrinaire judgments to actual clinical observation. And he must be willing and able to be completely honest with both his patients and himself.

It must not, however, be thought that the therapist alone can treat a child's personality disorder. The child is, for most of his waking life, in more or less intensive contact with a variety of persons and institutions that have a material influence on his current adaptation. Paramount among these are the family and the school, and it is necessary for the child therapist to be, at the very least, aware of the influences these institutions bring to bear on the child and to consider in all cases the possibility of using these institutions for therapeutic ends.

The school, for instance, is frequently a critical element in the child's life situation. For many children it is the focus of great anxiety, whether direct, as in the case of the child with a learning disorder, or displaced from other sources, as in school phobia. Problems in interpersonal relations characteristically manifest themselves in the child's involvements with his peers at school, and behavioral disturbances often manifest themselves in power struggles between the child and teacher as a displacement from the home. The therapist should, as a matter of course, maintain contact with the school, both as a source of information about the child's functioning and as a possible resource for appropriate modification of the child's reality situation.

Similarly, other community institutions, such as community centers, play groups, scouts, and the like, may frequently be called upon for adjuvant services in certain situations in the child's life. It is for this reason that the clinical team approach is often the most useful one in child therapy, permitting the use of the social worker's knowledge of community resources as an adjunct to therapeutic interventions.

Finally, an introductory word must be said about the role of the parents in child therapy. The recent emphasis in the child psychiatric literature on family diagnosis and family therapy (Ackerman, 1959; Ackerman & Behrens, 1955) is too familiar to require extensive restatement. It is certainly clear that in many, if not most, instances the child's pathology is symptomatic of family disturbance and that treatment of the family unit, either jointly or individually, is the necessary focus of therapeutic action. Like many truths, however, this one threatens to become a cliché, imposing arbitrary and inflexible procedures on clinical personnel. Experience indicates that there are a substantial number of cases in which pathology develops in a child whose family is not demonstrably pathological and that there are others in which treatment of the child alone is not only possible but clinically indicated. Each case, in short, must be evaluated on its own merits, and treatment plans must be devised not on the basis of current fashions or shibboleths but on the basis of sound diagnostic assessment.

MODALITIES OF CHILD THERAPY

In the treatment of the personality disorders of adults, the available modalities can be broadly grouped into those which can be used while the patient is in the community and those which are applicable when the patient requires hospitalization. The wider range of child pathology, bound as it is to the developmental flux of childhood, and the dependence of the child for care and survival on parents or parent surrogates necessitate a broader panoply of services, with more flexible arrangements and, in certain instances, less clearly defined relationship to the community. Thus, for instance, the residential treatment center, occupying an intermediate position, looms large in considerations of resource planning in child psychiatry, and treatment efforts directed at the parents frequently replace those aimed at the child himself. In the following paragraphs, we shall consider the principal treatment modalities customarily used in the management of childhood disorders, with their indications and contraindications, and shall describe certain technical aspects of their practical application. We shall not attempt a complete text of child therapy; reference to the literature will direct the interested reader to more comprehensive treatments of the material under discussion. Needless to say, none of these procedures should be attempted by an untrained professional except under close supervision.

Parent Guidance

Most hallowed by tradition is the approach to the child's disturbance through the intermediary of the parents. Until the advent of psychoanalysis, advice to parents on the part of physicians, clergymen, well-meaning relatives, and others was the principal modality available for the management of those disorders that did not require institutional placement. Even now, with the availability of direct therapeutic techniques, there is still an honorable place in the treatment armamentarium for parent guidance. Indeed, the traditional guidance clinic, as its name implies, relied and continues to rely largely on this method for its therapeutic work.

Parent guidance is defined as that mode of treatment of childhood pathology that involves the directive, educational counseling of one or both parents in techniques of care that will, it is believed, serve either to ameliorate the child's difficulty or to improve the parents' ability to cope with it.

In the first case, parent guidance is predicated on three basic assumptions:

1. That the child's pathology is based on environmental causes which are subject to modification by the parents or that the child's pathology is a response to an acute traumatic experience and can be relieved by proper supportive measures on the part of the parents

2. That the child's pathology is not fixed or internalized and that it is likely to respond to environmental changes

3. That the personality patterns of the parents are sufficiently flexible so that they can modify their ways of relating to the child or other environmental circumstances without suffering excessively severe disruption to their own equilibrium

In the second case, parent guidance is based on the assumption that the child's pathology is profound and fixed and that the parents require help in planning for, and carrying out, its proper management.

Parent guidance of the first type thus finds its most effective application in cases of disturbance in young children, particularly infants and those in the preschool period, with reactive disorders based on faulty child-rearing methods or acute situational traumata (Furman, 1957; Jacobs, 1949). In such cases the therapist, operating within the framework of a positive transference, attempts to clarify for the parent (most often the mother) the connections between the child's difficulties and the particular parental patterns that appear to be pathogenic, and he tries to help the parent to develop more effective ways of managing the relationship.

> Johnny, a 4-year-old boy, was the source of great concern to his parents because of his extremely aggressive behavior. He constantly attacked other children, was completely unable to play with them, often bit and spat at them, and was defiant to his mother. He also had nightmares and separation anxiety. His mother noted that his difficulties had become prominent shortly after the birth of a younger sister when he was 2½. Mrs. L, normally an easygoing and gentle person, was harassed by the competing demands of Johnny, his older sister Sally and the baby. She became irritable and authoritarian, demanding rather rigid compliance along lines laid down by her loving but somewhat obsessional husband. Johnny, faced with the problems of sharing his mother with an unwanted sibling and pressured into unwelcome conformity, became angry, displacing rage to peers and manifesting intense anxiety about abandonment and retaliatory punishment. Mrs. L was advised to lower her demands on Johnny, to permit more open expression of aggression at home, and to devote more time and attention to this child of whom she was basically very fond. Within two months Johnny's aggressiveness had subsided considerably, and his night fears, though not completely gone, had also moderated considerably, so that his parents were able to get an occasional night's sleep.

It must be emphasized, however, that such an approach requires a thorough evaluation of the child's developmental history and present emotional status as well as a searching scrutiny of the parent-child relationship. It can be applied only where there is evidence of flexibility on the part of the parent and where the therapist-parent relationship is itself one that allows for considerable directness and frankness in the guidance process. The mother must not, as Furman points out, have too great a stake in the child's pathology to allow for its modification or be limited to passive submission to, or imitation of, the therapist, only to revert to old patterns once treatment has ended. These problems can, unfortunately, not always be anticipated in advance.

Another type of case suitable for this approach is, as indicated above, the acute reaction to traumatic circumstances in a young child.

> Nancy, age 15 months, was hospitalized following an acute respiratory infection that led to closure of the larynx and emergency tracheotomy. Secondary pneumonia and the sequelae of the operation kept her, a previously warm, sunny and responsive toddler, hospitalized for a month. Her mother was in the hospital with her continuously throughout, as were several of her most treasured possessions. On her return home, she appeared fearful, woke repeatedly at night screaming and apparently confused, seemed to lack her old sparkle and was very timid with everyone outside her immediate family. Nancy's parents, an unusually sensitive, insightful and devoted couple, had already instituted certain necessary procedures; Mrs. R was devoting herself extensively to Nancy, while Mr. R was continuing the concentration on her older brother he had begun during Nancy's (and the mother's) hospitalization. They regularly reassured her that she was home to stay and that the sore place on her neck would go away, verbalizing her fears and concerns for her whenever possible. The therapist in this instance directed his attention primarily to the night fears, advising the parents that they respond immediately to Nancy's call and attempt to arouse her fully when she woke, rather than leaving her in a confused half-waking state. He reassured them that their approach was a generally sound one, and advised continuing in it. Nancy gradually but quickly responded, so that within a month her symptoms had largely subsided and she was well on the way to restoration of her previous personality.

The second group of cases for which parent guidance is indicated in certain instances is that of chronically impaired children—the organically damaged, mentally defective, or severely psychotic—where direct treatment is unfeasible or inappropriate or where the two processes are carried on concurrently. The objectives of such guidance procedures include helping the parent to grasp and accept the nature of the child's disorder; to learn modes of relating to, and coping with, such a child; and/or to plan for placement or other management measures. In cases such as these, a great deal of support is obviously necessary in addition to pure guidance procedures. In some cases group guidance methods have proved effective (Bauer & Gurevitz, 1952; Beck, 1952; Peck, Rabinovitch, & Cramer, 1949). In all cases, the narcissistic injury to the parents that such handicapped children cause must be given sensitive consideration; it characteristically represents the major difficulty to be overcome and the major focus of resistance in the therapeutic work.

Psychotherapy of the Child

There are many approaches to the psychotherapy of the child. Each therapist necessarily develops his own style, dependent on his own training and his own personality characteristics. Over the years, however, certain consistent lines of approach have emerged, geared in most instances to particular types of pathology and particular situational and cultural contexts. It must again be stressed that the application of one or another technique must be based on a thorough evaluation of the child's disturbance and of the familial, social, and cultural situations in which it has developed.

Release therapy. Levy (1938; 1939) has described a therapeutic technique based essentially on the early psychoanalytic principle of abreaction, or "emotional release." It involves the recreation in the therapeutic situation of the postulated traumatic situation which the therapist believes has engendered the child's disturbance, thereby permitting the child to express the emotions called up but repressed at the time and to achieve control over them, not only by expressing them, but also by replacing passive experience with active mastery (S. Freud, 1909b). This description makes it immediately evident that this technique is specifically indicated for acute traumatic disturbances, specific either to a single trauma or to the consequence of a particular type of traumatic interaction, where severe parental pathology does not exist and where the child is capable of verbal communication. It may or may not be combined with some guidance of the parents. It is usually a short-term procedure and is directed toward specific symptomatology of a rather discrete nature in most instances.

Implied, too, in Levy's description of his cases and his method is the requirement that the child be sufficiently well organized that his personality structure can withstand relatively direct confrontation with instinctual conflict material, without preparatory interpretation of defenses. This means that the diagnostic appraisal must be a careful one and that the therapist who wishes to use this method must be skilled in rapid evaluation of ego structure.

In Levy's view, release therapy is of particular value as a preventive measure, reinforcing or furthering normal developmental tendencies and seeking to avert premature consolidation of maladapative modes of response to traumatic experiences.

Supportive or relationship therapy. It is axiomatic in all psychotherapeutic procedures that the relationship between the patient and the therapist is the focus of the dynamic interactions that bring about change. From the pioneer investigations of Freud, we have learned of the power of the transference, the significance of countertransference, and the role of such elements as suggestion, identification, and the like in the therapeutic process.

There are certain types of therapy that employ the patient-therapist relationship itself as the principal, if not the sole, lever of therapy. In these approaches, little concern is given to interpretative interventions of the types used in child analysis and analytically oriented therapies (see sections below). Reliance is placed on the dynamic effect of various maneuvers in the relationship or on the supportive value that a positive, friendly contact with another human being (in our case, an adult) can have to a person who is troubled, confused, unhappy, or in need or who is suffering the consequences of disordered human relationships.

It is, again, axiomatic that the application of such therapeutic measures as will be detailed here requires a thorough dynamic understanding of the patient, his problem, and his human context. As in any mode of direct child-therapist interaction, concomitant work with parents will frequently, if not always, be necessary.

One of the most dramatic occasions for the use of a relationship therapy is in the severe disorders of infancy, such as those described by Spitz (1945), Ribble (1943), R. Lourie (1955), Provence and Lipton (1963), and others, in which the infant manifests the affective and developmental consequences of severe deprivation of mothering contact, particularly in the second half of the first year. Obviously verbal therapy is inapplicable in such cases; the child's need is for replenishment of the supplies of tactile, thermal, kinesthetic, and affective experience that have been missing. Such therapy can be carried out by almost anyone who is emotionally qualified to do so; no professional training is required, but an ample supply of warmth, interest, and concern is necessary. Holding the child during feedings and playing with him or carrying him about for a few hours a day serve, if done by one person who devotes himself consistently to the child, to redress the developmental lags that accompany severe affect deprivation in infancy.

Less dramatic but equally significant from the theoretical and practical standpoints are those cases of maternal deprivation seen during the preschool period, in which conventional psychotherapies have proved useless. For such children, many of whom appear to be psychotic or even autistic and who have in their histories prolonged experience of deprivation of maternal care as a result either of the loss of the mother and absence of an adequate substitute or of the emotional unavailability of the mother due to her own psychopathology, Alpert (1959; 1963; Alpert & Pfeiffer, 1963) has developed a therapeutic technique called "corrective object relations" (COR). In this technique the child is assigned to a "special teacher," who devotes herself to the child for an hour a day, four or five times a week. The child is permitted the opportunity to regress in the setting of an exclusive, need-satisfying relationship to the level of traumatic fixation. Gratification at this level, afforded without stint, encourages the establishment of "basic trust" (Erikson, 1961) and, in certain instances, permits a reversal of the developmental pathology, with progressive development ensuing and being similarly supported by the therapist. The child's verbalizations are used as clues but are not employed as the basis of communicated interpretations; rather, they are used as guides to the therapist's support and management of the regressive and progressive processes that occur during the course of the corrective relationship.

In those cases in which this method has proved successful, therapy has generally lasted from seven to nine months. In some instances it has been followed by more conventional, interpretative therapies. It will be noted that this technique is in many ways similar to that employed by Sechehaye (1951) with an adolescent psychotic girl.

It becomes apparent, then, that a major indication for therapy based primarily on relationship factors is severe impairment of the ego, affecting particularly the functions of object relations, reality testing, and verbal communication. In such cases, where the interpretation of unconscious conflict is of less significance than the provision of an atmosphere that will encourage ego growth and compensate for earlier experiences of deprivation, a variety of measures, ranging from active encouragement, reassurance, and clarification of reality to such total experiences as "symbolic realization," may be employed with profit. The therapist must in all cases be consistently accepting without being excessively permissive and must be firmly based in reality but ready to allow such regressive behavior as does not appear to undermine the child's fragile ego structure. The primary goal is the establishment of an object relationship that has the potentiality of progressing beyond the level of need satisfaction to that of true object constancy.

It is this aim—the establishment of a meaningful relationship—that is the basis for another major indication for this approach, that of the introductory phase of treatment of the severe behavior disorders of latency and their successors, the character disorders of adolescence. Eissler (1950), van Ophuijsen (1945), Aichorn (1935), and others have demonstrated the futility of attempting interpretative, verbal forms of therapy with aggressive, impulsive, suspicious children until a foundation has been laid down in the form of a relationship that will bear the strains of the child's limited frustration tolerance, rage reactions, and exploitative tendencies. As Eissler points out in his discussion of treatment of adolescent delinquents, much ingenuity and a certain measure of role playing may be needed in the preparatory, relationship-building phases of such therapy.

Allen (1942) describes a therapeutic approach which, in some quarters, is considered largely a relationship-centered, supportive therapy. Emphasizing the "creative" and self-restorative capacities of the patient, Allen, following the teaching of Rank, directs attention to the present problem, minimizing the genetic aspects and attempting through the establishment of a "projective identification" with the therapist to encourage him to "differentiate" himself and realize his own untapped resources. Interpretation, in the psychoanalytic sense, is not utilized; the therapist's interventions concern "what the individual can do about what . . . is wrong." Allen's view of the indications for this type of therapy is a broad one and includes all types of psychopathology.

Child analysis. In his classic paper *Analysis of a Phobia in a Five-year Old Boy,* Freud (1909a) demonstrated the possibility of applying a modified psychoanalytic method of treatment to an emotional disturbance in a child. Operating from this base, Anna Freud and Melanie Klein proceeded to develop two widely divergent treatment methods, each designating itself as child analysis. In the United States, Anna Freud's theoretical and practical approach has been by far the more influential, and our discussion of child analysis will concern itself with techniques that follow the lines she has delineated. The Kleinian system will also be described in less extensive detail.

Child analysis sets as its goal, as the analysis of adults does, the modification of the personality of the patient, and thus the relief of his symptoms, through systematically uncovering the unconscious elements of his mental activity and communicating them to him in verbal form. The objective of this procedure is so to strengthen the ego, vis-à-vis the superego on one hand and the id drives on the other, that it can function autonomously and with maximal adaptive efficiency (Kramer & Settlage, 1962). The theoretical foundations for child analysis are set forth by Anna Freud, while valuable technical contributions have been offered by many of her students and followers (Bornstein, 1945; Fraiberg, 1951; Mahler, 1945).

As in all child therapies, the approach to the child must be modified from that used with adults in order to meet the developmental characteristics of the immature patient. Thus in child analysis one meets the young child's inability to contribute verbal free associations by making use of his nonverbal communications, particularly those represented by his play activities and his drawings, as well as any verbal elements that he can offer in the form of fantasies and other types of communications. The Freudian child analyst makes use of these communications to derive inferences concerning the child's affects, defenses, and conflicts. These are communicated in turn to the child, emphasis being directed, as in adult analysis, at his ego defenses and their underlying affective states, at transference phenomena, and at resistances before instinctual conflicts are brought into consciousness.

It is in this respect that Freudian and Kleinian techniques differ most extensively. Kleinian child analysis directs itself to the child's instinctual life almost exclusively, bypassing ego elements and treating play activities and fantasies as free associations subject to direct symbolic interpretation. Similarly, where the Freudian analyst makes extensive use of information derived from corollary sources (parents, schools, etc.) and relates his constructions and interpretations to his knowledge of the child's life situation, the Kleinian analyst tends to ignore the external life of the child, concentrating exclusively on what he considers transference manifestations or his theoretically derived interpretations of the child's play activities. Thus, in the classic illustration, if a 5-year-old boy plays with two toy cars, constantly banging them into each other, the Kleinian would immediately interpret this to the child as a representation of his fantasies about his mother and father having sexual intercourse, while the Freudian analyst would attempt to elicit from the child some information concerning recent experiences that might have stimulated such play—anxiety-laden or excited observation of an actual collision, angry feelings toward a sibling, or something else—that would be more immediately available to the child's own awareness, even though the Freudian analyst might also consider that the primal scene fantasy might be operative at the deepest unconscious level. The Freudian, then, seeks to relate himself to the child's immediate conscious or preconscious experience and, through systematic interpretation of affects and defenses, to reach unconscious material, while the Kleinian goes directly to what he regards as the unconscious fantasy.

Freudian critiques of Kleinian methods are numerous (Bornstein, 1945; Glover, 1945; Zetzel, 1956). In general, Freudians consider Kleinian techniques a species of "wild" analysis which ignores the fruits of over thirty years of work in the field of ego psychology and which is potentially dangerous in its precocious confrontation of the child with his deepest unconscious impulses and conflicts, however correctly interpreted. Those interested in detailed expositions of Kleinian theory and methodology are referred to works by Isaacs (1952), Rosenfeld (1959), Segal (1964), and above all Klein (1961).

The child analyst must come to his work with a thorough grounding in the theory and technique of psychoanalysis with adults, a knowledge of normal child development, and specialized training in the application of the psychoanalytic method to children of various developmental phases. He must be prepared to give a great deal more of himself as a person than he is accustomed to do in the adult analytic situation and to allow considerably more gratification to his child patients than to his adults, in the form of food (Haworth & Keller, 1962), Christmas and birthday gifts, self-revelations, and even home visits, without being influenced by overidentification or other countertransference responses to transcend the bounds of the analytic relationship.

In child analysis the patient is seen four to five times a week. Depending on his age and general level of maturation, he is permitted to play and/or is encouraged to talk about his thoughts and feelings, but play is used not for catharsis or "release" but as a means of establishing a relationship with the child and as a vehicle for observing the nature of his defenses, adaptive functions, and fantasies. Transference and resistance manifestations are interpreted to the child in language he is capable of understanding and in a manner which he will be able to accept. Interpretations are frequently, especially with younger children, couched in stories or metaphors or in the third-person plural ("Some children feel . . ."). As the child passes into later latency, play begins to be a less conspicuous mode of communication, and his greater verbal facility permits him to deal more directly with, and with greater sustained attention to, the actual therapeutic work. At puberty and in early adolescence, the increased pressure of instinctual drives may induce some hyperactivity and diminish frustration tolerance; at this age some activity is often a necessary adjunct to the verbal communication, particularly since at this phase resistance to treatment is frequently at its most intense.

From mid-adolescence, technique is much like that used with adults, with certain modifications in the direction of greater presence on the part of the analyst (Erikson, 1958). In general, it is of the essence to design the technical approach to the phase of ego and instinctual development of the specific child under consideration; no universal prescription can deal with the protean range of individual variations seen in children.

As is apparent, child analysis is a technique of treatment that demands much of all concerned—child, therapist, and parents. The ego resources of the child must be at least sufficient to permit him to communicate verbally and to sustain a relationship which will become intense and which will undergo many vicissitudes. The parents in their turn must be prepared to accept the demands on their time—and, frequently, on their financial resources—that so intensive a form of treatment requires. They must also be able at least to cooperate with the therapist to the extent of providing necessary information about the child's past and present life situations and to avoid doing things that will grossly undermine the treatment. They must also be able to permit their child to involve himself in an intense relationship with another adult from which, to a considerable degree, they will be excluded.

Thus the indications for child analysis must necessarily be somewhat restrictive (Bernstein, 1957; A. Freud, 1946). Generally speaking, analysis is the treatment of choice for children with chronic neuroses or behavior disorders based on neurotic conflict. It is relatively contraindicated for children with little internalization of conflict or with severe ego disorders of the developmental type. Parents, too, must be fairly well organized and must be willing and able to participate to the necessary degree and to commit themselves to what will in most cases be a prolonged and rigorous course (Bernstein, 1958). In the older child and adolescent, who can inform us of much that is pertinent in his life himself and who is less dependent on his parents, treatment can often proceed relatively apart from parental participation; indeed, it is frequently the objective of the adolescent analysis to aid the child in separating himself from regressive ties to the parents (Blos, 1962).

Psychoanalytic psychotherapy. The boundaries of psychoanalytic psychotherapy have never been clearly delineated. Between pure relationship and manipulative therapy, on the one hand, and classical child analysis, on the other, lies a vast borderland in which a wide range of therapeutic practices flourish, not always well adapted to the needs of the population served therein. The literature dealing with this area is bewilderingly profuse, and innumerable variations of fundamental techniques have been proposed to meet varying clinical conditions (Lippman, 1956).

In general, psychoanalytic psychotherapy can be said to comprise all therapeutic approaches based on psychoanalytic understanding of the pathology and its development that utilize limited interpretations of preconscious or unconscious conflicts, along with greater or lesser degrees of supportive and directive measures, parent guidance and/or treatment, environmental manipulation, and the like, to achieve limited therapeutic goals. These may include symptom removal, behavioral modification, and interpersonal conflict resolution. Attention is focused on specific areas, rather than being widespread, as in child analysis, and in most instances interpretations are more superficial and less systematic (Bernstein, 1957).

It is obviously impossible to discuss all the variations in therapeutic technique subsumed under the designation of psychoanalytic psychotherapy. I shall limit myself to describing the indications for this mode of approach and shall refer to a few of the more important variants commonly employed in clinical practice.

Broadly speaking, psychoanalytic psychotherapy is indicated for those cases of psychoneurosis and primary behavior disorder that either are not severe enough to warrant psychoanalysis or cannot, for one reason or another, make use of it. Among the conditions included here are the acute neurotic reactions of a situational nature, chronic neuroses where the parents cannot comply with the requirements of analysis, severe behavior disorders of latency and adolescence where the demands of analysis transcend the child's capacity to tolerate delay of gratification or his ability to sustain a relationship, and the borderline and psychotic disorders, where extensive ego deficits make participation in a classical analytic relationship impossible (Rank, 1949).

It must be emphasized in all these cases not only that the treatment is properly guided by psychoanalytic principles and psychoanalytic understanding of the structural, dynamic, and genetic aspects of the problem, but also that in particular circumscribed areas, psychoanalytically informed interpretations may be utilized with considerable effect, provided they are appropriately timed (Anthony, 1964). In psychotherapy, however, they are more frequently founded on educated guesses than on solidly founded clinical inference from abundant material, and often data from parents and other accessory sources must be used in preference to material derived directly from the child.

> Susan, a very bright 8-year old, was brought for treatment because of nightmares, difficulties in school largely relating to her indifference and her need to talk in class, and intense and unremitting clashes with her mother about innumerable mundane details of life, like dressing in the morning, going to bed, combing her hair, etc. Significant in the history was an extremely close relationship with her father, whose behavior with her had been seductive and stimulating. Susan's general adaptation was quite sound; there were no indications of ego disorder. Diagnosis of primary behavior disorder with neurotic traits was made, and, particularly in view of Susan's eagerness to get rid of her terrifying nightmares, analysis was recommended. Her parents were not in a position immediately to accept this recommendation, however, and so Susan was taken into psychotherapy on a provisional basis, with the objective of alleviating her acute anxiety and attempting to promote her progress into latency. She immediately brought in accounts of her nightmares, relating vividly the images of gorillas coming to carry her away and her pre-sleep fantasies of kidnappers. She quite spontaneously associated to the gorilla her hirsute father, and it was easy at a very early phase of treatment to interpret oedipal conflict quite directly, relating it at the same time to her struggles with her mother. The excit-

ing quality of these struggles also came out very readily in her own associations. Little attention was given overtly to transference manifestations; a fairly positive relationship existed throughout the course of therapy.

Within a few months Susan's nightmares had disappeared. She began to show greater interest in schoolwork, along with a contemptuous disdain for childish activities as her rivalry with her mother shifted in the direction of an exaggerated identification. Though she still had some mild difficulty in falling asleep there were no further forays into the parental bedroom, and the general tone of the home atmosphere was greatly improved.

It was recognized that there had been no basic alteration in Susan's personality, and that at another developmental transition symptoms might again arise. It seemed, however, that a successful movement into latency had been fostered by interpretation of her oedipal conflicts, facilitated considerably by shifts in her mother's attitudes deriving from her own concurrent analysis, and that it was appropriate to interrupt treatment with the understanding that it could be resumed at any point necessary in the future.

This case illustrates some of the basic elements in psychoanalytic psychotherapy: it is goal-directed; it may be of relatively short duration; it utilizes focused interpretation in the context of a basically positive transference; it may often (as this case was not) be associated with direct environmental manipulations and other types of active intervention; it is frequently most successful when the parent or parents are concurrently in therapy (Mrs. B was seen by Susan's therapist for informational purposes only at weekly intervals for the first few months, and after that, irregular but frequent telephone contact was maintained); and it is properly considered to be "interrupted" rather than "terminated" at strategic points of development.

Psychotherapy of the psychotic child. Virtually every therapist who works seriously with psychotic and borderline children becomes aware in time of the necessity for modifying the basic psychotherapeutic technique to meet the special conditions obtaining in these disorders, i.e., the specific ego defects from which such children suffer. Conventional psychotherapies, which depend on normal capacities for verbal communication, reality testing, and impulse control, are obviously inapplicable to children for whom primary-process modes of thought and communication, inextricable penetration of fantasy into reality, and disorganized motor activity are the characteristic features of their illness.

As indicated earlier in this chapter, most workers in this field agree on the use of the child-therapist relationship as a therapeutic lever as the mode of treatment approach. Whatever the theoretical bent, from those who see the disorder as a basically organic one (Bender, 1947a) to those who view it as a consequence of severe maternal deprivation and/or inconsistency (Rank, 1949), all are agreed on the necessity of providing the child with a warm, consistent, accepting relationship in which he can behave as he must without fear of rejection, punishment, or object destruction. This is the sine qua non of treatment of the psychotic, and this basically relationship mode may go on for months or years before any verbal, interpretative therapy is instituted or may be used in place of such therapy (Rank, 1949).

Beyond this point, however, certain divergences occur. There are many therapists who believe that in the context of this sort of relationship, the child should be allowed virtually complete freedom to regress and act out any and all impulses so that he will attain a sense of total acceptance on the most primitive level as a precondition for progressive development. The therapist "follows" the child into his fantasies (Ekstein & Wallerstein, 1956), seeking to set up communication with him at whatever level of thought and reality evaluation is possible; the primary and crucial aim is to make contact with the child.

There are, however, others who take a somewhat different view. They consider the therapist's function to be primarily that of a representative of reality and a source of ego support. Such therapists (Des Lauriers, 1962) consider it essential that controls of a benign but firm sort be imposed on the child's regressive trends and that the therapist repeatedly and aggressively reflect to the child realistic standards of behavior and realistic assessment of his fantasy productions. This role of the auxiliary ego is identified with by the child and helps to repair the ego fragmentation typical of these children.

All variants of these approaches have been employed and advocated by various therapists

(Furman, 1956; Geleerd, 1958; Mahler & Gosliner, 1955). It is probable that variations in the particular types of psychotic children treated and/or their age, class, sex, and other variants dictate these varied recommendations as much as theoretical preferences do. The basic theme that runs throughout is the necessity to establish a stable relationship in which the child feels totally accepted and in the matrix of which ego growth can occur. Verbal interpretation of unconscious conflicts and symbolic communications takes second place and is frequently reserved for a period in treatment when ego growth and repair have already taken place [see the excellent review by Ekstein, Bryant, and Friedman, (1958)].

In cases of such severe pathology, prognosis is, of course, guarded. The therapist who chooses to treat such children must be prepared for a very long course of treatment, with many frustrations and much regressive behavior, which he must be sufficiently flexible and devoted to be able to accept (Christ, 1964).

Residential treatment. The great majority of emotionally disturbed children can and should be treated in the community, in close proximity to their normal environment and in contact and collaboration with parents and other significant figures in their everyday lives. There is, however, a substantial group of such children who cannot, for a variety of reasons, be so managed. For them a number of institutional settings have been devised over the years that offer—or purport to offer—one or another type of residential treatment.

The indications for residential treatment cover a wide range of pathology but tend to center on those children whose behavior is marked by a tendency toward the living out of their impulses and conflicts in ways that cannot be tolerated by the community or by their families. Such children include the intractable delinquent, whether of the neurotic or antisocial type, and the severely psychotic child, as well as children with less aggravated degrees of pathology whose family situations are so pathological as to require separation of the parties involved and protective care for the child during the period in which he cannot assume responsibility for his own management.

Among the latter type are some of those children, described by Johnson and Szurek (1952), in whom the acting-out behavior is fostered and sanctioned by the parents, either consciously or, more often, unconsciously. Others in this group are children whose parents are involved in intense marital conflicts or in whose families there is gross disorganization of role patterns (Esman, Kohn, & Nyman, 1959) that impairs the child's capacity to test reality or to develop a sense of self and where it is believed that such patterns are intractable to modification, at least while the child remains in the home as a focus for the parental acting out.

The objective of residential treatment as presently conceived by most authorities in this field is to provide "a setting in which the child's total experience is healthful as well as healing . . ." (Alt, 1960). This involves the design and implementation of a program that engages the child at every hour in situations that are intended to support his ego strengths, to reinforce his ego weaknesses (Redl & Wineman, 1952), and to enable him, through constructive interactions with adults and with peers, to develop new and more effective modes of behavior. It should be evident, therefore, that residential treatment means more than psychotherapy in a residential institution. It means the use of the milieu itself as a therapeutic instrument, leading to constructive identification and improved adaptation.

Types of residential treatment institutions. The variety of residential treatment institutions is as great as the range of disorders served therein and the philosophies of those who plan and direct them. Broadly, however, they can be divided into two types: hospitals and residential treatment centers.

Child psychiatry inpatient settings in hospitals range from short-term diagnostic centers to long-term custodial institutions such as those found in certain state hospitals. In neither of these settings is one likely to find residential treatment as presently defined (Noshpitz, 1962). One is more likely to find it in those small units located in general hospitals or psychiatric training centers where the freedom to select patients and to retain limited numbers for long periods permits the intensive programming necessary for the total care needed by the severely disturbed children for whom hospitalization is required.

Ordinarily, only the most disturbed children are placed in hospital wards. They are those who require the greatest degree of externally imposed structure as well as medical management which may involve intensive drug therapy as part of the total program. Severely psychotic children, brain-damaged children, children with suicidal and/or homicidal trends, chronic fire setters, and other grossly destructive children are generally those included, though, of course, some experimental settings may have populations of other sorts. Treatment programs for such units have been described by Benjamin and Howard (1947), Curran (1939), Gordon and Siegel (1957), Szurek (1947), Toolan (1955), and others. (For a discussion of the day hospital, see Day-care Programs, below.)

Residential treatment centers have traditionally concerned themselves with the care of delinquent adolescents; they grew out of the old correctional schools and, under the aegis of Aichorn and others, developed therapeutic milieu programs which, in many cases under the influence of psychoanalytic teachings, became infused with greater or lesser degrees of psychotherapeutic services. During the past two or three decades, the residential treatment concept has been extended to include the care of children with severe disorders of ego development—the psychotic or so-called "schizophrenic" child.

The treatment center for the psychotic child, whether of latency age (Bettelheim, 1950; Goldfarb, 1961) or adolescence (Alt, 1955), aims at providing a milieu which will offer to the child with severe ego disorders a life structure that will compensate for his own ego defects and an opportunity for a corrective type of object relationship that will serve to undo postulated deficiencies in this area in the child's early development. The "therapist" may be an untrained but intuitively sensitive nonprofessional (Orthogenic School), a highly skilled psychiatric social worker (Linden Hill), or a psychoanalytically oriented psychiatrist (Ittleson Center). In any event, the aim is the same: to provide a total life structure in which the psychotic ego can be reformed. In some cases, the distinction between the child who needs hospital care and the child who will be manageable in such institutions is hard to make; the decision is often based on such nonclinical factors as availability of service, economic considerations, special research interests, etc. Other variations relate to the degree of involvement of parents (ranging from Bettelheim's preference for almost complete separation to Goldfarb's insistence on almost total involvement).

In every residential institution certain basic principles of organization obtain. A panoply of therapeutic services, including schooling (Hirschberg, 1953), group recreational and group therapy programs (Goldsmith, 1958; Konopka, 1955), psychotherapy, pharmacotherapy, nursing, and/or child-care arrangements all must be built in both physically and in terms of program and personnel. The institution must meet as many of the child's needs as possible and must provide a milieu as close to that of a normal family organization as the patients' pathology and the realities of institutional design will permit.

It is essential to be aware of the role of the institution itself in the therapeutic process (Gardner, 1952). The child's treatment does not begin and end with his daily or weekly hour with his psychotherapist. It is his experiences and interactions with the total personnel of the institution and his peers that more frequently are critical in determining the outcome of his stay (N. Lourie & Schulman, 1952). This implies the necessity for all personnel, even those ostensibly involved in routine custodial tasks, to be aware of their roles in the milieu and the possibilities for therapeutic and nontherapeutic contact (Bettelheim & Wright, 1955).

The design of the institution will, of course, vary greatly according to the nature of the cases served; the history of its growth and development; and the attitudes, experiences, and personalities of those responsible for it. Although it is generally considered preferable for the institution to be small enough so that it can be easily supervised by the principal administrator, at least one major institution has functioned with a considerable measure of success with a far greater case load and staff population than are generally considered ideal (Alt, 1960). The trend, since the days of Aichorn, has been in the direction of open institutions with only the most essential security arrangements, but this must also often be modified to meet community or other pressures. All such considerations, however, will have significant influence on clinical practice and patterns of institutional life.

Finally, attention must be directed to the influence of the institutional peer culture. Recent studies have shown that this may be of far greater significance in shaping the outcome of the program than any other single factor (Bettelheim & Sylvester, 1947; Polsky, 1963). Particularly in those institutions serving a delinquent population, the peer culture may quickly come to approximate that in which the child's pathology flowered; administrative and therapeutic manipulation of this element in the institutional structure cannot be taken for granted and must be based on a clear and unclouded awareness of the nature of the patterns actually occurring.

The role of the therapist in the institution. In certain respects the role of the therapist in the institution deviates from the classical model of the psychoanalytic therapist. Usually a member of the institutional staff with a number of administrative, clinical, and perhaps investigative responsibilities, he is of necessity a more real figure to his patients than the therapist in noninstitutional practice. This set of circumstances has given rise to a number of practical problems, which in turn have led to a variety of structural arrangements designed to meet them (Noshpitz, 1962; Greenwood, 1955).

Perhaps the most difficult of the problems in question has been that of the conflict between therapist and administrator roles. It has often seemed that the necessity of making administrative decisions, relating to such issues as passes, discharges, on-ground privileges, etc., imposes a strain on the therapist's ability to deal with transference-countertransference issues; it makes him, for example, too real an authority figure in the child's life to permit a separation of reality issues from transference distortions.

Following the lead of some adult institutions, certain workers in the residential treatment field have sought to meet this problem by an institutionalized role separation, with one psychiatrist assuming the administrative role and another assuming the therapeutic role for each patient (Bloch & Silber, 1957). Others, however, regard this dichotomy as unnecessary and unrealistic, viewing the child's capacity to cope with this problem as a measure of his adaptive and ethical resources.

In any event, it is apparent that the therapist, in order to be truly effective, must be integrated into the operational structure of the institution. He must be aware not only of the content of the formal therapy "hour" but also of all details of the child's adaptation to the institution; of his peer relationships and his role in the peer culture; and of his relations with child-care personnel, teachers, group workers, and other significant adults. The psychotherapy must, that is, be a part of the total therapeutic design, and the therapist must be able so to relate himself to other staff members as to play his appropriate role therein (Gordon & Siegel, 1957). Beyond this, however, he must be prepared to relinquish his isolation from the child's everyday life experience (Noshpitz, 1957), and to intervene immediately in response to specific incidents, rather than waiting until the passage of time has clouded the immediate affective significance and even the factual data of the incident for the child with what Redl and Wineman (1952) call the "evaporation of self-contributed links in the causal chain." Redl's concept of the "life-space interview" represents an enormously valuable contribution to the technique of residential treatment.

Day-care Programs

Relatively new in the realm of treatment designs are the day-care programs for emotionally disturbed children. Deriving to a considerable extent from Cameron's (1958) experiments with the day hospital and from efforts at extension of the services of certain specialized schools for severely disturbed children, these newly developed services aim to provide a total treatment program for children who are able to live at home but who cannot function in the usual community resources and who require, in addition to specialized educational and recreational programs, therapeutic services of various kinds. Day-care centers may be found associated with psychiatric hospitals (Connell, 1961; LaVietes, Hulse, & Blau, 1960), residential treatment centers, or special schools, or they may be quite autonomous (Alt, 1955).

The rise of the day-care center is predicated on the increasing appreciation of the value of normal homelife situations for children and of the damaging consequences that unnecessary institutionalization may have on child development. It is also true that day care is considerably less expensive than residential treatment or total hospital care. Day care keeps the patient in touch with his community and obviates the extensive reorientation to normal community life so frequently necessary after prolonged residential institutionalization.

The day-care center must, of course, be community-based because parents must bring the child each morning and call for him each night, or at least they must provide transportation that is not too fatiguing. The frequent comings and goings of the parents offer the advantage of close contact between staff and family; in most such centers, treatment of parents is an integral aspect of the program. This is particularly true in those centers that care for preschool children, where the orientation is heavily preventive and where efforts are made to abort early developmental deviations.

Special Modalities of Therapy

Group therapy. The natural habitat of the child over the age of 3 or 4 is the peer group. As many of his normal growth trends are reinforced and nurtured by his group experiences, many of his conflicts and ego deficiencies are expressed in group situations. The group is, therefore, a natural medium for the observation of behavioral patterns and for treatment intervention with children.

The nursery group has been utilized for such purposes. Under the direction of trained nursery teachers, the group setting serves as an important adjuvant to psychotherapy (Alpert & Krown, 1953). Gratton (1962) reports the use of psychoanalytic group therapy as a primary modality with such children, based on Kleinian principles.

As a specialized form of therapy, however, group therapy is usually regarded as a significant instrumentality in the latency period. Slavson (1943; 1955) has developed a specific form of treatment for children of this age suffering from defective identifications (passivity and effeminacy in boys and "tomboyism" in girls), infantilization and overdependency, withdrawal and personality constriction, and for children defeated in sibling rivalry situations. It is particularly valuable for children who are primarily action-oriented rather than verbally oriented, for cultural or individual developmental reasons. Activity group therapy[1] is designed to provide an emotionally corrective experience for such children. It utilizes a highly permissive setting which encourages freedom of expression of pent-up feelings and which facilitates regression to earlier developmental levels. The group is presented to its members as a club. Arts-and-crafts materials are provided, but no conditions are placed on their use.

The generally defined role of the therapist is one of neutrality and passivity. He does not initiate discussions and does not intervene in or seek to mediate intragroup conflicts; rather, he seeks to afford members the fullest measure of personal and group autonomy. He enacts the role of a calm, giving, unconditionally accepting parental figure, but within this framework he may be highly active in responding to the unique dynamics of each member's personality. The group is a symbolic family to the child; as such, it offers a real living site for the working through of sibling rivalry. It provides for social rejects a group haven and social sanctuary.

Activity group therapy can, of course, be employed as an adjunct to individual psychotherapy as well as an exclusive modality. It is not suitable for children who lack the inner controls necessary to assimilate a permissive atmosphere (cf. Redl & Wineman, 1952) or for those who have been so severely deprived that they are unable to tolerate the experiences of group life.

In addition to activity group therapy, verbal or "interview" group methods have been widely utilized with adolescents, particularly with those adjudged to be inaccessible to individual contact and/or in settings in which individual therapy is impracticable. In practice, this generally involves delinquent and predelinquent children, though some work with nondelinquent middle-class children has been done. Slavson (1952) describes the methods used, while Stranahan, Schwartzman, and Atkin (1957), Tec (1956), and Kraft (1961) have presented illustrative material. In general, the groups consist of 10 to 15 adolescents, frequently of both sexes, with a mixture of clinical pictures, excluding only extremes of pathology. Discussions may range far and wide, involving not only individual problems of members and problems of group interaction but also general matters of relevance to the group such as social patterns, authority relationships, etc. In some cases, activity elements are introduced to reduce tensions, and refreshments are made available. The role of the

[1] This discussion of activity group therapy is adapted from a memorandum on the subject prepared by Leslie Rosenthal, Group Therapy Consultant, Jewish Board of Guardians, New York.

therapist also varies from relative passivity to active direction, with more or less use of cues derived from his own countertransference reactions. Those who have used this approach consider it ideally suited to the treatment of adolescents, who are in their nature peer-oriented and who often find the one-to-one, parent-child-like situation of individual psychotherapy intolerable. Special techniques for lower-class delinquents have been reported by Black and Rosenthal (1963).

Physiological therapies. Treatment of children with physiologically active agents has been a method of great importance, recently eliciting even greater interest and enthusiasm with the introduction of the new psychotropic drugs.

Bender and her associates (1947a) have for many years been treating psychotic children with electroshock therapy. This is perhaps the most intensely controversial form of treatment in the whole range of modern psychiatric therapies. Bender herself claims to have evidence of improvement in children treated in this manner, with reduction in impulsivity and improved "patterning" of behavior and with reduction in autism. Others, however (Clardy & Rumpf, 1954), are extremely skeptical about this method of treatment, reporting cases of brain damage at worst and complete lack of significant improvement at best. It is fair to say that only Bender and her associates retain any favorable view of EST in childhood pathology.

The great majority of the work in physiological therapy has been done in the realm of drug treatment. Again, Bender (Bender & Faretra, 1961) and her colleagues have been in the forefront of the investigations of psychopharmacological methods with children. Bakwin's (1948) early studies with Benzedrine in impulsive behavior disorders led to further investigations with Benadryl and anticonvulsive drugs and, more recently, with such drugs as chlorpromazine, meprobamate, and others.

Most effective and generally agreed upon (Fish, 1960a; Fish, 1960b; Nichtern, 1961) has been the use of amphetamine and its derivatives for impulsive, brain-damaged children; Benadryl for hyperactive children with behavior disorders; and chlorpromazine for severely agitated psychotic youngsters. Most recently Bender (Bender, Goldschmidt, & Siva Sankar, 1962) has reported encouraging results with the use of LSD in autistic children.

The use of drug therapy, though generally regarded as an important element in the treatment of the severely disturbed child, is seen by most workers as but one element in a total treatment program, which ideally should involve in addition psychotherapeutic and, in residential treatment, educational and other milieu therapy elements. It cannot in any event be more than an ameliorative measure, useful while other treatment modalities and/or maturational and normal developmental processes affect the basic pathological processes. Those who regard the psychoses of childhood in particular as fundamentally organic disorders are, of course, hopeful of a pharmacological or physiological measure that will directly affect the basic biochemical or neurophysiological disorder; no such remedy is, however, at hand.

It need hardly be mentioned that the use of any physiological therapy must be carried out by a physician who is aware of the nature of the biological action of the therapy in question as well as of its dangers and possible contra-indications.

Remedial instruction. Learning disturbance is a symptom that appears in a variety of pathological conditions, mild or severe. As with any symptom, its management depends on one's evaluation of its place in the child's total personal and interpersonal situation and may range from environmental manipulations in the home or school to intensive psychoanalytic psychotherapy (Ephron, 1953). In many cases it is necessary to institute specific measures directed to the learning difficulty itself. These procedures, falling under the designations of "tutoring" or "remedial instruction," are frequently of critical value in the treatment of such disturbances and are all too frequently ignored by therapists who feel committed to a "therapeutic" as opposed to an "educational" approach.

Since, after all, the learning disturbance is an ego difficulty which may or may not be due to specific emotional conflicts in the area of learning itself (Esman, 1962; Pearson, 1954), it is logical that psychotherapeutic resolution of conflict may not serve of itself to alleviate it. This is particularly the case in children who suffer from constitutional or organic impairment in their capacity to learn. For such children special techniques of teaching, geared to their limited attention span, perceptual difficulties, and need for concrete rather than abstract presentations of data, are necessary (Gallagher, 1960; Kirk, 1958; Strauss & Kephart, 1955).

Even where the learning difficulty is the product of emotional conflict, however, timely and intelligent introduction of remedial instruction concurrent with psychotherapy may be crucial. By enhancing the child's self-esteem, affording him experiences of success rather than failure in his school pursuits, and enlarging the range of his ego competence, successful tutoring or remedial instruction by an expert in this field may considerably advance the psychotherapeutic process. The psychotherapist must, however, avoid mechanical or arbitrary introduction of such procedures; the institution of remedial teaching must be carefully timed and is most useful when the child himself is able to express concern about his learning problem and openly to request help in dealing with it.

Discussions of the technique of remedial education may be found in works by Arthur (1946), Gillingham and Stillman (1940), and Fernald (1943).

ENVOI

The treatment of the personality disorders of children is a diverse, complex task which carries with it many rich rewards but which demands of its practitioner a full measure of flexibility and imaginativeness. It is a realm in which dogmas languish and stereotypes melt away, in which the race is to the clear in mind and the young in spirit. Above all else, it is the area of treatment which offers the best hope of prevention of future distress. It is, too, the field in which experimentation thrives and multiplies and in which the interaction with vital community interests is most active. Group methods, short-term therapies, family procedures, and a host of others flourish. It is a field into which none should enter without forethought but in which none can sojourn without profit.

REFERENCES

Ackerman, N. *Psychodynamics of family life.* New York: Basic Books, 1959.

Ackerman, N., & Behrens, Marjorie. Child and family psychopathology: problems of correlation. In P. Hoch & J. Zubin (Eds.), *Psychopathology of childhood.* New York: Grune & Stratton, 1955.

Aichorn, A. *Wayward youth.* New York: Viking, 1935.

Allen, F. *Psychotherapy with children.* New York: Norton, 1942.

Alpert, Augusta. Reversibility of pathological fixations associated with maternal deprivation in infancy. In *The psychoanalytic study of the child.* Vol. XIV. New York: International Universities Press, 1959. Pp. 169–185.

Alpert, Augusta. A special therapeutic technique for prelatency children with a history of deficiency in maternal care. *Amer. J. Orthopsychiat.,* 1963, **33**, 161–182.

Alpert, Augusta, & Krown, Sylvia. Treatment of a child with severe ego restriction in a therapeutic nursery. In *The psychoanalytic study of the child.* Vol. VIII. New York: International Universities Press, 1953. Pp. 333–354.

Alpert, Augusta, & Pfeiffer, Elsbeth. Treatment of an autistic child. *J. Child Psychiat,* in press.

Alt, H. *Forging tools for mental health.* New York: Jewish Board of Guardians, 1955.

Alt, H. *Residential treatment of the disturbed child.* New York: International Universities Press, 1960.

Anthony, E. J. Review of case studies. In G. Gardner (Ed.), Childhood emotional disabilities. *Int. J. Psychoanal.,* 1959, **40**, 69.

Anthony, E. J. Communicating therapeutically with the child. *J. Amer. Acad. Child Psychiat.,* 1964, **3**, 106–125.

Arthur, Grace. *Tutoring as therapy.* New York: Commonwealth Fund, 1946.

Bakwin, H. Benzedrine in the behavior disorders of young children. *J. Pediat.,* 1948, **32**, 215–216.

Bauer, I. & Gurevitz, S. Group therapy of parents of schizophrenic children. *Int. J. group Psychother.,* 1952, **2**, 344–357.

Beck, Helen. Casework with parents of mentally retarded children. *Amer. J. Orthopsychiat.,* 1962, **32**, 870–877.

Bender, Lauretta. Childhood schizophrenia. *Amer. J. Orthopsychiat.,* 1947, **17**, 40-56. (a)

Bender, Lauretta. One hundred cases of childhood schizophrenia treated with electric shock. *Trans. Amer. neurol. Ass.,* 1947, 165–169. (b)

Bender, Lauretta, & Faretra, Gloria. Organic therapy in pediatric psychiatry. *Dis. nerv. System, Monogr. Suppl.,* 1961, **22**.

Bender, Lauretta, Goldschmidt, L., & Siva Sankar, D. V. Treatment of autistic schizophrenic children with LSD-25 and UML-491. In *Recent advances in biological psychiatry*. Vol. IV. New York: Plenum Press, 1962.

Benjamin, Anne, & Weatherly, H. Hospital ward therapy of emotionally disturbed children. *Amer. J. Orthopsychiat.*, 1947, **17**, 665–674.

Bernstein, I. Panel report: indications and goals of child analysis as compared with child psychotherapy. *J. Amer. Psychoanal. Ass.*, 1957, **5**, 158–163.

Bernstein, I. The importance of characteristics of the parents in deciding on child analysis. *J. Amer. Psychoanal. Ass.*, 1958, **6**, 71–78.

Bettelheim, B. *Love is not enough*. New York: Free Press, 1950.

Bettelheim, B., & Sylvester, Emmy. Therapeutic influence of the group on the individual. *Amer. J. Orthopsychiat.*, 1947, **17**, 684–692.

Bettelheim, B., & Wright, B. Staff development in a treatment institution. *Amer. J. Orthopsychiat.*, 1955, **25**, 705–719.

Black, M., & Rosenthal, Leslie. Changes in treatment techniques in group therapy of delinquent boys. Paper read at Amer. Orthopsychiat. Ass., Washington, D.C., 1963.

Bloch, D., & Silber, E. The role of the administrator in relation to individual psychotherapy in a residential setting. *Amer. J. Orthopsychiat.*, 1957, **27**, 69–74.

Blos, P. *On adolescence*. New York: Basic Books, 1962.

Bornstein, Berta. Clinical notes on child analysis. In *The psychoanalytic study of the child*. Vol. I. New York: International Universities Press, 1945. Pp. 151–166.

Cameron, D. C. *The day hospital*. Washington, D.C.: American Psychiatric Association, 1958.

Christ, A. E. Sexual counter transference problems with a psychotic child. *J. Amer. Acad. Child Psychiat.* 1964, **3**, 298–316.

Clardy, E., & Rumpf, E. M. The effect of EST on children having schizophrenic manifestations. *Psychiat. Quart.*, 1954, **28**, 616–623.

Connell, P. H. The day hospital approach in child psychiatry. *J. ment. Sci.*, 1961, **107**, 969–977.

Curran, F. J. Organization of a ward for adolescents in Bellevue Hospital. *Amer. J. Psychiat.*, 1939, **95**, 1365–1388.

Des Lauriers, A. *The experience of reality in childhood schizophrenia*. New York: International Universities Press, 1962.

Eissler, K. Ego-psychological implications of the treatment of delinquents. In *The psychoanalytic study of the child*. Vol. V. New York: International Universities Press, 1950. Pp. 97–121.

Ekstein, R., Bryant, K. & Friedman, S. Childhood schizophrenia and allied conditions. In L. Bellak (Ed.), *Schizophrenia: a review of the syndrome*. New York: Logos Press, 1958. Pp. 555–693.

Ekstein, R., & Wallerstein, Judith. Observations on the psychotherapy of borderline and psychotic children. In *The psychoanalytic study of the child*. Vol. IX. New York: International Universities Press, 1956. Pp. 303–311.

Ephron, Beulah K. *Emotional difficulties in reading*. New York: Julian Press, 1953.

Erikson, E. The nature of clinical evidence. *Daedalus*, 1958, **87**, 65–81.

Erikson, E. Growth and crises of the healthy personality. In *Identity and the life cycle*. New York: International Universities Press, 1961.

Esman, A. H. The case of the underachiever. *N.Y. Times Mag.*, Sept. 23, 1962.

Esman, A. H., Kohn, M., & Nyman, L. Parents of "schizophrenic" children. *Amer. J. Orthopsychiat.*, 1959, **29**, 455–459.

Fernald, Grace M. *Remedial techniques in basic school subjects*. New York: McGraw-Hill, 1943.

Fish, Barbara. Drug treatment in child psychiatry: pharmacological aspects. *Comprehensive Psychiat.*, 1960, **1**, 212–227. (a)

Fish, Barbara. Drug treatment in child psychiatry: psychological aspects. *Comprehensive Psychiat.*, 1960, **1**, 55–61. (b)

Fraiberg, Selma. Clinical notes on the nature of transference in child analysis. In *The psychoanalytic study of the child*. Vol. VI. New York: International Universities Press, 1951. Pp. 286–306.

Freud, Anna. *The psychoanalytical treatment of children*. London: Imago Publishing Co., 1946.

Freud, Anna. Assessment of childhood disturbances. In *The psychoanalytic study of the child*. Vol. XVII. New York: International Universities Press, 1962. Pp. 149–158.

Freud, Anna. The concept of developmental lines. In *The psychoanalytic study of the child*. Vol. XVIII. New York: International Universities Press, 1963. Pp. 245–265.

Freud, S. Analysis of a phobia in a five-year old boy (1909). In *Standard edition.* Vol. X. London: Hogarth Press, 1955. (a)

Freud, S. Beyond the pleasure principle (1909). In *Standard edition.* Vol. XVIII. London: Hogarth Press, 1955. Pp. 16–17 (b)

Furman, Erna. An ego disturbance in a young child. In *The psychoanalytic study of the child.* Vol. IX. New York: International Universities Press, 1956. Pp. 312–335.

Furman, Erna. Treatment of under-5's by way of parents. In *ibid.* Vol. XII. 1957. Pp. 250-262.

Gallagher, J. J. *The tutoring of brain-injured mentally retarded children.* Springfield, Ill.: Charles C Thomas, 1960.

Gardner, G. The institution as therapist. *Child,* 1952, **16**, 70–72.

Geleerd, Elizabeth. Borderline states in childhood and adolescence. In *The psychoanalytic study of the child.* Vol. XIII. New York: International Universities Press, 1958. Pp. 279–295.

Gillingham, Anna, & Stillman, Bessie W. *Remedial reading for children with specific disability in reading, spelling and penmanship.* New York: Sackett & Wilhelms, 1940.

Glover, E. An examination of the Klein system of child psychology. In *The psychoanalytic study of the child.* Vol. I. International Universities Press, 1945. Pp. 75–118.

Goldfarb, W. *Childhood schizophrenia.* Cambridge, Mass.: Harvard Univer. Press, 1961.

Goldsmith, J. Clinical group work in a residential treatment center. In A. H. Esman (Ed.), *New frontiers in child guidance.* New York: International Universities Press, 1958. Pp. 93–107.

Gordon, G., & Siegel, L. The evolution of a program of individual psychotherapy for children with aggressive acting-out disorders in a new residential treatment unit. *Amer. J. Orthopsychiat.,* 1957, **27**, 59–68.

Gratton, L. Psychoanalytical group therapy for preschool children. *Canad. psychiat. Ass. J.,* 1962, **7**, 90–96.

Greenwood, E. D. The role of psychotherapy in residential treatment. *Amer. J. Orthopsychiat.,* 1955, **25**, 692–698.

Haworth, Mary, & Keller, Mary Jane. The use of food in the diagnosis and treatment of emotionally disturbed children. *J. Amer. Acad. Child Psychiat.,* 1962, **1**, 548–563.

Hirschberg, J. C. The role of education in the treatment of emotionally disturbed children through planned ego development. *Amer. J. Orthopsychiat.,* 1953, **23**, 684–690.

Isaacs, Susan. The nature and functions of phantasy. In *Developments in psychoanalysis.* London: Hogarth Press, 1952.

Jacobs, Lydia. Methods used in the education of mothers. In *The psychoanalytic study of the child.* Vols. III, IV. New York: International Universities Press, 1949. Pp. 409–422.

Johnson, Adelaide, & Szurek, S. The genesis of antisocial acting-out in children. *Psychoanal. Quart.,* 1952, **21**, 323–343.

Kirk, S. A. *Early education of the mentally retarded.* Urbana, Ill.: Univer. of Illinois Press, 1958.

Klein, Melanie. *The psychoanalysis of children.* London: Hogarth Press, 1932.

Klein, Melanie. *Narrative of a child analysis.* New York: Basic Books, 1961.

Konopka, Gisela. The role of the group in residential treatment. *Amer. J. Orthopsychiat.,* 1955, **25**, 679–684.

Kraft, I. Some special considerations in adolescent group psychotherapy. *Int. J. group Psychother.,* 1961, **11**, 196–203.

Kramer, Selma, & Settlage, C. On the concepts and technique of child analysis. *J. Amer. Acad. Child Psychiat.,* 1962, **1**, 509–535.

Kris, Marianne. The use of prediction in a longitudinal study. In *The psychoanalytic study of the child.* Vol. XII. New York: International Universities Press, 1957. Pp. 175–189.

LaVietes, Ruth, Hulse, W., & Blau, A. A psychiatric day treatment center and school for young children and their parents. *Amer. J. Orthopsychiat.,* 1960, **30**, 488–492.

Levy, D. Release therapy in young children. *Psychiatry,* 1938, **1**, 387–390.

Levy, D. Release therapy. *Amer. J. Orthopsychiat.,* 1939, **9**, 713–736.

Lippman, H. *The treatment of the child in emotional conflict.* New York: McGraw-Hill, 1956.

Lourie, N. V., & Schulman, Rena. The role of the residential staff in residential treatment. *Amer. J. Orthopsychiat.,* 1952, **22**, 798–808.

Lourie, R. Experience with treatment of psychosomatic problems in infants. In P. Hoch & J. Zubin (Eds.), *Psychopathology of childhood.* New York: Grune & Stratton, 1955.

Mahler, Margaret S. Child analysis. In N. Lewis & B. Pacella (Eds.), *Modern trends in child psy-*

chiatry. New York: International Universities Press, 1945. Pp. 262–290.

Mahler, Margaret S., & Gosliner, B. On symbiotic child psychosis. In *The psychoanalytic study of the child*. Vol. X. New York: International Universities Press, 1955. Pp. 195–212.

Nichtern, S. Chemotherapy in child psychiatry. In *Child psychiatry and the general practitioner*. Springfield, Ill.: Charles C Thomas, 1961.

Noshpitz, J. Opening phase in the psychotherapy of adolescents with character disorders. *Bull. Menninger Clin.*, 1957, **21**, 153–164.

Noshpitz, J. Notes on the theory of residential treatment. *J. Amer. Acad. Child Psychiat.*, 1962, **1**, 284–296.

Pearson, G. H. J. *Psychoanalysis and the education of the child*. New York: Norton, 1954.

Peck, H., Rabinovitch, R., & Cramer, J. A treatment program for parents of schizophrenic children. *Amer. J. Orthopsychiat.*, 1949, **19**, 592–598.

Polsky, H. *Cottage six*. New York: Russell Sage, 1963.

Provence, Sally, & Lipton, Rose. *Infants in institutions*. New York: International Universities Press, 1963.

Rank, Beata. Adaptation of the psychoanalytic technique for the treatment of young children with atypical development. *Amer. J. Orthopsychiat.*, 1949, **19**, 130–139.

Redl, F., & Wineman, D. *Controls from within*. New York: Free Press, 1952.

Ribble, Margaret. *The rights of infants*. New York: Columbia Univer. Press, 1943.

Rosenfeld, H. An investigation into the psychoanalytic theory of depression. *Int. J. Psychoanal.*, 1959, **40**, 105–129.

Ross, Helen. Diagnosis in terms of character structure as an indication for child analysis and psychotherapy. Cited in Bernstein, 1957.

Segal, H. *Introduction to the work of Melanie Klein*, New York: Basic Books, 1964.

Sechehaye, M. *Symbolic realization*. New York: International Universities Press, 1951.

Slavson, S. *Introduction to group therapy* (1943). New York: International Universities Press, 1950.

Slavson, S. *Fields of group psychotherapy*. New York: Columbia Univer. Press, 1952.

Slavson, S. *Fields of group psychotherapy*. New York: International Universities Press, 1955.

Spitz, Rene. Hospitalism. In *The psychoanalytic study of the child*. Vol. I. New York: International Universities Press, 1945. Vol. I. Pp. 53–74.

Stranahan, Marion, Schwartzman, Cecile, & Atkin, Edith. Group treatment for emotionally disturbed and potentially delinquent boys and girls. *Amer. J. Orthopsychiat.*, 1957, **27**, 518–527.

Strauss, A. A., & Kephart, N. C. *Psychopathology and education of the brain-injured child*. New York: Grune & Stratton, 1955.

Szurek, S. Psychiatric services in a children's hospital. *J. Pediat.*, 1947, **31**.

Tec, L. A psychiatrist as participant observer in a group of delinquent boys. *Int. J. group Psychother.*, 1956, **6**, 418–429.

Toolan, J. Female adolescent service in a psychiatric hospital. *Psychiat. Quart.*, 1955, **29**, 239–249.

van Ophuijsen, J. H. W. Primary conduct disturbances. In N. Lewis & B. Pacella (Eds.), *Modern trends in child psychiatry*. New York: International Universities Press, 1945. Pp. 35–52.

Zetzel, Elizabeth. An approach to the relation between concept and content in psychoanalytic theory. In *The psychoanalytic study of the child*. Vol. XI. New York: International Universities Press, 1956. Pp. 99–121.

49

Mental Hospitals

MILTON GREENBLATT AND DANIEL J. LEVINSON[1]

It is appropriate that the title of this chapter be in the plural rather than the singular. One could hardly write about "the" mental hospital. There is a remarkable diversity among mental hospitals today, and individual hospitals are, in most cases, undergoing an extensive process of change. The most apt analogy, perhaps, is to the so-called "underdeveloped" countries, which have been going through such drastic changes in national awareness, in technology and economic structure, in political and educational development, and in their relations with neighbors and the world community. The changes in mental hospitals, while on a smaller scale, are no less fundamental and dramatic. There are newly emerging conceptions of the nature and functions of mental hospitals; modifications in size, structure, and policy; technological developments in modes of patient care and therapy; redefinitions of the roles of staff as well as of patients; and so on. Generalizations derived from the literature on mental hospitals are likely to be at least ten years out of date and to neglect current developments and future potentialities. Therefore, rather than offer a static picture of the current scene, we shall present a historical view, starting with a brief sketch of the long-term development of American mental hospitals and then giving our main attention to contemporary directions of change.

For historical guidance, we are in great debt to two sources: *The Mentally Ill in America* (Deutsch, 1949) and *Moral Treatment in American Psychiatry* (Bockoven, 1963; see also Bockoven, 1956). The history of mental hospitals (and of psychiatry generally) in this country can be usefully divided into three major periods (Brown & Greenblatt, 1955): (1) the moral-treatment era, starting about 1817, with the first American mental hospital, and extending until roughly the time of the Civil War; (2) the period of the decline and fall of moral treatment, extending from the Civil War until the early twentieth century; and (3) what we shall call the "road back," covering roughly the last thirty to forty years, in which a slow but accelerating effort has been made to reassert the therapeutic impulse in mental hospitals.

THE MORAL-TREATMENT ERA

The pattern of early American psychiatry followed the steps taken as a result of the great upheavals and liberal reforms set in motion by the French Revolution. At the Bicêtre, Philippe Pinel transformed a prison into a hospital by taking the chains from the bodies of the mentally ill. In England, William Tuke built a retreat for the mentally ill along humanitarian lines. Similar reforms were produced in Italy, Germany, and America by Chiarurgi, Reil, and Rush, respectively.

The reforms in America pioneered by Benjamin Rush were not so extensive as those of Pinel but were based on the same source of inspiration. From 1817 on, a number of hospitals were built on the Eastern seaboard

[1] Preparation of this chapter was supported in part by a grant from the Foundations Fund for Research in Psychiatry.

which set the pattern of moral treatment in our nation. Included among these were the Friends' Asylum, built in Pennsylvania by Quakers; the McLean Hospital, in Waverly; Bloomingdale, in New York; and the Retreat, at Hartford. Among state hospitals, Manhattan State (New York, 1825), Western State Hospital (Virginia, 1828), South Carolina State Hospital (Columbia, 1828), and Worcester State Hospital (Massachusetts, 1833) led the march of psychiatric progress.

In many respects American soil was a suitable medium for the liberal ideas of the French Revolution, since American society in the 1830s and 1840s consisted of small well-knit communities, whose citizens were, for the most part, mutually interdependent and united by religious ties. A small village was in a sense an experiment in democratic government and in communal living, where the individual was held in high esteem. This was the time during which Emerson proclaimed: "The world is nothing, the man is all." Societies were being formed for the abolition of slavery, and the American pioneer saw himself as an independent, socially responsible individual striving for betterment of his lot both physically and intellectually. Moral treatment in psychiatry at this time involved compassionate understanding and treatment of innocent sufferers who were not entirely responsible for the ravages of their disease. Its treatment philosophy required close attention to personal needs of patients and detailed inquiry into their thinking, feeling, and behavior. There was also the expectation that proper attention by caretakers would result in improvement. Both the therapeutic atmosphere and the prognostic climate were favorable.

In the moral-treatment American hospital of this period, the superintendent played a mighty role. He was a man of distinction, and his job was highly regarded by society. He knew every patient in his care. He lived on the grounds and mingled with the mentally ill as though they were an extension of his family. How a good superintendent might function was cogently stated by Isaac Ray (1873):

> He constantly striveth to learn what is passing in the mind of his patient, by conversation and inquiry of those who see him in his unguarded moments. He also maketh diligent inquiry respecting the bodily and mental traits of his kindred, knowing full well that the sufferer is generally more beholden to them than himself for the evil that has fallen upon him. He endeavoreth so to limit the number committed to his care, as to obtain a personal knowledge of every wandering spirit in his keeping. He boasteth not of the multitude borne of his registers, but rather, if he boasteth at all, of the many whose experience he has discovered, whose needs he has striven to supply, whose moods, fancies, and impulses he has steadily watched. To fix his hold on the confidence and good will of his patients, he spareth no effort, though it may consume his time and tax his patience, or encroach, seemingly, on the dignity of his office. A formal walk through the wards, and the ordering of a few drugs, compriseth but a small part of his means of restoring the troubled mind (p. 67).

The success of moral treatment was vividly described by Charles Dickens (1842) in his *American Notes for General Circulation.* Here he discusses what he saw at the "institution at South Boston," now known as the Boston State Hospital. His fascinating description has been given wide currency in recent years:

> The state Hospital for the insane [is] admirably conducted on those enlightened principles of conciliation and kindness, which twenty years ago would have been worse than heretical. . . .
>
> Each ward in this institution is shaped like a long gallery or hall, with the dormitories of the patients opening from it on either hand. Here they work, read, play at skittles, and other games; and when the weather does not admit of their taking exercises out of doors, pass the day together. . . .
>
> Every patient in this asylum sits down to dinner every day with a knife and fork; and in the midst of them sits the gentleman [the superintendent]. . . . At every meal, moral influence alone restrains the more violent among them from cutting the throats of the rest; but the effect of that influence is reduced to an absolute certainty, and is found, even as a means of restraint, to say nothing of it as a means of cure, a hundred times more efficacious than all the strait-waistcoats, fetters, and hand-cuffs, that ignorance, prejudice, and cruelty have manufactured since the creation of the world.
>
> In the labour department, every patient is as freely trusted with the tools of his trade as if he were a sane man. In the

> garden, and on the farm, they work with spades, rakes, and hoes. For amusement, they walk, run, fish, paint, read, and ride out to take the air in carriages provided for the purpose. They have among themselves a sewing society to make clothes for the poor, which holds meetings, passes resolutions, never comes to fisty cuffs or bowie-knives as sane assemblies have been known to do elsewhere; and conducts all its proceedings with the greatest decorum. The irritability, which would otherwise be expended on their own flesh, clothes, and furniture, is dissipated in these pursuits. They are cheerful, tranquil, and healthy.
>
> Once a week they have a ball, in which the Doctor and his family, with all the nurses and attendants, take an active part. Dances and marches are performed alternately, to the enlivening strains of a piano; and now and then some gentleman or lady (whose proficiency has been previously ascertained) obliges the company with a song: nor does it ever degenerate, at a tender crisis, into a screech or a howl; wherein, I must confess, I should have thought the danger lay. At an early hour they all meet together for these festive purposes; at eight o'clock refreshments are served; and at nine they separate.
>
> Immense politeness and good-breeding are observed throughout. They all take their tone from the Doctor; and he moves a very Chesterfield among the company. Like other assemblies these entertainments afford a fruitful topic of conversation among the ladies for some days; and the gentlemen are so anxious to shine on these occasions, that they have been sometimes found "practicing their steps" in private, to cut a more distinguished figure in the dance.
>
> It is obvious that one great feature of this system, is the inculcation and encouragement, even among such unhappy persons, of a decent self-respect (pp. 105–111).

Thus we see that many of the achievements of recent decades which invite our admiration were in fact embodied in moral treatment 100 years ago: trust of the patient, interaction between patients and staff without paralyzing fear, little or no use of restraint, a diversity of occupations and recreations, and the expectation that behavior could become well modulated even in the severely deranged and that the future held out promise for these unfortunates if they were cared for properly.

Bockoven has traced a report written in 1893 by John Parks, at Worcester State Hospital, covering 1,173 patients discharged from that hospital between 1833 and 1846—a report that casts considerable bright light upon the issue of prognosis of the mentally ill in those times. Summarizing his data, we find that approximately 70 per cent of the patients were discharged improved or recovered within a year following admission. Substantially one-half of those discharged never returned to the hospital again, and of those who returned, a significant number remained for brief periods and were then able to be resettled in the community. Considering the fact that some of the patients suffered from irrecoverable neurosyphilis, the results are truly dramatic and challenge the best that can be achieved today, even in the most modern hospitals. Moral treatment proceeded in the absence of tranquilizers, antidepressants, shock treatment, insulin treatment, and psychoanalytic approaches. What was achieved through kindness, forbearance, attention to psychological needs, opportunities for expression of creative urges and satisfactions, liberty to work and to handle freely the tools of labor, and the maintenance of self-respect stands as a great lesson to us all: that it is not so much *modality* of treatment or *school of thought* that influences the result, but primarily humanism in an atmosphere of reasonable therapeutic optimism.

THE DECLINE OF MORAL TREATMENT

The breakdown of moral treatment can be attributed to a complex of factors which in their totality spelled the dehumanization of the individual and the loss of respect for the mentally ill. First, there was the Industrial Revolution, with its emphasis on mass production and the growing desire to run costly mental hospitals at a profit. There was also the rapid rise of the immigrant population, with crowding urbanization and overfilling of the mental hospitals by newcomers to our soil who were regarded as below the intellectual and moral level of the early settlers. A prime example of this latter attitude is contained in a state hospital trustee's report of 1854:

> The Hospital is fast becoming a Hospital for foreigners, and its doors are becoming practically closed against that class of persons who for many years enjoyed its advantages. . . . The intelligent yeomanry of

> Massachusetts who can afford to pay the cost of their board, and will not ask for charity . . . would have shrunk most sensitively from living next door even to a wretched hovel, and from intimate association with those who are accustomed to, and satisfied with filthy habitations and filthier habits. (Trustees of the State Lunatic Asylum at Worcester, 1854.)

To meet the population explosion of that time, hospitals were doubled and redoubled in size but without adequate provisions being made for personnel or even maintenance of pay schedules for ward attendants at the level found in general hospitals. Dorothea Dix was deeply moved by the plight of the mentally ill and did much to bring about increased construction of mental hospitals. Unfortunately, personnel complements of adequate size did not follow automatically. As the hospitals expanded, patients were removed further and further from those who were responsible for them. Administrators were now governing hospitals without knowing intimately the lives and problems of the various sick persons in their charge. Increasing neglect took the place of once proud concern with each individual. Hospital statistics of improvement and discharge rapidly declined. At Worcester, for example, the earlier discharge figure of 70 per cent reported by John Parks gave way, decade by decade, to a low of about 5 per cent in the latter part of the nineteenth century.

Concomitant with changes engendered by the Industrial Revolution were other interesting developments. For example, Pliny Earle, one of the early leaders in psychiatry on the Eastern seaboard, began to present facts and figures to substantiate the claim that mental illness was changing its form and was becoming increasingly malignant (see Sanborn, 1898). He was, of course, describing a social phenomenon of neglect but was attributing it to innate change in the nature of the disorder. At this time also, the sociologist William Graham Sumner postulated his philosophy of social Darwinism. He contended that the evolution of the social order is fixed by laws of nature precisely analogous to those of biological evolution. Illness is a form of unfitness. The unfit cannot expect to survive or to prosper. Man cannot alter these laws; the most he can do is to help the unfit to survive, shifting responsibility for their support upon future generations.

In many laboratories of pathology, which were highly esteemed in the medical profession, mental illness was being attributed to definitive brain lesions. This mistake of neuropathology was later rectified by studies which indicated that no apparent gross or microscopic brain lesion could account for the large body of mentally ill cases. However, the impact of such statements by great pathologists of that time was disastrous. If mental illness had been due to brain lesion, custodial care would probably have been the most suitable and economical arrangement for mentally ill individuals until such time as brain pathology could be corrected by devices still to be discovered.

Finally, none of the early moral psychiatrists developed schools of thought embodying their principles. In a sense this was unnecessary, since the principles were embodied in the daily life of the early American settler. Few could foresee how industrialization, urbanization, and the great growth of population would come to undermine the entire philosophy of moral treatment.

THE ROAD BACK

Thus we have been left with large hospitals, inadequate staff, low pay, and institutions geographically isolated from centers of population. Impressive numbers of chronic custodial cases have accumulated, whose chronicity is to a significant degree dependent upon forces of institutionalization rather than innate pathology; yet neglected wards and buildings require such large outlays for their upkeep as to strain the fiscal structure of the states. The full meaning of recent efforts to reduce and allay custodialism can be appreciated only in the light of the foregoing discussion of the history and heritage of mental hospitals.

We are now slowly moving on the way back to a more "moral" attitude toward the mentally ill patients. The responsibility rests firmly upon all of us because the mentally ill cannot, by the nature of their disorder, speak out on their own behalf. Efforts throughout our country to move in a favorable direction have been aided and abetted by a variety of forces which we may now briefly discuss.

The Wars

Two world wars have taught us the significance to our national efforts of the mental and physical health of our people. In World

War I, startling casualty rates from emotional disorder were reported, equal in fact to casualty rates from physical causes. However, the well-documented studies on shell shock and disordered heart function had no large impact because mobilization in our country concerned only a fraction of the male population. The war did not touch us in the sense of involving total industrial and manpower effort, and victory was won in a short time.

However, World War II made it impossible to overlook the fact that a very large percentage of our young men were impaired by emotional or neurological disease, that our rehabilitation efforts on their behalf were largely inadequate at the national level, and that the implications of adequate rehabilitation were so far-reaching and costly as to require Federal as well as state and local commitment to the cause of mental health.

The Depression

The great economic Depression of the 1930s, devastating to morale and to the health of the community, gave rise to the philosophy that every man is not necessarily his own master, that there are social and economic forces far beyond him that necessitate the intervention of Federal government. In our country, Roosevelt led a veritable social revolution much like that which England had undergone some two decades previously. Responsibility for the individual citizen, cradle to grave, became a serious slogan. There was a reaffirmation of the importance of the individual and recognition that without outside help, however rugged his personality, the individual could succumb to overwhelming forces.

Freudian Psychology

Also during this time important changes were occurring within the psychiatric profession. The Freudian influence was beginning to be felt. Gradually in America strong bands of enlightened Freudians developed their sway and began to instruct younger men in the importance of the inner life of the neurotic sufferer. Medical schools began to bring to their faculties men of psychodynamic persuasion. The new light was spread into every area of behavior and practice. It became proper to consider a patient's feelings and thinking as part of good management. Thus once again the physician was finding his way back to the individual.

Leadership

An important group of pathologists who originally entered medicine hoping to understand human behavior decided that pathology alone could not illuminate the complexity of relevant factors in mental illness. Many of these men turned to psychiatry and began to follow the lead of Freud, Meyer, Southard, White, Sullivan, Jelliffe, and others who postulated that experiential and social factors could produce psychological disorder.

Somatic Therapy

In the 1930s, several somatic therapies brought new hope to the treatment of the mentally ill. For example, the shock therapies demonstrated that extraordinary changes could be produced in depressed patients, some schizophrenics, and many involutional cases by means of a few electric discharges passed through the brain (Cerletti, 1954; Mezer & Solomon, 1954). In 1933 Sakel, in Vienna, demonstrated his insulin hypoglycemic technique, which apparently yielded remarkable improvements in some paranoid schizophrenics subjected to repeated comas. This method was brought to America and for many years was a highly respected therapeutic modality. Although there is now much doubt about the efficacy of insulin treatment, as such, it is acknowledged that many patients so treated did indeed improve greatly. It is not yet clear how much of the improvement was due to the hypoglycemic spells and the occasional convulsions and how much to the new climate of therapeutic optimism and the care given by a trained group of professionals.

Also in the 1930s we witnessed the rise of psychosurgery, a neurosurgical technique to help the mentally ill. Originated by Moniz (1936–1937) and Lima in Portugal and adopted in this country by Freeman (1955) and Watts, psychosurgery spread rapidly throughout many nations as a method of radical intervention. This approach depended on severing vast numbers of fibers connecting frontal lobes with the rest of the brain. Many patients undoubtedly were eased in their emotional tensions and were relieved of their depression and of their crippling compulsive ideas through this procedure (Greenblatt, Arnot, & Solomon, 1950; Greenblatt, Robertson, & Solomon, 1953; Greenblatt & Solomon, 1953). However, in America lobotomy soon waned as new methods and approaches, less destructive than surgery, were advocated for the severely mentally ill.

Drug Therapy

In the 1950s tranquilizer medications began to produce significant improvement in the behavior of psychotic patients and led to the discharge of many (Brill & Patton, 1959; Cole & Gerard, 1959). More recently, antidepressant drugs have been advanced as possible aids in the treatment of sadness, despondency, and hopelessness manifested in a large variety of cases (Greenblatt, Grosser, & Wechsler, 1963). All these treatments have helped psychiatry gain new respect from professional colleagues and the public.

Participation of Federal and State Government

Foremost among the helpful influences in recent years has been the decision of the Federal government to participate in the mental health program. In 1950, for example, some 8 million dollars were spent by the National Institute of Mental Health in support of research projects throughout the nation. In 1963, by contrast, approximately 190 million dollars was spent to further research. Support for *training* of professionals in the mental health field has grown extraordinarily. State funds have increased greatly as the states have begun to attack the problems locally. The passage of the late President Kennedy's omnibus mental health bill promises to extend Federal support into the area of *service* to the mentally ill. Two important governors' conferences have been held dealing with the issues of mental health and disease. In both, the group has committed itself solidly on the side of progress in mental therapy. State after state is reorganizing and revamping its program. The outlook for patients with mental retardation is much more hopeful, as this issue is gaining great support from the Kennedy family. The Vocational Rehabilitation Administration has applied its strength and financial resources to the problem of rehabilitating the mentally ill, making no distinction now between the mentally and the physically handicapped.

Participation of Citizens

Perhaps most heartening of all has been the fact that the average citizen has begun to change his attitude. Slowly there is acceptance of the idea that mental illness is everybody's business, that the risk of illness in any given family during one generation is great, and that the attitude in the home, in the community, and in the factory makes a world of difference in rehabilitation. Many citizens' organizations at the state and local levels are being formed; hospitals can now boast of supporting citizens' groups that form important humanistic bridges between the community and back wards.

THE CURRENT SITUATION AND DIRECTIONS OF CHANGE

The period since the end of World War II has been one of almost revolutionary change in mental hospitals. We shall not attempt here to review the large and still growing research literature on the mental hospital as a therapeutic organization.[2] It should be noted, however, that these studies have played an important part in instigating and directing the process of change. They have been carried out largely by psychiatrically oriented sociologists and anthropologists and by socially oriented psychiatrists and psychologists. The support of senior administrative figures (psychiatrists, nurses, government officials, and others) deserves greater attention than it has yet received. It takes considerable maturity and wisdom for an administrator to permit and facilitate research that brings into critical focus the shortcomings of an institution for which he has major responsibility. The openness of mental hospitals to critical examination, while far from complete, has nonetheless been greater than that of similar organizations such as general hospitals, prisons, business firms, and universities.

Among the many faults of the mental hospital system bequeathed to us by the late nineteenth century, the following may be singled out for emphasis: The social structure and component staff roles of the mental hospital were patterned largely after those of the

[2] For a comprehensive coverage of this work, see reports by Greenblatt, Levinson, and Williams (1957) and Pratt et al. (1960). A partial list of major hospital studies includes those by Barrabee (1951); Belknap (1956); Bettelheim (1949); Caudill (1958); Cumming and Cumming (1957); Dunham and Weinberg (1960); Gibson (1954); Gilbert and Levinson (1956); Goffman (1961); Greenblatt, Levinson, and Klerman (1961); Greenblatt, York, and Brown (1955); Henry (1957); Joint Commission on Mental Illness and Health (1961); Jones (1953); Kennard (1957); Parsons (1957); Stanton and Schwartz (1954); Von Mering and King (1957); Ward (1955); Wilmer (1958); Rapoport (1960); Levinson and Gallagher (1964).

general hospital. The institutional model of the general hospital, grossly inadequate even for its own purposes (Freidson, 1963), is inappropriate and therapeutically harmful for mental hospitals. In addition, the "custodial" version of the mental hospital has many features in common with massive prisons and other "total institutions" (Goffman, 1961). The traditional custodial hospital was a highly segregated organization, encapsulated and cut off from outside society. Its patients, and many of its staff as well, had only minimal contact with the community from which they came. At the same time, patients' relatives and other ordinary citizens were kept from intimate contact with the mental hospital. Mental illness, in general, and mental hospitals, in particular, were regarded with emotions of fear, revulsion, and disgust. Within the hospital there developed a rigidly hierarchical, castelike social structure. This had direct consequences for patients, who formed the lowest caste in the hospital society and who suffered the degradations inherent in that social position. There were hurtful consequences for staff as well, and these in turn had their effects on patient care. The tight, autocratic structure prevented experimentation, innovation, and redefinition of staff roles in ways that would utilize the therapeutic talents of individual staff members, regardless of formal occupational label.

The efforts at change in recent years are virtually countless; they have taken myriad forms and have led to numerous specific modifications of hospital organization and practice. Broadly speaking, we can discern three basic directions of change:

1. Efforts to move from custodial to therapeutic care within hospitals, that is, attempts to foster the development of "therapeutic communities" within the intramural social environment of the hospital. The goal here is to maximize the therapeutic potential of every individual—patient as well as staff member—in the system.

2. Efforts to make "community mental hospitals" out of relatively isolated institutions. Here the goal is to remove barriers between hospital and community and to develop mutual assistance and cooperation between the two for every phase of patient care.

3. Efforts to turn a relatively complacent extramural society into a therapeutic one. The goal is to maximize the therapeutic attitudes of citizens in the community so as to reduce psychological stresses upon vulnerable individuals and to enhance community adaptation of discharged patients.

We turn now to a discussion of problems and progress in each of the above directions. With the gradual freeing of human ingenuity to seek new and better solutions to old problems, it is not surprising to find diverse efforts, claims, and counterclaims in each area. Our concern here is not to evaluate or to pass judgment on the specific attempts that have been made or to describe all of them. Our primary intent is to convey a sense of the fundamental problems involved, of the enthusiasm and imaginativeness with which a great challenge is being confronted, and of the potential gains to be realized.

Toward a Therapeutic Community

In the early part of the twentieth century, the treatment of patients was mainly based on the security motif (Greenblatt et al., 1955). Because of overwhelming fear of the mentally ill, many measures were practiced to separate them from the staff as well as from the community. The windows were barred, and the ward doors were locked. Heavy sedation was used. There was also use of tubs, wet sheet packs, and physical restraint. In the name of "security," patients were stripped of their clothes and were relieved of their glasses, belts, shoes, and any other articles that might be used aggressively against themselves or others. The furniture was inadequate, and the wards were barren. Smoking privileges were rarely permitted, and then only under immediate supervision. Admission of patients was usually by legal commitment procedures which robbed them of basic civil rights. The admission process was often inhumane, the patient being forcibly undressed after manacles were removed, brought to the washroom, and treated as though he had every contagious disease. Thereafter, no systematic introduction to ward life was attempted, and the patient was forced to orient himself as best he could to an environment that was cold and repelling.

Reduction of restraint and seclusion. This state of affairs gradually diminished as methods of restraint and punitive practices came under specific examination. In the 1920s and 1930s, constant tub baths were gradually eliminated or were used less throughout the country. Seclusion by force was found to be unnecessary for most patients and for violent ones necessary for only short periods of time. Wet sheet packs were found dangerous, and heavy sedation by barbiturates was gradually eliminated. Reduction in the use of such measures was accompanied by greater attention to staff-patient relationships, by attempts to reduce the fear between staff and patients, and by encouragement of staff and patients to come together for discussions and mutual activities and to reach an understanding of the problems that beset both. As the barriers were lowered, many favorable effects were perceived. The staff began to appreciate better the patients' inner problems. They felt more secure in working with individuals whom they understood. They manifested less anxiety and, in turn, tended to produce less anxiety and fear in the patients.

As interpersonal relationships improved, the hospital staff began to take an active role in working with the patients in a constructive and creative fashion to improve the conditions of life. Much more attention was paid to the routine of admission and to orientation of patients upon the ward. The patient's rights and privileges were pointed out to him. He was introduced to patients and staff, much as if he were in a school dormitory, and a planned program of therapy was started as soon as possible to convince him that he was in a well-organized therapeutic environment and would not be neglected.

At this time also, group sessions with attendants were undertaken, led by psychiatrists, nurses, and psychologists (e.g., Jones, 1953; Hyde, 1955; Wilmer, 1958). These efforts were directed toward understanding the bizarre behavior of the patient and the relevance of the attendants' feelings to their management of him. The improvement of morale, especially among staff members in closest contact with patients, led to a quieter and more relaxed atmosphere everywhere in the hospital.

With greater interest in the patient's true feelings and individualization of patient needs, the person rather than the procedure became the chief object of concern. Communication between staff members and between staff and patients became especially emphasized as the social, psychological, and physiological needs of the patient were brought into focus.

Improvement of the physical environment. New interest in the details of the patients' lives led to concern with the physical environment of the ward. It was soon appreciated that the physical situation could be a most significant factor influencing the patient. Patients began to be regarded not as insensitive because of their illness but as supersensitive individuals who withdrew into a life of their own when the surroundings were uncomfortable, unattractive, and frightening. A great many attempts were made to improve the color and decor within the hospital, to render the wards more homelike, and to break down large wards into small units where the patients could enjoy all kinds of privileges, occupational and recreational activities, and the opportunity to eat together in small groups, making the mealtime a social activity. Also during this period, radios, television sets, paintings, and furniture were introduced into many hospitals.

Improvement in the social environment. Recently, much attention has been paid to the fact that the level of social activity and social interaction on a ward is very low. In part this is a function of the inner-directed energy of the patient, but it can also be attributed partly to the lack of social and recreational opportunities offered in many hospitals, especially those of the custodial type. Investigators have described the value of social interaction, competitive sports, recreation, music, dance, and the like (Barton, 1950; Hyde & Atwell, 1948; Niswander & Hyde, 1954). Occupational therapists have received new recognition for their part in bringing patients out of their turmoil or apathy and engaging them in outwardly directed tasks. A most remarkable change in many institutions has been the integration of men and women patients, who formerly had been completely separated, in social and recreational activities. There had been fear that the mixing of the sexes would result in serious misdemeanors. However, it has been shown that patients behave themselves as well, if not better, when properly supervised in mixed-sex activities than when kept separated. Not only were there no serious consequences, generally, but also the men became more concerned about their clothes, their behavior became less bizarre and more acceptable, their talk became less uncouth, and their interest in group work heightened. The women, correspondingly, became more interested in personal appearance, and crudities gave way to more wholesome, modulated interaction.

As concern for the patient's twenty-four-hour day came into focus, it was noted that activities were often lacking for many patients during the evening hours and on weekends. Hospitals have therefore made an effort to fill in these dull periods with new programs. In many institutions the staff has given extra time in the evenings to entertain patients or help them provide their own entertainment. Auxiliary and other types of citizens' organizations have in recent years made a fine contribution in this respect.

Patient government and self-help organizations. Another important advance in the development of the internal milieu of the mental hospital has resulted from efforts to develop patient councils, patient government, and other patient self-help organizations (Bierer & Haldane, 1941; Bridger, 1946; Hyde & Solomon, 1950). Many have appreciated the possibilities of mobilizing the patient to help himself and other patients through his participation in the life and business of the hospital. We are especially indebted to Maxwell Jones (1953) for developing patient participation at many levels of hospital life, from the simplest arrangements of ward living to involvement in limit setting for antisocial patients, enforcement of disciplinary measures, and even collaboration with staff in setting general policies for the institution. Perhaps the truest meaning of the phrase "therapeutic community," originated by Jones, pertains to the influence upon hospital life of the greater regard for patients and of the increased willingness of staff to harken to their collective voice. Patient government and patient councils offer patients many opportunities for self-development as well as a choice of roles involved in the democratic process. The patient may choose to listen passively to the group, or he may serve on a committee or try his wings as a responsible officer. Sometimes the activities of patient organizations have benefited not only the patients themselves and the hospital but the extramural community as well, for patients have adopted projects to help fellow patients in deprived circumstances elsewhere.

We sense a vast potential in manpower and in effective therapeutic action latent within the patient organization. However, our experience is limited, and research and social experimentation in this area have hardly begun.

The therapeutic potential of staff. The key to the elimination of restrictive measures such as tubs, packs, and seclusion was, as mentioned above, the elimination of psychological barriers existing between staff and patients. Recently, there has been recognition of the fact that in many respects staff is in a situation of stress almost as serious as that of patients. Staff members, too, may suffer from discrimination, neglect, job dissatisfaction, social ostracism, etc., which parallel the tensions suffered by patients. This can lead to low morale, poor communication, scapegoating, and sabotage of the hospital's program. The welfare of staff, therefore, becomes as important as that of patients, and since patients are primarily dependent on ward staff, it is imperative to improve staff morale wherever possible. A prime example of an occupational group under stress is the attendant-nurse echelon.

In most hospitals, attendants are entrusted with the direct care of patients at the ward level. They are in contact with patients for many hours each day. The patients depend upon them for orientation, guidance, privileges, and plain human amenities. An unhappy, prejudiced, or angry attendant can make life miserable for the mentally ill person. Yet, the attendant is lowest in the hierarchy of hospital workers. He receives the lowest pay and the least instruction; he is often socially rejected by workers at higher levels; and he is unable to attract the attention and interest of the administrative staff. It is small wonder that he should seek outlets for his dissatisfaction through acting out against patients. The only available channel for relief is too often against the individual in his charge and against the welfare of the institution.

It has become, therefore, a basic principle of good management to carry out measures for the alleviation of staff tensions at all levels. Within the course of a busy hospital life, such tensions arise anew wherever changes of any significance take place. Many studies have been made of the functions, values, and rewards characteristic of various occupational roles. Various efforts have been made to determine how these variables can be modified or manipulated to help employees and ultimately benefit patients. Efforts to raise salaries and to provide stimulating educational opportunities, chances for self-expression, possibilities for promotion, and involvement in planning in the treatment of patients have all been made, with encouraging effects upon morale. There still remains a very great deal to be done, and efforts to upgrade the therapeutic potential of staff will certainly occupy administrators for a long time in the future.

Hospital organization and ideology. In recent years, social psychologists, sociologists, and anthropologists have paid considerable attention to the structure and function of hospital organization (Greenblatt et al., 1957), an interest which parallels in many respects their earlier analysis of human relations in the factory and the relevance of these to factory production. Social scientists have clarified considerably the relation of hospital organization to patient welfare and particularly the role of institutionalism in fostering health or disease. The kind of therapeutic ideology held by various citizens in the hospital community—custodialism or humanism, for example—may affect treatment results, and the kinds of decisions made by management, not merely with respect to day-to-day crises, but also with respect to overriding general orientations, can profoundly affect the functioning of the system. For example, the attitudes toward open or closed communication systems, toward open or closed doors in hospitals, toward research, toward psychoanalysis, toward somatic therapy, and toward change itself and speed of change are vital determinants of the characteristics of a therapeutic climate (Greenblatt & Levinson, 1959a). The essential unity of the hospital organization and the effect of the relationships of principal norm setters and leaders upon the health and vitality of the social system have been sharply focused by these studies.

Discharge of patients and decentralization of large hospitals. The earliest pioneers in American mental hospitals put great stock in knowing each person in their charge personally, and they warned against building hospitals to accommodate more than 200 or 250 patients. They claimed that a population beyond that number made it extremely difficult for the superintendent to maintain the personal relationships necessary for good care. Unfortunately, as we have seen, the state hospitals in our country have reached enormous and unwieldy size. It has become necessary to reduce them to manageable proportions. Indeed, the Joint Commission on Mental Illness and Health (1961) has recommended that no new hospital exceed 1,000 beds and that old hospitals be reduced to such size as soon as possible.

Three methods are available to accomplish these desirable ends: First is reduction of hospital census by discharge of all patients who can possibly be managed at home or in nursing situations or who can be handled on an outpatient or day status. This has indeed been a trend throughout the nation. The population in residence in mental hospitals has generally fallen slowly in recent years. This is due in part to removal of symptoms by tranquilizers, to improvement in behavior through social and other therapeutic methods, to earlier and more liberal discharge of patients, and to greater receptivity toward patients on the part of the family and the community. There is evidence that census reduction is a function of staff-patient relations in hospitals and also of staff-patient ratio. Hospitals that have succeeded in adding measurably to their staffs have generally been able to discharge more patients then those who have not enjoyed such advantages.

A second approach has been to prevent admissions by earlier case detection and emergency management in the community (see below). In effect, fewer are admitted, and staff attention can then be directed more to the long-term resident population and to methods of effecting their discharge.

The third method has been to decentralize large hospitals into smaller, semiautonomous units. In effect, several small hospitals replace the larger unit. Each smaller hospital has its own admission and intensive treatment facility and makes its own provision for the care of the aged and the infirm. The identification and loyalty of the staff in this instance are directed more to its own treatment-unit team than to its professional group as such. There are many advantages to this system; however, in hard-pressed hospitals with less than a minimum staff, it may be difficult or impossible to accomplish this decentralization without undue strain.

Continuity of patient care. Linked to the general problems of decentralization is the problem of continuity of patient care. Two models are available here. One sees it desirable to categorize or classify patients into groups based on some behavioral index such as "eloper," "untidy," "assaultive," "quiet," or "incontinent," and patients are moved from one area to another as their reputation changes. The other model assumes that continuous contact between staff and patient is more important than superficial behavioral manifestation. Long-term contact and responsibility for the patient in all phases of his hospital career are seen as basic necessities for therapeutic progress. This school of thought would have patients admitted to one ward and discharged from the same ward, always allied with the same treatment team. Transfers between wards are discouraged. In its fullest development, this model proposes that treatment personnel have contact with patients before admission, during hospitalization, and through discharge and the aftercare phase. The current trend favors the second model as being more consistent with modern psychological theory and practice.

The therapeutic team. A basic problem in hospitals is integration of efforts of professionals and other workers who come in contact with the patient. In earlier times the so-called "treatment team" consisted of only doctor and nurse. Today a much larger number of trained persons must work together. Each has something special to offer. The members of this team include the psychiatrist, the nurse, the psychologist, the psychiatric social worker, the occupational therapist, the recreational therapist, the industrial therapist, and the rehabilitation counselor. To this could be added any and all others who play a significant role in the patient's life, for example, the chaplain, the attendant, the volunteer, the housekeeper, and the employer of patients in any of the activities to which they are assigned during the day.

Space does not permit delineation of all these staff roles. Numerous meetings and conferences, formal and informal, are necessary to meet the communication requirements for proper coordination of efforts, and mature, consistent leadership must be provided by the psychiatrist or by some other trained, experienced person (Wolman, 1964).

Toward a Community Mental Hospital

The concept of the community mental hospital is based on the recognition that a hospital cannot, in the long run, rise above the level of the public's acceptance of its program. Each hospital perforce must work toward improving its public image and cultivating community support. The hospital cannot wait for the public to become interested in it but must actively foster education of citizens and then seek to incorporate them into its program for patient care and rehabilitation. Moreover, all occupations represented in the mental hospital will have to educate themselves to the tasks involved here—something that will require a considerable broadening of perspective in all of them.

The open door. A great many recent developments in hospital management deserve to be included among the efforts to develop community mental hospitals. First, there is the trend toward open doors, where formerly patients were incarcerated under lock and key (Greenblatt & Levinson, 1959b). When patient behavior has become less bizarre and more acceptable, whether this is accomplished through use of tranquilizers, an improved social program, or increased trust by staff, it becomes natural to consider opening doors to the outside. In recent years, following the leadership of the better English hospitals, innumerable doors have been opened and generally with favorable consequences. Patients have more freedom, staff is less burdened, escapes and suicides are not increased, and relatives are usually relieved that the patients are treated more humanely. Along with the opening of doors have come more liberal discharge policies, greater trust in the therapeutic value of family and community, and easier admission and readmission procedures. With patients less frightened, many more have been admitted and hospitalized under voluntary arrangements, and fewer have had to suffer the indignities of loss of civil rights or the stigma of legal commitment.

Staff as hospital envoys. Formerly, employment in a mental hospital carried the implication that the employee, like the patient, was in retreat from society. Part of this assumption was based on the fact that many employees lived within the walls of the hospital, where life was much less complicated and demanding, where rent was low or free, where meals were prepared, where there was no problem in commuting, etc. Dependency upon the hospital was thus fostered in the employee as it was in the patient. Many employees were ashamed of their hospital connections, and the fact that they received low wages added to the social perception of low status. Not fully recognized or appreciated was the incredible devotion to patient welfare of many of these hospital employees, who often worked under the most trying conditions.

In recent years, however, there has been a tendency for staff to live off campus, especially in urban hospitals. This trend appears to be a healthy one, insofar as it teaches employees the practical problems of life that will be faced by patients upon their discharge and encourages the employees to face the community without feelings of inferiority due to their association with the hospital. Indeed, they may be proud of their work and their hospital, tell their friends and neighbors about the program and its needs, and encourage them to contribute to it. Thus, workers formerly in retreat may become ambassadors of good will, performing an important public relations task.

Volunteers. Once unwanted, volunteers have now become a significant part of the mental health effort (Hyde & Hurley, 1950; Kline, 1947; Malamud, 1955). It is recognized that adequate staffing of mental hospitals through paid employees is an impossible strain on the state budget. On the other hand, citizens giving of their time without compensation can make a meaningful bridge from patient to community, assist staff in numerous flexible ways, and provide much needed "friendship therapy" to neglected patients. They may function as aides to occupational and recreational therapists, social workers, and others; they may also conduct educational courses and help with discharge planning and the like. Their increasing familiarity with mental illness and the hospital gives them a kind of leadership training essential to further mobilization of community and legislature in behalf of the hospital. Many of the volunteers have organized themselves into groups to engage in fund raising or to undertake special programs that bring patients into the community, where they can learn again the fundamental social skills needed to navigate on the outside. Organizations devoted to facilitation of occupational and industrial rehabilitation of patients form an additional link to the workaday world.

Within the last ten years, an impressive development has been the movement of student volunteers into the mental hospital; this started with students at the college level and more recently has included those from the high school ranks (Greenblatt & Kantor, 1961; Umbarger, Dalsimer, Morrison, & Breggin, 1962). It is heartening to think how great may be the influence of these young people in the cause of the mentally ill within the next two decades, as maturity brings them into roles of greater and greater social responsibility.

Transitional facilities and outpatient services. Since the step from hospital to community is often too great for easy negotiation, attempts have been made recently to establish transitional facilities to ease the shock of cultural discontinuity and to reduce the need for twenty-four-hour hospitalization. Many arrangements could be called "transitional"; the most significant of these are the day hospital, the halfway house, and the social therapeutic club. In addition, one might include outpatient services as facilities which bridge the gap from hospital to community and which function to prevent twenty-four-hour, full hospitalization. Only a word about each of these facilities is possible here.

DAY HOSPITAL OR PARTIAL HOSPITALIZATION. The day hospital has been in use since the early 1930s (Kramer, 1962). Essentially, the patient who has community ties and a family to look after him at night goes to the hospital by day, participates in the treatment program designed for him, and returns home in the evening to his family. This arrangement can be used for discharged patients or for a new patient whose illness is such that he can be handled without full hospitalization. Almost all forms of therapy can be used in the day setting, and with greater experience, almost every variety of illness can be handled there. Day hospitals have gained greatly in popularity in this country and abroad.

THE HALFWAY HOUSE. This refers to a familylike group living arrangement, especially suitable for patients who have no home to go to or whose homes are not suitable for them (Landy & Greenblatt, 1965). These facilities of necessity handle small numbers of cases, but it is felt that the close group interaction under professional supervision possesses therapeutic advantages not possible in other settings.

SOCIAL THERAPEUTIC CLUBS. These are organizations of expatients banded together to ease the tensions of full community relationships (Blair, 1955). They share their social occasions until they are strong enough to face society at large. Clubs may be run by hospitals or by patients independently of hospitals. Often they become interested in self-help through group therapy, through self-education, or through fostering better attitudes in the public. Many social therapeutic clubs now exist in this country and abroad and appear to fill a definite need for patients who are shy or squeamish when in full public view.

OUTPATIENT SERVICES. Outpatient services may be for any variety of case which can be managed by occasional visits with professional staff such as psychiatrist, social worker, or psychologist. These services may be for expatients to help in community adjustment or to prevent relapse. They may be utilized as well by the new patient whose disorder is not overwhelming and does not necessitate a disruptive break with society. A healthy trend to outpatient department and aftercare services is manifest throughout the country today.

Family therapy. It has long been recognized that the family is of strategic importance both in the development of the patient's illness and in his recovery. However, there has been great confusion as to how to deal with the family: Are they, for example, therapeutic object or therapeutic ally? In earlier times the family was excluded from the hospital as much as possible; it was felt that the reminder of past irritations and tensions would be harmful to the patient. In modern times there is more and more interest in including the family in the therapeutic scene (Ackerman, 1958; Paul, 1963). How to make proper use of the family or how to reintegrate the patient into the family household has been the question. Should it be via psychiatric social work services, by direct psychotherapy with family members, or by group activities with families? Should family members be hospitalized together with the sick patient?

All these methods have in fact been tried. Hospitalization of children with sick mothers is now being experimented with, and with some success (Grunebaum, Weiss, Hirsch, & Barrett, 1963). Here the reasoning is that young children and babies need not be separated from their parents during the crucial months of early development and that indeed it may be better for the parents to work through their problems while caring for the child than to have a period of guilt-ridden separation. Family members and whole families have been hospitalized along with the mentally ill person. Much more experience needs to be accumulated in this area before firm conclusions can be drawn.

For certain patients who have failed to make adequate progress in individual therapy during their hospitalization, several pioneering workers have undertaken to do intensive total family therapy with patient and family members together. The claim is that many personal impasses are resolved through such maneuvers, especially the working through of long-suppressed feelings of mourning in relation to shared family losses.

The role of the social worker in treating the family has been most strategic. In her contacts she has helped in the past to accomplish much that is now being attempted by newer techniques. In addition, she has been the most valuable resource in changing the environment to make it more suitable for the patient.

Emergency services and prevention of hospitalization. To some extent in this country, attempts are under way to develop extramural services similar to those pioneered by the Amsterdam experiment. In the latter, mobile teams of professionals answer calls for help in the community, dealing with emergencies as they arise and trying always to handle them within the context of family and community without separation of the patient from his environment.

In Boston two such experiments have been tried with success: the Home Treatment Service of Boston State Hospital (Perry, 1963) and the Community Extension Service of Massachusetts Mental Health Center (Greenblatt, Moore, Albert, & Solomon, 1963). While the methods are somewhat different, the essential aims are the same—to strike illness when first recognized; to work in the community with family, referring physician, and friends; to mobilize community agencies in support of the patient; and to prevent hospitalization, if at all possible.

Roughly 40 to 50 per cent of patients seen in the community who would be destined for admission may be prevented from entering the hospital, and the maintenance of ties to the community appears to be a most desirable end. At the same time the professional team learns crisis management in a sense not possible within the hospital, and they become better acquainted with problems in the community before illness and attitudes have had a chance to become hardened. There is every indication that these methods will spread and that education of workers in all the mental health disciplines will in the future include such new sociopsychiatric approaches to mental disorder.

The Therapeutic Society

It is difficult to appreciate how much societal attitudes have changed toward the mentally ill unless one has had the opportunity to observe, firsthand, the reduction of fear and stigmatization attending mental illness over the last few decades. While prejudice and suspiciousness are still rampant in most segments of society, the gains have been remarkable. Those who have practiced over a span of years have witnessed earlier referrals of sick individuals for help, earlier discharges to family and community, voluntary participation in the mental health movement by citizens everywhere, and increasingly wider responsibility for improving the lot of the mentally ill.

To an extent, the mental hospital has actually fostered these changes by direct efforts to involve the community in its program, recognizing that severe limitations are imposed upon it by a standoff attitude on the part of the public. Public relations work in the family, factory, school, and church has therefore become a necessary function of the modern mental hospital. The goal of a therapeutic society, which only a few years ago appeared to be an unattainable dream, now looms as a significant end in itself, an end that will also serve to facilitate and simplify the work of the mental hospital.

THE CHANGING ROLE OF THE CLINICAL PSYCHOLOGIST

The present period of rapid change presents both opportunities and threats to every professional (and other) group represented in the mental hospital. No traditional form of role definition is sacrosanct. The question facing each profession is not *whether* to change but rather *what kind* of change to foster and with what degree of rational consideration. The issue is perhaps most dramatically evident in the case of hospital psychiatry. Hospital psychiatrists have shown an increasing readiness to adopt and combine diverse approaches in order better to deal with the many-sided problems of treatment and rehabilitation. Somatic, dynamic, and social viewpoints, formerly conceived of as separate and even antagonistic, are coming more and more to be seen as interrelated aspects of an over-all approach to mental illness. The techniques involved in home treatment, in various forms of aftercare, in emergency services, and in halfway houses and day programs all require the development of concepts and of professional roles for which there is little precedent in traditional psychiatry. Such innovations are, of course, not without their "role strains" for psychiatrists and related professionals.

Since the *Handbook* is devoted primarily to problems of clinical psychology, it is perhaps fitting to conclude with a brief comment on the relevance of the changes in mental hospital structure and practice for the clinical psychologist. The professional form of clinical psychology, largely shaped during and immediately after World War II, has been built upon the three primary functions of diagnosis, psychotherapy, and research. Its theoretical context has been primarily that of dynamic psychology, and its research has been directed chiefly toward the study of psychopathology: the psychodynamics of various forms of mental illness and ego dysfunction and the developmental origins of such dysfunction in early childhood. In their clinical work, psychologists have in recent years sought to minimize their diagnostic functions and to gain greater legitimacy for their endeavors as psychotherapists. History appears to be on their side in this effort; it seems clear that psychotherapy cannot be limited to those with medical training and that its practice is diffusing over a wide range of professions, including clinical psychology.

However, the historical situation and the key issues of the mental health field today are drastically different from what they were twenty years ago. The basic legitimacy of dynamic psychology and psychiatry has been established, and the various psychotherapies are flourishing. At the same time, it has become apparent that, like love, psychotherapy is not enough. Clinical psychologists will have to widen their theoretical and therapeutic horizons if they are to make a significant contribution to the over-all field. The current revolution in mental hospitals involves, as we have noted, a convergence of dynamic with social and somatic approaches. Constructive changes in the organizational structure of hospitals require an understanding both of therapeutic techniques and of administration and social context. Clinical work in the wider community and in particular organizations (such as schools and work settings) requires a sociocultural perspective that clinical psychologists have until now been loath to develop. What can be done to help those persons—the majority of the population at present—for whom one or another form of intensive psychotherapy is not the appropriate treatment? Questions of this kind must be confronted. Apart from their practical importance, they have considerable theoretical relevance, serving as they do to broaden the scope of thought in clinical psychology. The very concrete challenges of work in mental hospitals and other community settings may do more than the exhortations of academic colleagues to bring about theoretical syntheses of dynamic personality theory with social psychology and with biology.

REFERENCES

Ackerman, N. W. *The psychodynamics of family life.* New York: Basic Books, 1958.

Barrabee, P. S. *A study of a mental hospital: the effects of its structure on its functions.* Unpublished doctoral dissertation, Harvard Univer., 1951.

Barton, W. E. Occupational therapy for psychiatric disorders. In W. R. Dunton & S. H. Licht (Eds.), *Occupational therapy.* Springfield, Ill.: Charles C Thomas, 1950.

Belknap, I. *Human problems of a state mental hospital.* New York: McGraw-Hill, 1956.

Bettelheim, B. *Love is not enough.* New York: Free Press, 1949.

Bierer, J., & Haldane, F. P. A self-governed patients' social club in a public mental hospital. *J. Ment. Sci.*, 1941, **87**, 419–426.

Blair, D. The therapeutic social club: an important measure of social rehabilitation in the treatment of psychiatric cases. *Ment. Hyg.*, 1955, **39**, 54–62.

Bockoven, J. S. Moral treatment in American psychiatry. *J. nerv. ment. Dis.*, 1956, **124**, 167–194, 292–321.

Bockoven, J. S. *Moral treatment in American psychiatry.* Springfield, Ill.: Charles C Thomas, 1963.

Bridger, H. The Northfield experiment. *Bull. Menninger Clin.*, 1946, **10**, 71–76.

Brill, H., & Patton, R. S. Analysis of population reduction in New York State mental hospitals during the first four years of large scale therapy with psycnotropic drugs. *Amer. J. Psychiat.*, 1959, **116**, 495–509.

Brown, Esther & Greenblatt, M. Social treatment. In M. Greenblatt, R. H. York, & Esther Brown, *From custodial to therapeutic patient care in mental hospitals.* New York: Russell Sage, 1955.

Caudill, W. *The psychiatric hospital as a small society.* Cambridge, Mass.: Harvard Univer. Press, 1958.

Cerletti, U. Electroshock therapy. *J. clin. exp. Psychopath.*, 1954, **15**, 191–217.

Cole, J. O., & Gerard, R. W. (Eds.) Psychopharmacology: problems in evaluation. *Natl Acad. Sci., Natl Res. Council Publ.*, 1959, No. 583.

Cumming, J., & Cumming, Elaine. Social equilibrium and social change in the large mental hospital. In M. Greenblatt, D. J. Levinson, & R. H. Williams (Eds.), *The patient and the mental hospital.* New York: Free Press, 1957. Pp. 49–71.

Deutsch, A. *The mentally ill in America.* (2nd ed.) New York: Columbia Univer. Press, 1949.

Dickens, C. *American notes for general circulation.* (3rd ed.) Vol. 1. London: Chapman and Hall, 1842. Pp. 105–111.

Dunham, N. W., & Weinberg, S. K. *The culture of the state mental hospital.* Detroit: Wayne State Univer. Press, 1960.

Freeman, W. Psychosurgery. *Amer. J. Psychiat.*, 1955, **111**, 518–520.

Freidson, E. (Ed.) *The hospital in modern society.* New York: Free Press, 1963.

Gibson, W. *The cobweb.* New York: Knopf, 1954.

Gilbert, Doris, & Levinson, D. J. Ideology, personality, and institutional policy in the mental hospital. *J. abnorm. soc. Psychol.*, 1956, **53**, 263–271.

Goffman, E. *Asylums.* Garden City, N.J.: Doubleday, 1961.

Greenblatt, M., Arnot, R., & Solomon, H. C. (Eds.) *Studies in lobotomy.* New York: Grune & Stratton, 1950.

Greenblatt, M., Grosser, G. H., & Wechsler, H. Differential response of hospitalized depressed patients to somatic therapy. *Amer. J. Psychiat.*, 1964, **120**, 935–943.

Greenblatt, M., & Kantor, D. Student volunteers in mental health. *Penn. Psychiat. Quart.*, 1961, **1**, 43–48.

Greenblatt, M . Levinson, D. J., & Williams, R. H. (Eds.) *The patient and the mental hospital.* New York: Free Press, 1957.

Greenblatt, M., & Levinson, D. J. Issues in a therapeutic organization. *Psychiat. Res. Rep.*, 1959, **2**. (a)

Greenblatt, M., & Levinson, D. J. The open door: a study of institutional change. In H. C. B. Denber (Ed.), *Research conference on the therapeutic community.* Springfield, Ill.: Charles C Thomas, 1959. (b)

Greenblatt, M., Levinson, D. J. & Klerman, G. L. (Eds.) *Mental patients in transition.* Springfield, Ill.: Charles C Thomas, 1961.

Greenblatt, M., Moore, R. F., Albert, R. S., & Solomon, Maida. *The prevention of hospitalization.* New York: Grune & Stratton, 1963.

Greenblatt, M., Robertson, Emily, & Solomon, H. C. Five-year follow-up of one hundred cases of bilateral prefrontal lobotomy. *J. Amer. med. Ass.*, 1953, **151**, 200–202.

Greenblatt, M., & Solomon, H. C. (Eds.) *Frontal lobes and schizophrenia.* New York: Springer, 1953.

Greenblatt, M., York, R., & Brown, Esther. *From custodial to therapeutic care in mental hospitals.* New York: Russell Sage, 1955.

Grunebaum, H., Weiss, J., Hirsch, Linda, & Barrett, J. The baby on the ward. *Psychiatry*, 1963, **26**, 39–53.

Henry, J. Types of institutional structure. In M. Greenblatt, D. J. Levinson, & R. H. Williams (Eds.), *The patient and the mental hospital.* New York: Free Press, 1957. Pp. 73–90.

Hyde, R. W. *Experiencing the patient's day.* New York: Putnam, 1955.

Hyde, R. W., & Atwell, C. R. Evaluating the effectiveness of a psychiatric occupational therapy program. *Amer. J. occup. Ther.*, 1948, **2**, 332–349.

Hyde, R. W., & Hurley, Catherine. Volunteers in mental hospitals. *Psychiat. Quart. Suppl.*, 1950, **24**, 233–249.

Hyde, R. W., & Solomon, H. C. Patient government: a new form of group therapy. *Dig. Neurol. Psychiat.*, 1950, **18**, 207–218.

Joint Commission on Mental Illness and Health. *Action for mental health.* New York: Basic Books, 1961.

Jones, M. *The therapeutic community.* New York: Basic Books, 1953.

Kennard, E. A. Psychiatry, administrative psychiatry, administration: a study of a veterans hospital. In M. Greenblatt, D. J. Levinson, & R. H. Williams (Eds.), *The patient and the mental hospital.* New York: Free Press, 1957. Pp. 36–45.

Kline, N. S. Volunteer workers. *Occup. Ther. Rehabilit.*, 1947, **26**, 153–166. (Also included in W. H. Soden. *Rehabilitation of the handicapped.* New York: Ronald, 1949.)

Kramer, B. M. *Day hospital: a study of partial hospitalization in psychiatry.* New York: Grune & Stratton, 1962.

Landy, D., & Greenblatt, M. *Halfway house.* Washington, D.C.: Vocational Rehabilitation Administration, 1965.

Levinson, D. J., & Gallagher, E. B. *Patienthood in the mental hospital.* Boston: Houghton Mifflin, 1964.

Malamud, Irene T. Volunteers in community mental health work: the respective roles of laymen and professionally-trained persons. *Ment. Hyg.*, 1955, **39**, 300–309.

Mezer, R. R., & Solomon, H. C. Value of electric-shock treatment on outpatients. *New Engl. J. Med.*, 1954, **250**, 721–722.

Moniz, E. Prefrontal lobotomy in the treatment of mental disorder. *Amer. J. Psychiat.*, 1936–1937, **93**, 1379–1385.

Niswander, P. D., & Hyde, R. W. The value of crafts in psychiatric occupational therapy. *Amer. J. occup. Ther.*, 1954, **8**, 104–106.

Parsons, T. The mental hospital as a type of organization. In M. Greenblatt, D. J. Levinson, & R. H. Williams (Eds.), *The patient and the mental hospital.* New York: Free Press, 1957.

Paul, N. Workshop on perspectives in family therapy. Paper read at Amer. Orthopsychiat. Ass., Washington, D.C., March, 1963.

Perry, S. E. Home treatment and the social system of psychiatry. *Psychiatry*, 1963, **26**, 54–64.

Pratt, S., Scott, G., Treesh, E., et al. The mental hospital and the treatment field. *J. Psychol. Studies*, 1960, 11.

Rapoport, R. N. *Community as doctor.* Springfield, Ill.: Charles C Thomas, 1960.

Ray, I. Ideal characters of the officers of a hospital for the insane. *Amer. J. Psychiat.*, 1873, **30**, 67.

Sakel, M. The classical Sakel shock treatment: a reappraisal. *J. clin. exp. Psychopath.*, 1954, **15**, 255–316.

Sanborn, F. B. *Memoirs of Pliny Earle, M.D.* Boston: Donnell and Upham, 1898.

Stanton, A., & Schwartz, M. S. *The mental hospital.* New York: Basic Books, 1954.

Trustees of the State Lunatic Asylum at Worcester. *Twenty-second annual report.* Author, 1854.

Umbarger, C., Dalsimer, J., Morrison, A., & Breggin, P. *College students in a mental hospital.* New York: Grune & Stratton, 1962.

von Mering, O., & King, S. *Remotivating the mental patient.* New York: Russell Sage, 1957.

Ward, Mary Jane. *The snake pit.* New York: New American Library, 1955.

Worcester Insane Asylum. *Sixteenth annual report: 1893.* Boston: Wright and Potter, 1894.

Wilmer, H. A. *Social psychiatry in action.* Springfield, Ill.: Charles C Thomas, 1958.

Wolman, B. B. Non-participant observation on a closed ward. *Acta Psychother.*, 1964, **12**, 61–71.

50

Psychological Aspects of Physical Illness and Hospital Care

IRVING L. JANIS AND HOWARD LEVENTHAL

There has been a growing effort in recent years to deal with the various psychological problems arising from physical illness and hospitalization. The main purpose of this chapter is to indicate the nature of psychological changes observed in clinically normal personalities during illness and to call attention to preventive and corrective techniques for coping with the adjustment problems encountered in the medical and surgical wards of general hospitals. We shall present a set of theoretical concepts appropriate for analyzing stress reactions, together with brief summaries of pertinent research findings. In discussing these topics we shall emphasize "psychological" rather than "physical" or "physiological" factors that enter into adaptive and maladaptive reactions to life stress. We shall also attempt to suggest relevant research areas that can help to advance our theoretical understanding of the psychological impact of illness and hospitalization on normal personalities.

PROBLEMS OF DIAGNOSING SOMATO–PSYCHOLOGICAL DISORDERS

When a well-trained clinical psychologist or psychiatrist begins working in a large general hospital, before he acquires any special knowledge of stress reactions, he is likely to feel puzzled and even somewhat disoriented. He will be surprised at the extraordinary varieties of seemingly gross behavior pathology among physically ill patients and at subsequent changes in patient behavior that frequently turn out to be the opposite of what he had expected.

For certain cases, his diagnostic and perhaps pessimistic prognostic judgments will turn out to be quite correct. For example, on a large surgical ward, there will be an occasional patient who begins to display hallucinations, delusions, and other psychotic symptoms characteristic of schizophrenic disorders. Such cases can be readily identified as postoperative psychoses. On the basis of his training in psychopathology, a psychologist or psychiatrist can readily verify in his own experience the well-known generalization that such reactions cannot in any way be distinguished from the familiar pathological patterns seen in mental hospitals, the only difference being that the onset has been precipitated by the life stress of physical illness (cf. Abeles, 1937–1938; Miller, 1939; Preu & Guida, 1937; Titchener, Zwerling, Gottschalk, Levine, Culbertson, Cohen, & Silver, 1956; Washburne & Carns, 1935). So too with the cases of men and women suffering from cancer or other chronic diseases who develop psychotic depressions. Also quite familiar will be the somewhat more frequent cases of women on the obstetrical wards who develop a neurotic type of postpartum depression, for most of whom the current stress experience functions as a precipitating event.

The situation is quite different, however, for the vast majority of manifestly disturbed people seen on the hospital wards—people who are suffering from recurrent pains, the threat of mutilating treatment, confinement, separation from loved ones, and a variety of other stresses. Their emotional outbursts, preoccupation with bodily processes, and relative lack of interest in the social world might initially incline a naïve clinician to assume that the hospital experiences have precipitated in these people a severe neurosis or borderline withdrawal and hypochondriac reactions. If he makes a diagnosis of this type, the inexperienced clinician would certainly not predict that the psychological symptoms will clear up spontaneously when there is a change in environmental conditions. He might expect a relatively poor prognosis even if these patients were to be treated with prolonged psychotherapy.

The outlook for such cases is likely to seem all the more grave if they are given psychodiagnostic tests. On the Rorschach test, for example, these patients usually show a striking number of anatomical responses and related indications of regressive concentration of interest on the self. A study by Singeisen (1940) reported that among 40 chronic cardiac cases and 50 chronic pulmonary tuberculosis cases, the extraordinarily large number of anatomical and damaged-body responses (suggestive of pathological preoccupation with bodily processes) exceeded that found in cases of chronic hypochondriasis or anxiety neurosis. Similar results have also been reported in a Rorschach study of women hospitalized for gynecological surgery (Klatskin, 1952).

Further contact with convalescing patients will enable an alert observer to recognize the many serious deficiencies in applying to this population the diagnostic and prognostic criteria derived exclusively from investigations of chronic neurosis, psychosis, and psychosomatic disorders. In their monograph on adjustment to physical handicap and illness, Barker, Wright, Meyerson, and Gonick (1953) have suggested that the affective and behavioral symptoms seen in patients hospitalized for acute physical illnesses should be regarded as *somatopsychological* problems, which should be sharply differentiated from the more frequently discussed psychosomatic problems. One of the main differentiating criteria they discuss is the degree to which the symptoms are dependent on the current life stresses to which the patient is subjected.[1] A psychosomatic reaction, like the majority of chronic neurotic symptoms, is difficult to modify; when one symptom is apparently cured, another one will appear in its place. But a somatopsychological reaction is closely related to the objective conditions of the patient's current life situation and, unless it involves irreversible physical damage, will improve when the intensity of physical suffering or external stress decreases. The patient's egocentricity, hypochondriasis, regressive dependency, and affective symptoms are highly *reversible* and can sometimes be alleviated rapidly merely by eliminating a source of severe threat, discomfort, or frustration.

Ferraro (1948) pointed out that somatopsychological problems were being neglected by clinical investigators who were emphasizing the importance of psychogenic mechanisms in digestive disorders, heart disease, and other somatic pathology without paying much attention to the reverse type of causal sequence. A number of recent studies have begun to fill in the gap by elucidating the psychological effects of various types of illness, surgery, and hospitalization. One result of these studies has been the specification of criteria that help to differentiate somatopsychological problems into pathological and nonpathological reactions to stress. By a "pathological" reaction is meant maladaptive behavior that is based on a relatively fixed neurotic (or psychotic) personality predisposition. Whenever stress

[1] Somatopsychological disorders also include a large number of physical and chemical changes that occur during illness and treatment, which may lead to psychosis. The disease process may destroy important organs, including nerve tissue, and the structural alterations may have profound effects upon behavior. Moreover, infections, toxins, and drugs may alter the chemical balance of the organism, which can in turn generate acute behavioral alterations. Psychoses induced by somatopsychological factors have been extensively studied along with other "organic psychoses," and well-known criteria have been worked out for differential diagnosis. What have been neglected, however, are those somatopsychological disorders of a neuroticlike character, arising from chronic pain, confinement, separation, and other reversible features of illness and hospitalization.

stimuli of a given type are present, the person will repeatedly show a panic reaction or some other inappropriate or exaggerated response. A nonpathological stress reaction *may* be equally maladaptive, but it is *not* a fixed consequence of the individual's personality makeup, and it *can be prevented* if the appropriate situational factors are present. These contrasting terms should be regarded, of course, as extremes on a continuum that ranges from a high degree to a low degree of dependence on personality predisposition.

The psychiatric literature emphasizes the highly personal and pathological nature of nonadaptive stress reactions by focusing mainly on incapacitating anxiety and depressive reactions that are determined by differences in individual predispositions. But among people who are not pathologically disposed, much of the variability in stress reactions depends on differences in *situational factors*, including features of the hospital environment that can be altered by administrative policies and training of the staff. The presence of striking differences in the emotional reactions of the same person during different hospitalizations strongly suggests that environmental factors in the current life situation are important determinants of emotional control (cf. Janis, 1958). Parallel observations can be found in studies of civilian behavior in disasters (Glover, 1942; Janis, 1951; Schmideberg, 1942) and of military crews in combat (Hastings, Wright, & Glueck, 1944), all of which indicate that under relatively extreme conditions, situational variables account for a high degree of the variance in emotional control and in the occurrence of maladaptive behavior.

Modifiability, as a function of environmental events and interpersonal communications, is the first important characteristic denoting the nonpathological emotional states, such as grief, fear, guilt, and anger, that occur under exposure to stress stimuli. Such emotional reactions have been described as "reflective" in character, both in the sense of being highly influenced by deliberation or thoughtful anticipations and in the sense of reflecting the realities of the person's current life situation (see Janis, 1962). A second important characteristic of these reflective emotions is their potentially adaptive significance. A number of unique functional properties have been specified in some detail for "reflective fear," enabling us to differentiate such reactions from neurotic or psychotic anxiety. Similar differentiating characteristics remain to be worked out for reflective forms of grief, guilt, anger, and other emotional states in order to differentiate these reality-based reactions from their pathological counterparts.

In the section which follows, we shall give a preliminary account of the functional characteristics of reflective grief, emphasizing those features that differentiate it from neurotic grief and the acute psychiatric disorders diagnosed as "reactive depression." Special attention will be given to the positive value of reflective grief for preventing severe reactive depression and related incapacitating responses to severe deprivation. The distinction is of particular relevance for making correct prognostic assessments. In a later section on reflective fear, a similar positive consequence will also become apparent. Evidence will be cited from research studies of surgical patients which indicate that a moderate degree of reflective fear during the preoperative period tends to reduce the likelihood that a person will be overwhelmed by subsequent stress stimuli. To put it another way, if a person does *not* react to stress situations involving serious physical danger with reflective fear, or if he does not react to stress situations involving profound loss with reflective grief, there are likely to be adverse psychological consequences at a later time.

Underreactions to external stress, as we shall see, are often *nonpathological* in character; i.e., they do not imply a preexisting emotional disorder, since they occur in persons whose life histories indicate that they are clinically normal. But, although nonpathological, such underreactions are potentially *pathogenic* in that they can lead to subsequent emotional disorder. These pathogenic consequences are mentioned at this point because they highlight the second of two main types of diagnostic errors that might be made by a naïve clinician when he first observes patients on the medical and surgical wards of a general hospital. As we saw earlier, the first type consists of errors of *commission*, i.e., judging patients with intense emotional disturbances that are situationally determined as suffering from pathological disorders and therefore expecting the disturbed behavior to persist after the current stresses have been alleviated. The second type consists of errors of *omission*, i.e., failing to identify the patients with a calm and undisturbed facade whose underreactions to stress are *pathogenic* in character.

REFLECTIVE GRIEF AND THE WORK OF MOURNING

According to numerous psychological studies of illness and disaster, direct exposure to the danger of mutilation or annihilation gives rise to acute emotional shock, followed by preoccupation with disturbing memories of the traumatic events and related forms of emotional disturbance (see Janis, 1951; Janis, 1958; Wolfenstein, 1957). These studies indicate that among clinically normal persons who have no prior history of neurotic disturbance, the symptoms usually subside within a few days or weeks. The first signs of recovery usually do not appear until after a phase of acute grief. Especially in physically injured and diseased persons, there is a well-known sequence such that acceptance of the medical regimen and psychological readjustment during the course of normal convalescence gradually occurs following an initial period of overt grieving and preoccupation with loss (Blank, 1957; Cholden, 1954; Dembo, Levitan, & Wright, 1956; Wright, 1960).

While the most acute manifestations of grief occur in response to the death of a loved person, the same type of affective reaction is aroused by the temporary or permanent loss of any positively cathected object or activity that is regarded as part of the self. Thus, grief is to be expected whenever there is separation from one's family, a decline in one's social status, or a loss of any physical structure or bodily function that entails a marked change in one's body image. In addition to pessimism, crying, feelings of sadness, and other obvious manifestations of grief, there is likely to be generalized inhibition accompanied by a profound withdrawal of interest from daily life activities, with a corresponding concentration upon, or "mulling over," the loss.

To the extent that such grief reactions are reflective and nonpathological, their intensity and duration will appear to be roughly proportional to the perceived magnitude and importance of the loss. Thus, just as in the case of other reflective emotional reactions, the degree of arousal evoked in an ailing person is highly dependent upon external signs and information concerning the extent of his body damage and incapacitation. Among the effective external cues are the facial expressions and other expressive behaviors on the part of the hospital staff, as well as their verbal comments about the prospects for physical recovery.

Freud (1917) has drawn attention to the way in which reminiscences about a missing object repeatedly confront the mourner with painful comparisons between the richness of his past life when the beloved person was alive and the emptiness of the present and future. His theory of the work of mourning postulates that as the person engages in this form of bereavement, he gradually "works it through" so that he comes to accept the limitations imposed by the loss, regains his interest in daily activities, and ultimately is able to console himself. Freud applied his theoretical concept primarily to the process of recovering from the death of a loved person or the loss of an ideal that is a substitute for a parent. There are many indications from studies of psychological stress that essentially the same type of working through goes on in physically ill people when they are grieving over the loss of their former state of physical well-being or the loss of specific physical capabilities.

When suffering and the threat of annihilation extend over a period of many months, as in the case of a chronic disease, the process of working through evidently goes on gradually and gives rise to a profound change in personal outlook. Shands (1955) has described the characteristic phases and changes in attitude observed in cancer patients. When a person is first told—or strongly suspects—that he has a malignacy, his initial reaction usually consists of dazed emotional shock, apathetic numbness, feelings of depersonalization, and inhibition of action. Shands points out that the patient feels "empty" of purpose and unable to make plans for the future as a consequence of his alien, "doomed" status. After a short time, however, a second phase begins, characterized by intense preoccupation with the illness, combined with unsuccessful attempts to alleviate emotional tension by projecting the blame onto doctors or nurses. During this phase the patient strives to deny the obvious implications of the malignant disease. According to Shands, these unsuccessful attempts are followed by a third phase, in which the person *grieves* over his condition and then gradually readapts, overcoming the sense of emptiness by forming a new conception of himself which is facilitated by a process of identification. More specifically, the patient identifies himself with someone in the role of a "good helper" or a "good child," and in this adopted role he no longer shies away from people. He has now found a way of obtaining satisfaction from his interaction not only with doctors and nurses but also with his family, friends, and fellow patients. The crucial phase in this development, Shands asserts, is the grieving reaction, which is essential for replacing the initial alien outlook with a more constructive one:

> Grieving is a response to the loss of a whole system of assumptions and expectations upon which human beings build a view of the world. In some manner the weeping reaction . . . serves to "dissolve" the old system in such a way that it can be replaced by a new. Where the grieving is blocked for any reason, the patient has to adopt some precarious defensive sort of adaptation rather than attempting, after clearing the site, to make a new construction with the materials at hand.

This reorientation is regarded as "adaptive," since it enables the patient to take an interest in the social world again, to seek and obtain consolation from others, to plan his actions in a realistic way that maximizes his chances for survival, and to take account of various limitations imposed by his illness.

Observations of injured disaster victims, tuberculosis cases, and many other types of medical patients also suggest that poor adjustment during convalescence and subsequent emotional disturbances are more likely to ensue if the period of grief is postponed or evaded by means of continuous denial attempts (Cobb & Lindemann, 1943; Lindemann, 1944; Wright, 1960). Perhaps the most extreme examples of the pathogenic consequences of denial and the warding off of overt grief are to be found in pediatric wards and in institutions for chronically ill children. In children, prolonged separation from parents, combined with physical suffering and other stresses of hospitalization, can give rise to superficial acceptance and compliance involving an extreme degree of affective detachment (Bowlby, 1952; Robertson, 1958). The apparently "good" behavior of young children evidently is based on extreme denial mechanisms which have highly pathogenic consequences for subsequent personality development. Hospital policies can play a major role in determining whether or not appropriate situational supports will be available for fostering normal grief reactions in children. Such reactions are facilitated when parents are permitted to visit the wards frequently and when warm maternal treatment is given by the nurses. Solnit (1960) suggests that members of the pediatrics staff can benefit from training oriented toward making them more empathic and less competitive with the mothers of hospitalized children. The mothers, in turn, can be aided by special preparation procedures to help them gain confidence, understanding, and satisfaction in mothering their miserable, suffering children.

In adults, personality predispositions acquired from earlier experiences of separation and object loss probably make for more marked individual differences than in children, but similar situational factors enter in as determinants of grief reactions. Shands (1955) points out that a warm social environment and the availability of sympathetic listeners can greatly facilitate the reorientation process in stricken adults, provided that the personality of the patient is sufficiently "mature." In patients suffering from serious diseases, the completion of the work of mourning, as Shands suggests, apparently depends upon the availability of parent surrogates and appropriate role models with whom the patient can identify.

REFLECTIVE FEAR AND MALADAPTIVE REACTIONS TO THREAT

Freud distinguished between "neurotic anxiety" arising from inner dangers linked with the person's unconscious impulses and "normal fear" (or "objective anxiety") occurring when a person is aware of a known danger. He recognized, however, that the question of whether or not the person is aware of an external danger is not an entirely dependable criterion (1936, p. 148). Studies of people facing the threats of surgery, epidemics, accidents, and large-scale disasters bear out Freud's observations that reality-oriented fears are sometimes heavily overlaid with neurotic anxiety or neurotic guilt (Janis, 1958; Wolfenstein, 1959). Therefore, criteria other than the eliciting stimulus must be used to differentiate nonneurotic from neurotic reactions. Taking account of such studies, Janis (1962) has elucidated the distinction between neurotic anxiety and reflective fear by describing a number of functional properties that Freud alluded to implicitly but did not specify.

The construct "reflective fear" can be anchored to empirical observations by positing the following four functional properties:

1. In contrast to the relatively unmodifiable character of neurotic anxiety, the onset and intensity of reflective fear depend upon perceptions of actual threat stimuli, warning communications, and other environmental cues that convey information about impending danger.

2. A major behavioral consequence of reflective fear is a strong need for vigilance. In the average hospitalized patient, some of the dominant forms of vigilant activity consist in paying close attention to any new or unusual feelings of physical discomfort, requesting information from the staff, and becoming tense when injections or other distressing treatments are about to be administered.

3. Another consequence of reflective fear is a strong need for alleviating emotional tension by obtaining convincing reassurances. Like vigilance, the need for reassurance gives rise to changes in cognitions as well as affects and actions. For example, many hospitalized patients show selective retention of the staff's optimistic remarks that minimize the danger. Other manifestations of the heightened need for reassurance include the readiness with which patients adopt a fatalistic outlook, increase their faith in divine protection, and make use of magical or superstitious practices for warding off bad luck. The most extreme forms of reassurance are those involving anticipations of total invulnerability: the person feels convinced either that the danger will never materialize in his vicinity ("It can't happen here") or that, if it does, he will be completely protected from it ("Others may suffer, but I shall be safe"). Such extreme anticipations, referred to as "blanket reassurances," sometimes completely dominate vigilance tendencies, as is seen in certain cancer patients who fail to seek medical aid even though suffering from serious symptoms (cf. B. C. Cobb, Clark, McGuire, & Howe, 1954).

4. The two tendencies do not *necessarily* conflict every time both are aroused, and it is possible to develop *discriminative compromise defenses* which combine both vigilance (anticipating danger, remaining alert to signs of threat) and reassurance (expecting to be able to cope successfully with the danger or to be helped by others if the danger becomes extreme). A common type of compromise defense among chronic cardiac patients who learn to live with their illness involves *danger-contingent* reassurances. The person acknowledges his potential vulnerability to another attack and makes plans for carrying out protective actions that will help him to survive if acute symptoms recur. Such an attitude, combining discriminative vigilance with reassurance, is likely to be much more adaptive than an attitude of either blanket reassurance or indiscriminate vigilance.

Figure 1 shows the three alternative modes of responding when reflective fear is aroused in threat situations. The likelihood that one or another of the three modes of defense will occur depends upon a large number of situational as well as predispositional variables. For example, when a physician recommends a minor procedure or warns that a relatively unimportant physical defect is likely to occur,

Figure 1. Hypothetical consequences of the arousal of reflective fear (*Janis, 1962*).

a clinically normal person will tend to react with only a low degree of reflective fear. A mild emotional reaction of this type can be rapidly dissipated by a blanket reassurance (e.g., "There's nothing to it"), leaving the patient's behavior unaffected by the warning. Such reassurances will have adaptive value if the danger does not exceed that suggested by the warning, since time and energy will not have been wasted on useless preparation. If serious dangers were to materialize, however, the sequence would prove to be highly maladaptive.

When he receives warning of serious danger, the clinically normal person can be expected to show a moderate or high degree of reflective fear. This will generally induce either strong vigilance and reassurance-seeking responses—that are gradually reduced as the person develops reality-oriented compromise defenses of a discriminative nature—or overreactions that are maladaptive because they lead to useless expenditure of energy and impulsive or inefficient behavior. The latter type of reaction does not necessarily imply neurotic anxiety. Bard (1952) has described such overreactions in women who were hospitalized for the surgical removal of the breast. They were constantly alert, unable to sleep, subject to attacks of tachycardia, and extraordinarily watchful, as though mobilized to shield themselves from further injury. The available evidence suggests that any normal person, whether or not he is hypersensitive to a given threat, is capable of displaying panic and other manifestations of indiscriminate vigilance if he perceives an impending danger as being far greater than his limited resources for escaping it (see Janis, Chapman, Gillin, & Spiegel, 1955; Withey, 1962). The greater the positive disparity between the *perceived magnitude of the danger* and the *perceived capacity for coping with it*, the higher the probability of an indiscriminate vigilance reaction. (See Janis, in press.)

A different type of maladaptive outcome results from extreme underreactions to a serious threat. These underreactions, which leave the individual completely unprepared, sometimes resemble the denial symptoms encountered in bland psychotics, but they are not necessarily pathological, inasmuch as the exclusive use of a blanket-reassurance defense often depends upon lack of adequate warnings, misleading information, or other environmental conditions. Although nonpathological, i.e., occurring in persons whose life histories indicate that they are clinically normal, such reactions are potentially *pathogenic*, as is indicated by the series of research investigations to be discussed in the next two sections.

PREOPERATIVE AND POSTOPERATIVE REACTIONS OF SURGICAL PATIENTS

Janis's (1958) studies of surgical patients provide considerable preliminary evidence concerning the potentially positive consequences of a moderate degree of reflective fear and provide clues to a working-through process that can be initiated *before* actual exposure to danger stimuli. With the cooperation of the Surgery Department of the Yale Medical School, 23 typical patients on the surgical wards of the Grace–New Haven Hospital were interviewed intensively before and after undergoing major surgery. Hospital records, including the physicians' and nurses' daily notes on each patient's behavior, were also used. The patients were classified into three categories—high, moderate, and low preoperative fear—according to the available interview data and behavioral records concerning their preoperative emotional status.

The following conclusions from the case study series were also supported by correlational data from a survey research study conducted with about two hundred male adolescents who had undergone a recent surgical procedure.

1. Persons who were *extremely fearful* before the operation were *more* likely than others to be *anxiety-ridden* again afterward, and their excessive fears of body damage were linked with clinical signs of chronic neurotic disturbance.

2. Persons who displayed a *moderate* degree of preoperative fear were significantly *less* likely than others to display *any apparent form of emotional disturbance* during the stressful period of postoperative convalescence.

3. Persons who showed a relative *absence* of preoperative fear were *more* likely than others to display reactions of *anger* and *intense resentment* during postoperative convalescence.

Many additional observations contribute evidence in support of the following general theoretical proposition: The arousal of reflective fear prior to exposure to a stressful life situation is one of the necessary conditions for developing effective inner defenses that enable the person to cope psychologically with stress stimuli.

Some individuals (notably those who displayed excessively high anxiety before the operation) appear to benefit relatively little from mentally rehearsing the dangers in advance. Evidently they are neurotically predisposed persons of the type described in psychoanalytic reports; i.e., they tend to overreact to environmental threats and dangers because their displaced castration anxiety or masochistic wishes, arising from unconscious conflicts, are reactivated whenever they perceive either the remote or the imminent possibility of suffering actual body damage (see Fenichel, 1945).

The psychological situation appears to have been quite different among the patients in the "moderate preoperative fear" group. These people appeared to be highly responsive to reassurances from the hospital authorities and seemed to have developed discriminative compromise defenses that enabled them to cope effectively with the subsequent stresses of the postoperative period. Such patients would frequently report instances of successful self-reassurance in their postoperative interviews, for example, "I knew that there might be some bad pains, and so when my side started to ache I told myself that this doesn't mean anything has gone wrong."

Such self-reassurances appeared to be rare among the patients who had been relatively free from fear before the operation. During the period when they were able to deny the possibility of danger and suffering, they remained calm; when they began to experience the pains and other harassments that accompany the usual recovery from a major operation, they became extremely tense or angry and tended to assume that the hospital staff must be to blame for their suffering. In a few such cases, it seemed probable that this way of reacting to external dangers was a manifestation of a characteristic personality tendency and might be quite unrelated to any events occurring either before or after the operation. In most of the other cases, however, it seemed extremely likely that the individual's lack of fear beforehand—and the consequent lack of inner preparation for coping with the stresses of surgery—was the result of the *absence of adequate preparatory communications.*

From the survey of a large sample of male surgery cases, Janis (1958, pp. 354–360) obtained some relevant correlational evidence on this point. He found that the postoperative reactions of men who had been informed beforehand about specific unpleasant experiences that were in store for them differed significantly from those of men who were uninformed. The uninformed cases were more likely than the informed to indicate, when their attitudes were assessed many months after the operation, that (1) they were not at all fearful *before* the operation, (2) they became angry or emotionally upset during the postoperative convalescent period, and (3) they felt resentful or derogatory toward the doctors and nurses.

These correlational data are based on retrospective reports and therefore cannot be accepted as conclusively valid evidence. Nevertheless, they parallel the findings from the intensive case studies and add weight to the following conclusions: If no authoritative communications are given and if other circumstances are such that reflective fear is *not* aroused beforehand, the person will lack the motivation to undergo the learning process that enables him to build up effective compromise defenses (danger-contingent reassurances) before the onset of the crisis, and therefore he will have relatively low stress tolerance when the crisis situation is actually at hand.

ADDITIONAL STUDIES ON THE RELATIONSHIP BETWEEN PRESTRESS AND POSTSTRESS REACTIONS

A search of the literature on psychological effects of surgical operations, acute illness, physical disability, and hospitalization reveals a number of findings that are consistent with the general conclusions from the surgery studies summarized in the preceding section (cf. Cramond & Aberd, 1954; Deutsch, 1942; Drellich, Bieber, & Sutherland, 1956; Lindemann, 1941; Prugh, 1953; Titchener et al., 1957). For example, Drellich et al. (1956) report that patients who remain "carefree" during the preoperative period are more likely to lose emotional control and become panic-stricken when undergoing the stressful experiences that ensue from surgery.

Some systematic observations bearing on

the relationship between reflective fear and subsequent reactions during a related type of stressful crisis are presented by Cramond and Aberd (1954). These authors compared 50 women who had undergone normal labor with 50 who had developed severe uterine dysfunction during labor, a type of dysfunction which in most instances is assumed to be a somatic manifestation of acute anxiety in response to the stresses of childbirth. It was found that the women in the dysfunctional group were much more likely to have a history of "suppression or repression of feelings of tension." This antecedent characteristic was found in 54 per cent of the dysfunctional group, as compared with only 12 per cent of the normal control group. Thus a relative absence of fear during the precrisis period was found to be associated with high emotional disturbance during the crisis period.

A number of other studies of adult surgical patients provide pertinent findings (Deutsch, 1942; Lindemann, 1941; Titchener et al., 1957), some of which appear to bear out the previously cited findings, and some of which apparently do not. It is difficult to determine, however, the extent to which the findings are inconsistent, especially since the best of the available data come from group comparisons where unknown variables exert an influence and where the techniques for assessing the individual's preoperative and postoperative reactions differ from one study to the next. It should be noted, however, that none of the studies reported so far offers any impressive evidence negating the main conclusions concerning the relationship between preoperative fear and postoperative emotional disturbance.

In contrast to the necessarily ambiguous findings from purely correlational studies, clear-cut evidence is available from a few experimental studies which have tested the effects of giving preparatory information and related staff practices on stress tolerance. A laboratory experiment by Lazarus, Speisman, Mordkoff, and Davison (1962) indicates that orienting communications and preliminary information can markedly reduce the emotional reactivity of young men to frightening stimuli (a film depicting genital mutilation). A study by Prugh, Staub, Sands, Kirschbaum, and Lenihan (1953) indicates that it is possible to reduce the over-all incidence of severe emotional disturbances among hospitalized children by modifying the traditional practices of ward management so as to introduce special forms of preparation and reassurance designed to take account of the patients' emotional needs. In this study, two equated groups, each containing 100 cases of physically ill children, were selected as control and experimental groups. The control series, obtained over a period of four months, was exposed to traditional American practices of ward management. Then, after every one of the control cases had left the hospital, an experimental program of ward management was put into effect. This program placed considerable emphasis on psychological preparation and emotional support, including such features as (1) giving each parent a special pamphlet containing advice on what to tell the child and explaining the importance of the parent's role in the child's hospital care; (2) asking the parents to accompany the child to the ward, to introduce the child to the staff, and to arrange for daily visits; (3) encouraging the child to participate in free-play activities under the supervision of a nursery school teacher; and (4) giving the child special information and reassurances before injections, catheterizations, and other distressing treatments.

In the control series, especially among the younger children, there was a sizable incidence of acute panic states following departure of the parents. These children also showed symptoms of depression and withdrawal, resembling the varieties of severe separation reactions described by Bowlby (1952) and Robertson (1958). Such reactions were observed much less often in the experimental group. Only 14 per cent of the entire latter group showed extreme symptoms of anxiety or depression, as compared with 36 per cent of the control group. At the opposite extreme, 32 per cent of the experimental group showed excellent adaptation to stress (mild emotional reactions with rapid recovery), as compared with only 8 per cent of the control group.

It is also noteworthy that in the experimental group, aggressive reactions to medical procedures were only half as frequent and were less intense than in the control group, a difference which Prugh and his associates attribute partly to the consistent policy of preparing the child beforehand as well as giving him emotional support. This finding exactly parallels the previously cited relationship between low preoperative information and high postoperative aggression among adolescent and adult surgical patients.

Similar studies of hospitalized children at the Albany Medical College tend to bear out Prugh's main findings (Jackson, Winkley, Faust, Germak & Burtt, 1953; Winkley, 1953). But in all these quasi-experimental studies, the effects of preparatory communications on the children's emotional reactions are confounded with the effects of other important variables that were also included in the experimental programs (such as arranging to have the mother remain with the child during the most frightening periods). Moreover, the practical demands of the hospital setting evidently made it difficult to avoid unintentional errors from "observer contamination"; i.e., the research workers who rated the children knew which ones were receiving the special experimental treatment and which ones were not.

These methodological difficulties have apparently been surmounted in a recent experiment by Moran (1963), conducted under the auspices of the Yale School of Nursing. The patients were children awaiting tonsillectomy. In the experimental group, each parent, as well as each child, was given information on admission about ward procedures and a descriptive account of what the child would be likely to experience. An equated control group received only the standard hospital care. Nursing procedures and the presence of the parents were equivalent for both experimental and control groups. Observations on both groups were carried out by special observers using "blind" procedure, which avoided contamination. The children (and their parents) in the experimental group were found to have fewer signs of emotional disturbance during convalescence, not only while in the hospital but also at home after discharge.

Although this experiment provides clear-cut evidence concerning the positive value of preparatory communications, it does not exclude the possibility that the preparation procedure led to more favorable relationships with ward personnel, which could mediate the favorable outcome. Nevertheless, this experiment, together with the earlier studies just cited, adds considerable support to the correlational and clinical observations indicating that accurate predictions about impending physical pains and discomforts tend to reduce the incidence of subsequent emotional disturbances.

A KEY THEORETICAL CONSTRUCT: THE WORK OF WORRYING

The observed relationship between lack of preparatory information and subsequent emotional disturbance forms part of the empirical basis for a theoretical analysis of the consequences of reflective fear. A central postulate, suggested by the findings cited in the preceding two sections, is that there is a "work of worrying," which, like the "work of mourning," enables the person to cope more effectively in the long run with a painful reality situation (cf. Janis, 1958, pp. 374–388). The work of mourning does not usually begin until *after* the person has been stricken, whereas the work of worrying is assumed to begin as soon as one becomes aware of an *impending danger* that is perceived as potentially threatening to the self.

A person who has remained unworried is likely to find himself suddenly unable to ward off intense fright if danger materializes. This occurs not only because his blanket-reassurance defenses can no longer succeed but also because disappointment and distrust are aroused toward the authorities whom he had expected to protect him.

A frequent form of blanket reassurance displayed by a high percentage of hospitalized adult patients is a childlike dependency upon the medical authorities (Coser, 1956; Dichter, 1954; Wright, 1960). Many patients succeed in maintaining an attitude of unwarranted optimism in facing the threats of surgery by elevating the hospital authorities, particularly the surgeon, to the role of an omnipotent parent or diety (Janis, 1958; Marmor, 1953). But two significant problems ensue when this type of defense remains unmodified by the arousal of vigilance. First, any "error" or unexpected "harm" in treatment is likely to shatter the patient's unrealistic image of the authorities, leaving him in a helpless state at the time when he is most in need of environmental supports. This is one of the conditions that fosters panic reactions, phobic avoidances, and other persistent symptoms of psychological trauma. Second, the image of the physician as a magical protector will augment the patient's passivity, interfering with his own efforts to develop danger-contingent reassurances involving plans for protective action (see Szasz, 1956).

Reactions of irritability and resentment

have been observed in a number of surgical cases who, upon entering the operating room or after awakening from the anesthetic, suddenly realized for the first time that surgery entails real danger and suffering (cf. Janis, 1958, pp. 339–350). Their initial feelings of helplessness were immediately followed by intense fear and fantasies of hostile intentions on the part of those responsible for carrying out the operation [e.g., "I felt he could be sadistic if he wanted to . . . I was afraid he might do a hysterectomy" (instead of the scheduled appendectomy)].

At a moment of grave crisis, there seems to be a tendency to project blame upon the authorities for unexpected stress. Many observations of surgical patients suggest the following psychological sequence: Absence of mental rehearsal of the impending danger leads to feelings of helplessness when the danger materializes and disappointment in protective authorities, resulting in increased expectations of vulnerability. This sequence can be regarded as a prime consequence of the *failure to carry out the work of worrying*, whether the failure arises primarily from inadequate warnings or from a strong predisposition to ignore warnings. It provides a tentative explanation for the high frequencey of disturbances in the postoperative behavior of those people who, for one or another reason, had managed to ward off reflective fear almost completely, beforehand.

Failure to complete the work of worrying for *each source of stress* also seems to account for isolated instances of fright and rage behavior observed in persons who had displayed a moderate degree of preoperative fear. This is well illustrated by the case of a 29-year-old housewife who was somewhat apprehensive before her operation (lung lobectomy) but who was then uncomplaining, cooperative, and relatively free from emotional disturbances postoperatively. Having had a similar operation once before, she expected that there would be acute incision pains and various unpleasant postoperative treatments. She was caught completely by surprise, however, when, on the first day after the operation, a physician asked her to swallow a drainage tube. On this occasion, she could not get herself to relax and begged the physician to let her alone. She described herself as having been terribly upset because she had not been told there would be any such treatment and felt that something must have gone wrong. During this brief postoperative episode she was unable to dispel unfavorable thoughts about the physician—either he was withholding information about the seriousness of her condition, or he was unnecessarily imposing the "hideous" drainage treatment and was carrying it out "so badly it was practically killing me." At no other time during her long and painful convalescence did she entertain any similar doubts about this physician or any other member of the hospital staff, nor did she display any other instance of overt resistant behavior.

There are some indications, especially from intensive case observations, that if a person undergoes more suffering than he had expected, or was told to expect, the ensuing reaction is one of *acute aggrievement* (rage mixed with grief), which derives its intensity from the *reactivation of childhood disappointments in one's parents* (see Janis, 1958, pp. 159–178). According to this hypothesis, unexpectedly severe stress episodes in adult life tend to be unconsciously assimilated to early experiences during which the child had felt keenly disappointed in one or both parents. The reactivated childhood experiences include not only instances of exceptionally harsh punishment at the hands of the parents but also accidents, illnesses, and other such unavoidable episodes of suffering, which had been interpreted by the child as being caused by parental anger or neglect. When such emotional experiences are reactivated in adult life, intense feelings of resentment and depression are likely to occur. A child who has been neglected or overseverely punished by his parents is likely to protest against the maltreatment and to struggle against the incipient guilt feelings evoked by parental rejection (e.g., "I don't deserve this; why don't you take care of me?"). A similar attitude of childlike protest seems to characterize the anger, resentment, and resistant behavior displayed at times by hospitalized patients who, in the absence of authoritative preparatory communications, had remained overoptimistic and relatively free from reflective fear before the specific stress stimuli materialized.

In conclusion, three adverse effects are likely to occur whenever a person has not become sufficiently fearful to carry out the work of worrying in advance of being exposed to actual danger or loss:

1. The normal tendency to ward off fear by means of blanket reassurances remains dominant and results in failure to engage in the mental rehearsal essential for developing the following two types of danger-contingent reassurances (compromise defenses), which can reduce the probability of subsequent hypervigilance and disappointment: reality-based expectations about ways and means of surviving the impending danger situation, which can function as a source of hope and optimism at times when stress becomes maximal, and reality-based plans for taking effective actions in case various specific contingencies arise, the subsequent execution of which can reduce feelings of passive helplessness.

2. The person's denial fantasies and overoptimistic expectations remain uncorrected, and hence the chances are increased that there will be a marked disparity between the amount of suffering or loss experienced and the amount expected, thus increasing the probability of regressive aggrievement reactions (childlike rage or depression).

3. When the person subsequently realizes that the protective authorities failed to predict or give warnings about the dangers that were going to arise, childhood episodes of resentment against the parents (for unfair or unprotective treatment) are especially likely to be reactivated, thus increasing the likelihood that the physicians and nurses will lose their capacity to give reassurances and will be inappropriately blamed for inflicting suffering and deprivations.

All three reactions to objective danger situations would be expected whenever a person fails to engage in adequate work of worrying beforehand, whether the failure is attributable primarily to predanger environmental conditions or to exceptionally strong personality needs that predisposed the person to deny clear-cut signs of impending danger.

Thus, the work of worrying is conceived as a form of inner preparation that increases the level of tolerance for subsequent threat or danger stimuli. The more thorough the work of worrying, the more reality-tested the person's self-delivered reassurances are likely to be, and hence the more emotional control he will maintain under conditions of subsequent danger or deprivation.

PROBLEMS OF EMOTIONAL INOCULATION

A major implication of the research findings and theoretical conclusions bearing on the work of worrying is that it should be possible to develop successful techniques of emotional inoculation. That is to say, we should be able to reduce the incidence of maladaptive and pathogenic reactions to stress by giving hospitalized patients certain types of affectively potent information that provide appropriate cognitions and attitudes about what is in store for them.

The first important barrier to successful emotional inoculation is the tendency of the ill or stricken person to deny the seriousness of danger and to avoid thinking about it altogether. By interfering with spontaneous denial tendencies, realistic information can evoke some degree of fear, with a consequent arousal of vigilance, which increases the chances that the person will develop discriminative compromise defenses.

A second function of successful preparatory communication is to supplement the person's spontaneous protective measures by teaching him (1) what he can do to help ward off or minimize the objective danger (e.g., whom to call upon for help) and (2) what reassurances he can dependably count on for reducing his fears at times when the danger is actually at hand (e.g., the half-comforting thought that whenever very intense pains occur, they will be of short duration). By giving the person a correct cognitive appraisal of the danger situation, a preparatory communication can help to build an attitude of self-confidence which can be maintained if the crisis actually arises (e.g., "I know what it's all about; I can predict what will happen next") and which, at the same time, can help the person to develop realistic expectations that will have a reassuring effect (e.g., "If the pain doesn't stop soon, I will be given something to relieve it"). For such purposes, it is probably essential that the preparatory communications focus attention on the danger signs and events that will actually be *perceived* by the person. It would be unnecessary, however, and perhaps even detrimental, to give a vivid picture of disquieting aspects of the danger situation which will ordinarily remain outside the person's conscious perceptual or anticipatory experiences (e.g., details about physiological complications that can cause brain damage or death while one is unconscious on the operating table).

A third general function of preparatory communications is to facilitate a realistic attitude of reliance on the physicians and nurses. This is perhaps the most difficult effect for a hospital staff to achieve because it is likely to arouse deep-seated dependency conflicts. It requires a delicate balance between conveying unpleasant information about impending dangers (which could elicit disappointment and resentment toward the staff) and offering fear-reducing reassurances (which could be misconstrued in a way that reinforces indiscriminate faith in the staff's magical powers).

One important set of problems posed by the foregoing considerations has to do with the dosage of fear-arousing stimuli. In predisposed personalities, the stimulation of anticipatory fear can produce serious psychiatric complications. Some physicians have gone so far as to use elaborate subterfuges (e.g., keeping surgical patients from knowing the day on which a major operation will be performed) or to give patients heavy sedation during the days preceding the operation "as a recognition of the damage caused by preoperative anxiety" (Reichard, 1938). But we have seen that the research on surgical patients points to an opposite danger of failure to instigate the work of worrying in those who would be capable of developing effective defenses if their fears were aroused. In order to produce successful emotional inoculation, is seems to be essential to give unwelcome information that will convey a realistic picture of all the disturbing events that the patient is likely to experience. How can this be done without running the risk of provoking adverse reactions?

Some preliminary answers are beginning to emerge from systematic communication research on the effects of different dosages of fear-arousing material. A series of experimental studies by the authors and their coworkers (Janis & Feshbach, 1953; Janis & Feshbach, 1954; Janis & Terwilliger, 1962; Leventhal & Kafes, 1963) provide some pertinent results concerning the conditions under which emotionally arousing communications will lead to changes in beliefs and attitudes. One major implication of the research is that high levels of fear promote feelings of hopelessness or denial in many individuals. When threats are described and reflective fear is stimulated, impressive reassuring statements help keep the intensity of fear at a moderate or tolerable level.

At present we are able to formulate only a few tentative generalizations (as yet only partially tested) on how to select and organize the content of preparatory communications designed to produce emotional inoculation (see Janis, 1958). As more evidence becomes available from communication research, it should be possible to formulate dependable rubrics that can be applied to the average recipient or audience within our society. It is conceivable, however, that individual differences in sensitivity to fear-arousing material may prove to be so great that very few rubrics will hold true for "people in general." From what is already known about differences in personality predispositions, for example, it is apparent that different persons may require quite different forms of preparatory communications (see Caplan, 1961). In fact, one of the direct implications of the research findings on fear-arousing communications is that in order to attain a positive motivating effect, the threat content of a preparatory communication given to chronically anxious persons should be somewhat different from that of a communication given to relatively unanxious persons (see Janis & Feshbach, 1954). The latter, in contrast to the former, appear to require a more dramatic account of the threat (including vivid examples explicitly pointing out the ways in which the individual can be personally affected by the impending dangers) in order to overcome their higher threshold of responsiveness to fear stimuli. With such persons, the communicator probably can successfully employ a moderate or fairly strong fear appeal, whereas with persons who are exceptionally apprehensive about body damage, the dosage of fear material might have to be kept to a minimum in order to prevent the arousal of interfering responses. Obviously a great many more systematic research studies will have to be carried out on these and related predispositional factors, as well as content variables, before we can expect to have a dependable set of specific guiding principles concerning the effective use of preparatory communications for increasing stress tolerance. [A review and discussion of recent studies will be found in Janis (in press).]

POTENTIAL ROLE OF THE PSYCHOLOGICAL COUNSELOR

From what has just been said, it is apparent that any mental health program that attempts to provide psychological preparation for large numbers of hospitalized patients will entail many problems concerning the dosage of fear and the selection of appropriate reassurances. These problems are difficult to solve, especially because of the necessity to take account of personality differences among those for whom the preparatory communications are intended. It is for this reason, among others, that we must expect the messages presented via the mass media to be far less effective for purposes of emotional inoculation than those presented in situations of direct, face-to-face interaction between a professional counselor and the patient. Pamphlets, magazine articles, lectures, and films might be able to fulfill some limited role in preparing people to face the stresses of illness and hospitalization, but they have obvious disadvantages since they are essentially fixed, prepackaged messages. When there is direct verbal interchange with the recipient in a personal interview, a psychologically skilled communicator can make use of the opportunity to observe the effects his statements are having and can change his message accordingly. For example, he can temporarily curtail his intended description of the impending threat if he notes that the client is becoming exceptionally upset; he can "hand-tailor" his reassuring remarks to help alleviate specific sources of fear after hearing the client express his personal fantasies and expectations; and above all, he can take account of obvious misunderstandings and more subtle manifestations of resistance that prevent the client from absorbing the full significance of the message.

Many of the same interpersonal skills and strategic judgments that are essential for successful work in individual and group psychotherapy are undoubtedly required for successful work in emotional inoculation on the part of would-be practitioners of preventive psychiatry. It is probably a serious mistake to assume that all that is needed to expand this type of activity in modern society is to communicate a set of simple guiding principles to all interested professional workers who are in a position to make use of them, irrespective of their psychological talents, training, or experience.

In this respect, a psychologist affiliated with a general hospital could fulfill an important new role, namely, that of taking the lead in working out detailed procedures for the psychological preparation of various types of patients, participating in team research on the effectiveness of the new methods, and helping to train other hospital personnel to enable them to apply effective procedures with skill and understanding.

Barker et al. (1953, p. 164) call attention to the difficulties (and frequently the impossibility) of inducing tuberculosis patients to accept the prescribed treatment and to follow a special set of health rules. They assert: "There is no reason why the educational aspects of the physician's work need be left to his native understanding any more than the medical aspects. We must recognize that these problems can be investigated as satisfactorily as the medical aspects. . . ." The same point can be made for many other problems that arise in a medical clinic or hospital. In order to overcome the powerful emotional resistances encountered in seriously ill people, new methods of counseling will undoubtedly have to be worked out and tested.

When the disease itself or the prescribed treatment requires major alterations in the structural and functional capacities of the body, simply giving appropriate information may not ensure that the patient will develop the attitudes necessary for tolerating a prolonged convalescent regime. For example, cancer patients and amputees often "know" and are able to verbalize the change but are not able to accept it emotionally (Dembo et al., 1956; Shands, 1955; Titchener et al., 1956). The result is intractable resistance to medical treatments, reactive depression, and feelings of worthlessness. In such cases, psychotherapy or special forms of counseling are needed in order to help the patient accept painful aspects of reality and assimilate the change in his self-image.

Paradoxically, the reverse type of change—from illness to recovery—sometimes requires a similar type of psychological treatment. Unexpected recovery can create distress because the patient role is no longer appropriate, and because illness can no longer be used as a protection against other disturbing environmental demands (see Parsons, 1958). Among successful cases of cardiac surgery, the poorest psychological readjustment has been found in those patients who had fully accepted the limitations imposed by their heart disease presurgically (Kaplan, 1956).

The standard techniques of group therapy, as well as of individual psychotherapy, are obviously of potential use to a psychologist who is attempting to cope with the preventive and therapeutic tasks posed by the stresses of physical illness and hospitalization. There are, of course, many different types of group techniques currently in use with *psychiatric* patients, ranging from very superficial discussion groups to group psychoanalysis (see "Group Psychotherapy and Psychodrama" above). Although similar group methods have long been used with *nonpsychiatric* patients hospitalized for tuberculosis and other chronic diseases (Dunbar, 1959), little research has been done as yet concerning the most effective ways of adapting group techniques to the somatopsychological problems encountered in general hospitals. Probably different types of group methods will prove to be applicable to the various problems mentioned earlier in this chapter, such as (1) the readjusting of life goals by patients suffering from permanent disabilities, (2) alleviating feelings of hopelessness and promoting constructive identifications in cancer patients and others with poor prognoses, (3) preventing pathogenic reactions of excessive dependency upon the hospital staff in cases of chronic illness, and (4) promoting active participation in the medical regime on the part of all patients who are expected to display self-control in adhering to special diets, restrictions, unpleasant exercises, and the like. Research on effective group methods is likely to be of considerable theoretical as well as practical interest, since relevant data can be obtained bearing on such concepts as *social role expectations* imposed on hospitalized patients (Goffman, 1959; Parsons, 1958) and changes in *relative deprivation* produced by adopting a different *reference group* (see Davis, 1956; Merton & Kitt, 1950; Newcomb, 1950).

CREATING A THERAPEUTIC SOCIAL MILIEU

Another new development in which psychologists with research skills can be expected to play a major role involves setting up and maintaining a psychologically therapeutic milieu in the general hospital. It has become the practice in many mental hospitals to gear the entire social environment toward therapy (see "Mental Hospitals," above). Aides, nurses, and all personnel contacting patients are given special training in the hope that this will create a therapeutic atmosphere affecting all the patient's interpersonal contacts. Similar efforts are now under way in general medical hospitals (see Caplan, 1961). Attempts are being made to redefine the role of the staff members and the hospital administrators. With regard to nurses' training, for example, emphasis is being placed on creating appropriate social relationships with patients and increasing sensitivity to the sources of fear and conflict generated by life in a hospital ward (Hofling & Leininger, 1960). There is a new emphasis on listening to the patient, allowing him to express his feelings, and providing meaningful explanations to reduce his fears (Connolly, 1960; Elms, 1963; Gregg, 1955). There is no deemphasis on nursing techniques, but there has been a deemphasis on the paper work which seems to occupy so much of the nurses' time.

Brown and Fowler (1954) recommend that every medical, surgical, and convalescent ward be a "therapeutic environment," characterized by "an accepting, protective and permissive atmosphere which provides a testing ground for the establishment of new patterns of behavior." They propose that in addition to new administrative policies fostering prompt attention to individual patients' needs, a special training program for nurses and other members of the staff be initiated. One goal of the training is to increase the psychological skills of the staff, thus enabling them to engage in client-centered "therapeutic conversation" and to be aware of the impact of their facial expressions and other nonverbal communications.

Similarly, a strong emphasis is beginning to be placed on physician-patient relationships. Barker et al. (1953) call attention to the availability of valid techniques for assessing patients' attitudes and reactions to physicians' behavior. Romano's (1941) study of 100 unselected medical patients seen on ward rounds is cited as an example of how research can contribute to new developments in hospital policy affecting doctor-patient relationships. This study highlights the importance of arranging for a preliminary discussion between doctor and patient in preparation for the arrival of staff members and students on ward rounds. A vocabulary test indicated that many technical medical terms freely used by the physicians were grossly misunderstood by the patients. Romano's report also calls attention to common sources of embarrassment for the patient which can be avoided (e.g., disrobing or discussing personal problems before a group).

The entire hospital structure itself is currently being reexamined from the point of view of patient needs as well as of medical practice and economics. A program called "progressive patient care" (Haldeman & Abdellah, 1959) represents one effort to create an institution built around the patients' needs. Using specially built architectural units, the hospital is equipped with different sections to provide intensive care, standard ward care, self-service, and long-term care in coordination with a home-care program. The various units are designed to deal most effectively with the special needs posed by the different phases of hospitalization. For example, a self-service unit is used to house ambulatory patients undergoing diagnostic workups. It is also used as a self-help training station where the patient can have freedom of movement and can regain physical skills (see Lockward, Giddings, & Thoms, 1960). During the intense treatment phase, which is generally the time of maximum crisis, the patient is kept in an intensive-care unit. Here he is under continual observation by highly skilled nurses, and when awake, he can see for himself that protective authorities are at hand in case of emergency.

A recent psychological study (Leventhal, 1963), conducted under the auspices of the U.S. Public Health Service, used preoperative and postoperative interviews in order to compare the reactions of surgical patients treated in intensive-care units with those treated in standard surgical wards. While no differences were found in the patients' attitudes and concerns before the operation, a number of marked differences were observed a few days after the operation. Among the 46 intensive-care patients interviewed postoperatively, 35 per cent gave the highest possible rating to the importance of the nurse with respect to their postoperative care, in contrast to 13 per cent of the 31 patients receiving regular ward care. The patients in intensive-care units made significantly more favorable remarks concerning the nurse and reported that her presence made them feel less tense. Although this system entails numerous administrative and personnel difficulties, it appears to be very promising as another step in the direction of a supportive social milieu to help reduce the psychological stresses that beset hospitalized patients.

As the development toward creating a therapeutic hospital milieu proceeds, we can expect to see more and more psychologists, along with other specialists in the human sciences, being recruited as consultants and participants on the general hospital staff. In the long run, a cadre of experts in somatopsychological problems will be needed to select and train hospital personnel, to help invent new psychoprophylactic techniques, and to establish new administrative procedures and traditions that will improve the psychological atmosphere. Above all, those equipped to carry out systematic research can play a crucial role by objectively testing the effectiveness of new procedures and policies designed to enhance the patients' capacity for coping with stress.

REFERENCES

Abeles, M. M. Postoperative psychoses. *Amer. J. Psychiat.*, 1937–1938, **94**, 1187–1200.

Bard, M. Sequence of emotional reactions in radical mastectomy. *Public Health Repts.*, 1952, **67**, No. 11.

Barker, R. G., Wright, B. A., Meyerson, L., & Gonick, M. R. *Adjustment to physical handicap and illness: a survey of the social psychology of physique and disability.* New York: Social Research Council, 1953.

Blank, H. R. Psychoanalysis and blindness. *Psychoanal. Quart.*, 1957, **26**, 1–24.

Bond, D. *The love and fear of flying.* New York: International Universities Press, 1952.

Bowlby, J. Maternal care and mental health. *Bull. World Hlth Organization,* 1951, **3**, 355–533.

Brown, M., & Fowler, G. *Psychodynamic nursing.* Philadelphia: Saunders, 1954. Pp. 86–89.

Caplin, G. *An approach to community mental health.* London: Tavistock, 1961.

Cholden, L. Some psychiatric problems in the rehabilitation of the blind. *Bull. Menninger Clin.*, 1954, **18**, 107–112.

Cobb, B. C., Clark, R. L., Jr., McGuire, C., & Howe, C. D. Patient-responsible delay of treatment of cancer: a social psychological study. *Cancer,* 1954, **7,** 920–926.

Cobb, S., & Lindemann, E. Symposium on management of Cocoanut Grove burns at Massachusetts General Hospital: neuropsychiatric observations. *Ann. Surgery,* 1943, **117,** 814–824.

Connolly, M. G. What acceptance means to patients. *Amer. J. Nursing,* 1960, **60,** 1754–1757.

Coser, R. L. A home away from home. *Soc. Problems,* 1956, **4,** 3–17.

Cramond, W., & Aberd, D. Psychological aspects of uterine disfunction. *Lancet,* 1954, **2,** 1241–1245.

Davis, F. Definitions of time and recovery in paralytic polio convalescence. *Amer. J. Sociol.,* 1956, **61,** 582–587.

Dembo, T., Leviton, G. L., & Wright, B. A. Adjustment to misfortune: a problem of social-psychological rehabilitation. *Artif. Limbs,* 1956, **3,** 4–62.

Deutsch, H. Some psychoanalytic observations in surgery. *Psychosom. Med.,* 1942, **4,** 105–115.

Dichter, E. The hospital-patient relationship: what the patient really wants from the hospital. *Modern Hosp.,* 1954, **83,** 36, 51–54.

Drellich, M. G., Bieber, I., & Sutherland, A. M. The psychological impact of cancer and cancer surgery. IV. Adaptation to hysterectomy. *Cancer,* 1956, **9,** 1120–1126.

Dunbar, F. *Psychiatry in the medical specialties.* New York: McGraw-Hill, 1959. Pp. 166–169.

Elms, R. R. The effects of varied nursing approaches during elective admission to a surgical unit. Unpublished master's thesis, Yale Univer. School of Nursing, 1963.

Fenichel, O. *The psychoanalytic theory of neurosis.* New York: Norton, 1945.

Ferraro, A. Somato-psychic factors in anxiety neurosis. *J. nerv. ment. Dis.,* 1948, **107,** 228–242.

Freud, S. Mourning and melancholia (1917). In *Collected papers.* Vol. 4. London: Hogarth, 1925. Pp. 152–170.

Freud, S. *The problem of anxiety.* (Tr. by H. A. Bunker.) New York: Norton, 1936.

Glover, E. Notes on the psychological effects of war conditions on the civilian population. III. The blitz. *Int. J. Psychoanal.,* 1942, **23,** 17–37.

Goffman, I. *The presentation of the self in everyday life.* Garden City, N.J.: Doubleday, 1959.

Gregg, D. N. Reassurance. *Amer. J. Nursing,* 1955, **55,** 171–174.

Haldeman, J. C., & Abdellah, F. G. Hospitals. *J. Amer. med. Ass.,* 1959, **33,** 38–46, 142–144.

Hastings, D. W., Wright, D. G., & Glueck, B. C. Sodium amytal narcosis in treatment of operational fatigue in combat aircrews. *War Med.,* 1944, **5,** 368–372.

Hofling, C., & Leininger, M. *Basic psychiatric concepts in nursing.* Philadelphia: Lippincott, 1960. Pp. 78–79.

Jackson, K., Winkley, R., Faust, O., Germak, E., & Burtt, M. Behavior changes indicating emotional trauma in tonsillectomized children. *Pediatrics,* 1953, **12,** 23–28.

Janis, I. *The contours of fear.* New York: Wiley, in press.

Janis, I. *Air war and emotional stress.* New York: McGraw-Hill, 1951.

Janis, I. *Psychological stress.* New York: Wiley, 1958.

Janis, I. Psychological effects of warnings. In G. W. Barker and D. W. Chapman (Eds.), *Man and society in disaster.* New York: Basic Books, 1962.

Janis, I., Chapman, D. W., Gillin, J. P., & Speigel, J. P. The problem of panic. *Fed. Civil Defense Admin. Bull. TB–19–2,* 1955.

Janis, I., & Feshback, S. Effects of fear-arousing communications. *J. abnorm. soc. Psychol.,* 1953, **48,** 78–92.

Janis, I., & Feshbach, S. Personality differences associated with responsiveness to fear-arousing communications. *J. Pers.,* 1954, **23,** 154–166.

Janis, I., & Terwilliger, R. An experimental study of psychological resistances to fear-arousing communications. *J. abnorm. soc. Psychol.,* 1962, **65,** 403–410.

Kaplan, S. M. Psychological aspects of cardiac disease. *Psychosom. Med.,* 1956, **18,** 221–233.

Klatskin, E. An analysis of the effect of the test situation upon the Rorschach record: normal scoring characteristics. *J. proj. Tech.,* 1952, **16,** 193–199.

Lazarus, R. S., Speisman, J. C., Mordkoff, A. M., & Davison, L. A. A laboratory study of psychological stress produced by a motion picture film. *Psychol. Monogr.,* 1962, **76,** 1–350.

Leventhal, H. Patient responses to surgical stress in regular and intensive care units. *Progr. Rep. Div. hosp. med. Facilities, U.S. Publ. Hlth Serv.,* 1963. (mimeographed)

Leventhal, H., & Kafes, P. N. The effectiveness of fear-arousing movies in motivating preventive health measures. *N.Y. State J. Med.*, 1963, **63**, 867–874.

Lindemann, E. Observations on psychiatric sequelae to surgical operations in women. *Amer. J. Psychiat.*, 1941, **98**, 132–139.

Lindemann, E. Symptomatology and management of acute grief. *Amer. J. Psychiat.*, 1944, **101**, 141–148.

Lockward, H. J., Giddings, L., & Thoms, E. J. Progressive patient care: a preliminary report. *J. Amer. med. Ass.*, 1960, **172**, 132–137.

Marmor, J. The feeling of superiority: an occupational hazard. *Amer. J. Psychiat.*, 1953, **110**, 370–376.

Marmor, J. The psychodynamics of realistic worry. *Psychoanal. and soc. Sci.*, 1958, **5**, 155–163.

Merton, R. K., & Kitt, Alice. Contributions to the theory of reference group behavior. In R. K. Merton & P. F. Lazarsfeld (Eds.), *Studies in the American soldier*. New York: Free Press, 1950.

Miller, H. H. Acute psychosis following surgical procedures. *Brit. med. J.*, 1939, **1**, 558–559.

Moran, P. A. An experimental study of pediatric admission. Unpublished master's thesis, Yale Univer. School of Nursing, 1963.

Newcomb, T. *Social psychology*. New York: Dryden Press, 1950.

Parsons, T. Illness and the role of the physician: a sociological perspective. *Amer. J. Orthopsychiat.*, 1951, **21**, 452–460.

Parsons, T. Definitions of health and illness in the light of American values and social structure. In E. G. Jaco (Ed.), *Patients, physicians and illness*. New York: Free Press, 1958. Pp. 165–187.

Preu, P. W., & Guida, F. P. Psychoses and complicating recovery from extraction of cataract. *Arch. Neurol. Psychiat.*, 1937, **38**, 818–832.

Prugh, D., Staub, E., Sands, H., Kirschbaum, R., & Lenihan, E. A study of emotional reactions of children and families to hospitalization and illness. *Amer. J. Orthopsychiat.*, 1953, **23**, 70–106.

Reichard, J. Preventing psychic shock. *Modern Hosp.*, 1938, **50**, 47–48.

Robertson, J. *Young children in hospital*. London: Tavistock Publications, 1958.

Romano, J. Patients' attitude and behavior in ward round teaching. *J. Amer. med. Assoc.*, 1941, **117**, 664–667.

Schmideberg, M. Some observations on individual reactions to air raids. *Int. J. Psychoanal.*, 1942, **23**, 146–176.

Shands, H. C. An outline of the process of recovery from severe trauma. *Arch. Neurol. Psychiat.*, 1955, **73**, 403–409.

Singeisen, F. Rorschashbefunde bei chronisch lungentuberkulosen. *Nord. Med. (Hospitalstid.)*, 1940, **5**, 7–8.

Solnit, A. J. Hospitalization: an aid to psychological health in childhood. *J. Dis. Child.*, 1960, **99**, 155–163.

Szasz, T., & Hollender, M. A contribution to the philosophy of medicine. *Arch. intern. Med.*, 1956, **97**, 585–592.

Titchener, J., Zwerling, I., Gottschalk, L., Levine, M., Culbertson, W., Cohen, S., & Silver, H. Psychosis and surgical patients. *Surg. Gynecol. Obstet.*, 1956, **102**, 59–65.

Titchener, J. L., Zwerling, I., Gottschalk, L., Levine, M., Silver, H., Cowett, A., Cohen, S., & Colbertson, W. Consequences of surgical illness and treatment: interaction of emotions, personality and surgical illness, treatment, and convalescence. *Arch. Neurol. Psychiat.*, 1957, **77**, 623–634.

Washburne, A. C., & Carns, M. L. Postoperative psychosis: suggestions for prevention and treatment. *J. nerv. ment. Dis.*, 1935, **82**, 508–513.

Winkley, R. The case-worker's participation in preparation for tonsillectomy in children. *Ment. Hyg.*, 1953, **37**, 430–440.

Withey, S. B. Reaction to uncertain threat. In G. W. Baker & D. W. Chapman (Eds.), *Man and society in disaster*. New York: Basic Books, 1962, 93–123.

Wolfenstein, M. *Disaster: a psychological essay*. New York: Free Press, 1957.

Wright, B. A. *Physical disability: a psychological approach*. New York: Harper & Row, 1960.

51

The Prevention of Mental Illness

NEVITT SANFORD[1]

In the literature of clinical psychology and psychiatry, "prevention" has had an ambiguous and shifting position. Prevention is often said to be the ultimate aim of research—in psychiatry, in clinical psychology, and in various areas of social science—and it is evoked as a justification for practices in training, including training for psychotherapy; but it is treated as virtually an afterthought in textbooks and treatises on psychiatry and abnormal psychology.

The final report of the Joint Commission on Mental Illness and Health (1961) is of two minds about prevention. Four of the seven published studies of the Commission (excluding the final report) have to do mainly with prevention, in the largest sense of the term, and these are faithfully summarized in the final report, but the recommendations of the Commission have little to do with prevention. Instead, the "core problem" is said to be major mental illness—psychosis and other forms of chronic illness—and the mental hygiene movement is criticized for neglecting this problem in favor of an interest in prevention. But the mental hygiene movement seems not to have been altogether cowed by this criticism, as witness the rejoinder of Dr. René Dubos of the Rockefeller Foundation:

> The Final Report of the Joint Commission on Mental Health and Mental Illness states that humane treatment and rehabilitation of the mentally ill is the great unfinished business of the mental health movement. But the great unfinished business really is to do something about the social, psychological and other circumstances leading to this condition (1962).

The educated public in North America has, since the early years of this century, been consistently interested in prevention and consistently neglectful of the mentally ill in hospitals, as *Action for Mental Health*, the final report of the Joint Commission (1961), correctly points out. But this public has tended to follow the specialists, adopting whatever ideology of upbringing or early treatment the psychiatrists or psychologists advocated during a particular period and doing what it could to look after the mental health of itself and its children. For their part, the mental health specialists have tended to serve the interests of this public more than those of the less privileged segments of the population, from which most patients in mental hospitals come. The mental health specialists themselves have participated in the "diversion of attention from the core problem," for which *Action for Mental Health* criticizes the mental health movement.

HISTORY

We deal here with conflicts of value and interest that can be understood only in the light of what we know about the culture and social

[1] The writer is heavily indebted to Thomas Plaut for advice and helpful suggestions in all phases of the preparation of this chapter. Warm thanks also go to Eva Blum, Joseph Katz, and Max Levin, who read the manuscript and added substance as well as clarity to the presentation.

structure of the United States and about certain events of the last fifty or sixty years. This brief account of the mental hygiene movement may well start with the founding of the National Committee on Mental Hygiene, in 1909. This was largely a result of the writing and activity of Clifford Beers, whose book, *A Mind That Found Itself,* first appeared in 1908. Beers was out to reform the mental hospitals, but the leaders whom he aroused—men such as William James and Adolph Myer—were more interested in prevention of mental disease through eugenics and through improvement of the environment.

Beers was a catalyst. The soil for the flowering of a mental hygiene movement had already been prepared. Some writers, for example, Seeley (1953), trace the origins of the mental health movement to the breaking up of the settled order of the Middle Ages. When the church lost its position as the sole authority on questions of virtue and the good life, a power vacuum was created into which the mental health movement, along with a variety of competitors, could move. Other writers, for example, Rickman (1938), are content to begin their accounts of the movement with Darwin and his contemporaries, who shattered belief in the fixity of the species and who revolutionized ideas of human potentialities. By the time of Beers's writing it was understood that children could develop beyond their parents, and the "new psychology" had revealed some of the mechanisms by which the environment had its effects. Hence there was a general loss of faith in the traditional bases for the rearing of children and growth of the belief that it was up to parents and the community to provide an environment favorable to the child's welfare.

Proceeding in accordance with this spirit, the early mental hygiene movement in the United States inspired the establishment of child guidance clinics and programs of education for parents and the public.

Psychiatric experience during World War I provided fresh impetus to the movement. Not only was there some success in the early identification and treatment of potential psychiatric cases among soldiers, but also knowledge of the "war neuroses" led to increasing acceptance of the theory of the psychogenesis of mental disorders. During the 1920s there was a vast increase in the number of outpatient services, child guidance clinics, and programs of public education. All these activities were pervaded with a general air of optimism.

Meanwhile in Europe, psychoanalysis, with its heavy accent on childhood events as determinants of neurosis, led to much concern about the applications of psychoanalytic principles to education. Freud himself was not very optimistic about the possibilities in this area, believing as he did that neurosis is inevitable in highly civilized societies (1959, p. 217). Rather, he seems to have put his faith in what nowadays is called "secondary prevention," envisioning large numbers of psychoanalytically trained "secular pastoral workers" who would apply themselves to the early treatment of neurosis. He permitted himself this tongue-in-cheek remark: "Perhaps once more an American may hit on the idea of spending a little money to get the 'social workers'[2] of his country trained analytically and to turn them into a band of helpers for combating the neuroses of civilization" (1959, p. 250). But some of Freud's followers—for example, Siegfried Bernfeld, August Aichorn, and Anna Freud (of the Vienna group)—were very much interested in the preventive possibilities of psychoanalytic knowledge and wrote extensively on child training and education. Psychoanalysts of the English school—notably, Melanie Klein, Susan Isaacs, John Rickman, and Ella Sharpe—soon joined in the discussion, differing in important respects from the Vienna group (see Isaacs, 1933; Rickman, 1938). By the mid-1930s there had begun in the United States the outpouring of a more or less popular psychoanalytically oriented literature for parents and educators that has been a feature of the American scene ever since.

During the time when Freud was developing his ideas and starting his psychoanalytic movement, socialism was very much in the air. The Russian Revolution was having its impact on European intellectuals, including some of Freud's followers. There were "socially oriented" psychoanalysts almost from the start. Most of these, it seems, kept their psychoanalysis and their socialism in separate compartments; but some, perhaps most notably Alfred Adler, tried to integrate their psychological and their social theories. Adler became very much interested in education for cooperation and social responsibility; he wrote and

[2] In English in the original.

lectured widely on the subject and founded, in Vienna, in 1931, the Individual Psychology Experimental School, which was closed in 1934 "for political reasons" (Adler, 1930; Ansbacher & Ansbacher, 1956). As is well known, Adler developed a psychology that differed fundamentally from Freud's, and the two men went their separate ways.

The decade of the 1930s was a period of great ferment in American psychology and psychiatry. The Great Depression drew attention to the importance of broad economic and social processes in the determination of behavior. The assimilation of European ideas, which had been very gradual, was enormously speeded up by the great influx of psychologists, psychiatrists, and psychoanalysts—refugees from the Nazi oppression. All the great European systems of psychological thought, and a great variety of other ideas and points of view, were now strongly represented in this country. All received a hearing, but those which took root and flowered were those which could be most readily assimilated to trends in American culture. For example, this culture, traditionally, has accented self-improvement and adjustment rather than social change as the road to the good life. Hence the socially oriented psychology of Adler, Horney (1939), and Fromm (1942; 1947), though it could win many supporters, could never attain a dominating position in the mental health field. Freudian psychoanalysis, on the other hand, with its accent on individual psychodynamics, its appeal to the Puritan mentality, and its neutrality with respect to social questions—especially after it had found a home within American medicine—could attain to great power and influence. Again, the English school of psychoanalysis, with its emphasis on native factors, on the priority of aggression, and on the importance of the child's fantasies in the determination of neurosis, clashed with American optimism and empiricism and has never gained more than a foothold in this country. Freudian psychoanalysis, in contrast, proved more flexible. Accenting its environmentalist features—especially the role of the family in the determination of neurosis—sticking to medicine and embracing science (but not too closely), and developing an "ego psychology" that was congenial to American academic psychology, it found the going relatively smooth.

The newly imported European ideas combined with trends of thought already present in the United States to give the mental health movement an enormous push forward in the 1930s and early 1940s. A psychodynamic approach to the understanding and guidance of children became a part of American culture, being the basis not only for a great surge of popular literature but also for movies and for radio and television programs.

World War II led to even further public interest in mental illness and health. Psychiatric screening of recruits to the armed services, breakdowns in the services, and the adjustment problems of the returning servicemen were very much in the public eye, and after the war it was not difficult to persuade Congress to spend money for programs of service, training, and research in the field of mental illness and health.

This climate, and the availability of public funds for training and research—mainly through the National Institute of Mental Health and the Veterans Administration—made possible a great leap forward in clinical psychology. During the decade after 1945 this field of psychology made large gains in status, both within the universities and on the national scene; several thousand Ph.D.s were turned out, most of whom had had some training for psychotherapy. Psychotherapy, indeed, was the order of the day. The practice of psychotherapy, on the psychoanalytic model, had the highest prestige among workers in the mental health professions, and since from the point of view of the National Institute of Mental Health there could never be enough psychiatrists and psychologists to meet the demand for this service, social workers, counselors, and ministers found it not difficult to enter programs for training in this specialty.

During this period of prosperity for psychology, the prevention of mental disease received relatively little attention. There was, to be sure, some continuing attention to the early diagnosis and treatment of disorders in children, and there is no doubt that the understanding of children was broadened and deepened as compared with what it had been before 1930; but apparently the main trends of activity in psychiatry and clinical psychology were borne on the assumption that true prevention was to be achieved in the new generation through giving enough psychotherapy and enough knowledge of psychodynamics to parents and educators.

It was during this same period that the concept of "positive mental health" began to loom large in clinical psychology—a prelude to the present concern with creativity. Efforts to learn something of the determinants of the superior in personality functioning were begun by Murray and his associates (Murray et al., 1938) in the early 1930s, were carried forward by the OSS assessment teams during World War II (1948), and were continued in several centers after 1945. This trend in research was combined with the older concerns of some psychologists and psychiatrists with developmental tasks and the goals of psychotherapy in much new writing about the "positive"—writing that reached a kind of culmination in Jahoda's report (1958) for the Joint Commission on Mental Illness and Health. Although highly relevant to prevention in its most basic sense, this writing did not result in many suggestions for programs of action aimed at changing the social environment of the developing individual. Psychotherapy still seemed to be generally regarded as the means *par excellence* for attaining to the highest levels of development.

In the years since 1950, many of the assumptions and practices of psychodynamically oriented clinical psychologists and psychiatrists have been effectively challenged, mainly by social scientists and public health specialists newly arrived on the mental illness–mental health scene.

As early as 1938, Kingsley Davis (1938) argued that the mental hygiene movement in the United States was promoting under the guise of science the prevalent, middle-class values of our society—indeed that it defined mental health in terms of conformity with these values—and that because of its "psychologistic" bias, it failed to investigate the social and cultural determinants of behavior and tended to regard social norms as universal human traits. This line of argument has been put forward by sociologists and anthropologists ever since, but it was not until some of these social scientists actually entered the mental health field and conducted empirical investigations—most often at the invitation of psychiatrists—that their thrusts began finding their marks among exponents and practitioners of the traditional psychodynamic psychotherapy.

Meanwhile specialists in public health, having long since gained control over the communicable diseases, which were the first concern of community health departments, and having turned from a primary concern with mortality to concern with reducing rates of morbidity, were looking for new fields to conquer. In recent years, health departments have been engaged in programs, such as those having to do with maternal and child care and the control of syphilis, which have significant implications for mental illness or health. In some of the newer and current programs, such as those in the fields of alcoholism and chronic disease, the mental illness or health factor has been large. And since the passage of the National Health Act of 1946, an increasing number of specialists in public health have been interested in assuming greater responsibilities for problems in the field of mental illness itself.

Since public health programs have reference to the community—they arise out of community needs and consist of actions within the community—it was natural enough that public health workers should make common cause with social scientists. Thus by the mid-1950s there was a convergence. Sociologists, anthropologists, and social psychologists, no longer content to limit themselves to their function of criticism, were now taking part in research and action programs in the health fields, accepting positions on the staffs of medical schools—most often in departments of psychiatry—and schools of public health and finding kindred spirits among psychiatrists who saw mental illness as a community problem. Public health specialists, meanwhile, were moving into the mental health field, finding collaborators among social scientists and adopting social science techniques, while sticking to the basic public health strategies.

These developments were also in some part the fruits of the "culture and personality" movement, which has persisted since its origins in the early 1930s; of the steadily growing influence of British social psychiatry; and of the new chemotherapy, which, by reducing acute disturbance among hospital patients to a minimum, permitted sociological and sociopsychological experimentation on ward and hospital social organization and the changing of staff attitudes toward patients.

There was an outpouring of literature reflecting these developments. A committee of the Harvard Medical School (1962) was able to list, for the years from 1953 to 1960, over one thousand publications in the fields of community mental health and social psychiatry, many of them reports of large-scale empirical studies.

The entry of social scientists and public health specialists into the field of mental health brought not only new conceptions and strategies of prevention but also a shift in values and ideology; there was now a new emphasis upon the underprivileged, the acutely ill, the deviant, and the "mass" of people—in short, upon what used to be called the "socially significant."

It would be surprising, in the light of this history, if there were anything like unanimity in outlook on prevention among all the workers now active in the field. Owing to their different backgrounds and training and to their memberships in different intellectual traditions, mental health specialists today approach the problem of prevention with different theories of personality development and of social process, different conceptions of mental illness and different views respecting its determinants, different orientations to value, and, accordingly, different strategies of prevention. In the most general terms, the big difference is between those who focus on the individual and those who focus on social processes. The former see the determinants of mental disease as residing primarily in the individual, having there been set in motion very early in the individual's life, if not before that; and, consistent with this, they see prevention mainly as a matter of reaching the troubled child as early as possible or, better, of reaching parents so that they will start their children off right. The latter see mental illness mainly as a function of processes in society, and they see prevention mainly as a matter of intervention in these processes. At the present time, however, there is a movement toward convergence of views.

PLAN OF THIS CHAPTER

It seems well, then, to take up some of the philosophical and theoretical issues that loom large in the field before proceeding to a discussion of programs of preventive action. The following brief discussion of these issues begins with an effort to describe the public health approach and compare it with others and then goes on to a consideration of the interactions of this approach with psychological and social theory. The next section describes current programs and practices and begins with a scheme that attempts to lay out the major dimensions of the field of prevention: What is to be prevented, in whom, and by what methods? Finally, there is some discussion of the implications of what has been said for research, training, and practice in clinical psychology.

THEORETICAL CONSIDERATIONS

The Public Health Approach

The public health approach to prevention focuses upon a community or population rather than upon individuals, and it attempts to reduce the rate of mental illness by modifying factors believed to be affecting large segments of that community or population. The approach has grown out of the conviction, formed on the basis of public health experience, that no disease has ever been controlled by early diagnosis and treatment and that mental disease will be no exception (Lemkau, 1959; McGavran, 1962). This is partly a matter of logistics; with mental diseases, as with others, there can never be enough therapists to provide more than a drop in the bucket. Partly, also, this is a deduction from a theory of causation; all diseases, and perhaps particularly mental diseases, have multiple causes, some of which arise out of processes in the environment. Hence not all causative factors can be touched by treatment or other actions directed to individuals. It also follows from this view of causation that it is impossible to predict that, unless specific preventive steps are taken, a particular individual will develop a disease.

This line of reasoning holds even for organic diseases of which the causes are known. Just as the eradication of malaria was achieved by modifications of the environment, so the control of syphilis will eventually be achieved not merely by treating infected individuals but by actions designed to change behavior and attitudes throughout the whole community.

It is not necessary to know how a disease is caused in order to take effective preventive action. A famous example in the public health literature concerns the control of a cholera epidemic in London by the removal of a public water pump. This was long before there was any knowledge of infection by microorganisms. Someone noticed that the frequency of cases varied with the proximity to this pump, and so its removal seemed a good action and was—eventually—a sensationally effective one. Again, Bowlby and his associates (Bowlby, 1951; Bowlby, Ainsworth, Boston, & Rosenbluth, 1956) did not need to prove that a 2-year-old child's separation from his mother for periods of two weeks or longer is a cause of psychopathology in later years. His thesis was persuasive enough so that the British Ministry of Health issued a directive permitting and encouraging mothers to visit their children in hospitals for unlimited amounts of time. This administrative action might or might not prevent any specific mental disease, but it might lead to a reduction in the rate of mental illness in general; and, in any case, it seemed a humane thing to do.

Most characteristic of the public health approach, perhaps, is the idea of intervention at some point in a system—some interruption of the course of events—with a view to changing the system in such a way as to reduce the rate of mental illness. Consider, for example, a school system. From the point of view of individual psychodynamics, the proper approach to the prevention of mental illness in childhood would consist in actions such as hiring mentally healthy teachers, teaching them about mental illness and health in children, and training them to recognize signs of disturbance in children and to give psychological first aid. A spokesman for the sociological approach would express grave doubt that these measures would reduce the rate of mental illness among the children in that school system; he would suspect that the causes of their disturbances lay not only in the personality structures that they brought to school with them but also in the school system itself and that the problematic behavior of teachers and other school personnel sprang not so much from *their* neuroses as from the situation in which they worked. Accordingly, he would also suspect that proper preventive action would consist in efforts to change the system as a whole, so that everybody in it was happier, in less conflict, and more productive. A teacher of the writer's acquaintance is sure that a large step in this direction could be taken, in the system in which she works, by allowing school principals academic tenure.

Sociopsychological Theory

The public health approach can go quite a long way on the basis of knowledge or hypotheses about the correlations of broad social factors, such as unemployment or bad housing, with mental illness and on the basis of theory of social structures. Action for mental health would consist in removing or reducing the harmful or hazardous factors or in intervention at some point in a social structure—an organization, institution, or community—in such a way as to make for favorable change in the whole.

Actions of these kinds, however, always involve, at least implicitly, psychological assumptions or theories about how people in general will react to an environmental condition, how they are organized as personalities, and how they develop from birth onward.

The British Ministry of Health, in encouraging mothers to visit their children in hospitals, must have assumed that both mothers and children would be happier and less anxious if this were done and that doctors and nurses could adapt themselves to this change in routine without too much disturbance of their work. When large-scale social actions are based on wrong psychological assumptions, the results can be damaging to large numbers of individuals. In Poland for some years after World War II, the official word was "We have no delinquency because we have socialism"—this at a time when the police were all but overwhelmed by masses of disturbed and delinquent children, the products of broken homes, poverty, neglect, and general social disorganization. This was not merely official hypocrisy but an expression of the belief that a far-reaching change in the organization of society would immediately and automatically bring far-reaching changes in people, including children. Again, in England during the same period, large numbers of families were moved from bombed-out areas of the east end of London to clean and comfortable but rather sterile housing estates in the suburbs around the city. The assumption seems to have been made that these former slum dwellers would immediately begin living like middle-class people. They did not. Instead, they were unhappy; the women, especially, missed their family and community networks, and the kitchen, having become modern—small and electrified—could no longer be the center of life for the nuclear family. Many of these people made their way back to the true communities from whence they came.

In this last instance, more appropriate action would have had to be based on knowledge of culture, and of a particular subculture, as well as on knowledge of the general psychological laws according to which cultural values are acquired. Nowadays in this country specialists who would improve mental health by changing environments are very alert to cultural factors. This has been favored by public health experience, and, of course, it has been further promoted by the entrance of anthropologists and sociologists into the mental health field. For that matter, it is doubtful whether anywhere in the Western world today anyone interested in mental illness or health would seek to apply so doctrinaire a version of socialism as the Polish officials did or so class-bound a version of the good life as the British planners of the housing estates did. In Mexico, for example, when people are moved by the thousands into new housing developments, there is the closest attention to the requirements of family life and to what favors the psychological as well as the physical well-being of people.

Personality Theory

The public health approach also makes assumptions about the elements of personality and their organization in individuals. The idea of susceptibility to disease or to kinds of diseases and the idea of resistance must have reference to more or less enduring structures in people, structures which are built up over time and which stand ready to help determine what will happen when stimuli arrive. The public health specialist or the social scientist may or may not believe, with most personality theorists, that personality functions as a unit and that mental illness or mental health is a condition of the whole person. He may believe—and this with good reason—that problematic or deviant behavior can be a response to a momentary stimulus and is open to change without alteration in the structure of the person; but to take preventive actions aimed at particular conditions without giving attention to the complexity of personality, particularly to the interactions of its constituent processes, is to court trouble. Such an action might indeed affect a particular condition in the predicted way but might still do more harm than good if there is no theory to suggest other consequences of that action for other features or functions of the person. For example, the segregation and exposure to special educational procedures of slow learners or the gifted in school might result in more appropriate learning of content by children of these two groups, but it might also lead to a kind of labeling and to a kind of self-conception that would be, in the long run, most unfortunate from the point of view of mental health.

It may also be suggested that attention to personality theory, which deals with the complexity of processes inside the person, is a good safeguard against the extreme forms of collectivism which sometimes animate social planners and advocates of large-scale social actions. The frame of mind that permits enthusiasts for social action to concentrate on the group without attention to what goes on inside people would appear to be close to that which permits contemplating the sacrificing of individuals for the good of the group.

It seems that today most specialists who would reduce rates of mental illness by modifying the social environment are aware of these considerations. They are also aware of the great difficulties in the way of persuading people to take measures that might protect their health. Smoking, drinking too much, indulging indiscriminately in sexual relations, and driving without seat belts may be bad for the health, mental as well as physical, but people by and large do not seem to be on the point of changing their ways. Effective actions in areas of this kind will require at least as much knowledge of human motivation as knowledge of social processes.

Public health workers and social scientists who work in the mental health field also have their theories and assumptions about personality development, but, as suggested above, their notions tend to run counter to the general position of classical psychodynamic—typically Freudian psychoanalytic—theory. What is this theory? Most essential is the notion that personality exists in time and exhibits continuity over time. As with all living things, early events have lasting consequences; other things being equal, damage to the growing organism will be the more far-reaching in its consequences the earlier in the individual life that it occurs. Major features of the personality are formed in childhood, and childhood is the time when events that are most significant for the genesis of mental illness occur. This last follows from the fact—according to psychoanalytic theory—that childhood is preeminently the time for repression. Then the ego is relatively weak, while emotional strains are as great as at any time of life. Hence the child commonly adapts to strains with the use of unconscious mechanisms, and these, which are not open to modification through ordinary experience, become the basis of vulnerability to future strains; when these are met in a maladaptive way, pathology snowballs.

A mental health worker who takes this view of the matter naturally wishes to educate or otherwise intervene with parents so that the maladaptive reactions will not occur in the first place; or if, as seems likely, some such reactions are inevitable, then the thing to do is to reach the child as early as possible, using special techniques to modify his unconscious adaptive devices and to help make other more adequate devices available to him.

What is wrong with this picture, from the point of view of the social scientist or the public health specialist? One thing that is wrong—so runs the argument—is that the individual psychodynamic approach, after years of work and the expenditure of huge sums of money, has not succeeded in reducing rates of admission to mental hospitals. At least there is no evidence that this is the case. This may be because the early treatment was ineffective; children seen in child guidance clinics went on to become hospital patients anyway. More likely it is because people who are treated in child guidance clinics, or who are treated privately as children, and people who fill the mental hospitals are drawn from different populations (Forstenzer, 1961). As is well known from the work of Hollingshead and Redlich (1953) and others (see A. Rose & Stub, 1955), the highest rates of admission to mental hospitals are found in the lowest economic stratum of society, while there is a strong tendency, pointed to by Albee in his report for the Joint Commission (1959), for child guidance clinics, and outpatient clinics generally, to turn away or not to have referred to them people who have the most serious problems. These last, typically, are individuals from the lower economic classes; it is they, rather than individuals who can "benefit from psychotherapy," who from the start are more likely to be destined for the mental hospital. Hence the argument, often forcibly put by social scientists, that the most highly trained specialists in the mental health field, that is, the psychoanalytically oriented psychotherapists, are devoting themselves to the least ill members of the population affected by mental illness—and are training and otherwise encouraging more people to do the same thing.

This kind of critique often attributes wrong practices by psychiatrists, clinical psychologists, and social workers to the domination of the mental health field by psychodynamic theories, mainly those of the Freudian variety. There is a strong implication that practice is wrong because the theory is wrong and that everybody—particularly the mentally ill—would be better off if Freud had not saddled us with his theories about the determination of neurosis in childhood.

This may be doubted. Criticism of mental health practice is one thing; criticism of psychodynamic theories is something else. Various psychological theories besides the psychodynamic ones focus on individuals rather than on the mass of people, and the way mental health services in this country are organized would seem to depend more on the kind of society we are than on the kind of psychological theory favored by psychiatrists during a particular period.

The rewards for performing two-person psychotherapy with people who are not very sick—and particularly with people who can pay—are, by American standards, great compared with those for using other kinds of methods with very sick people in public institutions. These rewards are not primarily status and money, though these no doubt have their place; most important is the satisfaction of seeing an individual "improve" or benefit otherwise as a result of therapeutic efforts. This satisfaction is of the same kind as that experienced by devoted teachers or counselors of individuals; to observe a favorable change in the "statistics" for a population is not a substitute for it. We should expect what we in fact find—that professionals of various theoretical points of view, including modern behavioristic ones, prefer to practice individual psychotherapy and that the role is often chosen before there is commitment to a theoretical position.

No doubt there is interaction between theory and practice. People who are trained for the practice of psychoanalysis or for psychoanalytically oriented psychotherapy naturally tend to interpret Freudian theories in ways that lend support to what they do, and their practice often cuts them off from experiences that might broaden their horizons. When they are thus led to take narrow and stereotyped views of neurosis, to overgeneralize from their clinical experience, or to overaccent the role of childhood traumata in personality functioning, they become easy targets for the sociological critics. But these critics, if they are to attack Freudian psychodynamic theories effectively, must do more than suggest that belief in these theories has led to the poor allocation of our mental health resources.

These critics have, of course, done more. They have attacked the theories directly—both the theory of determination of neurosis in early childhood and the theory of personality change that underlies psychoanalytic psychotherapies.

With respect to the determination of mental illness, the social scientists critical of psychoanalysis have argued that broad social and economic factors such as social disorganization, unemployment, and bad housing may be more important then emotional crises arising in the context of relationships within the family. But this does not seem to touch the psychodynamic theories themselves, for however much one may be struck by bad cultural and social conditions and feel moved to change them, an explication of their role in psychopathology would still have to make clear the ways in which they affect the individual personality. And here the role of the family as mediator and the role of psychodynamic mechanisms of input and adaptation seem as important as ever.

Nor does the social scientist's accent upon events occurring later in the individual's life, rather than upon the events of childhood, lead to any great shaking of the psychodynamic position. It is possible for the psychoanalyst to be quite relaxed about this, agreeing readily that "later events are important too," for nothing has happened to threaten his view that in every neurotic or psychotic breakdown there was a predisposition laid down in early childhood. This view is not contradicted by evidence that such a breakdown would not have occurred but for severe strains arising in adult life. The psychoanalyst would say that people with neurotic or psychotic predispositions commonly find modes of life that serve their defensive needs or offer enough support so that a more or less adequate existence is possible. Breakdowns come when supports are withdrawn or when radical change in the individual's situation renders his defensive operations ineffective. This seems to have happened to thousands of young men when they were inducted into the armed services during World War II.

This is not to say that there are not environmentally determined strains of such severity or of such a character as to cause prolonged emotional disturbance, malfunctioning, or deviant behavior in anyone—regardless of predisposition or resistance. The psychoanalyst would say simply that these disturbances are not manifestations of neurosis in his sense of the term; and the fact that this is so, he would argue, helps to explain why so many people with severe psychological problems get well without benefit of professional help.

Sophisticated critics of psychodynamic theory have warned their colleagues in social science, who have thought they had psychoanalysis on the run, not to throw out the baby with the bath water. It may be suggested to enthusiastic social and situational determinists that they approach this whole baby-bath complex with caution. We are dealing here with differences in emphasis upon one or another aspect of what should be a total theory of causation. In particular cases there will always be a question of whether the situational or the predispositional factors were crucially important, and the psychoanalysts will often turn out to be right.

The psychodynamic theories, then, remain pretty much intact—so far—but when it comes to the question of what to do, the social scientists and the public health specialists have made a point. No psychodynamicist can deny the importance of precipitating factors in mental disease or of situational events in emotional disturbance. There are enough unnecessary strains and enough failures in support in the lives of enough people in this country to keep an army of preventers busy. And since the strains and lacks of support affect millions, it seems clear that actions that might modify these conditions in whole communities have a better chance of reducing rates of mental illness than psychotherapy does, with its very limited applicability.

The second major line of argument against psychoanalysis and the psychodynamic theory has to do with the nature of personality and the processes of personality change. Once again it seems well to separate arguments about practice from arguments about theory. Many psychologists, psychiatrists, and psychonanalysts, in addition to social scientists and public health specialists, have long been aware of the practical limitations of psychotherapy and have sought substitutes for it. The success of such substitutes as group psychotherapy or even the therapeutic community does not necessarily imply any criticism of the theory, nor does the fact that various kinds of psychotherapy besides psychoanalytic ones bring benefits to patients. Actions that induce changes in people and the explanation for those changes are two different things.

The same consideration holds generally for activities designed to effect changes in behavior without pretending to modify the structures of the personality. Certain types of alcoholism, for example, can be regarded as symptoms of underlying disturbances in the personality. Action which leads to the exchange of alcoholism for some other symptom but which involves no change in personality might be a great benefit both to the alcoholic patient and to the people around him.

The crucial theoretical question is: "How central or all-determining, within the personality, are the unconscious structures laid down in early childhood?" There is a tendency sometimes found among psychoanalysts, and often attributed to them by their critics, to suppose that personality formation is a matter of building unconscious defenses against instincts and that personality development is a matter of undoing, or having undone, these defenses and of contriving better ones. Some psychoanalysts and some psychologists sympathetic to psychoanalysis (e.g., Hartmann, Kris, & Loewenstein, 1947; Sanford, 1962b; White, 1952), as well as numerous writers of quite different persuasions (e.g., Allport, 1961; Kelly, 1953; Maslow, 1954), have argued and assembled evidence to show that this is not the whole story. There are parts of the personality that do not become involved in the child's unconscious complexes, and always there are parts of the personality which are not dominated by unconscious processes but which are open to modification through ordinary experience. Significantly, the best evidence for this view has been contributed not by psychotherapists, who focus on neurotic structures, but by investigators who have seen neurotic or mentally ill people in various settings other than psychotherapy. Most impressive has been evidence from work in mental hospitals that even the most seriously ill patients are still capable of functioning in organized groups and of responding to stimuli which in normal people raise or lower self-respect (Greenblatt, Levinson, & Williams, 1957; Milbank Memorial Fund, 1958).

The point is of enormous significance, both for the care of the mentally ill and for prevention. It means that much can be done for people in trouble, outside as well as inside mental hospitals, by less highly trained professionals and even by nonprofessionals, for, on this view of the matter, benefit to troubled people does not flow entirely from changes in their unconscious structure or even from psychological understanding of them. And where the concern is with the education and upbringing of children, it means that one makes no mistake when he devotes effort to the development of those parts of the personality that are free or relatively free of involvement with unconscious processes. It does *not* mean that those who have responsibility for troubled children can ignore the unconscious processes determining their symptoms; for although such children can respond to efforts to develop the unimpaired parts of their personalities, some of them will, if not understood, insist on acting out their unconscious motives in ways irreparably destructive to themselves or others. One may hope that with respect to facilities for troubled children, we will not always have to choose between those which adhere to rigid stereotypes of Freudian categories and those inspired by a blind optimism concerning what can be achieved by providing a favorable environment.

The final issue concerns the possibilities of modifying unconscious structures of the personality by means other than psychotherapy or its equivalents. The writer has argued elsewhere (Sanford, 1962b, pp. 628–629), on the basis of observations of college students, that in individuals with symptoms based on underlying neurotic structures developments in the unimpaired parts of the personality may so change the relationships between what is conscious and what is unconscious that the latter fades into relative insignificance. And the writer has also argued (Sanford, 1956, p. 354) that unconscious processes are not necessarily cut off from direct influence by social stimuli. A challenging question concerns the interaction of the conscious and the unconscious. The traditional and well-substantiated psychodynamic view is that unconscious processes have a heavy determining effect upon cognition; there is reason to believe that the determination may also be the other way around. This is a frontier area for research—although those who have no truck with concepts of the unconscious will not be intrigued by it.

Once again, this kind of liberalization of the psychodynamic view is consistent with the "new thinking" that supports the activities of social scientists and public health specialists who would reduce rates of mental illness by modifying the social environment. Some supporters of the "new thought" seem to have come by their liberal views too easily. It will be up to clinical psychologists to see to it that the practical orientation, and particularly the practical success, of the new breed of mental health workers does not impair investigation into the nature of personality organization and functioning. In the long run, knowledge of these matters will be essential if preventive work is to reach a high level of effectiveness.

Orientation to Value

All programs of preventive action have to be guided by values, that is, values over and above the simple faith that mental illness is bad. This follows from the fact that pathological conditions are not isolated in the person (a change in them might induce desirable or undesirable changes in other areas of the person) and from the consideration that actions deemed necessary to prevent an unhealthy condition may affect a person in various ways, some good and some bad.

The mental health specialist faces this issue as soon as he says, as he must, that he wants to be sure his preventive actions do not do more harm than good. The evaluation in such a case cannot possibly be limited to the single dimension of increased or decreased "mental health," for it is unthinkable that all virtues, all desiderata of human development, can be brought under the mental illness–mental health rubric. To be convinced of this, one has only to ask what a person who has achieved mental health should do with himself or whether one would be willing to give up our ideals of individualism in order to eliminate psychological strains and thus to reduce rates of mental illness. It would be hard to imagine circumstances in which the goal of reducing or preventing mental illness should take precedence over humanity, justice, or the fullest possible development of the individual's potential.

Critics of the efforts of psychologists to formulate positive goals for people—too often, unfortunately, under the banner of "positive mental health"—early critics such as Kingsley Davis (1938), and late ones such as Elaine Cumming (1963) do not berate the psychologists so much for having values as for having the wrong values, that is, values which these sociologists would not put very high in *their* hierarchy. Fundamentally, it seems, writers such as these want more "social conscience" and less "social desirability" or, more seriously, more attention to the welfare of people in general and less to what might be ideal for particular individuals.

In the literature on positive mental health, two conceptions of positive mental health may be differentiated. First, there is the conception of something, over and above freedom from illness, that stands as resistance to, or relative immunity from, mental illness. There would seem to be a place for this conception and for research that could specify what such a condition might be. The criticism that positive mental health is undefinable would not seem to apply with any great force here, for to define resistance and to specify it experimentally would seem to be no more difficult than to define susceptibility to illness and to specify it experimentally. The second conception embodies a set of ideals referring to what a person might become. This conception might easily come into conflict with the first one, for it may turn out that qualities such as insensitivity, for example, which contribute to resistance to illness, do not fit into conceptions of the ideal.

Particular conceptions of this second kind are always easy to criticize. Frequently they can be shown to be culture-bound or class-bound or to be expressions of particular historical periods. But the search for ideals must go on, and there is no reason why psychologists and social scientists should not take part in the quest. If these scientists are to assist in the designing of plans for the upbringing and education of children and youth, they must be guided by open-ended conceptions of what people can become. They need commit themselves only tentatively to particular systems of value, while continuing their efforts to improve thinking about values—by showing how values are arrived at and what will be the consequences of particular values. Perhaps they can make their greatest contribution by urging—and this flows directly from knowledge they now have—that where human beings are concerned, ends and means cannot be separated. In a humanistic approach to prevention, means as well as ends are humanistic. This is to say that long-range programs of discipline or deprivation aimed at the ultimate inculcation of some virtue cannot be supported. What is good for people in the long run is, by and large, good for them *now*, in the immediate situation. Actions that aim to develop people or to build resistance to mental illness in them can be evaluated in the momentary situation without waiting for long-range consequences. Such evaluation would take into account the motives, feelings, and behavior of the "helping" parent or professional as well as the immediate effects of their actions upon the object of their concern. If the helpers are well motivated and if their actions have good effects upon *them*, the chances are that the other will be benefited.

PROGRAMS AND PRACTICES

Concepts of Prevention

We may achieve some clarification of the concepts of prevention by asking what is to be prevented, in whom, and by what methods?

What is to be prevented? The goal is to prevent the development of disorders (primary prevention) and to prevent mild disorders from becoming acute or prolonged (secondary prevention).

Tertiary prevention consists in actions directed to preventable consequences of mental illness.

"Mental disease" is broadly interpreted to include psychogenic conditions as well as diseases of organic origin (i.e., diseases due in very large part to the destruction of brain tissue or to disturbances of the physiological functioning of the brain) and to include not only the psychoses and neuroses but also the so-called "special" phenomena, such as delinquency and alcoholism, with which society has a concern and which affect more people than the hard-core diseases.

What is to be prevented must also include not merely specific symptoms and patterns of behavior but also more general pathological or deviant states. We must allow for the possibility that actions directed to alcoholism, for example, may in some cases, through failure to deal with a more general underlying condition, lead to the substitution of other, less desirable manifestations.

Prevention in whom? Primary prevention is almost always directed to *populations of people*—sometimes the whole population of the nation or state. There might be, for example, action to improve the general quality of life or action to remove some harmful agent that might attack anyone. Efforts at prevention are also directed to *selected groups of individuals*, for instance, people in specially vulnerable age groups: the prenatal population, children, adolescents, and old people.

People in dangerous situations, "high-risk" groups (e.g., people of any age who are economically or socially disadvantaged or children who have lost a parent, who have a psychotic parent, or whose homes have been broken), are often targets for preventive effort.

It is further to be noted that all people, however free from external hazards they may be, go through periods of crisis involving threats to their mental health. At these times there is a place for preventive activity.

People of any age who are already in trouble—trouble of a kind that can be diagnosed and that can, hopefully, be remedied—can also be helped. Here there is, typically, some kind of therapeutic attention to the individual case. This is *secondary prevention*. But people who are already in trouble may benefit from primary preventive activities directed to the whole population. Indeed there is as yet no very good way of knowing which people *are* in trouble.

Prevention by what means? Services are often organized with particular kinds of people or particular problem areas as a focus of attention. Examples are centers for prenatal care and child guidance clinics. But it is useful to classify preventive activities in more general terms, according to the conditions in individuals and in society that are to be changed. For instance, one may think of reducing susceptibilities or building strengths in individuals and of removing hazards or building supports in society.

Actions of any or all of these kinds may be directed to populations at large or to selected groups of individuals, to people who are free of symptoms—whether or not they are in dangerous or critical situations—or to people who are in trouble.

Various services of institutional units—home, school, church, physicians, social agencies, courts, general hospitals, clinics, prisons, training schools, public health departments, recreational departments, employment agencies, civic organizations, etc.—may engage in these actions singly or in various combinations of two or more.

We may organize the remainder of this discussion by maintaining the fundamental distinction between primary and secondary prevention and then, for each of these two major areas, by grouping kinds of programs or actions according to whether they are undertaken by the nation, by the state, by private organizations that are national in scope, by public or private agencies of the local community, or by individuals who have some kind of personal interaction with the people who are the objects of concern.

Primary Prevention

At the national or state level. Here belong activities by national or state agencies—legislative or administrative—directed toward preventing the development of organic or psychological disorders in the general population or in selected groups of individuals; the activities may be directed toward reducing susceptibilities or building strengths in individuals or toward removing hazards or building supports in society. Most often, these programs seek to improve the quality of life for everybody by changing economic and social conditions, e.g., reducing unemployment and bad housing.

Not always, of course, are such programs carried forward in the name of mental health or mental health alone; they are also carried forward in the names of justice and the general welfare. Also, there seems to be increasing understanding of the fact that changes in the economic system, or in the economic well-being of citizens, does not automatically bring improvement in morale or psychological well-being. In order to give everybody a sense of having a fair chance and a sense of participation in the whole enterprise, it is necessary to look to public morality, to political and social arrangements, and to the system of rewards. Economic benefits to a depressed area, for example, would accomplish little unless something were done to reduce the inhabitants' suspicion of officialdom or to change the system whereby local leaders or authority figures lined their pockets at the expense of the community.

Also, there is increased understanding of the fact that the conditions of life in modern society are psychologically difficult for many people, including middle-class people, who have economic security—at least at a minimal level. As early as 1936, Frank put forward the notion of "society as the patient," and there have since been numerous efforts at "community diagnosis," that is, efforts to understand how changes in our society and in our national life affect the psychological well-being of people in general. For example, Burgess (1955, p. 14) calls attention to the threats to mental health implicit in the complexity, mechanization, and standardization of living in our society—circumstances which lead to the substitution of impersonal relations among people for personal ones. Analyses of this kind do not usually lead to suggestions for action in particular situations; rather, they seek to promote the kind of understanding that helps to make all actions affecting the great mass of people more humane.

More directly aimed at prevention are Federal and state programs of education respecting mental illness and mental health. For example, the Children's Bureau has for many years sought to make available to parents current knowledge and ideas regarding child rearing; and the 1950 White House Conference on Children and Youth had effects which, according to Rosen (1961), have "reverberated throughout the past decade," speeding the process by which mental health concepts become part of the professional equipment of workers concerned with children and their families. Similarly, the 1948 White House Conference on Education did much to encourage schools at all levels to take an interest in the healthy personality development of students.

State departments of health, of mental health, and of education generally, and increasingly, have educational programs designed to spread the word about mental illness and health among the general public and among members of various professions that have responsibilities for people. Many states require that instruction in hygiene, including aspects of mental hygiene (e.g., instruction regarding alcohol and narcotics), be offered in public schools.

Federal and state departments of health often rely upon laws and administrative directives as means for inducing people to take necessary actions to help remove hazards or to immunize themselves. The same approach holds for mental diseases of known organic origin, for example, those due to infections or to nutritional deficiencies.

It is in this area that efforts to control mental disease have met with the most success. Although the number of people affected by mental diseases of organic origin is not nearly so great as the number of those with psychogenic conditions, the number is still large, and much remains to be done before preventable organic diseases are brought under control. Here psychologists—particularly social psychologists—have an opportunity to play important roles (Rosenstock, 1963). Although a single factor, e.g., syphilitic infection, may dominate the system of causation, there is nonetheless a *system* in which psychological and social factors play their parts. In the last analysis, the prevention of general paresis will involve understanding and control of abnormal sexual behavior and of attitudes and practices having to do with reporting, and accepting treatment for, syphilitic infection.

The use of laws to change the behavior of the great mass of people, in the interests of prevention, raises highly complicated ethical and psychological issues. How far can a government go in making laws to induce people to do "what is good for them" without infringing too much upon individual liberties? How much are people willing to sacrifice in order to increase the likelihood that they or those close to them will be spared some impairment of their mental health? What diverse consequences may flow from a hard-to-enforce law aimed at some particular hazard to health?

The Eighteenth Amendment was thought by some to be a means for controlling the "toxic agent" in alcoholism. But ever since its passage, this "prohibition law" and its aftermath have been cited in efforts to show how an unenforceable law, or a law that is based on too narrow a view of the phenomena it is intended to affect, can do more harm than good because of its unanticipated consequences. Certainly the experience of the prohibition era in this country generated attitudes and beliefs that have severely hampered rational efforts to deal with the sale and distribution of alcohol. Only in recent years has evidence emerged that national prohibition was not a total failure; and only in recent years have we had the kind of social analysis that can suggest what kinds of legal actions might be expected to modify social practice in constructive ways (Chafetz & Demone, 1962, pp. 175ff.; Jellinek, 1945; McCarthy, 1959).

The view that passage of a law that affects the interests and behavior of the great mass of people ought to wait until attitudes and beliefs are such that the law will be universally welcomed and obeyed was challenged by the Supreme Court's 1954 decision concerning the desegregation of public schools. This decision took into account evidence, supplied by social scientists, that segregation impaired the mental health of Negro children. The events that followed the decision show what a powerful instrument of cultural change the law can be; they also suggest that there are optimum times and conditions for recourse to sweeping legal remedies. It seems that the legal action should be in keeping with a cultural trend that is already to be discerned, that there should be enough readiness among the people so that the action will be generally accepted, and that there should remain enough resistance to it, so that the action can play an important role in further educating the people and speeding the desired cultural change.

This discussion of primary prevention at the state or national level has so far dealt with actions that affect people in general. There are also, at these levels, legislative or administrative actions aimed at improving the lot of people in special situations of danger. Here belong child labor laws and social welfare legislation generally, e.g., provision for special educational facilities for children in "impacted areas" or actions to provide job opportunities or work-study programs for youth. Psychologists and other social scientists have opportunities here for "community diagnosis," calling attention to groups of people who are in special danger, e.g., alienated youth (Keniston, 1962), or to social practices, e.g., the racial segregation of schools, that are damaging to large segments of the population. These scientists may also serve as consultants to officials who have responsibility for groups of people in dangerous situations; for example, Lindemann and Caplan (1963) tell the story of how a minimum of psychiatric consultation with Israeli authorities led to highly constructive changes in methods of caring for immigrants.

At the community level. As Kahn (1963, p. 62) says: "A local community is in a position to interpose itself between the general social environment and the family or individual." There are from time to time actions by whole communities designed to improve themselves generally and to affect in a positive way all their families. Here would belong large-scale redevelopment projects and community-wide programs for reducing unemployment, improving intergroup relations, or promoting more gratifying use of leisure. Actions of these kinds, starting with a focus on some particular problem, such as juvenile delinquency, may have the effect of improving the morale of the whole community, generating a sense of direction and a sense of pride. From what we know of social factors in mental disorder, such actions might be presumed to reduce rates of morbidity in the community's population.

There are numerous community programs that aim to bring enlightenment respecting mental illness and health to parents and others who have responsibility for the young. Agencies of the community, such as mental health associations, PTAs, and professional organizations, arrange for lectures, discussions, institutes, courses, and uses of the mass media to acquaint parents and others with current knowledge and wisdom concerning the rearing of children. Guidance programs for parents have been set up in clinics, day-care centers, and nursery schools. Brim (1959) has reported on numerous efforts to educate parents for mental health and pointed to how little is known about the effects of these efforts.

It is also common for mental health specialists working through local organizations and institutions to try to modify the behavior of various professionals who deal with children, e.g., pediatricians (Caplan, 1959; Richmond, 1959; J. A. Rose & Ross, 1960), obstetricians, nurses, and nursery school teachers (Brody, 1961; Murphy, 1961; Waldfogel & Gardner, 1961). Then there are community-supported efforts to promote mental health in schools. Here belong efforts to give teachers a fuller understanding of the children they teach (Allinsmith & Goethals, 1962, pp. 134–135; Ojemann, 1958; Prescott, 1957 and efforts to help teachers to understand themselves so that they will be able to provide a more favorable experience for children (Frank, 1962). There are also efforts to influence the curriculum, methods of teaching, and the social organization of schools in such a way that individual development, with its implications for mental health, is favored (Biber, 1962). It is in this last area that conflict between educators interested in mental health and educators who accent learning of traditional school subjects often becomes acute. Allinsmith and Goethals (1962) report in detail on this matter but are unable to suggest that resolution of the conflicts is in sight. Biber (1961), like the writer (Sanford, 1962a), has sought to restate the issues around "life adjustment" versus fundamentalism in education by pointing out that cognitive or intellectual development cannot be separated categorically from the rest of the personality and by urging that development of the total individual rather than either positive mental health or learning of content should be the educational goal.

There are also community actions directed to presumably symptom-free people in situations of danger or unusual stress and to people in situations that are likely to be stressful, for example, populations in depressed areas, immigrants or refugees in search of jobs, and middle-class people assembled in housing developments where there is no community.

Glass (1963) offers a good example of this kind of action on the part of military establishments, where efforts have been made to improve the conditions under which men work, live, and fight. He recommends that such efforts be followed by epidemiological work that would note the frequencies with which problems appeared within different units.

Lindemann and Caplan (1963) offer an example of how psychiatric consultation might have improved matters and reduced rates of delinquency in a housing project in the Boston area. They note that the screening procedures for admission to this low-rental housing development made it inevitable that too high a proportion of "unhealthy families" were admitted and had an unfavorable effect upon the healthy families. Consultation by psychiatrists or social scientists with those who had administrative responsibility might very well have led to working out a better balance.

Perhaps the best examples of primary prevention directed to people in dangerous situations are the "higher horizons" projects that aim to raise the level of the cultural aspirations of the underprivileged youth. In New York City, for example, the program that goes forward under this heading undertakes to speed racial integration; to speed construction of school facilities; to offer more guidance, better teaching, and smaller classes in the schools; and, by direct action, to stimulate the less motivated and more culturally deprived youth (New York State Youth Commission, 1959; Wrightstone, 1958). Other cities have instituted "special-service schools," designed to give the less privileged children the best in education and counseling. Downing (1959) describes a program designed to enrich the lives of deprived children through outings and recreational programs and by helping socially isolated families become a part of their neighborhood. Other communities have programs for school dropouts, for unemployed youth, and for young people who do not fit the educational lockstep.

At the level of personal interaction. This is intervention by the mental health specialist either through face-to-face relations with the individual involved (direct services) or through close consultation with people such as parents or teachers who have immediate responsibility for the threatened individual (indirect services). Concerning indirect personal interaction, there is a distinction to be made between the activities described above, in which the effort is made to educate parents or teachers in a general way and to provide generally improved conditions for deprived individuals, and activities in which the mental health specialist works closely with parents or educators in programs designed to meet particular conditions. Pavenstedt (1961), for example, describes a program of special counseling for immature mothers, and J. A. Rose (1961) describes a program of counseling for mothers of children with physical abnormalities. Here would belong also Ojemann's (1958; 1961) program for teaching teachers to use educational techniques designed to induce children to adopt a "causal" instead of a judgmental approach to problems.

When Ojemann, however, or a specially educated teacher, works directly with children in an effort to induce them to think in causal terms, this is direct interaction. The same is true of Seeley's (1959) program of human relations classes, in which students are prepared for forthcoming crises, are given reassurance, and are made aware of feelings.

This kind of direct approach has been carried furthest by Lindemann and by Caplan and their colleagues (Caplan, 1961; Klein & Lindemann, 1961; Lindemann, 1944; Lindemann & Dawes, 1952). This work is based on what these workers have termed "crisis theory" (Caplan, 1961, pp. 12–14). The essential idea is that people normally during the course of their development reach certain periods of crisis during which they are particularly open to change. Depending upon the quality and intensity of the crisis, the individual may either take a step forward developmentally or fall back upon coping devices that are maladaptive in the long run. The aim of intervention at such periods is to supply the sort of help that would enable the individual to avoid this latter kind of response and to make of the crisis an occasion for a developmental gain. This method is based on psychodynamic theory (Lindemann, 1944), but it represents an effort by Lindemann and Caplan and their colleagues to integrate psychodynamic and public health approaches to prevention. Although the theory of change is an individual psychodynamic theory, the argument is that crises occur very commonly in populations and that a minimum of professional intervention at the right times and places can result in reducing rates of mental illness. A number of different kinds of crises have been studied, for example, entering school (Klein & Ross, 1958), entering college (Silber, Hamburg, & Coelho, 1961), entering professional training (Rosenberg & Fuller, 1957), experiencing loss or a death in the family (Lindemann, 1944), and suffering a serious illness (Lindemann & Caplan, 1963).

Few primary preventive activities at any level have been carefully evaluated, and where evaluations have been made, positive results have only rarely been demonstrated. Brim (1959) has pointed up the state of our ignorance concerning the effects of programs of education for child training. With respect to preventive efforts in the schools, the situation is not much better. Ojemann, Levitt, Lyle, and Whiteside (1955), in one of the few adequate studies, were able to produce some evidence of the effectiveness of projects for education in causal thinking. It is not surprising, in view of the great difficulties, that large-scale programs for changing the social environment in the state or in the community have not been evaluated in ways that would be satisfactory to a psychologist. It must be considered, however, that programs designed to benefit large groups of people probably never will be evaluated in the way that psychologists are accustomed to evaluate pychotherapeutic procedures or particular educational devices. "Social experiments" do not permit of the same kinds of controls that can be maintained in the laboratory, but humane considerations and good sense still argue that such experiments be carried out. One may hope that those who do the carrying out will recognize the obligation to evaluate and to do the best they can in their circumstances.

Secondary Prevention

The early diagnosis and treatment of individuals who exhibit some kind of mental disorder are the stock-in-trade of clinical psychologists, and this practice need not be considered in any detail here. The clinical psychologist will, of course, be concerned to see to it that programs of primary prevention do not lead to the neglect of children who are plainly already in trouble. The case for secondary prevention has recently been well put by Kahn (1963), and, as was suggested earlier in this chapter, it has been well put by psychologists and psychiatrists over the years. Glass (1963) has reported on how prompt treatment of soldiers at the front seems to have been effective. Waldfogel, Hahn, and Landy (1955) have reported that good results were had with children with school phobias when referral was made early, and Fraiberg (1954) and Bower (1959) have given evidence that children who will have difficulty in learning can be identified in nursery school and that steps to avoid serious difficulty can be taken at that early stage. College psychiatrists, e.g., Wedge (1958) and Funkenstein (1959), have argued convincingly that relatively little counseling of students in trouble, if it is begun at the right time, can keep the students functioning in the educational system so that the normal educational influences can do their work of building internal strength. Allinsmith and Goethals (1962) have shown that schools are the most natural place for early detection, for first aid, for referral, and for rehabilitation and follow-up.

A serious question concerning early detection has to do with the dangers of premature labeling. This can lead children to conceive of themselves as "problems" and then to behave as such, and it can lead people responsible for children to perceive them as disturbed and then to act toward them in ways that encourage their further disturbance. Kahn (1963) has pointed out that "delinquency scales" tend to overpredict delinquency. He urges that, at this stage of our knowledge, scales should be used only in efforts to understand and not to sort out the sheep and the goats. He suggests that dropping out of school is probably a better sign of trouble ahead than an extreme score on a scale for measuring delinquency. It is perhaps generally true that a preoccupation with early detection can lead to a tendency to find something wrong with everybody or even to efforts at therapy in cases where doing nothing might have been the treatment of choice.

A fundamental issue that has to be faced by authorities responsible for the mental health of large segments of the population has to do with how limited resources are to be allocated. There is no question but that during the past thirty years, the major commitment of resources has been to individual diagnosis and treatment. We are now entering a phase in which primary preventive activities are beginning to participate more fully in budgets for mental health activities. To find and to maintain a proper balance will be a continuing problem for mental health specialists.

Another continuing problem has to do with the coordination of services for people in trouble. There is still competition among agencies for the "good referral," and there is still neglect of people who have "low-status" diseases. Further, there is a problem of how to ensure that people with mental disorders will be regarded as people and not as "cases" of this or that disease. Troubled people are too often totally defined in terms of their disease or affliction and are managed according to procedures that are suited to agencies rather than to the needs of human beings. It will take an enormous amount of social engineering to arrange things so that the troubled individual who needs several kinds of help will be served either by a single broad-purpose agency or by several agencies that can coordinate their efforts, and so that no individual will be pulled apart by conflicts among specialized agencies that either lay claim to his total being or else accept responsibility for only a part of his total problem.

CONCLUSION

In conclusion we may consider some implications of what has been said in this chapter for the work of the clinical psychologist. There are implications for his practice, his research, and his training.

Practice

Despite all that has been said about primary prevention, the fact remains that there are and there will be in the future people in trouble who need the help of the clinical psychologist. Indeed there are at the present time far more such people than all available psychotherapists could possibly take care of. We cannot turn away from those who present themselves to us for help just because our helping them would not seem to contribute much to the total effort to reduce mental illness.

On the other hand, the clinical psychologist should be well aware of the fact that times are changing. It seems not unlikely that the present generation of psychotherapists will be the last to devote themselves primarily to the private practice of psychotherapy. One may easily envision a time when the expensive psychoanalyst in private practice not only will have lost his top status in the mental health hierarchy but also will be regarded more or less as a retainer in a small community of the very rich.

But lest this picture be overdrawn, let us remember that psychotherapy still has, and should have, a highly important place in the training and in the work of the clinical psychologist. To perform psychotherapy or to take responsibility for individuals in trouble is still the best way to learn about people. Not only is it the best way for the individual psychologist to acquire a knowledge of acquaintance respecting the functioning of the person as a whole, but it also remains a major source of hypotheses for subsequent testing by rigorous methods. Moreover, experience designed to give the individual insight into his own functioning is still an invaluable part of preparation for psychological work in various settings. This means, then, that an important function of the most highly trained mental health specialist—that is, the psychoanalytic psychotherapist—will continue to be the training of, and consultation with, other specialists and the advancement of knowledge through observations from his special vantage point.

In order to realize the benefits of this special training, the psychoanalytic psychotherapist must work in other settings besides that of the two-person therapeutic one. If he is to make his full contribution to the prevention of mental illness, he must work in various settings—educational, industrial, medical, correctional, and social welfare—in which service to the vulnerable is offered and in which developmental crises occur.

It is difficult to see why the management of a ward in a mental hospital—a complex community of complex people—or, for that matter, the management of the mental hospital itself should not be as challenging, as prestigeful, and as rewarding otherwise as practice with a handful of private patients. The same holds for a variety of other settings in which opportunities for studying the dynamics of social structures are added to opportunities for studying the functioning of individuals within these structures. One is forced to conclude that the relatively low status, within the mental health professions, of positions in these settings has less to do with the responsibilities and intellectual challenges they offer than with the social organization of the professions and with economic and social processes of the larger society. The situation prevailing at the moment is bound to change; this will involve fresh opportunities for the clinical psychologist. One may hope that he will be flexible, forward looking, and enterprising enough so that he can move into new kinds of settings of psychological practice.

In sum, although in the foreseeable future there will be a place for individual diagnosis and treatment, the clinical psychologist who would be maximally useful socially and constantly challenged intellectually must broaden his horizons and must be prepared to utilize his special knowledge of people in various settings where actions for human welfare are carried out.

Research

The research function of the clinical psychologist, where prevention is the ultimate objective, becomes more important every day. We have seen that those workers who would prevent mental disorder by modifying the social environment have to be guided by information concerning how people are to be motivated and how social conditions—and changes in these conditions—actually affect people. In addition, they will have to have help in the evaluation of their programs. We have seen that social scientists and public health specialists may take preventive action affecting many people without explicitly making use of psychological knowledge. It might sometimes appear that they can get along without such knowledge. This is an illusion sustained by the fact that such knowledge is all around them, a part of their culture created by personality psychologists over the years. If the wellsprings of such knowledge should dry up and if the knowledge that we now have should be forgotten, the results could, in the long run, be catastrophic. Our social scientists could then act with as much blindness, or even inhumanity, as some of the more doctrinaire social planners of the last fifty years.

The kind of research that is most needed concerns the functioning of the total personality. Nowadays the *person* tends to disappear in psychological as well as in social research. The person falls, as it were, between two chairs—on the one hand, psychological researchers (including, alas, many who call themselves "clinical") do not study persons but fragments or part functions of persons; on the other hand, many social scientists regard the person as an empty organism or as a "point region" or, as popular writers have it, a "statistic."

The situation in psychology is at the moment particularly unfortunate. Laboratory research aimed at the accumulation of precise information about particular part functions of the person enjoys the highest prestige and is best rewarded. Accordingly it tends to be imitated by clinical psychologists in the universities, and their work comes to resemble more and more that of the experimentalists. Psychologists, including clinical ones, state their research problems on the basis of a reading of the journals rather than on the basis of their own experience or the observation of people in natural situations. And their work shows it. The psychological journals are filled with papers which not only lack relevance, in the sense that they have little or nothing to do with the functioning of human beings, but also are wrong in their conclusions because their authors failed to see that the variables with which they were concerned actually operate in contexts of personality and cannot be accurately appraised without attention to these contexts. Somebody will have to get back to the person; no one is in a better position to do it than the clinical psychologist.

Interestingly enough, sociologists seem to divide themselves in much the same way that psychologists do. On the one side, there are the experimentalists, who would like to match—in their work on small groups, for example—the niceties of experimental design and the precision in quantification achieved in some psychological experiments. On the other side, there are the sociologists, who are interested in people. Perhaps these last and the humanistic clinical psychologists can make common cause in building a social science and a practice respecting prevention based on increasingly deep-going knowledge of the interaction of the person and the social structure.

Training

The question of why there have been so few significant contributions to psychoanalytic theory after Freud is often raised. The answer often given is that psychoanalysis is not science but dogma and is carried forward by institutions that require conformity and discourage creativity. This could hardly be the whole story, however, because for many years psychoanalytically trained practitioners have been free of institutes and have worked in other settings besides that of private practice. There is reason to believe that much of the fault lies with medical education. For a long time now, the practitioner of psychoanalysis has specialized in biological science long before he went to medical school, and often he finally emerges from his psychoanalytic training a narrowly educated man. There is a striking contrast with men of Freud's generation, who usually not only were broadly educated from early periods in their lives but also had prepared themselves for one or more other professions before they ever went into psychoanalysis. Able to view psychological problems against a broad background of knowledge and experience, they were able to see relationships in a way that the narrowly educated specialist could not. For a long time now, no one has expected much, in the way of additions to knowledge, from the medically educated practitioner of psychoanalysis. Thus it is somewhat alarming to contemplate that training in clinical psychology is, in important respects, going the same way as training in medicine.

For some time now, people have been recruited for clinical psychology not on the basis of their curiosity about people or their curiosity and concern about themselves but on the basis of the fact that they had a conception of a social role for which they wanted to prepare themselves in the most efficient way possible. It seems that training in graduate schools of psychology has tended to give these recruits what they wanted. Practice respecting admission to graduate school puts more and more pressure on the young person to specialize early; and once he is in graduate school, he is under pressure to professionalize himself as soon as possible by taking a large offering of required courses in methods and techniques. The days when graduate students in psychology fraternized easily with anthropologists, sociologists, philosophers, and students of literature seem to have passed. The clinical psychologist who sticks to the academic setting tends to acquire a professional identity more and more like that of the general psychologist, while those who break out of this setting, once they have their Ph.D.s, tend to be more and more like private practitioners of psychiatry or psychoanalysis.

As we think of the future and of the new roles for the clinical psychologist that are emerging, the deficiencies of present training programs become apparent. To meet the needs and to take advantage of the opportunities the future will present, existing programs must be revised, and totally new programs should be developed. One may hope that various departments of psychology—or new departments or centers within the university—will innovate in their own ways and that as they do, they will pay attention to the following suggestions.

First, selection. It is essential that the clinical psychologist of the future be a broadly educated person. Admission to a graduate program of training should depend little upon how much psychology a student "has had" and how well he did with it but much upon what he shows of the best effects of general education at the undergraduate level: clarity of thinking, richness of imagination, breadth of interests, openness to experience.

The graduate program should be focused upon personality theory and social theory—as much of one as of the other. Personality theory will provide the basis for understanding the conditions and processes of change in individuals, and social theory will provide the basis for understanding change in social organizations and institutions; a combination of the two is necessary for a grasp of how changes in the social environment tend to promote or to prevent mental disorders in individuals.

Knowledge of theory must, of course, go hand in hand with practical experience. Just as the didactic part of the training should include personality *and* social theory, so should the practical part include work with people in various kinds of social situations. Each student should have some experience not only in mental hospitals and clinics but also in several other kinds of settings such as general hospitals, schools, probation departments, social welfare agencies, and summer camps—settings where people in trouble or in dangerous situations are given help or where people are influenced by a social organization or institution set up for that purpose. Experience with psychotherapy is, as indicated above, vitally important as a means for achieving depth of understanding. But the two-person psychotherapeutic relationship is only one kind of social situation in which personality is modified. The psychologist who is to serve as a consultant to various kinds of "helpers" who work directly with individuals or who have responsibility for social organizations must have some knowledge of the total range of personality and social processes. His goal should be not so much the mastery of particular therapeutic techniques but the basic understanding of people in social situations. He should be as much a diagnostician of bad situations as a diagnostician of individual pathology.

Finally, it should be recognized that graduate training programs can at best offer only a beginning toward the kind of understanding of people that the clinical psychologist needs. The major function of his graduate education should be to supply the basic approach to psychological understanding, the basic attitudes and inclinations, and the knowledge of how to learn that will set in motion and give direction to a lifelong quest.

REFERENCES

Adler, A. *The education of children.* New York: Greenberg, 1930.

Albee, G. *Mental health manpower trends.* New York: Basic Books, 1959.

Allinsmith, W., & Goethals, G. W. *The role of the schools in mental health.* New York: Basic Books, 1962.

Allport, G. W. *Pattern and growth in personality.* New York: Holt, 1961.

Ansbacher, H. L., & Ansbacher, Rowena R. (Eds.) *The individual psychology of Alfred Adler.* New York: Basic Books, 1956.

Beers, C. *A mind that found itself.* Garden City, N.J.: Doubleday, 1921.

Biber, Barbara. Integration of mental health principles in the school setting. In G. Caplan (Ed.), *Prevention of mental disorders in children.* New York: Basic Books, 1961.

Biber, Barbara, Gilkeson, E., & Winsor, C. Basic approaches to mental health: teacher education at Bank Street College. *Personnel Guidance J.*, 1959, **38**, 558.

Board of Education of the City of New York. *Toward greater opportunity.* New York: Board of Education, 1960.

Bower, E. M. *Early identification of emotionally handicapped children in school.* Springfield, Ill.: Charles C Thomas, 1960.

Bowlby, J. *Maternal care and mental health.* Geneva: World Health Organization, 1951.

Bowlby, J., Ainsworth, Mary, Boston, M., & Rosenbluth, D. The effects of mother-child separation: a follow-up study. *Brit. J. med. Psychol.*, 1956, **29**, 211.

Brim, O. G., Jr. *Education for child rearing.* New York: Russell Sage, 1959.

Brody, Sylvia. Preventive intervention in current problems of early childhood. In G. Caplan (Ed.), *Prevention of mental disorders in children.* New York: Basic Books, 1961.

Burgess, E. W. Mental health in modern society. In A. Rose (Ed.), *Mental health and mental disorder: a sociological approach.* New York: Norton, 1955.

Caplan, G. Practical steps for the family physician in the prevention of mental disorder. *J. Amer. med. Ass.*, 1959, **170**, 1497–1506.

Caplan, G. (Ed.) *Prevention of mental disorders in children.* New York: Basic Books, 1961.

Chafetz, M., & Demone, H. *Alcoholism and society.* New York: Oxford Univer. Press, 1962.

Clausen, J. A., & Straus, R. (Eds.) Medicine and society. *Ann. Amer. Acad. polit. soc. Sci.*, 1963, **346**, 1–210.

Cumming, Elaine. Pathways to prevention. In *Key issues in the prevention of alcoholism: a report of the Northeast conference.* Harrisburg, Pa.: Pennsylvania Department of Health, 1963.

Cumming, J., & Cumming, Elaine. Mental health education in a Canadian community. In B. D. Paul (Ed.), *Health, culture and community.* New York: Russell Sage, 1955.

Davis, K. Mental hygiene and the class structure. *Psychiatry,* 1938, **1**, 55–65.

Downing, Ruth. A cooperative project of an elementary school and a family agency. *Soc. Casewk,* 1959, **25**, 84.

Dubos, René. Paper read at Natl Ass. Ment. Hlth, Miami, 1962.

Eliot, T. D. Interactions of psychiatric and social theory prior to 1940. In A. Rose (Ed.), *Mental health and mental disorder: a sociological approach.* New York: Norton, 1955.

Faris, R. E., & Dunham, H. W. *Mental disorders in urban areas: an ecological study of schizophrenia and other psychoses.* Chicago: Univer. of Chicago Press, 1939.

Forstenzer, H. Problems in relating community programs to state hospitals. *Amer. J. publ. Hlth,* 1961, **51**, 1152.

Fraiberg, Selma. Counseling for the parents of the very young child. *Soc. Casewk,* 1954, **35**, 47.

Frank, L. K. Society as the patient. *Amer. J. Sociol.*, 1936, **42**, 335–344.

Frank, L. K. *Introductory remarks to a panel discussion on ideals and realities in modern education.* New York: Bank Street College of Education, 1955. Cited in Allinsmith & Goethals, 1962.

Freud, S. The question of lay analysis. In *Standard Edition of Freud's Collected Works.* Vol. XX. London: Hogarth Press, 1959. Pp. 176–258.

Fromm, E. *The fear of freedom.* London: Routledge, 1942.

Fromm, E. *Man for himself.* New York: Holt, 1947.

Funkenstein, D. H. (Ed.) *The student and mental health: an international view.* Cambridge, Mass.: Riverside Press, 1959.

Glass, A. J. Military psychiatry. In A. Deutsch (Ed.), *The encyclopedia of mental health,* New York: F. Watts, 1963.

Green, S. L., & Rothenberg, A. B. *A manual of first aid for mental health.* New York: Julian Press, 1953.

Greenblatt, M., Levinson, D. J., & Williams, R. H. (Eds.) *The patient and the mental hospital.* New York: Free Press, 1957.

Hartmann, H., Kris, E., & Loewenstein, R. Comments on the formation of psychic structure. In *The psychoanalytic study of the child.* Vol. 2. New York: International Universities Press, 1947.

Harvard Medical School and Psychiatric Service. *Community mental health and social psychiatry.* Cambridge, Mass.: Harvard Univer. Press, 1962.

Hollingshead, A. B., & Redlich, F. Social stratification and psychiatric disorders. *Amer. sociol. Rev.,* 1953, **18,** 163–169.

Horney, Karen. *New ways in psychoanalysis.* New York: Norton, 1939.

Isaacs, Susan. *Social development in young children.* London: Routledge, 1933.

Jahoda, Marie. Toward a social psychology of mental health. In M. Senn (Ed.), *Problems of infancy and childhood.* New York: Josiah Macy, Jr. Foundation, 1950.

Jahoda, Marie. *Current concepts of positive mental health.* New York: Basic Books, 1958.

Jellinek, E. M. The problems of alcohol. In *Alcohol Sci. Soc., quart. J. Stud. Alcohol,* 1945.

Joint Commission on Mental Illness and Health. *Action for mental health.* New York: Basic Books, 1961.

Kahn, A. J. *Planning community services for children in trouble.* New York: Columbia Univer. Press, 1963.

Kelly, G. *The psychology of personal constructs.* Vol. 1. New York: Norton, 1953.

Keniston, K. Social change and youth in America. *Daedalus,* 1962, **91,** 145–171.

Klein, D., & Lindemann, E. Preventive intervention in individual and family crisis situations. In G. Caplan (Ed.), *Prevention of mental disorders in children.* New York: Basic Books, 1961.

Klein, D., & Ross, A. Kindergarten entry: a study of role transition and its effects on children and their families. In M. Krugman (Ed.) *Orthopsychiatry and the school.* New York: American Orthopsychiatric Association, 1958.

Lemkau, P. V. Mental hygiene. In S. Arieti (Ed.), *American handbook of psychiatry.* Vol. II. New York: Basic Books, 1959. Pp. 1948–1949.

Lindemann, E. Symptomatology and management of acute grief. *Amer. J. Psychiat.,* 1944, **101,** 141.

Lindemann, E., & Caplan, G. Explorations in preventive psychiatry, unpublished manuscript, 1963.

Lindemann, E., & Dawes, L. The use of psychoanalytic constructs in preventive psychiatry. In *The psychoanalytic study of the child.* Vol. 7. New York: International Universities Press, 1952.

Lippitt, R., & Gold, M. Classroom social structure as a mental health problem. *J. soc. Issues,* 1959, **15,** 40.

McCarthy, R. G., & Douglass, E. M. Prohibition and repeal. In R. G. McCarthy (Ed.), *Drinking and intoxication.* New York: Free Press, 1959.

McGavran, E. G. Facing reality in public health. In *Key issues in the prevention of alcoholism: a report of the Northeast conference.* Harrisburg, Pa.: Pennsylvania Department of Health, 1963.

Maslow, A. H. *Motivation and personality.* New York: Harper & Row, 1954.

Milbank Memorial Fund. *An approach to the prevention of disability from chronic psychoses: the open mental hospital within the community.* New York: Milbank Fund, 1958. 80 pp.

Murphy, Lois. Preventive implications of development in the preschool years. In G. Caplan (Ed.), *Prevention of mental disorders in children.* New York: Basic Books, 1961.

Murray, H. A., et al. *Explorations in personality.* New York: Oxford Univer. Press, 1938.

New York State Youth Commission. *Program for youth.* Albany, N.Y., 1959.

Ojemann, R. H. Basic approaches to mental health: the human relations program at the State University of Iowa. *Personnel Guidance J.,* 1958, **37,** 198.

Ojemann, R. H. Investigations on the effects of teaching an understanding and appreciation of behavior dynamics. In G. Caplan (Ed.), *Prevention of mental disorders in children.* New York: Basic Books, 1961.

Ojemann, R. H., Levitt, E. E., Lyle, W. H., Jr., & Whiteside, M. F. The effects of a "causal" teacher-training program and certain curricular changes on grade school children. *J. exp. Educ.,* 1955, **24,** 95.

Opler, M. K. Anthropological aspects of psychiatry. In J. H. Masserman & J. L. Moreno (Eds.), *Progress in psychotherapy.* New York: Grune & Stratton, 1959.

OSS Assessment Staff. *Assessment of men.* New York: Holt, 1948.

Paul, B. (Ed.) *Health, culture and community: case studies of public reactions to health programs.* New York: Russell Sage, 1955.

Pavenstedt, Eleanor. A study of immature mothers and their children. In G. Caplan (Ed.), *Prevention of mental disorders in children.* New York: Basic Books, 1961.

Prescott, D. A. *The child in the educative process.* New York: McGraw-Hill, 1957.

Richmond, J. B. Some observations on the sociology of pediatric education and practice. *Pediatrics,* 1959, **23,** 1175.

Rickman, J. *On the bringing up of children.* London: Routledge, 1938.

Rose, A., & Stub, H. Summary of studies on the incidence of mental disorders. In A. Rose (Ed.), *Mental health and mental disorder: a sociological approach.* New York: Norton, 1955.

Rose, J. A. The prevention of mothering breakdown associated with physical abnormalities of the infant. In G. Caplan (Ed.), *Prevention of mental disorders in children.* New York: Basic Books, 1961.

Rose, J. A., & Ross, D. C. Comprehensive pediatrics: post-graduate training for practicing physicians. *Pediatrics,* 1960, **135,** 144.

Rosen, G. (Ed.) Public health and mental health: converging trends and emerging issues. In *Mental health teaching in schools of public health: a report of a conference sponsored by the Association of Schools of Public Health.* New York: Columbia Univer. School of Public Health and Administrative Medicine, 1961. Pp. 1–75.

Rosenberg, Pearl, & Fuller, Myrtice. Human relations seminar for nursing students. *Nursing Outlook,* 1957, **5,** 724.

Rosenstock, I. M. The motivation of health behavior. In *Key issues in the prevention of alcoholism: report of the Northeast conference.* Harrisburg, Pa.: Pennsylvania Department of Health, 1963.

Sanford, N. Surface and depth in the individual personality. *Psychol. Rev.,* 1956, **63,** 349–359.

Sanford, N. Ends and means in higher education. In G. K. Smith (Ed.), *Current issues in higher education.* Washington, D.C.: Association for Higher Education, 1962. (a)

Sanford, N. What is a normal personality? In J. Katz, P. Nochlin, & R. Stover (Eds.), *Writers on ethics.* Princeton, N.J.: Van Nostrand, 1962. (b)

Schwartz, M. S. Social research in the mental hospital. In A. Rose (Ed.), *Mental health and mental disorder: a sociological approach.* New York: Norton, 1955.

Seeley, J. R. Social values, the mental health movement, and mental health. *Ann. Amer. Acad. polit. soc. Sci.,* 1953, **286,** 15–24.

Seeley, J. R. The Forest Hill Village human relations classes. In *Basic approaches to mental health in the schools.* Washington, D.C.: American Personnel and Guidance Association, 1959.

Silber, E., Hamburg, D. A., & Coelho, C., Murphey, E. B., Rosenberg, M., & Pearlin, L. I. Adaptive behavior in competent adolescents: coping with anticipation of college. *Arch. general Psychiat.,* 1961, **5,** 354–365.

Stanton, A. H., & Schwartz, M. S. *The mental hospital.* New York: Library of Behavior Sciences, 1954.

Waldfogel, S., & Gardner, G. E. Intervention in crisis as a method of primary prevention. In G. Caplan (Ed.), *Prevention of mental disorders in children.* New York: Basic Books, 1961.

Waldfogel, S., Hahn, Pauline, & Landy, E. School phobias: causes and management. *Sch. Counselor,* 1955, **3,** 19.

Wedge, B. M. (Ed.) *Psychosocial problems of college men.* New Haven, Conn.: Yale Univer. Press, 1958.

White, R. W. *Lives in progress.* New York: Dryden Press, 1952.

Wootton, Barbara. *Social science and social pathology.* New York: Macmillan, 1959.

Wrightstone, J. W. Discovering and stimulating culturally deprived talented youth. *Teach. Coll. Rec.,* 1958, **60,** 23–27.

part 6

Clinical Psychology as a Profession

52

Graduate Education in Clinical Psychology

GORDON F. DERNER

When the interest of psychology turned toward applications of understanding, predicting, and controlling human motivation and behavior, the need for specialized programs of preparation in these areas began. Historically, the concern can be shown in the writings of the ancient Greeks and in the Bible. More pertinent, however, have been the developments since Freud and Breuer originated "talking treatment" for emotional disorders and since Binet and Simon, after Galton, measured intelligence.

Most modern historians of the development of clinical psychology use the two world wars as identification marks. During World War I, the use of psychological tests, particularly intelligence tests, demonstrated the value of psychological practice in academic and personnel identification and selection. Programs of study following the psychometric advances focused on testing and its applications.

The impetus to practice psychotherapy which was building up prior to World War II and which became particularly manifest during the war extended the psychologist's service function. Professional activity, however, was somewhat apart from the central goal of university programs. Psychology, within the university, was seen as a research science akin to the natural or pure sciences.

The earliest practical applications of psychology were found more often in schools and departments of education. The first psychological clinic in the United States was established by Witmer at the University of Pennsylvania in 1896, but he emphasized the applications of psychology to school learning problems, not emotional problems. His second case, with which he opened the clinic, was a boy with whom he studied the causes and treatment of poor spelling (Brotemarkle, 1931). In connection with his clinic, Witmer proposed a training program for a new profession of psychological expert. He saw this expert working in a school system examining and treating mentally and morally retarded children or functioning within the profession of medicine.

After Witmer, the major function of the clinical psychologist was the examination of retarded children. The training programs most often attracted teachers who took special courses in intelligence testing, generally learning the administration of one or another form of the Binet test. With World War I and the development of the Army Alpha Examination, training programs focused on developing expertness in the development and use of a wide variety of educational achievement tests. Psychologists devised the tests, but they were used by teachers.

In a book published in 1934, Stevenson reviewed the function of the psychologist in the child guidance clinic, which indicates the kind of training the psychologist received. He was trained as an educational specialist with knowledge of learning and teaching, school practices, and school remediation measures. In 1938 a shift became apparent with several papers which appeared in vol. 1 of the *Journal of Consulting Psychology*. These papers discussed training of clinical psychologists and the development of an internship year. The very first paper in the *Journal* was by Poffenberger (1938) and was devoted to the topic of training and the new American Association of Applied Psychology. The doctorate was set as the prerequisite to membership in the newly formed association, but a new type of doctorate, the Doctor of Psychology (Ps.D.), was suggested. The chief emphasis in the program for the new degree would be preparation for clinic service and less emphasis on academic research. In 1938, Shakow described the features of the internship as part of the training for clinical psychologists. The values listed for the supervised year, which was directly modeled after the medical internship, are several. The psychologist acquires skill in the use of psychological techniques; he becomes immersed in the problems of psychopathology; he develops an objective attitude; and he gets to know how psychiatrists and social workers think and feel.

Rogers (1939) outlined a program in clinical psychology in which he noted the lack of a suitable curriculum in university training and in which he recommended academic involvement. He also supported the internship and, in addition, indicated that a psychologist must be given an opportunity in his program for self-insight.

When Shakow (1945) prepared a paper on trends in training in clinical psychology, he recommended that careful thought be given to requiring a psychoanalysis as part of the training of a clinical psychologist. While it is doubtful that Rogers was recommending analysis, as Shakow did, the need for self-study became increasingly considered a part of the training process.

Official action on clinical psychology training began in 1946 with a request from the U.S. Public Health Service and the Veterans Administration to the APA. The board of directors established a committee on training in clinical psychology in March, 1947, following the request for a list of universities giving training in clinical psychology. This committee subsequently presented a report in September, 1947. The report, entitled "Recommended Graduate Training Program in Clinical Psychology" (Shakow, 1947), subsequently became known as the "Shakow report." Members of Shakow's committee were Drs. Ernest R. Hilgard, E. Lowell Kelly, Bertha Luckey, R. Nevitt Sanford, and Laurance F. Shaffer. These distinguished people set the stage for professional clinical psychology training in the context of university education. The report established general goals and principles but also gave direction to program development. It defined clinical psychology as a method of acquiring systematic knowledge of human personality and of developing techniques to use the knowledge for the betterment of the individual's mental well-being. It therefore emphasized both the scientific and the professional aspects of clinical psychology. Three major areas were identified: diagnosis, therapy, and research. Training in one area only was considered inadequate for full functioning.

A long list of personal qualifications for potential students was included. They included superior intellectual ability, versatility, interest in people, self-insight, an ability to establish effective interpersonal relationships, a sense of responsibility, and special interest in clinical aspects of psychology. Recruitment of enough persons with these and the other attributes was viewed as a major task. The actual selection does remain a major task, but the pool of prospective students for clinical psychology continues to be greater than the number of training slots available in the universities.

Undergraduate education was recommended in broad terms. Major emphasis for the psychology courses was to be in dynamic psychology, with crucial human problems studied with scientific rigor. The optimum of undergraduate psychology recommended was twenty semester hours. The student would have sufficient opportunity to get a full awareness of the area of psychology but still have breadth of education in other areas. Biological and physical sciences; mathematics and statistics; education with practice teaching, if possible; social sciences; history of culture; literary psychology; and foreign languages were considered to be the other areas which should be included.

The report established 14 general principles, including the following: The clinical psychologist should have a core of knowledge and training common to all psychologists; the program would be of four years' duration, combining academic and clinical training, including an internship; preparation should be broadly directed toward research and professional goals rather than simply technical skills; courses should be developed in a sequence and should be complementary rather than overlapping; the faculty should not be overdominated by the academy, nor should it be simply practical; continued contact throughout the four years with clinical material is necessary, and the range should extend from the normal to the severely abnormal; a sense of professional responsibility and professional obligation should be instilled; cooperative work with persons of related disciplines and sensitivity to social implications of the psychologist's activities is essential; and throughout the course of training, research issues should be emphasized. Clearly, the clinical psychologist would be a professional trained in a research tradition.

The graduate program was divided into six major areas of instruction: general psychology, psychodynamics of human behavior, diagnostic methods, therapy, research methods, and related disciplines. A full program of studies was conceived with more semester hours of teaching contact than had been typical in graduate psychology education. It did not, however, specify courses as such but material to be covered in the several areas.

In the area of general psychology, courses in general psychology, physiological and comparative psychology, history of psychology, developmental psychology, and social psychology were recommended. Psychodynamic theory was viewed as central to the program and was to be presented in academic as well as field courses. The fundamental theories of personality and motivation were to be taught as theory and in experimental work. A series of experiments starting with classical research and extending to experiments on personality, with critical study of published research in the clinical area, was recommended. Psychopathology would include actual case presentations so that the mechanisms and dynamics of personality disorder as well as pathognomics would be understood.

Diagnosis was viewed very broadly. It was concerned with etiology, genesis, characteristics, dynamics, and prognosis under varying circumstances. Training, therefore, required an intensive sequence of experiences. Theoretical presentations would be followed by laboratory experience with fellow students as subjects, clerkships called "practicums" for intensive although limited functions for short-term periods, and an internship for a full-time extended period with broad functions. This sequence of didactic presentations and supervised practice was also recommended for therapy training. The diagnostic training would begin in the first year with observation and reporting. Learning techniques of anamnesis taking, interviewing, and preparing an autobiography was to be part of the first-year diagnostic experience. Theoretical presentation on test development and acquaintance with a broad range of clinical instruments, including projective techniques, would lead naturally into practicum experience. These clerkships were recommended for at least four types of clinical settings, such as schools, guidance clinics, psychiatric hospitals, vocational guidance centers, prisons, industrial plants, schools for the retarded, educational clinics, general medical hospitals, and rehabilitation centers. Throughout, the training would emphasize the person rather than the techniques. A balanced understanding of the limits and the values of the psychological appraisal would be the goal.

Psychotherapy training was considered an absolute requirement. It was expected that many more psychologists than previously would be devoting at least part of their time to psychotherapy practice.

Therapy training, like diagnostic training, would start with theoretical courses and didactic experience, followed by supervised experience in practicums and the internship.

Research was considered of paramount importance, and universities were encouraged to assume responsibility for developing research interest and skills. A research atmosphere was to permeate all courses and experiences, including diagnostics and therapy. Research areas included experimental psychology, statistics, research in dynamic psychology, and a dissertation. The dissertation was to be developed in the second year, data collected during the third-year internship, and final work completed during the fourth year.

Related disciplines recommended included physiological sciences, especially neuropsychology and clinical medicine. Sociological sciences recommended were social organization, social pathology, and cultural anthropology.

The program was summarized for the four years. The first year was to be used to give a foundation in general psychology, physiological sciences, and basic clinical skills. The second year would consist mainly of practicums in diagnostics, therapy, and research. The third year would be an internship. The fourth year would allow for the completion of the dissertation, cross-discipline seminars, additional psychology or other related courses, a seminar on professional problems, advanced therapy practicum, and personal therapy.

The internship was suggested for the third year. The rationale was that the student could thus complete his dissertation at the university; unity of practice and theory would be achieved; there would be the enrichment of faculty and students at the university from the experiences of the returning intern; and employment service was more available at the university. A full-year block assignment without rotation was encouraged. Other patterns of the internship arrangement were encouraged, however, and a frequent plan has been a half-time placement at a clinical setting such as the Veterans Administration hospitals or clinics, the other half of the student's time to be spent at the university. The major value of the internship was the opportunity for extended clinical experience under competent supervision. Diagnosis, therapy, research, seminars, and interdisciplinary conferences would all be included.

The proposed program also recommended self-evaluation for the student. Several ways were suggested, including intensive supervision with opportunity for the student to do some self-examination, self-examination in therapy, or some form of psychoanalysis.

Finally, the report listed in sequence the steps in professional development of the clinical psychologist. First would be the four-year course of professional preparation; second would be membership in the Clinical Division of the American Psychological Association. Then would follow legal certification or licensure after one additional year of supervised experience taken postdoctorally. Finally, with five years of professional experience, the psychologist would be examined for diplomate status by the American Board of Examiners in Professional Psychology in the specialty of clinical psychology. This examination would include evaluation of the candidate's education and experience and extensive written, oral, and clinical practice examinations.

In order to ensure potential students that a particular university offered a program in keeping with the committee recommendations, an evaluation procedure was established. The evaluation team also planned to accredit field placement centers.

The very substantial Shakow report has continued to be a monumental statement of recommended education in clinical psychology. The several conferences which have followed since have not substantially altered the basic concepts of the Shakow report, although it will be seen that professional emphasis has frequently been underplayed in many universities. Although no university has delimited research training, many have felt that service interests on the part of students were to be discouraged. As a result, the Shakow report has never been fully implemented by a large number of universities.

Shortly before the Shakow report appeared, a conference had been held under the auspices of the Josiah Macy, Jr., Foundation (Harrower, 1947). The Macy conference brought together representatives from many professions. Many excellent and broadly focused programs were recommended. For example, Kubie recommended a program which combined the first two years of medical school with clinical training, combining psychology and psychiatry. The Kubie program would eliminate those aspects of medical programs which were noncontributing to psychological service and would also focus on practice rather than on clinical research. The program would offer a doctorate in medical psychology. This novel program was so unlike the mold in either medicine or psychology that its impact as a heroic attempt to straddle the complexities of professional education in mental health has never been implemented. The Macy conference, probably because of the diversity of professional backgrounds of the participants, has had limited impact on psychology education.

The Shakow report was not accepted at that time, nor is it now, without negative criticism. Often the criticism was phrased as a defense of academic freedom and support for protection of scientific development of psychology. Many university faculties saw any program recommendations as leading to loss of university autonomy and therefore as a limitation on free development in psychology's research efforts. One critic (Paterson, 1948) felt that the Shakow report was unrealistic in its construction and was too dogmatic.

The Shakow report did furnish a comprehensive outline that served to identify university programs that had clinical psychology programs. To meet the need which led to the committee, an evaluation of clinical psychology programs was done to advise the U.S. Public Health Service and the Veterans Administration. The committee on clinical training evaluated programs in 1947, 1948, and 1949. Part of the 1947 evaluations was published (Sears, 1947), but because of grave concern about the implications to be drawn from the published list, the 1948 and 1949 evaluations were not published.

The hazards in accreditation had to be carefully weighed against the advantages. Accreditation brought about raised standards; departments and their offerings were improved, and university administrations became cognizant of training issues in clinical psychology. Accreditation also brought about concern over arbitrary judgments possible with a small committee, too early overcrystallization of training, and an overslavish adherence to minimal standards, with little attempt to try necessary alternatives. Members of the many accrediting committees, however, have almost universally stood for genuine experimentation in training and have not felt that the inherent dangers in accreditation have become a reality. A final problem has been the frequent confusion of clinical psychology with medicine and medical models. The problem has been only partially resolved. The closer identification of clinical psychology with other applied psychology activities, particularly in counseling and school psychology, along with a growing development in community psychological service appears to be helping clarify the more limited point of view.

Two years after the Shakow report, the second major milestone in clinical psychology training appeared. In August, 1949, 71 representatives from universities, service agencies, and allied professions met in Boulder, Colorado, to consider training in clinical psychology (Raimy, 1950).

The Boulder conference permitted a reconsideration of the Shakow report by a large group after several years of implementation. Approximately seventy propositions were voted on. The large group and the extended experience made votes on the propositions carry serious meaning for professional education. In the main, the Shakow recommendations were approved. They were extended and sometimes spelled out, but no important consensual difference arose about the report. It is interesting to note that considerable thought was given to the problem of combined training in practice and research. The emphasis at first appeared to focus on straight practitioner training. In listing the social goals of clinical psychology, equal weight was given to professional services in diagnosis, therapy, community mental health, and public information and to research contributions toward better understanding of human behavior, better diagnostic instruments, more efficient therapy procedures, and promotion of mental health. "The conference made an important decision when it recommended that research be given a place of equal and coordinate importance with practice in the education of graduate students in the clinical area" (Raimy, 1950, p. 23).

The conference reaffirmed the Shakow recommendations for training in general psychology, clinical core, and fieldwork, including the internship and research. Diversified programs were encouraged, although a basic core of general and clinical psychology was considered necessary. The training was to take a minimum of four years of graduate study, and only those persons possessing the doctorate in clinical psychology would qualify for the title "clinical psychologist." The identification of clinical psychology with the doctorate has continued, although the Boulder conference, as well as the Miami Beach conference in 1959 (Roe, 1959), encouraged the development of subdoctoral programs for psychological technicians. Courses in diagnostic or other clinical techniques were to be offered on the graduate level only. Specifically, courses in psychological test administration, projective techniques, and psychotherapy were not to be taught on the undergraduate level.

The core curriculum of the Shakow report was approved. The goals were to teach content, skills, and attitudes. Twelve areas for study were listed: human physiology, personality theory, developmental psychology, social relations, psychopathology, personality appraisal, clinical medicine and clinical psychiatry, psychotherapy and remedial measures, clinical research methodology, professional and interprofessional relationships, community resources and organization, and practicum and internship experiences.

The explicit reasons for research training were carefully surveyed. The conference did have a difference of opinion on whether service or research would be emphasized or whether there would be some combination of the two. The resolution of the opposing points of view were made on the basis of five points: (1) Training should be in both research and practice so that interest and background are developed in both and so that future activity can be in one or the other or in both; (2) there is vital need for research because of the limited knowledge in clinical psychology; (3) there is little evidence that a person cannot have combined interest and competence in both; (4) service functions provide contact for developing research problems; and (5) effective service functioning can be used as a basis for obtaining research funds. Further experience with graduate programs which stressed both research and service was considered necessary before the research and service question could be answered.

Psychotherapy training was viewed as a requirement in the program of study, even though not every graduate would be a therapy practitioner. Postgraduate training was indicated for full competence. The view of postgraduate training as necessary for full responsibility in psychotherapy continues to be widely held.

Even in programs such as those described by Derner (1960a; 1963), which emphasize the nonmedical nature of psychotherapy, postdoctoral training is necessary. The conference also concerned itself with the interprofessional rivalry with psychiatry over psychotherapy, which it felt was improving; the affirmation of agreement on the developing code of ethics; and the focusing in practicum agencies on the quality of supervision, student selection, staff training, support of accreditation of clinical programs by the APA, and encouragement of APA efforts in furtherance of legislation for psychology. The conference recommended that evaluation of programs be made by a committee on accreditation and that its results be published. Such a group has been established as the Education and Training Board, with a Committee on Evaluation. The standards for evaluation were brought up to date in 1958 (American Psychological Association). The APA publishes a list of approved programs in clinical and counseling psychology each year in the *American Psychologist*. The *American Psychologist* also publishes an annual list of accredited internship centers and a detailed roster of graduate programs in psychology.

The Boulder conference suggested that there be continuing conferences on clinical training. Nonetheless, no conference on clinical psychology per se has been held since, although one is planned for 1965. In 1955 a meeting was held at Stanford University on the broad topic of psychological contributions to mental health (Strother, 1957).

Between the Boulder and the Stanford conferences, two conferences were held which, although not concerned with clinical psychology training, were nonetheless related. In 1951 a conference on counseling psychology training was held at Northwestern University (Committee on Counselor Training, 1952), and in 1954 a conference on school psychology was held at Hotel Thayer, at West Point (Cutts, 1955). Both conferences outlined programs of specialized training, but a clear overlap with clinical psychology was evidenced. At the Stanford conference (Strother, 1957) a discussion resulted in subsuming clinical, counseling, and school psychology under an area broadly defined as "clinical psychology." The emphasis that clinical psychology had often had as medical psychology was an important deterrent to agreement. At the Miami Beach conference (Roe, 1959), again the overlap of the three applied specialities was discussed. A generic term to cover the psychological specialities concerned with a helping relationship with people was proposed. The term, "synergetic," has not been widely used, but the attempt to find a meaningful way of combining the several specialties by name follows very much the practice in the training. Paterson and Lofquist (1960) did a survey of overlap between programs at universities which had both approved clinical and approved counseling programs. Of the twenty-four institutions, only eight made a clear differentiation in courses required, and only three differentiated on the preliminary exams. It was concluded that there was very little differentiation between programs at the major training institutions. There is no survey comparing clinical with school psychology training programs, but a perusal of the program considered at Thayer seems to indicate a substantial overlap, except for the recommendation that some courses in education be taken and that at least one semester of the internship be spent in a school setting.

The Stanford conference made no recommendations but focused on training problems in community mental health, practicum training, therapy, research, and university department organization. It is interesting that no paper was given on diagnostic training, although research and therapy were specific topics. No particular new directions in clinical psychology emerged from the Conference except in reference to general training in mental health.

In 1958 a conference was held at Miami Beach on graduate education in psychology. The coverage was much broader than clinical psychology training, and there was a large group of nonclinical psychologists among the participants. There was a return to an older training idea in the recommendation that psychological preparation be offered at the nondoctoral level, which would be essentially nonresearch. The report is not specific as to what particular positions the nondoctoral personnel would fill, except that they could fill junior college teaching positions and do the routine service work of the doctoral psychologist, such as testing, interviewing, and report writing. Generally, the conference took a very conservative view toward the universities' prerogatives in curriculum. There was agreement that there was a common core of subject matter, but the participants were unable to agree on its specifications. The training goal emphasized was research. It considerably broadened the concept of research to include hypothesis formulation and naturalistic observation, as well as empirical studies. Specialization training was approved unless it interfered with an understanding of basic psychological principles, which were left undefined. Specialization was seen as a threat to the development of psychology when it takes the form of training for service functions rather than being the basis for scientific inquiry. The conference was not planned as a conference on clinical psychology training by design or selection of participants. It therefore has had limited impact on clinical psychology training. The most marked effect the conference could have had would have been the encouragement of nondoctoral education in psychology, which many felt was a downgrading in the applied areas; this has yet to be seen.

The Miami Beach conference, like the Stanford conference, by not focusing on clinical psychology training leaves for the future a renewed look at the Shakow report and the Boulder conference. In 1962, a limited conference at Princeton (Blank & David, 1962) considered manpower needs in clinical psychology. In the report of the conference appears a review of the several training conferences with a focus on agency views. Blank (1964) covers the major training issues, such as undergraduate background, subdoctoral training, field training, training for psychotherapy, and training for research in a cohesive fashion. The view of service and research as complementary goals is often not evident. Bobbitt (Roe, 1959), in his opening address to the Miami Beach conference, noted the problem, but the conference left it unsolved. The emphasis in the majority of clinical psychology programs fits the model of the research scientist rather than that of the practitioner:

> The educators still want to produce something identifiable as scientists and scholars (or in other words, psychologists). . . . The time has passed, though, when the vocational activities of the psychologist they are teaching can be ignored. The educators must listen to the needs of the employers and the aspirations of the students (Bobbitt, in Roe, 1959, p. 22).

University professors of clinical psychology, however, tend to set their model as a basis for training.

Many programs tend to focus on the limitations of diagnostic procedures and the lack of research demonstrations of the effectiveness of psychotherapy, and they discourage the student from considering a clinical practice career. A recent report from 39 graduates of the University of Michigan (Pottharst & Kovacs, 1962) outlines the problem as seen by consumers of one particularly distinguished university program. Their alma mater has a first-rate faculty with a number of distinguished clinicians on the staff. Nonetheless, they are able to identify problems which are prevalent in clinical psychology training. They felt that there has been a deemphasis on clinical psychology in many universities, and they particularly disagreed with training clinicians on a subdoctoral level. They felt that even the doctoral programs were often inadequate unless more actual clinical experience was included in the doctoral program. They disagreed with the oft-repeated idea of reserving specialization training until a postdoctoral period. Postdoctoral programs are scarce, and so many new Ph.D.s may be forced to begin their careers in spite of their deficient training. Further, a split between the academic and the research scientists and the service-oriented clinical psychologists, along with difficulty in securing adequate clinical training, could drive prospective students into other professions. Some respondents in the report, however, saw the training programs as broadening rather than limiting the education of the clinical psychologists.

The Michigan alumni analysis of the problem of training in clinical psychology even includes a clinical evaluation of the anxiety-provoking consequences of clinical work and suggests that people may turn to teaching and research for the purpose of anxiety reduction! In turn, the clinical psychologist has come to feel inferior to research psychologists. Less clinical, is their identification of the sticky reality that very few full-time professors are actively involved in, and dedicated to, clinical work. Clinical supervision and teaching are often done by younger and clinically inexperienced professors.

The Michigan alumni suggested several remedies, among them tailoring graduate clinical psychology programs to focus on individual aptitudes of particular students. Thus for some, the emphasis would be research if interests and skills were shown in that activity; for some with a high degree of empathy and less research ingenuity, the program emphasis could be therapy service. Greater synthesis of theoretical, experimental, and clinical training should be developed, rather than setting clinical training into a separated experience of the internship. More emphasis on the humanities and social sciences is recommended. A knowledge of the history and culture of mankind was seen as at least equally important for the clinical psychologists as research methods, statistics, and the hard sciences. The clinical training should occur in psychology settings rather than medical settings so that the student would have opportunity to identify with his profession. Interdisciplinary experience would be reserved for the later phases of training. The Michigan group also recommended that the philosophy of the clinical training program of each university be made clear so that the prospective student would have a basis for matching his goals with that of the university.

A committee of the Clinical Division of the New York State Psychological Association, chaired by Dr. Rueben Fine (1960), was even more specific in its recommendations to universities. The committee envisioned a doctoral program in psychotherapy. The program was carefully spelled out with a core of basic psychology, personal therapy, and extensive supervised therapy practicums. The program was viewed very favorably by many clinical psychologists who favor increasing university responsibility for clinical practice training. One important difficulty in the proposal outlined by Fine, unrelated to any philosophical questions, was the administrative infeasibility of including all the academic subjects recommended for the first year of the program. The overinclusive list gave the appearance of greater general psychology depth than could be reasonably possible. This problem emphasizes the difficulty of including the extensive amount of psychology in the relatively brief period of the graduate program.

The model of the combination of research trained and professionally trained clinical psychologist continues to be the most admired and desired. Cook (1958), after a studied view of the state of affairs in clinical psychology, stated: "The professional side [clinical psychology] of training has been restricted and superficial." He encourages the model of the scientist-professional, however. Derner (1960b) reviewed the views of the public, the prospective student, the professor, and the clinical practitioner concerning which was the appropriate model. He also concludes that the scientist-practitioner model affords the best structure for clinical psychology training. The scientist's goal, however, need not imply published research from every psychologist. It would imply training in scientific methods and thinking, development of critical-mindedness, development of ability to evaluate research literature, skill in research consultation, and, for the ingenious, the production of research which extends the frontiers of knowledge.

In light of the Shakow report and the Boulder conference, programs akin to professional schools in clinical psychology would seem likely. Development of professional schools, however, even along the scientist-practitioner model, has been slow. McGill University, in Montreal, established a professional program with a professional degree, Doctor of Psychology, as a companion program to the Ph.D.

program in psychology in the late 1940s, but the program was soon abandoned. The professional programs for psychotherapy practice have been developed outside the university, except for recent postdoctoral programs offered by New York University, which began its postdoctoral program in 1961, and by Adelphi University, which began its postdoctoral program in 1963.

The Los Angeles Society for Clinical Psychologists suggests that the impetus for professional schools will need to come from outside the university. "Professional schools in medicine, law and social work all had their beginnings outside the university, and there is not reason to believe that the story will be any different in the field of psychology" (Michael, 1963, p. 38).

It is possible to approach the professional school model while still emphasizing research as well as clinical practice, with clinical practice as a primary training goal. A program which follows the Shakow and Boulder recommendations is shown in Table 1. The program does not make an artificial separation of clinical and school psychology but requires students in both areas to have both school experience and clinic and hospital experience. For those students who wish to function as school psychologists, additional courses in educational philosophy and curriculum round out the education background. The Thayer report (Cutts, 1955), although more education-oriented than the above program, recommends essentially the same kind of training.

The student gets breadth of training in psychological theory, research methods and statistics, and personality and clinical theory and extensive supervised clinical experience. During the first year, the two diagnostic courses are taught as a combined sequence each semester and also have a practicum of one full day a week in a school psychology setting with an additional half-day on alternate weeks in a mental hospital. In the beginning the student first observes, then interviews, and finally does psychological testing under supervision. In the second year, he spends two days a week in intensively supervised clinical practice in diagnostics. One semester is spent in a mental hospital, and the other semester is spent in an outpatient clinic which has social work, speech and hearing, and school remediation services. In the third year, 2½ days a week are spent in an out-patient clinic in psychotherapy service. All therapy is supervised by analytically trained supervisors on an hour-for-hour basis. Students attend weekly case conferences for the second and third years. In addition, a diagnostic case seminar is held weekly for second-year students, and a therapy case seminar for third-year students. Since the clinical faculty are all practicing clinical psychologists, some with major activities in a school, clinic, hospital, or private practice, and since others are primarily at the university, a professional air permeates the program. Professional values are stressed throughout and are specifically covered in a course in forensic psychology and ethics. Personal group psychotherapy is also available and is encouraged for students throughout their three years in residence.

General psychology and research also are begun in the first year and are continued throughout the program. Students are also encouraged to begin work on their doctoral dissertations during their second year. All courses in theory and clinical practice emphasize research problems; therefore the student is immersed in a research-minded setting. The weekly colloquium, while required for one year only, is generally attended throughout the student's residency, so that he has a continuing opportunity to hear of the research at the frontiers of knowledge as presented by fellow students, professors, and visiting psychologists.

The qualifying examination and the language examination come at the end of the first year. The successful student can then devote himself full time to his clinical, research, and course-work activities.

The internship is taken in the fourth year as a full-time culminating experience. If the student has progressed according to schedule, he will complete his dissertation oral examination during the fourth year and will have met all the doctoral degree requirements within a four-year period.

A particular feature of the program is a series of interrelated offerings of an interdisciplinary nature. They include biological and medical courses as well as sociological, anthropological, and education courses. A rounded training experience with clear professional goals is possible within the framework of a research-minded and scholarly program. Preparation for full independent practice, privately or in an institution, necessitates additional postdoctoral training (Derner, 1959) and ex-

TABLE 1

Year	Semester	Clinical training technique courses and practicums	Research and experimental	Theory: general and clinical	Biological and social bases
1	Fall	Advanced clinical psychology I Rorschach I	Advanced experimental psychology I Advanced psychological statistics	Psychodynamics of behavior Scientific methods in psychology	
	Spring	Advanced clinical psychology II Rorschach II	Research problems in clinical psychology I Design and analysis of experiments	Behavior theory and research (Qualifying examination)	Human physiology (Language examination)
2	Fall	Clinical practice I (Diagnostic clinic) Clinical case conference	Research problems in clinical psychology II	Developmental psychology Clinical psychopathology	Neuropsychology
	Spring	Clinical practice II (Diagnostic hospital) Clinical case conference Techniques of psychotherapy	Colloquium	Advanced social psychology	Clinical neurology
3	Fall	Clinical practice III (Therapeutic clinic) Clinical case conference Remedial reading	Colloquium	Theories of personality	Forensic psychology and ethics Social forces and the individual
	Spring	Clinical practice IV (Therapeutic clinic) Clinical case conference	(Prefinal oral examination)	Clinical psychodynamics	Clinical medicine Cultural anthropology Social philosophy
4	One full year	Resident clinical internship	(Final oral examination)		

perience. Essential to the clinical program is an attitude of both professional and research clarity on the part of the faculty and students.

In summary, the Shakow report of 1947 and the follow-up conference at Boulder set the sights for clinical psychology training. This training requires a minimum of four years of graduate training. It includes training in general psychology, psychodynamic theory, research, diagnostics, and psychotherapy. The internship of one year is an integral experience. For independent practice, postdoctoral training and experience are required. The recommended program of 1947 has seen only minor substantive changes since its inception, although some universities would prefer to focus on research training within the university rather than offer the scientist-professional training recommended by Shakow and confirmed at Boulder. Research is sorely needed, and such training should be available; in like manner, training for professional service is a part of university teaching responsibility. By continuing substantial simultaneous training in both areas, clinical psychology can make its maximum educational impact. The school of psychology for professional training that is research-oriented but practice-directed is sure to come. A comprehensive view of university responsibility clearly points in such a direction.

REFERENCES

American Association for Applied Psychology, Committee on Training in Clinical (Applied) Psychology (B. V. Moore, Chairman). Proposed program of professional training in clinical psychology. *J. consult. Psychol.*, 1943, **7**, 23–26.

American Psychological Association and American Association for Applied Psychology, Committee on Graduate and Professional Training (D. Shakow, Chairman). Sub-committee report on graduate internship training in psychology. *J. consult. Psychol.*, 1945, **9**, 243–266.

American Psychological Association, Committee on Training in Clinical Psychology. Recommended graduate training program in clinical psychology (Shakow report). *Amer. Psychologist*, 1947, **2**, 539–558.

American Psychological Association, Committee on Counselor Training, Division of Counseling and Guidance. Recommended standards for training counseling psychologists at the doctorate level (Northwestern conference). *Amer. Psychologist*, 1952, **7**, 175–181.

American Psychological Association, Education and Training Board. Criteria for evaluating training programs in clinical or counseling psychology. *Amer. Psychologist*, 1958, **13**, 59–60.

Blank, L. An overview of clinical psychology training. In L. Blank & H. P. David, *Sourcebook for training in clinical psychology*. New York: Springer, 1964.

Blank, L., & David, H. P. *Sourcebook for training in clinical psychology*. New York: Springer, 1964.

Brotemarkle, R. A. (Ed.) *Clinical psychology: studies in honor of Lightner Witmer to commemorate the thirty-fifth anniversary of the founding of the first psychological clinic*. Philadelphia: Univer. of Pennsylvania Press, 1931.

Brown, A. W., et al. Report of committee of clinical section of American Psychological Association. I. The definition of clinical psychology and standards of training for clinical psychologists. II. Guide to psychological clinics in the United States. *Psychol. Clin.*, 1935, **23**, 1–140.

Cook, S. W. The psychologist of the future: scientist, professional or both. *Amer. Psychologist*, 1958, **13**, 635–644.

Cutts, Norma E. (Ed.) *School psychologists at mid-century* (Thayer conference). Washington, D.C.: American Psychological Association, 1955.

Dellis, N. P., & Stone, H. K. (Eds.) *The training of psychotherapists*. Baton Rouge, La.: Louisiana State Univer. Press, 1960.

Derner, G. F. The university and clinical psychology training. In M. H. P. Finn & F. Brown (Eds.), *Training for clinical psychology*. New York: International Universities Press, 1959. Pp. 55–66.

Derner, G. F. An interpersonal approach to training in psychotherapy. In N. P. Dellis & H. K. Stone (Eds.), *The training of psychotherapists*. Baton Rouge, La.: Louisiana State Univer. Press, 1960. Pp. 130–146. (a)

Derner, G. F. Presidential address: many views of psychology. *N.Y. State psychol. Ass. annu. Proc.*, 1960. (b)

Derner, G. F. Specialized training for psychotherapy. In L. Blank & H. P. David, *Sourcebook for training in clinical psychology*. New York: Springer, 1964.

Fine, R. The Ph.D. in psychotherapy. *N.Y. State psychol. Ass. annu. Proc.*, 1960.

Finn, M. H. P., & Brown, F. (Eds.) *Training for clinical psychology*. New York: International Universities Press, 1959.

Harrower, Molly R. (Ed.) *Training in clinical psychology: minutes of the first conference*. New York: Josiah Macy, 1947.

Michael, Ethel Anne. *The development of a post-doctoral training program.* As recorded in the minutes of the Educational and Planning Committee of the Los Angeles Society of Clinical Psychologists, 1959–1960, 1960–1961. Committee on Relations with Local Clinical Groups (M. Siegel, Chairman), April, 1963.

Paterson, D. G. Comments on the Shakow report on training in clinical psychology. *J. clin. Psychol.*, 1948, **4**, 298–300.

Paterson, D. G., & Lofquist, L. H. A note on training of clinical and counseling psychologists. *Amer. Psychologist*, 1960, **15**, 365–366.

Poffenberger, A. T. The training of a clinical psychologist. *J. consult. Psychol.*, 1938, **1**, 1–6.

Pottharst, K., & Kovacs, A. Memo to University of Michigan clinical alumni and faculty, June 15, 1962.

Raimy, V. C. (Ed.) *Training in clinical psychology* (Boulder conference). Englewood Cliffs, N.J.: Prentice-Hall, 1950.

Roe, Anne (Ed.) *Graduate education in psychology.* Washington, D.C.: American Psychological Association, 1959.

Rogers, C. R. Needed emphasis in the training of clinical psychologists. *J. consult. Psychol.*, 1939, **3**, 141–143.

Sears, R. R. Clinical training facilities: 1947. *Amer. Psychologist*, 1947, **2**, 199–205.

Shakow, D. An internship year for psychologists (with special reference to psychiatric hospitals). *J. consult. Psychol.*, 1938, **2**, 73–76.

Shakow, D. Training in clinical psychology: a note on trends. *J. consult. Psychol.*, 1945, **9**, 240–242.

Stevenson, G. S., & Smith, G. *Child guidance clinics: a quarter century of development.* New York: Commonwealth Fund, 1934.

Strother, C. R. (Ed.) *Psychology and mental health.* Washington, D.C.: American Psychological Association, 1957 (Stanford Conference).

53

Postdoctoral Training in Clinical Psychology

IRVING E. ALEXANDER

As Watson, in his brief historical review, points out, clinical psychology in this country is not a new phenomenon; it dates back at least to the turn of the century (1953). However, from the standpoint of growth and development, especially with regard to training, the past twenty years may be considered its most critical period.

During this time, when the major effort has been devoted to the problems of predoctoral education, a new, almost unnoticed set of training resources have appeared on our scene. These postdoctoral centers, largely divorced until now from consideration in the preparation of clinical psychologists, are beginning to make their impact known to the field and are likely to play an increasingly important role in the future. It will be the task of this chapter to trace some of the precipitating conditions that led to postdoctoral training efforts, to review the major opportunities for training that exist at present, and to indicate some trends for the future. It should be recognized that we are "tuning in" on a development very early in its history and that any attempts to impose undue order on an emerging phenomenon is subject to misplaced emphasis and error.

The story of the struggle to prepare both a scientist and a professional person in the few short years of graduate training has been chronicled in the proceedings of the various national conferences dedicated to the problems of training (Raimy, 1950; Roe, 1959; Strother, 1956) and is further elucidated in "Graduate Education in Clinical Psychology," above. For our purposes, we may note what appears to be a major dilemma. Psychology as a science is growing in its accumulated body of knowledge and in its research sophistication at a rapid pace. At the same time, the professional role of the clinical psychologist is broadening at a similar rate as a function of the demands and expectations of a society much more alerted to the problems of mental health. The attempt to resolve this dilemma insofar as training is concerned has been the focus of many policy discussions in departments of psychology and in wider professional circles. Departmental resolutions are always tempered somewhat by concerns about what the Ph.D. degree stands for in American education, particularly in psychology; the history of psychology's struggle to present itself as a science is also taken into account. These considerations have led, in most instances, to a uniform policy reaffirming the research training function of university education and leaving the professional aspects to field training centers. That the consequences have not been entirely satisfactory is attested to by the increasing clamor for postdoctoral training opportunities by both students of clinical psychology and the institutions and settings that have need of their services.

It was already recognized in 1949 by the thoughtful group of psychologists who gathered at Boulder to discuss training in clinical psychology that graduate training, no matter how well conceived, could not adequately cover the specialized skills and competences that were already extant in this field. Two sentences from that report appear to present the underlying rationale for a great deal of the impetus for postdoctoral training in recent years: "Mature diagnostic ability and full competence in clinical research cannot be assumed as a general result of present doctoral training. Therapy can be presented only in an introductory manner" (Raimy, 1950, p. 192).

The implications to be drawn from these statements seem to point to the need for further preparation before a student emerging from Ph.D. training in clinical psychology can take his place in the professional world. As we shall see in a later examination of present postdoctoral opportunities, these implications served as the basis for the implicit philosophy of many active programs.

The Boulder report also listed five emerging areas of activity for clinical psychologists in which further training might reasonably be demanded beyond the doctorate. It would be well to examine each of these, since what seemed like possibilities only a scant decade ago are the realities of today.

The first concerns the role of psychology in medical schools. The past few years have seen a tremendous increase in the numbers of psychologists employed on medical school staffs. In addition, the functions of the psychologist in such settings have changed considerably. Teacher, research consultant, and administrator are all roles beyond the traditional ones which psychologists engage in today. While almost all psychiatry departments include sections of psychology, other departments as well have begun to employ psychologists; indeed, the University of Oregon Medical School has established its own independent department of psychology.

A frequent complaint voiced by senior psychologists in medical settings is that Ph.D. training, as presently conceived, does not adequately prepare a job candidate to fulfill the functions expected of him in a staff position. This set of circumstances has prompted several institutions to initiate postdoctoral programs. The search for more appropriately trained people and the trend toward training them as postdoctoral fellows, rather than through in-service staff training programs, stems not only from altruistic motives but also from the historic status battle that psychologists have waged, and are still waging, in medical schools. The hard-won increases are jealously guarded by those who fought to attain them, and there is little wish to risk the gains by adding inadequately trained people at staff levels.

A second need arises from the demand for trained people to man the burgeoning graduate training programs in clinical psychology in the university departments of psychology. At a recent count, there were some sixty programs approved for such training by the APA Education and Training Board, and a fair number of other groups are known to be preparing themselves for accreditation. A typical source in psychology has been the new Ph.D. Yet, these are the very people whose clinical training typically has not been intensive enough to permit them to assume the role of teachers in clinical programs. Here again one might assume that this is a temporary state of affairs which would be remedied in a short period of time as the new appointee gains experience. However, the probabilities that further clinical experience will be gained after academic appointment tend to be small. The academic hierarchy of values emphasizes research productivity, and an all too frequent result is a tendency for the new appointee to lose his clinical skills and interests rapidly. As a consequence, some departments are beginning to urge promising students to seek postdoctoral training before committing themselves to an academic career, and many departments are beginning to weigh heavily such experience in appointing people to the clinical staff.

The recent increase in research support for the field of mental health is still another reason for training beyond the doctorate. Although research skills are taught in every graduate program, students infrequently have the opportunity to learn those which are most relevant to mental health research. As Garmezy points out, laboratory investigation, with its particular methodology, remains the most highly valued route to fulfilling the dissertation requirement (1960). All too frequently, clinical students do theses problems outside their area of interest because no one on the staff is working on clinically relevant research problems or because the ratio of clinical staff to clinical students is so low that students are forced to seek research sponsors in areas that may be only tangentially related to their central interest. Clinical research often is group research or interdisciplinary research, and opportunities for this kind of experience do not abound in university psychology departments where clinical facilities are limited.

Still another development in the recent past, the expansion of state mental health programs, has created a pressure for training beyond the doctoral level. In many regions where trained personnel are few in number, the traditional mental health clinic, with its prescribed professional roles, is hardly adequate to meet general community needs. Community mental health consultation to teachers, ministers, nurses, and social service agency workers—in fact to all responsible community resources dealing on some level with problems of mental health—has become, in the minds of many, the path of the future. The state of New Mexico has been a pioneer in this respect, and the reports of Libo at recent APA symposia (in 1961 and 1962) have been of special interest. The problem outlined above is not restricted to states with limited mental health resources; it exists even in those states in which large concentrations of psychologists tend to live and work. The manpower picture is such that we are forced to examine new approaches to mental health consultation beyond that of the patient-professional interaction. Training in these new approaches has been conducted largely at the postdoctoral level and has been led by the group at the Massachusetts General Hospital, in conjunction with the Harvard School of Public Health.

The most powerful appeal for advanced training comes from those psychologists concerned with the practice of psychotherapy. The struggle with psychiatry over who shall do psychotherapy seems to be receding into the background for a number of reasons, including the overwhelming demand for this service, the inability of the medical profession to meet this demand, the demonstrated competence of psychologists to assume this role, and the legislative programs that have been fought through in various states to assure the status of the psychologist in professional life. Perhaps the beginning of the end of this struggle was expressed in one of the recommendations of the Joint Commission on Mental Health and Illness, to the effect that adequate training and demonstrable competence be the principal requisites for the practice of psychotherapy, independent of the primary professional discipline in which one was trained (1961).

That large numbers of clinical psychologists are engaged in the practice of psychotherapy is attested to by Kelly's (1961) data reported in his presidential address to Division 12 in 1960. Although his figures represent less than half of the division membership (and perhaps no more than one out of every three clinicians are affiliated with the division), they can give us some estimate of the information with which we are concerned. Intensive psychotherapy is listed as one of their functions by 54 per cent of the respondents. Of this group 31 per cent regard it as their primary function.

The increasing interest in the private practice of psychotherapy is also indicated by Kelly's data. In the sample reported, 17 per cent listed private practice as their primary work setting. If this activity continues to remain a rather large source of motivation for students to enter the field of clinical psychology and a reasonably large source of employment for practitioners of clinical psychology, it seems evident that sources of training beyond the minimal ones offered in doctoral programs will have to become available if psychologists are to achieve the levels of competence necessary to enter private, unsupervised therapeutic practice. In a sense it is paradoxical that a field which has argued so vigorously for the right to engage in psychotherapy has done so little to provide adequate training opportunities for its members.

It would be unfair to intimate that the problems relating to psychotherapy and other clinical skills have gone largely unrecognized. Some attempts to approach the problems of general clinical competence within the context of formal professional training were made at the Miami Beach Conference on Graduate Education in Psychology, held in 1958 (Roe, 1959). By this time, almost a decade had passed since the Boulder conference had been held. During this period, enough experience had been gained to begin an assessment of graduate training in clinical psychology. At Miami Beach, questions were raised especially with regard to whether an adequate clinical product could be turned out in the period of time allotted for graduate training. The increasing separation between university and field training experience was noted, and a somewhat radical solution, important for considerations of postdoctoral training, was offered by a small group of participants. The proposal, originally mentioned in the proceedings of the Stanford conference (Strother, 1956), essentially involved a three- or four-year university program, including practicum experience in diagnosis and therapy and a concentration in personality research. The Ph.D. would be granted when all requirements were fulfilled. This program would serve as a prelude to training in clinical psychology, and a person completing this stage would not be recognized as a qualified clinician. To assume this status a two-year postdoctoral residency would have to be served in an accredited training center where the traditional areas of diagnosis, therapy, and clinical research would be treated much more intensively. Upon completion of this two-stage program, a candidate would be ready for minimal certification as a clinical psychologist. While the proposal did not gain extended support among the conference members, it did serve as a focus for discussion about issues of postdoctoral training. Did adequate centers exist for training large numbers of people postdoctorally? How would they be financed? What are the responsibilities of university departments vis-à-vis field training centers? One central feature of the proposal which brought forth considerable negative comment concerned lengthening the required training period for clinical psychologists. At a time when many voices in education had been raised to reduce the apparent interminable length of graduate education, this aspect of the proposal seemed to fly in the face of the *Zeitgeist*.

The establishment of formal postdoctoral training programs has been undertaken cautiously for a variety of understandable reasons. In addition to the wish to avoid lengthening the required period of training already mentioned, we find that the conflict of training models also presents a problem. Psychology stems from a tradition that dictates the particular route toward scholarly activity. Its allegiance is to science. Control has always been vested in the hands of the degree-granting institution, and the apprentice relationship has been the dominant mode of operation. Clinical psychology has been caught, in a sense, between its loyalty to this model and that of medical training, to which it finds itself so often allied. "Clerkship," "practicum," "internship," and "residency" are all terms borrowed from the medical educational lexicon with little further applicability to general Ph.D. training. Medicine is a clinical discipline, and as such, with its independent departmental specialization and control of clinical facilities, it has no difficulty providing continuity between predoctoral and postdoctoral training. The same state of affairs has not existed in the past for clinical psychology. Most postdoctoral opportunities exist in institutions which are not primarily educational in character, and official recognition of their activities by national accrediting groups has not yet been attempted. Without formal ties, either directly or through the national professional organization, between predoctoral and postdoctoral training centers, postdoctoral education is likely to progress slowly.

Still another important aspect in the growth of postdoctoral training centers concerns the problem of funding. Medicine, with its culturally established routes to specialization, has found particular ways to fund this operation. Because it is a sanctioned activity, this item has found its way into hospital budgets and into the considerations of government-support programs. Indeed, without internship and residency training programs, most large-scale medical facilities could not possibly carry out their service responsibilities. Clinical psychology has not generally benefited from this kind of support, partly because postdoctoral training has not yet become a significant aspect of its cultural tradition. How close we are to reaching this stage is difficult to assess. Certainly attitudes toward such training, even by those engaged in it, differ markedly. Some see advanced training as a general solution to the problem of minimum competence levels in all aspects of clinical practice established during predoctoral work. Others see this as an opportunity for specialization in areas which command the attention of clinicians in the work setting but which are inadequately treated in graduate work. Without clear-cut expressions from the field on the necessity for postdoctoral training and its importance in the development of mature professional people, funding is likely to remain a problem.

To trace the extent of postdoctoral training opportunities at our present stage of development is an almost impossible task. The only central source to which one can go is the annual December issue of the *American Psychologist,* which lists educational facilities and financial assistance for graduate students for the coming year. Yet this proves to be somewhat of a misleading enterprise. For one thing, only university programs are listed, which excludes the most significant source of postdoctoral training, the field training centers. A perusal of such listings over a four-year period, 1958 to 1962, finds them unusually stable, especially for clinical psychology. Thirty-two departments in 1958 listed postdoctoral opportunities, and a similar group gave this same information in 1962. Now what precisely does this mean? Is it really the case that if one wished further training in diagnostics, therapy, community mental health practices, or mental retardation, he could choose from among these 32 institutions the one at which he would like to train? Are there established programs of advanced study within these institutions which could be assessed or evaluated by the prospective student? Are there funds available for the support of advanced students during their period of study? The answer to these questions, for the most part, is "no." What is meant typically by such information is that an advanced research apprenticeship with individual faculty members is possible, providing the student can find some means of support. Usual avenues for such arrangements are the research fellowship programs supported by the National Science Foundation and the National Institutes of Health. While no available data exist on the number of such appointments made each year to students of clinical psychology, it is this writer's impression, from having had contact with all but four of the listed institutions on training matters within the past few years, that no more than five to ten clinical students receive training each year under these particular auspices.

In 1960, in a symposium report, Alexander and Little estimated after brief survey of this problem that there were between 80 and 100 postdoctoral stipends available for clinical training each year. They traced the bulk of postdoctoral support to two government sources, NIMH and the VA, which together accounted for 65 to 70 stipends per year. However, some forty VA stipends were awarded to people whose doctoral training was taken in some other specialty area and whose interest had now turned to clinical psychology. In most instances the training that these people receive is identical to that of the predoctoral clinical interns. This serves as a very effective and desirable recruiting device for clinical psychology, but the term "postdoctoral" is used in this connection in its literal sense rather than in the commonly accepted sense of advanced or higher-level training. Thus if one eliminates these from consideration, the 25 or 30 stipends emanating from the NIMH become the core support for stable, ongoing programs. The remaining figure of perhaps 15 to 30 stipends, largely unaccounted for as far as any central literature source is concerned, were attributed to private foundation, state, and individual institutional awards.

Since NIMH has turned out to be the major source of funding for postdoctoral training, it may be worthwhile to trace the experience of this group with regard to its program of support. Close upon the heels of the Boulder report, the training branch of NIMH explored the possibility of extending funds for advanced training. The first applications were received in 1950 and were funded in 1951. Recognizing the strong need for establishing criteria for support, institutions were asked to delineate formal programs and not simply opportunities for training. This attitude toward evaluating *programs* of training has remained a central feature of NIMH support. In 1960, summary material became available for the previous decade, and an examination of this material may give us some insight into the nature and character of postdoctoral training at present.

Seventeen institutions were approved for support during that period. Not all these, however, continued their postdoctoral programs after an initial attempt. Some had extreme difficulty in attracting students because stipend levels at this time were not at all commensurate with beginning salaries in clinical jobs. New, promising Ph.D.s, greatly in demand, were lured away from further training opportunities by good job placements. More established people found it difficult financially to seek additional training. Toward the end of this period, a change in postdoctoral stipend levels to $6,000 and $7,000 resulted in renewed interest on the part of training institutions and students in advanced training possibilities. A second factor that caused some institutions to drop postdoctoral training was the continuously increasing number of attractive job opportunities that became available for people with experience and the consequent effect this had on staff stability. Since postdoctoral training demands senior supervisory personnel and since these people were highly marketable, it was not always possible for institutions to maintain acceptable programs.

In all, 71 people received postdoctoral training in these 17 institutions for periods of one or two years. Roughly one-third of the programs were designated as two years in length, one-third called for a one-year period of training, and the remainder fixed a one-year required period with a second year optional. Twenty-seven of the trainees completed two years of postdoctoral work.

Examining the characteristics of the people who were trained, we find that more than half began their training immediately upon completion of the Ph.D. and that approximately 90 per cent of the sample had initiated their training within three years of the doctorate. Of the remaining group, the heavy majority were women or people who were foreign-trained. Within the total sample, the ratio of males to females was 3:1, a figure probably not too much different from that existing in predoctoral programs.

Some attempt was made to trace the later career development of the trainees up to and including the most recent issue of the APA Directory. More than 50 per cent of the sample are to be found in hospital and clinical settings, and a significant number of these carry the title "chief" next to their name. Approximately 30 per cent, about equally distributed, can be found in university departments of psychology or in medical school departments of psychiatry. Among this group are people who have assumed important research and training roles. Roughly 10 per cent are located in full-time research positions in academic, government, and clinical settings, while the remaining 10 per cent list private practice as their chief occupational role. Without comparable figures for a similar population who did not take postdoctoral training, it is difficult to assess whether this experience significantly influenced placement selection, performance, or rate of progress in the job. However, it does seem clear that advanced training does not lure large numbers of people into the private practice of psychotherapy, a concern which has been repeatedly expressed in discussions about the future of postdoctoral training.

Two further characteristics of the data are interesting to consider. One involves the extent to which this population goes on to acquire other indications of professional recognition, such as the ABEPP diploma. The other refers to the geographical location of the trainees after completion of the postdoctoral work.

Through August of 1962, seventeen, or roughly 25 per cent of the group, had been awarded diplomate status by ABEPP, even though by this time it was highly likely that almost all were eligible for examination. Of the total number of diplomates in the sample, 42 per cent had been trained in one institution which had, over all, trained 22 per cent of the sample. The possible interpretations of these figures are numerous and must include the variety of attitudes held by clinical psychologists toward the diplomate concept. However, it does seem likely that the attitude of the training institution is a significant factor in the later behavior of its trainees with regard to ABEPP. In the institution just described, a large proportion of the training staff were people who had received ABEPP recognition.

An examination of where people find employment after postdoctoral training reveals that a good many tend to stay in the immediate vicinity of the institution in which they were trained. Slightly more than 50 per cent of the sample are located occupationally in close proximity to the source of their training. This figure seems especially significant, since not all the training institutions are located in urban centers. What seems to have been the case, at least for this group, is that postdoctoral training was used, in part, as a recruitment device. Many of the institutions enjoyed staff expansion during this period of time and tended to select new appointees from the people they had trained.

Any attempt to summarize the nature of the program in the identifiable institutions offering postdoctoral work is fraught with difficulty. Each one offers, by its own admission, its particular staff, its clinical population, and—by the special features of its mission—something unique. Yet there are some arbitrary categorical divisions which can be set up to describe the general situation. In preparation for this task, this writer corresponded with all centers he could locate which either were known or were suspected to be offering postdoctoral programs primarily for psychologists. From this source and from personal experience in visiting various training centers as a representative of NIMH in the recent past, it was possible to get a subjective picture of the kind of facilities that exist.

Excluding the VA installations, there are perhaps 22 institutions offering continuing one- or two-year programs of study, with an additional 10 that have trained students sporadically over the years as the occasion arose. Of the group, 16 can be clearly identified as offering opportunities for training in diagnosis, therapy, and research (although emphasis on one or another of these skills may differ), while the remaining six programs are more highly specialized. Four of these are centrally concerned with training in psychotherapy, one with research in psychotherapy and the others with training in community mental health. Fifteen of the programs are primarily devoted to training with adult populations, four deal almost exclusively with children, and the remaining three offer options to the students to work with either or both populations. Eight programs are located in medical schools, while five are in private clinical facilities. Most of the remainder are to be found in joint hospital, clinical, or medical school settings. Two unique facilities are a school for exceptional children and a university department of psychology.

At the risk of minimizing some of the inherent flexibility in these programs so that the particular needs of students may be met, it may be worthwhile to identify and characterize each one briefly.[1]

Albert Einstein College of Medicine. A two-year program is offered in a psychoanalytically oriented department of psychiatry. Major emphasis in the first year is on diagnostic practice. In the second year, the student may specialize in further diagnostic work with particular populations, psychotherapy, research, or teaching. A two-year research training program is also possible. One or two students are admitted each year.

Austen Riggs Center. A two-year program is offered in a small, open, private hospital whose treatment orientation is psychoanalytic. Thorough training in psychological evaluation procedures is stressed, especially as it relates to theory and to treatment plans. Psychotherapy training is given both at the center and in a local community outpatient facility. Experience with milieu therapy and ward management problems is also part of the training plan. One or two students are accepted each year.

University of Colorado School of Medicine. Typically a one-year program in a department of psychiatry is offered. Ego psychology and psychoanalytic theory provide the conceptual framework for the various clinical experiences. A general program of training in psychodiagnosis, psychotherapy, and teaching is offered. The candidate may elect to focus his work either with children or adult populations. Research opportunities are readily available although participation is optional for the student. Two or three candidates are accepted each year.

Devereux Foundation. A 1- or 2-year program in a residential educational setting consisting primarily of children and adolescents with emotional adjustment problems and those who are mentally retarded. Training in psychodiagnostics, psychotherapy (individual, group, and milieu), research, administration, and psychoeducational procedures are all available. Training emphases are adjusted to fit the goals of particular students. Three to five students are accepted each year.

Judge Baker Guidance Center. A 1-year program carried on in conjunction with the Department of Psychiatry in the Children's Hospital Medical Center. Diagnosis and therapy with a wide variety of child and adolescent problems constitute the core of the training. These include inpatient and outpatient services. Specialization either in research, a particular type of therapeutic approach, or a par-

[1] One institution in our sample, the Postgraduate Center for Mental Health, will not be dealt with in this manner but will be discussed in a later section devoted to training institutes for psychotherapists.

Brochures are available from each of the institutions described.

Immediately prior to the publication of the *Handbook*, Adelphi University announced the beginning of a four-year program to train psychotherapists in short-term and intensive psychotherapy. Ten students were accepted in the initial class.

ticular age or symptom group is also expected of students. Opportunities are offered for one or two students each year.

Lafayette Clinic. A 1- or 2-year program in a state-supported psychiatric research and training center affiliated with a local medical school and a University department of psychology. Training in diagnosis and therapy is offered within the context of a heavy research emphasis. One or two students are accepted each year.

Massachusetts General Hospital. A 1- or 2-year program in community mental health theory and practice sponsored by a medical school department of psychiatry and carried out in a general hospital and its affiliated field stations. Seven training areas are delineated in the program: (1) research; (2) special clinical services and intervention; (3) group methods; (4) consultation; (5) communication and public education; (6) administration; and (7) community organization. The 2-year program is designed for people with little or no previous community mental health experience. In the first year the student is exposed to knowledge in the seven areas listed above, with appropriate field experience in four of them. The second year calls for extensive training in the one area of the student's choice. A 1-year specialty program, similar to that described for the second year of the 2-year program, is offered for people with previous experience in community mental health practice. A 1-year academic program for senior people in university teaching positions is also provided. The program accepts psychiatrists, psychologists, and social workers for training. One or two placements for psychologists are typically available each year.

Menninger Foundation. A 2-year program in a private psychiatric setting whose basic orientation is psychoanalytic. This is one of the oldest and best established postdoctoral training programs. Training is offered in diagnosis, therapy, and research, with emphasis on personality evaluation. Experience is gathered with both inpatient and outpatient populations. For those interested in problems of childhood, training in the Southard School is also available. Two to three placements are offered yearly.

Michael Reese Hospital. A 2-year program in a private psychiatric facility with a distinguished interdisciplinary research history. Two major training options are offered, one in research, the other in problems of childhood and adolescence. In research the problems and methods of multidisciplinary research are stressed. Psychodiagnosis and psychotherapy form the core of the training in the child and adolescent area. One or two appointments are made each year.

Mt. Sinai Hospital, Los Angeles. A 1- or 2-year program located in the psychiatry department of a large general hospital. Training is offered in diagnosis, therapy, and research, with a widely varied population. Child and adult training are both available. Research centers around problems of psychotherapy and psychosomatic disorders. One or two placements are available each year.

Mt. Zion Hospital and Medical Center. A 1-year program with the possible option of a second year of appointment. This program under the administrative aegis of Mt. Zion Hospital is actually a flexible confederation of four participating groups. Included are the Department of Psychiatry at Mt. Zion, the Department of Psychiatry at Stanford University School of Medicine, the Department of Psychology at Stanford University, and the Langley Porter Neuropsychiatric Institute at the University of California School of Medicine. The number of training arrangements possible within this complex of settings is numerous. Mount Zion offers essentially diagnostic and therapeutic experience with children and adults in an outpatient setting. The emphasis here is on therapy training. Langley Porter and the Stanford Medical School offer training in diagnosis, therapy, and research with adults and children in both inpatient and outpatient settings. Stanford's department of psychology offers specialization in research utilizing clinical methods in the study of personality development and parent-child interactions. A student may arrange a program to include training in one or more of these installations. One or two placements are available each year.

New York University, All-University Department of Psychology. This program is a relatively new venture, just finishing its second year of operation. It appears to be the first full-scale effort to bring postdoctoral clinical training under the sponsorship of a university department of psychology. It was conceived to consist of three separate parts, two of which have already been initiated. The first is a two-year intensive training schedule in psychotherapy, based on the psychoanalytic institute model. This consists of a series of didactic courses, supervised practice of psychotherapy, and personal analysis. The second is termed a "refresher and modernization program," which includes a series of courses on recent developments in various fields of psychology. These cover such topics as automated teaching, computer applications to psychology, statistical design and methodology, research problems in ego psychology, etc., and are designed for trained psychologists who wish to keep abreast in fields related to their interests. The third aspect, which will include opportunities for research consultation and the use of facilities for practicing clinicians wishing to continue individual research, is in the offing. Fifteen appointments were made to the therapy specialization program in the first year of operation.

University of Oregon Medical School. A one- or two-year program is conducted by an independent department of psychology in a medical school. Training in diagnosis, therapy, and research is offered. Particular emphasis is given to the role of the psychologist in a general medical setting. Both diagnostic training and therapy training are conceptualized within the framework of a social-learning approach. Two appointments are typically made each year.

Philadelphia Child Guidance Clinic. A two-year program is offered in a community-supported outpatient clinic and affiliated children's settings. Primary training emphasis is placed on psychotherapy. Clinical practice is family- and community-oriented. One or two students are accepted for training each year.

Reiss-Davis Clinic for Child Guidance. A two-year program is offered in a private, nonprofit clinic. The basic treatment orientation is psychoanalytic. Training emphasis is on diagnostic evaluation and treatment. Clinical research training is also available. One or two students are admitted to the program each year.

University of Rochester School of Medicine. A one-or two-year program is offered in a department of psychiatry in a medical school. Training in diagnosis, therapy, and research is available, with a wide variety of clinical case material. Teaching opportunities in medical education are also available. One or two placements are made each year.

University of Wisconsin Psychiatric Institute. A one- or two-year program is offered, sponsored by a research group, specifically designed to produce trained researchers in the area of psychotherapy. Training is provided in research methodology, personality theory, and the practice of psychotherapy. Students are expected to participate in the ongoing research program and to design their own independent problems. Two students are accepted yearly.

University of Wisconsin Medical School. A two-year program in a department of psychiatry is offered. Particular emphasis is placed on psychotherapy training and on psychodiagnostic evaluation. The didactic program coincides closely with that set up for second- and third-year psychiatric residents. One or two students are accepted each year.

Worcester State Hospital. A two-year program is offered, although appointment for one year is possible, jointly sponsored by the Worcester State Hospital and Clark University's Institute of Human Development. The basic intention of the program is to prepare people for clinical research careers. Training in clinical diagnostic and therapeutic skills is adjunctive to this goal. Programs are individually arranged to help further the student's particular research interests within the framework of what is possible in this large and complex clinical research setting. Two appointments are made each year.

Yale University School of Medicine. A one- or two-year program located within a department of psychiatry is offered; a large number of clinical resources are also available. The basic objectives are to help the student develop further skills in clinical practice, including diagnosis and therapy, teaching, and research. The program has taken one or two students each year but has restricted the appointments for the most part to graduates of the Yale clinical program.

Postdoctoral training opportunities have been available also, at various times over the years, at the University of Minnesota Medical School, the University of Illinois College of Medicine, Baylor University School of Medicine, Connecticut Valley State Hospital, the University of California (Berkeley) Student Health Center, and the Nebraska Psychiatric Institute. For the most part, these have all followed the general pattern of training in the traditional skills of diagnosis, therapy, and research.

In recent years, as a result of the growing interest among psychologists in participating in the independent practice of psychotherapy, still another resource for postdoctoral training has been brought into focus: the nonacademic private institutes. The oldest and best known of these are, of course, the psychoanalytic training institutes affiliated with the American Psychoanalytic Association. These, however, still maintain the attitude that the practice of psychoanalysis should be restricted to physicians trained in this method, and they have generally excluded psychologists from their training programs. Only in recent years have some admitted psychologists as research candidates. The usual condition stipulated for such appointments is that the trainee has to agree not to engage in the clinical practice of psychoanalysis upon the completion of his training.

Over the last twenty years, partly as a function of the influx of European-trained analysts who were not quite as mindful of the medical-nonmedical distinction, and partly as a function of the growth of groups who had split off from the orthodox psychoanalytic tradition, new training institutes open to both physicians and nonphysicians have sprung up. Gertrude Blanck, in her monograph surveying education for psychotherapy, has identified eight of these, with no pretense that this list is necessarily inclusive (1962). For the most part, they are located in one urban area, New York City, and each can be identified by its allegiance to one particular theoretical position. As training institutes they typically follow the part-time, long-term model, with personal analysis and intensive case supervision as requirements. Because of the great expense involved, their cost tends to be prohibitive for people with newly acquired or recent Ph.D. degrees. One possible exception might be the program of the Postgraduate Center for Mental Health, formerly known as the Postgraduate Center for Psychotherapy, which has its own continuously operating clinical facilities, a full-time training program, and fellowship awards to defray some of the costs of training. Four psychologists on a full-time basis and from six to ten on a part-time basis are admitted each year. In the future, with the development of similar facilities under university sponsorship, as has already taken place at New York University and is just beginning at Adelphi University, this avenue of training may become a more feasible one for psychologists in an earlier phase of career development.

What can we say, by way of summary, about the present state of postdoctoral training and its future? It seems fair to conclude that, for the most part, opportunities for advanced general-skills training exist in sufficient number to meet present demands. Most programs report little difficulty in filling their available openings with qualified candidates. Few indicate that they have to turn away especially desirable applicants. The great hiatus exists for people seeking highly specialized training of the sort that seems to be increasingly in demand in the mental health field. Only one program is set up to offer training in community mental health practice, although the need for people with such skills appears to be great. None of the present programs are geared toward training in special problems such as mental retardation, alcoholism, and juvenile delinquency, despite the fact that these have been clearly identified as major areas of need to which psychologists can make a valuable contribution. The demand for highly skilled psychotherapists, especially for work with children, remains high, and yet all too few practicable opportunities for training are available. What, then, appear to be reasonable solutions?

With the continuing realistic objections to extending the required period of time for minimum professional recognition, it seems obvious that some of the present functions assigned to postdoctoral training may have to be reconsidered in terms of predoctoral preparation. This would serve to free the postdoctoral years for highly specialized endeavor. A proposed change of this sort may well intensify the scientist-practitioner controversy in graduate education but may also serve as an impetus to attempt new solutions. Perhaps it is time, as many have suggested, to consider alternative routes to preparation for clinical psychology in addition to the Ph.D. This, by no means, is an attempt to deny the critical need for research in clinical psychology but is rather a recognition of the fact that of all the people who have a contribution to make to the clinical field, only a limited number will make it in research.

Another possible future direction for postdoctoral training involves an extension in the meaning of this term. In some fields, of which engineering is a good example, beginning professionals are not expected to have acquired the specialized skills needed for a particular kind of work. Employers are willing to structure the initial phase of employment as a training period during which intensive instruction and supervision take place. Psychologists have generally tended to avoid such a model. This kind of postdoctoral in-service training could do much to raise the competence level of new Ph.D.s in a variety of specialized fields and could reduce considerably the search for formal postdoctoral opportunities.

A third course for the future is one which has already been initiated with some success. What is referred to here is the short-term, intensive postdoctoral institutes of the kind that Division 12 has been sponsoring for a number of years, offered just prior to the APA meetings. It has been possible to gather together highly qualified instructors to present, in workshop fashion, topics of interest and value to clinical psychologists. The workshop model holds the promise of being able to offer advanced work in time periods that are much more convenient for people with professional work schedules, thus making it more feasible for larger numbers of people to participate.

Intensive training in summer laboratories is another method that has been tried with some success. An outstanding example is the annual offering of the National Training Laboratories in group dynamics and sensitivity training. Other efforts have included mathematics training for psychologists, sponsored by the Social Science Research Council, and training for research in gerontology, sponsored by the National Institute of Mental Health. Again it seems reasonable to believe that this type of approach may reach more people interested in a specific type of training and that it may have the further benefit of being able to secure outside support for its funding.

One final resource comes to mind in considering new avenues for postdoctoral training: the local psychological societies. An active effort in this direction has been made by the New York Society of Clinical Psychologists over a number of years and more recently by the Los Angeles Society for Clinical Psychology, which has sponsored both intensive workshops and year-long courses in its educational program for members. An extension of this model to similar groups throughout the country might help to alleviate present advanced-training needs.

It appears reasonable to believe that the future of postdoctoral training will best be served by strengthening the present Ph.D. programs. If students emerging from these programs have had sufficient training in clinical skills and a proper introduction to clinically relevant research, the problem of preparing a minimally competent clinical psychologist through postdoctoral training will disappear. These excellent clinical facilities can then truly turn to the task for which they are best suited, namely, offering relatively long-term, specialized training to a limited number of highly promising people.

Beyond this, there will always remain in a continuously expanding field a need for training opportunities beyond the doctorate. The educational process for professional people cannot stop at the end of a formal period of training, and provision to meet this need must be made. It is in this direction, the development of short-term professional educational resources, that we may most profitably turn.

REFERENCES

Alexander, I. E., & Little, K. B. Post-doctoral training in clinical psychology. *Proc. N.Y. psychol. Ass.*, 1960, 21–22.

Blanck, Gertrude. Education for psychotherapy. *Inst. psychoanal. Training Res., Res. Monogr. Ser.*, 1962, No. 1.

Garmezy, N. Postdoctoral programs and their relation to graduate training. Paper read at Amer. Psychol. Ass., Chicago, September, 1960.

Joint Commission on Mental Health and Illness.

Action for mental health. New York: Basic Books, 1961.

Kelly, E. L. Clinical psychology: 1960. *Newsltr Div. clin. Psychol.*, 1961, **14**, 1–11.

Raimy, V. (Ed.) *Training in clinical psychology.* Englewood Cliffs, N.J.: Prentice-Hall, 1950.

Roe, Anne (Ed.) *Graduate education in psychology.* Washington, D.C.: American Psychological Association, 1959.

Strother, C. R. (Ed.) *Psychology and mental health.* Washington, D.C.: American Psychological Association, 1956.

Watson, R. I. A brief history of clinical psychology. *Psychol. Bull.*, 1953, **50**, 321–346.

54

The Profession of Clinical Psychology

ERASMUS L. HOCH

While Nero fiddled, Rome burned. Clinical psychology will doubtless have none of that, partly because it does not intend to stand idly by while history marches on and partly because the outside world, come what may, is in one way or another involving the clinical psychologist in its problems.

HERE AND NOW

> Lest the jury be misled into relying on opinions which are not based upon relevant learning and experience, we must examine the reality behind the title "psychologist." Many psychologists may not qualify to testify concerning mental disease or defect. Their training and experience may not provide an adequate basis for their testimony. Some psychologists, for example, teach and engage in theoretical research in fields unrelated to the diagnosis and treatment of mental disease.
>
> On the other hand, the Ph.D. in Clinical Psychology involves some—and often much—training and experience in the diagnosis and treatment of mental disorders. Typically, candidates are trained, *inter alia,* in general psychology, theory of personality and psychodynamics, psychopathology, diagnostic methods, therapeutic techniques, selected aspects of physiology and anatomy, and clinical methods. A one-year internship in a mental hospital is required for this degree. . . .
>
> The determination of a psychologist's competence to render an expert opinion based on his findings as to the presence or absence of mental disease or defect must depend upon the nature and extent of his knowledge. It does not depend upon his claim to the title "psychologist."

This was not the American Psychological Association telling the community how to recognize a qualified psychologist. It was the United States Court of Appeals, with Circuit Judge Bazelon writing the majority opinion, in the case of *Jenkins v. U.S.* (Hoch & Darley, 1962). If ever the legal status of psychology in general and clinical psychology in particular was literally at issue, it was in the historic decision handed down on June 7, 1962.

Elsewhere other opinions get writ large as well, again not directly by psychology's own pen:

> And, all mental health professions should recognize . . . that psychoanalysis and allied forms of deeply searching and probing "depth psychotherapy" must be practiced only by those with special training, experience, and competence in handling these techniques without harm to the patient—namely, by physicians trained in psychoanalysis or intensive psychotherapy plus those psychologists or other professional persons who lack a medical education but have an aptitude for, training in, and demonstrable competence in such techniques of psychotherapy. . . .

This time the words are those of the Joint Commission on Mental Illness and Health (1961), with a mandate from Congress to make recommendations for combating mental illness in the United States.

To be sure, psychology is in the business of writing laws too. But more of that later. Part of our thesis for the moment is simply that, whether it wills it or not, clinical psychology is having its status defined in a number of ways. Indeed, at another level of discourse, psychologists themselves have at one meeting or another (Albee, 1960) invariably organized symposia around the topic of whether the shape of psychology should allow itself to be molded by societal needs, pressures, and possibly whims or whether it should take the clay more vigorously into its own hands.

Here it is largely clinical psychology that gets talked about, or at most the more applied branches of psychology. For, at the moment at least, it is to these areas of the field that the community turns for help with its mental health and consultation on its "problem children"—whether, literally, the slow learner, the withdrawn, or the delinquent or, more generally, the alcoholic, the amputee, or the criminal, not to mention the reckless driver, the absentee worker, and the errant spouse. But the clinical psychologist does not want for company. The cry for services has carried over the ivy walls, into the laboratory, to the academic experimentalist and the basic researcher. If Tryon is even only partially correct as he talks about "psychology in flux" (1963), the organization of branches other than clinical is being determined in some very real ways by this pressure and that:

> Paradox of paradoxes, professionalization of experimental psychology itself is now suddenly on the rise—a phenomenon with which the traditionalist is unprepared to cope. The reason is simple: Industry and the military services have discovered that the laboratory methods and the experimental logic of experimental psychology have great use in tackling many concrete problems that confront them. . . .

Or, to heed Tryon again:

> The experimental psychologist in industry, in military, and in other "systems programs" seems as surely to be coming under the administrative dominance of the engineer as has the applied clinical psychologist been professionally subordinated to the physician. . . . I have selected for special treatment the clinical psychologist and the experimental psychologist. But the professionalization problem is a *common* problem to the academic psychologist, whatever his field, and it must be met by the joint cooperation of all varieties of psychologists.

As if to bear out Tryon's thesis, a couple of social psychologists have recently reminded their colleagues—clinical psychologists and whoever else would listen—that the legal status of whatever breed of psychologist venturing forth into the market place is being daily fashioned in a number of quarters, not always at psychology's own behest or always on its own terms. This time the judicial forum was the Federal Trade Commission, and the issue was disclosure or nondisclosure of information obtained in the course of survey research. As King and Spector (1963) put it:

> The application of social science techniques, and of social scientists themselves, in studies beyond the academic laboratory brings into being new questions of the public and professional responsibilities of the scientist on new environments. Psychologists in recent years have worked assiduously to develop a code of ethics that would cover circumstances they might encounter in private or public practice of clinical psychology, in the use and distribution of psychological tests, in the treatment of human and animal subjects of experimentation, etc. These standards serve many purposes, including protection of the public against unprofessional conduct by practitioners of psychology; they provide a basis for the public's expectations and image of psychologists, and also furnish guidelines for the psychologists who are in doubt about proprieties in a given situation.

But, King and Spector go on:

> With the increasing use of survey techniques for basic and applied research studies, social scientists find themselves in situations in which the legal and ethical implications are not clear, and for which our professional associations have not codified the expected behaviors. . . .

As for the clinical psychologist, who started the whole thing some time ago, Jones and Levine (1963) feel that even he needs to be reminded that the legal status, roles, and functions of his profession are in a constant process of being spelled out, in part by many forces:

The notion of the clinical psychologist as a technician who aids in pinning a psychiatric label on a patient is giving way to the notion of the psychologist as a consultant who aids in the overall evaluation of persons with many different kinds of problems in many kinds of situations. He is called on by teachers, attorneys, judges, rehabilitation counselors, parents, wardens, institution heads, the police, executives, military officers, and many other groups to evaluate people and aid in making decisions involving these people. . . .

STEPPING BACK A PACE

It is not only the "teachers, attorneys, judges," etc., who are helping to determine the shape and weight of clinical psychology. There are society's lawyers, but there are others, equally articulate, as well. It is a staggering assortment of influences at work, some obvious, some subtle; some of our own making and choosing, some of others'. Some are simple, straightforward, and easily dealt with; others are exquisitely complex in their workings.

Innocently enough, the American Psychological Association, several years ago, appointed a committee to look into the effects of the kind of legislation (in the form of licensing and certification laws) it was responsible for, by way of clarifying the legal status of psychologists in general and of applied psychologists in particular. Even if one hesitates to say that the committee solved the problem, it must be admitted that it succeeded in showing that it was a bigger one than had been thought. The problem seemed to extend far beyond relations between a couple of professions, indoctrination of legislators, or education of the public. Indeed, the committee on scientific and professional responsibility, as it more aptly came to be called under the chairmanship of Miller (Bauer, 1964), could see no less than 26 influences playing on six major functions that psychologists serve. In the 6-by-26 table visualized by the committee to show the interaction between functions and influences, the clinical psychologist need not stretch his imagination very far to find himself sitting in many a cell where influence x (be it peers, clients, or the public) interacts with function y (be it teaching, research, or practice).

On a less conceptual level, the clinical psychologist might (and apparently does) give some thought to how a particular television program—in this case "The Eleventh Hour" (Amrine, 1963)—shapes his role (at least in the public eye) perhaps as much as some of the "formal regulatory influences" outlined by the Miller committee do. One need only dwell on cell 8*e* a bit (where the public and professional relations interact) to come to the realization that it *can* happen here—and does. A few million television viewers watching Dr. Graham, the "young psychologist," each week come away with an image of the clinical psychologist quite as vivid as that which emerges from the *Handbook*.

Somewhat as a trial balloon, the Miller committee "blew up" cell 7*a*, where the influence of fund-granting agencies plays upon the research function. If there is a clinical psychologist who feels that he maps his own destiny, it would behoove him to think about this cell in which he, like many a colleague, daily sits if his forte is research. For it turns out that the nature, direction, and focus of his projects are in no small measure determined by what the sponsor is willing to support. Whether clinical psychology should be having a good share of its research effort thus influenced, dare we say determined, by outside sources can be debated; that it is the case cannot.

One given to ruing the fact that sponsors in the mass media all too strongly influence the public's bill of fare might be allowed to feel a bit sorry for himself as a clinical or other psychologist in the business of research. Let him who is without qualms be the first to reread "Pigeons in a Pelican," in which Skinner (1960) recounts his efforts to train birds to steer missiles during World War II. It deals not only with an intriguing research notion but even more with the unnerving extent to which outside influences affect the work and role of the psychologist and, most of all, with the implications thereof. And implications there are—with respect to the legal status, organization, and all the rest of clinical psychology.

MOLDERS AND SHAPERS, MOVERS AND SHAKERS

If behavior is multidetermined and if organisms become what they are as the result of many influences, inner and outer, psychology itself is no exception, and clinical psychology is a prime example. Which forces influence it? Or, to take the easier way out, which ones do not?

Religion

It is not only civil and criminal law that has had something to say about the status of psychology (Louisell, 1955). Those who know moral law have also felt impelled to make pronouncements about psychology's place in the sun:

> It is immoral to penetrate into the conscience of someone; but this act becomes moral if the person involved gives his valid consent. It can also happen that certain actions lay a person open to the dangers of violating a moral law: thus, for instance, the use of tests can in certain cases engender immoral impressions, but this action becomes moral when proportionate motives justify the danger incurred.
>
> One can therefore establish three kinds of immoral actions which can be judged as such by referring to the three basic principles: whether they are immoral either in themselves, or because the person who enacts them lacks the right to do so, or because of the dangers they provoke without sufficient motive.

So said no less a personage than Pope Pius XII to the Rome Congress of the International Association of Applied Psychology on April 10, 1958. Nor was His Holiness concerned only with abstract theological issues. Referring specifically to the *Ethical Standards of Psychologists* (American Psychological Association, 1953), he dealt with concrete aspects of both diagnostic and psychotherapeutic work. Happily, he wound up, after a series of cautions, giving clinical efforts his blessing:

> It is our wholehearted wish that your work may ever increasingly penetrate into the complexities of the human personality, that it may help it remedy its weaknesses and meet more faithfully the sublime designs which God, its Creator and Redeemer, formulates for it and proposes to it as its ideal.

Government

While we are concerned here primarily with the clinical psychologist, he is not without company when questions of status are being decided outside the clinic and the laboratory. Thus, a few years ago, as the result of some overnight publicity, the community became alarmed at the prospect of having 1984 already upon us. James Vickery and the company with which he was associated had allegedly succeeded in boosting popcorn and soft-drink sales appreciably in a New Jersey movie house through the medium of "subliminal advertising." With understandable concern, parts of the public and the press asked where such techniques might lead. Indeed, had the event been publicized a bit earlier, the papal message referred to above could well have made an issue of it.

Equally concerned, the Federal Communications Commission held a press conference in Washington, D.C., at which were present Mr. Vickery and officials of his company and their cinematic apparatus. Governmental concern was straightforward: Can psychologists, through the device of subliminal perception, influence a person's behavior to get him to do something he is not aware of having been influenced to do? Clearly many breeds of psychologist had a stake here—clinical, experimental, social, industrial. Just as clearly, there was the possibility that, taken precipitately, governmental action could have chiseled more than a few chips out of the image of psychology as it was being hewn by community forces. Fortunately, government took no rash action to impose legal restraints on the profession. Organized psychology had time to commission a paper (McConnell, Cutler, & McNeil, 1958) on both the status and the ethics of subliminal perception, and clinical psychology and its colleagues emerged with wings unclipped.

Would that clinical psychology had enough basic knowledge at this point to reciprocate by contributing to the solution of major social problems to the degree it would like. Again, cases in point are close at hand. Officials of the U.S. Post Office Department bring to the office of the American Psychological Association a device being offered for sale on therapeutic grounds which, on other grounds, might seem offensive. Would clinical psychology be so good as to evaluate the particular promotional literature in terms of its effect on possible teen-age recipients? The invitation is flattering, the task frightening. Clinically it is not all that easy; experimentally the problem is almost too real for the research designs grown out of more synthetic, albeit basic, concerns.

Not about to be hoist by its own petard, however, psychology could counter that precisely because the "research" of the subliminal advertising proponents was not so rigorous as that of the professor's laboratory, claims made on the basis thereof were not necessarily to be taken at face value. As McConnell et al. (1958) were quick to point out:

> Despite the likelihood of serious methodological and technical defects (exposure time was reported as 1/3,000 sec., far faster than any previously reported stimulation), this demonstration has been the one which has caused the most stir in both the fields of advertising and psychology. There were no reports, however, of even the most rudimentary scientific precautions, such as adequate controls, provision for replication, etc., which leaves the skeptical scientist in a poor position to make any judgment about the validity of the study.

In their carefully reasoned but fairly nontechnical article, written to be understood by intelligent laymen (policy makers among them), McConnell et al. were concerned that psychology be properly perceived:

> The furor which promises to accompany the further application of a variety of devices involving subliminal perception is certain to embroil psychology in a dispute not of its own choosing. The indiscriminate and uncontrolled application of psychological principles is increasing at a fearsome rate in the form of motivation research, propaganda, public relations, and a host of other "useful" practices based on the work of psychologists. In a very real sense this era of applied psychology will be a test of the workability of the psychologist's code of ethics and promises to stimulate the profession to give further consideration to its responsibility for assisting society to use its findings wisely.

In all this, it is perhaps the clinical psychologist who needs most to worry about his status, legal or quasi-legal, as it emerges out of the interaction of historical accident, temper of the times, society's needs, and psychologists' own vices and virtues.

The Press

Time was when psychology worried little about its press notices. Indeed, very likely the press did *not* note experiments on learning, perception of JNDs, or curves of forgetting. If such anonymity was a good thing (though some would dispute it), perhaps clinical psychologists are the villains of the piece for having won for psychology its quota of inches of space in today's newspapers and magazines and gallons of printer's ink used for today's books. Even where the experimental psychologist is doing research of a fairly basic kind, it is its clinical aspects that the public seems concerned with.

The implications of sensory-deprivation research for neurological models notwithstanding, science writers seem more interested in the fact that the subjects started hearing voices. And while experiments with LSD might be calculated to get at the biochemistry of mental illness, the public is most concerned with weapons in the hands of scientists which can induce psychosis à la carte. Now, if best-seller lists reflect at all the tenor of the times, there is more than a little concern with defining the status of the clinical and other psychologists more precisely, if not hedging them in by laws written or unwritten. Whyte (1956) set the process in motion, going so far as to offer gratuitous advice to the defenseless citizen on how he could "beat" the personality tester at his own game. Vance Packard (1957) kept up the momentum in a two- or three-phased tocsin-sounding operation. Most recently, Banesh Hoffman (1961) and Martin Gross (1962) have forcefully, if exaggeratedly, continued to insist that the clinical psychologist and others like him bear watching, containing, and perhaps more formal restricting.

Publishers generally, though this is not to indict them as a group, have had no small part in helping define the status of clinical psychology in more ways than one, salable as the more applied products of the field have become. The clinician's books have appeal—whether they are on the subject of call girls, self-analysis, or child rearing. So do the clinician's products—whether they are intelligence tests, devices for handling infants, or personality inventories. Publishers are intent on selling their wares. In the process, psychologists find their products "plugged"; fellow psychologists (sometimes with competing products) wonder about the ethics, or at least the good taste, of some of the promotional efforts; and the APA writes into its revised code of ethics sections intended specifically to handle the issues. Meanwhile, the status of clinical psychology keeps being further defined.

Politics

It may well be that in the end, the unwritten or quasi-legal definitions of clinical psychology will turn out cumulatively to have had as much impact on the status of the profession as the formal, legal attempts to go on record, if not more. Examples of the former variety are neither rare nor academic, and they attest, if anything, to the fact that if the efforts of clinical psychologists have been misunderstood, they have not gone unnoticed.

So much has clinical work been in the public eye, that the Republican party in the state of Washington took pains to write into its platform a plank assuring the voters that it was mindful that administration of certain psychological tests to schoolchildren needs to be curtailed, if not prohibited. At about the same time, the school board of Hicksville, Long Island (New York State Psychologist, 1962) was demanding to see the Blacky Pictures and to hear from the clinical psychologists good reasons why the materials should not be judged offensive and hence not used with their schoolchildren. Another school board, this time in Texas, made shorter shrift of the whole business—it literally burned the personality tests being used in connection with Project Talent (Nettler, 1959).

It is at this point that quasi-legal actions either begin to resemble legal ones or else promise to lead to them. The moral of the story, if it needs one, seems again to be that the status of clinical psychology, legal and otherwise, is defined in many quarters, in lots of ways, by all kinds of people. It behooves clinical psychology to be mindful of the fact, to reckon with it, and perhaps to treat the problem as only clinicians can.

To be sure, the situation has its positive side too. If some are determined to keep a wary eye on the psychologist, others are eager to make use of his services. In a number of states, legislation is in force which requires, among other things, that before a child may be placed in a class for the retarded, he must have been duly tested by a psychologist qualified to make a valid estimate of his intellectual status. By the same token, the National Defense Education Act contains provisions which depend heavily upon the contributions of psychology. With psychologists in comparatively short supply in relation to demands made upon them, the requests are not always an unmixed blessing.

Directories and Diplomas

If it is true that a man may be known by the company he keeps, psychologists, at least in telephone directories, have bedfellows who are at best strange, at worst shoddy. Again, legally the telephone directory, as such, probably has little status; as a quasi-legal document, however, it may help more people find their way to psychologists or "psychologists" than some of the more reputable, but often less accessible, directories put out by psychologists themselves or by bodies which have duly certified, licensed, or in other ways passed upon them.

The problem has seemed real enough so that David (1963), among others, has done a running survey on what has proved a running sore. As he puts it, in the third of a series of articles on the subject: "While the psychology sections in classified telephone directories are now dominated by APA members, the minority of 'phonies' continues to be a source of embarrassment to our professional image."

Regardless of the merits of having psychology defined legally, leaving the untrained or ill-trained "psychologist" undefined or ill-defined is not without its price:

> Between 1947 and 1952 there is popularly reported to have been such an increase in the number of unqualified psychological practitioners that their total in the nation rose to 25,000 and their "take" amounted to $375,000,000 annually, an amount said to approximate about five percent of the nation's total medical care bill (Illinois Legislative Council, 1956).

In all these areas—religion, government, the press, politics, and the courts, among others—no foothold was gained cheaply or always held securely. In some cases, psychology was being pushed toward climbing the particular mountain; in others it was pulled up by its own bootstraps. Sometimes, of course, psychologists themselves took the initiative. In any, and every, case, new paths were being blazed.

PSYCHOLOGY FROM THE INSIDE

The burden of our argument thus far has been that psychology in general and clinical psychology in particular keep being pointed to, talked about, and defined in a lot of quarters by a lot of events—sometimes legally, more often quasi-legally, always for better or worse, and never without consequences or implications. Hardly inarticulate, organized psychology has helped do its own share of defining. In what was for it pretty much virgin territory, it made a commendable effort at reconnaisance (American Psychological Association, 1955) and then sallied forth.

Legislation—Psychological Style

> Your decision in favor of legislation for psychologists will . . . for better or for worse, permanently entwine psychologists in your state with the executive, legislative, and judicial branches of government; of necessity it will tend to sharpen the local definition of "psychology" and of "psychologists"; and it will give cause for the occasional public suspicion which all of us experience at times toward "protected" occupations (American Psychological Association, nd).

The memorandum from the APA central office goes on to sound neither like Cassandra nor like Pollyanna, while at the same time calling a spade a spade. Speaking of the general problem of freedom and restraint, Gellhorn (1956) had something to say on the subject:

> In occupational licensing, the choice is not between some regulation and none. The choice is between licensing for the sake of the occupations and, on the other hand, licensing for the sake of the public at large. As matters stand, the citizen's right to use his faculties in a freely chosen career has been squeezed beyond justification. What we need now is fewer but better designed bindings on that right.

As of March, 1963, the 23-state roster of laws which either certify or license psychologists included Arkansas, California, Colorado, Connecticut, Delaware, Florida, Georgia, Idaho, Illinois, Kentucky, Maine, Maryland, Michigan, Minnesota, Nevada, New Hampshire, New Mexico, New York, Oregon, Tennessee, Utah, Virginia, and Washington. The typical requirement is the Ph.D. degree and two years of supervised experience. The laws generally control the title "psychologist" and its variants as well as the description of services as psychological. In New York, the definition of psychological practice began as follows:

> A person practices psychology within the meaning of this Act when he renders to individuals, organizations, or the public any service involving the application of principles, methods or procedures of understanding, predicting, or influencing behavior, such as the principles pertaining to learning, perception, motivation, thinking, emotions, or interpersonal relationships; or of the methods and procedures of interviewing, counseling, and psychotherapy; or of constructing, administering, or interpreting tests of mental abilities, aptitudes, interests, attitudes, personality characteristics, emotions, or motivation; or of assessing public opinion. The application of said principles and methods includes, but is not restricted to: the diagnosis, prevention, and amelioration of emotional disorders and adjustment problems of individuals and groups; educational and vocational planning; personnel selection and management; the arrangement of effective work and learning situations; advertising and market research; the resolution of interpersonal and social conflicts; lecturing on or teaching of psychology; and the design and conduct of applied psychological research.

Even more states had "nonstatutory" programs, the certification requirements being administered by the state psychological association rather than by the state government. Here the roster read: Alabama, Arizona, District of Columbia, Hawaii, Iowa, Kansas, Louisiana, Massachusetts, Missouri, Montana, Nebraska, New Jersey, North Dakota, Ohio, Pennsylvania, Rhode Island, South Carolina, South Dakota, Texas, and West Virginia.

The remaining states are in the process of introducing bills in the legislature, are thinking about so doing, or else are planning their own nonstatutory programs. Meanwhile, four Canadian provinces—Alberta, Ontario, Quebec, and Saskatchewan—have laws on their books as well.

All this has not proceeded without incident. The course of interprofessional relations, like that of true love, has not always run smooth; intraprofessionally it has been no less rough, on occasion (Deutsch, 1958; Katzell & Thompson, 1958). Some have speculated about the "hidden issues" (Ausubel, 1956). Others have gathered jointly around the committee table (American Psychological Association, 1955).

Indeed, the joint efforts of the APA and CSPA committees on legislation, commissioned by the APA board of directors in 1954, were not directed at the short-range consideration of legislative tactics and strategy. Of primary concern was the thoughtful searching out of long-term implications which policies on legislative and social controls were to have for the profession. The ensuing report was remarkable for its grasp of the broader issues and its reasoned and statesmanlike weighing of pros and cons.

On Growing Up

Clinical psychology seemed just to have grown so quickly that as the organization adapted to one phase of the specialty's development, the latter had already moved into the next. When minority groups become majority groups as fast as happened here, some dislocation can come about—and did. And if there is a psychological system as there is a political system, adjustments in one part of the system will require comparable adjustments in others. Conveniently, psychologists are, among other things, systems theorists. Whether having such a doctor in the family is a happy coincidence or whether it will prove anew that one cannot really treat one's own family remains to be seen. In either case, there will be a lot of psychologists, clinical and nonclinical, sitting in the amphitheater watching the operation.

A decade ago one *could* tell a clinical psychologist without a scorecard. His training was all of a piece; he performed certain functions, and the types of places in which he worked could in fact be counted on the fingers of one hand. Time marches on. What a few years ago seemed the ultimate in having "arrived"—the privilege of doing individual psychotherapy—is already in some quarters looked upon as an effete, or at least a shortsighted, notion of what the clinical psychologist is or should be equipped to contribute. While clinical psychologists at work and the APA at the conference table have fought the good fight for inalienable rights, other clinical psychologists, having turned 90 or 180 degrees, are describing roles more glamorous than those of the therapist and more befitting the research-minded consultation that clinical psychologists are uniquely equipped to take on. Why fight for a small piece of barren land, some are asking, when in this boundless space age of professional possibilities one can literally shoot for the moon (with all due respect to social needs)? Indeed, some of the flavor of the more *avant-garde* thinking was already evident in the report of a special committee of the APA created precisely for the purpose of looking at the role of psychology in mental health (1959).

If imaginativeness exacts its price in the form of still newer problems to face, so does flexibility in the training of clinical and other psychologists. In 1950 one knew a clinical psychologist when one saw one, often by the company he kept. Today he is—fortunately, albeit exasperatingly—not nearly so easy to spot; by the same token, organizationally he poses new and different problems. If, curricularly speaking, it is difficult to triangulate the psychologist who moves in the experimental psychology–mathematics–engineering plane, it is perhaps even harder to track his colleague who orbits the clinical psychology–personality–social sphere. Neither stays put long enough to let us get our sights on him, and surveyors are the more harried, and surveys the more complicated, for it.

Spring and Psychology Are Busting Out All Over

Doubtless every psychologist worth his salt sees his own specialty as the keystone in the arch through which march the minions of science on their way to the behaviorally engineered world of tomorrow. The engineering psychologist makes no bones about it; his is the area of human performance—and what branch of psychology cannot be subsumed thereunder? No shrinking violet, the clinical psychologist asserts with equal candor the dependence of all psychology on that branch, which traffics in motives, aspirations, anxieties, and indeed the very stuff of life.

When the APA education and training board allowed itself some "anticipations of developments during the next decade which will influence psychology" (Bordin, 1956), it could not help concluding that, whether we willed it or not, the world, in marching on, would bring about an increased demand for psychologists and their services—all psychologists, all services. Automation was a phenomenon to be reckoned with; population growth would bring its own share of psychological problems, and rapid scientific and technological developments were already presenting theirs.

Many things are happening outside psychology that have repercussions inside psychology or, at the very least, implications for psychology. And many things are happening within psychology which, for better or worse, promise to affect its capacity to play the role on the scientific and professional stage for which it has applied or in which it finds itself cast. Since it is the developments within its ranks which are perhaps more under its control, it behooves us to take a closer look at them, particularly as they affect the present and future organization of clinical psychology.

The Latent and the Manifest

When in the 1950s the Conference of State Psychological Associations (CSPA) made its bid for recognition, clinical psychologists were well represented in the battle for states' rights, and in 1957 a major portion of the APA business meeting (and separate caucuses) came to be devoted to preserving peace in the association and goodwill toward psychologists (Carter, 1957). By the same token, this time on the nonclinical side, it took a survey of the members of the APA Division of Experimental Psychology to reassure the founding fathers that members of that respectably scientific camp were not so disenchanted with the association as one could have been led to believe. In both cases, the rise and fall of the CSPA and the soul-searching of Division 3, the articulated discontent, if not seething, was at least manifest.

Other organizational developments, again manifest, in each of which clinical psychology had a large stake, are not hard to find. Cook's memorable address (1958) as president of the Eastern Psychological Association laid the issue on the line, as he pondered the question: "psychology: science or profession or both?" The so-called Miami Beach conference (Roe, 1959) very consciously raised and debated the issues of practicum training, the professional degree in psychology, legislation, and independent practice, among others. In 1960, after a special committee had given the matter long, hard thought, the APA adopted its *Standards for APA Directory Listings of Private Practice* (American Psychological Association, 1960). And in 1961, the association, in revising its bylaws, gave explicit recognition to the demonstrated viability of its clinical wing by spelling out APA's "objects" so as to embrace the "encouragement of psychology in all its branches in the broadest and most liberal manner."

Without pushing the manifest-latent analogy too hard, and while recognizing that many of the developments may fall somewhere along the continuum rather than at one of its end points, we might turn for a moment to some of the less manifest and more latent developments. In either case, clinical psychology and clinical psychologists have been wont to ask that they be listened to—sometimes entreatingly, sometimes threateningly, always earnestly.

Psychology's DEW Line

If psychology has its distant early warning line to alert it to dissatisfaction in the ranks, it is doubtless most often the clinical psychologist who appears as blips on the profession's radar screen. True, the experimental psychologists have formed their own Psychonomic Society—with membership by invitation only—avowedly to provide a forum for the presentation of research but actually as much by way of being an unwritten expression of dissatisfaction with some trends in the association. But the clinical psychologists can match their experimental colleagues ten to one. Within the span of a few years, literally dozens of special clinical groups have flowered, so much so that when the Committee on Relations with Local Organizations of Clinical Psychologists met in St. Louis on August 30, 1962, more than a score of organizations were represented (Lebo, 1962). It is perhaps not unfair to say that in both cases—whether clinical or experimental—there has sometimes been a note of threatening to pick up one's marbles and go home unless demands were granted or at the very least recognized.

The proliferation of clinical groups is noteworthy. Whether the development augurs well or ill, the fact is that they have come to exert an influence within the organization which would not have been predicted ten years ago. While there were then some small interest groups (and, of course, the state psychological associations), there are today some major pressure groups (we use the term descriptively rather than pejoratively). Psychologists in Private Practice (PPP) publishes a regular newsletter, which leaves few stones unturned with respect to recent developments in the profession. Psychologists Interested in the Advancement of Psychotherapy (PIAP), a group best defined by its name, nonetheless is equally concerned with the professional status and organization of psychology as a whole and of clinical psychology as a specialty, having a newsletter of its own as well. The National

Clinical Liaison Committee (NCLC), nonexistent just a few years ago, takes more simply to the mimeograph machine and yet reaches an impressive number of clinical psychologists. It has, in fact, been represented at a meeting of the APA board of professional affairs. However clinical psychology as a whole may view its PPPs, PIAPs, and NCLCs, the fact is that such articulate, vigorous groups have come into being, seem viable, and will no doubt be joined by yet others, most of which, alone or in concert, promise to contribute in one way or another to the shaping of clinical psychology in the years ahead.

1957

Children of fortune have their troubles, and clinical psychology is no exception. Its lot, as Shoben (1959) points out, is not uneventful:

> Thus clinical psychology is subject to such intraprofessional bipolarities as science versus research and scholarship, intuition and improvisation versus verification and system, the cultivation of heuristic doctrines of considerable breadth versus the cultivation of rigorous theories of considerable narrowness, and the development of productive skepticism.

The phenomenologists among us might well put ourselves in the clinical psychologist's shoes for a while to see how they feel. The APA did not think of doing so spontaneously, but someone slipped it a shoehorn, so to speak, and in the last seven years it has managed to squeeze its larger academic foot into something that has not always felt or looked like Cinderella's slipper. At any rate, after the ball was over in 1957, a couple of new boards had made their debut at the annual business meeting. Aptly named the Board of Scientific Affairs (BSA) and the Board of Professional Affairs (BPA), they symbolized the organization's concern with just the kinds of "bipolarities" that Shoben was talking about. The two boards were meant to act as governors on the psychological machine as it continued to rev up to higher speeds, pulling the heavier load the intervening years had hung on it. The Board of Scientific Affairs was neither surprising nor hard to figure out; the Board of Professional Affairs, to some at least, was both. For this reason, it may be well to look at the BPA in some detail.

The Board of Professional Affairs

Whether maverick (in the political sense) or bastard (in the genealogical sense), the Board of Professional Affairs has raised many issues and some eyebrows. To clinical psychologists and others concerned about APA's taking a "proper" role in the professional side of things, it has seemed long in coming. To others, who wonder whither professionalization might lead, it hardly comes as the Messiah. Indeed, the new board itself was not without an appreciation of both sides of the argument, as it held its first meeting in 1957.

Under the caption "Issues Referred to the Board of Professional Affairs," one finds in the account of the board's meeting (its first report to the APA board of directors) the following: status and privileges of psychologists in the Air Force; nature of APA directory listings; survey of scope and nature of psychological services rendered in a variety of settings; review of staffing ratios employed in clinical settings; invitation to appoint a representative to the National Tuberculosis Association; and tax status of fees paid for psychological services.

In almost every case, clinical psychologists were injecting the issues into the discussion, having long waited to "shoot the mainstream" of the organization rather than shooting simply the rapids of their divisional tributary. One case, destined to become a bête noire, actually started life as an inconspicuous note in the report of the November, 1958, meeting of the Board of Professional Affairs: "A preliminary survey had disclosed that, as a rule, either psychological services are omitted from health insurance coverage (except when authorized by a physician, and not even always then) or else insurance firms have an inconsistent and sometimes contradictory policy with regard to such claims."

Because the particular issue reflects so pointedly the extent and kind of influence that clinical psychologists find themselves able to exert organizationally, it is well to trace its course of development as a case in point.

"Project Insurance"

It all began innocently enough. A clinical psychologist here and there noted that one of his clients was not reimbursed under the latter's health insurance plan for fees paid to his psychologist. The issue was raised in the local psychological association, in the state association, and eventually in the APA. Its proportions were at first not appreciated. Beyond economic considerations, clinical psychologists saw matters of principle at issue. Did psychological difficulties constitute "illness," with the implication that they therefore required the services of a medical specialist? Should clients with such problems need to be referred to the psychologist through a physician in order to be considered "legitimate" clients of the clinical psychologist for insurance purposes? Should insurance companies be making decisions in the first place about who may rightfully provide "treatment"?

By May, 1959, the Board of Professional Affairs had asked its *ad hoc* committee to meet with a committee of the Health Insurance Council in order to discuss the problems directly. The story continued to unfold, and in May, 1960, the Board of Professional Affairs reported as follows:

> BPA voted to recommend to the Board of Directors that future efforts should be directed not at changing the basic principle of insurance policies with regard to determination of need for treatment but rather at gaining general acceptance of provisions for covering psychological services when deemed necessary by those having medical responsibility for the treatment of the claimant.

The board of directors concurred in the recommendation, the council of representatives adopted it, the action (along with a report by the chairman of the *ad hoc* committee) was published in the *American Psychologist* (Wallace, 1960)—and the storm broke! The letters and telegrams which rained down on the APA central office and its board of directors are significant not for their reactions to a particular action by the association on a particular issue but as tangible evidence of the voice that clinical psychologists had become able to raise in concert. The insurance problem had turned out to be the *cause célèbre*. Had it not, another issue was doubtless destined for the role, an issue which could have afforded a similar rallying point for the expression of sentiment, the assertion of rights, and, perhaps most to the point, the bid for a place at the conference table.

The invitation was issued literally, and at its spring meeting in 1961, the board was joined by two clinical psychologists representing, respectively, the New York State Psychological Association, on the one hand, and the California State Psychological Association and Los Angeles Society of Clinical Psychologists, on the other. The issues were joined too as the visitors sought to present the case from the clinical psychologist's point of view.

The practice of "inviting to its meetings such members of the Association as could best speak to the issues" (American Psychological Association, 1962) was continued, and at its meeting in May, 1962, the Board of Professional Affairs was joined by a member of its *ad hoc* committee on insurance together with the executive secretary of the Eastern branch of the National Clinical Liaison Committee. The latter invitation is as symbolically significant now as it was precedent-setting then. With NCLC represented at the conference table, the voice of a loosely federated organization of a large number of clinical psychologists throughout the country was being afforded a direct chance to participate in the policy-making deliberations of the parent organization.

The issue moved forward, there was an attempt at a definition of "psychologist" for insurance purposes, the Board of Professional Affairs made its recommendations, the board of directors concurred in them with some modifications, and in September, 1962, the council of representatives (Newman, 1962) adopted as official policy the statement in which many had had a hand. It read, in part:

> The properly qualified professional psychologist has specialized knowledge and skills with which to render psychological services to clients with appropriately selected problems without routinely involving other professions or service groups in order to accomplish the maximum benefit for clients with such selected problems. In taking this position, it is recognized that such a policy is to be carried out in conformity with principles set forth in Ethical Standards of Psychologists, Psychology and Its Relations with Other Professions, the policies of the APA Education and Training Board governing evaluation of training programs, and of ABEPP with respect to its diploma. . . .

What earlier might have looked like the end of a short story turns out to be only the beginning of a longer one, insurance actuaries being leery of psychotherapy by whatever profession. But that is another matter.

The Grass Roots

Possibly psychology's "movements," like chemistry's "seed crystals," need issues around which to agglutinate. Possibly not. The historians of the profession, better able to stand back from the problems some time hence, can decide. There is no gainsaying the fact, however, that the past decade has witnessed the birth and felt the presence of newer members of the family.

Columns of "Psychology in the States" in the *American Psychologist* have been devoted to the exploits of local societies, which in numbers and possibly in influence, rival, if not exceed, the efforts of some state psychological associations. NYSCP and LASCP, the New York Society of Clinical Psychologists and the Los Angeles Society of Clinical Psychologists, respectively, have gained an audience, both literally and figuratively. PPP (Psychologists in Private Practice), PIAP (Psychologists Interested in the Advancement of Psychotherapy), and NCLC (National Clinical Liaison Committee), only initials a short while ago, are now messages, newsletters, statements of position, and even new journals. PPP and PIAP embrace psychology's practitioners in many quarters; the NCLC serves as a national channel of communication for issues and concerns that many feel have not been accorded their due. All three represent new organizational kinfolk joining local, state, and national elders at the bigger family reunions of today.

"Clinical" Issues

In the old days, psychology could look forward to how Guthrie would reply to Tolman, or Köhler to Spence. As the issues got more lifelike, Skinner and Rogers had it out on the question of controlling people (Rogers & Skinner, 1956). One thing led to another, and gradually the voice of clinicians, like that of the turtle, was heard throughout the land—sometimes on issues smacking more of the community than of the classroom or the clinic.

The Board of Professional Affairs had evolved neither as a "sport" nor as an accident of the rhythm method; planned parenthood had worked to produce this particular offspring at the time the family seemed ready for it. And as the BPA started to talk, it was evident from the beginning that its topics of conversation might be a bit out of keeping with those one was used to but that they would never be dull.

The chips have always been down, and dander sometimes up, whenever this board has met. If clinical psychologists have not used it as a mouthpiece, they have at least availed themselves of the privilege of writing letters to its nine congressmen to suggest which events bear watching, and which questions airing.

What should be the APA's official statement of position in the field of mental health? How should the APA advise state associations, if at all, with respect to incorporating in certification bills clauses which would take into account sociologists' claims to the title "social psychologist"? Should the APA suggest to the United States Civil Service Commission that the ABEPP diploma be considered a type of evidence of superior qualifications and performance for promotion to certain positions? Is it within the board's province to make recommendations about instances in which psychologists feel themselves under duress to slant their testimony on controversial issues (such as desegregation)? What, if anything, should the board attempt to do about "cleaning up" the area of marriage counseling? Should the APA take active steps with respect to the practice, teaching, and study of hypnosis, possibly setting up a procedure for "boarding" qualified psychologists in the manner of the ABEPP? Should the APA intercede with the Internal Revenue Service to clarify the status of income tax deductions for the cost of didactic analysis? Should the association go on record with a resolution approving the constructive attitude adopted by an AMA Committee to Study the Relationships of Medicine with Allied Health Professions and Services? Should the APA concern itself with the admission requirements (or lack of requirements) set by universities for enrollment in courses on psychological testing? Should it encourage, assist, or possibly direct the state associations in issuing directories of psychological services?

To Act or Not to Act

Time was when the canons of science encouraged the spirit of forthright inquiry and vigorous disputation but led to few altercations with the world outside. Playing newer and different roles, clinical psychologists have tended to confront organized psychology with that world on many a recent occasion.

When a state education department issues a ruling which would require that psychological records and reports be furnished on request to parents of pupils who had received psychological services, organized psychology cannot well ignore the affair. Whether the association should attempt to influence developments can be debated; whether some members will urge strongly that it do so cannot. They invariably do. In this particular case, the APA did move—with the blessing of the Board of Professional Affairs and in concert with the New York State Psychological Association.

The confluence of state and national courses of action exemplifies the multidetermined character of clinical psychology. The latter has, however, hardly sat quietly by while its fate was decreed on high. Quite aware of the influence they wield, clinical psychologists have gone earnestly about their business, partly in their own associations, largely in their own division, usually shaking hands, occasionally shaking fists.

Division 12

To brand the Division of Experimental Psychology as orthodox, conservative, and staid, and the Division of Clinical Psychology as radical, lusty, and forward-looking, would be like saying that all Chinese look alike and eat only rice. Members of Division 3 are working on the latest model of ataractic drug, helping put astronauts in space, and drawing fancy prices as consultants to industry; members of Division 12 are not all engaged in a thriving private practice, swearing by the Rorschach, or failing to read the Sigmund Koch series. It is not as simple as separating the men from the boys.

Back in 1952, division president O. H. Mowrer (soon to be the APA president as well) remarked: "We should not think of the Division as wholly abandoning its concern with the more strictly professional type of issue." History has given the president little occasion for worry on any score. The most recent issues of the *Newsletter* of the Division of Clinical Psychology have dealt, among other things, with such "professional" issues as private practice and such "scientific" issues as the proportion of research papers to clinical and theoretical papers on the program of the division at the annual convention of the association. (The research papers, incidentally, outnumbered the latter by a ratio of 9:1 in 1961.)

If there is any division which has neither hesitated to free-associate, and quite publicly, nor to air its differences of opinion, again quite publicly, it is Division 12. There is real concern with doing the right thing, whatever that may prove to be. As a recent president of the division put it (Hobbs, 1961):

> Can a professional group, such as Division 12, shape the character of the profession it represents, or does it serve merely to tidy up the situation after major social forces have already wrought a change?
>
> I should like to see us mounting some debates, publishing some manifestoes, with the assumption that what we think our profession *should* become may have some influence on what it does in fact become. I assume too that there are both multiple and alternate courses open to us. We do and should have a pluralistic profession. . . .

Perhaps precisely because the clinical psychologist is so much in the public eye, Division 12 has continued to worry constructively about forestalling any image of the "ugly psychologist." Martin Gross (1962) accuses him of testing people into submission, Vance Packard (1957) of selling people things they do not really want, and William H. Whyte, Jr. (1956), of being just generally perverse. When they are not portrayed as dangerous, they may wind up looking like "characters." Back in 1955, the *Newsletter* carried the plea of a member that the division express its concern to the Columbia Broadcasting System over a new weekly television comedy entitled "Professional Father," which would recount the plight of a "child psychologist father proficient in guiding the children of other parents but unable to cope with his own children." That this war has hardly been won is evidenced by the amount of feeling engendered by the more recent "Eleventh Hour."

Small wonder, then, that Division 12 should try to worry as constructively as it does about "defining" the "compleat clinical psychologist." One psychologist (Carson, 1962) would "not view the Ph.D. as *necessarily* indicating special competence in clinically relevant skills." He would feel it "not unfair to say, however, that as a group people having the doctorate are more generally competent than those who do not have it." His colleague (Thorne, 1962) reminds him, nevertheless: "In many cases, psychologists with only a Master's Degree, but with high levels of experience and competence, are responsibly directing state, municipal, institutional and agency programs."

On the issues, President Holt of the division felt moved to reply at the time (1962):

> What bothers me about the processes of definition that are already going on is that they are forcing clinical psychology to crystallize prematurely into a standard, procrustean pattern. . . . We must guard against becoming a vested-interest group, so intent on maintaining obsolescent standards that we begin to oppose the best interests of the public welfare and of science alike.

He who may have thought the millennium had arrived in 1944, when the APA voted to adopt a new constitution and the AAAP moved to end its separate existence and join forces, must have had some second thoughts in the years between. As Wolfle (1946) opined at the time, the event marked "in some respects a radical break with the old pattern. Instead of having one undifferentiated whole, interest differences have been recognized by the creation of eighteen APA divisions." There were, and are, strong hopes. As Wolfle put it then: "Strong divisions will remain. Weak ones . . . may go out of existence. If an important and distinctive group is not now represented, it may petition for the formation of a new division. The divisional structure is sensitive to interest differences and can keep step with changing needs."

Thus it was then. Thus it still is.

Long Past, Short History, or Vice Versa

If those who grew up with clinical psychology occasionally get the feeling that "this is where I came in," it is perhaps because the *déjà vu* experience is just that—the particular issue *has* come up before. Many of the problems persist, now joined by new ones. Hence, in a thoroughgoing survey of the attitudes, opinions, and feelings of division members, former President E. Lowell Kelly sought the facts of life in 1960 with respect to such topics as professional background and identification, work settings and experiences, theoretical orientation, perceived functions of Division 12, and "basic issues confronting the profession."

"With the full knowledge that I am taking positions not shared by the majority of the Division," Kelly concluded (1961), "I wish to comment on what are three important issues: two confronting our profession and one confronting the Division." As conductor of the most recent large-scale survey of clinical psychologists, not to mention his former presidency of both the division and the association, Kelly's triangulation of the issues is worth noting.

The first issue, as he sees it, has to do with the public image psychology develops for itself. As Kelly puts it:

> I think we must decide and decide soon whether, on the one hand, we wish clinical psychology to be perceived as one of the healing arts professions (and ourselves as doctors treating sick people) or alternatively a new type of profession—a unique profession which while contributing to the treatment of the sick (under conditions of genuine collaboration with the medical profession) is also a profession equally concerned with and capable of contributing a wide range of useful services to all sorts of people in widely varied settings, a profession unique in that it is also deeply committed to and active in the creation of new knowledge and new methods.

Having said the first mouthful, Kelly continues with his second concern, certain "imbalances" within the profession:

> Only a few years ago, we argued that clinical psychologists were badly needed in the mental health field because they would bring to it a set of critical attitudes and the research skills needed to develop new knowledge, to evaluate old methods and to develop new ones, to increase the efficiency of therapeutic procedures, etc. It is my impression a great many of us have been all too content to adopt uncritically the current modes of thought and practice of psychiatry and social work. . . . Surely we don't really believe that we now have all the answers or that our methods cannot be improved!

The third of the three "basic" issues, as Kelly sees them, has to do with the kind and degree of professionalism which the division should or should not foster. Here he adds, among other things:

> Now, I am most sympathetic with the desire of the membership to feel that they belong to a strong professional organization. . . .

> Personally, I am convinced that the APA has been just this sort of professional organization for clinical psychology. Admittedly, Division 12 has had but little direct part in those extensive and effective APA activities concerned with the development and protection of psychology as a profession. . . . As for the professional functions of Division 12, I believe that it should take the lead in studying the special professional problems of clinical psychology, recommending action to BPA and working collaboratively with APA for the profession of psychology as a whole.

Action, Reaction, and Synthesis

As if heeding Kelly's words, Division 12, through its Committee on Relations with Local Clinical Groups, arranged for the 1962 annual convention of the APA in St. Louis, a conference of local organizations of clinical psychologists. There were 22 psychological interest groups represented, the president of Division 12 addressed the assembly, papers on key issues were read, members of the APA central office staff participated, and, withal, the evolving character of the profession seemed the better for it.

It is not as if anything represents the final act in the ongoing professional drama of clinical themes played off against the backdrop of social needs. But perhaps the communion of spirit and meeting of mind sought by clinical psychologists thus assembled go far toward realizing the "aspirations for the good profession of psychology" set forth by the American Psychological Association (1954):

> Since no society yet devised has achieved perfection in advancing and protecting the integrity of the individual, a good profession must do more than adjust passively to the explicitly stated preferences of a society; the contribution of the good profession must be creative rather than passive, for perfect adjustment to an imperfect social reality can be stagnating. The good profession of psychology will seek through investigation, practice, and teaching to improve the society which supports it.

REFERENCES

Ad Hoc Planning Group on the Role of the APA in Mental Health Programs and Research. Mental health and the American Psychological Association. *Amer. Psychologist,* 1959, **14,** 820–825.

Albee, G. W. Social need and graduate education in psychology. Paper read at Pa. Psychol. Ass., May 13, 1960.

American Psychological Association. Legislation for psychologists, Memo No. 1, nd.

American Psychological Association. *Ethical standards of psychologists.* Washington, D.C.: Author, 1953.

American Psychological Association. *Psychology and its relations with other professions.* Washington, D.C.: Author, 1954.

American Psychological Association, Board of Professional Affairs. Report of meeting of November 15–16, 1958.

American Psychological Association, Board of Professional Affairs. Report of BPA to board of directors and council of representatives, May, 1962.

American Psychological Association, Board of Professional Affairs, Committee on Private Practice. Proposed standards for APA Directory listings of private practice. *Amer. Psychologist,* 1960, **15,** 110–112.

American Psychological Association, Committee on Legislation, Conference of State Psychological Associations. Joint report of the APA & CSPA Committees on Legislation. *Amer. Psychologist,* 1955, **10,** 727–756.

Amrine, M. Psychology in the news. *Amer. Psychologist,* 1963, **18,** 74–78.

Ausubel, D. P. Relationships between psychology and psychiatry: the hidden issues. *Amer. Psychologist,* 1956, **11,** 99–105.

Bauer, R. A., et al. Social influences on the standards of psychologists. *Amer. Psychologist,* 1964, **19,** 167–173.

Bobbitt, J. M. & Hoch, E. L. Psychology in the states. *Amer. Psychologist,* 1961, **16,** 151–153.

Bordin, E. S. Anticipations of developments during the next decade which will influence psychology. Unpublished summary of meeting of Education and Training Board, American Psychological Association, February 1, 1956.

Carson, R. C. Membership and competence. *Newsltr Div. clin. Psychol., Amer. psychol. Ass.* 1962, **15,** 10–11.

Carter, L. F. Report of the recording secretary: proceedings of the sixty-fifth annual business meeting of the American Psychological Association, Inc. *Amer. Psychologist,* 1957, **12,** 690–706.

Cook, S. W. The psychologist of the future: scientist, professional, or both. *Amer. Psychologist,* 1958, **13,** 635–644.

David, H. P. Phones, phonies, and psychologists. *Amer. Psychologist,* 1963, **18,** 144–148.

Deutsch, C. P. After legislation—what price psychology? *Amer. Psychologist,* 1958, **13,** 645–652.

Gellhorn, W. *Individual freedom and governmental restraints.* Baton Rouge, La.: Louisiana State Univer., 1956.

Gross, M. *The brain watchers.* New York: Random House, 1962.

Hobbs, N. From the president. *Newsltr Div. clin. Psychol., Amer. psychol. Ass.,* 1961, **14,** 4.

Hoch, E. L., & Darley, J. G. A case at law. *Amer. Psychologist,* 1962, **17,** 623–654.

Hoffman, B. The tyranny of multiple-choice tests. *Harper's,* 1961, **222,** 37–44.

Holt, R. R. What is a clinical psychologist? *Newsltr Div. clin. Psychol., Amer. psychol. Ass.,* 1962, **15,** 4–5.

Illinois Legislative Council. State regulation of psychologists. *Bull.* 2-580, 1956.

Joint Commission on Mental Illness and Health. *Action for mental health.* New York: Basic Books, 1961.

Jones, M. R., & Levine, D. Graduate training for community clinical psychology. *Amer. Psychologist,* 1963, **18,** 219–223.

Katzell, R. A., & Thompson, A. S. Some comments on "After Legislation. . . ." *Amer. Psychologist,* 1958, **13,** 652–654.

Kelly, E. L. Clinical psychology—1960: report of survey findings. *Newsltr Div. clin. Psychol., Amer. psychol. Ass.,* 1961, **14,** 1–11.

King, A. J., & Spector, A. J. Ethical and legal aspects of survey research. *Amer. Psychologist,* 1963, **18,** 204–208.

Langhorne, M. C., & Hoch, E. L. Psychology in the states. *Amer. Psychologist,* 1960, **15,** 632–634.

Lebo, D. *Proceedings of conference of local organizations of clinical psychologists.* St. Louis, Mo., August 30, 1962. (Mimeographed)

Louisell, D. W. The psychologist in today's legal world. *Minn. Law Rev.,* 1955, **39,** 237–272.

McConnell, J. V., Cutler, R. L., & McNeil, E. B. Subliminal stimulation: an overview. *Amer. Psychologist,* 1958, **13,** 229–242.

Nettler, G. Test burning in Texas. *Amer. Psychologist,* 1959, **14,** 682–683.

Newman, E. B. Report of the recording secretary: proceedings of the seventieth annual business meeting of the American Psychological Association, Inc. *Amer. Psychologist,* 1962, **17,** 843–864.

New York State Psychologist. Hicksville schoolboard attacks Blacky test. *Newsltr,* 1962, **14,** 1.

Packard, V. *The hidden persuaders.* New York: McKay, 1957.

Pope Pius XII. Applied psychology. Paper read at Int. Ass. appl. Psychol., Rome, April, 1958. Washington, D.C.: National Catholic Welfare Conference.

Roe, A. (Ed.) *Graduate education in psychology.* Washington, D.C.: American Psychological Association, 1959.

Rogers, C. R., & Skinner, B. F. Some issues concerning the control of human behavior. *Science,* 1956, **124,** 1057–1066.

Shoben, E. J., Jr. Conflict and identification in the training process. In M. H. P. Finn & F. Brown (Eds.), *Training for clinical psychology.* New York: International Universities Press, 1959.

Skinner, B. F. Pigeons in a pelican. *Amer. Psychologist,* 1960, **15,** 28–37.

Thorne, F. C. Unrealistic membership standards. *Newsltr Div. clin. Psychol., Amer. psychol. Ass.,* 1962, **15,** 11.

Tryon, R. C. Psychology in flux: the academic-professional bipolarity. *Amer. Psychologist,* 1963, **18,** 134–143.

Wallace, S. R. Psychological services in relation to health insurance plans. *Amer. Psychologist,* 1960, **15,** 824–826.

Whyte, W. H., Jr. *The organization man.* New York: Simon and Schuster, 1956.

Wolfle, D. The reorganized American Psychological Association. *Amer. Psychologist,* 1946, **1,** 3–6.

55
Clinical Psychologists at Work

MOLLY HARROWER

BACKGROUND

The reader who scans the table of contents or who has read systematically to this point may be aware from the title that this chapter makes a rather abrupt departure from the preceding ones. It suggests that we are about to leave the realm of scholarship, basic research, theories, and methodology and deal with people holding jobs—with clinical psychologists at work.[1]

Because of this shift of emphasis, we shall proceed in a somewhat prosaic fashion to examine, first, who clinical psychologists in the 1960s really are. Second, we shall consider some job descriptions, moving from the more general ones characteristic of various types of institutions to the highly specific and individual programs of psychologists in private practice. By such contrasts, we may sharpen the different frames of reference characteristic of employment versus self-employment. Third, we shall make some comment on what we feel to be the core of experience and personal development necessary for competent and responsible functioning in psychodiagnostics and therapy, regardless of whether the setting is within an institution or not.

It should be stated at the outset that it is our belief that hospitals and clinics, on the one hand, and private practice, on the other, admittedly present some different problems and may satisfy somewhat different professional needs. But the tasks performed by clinical psychologists, whether employed or self-employed, are not basically different. They require comparable backgrounds in our profession's basic subject matter and demand comparable standards of excellence in performance. Moreover, in present-day clinical psychology, it is hardly a question of either-or—institution or private practice—rather, as we shall see from numerous examples, it is a question of what percentage of an individual's time is given to work that he may program essentially according to his own interests and what percentage is given to work that is programmed according to hospital or clinic schedules.

Most chapters have included a section on the history of the topic to be discussed; in this instance, a few paragraphs will suffice. The first psychological clinic, as is well known, was founded in 1896 by Lightner Witmer in a university setting for the dual purpose of providing a service to individuals and training graduate students. We then jump several decades, to the time when the emergence of the projective techniques gave psychologists new tools for diagnostic and prognostic studies. However, prior to World War II, psychologists in hospitals and clinics were rarities. In 1938, for example, the Rockefeller Medical Foundation awarded its first fellowship to an experimental psychologist for exploratory work within a hospital setting. And it is an interesting comment on how dramatically the climate

[1] This chapter describes the functions of clinical psychologists and does not include a discussion of the valuable work of other psychologists whose functions border on those of clinical psychologists, such as school psychologists, consulting psychologists, and certain industrial psychologists.

of opinion can change to record the fact that the topic suggested by the applicant, the psychological effects of surgical shock, was assumed by one member of the evaluating committee to have been a typographical error; it should have read, according to that authority, "the physiological effects of surgical shock," since there could be no possible connection between psychology and this organic phenomenon!

Lowell Kelly has epitomized the pre-World War II situation as follows:

> To those of us who were clinicians in the 30's, the growth and development of our professional specialty during the last 15 years is well nigh phenomenal. Before World War II clinical psychologists were few in number, poorly paid and had but little status. Primarily as the result of the decision of the VA to make the clinical psychologist a full fledged professional in staffing its NP facilities, and the creation of a training program to produce the needed but then non-available Ph.D. level personnel, clinical psychology has become a respected and prestigeful professional specialty. Nurtured by substantial training and research grants from the NIMH, in a public climate sensitive to the problems of mental health, and through the efforts of often understaffed university departments of psychology, clinical psychologists began to be produced in ever increasing numbers. A few pessimists were sure that the market would soon be glutted but such was not to be the case. No matter how many clinical psychologists were produced, there were never enough to fill the openings which had been created for the product—first in the VA but soon in other agencies of the federal and state government, in private agencies and elsewhere. We have grown rapidly not only in numbers but also in status, in the opportunity to serve and in income. By these criteria, ours is a success story without counterpart in the history of professions.

THE KELLY REPORT

So much for background; now let us see what is known about clinical psychologists of the present day. Several attempts have been made to discover what kind of people practicing clinical psychologists are. The most exhaustive was made by Kelly, who sent out a questionnaire to the members of the Clinical Division of the APA, Division 12.

Kelly (1960) summarized his findings in terms of where clinical psychologists work, what they do, and whom they serve, as follows:

> **Where Do Clinical Psychologists Work?**
>
> Almost exactly half of the respondents reported that their primary work setting is what might be labeled a medical one: general hospitals, mental hospitals, and clinics each account for approximately 15% of our membership and medical schools for another 7%. The next most common setting is a university or college, accounting for one-fifth of our members. Third in order of frequency is the private practice setting with 17%. At the other end of the scale, Division members are least likely to be found in a public school (3%), industry (3%), or the Armed forces (1½%). The remaining fifth of our respondents checked "other" work settings: including such varied things as School or Hospital for Mentally Retarded, a city, county, state or federal agency, nursery school, counselling office, residential treatment center, psychoanalytic institute, juvenile court, Salvation Army, correctional institution, Highway Patrol School and a publishing company.
>
> In view of the fact that the modal clinical psychologist holds two or more remunerative positions it is of interest to combine the responses of those indicating primary, secondary, or tertiary appointments for each type of setting. Nearly three-fourths of all respondents report some type of work appointment involving clinical psychology in a medical setting (clinics 28%, mental hospitals 18%, medical schools 13%, and general hospitals 12%).
>
> Slightly over half of our members (54% to be exact) list private practice as their primary, secondary, or tertiary work setting. For about a third of these it is primary and for the other two-thirds secondary or tertiary. Forty percent of our members have some association with the faculty of the college or university; about half of these hold a primary appointment in such a setting and the other half are on a part-time appointment. Only 6% of our membership indicate any contact with public schools, only 4% with industry and only 3% with the Armed Forces.

What Do Clinical Psychologists Do?

With this background let us now turn to the question of the distribution of professional time among the several functions performed by our members. Here again we asked respondents to indicate the role or function to which they devoted the highest proportion of their time, the second highest, and the third highest. At the top of the list is intensive psychotherapy: 54% of all members reporting this as one of their functions; for 31% it is their primary function. (The corresponding figures for Counseling are 11% and 5%.) Next in order of frequency is diagnosis and clinical assessment. Exactly half of the respondents indicated that they spend some time in diagnosis or assessment; for one out of six this is the function to which they devoted the largest share of their time. Supervision is reported as an activity by ¼ of our colleagues but for only 5% or one out of twenty is it a primary function. Experimental research is also reported as an activity by one out of four members; it is a primary function for only one out of ten. About 5% of all respondents reported still other types of functions including: scholarly writing, clinical research, milieu therapy, program development, systems training, factory management, editorial, advising and consulting.

Whom Do Clinical Psychologists Serve?

Because of the variety of work settings and different role functions of clinical psychologists, we asked respondents to indicate the types of clients or patients with whom they spend the most time, next most and third most. The results are unequivocal. The services of the majority of clinical psychologists (55%) are directed primarily toward the adults in our society. By contrast only 17% work primarily with children. Another 9% of the respondents report college students are the most typical clients. Just as we found relatively few clinicians reporting the public school as their primary work setting, only 4% reported school children as their primary type of client and a bare 1% of our psychologists serve primarily alcoholics, juvenile delinquents, and criminals in our society. When we combine the three categories of patients seen most, next most, and third most, the rank ordering of the different types of clients remains essentially the same. Nearly 15% of all respondents felt it necessary to check "other" types of patients or clients. These included "normal," pre-school, management personnel, physically handicapped, mentally retarded, adolescents and workers.

Summarizing the data with respect to work settings, functions and types of clients, we may say that the members of Division 12 are most likely to be found in a medical setting (clinic, general hospital, mental hospital, or medical school), to be working primarily with the adult patients and to be primarily engaged in intensive therapy, diagnosis or administration. On the other end of the scale members of Division 12 are least likely to be found in the Armed Forces, industry or public schools, least likely to be primarily concerned with undergraduate teaching or scholarly writing and least likely to be primarily concerned with alcoholics, juvenile delinquents, criminals, or school children. Unfortunately, comparable information regarding the pattern of practice among the present day psychiatrists is not available but I strongly suspect that a similar pattern would characterize the professional activities of our psychiatric colleagues. If this surmise is correct, it is not surprising that the emergence of clinical psychology as a profession has been accompanied by considerable interprofessional conflict.

CLINICS

Let us turn now to a consideration of some of the day-by-day activities of psychologists in clinics, hospitals, and private practice.

A general statement of the activities of psychologists in clinics has recently been given by Greening and Bugental (1962):

> Since the early days of clinical psychology, members of this profession have found themselves continually presented with new roles to fill, roles for which formal training programs could not always prepare them adequately. In fact, it might be maintained that the one major task of a clinical psychologist in a clinic is continually to redefine his responsibilities and ways of fulfilling them on the basis of newly discovered knowledge and problems.
>
> Having stressed the importance of this general function, let us now attempt to list the specific functions of psychologists in clinics:
>
> Psychodiagnosis
> Psychotherapy
> Research
> Training and teaching
> Analysis and facilitation of intrastaff group dynamics
> Administration and policy making
> Personnel selection
> Community relations and education
> Participation in professional organizations
> Learning and self-development

It is hoped that this is a comprehensive and up-to-date list, but probably somewhere there are resourceful psychologists who have already thought of even more functions to include in their busy schedules.

It would seem quite unnecessary to spell out the activities involved in most of the functions listed above. However, those described as "analysis and facilitation of intrastaff group dynamics" and as "community relations and education" may merit more detailed comment. Greening and Bugental describe their experiences in these areas as follows:

> Clinical psychologists traditionally focus on individual personality dynamics. Yet they usually do this while working as part of a group, such as groups of colleagues in a clinic. The convenient assumption is easily made that psychologists are mature people whose understanding of human nature enables them to get along well with co-workers. The combination of their individualistic orientation and a group setting, however, can lead to some surprising disruptions of smooth clinic functions. Although the knowledge and skills of clinical psychologists pertaining to personality dynamics may be valuable in this context, they may not be enough to deal with the explicit and implicit group forces that derive from more than individual personalities. When such forces disrupt the efficiency of a clinic, *psychologists who specialize in group dynamics and social psychology can be of great use.* They can bring to bear results and methods drawn from studies of leadership, decision-making processes, and small-group interaction.
>
> A realistic analysis of role and status patterns in a clinic may reveal an organizational and social structure that has profound but unrecognized influence on clinic functioning (Grusky, 1957). Well-designed "gripe sessions" may help reveal and solve some group tensions; a reorganization of authority and communications channels may help create greater congruence between supposed and actual procedures.
>
> There are many of these elusive variables that affect the harmony and efficiency of a clinic. When a clinic has representatives of several professions, complications may indeed arise (Zander et al., 1957). Pride and prestige are sometimes easily threatened in a field like mental health, which presents such difficult and complex problems. To reap the benefits of the often praised "team approach," special efforts are required. Because of the broad training available in graduate psychology programs in nonclinical as well as clinical areas, psychologists are here again in the unique position of having the flexibility but also the responsibility to contribute in a variety of ways to a clinic's functioning. However, it must be recognized that in the solution of delicate intrastaff tensions, the psychologist who is a member of that staff cannot serve as an impartial expert. In such instances, outside consultants are necessary.

How the staff of a clinic relates to the community is of great importance, for "clinics are not islands," as these authors conclude. They are located in communities and are designed to serve them. To maximize the effectiveness of this service, a clinic must make clear what it has to offer and how this can be of value to people. Effective treatment is greatly aided by early detection of problems and intelligent referral to an appropriate agency. *It is therefore necessary for the psychologist to function at times as an interpreter of clinic services to the general public, by means of talking to local groups, community leaders, and referral sources, such as teachers, physicians, and clergymen.* His aim should be to educate the public, not only concerning clinics, but also concerning psychological knowledge and techniques in general. Many psychologists come to recognize speaking on mental hygiene topics as a regular part of their professional lives and as a worthwhile community contribution (Greening and Bugental, 1962).

INSTITUTIONS AND HOSPITALS

Is the distinction between a clinic, on the one hand, and institutions or hospitals, on the other, a valid one? Certain essential differences have been noted by Klebanoff (1962):

> The psychologist in an institution performs essentially the same major functions as his colleague in a clinic: he assesses personality, he attempts to modify behavior, and he carries out research. There are, however, two important differences between most clinics and most institutions. The inmate of an institution is just that: resident twenty-four hours a day during a variable period of confinement. The clinic patient lives at home, and, even if he is receiving intensive

psychotherapy, spends only a small proportion of his time in the clinical setting. The second significant difference is related to the first. Most inmates of institutions occupy their roles involuntarily, as a result of antisocial behavior or because of the seriousness of their malfuctioning. The clinic patient seeks the services of the clinic voluntarily and is able to terminate them at will. Many of the specific variations in the general functions performed by psychologists in both clinical and institutional settings arise out of these differences between their client populations.

In the interests of specificity, we include here descriptions of the functions of the psychologist in three types of institutions: (1) a training and research mental hospital, (2) a neurological institute, and (3) a rehabilitation institute.

Functions of a Psychologist in a Training and Research Mental Hospital

The activities of the psychologist are in the following five general categories.

Service. Service activities include both psychological testing and psychotherapy. Psychological testing is done at the request of the patient's psychotherapist. Referral is made by means of the attached referral form. Services are not available for routine testing of all patients. A written report is submitted by the psychologist, although the findings are also discussed personally with the referring source and are presented in staff conferences. The written report becomes part of the patient's permanent record.

Both individual and group psychotherapy are conducted by psychologists. Responsibility for the medical care of the patient is delegated to a resident psychiatrist. Psychotherapy is supervised by supervising psychiatrists of the hospital staff. Patients are generally seen for two to three hours per week.

Training. Since the institute is an active training center for psychiatric residents, psychology interns, and medical students, a large proportion of the staff psychologist's function concerns teaching and training.

Intradepartmentally, he is responsible for supervision of intern training and of junior psychologists. Extradepartmentally, he is responsible for instructing psychiatric residents in the nature of psychological tests and for giving lectures in clinical psychology in the postgraduate training course in neurology and psychiatry. Both senior psychologists also engage in medical school teaching, particularly in a second-year course in psychopathology.

Research. Psychologists carry on both individual and collaborative research. An example of collaborative research is an ongoing study on diverse overt psychopathology in identical twins, which involves a senior psychiatrist, a resident psychiatrist, and a clinical psychologist. One psychologist is also collaborating with a psychiatrist on a monograph pertaining to psychopathology for medical students.

Administration. Administrative activities include assigning referrals and preparing routine administrative reports, annual progress reports, etc.

Professional activities. Some proportion of the psychologist's time also involves professional activities outside the hospital setting, e.g., participation in conventions, ABEPP certification, and program planning for professional societies (Carr, 1963).

Functions of a Psychologist in a Neurological Institute

Psychological responsibilities at the Neurological Institute of the Presbyterian Hospital, Columbia Presbyterian Medical Center, are in four major areas: service, training, teaching, and research.

Service to patients. Service to patients includes the administration of psychological tests and the interpretation of test data for the purposes of diagnosis, prognosis, and recommendations for treatment. The kind of psychological evaluation which is given to each patient depends on the particular referral problem. Patients are referred by a staff physician, who states the presenting problem on a special psychological referral form. Among the referral problems frequently encountered are the question of differential diagnosis, usually between functional and organic states; the amount of interference in functioning attributable to organic factors; the identification of special emotional, sensory, motor, verbal, and experiential handicaps; and the suitability of the patient for possible psychotherapy.

The age range of the patients is extremely wide, extending from infants to advanced geriatric cases. Their problems include birth injuries, brain tumors and other chronic neurological disorders, mental deficiency, various types of convulsive disorders, alcoholism, and cerebral arteriosclerosis, as well as various organic and nonorganic neurotic and psychotic states.

Psychological services are available to both inpatients and outpatients from various sources, including the Child and Adult Neurological and Seizure Clinics, the Speech and Hearing Clinic, the Plastic Surgery Clinic, and the Private Pavillion. Patients are also seen from the hospital's private psychiatric service.

Training. For the most part, psychological tests at the Neurological Institute are administered by junior psychologists, each of whom is individually supervised on each case by a certified psychologist. Training is also provided for the interns in the predoctoral training program in clinical psychology conducted in the department of psychiatry. Each intern spends approximately three months of the training year at the Neurological Institute, where he evaluates both children and adults under careful, individual supervision. Training facilities include three testing rooms with large one-way-vision screens, which are audio-equipped. This equipment is also available for use in the medical, nursing, social work, and occupational and physical therapy training programs.

Teaching. The chief psychologist at the Neurological Institute teaches a formal course in the department of physical medicine and rehabilitation, in which the purpose and interpretation of clinical tests are stressed. In addition to her teaching role with the psychologists, she also participates in a number of teaching programs with various allied disciplines.

Research. The chief psychologist and a number of others assigned to the Neurological Institute are connected with an extensive investigation into the incidence of neurological abnormalities in infants and young children. They are also participating in a continuing study of the personality features associated with conversion hysteria, migraine, and various types of ulcers. At present, areas of major research interest also include studies of the learning behavior of retarded children and the construction and development of special test procedures for evaluating abilities in children with severe physical, mental, and emotional handicaps (Schucman, 1963; Thetford, 1963).

Functions of a Psychologist in a Rehabilitation Institute

Psychologists are employed to give psychological services as part of a social adjustment program. The duties here are almost indentical to those listed in connection with research and training in a mental hospital. This is necessitated by the fact that 50 per cent of the physically disabled are in need of adjustment services more than services related to physical restoration.

Psychologists are employed on a mental hygiene research project. There are no administrative or teaching duties associated with this. They are, however, responsible for (1) research methodology and (2) staff in-service training.

A director of research is responsible for (1) reviewing the service program for researchable leads which may point the way to better services, (2) consulting with any staff member interested in research, (3) formulating research proposals and directing research activities, and (4) lecturing on research in rehabilitation when nationwide seminars are held.

A director of professional education has the following program: (1) He coordinates all training programs offered in medical, vocational, and social adjustment services; these programs may be formal courses in conjunction with affiliating universities, clinical traineeships, fieldwork observation, on-the-job training, internships at the graduate level, and workshops in specialized areas; (2) he analyzes current programs in terms of the special needs of participants and the optimum use of staff facilities, and he develops long-range training plans consistent with the expanding demands of rehabilitation and the planned expansion of institute resources; (3) he integrates the services of the institute with the affiliated university; (4) he coordinates arrangements for joint programs with universities, government agencies, and other rehabilitation facilities; and (5) he serves as an instructor when appropriate and when he is competent to do so, and he orients foreign visitors to the institute's role in rehabilitation in the United States (Robinault, 1963).

PRIVATE PRACTICE

In an attempt to discover how the private practitioner divided his time, to what extent his services were diagnostically or therapeutically oriented, and what proportion of his day went to clinic services despite his "independent" status, Harrower (1961) sent a questionnaire to 70 colleagues in the New York City area. This questionnaire was concerned with many facets of the practitioner's life, but the question relevant to our topic here was: "Can you give a brief sketch of your workday or workweek?"

It will be seen from the brief reports that follow that the schedules are highly individualistic or "custom-made." One can say that no two are really alike, despite the fact that the same basic services are rendered by all concerned.

It is our belief that the differences between independent practice and work within institutions and clinics have to do essentially with *greater flexibility in the work schedule.* The individual chooses to go into independent practice on the basis of his particular needs, and he is willing to accept certain uncertainties, both financial and professional.

Opportunities for service and for research exist in both frames of reference, but only within the "independent" setting can the individual choose how to distribute his time and efforts.

The following answers were given to the question: "Can you give a brief sketch of your workday or workweek?"

> During the past few years, I have been more and more involved in my full-time job at the Clinic, so that at the moment, I have only evening hours and weekends available as psychotherapist and consultant in private practice [in practice more than thirty-five years].

> Analytic patients from six to seven hours daily; conferences with parents a few times a week, perhaps two or three hours weekly but varies with type of problem. Recently half of the patients are adult, the others—children or adolescents. Previously one-third were adults; Freudian Psychoanalysis is the method. But with children, where necessary, educational help given during resistance period when demanded. Occasionally now, a parent may report a child's progress in "normal" growth process and advice and insight is worked out to help over the difficulties that arise. A few hours a day during the week given to supervision of psychologists' work with their patients. Usually the regular patient comes from five to three hours weekly; adults come five or four hours. In recent years, I have made rare exceptions for children who live at a distance or are at boarding school and have seen them once or twice a week [in practice thirty-one years].

> I spend about eight hours a week with a private agency where I primarily train Fellows in Psychology as well as trainees in Psychiatry and Social Work for whom I give a series of seminars. I also test infants several hours a week for two adoption agencies. The balance of my time is given over to private work with patients, some of it diagnostic evaluation and some of it in a therapeutic relationship. Also research whenever possible [in practice twenty-seven years].

> Two afternoons and one evening a week (approximately 14 hours) are devoted to community clinic work. In one clinic I conduct group psychotherapy. In the second clinic I coordinate and supervise a group psychotherapy program. At least six to eight hours a week are devoted to teaching in the graduate psychology department of a local university. Three afternoons and three mornings a week are spent in my private office practicing both individual and group psychotherapy. My patient load is diversified. I carry patients on a three times a week and on a twice a week basis [in practice twenty-six years].

> One morning a week testing. The other mornings I keep free for writing and research. Afternoons I see patients for therapy and psychoanalysts in training for supervision. Some evenings I teach but not more than once a week [in practice twenty-four years].

> Over the years changes in schedules always adjusted to the needs of the family (such as extremes working from 6–12:00 PM daily or three days on and three days off). At present three long days, two short days, two days off. Work at present: fifty per cent individual analysis (including therapy and guidance); ten per cent group analytic therapy; twenty-five per cent supervision, teaching, leadership of professional work-

shop; fifteen per cent professional organization—administration and research [in practice twenty-two years].

My private practice is exclusively psychodiagnostic, and when self-referred patients are seen it is with the understanding that they will be referred to a psychotherapist if indicated. I see an average of six patients a week and make it a rule to submit a report within three days. Three-quarters of my week are devoted to teaching and training activities within the organization (six hours of lectures and seminars with psychologists and psychiatric residents and fellows) involving direct supervision of cases, progress interviews, administrative functions, and participation in therapy and research conferences. Outside activities comprise consultation work with VA, public speaking, and participation in community activities by serving on boards and committees [in practice twenty-one years].

Mine is a very small private practice. I spend an average of about two to three hours per week, mostly Saturday morning and an occasional evening; usually one or two patients in once a week therapy; occasional diagnostic testing or a consultation [in practice twenty-one years].

Two days are spent at the clinic. The other three days are devoted half to private patients and half to group patients. New patients are given psychological tests. I try to keep some time for my family of four children and nine grandchildren and always serve my husband's needs when necessary [in practice twenty-one years].

Currently 16 "regular" patient hours, scattered; sporadic counseling and testing cases; articles, lectures, etc. For the first time in years no continuing research or teaching [in practice twenty-three years].

Psychotherapy hours: 8:30–12:15; reading, correspondence, etc.: 1:00–3:00; psychotherapy hours: 3:00–6:15 PM. Work week: Three days in New York City, three days in suburbs, alternate days [in practice over twenty years].

My work is principally in large national programs. My private practice is "week-end" for the most part—largely diagnostic but occasionally I do supportive therapy when requested by physician [in practice over twenty years].

My supervisory position at the hospital with which I have been associated all of my professional career, occupies most of the midweek day hours. I am involved in teaching, and supervision of diagnostic, therapy, and research activities. I devote about fifteen hours weekly to therapy and occasional consultation—in private practice. I am always involved in research and correlated reading, that is very time consuming. Some time is spent in resolving to cut down schedule and relax [in practice over twenty years].

Each day at least one patient is examined with parts of a comprehensive psychodiagnostic test battery, with five or six others seen in psychotherapeutic sessions. Two mornings are devoted to teaching a course to student nurses on behavioral sciences; two mornings to writing reports and a book and to interdisciplinary researches [in practice twenty years].

Approximately seven patients twice a week. Two groups. Half day teaching and supervising [in practice twenty years].

My work week is quite involved. The major part of my time I spend as the University Director of a clinical psychology training program. In this program I teach courses and seminars, supervise theses, diagnosis and therapy. I do considerable amount of consulting to the VA, private clinics and schools. I conduct a small amount of research and maintain private practice of about two diagnostic workups a month and about a ten patient load in therapy. I am also quite involved and busy in professional organizations including the presidency of a national organization and a state organization [in practice nearly twenty years].

Three days a week I carry a group therapy session of one hour-and-a-half, in addition to about seven individual hours of therapy; two and one-half days of individual therapy, so that work week averages thirty-two individual hours and three group sessions [in practice almost twenty years].

Pattern is fairly stable. I see about five patients in the morning and five in the afternoon. I begin about 8:30 AM and end about 6:30 PM. Between 12 noon and 2:30 on four days and the entire fifth day (Wednesday) I spend my time at an analytic treatment and training center where I hold a high administrative office. A two-hour period every other Friday is devoted to consultation in a VA hospital. Patients generally come three times a week, for psychoanalytic psychotherapy [in practice nineteen years].

Work day runs about fourteen hours—six to eight hours in clinic work and teaching. Rest of time either in diagnostic testing or therapy [in practice eighteen years].

Since no two work days are alike, it is not possible to answer this question. Approximately three patients are seen for diagnostic evaluation and a report submitted within two weeks. Four patients are seen on a once-a-week basis for therapy (children). Saturday mornings are devoted to emotionally disturbed blind children. Mornings and the major portion of the afternoons are devoted to the community hospital clinic [in practice over fifteen years].

During the week I have thirty-two patients in therapy hours; five hours of supervision of therapy trainees; four hours of meetings in a clinic and training school; five hours administration and one-and-a-half hours teaching in the same clinic and training school; one day is spent writing [in practice fifteen years].

This fall I start with a Negro group, a white group (therapy), two nights of teaching (Adult Education, Personality Development and Basic Psychology); psychoanalytic patients and marriage counseling couples in day. Also do research, publish technical and popular articles in psychotherapy and marriage counseling fields—two books so far [in practice fifteen years].

Approximately seven patients a day for analysis or therapy Monday through Friday. Once a week teaching in a psychoanalytic training school. Very rarely (if time allows) diagnostic work-up for other analysts. Whenever time permits—research work and writing on the basis of my own material [in practice fifteen years].

The pattern is a relatively consistent one, since most of my work involves long-term psychotherapy: My work day, Monday through Friday, is from nine to six, with some variation, at times, according to patient needs. One evening is devoted to teaching a graduate course in psychology, and one evening to attending a therapy group. I am at the college, doing counseling and administrative work about four hours each day, and see patients for about the same average amount of time, plus carrying one therapy group [in practice about fifteen years].

Psychoanalytic therapy only. Three or four morning sessions. Three or four late afternoon-evening sessions. Flexibility of schedule and frequency is encouraged for mutual personal conveniences and on principle of patient's self-pacing of his therapy [in practice fifteen years].

My time is taken up with psychoanalytic work. I carry an average of forty weekly sessions. In addition, I do supervision and control three to five hours weekly. I teach psychoanalysis in a seminar two hours weekly. About three hours weekly are devoted to work with schizophrenic children. The balance are adults [in practice over fourteen years].

On the average: about thirty hours of doing treatment, about five hours of doing supervision and control work. When teaching about two hours a week plus about two hours of preparation. The rest of the time (about 35–40 hours of routine work) is spent in reading, writing, housekeeping, entertainment [in practice fourteen years].

Two days weekly are spent as consultant (examination, interviews, analysis of personnel files) to two large community agencies; one is spent in research with an alcoholic-vocational project; the remaining time goes to whatever diagnostic work, interviewing and counseling come up; if at all possible, I keep the weekends free; often, however, appointments must be made for at least Saturday mornings [in practice fourteen years].

One day a week is devoted to my work as supervising psychologist at Postgraduate Center for Psychotherapy. Two mornings are devoted to research, teaching and occasional diagnostic testing. The rest of my time, i.e., sixteen hours per week, are devoted to patient-sessions [in practice fourteen years].

My teaching contract, full time, grants me two afternoons for private practice. Besides, I carry some evening patients [in practice fourteen years].

One to two days per week averaging seven to fourteen hours are reserved for private practice. One diagnostic interview with follow-up parent interview, phone calls and recording fill the time [in practice thirteen years].

I spend six to eight hours, four days a week in doing psychotherapy. The fifth day I use for diagnostic testing and for increased visits for those who need them. Usually patients are seen twice a week unless otherwise indicated when they may be seen as many as seven. Mornings are spent in study of cases or readings, in the field, out of the field, and just keeping up with the news. Until now my private practice was at a minimum of twenty hours a week because I had an extensive teaching program which sometimes was a full morning program. I taught all the psychologies, mental hygiene, testing, and a few educational subjects [in practice thirteen years].

Usually I have six or seven analytic sessions per day five days a week. In the course of my work day I keep two hours free for preparation of courses, reading and some writing. I also teach on a part time basis in a doctoral clinical training program. Usually I give one clinical seminar and another more theoretical course in the area of psychotherapy during the course of the year [in practice thirteen years].

Seeing patients takes up some forty hours per week. Of these, about forty percent are spent with children and adolescents, the remainder with adults. Administrative and research activities at the Clinic take up some fifteen to twenty additional hours [in practice twenty years].

The working schedule changed over the years with more and more time spent in private testing and especially therapy as the years went by until part time clinic job abandoned altogether. In last few years, two full days a week spent in doing therapy (average of 15 to 20 patient hours. Four days spent in testing (2 to 3 patients tested a week), report writing and conferences with parents of children tested. One evening a week teaching at the University and one evening correcting papers, etc. One afternoon (approximately 4 hours a week) doing paid research for private persons (grant basis) [in practice twelve years].

I carry on a full work day in a combined hospital-clinic setting five days a week. My private practice is conducted about twenty hours a week, evenings and Saturday. I do psychotherapy, diagnosis by testing and consultation in private practice. Additional hours are required for report writing. In addition I have two hours of therapy supervision and about six hours of clinical coursework [in practice twelve years].

Half-time consultant to the United Epilepsy Association as Director of Program; duties primarily administrative and planning public education and community service programs in epilepsy. Private practice limited to psychotherapy [in practice eleven years].

The basic work week involves approximately twenty hours of psychotherapy, ten to twenty hours a week of psychodiagnostic testing, evaluation and report writing. Approximately five hours a week of consultation —usually with parents around diagnostic studies of children or adolescents. Approximately five hours a week to outside project activity usually of a research nature, although at some times involving direct consultation to agencies. Approximately twelve hours a week to a public clinic. Other time is spent in pursuing a research interest in delinquency psychotherapy and in participating in developing a training institute in this field [in practice eleven years].

Thirty-five hours of private practice of which about six are in diagnostic testing, the rest in individual psychotherapy. Six hours (two mornings) testing and consulting, and some research for a private social agency. Four hours weekly supervising therapists (of all disciplines) in the psychiatric division of a public hospital [in practice eleven years].

I devote about fifteen hours weekly to my private practice which is largely a therapy practice, with occasional referrals for psychodiagnostics and personality evaluation. Another sixteen hours of my time is spent at an out-patient middle-income clinic, where the division in terms of hours of therapy and testing is similar to that in my own office [in practice eleven years].

Mornings are devoted to some university teaching as well as supervision of psychotherapy practice in a community agency. One morning I spend as consultant in a multidisciplinary research undertaking in the field of juvenile delinquency. Afternoons are used for the private practice of psychotherapy [in practice eleven years].

I work eight to nine hours daily. My patients come from five to twice a week. They are mostly adults but I also see a few children [in practice over ten years].

Administration and supervision of psychology department at hospital; individual diagnostic and therapy consultations; lead two therapy seminars; consultation and writing in re two research projects; average of four to five therapy patients four evenings per week in private office; occasional consultations; administration clinical psychology teaching program for medical students; lecture one hour weekly to psychiatric residents; lead staff conferences [in practice over ten years].

Approximately thirty-five analytic hours; about one diagnostic a month; teaching about two to four hours a week; supervision of trainees, two hours a week [in practice over ten years].

Most typically six or seven therapeutic hours with patients, a couple of hours of driving to offices and return. Some time spent on phone with patients or relatives, referring psychologists or collaborating practitioners. Several times per week have session with control analyst. One evening per week typical for committee or professional activity. Also teach psychology at local college one night per week [in practice over ten years].

Usually about ten patients are seen three or four times a week on a regular basis. Two beginning analysts are seen for an hour once a week for control. Two evening hours a week are devoted to teaching a course in an analytic training program [in practice over ten years].

I have devoted approximately half-time to private practice, doing psychoanalytic therapy with adults, and group therapy. I have about twenty patients in private practice. Half-time has been devoted to clinic patients for individual and group therapy, and to the program of courses, seminars, lectures, supervision, and controls, on a formal, organized basis. I have currently about ten hours of clinic work with patients, and five hours of supervision. It is a long day to have a combined private and clinic practice, and my hours begin at 7:00 AM and do not usually end till 9:00 PM [in practice over ten years].

10:00 AM–5:00 PM (Daily except Tuesdays and weekends): Director and Clinical Psychologist of Mental Retardation Diagnostic Clinic. About 20 per cent of time in clinical diagnostic work; ten per cent parent counseling; seventy per cent administration and supervisory. Tuesdays, evenings and/or Saturdays: About ten hours private practice; about fifty per cent therapy cases and fifty per cent diagnostic [in practice over ten years].

Half time (twenty hours) in a hospital setting attached to medical school doing teaching and research; twenty hours in private therapy; ten hours a week supervision and consultation (latter varies with referrals) [in practice ten years].

Variable. I limit practice to eight hours per week. Teaching, research, editing and writing, and commitments to professional associations more than fill up the balance [in practice ten years].

I am employed full time in a large mental hygiene clinic, where fifty per cent of my time is taken up with seeing patients in therapy and diagnostic testing. The remainder of my time is devoted to the directing of a training program in clinical psychology for a yearly average of ten to twelve trainees at the third and fourth year levels. Privately, I see an average of two patients twice a week, on two evenings a week, for therapy, and diagnostic batteries as time and demand permit [in practice about ten years].

The major proportion of my time is spent in research and clinical activity in the clinic with which I am affiliated. At the present time no therapy cases are being carried; diagnostic evaluations and consultations may vary between one a week and one in several weeks [in practice ten years].

Four patients are seen twice a week. I reserve two weekday mornings for my private practice. The remainder of the week is devoted to teaching and clinic practice at the University [in practice ten years].

Testing and diagnostic referral for school. Patients on a weekly and some on a biweekly basis [in practice about ten years].

I am in my office from 11:00 AM until 6:00 PM seeing either individual patients or conducting groups. (My practice is solely therapeutic.) In open hours, I try to catch up on the literature or I prepare a paper for publication or for a meeting. I am on several committees in membership organizations which takes more time than I like [in practice nine years].

I see patients, one, two or three times a week: two groups. Since my clientele mostly work in the daytime, it is a long day, with holes in the middle. One day a week at a Clinic, for research and some patients; meetings. Collaborative research with interdisciplinary groups, evening, weekend. Professional meetings often pile up [in practice eight to nine years].

Three full days and Saturday mornings and two late evenings per week are spent seeing patients. Remainder of time devoted to directing research project of which I am principal investigator at university and to professional meetings, etc. Occasional consulting at clinics and home for disturbed children [in practice eight years].

I consider my position a full-time one. It involves supervision of other psychologists and particularly psychology interns in diagnostic evaluations; group therapy; opportunity for clinical research; and some teaching in a large medical school. While my responsibilities extend to all these areas, there is great flexibility in my schedule [in practice eight years].

The pattern is constant. Morning hours are devoted to teaching or clinic work, (supervision-administration). Afternoons and early evening to private practice of psychotherapy. This occurs five days per week [in practice eight years].

I work four days a week, usually making my first appointment at 10:00 AM and my last at 7:00 PM—with breaks in between, of course. I do no diagnostic work, but chiefly long-term psychoanalytically-oriented therapy, plus occasional consultations and short-term contacts. I have two groups meeting once a week for 100 minutes each, one being a co-group which I conduct with a male therapist. In addition, I give four hours a week without remuneration to supervising beginning therapists at two community clinics where the therapists are unpaid trainees. I teach a course in psychoanalytic theory at a training institute [in practice seven years].

Part of my day is occupied in clinical and administrative work in a college setting. The balance of each day is occupied in several therapy sessions with patients, and with two or more hours devoted to service to organizational work for professional associations in psychology. Therapy sessions are generally of an hour's duration, and cover from sixteen to twenty hours a week [in practice seven years].

I spend about two hours each morning at the hospital doing clinical work and teaching. One afternoon is devoted to out-patient psychiatric clinic work (about four hours). In addition, I teach one course in psychotherapy training school. The remainder of the week is devoted to private practice, professional organizational activities, etc. [in practice about seven years].

Half-time in a private out-patient psychiatric clinic, the second half in private practice, diagnostic work-up and therapy [in practice over five years].

Four full days at Community Clinic (children and adults). Two to four hour evenings in private practice. At least one evening per week for professional meeting or consultation with psychiatrist. One day per week—education, research or consultation with psychologist [in practice five years].

I see about thirty patients a week for from one to two hours each, for marriage counseling. In addition, I teach one or more classes a week in preparation for marriage, and conduct seminars for ministers and adult community leaders in marital counseling techniques and sex education. I also write for approximately one day a week [in practice five years].

Most of every day is spent doing basic research on interpersonal processes. I see patients two to three evenings a week and on Saturday mornings. Some of my patients I see three times a week, some two times a week, and some once a week [in practice five years].

Approximately twenty hours a week are spent at the university in a clinic setting with patients, students and colleagues. Approximately fifteen to twenty hours are in my office with patients in therapy. I have arranged to divide my week by having two full days at the university clinic, and two days at my office. The fifth day I spend one-half day at each place. Currently I am seeing at my office two patients, three times a week; four patients, twice a week; two patients, once a week [in practice four years].

Three mornings a week are currently devoted to work in two private schools. In one, I serve as "Coordinator" of the interdisciplinary guidance department, in another as consultant to teachers and parents about problems of children. Remainder of time (including one evening) is devoted to regularly scheduled hours with adults in psychotherapy or analysis . . . approximately 20 hours per week as a maximum. . . . I find it imperative not to overload my scheduling of clients. At least one evening per week for professional meetings or seminar work [in practice four years].

Have been working two days at a college, one day to two at consulting firm, remainder of time writing a book and seeing few therapy patients, not more than two concurrently. Teach two nights per week at another college [in practice three years].

I have a full-time position at which I work five days a week. Two evenings a week are spent at a clinic where I obtain wider experience in psychotherapy and am supervised. I have a few hours during the week (including some on Saturday) for individual psychotherapy sessions with patients seen once or twice weekly. I also participate in a research project, involving three or four diagnostic appraisals per month [in practice three years].

THE ROLE OF THE PSYCHODIAGNOSTICIAN

Certain core experiences that are imperative for optimum functioning as a *psychodiagnostician,* regardless of the setting, may be summarized as follows:

1. He should be able to establish graceful and appropriate rapport with the individual he is testing—his partner in the diagnostic situation. He should feel equally at home with old and young, rich and poor, native and foreign-born, and he should have become used to experiences involving persons out of touch with reality and should have adapted his own procedures in various ways to meet the difficulties imposed by illness or disability which may confront the patient.

2. He should have at his command a wide variety of test instruments. He should be sufficiently well versed in these and sufficiently familiar with their procedure so that he conducts them effortlessly and so that he may make, without feeling that he is trespassing, certain minor alterations or adaptations to meet particular situations. He should also have developed a core battery of his own with which he is particularly happy and satisfied and which he can use sufficiently frequently so that, for comparative or research purposes, he begins to build up a backlog of uniform material.

3. He should know himself to the extent that this is possible; certainly he should be aware of his own biases and preferences and of his own particular sources of anxiety, the kind of self-knowledge which comes from some kind of experience in insight-giving therapeutic sessions. He should, furthermore, know his own performance in the projectives, so that he will not unconsciously ally himself with patients with similar psychodiagnostic patterns or, conversely, react with undue severity to the producers of test protocols diametrically opposite to his own. The point is rarely emphasized, but this author considers it of prime importance. The psychodiagnostician badly needs to understand his own productions on all the test instruments that he uses. Moreover, he should have the opportunity to go over and to discuss a report written on his test production by an experienced and wise psychodiagnostic practitioner. Unless this is done, he will find himself automatically assuming that somehow or other his own productions constitute a base line of normality. He will too readily read pathology into test profiles that are dissimilar to his own and, conversely, will find condoning circumstances where striking similarities pertain.

4. The psychodiagnostician should have evolved a method of scoring, handling, and reporting his cases which can be done in a reasonable amount of time and without including and covering every possible angle of the case. He should find his own peculiar mode of expression, so that in writing a report he feels no more strain than he would in writing a letter to a good friend. He should be acutely aware that the purpose of the report is to communicate information. He should, in fact, to use a metaphor, be playing to an audience and not practicing his instrument in isolation.

Finally, he should be constantly aware of what meaning his words will have to the individual to whom they are addressed. He should steer clear of explicit psychological or projective jargon but, conversely, not rush headlong into medical terminology, which may not really be a meaningful mode of expression for him.

THE ROLE OF THE THERAPIST

It is much less easy to epitomize the prototype of the *psychologist as therapist,* for, as Greening and Bugental have stated:

> The role of psychologists in the practice of psychotherapy has been the focus of much discussion and controversy. At one extreme there has been the position that psychotherapy should be practiced by psychologists only under strict medical supervision; at the other extreme has been the claim for complete autonomy by the psychologist in the practice of psychotherapy. At least three points can be noted: (1) it has been increasingly demonstrated that psychologists can make valuable and sometimes unique contributions to psychotherapy; (2) psychologists are actively involved in psychotherapy

in a wide variety of hospital, clinic, and independent practice settings; and (3) effective collaborative relationships have been worked out between psychologists and physicians in numerous instances. Effective collaboration requires the psychologist to keep in mind the stated policies of the APA that he is ". . . expected to establish and maintain effective intercommunication with a psychologically oriented physician" but ". . . should not compromise the professional standards of psychology or his freedom to pursue his profession."

As long as concepts of "disease" and "illness" predominate in our thinking about problems of emotional adjustment, medical training or supervision may seem essential in the practice of psychotherapy. Many medical as well as nonmedical therapists, however, have cast doubt on the meaningfulness of concepts such as mental "illness" and on the value of a medical monopoly in the field of psychotherapy (Saul, 1958; Szasz, 1960). The fact is that psychologists are actively and permanently involved in psychotherapy, and therefore the problem to be dealt with realistically is how to bring their competence to its highest possible level (Blau, 1959; Cook, 1957; Grossman et al., 1954).

Not only has the rapid growth of the therapeutically minded clinical psychologist evoked interprofessional tensions, but also there is a real danger of rift between the academically oriented and the service-oriented psychologist within psychology itself. The interests of psychologists involved in the science of their discipline and in basic research and of those concerned with the problems of a growing service-oriented profession have at times clashed head on. Academicians and clinicians have looked at each other and asked the same question: "Are you also a psychologist?"

The future activities of clinical psychologists in their therapeutic role, both in private practice and in institutions, will, to some extent, depend on the direction the training for psychotherapy takes in the coming years. Many highly competent therapists are at work, but their training has, to some extent, been catch-as-catch-can. In the "early" years, that is, the late 1930s and early 1940s, it was virtually impossible to secure analytic training, for example, except in a somewhat black-market fashion. Yet, almost all would agree that some form of personal analysis is imperative, perhaps even more so for the independent practitioner, who must always contend with a certain isolation which could increase his own vulnerability under certain conditions. The private practitioner must also cope much more directly with the question of fee, an important area, which must frequently be worked through analytically.

Somehow maturity must be attained in the sense of having met up with, and lived through, some inevitable experiences which fall to the lot of human beings, or, as has been well described elsewhere, the therapist must somehow attain a "clinical orientation with a respect for and first hand familiarity with the major crises of life (for example, birth, bereavement, suffering, death)" combined with a "deep ethical sense of responsibility for the patient's welfare, desire to help others, sympathy and reflective understanding of motivations" (Holt, 1963).

How are such persons to be found, created, or allowed to develop? It is clear that the training of psychotherapists is one of the central issues facing clinical psychologists, regardless of where they work.

The acute realization of this led Holt and others to organize a conference on an ideal training program for psychotherapists, in which the fields of clinical psychology, social work, psychiatry, and psychoanalysis were represented. Since this conference may well be one of the foundation stones for future training of psychotherapists, a statement put out by its members is reproduced here:

Report of Conference on an Ideal Training Program for Psychotherapists[2]

The conference unanimously recognized the tremendous and growing social need and demand for psychotherapeutic services, which far outstrip the combined capacity of the existing mental health professions to satisfy them, either at present or in the foreseeable future. In the judgment of the conferees, this problem cannot be met only by means of attempts to increase the supply of psychotherapists; it was agreed that constructive social action to change the pathogenic aspects of society and other types of

[2] The conference on an ideal training program for psychotherapists was held under the auspices of New York University and with the support of the Aaron E. Norman Fund, at the Frank Jay Gould House, Ardsley-on-Hudson, N.Y., March 21–24, 1963. Thirty-two representatives of the fields of clinical psychology, social work, psychiatry, and psychoanalysis discussed a set of 14 working papers, and agreed on the following statements.

social-psychiatric public health measures were necessary, as well as further research into methods of prevention. Nevertheless, it is the duty of the professions concerned to do whatever possible to alleviate human suffering and facilitate the most creative functioning of the greatest number of persons. It was agreed that current methods of training psychotherapists are unsatisfactory both quantitatively and qualitatively: current types of professional preparation for the psychotherapeutic role are not only incomplete but contain elements that are at best redundant, at worst wasteful and interfering, besides providing an inadequate supply of competent therapists. Even so, there are all too many "psychotherapists" practicing today with a minimum of training of any relevant kind. The conferees were divided on whether first priority should be given to attempts to increase the numbers of psychotherapists or to attempt to raise the level of training.

There are three principal preparations for psychotherapeutic practice today: Psychiatric residency (preceded by medical school and often followed by psychoanalytic training); doctoral and post-doctoral programs in clinical psychology; and social work school (leading to the M.A. or Ph.D.) plus supervised work in social agency. It was agreed that each of these has valuable contributions to make to psychotherapeutic training, and that a program combining the best of each existing types would probably be preferable to anything that currently exists. A minority of the participants, including someone from each profession represented, found enough practical or theoretical objections to such a combined program to judge that present efforts should be concentrated on reorganizing and strengthening existing schools with more cross-disciplinary assistance and interaction.

It was unanimously agreed, however, that the case for a new, improved type of training was good enough to warrant its early trial in several pilot programs, in which psychoanalysts, social workers, psychiatrists, and clinical psychologists would form integrated faculties. Several types of pilot plans were proposed as being worth trying:

(a) An extended program involving *at least* 4 years of full-time graduate study and supervised experience, leading to a new doctoral degree and aiming at the highest level of competence.

(b) A briefer (about 2 years) and more modest program for older students producing graduates who could function in an institutional setting under supervision, as exemplified by the pioneering experiment at the National Institute of Mental Health by Margaret Rioch and her co-workers, which was the subject of a great deal of favorable discussion at the conference.

(c) A school that would stratify its offerings in several successive levels, the first bringing the student to approximately the degree of competence described in (b), the second producing a "general practitioner" of psychotherapy with a doctoral degree and facility in several techniques, and higher levels branching off into training for research, scientific and academic careers, or for such specialties as psychoanalysis or child psychotherapy. The point at which training in psychoanalytic technique should be introduced, however, was the subject of considerable discussion and several opinions.

The conference considered it important that all pilot projects operate in a flexible, experimental spirit, evaluating the effects of each innovation by means of systematic self-study, and continually exchanging experiences.

Several kinds of potential institutional settings for such programs were considered, the most seriously discussed being 1) a separate professional school in a university, 2) a cooperative joint endeavor by a department of psychiatry in a medical school, a graduate department of psychology, and a social work school, 3) a program primarily based in a medical school and teaching hospital. Though each of these possibilities had its supporters, the great majority of participants favored the first; and there was unanimity that the setting should be somewhere in a university containing a medical school, a graduate school with a psychology department, and a school of social service. A few conferees would require (at least for the first few classes in an experimental school for psychotherapy) a prerequisite graduate degree in social work, medicine, or psychology; a few considered graduation from a liberal arts college sufficient; and some wanted training in psychotherapy to be deferred until after a period of work following a bachelor's degree, such as in the Peace Corps or in some profession.

As far as curriculum was concerned, there was unanimous agreement that supervised experience in doing psychotherapy was of primary importance. The conference agreed that a substantial body of skills and knowledge from the biological and behavioral sciences and the humanities needed to be taught in courses. It was explicitly recognized that an important additional effect of course work and contact with faculty was the development of professional attitudes or sets, and that it was vital to produce in the students a clinical orientation with a respect for and first-hand familiarity with the major crises of life (for example, birth, bereavement, suffering, death) and with the body, a deep ethical sense of responsibility for the patient's welfare, desire to help others, empathy, and reflective understanding of motivation. The majority strongly favored personal treatment, at least for students in the more prolonged and intensive types of training. The attitudes of open-mindedness, curiosity, and search for improved ways of doing things, commonly associated with research, were generally considered highly desirable but it was the judgment of most of the conferees that formal research training was not necessarily the way to produce them. The emphasis of any new training program should be on turning out competent clinicians. It would be advantageous, however, to have research actively going on in the training institution, creating an atmosphere of inquiry, stimulating interest and providing opportunities for training those students who have relevant talent and desire.

It was recognized that schools of psychotherapy could and should be set up with various types of theoretical orientation, including the eclectic. Although most of the participants favored a curriculum built around psychoanalytic theory, everyone agreed that all major theories of personality, psychopathology and treatment should be included in the curriculum of every school.

Finally, there was discussion of the possibility that a new and independent profession of psychotherapy was coming into existence, and that founding professional schools outside the domain of any one contemporaneous profession might speed this process. Since many difficult problems would be entailed in the emergence of psychotherapy as a recognized profession, the conference concluded that consideration of these issues should go on without prejudgment one way or another and concurrently with accumulation of experience with experimental schools of the types described above.

REFERENCES

Blau, T. H. *Private practice in clinical psychology.* New York: Appleton-Century-Crofts, 1959.

Carr, A. C. Personal communication, 1963.

Cook, S. W. Beyond law and ethics: a proposal for collaboration in psychological practice. *Amer. Psychologist,* 1957, **12**, 267–272.

Finger, F. W. Psychologists in colleges and universities. In *The profession of psychology.* New York: Holt, 1962.

Fruchter, B. Psychologists in government agencies. In *The profession of psychology.* New York: Holt, 1962.

Greening, T., & Bugental, J. F. T. Psychologists in clinics. In *The profession of psychology.* New York: Holt, 1962.

Grossman, D., Rapkin, M., & Shapiro, S. Psychological service center. In E. A. Rubinstein & M. Lorr, *Survey of clinical practice in psychology.* New York: International Universities Press, 1954. Pp. 173–185.

Grusky, O. A case for the theory of familial role differentiation in small groups. *Soc. Forces,* 1957, 35, 209–217.

Harrower, Molly. *The practice of clinical psychology.* Springfield, Ill.: Charles C Thomas, 1961.

Harrower, Molly. Psychologists in independent practice. In *The profession of psychology.* New York: Holt, 1962.

Holt, R. Preliminary report of conference on an ideal training program for psychotherapists. Unpublished manuscript, 1963.

Huber, J. T. *Report writing in psychology and psychiatry.* New York: Harper & Row, 1961.

Katzell, R. A. Psychologists in industry. In *The profession of psychology.* New York: Holt, 1962.

Kelly, E. L. *Newsltr. Div. clin. Psychol., Amer. psychol. Ass.,* 1961, **14** (1), 1–12.

Klebanoff, S. G. Psychologists in institutions. In *The profession of psychology.* New York: Holt, 1962.

Klopfer, W. G. *The psychological report: use and communication of psychological findings.* New York: Grune & Stratton, 1960.

Newland, T. E. Psychologists in the schools. In *The profession of psychology.* New York: Holt, 1962.

Robinault, Isabel. Personal communication, 1963.

Saul, L. J. *Technique and practice of psychoanalysis.* Philadelphia: Lippincott, 1958.

Schucman, Helen. Personal communication, 1963.

Szasz, T. S. The myth of mental illness. *Amer. Psychologist,* 1960, **15** (2), 113–118.

Thetford, W. N. Personal communication, 1963.

Zander, A., Cohen, A. R., & Stotland, E. *Role relations in the mental health professions.* Ann Arbor, Mich.: Univer. of Michigan Press, 1957.

56

Relations with Other Professions

WILLIAM A. HUNT

Inevitably, in the development of any scientific discipline there comes a time when the body of knowledge that forms the content of that discipline becomes applicable to the practical affairs of man. At this point a profession is born. This development was rapid and inevitable in the science of psychology, dealing as it does with the gross, molar, and socially significant behaviors of man (as opposed, let us say, to the molecular and less immediately socially applicable findings of a discipline such as physiology). As Sanford has so aptly stated (1952), psychologists have always tended toward "skepticism about knowledge for its own sweet savor and to enthusiasm for the ideal of knowledge as a servant of man." The tendency was there at the turn of the century in the militant interest of American functionalism not only in the *what* but also in the *how* and *why* of human behavior and in its bold desire to establish psychological foundations for logic, ethics, and esthetics (Hunt, 1956). It is there in the latent utopianism of Watsonian behaviorism and currently in the overt utopianism of Skinner. It is peculiarly American that John Dewey began as a psychologist, made a distinguished contribution as a philosopher, and ended up among the patron saints of education. This trend toward the application of psychological knowledge has given us industrial psychology, child psychology, legal psychology, educational psychology, social psychology, clinical psychology, and a host of other specialties.

The development of specialty areas for the application of scientific knowledge, however, does not guarantee the emergence of a profession. That clinical psychology has been foremost in developing the characteristics, organization, and problems of a profession is due not only to the extent of its activities (there are probably more psychologists involved in applying psychological techniques of measurement in education, industry, opinion polling, etc., than in applying these techniques to problems of therapeutic management), but also to the fact that its activities have been such as to involve psychologists more immediately in matters of social control. To label someone as intellectually superior, an introvert, authoritarian, or suited for employment as a typist is of course significant and has implications for his living, but it has nowhere near the social impact of calling him mentally retarded, maladjusted, or schizophrenic.

In his discussion of psychology as a profession, Hughes (1952) distinguishes between a science, a business, and a profession. Science is engaged in the discovery, sytematization, and communication of knowledge. While business and the professions both offer services for hire, business tends to be viewed as a kind of a game in which everything is fair and the principle of *caveat emptor* governs, whereas it is assumed that with professional services, the public is not sufficiently knowledgeable to make an intelligent decision and must be protected by some kind of social control such as licensing. While the distinction between business and profession blurs with the current trend toward exclusionary trade organizations and increasing Federal control in business and with the recent phenomenon of doctors "striking" and refusing to serve, the imposition of social controls, with their implication of the social importance and significance of the activities to be regulated, remains a major characteristic of a profession. Certainly it is in this area of social controls such as certification and licensing that the profession of clinical psychology has had its greatest difficulties in relating with other professions. There are other characteristics of a profession, such as the high level of skill usually involved and the greater educational preparation necessary, but these are matters of professional tension only when they concern the adoption of internal or external social controls.

Another way of approaching this problem of social control, with all its interprofessional rivalries concerning the right to practice certain professional techniques and procedures, is to look at the behavior to be controlled. In general, professions acquire their activities and duties in three ways (Hunt, 1956):

1. They may develop from the peculiar and indigenous skills and knowledge of the discipline from which the profession sprang. Thus there is little question about the essential and basic contribution of the science of psychology to the development of psychological testing in general and of diagnostic testing in particular, and there is little opposition to the delegation of such duties to the clinical psychologist as his professional right. There is, however, much medical opposition to permitting the psychologist the legal, administrative, and official professional privilege of diagnosis in the field of mental disorder, since this is usually viewed as a medical function necessary to medical responsibility for the patient concerned. Thus a psychologist may say that a patient behaves like a psychotic, but to label him as "psychotic" for purposes of social or therapeutic management may be viewed as a medical function.

The peculiar importance of psychological testing in establishing the presence and amount of mental retardation has resulted in exceptions to this principle, and many states and courts have recognized the competence of the psychologists in this area and have accorded him the official professional privileges of diagnosis in this field. Medical resistance to this practice remains strong, however, and the professional right to such diagnostic functions is by no means universally accepted.

2. The activities and duties of a profession are also acquired heuristically, by the fortuitous demands and exigencies of social need. Irrespective of the psychologist's claim that his right to practice psychotherapy is justified by the contribution his discipline has made to the understanding of the psychotherapeutic process and to the development of techniques for its facilitation, many psychologists have been admitted to the practice of psychotherapy because of the tremendous demand for such services and the inability of the medical profession to supply trained personnel in adequate numbers to meet this demand. It is no exaggeration to say that many child behavior clinics would be unable to function and that the psychotherapeutic facilities of the Veterans Administration, the armed services, medical school clinics, and private hospitals would be seriously handicapped if the practice of psychotherapy were forbidden to the psychologist. The concept of medical responsibility with the practice of some medical supervision, however tenuous, is invoked to handle this embarrassing situation, but it remains difficult for the psychologist to accept the fact that in dedicating his life to the filling of this social need, he must of necessity relegate himself to the position of a second-class citizen. On the other hand, some medical men long used to responsibility for the treatment of the ill are not happy at being asked to share it with a relative newcomer. This leads us to the third point.

3. After a profession includes a technique or procedure in its practice and maintains this service over a period of time, custom and precedent establish the right of that profession to that practice. Theoretically, a profession might preempt a service not indigenous to its discipline or demanded by social need, and, after the passage of time, claim this service as a professional right. Actually, cases of pure preemption are difficult to find, and custom and precedence usually interact with the first two principles to confirm and strengthen practices based on indigenous factors or of heuristic origin. But it must be remembered that the peculiar or indigenous nature of a service is hard to establish, as are the reality and validity of social need. Thus to clinical psychology, the practice of psychotherapy or the application of psychological procedures to the modification of human behavior is a peculiarly psychological function, drawing heavily upon the schol-

arly contribution of psychology to the understanding and control of behavior. To many psychiatrists this is nonsense, and the psychologists' therapeutic activities are purely opportunistic preemption to be resisted on every front. In the same vein, vocational and educational guidance, which to the psychiatrist may seem a reasonable and integral part of his therapeutic practice, may be viewed as a preemptive intrusion by the vocational counselor or educator.

In any case, this principle of custom and precedent, while often overlooked, has important implications for professional development. Many psychiatrists, while admitting the necessity of permitting the clinical psychologist to do psychotherapy because of the present shortage of psychiatric personnel, wonder: "How do we get rid of them when we cease to need them?" and many psychologists viewing the occasional use of psychological tests by relatively untrained psychiatrists wonder how long this duty may remain their professional right.

Clinical psychologists classically have defined their duties as consisting of diagnostic evaluation (including interviewing and testing), research, and therapy. To these may be added teaching and that ever-present bugaboo of modern science, administration. Their duties in the field of evaluation are recognized, and their peculiar right to this function is rarely challenged. Their research activities are recognized and accepted, although the universal position of research in science excludes the claiming of any preemptive rights. In their relations with medicine, their research position is reinforced by the prominent position that training in research occupies in the graduate psychological curriculum and by the still relatively small, though increasing, part it plays in medical education. Administrative functions are sometimes a source of local irritation but have received little attention at the level of organized interprofessional adjudication. The teaching function is widely accepted, a recognition of the contribution of the basic science of psychology to the practice of medicine in general and of psychiatry in particular. It is the practice of psychotherapy that poses the primary source of professional friction between medicine and psychology.

Before discussing this further and noting the forms of professional interaction that attempt to solve this conflict, it will be wise to note three further points about professional practice that influence the relation of clinical psychology to other professions. The relations of one profession to another are governed by whether the duties of that profession (1) merely contribute to another profession, (2) complement another profession, or (3) compete with another profession. Admittedly the difference between contribution and complementation is vague, but we shall define it by saying that in contribution, one profession, as an external entity, offers something to another profession that the second profession independently incorporates into its service functions, whereas in complementation, both professions act in concert to the attainment of a common goal.

In its teaching activities, clinical psychology makes a contribution to many other professions. It teaches nurses the basic principles of human behavior, which nursing then incorporates into its activities in patient management. It does the same for dentistry and for medicine and its specialties. Such contributory activities rarely cause any friction, nor are any interprofessional formalities involved.

Diagnostic evaluation is an example of a complementary activity. Here the clinical psychologist functions as a member of a team, complementing through his special testing abilities the work of the psychiatrist, pediatrician, neurologist, etc. Friction here tends to be minimal, as the ultimate patient responsibility resides with the physician. Nevertheless, as we have mentioned above, there remain many issues of diagnostic responsibility that pose some problems. Some of these are semantic and some ridiculous, such as the discussion of whether a psychologist who has tested a patient has the right to communicate his findings to a medical colleague by using a diagnostic label such as "psychotic." They become serious when formal matters such as official records, patient management, and legal questions of commitment are involved as a consequence. In general these problems are absorbed under the general question of who has the responsibility for the patient. In a medical setting, medical practice places this upon the physician, although he may delegate authority while maintaining ultimate responsibility.

It is when two professions compete by offering the same service that trouble arises, and psychotherapy provides an outstanding example of this. The problem involves the many complexities introduced by the advent of the dynamic approach in psychiatry. Clinical psychology had little conflict with psychiatry during the first part of the century. True, there were far fewer clinical psychologists, although the number of psychologists offering clinical services was far greater than the number of those formally on record (Hunt, 1956). Psychiatry during this period, however, was organically oriented, and no psychologist aspired to the therapeutic techniques of choice—pharmaceutical or surgical interference. This period was the heyday of testing and of the development of its diagnostic potentiality. When the influence of Freud and of what Watson (1953) has called the "Boston group" of James, Hall, Prince, Hoch, Sidis, and Meyer first began to make itself felt and "dynamics" began to attract attention, the psychologist was welcomed as a partner in a new and exciting exploration into the mysteries of the human personality, an exploration that might or might not pay off. With the later domination of the dynamic approach in psychiatry and with dynamic techniques playing the leading part in psychotherapy, the participation of psychology was no longer as welcome, and the competition became pronounced.

In the team situation where the psychologist works with the psychiatrist in a medical setting such as a medical school, hospital, or clinic or in group practice, these conflicts are minimal. Medical responsibility is usually taken for granted, and the delegation of authority or function is easy and natural, since the close working contacts within the team provide the knowledge of, and confidence in, the personnel concerned that facilitate delegation. Occasional tensions may arise, but these are more apt to be clashes of personality between two human beings than conflicts of professional policy. There is the amusing story of the psychiatrist who refers patients for therapy to "his" psychologist, while opposing the right of psychologists in general to practice psychotherapy, and of the psychologist who accepts (and may not even be conscious of) the vesting of medical responsibility for the patient in the physicians with whom he is working from day to day, while objecting to it as a principle.

Private practice is another matter, of course, and constitutes the real problem area. Yet here again it is fair to ask just how much private practice is really private and independent and how much of it is actually, through the process of cross-referral, a loose type of group activity where mutual control and cooperation are latent and implicit although not obvious at first. As a result, there is occasionally a curious quality of unreality about the jockeying of rights and privileges between professions. This is as true of the relations between medicine and dentistry as it is of the relations between psychology and psychiatry, although the greater maturity of the former has perhaps resulted in medicine and dentistry adjudicating their differences in a more adult and practical fashion than is true of the less experienced psychiatry and psychology. The discussions here still have a heavily academic flavor. Conflicts arise over the wording of a phrase, and at times one gets the feeling that patient care and the social need for it, which after all are the realities in the situation, get lost in a welter of verbal maneuvering that is more appropriate to a contest in sophistry than to the settling of practical issues affecting the public health. The amount of committee time that may be given to the weighty discussion of whether the disciplines related to medicine should be designated as allied, supportive, adjunctive, or ancillary is at times appalling (Hunt, 1962).

Yet there is a very real semantic problem here. The primary conflict between clinical psychology and organized medicine has always been over the *independent* practice of *psychotherapy* with the *mental disorders* by psychologists. Few psychologists are willing to carry their claims this far, and the public statements of the American Psychological Association usually support some collaborative setting distinguished by the process of cross-referral. But is this independence? Medicine holds out for medical supervision, but supervision is difficult to implement. Psychotherapy itself is not open to any exact definition (which may be one of the reasons why it is so difficult to give its consequences any very exact validation), and it is impossible to define it as an obvious medical procedure that does not encroach upon such clearly nonmedical functions as pastoral counseling, educational advising, etc., because of our relative ignorance of just what is going on in the psychotherapeutic process. And where does one draw the line between illness and health?

For many years, the American Psychological

Association's Committee on Relations with the American Psychiatric Association and the American Psychiatric Association's Committee on Relations with the American Psychological Association labored over such semantic problems in the attempt to draw up a statement or charter agreeable to both professions, a statement which would define the nature, rights, and functions of both professions and forever end their conflicts with each other. There was an atmosphere of academic naïveté about these attempts, however well intentioned. History has shown the illusory nature of the peace treaty as an ultimate solution for social conflict. Treaties are made to be amended and are superseded or supplemented by boundary commissions and arbitration commissions or, at best, by supranational courts for the adjudication of recurrent differences. The reality is one of a state of armistice rather than peace, but it is infinitely better than open military conflict.

Of late, the thinking of both associations seems to be tending in this more realistic direction. The idea of the final charter, the ultimate constitution which settles all conflict of interest by reference to the letter of the law, is slowly disappearing and is being replaced by the concept of specific adjudication of the most threatening problems as they arise. Professional survival of one profession at the expense of the other is being replaced by the goal of mutual coexistence—of cold war, if you will—while time is gained for further mutual education, for the development of mutual tolerance, and for the experimental testing of varying patterns of interaction and social control. This is the history of the development of most conflicts between professions. The war is never won. Professions learn to live with one another and to spend increasing time in cooperation rather than in conflict. But the peace is never complete. Conflicts are minimized and civilized, and a mature relationship is attained, but never is the millennium achieved.

Unfortunately, the lessons learned so painfully at the national level often must be relearned at the local level. The recent pressure for certification and licensing by psychologists has transferred many of the problems to the state level, where they must be lived through again. The evil genie of semantics appears again and again in the writing of state legislation, and all the old wounds are reopened, and the old phrases are argued about again, to the neglect of professional acceptance of some tentative patterns of interaction which can be tested further by trial for their efficacy.

Because patterns of professional relations and interaction appear most vividly in those areas where the problem of social control arises, we have dealt at length with the questions of the practice of psychotherapy by psychologists and with the conflicts generated with medicine and with psychiatry over this issue. It would be unfortunate, however, to create the impression that clinical psychology lives only in conflict with psychiatry. It lives cooperatively as well. At the national level, it was represented on the Joint Commission on Mental Illness and Health and since has been important in helping to develop the commission's report and in pushing for its implementation by the Congress. Psychologists work with physicians on various governmental and civic panels. They cooperate with medicine at the state level in supporting programs to benefit the public health. They consult with medical faculties in the development of medical school curriculums. The two professions labor side by side in the area of research, as they mutually attack the problem of the causes of mental disorder and the discovery of techniques for its amelioration. It is unfortunate that the acrimony generated in the area of psychotherapy tends to becloud a relationship that is essentially more positive than negative and to conceal the tremendous accomplishment that has been made by cooperative action in the whole area of public health.

Nor is it fair to assume that only in clinical psychology does psychology relate to, and interact with, medicine. While the psychologist as human engineer has been relatively slow in contributing to the design of surgical and medical equipment, the social psychologist has become involved in studying the patterning of human relations in the hospital in general and on the hospital ward as a specific microcosm. Working with the anthropologist and sociologist, he studies the social climate of the hospital and manipulates it for the improvement of patient care. Educational and personnel psychologists are utilizing their knowledge and skill in developing tests for the selection of hospital aides and for the selection of students for medical schools and for schools of nursing. Physiological and comparative psychologists are assisting in the evaluation of new drugs. The psychologist also contributes his knowledge of group behavior to the understanding and betterment of communication chains in the hospital staff and to the solution of problems of employee relations and evaluation.

In all these activities, no clear line demarcates the clinical psychologist from his nonclinical colleagues, for the clinical psychologist is trained in basic psychology as a preliminary to specialization in peculiarly clinical skills. It is therefore necessary to realize that the clinical psychologist is possessed of and practices psychological skills far beyond those usually viewed as "clinical." This is frequently overlooked by the medical man when he asks for complete supervision and control over *all* the activities of the clinical psychologist. When asking for representation on the examining board of a state that certifies psychologists, it is well for the physician to realize that such certification bills usually limit the right to the use of the title "psychologist" and that psychotherapy is only one of the many fields covered under the discipline of psychology. Since these boards have an important influence on training programs in psychology, the physician may find himself in the embarrassing position of seeking control over higher education in a discipline with which his acquaintance is often minimal.

The usual pattern of training, which builds the specific skills of the clinical area on a fundamental basis of research methodology and findings in all the important areas of psychology such as experimental, social, personality, developmental, etc., recognizes the importance of a broad grounding in basic psychology. A very common curriculum pattern puts the first-year graduate student in clinical psychology through a basic core program (sometimes organized as a proseminar) in psychology, with specialization in the clinical area beginning only in the second year, to be followed by an internship in the third year and possible further specialization in some specific clinical area during the fourth and final year of his training. This complicates the picture of interrelationship with other professions, since the clinical psychologist is relating as generalist as well as specialist.

This confusion in relationships is further complicated by the fact that owing to the above (plus the fact that in union there is strength), the organized mechanisms for professional interaction are largely focused in the American Psychological Association itself rather than in its Division of Clinical Psychology. Sometimes the interrelationship is at the personal, individual level, as in the various governmental and military panels and advisory boards. Here a man may represent his profession, but he is not selected through a professional organization, and he is not under its direct control. Another example is the American Board of Examiners in Psychological Hypnosis, which, as a section of the American Board of Clinical Hypnosis, was organized so that psychologists might cooperate with their medical and dental colleagues in the control and development of this technique. Sometimes the individual and professional relating goes on side by side, as in the National Research Council, the hard core of whose members are members of the National Academy of Science. Individuals elected to the National Academy of Science are selected on the basis of their excellence by their distinguished colleagues within the academy. Yet the National Research Council also has a provision for council members who are elected by and who officially represent their various professional organizations. Thus each year the American Psychological Association elects representatives for a limited tenure of office to serve as its official representatives on the council.

Such examples are limitless, and we must confine ourselves here to those patterns typical of the American Psychological Association (Hunt, 1962), recognizing that even here we must be selective. These relationships take place through committees, commissions, and associations organized at an interprofessional or supraprofessional level between professions and at an intraprofessional level through the association's own internally organized committees and task forces. The interprofessional mechanisms are again of two kinds; the association may participate actively in the formation and direction of the joint organization, or it may furnish a representative to a previously established and independent group. In some cases this may be another professional organization, such as when we have an official representative to the American Speech and Hearing Association, in recognition of overlapping interests and functions as well as membership. The intraprofessional committees may be standing committees, or they may be *ad hoc* committees appointed temporarily for a specific mission. The number of such activities and their extent have necessitated placing them under the Board of Professional Affairs, which is responsible for them to the board of directors and ultimately to the council of representatives of the American Psychological Association.

As examples of interprofessional structures, let us take the proposed Congress of Allied Health Services and the Interprofessional Research Commission on Pupil Personnel Services. The Congress of Allied Health Services was proposed as a means of unifying those scholarly disciplines granting the Ph.D. degree whose activities are in some instance related to the medical arts. Thus the American Chemical Society, particularly through its specialty of clinical chemistry, and the American Psychological Association, through its various research and clinical functions, expressed interest in joining with biologists, bacteriologists, pathologists, etc., in an organization which could focus and unify the activities of those sciences related to medicine in their official contacts with the medical profession. Modern medicine faces a tremendous problem in understanding the rapid developments in chemistry, physics, physiology, genetics, the behavioral sciences, etc.; in grasping their implications for medicine; and in adapting their findings to patient care. The problems of mutual education are vast, and the question of social controls of practice are bound to be more pressing (and vexing) as medicine inevitably increases its reliance on the basic sciences. The importance of some unified front for educational and adjudicative action among the related disciplines is obvious.

The Interprofessional Research Commission on Pupil Personnel Services, in whose creation the American Psychological Association played a prominent part, was established to facilitate and conduct research and to initiate pilot demonstration projects in this increasingly important area. It unites psychologists with many other professional groups involved in pupil personnel services for promoting effective action toward maximal mental health for children and youth.

Where the mechanism of interaction is the appointment of a representative to some other organized body, either professional or interprofessional, the participation is less active and certainly less direct, but the procedure represents a vital link in professional communication and assures the necessary basis for ready action and further organizational implementation should this become desirable or necessary. Among others, the American Psychological Association has official representatives to the American Association of Marriage Counsellors, the American Public Health Association's Committee on Public Health and the Behavioral Sciences, the World Federation for Mental Health, and the National Commission on Accrediting, an organization whose constituent members include the Association of American Colleges, the Association of American Universities, the Association of Teacher Education Institutions, and other groups interested in the accreditation process.

This last points up the increasing importance of the American Psychological Association's own accrediting procedures in which clinical psychology is intimately involved. Such interaction and mutual education are increasingly necessitated by the discipline-oriented accrediting functions assumed as the professionalization of psychology proceeds. University, college, and school administrations do not look kindly on what they feel is an intrusion on the part of the professional societies in setting up and attempting to enforce their own standards, and the friction will not lessen as the rapid spread of state certification procedures increasingly involves professional demands on, and controls over, the curriculums in institutions of higher learning. The conflict is particularly intense in psychology, where the academic, scholarly functions of the discipline still outweigh its professional service functions.

The intraprofessional committee structure of the American Psychological Association may serve as a means of direct communication with another profession, as is true of the Committee on Relations with the American Psychiatric Association, which serves both a communicatory and an adjudicative role with the American Psychiatric Association's Committee on Relations with the American Psychological Association and which may even have joint meetings with it; it may also serve as a means of generating policies and standards which will indirectly influence another profession, as in the case of the Ad Hoc Committee on Private Practice, which was defining standards for directory listing of private practice, standards which will immediately be reflected in our relations with psychiatry.

Such committees may be continuing, standing committees, such as the one on psychiatry, or they may be *ad hoc*, temporary committees dedicated to a limited goal, such as the committee on private practice. The Committee on Relations with the Social Work Profession is a continuing committee, recognizing a continuing need for interaction with a complementary profession in the field of mental health. The Committee on Relations with Sociology was an *ad hoc* committee which arose in connection with certification legislation and the threat to sociology if psychology preempted the right to the words "psychology" and "social psychology." Sociologists are trained in social psychology, and as consultants they may be said to practice social psychology. Careless phrasing of a certification or a licensing law might well do them a grave injustice. Apart from this specific crisis, however, it is difficult to see where our relations with this sister discipline would demand continuing committee actions.

These patterns of interaction are repeated at the local, state, and regional levels. Thus there is a Chicago Psychology Club, an Illinois Psychological Association, and a Midwestern Psychological Association, and this structure is duplicated across the country. The local and regional associations are largely cultural in their functions and tend historically to antedate the large-scale professionalization of psychology. Their ties to the American Psychological Association are loose.

Maintenance of interprofessional relations and the implementation of social controls, however, are important functions of the various state associations, as is demanded by our American legislative organization, with the state as its unit. The ties with the parent association are close but, as in medicine, never complete. General interprofessional policies are usually arbitrated by the American Psychological Association, perhaps because the bigger the question, the greater the status necessary to back an answer; perhaps because the higher the policy, the higher the body that best promulgates it; perhaps because the broader the category, the more inclusive and representative it becomes; and perhaps even because the larger the sample, the less the influence of error. There is a duplication of function, however, and there are local revolts as well, all of which complicate the relational problem.

We have suggested that the relations of any profession with others are a function of that profession's activities. If these activities are indigenous to the profession or the discipline from which it sprang, the profession is in a clearly defensible position, its duties are not apt to be challenged, and interprofessional irritations usually are minor. If the duties have been assumed heuristically, the profession's position is not clear, conflicts may arise, and social need tends to be the major argument advanced in defense of the activity in question. Where practice over a period of time adds the rationale of custom and precedent, the profession's position is strengthened legally, legislatively, and in public opinion.

These factors do not act in isolation but interact with others. Thus it is important in understanding professional group behavior to know whether the profession's activities are contributory to the activities of another profession, complementary to them, or competitive with them. If the services rendered are contributing to the activities of another profession, the situation is one in which assistance or aid is offered from the outside, and friction is minimal. If the activities are complementary, the setting is again one of assistance, but where two professions are working together in a team relationship, as they are in the complementary situation, conflict may arise over relative status, ultimate task responsibility, or administrative control. An ameliorating factor here, however, is the necessary presence of each profession if the common goal is to be attained. When the services are competitive, conflict tends to be frequent and open, since neither profession may feel the need of tolerating the other.

Of the various combinations, the indigenous-contributory one offers the greatest possibility for harmonious interprofessional relations, as in the case of the teaching function of clinical psychology, and the heuristic-competitive combination, represented by psychotherapy, augurs least well for amicable relations. In teaching, the psychologist has a clear right to the communication of the content of his discipline, and the content usually is of real value to the second profession. In psychotherapy, the right to use psychotherapeutic procedures is less clear because both psychiatry and psychology have contributed to their development, and the therapeutic services of each profession tend to preclude or render minimal the potential therapeutic opportunities of the other.

This is not the place for a detailed analysis

of the contributions of individual personality dynamics to group behavior, but it is only fitting to point out in passing that the human beings who constitute any profession carry into their professional behavior all the human emotions and strivings that characterize them as individuals. Insecurity, aggression, compensation, and displacement are all common human behaviors that can be recognized in professional interaction. Thus indigenous-contributory activities are usually requested by the second profession and place the contributing profession in a pleasant, nurturant role, with the implicit admission of at least some dependency on the part of the second profession. If, on the other hand, the activity is heuristic-competitive, the goal of interaction may be the hostile exclusion of one participant. Moreover, since heuristic "rights" are seldom historically clear, the security of moral certainty is usually missing as a support.

Professions also may inculcate ideals and standards in training that are opposed to the subsequent realities of actual professional practice. This may produce personal conflict, which may be expressed in irrational professional behavior. Thus the nursing profession in its classical training pattern stresses the bedside care of the patient as basic and primary among the nurse's duties, and yet more and more the realities of medical care delegate supervisory and administrative functions to the nurse, at the cost of time for bedside patient care. Many nurses complain about being isolated from what they consider to be their professional *raison d'être*, but as Reissman and Rohrer (1957) have shown in one hospital, when supervisory and administrative duties are lacking, the nurse does not hurry to a patient's bedside but remains marking time in the nursing station. Such attitudinal conflicts often accentuate the nurse's resistance to encroachments that the nursing aide may make upon the traditional nursing functions as well as increase her resistance to the further delegation of greater responsibility by the doctor or the hospital administration.

Clinical psychology is no stranger to such conflicts, and they are exacerbated by the fact that only relatively recently has clinical psychology developed as a service profession. The basic scholarly and research orientations of psychology as a science make many psychologists suspicious of the service function and reluctant to see the growth of psychology as a profession. As Borden (1963) has said, speaking for the clinician: "Many of us are worried by suspicions that academic psychologists are not yet ready to come to terms with psychology as a responsible service profession." It might also be added that there is reason for suspicion that clinical psychology is not yet mature and secure enough to come to terms with its parent, the science of psychology, whose roots must necessarily remain in research and scholarship. The resulting *intra*professional tensions often express themselves in conflictful *inter*professional behavior. Such problems are not the exclusive property of any one profession, and their very universality offers hope for their understanding and amelioration.

In summary, the relations of clinical psychology with other professions are in general good. The formal patterns are somewhat difficult to trace, as they often are masked in the activities of the American Psychological Association per se. A further complication arises owing to the tendency of the clinical psychologist to wear two hats, one as a generalist when he represents psychology as a whole and one as a specialist when he represents his own subspecialty. Much of the interaction is informal, which may well attest to its excellence, since conflict is a well-known source of structured behavior.

The contest with psychiatry in the area of psychotherapy should not conceal the generally pleasant relationships with medicine in the area of teaching, where each group contributes to the education of the other; in research, where a mutual attack upon the problem of etiology and control is proving profitable; and in the area of public education and promotional support, where closed ranks and combined effort are accomplishing much in furthering the cause of mental health. The psychotherapy issue will not be settled for some time, and both professions must learn to live with it gracefully.

With dentistry, relations are pleasant, as might be expected with professions engaging in such different, noncompetitive activity. Psychology performs some teaching functions; there is occasional collaborative research; and in the area of hypnosis, there is participation in an interprofessional structure to further the social control of a jointly, but noncompetitively, practiced technique.

With nursing, the relationship is largely a

one-way contributory process of providing teaching services, although there is interaction at the level of interprofessional panels, committees, and commissions in the public health areas.

Sociology's relations with clinical psychology are usually at the academic level, involving some joint programs in training social scientists for work in mental health, some collaborative research, and the numerous campus collaborations typical of sister scientific disciplines. It is interesting to note that the relationship did become structured through mutual committees of each professional organization when the question of certification of psychologists raised certain possibilities of professional preemption of the field of social psychology.

The relation of clinical psychology to the social work profession, since it involves a complementary relationship in the area of mental health, must be a continuing one. It is structured through a continuing committee of the American Psychological Association.

Relations with education are many and complex. The teaching of the psychology of adjustment and of social relations is being introduced in secondary schools. Clinical psychology will have an interest in this. The increasing importance of the school psychologist will raise many problems of a professional nature within the structure of primary and secondary education. In the field of higher education, the social control of graduate training programs is presenting increasing problems. The conflicts inherent here are largely latent, but it will take a great deal of tolerance and understanding of the historical inevitability of professional development and of justifiable professional concern with professional training if they are to be handled smoothly.

Perhaps the most important need is for clinical psychology to realize, as any profession must, that interprofessional relations are a continuing responsibility. They furnish a constant and necessary background to all professional practice. Fortunately, they are a more frequent source of satisfaction than of irritation. With tolerance, with understanding, and with a sense of mutual justice, the irritations can be kept minimal. However, they are the inevitable accompaniment of professional existence.

REFERENCES

Borden, E. Clinical psychology at the crossroads. *Newsltr Div. clin. Psychol. Amer. psychol. Ass.*, 1963, **16** (2), 3–4.

Hughes, E. C. Psychology: science and/or profession. *Amer. Psychologist,* 1952, **7,** 441–443.

Hunt, W. A. *The clinical psychologist.* Springfield, Ill.: Charles C Thomas, 1956.

Hunt, W. A. Education—the dream and the reality. *Nursing World,* 1958, No. 2, 132.

Hunt, W. A. Professional interaction between psychology and medicine. *Pre-Med.,* 1962, **2,** 18–24.

Lockman, R. F. Characteristics of APA members in the 1962 National Scientific Register. *Amer. Psychologist,* 1962, **17,** 789–792.

Reissman, L., & Rohrer, J. H. (Eds.) *Change and dilemma in the nursing profession.* New York: Putnam, 1957.

Sanford, F. Annual report of the executive secretary: 1952. *Amer. Psychologist,* 1952, **7,** 686–696.

Watson, R. I. A brief history of clinical psychology. *Psychol. Bull.,* 1953, **50,** 321–346.

Watson, R. I. *Psychology as a profession.* Garden City, N.Y.: Doubleday, 1954.

57

International Trends in Clinical Psychology

HENRY P. DAVID[1]

Clinical psychology transcends geographic boundaries. It is the purpose of this chapter to survey, insofar as is feasible, the general situation, professional roles, emerging trends, and legislation pertaining to clinical psychology in 57 countries outside the United States. The material presented is based primarily on extensive communications from correspondents abroad, whose names are cited in the footnotes and in a separate listing at the end of the chapter. Observations gathered on personal travels and in discussions with colleagues are also included.[2]

Following an overview, the reports are grouped according to major geographic areas and are then arranged alphabetically by country. Most of the larger sections are prefaced by brief introductory commentaries. Although 57 countries are represented, individual contributions vary in length and scope. While translations and edited papers were resubmitted for revision to the many correspondents, it is inevitable that some errors have been made. Corrections and additional information would be very welcome for future editions.

If this chapter renders a service, it will be because of the dedication of colleagues who share the ideal of international cooperation.

OVERVIEW

As will be apparent from the 57 reports to follow, standards for clinical psychology differ from country to country. The model of an accredited doctoral-level graduate training program with an approved internship, enjoying massive governmental and private support, appears unique to the United States.

One of the difficulties in making comparisons has to do with the varying approaches to training and with the problem of equating degrees obtained in one country with those awarded in another. For many clinical positions abroad, subdoctoral training is deemed appropriate. Doctoral requirements may be less systematized and of either shorter or longer duration than in the United States. Patterns of education differ, and the stage at which professional practice in psychology begins varies widely. A knowledge of local conditions is essential in evaluating academic credentials from abroad.

Demand for professional services is growing at such a rapid rate all over the world that many countries are exploring expanded uses of nonmedical personnel. Psychologists are assuming additional administrative responsibili-

1 It is gratifying to acknowledge the encouragement of Dr. Roger W. Russell, Secretary-General of the International Union of Scientific Psychology, and the assistance of Dr. Victor D. Sanua, Secretary-General of the Interamerican Society of Psychology, who facilitated reports from Latin America. Special thanks are expressed to the Human Ecology Fund for its continuing support.

2 Collection of these and other data on clinical psychology abroad was stimulated by Dr. Benjamin Wolman's invitation to contribute a chapter to the *Handbook*. When it became apparent that the information elicited far exceeded the allotted chapter space, permission was graciously given for the publication of a separate monograph (McGraw-Hill, 1964). Details on graduate university training and supervised practicum facilities, including names and addresses, also appear in the *Sourcebook for Training in Clinical Psychology* (Springer, 1964). Most of the material was collected in early 1963.

ties. In Japan they frequently head clinics for children and provide the major professional resource in rehabilitation and correctional centers. In the emerging countries of Africa, psychologists have been assigned a leading role in social and industrial planning and in the selection and training of candidates for higher education. Where resources are limited, professional personnel tend to be characterized by the breadth of their activities rather than by narrow specialization.

While the use of tests continues to be viewed as a primary responsibility of the clinical psychologist, particularly in diagnostic work and assessment of training capabilities, there is growing recognition that the application of techniques standardized in one country to a totally different population on another continent is questionable at best. Efforts to translate or adapt Western instruments have been initiated in many lands. The importance of local standards and norms has been demonstrated by the work of the American Institute for Research in Ghana and Nigeria.

Individual psychotherapy and group psychotherapy by qualified psychologists are more often encouraged than not, especially in children's centers and in working with delinquent or disturbed youth. Freud's theories have long divided academicians and professionals. Increasingly, emphasis has been placed on neo-Freudian and other depth therapies, such as phenomenology and existentialism, and on learning theory–oriented behavior therapies. In most countries psychoanalysis is associated with private institutes which do not necessarily restrict membership to any one profession. There is, however, growing recognition that traditional one-to-one therapist-patient relationships are unlikely to resolve major mental health problems and that manpower shortages alone demand more training in the areas of mental health consultation and working with other groups. In the emerging countries, the basic question is likely to center on who can be of service now, on what basis, and with whom, rather than on who has had what traditional prerogatives.

Many of the reports suggest that clinical psychology has not yet attained official recognition as a discipline or a profession. Efforts to promulgate standards and legislation governing professional practice are worldwide, with major emphasis in those countries where psychology has made considerable progress or where organized medicine wishes to emphasize its priority to psychotherapy. Some unusual aspects include the provision in the Egyptian legislation which requires physicians to make reports to referring psychologists, who are not permitted to treat severely disturbed patients. The tendency toward equivalence with psychiatrists in public service is suggested in such diverse countries as Poland and South Africa, where some psychologists' salaries are on a par with those of physicians. The Israeli Psychological Association is incorporated in the Academic Section of the General Labor Organization, which protects psychologists' rights and attempts to obtain better working conditions, as it would for any affiliated professional group. Legislation on a regional basis is encouraged by the Scandinavian Psychological Association, in collaboration with the Northern Council.

In viewing the international scene, American psychologists are not always fully aware of their own role. According to the 1957 *International Directory of Psychologists* (now in revision), some 70 per cent of all self-styled psychologists live and work in the United States, and the total rises to 85 per cent if only Ph.D.s are counted. As of 1957, and probably as of this writing, six out of seven Ph.D. psychologists work in the United States. It is hardly surprising that American psychology is perceived as a Goliath and that colleagues abroad are sensitive about the attention, if any, their contributions receive.

EUROPE

Just as there is no one American brand of clinical psychology, European approaches vary according to local interests and academic traditions. Except for childhood studies, European universities rarely offer professional programs. Few provide opportunities for practicum training, and some are still bound to philosophy. In the absence of academic leadership, independent schools and professional societies have assumed a major role in clinical training, certification, and legislative efforts, particularly in Switzerland. Interested students study English and avidly discuss American publications when their own country offers less opportunity.

While numerous psychiatrists hold that psychotherapy should be restricted to medical practitioners, psychologists are often encouraged to engage in therapeutic activities, especially with children and adolescents. In Poland they have been invited to join the psychiatric association.

In contrast to the United States, many European countries place less emphasis on the doctorate as a requirement for clinical positions. For example, few Scandinavian psychologists have a Ph.D., which is generally considered a research or scholarly degree. In the Soviet Union, the Ph.D. is awarded in recognition of major contributions, often in midcareer. Occasionally, the nonmedical doctorate is more easily obtained and may be equivalent to an American M.A. A knowledge of local standards is essential to evaluate fully a European psychologist's credentials.

In sum, there is much diversity, as the following reports from twenty-one countries will reflect.

Austria[3]

General situation. Clinical psychology, as it is understood in the United States, is in only its early stages of development in Austria. While the postwar period has revitalized the universities, fostered social services, and generated a demand for professional facilities, psychology departments have retained their primarily academic and experimental research orientation. Freud's contributions continue to be considered more appropriate to medicine and psychiatry than to psychology.

Professional roles. Psychotherapy is considered an exclusively medical function, and "clinical" psychological activities are generally restricted to intelligence testing, differential diagnosis, school counseling, character appraisals for forensic purposes, and research. Independent private practice by psychologists is rare.

Emerging trends. As is the case in Germany, the title "psychologist" is not protected by law, and the Austrian Psychological Society has been concerned over professional practices. Outside Vienna, relations with psychiatry are largely determined by the strong organic orientation of most Austrian psychiatrists, who seldom view psychology as anything other than a testing and research service. As in many other countries of Europe, dynamically oriented clinical psychologists frequently tend to be physicians who rarely identify with a separate profession of clinical psychology.

[3] John L. Wallace (St. Cloud, Minn.).

Belgium[4]

General situation. Until a few years ago, clinical psychology and psychoanalysis were not particularly popular in Belgium. Because of limited demand and a shortage of psychologically trained psychiatrists, psychotherapy with adults is still practiced on only a very small scale. However, outpatient clinics have been opened, and special seminars and psychology courses have been developed in the four Belgian universities (Brussels, Ghent, Liége, and Louvain).

Services for children and adolescents are far better established. Since the end of the last century, there has been much emphasis on psychological examination, treatment, and rehabilitation of difficult, delinquent, deficient, and seriously disturbed children. For example, schools for the retarded were opened in 1897, and the first European juvenile courts were created in Belgium in 1912. Child guidance centers, in which the psychiatrist, psychologist, social worker, and educator work as a team, have long been established in the major Belgian cities.

Particularly advanced and accepted are vocational guidance and school psychology, officially sponsored and encouraged by the Ministry of Public Instruction and by voluntary organizations. There are more than fifty centers for vocational and school guidance supported by the Christian Social Association, and there are 35 such centers administered by the state, provinces, and townships. Psychologists frequently head guidance services in the public secondary schools and join with physicians and social workers in providing team services in private high schools. (In Belgium, more than 50 per cent of high school students go to Catholic institutions, which are financially supported by the state.)

Professional roles. When working in a psychiatric or psychomedical clinic as a team member, the psychologist devotes most of his time and energy to diagnostic evaluations. Psychologists are, however, increasingly engaged in group therapy with adults and play therapy with children.

Emerging trends and legislation. While there is no legal protection for the profession of

[4] Joseph R. Nuttin (Louvain).

clinical psychology in Belgium, most state-supported services and private clinics accept only university-trained psychologists. The Belgian Psychological Association has repeatedly expressed its support of basic standards of training to the official authorities.

Czechoslovakia[5]

General situation. Clinical psychology in Czechoslovakia has a relatively short history. Its development did not begin until after World War II. At that time, some psychologists were interested in solving certain research tasks in the field of psychopathology. They worked in research teams under the supervision of psychiatrists. In the process of this collaboration, there appeared the need for psychological examination of psychiatric patients. In these cases, more detailed information about the mental ability and the personality of the patient was expected, and clinical psychologists could help in making the diagnosis more precise. In about 1950 the profession of clinical psychology was, for the first time, officially recognized in Czechoslovak hospitals and clinics. Since that time, the number of psychologists working in medical settings has risen to more than one hundred, indicating the growing need for specialized psychological services. Czechoslovak medicine follows with increasing consistency the principle of mutual interrelation between psychic and somatic factors. This principle is also reflected in the fact that psychologists are employed in other branches of medicine, including neurology, pediatrics, internal medicine, gynecology, sexology, surgery, etc.

Professional roles. The professional responsibilities of the clinical psychologist depend to a great degree upon the institution where he works, but they are focused chiefly upon diagnostic procedures. In addition to psychological interviews and various psychological tests, experimental techniques (special apparatuses) are used. The psychologist usually examines only those patients who are referred to him by the psychiatrist, and the examination then depends on the special problem presented. The main tasks of the clinical psychologist include detailed study of the patient's personality, quantitative evaluation of certain psychological functions, and assistance in solving differential diagnostic problems.

Psychotherapy is usually practiced by the clinical psychologist through indirect efforts; that is, the psychologist frequently arranges the environment of the patient and by cultural means and work therapy contributes to an effective organization of the patient's schedule. He may often take the leading role in developing such therapeutic progress. In group therapy he is usually a member of the therapeutic team. In individual psychotherapy the psychologist uses chiefly educational methods; other approaches are used only rarely, in special cases recommended by the psychiatrist who supervises the progress of the therapy.

Psychologists working in clinics take an active part in the training of medical students and psychology trainees. They are also engaged in medical research, either individually or in research teams. In the latter case, they are oriented especially to methodological aspects.

Emerging trends and legislation. The work of clinical psychologists has been evaluated positively on the basis of experience. The profession of clinical psychology is socially as well as legally acknowledged. The recent document of the Czechoslovak government (March, 1962) dealing with the "measures for the progress of psychiatric care" contains the following instructions: "The psychologists are to be appropriately employed in the complex therapy and diagnostics, and thus to be directly associated with the practical work in out-patient and in-patient care." After the initial controversy regarding the definition of the competence and optimal use of the clinical psychologist in the field of psychiatry, a period of fruitful collaboration between clinical psychologists and psychiatrists has begun. The results of the psychological examination are now used also for educational, forensic, and other purposes.

Clinical psychology in Czechoslovakia is still in the process of development. The possibilities and limitations of the application of psychology in psychodiagnosis and psychotherapy are gradually crystallizing. Methodological equipment is being improved with regard to special cultural and social conditions. The fur-

[5] J. Hoskovec (Charles University, Prague) and J. Diamant (Charles University Psychiatric Clinic, Prague).

ther improvement of psychological work in medicine would be speeded by a more intensive exchange of experiences on an international level.

Denmark[6]

Clinical psychology in Denmark is in a period of notable growth and rapid development. Danish authorities have shown increasing interest in assigning psychologists to varied medical and social institutions. More than one hundred psychologists, about one-third of the membership of the Danish Psychological Association, are active in psychiatric clinics and hospitals and in institutions for children, adolescents, and adults. They have developed particular skill in working with psychiatric and neurological cases; mental retardates; crippled, maladjusted, and delinquent children; and criminals.

Professional roles. In most psychiatric teams, the main activity of the clinical psychologist is diagnostic testing. In child guidance clinics, institutions for maladjusted children, and centers for alcoholics, criminals, etc., there is more emphasis on psychotherapy. The type of psychotherapeutic techniques used depends on the setting served and on the training and theoretical orientation of the psychologist, ranging from strictly psychoanalytic procedures to a combined pedagogical-psychological approach.

In university clinics, psychologists participate in research programs, either as team members or independently. They also join in the training of other mental health professions. In other centers, psychologists engage in group activities or function as consultants.

Emerging trends and legislation. In 1958, the Joint Committee of the Scandinavian Psychology Association asked the Northern Council, an official body for the Scandinavian countries, to consider the problems of the legal registration of psychologists, protection of the title "psychologist," protection against misuse of test material, and the possibility of coordinating university training. The Northern Council accepted the proposal and asked the individual countries to establish national subcommittees. Shortly, it is expected that all the national subcommittees will have ended their work and reported back to the Northern Council, which then has to coordinate the suggestions and propose standards for Scandinavia.

In 1961, the Cultural Commission of the Northern Council asked the Joint Committee of the Scandinavian Psychology Association to appoint a subcommittee to develop proposals for arranging courses and common training for psychologists on the postgraduate level. This subcommittee hopes to complete its work in the near future.

Relations between clinical psychologists and psychiatrists have progressed satisfactorily. In the past decade, medical authorities have evidenced increasing interest in attaching clinical psychologists to hospitals and institutions. In Denmark psychologists can obtain proper psychoanalytic training, and in those psychiatric clinics where psychotherapy is offered, qualified psychologists participate in this activity on equal terms with medical psychotherapists.

Federal Republic of West Germany[7]

General situation. Clinical psychology is still in its infancy in the Federal Republic of West Germany. The very name "clinical psychology" has aroused considerable conflict with the medical profession, which is generally unwilling to accept the term "clinical" in the title of a nonmedical psychologist. Training in professional psychology is relatively new and has been handicapped by the absence of a widely accepted image. The few university departments offering some training tend to concentrate on psychodiagnosis, at the expense of both research and psychotherapy. Psychologists working in clinics usually function as assistants to physicians and have only rarely attained the role of professional colleague or consultant. Independent private practice tends to be limited to psychodiagnostics, usually for vocational or forensic purposes.

Most psychologists begin their professional careers immediately after leaving the university. If they work in one of the many new "educational counseling centers," their primary responsibility is usually for the diagnostic study of children or adults. Only rarely is a psychologist trained to do therapy, and re-

[6] Karen Berntsen (Copenhagen) and Lise Østergaard (University of Copenhagen).

[7] Hildegard Hiltmann (Freiburg) and Hans J. Priester (Princeton, N.J.).

search is generally considered the function of the university. The team approach is still viewed with skepticism.

Emerging trends and legislation. There is a subcommittee on clinical psychology in the German Psychological Society working jointly with the Professional Association of German Psychologists which is attempting to raise standards and obtain legislation. There are many obstacles, and progress has been slow. Considerable work has been done toward evolving ethical standards for clinical psychologists, but no agreement has been reached so far. Over 40 per cent of practicing psychologists are licensed in graphology.

There has been considerable resistance from the medical profession to the notion of a "clinical" psychology. Professional psychological services are handicapped by the continuing preference of most German psychiatrists for an organic orientation. There is an almost complete absence of a dynamic approach. Community mental health is in its infancy. Psychologists do, however, enjoy increasingly good relations with psychiatric colleagues in many university clinics and research centers, which offers much hope for the future.

Clinical psychology is emerging in the Federal Republic of West Germany amid many difficulties. As standards for training become accepted within psychology itself and as public service demands grow, the profession of psychology will make its contribution here as it has in other lands.

Finland[8]

General situation. While the profession of clinical psychology is of relatively recent origin in Finland, demands for services and training have grown considerably in the past decade. Most of the approximately seventy-five clinical psychologists serve in public hospitals and clinics; only a small number are in private practice (mainly psychoanalysis).

Finland is divided into 18 districts for public health services. According to present plans, each district will have an A hospital (for acute cases), several B hospitals (mainly for chronic cases), and community clinics for children and adults. When this report was written, psychologists were on the staffs of 23 child guidance centers. Costs are jointly defrayed by the state and the communities.

[8] Martti Takala and Isto Ruoppila (Center for Educational Research, Jyväskylä).

Professional roles. Although no uniform legislation has been enacted, steps have been initiated to define psychological roles and professional responsibility. This responsibility has been dependent partly on the (special) training received by clinical psychologists and partly on the availability of psychiatrists. According to law, the institutional psychiatrist is responsible for diagnosis and therapy. In practice, however, it has often been left to the clinical psychologist to render diagnoses, especially in cases of mentally defective persons. In Finland there is limited psychotherapy outside of private practice, so that it is difficult to write much about this matter. Aside from selection studies in psychiatric nursing, there is little research.

Emerging trends and legislation. A bill now under consideration reserves the title "psychologist" for individuals who have completed a stipulated training program leading to the equivalent of an M.A. degree. The bill follows legislation already enacted in other Scandinavian countries and contains statutes regarding training, professional ethics, and psychological evaluation. Training will take about six years, including eighteen months of practicum.

France[9]

General situation. France, with its long tradition of intelligence testing (Binet) and advances in psychopathology (Pinel), offers little impetus for the development of a separate profession of clinical psychology. Indeed, the very term "clinical psychology" has given rise to much controversy, with many physicians maintaining that the connotation of "bedside psychology" encroaches on the medical domain.

Numerous well-known French psychologists are primarily philosophers who continue to espouse a strong relationship to philosophy and who have not been receptive to a more scientific orientation. Many eminent clinical psychologists tend to be psychiatrists, one of whom (Pichot) wrote the first modern French text on psychological testing in 1949.

Professional roles. As already noted, the work of nonmedical French clinical psychologists is largely limited to diagnostic contributions.

[9] Victor D. Sanua (Yeshiva) and Emory L. Cowen (Rochester).

Psychotherapy by nonphysicians is strongly resisted by psychiatrists. Although in 1953 the Paris Court of Appeals convicted a nonmedical analyst for the illegal practice of medicine, psychologists have continued to practice therapy, particularly with children and delinquent youths and in psychological counseling services.

Emerging trends and legislation. Professional problems are complicated by the lack of legal protection for clinical psychologists and by the claim to the title "psychologist" by many unqualified individuals. The French Psychological Association recently adopted a code of ethics and is further exploring the situation.

The relationship between psychiatry and psychology is a relatively old one in France. A strong psychopathological tradition was established at the time of Charcot, and the memorable work of Binet created much interest in psychological evaluation. While psychiatrists have fostered a program leading to the diploma in pathological psychology at the Sorbonne Institute of Psychology, they are generally of the opinion that the psychologist should be restricted to administering and interpreting tests. At this time French psychiatry is still intimately associated with neurology, treatment is most frequently along classical lines, and interest in psychodynamics is emerging only slowly.

Despite its early start and long tradition, French clinical psychology has still to emerge as an accepted science and profession.

German Democratic Republic[10]

Professional training and specialization in medical psychology may be obtained at the Psychological Institutes of Humboldt University in East Berlin and at the Universities of Leipzig and Dresden. A fourth institute is to be established at the University of Jena. Allowing for individual differences in the personal orientation of the respective directors, academic requirements in all three institutes are largely similar and follow the pattern of other German universities. Primary focus is on training for research. The diploma course lasts five years and is followed by an additional four years for those relatively few who continue to the doctorate.

Training in medical psychology at Humboldt University is facilitated by extensive modern laboratories and by a kindergarten for disturbed children, who can be continually observed and studied through one-way screens and other recording media. A nonmedical director is in charge, with a psychiatrist available for consultation. Much of the research is topological and Lewinian in orientation, with a modified gestalt methodology prevailing. The majority of students, after receiving their diplomas, go into clinics, industry, or some form of teaching. Research is emphasized as an integral part of their responsibilities.

The Institute of Cortical-Visceral Pathology and Therapy of the German Academy of Science in East Berlin is engaged in efforts to integrate clinical and experimental techniques within a framework of Pavlovian physiology and psychology. Recognizing that Pavlov was concerned with all forms of activities, not just conditioning, in his attempts to formulate the principles of higher nervous functioning, Pavlovian concepts have been applied at a variety of physiological and psychological levels. Sleep therapy, which in accord with these principles is regarded as a form of protective inhibition, is practiced extensively. At first, sleep is induced by means of barbiturates and similar agents; then, using placebos and a variety of pleasant conditioned stimuli (interspersed by drug reinforcements from time to time), a conditioned sleep response pattern is gradually introduced.

Medical psychology in the German Democratic Republic is part of the state service; there is no private practice. Communication with colleagues is facilitated through the German Psychological Society and other professional associations whose activities transcend the borders between East and West.

Greece[11]

There is practically no training in clinical psychology being conducted in Greece. Of the small number of professional psychologists in the country, most were trained elsewhere in Europe and a few in the United States. Only one holds a Ph.D. in clinical psychology, awarded by an American university. The recently founded Hellenic Psychological Association has 22 members; approximately one-half are involved in clinical work. There is no

10 Cyril M. Franks (Princeton, N.J.).

11 Vasso Vassiliou (Athens).

legislation recognizing the profession of clinical psychology, and professional standards and requirements are in only the developmental stage.

The major function of clinical psychologists in Greece is psychodiagnosis, and most patients are referred for psychometric evaluation. A few do psychotherapy. One of the initial aims of the Hellenic Psychological Association is to establish standards of professional practice. The prevailing psychiatric orientation continues to be largely organic, although the dynamic approach is rapidly growing in popularity.

Ireland[12]

General situation. While applications of psychology in educational, clinical, and industrial areas are still in their infancy in Ireland, the 1960s have initiated a period of more rapid development. The Minister of Health has appointed two commissions of inquiry, one in the area of mental retardation and one in the area of mental illness. An Irish branch of the Association of Child Psychology and Psychiatry has been organized, a National Association for the Mentally Handicapped is flourishing, and an Irish Psychological Society is in the discussion stage.

Professional roles. There are about four psychologists in full-time employment in clinical situations in Ireland, and their major assignment is diagnosis. Although therapy is considered the principal function of psychiatrists, there is no rigid delimitation of roles, and some psychologists may have a large case load of practically every type of therapy. In education there are three full-time psychologists, and in industry there are two.

Emerging trends and legislation. As of 1963, Ireland had no state certification for psychologists and no statutory requirements for their training or professional employment. However, the increasing number of psychology teaching appointments in the universities of Dublin and Cork bodes well, and the eventual emergence of an Irish Psychological Society may supply the impetus needed for the advancement of professional endeavors.

[12] John McKenna (Dublin).

Italy[13]

General situation. Psychology as a science and profession is rather underdeveloped in Italy, mainly as the result of idealistic philosophical traditions. The only avenues of specialization have been either in departments of philosophy or in institutes of psychology, where individuals with any degree (mostly M.D.) are admitted for postgraduate training, sometimes in conjunction with a residency in psychiatry. This is one reason for the production of physicians with training in clinical psychology amid a sprinkling of a few Ph.D.s. Another approach to clinical psychology is via a few schools of education, where there is some overlap with clinical psychology in the area of psychometric work with children.

Clinical psychology as an area of specialization is only second in importance to vocational guidance and industrial psychology. The wide range and variety of interests are further exemplified by the psychoanalysts, one of whose recent presidents held a degree in chemistry.

Among the approximately 250 qualified psychologists recognized by the Italian Psychological Association, nearly one-third are engaged in part-time clinical activities, while about fifty are engaged full time. Clinical psychologists are generally found in the newly established child guidance centers, using a team approach; in special training schools; in state hospitals; and in the Bureau of Correction of the Department of Justice, where they participate in medicolegal expert opinions for criminal and legal cases.

Professional roles. In addition to private practice, qualified clinical psychologists frequently hold part-time positions in institutions, such as (in decreasing frequency) child guidance clinics, juvenile courts and prisons, mental hospitals, universities (only teaching), public schools, the armed forces, and research centers. Their work is primarily psychodiagnostic, rarely psychotherapeutic. Qualified psychotherapists are almost exclusively Freudian psychoanalysts. Of the many physicians who claim to do psychotherapy, few have adequate training.

Emerging trends and legislation. Present legislation recognizes the title "specialist in psy-

[13] Franco Ferracuti (Puerto Rico), Luciano L'Abate (Atlanta), and Luigi Meschieri (Rome).

chology" for only two categories of persons: (1) those who have graduated from the specialization (postgraduate) schools of psychology, officially recognized by the state, and (2) those who have the title "libero docente," i.e., those who have passed a careful examination by a state-appointed commission and who have presented a good deal of original research work.

Owing to the small number and recent establishment of the specialization schools in psychology and to their limited output, as well as to the difficulty of the examination for the Libera Docenza, the total number of specialists is currently about fifty.

The professional title "psychologist" is not restricted by law. Outside the statutes regulating medical practice, there is no special legislation to protect the public from improper or unethical practices. The Italian Psychological Association in 1960 established stringent membership requirements and criteria for recognizing clinical psychologists.

The traditional psychiatric approach in Italy is largely organic. In recent years, many psychiatrists have tended to identify more with clinical psychology than with medicine. However, it is essential to remember that most Italian clinical psychologists are psychiatrists. As a result, it is at times difficult for a nonmedically trained clinical psychologist to achieve recognition at a medical school or even in an institute of psychology directed by a nonclinical psychologist who also holds a medical degree.

In Italy, as elsewhere in Europe, there has been a strong American influence since the end of World War II. There is a growing public demand for clinical psychological services. Fulbright-sponsored American psychologists have made an impact on Italian universities. While philosophical and political opposition to psychology and other social sciences is slowly fading away, implementation of new psychological concepts will require further patience.

The Netherlands[14]

General situation. Clinical psychology in the Netherlands, in both theory and practice, is strongly influenced by the meaning inherent in the term "clinical." Most clinical psychologists work in psychiatric or general hospitals and in institutions. They are usually members of the Netherlands Institute for Practicing Psychologists, an organization similar to the American Psychological Association, and maintain contact with their colleagues in the Clinical Section. If their interests are primarily in child or vocational guidance, their main connection with NIPP is through the Section of Child and Adolescent Psychology.

Nearly every Dutch psychiatric institution or clinic has one or more clinical psychologists. One of the requirements for training psychiatric residents is that a qualified psychologist be on the staff of the training facility. While the present supply of adequately trained clinical psychologists is insufficient to meet the demand, this situation is likely to change with the increasing number of psychology students.

Professional roles. Perhaps the most important role for clinical psychologists in the Netherlands is that of a psychodiagnostician who attempts to supply insights into the individual's personality in answer to questions posed by the psychiatric staff. The function of the psychologist may be seen as somewhat more socially than scientifically oriented; the major responsibility is to describe the patient in terms which will help the psychiatrist to stabilize his opinions and diagnosis. Thus, the psychologist often has little chance to do independent research or to test his hypotheses and insights. Some psychologists are presently endeavoring to lessen their dependency ties with the psychiatrist. They are seeking respectability through utilizing and formulating more authentic psychological theories and objective test methods. Although many of the projective techniques are believed to be of dubious value, they are still widely used because more exact methods do not often offer information with which clinically formulated questions can be answered.

In several clinics the clinical psychologist also provides instruction for nurses and work therapists. In the university hospitals his most important task is the training of psychology students in the practice of clinical psychology. In some cases this may also include instructing psychiatric residents.

The University of Utrecht has introduced to its staff an associate professor in nonmedical psychotherapy, and at present Utrecht is the only university in the Netherlands to have

[14] J. T. Barendregt and A. Gravestein (Amsterdam).

such a position. At most universities preparations are made to involve some aspects of nondirective therapy techniques into the training program for psychology students. Neither inside nor outside the universities are there centers where systematic training in psychotherapy can be obtained, except for the international and national psychoanalytic associations, which in principle are open to psychologists. Despite these uncontrolled conditions, many individual clinical psychologists do attempt psychotherapy. Their efforts take the form of classical or nonclassical psychoanalysis, nondirective therapy, group therapy, behavior therapy, and movement and creative therapy. Some progress toward a more organized and scientific approach to psychotherapy is evident in the growing research studies and in a recently formed Rogerian work group, which is composed of psychologists and representatives from allied disciplines. It should also be noted that many clinical psychologists are directly involved in therapy in psychiatric clinics through their participation in work and creative therapy programs.

Since the training received by the clinical psychologist is directed more toward the analyses of methodological problems and their importance in research, he is usually called upon to play a major role in research conducted in psychiatric institutions.

Emerging trends and legislation. There is no legislative control, certification, or licensing of the profession of psychology in the Netherlands. Some preparations in this direction have been initiated, but it may be a long time before they are realized. Although the universities have eradicated their major differences, they have not yet agreed upon standardized training programs for specialization purposes, including clinical psychology.

It is difficult to find a common denominator for the psychiatric orientation found in the Netherlands since viewpoints from a variety of origins, such as psychoanalysis, phenomenology, anthropological philosophy, sociology, biology, and neuropathology, have all made their contributions and have become integrated into a broad, somewhat collective whole. The clashes of personality and the often-perceived mutual deafness and ability for misunderstanding between the worlds of psychiatry and psychology have all but vanished in the practical clinical situation. However, if clinical psychology is to mature in the Netherlands, it must focus on progress in theory formation, methodology, and research as well as on advances in training.

Norway[15]

General situation. Clinical psychology in Norway is in a period of rapid expansion. Clinicians represent the largest single group within the Norwegian Psychological Association; about 50 per cent of the 260 members are engaged in some clinical psychological work. There is also a clear tendency among graduate students to choose clinical psychology as their main field of study.

The great majority of Norwegian clinical psychologists hold official positions in national or local services; only a few are in private practice. The range of activities is very wide, including correctional centers, public child welfare stations, neurological departments, school psychology facilities, psychiatric clinics, and mental hospitals. The clinical psychologist is viewed as a necessary and natural participant on the staff of every psychiatric institution.

Professional roles. It is commonly accepted that psychologists do both diagnostics and psychotherapy as part of their clinical work. The distribution of time and energy between these two main activities depends on the institution's needs and on the particular psychologist's interest and background. Within the field of child treatment, by and large, only psychologists engage in long-range, intensive psychotherapy.

For the most part, psychotherapy is conducted by psychologists within or in close contact with medical institutions. A small group, composed mainly of psychoanalytically oriented psychologists, is in purely private practice. The only accredited training analysts in Norway are psychologists; they provide therapeutic training and act as controls for both psychiatrists and clinical psychologists.

Emerging trends and legislation. While there is no legal protection for the title "psychologist" in Norway, a state-appointed committee is considering the problem of licensing, working in cooperation with similar committees in Sweden, Finland, and Denmark.

15 William Rabinowitz (Pennsylvania State) and Bjørn Killingmo (Oslo).

The Norwegian Psychological Association (NPF) has established regulations with approved standards for "specialist in clinical psychology, NPF." This title is commonly known and publicly accepted and provides a foundation for, among other things, salary schedules in official positions. NPF has also developed regulations for approving competence to conduct intensive psychotherapy on an independent basis. These standards await formal adoption.

A variety of professional orientations may be found among and within institutions. While there may be occasional local differences and problems in interprofessional communication, these have not hindered the expansion of clinical psychology in society. In a general sense, there is mutual respect and acceptance between psychiatry and clinical psychology in Norway.

Poland[16]

General situation. Before World War II, Polish psychology, while separate from philosophy, was still combined with it in a common curriculum and philosophical approach to some general problems of psychology as a science of mental phenomena. Although educational and developmental psychology blossomed with the establishment of child guidance centers and child welfare stations, neither industrial nor clinical psychology was included in university curriculums, and statistical studies were relatively rare. During World War II, Polish universities were closed, and journals and publications were suspended. In the postwar reconstruction period, when Pavlovian theories prevailed in the universities, clinical psychologists began to be employed in outpatient clinics, hospitals for the mentally ill, and rehabilitation centers. The most recent period of progress followed the 1956 Convention of Polish Psychologists.

Training of clinical psychology and its postwar expansion were greatly facilitated by the existence of the Institute of Mental Hygiene, established in 1935, and its affiliated Higher School of Mental Hygiene, organized in 1942 and underground until the end of the war. Both centers were founded by Prof. Kazimierz Dabrowski, foremost pioneer of the mental hygiene movement in Poland. Several hundred clinical psychologists were trained before the institutes were closed in 1952. Closely related to clinical psychology are some of the endeavors of the Institute of Special Education, founded in 1921 through the efforts of Prof. Maria Grzegorzewska and headed by her to the present day.

Clinical psychology is numerically the best-developed field in Polish psychology. More than two hundred psychologists work in psychiatric hospitals and outpatient clinics; about fifty are in rehabilitation, neurology, pediatrics, tuberculosis, and other hospitals; and perhaps twenty more are in correctional centers. It is estimated that approximately 40 per cent of all professional psychologists in Poland are involved in clinical endeavors. The Conference of Clinical Psychologists, organized in 1962 by the Committee of Applied Psychology of the Polish Psychological Association and the Department of Prophylaxis and Therapeutics of the Ministry of Health and Social Care, has attracted more than seven hundred persons, including clinical and other psychologists, physicians, sociologists, and teachers.

Professional roles. The roles of clinical psychologists in Poland differ according to their qualifications and local needs. The main duties are interviewing and diagnostic testing, and very rarely psychotherapy. Among the tests used most often are the Wechsler-Bellevue and the WISC, the Stanford-Binet, the Rorschach, the TAT, the MMPI, incomplete sentences tests, the Graham-Kendall Memory for Designs Test, and the Bender-Gestalt. However, these tests are not yet properly adapted, and much effort is being devoted to their validation and standardization.

In centers such as the Babinski Hospital, where, thanks to its good equipment and professionally responsible approach, psychology gained prestige and confidence, all patients with diagnostic problems are psychologically examined. In other places the contributions of psychologists to diagnosis may be greater or smaller; in some, their duties are more similar to those of psychiatric social workers in the United States. In university hospitals and at the Psychoneurological Institute in Pruszkow, psychologists participate in research.

Psychotherapy by psychologists is usually challenged by psychiatrists, many of whom assume that professionally adequate psychotherapy can be practiced only by physicians. There is no private practice. However, psy-

[16] M. Choynowski (Warsaw) and Zenomena Pluzek (Krakow).

chologists are paid by the state on the same basis as physicians. Salary bonuses depend on years of service and attaining graduate degrees.

Emerging trends and legislation. While clinical psychology has clearly emerged as a profession, it has not yet attained formal recognition. The Polish Psychological Association, with its more than seven hundred members, has endeavored to facilitate progress through its Committee of Applied Psychology, chaired by Prof. Janina Budkiewicz. A preliminary draft of a legislative bill for the profession of psychology has been completed. Although medical institutes, as indicated, employ psychologists on the same basis as physicians and at a similar rate of remuneration, professional prestige in the field of medical care is not always equal.

While there is good cooperation between psychology and psychiatry in the field of psychodiagnosis, there are still some psychiatrists who would prefer to limit psychologists' roles to the functions of a social worker. Although there continue to be differences of opinion regarding psychotherapy, since 1959 psychologists have been invited to become members of the Polish Psychiatric Association. Relations with other physicians, especially in the area of physical rehabilitation, are encouraged; this may be because there is a clearer division of roles and no collision of competence, interests, and ambition. Supported by the very favorable attitude of the Ministry of Health and Social Care, most physicians welcome cooperation with psychologists and are eager to employ them in medical institutions.

There is an ever-growing interest in clinical psychology among Polish university students, and the number of clinical psychologists is rapidly expanding. While the level of professional training at the universities is improving less quickly, the recent creation of a chair and of two new departments of clinical psychology offers hope for further development. The lack of ready-to-use tests and professional literature is slowly being overcome through research and translation efforts, facilitated by international contacts.

Portugal[17]

General situation. Clinical psychology has been accepted as a field of professional specialization in Portugal, requiring postgraduate training. Psychologists usually acquire training through personal initiative under organized or private supervision, which may be recognized by professional societies, or through "public service examinations." The past decade has witnessed an explosive demand for psychological service, in both diagnosis and treatment. Schools and industry are clamoring for trained professionals.

Professional roles. Portuguese state civil service examinations define the status of most practicing clinical psychologists independently of their graduation in medicine or in philosophy (psychology). As in many other countries, the work of professional nonmedical psychologists is often considered controversial.

Some institutions use less adequately trained individuals to provide certain diagnostic procedures, for example, specialized teachers working under supervision, physicians with the "civil service exam" for school health, social workers, and engineers with in-service training in "human relations."

Emerging trends and legislation. The three responsible associations dealing with clinical psychology (the Society for Neurology and Psychiatry, the Portuguese Society for Psychology, and the Luso-Spanish Society for Psychoanalysis) have accepted, in principle, the need for close cooperation of different professionals in the study and treatment of human beings. Although there is less emphasis on formal status, there is considerable concern about enforcing standards.

While the decisions of these societies apply only to members and do not have statutory force, they exert valuable influence on the evolution of opinion and practice. In some centers, such as the Group Analytic Section of the Portuguese Society of Neurology and Psychology, the concepts of status, standards, and teamwork among psychiatrists, psychologists, and specialized social workers have been particularly successfully interwoven.

Spain[18]

An independent nonmedical profession of clinical psychology is only beginning to emerge in Spain. Professional roles are clouded by the fact that there are very few clinical psychologists who are not psychiatrists.

17 Maria Rita Mendes Leal (Lisbon).

18 Jose L. Pinillos (Valencia).

There is no legislation pertaining to psychological practices. The Spanish Psychological Society has a Section on Clinical Psychology, which is attempting to develop professional standards.

Sweden[19]

General situation. Although the profession of psychology is very new to Sweden, clinical psychology is making rapid advances. Practice was limited largely to children and adolescents in the 1940s, but in the subsequent decade increasing opportunities arose in mental hospitals and in work with adults in special settings. Membership in the Swedish Psychological Association has grown from about thirty in 1950 to over eight hundred in 1962.

Professional roles. Professional responsibilities assumed by Swedish psychologists depend on their training and experience as well as on the functions of the institutions in which they work. Psychodiagnosis is practiced by nearly all and usually includes interviewing, testing of mental level, and differential diagnosis, generally performed in cooperation with medical colleagues. In the absence of training facilities, few psychologists undertake psychotherapy with institutionalized adult patients. However, psychotherapy with children and adolescents is conducted mainly by psychologists, most of whom are trained at the Erica Foundation. Many psychologists engage in part-time research, which consists mostly of test validation and psychopharmacological investigations; a few are exploring aspects of psychotherapy. A number of psychologists serve as consultants to social welfare institutions, courts, and other centers.

There are about two hundred licensed clinical psychologists in Sweden; two-thirds work with children and most of the rest with adults, either at psychiatric clinics or at mental hospitals. Eight psychologists are members, and ten are associates of the Swedish Psycho-Analytical Society. While some are assistant psychologists, since 1954 the status of "psychologist" has been required for acceptance in psychoanalytic training by nonmedical personnel.

Emerging trends and legislation. A committee of the Swedish Psychological Association is reconsidering the problems of specialist education, while another group is studying matters of confidentiality and state certification. Both committees work in close cooperation with similar groups in Denmark, Norway, and Finland, with the aim of establishing Scandinavian standards for professional psychology.

The Royal Swedish Medical Board has ruled that assistant psychologists in the health services must have at least six months of supervised clinical experience, which is similar to the practicum standard of the Swedish Psychological Association. To become a certified psychologist requires at least one year's supervised practicum or a year's service as assistant psychologist.

After a period of marked uneasiness and a certain aloofness evinced by the medical profession, interprofessional relations can now be said to be quite satisfactory. Where tension still prevails, it seems to be individually, not organizationally, motivated.

The growth curve of the Swedish Psychological Association reflects the rapid progress of the science and profession of psychology. With the eventual acceptance of Scandinavian standards, the stage will be set for further advances in professional practice.

Switzerland[20]

The beginnings of Swiss clinical psychology coincided with the development of psychoanalysis in the first decade of the century at the Burgholzli Clinic in Zurich and at the University of Geneva. Significant contributions to psychoanalysis and psychodiagnosis were made not only by such outstanding psychiatrists as Bleuler, Jung, Maeder, Binswanger, Rorschach, and others but also by distinguished nonmedically trained individuals, including the Protestant minister Oscar Pfister and the elementary school teacher Hans Zulliger. They, their students, and their followers rooted the scientific bases for their activities in their initially secondary, and later often primary, private practice of psychotherapy and counseling. To this day, a relatively large percentage of Swiss clinical psychologists are in private practice rather than clinics. The term "clinical" is used more for comparison with the activities of colleagues abroad than as a description of local trends.

Despite the early interest in certain academic circles, only a few research and training

[19] Gösta Fröbärj (Göteborg) and Margareta Garai (Stockholm).

[20] Fred Schmid (Zurich).

centers for clinical psychology have developed in university departments outside the medical faculties. Many of the most renowned analysts and researchers either were called to teach in an academic setting only late in life or were never called at all. Even today, clinical psychology is only beginning to attain some standing in Swiss universities. General recognition of a separate discipline or systematic development of training centers has hardly begun.

Even stronger resistance to the emergence of a nonmedical clinical psychology has arisen in the Swiss psychiatric hospitals and clinics. These centers have remained almost entirely closed to the professional psychologist and offer very limited opportunities for service, training, and research. Only in the last several years have a few of these centers established permanent positions for psychologists.

An important exception is that branch of clinical psychology which is primarily concerned with children and adolescents. Almost from the beginning, the canton- and city-supported educational guidance centers, school psychological services, medicopedagogic services, child psychiatric centers, and institutions have employed clinical psychological techniques and assigned responsibilities to nonmedical psychologists and therapists (as well as to physicians, social workers, remedial teachers, and other staff members). This tradition is also reflected in the universities, where child-centered clinical psychology has had a much better reception than clinical psychology in general.

Vocational guidance, counseling, and industrial psychology have a much stronger clinical orientation in Switzerland than in many other countries. Before World War II, the Institute of Applied Psychology in Zurich took the lead in adopting a total, personality-oriented "clinical" approach and in establishing the Psychologisches Seminar, a training center at which many psychologists in business and industry received their professional education. While it may appear paradoxical, it is characteristic of Switzerland that clinical psychology has made far greater advances in the primarily nonclinical areas of applied psychology, while the clinics have largely remained closed and research and training have progressed very slowly in the universities. This trend is also reflected in the current status of Swiss clinical psychology; it is strongly reality-focused and very creative in practical areas, while at the same time it is relatively weak in advancing theory, methodology, and psychopathology.

Professional roles. The majority of Swiss clinical psychologists are engaged in psychological counseling and psychotherapy and also practice psychodiagnosis (including graphology). Some specialize in graphology alone. Most prefer independent private practice. Their next choice is to work in institutions for children and adolescents. Only a few clinical psychologists hold senior positions in large public institutions.

There are quite a number of national and regional professional organizations. The coordinating body for all Swiss psychology is the Swiss Society for Psychology and Its Applications (SGPA). Federated with it are, among others, the Swiss Graphological Society, the Swiss Rorschach Commission, the International Rorschach Society, and the Szondi Commission. To obtain individual membership in the Swiss society, a candidate must have completed his university training.

Many graduates of the Psychologisches Seminar and similar schools—especially those active in industrial psychology, but also several clinical psychologists—are members of the Swiss Professional Organization for Applied Psychology (SBAP).

Emerging trends and legislation. Currently there are no federal statutes regarding the activities of clinical psychologists in Switzerland. Protection of titles or admission procedures for practice are nonexistent. The only exceptions are in the cantons of Baselland and Neuenburg. Baselland requires sanction by the Department of Health of educational guidance activities, and Neuenburg insists that examination and treatment of psychological conditions be supervised by a medical specialist. In other cantons, medical practice acts are interpreted so liberally that clinical psychologists are hardly aware of any limitations on their professional practice.

The professional liability of clinical psychologists, especially psychotherapists, is guarded by Swiss professional societies, e.g., the Swiss Society for Psychoanalysis, the Swiss Society for Practical Psychology, etc. These professional organizations accept as members physicians and nonphysicians on a basis of equality. Efforts have been initiated, particularly by the Swiss Professional Organization for Applied

Psychology, to revise statutes and to accept as members only those persons who satisfy basic criteria of training and supervised experience.

To date, Swiss psychiatry has neither participated in nor supported efforts to develop clinical psychology. While public debates regarding the legitimacy of nonmedical psychodiagnosis and psychotherapy, so common in the 1930s, have not occurred in recent years, certain medical circles insist that the practice of clinical psychology should be reserved for physicians. There is little likelihood that this view will prevail, particularly in the face of the growing strength of psychotherapeutic specialty organizations, which currently train more nonphysicians than physicians.

The prospect is good that clinical psychology will continue to grow and develop in Switzerland. Progress is particularly likely in practical applications. It may be expected that the number of clinical psychologists will increase in private and public institutions, including schools, homes and clinics, industry, and administration. From a qualitative point of view, however, a decisive breakthrough is unlikely until the current splintering in the training area has been resolved. Swiss clinical psychology will have to recognize the desirability and necessity of working toward unification and creation of training and research centers that correspond to the most modern standards.

Union of Soviet Socialist Republics[21]

General situation. Much has been said and written about Soviet psychology, its adherence to Pavlovian concepts of higher nervous activity, and its relation to the Marxist philosophy of dialectical materialism. On his 1960 visit to the United States, Professor Luria defined Soviet psychology as the "science of voluntary behavior in man." He reported that one of the focuses of current research is Pavlov's second signal system, involving aspects of physiology, conditioning, and speech in relation to problem solving. However, "speech" is not purely motor or verbal; it includes culturally derived meanings and concepts. Unconscious processes are also studied, and much of the work done in Soviet physiological laboratories would be labeled "psychological" in the United States. Russian psychology also emphasizes the importance of social interaction in man's historical development, and studies in social psychology have been initiated by the Institute of Philosophy of the USSR Academy of Sciences.

"Work in the field of pathological or clinical psychology is an essential part of Soviet psychology." So wrote Luria some years ago, when he described the work of Soviet researchers as "mainly directed to the study of pathological change in the dynamics of the nervous processes which lie behind disturbances in mental activity." Luria emphasizes the importance of "exact methods" of psychological experimentation "to put the diagnosis of nervous and mental ailments on a scientific basis, and to elaborate scientific methods of restoring impaired function." However, it should be noted that the term "clinical psychology," when applied to the Soviet Union, usually refers to "psychopathology." Work in this field is generally in medicine or pathophysiology under the primary direction of physicians. Luria is both an M.D. and a Ph.D.

Professional roles. The assignments, responsibilities, and remuneration of Soviet "clinical psychologists" are determined by the Ministry of Health, often in association with the Academy of Medical Sciences. Activities in psychopathology follow a Pavlovian orientation, which usually means that major interest is focused on studies of pathological changes in the higher nervous processes believed to lie behind mental disturbances.

In 1960 there were about seventy medical psychologists in major Soviet psychiatric centers. Their activities are largely limited to diagnosis, particularly in regard to questions of organic involvement and rehabilitation. As "psychoneurologists," they work in neurological, psychiatric, and neurosurgical hospitals and clinics, usually organized into teams with colleagues from the medical professions, educators, defectologists, or teachers who may be concerned with the recommendations. One of the senior clinical psychologists is Madame B. V. Zeigarnik, well known for her earlier work with Lewin. She teaches psychopathology at the University of Moscow and heads the Psychology Laboratory at the Institute of Psychiatry, affiliated with the Academy of Medical Sciences.

Psychological tests were severely criticized during the 1930s and were condemned in a 1936 Communist Party decree as unscientific,

[21] A. R. Luria (Moscow) and Ivan P. London (Brooklyn).

detrimental to public education, and "in conflict with both dialectical materialism and the practical experience of Soviet Society." It is generally held that tests do not reveal underlying processes and ignore the possibilities of increasing abilities through training. On our visit to the USSR, we frequently heard the argument: "Quantitative scores are meaningless if different children can achieve the same results in quite different ways."

There is evidence that psychological tests have been and are being used. For example, Yvonne Brackbill was told at the Institute for Defectology that children suspected of mental retardation are asked to "classify pictures, draw proper conclusions, match colors and forms, describe a story shown in pictures, etc." Professor London has noted that the Binet-Simon tests were sketched and recommended for use on pages 62 to 64 of A. A. Barsuk's *Brief Manual on Psychiatry for Divisional Doctors,* published by the Administration of Moscow Psychiatry in 1949.

While projective techniques are little known, the Rorschach is cited in Soviet literature and is occasionally used as a diagnostic aid in the evaluation of suspected organic brain damage. Despite the growing interest in psychodynamics, one Soviet colleague told us: "We are not so much interested in probing man's depths as in the heights to which he can rise."

Psychotherapy is weakly developed and has only lately come into growing favor, presumably as an application of Pavlov's second signal system. While a Psychoanalytic Society was established in the Soviet Union, it was banned in about 1930, when Freudian concepts were declared to be unscientific, nonexperimental, idealistic, and capable of leading to political reaction. By 1958 the view was held that the problems explored by Freud were important but that they should be considered in Pavlovian terms. Current Soviet professional literature indicates increasingly frequent discussion of unconscious motivation, conflicts, etc.; the possibility of psychogenic disorders is acknowledged. Published protocols reflect efforts to delve into childhood experiences and family influences.

Whatever psychotherapy is practiced is generally considered a medical function. However, psychologists are encouraged to explore applications of brief rational therapy, hypnotherapy, and work therapy.

Emerging trends and legislation. It may be pertinent to recall that Pavlov's views, pointing to a physiological rather than a psychological basis of disorders, are particularly acceptable to Party theorists, who stress the material and rational (which fits the Soviet Marxist concept of man as responsible for his behavior). Freud, on the other hand, emphasized the psychological and irrational, while assuming physiological correlates and bases. Soviet psychiatry endeavors to localize events in the brain, not in the mind. It is frequently held that behind every human action there is a definite physiological occurrence, effecting a state of excitation or inhibition in the brain.

Every Soviet psychologist belongs to the Soviet Psychological Society, whose current membership is about 1,100. The society has approximately twenty branches with special-interest sections, some of which may hold regional conferences on particular topics. Some Soviet clinical psychologists are members of the Soviet Society of Neurology and Psychiatry, which has local branches and its own conferences. Psychological workers, like all others, follow official directives and are paid at state-established rates.

About 70 per cent of all psychiatrists are women, most of whom receive six years of medical school training after graduating from high school, followed by two or three years as general physicians and a year's training in adult and child psychiatry. The medical school curriculum has no courses in psychological theory. The Soviet Ministry of Health is responsible for training, hires all physicians, and makes assignments throughout the country on the basis of needs and priorities. Beginning state salaries are about the same as those for skilled factory workers.

Within the centers we visited, the basic orientation in psychiatry was biochemical. The view was expressed that most mental illness, especially schizophrenia, was probably organically caused and that, in time, continued research would provide the evidence. It was postulated that organic changes may occur without psychotic components, which suggests that organicity may not be the sole basis for psychoses and that environmental stresses can function as trigger mechanisms. Neuroses are considered to be largely due to a weak nervous system or a faulty environment, and so, as one approach, the environment may be changed. There appears to be less reluctance in the Soviet Union to refer neurotic patients to outpatient centers or even to hospitalize them; authorities can refuse admission if they disagree with the diagnosis. Psychopharmacological preparations are widely used, and electric shock appears to be applied more than insulin or sleep therapy.

Soviet psychology, like everything else in the USSR, is interwoven with local conditions and state plans. Assigned roles and responsibilities are likely to determine future developments. Despite the considerable differences between our societies, opportunities have never been more propitious for communication and exchange.

United Kingdom[22]

General situation. Clinical psychology in the United Kingdom is largely a postwar development. Before 1948, the number of clinical psychologists was small, and their activities were limited. Subsequent growth was stimulated within the context of the 1948 National Health Services. Qualifications, standards, and salaries were developed with the counsel of the British Psychological Society, whose clinical representatives sat on the national and regional advisory bodies responsible for mental health. An interesting professional trend may be reflected in the 1957 founding of the (British) Association for Child Psychology and Psychiatry, with its equal number of medical and nonmedical board members. As of 1962, there were about three hundred psychologists working in the National Health Service and about 215 in the Education Service, whose activities are along clinical lines.

There have been two main trends in the development of clinical psychology. At one extreme has been a trend which is very similar to that which dominates the American scene, in which the psychologist makes use of methods and measures which are largely unvalidated or which, at best, have only an attenuated relationship with the relevant criteria. Such psychologists are usually involved in conventional forms of psychotherapy and practice clinical psychology essentially as an art. At the other extreme has been a trend which considers the psychologist an applied scientist whose role is to apply the methods and findings of psychology to the solution of psychological problems in the field of medicine, defined as broadly as possible. The variety of applications and of possible methods is extremely wide.

Professional roles. On the whole, it appears that there is no limit to the roles psychologists can play in psychodiagnosis and psychotherapy, training, and research. There is a substantial proportion of psychiatrists in Britain who have a good understanding of scientific method and who welcome the participation of the psychologist as an applied scientist. Although the National Health Service does not provide or employ nonmedical psychotherapists, clinical psychologists can engage in private practice.

Emerging trends. Current attitudes toward clinical psychology in Britain tend to reflect a steadily growing interest. Requests for clinical psychologists from industry, civil service, and the armed forces far exceed the available supply. There are increasing opportunities for psychotherapy, usually child referrals from psychiatrists. The (British) Association for Child Psychology and Psychiatry, formed in 1957, has an equal number of medical and nonmedical board members.

The outstanding development in the United Kingdom is that the mental health service is going to be taken out of specialized mental hospitals and made part of the general health service. This will mean that each hospital will have its own psychiatric department. It will also mean that psychologists will be involved with medical practice of all kinds. On the whole there is no wish to have the extension of psychological services take place under the wing of a psychiatrist; rather, psychologists will want their own connections directly with each aspect of medical practice, of which psychiatry will be only one. However, whether or not it is in the interest of mental health that this development occur is open to question.

The orientation of psychiatrists in the United Kingdom is mixed. On the one hand, there is the "scientific" wing, which can shield a wide variety of attitudes ranging from hostility to all new developments in the name of caution to a highly imaginative, many-sided approach which some psychiatrists are capable of practicing. At the other extreme, there are psychiatrists who work under general theoretical labels, such as a particular brand of psycho-

22 M. B. Shapiro (London).

analysis, and they too can be very varied in their degree of flexibility and interest in objective facts. Psychiatrists are like psychologists in all these respects.

Relationships between the psychiatrist and the psychologist have been affected by two factors. Many psychologists entering into the field of mental health have been horrified by the looseness with which some psychiatrists appear to make their psychological observations, by the apparent lack of distinction between interpretation and observation, and by the general methodological naïveté. On the other hand, psychiatrists have been quite understandably disturbed by the care with which psychologists measure variables which are apparently irrelevant to clinical requirements or which are very obscurely related to them. There is sufficient basis for the development of misunderstanding. This is exemplified by the fact that there are a few well-known clinical psychologists in Britain who have no clinical responsibilities whatever and who are completely involved in what they consider to be research.

Fortunately, this position is changing in a number of places. At the Maudsley, intimate working relations are developing between psychiatrists and psychologists in both clinical work and research. For example, a particular pair, psychiatrist and psychologist, will be doing both their clinical and their research work together, each kind of work informing the other. In such a case the psychologist is capable of assessing a patient's mental state in an interview, while the psychiatrist is capable of deciding what tests should be done. When it comes to the consideration of psychological dysfunction, there is a considerable area of overlap between the good psychiatrist and the good psychologist, and each continues to teach and inform the other. The difference lies in the fact that in the last analysis, the psychologist is primarily concerned with introducing control into the methods of psychological observation, with validating all psychological procedures of both measurement and treatment, and with applying the methods and findings of psychology, while the psychiatrist is primarily concerned with bringing together all disciplines in the effective treatment of an individual patient and with relating these to psychiatric knowledge, which is the systematized experience of psychiatric disorder.

Yugoslavia[23]

General situation. The present status of clinical psychology in Yugoslavia can perhaps be best understood in the light of the general development of Yugoslav scientific psychology. It is not always realized that Yugoslav psychology is composed of three distinct and almost independent units—the Serbian, the Croatian, and the Slovene. Serbian psychology is primarily clinically oriented; Croatian and Slovene interests are more experimentally inclined. While American and French psychology have had considerable influence on Croatian work, the Slovenes have looked more to Austria and Germany.

It should also be noted that Yugoslav psychology has passed through three distinct phases in its development. Until World War II, Yugoslav psychology was primarily academic, although there were a few attempts to apply psychological principles to everyday problems, e.g., in the selection and orientation of schoolchildren and in the testing of mentally retarded adults. After World War II, Yugoslav psychology tried unsuccessfully to adjust to the then prevailing Soviet psychology. Since 1948, applied psychology has been emphasized, especially industrial endeavors. It was in this third phase that Yugoslav clinical psychology was born.

Professional roles. Yugoslav clinical psychologists conduct research in mental hospitals and clinics and provide diagnostic services. Although group psychotherapy and individual psychotherapy are still largely in the hands of psychiatrists, well-qualified clinical psychologists are doing an increasing amount of therapy, particularly with children. There is no private practice. The considerable variety of clinical research is apparent from the extensive programs presented at the congresses of the Yugoslav Psychological Association, ranging from the correlation between IQs of parents and children, and psychological selection, to studies in the prevention of suicide.

Emerging trends and legislation. The training of Yugoslav clinical psychologists does not differ significantly from that of psychologists in general. Specialist training is beginning, and, in part through the efforts of the Yugoslav Psychological Association, clinical psycholo-

[23] Nicholas Kopatic (Vineland, N.J.).

gists are beginning to have a recognized role. Indeed, a number of physicians are now seeking doctorates in psychology. With the promulgation of higher standards and the potential influence of the 1964 International Congress of Applied Psychology, held in Ljubljana, clinical psychology is progressing.

THE MIDDLE EAST AND NORTH AFRICA

Among the Arab countries of the Middle East and North Africa (Algeria, Egypt, Iraq, Jordan, Kuwait, Lebanon, Lybia, Morocco, Saudi Arabia, Syria, Sudan, Tunis, and Yemen), only Egypt offers formal training in clinical psychology. While the American University in Beirut, Lebanon, has an active psychology department, primary interest is in traditional experimental areas. There is increasing research in mental measurement. Graduate psychology training in the other Arab countries is strongly influenced by European traditions and emphasizes educational services.

Egypt (United Arab Republic)[24]

General situation. Influenced by both British and French psychology, the development of academic psychology in Egypt accompanied the post-World War I spurt in higher education. Graduate degrees in psychology were awarded in departments of philosophy until the entire educational system was revised following the July, 1952, revolution. Subsequent emphasis on industrial and social planning has fostered research in all areas, including clinical psychology, with particular emphasis on professional services. Egyptian psychologists holding Ph.D. degrees generally obtain their graduate training abroad, most frequently in England and the United States and occasionally in France or Switzerland.

Professional roles. Properly trained professional psychologists are overwhelmed with demands for clinical services, ranging from psychodiagnosis and psychotherapy in correctional centers and schools to research in social planning, mental health, and rehabilitation. While the two state hospitals in Cairo have no staff psychologists at present, it is anticipated that positions will be established in the near future. Private hospitals have set an example in the employment of part-time consultants in psychology. The Egyptian Psychological Association takes considerable interest in the development of psychological services, especially in government centers for emotionally disturbed, delinquent, or retarded children. The Egyptian Society for Non-Medical Psychotherapists has been organized to facilitate supervised training.

Emerging trends and legislation. The question of psychotherapy has long been debated among Egyptian psychiatrists and psychologists. Following considerable publicity and some acrimony, a law was promulgated in 1956 stipulating the conditions and qualifications for the practice of psychotherapy. A psychotherapist is one who holds a diploma in psychological medicine (DPM) from Egypt or abroad, who is a university graduate with postgraduate work and a diploma in psychotherapy from a recognized training institute (which does not currently exist in Egypt), who is a member of a recognized association of psychotherapists and who passes an examination held by a committee, or who is a graduate of a university psychology department and who has had at least two years of training in psychotherapy in an institute recognized by the committee. Nonmedical therapists are specifically instructed to refrain from treating any patient who shows signs of severe psychopathology accompanied by physical symptoms or psychotic disturbances. Such individuals are to be referred to physicians, who are required to make reports to the referring source. The law recognizes the independent practice of professional psychology, but this was the most effective way of fighting quackery in a land where illiteracy is still a major social problem.

Israel[25]

During the 1930s, several psychologists with European or American training settled in Israel (Palestine at that time), among them J. Levy, H. Ormian, B. Wolman, and others. Clinical psychologists cooperated with psychiatrists and were employed by education and welfare departments. Most clinical psychologists were engaged in diagnostic and therapeutic work with children in institutional settings or in private practice. The first mental health clinic run by a psychologist was opened in 1933 under the supervision of the Social

[24] A. Moneim El-Meligi (Cairo).

[25] Edith Falik (Tel Aviv).

Welfare Department of the Vaad Leumi. The director of the clinic was Dr. B. Wolman.

During World War II, Israeli psychologists participated in child guidance for the families of servicemen, while others continued their services in clinics and guidance centers as well as in private practice. During the Israel War of Independence (1948 to 1949), Israeli clinical psychologists served the armed forces in testing, screening, and other clinical assignments.

Israeli psychologists were as divided as their European or American colleagues; one could find among the small group of Israeli psychologists disciples of several schools of thought.

With the establishment of the state of Israel and its mental health institutions, the situation has rapidly changed. Several trained psychologists immigrated to Israel, while many Israelis went abroad to study and brought back their new knowledge.

At a relatively early date, the Association of Clinical Psychologists emerged with few members but with high professional standards, which were subsequently adopted when the clinical psychologists merged with the Society for Psychology in 1958 to form the Israel Psychological Association. These standards, which became a condition for membership, included an M.A. or a Ph.D. degree from a recognized university. At least two years of clinical training or experience was required for membership in the Clinical Psychology Section of the Israel Psychological Association. The association has 142 members, of whom 43 also belong to the Section of Clinical Psychology.

Presently, clinical psychology is a well-appreciated and much demanded profession in Israel. The major problem of the Israeli clinical psychologists, who come from many countries and various cultures and who have nonequated professional backgrounds, is to find common grounds for integrating methods and training.

The Ministry of Health and the Sick Fund of the General Labor Federation share in supporting the main medical and psychiatric settings which employ clinical psychologists; the Youth Department of the Jewish Agency, the Ministry of Welfare, and to a certain extent the Ministry of Education are the educational and guidance settings which also employ clinical psychologists, though to a lesser degree. Only a very few psychologists are in private practice exclusively. Opportunities are limited because Israeli medicine is being rapidly socialized. Moreover, only in recent years has the public become aware of mental health implications, with growing demands for professional psychological services by teachers, general physicians, psychiatrists, and lawyers.

Professional roles. Clinical psychologists are employed as members of the psychiatric team in various hospitals, mental health departments, and rehabilitation centers. Within the Ministry of Health and at the Guidance Clinic of the Youth Immigration Department in Jerusalem, as well as at the Mental Health Center of the Oranim Kibbutz Seminary near Haifa, clinical psychologists direct the mental health clinics for children and youth. Within the Ministry of Health psychiatric institutions, psychiatric wards for children, and mental health clinics and within the Sick Fund psychiatric hospitals and mental health clinics, psychologists are members of a staff which is always directed by a psychiatrist.

When they are directors of various mental health settings, clinical psychologists develop policies, supervise staff, and are legally and professionally responsible for therapeutic measures taken. When they are members of a psychiatric staff, clinical psychologists serve as psychodiagnosticians and therapists. While few clinical psychologists are fully trained psychoanalysts, most use the psychoanalytic approach in their therapeutic activities. Clinical psychologists were among the most active initiators and founders of the group therapy movement in Israel.

Research is handicapped by the limited funds available from official institutions. Many clinical psychologists are employed as lecturers at Hebrew University (Jerusalem), Bar-Ilan University (Ramat-Gan), and Tel Aviv University. They also participate in interdisciplinary professional training and serve as consultants for the probation office, law courts, social agencies, rehabilitation centers, the armed forces, and the rabbinical courts.

Emerging trends and legislation. Despite urgent necessity, there is no legal licensing of clinical psychologists in Israel. While a special commission is preparing suitable suggestions for the Minister of Health, the official body recognizing clinical psychologists is the Clinical Section of the Israel Psychological Association. The IPA is incorporated in the academic section of the General Labour Organization, which comprises all the trade unions. This arrangement makes it possible for the relatively small number of psychologists to be protected in their professional rights together with other academic workers in the country. However, the small size also limits the possibility of imposing professional policy. To support its request for licensing, the IPA Clinical Section is preparing a three-year postgraduate training program, including a supervised internship, in a recognized institution.

Turkey[26]

General situation. In comparison with its professional status in many other countries of the world, the scientific and professional status of clinical psychology in Turkey is in its earliest stage of development. This is in part because psychology itself still tends to be perceived as closely related to philosophy. Another reason for the limited progress is the traditional psychiatric orientation of Turkish medical authorities. Kraepelinian concepts prevail; the importance of dynamic sociopsychological forces in the formation of emotional disorders is not yet widely accepted. The interpretation of most mental disturbances in terms of neurological, organic, physiological, or hereditary factors, to some extent at least, undermines the role of the clinical psychologist and places limitations on his services.

Until about a decade ago, psychology was taught in Turkish universities as a course or certificate in philosophy departments. The only job opportunities available to the graduates were in teaching logic, philosophy, or psychology in a lyceum or university. This still holds true for one of the three main graduate schools in Turkey, Ankara University, where psychology is offered as a certificate in the philosophy department. Lack of appropriate and challenging positions for training and research in several areas of psychology has, in turn, led to the unfortunate situation where intelligent, highly motivated, scholarly students refrain from selecting psychology as a profession, preferring instead to go into more prestigious and established fields of specialization.

Professional roles. When a position is available for a clinical psychologist in a newly opened institution, the applicant has to be trained in the techniques of testing, interviewing, and counseling. The professional duties of such a specially trained psychologist would be diagnosis on the basis of test results, intellectual evaluation, interviewing, counseling, and guidance.

There are institutions in Turkey where the medical staff is open to modern concepts of psychiatry and where a clinical psychologist can gain acceptance and prestige. Psychological services are encouraged, and mutual collaboration is possible. However, there are very few well-trained clinical psychologists in the country. While qualifications for practice remain legally ill-defined, establishing a reputation is often hampered by misunderstandings and wrong judgments concerning professional services rendered.

Emerging trends and legislation. At present, most students apply to university psychology departments with the intention of gaining experience in both testing and psychotherapy. However, according to the Medical Code, treatment and therapy are restricted to physicians. The law prohibits any other individual from engaging in therapeutic activities. While psychotherapy may be practiced only by those who hold a degree in medicine, there is no legal requirement for specialization in psychiatry. However, a graduate of the psychology department, who may be regarded as a laboratory technician, can practice psychoanalysis, provided the psychiatrist assumes all responsibility for any difficulties that may arise. Counseling is not subject to any statutory prohibitions, and any individual is legally free to open a counseling service.

MIDDLE AND SOUTH AFRICA

Middle Africa, as it is defined by UNESCO, actually includes most of Africa, that is, all except the Arab countries to the north (Egypt, Lybia, Tunisia, Algeria, and Morocco) and the Portuguese territories and the Republic of South Africa to the south.

In Middle Africa, a vast area encompassing about thirty countries, many of them newly independent, there were 19 universities in 1960. Over 70 per cent of the faculty members were born and trained abroad, mostly in Great Britain, France, Belgium, and the United States (in that order). The African

26 Gökçe Cansever (Istanbul).

nations are making extraordinary efforts and sacrifices to expand their educational facilities, to teach all their children at least to read and write, to send increasing numbers through secondary schools, and to provide university training for their ablest students.

While education is vital to economic and social development plans, primary emphasis is on producing educators, engineers, managers, agricultural experts, and physicians. Psychology has priority only to the extent to which it contributes to state plans and the development of talented manpower.

The Cameroons

It was reported at the 1962 La Napoule conference that the reunited former British and French Cameroons have as yet no institution of higher learning. While English and French are both considered official languages, it appears that French will predominate. Financial resources are very limited, and initial educational efforts are focusing on teacher training, with some interest in psychological testing and measurement.

The Congo

In June, 1960, independence came to a country (900,000 square miles) nearly equivalent in size to Western Europe. Among the native population of 14 million, there was not a single Congolese physician, lawyer, or engineer; indeed, there were only 14 college graduates.

At the time of our visit in 1961, there were no psychiatric facilities for non-Europeans. Psychotic Congolese remained in their villages. Juvenile delinquency was increasing, fostered by large-scale unemployment, ineffective government controls, and loosening family ties. While Belgian psychologists had taught in Elisabethville and Léopoldville, their activities focused mainly on personnel selection and socioanthropological studies. One Belgian missionary psychologist has returned to Louvanium University in Léopoldville; there is no information about Elisabethville. While there are no present prospects for establishing a clinical psychology training program, the Congo and other emerging African countries constitute a vast laboratory for studies in the public health approach to mental health, particularly as individuals leave a relatively sheltered tribal community for the rapidly industrializing but impersonal and frequently stress-inducing cities.

Ghana[27]

As of January, 1963, there was no undergraduate or graduate training in any field of psychology in Ghana. Psychological activities at the University of Ghana in Legon are generally limited to teaching in the education and sociology departments, psychological testing, and research. Trained by the American Institute of Research, the Psychological Testing Unit at the university participates in the West African Aptitude Test Development Program and in the screening and selection of candidates for government, education, and training schemes. It is staffed by an M.A. psychologist, aided by two assistants and a $20,000 Ford Foundation grant for a two-year period. In late 1963, four Ghanaians completed their M.A. training at the University of Pittsburgh and returned home to facilitate national standardization for Ghana of aptitude tests developed in Nigeria by the American Institute of Research. At the same time, the current M.A. psychologist was sent to the United States for Ph.D. training. Meanwhile, through the United States Agency for International Development, recruitment had been initiated for a professor of psychology to direct the department in Legon.

While Ghana has a mental hospital with three well-trained psychiatrists, to date there is no clearly established role for clinical psychologists. Interprofessional relations are cordial. Psychiatrists, sociologists, and other behavioral scientists participate in the meetings of the Ghana Psychological Association. At the National Medical Research Council, there are two fully trained social and experimental psychologists who conduct research on perceptual modes and the EEG.

The main focus of psychology in Ghana is on facilitating management and supervisory training plans and on research into, and the introduction of, radically different training methods for secondary schools and technical institutes. There is much interest in programmed learning, which appears to be particularly appropriate where good teachers are scarce and where pupil motivation is uncertain. Clinical psychology in Ghana will have to grow with the national development.

Nigeria[28]

The primary focus of university programs in Nigeria is on training teachers. At the Uni-

[27] George Soloyanis (Accra).

[28] Thomas A. Wickes (Enugu).

versity College in Ibadan, psychology is taught at the undergraduate level, and there is an active testing program; postgraduate research emphasizes developmental and educational approaches. Provision for psychological courses has been made at the University of Nigeria in Nuukka, where there is a psychological testing program under the office of the dean of students.

Psychologists from the American Institute of Research standardized a series of vocational aptitude tests in Nigeria and have contributed to the construction and validation of tests in the school system. Other psychologists with clinical experience are devoting their energies to programmed learning, psychological testing, management development, and training, aided by grants from the Ford Foundation, the Agency for International Development, etc.

There are no clinical psychologists in the strict sense of the word in Nigeria. Neither a graduate training program nor traditional practicum facilities have been established. However, the Neuro-Psychiatric Centre at Aro Hospital, located just outside Abeokuta, has become well known for its "village system" of community care for the mentally ill, established by Dr. T. Adeoye Lambo in 1954. Only 200 patients are in the hospital, whereas 300 are boarded out. The First Pan-African Psychiatric Conference was held at Aro Hospital in November, 1961, highlighting the possibilities for a scheme which keeps patients in touch with families and which avoids lengthy institutionalization.

Although there are only three psychiatrists in Nigeria, their contributions have far exceeded their number. The medical school at the University College in Ibadan established a chair of psychiatry in 1962, with Dr. Lambo as the first professor. Professional contributions of clinical psychology are invited.

South Africa[29]

General situation. Clinical psychology in this country is in a state of flux, transition, and rapid development. It was only in January, 1959, that the first formal course of training in clinical psychology was instituted, and from the amount of debate and controversy which problems in this field have generated, it is certain that by now, many of the trends and tendencies here reported have crystallized into specific policies and programs of action. As with nearly every activity in South Africa—industrial, cultural, professional, scientific—a distinction must be made between technical and professional standards and attainments, on the one hand, and the directions or mold which these developments are obliged to take as a result of the reigning political doctrine of apartheid, or separate development, on the other. On the purely professional level, clinical psychology in this country is characterized by enlightened and progressive principles which many older and larger countries might do worse than emulate. On the political level, we have just witnessed a fundamental ideological rift within the psychological profession, with the lamentable result that there are now two separate bodies serving the same purpose, the original South African Psychological Association (SAPA), which (like its legal and medical counterparts) has no color bar, and the schismatic Psychological Institute of the Republic of South Africa, which limits membership to whites only. That the matter is not going to rest here is evident from recent statements suggesting the government's disapproval of nonsegregated professional and scientific bodies.

Professional roles. The South African clinical psychologist who is registered with the Medical Council enjoys prerogatives which many of his overseas colleagues are denied. Provided that he works in conjunction with a medical practitioner (which means in practice that the latter takes responsibility for the patient's physical health), he is empowered, even encouraged, to undertake the full gamut of psychodiagnosis and psychotherapy. There are, however, very few full-time registered clinical psychologists in private practice. Johannesburg, with a population of 1 million, has only one private practitioner dealing with adult patients. In hospitals, clinical psychologists undertake psychometry, psychodiagnosis, individual psychotherapy, group psychotherapy, and teaching, and they also assist team research programs.

Emerging trends and legislation. An outstanding characteristic of clinical psychology in South Africa is the close cooperation which is maintained with the medical profession and the relatively high status which the dual registration system accords to psychologists. The South African Medical and Dental Council and the SAPA each have their own registers of clinical psychologists. For the medical register,

29 Arnold Abramovitz (Cape Town).

the criteria are (1) the possession of a Master of Arts or Master of Science degree in psychology and (2) eighteen months of internship at an approved institution. For the psychological register, the academic criteria are the same, but the minimum practical training is twelve months of experience at an approved center serving a variety of patients.

At the moment there is no legislation to prevent unqualified persons from practicing as psychologists, but definite moves are afoot to introduce a bill which will at least protect the name "psychologist." A medical practitioner may not, of course, collaborate with anyone who is not registered with the Medical Council.

The relationship between psychologists and the medical profession is, on the whole, one of friendly reciprocity. The bitter rivalry between psychology and psychiatry which seems to prevail in some countries is hardly in evidence here. In many centers the registered clinical psychologist enjoys about the same status and salary scale as the psychiatrist, who is usually not slow to recognize the former's special competence, particularly in psychodiagnosis.

Clinical psychology in South Africa is still in its early developmental stages, and it has to face certain formidable sociopolitical problems of the type which recur in many contexts in this country. As of 1962, there were only about seventy (European) clinical psychologists registered with the Psychological Association, of whom about twenty were also registered with the Medical Council. They serve a population of 15 million, of whom 12 million are non-Europeans. There is clearly a great need for nonwhite psychologists, and yet SAPA's decision in 1961 to admit nonwhites to membership resulted in unprecedented professional dissension and disruption. Although there are fewer than a dozen non-European psychologists in all fields at present, governmental policy favors separate associations for the different races. It is principally that issue which clouds the otherwise promising picture of clinical psychology in South Africa.

SOUTHEAST ASIA[30]

Many developments in Hong Kong, Indonesia, Malaya, Singapore, Taiwan, and Vietnam have been influenced by the psychology prevailing in the European countries which, until recently, controlled a large part of Southeast Asia. Indonesian psychologists have been deeply influenced by the Dutch, and those in Malaya have drawn on the experience of the British; French influences are still reflected in Vietnam. Hong Kong shows both British and Chinese influences, while Taiwan has retained little from the Japanese because psychology is largely in the hands of those who came from the mainland more than a decade ago.

At their state of development, these countries do not have professional groups with sharply circumscribed roles, as is the case in the United States. The result is that anyone who was trained as a clinical psychologist may work in many phases of psychology or outside of psychology completely. Likewise, someone with limited training in psychology but extensive training in quite another discipline might be found working as a psychologist. Professional persons are characterized by their breadth of activities rather than by their narrow specialization since this is the only way they can earn a living.

Finally, clinical psychology, such as it is, seems to be getting its start in the educational setting in much the same way as it did in the United States. At the present time, the contribution is primarily in the assessment of ability. In most of these countries, there is also some attempt to use psychological tests in the armed forces, but only now is an attempt being made to develop tests appropriate to the cognitive processes of the subjects concerned. This is made more difficult by the presence of many dialects in each of these countries. Using tests developed in other countries has never been satisfactory, a realization that is becoming increasingly clear. In Indonesia, at least, this realization has been extended to questioning the validity of psychodynamic formulations in Western cultures. The picture, then, is of a limited number of psychologists in each of these countries who have received their graduate training abroad and who are performing a wide range of psychological activities using Western instruments. Diagnostic work is their principal concern, with little opportunity for, or tradition of, either psychotherapy or research.

Burma[31]

General situation. While psychology has a long history in the Union of Burma, clinical

[30] George M. Guthrie (Pennsylvania State).

[31] Julian Wohl (Toledo) and Hla Thwin (Rangoon).

psychology is in a very early, pioneering phase. The university departments of psychology are working hard for this development, which is proceeding in the midst of a general governmental reappraisal of education, medical and social service institutions, and facilities and functions.

Professional roles. The prevailing psychiatric orientation can be characterized as dynamic and social on the diagnostic side, with treatment focused on medical and physical approaches, primarily electric shock. There is particular interest in social, psychological, and cultural research as related to mental illness. The underemphasis on nonorganic treatment is due mainly to limitations in hospital facilities and psychiatric staff, plus the relatively heavy patient load. An increase in psychotherapy is favored by the psychiatrists, and psychotherapeutic activities by psychologists would be welcome. The trained psychologist could engage in all three traditional areas—diagnosis, research, and therapy—in addition to teaching and consulting. All that is needed is more trained people and better facilities.

Emerging trends. Vast possibilities exist for expansion in psychological and psychiatric training and research. Although psychology, particularly in its applications, is new in Burma, both the public and the government are increasingly aware of its utility and capabilities. With this awareness will come an increasingly strong demand for more services than can be adequately rendered at any of these early growth stages. To maintain standards, psychology will find it necessary to resist pressures to supply services where trained qualified people are not yet available.

As of mid-1962, there were five psychiatrists on the staff of the Government Mental Hospital, who had obtained their training in England or India. They are keenly interested in working in collaboration with clinical psychologists and have expressed their desire to establish closer relations between the universities and mental hospitals to facilitate mutual training, promote research, and improve both quality and quantity of service.

With the growing demand for mental health services, the strengthening of university psychology departments in response to student and professional interest, and government dedication to expansion in social welfare and education, clinical psychology in Burma is likely to continue its rapid development.

China

Direct communication with psychologists in the People's Republic of China is difficult from the United States. However, Chinese medical and psychological journals are available in the Library of the Academy of Medicine. in New York City, and elsewhere. Articles are frequently published in English and less commonly in Russian; Chinese contributions generally have English and Russian summaries. A report of trends in Chinese psychology has also appeared in *Psychologia*, an English-language journal dedicated to psychology in the Orient and edited by Prof. Koji Sato in Japan. Written by Prof. Pan Shu (Ph.D., University of Chicago), Director of the Institute of Psychology, Academia Sinica, Peking, and former President of the Chinese Psychological Association, this report makes the following general observation:

> Since the Liberation, psychologists in China have been intensively studying Marxism as well as the Soviet psychology of Pavlov's theory. Profiting by the experience of Soviet psychologists in building up the dialectic Materialist Psychology, Chinese psychologists fully realized that in order to shake off the ideological and methodological influence of the Idealistic Psychology of Capitalist countries, and in order for psychology to take up its share of important tasks in Socialist Reconstruction, it is necessary to reconstruct a scientific psychology upon the basis of Pavlov's theory in accordance with Marxist principles.

In considering the Chinese scene, it must be recalled that many senior Chinese psychologists received their training in the United States and that few know the Russian language or are very familiar with Soviet psychology. Efforts toward Pavlovianization are apparent in the following observations, quoted from Pan Shu:

> To the higher nervous activity of psychotics close attention was paid by Chinese medical workers, especially by psychiatric workers. With psychotics and neurotics they used the method of conditioned motor reflex with verbal reinforcements as well as the method of electro-encephalography and galvanic skin reflex recordings respectively in investigating

the formation, the extinction, and the re-formation of conditioned reflexes, and the mutual transposition of the two kinds of signal systems. They studied some emotional reactions of the patients and the type characteristic of schizophrenia as well as the effects of the environment on the occurrence of the disease by analyzing the patient's case history and clinical observations.

More recent Chinese publications suggest considerable competition between Western and traditional Chinese medicine, with the latter apparently gaining the upper hand. Particularly popular at the moment are traditional acapuncture (needle therapy) and cauterization, modernly viewed as a form of shock treatment.

While there is no current information on clinical psychology training and practicum facilities, it is known that China is experiencing a great shortage of professional personnel. Conceivably, the traditional Chinese methods of treatment are attractive because far less time is required for training than in the West. That Chinese psychologists have good relationships with Chinese psychiatrists may be deduced from the comment of Pan Shu, whose style perhaps reflects more an ideal than a reality.

> In our psychologists' opinion, in Socialistic countries all medical doctors and psychological workers as well as patients have the Communist spirit of cooperation to a high degree and their relationships are those of comrades, so that it is possible for their respective roles to get coordinated, and for the subjective activeness to become manifest through mutual influences. Besides, they have all other favorable conditions for the therapy (e.g., medicines and favorable environment, etc.).

What is happening in China is of general interest, and it is to be hoped that, in time, direct channels of scientific communication will be reopened.

Hong Kong[32]

The University of Hong Kong offers some training in psychology as part of its program in education. At least one staff member has an M.A. degree from an American university; a second was trained in England. They have been conducting a small child guidance clinic in conjunction with their offerings in developmental psychology. The Chung Chi College in the New Territories also offers courses in psychology.

India[33]

General situation. Psychology as it is understood in the English-speaking countries has been studied in India for over fifty years, usually as part of the B.A. or the M.A. degree in philosophy. The British system and textbooks exerted considerable influence on the development of psychology in Indian universities. Since the political independence of 1947, separate departments of psychology have been established. Clinical psychology is a well-recognized and firmly established branch of applied psychology.

Professional roles. In India, clinical psychologists are mainly entrusted with psychodiagnostic work, including history taking, mental examination, and psychometry. Some also do psychotherapy, either in collaboration with, or independently of, the psychiatrist or the medical personnel in charge of the team. A few centers for psychotherapy and mental clinics are administered by clinical psychologists. In the undergraduate and the postgraduate courses offered by the various universities, clinical psychologists shoulder the major burden of teaching and research in clinical and abnormal psychology, personality, and psychometry.

Although at present, clinical psychologists in India have to depend upon tests mainly standardized in the United States and the United Kingdom, as they are preoccupied with routine clinical work and teaching, there is an ever-growing demand to standardize tests suitable for Indian conditions. A number of tests have been standardized or adapted for the 13 most frequently spoken Indian languages, but, as most of them remain unpublished, Indian and foreign workers are not generally aware of them. There is also considerable duplication of work in test construction.

Because of the paucity of clinical psychology posts in mental hospitals and the inadequate remuneration, most trained clinical psychologists have to seek employment in colleges, universities, medical colleges, child guidance clinics, private clinical facilities,

32 George M. Guthrie (Pennsylvania State).

33 N. N. Sen (Delhi).

army selection boards, industry, vocational guidance bureaus, etc. As a consequence of this situation, the clinical approach is generally gaining ground in those areas, with proper emphasis on emotional and personality factors.

Emerging trends and legislation. In psychodiagnostic work there is relatively greater stress on objective tests, ratings, and questionnaires. Although projective techniques are used, not much reliance is placed on them. Most Indian clinical psychologists are eclectic in their approach to psychotherapy and do not lean toward any particular dynamic approach. While the writings of psychoanalysts are widely read, there are not many adherents of psychoanalysis.

Currently there is no law regarding professional practices, and none are proposed. In the opinion of some clinical psychologists, appropriate legislation could be postponed until the profession develops further and a definite pattern of clinical practice emerges.

Indonesia[34]

Indonesia has made great strides in clinical psychology. There is an active graduate training program at the University of Indonesia in Djakarta. This program is directed by Dr. Slamet Inam Santoso, a psychiatrist who also directs the psychiatric ward of the university hospital. Members of his staff have received doctorates from European universities. Their techniques include European and American tests which have been, in part at least, standardized on Indonesian populations. Other universities offering work in psychology include Gadjah Mada in Jogjakarta and medical schools in Bandung and Surabaya. There is also some concern with psychological research at the Institute for Pedagogical Research at the University of Padjadjaran in Bandung.

The armed forces of Indonesia employ a number of psychologists, at least one of whom has taken some training in the United States. Their testing program makes use of tests developed by the Dutch. There have been a number of modifications of these tests since their independence.

Psychologists have experienced difficulty in Indonesia obtaining journals and instruments from abroad because of severe currency restrictions. In spite of these difficulties they have maintained serious efforts to continue psychological research. They have been quite alert to the question of the appropriateness of foreign psychological techniques and theories when applied to Indonesian problems.

[34] George M. Guthrie (Pennsylvania State).

Japan[35]

General situation. Already well established in the 1930s, Japanese psychology has perhaps responded most actively to the post-World War II stimulus from the United States. Prof. Koji Sato indicated at the 1960 Bonn International Congress that the number of Japanese psychologists exceeds 2,500 and that about five hundred papers are read at conventions of the Japanese Psychological Association. There are 20 universities awarding Ph.D. degrees (usually five years after the B.A.).

Clinical psychology in Japan developed mainly after World War II. With the passage of the 1947 Child Welfare Laws and the 1948 Juvenile Act, demand for psychological services arose in the newly established child guidance centers, welfare agencies, family courts, and juvenile homes. Psychologists also assumed increasingly important roles in correctional centers, training schools, and social and rehabilitative agencies.

Although Japanese psychiatry was long dominated by German biological traditions, a more dynamic approach has gradually evolved, accompanied by more requests for psychologists in mental hospitals, both public and private. The major research and training center of Japanese clinical psychology is the National Institute of Mental Health, established in 1952.

Professional roles. Japanese psychologists participate in the activities of most social welfare agencies, including child guidance clinics, court clinics, mental health clinics, school clinics, correctional and rehabilitation centers, etc. Less than one hundred work in mental hospitals. In 1962, the 126 public child guidance and welfare centers had 239 full-time professional staff members, of whom 161 were graduates in clinical psychology. Because of the great shortage of psychiatrists and qualified psychiatric social workers, psychologists frequently constitute the majority of the clinical staff, carry the diagnostic load, and assume some social work responsibilities. They do psychological testing, interviewing, counseling,

[35] Keiichi Mizushima (Tokyo).

and psychotherapy. Similarly, in correctional centers and court clinics, psychologists provide most of the professional services. In the absence of clearly defined qualifications, some individuals with limited background in psychology perform professional services, although by American standards they might not be considered "clinical psychologists."

Emerging trends. Clinical psychology, along with educational, counseling, and industrial psychology, is making rapid strides in Japan. A major problem now is the development of adequate standards for training and professional positions. Such efforts have been initiated by the Japanese Psychological Association and by the newly established Japanese Association of Clinical Psychologists. Progress is reported in the newly founded *Japanese Journal of Clinical Psychology,* which carries English-language abstracts; occasionally in *Psychologia,* the English-language international journal edited by Prof. Sato at Kyoto University; and in the *Japanese Journal of Mental Health,* published by the National Institute of Mental Health in Tokyo.

Malaya and Singapore[36]

The University of Malaya in Singapore, like the University of Hong Kong, offers some training in psychology oriented to teacher training. There is a Malaysian Social Research Institute, but it is concerned primarily with topics outside the distinct domain of psychology. The Chinese community in Singapore opened a new university, Nanyang University, very recently with plans to offer instruction in Mandarin and in English. As of 1960 they had no offering in psychology.

The Federation of Malaya built a new university in Kuala Lumpur, but as of 1960 no work was being offered in psychology. Dr. Guthrie noted a good deal of interest in the Ministry of Education in problems of measurement.

Pakistan[37]

General situation. Development of psychology in Pakistan, as in many other Asian lands, has been impeded by the slow attainment of an independent academic status, separate from philosophy. The application of scientific methods to problems of the "mind" is not always palatable to those more mystically or metaphysically inclined. Since their independence, however, the situation has gradually improved. Presently almost every university has a department of psychology, with growing demand for more professional training.

Professional roles. Opportunities for psychologists outside the universities are very limited in Pakistan. Openings in government or industry are almost entirely absent. The few students who qualify for M.A. degrees in psychology every year seek employment in other areas. A small number are absorbed in the armed forces as personnel psychologists. Institutes for education and research have recently been established at Lahore, in West Pakistan, and in Dacca, in East Pakistan, but programs have barely begun.

Opportunities for private practice, counseling, guidance, and psychotherapy, even for those who receive training abroad, are practically nonexistent. People in need of psychiatric help are usually considered the family's responsibility, with little demanded from the state. Only those who are severely affected or dangerous are committed.

Emerging trends. While the present status of psychology in Pakistan offers some promise, conditions are far from satisfactory for the development of professional clinical training and service. It is up to the newly emancipated psychologists to shape their future course of action, led by the Pakistan Psychological Association (affiliated with the British Psychological Society).

The Philippines[38]

General situation. Clinical psychology in the Philippines advanced significantly in 1959, when a psychiatric team approach was pioneered by the Neuropsychiatric Section of the V. Luna General Hospital, Philippine Armed Forces, in Quezon City. Many psychologists trained there subsequently joined the staffs of the National Mental Hospital, Veterans Memorial Hospital, and other Philippine psychiatric facilities.

Before 1949, psychologists were employed in various centers, schools, and industrial plants, but not in psychiatric team settings. Even at this writing, there are relatively few psychologists trained in psychiatric teamwork.

[36] George M. Guthrie (Pennsylvania State).

[37] S. K. Ahmad (Lahore).

[38] Belen L. Garcia (Quezon City).

Most psychology graduates seek opportunities in nonmedical endeavors; they hold academic positions, work in industry, or are active as researchers and guidance counselors. Psychologists with a doctorate are very few (approximately a dozen); most have M.A. or B.A. degrees in psychology.

Professional roles. The Philippine Society of Psychiatry and Neurology has been vigorously opposed to the independent practice of psychologists working with psychiatric or emotionally disturbed patients. They are of the opinion that clinical psychologists should associate closely with psychiatrists and representatives of allied professions in the ideal "team approach." The implication is that clinical psychologists should limit their activities to diagnostic testing, research, training of other psychologists, and psychiatrically supervised psychotherapy.

There is a mental hospital which serves the whole Philippines, located on the outskirts of Manila. This hospital has a staff of about eight psychologists, none of whom has training beyond the M.A. degree. In all too many instances, the professional image of the clinical psychologist in the Philippines is that of a technician.

Emerging trends. In about 1960, the Philippine Society of Psychologists introduced in the Philippine Congress a bill to legalize the independent practice of psychology. The proposed bill failed because of the strong opposition of the Philippine Society of Psychiatry and Neurology, which maintained its stand that diagnosis and psychotherapy with patients are medical procedures and should be done only under medical supervision.

Taiwan[39]

A department of psychology was established at National Taiwan University in 1949. Research and student interest have concentrated on measurement of ability and of personality. Projective techniques have been used in studies of aboriginal groups on Formosa. There has also been an extensive effort in testing of aptitudes and achievement in the armed forces. Mental health activities and guidance programs have been established.

At Taiwan Normal University there is considerable interest in child development, and an extensive training and research program has been established. At both of these universities American influences are quite apparent, as is true in the armed forces.

Thailand[40]

General situation. Clinical psychology in Thailand is virtually nonexistent. A few psychologists, partially trained abroad, work in the juvenile courts and the Hospital for Nervous Disorders.

Professional roles. Clinical psychologists in Thailand generally limit their activities to psychodiagnostic studies. Psychotherapy is usually restricted to psychiatrists. Some psychologists are beginning to be used in student personnel administration on the university level. There are no school psychologists.

Emerging trends and legislation. There are no restrictions on the title "psychologist" in Thailand, and no legislation has been enacted. Mental health legislation favors (almost too much) the psychological approach. For example, male homosexuality, which includes transvestism (long an acceptable fragment of Thai culture), was a few years ago made cause for mandatory commitment to the mental hospital. Since the hospital clinicians could find no valid symptoms of maladjustment within the cultural mores, they consistently released such patients after one or two days.

At present, all personnel in the psychological-psychiatric field have been trained abroad, and little research has been done to relate to Thai cultural norms. The climate is good, and as the throes of rapid development wear off, trained psychologists—mostly in educational, developmental, and guidance branches—will be able to provide the research necessary for building strength in clinical psychology. On a per capita and per dollar income basis, Thailand is probably the best-endowed nation in Southeast Asia, offering many opportunities for the further development of clinical psychology.

Vietnam[41]

The division of Vietnam resulted in the loss of the principal educational resources, which were located in Hanoi. There is some concern with psychological problems on the part of

39 George M. Guthrie (Pennsylvania State).

40 Frederic L. Ayer (Bangkok).

41 George M. Guthrie (Pennsylvania State).

persons concerned with education in Saigon. The French influence remains strong and is not particularly congenial to American testing traditions. United States aid programs are bringing many Vietnamese to the United States for training.

AUSTRALIA[42]

General Situation

Clinical psychology in Australia is emerging as a professional field. It has had an uneven development, with considerable variation among the states as to the qualifications and standards required and professional roles undertaken. Only two universities, Western Australia and Sydney, offer postgraduate training programs; proposals for training at the universities of Melbourne and New South Wales are being considered.

The past decade has seen a marked increase in the number of psychologists entering the clinical and allied fields, and there is a growing demand for their services. In most Australian states, the employment areas are the usual ones of mental hospitals, clinics, child welfare agencies, mental deficiency centers, and honorary positions in the larger public hospitals. As yet there are no separate departments of psychology within these settings, and the clinical psychologist most often functions within the traditional psychiatric team framework. Private practice would constitute a very small percentage of the total numbers.

At present only a small percentage of psychologists have had postgraduate training in clinical psychology as such, although a number hold higher degrees in psychology. The qualifications usually required by employers are the B.A. degree with a major in psychology, and some employing authorities, such as the Army, require also professional status at the level of associateship in the British Psychological Society. Only in Western Australia has it been accepted by the State Public Service Authority that psychologists must have postgraduate qualifications in clinical psychology from a recognized university before using the title and carrying out clinical duties in government agencies. What has been mentioned in another context as "premature professionalism" is also of concern here. Thus, as of 1962, there are no nationally accepted qualification requirements beyond the B.A. degree, and most psychologists entering the clinical field depend on informal in-service training schemes, where available, to extend their professional competence.

This lack of agreed-upon national standards and the paucity of university postgraduate training programs (not only in clinical but also in all applied areas of psychology) would be seen by the majority of practicing psychologists as a pressing concern, and most would agree that there is an urgent need to develop and extend the clinical training resources.

Professional Roles

The responsibilities assigned to, and assumed by, clinical psychologists are varied throughout the country. In general, the psychologist functions as a member of a medically and psychiatrically led team in public agencies and only infrequently in nonmedical settings or in private practice. At this time of expansion in these agencies, it often happens that the psychologist finds himself filling the first position there and that the employing authority has little real understanding of the contribution he can make, apart from the usual expectation that he will test intelligence. In these frequent pioneering positions, it is often up to the psychologist to assume and perform duties which in time become acceptable to the agency. Where the psychologist finds that the medical administration assigns him a technician's role, he is faced with the problems of educating the medical hierarchy concerning the broader responsibilities he can assume. Not until the standards and qualifications of clinical psychologists become more uniformly established and are known by the other professions will these inconsistencies diminish.

Turning more specifically to the main areas of responsibility, the major one is *psychodiagnosis*. At present this remains the principal function, particularly in mental hospital settings and child guidance units. In most of these agencies the staff psychologist faces continuous pressure in coping with the diagnostic requirements, and in some settings, few other duties are undertaken. In some states, such as Victoria, the psychologist works predominantly with children and reports to the psychiatric team. In Western Australia this diagnostic function has been established for over ten years in the mental hospitals and in prison

[42] A. F. Bownes (Western Australia, Nedlands) and colleagues.

and court work and in the general hospitals. The procedure that is followed here is to try to get away from purely routine testing and to carry out a selective examination based on the specific questions and queries posed by the psychiatrist. This again has meant considerable emphasis on explaining the psychologist's role in psychodiagnosis to the referring medical specialists.

One indication of the growing professional responsibility in psychodiagnosis is the increasing participation of clinical psychologists in courts of law as expert witnesses. While the kinds of cases dealt with still have to do largely with questions of insanity in criminal court hearings and with questions arising in children's courts, there is likely to be an extension into civil court issues in the near future.

The *psychotherapeutic* function is the one concerning which there is most ambivalence, disagreement, interprofessional wrangling, and general insecurity. As has been stated, some of the university training programs include courses on counseling and guidance, but no one would pretend that these provide an adequate basis for intensive individual treatment.

The majority of psychologists working in clinical areas do, however, undertake therapeutic responsibilities, and for the most part, the agencies accept and support this practice. One reason is that the limited supervised experience the psychologist has is often a lot more extensive than that of the medical specialist. In some child guidance units the psychiatrist interviews the parents, and the psychologist treats the child. The dictum "under psychiatric supervision" is always appended, although this is often minimal in reality.

The *training* and *research* functions have not yet developed to any significant degree, apart from teaching centers. In the various hospitals, child welfare agencies, etc., staff psychologists participate to a limited extent in courses for psychiatric nurses, probation officers, and other staff, but most programs are of an informal nature through case conferences and seminars. In teaching hospitals, clinical psychologists participate in the clinical teaching of medical students, speech therapists, occupational therapists, etc., at particular stages in their courses.

Research, by and large, still remains within the university setting. Individual psychologists will undertake projects, but there are no signs as yet of research positions or centers being established in the field. Few contributions to the journals come from the clinical psychologist. The reason given for this dearth of research activity is usually the pressure of everyday service needs of the agency rather than a lack of official acceptance of this activity. Another major reason would be the lack of research training in the past in the preparation of the clinical psychologist. Few university programs have specialized courses directly relevant to the research problems the clinical psychologist will face later.

Emerging Trends and Legislation

Australia currently has no state legislation governing the practice of psychology as a profession. From time to time over the last few years, moves have been made to establish the pros and cons of moving for state registration, but as yet no definite decisions have been reached. At the 1962 general meeting of the Australian Branch of the British Psychological Society in Perth, a resolution was carried which stated that as there now seemed to be no obstructions to the registration of psychologists as such, the executive committee should examine the matter and report next year.

In this regard, close attention has been paid to the experiences on the American scene, and the obstacles, moves, and countermoves that have been documented have been well studied in Australia. Most professional psychologists feel that closely related to the registration issue is the need to raise the professional qualifications and standards well beyond their present level in most states so that registration will genuinely mean the provision of adequate professional psychological services to the community.

NEW ZEALAND[43]

There are four universities in New Zealand—Auckland, Victoria (in Wellington), Canterbury (in Christchurch), and Otago (in Dunedin)—all of which offer graduate courses in psychology. The course at Otago does not go beyond the first year, but a chair is soon to be established, and Otago will offer a B.A. degree in psychology, as the other universities do.

While the University of Canterbury offers a postgraduate diploma in clinical psychology, standards meeting British or American criteria

[43] Harold Bourne (Dunedin).

have still to be established. The department of psychological medicine in Otago cannot as yet offer any postgraduate training in psychology or psychiatry; however, together with certain other facilities in Dunedin, it is the only center in New Zealand where clinical work in psychology approaches anything that would be academically recognizable elsewhere.

Although training and facilities for attaining a proper level of professional psychological practice are still inadequate, it remains true that work in the field of clinical psychology is undertaken by persons in New Zealand designated as "clinical psychologists." Usually they have majored in psychology or education. Among the small number employed in the state mental hospital system and schools, there are few with full or partial professional training in clinical psychology obtained overseas. There are no legal restrictions, and some people practice psychotherapy and a kind of industrial psychology, but seldom with any acceptable qualifications.

THE AMERICAS

Canada[44]

General situation. While there is no distinctively Canadian psychology, psychology in Canada is varied and eclectic, reflecting British and continental European as well as American traditions. The strong influence of American psychology is readily apparent from the fact that one-third of Canadian Psychological Association members also belong to the American Psychological Association. (Not quite one in three hundred APA members belongs to the CPA.) Canadian psychologists suffer and benefit from the same kind of pressures for psychological services which exist in the United States, but they have fewer training and research resources with which to meet these needs.

Canadian psychologists as a group seem to be considerably less home-trained and inbred than psychologists in most other countries. For example, only 55 per cent of the teachers of psychology in Canadian universities were trained in Canada, 30 per cent were trained in the United States, and 10 per cent were trained in the United Kingdom. One of the "unhappy consequences" of the close proximity to the United States is the loss of graduate students, many of whom do not return to Canada after completing their graduate work in American universities. Canada's main influence in American psychology has thus been through the export of high-quality material for the making of psychologists.

Professional roles. Clinical psychologists are employed in a variety of settings in Canada—in mental hospitals, psychiatric units, mental health clinics, private practice, social service, and industry. Many, in association with psychiatrists and other physicians, are engaged in research studies supported by federal-provincial health research grants devoted to the prevention and treatment of mental illness. Others in the various treatment centers are engaged in psychodiagnostic testing, staff training, group and milieu psychotherapy, rehabilitation counseling, and training. Still others have administrative responsibilities for the planning or direction of clinical training and research programs. A small but increasing number are becoming involved in advisory, research, and administrative roles in forensic clinics, alcoholic treatment and drug addiction centers, and penal institutions. The creation of several new Canadian universities and the expansion of established ones are drawing many experienced and senior clinical psychologists onto the staffs of psychology teaching and research departments.

Emerging trends and legislation. Presently about 20 per cent of Canadian psychologists (approximately two hundred) are employed in clinical work, which is not far short of the 23 or 25 per cent on university staffs and the similar number engaged in counseling and personnel work. Of those employed as clinical psychologists, some 8 to 10 per cent have a B.A. degree, about 50 per cent an M.A., and about 40 per cent a Ph.D. At a recent (1960) conference of Canadian psychologists, arranged by the Canadian Psychological Association to review the nature and adequacy of psychological training in Canada, there was general agreement on the desirability of having all psychologists, including clinical, trained in research and qualified at the Ph.D. level; this is likely to become an increasingly insistent requirement in certification and registration regulations.

[44] C. Roger Myers (Toronto) and Craig M. Mooney (Ottawa).

Legislation providing for the certification and registration of qualified psychologists now exists in the provinces of Quebec, Ontario, Saskatchewan, and Alberta, and similar enactments may be expected in the remaining provinces. The main purpose of such legislation is to limit the use of the term "psychologist" to persons with specified academic and professional qualifications. One difficulty in bringing about these enactments has been the uncertainty among psychologists concerning the minimum academic criteria to be specified. The tendency is to aim at the Ph.D. as an ultimate requirement, while making reasonable interim provision for those with the M.A.

The issue of standards reflects practical difficulties of an almost circular nature, which are not unique to Canadian psychology but which are intensified by the proximity of the United States. The salaries offered to Canadian psychologists, especially in clinical fields, are not predicated on high qualifications. There is, moreover, a serious and continuing shortage of competent clinical psychologists, aggravated by the fact that the experienced and highly qualified can command more compatible salaries in the United States. In these circumstances it is difficult to evolve the best strategy for bringing good salaries and high qualifications into line, while meeting the need for at least minimally trained personnel, and until this is accomplished, Canadian psychologists cannot assuredly enjoy professional parity with medical, psychiatric, and other scientific colleagues.

In sum, it may be said that graduate training in clinical psychology in Canada is not lightly undertaken in any of the universities, and where it is offered it is academically thorough and scientifically oriented. Working relationships with physicians, psychiatrists, social workers, and others are notably good by virtue of the sound training given clinical psychologists and because their competence is grounded in psychodiagnostic and research fields rather than in analysis and therapy. Professional working conditions are becoming more varied and attractive by virtue of the premium being placed upon high qualifications and the underwriting of professional standards under the new certification and registration regulations being adopted by the various provinces.

LATIN-AMERICAN OVERVIEW[45]

The development of clinical psychology in Latin America has been greatly stimulated by the increasing communication fostered by the Interamerican Society of Psychology, founded in December, 1951, during the International Congress of Mental Health in Mexico. The first Interamerican Congress of Psychology was held two years later, in December, 1953, in the Dominican Republic at the University of Santo Domingo, the oldest university in the Americas. Information is not always readily obtainable, and diverse details need to be properly understood in terms of prevailing trends and conditions.

First, there are the psychiatrists who work in mental hospitals almost exclusively and who have a largely "nondynamic" orientation. Although not directly involved in psychological training, they participate to some extent in practicum supervision.

Second, there are physician-psychologists who are M.D.s with experience in psychoanalysis or psychotherapy and who sometimes also have additional training in the behavioral sciences. They are presently one of the dynamic forces behind the training of clinical psychologists. Among the analysts, there are some Ph.D. psychologists who play a very similar role and who identify themselves as medical psychologists.

Third, there is a small group of academic psychologists who are very rarely concerned with training for professional work. Harking back to a European psychology of over thirty years ago, they are deeply involved with theoretical contributions and are rarely interested in statistical research design or systematic methodological efforts.

Fourth, there are the "educationalists," who constitute another segment of the dynamic forces in clinical psychology training. Led by relatively few Ph.D.s in educational settings, they train a large number of students, many of whom obtain certification by what might be equivalent to an M.A. degree in the United States.

Leadership for clinical training has long been under the aegis of the physician-psychologists but is contested by the educationalists. Since the more traditional psychologists do not take much interest in clinical

[45] Ernst Beier (Utah) and Victor D. Sanua (Yeshiva).

programs, the directions and goals of training frequently differ from the United States standard of endeavoring to produce a well-rounded psychologist with a research orientation as well as professional skills.

One of the major problems faced by the universities in staffing departments of psychology is the fact that many of the department heads and most of the faculty were trained in other disciplines, such as psychoanalysis, psychiatry, and philosophy. Only a few staff members in the departments of psychology received some training in the United States, and that usually at the M.A. level. Some others trained in Europe and immigrated to Latin America before World War II.

In all the larger South American countries from whom responses were received for the 1963 La Plata Congress Symposium on Clinical Training, there seems to be a genuine public demand for applied psychological services, particularly with regard to psychodiagnostic testing and psychotherapy. With the establishment of many new governmental agencies, there is an ever-growing need for professional personnel. Most of the students are young women (85 to 90 per cent). They usually obtain an equivalent of a B.A. or an M.A., with little emphasis on research or methodology. After completing their training with a good deal of practicum experience, obtained in a variety of clinical settings, they are certified as psychologists and work under the direction of a physician-psychologist, a medical psychologist, or an educationalist.

Because of the recency of psychology as a profession, Latin-American males still prefer to go into the old, established professions of medicine, law, and engineering. In Argentina, for example, one-third of the student body studies medicine. The fact that so few males pursue psychology as a career will undoubtedly affect the development of that field, particularly since women still are perceived as inferior in much of Latin America.

The certified psychologists on the B.A. or M.A. level are very much concerned about their professional standing and independence. Their struggles are reminiscent of the efforts of clinical psychologists in the United States, who twenty years ago tried to discover their role in society. For example, psychotherapy is a major issue in most Latin-American countries. The physician-psychologists, who have a leading role in clinical training, by and large do not want to give the subdoctoral professionals the right to do psychotherapy. However, efforts have been initiated to establish doctoral-level clinical psychology training programs in several countries, generally following the United States model and requiring five years of training but with less emphasis on methodology and statistics.

While the educationalists appear more willing to permit young professionals to do psychotherapy, they are also involved in upgrading training programs, hopefully toward the Ph.D. degree, but emphasizing professional rather than academic preparation. It should be noted, however, that the actual number of students who have so far graduated from these Ph.D. programs is very small (compared with the production-line efforts of some United States universities), while literally hundreds of students obtain certifiable psychological training on the lower levels.

In view of these remarks, the descriptions of clinical training in Latin-American countries must be read with caution. In some instances they reflect only one of several forces acting upon clinical training and may not be representative of the entire situation in that country. Beyond these professional differences, each university takes much pride in differing significantly from all others in its training curriculum and goals. In the absence of widely accepted standards, the following reports represent an important aspect but not the total picture. It is hoped that future editions will contain more extensive coverage of the countries only briefly cited.

Argentina[46]

General situation. Clinical psychology in Argentina emerged long before formal training in psychology separated from philosophy. The interest in, and demand for, psychological services, together with the impact of psychoanalysis, greatly influenced the development of psychology courses and the establishment of independent training centers. Although until recently there has been limited international exchange, several Argentine psychologists trained in Europe or the United States hold teaching or other responsible positions at universities and private institutions.

Professional roles. The Argentine Medical Association is opposed to the practice of psy-

[46] Fernanda Monasterio (La Plata).

chotherapy by psychologists. Clinical psychologists usually work in professional teams, doing psychological evaluation and making recommendations for treatment to psychiatrists, who, with the exception of psychoanalysts, generally receive no training in psychotherapy as part of their medical education. In the opinion of most psychiatrists, clinical psychologists are not qualified to practice independently. Yet in many instances, psychologists have actually more training in psychodiagnosis and psychotherapy than their medical colleagues. No resistance is encountered in applying clinical psychological training in educational and industrial settings.

Emerging trends and legislation. A law for the practice of psychology has been introduced in the legislature which is expected to restrict psychotherapy to physicians. The Argentine Psychological Society, founded in 1910, is attempting to establish standards for training.

While relations between clinical psychologists and the Argentine Medical Association have not been altogether satisfactory, they are improving. The focal point of friction is the practice of psychotherapy, which is strongly opposed by the Medical Association.

Despite the professional and legal limitations of clinical psychology, it continues to attract the largest number of graduate students in the university psychology departments.

Brazil[47]

Clinical psychology began to develop in Brazil in response to a demand for training primary and secondary school teachers. With the start of World War II, university teachers of psychology interested in clinical work went to study abroad, and in 1945 the Service of Mental Hygiene for Schools created the post of psychologist.

Psychologists work in schools and clinics, often in collaboration with social workers, psychiatrists, and neurologists. There is much interest in retarded children, and the Pestallozi Society has sponsored both psychological training and psychological research.

The profession of psychology was officially recognized by law in August, 1962, when the necessary requirements for obtaining the title "psychologist" were established. Professional practice is now restricted to those who have graduated with a degree in psychology from a university. Until the passage of the law, students of related studies who had graduated in education or philosophy could also practice psychology.

47 Arrigo L. Angelini (São Paulo).

Chile[48]

The University of Chile in Santiago has started a regular program in psychology under the chairmanship of Dr. Manuel Poblete. Dr. Carl Hereford of Texas University has been appointed by the Interamerican Society of Psychology as chairman of a committee to study standards of education, training, and professional psychology. A well-known figure in the field of psychology in Chile is Dr. Carlos Nassar, who teaches abnormal psychology and mental hygiene at the university.

Colombia[49]

With its long tradition of social welfare, Colombia has developed graduate training in clinical psychology at the National University and the Catholic University Javeriana, both in Bogotá.

The few clinical psychologists active at the present time are mostly involved with psychodiagnosis and supportive psychotherapy. They work in close contact with a small group of psychiatrists and have good professional standing but a lower income than industrial psychologists.

There is no legislation pertaining to professional psychological services. It is hoped that eventually it may be feasible to build a program in accordance with the American Psychological Association model.

Cuba[50]

Clinical psychology has been developing in Cuba for more than two decades, particularly in children's services. Although there have been considerable changes since January, 1959, and although many clinical psychologists have left the island, work continues.

Cuban clinical psychologists work primarily in the area of psychodiagnosis, usually in association with psychiatrists. While some are engaged in psychotherapy, there is very little private practice. Whereas many psychiatrists continue to insist that therapy with adults is

48 Victor D. Sanua (Yeshiva).

49 Guido Wilde (Bogotá).

50 Ines Segura Bustamante (Miami).

exclusively their responsibility, clinical psychologists encounter almost no opposition in psychotherapy with children.

Most clinical psychologists remaining in Cuba are in the service of the state. Traditional university training has ceased. Neither before nor after 1959 was there any legislation protecting the title "psychologist" or regulating professional practice.

Ecuador[51]

A school of psychology is connected with the Universidad Central del Ecuador. The Faculty of Judicial and Social Sciences publishes a journal, *Archives of Criminology, Neuropsychiatry, and Related Disciplines,* under the editorship of Dr. Julio Endara.

Guatemala[52]

Guatemala has nine applied psychologists, three with Ph.D.s and six at the licentiate level. While the Psychology Department at San Carlos University has been only recently established, the number of students in the four-year program is rapidly increasing. Practicum facilities are available at private and state clinics. Attainment of a university degree is required for professional practice.

Mexico[53]

General situation. There are from 500 to 600 psychologists in Mexico, not more than twelve of whom hold doctorates and of whom approximately fifty have M.A. degrees. The situation reflects the absence of an official or acceptable definition of a psychologist. Any individual who has completed requirements for any of the three levels of training for which psychology degrees are presently granted at the National University of Mexico can call himself a "psychologist," and most people will accept him as such. Occasionally, even students in the second year of training may be employed as psychologists.

Professional roles. Clinical psychologists in Mexico are employed primarily in general or psychiatric hospitals, government nurseries, and private psychiatric clinics, where they are engaged mostly in psychodiagnostic evaluation of children and, on occasion, in supervised or nonsupervised counseling with parents. A good number have their own private practices for psychodiagnosis and therapy. Psychologists with teaching certificates are active in private and public schools. A few clinical psychologists work for the courts and correctional centers, particularly in counseling juvenile delinquents.

Emerging trends and legislation. Although many "pasantes," who have completed all academic requirements except a dissertation, are on the staffs of schools or in private practice, there has been a growing tendency for governmental institutions and particularly for universities to require one of the three degrees granted at the National University as a condition of employment. The regulations of the Faculty of Philosophy, which includes psychology, have been revised to indicate that the degree of psychotechnician is a minimum requirement for engaging in professional practice. An M.A. degree is needed for teaching appointments at the university level.

A major effort has been made by the recently reorganized Mexican branch of the Interamerican Society of Psychology to establish criteria for official recognition. The first move has been to grant full status in the society only to those members who have one of three degrees. While "pasantes" will be accepted, they will not have the right to vote, nor can they hold positions as officers.

At present Mexico still has no federal or state legislation protecting the title "psychologist." This implies an absence of legal rights and responsibilities. However, the Mexican Constitution defends the right of any individual to earn an honest living, and so any psychologist can practice, though undifferentiated from the ill-trained quack.

As in many other Latin-American countries, psychiatrists generally hold to the view that psychologists should limit their professional activities to diagnostic studies and superficial therapy. Nevertheless, psychiatrists actively participate in the training of clinical psychologists and hold faculty rank in the department of psychology at the National University.

As the first Latin-American country to offer a Ph.D. in psychology, Mexico has made many advances. Implementing the much-needed clinical psychology training program is mostly a matter of obtaining more adequate financing and of strengthening the National University, where currently only one out of fifty-nine fac-

[51] Victor D. Sanua (Yeshiva).

[52] Elisa Fernandez B. (San Carlos).

[53] Rogelio Diaz-Guerrero (Mexico City).

ulty members is employed full time and where three are employed half time.

Panama[54]

As of 1962, there were three professional psychologists in Panama; two had a doctorate. There is no psychological association, and no efforts have been made toward legislation. While the University of Panama has no graduate psychology program, plans have been initiated to develop a seven-year curriculum for the doctorate degree and another of four years for the licentiate degree. Practicum facilities are available but are seldom used.

Peru[55]

Ph.D. degrees with specialization in psychology are awarded by the San Marcos University and by the Pontifical Catholic University, both located in Lima. Training programs are developed by the respective department heads, with practicum facilities provided by private and state agencies. The university degree is required for professional practice, teaching, and guidance positions in school systems. One of the leading figures in the Interamerican Society of Psychology is Prof. Dr. Carlos Alberto Sequin, who is presently head of the department of psychiatry at the Hospital Obrera. He is trained both as a psychiatrist and as a psychologist, as is Dr. A. Cano, who teaches at the Catholic University.

San Salvador, Uruguay, and Venezuela[56]

A five-year program in psychology is offered by the Faculty of Humanities at the University of El Salvador. The Uruguayan Society of Psychology is a member of the International Union of Scientific Psychology. Prof. Magda Lauzan is the president and teaches child psychology and testing methods at the Instituto Normal de Montevideo.

The department of psychology at the central University of Venezuela was reorganized in 1958. Some clinical psychology is taught at the National Institute of Pedagogy under the directorship of Father Manuel Montaner. Dr. Francisco del Olmo, who works for the Creole Petroleum Corporation, teaches measurements in the department of education of the Central University of Caracas and has been developing new tests for use in Venezuela.

[54] Carlos M. Malgrat (Panama City).
[55] Miguel A. Sardon (Lima).
[56] Victor D. Sanua (Yeshiva).

CORRESPONDENTS

Abramovitz, Arnold. University of Cape Town, Rondebosch, Cape Town, South Africa.

Ahmad, Dr. S. K. T/7 St. John Park, Sir Hugh Rose Road, Lahore, West Pakistan.

Angelini, Dr. Arrigo L. University of São Paulo, Rua Maria Antonia, Brazil.

Ayer, Dr. Frederic L. Business Research Ltd., 66 Rajdamri Road, Banekok, Thailand.

Barendregt, Dr. J. T. University of Amsterdam, Binnengasthuis, Amsterdam, Netherlands.

Beier, Dr. Ernst G. University of Utah, Salt Lake City, Utah, USA.

Berntsen, Karen. Violvej 8, Gentofte, Denmark.

Bourne, Dr. Harold. University of Otago Medical School, Dunedin, C.I., New Zealand.

Bownes, A. F. University of Western Australia, Nedlands, W. A., Australia.

Bustamante, Dr. Ines Segura. 1566 Coral Way, Apt. 3, Miami 45, Fla., USA.

Cansever, Dr. Gökçe. Bakirköy Mental Hospital, Istanbul, Turkey.

Choynowski, Dr. M. Psychometrical Laboratory, Polish Academy of Sciences, Warsaw, Poland.

Cowen, Dr. Emory L. University of Rochester, Rochester, N.Y., USA.

David, Dr. Henry P. World Federation for Mental Health, 1 Rue Gevray, Geneva, Switzerland.

Diamant, Dr. J. Psychiatric Clinic, Ke Karlovu 11, Prague 2, Czechoslovakia.

Diaz-Guerrero, Dr. Rogelio. Georgia 123, Mexico 18, D.F., Mexico.

El-Meligi, Dr. A. Moneim. N.J. Neuropsychiatric Institute, Princeton, N.J., USA.

Falik, Mrs. Edith. 6 Weisel Str., Tel-Aviv, Israel.

Fernandez B., Prof. Elisa. University of San Carlos, Guatemala City, Guatemala.

Ferracuti, Dr. Franco. Social Science Research Center, University of Puerto Rico, Rio Pedros, Puerto Rico.

Franks, Dr. Cyril M. N.J. Neuropsychiatric Institute, Princeton, N.J., USA.

Fröbärj, Dr. Gösta. Hjo, Sweden.

Garai, Mrs. Margareta. Södersjukhuset, Stockholm, Sweden.

Garcia, Dr. Belen. Trenton State Hospital, Trenton, N.J., USA.

Gravestein. A. Valeriuskliniek, Amsterdam, Netherlands.

Guthrie, Dr. George M. Pennsylvania State University, University Park, Pa., USA.

Hiltmann, Prof. Dr. Hildegard. University of Freiburg, Freiburg i. Br., Germany.

Hla Thwin, Dr. University of Rangoon, Rangoon, Burma.

Hoskovec, Dr. J. Charles University, Hradcanske Nam. 5, Prague 1, Czechoslovakia.

Killingmo, Bjørn. University of Oslo, Lokkeveien 7, Oslo, Norway.

Kopatic, Nicholas. Vineland State School, Vineland, N.J., USA.

L'Abate, Dr. Luciano. Emory University Children's Clinic 1317 Clifton Road, N.E., Atlanta 7, Ga. USA.

Leal, Dr. Maria Rita Mendes. Hospital Miguel Bombarda, Lisbon, Portugal.

London, Dr. Ivan P. Institute for Political Psychology, Brooklyn College, Brooklyn 10, N.Y., USA.

Luria, Prof. A. R. 13 Frunze St., Apt. 29, Moscow G 19, USSR.

McKenna, Dr. John. University College, Dublin, Ireland.

Malgrat, Dr. Carlos M. University of Panama, Panama City, Panama.

Meschieri, Dr. Luigi. Instituto Nazionale di Psicologia, Piazza della Scienze 7, Rome, Italy.

Mizushima, Keiichi. 23, 1—Chrome, Inokashira Mitaka, Tokyo, Japan.

Monasterio, Dr. Fernanda. National University of La Plata, La Plata, Argentina.

Mooney, Dr. Craig M. Department of National Health and Welfare, Ottawa, Ontario, Canada.

Myers, Dr. C. Roger. University of Toronto, Toronto, Ontario, Canada.

Nuttin, Prof. Joseph R. University of Louvain, Louvain, Belgium.

Østergaard, Lise. University of Copenhagen, Copenhagen, Denmark.

Pinillos, Dr. Jose L. University of Valencia, Valencia, Spain.

Pluzek, Dr. Zenomena. Babinski Hospital, Krakow, Poland.

Priester, Dr. Hans J. Child Guidance Center of Mercer County, 253 Nassau Street, Princeton, N.J., USA.

Rabinowitz, Dr. William. Pennsylvania State University, University Park, Pa., USA.

Ruoppila, Isto. Jyväskylä Kasvatusopillinen, Jväskylä, Finland.

Sanua, Dr. Victor D. Yeshiva University, 110 West 57 Street, New York, N.Y., USA.

Sardon, Prof. Miguel A. National Psychopedagogic Institute, Lima, Peru.

Schmid, Dr. Fred. Freiestrasse 155, Zurich, Switzerland.

Sen, Dr. N. N. Department of Psychological Foundations H2/6 Model Town, Delhi 9, India.

Shapiro, Dr. M. B. Institute of Psychiatry, Maudsley Hospital, London S.E. 5, England.

Soloyanis, Dr. George. Office of the Planning Commission, P.O. Box M76, Accra, Ghana.

Takala, Dr. Martti. Center for Educational Research, Jyväskylä, Finland.

Vassiliou, Dr. Vasso. 17 Yannarou Str., Kalamaki, Athens, Greece.

Wallace, John L. Box 713, St. Cloud, Minn., USA.

Wickes, Dr. Thomas A. Office of the Premier, Institute of Administration, Enugu, Nigeria.

Wilde, Dr. Guido. Apartado Aereo 11228, Bogotá D.E., Colombia.

Wohl. Dr. Julian. University of Toledo, Toledo, Ohio, USA.

58

Ethics in Clinical Psychology

NICHOLAS HOBBS

PHILOSOPHICAL PROBLEMS

Changing Conceptions of the Nature of Science

It has been said that science is ethically neutral. This aseptic view, which maintained that the process of science could be separated from the uses to which men put its product, prevailed without effective challenge up to the dreadful day of Hiroshima. The fiction that scientists were not responsible participants in the chain of events that led to that day broke down in the face of the enormity of its horror. Scientists rejoined the human race; the holocaust of that day welded them again to the common lot of the common man. More importantly, and ironically, the holocaust of Hiroshima destroyed the Cartesian dichotomy of *res cogitans* and *res extensa,* a fiction that had to be invented in the seventeenth century to make possible the emergence of modern science out of medieval theology. Thus the scientist's sense of responsibility for Hiroshima was not simply a tactical response to a situation gone out of hand; the resolution was philosophical in character, not simply pragmatic. After 1945, the scientist could no longer maintain the philosophical position of apartness from the knowledge he creates; he could no longer maintain that the scientist deals with something "out there." He had to accept his oneness with the subject of his experiments and observations. The questions he asks determine the answers he gets.

To be more accurate, the explosion of Hiroshima dramatized and focused attention of scientists and philosophers alike on a revolution in scientific thought that had been going on quietly and in limited circles for some time, interestingly enough among the very people—Planck, Heisenberg, Bohr, Schrödinger, Einstein—whose work made atomic fission possible. The years of decision were 1926 and 1927, in Copenhagen, and the struggle for a more adequate way of conceiving reality was most difficult. Heisenberg writes:

> I remember discussions with Bohr which went through many hours till very late at night and ended almost in despair; and when at the end of the discussion I went alone for a walk in the neighboring park I repeated to myself again and again the question: Can nature possibly be as absurd as it seemed to us in these atomic experiments?

The Copenhagen discussions resulted in such sentences as these:

> The observation plays a decisive role in the event and . . . reality varies, depending on whether we observe it or not; we have to remember that what we observe is not nature itself but nature exposed to our method of questioning (Heisenberg, 1958).

Implication for Psychology

The topic of this chapter is supposed to be "ethics in clinical psychology." I have chosen to get to this issue through these paragraphs on the history and philosophy of science because I believe that there are no ethical standards for clinical psychologists apart from all psychology, all science, and all ethics. If the ethics of clinical psychologists are to amount to anything, they must be more than a compendium of approved and disapproved ways of handling fees, referrals, advertising, and countertransference. It seems to me especially important not to think of ethics as a book of rules to govern the professional conduct of the applied psychologist. Ethical standards may be expressed in some guides to conduct, but these guides should be more than *ad hoc* admonitions; they should reflect a mature consideration of the assumptions underlying the psychological relationship, whether between clinician and client, experimenter and subject, teacher and student, or writer and audience.

Let us take seriously, then, the idea that the clinician is first of all a psychologist, that the psychologist is a scientist, and that the scientist is a responsible citizen accountable for the consequences of his work. The lesson of Hiroshima and of Copenhagen is that the scientific enterprise is intrinsically an ethical enterprise, both with respect to the uses of its product (this was the lesson of Hiroshima) and with respect to its process (this was the lesson of Copenhagen). The psychologist as scientist who scorns ethics as merely a guide for practitioners or a vestigial involvement with philosophy is maintaining a conception of science that is no longer tenable. Science and ethics are inextricably intertwined, both as pragmatic (Hiroshima) and as philosophical (Copenhagen) concerns.

The centrality of ethics to science is perhaps a position that will not command immediate acceptance; it has to be argued and won against a centuries-old assumption that the scientist is a detached and uncommitted observer of a reality that unfolds independently of him. But when one moves to a consideration of the clinical relationship, there would seem to be no need to argue the point. The clinical relationship, in all its inwardness, is a moral and ethical engagement. Ethical considerations are at the very heart of the matter.

The Ethical Character of the Clinical Relationship

When the clinical psychologist was emulating the physician, there might have been some question about this issue. The physician, for the most part, has followed the tradition of Cartesian science. His concern has been with things and events "out there." Ethical standards, as embodied in the *Principles of Medical Ethics*, govern relationships with patients and among physicians, and his has been among the most honorable of professions. But in medicine, ethics are not central to the healing process. In clinical psychology, ethics are not just a guide to conduct but are the very essence of the treatment process itself.

Clinical psychologists have responded enthusiastically to the brilliant paper by Thomas Szasz in which he rejects the medical model for the conceptualization of psychological disorders. There is some danger that Szasz's thesis may be espoused because of its effectiveness as a ploy in the trivial struggle for hegemony between psychology and psychiatry, and this would be a pity, for Szasz's thesis is much more demanding. It requires the psychologist to examine the adequacy of his model in the light of the demands that his clinical responsibility will make upon it. Here, in essence, is Szasz's perceptive and demanding thesis:

> The concept of illness, whether bodily or mental, implies *some deviation from some clearly defined norm*. . . . What is the norm deviation from which is regarded as mental illness? This question cannot be easily answered. But whatever this norm might be, we can be certain of only one thing: namely, that it is a norm that must be stated in terms of *psychosocial, ethical,* and *legal* concepts. . . .
>
> My aim [is] to suggest that the phenomena now called mental illness be looked at afresh and more simply, that they be removed from the category of illness, and that they be regarded as the expression of man's struggle with the problem of *how* he should live. The last mentioned problem is obviously a vast one, its enormity reflecting not only man's inability to cope with his environment, but even more his increasing self-reflectiveness (1960).

Personality theorists, their thinking maturing quite independently of Szasz, have recognized the need to cast the clinical problem in ethical and moral terms, adopting for heuristic reasons an idiom, a phraseology, long absent from scientific psychology. Thus Hobart Mowrer and George Kelly find it useful to talk in terms of sin, and Henry Murray finds the metaphor of Satan a productive one in trying to conceptualize "certain definable human dispositions or complexes . . . within a scientific framework" (1962).

In what specific respects is the clinical relationship an ethical matter? If you start with the raw data of the clinical interview, whether for diagnostic or therapeutic purposes, much of the content will bear upon issues that fall in the domain of ethics in a classical (not professional) sense. Clients talk about their distress in personal terms that can be described generally as a product of a perceived discrepancy between the way they describe themselves or the way they behave and some ideal self or some desired standard of conduct, usually involving other people. Guilt may be conceptualized as an awareness of these discrepancies in acts already committed, and anxiety as a diffused fear of punishment or alienation that may result from being found out. Hostility is most often described by a client in terms of his (to himself) justifiable reaction to a moral transgression on the part of some other person. The behavior of the other person is often distorted to make it a clear and appropriately punishable violation of some widely accepted ethical standard. Psychotherapy may be described as an intimate dialogue about moral issues as lived by the client.

It further seems reasonable to assume that the conduct of the psychologist toward his client must be ethical to be effective. In contrast with the practice of medicine or law, where the function of ethical standards is to protect the patient or client, the practice of psychotherapy requires adherence to exemplary conduct not solely to protect the client when he is in a vulnerable position but more importantly to provide the client with a concrete experience of an intrinsically moral relationship with another human being. It is commonplace to note that the character of the relationship between the therapist and his client is a major source of therapeutic gain; the relationship must be a living, immediate act of ethical discovery.

The Antinomy of Determinism

To assert that a clinical psychologist is a scientist who has a hard time shaking off the weight of scientific tradition (the hand of Descartes is on one shoulder and the hand of Comte on the other) and then to add that the clinical engagement is a moral and ethical enterprise at its center is to lay bare the clinical psychologist's most exquisite dilemma. He has got to make up his mind about the issue of determinism. He will not solve the problem because it is probably not solvable, but if he is conscientious he will live with the problem examined and unresolved as one of the existential impossibilities in his chosen profession. Sisyphus-like, he will advance the stone uphill one day, only to have it roll back the next. His dilemma is this: As a scientist, he assumes that behavior is orderly, that cause-and-effect sequences can be discovered, and that definable interventions will be followed by predictable outcomes. He will of course allow for some slippage as a result of imperfect knowledge and for some randomness perhaps because of entropy and the Heisenberg type of indeterminacy, but these are technical and not philosophical difficulties. He assumes that behavior is lawful and, with all facts known, predictable. On the other hand, as a clinician, he is dealing with a client who talks of anxiety and guilt and choice and responsibility. The assumption of determinism renders these terms meaningless, however poignant may be their expression.

Here is a Kantian antinomy of magnificent proportion. The personality theorist, the child development specialist, and the practicing clinician rebel at its absurdity. Gordon Allport (1955) protests vehemently against it and then bows to its logic. Daniel Prescott (1957) finds illusory comfort in Heisenberg's principle of indeterminacy, equating it with the freedom of the individual to choose the better or worse part. George Kelly (1955), with some verbal legerdemain, solves the problem of freedom of choice by redefining it as degrees of freedom or richness of response repertoire. Isador Chein (1962) asserts that he is a determinist who believes in free choice. Each is Sisyphus, as I am. And so must you be also, for this is the point of origin of ethics in psychology.

Criteria for Ethics

There is a final philosophical issue that must be examined before moving on to a consideration of problems of applied ethics or of ethical standards for the clinical psychologist. The issue is this: By what criterion can one establish the validity of any system of ethics? Here again is a problem that probably has no satisfactory solution. None of the various criteria for the adequacy of ethical systems is entirely satisfactory in the absence of a criterion for criteria, and of course this ultimate is even harder, if not impossible, to come by. Nonetheless, it is a good exercise to take a look at several of the criteria that have been suggested from time to time.

Conformity with the natural law has been suggested as the essential requirement of any ethical system. The difficulty here, of course, is that not all people agree with those who are sure that they know what the natural law is. When the *Ethical Standards of Psychologists* was being developed, there was a counterproposal that psychologists should have a code built on the natural law. This seemed like a good idea as a source of enrichment of thinking about ethics. Unfortunately, the project did not come to fruition.

Survival of the species has frequently been suggested as the ultimate criterion for an ethical system. This certainly has a ring of authority about it, though its species-centric character is evident, and it is possible to imagine circumstances under which survival would be an ignoble accomplishment.

That which leads to better organization promoting greater individuation has been proposed as a more immediate criterion for an ethical system. This is the evolutionist's view, admirably stated by George Gaylord Simpson.

A pragmatic criterion for an ethical system, reflecting Peirce, James, and Dewey, is the one that fits most comfortably for most Americans and is doubtlessly the reference point that has had most influence in determining the directions taken by ethics committees.

The criterion of consensus among informed persons is a crosscutting standard that is, operationally at least, the criterion actually employed when psychologists try to be explicit about their ethical commitments. This has worked reasonably well, though it is clear that the procedure begs the question. It leaves in obscurity the basis of judgment used by the respondents; it assumes, and the assumption is not a bad one, that a group of decent men and women will come up with a decent code for professional conduct.

These are some of the fundamental issues the clinical psychologist must work with, quite possibly without ever reaching a satisfactory resolution. The argument here is that the problem is much more than one of finding a basis for a code of professional conduct; it is a problem of discovering the full meaning of the proposition that the clinical relationship is in its essence an ethical enterprise.

PRACTICAL PROBLEMS

The philosophical problems involved in ethics and clinical psychology may be at once more interesting and more practical than the delineation of principles that might be involved in a code of ethics. In any event, it seems unnecessary here to repeat or even summarize the principles of conduct that are presented in the *Ethical Standards of Psychologists*. What may be useful is a consideration of two major issues: (1) What is the best practical resolution of the conflict of the psychologist as scientist and as clinician with respect to the issue of determinism? (2) What are some of the characteristics of a good statement of ethical standards, and what difficulties are likely to be involved in working out such a statement?

A Pragmatic Resolution of the Determinism Issue

Psychologists who work with rats or pigeons or people at a distance are never really troubled by the determinism issue. They have known since Psychology 201 that behavior is wholly determined and would rather not hear any more about it. It is the clinician and the personality theorists who are uncomfortable with this easy formulation, who fret and produce opinions from sources even more pristine than experimental psychology, from microphysics, to lend an air of respectability to the palpable sense of freedom and responsibility they live with every anguished hour in the clinic.

A working solution to the unsolvable problem of determinism is a pragmatic one: Do not contend for the ultimate truth of the matter or even for logical consistency; instead, adopt the position that will get you ahead with the business at hand. Any solution to the problem of determinism is ultimately arbitrary. I freely chose to compose this sentence, or this sentence was strictly determined by my present circumstance and past experience. Both statements are equally true; choice between them will depend on one's purpose.

I came to this pragmatic position through an admiration for the forthright way in which the law dispenses with the matter. Before a particular birthday, a child's behavior is the responsibility of his family and of society; after that birthday, the child himself is responsible. The law is especially charming and instructive in that the age of transition from determined to free behavior varies from state to state. Freedom and responsibility are achieved two years earlier in North Carolina than in Kentucky. In four states, boys become responsible one or two years earlier than girls.

The law is even more instructive in its emerging tests for adult culpability. The clinical psychologist who testifies before some courts today will find his task more demanding than ever before, a consequence of what Szasz has identified (see page 1508) as our increasing self-reflectiveness. Formerly, under the M'Naghten Rule the expert (psychiatrist, psychologist) was asked to testify simply on the issue of whether or not the defendant, at the time of the act, was able to distinguish between right and wrong. In some courts today this criterion is regarded as insufficient. The Durham Rule (1954) states "that the accused shall not be held criminally responsible for his act if it was the product of a mental disease or a mental defect." That this is considerably more than a play on words is evident in the interpretation by Judge David Bazelon of what this new test requires:

> I see *Durham*—or any proper test—as a conceptual vehicle through which the jury will be presented with detailed and comprehensive testimony casting light on *why* the accused acted as he did. We need to know as much as we can about how and why he got the way he is. With such knowledge, the jury has the essential information for its moral judgment of responsibility. For any judgment which ignores the realities of mental life cannot be moral.
>
> As you will readily perceive, the task of the expert witness under the *Durham* concept is great. He must delve deep into the background of the accused. He must study, analyze and co-ordinate reports of physical, neurological and psychological examinations. He must do all this to provide the best explanation of the dynamics of the behavior to a lay jury. He cannot fulfill his duty merely by attaching—or refusing to attach—a few classificatory labels denoting mental disorder —or by reciting the report of an IQ score. As our Court emphasized in 1957: "Unexplained medical labels—schizophrenia, paranoia, psychosis, neurosis, psychopathy— are not enough. . . . The chief value of an expert's testimony in this field, as in all other fields, rests upon the material from which his opinion is fashioned and the reasoning by which he progresses from his material to his conclusion; in the explanation of the disease and its dynamic, that is, how it occurred, developed, and affected the mental and emotional processes of the defendant; it does not lie in his mere expression of conclusion (1962).

Judge Bazelon underscores the pragmatic character of the legal test for responsibility by endorsing a change of rules to reflect developments of knowledge in the behavioral sciences and by asserting that even further changes may be expected as the behavioral sciences become more precise.

The implications of Judge Bazelon's position with respect to the issue of freedom and responsibility suggest a sensible way out for the clinical psychologist. In spite of the straining and pulling of such writers as Allport, Chein, and Kelly, I can find no convincing statement to resolve the inherent and abiding contradictions in the situation. The jurist takes a position on the issue that will make justice a bit more responsive to new developments in knowledge; he asserts not a truth but a working proposition. The physicist makes a comparable theoretical accommodation to get on with his business; for some purposes, light is assumed to be made up of waves, for other purposes of particles. The jurist and the physicist set us a good example. The clinical psychologist's choice of position with respect to the issue of determinism should be determined pragmatically by the requirements of the problem at hand and by his own role at a particular time.

The clinical psychologist as scientist must assume that behavior is determined in order to get about his business. Whether or not behavior is actually determined is irrelevant; indeed, the proposition in the abstract is meaningless. For purposes of research, behavior is determined. We have no tactics of confirmation to permit any other assumption. Furthermore, the researcher commonly makes another arbitrary and pragmatic assumption, i.e., that he is dealing with something "out there."

The clinical psychologist as diagnostician also assumes that behavior is determined, although he tends to use the idiom and the vocabulary of free choice in describing behavior: "The patient refused to talk about his father." In the diagnostic role, the psychologist takes a mixed position on the "out there" issue. For some purposes, such as administering a test, he assumes that the relationship between examiner and client is not central; in a diagnostic interview, interpersonal interactions become as important as content. The concept of participant-observer expresses the duality of the solution in diagnostic work. The examinee is sometimes "out there" and sometimes not.

The clinical psychologist as therapist takes a mixed and varying stance on these issues, probably best described, after William James, as a "soft determinism." He assumes that the therapeutic process is lawful and that particular kinds of interventions have a better than chance probability of producing expected results. On the other hand, he adopts for the most part the client's metaphor, which assumes freedom of choice, responsibility, and guilt as substantial realities. Most therapists explicitly reject the "out there" position and assume that the relationship is paramount.

There is no profit in asking whether man's behavior is determined or free; the useful question is: "What assumption is required by the task at hand?"

Practical Requirements for a Code of Ethics

The *Ethical Standards of Psychologists* gains its strength and its unique character from the fact that it was empirically derived from actual problem situations that psychologists considered to be of ethical significance. Major problem areas were defined, principles derived, and illustrative material obtained from hundreds of critical incidents that were submitted by psychologists to a committee that began its work in 1948. Earlier efforts to develop a code of ethics for psychologists had been bound by existing codes of other professions, notably medicine, or by some special theoretical position, such as nondirective counseling.

These derivative efforts lacked authenticity and relevance and were thus unable to gain the kind of acceptance that is prerequisite for a statement of ethical standards to have an influence on conduct. What the ethical standards committee did essentially was to speed up the process of creating common law. Effective codes of professional ethics are those which reflect standards of conduct already substantially established in the mores of the professional group. The ineffective codes of ethics are the rootless ones that are drawn up, usually by a committee of elders, with the more or less explicit objective of increasing the prestige of the profession or of allaying public distrust. Psychologists took the pains to find out how ethical problems actually arise in the practice of their profession and what kinds of solutions represented the best aspirations of informed members of the profession.

Such a solution presents difficulties. First of all, psychologists differ in their assumptions of what constitutes an ethical problem; some would include relatively minor sources of potential conflict that might best be called problems of "professional courtesy," while others would limit a statement of ethical standards to problems where clearly moral issues are joined. I think clinical psychology is well-advised to take a broader view of what constitutes an ethical problem. At least three levels of seriousness may be identified: the level of courtesy, the level of good professional practice, and the level of clear moral responsibility. While the last is surely the most important, the first and second are not trivial and may, indeed, be of considerable importance to the welfare of the people served by the profession.

Another difficulty that has arisen, though it need not have done so, is that an empirically derived statement of ethical standards tends to become out of date. The *Ethical Standards of Psychologists* is now inadequate in its coverage because it is based on incidents that reflected the practice of psychology almost two decades ago. Psychologists interested in problems of children, in problems of private practice of clinical psychology, and in problems of survey methods—these and others have voiced their concern over the incomplete coverage of the present code. Other areas are skimpily treated, notably, industrial practice and forensic psychology. To be effective the psychologist's code of ethics must be continually revised and brought up to date. The parameters of morality may be deep-rooted in the nature of man and the character of the societies he creates, but their expression in requirements for ethical conduct are as immediate as the next telephone call from a prospective client.

The contention that a code of professional ethics should be under constant revision does make some trouble for ethics committees. Their difficult task is made easier when they have *a* code to go by, when they can cite numbered principles and paragraphs in confronting a recalcitrant offender. But such people are few, and the code of ethics of a profession should not be limited by requirements of dealing with the gross transgressor. A code of ethics should be addressed (as is the code of the APA) to the *ethical* practitioner, to the person with strong ethical sensitivities who is seeking the guidance of his fellow psychologists in a constant effort to improve his conduct. The formal decisions of ethics committees of the APA and of state associations are now being collected to build up a body of common law; however, these decisions will perforce deal with gross violations calling for reprimand or for punitive action and not with the more important edge of the problem, the kinds of choices confronting the psychologist who is already explicitly committed to the maintenance of highest ethical standards.

Let me give an example of the level at which the continuing debate on ethical issues should be pitched to be most effective in improving the ethical standards of psychologists. In their research with human subjects, psychologists often engage in deception. For the purpose of an experiment it may be necessary to make the subject believe something that is different from what the experimenter knows the situation to be; e.g., associates are presented as colleagues of the subjects rather than as confederates of the experimenter; ratings prepared by the experimenter are presented as ratings by friends of the subject. These procedures may be called "creating a set." They may also be called "lying." In reference to the clinical relationship, the *Ethical Standards of Psychologists* (principle 2.31–1) states:

> The psychologist is obligated to inform his client of those aspects of the clinical relationship that might reasonably be considered important factors in the client's decision to enter the relationship. Candor in describing such circumstances and scrupulous adherence to understandings worked out with the client are essential.

Is it unreasonable to expect that the same standard should apply to the relationship of experimenter to subject? I am not ready to take this position, but I do feel that it should be debated carefully. The losses from such an ethical policy would be great: many experiments in clinical and social psychology especially would be made impossible. Ethics aside, there are pragmatic arguments in favor of the policy. With growing public sophistication, the supply of naïve subjects will diminish. Soon, perhaps, the public will come to regard all psychological experiments involving human subjects as situations in which deception is to be expected. At this point even truth is suspect. The problem is not simple, nor is it unimportant.

TRAINING

What are the implications of this discussion for the training of the clinical psychologist? Two programmatic emphases, reflecting the two major divisions of this chapter, seem called for.

The first suggestion is that the undergraduate preparation of the clinical psychologist be broadly humanistic in emphasis. My bias is that the formal study of psychology should be held to a minimum—just enough courses for the student to see whether he is interested in the psychologist's mode of approach to the problem of human behavior. Education in science and mathematics should be extensive, especially as a study of systems developed by man to give cognitive and esthetic order to his world. But the main thrust of undergraduate preparation for the clinical psychologist (perhaps I should again add the phrase "according to my bias") should be in the humanities: some social science and history, some philosophy, some fine arts, much literature. The central query should be: "How have men, other than psychologists, attempted to make sense of man?" I should add that a respect for the artist, poet, novelist, theologian, and philosopher as interpreters of man to men should be a career-long source of nourishment for the clinical psychologist who takes seriously the thesis that his professional work is at its heart an ethical matter.

In the professional training of the clinical psychologist in the graduate school, there should certainly be formal instruction in professional ethics. Perhaps an introduction to the problem can be achieved early in a course or seminar. This will perhaps suffice to get the student acquainted with the rule book and with the challenge to learn that is before him. He can then move ahead to what should become a career-long engagement, to a continuous inquiry into the ethical component of the clinical relationship.

REFERENCES

Allport, G. *Becoming*. New Haven, Conn.: Yale Univer. Press, 1955.

Bazelon, David L. The responsibility of the accused —and the *psychiatrist.* Paper delivered to the New York Society for Clinical Psychiatry, January 11, 1962.

Chein, I. The image of man. *J. soc. Issues,* 1962, **18** (4), 1–35.

Heisenberg, W. *Physics and philosophy.* New York: Harper & Row, 1958.

Kelly, G. *The psychology of personal constructs.* New York: Norton, 1955.

Murray, H. A. The personality and career of satan. *J. soc. Issues,* 1962, **18** (4), 36–54.

Prescott, D. *The child in the educative process.* New York: McGraw-Hill, 1957.

Szasz, T. S. The myth of mental illness. *Amer. Psychologist,* 1960, **15**, 113–118.

Name Index

Page numbers in *italics* refer to the bibliographic section at the end of each chapter.

Subject Index